Elkouri & Elkouri

HOW ARBITRATION WORKS

Sixth Edition

BNA Books Authored by the
ABA Section of Labor and Employment Law

Covenants Not to Compete: A State-by-State Survey

The Developing Labor Law

Discipline and Discharge in Arbitration

Elkouri & Elkouri: How Arbitration Works

Employee Benefits Law

Employee Duty of Loyalty: A State-by-State Survey

Employment Discrimination Law

Employment Termination: Rights and Remedies, 2003 Supplement

Equal Employment Law Update

The Fair Labor Standards Act

How ADR Works

How to Take a Case Before the NLRB

International Labor and Employment Laws

Labor Arbitration: A Practical Guide for Advocates

Labor Arbitration: Cases and Materials for Advocates

Labor Arbitrator Development: A Handbook

Labor Union Law and Regulation

Occupational Safety and Health Law

The Railway Labor Act

Trade Secrets: A State-by-State Survey

For details on these titles, visit BNA Books' home page on the Internet at **http://www.bnabooks.com** or call **800-960-1220** to request a catalog. All BNA books are available on a 30-day free-examination basis.

Elkouri & Elkouri

HOW
ARBITRATION
WORKS

Sixth Edition

Editor-in-Chief
Alan Miles Ruben

Emeritus Professor of Law
Cleveland-Marshall College of Law
Cleveland State University
Cleveland, Ohio

Advisory Professor of Law
Fudan University
Shanghai, PRC

Committee on ADR in Labor & Employment Law

American Bar Association
Section of Labor and Employment Law

The Bureau of National Affairs, Inc., Washington, D.C.

Library of Congress Cataloging-in-Publication Data

Elkouri, Frank.
  How arbitration works / Elkouri and Elkouri.-- 6th ed. / editor-in-chief, Alan Miles Ruben.
    p. cm.

  "Committee on ADR in Labor and Employment Law, Section of Labor and Employment
Law, American Bar Association."
  Includes index.
  ISBN 1-57018-335-X
  1. Arbitration, Industrial--United States.   I. Elkouri, Edna Asper.   II. Ruben, Alan Miles.
III. American Bar Association. Committee on Alternative Dispute Resolution in Labor and
Employment Law. IV. Title.

KF3424.E53 2003
344.7301'81943--dc22

                                                                            2003063598

Published by BNA Books
1231 25th St., NW, Washington, DC, 20037
http://www.bnabooks.com

Printed in the United States of America
International Standard Book Number: 1-57018-335-X

Board of Editors

Jeffrey A. Blevins
Richard Bloch
Christopher R. Bloom
Lance A. Bowling
Seth P. Briskin
Robert G. Brody
Timothy C. Burke
Gust Callas
Robert W. Capobianco
Arthur T. Carter
Lawrence J. Casazza
Christine E. Cervasio
Leonard E. Cohen
Frederick W. Cory
Kevin L. Coulson
Mark Antoin Crawford
Jerry M. Cutler
Dale L. Deitchler
Isabel DeMoura
Fredric Dichter
Joshua L. Ditelberg
Robert L. Douglas
John Deaver Drinko
James J. DuBois
Theodore M. Eisenberg
John A. Entenman
Ali Farhang
Peter N. Farley
Guy O. Farmer II
Richard D. Faulkner
Peter Feuille
Pasquale A. Fioretto
B. Frank Flaherty
Paul A. Flannigan
Edna E.J. Francis
Steven M. Friedland
Puja Gakhar
Joseph D. Garrison
Thomas F. Gibbons
Thomas P. Gies
Matthew J. Gilley
Courtney E. Goddard
Jerold E. Glassman
Edward P. Goggin
Brian Gold
Jodi P. Goldman
Corbett Gordon
Amedeo Greco
David L. Gregory

Lyle J. Guilbeau
Richard Hafets
Robert K. Haderlein
Rick D. Hampton
Joseph Hegedus
J. Kevin Hennessy
Lynne Hicks
Melinda Holmes
C. John Holmquist, Jr.
David L. Hoskins
Richard C. Hunt
Aaron M. Hurvitz
Annette A. Idalski
LeAnne K. Jabs
Joshua Javits
John Kagel
Gary W. Klotz
Barbara Kraft
Jennifer J. Kukac
Frank J. Kundrat
Leslie Iams Kuntz
Michael T. Lamb
James F. Lamond
Carl B.A. Lange III
John B. LaRocco
Michael H. LeRoy
Eric Levine
Alexandra Oberdorfer Liner
Jeffrey M. Linihan
Gene M. Linkmeyer
Andrea G. Lisenbee
Jonathan L. Lister
Gregory T. Lodge
Margaret A. Lyons
Tiffany S. Madsen
William E. Mahoney
Alison J. Maki
Stefan Jan Marculewicz
Charles J. Marino
Arthur J. Martin
Jordan D. Mathies
Kenneth May
John T. McBroom
Patrick J. McCarthy
Brian L. McDermott
Cindie K. McMahon
Ronald E. Meisburg
Devjani Mishra
Steven Moore

Foreword

Since 1945 the ABA Section of Labor and Employment Law has expanded its stated purposes in response to the evolution of the field. Currently, they include the following: (a) to study and report upon continuing developments in the field of labor and employment law; (b) to provide a discussion forum for members of the Association, and other lawyers and law students interested in the field of labor and employment law; (c) to assist the professional growth and development of practitioners in the field of labor and employment law by providing educational seminars, forums, publications, and other programs that advance knowledge and practice in this field of law; (d) to establish and maintain working liaison with state, federal, and, where applicable, multi-national agencies having jurisdiction over labor and employment law matters in order to influence development of the law, workable procedures, and administrative due process; (e) to study and report upon proposed or desirable legislation and rule making within the field encompassed by the jurisdiction of this Section; (f) to promote justice, human welfare, workplace harmony, and the recognition of the importance of the rule of law in labor-management relations and the employment relationship; and (g) to provide consensus views on balanced and diverse perspectives to law makers, courts, administrative agencies, employers, and unions, which make or influence labor and employment policy.

Through the publication of books such as *Elkouri & Elkouri: How Arbitration Works* and through annual and committee meeting programs designed to provide a forum for the exchange of ideas, the Section has pursued these stated goals. Gradually, the Section has built a library of comprehensive legal works intended for the use of the Section membership as well as the bar generally.

The Section of Labor and Employment Law is pleased to provide this new edition of the classic treatise on labor arbitration as part of its library of books published by BNA Books, a Division of The Bureau of National Affairs, Inc. The combined efforts of many individual authors from the Committee on ADR in Labor and Employment Law of the Section are reflected in this work.

The Section wishes to express its appreciation to the committee, and in particular to the editor-in-chief, Alan Miles Ruben. This group has tried to accomplish two primary objectives: (1) to be equally balanced and nonpartisan in its viewpoints, and (2) to ensure the book is of significant value to the practitioner, student, and sophisticated nonlawyer. The views expressed herein do not necessarily represent the views of the American Bar Association, or its Section of Labor and Employment Law, or any other organization, but are simply the collective, but not necessarily the individual, views of the authors. Information on the affiliation of government employees who contributed to this work is for informational purposes and does not constitute any official endorsement of the information provided herein.

STEPHEN D. GORDON
Chair

HOWARD SHAPIRO
Chair-Elect

Section of Labor
and Employment Law
American Bar Association

October 2003

Preface to the Sixth Edition

Since its inception a half a century ago, *How Arbitration Works* has been justly acclaimed as the most comprehensive, definitive, and authoritative treatise on labor arbitration.

Beginning with the Fifth Edition, the responsibility for continuing the creative scholarship of Frank and Edna Asper Elkouri passed to the Committee on ADR in Labor & Employment Law of the Section of Labor and Employment Law of the American Bar Association. The proper discharge of that responsibility requires that the present Sixth Edition begin the process of reorganizing and expanding the text to more fully consider several major developments.

Perhaps the most significant of these is the growth of public-sector collective bargaining and the arbitration of contract disputes in the federal service and state and local government employment. These involve important constitutional and statutory issues that have no private-sector counterpart and require extended treatment.

Second in importance is the increasing reliance by arbitrators upon federal and, to a somewhat lesser extent, state statutory employment regulations to resolve an ever-widening array of grievance issues. These regulations must be considered if arbitration awards are to continue to receive great deference by the courts.

A third development is the judicially approved extension of the Federal Arbitration Act and the compatible provisions of the original and revised Uniform Arbitration Act to arbitrations arising under contracts of employment. These statutes set standards for pre-hearing discovery, admissibility of evidence, and the enforcement or vacatur of arbitration awards.

Thus, *How Arbitration Works* is, and should always remain, a work in progress.

I would like to acknowledge the invaluable assistance of several non-Section members in the formulation of this edition.

My Administrative Assistant, Ms. Laura Gardner, was responsible for the transcription of the manuscript, and patiently endured and successfully dealt with the countless revisions.

My many abstruse queries, requiring in some cases the equivalent of archeological excavation, were unfailingly answered by the Cleveland-Marshall College of Law's Research Librarian, Mr. Schuyler Cook, upon whose good nature I imposed shamelessly.

My wife, Judge Betty Willis Ruben, shared the tedious task of proofing the galleys. (Of course, she received a cruise for compensation.)

I was fortunate to have the benefit of the services of the country's best Book Editor, BNA's Renee Brown, who corrected my errors and made valuable suggestions for improving the text.

It is perhaps inevitable that in a treatise of such scope, blending as it does the contributions of so many distinguished members of the Section, errors of commission and omission will occur. The criticism of readers, all of which are undoubtedly valid, as well as suggestions for future supplementation, are invited and welcomed.

I must confess that in each Chapter I have trespassed beyond the borders of editorship into the realm of authorship. For this I ask pardon.

Alan Miles Ruben
Editor-in-Chief
September 30, 2003

Overview

Long considered by labor law and dispute resolution professionals to be the standard text on labor arbitration, *Elkouri & Elkouri: How Arbitration Works* is the most comprehensive and authoritative treatise available on this subject. The reference of first resort, it has been relied upon and cited by advocates, arbitrators, and judges more than any other arbitration book published.

The text in the new *Sixth Edition* has been contributed by more than two hundred distinguished experts in labor relations under the editorship of Professor Alan Miles Ruben. The *Sixth Edition* provides a thorough revision to this classic, incorporating all major developments of interest to labor relations practitioners and expanding coverage to discuss over one hundred new topics in depth. It also provides citations to over 12,000 arbitration awards and over 2,500 important judicial and administrative decisions, as well as references to academic and professional commentary, administrative agency regulations and opinions, and federal and state legislation.

Significant changes in the new edition include:

- Chapters on "Interpreting Contract Language" and "Evidence" have been thoroughly revised to reflect the trend of modern critical thought concerning issues such as ambiguity in contract interpretation, hearsay, and after-acquired evidence.
- A new chapter on "Remedies" analyzes changing views on the availability of non-traditional remedies such as attorneys' fees and interest awards.
- Extended discussion of legislation, regulations, and judicial decisions that bear upon labor arbitration issues is provided, since collective bargaining agreements increasingly incorporate federal and state statutory standards in contract language.
- Analysis of the Federal Arbitration Act and the new Revised Uniform Arbitration Act is provided because of recent judicial decisions recognizing their applicability, along with a discussion of the implications of their provisions for pre-arbitration discovery and other procedural matters.

• Separate chapters on federal labor arbitration issues and state and local government labor arbitration issues have been added, reflecting the growing importance of public-sector arbitration.

Among the new topics covered by the *Sixth Edition* of *Elkouri & Elkouri: How Arbitration Works* are:

• jurisdictional disputes;
• last-chance agreements;
• ethical obligations of arbitrators and advocates;
• mental distress damages;
• admissibility of employee surveillance and post-discipline acquired evidence;
• recent federal employment-related statutes;
• workplace rules validity;
• a state-by-state summary of public-sector interest arbitration statutes, and more.

The *Sixth Edition* adds new reference materials to enhance the usefulness of the volume. A table of arbitration awards has been included for all awards, whether discussed in text or cited in footnotes. There is also a table of arbitrators that can be used to research references to a particular arbitrator in the book. A table of statutory authorities also has been provided. In addition, topics in the chapters are identified by BNA's *Labor Arbitration Reports Cumulative Digest Index* (LA CDI) classification numbers, making it easier to do additional research in that reference service. As in past editions, there will be a table of cases, which will now include both court and administrative cases, and a comprehensive index.

Key to Arbitral Reporter Abbreviations

ALAA   *American Labor Arbitration Awards*, published by Prentice Hall
ARB   *Labor Arbitration Awards*, published by Commerce Clearing House
LA   *Labor Arbitration Reports*, published by the Bureau of National Affairs
LAIS   *Labor Arbitration Information System*, published by LRP Publications
WAR. LAB. REP. *War Labor Reports*, published by the Bureau of National Affairs
WL   Unpublished arbitration award, available on Westlaw

How to Use LA CDI Classification Numbers

Topic subheads in *How Arbitration Works* are followed by the relevant classification number in volumes of BNA's *Labor Arbitration Reports* (LA) *Cumulative Digest Index* (CDI), where such a classification number exists. Headnotes of awards published in LA are organized in the CDI volumes according to these classification numbers. For instance, CDI number 94.60525, "Hearsay evidence and other exclusionary rules," includes headnotes describing rulings on hearsay evidence in awards published in volumes of LA. Thus, where an LA CDI number is provided in a topic subhead of *How Arbitration Works*, readers may conduct further research to supplement the text and awards cited therein by referring to headnotes under that CDI number in volumes of the LA CDI to find summaries of additional awards involving the relevant issue. Readers may review the full text of those cases, should they wish to do so, using the LA citation provided in the headnote (or hyperlink in the electronic version) to locate the text of the award.

Summary Contents

Table of Contents

Chapter 1

Arbitration and Its Setting

The labor dispute is a characteristic of our free enterprise system and a natural outgrowth of collective bargaining. Whether such conflict between unions and employers is harmful, necessary, or even inevitable, is not the concern here. What is important is that unions, employers, and the public all recognize that production stoppages resulting from disputes should be minimized, and that an effective means of accomplishing this end is arbitration. The national policy favoring arbitration was explained by Justice Arthur J. Goldberg:

> In the United States Arbitration Act, the Labor-Management Relations Act and in numerous state statutes, our legislative bodies have voiced their conviction that voluntary arbitration of disputes is favored and has an important role in a society which seeks the peaceful, prompt and just disposition of controversies involving our citizens.[1]

The significance of the arbitration profession was emphasized by a former member of the National Labor Relations Board (NLRB), Joseph A. Jenkins: "I call arbitrators 'peacemakers' because they have it within their power to contribute more to the maintenance of good relations between conflicting forces in our society than any other group, whether public or private."[2]

That arbitration is a distinct dispute resolution institution was recognized in *Teamsters Local 657 v. Stanley Structures:*[3]

> When an employer and a union contract that all disputes and controversies that may arise between them shall be settled by arbitration, they do not simply substitute an arbiter for a judge. They adopt a different method of dispute resolution. They alter pretrial procedures, the method of trial, the standards for admissibility of evidence, and the method of rendering a decision, and they limit the scope of judicial review of the arbitration award.[4]

While arbitration is a distinct institution, however, it would be totally unrealistic to deny the close relationship now existing between it, especially

---

[1]Goldberg, *A Supreme Court Justice Looks at Arbitration,* 20 ARB. J. 13, 13 (1965). In urging wider use of arbitration for certain other types of disputes, former Chief Justice Warren E. Burger of the U.S. Supreme Court acknowledged that the relatively "simple and informal" arbitration procedures have made "incalculable contributions to commerce and trade and labor peace." AAA, NEWS & VIEWS, No. 4 (1977). Professor Benjamin Aaron, looking back to 1939 when he began his formal study of labor law while at Harvard Law School, noted in remarks to an American Bar Association Annual Meeting that while the American labor movement had fallen on hard times due in part to employer opposition, the "one outstanding exception to the opposition by employers to collective bargaining" was the institution of arbitration. Aaron, *A Half-Century of Labor Relations Law,* 13 LAB. LAW. 551, 557 (1998).

[2]Jenkins, *The Peacemakers,* 47 GEO. L.J. 435, 436 (1959).

[3]735 F.2d 903, 117 LRRM 2119 (5th Cir. 1984).

[4]*Id.* at 904, 117 LRRM at 2120.

"rights" arbitration, and our formal legal system. Indeed, labor arbitration has drawn heavily from the standards and techniques of that system. However, fears that the labor arbitration process would become "'over-legalized" have proven unfounded. Indeed, such formalization may have run its course.[5]

The increased use of interest arbitration, principally by governmental entities, together with the continued vitality of "rights" arbitration, is a cause for optimism about labor arbitration as an institution.[6]

This book deals with the workings of labor-management arbitration, and with the numerous questions and problems that have confronted the parties and their arbitrators. The most realistic picture of how arbitration works, and the most practical answers to the issues arbitrators face, it is believed, can be obtained through analysis of actual awards rendered by arbitrators. So it is those awards that form the primary source material for most of the chapters.

1. Arbitration Defined—Historical Background [LA CDI 94.03; 100.06]

Arbitration, to use the words of one writer, is a "simple proceeding voluntarily chosen by parties who want a dispute determined by an impartial judge of their own mutual selection, whose decision, based on the merits of the case, they agree in advance to accept as final and binding."[7]

Submission of disputes to arbitration may be made compulsory by law. However, except as otherwise indicated, the use of the term "arbitration" in this book refers to voluntary arbitration. When parties voluntarily agree to arbitrate their differences, it thereafter becomes "obligatory" on either party to arbitrate at the request of the other. Although both parties have voluntarily agreed to arbitrate, arbitration will not be resorted to unless at least one of them thereafter so wishes.

Arbitration as an institution is not new, having been in use many centuries before the beginning of the English common law.[8] Indeed, one court has called arbitration "the oldest known method of settlement of disputes between men."[9]

King Solomon was an arbitrator[10] and the procedure he used was in many respects similar to that used by arbitrators today. Phillip II of Macedon, the

---

[5]Nolan & Abrams, *The Future of Labor Arbitration,* 37 Lab. L.J. 437, 439–40 (1986).

[6]A majority of states provide by statute for arbitration of interest disputes arising in public-sector employment. However, only a small percentage of the awards rendered in such arbitrations ever reach the reporting services. Therefore, the practitioner's perceptions of its use may be somewhat skewed. Doherty, *Trends and Strikes and Interest Arbitration in the Public Sector,* 37 Lab. L.J. 473 (1986).

[7]Chappel, *Arbitrate . . . and Avoid Stomach Ulcers,* 2 Arb. Mag., Nos. 11–12, at 6, 7 (1944). For a similar definition by a court, see *Gates v. Arizona Brewing Co.,* 95 P.2d 49, 50 (Ariz. 1939). For a discussion of the perils of contracting for judicial review of arbitral awards, see Younger, *Agreements to Expand the Scope of Judicial Review of Arbitration Awards,* 63 Alb. L. Rev. 241 (1999).

[8]For some ancient sources and early developments of arbitration, see Murray, *Arbitration in the Anglo-Saxon and Early Norman Periods,* 16 Arb. J. 193 (1961).

[9]McAmis v. Panhandle Pipe Line Co., 23 LA 570, 574 (Kan. Ct. App. 1954).

[10]1 *Kings* 3:16–28.

father of Alexander the Great, in his treaty of peace with the city-states of southern Greece circa 338–337 B.C., specified the use of arbitration in disputes "between members over vexed territory."[11] Another great man of history, George Washington, was a staunch believer in arbitration. Although he exercised all possible caution in writing his last will and testament, he did not overlook the possibility of disputes as to its intent. For this eventuality, he specified arbitration:

> But having endeavored to be plain and explicit in all the Devises—even at the expense of prolixity, perhaps of tautology, I hope, and trust, that no disputes will arise concerning them; but if contrary to expectation the case should be otherwise from the want of legal expression, or the usual technical terms or because too much or too little; has been said on any of the devises to be consonant with law, my will and direction expressly is, that all disputes (if unhappily any should arise) shall be decided by three impartial and intelligent men, known for their probity and good understanding; two to be chosen by the disputants, each having the choice of one, and the third by those two—which three men thus chosen, shall unfettered by Law, or legal constructions, declare their sense of the Testator's intention; and such decision is, to all intents and purposes to be as binding on the Parties as if it had been given in the Supreme Court of the United States.[12]

Commercial arbitration has long been used as a substitute for court action in the settlement of disputes between businessmen.[13] International arbitration has been used for the settlement of differences between nations; differences which, if not removed, might lead to war. International commercial arbitration has been used with increasing frequency.[14]

---

[11]Fox, The Search for Alexander 113–14 (1980).

[12]AAA, Arbitration News, No. 2 (1963) (also explaining that the quoted lines of the will are reproduced from a document published many years ago by the federal government).

[13]Gilmer v. Interstate/Johnson Lane Corp., 500 U.S. 20, 55 FEP Cases 1116 (1991); Rodriguez de Quijas v. Shearson/American Express, 490 U.S. 477 (1989); Shearson/American Express v. McMahon, 482 U.S. 220 (1987). See Billings, Handling Automobile Warranty and Repossession Cases ch. 4 (2d ed. 1992). For the historical development of commercial arbitration, see Keller, Arbitration and the Legal Profession (AAA 1952).

[14]Regarding international commercial arbitration, in 1970 the United States ratified the United Nations (UN) Convention on the Recognition and Enforcement of Foreign Arbitral Awards, under which courts of the signatory nations are to enforce arbitration clauses and awards on the same basis as they would domestic arbitration proceedings. For explanation and discussion, see McMahon, *Implementation of the UN Convention on Foreign Arbitral Awards in the U.S.*, 26 Arb. J. 65 (1971). Illustrating enforcement of an agreement to arbitrate international commercial disputes under the Convention, see *Mitsubishi Motors v. Soler Chrysler-Plymouth*, 473 U.S. 614 (1985) (arbitration of an antitrust claim raised in an international contract dispute); *Sherk v. Alberto-Culver Co.*, 417 U.S. 506 (1974), and illustrating enforcement of an award under the Convention, see *Island Territory of Curacao v. Solitron Devices*, 356 F. Supp. 1 (S.D.N.Y. 1973). In 1976, the UN endorsed worldwide use of the UNCITRAL Arbitration Rules for international commercial arbitration. "It was felt that rules under UN sponsorship would assist international trade by promoting use of arbitration in all parts of the world and by helping to end the confusing proliferation of rules, each designed for a single region or institution." AAA, News & Views, No. 3 (1976). For a discussion of recent developments, see Comment, *Recognition and Enforcement of International Arbitral Awards Under the U.N. Convention of 1958: The Refusal Provisions,* 24 Int'l Law. 487 (Summer 1990). *See also* Marchac, *Note and Comment, Interim Measures in International Commercial Arbitration Under the ICC, AAA, LCIA and UNCITRAL Rules,* 10 Am. Rev. Int'l Arb. 123 (1999); Baker & Davis, *Establishment of an Arbitral Tribunal Under the UNCITRAL Rules: The Experience of the Iran-United States Claims Tribunal,* 23 Int'l Law. 81 (1989). For a discussion of the conflict between policies of recognizing foreign

Development of labor arbitration in the United States began during the latter part of the nineteenth century and advanced rapidly after the United States became involved in World War II.[15]

The development of labor-management arbitration generally has followed the development of collective bargaining. One of the more recent examples is professional athletics, where use of arbitration quickly followed the introduction of collective bargaining.[16] Arbitration has been most successful where collective bargaining has been successful.[17]

2. Collective Bargaining, Mediation, Factfinding, and Arbitration
[LA CDI 94.03; 100.06]

The process of collective bargaining, mediation, factfinding, and arbitration, and the differences among them, can be better understood if one

---

judgments and enforcing arbitral awards, see Park, *Duty and Discretion in International Arbitration,* 93 Am. J. Int'l L. 805 (Oct. 1999). *See also* Cogan & Sifre, *United States Federal Courts: No Longer Available to Compel Discovery in Connection With Non-United States Arbitrations,* 10 Am. Rev. Int'l Arb. 19 (1999).

[15]Commercial arbitration grew up as an alternative to court action, while labor arbitration evolved primarily as a substitute for strikes. For the historical development of labor arbitration in the United States, see Morris, *Historical Background of Labor Arbitration: Lessons From the Past, in* Labor Arbitration: A Practical Guide for Advocates 3 (Zimny, Dolson & Barreca eds., BNA Books 1990). *See also* Fleming, The Labor Arbitration Process 1–30 (Univ. of Ill. Press 1965); Stessin, Employee Discipline 8–12 (BNA Books 1960); Witte, Historical Survey of Labor Arbitration (Univ. of Pa. Press 1952); Keller, Arbitration and the Legal Profession; Fleming, *Reflections on Labor Arbitration, in* Arbitration 1984: Absenteeism, Recent Law, Panels, and Published Decisions, Proceedings of the 37th Annual Meeting of NAA 11 (Gershenfeld ed., BNA Books 1985); Nolan & Abrams, *American Labor Arbitration: The Early Years,* 35 U. Fla. L. Rev. 373 (1983); Witte, *The Future of Labor Arbitration—A Challenge, in* The Profession of Labor Arbitration, Selected Papers From the First Seven Annual Meetings of NAA 1, 3–11 (McKelvey ed., BNA Books 1957); Oliver, *The Arbitration of Labor Disputes,* 83 U. Pa. L. Rev. 206 (1934).

[16]*See* Conti, *The Effect of Salary Arbitration on Major League Baseball,* 5 Sports Law. J. 221 (Spring 1998); Roberts, *Sports Arbitration,* 10 Indus. Rel. L. Rev. 8 (1988); Dworkin, *Salary Arbitration in Baseball: An Impartial Assessment After Ten Years,* 41 Arb. J. 63 (1986); Wong, *A Survey of Grievance Arbitration Cases in Major League Baseball,* 41 Arb. J. 42 (1986); Stark, *The Presidential Address: Theme and Adaptations, in* Truth, Lie, Directors, and Other Problems in Labor Arbitration, Proceedings of the 31st Annual Meeting of NAA 1, 19–20 (Stern & Dennis eds., BNA Books 1979) (other new uses of arbitration are noted); Comment, *Arbitration of Grievance and Salary Disputes in Professional Baseball: Evolution of a System of Private Law,* 60 Cornell L. Rev. 1049 (1975).

[17]In the full-fashioned hosiery industry, for example, where the use of collective bargaining has been highly successful, over 1,500 disputes were decided over a 10-year period by the industry's impartial chairman without a single reported instance of noncompliance with or nonacceptance of an award. Millis, How Collective Bargaining Works 460 (1942). For a comprehensive summary of the development of collective bargaining and its effect on arbitration, see *id.* at 891–907. For a later study made after some dramatic changes had occurred in the economic setting, collective bargaining, and in the percentage of the work force that is unionized, see Kochan, *Labor Arbitration and Collective Bargaining in the 1990s: An Economic Analysis: The Future of Collective Bargaining and Its Implications for Labor Arbitration, in* Arbitration 1986: Current and Expanding Roles, Proceedings of the 39th Annual Meeting of NAA 44, 57 (Gershenfeld ed., BNA Books 1987) ("[T]he future of grievance arbitration will depend heavily on both the future scope and nature of the collective bargaining process and on how the arbitration profession chooses to adapt to these changes. As well, the future of arbitration depends on which of a number of possible scenarios dominate the future of collective bargaining.").

considers each a stage in the relationship between unions and management. Collective bargaining is the first stage and arbitration the last. Conciliation or mediation, and factfinding, occupy intermediate stages.

Conciliation or mediation may be resorted to as an aid to negotiations.[18] Technically, conciliation is carried on without the intervention of a third party, while mediation implies the intervention of an outside person, but the two terms are commonly used interchangeably.[19] The essence of mediation and conciliation is compromise. The mediator does not make a decision. Rather, the mediator's aim is to persuade negotiators to come to voluntary agreement by formulating mutually acceptable proposals or reasons for the adoption of existing proposals.[20]

Mediation has received increased attention in recent years as a useful form of alternative dispute resolution.[21] The proliferation of inconsistent state laws regulating mediation procedures has led the American Bar Association (ABA) and the National Conference of Commissioners on Uniform State Laws to propose a Uniform Mediation Act.[22]

"Factfinding," as the term is most commonly used, refers to a method of handling labor-management disputes that prohibits strikes and lockouts until an official agency, usually a factfinding board, or a designated private neutral, has had the opportunity to investigate and report. Changes in the status quo, except when made by mutual consent of the parties, are prohibited during the "cooling-off" period, which runs concurrently with the period of investigation and report. The function of factfinders is to investigate and assemble all facts surrounding disputes. After the investigation, a report is

---

[18]Another possible device is the private use of independent third parties as neutral "consultants" or participants in the collective bargaining process itself. *See* Chamberlain, *Neutral Consultants in Collective Bargaining, in* Collective Bargaining and the Arbitrator's Role, Proceedings of the 15th Annual Meeting of NAA 83 (Kahn ed., BNA Books 1962); Wirtz, *Role of Federal Government in Labor Relations*, 51 LRRM 70, 78 (1962); Hildebrand, *The Use of Neutrals in Collective Bargaining, in* Arbitration and Public Policy, Proceedings of the 14th Annual Meeting of NAA 135 (Pollard ed., BNA Books 1961).

[19]Mills & Montgomery, Organized Labor 719 n.2 (1945). It should be noted that these definitions are not necessarily recognized by all legislatures and courts. For example, the "conciliator" appointed under Ohio law to resolve disputes between unions representing safety forces and their governmental employers over terms and conditions of employment must choose "on an issue-by-issue basis, from between each of the party's final settlement offers . . . ." See Ohio Rev. Code §4117.14(G)(7) for the factors the conciliator must consider in rendering his award.

[20]For a short yet highly informative and interesting explanation of the mediation process, see Gold, *Mediation of Interest Disputes, in* Arbitration 1988: Emerging Issues for the 1990s, Proceedings of the 41st Annual Meeting of NAA 9 (Gruenberg ed., BNA Books 1989). For excellent treatises of mediation, see Kagel & Kelly, The Anatomy of Mediation: What Makes It Work (BNA Books 1989); Simkin & Fidandis, Mediation and the Dynamics of Collective Bargaining (BNA Books 2d ed. 1986); Maggiolo, Techniques of Mediation (Oceana 1985). A shorter study is Fuller, *Mediation—Its Forms and Functions*, 44 S. Cal. L. Rev. 305 (1971). *See also* Zirkel & Lutz, *Characteristics and Functions of Mediators: A Pilot Study*, 36 Arb. J. No. 2, at 15 (1981) (citing many other articles on mediation).

[21]*See* Gatter, *Unnecessary Adversaries at the End of Life: Mediating End-of-Life Treatment Disputes to Prevent Erosion of Physician-Patient Relationships*, 79 B.U. L. Rev. 1091 (1999); Eisen, *Are We Ready for Mediation in Cyberspace?*, 1998 BYU L. Rev. 1305.

[22]*See generally* Hoy, *Comment, The Draft Uniform Mediation Act in Context: Can It Clear Up the Clutter?*, 44 St. Louis U. L.J. 1121 (1993). Updated drafts may be obtained via the Internet at <http:www.pon.harvard.edu/guests/uma/>.

made that may include recommendations (except under the emergency dispute provisions of the Labor Management Relations Act (LMRA))[23] and which, unlike the findings of an arbitrator, the disputants have a choice of accepting or rejecting.[24]

In arbitrating, parties are compelled by their own agreement to accept the decision of an arbitrator as final and binding. The objective of arbitration is adjudication, not compromise. Resort to arbitration usually occurs after the techniques of conciliation or mediation (and possibly factfinding) have failed to produce agreement.

3. GRIEVANCE MEDIATION [LA CDI 94.03; 100.06]

A hybrid variation involving a cross between mediation and arbitration has been advanced in recent years as a response to situations in which arbitration is perceived to have become excessively delayed, expensive, or formalistic.[25] Labeled as grievance mediation, it proposes that, after the final step of the internal grievance procedure, unresolved grievances will be referred to mediation rather than directly to arbitration, with arbitration reserved for those grievances that cannot be resolved through mediation. The mediator may not act as the arbitrator, and nothing said or done in the grievance mediation proceedings is admissible in the arbitration.[26] The device was tested with significant positive results in the bituminous coal industry during an experiment lasting 2½ years.[27]

The arbitration process also found a place in public-sector bargaining. With the expansion of collective bargaining in the public sector, state statutes authorizing such bargaining frequently make provision for the use of mediation, factfinding, and interest arbitration as means for resolving im-

---

[23]29 U.S.C. §§206–210.

[24]Boards of Inquiry under LMRA §213 enacted in 1974 for the health care industry do make recommendations. For a discussion of factfinding, see Simkin, *Fact-Finding: Its Values and Limitations, in* ARBITRATION AND THE EXPANDING ROLE OF NEUTRALS, PROCEEDINGS OF THE 23D ANNUAL MEETING OF NAA 165 (Somers & Dennis eds., BNA Books 1970).

[25]SIMKIN & FIDANDIS, MEDIATION AND THE DYNAMICS OF COLLECTIVE BARGAINING 178–79 (BNA Books 2d ed. 1986); Brett & Goldberg, *Grievance Mediation in the Coal Industry: A Field Experiment*, 37 INDUS. & LAB. REL. REV. 49 (1983).

[26]Goldberg, *Mediation of Grievances Under a Collective Bargaining Agreement*, 77 Nw. U. L. REV. 270, 281 (1982). For a discussion of private-sector grievance mediation, see Quinn, Rosenbaum & McPherson, *Grievance Mediation and Grievance Negotiation Skills: Building Collaborative Relationships*, 41 LAB. L.J. 762 (1990). A constructive discussion of public-sector grievance mediation from a neutral's perspective is Caraway, *Grievance Mediation: Is It Worth Using?*, 18 J.L. & EDUC. 495 (Fall 1989). *See also* Chapter 5, section 6.C., "Grievance Mediation."

[27]Of 300 coal industry grievances and 25 grievances from other industries, 275 (85%) were reported resolved without arbitration, 50% by compromise. In 25% of the cases the mediator gave an advisory opinion, which was accepted by the parties 50% of the time. When grievances went to formal arbitration after mediation, the award was the same as the advisory opinion in 75% of the disputes. The average cost for the mediation of a grievance was $200. *See* Goldberg, *Grievance Mediation: I. The Coal Industry Experiment, in* ARBITRATION—PROMISE AND PERFORMANCE, PROCEEDINGS OF THE 36TH ANNUAL MEETING OF NAA 128, 131 (Stern & Dennis eds., BNA Books 1984).

passes that arise during contract negotiations.[28] The constitutionality of such statutes when challenged has usually been upheld.[29]

4. Uses of Arbitration

A. Arbitration as a Substitute for Work Stoppages [LA CDI 80.555]

It has been said that the "most important difference between civilization and savagery is the habitual willingness of civilized men and nations to submit their differences of opinion to a factual test," and that "it is a mark of civilization to present reasons rather than arms."[30] Again, "industrial peace is not a God-given product. It must be cultivated and worked for constantly. . . . Conciliation, mediation and voluntary arbitration are the marks of civilization. They are the enemies of distrust and force. They do away with the fang and the claw."[31] Moreover, "if the rules and standards of orderly social behavior accepted for society at large are to be valid also for industrial relations, it would seem that settlement of labor disputes on rights should be sought as far as possible through judicial methods rather than through strikes and lockouts."[32] One method of settling labor-management differences without resort to strike or lockout is voluntary arbitration. As recognized by the U.S. Supreme Court, arbitration "is the substitute for industrial strife.[33]

In the United States, the right to strike is looked on as an essential economic freedom. Like all freedoms, however, it can be abused; it can be used unwisely and without sufficient justification. Many times, for example, strikes or lockouts have occurred not because of a real difference between the parties, but because one of them could not, or would not, willingly recede from a position irrevocably taken.[34] Here, of course, there is no social justifi-

---

[28]Ackerman, *Arbitration Forums Revisited: I.B. Interest Arbitration, in* Arbitration 1990: New Perspectives on Old Issues, Proceedings of the 43d Annual Meeting of NAA 179 (Gruenberg ed., BNA Books 1991); Anderson & Krause, *Interest Arbitration: The Alternative to Strike,* 56 Fordham L. Rev. 153, 155 n.16–17 (1987); Rehmus, *Report of the Committee on Public Employment Disputes Settlement, in* Arbitration 1986: Current and Expanding Roles, Proceedings of the 39th Annual Meeting of NAA 174 (Gershenfeld ed., BNA Books 1987). *See* Chapter 21, "Issues in State and Local Government Sector Arbitration," and Chapter 22, "Arbitration of Interest Disputes."

[29]Anderson & Krause, 56 Fordham L. Rev. at 169. *See also* Aaron, Najita & Stern, Public-Sector Bargaining 252–61 (BNA Books 1988); Chapter 22, "Arbitration of Interest Disputes."

[30]Boland, *Labor Disputes: The Preventive and Cure,* Arbitration in Action, at 6 (Dec. 1943).

[31]McGrady, *Industrial Peace: A Joint Enterprise,* 2 Arb. J. 339, 343 (1938). In *Steelworkers v. NLRB (Dow Chem. Co.),* 530 F.2d 266, 276, 91 LRRM 2275 (3d Cir. 1976), the court similarly stressed use of arbitration instead of "the tooth and claw of industrial warfare."

[32]Spielmans, *Labor Disputes on Rights and on Interests,* Am. Econ. Rev. 299 (June 1939).

[33]Steelworkers v. Warrior & Gulf Navigation Co., 363 U.S. 574, 578, 46 LRRM 2416 (1960).

[34]For views on use of arbitration for purposes of "face saving," see Eaton, *Labor Arbitration in the San Francisco Bay Area,* 48 LA 1381, 1389–90 (1967); Warren & Bernstein, *A Profile of Labor Arbitration,* 16 LA 970, 979 (1951).

cation for a work stoppage. Even where a real difference exists, possibilities for a peaceful solution may make resort to force uncalled for. A basic tenet of arbitration is that the arbitrator will be able to look at the issue objectively; accordingly, a reasonable decision based on the true merits of the dispute can be expected.

An agreement to arbitrate effects a complete surrender of any right of the employer to determine the controversy by unilateral action and of any right of both parties to support their contentions by a show of economic strength.[35] This surrender on occasion has been the basis of distrust of arbitration. One management argument against arbitration is that it substitutes for the experienced, responsible judgment of management the judgment of an outsider who lacks the responsibility for conducting the business. Labor, in turn, sometimes feels that giving up its freedom to strike, in reliance on the understanding of an outsider who might prove to be not so understanding, involves too great a risk.[36] The answer to such fears is that the initially uninformed outsider is soon enlightened, for both parties have adequate opportunity to present their views, and the outsider carries a decisional responsibility akin to that of a judge in a court of law.[37]

Contracts that make arbitration the final step in the grievance procedure generally prohibit strikes and lockouts over arbitrable issues.[38] Moreover, the Supreme Court has held that a no-strike obligation is implied in those issues that are subject to binding arbitration under the agreement, and that a strike over such an issue violates the agreement despite the absence of an express no-strike clause.[39]

There is a general disposition on the part of labor and management to provide, as the final grievance step, for the arbitration of contract interpre-

---

[35]Pan Am. Airways, 5 LA 590, 594–95 (Cahn, 1946).

[36]That these arguments are heartfelt and longstanding is evidenced by union and management resistance to any kind of labor relations law in the latter part of the nineteenth and early twentieth centuries. Zakson, *Railway Labor Legislation 1888 to 1930: A Legal History of Congressional Railway Labor Relations Policy*, 20 Rutgers L.J. 317, 330–32 (1989).

[37]*See* Stone, *The Legacy of Industrial Pluralism: The Tension Between Individual Employment Rights and the New Deal Collective Bargaining System*, 59 U. Chi. L. Rev. 575, 622–23 (1992) (explaining the theoretical underpinnings for the use of grievance arbitration as the judicial arm of industrial self-government).

[38]Of 1,717 contracts analyzed in one study, 1,527 contained restrictions on strikes and lockouts. Many of these specified an absolute ban, but many limited the ban to disputes subject to grievance and/or arbitration procedures; some permitted strikes after exhaustion of the grievance procedure where there was no provision for arbitration or where mutual consent was required for arbitration. *Major Collective Bargaining Agreements: Arbitration Procedures*, at 83 (U.S. Dep't of Labor Bull. No. 1425-6, 1966). A later but less detailed study revealed a 93% frequency of no-strike and no-lockout clauses. *Characteristics of Major Collective Bargaining Agreements, July 1, 1976*, at 83 (U.S. Dep't of Labor Bull. 2013, 1979). That the no-strike ban and the no-lockout ban are not always coextensive is illustrated by *General Electric Co.*, 54 LA 660, 673 (Wildebush, 1971). For a study and discussion of public strike bans and the possibility of resultant increases in grievance arbitration, see Hebdon & Stern, *Tradeoffs Among Expressions of Industrial Conflict: Public Sector Strike Bans and Grievance Arbitrations*, 51 Indus. & Lab. Rel. Rev. 204 (Jan. 1998).

[39]Teamsters Local 174 v. Lucas Flour Co., 369 U.S. 95, 49 LRRM 2717 (1962). *See* Litton Fin. Printing Div. v. NLRB, 501 U.S. 190, 205, 137 LRRM 2441 (1991) (the implicit no-strike clause survives the expiration of the agreement, but only to the extent the grievance arbitration provision survives).

tation and application disputes. A study made by the Bureau of Labor Statistics of agreements in effect on or after July 1976 indicated that almost 96 percent of the collective bargaining agreements in the nation's important industries provided for arbitration as the terminal point of the grievance machinery.[40] It is significant that during the widespread concession bargaining of the 1980s, resulting in wage reductions, wage freezes, elimination or adjustments in cost-of-living clauses, and substantial modification of many other contract provisions, there was not a single reported case of the elimination of grievance arbitration from a major contract. Indeed, there is no reported instance of any employer demanding this in negotiations.[41]

In contrast to the overwhelming acceptance of arbitration for contract interpretation and application disputes, the proportion of collective agreements with specific provision for the arbitration of disputes over the terms and conditions of employment continued to hover at about 2 percent from 1949 to 1966.[42] In some quarters, however, it is suspected that the strike is becoming outmoded even for contract negotiation disputes, and that the use of voluntary arbitration with proper safeguards may be preferable.[43] In the

---

[40]*Characteristics of Major Collective Bargaining Agreements*, at 82. A BNA study had similar results. BASIC PATTERNS IN UNION CONTRACTS 33 (BNA Books 14th ed. 1995) (survey of 400 contracts showed that about 80% had arbitration of issues involving interpretation and application of collective bargaining agreement). Earlier studies made by BNA in 1944, 1949, 1952, and 1966 showed percentages of 73, 83, 89, and 94, respectively. *Major Collective Bargaining Agreements: Arbitration Procedures*, at 5 (U.S. Dep't of Labor Bull. No. 1425-6, 1966).

[41]Stieber, *The Future of Grievance Arbitration, in* ARBITRATION 1986: CURRENT AND EXPANDING ROLES, PROCEEDINGS OF THE 39TH ANNUAL MEETING OF NAA 205 (Gershenfeld ed., BNA Books 1987).

[42]*Major Collective Bargaining Agreements: Arbitration Procedures*, at 95. The Bureau of Labor Statistics' study of agreements in effect on July 1976, cited above, did not report on use of arbitration for contract negotiation disputes. There are marked differences between the United States and Great Britain in the use of arbitration. In Great Britain, arbitration has been used less for grievances than for contract negotiation disputes. Handsaker & Handsaker, *Arbitration in Great Britain*, 1 INDUS. REL. 117, 135 (1961). For more on the extent of use of arbitration in Great Britain and some European countries, see Beaumont, *Arbitration & the Extension of Terms in Britain*, 34 ARB. J. 32 (1979); Blanpain, *Appendix E. Arbitration and Settlement of Labor Disputes in Some European Countries, in* ARBITRATION—1976, PROCEEDINGS OF THE 29TH ANNUAL MEETING OF NAA 355 (Dennis & Somers eds., BNA Books 1976); Wood, *Appendix E. Conciliation and Arbitration in Great Britain, 1974–1975, id.* at 350; Johnston, *Appendix C. Report of the Committee on Overseas Correspondents: Labor Dispute Settlement in the United Kingdom, 1972, in* ARBITRATION OF INTEREST DISPUTES, PROCEEDINGS OF THE 26TH ANNUAL MEETING OF NAA 233 (Dennis & Somers eds., BNA Books 1974); Fairweather, *American and Foreign Grievance Systems: I. A Comparison of British and American Grievance Handling, in* DEVELOPMENTS IN AMERICAN AND FOREIGN ARBITRATION, PROCEEDINGS OF THE 21ST ANNUAL MEETING OF NAA 1 (Rehmus ed., BNA Books 1968).

[43]*See* Anderson, *Lessons From Interest Arbitration in the Public Sector: The Experience of Four Jurisdictions, in* ARBITRATION—1974, PROCEEDINGS OF THE 27TH ANNUAL MEETING OF NAA 59, 69 (Dennis & Somers eds., BNA Books 1975); Loewenberg, *Lessons From Interest Arbitration in the Public Sector: What the Private Sector Can Learn From the Public Sector in Interest Arbitrations: The Pennsylvania Experience, id.* at 69, 77; Fleming, *Interest Arbitration Revisited, in* ARBITRATION OF INTEREST DISPUTES, PROCEEDINGS OF THE 26TH ANNUAL MEETING OF NAA 1, 5–7 (Dennis & Somers eds., BNA Books 1974); Howlett, *Contract Negotiation Arbitration in the Public Sector*, 42 CIN. L. REV. 47, 49, 74 (1973); Taylor, Chair, *Making Arbitration Work: A Colloquium, in* CHALLENGES TO ARBITRATION, PROCEEDINGS OF THE 13TH ANNUAL MEETING OF NAA 101, 104–07 (McKelvey ed., BNA Books 1960). In 1970, the American Federation of Labor-Congress of Industrial Organizations (AFL-CIO) announced a joint labor-

public sector, many states have enacted statutes authorizing or requiring arbitration of contract negotiation disputes remaining unresolved after mediation or other bargaining aids have failed.[44]

B. Advantages of Arbitration Over Litigation

Arbitration claims among its advantages the expertise of a specialized tribunal and the saving of time, expense, and trouble. While it is true that the courts of some jurisdictions have recognized that parties to collective bargaining agreements have legally enforceable rights thereunder, the costly, prolonged, and technical procedures of courts are not well adapted to the peculiar needs of labor-management relations. Arbitration is more satisfactory "where a speedy decision by men with a practical knowledge of the subject is desired."[45]

The Supreme Court has acknowledged that arbitration, rather than court litigation, is the superior method of resolving disputes under collective bargaining agreements:

> The labor arbitrator performs functions which are not normal to the courts; the considerations which help him fashion judgments may indeed be foreign to the competence of courts.
>
> . . .
>
> The parties expect that his judgment of a particular grievance will reflect not only what the contract says but, insofar as the collective bargaining agreement permits, such factors as the effect upon productivity of a particular result, its consequence to the morale of the shop, his judgment whether tensions will be heightened or diminished. For the parties' objective in using the arbi-

---

management effort, under the aegis of the American Arbitration Association (AAA), to explore the possibility of voluntary arbitration as a substitute for strikes in bargaining. *Labor-Management Plans for Voluntary Arbitration Study,* 75 LRR 280 (1970). A large-scale experimental program began in 1974 when the United Steelworkers entered into the Experimental Negotiating Agreement (ENA) with 10 steel companies, waiving the right to strike and agreeing to submit unresolved bargaining issues to binding arbitration. The ENA and its background are explained in *Aiken v. Abel,* 73 Lab. Cas. (CCH) ¶14,414 (D.C. Cir 1974); Fischer, *Updating Arbitration, in* ARBITRATION OF INTEREST DISPUTES, PROCEEDINGS OF THE 26TH ANNUAL MEETING OF NAA 62, 78–79 (Dennis & Somers eds., BNA Books 1974); Stoner, *Comment, id.,* at 88. *See* Stark, *The Presidential Address: Theme and Adaptations, in* TRUTH, LIE DETECTORS, AND OTHER PROBLEMS IN LABOR ARBITRATION, PROCEEDINGS OF THE 31ST ANNUAL MEETING OF NAA 1, 16 (Stern & Dennis eds., BNA Books 1979). A case using the public-sector principles of parity in a purely private context is *St. Joseph's Med. Ctr.,* 98 LA 98 (Jacobowski, 1991).

[44]See Chapter 22, section 5., "Public-Sector Interest Arbitration Legislation." A study of experience in certain states disclosed that the percentage of public-sector contracts being settled by arbitration ranged from 5% in Iowa to a high of 28% in Pennsylvania (where mediation was not a required step). Anderson, *Interest Arbitration as Strike Alternative,* 101 LRR 283 (1979). *See also* Currie & McConnell, *The Impact of Collective-Bargaining Legislation on Disputes in the U.S. Public Sector: No Legislation May Be the Worst Legislation,* 37 J.L. & ECON. 519 (Oct. 1994).

[45]Webster v. Van Allen, 216 N.Y.S. 552, 554 (1926). For detailed explanations of labor arbitration's advantages over litigation, see Edwards, *Advantages of Arbitration Over Litigation: Reflections of a Judge, in* ARBITRATION 1982: CONDUCT OF THE HEARING, PROCEEDINGS OF THE 35TH ANNUAL MEETING OF NAA 16 (Stern & Dennis eds., BNA Books 1983); Coulson, *Certification and Training of Labor Arbitrators: Should Arbitrators Be Certified? Dead Horse Rides Again, in* ARBITRATION—1977, PROCEEDINGS OF THE 30TH ANNUAL MEETING OF NAA 173, 181–82 (Dennis & Somers eds., BNA Books 1978). *See also* Berger, *Realizing the Potential of Arbitration in Federal Agency Dispute Resolution,* 46 ARB. J. 35 (1991).

tration process is primarily to further their common goal of uninterrupted production under the agreement, to make the agreement serve their specialized needs. The ablest judge cannot be expected to bring the same experience and competence to bear upon the determination of a grievance, because he cannot be similarly informed.[46]

Parties to an industrial dispute must "live with" the judgment or award rendered by the adjudicator. Courts of general jurisdiction are not often versed in labor relations problems. This recognized, some countries have established labor courts as a part of the judicial system. Scholars have noted that European labor courts serve different and broader purposes than do American arbitration tribunals, and they have advised that labor courts do not offer a ready alternative to grievance arbitration in America.[47] However, one of the

---

[46]Steelworkers v. Warrier & Gulf Navigation Co., 363 U.S. 574, 581–82, 46 LRRM 2416. Not everyone agrees that arbitration is the superior process for grievances. In 1964, U.S. Court of Appeals Judge Paul R. Hays (a former arbitrator) launched a massive assault on the institution of labor arbitration. HAYS, LABOR ARBITRATION: A DISSENTING VIEW (Yale Univ. Press 1966). For responses to the critics of arbitration, see Luskin, *The Presidential Address: Arbitration and Its Critics, in* DEVELOPMENTS IN AMERICAN AND FOREIGN ARBITRATION, PROCEEDINGS OF THE 21ST ANNUAL MEETING OF NAA 125 (Rehmus ed., BNA Books 1968); Smith, *The Presidential Address, in* PROBLEMS OF PROOF IN ARBITRATION, PROCEEDINGS OF THE 19TH ANNUAL MEETING OF NAA 74 (Jones ed., BNA Books 1967); Straus, *Labor Arbitration and Its Critics*, 20 ARB. J. 197 (1965). An overwhelming majority of union and management officials contacted in one survey prefer the arbitration process to the available alternatives as a method of ultimate resolution of grievance disputes. Jones & Smith, *Management and Labor Appraisals and Criticisms of the Arbitration Process: A Report With Comments*, 62 MICH. L. REV. 1115, 1116–17 (1964). For a survey of opinions concerning arbitration's faults, see Zinkel & Krahmal, *Creeping Legalism in Grievance Arbitration: Fact or Fiction?*, 16 OHIO ST. J. ON DISP. RESOL. 243, 244 n.4 (2001); Graham, Heshizer & Johnson, *Grievance Arbitration: Labor Officials' Attitudes*, 33 ARB. J. 21 (1978) (78% of union officials responding in this survey consider arbitration "the best method of resolving unsettled grievances"); Davey, *What's Right and What's Wrong With Grievance Arbitration: The Practitioners Air Their Views*, 28 ARB. J. 209 (1973). *See also* Abrams, *The Integrity of the Arbitral Process*, 76 MICH. L. REV. 231 (1977). Of course arbitration does not work perfectly. No human mechanism of its scope and variety of uses, confronted with such demands and challenges as arbitration faces, can function without problems. But no system has yet been offered that is as mutually acceptable as a means of labor-management grievance settlement. Moreover, neither the courts nor any governmental administrative tribunal offers any realistic possibility of equaling private labor-management arbitration for the purposes it has served since World War II. The use of arbitration continued to increase from year to year until about the mid-1980s. From 1986 through 2002, the number of panels requested declined from 31,515 in 1986 to 17,282 in 2002, a 45.2% decrease. The total number of panels issued during the 1986–2002 period declined about 42.6%, from 32,935 in 1986 to 18,891 in 2002. During the same period, the number of arbitrator appointments ranged from 10,638 in 1986 to 8,335 in 2002, with a high of 13,037 in 1992. *See* FEDERAL MEDIATION AND CONCILIATION SERVICE (FMCS), 46TH ANN. REP., FISCAL YEAR 1993; FMCS 55TH ANN. REP., FISCAL YEAR 2002.

[47]Aaron, Labor Courts: Western European Models and Their Significance for the United States, 16 UCLA L. REV. 847, 876 (1969); Fleming, The Presidential Address: The Labor Court Idea, in THE ARBITRATOR, THE NLRB, AND THE COURTS, PROCEEDINGS OF THE 20TH ANNUAL MEETING OF NAA 229, 246 (Jones ed., BNA Books 1967). For other discussions of labor courts, see Vranken, Specialisation and Labour Courts: A Comparative Analysis, 9 COMP. LAB. L.J. 497 (1988); Handsaker, Labor Courts in Germany, 8 ARB. J. (N.S.) 131 (1953); Lenhoff, Some Basic Features of American and European Labor Law: A Comparison, 26 NOTRE DAME LAW. 389 (1951). In Canada, there have been two major legislative reforms of note. Great controversy has surrounded the abolition of the British Columbia Labour Code, a 1973 statute greatly influenced in the drafting by Professor Paul Weiler, who subsequently administered its provisions as Chairman of the British Columbia Labour Relations Board. The Industrial Relations Reform Act abolishes the old Board and makes sweeping changes in the 1973 Code, which was generally seen as legislation highly favorable to collective bargaining.

similarities between the two systems should be noted: like labor courts, arbitrators are presumed to be familiar with the needs and techniques of industrial relations, so parties generally will be able to "live with" their awards.

In predicting expanded use of arbitration beyond industry to cover a broad range of conflicts in our society, the critical role of arbitration was explained in another light:

> The courts cannot handle all of the load now, and even if they could handle all of it well, the judicial process is too slow and too costly. Courts are better at setting principles and establishing procedures in test cases. Private mechanisms need to carry the bulk of the caseload if the whole dispute-settling process is not to break down with serious consequences. This is one of the great lessons to be derived from the handling of grievances in industrial relations.[48]

Under the new statute, both the Labour Board and the Ministry of Labour's mediation services are abolished and replaced by an Industrial Relations Council, which has both adjudicative and mediative divisions. Plainly conservative in outlook, the new Industrial Relations Reform Act adds to the objective of effective industrial relations the need to have regard for the rights of individuals and the value of "a competitive market economy." It also authorizes the Minister of Labour to ban a strike or lockout for a 40-day "cooling off" period or to direct the Council to designate certain services as essential, thereby eliminating the rights of strike and lockout. Arbitrators appointed to boards of interest arbitration in the public sector are statutorily required to recognize the government's ability to pay as "the paramount factor," with the right reserved to the Legislature to disallow the result in any interest arbitration.

Other controversial provisions include restrictions on picketing and the imposition of notice and vote requirements as preconditions to any lawful strike. The replacement of the old statutory definition of "common employer" with a narrower test of "some control and direction" is expected to facilitate "double breasting" by employers who seek to separate into unionized and nonunionized operations. The Industrial Relation Reform Act also narrows the successor rights protections of unions. With the exception of the powers of the Cabinet and Legislature to intervene in essential service disputes and repudiate arbitration awards, which powers may yet be invoked, the Industrial Relations Reform Act was proclaimed in force on July 27, 1987. For an earlier review of the Labour Board, see Weiler, *Avoiding the Arbitrator: Some New Alternatives to the Conventional Grievance Procedure: I. The Role of the Labour Board as an Alternative to Arbitration, in* ARBITRATION—1977, PROCEEDINGS OF THE 30TH ANNUAL MEETING OF NAA 72 (Dennis & Somers eds., BNA Books 1978). For more on dispute resolution in Canada, see LYON, REINER & TEPLE, THE LABOR RELATIONS LAW OF CANADA (BNA Books 1977); Woods, *The Presidential Address: Shadows Over Arbitration, id.* at 1; Carrothers, *The Cuckoo's Egg in the Mare's Nest—Arbitration of Interest Disputes in Public-Service Collective Bargaining: Problems of Principle, Policy, and Process, id.* at 15. For studies sponsored by the National Academy of Arbitrators (NAA) surveying different types of tribunals and systems utilized by several countries for interest disputes and for grievance disputes, see *Comparative Overview of the Role of Third Party Intervention in Resolving Interests Disputes*, 10 COMP. LAB. L.J. 271 (1989); *The Role of Neutrals in the Resolution of Shop Floor Disputes*, 9 COMP. LAB. L.J. 1 (1987). For a summary of the latter study and comments thereon, see Loewenberg, *International Comparison of the Role of Neutrals in Resolving Shop Floor Disputes: Lessons for Arbitrators, in* ARBITRATION 1988: EMERGING ISSUES FOR THE 1990s, PROCEEDINGS OF THE 41ST ANNUAL MEETING OF NAA 247 (Gruenberg ed., BNA Books 1989); Stieber, *Comment, id.* at 249.

[48]Kerr, *More Peace—More Conflict, in* ARBITRATION—1975, PROCEEDINGS OF THE 28TH ANNUAL MEETING OF NAA 8, 14 (Dennis & Somers eds., BNA Books 1976). Chief Justice William H. Rehnquist of the U.S. Supreme Court has stated: "With the increasing load on courts at all levels in state and federal judicial systems . . . the prospects of increased use of arbitration as a means of settlement of disputes must never have been better." Rehnquist, *A Jurist's View of Arbitration*, 32 ARB. J. 1, 2 (1977). For an excellent overview combined with pinpointing of the potential benefits and limitations of alternative dispute resolution (ADR) mechanisms, quickly bringing the subject of ADR into sharp focus, see Edwards, *Alternative Dispute Resolution: Panacea or Anathema?*, 99 HARV. L. REV. 668 (1986).

The parties can make arbitration, as compared with litigation, relatively quick and inexpensive. Sometimes it takes only a few days from the appointment of the arbitrator until the issuance of the award. For example, one company obtained an arbitrator's reasoned and documented decision on a bargaining-unit accretion question (decided by National Labor Relations Act (NLRA)[49] standards and decisions as the arbitrator was directed) within 11 days after the company requested arbitration with the incumbent union by a telegram declaring that the "Company is incurring inordinate expense and potential disruption of its business as a result of NLRB scheduling of hearings re representation claim of another union."[50] However, in the bulk of the cases, several weeks or even several months are required. The issues taken to arbitration have become increasingly complex and the time required for arbitration has naturally tended to increase as a result of this complexity of issues. Also, it frequently happens that the arbitrator chosen by the parties cannot be quickly available because of existing commitments to other parties. Nor are the parties themselves always quickly available for the arbitration hearing. Nonetheless, arbitration continues to be relatively speedy as compared to litigation.[51]

Because the parties arbitrate voluntarily, prompt compliance with the award is obtained in most cases. Only infrequently is court action required for the enforcement or vacation of awards.[52] Of course, there are some drawbacks to pursuing the arbitration process rather than judicial litigation. Judicial discovery rights may be more expansive, and traditional remedies, such as attorneys' fees, punitive damages, and supervised equity relief may not be available in arbitration. Furthermore, arbitration awards, as private settlements, unlike judicial decisions, lack precedential value for the jurisprudential development of the law of collective bargaining as would judicial judgments. Also, faulty arbitral decisions, being "final and binding" on the parties, may not be subject to review and correction as would trial judge errors.

---

[49]29 U.S.C. §§151–169.

[50]Hartford Jai-Alai, 71 LA 1155, 1155 (Rubenstein, 1978). For considerations relating to finality of the decision in such situations, see Chapter 10, Section 3.A.v., "The NLRA, the Arbitrator, and the NLRB."

[51]Stieber, Block & Nichol, *New Perspectives on Old Problems: Part I. Elapsed Time in Grievance Arbitration, in* Arbitration 1990: New Perspectives on Old Issues, Proceedings of the 43d Annual Meeting of NAA 128 (Gruenberg ed., BNA Books 1991). For statistics and discussions of the time required for grievance processing and/or arbitration, see FMCS 50th Ann. Rep., Fiscal Year 1997 (reporting that for cases administered by the FMCS, the average number of days required from the time a grievance was filed until an arbitrator's award was rendered was 317.7 in 1993, 342.88 in 1994, 334.59 in 1995, 318.58 in 1996, and 311.50 in 1997. The reports show that during the period the major portion of the time was consumed in the prehearing phase, ranging from a low of 244.50 days in 1997 to a high of 266.01 days in 1994. The annual reports also show that the time between the date of the hearing and the date award was rendered by the arbitrator was 66.28 in 1993, 76.87 in 1994, 72.71 in 1995, 73.74 in 1996, and 67.00 in 1997. FMCS posts Annual Reports as they become available on its web site, at <http://www.fmcs.gov>.

[52]For statistics, see Chapter 2, "Legal Status of Arbitration in the Private Sector."

C. Arbitration of Public Employee Disputes [LA CDI 100.01 et seq.]

Since 1960, the tremendous growth of employee and collective bargaining in the public sector has been accompanied by the rapidly expanding use of arbitration for public-employee disputes. This development has been particularly important because federal and state employees generally continue to be restricted by the traditional prohibition against strikes by public employees.[53] Neutral dispute settlement machinery is essential in the public sector if organizational and bargaining rights are to have any real substance.[54]

Studies of grievance arbitration indicate that most issues in public-sector arbitration do not differ from private-sector issues and that arbitrators tend to apply the same standards in both areas.[55] This same conclusion can be drawn from the observation that principles and precedents from private-sector arbitration are often being considered and utilized in public-sector

---

[53]Often, prohibitions of strikes are coupled with compulsory arbitration in imitation of the bargain contained in most voluntary private-sector agreements. *See* Chapter 20, "Legal Status of Arbitration in the Federal Sector," and Chapter 21, "State and Local Government Issues in Sector Arbitration." *See also* Hodges, *The* Steelworker Trilogy *in the Private Sector*, 66 CHI.-KENT L. REV. 631, 633 & n.11 (1990) (citing illustrative statutes).

[54]The Administrative Dispute Resolution Act of 1990, Pub. L. No. 101-552, 104 Stat. 2436 (codified as amended in scattered sections of the U.S. Code), contains amendments to the LMRA and the Administrative Procedure Act, 5 U.S.C. §551 et seq., relative to the use of alternative means of dispute resolution. On the special need for neutral dispute machinery, see Zack, *Why Public Employees Strike*, 23 ARB. J. 69 (1968); *Triborough Bridge & Tunnel Auth.*, 49 LA 1212, 1224–28 (Wolf, Feinberg, & Stockman, 1968).

[55]"That the skills used by arbitrators were transferable from the private to the public sector was never doubted by arbitrators or the practitioners. The history of arbitration has shown a great ability of arbitration and arbitrators to accommodate to the differing needs and desires of the parties for the use of neutrals in dispute settlement." Anderson, *The Presidential Address: Labor Arbitration Today, in* ARBITRATION 1988: EMERGING ISSUES FOR THE 1990S, PROCEEDINGS OF THE 41ST ANNUAL MEETING OF NAA 1, 3 (Gruenberg ed., BNA Books 1989); Krislov & Peters, *Grievance Arbitration in State and Local Government: A Survey*, 25 ARB. J. 196, 205 (1970) ("The parties in state and local government have leaned heavily upon private industry's arbitration experience. A formidable case could be made that the parties have virtually adopted the grievance arbitration mechanism from private industry."). *See also* Pegnetter & Hayford, *State Employee Grievances and Due Process: An Analysis of Contract Arbitration and Civil Service Review Systems*, 29 S.C. L. REV. 305, 313 (1978); DeWolf, *The Enforcement of the Labor Arbitration Agreement in the Public Sector—The New York Experience*, 39 ARB. L. REV. 393, 398 (1975) ("the law applicable to private sector labor arbitration is for the most part applicable to the public sector"); Krinsky, *Municipal Grievance Arbitration in Wisconsin*, 28 ARB. J. 50, 61 (1973) ("Wisconsin municipal grievance arbitration experience shows great similarities to private sector arbitration experience both procedurally and in terms of the issues arbitrated"); Howlett, *Arbitration in the Public Sector, in* SOUTHWEST LEGAL FOUNDATION 15TH ANNUAL INSTITUTE ON LABOR LAW 231, 268–69 (1969).

cases.[56] Of course, public-sector arbitration in turn no doubt will influence future developments in the private sector.[57]

D. Other Important Roles of Arbitration

It has been noted that arbitration is a substitute for work stoppages and for litigation. But it is much more than a substitute:

> To consider . . . arbitration as a substitute for court litigation or as the consideration for a no-strike pledge is to take a foreshortened view of it. In a sense it is a substitute for both—but in the sense in which a transport airplane is a substitute for a stagecoach. The arbitration is an integral part of the system of self-government. And the system is designed to aid management in its quest for efficiency, to assist union leadership in its participation in the enterprise, and to secure justice for the employees. It is a means of making collective bargaining work and thus preserving private enterprise in a free government.[58]

---

[56]*See, e.g.,* City of Chi., 97 LA 20 (Goldstein, 1990); Roseville Cmty. Sch., 96 LA 1144 (Borland, 1990); Carbon County, Pa., 73 LA 1305, 1307 (Handsaker, 1980); Ogden Air Logistics Ctr., Utah, 73 LA 1100, 1104 (Hays, 1979); San Antonio Air Logistic Ctr., Tex., 73 LA 1074, 1083 (Caraway, 1979); State of Alaska, 73 LA 990, 991–92 (Hauck, 1979); Lake Orion Cmty. Sch., 73 LA 707, 709–11 (Roumell, Jr., 1979); Commonwealth of Pa., 73 LA 556, 561 (Gerhart, 1979); Individual Grievant, 73 LA 464, 475 (Ellmann, 1979); San Antonio Air Logistics Ctr., Tex., 73 LA 455, 463 (LeBaron, 1979); Capital Dist. Transp. Auth., 72 LA 1313, 1316, 1318 (Cutler, 1979); Le Mars Cmty. Sch. Dist., 72 LA 1135, 1141 (Smith, 1979); Illinois Dep'ts of Pers. & Corr., 72 LA 941, 946–47 (Rezler, 1979); Superior Sch. Dist., 72 LA 719, 723 (Pieroni, 1979); County of Genesee, 72 LA 564, 566–67 (Kanner, 1979); Muskegon County Bd. of Comm'rs, 71 LA 942, 947–48 (Allen, Jr., 1978); Bethel Sch. Dist. No. 403, 71 LA 314, 319–20 (Beck, 1978); Fitas, Mahoning County Eng'r, 70 LA 895, 897–98 (Cohen, 1978); Veterans Admin. Reg'l Office, 70 LA 514, 517 (Denson, 1978). For a scholarly perspective, see former Federal Labor Relations Authority Chair J. McKee, *Federal Sector Arbitration, in* ARBITRATION 1991: THE CHANGING FACE OF ARBITRATION IN THEORY AND PRACTICE, PROCEEDINGS OF THE 44TH ANNUAL MEETING OF NAA 187 (Gruenberg ed., BNA Books 1992).

[57]*See, e.g.,* Bekins Moving & Storage Co., 98 LA 1087 (Madden, 1992); Pepsi-Cola Bottling Co., 97 LA 1011 (DiLauro, 1991); Allen Dairy Prods. Co., 97 LA 988 (Hoh, 1991). Many arbitration decisions from the public sector (state and federal) are cited throughout this book. Arbitration issues pertinent to the federal, state, and local government sectors are dealt with extensively in Chapter 20, "Legal Status of Arbitration in the Federal Sector," and Chapter 21, "Issues in State and Local Government Sector Arbitration." Public-sector interest arbitration is discussed in Chapter 22, "Arbitration of Interest Disputes."

[58]Shulman, *Reason, Contract, and Law in Labor Relations,* 68 HARV. L. REV. 999, 1024 (1955), *reprinted in* MANAGEMENT RIGHTS AND THE ARBITRATION PROCESS, PROCEEDINGS OF THE 9TH ANNUAL MEETING OF NAA 169, 198 (McKelvey ed., BNA Books 1956). One observer believes that this self-government system is threatened by encroachment of laws dealing with employment relations (such as the Equal Pay Act, 29 U.S.C. §206, Title VII of the Civil Rights Act of 1964, 42 U.S.C. §2000e et seq., the Occupational Safety and Health Act (OSHA), 29 U.S.C. §651 et seq., and the Employee Retirement Income Security Act (ERISA), 29 U.S.C. §1001 et seq.), with a future fading of the "Golden Age" of arbitration as the parties' self-governance court of last resort. Feller, *The Coming End of Arbitration's Golden Age, in* ARBITRATION—1976, PROCEEDINGS OF THE 29TH ANNUAL MEETING OF NAA 97 (Dennis & Somers eds., BNA Books 1976). But other observers have responded with expressions of optimism for the future of labor arbitration. *See* Jaffe, *The Arbitration of Statutory Disputes: Procedural and Substantive Considerations, in* ARBITRATION 1992: IMPROVING ARBITRAL AND ADVOCACY SKILLS, PROCEEDINGS OF THE 45TH ANNUAL MEETING OF NAA 110 (Gruenberg ed., BNA Books 1993); Heinsz, *Judicial Review of Labor Arbitration Awards: The* Enterprise Wheel *Goes Around and Around,* 52 MO. L. REV. 243, 298 (1987); Stark, *The Presidential Address: Theme and Adaptations, in* TRUTH, LIE DETECTORS, AND OTHER PROBLEMS IN LABOR ARBITRATION, PROCEEDINGS OF THE 31ST ANNUAL MEETING OF NAA 1, 29 (Stern & Dennis eds., BNA Books 1979) (the "future is bright and challenging"); Smith, *The Search for Truth: I. The Search for Truth— The Whole Truth, id.* at 40, 48; Eisenberg, *New Dimensions in Public-Sector Grievance Arbitration: II. Some Recent Developments in Public-Sector Grievance Arbitration: A View*

George W. Taylor observed that, "In a very real sense, the parties who establish their own labor arbitration machinery create a judicial procedure where none has existed."[59] In this connection, not all jurisdictions hold that collective bargaining agreements give rights that are enforceable in the courts. Moreover, the NLRB lacks jurisdiction over contract-interpretation disputes that do not involve unfair labor practice aspects, and it possibly may refuse to exercise jurisdiction over interpretation disputes that do involve unfair labor practice allegations if the dispute is covered by an arbitration clause.[60]

Then, too, insofar as contract-negotiation disputes are concerned, arbitration provides essentially the only available tribunal for the final and binding resolution of such disputes after negotiations and mediation have failed to produce a settlement. Thus, it is obvious that even aside from any consideration of work stoppages and their avoidance, cases are taken to arbitration simply to obtain an answer to the dispute.

Another role of arbitration was recognized by the Supreme Court in emphasizing that the "processing of even frivolous claims may have therapeutic values. . . ."[61] This role was described in a manner that portrays realistically the spirit of the arbitration hearing:

> Arbitration . . . is a school, an arena, a theater. Everyone both participates and observes. The whole company of actors—arbitrator, union and employer officials, the . . . [grievant], and the witnesses (mostly employees)—sits at one table. Argument, assertion, testimony, charge and countercharge, even angry abuse—sometimes spontaneous, sometimes "for the record"—flow freely in

---

From New York, id. at 240, 263–64; St. Antoine, *Judicial Review of Labor Arbitration Awards: A Second Look at* Enterprise Wheel *and Its Progeny, in* ARBITRATION—1977, PROCEEDINGS OF THE 30TH ANNUAL MEETING OF NAA 29, 36 (Dennis & Somers eds., BNA Books 1978) ("we are actually entering a new 'golden age' for the arbitration process"); Edwards, *Labor Arbitration at the Crossroads: The "Common Law of the Shop" v. External Law*, 32 ARB. J. 65, 85–88 (1977). Whichever group is ultimately right, it is true that situations where the arbitrator is asked to, or simply does, refer to external law are increasing and, especially in the public sector, have generated considerable controversy. Hodges, *The* Steelworkers Trilogy *in the Public Sector*, 66 CHI.-KENT L. REV. 631, 674-75 & nn.234–39 (1990). *See also* Stone, *The Legacy of Industrial Pluralism: The Tension Between Individual Employment Rights and the New Deal Collective Bargaining System*, 59 U. CHI. L. REV. 575, 595 & nn.72–73 (1992). While the role of the courts and governmental administrative tribunals will always be critically important in our increasingly complex society, so will that of arbitration. The courts and administrative tribunals such as the NLRB and the Equal Employment Opportunity Commission (EEOC) already have overburdening caseloads and must not be further strained unnecessarily by the restricted and *mass* use of such forums for resolution of grievances of the type for which the contractual grievance and arbitration procedures have been designed. Furthermore, these facts remain even though it is accepted that some limited types of situations will arise (such as the arbitrator exceeding his or her jurisdiction) and some limited types of issues will exist (such as certain statutory issues) for which the contractual grievance and arbitration procedures need not be the final word and for which resort to the administrative tribunals or courts will be permitted.

[59]*Preface, in* FREIDIN, LABOR ARBITRATION AND THE COURTS (1952).

[60]For discussion of the Board's policy and practice in regard to deferring to arbitration, see Chapter 10, section 3.A.v.b., "NLRB Policy on Deferral to Arbitration." The Supreme Court emphasized that it is the arbitrator and not the NLRB that has the principal responsibility and authority to interpret the agreement. Litton Fin. Printing Div. v. NLRB, 501 U.S. 190, 205, 137 LRRM 2441 (1991).

[61]Steelworkers v. American Mfg. Co., 363 U.S. 564, 568, 46 LRRM 2414 (1960). The Supreme Court again recognized the "therapy" of arbitration in *Alexander v. Gardner-Denver Co.*, 415 U.S. 36, 50 n.13, 7 FEP Cases 81 (1974).

quick, continuous intercourse. The arbitrator may let the discussion take its head for a moment, then rein it in; an occasional question, a request for clarification. Because the process is relatively free, it may assume many forms, some quiet and orderly, some volatile and discordant. The form is in fact a function of the general labor relations—of the maturity, the degree of mutual understanding and respect, the intelligence, of the opposing officials. . . .

Arbitration takes its stand in the very current of industrial life. The scene, the dramatis personae, the vocabulary, being familiar, raise no barriers to comprehension. The worker sees his case analyzed by his leaders, among whom I include employer as well as union officials. They reveal the clashing propositions at the heart of the grievance. The arbitrator relates his answer to basic industrial premises. . . . [62]

Finally, it may be noted that a union might arbitrate a dispute because the employees or subordinate union officers directly involved simply could not be convinced that they were wrong; the company might do likewise in regard to its own subordinate officials. In either instance, higher officials may find it preferable to let an arbitrator make it clear to such persons that they were wrong.[63] However, while this may be justified in isolated instances, caution must be exercised against overburdening the arbitration machinery. A central theme at labor-management seminars conducted in 1979 by the President's Commission on Coal was that the flood of coal industry wildcat strikes in the 1970s resulted from lost employee confidence in the grievance procedure and arbitration, caused by too little reliance on the grievance procedure and too much reliance on arbitration.[64]

5. ARBITRATION AND THE NATIONAL WAR LABOR BOARD

The legitimacy of labor arbitration and the impetus for its use resulted from the policies of the National War Labor Board during World War II. The National War Labor Board was created by Executive Order in 1942 and was given statutory authority by the War Labor Disputes Act in 1943.[65] Most of the 20,000 labor dispute cases determined by the National War Labor Board during the war emergency were disputes over the terms of collective bargaining agreements. Of special importance was the National War Labor

---

[62]Jaffe, *Labor Arbitration and the Individual Worker, in* ANNALS OF THE AMERICAN ACADEMY OF POLITICAL AND SOCIAL SCIENCE 34, 40–41 (May 1953).

[63]*See* Ahner, *Arbitration: A Management Viewpoint, in* THE ARBITRATOR AND THE PARTIES, PROCEEDINGS OF THE 11TH ANNUAL MEETING OF NAA 76, 80 (McKelvey ed., BNA Books 1958); Killingsworth, *Arbitration: Its Uses in Industrial Relations*, 21 LA 859, 865 (1953).

[64]*See* THE PRESIDENT'S COMMISSION ON COAL, LABOR-MANAGEMENT SEMINAR III, WILDCAT STRIKES (Apr. 27, 1979), at 6, 26–30 (Gov't Printing Office 1979, No. 0-302-758); THE PRESIDENT'S COMMISSION ON COAL, LABOR-MANAGEMENT SEMINAR IV, GRIEVANCE AND ARBITRATION PROCEDURES (June 20, 1979), at 39 (Gov't Printing Office 1979, No. 0-302-759); City of Taylor, Mich., 85 LA 647, 648 (Keefe, 1985). Grievance and arbitration machinery in the coal industry subsequently has been revamped to correct the problem. Sharpe, *A Study of Coal Arbitration Under the National Bituminous Coal Wage Agreement Between 1975 and 1990*, 93 W. VA. L. REV. 498 (1991). Regarding labor arbitration in general, it was pointed out that there "appears to be an increasing tendency by both parties to the grievance process to pass the buck to the arbitrator." Zack, *Suggested New Approaches to Grievance Arbitration, in* ARBITRATION—1977, PROCEEDINGS OF THE 30TH ANNUAL MEETING OF NAA 105, 107 (Dennis & Somers eds., BNA Books 1978). *See also* Seward, *Labor Arbitration: The Early Years in Retrospect: The Twenty-Five Year Milestone, in* LABOR ARBITRATION AT THE QUARTER-CENTURY MARK, PROCEEDINGS OF THE 25TH ANNUAL MEETING OF NAA 61, 63–64 (Dennis & Somers eds., BNA Books 1973).

[65]57 Stat. 163 (1943).

Board's policy of requiring the use of clauses providing for arbitration of future disputes over the interpretation or application of the agreement. This policy laid the foundation for the popular practice today of terminating the contract grievance procedure with the final step of arbitration.[66]

6. RECOMMENDATIONS OF THE PRESIDENT'S NATIONAL LABOR-MANAGEMENT CONFERENCE OF 1945

The President's National Labor-Management Conference of 1945 was called for the purpose of laying the groundwork for industrial peace by studying the major causes of industrial strife and possibilities for their elimination. It was attended by delegates representing the AFL, the U.S. Chamber of Commerce, the CIO, the National Association of Manufacturers, the United Mine Workers of America, and the Railway Brotherhoods.

In regard to the setting of new contract terms, the Conference recommended that parties first undertake good-faith collective bargaining and thereafter, if necessary, conciliation and consideration of voluntary arbitration. It recommended, however, that, before voluntary arbitration is accepted, the parties should agree on the precise issues to be decided, the terms of the submission, and principles or factors by which the arbitrator is to be governed.[67]

As to the settlement of grievances or disputes involving the interpretation or application of the agreement, the Conference recommended:

4. The parties should provide by mutual agreement for the final determination of any unsettled grievances or disputes involving the interpretation or application of the agreement by an impartial chairman, umpire, arbitrator, or board. In this connection the agreement should provide:

(a) A definite and mutually agreed-upon procedure of selecting the impartial chairman, umpire, arbitrator, or board;

(b) That the impartial chairman, umpire, arbitrator, or board should have no power to add to, subtract from, change, or modify any provision of the agreement, but should be authorized only to interpret the existing provisions of the agreement and apply them to the specific facts of the grievance or dispute;

(c) That reference of a grievance or dispute to an impartial chairman, umpire, arbitrator, or board should be reserved as the final step in the procedure and should not be resorted to unless the settlement procedures of the earlier steps have been exhausted;

(d) That the decision of the impartial chairman, umpire, arbitrator, or board should be accepted by both parties as final and binding;

(e) That the cost of such impartial chairman, umpire, arbitrator, or board should be shared equally by both parties.

5. Any question not involving the application or interpretation of the agreement as then existing but which may properly be raised pursuant to agreement provisions should be subject to negotiation, conciliation, or such other means of settlement as the parties may provide.[68]

---

[66]*See* Freidein & Ulman, *Arbitration and the War Labor Board*, 58 HARV. L. REV. 309 (1945). Another informative discussion of the National War Labor Board came much later in *Symposium: An Oral History of the National War Labor Board and Critical Issues in the Development of Modern Grievance Arbitration*, 39 CASE W. RES. L. REV. 505 (1989), featuring articles by Sharpe, Day, Aaron, Gill, and Garrett.

[67]*The President's National Labor-Management Conference, Nov. 5–30, 1945*, at 42–43 (U.S. Dep't of Labor, Div. of Labor Standards, Bull. No. 77, 1946).

[68]*Id.* at 46–47.

7. TYPES OF ARBITRATION

A. Compulsory Arbitration [LA CDI 94.08]

Although there are obvious and fundamental differences between voluntary and compulsory arbitration, many of the considerations involved in the use of compulsory arbitration are helpful in an analysis of voluntary arbitration. These considerations help define the usefulness but also the pitfalls that may be faced in the use of arbitration generally.

"Compulsory arbitration" has been defined by the Department of Labor to mean a "process of settlement of employer-labor disputes by a government agency (or other means provided by government) which has power to investigate and make an award which *must* be accepted by all parties concerned."[69] Stated otherwise, compulsory arbitration "is that required by law."[70]

Thus, even where neither party wishes to arbitrate, both may be required to do so under compulsory arbitration. At times there has been agitation for legislation to subject all types of labor-management disputes to compulsory arbitration where settlement by any but a peaceful procedure would result in severe loss or hardship to third persons or the general public. While there is considerable support for use of compulsory arbitration in such situations, its use otherwise is generally opposed in the private sector by labor and management alike.[71]

The principal argument in favor of compulsory arbitration is that unions and industries have grown so large and the economy has become so intermeshed that one strike can paralyze a large part of the nation. This consideration is particularly urgent where the strike interferes with national defense. Moreover, local critical disputes, such as those in transportation and public utility enterprises, can severely burden the general public. Proponents of compulsory arbitration contend that in such cases governmental action is warranted to protect the general welfare; that, when collective bargaining, mediation, and all other steps have failed, the government should step in as a last resort to prevent ruinous strikes, and, as a quid pro quo, provide for the settlement of the issues on their merits.[72]

---

[69]*Should the Federal Government Require Arbitration of Labor Disputes in All Basic American Industries?*, 26 CONG. DIG. 193, 195 (1947).

[70]C.C.H. DICTIONARY OF LABOR TERMS. For discussions of the development of compulsory arbitration in the United States and abroad, see NORTHRUP, COMPULSORY ARBITRATION AND GOVERNMENT INTERVENTION IN LABOR DISPUTES 9–50 (Labor Policy Ass'n 1966); Williams, *The Compulsory Settlement of Contract Negotiation Labor Disputes*, 27 TEX. L. REV. 587 (1949).

[71]Opposition was voiced to substituting compulsory arbitration for the strike in private-sector collective bargaining at the AAA's 1977 "Arbitration Day" in New York. 95 LRR 14 (1977). The general opposition also is reflected in, for example, Farmer, *Compulsory Arbitration—A Management Lawyer's View*, 51 VA. L. REV. 396 (1965); Feller, *Compulsory Arbitration—A Union Lawyer's View*, 51 VA. L. REV. 410 (1965); *Report of American Bar Association Sub-Committee on Labor Arbitration Law*, 35 LA 949, 949–51 (1960). *See also* Warren & Bernstein, *A Profile of Labor Arbitration*, 16 LA 970, 972–73 (1951).

[72]*Should the Federal Government Require Arbitration of Labor Disputes in All Basic American Industries?*, 26 CONG. DIG. at 208. *See also* Richberg, *Industrial Disputes and the Public Interest*—I, Inst. of Indus. Rel., U. Cal. 59, 60 (1947); Huebner, *Compulsory Arbitration of Labor Disputes*, 30 AM J. JUD. SOC'Y 123 (1946).

It also has been urged that compulsory arbitration is necessary in a relationship where workers are not free to engage in collective bargaining in its fullest sense, namely, in the area of public employment.[73] In fact, a majority of states have legislated compulsory arbitration of contract negotiation disputes for specified classes of public employees.[74] In federal employment, the Federal Service Impasses Panel can impose settlement terms for contract negotiation disputes under the Civil Service Reform Act of 1978,[75] and compulsory arbitration of such disputes is a possibility in the postal service under the Postal Reorganization Act of 1970.[76]

The arguments against compulsory arbitration as revealed in literature on the subject, are, broadly stated, that (1) it is incompatible with free collective bargaining, (2) it will not produce satisfactory solutions to disputes, (3) it may involve great enforcement problems, and (4) it will have damaging effects on the economic structure.[77] These arguments are set forth in greater detail below:

1. Compulsory arbitration is the antithesis of free collective bargaining. Each party will be reluctant to offer compromises in bargaining for fear that they may prejudice its position in arbitration. Elimination of the strike from collective bargaining will eliminate the strongest incentive the parties now have to reach agreement. One or both of the parties may make only a pretense at bargaining in the belief that more desirable terms may be obtained through the arbitration that is assured if bargaining fails. Because compulsory arbitration will be used to resolve unknown future disputes, both sides may list many demands and drop few in bargaining, believing that little will be lost if some of the "chaff" is denied by an arbitrator (who the party may believe would then be more inclined to favor that party on major issues in order to appear fair).

2. Compulsory arbitration is a dictatorial and imitative process rather than a democratic and creative one. The parties may not be allowed

---

[73]Schwartz, *Is Compulsory Arbitration Necessary?*, 15 ARB. J. 189, 200 (1960) ("The most significant arguments against compulsory arbitration are inapplicable in the area of public employment." *Id*. at 194).

[74]See Chapter 22, section 5., "Public-Sector Interest Arbitration Legislation," and section 6., "Constitutionality of Binding Interest Arbitration," where numerous articles dealing with compulsory arbitration in the public sector are also cited.

[75]5 U.S.C. §7119. *See* Chapter 20, "Legal Status of Arbitration in the Federal Sector."

[76]39 U.S.C. §1206. *See* Chapter 20, "Legal Status of Arbitration in the Federal Sector."

[77]For writings in which various of these and related arguments are asserted or noted, see Kennedy, *Freedom to Strike Is in the Public Interest*, HARV. BUS. REV., July–Aug. 1970, at 45; Farmer, *Compulsory Arbitration—A Management Lawyer's View*, 51 VA. L. REV. 396 (1965); Feller, *Compulsory Arbitration—A Union Lawyer's View*, 51 VA. L. REV. 410 (1965); Van de Water, *Involuntary Arbitration and National Defense*, 18 ARB. J. 96 (1963); Keel, THE PROS AND CONS OF COMPULSORY ARBITRATION 18–24 (N.Y. Chamber of Commerce 1961); Dash, *The Academy and Public Opinion, in* CHALLENGES TO ARBITRATION, PROCEEDINGS OF THE 13TH ANNUAL MEETING OF NAA 1, 8–12 (McKelvey ed., BNA Books 1960) (summarizing arguments of George W. Taylor, John T. Dunlop, and Thomas Kennedy against compulsory arbitration); Schwartz, *Is Compulsory Arbitration Necessary?*, 15 ARB. J. 189, 200 (1960); *Should the Federal Government Require Arbitration of Labor Disputes in All Basic American Industries?*, 26 CONG. DIG. 193, 203–21 (1947) (strong opposition to compulsory arbitration in the private sector was voiced by high government, labor, and management officials).

to select the arbitrator and cannot specify the standards or criteria for the decision. If terms of employment are determined by legislation or by arbitration required by law, rules may emerge for uniform application to all parties regardless of their individual character and needs. Compulsory arbitration means an imposed decision that will often fail to satisfy either party, rather than an acceptable settlement based on a meeting of the minds.

3. Compulsion generates resistance and is a source of further conflict. There may be serious difficulty of enforcement of compulsory orders, with the attendant danger of exposing the impotence of government.

4. Compulsory arbitration means governmental—politically influenced—determination of wages and will inevitably lead to governmental regulation of prices, production, and profits; it threatens not only free collective bargaining, but also the free market and enterprise system.

Australia has the most extensive experience (over 70 years) with compulsory arbitration. Writers who have studied the Australian system are by no means in agreement as to its degree of success, but they all agree that it has not eliminated strikes.[78] Indeed, an extensive study of compulsory arbitration experience in various countries led to the unqualified conclusion that compulsory arbitration "does not insure industrial peace, but rather can breed strikes, especially short ones."[79]

In 1920, Kansas enacted a compulsory arbitration act that set up a court of industrial relations for disputes in industries affecting the public interest. Broad interpretation of the Kansas law led to its application to industries other than public utilities. In 1923, the Supreme Court[80] declared the

---

[78]See NORTHRUP, COMPULSORY ARBITRATION AND GOVERNMENT INTERVENTION IN LABOR DISPUTES 35–44 (Labor Policy Ass'n 1966); Morris, *The Role of Interest Arbitration in a Collective Bargaining System, in* THE FUTURE OF LABOR ARBITRATION IN AMERICA 197, 209–26 (AAA 1976); Sykes, *Labor Regulation by Courts: The Australian Experience,* 52 NW. U. L. REV. 462 (1957); Merrifield, *Wage Determination Under Compulsory Arbitration: Margins for Skill in Australia,* 24 GEO. WASH. L. REV. 267 (1956); Oxnam, *Industrial Arbitration in Australia,* 9 INDUS. & LAB. REL. REV. 610 (1956). The number of strikes in Australia in 1974 exceeded all records for that country. Isaac, *Appendix E. Reports of Overseas Correspondents: Labor Relations Development in Australia, 1974, in* ARBITRATION—1975, PROCEEDINGS OF THE 28TH ANNUAL MEETING OF NAA 361 (Dennis & Somers eds., BNA Books 1976). For a comprehensive assessment of the use of compulsory arbitration in Australia, Canada, Great Britain, the United States, and Jamaica, see COMPULSORY ARBITRATION: AN INTERNATIONAL COMPARISON (1976). *See also* Forkosch, *Compulsion in Collective Bargaining and Arbitration: A Comparison of American and Australian Industrial Law,* 7 U. TOL. L. REV. 457, 498 (1976) (the "major conclusion reached" was that "the Australian and American systems of industrial law are different, quite different, in their methods and procedures . . . ."). Recent discussions of Australian arbitration are Stewart, *Arbitration in International and Comparative Perspective: Part I. A View From Abroad: Compulsory Arbitration in Australia, in* ARBITRATION 1994: CONTROVERSY AND CONTINUITY, PROCEEDINGS OF THE 47TH ANNUAL MEETING OF NAA 293 (Gruenberg ed., BNA Books 1994); Isaac & McCallum, *The Neutral and Public Interests in Resolving Disputes in Australia,* 13 COMP. LAB. L.J. 380 (1992); Nolan, *Regulation of Industrial Disputes in Australia, New Zealand and the United States,* 11 WHITTIER L. REV. 761–82 (1990).

[79]NORTHRUP, at 206. Professor Northrup also stated the conclusions that compulsory arbitration does not necessarily further the economic or social policies of government, but in fact may work against such policies; that it enhances union power and growth, especially through political action; and that it discourages collective bargaining.

[80]Chas. Wolff Packing Co. v. Court of Indus. Relations of Kan., 262 U.S. 522 (1923).

wage-fixing provisions of the statute unconstitutional as violating the due process clause of the Fourteenth Amendment. In light of later decisions of the Supreme Court, however, it seems possible that the exercise of similar power by the states now would withstand constitutional challenge (apart from federal preemption).[81] Some of the state statutes making arbitration of public-sector disputes compulsory and binding have been challenged on constitutional grounds; the challenge has occasionally succeeded, but more often has failed.[82]

Some states have enacted compulsory arbitration statutes for their public utilities. These statutes prohibit work stoppages and either provide for outright compulsory arbitration or require the use of settlement procedures that amount to compulsory arbitration. This legislation, much of which was adopted about 1947, evidenced a growing public concern over work stoppages that cause hardship to the general consuming public. However, in 1951 the Supreme Court held that state power in this field must fall where the state law conflicts with the LMRA.[83] Thus, the supremacy of federal regulation constitutes a potent barrier to the application of state compulsory arbitration laws to workers covered by the federal statute.

In 1963, Congress enacted a highly visible compulsory arbitration law,[84] providing for the compulsory arbitration of diesel firemen and crew consist issues in the railroad industry. The neutral members of that compulsory arbitration board expressed regrets that this congressional action was required:

> We write this opinion as the neutral members of a statutory arbitration board—a board whose creation was virtually forced upon Congress as the only way of avoiding a nationwide railroad strike. Never before in peacetime has Congress found it necessary to take such action. We wish at the very outset to record our regret that in this case the leaders of the railroad industry and the railroad operating unions were unable to agree upon some method of resolving their differences which would avoid the need for Congressional intervention. The great virtue of arbitration as it has developed in this country's labor relations has been the fact that it was a *voluntary* procedure, created and shaped by the disputing companies and unions themselves and thus responsive to their

---

[81]For a survey of decisions that bear on the matter, see *Fairview Hosp. v. Hospital Employees*, 22 LA 279, 282–89 (Minn. 1954). *See also* Spruck, *Compulsory Arbitration of Labor Disputes*, 47 MICH. L. REV. 242 (1948).

[82]*See* Chapter 22, section 5., "Public-Sector Interest Arbitration Legislation," and section 6., "Constitutionality of Binding Interest Arbitration."

[83]Street, Elec. Ry. & Motor Coach Employees Div. 998 v. Wisconsin Employment Relations Bd., 340 U.S. 383, 27 LRRM 2385 (1951). A state "plant seizure" statute was similarly invalidated on federal preemption grounds in *Street, Elec. Ry. & Motor Coach Employees Div. 1287 v. Missouri*, 374 U.S. 74, 53 LRRM 2394 (1963). For a discussion of experience under the state public utility statutes prior to these decisions, see NORTHRUP, COMPULSORY ARBITRATION AND GOVERNMENT INTERVENTION IN LABOR DISPUTES 24–33 (Labor Policy Ass'n 1966). Some of the statutes have subsequently been repealed.

[84]This was apparently the first time *Congress* ever ordered a specific dispute to compulsory arbitration during peacetime. However, in the 1920 Transportation Act, 41 Stat. 457 (1920), Congress created a Railroad Labor Board to engage in wholesale compulsory interest arbitration of wage and other disputes in the railroad industry. Zakson, *Railway Labor Legislation 1888 to 1930: A Legal History of Congressional Railway Labor Relations Policy*, 20 RUTGERS L.J. 317, 355–56 (1989). Both parties soon rejected this scheme, as, eventually, did Congress. *Id.* at 365–66.

peculiar problems, values, and needs. It is unfortunate that the parties in this case, though finally agreeing in principle to arbitration, failed to agree upon the terms and procedures of an arbitration agreement and thereby abandoned to Congress an opportunity and responsibility that should rightly have been theirs.[85]

Congress next enacted special legislation for the compulsory arbitration of a specific dispute (railroad shopcrafts) in 1967. This approach of using ad hoc compulsory arbitration by special congressional action (and only infrequently) is viewed in some quarters as less damaging and potentially more beneficial than any general provision for compulsory arbitration.[86] It has been suggested that an ad hoc compulsory arbitration procedure might be included as one of a so-called "arsenal of weapons" to be made available by Congress for use within the president's discretion in critical industrial disputes.

Finally, it may be noted that Congress by Section 302(c)(5)(B) of LMRA has mandated the use of impartial umpires for resolving deadlocks between trustees of jointly administered employee pension or welfare plans over the administration of the plan.[87]

---

[85]Railroads, 41 LA 673, 680 (Aaron, Healy, & Seward, 1963) (emphasis in original). This dispute is discussed in Levinson, *The Locomotive Firemen's Dispute*, 17 Lab. L.J. 671 (1966); Kaufman, *The Railroad Labor Dispute: A Marathon of Maneuver and Improvisation*, 18 Indus. & Lab. Rel. Rev. 196 (1965).

[86]*See* Farmer, *Compulsory Arbitration—A Management Lawyer's View*, 51 Va. L. Rev. 396, 405–06 (1965). But in other quarters the ad hoc approach is viewed as discriminatory and not to be preferred. *See* Wyle, *Compulsory Labor Arbitration and the National Welfare*, 19 Arb. J. 98 (1964).

[87]For examples of the use of neutrals under this provision, see *Association Trs. of the United Auto. Ass'n of St. Louis*, 96 LA 222, 223 (McAlpin, 1990); *Carpenters' Funds Trs.*, 90 LA 1097, 1103 (Nicholas, Jr., 1988) (arbitrator lacked jurisdiction to consider merits of case); *San Diego Plasterers Pension, Group Ins., & Vacation Trusts*, 83 LA 662, 664 (Weckstein, 1984) (qualifications for serving as trustee); *Trustees Designated by Sailors' Union of the Pac., SIU-PD*, 73 LA 590 (Hoffman, 1979) (deadlock over investment of trust funds); *Trustees of Resilient Floor Covering Welfare Trust*, 72 LA 695 (Koven, 1979) (removal of trust administrator); *Union-Appointed Trustees*, 70 LA 841 (Miller, 1978) (selection of trust administrator). Another statute, ERISA, is also relevant to arbitration under LMRA §302(c)(5)(B), as it is to certain other uses of arbitration in connection with employee benefit plans:

> Under the Employee Retirement Income Security Act of 1974 (ERISA), arbitrators may be called upon to resolve a variety of disputes involving collectively bargained employment benefit plans, including: (1) disputes between parties over a clause that affects a benefit plan; (2) disputes in which the plan trustees are deadlocked and the plan document calls for arbitration; (3) disputes between plan participants or beneficiaries and plan officials over benefit entitlement; and (4) disputes about employer liability following withdrawal from multiemployer plans.

AAA Study Time, July 1983. For discussion of arbitration under LMRA §302(c)(5)(B) and under ERISA, see Gregory, *Mandatory Arbitration and Wealth Distribution: The Policies and Politics of the Multiemployer Pension Plan Amendments Act*, 24 U.C. Davis L. Rev. 195–225 (1990); Tilove, *The Arbitration of Pension Disputes*, 34 Arb. J. No. 4, at 28 (1979); Brauer, *Limitations on Use of an Impartial Umpire to Resolve Deadlocked Disputes Between Taft-Hartley Trustees*, 30 Lab. L.J. 741 (1979); Murphy, *The Impact of ERISA on Arbitration*, 32 Arb. J. 123, 132 (1977); Fasser, *New Pension Reform Legislation*, in Arbitration—1975, Proceedings of the 28th Annual Meeting of NAA 138 (Dennis & Somers eds., BNA Books 1976). Dealing with the interaction of LMRA §302(c)(5)(B) and ERISA, see *Cutaiar v. Marshall*, 590 F.2d 523 (3d Cir. 1979). For related discussion, see Chapter 4, section 9.G., "Arbitrator's Immunity From Civil Liability."

B. Employer-Sponsored Arbitration of Statutory Claims in the Nonunionized Employment Context [LA CDI 24.111]

The "default" legal rule of the employment relationship is "employment at will."[88] Under this doctrine, employees in the private sector who are not covered by a collective bargaining agreement and who do not have an enforceable contract of employment may be discharged for any reason, good or bad, so long as the reason is not illegal.[89] Though often criticized,[90] the doctrine is strongly entrenched in the nonunion workplace.[91]

Until the 1990s, labor arbitrators were minimally active in the nonunion sector.[92] One survey revealed that fewer than 8 percent of the leading nonunion companies under the umbrella of the National Association of Manufacturers used the services of arbitrators.[93] The methods used for selecting arbitrators at these companies included the following: (1) management chose "at random" from a list of three names supplied by a "recognized" arbitration association, (2) the grievant chose from a list provided by the American Arbitration Association (AAA), (3) management and the grievant alternately struck names from a list of five arbitrators supplied by "an appropriate source," and (4) an arbitrator was designated by the AAA when management and the grievant failed to agree.[94] In each case reflected in the survey, management paid the arbitrator's fee, but at one company employees were required to pay $25 toward the fee if their grievances were denied.[95]

Recent decades, however, have witnessed a proliferation of federal[96] and state[97] statutes regulating the workplace. At the same time, state courts have

---

[88]*See* Summers, *Employment at Will in the United States: The Divine Right of Employers*, 3 U. PA. J. LAB. & EMP. L. 65 (2000).

[89]Payne v. Western & Atl. R.R., 81 Tenn. 507, 519–20 (1884) ("All [employers] may dismiss their employees at will, be they many or few, for good cause, for no cause or even for cause morally wrong, without being thereby guilty of legal wrong.").

[90]*See, e.g.*, Summers, *Individual Protection Against Unjust Dismissal: Time for a Statute*, 62 VA. L. REV. 481 (1976); Howlett, *Due Process for Nonunionized Employees: A Practical Proposal*, 32 PROC. ANN. MEETING INDUS. REL. RES., A. 164 (1979). *See also* Model Employment Termination Act §3(a)–(b), 7A U.L.A. 428 (1991) (prohibiting discharges without "good cause" for employees with at least 1 year's tenure).

[91]*See* Schwab, *Predicting the Future of Employment Law: Reflecting or Refracting Market Forces?*, 76 IND. L.J. 29, 36–37 (2001). To date, only one state, Montana, has rescinded at-will employment. MONT. CODE ANN. §39-2-901 to -915 (1999).

[92]Bognanno & Smith, *The Arbitration Profession: Part I. The Demographic and Professional Characteristics of Arbitrators in North America, in* ARBITRATION 1988: EMERGING ISSUES FOR THE 1990S, PROCEEDINGS OF THE 41ST ANNUAL MEETING OF NAA 266 (Gruenberg ed., BNA Books 1989).

[93]McCabe, *Corporate Nonunion Grievance Arbitration Systems: A Procedural Analysis*, 40 LAB. L.J. 432 (1989).

[94]*Id.*

[95]*Id.*

[96]Examples include Title VII of the Civil Rights Act of 1964, 42 U.S.C. §2000e-2 et seq. (prohibiting workplace discrimination on the basis of race, color, religion, sex, or national origin); the Age Discrimination in Employment Act (ADEA), 29 U.S.C. §§621–634; and the Americans with Disabilities Act (ADA), 42 U.S.C. §§12101–213.

[97]Examples include statutes that prohibit retaliatory dismissal for filing a workers' compensation claim, that protect whistleblowers, and that regulate the administration of polygraph tests.

applied contract and tort principles to open gaping holes in the doctrine of employment at will.[98] Most of these new individual employment rights (as opposed to the collective rights conferred by collective bargaining) are enforceable through civil lawsuits. As the number of such suits and the cost of defending them have increased, employers have sought refuge in a familiar dispute resolution forum: arbitration.[99] An increasing number of employers have begun to require their nonunion employees to submit any dispute regarding the termination of their employment—and in many cases other disputes—to final and binding arbitration.[100]

---

[98]Examples include the use of contract doctrines to bind employers to promises (oral or in handbooks) of job security and the use of tort doctrines to create a public policy exception to employment at will.

[99]*See, e.g.,* Pratt & Whitney Aircraft Group, 91 LA 1014, 1015 (Chandler, 1988); Burlington N. Motor Carriers, 90 LA 585, 589–90 (Goldstein, 1987); American Sunroof Co., 86 LA 390, 391 (Kates, 1985); Ohio Power Co., 79 LA 1, 1–2 (Feldman, 1982); Donn Prods., 70 LA 430, 430 (Siegel, 1978); Cardinal Operating Plant, 52 LA 688, 690, 693 (Leach, 1969); Pittsburgh Plate Glass, 49 LA 370, 371–72 (Dworkin, 1967); Mohawk Airlines, 49 LA 290, 291 (McKelvey, 1967); Ohio Power Co., 48 LA 299, 301–02 (Leach, 1967). In *Fregara v. Jet Aviation Business Jets,* 764 F. Supp. 940, 6 IER Cases 854 (D.N.J. 1991), the court held that a discharged employee who failed to exhaust a detailed handbook grievance procedure could not pursue a breach of contract action. For a scholarly discussion, see Gould, *The Employment Relationship Under Siege: A Look at Recent Developments and Suggestions for Change,* 22 Stetson L. Rev. 15, 21–22 (1992); Guidry & Huffman, *Legal and Practical Aspects of Alternative Dispute Resolution in Non-Union Companies,* 6 Lab. Law. 1 (Winter 1990); Keppler, *Nonunion Grievance Procedures: Union Avoidance Technique or Union Organizing Opportunity?,* 41 Lab. L.J. 557 (1990); McCabe, *Corporate Nonunion Grievance Procedures: Open Door Policies— A Procedural Analysis,* 41 Lab. L.J. 551 (1990); Baxter & Hunt, *Alternative Dispute Resolution: Arbitration of Employment Claims,* 15 Emp. Rel. L.J. 187 (1989). For discussion of one employer's long and favorable experience with such a program, see Wolf, *Novel Roles for Arbitration and the Arbitrator: I. Trans World Airlines' Noncontract Grievance Procedure, in* Arbitration 1986, Current and Expanding Roles, Proceedings of the 39th Annual Meeting of NAA 27 (Gershenfeld ed., BNA Books 1987), and for a discussion based on the experiences of the three Canadian jurisdictions that have experimented with mandatory arbitration in many nonunion settings, see Heenan & Brady, *Arbitrating Dismissals of Nonunion Employees: A Canadian Perspective,* 13 Comp. Lab. L.J. 273 (1992). For views on the use of employer-promulgated arbitration, see Walt, *Arbitration Forum Revisited: Part II.A. Employer-Promulgated Arbitration, in* Arbitration 1990: New Perspectives on Old Issues, Proceedings of the 43d Annual Meeting of NAA 189 (Gruenberg ed., BNA Books 1991); Rentfro, *Part II.B, id.* at 192; Das, *Part II.C., id.* at 199.

[100]St. Antoine, *The Changing Role of Labor Arbitration,* 76 Ind. L.J. 83, 83–84 (2001). Experience with the arbitration of grievances of unorganized employees is described in Hepple, *Arbitration of Job Security and Other Employment-Related Issues for the Unorganized Worker: I. The British Experience With Unfair Dismissals Legislation, in* Arbitration Issues for the 1980s, Proceedings of the 34th Annual Meeting of NAA 18 (Stern & Dennis eds., BNA Books 1982); Littrell, *II. Grievance Procedure and Arbitration in a Nonunion Environment: The Northrop Experience, id.* at 35; St. Antoine, *III. Protection Against Unjust Discipline: An Idea Whose Time Has Long Since Come, id.* at 43; Epstein, *Comment, id.* at 62. *See also* 3 Bornstein & Gosline, Labor and Employment Arbitration ch. 72, §72.02(b) et seq. (1989) (discussing the use and effect of nonunion arbitration procedures and awards); Morris, *EGAPS—Arbitration Plans for Nonunion Employees,* 14 Pepperdine L. Rev. 827 (1987); *Employment at Will, in* 1A West's Federal Practice Manual Ch. 21.16, §1475.9. The National Conference of Commissioners on Uniform State Laws drafted a proposed Uniform Employment Termination Act, which provides that nonunion employees can demand arbitration of their discharge. The *Draft Employment Termination Act* is reproduced at 138 Daily Lab. Rep. (BNA), at D-1 (Aug. 30, 1989). For a discussion of the Model Act, see Note, *The Model Employment Termination Act: Fruitful Seed or Noxious Weed,* 31 Duq. L. Rev. (1992).

Arbitration agreements come in all shapes and sizes. A few are post-dispute attempts to find an inexpensive and amicable way to resolve existing disputes.[101] Others are predispute agreements negotiated between employers and executive employees, often as part of an overall employment agreement that includes provisions on salary, stock options, and the like. A third type of arbitration agreement is a predispute agreement that is drafted exclusively by the employer and presented (often in a handbook or in a stand-alone arbitration agreement) to middle- or lower-level employees. Often, the employer requires new employees to sign the agreement as a condition of hire and requires existing employees to sign the agreement as a condition of continued employment. This type of agreement has proven most controversial,[102] because there is little to prevent an employer from "stacking the deck" against the employee, except for a self-imposed sense of fairness and the possibility that the procedure may be subjected to judicial review. Historically, organized labor has tended to view these agreements as union-avoidance devices[103] and has questioned whether it is realistic to expect employers to establish and follow procedures that are balanced and fair.[104]

i. Federal Arbitration Act [LA CDI 94.07]

While the statutory basis for labor arbitration is Section 301 of the LMRA, the statutory basis for employment arbitration is the Federal Arbitration Act,[105] and, to the extent it is not inconsistent with the Federal Arbitration Act,[106] in the 37 states that have adopted it, the similar Uniform Arbitration Act.[107] Section 2 of the Federal Arbitration Act provides that arbitration agreements "shall be valid, irrevocable and enforceable, save upon such grounds as exist at law or in equity for the revocation of any contract." Section 3 permits a party to an arbitration agreement to obtain a stay of proceedings in federal court when an issue is referable to arbitration. Section 4 permits such a party to obtain an order compelling arbitration when another party has failed, neglected, or refused to comply with an arbitration agreement, and authorizes judicial enforcement of arbitration awards.

---

[101]See Estreicher, *Saturns for Rickshaws: The Stakes in the Debate Over Predispute Employment Arbitration Agreements*, 16 OHIO ST. J. DISP. RESOL. 559 (2001) (explaining the rarity of postdispute employment arbitration agreements).

[102]See Van Wezel Stone, *Mandatory Arbitration of Individual Employment Rights: The Yellow Dog Contract of the 1990s*, 73 DENV. U. L. REV. 1017 (1996).

[103]In 1987, the AFL-CIO's Executive Council went on record supporting the enactment of wrongful discharge legislation to overcome the employment-at-will doctrine. 34 Daily Lab. Rep. (BNA), at E-8 (Feb. 23, 1987). The proposed bill never made it out of committee.

[104]Bank, *The Future of Collective Bargaining and Its Impact on Dispute Resolution: Labor Response, in* ARBITRATION 1999: QUO VADIS? THE FUTURE OF ARBITRATION AND COLLECTIVE BARGAINING, PROCEEDINGS OF THE 52D ANNUAL MEETING OF NAA 30, 30 (Grenig & Briggs eds., BNA Books 2000).

[105]9 U.S.C. §§1–16 (1994) (original version at 43 Stat. 883 (1925)).

[106]For discussion of federal preemption of state arbitration laws, see Chapter 2, section 2.A.i., "The Federal Arbitration Act."

[107]7 U.L.A. 281–283 (1997); Ware, ALTERNATIVE DISPUTE RESOLUTION §2.5 (2001).

a. Applicability: Gilmer v. Interstate/Johnson Lane Corp.

For years, courts assumed that the Federal Arbitration Act was inapplicable to statutory employment claims, such as claims arising under federal and state antidiscrimination statues.[108] This changed, however, with the 1991 decision of *Gilmer v. Interstate/Johnson Lane Corp.*[109] In *Gilmer,* the Supreme Court enforced an employee's agreement to submit all future claims against his employer to arbitration and required the employee to arbitrate, rather than litigate, his age discrimination claim. The Court rejected arguments that arbitration was inadequate to protect statutory rights and that arbitration was inconsistent with the statutory purposes and framework of the Age Discrimination in Employment Act (ADEA). Instead, the Court emphasized its "current strong endorsement" of arbitration. The Court also stated that arbitration agreements would not be voided merely because they were entered into under conditions of unequal bargaining power between employers and employees.

Gilmer raises as many issues as it answers. One issue is whether the *Gilmer* rationale applies only to ADEA claims.[110] Lower courts have consistently compelled arbitration of claims arising under other federal antidiscrimination statutes,[111] state antidiscrimination statutes,[112] and state common law.[113]

b. Applicability of "Contracts of Employment Exclusion"

A second issue is the applicability of the Federal Arbitration Act's "contracts of employment" exclusion. Section 2 of the statute excludes "contracts of employment of seamen, railroad employees, or any other class of workers engaged in foreign or interstate commerce." Until recently, there was an

---

[108]*See, e.g.,* Utley v. Goldman Sachs & Co., 883 F.2d 184, 187, 50 FEP Cases 1087 (1st Cir. 1989). *See also* Alexander v. Gardner-Denver Co., 415 U.S. 36, 7 FEP Cases 81 (1974) (holding that an employee does not forfeit a Title VII discrimination claim by first pursuing a grievance to final arbitration under the nondiscrimination clause of a collective bargaining agreement). See related discussion of de novo litigation of statutory claims following an arbitration award pursuant to a collective bargaining agreement in Chapter 2, section 2.A.ii.d., "De Novo Litigation Following Arbitration."

[109]500 U.S. 20, 55 FEP Cases 1116 (1991).

[110]*See also Developments in the Law—Employment Discrimination,* 109 Harv. L. Rev. 1569, 1670, 1672, 1675–77 (1996); Van Wezel Stone, *Mandatory Arbitration of Individual Employment Rights: The Yellow Dog Contract of the 1990s,* 73 Denver U. L. Rev. 1017, 1033–34 (1996); Bales, *Compulsory Arbitration of Employment Claims: A Practical Guide to Designing and Implementing Enforceable Agreements,* 47 Baylor L. Rev. 591, 604–05 (1995); Biretta, *Comment, Prudential Insurance Company of America v. Lai: The Beginning of the End for Mandatory Arbitration?,* 49 Rutgers L. Rev. 595, 596–600, 614–18 (1997).

[111]*See, e.g.,* Koveleskie v. SBC Capital Mkts., 167 F.3d 361, 362, 79 FEP Cases 73 (7th Cir. 1999) (Title VII); Pritzker v. Merrill Lynch, Pierce, Fenner & Smith, 7 F.3d 1110, 1112 (3d Cir. 1993) (ERISA). *See also* Adams, *Compulsory Arbitration of Discrimination Claims and the Civil Rights Act of 1991: Encouraged or Proscribed?,* 44 Wayne L. Rev. 1619 (1999); Halverson, *Arbitration and the Civil Rights Act of 1991,* 67 U. Cin. L. Rev. 445 (1999).

[112]*See, e.g.,* Willis v. Dean Witter Reynolds, Inc., 948 F.2d 305, 308, 57 FEP Cases 386 (6th Cir. 1991). *See also* Circuit City Stores v. Adams, 532 U.S. 105, 122, 85 FEP Cases 266 (2001) (reaffirming "that Congress intended the FAA [Federal Arbitration Act] to apply in state courts, and to pre-empt state antiarbitration laws to the contrary").

[113]*See, e.g.,* Bender v. A.G. Edwards & Sons, 971 F.2d 698, 699, 59 FEP Cases 1231 (11th Cir. 1992).

open issue as to whether this exclusion applies to all employment contracts, or whether it applies only to employees in the transportation industry such as seamen and railroad employees.[114] The *Gilmer* Court sidestepped this issue by noting that the arbitration agreement at issue in that case was between the plaintiff and an industry association, not between the plaintiff and his employer. In *Circuit City Stores v. Adams*,[115] the Supreme Court, in a 5–4 decision, ruled that the exclusion should be interpreted narrowly, to apply only to transportation workers.

c. *Precondition to Judicial Enforcement*

A third issue is the extent to which arbitration procedures must meet some minimum threshold of procedural fairness as a precondition to judicial enforcement. For example, in *Hooters of America v. Phillips*,[116] the U.S. Court of Appeals for the Fourth Circuit refused to enforce an arbitration agreement that, among other things, gave the employer complete control over the pool from which arbitrators were selected. Beyond an agreement that the employee should have some say in the selection of arbitrators, however, there is little judicial consensus on issues such as assent,[117] waiver,[118] arbitrator qualification and neutrality,[119] access to discovery,[120]

---

[114]*See* Feller, *Putting* Gilmer *Where It Belongs: The FAA Labor Exemption*, 18 HOFSTRA LAB. & EMP. L.J. 253 (2000) (arguing that the clause should be construed broadly to preclude application of the Federal Arbitration Act to any employment relationship); BALES, COMPULSORY ARBITRATION: THE GRAND EXPERIMENT IN EMPLOYMENT 32–48 (1997); Estreicher, *Pre-dispute Agreements to Arbitrate Statutory Employment Claims*, 72 N.Y.U. L. REV. 1344, 1363–72 (1997).

[115]532 U.S. 105, 85 FEP Cases 266 (2001).

[116]173 F.3d 933, 79 FEP Cases 629 (4th Cir. 1999).

[117]*See, e.g.*, Prudential Ins. Co. of Am. v. Lai, 42 F.3d 1299, 66 FEP Cases 933 (9th Cir. 1994) (refusing to enforce employment arbitration agreement that was not knowingly entered into by the employee); Prevot v. Phillips Petroleum Co., 133 F. Supp. 2d 937 (S.D. Tex. 2001) (refusing to enforce English-language agreement signed by Spanish-speaking employees); Maye v. Smith Barney Inc., 897 F. Supp. 100, 68 FEP Cases 1648 (S.D.N.Y. 1995) (enforcing arbitration agreement despite employees' complaint that they were given an inadequate amount of time to read and consider the agreement before they signed it); Romo v. Y-3 Holdings, 87 Cal. App. 4th 1153, 105 Cal. Rptr. 2d 208 (Cal. Ct. App. 2001) (an employee's signature acknowledging that she received, understood, and agreed to the terms in an employee handbook did not bind her to an arbitration agreement contained in the handbook).

[118]*See, e.g.*, Dexter v. Prudential Ins. Co. of Am., 215 F.3d 1336 (table), 2000 WL 728821 (10th Cir. 2000) (holding that an employer's failure to invoke its right to arbitration in proceedings before the EEOC and a state human rights commission did not waive the employer's right to arbitration).

[119]*See* Geiger v. Ryan's Family Steak Houses, 134 F. Supp. 2d 985, 85 FEP Cases 469 (S.D. Ind. 2001); Malin, *Privatizing Justice—But By How Much? Questions* Gilmer *Did Not Answer*, 16 OHIO ST. J. DISP. RESOL. 513 (2001).

[120]*Compare, e.g.*, Continental Airlines v. Mason, 87 F.3d 1318, 12 IER Cases 160 (9th Cir. 1996) (table) (enforcing arbitration agreement that did not provide for any discovery), *with* Kinney v. United Healthcare Serv., 70 Cal. App. 4th 1322, 83 Cal. Rptr. 2d 355 (Cal. Ct. App. 1999) (noting that restrictions on discovery "work to curtail the employee's ability to substantiate any claim against" the employer). *See also* Geiger v. Ryan's Family Steak Houses, 134 F. Supp. 2d 985, 996, 85 FEP Cases 469, 476 (S.D. Ind. 2001) ("limited discovery, controlled by a potentially biased arbitration panel," creates unfairness that renders an arbitration agreement unenforceable).

payment of arbitration fees,[121] representation by attorneys,[122] and restrictions on remedies.[123]

In *Morrison v. Circuit City Stores*,[124] the U.S. Court of Appeals for the Sixth Circuit, while otherwise upholding a mandatory arbitration agreement, invalidated a sharing provision. It held

> [P]otential litigants must be given an opportunity, prior to arbitration on the merits, to demonstrate that the potential costs of arbitration are great enough to deter them and similarly situated individuals from seeking to vindicate their federal statutory rights in the arbitral forum.[125]

The court also held unenforceable provisions in the arbitration agreement limiting the amount of damages available to an employee who prevails on a statutory claim. The remedies available to the employee under the arbitration agreement, the court concluded, must be the same as would be available through the judicial process.[126]

d. Scope of Judicial Review: Vacation of Award

A fourth issue is the scope of judicial review. Traditionally, judicial review of arbitration awards under the Federal Arbitration Act has been extremely limited. The Federal Arbitration Act permits a reviewing court to vacate an arbitration award in limited circumstances, including "[w]here the award was procured by corruption, fraud or undue means"; "[w]here there [existed] evident partiality or corruption [by] the arbitrators"; where there existed specified misconduct by the arbitrators, or "[w]here the arbitrators exceeded their powers."[127] Courts also will vacate an arbitration award if the

---

[121]*See, e.g.*, Bradford v. Rockwell Semiconductor Sys., 238 F.3d 549, 84 FEP Cases 1358 (4th Cir. 2001) (fee-splitting provision that required employee to share costs of arbitration does not per se render an arbitration agreement unenforceable); Williams v. CIGNA Fin. Advisors, 197 F.3d 752, 81 FEP Cases 747 (5th Cir. 1999) (enforcing arbitral award that, among other things, imposed a $3,150 "forum fee" on plaintiff); Shankle v. B-G Maint. Mgmt. of Colo., 163 F.3d 1230, 78 FEP Cases 1057 (10th Cir. 1999) (refusing to enforce arbitration agreement that required employee to pay for one-half of the arbitration fees). The Supreme Court may have given some indirect guidance on this issue when it held, in a case brought under the Truth in Lending Act, 15 U.S.C. §§1601–1667f, that an arbitration agreement that does not mention arbitration costs and fees is not per se unenforceable. Green Tree Fin. Corp.—Ala. v. Randolph, 531 U.S. 79, 84 FEP Cases 769 (2000).

[122]Most employment arbitration agreements permit an employee to be represented by an attorney; some employers even pay for the employee's attorney. Some agreements contain a clause similar to the following: "If the employee elects not to bring a attorney to the arbitration hearing, the Company also will agree not to bring an attorney to the hearing." Such a clause, however, may be misleading, because the employer may use attorneys extensively in the preparation of its case, even if the attorneys do not attend the hearing itself.

[123]*See, e.g.*, Paladino v. Avnet Computer Tech., 134 F.3d 1054, 76 FEP Cases 1315 (11th Cir. 1998); Great W. Mortgage Corp. v. Peacock, 110 F.3d 222, 232, 73 FEP Cases 856 (3d Cir. 1997); DiCrisci v. Lyndon Guar. Bank of N.Y., 807 F. Supp. 947, 953–54, 61 FEP Cases 279 (W.D.N.Y. 1992).

[124]317 F.3d 646, 90 FEP Cases 1697 (6th Cir. 2003) (en banc).

[125]*Id.* at 663. Two judges dissented on the ground that the "complicated pre-arbitration quasi-class action litigation scheme . . . raises questions for which it provides no answers." *Id.* at 681, 683.

[126]*Id.* at 674.

[127]9 U.S.C. §10 (1994).

arbitrator acted in "manifest disregard of the law."[128] More recently, however, some legal commentators have argued for expanded review of cases involving statutory claims,[129] and some courts appear to be headed in that direction.[130]

(1) Evident Partiality [LA CDI 94.68]

Under both the Federal Arbitration Act and the Revised Uniform Arbitration Act, the award of a neutral arbitrator also can be vacated because of the arbitrator's "evident partiality."[131] A presumption of evident partiality arises when a neutral arbitrator fails to disclose "a known, direct, and material interest in the outcome, or a known, existing, and substantial relationship with a party."[132] In such event, the nonobjecting party has the burden to rebut the presumption by showing absence of taint in the award or a lack of prejudice.[133] Nevertheless, courts have generally required a party seeking vacatur to meet a high burden.[134]

However, the U.S. Court of Appeals for the Ninth Circuit has held that, before a court can vacate an arbitration award because of evident partiality on the part of an arbitrator, the party alleging bias must only establish facts that create a reasonable impression of partiality.[135] The court found that the joining of an arbitrator as a party to the employer's suit to enjoin the arbitration on grounds that it was untimely requested, and the arbitrator's subsequent filing for sanctions against the employer's attorney under Rule 11 of

---

[128]For a thorough discussion of how courts apply both the statutory (e.g., bias, misconduct, or corruption on the part of the arbitrator) and nonstatutory (e.g., manifest disregard) grounds for judicial review of arbitration awards, see Hayford, *A New Paradigm for Commercial Arbitration: Rethinking the Relationship Between Reasoned Awards and the Judicial Standards for Vacatur*, 66 GEO. WASH. L. REV. 443 (1998).

[129]*See, e.g.,* Moohr, *Arbitration and the Goals of Employment Discrimination Law*, 56 WASH. & LEE L. REV. 395, 447–54 (1999).

[130]*See, e.g.,* Halligan v. Piper Jaffray, Inc., 148 F.3d 197, 77 FEP Cases 182 (2d Cir. 1998); Cole v. Burns Int'l Sec. Servs., 105 F.3d 1465, 1486–87, 72 FEP Cases 1775 (D.C. Cir. 1997).

[131]7 U.L.A. §23(a)(2)(A) (2000). Nonneutral arbitrators are treated under a different standard.

[132]*Id.* §23(a)(2).

[133]Drinane v. State Farm Mut. Auto. Ins. Co., 152 Ill. 2d 207, 214–26, 606 N.E. 2d 1181, 1184–85 (1992).

[134]Merit Ins. Co. v. Leatherby Ins. Co., 714 F.2d 673, 681 (7th Cir. 1983) (evidence of partiality must be "powerfully suggestive of bias"); Artists & Craftsmen Builders v. Schapiro, 232 A.D.2d 265, 668 N.Y.S.2d 550 (N.Y. App. Div. 1996). There is a division of authority on this issue that stems from the Supreme Court's split decision in *Commonwealth Coatings Corp. v. Continental Casualty Co.,* 393 U.S. 145 (1968). In the four-justice plurality opinion, it was stated that undisclosed "dealings that might create an impression of possible bias" or "even the appearance of bias" would amount to evident partiality. *Id.* at 149. Two other justices applied a more limited test that requires disclosure of "a substantial interest in a firm which has done more than trivial business with a party." *Id.* at 151–52. The dissenting justices sought to raise a rebuttable presumption for failing to disclose certain relationships. Because of this mixed analysis, some courts have applied "the appearance of bias" tests. Sanko S.S. Co. v. Cook Indus., 495 F.2d 1260, 1263 (2d Cir. 1973). Other courts review the conduct from the viewpoint of a reasonable person aware of all the circumstances. Ceriale v. AMCO Co., 48 Cal. App. 4th 500, 55 Cal. Rptr. 2d 685 (1996).

[135]Toyota of Berkeley v. Automobile Salesman's Union Local 1095, 834 F.2d 751, 127 LRRM 2112, 2116 (9th Cir. 1987), *cert. denied,* 486 U.S. 1043 (1988).

the Federal Rules of Civil Procedure, did not create a reasonable impression of partiality. The district court order vacating the arbitration award accordingly was reversed.[136]

The U.S. Court of Appeals for the Sixth Circuit applied a similar analysis to hold that the participation of a co-chair on the employer side of a committee deciding a grievance in which his former law partners were involved during their partnership did not create a reasonable impression of partiality in the arbitral setting,[137] although it would raise an appearance of impropriety requiring a federal judge's recusal from a case. In another opinion, however, the Sixth Circuit held that, where the employer and union act jointly to procure an arbitrator whom they think will be biased against a grievant, fundamental fairness required that the arbitration decision be set aside even in the absence of a finding of arbitral bias.[138]

Likewise, a dispute over a union's attempted dismissal of a permanent impartial arbitrator for an industrywide grievance-arbitration procedure was deemed arbitrable[139] when the court found that the impartial arbitrator's clear personal interests in the outcome of the dispute, arising from his unilateral termination by the union, disqualified him from hearing the dispute as an arbitrator. It directed the parties to appoint another arbitrator, in accordance with the contract, for purposes of hearing and deciding the issue.[140]

But, in another case, a neutral arbitrator's failure to disclose a prior business relationship with a principal of one of the parties to an arbitration did not justify a district court's use of its powers under Rule 60(b) of the Federal Rules of Civil Procedure and the Federal Arbitration Act to set aside the award.[141] The court stated that the test to be applied is whether, having due regard for the different expectations regarding impartiality that parties bring to arbitration, the relationship with the party's principal was so personally, socially, professionally, or financially intimate as to cast serious doubt on the arbitrator's impartiality.[142] In this case, although the president of one party to the arbitration had been the neutral arbitrator's supervisor for 2 years and was a key witness in the arbitration, their relationship had ended 14 years before, the arbitrator had no possible financial stake in the outcome

---

[136]*Id.*, 127 LRRM at 2116–17. For additional cases rejecting claims of arbitrator bias, see *Teamsters Local 814 v. J&B Sys. Installers & Moving,* 878 F.2d 38, 131 LRRM 2799 (2d Cir. 1989); *Broadcast Employees v. NBC,* 707 F. Supp. 124, 131 LRRM 2995 (S.D.N.Y. 1988); *Sanford Home for Adults v. Health Prof'ls Local 6,* 665 F. Supp. 312, 126 LRRM 3149 (S.D.N.Y. 1987).

[137]Apperson v. Fleet Carrier Corp., 879 F.2d 1344, 1360–61, 131 LRRM 3079 (6th Cir. 1989).

[138]Allen v. Allied Plant Maint. Co. of Tenn., 881 F.2d 291, 132 LRRM 2021, 2027 (6th Cir. 1989).

[139]Pitta v. Hotel Ass'n of New York City, 806 F.2d 419, 420, 124 LRRM 2109, 2110 (2d Cir. 1986). The collective bargaining contract clause provided for arbitration of all complaints and disputes involving "any acts, conducted or relations between the parties." *Id.* at 422.

[140]*Id.* at 423–25, 124 LRRM at 2112–14.

[141]Merit Ins. Co. v. Leatherby Ins. Co., 714 F.2d 673 (7th Cir.), *cert. denied,* 464 U.S. 1009 (1983).

[142]*Id.* at 680.

of the arbitration, and his relationship with that corporate officer during their tenure together at another company had been distant and impersonal.[143]

A more stringent and questionable standard was utilized by the New York Supreme Court, Appellate Division, in vacating an arbitration award where a sole arbitrator's undisclosed contractual arbitral relationship with the parent organization of one of the parties was held to be substantial enough to create an inference of bias.[144] The arbitrator was one of a panel of eight arbitrators designated to hear and determine disputes between the parent organization and its field representatives.[145]

However, in the same year, the Appellate Division came to a seemingly inconsistent conclusion in a case where a party to an arbitration under the Federal Arbitration Act had fully disclosed a past relationship with the arbitrator involving some insubstantial business dealings prior to commencement of the hearing, the arbitration council had examined the relationship and determined that the arbitrator should remain on the panel, and nothing in the record demonstrated that the opposing party was prejudiced. The court there, utilizing the evident partiality standard, found no bias on the part of the arbitrator and confirmed the arbitration award.[146]

The U.S. Court of Appeals for the Second Circuit, while refusing to require of an arbitrator the same demanding level of impartiality as that required for judges,[147] nevertheless concluded that a father-son relationship between an arbitrator and an officer of the international union of which the party to the arbitration was a local, gave rise to a presumption of filial loyalty that satisfied the standard of evident partiality required for vacating the arbitration award.[148]

As a general rule, a grievant must object to an arbitrator's partiality at the arbitration hearing before such an objection will be considered by the federal courts. The exception to this rule is when all facts as to the alleged bias are not known at the time of the hearing.[149] Thus, where an employer

---

[143]*Id.* at 676–78.

[144]City Sch. Dist. v. Oswego Classroom Teachers, 100 A.D.2d 13, 473 N.Y.S.2d 284 (N.Y. App. Div. 1984).

[145]*Id.*, 473 N.Y.S.2d at 287–88.

[146]Milliken & Co. v. Tiffany Loungewear, 99 A.D.2d 993, 473 N.Y.S.2d 443 (N.Y. App. Div. 1984).

[147]Morelite Constr. Corp. v. District Council of Carpenters Benefit Funds (New York City), 748 F.2d 79, 81, 117 LRRM 3009 (2d Cir. 1984).

[148]*Id.* at 84, 117 LRRM at 3012. See standards under which an award may be vacated. Federal Arbitration Act, 9 U.S.C. §10. The court defined "evident partiality" to mean "where a reasonable person would have to conclude that an arbitrator was partial to one party to the arbitration." *Morelite,* 748 F.2d at 84, 117 LRRM at 3012. This "reasonable person" standard has been adopted by other courts. *See* Apperson v. Fleet Carrier Corp., 879 F.2d 1344, 1360–61, 131 LRRM 3079 (6th Cir. 1989); Teamsters Local 814 v. JB Sys. Installers, 878 F.2d 38, 131 LRRM 2799 (2d Cir. 1989); Broadcast Employees v. NBC, 707 F. Supp. 124, 131 LRRM 2995 (S.D.N.Y. 1988). Any arbitrator, nevertheless, should adhere to a policy of disclosing any circumstance likely to create a "presumption of bias" or that the arbitrator believes "might disqualify" him or her as an impartial arbitrator. *See* AAA Labor Arbitration Rules 11 & 17; FMCS Regulations, 29 C.F.R. §1404; CODE OF PROFESSIONAL RESPONSIBILITY §2.B.

[149]Apperson v. Fleet Carrier Corp., 879 F.2d 1344, 1358–59, 131 LRRM 3079 (6th Cir. 1989).

failed to object to the selection of members of a contractually established joint arbitration committee at the time they were seated, the employer's objection to the committee's award based on the alleged partiality of the committee members was found to have been waived.[150]

(2) Injustice

The courts retain the equitable power to intervene in an arbitration proceeding before an award is rendered where there is "a real possibility that injustice will result," and one court has held that plaintiffs were not required to arbitrate their claims, as required by the bylaws of an organization of which all parties were members, in a charged atmosphere where the appearance of bias permeated the panel of arbitrators from which the arbitrators had been selected.[151] Overall, it is a tribute to the effectiveness of professional self-policing that both state and federal courts regularly reject challenges to arbitration awards on the ground of arbitrator bias or prejudice.[152]

(3) Manifest Disregard of the Law

In addition to "partiality," an arbitrator's award can be vacated if it is in "manifest disregard of the law." The "manifest disregard of the law" standard "'clearly means more than error or misunderstanding with respect to the law.'"[153] "[A] party seeking to vacate an arbitration award on the ground of manifest disregard of the law may not proceed by merely objecting to the results of the arbitration."[154] As a result, courts will vacate an award on this ground only after concluding that the arbitrator knew the correct legal standard, but "made a conscious decision" to ignore it.[155]

(4) Corruption and Misconduct [LA CDI 94.68]

Finally, it should be noted that "corruption" and "misconduct" are obviously grounds for vacating awards by both neutral and nonneutral arbitrators. Oddly enough, while prejudice need not be shown by a party seeking vacatur due to "corruption" by an arbitrator, neutral or otherwise,[156] courts

---

[150]Electrical Workers (IBEW) Local 2 v. Gerstner Elec., 614 F. Supp. 874, 121 LRRM 3042, 3044 (E.D. Mo. 1985).

[151]Rabinowitz v. Olewski, 100 A.D.2d 539, 473 N.Y.S.2d 232, 234 (N.Y. App. Div. 1984).

[152]See Northwestern Nat'l Ins. Co. v. Generali Mex. Compania de Seguros, 2000 U.S. Dist. LEXIS 5586, 2000 WL 52063. (S.D.N.Y. May 1, 2000); Eckstein v. Preston, 41 V.I. 130 (1999). See also Chapter 4, section 10., "Formulation and Enforcement of Ethical Obligations of Arbitrators and Advocates."

[153]Carte Blanche (Singapore) PTE v. Carte Blanche Int'l, 888 F.2d 260, 265 (2d Cir. 1989) (quoting Merrill Lynch, Pierce, Fenner & Smith v. Bobker, 808 F.2d 930, 933–34 (2d Cir. 1986)).

[154]D.R. Sec. v. Professional Planning Assocs., 857 F.2d 742, 747 (11th Cir. 1988).

[155]M&C Corp. v. Erwin Behr Gmbh & Co., 87 F.3d 844, 851 (6th Cir. 1996). See Hayford, Reining in the Manifest Disregard of the Law Standard: The Key to Stabilizing the Law of Commercial Arbitration, 1999 J. Disp. Resol. 117.

[156]Egan & Sons Co. v. Mears Park Dev. Co., 414 N.W.2d 785 (Minn. Ct. App. 1987); Northwest Mech. v. Public Util. Comm'n, 283 N.W.2d 522 (Minn. 1979); Gaines Constr. Co. v. Carol City Util., 164 So. 2d 270 (Fla. Dist. Ct. App. 1964).

require an objecting party to show prejudice in order to vacate an award due to arbitral misconduct.[157]

ii. Due Process Protocol for Mediation and Arbitration of Statutory Disputes

In 1995, representatives of the American Bar Association (ABA), the Society of Professionals in Dispute Resolution (SPIDR), the NAA, the FMCS, the National Employment Lawyers' Association, the American Civil Liberties Union, and the International Ladies' Garment Workers' Union drafted the Due Process Protocol for Mediation and Arbitration of Statutory Disputes Arising Out of the Employment Relationship.[158] This protocol set minimum procedural safeguards for inclusion in all employment arbitration agreements. This protocol is not, however, legally enforceable. In 1999, the AAA adopted its National Rules for the Resolution of Employment Disputes. These rules, which incorporate many of the principles set forth in the protocol,[159] are contractually enforceable when they are incorporated by reference into the underlying arbitration agreement.

Under its National Rules, the AAA may decline to administer the arbitration of disputes under an employer's arbitration program it deems "on its face substantially and materially deviates from the minimum due process standards" of its rules and the Due Process Protocol.[160]

An argument can be made that it is in an employer's best interests to draft a scrupulously fair arbitration agreement, because it is only by doing so that an employer may assure itself of judicial enforcement, and, thereby, the benefits of arbitration.[161] Nonetheless, as the *Hooters*[162] case illustrates, not all employers have drafted sustainable agreements. This has led many

---

[157]Creative Homes & Millwork v. Hinkle, 426 S.E.2d 480 (N.C. Ct. App. 1993).

[158]*See* 9A IER MANUAL (BNA) 534:401 (May 9, 1995); DISCIPLINE & DISCHARGE IN ARBITRATION app. A, at 149 (Draznin ed., BNA Books Supp. 1991).

[159]*See Appendix B. A Due Process Protocol for Mediation and Arbitration of Statutory Disputes Arising Out of the Employment Relationship, in* ARBITRATION 1995: NEW CHALLENGES AND EXPANDING RESPONSIBILITIES, PROCEEDINGS OF THE 48TH ANNUAL MEETING OF NAA 298 (Najita ed., BNA Books 1996), for a copy of the protocol and a list of the organizations subscribing to it. The NAA currently has under consideration a proposed change in its membership criteria. If adopted, the change would continue the requirement that an applicant demonstrate substantial and current experience and acceptability as an arbitrator of labor-management disputes, but give some consideration to experience as an arbitrator of employment disputes of this type, provided the procedures followed afforded protections equivalent to those contemplated by the due process protocol and NAA guidelines. *See* Fazzi, *The NAA Wrestles With the Issue of Expansion*, 55 DISP. RESOL. J. No. 4, at 489 (Nov. 2000–Jan. 2001).

[160]National Rules, AAA's Policy on Employment ADR (2002). The protocol identifies the minimum standards of an agreement to arbitrate to consist of: (1) the right to choose one's representative; (2) a method of fee reimbursement "in accordance with applicable law or in the interests of justice'" (3) access to information and discovery; and (4) the use of impartial arbitrators with "skill in the conduct of hearings, knowledge of the statutory issues at stake in the dispute, and familiarity with the workplace and employment environment." *Due Process Protocol*, NAA 48TH PROCEEDINGS.

[161]Bales, *Compulsory Arbitration of Employment Claims: A Practical Guide to Designing and Implementing Enforceable Agreements*, 47 BAYLOR L. REV. 591, 618 (1995).

[162]Hooters of Am. v. Phillips, 173 F.3d 933, 79 FEP Cases 629 (4th Cir. 1999).

experienced labor arbitrators to refuse to serve on employment cases.[163] It can be argued, however, that it is desirable that experienced arbitrators make themselves available to serve in such cases, because of the special expertise they possess.[164]

iii. Mandatory Arbitration

Proponents of mandatory arbitration of statutory employment claims note its potential for reducing the high number of employment bias cases currently being litigated, its lower cost and speed as compared with litigation, and its potential to increase access to a system of dispute resolution for lower-income employees.[165] Critics of mandatory arbitration of statutory employment claims point to the procedural differences between arbitration and litigation—that is, the absence of discovery rules in arbitration—as potentially placing employees at a greater disadvantage than employers,[166] and they assert that even experienced arbitrators are not well versed in employment law.[167]

Critics of mandatory arbitration of employment claims include the EEOC, the NLRB, the NAA, and the Commission on the Future of Worker-Management Relations (CFWMR).[168] The chairman of the NLRB

---

[163]Part 1.A.2. of the Code of Professional Responsibility for Arbitrators of Labor-Management Disputes states, in relevant part, that "[a]n arbitrator must be as ready to rule for one party as for the other on each issue, either in a single case or a group of cases." The 1996 amendments to the code, extending its coverage to employment disputes, state in Part 2.A.3. that "an arbitrator who is asked to arbitrate an [employment] dispute under a procedure established unilaterally by an employer . . . has no obligation to accept such appointment." In May 1997, the NAA adopted a policy statement opposing mandatory employment arbitration as a condition of employment when it requires a waiver of direct access to a judicial or administrative forum for the pursuit of statutory rights. *Appendix B. Statement of the National Academy of Arbitrators on Condition of Employment Agreements, in* Arbitration 1997: The Next Fifty Years, Proceedings of the 50th Annual Meeting of NAA 312 (Najita ed., BNA Books 1998) [hereinafter *1997 NAA Statement*].

[164]*Cf.* Gerhart & Crane, *Wrongful Dismissal: Arbitration and the Law*, 48 Arb. J. 56, 59 (June 1993). The policy statement adopted by the NAA in May 1997, opposing mandatory employment arbitration as a condition of employment, recognizes that, under the current state of the law, its members may choose to participate in such procedures, but requires them to evaluate the fairness of the procedures in light of detailed guidelines. *See 1997 NAA Statement,* at 312.

[165]*Developments in the Law—Employment Discrimination*, 109 Harv. L. Rev. 1569, 1670, 1672–73 (1996).

[166]*Id.* at 1674. The NAA, the AAA, and the ABA have each published procedural guidelines to assist members who are appointed to hear individual claims alleging violations of federal and state employment statutes. *NAA Opposes Mandatory Arbitration Restricting Statutory Rights*, Report No. 1878 Lab. Arb. Awards (CCH) 3–4 (June 10, 1997); *Arbitrators' Academy Votes to Oppose Mandatory Arbitration of Job Disputes*, 103 Daily Lab. Rep. (BNA), at A-3 (May 29, 1997); *National Academy of Arbitrators' Statement and Guidelines Adopted May 21, 1997*, 103 Daily Lab. Rep. (BNA), at E-1 (May 29, 1997); *American Arbitration Association Rules for Resolution of Employment Disputes*, 102 Daily Lab. Rep. (BNA), at E-17–E-26 (May 28, 1997); *Biretta, Comment,* Prudential Insurance Company of America v. Lai: *The Beginning of the End for Mandatory Arbitration?,* 49 Rutgers L. Rev. 595, 599 n.18 (1997).

[167]*Developments in the Law*, 109 Harv. L. Rev. at 1680.

[168]In August 1997, the National Association of Securities Dealers Inc. (NASD) voted to eliminate mandatory arbitration of statutory employment discrimination claims for registered brokers. The Securities and Exchange Commission (SEC) approved the new rule on June 23, 1998. *SEC Approves NASD Proposal to End Mandatory Arbitration of Bias Claims*, 121 Daily Lab. Rep. (BNA), at A-10 (June 24, 1998). *See also* <http://www.sec.gov/news/press/98-61.txt>.

questioned whether deference should be given by the NLRB to mandatory arbitration in nonunion settings because the system is set up and paid for by management.[169] The NAA released a statement opposing mandatory employment arbitration as a condition of employment when it requires waiver of direct access to either a judicial or administrative forum for the pursuit of statutory rights.[170] The CFWMR emphasized in its 1995 Report and Recommendations to the Secretary of Labor that, while it strongly supports the expansion and development of alternative dispute resolution (ADR) mechanisms in the workplace, it does not favor compulsory arbitration of employment claims as a condition of employment.[171]

iv. Alternative Dispute Resolution

It should be noted, however, that state and federal agencies charged with the enforcement of statutory employment laws have begun to offer ADR options to parties litigating charges before their respective agencies. For example, the Massachusetts Commission Against Discrimination launched an ADR program in 1996 that offers voluntary arbitration of employment discrimination charges, and the New York State Human Rights Commission has offered voluntary arbitration since 1993.[172] Colorado has authorized its Civil Rights Commission to utilize ADR in conjunction with other public agen-

---

Bills were introduced in both houses of the U.S. Congress to eliminate mandatory arbitration of federal employment discrimination claims. *See Senate Subcommittee Hears Testimony on Arbitration of Employment Bias Disputes*, 42 Daily Lab. Rep. (BNA), at A-10 (Mar. 2, 2000); Press Release, Securities & Exchange Comm'n, *SEC Approves Proposal by the NASD Which Eliminates Requirement That Employees Must Arbitrate Statutory Discrimination Claims* (June 23, 1998); *Feingold Urges SEC to Advise Industry to End Mandatory Arbitration of Job Claims*, 68 Daily Lab. Rep. (BNA), at A-7 (Apr. 9, 1997); Biretta, 49 RUTGERS L. REV. at 597; *Schroeder Bill Would Bar Enforcement of Mandatory Arbitration Contracts*, 128 Daily Lab. Rep. (BNA), at A-1–A-2 (July 3, 1996); Van Engen, *Note, Post*-Gilmer *Developments in Mandatory Arbitration: The Expansion of Mandatory Arbitration for Statutory Claims and the Congressional Effort to Reverse the Trend*, 21 IOWA J. CORP. L. 391, 410–12 (1996).

[169]*NLRB Chairman Questions Impartiality of Arbitration in Nonunion Workplaces*, 72 Daily Lab. Rep. (BNA), at A-2 (Apr. 15, 1997); *NLRB Chairman Outlines Growing Use of Arbitration Among Nonunion Employers*, 69 Daily Lab. Rep. (BNA), at A-2, E-1 to E-6 (Apr. 10, 1997).

[170]*Arbitrators' Academy Votes to Oppose Mandatory Arbitration of Job Disputes*, 103 Daily Lab. Rep. (BNA), at A-3 (May 29, 1997); *National Academy of Arbitrators' Statement and Guidelines Adopted May 21, 1997*, 103 Daily Lab. Rep. (BNA), at E-1, E-2 (May 29, 1997); *NAA Opposes Mandatory Arbitration Restricting Statutory Rights*, Report No. 1878 Lab. Arb. Awards (CCH) 3–4 (June 10, 1997).

[171]Dunlop, *Employment Litigation and Dispute Resolution: The Dunlop Commission Report: I. The Industrial Relations Universe Revisited, in* PROCEEDINGS OF THE 48TH ANNUAL MEETING OF NAA 124 (Najita ed., BNA Books 1996); *Report and Recommendations of the Commission on the Future of Worker-Management Relations (January 9, 1995), reproduced in* Daily Lab. Rep. Supp. (BNA), at S-42, S-48 (Jan. 10, 1995) (Special Supplement); *Dunlop Commission Panel Strongly Endorses Use of ADR, But Opposes Mandatory Arbitration*, 6 Daily Lab. Rep. (BNA), at AA-4 (Jan. 10, 1995).

[172]*Massachusetts Rights Agency Launches ADR Program to Arbitrate Bias Disputes*, 33 Daily Lab. Rep. (BNA), at A-1 (Feb. 20, 1996); *Lawyers Urged to Consider Arbitration as Alternative in Employment Disputes*, 26 Daily Lab. Rep. (BNA), at A-9, A-10 (Feb. 8, 1996); Spelfogel, *Legal and Practical Implications of ADR and Arbitration in Employment Disputes*, 11 HOFSTRA LAB. L.J. 247, 256–57 (1993).

cies and private organizations in the resolution of disputes.[173] The EEOC requires its agencies to provide ADR programs in their pre-complaint and formal complaint processes.[174] The Department of Labor is also exploring the use of arbitration and other forms of ADR as a vehicle to resolve certain "whistleblower," FMLA, Fair Labor Standards Act (FLSA),[175] and Office of Federal Contract Compliance Programs claims.[176]

8. THE EXPANDING ROLE OF ARBITRATION IN THE RESOLUTION OF STATUTORY EMPLOYMENT CLAIMS UNDER COLLECTIVE BARGAINING AGREEMENTS [LA CDI 94.553; 100.30]

Commentators have noted a growing tendency of collective bargaining agreements to incorporate by reference requirements to abide by statutes such as the Americans with Disabilities Act (ADA), the ADEA, and the Family and Medical Leave Act (FMLA),[177] thus, in effect, bringing these statutory claims within the four corners of the agreement for an arbitrator's consideration and interpretation.[178] This trend is not limited to the collective bargaining context.

As has been seen in *Gilmer v. Interstate/Johnson Lane Corp.*,[179] the Supreme Court held that an ADEA claim can be subjected to mandatory arbitration. The *Gilmer* case marked the first time that the Supreme Court had ruled on the arbitrability of an individual employee's statutory claims outside the collective bargaining context,[180] and it sparked the beginning of an ongoing national debate. There has been some disagreement among the courts regarding the applicability of *Gilmer* in the context of collective bargaining agreements. Most courts that have considered this issue have drawn a distinction between the enforceability of mandatory arbitration clauses contained within individual employment contracts and mandatory arbitration clauses contained within collective bargaining agreements. These courts have followed the reasoning of the Supreme Court in *Alexander v. Gardner-Den-*

---

[173]*State Labor Laws Aimed at Social Concerns Among Measures Adopted in 1999*, 46 Daily Lab. Rep. (BNA), at S-5, S-13 (2000).

[174]29 C.F.R. §1614.102(b)(2).

[175]29 U.S.C. §201 et seq.

[176]*DOL Seeks to Expand Use of Mediators to Resolve Disputes Under Employment Laws*, 1 Daily Lab. Rep. (BNA), at AA-1 (2001); *Lawyers Urged to Consider Arbitration as Alternative in Employment Disputes*, 26 Daily Lab. Rep. (BNA), at A-9, A-10 (Feb. 8, 1996).

[177]29 U.S.C. §2601 et seq.

[178]*Academy Board Endorses ADR Task Force Prototype*, 104 Daily Lab. Rep. (BNA), at A-4, A-5 (May 31, 1995).

[179]500 U.S. 20, 55 FEP Cases 1116 (1991). *See also* Van Wezel Stone, *Mandatory Arbitration of Individual Employment Rights: The Yellow Dog Contract of the 1990s*, 73 DENV. U. L. REV. 1017, 1036 (1996). For a more complete discussion of the *Gilmer* decision, see Chapter 10, section 2.B., "U.S. Supreme Court Statements Regarding Arbitral Consideration of External Law."

[180]Van Engen, Note, *Post*-Gilmer *Developments in Mandatory Arbitration: The Expansion of Mandatory Arbitration for Statutory Claims and the Congressional Effort to Reverse That Trend*, 21 J. CORP. L. 391, 401–02 (1996).

ver Co.,[181] to hold that arbitral remedies contained within collective bargaining agreements do not preclude individual employees subject to these agreements from bringing statutory employment claims in court in addition to or in lieu of arbitration.[182] Nonetheless, some courts have expanded *Gilmer* to require individual employees to exhaust mandatory arbitral remedies contained within collective bargaining agreements before filing a statutory action in court.[183] The Supreme Court declined to decide the circuit split with finality in *Wright v. Universal Maritime Service Corp.*[184] The Court stated that "we find it unnecessary to resolve the question of the validity of a union-negotiated waiver, since it is apparent to us, on the facts and arguments presented here, that no such waiver has occurred."[185] The Court found that the collective bargaining agreement's waiver was not "clear and unmistakable," but declined to rule on "the question of whether such a [clear and unmistakable] waiver would be enforceable."[186]

Lower courts have relied on *Gilmer* to enforce employment agreements requiring mandatory arbitration of claims brought under various federal and state employment statutes.[187]

9. ARBITRATION COSTS [LA CDI 94.65; 100.0780]

A number of factors or elements may contribute to the ultimate cost of any given arbitration.[188] Some of the factors are largely within the control of

---

[181]415 U.S. 36, 7 FEP Cases 81 (1974).

[182]Pryner v. Tractor Supply Co., 109 F.3d 354, 154 LRRM 2806 (7th Cir.), *cert. denied*, 522 U.S. 912 (1997); Ryan v. City of Shawnee, 13 F.3d 345 (10th Cir. 1993); Bates v. Long Island R.R., 997 F.2d 1028, 143 LRRM 2767 (2d Cir.), *cert. denied*, 510 U.S. 992 (1993). *See also* Cole v. Burns Int'l Sec. Servs., 105 F.3d 1465, 72 FEP Cases 1775 (D.C. Cir. 1997) (provides a comprehensive analysis in which enforcement of a mandatory arbitration provision dealing with statutory claims contained in an individual employment agreement is forcefully distinguished from enforcement of such a provision in a collective bargaining agreement).

[183]Reece v. Houston Lighting & Power Co., 79 F.3d 485, 151 LRRM 2936 (5th Cir.), *cert. denied*, 519 U.S. 864 (1996); Austin v. Owens-Brockway Glass Container, 78 F.3d 875, 151 LRRM 2673 (4th Cir.), *cert. denied*, 519 U.S. 980 (1996).

[184]525 U.S. 70, 159 LRRM 2769 (1998).

[185]*Id.* at 77.

[186]*Id.* at 82.

[187]Recent cases upholding mandatory arbitration clauses in nonunion employment agreements include the following: Koveleskie v. SBC Capital Mkts., 167 F.3d 361, 79 FEP Cases 73 (7th Cir.), *cert. denied*, 528 U.S. 811 (1999); Rosenberg v. Merrill Lynch, Pierce, Fenner & Smith, Inc., 170 F.3d 1, 79 FEP Cases 707 (1st Cir. 1999); Seus v. John Nuveen & Co., 146 F.3d 175, 77 FEP Cases 751 (3d Cir. 1998); Patterson v. Tenet Healthcare, 113 F.3d 832, 73 FEP Cases 1822 (8th Cir. 1997), *cert. denied*, 525 U.S. 1139 (1999).

[188]For discussion and statistics regarding the cost of arbitration, see *FMCS Viewpoint*, *FMCS Arbitration Statistics, Fiscal Year 1993*, 145 LRR 178 (1994); Jennings & Allen, *Labor Arbitration Costs and Case Loads: A Longitudinal Analysis*, 41 LAB. L.J. 88 (1990); Ver Ploeg, *Labor Arbitration: The Participants' Perspective*, 43 ARB. J. 36 (1988); Veglahn, *Arbitration Costs/Time: Labor and Management Views*, 30 LAB. L.J. 49 (1979); Peterson & Rezler, *Fee Setting and Other Administrative Practices of Labor Arbitrators*, 68 LA 1383 (1977). For formal rules concerning arbitrator fees or certain other expenses of arbitration, see the CODE OF PROFESSIONAL RESPONSIBILITY FOR ARBITRATORS OF LABOR-MANAGEMENT DISPUTES, 2.K. (2000); AAA Labor Arbitration Rules 43 & 44; FMCS Regulations §1404.16 (29 C.F.R. pt. 1404).

the parties, who have it within their power to reduce costs by avoiding unnecessary delays, making thorough preparation for the hearing, using stipulations, and waiving preparation of transcripts and filing of post-hearing briefs. (This is not to suggest that the use of transcripts and briefs in proper cases is not justified and desirable.)

The total cost of arbitration can be (and often is) considerably less than the cost of taking the dispute to court, just as the time required for the arbitration process to run its course can be (and often is) considerably less than would be required to reach judgment in a court action.[189] Of course, arbitration costs have increased with the increased complexity of the issues being taken to arbitration. Likewise, arbitration costs have naturally risen along with the rise in the consumer price index. Nevertheless, there has been no complaint from the parties that arbitration is not still well worth its dollar cost.

In some instances the arbitrator's fee and expenses constitute the primary cost of arbitration. The parties and the arbitrator should always agree in advance, and usually do, as to compensation or the basis on which it is to be determined. Ad hoc arbitrators typically charge on a per diem basis for hearing time, travel time, and time spent studying the case and preparing the decision (permanent arbitrators may be employed on a retainer basis).[190] The idea that there should be a fixed ratio of study days to hearing days is unrealistic:

> The ratio theory has a surface plausibility; if the hearing lasts for only one day or less, it may seem reasonable to assume that the arbitrator will need no more than one or two days to dispose of it. Unfortunately for the theory and its proponents, however, the fact is that some of the knottiest problems are most easily presented. Again, two experienced practitioners can, in a day's time . . . build a record that will keep the most conscientious arbitrator working for a week.[191]

If counsel is retained, then of course counsel fees are involved. Additional costs also are entailed when a neutral hearing site and a transcript of the proceedings are desired.[192] However, there are no court costs.[193] Arbitration costs, except for attorneys' fees and transcripts, generally are shared by the parties. Even where the parties have reached no agreement as to costs, arbitrators have required equal division since such "is common practice in arbitration."[194] Occasionally the collective bargaining agreement will pro-

---

[189]*E.g.*, Mahoning County Bd. of Mental Retardation v. Mahoning County Educ. Ass'n, 22 Ohio St. 3d 80, 83, 488 N.E.2d 872, 875 (1986).

[190]For statistics on arbitrator fees, see Bognanno & Smith, *The Arbitration Profession: Part I. The Demographic and Professional Characteristics of Arbitrators in North America, in* Arbitration 1988, Emerging Issues for the 1990s, Proceedings of the 41st Annual Meeting of NAA 266 (Gruenberg ed., BNA Books 1989). *See also* Bognanno & Coleman, Labor Arbitration in America: The Profession and Practice (1992). For related discussion, see Chapter 7, section 3.K., "Arbitrator's Charges When Case Is Cancelled."

[191]Aaron, *Labor Arbitration and Its Critics*, 10 Lab. L.J. 605, 645 (1959).

[192]*See* Chapter 7, section 4.F., "Transcript of Hearing."

[193]Both the AAA and the FMCS charge parties an administrative fee for use of their services.

[194]P.P. Williams Co., 24 LA 587, 592 (Reynard, 1955). In *Schott's Bakery*, 61-3 ARB ¶8675 (McSwain, 1961), the arbitrator ruled that, unlike a court, he did not have power to award costs against a party who had unnecessarily caused an increase in arbitration costs. But in

vide that the loser in arbitration shall pay all of the costs. This is contrary to the recommendation of the President's National Labor-Management Conference that the cost of the neutral "should be shared equally by both parties." It is highly undesirable from the standpoint of the arbitrator and, it would seem, from the standpoint of the best interests of the parties.[195]

10. ORGANIZATIONS INVOLVED IN ARBITRATION

A. National Academy of Arbitrators

The NAA is a nonprofit, professional, and honorary association of arbitrators.[196] While many of the most experienced arbitrators are included among the NAA's members, the Academy is not an agency for the selection of arbi-

---

limited situations, some other arbitrators have awarded costs against a party or have recognized an arbitrator's power to do so. See General Servs. Admin., 91 LA 1357 (Lumbley, 1988); Tenneco Chems., 77 LA 999, 1001 (Geltman, 1981); Cameron Iron Works, 73 LA 878, 882 (Marlatt, 1979); Dan's Mkt., 72 LA 706, 712 (Harter, 1979) (the power "should be reserved only for unusual cases"); Ralph Rogers & Co., 48 LA 40, 43 (Getman, 1966). For statistics on arbitrator fees, see Bognanno & Smith, NAA 41ST PROCEEDINGS, at 266; BOGNANNO & COLEMAN, LABOR ARBITRATION IN AMERICA. For related material, see Chapter 18, section 3.G., "Attorneys' Fees and Arbitration Expense," and section 3.I., "Other Avoidable Damages; Delayed Arbitration."

[195]In some instances under such provisions the arbitrator has assessed the costs against one party as the loser. See Servco Automatic Mach. Prods. Co., 100 LA 882 (Ellmann, 1993); Jackson Crankshaft Co., 71 LA 1161, 1165 (Howlett, 1978) (if this had not been required by the agreement, the arbitrator would have ordered that his fee be "shared equally" by the parties as a "fair" order in this case); Tag Container Co., 53 LA 1298, 1301 (Hon, 1969); Dietz Mach. Works, 52 LA 1023, 1026 (Jaffee, 1969); Hoover Chem. Prods. Div., Hoover Ball & Bearing Co., 48 LA 373, 379 (Keefe, 1967); Tyson Bearing Co., 38 LA 385, 388–89 (Dworkin, 1962). See also City of Roseburg, Or., 97 LA 262 (Wilkinson, 1991) (awarding all expenses to union as prevailing party, without adverse comment, despite closeness of case). In other cases, however, the arbitrator divided the costs equally because neither party lost all aspects of the case. See Stone Container Corp., 95 LA 729, 737 (Nolan, 1990); Grossmont Union High Sch. Dist., 91 LA 917 (Weiss, 1988); Northern Ohio Red Cross Blood Serv., 90 LA 393, 398–99 (Dworkin, 1988); National Archives & Records Serv., 73 LA 138, 141 (Jaffee, 1979); Fisher & Wright, 71 LA 994, 997 (Beitner, 1978); Dura Steel Prods. Co., 27 LA 611, 613 (Pollard, 1956); East Tex. Salt Water Disposal Co., 22 LA 484, 489 (Emery, 1953). In W.O. Larson Foundry Co., 42 LA 1286, 1293 (Kates, 1964), the arbitrator assessed his fee 80% against the union and 20% against the company. It may be noted that the common law has long recognized that: (1) the parties are jointly and severally liable for the arbitrator's fee, and this is so regardless of the parties' agreement concerning payment of the fee because the arbitrator is not a party or privy to that agreement; (2) a party who is compelled to pay the full fee is entitled to a contribution from the other party for his or her proportionate share, absent any agreement to the contrary. For cases stating one or more of these points, see Alexander v. Vollins, 2 Ind. App. 176, 179–80 (1891); Russel v. Page, 147 Mass. 282, 286 (1888); Carpenter v. Bloomer, 54 N.J. Super. 157 (1859); Young v. Starkey, 1 Cal. 426, 427 (1851). See also Theofano Maritime Co. v. 9,551.19 Tons of Chrome Ore, 122 F. Supp. 853, 858 (D.C. Cir. 1954) (a case under the Federal Arbitration Act). Discussing the above cases, see Cahn, Who Shall Pay the Piper?, AAA Study Time, July 1980, 7–8. See also 3 AM. JUR., Arbitration & Award §§98, 99. Following the arbitration hearing in Pacific Southwest Airlines, 77 LA 320, 330 (Jones, Jr., 1981), the arbitrating union was displaced by another union as bargaining representative, in view of which fact the arbitrator specified in the award that his fee was "a joint and several obligation of the parties for the full payment of which either is liable with a right of subrogation against the other," and that "the Company shall presently pay that sum in full with the right to reimbursement for one-half thereof against the Union."

[196]For discussion of the Academy and its history, see Killingsworth, Twenty-Five Years of Labor Arbitration—And the Future: I. Arbitration Then and Now, in LABOR ARBITRATION AT THE QUARTER-CENTURY MARK, PROCEEDINGS OF THE 25TH ANNUAL MEETING OF NAA 11 (Dennis &

trators. Rather, it was founded in 1947 to establish and foster high standards of conduct and competence for labor-management arbitrators and to promote the study and understanding of the arbitration process.[197] The Academy conducts an extensive and highly important educational program through its various committees, study groups, fall educational conferences, and annual meetings.[198]

B. Government Agencies Serving Arbitration

Part of the FMCS's responsibility since its creation has been the provision of panels of arbitrators experienced in dealing with labor matters. The FMCS's Office of Arbitration Services administers this function, maintaining rosters of arbitrators screened and qualified to make decisions in labor-management disputes. Panels of arbitrators are submitted to the parties involved in collective bargaining, and those arbitrators selected by the parties are appointed. The names and qualifications of arbitrators are kept in FMCS's computerized arbitration retrieval system, allowing them to be retrieved by geographic location, professional affiliation, occupation, experience in particular industries, or other specified criteria.[199]

The National Mediation Board performs important functions in the promotion of arbitration and the selection of arbitrators for the railroad and airline industries under the Railway Labor Act.[200]

The various state mediation agencies likewise perform services in the furtherance and assistance of arbitration. The New York State Board of Mediation, for instance, maintains a panel of private arbitrators, and the Board's members and staff also serve as arbitrators.

Somers eds., BNA Books 1973); McDermott, *II. Some Developments in the History of the National Academy of Arbitrators, id.* at 27; Myers, *III. Arbitration in the Future, id.* at 35; Valtin, *The National Academy After Twelve Years: A Symposium: What I Expect of the Academy, in* CHALLENGES TO ARBITRATION, PROCEEDINGS OF THE 13TH ANNUAL MEETING OF NAA 13 (McKelvey ed., BNA Books 1960); Loucks, *Arbitration—A Profession?, id.* at 20; McKelvey, *Discussion, id.* at 31; Scheiber, *Discussion, id.* at 35; Larkin, *Introduction: The First Decade, in* CRITICAL ISSUES IN LABOR ARBITRATION, PROCEEDINGS OF THE 10TH ANNUAL MEETING OF NAA viii (McKelvey ed., BNA Books 1957). The Academy's Constitution and By-Laws as amended in 1995 (there have been subsequent amendments) are published in GRUENBERG ET AL., THE NATIONAL ACADEMY OF ARBITRATORS: FIFTY YEARS IN THE WORLD OF WORK app. B, at 329 (BNA Books 1998), and are also available on the Academy's web site, at <http://www.naarb.org>. Another organization is the Association for Conflict Resolution, or ACR, whose membership is not limited to neutral arbitrators but also includes mediators, factfinders, government and private administrators, and party advocates in dispute resolution.

[197]For a discussion of how well the NAA is meeting its goals, see Briggs, *New Voices in the Academy: Part II. The National Academy of Arbitrators: Trade Organization or Professional Society?, in* ARBITRATION 1990: NEW PERSPECTIVES ON OLD ISSUES, PROCEEDINGS OF THE 43D ANNUAL MEETING OF NAA 263 (Gruenberg ed., BNA Books 1991).

[198]The proceedings of the annual meetings, including all important committee reports, have been published by The Bureau of National Affairs, Inc., and thus are easily available to all persons interested in arbitration. Many of those published volumes have been cited extensively throughout this book.

[199]FMCS 46TH ANN. REP., FISCAL YEAR 1993; FMCS 47TH ANN. REP., FISCAL YEAR 1994. For illustrative purposes, see, e.g., 29 C.F.R. §1404.2.

[200]45 U.S.C. §151 et seq. These functions are described in detail in Chapter 4, "The Arbitration Tribunal."

C. American Arbitration Association

The AAA is a private, nonprofit organization that offers services, procedures, and facilities for voluntary arbitration.[201] As an administrator, its activities include listing panels of qualified arbitrators from which parties can select a neutral and providing case administrators who oversee the handling of cases under its rules.[202]

The AAA has recently developed Grievance Mediation Procedures, which are intended to assist the labor-management community. In addition, the AAA maintains a Library and Information Center on the Resolution of Disputes that assists researchers and professionals. Seminars and training programs for advocates and arbitrators are provided by the AAA nationwide.

---

[201]The AAA maintains a web site on which it posts updated rules and procedures. *See* <http://www.adr.org/>.

[202]Rules, pamphlets, and materials are available directly from the AAA. In addition, the AAA's Labor Arbitration Rules, Employment Dispute Resolution Rules, Grievance Mediation Procedures, Rules for Impartial Determination of Union Fees, and Model for Sexual Harassment Claims Resolution Process are reprinted in BNA's Labor Arbitration binder, 1-71 (1994).

Chapter 2

Legal Status of Arbitration
in the Private Sector

1. Introduction—Arbitration and the Law

In the private sector of the United States, labor arbitration has been, and still is, predominantly a product of private contract between unions and management.[1] So it is that through the years private contract, along with workplace custom, has shaped the principal features of labor arbitration. Having chosen arbitration as the best means of resolving their differences, employers and unions in the vast majority of cases have honored their agreement to arbitrate by proceeding faithfully to arbitration, by presenting their case informally but fully to the arbitrator, and by carrying out the award as the final disposition of the dispute—probably giving little or no thought to the legal status of arbitration at any time during the entire process.[2] In any event, in only a very small percentage of cases has court action been instituted in connection with any aspect of the arbitration.[3]

---

[1]"The uniqueness enjoyed by arbitration as a system of industrial jurisprudence is that it is the creature of the parties. It is created by them, and its limits, rules and regulations are established and may be changed by them." McDermott, *Arbitrability: The Courts Versus the Arbitrator*, 23 Arb. J. 18, 19 (1968). See section 2.A., "Federal Law: Private Sector," below. One authority concluded that court decisions have not changed "the fact that grievance arbitration is basically a private system of jurisprudence," though federal court decisions have had an important effect in making both the arbitration agreement and the award enforceable and have set the stage for the establishment of other rules by court action. Fleming, The Labor Arbitration Process 28 (Univ. of Ill. Press 1965).

[2]"The efficacy of grievance arbitration is founded on the pledge of the disputing parties that the arbitrator's award would be final and binding." *Major Collective Bargaining Agreements: Arbitration Procedures*, at 73 (U.S. Dep't of Labor Bull. No. 1425–6, 1966). In *Piggly Wiggly Operators' Warehouse Indep. Truck Drivers Local 1 v. Piggly Wiggly Operators' Warehouse*, 611 F.2d 580, 581, 103 LRRM 2646, 2646 (5th Cir. 1980), the court stated that, "The relatively small number of reported cases contesting the countless arbitration proceedings convened to resolve labor-management disputes attests to the parties' general satisfaction with this method of resolving industrial problems."

[3]For the 40-year period 1960–2001, an empirical study located only 1,244 federal district court decisions and 543 appellate court decisions (less than 1% of all private sector awards) that compelled or denied arbitration, or that enforced or vacated an arbitrator's award in whole or in part. LeRoy & Feuille, *Final and Binding, But Appealable to Courts: Empirical Evidence of Judicial Review of Labor and Employment Arbitration Awards, in* Arbitration 2001: Arbitrating in an Evolving Legal Environment, Proceedings of the 54th Annual Meeting of NAA 49, 62 (Grenig & Briggs eds., BNA Books 2002). That study found:

In turn, the courts and the legislatures generally have honored the "private contract" nature of arbitration by wisely limiting their roles in the process. Indeed, the role of the government in the private sector has been largely limited to the preliminaries and the "post-liminaries" of the arbitration process. That is, the law has been concerned primarily with the enforceability of agreements to arbitrate, at the outset, and with the review and enforcement of awards at the close. The heart of the arbitration process, from the time the arbitrator is selected until the award has been issued, has been left largely within the exclusive control of and determination by the parties and their arbitrator. The temperance of the law, avoiding undue interference with the arbitration process, has permitted the high degree of flexibility essential to the success of the process.

Turning to the public sector, the law has tended to play a more active role in the arbitration of disputes between public employers and employees. This is hardly a surprise, the government itself being the employer. The more surprising fact is that many jurisdictions permit public employers and employees fairly free rein to shape their labor relations, leaving much for determination by collective bargaining. On the whole, it cannot be said that arbitration (where permitted at all in the public sector) is unduly circumscribed by law. Particularly in reference to arbitration of grievances, the parties are relatively unrestricted in choosing and utilizing arbitration machinery.[4]

---

1. Courts have confirmed awards at a consistent rate throughout this 41-year history. District courts confirmed 71.8 percent of the 1,008 cases decided from 1960–1991, and 70.3 percent of the 232 decisions in the past decade. Appellate courts behaved about the same, confirming 70.5 percent of awards from 1960–1991, and 66.4 percent in the recent period.

2. Comparing recent to earlier decisions, the award confirmation rate dropped substantially in district courts in the Fourth and Eighth Circuits but rose in the Ninth Circuit. Although federal courts in the aggregate are consistent in their tendency to confirm awards, their behavior varies by region. This is most evident among district courts in circuits with large subsamples. In the past decade the confirmation rate for these courts increased in the Ninth Circuit by 13 percent. Although the Tenth Circuit had only seven award confirmation cases from 1991–2001, it confirmed all of them. Even adjusting for this very small sample size, the 45.8-percent increase in the confirmation rate by courts in this circuit is noteworthy. Conversely, the confirmation rate dropped by 15.5 and 19.2 percent in the Fourth and Eighth Circuits, respectively. Meanwhile, district courts in two circuits where a high number of cases occur had fairly constant rates over these periods. Confirmation rates for courts in the Second and Third Circuits increased by 4.7 and 4.2 percent, respectively.

3. Awards that were challenged in federal courts almost always ruled in favor of a union. Unions prevailed in 84.9 percent of the arbitration awards.

4. During the more recent period surveyed, confirmation rates varied only moderately by the type of issue on which awards were challenged. The most effective argument for contesting an award was that it failed to draw its essence from the agreement. District courts confirmed 70.4 percent of these awards. The least effective argument for vacating an award was that the arbitrator made a fact-finding error. In cases raising this argument, the award enforcement rate was 82.1 percent. The confirmation rate for awards challenged on public policy grounds fell in this range. District courts confirmed 71.4 percent of these awards. The range between these extremes was not large.

Id. at 62–64 (footnotes and tables omitted). *See also* Feuille & LeRoy, *Grievance Arbitration Appeals in the Federal Courts: Facts and Figures*, 45 ARB. J. No. 1, at 35 (1990).

[4]Use of arbitration for interest disputes in the public sector has tended to be more closely regulated by statute, including some procedural details. *See* Chapter 22, "Arbitration of Interest Disputes." But, demonstrating that public-sector arbitration often is conducted under rules widely utilized for private-sector cases, note that of the 2,669 awards reported to the

Collective bargaining and the arbitration of grievances filed over contract disputes had reached maturity and proven their value in the private sector long before employee organization in the public sector began to find acceptance in the 1960s. This maturity and this proven value are two of the reasons why a majority of jurisdictions ultimately accepted collective bargaining and dispute resolution through the arbitral process for public employment, why they permit the parties meaningful freedom of choice without undue interference by the law, and why the public jurisdictions and their parties have borrowed extensively from private-sector arbitration.

However, consideration of the law, or at least legal principles, enters the arbitration process in many guises. For example, in interpreting contracts arbitrators rely on principles developed at common law. Issues over admissibility of evidence at arbitral hearings are often resolved by reference to judicial or administrative rules of evidence. Disciplinary disputes frequently involve considerations of "due process" and myriad federal or state statutory provisions governing the employment and bargaining relationships. Indeed, references to statutory law in the adjudication of nondisciplinary contract questions have increased markedly in recent years. Many collective bargaining contracts expressly or implicitly incorporate federal and state regulations dealing with such subjects as equal employment opportunity, sexual harassment, and disability accommodation. Moreover, the National Labor Relations Board (NLRB) will often defer consideration of an unfair labor practice charge pending arbitral resolution of the underlying grievance.

The present book deals primarily with that part of the arbitration process that falls largely within the exclusive determination of the parties and their arbitrator. This chapter will consider federal and state law relating to the private sector.[5]

Federal Mediation and Conciliation Service by arbitrators appointed by that agency, 568 were public-sector cases (283 federal-sector cases and 285 sub-federal public-sector cases), or 21.3%. *See* Annual Report for 2002 (October 1, 2001–September 30, 2002), Office of Arbitration Services. (Preliminary statistics supplied by Honorable Vella M. Traynham, Director). Of the 13,287 labor cases filed in 2002 with the American Arbitration Association by arbitrators appointed by that agency, 5,554 were public-sector, or 41.8% (resulting in the issuance of 1,677 awards). Statistics supplied by Katherine Burton of the AAA.

A survey of the number of awards issued by members of the National Academy of Arbitrators during the 3-year period 1996–1998 reported that 74,000 cases were arbitrated by the 462 responding members of the then total of 535 who were actively engaged in arbitrating. Approximately 38% of the cases arose in the public sector and primarily involved "rights" or grievance disputes. *See* Picher, Seeber & Lipsky, *The Arbitration Profession in Transition, Appendix B, in* Arbitration 2000: Workplace Justice and Efficiency in the Twenty-First Century, Proceedings of the 53d Annual Meeting of NAA 267, 280–81 (Briggs & Grenig eds., BNA Books 2001). Those private-sector rules cover various (but not all) aspects of the process, from the initiation of arbitration through issuance of the award, and they apply equally to private-sector and public-sector cases. Although several of the rules expressly envision variations "required by law," as to many aspects (particularly in grievance arbitration), public-sector parties who choose to arbitrate under the AAA rules enjoy the same options and are bound by the same limitations that apply to private-sector parties.

[5]The regulation of federal employment and state and federal regulation of state and local government employment are considered in Chapter 20, "Legal Status of Arbitration in the Federal Sector," and Chapter 21, "Issues in State and Local Government Sector Arbitration."

2. PRIVATE SECTOR ARBITRATION

A. *Federal Law: Private Sector* [LA CDI 94.553]

Federal statutes of significance to arbitration in the private sector are the Federal Arbitration Act (also called the United States Arbitration Act),[6] the Labor Management Relations Act (LMRA),[7] and the Railway Labor Act (RLA).[8] The RLA deals extensively with arbitration and is discussed elsewhere in this book.[9]

i. *The Federal Arbitration Act* [LA CDI 94.07]

The Federal Arbitration Act by its terms does not apply "to contracts of employment of seamen, railroad employees, or any other class of workers engaged in foreign or interstate commerce."[10]

The courts of appeals had previously disagreed over the scope of the Federal Arbitration Act, with some courts holding that all employees involved in interstate commerce were exempt. The issue was resolved by the Supreme Court in *Circuit City Stores v. Adams*.[11] There, the Court held that the Federal Arbitration Act gives federal court jurisdiction over the arbitration of employment disputes involving workers in private industry, excluding only those engaged directly in transportation such as railroad, airline, and truck-

---

[6]The Federal Arbitration Act was passed in 1925 and codified in 1947. 9 U.S.C. §§1–14. For discussion of the Federal Arbitration Act, see Burnstein, *The United States Arbitration Act—A Reevaluation*, 3 VILL. L. REV. 125, 9 LAB. L.J. 511 (1958). *See also* Valtin, *The Presidential Address: Judicial Review Revisited—The Search for Accommodation Must Continue*, in ARBITRATION—1976, PROCEEDINGS OF THE 29TH ANNUAL MEETING OF NAA 1, 7 (Dennis & Somers eds., BNA Books 1976); Cox, *Grievance Arbitration in the Federal Courts*, 67 HARV. L. REV. 591 (1954). *See also* Holcomb, *The Demise of the FAA's "Contract of Employment" Exception?* (Gilmer v. Interstate/Johnson Lane Corp.), 1992 J. DISP. RESOL. 213 (1992).

[7]29 U.S.C. §§141–187.

[8]45 U.S.C. §§51–163, 181–188.

[9]*See* Chapter 3, "Scope of Labor Arbitration," and Chapter 4, "The Arbitration Tribunal."

[10]9 U.S.C. §1.

[11]532 U.S. 105, 85 FEP Cases 266 (2001). *Accord* EEOC v. Waffle House, 534 U.S. 279, 12 AD Cases 1001 (2002). "In 1995, Saint Clair Adams applied for a job at Circuit City Stores. Adams signed an employment application that included an arbitration provision for any and all disputes relating to 'application or candidacy for employment, employment and/or cessation of employment with Circuit City.'" *Circuit City*, 532 U.S. at 110. The provision covered state law claims and specifically named the Age Discrimination in Employment Act (ADEA), 29 U.S.C. §621 et seq., Title VII of the Civil Rights Act of 1964, 42 U.S.C. §2000e et seq., and the Americans with Disabilities Act (ADA), 29 U.S.C. §706 et seq. Adams was hired as a sales counselor in Circuit City's store in Santa Rosa, California. In 1997, Adams filed suit against Circuit City in state court, asserting claims under California's Fair Employment and Housing Act and other tort claims under California law. Circuit City filed suit in the district court, seeking to enjoin the state-court action and to compel arbitration pursuant to the Federal Arbitration Act. The district court entered the requested order. While the appeal was pending in the U.S. Court of Appeals for the Ninth Circuit, the court ruled on the key issue in an unrelated case. The court held that the Federal Arbitration Act does not apply to contracts of employment. The court of appeals held the arbitration agreement between Adams and Circuit City was contained in a "contract of employment," and so was not subject to the Federal Arbitration Act. In reversing the Ninth Circuit, the Supreme Court did not address the issues relating to the application of the Federal Arbitration Act in the context of a dispute arising under a collective bargaining agreement.

ing employees.[12] Even as to cases involving transportation industry employees, courts may look to the Federal Arbitration Act as a guide in fashioning the body of law for labor arbitrations.[13]

The consequence is that state private-sector employment laws restricting the use of arbitration agreements are preempted. The Court reaffirmed its decision in *Southland Corp. v. Keating*,[14] holding that Congress intended the FAA to apply in state courts and to preempt conflicting state arbitration laws.

The Federal Arbitration Act allows concurrent state court jurisdiction if so designated by the parties,[15] provides for a stay of judicial proceedings where the issue is referable to arbitration,[16] authorizes the issuance of an order directing arbitration,[17] and allows for court appointment of an arbitrator on default of the parties.[18] The arbitrators are given the power to compel the attendance of witnesses and the production of documents.[19] Any award is subject to judicial confirmation,[20] but may be vacated on proof that the award was "procured by corruption, fraud, or undue means," or that there was "evident partiality" on the part of the arbitrator, or the arbitrator refused "to postpone the hearing upon sufficient cause shown" or "to hear evidence pertinent and material to the controversy," or engaged in misbehavior prejudicial to the rights of a party, or exceeded the arbitrator's powers or so imperfectly executed them that a "final and definite" award was not made.[21]

To the extent that state arbitration statutes do not conflict with the provisions, purpose, or policy of the Federal Arbitration Act, and when parties explicitly agree to have their arbitration proceedings conducted under such statutes, it appears that they will not be preempted.[22]

---

[12]Employees working in interstate commerce who fall within the FAA exemption as construed by the Supreme Court in *Circuit City* may not be held to mandatory arbitration agreements. Harden v. Roadway Package Sys., 249 F.3d 1137, 85 FEP Cases 1604 (9th Cir. 2001).

[13]*See* Textile Workers v. Lincoln Mills, 353 U.S. 448, 466, 468, 40 LRRM 2113 (1957) (Frankfurter, J., dissenting). For an illustration of such use of the Federal Arbitration Act, see *Pizzuto v. Hall's Motor Transit Co.*, 409 F. Supp. 427, 429 (E.D. Va. 1976). Furthermore, the Federal Arbitration Act gives federal substantive rights rather than merely providing federal enforcement of state-created rights. *See* Southland Corp. v. Keating, 465 U.S. 1, 12, 10 (1984) (stressing that "the substantive law the Act created was applicable in state and federal courts," and that by the Federal Arbitration Act, "Congress declared a national policy favoring arbitration and withdrew the power of the states to require a judicial forum for the resolution of claims which the contracting parties agreed to resolve by arbitration"). *See also* Coulson, Prima Paint: *An Arbitration Milestone*, 22 Arb. J. 237 (1967) (discussing *Prima Paint Corp. v. Flood & Conklin Mfg. Co.*, 388 U.S. 395 (1967)).

[14]465 U.S. 1 (1984). *See* Borg-Warner Protective Servs. Corp. v. EEOC, 245 F.3d 831, 85 FEP Cases 673 (D.C. Cir. 2001).

[15]9 U.S.C. §9. *See* Mastrobuono vs. Shearson Lehman Hutton, Inc., 514 U.S. 52 (1995) (parties may contract to conduct arbitration under state law rules).

[16]9 U.S.C. §3.

[17]*Id.* §4.

[18]*Id.* §5.

[19]*Id.* §7.

[20]*Id.* §9.

[21]*Id.* §10.

[22]*See* Ferro Corp. v. Garrison Indus., 142 F.3d 926 (6th Cir. 1998); Flexible Mfg. Sys. Pty Ltd. v. Super Prods. Corp., 874 F. Supp. 247 (E.D. Wis. 1994), *aff'd*, 86 F.3d 96 (7th Cir. 1994). The Federal Arbitration Act has been held, however, not to apply to suits under the LMRA. Coca-Cola Bottling Co. of N.Y. v. Teamsters Local 812, 242 F.3d 52 (2d Cir. 2001).

ii.   The Labor Management Relations Act

The Labor Management Relations Act of 1947 (LMRA) declares in Section 203 that final adjustment by a method agreed on by the parties is the most desirable way to settle disputes over the interpretation and application of collective agreements.

Section 301 of the LMRA authorizes suits in the federal courts for violation of collective bargaining agreements in industries affecting interstate commerce. In *Lincoln Mills*, the Supreme Court held that Section 301 authorizes the federal courts to fashion a body of federal law for the enforcement of arbitration provisions in collective bargaining agreements.[23]

a.   The Lincoln Mills *Case*

In *Lincoln Mills*, the Court declared that it was clear "that Congress adopted a policy which placed sanctions behind agreements to arbitrate grievance disputes, by implication rejecting the common-law rule . . . against enforcement of executory agreements to arbitrate."[24]

As to the substantive law to be applied in Section 301 suits, the Court stated:

> We conclude that the substantive law to apply in suits under § 301 (a) is federal law, which the courts must fashion from the policy of our national labor laws . . . . The Labor Management Relations Act expressly furnishes some substantive law. It points out what the parties may or may not do in certain situations. Other problems will lie in the penumbra of express statutory mandates. Some will lack express statutory sanction but will be solved by looking at the policy of the legislation and fashioning a remedy that will effectuate that policy. The range of judicial inventiveness will be determined by the nature of the problem. . . . Federal interpretation of the federal law will govern, not state law. . . . But state law, if compatible with the purpose of § 301, may be resorted to in order to find the rule that will best effectuate the federal policy. . . . Any state law applied, however, will be absorbed as federal law and will not be an independent source of private rights.[25]

b.   The Trilogy

After *Lincoln Mills* came the *Steelworkers Trilogy* of 1960.[26] Some of the significant teachings of these cases are summarized in the following sections.

---

[23]*See* discussion in Pfander, *Judicial Purpose and the Scholarly Process: The* Lincoln Mills *Case*, 69 WASH. U. L.Q. 243 (1991).

[24]Textile Workers v. Lincoln Mills, 353 U.S. 448, 456, 40 LRRM 2113 (1957) (footnote and citation omitted).

[25]*Id.* at 456–57 (citations omitted). Included among the many articles on *Lincoln Mills* are Gregory, *The Law of the Collective Agreement*, 57 MICH. L. REV. 635 (1959); Kramer, *In the Wake of* Lincoln Mills, 9 LAB. L.J. 835 (1958); Bickel & Wellington, *Legislative Purpose and the Judicial Process: The* Lincoln Mills *Case*, 71 HARV. L. REV. 1 (1957); Feinsinger, *Enforcement of Labor Agreements—A New Era in Collective Bargaining*, 43 VA. L. REV. 1261 (1957); American Bar Ass'n Comm. on Arbitration, *Report on Labor Arbitration*, 28 LA 913, 914–22 (1957).

[26]Steelworkers v. American Mfg. Co., 363 U.S. 564, 46 LRRM 2414, 34 LA 559 (1960); Steelworkers v. Warrior & Gulf Navigation Co., 363 U.S. 574, 46 LRRM 2416, 34 LA 561 (1960); Steelworkers v. Enterprise Wheel & Car Corp., 363 U.S. 593, 46 LRRM 2423, 34 LA 569 (1960). For an extensive survey of the impact of these and other Supreme Court decisions on arbitration, see Smith & Jones, *The Impact of the Emerging Federal Law of Griev-*

(1) Determining Arbitrability and Compelling Arbitration

Unless the parties expressly provide that the arbitrator is to determine arbitrability, the final determination rests with the courts (if such issue is presented for judicial determination).[27] The courts must compel arbitration where the party seeking it is making a claim that on its face is governed by the contract, even though the court might otherwise conclude that the grievance is frivolous or baseless. Doubts should be resolved in favor of arbitrability, and arbitration should be compelled unless it may be said with "positive assurance" that the arbitration clause is not susceptible to an interpretation that covers the dispute.[28]

---

ance Arbitration on Judges, Arbitrators, and Parties, 52 VA. L. REV. 831 (1966). *See also* Nelson, *Preemption*, 86 VA. L. REV. 225, 305 (2000); Corrada, *The Arbitral Imperative in Labor and Employment Law*, 47 CATH. U. L. REV. 919, 940 (1998); Feller, Taft *and* Hartley *Vindicated: The Curious History of Review of Labor Arbitration Awards*, 19 BERKELEY J. EMP. & LAB. L. 296, 306 (1998); Clark, *Federal Common Law: A Structural Reinterpretation*, 144 U. PA. L. REV. 1245, 1376 (1996); Holden, *Arbitration of State Law Claims by Employees: An Argument for Containing Federal Arbitration Law*, 80 CORNELL L. REV. 1695, 1755 (1995); Feller, *End of the* Trilogy: *The Declining State of Labor Arbitration*, 48-SEP ARB. J. 18, 25 (1993); Howard, *The Evolution of Contractually Mandated Arbitration*, 48-SEP ARB. J. 27, 36 (1993); Zablotsky, *The Continuing Availability of Retaliatory Discharge and Other State Tort Causes of Action to Employees Covered by Collective Bargaining Agreements*, 56 ALB. L. REV. 371, 402 (1992); Harper, *Limiting Section 301 Preemption: Three Cheers for the* Trilogy, *Only One for* Lingle *and* Lueck, 66 CHI.-KENT L. REV. 685, 752 (1990); Hodges, *The* Steelworkers Trilogy *in the Public Sector*, 66 CHI.-KENT L. REV. 660 (1990); Malin, *Forward: Labor Arbitration Thirty Years After the* Trilogy, 66 CHI.-KENT L. REV. 551 (1990); St. Antoine, *Afterward: Labor Arbitration Thirty Years After the* Trilogy, 66 CHI.-KENT L. REV. 845 (1990); White, *Section 301's Preemption of State Law Claims: A Model For Analysis*, 41 ALA. L. REV. 377, 434 (1990); Budd, *Public Policy and Preemption: Union Employees' State Wrongful Discharge Actions*, 18 U. BALT. L. REV. 570 (1989); Gardner, *Federal Labor Law Preemption of State Wrongful Discharge Claims*, 58 U. CIN. L. REV. 491 (1989); Morris, *Twenty Years of* Trilogy: *A Celebration, in* DECISIONAL THINKING OF ARBITRATORS AND JUDGES, PROCEEDINGS OF THE 33D ANNUAL MEETING OF NAA 331 (Stern & Dennis eds., BNA Books 1981); Smith & Jones, *The Supreme Court and Labor Dispute Arbitration: The Emerging Federal Law*, 63 MICH. L. REV. 751 (1965); Aaron, *Arbitration in the Federal Courts: Aftermath of the* Trilogy, 9 UCLA L. REV. 360 (1962); Gregory, *Enforcement of Collective Agreements by Arbitration*, 48 VA. L. REV. 883 (1962); Meltzer, *The Supreme Court, Arbitrability, and Collective Bargaining*, 28 U. CHI. L. REV. 464 (1961).

[27]Howsam v. Dean Witter Reynolds, 537 U.S. 79 (2002); AT&T Techs v. Communications Workers, 475 U.S. 643, 121 LRRM 3329 (1986). In *Howsam*, the Court noted that procedural issues that grow out of the dispute, such as time limit defenses, are for the arbitrator, not the court, to decide. Questions of arbitrability are limited to "gateway disputes"—the kind of narrow circumstances "where contracting parties would likely have expected a court to have decided the gateway matter, where they are not likely to have thought that they had agreed that an arbitrator would do so, and, consequently, where reference of the gateway dispute to the court avoids the risk of forcing parties to arbitrate a matter that they may well not have agreed to arbitrate." 537 U.S. at 83–84.

[28]In *Gateway Coal Co. v. Mine Workers Dist. 4, Local 6330*, 414 U.S. 368, 377, 85 LRRM 2049 (1974), the Supreme Court stated that in the *Trilogy*, the "Court enunciated the now well-known presumption of arbitrability for labor disputes." In *Nolde Bros. v. Bakery & Confectionery Workers Local 358*, 430 U.S. 243, 254, 94 LRRM 2753 (1977), the Court reaffirmed the "strong presumption favoring arbitrability," and it expanded the scope of the presumption. *Nolde* is discussed in Chapter 3, section 3.C.i., "Precontract and Post-Contract Grievances." More recently, in *Major League Baseball Players Ass'n v. Garvey*, 532 U.S. 504, 167 LRRM 2134 (2001), the Supreme Court reversed a decision of the U.S. Court of Appeals for the Ninth Circuit that had vacated an arbitral award and, adjudicating the merits of the dispute, ordered payment of Garvey's claim. In a per curiam opinion, the Court reaffirmed the *Trilogy* principles. The presumption of arbitrability does not extend to grievances that arise after the expiration of the collective bargaining agreement unless the acts occurred prior to expiration. Litton Fin. Printing Div. v. NLRB, 501 U.S. 190, 137 LRRM 2441 (1991).

(2) Enforcement and Review of Arbitration Award [LA CDI 94.63]

When arbitration awards are brought before courts for review and enforcement, questions of contract interpretation are for the arbitrator, and the courts "have no business overruling him because their interpretation of the contract is different from his."[29] This deference to arbitral judgment, however, is not without its limitation. An award "is legitimate only so long as it draws its essence from the collective bargaining agreement. When the arbitrator's words manifest an infidelity to this obligation, courts have no choice but to refuse enforcement of the award."[30] But the Court is unwilling to "assume" that an arbitrator has "abused the trust the parties confided in him" or "has not stayed within the areas marked out for his consideration,"[31] and courts should not reject an award unless it is clear that the arbitrator has exceeded his or her authority. The Court has not decided whether an award made in contravention of positive law is within the "essence" harbor.

The Supreme Court suggested that, under the Federal Arbitration Act, courts might set aside an arbitral award made in "manifest disregard" of the law. Thus, in *Wilko v. Swan*,[32] involving an arbitration clause in a contract between a securities house and a customer, the Court wrote:

Also, the presumption of arbitrability of disputes between a union and an employer does not apply in determining whether parties agreed to require arbitration of disputes between employers and trustees of employee-benefit funds. In *Schneider Moving & Storage Co. v. Robbins*, 466 U.S. 364, 115 LRRM 3641 (1984), the Supreme Court stated:

> Arbitration promotes labor peace because it requires the parties to forgo the economic weapons of strikes and lockouts. Because the trustees of employee-benefit funds have no recourse to either of those weapons, requiring them to arbitrate disputes with the employer would promote labor peace only indirectly, if at all. We conclude, therefore, that the presumption of arbitrability is not a proper rule of construction in determining whether arbitration agreements between the union and the employer apply to disputes between trustees and employers, even if those disputes raise questions of interpretation under the collective-bargaining agreements.

Id. at 372 (footnotes omitted).

[29]*Enterprise Wheel*, 363 U.S. at 599, 46 LRRM at 2425, 2426. In its 1983 *Grace* decision, the Supreme Court summarized as follows (citing *Enterprise Wheel*, 363 U.S. at 596, 597, 598, at several points):

> Under well-established standards for the review of labor arbitration awards, a federal court may not overrule an arbitrator's decision simply because the court believes its own interpretation of the contract would be the better one. . . . When the parties include an arbitration clause in their collective-bargaining agreement, they choose to have disputes concerning constructions of the contract resolved by an arbitrator. Unless the arbitral decision does not "dra[w] its essence from the collective bargaining agreement," . . . a court is bound to enforce the award and is not entitled to review the merits of the contract dispute. This remains so even when the basis for the arbitrator's decision may be ambiguous.

W.R. Grace & Co. v. Rubber Workers Local 759, 461 U.S. 757, 764, 113 LRRM 2641, 2644 (1983). In *Grace*, the Court stated that conclusions by the arbitrator there did "draw their 'essence' from the provisions of the collective-bargaining agreement," *id.* at 765, and accordingly that: "Regardless of what our view might be of the correctness of [the arbitrator's] contractual interpretation, the Company and the Union bargained for that interpretation. A federal court may not second-guess it." *Id.* For more on the *Grace* decision, see Chapter 14, section 2.A.iv., "Seniority Systems and the Arbitral Enforcement of Antidiscrimination Clauses Resulting in 'Reverse Discrimination' Claims." In *Garvey*, 532 U.S. 504, the Court opined that even "serious error" by the arbitrator affords insufficient grounds to vacate an award so long as the interpretation of the contract falls within the scope of the arbitrator's authority.

[30]*Enterprise Wheel*, 363 U.S. at 597.

[31]*Id.* at 598.

[32]346 U.S. 427 (1953). *See also* Bernhardt v. Polygraphic Co. of Am., 350 U.S. 198, 203 n.4, 25 LA 693, 695 (1956) ("Whether the arbitrators misconstrued a contract is not open to judicial review.").

While it may be true . . . that a failure of the arbitrators to decide in accordance with the provisions of the Securities Act would "constitute grounds for vacating the award pursuant to [FAA §10]," that failure would need to be made clearly to appear. In unrestricted submissions, such as the present margin agreements envisage, the interpretations of the law by the arbitrators in contrast to manifest disregard are not subject, in the federal courts, to judicial review for error in interpretation. The [FAA] contains no provision for judicial determination of legal issues such as is found in the English law.[33]

Whether the FAA applies to arbitrations conducted under collective bargaining contracts is, however, an unanswered question.

(3) Arbitral Modification of Incomplete or Deficient Awards
[LD CDI 94.63]

The early common law rule that a court action to enforce an award must be dismissed in its entirety if any deficiency exists in the award was rejected by the Supreme Court. The Court held that an award need not be set aside for incompleteness. Thus, if the arbitrator has neglected to calculate the amount of back pay due a grievant, the award should be returned to the parties for a determination of the amount by arbitration.[34]

c. Post-Trilogy: Enforcement of Agreements to Arbitrate and Review of Arbitration Awards

(1) Arbitrability

The initial responses of the courts to the *Trilogy* teachings was studied by the Law and Legislation Committee of the NAA in 1967 and produced the following finding: "Because of the presumption favoring the arbitrability of labor disputes, courts have continued to compel arbitration in most cases where the arbitrability of the dispute has been challenged."[35]

About a decade later, the Committee reported that "[t]he health of the arbitration process is graphically illustrated by the large number of cases wherein the courts hold in favor of a party who is seeking to compel arbitration or who is resisting a stay of arbitration, compared with the small number of decisions where arbitration is denied."[36]

---

[33]*Wilko*, 346 U.S. at 436–37 (footnotes omitted).

[34]For rejection of the common law rule by a court of appeals, see *Enterprise Wheel & Car Corp. v. Steelworkers*, 269 F.2d 327, 332, 44 LRRM 2349 (4th Cir. 1959).

[35]*Appendix B. Arbitration and Federal Rights Under Collective Agreements in 1967: Report of the Committee on Law and Legislation for 1967, in* DEVELOPMENTS IN AMERICAN AND FOREIGN ARBITRATION, PROCEEDINGS OF THE 21ST ANNUAL MEETING OF NAA 201, 214–15 (Rehmus ed., BNA Books 1968).

[36]Kurtz, *Appendix B. Arbitration and Federal Rights Under Collective Agreements in 1976, in* ARBITRATION—1977, PROCEEDINGS OF THE 30TH ANNUAL MEETING OF NAA 265, 280 (Dennis & Somers eds., BNA Books 1978). "For arbitration to be denied or stayed, the language of the contract must clearly rebut the strong presumption of arbitrability, and the courts will restrictively interpret any exclusionary clause." Kurtz, *Appendix B. Arbitration and Federal Rights Under Collective Agreements in 1975, in* ARBITRATION—1976; PROCEEDINGS OF THE 29TH ANNUAL MEETING OF NAA 233, 251 (Dennis & Somers eds., BNA Books 1976). A more recent study found that arbitral awards were confirmed in more than 70% of the cases in which vacatur or enforcement was sought. LeRoy & Feuille, *Final and Binding, but Appealable to Courts: Empirical Evidence of Judicial Review of Labor and Employment Arbitration Awards, in* ARBITRATION 2001: ARBITRATION IN AN EVOLVING LEGAL ENVIRONMENT, PROCEEDINGS OF THE 54TH ANNUAL MEETING OF NAA (Grenig & Briggs eds., BNA Books 2001).

"In general, if the arbitration award is not [in] manifest disregard of the contract and draws its essence from the contract, it will be enforced by the courts in routine fashion."[37] The U.S. Court of Appeals for the First Circuit, for instance, found that both the employee's underlying grievance and the employer's arbitration defenses were arbitrable and affirmed a lower court's refusal to rule on the employer's defenses.[38]

In *John Wiley & Sons v. Livingston*,[39] the Supreme Court ruled that once it is determined that the subject matter of a dispute is arbitrable, pro-

---

[37]*Arbitration and Federal Rights Under Collective Agreements in 1976*, NAA 21ST PROCEEDINGS, at 288. For other studies and views concerning court review of awards under the *Trilogy*, see ROTHSCHILD, MERRIFIELD & EDWARDS, COLLECTIVE BARGAINING AND LABOR ARBITRATION 342–61 (1979); GORMAN, BASIC TEXT ON LABOR LAW 584–603 (1976); Berger, *Judicial Review of Labor Arbitration Awards: Practices, Policies and Sanctions*, 10 HOFSTRA LAB. L. REV. 245 (1992); Feller, *Court Review of Arbitration*, 43 LAB. L.J. 539 (1992); Borong, *Judicial Review by Sense and Smell: Practical Application of the Steelworkers Essence Test in Labor Arbitration Awards*, 65 U. DET. L. REV. 643 (1988); Jones, Jr., *Presidential Address: A Meditation on Labor Arbitration and "His Own Brand of Industrial Justice," in* ARBITRATION 1982: CONDUCT OF THE HEARING, PROCEEDINGS OF THE 35TH ANNUAL MEETING OF NAA 1 (Stern & Dennis eds., BNA Books 1983); Morris, *Twenty Years of* Trilogy: *A Celebration, in* DECISIONAL THINKING OF ARBITRATORS AND JUDGES, PROCEEDINGS OF THE 33D ANNUAL MEETING OF NAA 331, 355–72 (Stern & Dennis eds., BNA Books 1981); Kaden, *Judges and Arbitrators: Observations on the Scope of Judicial Review*, 80 COLUM. L. REV. 267 (1980); St. Antoine, *Judicial Review of Labor Arbitration Awards: A Second Look at* Enterprise Wheel *and Its Progeny*, 75 MICH. L. REV. 1137 (1977), *reprinted in* ARBITRATION—1977, PROCEEDINGS OF THE 30TH ANNUAL MEETING OF NAA 29 (Dennis & Somers eds., BNA Books 1978) (the arbitrator is the parties' officially designated "reader" of the contract, and courts will ordinarily treat an award as final and binding because the parties have *agreed* on such treatment); Adams, *Comment, id.* at 52; Katz, *Comment, id.* at 61; Christensen, *Judicial Review: As Arbitrators See It: I. The Disguised Review of the Merits of Arbitration Awards*, *in* LABOR ARBITRATION AT THE QUARTER-CENTURY MARK, PROCEEDINGS OF THE 25TH ANNUAL MEETING OF NAA 99 (Dennis & Somers eds., BNA Books 1973); Gould, *II. Judical Review of Employment Discrimination Arbitrations, id.* at 114; Roberts, *III. Judicial Review of "Misconduct" Cases, id.* at 150; Bailer, chair, *Panel Discussion: Judicial Review: As the Parties See It, id.* at 176; Meltzer, *Ruminations About Ideology, Law, and Labor Arbitration, in* THE ARBITRATOR, THE NLRB, AND THE COURTS, PROCEEDINGS OF THE 20TH ANNUAL MEETING OF NAA 1, 7–19 (Jones ed., BNA Books 1967); Note, *Judicial Review of Labor Arbitration Awards Which Rely on the Practices of the Parties*, 65 MICH. L. REV. 1647 (1967); Comment, *Judicial Enforcement of Labor Arbitrators' Awards*, 114 U. PA. L. REV. 1050 (1966). For a discussion of possibilities for achieving the review of arbitration decisions short of going to court, see Jones & Smith, *Management and Labor Appraisals and Criticisms of the Arbitration Process: A Report With Comments*, 62 MICH. L. REV. 1115, 1119–27 (1964). For actual efforts along this line by arbitrators or parties, see Progress-Bulletin Publ'g Co., 47 LA 1075, 1078 (Jones, Jr., Levin, Whaley, Edward, & Nevins, 1966); Bemis Bros. Bag Co., 44 LA 1139, 1139 (Stix, 1965); U.S. Indus. Chems. Co., 43 LA 824 (Stix, 1964); Allis-Chalmers Mfg. Co., 42 LA 193 (Sullivan, 1964). For a sampling of court determinations of whether an arbitral award drew its essence from the contract, see, e.g., Litvak Packing Co. v. Food & Commercial Workers Local 7, 886 F.2d 275, 132 LRRM 2383 (10th Cir. 1989); Geo. A. Hormel & Co. v. Food & Commercial Workers Local 9, 879 F.2d 347, 131 LRRM 3018 (8th Cir. 1989); *In re* Marine Pollution Serv., 857 F.2d 91, 129 LRRM 2472 (2d Cir. 1988); New Jeiji Mkt. v. Food & Commercial Workers Local 905, 789 F.2d 1334, 122 LRRM 2961 (9th Cir. 1986).

[38]Bechtel Constr. v. Laborers, 812 F.2d 750, 124 LRRM 2785 (1st Cir. 1987). *See also* National R.R. Passenger Corp. v. Boston & Maine Corp., 850 F.2d 756 (D.C. Cir. 1988); Ryan v. Liss, Tenner & Goldberg Sec. Corp., 683 F. Supp. 480 (D.N.J. 1988).

[39]376 U.S. 543, 55 LRRM 2769 (1964). *See also* Operating Eng'rs Local 150 v. Flair Builders, 406 U.S. 487, 80 LRRM 2441 (1972). In *Wiley*, the Court also held that under appropriate circumstances the successor employer must honor the arbitration agreement of a company acquired by merger. The successor, however, was not required to honor the entire agreement of the predecessor employer in *NLRB v. Burns International Security Services*, 406 U.S. 272, 80 LRRM 2225 (1972). *See also* Howard Johnson Co. v. Hotel & Restaurant Employees, 417 U.S. 249, 86 LRRM 2449 (1974).

cedural questions that grow out of the dispute and bear on its final disposition should be left to the arbitrator. The Court stated that procedural questions, such as whether the preliminary steps of the grievance procedure have been exhausted or excused, ordinarily cannot be answered without consideration of the merits of the dispute. Respecting this wisdom, the U.S. Court of Appeals for the Fifth Circuit held that the issue of timely compliance with grievance procedures is arbitrable.[40] Although a panel of the U.S. Court of Appeals for the Sixth Circuit affirmed a lower court's contrary ruling that the issue of timely compliance with grievance procedures was not arbitrable, the panel did so in the belief that it was bound to follow its Circuit precedent and unsuccessfully recommended that a full en banc panel overrule the precedent as contrary to Supreme Court decisions.[41]

In *Nolde Bros. v. Bakery & Confectionery Workers Local 358*,[42] the Supreme Court held that an issue over severance pay arose under the collective bargaining agreement and was subject to arbitration even though it arose after the agreement had been terminated. But, in *Litton Financial Printing Division v. NLRB*,[43] the Court held, at least in the context of an NLRB proceeding, that there was no duty to arbitrate disputes occurring after expiration of the collective bargaining agreement, because a party cannot be forced to "'arbitrate the arbitrability issue.'"[44]

Even work jurisdiction questions, such as whether a nonbargaining-unit supervisor could be assigned to do production work, were held to be arbitrable.[45]

The U.S. Court of Appeals for the Ninth Circuit concluded that an arbitrator's determination of the nature of the issue to be decided is entitled to the same deference as his or her interpretation of the contract.[46]

---

[40]Oil, Chem. & Atomic Workers Local 4-447 v. Chevron Chem. Co., 815 F.2d 338, 125 LRRM 2232 (5th Cir. 1987). *See also* Teamsters Local 682 v. Ed Jefferson Contracting, 768 F. Supp. 691 (E.D. Mo. 1991). In *Weber Aircraft v. General Warehousemen Local 767*, 253 F.3d 821, 167 LRRM 2321 (5th Cir. 2001), the court reversed the district court's vacation of an arbitral award reinstating an employee who had committed an offense listed in the collective bargaining agreement as potentially subjecting an offender to discharge without warning.

[41]Raceway Park v. Service Employees Local 47, 167 F.3d 953, 160 LRRM 2274 (6th Cir. 1999).

[42]430 U.S. 243, 94 LRRM 2753 (1977).

[43]501 U.S. 190, 137 LRRM 2441 (1991).

[44]*Id*. at 209 (quoting AT&T Techs. v. Communications Workers, 475 U.S. 643, 651, 121 LRRM 3329 (1986)).

[45]Service Employees Local 106 v. Evergreen Cemetery, 708 F. Supp. 917, 133 LRRM 2336 (N.D. Ill. 1989). However, in discussing whether disability benefits are arbitrable, the U.S. Court of Appeals for the District of Columbia emphasized that this issue was to be decided by the court, not the arbitrator. Air Line Pilots v. Delta Air Lines, 863 F.2d 87, 130 LRRM 2165 (D.C. Cir. 1988), *cert. denied*, 493 U.S. 821 (1989).

[46]Pack Concrete v. Cunningham, 866 F.2d 283, 130 LRRM 2490 (9th Cir. 1989). *See also* Mobil Oil Corp. v. Oil, Chem. & Atomic Workers Local 4-522, 777 F. Supp. 1342 (E.D. La. 1991) (summary of circuit courts' agreement on the scope of issue to be arbitrated).

(2)   Concurrent Arbitral and NLRB Jurisdiction [LA CDI 94.553]

The presumption of arbitrability extends even to disputes over which the NLRB has jurisdiction.[47] In *Carey v. Westinghouse Electric Corp.*,[48] the Supreme Court held that the use of arbitration to resolve work-assignment jurisdictional disputes that involve questions of representation is not preempted by the superior authority of the NLRB, though the Board's processes may be invoked at any time and a Board decision would control in the event of disagreement with that of the arbitrator. In requiring the employer to arbitrate on demand by one of the unions, the Court spoke to "the blurred line" that often exists between work-assignment disputes and representation disputes:

> If it is a work assignment dispute, arbitration conveniently fills a gap and avoids the necessity of a strike to bring the matter to the Board. If it is a representation matter, resort to arbitration may have a pervasive, curative effect even though one union is not a party.
> . . . The superior authority of the Board may be invoked at any time. Meanwhile the therapy of arbitration is brought to bear in a complicated and troubled area."[49]

In order to conserve and efficiently allocate its resources, the Board has adopted a policy allowing it to defer consideration of unfair labor practice charges filed with it until an available arbitration procedure has been exhausted where the statutory claim was implicated in the contractual issue subject to arbitration. However, as to any res judicata, collateral estoppel, or issue preclusion effect of an arbitral award, the U.S. Court of Appeals for the Fifth Circuit ruled that the NLRB was not required to defer to the decision of an arbitration panel upholding an employee's discharge where the arbitration proceedings addressed only the issue of whether the employer had good cause to discharge the employee under the collective bargaining agreement, and did not consider whether the employee had been impermissibly discharged for exercising his statutorily protected grievance-filing activity.[50]

The U.S. Court of Appeals for the Ninth Circuit set forth guidelines outlining when the NLRB should defer to the judgment of an arbitrator on contractual claims that also form the predicate for unfair labor practice charges.[51] Deferral is appropriate where (1) the proceedings are fair and regular, (2) the parties agree to be bound, (3) the decision is not repugnant to the purposes and policies of the act, (4) the contractual issue is factually parallel to the unfair labor practice issue, and (5) the arbitrator is presented generally with the facts relevant to resolving the unfair labor practice.[52]

---

[47]Communications Workers v. U.S. W. Direct, 847 F.2d 1475, 128 LRRM 2698 (10th Cir. 1988).

[48]375 U.S. 261, 55 LRRM 2042 (1964).

[49]*Id.* at 272, 55 LRRM at 2047.

[50]NLRB v. Ryder/P.I.E. Nationwide, 810 F.2d 502, 124 LRRM 3024 (5th Cir. 1987).

[51]Garcia v. NLRB, 785 F.2d 807, 121 LRRM 3349 (9th Cir. 1986).

[52]*Id.*, 121 LRRM at 3351. *See also* Olin Corp., 268 NLRB 573, 115 LRRM 1056 (1984) (Board will not engage in de novo examination of arbitrator's findings and will defer to arbitrator's judgment so long as conditions reiterated in *Garcia* are met); Bakery & Confectionery Workers Local 25 v. NLRB (Pet, Inc., Bakery Div.), 730 F.2d 812, 115 LRRM 3390 (D.C. Cir. 1984) (approves *Olin* standard). *But see* NLRB v. Babcock & Wilcox Co., 736 F.2d

(3) Arbitration and Section 301 Suits

In *Republic Steel Corp. v. Maddox*,[53] the Supreme Court held that an employee must attempt to exhaust a contractual grievance and arbitration procedure prior to resorting to court action under Section 301 of the LMRA. In *Teamsters Local 89 v. Riss & Co.*,[54] the Supreme Court concluded that an award of a joint labor-management grievance committee, though the procedure was not styled "arbitration," is enforceable by court action under Section 301 *if* the award was to be final and binding under the terms of the collective agreement.

Timely Section 301 suits for damages must be stayed by the court pending arbitration where the arbitration clause is sufficiently broad to contemplate submission of the employer's claim for damages for breach of a no-strike clause.[55] But, where the agreement limits arbitration to employee grievances, an employer's damage suit for breach of a no-strike clause may not be dismissed or stayed pending arbitration.[56]

1410, 116 LRRM 2748 (10th Cir. 1984) (unfair labor practice issue was put before arbitrator but he expressly refused to rule on it; NLRB was right in declining to defer the award). For deferral to the arbitration process, see *Spann Bldg. Maint. Co.*, 275 NLRB 971, 119 LRRM 1209 (1985) (deferral to arbitration mechanism appropriate even where hearing had not been scheduled and it appeared that union was not pursuing grievance); *United Techs.*, 268 NLRB 557, 115 LRRM 1049 (1984) (where agreement contains a broad arbitration clause, and there are reasons to believe dispute can be successfully handled by arbitrator, NLRB will let arbitrator decide). For a fuller treatment of the NLRB's policy of deferring to both arbitral awards and the arbitral process in general, and of the court's review of the Board's power to defer, see Comment, *The National Labor Relations Board's Policy on Deferring to Arbitration*, 13 Fla. St. U. L. Rev. 1141 (1986).

[53]379 U.S. 650, 58 LRRM 2193 (1965). The *Maddox* rule was extended to railroad employees in *Andrews v. Louisville & Nashville R.R.*, 406 U.S. 320, 80 LRRM 2240 (1972). *Cf.* Glover v. St. Louis-San Francisco Ry., 393 U.S. 324, 70 LRRM 2097 (1969). The *Maddox* rule does not apply to a seaman's wage claims, which can be taken directly to federal court under an early statute or to arbitration under §301. United States Bulk Carriers v. Arguelles, 400 U.S. 351, 76 LRRM 2161 (1971). Also, in *Alexander v. Gardner-Denver Co.*, 415 U.S. 36, 52, 7 FEP Cases 81 (1974), the Supreme Court said that both the employee's statutory right to proceed in court under Title VII and the contractual right to submit a claim to arbitration "have legally independent origins and are equally available to the aggrieved employee." It is apparent that this is also true in regard to rights under the Fair Labor Standards Act, 29 U.S.C. §201 et seq. Barrentine v. Arkansas Best Freight Sys., 450 U.S. 728, 740–41, 24 WH Cases 1284 (1981). For more on these cases, see section 2.A.ii.d.(1), "De Novo Litigation of Statutory Claims," below. However, in *Emporium Capwell Co. v. Western Addition Community Organization*, 420 U.S. 50, 70, 88 LRRM 2660 (1975), the Court refused to sanction picketing by black employees as an alternative to relying on the union's efforts as exclusive bargaining representative to resolve their racial discrimination complaint against the employer through the grievance and arbitration procedures. *See* Citron, *Deferral of Employee Rights to Arbitration: An Evolving Dichotomy by the Burger Court?*, 27 Hastings L.J. 369, 372–73 (1975).

[54]372 U.S. 517, 52 LRRM 2623 (1963).

[55]Drake Bakeries v. Bakery & Confectionery Workers Local 50, 50 LRRM 2440 (1962). *See also* Packinghouse Workers Local 721 v. Needham Packing Co., 376 U.S. 247, 253, 55 LRRM 2580, 2582 (1964) (Breach of a no-strike clause not a repudiation of the agreement so as to relieve the employer of its obligation to arbitrate grievances over discharge of the strikers. The Court implied a different result might be reached in other instances, saying that it did not decide "[w]hether a fundamental and long-lasting change in the relationship of the parties prior to the demand for arbitration would be a circumstance which, alone or among others, would release an employer from his promise to arbitrate . . . .").

[56]Atkinson v. Sinclair Ref. Co., 370 U.S. 238, 50 LRRM 2433 (1962) (where a union is liable for such breach of contract, its officers and members are not liable). In *Boys Markets v. Retail Clerks Local 770*, 398 U.S. 235, 74 LRRM 2257 (1970), the Court held that strikes that

In *Smith v. Evening News Ass'n*,[57] the Supreme Court held that the NLRB's authority to deal with conduct constituting an unfair labor practice that also violates a collective bargaining agreement is not exclusive and does not destroy the jurisdiction of the courts in Section 301 suits. The Court further held that individual employees can sue under Section 301 to enforce their individual rights under a collective bargaining agreement that did not contain an arbitration clause. In a companion case, *Dowd Box Co. v. Courtney*,[58] the Supreme Court also decided that Section 301 did not divest state courts of jurisdiction over suits to enforce the collective bargaining agreement. The result is that both state and federal courts have concurrent jurisdiction over such suits, including suits to enforce an arbitration clause. But, the Court made it clear in *Teamsters Local 174 v. Lucas Flour Co.*[59] that although both state and federal courts can enforce collective bargaining agreements, state courts exercising jurisdiction over cases within the purview of Section 301 must apply principles of federal substantive law rather than state law.

---

breach the collective bargaining agreement's no-strike clause may be enjoined despite the Norris-LaGuardia Anti-Injunction Act (Norris-LaGuardia Act), 29 U.S.C. §§101–115, but only within the bounds of certain principles: When a strike is sought to be enjoined because it is over a grievance that both parties are contractually bound to arbitrate, the district court may not issue an injunctive order until it first holds that the contract *does* have that effect; and the employer should be ordered to arbitrate, as a condition of its obtaining an injunction against the strike. Beyond this, the district court must, of course, consider whether issuance of an injunction would be warranted under principles of equity—whether breaches are occurring and will continue, or have been threatened and will be committed; whether they have caused or will cause irreparable injury to the employer, and whether the employer will suffer more from the denial of an injunction than will the union from its issuance. *Boys Mkts.*, 398 U.S. at 253–55, 74 LRRM at 2264. The Supreme Court expressly overruled its decision in *Sinclair Refining Co. v. Atkinson*, 370 U.S. 195, 50 LRRM 2420 (1962). The Supreme Court has held that state courts also have jurisdiction over §301 suits to enjoin strikes violating no-strike clauses of agreements containing binding settlement procedures. *See* William E. Arnold Co. v. Carpenters Dist. Council (Jacksonville & Vicinity), 417 U.S. 12, 86 LRRM 2212 (1974) (injunction may be issued even where the strike arguably is an unfair labor practice under the National Labor Relations Act (NLRA), 29 U.S.C. §§151–169). In *Buffalo Forge Co. v. Steelworkers*, 428 U.S. 397, 92 LRRM 3032 (1976), the Supreme Court held that a court could not issue a *Boys Markets* injunction against a sympathy strike. The agreement contained a no-strike clause and a broad arbitration provision, thus, the question whether the strike violated the no-strike clause would be subject to arbitration. However, since the strike itself was not *over* any issue subject to arbitration, it could not be enjoined pending such arbitration. For discussion, see Gould, *On Labor Injunctions Pending Arbitration: Recasting* Buffalo Forge, 30 Stan. L. Rev. 533 (1978); Lowden & Flaherty, *Sympathy Strikes, Arbitration Policy, and the Enforceability of No-Strike Agreements—An Analysis of* Buffalo Forge, 45 Geo. Wash. L. Rev. 633 (1977); Smith, *The Supreme Court*, Boys Markets *Labor Injunctions, and Sympathy Work Stoppages*, 44 U. Chi. L. Rev. 321 (1977). *See also* Longshoremen (ILA) Local 1814 v. New York Shipping Ass'n, 965 F.2d 1224, 140 LRRM 2489 (2d Cir. 1992) (Upholding district court's decision to enjoin arbitration of grievance alleging that association would violate labor agreement by entering into consent judgment with federal government in Racketeer Influenced and Corrupt Organization's Act (RICO), 18 U.S.C. §§151–169, action. The Norris-LaGuardia Act's prohibition against injunctions in labor disputes is overcome by the government's compelling interest in eliminating organized crime's hold on labor unions.).

[57]371 U.S. 195, 51 LRRM 2646 (1962).

[58]368 U.S. 502, 49 LRRM 2619 (1962).

[59]369 U.S. 95, 49 LRRM 2717 (1962). The rule that there is an implied no-strike obligation as to issues subject to arbitration was held to apply to safety disputes in *Gateway Coal Co. v. Mine Workers Dist. 4, Local 6330*, 414 U.S. 368, 85 LRRM 2049 (1974). The Court did say it "would be unusual, but certainly permissible, for the parties to agree to a broad mandatory arbitration provision yet expressly negate any implied no-strike obligation." *Id.* at

The concurrent jurisdiction of state courts and their obligation to follow federal law extends to suits by employees against their union for refusing to arbitrate their grievances.[60] Under federal standards, however, mere negligence, even in enforcement of the collective bargaining agreement, does not state a claim for breach of duty of fair representation. Such a breach occurs only when the union's conduct toward members of the collective bargaining unit is arbitrary, discriminatory, or in bad faith. [61]

(4) Vacatur of Arbitration Awards—General Principles

Awards that conflict with the standards set forth in the *Steelworkers Trilogy*[62] are subject to judicial nullification.[63] Despite their broad language, the *Trilogy* standards left significant room for courts to set aside arbitral rulings. In this connection, one arbitrator stated: "Expectably, the lower courts in applying *Enterprise* have reflected the Supreme Court's ambivalence toward finality."[64]

Indeed, several courts that purport to follow the Supreme Court's *Enterprise Wheel* pronouncement that an arbitration award must draw its essence from the collective bargaining agreement[65] have interpreted the "essence" concept broadly. Thus, the U.S. Court of Appeals for the Eighth Circuit refused to enforce an arbitrator's decision that an employer's "no-beards" policy was an unreasonable standard of appearance.[66] Yet, in another case, the same court found that an arbitration award reinstating an employee without back

---

382. However, expressly rescinding no-strike clauses contained in prior agreements (leaving none in the current agreement) did not suffice to negate an implied no-strike obligation. *Id.* at 383–85. *Gateway Coal* also held that the *Trilogy* presumption of arbitrability applies to safety disputes.

[60]Vaca v. Sipes, 386 U.S. 171, 64 LRRM 2369 (1967). See also discussion of *Hines v. Anchor Motor Freight*, 424 U.S. 554, 91 LRRM 2481 (1976), in section 2.A.ii.d.(2), "De Novo Litigation of Claims Cognizable Under the Labor Management Relations Act," below. In *Electrical Workers (IBEW) v. Foust*, 442 U.S. 42, 101 LRRM 2365 (1979), the Supreme Court held that punitive damages may not be assessed against a union that breaches its duty of fair representation under the RLA, and the decision was clearly intended to apply also to unions under the NLRA. In *Humphrey v. Moore*, 375 U.S. 335, 55 LRRM 2031, *reh'g denied*, 376 U.S. 935 (1964), the Supreme Court held that federal and state courts had concurrent jurisdiction under §301 over an employee's suit for alleged breach of a collective agreement by a joint union-employer committee in dovetailing the seniority lists of two companies. The improper representation claim against the union could be resolved as part of the §301 breach of contract claim against the employer. Even if an unfair labor practice within the NLRB's jurisdiction was involved, the courts could entertain the §301 suit.

[61]Steelworkers v. Rawson, 495 U.S. 362, 134 LRRM 2153 (1990).

[62]Steelworkers v. American Mfg. Co., 363 U.S. 564, 46 LRRM 2414, 34 LA 559 (1960); Steelworkers v. Warrior & Gulf Navigation Co., 363 U.S. 574, 46 LRRM 2416, 34 LA 561 (1960); Steelworkers v. Enterprise Wheel & Car Corp., 363 U.S. 593, 46 LRRM 2423, 34 LA 569 (1960).

[63]*Report of the Committee on Labor Arbitration and the Law of Collective Bargaining Agreements*, 1977 LAB. REL. L. COMM. REP. 5, 12 (ABA, 1977).

[64]St. Antoine, *Judicial Review of Labor Arbitration Awards: A Second Look at Enterprise Wheel and Its Progeny*, 75 MICH. L. REV. 1137, 1148 (1977), *reprinted in* ARBITRATION—1997, PROCEEDINGS OF THE 30TH ANNUAL MEETING OF NAA 29, 40 (Dennis & Somers eds., BNA Books 1978).

[65]*Enterprise Wheel*, 363 U.S. 574, 46 LRRM 2423, 34 LA 569 (1960).

[66]Trailways Lines v. Trailways Joint Council, 807 F.2d 1416, 124 LRRM 2217 (8th Cir. 1986), *reh'g denied*, 817 F.2d 1333, 125 LRRM 2364 (8th Cir. 1987).

pay did draw its essence from the collective bargaining agreement,[67] reasoning that the award was an "obviously well-considered attempt to balance the conduct of the parties in light of the terms of the existing labor contract."[68]

One problem is that courts, under the guise of 'interpretation," often cannot resist the impulse to "do justice" when they perceive the arbitrator's award to be wrong on the merits. Merit review of arbitral awards not only fails to accord grievance-arbitration the semiautonomous status sanctioned by the *Trilogy*, but it also undermines the attribute of arbitral finality. For example, in *Bruce Hardwood Floors v. UBC, Southern Council of Industrial Workers Local 2713*,[69] the U.S. Court of Appeals for the Fifth Circuit reversed the district court's enforcement of an arbitration award finding a discharge unreasonable because the grievant's behavior constituted "immoral conduct" under a contractual provision permitting immediate discharge for the offense. In that case, the dissent accused the majority of usurping the function of the arbitrator by interpreting the "immoral conduct" term.[70]

In *Bruce Hardwood Floors*, a production employee secured permission from her supervisor to leave work in order to "take her truck to her daughter who needed it to go to the doctor." The supervisor learned after approving the request that the employee actually needed the time off to pay an electric bill. The following day, the employee admitted to her supervisor that she had fabricated the story about the daughter's doctor's appointment. The supervisor summarily discharged the employee "for obtaining time off from work under false pretenses," without using progressive discipline. While the agreement provided for immediate discharge for "immoral conduct," it required progressive discipline for other offenses. The question was whether her conduct was subject to summary discharge or progressive discipline under the contract. The arbitrator found the discharge unreasonable, because the employer should have applied the progressive discipline rather than the summary discharge provisions. Although the district court enforced the award, the Fifth Circuit reversed, holding that the arbitrator exceeded his authority under the contract. In the court's view, the award did not draw its essence from the contract, because it viewed the employee's lying as "immoral conduct" and the provision calling for immediate discharge as a limitation on the arbitrator's authority. Noting the plausibility of the arbitrator's interpretation of the employee's lying as more analogous to the progressive discipline offenses than the immediate discharge offenses, the dissent argued that the majority substituted its own interpretation of the agreement for that of the arbitrator's.

---

[67]Walsh v. Union Pac. R.R., 803 F.2d 412, 123 LRRM 2789 (8th Cir. 1986), *cert. denied*, 482 U.S. 928 (1987).

[68]*Id.* at 414, 123 LRRM at 2791. For a fuller overview of U.S. Court of Appeals for the Eighth Circuit cases, see Note, *Judicial Review of Labor Arbitration Awards: Refining the Standard of Review*, 11 Wm. Mitchell L. Rev. 993 (1985).

[69]103 F.3d 449, 154 LRRM 2207 (5th Cir. 1997).

[70]*See generally* Sharpe, *Judicial Review of Labor Arbitration Awards: A View From the Bench*, *in* Arbitration 1999: Quo Vadis? The Future of Arbitration and Collective Bargaining, Proceedings of the 52d Annual Meeting of NAA 126 (Briggs & Grenig eds., BNA Books 1999).

Bruce Hardwood Floors is not an isolated instance in the Fifth Circuit's recent arbitral review jurisprudence.[71] Recent data show that in 11 years of post-*Misco*[72] cases, 73.97 percent of the appealed awards were enforced and only 26.03 percent were overturned. Circuits varied in their enforcement rates from the lowest Tenth Circuit reversal rate of 10.53 to the highest Fifth Circuit reversal rate of 42.86.[73] The Fifth Circuit's outlier status might be explained by its reformulation of *Enterprise Wheel*'s essence standard as follows:

> [A]n arbitration award "must have a basis that is at least rationally inferable, if not obviously drawn, from the letter or purpose of the collective bargaining agreement . . . . [T]he award must, in some logical way, be derived from the wording or purpose of the contract."[74]

This reformulated standard seems to invite a review of the merits of an award that is impermissible under *Enterprise Wheel*.[75] It may be part of a judicial mood in the Fifth Circuit toward intervention in arbitration outcomes.[76]

The Fourth Circuit also seems particularly prone to use the "essence" standard of *Enterprise Wheel* as the justification for setting aside awards with which they disagree.[77]

---

[71]*See, e.g.*, Houston Lighting & Power Co. v. Electrical Workers (IBEW) Local 66, 71 F.3d 179, 151 LRRM 2020 (5th Cir. 1995) (reversing an award, enforced by the district court, based on the court's contrary interpretation of the relevant contractual provision); Operating Eng'rs Local 351 v. Cooper Natural Res., 163 F.3d 916, 160 LRRM 2241 (5th Cir. 1999) (refusing to enforce the arbitrator's award because of its disagreement on a garden variety issue of interpretation of notice requirement).

[72]Paperworkers v. Misco, Inc., 484 U.S. 29, 126 LRRM 3113 (1987).

[73]*See* Sharpe, *Judicial Review of Labor Arbitration Awards: A View From the Bench, in* Arbitration 1999: Quo Vadis? The Future of Arbitration and Collective Bargaining, Proceedings of the 52d Annual Meeting of NAA 126, 142 (Briggs & Grenig eds., BNA Books 1999) (citing data produced by Professor Paul Barron in a study of judicial review). These results are generally consistent with those found in LeRoy & Feuille, *Private Justice in the Shadow of Public Courts: The Autonomy of Workplace Arbitration Systems*, 17 Ohio St. J. Disp. Res. 19 (2001), analyzing judicial review of labor arbitration awards from 1960–2001. This study found that district courts confirmed 71.8% of the 1,008 cases decided from 1960–1991, and 70.3% of the 232 decisions in the past decade, while appellate courts confirmed 70.5% of the awards from 1960–1961 and 66.4% from 1991–2001. Interestingly, this study showed that the confirmation rate dropped substantially in district courts in the Fourth and Eighth Circuits, but rose in the Ninth Circuit. Also consistent with the Barron data was the variance by region, with confirmation rates increasing among district courts in circuits with high volume, e.g., the Ninth Circuit by 13%. By contrast, the confirmation rate dropped by 15.5% and 19.2% in the Fourth and Eighth Circuits. However, they remained fairly constant for courts in the Second and Third Circuits.

[74]Executone Info Sys. v. Davis, 26 F.3d 1314, 1325 (5th Cir. 1994) (quoting Railroad Trainmen v. Central of Ga. Ry., 415 F.2d 403, 412, 71 LRRM 3042 (5th Cir. 1969)).

[75]*See* Sharpe, *Integrity Review of Statutory Arbitration Awards*, 54 Hastings L.J. 311 (2003) (distinguishing between procedural and substantive integrity review standards, the former applicable to private contractual awards and not involving a review of the merits, and the latter applicable to statutory awards and involving a limited review of the merits).

[76]*See, e.g.*, Houston Lighting & Power Co. v. Electrical Workers (IBEW) Local 66, 71 F.3d 179, 182, 151 LRRM 2020 (5th Cir. 1995) (quoting Delta Queen Steamboat Co. v. Marine Eng'rs Dist. 2, 889 F.2d 599, 604, 133 LRRM 2077, 2081 (5th Cir. 1989) ("[The] rule in this circuit, and the emerging trend among other courts of appeals, is that arbitral action contrary to express contractual provisions will not be respected.").

[77]*See generally* Woody, Clinchfield Coal v. District 28, United Mine Workers; *A New Standard for Judicial Review of Labor Arbitration Awards?*, 88 W. Va. L. Rev. 605 (1985–1986).

In addition to vacating an award that is utterly unsupported by the evidence,[78] or is contrary to the express language of the agreement,[79] the U.S. Court of Appeal for the Fourth Circuit's two *Clinchfield* decisions[80] also reveal the court's willingness to scrutinize both the arbitrator's treatment of the evidence and the arbitrator's reasoning. *Clinchfield I* apparently imposes on the arbitrator requirements that the decision be "reasonable" and that the arbitrator explain his or her stance on the issues crucial to resolving the dispute before the arbitrator.[81]

Clinchfield II represents yet another interference with finality of an arbitrator's award, holding that, even though the award is reasonable, it will still be reversed if the court has already ruled on the issue and the facts that the arbitrator is called on to consider.[82]

Other courts of appeals have been more faithful to the limited review contemplated by *Enterprise Wheel*. The U.S. Court of Appeals for the Seventh Circuit, in *Hill v. Norfolk & Western Railway*,[83] affirmed the principle that a court may not substitute its interpretation of the agreement for that of an arbitrator in a railroad case, holding that the arbitrator's interpretation is conclusive even if it is a gross error.[84] In *Auto Workers v. Dana Corp.*,[85] the U.S. Court of Appeals for the Sixth Circuit concluded that the arbitrator's award drew its essence from the agreement, because his interpretation

> on its face does not appear to: (1) conflict with the express terms of the agreement; (2) impose additional requirements not expressly provided for in the agreement; (3) fail to be rationally supported by or derived from the agreement; or (4) be based on general terms of fairness and equity instead of the exact terms of the agreement. Instead, the interpretation seems to be a reasonable construction of ambiguous terms.[86]

In *Madison Hotel v. Hotel Employees Local 25*,[87] the U.S. Court of Appeals for the D.C. Circuit used the following reasoning to reverse a district court's decision vacating an arbitrator's award:

> That the arbitrator gave more weight to some provisions—such as the seniority and classification provisions—and less weight to others—such as the Management Rights Clause—than the district court or the Hotel might have preferred is not a permissible basis for vacating the award. It should hardly need repeating that "courts have no business overruling [an arbitrator] because their

---

[78]Clinchfield Coal Co. v. Mine Workers Dist. 28, 720 F.2d 1365, 1371, 114 LRRM 3053 (4th Cir. 1983) (Sprouse, J., concurring) (*Clinchfield I*).

[79]*Id.* at 1372.

[80]*Id.*; Clinchfield Coal Co. v. Mine Workers Dist. 28, 736 F.2d 998, 116 LRRM 2884 (4th Cir. 1984) (*Clinchfield II*).

[81]*Clinchfield I*, at 1369. *See also* Woody, 88 W. VA. L. REV. at 608–10.

[82]For a critical analysis of the *Clinchfield* decisions, see Trumka, *Keeping Miners Out of Work: Cost of Judicial Revision of Arbitration Awards*, 86 W. VA. L. REV. 705 (1984).

[83]814 F.2d 1192, 124 LRRM 3057 (7th Cir. 1987).

[84]More recently, see *Northern Indiana Public Service Co. v. Steelworkers*, 243 F.3d 345, 348, 166 LRRM 2808 (7th Cir. 2001), holding that the award drew its essence from the agreement because "although the arbitrator was not empowered under the CBA to add terms to the [agreement], the arbitrators are empowered to fill gaps left in contracts."

[85]278 F.3d 548, 169 LRRM 2193 (6th Cir. 2002).

[86]*Id.* at 557–58. It should be noted that like the reformulated Fifth Circuit standard, this Sixth Circuit standard would seem to invite an impermissible review of the merits in some cases.

[87]144 F.3d 855, 158 LRRM 2398 (D.C. Cir. 1998).

interpretation of the contract is different from his." *Enterprise Wheel*, 363 U.S. at 599. The "parties having authorized the arbitrator to give meaning to the language of the agreement," courts cannot "reject [the] award on the ground that the arbitrator misread the contract." *Misco*, 484 U.S. at 38.[88]

The U.S. Court of Appeals for the First Circuit, in *Kraft Foods, Inc. v. Office & Professional Employees Local 1295*,[89] refused to set aside the award without a showing that it violated a specific prohibition in the agreement. The Eighth Circuit, in *Trailmobile Trailer, LLC v. Electronic Workers Local 1149*,[90] upheld the arbitrator's award, despite contractual provisions that suggest error.[91]

Even courts that evince a respect for the *Enterprise Wheel* standard sometimes have difficulty applying the standard. The inherent ambiguity of the standard seems to combine with the courts' irresistible focus on the merits to produce an aberrant decision. For example, in *Appalachian Regional Healthcare v. Steelworkers Local 14398*,[92] the Sixth Circuit upheld the district court's vacating of an arbitrator's award that had required the reinstatement of three discharged employees. The reviewing court articulated the appropriately narrow scope of review of arbitral awards as follows:

> A reviewing court will not replace an arbitrator's construction of the Agreement with its own interpretation. "The Supreme Court has made clear . . . that courts must accord an arbitrator's decision substantial deference because it is the arbitrator's construction of the agreement, not the court's construction, to which the parties have agreed."[93]

Yet, in this case, where the outcome turned on the interpretation of a workweek provision, the court examined the intent of the parties and determined that the arbitrator was "wrong" in his conclusion about the applicability of the provision. The dissent noted that even though the majority had articulated the appropriate standard that a reviewing court will not replace an arbitrator's construction of the agreement with its own interpretation,

---

[88]*Id.* at 859 (citation omitted).

[89]203 F.3d 98, 163 LRRM 2526 (1st Cir. 2000).

[90]223 F.3d 744, 164 LRRM 3100 (8th Cir. 2000). However, in *Alvey, Inc. v. Teamsters Local 688*, 132 F.3d 1209, 157 LRRM 2018 (8th Cir. 1997), the court vacated the arbitrator's award because it did not purport to construe the contract. Rather, "the arbitrator adopted his own, hyper-technical meaning derived from a contextually inapposite source in state law." *Id.* at 1213.

[91]*But see* Leroy & Feuille, *Private Justice in the Shadow of Public Courts: The Autonomy of Workplace Arbitration Systems*, 17 OHIO ST. J. DISP. RES. 19, 50 (citing data that show a substantial drop in confirmation rates in the Eighth Circuit from 1991–2001). *See also* Rubbermaid Office Prods., Inc. v. Steelworkers Local 451, 168 F.3d 501 (9th Cir. 1999) (affirming arbitrator's award over company's objection that the award contradicted the terms of the agreement); Kennecott Utah Copper Corp. v. Becker, 195 F.3d 1201, 162 LRRM 2641 (10th Cir. 1999) (sustaining under essence review an arbitration award reinstating employee discharged for testing positive for marijuana); Yuasa, Inc. v. Electronic Workers (IUE) Local 175, 224 F.3d 316, 165 LRRM 2016 (4th Cir. 2000) (confirming the award while expressing doubt about its merits; noting that the award was within the scope of the grievance and drew its essence from the agreement); Consolidation Coal Co. v. Mine Workers (UMW) Dist. 12, Local 1545, 213 F.3d 404, 164 LRRM 2321 (7th Cir. 2000) (Judge Posner pointing out that the courts cannot second-guess the arbitrator's decision).

[92]245 F.3d 601, 166 LRRM 3011 (6th Cir. 2001).

[93]245 F.3d at 604 (quoting Beacon Journal Publ'g Co. v. Akron Newspaper Guild Local 7, 114 F.3d 596, 599, 155 LRRM 2482 (6th Cir. 1997)).

the majority had done precisely that.[94] Similarly, the U.S. Court of Appeals for the Ninth Circuit in *Hawaii Teamsters & Allied Workers Union Local 996 v. United Parcel Service*[95] reversed the district court's enforcement of an award sustaining a discharge. The court disagreed with the arbitrator's interpretation of a provision permitting summary discharge.[96]

The philosophy underlying these decisions may have to be re-examined in light of the Supreme Court's decision in *Major League Baseball Players Ass'n v. Garvey*,[97] concluding that even "serious error" by the arbitrator does not justify vacating the award so long as he or she acts honestly and within the scope of his or her authority. In *Garvey v. Roberts*,[98] the Ninth Circuit had rejected an arbitrator's factual determination leading to his denial of a baseball player's grievance that had asserted that club owners had conspired to deny him a new contract, and proceeded to resolve the merits of the dispute. The Supreme Court reversed:

> We recently reiterated that if an "'arbitrator is even arguably construing or applying the contract and acting within the scope of his authority,' the fact that 'a court is convinced he committed serious errors does not suffice to overturn his decision.'"[99]

The U.S. Court of Appeals for the Tenth Circuit, in an important 1989 case,[100] upheld an award rescinding the discharge of an employee with 23 years of service for failure to perform a job duty. The arbitrator found the employee's carelessness, laziness, and neglect failed to satisfy the "just and sufficient cause" standard. The arbitrator stated that only dereliction of duty involving extreme carelessness and resulting in serious economic damage could justify discharge. The court held that the findings and conclusions of the arbitrator, "correct or not," were rooted in the agreement and the court could not substitute its own interpretation.

Although the courts have failed to develop a uniformly recognized set of reasons for vacating or refusing to enforce awards,[101] there are some gener-

---

[94]As previously noted, the standard articulated in *Auto Workers v. Dana Corp.*, 278 F.3d 548, 169 LRRM 2193 (6th Cir. 2002), and applied in this case may well have caused the court to improperly consider the merits in this case.

[95]229 F.3d 847, 165 LRRM 2200 (9th Cir. 2000)

[96]Typical of the appellate decisions that disagree on the merits of awards the Ninth Circuit expressed a preference for the authority not relied upon by the arbitrator rather than that relied upon. *See Hawaii Teamsters*, 229 F.3d at 851–52. *Cf.* Madison Hotel v. Hotel Employees Local 25, 144 F.3d 855, 158 LRRM 2398 (D.C. Cir. 1998).

[97]Major League Baseball Players Ass'n v. Garvey, 532 U.S. 504, 167 LRRM 2134 (2001).

[98]203 F.3d 580, 1636 LRRM 2449 (9th Cir. 2000).

[99]*Major League Baseball Players Ass'n*, 532 U.S. at 509 (quoting Eastern Assoc. Coal Corp. v. Mine Workers, 531 U.S. 57, 62, 165 LRRM 2865 (2002), in turn quoting Paperworkers v. Misco, 484 U.S. 29, 38, 126 LRRM 3113 (1987)).

[100]Litvak Packing Co. v. Food & Commercial Workers Local 7, 886 F.2d 275, 132 LRRM 2383 (10th Cir. 1989). *See also* Electrical Workers (IBEW) Local 611 v. Public Serv. Co. of N.M., 980 F.2d 616, 141 LRRM 2915 (10th Cir. 1992); Polk Bros. v. Chicago Truck Drivers, 973 F.2d 593, 141 LRRM 2172 (7th Cir. 1992); Clean Coverall Supply Co. v. Construction, Bldg. Material, Ice & Coal Local 682, 688 F. Supp. 1364 (E.D. Mo. 1988).

[101]*See* ROTHSCHILD, MERRIFIELD & EDWARDS, COLLECTIVE BARGAINING AND LABOR ARBITRATION 342–61 (1979); GORMAN, BASIC TEXT ON LABOR LAW 584–603 (1976); Kaden, *Judges and Arbitrators: Observations on the Scope of Judicial Review*, 80 COLUM. L. REV. 267 (1980); St. Antoine, *Judicial Review of Labor Arbitration Awards: A Second Look at Enterprise Wheel and Its Progeny*, 75 MICH. L. REV. 1146–57 (1977), *reprinted in* ARBITRATION–1977, PROCEEDINGS OF THE 30TH ANNUAL MEETING OF NAA 29, 38–48 (Dennis & Somers eds., BNA Books 1978); Yarowsky,

ally accepted individual grounds. Enforcement of an award ordinarily will be denied if the award (1) is in manifest disregard of the law, (2) sustains or orders conduct that is illegal, (3) is contrary to a well-defined and established public policy, or (4) concludes that, in the eyes of the court, the arbitrator lacked jurisdiction over the dispute.[102] In addition, there have been a few isolated cases where courts have struck down awards on other grounds set forth in the Federal Arbitration Act, such as evident bias or partiality by the arbitrator;[103] prejudicial exclusion of evidence; gross error of fact underlying the award; or violation of a contractual limitation on the arbitrator's authority to rule on some particular issue, or on the arbitrator's remedy power.[104] The Sixth Circuit summarized the following four types of cases where it has vacated arbitration awards as follows: "(1) an award conflicts with express terms of the collective bargaining agreement," "(2) an award im-

---

Judicial Deference to Arbitral Determinations: Continuing Problems of Power and Finality, 23 UCLA L. Rev. 936 (1976); Note, *Judicial Review of Labor Arbitration Awards After the Trilogy*, 53 Cornell L. Rev. 136 (1967). Even apart from other considerations, it may be that the total number of awards struck down over the years has not been large enough to reflect a clearly defined and generally accepted set of grounds. But consider the conclusion of one court that made an extensive survey of court decisions under the RLA, the NLRA, and the Federal Arbitration Act:

> In recognition of the limited judicial role in the arbitration process, courts have typically confined their scrutiny of awards to the broad contours of procedural fairness and arbitral impartiality. . . . It is thus firmly established that courts will not review the substance of a labor arbitration award for ordinary error and that courts will not vacate an award because a judge might have reached a different result. . . .
>
> The substantive grounds for vacating labor arbitral awards that do exist are extremely narrow. . . . As exposited by the courts, there appear to be three interrelated grounds for such substantive review of arbitral awards:
>
> (1) whether the award is irrational . . . [as, for example, where an award is "wholly baseless and completely without reason," or as where "no judge, or group of judges, could ever conceivably have made such a ruling"]; . . .
>
> (2) whether the award draws its essence from the letter or purpose of the collective bargaining agreement . . . ; and
>
> (3) whether the arbitrator conformed to a specific contractual limitation upon his authority . . . .

Loveless v. Eastern Air Lines, 681 F.2d 1272, 1275–76, 111 LRRM 2001, 2003–04 (11th Cir. 1982) (quoting Gunther v. San Diego & Ariz. Ry., 382 U.S. 257, 261, 60 LRRM 2496 (1965); Safeway Stores v. Bakery & Confectionery Workers Local 111, 39 F.2d 79, 82, 67 LRRM 2646 (5th Cir. 1968); Steelworkers v. Enterprise Wheel & Car Corp., 363 U.S. 593, 597, 46 LRRM 2423, 34 LA 569 (1960)) (other citations omitted). *See also* Chapter 11, section 4., "Judicial Treatment of the Precedential Value of Arbitration Awards."

[102]*See* Montes v. Shearson Lehman Bros., 128 F.3d 1456, 1460–61 (11th Cir. 1997). *See also* M&C Corp. v. Erwin Behr GmbH & Co., KG, 87 F.3d 844, 850–51 (6th Cir. 1996); Barnes v. Logan, 122 F.3d 820, 821 (9th Cir. 1997). For a discussion on the evolution of the "manifest disregard for the law" standard and when courts will vacate arbitration awards based on the standard, see Milam, *A House Built on Sand: Vacating Arbitration Awards for Manifest Disregard of the Law*, 29 Cumb. L. Rev. 705 (1999).

[103]See discussion of the scope of judicial review of awards under the Federal Arbitration Act in Chapter 1, section 7.B.i.d., "Scope of Judicial Review: Vacation of Award." *See also* Flexsys Am., L.P. v. Steelworkers Local 12601, 88 F. Supp. 2d 600, 164 LRRM 2985 (S.D. W. Va. 2000) (after hearing, arbitrator had ex parte conversation with employer advocate requesting that company reopen hearing to investigate whether discharged employee's supervisor was "gay," and indicating that if the employee thought he was, he would overturn the discipline).

[104]*See* Carpenters Local 1027 v. Lee Lumber & Bldg. Material Corp., 2 F.3d 796, 144 LRRM 2199 (7th Cir. 1993) (although contract defined grievance as claim against employer, arbitrator entered back-pay order against the union in reinstating discharged employee).

poses additional requirements that are not expressly provided in the agreement," "(3) an award is without rational support or cannot be rationally derived from the terms of the agreement,"[105] and "(4) an award is based on general considerations of fairness and equity instead of the precise terms of the agreement."[106]

One of the most often cited explanations for a court's refusal to uphold an award is that the arbitrator's award violates the clear language of the agreement (the "plain meaning" standard of contract interpretation). The U.S. Court of Appeals for the Tenth Circuit affirmed a remand decision of a district court on this basis.[107] There the agreement between the union and the company required the employer to pay damages to the aggrieved employees or the union if the employer failed to properly man its compressors. The arbitrator found such a violation and ordered the employer to man the particular set of compressors in the future, but refused to award damages. The district court remanded the case to the arbitrator for a calculation of the lost earnings. The court affirmed, reasoning that because the arbitrator found that the employer had violated the agreement, he was compelled by the express terms of the agreement to award damages sustained as a result of the violation.

Greater uniformity among circuits in adopting standards for vacatur of awards may result because of the Supreme Court's *Circuit City* decision,[108] declaring the Federal Arbitration Act applicable to employment contracts covering virtually all private sector employees except those engaged directly in transportation, although reserving the issue whether the Act applies to collectively bargained contracts. Section 10 of the Federal Arbitration Act sets forth six grounds on which a court may vacate an arbitration award:

1. The award was procured by corruption, fraud, or undue means;
2. The arbitrator was guilty of evident partiality;
3. The arbitrator refused to "postpone the hearing, upon sufficient cause shown";
4. The arbitrator refused "to hear evidence pertinent and material to the controversy";
5. The arbitrator engaged in misbehavior prejudicial to the rights of a party; and
6. The arbitrator exceeded his or her powers or so imperfectly executed them that a "final and definite" award was not made.[109]

---

[105]It should be reiterated that this particular basis for vacatur may create an unacceptable risk of judicial noncompliance with the *Enterprise Wheel* mandate.

[106]Appalachian Regional Healthcare v. Steelworkers Local 14398, 245 F.3d 601, 604–05, 166 LRRM 3011 (6th Cir. 2001). *See* Wyandot, Inc. v. Food & Commercial Workers Local 227, 205 F.3d 922, 163 LRRM 2705 (6th Cir. 2000) (where the court found that the arbitrator's award violated all four *Dobbs* factors).

[107]Operating Eng'rs Local 9 v. Shank-Artukovich, 751 F.2d 364, 118 LRRM 2157 (10th Cir. 1985). *See also* Morgan Servs. v. Clothing & Textile Workers Local 323, 724 F.2d 1217, 115 LRRM 2368 (6th Cir. 1984) (arbitrator erred in ordering reinstatement of employee after finding insubordination, where contract permitted employer to discharge employee for insubordination).

[108]Circuit City Stores v. Adams, 532 U.S. 105, 85 FEP Cases 266 (2001).

[109]9 U.S.C. §10. See the discussion of the scope of judicial review of awards under the Federal Arbitration Act in Chapter 1, section 7.B.i.d., "Scope of Judicial Review: Vacation of Awards."

The extent to which this last vacatur ground—that the arbitrator exceeded his or her powers—will be interpreted elastically by the courts to subsume other asserted defects, such as gross errors of law or lack of rationality, remains to be seen. However, the Supreme Court's summary reversal of the U.S. Court of Appeals for Ninth Circuit in the *Garvey* case[110] perhaps serves as a potent reminder that judicial disagreement with an arbitrator's interpretation does not provide a basis for setting it aside. It should be remembered, nevertheless, that the parties may be able to alter the standard of review in their arbitration agreement, as for example, by providing that each party retains the right to appeal "any questions of law."[111]

(5) Vacatur Based on Improper Remedies [LA CDI 94.559; 118.03]

In many disciplinary cases, the focus is on the arbitrator's authority to convert a greater penalty into a lesser one once a grievant has been found to have committed a violation. In a pair of cases decided in 1988, the U.S. Court of Appeals for the First Circuit upheld the employer's assertion that once a violation of a disciplinary standard is proven, the express language of the contract may give the employer the exclusive right to determine the penalty.[112] There, the court overruled the arbitrators' conclusions that the contractual language on penalty was ambiguous, but held rather that the fixed sanction system set forth in the work rules had been incorporated into the contract. Whether this decision can survive the Supreme Court's *Garvey* decision is questionable.[113] As the U.S. Court of Appeals for the Eleventh Circuit tartly observed, quoting *Trilogy*[114] doctrine, an award cannot simply reflect the arbitrator's own notions of industrial justice.[115]

The concept that the parties may limit the discretion of arbitrators in fashioning a remedy is supported by the statement of the Supreme Court in *Misco*[116] that a contract may vest unreviewable discretion in management to discharge an employee once a disciplinary offense has occurred. A decade earlier, anticipating this pronouncement, a U.S. Court of Appeals for the

---

[110]Major League Baseball Players Ass'n v. Garvey, 532 U.S. 504, 167 LRRM 2134 (2001).

[111]Harris v. Parker Coll. of Chiropractic, 286 F.3d 790, 88 FEP Cases 663 (5th Cir. 2002).

[112]S.D. Warren Co. v. Paperworkers Local 1069, 846 F.2d 827, 128 LRRM 2432 (1st Cir.), *cert. denied*, 488 U.S. 992 (1988); S.D. Warren Co. v. Paperworkers Local 1069, 845 F.2d 3, 128 LRRM 2175 (1st Cir.), *cert. denied*, 488 U.S. 992 (1988). *See also* Paperworkers Local 369 v. Georgia Pac. Corp. 841 F.2d 243, 127 LRRM 3112 (8th Cir. 1988).

[113]Major League Baseball Players Ass'n v. Garvey, 532 U.S. 504, 167 LRRM 2134 (2001).

[114]Steelworkers v. American Mfg. Co., 363 U.S. 564, 46 LRRM 2414, 34 LA 559 (1960); Steelworkers v. Warrior & Gulf Navigation Co., 363 U.S. 574, 46 LRRM 2416, 34 LA 561 (1960); Steelworkers v. Enterprise Wheel & Car Corp., 363 U.S. 593, 46 LRRM 2423, 34 LA 569 (1960).

[115]Bruno's, Inc. v. Food & Commercial Workers Local 1657, 858 F.2d 1529, 129 LRRM 2815 (11th Cir. 1988). *See also* Pennsylvania Power Co. v. Electrical Workers (IBEW) Local 272, 886 F.2d 46, 132 LRRM 2388 (3d Cir. 1989); Georgia-Pacific Corp. v. Paperworkers Local 27, 864 F.2d 940, 130 LRRM 2208 (1st Cir. 1988); *In re* Marine Pollution Serv., 857 F.2d 91, 129 LRRM 2472 (2d Cir. 1988).

[116]Paperworkers v. Misco, Inc., 484 U.S. 29, 126 LRRM 3113, 3118 (1987). See discussion in text beginning in section 2.A.ii.c.(8), "Vacatur and Refusals to Enforce Awards Based on Public Policy Grounds," below.

Tenth Circuit decision declared that an arbitrator had departed from the contract by grafting principles of progressive discipline onto perfectly unambiguous language that vested total discretion over remedies in the employer.[117]

Subsequent to *Misco*, the U.S. Court of Appeals for the Fifth Circuit approved the vacation of an award reinstating a riverboat captain who had been discharged because his carelessness had almost caused a riverboat collision.[118]

In a few cases, attorneys' fees assessed by an arbitrator have been upheld. In one, the U.S. Court of Appeals for the Second Circuit noted that while counsel fees are not routinely awarded in labor disputes, they were justified under the egregious circumstances there present. Acknowledging that an arbitrator is not authorized to award punitive damages as a matter of public policy under New York law, the court distinguished the shifting of counsel fees as a nonpunitive permissible sanction.[119]

A U.S. Court of Appeals for the Tenth Circuit decision established a novel remedial precedent in awarding the lion's share of a back-pay award against the union, where the employer had failed to properly recall an employee under the labor agreement.[120] The arbitrator held the union responsible for a 2-year delay in bringing the case to arbitration. The award was premised on the breadth of the parties' issue stipulation.[121]

The U.S. Court of Appeals for the Second Circuit reinstated an award that had been vacated by a lower court because the arbitrator had awarded $50,000 to the union, when no evidence of money damages had been adduced at the hearing. There, in anticipation of a strike, the employer had locked out bargaining-unit employees. The Second Circuit reasoned that "the arbitrator was nonetheless entitled to conclude that the Employer's preemptive lockout weakened the Union's bargaining position both at that juncture of the ongoing labor controversy and in the aftermath, with resultant economic damage to the Union, and to approximate that damage as the circumstances allowed."[122]

---

[117]Mistletoe Express Serv. v. Motor Expressmen's Union, 566 F.2d 692, 96 LRRM 3320 (10th Cir. 1977).

[118]Delta Queen Steamboat Co. v. Marine Eng'rs Dist. 2, 889 F.2d 599, 133 LRRM 2077 (5th Cir. 1989). *See also* E.I. DuPont de Nemours & Co. v. Chemical Workers Local 900, 803 F. Supp. 1223 (S.D. Tex. 1991), *aff'd*, 968 F.2d 456, 141 LRRM 2204 (5th Cir. 1992).

[119]Synergy Gas Co. v. Sasso, 853 F.2d 59, 129 LRRM 2041 (2d Cir.), *cert. denied*, 488 U.S. 994 (1988). *See also* Gilling v. Eastern Airlines, 680 F. Supp. 169 (D.N.J. 1988); Ultracashmere House v. Nordstrom, Inc., 123 F.R.D. 435 (S.D.N.Y. 1988).

[120]Food & Commercial Workers Local 7R v. Safeway Stores, 889 F.2d 940, 132 LRRM 3090 (10th Cir. 1989). *But see* Carpenters Local 1027 v. Lee Lumber & Bldg. Material Corp., 2 F.3d 796, 144 LRRM 2199 (7th Cir. 1993).

[121]*Cf.* Bowen v. U.S. Postal Serv., 459 U.S. 212, 112 LRRM 2281 (1983) (a union that breaches its duty of fair representation by failing to take a meritorious grievance to arbitration will be liable for a portion of the grievant's back-pay damages).

[122]Hygrade Operators v. Longshoremen (ILA) Local 333, 945 F.2d 18, 24, 138 LRRM 2517 (2d Cir. 1991).

(6) Awards Based on, or Inconsistent With, Statutory Law
[LA CDI 94.553]

The U.S. Court of Appeals for the Seventh Circuit, adopting what may be viewed as a perverse rationale, held that an arbitrator's decision must be based on the contract, even if the resulting decision conflicts with federal statutory law,[123] and vacated an award based on provisions of the NLRA. Even when an arbitrator relied on previous interpretations of a contract provision by a federal judge, his award was ruled defective on the theory that he should have made his own interpretation.[124]

The U.S. Court of Appeals for the Fifth Circuit in a 1988, and now questionable, pre-*Circuit City*[125] decision held that an award was not final and binding to the extent that it purported to resolve discrimination issues.[126] The notion seems to have been that any award arising out of a discrimination claim would be against public policy because the mandate of Title VII and analogous state statutes could be thwarted.[127]

(7) Procedural or Evidentiary Errors as Bases for Vacatur and Refusal to Enforce Arbitration Awards

Objections to the confirmation or enforcement of arbitration awards, and corresponding actions seeking vacatur based on alleged procedural irregularities or evidentiary errors, typically fail.[128] For example, an award was confirmed even though it was issued 3 days beyond the time allowed in the contract, where the request for an extension had gone unanswered. The court based its decision on the losing party's waiver of objection and the lack of prejudice.[129]

In another case, an arbitrator's award issued after his term had expired nevertheless was upheld where the hearing had been concluded prior to the expiration of the term.[130] Even where the same arbitrator, under the same contract and similar facts, rendered a subsequent award arguably inconsistent with his prior decision, the award was nevertheless enforced. The arbitrator's explanation for the apparent discrepancy was held to be sufficient.[131]

---

[123]Roadmaster Corp. v. Laborers Local 504, 851 F.2d 886, 129 LRRM 2449 (7th Cir. 1988). *See also* Polk Bros. v. Chicago Truck Drivers, 973 F.2d 593, 141 LRRM 2172 (7th Cir. 1992). Supervening law had always been held to constitute grounds for the dissolution of a contractual obligation. *See* RESTATEMENT (SECOND) OF CONTRACTS §264 (1979).

[124]Union Appointed Trus. Funds v. Employer Appointed Trus. of Tapers Indus., 714 F. Supp. 104 (S.D.N.Y. 1989).

[125]Circuit City Stores v. Adams, 532 U.S. 105, 85 FEP Cases 266 (2001).

[126]Owens v. Texaco, 857 F.2d 262, 129 LRRM 2925 (5th Cir. 1988), *cert. denied*, 490 U.S. 1046 (1989).

[127]Swenson v. Management Recruiters Int'l, 872 F.2d 264, 49 FEP Cases 760 (8th Cir.), *cert. denied*, 493 U.S. 848 (1989).

[128]Mutual Redevelopment Houses v. Service Employees Local 32B-32J, 700 F. Supp. 774 (S.D.N.Y. 1988).

[129]McMahon v. RMS Elecs., 695 F. Supp. 1557 (S.D.N.Y. 1988).

[130]Pelham Parkway Nursing Home v. Service Employees Local 144, 132 LRRM 2744 (S.D.N.Y. 1989).

[131]Hotel & Restaurant Employees Local 54 v. Adamar, Inc., 682 F. Supp. 795, 126 LRRM 3029 (D.N.J. 1987).

There are, of course, limitations. An arbitrator cannot award reinstatement and back pay to an employee beyond the expiration date of the contract.[132] Indeed, the U.S. Court of Appeals for the Tenth Circuit found this issue to be jurisdictional.[133]

(8) Vacatur and Refusals to Enforce Awards Based on Public Policy Grounds [LA CDI 94.64]

The public policy exception to the enforcement of arbitration awards was given a narrow reading by the Supreme Court in *Paperworkers v. Misco, Inc.*[134] In *Misco*, the arbitrator had reinstated a discharged employee after refusing to consider evidence, unavailable at the time of the termination decision, that the grievant's car while parked on company property was found to have contained marijuana.[135] The court of appeals held that the evidence of marijuana in the grievant's car required that the award be set aside on public policy grounds.[136] The Supreme Court reversed because the public policy standard followed by the court of appeals did not comply with the standard the Supreme Court had adopted in its earlier *W.R. Grace & Co. v. Rubber Workers Local 759*:[137]

> [A] court's refusal to enforce an arbitrator's *interpretation* of such contracts is limited to situations where the contract as interpreted would violate "some explicit public policy" that is "well defined and dominant, and is to be ascertained 'by reference to the laws and legal precedents and not from general considerations of supposed public interests.'"[138]

The Supreme Court revisited the public policy exception in *Eastern Associated Coal Corp. v. Mine Workers District 17*[139] and reaffirmed this standard by holding that an arbitrator's reinstatement of a truck driver, who had been discharged under a company's substance abuse policy because he had twice tested positive for marijuana use, did not violate any explicit, well-defined, and dominant public policy. Rejecting the employer's action to vacate the award, the Supreme Court ruled:

> To put the question more specifically, does a contractual agreement to reinstate Smith with specified conditions . . . run contrary to an explicit, well de-

---

[132]Laborers Local 1273 v. Deaton Hosp., 671 F. Supp. 1049, 125 LRRM 2964 (D. Md. 1986).

[133]Barnard v. Commercial Carriers, 863 F.2d 694, 130 LRRM 2073 (10th Cir. 1988).

[134]484 U.S. 29, 126 LRRM 3113 (1987).

[135]*Id.* at 33–34, 126 LRRM at 3115.

[136]Misco, Inc. v. Paperworkers, 768 F.2d 739, 120 LRRM 2119 (5th Cir. 1985).

[137]461 U.S. 757, 113 LRRM 2641 (1983).

[138]Paperworkers v. Misco, 484 U.S. 29, 43, 126 LRRM 3113, 3119 (1987) (quoting Muschany v. United States, 324 U.S. 49, 66 (1945) (emphasis in original)). Where an employee operated potentially hazardous electrical equipment and was found by an arbitrator to be a chronic heavy drug user and intoxicated at the time of his drug screen, the district court vacated an arbitrator's decision to reinstate the employee. The court distinguished *Misco*, which involved smoking marijuana in a car in a parking lot, and observed that if the employer permitted this activity it would be an accessory to the wrongdoing. Georgia Power v. Electrical Workers (IBEW) Local 84, 707 F. Supp. 531, 130 LRRM 2419 (N.D. Ga. 1989), *aff'd*, 896 F.2d 507, 133 LRRM 2856 (11th Cir. 1990).

[139]531 U.S. 57, 165 LRRM 2865 (2000). *See* George Wath & Son v. Tiffany & Co., 248 F.3d 577, 580 (7th Cir. 2001) ("manifest disregard of law" standard to be narrowly interpreted as a result of this decision).

fined, and dominant public policy, as ascertained by reference to positive law and not from general considerations of supposed public interests?

. . .

We agree, in principle, that courts' authority to invoke the public policy exception is not limited solely to instances where the arbitration award itself violates positive law. Nevertheless, the public policy exception is narrow and must satisfy the principles set forth in *W.R. Grace* and *Misco*. Moreover, in a case like the one before us, where two political branches have created a detailed regulatory regime in a specific field, courts should approach with particular caution pleas to divine further public policy in that area.[140]

The teaching of these cases is that a court may vacate an arbitrator's award as contrary to public policy only when the policy is defined in, and ascertainable by reference to, laws and legal precedents, as distinguished from general considerations of supposed public interests.[141]

However, the U.S. Court of Appeals for the Eleventh Circuit, in *Delta Airlines v. Air Line Pilots*,[142] held that *Misco*'s public policy standards were met where a pilot operated an aircraft while intoxicated. The court observed that every state, as well as the federal government, made driving while intoxicated illegal. In addition, the U.S. Court of Appeals for the Eighth Circuit overturned the reinstatement of an employee discharged for leaving his post too early because of the jeopardy to a nuclear reactor safety system. The court cited what it considered a well-defined national policy requiring strict adherence to nuclear safety rules.[143]

In *Stead Motors of Walnut Creek v. Machinists Lodge 1173*,[144] the U.S. Court of Appeals for the Ninth Circuit followed and perhaps expanded the *Misco* doctrine, while also emphasizing the extremely narrow scope of judicial review. In *Stead*, the arbitrator had reinstated an employee who, on several occasions, had been found negligent in maintaining vehicles. The court held that state statutes prohibiting the operation of unsafe vehicles and providing for the inspection and certification of auto repair facilities were insufficient to establish the existence of an explicit, well-defined, and dominant public policy that would be contravened by reinstatement of the employee. The court went on to opine that to overturn the award, the public policy would have to go beyond merely penalizing certain kinds of careless

---

[140]*Eastern Associated Coal*, 531 U.S. at 63.

[141]*See, e.g.*, Hamilton & Veglahn, *Public Policy Exceptions to Arbitration Awards*, 42 Lab. L.J. 366 (1991); Gould, *Judicial Review of Labor Arbitration Awards—Thirty Years of the Steelworkers Trilogy: The Aftermath of AT&T and* Misco, 64 Notre Dame L. Rev. 464 (1989); Hexter, *Judicial Review of Labor Arbitration Awards: How the Public Policy Exception Cases Ignore the Public Policies Underlying Labor Arbitration*, 24 St. Louis U. L.J. 77 (1989); Parker, *Judicial Review of Labor Arbitration Awards:* Misco *and Its Impact on the Public Policy Exception*, 4 Lab. L.J. 683 (1988); Edwards, *Judicial Review of Labor Arbitration Awards: The Clash Between the Public Policy Exception and the Duty to Bargain*, 64 Chi-Kent L. Rev. 3 (1988); *Protecting the Parties' Bargain After* Misco: *Court Review of Labor Arbitration Awards*, 64 Ind. L. Rev. 1 (1988); Note, *Judicial Review of Arbitration Awards on Public Policy Grounds:* United Paperworkers v. Misco, Inc., 30 B.C. L. Rev. 130 (1988).

[142]861 F.2d 665, 130 LRRM 2014 (11th Cir. 1988), *cert. denied*, 491 U.S. 871 (1989).

[143]Iowa Elec. Light & Power v. Electrical Workers (IBEW) Local 204, 834 F.2d 1424, 127 LRRM 2049 (8th Cir. 1987).

[144]843 F.2d 357, 127 LRRM 3213 (9th Cir. 1988), *reh'g en banc*, 886 F.2d 1200, 132 LRRM 2689 (9th Cir. 1989), *cert. denied*, 495 U.S. 946 (1990).

behavior and specifically bar the reinstatement of offending employees. Thus, to overturn an award the asserted public policy must specifically militate against the relief ordered by the arbitrator. In effect, the *Stead* court interpreted *Misco* as recognizing that an arbitral judgment of an employee's amenability to discipline is a factual determination that cannot be judicially questioned or rejected.[145] In so ruling, the Ninth Circuit rejected the Eleventh Circuit's *Delta Air Lines*[146] decision and the Eighth Circuit's *Iowa Electric Light & Power*[147] opinion where contrary results were reached for similar violations, respectively, of the Federal Aviation Administration rules and those of the Nuclear Regulatory Commission. The court in *Stead* concluded that there was no legal proscription against the reinstatement of drug users such as the grievant in this case, and that the award did not otherwise have the effect of mandating any illegal conduct.

In the same year as its *Delta Airlines* ruling, the Eleventh Circuit upheld the arbitral reinstatement of a discharged employee who had been arrested on drug charges away from the plant although he worked in a sensitive position.[148] Also, in the year following its *Iowa Electric* decision, the Eighth Circuit reversed the district court and affirmed an arbitral award reinstating with back pay employees who were discharged in violation of a project agreement for failing an invalid test, despite the claim that the Nuclear Regulatory Commission should have decided whether the safety plan was consistent with regulatory standards.[149]

The U.S. Court of Appeals for the Third Circuit similarly criticized a district court for second-guessing the arbitrator's evidentiary conclusions and construction of a contract[150] in the case of an employee who had been discharged for firing gunshots into his supervisor's unoccupied vehicle.

(9) Vacatur Because of "Evident Partiality," "Misconduct," "Corruption," and "Manifest Disregard of the Law" [LA CDI 94.68]

An award of a neutral arbitrator in a commercial and employment context, and, presumably, in a collective bargaining context as well, can be vacated because of the arbitrator's "evident partiality."[151] There is no general

---

[145]*Id.*, 886 F.2d at 1216, 132 LRRM at 2701.

[146]861 F.2d 665, 130 LRRM 2014 (11th Cir. 1988).

[147]834 F.2d 1424, 127 LRRM 2049 (8th Cir. 1987). A district court also overturned an arbitration award on public policy grounds because safety issues were involved. "Where public policy considerations concern public safety, as in this case, courts should decide the public policy matters instead of deferring them to arbitrators by cloaking them as arbitration issues. Where public safety is the public policy at issue, courts should err on the side of scrutinizing arbitration findings more closely and vacating arbitration awards which violate well defined and dominant public policies." Exxon Shipping Co. v. Exxon Seamen's Union, 801 F. Supp. 1379, 1388, 141 LRRM 2185 (D.N.J. 1992). *See also* Union Pac. R.R. v. Transportation Union, 3 F.3d 255, 144 LRRM 2027 (8th Cir. 1993), *cert. denied*, 510 U.S. 1072 (1994); Exxon Shipping Co. v. Exxon Seamen's Union, 788 F. Supp. 829, 140 LRRM 2096 (D.N.J. 1992).

[148]Florida Power Corp. v. Electrical Workers (IBEW), 847 F.2d 680, 128 LRRM 2762 (11th Cir. 1988).

[149]Daniel Constr. Co. v. Electrical Workers (IBEW) Local 257, 856 F.2d 1174, 129 LRRM 2429 (8th Cir. 1988), *cert. denied*, 489 U.S. 1020 (1989).

[150]U.S. Postal Serv. v. Letter Carriers, 839 F.2d 146, 127 LRRM 2593 (3d Cir. 1988). *See also* Exxon Shipping v. Exxon Seamen's Union, 788 F. Supp. 829 (D.N.J. 1992).

[151]*See* Federal Arbitration Act, 9 U.S.C. §10; Revised Uniform Arbitration Act (RUAA), 7 U.L.A. (2000) §23(a)(2)(A).

agreement on the standard of proof necessary to establish such evident bias.[152] A presumption of evident partiality arises when a neutral arbitrator fails to disclose "a known, direct, and material interest in the outcome or a known, existing, and substantial relationship with a party."[153] In such event, the nonobjecting party has the burden to rebut the presumption by showing absence of taint in the award or a lack of prejudice.[154]

Obviously, however, disqualification is appropriate when the arbitrator has a personal stake in the outcome of the arbitration. Thus, when a union's attempt to dismiss a permanent impartial arbitrator for an industrywide grievance-arbitration procedure was deemed arbitrable,[155] the U.S. Court of Appeals for the Second Circuit found that the impartial arbitrator's clear personal interest in the outcome of the dispute disqualified him from hearing the dispute as an arbitrator. The court directed the parties to appoint another arbitrator, in accordance with the contract, to hear and decide the issue.[156]

Similarly, a failure to disclose an interest could be evidence of corruption or misconduct. "Corruption and misconduct" provide grounds to vacate awards whether issued by a neutral arbitrator or nonneutral arbitrators representing one of the parties. Oddly enough, while prejudice need not be shown by a party seeking vacatur due to corruption or evident partiality by an arbitrator, neutral or otherwise,[157] courts require an objecting party to show prejudice in order to vacate an award due to misconduct.[158]

The U.S. Court of Appeals for the Ninth Circuit has held that "[b]efore a court can vacate an arbitration award because of 'evident partiality' on the part of an arbitrator, the party alleging bias must establish facts that create 'a reasonable impression of partiality.'"[159] The court found that the joining of

---

[152]Merit Ins. Co. v. Leatherby Ins. Co., 714 F.2d 673, 681 (7th Cir. 1983) (evidence of partiality must be "powerfully suggestive of bias"); Artists & Craftsmen Builders v. Schapiro, 232 A.D.2d 265, 648 N.Y.S.2d 550 (N.Y. App. Div. 1996). The division of authority on this issue stems from the Supreme Court's split decision in *Commonwealth Coatings Corp. v. Continental Casualty Co.*, 393 U.S. 145 (1968). In the four-justice plurality opinion, Justice Black wrote that undisclosed "dealings that might create an impression of possible bias," or "even an appearance of bias," would amount to evident partiality. *Id.* at 149. Justices White and Marshall applied a more limited test that requires disclosure of "a substantial interest in a firm which has done more than trivial business with a party." *Id.* at 150. The dissenting justices sought to raise a rebuttable presumption for failing to disclose certain relationships. Because of this mixed analysis, some courts have applied "the appearance of bias" tests. Steamship Co. v. Cook Indus., 495 F.2d 1260, 1263 (2d Cir. 1973). Other courts review the conduct from the viewpoint of a reasonable person aware of all the circumstances. Ceriale v. AMCO Ins. Co., 48 Cal. App. 4th 500, 55 Cal. Rptr. 2d 685 (1996).

[153]RUAA, 7 U.L.A. (2000) §23(a)(2).

[154]Drinane v. State Farm Mut. Auto. Ins. Co., 152 Ill. 2d 207, 214–26, 606 N.E.2d 1181, 1184–85 (1992).

[155]Pitta v. Hotel Ass'n of New York City, 806 F.2d 419, 420, 124 LRRM 2109, 2110 (2d Cir. 1986). The collective bargaining contract clause provided for arbitration of all complaints and disputes involving "any acts, conduct or relations between the parties."

[156]*Id.* at 423–25, 124 LRRM at 2112–14.

[157]Egan & Sons Co. v. Mears Park Dev. Co., 414 N.W.2d 785 (Minn. Ct. App. 1987); Northwest Mech. v. Public Utils. Comm'n, 283 N.W.2d 522 (Minn. 1979); Gaines Constr. Co. v. Carol City, Ut., Inc., 164 So. 2d 270 (Fla. Dist. Ct. 1964).

[158]Creative Homes & Millwork v. Hinkle, 426 S.E.2d 480 (N.C. Ct. App. 1993).

[159]Toyota of Berkeley v. Automobile Salesmen's Union Local 1095, 834 F.2d 751, 756, 127 LRRM 2112, 2116 (9th Cir. 1987), *cert. denied*, 486 U.S. 1043 (1988) (quoting Sheet Metal Workers Local 420 v. Kinney Air Conditioning Co., 756 F.2d 742, 745, 118 LRRM 3398 (9th Cir. 1985)).

an arbitrator as a party to the employer's suit to enjoin the arbitration on grounds that it was untimely requested, and the arbitrator's subsequent filing for sanctions against the employer's attorney under Rule 11 of the Federal Rules of Civil Procedure, did not create a reasonable impression of partiality. The district court order vacating the arbitration award was accordingly reversed.[160]

The U.S. Court of Appeals for the Sixth Circuit applied a similar analysis to hold that the participation of an employer-appointed cochair on a committee deciding a grievance, in which his former law partners had been involved during their partnership, did not create a reasonable impression of partiality in the arbitral setting,[161] although it would raise an appearance of impropriety requiring a federal judge's recusal. In another opinion, however, the Sixth Circuit held that, where the employer and union acted jointly to procure an arbitrator who they thought would be biased against a grievant, fundamental fairness required that the arbitration decision be set aside, even in the absence of a finding of arbitral bias.[162]

The U.S. Court of Appeals for the Seventh Circuit held that a neutral arbitrator's failure to disclose a prior business relationship with a principal of one of the parties to an arbitration did not justify a district court's use of its powers under Rule 60(b) of the Federal Rules of Civil Procedure and the Federal Arbitration Act to set aside the award.[163] The court stated that the test to be applied is whether, having due regard for the different expectations regarding impartiality that parties bring to arbitration, the relationship with the party's principal was so personally, socially, professionally, or financially intimate as to cast serious doubt on the arbitrator's impartiality.[164] In this case, although the president of one party to the arbitration had been the neutral arbitrator's supervisor for 2 years and was a key witness in the arbitration, their relationship had ended 14 years before, the arbitrator had no possible financial stake in the outcome of the arbitration, and his relationship with that corporate officer during their tenure together at another company had been distant and impersonal.[165]

A less stringent and questionable standard was utilized by the New York Supreme Court, Appellate Division, in vacating an arbitration award where a sole arbitrator's undisclosed contractual arbitral relationship with the parent organization of one of the parties was held to be substantial enough to create an inference of bias.[166] The arbitrator was one of a panel of eight arbi-

---

[160]*Id.* at 756–57, 127 LRRM at 2116–17. For additional cases rejecting claims of arbitrator bias, see *Teamsters Local 814 v. J&B Sys. Installers & Moving,* 878 F.2d 38, 131 LRRM 2799 (2d Cir. 1989); *Broadcast Employees v. NBC,* 707 F. Supp. 124, 131 LRRM 2995 (S.D.N.Y. 1988); *Sanford Home for Adults v. Health Professionals Local 6,* 665 F. Supp. 312, 126 LRRM 3149 (S.D.N.Y. 1987).

[161]Apperson v. Fleet Carrier Corp., 879 F.2d 1344, 1360–61, 131 LRRM 3079 (6th Cir. 1989).

[162]Allen v. Allied Plant Maint. Co., 881 F.2d 291, 132 LRRM 2021, 2027 (6th Cir. 1989).

[163]Merit Ins. Co. v. Leatherby Ins. Co., 714 F.2d 673 (7th Cir.), *cert. denied,* 464 U.S. 1009 (1983).

[164]*Id.* at 680.

[165]*Id.* at 676–78.

[166]City Sch. Dist. v. Oswego Classroom Teachers, 100 A.D.2d 13, 473 N.Y.S.2d 284 (N.Y. App. Div. 1984).

trators designated to hear and determine disputes between the parent organization and its field representatives.[167]

However, where prior to the arbitral hearing conducted under the Federal Arbitration Act, a party fully disclosed a past relationship with the designated panel arbitrator that involved some insubstantial business dealings, the contractually created arbitration council examined the relationship and determined that the arbitrator should remain on the panel. Because nothing in the record demonstrated that the opposing party was prejudiced, or that there was evident partiality on the part of the arbitrator, the arbitration award was confirmed.[168]

The U.S. Court of Appeals for the Second Circuit, in examining whether a father-son relationship between an arbitrator and an officer of the international union to which the party, a local union, belonged, expressed its traditional reluctance to inquire into the merits of an arbitrator's award, or to require of an arbitrator the same demanding level of impartiality as that required for judges,[169] but nevertheless concluded that in the absence of evidence of estrangement between the arbitrator and his father, a presumption of filial loyalty satisfied the standard of evident partiality required for vacating the arbitration award.[170]

As a general rule, a party must object to an arbitrator's partiality at the arbitration hearing before such an objection will be considered by the federal courts. The exception to this rule is when all facts as to the alleged bias are not known at the time of the hearing.[171] Thus, where an employer failed to object to the selection of members of a contractually established joint arbitration committee at the time they were seated, the employer's objection to the committee's award based on the alleged partiality of the committee members was found to have been waived.[172]

The courts retain the equitable power to intervene in an arbitration proceeding before an award is rendered where there is "a real possibility that injustice will result." In one case,[173] the bylaws of an organization, of which all parties were members, provided for arbitration of all member claims. The

---

[167]*Id.*, 473 N.Y.S.2d at 287–88.

[168]Milliken & Co. v. Tiffany Loungewear, 99 A.D.2d 993, 473 N.Y.S.2d 443 (N.Y. App. Div. 1984).

[169]Morelite Constr. Corp. v. New York City Dist. Council Carpenters Benefit Funds, 748 F.2d 79, 81, 117 LRRM 3009 (2d Cir. 1984).

[170]*Id.* at 84, 117 LRRM at 3012. See standards under which an award may be vacated, Federal Arbitration Act, 9 U.S.C. §10. The court defined "evident partiality" to mean "where a reasonable person would have to conclude that an arbitrator was partial to one party to the arbitration." *Id.* This "reasonable person" standard has been adopted by other courts. *See* Apperson v. Fleet Carrier Corp., 878 F.2d 1344, 1360–61 (6th Cir. 1989); Teamsters Local 814 v. J&R Sys. Installers, 878 F.2d 38 (2d Cir. 1989); Broadcast Employees v. NBC, 707 F. Supp. 124, 131 LRRM 2995 (S.D.N.Y. 1988). Any arbitrator, nevertheless, should adhere to a policy of disclosing any circumstance likely to create a "presumption of bias" or that the arbitrator believes "might disqualify" him or her as an impartial arbitrator. *See* American Arbitration Ass'n, LABOR ARBITRATION RULES, RULES 11 & 17; Federal Mediation & Conciliation Serv. Regulations, 29 C.F.R. §1404; CODE OF PROFESSIONAL RESPONSIBILITY §2.B.

[171]Apperson v. Fleet Carrier Corp., 879 F.2d 1344, 1358–59, 131 LRRM 3079 (6th Cir. 1989).

[172]Electrical Workers (IBEW) Local 2 v. Gerstner Elec., 614 F. Supp. 874, 121 LRRM 3042, 3044 (E.D. Mo. 1985).

[173]Rabinowitz v. Olewski, 100 A.D.2d 539, 473 N.Y.S.2d 232, 234 (N.Y. App. Div. 1984).

court held that the plaintiffs could not be compelled to exhaust the arbitral procedure because of the charged atmosphere where the appearance of bias permeated the panel from which the arbitrators had been selected.

It is perhaps a tribute to the effectiveness of professional self-policing that both state and federal courts regularly reject challenges to arbitration awards on the ground of arbitrator prejudice.[174] Vacatur of a commercial arbitration award can be based on an arbitrator's "manifest disregard of the law." But it is questionable whether the standard is applicable to a labor arbitration award. [174a] Manifest disregard of the law "clearly means more than error or misunderstanding with respect to the law."[175] "A party seeking to vacate an arbitration award on the ground of 'manifest disregard of the law' may not proceed by merely objecting to the results of the arbitration."[176] Thus, courts have included a "conscious disregard" element to vacating awards under this standard. As a result, courts will vacate an award on this ground only on concluding that the arbitrator knew the correct legal standard, but "made a conscious decision" to ignore it.[177] Certainly, proof of bias that arises from an undisclosed interest could go far in helping to establish the element of "conscious disregard" for purposes of vacating an award based on the manifest disregard of the law standard.

(10) Sanctions and Costs for Frivolous Post-Arbitration Litigation

The courts in one important respect have acted to encourage voluntary compliance with arbitration awards and to discourage frivolous and unjustified post-arbitration litigation. The courts have penalized obstinate parties that bring frivolous actions to set aside an award, or without justification refuse to comply with an award and thereby force the other party to resort to court action for its enforcement. An obstinate party may be required to pay the other party's court costs and attorneys' fees in the post-arbitration litigation.[178] As one court declared: "We refuse to countenance frivolous and wasteful judicial challenges to conscientious and fair arbitration decisions."[179]

---

[174]*See* Northwestern Nat'l Ins. Co., 2000 U.S. Dist. Lexis 5586 (S.D.N.Y. May 1, 2000); Matthias Eckstein dba Irie Assocs. v. Preston & Preston, 41 V.I. 130 (V.I. 1999).

[174a]*See* Roadmaster Corp. v. Laborers Local 504, 851 F.2d 886, 129 LRRM 2449 (7th Cir. 1988). *See also* Polk Bros. v. Chicago Truck Drivers, 973 F.2d 593, 141 LRRM 2172 (7th Cir. 1992).

[175]Carte Blanche PTE Ltd. v. Carte Blanche Int'l, 888 F.2d 260, 265 (2d Cir. 1989).

[176]D.R. Sec. v. Professional Planning Assocs., 857 F.2d 742, 747 (11th Cir. 1988).

[177]M&C Corp. v. Erwin Behr & Co., 87 F.3d 844, 851 (6th Cir. 1996). *See* Hayford, *Reining in the Manifest Disregard of the Law Standard: The Key to Stabilizing the Law of Commercial Arbitration*, 1999 J. DISP. RESOL. 117.

[178]See section 2.A.ii.c.(5), "Vacatur Based on Improper Remedies," above. *See also* Typographical Union Local 16 (Chicago) v. Chicago Sun-Times, 935 F.2d 1501, 137 LRRM 2731 (7th Cir. 1991); Food & Commercial Workers Local 400 v. Marval Poultry Co., 876 F.2d 346, 131 LRRM 2465 (4th Cir. 1989); Posadas de P.R. Assocs. v. Asociacion de Empleados de Casino de P.R., 821 F.2d 60, 125 LRRM 3137 (1st Cir. 1987); Bailey v. Bicknell Minerals, 819 F.2d 690, 125 LRRM 2317 (7th Cir. 1987); Hill v. Norfolk & W. Ry., 814 F.2d 1192, 124 LRRM 3057 (7th Cir. 1987); Machinists Dist. 776 v. Texas Steel Co., 538 F.2d 1116, 93 LRRM 2285, 2289 (5th Cir. 1976) (citing several other cases); Union de Trabajadores Petroquimicos v. Union Carbide Caribe, 440 F. Supp. 310, 312 (D.P.R. 1977) (union to so pay because it had been "obstinate" in filing its unsuccessful suit to set aside an award).

[179]Machinists Dist. 776 v. Texas Steel Co., 538 F.2d 1116, 1122, 93 LRRM 2285, 2289 (5th Cir. 1976).

In furtherance of this policy, the U.S. Court of Appeals for the Seventh Circuit[180] awarded a union attorneys' fees where the employer's suit to vacate an arbitration award was barred by the statute of limitations and was otherwise meritless. The court emphasized that an employer that includes an arbitration clause in its collective bargaining agreement "will not be permitted to nullify the advantages to the union by spinning out the arbitral process unconscionably through the filing of meritless suits and appeals."[181] Again, in awarding a union full costs and attorneys' fees incurred on appeal, the same court[182] stated, "reluctance to see the benefits of arbitration smothered by the costs and delay of litigation explains the increasing tendency of courts to order a party feebly opposing arbitration (or its outcome) to pay the winner's legal fees."[183] The U.S. Court of Appeals for the Fourth Circuit also awarded attorneys' fees when it found that a company's attempt to overturn an arbitration decision was completely unjustified.[184]

The award of costs and fees favors no particular side. A union's attempt to relitigate an arbitrator's decision as to the amount of a monetary award resulted in the imposition of sanctions requiring the union to pay the employer's litigation costs and attorneys' fees.[185]

d. De Novo Litigation Following Arbitration

Under both federal law and state common law, the issuance of an arbitration award ordinarily bars any subsequent, independent court action on the merits of the original claim.[186] Thus, judicial recourse is limited in most instances to the review of arbitration awards, the scope of which is exceedingly narrow.[187] For example, the U.S. Court of Appeals for the Sixth Circuit dismissed an employee's state law-based retaliatory discharge action. Side-stepping the question of whether the retaliatory discharge action was preempted by federal labor law, the court reasoned that the arbitrator's decision that the employee had been fired for absenteeism was res judicata.[188]

---

[180]Dreis & Krump Mfg. Co. v. Machinists Dist. 8, 802 F.2d 247, 123 LRRM 2654 (7th Cir. 1986).

[181]Id. at 255, 123 LRRM at 2661.

[182]Laborers Local 504 v. Roadmaster Corp., 916 F.2d 1161, 135 LRRM 2831 (7th Cir. 1990).

[183]Id. at 1163, 135 LRRM at 2833.

[184]Food & Commercial Workers Local 400 v. Marval Poultry Co., 876 F.2d 346, 131 LRRM 2465 (4th Cir. 1989).

[185]Teamsters Local 760 v. United Parcel Serv., 921 F.2d 218, 136 LRRM 2114 (9th Cir. 1990).

[186]See Vacca v. Viacom Broad. of Mo., 875 F.2d 1337, 131 LRRM 2478 (8th Cir. 1989); Kroger v. U.S. Postal Serv., 865 F.2d 235 (Fed. Cir. 1988); Kaplan v. Long Island Univ., 1978 WL 1709, 85 Lab. Cas. (CCH) ¶10,942 (S.D.N.Y. 1978); Piper v. MECO, Inc., 412 F.2d 752, 71 LRRM 2655 (6th Cir. 1969); Haynes v. United States Pipe & Foundry Co., 362 F.2d 414, 62 LRRM 2389 (5th Cir. 1966); Howard v. U.S. Rubber Co., 190 F. Supp. 663, 36 LA 62 (D. Mass. 1961). Extensive discussion of this subject is included in Vestal & Hill, *Preclusion in Labor Controversies*, 35 OKLA. L. REV. 281 (1982).

[187]See AT&T Techs. v. Communications Workers, 475 U.S. 643, 121 LRRM 3329 (1986); Steelworkers v. Warrior & Gulf Navigation Co., 363 U.S. 574, 46 LRRM 2416, 34 LA 561 (1960).

[188]Fisher v. Martin Marietta, 815 F.2d 703 (6th Cir. 1987), *aff'd without a published opinion.*

There are, however, some important exceptions to this claim preclusion doctrine.

(1) De Novo Litigation of Statutory Claims

In 1974, the Supreme Court held in *Alexander v. Gardner-Denver Co.*[189] that a discharged employee's statutory right to a trial de novo on his discrimination claim under Title VII of the Civil Rights Act of 1964 was not

---

[189]415 U.S. 36, 7 FEP Cases 81 (1974). Harrell Alexander, an African American steelworker employed by Gardner-Denver Co., was discharged for producing "too many defective or unusable parts." *Id.* at 38. Alexander filed a grievance under the collective bargaining agreement, making no claim of discrimination. During the final step of the grievance arbitration process, Alexander claimed that his termination was the result of racial discrimination. At the arbitration, the arbitrator found that Alexander had been discharged for just cause, making no reference to his claim of discrimination. Alexander proceeded on to the litigation process, and on summary judgment the district court found for Gardner-Denver, holding the "claim of racial discrimination had been submitted to the arbitrator and resolved adversely to petitioner." *Id.* at 43. It further ruled that Alexander's decision to voluntarily pursue his grievance into arbitration bound him to that decision and precluded petitioner from making a claim of discrimination under the provisions of Title VII. The U.S. Court of Appeals for the Tenth Circuit affirmed the findings of the district court but the Supreme Court reversed, allowing the statutory claim to go forward.

The *Gardner-Denver* principle was applied in *Barrentine v. Arkansas-Best Freight System*, 450 U.S. 728, 24 WH Cases 1284 (1981) (right to sue under Fair Labor Standards Act not waived by arbitration award under collective bargaining contract claim arising from same facts), and *McDonald v. City of West Branch, Mich.*, 466 U.S. 284, 115 LRRM 3646 (1984) (right to bring civil rights claim under §1983 not waived by arbitration of collective bargaining contract claim based on same facts). In *City of West Branch*, the Supreme Court, reiterating its *Gardner-Denver* reasoning, held that, in an action under the Civil Rights Act of 1964, 42 U.S.C. §1983, a federal court should not give res judicata or collateral estoppel effect to an award in an arbitration proceeding brought pursuant to the terms of a collective bargaining agreement. In *Barrentine*, the Supreme Court clearly extended its *Gardner-Denver* holding to individuals who seek recovery under the Fair Labor Standards Act following an adverse decision in arbitration proceedings arising from the same event. In doing so, the Court stated that: "While courts should defer to an arbitral decision where the employee's claim is based on rights arising out of the collective-bargaining agreement, different considerations apply where the employee's claim is based on rights arising out of a statute designed to provide minimum substantive guarantees to individual workers." *Id.* at 737. The impact of *Gardner-Denver* on arbitration in relation to the Occupational Safety and Health Act (OSHA), 29 U.S.C. §553 et seq., and the Employee Retirement Income Security Act of 1974 (ERISA), 29 U.S.C. §1001, may still be uncertain. *See* Edwards, *Labor Arbitration at the Crossroads: The "Common Law of the Shop" v. External Law*, 32 ARB. J. 65, 83–84 (1977). It is said that the Supreme Court's *Gateway Coal Co. v. Mine Workers Dist. 4, Local 6330*, 414 U.S. 368, 85 LRRM 2049 (1974), decision, decided contemporaneously with *Gardner-Denver*, "suggests that, whatever the applicability of the *Gardner-Denver* rationale to other federal statutory rights, that rationale will not extend to matters of health and safety." Edwards, 32 ARB. J. at 83. *See also* Citron, *Deferral of Employee Rights to Arbitration: An Evolving Dichotomy by the Burger Court?*, 27 HASTINGS L.J. 369 (1975). Note, however, the Supreme Court's subsequent decision in *Whirlpool Corp. v. Marshall*, 445 U.S. 1, 8 OSH Cases 1001 (1980), upholding the Secretary of Labor's OSHA regulation stating the right of an employee, with no reasonable alternative, to choose not to perform an assigned task because of a reasonable apprehension of death or serious injury. Although *Whirlpool* does not refer to grievance procedures or arbitration, it seems apparent that an arbitration award against an employee at least would not bar de novo litigation by the Secretary of Labor pursuant to that regulation. Regarding ERISA, see Murphy, *The Impact of ERISA on Arbitration*, 32 ARB. J. 123, 126–27 (1977), discussing the possibility that some issues resolved by arbitration may be relitigated under ERISA. *See also* Mahan v. Reynolds Metals Co., 569 F. Supp. 482 (E.D. Ark. 1983), where the court stated in reference to *Gardner-Denver* and ERISA:

> When an employee brings a suit under ERISA with respect to §1132(a)(1)(B), he is seeking to remedy alleged violations of rights accorded him under the *terms of a benefit plan*. Congress did not accord him any right to receive retirement or disability benefits,

foreclosed by the prior submission of his claim to final and binding arbitration under a collective bargaining agreement. In so holding, the Court noted the distinctly separate nature of contractual and statutory rights.[190] The Court determined that the arbitration process was intended to address the employee's contractual rights under the collective bargaining agreement, but not the affected employee's statutory rights.[191] The Court stated:

> [T]he federal policy favoring arbitration of labor disputes and the federal policy against discriminatory employment practices can best be accommodated by permitting an employee to pursue fully both his remedy under the grievance-arbitration clause of a collective-bargaining agreement and his cause of action under Title VII. The federal court should consider the employee's claim *de novo*. The arbitral decision may be admitted as evidence and accorded such weight as the court deems appropriate.[192]

---

but simply allowed him to bring a civil action to enforce *already existing contractual rights,* much in the way other collective bargaining rights can be judicially enforced under §301 of the LMRA. On the other hand, some provisions of ERISA itself create rights that may not exist under a collective bargaining agreement. . . .

This Court concludes that a civil suit brought under ERISA for the purpose of vindicating an individual right created by a pension plan or collective bargaining agreement is not a claim which requires *de novo* consideration as would a claim brought under Title VII, but is instead similar to a suit brought under §301 of LMRA and therefore must be treated as such with respect to the treatment of an arbitration decision already rendered on issues presented to the Court.

Id. at 490 (citations omitted). Regarding the relationship between arbitration and the NLRA since *Gardner-Denver*, see Chapter 10, section 3.A.v., "The NLRA, the Arbitrator, and the NLRB." *See also* Electrical Workers (IUE) Local 790 v. Robbins & Myers, 429 U.S. 229, 13 FEP Cases 1813 (1976) (utilization of grievance or arbitration procedures under the collective bargaining agreement does not toll the running of the statute of limitations for filing a claim); Caldeira v. County of Kauai, 866 F.2d 1175 (9th Cir. 1989); Rider v. Pennsylvania, 850 F.2d 982 (3d Cir. 1988) (once an award is reviewed by, and becomes a judgment of, a court, it is entitled to full faith and credit in subsequent Title VII litigation). For a discussion of *Gardner-Denver* and the use of multiple forums (arbitration and judicial) in discrimination cases, see Wolkinson & Nichol, *The Arbitration of Discrimination Claims in Employment Cases*, 47 ARB. J. No. 3, at 20 (1992).

[190]Alexander v. Gardner-Denver Co., 415 U.S. 36, 50, 7 FEP Cases 81 (1974).

[191]*Id.*

[192]*Id.* at 59–60, 7 FEP Cases at 90. The Court rejected application of the doctrines of election of remedies, waiver, res judicata, and collateral estoppel. *Id.* at 51–52 n.10. In contrast, in *Kremer v. Chemical Construction Co.*, 456 U.S. 461, 28 FEP Cases 1412 (1982), the Supreme Court did give res judicata and collateral estoppel effect to a state court decision disposing of an employment discrimination claim, thus precluding relitigation of the same question in federal court under Title VII. The Court did suggest in *Gardner-Denver* that an employee can waive a Title VII claim if he or she voluntarily and knowingly accepts a settlement that provides relief that is equivalent to that provided under Title VII. The Court also said that "if the relief obtained by the employee at arbitration were fully equivalent to that obtainable under Title VII, there would be no further relief for the court to grant and hence no need for the employee to institute suit." *Gardner-Denver*, 415 U.S. at 51 n.14. For cases applying these guidelines, see *EEOC v. McLean Trucking Co.*, 525 F.2d 1007, 11 FEP Cases 883 (6th Cir. 1975) (no preclusion of an Equal Employment Opportunity Commission (EEOC) action against the employer in the public interest for changes from which the employee might benefit); *Strozier v. General Motors Corp.*, 442 F. Supp. 475, 16 FEP Cases 363 (N.D. Ga. 1978). An employee instituting a baseless suit under Title VII risks having to pay the defendant's attorney fees. *See* Obin v. Machinists Dist. 9, 487 F. Supp. 368, 22 FEP Cases 815 (E.D. Mo. 1980) (requiring an employee with a net worth of nearly $200,000 to pay $44,295 to the defendants (employer and union) for their attorney fees). *See also* Bugg v. Industrial Workers (AIW) Local 507, 674 F.2d 595, 28 FEP Cases 40, 44 (7th Cir.), *cert. denied*, 495 U.S. 805 (1982) (appeal of a trial court decision against the employee was frivolous); Coleman v. General Motors Corp., 667 F.2d 704, 27 FEP Cases 1009, 1012 (8th Cir. 1981).

In its now famous "Footnote 21," the Supreme Court indicated the terms under which lower courts in Title VII discrimination actions "may properly accord [a prior arbitration decision] great weight." Footnote 21 reads:

> We adopt no standards as to the weight to be accorded an arbitral decision, since this must be determined in the court's discretion with regard to the facts and circumstances of each case. Relevant factors include the existence of provisions in the collective-bargaining agreement that conform substantially with Title VII, the degree of procedural fairness in the arbitral forum, adequacy of the record with respect to the issue of discrimination, and the special competence of particular arbitrators. Where an arbitral determination gives full consideration to an employee's Title VII rights, a court may properly accord it great weight. This is especially true where the issue is solely one of fact, specifically addressed by the parties and decided by the arbitrator on the basis of an adequate record. But courts should ever be mindful that Congress, in enacting Title VII, thought it necessary to provide a judicial forum for the ultimate resolution of discriminatory employment claims. It is the duty of courts to assure the full availability of this forum.[193]

---

[193]*Gardner-Denver*, 415 U.S. at 60 n.21, 7 FEP Cases at 90 n.21. The Supreme Court reaffirmed Footnote 21 in its Fair Labor Stanards Act *Barrentine* decision. Barrentine v. Arkansas Best Freight Sys., 450 U.S. 728, 743 n.22 (1981). Illustrating the willingness of courts to give significant weight to arbitration decisions meeting the Footnote 21 terms, see *Washington v. Johns-Manville Prods. Corp.*, 17 FEP Cases 606, 607–08 (E.D. Cal. 1978); *Burroughs v. Marathon Oil Co.*, 446 F. Supp. 633, 636–37, 17 FEP Cases 612 (E.D. Mich. 1978). Also regarding the possible impact of *Gardner-Denver* and its Footnote 21 on arbitration, see Chapter 10, section 2.B., "U.S. Supreme Court Statements Regarding Arbitral Consideration of External Law," and section 3.A.i., "Title VII of the Civil Rights Act." For other writings containing discussion of *Gardner-Denver*, some making special proposals regarding arbitration in light of the decision, see FAIRWEATHER'S PRACTICE AND PROCEDURE IN LABOR ARBITRATION 646–88 (Schoonhoven ed., BNA Books 4th ed. 1999); Fletcher, *How Others View Us and Vice Versa: Administrative and Judicial Critiques of the Arbitration Process: I. Arbitration of Title VII Claims: Some Judicial Perceptions, in* ARBITRATION ISSUES FOR THE 1980S, PROCEEDINGS OF THE 34TH ANNUAL MEETING OF NAA 218 (Stern & Dennis eds., BNA Books 1982); Clark, *III. The Legitimacy of Arbitrating Claims of Discrimination, id.* at 235; Murphy, *Arbitration of Discrimination Grievances, in* DECISIONAL THINKING OF ARBITRATORS AND JUDGES, PROCEEDINGS OF THE 33D ANNUAL MEETING OF NAA 285 (Stern & Dennis eds., BNA Books 1981); Adair, *Comment, id.* at 295; Ashmore, *Comment, id.* at 300; Jacobs, *Confusion Remains Five Years After* Alexander v. Gardner-Denver, 30 LAB. L.J. 623 (1979); Oppenheimer & La Van, *Arbitration Awards in Discrimination Disputes: An Empirical Analysis*, 34 ARB. J. No. 1, at 12 (1979); Edwards, *Arbitration as an Alternative in Equal Employment Disputes*, 33 ARB. J. No. 4, at 22 (1978); Webster, *Arbitrating Title VII Disputes: A Proposal*, 33 ARB. J. No. 1, at 25 (1978); Hill & Sinicropi, *Excluding Discrimination Grievances From Grievance and Arbitration Procedures: A Legal Analysis*, 33 ARB. J. No. 1, at 16 (1978); Hill, *The Authority of a Labor Arbitrator to Decide Legal Issues Under a Collective Bargaining Contract: The Situation After* Alexander v. Gardner-Denver, 10 IND. L. REV. 899 (1977); Robinson & Neal, *Arbitration and Discrimination: I. Arbitration of Employment Discrimination Cases: A Prospectus for the Future, in* ARBITRATION—1976, PROCEEDINGS OF THE 29TH ANNUAL MEETING OF NAA 20 (Dennis & Somers eds., BNA Books 1976); Williams, *II. A Modest Proposal for the Immediate Future, id.* at 34; Meltzer, *III. The Parties' Process and the Public's Purposes, id.* at 46; Jones, *What Price Employment? Arbitration, the Constitution and Personal Freedom: Comment, id.* at 85; Feller, *The Coming End of the Arbitration's Golden Age, id.* at 97; Sachs, *Comment, id.* at 127; Shaw, *Comment, id.* at 139; Youngdahl, *Arbitration of Discrimination Grievances: A Novel Approach Under One Collective Agreement*, 31 ARB. J. 145 (1976); Edwards, *Arbitration of Employment Discrimination Claims, in* ARBITRATION—1975, PROCEEDINGS OF THE 28TH ANNUAL MEETING OF NAA 59 (Dennis & Somers eds., BNA Books 1976); Aksen, *Post*-Gardner-Denver *Developments in Arbitration Law, id.* at 24; Richards, Alexander v. Gardner-Denver: *A Threat to Title VII Rights*, 29 ARK. L. REV. 129 (1975); *Citron*, 27 HASTINGS L.J. 369; Cone & Henry, Alexander v. Gardner-Denver *and Deferral to Labor Arbitration, id.* at 403; Oppenheim, Gateway *and* Alexander—*Whither Arbitration*, 48 TUL. L. REV. 973 (1974). In 1978, the AAA announced its new system of rules and procedures designed especially for arbitration of equal employment opportunity disputes. The AAA President stated that the arbitration would

However, in subsequent cases, the Court held a variety of non–civil rights statutory claims subject to mandatory arbitration where the parties had in some fashion agreed to resolve the underlying dispute through an arbitration process.[194]

The reach of *Gardner-Denver* was narrowed by subsequent Court holdings that, under certain circumstances, victims of discrimination could be compelled to arbitrate their claims. In *Gilmer v. Interstate / Johnson Lane Corp.*,[195] the employee, a financial services manager, had, as a term of his employment, registered as a securities representative with the New York Stock Exchange (NYSE) under an agreement requiring arbitration of disputes.[196] Thereafter, he filed a charge with the EEOC and brought suit in federal court, alleging that he had been discharged in violation of the ADEA.[197] The employer then moved to compel arbitration.

In framing the basis of its decision, the Supreme Court turned to the "'liberal federal policy favoring arbitration agreements'" and seemingly backtracked from its *Gardner-Denver* position that the arbitral forum, as a general matter, was not adequate to address the policies and intricacies of civil rights legislation.[198] Relying on *Mitsubishi Motors Corp v. Soler Chrysler-*

---

be based not on a collective bargaining agreement, but on "a submission agreement drafted by an attorney representing an employee and an attorney for an employer, a stipulation that creates a lawyer-like system of arbitration, to be used in preference to the statutory procedures of enforcement agencies or courts." He offered the new AAA system to parties desiring to avoid the delays and costs of litigation in the courts. Coulson, *Fair Treatment: Voluntary Arbitration of Employee Claims*, 33 ARB. J. No. 3, at 23 (1978).

[194]*See, e.g.*, Shearson/American Express v. McMahon, 482 U.S. 220 (1987) (holding enforceable an arbitration agreement for claims arising under the Securities Exchange Act, 15 U.S.C. §78a et seq.); Mitsubishi Motors Corp. v. Soler Chrysler-Plymouth, Inc., 473 U.S. 614 (1985) (holding enforceable an arbitration agreement for claims arising under federal antitrust laws).

[195]500 U.S. 20, 55 FEP Cases 1116 (1991).

[196]*Id.* at 23. In relevant part the agreement stated that Gilmer "'agree[d] to arbitrate any dispute, claim or controversy' arising between him and [the employer] 'that is required to be arbitrated under the rules, constitutions or by-laws of the organizations with which I register.'" *Id.* The court also found that NYSE Rule 347 provides for the arbitration of "'[a]ny controversy between a registered representative and any member or member organization arising out of the employment or termination of employment of such registered representative.'" *Id.* Thus, the registration application signed by Gilmer with the NYSE extended to cover any disputes with his employer. For a general discussion of *Gilmer*, see Covington, *Employment Arbitration After* Gilmer: *Have Labor Courts Come to the United States?*, 15 HOFSTRA LAB. & EMP. L.J. 345 (1998); Bingham, *Employment Arbitration: The Repeat Player Effect*, 1 EMPLOYEE RTS. & EMP. POL'Y J. 189 (1997). *See also* Hardin, *Sacrificing Statutory Rights on the Alter of Pre-dispute Employment Agreements Mandating Arbitration*, 28 CAP. U. L. REV. 455 (2000); Cooper, *Where Are We Going With* Gilmer? *Some Ruminations on the Arbitration of Discrimination Claims*, 11 ST. LOUIS U. PUB. L. REV. 203 (1992); Sweeney, *Employment Arbitration—Age Discrimination in Employment Act—Arbitrability of Claims Under Age Discrimination in Employment Act Upheld Pursuant to Arbitration Agreement—* Gilmer v. Interstate Johnson Lane Corp., 22 SETON HALL L. REV. 540 (1992); Berkeley & McDermott, *The Second Golden Age of Employment Arbitration*, 43 LAB. L.J. 774 (1992); Duston, Gilmer v. Interstate/Johnson Lane Corp.: *A Major Step Forward for Alternative Dispute Resolution, or a Meaningless Decision?*, 7 LAB. LAW. 823 (1991).

[197]*Gilmer*, 500 U.S. at 23–24.

[198]*Id.* at 25–27 (quoting Moses H. Cone Mem'l Hosp. v. Mercury Constr. Corp., 460 U.S. 1, 24 (1983)). This rationale raises the issue of whether the lack of a procedural right in arbitration equates to a denial of a substantive right. In the context of collective bargaining agreements, the absence of the judicial discovery process in the arbitration forum may not be a significant issue because the arbitration statutes and the NLRA provide possible alternative methods to obtain from the other party information relevant to the dispute. The union

Plymouth, Inc.,[199] the Court found that agreements to arbitrate employment disputes were enforceable pursuant to the Federal Arbitration Act. It held that "[b]y agreeing to arbitrate a statutory claim, a party does not forego the substantive rights afforded by the statute; it only submits the resolution in an arbitral, rather than judicial forum."[200] Here, the Court found that arbitration would not undermine the broader social policies that the ADEA was designed to further, that EEOC enforcement would not be affected, and that Congress did not intend to preclude a nonjudicial forum for the resolution of claims under the ADEA.[201]

Again, relying on *Mitsubishi*, the Supreme Court rejected Gilmer's due process arguments, reasoning that one trades the judicial forum for the simplicity and efficiency of the arbitral process.[202] In responding to Gilmer's contention that the limited discovery process in arbitration would prejudice a party's ability to prove discrimination, the Court pointed out that the NYSE's arbitration process allowed for document production, information requests, depositions, and subpoenas.[203] As a countervailing consideration, the Court also relied on the NYSE requirement that decisions be published and made available to the public.[204] While acknowledging the necessity to be "'attuned'" to "'fraud'" or "'overwhelming economic power'" over an employee who signs an arbitration agreement, the Court quickly discounted the possibility in the situation presented.[205] The Court found Gilmer to be an experienced businessman who was neither coerced nor defrauded into agreeing to the arbi-

---

may make an informational demand on the employer, and if the employer refuses to produce information, the union can contest it with an unfair labor practice charge before the NLRB. Furthermore, the law of collective bargaining agreements, as a general rule, precludes parties from presenting for the first time in an arbitration hearing information that was not supplied to the other party during prior steps of the grievance and arbitration procedure. This combination of federally enforceable rights and obligations under the NLRA, coupled with a discovery process that occurs during prearbitration grievance steps, which process is typically enforced by arbitrators, provides an effective alternative to formal discovery. There is also no res judicata or collateral estoppel effect of arbitration award on the NLRB. NLRB v. Yellow Freight Sys., 930 F.2d 316, 137 LRRM 2045 (3d Cir. 1991) (full faith and credit statute did not require the NLRB to accord preclusive effect in unfair labor practice proceeding to arbitrator's finding that discharged employee assaulted his supervisor). For an individual, however, the lack of formal discovery could amount, in some contexts, to a deprivation of substantive rights. A scope of review that might limit the right of a party to have mistakes of law regarding substantive rights guaranteed under the statute reviewed on appeal may eliminate a substantive right guaranteed by statute. Chisolm v. Kidder, Peabody Asset Mgmt., 966 F. Supp. 218 (S.D.N.Y. 1997). It may be argued that, where the arbitrator misapplies the law when arbitrating a statutory claim, the award does not draw its essence from the arbitration agreement and, hence, the arbitrator exceeded his or her authority. For commentary on substantive rights issues in arbitration, see Tyre, *Arbitration: An Employer's License to Steal Title VII Claims?*, 52 ALA. L. REV. 1359 (Summer 2001); Flanagan, *Expanded Grounds for Judicial Review of Employment Arbitration Award*, 67 DEFENSE COUNSEL J. 488 (2000).

[199]473 U.S. 614 (1985).

[200]*Gilmer*, 500 U.S. at 26 (quoting *Mitsubishi*, 473 U.S. at 628).

[201]*Id.* at 27.

[202]*Id.* at 29–31.

[203]*Id.* at 31–32.

[204]*Id.*

[205]*Id.* at 33 (quoting Mitsubishi Motors Corp. v. Soler Chrysler-Plymouth, Inc., 473 U.S. 614, 627 (1985)). Thus, the Court recognized that defenses other than those listed in the Federal Arbitration Act are available to contest the enforceability of an arbitration clause.

tration clause in the registration agreement.[206] In sum, the Court held that an employee who had agreed individually to waive his right to a federal forum could be compelled to arbitrate an age discrimination claim.[207]

The Court did not overrule *Gardner-Denver* sub silentio. Rather, it distinguished *Gilmer* from its earlier decision. First, the Court stated that *Gardner-Denver* did not involve the enforceability of an agreement to arbitrate statutory claims, but instead raised the issue as to whether arbitration of contract-based claims precluded subsequent judicial resolution of statutory claims.[208] The Court then noted that because the plaintiff in *Gardner-Denver* had not agreed to arbitrate his statutory claims, the arbitrator was not allowed to resolve those claims, and thus arbitration in those cases "understandably was held not to preclude subsequent statutory actions."[209] Moreover, the Court stated that *Gardner-Denver* portrayed the "tension between collective representation and individual statutory rights, a concern not applicable to the present case."[210] Finally, the *Gilmer* Court noted that *Gardner-Denver* was not decided under the Federal Arbitration Act, which embodies the federal policy favoring arbitration.[211]

However, the Court did indicate that there might be some cases in which the arbitral setting provides an inappropriate forum for the resolution of statutory claims, but placed the burden of proving inappropriateness on the party attempting to avoid arbitration.[212]

So far, the only limitation on the enforceability of a mandatory employment dispute arbitration clause appears to be whether it is fair.[213] Specifi-

---

[206]*Id*. at 33.

[207]*Id*.

[208]*Id*. at 33–34.

[209]*Id*. at 35.

[210]*Id*. The concern is that a situation could arise where the interests of the individual members would be subordinated by the union to the interests of the unit as a whole. Thus, if a union chose to settle a discrimination grievance in order to further another goal of the bargaining unit, an employee subject to a collective bargaining agreement would be denied all avenues to a forum for resolution of a discrimination claim. In *Air Line Pilots v. Northwest Airlines*, 199 F.3d 477, 484, 163 LRRM 2072 (D.C. Cir. 1999), the U.S. Court of Appeals for the District of Columbia Circuit held that "a union may not use the employees' individual statutory right to a judicial forum as a bargaining chip to be exchanged for some benefit to the group."

[211]*Gilmer*, 500 U.S. at 35.

[212]*Id*. Specifically, the Court stated that a party, having made the bargain to arbitrate, should be held to it "unless Congress itself has evinced an intention to preclude a waiver of judicial remedies for the statutory rights at issue. . . . If such an intention exists, it will be discovered in the text of the ADEA, its legislative history, or an 'inherent conflict' between arbitration and the ADEA's underlying purposes." *Id*. at 26 (citations omitted). In *Gilmer*, the Court concluded that nothing in the text, legislative history, or statutory framework and purposes of the ADEA was inconsistent with compulsory arbitration pursuant to agreement. *See also* Bercovitch v. Baldwin Sch., 133 F.3d 141, 143 (1st Cir. 1998) (a plaintiff could be compelled to arbitrate claims under the ADA, "where the plaintiff had voluntarily signed an agreement requiring arbitration"); Miller v. Public Storage Mgmt, 121 F.3d 215, 218 (5th Cir. 1997) (ADA claim subject to arbitration and the explicit language of the ADA "persuasively demonstrates Congress did not intend to exclude the ADA from the scope of the FAA [Federal Arbitration Act]"). *But see* Penny v. United Parcel Serv., 128 F.3d 408, 156 LRRM 2618 (6th Cir. 1997) ("[A]n employee whose only obligation to arbitrate is contained in a collective bargaining agreement retains the right to obtain a judicial determination of his rights under a statute such as the ADA.").

[213]Cole v. Burns Int'l Sec. Servs., 105 F.3d 1465, 1484–85, 72 FEP Cases 1775 (D.C. Cir. 1997) (an employee seeking to vindicate statutory rights can be compelled to arbitrate, but

cally, the fact that an employee may not be able to afford the costs of arbitration may cause a court to deny the employer's motion to compel arbitration under an employment agreement.[214] Courts appear to be more solicitous of statutory rights than nonstatutory state law claims when evaluating an employee's claim that an assessment of arbitration costs is unfair.[215]

Thus, in *Shankle v. B-G Maintenance Management of Colorado*,[216] a janitor signed an arbitration agreement stating that any claim filed against the company would be subject to arbitration. But, the agreement required Shankle to pay for half of the cost associated with the arbitral process. The U.S. Court of Appeals for the Tenth Circuit held that neither Shankle nor other similarly situated employees could afford the outlay. Therefore, although the plaintiff "agree[d] to mandatory arbitration as a term of continued employment, yet [B-G Maintenance] failed to provide an accessible forum in which he could resolve his statutory rights."[217] In consequence, limiting the plaintiff's recourse to this private tribunal would undermine "the remedial and deterrent functions of the federal anti-discrimination laws."[218]

In *Green Tree Financial Corp. v. Randolph*,[219] the Supreme Court rejected an employee's challenge to an agreement to arbitrate that did not allocate arbitration costs between the employer and the employee. The Court decided that, absent evidence of how much the employee would be required to pay, it would not void the entire agreement, although it noted, perhaps impractically, that a party could obtain prearbitration discovery in a judicial proceeding, if necessary, to ascertain the cost of arbitration.

An agreement expressly providing that each party bear half the costs of arbitration may nevertheless be unenforceable where it unlawfully limits the arbitrator's authority to grant the type of relief Congress envisioned for violations of statutory rights, including Title VII.[220] Absent a severability

---

must not be required to pay costs in arbitration employee would not be responsible for in court); Ball v. SFX Broad., 165 F. Supp. 2d 230, 86 FEP Cases 991 (N.D.N.Y. 2001) (affirming state courts' denial of stay of arbitration and subsequent arbitration decision relating to one plaintiff's claims even though she did not attend arbitration hearing, but holding that another plaintiff could not be compelled to arbitrate statutory claims where she demonstrated that she could not afford arbitrator fees); Neal v. Lanier Prof'l Servs., 2001 U.S. Dist. LEXIS 15719 (N.D. Tex. Sept. 28, 2001).

[214]*Cole*, 105 F.3d at 1484–85; *Ball*, 165 F. Supp. 2d 230. *But see* LaPrade v. Kidder, Peabody & Co., 246 F.3d 702, 85 FEP Cases 779 (D.C. Cir. 2001) (upholding assessment of portion of fee in arbitration of statutory claims). *Cf.* Armendariz v. Foundation Health Psychcare Servs., Inc., 24 Cal. 4th 83, 6 P.3d 669, 83 FEP Cases 1172 (2000) (mandatory employment arbitration agreement requiring employee to arbitrate wrongful termination or employment discrimination claims rather than filing suit in court is unenforceable unless contract permits employee to vindicate statutory rights). *See* Isbell, *Compulsory Arbitration of Employment Agreements: Beneficent Shield or Sword of Oppression*? Armendariz v. Foundation Health Psychcare Services, Inc., 22 WHITTIER L. REV. 1107 (2001).

[215]Brown v. Wheat First Sec., 257 F.2d 821, 17 IER Cases 1410 (D.C. Cir. 2001).

[216]163 F.3d 1230, 1230–31, 78 FEP Cases 1057 (10th Cir. 1999).

[217]*Id.* at 1235.

[218]*Id.*

[219]531 U.S. 79, 84 FEP Cases 769 (2000).

[220]Perez v. Globe Airport Sec. Servs., 253 F.3d 1280, 86 FEP Cases 613 (11th Cir. 2001). In the consumer context, the U.S. Court of Appeals for the Eleventh Circuit held that a manufacturer that was a third-party beneficiary of a contract of sale could not compel binding arbitration of a buyer's breach of warranty claim against a seller if the manufacturer's warranty itself did not require arbitration.

clause, the U.S. Court of Appeals for the Eleventh Circuit declined to reform or enforce such an agreement.[221] But, the U.S. Court of Appeals for the Eighth Circuit had no such qualms and held that an invalid clause limiting punitive damages did not render a mandatory arbitration agreement unenforceable.[222]

The U.S. Court of Appeals for the Ninth Circuit has held that arbitration may not be compelled if the employee is required to sign an arbitration agreement or be fired, because the agreement to arbitrate under such compulsion is neither fair nor voluntary.[223] However, following the Supreme Court's decision in *Circuit City Stores, Inc. v. Adams*,[224] the Ninth Circuit reversed itself and held that employers may require employees to sign agreements to arbitrate Title VII claims as a condition of employment.[224a]

The *Gardner-Denver*[225] ruling was arguably further limited by the Supreme Court's decision in *Wright v. Universal Maritime Service Corp.*,[226] which has been interpreted to suggest that, under certain circumstances, a union-negotiated waiver of an employee's statutory right to a judicial forum may be enforceable. In *Wright*, the Court did not address the issue of enforceability. It held that, unlike employment contracts executed by individual employees, collective bargaining agreements that purport to waive an employee's

---

[221]*Id.* at 1286–87.

[222]Gannon v. Circuit City Stores, 262 F.2d 677, 86 FEP Cases 755 (8th Cir. 2001).

[223]Duffield v. Robertson Stephens & Co., 144 F.3d 1182, 76 FEP Cases 1450 (9th Cir. 1998); Lelouis v. Western Directory Co., 230 F. Supp. 2d 1214 (D. Or. 2001) (even after *Circuit City*, a court may, consistent with the Federal Arbitration Act, refuse to compel arbitration if the agreement to arbitrate is unfair).

[224]532 U.S. 105, 85 FEP Cases 266 (2001).

[224a]EEOC v. Luce, Forward, Hamilton & Scripps, 303 F.3d 994, 997, 89 FEP Cases 1134 (9th Cir. 2002).

[225]Alexander v. Gardner-Denver Co., 415 U.S. 36, 7 FEP Cases 81 (1974).

[226]525 U.S. 70, 159 LRRM 2769 (1998). Caesar Wright was a member of the International Longshoreman's Association Local 1422. Local 1422 functioned as a hiring hall that provided stevedores to various companies represented by the South Carolina Stevedore Association (SCSA). While working as a stevedore, Wright was injured and sought compensation for a permanent disability under the Longshore and Harbor Workers' Compensation Act, 33 U.S.C. §901 et seq. The claim was ultimately settled, awarding him damages and social security benefits. Three years later, after receiving clearance from his doctor to return to work, Wright requested that the union refer him out of the hiring hall to work. During a 9-day period Wright worked for four stevedoring companies, none of which complained about his performance. However, on learning that Wright had previously settled a permanent disability claim, the employers claimed that "they would not accept Wright for employment, because a person certified as permanently disabled is [was] not qualified to perform longshore work under the CBA [collective bargaining agreement]." *Wright*, 525 U.S. at 74. It was the union's position that the ADA entitled Wright to return to work if he could perform his duties. When Wright learned of this information he attempted to file a grievance with the union. The union, however, told him to file a claim under the ADA. At some point after that, Wright hired an attorney and filed a claim with the EEOC. In 1995, the EEOC issued a "right to sue" letter, and in early 1996 Wright filed a complaint in district court. The district court judge dismissed the case, stating that Wright had failed to pursue the grievance procedure. Wright v. Universal Maritime Serv. Corp., 157 LRRM 2601 (D.S.C. 1996). The U.S. Court of Appeals for the Fourth Circuit affirmed this decision. Wright v. Universal Maritime Serv. Corp., 121 F.3d 702, 157 LRRM 2640 (4th Cir. 1997) (table). The Fourth Circuit relied on precedent set under *Gilmer v. Interstate/Johnson Lane Corp.*, 500 U.S. 20, 55 FEP Cases 1116 (1991), concluding that "the general arbitration provision in the CBA [collective bargaining agreement] . . . was sufficiently broad to encompass a statutory claim arising under the ADA, and that such a provision was enforceable." *Wright*, 525 U.S. at 75.

right to bring discrimination claims in federal court must be clear and unmistakable as a prelude to consideration of enforceability.[227]

Wright involved a longshoreman's suit against his employer under the ADA.[228] The plaintiff was a member of a union and subject to a collective bargaining agreement governing his employment. The contract provided that disputes arising out of the collective bargaining agreement would be arbitrated.[229] Noting that the collective bargaining agreement did not specifically incorporate pertinent statutory antidiscrimination requirements and make compliance therewith a contractual commitment, the Court concluded that the waiver of the right to a federal forum was not clear and unmistakable.[230] Therefore, because the waiver was not explicit, the Court pointedly declined to consider whether such a purported waiver would be enforceable.[231]

There are two passages in *Wright* that suggest guidelines for determining whether a given collective bargaining agreement may fairly be read as waiving the right to bring a Title VII action de novo after having submitted the underlying discrimination claim to arbitration pursuant to provisions of the agreement. First, the Supreme Court suggested that "ordinary textual analysis" of the agreement may "show that matters which go beyond the interpretation and application of contract terms are subject to arbitration . . . ."[232] Second, the *Wright* Court made clear that it did not regard union-negotiated compulsory arbitration of employment discrimination claims to be objectionable as a matter of law or principle:

> [W]e will not infer from a general contractual provision that the parties intended to waive a statutorily protected right unless the undertaking is "explicitly stated." More succinctly, the waiver must be clear and unmistakable. . . .
>
> We think the same standard applicable to a union-negotiated waiver of employees' statutory right to a judicial forum for claims of employment discrimination. Although that is not a substantive right . . . and whether or not *Gardner-Denver*'s seemingly absolute prohibition of union waiver of employees' federal forum rights survives *Gilmer*, *Gardner-Denver* at least stands for the proposition that the right to a federal judicial forum is of sufficient importance to be protected against less-than-explicit union waiver in a CBA [collective bargaining agreement].[233]

However, like *Gilmer*, while *Wright* may have called *Gardner-Denver* into question, it clearly did not overrule it.[234] Moreover, in *EEOC v. Waffle House*,[235] the Court ruled 6-3 that an arbitration agreement that binds an employee does not preclude suit on the employee's behalf by the EEOC.

---

[227]*Wright*, 525 U.S. at 80, 159 LRRM at 2772. *See also* Turner, *Employment Discrimination, Labor and Employment Arbitration, and the Case Against Union Waiver of the Individual Worker's Statutory Right to a Judicial Forum*, 49 EMORY L.J. 135 (2000); Mitchell, *When Do Employees Waive Their Rights?*, 14 BYU J. PUB. L. 83 (1999).

[228]*Wright*, 525 U.S. at 72–75, 159 LRRM at 2772–73.

[229]*Id.* at 73, 159 LRRM at 2772.

[230]*Id.* at 82, 159 LRRM at 2775.

[231]*Id.*

[232]*Id.* at 79, 159 LRRM at 2774.

[233]*Id.* at 80, 159 LRRM at 2774 (quoting Metropolitan Edison Co. v. NLRB, 460 U.S. 693, 708, 112 LRRM 3265 (1983)).

[234]*See* Rogers v. New York Univ., 220 F.3d 73, 75, 164 LRRM 2854 (2d Cir. 2000).

[235]534 U.S. 279, 12 AD Cases 1001 (2002).

The U.S. Court of Appeals for the Fourth Circuit has loosely applied the "clear and unmistakable waiver" principle,[236] but the rest of the circuits that have considered the issue have more strictly scrutinized the language within collective bargaining agreements said to constitute a clear and unmistakable waiver.[237]

Most of the circuit courts have concluded that a waiver of statutorily conferred rights contained in a collective bargaining agreement is sufficiently explicit and unmistakable if either of two conditions is met. First, a waiver is sufficiently explicit if the arbitration clause contains a provision whereby employees specifically agree to submit all federal causes of action arising out of their employment to arbitration.[238] Second, a waiver may be sufficiently clear and unmistakable when the collective bargaining agreement contains explicit incorporation of the statutory antidiscrimination requirements in addition to a broad and general arbitration clause.[239] Thus, "[i]f another provision, like a nondiscrimination clause, makes it unmistakably clear that the discrimination statutes at issue are part of the agreement, employees will be bound to arbitrate their federal claims."[240] To satisfy the "specific incorporation" requirement, the antidiscrimination statutes must be identified by name or citation.[241] Moreover, as the Supreme Court stated in *Wright*, the collective bargaining agreement should make compliance with the named or cited statute a contractual commitment that is subject to the arbitration clause.[242]

Following *Gilmer*'s lead, most lower courts have focused their inquiry on whether the claimed waiver of rights originated in a bargaining context.[243]

---

[236]Safrit v. Cone Mills Corp., 248 F.3d 306, 167 LRRM 2070 (4th Cir. 2001).

[237]Air Line Pilots v. Northwest Airlines, 199 F.3d 477, 163 LRRM 2072 (D.C. Cir. 1999), *judgment reinstated en banc*, 211 F.3d 1312, 164 LRRM 2632 (D.C. Cir.), *cert. denied*, 531 U.S. 1011 (2000); Albertson's Inc. v. Food & Commercial Workers, 157 F.3d 758, 159 LRRM 2452 (9th Cir. 1998), *cert. denied*, 528 U.S. 809 (1999); Penny v. United Parcel Serv., 128 F.3d 408, 156 LRRM 2618 (6th Cir. 1997); Harrison v. Eddy Potash, Inc., 112 F.3d 1437, 156 LRRM 2033 (10th Cir. 1997), *vacated on other grounds*, 524 U.S. 947, 159 LRRM 2576 (1998); Brisentine v. Stone & Webster Eng'g Corp., 117 F.3d 519, 155 LRRM 2858 (11th Cir. 1997); Pryner v. Tractor Supply Co., 109 F.3d 354, 154 LRRM 2806 (7th Cir.), *cert. denied*, 522 U.S. 912 (1997); Varner v. National Super Mkts., 94 F.3d 1209 (8th Cir. 1996), *cert. denied*, 519 U.S. 1110 (1997).

[238]*See* Kennedy v. Superior Printing Co., 215 F.3d 650, 654, 164 LRRM 2609 (6th Cir. 2000); Bratten v. SSI Servs., 185 F.3d 625, 631, 161 LRRM 2985 (6th Cir. 1999) (discussing *Wright* test); Carson v. Giant Food, 175 F.3d 325, 331–32, 161 LRRM 2129 (4th Cir. 1999); Giles v. City of New York, 41 F. Supp. 2d 308, 160 LRRM 2879 (S.D.N.Y. 1999).

[239]Carson v. Giant Food, 175 F.3d 325, 332, 161 LRRM 2129 (4th Cir. 1999).

[240]*Id.*

[241]Bratten v. SSI Servs., 185 F.3d 625, 631, 161 LRRM 2985 (6th Cir. 1999); Prince v. Coca-Cola Bottling Co. of N.Y., 37 F. Supp. 2d 289, 293, 160 LRRM 2740 (S.D.N.Y. 1999). Courts holding that no waiver existed include: Rogers v. New York Univ., 220 F.3d 73, 164 LRRM 2854 (2d Cir. 2000); Kennedy v. Superior Printing, 215 F.3d 650 (6th Cir. 2000); *Bratten*, 185 F.3d 625; Brown v. ABF Freight Sys., 183 F.3d 319, 161 LRRM 2769 (4th Cir. 1999); *Carson*, 175 F.3d 325; Quint v. A.E. Stanley Mfg., 172 F.3d 1 (1st Cir. 1999). Court holding that waiver existed: Safrit v. Cone Mills Corp., 248 F.3d 306, 167 LRRM 2070 (4th Cir. 2001).

[242]Wright v. Universal Maritime Serv. Corp., 525 U.S. 70, 77–79, 59 LRRM 2769, 2774–75 (1998); *Prince*, 37 F. Supp. 2d at 293 (citing *Wright*, 525 U.S. at 80).

[243]A detailed discussion of the many decisions, sometimes conflicting, by the federal courts of appeals and district courts is beyond the scope of this work. For additional information on these decisions, see recent volumes of the proceedings of the annual meetings of the NAA; editions of SEYMOUR & BERISH BROWN, and SEYMOUR & ASLIN, EQUAL EMPLOYMENT LAW UPDATE

Consequently, when the arbitration provision has been negotiated by a union in a collective bargaining agreement, the majority view is that the *Gardner-Denver* principles apply.[244] The flip side of the coin is that an increasing number of circuit courts have held that individual predispute agreements to arbitrate Title VII claims, as well as other statutory claims, are enforceable.[245]

---

ch. 28 "Pre-Dispute Arbitration Agreements" (BNA Books 1996, 1998, 2001, 2003); LINDEMANN & GROSSMAN, EMPLOYMENT DISCRIMINATION LAW ch. 32 "Election and Exhaustion of Remedies" (BNA Books 3d ed. 1996 & supplements thereto).

[244]Appellate courts finding that unions cannot prospectively waive statutory rights include: Rogers v. New York Univ., 220 F.3d 73 (2d Cir. 2000) (*Alexander v. Gardner-Denver Co.*, 415 U.S. 36, 7 FEP Cases 81 (1974), was not overruled by *Wright* and the employee was not barred from filing an ADA claim and a Family and Medical Leave Act (FMLA), 29 U.S.C. §2601 et seq., action under *Gardner-Denver*); Air Line Pilots v. Northwest Airlines, 199 F.3d 477, 163 LRRM 2072 (D.C. Cir. 1999), *judgment reinstated en banc*, 211 F.3d 1312, 164 LRRM 2632 (D.C. Cir.), *cert. denied*, 531 U.S. 1011 (2000) (union may not use employees' individual statutory right to a judicial forum as a bargaining chip to be exchanged for some benefit to the group); Albertson's v. Food & Commercial Workers, 157 F.3d 758, 762, 159 LRRM 2452 (9th Cir. 1998), *cert. denied*, 528 U.S. 809 (1999) ("Employees are entitled to take their FLSA [Fair Labor Standards Act] claims to court regardless of whether those claims may also be covered by the grievance-arbitration procedure"); Penny v. United Parcel Serv., 128 F.3d 408 (6th Cir. 1997) (labor union may not prospectively waive an employee's right to choose a judicial forum for an individual statutory claim); Brisentine v. Stone & Webster Eng'g Corp., 117 F.3d 519, 155 LRRM 2858 (11th Cir. 1997) (union cannot bind employees to arbitrate individual federal statutory claims under a collective bargaining agreement); Harrison v. Eddy Potash Inc., 112 F.3d 1437, 1453, 156 LRRM 2033 (10th Cir. 1997), *vacated on other grounds*, 524 U.S. 947, 159 LRRM 2576 (1998) ("'Statutory employment claims are independent of a collective bargaining agreement's grievance and arbitration procedure.'") (citing Malin, *Arbitrating Statutory Employment Claims in the Aftermath of Gilmer*, 40 ST. LOUIS U. L.J. 84 (1996)), *vacated on other grounds*, 524 U.S. 947, 159 LRRM 2576 (1998); Pryner v. Tractor Supply Co., 109 F.3d 354, 363, 154 LRRM 2806 (7th Cir.), *cert. denied*, 522 U.S. 912 (1997) (a union cannot consent to arbitration for the employee "by signing a collective bargaining agreement that consigns the enforcement of statutory rights to the union-controlled grievance and arbitration machinery created by the agreement"); Varner v. National Super Markets, 94 F.3d 1209, 1213 (8th Cir. 1996), *cert. denied*, 519 U.S. 1110 (1997) (court has "an absolute right to adjudicate suits under Title VII" and employees have the right to bring such actions regardless of the existence of grievance procedures in a collective bargaining agreement). Appellate courts finding that union may waive individual statutory rights: Austin v. Owens-Brockway Glass Container, 78 F.3d 875, 151 LRRM 2673 (4th Cir. 1996) (relying on *Gilmer* as opposed to *Gardner-Denver*, union may waive unit employees' rights to a judicial forum for a statutory claim); *Safrit*, 248 F.3d 306 (union made a clear and unmistakable waiver). *See Northwest Airlines*, 199 F.3d at 481–86 (under RLA no duty to bargain over arbitration of statutory discrimination claims).

[245]*See, e.g.*, Seus v. John Nuveen & Co., 146 F.3d 175, 179, 182–83, 77 FEP Cases 751 (3d Cir. 1998), *cert. denied*, 525 U.S. 1139 (1999); McWilliams v. Logicon, Inc., 143 F.3d 573, 576 (10th Cir. 1998) (employment contracts are not outside the purview of the Federal Arbitration Act); Paladino v. Avnet Computer Techs., 134 F.3d 1054, 1062, 76 FEP Cases 1315 (11th Cir. 1998); Gibson v. Neighborhood Health Clinics, 121 F.3d 1126, 1130 (7th Cir. 1997); O'Neil v. Hilton Head Hosp., 115 F.3d 272, 274 (4th Cir. 1997) (employment contracts may be subject to the Federal Arbitration Act); Patterson v. Tenet Healthcare, 113 F.3d 832, 837, 73 FEP Cases 1822 (8th Cir. 1997); Cole v. Burns Int'l Sec. Servs., 105 F.3d 1465, 1467–68, 72 FEP Cases 1775 (D.C. Cir. 1997); Austin v. Owens-Brockway Glass Container, 78 F.3d 875, 882 (4th Cir. 1996); Metz v. Merrill Lynch, Pierce, Fenner & Smith, 39 F.3d 1482, 1487, 66 FEP Cases 439 (10th Cir. 1994); Willis v. Dean Witter Reynolds, Inc., 939 F.2d 229, 230 (5th Cir. 1991). Statistical studies show that a sizable number of these claims are arbitrated and that the number of cases processed by arbitrators is on the rise. *See* Hauck, *The Efficacy of Arbitrating Discrimination Complaints*, 35 LAB. L.J. 175 (1984). This prompted the EEOC to issue a policy statement discouraging the use of predispute arbitration agreements. *See* EEOC Notice No. 915.002 (July 10, 1997), *reprinted in Excerpts From Text: EEOC Rejects Mandatory Binding Employment Arbitration*, 52 DISP. RESOL. J. 11 (1997). Not surprisingly, supporters of arbitration have criticized the EEOC statement. *See, e.g.*, Oppenheimer & Johnstone, *Con: A Management Perspective: Mandatory Arbitration Agreements Are an Effective Alternative to Employment Litigation*, 52 DISP. RESOL. J. 19, 19–20 (1997).

The U.S. Court of Appeals for the Ninth Circuit in *Duffield*[246] had reached a contrary conclusion based in substantial part on its reading of the Civil Rights Act of 1991 and without consideration of the Federal Arbitration Act. However, finding that the Supreme Court's supervening opinion in *Circuit City Stores, Inc. v. Adams*[246a] had implicitly overruled *Duffield*, a panel of the Ninth Circuit in *EEOC v. Luce, Forward, Hamilton & Scripps*[246b] held that "employers may require employees to sign agreements to arbitrate Title VII claims as a condition of employment.[246c]

(2) De Novo Litigation of Claims Cognizable Under the Labor Management Relations Act

Federal labor policy generally requires deference to the decision by an arbitrator that a company has not violated its collective bargaining agreement in firing an employee.[247] However, this deference can result in "an unacceptable injustice" when the employee's assertion of his or her rights under the collective bargaining agreement has been compromised by the failure of the union to fulfill its duty of fair representation.[248] Under these cir-

---

[246]Duffield v. Robertson Stephens & Co., 144 F.3d 1182 1185, 76 FEP Cases 1450 (9th Cir.), *cert. denied*, 525 U.S. 982 (1998) (The holding was broad: "[W]e hold that, under the Civil Rights Act of 1991, employers may not by [conditioning employment on the execution of mandatory arbitration agreements] compel individuals to waive their Title VII right to a judicial forum."). The Supreme Court, in *Circuit City Stores v. Adams*, 532 U.S. 105, 85 FEP Cases 266 (2001), reversed the decision of the Ninth Circuit in that case, *Circuit City Stores v. Adams*, 194 F.3d 1070, 81 FEP Cases 720 (9th Cir. 1999), and held that contracts of employment that do not involve transportation workers are within the reach of the Federal Arbitration Act, which validates agreements to arbitrate claims. *Compare* Shankle v. B-G Maint. Mgmt. of Colo., 163 F.3d 1230, 1235, 78 FEP Cases 1057 (10th Cir. 1999) (a predispute agreement is not effective if an individual is prevented from vindicating statutory rights). Other circuits rejected the Ninth Circuit analysis: Armendariz v. Foundation Health Psychiatric Serv., 24 Cal. 4th 83, 6 P.3d 669, 83 FEP Cases 1172 (2000) (the reasoning in *Duffield* unpersuasive); Rosenberg v. Merrill Lynch, Pierce, Fenner & Smith, 170 F.3d 1, 10, 79 FEP Cases 707 (1st Cir. 1999) (specifically considering and rejecting *Duffield's* analysis). *See, e.g.*, Craine, *The Mandatory Arbitration Clause: Forum Selection or Employee Coercion?*, 8 B.U. Pub. Int. L.J. 537 (1999). *See also* Morrow, Austin v. Owens-Brockway Glass Container, Inc.: *Shattering Discrimination Union Members' Choice of Judicial Forum*, 14 Lab. Law. 143 (1998).

[246a]532 U.S. 105, 85 FEP Cases 266 (2001).

[246b]303 F.3d 994, 89 FEP Cases 1134 (9th Cir. 2002).

[246c]*Id.* at 997.

[247]DelCostello v. Teamsters, 462 U.S. 151, 113 LRRM 2737 (1983). *See also* Ash v. United Parcel Serv., 800 F.2d 409, 411, 123 LRRM 2541 (4th Cir. 1986).

[248]Hines v. Anchor Motor Freight, 424 U.S. 554, 91 LRRM 2481 (1976); Vaca v. Sipes, 386 U.S. 171, 64 LRRM 2369 (1967). Regarding a union's duty of fair representation, there is no definitive answer about what constitutes actionable arbitrariness on the part of the union. For a good overview of the fair representation doctrine, see Kirschner, *Duty of Fair Representation: Implications of* Bowen, 1 Lab. Law. 19 (1985); Note, *Adding Injury to the Insult:* Bowen *and the Duty of the Fair Representation*, 67 Marq. L. Rev. 317 (1984). A majority of courts agree that the union has to be more than negligent in order to breach the duty of fair representation. *See* Note, *Breaching the Duty of Fair Representation*, 17 J. Marshall L. Rev. 415, 420–24 (1986) (and accompanying footnotes). Some courts, however, do hold that negligence might, in at least some instances, constitute a violation of the duty. Dutrisac v. Caterpillar Tractor Co., 749 F.2d 1270, 113 LRRM 3532 (9th Cir. 1983) (negligent failure to perform a ministerial act, such as filing a timely application for an arbitration that results in eliminating one of the employee's remedies and potentially subjects the employee to a severe sanction, constitutes actionable breach of fair representation). *See also* Slevira v. Western Sugar Co., 200 F.3d 1218, 163 LRRM 2385 (9th Cir. 2000); Caputo v. Letter Carriers, 730 F. Supp.

cumstances, the employee is entitled to relitigate the decision if he or she can prove: (1) that the termination of employment was erroneous, and (2) that the union's breach of its duty of fair representation seriously undermined the arbitral process. This limited exception to the general rule of arbitral finality originated with *Hines v. Anchor Motor Freight*.[249]

The employees in *Hines* had been discharged for seeking "reimbursement for motel expenses in excess of the actual charges sustained by them."[250] Their union carried their grievance to arbitration, and the arbitration committee ruled in the employer's favor.[251] When evidence later surfaced that a third party was in fact the culprit, the employees sued their employer and their union.[252] The employees filed a hybrid claim[253] under Section 301 of the LMRA against their employer, alleging that their discharge violated the collective bargaining agreement, and against their union, alleging breach of its duty of fair representation.[254]

The U.S. Court of Appeals for the Sixth Circuit held that the claim against the union could be maintained, but, in the absence of evidence of misconduct by the employer, or of a conspiracy between the employer and the union, the action against the employer was barred by the arbitration finality provision of the collective bargaining agreement.[255] The Supreme Court reversed, rejecting the Sixth Circuit's conclusion that the award's finality was preserved by the employer's good faith. As the Supreme Court viewed the matter, the correct question was "whether the contractual protection against relitigating an arbitral decision binds employees who assert that the process has fundamentally malfunctioned by reason of the bad-faith performance of the union . . . ."[256] The answer given by the Court was that a breach of the union's duty

---

1221, 133 LRRM 2704 (E.D.N.Y. 1990); Ince v. National R.R. Passenger Corp., 693 F. Supp. 1466, 130 LRRM 3068 (S.D.N.Y. 1988). In *Electrical Workers (IBEW) v. Hechler*, 481 U.S. 851, 125 LRRM 2353 (1987), the Supreme Court held that any duty of care owed by a union to a member as a result of a contractual arrangement is not sufficiently independent of the collective bargaining agreement to withstand federal preemption.

[249]424 U.S. 554, 91 LRRM 2481 (1976). *See also* Cruz v. Electrical Workers (IBEW) Local 3, 34 F.3d 1148, 1152, 147 LRRM 2176 (2d Cir. 1994). *But see* Fleming v. Stop & Shop Supermarket Co., 36 F. Supp. 2d 87 (D. Conn. 1999) (where employees do not avail themselves of all collective bargaining grievance procedures, a union cannot be found to have wrongly refused to process their grievances).

[250]*Hines*, 424 U.S. at 556.

[251]*Id.* at 557–58.

[252]*Id.* at 558.

[253]The type of suit authorized by *Hines*, *Vaca*, and *DelCostello* is a "hybrid" action under §301, 29 U.S.C. §185, because it combines two conceptually independent causes of action, the first against the company for breach of the contract (a standard §301 claim) and the second against the union for breach of the duty of fair representation (a claim implied by operation of a union's status under federal law as the sole bargaining representative of the employee). To prevail against a former employer under this hybrid §301/duty of fair representation cause of action, a discharged worker must prove three elements: (1) some conduct by the worker's union that breached the duty of fair representation, (2) a causal connection showing that the union's breach affected the integrity of the arbitration process, and (3) a violation of the collective bargaining agreement by the company. *See Hines*, 424 U.S. at 570–71.

[254]*Hines*, 424 U.S. at 558–60.

[255]Hines v. Teamsters Local 377, 506 F.2d 1153, 87 LRRM 2971 (6th Cir. 1974).

[256]Hines v. Anchor Motor Freight, 424 U.S. 554, 569, 91 LRRM 2481 (1976).

of fair representation "relieves the employee of an express or implied requirement that disputes be settled through contractual grievance procedures," and that "if it seriously undermines the integrity of the arbitral process the union's breach also removes the bar of the finality provisions of the contract."[257] The Court stated: "Congress has put its blessing on private dispute settlement arrangements provided in collective agreements, but it was anticipated, we are sure, that the contractual machinery would operate within some minimum levels of integrity."[258] If the union's misconduct caused a "fundamental malfunction" in the arbitration, the arbitration decision need not stand, "for in that event error and injustice of the grossest sort would multiply."[259]

---

[257]*Id.* at 567. For discussion of *Hines* and litigation de novo following arbitration, see Sarno, *Preemption, by §301(a) of Labor-Management Relations Act of 1947, (29 USCS sec. 185(a)), of Employees State-Law Action for Infliction of Emotional Distress*, 101 A.L.R. FED. 395 (2000); Turner, *Employment Discrimination, Labor and Employment Arbitration, and the Case Against Union Waiver of the Individual Worker's Statutory Right to a Judicial Forum*, 49 EMORY L.J. 135 (2000); Moss, *The Fate of Arbitration in the Supreme Court: An Examination*, 9 LOY. U. CHI. L.J. 369 (1978); Kurtz, *Appendix B. Arbitration and Federal Rights Under Collective Agreements in 1975, in* ARBITRATION—1976, PROCEEDINGS OF THE 29TH ANNUAL MEETING OF NAA 233, 235–43 (Dennis & Somers eds., BNA Books 1976). For related discussion, see Chapter 5, section 9., "Grievance Adjustment by Individual Employees." Any fear that the *Hines* decision would impede settlement negotiations because of concern about future liability has not been demonstrated. Attacks on the finality of the grievance procedure have not fared well because of decisions narrowly interpreting *Hines*. Hoffman v. Lonza, Inc., 658 F.2d 519, 108 LRRM 2311 (7th Cir. 1981) (construing *Hines* as only narrowly opening the door to attacks on the finality of the grievance procedure). However, *Hoffman's* definition of duty of fair representation was rejected as too narrow by the Supreme Court in *Air Line Pilots v. O'Neill*, 499 U.S. 65, 136 LRRM 2721 (1991). *See also* Garcia v. Zenith Elecs. Corp., 58 F.3d 1171, 149 LRRM 2740 (7th Cir. 1995).

[258]*Hines*, 424 U.S. at 571. The Court further explained: "[W]e cannot believe Congress intended to foreclose the employee from his § 301 remedy otherwise available against the employer if the contractual processes have been seriously flawed by the union's breach of its duty to represent employees honestly and in good faith and without invidious discrimination or arbitrary conduct." *Id.* at 570. The Court also stated that its *Vaca v. Sipes*, 386 U.S. 171, 64 LRRM 2369 (1967), decision had accepted the proposition that "'a union may not arbitrarily ignore a meritorious grievance or process it in a perfunctory fashion.'" *Hines*, 424 U.S. at 569 (quoting *Vaca*, 386 U.S. at 191). But note, the LMRA, which governs disputes involving the interpretation of collective bargaining agreements, expressly exempts state and municipal government employers from coverage. 29 U.S.C. §152(2).

[259]*Hines*, 424 U.S. at 571.

*(3) State Law Tort Claims Arising From Wrongful Discharges:
      Federal Preemption and the Exhaustion of Arbitral Remedies
      Requirement*

Decisions over whether state tort claims arising out of an employee's allegedly wrongful discharge are preempted by federal labor law tend to be highly context dependent.[260] In *Allis-Chalmers v. Lueck*,[261] the Supreme Court made it clear that such a claim is preempted by LMRA Section 301 if it involves an interpretation of the employee's contractual rights.[262] Nevertheless, the Court did observe that the outcome might be different if the claim were based on a state rule that "proscribe[s] conduct, or establish[es] rights and obligations independent of a labor contract."[263] The Supreme Court approved this rationale in *Lingle v. Magic Chef Norge Division*,[264] where it allowed an employee to maintain a claim of retaliatory discharge by her employer for exercising her rights under the Illinois workers' compensation laws. The Court reasoned that the state law remedy did not require interpreting the collective bargaining agreement for Section 301 preemption purposes.[265]

The Supreme Court followed the same logic in *Caterpillar, Inc. v. Williams*,[266] where employees who had been promoted to other positions outside the bargaining unit were downgraded to unionized positions and subsequently laid off, despite assurances that their downgrades were temporary and that if the plant were ever closed they would be employed at other facilities. The

---

[260]*See generally* Christopher, McCormick v. AT&T Technologies, Inc., *and Section 301 Preemption: The Fourth Circuit Makes a Federal Case out of Workplace Torts*, 70 N.C. L. Rev. 377 (1990); White, *Section 301's Preemption of State Law Claims: A Model for Analysis*, 4 Ala. L. Rev. 377 (1990); Harper, *Limiting Section 301 Preemption: Three Cheers for the* Trilogy, *Only One for* Lingle *and* Lueck, 66 Chi.-Kent L. Rev. 685 (1990); Lane, *Labor Law Preemption Under Section 301: New Rules for an Old Game*, 40 Syracuse L. Rev. 1279 (1989); American Arbitration Association, *Implications of State Wrongful Discharge Actions on the Grievance Arbitration Remedy*, Law. Arb. Letter (June 1987); Lindau, Crawford, Hathaway & Hyde, *Arbitral Awards Versus Public Policy: The Continuing Conflict*, 39 N.Y.U. Nat'l Conf. on Lab. §§13.01–13.04 (1986); Jauvtis, *The Impact of Wrongful Discharge Suits on Grievance-Arbitration Procedures in Collective Bargaining Agreements*, 36 Lab. L.J. 307 (1985); Murphy, *Labor Arbitration and the State Public Policy:* Garibaldi v. Lucky Food Stores, 38 N.Y.U. Nat'l Conf. on Labor §§13.01–13.06 (1985).

[261]471 U.S. 202, 118 LRRM 3345 (1985) (whether federal law preempts a state law establishing a cause of action is a question of congressional intent), *rev'g sub nom.* Lueck v. Aetna Life Ins. Co., 116 Wis. 2d 559, 342 N.W.2d 699, 115 LRRM 3002 (Wis. 1984), *rev'g* 112 Wis. 2d 675, 333 N.W.2d 733 (Wis. Ct. App. 1983).

[262]*See* Electrical Workers (IBEW) v. Hechler, 481 U.S. 851, 125 LRRM 2353 (1987). *See also* Angst v. Mack Trucks, 969 F.2d 1530, 140 LRRM 2835 (3d Cir. 1992) (resolution of employee's ERISA claims required interpretation of the contract).

[263]*Allis-Chalmers*, 471 U.S. at 212, 118 LRRM at 3349 (footnote omitted).

[264]486 U.S. 399, 128 LRRM 2521 (1988). *See also* Hawaiian Airlines v. Norris, 512 U.S. 246, 146 LRRM 2577 (1994) (the RLA did not preempt aircraft mechanic's state law causes of action against air carrier for wrongful discharge).

[265]*Lingle*, 486 U.S. at 408–09, 128 LRRM at 2525. *See also* Owen v. Carpenters' Dist. Council, 161 F.3d 767, 159 LRRM 2897 (4th Cir. 1998) (wrongful discharge claim not preempted by §301); Miller v. AT&T Network Sys., 850 F.2d 543, 128 LRRM 2987 (9th Cir. 1988) (wrongful discharge case based on Oregon statute prohibiting firing of employee for physical handicap created mandatory and independent state right not preempted by §301); Baldracchi v. United Techs. Corp., 814 F.2d 102, 125 LRRM 3363 (2d Cir. 1987), *cert. denied*, 486 U.S. 1054 (1988) (upholding action based on Connecticut statute prohibiting employers from discharging employee in retaliation for filing workers' compensation claim).

[266]482 U.S. 386, 125 LRRM 2521 (1987).

employees then filed a state law action alleging that the company had breached their individual employment contracts. The Court held that employees covered by a collective bargaining agreement were permitted to assert their state law contract rights, as long as the contracts relied upon were not dependent on interpretation of the collective bargaining agreement.

The U.S. Court of Appeals for the Tenth Circuit had initially held that intentional infliction of emotional distress tort claims arising from a discharge context were preempted.[267] However, in *Albertson's Inc. v. Carrigan*,[268] the Tenth Circuit changed its position and decided that a bargaining-unit employee's claim of emotional distress is not preempted by Section 301 if it can be shown not to be dependent on the provisions of the collective bargaining agreement.

The U.S. Court of Appeals for the Fourth Circuit, however, reached a contrary result, declaring that state law tort claims of intentional infliction of emotional distress are preempted by Section 301 so long as the plaintiffs are members of a bargaining unit covered by a collective bargaining agreement.[269] The U.S. Courts of Appeals for the Seventh and Ninth Circuits joined the Fourth Circuit in holding that the allegedly wrongful acts forming the predicate for the tort claims are directly related to the terms and conditions of employment, so that resolution of the claims "'will be substantially dependent on an analysis' of the (implicit or explicit) terms and conditions of the collective bargaining agreement."[270]

One recognized exception to federal preemption of state wrongful discharge claims occurs where an employee's discharge involves a violation of a clearly defined state public policy.[271] This public policy exception was recognized in a case where an employee was fired after reporting a shipment of spoiled milk to health authorities.[272] He grieved his discharge, but an arbi-

---

[267]Mock v. T.G.&Y. Stores Co., 971 F.2d 522, 140 LRRM 3028 (10th Cir. 1992); Johnson v. Beatrice Foods Co., 921 F.2d 1015, 136 LRRM 2076 (10th Cir. 1990); Viestenz v. Fleming Cos., 681 F.2d 699, 110 LRRM 2935 (10th Cir. 1982), *cert. denied*, 459 U.S. 972 (1982).

[268]982 F.2d 1478, 142 LRRM 2220 (10th Cir. 1993). *See also* Garley v. Sandia Corp., 236 F.3d 1200 (10th Cir. 2001); Carter v. Ford Motor Co., 121 F.3d 1146, 1149, 155 LRRM 2914 (8th Cir. 1997) (state tort action for intentional infliction of emotional distress is preempted where a determination on the merits "would require the court to determine whether [plaintiff's] discharge was warranted under the terms of the collective bargaining agreement"); Flibotte v. Pennsylvania Truck Lines, 131 F.3d 21, 27, 156 LRRM 3132 (1st Cir. 1997) ("[The defendant's] rights and obligations under the collective bargaining agreement are obviously central not only to an inquiry into [its] intentions, but also to an inquiry into whether [it] conducted itself in a sufficiently outrageous manner to give rise to liability under state tort law.").

[269]McCormick v. AT&T Techs., 934 F.2d 531, 137 LRRM 2453 (4th Cir.), *cert. denied*, 502 U.S. 1048 (1991). *See also* Shiflett v. I.T.O. Corp. of Baltimore, 202 F.3d 260 (4th Cir. 2000) (unpublished).

[270]*McCormick*, 934 F.2d at 537 (quoting Douglas v. American Info. Techs. Corp., 877 F.2d 565, 573, 131 LRRM 2846 (7th Cir. 1989)). *See also* Newberry v. Pacific Racing Ass'n, 854 F.2d 1142, 129 LRRM 2047 (9th Cir. 1988).

[271]*See, e.g.*, Hawaiian Airlines v. Norris, 512 U.S. 246, 146 LRRM 2577 (1994) (employee's state law whistleblower and public policy claims are not preempted by RLA's grievance provisions).

[272]Garibaldi v. Lucky Food Stores, 726 F.2d 1367, 115 LRRM 3089 (9th Cir. 1984), *cert. denied*, 471 U.S. 1099 (1985). *See also* Garcia v. NLRB, 785 F.2d 807, 121 LRRM 3349 (9th Cir. 1986) (court refused to uphold NLRB's decision enforcing arbitral committee's order to suspend an employee for declining to honk his horn in violation of state traffic laws).

trator ruled that he had been discharged for cause. The employee then filed a state action claiming that his termination was prompted by his "whistleblowing," and therefore was in violation of California public policy. The court ruled that the arbitration award did not preclude the employee from raising his statutory claim under California law, because the claim "poses no significant threat to the collective bargaining process" and furthers a state interest in protecting the general public that transcends the employment relationship.[273]

Turning to consider whether pursuit of an available arbitral remedy is required before a state law tort claim may be brought, state courts have disagreed on whether exhaustion of the grievance arbitration procedure must be pleaded prior to filing a retaliatory discharge action. The Illinois Supreme Court ruled that exhaustion of the grievance arbitration procedure was not required,[274] but, the U.S. Court of Appeals for the Fourth Circuit, applying Maryland law, came to the opposite conclusion and held that an employee subject to a collective bargaining agreement must exhaust contractual and federal remedies before initiating a state tort action for wrongful discharge.[275] In a case initially filed in state court and removed under Section 301, the Fourth Circuit determined that it has jurisdiction to consider alleged state law claims during the course of its preemption inquiry, and should remand action to a state court if the claim was not preempted, but dismiss it if the complaint plainly failed to state a cause of action under state law.[276]

B. State Law: Private Sector

State arbitration law is derived from both state common law and legislation.[277] While all 50 states and the District of Columbia have some type of

---

[273]*Garibaldi*, 726 F.2d at 1375. *See also* Vincent v. Trend W. Tech. Corp., 828 F.2d 563, 126 LRRM 2451 (9th Cir. 1987) (wrongful discharge case of employee fired in retaliation for reporting perceived illegalities stemming from sources other than collective bargaining agreement and thus was not preempted by §301); Paige v. Henry J. Kaiser Co., 826 F.2d 857, 126 LRRM 2145 (9th Cir. 1987), *cert. denied*, 486 U.S. 1054 (1988) (wrongful discharge claim based on violation of a state public policy is not preempted because it is a nonnegotiable independent state law right); Rosen v. Transx Ltd., 816 F. Supp. 1364, 143 LRRM 2142 (D. Minn. 1993).

[274]Gonzalez v. Prestress Eng'g Corp., 503 N.E.2d 308, 124 LRRM 2252 (Ill. 1986), *cert. denied*, 483 U.S. 1032 (1987). *See also* Puchert v. Agsalud, 67 Haw. 225, 677 P.2d 449 (Haw. 1984), *appeal dismissed sub nom.* Pan Am. World Airways v. Puchert, 472 U.S. 1001 (1985). For an exhaustive discussion of Illinois cases addressing federal preemption and retaliatory discharge issues, see Green, *Federal Preemption of Suits for Wrongful Discharge under Illinois State Law*, 41 ARB. J. 46 (1986). *See also* Yonover, *Preemption of State Tort Remedies for Wrongful Discharge in the Aftermath of* Lingle v. Norge: *Wholly Independent or Inextricably Intertwined?*, 34 S.D. L. REV. 63 (1988–1989).

[275]Childers v. Chesapeake & Potomac Tel. Co., 881 F.2d 1259, 1265, 131 LRRM 3217 (4th Cir. 1989); Owen v. Carpenters' Dist. Council, 161 F.3d 767, 159 LRRM 2897 (4th Cir. 1998).

[276]*Childers*, 881 F.2d at 1262.

[277]The concept of "common law" has been explained as follows: "When [a court has] no written law [constitution or statute] on which to base the decision in a particular controversy, it decides the case on the basis of custom and general principles of right and wrong. These decisions create precedents or rules, which are applied to similar future controversies. The body of law created in this fashion is spoken of as the common law." KAGEL, ANATOMY OF A LABOR ARBITRATION 131 (BNA Books 2d ed. 1986).

arbitration statute, some, by their terms, exclude arbitration of labor disputes from their coverage. Moreover, many of those that are applicable to labor arbitration are very general in nature, leaving important details to be filled in through the judicial process. Even where an arbitration proceeding is within the coverage of a state statute, it has usually been held that the statute does not supersede, but merely supplements, the common law.[278] While one state, Washington, has held that its arbitration statute completely supersedes the common law, its courts have indicated that the parties may in their contracts elect to establish their own arbitration procedures.[279]

i.   *State Common Law*

Obviously, the common law of any given jurisdiction is unlikely to accord in all respects with that of any other. Nevertheless, the following general summary of common law arbitration and its relation to statutory arbitration prepared by the U.S. Department of Labor provides a useful overview:

> Common law arbitration rests upon the voluntary agreement of the parties to submit their dispute to an outsider. The submission agreement may be oral and may be revoked at any time before the rendering of the award. The tribunal, permanent or temporary, may be composed of any number of arbitrators. They must be free from bias and interest in the subject matter, and may not be related by affinity or consanguinity to either party. The arbitrators need not be sworn. Only existing disputes may be submitted to them. The parties must be given notice of hearings and are entitled to be present when all the evidence is received. The arbitrators have no power to subpoena witnesses or records and need not conform to legal rules of hearing procedure other than to give the parties an opportunity to present all competent evidence. All arbitrators must attend the hearings, consider the evidence jointly and arrive at an award by a unanimous vote. The award may be oral, but if written, all the arbitrators must sign it. It must dispose of every substantial issue submitted to arbitration. An award may be set aside only for fraud, misconduct, gross mistake, or substantial breach of a common law rule. The only method of enforcing the common law award is to file suit upon it and the judgment thus obtained may be enforced as any other judgment. Insofar as a State arbitration statute fails to state a correlative rule and is not in conflict with any of these common law rules, it may be said that an arbitration proceeding under such statute is governed also by these rules.[280]

---

[278]*See* 20 Samuel Williston & Richard A. Lord, A Treatise on the Law of Contracts §56.4 (4th ed. 2000); Jones, *Judicial Review of Arbitral Awards—Common-Law Confusion and Statutory Clarification*, 31 S. Cal. L. Rev. 1, 2 (1957); Gregory & Orlikoff, *The Enforcement of Labor Arbitration Agreements*, 17 U. Chi. L. Rev. 233, 254–55 (1950).

[279]Puget Sound Bridge & Dredging Co. v. Lake Wash. Shipyards, 96 P.2d 257, 259, 261 (Wash. 1939). This right of election was reaffirmed in *Greyhound Corp. v. Motor Coach Employees*, 271 P.2d 689, 22 LA 555 (Wash. 1954). In Pennsylvania, the common law applies unless the parties elect to come under the statute. Thus, in *Guille v. Mushroom Transportation Co.*, 229 A.2d 903, 904, 65 LRRM 2524 (Pa. 1967), the court noted that where neither the agreement nor the arbitration conducted pursuant thereto made any reference to the state statute, "rules governing common law arbitration are applicable . . . except to the extent that these rules themselves have been pre-empted by federal common labor law."

[280]Ziskind, *Labor Arbitration Under State Statutes* 3 (U.S. Dep't of Labor 1943). As noted in the text accompanying note 288, below, many jurisdictions hold, both under the common law and under statute, that awards ordinarily may not be set aside for a mistake of law.

As the summary points out, the common law provides very little support for executory agreements to arbitrate (executory in the sense that the arbitration has not proceeded as far as issuance of an award). Either party may repudiate or withdraw from arbitration at any time prior to issuance of an award, because executory agreements to arbitrate future disputes have no binding effect and will not be enforced either by way of damages or specific enforcement. Moreover, executory agreements to arbitrate existing disputes likewise will not be specifically enforced (although in some jurisdictions breach of the latter agreements may be the basis of suit for nominal damages).[281] This common law rule against enforceability of executory agreements to arbitrate still prevails in some states.[282]

Although executory agreements to arbitrate are not specifically enforceable at common law, once an arbitration proceeding has been conducted and an award issued, the courts will take jurisdiction to enforce or vacate the award.[283] A party that is dissatisfied with an award may initiate action for court review or may challenge the award when the satisfied party seeks court enforcement.[284] At common law, the issuance of an award generally bars any subsequent action on the original claim, but suit may be filed for enforcement of the award itself to the same extent as any contract.[285] The grounds for attacking awards at common law are generally limited to:[286]

1. Fraud, misconduct, or partiality by the arbitrator, or gross unfairness in the conduct of the proceedings;
2. Fraud or misconduct by the parties affecting the result;
3. Complete want of jurisdiction in the arbitrator, or action beyond the scope of the authority conferred on the arbitrator or failure of the arbitrator to fully carry out his or her appointment (i.e., the arbitrator decides too much or too little); and

---

[281]*See* FREIDIN, LABOR ARBITRATION AND THE COURTS 2 (1952); Gregory & Orlikoff, 17 U. CHI. L. REV. at 236, 241.

[282]American Bar Association Committee on Arbitration, *Report on Labor Arbitration*, 28 LA 913, 929 (1957); Gregory & Orlikoff, 17 U. CHI. L. REV. at 234, 254.

[283]Because the arbitrator's authority terminates under the common law on issuance of the award, any review and enforcement of the award must be left to the courts, except to the extent that the parties or applicable statute give the arbitrator authority to interpret or otherwise deal with the award after its issuance. Regarding termination of the arbitrator's authority, see Chapter 7, section 5.E., "Reconsideration and Clarification of Award and Retention of Jurisdiction"; UPDEGRAFF, ARBITRATION AND LABOR RELATIONS 279–83 (BNA Books 1970); UPDEGRAFF & McCOY, ARBITRATION OF LABOR DISPUTES 211–15 (2d ed. 1961) (discussing also the question of power in the arbitrator to correct obvious mistakes and clerical errors in the award).

[284]*See* Justin, *Arbitration: Proving Your Case*, 10 LA 955, 967 (1948); UPDEGRAFF, at 285; UPDEGRAFF & McCOY, at 216.

[285]20 SAMUEL WILLISTON & RICHARD A. LORD, A TREATISE ON THE LAW OF CONTRACTS §56.4 (4th ed. 2000). *See also* Dowell, *Judicial Enforcement of Arbitration Awards in Labor Disputes*, 3 RUTGERS L. REV. 65, 70–72 (1949).

[286]*See When May an Arbitrator's Award Be Vacated?*, 7 DEPAUL L. REV. 236 (1958); Rothstein, *Vacation of Awards for Fraud, Bias, Misconduct and Partiality*, 10 VAND. L. REV. 813 (1957); FREIDIN, LABOR ARBITRATION AND THE COURTS 31 (1952); UPDEGRAFF, at 275, 278, 288–89; UPDEGRAFF & McCOY, at 208, 210–11, 216–17.

4. Violation of public policy as by ordering the commission of an unlawful act.[287]

Under the common law, awards generally will not be set aside for mistake of law or fact. As the Pennsylvania Supreme Court has stated: "Unless they are restricted by the submission [agreement], the arbitrators are the final judges of both law and fact and their award will not be disturbed for a mistake of either."[288]

ii.   State Arbitration Statutes [LA CDI 94.08]

State arbitration statutes are of three general types: (1) general statutes designed primarily for commercial disputes, but some of which may be used for labor disputes; (2) special labor arbitration statutes, which contain some detail as to procedure; and (3) statutes that merely "promote" arbitration by charging a state agency to encourage its use.[289]

One of the most detailed and most utilized statutes is that of New York, which was amended in 1940 for the specific purpose of covering labor arbitration, and which was revised and modernized in 1963.[290]

The California statute, enacted in 1961, supplanted an earlier act and introduced a number of innovations.[291] Other major industrial states with modern arbitration statutes applicable to labor arbitration include Illinois, Massachusetts, Michigan, New Jersey, and Ohio.

---

[287]Regarding this fourth ground, see Sturges, Commercial Arbitrations and Awards §61, at 202 (1930). See also Smith & Jones, *The Supreme Court and Labor Dispute Arbitration: The Emerging Federal Law*, 63 Mich. L. Rev. 751, 803–07 (1965); Cox, *The Place of Law in Labor Arbitration*, in The Profession of Labor Arbitration, Selected Papers From the First Seven Annual Meetings of NAA 76, 78–79 (McKelvey ed., BNA Books 1957).

[288]Newspaper Guild v. Philadelphia Daily News, 164 A.2d 215, 220 (Pa. 1960). For large collections of cases to the same general effect, see 6 C.J.S., *Arbitration and Award* §105, at 251 (1975); 4 Am. Jur. 2d (rev.), *Alternate Dispute Resolution* §92, at 923–24 (1995). Regarding the use of substantive law in arbitration, see Chapter 10, "Use of Substantive Rules of Law."

[289]See Ziskind, *Labor Arbitration Under State Statutes* (U.S. Dep't of Labor 1943). See also *Legislation Advances ADR Techniques: States Enact Arbitration Laws*, Arb. Times, Winter 1991/92, at 5; Matto, *The Applicability of State Arbitration Statutes to Proceedings Subject to LMRA Section 301*, 27 Ohio St. L.J. 692 (1966); Lillard, *State Arbitration Statutes Applicable to Labor Disputes*, 19 Mo. L. Rev. 280, 282–86 (1954). For extensive lists of citations to state arbitration statutes, see Updegraff, Arbitration and Labor Relations 385–88 (BNA Books 1970); Bedikian, *Use of Subpoenas in Labor Arbitration: Statutory Interpretations and Perspectives*, 1979 Det. C. L. Rev. 575, 576–77 (1979).

[290]See *An Outline of Procedure Under the New York Arbitration Law*, 20 Arb. J. 73 (1965); *The New York Arbitration Law*, 18 Arb. J. 132 (1963). The California and New York arbitration statutes as enacted in 1961 and 1962 respectively have remained in force without material change, but with some minor amendments not here germane relating to such matters as disclosure of potential bias or conflict of interest, which topics have been covered elsewhere. Statutes pertaining to arbitration of public sector labor disputes are discussed in Chapter 22, "Arbitration of Interest Disputes."

The decision in *Armendariz v. Foundation Health Psychcare Services, Inc.*, 24 Cal. 4th 83, 6 P.3d 669, 83 FEP Cases 1172 (2000), relates to mandatory employment agreements that purport to waive statutory rights, in section 2.A.ii.d.(1), "De Novo Litigation of Statutory Claims," above.

[291]See *Appendix C. Report of NAA Committee on Law and Legislation*, in Collective Bargaining and the Arbitrator's Role, Proceedings of the 15th Annual Meeting of NAA 249, 252–53 (Kahn ed., BNA Books 1962).

In 1955, a Uniform Arbitration Act was promulgated by the National Conference of Commissioners on Uniform Laws, and enacted in whole or substantial part in a majority of jurisdictions.[292] As of 2002, "all 50 states, as well as the District of Columbia," had a form of arbitration statute applicable to disputes arising under labor agreements.[293]

While the statutes vary in detail, and a full exploration of their terms is beyond the scope of this treatise, it may be noted that they usually contain the following provisions:

1. Agreements to arbitrate existing and future disputes are valid and may be judicially enforced, and courts are given jurisdiction to compel arbitration, or, if no agreement to arbitrate exists, to stay arbitration proceedings.
2. Courts are given jurisdiction to stay litigation when one party to an arbitration dispute attempts, instead, to have the dispute judicially resolved.
3. Courts may appoint arbitrators where the parties fail to provide a method for appointment.
4. Arbitration boards may render decisions by majority vote of their members.
5. Unless waived by the parties, arbitrators and witnesses are to be placed under oath.
6. Proceedings in the absence of a party and the rendering of default awards are allowed under certain circumstances.
7. Hearings may be continued and adjourned.
8. The right to be represented by counsel may be waived.
9. Arbitrators are given subpoena power.
10. Awards are required to be in writing, signed by the arbitrators, and issued within a specific time.
11. Arbitrators may, within specified limitations, modify or correct awards on timely application by a party. (The Uniform Arbitration Act additionally permits the arbitrator to clarify the award on application from a party.)
12. Court confirmation of awards and court vacation, modification, or correction of awards on limited grounds set forth in the statute may be pursued through summary procedures.
13. Courts may enter judgment on awards as confirmed, modified, or corrected, and the judgment is then enforceable as in normal course.
14. Appeals from court orders and judgments are permitted.

---

[292]The original Uniform Arbitration Act is published in 24 LA 886–89 (1955). The Uniform Arbitration Act, as amended, is published in 27 LA 909–12 (1956). For discussions of court decisions under various sections of the Uniform Arbitration Act, see Hunt, Ratcliffe, Williams & Yates, *Recent Developments: The Uniform Arbitration Act*, 1999 J. DISP. RESOL. 219 (1999); Berge, *The Uniform Arbitration Act: A Retrospective on its Thirty-Fifth Anniversary*, 14 HAMLINE L. REV. 301 (1991); *The Uniform Arbitration Act*, 48 MO. L. REV. 137 (1983).
[293]FAIRWEATHER'S PRACTICE AND PROCEDURE IN LABOR ARBITRATION 3 (Schoonhoven ed., BNA Books 4th ed. 1999).

The grounds for setting aside awards under many of the state statutes tend to track those in the Federal Arbitration Act and differ little from those available at common law:[294]

1. The award was procured by corruption, fraud, or other undue means.
2. The arbitrator was guilty of evident partiality, corruption, or misconduct (some statutes expressly limit the impartiality requirement to the neutral arbitrators serving on tripartite boards).[295]
3. The arbitrator refused to postpone the hearing on sufficient cause shown, or refused to hear material evidence, or otherwise so conducted the hearing as to prejudice substantially the rights of a party.
4. The arbitrator exceeded his or her powers, or so imperfectly executed them that a mutual, final, and definite award on the subject matter submitted was not made.[296]
5. There was no valid agreement to arbitrate (and it has not been determined otherwise by an action to compel or stay arbitration), and objection based on this ground was properly raised.

The Uniform Arbitration Act and the statutes of California, Florida, New York, and some other states provide that on vacation of an award, the court may order a rehearing before new arbitrators or, in some cases, before the original arbitrators. Some state statutes, and the Federal Arbitration Act, authorize the courts to modify or correct awards on grounds essentially as follows (some statutes also authorize the arbitrator to modify or correct an award on these grounds):[297]

1. Where there was an evident miscalculation of figures, or an evident mistake in the description of any person, thing, or property referred to in the award.
2. Where the arbitrators have awarded on a matter not submitted to them, and not affecting the merits of the decision on the matter submitted.

---

[294]*See Uniform Arbitration Act*, 27 LA 909, 910–11 (1956); Federal Arbitration Act, 9 U.S.C. §10; Lillard, *State Arbitration Statutes Applicable to Labor Disputes*, 19 Mo. L. Rev. 280, 293 (1954).

[295]The Supreme Court has stated that under the Federal Arbitration Act, the arbitrator "must not only be unbiased but also must avoid even the appearance of bias." Commonwealth Coatings Corp. v. Continental Cas. Co., 393 U.S. 145, 150 (1968), *reh'g denied*, 393 U.S. 112 (1969). *See also* Apperson v. Fleet Carrier Corp., 879 F.2d 1344, 131 LRRM 3079 (6th Cir. 1989); Toyota of Berkeley v. Automobile Salesmen's Union Local 1095, 856 F.2d 1572, 129 LRRM 2732 (9th Cir. 1988); Concourse Beauty Sch. v. Polakov, 685 F. Supp. (S.D.N.Y. 1988); Electrical Workers (IBEW) Local 323 v. Coral Elec., 104 F.R.D. 88 (S.D. Fla. 1985). For a discussion of arbitral bias, see Zirkel & Winebrake, *Legal Boundaries for Partiality and Misconduct of Labor Arbitrators*, 1992 Det. C. L. Rev. 679 (1992).

[296]Some of the statutes, such as California's, provide for vacation of the award where the arbitrator exceeded his or her powers, and the award cannot be corrected without affecting the merits of the decision.

[297]*See* Matto, *The Applicability of State Arbitration Statutes to Proceedings Subject to LMRA Section 301*, 27 Ohio St. L.J. 692, 713–14 (1966); Lillard, 19 Mo. L. Rev. at 294; *Uniform Arbitration Act*, 27 LA 909, 911; Federal Arbitration Act, 9 U.S.C. §11. Courts acting only under state common law may not be permitted to modify awards. *See* Updegraff, Arbitration and Labor Relations 289 (BNA Books 1970); Updegraff & McCoy, Arbitration of Labor Disputes 217–18 (2d ed. 1961); Enterprise Wheel & Car Corp. v. Steelworkers, 269 F.2d 327, 332, 44 LRRM 2349 (4th Cir. 1959).

3. Where the award is imperfect in a matter of form not affecting the merits of the controversy.

State statutes, following the common law tradition, generally provide no right of court review for errors of law or errors as to findings of fact.[298]

The RUAA (2000) attempts to fill in the procedural gaps and address other issues not considered in the original[299] as follows:

1. Providing for the issuing of orders for provisional remedies to protect the effectiveness of the arbitration proceeding.[300]
2. Creating a presumption that neutral arbitrators who do not disclose conflicts of interest "act with evident partiality," and making their awards subject to vacatur.[301]
3. Immunizing the arbitrator from civil liability to the same extent as judges.[302]
4. Establishing hearing procedures.[303]
5. Allowing prehearing discovery, the taking of depositions, and the issuing and enforcing of subpoenas.[304]
6. Authorizing the award of punitive damages and attorneys' fees.[305]
7. Allowing the correction, modification, or clarification of an award under certain circumstances.[306]
8. Incorporating substantially the same grounds for vacatur of awards as set forth in the original, 1955, Uniform Arbitration Act and the Federal Arbitration Act.[307]

Some courts have held that under the Federal Arbitration Act, arbitrators do not have authority to compel discovery from nonparties to a dispute.[308] Section 17 of the RUAA (2000) not only allows the arbitrator to subpoena witnesses and testimony from nonparties in appropriate circumstances, but also authorizes the arbitrator to compel out-of-state witnesses to attend the hearing.

C. Jurisdictional Limits on State Arbitration Law

State common law and state statutory law control only the arbitration of labor-management disputes involving private-sector concerns not affecting interstate commerce and thus not falling within the purview of Section

---

[298]*See also* Justin, *Arbitration: Proving Your Case*, 10 LA 955, 967 (1948).

[299]As of the middle of 2002, six states—Arizona, Hawaii, Nevada, New Jersey, New Mexico, and Utah—have adopted the 2000 Act. *See* Heinsz, *The Revised Uniform Arbitration Act; An Overview*, 56 J. DISP. RESOL. 28 (2000).

[300]7 U.L.A. (2000) §8.

[301]*Id*. §12.

[302]*Id*. §14.

[303]*Id*. §15.

[304]*Id*. §17.

[305]*Id*. §21.

[306]*Id*. §§20, 24.

[307]*Id*. §23.

[308]COMSAT Corp. v. National Sci. Found., 190 F.3d 269 (4th Cir. 1999).

301 of the LMRA and the Federal Arbitration Act.[309] However, as has been noted, the provisions of state law may be resorted to when the parties so agree in the arbitration clause of their labor agreement and where their terms are not inconsistent with the provisions and policies of the Federal Arbitration Act.

When the federal courts have only diversity jurisdiction over an action arising under state law concerning an arbitration provision or award, "the federal court enforcing a state-created right in a diversity case is . . . 'only another court of the State'"[310] and must decide the case on the basis of state law. State courts, however, have concurrent jurisdiction to enforce the Federal Arbitration Act and Section 301.

The bulk of labor-management arbitrations in the private sector no doubt falls within the purview of Section 301. As has been pointed out, however, such cases in state courts are to be governed by federal substantive law.[311] As state courts have recognized:[312] "Congress intended doctrines of federal labor law uniformly to prevail over inconsistent local rules."[313] Nevertheless, there is obvious validity in the comment that the "grant of concurrent jurisdiction gives the state courts an important role in assisting in the formulation of the federal substantive law under section 301."[314] Thus, while noting

---

[309]For disputes covered by the RLA, the federal statute provides the applicable law and is treated in Chapter 3, "Scope of Labor Arbitration," and Chapter 4, "The Arbitration Tribunal." Regarding public-sector employment, federal law governs the federal public sector and state law governs the state public sector. These areas are treated in Chapter 20, "Legal Status of Arbitration in the Federal Sector," and Chapter 21, "Issues in State and Local Government Sector Arbitration."

[310]Bernhardt v. Polygraphic Co. of Am., 350 U.S. 198, 203, 25 LA 693, 695 (1956) (quoting Guaranty Trust Co. v. York, 326 U.S. 99, 108 (1945) (enforceability of agreements to arbitrate must be decided by state law in such diversity cases).

[311]See section 2.A., "Federal Law: Private Sector," above. A clause stating that a contract was to be governed by New York law was held of no effect in a §301 action. Carey v. General Elec. Co., 213 F. Supp. 276, 50 LRRM 2119 (S.D.N.Y. 1962), *modified on other grounds*, 315 F.2d 499, 52 LRRM 2662 (2d Cir. 1963). *Cf.* Teamsters Local 117 v. Washington Employers, 557 F.2d 1345, 96 LRRM 2096 (9th Cir. 1977).

[312]*See, e.g.*, Meat Cutters Local 229 v. Cudahy Packing Co., 428 P.2d 849, 65 LRRM 2820 (Cal. 1967).

[313]Teamsters Local 174 v. Lucas Flour Co., 369 U.S. 95, 104, 49 LRRM 2717 (1962). Cases may be removed from state to federal court by virtue of §301 coverage. Johnson v. England, 356 F.2d 44, 61 LRRM 2635 (9th Cir.), *cert. denied*, 384 U.S. 961 (1966); Kracoff v. Retail Clerks Local 1357, 244 F. Supp. 38, 59 LRRM 2942 (E.D. Pa. 1965).

[314]Smith & Clark, *Reappraisal of the Role of the States in Shaping Labor Relations Law*, 1965 Wis. L. Rev. 411, 421 (1965). "Furthermore, it may be that procedural and remedial matters in the enforcement of labor agreements remain to be determined by the law of the forum." *Id.* at 421. *See also* Jiang, *Federal Arbitration Right, Choice-of-Law Clauses and State Rules and Procedure*, 22 Sw. U. L. Rev. 159 (1992). In *Machinists Local 1416 v. Jostens, Inc.*, 250 F. Supp. 496 (D. Minn. 1966), the court stated that while the *Textile Workers v. Lincoln Mills*, 353 U.S. 448, 40 LRRM 2113 (1957), mention of resort to state law was undoubtedly referring to principles of substantive law, there should be no impediment to the use of state procedure, in the absence of a contrary or inconsistent federal statute or rule. In *Machinists W. Rock Lodge 2120 v. Geometric Tool Co. Div., United-Greenfield Corp.*, 406 F.2d 284, 70 LRRM 2228, 51 LA 1156 (2d Cir. 1968), a 60-day time limit specified by state statute for rendering awards was deemed contrary to federal labor policy and could not be strictly enforced where the case was covered by LMRA §301. *But see* Huntington Alloys v. Steelworkers, 623 F.2d 335, 104 LRRM 2958, 2961 (4th Cir. 1980). In *Teamsters Local 671 v. United Parcel Service*, 526 F. Supp. 1044, 108 LRRM 3216, 3217 (D. Conn. 1981), the *Geometric Tool* reasoning was applied by the court in rejecting the applicability of a state provision regarding the arbitrator's oath.

that "the controlling substantive law is Federal law," the Minnesota Supreme Court emphasized that "state law, if compatible with the purposes of Section 301, may be resorted to in order to find the rule that will best effectuate the Federal policy."[315]

---

[315]Fischer v. Guaranteed Concrete Co., 276 Minn. 510, 151 N.W.2d 266, 269, 65 LRRM 2493 (1967). However, it has been observed, for instance, that state courts "have not faced the problem of the applicability of their arbitration statutes to proceedings subject to section 301 to any great extent." The reason may be that "it is easy to look to the state statute and not attempt to determine what the federal policy is and whether any conflict exists." Matto, *The Applicability of State Arbitration Statutes to Proceedings Subject to LMRA Section 301*, 27 OHIO ST. L.J. 692 (1966). This excellent article discusses certain common features of state arbitration statutes and evaluates their compatibility with the federal labor policy. For related discussion of the preemption of state law under Section 301, see Stein, *Preserving Unionized Employee's Individual Employment Rights: An Argument Against Section 301 Preemption*, 17 BERKELEY J. EMP. & LAB. L. 1 (1996); Grabar, Antol v. Esposto: *The Third Circuit Expands Preemption Under The Labor Management Relations Act*, 42 VILL. L. REV. 1995 (1997) (Issues in the Third Circuit: Casebrief: Labor Law).

Chapter 3

Scope of Labor Arbitration

1. INTRODUCTION

While many labor disputes are clearly suitable for arbitration, one of the potential hazards of labor arbitration has been said to be an "overoptimistic estimate" of its effective scope, "which tends to consider it an all-purpose tool or panacea for the resolution of any and all disputes which the parties fail to settle privately."[1] Before a dispute even reaches arbitration, the parties must decide whether the subject matter of the dispute is suitable for arbitration. Most collective bargaining agreements contain an arbitration clause that outlines the "scope of arbitration." When a collective bargaining agreement contains an arbitration clause and a dispute is submitted to arbitration, there is a presumption of arbitrability.[2]

Even if a dispute is of a type generally suitable for arbitration and is arbitrable under the collective bargaining agreement, judgment must be exercised in deciding whether to arbitrate the particular dispute.[3] Included

---

[1]Davey, *Hazards in Labor Arbitration*, 1 INDUS. & LAB. REL. REV. 386, 387 (1948). For related discussion, see Chapter 1, section 4.D., "Other Important Roles of Arbitration."

[2]AT&T Techs. v. Communications Workers, 475 U.S. 643, 121 LRRM 3329 (1986).

[3]Courts may overturn arbitration decisions if the arbitrator's interpretation of the contract would violate an explicit public policy. *See* Eastern Associated Coal Co. v. Mine Workers Dist. 17, 531 U.S. 57, 165 LRRM 2865 (2000); W.R. Grace & Co. v. Rubber Workers Local 759, 461 U.S. 757, 113 LRRM 2641 (1983); Delta Air Lines v. Air Line Pilots, 861 F.2d 665,

among the factors to be considered in this regard are the merits of the case, the importance of the issue, the effect of winning or losing, the possibilities of settlement, internal policies and politics within the union or the company, psychological and face-saving considerations, and public relations policies.[4] Some parties have adopted grievance mediation processes in their collective bargaining agreements either as a prior step or as a means of avoiding arbitration altogether.[5]

Certainly not all disputes are equally suitable for arbitration. The most popular use of labor arbitration concerns disputes involving the interpretation or application of the collective bargaining agreement. There is much less enthusiasm for its use, even on a voluntary basis, as a means of resolving disputes over terms of new or renewal contracts.[6] There are some matters, too, that are so delicate, or are considered to belong so intimately to one or the other of the parties, that they are not readily submitted to arbitration.[7] This has been suggested as a reasonable explanation for many of the specific exclusions from arbitration clauses studied by the U.S. Department of Labor in one survey:

> The reasons for such exclusions usually were not indicated by the agreements and, although they may have been fully understood by the parties, they are not always clear to outsiders reading the agreements. Some exclusions undoubtedly were intended to preserve certain management prerogatives, others to preserve union prerogatives. Some were necessary because the parties had agreed upon other methods of handling certain problems, and possibly some were motivated by a mutual desire not to overburden the arbitration machinery with trivialities. Exclusions in some cases appeared to represent a signal to workers in the bargaining unit that it would be pointless to raise a grievance over the designated issue. It seems reasonable to assume, however, that underlying many exclusions was a strongly held belief of one or both parties that

---

130 LRRM 2014 (11th Cir. 1988) (arbitration of just cause termination of a pilot who was intoxicated while flying was contrary to public policy. "The existence of public policy denouncing the operation of any aircraft, even those not occupied by passengers, while intoxicated is 'explicit'. . . ."); Pettway v. American Cast Iron Pipe Co., 411 F.2d 998 (5th Cir. 1969) (holding that public policy forbids the enforcement of a contract that submits to arbitration whether a complaint to the Equal Employment Opportunity Commission (EEOC) for racial discrimination constitutes just cause for discharge).

[4]*See* Kagel, Anatomy of a Labor Arbitration 20–21 (BNA Books 2d ed. 1986); Fleming, The Labor Arbitration Process 205–08 (Univ. of Ill. Press 1965); O'Hara, *Prehearing Arbitration Problems: A Panel Discussion: Strategy: To Settle or to Arbitrate?, in* The Arbitrator, the NLRB, and the Courts, Proceedings of the 20th Annual Meeting of NAA 341 (Jones ed., BNA Books 1967).

[5]*See Alternative Dispute Resolution Symposium Issue: In Praise of Party Empowerment and of Mediator Activism*, 33 Willamette L. Rev. 501, 518 (1997) (grievance mediations are often conducted by a practicing arbitrator, who will commonly predict the possible determination of the matter if it is taken to arbitration).

[6]For extent of acceptance of the various uses of arbitration, see Chapter 1, section 4.A., "Arbitration as a Substitute for Work Stoppages." For earlier data, see *Basic Patterns in Labor Arbitration Agreements*, 34 LA 931, 939 (1960); Warren & Bernstein, *A Profile of Labor Arbitration*, 16 LA 970, 971–73 (1951).

[7]*See* Lapp, Labor Arbitration 44 (1942); Moore & Mix, *Arbitration Provisions in Collective Agreements*, 76 Monthly Lab. Rev. 261–64 (1953). For surveys of matters that might be excluded from the collective agreement arbitration clause, see *Characteristics of Major Collective Bargaining Agreements, July 1, 1976*, at 82 (U.S. Dep't of Labor Bull. No. 2013, 1979); *Major Collective Bargaining Agreements: Arbitration Procedures* 6–22 (U.S. Dep't of Labor Bull. No. 1425-6, 1966); *Basic Patterns in Labor Arbitration Agreements*, 34 LA at 939.

the issue in question was too important or too subtle to be entrusted to a decision of a third party.[8]

Management naturally hesitates to submit to arbitration issues involving its normal prerogatives in the conduct of the business, such as the determination of methods of operation, operation policies, and finances. Labor usually considers that the settlement of an internal union conflict is "a matter in which management should not be permitted to participate, and it would be undesirable to permit the company to become involved in this question indirectly or in any manner whatsoever."[9] The alleged improper activities of union officials in the administration of grievances have been held to be improper subjects for arbitration, because a contrary approach "might well result in a form of policing of internal union affairs by a third party who clearly was not intended nor competent to accomplish such a purpose... The remedy lies with the union membership, which has the ultimate power, through democratic means, to control the selection of their representatives."[10] It may be noted, however, that arbitrations between the company and the union do sometimes reach internal union disputes.[11] Furthermore, internal union disputes may be arbitrated without management involvement.[12] Agency fee disputes[13] and interunion jurisdictional disputes[14] are two examples.

---

[8]*Major Collective Bargaining Agreements*, at 11.

[9]Babcock & Wilcox Co., 8 LA 58, 61 (Dworkin, 1947).

[10]Spencer Kellogg & Sons, 1 LA 291, 294 (Miller, 1945). *Cf.* North Am. Aviation, 17 LA 199, 204 (Komaroff, 1951).

[11]*See* Houston Chronicle Publ'g Co. v. Typographical Union No. 87 (Houston), 272 F. Supp. 974 (D.C. Cir. 1966) (union action against a member acting as foreman: union refused to submit the dispute to arbitration, characterizing its actions as union conduct; court ordered arbitration on the basis of a broad arbitration clause).

[12]*See* Alpha Beta Co., 93 LA 855 (Horowitz, 1989); Cook County Coll. Teachers Union, 71 LA 1057 (Nathan, 1978); Royal Indus. Union, 51 LA 642 (Johnson, Sirabella, & Reama, 1968); Screen Extras Guild, 46 LA 169 (Bernstein, 1966). Some unions utilize public review boards for such arbitration. "In the context of UAW [United Auto Workers] governance, the public review board represents essentially a group of arbitrators in whom the union has reposed ultimate authority to interpret its constitution and ethical practices codes and to decide disputes arising thereunder." Klein, *The Public Review Boards: Their Place in the Process of Dispute Resolutions, in* ARBITRATION—1974, PROCEEDINGS OF THE 27TH ANNUAL MEETING OF NAA 189, 191 (Dennis & Somers eds., BNA Books 1975). *See also* Linn, *The American Federation of Teachers Public Review Board, id.* at 205; Feller, *The Association of Western Pulp and Paper Workers Public Review Board, id.* at 221.

[13]*See* American Fed'n of Teachers Union Local 1 (Chicago) v. Hudson, 475 U.S. 292, 121 LRRM 2793 (1986). The *Hudson* Court held that union procedures used in determining agency fee disputes must provide for "a reasonably prompt decision by an impartial decisionmaker." *Id.* at 309. "[W]e think that an expeditious arbitration might [satisfy this requirement] so long as the arbitrator's selection did not represent the Union's unrestricted choice." *Id.* at 308 n.21. *See also* Montana Educ. Ass'n, 91 LA 1228 (Corbett, 1988) (applying *Hudson* in the arbitral setting); National Educ. Ass'n, 90 LA 973 (Concepcion, 1988) (applying *Hudson* in deciding what percentage of agency fees may properly be charged to the participants (objecting fee payers) for the 1987–88 school year as their pro-rata share of local, chargeable union expenses under applicable constitutional and statutory principles). *But see* Air Line Pilots v. Miller, 523 U.S. 866, 158 LRRM 2321 (1998) (agency-fee objectors, who have not agreed to the arbitration process adopted by the union to comply with *Hudson*, need not exhaust arbitral remedy before challenging union's agency-fee calculations).

[14]*E.g.,* Service Employees, 91 LA 530 (Weiler, 1987); Transit Union, 89 LA 263 (Weiler, 1987); Retail, Wholesale & Dep't Store Union, 88 LA 921 (Lesnick, 1986); Bricklayers, 87 LA 970 (Lesnick, 1985); Building Serv. Employees, 46 LA 28 (Cole, 1965); Retail, Wholesale & Dep't Store Union, 45 LA 69 (Taft, 1965); Upholsterers' Union, 23 LA 827 (Cole, 1955). For discussion, see Krislov & Mead, *Arbitrating Union Conflicts: An Analysis of the AFL-CIO*

Similarly, intermanagement disputes may be arbitrated without labor involvement.[15]

Unions ordinarily would not consider their statutory right to strike a proper subject for arbitration. However, the right to strike is frequently arbitrated in disputes involving the interpretation of contractual no-strike clauses,[16] and in such proceedings the question of the right to strike under legislative enactments may be brought into play.[17]

Some doubt exists as to the suitability of labor-management arbitration for resolving racial discrimination grievances for which statutory remedies are available, but proposals have been made to adapt the process to the needs of such grievances.[18]

While it has been suggested that "[a]rbitration is most effective when used sparingly,"[19] it has also been suggested that "it would hardly be right to judge the effectiveness or worth of an arbitration system or the health of a labor-management relationship by the number of cases" arbitrated each year.[20]

2. Disputes of Rights and Interests

The distinction between "rights" and "interests" is basic to the classification of labor disputes and to gaining an understanding of which kinds of disputes may be arbitral. Disputes as to rights comprehend the interpretation or application of laws, agreements, or customary practices, whereas disputes as to interests involve the question of what shall be the basic terms and conditions of employment. This nomenclature is derived from the Scandinavian countries, which have treated the distinction between rights and interests as basic in their labor legislation. Sweden, for instance, established

---

Internal Disputes Plan, 36 Arb. J. No. 2, at 21 (1981); Stark, *The Presidential Address: Theme and Adaptations, in* Truth, Lie Detectors, and Other Problems in Labor Arbitration, Proceedings of the 31st Annual Meeting of NAA 1, 28 (Stern & Dennis eds., BNA Books 1979); Cole, *Arbitration of Jurisdictional Disputes: The AFL-CIO No-Raiding Agreement, in* Arbitration Today, Proceedings of the 8th Annual Meeting of NAA 149 (McKelvey ed., BNA Books 1955); Feinsinger, *The Arbitration of CIO Organizational Disputes, id.* at 155; Dunlop, *The Arbitration of Jurisdictional Disputes in the Building Industry, id.* at 161. The U.S. Supreme Court has upheld the use of arbitration for resolving representation disputes; "the therapy of arbitration" may thus be brought to bear, though any subsequent decision by the National Labor Relations Board (NLRB, or the Board) would take precedence over that of the arbitrator. Carey v. Westinghouse Elec. Corp., 375 U.S. 261, 272, 55 LRRM 2042 (1964).

[15]Plumbing, Heating & Piping Employers Council, 39 LA 513 (Ross, 1962).

[16]*See* Washington Hosp. Ctr., 112 LA 495 (Liebowitz, 1999). *See also* Children's Hosp. Med. Ctr. v. California Nurses Ass'n, 163 LRRM 2724 (N.D. Cal. 2000).

[17]*See* General Elec. Co., 42 LA 1255, 1264–66 (Koretz, 1964).

[18]*See* Alexander v. Gardner-Denver Co., 415 U.S. 36, 7 FEP Cases 81 (1974). See also discussion of *Gardner-Denver* in Chapter 2, section 2.A.ii.d.(1), "De Novo Litigation of Statutory Claims," where other writings are also cited.

[19]Davey, *Labor Arbitration: A Current Appraisal*, 9 Indus. & Lab. Rel. Rev. 85, 90 (1955).

[20]Platt, *The Chrysler-UAW Umpire System: Discussion, in* The Arbitrator and the Party, Proceedings of the 11th Annual Meeting of NAA 111, 142–43 (McKelvey ed., BNA Books 1958) (labor relations at Ford were "at least as good as at Chrysler" even though Ford arbitrated many more cases than Chrysler; explanations and justifications for the heavier caseload at Ford are offered).

permanent national labor courts with jurisdiction carefully restricted to disputes concerning rights under collective bargaining agreements.[21]

The Supreme Court has explained the fundamental distinction between interest disputes and rights disputes in this manner:

> The first relates to disputes over the formation of collective agreements or efforts to secure them. They arise where there is no such agreement or where it is sought to change the terms of one, and therefore the issue is not whether an existing agreement controls the controversy. They look to the acquisition of rights for the future, not to assertion of rights claimed to have vested in the past.
>
> The second class, however, contemplates the existence of a collective agreement already concluded or, at any rate, a situation in which no effort is made to bring about a formal change in terms or to create a new one. The dispute relates either to the meaning or proper application of a particular provision with reference to a specific situation or to an omitted case. In the latter event the claim is founded upon some incident of the employment relation, or asserted one, independent of those covered by the collective agreement . . . . In either case the claim is to rights accrued, not merely to have new ones created for the future.[22]

Disputes as to rights are adjudicable under the laws or agreements on which the rights are based, and are readily adaptable to settlement by arbitration. Disputes as to interests, on the other hand, involve questions of policy that, for lack of predetermined standards, have not been generally regarded as justiciable or arbitrable. Yet many interest disputes are settled by arbitration, and, as was seen in Chapter 1, some states have concluded that public utility interest disputes involve such serious risk of public harm that a requirement of compulsory arbitration of such disputes is justified. Also, as discussed in Chapter 22, "Arbitration of Interest Disputes," many states by statute provide for the use of mediation and factfinding in the resolution of interest disputes in public-sector employment, and frequently these statutes provide for the use of arbitration (some making it compulsory) for disputes that have not been resolved by mediation or factfinding.

The distinction between these two basic types of disputes must not be overlooked in considering methods of settlement. Thus, the full-fashioned hosiery industry adopted one method of procedure for rights disputes and another for interest disputes:

> The jurisdiction of the Impartial Chairman does not extend to disputes regarding the general level of wages in the industry. Since decisions of this type would involve changing all the rates specified in the Agreement, they are excluded from his jurisdiction by the provision which denies him the right to change any of the terms of the contract. Furthermore, the parties have established in the Agreement a special procedure for handling disputes over general wage-level changes. The "flexibility clause" permits either party to seek a change in the general wage level at any time during the life of the agreement and

---

[21]Spielmans, *Labor Disputes on Rights and on Interests*, 29 AM. ECON. REV. 299 (1939).

[22]Elgin, Joliet & E. Ry. v. Burley, 325 U.S. 711, 723, 16 LRRM 749 (1945) (Railway Labor Act). The Court noted that the two basic types of disputes are traditionally called "major" and "minor" disputes in the railroad industry. *Id.* The Railway Labor Act is discussed below.

provides for the establishment of a special wage tribunal in case the parties cannot agree on the percentage change to be made.[23]

Because there is no uniformly accepted body of principles for determining wage levels, one or both of the parties is likely to feel that a given interest decision is grossly inequitable. Recognition of this fact by both labor and management in the full-fashioned hosiery industry led to the use of one set of procedures for the arbitration of rights disputes and another for interest disputes. Ill-feeling against an arbitrator after an interest decision may be so general and so severe that just one decision will destroy that arbitrator's usefulness to the industry.

Of the first six arbitrators chosen to determine general wage-level changes under the flexibility clause in the hosiery industry, not one was invited to serve a second time. Because it is not easy to find a person who combines the specialized knowledge of the industry and the type of personality that is necessary for success as an impartial chairman, the parties, in order to avoid the risk of losing a good impartial chairman over decisions on general wage-levels and other new contract issues, farmed those disputes out to other arbitrators.[24]

Federal legislation governing labor relations in the railroad industry reflected the distinction between rights disputes and interest disputes. The first three federal acts did not differentiate between them,[25] but the Transportation Act of 1920[26] provided for special treatment of the two types of disputes. Ever since then the two types of disputes have received different treatment.

The Railway Labor Act of 1926,[27] as amended in 1934, created the National Railroad Adjustment Board (NRAB), which, on submission of a complaint by either party, takes jurisdiction over "disputes between an employee or group of employees and a carrier or carriers growing out of grievances or out of the interpretation or application of agreements concerning rates of pay, rules, or working conditions . . ." after they have been "handled in the usual manner up to and including the chief operating officer of the carrier designated to handle such disputes."[28] Disputes concerning "changes in rates of pay, rules, or working conditions not adjusted by the parties in conference" and "[a]ny other dispute not referable to the National Railroad Adjustment Board and not adjusted in conference between the parties or where conferences are refused"[29] are handled by the National Mediation Board (NMB).

---

[23]Kennedy, Effective Labor Arbitration 37 (1948). This is a comprehensive treatise on the impartial chairmanship of the full-fashioned hosiery industry. As to this industry, see also Fleming, The Labor Arbitration Process 10–11 (Univ. of Ill. Press 1965).

[24]Kennedy, at 38–39.

[25]Arbitration Act of 1888, ch. 1063, 25 Stat. 501; Erdman Act, ch. 370, 30 Stat. 424 (1898); Newlands Act, ch. 6, 38 Stat. 103 (1913).

[26]54 Stat. 898, Act of Sept. 18, 1940, ch. 722.

[27]45 U.S.C. §151 et seq.

[28]Railway Labor Act, 45 U.S.C. §153(i).

[29]Id., 45 U.S.C. §155(a).

The function of the NRAB is to interpret and apply collective bargaining agreements, not to make or modify them. The NMB, on the other hand, is directed to help the parties, through mediation, to reach agreement on the terms of collective bargaining agreements, and, on failure to bring about an agreement, attempt to induce the parties to submit their dispute to voluntary arbitration.[30]

When requested by the parties to provide assistance in the selection of an arbitrator, the various appointing agencies consider whether the dispute is one over rights or interests. Some disputes, however, involve elements of each type, and cannot be clearly classified as falling exclusively within either of the two categories. In such cases, arbitrability depends on whether the arbitration clause or submission agreement is broad enough to cover the dispute. The subject of interest arbitration is considered in Chapter 22, "Arbitration of Interest Disputes."

3. Rights Arbitration

A. Subject Matter of Rights Arbitration [LA CDI 94.101 et seq.]

The sources of the subject matter of rights disputes are usually agreements, laws, and customary practices. Among the infinite number of matters that may be the subject of rights arbitration are questions with respect to seniority rights, vacations, holidays, discharge and discipline, layoffs, and job classifications. But not all issues that are taken to arbitrators fall into such commonly recognized categories. This is illustrated by the historical "Case of the Lady in Red Slacks." A Ford Motor Company employee was reprimanded and docked one-half hour because she wore slacks described as bright red in color. The objection was to the color, not to the slacks, which female employees were required to wear. The issue was whether a lady's red slacks constituted a production hazard because of a tendency to distract male employees. The umpire stated that "it is common knowledge that wolves, unlike bulls, may be attracted by colors other than red and by various other enticements in the art and fit of female attire."[31] The reprimand was expunged and the employee was reimbursed for the pay that she had been docked.[32]

---

[30]For additional discussion, see Chapter 4, section 6., "Tribunals Under the Railway Labor Act"; Lecht, Experience Under Railway Labor Legislation (1955); Jones, Handling of Railroad Labor Disputes 1888–1940 (1941). "[V]irtually every major carrier and labor organization in the railroad industry has participated in at least one major interest arbitration. The same is true in the airline industry." Stark, *The Presidential Address: Theme and Adaptations, in* Truth, Lie Detectors, and Other Problems in Labor Arbitration, Proceedings of the 31st Annual Meeting of NAA 1, 16 (Stern & Dennis eds., BNA Books 1979).

[31]Shulman, Opinions of the Umpire, Opinion A-117 (June 30, 1944).

[32]*See also* Cooper, *Arbitral Continuity: Part II. Harry Shulman: Deciding Women's Grievances in Wartime, in* Arbitration 1994: Controversy and Continuity, Proceedings of the 47th Annual Meeting of NAA 153 (Gruenberg ed., BNA Books 1994). Other disputes about female attire were resolved by *Mitchell-Bentley Corp.*, 45 LA 1071, 1073 (Ryder, 1965) (female could not be punished for wearing "short shorts"); *Lawrence Bros.*, 28 LA 83, 87 (Davis, 1957). In later years, personal appearance has emerged as a frequently arbitrated subject. *See* Chapter 17, section 5., "Personal Appearance: Hair and Clothes."

B. Arbitrator's Function in Rights Disputes

Unlike the arbitrator's quasi-legislative role in interest disputes, the arbitrator's function in rights disputes is limited to interpretation of the bargained-for agreement.[33] Indeed, the parties very frequently provide that the arbitrator shall have no power to add to, subtract from, or modify any provision of the agreement.[34] Beginning with its *Enterprise Wheel* decision,[35] the Supreme Court limited the arbitrator's role in rights disputes to interpretation and application of the collective bargaining agreement.[36] The Court held that although an arbitrator could look outside the contract for guidance, "he does not sit to dispense his own brand of industrial justice,"[37] and the arbitrator's award is therefore legitimate only insofar as it "draws it essence" from the collective bargaining agreement.[38] Along with the federal courts, "'arbitrators . . .are still the principal sources of contract interpretation.'"[39]

---

[33]The function of the rights arbitrator in the interpretation and application of collective agreements is treated in detail in Chapter 9, particularly in section 2., "Ambiguity and the Exclusion of Extrinsic Evidence" and section 3., "'Legislation' Versus 'Interpretation.'" The reader is urged to consult those topics concerning the arbitrator's function in rights disputes.

[34]Of 400 agreements included in one study,

> restrictions [were] placed on arbitrators in 82 percent of agreements studied. Of these, 92 percent apply a general restriction prohibiting the arbitrator from adding to, subtracting from, or in any way altering contract language. Twenty-six percent of restrictive clauses specify that arbitrators must submit their decisions in writing, and 38 percent require that decisions be rendered within a specified time period, usually 30 days.

BASIC PATTERNS IN UNION CONTRACTS 38 (BNA Books 14th ed. 1995).

[35]Steelworkers v. Enterprise Wheel & Car Corp., 363 U.S. 593, 46 LRRM 2423 (1960). The *Enterprise Wheel* decision was part of the famous *Steelworkers Trilogy* (Steelworkers v. American Mfg. Co., 363 U.S. 564, 46 LRRM 2414 (1960); Steelworkers v. Warrior & Gulf Navigation Co., 363 U.S. 574, 46 LRRM 2416 (1960)), in which the Court outlined the significance of arbitration in the labor-management context. For a discussion of the *Steelworkers Trilogy*, see Chapter 2, section 2.A.ii.b., "The *Trilogy*."

[36]*Enterprise Wheel*, 363 U.S. at 597, 46 LRRM at 2425.

[37]*Id.*

[38]*Id.* For an informative discussion arguing that limited judicial review has properly fostered the development and expansion of grievance arbitration as an efficient, fair, and inexpensive system of private industrial jurisprudence, see Morris, *Twenty Years of* Trilogy: *A Celebration, in* DECISIONAL THINKING OF ARBITRATORS AND JUDGES, PROCEEDINGS OF THE 33D ANNUAL MEETING OF NAA 331 (Stern & Dennis eds., BNA Books 1981).

[39]Litton Fin. Printing Div. v. NLRB, 501 U.S. 190, 202, 137 LRRM 2441 (1991) (quoting NLRB v. Strong, 393 U.S. 357, 360–61, 70 LRRM 2100 (1969)). *See also, e.g.,* Conoco Inc. v. NLRB, 91 F.3d 1523, 1525, 153 LRRM 2007 (D.C. Cir. 1996) ("we have held that 'under federal labor laws, arbitrators and the courts, rather than the [National Labor Relations] Board, are the primary sources of contract interpretation'" (quoting NLRB v. U.S. Postal Serv., 8 F.3d 832, 837, 144 LRRM 2691 (D.C. Cir. 1993)).

In 1981,[40] 1983,[41] and again in 1984,[42] the Supreme Court reaffirmed both *Enterprise Wheel* and the "primacy and exclusivity of arbitration within its proper sphere of contract interpretation":[43]

> [E]ven though a particular arbitrator may be competent to interpret and apply statutory law, he may not have the contractual authority to do so. An arbitrator's power is both derived from, and limited by, the collective-bargaining agreement. He "has no general authority to invoke public laws that conflict with the bargain between the parties." His task is limited to construing the meaning of the collective-bargaining agreement so as to effectuate the collective intent of the parties.[44]

Lower courts have followed the Supreme Court's lead and have uniformly restricted the arbitrator's function in rights disputes to the role of contract

---

[40]Barrentine v. Arkansas-Best Freight Sys., 450 U.S. 728, 24 WH Cases 1284 (1981).

[41]W.R. Grace & Co. v. Rubber Workers Local 759, 461 U.S. 757, 113 LRRM 2641 (1983). In *Grace,* the Court issued its oft-cited statement that "a federal court may not overrule an arbitrator's decision simply because the court believes its own interpretation of the contract would be the better one." *Id.* at 764, 113 LRRM at 2644. For an in-depth discussion of the Supreme Court's opinion in *Grace,* see Christensen, *Recent Law and Arbitration: I. W.R. Grace and Co.: An Epilogue to the* Trilogy?, *in* Arbitration 1984: Absenteeism, Recent Laws, Panels, and Published Decisions, Proceedings of the 37th Annual Meeting of NAA 21 (Gershenfeld ed., BNA Books 1985).

[42]McDonald v. City of West Branch, 466 U.S. 284, 115 LRRM 3646 (1984). In *McDonald,* the Court upheld the res judicata or collateral estoppel effect of an arbitration award rendered in a discrimination case under 42 U.S.C. §1983. The Court reiterated its stance that the arbitrator's authority "derives solely from the contract." *Id.* at 290, 115 LRRM at 3648.

[43]Nolan & Abrams, *The Future of Labor Arbitration,* 37 Lab. L.J. 437, 438–39 (1986). *See also* Heinsz, *Judicial Review of Labor Arbitration Awards: The* Enterprise Wheel *Goes Around & Around,* 52 Mo. L. Rev. 243 (1987); Dunsford, *The Role and Function of the Labor Arbitrator,* 30 St. Louis U. L.J. 109, 119 (1985) ("In the first great debate about the role of the arbitrator, the prevailing judgment has been to consider the arbitrator an adjudicator and not a mediator or problem solver.").

[44]Barrentine v. Arkansas-Best Freight Sys., 450 U.S. 728, 744, 24 WH Cases 1284 (1981) (quoting Alexander v. Gardner-Denver Co., 415 U.S. 36, 53, 7 FEP Cases 81 (1974)). *See also Gardner-Denver,* 415 U.S. at 53–54, 7 FEP Cases at 87 ("the arbitrator has authority to resolve questions of contractual rights"). *But see* Korn, *Changing Our Perspective on Arbitration: A Traditional and a Feminist View,* 1991 U. Ill L. Rev. 67, 91 (arguing not only that if parties to a contract agree to arbitrate their statutory claims, an arbitrator has contractual authority to apply federal statutes, but furthermore that arbitration of statutory claims should preclude judicial examination of those same claims). *See also* Gilmer v. Interstate/Johnson Lane Corp., 500 U.S. 20, 55 FEP Cases 1116 (1991) (holding that a claim under the Age Discrimination in Employment Act (ADEA), 29 U.S.C. §621 et seq., can be subjected to compulsory arbitration under the Federal Arbitration Act, 9 U.S.C. §1 et seq. This decision extended the scope of arbitrators' authority in the context of employment agreements enforceable pursuant to the Federal Arbitration Act. Whether this expanded authority will be extended to cover collective bargaining agreements in the labor context is unclear, but a majority of federal appellate courts have found it does not, leaving the choice of forum to the aggrieved employee. See section 3.B.i., "Expansion of the Arbitrator's Role," below. The Supreme Court avoided resolving this issue in *Wright v. Universal Mar. Serv. Corp.,* 525 U.S. 70, 77, 159 LRRM 2769 (1998) (it is "unnecessary to resolve the question of the validity of a union-negotiated waiver [of the right to bring a federal statutory claim in court], since it is apparent to us . . . that no such waiver occurred").

interpreter.[45] The lower courts are routinely called on to define the arbitrator's function in the context of reviewing arbitration awards. The arbitrator's role as contract interpreter is evidenced by the Supreme Court's reluctance to vacate or modify an award that "draws its essence" from the contract.[46] The Court has now reconfirmed the principle that

> the arbitrator's award . . . must draw its essence from the contract and cannot simply reflect the arbitrator's own notions of industrial justice. But as long as the arbitrator is even arguably construing or applying the contract and acting within the scope of his authority, that a court is convinced he committed serious error does not suffice to overturn his decision.[47]

---

[45]*See, e.g.*, Teamsters Local 42 v. Supervalu, Inc., 212 F.3d 59, 69, 164 LRRM 2296 (1st Cir. 2000) (upholding award because it drew its essence from the agreement and "stemmed rationally, if not inevitably, from the arbitrator's construction of the CBA [collective bargaining agreement]"); Wyandot, Inc. v. Food & Commercial Workers Local 227, 205 F.3d 922, 163 LRRM 2705 (6th Cir. 2000) (arbitrator's decision departed from the essence of the agreement because the award conflicted with and was not rationally based on the agreement, imposed additional requirements not included in the agreement, and was not based on considerations of fairness and equity); American National Can Co. v. Steelworkers Local 3628, 120 F.3d 886, 155 LRRM 2905 (8th Cir. 1997) (determining that award draws its essence from agreement and finding that the arbitrator was not bound by previous arbitration awards concerning the application of the same clause of the collective bargaining agreement); Bruce Hardwood Floors v. UBC, Southern Council of Indus. Workers Local 2713, 103 F.3d 449, 154 LRRM 2207 (5th Cir. 1997) (vacating award that mitigated discharge penalty where agreement expressly permitted discharge for immoral conduct); Excel Corp. v. Food & Commercial Workers Local 431, 102 F.3d 1464, 154 LRRM 2154 (8th Cir. 1996) (vacating award reinstating employees because it ignored plain language of agreement); Amax Coal Co. v. Mine Workers, 92 F.3d 571, 574, 153 LRRM 2011 (7th Cir. 1996) (vacating award because "an arbitrator cannot grant a remedy when he finds that there is no breach of the collective bargaining agreement"); Island Creek Coal Co. v. Mine Workers Dist. 28, 29 F.3d 126, 146 LRRM 2773 (4th Cir. 1994) (vacating award of punitive damages); Typographical Union No. 16 (Chicago) v. Chicago Sun-Times, 935 F.2d 1501, 1505, 137 LRRM 2731 (7th Cir. 1991) (award upheld where arbitrator interpreted contract without injecting his personal opinions); Upshur Coals Corp. v. Mine Workers Dist. 31, 933 F.2d 225, 137 LRRM 2397 (4th Cir. 1991) (confirming award that employer was required to provide accrued health benefits to laid-off employees even after agreement expired); NCR Corp. v. Machinists Dist. 70, 906 F.2d 1499, 134 LRRM 2694 (10th Cir. 1990) (confirming award that employer subcontracting violated agreement); Jersey Nurses Econ. Sec. Org. v. Roxbury Med. Group, 868 F.2d 88, 130 LRRM 2680 (3d Cir. 1989) (award unenforceable because it did not draw its essence from collective bargaining agreement); *In re* Marine Pollution Serv., 857 F.2d 91, 129 LRRM 2472 (2d Cir. 1988) (arbitrator failed to satisfy requirement that award be drawn from essence of collective bargaining agreement); Northwest Airlines v. Air Line Pilots, 808 F.2d 76, 124 LRRM 2300 (D.C. Cir. 1987); Morgan Servs. v. Clothing & Textile Workers Local 323, 724 F.2d 1217, 115 LRRM 2368 (6th Cir. 1984) (award vacated because arbitrator exceeded authority given him by the contract); Super Tire Eng'g Co. v. Teamsters Local 676, 721 F.2d 121, 114 LRRM 3320 (3d Cir. 1983) (reversing district court decision vacating award because award was based on the contract and was not irrational). *But see* High Concrete Structures v. Electrical Workers (UE) Local 166, 879 F.2d 1215, 131 LRRM 3152 (3d Cir. 1989) (recognizing arbitrator's authority to go beyond express terms of collective bargaining agreement where so agreed by the parties either through an interest- or rights-arbitration clause in the agreement or through a separate agreement). For additional cases and discussion, see *Labor Arbitration and the Law of Collective Bargaining Agreements,* 7 Lab. Law. 747, 747–54 (1991). The U.S. Court of Appeals for the Second Circuit had put a gloss on the *Steelworkers Trilogy* that "an arbitration award will not be vacated when the arbitrator explains his decision in terms that offer even a barely colorable justification for the outcome reached . . . ." Pinkerton's N.Y. Racing Sec. Serv. v. Service Employees Local 32E, 805 F.2d 470, 473, 123 LRRM 3090, 3092 (2d Cir. 1986) (and cases cited therein).

[46]Steelworkers v. Enterprise Wheel & Car Corp., 363 U.S. 593, 597, 46 LRRM 2423 (1960). See also cases cited in note 45, above.

[47]Paperworkers v. Misco, Inc., 484 U.S. 29, 38, 126 LRRM 3113 (1987).

At the same time, the Supreme Court endorsed an exception, albeit a narrow one, to the usual judicial deference paid to arbitrators by the "essence" standard—when the award violates well-defined and dominant public policy.[48] That is, even though the arbitrator's award may "draw its essence" from the contract, it may at the same time be unenforceable because it violates established law or seeks to compel unlawful action.[49] After over a decade and a half of interpretation by the lower courts,[50] the limits of the

---

[48]*Id.* at 43.

[49]W.R. Grace & Co. v. Rubber Workers Local 759, 461 U.S. 757, 113 LRRM 2641 (1983). The Supreme Court in *Grace* first recognized that an arbitrator's award may be unenforceable because it violates public policy. The Court explained that the basis for the public policy exception must be "well defined and dominant" and ascertained "'by reference to the laws and legal precedents and not from general considerations of supposed public interests.'" *Id.* at 766, 113 LRRM at 2645 (quoting Muschany v. United States, 324 U.S. 49, 66 (1945). The Court in *Misco* recognized that *Grace* did not "sanction a broad judicial power to set aside arbitration awards as against public policy." *Misco*, 484 U.S. at 43. The breadth of this exception received immediate scholarly attention. *See generally* Meltzer, *After the Labor Arbitration Award: The Public Policy Defense*, 10 INDUS. REL. L.J. 241 (1988); Edwards, *Judicial Review of Labor Arbitration Awards: The Clash Between the Public Policy Exception and the Duty to Bargain*, 64 CHI.-KENT L. REV. 3 (1988). *See also* Dunsford, *The Judicial Doctrine of Public Policy: Misco Reviewed*, 4 LAB. LAW. 669 (1988) (reviews arguments both for and against invocation of public policy in arbitration and provides alternative bright-line rules the Supreme Court could adopt to resolve issue); Parker, *Judicial Review of Labor Arbitration Awards: Misco and Its Impact on the Public Policy Exception*, 4 LAB. LAW 683, 685 (1988) ("It is the author's conclusion that the judicial adoption of an expansive public policy exception flies in the face of well-established federal labor policy; ignores the mandate issued by the Supreme Court in *Misco*; and undermines the process of grievance arbitration.").

[50]Since the *Misco* decision, the lower courts have developed the exception thoroughly. *See, e.g.*, Pierce v. Commonwealth Edison Co., 112 F.3d 893, 155 LRRM 2146 (7th Cir. 1997) (rejecting public policy argument); Exxon Corp. v. Baton Rouge Oil & Chem. Workers, 77 F.3d 850, 151 LRRM 2737 (5th Cir. 1996) (public policy exception applies both to bar reinstatement of a drug-abusing employee and to bar an award to him of back pay); Food & Commercial Workers Local 588 v. Foster Poultry Farms, 74 F.3d 169, 151 LRRM 2013 (9th Cir. 1995) (rejecting public policy defense against reinstatement of drug-using drivers); Exxon Shipping Co. v. Exxon Seamen's Union, 73 F.3d 1287, 151 LRRM 2161 (3d Cir. 1996) (and cases discussed therein) (reinstatement of transportation employee who refused drug test would violate public policy); Postal Workers v. U.S. Postal Serv., 52 F.3d 359, 362, 149 LRRM 2070 (D.C. Cir. 1995) ("the Supreme Court has made clear that to overturn a labor arbitration award as contrary to public policy is a daunting task"); Transportation Union Local 1589 v. Suburban Transit Corp., 51 F.3d 376, 382, 148 LRRM 2796 (3d Cir. 1995) (the public policy "exception is available only when 'the arbitration decision and award create an explicit conflict with an explicit public policy.'"); Newsday, Inc. v. Typographical Union No. 915 (Long Island), 915 F.2d 840, 135 LRRM 2659 (2d Cir. 1990), *cert. denied*, 499 U.S. 922 (1991) (vacated reinstatement award as violative of public policy against sexual harassment); Interstate Brands Corp. v. Teamsters Local 135, 909 F.2d 885, 135 LRRM 2006 (6th Cir. 1990), *cert. denied*, 499 U.S. 905 (1991) (reinstatement award allowed—although grievant's off-duty drug and alcohol offenses themselves violated public policy, it does not necessarily follow that reinstatement of said grievant itself violates public policy). *See also* Stead Motors of Walnut Creek v. Machinists Lodge 1173, 886 F.2d 1200, 132 LRRM 2689 (9th Cir. 1989), *cert. denied*, 495 U.S. 946 (1990); E.I. DuPont de Nemours & Co. v. Grasselli Employees Indep. Ass'n of E. Chicago, 790 F.2d 611, 122 LRRM 2217 (7th Cir. 1986); Postal Workers v. U.S. Postal Serv., 789 F.2d 1, 122 LRRM 2094 (D.C. Cir. 1986). The recent trend has been to focus only on whether the arbitrator's award, not the arbitrator's reasoning, offends public policy. Eastern Associated Coal Co. v. Mine Workers Dist. 17, 188 F.3d 501, 165 LRRM 2864 (4th Cir. 1999) (per curiam) (table) (affirming district court reasoning that there may be a public policy against drug use by those in safety-sensitive positions, but no such policy exists against reinstating employees who used illegal drugs in the past), *aff'd*, 531 U.S. 57, 165 LRRM 2865 (2000); Tennessee Valley Auth. v. Tennessee Valley Trades & Labor Council, 184 F.3d 510, 520–21, 161 LRRM 2844 (6th Cir. 1999) (finding arbitrator's award reinstating employee at nuclear power plant after testing positive for marijuana in a random drug screen and failing to meet fitness for duty requirements did not violate public

public policy exception were recently more clearly defined by the Supreme Court in *Eastern Associated Coal Co. v. Mine Workers*,[51] in which the Court held that an arbitrator's decision reinstating a mobile equipment operator who twice tested positive for drug use was not violative of public policy.

Even as the courts generally limit arbitrators to interpretation of the collective bargaining agreement with certain exceptions, the arbitrator's authority to construe the agreement also depends on the scope of the arbitration clause.[52] The Supreme Court held that an order to arbitrate should not be denied unless it could be said that arbitration of a particular grievance is outside the scope of the collective bargaining agreement.[53] Arbitration is a creation of the bargained-for agreement, and the arbitrator is limited by its terms.[54] Thus, broad arbitration clauses give an arbitrator expansive authority to decide a multitude of disputes. The lower courts have not hesitated to support arbitration of an issue (unless they are convinced that the contract specifically excludes that issue),[55] since the Supreme Court ruled that a broad grievance-arbitration provision should be held to encompass all disputed matters not specifically excluded. "'[Arbitration] should not be denied unless it may be said with positive assurance that the arbitration clause is not susceptible of an interpretation that covers the asserted dispute. Doubts should be resolved in favor of coverage.'"[56]

---

policy where employee was to undergo a hearing for fitness on reinstatement); Electrical Workers (IBEW) Local 97 v. Niagara Mohawk Power Corp., 143 F.3d 704, 716–19, 158 LRRM 2198 (2d Cir. 1998) (determining that "nothing within the [Nuclear Regulatory Commission] regulations prohibits the re-employment of an employee who yields a first positive on a drug test, provided that adequate insurance of the employee's rehabilitation is obtained.").

[51]Eastern Associated Coal Co. v. Mine Workers Dist. 17, 531 U.S. 57, 165 LRRM 2865 (2000).

[52]Safeway Stores v. Food & Commercial Workers Local 400, 621 F. Supp. 1233, 118 LRRM 3419 (D.D.C. 1985) (arbitration is a matter of contract and arbitrator's authority is defined by agreement).

[53]AT&T Techs. v. Communications Workers, 475 U.S. 643, 649–50, 121 LRRM 3329 (1986).

[54]*Id.* at 648 ("'arbitration is a matter of contract,'" (quoting Steelworkers v. Warrior & Gulf Navigation, 363 U.S. 574, 582, 46 LRRM 2416 (1960)). *See also* Leed Architectural Prods. v. Steelworkers Local 6674, 916 F.2d 63, 65, 135 LRRM 2766 (2d Cir. 1990) (an arbitrator's authority is "limited to the powers that the agreement confers"); Seafarers v. National Marine Servs., 639 F. Supp. 1283, 1290 (E.D. La. 1986) ("arbitration is a creature of contract with no life independent of its collective bargaining agreement"), *overruled on other grounds by* Litton Fin. Printing Div. v. NLRB, 501 U.S. 190, 137 LRRM 2447 (1991). The arbitrator's role as contract interpreter is further evidenced by the court's role in LMRA §301 (29 U.S.C. §185 (1982)) suits to compel arbitration. In actions to compel arbitration, the court's role is to ascertain "'whether the party seeking arbitration is making a claim which on its face is governed by the contract.'" Graphic Communications Local 680 v. Nabisco Brands, 649 F. Supp. 253, 256 (N.D. Ill. 1986) (quoting Steelworkers v. American Mfg. Co., 363 U.S. 564, 568, 46 LRRM 2414, 2415 (1960)). Congress has also defined the arbitrator's function as contract interpreter. The NLRA provides in part: "Final adjustment by a method agreed upon by the parties is hereby declared to be the desirable method for settlement of grievance disputes arising over the *application or interpretation of an existing collective-bargaining agreement.*" 29 U.S.C. §173(d) (emphasis added).

[55]For an example of a contract that very specifically narrowed the scope of arbitration, see *Machinists Local 2725 v. Caribe Gen. Elec. Prods.*, 108 F.3d 422, 154 LRRM 2765 (1st Cir. 1997).

[56]*AT&T*, 475 U.S. at 650 (quoting *Warrior & Gulf*, 363 U.S. at 582–83). "In the absence of any express provision excluding a particular grievance from arbitration, . . . only the most forceful evidence of a purpose to exclude the claim from arbitration can prevail." *Warrior &*

Moreover, the issue of arbitrability is one that is to be finally resolved by the courts, not by an arbitrator.[57] In ruling on arbitrability, however, the court "is not to rule on the potential merits of the underlying claims."[58] In some cases, however, a determination that a dispute is or is not arbitrable is effectively a determination of the underlying dispute as well. The Court has strongly indicated that the judicial obligation to determine arbitrability must prevail, even if it requires an interpretation of the agreement that would leave an arbitrator with virtually nothing to do. The Court stated: "Although '[d]oubts should be resolved in favor of [arbitrability],' we must determine whether the parties have agreed to arbitrate this dispute, and we cannot avoid that duty because it requires us to interpret a provision of a bargaining agreement."[59] As one appellate court explained, " '[i]t appears that the rule that courts must decide arbitrators' jurisdiction takes precedence over the rule that courts are not to decide the merits of the underlying dispute. If the courts must, to decide the arbitrability issue, rule on the merits, so be it.' "[60]

i. Expansion of the Arbitrator's Role [LA CDI 94.551]

While the courts generally limit the scope of the arbitrator's authority to the terms of the collective bargaining agreement, the NLRB expanded the role of arbitrators by deferring cases alleging violations of individuals' basic Section 7 rights to the grievance arbitration machinery.[61] Their role has taken

---

Gulf, 363 U.S. at 584–85. *See also* Daniel Constr. Co. v. Electrical Workers (IBEW) Local 257, 856 F.2d 1174, 129 LRRM 2429 (8th Cir. 1988), *cert. denied*, 489 U.S. 1020 (1989) (where arbitration clause broadly refers to "any dispute over interpretation," only the most forceful evidence of purpose to exclude claim from arbitration can prevail); Pervel Indus. v. TM Wallcovering, 675 F. Supp. 867 (S.D.N.Y. 1987), *aff'd*, 871 F.2d 7 (2d Cir. 1989) (doubts concerning scope of arbitrable issues should be resolved in favor of arbitration).

[57]First Options of Chicago v. Kaplan, 514 U.S. 938 (1995).

[58]AT&T Techs. v. Communications Workers, 475 U.S. 643, 649, 121 LRRM 3329 (1986).

[59]Litton Fin. Printing Div. v. NLRB, 501 U.S. 190, 209, 137 LRRM 2441 (1991) (quoting *AT&T*, 475 U.S. at 650). The lower courts endorsed this view in a number of instances. *See e.g.*, Teamsters Local 744 v. Hinckley & Schmitt, Inc., 76 F.3d 162, 165, 151 LRRM 2758 (7th Cir. 1996); Typographical Union No. 3 Local 14519 (Cincinnati) v. Gannett Satellite Info. Net., 17 F.3d 906, 910–11, 145 LRRM 2622 (6th Cir. 1994); Independent Lift Truck Builders Union v. Hyster Co., 2 F.3d 233, 236, 144 LRRM 2015 (7th Cir. 1993); Typographical Union No. 244 (Cumberland) v. Times & Alleganian Co., 943 F.2d 401, 404–05, 139 LRRM 2838 (4th Cir. 1991). The U.S. Court of Appeals for the Third Circuit, however, avoided the issue through the "implied in fact" doctrine. In *Luden's Inc. v. Bakery, Confectionery & Tobacco Workers Local 6*, 28 F.3d 347, 355–56, 146 LRRM 2586 (3d Cir. 1994), the court held that where a collective bargaining agreement expires and the parties continue to act in accordance with the terms of the agreement, a presumption arises under the federal common law of contracts that the parties entered into an implied-in-fact agreement containing the terms of the expired contract. This doctrine has not been embraced by other courts, with the others instead focusing on *Litton*. Moreover, other courts rejected the doctrine outright. Williamsbridge Manor Nursing Home v. Service Employees Local 144, 107 F. Supp. 2d 222, 165 LRRM 2185 (S.D.N.Y. 2000); Teamsters Local 122 v. August A. Busch & Co. of Mass., 932 F. Supp. 374, 380–81, 153 LRRM 2249 (D. Mass. 1996) (noting that a party's post-expiration conduct may reflect compliance with the unilateral change doctrine rather than an intent to extend contract terms).

[60]Teamsters Local 744 v. Hinckley & Schmitt, Inc., 76 F.3d 162, 165, 151 LRRM 2758 (7th Cir. 1996) (quoting *Hyster*, 2 F.3d at 236).

[61]Prior to 1977, the Board showed a reluctance to defer to arbitration grievances, alleging a violation of an individual's basic rights under §7 of the NLRA. General Am. Transp. Corp., 228 NLRB 808, 94 LRRM 1483 (1977). This posture was consistent with §10(a) of the

on new dimensions as the NLRB has thrust upon them new authority to apply and interpret legal issues and statutes clearly outside the four corners of the parties' bargained-for agreement. Nonetheless, the boundary line between interpretation and legislation cannot be drawn absolutely, and it is inevitable that the line will be crossed, in greater or lesser degree, fairly often. As is true of a court, an arbitrator may apply either a liberal or a strict construction to the provisions of an agreement, depending on the question and circumstances involved, the attitude of the parties, and, of course, the general attitude of the arbitrator.

Section 7, however, is not the only statute that may be subject to arbitral interpretation. Perhaps because it seems so at odds with the traditional, overriding role of arbitrators as contract interpreters, a degree of controversy has emerged over the question of vesting the resolution of statutory discrimination charges with labor arbitrators. This tension essentially stems from two Supreme Court decisions.

Since the Supreme Court's decision over two decades ago in the first of the two cases, *Alexander v. Gardner-Denver Co.*,[62] many practitioners had reasonably concluded that Title VII and other federal statutory employment discrimination claims could not be foreclosed by a plaintiff's access, or resort, to grievance-arbitration procedures. In *Gardner-Denver*, the Supreme Court observed that "the federal policy favoring arbitration of labor disputes

---

NLRA, which gives the Board jurisdiction to hear unfair labor practice issues. However, in *United Technologies Corp.*, 268 NLRB 557, 115 LRRM 1049, 1051 (1984), the Board overruled *General American* and held that it would begin deferring to arbitration cases in which individuals alleged violations of §§8(a)(1), 8(a)(3), 8(b)(1)(A), and 8(b)(2) of the NLRA. The Board believed that "[w]here an employer and a union have voluntarily elected to create dispute resolution machinery culminating in final and binding arbitration, it is contrary to the basic principles of the Act for the Board to jump into the fray prior to an honest attempt by the parties to resolve their disputes through that machinery." *United Techs.*, 268 NLRB at 559. *See also* Chevron, U.S.A., 275 NLRB 949, 119 LRRM 1238 (1985) (Board ordering deferral to arbitration of alleged violations of §8(a)(3)); Spann Bldg. Maint. Co., 275 NLRB 971, 972, 119 LRRM 1209 (1985) (Board reaffirming *United Techs.* and upholding deferral unless grievance procedure "has been or is likely to be unfair or irregular").

Similarly, in *Olin Corp.*, 268 NLRB 573, 574, 115 LRRM 1056, 1058, 1063 (1984), the Board held that it would defer to an arbitrator's award that ruled on an unfair labor practice charge if "(1) the contractual issue is factually parallel to the unfair labor practice issue, and (2) the arbitrator was presented generally with the facts relevant to resolving the unfair labor practice" (footnote omitted). Member Zimmerman dissented because he believed that the Board would begin deferring to an arbitrator's award based on a presumption that an unfair labor practice issue has been resolved, without actually knowing if the issue was presented to or considered by the arbitrator. *See also* United Parcel Serv. of Ohio, 305 NLRB 433, 138 LRRM 1243 (1991) (Board deferred to arbitration award ruling on violation of §8(a)(1) and (3)); Ohio Edison Co., 274 NLRB 128, 118 LRRM 1429 (1985) (Board deferred to arbitration panel case in which it was alleged that employer violated §8(a)(3) of the NLRA); Northrop, *Distinguishing Arbitration and Private Settlement in NLRB Deferral Policy*, 44 U. Miami L. Rev. 341 (1989); Henkel & Kelly, *Deferral to Arbitration After* Olin *and* United Technologies: *Has the NLRB Gone Too Far?*, 43 Wash. & Lee L. Rev. 37 (1986); Comment, *The National Labor Relations Board's Policy of Deferring to Arbitration*, 13 Fla. St. U. L. Rev. 1141 (1986); Shank, *Deferral to Arbitration: Accommodation of Competing Statutory Policies*, 2 Hofstra Lab. L.J. 211 (1985); National Labor Relations Board Office of the General Counsel Memorandum GC 84-5, 115 LRR 334, 344–45 (1984) (interpreting *United Techs.* as allowing deferral to grievance-arbitration procedure alleged violations of §§8(a)(1), 8(a)(3), 8(a)(5), 8(b)(1)(A), 8(b)(1)(B), 8(b)(2), and 8(b)(3) of the NLRA).

[62]415 U.S. 36, 7 FEP Cases 81 (1974).

and the federal policy against discriminatory employment practices can best be accommodated by permitting an employee to pursue fully both his remedy under the grievance-arbitration clause of a collective-bargaining agreement and his cause of action under Title VII."[63] The widespread assumption that this language had more or less irretrievably ensconced employees and employers in a Balkanized system of concurrent, overlapping procedural avenues for prosecuting and defending discrimination claims was later called into question by the Supreme Court with its decision in *Gilmer v. Interstate/ Johnson Lane Corp.*,[64] where the Court, affirming the U.S. Court of Appeals for the Fourth Circuit, held that the federal courts *would* enforce private arbitration agreements to adjudicate federal ADEA claims solely in private arbitration.[65] Still, *Gilmer* was not decided in the context of a collective bargaining agreement grievance-arbitration clause, and *Gilmer* did not expressly overrule *Gardner-Denver*. Therefore, doubts remained about just how far *Gilmer* had altered the *Gardner-Denver* landscape,[66] and the U.S. Court of

---

[63]*Id.* at 59–60. *See also* Barrentine v. Arkansas-Best Freight Sys., Inc., 450 U.S. 728, 24 WH Cases 1284 (1981); McDonald v. City of W. Branch, 466 U.S. 284, 115 LRRM 3646 (1984).

[64]500 U.S. 20, 55 FEP Cases 1116 (1991).

[65]*See id.* at 35. After *Gilmer*, courts have repeatedly held that Title VII claims, like ADEA claims, are subject to mandatory arbitration. *See, e.g.*, Austin v. Owens-Brockway Glass Container, Inc., 78 F.3d 875, 151 LRRM 2673 (4th Cir. 1996); Metz v. Merrill Lynch, Pierce, Fenner & Smith, 39 F.3d 1482 (10th Cir. 1994); Nyhiem v. NEC Elec., 25 F.3d 1437 (9th Cir. 1992); Willis v. Dean Witter Reynolds, Inc., 948 F.2d 305 (6th Cir. 1991); Alford v. Dean Witter Reynolds, Inc., 939 F.2d 229 (6th Cir. 1991). In each of these decisions except *Austin*, the courts considered whether Title VII of the Civil Rights Act of 1964, 42 U.S.C. §2000e et seq., can be subjected to compulsory arbitration under an employee's noncollective bargaining agreement. Courts have also expanded the scope of arbitration agreements to cover Americans with Disabilities Act (ADA), 29 U.S. §706 et seq., claims. *See, e.g.,* Bercovitch v. Baldwin Sch., 133 F.3d 141, 151 (1st Cir. 1998) (holding ADA subject to arbitration under *Gilmer* and the Federal Arbitration Act's "strong federal policy favoring arbitration"); Miller v. Public Storage Mgmt., 121 F.3d 215, 218 (5th Cir. 1997) (holding the ADA subject to arbitration and that the ADA language shows Congress did not intend to exclude the ADA from the Federal Arbitration Act's scope).

　　Nevertheless, it is too soon to conclude that any and all arbitration clauses in the non-union setting will be enforced in the courts to dismiss statutory discrimination claims. For instance, in *Cole v. Burns International Security Services*, 105 F.3d 1465, 1482, 72 FEP Cases 1775 (D.C. Cir. 1997), a majority of the court refused to read *Gilmer* "as holding that an arbitration agreement is enforceable no matter what rights it waives or what burdens it imposes." The court affirmed the dismissal of a Title VII case differentiating a "take-it-or-leave-it" individual employment contract that required arbitration under the rules of the American Arbitration Association for collectively bargained agreements. The court found the fairly one-sided arbitration clause in the individual employment agreement required of the plaintiff-employee to be valid by judicially imposing the additional requirement that the employer pay all of the arbitrator's fees, stating that, "In our view, an employee can never be required, as a condition of employment, to pay an arbitrator's compensation in order to secure the resolution of statutory claims under Title VII . . . ." *Id.* at 1468. On a related note, the EEOC has recently announced its view that employment agreements that not only require alternative dispute resolution but which prevent employees from filing discrimination charges with the EEOC or assisting the agency, or participating in an EEOC investigation, "are null and void as a matter of public policy."

[66]*Compare* Austin v. Owens-Brockway Glass Container, Inc., 78 F.3d 875, 151 LRRM 2673 (4th Cir. 1996) (the arbitration pledge in a collective bargaining agreement precludes a union member from bringing a Title VII and ADA claim in federal court), *with* Pryner v. Tractor Supply Co., 109 F.3d 354, 363, 154 LRRM 2806 (7th Cir. 1997), Varner v. National Super Mkts., 94 F.3d 1209 (8th Cir. 1996), *and* Martin v. Dana Corp., 114 F.3d 421, 155 LRRM 2525, *vacated and reh'g en banc granted*, 124 F.3d 590, 155 LRRM 2762 (3d Cir. 1997) (on rehearing, the panel did not address the question of whether a grievance provision can preclude a worker from bringing a Title VII claim in court).

Appeals for the Fourth Circuit was once again the first to jump into the fray. In *Austin v. Owens-Brockway Glass Container, Inc.*,[67] the majority of the Fourth Circuit court held that the arbitration pledge in a collective bargaining agreement precluded the union member plaintiff from bringing both a Title VII and an Americans with Disabilities Act (ADA) claim in federal court.

Almost immediately, the *Austin* decision attracted attention. It was followed and relied on heavily by district courts in Kentucky[68] and North Carolina,[69] and was mentioned favorably but not followed in Illinois.[70] But one federal district court judge ventured quite deliberately out on the proverbial limb, predicting "that *Austin* is not an accurate interpretation of federal law as it presently stands and that the reasoning of the majority [in *Austin*] would not be adopted by the Seventh Circuit."[71] Shortly thereafter, in an opinion representative of the majority of the federal circuit courts, the U.S. Court of Appeals for the Seventh Circuit proved him correct, paying scant attention to the *Austin* decision.[72]

In *Pryner v. Tractor Supply Co.*,[73] the Seventh Circuit decided a consolidated appeal of two cases where district court judges had refused defense motions to stay statutory discrimination cases (brought variously under Title VII, the ADA, the Civil Rights Act of 1870,[74] and the ADEA).[75] After an extensive discussion—of peripheral concern here—of its appellate jurisdiction under the Federal Arbitration Act, the court held that "workers' statutory rights . . . are arbitrable if the worker consents," but that "the union cannot consent *for* the employee by signing a collective bargaining agreement that

---

[67]78 F.3d 875, 151 LRRM 2673 (4th Cir. 1996), *cert. denied,* 519 U.S. 980 (1996).

[68]Jessie v. Carter Health Care Ctr., 930 F. Supp. 1174, 1176, 152 LRRM 3054 (E.D. Ky. 1996) ("The court believes that the law as stated in *Austin* is sound.").

[69]Moore v. Duke Power Co., 971 F. Supp. 978, 155 LRRM 2412 (N.D.N.C. 1997).

[70]Baert v. Euclid Beverage, 954 F. Supp. 170, 173, 8 AD Cases 668 (N.D. Ill. 1997) ("While the reasoning supporting waiver in both *Gilmer* and *Austin* is persuasive, and would easily support reversing *Alexander [v. Gardner-Denver]*, nevertheless the Court in *Gilmer* took pains to distinguish *Alexander*. This means there is enough life left in *Alexander* to bind a federal district court.").

[71]Pryner v. Tractor Supply Co., 927 F. Supp. 1140, 1145, 154 LRRM 2845 (S.D. Ind. 1996).

[72]*See* Pryner v. Tractor Supply Co., 109 F.3d 354, 154 LRRM 2806 (7th Cir. 1997). *See also* Rogers v. New York Univ., 220 F.3d 73, 75, 164 LRRM 2854 (2d Cir. 2000) (adopting the majority view and emphasizing that "[w]hen the arbitration provision has been negotiated by a union in a CBA [collective bargaining agreement], [the lower courts other than the Fourth Circuit] have held that *Gardner-Denver* applies"); Air Line Pilots v. Northwest Airlines, 199 F.3d 477, 481–86, 163 LRRM 2072 (D.C. Cir. 1999), *judgment reinstated,* 211 F.3d 1312, 164 LRRM 2632 (D.C. Cir. 2000) (en banc); Bratten v. SSI Servs., 185 F.3d 625, 630–32, 161 LRRM 2985 (6th Cir. 1999); Albertson's, Inc. v. Food & Commercial Workers, 157 F.3d 758, 760–62, 159 LRRM 2452 (9th Cir. 1998), *cert. denied,* 528 U.S. 809 (1999); Brisentine v. Stone & Webster Eng'g Corp., 117 F.3d 519, 522–27, 155 LRRM 2858 (11th Cir. 1997); Harrison v. Eddy Potash, Inc., 112 F.3d 1437, 1453, 156 LRRM 2033 (10th Cir. 1997) (although determining that nothing in *Gilmer* indicates that the Supreme Court abandoned its concern with the conflicts between group and individual goals in the collective bargaining process), *vacated on other grounds,* 524 U.S. 947, 159 LRRM 2576 (1998); Varner v. National Super Mkts., 94 F.3d 1209, 1213 (8th Cir. 1996), *cert. denied,* 519 U.S. 1110 (1997).

[73]109 F.3d 354, 154 LRRM 2806 (7th Cir. 1997).

[74]42 U.S.C. §1981.

[75]*Pryner,* 109 F.3d at 357. Both plaintiffs in these cases pursued their grievance-arbitration remedies prior to filling suit, but those arbitration processes were either abandoned or unresolved. *Id.*

consigns the enforcement of statutory rights to the union-controlled griev-ance and arbitration machinery created by the agreement."[76]

In reaching this decision, the court pointed out that unions have "broad discretion as to whether or not to prosecute a grievance" and expressed re-luctance about granting unions the ability to control the vindication of indi-vidual statutory rights, stating that "[t]he statutory rights at issue in these two cases are rights given to members of minority groups because of concern about the mistreatment (of which there is a long history in the labor move-ment . . .) of minorities by majorities."[77] The court reasoned that "deliver[ing] the enforcement of the rights of these minorities into the hands of the major-ity [i.e., a union] is [not] consistent with the policy of these statutes or justi-fied by the abstract desirability of allowing unions and employers to cut their own deals."[78] Turning to *Gardner-Denver* and *Gilmer*, the *Pryner* court also declined to find *Gardner-Denver* impliedly overruled by *Gilmer*: "The con-servative reading of *Gilmer* is that it just pruned some dicta from *Gardner-Denver*—and it certainly cannot be taken to hold that collective bargaining agreements can compel the arbitration of statutory rights."[79]

The Supreme Court in *Wright v. Universal Maritime Service Corp.*[80] had an opportunity to address the conflict between the U.S. Court of Appeals for the Fourth Circuit and the majority view as represented in *Pryner*. In the *Wright* case, rather than address the debate surrounding the mandatory ar-bitration of statutory claims under a collective bargaining agreement, the Court instead narrowed the role of arbitration, even in situations where the employee arguably consented to arbitration of certain statutory rights. In so doing, the Court set forth two standards that will aid an employee's effort to bring statutory claims in federal court: (1) the presumption of arbitrability does not apply to an employee's statutory claim,[81] and (2) a union-negotiated waiver of a worker's statutory right must be "clear and unmistakable."[82] Applying these rules, the Court did not find a clear and unmistakable waiver in the agreement and thus did not reach the issue of the validity of a union-negotiated waiver.[83] Only in a future case, where the collective bargaining

---

[76]*Id.* at 363 (emphasis in original).

[77]*Id.* at 362 (citation omitted).

[78]*Id.* at 363.

[79]*Id.* at 365. *See* Adams v. Circuit City Stores, 532 U.S. 105, 85 FEP Cases 266 (2001) (the Court held that the Federal Arbitration Act does apply to labor and employment con-tracts except those covering transportation workers).

[80]525 U.S. 70, 159 LRRM 2769 (1998).

[81]*Id.* at 75–77. The Supreme Court stated that, even if a collective bargaining agreement's arbitration clause incorporates a statutory claim by reference, "the ultimate question for the arbitrator would be not what the parties have agreed to, but what federal law requires; and that is not a question which should be *presumed* to be included within the arbitration re-quirement." *Id.* at 79 (emphasis in original).

[82]*Id.* at 80. The Supreme Court adopted this standard from *Metropolitan Edison Co. v. NLRB*, 460 U.S. 693, 112 LRRM 3265 (1983), where the Court asserted that a union may waive an officer's statutory right under §8(a)(3) of the NLRA only if the waiver is clear and unmistakable.

[83]*Wright*, 525 U.S. at 81. The collective bargaining agreement included the following provisions that to the Court did not add up to a clear and unmistakable waiver: (1) Clause 15(f)—"Agreement is intended to cover all matters affecting wages, hours, and other terms and conditions of employment," *id.* at 81; (2) Clause 15(f)—"[a]nything not contained in this Agreement shall not be construed as being part of this Agreement," *id.*; and (3) Clause 17—

agreement in question contains a sufficiently clear waiver of a statutory right, might the Supreme Court specifically address this conflict between the appellate courts.[84]

Subsequent to *Wright*, lower courts have determined that a collective bargaining agreement is sufficiently clear if two conditions are met: (1) "the arbitration clause contains a provision whereby employees specifically agree to submit all federal causes of action arising out of their employment to arbitration"; and (2) "the CBA [collective bargaining agreement] contains an explicit incorporation of the statutory anti-discrimination requirements in addition to a broad and general arbitration clause."[85]

Moreover, if an arbitration award issues, the *Pryner* opinion provides support for the notion that the arbitrator's award ends the matter.[86] This is so because the *Pryner* court observed that "the arbitrator's award, whether or not confirmed, . . . can—this is implicit in the notion of binding arbitration—be pleaded as res judicata in the worker's federal district court suit."[87] The effectiveness of such a defense is not, however, a foregone conclusion, as the defendants in the case conceded that, if a stay were granted pending arbitration, the plaintiffs could resume the suit if the arbitrator's decision failed to vindicate all of the plaintiff's statutory rights.[88] But, as *Pryner* further noted: "the findings made by the arbitrators might be entitled to collateral estoppel effect in the [federal] suits. . . . We say 'might' to emphasize the readiness of courts to deny that effect to arbitral awards when the arbitrator has failed to explain his findings adequately or to follow procedures likely to lead to reliable findings . . . ."[89]

"[i]t is the intention and purpose of all parties hereto that no provision or part of this Agreement shall be violative of any Federal or State Law," *id*. *See also* Bedwell v. Mack Trucks, Inc., 173 F.3d 423 (4th Cir. 1999) (table) (dismissing a clause as "very broad and similar to the arbitration clause addressed in *Wright*").

[84]It should be noted that in *Equal Employment Opportunity Commission v. Waffle House*, 534 U.S. 279, 12 AD Cases 1001 (2002), the Court ruled 6-3 that an arbitration agreement that binds an employee does not preclude suit on the employee's behalf by the EEOC.

[85]Rogers v. New York Univ., 220 F.2d 73, 76, 164 LRRM 2854 (2d Cir. 2000) (citing Carson v. Giant Food, 175 F.3d 325, 331–32, 161 LRRM 2129 (4th Cir. 1999)). The U.S. Court of Appeals for the Second Circuit further noted that courts "[a]gree that specific incorporation requires identifying the antidiscrimination statutes by name or citation." *Rogers*, 220 F.2d at 76 (citing Bratten v. SSI Servs., 185 F.3d 625, 631, 161 LRRM 2985 (6th Cir. 1999); Prince v. Coca-Cola Bottling Co. of N.Y., 37 F. Supp. 2d 289, 293, 160 LRRM 2740 (S.D.N.Y. 1999)).

[86]The stance taken by *Pryner* in this regard may contradict the view of other courts. For instance, in a decision issued the same year as *Pryner*, the District Court for the Middle District of Tennessee relied on other courts that held that a Title VII action by employees in federal court should not be barred by prior arbitration of the discrimination claim. Gray v. Toshiba Am. Consumer Prods., 959 F. Supp. 805, 810, 155 LRRM 2346 (D.C. Tenn. 1997) (citing Humphrey v. Council of Jewish Fed'ns, 901 F. Supp. 703 (S.D.N.Y. 1995)). The court adopted the view that contractual rights under a collective bargaining agreement are "'legally independent from statutory rights under Title VII.'" *Toshiba*, 959 F. Supp. at 810 (quoting *Humphrey*, 901 F. Supp. at 709; Frank v. New York State Elec. & Gas, 871 F. Supp. 167, 172 (W.D.N.Y. 1994)).

[87]Pryner v. Tractor Supply Co., 109 F.3d 354, 361, 154 LRRM 2806 (7th Cir. 1997) (citations omitted).

[88]*Id*.

[89]*Id*. (citation omitted).

In addition, the developed body of federal antidiscrimination law will still continue to have great significance in the arbitration of employment discrimination claims arising under collective bargaining contracts. While the sufficiency or depth of arbitral legal analysis has been questioned,[90] most labor arbitrators do resort to federal Title VII precedent in deciding the employment discrimination claims presented to them.[91] Furthermore, the prospect of post-arbitration appeals to the federal courts from the arbitrator's award is dim under existing precedent. It has long been difficult to state adequate grounds for judicial review of an arbitrator's award,[92] and in recent

---

[90]*See, e.g.,* Block & Barasch, *Practical Ramifications of Arbitration of Employment Discrimination Claims, in* PROCEEDINGS OF N.Y.U. 4TH ANNUAL CONFERENCE ON LABOR 281, 294 (1995); Edwards, *Arbitration of Employment Discrimination Cases: An Empirical Study, in* ARBITRATION—1975, PROCEEDINGS OF THE 28TH ANNUAL MEETING OF NAA 59 (Dennis & Somers eds., BNA Books 1976).

[91]*See* Chapter 10, section 3.A.i., "Title VII of the Civil Rights Act." *See also* Wright v. Universal Maritime Serv. Corp., 525 U.S. 70, 79, 159 LRRM 2769 (1998) ("the ultimate question for the arbitrator would be not what the parties have agreed to, but what federal law requires").

[92]Limited grounds for vacating an award are found in Section 10 of the Federal Arbitration Act. Section 10 permits the court to vacate an arbitration award only:
  (a) where the award was procured by corruption, fraud, or undue means;
  (b) where there was evident partiality or corruption in the arbitrators, or either of them;
  (c) where the arbitrators were guilty of misconduct in refusing to postpone the hearing, upon sufficient cause shown, or in refusing to hear evidence pertinent and material to the controversy; or of any misbehavior by which the rights of any party may have been prejudiced;
  (d) where the arbitrators exceeded their powers, or so imperfectly executed them that a mutual, final, and definite award upon the subject matter was not made.
9 U.S.C. §10. The language of paragraph (d) is not really as broad as it might seem. Indeed, it has been held: (1) that courts will not substitute their view of the facts or the law for that of the arbitrator, *Shearson Hayden Stone, Inc. v. Liang,* 493 F. Supp. 104, 107 (N.D. Ill. 1980) (the courts "cannot set aside an award on the grounds of erroneous findings of fact or misinterpretation of the law"), *aff'd,* 653 F.2d 310 (7th Cir. 1981); (2) that courts will not overturn the arbitrator's interpretation of an agreement, even if the court might have decided the matter differently if presented with the issue in the first instance, *E.I. DuPont de Nemours & Co. v. Grasselli Employees Indep. Ass'n of E. Chicago,* 790 F.2d 611, 615, 122 LRRM 2217 (7th Cir.), *cert. denied,* 479 U.S. 853 (1986); *Ethyl Corp. v. Steelworkers,* 768 F.2d 180, 119 LRRM 3566 (7th Cir. 1985), *cert. denied,* 475 U.S. 1010 (1986); (3) that courts do not require arbitrators to explain their awards, *Shearson Hayden Stone, Inc. v. Liang,* 653 F.2d 310, 312 (7th Cir. 1981); *Stroh Container Co. v. Delphi Indus.,* 783 F.2d 743, 750 (8th Cir. 1986), *cert. denied,* 476 U.S. 1141 (1986); and (4) that an alleged lack of evidence to support an award does not constitute a basis for concluding that the arbitrator exceeded his powers; courts have frequently rejected challenges to awards based on an assertion that no evidence was presented to an arbitrator on which the award could be based, *Liang,* 653 F.2d at 312 ("lack of evidence to support the award is not among [the grounds set forth in Section 10 of the Federal Arbitration Act]."). *See also* Fontainbleau Hotel Corp. v. Hotel & Restaurant Employees Local 225, 328 F.2d 310, 55 LRRM 2439 (5th Cir. 1964).
    In short, in the context of an action to vacate an arbitration award, the arbitrator has generally been deemed the final judge of both fact and law, and arguments that an arbitrator erroneously excluded evidence, incorrectly weighed the evidence, or failed to credit certain testimony have all been unavailing. *See, e.g.,* Jenkins v. Prudential-Bache Sec., 847 F.2d 631 (10th Cir. 1988); Meat Cutters Local 641 v. Capitol Packing Co., 413 F.2d 668, 71 LRRM 2950 (10th Cir. 1969). While courts have not set aside awards on the grounds of erroneous findings of fact or misinterpretation of the law (*see, e.g.,* Northrop Corp. v. Triad Int'l Mktg S.A., 811 F.2d 1265 (9th Cir.), *cert. denied,* 484 U.S. 914 (1987) (enforcing arbitral interpretation of contract despite erroneous findings of fact)), if the arbitrator does not merely misinterpret the law but, instead and much more egregiously, demonstrates a deliberate and manifest disregard of the law, the award may be subject to challenge. *See* First Options of Chicago v. Kaplan, 514 U.S. 938, 942 (1995) (awards may be vacated if in "manifest disre-

years many courts have evinced a decided lack of enthusiasm for actions to vacate arbitration awards. For instance, as the U.S. Court of Appeals for the Seventh Circuit has bluntly observed, "there is a federal bias in favor of arbitration," the corollary of which "is that judicial review of an arbitration award is extremely limited."[93] The Seventh Circuit and other courts have followed this principle "to prevent arbitration from becoming merely an added preliminary step to a judicial resolution rather than a true alternative."[94] If this view continues, an arbitrator's resolution of a statutory discrimination claim referred to arbitration will likely be final and effectively unappealable in most cases.

ii. Arbitrator's Function in Various Industries
[LA CDI 103.101 et seq., for awards under Railway Labor Act]

Helpful insight into rights arbitration, and in particular in regard to the function of the arbitrator, is provided by observing the role of one of the nation's most experienced arbitration agencies—the National Railroad Adjustment Board (NRAB). The Railway Labor Act gives the NRAB jurisdiction over "disputes between an employee or group of employees and a carrier or carriers growing out of grievances or out of the interpretation or application of agreements concerning rates of pay, rules, or working conditions . . . ."[95] While the word "Adjustment" in the name might suggest that under this grant of jurisdiction the NRAB was intended to serve as an extension and

---

gard of the law"); Paperworkers v. Misco, Inc., 484 U.S. 29, 43 126 LRRM 3113 (1987) (quoting W.R. Grace & Co. v. Rubber Workers Local 759, 461 U.S. 757, 766, 113 LRRM 2641 (1983), quoting in turn Muschany v. United States, 324 U.S. 49, 66 (1945) (award may be set aside if contrary to "'some explicit public policy'" that is "'well defined and dominant'" and ascertained "'by reference to the laws and legal precedents'"); National Wrecking Co. v. Teamsters Local 731, 990 F.2d 957, 961, 143 LRRM 2046 (7th Cir. 1993) ("In order to vacate an award for manifest disregard of the law, the party challenging the award must demonstrate that the arbitrator deliberately disregarded what the arbitrator knew to be the law in order to reach a particular result.").

In sum, then, depending on the jurisdiction, there are a number of narrow situations in which an arbitrator's award may be overturned on appeal. As succinctly stated by the U.S. Court of Appeals for the Fifth Circuit in *Williams v. Cigna Financial Advisors*, 197 F.3d 752, 757–58 (5th Cir. 1999) (citing Wilner, 1 Domke on Commercial Arbitration §34.07, at 14 (rev. ed. 1998)), "[m]ost state and federal courts recognized one or more nonstatutory grounds warranting vacatur of an arbitral award, including (1) the arbitrator's manifest disregard of the law; (2) the award's conflict with a strong public policy; (3) the award being arbitrary and capricious; (4) the award being completely irrational; or (5) the award's failure to draw its essence from the underlying contract."

[93]Moseley, Hallgarten, Estabrook & Weeden v. Ellis, 849 F.2d 264, 267 (7th Cir. 1988) (quoting *Grasselli*, 790 F.2d at 614). *See also* Eijer Mfg. v. Kowin Dev. Corp., 14 F.3d 1250, 1253 (7th Cir. 1994) ("our scope of review of a commercial arbitration award is grudgingly narrow"), *cert. denied*, 512 U.S. 1205 (1994); Baravait v. Joseph Thal, Lyons & Ross, Inc., 28 F.3d 704, 706 (7th Cir. 1994) ("Judicial review of arbitration awards is tightly limited; perhaps it ought not be called 'review' at all").

[94]*Grasselli*, 790 F.2d at 614. Indeed, in apparent frustration that the bar had not taken its pronouncements in this regard seriously enough, the U.S. Court of Appeals for the Seventh Circuit imposed sanctions in *Dreis & Krump Manufacturing Co. v. Machinists District 8*, 802 F.2d 247, 256, 123 LRRM 2654 (7th Cir. 1986), in an action to vacate an arbitration award, finding it frivolous and stating quite plainly and emphatically: "Lawyers practicing in the Seventh Circuit, take heed!"

[95]Railway Labor Act, 45 U.S.C. §153(i).

continuation of the bargaining process,[96] in actual practice the function of the NRAB is much like true adjudication:

> In hearing and deciding the cases which come before the [Adjustment] Board [the Board members] do not act as negotiators or adjusters. Whatever may have been the intent of the law in setting up an Adjustment Board, there has been no trace in the history of the Board of any view on its part that its function is to iron out differences by taking into account the situation and needs of the parties and the practical effect of their respective demands, and on the basis of such consideration making concessions to one party in return for concessions by it for the good of the industry as a whole. The [Adjustment] Board has never taken this view of its function. Instead it has assumed with the strictest legalistic viewpoint that the loosely drawn and often vague terms of the schedules and agreements which come before it have a rigid technical meaning, and that this meaning is to be discovered by a process of purely technical reasoning. The most cursory examination of the nature of the arguments put up to the [Adjustment] Board and the grounds of its decisions, where these are given, conclusively demonstrates that it regards its function as one of strict legal interpretation rather than compromise and adjustment.[97]

Most persons familiar with the activities of the NRAB would likely agree that the just-quoted statement is basically accurate and applies with equal force today. Certainly, when a referee is called in to sit as a member of the NRAB in deadlocked cases, the function of the NRAB is adjudication. But even in adjudication some rulemaking is inevitable:

> Even on the assumption that the Adjustment Board is strictly confined to the interpretation and application of existing rules, it is inescapable, particularly in deadlocked cases, that it will exercise a greater or less influence on the nature and scope of agreements between carriers and labor organizations. The Constitution of the United States is a small compact document; but one can gain no appreciation of its meaning and scope without examining the thousands of decisions in which the Supreme Court, in its interpretation, has molded and modified it. In a similar manner, it is inevitable that the Adjustment Board, subject to judicial review, will mold and modify railway collective agreements.[98]

In industries that use the permanent umpire or chairman device, the scope of arbitral authority carries. The jurisdiction of the impartial umpire for the Ford Motor Company and the UAW has been limited generally to "alleged violations of the terms" of the parties' agreements. By specific provision, power has been denied to "add to or subtract from or modify any of the terms of any agreement," or to "substitute his discretion for the company's discretion in cases where the company is given discretion" by an agreement,

---

[96]The labor members of the NRAB at one time expressed the view that this was the intended function of the NRAB. See statement of labor members submitted to the Attorney General's Committee on Administrative Procedure, in RAILWAY LABOR 9–10 (1940), *reprinted in* JONES, NATIONAL RAILROAD ADJUSTMENT BOARD 226 (1941). Those "who were mainly responsible for the statutory creation of the Board in 1934 hoped and doubtless believed that the Board would grow up to live chiefly as a collective bargaining agency . . . rather than as a real arbitration tribunal of last resort. . . . [T]his hope has not been fulfilled for many years. . . ." Daughterty, *Arbitration by the National Railroad Adjustment Board*, ARB. TODAY 93, 94 (1955).

[97]RAILWAY LABOR, at 910. The quotation is the statement of a carrier spokesman before the Attorney General's Committee.

[98]SPENCER, THE NATIONAL RAILROAD ADJUSTMENT BOARD 31 (1938), *reprinted in* JONES, app. at 181.

or to "provide agreement for the parties in those cases where they have in their contract agreed that further negotiations shall or may provide for certain contingencies to cover certain subjects."[99] The General Motors-UAW agreement states that the umpire "shall have no power to add to or subtract from or modify any of the terms" of the agreement; the agreement further states that "[a]ny case appealed to the umpire on which he has no power to rule shall be referred back to the parties without decision." However, the agreement gives the umpire "full discretion" in certain discipline cases.[100] Conversely, the impartial chairman of the full-fashioned hosiery industry was given authority to determine all disputes except those involving new or renewal contract terms.[101]

iii. Arbitrator as Mediator in Rights Disputes

This subject should not be discussed without noting the view, as expressed by the late Professor George W. Taylor, former Chairman of the National War Labor Board and a former impartial chairman of the full-fashioned hosiery industry, that grievance settlement often becomes an integral part of agreement making. In an address before the NAA, he said:

> A third important characteristic of grievance arbitration should be mentioned. Contrary to the views of many arbitrators, grievance settlement is not simply a process of contract interpretation. . . . [T]he difficult grievances arise because the labor contract reflects only a partial or an inconclusive meeting of minds. It doesn't give the reasonably clear answer to a dispute. In such cases, grievance settlement becomes an integral part of agreement-making. At any event, the manner in which the grievances are settled provides understandings that are as durable, or more so, than the actual terms of the labor contract themselves. No one need amplify to this audience the weight of "established practices."[102]

The Taylor view has been approved by some, but severely criticized by others.[103] In one case, the Supreme Court appears to have considered arbitration a part of "the continuous collective bargaining process":

---

[99]See Ford Motor Co., 6 LA 952, 953 (Shulman, 1944).

[100]Alexander, *Impartial Umpireships: The General Motors-UAW Experience*, in Arbitration and the Law 157 (1958).

[101]Kennedy, Effective Labor Arbitration 34–36 (1948). In this industry, all disputes arising during the life of the contract "including but not limited to the interpretation, construction or application of the terms of this agreement" are "submitted to the Impartial Chairman for final and binding decision by him." He or she is denied the power to "alter, modify, or change" the "Agreement or any of the terms or provisions thereof," but there is no denial of power to add to the agreement, and the grant of power to decide issues not covered by the agreement can be viewed as giving him or her authority to add, by decisions, to the agreement. *Id.*

[102]Taylor, *Effectuating the Labor Contract Through Arbitration*, in The Profession of Labor Arbitration, Selected Papers From the First Seven Annual Meetings of NAA 20, 21 (McKelvey ed., BNA Books 1957). In *Standard Gravure Corp.*, 62-3 ARB ¶8927 (Platt, 1962), the company argued that the arbitrator's function was adjudication while the union argued that it was an instrument of collective bargaining. The arbitrator responded: "But in the Chairman's opinion, neither approach alone adequately represents the arbitration function in manning cases; together they mark the bounds within which an award should fall."

[103]For various reactions to the Taylor view, see O'Connell, *Should the Scope of Arbitration Be Restricted?*, in Proceedings of the 18th Annual Meeting of NAA 102, 103–10 (Jones ed., BNA Books 1965); Garrett, *The Presidential Address: Some Potential Uses of the Opin-*

Apart from matters that the parties specifically exclude, all of the questions on which the parties disagree must therefore come within the scope of the grievance and arbitration provisions of the collective agreement. The grievance procedure is, in other words, a part of the continuous collective bargaining process. It, rather than a strike, is the terminal point of a disagreement.

The labor arbitrator performs functions which are not normal to the courts; the considerations which help him fashion judgments may indeed be foreign to the competence of courts.

. . .

The labor arbitrator's source of law is not confined to the express provisions of the contract, as the industrial common law—the practices of the industry and the shop—is equally a part of the collective bargaining agreement although not expressed in it. The labor arbitrator is usually chosen because of the parties' confidence in his knowledge of the common law of the shop and their trust in his personal judgment to bring to bear considerations which are not expressed in the contract as criteria for judgment. . . . The ablest judge cannot be expected to bring the same experience and competence to bear upon the determination of a grievance, because he cannot be similarly informed.[104]

But in dictim in another case, contemporaneous with the statement quoted above, the Supreme Court bluntly confined arbitrators to the function specified by the parties:

When an arbitrator is commissioned to interpret and apply the collective bargaining agreement, he is to bring his informed judgment to bear in order to reach a fair solution of a problem. This is especially true when it comes to formulating remedies. . . . Nevertheless, an arbitrator is confined to interpretation and application of the collective bargaining agreement; he does not sit to dispense his own brand of industrial justice. He may of course look for guidance from many sources, yet his award is legitimate only so long as it draws its essence from the collective bargaining agreement. When the arbitrator's words manifest an infidelity to this obligation, courts have no choice but to refuse enforcement of the award.[105]

In apparently denying that there can be "a single generalized concept of the arbitration process which would be valid for all purposes,"[106] Impartial Chairman Sylvester Garrett explained:

There is infinite variety among arbitrators and arbitration systems, just as there are all kinds of judges and other tribunals. What one man will believe proper and practical in the interpretation of language will seem visionary to another under the same circumstances. One man's flair for mediation can be matched by another's distaste for it.[107]

Chairman Garrett explained further that some judges, like some arbitrators, have sought to induce settlements; he stated that critics of the "judi-

---

ion, in Proceedings of the 17th Annual Meeting of NAA 114, 122 (Kahn ed., BNA Books 1964); Garrett, *The Role of Lawyers in Arbitration, in* Arbitration and Public Policy, Proceedings of the 14th Annual Meeting of NAA 102, 115–22 (Pollard ed., BNA Books 1961).

[104]Steelworkers v. Warrior & Gulf Navigation Co., 363 U.S. 574, 581–82, 46 LRRM 2416 (1960). For extensive discussion of past practice in arbitration, see Chapter 12, particularly section 1., "Custom and Practice as a Term of the Contract."

[105]Steelworkers v. Enterprise Wheel & Car Corp., 363 U.S. 593, 597, 46 LRRM 2423 (1960).

[106]Garrett, *The Role of Lawyers,* at 122.

[107]*Id.*

cial process" theory of grievance arbitration have proceeded on the false assumption that all judges take a mechanical and sterile approach to agreement interpretation.[108]

The adjudicative role remains an arbitrator's foremost priority. For example, historically an arbitrator also acted as mediator: someone who would resolve disputes through settlement and compromise.[109] But today, even though arbitrators are frequently called on to mediate disputes, their role as mediator is cautioned against.[110] Moreover, arbitrators themselves are now viewing their function as more adjudicative: "Arbitration more and more resembles litigation, arbitrators think of themselves as contract interpreters rather than as 'labor relations physicians. . . .'"[111]

C. Rights Arbitration Contract Clauses [LA CDI 94.551 et seq.]

Although the courts limit arbitrators to interpretation of the collective bargaining agreement, arbitration is a creation of the contract, and the contract defines the scope of the arbitrator's authority.[112] Thus, the authority to interpret the agreement depends on the scope of the arbitration clause. Broad arbitration clauses give an arbitrator expansive authority to decide a multitude of disputes.[113] Broad arbitration clauses use terminology such as "all

---

[108]*Id.* at 114, 120, 122.

[109]Dunsford, *The Role and Function of the Arbitrator*, 30 St. Louis U. L.J. 109, 115 (1985).

[110]Code of Prof'l Responsibility for Arbitrators of Labor-Management Disputes pt. II, §F, ¶2(b)(c):

> If one party requests that the arbitrator mediate and the other party objects, the arbitrator should decline the request.
>
> An arbitrator is not precluded from suggesting mediation. To avoid the possibility of improper pressure, the arbitrator should not so suggest unless it can be discerned that both parties are likely to be receptive. In any event, the arbitrator's suggestion should not be pursued unless both parties readily agree.

The Code is found in 3 Lab. Arb. & Dispute Settlements (nondecisional material) 201.

[111]Nolan & Abrams, *The Future of Labor Arbitration*, 37 Lab. L.J. 437, 437 (1986). *See also* Dunsford, 30 St. Louis U. L.J. at 119 ("In sum, if an arbitrator ventures into mediation, he may learn things and evoke confidences which, should he later be forced to adjudicate, will seriously impair the integrity of the later process.").

[112]See note 54, above, and accompanying text. *See also* First Options of Chicago v. Kaplan, 514 U.S. 938, 943 (1995) ("arbitration is simply a matter of contract between the parties; it is a way to resolve those disputes—but only those disputes—that the parties have agreed to submit to arbitration"); Seafarers v. National Marine Servs., 639 F. Supp. 1283, 1290 (E.D. La. 1986) ("arbitration is a creature of contract with no life independent of its collective bargaining agreement"), *rev'd on other grounds*, 820 F.2d 148, 125 LRRM 3069 (5th Cir. 1987); Safeway Stores v. Food & Commercial Workers Local 400, 621 F. Supp. 1233, 118 LRRM 3419 (D.D.C. 1985) (arbitration is a matter of contract and the arbitrator's authority is defined by agreement).

[113]*See, e.g.*, Auto Workers v. United Screw & Bolt Corp., 941 F.2d 466, 138 LRRM 2163 (6th Cir. 1991) (broad arbitration clause covers dispute over wage premiums not specifically discussed); Service Employees Local 106 v. Evergreen Cemetery, 708 F. Supp. 917, 133 LRRM 2336 (N.D. Ill. 1989) (broad arbitration clause authorized arbitration regarding the type of work that can be assigned to a supervisor not covered by the collective bargaining agreement); Simkins Indus., 81 LA 592 (Carter, 1983) (broad grievance-arbitration clause covers dispute over job rotation even though job rotation not specifically mentioned in contract, because grievance-arbitration clause did not limit grievances to only those specific conditions of employment set forth in written agreement); Trans World Airlines, 81 LA 524 (Heinsz, 1983) (broad arbitration clause covers arbitration over award of attorneys' fees). For an example of a broad arbitration clause, see *E.M. Diagnostic Sys. v. Teamsters Local 169*, 812

disputes" or "any difference" between the parties.[114] Such clauses often expressly exclude stated types of interest disputes, and sometimes exclude stated types of rights disputes.[115]

Courts do not hesitate to support arbitration of an issue unless they are convinced that the arbitration clause specifically excludes that issue.[116] For example, the U.S. Court of Appeals for the Second Circuit held that a broad arbitration clause gave an arbitrator the authority to resolve a grievance that required him to interpret a separate employment contract and determine whether the impartial chairman had been properly dismissed.[117] The Second Circuit held that even if the separate employment contract was wholly distinct from the collective bargaining agreement, the dispute would be arbitrable under the broad language of the arbitration provision.[118] In addition, where an exclusionary clause conflicts with a broad arbitration clause, courts will generally rule in favor of coverage.[119]

In 400 sample contracts,

F.2d 91, 92, 124 LRRM 2633, 2634 (3d Cir. 1987): "*Any dispute arising out of a claimed violation of this Agreement* shall be considered a grievance . . ." (emphasis in original).

[114]Examples of disputes held arbitrable though not involving interpretation or application of the agreement are: claim against employer for assault upon employee by employer's agent: Goldstein v. Corbin, 63 LRRM 2248 (N.Y. Sup. Ct. 1966); compulsory retirement: Communications Workers v. Southwestern Bell Tel. Co., 415 F.2d 35, 71 LRRM 3025 (5th Cir. 1969); claim based on alleged oral agreement: Labib v. Younan, 755 F. Supp. 125 (D.N.J. 1991); United Eng'g & Foundry Employees Ass'n v. United Eng'g & Foundry Co., 389 F.2d 479, 67 LRRM 2168 (3d Cir. 1967); issue of contract termination by abandonment: Painters Local 1176 v. Bay Area Sealers, 577 F.2d 609, 99 LRRM 2313 (9th Cir. 1978); safety dispute: Gateway Coal Co. v. Mine Workers Dist. 4, Local 6330, 414 U.S. 368, 85 LRRM 2049 (1974); right to Christmas bonus: Newspaper Guild Local 26 (Buffalo) v. Tonawanda Publ'g Corp., 245 N.Y.S.2d 832, 55 LRRM 2222 (N.Y. Sup. Ct. 1964); pension plan: Electrical Workers (IBEW) Local 2020 v. AT&T Network Sys. (Columbia Works), 879 F.2d 864 (6th Cir. 1989) (table). For other examples, but involving arbitrability rulings by arbitrators, see *Munising Wood Prods. Co.*, 22 LA 769, 771 (Ryder, 1954); *Best Mfg. Co.*, 22 LA 482, 483–84 (Handsaker, 1954); *Rock Hill Printing & Finishing Co.*, 19 LA 872, 874 (Jaffee, 1953); *John Morrell & Co.*, 17 LA 81, 84 (Gilden, 1951); *Kendall Mills*, 8 LA 306 (Lane, 1947); *Warren City Mfg. Co.*, 7 LA 202, 217 (Abernethy, 1947); *F.H. Hill Co.*, 6 LA 661, 662–63 (Whiting, 1947). In *Operating Engineers Local 150 v. Flair Builders*, 406 U.S. 487, 80 LRRM 2441 (1972), the Supreme Court broadly interpreted the term "any difference," and allowed a laches defense to be decided in arbitration.

[115]A clause excluding disputes concerning the "general subject of wages, hours and working conditions" was construed to exclude interest disputes but not rights disputes. Standard Oil Co. of Cal., 52 LA 151, 153 (Koven, 1968).

[116]*See* Food & Commercial Workers v. Morgans Holiday Mkts., 202 F.3d 280 (9th Cir. 1999) (unpublished disposition) (because there is no specific exclusion of alter ego disputes in a broad arbitration clause, the clause therefore encompasses such disputes).

[117]Pitta v. Hotel Ass'n of New York City, 806 F.2d 419, 422, 124 LRRM 2109, 2112 (2d Cir. 1986). *See also* Ceres Terminals, 92 LA 735 (Malin, 1989) (arbitrator has authority to consider master contract provisions in interpreting local's contract). *But see* FMC Corp., 92 LA 1246 (Stoltenberg, 1989) (interpretation of sales agreement outside scope of arbitrator's authority).

[118]*Pitta*, 806 F.2d at 423, 124 LRRM at 2112. However, the court directed the parties to appoint another arbitrator because of the impartial chairman's clear personal interest in the outcome of the issue. *But see* Cornell Univ. v. Auto Workers Local 2300, 942 F.2d 138, 138 LRRM 2427 (2d Cir. 1991) (holding dispute over letter contract collateral to agreement and not covered by arbitration clause).

[119]H.C. Lawton, Jr., Inc. v. Teamsters Local 384, 755 F.2d 324, 118 LRRM 2825 (3d Cir. 1985); Hahnemann Univ. v. Hospital Employees Dist. 1199C, 596 F. Supp. 443 (E.D. Pa. 1984), *aff'd*, 765 F.2d 38, 119 LRRM 3018 (3d Cir. 1985).

The scope of arbitration is specified in 98 percent of the sample. Of these provisions, 98 percent provide for arbitration of any dispute not resolved through the grievance procedure. Specific issues are excluded from arbitration procedures in 32 percent of these contracts; specific issues are included in 43 percent. In 6 percent of provisions specifying scope of arbitration, certain matters bypass the grievance procedure and go directly to arbitration.[120]

Agreements with narrow clauses typically restrict arbitrators' authority further by expressly prohibiting them from adding to, subtracting from, or altering the agreement. Sometimes additional restrictions are added by the express exclusion of stated types of interpretation or application disputes. Under narrow arbitration clauses, a dispute may be held nonarbitrable unless it involves rights traceable to the agreement.[121] However, disputes are sometimes held arbitrable under such clauses even though the agreement contains no specific provision on the subject of the alleged right, as where the claimed right may be inherent in clauses on other subjects.[122] Furthermore, the "presumptive arbitrability" standard of the Supreme Court must be kept in mind in considering whether a court or an arbitrator might hold any given dispute to be arbitrable.[123]

Even though courts generally resolve a disputed question of coverage in favor of arbitration, where the arbitration provision expressly excludes certain issues, the courts will enforce the exclusion and exclude those issues from arbitration. For example, the U.S. Court of Appeals for the Eighth Cir-

---

[120]Basic Patterns in Union Contracts 37 (BNA Books 14th ed. 1995).

[121]See, e.g., Cornell Univ., 942 F.2d 138; Machinists Lodge 1000 v. General Elec. Co., 865 F.2d 902, 130 LRRM 2464 (7th Cir. 1989); Anderson-Tully Co., 88 LA 7 (Hart, 1986); WJLA v. Broadcast Employees, 103 LRRM 2952 (D.D.C. 1980); Safeway Stores, 71 LA 102 (Stephens, 1978). Where arbitration was limited to "alleged violation of the terms of the agreement," and where the agreement was silent on subcontracting, a grievance protesting subcontracting was not arbitrable. Independent Petroleum Workers v. American Oil Co., 324 F.2d 903, 54 LRRM 2598 (7th Cir. 1963), aff'd by equally divided Court, 379 U.S. 130, 57 LRRM 2512 (1964). Where the agreement limited arbitration to grievances involving "the interpretation and application of the specific provisions of this agreement," a grievance over the employer's decision to discontinue the distribution of Christmas turkeys was held nonarbitrable. Boeing Co. v. Auto Workers, 349 F.2d 412, 59 LRRM 2988 (3d Cir. 1965). See also Los Angeles Unified Sch. Dist., 85 LA 905 (Gentile, 1985). For cases in which arbitrators have denied or dismissed grievances as being beyond the scope of their authority, see Chapter 18, section 1.C., "Scope of Remedy Power Limited by the Agreement."

[122]See Virginia-Carolina Chem. Corp., 23 LA 228 (Marshall, 1954); Atwater Mfg. Co., 13 LA 747 (Donnelly, 1949); General Elec. Co., 9 LA 757 (Wallen, 1948). See also Levi Strauss & Co., 69 LA 1 (Goodstein, 1977); General Aniline & Film Corp., 25 LA 50 (Shister, 1955); National Vulcanized Fibre Co., 3 LA 259 (Kaplan, 1946). In Camden Indus. Co. v. Carpenters Local 1688, 246 F. Supp. 252, 60 LRRM 2183 (D.N.H. 1965), the court took the view that arbitration should be ordered if there is a possibility that an arbitrator may be able to resolve the dispute by interpreting existing provisions of the agreement; if the arbitrator subsequently finds that the dispute cannot be resolved by interpreting existing provisions, it is the arbitrator's responsibility then to hold the dispute to be nonarbitrable.

[123]See Chapter 2, section 2.A.ii.b., "The Trilogy," and Chapter 6, section 2., "Determination by the Courts," and section 3., "Determination by the Arbitrator." Matters expressly excluded from the arbitration clause will ordinarily be held nonarbitrable. See Mine Workers Dist. 50 v. Chris-Craft Corp., 385 F.2d 946, 67 LRRM 2124 (6th Cir. 1967). In Oil, Chem. & Atomic Workers Local 4449 v. Amoco Chem. Corp., 589 F.2d 162, 100 LRRM 2646 (5th Cir. 1979), the collective bargaining agreement made the employer's decision on a certain matter "final," and this was held to constitute a specific exclusion of the matter from arbitration. Cf. Los Angeles Paper Bag Co. v. Printing Pressmen Dist. Council 2, 345 F.2d 757, 59 LRRM 2427 (9th Cir. 1965).

her the determination of contract duration
ovision that was limited to "employee griev-
ough such an issue could be covered under a
d not be arbitrated under a narrow clause
.[24] In another example, a court held that an
lly excluded jurisdictional disputes from its
rator's authority the ability to resolve a dis-
on locals over work at a particular job site.[125]
arbitration clause may be limited by lan-
greement. In one case, a court held that al-
as "broadly worded," an exclusionary clause
ibiguous" will be given effect to negate the
Similarly, an arbitrator lacks authority to
ct is silent as to the disputed rights involved
lause limits the arbitrator to interpretation
agreement.[127] However, in another case the
Third Circuit held that a broad arbitration
ority to arbitrate a dispute over subcontract-
t contained an express right of management
.[128] The court rejected the employer's position
granted the employer an absolute right to
ork because the subcontracting clause stated
contract was "subject to" the restrictions con-
court held that because of the scope of the
iad "no difficulty concluding that the subject
comes within the zone of its protected inter-
ining agreement."[129]

al 618, 705 F.2d 274, 277, 112 LRRM 3433, 3436 (8th

nters Local 845, 585 F. Supp. 102 (E.D. Pa. 1984).
Service Employees Local 144, 788 F.2d 894, 898, 122
me arbitrators have also looked outside the contract for
sue is arbitrable. *See, e.g.*, John Morrell & Co. v. Food &
13 F.2d 544, 135 LRRM 2233 (8th Cir. 1990), *cert. de-*
rbitrator's authority according to conduct of the parties,
e dispute); Bridgestone/Firestone, Inc. v. Rubber Workers
Okla. 1990) (dispute over employee suggestion system
exclusion clause existed, but where system was not prod-
nications Corp. v. Teamsters Local 111, 719 F. Supp. 1,
re exclusionary clause is ambiguous, parol evidence can
). *But see* Westinghouse Hanford Co. v. Hanford Atomic
138 LRRM 2144 (9th Cir. 1991) (where a broad arbitra-
clusionary clauses, court refused to look to externalities
rable).
A 598 (Harkless, 1986).
asters Local 169, 812 F.2d 91, 124 LRRM 2633 (3d Cir.

In a dissent, Judge Garth believed that the parties had
from the arbitration clause. He found that the record
ul evidence" of intent to exclude subcontracting from ar-
bitration so that, regardless of the scope of the arbitration clause, the issue of subcontracting
was not arbitrable. *See also* Dallas Power & Light Co., 87 LA 415 (White, Keller, & Young,
1985) (holding grievance over right not specifically contained in contract arbitrable under

Even when an employee may be ineligible to utilize the grievance machinery, the union may be able to press the claim. One arbitrator adopted this option in allowing a union to seek arbitration when the affected probationary employee was not entitled to resort to the grievance process. In *Marathon Oil Co.*,[130] the arbitration and grievance procedure stated "[a]ny aggrieved employee or employees may . . . present a complaint, either individually or with the assistance of a Union Representative . . . ."[131] However, probationary employees were not eligible to invoke the procedure. The arbitrator held the union may initiate and arbitrate a grievance on behalf of a probationary employee.

i. *Precontract and Post-contract Grievances* [LA CDI 94.02]

Under the narrow "interpretation and application" arbitration clauses, disputes that arise prior to execution of a collective bargaining agreement have been held nonarbitrable, even though the grievance is filed after execution of the agreement.[132] As to grievances that arise in the interim between the expiration of one collective agreement and the execution of a new one, the situation as it stood prior to the Supreme Court's 1977 decision in *Nolde Bros. v. Bakery & Confectionery Workers Local 358*[133] was summarized as follows:

> [M]ost courts have held that a grievance which arises after a contract terminates is not subject to the expired arbitration provisions of that contract, and that the court must thus determine whether the contract on which suit is brought has indeed expired. . . .
>
> When the grievance arises during the contract term but arbitration is not demanded until after its termination, the theory just developed might point toward denying arbitration, but the few cases on the issue hold to the contrary. . . . In effect, the right of access to the grievance procedure is deemed "vested" as of the date the alleged grievance arises.[134]

In its *Nolde* decision, the Court recognized that grievances that arise during the life of the collective bargaining agreement, and are arbitrable under the agreement, do not become nonarbitrable merely because the agreement is terminated before arbitration is requested or commences. The Court then went further and held that a grievance is arbitrable although it arises

---

grievance-arbitration clause even though clause provided that, to be arbitrable, grievance must be covered by a specific provision of agreement, and disputes over matters not referred to in agreement would not be subject to arbitration).

[130]110 LA 124 (Allen, Jr., 1998).

[131]*Id.* at 125.

[132]*See* Cone Mills Corp., 25 LA 772, 773 (Wettach, 1956); International Harvester Co., 20 LA 850, 851–52 (Platt, 1953); Tennessee Prods. & Chem. Corp., 20 LA 207, 210 (Millar, 1953); Goodyear Clearwater Mills, 8 LA 66, 67 (McCoy, 1947); Merrill-Stevens Drydock & Repair Co., 6 LA 460, 461 (Marshall, 1947). *Cf.* Tuscarora Contractors, 33 LA 390 (Shister, 1959). Similarly, a promise made to persons before they became covered by the collective bargaining agreement was not arbitrable under an "interpretation and application" clause. Ranco, Inc., 50 LA 269, 273 (Klein, 1968).

[133]430 U.S. 243, 94 LRRM 2753 (1977).

[134]Gorman, Basic Text on Labor Law, Unionization, & Collective Bargaining 563–64 (1976). *See also* City of Detroit, 71 LA 340, 341 (Munger, 1978) (illustrative cases are cited).

after termination of the collective bargaining agreement, so long as the grievance was based on a right that arguably had "accrued" or become "vested" under the agreement prior to its termination. In the grievance at issue before it, the union sought severance pay for workers laid off following a plant closure that occurred after the agreement expired.

On the ground that the claimed severance benefits had accrued or become vested during the term of the agreement (though payable only when employment terminated),[135] the grievance would clearly have been arbitrable under the broad "all grievances" clause had it arisen during the life of the agreement.

The Court stated that the dispute, "although arising *after* the expiration of the collective-bargaining contract, clearly arises *under* that contract."[136] Reaffirming its position favoring the arbitration of such employment disputes, the Court concluded that "where the dispute is over a provision of the expired agreement, the presumptions favoring arbitrability must be negated expressly or by clear implication."[137]

---

[135]Nolde Bros. v. Bakery & Confectionery Workers Local 358, 430 U.S. 243, 94 LRRM 2753 (1977). The employer had paid accrued vacation pay under the expired agreement but refused to pay severance pay. Because the union promptly sought arbitration, the Court said it "need not speculate as to the arbitrability of post-termination contractual claims which, unlike the one presently before us, are not asserted within a reasonable time after the contract's expiration." *Id.* at 255 n.8. For related discussion, see Chapter 5, section 7., "Time Limitations."

[136]*Nolde*, 430 U.S. at 249 (emphasis in original). The Court explained: "Of course, in determining the arbitrability of the dispute, the merits of the underlying claim for severance pay are not before us. However, it is clear that . . . the resolution of that claim hinges on the interpretation ultimately given the contract clause providing for severance pay." *Id.* For a discussion of *Nolde* and its subsequent application, see Bosanac, *Expiration of the Collective Bargaining Agreement: Survivability of Terms and Conditions of Employment*, 4 Lab. Law. 715 (1988). In *Bunn-O-Matic Corp.*, 70 LA 34, 39–40 (Talent, 1978), a post-contract claim for severance pay was sustained, the arbitrator discussing *Nolde* along with arbitral precedents in which severance pay had been held to be an accrued benefit surviving the agreement's expiration. Regarding court action to preserve employer assets pending arbitration, see *Teamsters Local 71 v. Akers Motor Lines*, 582 F.2d 1336, 99 LRRM 2601 (4th Cir. 1978); *Teamsters Local 299 v. U.S. Truck Co. Holdings*, 87 F. Supp. 2d 726, 736–37, 163 LRRM 2412 (E.D. Mich. 2000) ("[h]arm lies in the fact that the company here would not be able to fully comply with an order of backpay if it continues to liquidate its assets." On a union's right to arbitrate grievances after it has lost its majority status or has been decertified, see *Longshoremen (ILWU) Local 142 v. Land & Constr. Co.*, 498 F.2d 201, 86 LRRM 2874 (9th Cir. 1974); *Machinists Lodge 1652 v. International Aircraft Servs.*, 49 LRRM 2976 (4th Cir. 1962); *Trumbull Asphalt Co.*, 38 LA 1093 (Elson, 1962). *See also* Note, *Union's Right to Assert Grievances Subsequent to Its Decertification and Change of Corporate Employers*, 16 Kan. L. Rev. 552 (1968). In *Chemical Workers v. E.I. DuPont de Nemours & Co.*, 615 F.2d 187, 103 LRRM 3111 (5th Cir. 1980), an employer was compelled to arbitrate with a successor union under the predecessor union's agreement.

[137]*Nolde*, 430 U.S. at 255. In *Typographical Union No. 23 (Milwaukee) v. Madison Newspapers*, 444 F. Supp. 1223, 97 LRRM 2950 (W.D. Wis. 1978), certain matters raised by the union after the agreement expired were held nonarbitrable, the court stating that, unlike *Nolde*, it was not alleged that the matters "arose" out of the agreement. A post-contract discharge also was nonarbitrable where evidence negated any mutual intent to keep the terms of the old agreement in effect during negotiations. Mid-Hudson Publ'ns v. Newspaper Guild Local 180 (Kingston), 103 LRRM 2050 (S.D.N.Y. 1980). *See also* Westwood Prods., 77 LA 396, 398–99 (Peterschmidt, 1981). Intent not to extend the arbitration procedure beyond the life of the agreement was adequately indicated where the agreement defined grievances subject to the grievance procedure as those "arising under *and during* the term of the agreement." Teamsters Local 636 v. J.C. Penney Co., 484 F. Supp. 130, 103 LRRM 2618, 2622 (W.D. Pa. 1980) (emphasis added). However, actions of the parties after the term of the agreement has expired may be important to a finding of arbitrability. *See* Dura-Vent Corp.,

As a result of the *Nolde* decision, termination of the collective bargaining agreement no longer necessarily extinguishes a party's duty to arbitrate grievances "arising under" the contract. Yet the Court's holding in *Nolde* was imprecise. The opinion, though containing a narrow holding,[138] embraced two disparate, inconsistent propositions: (1) the obligation to arbitrate survives the expiration of a collective bargaining agreement where the dispute is over a right "arguably created" by the expired agreement,[139] and (2) a "presumption of arbitrability" arises when the parties do not clearly express their desire that the duty to arbitrate terminates with the contract.[140]

It is not surprising, therefore, that the decision caused confusion in the lower courts and led to the taking of conflicting positions over the scope of the obligation to arbitrate post-contract grievances.[141] The majority of federal courts have read *Nolde* narrowly, holding that for a grievance to be arbitrable after the expiration of the contract, it must involve either rights that accrued or vested during the term of the agreement, or disputes that arose under the agreement while it was still in effect.[142] Specifically, the U.S. Court

---

77 LA 399, 400–01 (Griffin, 1981); Santa Cruz City Sch. Dist., 73 LA 1264, 1269 (Heath, 1979) (parties recognized continued existence of the grievance procedure by their conduct); Mason County Rd. Comm'n, 70 LA 234, 237–38 (Allen, Jr., 1978); Buffalo Bd. of Educ., 68 LA 921, 922 (Dennis, 1977) (parties had continued the contract on a day-to-day basis).

[138]Nolde Bros. v. Bakery & Confectionery Workers Local 358, 430 U.S. 243, 255, 94 LRRM 2753, 2756 (1977). The Court held only that severance pay disputes were arbitrable under the expired agreement.

[139]*Id.* at 252.

[140]*Id.* at 254.

[141]*See, e.g.,* Litton Fin. Printing Div. v. NLRB, 501 U.S. 190, 197 n.1, 137 LRRM 2441, 2444 n.1 (1991) (recognizing and summarizing the disagreements among lower courts on the proper interpretation of *Nolde*); George Day Constr. Co. v. Carpenters Local 354, 722 F.2d 1471, 115 LRRM 2459 (9th Cir. 1984) (court declining to interpret holding in *Nolde* or reconcile conflicting opinions); Zirkel, *Does Grievance Arbitration Survive After Contract Expiration?,* 3 Det. C. L. Rev. 843 (1989); Zirkel & Koff, *Grievance Arbitration After Contract Expiration,* 39 Lab. L.J. 379 (1988); Ogden, Lees & Gasperini, *The Survival of Contract Terms: The Quagmire Expands,* 36 Lab. L.J. 688, 693 (1985).

[142]*See, e.g.,* Food & Commercial Workers Local 7 v. Gold Star Sausage Co., 897 F.2d 1022, 133 LRRM 2765 (10th Cir. 1990) (post-contract arbitration required only if grievance involves either conduct that occurred partially during contract term or employee rights that accrued or vested during that period); Mine Workers Local 2487 v. Blue Creek Mining Co., 806 F.2d 1552, 1555, 124 LRRM 2294, 2296 (11th Cir. 1987) (grievants' right to be placed on panel for employment accrued at time they were laid off, and thus "accrued" during contract period); Teamsters Local 238 v. C.R.S.T., Inc., 795 F.2d 1400, 122 LRRM 2993 (8th Cir. 1986) (right to be discharged for just cause is strictly creature of contract and as such does not survive beyond contract expiration); Graphic Communications Local 2 v. Chicago Tribune Co., 794 F.2d 1222, 123 LRRM 2488 (7th Cir. 1986) (grievance did not arise under expired collective bargaining agreement because it dealt with a future practice to be instituted by employer); Electrical Workers (IBEW) Local 22 v. Nanco Elec., 790 F.2d 59, 122 LRRM 2826 (8th Cir. 1986) (dispute over post-expiration contributions to trust fund did not arise under contract); Teamsters Local 807 v. Brink's, Inc., 744 F.2d 283, 286, 117 LRRM 2306 (2d Cir. 1984) (*Nolde* limited to grievances which "arise under the collective bargaining agreement"); Glover Bottled Gas Corp. v. Teamsters Local 282, 711 F.2d 479, 113 LRRM 3211 (2d Cir. 1983) (expiration of contract did not preclude arbitration of discharge when activity giving rise to discharge occurred prior to expiration); O'Connor Co. v. Carpenters Local 1408, 702 F.2d 824, 825, 122 LRRM 3316 (9th Cir. 1983) (post-expiration dispute over hiring of nonunion employees not arbitrable because it is not "covered" by expired contract); Chicago Web Printing Pressmen Local 7 v. Chicago Tribune, 657 F. Supp. 351, 125 LRRM 2137 (N.D. Ill. 1987) (dispute concerning calculation of vacation pay is arbitrable under expired collective bargaining agreement, even though events triggering grievance occurred more than 6 months after expiration of contract because such rights accrued under contract).

of Appeals for the Tenth Circuit defined the term "arises under" as a dispute that either involves "rights which to some degree have vested or accrued during the life of the contract and merely ripened after termination, or relate to events which have occurred at least in part while the agreement was still in effect."[143]

A good discussion of the narrow view can be found in *Oil, Chemical & Atomic Workers Local 4-23 v. American Petrofina Co. of Tex.*, 586 F. Supp. 643, 117 LRRM 2034 (E.D. Tex. 1984), *rev'd on other grounds*, 759 F.2d 512, 119 LRRM 2395 (5th Cir. 1985), *vacated and remanded on other grounds*, 476 U.S. 1180, 122 LRRM 2655 (1986), in which the court dismissed the broad view as a "misinterpretation" of *Nolde*. The court rejected the union's argument that the "duty to arbitrate survives independent of contract expiration unless (1) there is language clearly to the contrary in the collective bargaining agreement; or, (2) there is conduct of the parties that is so clear that a contrary intent is established." *Id.* at 648. The court noted that "[o]ther decisions have limited *Nolde* to apply only to accrued rights and benefits; and this Court believes this is the proper view. Otherwise, almost every clause and term of a collective bargaining agreement would stay in effect after agreement was terminated. This certainly would not reflect the intention of the parties; but it certainly would lead to a raft of litigation." *Id.* at 648–49.

For arbitrators accepting the narrow view, see *Basic Inc.*, 82 LA 1065 (Dworkin, 1984) (Christmas bonus "vested" under prior contract and therefore was payable even though new contract expressly excluded Christmas bonus provision); *Shieldalloy Corp.*, 81 LA 489 (Talmadge, 1983) (right to vacation pay is a right "established by the contract" and is arbitrable even though grievance arises after expiration of agreement); *Bekins Moving & Storage Co.*, 81 LA 1198 (Brisco, 1983) (grievance over birthday holiday pay when birthdays occurred after expiration of contract not arbitrable).

Several courts have focused not on whether the dispute arose under the contract or whether the rights were accrued or vested but on the *Nolde* Court's statement that it would reserve judgment on "the arbitrability of post-termination contractual claims which, unlike the [claim in *Nolde*] are not asserted within a reasonable time after the contract's expiration." *Nolde,* 430 U.S. at 255 n.8. These courts appear to read *Nolde* as allowing post-contract arbitration as long as the grievance is filed within a reasonable time after the expiration of the contract. In *Teamsters Local 703 v. Kennicott Bros.*, 771 F.2d 300, 120 LRRM 2306 (7th Cir. 1985), the U.S. Court of Appeals for the Seventh Circuit held that a grievance filed over 6 months after the expiration of the contract was not filed within a reasonable time and was therefore not subject to arbitration. *But see* Chicago Web Printing Pressmen v. Chicago Trib., 657 F. Supp. 351, 125 LRRM 2137 (N.D. Ill. 1987) (holding that *Kennicott* cannot be read to preclude *Nolde's* presumption of arbitrability when the dispute involves a right that accrued under contract but did not ripen until after contract expired). *See also* Auto Workers v. Young Radiator Co., 904 F.2d 9, 134 LRRM 2442 (7th Cir. 1990) (arbitration ordered 11 months after contract expiration where dispute arose solely due to employer's refusal to pay benefits accrued under contract); Federated Metals Corp. v. Steelworkers, 648 F.2d 856, 107 LRRM 2271 (3d Cir.), *cert. denied*, 454 U.S. 1031 (1981) (grievance filed over 9 months after expiration of agreement not unreasonable where grievances arose while union was negotiating for a new agreement after old agreement had expired).

One court held termination of the collective bargaining agreement due to decertification of the union, while changing relations between and among the employer, union, and employees, does not deprive the union of the use of the arbitration procedure and the right to redress under the terminated contract. *See* Auto Workers v. Telex Computer Prods., 816 F.2d 519, 125 LRRM 2163 (10th Cir. 1987). In *Quinn v. Police Officers Labor Council*, 465 Mich. 478, 486, 572 N.W.2d 641, 644 (Mich. 1998), the court held the grievance arose and was pursued under the collective bargaining agreement while the Labor Council was the exclusive representative, and thus had the obligation to process the grievance to its completion, not the new representative. For a discussion of the obligation to arbitrate disputes after a rejection of the collective bargaining agreement in bankruptcy, see Simon & Bishop, *Bankruptcy and Its Impact on Arbitration: A Union View*, 39 N.Y.U. Nat'l Conference on Labor (1986).

[143]Food & Commercial Workers Local 7 v. Gold Star Sausage, 897 F.2d 1022, 1024–25, 133 LRRM 2765 (10th Cir. 1990).

However, several courts, interpreting *Nolde* broadly, have held that regardless of whether the rights in dispute "arose under" the contract, or "accrued" or "vested" during the term of the contract, there is a presumption that the parties intended their arbitration obligation to survive beyond the expiration of the agreement unless its survival is expressly negated.[144] These courts rely on the *Nolde* dictim that, "in the absence of some contrary indication, there are strong reasons to conclude that the parties did not intend their arbitration duties to terminate automatically with the contract."[145] For example, the U.S. Court of Appeals for the Ninth Ciricuit held that notwithstanding the fact that the agreement had terminated, courts "must presume that the parties intended the arbitration duty to survive" where no evidence existed to negate the presumption.[146] Therefore, unless proved otherwise, all post-expiration disputes arguably touching on the collective bargaining agreement are subject to arbitration.[147]

Similarly, the U.S. Court of Appeals for the Third Circuit held that a narrow arbitration clause does not provide sufficient indication of an intent to exclude post-contract disputes.[148] The court expressly rejected the distinction between vested and nonvested rights: "We do not believe that the somewhat esoteric determination that the disputed right to a particular benefit

---

[144]*See, e.g.*, Culinary Workers Local 226, Las Vegas Joint Executive Bd. v. Royal Ctr., 796 F.2d 1159, 123 LRRM 2347 (9th Cir. 1986) (holding that arbitration clause survived termination of collective bargaining agreement because broad arbitration clauses presumptively survive termination); Federated Metals Corp. v. Steelworkers, 648 F.2d 856, 107 LRRM 2271 (3d Cir.) *cert. denied*, 454 U.S. 1031 (1981) (even narrowness of arbitration clause does not foreclose post-contract grievance arbitration); Paperworkers v. Wells Badger Indus., 124 LRRM 2658 (E.D. Wis. 1987) (evidence reveals parties' intent to arbitrate post-contract disputes even though such disputes did not arise under contract); Trustees of Graphic Communications Local 229 v. Rapid Copy, 620 F. Supp. 202 (D. Minn. 1985) (holding arbitration clause survives termination of contract because presumption is that parties intended clause to survive). *See also* Emery Air Freight Corp. v. Teamsters Local 295, 786 F.2d 93, 121 LRRM 3240 (2d Cir. 1986) (applying broad reading of *Nolde*). For an example of an arbitrator accepting the broad view, see *MGM Grand Hotels*, 86 LA 765 (Rothschild, 1986) (grievances protesting employer's failure to obtain replacements through union's hiring hall are arbitrable even though replacements were hired during strike that occurred after contract expired). For a critical discussion of the broad view of *Nolde*, see Jauvtis, *The Liminal Period: Obligations of Parties Upon Expiration of a Collective Bargaining Agreement*, 58 N.Y. St. B.J. 30 (Nov. 1986); Geslewitz, *Case Law Development Since* Nolde Brothers*: When Must Post-Contract Disputes Be Arbitrated?*, 35 Lab. L.J. 225 (1984); Leonard, *Post-Contractual Arbitrability After* Nolde Brothers: *A Problem of Conceptual Clarity*, 28 N.Y.L Sch. L. Rev. 257 (1983).

[145]Nolde Bros. v. Bakery & Confectionery Workers Local 358, 430 U.S. 243, 253, 94 LRRM 2753, 2756 (1977).

[146]Culinary Workers Local 226, Las Vegas Joint Executive Bd. v. Royal Ctr., 796 F.2d 1159, 1161, 123 LRRM 2347, 2349 (9th Cir. 1986). *See also* NLRB v. Litton Fin. Printing Div., 893 F.2d 1128, 133 LRRM 2354 (9th Cir. 1990) (reaffirming its interpretation of *Nolde*); Mississippi Ins. Managers v. Providence Wash. Ins. Co., 72 F. Supp 689, 695 (S.D. Miss. 1999) (recognizing the abrogation of Seafarers by *Litton* and stating, "[n]o provision of the new [agreement] nullifies the duty to arbitrate indemnification disputes or any other disputes where the conduct of a party giving rise to a dispute occurred while the old general agency was still in effect").

[147]Culinary Workers Local 226, Las Vegas Joint Executive Bd. v. Royal Ctr., 796 F.2d 1159, 1162–63, 123 LRRM 2347, 2350 (9th Cir. 1986).

[148]Federated Metals Corp. v. Steelworkers, 648 F.2d 856, 107 LRRM 2271 (3d Cir), *cert. denied*, 454 U.S. 1031 (1981). *See also* Seafarers v. National Marine Servs., 820 F.2d 148, 125 LRRM 3069 (5th Cir.), *cert. denied*, 484 U.S. 953 (1987) (rejecting narrow interpretation of *Nolde*).

has vested or accrued should control the decision whether the duty to arbitrate the dispute survives contract termination."[149]

The NLRB initially adopted a broad interpretation of the Court's *Nolde* opinion, holding in one case that the parties' duty to arbitrate survived the termination of the contract when the dispute arose over an obligation created by the contract,[150] and that the employer was obligated to arbitrate the discharge of an employee whose termination occurred after the contract term.[151] The Board read *Nolde* to mean:

> [W]here the parties to a collective-bargaining agreement have agreed to subject certain matters to a grievance and arbitration process, "the parties' obligation under their arbitration clause survive[s] contract termination when the dispute [is] over an obligation arguably created by the expired agreement." That obligation is not terminated merely by the parties' failure to expressly cover this situation. As the Court stated generally in *Nolde*, in the "absence of some contrary indication, there are strong reasons to conclude that the parties did not intend their arbitration duties to terminate automatically with the contract."[152]

Consistently, in another case,[153] the Board found arbitrable the discharge of an employee after the contact had expired when the conduct on which the discharge was based had occurred at least in part before expiration of the contract.[154] However, in a later decision the Board specifically adopted the narrow interpretation of *Nolde*:

> We acknowledge that *Nolde* contains language with a broader sweep than its narrow holding that a claim to severance pay arguably accruable under the contract is arbitrable even though the plant closed after the contract expired.

---

[149]*Federated Metals*, 648 F.2d at 861. Parties that wish to avoid a broad reading of *Nolde* have added to the collective bargaining agreement a provision that only disputes arising "under and during the term of the Agreement" will be arbitrable. *See, e.g.*, Teamsters Local 636 v. J.C. Penney Co., 484 F. Supp. 130, 132 n.1, 103 LRRM 2618 (W.D. Pa. 1980); Gates Can., 82 LA 480 (Brown, 1984) (grievance seeking health benefits for employee who had surgery after contract expired not arbitrable where expired contract had provision that provided for arbitration of grievances solely under "the collective bargaining agreement then in effect"). Such provisions clearly negate any presumption that the parties intended that all post-contract disputes be arbitrable.

[150]American Sink Top & Cabinet Co., 242 NLRB 408, 101 LRRM 1166 (1979).

[151]*Id.* at 408, 101 LRRM at 1167.

[152]*Id.* at 408, 101 LRRM at 1166 (quoting Nolde Bros. v. Bakery Confectionery Workers Local 358, 430 U.S. 243, 252, 253, 94 LRRM 2753 (1977)).

[153]Digmar Equip. & Eng'g Co., 261 NLRB 1175, 110 LRRM 1209 (1982).

[154]*Id.*, 110 LRRM at 1210. Several commentators and at least one court have criticized the Board's position on ordering arbitration when a discharge might have been based on events that occurred prior to the contract's expiration. County of Ottawa v. Jaklinski, 423 Mich. 1, 377 N.W.2d 668, 120 LRRM 3260 (1985); Geslewitz, *Case Law Development Since Nolde Brothers: When Must Post-Contract Disputes Be Arbitrated?*, 35 Lab. L.J. 225, 230–32 (1984); Kirkscium, *Post Contract Arbitrability Since* Nolde Brothers, 54 U. Colo. L. Rev. 103, 107 (1982). These commentators believe that under the Board's reading of *Nolde*, the substantive "just cause" right of a collective bargaining agreement would continue indefinitely. Also, the Board's position may require courts to examine the causes for the disputed discharge, and "the risk that courts would decide the merits of a case in the guise of deciding arbitrability would be enhanced." *Jaklinski*, 377 N.W.2d at 679, 120 LRRM at 3268. Finally, indefinite arbitration under the Board's position is likely because almost all discharged employees can arguably allege that their discharge was due at least in part to conduct occurring during the term of the collective bargaining agreement.

We conclude, however, in agreement with the circuit courts that have addressed the issue, that a dispute based on postexpiration events "arises under" the contract within the meaning of *Nolde* only if it concerns contract rights capable of accruing or vesting to some degree during the life of the contract and ripening or remaining enforceable after the contract expires.[155]

In this case, the collective bargaining agreements at several of the employer's facilities had expired. Immediately after expiration, the employer sent a letter to the union stating that it would not abide by the grievance-arbitration procedure under the expired contract for "grievances filed during the time we are without an agreement."[156] During the interim period between the two contracts, the union filed nine grievances. The employer refused to arbitrate each one, stating by letter that it would not "arbitrate grievances based on alleged violations of the contract which occurred during the contractual hiatus."[157]

In the ensuing unfair labor practice proceeding, the Board addressed the issue of whether the employer's repudiation of the grievance-arbitration process in the expired contract constituted a violation of the employer's duty to bargain under Section 8(a)(5) of the NLRA. It found that the employer's refusal amounted to a "wholesale repudiation of its contractual obligation to arbitrate," and that the employer therefore violated Section 8(a)(5) and 8(a)(1) of the NLRA.[158] The Board held that neither party may unilaterally abandon a procedure by which they have customarily resolved day-to-day worksite disputes.[159]

Although the Board found that an employer could violate federal law by a blanket repudiation of the obligation to arbitrate post-contract grievances, it nevertheless held that *Nolde* did not require that every post-contract grievance be arbitrated.[160] The employer had a duty to arbitrate only those disputes concerning rights that accrued or vested under the prior contract.[161] Because the Board found that the nine grievances filed by the union neither

---

[155]Indiana & Mich. Elec. Co., 284 NLRB 53, 60, 125 LRRM 1097, 1103 (1987). *See also* Rose Printing Co. v. Graphic Communications Local 241-B, 289 NLRB 252, 131 LRRM 1420 (1988) (refusal to arbitrate any grievances after expiration of contract is unlawful based on rationale of *Indiana & Mich. Elec.*).

[156]*Indiana & Mich. Elec. Co.*, 284 NLRB at 53, 125 LRRM at 1097.

[157]*Id.*

[158]*Id.* at 59, 125 LRRM at 1103.

[159]*Id.* at 59, 125 LRRM at 1099. The Board reasoned that permitting either party to unilaterally abandon its grievance procedure would not serve the interest of preserving industrial peace. Answering dissenting Chairman Dotson, the majority of the Board explained that it was not insisting "upon rigid adherence to an expired and truncated contractual dispute resolution system," but merely insisting "that changes in that dispute resolution system be made only after the parties concerned have agreed to them or otherwise adequately bargained over the matter." *Id.*

[160]*Id.* at 60, 125 LRRM at 1103. The Board held that "whether the nine hiatus grievances are arbitrable under *Nolde* turns on whether they 'arise under' the expired agreements." *Id.*

[161]*Id.* Not only did the Board choose to follow the courts that accept the narrow view of *Nolde*, it expressly declined to follow *American Sink Top & Cabinet Co.*, 242 NLRB 408, 101 LRRM 1166 (1979), to the extent that it could be read to hold that "the mere invocation of any term of the expired contract triggers the postexpiration duty to arbitrate under *Nolde* . . . ." *Indiana & Mich. Elec. Co.*, 284 NLRB at 60 n.9, 125 LRRM at 1104 n.9.

arose under the expired contracts nor involved rights that accrued or vested under the expired contracts, it declined to order the employer to arbitrate the grievances.[162]

In 1991, the Supreme Court resolved some of these post-expiration arbitration issues in *Litton Financial Printing Division v. NLRB*.[163] The Court in *Litton* agreed with the Board and those courts that applied the narrow view of *Nolde*, stating that post-expiration arbitration is strictly limited to "disputes arising under the contract."[164] The *Litton* Court went on to explain that such contract disputes arise in only three situations: (1) where the dispute involves events that occurred before expiration, (2) where post-expiration conduct "infringes a right that accrued or vested under the agreement,"[165] or (3) where the right survives the contract's expiration.

In the aftermath of *Litton* the federal courts have attempted to apply the reinterpreted *Nolde* doctrine. In *South Central Power Co. v. Electrical Workers (IBEW) Local 2359*,[166] some, but not all, of the facts and occurrences involved in a grievance arose prior to the expiration of the collective bargaining agreement. Therefore, the case did not fit neatly into either the *Nolde* or *Litton* mold. The U.S. Court of Appeals for the Sixth Circuit rejected the union's view that arbitration was required so long as *any* fact or occurrence arose prior to the expiration of the old agreement. Extrapolating the *Litton* decision, the court held a dispute arises under the contract when a "majority of the material facts and occurrences arise before expiration of the collective bargaining agreement."[167]

Another court made it clear that for an employer to be bound by the arbitration clause of an expired contract, there must be an affirmative manifestation of the intent to be so bound. In *Williamsbridge Manor Nursing Home v. Service Employees Local 144*,[168] a New York district court refused to find an implied-in-fact contract based on the expired collective bargaining agreement. For an implied-in-fact contract, the court noted, there must be mutual assent of the parties, and such assent will not be inferred. The court expressly rejected the test used by the U.S. Court of Appeals for the Third

---

[162]The nine grievances in *Indiana & Mich. Elec. Co.* involved the following events: (1) an employee's "suspension for excessive absenteeism"; (2) an employee's "suspension for improper job performance and sleeping on company time"; (3) the employer's failure to assign an employee "overtime, [and] giving the work to a supervisor instead"; (4) the employer's failure to provide an employee with "proper working conditions and compensation when he was assigned to a job away from his normal work location"; (5) the employer's "request that [an employee] report to his new job 2 days before the date he was told he would be transferred"; (6) the employer's failure to pay an employee line mechanic wages for the "time he spent working as a leadman"; (7) "the manner in which the [employer] assigned routes to [an employee] and other meter readers"; (8) "an oral warning given to meter readers for failure to read enough meters in a day"; and (9) "a supervisor's acquisition of an employee's telephone number and use of it to contact her at home." *Id.* at 53 n.2, 125 LRRM at 1098 n.2. After examining the grievances, the Board concluded that rights invoked in each grievance did not arise under the expired contracts within the meaning of *Nolde*.

[163]501 U.S. 190, 137 LRRM 2441 (1991).

[164]*Id.* at 205, 137 LRRM at 2447.

[165]*Id.* at 206.

[166]186 F.3d 733, 161 LRRM 2998 (6th Cir. 1999).

[167]*Id.* at 740.

[168]107 F. Supp. 2d 222, 165 LRRM 2185 (S.D.N.Y. 2000).

Circuit that when a contract expires, and the parties "'continue to act, as if they are performing under a contract, the material terms of the prior contract will survive intact unless either one of the parties clearly and manifestly indicates, through words or conduct, that it no longer wishes to continue to be bound.'"[169] The court ultimately held the union could not unilaterally, on the basis of the expired agreement, demand the arbitration.

Litton's "arising under" test appears to have resolved the ambiguities left by *Nolde*, but as new cases come to the courts with varying fact patterns they pose new questions that must be answered.[170]

---

[169] *Id.* at 226 (quoting Luden's Inc. v. Bakery, Confectionery & Tobacco Workers, 28 F.3d 347, 355–56, 146 LRRM 2586 (3d Cir. 1994)).

[170] *See* Hacienda Hotel Inc. Gaming Corp., 331 NLRB 665, 164 LRRM 1273 (2000) (holding an employer's dues check-off obligation does not survive contract expiration); CPR (USA) Inc. v. Spray, 187 F.3d 245 (2d Cir. 1999) (dispute over whether agreement had expired involves dispute over the interpretation of the agreement, which the agreement specifically provides is arbitrable); In the matter of National Basketball Players Association and National Basketball Association (Lockout Arbitration, Opinion and Award), 548 PLI/Pat 87 (1999) (the fact that the National Basketball Association decided not to play players during the period of impending lockout arose before the expiration of the agreement and infringed on a right that accrued or vested under that agreement); *Expired Arbitration Agreement Still Applies to Pre-Expiration Disputes*, 10 World Arb. & Mediation Rep. 302 (1999) (discussing the National Basketball Association lockout. *See also* AlliedSignal Aerospace, 330 NLRB 1216, 167 LRRM 1226 (2000); Coast Hotels & Casinos v. Culinary Workers Local 226, 35 F. Supp. 2d 765, 161 LRRM 2507 (D. Nev. 1999) (recognizing limits *Litton* placed on *Nolde*); Typographical Union Local 18 (Detroit) v. Detroit Newspaper Agency, 157 LRRM 2742 (E.D. Mich. 1998); *Enforceability of Arbitral Clause Not Affected by Expiration of Contract*, 11 World Arb. & Mediation Rep. 12 (2000).
In a related issue, a request to "open" a contract that was subject to automatic annual renewal was held not to bar arbitration of a worker's grievance filed during the ensuing bargaining impasse. Oil, Chem. & Atomic Workers Local I-369 v. Sandvik Special Metals Corp., 10 P.3d 470, 165 LRRM 2544 (Wash. App. 2000). The agreement contained a general arbitration clause that allowed an employee, the union, or the employer to demand arbitration "for any asserted violation of the specific terms or provisions of this Agreement." *Id.* at 472. The contract expiration date was May 31, 1996, after which the agreement was to be automatically renewed from year to year. The contract also provided that the agreement would remain in effect during negotiations over any proposed modification. In March 1996 the union announced its intention to "open" the contract, and negotiations started. In September 1997, during a period of impasse, an employee was fired. The company contended that the discharge was not arbitrable, and the employee and the union sought to compel arbitration. The Washington State Court of Appeals observed that the union simply wanted to open the contract and that, "[Whatever open] might mean, it does not mean terminate. In fact, the terms *open* or *reopen* refer to discussions regarding the terms of an ongoing contract." *Id.* at 474 (citing KCW Furniture v. NLRB, 634 F.2d 436, 439, 106 LRRM 2112 (9th Cir. 1980)) (emphasis in original). In consequence, the court concluded that the the the contract continued in effect, and therefore the grievance was arbitrable.

Chapter 4

The Arbitration Tribunal

In the absence of statutory mandates, parties choose the composition of the arbitral tribunal and the method of selecting the arbitrator or arbitrators in accordance with their assessment of their needs. A description of the commonly utilized forum structures and arbitrator selection criteria and methodology follow.

1. Single Arbitrator Versus Arbitration Board

Parties most often decide to use a single neutral arbitrator, though in given industries boards of arbitration frequently are employed.[1] Arbitration boards may be composed entirely of neutrals or the membership may be tripartite—that is, one arbitrator who represents management, one who represents the union, and the third, a neutral, who is selected either by the parties directly or by their representative arbitrators. Of the two types, the tripartite board is used much more frequently than the board of neutrals.[2]

A board of neutrals ordinarily will have three members. Sometimes an alternate also is designated.[3] Under one format, only one member hears the case and makes findings of fact; then a decision based on such findings is made by the full board.[4] Under another arrangement, the case is heard by a board of two neutrals, with a third neutral to be selected subsequently if the first two cannot agree on a decision.[5]

---

[1]The Bureau of Labor Statistics of the Department of Labor studied 1,717 labor agreements in 1952 and found that 46% provided for tripartite arbitration boards, but that the percentage declined steadily to reach 38% in 1965. Fairweather's Practice and Procedure in Labor Arbitration 99 (Schoonhoven ed., BNA Books 4th ed. 1999) (citing *Major Collective Bargaining Agreements*, at 36 (U.S. Bureau of Labor Statistics, Dep't of Labor Bull. No. 1425-26, 1966)). *See also* Basic Patterns in Union Contracts (BNA Books 14th ed. 1995); *Basic Patterns in Labor Arbitration Agreements*, 34 LA 931, 938 (1960 survey); *Procedural Aspects of Labor-Management Arbitration*, 28 LA 933, 934–35 (1954 survey).

[2]For discussion of tripartite boards, see section 5., "Tripartite Arbitration Board," below.

[3]*See* Southern Bell Tel. & Tel. Co., 25 LA 85, 86 (Alexander, McCoy, Schedler, & Whiting, 1955).

[4]*Id.*

[5]*See* Fairmont Auto Supply Co., 43 LA 369, 369 (Lugar & Furbee, 1964) (the two neutrals who heard the case did agree on a decision).

2. TYPES OF ARBITRATORS

A. "Temporary" or "Ad Hoc" Arbitrators [LA CDI 94.45]

The "temporary" or "ad hoc" arbitrator is selected after the dispute arises.[6] The individual is named to arbitrate a specific dispute or a specific group of disputes, and there is no commitment to select that arbitrator again. Most interest arbitrations involve temporary arbitrators. The arbitration clause in the collective bargaining agreement also usually will specify the use of temporary arbitrators in "rights" or "grievance" arbitrations. The details of such clauses vary considerably from agreement to agreement, but it is customary to state at least: (1) what grievances may be submitted to arbitration, (2) the procedure for selecting an arbitrator, and (3) the scope of the arbitrator's jurisdiction and the binding effect of the award.

i. Advantages

The possibility of easily changing arbitrators is one of the chief advantages of the use of temporary arbitrators. At the same time, as long as an arbitrator continues to be satisfactory to the parties, that arbitrator can be selected again and again, if available, for cases as they arise. When parties first begin to arbitrate, the use of temporary arbitrators makes experimentation possible. Thus, they may become acquainted with arbitration and, at the same time, better determine their particular needs. Later, the parties might graduate to the use of a permanent system.

Use of temporary arbitrators permits the selection, in each case, of an arbitrator with qualifications appropriate for deciding the particular dispute. While the use of a specialist, as such, may not be required often, some issues are of such technical nature that it is advisable to select an arbitrator who has special training or knowledge.[7]

Finally, it is probable that a temporary arbitrator, not being personally acquainted with either party, will not be swayed too far by the personalities of the parties. In other words, brief tenure in office makes it less likely that a temporary arbitrator will acquire a bias in favor of either party.

For those parties who find themselves with relatively few disputes, the appointment of arbitrators only as needed is generally more economical.

ii. Disadvantages

The selection of an arbitrator after a dispute has arisen may involve as much difficulty as the dispute itself. Much time and effort may be lost because parties that are no longer friendly find themselves unable to agree on an arbitrator, or even on a method of selecting one. In the meantime, the

---

[6]Over four-fifths of the agreements in the aforementioned survey by the Department of Labor provided for selection of the arbitrator on an ad hoc basis. *Major Collective Bargaining Agreements: Arbitration Procedures*, at 33 (U.S. Dep't of Labor Bull. No. 1425-6, 1966).

[7]*See* Ferguson v. Writers Guild of Am., 277 Cal. Rptr. 450 (Ct. App. 1991).

dispute remains unsettled, which may result in additional damage to the parties' relationship.

An arbitrator who is chosen for only one dispute, or a specific group of disputes, may not be familiar with the general circumstances of the parties and may know little of the background of the dispute or the setting in which the collective bargaining agreement operates. The parties may seek to educate the arbitrator as to these matters; even so, the arbitrator's knowledge of the parties' relationship may be shallow. The most successful arbitration is that which sets a smooth course for future operations. Thorough knowledge of the past relationship of the parties is an invaluable aid to one who would pursue this end. Moreover, since temporary arbitrators sometimes are selected on somewhat of an emergency basis, the parties may not have adequate opportunity to check the qualifications of the arbitrator.[8] Thus, there is the potential that the parties may have chosen inappropriately and will be forced to accept a decision that leaves their relationship in a weaker condition than that which existed prior to the rendition of the award.

Another disadvantage of the use of temporary arbitrators is the possibility that divergent and even conflicting interpretations of the same contractual provision may be given.[9] In fact, it is not uncommon for a losing party to take the very same issue to arbitration again if it is thought that there is any possibility of obtaining a different ruling. An award by one temporary arbitrator may be accorded little precedential force when a subsequent arbitrator is called upon to decide a similar dispute.

Because it is easy to change temporary arbitrators, losing parties frequently will demand a change of arbitrators even though there may be no reasonable cause for a change. Thus, the parties may be deprived of future valuable service of the eliminated arbitrator. Moreover, frequent and indiscriminate change of arbitrators permits none to become truly acquainted with the long-term needs of the parties. This means that the parties may deprive themselves of the best possible arbitration services.[10]

B. "Permanent" Arbitrators [LA CDI 94.45]

A "permanent" arbitrator is one who is selected to serve for a period of time, rather than for just one case or a specific group of cases. The arbitrator may be selected to serve for the term of the collective bargaining agreement, for some other specific period, or even at the pleasure of the parties. Gener-

---

[8]Although an arbitrator's qualifications are an important consideration in the selection process, one study suggests a lack of significant relationships between the characteristics of arbitrators and their decisions, thus calling into question the usefulness of investigating arbitrators' backgrounds as part of the selection process. Bemmels, *Arbitrator Characteristics and Arbitrator Decisions*, 11 J. LAB. RES. 181 (1990).

[9]See results of study and discussion in Thornton & Zirkel, *The Consistency and Predictability of Grievance Arbitration Awards*, 43 INDUS. & LAB. REL. REV. 294 (1990).

[10]For a discussion of the advantages and disadvantages of using temporary arbitrators, see Simkin & Kennedy, *Arbitration of Grievances* (U.S. Dep't of Labor, Div. of Labor Standards, Bull. No. 82, 1946). *See also* Grenig, *Arbitration: The Arbitration Agreement, Commencing the Arbitration, and Arbitrators, in* ALTERNATIVE DISPUTE RESOLUTION WITH FORMS §4.42 (2d ed. 1997); Warren & Bernstein, *A Profile of Labor Arbitration*, 16 LA 970 (1951); *Labor Arbitration Today: Accomplishments and Problems*, 16 LA 987 (1951).

ally, the removal of a permanent impartial arbitrator requires the consent of both parties, and the process of removal is subject to the provisions of the collective bargaining agreement.[11] The arbitrator's responsibilities and functions are determined by the contract by which the office is created. (The terms of permanent-arbitrator contracts vary widely, especially as to the precise jurisdiction of the arbitrator, because each such contract is carefully tailored to meet the special needs and wishes of the parties.[12]) While some arbitrators are employed on a full-time basis, most are employed on a part-time basis, subject to call when needed. The use of a permanent arbitrator in an industry is evidence that labor-management relations have reached a relatively high degree of maturity. One arbitrator noted that in his experience permanent umpireships and mature collective bargaining relationships are related, but that it is unclear which is cause and which is effect.[13]

In a presentation at the Fiftieth Annual Meeting of the National Academy of Arbitrators, Abe Rosner, National Representative, Canadian Auto Workers Union, Montreal, Quebec, discussed the unique process of handling disputes under the Canadian Railway System.[14] Mr. Rosner noted that over a 30-year period his union has relied on the arbitral skills of two "permanent" arbitrators.

---

[11]For example, the permanent umpire under the 1979 General Motors-United Auto Workers (GM-UAW) agreement "shall serve during the term of his contract for as long as he continues to be acceptable to both parties," where the Ford-UAW agreement provided that the umpire "shall continue to serve only so long as he continues to be acceptable to both parties." *Pitta v. Hotel Ass'n of New York City*, 806 F.2d 419, 124 LRRM 2109 (2d Cir. 1986); *Gallagher & Burk*, 91 LA 1217, 1221 (Richman, 1988). For factors that might affect the tenure or "survival" of a permanent arbitrator, see FLEMING, THE LABOR ARBITRATION PROCESS 219–20 (Univ. of Ill. Press 1965). In *Greater N.Y. Health Care Facilities Ass'n v. Service Employees Local 144*, 492 F. Supp. 578, 106 LRRM 2176 (S.D.N.Y. 1980), the collective bargaining agreement defined the permanent arbitrator's jurisdiction very broadly, and the court held that he was the proper arbitrator to interpret the agreement's termination-of-arbitrator clause and rule on one party's effort to terminate him against the wishes of the other party. The court rejected the contention that his pecuniary interest in continued employment disqualified him from ruling on his own termination.

[12]In the 1986 Agreement between the American Federation of Labor-Congress of Industrial Organizations (AFL-CIO) Building and Construction Trades Department and Ohbayashi Corporation for the construction of the $800 million automobile assembly plant built for the Toyota Motor Corporation in Georgetown, Kentucky, the parties provided for the selection of two permanent arbitrators to avoid any work interruptions. Under the agreement, the parties agreed that all jurisdictional disputes would be submitted to one of the permanent arbitrators within 72 hours. The agreement also provided that the decision of the permanent arbitrator would be rendered within 24 hours after the conclusion of the expedited hearing and would be final and binding on the parties. The parties included the same arbitration procedure in several subsequent Toyota construction contracts in the Georgetown, Kentucky, area.

[13]Sherman, *Unique Problems and Opportunities of Permanent Umpireships—A Panel Discussion: Part III., in* ARBITRATION 1989: THE ARBITRATOR'S DISCRETION DURING AND AFTER THE HEARING, PROCEEDINGS OF THE 42D ANNUAL MEETING OF NAA 185, 188 (Gruenberg ed., BNA Books 1990).

[14]Rosner, *By Land and by Air: Two Models of Expedited Grievance Resoluton: II. Ad Hoc Arbitration on Canadian Railways, in* ARBITRATION 1997: THE NEXT FIFTY YEARS, PROCEEDINGS OF THE 50TH ANNUAL MEETING OF NAA 115 (Najita ed., BNA Books 1998). In this discussion of the method in which grievances are arbitrated by the Canadian Auto Workers in the Canadian Railway System, Rosner points out the virtue of consistently naming the same group of ad hoc arbitrators in order to decrease the learning curve in the complicated railway industry. Rosner highlighted the prearbitration process, which requires extensive prehearing preparation by the parties. At the hearing, each party arrives with a written brief that contains evidence, argument, and references to authorities. *See also* NAA 50TH PROCEEDINGS, ch. 6.

A permanent arbitrator usually is called either an "impartial umpire" or "impartial chairman." The impartial umpire usually sits alone and has a function similar to that of a temporary arbitrator, except that the umpire is appointed to consider all arbitrable disputes that arise during the span of his or her tenure. The umpire generally is not commissioned to mediate, but has a quasi-judicial function in the sense that the umpire is charged with adjudicating contract disputes.[15]

An impartial chairman, however, usually sits as the only impartial member of an arbitration board. Often the impartial chairman is commissioned to be something more than an arbitrator, although the functions vary considerably from industry to industry. The impartial chairman may be authorized to mediate, and, where this is the case, will arbitrate only as a last resort after other methods for resolving the dispute have failed. But when the impartial chairman does find it necessary to assume the role of an arbitrator, he or she may then be restricted to contract interpretation and application.

The type of situation to which the use of a permanent arbitrator is especially well adapted is indicated in the recommendation of the factfinding board appointed by the Secretary of Labor to serve in connection with an International Harvester Company dispute:

> While the Board believes that a permanent umpire system of arbitration would be more desirable here because of the complexity of the issues involved in the numerous grievances which have arisen under the recently expired contract, as witnessed by cases involving these grievances which have come before the National War Labor Board, we hesitate to recommend provision for a permanent umpire system in the contract unless by agreement of the parties. We recommend that the parties give serious consideration to naming an arbitrator in the contract, whose term of office would extend for the life of the agreement unless otherwise changed by mutual agreement. We believe that the value of the services of an arbitrator to the industrial relations welfare of the parties may be considerably enhanced by the experience gained through more frequent contact with the shop practices prevailing in the various International Harvester plants and the characteristics of the company's wage and incentive system than would be possible under an ad hoc arrangement.[16]

Accepting the above recommendation, the parties established a permanent umpire system at International Harvester. One informed observer has been quoted as saying that it "proved to be the turning point in bringing order out of chaos in the field of contract interpretation."[17]

The use of permanent labor-management arbitrators in the United States has its roots in industries where justice had to be dispensed on a large scale, such as the clothing and manufacturing industries of the 1920s, and later the mass production industries organized by the CIO unions in the 1930s.[18]

---

[15]Exceptions to this general rule are noted in Sherman, NAA 42D Proceedings, at 188. An interesting variation is the "Impartial Advisor," whose authority is not only restricted to agreement interpretation but is also limited to making findings and recommendations only. New York City Transit Auth., 27 LA 838 (Stark, 1955).

[16]International Harvester Co., 1 LA 512, 522 (Marshall, Spencer, & Holly, 1946).

[17]Reilly, *Arbitration's Impact on Bargaining*, 16 LA 987, 990 (1951).

[18]Goldstein, *Unique Problems and Opportunities of Permanent Umpireships—A Panel Discussion: Part II., in* Arbitration 1989: The Arbitrator's Discretion During and After the Hearing, Proceedings of the 42D Annual Meeting of NAA 178, 180 (Gruenberg ed., BNA

Cases heard before permanent arbitrators could be handled in less time than cases before ad hoc arbitrators because the procedural ground rules had already been set, and consistency of result could be expected by the parties.[19]

Some industries have had umpire systems since the turn of the twentieth century. The anthracite coal industry, for instance, established a permanent system in 1903. However, permanent arbitrator provisions appear rather infrequently in collective bargaining agreements.[20] Sometimes, though, particular industries, such as the full-fashioned hosiery industry, have selected permanent arbitrators.[21]

The Daimler-Chrysler Corporation uses an appeal board consisting of two representatives of each of the parties and an impartial chairman. The partisan members of the appeal board first attempt to settle all grievances properly referred to the board. If the partisan members are unable to settle a matter, it is decided by the impartial chairman.[22]

Sometimes permanent umpire panels are maintained, as, for instance, in the case of United States Steel.[23] Umpires are called in turn from these panels. Sometimes recommended decisions are made by individual members of a panel, subject to approval by another member thereof.[24]

Books 1990). *See also* Nolan & Abrams, *American Labor Arbitration: The Early Years*, 35 U. Fla. L. Rev. 373 (1983).

[19]Goldstein, NAA 42D Proceedings, at 181.

[20]A study of 400 sample collective bargaining agreements found that only 4% had permanent arbitrator provisions. Basic Patterns in Union Contracts 38 (BNA Books 14th ed. 1995).

[21]*See* Kennedy, Effective Labor Arbitration 20, 24 (1948).

[22]For a detailed discussion of the appeal board, see Wolff, Crane & Cole, *The Chrysler-UAW Umpire System, in* The Arbitrator and the Parties, Proceedings of the 11th Annual Meeting of NAA 111 (McKelvey ed., BNA Books 1958). The discussion is followed by comments comparing the Ford and GM umpire systems with that at Chrysler. Platt, *The Chrysler-UAW Umpire System: Discussion, id.* at 141; Feinsinger, *id.* at 146. *See also* Killingsworth & Wallen, NAA 17th Proceedings, at 56 (comparing Ford, Chrysler, and GM); *Chrysler Procedure*, 29 LA 885 (1958). In 1963, the Chrysler procedure of using only signed written statements as evidence was changed to receive evidence in a manner customary in most arbitration proceedings. *See* Jones & Smith, *Management and Labor Appraisals and Criticisms of the Arbitration Process: A Report With Comments*, 62 Mich. L. Rev. 1115, 1129 (1964).

[23]*See* Fischer, *The Fine Art of Engineering an Arbitration System to Fit the Needs of the Parties: IV. The Steelworkers Union and the Steel Companies, in* Arbitration of Subcontracting and Wage Incentive Disputes, Proceedings of the 32D Annual Meeting of NAA 198 (Stern & Dennis eds., BNA Books 1980); Killingsworth, *Arbitration: Its Uses in Industrial Relations*, 21 LA 859, 860 (1953).

[24]*See, e.g.,* Bethlehem Steel Corp., 91 LA 789 (Oldham, 1988); Arch on the Green, 89 LA 895, 895–96 (Seidman, 1987); North River Energy Co., 88 LA 447, 451–53 (Witney, 1987); United States Steel Corp., 68 LA 1094 (Rimer, Jr., 1977); Bethlehem Steel Co., 47 LA 270 (Gill & Seward, 1966). In certain circumstances the parties waive the review and approval requirement. *See* Bethlehem Steel Co., 37 LA 143, 144 (Valtin, 1961). The newspaper industry has utilized a procedure for appellate review of local arbitrators' awards. *See* Stark, *The Presidential Address: Theme and Adaptations, in* Truth, Lie Detectors, and Other Problems in Labor Arbitration, Proceedings of the 31st Annual Meeting of NAA 1, 12–13 (Stern & Dennis eds., BNA Books 1979); McLellan, *The Appellate Process in the International Arbitration Agreement Between the American Newspaper Publishers Association and the International Printing Pressmen, in* Arbitration of Interest Disputes, Proceedings of the 26th Annual Meeting of NAA 53 (Dennis & Somers eds., BNA Books 1974); Newspaper Agency Corp., 43 LA 1233 (Platt, 1964). The coal industry similarly has utilized arbitral appellate review procedures. *See* Selby, *The Fine Art of Engineering an Arbitration System to Fit the Needs of the Parties: IV. The United Mine Workers and Bituminous Coal Operators' Association, in* Arbitration of Subcontracting and Wage Incentive Disputes, Proceedings of the 32D Annual Meeting of NAA 181 (Stern & Dennis eds., BNA Books 1980); Valtin, *The Bituminous Coal*

i. Advantages

Many persons active as arbitrators or as students of arbitration feel that great value is to be realized from the use of a permanent arbitrator. One arbitrator, for instance, urged that ad hoc arbitration should be looked upon, at best, as a transitory method and as entailing comparative disadvantages. "As a support for industrial relations stability, a permanent arbitrator is a prime requisite. Out of the continuing relationship, consistent policy and mutually acceptable procedures can gradually be evolved."[25]

Because a permanent arbitrator is appointed in advance, no time need be lost in selecting one after a dispute arises. Moreover, advance selection permits time for careful consideration of the arbitrator's qualifications of impartiality, skill, and knowledge of labor-management relations. The permanent arbitrator usually is selected by the highly desirable method of mutual choice of the parties, rather than by some outside person or agency.

A permanent arbitrator becomes familiar with the provisions of the parties' agreement and comes to know the parties' day-to-day relationships and their circumstances, personalities, and customary practices. The importance of this knowledge was emphasized by Umpire Harry Shulman:

> An opportunity should be provided, if possible, for the arbitrator by continuous association with the parties, or at least by repeated association with the parties, to get to know them better. A good many disputes that come to arbitration are deceptive. . . . Some are deceptive even because they don't really portray what the parties are concerned about. They seem to be fighting about one thing, and actually it is something else which is bothering them. That kind of thing happens, at least in my experience, quite frequently. A grievance is filed partly as a sort of pressure technique. It is filed partly in order to lay a foundation for a claim subsequently to be made. An arbitrator who doesn't know and doesn't sense what he is getting into, what a decision one way or the other will lead to in the developing strategy, might find himself regretting subsequently, when he finds out what the parties were really after—regretting he made that kind of determination. And so an arbitrator who is in continuous association with the parties may be in a better position to realize what the parties are really fighting for rather than what they appear to be fighting for.[26]

Economic considerations favor the use of a permanent umpire, particularly if the parties generate a large number of disputes that must be arbitrated. With increased knowledge of the parties' relationship, the perma-

---

Experiment, 29 Lab. L.J. 469 (1978). However, that industry ultimately abandoned use of its Arbitration Review Board. Valtin, *The Coal Mediation Experiment: What's It About and What's Happened?, in* Proceedings of 4th Annual Seminar, Arbitration in the Coal Industry 4 (1981) (examination of the grievance mediation experiment that was subsequently commenced by some areas of the industry). Although the Arbitration Review Board was abandoned, pursuant to Article XXIII, Section (k) of the 1981 and subsequent agreements, the 207 awards decided under the 1974 and the 1978 agreements have precedential effect and have been followed by the panel arbitrators. Sharpe, *A Study of Coal Arbitration Under the National Bituminous Coal Wage Agreement Between 1975 and 1990*, 93 W. Va. L. Rev. 497, 503 (1991).

[25]Taylor, *Effectuating the Labor Contract Through Arbitration, in* The Profession of Labor Arbitration, Selected Papers From the First Seven Annual Meetings of NAA 20, 40 (McKelvey ed., BNA Books 1957).

[26]Conference on Training of Law Students in Labor Relations: Vol. III. Transcript of Proceedings 710–11 (1947).

nent arbitrator is able to shorten hearings, knows many details from the outset, and does not require time to establish or debate procedural ground rules.[27] Being familiar with the parties and the industry in which they operate, the arbitrator needs less time for investigating. For the same reason, time is saved in the preparation of opinions. Naturally, the saving of time results in a reduction of costs.

Permanent arbitrators make their awards available for the guidance of the parties. Cases that do not involve new issues or new situations are likely to be settled at early stages of the grievance procedure, because the parties know how the arbitrator has decided similar disputes. Thus, one effect of a decision covering a disputed point may be its application by the parties themselves to other disputes involving the same issue. The awards of a permanent arbitrator generally will be consistent with one another, thus avoiding the confusion that sometimes results from having two or more temporary arbitrators rule on similar issues.[28]

Permanent arbitrators have special reason for concern regarding the ultimate effect of each decision. They expect to continue to serve the parties after each decision is rendered and expect to be confronted time and again by their own decisions. The situation is somewhat different with temporary arbitrators, who, while in good conscience are eager to render sound awards, serve with the realization that they may never again have contact with the parties.

ii. Disadvantages

If not a disadvantage, then certainly the limited number of mutually acceptable, highly qualified, and available arbitrators presents a problem to be faced by parties electing to employ a permanent arbitrator. Any arbitrator given tenure of office should not only be thoroughly experienced but also should be able to inspire a high degree of confidence in both parties. The field is necessarily limited.

The establishment of a permanent umpire system may tempt the parties to take a short-cut route to dispute settlement. There is a danger that the parties will be too quick to turn to the permanent arbitrator,[29] who, once

---

[27]Goldstein, *Unique Problems and Opportunities of Permanent Umpireships—A Panel Discussion: Part II., in* Arbitration 1989: The Arbitrator's Discretion During and After the Hearing, Proceedings of the 42d Annual Meeting of NAA 178, 180–85 (Gruenberg ed., BNA Books 1990). Permanent umpireships are inherently better able to maintain the simple and expeditious procedure that is the hallmark of arbitration than ad hoc arbitration, which faces ever-growing legalism and a resulting increase in cost and time before the final decision. *Id.* at 182–83.

[28]*Id.* at 181.

[29]Concerning the serious effort by the UAW to screen grievances headed for the umpire at GM, see Dunne, *The UAW Board of Review on Umpire Appeals at General Motors*, 17 Arb. J. 162 (1962). *See also* Stark, *The Presidential Address: Theme and Adaptations, in* Truth, Lie Detectors, and Other Problems in Labor Arbitration, Proceedings of the 31st Annual Meeting of NAA 1, 5 (Stern & Dennis eds., BNA Books 1979). Stark explained that many of the grievances that are sent to arbitration by the UAW are settled in an "unwritten 'shakeout' step" at which GM and UAW staff representatives and officers "whittle away at the arbitration docket"; in 1 year, 214,000 grievances were filed, of which 1,150 were sent to arbitration and fewer than 50 were actually arbitrated.

selected, is easily available. Arbitration should not be substituted for negotiation—the labor relations process is harmed when the parties fail to exhaust all possibilities of settlement at the prearbitration steps of the grievance procedure.

The use of a permanent arbitrator may obligate the parties in advance
of need to substantial expense. The arbitrator may charge a retainer fee that
must be paid regardless of whether the arbitration services are utilized.[30]
Other disadvantages where permanent arbitrators are used include a tendency by management and labor to "keep score" of arbitral results and make
decisions regarding the arbitrator's retention on that basis rather than on
the fairness of the awards.[31]

3. Danger of Favoritism or of "Splitting" Awards

Whether a permanent or temporary arbitrator system is chosen, both
labor and management should be quick to disown any arbitrator who appears to be playing favorites or appears to have the faintest taint of prejudice in favor of either party.[32] Arbitration maintains its legitimacy only if
decisions are rendered on the merits. There is a danger that the arbitrator
might acquire a bias in favor of one side or the other, or go to the other
extreme and, in a desire to please both parties, render approximately the
same number of awards for each side. In common parlance, this is known as
"splitting" awards.[33]

Some believe that a temporary arbitrator is less likely to acquire a bias
in favor of either side and is in a better position to decide cases impartially
on the merits. But, it is also argued that the relative stability of the permanent arbitrator relationship is the best insurance for decisions on the merits.
Each of these conclusions is debatable.[34]

---

[30]Sometimes a retainer is provided in addition to a certain sum per case. For a discussion of the pros and cons of the use of permanent arbitrators, see Simkin & Kennedy, *Arbitration of Grievances* (U.S. Dep't of Labor, Div. of Labor Standards, Bull. No. 82, 1946).

[31]Zack, *Unique Problems and Opportunities of Permanent Umpireships—A Panel Discussion, Part I.,* in Arbitration 1989: The Arbitrator's Discretion During and After the Hearing, Proceedings of the 42d Annual Meeting of NAA 176, 177 (Gruenberg ed., BNA Books
1990); Goldstein, *Part II., id.* at 178, 179; Sherman, *Part III., id.* at 185, 187.

[32]Balancing the number of awards in favor of labor against the number of awards in
favor of management is not necessarily a valid indicator of whether the arbitrator is playing
favorites or is prejudiced in favor of either party. *See* Dilts & Deitsch, *Arbitration Win/Loss
Rates as a Measure of Arbitrator Neutrality,* 44 Arb. J. 42 (1989).

[33]As a group, arbitrators reject any suggestion of splitting awards, though the possibility
has been recognized. *See* Jones & Smith, *Management and Labor Appraisals and Criticisms
of the Arbitration Process: A Report With Comments,* 62 Mich. L. Rev. 1115, 1148–49 (1964).

[34]Shaw, *The National Labor Relations Act: 1935–1985: II. The Pendulum Swings,* in
Arbitration 1985: Law and Practice, Proceedings of the 38th Annual Meeting of NAA 67,
79–80 (Gershenfeld ed., BNA Books 1986); Davey, *Hazards in Labor Arbitration,* 1 Indus. &
Lab. Rel. Rev. 386, 394 n.22 (1948). One survey indicated that among those parties that do
believe that cases are not always decided on their merits, "the fear of excessive compromise
is greatest in a series of cases tried in succession before the same arbitrator, or where there
is a permanent arbitrator." Eaton, *Labor Arbitration in the San Francisco Bay Area,* 48 LA
1381, 1387 (1967). Danger of splitting awards has been rejected as grounds for resisting the
simultaneous arbitration of several grievances before the same arbitrator. Koehring Div., 46
LA 827, 830 (King, 1966).

Of course, arbitrators themselves have an affirmative obligation to disclose dealings or relationships that might affect their impartiality.[35] Possibly, there has been too much concern over this matter. Faith in the integrity and sound judgment of arbitrators, and in their ability to "see through" attempts to obtain decisions not based on the merits, generally has been justified. If adequate evidence is produced showing that an arbitrator is not deciding issues on the merits, the parties need lose no time in terminating his or her services. This matter was given special consideration by the late Harry Shulman. His splendid analysis and expression of views leaves little more to be said:

> Another, and perhaps less lofty thought, should be expressed. There seems to be a feeling on the part of some that a party can win a greater number of cases if it presents a greater number for decision, the assumption being that some purposeful percentage is maintained. There are many reasons why this point of view is wholly unsound. No umpire should be retained in office if he is really believed to be making decisions on such a basis. An umpire should be employed only so long as he renders decisions on the basis of his best and honest judgment on the merits of the controversies presented, and only so long as both parties believe that he does so. If he is believed to be making his decisions on a percentage basis, the remedy is to put him out of office rather than to give him more cases for arbitrary decision.
>
> Moreover, as anyone concerned with industrial relations thoroughly knows, there is a great deal of room in the relation between a company and its employees for honest and reasonable differences of opinion on important questions of interpretation and application. If only such questions were brought to an umpire, their normal, honest determinations could fairly be expected in proper course to fall on both sides of the line. A purposeful percentage would be as unnecessary as it would be dishonest.
>
> From the selfish point of view of a party, there is a great advantage in appealing only cases believed to be entirely good rather than indiscriminately appealing many cases for the purpose of winning a percentage. When a party brings only strong cases, it breeds in others a feeling of confidence in its judgment and in its reasonableness which may tip the scales in cases of doubt and give it a considerable advantage at the start. If, on the other hand, a party brings

---

[35]Commonwealth Coatings Corp. v. Continental Cas. Co., 393 U.S. 145 (1968) (business dealings); Morelite Constr. Corp. v. Carpenters Benefit Funds New York City Dist. Council, 748 F.2d 79, 117 LRRM 3009 (2d Cir. 1984) (family relationship); CODE OF PROF'L RESPONSIBILITY FOR ARBITRATORS OF LABOR-MANAGEMENT DISPUTES §2.B (2000) (CODE OF PROF'L RESPONSIBILITY); AMERICAN ARBITRATION ASSOCIATION (AAA), LABOR ARBITRATION RULES, Rules 11, 17 (2000); Revised Uniform Arbitration Act (RUAA) (2000), 7 U.L.A. §12 (Supp. 2001). *See also* Gershenfeld, *Professional Responsibilities of Arbitrators: Part II. Disclosure and Recusement— When to Tell and When to Leave, in* ARBITRATION 1991: THE CHANGING FACE OF ARBITRATION IN THEORY AND PRACTICE, PROCEEDINGS OF THE 44TH ANNUAL MEETING OF NAA 218 (Gruenberg ed., BNA Books 1992); Porter, *Professional Responsibilities of Arbitrators: Part III. Arbitral Neutrality and Accounts Receivable, id.* at 230; Caraway, *The Arbitrator's Responsibility to the Parties: Part I. The Duty to Disclose, in* ARBITRATION 1990: NEW PERSPECTIVES ON OLD ISSUES, PROCEEDINGS OF THE 43D ANNUAL MEETING OF NAA 215 (Gruenberg ed., BNA Books 1991); Page, *The Arbitrator's Duty to Disclose:* Morelite Construction v. Carpenters Benefit Funds, *in* PROCEEDINGS OF NEW YORK UNIVERSITY 38TH ANNUAL NATIONAL CONFERENCE OF LABOR 14-1 (Adelman ed. 1985). *But see* Umana v. Swidler & Berlin, 745 A.2d 334, 341 (D.C. Cir. 2000) (following a narrow interpretation of *Commonwealth* and finding that without "concrete, current or close links" to a party, the court should be reluctant to set aside arbitration awards for reasons of bias); Kiewit v. Electrical Workers (IBEW) Local 103, 76 F. Supp. 2d 77, 80 (D. Mass. 1999) (interpreting the *Commonwealth* decision to apply only to direct business dealings, where the instance in *Kiewit* dealt with alleged bias that was one level removed).

cases carelessly, without substantial evidence and without apparent judgment in selection, it tends to breed in others a lack of confidence in its judgment which starts it off with a considerable disadvantage. This is particularly true in the "did or didn't he" type of case. In such cases where the evidence is not conclusive, there is little to go on except the conflicting testimony of witnesses and the confidence in the parties developed over a period of time as a result of the record of their own selections.[36]

4. MEDIATION BY PERMANENT ARBITRATORS [LA CDI 94.03; 100.06]

As previously noted, impartial chairmen often are commissioned to try to bring about settlement of differences through mediation. Sometimes an impartial umpire also exercises this function. The impartial chairman for the full-fashioned hosiery industry has acted as a mediator as well as an arbitrator.[37] The impartial chairman for the men's clothing industry in New York City has had the duty of continuing negotiations concerning disputes and of deciding issues only if agreement is not reached through such negotiations.[38]

During his tenure with the Ford Motor Company, Umpire Harry Shulman performed some mediation functions, as he once explained:

> The Umpire's contractual jurisdiction is limited to the interpretation, application or alleged violation of the terms of the parties' written agreements, with few exceptions. But, as the parties and I came to know each other better, my actual functions were greatly expanded. With the full consent of both sides, I conferred with the parties separately and jointly on diverse problems outside that contractual jurisdiction, sat with them as mutual friend and adviser in their negotiations of amendments and supplements, spoke at educational classes and other union meetings, and was generally available for such help as a well-intentioned mutual friend could give in the interest of the total enterprise.[39]

---

[36]Ford Motor Co., 1 ALAA ¶67,274 at 67,620 (Shulman, 1945). *See also* National Mine Serv. Co., 69 LA 966, 969 (Amis, 1977); Servel, Inc., 1 LA 163, 165 (Ferguson, 1945). Summarizing the results of a study by Geoffrey R. King to determine the extent of union success in arbitration, see Note, *Union Success in Arbitration*, 33 ARB. J. 45 (June, 1978), in which of 4,990 cases reported between 1960 and 1970 in *LA Reports* and germane to the study (interest disputes, split decisions, and interunion disputes were excluded as not germane), the union won 42.7%. For a broad discussion of the need for joint acceptability of arbitrators by the parties and its influence on the arbitration process, see Ryder, *The Impact of Acceptability on the Arbitrator*, in DEVELOPMENTS IN AMERICAN AND FOREIGN ARBITRATION, PROCEEDINGS OF THE 21ST ANNUAL MEETING OF NAA 94 (Rehmus ed., BNA Books 1968); Prashker, *Discussion, id.* at 108; Kleiman, *id.* at 112; Platt, *id.* at 118.

[37]KENNEDY, EFFECTIVE LABOR ARBITRATION 20, 57 (1948).

[38]MORGAN, ARBITRATION IN THE MEN'S CLOTHING INDUSTRY IN NEW YORK CITY 1, 5 (1940). For a discussion of the impartial chairman in the men's clothing industry, see Nolan, *The Labor Arbitrator's Several Roles*, 44 MD. L. REV. 873, 874–79 (1985). *See also* Nolan & Abrams, *American Labor Arbitration: The Early Years*, 35 U. FLA. L. REV. 373, 393–94 (1983).

[39]SHULMAN, OPINIONS OF THE UMPIRE 3 (1943–1946). Describing the varied role of permanent arbitrator Richard Mittenthal and his close relationship with the parties, see Meyer, *The Fine Art of Engineering an Arbitration System to Fit the Needs of the Parties: II. The Teamsters and Anheuser-Busch*, in ARBITRATION OF SUBCONTRACTING AND WAGE INCENTIVE DISPUTES, PROCEEDINGS OF THE 32D ANNUAL MEETING OF NAA 174, 179 (Stern & Dennis eds., BNA Books 1980). Stressing the value of neutrals who have been "mediator-arbitrator-advisers to the parties," one arbitrator expressed concern that "the rise of professional staff in labor and management organizations, and the growing legalisms of many aspects of industrial relations, have led to much more limited roles for most neutrals" in recent years. Dunlop, *The Industrial Relations Universe, in* ARBITRATION—1976, PROCEEDINGS OF THE 29TH ANNUAL MEETING OF NAA 12, 15 (Dennis & Somers eds., BNA Books 1976).

Shulman also observed that sometimes the parties may press the umpire to decide issues that might be left undecided, or at least delayed, until time and experience provide greater assurance of wise judgment. "In cases of this character, and others in which the arbitrator conscientiously feels baffled, it may be much wiser to permit him to mediate between the parties for an acceptable solution."[40] Mediation also has been advocated as an effective problem-solving technique in labor-management relations by some commentators.[41]

One of the strongest advocates of mediation by permanent arbitrators was Dr. George W. Taylor. It was his belief that collective bargaining should be carried on through the arbitration step and that the essential task of most chairmen is to bring about a meeting of minds, if possible.[42] His view of the impartial chairman's office was expressed as follows:

> An impartial chairman, then, is first of all a mediator. But he is a very special kind of mediator. He has a reserve power to decide the case either by effectuating his own judgment or by joining with one of the partisan board members to make a majority decision, depending upon the procedure designated by the agreement. A new reason for labor and management to agree is introduced—to avoid a decision. By bringing in a fresh viewpoint, moreover, the impartial chairman may be able to assist the parties in working out their problem in a mutually satisfactory manner. To me, such a result has always seemed to be highly preferable to a decision that is unacceptable to either of the parties. What's wrong per se about an agreement when agreeing is the essence of collective bargaining?[43]

Taylor recognized the widespread belief among labor relations professionals that an arbitrator should not mediate, and he hastened to warn that the impartial chairman approach is not universally applicable; "it is only usable when both parties see eye-to-eye on the point."[44] It is interesting to note that over one-third of all problems presented to Taylor as impartial chairman of the full-fashioned hosiery industry were settled by agreement of the parties.[45] A criticism of that office after Taylor stepped down was in regard to the decreased number of such voluntary settlements.[46]

The combination of arbitration and mediation functions has been criticized by those who believe that there should be a clear distinction between the two, and that the usefulness of arbitrators is reduced when they attempt

---

[40]Shulman, *Reason, Contract, and Law in Labor Relations*, 68 HARV. L. REV. 999, 1022–23 (1955), *reprinted in* MANAGEMENT RIGHTS AND THE ARBITRATION PROCESS, PROCEEDINGS OF THE 9TH ANNUAL MEETING OF NAA 169, 197 (McKelvey ed., BNA Books 1957). *See also* Schlossberg, *Challenge and Change, in* ARBITRATION 1987: THE ACADEMY AT FORTY, PROCEEDINGS OF THE 40TH ANNUAL MEETING OF NAA 13 (Gruenberg ed., BNA Books 1988).

[41]Dunlop, *The Neutral in Industrial Relations Revisited, in* ARBITRATION 1991: THE CHANGING FACE OF ARBITRATION IN THEORY AND PRACTICE, PROCEEDINGS OF THE 44TH ANNUAL MEETING OF NAA 26 (Gruenberg ed., BNA Books 1992); Silberman, *Breaking the Mold of Grievance Resolution: A Pilot Program in Mediation*, 44 ARB. J. 40 (Dec. 1989).

[42]Taylor, *Effectuating the Labor Contract Through Arbitration, in* THE PROFESSION OF LABOR ARBITRATION, SELECTED PAPERS FROM THE FIRST SEVEN ANNUAL MEETINGS OF NAA 20, 35 (McKelvey ed., BNA Books 1957).

[43]*Id.*

[44]*Id.* at 36.

[45]KENNEDY, EFFECTIVE LABOR ARBITRATION 28 (1948).

[46]*Id.* at 216.

to mediate.[47] One problem is that often disclosures will be made by a party in the course of mediation that would not be made to the neutral functioning solely as arbitrator.

In some umpire systems, neither party wishes the umpire to act as a mediator at any time.[48] Furthermore, an umpire system might utilize mediation for a time but the parties ultimately might come to favor the adjudication approach to decisionmaking rather than the mediation approach, as has been said to be true both at GM and at Ford.[49]

With respect to temporary arbitrators, it appears reasonably clear that most parties ordinarily prefer that the arbitrator not attempt mediation.[50] At least one commentator, however, offered the opinion that the mediation of interest disputes is "the way of the future in industrial relations."[51]

The *Code of Professional Responsibility* for arbitrators recognizes that (1) an arbitrator may be appointed on the basis that some mediation role is expected, and (2) an arbitrator may undertake mediation after arbitration has been "invoked" if neither party objects, either at the request of a party or at the arbitrator's own suggestion, provided it can be discerned that both parties are likely to be responsive.[52]

---

[47]For a collection of views expressed in opposition to Taylor's, see Braden, *The Function of the Arbitrator in Labor-Management Disputes*, 4 Arb. J. (N.S.) 35 (1949). For very strong criticism of the Taylor view, see O'Connell, *Should the Scope of Arbitration Be Restricted?*, in Proceedings of the 18th Annual Meeting of NAA 102, 103–04 (Jones ed., BNA Books 1965).

[48]*See, e.g.*, Davey, *The John Deere-UAW Permanent Arbitration System*, in Critical Issues in Labor Arbitration, Proceedings of the 10th Annual Meeting of NAA 161, 162, 185 (McKelvey ed., BNA Books 1957).

[49]*See* Killingsworth & Wallen, *Constraint and Variety in Arbitration Systems*, in Labor Arbitration Perspectives and Problems, Proceedings of the 17th Annual Meeting of NAA 56, 64, 68, 75–76 (Kahn ed., BNA Books 1964).

[50]For statistical surveys of views on the desirability of mediation by arbitrators, see Simkin & Fidandis, Mediation and the Dynamics of Collective Bargaining 179–90 (BNA Books 2d ed. 1986); Eaton, *Labor Arbitration in the San Francisco Bay Area*, 48 LA 1381, 1384 (1967); Warren & Bernstein, *A Profile of Labor Arbitration*, 16 LA 970, 981–82 (1951). For further discussion of the pros and cons of mediation by arbitrators, see LaRue & Lesnick, *Novel Roles for Arbitration and the Arbitrator: II. Transferring Arbitral Experience to Mediation: Opportunities and Pitfalls*, in Arbitration 1986: Current and Expanding Roles, Proceedings of the 39th Annual Meeting of NAA 34 (Gershenfeld ed., BNA Books 1987); Krislov, *Reports of the Research Committee: I. Academy Members' Experience With Tripartite Arbitration in the Early 1980s*, in Arbitration 1985: Law and Practice, Proceedings of the 38th Annual Meeting of NAA 255, 260–61 (Gershenfeld ed., BNA Books 1986) [hereinafter *Krislov*]; Jaffee, chair, *The Arbitration Hearing—Avoiding a Shambles: A Panel Discussion*, in Proceedings of the 18th Annual Meeting of NAA 75, 94–101 (Jones ed., BNA Books 1965); Fuller, *Collective Bargaining and the Arbitrator*, in Collective Bargaining and the Arbitrator's Role, Proceedings of the 15th Annual Meeting of NAA 8, 24–54 (Kahn ed., BNA Books 1962); Raffaele, *Needed: A Fourth Party in Industrial Relations*, 13 Lab. L.J. 230 (1962).

[51]Gold, *Mediation of Interest Disputes*, in Arbitration 1988: Emerging Issues for the 1990s, Proceedings of the 41st Annual Meeting of NAA 9 (Gruenberg ed., BNA Books 1989). See also discussion advocating mediation of interest disputes in Sigler, *Mediation of Grievances: An Alternative to Arbitration?*, 13 Employee Rel. L.J. 266 (Autumn 1987).

[52]Code of Prof'l Responsibility §2.F.; Lloyd W. Aubry Co., 91 LA 679 (Millious, 1988). *See* Hoellering, *Mediation and Arbitration: A Growing Interaction*, 52 Disp. Resol. J. 23 (1997) (discussing the growing trend among parties to arbitrations, particularly in the construction industry, to provide for a period to mediate issues prior to their arbitration). For arbitration-mediation techniques that have been generally successful for one highly regarded arbitrator, see Zack, *Avoiding the Arbitrator: Some New Alternatives to the Conventional Grievance Procedure: III. Suggested New Approaches to Grievance Arbitration*, in Arbitration—1977, Proceedings of the 30th Annual Meeting of NAA 105, 112–17 (Dennis & Somers eds., BNA Books 1978). Many state agencies established primarily to mediate interest disputes also

5. TRIPARTITE ARBITRATION BOARD

As we have seen, a tripartite arbitration board, which may be either temporary or permanent, is one made up of one or more members selected by management, an equal number selected by labor, and a neutral member who serves as chairman.[53] Because the partisan members may fail to agree on the neutral, the agreement should provide alternate methods of selection.[54]

The labor and management members generally are partisans and act as advocates for their respective sides.[55] The original *Code of Ethics and Procedural Standards for Labor-Management Arbitration* did not impose an obli-

---

provide mediation assistance for grievances. *See* O'Grady, *Grievance Mediation Activities by State Agencies*, 31 ARB. J. 125 (1976). In Canada, the British Columbia Labour Board, with centralized authority to administer the entire body of labor law, has an arbitration procedure primarily utilizing mediation rather than adjudication. Weiler, *Avoiding the Arbitrator: Some New Alternatives to the Conventional Grievance Procedure: I. The Role of the Labour Board as an Alternative to Arbitration*, NAA 30TH PROCEEDINGS, at 72, 79 (Dennis & Somers eds., BNA Books 1978). Regarding the potential for greater use of grievance mediation in the United States, see Sigler, *Mediation of Grievances: An Alternative to Arbitration?*, 13 EMPLOYEE REL. L.J. 266 (1987); Goldberg, *The Mediation of Grievances Under a Collective Bargaining Contract: An Alternative to Arbitration*, 77 NW. U. L. REV. 270 (1982).

[53]For discussion of tripartite boards, see Veglahn, *Grievance Arbitration by Arbitration Boards: A Survey of the Parties*, 42 ARB. J. 47 (1987); *Krislov, supra* note 50, at 260–61; Zack, *Tripartite Interest and Grievance Arbitration: I. Tripartite Panels: Asset or Hindrance in Dispute Settlement?*, *in* ARBITRATION ISSUES FOR THE 1990S, PROCEEDINGS OF THE 34TH ANNUAL MEETING OF NAA 273 (Stern & Dennis eds., BNA Books 1982); Rehmus, *II. Tripartite Arbitration: Old Strengths and New Weaknesses, id.* at 284; Gromfine, *Comment, id.* at 288; Schnapp, *Comment, id.* at 295; Smith, *The Search for Truth: I. The Search for Truth—The Whole Truth, in* TRUTH, LIE DETECTORS, AND OTHER PROBLEMS IN LABOR ARBITRATION, PROCEEDINGS OF THE 31ST ANNUAL MEETING OF NAA 40, 57–59 (Stern & Dennis eds., BNA Books 1979); Davey, *The Uses and Misuses of Tripartite Boards in Grievance Arbitration, in* DEVELOPMENTS IN AMERICAN AND FOREIGN ARBITRATION, PROCEEDINGS OF THE 21ST ANNUAL MEETING OF NAA 152–79 (Rehmus ed., BNA Books 1968). *See also* Spitko, *Gone but Not Conforming: Protecting the Abhorrent Testator From Majoritarian Cultural Norms Through Minority-Culture Arbitration*, 49 CASE W. RES. L. REV. 275, 312 (1990). For the views of other observers, see *The Uses and Misuses of Tripartite Boards in Grievance Arbitration: Workshop Sessions*, NAA 21ST PROCEEDINGS, at 180–97.

[54]In *Sam Kane Packing Co. v. Meat Cutters Local 171*, 477 F.2d 1128, 83 LRRM 2298 (5th Cir. 1973), the employer arbitrator refused to participate in the selection of a neutral and the union arbitrator thereupon issued an award; the court vacated the award, stating that the proper remedy was an action to secure appointment of a neutral rather than an ex parte award by a party member. For commentary, see also Rios, *Mandatory Arbitration Agreements: Do They Protect Employers From Adjudicating Title VII Claims?*, 31 ST. MARY'S L.J. 199, 239 (1999) (citing *Kane* in discussion of structural bias in arbitration procedures).

[55]University of Cincinnati, 99 LA 1060, 1062 (Ferree, 1992). Sometimes they even present the evidence and argument for their respective sides, no other representatives being used. *See* Pfeiffer Brewing Co., 16 LA 89, 90 (Smith, 1951). When they thus serve as counsel, they might agree to make the neutral the sole arbitrator. *See* United Tavern, 16 LA 210, 211 (Slavney, 1951). In *Edmund E. Garrison, Inc. v. Operating Engineers Locals 137, 137A & 137B*, 283 F. Supp. 771, 68 LRRM 2249 (S.D.N.Y. 1968), the employer's appointees to the arbitration board were himself and his attorney (who the court said was as closely related to the dispute as the employer). The union would not voluntarily accept such complete merger of roles and the court would not compel it to do so. The court said that party arbitrators need not be neutral, but a party could not appoint himself. Even aside from the fact that one of the relevant agreements prohibited parties to the dispute from serving on the board, the court believed that such a limitation applies by arbitration custom. Additionally, a system board member may not serve as a witness in the same case. Northwest Airlines, 89 LA 484, 487 (Flagler, 1987). It has also been held that an award issued by a joint arbitration board will not be vacated if the "parties" member does not vote for the "parties interest." Teamsters Local 814 v. J&B Sys. Installers & Moving, 878 F.2d 38, 131 LRRM 2799 (2d Cir. 1989); Tongay v. Kroger Co., 860 F.2d 298, 129 LRRM 2752 (8th Cir. 1988).

gation of strict neutrality on the party members of tripartite boards, and the *Code of Professional Responsibility* which superseded it "does not apply to partisan representatives on tripartite boards."[56]

Thus, the impartial member is in some respects a single arbitrator, and it is something of a misnomer to call the partisan members "arbitrators." Some writers believe it would be more realistic to call them "representatives in arbitration" or use some other such title to acknowledge that the dispute is to be submitted to the neutral member, who is to act as sole arbitrator.[57] In this connection, some agreements provide that the party representatives shall be "advisory" members without voting rights, thus leaving the decision solely to the neutral.[58]

Tripartite boards often do not reach unanimous decisions.[59] In this regard, the collective bargaining agreements, statutes, and other instruments under which tripartite boards are established usually provide that a majority award of the board shall be final and binding.[60] The side whose position is favored by the neutral member generally joins the neutral in a majority award. Some agreements give the neutral member the right and responsibility of making the final decision, regardless of whether it is a majority award.[61]

---

[56]*See Code of Ethics and Procedural Standards for Labor-Management Arbitration*, 15 LA 961, 962–63, 965; *Code of Professional Responsibility for Arbitrators of Labor-Management Disputes: Preamble,* 64 LA 1319. Some state arbitration statutes expressly limit the impartiality requirement to neutrals. Similarly, party members of tripartite boards under the Railway Labor Act (RLA), 45 U.S.C. §151 et seq., "are not in legal contemplation, or in fact, supposed to be neutral arbitrators." Arnold v. United Air Lines, 296 F.2d 191, 195, 49 LRRM 2072 (7th Cir. 1961). *Accord* Steelworkers Local 1913 v. Union R.R., 648 F.2d 905, 913, 107 LRRM 2579 (3d Cir. 1981). In *Yorkaire, Inc. v. Sheet Metal Workers Local 19*, 758 F. Supp. 248, 257–58, 137 LRRM 2376 (E.D. Pa. 1990), *aff'd without opinion*, 931 F.2d 53, 137 LRRM 2384 (3d Cir. 1991), the court cited *Arnold* and *Steelworkers Local 1913* in holding that although there is an element of partiality in a panel composed of an equal number of representatives chosen by the union and the employer, it is permissible if their partiality is no more than inheres in the tripartite method of dispute resolution chosen by the parties.

[57]UPDEGRAFF & MCCOY, ARBITRATION OF LABOR DISPUTES 27 (1946). *See also* Reynard, *Drafting of Grievance and Arbitration Articles of Collective Bargaining Agreements*, 10 VAND. L. REV. 749, 757 (1957).

[58]*See Tri-Partite Arbitration: Comment From Readers*, 15 ARB. J. 49, 95 (1960). *See also* Fleming, *Reflections on the Nature of Labor Arbitration*, 61 MICH. L. REV. 1245, 1267–68 (1963).

[59]See statistics in *Procedural Aspects of Labor-Management Arbitration*, 28 LA 933, 935 (1957) (1954 statistics). Whether the decision is unanimous is irrelevant, because a majority award is always valid. FAIRWEATHER'S PRACTICE AND PROCEDURE IN LABOR ARBITRATION 515 (Schoonhoven ed., BNA Books 4th ed. 1999) (citing generally GRENIG, ALTERNATIVE DISPUTE RESOLUTION WITH FORMS §6.2 (2d ed. 1997)). *See also* LABOR AND EMPLOYMENT ARBITRATION §7.04[3] (Bornstein, Gosline, & Greenbaum eds., 2d ed. 2002).

[60]Thus, in most cases the common law rule requiring a unanimous decision does not apply. Furthermore, the U.S. Supreme Court has held that the common law unanimity rule does not apply "when the submission is one which concerns the public." City of Omaha v. Omaha Water Co., 218 U.S. 180, 192 (1909). In *LaStella v. Garcia Estates*, 331 A.2d 1, 5 (N.J. 1975), the common law unanimity rule was rejected for the private sector in New Jersey, the court holding a majority award sufficient unless the agreement to arbitrate specifies otherwise. AAA Rule 25 specifies awards by majority vote unless unanimity is expressly required. Of course, all members of a tripartite board are entitled to full participation in its deliberations and no member should be excluded without fault on its part. *See* Simons v. News Syndicate, 152 N.Y.S.2d 236, 26 LA 281 (N.Y. Sup. Ct. 1956).

[61]*See* Warren & Bernstein, *A Profile of Labor Arbitration*, 16 LA 970, 977 (1951). Similarly, a fairly common provision is that the decision of a majority of the board, or of the neutral member if a majority decision cannot be reached, shall be final and binding. *See Major Collective Bargaining Agreements: Arbitration Procedures*, at 76 (U.S. Dep't of Labor Bull. No. 1425-6, 1966).

Even where the agreement does not give the neutral this right, the parties may agree at the hearing that the neutral shall write the opinion and award, and that the same shall be final and binding on the parties (the right to dissent may be reserved),[62] or, they may agree that if no majority award is reached, the award of the neutral shall be final and binding.[63] Indeed, when arbitration commences the parties frequently agree to waive the collective bargaining agreement provision for a tripartite board and agree that the neutral is to act as sole arbitrator from the outset.[64]

A neutral member of a tripartite board who is not given authority to render a binding award without a majority vote might be faced with the necessity of compromising his or her own views, or even accepting the extreme position of one side or the other, in order to achieve a majority award.[65]

---

[62]See Schlitz Brewing Co., 51 LA 41, 42 (Bothwell, 1968); Mobil Oil Co., 46 LA 140, 140 (Hebert, 1966); Olin-Mathieson Chem. Corp., 24 LA 116, 117 (Reynard, 1955); Servel, Inc., 20 LA 684, 684 (Ferguson, undated); Detroit Bakery Employers Labor Council, 16 LA 501, 501 (Feinsinger, 1951); Republic Oil Ref. Co., 15 LA 608, 608 (Ralston, 1950).

[63]See Marathon S. Corp., 35 LA 249, 250 (Maggs, 1960); Missouri Pub. Serv. Co., 23 LA 429, 430 (Howard, 1954); Safe Bus Co., 21 LA 456, 457 (Livengood, 1953).

[64]See Transit Auth. of River City, 95 LA 137, 138–39 (Dworkin, 1990); Van Nuys Communications Co., 84 LA 881, 882 (Gentile, 1985); ITT Cont'l Baking Co., 84 LA 41 (Traynor, 1984); FMC Corp., 70 LA 683, 685 (Johannes, 1978); Monsanto Co., 68 LA 101, 103 (Dworkin, 1977); Schaefer Super Mkts., 46 LA 115, 116 (Geissinger, 1966); Perth Amboy Evening News Co., 46 LA 111, 112 (Yagoda, 1966); Mead Corp., 46 LA 70, 70 (King, 1966); Danbury Cemetery Ass'n, 42 LA 446, 446 (Stutz, 1964); United States Potash Co., 19 LA 658, 659 (Abernethy, 1952); United Tavern, 16 LA 210, 211 (Slavney, 1951). This was also done in *Food Employers Council*, 20 LA 724, 725, 730 (Van de Water, 1953), but the neutral was also authorized to call on counsel for the parties for a joint discussion of the issues brought out at the hearing. In a 1983 survey of National Academy of Arbitrators (NAA) members, about three-fourths of the respondents indicated that they were chosen as the single neutral at least once during the preceding 3 years, despite the fact that the contract called for a tripartite panel. Overall survey results showed that if the parties had not waived panels, the number of tripartite cases would have increased by about one-fourth. *Krislov, supra* note 50, at 257–58. Where the agreement called for a tripartite board but where the neutral acted throughout as sole arbitrator without a waiver of the board requirement, a court refused to enforce the award of the neutral as sole arbitrator. Hod Carriers Local 227 v. Sullivan, 221 F. Supp. 696, 54 LRRM 2548 (E.D. Ill. 1963). A waiver was found and the award of the neutral as sole arbitrator was upheld in *Minot Builders Supply Ass'n v. Teamsters Local 123*, 703 F.2d 324, 112 LRRM 3300, 3303 (8th Cir. 1983). In *Meat Cutters Local 195 v. Cross Bros. Meat Packers*, 518 F.2d 1113, 1121, 89 LRRM 2594 (3d Cir. 1975), the court held that factual issues regarding waiver of a tripartite board are for the arbitrator, and the neutral's award was upheld although it was silent concerning such waiver. In *Houston Publishers Ass'n*, 71 LA 667, 667 (Traynor, 1978), the agreement specified arbitration by a joint standing committee (two union members and two company members) and an impartial chairman, but based on the manner in which the case was submitted to him, the arbitrator "presumed" that: (1) the parties had waived the contractual provision for a tripartite board, and (2) his decision was to be final. As a precaution he added: "In the event these presumptions are incorrect then there should be appended to this award by the parties a statement as to their concurrence or non-concurrence with the award signed by the members of the joint standing committee." Similarly, in *Adams Business Forms*, 96 LA 841, 844 (Thornell, 1991), the arbitrator rejected the company's claim that the union failed to comply with the contractual requirement that the parties each select arbitrators who then select the neutral. The arbitrator noted that this requirement historically has been waived and that the obligation to form a board fell equally on both parties. Because neither the company nor the union made any effort to comply with the contractual selection requirement, the arbitrator found that it had been waived.

[65]In *Publishers' Ass'n of New York City*, 36 LA 706, 711–12 (Seitz, Bradford, Mortimer, Danielson, & Schlosser, 1961), the arbitrator thus had to compromise his own best judgment. In *Remington Rand, Inc.*, 20 LA 799, 800 (Lehoczky, Jones, & Carney, 1953), the arbitrator withdrew his first proposed award (*Remington Rand, Inc.*, 20 LA 271 (Lehoczky, 1953)) and issued an amended award that attained a majority vote.

Sometimes neither party will vote with the neutral in favor of an award based on the true merits of the case.

At least one commentator has criticized the use of tripartite arbitration panels convened under the Federal Arbitration Act[66] and the rules of the American Arbitration Association (AAA) in a nonlabor context:

> In at least one form of dispute resolution sanctioned by the federal courts, neutrality and impartiality are not only ignored but denounced as hindering its effectiveness. In tripartite panel arbitrations, under the rules of the American Arbitration Association (AAA), party-appointed arbitrators are permitted and even encouraged to be predisposed toward the position of their nominating party.
> . . .
> The courts' approach toward challenges to arbitral awards on the basis of arbitrator relationships or misconduct suggests an unwillingness to restrain, in any meaningful way, an arbitrator's behavior. Rather, it denotes a willingness to apply a lesser standard of ethical behavior to arbitrators than is applied to judicial officers. This approach permits a court to use arbitration to reduce its docket while neglecting to monitor the arbitration process itself.[67]

A. Advantages

One advantage of using a tripartite board is that the neutral member may get valuable advice and assistance from the partisan members.[68] The usual practice is for the parties to select persons from their own ranks who are familiar with the background of the dispute. The technical assistance that such persons may give to the neutral member may be of special value. Moreover, use of the tripartite board gives the parties a better opportunity to keep the neutral arbitrator informed as to their "real" positions, which may not be exactly the same as their formal positions.

The tripartite board has its greatest utility in the arbitration of interest disputes.[69] In this regard, the tripartite composition of the National War Labor Board was considered in reality to be a substitute for the lack of completely satisfactory guiding principles and points of reference.[70] In the arbi-

---

[66]9 U.S.C. §1 et seq.

[67]Kennedy, *Predisposed With Integrity: The Elusive Quest for Justice in Tripartite Arbitrations*, 8 GEO. J. OF LEGAL ETHICS 749, 750, 781 (1995).

[68]*See, e.g.*, Diamond State Tel. Co., 32 LA 200, 212 (Seward, Lindell, Jr., McNeil, Feiler, & Carroll, 1959); Bell Aircraft Corp., 13 LA 813, 820–21 (Day, Andrews, Capen, Garside, & Herrick, 1950).

[69]*See Krislov, supra* note 50, at 263, in which three predominant advantages are cited by NAA members: (1) the presence of company/union arbitrators to present each side's view is helpful in negotiations; (2) the presence of an advocate for each side is helpful to fully explain the facts; and (3) interest arbitration affords more opportunities for mediation, and the presence of company/union representatives facilitates mediation. See also discussion by FREIDIN, LABOR ARBITRATION AND THE COURTS 44–46 (Univ. of Pa. Press 1952). Stating that a "vital characteristic of successful" interest arbitration is "tripartite determination," an attorney explained: "The tripartite executive session produces the result that can come no other way." Sternstein, *Arbitration of Interest Disputes in the Local Transit and Newspaper Publishing Industries: Arbitration of New Contract Terms in Local Transit: The Union View, in* ARBITRATION OF INTEREST DISPUTES, PROCEEDINGS OF THE 26TH ANNUAL MEETING OF NAA 10, 19 (Dennis & Somers eds., BNA Books 1974). Interest arbitration statutes in the public sector commonly specify use of tripartite boards. For an indication of how such boards may function in executive session, see Anderson, MacDonald, & O'Reilly, *Impasse Resolution in Public Sector Collective Bargaining—An Examination of Compulsory Interest Arbitration in New York*, 51 ST. JOHN'S L. REV. 453, 472, 481, 513 (1977).

[70]*See* Taylor, *The Arbitration of Labor Disputes*, 1 ARB. J. (N.S.) 409, 413 (1946).

tration of interest disputes, it is of the utmost importance that clear understanding of the underlying needs and requirements of the parties be obtained. To this end, the assistance of the partisan members may serve to prevent serious errors of judgment by the neutral member.[71]

Awards of tripartite boards, when they are unanimous, tend to be more acceptable than awards by single arbitrators. As one workshop discussion concluded:

> A principal feature of the tripartite system, as expressed during the workshop discussion, is that it promotes acceptability of the award on the part of both management and union and provides an opportunity for practical compromise. This result was not viewed as objectionable, and several responsible industry and union representatives voiced the opinion that compromise is not improper in some cases. It guards against an award which, although correct, may be impracticable for reasons not readily apparent to the neutral member.[72]

B. Disadvantages

Tripartite boards often cause delay not only in the initial appointment of the partisan members, but also both at hearings and afterwards.[73] The members selected by the parties may insist on complete reargument of the case after the hearing is concluded, thereby extending the session. Also, time may be lost in waiting for dissenting opinions to be written. Any additional time required of the neutral necessarily adds to the costs.[74]

The task of the impartial member can be unhappy and difficult. Too frequently the impartial member must act as conciliator for the other members and may be forced to compromise his or her own best judgment in order to secure a majority vote, where such vote is required.

It also has been suggested by some that tripartite panels tend to cause the transgressing of ethical boundaries. While courts are required to overturn arbitration awards if they find that there has been evident partiality, two of the arbitrators of a tripartite panel are, by their very nature, biased:

> Maintaining the goals of arbitration—speed, efficiency, and economy—is hindered rather than helped by the participation of party-appointed arbitrators. Uncertainty exists as to what behavior the courts will tolerate from arbitrators as well as which relationships are taboo. It is clear, however, that fed-

---

[71]*See* Davey, *Hazards in Labor Arbitration*, 1 INDUS. & LAB. REL. REV. 386, 399 (1948). The same precaution is served by tripartite boards for grievances. *See* Dworkin, chair, *The Uses and Misuses of Tripartite Boards in Grievance Arbitration*: *Workshop Sessions: Summary of Workshop C., in* DEVELOPMENTS IN AMERICAN AND FOREIGN ARBITRATION, PROCEEDINGS OF THE 21ST ANNUAL MEETING OF NAA 190–92 (Rehmus ed., BNA Books 1968) (other advantages of tripartite boards for grievances are enumerated).

[72]Dworkin, NAA 21ST PROCEEDINGS, at 193.

[73]Regarding the problem of delay and possibilities of minimizing it, see *Bell Aircraft Corp.*, 13 LA 813, 820–21 (Day, Andrews, Capen, Garside, & Herrick, 1950).

[74]Almost two-thirds of the respondents in a 1983 survey of NAA members stated their belief that tripartite arbitration is not worth the expense and delay it may cause, "some rather violently so!" *Krislov, supra* note 50, at 261–62. Moreover, a clear majority of the respondents indicated their belief that tripartition had little effect on the quality of the opinion and award, the acceptability of the award, or the orderliness and expedition of the hearing. *Id.* at 261.

eral appellate courts are not inclined to set aside arbitral awards for inappropriate arbitrator behavior for fear of creating a tide of continually relitigated cases. The judiciary's unwillingness to upset arbitral awards almost certainly leads parties and their counsel to push the limits of party-appointed arbitrator behavior as far as possible to assist the nominating parties in arising victoriously from the arbitration. Unfortunately, it is the repeat, experienced, and more savvy users of arbitration who best realize how elastic the boundaries of accepted arbitrator conduct can be.[75]

Because of such disadvantages, many parties prefer not to use tripartite boards for rights disputes. A survey of 1,717 collective bargaining agreements indicated that slightly more than one-third specified use of tripartite boards.[76]

The extinction of tripartite arbitration boards predicted by some neutral arbitrators has not occurred. A 1987 study suggests that such boards continue to be used in grievance arbitration for three reasons: (1) the tradition of tripartite grievance resolution ingrained into the labor-management relationship in industries such as those covered under the Railway Labor Act (RLA), (2) distrust of neutral arbitrators, and (3) inertia.[77] It also has been suggested that labor and management support for tripartite arbitration boards could indicate a desire to mediate grievances.[78]

C. Procedure Following the Hearing

The inherent nature of tripartite boards raises procedural issues regarding the extent of consultation and discussion between the impartial chairman and the partisan members following the arbitration hearing.[79] The members of tripartite boards in many cases meet in executive session to discuss the case at some point after the hearing has been completed.[80] The conduct of executive sessions follows no specific pattern. Rather, neutrals are free to choose the course of the procedure and to vary their practice in accordance with their evaluation of the parties, the circumstances of the case, and the time when the session is held.[81]

Customarily the impartial chairman of the board will inquire as to the wishes of the partisan members to meet in executive session. In some cases the partisan members will agree to omit the executive session and allow the

---

[75]Kennedy, *Predisposed With Integrity: The Elusive Quest for Justice in Tripartite Arbitration,* 8 GEO. J. LEGAL ETHICS 749, 788 (1995) (footnote omitted).

[76]*See* FAIRWEATHER'S PRACTICE AND PROCEDURE IN LABOR ARBITRATION 99 (Schoonhoven ed., BNA Books 4th ed. 1999).

[77]Veglahn, *Grievance Arbitration by Arbitration Boards: A Survey of the Parties,* 42 ARB. J. 47 (1987).

[78]*Id.*

[79]For discussion of arbitration procedure generally, see Chapter 7, "Arbitration Procedures and Techniques."

[80]Only one in seven respondents in a 1983 survey of NAA members indicated not holding an executive session. Among the remaining, about one-half reported that they had held executive sessions in over three-quarters of their cases. About a one-fourth reported executive sessions in one-half to three-quarters of their cases. *Krislov, supra* note 50, at 258. Sometimes it is agreed that counsel for the parties may attend the session. Safeway Stores, 22 LA 466, 467 (Hildebrand, 1954).

[81]See explanations in *Procedural Problems in the Conduct of Arbitration Hearings: A Discussion, in* LABOR ARBITRATION: PERSPECTIVES AND PROBLEMS, PROCEEDINGS OF THE 17TH ANNUAL MEETING OF NAA 1, 14–16 (Kahn ed., BNA Books 1964).

neutral to write the opinion and award, reserving, however, the right to file a dissent.[82] Alternatively, the neutral will prepare a tentative opinion and award, followed by an executive session to review the draft decision.[83] Or, it may be agreed that an executive session will be held only if a party requests one after the neutral has issued a tentative award.[84]

Perhaps the most frequently followed procedure calls for the tripartite board to meet in executive session prior to the preparation of any proposed award.[85] But while the session ordinarily gives the neutral a better insight into the dispute, only infrequently does it produce a unanimous decision. When the executive session fails to resolve the dispute, it is typically understood that the neutral will prepare a proposed award without further conference or communication with the partisan members other than to submit the award to them for concurrence or dissent.[86]

Usually the neutral prepares an opinion to accompany the proposed award, but in signing an award, a partisan member does not necessarily indicate concurrence with any or all of the statements made in the neutral's opinion.[87] Where an executive session produces a unanimous decision, the responsibility for preparing a supporting opinion usually is placed solely on the neutral member.[88]

Under some circumstances the neutral member of a tripartite board might not be compelled to meet in executive session with the partisan mem-

---

[82]*See* Texas Co., 24 LA 240, 241 (White, 1955). Upholding this procedure, see *Davey Tree Surgery Co. v. Electrical Workers (IBEW) Local 1245*, 65 Cal. App. 3d 440, 135 Cal. Rptr. 300, 94 LRRM 2905 (1976). When this procedure is followed, it also may be agreed that if the award prepared by the neutral does not receive a majority vote, the board will then meet in executive session to discuss the case further. *See* Kraft Foods Co., 15 LA 38, 39 (Updegraff, 1950). *See also* Hillbro Newspaper Printing Co., 48 LA 1304, 1321 (Jones, Jr., 1967).

[83]*See* Northwest Airlines, 41 LA 360, 361 (Rohman, 1963). Such tentative decision by the neutral is not final and binding. *See* Food & Commercial Workers Local P-9 v. George A. Hormel & Co., 776 F.2d 1393, 120 LRRM 3283 (8th Cir. 1985); Air Line Pilots v. Northwest Airlines, 498 F. Supp. 613, 618–19 (D. Minn. 1980). Nonetheless, where this procedure is used, "the neutral obviously has committed himself and normally it will take a good deal of persuasion to induce him to change his mind." Smith, *The Search for Truth: The Search for Truth—The Whole Truth, in* TRUTH, LIE DETECTORS, AND OTHER PROBLEMS IN LABOR ARBITRATION, PROCEEDINGS OF THE 31ST ANNUAL MEETING OF NAA 40, 58 (Stern & Dennis eds., BNA Books 1979). In *City of Renton*, 71 LA 271, 272 (Snow, 1978), the neutral's tentative award covering a police interest dispute was announced in a conference telephone call (which he would not permit to be recorded), and this was followed by written comments from the party members and then by issuance of the final award.

[84]*See* Chevron Oil Co., 70 LA 572, 573 (Davis, 1978).

[85]About 40% of the respondents in a 1983 survey of NAA members indicated that they prepared their draft decisions after the executive session; 20% indicated that they prepared their decisions immediately after the hearing. The remaining 40% reported a varied practice, with some decisions prepared immediately after the hearing and others after the executive session. *Krislov, supra* note 50, at 259.

[86]*See, e.g.*, Fruehauf Trailer Co., 26 LA 477, 478 (Tatum, 1956); Chesapeake & Potomac Tel. Co. of W. Va., 21 LA 367, 369 (Dworkin, 1953); Cities Serv. Oil Co., 17 LA 335, 341 (Larkin, 1951).

[87]Sometimes the neutral emphasizes the latter fact. *See* Transamerica Airlines Pilots' Fixed Benefit Ret. Plan, 87 LA 1167, 1167 (Kahn, 1986); U.S. Postal Serv., 83 LA 1105, 1110 (Kerr, 1984); American Airlines, 48 LA 705, 705 (Seitz, 1967); Needham Packing Co., 44 LA 1057, 1059, 1089 (Davey, 1965); Baugh & Sons Co., 23 LA 177, 177 (Dash, 1954); Pennsylvania Greyhound Lines, 20 LA 625, 625 (Smith, 1953); Pittsburgh Rys. Co., 17 LA 152, 153 (Pierson, Scharff, & Zimring, 1951).

[88]*See* Shenango Valley Transit Co., 21 LA 356, 357 (Brecht, 1953).

bers, even though the latter members have not expressly waived the session. For instance, in arbitration by a tripartite board under the RLA, a U.S. District Court declared that the provisions of the Act "necessarily recognize that the partisan members [of the tripartite board] will champion the position of their respective employers."[89] Because members of the board had attended the arbitration hearing, the court held that the failure of the neutral member to call the board together after his proposed findings had been submitted to them should, at most, "be considered as a mere irregularity and not sufficient to vitiate the action of the majority of the Board."[90] In that case there was no showing that the members of the board had ever so convened, or that such consultation had been requested by either party. The court said:

> The amenities of the situation might well have suggested to the Chairman that the other two members be advised that he would call the Board together for a conference if it was deemed desirable after the draft of the findings and award had been submitted to them. But, realistically considered, it must be recognized that such gesture would have accomplished nothing.[91]

The neutral's findings and award, when submitted to the partisan members, were concurred in by the company member, and accordingly became a binding award by a majority of the board.[92]

Neither the refusal of a partisan member of a tripartite board to attend a board's executive session, nor the resignation or withdrawal of a partisan member prior to issuance of the award defeats the proceedings or prevents the issuance of a binding majority award by the other members of the board.[93]

---

[89]*In re* Duluth, Missabe & Iron Range Ry., 124 F. Supp. 923, 928, 34 LRRM 2891 (D. Minn. 1954).

[90]*Id.* at 929.

[91]*Id.* at 928.

[92]The opposite result was reached under state law in *Simons v. News Syndicate*, 26 LA 281 (N.Y. Sup. Ct. 1956). Failure of the neutral to call an executive session prior to issuance of his proposed award was strongly criticized by one party in *Northwest Airlines*, 29 LA 541, 545–46 (Schedler, 1957). In *Jones v. St. Louis-San Francisco Railway*, 728 F.2d 257, 115 LRRM 2905 (6th Cir. 1984), the court stated that "although an arbitration board need not be impartial, certain minimal procedural considerations must be afforded the parties," *id.* at 263, 115 LRRM at 2909 (footnote omitted); this requirement was not met where two of the three members of a special board of adjustment that issued an award under the RLA failed both to "*hear* the proof in evidence submitted by the parties and to consult with each other for the purpose of determining the proper resolution," *id.* at 264, 115 LRRM at 2909–10 (emphasis in original). In *Hayes v. Western Weighing & Inspection Bureau*, 838 F.2d 1434, 127 LRRM 300 (5th Cir. 1988), the court held that if lies or misstatements were proven, that would constitute fraud or corruption sufficient to justify nullifying the decision of the National Railroad Adjustment Board (NRAB). *See also* Northwest Airlines, 89 LA 484, 487 (Flagler, 1987) (the neutral chair held that in order to preserve both the fact and appearance of integrity, a witness in a proceeding before the System Board cannot serve as board member in the same case).

[93]*See* Publisher's Ass'n of New York City v. Stereotypers Union No. 1, 181 N.Y.S.2d 527, 31 LA 871 (Sup. Ct. 1959), *aff'd*, 8 N.Y.2d 414, 208 N.Y.S.2d 981 (N.Y. 1960); Shoeworkers Ass'n v. Federal Shoe, 24 LA 573, 576 (Me. 1955); Street, Elec. Ry. & Motor Coach Employees v. Connecticut Co., 24 LA 107, 108–10 (Conn. 1955). *Cf.* Fromer Foods v. Edelstein Foods, 181 N.Y.S.2d 352 (Sup. Ct. 1958) (involving death of a partisan member). *See also* West Towns Bus Co. v. Street, Elec. Ry., & Motor Coach Employees Div. 241, 168 N.E.2d 473 (Ill. App. Ct. 1960); Consumers Power Co., 24 LA 581, 582 (Smith, Howlett, & Sorensen, 1955). For a related discussion, see Chapter 7, section 5.D.i., "Default Awards in Ex Parte Proceedings."

Even assuming the applicability of statutory provisions or common law doctrine that permit either party to withdraw from arbitration at any time prior to issuance of an award, one commentator has pointed out that where an arbitrator orally "announces what his decision will be, it is doubtful whether a party could withdraw between the time of that announcement and the formal written rendition."[94]

6. TRIBUNALS UNDER THE RAILWAY LABOR ACT [LA CDI 103.50]

One of the nation's most extensive experiences in labor-management arbitration has resulted from the arbitration provisions of the Railway Labor Act of 1926.[95] Because it sometimes has been suggested that arbitration tribunals of the RLA variety be used for other industries, consideration is given here to the basic features of those tribunals. As was seen in Chapter 3, "Scope of Labor Arbitration," the present railroad labor legislation of the United States recognizes the distinction between disputes as to "rights" called "minor disputes," and those as to "interests," called "major disputes." The National Mediation Board (NMB) is concerned primarily with interest disputes, while the National Railroad Adjustment Board (NRAB, or Adjustment Board) is concerned with rights disputes.

A. Railroad Interest Disputes

The NMB has jurisdiction over any "dispute concerning changes in rates of pay, rules, or working conditions not adjusted by the parties in conference,"[96] or "[a]ny other dispute not referable to the National Railroad Adjustment Board and not adjusted in conference between the parties or where conferences are refused."[97] Either party may invoke the services of the NMB, or the NMB may proffer its services if a labor emergency is found to exist. One of the three primary functions of the NMB is to help the parties, through mediation, to reach agreement. On failure to bring about an amicable settle-

---

[94]UPDEGRAFF & McCOY, ARBITRATION OF LABOR DISPUTES 122 (1946). *See also* UPDEGRAFF, ARBITRATION AND LABOR RELATIONS 280 (BNA Books 1970). For related matter, see Chapter 2, "Legal Status of Arbitration in the Private Sector."

[95]45 U.S.C. §§151–163, 181–188; 1 LRRM 843. The arbitration provisions of the 1926 RLA (44 Stat. 577) were amended and expanded in 1934 (48 Stat. 1185), in 1936 (49 Stat. 1189), and in 1966 (80 Stat. 208). For extensive discussion of the RLA, see GOHMANN, ARBITRATION AND REPRESENTATION: APPLICATIONS IN AIR AND RAIL LABOR RELATIONS (1981); GOHMANN, AIR AND RAIL LABOR RELATIONS: A JUDICIAL HISTORY OF THE RAILWAY LABOR ACT (1979); REHMUS, THE RAILWAY LABOR ACT AT FIFTY: COLLECTIVE BARGAINING IN THE RAILROAD AND AIRLINE INDUSTRIES (1976); LECHT, EXPERIENCE UNDER RAILWAY LABOR LEGISLATION (1955); *U.S. Labor Law and the Future of Labor-Management Cooperation*, at 134 (U.S. Dep't of Labor, Bureau of Labor-Management Relations Final Report 35-133, 1989); Witt, *Improvements in Procedures Speed Rail and Air Grievance Resolution*, THE CHRONICLE, at 6 (NAA, Oct. 1988). *See also* CLEARED FOR TAKEOFF: AIRLINE LABOR RELATIONS SINCE DEREGULATION (McKelvey ed., ILR Press 1988); Roukis, *Should the Railway Labor Act Be Amended?*, 38 ARB. J. No. 1, at 16 (1983); *Procedures Under the Railway Labor Act: A Panel Discussion, in* PROCEEDINGS OF THE 18TH ANNUAL MEETING OF NAA 27 (Jones ed., BNA Books 1965).

[96]RLA, 45 U.S.C. §155, First (a).

[97]*Id.* §155, First (b).

ment through mediation, however, the NMB seeks to induce the parties to submit the controversy to voluntary arbitration.

The award of the NMB, when signed by a majority of the members, may be filed with the clerk of the federal district court for the district in which the controversy arose or the arbitration is entered into. When so filed, it is conclusive on the parties as to the merits and facts of the controversy, and, unless within 10 days a petition to impeach it on grounds specifically set out in the RLA is filed with the court, judgment will be entered on the award.

B. National Railroad Adjustment Board [LA CDI 103.50]

On submission of a petition by either side, the NRAB takes jurisdiction over "disputes between an employee or group of employees and a carrier or carriers growing out of grievances or out of the interpretation or application of agreements concerning rates of pay, rules, or working conditions," after they have been "handled in the usual manner up to and including the chief operating officer of the carrier designated to handle such disputes."[98] Thus, it is seen that the NRAB handles rights disputes. It assumes jurisdiction only if at least one of the parties wishes it to do so.[99] But, individual employees can take their cases to the NRAB without the union.

The following circumstances were found not to be sufficient to exempt an employee from the exhaustion-of-remedies requirement under the RLA: (1) where the union "grievor" stated that he believed the grievance of the railroad employee had little merit or hope for success; (2) where the employee was not required to use the union "grievor," in whom he had little faith, to ensure that pursuing and exhausting administrative remedies under the RLA would not be wholly futile; and (3) where the employee claimed that due process rights under federal and state law were violated by the discharge.[100]

The U.S. Court of Appeals for the Eight Circuit, however, has held that the district court should exercise its jurisdiction without requiring exhaustion of remedies before the NRAB in cases in which the primary question is the interpretation of a Federal Employers' Liability Act[101] release, and questions of interpretation of a railroad industry collective bargaining agreement are only incidental.[102]

The NRAB is strictly bipartisan. It is composed of 34 members, 17 of whom are selected and compensated by the carriers and 17 by the railroad

---

[98]*Id.* §153, First (i).

[99]Railroad employees no longer have any option to take their grievance under the collective bargaining agreement to court without exhausting the NRAB remedy. Andrews v. Louisville & Nashville R.R., 406 U.S. 320, 80 LRRM 2240 (1972). *Cf.* Glover v. St. Louis-San Francisco Ry., 393 U.S. 324, 70 LRRM 2097 (1969).

[100]Kozina v. Chicago Terminal R.R., 609 F. Supp. 53 (N.D. Ill. 1984). *See also* Rader v. Transportation Union, 718 F.2d 1012, 114 LRRM 3127 (11th Cir. 1983); Kaschak v. Consolidated Rail Corp., 707 F.2d 902, 113 LRRM 2760 (6th Cir. 1983).

[101]45 U.S.C. §51 et seq.

[102]Tello v. Soo Line R.R., 772 F.2d 458, 460, 120 LRRM 2343, 2345 (8th Cir. 1985).

labor organizations.[103] The NRAB is organized into four divisions, each division having jurisdiction over specified classes of railroad employees. The NRAB functions almost entirely through the individual divisions, and each division for all practical purposes is independent of the others. Each division really amounts to a distinct arbitration tribunal, bipartisan in nature, with equal representation from the carriers and the labor organizations. The First Division has 8 permanent members, the Second and Third Divisions have 10 each, and the Fourth Division has 6.

When a dispute is referred to one of the divisions, a hearing is held, unless waived. At the hearing the parties may be heard either in person, by counsel, or by other representatives. After the hearing, the Division proceeds to decide the case. As a matter of practice the divisions frequently hold successive hearings on a group of cases, then hold sessions for deliberation and decision of the cases. Because each division is equally represented by labor and management and because the representatives of each side almost always tend to vote the same way, a unanimous vote generally is necessary to decide a case. While many cases do receive the required vote, numerous others do not. Deadlocks are inevitable and frequent. The RLA provides for the selection of referees in such cases. Referees sit with the division as temporary members and decide the cases for which they are appointed. Usually a referee's appointment will be for a group of cases. Deadlocked cases are set aside until a sufficient number have accumulated on a docket to warrant calling in a referee.[104]

Divisions, which have the initial responsibility for the selection of a neutral person to serve as a referee, generally speaking have not been able to agree on a selection. Consequently, the primary responsibility for the appointment of referees has been with the NMB. The selection by the NMB is within 10 days after a division certifies its inability to agree on a referee. All referees are compensated by the NMB.

Cases assigned to a referee are presented by division members. Occasionally, if request is made, some divisions permit oral argument by the parties before the referee. Generally, however, the referee's knowledge of a case comes from the parties' written submissions and from briefs and arguments of division members.[105] Each division has both labor and management members highly skilled in presenting cases to the referees. The referee is given the opportunity to study case records prior to meeting with division members. Division members often present written briefs to the referee and the referee always has the opportunity to ask questions.

---

[103]Prior to amendment of the RLA in 1970, the NRAB had 36 members, 18 selected by each side. The 1970 amendment, Pub. L. No. 91-234, reduced from 10 to 8 the number of members on the NRAB's First Division. This was made necessary by the merger of four unions representing the trainmen, firemen, conductors, and switchmen into a single union, the United Transportation Union. Although each side now has four members on the First Division, only two members from each side are entitled to vote.

[104]Stieber, *Appendix E. The Future of Grievance Arbitration, in* Arbitration 1986: Current and Expanding Roles, Proceedings of the 39th Annual Meeting of NAA 205, 211–12 (Gershenfeld ed., BNA Books 1987).

[105]The NRAB is essentially an appellate tribunal. Rejecting a due process challenge related to one aspect of this fact, see *Edwards v. St. Louis-San Francisco R.R.*, 361 F.2d 946, 62 LRRM 2300 (7th Cir. 1966).

The referee then takes the cases under advisement, makes findings, and writes the proposed opinions and awards. Practice varies as to the length of opinions. The Third Division, for instance, has expected its referees to write relatively long opinions. The First Division has preferred brevity. The referee discusses proposed awards with the division and voting follows. The side in whose favor an award is rendered generally will vote with the referee to provide the required majority vote.[106]

The RLA as amended in 1966 provides that Adjustment Board awards "shall be final and binding upon both parties to the dispute" (though, as noted below, limited right of court review does now exist).[107] If a dispute arises over the interpretation of an award, the RLA directs the division to interpret the award on request by either party.[108]

If an award is in favor of the employees, the division is directed by the RLA to issue an order requiring the carrier to make the award effective.[109] After such order is issued, the division has nothing to do with its enforcement. When a denial award is issued, the division is directed by the RLA to issue "an order to the petitioner stating such determination."[110]

Prior to the 1966 amendments, only the winning party could take the award to court, and only for the purpose of seeking court enforcement. Under the amendments the loser also has a right to take the award to court, for review. In either instance the court may not set the award aside except on limited grounds: (1) failure of the division to comply with requirements of the RLA, (2) failure of the division to confine itself to matters within the scope of its jurisdiction, or (3) fraud or corruption by a member of the division making the order.[111]

If a carrier does not comply with an order implementing an award, the party in whose favor it stands may sue on it for enforcement by the appropri-

---

[106]For other studies and discussions of the Adjustment Board, see LAZAR, DUE PROCESS IN DISCIPLINARY HEARINGS: DECISIONS OF THE NATIONAL RAILROAD ADJUSTMENT BOARD (University of Cal., Los Angeles, Inst. of Indus. Relations 1980); GOHMANN, AIR AND RAIL LABOR RELATIONS: A JUDICIAL HISTORY OF THE RAILWAY LABOR ACT 141 et seq. (1979); LECHT, EXPERIENCE UNDER RAILWAY LABOR LEGISLATION 10–11, 83, 163, 171, 191–92 (1955); JONES, NATIONAL RAILROAD ADJUSTMENT BOARD (1941); SPENCER, THE NATIONAL RAILROAD ADJUSTMENT BOARD (1938); Lazar, *Arbitration in the Railroad Industry, in* LABOR AND EMPLOYMENT ARBITRATION ch. 89 (Bornstein & Gosline eds., Bender 1988); Mangum, *Railroad Grievance Procedures*, 15 INDUS. & LAB. REL. REV. 491 (1962); Kaufman, *Grievance Arbitration in the Railroad Industry*, 9 LAB. L.J. 244 (1958); Daugherty, *Arbitration by the National Railroad Adjustment Board, in* ARBITRATION TODAY, PROCEEDINGS OF THE 8TH ANNUAL MEETING OF NAA 93 (McKelvey ed., BNA Books 1955); Whiting, *Discussion, id.* at 120; Guthrie, *Discussion, id.* at 122; Garrison, *The National Railroad Adjustment Board; A Unique Administrative Agency*, 46 YALE L.J. 567 (1937). NRAB Rules of Procedure are published in 29 C.F.R. pt. 301.

[107]RLA, 45 U.S.C. §153(m). As to the permissible scope of court review under the language of the RLA prior to the 1966 amendments, see *Gunther v. San Diego & Ariz. E. Ry.*, 382 U.S. 257, 60 LRRM 2496 (1965).

[108]RLA, 45 U.S.C. §153(m).

[109]*Id.* §153(o).

[110]*Id.*

[111]*Id.* §153(p). These three grounds for setting awards aside are part of the 1966 amendments. As to the court's right to "interpret" awards, see *Sweeney v. Florida E. Coast Ry.*, 389 F.2d 113, 67 LRRM 2263 (5th Cir. 1968). The burden of seeking court enforcement of awards is reduced by a provision of the RLA that relieves the petitioner from some of the court costs and that allows a petitioner who prevails in the action reasonable attorneys' fee.

ate federal district court within 2 years. In such suit the findings and order of the Adjustment Board division "shall be conclusive on the parties."[112]

Under the 1966 amendments, any party that is aggrieved by an NRAB award (i.e., a loser, whether an employee or carrier) may obtain review thereof by petitioning the appropriate federal district court. Here again, the action must be instituted within 2 years and the findings and order of the Adjustment Board division "shall be conclusive on the parties," except that the court may set the order aside or remand it to the division for any of the three reasons noted above.[113] The Supreme Court has stressed that judicial review is limited to these three specific grounds.[114]

Finally, it should be noted that sometimes neither party to a dispute will submit it to the Adjustment Board even though the dispute is a "rights" or "minor" dispute of the type for which the Adjustment Board was established. The Supreme Court has held that railroad employees may not strike over disputes that are actually pending before the NRAB, and that the federal courts may enjoin such strikes.[115] However, strikes over such disputes apparently may not be enjoined if the dispute is not actually pending before the NRAB.[116]

C. Railroad Special Boards of Adjustment [LA CDI 103.50]

Even prior to the 1966 amendments, the RLA authorized the establishment of system, group, or regional boards of adjustment by mutual consent

---

[112]RLA, §153. The 2-year limitation is stated in §153(r).

[113]*Id.* §153(q). Prior to the 1966 amendments, the party against whom an award was directed had no right to take it to court for review. Essentially, the only way an award could be tested was for it to be in favor of the employees, for the carrier to refuse to comply with the award, and for the employees then to take it to court for enforcement. Theoretically, the carrier needed no right to go to court on its own initiative because it could refuse to comply with an award in favor of employees and let them take it to court. However, employees at times chose to strike instead of suing to force carrier compliance, thus depriving the carrier of an opportunity for court review. The carrier's right of court review was ultimately assured by the Supreme Court ruling that strikes cannot be used to enforce Adjustment Board awards, *Locomotive Eng'rs v. Louisville & Nashville R.R.*, 373 U.S. 33, 52 LRRM 2944 (1963), and by the 1966 amendment giving any party aggrieved by an NRAB award the right to take it to court for review.

[114]Union Pac. Ry. v. Sheehan, 439 U.S. 89, 93, 99 LRRM 3327 (1978). In *Curtis v. Transportation Union*, 102 LRRM 2961, 2963 (E.D. Ark. 1979), the district court concluded that the doctrine specified by the Supreme Court in *Hines v. Anchor Motor Freight*, 424 U.S. 554, 91 LRRM 2481 (1976), applies also under the RLA. For that doctrine, see Chapter 2, section 2.A.ii.d., "De Novo Litigation Following Arbitration."

[115]Railroad Trainmen v. Chicago River & Ind. R.R., 353 U.S. 30, 39 LRRM 2578 (1957). The carriers sometimes submit disputes to the Adjustment Board as a means of avoiding strikes. While strikes may thus be enjoined, however, the Supreme Court has held that the district court may impose conditions requiring maintenance of the status quo as the "price of relief" when the injunctive powers of the court are invoked; thus, the employees would be protected against a harmful change in working conditions during pendency of the dispute before the Adjustment Board. Locomotive Eng'rs v. Missouri-Kansas-Texas R.R., 363 U.S. 528, 46 LRRM 2429 (1960).

[116]A state court injunction against one such strike was vacated by the Supreme Court where the dispute was not pending before the Adjustment Board. Manion v. Kansas City Terminal Ry., 353 U.S. 927, 39 LRRM 2641 (1957).

of the parties.[117] The 1966 amendments added a provision for establishment of special boards of adjustment, at the request of either party, "to resolve disputes otherwise referable to the Adjustment Board, or any dispute which has been pending before the Adjustment Board for twelve months from the date" when the dispute was submitted to the NRAB.[118] Thus, disputes in some instances may be withdrawn from the NRAB and submitted to a special board.

The RLA directs the NMB to aid in the establishment of these special boards (which have three members) and in the designation of the neutral member.[119] The RLA makes awards of the special boards of adjustment "final and binding upon both parties" and provides that the awards shall be enforceable in federal district courts in the same manner as awards of the NRAB.[120]

The U.S. Court of Appeals for the Sixth Circuit has found that a public law board failed to comply with the requirements of the RLA because the board had acted improperly in rendering an award that was not fully considered by a majority of its members in the manner required by the RLA. The two substitute arbitrators were not present on the date of the hearing, did not have the opportunity to hear a tape or read a transcript of the proceedings, did not discuss the award with each other or with the neutral board member who was present at the hearing, and, thus, a majority of the board did not fully consider appellant's claims because they did not have an opportunity to participate in or consider the oral proceedings.[121]

D. Airline System Boards of Adjustment [LA CDI 103.50]

Amendment of the Railway Labor Act in 1936 made provision for the establishment of a national board of adjustment for the airlines when it shall

---

[117]Discussing such private, mutually voluntary boards and holding their awards to be subject to judicial review, see *Merchants Despatch Transp. Corp. v. System Fed'n No. 1 Ry. Employees Dep't*, 551 F.2d 144, 94 LRRM 3119 (7th Cir. 1977).

[118]RLA, 45 U.S.C. §153, Second.

[119]The NMB's rules for setting up special boards of adjustment under the 1966 amendments are published in 29 C.F.R. pt. 1207. The NMB calls the special boards "PL Boards" under Pub. L. No. 89–456. For discussion of these special boards, see *Atchison, Topeka & Santa Fe Ry.*, 50 LA 1057 (Jones, 1968) (also contains rulings as to procedural matters before PL Boards); *Western Pac. R.R.*, 50 LA 1013 (Wyckoff, 1968). It has been held that a special board considering a case that has been withdrawn from the NRAB should not be limited to a consideration of the evidence contained in the parties' submissions to the NRAB—the parties may proffer such oral testimony or written evidence as they wish, and the special board may request additional evidence from either party. Illinois N. Ry., 53 LA 767, 769–70 (Sembower, 1969). It has been pointed out, however, that "[a]lthough the public law boards now hear witnesses, the underlying concept remains that of an appellate rather than a *de novo* proceeding." Stark, *The Presidential Address: Theme and Adaptations*, in TRUTH, LIE DETECTORS, AND OTHER PROBLEMS IN LABOR ARBITRATION, PROCEEDINGS OF THE 31ST ANNUAL MEETING OF NAA 1, 15 (Stern & Dennis eds., BNA Books 1979).

[120]RLA, 45 U.S.C. §153, Second. Awards of these boards are subject to judicial review. Transportation Union v. Indiana Harbor Belt R.R., 540 F.2d 861, 93 LRRM 2130 (7th Cir. 1976). However, a public law board's decision, which is based on the relevant bargaining agreement and which is conclusive, is not subject to judicial review. Hill v. Norfolk & W. Ry., 814 F.2d 1192, 124 LRRM 3057 (7th Cir. 1987).

[121]Jones v. St. Louis-San Francisco Ry., 728 F.2d 257, 115 LRRM 2905, 2910 (6th Cir. 1984).

be necessary "in the judgment of the National Mediation Board."[122] Pending establishment of such national board, which the NMB has not seen fit to do, the airlines and their employees are directed to establish system boards of adjustment for the resolution of grievances.[123] System boards of adjustment have been established by each airline pursuant to this mandate and have functioned very effectively on the whole.[124] A system board of adjustment has jurisdiction to consider whether a rule was reasonable and reasonably applied, not merely to decide whether a safety rule, for example, has been violated.[125] In order to avoid possible inadvertent additional "testimony" during executive sessions and to preserve the board's integrity both in appearance and in fact, a witness in a proceeding before a system board of adjustment may not serve as a partisan board member in the same case.[126]

A system board of adjustment also has authority to determine the appropriateness of discipline where the degree of discipline is challenged as being disparate and dissimilar, even though such determination was not specifically encompassed in the request for a ruling on the existence of just cause.[127]

Awards of these airline boards are governed and enforceable by federal law, in the federal courts.[128]

The NMB aids in the designation of neutrals for service and the parties compensate the neutrals who serve with airline system boards of adjustment. In sharp contrast, the RLA provides that the NMB shall compensate the neutrals who serve with the NRAB or with railroad special boards of adjustment. Requiring the parties to compensate the neutrals tends to reduce the number of meritless grievances that will be taken to arbitration, and this in turn contributes significantly to the success of any dispute settlement program or tribunal.[129]

7. STATUTORY TRIBUNALS FOR CRITICAL INDUSTRIAL DISPUTES

Both the RLA and the Labor Management Relations Act (LMRA) of 1947[130] contain provisions for special tribunals for critical industrial dis-

---

[122]RLA, 45 U.S.C. §185.

[123]For informative discussions of airline system boards, see Bernstein, *Arbitration Without Neutrals: IV. Bipartite Airline System Boards, in* ARBITRATION 1984: ABSENTEEISM, RECENT LAW, PANELS, AND PUBLISHED DECISIONS, PROCEEDINGS OF THE 37TH ANNUAL MEETING OF NAA 153 (Gershenfeld ed., BNA Books 1985); Nichols, *Arbitration Without Neutrals: IV. Bipartite Airline System Boards of Adjustment, id.* at 161.

[124]For general discussion of these boards, see CLEARED FOR TAKEOFF: AIRLINE LABOR RELATIONS SINCE DEREGULATION (McKelvey ed., ILR Press, 1988); Eischen & Kahn, *Grievances Growing Among Airline Employees*, 132 LRR 312 (1989); Kahn, *Airline Grievance Procedures: Some Observations and Questions*, 35 J. AIR L. & COM. 313 (1969).

[125]Delta Air Lines, 89 LA 408 (Kahn, 1987).

[126]Northwest Airlines, 89 LA 484 (Flagler, 1987).

[127]Trans World Airlines, 93 LA 167 (Eisler, 1989).

[128]Machinists v. Central Airlines, 372 U.S. 682, 52 LRRM 2803 (1963).

[129]For related discussion, see Vernon, *Public Funding for the Arbitration of Grievances in the Railroad Industry*, 38 ARB. J. No. 3, at 22 (1983); Fletcher, *Backlog Not the Issue—Public Funding Is; User Fees Questioned, id.* at 34; Hopkins, *Public Funding Not the Issue—Backlog Is; Cost Sharing Supported, id.* at 38.

[130]29 U.S.C. §141 et seq.

putes, and both acts contain provisions for requiring the parties to maintain the status quo without work stoppages pending investigation and report by the special tribunal. These tribunals should be noted briefly in passing even though, technically speaking, they are not arbitration tribunals.

Section 160 of the RLA provides that if "a dispute between a carrier and its employees" is not settled by use of the RLA's other machinery, and if the NMB finds that the dispute threatens a substantial interruption of interstate commerce, the president has discretion to create an emergency board to investigate and report the facts and circumstances of the dispute and make recommendations as to its settlement.[131]

Section 206 of the LMRA provides that in national emergency disputes imperiling the "national health or safety," the president "may appoint a board of inquiry to inquire into the issues involved in the dispute and to make a written report" that "shall include a statement of the facts with respect to the dispute, including each party's statement of its position but shall not contain any recommendations."[132]

Section 213 of the LMRA was added in 1974 and authorizes the director of the Federal Mediation and Conciliation Service (FMCS) to establish a board of inquiry, whose report shall contain findings of fact together with recommendations, when "a threatened or actual strike or lockout affecting a health care institution" threatens to "substantially interrupt the delivery of health care in the locality concerned."[133]

Boards of inquiry also may be established under state statute. The function of one such board, which had authority to make recommendations, was

---

[131]RLA, 45 U.S.C. §160. For detailed discussion of these boards, see *Railroads v. Nonoperating Unions*, 17 LA 833, 841, 843 (Cole, Horvitz, & Osborne, 1952); Lecht, Experience Under Railway Labor Legislation 6, 11–12, 53–54, 176, 190–91 (1955); Kaufman, *Emergency Boards Under the Railway Labor Act*, 9 Lab. L.J. 910 (1958). For statement of the functions of emergency boards, see Chapter 22, section 3., "The Arbitrator's Function in Interest Disputes"; Witt, *Resolution of Major Disputes in the Railroad and Airline Industries, in* Labor and Employment Arbitration ch. 90 (Bornstein & Gosline eds., Matthew Bender 1988). In 1981, the RLA was amended to provide special emergency board procedures for disputes "between a publicly funded and publicly operated carrier providing rail commuter service (including the Amtrak Commuter Services Corporation) and its employees." RLA, 45 U.S.C. §159a(a). At one stage a second emergency board may be established to receive and select between the "final offers" of the parties. *Id.* §159a(e) & (f). Employees refusing to honor the board's final-offer selection become ineligible for certain statutory unemployment benefits. *Id.* §159a(i). Employers refusing to honor the board's selection become ineligible to "participate in any benefits of any agreement between carriers which is designed to provide benefits to such carriers during a work stoppage." *Id.* §159a(j).

[132]29 U.S.C. §206. For the reports of some of these boards, see *Steel Indus.*, 33 LA 236 (Taylor, Perkins, & Lehoczky, 1959); *Maritime Indus. of the Atl. & Gulf Coasts*, 33 LA 255 (Farmer, Frankenthaler, & Sembower, 1959); *Atlantic Coast Maritime Indus.*, 21 LA 489 (Cole, Carman, & Comey, 1953); *Atlantic Coast Maritime Indus.*, 21 LA 189 (Cole, Carman, & Comey, 1953); *American Locomotive Co.*, 19 LA 532 (Harris, Cheney, & Levy, 1952). For general discussion, see Dunlop, Dispute Resolution: Negotiation and Consensus Building 147–72 (1984); Cole, *Major Labor Disputes—Reexamination and Recommendations, in* The Profession of Labor Arbitration, Selected Papers From the First Seven Annual Meetings of NAA 90 (McKelvey ed., BNA Books 1957). *See also* Foster, *Final Offer Selection in National Emergency Disputes*, 27 Arb. J. 85 (1972).

[133]29 U.S.C. §213. For discussion, see *Sinai Hosp. of Balt. v. Horvitz*, 621 F.2d 1267, 104 LRRM 2171, 2174 (4th Cir. 1980) (the FMCS director's decision to establish a health care board of inquiry is not subject to judicial review).

deemed by its members to "contain elements both of mediation and arbitration," because,

> [L]ike a mediator, the Board must think about the acceptability of its proposals. Like an arbitrator, it is concerned with the weight of the evidence and with the merits of the questions before it. As a statutory Board appointed by the State of New York, the Board has the additional function of serving a public interest which is not necessarily present in private proceedings.[134]

While the parties are not legally compelled to accept the findings of emergency boards and boards of inquiry, public pressure may strongly motivate them to do so, especially where the board has authority to make recommendations and actually does so.

8. METHODS OF SELECTING ARBITRATORS

Selection of an arbitrator satisfactory to both parties often entails difficulties. No part of the arbitration process is more important than that of selecting the person who is to render the decision. Generally, the parties will be held to the time limits governing the arbitrator selection process established in their contract.[135] Where a contract does not contain a limitation of time or specify a method of selection, the parties' past practice may govern the process.[136]

It is generally assumed that selection by mutual agreement of the parties is the most desirable method. This may certainly be true in terms of ensuring acceptance of the award, although there is no inherent reason why an equally if not more competent arbitrator might not be selected by a third party. However, there does appear to be more justification for mutual selection of permanent arbitrators because they ordinarily have some tenure of office.

Collective bargaining contracts often provide for arbitrator selection by agreement of the parties,[137] and, in default of such agreement within a given period, specify alternative methods to be used. Provision for alternative methods of appointment always should be made in the labor agreements to avoid the necessity of resort to the courts to remedy the situation.[138] Modern arbi-

---

[134]Rochester Transit Corp., 19 LA 538, 542 (Tolley, McKelvey, & Turkus, 1952). *See also* statement of functions in *Steel Industry*, 33 LA 236, 236 (Taylor, Perkins, & Lehoczky, 1959).

[135]W.J. Bullock, Inc., 93 LA 33 (Clarke, 1989); Trumbull County, Ohio, Dep't of Human Servs., 90 LA 1267 (Curry, Jr., 1988).

[136]Gallagher & Burk, 91 LA 1217 (Richman, 1988); City of Oregon, Ohio, 90 LA 431 (Stieber, 1988).

[137]Under some circumstances, this step may be held to have been waived. *See* Werner-Continental, 72 LA 1, 7 (LeWinter, 1978); Barbet Mills, 16 LA 563 (Livengood, 1951). *But see* Hartford Gas Co., 49 LA 630, 631–33 (Summers, 1967).

[138]See discussion by board of inquiry in *Rochester Transit Corp.*, 19 LA 538, 558 (Tolley, McKelvey, & Turkus, 1952). For a survey of collective bargaining agreement provisions on selecting the arbitrator, see *Major Collective Bargaining Agreements: Arbitration Procedures*, at 36–46 (U.S. Dep't of Labor Bull. No. 1425-6, 1966). While many agreements provide alternative methods of appointment, this precaution is by no means universal. *Id.* at 36.

tration statutes specify court appointment of an arbitrator if the parties cannot agree on one, or on a method of appointment.[139]

An award will not be enforced if the arbitrator is not chosen in accordance with the method agreed to by the parties. In a case in which an arbitrator's appointment did not conform to the agreement on which he based his jurisdiction, the defect was held to have rendered him powerless to act.[140] Similarly, where a grievance was not appealed to arbitration in accordance with AAA rules incorporated into the collective bargaining agreement, the arbitrator held that the grievance was not arbitrable.[141]

Many cases turn on the specific language of the collective bargaining agreement at issue. In one case, management argued that the grievance was not arbitrable because the union did not seek to strike arbitrators from a list provided by the FMCS, and thus delayed the arbitration. The collective bargaining agreement imposed only a mutual obligation to meet and select an arbitrator, and did not require recourse to the FMCS procedure. The arbitrator held that in the absence of any such specific duty, or substantial evidence that the union solely had caused the arbitrator selection process to be tardy, management's objection would be overruled.[142]

In *Rhone-Poulenc Basic Chemicals Co.*,[143] the union sent a letter to the FMCS asking for a panel of arbitrators. However, the union did not send a copy of the letter to the company. When more than 4 months had passed and the union had received no response from the FMCS, the union again wrote to the FMCS, but again did not inform the company. After a delay of almost 6 months, the FMCS finally submitted a panel of arbitrators. Because the union had failed to notify the company of any of its requests, the arbitrator upheld the company's jurisdictional challenge and ruled that the arbitration request was untimely and thus not arbitrable.

A contrary result was reached, however, in another case where the union unilaterally waited 4 months to request a list of arbitrators from the FMCS. The arbitrator held that because the collective bargaining agreement in ques-

---

[139]For example, a New York statute provides: "If the arbitration agreement does not provide for a method of appointment of an arbitrator, or if the agreed method fails or for any reason is not followed, or if an arbitrator fails to act and his successor has not been appointed, the court, on application of a party, shall appoint an arbitrator." N.Y. C.P.L.R. §7504 (McKinney 1998). *See also* Uniform Arbitration Act, 7 U.L.A. §3; Revised Uniform Arbitration Act (2000), 7 U.L.A. §11 (Supp. 2001); Federal Arbitration Act, 9 U.S.C. §5 (1999). In *Bethlehem Mines Corp. v. Mine Workers*, 344 F. Supp. 1161, 80 LRRM 3069 (W.D. Pa. 1972), the court concluded that it had authority under LMRA §301 (29 U.S.C. §185) to determine how an arbitrator shall be selected if the parties cannot agree.

[140]Avis Rent A Car Sys. v. Garage Employees Local 272, 791 F.2d 22, 122 LRRM 2861, 2864 (2d Cir. 1986). For a general discussion on the role of the arbitrator, see Dunsford, *The Role and Function of the Labor Arbitrator*, 30 ST. LOUIS U. L.J. 109 (1985).

[141]Inland Container Corp., 90 LA 532 (Ipavec, 1987). In *Supermarkets General Corp. v. Food & Commercial Workers Local 919*, 645 F. Supp. 831, 123 LRRM 3181 (D. Conn. 1986), the court held, in confirming an arbitrator's award, under an agreement permitting the parties to arbitrate either through the AAA or the Connecticut State Board of Mediation and Arbitration, that the arbitrator, selected by the company through AAA, had properly found that only the company had complied with the contract requirements for the selection of an arbitrator.

[142]Martin-Brower Co., 102 LA 673 (Dilts, 1994).

[143]103 LA 791, 793 (Darrow, 1994).

tion set no specific deadline for requesting a panel from the FMCS, the delay was not a violation and thus the grievance was timely presented for arbitral review.[144]

The U.S. Court of Appeals for the Tenth Circuit has held that failure to observe the contractual time limit for processing grievances deprived a special subcommittee of any jurisdiction it might otherwise have had to entertain a grievance.[145] But where no time limits are contained in the parties' contract,[146] arbitration awards generally have held that delays in demanding arbitration or selecting the arbitrator do not bar arbitration.

Aid from an outside agency, whether requested at the outset or after the parties have failed to agree on an arbitrator, generally takes one of two forms: (1) a list is submitted from which, often by a process of elimination by alternately striking names, the parties select an arbitrator;[147] or (2) direct appointment of the arbitrator by the agency. An agreement may designate the FMCS, a state agency, the AAA, a judge, some public official, or any other impartial agency.[148]

---

[144]Mercury Consol., 101 LA 309, 314 (Schubert, 1993) (citing Operating Eng'rs, Stationary Local 39 (Kennedy, 1988, unpublished)).

[145]Barnard v. Commercial Carriers, 863 F.2d 694, 130 LRRM 2073 (10th Cir. 1988). But see Kennecott Utah Copper Corp. v. Becker, 186 F.3d 1261, 1267, 162 LRRM 2010 (10th Cir. 1999) (finding that Barnard was not applicable to Kennecott because the employee in Kennecott expressly agreed to submit his timeliness dispute to arbitration, while, in Barnard, the employee had not); Robinson v. Union Pac. R.R., 98 F. Supp. 2d 1211, 1217 (D. Colo. 2000) (clarifying that the decision in Barnard was made under the National Labor Relations Act, 29 U.S.C. §§151–169, and therefore does not apply to cases arising under the RLA because the Railway Labor Act does not establish mandatory arbitration procedures).

[146]See, e.g., W.J. Bullock, Inc., 93 LA 33 (Clarke, 1989); Trumbull County, Ohio, Dep't of Human Servs., 90 LA 1267 (Curry, Jr., 1988); City of Maumee, Ohio, 90 LA 946 (Graham, 1988); City of Oregon, Ohio, 90 LA 431 (Stieber, 1988); Social Sec. Admin., 89 LA 457 (Feigenbaum, 1987).

[147]For an examination of how the FMCS and the AAA decide which names to place on the list for a given case, see Jones & Smith, Management and Labor Appraisals and Criticisms of the Arbitration Process: A Report With Comments, 62 MICH. L. REV. 1115, 1138–39 (1964). See also FMCS REGULATIONS §1404.11(a) (providing a summary of factors (known as a biographical sketch) the FMCS considers when selecting names for inclusion on a panel); Report by FMCS, AAA on Arbitration Panels, 1967 LABOR RELATIONS YEARBOOK 225, 226 (BNA Books 1968).

[148]For statistics as to the use of various appointing agencies, see FMCS ARBITRATION AND STATISTICS, FISCAL YEAR 1993. FMCS statistics indicate that, during fiscal years 1998–2002, the number of panels requested declined from 17,357 (1998) to 17,282 (2002), and the number of arbitrator appointments decreased from 10,391 (1998) to 8,335 (2002). FMCS 55TH ANN. REP., FISCAL YEAR 2002. Yet, according to the FMCS 55TH ANN. REP., FISCAL YEAR 2002, 18,891 arbitration panels were issued in 2002. At the midwinter meeting of the ABA Committee on Labor Arbitration and Collective Bargaining Agreements, February 7, 1994, Robert Coulson, then President of AAA, observed that there had been a "plateauing off" of cases in the last few years. He also indicated that AAA provides panels of arbitrators for about 16,000 labor cases per year, and that about half of the cases go to award. Coulson also noted that AAA had a roster of 3,500 names on the Labor Panel, 890 of whom had cases in 1993. LRR 177–78 (BNA, Feb. 14, 1994). See also Appendix D. Survey of Arbitration in 1964, in PROCEEDINGS OF THE 18TH ANNUAL MEETING OF NAA 243, 245, 251–52 (Jones ed., BNA Books 1965); Appendix C. Survey of Arbitration in 1962, in LABOR ARBITRATION: PERSPECTIVES AND PROBLEMS, PROCEEDINGS OF THE 17TH ANNUAL MEETING OF NAA 292, 296 (Kahn ed., BNA Books 1964); Warren & Bernstein, A Profile of Labor Arbitration, 16 LA 970, 974–75 (1951). In one survey, 203 arbitrators reported that 55.1% of their ad hoc appointments came from appointing agencies, 42.5% came directly from the parties, and 2.5% came from other sources. McDermott, Appendix F. Survey on Availability and Utilization of Arbitrators in 1972, in ARBITRATION OF INTEREST DISPUTES, PROCEEDINGS OF THE 26TH ANNUAL MEETING OF NAA 261, 297 (Dennis & Somers eds., BNA Books 1974).

The FMCS Regulations relating to the selection and appointment of arbitrators provide in Section 1404.12 that:

(a) After receiving a panel of names, the parties must notify the OAS [Office of Arbitration Services] of their selection of an arbitrator or of the decision not to proceed with arbitration. Upon notification of the selection of an arbitrator, the OAS will make a formal appointment of the arbitrator. The arbitrator, upon notification of appointment, is expected to communicate with the parties within 14 days to arrange for preliminary matters, such as the date and place of hearing. Should an arbitrator be notified directly by the parties that he or she has been selected, the Arbitrator must promptly notify the OAS of the selection and his or her willingness to serve. If the parties settle a case prior to the hearing, the parties must inform the arbitrator as well as the OAS. Consistent failure to follow these procedures may lead to a denial of future OAS service.

(b) If the parties request a list of names and biographical sketches rather than a panel, they may choose to appoint and contact an arbitrator directly. In this situation, neither the parties nor the arbitrator is required to furnish any additional information to FMCS and no case number will be assigned.

(c) Where the parties' collective bargaining agreement is silent on the manner of selecting arbitrators, the parties may wish to consider any jointly determined method or one of the following methods for selection of an arbitrator from a panel:

(1) Each party alternately strikes a name from the submitted panel until one remains, or

(2) Each party advises the OAS of its order of preference by numbering each name on the panel and submitting the numbered lists in writing to the OAS. The name that has the lowest combined number will be appointed.

(3) In those situations where the parties separately notify the OAS of their preferred selections, once the OAS receives the preferred selection from one party, it will notify the other party that it has fourteen (14) days in which to submit its selections. If that party fails to respond within the deadline, the first party's choice will be honored. If, within 14 days, a second panel is requested and is allowed by the collective bargaining agreement, the requesting party must pay a fee for the second panel.

(d) The OAS will make a direct appointment of an arbitrator only upon joint request unless authorized by the applicable collective bargaining agreement.

(e) The issuance of a panel of names or a direct appointment in no way signifies a determination on arbitrability or an interpretation of the terms and conditions of the collective bargaining agreement. The resolution of such disputes rests solely with the parties.

Regarding access to additional panels, Section 1404.11(d) states that:

(5) If the parties do not agree on an arbitrator from the first panel, the OAS will furnish a second and third panel to the parties upon joint request and payment of an additional fee. Requests for a second or third panel should be accompanied by a brief explanation as to why the previous panel(s) was inadequate. If parties are unable to agree on a selection after having received three panels, the OAS will make a direct appointment upon joint request.

Similarly, the AAA sends lists of names to the parties. The parties have the privilege of crossing off names to which they object. The AAA then makes the appointment from the names remaining on the lists, in order of preference.[149] If the parties fail to agree on any of the names submitted, they may request additional lists. If they still cannot agree, the AAA appoints an arbitrator whose name has not appeared on the lists.[150]

While the rules of the FMCS and the AAA provide for direct appointments by the agency,[151] both agencies prefer selection by the parties. It has been said that the agencies will make the selection "only when the parties are adamant."[152]

A. Arbitrator's Acceptance or Withdrawal

The *Code of Ethics for Arbitrators* included the following statement on acceptance, refusal, or withdrawal from office: "The arbitrator, being appointed by voluntary act of the parties, may accept or decline the appointment. When he accepts he should continue in office until the matter submitted to him is finally determined. When there are circumstances which, in his judgment, compel his withdrawal, the parties are entitled to prompt notice and explanation."[153] The *Code of Professional Responsibility*, which succeeded the *Code of Ethics*, has no general provision on acceptance or withdrawal, but does state that an invitation to serve "should be declined if the arbitrator is unable to schedule a hearing as soon as the parties wish," unless "the parties, nevertheless, jointly desire to obtain the services of the arbitrator" and arrangements can be agreed on "that the arbitrator confidently expects to fulfill."[154]

AAA Rule 18 provides that "[i]f an arbitrator should resign, die, or otherwise be unable to perform the duties of the office, the AAA shall, on proof

---

[149]AAA LABOR ARBITRATION RULES rule 12. The AAA may aid in the selection of the arbitrator even where it is not administering other aspects of the case. *See* Celotex Corp., 24 LA 369, 370 (Reynard, 1955).

[150]*Labor Arbitration* 14–15 (AAA 1957). The AAA's formal rules have not actually provided for additional lists. *See Voluntary Labor Arbitration Rules of the American Arbitration Ass'n*, 43 LA 1292, 1293 (1965 Rules); *Labor Arbitration Rules of the American Arbitration Ass'n*, 28 LA 908, 909 (1952 Rules).

[151]*See* FMCS REGULATIONS, 29 C.F.R. §1404.12(d), above. Rule 12 of the AAA LABOR ARBITRATION RULES states: "If the parties fail to agree upon any of the persons named, if those named decline or are unable to act, or if for any other reason the appointment cannot be made from the submitted lists, the administrator shall have the power to make the appointment from among other members of the panel without the submission of any additional list."

[152]*Basic Patterns in Labor Arbitration Agreements*, 34 LA 931, 939 (1960). The FMCS indicates that its office of arbitration services made the selection in less than 1% of the cases (i.e., in the 1993 fiscal year, only 36 of 12,231 selections were made by the agency, and in the 1994 fiscal year, only 37 of 11,640 selections were made by the agency). FMCS, 46TH ANN. REP. FISCAL YEAR 1993; FMCS, 47TH ANN. REP. FISCAL YEAR 1994.

[153]Part 1, §6, 15 LA 961, 963.

[154]CODE OF PROF'L RESPONSIBILITY §2.J.2.b. The CODE also provides that: "When an arbitrator decides that a case requires specialized knowledge beyond the arbitrator's competence, the arbitrator must decline appointment, withdraw, or request technical assistance." *Id.* §1.B.1.

satisfactory to it, declare the office vacant. Vacancies shall be filled in the same manner as that governing the making of the original appointment, and the matter shall be reheard by the new arbitrator."[155]

9. ARBITRATORS AND THEIR QUALIFICATIONS

A. Background, Training, and Supply of Arbitrators

With the rapid expansion of labor-management arbitration during and since World War II, a large body of experienced professionals available for arbitration service has developed. No special educational or technical training is required for arbitrators except as may be specifically required by the parties. It is not surprising, then, that arbitrators come from a wide variety of backgrounds. Indeed, the group includes professors, lawyers, judges, public office holders, ministers, accountants, and economists.[156]

---

[155]AAA, LABOR ARBITRATION RULES. *But see* Belleville Shoe Mfg. Co., 84 LA 337, 340 (Pratte, 1985) (the parties agreed to allow the deceased arbitrator's law partner, who had available a transcript and briefs, to finish writing the decision).

[156]Arbitrators Ralph T. Seward, Eva Robins, and Clare B. McDermott each answered "no" when asked the following question: "Most of today's arbitrators entered the profession by way of highly diverse paths. Do you believe it is beneficial to standardize a method of training future arbitrators?" Seward answered in part: "Most emphatically not. The wide variety of background and training that arbitrators have brought to the process has immeasurably enriched it." *An Interview With Three Distinguished Arbitrators,* THE CHRONICLE (NAA) (May 1980), at 12. For "vital statistics" concerning arbitrators (education, background, arbitration training, arbitration income, and the like), see Picher, Seeber, & Lipsky, *Appendix B. The Arbitration Profession in Transition, in* ARBITRATION 2000: WORKPLACE JUSTICE AND EFFICIENCY IN THE TWENTY-FIRST CENTURY, PROCEEDINGS OF THE 53D ANNUAL MEETING OF NAA 267 (Briggs & Grenig eds., BNA Books 2001); Bognanno & Smith, *The Arbitration Profession, in* ARBITRATION 1988: EMERGING ISSUES FOR THE 1990S, PROCEEDINGS OF THE 41ST ANNUAL MEETING OF NAA 266 (Gruenberg ed., BNA Books 1989); Herrick, *Profile of a Labor Arbitrator,* 37 ARB. J. No. 2, at 18 (1982); *Appendix F. Report of the Special Committee to Review Membership and Related Policy Questions of the Academy—Otherwise Known as the Reexamination Committee, in* ARBITRATION—1976, PROCEEDINGS OF THE 29TH ANNUAL MEETING OF NAA 361, 376–81 (Dennis & Somers eds., BNA Books 1976); *Appendix C. Survey of the Arbitration Profession in 1969, in* ARBITRATION AND THE PUBLIC INTEREST, PROCEEDINGS OF THE 24TH ANNUAL MEETING OF NAA 275 (Somers & Dennis eds., BNA Books 1971); *Appendix C. Survey of Arbitration in 1962, in* LABOR ARBITRATION: PERSPECTIVES AND PROBLEMS, PROCEEDINGS OF THE 17TH ANNUAL MEETING OF NAA 292, 292–94, 304–16 (Kahn ed., BNA Books 1964); *Appendix E. Survey of the Arbitration Profession (January 15, 1954), in* THE PROFESSION OF LABOR ARBITRATION, SELECTED PAPERS FROM THE FIRST SEVEN ANNUAL MEETINGS OF NAA 176 (McKelvey ed., BNA Books 1957); *Procedural Aspects of Labor-Management Arbitration,* 28 LA 933, 936 (1957) (1954 statistics); Warren & Bernstein, *A Profile of Labor Arbitration,* 16 LA 970, 973–74 (1951). For general discussions of arbitrators and the qualities essential to their success, see Lawson, *Arbitrator Acceptability: Factors Affecting Selection,* 36 ARB. J. No. 4, at 22 (1981); Kelliher, *The Presidential Address, in* PROCEEDINGS OF THE 18TH ANNUAL MEETING OF NAA 66, 68–71 (Jones ed., BNA Books 1965); Loucks, *The National Academy After Twelve Years: A Symposium: Arbitration—A Profession, in* CHALLENGES TO ARBITRATION, PROCEEDINGS OF THE 13TH ANNUAL MEETING OF NAA 20 (McKelvey ed., BNA Books 1960); Cole, Freidin & Oliver, *The Status and Expendability of the Labor Arbitration: A Panel Discussion, in* THE PROFESSION OF LABOR ARBITRATION, SELECTED PAPERS FROM THE FIRST SEVEN ANNUAL MEETINGS OF NAA 42, 65 (BNA Books 1957). Suggesting that "we have moved from expendability to interchangeability of arbitrators," see Killingsworth, *Twenty-Five Years of Labor Arbitration—And the Future, in* LABOR ARBITRATION AT THE QUARTER-CENTURY MARK, PROCEEDINGS OF THE 25TH ANNUAL MEETING OF NAA 11, 21 (Dennis & Somers eds., BNA Books 1973).

Numerous studies have been conducted into the demographics of the arbitration profession. In one such study covering an 8 year period, 1987–1994,[157] it was found that approximately 60 percent of arbitrators are attorneys, and 90 percent are male:

> Overall, the most striking point in the year by year review of arbitrator biographical characteristics is therefore not the difference but the sameness of the look of the pool. It is remarkable because there was an increase of approximately 300+ persons in the total numbers of arbitrators over this same eight year time span. In 1987, there were a total of 1145 active arbitrators in the pool, 1035 or 90.4% of which were men and 110 or 9.6% of which were women. By 1994, the total numbers had increased considerably. Of a total of 1457 active arbitrators nominated for appointment during the fiscal year, 1287 or 88.3% were men and 170 or 11.7% were women.[158]

The most frequently requested arbitrators, and thus the busiest, are those who have the most experience. These individuals have been elected to membership in the National Academy of Arbitrators (NAA), and they are in an older age group.[159] Indeed, another study reveals that the typical arbitrator is about 63 years old.[160]

Because a large percentage of labor arbitrators will likely have retired from practice by the year 2010, there is a continuing need to develop a future supply to fill the inevitable void that will be created.[161] An American Bar Association (ABA) panel has found that, while there is interest in the possibility of training attorneys to be arbitrators, there is also skepticism regarding the need for such training: "Arbitration, negotiation, and mediation are what lawyers do every day."[162] Although an individual must first be registered by a neutral arbitrator listing agency, such as the AAA or the FMCS, the arbitrator ultimately must be selected by the parties.[163] Designating one-

---

[157]Draznin, *Debunking the Myths About Gender Factors in Labor Arbitrator Selection*, Paper Presented at the ADR in Employment Law Committee of the Section of Labor and Employment Law of the American Bar Association, Midwinter Meeting, Feb. 16, 1998.

[158]*Id.* at 12–13 (footnote omitted).

[159]Kauffman & McKee, *Labor Arbitrator Selection and the Theory of Demand*, 42 ARB. J. 35, 38 (1987). *See also* Bognanno & Smith, *The Arbitration Profession: Part I. The Demographic and Professional Characteristics of Arbitrators in North America, in* ARBITRATION 1988: EMERGING ISSUES FOR THE 1990S, PROCEEDINGS OF THE 41ST ANNUAL MEETING OF NAA 266 (Gruenberg ed., BNA Books 1989); Berkeley, *The Arbitration Profession: Part II. Arbitrators and Advocates: The Consumers' Report, id.* at 290; Fleischli, *Comment, id.* at 302.

[160]Picher, Seeber, & Lipsky, *Appendix B. The Arbitration Profession in Transition, in* ARBITRATION 2000: WORKPLACE JUSTICE AND EFFICIENCY IN THE TWENTY-FIRST CENTURY, PROCEEDINGS OF THE 53D ANNUAL MEETING OF NAA 267, 275 (Briggs & Grenig eds., BNA Books 2001). *See also* Allen & Jennings, *Sounding Out the Nation's Arbitrators: An NAA Survey*, 39 LAB. L.J. 423 (1988).

[161]LABOR ARBITRATION: A PRACTICAL GUIDE FOR ADVOCATES (Zimny, Dolson, & Barreca eds., BNA Books 1990); Allen & Jennings, 39 LAB. L.J. 423. *See also* Berkeley, *The Other Side of the Mirror: Advocates Look at the Future for Female Arbitrators*, 40 LAB. L.J. 370, 371 (1989) (advocates responding to 1987 survey expressed overwhelming agreement with the statement that there is a shortage of newer, acceptable arbitrators).

[162]Steen, *The Multi-Door Courthouse Project: Examining the Arbitration Door, in* ARBITRATION BIG CASE: ABC'S OF DISPUTE RESOLUTION 84 (American Bar Ass'n 1986).

[163]Buonocore, *Resurrecting a Dead Horse—Arbitrator Certification as a Means to Achieve Diversity*, 76 U. DET. MERCY L. REV. 483 (1999).

self an arbitrator is easy enough but obtaining cases is a difficult task, and the ability to obtain cases is the true validation of one's status as an arbitrator.[164] Once new arbitrators have received training in the basic substantive and procedural skills of the profession, labor and management must be willing to provide them with opportunities to serve in order to assure an adequate supply of arbitrators in the future.[165]

To help alleviate the problem, the AAA, the FMCS, and the NAA have cooperated in programs to give training and experience to new arbitrators.[166] In this regard, the FMCS Regulations expressly state that, to increase exposure for new arbitrators, those arbitrators who have been listed on the Roster of Arbitrators for a period of 5 years or less automatically will be placed on expedited panels submitted to the parties. However, all panels also will contain the names of at least two more senior arbitrators.[167]

---

[164]Lawson & Rinaldo, *Improving Arbitrator Performance: A Modest Proposal*, 39 ARB. J. 49 (1984). *See also* Kauffman & McKee, *Labor Arbitrator Selection and the Theory of Demand*, 42 ARB. J. 35 (1987).

[165]Nowlin, *Arbitrator Development: Career Paths, a Model Program, and Challenges*, 43 ARB. J. 3, 4 (1988).

[166]Descriptions and explanations of these and other training programs, sometimes with indications of their degrees of success, are provided in the proceedings of the annual meetings of the NAA, which are published by the Bureau of National Affairs, Inc. *See* Teple, *Appendix D. 1979 Report of the Committee on the Development of Arbitrators*, *in* ARBITRATION OF SUBCONTRACTING AND WAGE INCENTIVE DISPUTES, PROCEEDINGS OF THE 32D ANNUAL MEETING OF NAA 275 (Stern & Dennis eds., BNA Books 1980); Teple, *Appendix C. 1978 Report of the Committee on Development of Arbitrators*, *in* TRUTH, LIE DETECTORS, AND OTHER PROBLEMS IN LABOR ARBITRATION, PROCEEDINGS OF THE 31ST ANNUAL MEETING OF NAA 397 (Stern & Dennis eds., BNA Books 1979); Teple, *Appendix D. 1977 Report of Committee on Development of Arbitrators*, *in* ARBITRATION—1977, PROCEEDINGS OF THE 30TH ANNUAL MEETING OF NAA 357 (Dennis & Somers eds., BNA Books 1978); Teple, *Appendix D. 1976 Report of Committee on Development of Arbitrators*, *in* ARBITRATION—1976, PROCEEDINGS OF THE 29TH ANNUAL MEETING OF NAA 327 (Dennis & Somers eds., BNA Books 1976) (this report is particularly interesting in that it indicates how persons admitted to NAA membership between 1970 and 1975 had initially gotten into arbitration); McDermott, *Appendix D. Entry Into Labor Arbitration and the Effectiveness of Training Programs for Such Entry*, *in* ARBITRATION—1975, PROCEEDINGS OF THE 28TH ANNUAL MEETING OF NAA 335 (Dennis & Somers eds., BNA Books 1976) (another particularly interesting report); McDermott, chair, *Appendix D. Evaluation of Programs Seeking to Develop Arbitrator Acceptability*, *in* ARBITRATION—1974, PROCEEDINGS OF THE 27TH ANNUAL MEETING OF NAA 329 (Dennis & Somers eds., BNA Books 1975); McDermott, chair, *Appendix E. Progress Report: Programs Directed at the Development of New Arbitrators*, *in* ARBITRATION OF INTEREST DISPUTES, PROCEEDINGS OF THE 26TH ANNUAL MEETING OF NAA 247 (Dennis & Somers eds., BNA Books 1974); McDermott, chair, *Appendix C. Activities Directed at Advancing the Acceptability of New Arbitrators*, *in* LABOR ARBITRATION AT THE QUARTER-CENTURY MARK, PROCEEDINGS OF THE 25TH ANNUAL MEETING OF NAA 331 (Dennis & Somers eds., BNA Books 1973). For other discussions of programs for training new arbitrators, see Sinicropi, *Arbitrator Development: Programs and Models*, 37 ARB. J. 24 (1982); Cahn, *Labor Arbitration Training Programs: Participant Perceptions*, *id.* at 33; Robins & Seitz, *Not Training but Sharing (The Rewarding Experiences of Two Veteran Arbitrators)*, *id.* at 41; Douglas, *Arbitrators, Apprentices, and Arbitration*, *id.* at 46. A training program manual is that by BARRECA, MILLER & ZIMNY, LABOR ARBITRATOR DEVELOPMENT: A HANDBOOK (BNA Books 1983). In 1977, Montana *by statute* authorized the establishment of a course of study for training arbitrators and factfinders. The CODE OF PROF'L RESPONSIBILITY provides that experienced arbitrators "should cooperate in the training of new arbitrators." §1.C.2. Regarding arbitrator use of assistants, see CODE §2.H. *See also* Dorr, *Labor Arbitrator Training: The Internship*, 36 ARB. J. No. 2, at 4 (1981). For an explanation of how the steel industry obtained many new arbitrators for its expedited arbitration program, see Fischer, *Updating Arbitration*, *in* ARBITRATION OF INTEREST DISPUTES, PROCEEDINGS OF THE 26TH ANNUAL MEETING OF NAA 62, 70–71 (Dennis & Somers eds., BNA Books 1974).

[167]FMCS REGULATIONS, 29 C.F.R. §104.20.

Internship programs provide another method to train new arbitrators. Under such programs, an experienced arbitrator (the mentor) assumes responsibility for training a potential arbitrator (the intern).[168] Initially, the intern is usually limited to observing the mentor conduct hearings, reading the mentor's opinions, and discussing the nuances of the cases with the mentor.[169] When the intern progresses to the next level, the intern drafts opinions for the mentor and sits as a hearing officer under the mentor's supervision.[170] The candidate enters the final stage of an internship once the parties accept the intern as an arbitrator. At this point, the intern conducts the hearing alone, consulting with the mentor only when necessary.[171] However, simply investing the time and effort to participate in an internship program does not guarantee that an intern will be chosen by the parties, or that the intern will be placed on any agency rosters.[172]

Studies and surveys involving the decisionmaking processes of arbitrators reflect a difference in the perception of parties and actual performance. In one survey, the parties indicated they had found that arbitrators' decisions were significantly related to age and experience.[173] Analytic studies, however, indicate that age, experience, education, gender, attorney status, and NAA membership have no apparent relationship to arbitrators' decisions.[174] Although the parties in one survey said that they did not necessarily select arbitrators who were most likely to decide in their favor,[175] another survey concluded that evaluation of arbitrator performance is affected by whether the arbitrator's award was favorable.[176] A 1987 study suggested that parties seek in an arbitrator characteristics that they themselves possess.[177]

---

[168]Buonocore, *Resurrecting a Dead Horse—Arbitrator Certification as a Means to Achieve Diversity*, 76 U. DET. MERCY L. REV. 483, 486 (1999) (citing Dorr, 36 ARB. J. No. 2, at 4, 5).

[169]*Id.*

[170]*Id.*

[171]*Id.*

[172]Training programs also have been used as another tool to help new arbitrators break into the field of arbitration. Under one such plan, General Electric and the International Union of Electrical Workers (IUE) sponsored a training program at the University of Michigan Law School. Under General Electric's training program, new arbitrators were appointed by the arbitrator-listing agencies and selected by the arbitrating parties. Once selected, the new arbitrator received training from expert arbitrators. The training program also provided actual experience as an arbitrator. Awards recognizing the participants' abilities were published, thereby increasing the participants' name recognition and acceptance. *See* Buonocore, 76 U. DET. MERCY L. REV. at 457.

[173]Thornton & Zirkel, *The Consistency and Predictability of Grievance Arbitration Awards*, 43 INDUS. & LAB. REL. REV. 294 (1990); Nelson, *The Selection of Arbitrators*, 37 LAB. L.J. 703 (1986).

[174]Thornton & Zirkel, 43 INDUS. & LAB. REL. REV. 294; Deitsch & Dilts, *An Analysis of Arbitrator Characteristics and Their Effects on Decision Making in Discharge Cases*, 40 LAB. L.J. 112 (1989); Scott & Shadoan, *The Effect of Gender on Arbitration Decisions*, 10 J. LAB. RES. 429 (1989).

[175]Nelson, 37 LAB. L.J. at 703.

[176]Crane & Miner, *Labor Arbitrators' Performance: Views From Union and Management Perspectives*, 9 J. LAB. RES. 42 (1988).

[177]Berkeley, *The Arbitration Profession: Part II. Arbitrators and Advocates: The Consumers' Report, in* ARBITRATION 1988: EMERGING ISSUES FOR THE 1990S, PROCEEDINGS OF THE 41ST ANNUAL MEETING OF NAA 290 (Gruenberg ed., BNA Books 1989).

B. Qualifications Set Forth in Agreement or by Regulation
[LA CDI 94.56]

The collective bargaining agreement may specify qualifications that must be possessed by an arbitrator.[178] The selection of an arbitrator may be hampered seriously, however, if the qualifications are excessively demanding. It may be impossible to obtain an arbitrator who meets the specified qualifications. Although the determination of the requisite qualifications generally is left to the parties, a few state arbitration statutes do prescribe qualifications designed to ensure impartiality. The *Code of Professional Responsibility* states that the essential qualifications of an arbitrator "include honesty, integrity, impartiality and general competence in labor relations matters."[179] Both the FMCS[180] and the AAA[181] have adopted standards and procedures relating to the qualifications needed to be placed on a prospective panel.

Proposals for the licensing of arbitrators often have been advanced, but have been criticized heavily by informed students of arbitration.[182] It also has been suggested that arbitrators should be required to undergo an examination similar to that required of lawyers for admission to the bar. Such an examination would aim at creating an objective standard for evaluating potential arbitrators.[183] A report of the Society of Professionals in Dispute Resolution Commission on Qualifications maintained that any arbitrator qualification system should follow three central principles: (1) no single entity, but rather a variety of organizations, should establish qualifications for neutrals; (2) the greater degree of choice the parties have over the dispute-resolution process, program, or neutral, the less mandatory the qualification

---

[178]Keebler Co., 86 LA 963, 967–68 (Nolan, 1986). This is not the usual practice. *See Major Collective Bargaining Agreements: Arbitration Procedures*, at 50–51 (U.S. Dep't of Labor Bull. No. 1425-6, 1966).

[179]Section 1.A.1. *See also Report of the SPIDR Commission on Qualifications, in* DISPUTE RESOLUTION FORUM 9 (National Institute for Dispute Resolution May, 1989); Seward, *Appendix B. Report of the Special Committee on Professionalism, in* ARBITRATION 1987: THE ACADEMY AT FORTY, PROCEEDINGS OF THE 40TH ANNUAL MEETING OF NAA 221 (Gruenberg ed., BNA Books 1988). A President of the NAA summarized the essential qualifications of arbitrators as follows: "We must be competent, honest, fair minded, objective, courteous, patient and, I suggest, capable of a perspective on the matters before us that permits the leavening of humor, the lighter touch I urge upon you in your work." Fallon, *The Presidential Address: The Role of Humor in Arbitration, in* ARBITRATION 1986: CURRENT AND EXPANDING ROLES, PROCEEDINGS OF THE 39TH ANNUAL MEETING OF NAA 1, 5 (Gershenfeld ed., BNA Books 1987). Asked whether there should "be significant differences in the type of qualifications required of arbitrators as between the private and public sectors," over two-thirds of the respondents in an extensive ABA survey tended to believe or strongly believed that there should not be. *Report of Subcommittee on Qualifications and Training of Arbitrators*, Labor and Employment Law Committee Reports 303, 309 (American Bar Ass'n 1979).

[180]FMCS REGULATIONS, 29 C.F.R. §§1404.4, 1404.5.

[181]AAA LABOR ARBITRATION RULES rules 5 and 12 (Jan. 1, 1996).

[182]*See* Coulson, *Certification and Training of Labor Arbitrators: Should Arbitrators Be Certified? Dead Horse Rides Again, in* ARBITRATION—1977, PROCEEDINGS OF THE 30TH ANNUAL MEETING OF NAA 173 (Dennis & Somers eds., BNA Books 1978); Barreca, *Comment, id.* at 192; Gilliam, *Comment, id.* at 199; Greenbaum, *Comment, id.* at 202; Aaron, *Should Arbitrators Be Licensed or "Professionalized"?, in* ARBITRATION—1976, PROCEEDINGS OF THE 29TH ANNUAL MEETING OF NAA 152 (Dennis & Somers eds., BNA Books 1976).

[183]Kalet, *Training New Arbitrators*, 39 ARB. J. 73 (1984).

requirements should be; and (3) qualifications criteria should be based on performance, rather than paper credentials.[184] The report advocated incorporation of performance-based testing into training and apprenticeship programs.[185] It also concluded that neutrals and their appointing agencies "have an ongoing obligation to maintain and improve acquired knowledge and skills through additional training, practice, and study."[186] The NAA inaugurated annual "Fall Education Conferences" to serve this purpose, and the AAA now requires arbitrators lised on its rosters to attend an annual continuing education program.

One commentator has suggested that the AAA and FMCS establish a review committee to examine applications from individuals whose work brings them into daily contact with labor relations in a nonadvocacy capacity, because they may have a more substantial grounding in the labor relations field than part-time arbitrators. Candidates would include writers on labor and related legal issues employed by publishing companies. The AAA/FMCS committee would have the discretion to approve the listing of these individuals on an arbitration panel, or to authorize them to take a certification examination.[187]

Many seasoned arbitrators have argued that certification of arbitrators would not guarantee competence. The belief is that an arbitrator's quality is best reflected by his or her acceptance among arbitrating parties, and that certification would not guarantee even a minimal level of acceptance. Some commentators also argue that certification would interfere with the parties' longstanding freedom to choose their own arbitrators. Finally, critics argue that certification would burden arbitrator-listing agencies and increase arbitration costs.

On the other side of the debate, a survey reported that a vast majority of ABA-member respondents favored an examination process for arbitrators, from which, however, attorneys would be exempt. Two out of three of the respondents thought that the ABA should certify arbitrators. The Federal Judiciary, in a model plan for reducing the expense and delay of civil cases, also recommended arbitrator certification. Given the sharp differences of opinion in the arbitration community, a consensus remains unlikely.

Perhaps a majority of commentators, advocates, and arbitrators believe that the most effective evaluation procedure is market based—the parties' choice of arbitrators informed by the arbitrator's past performance. It has been suggested that inclusion of the following three data items in arbitrator biographies by appointing agencies such as the AAA and the FMCS would provide additional assistance in selecting arbitrators based on their performance: "(1) Issues award: within ____ days after close of hearing record; (2) Study time: ____ days per hearing day; (3) Waiting period for first available hearing date: ____ weeks."[188]

---

[184]*Qualifying Neutrals: The Basic Principles*, 44 ARB. J. 48 (1989).
[185]*Id.*
[186]*Id.* at 49.
[187]Kalet, 39 ARB. J. 73. *See* Chapter 1, section 10.A., "National Academy of Arbitrators."
[188]Berkeley, *The Most Serious Faults in Labor-Management Arbitration Today and What Can Be Done to Remedy Them,* 40 LAB. L.J. 728, 731 (1989).

The most common complaint voiced by parties is the undue delay in the rendering of arbitration awards. It has been suggested that, if appointing agencies such as the AAA and the FMCS do not take a more active internal policing role to remedy this situation, external remedies may be imposed.[189] The AAA and the FMCS currently stress the timeliness of arbitration awards. Under the AAA rules, awards are due within 30 days,[190] and under the FMCS rules, awards are due within 60 days after the close of the hearing.[191] In FY 1993, the average number of days between hearing and award in FMCS cases was 66.28 days.[192] If arbitrators consistently fail to issue timely awards, they may be removed from the agencies' list.

In the early 1970s, the steel industry was inundated with complaints not only about the length of time required for resolution of cases, but also the high costs, the "technicalities" of the procedure, and the lack of satisfaction for the grievants. As a result, the industry initiated expedited arbitration. New arbitrators were included on the steel panels to hear routine and not precedent-setting grievances. The new procedure gave employers and union leaders an opportunity to evaluate novice arbitrators and provided a qualified pool of neutrals that could be drawn on for cases involving issues of major importance. Similarly, the U.S. Postal Service appoints arbitrators to its expedited panels before appointing them to hear the more complex cases, although it generally uses experienced arbitrators even on its expedited panels.[193]

C. Impartiality

No qualification is more important than that of impartiality. It may well be that no person can be absolutely free from bias or prejudice of any kind, but it is not too much to expect an arbitrator to be able to put aside any personal inclinations and stand between the parties with an open mind. This does not mean, however, that the decision should be contrary to the arbitrator's own best judgment. Indeed, the element of honesty is not satisfied unless the arbitrator fully believes that he or she is doing what is right. To be worthy of the name, arbitrators must always be ready and able to "call 'em as they see 'em." As long as both parties believe that is the case, they will respect the arbitrator whether or not they "see 'em" in the same way.[194]

---

[189]Dilts, *Timeliness of Arbitration Awards: Some Ethical Considerations*, 43 Arb. J. 62 (1988).

[190]AAA Labor Arbitration Rules rule 37.

[191]FMCS Regulations, 29 C.F.R. §1404.3(c).

[192]FMCS Arbitration Statistics Fiscal Year 1993.

[193]Kauffman & McKee, *Labor Arbitrator Selection and the Theory of Demand*, 42 Arb. J. 35 (1987).

[194]Some parties remain unconvinced that the typical arbitrator is consistently objective. *See* Jones & Smith, *Management and Labor Appraisals and Criticisms of the Arbitration Process: A Report With Comments*, 62 Mich. L. Rev. 1115, 1146–47 (1964). However, many parties apparently believe that awards are generally fair and objective. *See* Eaton, *Labor Arbitration in the San Francisco Bay Area*, 48 LA 1381, 1387 (1967). For the view that a well-crafted opinion dispels concerns about neutrality, see Munsell, *Note: Judicial Review of Contract Interpretation by Labor Arbitrators: Whose Brand of Industrial Justice?*, 1996 J. Disp. Resol. 477 (1996).

When asked about impartiality in arbitration and absence of misconduct in the profession, Dean Eric J. Schmertz stated that there

> has not been a single instance in which an arbitrator has been accused and proved of having committed misconduct. . . . And one of the reasons is that we serve in a "fish bowl." Everything that is done is seen. And we serve on acceptability. We are not appointed by the government, and we don't have lifetime tenure like a judge. . . . And we police our own profession. The parties do too; when someone does a poor job, he or she is not acceptable anymore.[195]

One survey suggested that a party's evaluation of arbitrator performance is affected by whether the arbitrator's award was favorable to the party.[196] Parties are cautioned against measuring an arbitrator's neutrality based on the percentage of awards in favor of management or labor. "[T]here is no simple method of determining arbitrator neutrality—that is, no substitute for a case-by-case examination of the arbitrator's knowledge and reasoning. Applying the 50/50 measure will only harm the parties, the arbitrator, and the arbitration process."[197]

A number of methods are used in screening arbitrators to eliminate potential bias. In some jurisdictions, arbitrators are selected on an entirely random basis. In others, a panel of arbitrators is chosen, consisting of one attorney generally perceived to be a "plaintiff's lawyer" and another attorney generally perceived to be a "defendant's lawyer." In the case of a single arbitrator, a formal process is sometimes used to select a pool of "neutral" neutrals, from which a random selection may be made.[198] Despite best efforts to ensure impartiality, some longstanding societal prejudices may linger. For example, one study suggests that women receive more favorable treatment from arbitrators than men,[199] while another found no such bias.

On August 3, 2000, the National Conference of Commissioners on Uniform State Laws approved the Revised Uniform Arbitration Act (RUAA), which the states are considering for adoption.[200] Section 12(a) of RUAA imposes a more substantive and objective disclosure standard for arbitrators. They are required to notify the parties of "facts that a reasonable person would consider likely to affect the impartiality of the arbitrator."[201] Such facts would include any personal or financial interest in the outcome of a

---

[195]Friedman, *Arbitrators in Oral History Interviews: Looking Back and Ahead*, 12 EMPLOYEE REL. L.J. 424, 444–45 (1986).

[196]Crane & Miner, *Labor Arbitrators' Performance: Views From Union and Management Perspectives*, 9 J. LAB. RES. 42 (1988).

[197]Dilts & Deitsch, *Arbitration Win / Loss Rates as a Measure of Arbitrator Neutrality*, 44 ARB. J. 42, 47 (1989).

[198]Steen, *The Multi-Door Courthouse Project: Examining the Arbitration Door*, in ARBITRATION/BIG CASE: ABC's OF DISPUTE RESOLUTION (American Bar Ass'n 1986).

[199]*See, e.g.*, Scott & Shadoan, *The Effect of Gender on Arbitration Decisions*, 10 J. LAB. RES. 429 (1989) (study indicates that the gender of grievants in discipline and discharge cases does not influence the arbitrator's decision); Bemmels, *The Effect of Grievants' Gender on Arbitrators' Decisions*, 41 INDUS. & LAB. REL. REV. 251 (1988) (study of discharge cases in Canada suggests that women received more favorable treatment by arbitrators than did men).

[200]*Uniform Law Commissioners Adopt Revised UAA*, ADR CURRENTS (Sept.–Nov. 2000).

[201]*Id.*

case, and an existing or past relationship with the parties, representatives, or counsel.[202]

On January 1, 1999, the AAA announced its National Rules for the Resolution of Employment Disputes, which set forth the standards to be used in determining an arbitrator's experience and neutrality in the field of employment law. Specifically, the rules states in relevant part:

> (ii) Arbitrators serving under these rules shall have no personal or financial interest in the results of the proceedings in which they are appointed and shall have no relation to the underlying dispute or to the parties or their counsel that may create an appearance of bias.[203]

The rule goes on to state the standards of disclosure to which an arbitrator must adhere:

> Prior to accepting appointment, the prospective arbitrator shall disclose all information that might be relevant to the standards of neutrality set forth in this Section, including but not limited to service as a neutral in any past or pending case involving any of the parties and/or their representatives or that may prevent a prompt hearing.[204]

Finally, if an arbitrator fails to meet the requisite standards of experience and neutrality, he or she can be disqualified in one of the following two ways:

> (i) No later than ten (10) days after the appointment of the arbitrator, all parties jointly may challenge the qualifications of an arbitrator by communicating their objection to the AAA in writing. Upon receipt of the objection, the arbitrator shall be replaced.
>
> (ii) Any party may challenge the qualifications of an arbitrator by communicating its objection to the AAA in writing. Upon receipt of the objection, the AAA either shall replace the arbitrator or communicate the objection to the other parties. If any party believes that the objection does not merit disqualification of the arbitrator, the party shall so communicate to the AAA and to the other parties within ten (10) days of the receipt of the objection from the AAA. Upon objection of a party to the service of an arbitrator, the AAA shall determine whether the arbitrator should be disqualified and shall inform the parties of its decision, which shall be conclusive.[205]

D. Integrity

The integrity of arbitrators generally is, and should be, beyond question. Appointed judges sometimes are criticized for allegedly receiving political "plums." Elected judges sometimes are accused of being politicians. But, arbitrators ordinarily are not open to such criticism because they are selected by free choice of the parties or their agents. But how may a prospective arbitrator be tested for integrity and impartiality? Careful consideration of personal and business background and affiliations is enlightening in

---

[202]*Id.*
[203]AAA National Rules for the Resolution of Employment Disputes rule 11.a.
[204]*Id.* rule 11.b.
[205]*Id.* rule 11.c.

this respect. Has the arbitrator any financial or business interest in the affairs of either party?[206] Has there been any such interest in the past? Is there any personal affiliation, either direct or indirect, with either of the parties?[207] Does the arbitrator have strong opinions in favor of either labor or management?[208] What has been the past record of the arbitrator?[209] The parties may review some past awards of the arbitrator, but, as previously stated, the number of awards rendered in favor of each side should not be used as a test of impartiality.[210] It is the arbitrator's fairness and good judgment, as indicated by past awards and general reputation, with which the parties should be concerned.[211]

E. Ability and Expertise

Naturally, extensive arbitration experience is one indication of ability. But at the outset, a labor-management arbitrator should have a broad back-

---

[206]Arbitrators must disclose to parties any dealings that might create an impression of possible bias. Commonwealth Coatings Corp. v. Continental Cas. Co., 393 U.S. 145 (1968). *But see* Asbestos Workers Local 12 v. Insulation Quality Enters., 675 F. Supp. 1398, 128 LRRM 2865 (E.D.N.Y. 1988). The CODE OF PROF'L RESPONSIBILITY requires disclosure of "any current or past managerial, representational, or consultative relationship with any" party to the case; of "any pertinent pecuniary interest"; and of "any close personal relationship or other circumstance . . . which might reasonably raise a question as to the arbitrator's impartiality." CODE §2.B.1. & 3. The CODE also provides that: "After appropriate disclosure, the arbitrator may serve if both parties so desire. If the arbitrator believes or perceives that there is a clear conflict of interest, the arbitrator should withdraw, irrespective of the expressed desires of the parties." *Id.* §2.B.5. For an extensive survey of views concerning the scope of arbitrators' duty to disclose information concerning their background, associations, previous and current contacts with a party, and the like, see Sherman, *The Duty of Disclosure in Labor Arbitration*, 25 ARB. J. 73 (1970). *See also* Ver Ploeg, *Labor Arbitration: The Participants' Perspective*, 43 ARB. J. 36 (1988); Sherman, *Ethical Responsibilities of the Arbitrator: II. Arbitrator's Duty of Disclosure—A Sequel, in* ARBITRATION AND THE PUBLIC TRUST, PROCEEDINGS OF THE 24TH ANNUAL MEETING OF NAA 203 (Somers & Dennis eds., BNA Books 1971); Elson, *Ethical Responsibilities of the Arbitrator: The Case for a Code of Professional Responsibility for Labor Arbitrators, id.* at 194.

[207]The degree of formality in the arbitrator's personal relationships with the parties is essentially a matter of joint choice by the parties themselves. *See* CODE OF PROF'L RESPONSIBILITY §2.D.

[208]A New York court was upheld in removing an arbitrator it had appointed but who, the court later learned, was partisan toward labor, although his integrity and honesty were not questioned. Western Union, 2 LA 688 (N.Y. Ct. App. 1946). *See also In re* Steuben, 14 LA 541 (N.Y. Sup. Ct. 1950); *In re* Culinary Bar & Grill Employees, 11 LA 1119 (N.Y. Sup. Ct. 1949). An award was vacated on the ground of bias on the part of the arbitrator. Holodnak v. Avco Corp., 387 F. Supp. 191, 88 LRRM 2950 (2d Cir. 1975). The *Holodnak* decision is strongly criticized in Valtin, *The Presidential Address: Judicial Review Revisited—The Search for Accommodation Must Continue, in* ARBITRATION—1976, PROCEEDINGS OF THE 29TH ANNUAL MEETING OF NAA 1, 5–9 (Dennis & Somers eds., BNA Books 1976).

[209]For helpful suggestions to aid parties in obtaining information concerning any particular arbitrator, and suggestions to aid in evaluating the arbitrator's thinking and methods, see Jaffee, *Have Gavel, Will Travel*, 18 ARB. J. 235 (1963).

[210]*See, e.g.,* General Contractors Ass'n of N.Y. v. Teamsters Local 282, 98 LRRM 2135 (S.D.N.Y. 1978).

[211]For commentary on the possible appearance of impropriety arising from discretionary evidentiary rulings, see Schwartz, *From Star to Supernova to Dark, Cold, Neutron Star: The Early Life: The Explosion and the Collapse of Arbitration*, 22 W. ST. U. L. REV. 1, 32 (1994). *See also* Fiotto, *Note: The United States Arbitration Act and Preliminary Injunctions: A New Interpretation of an Old Statute*, 66 B.U. L. REV. 1041, 1061 (1986).

ground of social and economic study or experience. An arbitrator should have an analytical mind and should be able to quickly grasp new subject matter. Maturity of judgment is indispensable. Diplomacy helps, too.

Must an arbitrator be something of a specialist in the subject matter that is to be considered? Generally speaking, no. While neither side cares to appoint persons completely unfamiliar with industrial matters, arbitrators generally will not be disqualified merely because they are not experts in the subject of the dispute. An acceptable expert may be difficult or impossible to secure. Moreover, the parties often prefer an arbitrator who has general business or financial experience or who is versed in law. Arbitrators, as judges, generally should be selected for their ability to understand all sorts of problems. But in some disputes a specialist may be considered essential.[212] Thus, the parties may seek an industrial engineer, or a doctor, or some other type of specialist, depending on the technical matter involved. For many lawyers, an arbitrator's expertise is one of the positive aspects of the arbitration system: "Having lawyers or physicians on the panel in products liability or medical malpractice cases may save your client the cost of rebuilding the wheel each time a case is heard."[213]

Not all commentators find that such expertise is among the desirable qualities to be sought in selecting an arbitrator. An impartial arbitrator may be harder to find than one who is an expert. Furthermore, it has been asked: "[E]ven in intra-industry disputes, is it always desirable to have a decision maker whose mind is filled with preconceived notions about industry reputations and practices?"[214] Others have observed that expertise in the field may serve to handicap the proceedings if the parties look to the arbitrator as an advice giver.[215]

There is, of course, "a tradeoff between impartiality and expertise," according to the U.S. Court of Appeals for the Seventh Circuit:

> The expert adjudicator is more likely than a judge or juror not only to be precommitted to a particular substantive position but to know or have heard of the parties (or if the parties are organizations, their key people).
>   ... [P]eople who arbitrate do so because they prefer a tribunal knowledgeable about the subject matter of their dispute to a generalist court with its austere impartiality but limited knowledge of subject matter. "The professional competence of the arbitrator is attractive to the businessman because a com-

---

[212]Keebler Co., 91 LA 559, 562 (Fox, Jr., 1988) (parties' agreement specified Blue Ribbon Panel for work measurement disputes). For pros and cons as to use of arbitrators with "specific expertise" for the given dispute, see Eaton, *Labor Arbitration in the San Francisco Bay Area*, 48 LA 1381, 1381 (1967). Regarding need for technical expertness of arbitrators, see Warren & Bernstein, *A Profile of Labor Arbitration*, 16 LA 970, 975 (1951). *See also* Code of Prof'l Responsibility §2.J.2.b., quoted in section 8.A., "Arbitrator's Acceptance or Withdrawal," above. Some agreements provide for specialists for certain types of cases, or for employment of technical experts to assist the arbitrator when needed. *See Major Collective Bargaining Agreements: Arbitration Procedures*, at 47–50 (U.S. Dep't of Labor Bull. No. 1425-6, 1966).

[213]Meyerowitz, *The Arbitration Alternative*, 71 A.B.A. J. 78, 79 (1985).

[214]Bayer & Abrahams, *The Trouble With Arbitration*, 11 Litig. 30 (Winter 1985) (quoting Hart & Sacks, The Legal Process 342 (1958)).

[215]*Cf.* Phillips & Piazza, *How to Use Mediation*, 10 Litig. 31, 33 (Spring 1984) (discussing choosing a mediator).

mercial dispute arises out of an environment that usually possesses its own folkways, mores, and technology. Most businessmen interviewed contended that commercial disputes should be considered within the framework of such an environment. No matter how determinedly judge and lawyer work to acquire an understanding of a given business or industry, they cannot hope to approximate the practical wisdom distilled from 30 or 40 years of experience."[216]

The desire of appointing agencies to accommodate the special needs of parties is illustrated by the following statement in annual reports of the FMCS:

> The Office of Arbitration Services (OAS) has a computerized arbitration retrieval system. This system enables OAS to produce data pertinent for rapid and accurate panel selections and arbitrator appointments. Upon receiving a request for a panel of arbitrators, panels can be selected on the basis of geographical location, professional affiliation, occupation, experience in various industries and issues or other specified criteria requested by the parties.[217]

F. Legal Training

Persons trained in law often make able arbitrators, although legal training is not indispensable. Many parties prefer lawyers as arbitrators,[218] and lawyers are considered especially desirable for the position of neutral chairman of arbitration boards.[219]

Legal training helps an arbitrator to be objective. It improves the ability to analyze and evaluate facts. This means that the arbitrator who has had legal training may be less likely to be moved by personal bias or by extraneous evidence. By no means, however, do all lawyers make good arbitrators. Especially ineffective is the lawyer who is so concerned with technical rules of evidence and procedure that the arbitration process is made unduly complicated. Such concern also may result in an award that fails to give sufficient consideration to the real merits of the dispute. Legal training alone is not enough to make an able arbitrator, but if a person possesses the other qualifications, legal training helps to make an arbitrator even better.[220]

---

[216]Merit Ins. Co. v. Leatherby Ins. Co., 714 F.2d 673, 679 (7th Cir. 1983) (quoting RESOLVING BUSINESS DISPUTES 51 (American Medical Ass'n 1965)).

[217]FMCS 46TH ANN. REP. FISCAL YEAR 1993; FMCS 47TH ANN. REP. FISCAL YEAR 1994. FMCS Regulations state that: "A brief statement of the issues in dispute should accompany the request [for a panel of arbitrators] to enable the Service to submit the names of arbitrators qualified for the issues involved." 29 C.F.R. §1404.10(c). See also 29 C.F.R. §1404.12(c)(4). AAA LABOR ARBITRATION RULES, Rules 7 and 9 require parties seeking arbitration to indicate "the nature of the dispute."

[218]See Eaton, Labor Arbitration in the San Francisco Bay Area, 48 LA 1381, 1381 (1967). A survey asking whether parties preferred arbitrators who have a law degree indicated that if a union or management "selector has a law degree, it is highly likely that an arbitrator with a law degree will be sought. Conversely, those selectors lacking a law degree did not exhibit a marked preference for arbitrators with law degrees, and a number in this group recorded a preference for arbitrators without a law degree." Berkeley, The Arbitration Profession: Part II. Arbitrators and Advocates: The Consumers' Report, in ARBITRATION 1988: EMERGING ISSUES FOR THE 1990S, PROCEEDINGS OF THE 41ST ANNUAL MEETING OF NAA 290, 299 (Gruenberg ed., BNA Books 1989).

[219]See Gotshal, The Lawyer's Place in Arbitration, 1 ARB. J. (N.S.) 367 (1946).

[220]Cf. Raffaele, Lawyers in Labor Arbitration, 37 ARB. J. No. 3, at 14 (1982).

Participants in an arbitration workshop sponsored by the National Institute for Dispute Resolution and the ABA Special Committee on Dispute Resolution agreed that only attorneys who possessed a minimum legal experience should be allowed to serve as arbitrators.[221]

In a survey yielding 1,040 usable replies from persons on AAA's national list of labor arbitrators, over half of the respondents had degrees in law.[222] In another study involving 74 usable responses to a survey sent to arbitrators, 68.9 percent of the respondents had law degrees.[223]

G. Arbitrator's Immunity From Civil Liability [LA CDI 94.56]

Arbitrators acting in their official capacity perform quasi-judicial duties and, like judges, are immune from civil liability for acts done in their arbitral capacity.[224] In recognizing this immunity, it is considered that arbitrators "must be free from the fear of reprisals" and "must of necessity be uninfluenced by any fear of consequences for their acts."[225] Indeed, in light of the

---

[221]Steen, *The Multi-Door Courthouse Project: Examining the Arbitration Door, in* Arbitration/Big Case: ABC's of Dispute Resolution 80 (American Bar Ass'n 1986).

[222]Sprehe & Small, *Members and Nonmembers of the National Academy of Arbitrators: Do They Differ?*, 39 Arb. J. 25, 28 (1984).

[223]Nelson, *The Selection of Arbitrators*, 37 Lab. L.J. 703, 705 (1986).

[224]Massachusetts Mut. Life Ins. Co. v. Russell, 473 U.S. 134, 6 EB Cases 1733 (1985); Auto Workers v. Greyhound Lines, 701 F.2d 1181 (6th Cir. 1983); Larry v. Penn Truck Aids, 567 F. Supp. 1410 (E.D. Pa. 1983); Calzaron v. Liebowitz, 550 F. Supp. 1389 (S.D.N.Y. 1982); Locomotive Eng'rs v. New York Dock R.R., 94 Lab. Cas. (CCH) ¶13,704 (E.D.N.Y. 1981); Yates v. Yellow Freight Sys., 501 F. Supp. 101, 106 LRRM 2438 (S.D. Ohio 1980); Merchants Despatch Transp. Corp. v. System Fed'n No. 1 Ry. Employees Dep't, 444 F. Supp. 75, 97 LRRM 2644 (N.D. Ill. 1977) (dismissing RLA Special Board of Adjustment members and referee (as parties defendant) in a suit to review an award); Cahn v. Ladies' Garment Workers (ILGWU), 311 F.2d 113, 51 LRRM 2186 (3d Cir. 1962). The Supreme Court strongly reaffirmed the doctrine of judicial immunity. Stump v. Sparkman, 435 U.S. 349 (1978).

[225]Babylon Milk & Cream Co. v. Horvitz, 151 N.Y.S.2d 221, 26 LA 121, 122 (N.Y. Sup. Ct. 1956). The AAA Legal Department has defended suits against arbitrators and has helped arbitrators fend off moves to involve them in post-arbitration litigation. *See* Page, *Representing the Arbitrator*, The Chronicle (NAA), at 12 (Aug. 1978); AAA Study Time, Jan. 1977, at 1. Based on an extensive examination of court decisions, the AAA has offered the following summary:

> The cases are unanimous in holding that arbitrators are quasi-judicial officers and as such are immune from civil liability when acting in their official capacity. This concept has been expanded by one federal court to include challenges to the authority of the arbitrators to hear the dispute. [Tamari v. Conrad, 552 F.2d 778 (7th Cir. 1977).]
>
> In general, the courts have held that an arbitrator may not be deposed or required to testify in order to impeach, clarify or otherwise show that the award resulted in an unintended outcome. [For example, see Fukaya Trading Co., S.A. v. Eastern Marine Corp., 322 F. Supp. 278 (E.D. La. 1971).] There have been only a few exceptions to this rule such as the admissibility of testimony of a dissenting arbitrator or admissibility of testimony to show arbitrator misconduct. However, in those cases the testimony was admitted primarily to show what matters were considered or to show misconduct by the arbitrators. Therefore, while few jurisdictions have allowed the limited use of arbitrators' testimony, none have allowed it for the express purpose of impeaching the award through a general inquiry into the manner in which the award was arrived at.

Arbitrators' Immunity From Civil Liability—Deposition of Arbitrators, Lawyers' Arbitration Letter (AAA Dec. 1977), at 6. *See also Arbitral Immunity*, Lawyers' Arbitration Letter (AAA Dec. 1990); Nolan & Abrams, *Arbitral Immunity*, 11 Indus. Rel. L.J. 228 (1989); Nolan & Abrams, *The Arbitrator's Immunity From Suit and Subpoena, in* Arbitration 1987: The Academy at Forty, Proceedings of the 40th Annual Meeting of NAA 149, 180 (Gruenberg ed., BNA Books 1988).

national policy that encourages arbitration, it is said that the common law rule protecting arbitrators from liability "ought not only to be affirmed, but, if need be, expanded."[226]

In a case in which an arbitrator's award caused an employee to lose a promotion and his place on a recall list, the arbitrator was found to be absolutely immune from suit for damages despite the employee's contention that the arbitrator had intentionally acted to adjudicate his rights without giving him notice or the opportunity to be present or represented because the employee had acknowledged that the arbitrator had jurisdiction to determine his employment status.[227]

However, where the parties to an arbitration proceeding brought an action against the arbitrator, as well as the organization sponsoring the arbitration for the arbitrator's breach of a contractual obligation to render a timely award, the California Court of Appeals reversed a lower court's dismissal of the complaint and declined to grant quasi-judicial immunity to the arbitrator.[228] As noted by the California Court of Appeals in a subsequent case, this decision was superseded by legislation.[229]

It may be noted that when neutrals serve as umpires under LMRA §302(c)(5)(B) for the purpose of resolving deadlocks between the trustees of employee benefit trusts, the provisions of the Employee Retirement Income Security Act of 1974 (ERISA)[230] become relevant. There is the possibility that, in certain arbitration cases under ERISA, the neutral may be subject to liability as a fiduciary. In any event, it has been suggested[231] that arbitrators may be more willing to serve on ERISA cases as the result of the 1983 *Greyhound Lines*[232] decision, in which the U.S. Court of Appeals for the Sixth Circuit concluded that immunity did extend to an arbitrator who performed functions that arguably come within ERISA's definition of a fiduciary.[233]

---

[226]Hill v. Aro Corp., 263 F. Supp. 324, 64 LRRM 2315 (N.D. Ohio 1967). For related discussion, see Douglas, *The Scope of Arbitrator Immunity*, 36 ARB. J. No. 2, at 35 (1981); Domke, *The Arbitrator's Immunity From Liability: A Comparative Survey*, 3 U. TOL. L. REV. 99 (1971); Glick, *Bias, Fraud, Misconduct and Partiality of the Arbitrator*, 22 ARB. J. 161 (1967).

[227]Durden v. Lockheed-Georgia Co., 123 LRRM 2262 (N.D. Ga. 1985).

[228]Baar v. Tigerman, 140 Cal. App. 3d 979, 211 Cal. Rptr. 426, 41 A.L.R. 4th 1004 (1983). For articles discussing this case, see Daugherty, *Quasi-Judicial Immunity Lost by the Arbitrator Who Sat on the Award:* Baar v. Tigerman, 22 AM. BUS. L.J. 583 (1985); Note: Baar v. Tigerman: *An Attack on Absolute Immunity for Arbitrators!*, 21 CAL. W. L. REV. 564 (1985); Note: *Arbitrator Potentially Liable for Failure to Render a Decision*, 67 MARQ. L. REV. 147 (1983). For an analogous discussion of mediator liability, see Chaykin, *Mediator Liability: A New Role for Fiduciary Duties?*, 53 U. CIN. L. REV. 731 (1984). *See also* Note: *The Sultans of Swap: Defining the Duties and Liabilities of American Mediators*, 99 HARV. L. REV. 1876 (1986).

[229]*See* Coopers & Lybrand v. Superior Court, 212 Cal. App. 3d 524, 260 Cal. Rptr. 713, 720 (1989) (the purpose of CAL. CODE CIV. PROC. §1280.1 was to supersede the holding in *Baar* and to expand arbitral immunity to conform to judicial immunity when the arbitrator is acting under any statute or contract).

[230]29 U.S.C. §1001 et seq. For more on arbitration under LMRA §302(c)(5)(B) and on ERISA, see Chapter 1, section 7.A., "Compulsory Arbitration."

[231]*An Arbitrator's Fiduciary Responsibility in Pension Cases*, AAA STUDY Time, July 1983.

[232]Auto Workers v. Greyhound Lines, 701 F.2d 1181 (6th Cir. 1983).

[233]*See* BASF Wyandotte Corp., 85 LA 602, 606 (Nicholas, Jr., 1985) (the arbitrator indicates in footnote 3 that as a result of the *Greyhound Lines* decision, the Labor Department reversed its position).

H. The Arbitrator's Accountability

Regardless of qualifications at the outset, the more important ultimate consideration is how well has the person performed as an arbitrator. As is no doubt generally typical of the appointing agencies, it is the policy of the FMCS to maintain on its roster only those arbitrators who "conform to the ethical standards and procedures" of the *Code of Professional Responsibility*, and who:

> (1) Are experienced, competent and acceptable in decision-making roles in the resolution of labor disputes; or
> (2) Have extensive experience in relevant positions in collective bargaining; and
> (3) Are capable of conducting an orderly hearing, can analyze testimony and exhibits and can prepare clear and concise findings and awards within reasonable time limits."[234]

The FMCS Arbitrator Review Board is guided by the above criteria not only when it reviews applications for listing on the FMCS Roster of Arbitrators *but also when it reviews the status of arbitrators whose eligibility for continued listing on the Roster has been questioned.*[235]

An arbitrator is indeed accountable, as was emphasized by a president of the NAA:

> The arbitrator functions in a glass bowl. The conduct of the hearing is closely observed by sophisticated, knowledgeable advocates. An arbitrator who exhibits a lack of understanding of the process and who fails to conduct a hearing in an orderly fashion will usually find himself unacceptable to the parties for a subsequent hearing. The *ad hoc* arbitrator has no tenure; an umpire has limited tenure, and nothing is so impermanent as the permanent arbitrator. The arbitrator is selected by the parties either directly or through the offices of the AAA, the FMCS, or state mediation agencies. His decisions are read and reread, not only by the parties, but by hundreds of company and union representatives who have access to his awards through their own systems of distribution. Awards that are not based upon logical, sound interpretation of the provisions of the agreement will very quickly make the arbitrator responsible unacceptable to companies and unions alike.
>
> Sophisticated companies and unions do not keep a box score. They are primarily concerned with the quality of decisions. The companies and unions which submit a dispute to arbitration have complete freedom of choice in the selection of the arbitrator. The arbitrator is almost never foisted upon the parties. We are all aware of the fact that unions and companies, and those who represent them, effectively utilize their private pipelines of information. An arbitrator's reputation precedes him, and a series of poorly reasoned or poorly written decisions will very quickly read that arbitrator out of the profession. Major companies and major unions have their own "don't use" list. That is a fact of life . . . .[236]

---

[234]FMCS Regulations, 29 C.F.R. §§1404.4(b), 1404.5(a).

[235]*Id.* §1404.3(c).

[236]Luskin, *The Presidential Address: Arbitration and Its Critics, in* Developments in American and Foreign Arbitration, Proceedings of the 21st Annual Meeting of NAA 125, 134 (Rehmus ed., BNA Books 1968). *See also* Jones, Jr., *The Presidential Address: A Meditation on Labor Arbitration* and *His Own Brand of Industrial Justice, in* Arbitration 1982: Conduct of the Hearing, Proceedings of the 35th Annual Meeting of NAA 1, 8–11 (Stern & Dennis eds., BNA Books 1983). At the end of 1987, the AFL-CIO began compiling data on individual

I.　Data on Arbitrators

Information concerning the qualifications of some of the more active arbitrators may be had by consulting the *Labor Arbitration Cumulative Digest and Index* volumes of the Bureau of National Affairs, Inc., or the *Arbitrators' Biographies* in the looseleaf *Labor Arbitration* volume of Commerce Clearing House. This information includes the name, age, address, education, occupation, affiliations, experience, articles or books written, awards published, and other miscellaneous information concerning the arbitrator.

The AAA and the FMCS provide biographical data on the arbitrators whose names are supplied to the parties for selection, and most other designating agencies follow the same practice.

10. Formulation and Enforcement of Ethical Obligations of Arbitrators and Advocates

The *Code of Professional Responsibility for Arbitrators*,[237] the RUAA,[238] and the ABA's *Model Rules of Professional Conduct*[239] each address the ethical responsibilities of arbitrators.

A.　Professional Responsibility in Accepting Appointment

Under the *Code of Professional Responsibility*, arbitrators are required to assure that their selection is appropriate. An "arbitrator must decline appointment, withdraw, or request technical assistance" when he or she de-

---

arbitrators. 126 LRR 267 (1987). For various factors that parties might consider in accepting or rejecting an arbitrator, see Berkeley, *The Arbitration Profession: Part II. Arbitrators and Advocates: The Consumers' Report, in* Arbitration 1988: Emerging Issues for the 1990s, Proceedings of the 41st Annual Meeting of NAA 290, 297–302 (Gruenberg ed., BNA Books 1989); Dilts & Deitsch, *Arbitration Win / Loss Rates as a Measure of Arbitrator Neutrality*, 44 Arb. J. 42 (1989); Ver Ploeg, *Labor Arbitration: The Participants' Perspective*, 43 Arb. J. 36 (1988); Eaton, *Labor Arbitration in the San Francisco Bay Area*, 48 LA 1381, 1382 (1967); Fleming, The Labor Arbitration Process 209–10 (Univ. of Ill. Press 1965). One study based on in-depth interviews with labor and management representatives regularly involved in arbitrator selection revealed that:

> [E]xperience of an arbitrator is the single most important factor in selection. However, it is closely followed by the consideration of the arbitrator's suitability to the issue involved in the case. Familiarity with the arbitrator ranked third. All other factors lagged far behind the first three criteria, with the combined background of the arbitrator and his availability being fourth and fifth. Obviously, the geographical proximity of the arbitrator, a factor of overall costs, and the arbitrator's fee do not carry much weight in the selection process.

Rezler & Petersen, *Strategies of Arbitrator Selection*, 70 LA 1307, 1315 (1978).

[237]This Code has been approved by the NAA, the AAA, and the FMCS, and supersedes the Code of Ethics and Procedural Standards for Labor-Management Arbitration, approved in 1951.

[238]Its precursor, the Uniform Arbitration Act (UAA), has been fully adopted by 35 states, and partially adopted in substantial form by 14. Revised Uniform Arbitration Act, Prefatory Note (2000), 7 U.L.A. (Supp. 2001).

[239]The ABA's Model Rules of Prof'l Conduct have been adopted in whole or substantial part in three-quarters of the states. The predecessor Model Code of Prof'l Responsibility, as modified, remains in force in a handful of jurisdictions.

cides that a case is "beyond the arbitrator's competence."[240] An arbitrator is also expected to consider the procedures governing the arbitration on those occasions when procedures have been "established unilaterally" and to reject an appointment in the event he or she deems the procedures inadequate.[241] This obligation coincides with the arbitrator's general obligation to "provide a fair and adequate hearing which assures that both parties have sufficient opportunity to present their respective evidence and argument."[242] In accepting his or her selection, the arbitrator also must be confident that the purpose of the arbitration is not for any "collusive" or "improper purpose."[243] "An arbitrator should conscientiously endeavor to understand and observe . . . the significant principles governing each arbitration system in which the arbitrator serves."[244]

B. Disclosing Conflicts

The *Code of Professional Responsibility* provides that an arbitrator's personal qualifications must include "honesty, integrity, impartiality and general competence in labor relations matters."[245] To that end, an arbitrator must be willing to disclose any relationship "which might reasonably raise a question as to the arbitrator's impartiality."[246] The *Code of Professional Responsibility* includes within such relationships any "current or past managerial, representational, or consultative relationship with any company or union involved . . . ."[247]

Although the "burden of disclosure rests on the arbitrator," not all friendships and associations need be disclosed.[248] While "[t]here should be no at-

---

[240]Code of Prof'l Responsibility §1.B.1.

[241]*Id.* §2.A.3.

[242]*Id.* §5.A.1. The ethical canons for commercial arbitrators similarly provide that an "arbitrator should uphold the integrity and fairness of the arbitration process," but say nothing on competency in accepting an appointment. Canon I.

[243]Code of Prof'l Responsibility §2.A.2.

[244]*Id.* §2.A.1.

[245]*Id.* §1.A.1. *See also* Code of Ethics for Commercial Arbitrators canon I ("arbitrator should uphold the integrity and fairness of the arbitration process").

[246]Code of Prof'l Responsibility §2.B.3. *See also* Code of Ethics for Commercial Arbitrators canon II; RUAA §12; ANR Coal Co. v. Cogentrix of N.C., 173 F.3d 493 (4th Cir. 1999) (attenuated business relationship between arbitrator and party does not reasonably raise questions of impartiality, even if undisclosed); Beebe Med. Ctr. v. Insight Health Servs. Corp., 751 A.2d 416 (Del. Ch. 1999) (attorney-client relationship between arbitrator and party's counsel involving an unrelated matter raises question of impartiality). The parties may also agree to follow a higher or lower standard for disclosure, provided the standard does not "unreasonably restrict the right to disclose." RUAA §4(b)(3). Indeed, the Code of Prof'l Responsibility expressly recognizes that the field of labor arbitration often involves ongoing relationships among arbitrators and the parties. Code §2.B.3.

[247]Section 2.B.1. The extent of involvement is defined to reach an arbitrator's membership on the Board of Directors, current stock or bond ownership (other than in mutual funds or trust arrangements), full or part-time service as a representative or advocate, "or any other pertinent form of managerial, financial or immediate family interest in the company or union involved." *Id.* §2.B.1.a. Further, the arbitrator must disclose "any close personal relationship or other circumstance . . . which might reasonably raise a question as to the arbitrator's impartiality." *Id.* §2.B.3.

[248]*Id.* §2.B.5.

tempt to be secretive about such friendships or acquaintances," disclosure "is not necessary unless some feature of a particular relationship might reasonably appear to impair impartiality."[249] Courts have similarly adopted this disclosure requirement.[250]

Disclosure is to occur once the "circumstances become known to the arbitrator."[251] Upon disclosure, the arbitrator may continue to serve "if both parties so desire." However, "[i]f the arbitrator believes or perceives that there is a clear conflict of interest, the arbitrator should withdraw, irrespective of the expressed desire of the parties."[252] Still, a party's failure to object to an arbitrator upon disclosure of a disqualifying interest constitutes a waiver.[253]

Where the arbitrator is an attorney, he or she also is governed by the *Rules of Professional Conduct* under an amendment to the Model Rules adopted by the ABA. An arbitrator/attorney is restricted from representing "anyone in connection with a matter in which the lawyer participated personally and substantially . . . as an arbitrator, mediator or other third-party neutral, unless all parties to the proceedings give informed consent, confirmed in writing."[254] A lawyer disqualified from such representation also disqualifies the firm with which the lawyer is associated "unless: (1) the disqualified lawyer is timely screened from any participation in the matter and is apportioned no part of the fee therefrom, and (2) written notice is promptly given to the parties and any appropriate tribunal to enable them to ascertain compliance with provisions of this rule."[255] Under another amendment, a "lawyer shall not negotiate for employment with any person who is in-

---

[249]*Id.* §2.B.3.a. Under the CODE OF ETHICS FOR ARBITRATORS IN COMMERCIAL DISPUTES, arbitrators should disclose the existence of "any interest or relationship likely to affect impartiality or which might reasonably create the appearance of partiality or bias." Canon II.

[250]William C. Vick Constr. Co. v. North Carolina Farm Bureau Fed'n, 123 N.C. App. 97, 100–01, 472 S.E.2d 346, 348 (1996) (numerous social, business, and professional relationships with law firm representing the Farm Bureau impaired impartiality and failure to disclose warrants vacatur); Safeco Ins. Co. of Am. v. Stariha, 346 N.W. 2d 663, 666 (Minn. Ct. App. 1984) (arbitrator's unrelated and remote attorney-client relationship with firm representing claimant did not impair impartiality).

[251]CODE OF PROF'L RESPONSIBILITY §2.B.4. *See also* CODE OF ETHICS FOR COMMERCIAL ARBITRATORS canon II(C) (duty to disclose is a "continuing duty").

[252]CODE OF PROF'L RESPONSIBILITY §2.B.5. For ethical problems arising from ex parte mediation efforts, see Fowler, *Court Ordered Arbitration in North Carolina: Selected Issues Practice and Procedure*, 21 CAMPBELL L. REV. 191, 211–12 (1999).

[253]Bernstein Seawell & Kove v. Bosarge, 813 F.3d 726 (5th Cir. 1987) (failure to raise arbitrator's former fractional interest in partnership involved in arbitration at hearing constitutes waiver); Bossley v. Mariner Fin. Group, 11 S.W.3d 349, 351 (Tex. Ct. App. 2000) (no waiver as party did not have knowledge of conflict). Nonneutral arbitrators serve as representatives of the parties appointing them and are not expected to be impartial in the same manner as neutral arbitrators. Thus, they are not subject to the same disclosure duty. Instead, nonneutral arbitrators have a duty to disclose interests based on the "reasonable person" standard for someone in the position of a party, not as a neutral arbitrator. Nasca v. State Farm Mut. Auto. Ins. Co., 12 P.3d 346 (Colo. Ct. App. 2000) (nonneutral arbitrator had a duty to disclose substantial business ties with a party).

[254]ABA MODEL RULE OF PROF'L CONDUCT 1.12(a) [hereinafter ABA MODEL RULES].

[255]*Id.* Rule 1.12(c). MODEL RULE 1.12 addresses conflicts of interest issues of an attorney in connection with his or her work as an arbitrator. This contrasts with ABA MODEL RULE 1.9, which addresses conflict issues between an attorney acting in a representational capacity and former clients.

volved as a party or as a lawyer for a party in a matter in which the lawyer is participating personally and substantially . . . as an arbitrator, mediator or other third-party neutral."[256]

The ABA Commission on Evaluation of the Rules of Professional Conduct drafted a new Rule, 2.4, for lawyers serving as third-party neutrals in alternative dispute resolution (ADR) settings. Under Rule 2.4, lawyers serving as neutrals, which "may include service as an arbitrator," must make clear the nature of their role in the matter to the parties. This becomes particularly significant when a party in the ADR forum is unrepresented. "When the lawyer knows or reasonably should know that a party does not understand the lawyer's role in the matter, the lawyer shall explain the difference between the lawyer's role as a third-party neutral and a lawyer's role as one who represents a client."[257]

C. Advertising and Solicitation

In addition to an arbitrator's responsibility to hold a fair and adequate hearing and maintain impartiality, an "arbitrator must uphold the dignity and integrity of the office."[258] To that end, arbitrators were prohibited by the *Code of Professional Responsiblity* from advertising or soliciting assignments,[259] including the "making of requests for arbitration work through personal contacts with individual parties, orally or in writing."[260] Arbitrators were allowed only to provide biographical information (including fees and expenses for inclusion in administrative agency arbitration rosters), dispute resolution directives, and their names, addresses, phone numbers, and identification as an arbitrator in telephone directories, and to use the title "Labor Arbitrator" on professional letterheads, cards, and announcements.[261]

In response to concerns that the restrictions on advertising were anticompetitive and unenforceable, however, the NAA, a party to the *Code*, took the lead in eliminating the ban and substituting in its place the admonition that "An arbitrator shall not engage in false or misleading advertising."

Subsequently, in May 2002, the NAA was notified by the Federal Trade Commission (FTC) that "it was preparing to bring an action against the Academy directed against the existing ban on solicitation in the Code of Professional Responsibility." The FTC stated in part:

> NAA's flat ban on solicitation in its Code of Professional Responsibility raises serious questions under the anti-trust laws since it and certain related advisory opinions or parts thereof appear to be broader than necessary to deal with the asserted rationale for them: that solicitation can compromise or appear to compromise the impartiality of neutral arbitrators.

---

[256]*Id.* Rule 1.12(b).
[257]*Id.* Rule 2.4.
[258]Code of Prof'l Responsibility §1.C.1.
[259]*Id.* §1.C.3. & 4.
[260]*Id.* §1.C.4.a. The Code of Ethics for Commercial Arbitrators has no specific advertising or solicitation restrictions.
[261]*Id.*

The matter was resolved by the entry of a Consent Order in December 2002, stating in relevant part:

> The Federal Trade Commission . . . having initiated an investigation of certain acts and practices of the National Academy of Arbitrators . . . and having proposed to charge Respondent with violations of Section 5 of the Federal Trade Commission Act, as amended, 15 U.S.C. Section 45; and . . . having accepted the executed Consent Agreement, . . . [orders the Academy to cease and desist from]:
>
> A. Regulating, restricting, impeding, declaring unethical, interfering with, or advising against the advertising or publishing by any person of the prices, terms or conditions of sale of Arbitrators' services, or of information about Arbitrators' services that are offered for sale or made available by Arbitrators or by any organization with which Arbitrators are affiliated;
>
> B. Regulating, restricting, impeding, declaring unethical, interfering with, or advising against solicitation of arbitration work, through advertising or other means, by any Arbitrator or by any organization with which Arbitrators are affiliated.
>
> Provided that nothing contained in this Part shall prohibit Respondent from formulating, adopting, disseminating to its members, and enforcing reasonable ethics guidelines governing the conduct of its members with respect to representations that Respondent reasonably believes would be false or deceptive within the meaning of Section 5 of the Federal Trade Commission Act, and
>
> Provided further that nothing contained in this Part shall prohibit Respondent from formulating, adopting, disseminating to its members and enforcing reasonable ethics guidelines governing conduct that Respondent reasonably believes would compromise or appear to compromise the impartiality of Arbitrators. Such guidelines shall not prevent Arbitrators from disseminating or transmitting truthful information about themselves through brochures and letters, among other means; provided further, however, that in the event that the NAA determines that the dissemination or transmission of such material may create an appearance of partiality, the NAA may promulgate reasonable guidelines that require, in a manner that is not unduly burdensome, that such material and information be disclosed, disseminated or transmitted in good faith to representatives of both management and labor.[262]

D. Advocate's Responsibilities in Arbitration

The ABA's *Model Rule of Professional Conduct* 3.3 expands the ethical obligations of lawyers to ensure candor toward a tribunal. "Tribunal" is defined to include "binding arbitration proceedings."[263] Lawyers are prohibited from knowingly making false statements of law or fact to an arbitrator, failing to correct a false statement, or offering false evidence. The lawyer must not knowingly "fail to disclose to the . . . [arbitrator] legal authority in the controlling jurisdiction known to the lawyer to be directly adverse to the position of the client and not disclosed by opposing counsel."[264] If the lawyer's client or a witness the lawyer has called "offered material evidence" that the

---

[262]Agreement Containing Consent Order, Dec. 3, 2002, Fed. Trade Comm'n-Nat'l Academy of Arbitrators, available at <www.naarb.org> and <www.ftc.gov/os/caselist/0110242.htm>.

[263]ABA MODEL RULE 1.0(m).

[264]*Id.* Rule 3.3.

lawyers learn is false, "the lawyer shall take reasonable remedial measures, including, if necessary, disclosure to the tribunal."[265]

Although expanding *Rule* 3.3, the ABA proposed no change to *Model Rule* 4.1, which addresses the lawyer's general responsibility "to not knowingly . . . make a false statement of material fact or law" when dealing with others on a client's behalf. Under that *Rule*, the lawyer "generally has no affirmative duty to inform an opposing party of relevant facts."[266]

E. Sanctions for Violations of Codes of Conduct

The mere violation of a code of conduct does not necessarily expose an arbitrator to liability. Arbitrators, as we have seen, have been afforded immunity in their function "of resolving disputes between parties or of authoritatively adjudicating private rights."[267] Extending judicial immunity to arbitrators is premised on the "functional comparability" between arbitrators and judges.[268] Some states have encoded this immunity in their statutes.[269]

Such immunity extends to testifying in subsequent proceedings regarding an arbitrator's conduct.[270] Indeed, some states prohibit calling an arbitrator as a witness in a subsequent proceeding.[271] Still, courts will require arbitrators who allegedly have engaged in corruption, fraud, partiality, or other misconduct to present testimony or other evidence on the issue, provided the objecting party has made a sufficient objective, independent showing of such misconduct.[272]

---

[265]*Id.*

[266]These rules apply solely to attorneys. Thus, they do not apply to union and/or company representatives who often are present at arbitration hearings. With respect to those representatives, there is no available sanction for lack of candor.

[267]Antoine v. Byers & Anderson, Inc., 508 U.S. 429, 435–36 (1993).

[268]Butz v. Economou, 438 U.S. 478, 511–12 (1978).

[269]*E.g.*, FLA. STAT. ANN. §844.107 (West 1995); N.C. GEN. STAT. §7A-37 (1995); UTAH CODE ANN. §78-31b.4 (1994).

[270]Andros Compania Maritima, S.A. v. Marc Rich & Co., A.G., 579 F.2d 691 (2d Cir. 1978); Gramling v. Food Mach. & Chem. Corp., 151 F. Supp. 853 (W.D.S.C. 1957).

[271]*See* CAL. EVID. CODE §703.5; N.J. SUPER. CT. R. 4:21 A-4; N.Y. CT. R. §28.12.

[272]Carolina-Virginia Fashion Exhibitors v. Gunter, 230 S.E.2d 380, 388 (N.C. 1976).

Chapter 5

Grievances: Prelude to Arbitration

Arbitration generally is the last step or terminal point of dispute settlement under union contracts. A happy situation exists when the preliminary steps of dispute-settlement machinery function effectively, resulting in settlement of a high percentage of disputes prior to the arbitration stage. If the preliminary steps do not function smoothly, the arbitration forum may be overburdened with cases, leading, in turn, to loss of faith in the dispute-resolution system, the overhang of festering problems, and an unhealthy work environment. It is generally agreed that no dispute should be taken to arbitration until all possibilities of settlement at the negotiation stages of the grievance procedure have been exhausted. A positive attitude of the participants toward the grievance procedure, and an orderly methodology in processing grievances play important roles in achieving grievance resolution.[1] However, once the preliminary steps have been exhausted without success, resort to arbitration should be prompt.

1. The Grievance Procedure [LA CDI 93.01; 100.0730]

Collective bargaining is not confined to the periodic negotiations that lead to a written contract, but is a day-to-day process in which the grievance procedure plays a very important role.[2] "The grievance procedure is, in other words, a part of the continuous collective bargaining process."[3] Thus, an

---

[1]Lurie, *The 8 Essential Steps in Grievance Processing*, 54 Disp. Resol. J. No. 4, at 61-5 (Nov. 1999).
[2]Chrysler Corp., 10 War Lab. Rep. 551, 554 (1943).
[3]Steelworkers v. Warrior & Gulf Navigation Co., 363 U.S. 574, 581, 46 LRRM 2416 (1960).

employer's refusal to process employee grievances is a violation of the National Labor Relations Act (NLRA).[4] Some writers declare the grievance procedure to be the core of the collective bargaining agreement.[5] Professor Harry Shulman put it this way:

> In labor negotiations there are factors peculiar to them which affirmatively press for almost deliberate incompleteness and uncertainty in the agreement; but, even if it were otherwise, it surely is true that no collective agreement has been or can be written which covers in detail all the exigencies with which the parties may be confronted in the contract period, or which makes crystal-clear its meaning with respect to the matters that it does cover.
> ... It is this that makes collective bargaining an unending process in labor relations, and it is this that makes the grievance procedure the heart of the collective agreement.[6]

The extreme importance of a good grievance procedure in large companies was emphasized by an arbitrator who called the grievance machinery the "life-blood of a collective bargaining relationship."[7] In the coal mining industry the grievance procedure was said "to be the 'safety-valve' in industrial relations, the procedure which gives a vital flexibility to the whole system of collective bargaining."[8] When parties in that industry ceased to make a serious effort to utilize the grievance procedure properly, a flood of wildcat strikes ensued.[9]

The President's National Labor-Management Conference of 1945 recommended that every collective bargaining agreement contain provisions for an effective grievance procedure. The Conference outlined some of the standards that a grievance procedure, to be "effective," should meet:

1. Collective bargaining agreements should contain provisions that grievances and disputes involving the interpretation or application of the terms of the agreement are to be settled without resort to strikes, lockouts, or other interruptions to normal operations by an effective grievance procedure with arbitration as its final step.
2. To be effective, the procedure established for the settlement of such grievances and disputes should meet at least the following standards:
   (a) The successive steps in the procedure, the method of presenting grievances or disputes, and the method of taking an appeal from one step to another should be so clearly stated in the agreement as to be readily understood by all employees, union officials, and management representatives.
   (b) The procedure should be adaptable to the handling of the various types of grievances and disputes which come under the terms of the agreement.

---

[4]29 U.S.C. §§151–169. *See* Storall Mfg. Co., 1986–87 NLRB Dec. (CCH) ¶18,147 (1986).

[5]HILL & HOOK, MANAGEMENT AT THE BARGAINING TABLE 199 (1945).

[6]CONFERENCE ON TRAINING OF LAW STUDENTS IN LABOR RELATIONS, Vol. III: TRANSCRIPT OF PROCEEDINGS 669 (1947). The U.S. Supreme Court expressed a similar view in *Warrior & Gulf,* 363 U.S. at 581.

[7]North Am. Aviation, 16 LA 744, 747 (Komaroff, 1951).

[8]Somers, *Grievance Settlement in Coal Mining* 43 (West Virginia Univ. Bull., Series 56, No. 12-2, 1956).

[9]*See* THE PRESIDENT'S COMMISSION ON COAL, LABOR-MANAGEMENT SEMINAR III, WILDCAT STRIKES (Apr. 27, 1979) (No. 0-302-758, Gov't Printing Office 1979); THE PRESIDENT'S COMMISSION ON COAL, LABOR-MANAGEMENT SEMINAR IV, GRIEVANCE AND ARBITRATION PROCEDURES (June 20, 1979) (No. 0-302-759, Gov't Printing Office 1979). These reports are cited in Chapter 1, section 4.D., "Other Important Roles of Arbitration."

    (c)   The procedure should be designed to facilitate the settlement of grievances and disputes as soon as possible after they arise. To this end:

        (1)   The agreement should provide adequate stated time limits for the presentation of grievances and disputes, the rendering of decisions, and the taking of appeals.

        (2)   Issues should be clearly formulated at the earliest possible moment. In all cases which cannot be settled in the first informal discussions, the positions of both sides should be reduced to writing.

        (3)   Management and union should encourage their representatives to settle at the lower steps grievances which do not involve broad questions of policy or of contract interpretation and should delegate sufficient authority to them to accomplish this end.

        (4)   The agreement should provide adequate opportunity for both parties to investigate grievances under discussion.

        (5)   Provision should be made for priority handling of grievances involving discharge, suspension, or other disciplinary action.

    (d)   The procedure should be open to the submission of grievances by all parties to the agreement.

3.   Managements and unions should inform and train their representatives in the proper functioning of the grievance procedure and in their responsibilities under it. In such a program, it should be emphasized:

    (a)   That the basic objective of the grievance procedure is the achievement of sound and fair settlements and not the "winning" of cases;

    (b)   That the filing of grievances should be considered by foremen or supervisors as aids in discovering and removing causes of discontent in their departments;

    (c)   That any tendency by either party to support the earlier decisions of its representatives when such decisions are wrong should be discouraged;

    (d)   That the willingness of management and union officials to give adequate time and attention to the handling and disposition of grievances and disputes is necessary to the effective functioning of the procedure;

    (e)   That for the sound handling of grievances and disputes both management and union representatives should be thoroughly familiar with the entire collective bargaining agreement.[10]

Most collective bargaining agreements give recognition to at least some of those standards, and arbitrators of interest disputes have been known to direct the parties to "spell out" the details of their grievance procedures in accordance with the recommendations of the National Labor Management Conference.[11]

In recent years, arbitration has been extended beyond the company/union spectrum, and other forms of alternative dispute resolution have been developed. Because of the high cost of litigation, a fair number of companies, whose employees are not represented by unions, have adopted arbitration as a vehicle for providing employees with a mechanism for resolving workplace disputes. One company, General Electric Co., adopted a peer review system as

---

[10]*The President's National Labor-Management Conference, Nov. 5–30, 1945*, at 45–46 (U.S. Dep't of Labor, Div. of Labor Standards, Bull. No. 77, 1946).

[11]*See* New York Shipping Ass'n, 1 LA 80, 84, 87–88 (Davis, 1945). *See also* Jonco Aircraft Corp., 20 LA 211, 212 (Merrill, 1953). For general discussion of grievance procedures, see Lewin & Peterson, The Modern Grievance Procedure in the United States (1988); The Grievance Process (Mich. State Univ. Lab. & Indus. Relations Ctr. 1956); Reynard, *Drafting of Grievance and Arbitration Articles of Collective Bargaining Agreements*, 10 Vand. L. Rev. 749 (1957).

the third step for resolving employee disputes. The peer panel consists of two management and three nonmanagement or peer members. The first two steps of the procedure are similar to the traditional grievance procedure. At the third step the peer members are chosen at random by the grievant pulling names out of a box. The grievants may receive assistance from someone in the employee-relations group or they may represent themselves. The supervisor's side of the situation is presented separately. The panel's decision is by secret ballot and is final and binding on all parties.[12]

2. GRIEVANCES DEFINED [LA CDI 93.05, 100.0710]

What is a "grievance"? Comprehensively, it is that which the parties to a particular collective bargaining agreement say it is. Such a definition, of course, does no more than apprise one of the fact that labor relations authorities disagree widely as to the precise meaning of the term and that collective bargaining agreements reflect this lack of accord. The term connotes conflict and irritation, and thus could be defined as any "gripe" or type of complaint by an employee or a union against the employer or by an employer against its employee or the union. It is generally understood, however, that disputes involving demands for changes in the terms of a collective bargaining agreement ("interest" disputes) and disputes arising out of representation issues are not grievances.

Grievances may arise from an infinite number of causes, which may be either real or imaginary. This suggests inquiry as to what determines when a person has a grievance. Must there have been a wrong done? One employer has urged that a grievance does not come into existence so as to be subject to the grievance procedure until some harmful or disciplinary action has been taken against the complainant. The arbitrator who considered this view rejected it as being too narrow. He said: "Whether a man has a grievance or not is primarily his own feeling about the matter. Generally speaking, if a man thinks he has a grievance, he has a grievance."[13]

From a more technical standpoint, however, an arbitrator has stated that the term "grievance" as it appears in the average contract refers to "a formal complaint" by persons who believe they have been wronged.[14]

---

[12]*Focus on . . . Peer Review System*, IER Newsletter (BNA), at 4 (Nov. 22, 1988). *See also* Swartout v. Precision Castparts Corp., 730 P.2d 1270 (Or. Ct. App. 1986).

[13]Cudahy Packing Co., 7 LA 645, 646 (Fisher, 1947). *See also* Northwest Airlines, 45 LA 565, 569–70 (Shister, 1965) (inchoate harm from a new management policy sufficed for a "grievance"); Vulcan Mold & Iron Co., 41 LA 59, 61 (Brecht, 1963) ("A grievance, real or imaginary, is nevertheless a grievance."); Standard Oil Co., 62–3 ARB ¶8885 (Coffey, 1962); Wyandotte Chems. Corp., 35 LA 783, 786–87 (Wollett, 1960). *Cf.* North Am. Aviation, 16 LA 744, 747–48 (Komaroff, 1951). In *Forrest Indus. v. Woodworkers Local 3–436*, 381 F.2d 144, 146, 65 LRRM 3061 (9th Cir. 1967), the court explained that "a liberal and broad construction should be given to the term 'grievance' in the interest of encouraging the use of machinery which the parties themselves have set up for the peaceful settlement of disputes."

[14]E.I. DuPont de Nemours & Co., 29 LA 646, 650 (Gregory, Reilly, & Barrett, 1957). *But cf.* Braniff Airways, 27 LA 892, 896–98 (Williams, 1957).

3. Attitude of Parties to the Grievance Procedure

The parties' attitude in handling grievances, probably more than in any other aspect of the labor-management relationship, indicates their good faith. Nowhere in that relationship is mutual good faith more important.[15] The attitude of the parties is even more important than the type of grievance provisions contained in the agreement. This view has been shared by unions and management alike, not only in cases in which the grievance procedure has been considered successful, but also in the majority of cases in which the procedure has broken down.[16] Good grievance machinery is important, but such machinery alone will not ensure success. The attitude, judgment, experience, and training of the individuals involved are of prime importance. Moreover, a desire to settle grievances, rather than to win them, is essential.

The attitude of the parties becomes clear as the grievance moves through the grievance machinery. The terms and provisions of the collective bargaining agreement may provide for full, partial, or no disclosure.[17] However, unless there are contractual prohibitions, both parties should make a complete disclosure of all the facts, positions taken, and provisions of the agreement relied on at the earliest possible step in the grievance procedure.[18] For "[n]owhere in the relationship between Employer and Union is mutual good faith more important than in handling grievances. . . . Accordingly, settlements at the first steps of the grievance procedure will be facilitated by honest and open disclosure of each party's position and its basis."[19] The absence of such disclosure, with its inherent lack of good faith, is not only unfair but unwise.

No grievance should be presented unless there is a real basis for complaint or need for decision. Much responsibility belongs directly to the union stewards, and indirectly to the union, to screen out complaints that have no real merit. The U.S. Department of Labor has suggested that persons responsible for the preparation of stewards' manuals give serious thought to the inclusion of the following instructions to stewards:

---

[15]Crane & Jedel, *Arbitration Forums: Part II. Mature Collective Bargaining Relationships, in* Arbitration 1988: Emerging Issues for the 1990s, Proceedings of the 41st Annual Meeting of NAA 346, 350–51 (Gruenberg ed., BNA Books 1989). *See also* Luskin, *The Presidential Address: Arbitration and Its Critics, in* Developments in American Foreign Arbitration, Proceedings of the 21st Annual Meeting of NAA 125, 133 (Rehmus ed., BNA Books 1968); Hunt Foods & Indus., 44 LA 664, 669 (Jenkins, Thomas, & Leasman, 1965).

[16]*Grievance Procedure Under Collective Bargaining*, 63 Monthly Lab. Rev. 175 (1946).

[17]*See, e.g.*, Simmons Indus., 101 LA 1201 (Stephens, 1993) (employer that failed to furnish list of proposed witnesses and exhibits to union as required by the collective bargaining agreement is prohibited from using such evidence at hearing).

[18]Michigan Dep't of Corr., 103 LA 37 (Sugarman, 1994) (employer violated collective bargaining agreement by refusing to furnish union with requested information); Central Pa. Water Supply Co., 101 LA 873 (Talarico, 1993) (employee's grievance sustained due to employer's lack of candor in providing inaccurate and false information during grievance proceeding). *See also* Spectrulite Consortium, 101 LA 1134, 1140 (Hilgert, 1993) (in holding that it was not unduly burdensome to reschedule an investigatory meeting before discharging the employee who had failed to appear, "employees should be afforded all due process that can reasonably be made available to them, even if this causes some inconvenience on the part of either or both parties").

[19]Central Pa. Water Supply Co., 101 LA 873, 876 (Talarico, 1993).

Use your best judgment in deciding whether or not a grievance is justified.—If you are convinced that the worker does not have a real case it is better to tell him so right from the beginning. Taking up a lot of poor cases will cost you the respect of all concerned. On the other hand, don't forget that you are the worker's representative. If the case is a borderline one but you feel that the worker has considerable justice on his side, tell him frankly that you are not sure what is the correct answer. Then take the case up and get a definite ruling through the grievance procedure.[20]

Suggestions have also been made concerning the responsibility of foremen:

Greater emphasis should be placed on training foremen in the human relations aspects of their jobs. Many times a man simply wants a relief hour or perhaps a sympathetic listener. Foremen must be given better training, on the importance of fully hearing out rather than prematurely debating with their employees. They must acquire the ability of [noting] what is being said, rather than the manner in which the problem is being presented. Only in this way can gripes be separated from grievances, or can gripes be kept from becoming grievances.[21]

Grievances become magnified in importance and increasingly difficult to settle as they progress toward the top.[22]

Settlements at the first steps of the grievance procedure often will be facilitated by honest and open disclosure of each party's position and its basis.[23] Moreover, the Supreme Court has held that a company had a legal duty to provide information to explain certain of its actions, and thus enable the union to determine whether to process a grievance: "Arbitration can function properly only if the grievance procedures leading to it can sift out unmeritorious claims. For if all claims originally initiated as grievances had to be processed through to arbitration, the system would be woefully overburdened."[24]

---

[20]*Preparing a Steward's Manual*, at 7 (U.S. Dep't of Labor, Div. of Labor Standards, Bull. No. 59, 1943). *See also* Buddy-L Corp., 41 LA 185, 188 (Sembower, 1963).

[21]Comments of management spokesman Harry W. Lacey, *in* PROCEEDINGS OF THE CONFERENCE ON IMPROVING THE RELATIONS BETWEEN THE PARTIES 29 (Univ. of Notre Dame Press 1960). *See also* MILLS, LABOR RELATIONS FOR SUPERVISORS—A MANUAL FOR DAY-TO-DAY LIVING WITH EMPLOYEE ORGANIZATIONS (1977); Walker & Robinson, *The First-Line Supervisor's Role in the Grievance Procedure*, 32 ARB. J. 279 (1977); *Grievance Handling: 101 Guides for Supervisors* (AAA 1970). The BNA Editorial Staff offers a useful guide for stewards and supervisors alike, in GRIEVANCE GUIDE (BNA Books 11th ed. 2003).

[22]For discussion, see Fischer, *Updating Arbitration, in* ARBITRATION OF INTEREST DISPUTES, PROCEEDINGS OF THE 26TH ANNUAL MEETING OF NAA 62, 64–65 (Dennis & Somers eds., BNA Books 1974); statement of G.A. Moore, *Twenty-Five Years of Labor Arbitration—And the Future: Discussion, in* LABOR ARBITRATION AT THE QUARTER CENTURY MARK, PROCEEDINGS OF THE 25TH ANNUAL MEETING OF NAA 39, 42 (Dennis & Somers eds., BNA Books 1973).

[23]*See* Sebastiani Vineyards, 85 LA 371, 377 (Rothstein, 1985); Sperry-Rand Corp., 46 LA 961, 965–66 (Seitz, 1966). *See also* Zack, *Avoiding the Arbitrator: Some New Alternatives to the Conventional Grievance Procedure: III. Suggested New Approaches to Grievance Arbitration, in* ARBITRATION—1977, PROCEEDINGS OF THE 30TH ANNUAL MEETING OF NAA 105, 110–11 (Dennis & Somers eds., BNA Books 1978).

[24]NLRB v. Acme Indus. Co., 385 U.S. 432, 438, 64 LRRM 2069 (1967). In *North American Coal Co.*, 84 LA 150 (Duda, Jr., 1985), because the information needed to decide the merits of the union claim and the factual basis of the company defense was available only to the company, the arbitrator ruled that because the company was obligated by its commitment to the grievance procedure it was required to provide the information to the union unless doing so was unreasonably burdensome. In *Vickers, Inc.*, 43 LA 1256, 1261 (Bothwell,

When approached with the proper attitude, grievance machinery serves the mutual advantage of employer, employees, and union. It helps management discover and correct sore spots in plant operations before they cause serious trouble. Grievances constitute a channel of communication, informing top management of matters about which employees or the union feel strongly.[25] It is to the employer's advantage to make presentation of grievances as easy as possible, and employees should be encouraged not only to present their complaints, but also to present them while they are still "warm." Grievance machinery provides a mechanism for the union to enforce the rules it has worked for and achieved through collective bargaining.

Moreover, through use of grievance machinery the union performs a service to the employees, thereby increasing their loyalty to the union. The Department of Labor made an enduring observation about the significance of the grievance machinery:

> To the individual worker, grievance procedure provides the means of enforcing the terms of the contract and . . . a democratic method of appeal against any one person's arbitrary decision affecting his wages or working conditions. It protects the democratic rights of the individual in industry in the same way that our judicial system protects his democratic rights in civil life.[26]

A. Abuse and Misuse of Grievance Procedure

An "irresistible impulse to file grievances" is not a dischargeable offense, though the purposeful filing of deliberately untruthful grievances may be.[27] However, the National Labor Relations Board (NLRB, or the Board) has held that an employer's threat to sue an employee who filed grievances and unfair labor practice charges is unlawful. Such a threat involves a form of retaliation by the official within the framework of supervisory responsibilities that cannot be a part of the official role as the employer's grievance adjustment representative.[28]

1964), the provisions of the grievance procedure were held to imply an obligation by the company to provide the union with certain minimum information relevant to the validity of a grievance. For related discussion, see Chapter 8, section 3.C., "Requiring the Production of Evidence."

[25]Hill & Hook, Management at the Bargaining Table 199 (1945).

[26]*Settling Plant Grievances*, at 1 (U.S. Dep't of Labor, Div. of Labor Standards, Bull. No. 60, 1943).

[27]National Lead Co. of Ohio, 37 LA 1076, 1079 (Schedler, 1962). Also illustrating the strong inclination of arbitrators to protect employees against reprisals for filing grievances, see *Tyson Foods*, 105 LA 1119, 1123 (Moore, 1996) ("an employer may not unilaterally determine that a grievance was filed in bad faith and discipline an employee for doing so").

[28]Consolidated Edison Co. of N.Y., 286 NLRB 1031, 126 LRRM 1305 (1987). *See also* NLRB v. U.S. Postal Serv., 906 F.2d 482, 134 LRRM 2545 (10th Cir. 1990); Kuhlman, Inc., 305 NLRB 481, 139 LRRM 1296 (1991); U.S. Postal Serv., 290 NLRB 20, 129 LRRM 1043 (1988). *But see* Longshoremen (ILWU) Local 13 v. NLRB (Sea-Land Serv.), 884 F.2d 1407, 132 LRRM 2556 (D.C. Cir. 1989) (court held that the union unlawfully filed grievances protesting the employer's assignment of work to a rival union that represented the employers whom the NLRB had awarded the work under §10(k) of the NLRA); Teamsters Local 952 (Pepsi Cola Bottling Co.), 305 NLRB 268, 139 LRRM 1206 (1991) (the Board found that the union filed three grievances in retaliation for certain employees having voted to decertify it and another union, and that the union's action was an unlawful attempt to apply the collective bargaining agreement to employees other than those for whom the agreement was nego-

The more serious threat to the health and integrity of the grievance procedure (including arbitration) comes from other causes. A valuable study of distressed grievance procedures and their rehabilitation reveals various impediments to a healthy grievance procedure, including such factors as: the failure to screen grievances; factional strife within the union; the desire of the union shop committee to perpetuate itself (by the indiscriminate filing of grievances); poor investigation of grievances; poor steward training; an intransigent position taken by the company on practically all grievances; the failure of top management to back up industrial relations personnel, and their inclination to pass the buck to an arbitrator; overgenerous grievance pay; and the availability of free or subsidized arbitration.[29] Identifying another impediment, a management representative stated that foremen are generally well trained but that they should be better trained in the human relations aspects of their job and should not automatically assume a defensive attitude in favor of the company.[30]

i. *Remedies for Distressed Grievance Procedures*
[LA CDI 93.47; 93.48; 100.0738]

Among the remedial devices suggested to rehabilitate distressed grievance procedures are mass grievance settlements, screening of grievances, direct negotiations between management and union officials at higher levels of authority, and procedural changes.[31] It generally is agreed that screening of grievances is a most beneficial remedy, though this remedy may not be fully available due to internal union politics and union fears of legal liability to employees for failure to process grievances.[32]

---

tiated); Teamsters Local 705 (Emery Air Freight Corp.), 278 NLRB 1303, 122 LRRM 1050 (1986), *enforcement denied*, 820 F.2d 448, 125 LRRM 2705 (D.C. Cir. 1987) (the Board held that *Bill Johnson's Restaurants v. NLRB*, 461 U.S. 731, 113 LRRM 2647 (1983), does not apply where the objective of filing the grievance is illegal under federal law).

[29]Ross, *Distressed Grievance Procedures and Their Rehabilitation, in* LABOR ARBITRATION AND INDUSTRIAL CHANGE, PROCEEDINGS OF THE 16TH ANNUAL MEETING OF NAA 104, 107–08 (Kahn ed., BNA Books 1963).

[30]Comments of Harry W. Lacey, *in* PROCEEDINGS OF THE CONFERENCE ON IMPROVING THE RELATIONS BETWEEN THE PARTIES 29 (Univ. of Notre Dame Press 1960).

[31]For the pros and cons of these and other suggested remedies, see *Changes Needed in Grievance Process*, 135 LRR 334 (1990); Ross, NAA 16TH PROCEEDINGS, at 111 et seq. Also dealing with revival of distressed procedures, see Luskin, *The Presidential Address: Arbitration and Its Critics, in* DEVELOPMENTS IN AMERICAN FOREIGN ARBITRATION, PROCEEDINGS OF THE 21ST ANNUAL MEETING OF NAA 125, 132–34 (Rehmus ed., BNA Books 1968). Warning against "grab bag" settlements, where some individual employee grievances of possible merit are abandoned by the union in exchange for the allowance of other grievances, see Summers, *The Individual Employee's Rights Under the Collective Agreement: What Constitutes Fair Representation, in* ARBITRATION—1974, PROCEEDINGS OF THE 27TH ANNUAL MEETING OF NAA 14, 27–28 (Dennis & Somers eds., BNA Books 1975).

[32]*See* Jones & Smith, *Management and Labor Appraisals and Criticisms of the Arbitration Process: A Report With Comments*, 62 MICH. L. REV. 1115, 1152–53 (1964). As to extent of concern, by union officials, regarding possible legal liability, see Kleeb, *The Individual Employee's Rights Under the Collective Agreement: What Constitutes Fair Representation: Comment, in* NAA 27TH PROCEEDINGS, at 41, 42; *A Colloquium on the Arbitration Process, in* LABOR ARBITRATION PERSPECTIVES AND PROBLEMS, PROCEEDINGS OF THE 17TH ANNUAL MEETING OF NAA 82, 100–02, 106, 109 (Kahn ed., BNA Books 1964) (panel discussion). United Mine Workers' counsel Harrison Combs explained that even when a union is convinced that an employee's grievance is meritless, "when you get to the question of onsite settling of griev-

B. Failure to Comply Strictly With Technical Requirements of the Grievance Procedure   [LA CDI 93.4667; 93.467; 100.0733; 100.0735]

A general presumption exists that favors arbitration over dismissal of grievances on technical grounds.[33] Applying this presumption to a situation where the grievant did not testify in the preliminary stages of the proceeding, one arbitrator found a grievance arbitrable because the specific language of the contract surrounding the grievance procedure did not require such testimony and thus implied informality.[34]

However, where the parties' collective bargaining agreements contain specific language and requirements regarding the filing of grievances, arbitrators will deny a grievance where the procedure is not followed,[35] at least in the absence of mitigating circumstances.[36] Arbitrators also will sustain a union's grievance against an employer if the employer likewise fails to follow the proper grievance procedure.[37]

Finally, regardless of the procedure followed during the steps leading to arbitration, if a party does not timely object to the arbitrability of the grievance, but instead waits until the hearing or shortly before the hearing to object, some arbitrators hold that the party waived the objection.[38]

4. Should Grievance Machinery Be Open to All Complaints?
[LA CDI 93.29; 100.0718]

Professor Harry Shulman urged that every grievance should be received, heard, and considered seriously and sympathetically, and that, to the extent

---

ances, it isn't as free as you might think"; that the union "may get slapped with a charge of failure to fairly represent"; and that "it's a real danger." Thus, the meritless grievance may be taken to arbitration because of overcaution by the union. The President's Commission on Coal, Labor-Management Seminar I, Collective Bargaining (Mar. 21, 1979), at 71 (No. 0–302–756, Gov't Printing Office 1979). He pointed in particular to the Supreme Court's *Hines v. Anchor Motor Freight*, 424 U.S. 554, 91 LRRM 2481 (1976), decision on the duty of fair representation. Discussing *Hines* and related decisions, see section 9., "Grievance Adjustment by Individual Employees," below, and see Chapter 2, section 2.A.ii.d.(2), "De Novo Litigation of Claims Cognizable Under the Labor Management Relations Act." Although, as noted above, the Supreme Court, in *NLRB v. Acme Industrial Co.*, 385 U.S. 432, 64 LRRM 2069 (1967), emphasized the necessity of sifting out unmeritorious claims, it is apparent that other considerations may impede the attainment of this objective. Nonetheless, some parties have been very successful in resolving grievances short of arbitration. See Chapter 4, section 2.B., "'Permanent' Arbitrators," noting the successful efforts of General Motors and the United Auto Workers.

[33]Rodeway Inn, 102 LA 1003, 1013 (Goldberg, 1994).

[34]*Id.*

[35]Monroe Mfg., 107 LA 877, 879 (Stephens, 1996).

[36]For example, in *Teamsters Local 89 (Frito Lay)*, 00-1 ARB ¶3278 (Weisheit, 1999), the arbitrator excused the aggrieved employee's failure to comply with the contractual requirement to cite the specific provision of the contract as the basis for the grievance, because the requirement was relatively recent and the parties had agreed to ease into the requirement. *See also* Sterling Chems., 114 LA 269 (Baroni, 2000) (a letter from a private attorney protesting the discharge of an employee qualified as a grievance—the parties had handled grievances informally in the past and the letter otherwise substantially satisfied the requirements for grievance filing).

[37]USS, Div. of USX Corp., 107 LA 772, 775 (Neyland, 1996); Wisconsin Tissue Mills, 102 LA 601, 605 (Jacobs, 1994).

[38]Ardco, Inc., 108 LA 326, 330 (Wolff, 1997); Stone Container Corp., 105 LA 385, 388–89 (Berquist, 1995); Masolite Concrete Prods., 103 LA 10, 14 (Keenan, 1994).

possible, every grievance should be made the occasion for additional education of the parties and for a little more smoothing out of the wrinkles in their relationship.[39]

Some agreements do open the door of the grievance machinery to any complaint. The clause to this effect may take the following form:

> In the event of any complaints, grievances, difficulties, disagreements or disputes arising between the Company, its employees within the collective bargaining unit herein above defined, or the Union, there shall be no suspension of plant operations but an earnest effort shall be made to settle such difference, complaints, grievances, difficulties, disagreements, or disputes forthwith in the following manner [the particulars of the grievance procedure are set forth].[40]

Many agreements, however, limit the grievance procedure to complaints involving the "interpretation or application" of the agreement, or otherwise state exclusions from the grievance procedure.[41] The question of whether a complaint is subject to the grievance procedure may itself be processed through the grievance procedure and arbitration. As a rule, grievance statements should not be too general in nature.

For example, an arbitrator may not consider an employer's entire substance abuse policy, but rather only that provision of the policy to which the grievant was subjected, where the policy was part of the employer's final contract offer, the union did not grieve the implementation of the policy as a whole, and the union had not filed an unfair labor practice charge.[42] However, failure to cite the relevant contract provisions in the grievance will not necessarily prevent an arbitrator from considering such provisions.[43]

Whether an arbitrator may decide an issue that raises a question under labor or employment laws depends on the nature of the issue and the underlying facts.[44] Where the contract contains a nondiscrimination clause, an

---

[39]CONFERENCE ON TRAINING OF LAW STUDENTS IN LABOR RELATIONS, VOL. III: TRANSCRIPT OF PROCEEDINGS 702–03 (1947). Regarding the scope of the right of public-sector employees to express complaints to their employer under the First Amendment, see *Givhan v. Western Line Consol. Sch. Dist.*, 439 U.S. 410, 18 FEP Cases 1424 (1979).

[40]From an agreement between Windsor Mfg. Co. and Textile Workers Union. *See also* NLRB Prof'l Ass'n, 86 LA 689 (Bowers, 1986).

[41]*See Major Collective Bargaining Agreements: Arbitration Procedures*, at 6, 9 (U.S. Dep't Lab. Bull. No. 1425-6, 1966); *Major Collective Bargaining Agreements: Grievance Procedures*, at 2, 6 (U.S. Dep't Lab. Bull. No. 1425-1, 1964).

[42]Jefferson Smurfit Corp., 106 LA 306, 311–12 (Goldstein, 1996).

[43]Consolidated Drum Reconditioning, 108 LA 523, 524 (Richman, 1997) (union did not waive contention that employee was not in probationary status, even though union's grievance did not cite contract provision dealing with the employer's probation policy); Motion Picture & Television Fund, 103 LA 988, 991 (Gentile, 1994) (union may discuss contractual article not cited in original grievance where article is subsumed in any consideration of management's policy at issue).

[44]Southern Bag Corp., 108 LA 348, 353–54 (Overstreet, 1997) (arbitrator will decide whether NLRA was violated when the 6-month statute of limitations for filing charge with NLRB has run); Arizona Opera Co., 105 LA 1126, 1130–31 (Wyman, 1996) (arbitrator has authority to decide violation of NLRA where union has not filed unfair labor practice charge); Steelworkers, 105 LA 961, 963 (Lesnick, 1995) (arbitrator need not defer determination of issue pending NLRB decision where there is no showing that such decision will illuminate issue of whether contract violation occurred). *Cf.* Laborers v. Food & Commercial Workers (Smithfield Packing Co.), 107 LA 503, 505 (Fraser, 1996) (arbitrator will not withhold award due to alleged NLRA violation that should be dealt with before NLRB); Swift Cleaning & Laundry, 106 LA 954 (Nelson, 1995) (arbitrator does not have authority to hear question of

arbitrator may consider issues of discrimination based on age, race, gender or pregnancy, national origin, disability, or religion.[45]

A. Former Employees' Access to the Grievance Machinery

i. Retirees' Status as Grievants

Sometimes former employees may utilize the grievance procedure to file grievances arising from their previous employment status.

In *Allied Chemical & Alkali Workers Local 1 v. Pittsburgh Plate Glass Co.*,[46] the Supreme Court held that retired employees were not employees within the meaning of the NLRA, and that there was no requirement that an employer bargain regarding the benefits received by employees who had retired. As a corollary proposition, the U.S. Court of Appeals for the Eight Circuit,[47] in dealing with "duty of fair representation" matters, held that because retirees were not employees covered in the bargaining unit, the union did not have to represent the retirees. Thus, absent a clear and unmistakable inclusion of retirees under the grievance procedure, they are not covered by the grievance procedure and their benefits, as retirees, are not subject to arbitration.

One arbitrator, after examining the language in the collective bargaining agreement, did find that the definition of a grievance was expansive enough to include former employees' complaints[48] and allowed them to file and process a grievance.

ii. Status of Employees Who Have Resigned as Grievant

Employees who have resigned may subsequently claim that their resignation was, in reality, a constructive discharge and, in that context, is subject to the "just cause" and grievance provisions applicable to all employees. Whether a resignation was, in fact, a forced decision equivalent to a termination is obviously a factual matter.

The NLRB has developed standards for determining whether an apparent voluntary quit is, in reality, a constructive discharge. In *Crystal Princeton Refining Co.*, [49] the Board held that:

---

representation or appropriateness of unit); Norfolk Shipbuilding & Drydock Corp., 105 LA 529, 533 (Hockenberry, 1995) (*Weingarten* (NLRB v. J. Weingarten, Inc., 420 U.S. 251, 88 LRRM 2689 (1975)) issue not reviewable by arbitrator, where NLRB has not deferred on issue but rather settled matter without issuing complaint).

[45]Flamingo Hilton-Laughlin, 108 LA 545 (Weckstein, 1997) (disability); Champion Int'l Corp., 106 LA 1024 (Howell, 1996) (same); Clallam County Pub. Hosp., 105 LA 609 (Calhoun, 1995) (religion); San Francisco Unified Sch. Dist., 104 LA 215 (Bogue, 1995) (disability); Motion Picture & Television Fund, 103 LA 988 (Gentile, 1994) (national origin); Minnegasco, Inc., 103 LA 43 (Bognanno, 1994) (pregnancy).

[46]404 U.S. 157, 78 LRRM 2974 (1971).

[47]Anderson v. Alpha Portland Indus., 727 F.2d 177, 115 LRRM 2249 (8th Cir. 1983).

[48]Marion County, Or., 108 LA 698, 701 (Downing, 1997).

[49]222 NLRB 1068, 91 LRRM 1302 (1976).

There are two elements which must be proven to establish a "constructive discharge." First, the burden imposed upon the employee must cause, and be intended to cause, a change in his working conditions so difficult or unpleasant as to force him to resign. Second, it must be shown that those burdens were imposed because of the employee's union activities.[50]

Obviously, the second part of the test would not necessarily be applicable to an arbitration proceeding charging a violation of an existing collective bargaining agreement rather than the labor law. In the absence of proof that an employee had not voluntarily resigned, the former employee is foreclosed from access to the contractual grievance procedure.[51]

iii. Status of Grievance Filed by Subsequently Deceased Employees

There are no published arbitration decisions relating to the continuing arbitrability of a pending grievance after the grievant has died. In an unpublished decision,[52] an arbitrator found that the death of an employee who had grieved his discharge did not preclude arbitration of his grievance.

The employer had argued that the benefit sought in the arbitration would belong to the grievant's estate, a party not covered by the collective bargaining agreement, and therefore could be pursued only through an independent action by the decedent's representative. The arbitrator found that the grievance procedure belonged to the union, and that the grievance survived the death of the grievant. Obviously, while reinstatement was not possible, if the arbitrator found merit in the grievance, a compensatory, "make-whole" remedy was available covering the period between the date of discharge to the date of the grievant's death.[53]

In contrast, controversies over the benefits that employees will receive when they retire is an arbitrable matter because it affects the interests of employees presently in the unit.[54]

B. Management and Union Grievances [LA CDI 93.90; 100.0748]

Express provision is sometimes made for the initiation of management grievances at some stage of the grievance procedure.[55] Absent an express provision on the matter, the company's right to submit grievances depends

---

[50]*Id.* at 1069.

[51]Chivas Prods., 101 LA 546, 548 (Kanner, 1993).

[52]AAA Case No. 16-300-00014-93 (Aronin, Aug. 9, 1996) (unpublished).

[53]The arbitrator, in part, relied on the NLRB's doctrine of allowing an unfair labor practice case to continue when the charging employee had died and providing for any back pay due the employee to go to the employee's estate. St. Regis Paper Co., 285 NLRB 293, 126 LRRM 1017 (1987).

[54]*See* Independent Lift Truck Builders Union v. NACCO Materials Handling Group, 202 F.3d 965, 163 LRRM 2321 (7th Cir. 2000).

[55]Of 400 agreements examined in one survey, 26% provided for company grievances. BASIC PATTERNS IN UNION CONTRACTS 34 (BNA Books 14th ed. 1995). *See* Veterans Admin. Med. Ctr., 90 LA 964, 968 (Byars, 1988).

on the interpretation of the particular agreement.[56] The presence of a no-lockout clause may be a very significant factor in an arbitrator's conclusion that company grievances are permitted where the agreement does not deal expressly with the question.[57]

A union grievance against a company may also be cognizable under certain circumstances. For example, the U.S. Court of Appeals for the Eighth Circuit held that two union grievances against an employer were arbitrable because the dispute concerned the interpretation and application of the collective bargaining agreement, the arbitration clause was broad, and the agreement did not contain exclusionary language.[58]

5. Procedural Requirements

A. Signature of Grievant [LA CDI 93.309]

Sometimes an agreement will require, either specifically or by implication, that employee grievances be signed or otherwise presented by the aggrieved employee or employees.[59] One purpose of such requirements is to aid the employer in evaluating and responding to the grievance.[60] Arbitrators who strictly enforce such requirements have held that complaints signed

---

[56]*See* Meletron Corp., 36 LA 315, 317–19 (Jones, Jr., 1961). *See also* Lehigh Portland Cement v. Cement Workers, 849 F.2d 820, 128 LRRM 2766 (3d Cir. 1988); Kessler, Inc., 88 LA 1273, 1275–76 (Glazer, 1987); Chase Bag Co., 42 LA 153, 154 (Elkouri, 1963). Earlier cases appeared to require clear language authorizing company grievances in order to open the grievance procedure to the company. *See* Bassick Co. v. Bassick (IUE) Local 229, 24 LA 59 (D. Conn. 1954); Hinson Mfg. Co., 20 LA 688, 690 (Davey, 1953). In contrast, an arbitrator would require "clear and unambiguous language" in the collective agreement to bar federal agency management from filing grievances. Navy Exch., Naval Station, 73 LA 1016, 1019–20 (Bailer, 1979). A similar result for the private sector, at least for some cases, may be indicated by *Eberle Tanning Co. v. Food & Commercial Workers Section 63L*, 682 F.2d 430, 110 LRRM 3136, 3139 (3d Cir. 1982). By discussing a company grievance through the grievance procedure up to arbitration, the union waived any right to object that the contract made no provision for company grievances. Whitlock Mfg. Co., 19 LA 234, 236 (Stutz, 1952).

[57]*See* Schofield Mfg. Co., 45 LA 225, 226–27 (Duff, 1965); Chase Bag Co., 42 LA 153, 154–55 (Elkouri, 1963); Meletron Corp., 36 LA 315, 317–19 (Jones, Jr., 1961).

[58]Steelworkers v. Titan Tire, 204 F.3d 858, 163 LRRM 2644 (8th Cir. 2000).

[59]In nearly half of labor contracts, an employee is given the option of either filing a grievance alone or in the presence of a union representative. Basic Patterns in Union Contracts 33–34 (BNA Books 14th ed. 1995). A requirement for the signatures of individual employees on grievances has been held not to be a mandatory subject of bargaining. Bethlehem Steel Co., 136 NLRB 1500, 50 LRRM 1013 (1962), *enforcement denied on other grounds*, 320 F.2d 615, 53 LRRM 2878 (3d Cir. 1963). *See* U.S. Steel Corp., 89 LA 300, 305–06 (Dybeck, 1987).

[60]*See* Geigy Chem. Corp., 34 LA 102, 104–05 (Morvant, 1960); John Deere Harvester Works, 10 LA 778, 782 (Updegraff, 1948). Where this purpose is otherwise adequately achieved, an arbitrator might feel less strictly bound by the employee signature requirement. *See* Republic Steel Corp., 11 LA 691, 694–95 (McCoy, 1948).

only by a union steward do not qualify as grievances.[61] In some of these cases, the grievance was of a personal nature (as distinguished from a "policy" or a "general" grievance), but even policy grievances have been held to be subject to the employee signature requirement.[62] However, some arbitrators have viewed the provision for employee signatures to initiate the grievance process as a mere formality,[63] or have otherwise indicated a strong inclination to find in favor of the union's right to initiate grievances.[64]

B. Group Grievances [LA CDI 93.305; 100.0720]

In general, a member of a bargaining unit does not have standing to file a grievance without a showing that he or she has been adversely affected by the claimed violation and has a personal interest in the outcome. The situation is different, of course, if the grievance is presented as a "group grievance" (sometimes referred to as a "class action") or when its sponsor is an official of the union.[65]

----

[61]*See* Hillsborough Area Reg'l Transit Auth., 80 LA 644, 645–46 (von Rohr, 1983) (union president's signature not sufficient); Vogue Coach Corp., 72 LA 1156, 1159 (Gentile, 1979); Combustion Eng'g, 54 LA 1118, 1120 (Erbs, 1971); True Temper Corp., 53 LA 1230, 1233–34 (Eigenbrod, 1969); U.S. Steel Corp., 49 LA 278, 279–80 (Dybeck, 1967); M&E Co., 44 LA 76, 82 (Lennard, 1965); Joyce-Cridland Co., 41 LA 947, 952 (Seinsheimer, 1963); Howell Elec. Motors Co., 38 LA 580, 582–83 (Kahn, 1961); Caterpillar Tractor Co., 37 LA 659, 661 (Larkin, 1961); John Deere Harvester Works, 10 LA 778, 782 (Updegraff, 1948); Ford Motor Co., 3 LA 840, 841 (Shulman, 1946). *See also* International Harvester Co., 23 LA 64, 65 (Cole, 1954). Where there are multiple grievants, each may be required to sign to be included. *See* Independent Sch. Dist., 68 LA 325, 330–31 (Conway, 1977); True Temper Corp., 53 LA 1230, 1233–34 (Eigenbrod, 1969); M&E Co., 44 LA 76, 82 (Lennard, 1965); Geigy Chem. Corp., 34 LA 102, 104–05 (Morvant, 1960); Vulcan Corp., 28 LA 633, 634 (Howlett, 1957); John Deere Harvester Works, 10 LA 778, 782 (Updegraff, 1948). As to any need to verify the grievant's signature, see *American Airlines*, 46 LA 440, 442–43 (Sembower, 1966). In *Sohio Chem. Co.*, 141 NLRB 810, 52 LRRM 1390, 1391 (1963), the NLRB strictly construed a provision for signature by "the employee or the employee and his steward" to require the assent of the aggrieved employee to the filing of a grievance. *But see* Roadmaster Corp. v. NLRB, 874 F.2d 448, 131 LRRM 2483 (7th Cir. 1989) (court affirmed the Board's holding that it was unlawful to discharge a union official for signing an employee's name when the action was taken to ensure the grievance was timely filed and to protect the union from a duty of fair representation claim).

[62]*See* Joyce-Cridland Co., 41 LA 947, 952 (Seinsheimer, 1963); Howell Elec. Motors Co., 38 LA 580, 582–83 (Kahn, 1961); Caterpillar Tractor Co., 37 LA 659, 661 (Larkin, 1961).

[63]*See* Magic Chef, 88 LA 1046, 1049 (Caraway, 1987) (a group grievance was arbitrable without requiring a list of aggrieved employees or a specific description of the occurrence, but, on request, the union must provide the company with specific information prior to a hearing on the merits); Von Weise Gear Co., 51 LA 714, 715 (Bernstein, 1968); Industrial Gasket & Packing Co., 45 LA 847, 848–49 (Coffey, 1965) (omission of employee signature was not a defect as to substance and signature by a union representative will suffice).

[64]*See* BP Oil, 73 LA 347, 349 (Berkowitz, 1979); Brush Beryllium Co., 55 LA 709, 714 (Dworkin, 1970); Ohio Power Co., 45 LA 1039, 1044 (Leach, 1965); Sinclair Ref. Co., 42 LA 376, 384 (Willingham, 1964); Great W. Sugar Co., 40 LA 652, 658 (Seligson, 1963) (under public policy there is a presumption of union right to initiate grievances). *See also* City of Pawtucket Police Dep't, 88 LA 356, 358 (McAuliffe, 1986); Standard Oil Co. of Cal., 69 LA 164, 167–68 (Anderson, 1977); Frederick J. Dando Co., 69 LA 48, 51 (Di Leone, 1977); A.E. Moore Co., 62 LA 149, 151–53 (Greco, 1974).

[65]Cyprus Emerald Res. Corp., 101 LA 1053, 1055 (Ipavec, 1993) (citing Case No. EMC/D 22-86-43 (Feldman)). *See also* UPS Inc., 110 LA 1204 (Baroni, 1998) (grievant, a driver, had no standing to grieve the use of supervisors to assist with cleanup work, because driver was not a member of adversely affected classifications).

It is widely accepted that a union has standing to file a group grievance that affects a significant portion of the bargaining unit.[66] A grievance submitted by a union was found to be arbitrable although the contract did not expressly include the union within the definition of a "grievant," because the provision allowing for the filing of group grievances implied that the union could be a party.[67] A grievance filed by the union need not be signed by an employee member of the bargaining unit.[68]

Even when a provision in an agreement requires the employees themselves to file grievances, the requirement may be deemed waived if the employer had notice of the grievances and an opportunity to be heard.[69]

C. Waiver of Procedural Requirements and Substantive Rights
[LA CDI 93.47; 93.48; 100.0738; 100.0760]

Waivers, because they result in defeat of the rights of the parties without consideration of the merits of the dispute, are not lightly inferred by arbitrators. Thus, two grievances filed in a dispute over the issuance of reprimands and involuntary transfers were held to be arbitrable, despite the contention that the union had waived the right to process them in the course of responding to the employer's request for clarification, because the union never explicitly withdrew them.[70]

Questions arise (1) whether individual employees may waive their rights under the collective bargaining agreement, and (2) whether the employer may waive a contractual requirement that grievances be signed by the aggrieved employee or a requirement that the aggrieved employee be named. As to the latter question, arbitrators usually hold that a employer who fails to make timely objection to the noncompliance with the requirement has waived its right to complain.[71] Similarly, the requirement may be held unen-

---

[66]Cyprus Emerald Res. Corp., 101 LA 1053, 1055 (Ipavec, 1993).

[67]Los Angeles Cmty. Coll. Dist., 103 LA 1174, 1178 (Kaufman, 1994).

[68]Teamsters Local 744 v. Skokie Valley Beverage Co., 644 F. Supp. 213, 123 LRRM 3175 (N.D. Ill. 1986); Klosterman Baking Co., 95 LA 1224 (Bell, 1990); Texas Utils. Mining Co., 94 LA 160 (Baroni, 1990) (grievance arbitrable even where the employee filing the grievance elected not to pursue matter, where grievant testified grievance was filed on behalf of entire bargaining unit); Allegheny Ludlum Steel Corp., 86 LA 492 (Mullin, 1986) (grievance signed by only 20 of the 150 employees affected by closed department was treated by the arbitrator as a "general character" grievance under the agreement); Niagara Frontier Transp. Auth., 85 LA 229 (Lawson, 1985); District of Columbia Metro. Police Dep't, 82 LA 701 (Feigenbaum, 1984).

[69]Teamsters Local 657 v. Stanley Structures, 735 F.2d 903, 117 LRRM 2119 (5th Cir. 1984).

[70]Astro-Valcour, 93 LA 91 (Rocha, Jr., 1989) (no waiver where grievant bypassed the first two steps of the grievance procedure and timely filed written grievance at the third step where the contract provides that a grievance arising from suspension or discharge will automatically go to the third step); Grossmont Union High Sch. Dist., 91 LA 909 (Weiss, 1988). *But see* Ball Corp., 98 LA 233 (Duff, 1991) (12 outstanding grievances are sustained on ground that employer's step 4 responses were untimely, notwithstanding longstanding practice of granting extensions; where extensions were always in response to requests, employer failed to make such request, and prior awards sustained grievances on same ground under same language); Metropolitan Tulsa Transit Auth., 98 LA 205 (Goodman, 1991) (employer waived right to raise procedural arbitrability defense based on union failure to schedule required step 2 meeting).

[71]*See* Ren Elecs. Corp. v. Electrical Workers (UE) Local 208, 665 F. Supp. 77, 127 LRRM 2173 (D. Mass. 1989); Snap-on Tools, 50 LA 167, 169–70 (Dolnick, 1968); Perfection Biscuit, 49 LA 1095, 1096–97 (Kates, 1967); Berg Airlectro Prods. Co., 43 LA 140, 144–45 (Larkin,

forceable (for the case under advisement) because the employer's previous tolerance of noncompliance has been deemed to have resulted in a "past practice."[72]

An individual employee whose contract rights personal to him or her allegedly have been violated may refuse to file or prosecute a grievance.[73] But arbitrators have held that the union, as a party to the contract, may step in and press the issue, if it is one affecting employees generally, in order to assure observance by the employer of the provisions in question.[74] In upholding the right of the union to police the agreement, arbitrators have recognized that the interests of the union and those of an individual employee do not always coincide.[75] Thus, the consequence is that an employee may waive a purely personal right under the agreement (such as the right to a promotion), but that the employee may not waive other rights (which affect the interests of other employees or the union) against the wishes of the union.[76]

6. STEPS IN GRIEVANCE PROCEDURE [LA CDI 93.45, 100.0730]

A. Overview

The grievance machinery usually consists of a series of procedural steps to be taken within specified time limits.[77] The nature of the procedure will

---

1964). *But see* Vogue Coach Corp., 72 LA 1156, 1159 (Gentile, 1979).

[72]*See* Snap-on Tools, 50 LA 167, 169–70 (Dolnick, 1968); Marsco Mfg. Co., 49 LA 817, 818, 820–21 (Sembower, 1967); Fairbanks Morse, Inc., 47 LA 224, 226 (Fisher, 1966); Berg Airlectro Prods. Co., 43 LA 140, 144–45 (Larkin, 1964).

[73]Atlantic Seaboard Corp., 42 LA 865, 869 (Lugar, 1964). *See also* Von Weise Gear Co., 51 LA 714, 715 (Bernstein, 1968); U.S. Steel Corp., 44 LA 168, 174 (Garrett, 1965).

[74]Whiteway Stamping Co., 41 LA 966, 968 (Kates, 1963); Baur Bros. Bakery, 36 LA 1422, 1423 (Joseph, 1961). *Cf.* Cardinal Am. Corp., 74 LA 1296, 1296 (Perry, 1980); U.S. Air Force, 73 LA 185, 187 (Graham, 1979).

[75]*See* Pittston, Pa., Sch. Dist., 93 LA 117, 118–19 (Zirkel, 1989) (sustaining the union's right to file a grievance where the school district improperly permitted a chemistry teacher, over the objection of the union, to voluntarily use scheduled study-hall periods to help advanced placement students on request); Gulf Atl. Distribution Servs., 88 LA 475, 480 (Williams, 1986) (union has strong reason to object to the employer asking job applicants to waive a contract right); Food Mktg. Corp., 88 LA 98, 103–04 (Doering, 1986) (where uncertainty exists as to whether a dispute involves a purely personal right or a right affecting others, the employer should keep the union informed even though the employee has declined the offer of union participation); Great W. Sugar Co., 40 LA 652, 658 (Seligson, 1963) (recognizing possible diverse interests); Eastern Shore Pub. Serv. Co., 39 LA 751, 756–58 (Frey, 1962) (recognizing right to police).

[76]United States Borax & Chem. Corp., 41 LA 1200, 1203 (Leonard, 1963). As to personal rights, see also *U.S. Air Force*, 73 LA 185, 187 (Graham, 1979); as to other rights, see also *W.R. Grace & Co.*, 91 LA 170 (Taylor, 1988); *Georgia-Pac. Corp.*, 90 LA 573 (Crane, 1988); *Pride Prof'l Servs.*, 88 LA 229, 231–32 (Gallagher, 1986); *Trew-Craft Corp.*, 87 LA 1113, 1116 (Kanner, 1986); *Chilstrom Erecting Co.*, 87 LA 721, 724 (Redel, 1986); *Bliss & Laughlin Indus.*, 73 LA 72, 73 (Belshaw, 1979); *Lady Balt. Bakery Co.*, 47 LA 8, 10 (Koven, 1966). For related discussion, see Chapter 10, section 9., "Waiver and Estoppel."

[77]Precise pleadings in moving from step to step ordinarily should not be required. *See* Henry Vogt Mach. Co., 46 LA 654, 657 (Stouffer, 1966). One arbitrator has taken the view that a grievance alleging violation of a prior agreement but filed during the term of the subsequent agreement is to be processed under the procedures designated in the prior agreement. Dover Corp., 48 LA 965, 968 (Volz, 1966). *See also* Columbia Portland Cement Co. v. NLRB, 915 F.2d 253, 135 LRRM 2607 (6th Cir. 1990).

depend on the structure of the company and on the needs and desires of the parties, but there is a tendency to follow a fairly definite pattern. Grievances ordinarily are taken by the aggrieved employee, either with or without a union representative, to the first-line supervisor,[78] and, if no settlement is reached, may be appealed through successive steps of the management hierarchy and, in most cases, then taken to arbitration. The aggrieved may be represented successively by the shop steward, the business agent, the union shop committee, and international union representatives.[79]

Small companies can be expected to have short, simple grievance procedures, sometimes with only one or two steps. Larger companies usually have multistep procedures. Three-step and four-step procedures probably are most common,[80] but procedures with five or six steps are sometimes used, especially in workplaces that are units of a multiplant company.[81] The employee often is represented by the union grievance committee at the intermediate steps and by an international union representative at the next to last step and also at the last step.[82] The more steps in a grievance procedure, the more formal it can be expected to be. There is such variation in multistep procedures that no one plan may be said to be really typical. An indication, however, of what might be found in a multistep procedure is provided by the following illustration:

> Should any employee, subject to this agreement, believe he has been unjustly dealt with, or that any of the provisions of this agreement have been violated, he shall present his alleged grievance to the Foreman of his department within five (5) days of the occurrence of such grievance.
>
> In case the grievance is not adjusted by the foreman it shall be reduced to writing upon forms provided by the Company and signed and dated by the aggrieved employee and his department committeeman and three copies furnished the foreman. The foreman will have inserted in the proper place on the form his disposition of the matter and will sign and date the same returning one (1) copy to the aggrieved employee and one (1) copy to the department committeeman representing the employee within five (5) days.
>
> If satisfactory adjustment is not made the department committeeman or his representative shall then take up the grievance with the General Foreman and General Superintendent in their respective order, within ten (10) days.
>
> If no satisfactory adjustment is then reached it shall be submitted for consideration and handling to the Manager of Works, or his representative, by the duly authorized General Committee or their representative, within ten (10) days.

---

[78]The absence of a readily accessible "first step" may lead an employee to resort to self-help. Also, when the parties had not established a grievance committee, an informal discussion of the grievance with the plant superintendent and the purchasing director, who was in charge of labor relations, was held to have satisfied step 1 and step 2 of the grievance procedure. Elyria Foundry Co., 87 LA 1129, 1133 (Duda, Jr., 1986). *See* Millage Produce, 45 LA 211, 214–15 (Miller, 1965) (discharge for insubordination was set aside). For related discussion, see section 8.B., "Right to Union Representation at Early Stage," below.

[79]*See also* BASIC PATTERNS IN UNION CONTRACTS 35–36 (BNA Books 14th ed. 1995). It has been suggested that the representative of each party at each succeeding step should be a different person, with higher authority than the representative at the preceding step. Manning, Maxwell & Moore, Inc., 37 LA 475, 480 (Stutz, 1961).

[80]*See* BASIC PATTERNS IN UNION CONTRACTS, at 33.

[81]*Grievance Procedure Under Collective Bargaining*, 63 MONTHLY LAB. REV. 175, 179 (1946).

[82]*Id.* at 180.

If after such consideration by the General Committee and the management, the grievance shall be unsettled, then the question shall be jointly submitted to the Chief Executive of the Company and the Chief Executive of the Brotherhood of Railway Carmen of America (or their representative) for joint conference within ten (10) days.[83]

B. Advanced Step Filing [LA CDI 93.45; 100.0730]

There are certain issues that by their nature are not capable of being settled at the preliminary stages of the procedure. Such grievances may include, for instance, those filed on behalf of the bargaining unit itself, where the nature of the grievance has unitwide, not individual, consequences.[84] Provision sometimes is made for filing such grievances at an advanced step of the procedure.[85]

The question might be raised whether, in the absence of such provision, it should be permissible to file grievances at an advanced step where it is obvious that they cannot be settled at preliminary steps. The view has been expressed that there should be strict conformity with the agreement lest the exception be used to short-circuit the first steps in all cases.[86]

But a contrary position was taken by one arbitrator who held that a grievance concerning veterans' vacation rights was properly initiated at the third step of the grievance procedure without presentation to the foreman at an earlier step.[87] The arbitrator denied the union's contention that it had the right to enter an advanced step "at any time they choose," but nevertheless held that it could do so in proper cases. He stated that it is well recognized in the practice of industrial relations that certain disputes of a general nature can only be resolved at a high level in the union and management official hierarchy:

> Then, again, particular circumstances may make it impractical to begin processing a grievance at the first step. . . .
>   It would seem to be quite proper for this grievance to be processed at the third-step level, for only at this level are all negotiators of the contract, those officers of company and union who knew the meaning and intent of the language of the contractual provision controlling, required to appear.[88]

---

[83]From an agreement between the Pullman-Standard Car Mfg. Co. and Brotherhood of Ry. Carmen.

[84]*See* City of Toledo, 109 LA 518 (Borland, 1997).

[85]Bypassing one or more steps in certain cases is permitted by 79% of the 400 agreements covered by one survey, where types of cases included in these provisions are also indicated. BASIC PATTERNS IN UNION CONTRACTS 354 (BNA Books 14th ed. 1995). *See* Astro-Valcour, 93 LA 91 (Rocha, Jr., 1989); Fort Frye Sch. Dist., 91 LA 1140 (Dworkin, 1988); U.S. Army Forces Command, 84 LA 1093, 1095, 1099 (Alsher, 1985).

[86]LAPP, HOW TO HANDLE LABOR GRIEVANCES 95–96 (1945). Holding that all grievances must go the prescribed route, including group and policy grievances, one arbitrator stated that it is not for the arbitrator to say that required steps can be ignored. Tenneco Oil Co., 40 LA 707, 710–12 (Abernethy, 1963).

[87]Manion Steel Barrel Co., 6 LA 164 (Wagner, 1947).

[88]*Id.* at 168. *See also* Bechtel Constr. v. Laborers, 812 F.2d 750, 124 LRRM 2785 (1st Cir. 1987) (whether a grievance has been properly processed is a question of procedural arbitrability for the arbitrator to decide). For similar comments, see *McCarthy Bros. Constr. Co.*, 83 LA 147, 151 (Heinsz, 1984); *Trane Co.*, 44 LA 212, 215 (Markowitz, 1965); *Advance Window Cleaning Co.*, 43 LA 695, 699 (Kates, 1964). Advanced step filing under proper cir-

In any event, the right to object to the lack of discussion of a grievance at a preliminary step may be held waived by failure to make a timely objection.[89] In addition, earlier steps of the grievance procedure will be considered to have been waived if a company official, other than the one specified in the agreement, accepts and processes the grievance.[90]

C. Grievance Mediation [LA CDI 100.06]

In recent years, the concept of "grievance mediation" has gained acceptance by the parties, and it has been added as a step to the grievance procedure in a growing number of collective bargaining agreements.[91] The neutral party or "mediator" does not decide the case nor is he or she given the authority to do so. Unlike an arbitrator, the mediator has no binding power over either of the parties to a grievance. The mediator generally attempts to elicit the facts of the dispute with as little formality as possible. Using creative suggestions, thoughtful questioning, and gentle persuasion, the mediator attempts to guide the two sides toward a mutually acceptable agreement. The major advantage of mediation is the spirit of cooperation that can result from mediatory efforts. Both sides come to the mediation table of their own free will; both sides compromise to develop a solution that is acceptable to both parties. A solution reached by such a method is more likely to work than a binding arbitration decision, which, by its very nature, is imposed on the losing party in a grievance dispute. Winners and losers are not produced by the mediation process; partners, however, often are.

If the grievance cannot be resolved by mediation, the mediator may deliver an immediate advisory, nonbinding, and confidential opinion as to how

---

cumstances was also permitted in *Redmer Plastics*, 79 LA 351, 355–56 (Eagle, 1982); *Sunshine Mining Co.*, 73 LA 540, 542 (O'Neill, 1979); *Folding Carrier Corp.*, 53 LA 784, 788–89 (Gorsuch, 1969); *Todd Shipyards Corp.*, 50 LA 645, 655 (Prasow, 1968); *Babcock & Wilcox Co.*, 48 LA 1234, 1237 (Gibson, 1967); *Combustion Eng'g*, 46 LA 289, 290 (Murphy, 1966); *Babcock & Wilcox Co.*, 42 LA 449, 453 (Dworkin, 1963); *Todd Shipyards Corp.*, 27 LA 153, 155–56 (Prasow, 1956); *Mercury Eng'g Corp.*, 14 LA 1049, 1053 (Kelliher, 1950). See also Sunshine Mining Co., 72 LA 479, 483–84 (Flagler, 1979).

[89]*See* Los Angeles County Prob. Dep't, 68 LA 1373, 1378 (Rothchild, 1977); Celluplastic Corp., 28 LA 659, 663 (Callaghan, 1957); General Baking Co., 28 LA 621, 622 (Donnelly, 1957); International Shoe Co., 20 LA 618, 619 (Kelliher, 1953); Celanese Corp. of Am., 17 LA 187, 189–90 (Jaffee, 1951).

[90]Peabody Coal Co., 87 LA 1002 (Volz, 1986).

[91]Ury, Brett & Goldberg, GETTING DISPUTES RESOLVED: DESIGNING SYSTEMS TO CUT THE COSTS OF CONFLICT (1988); Kauffman, *Expedited Arbitration and Other Innovations in Alternative Dispute Resolution*, 43 LAB. L.J. 382 (1992); Roberts, Wolters, Holley & Feild, *Grievance Mediation: A Management Perspective*, 45 ARB. J. No. 3, at 15 (1990); Silberman, *Breaking the Mold of Grievance Resolution: A Pilot Program in Mediation*, 44 ARB. J. No. 4, at 40 (1989); Goldberg, *AT&T Pacts Include Grievance Mediation*, 131 LRR 305 (1989) (agreements with Communications Workers and Electrical Workers (IBEW) provide for prearbitration of grievances in an experimental program); Schmedemann, *Reconciling Differences: The Theory and Law of Mediating Labor Grievances*, 9 INDUS. REL. L.J. No. 4, at 523 (1987); Sigler, *Mediation of Grievances: An Alternative to Arbitration*, 13 EMPLOYEE REL. L.J. No. 2, at 266 (1987); Goldberg, *The Rise in Grievance Mediation*, PROCEEDINGS OF THE NYU 37TH ANNUAL NAT'L CONFERENCE ON LABOR §13-1 et seq. (1984); Goldberg, *The Mediation of Grievances Under a Collective Bargaining Contract: An Alternative to Arbitration*, 77 NW. U. L. REV. 270 (1982).

the issue should be decided under the terms of the agreement. The parties can then use the advisory opinion as the basis for further settlement discussions, or they can submit the grievance to arbitration.

The three major requirements for effective "grievance mediation" are: "(1) the mediator must be selected from a source outside the company; (2) the mediator must be a person in whose competence and impartiality both sides can place their trust and respect; and (3) each party must approach the mediation with an open mind and a sincere resolve to reach agreement."[92] While grievance mediation is still a new and relatively untested method of settling labor disputes, its potential for success is unlimited.[93]

To illustrate the growing popularity of prearbitration grievance mediation, it is being used by, or has been provided for, in agreements between AT&T/Communications Workers (CWA); AMAX/Mine Workers; Amoco Oil Company/Oil, Chemical, Atomic Workers (OCAW); Bell South Corporation/ CWA; Boston Edison Company/Utility Workers (UWUA); Cleveland Cliffs, Inc./Steelworkers; Consumers Power (Michigan)/UWUA; Naval Ordinance Station (Louisville)/ Machinists; New England Telephone Company/Electrical Workers (IBEW); United Airlines/Air Line Pilots; United Airlines/Flight Attendants (AFA); University of Cincinnati/University Professors, CWA, and IBEW; Southwestern Bell/CWA, District 6; Southern Bell/CWA; Continental Telephone Co./IBEW; Thrifty Corp./Food & Commercial Workers; Conoco, Inc./OCAW; and several Washington State School Boards and the Washington Education Association.

7. TIME LIMITATIONS

A. Filing Grievances

i. In General [LA CDI 93.4661; 100.0733]

In the vast majority of cases, arbitrators strictly enforce contractual limitations on the time periods within which grievances must be filed, responded to, and carried through the steps of the grievance procedure where the parties have consistently enforced such requirements.[94] Untimely grievances will be refused a hearing.[95] Untimely responses will result in the grievance

---

[92]Conti, *Mediation of Work-Place Disputes: A Prescription for Organizational Health*, 11 EMPLOYEE REL. L.J. 291, 296 (1985).

[93]*See generally* Power, *Targeting a New Dimension to Dispute Resolution*, 37 LAB. L.J. 524 (1986); Bierman & Youngblood, *Resolving Unjust Discharge Cases: A Mediatory Approach*, 30 ARB. J. 48 (1985); Loewenberg, *Structure of Grievance Procedures*, 35 LAB. L.J. 44 (1984); Brett & Goldberg, *Grievance Mediation in the Coal Industry: A Field Experiment*, 37 INDUS. & LAB. REL. REV. 49 (1983); Bowers, Seeber & Stallworth, *Grievance Mediation: A Route to Resolution for the Cost-Conscious 1980's*, 33 LAB. L.J. 459 (1982).

[94]Protection Tech. Los Alamos, 104 LA 23, 29–30 (Finston, 1994).

[95]Cosmic Distribution, 92 LA 205 (Prayzich, 1989); Louie Glass Co., 85 LA 5 (Hart, 1985); Dana Corp., 83 LA 1053 (King, 1984); Mobile Video Servs., 83 LA 1009 (Hockenberry, 1984); Kansas Gas & Elec. Co., 83 LA 916 (Thornell, 1984). *Compare* Phillips 66 Co., 92 LA 1037 (Neas, 1989) (employer did not sustain burden of proof by preponderance of the evidence that union did not timely file grievance; overwhelming arbitral precedent supports resolving doubts as to compliance with time limits in favor of arbitrability).

being automatically sustained.[96] When the agreement does not specify any time limitations on the filing or processing of grievances, objections to timeliness may be overruled.[97] Similarly, the grievance may be allowed to proceed where the date of the event giving rise to the grievance is difficult to determine.[98] Some arbitrators conclude, however, that a requirement for filing a grievance within a reasonable time is inferred by the establishment of a grievance procedure.[99] Where the contract fails to state a time limit for filing grievances, but does provide specific time limits for taking grievances to the various steps of the procedure, the evident intent of the contract is that grievances must be filed with reasonable promptness.[100] Certain situations, however, are not subject to contractual time limits.

ii. Continuing Violations [LA CDI 93.4663]

Many arbitrators have held that "continuing" violations of the agreement (as opposed to a single isolated and completed transaction) give rise to "continuing" grievances in the sense that the act complained of may be said

---

[96]Huron Lime Co., 106 LA 997, 1003–04 (Bowers, 1996); Wisconsin Tissue Mills, 102 LA 601, 615 (Jacobs, 1994).

[97]Clougherty Packing Co., 85 LA 1053 (Richman, 1985); Mesker Indus., 85 LA 921 (Mikrut, 1985). See Gaylord Container Corp., 93 LA 465, 468 (Abrams, 1989); Dow Jones & Co., 66 LA 1271, 1273–74 (Siegel, 1976); Walgreen Co., 66 LA 443, 445 (Larkin, 1976); Penn-Dixie Cement Corp., 47 LA 601, 602 (Shister, 1966); Capital Times, 44 LA 585, 589 (Gundermann, 1965) (but recognizing an exception where undue hardship results to the other party from delayed filing); Marathon Rubber Prods. Co., 6 LA 238, 260 (Gilden, 1947) (grievance may be filed at any time during the contract term); Crosby Co., 5 LA 477, 478 (Whiting, 1946); Lapham-Hickey Co., 3 LA 327, 333 (Gilden, 1946). See also Food Employers Council, 87 LA 514, 516 (Kaufman, 1986); Warwick Mfg. Co., 26 LA 688, 692 (Havighurst, 1956); Raybestos-Manhattan, Inc., 21 LA 788, 792 (Copelof, 1954). Where an agreement did not contain any time limit for filing grievances, it was held that a grievance that was dismissed on procedural grounds could be refiled and processed to arbitration. Electrical Workers (IUE) Local 616 v. Byrd Plastics, 428 F.2d 23, 74 LRRM 2550 (3d Cir. 1970). Cases relating to delay as grounds for finding a waiver of contractual right to arbitration are collected in Spain v. Houston Oilers, 593 S.W.2d 746 (Tex. Ct. Civ. App. 1979).

[98]Colwell Gen., 104 LA 1036, 1041 (Brunner, 1995) (grievance timely where collective bargaining agreement does not specify triggering event); Regional Transp. Dist., 107 LA 813, 819 (Finston, 1996) (although triggering data difficult to determine, grievance found timely by resolving doubts as to timeliness in favor of processing grievance).

[99]See Roadway Express, 87 LA 224, 226–27 (Cooper, 1986); Nickel's Pay-Less Stores of Tulare County, 47 LA 1153, 1156–57 (Killion, 1966) (an unreported decision by Edgar A. Jones, Jr., is quoted to the same effect); New York Racing Ass'n, 43 LA 129, 134–37 (Scheiber, 1964); Bell Aircraft Corp., 24 LA 324, 330 (Somers, 1955). See also Drexel Univ., 85 LA 579, 580–81 (Kramer, 1985); Telescope Folding Furniture Co., 49 LA 837, 840–41 (Cox, 1967).

[100]See Veterans Admin., 90 LA 350 (Wilcox, 1987); Huber Pontiac, Inc., 47 LA 767, 775–76 (Traynor, 1966); Riverside Paper Co., 66-1 ARB ¶8185 (Greenwald, 1966); Management Servs., 26 LA 505, 507 (Williams, 1956); Barbet Mills, Inc., 19 LA 677, 681 (Maggs, 1952); Durham Hosiery Mills, 12 LA 311, 316 (Maggs, 1949). But see Chrysler Corp., 32 LA 274, 276 (Smith, 1959). A requirement for reasonably prompt filing was held to exist under a provision calling for expeditious grievance settlement. Kennecott Copper Corp., 35 LA 412, 413–14 (Ross, 1960). In American Bakeries Co., 44 LA 156, 160–61 (Jones, Jr., 1965), the arbitrator held that the union could file a grievance and hold its further processing in abeyance pending the occurrence of a similar incident, because the contract did not set time limits for processing grievances from step to step.

to be repeated from day to day, with each day treated as a new "occurrence."[101] These arbitrators permit the filing of such grievances at any time, although any back pay would ordinarily accrue only from the date of filing.[102] For example, where the agreement provided for filing "within ten working days of the occurrence," it was held that where employees were erroneously denied work, each day lost was to be considered an "occurrence" and that a grievance presented within 10 working days of any such day lost would be timely.[103]

iii. Untimely Filings [LA CDI 93.48; 100.0760]

If the parties allow a grievance to move from step to step in the procedure without making objections of untimeliness, the right to object may be deemed to have been waived.[104]

---

[101]Consolidation Coal, 112 LA 407, 408 (West, 1999); Tendercare Inc., 111 LA 1192 (Borland, 1998); Municipality of Anchorage, Alaska, 108 LA 97, 99 (Landau, 1997); Kuhlman Elec. Corp., 106 LA 429, 436 (Duda, Jr., 1996); Larry's Mkts., 105 LA 795, 799 (Lehleitner, 1995); Harding Galesburg Mkts., 103 LA 1158, 1163 (Daniel, 1994); U.S. Silica Co., 102 LA 342, 344–45 (Goodstein, 1994); Stone Container Corp., 102 LA 219, 220 (Thornell, 1994); Dyncorp Wallops Flight Facility, 101 LA 1033, 1036 (Jones, 1993); Hacienda Health Care, 101 LA 550, 552 (Levy, 1993); Klosterman Baking Co., 95 LA 1224 (Bell, 1990); Celina, Ohio, City Sch. Bd. of Educ., 94 LA 1001 (Dworkin, 1990); Friedland Indus., 94 LA 816 (Daniel, 1990); County of Oakland, Mich., 94 LA 451 (Daniel, 1990).

[102]E.g., City of Buffalo, N.Y., 93 LA 5, 8–9 (Pohl, 1989); Cleveland Pneumatic, 91 LA 428, 430–31 (Oberdank, 1988); Plain Dealer Publ'g Co., 90 LA 1042, 1044–45 (Kates, 1988); Hillel Day Sch., 89 LA 905, 907–08 (Lipson, 1987); Cincinnati Post, 89 LA 901, 903–04 (McIntosh, 1987); Jim Walter Res., 87 LA 857, 861 (Nicholas, Jr., 1986); Board of Educ. Special Dist. 1, 81 LA 41, 48 (Rotenberg, 1983); Hartley & Hartley, Inc., 74 LA 196, 198 (Daniel, 1980); Neville Chem. Co., 73 LA 405, 409 (Richman, 1979); Wallace Murray Corp., 72 LA 470, 473 (Abrams, 1979); Washington Mack Trucks, 71 LA 412, 418 (Cushman, 1978); Aeronca, Inc., 70 LA 1243, 1245 (Morgan, 1978); Brockway Co., 69 LA 1115, 1121 (Eischen, 1977); Mississippi Valley Structural Steel Co., 55 LA 23, 25 (Boothe, 1970); Miller Brewing Co., 49 LA 1028, 1033–34 (Slavney, Anderson, & Rice II, 1967); Dow Chem. Co., 49 LA 480, 481–82 (Shister, 1967); Nashville Bridge Co., 48 LA 44, 45–46 (Williams, 1967); Eaton Mfg. Co., 47 LA 1045, 1048 (Kates, 1966); H.K. Porter Co., 47 LA 408, 413 (Altrock, 1966); Line Materials Indus., 46 LA 1106, 1109–10 (Teple, 1966); Combustion Eng'g, 46 LA 289, 290–91 (Murphy); Steel Warehouse Co., 45 LA 357, 360–61 (Dolnick, 1965); Cornish Wire Co., 45 LA 271, 275 (1965); Kerr-McGee Oil Indus., 44 LA 701, 703 (Hayes, 1965); Avco Corp., 43 LA 765, 767–68 (Kornblum, 1964); Leland Airborne Prods., 62-2 ARB ¶8504 (Stouffer, 1962); Sears, Roebuck & Co., 39 LA 567, 570 (Gillingham, 1962); American Suppliers, 28 LA 424, 428 (Warns, 1957); Republic Steel Corp., 27 LA 262, 264–65 (Platt, 1956); Bethlehem Steel Co., 23 LA 538, 540 (Seward, 1954); Celanese Corp. of Am., 17 LA 303, 309 (Justin, 1951); Robertshaw-Fulton Controls Co., 15 LA 147, 149 (Gregory, 1949); Pacific Mills, 14 LA 387, 388 (Hepburn, 1950). Cf. PYA/Monarch Foodservice, 86 LA 694, 697 (Smith, 1985); Square D Co., 47 LA 382, 383–84 (Larkin, 1966); Truitt Mfg. Co., 27 LA 157, 159 (Livengood, 1956); Consolidated Vultee Aircraft Corp., 12 LA 786, 793–94 (Aaron, 1949). Retroactivity is not always limited to the date of filing. See Blaw-Knox Co., 50 LA 1086, 1089 (Meltzer, 1968). See also Automotive Finishes, 69 LA 897, 899–900 (Brown, 1977).

[103]Pacific Mills, 14 LA 387, 388 (Hepburn, 1950). See also Sevako v. Anchor Motor Freight, 792 F.2d 570, 122 LRRM 3316 (6th Cir. 1986); Dep't of Air Force, Warner Robins Air Logistics Ctr., 91 LA 1265, 1268 (Holley, Jr., 1988). But see Chemung Contracting Corp., 291 NLRB 773, 129 LRRM 1305 (1988); Southeastern Pa. Transp. Auth., 91 LA 1382, 1384 (Lang, 1988).

[104]Crestline Exempted Village Sch., 111 LA 114 (Goldberg, 1998) (stating "arbitration principle" that timeliness issues must be raised early in the grievance process, otherwise the argument is considered to be waived); Liquid Transporters, 99 LA 217 (Witney, 1992) (arbitration is not the place to raise timeliness issue for first time; grievance timely filed and to be heard on merits); Autoquip Corp., 98 LA 538 (Chumley, 1992) (grievance timely filed since no time limit was stated and the issue of timeliness was raised for first time at arbitration); Camp Lejeune Marine Corps Base, 90 LA 1126 (Nigro, 1988) (grievance filed 5 years after

Where the absence of strict time limits results in the acceptance of grievances notwithstanding delayed filing, the arbitrator may make the grievance adjustment retroactive only to the date on which the grievance was filed or to some other date short of full retroactivity.[105] In particular, arbitrators can be expected to deny that part of a claim that, if allowed, would result in a loss to one party caused by the negligent delay of the other party in asserting the claim. Whether the arbitrator calls such delay laches, acquiescence, or sleeping on one's rights, the principle involved appears to be generally recognized and applied.[106]

If the agreement does contain clear time limits for filing and prosecuting grievances, failure to observe them generally will result in dismissal of the grievance if the failure is protested.[107] Thus, the practical effect of late

---

alleged wrongful failure to promote is arbitrable where employer processed grievance and did not assert timeliness objection until arbitration); Mid-America Canning Corp., 85 LA 900 (Imundo, 1985); Polygram Distribution, 83 LA 249 (Gibson, 1984). *See also* New Orleans Pub. Facility Mgmt., 93 LA 681 (McDermott, 1989) (failure to process dispute through separate grievance steps does not preclude arbitration where employer rejected grievance in writing and arbitration was invoked according to established procedure).

[105]*See* American Welding & Mfg. Co., 45 LA 812, 816 (Dworkin, 1965); AIC Corp., 45 LA 517, 521–22 (Larkin, 1965); Borden Ice Cream Co., 37 LA 140, 143 (Markowitz, 1961); Lavoris Co., 16 LA 156, 160–61 (Lockhart, 1951); F.G. Candy Mfg. Co., 9 LA 139, 140 (Davey, 1947); Keystone Reamer & Tool Co., 7 LA 785, 787 (Brandschain, 1947); Inland Steel Co., 2 LA 655, 659–60 (Gilden, 1945). *But see* Aero Supply Mfg. Co., 20 LA 183, 188–89 (Appleby, 1953). Of course the agreement may expressly limit retroactivity. *See* Hekman Furniture Co., 39 LA 1148, 1153 (Cole, 1963); New York Shipbuilding Corp., 37 LA 1046, 1047 (Crawford, 1961).

[106]*See* Lavoris Co., 16 LA 156, 160–61 (Lockhart, 1951). For other arbitrators applying the principle, see *Eaton Mfg. Co.*, 47 LA 1045, 1048 (Kates, 1966); *American Welding & Mfg.*, 45 LA 812, 816 (Dworkin, 1965); *Steel Warehouse Co.*, 45 LA 357, 361 (Dolnick, 1965); *Borden Ice Cream*, 37 LA 140, 143 (Markowitz, 1961); *Hale Bros. Stores*, 32 LA 713, 719 (Ross, 1959); *Warner Elec. Brake & Clutch Co.*, 31 LA 219, 220 (Kelliher, 1958); *Curtiss-Wright Corp.*, 12 LA 482, 483–84 (Cornsweet, 1949); *Hanscom Baking Corp.*, 10 LA 288, 293–94 (Wolff, 1948); *Neon Prods.*, 9 LA 659, 660 (Lehoczky, 1948); *Keystone Reamer & Tool Co.*, 7 LA 785, 787 (Brandschain, 1947); *Great Atl. & Pac. Tea Co.*, 2 LA 608, 612 (Gilden, 1945). *See also* C. Iber & Sons, 69 LA 697, 705 (Gibson, 1977); Dolan Steel Co., 49 LA 197, 199 (Seitz, 1967); Paul Mueller Co., 40 LA 780, 784 (Bauder, 1963); Dayton Steel Foundry Co., 37 LA 231, 234 (Stouffer, 1961). *Cf.* H.K. Porter Co., 38 LA 1031, 1040–41 (Murphy, 1962).

[107]*E.g.*, Wyandot, Inc. v. Food & Commercial Workers Local 227, 205 F.3d 922, 163 LRRM 2705 (6th Cir. 2000) (court reversed arbitrator's award reinstating discharged union member because grievance was not timely filed and thus award departed from essence of collective bargaining agreement); Perfection-Cobey Co., 88 LA 257 (Duda, Jr., 1987). *See also* Bowers v. Transportation Mexicana, 901 F.2d 258 (2d Cir. 1990); Barnard v. Commercial Carriers, 863 F.2d 694, 130 LRRM 2073 (10th Cir. 1988); Teamsters Local 89 v. Moog Louisville Warehouse, 852 F.2d 871, 128 LRRM 3100 (6th Cir. 1988); Steelworkers v. Cherokee Elec. Coop., 829 F.2d 1131, 128 LRRM 2223 (11th Cir. 1987), *cert. denied*, 485 U.S. 1038 (1988); Detroit Coil Co. v. Machinists Lodge 82, 100 LRRM 3138 (6th Cir. 1979); Trippey v. Rock Island Motor Transit Co., 78 Lab. Cas. (CCH) ¶11,249 (N.D. Ill. 1976); Department of Health & Human Servs., Social Sec. Admin, 35 FLRA 1167 (1990); Tinker Air Force Base, Okla., 34 FLRA 203 (1990); Department of Housing & Urban Dev., 33 FLRA 883 (1989). *Cf.* Berklee Coll. of Music v. Teachers Local 4412, 858 F.2d 31, 129 LRRM 2465 (1st Cir. 1988); Iron Workers Local 539 v. Mosher Steel, 796 F.2d 1361, 123 LRRM 2428 (11th Cir. 1986); Guidry v. Operating Eng'rs Local 406, 784 F.2d 1262, 121 LRRM 3282 (5th Cir. 1986); Teamsters Local 744 v. Metropolitan Distribs., 763 F.2d 300, 119 LRRM 2955 (7th Cir. 1985); Nursing Home & Hosp. Union 434 v. Sky Vue Terrace, 759 F.2d 1094, 119 LRRM 2097 (3d Cir. 1985); Slavin & Sons, Ltd., 114 Lab. Cas. (CCH) ¶12,007 (E.D.N.Y. 1989); Boilermakers v. Delta S. Co., 602 F. Supp. 625 (M.D. La. 1985); Naval Plant Representative Office, 34 FLRA 234 (1990). *See* Stipanowish, *Of "Procedural Arbitrability": The Effect of Noncompliance With Contract Claims Procedures*, 40 S.C. L. Rev. 847–81 (1989).

filing in many instances is that the merits of the dispute are never decided.[108] But where there are ambiguities in the wording of contractual time limits, or uncertainty as to whether time limits have been met, all doubts should be resolved against forfeiture of the right to process the grievance.[109] Moreover, even if time limits are clear, late filing will not result in dismissal of the grievance if the circumstances are such that it would be unreasonable to require strict compliance with the time limits specified by the agreement.[110]

---

[108]For discussion, see Benewitz, *On Timely Grievances and Arbitrability*, 34 ARB. J. No. 2, at 6 (1979). One of the relatively few cases in which the merits were reached by the arbitrator in spite of his ruling against the grievant on the time issue is *Northeast Airlines*, 37 LA 741, 745 (Wolff, 1961), where a ruling on the merits was issued in the belief that the parties would be aided by the arbitrator's views. In several cases the arbitrator has addressed the merits of the case, finding it unnecessary to address the issue of arbitrability, *H. Olson Distrib.*, 85 LA 302, 304 (Weiss, 1985), or timeliness, *Magic Chef*, 84 LA 15, 17 (Carver, 1984). *See also* Carolina Concrete Pipe Co., 76 LA 626, 631 (Foster, 1981) (dismissing the grievance because of time limitations but issuing an "advisory opinion" on the merits). In *American Zinc Co.*, 46 LA 645, 650 (Abernethy, 1966), the company asserted late filing but nonetheless agreed to have a ruling on the merits first, the time limit issue to be ruled on only if the company should lose on the merits. In *Hoffman v. Lonza, Inc.*, 658 F.2d 519, 108 LRRM 2311, 2314 (7th Cir. 1981), arbitration of a grievance was barred because the union forgot to file a notice of intent to arbitrate within the time limit specified by the agreement; the court held that an action for breach of the duty of fair representation "cannot be based solely on an allegation that a union unintentionally failed to file" a notice within the specified period. There was no finding of a breach of the duty of fair representation where the union forgot to act within the time specified by the agreement. Graf v. Elgin, Joliet & E. Ry., 697 F.2d 771, 112 LRRM 2462, 2466–68 (7th Cir. 1983). *But see* Dutrisac v. Caterpillar Tractor Co., 749 F.2d 1270, 113 LRRM 3532, 3535 (9th Cir. 1983); Ruzicka v. General Motors Corp., 649 F.2d 1207, 107 LRRM 2726 (6th Cir. 1981). For related discussion, see section 9., "Grievance Adjustment by Individual Employees," below.

[109]*See* Amana Refrigeration, 93 LA 249 (Mikrut, Jr., 1989); Astro-Valcour, 93 LA 91 (Rocha, Jr., 1989); W.J. Bullock Inc., 93 LA 33, 36–37 (Clarke, 1989); County of Ventura, Cal., 91 LA 107 (Knowlton, 1988); Children's Aid Soc'y, 87 LA 459, 463–65 (Daniel, 1986); King & Am. Ambulance Co., 87 LA 78, 82–83 (Concepcion, 1986); Bonita Unified Sch. Dist., 79 LA 207, 214–15 (Fiering, 1982); Hayes-Albion Corp., 73 LA 819, 823 (Foster, 1979); National Cleaning Contractors, 70 LA 917, 919 (Dworkin, 1978); Belknap, Inc., 69 LA 599, 601 (1977); Technical Serv. Corp., 36 LA 148, 151 (LaDriere, undated); Globe-Wernicke Co., 33 LA 553, 555 (Sanders, 1959). In *Miami Industries*, 50 LA 978, 984 (Howlett, 1968), the arbitrator stated that in raising time issues a party raises an affirmative defense that he or she has the burden of proof to establish by a preponderance of the evidence. In *Fort Frye School District*, 91 LA 1140, 1144 (Dworkin, 1988), the arbitrator noted that timeliness is an affirmative defense that can be waived by an employer either intentionally or by failure to assert the defense at the appropriate time.

[110]Berklee Coll. of Music v. Teachers Local 4412, 858 F.2d 31, 129 LRRM 2465 (1st Cir. 1988). *See* City of Melbourne, Fla., 91 LA 1210, 1212–13 (Baroni, 1988); Hughes Aircraft, 89 LA 205, 208–09 (Richman, 1987); Blue Creek Mining Co., 88 LA 730, 733 (Eyraud, 1987); Dunlop Tire Corp., 88 LA 262, 263–64 (Gentile, 1987); Stark County, Ohio, Sheriff, 88 LA 65, 71–74 (Richard, 1986); Sugardale Foods, 87 LA 18, 20–21 (DiLauro, 1986); Dillingham Shipyard, 86 LA 811 (Tsukiyama, 1986); Kent County, Mich., 75 LA 948, 951 (Kruger, 1980); Tennessee Dressed Beef Co., 74 LA 1229, 1236 (Hardin, 1980); Quality Beer Distrib., 73 LA 669, 671 (Ziskind, 1979); Eberle Tanning Co., 71 LA 302, 303 (Sloane, 1978); Mahoney Plastics Corp., 69 LA 1017, 1021 (King, 1977); Teledyne Still-Man Mfg., 68 LA 188, 191 (Jewett, 1977); Amoco Chem. Corp., 63 LA 1196, 1202 (Schedler, 1974); Bethlehem Steel Corp., 47 LA 524, 525 (Porter, 1966); E.F. Hauserman Co., 42 LA 1076, 1082 (Klein, 1964); Murphy Div., 66-2 ARB ¶8699 (Hardy, 1966); Lehigh Portland Cement Co., 66-3 ARB ¶9060 (Duff, 1966); Levinson Steel Co., 23 LA 135, 136 (Reid, 1954); Carnegie-Illinois Steel Corp., 16 LA 794, 800 (Sturges, 1951); A.D. Juilliard & Co., 15 LA 934, 935 (Maggs, 1951).

If both parties have been lax as to observing time limits in the past, an arbitrator will hesitate to enforce them strictly until prior notice has been given by a party of intent to demand strict adherence to the contractual requirements.[111]

iv. Waiver of Time Limits [LA CDI 93.4665]

Time limits may be extended or waived by a special agreement in writing. Oral agreements also have sufficed for this purpose.[112] Even where an agreement expressly required time limit waivers to be in writing, it was held that the parties' actions may produce a waiver without it being in writing.[113]

In many cases time limits have been held waived by a party who had recognized and negotiated a grievance without making clear and timely objection.[114] But there are some cases holding to the con-

---

[111]See Guayana Res., 90 LA 855, 856 (Feldman, 1987); Pea River Elec. Coop., 89 LA 1054, 1060–61 (Clarke, 1987); Sanford Corp., 89 LA 968, 971 (Wies, 1987); Fruehauf Corp., 88 LA 366, 369–70 (Nathan, 1986); CBS Inc., 75 LA 789, 792 (Roberts, 1980); Peru Foundry Co., 73 LA 959, 960 (Sembower, 1979); Collis Co., 50 LA 1157, 1158 (Doyle, 1968); National Distillers Prods. Co., 42 LA 884, 888 (Kesselman, 1964); Mosaic Tile Co., 9 LA 625, 626 (Cornsweet, 1948); Anchor Rome Mills, 9 LA 595, 596 (Biscoe, 1947); Four Wheel Drive Auto Co., 4 LA 170, 173 (Rauch, 1946). See also Bethlehem Steel, 19 LA 186, 187 (Killingsworth, 1952). Cf. Navy Exch., 85 LA 1006, 1007–08 (Alsher, 1985).
[112]See Technocast, Inc., 91 LA 164 (Miller, 1988); Farrell Lines, 86 LA 36, 39 (Hockenberry, 1986); Miami Indus., 50 LA 978, 984 (Howlett, 1968); Jackson Elec. Instrument Co., 42 LA 740, 745 (Seinsheimer, 1964); Bagwell Steel Co., 41 LA 303, 304 (Dworet, 1963). See also Naval Air Rework Facility, 86 LA 1129, 1131 (Hewitt, 1986); Alliance Mach. Co., 74 LA 1058, 1060 (Feldman, 1980).
[113]Jackson Elec. Instrument Co., 42 LA 740, 745 (Seinsheimer, 1964). See also Lear Siegler, Inc., 75 LA 612, 614 (Greer, 1980); Continental Tel. Co., 71 LA 1244, 1246 (Caraway, 1979); California Metal Trades Ass'n, 68 LA 876, 880 (Eaton, 1977).
[114]E.g., Iron Workers Local 539 v. Mosher Steel, 796 F.2d 1361, 123 LRRM 2428 (11th Cir. 1986); Coblentz Sch. Dist., 93 LA 80, 81–82 (Kates, 1989); Consolidation Coal Co., 91 LA 1011, 1013 (Stoltenberg, 1988); Hampton Township, Pa., Sch. Dist., 91 LA 476, 480 (Dissen, 1988); Camp Lejeune Marine Corps Base, 90 LA 1126, 1128 (Nigro, 1988); Reliance Elec. Co., 90 LA 641, 647 (Wolff, 1988); Lufkin Indus., 90 LA 301, 305 (Nicholas, Jr., 1988); Hayes Int'l Corp., 79 LA 999, 1003–04 (Valtin, 1982); Plumbers & Pipe Fitters Local 636, 75 LA 449, 453 (Herman, 1980); Aeolian Corp., 72 LA 1178, 1180 (Eyraud, 1979); Levi Strauss & Co., 69 LA 1, 5 (Goodstein, 1977); Crown Cork & Seal Co., 68 LA 240, 241 (Carson, 1977); Produce, Inc., 50 LA 453, 453 (Keefe, 1968); United Eng'g & Foundry Co., 49 LA 1036, 1039 (Wagner, 1967); Hughes Aircraft Co., 49 LA 214, 218 (Roberts, 1967); U.S. Steel Corp., 48 LA 1085, 1087 (Dybeck, 1967); Billingsley, Inc., 48 LA 802, 805–06 (Krimsly, 1967); Columbian Carbon Co., 47 LA 1120, 1125 (Merrill, 1967); Cornish Wire Co., 45 LA 271, 275–76 (Fallon, 1965); National Annealing Box Co., 45 LA 196, 201 (Teple, 1965); Mount Mary Coll., 44 LA 66, 72 (Anderson, 1965); Sanna Dairies, 43 LA 16, 18 (Rice, 1964); Lagomarcino-Grupe Co., 43 LA 453, 458 (Davey, 1964); Philips Indus., Inc., 63-1 ARB ¶8358 (Stouffer, 1963); General Tire & Rubber Co., 62-2 ARB ¶8464 (Willingham, 1962); Denver Post, 41 LA 200, 203–05 (Gorsuch, 1963); Patterson Steel Co., 38 LA 400, 403 (Autrey, 1962); Johnson Bronze Co., 32 LA 216, 219 (Wood, 1959); Ironrite, Inc., 28 LA 398, 400 (Whiting, 1956); Republic Steel Corp., 27 LA 685, 687 (Platt, 1956); Flexonics Corp., 24 LA 869, 873 (Klamon, 1955); American Smelting & Ref. Co., 24 LA 857, 859 (Ross, 1955); Harbison-Walker Refractories, 22 LA 775, 778 (Day, 1954). Cf. Bethlehem Steel Corp., 75 LA 353, 361–62 (Sharnoff, 1980); John Deere Waterloo Tractor Works, 18 LA 497, 504 (Davey, 1952). While parties gave persistent and prolonged consideration to a grievance over a period of 3 years, the contractual time limit was held not to bar the claim. Grace Lines, Inc., 39 LA 633, 635–36 (Shaughnessy, 1962). See also Interscience Encyclopedia, 55 LA 210, 216–17 (Roberts, 1970). As long as the parties are still discussing the possibilities of settling a grievance at a given step, the time for proceeding to the next step of the grievance procedure might be held not to have started running. See Montgomery Ward & Co., 48 LA 1171, 1172–73 (Updegraff, 1967). However, management's expression of opinion that employees had no valid basis for complaint did not

trary.[115] When clear and timely objection is made to time-limit violations, no waiver will result from subsequent processing of the grievance on the merits.[116] Indeed, it has been suggested that on making timely objection to a delayed filing, the objecting party ordinarily should then discuss the grievance on the merits so that all issues will be ready for presentation to an arbitrator if the case reaches that stage.[117] Under a less expeditious procedure, the objecting party may refuse to entertain the grievance on the ground that it is null and void, forcing the grievant to file a second grievance involving the time issue alone; discussion of the original dispute on the merits would thus be delayed pending final resolution of the timeliness issue.[118]

v. *Computation of Time* [LA CDI 93.4661; 93.4665]

The contract may specify whether Saturdays, Sundays, holidays, and the day of the occurrence are to be counted in computing time.[119] An arbitrator might be inclined toward flexibility in applying a short time limit within which a holiday falls, provided the basic objective of prompt grievance processing is not seriously jeopardized.[120] One arbitrator similarly believed that flexibility was needed where the agreement required grievances to be signed by the grieving employee and filed within 2 "working days." The arbitrator said the definition of the term "working days" may vary depending, inter alia, on the work schedule of the person who is being required to act.[121]

The events that give rise to a grievance are not always discovered at the time they occur. Some agreements provide specifically that grievances are to be filed within a certain number of days after the triggering event occurs or is discovered.[122] Even without such specific provision, arbitrators have held

---

suffice to relieve them of the contractual time limit for filing their grievance. Kroger Co., 36 LA 270, 272 (Stouffer, 1960).

[115]*See* Gilman Paper Co., 47 LA 563, 566 (Tatum, 1966); Joy Mfg. Co., 44 LA 304, 306–07 (Sembower, 1965); Publishers' Ass'n of New York City, 39 LA 379, 381–82 (Schmertz, 1962).

[116]*See* Hercules Powder Co., 47 LA 336, 339 (Boothe, 1966); New York Racing Ass'n, 43 LA 129, 136 (Scheiber, 1964); Chase Bag Co., 42 LA 153, 156 (Elkouri, 1963). *Cf.* City of S. Daytona, Fla., 84 LA 21, 23 (McCollister, 1984).

[117]North Am. Aviation, 17 LA 715, 719 (Komaroff, 1951).

[118]Square D Co., 25 LA 225, 230 (Prasow, 1955).

[119]*See* Grossmont Union High Sch. Dist., 91 LA 909, 913 (Weiss, 1988); Transport Body Serv., 65 LA 894, 895 (Raffaele, 1975); Republic Oil Ref. Co., 15 LA 640, 642–43 (Ralston, 1950); Chrysler Corp., 11 LA 732, 737 (Ebeling, 1948); Ford Motor Co., 1 ALAA ¶67,040 (Shulman, 1945). In *Belknap, Inc.*, 69 LA 599, 601 (Teple, 1977), the arbitrator was "convinced that the 10-day period [specified by the agreement] was meant to indicate calendar days, which is the normal construction of 'day' unless the word is limited in some way, as when the labor contract refers to 'working days.'"

[120]*See* Eimco Corp., 41 LA 1184, 1186–87 (Dykstra, 1963). In *Kent County, Mich.*, 75 LA 948, 951 (Kruger, 1980), the arbitrator applied a "rule of reason" in counting time during the Christmas holiday season.

[121]Indian Head, Inc., 71 LA 260 (Weiss, 1978). An employee was disciplined on Saturday and filed his grievance the following Wednesday, which was his next regularly scheduled workday. In holding the grievance timely, the arbitrator stated: "[T]he contract places the obligation on the grieving employee. He instigates the complaint and is required to sign it. The term 'working days' must then apply to his own work schedule." *Id.* at 262.

[122]*See* International Minerals & Chem. Co., 3 LA 405, 406 (Dwyer, 1946). *See also* Naval Plant Representative Office, 91 LA 964, 967–68 (Abrams, 1988); Kelsey-Hayes Co., 85 LA 774, 779 (Thomson, 1985); Aeronca, Inc., 84 LA 1045, 1049 (Katz, 1985); Bethlehem Steel Corp., 46 LA 767, 768 (Strongin, 1966).

that one cannot be expected to file a grievance until one is aware, or should be aware, of the action on which the grievance is based.[123] But time limits "cannot be extended by the excuse that the grievant just didn't think of it sooner."[124] Furthermore, where the employee had knowledge of the adverse action but did not speak up, the union will not be heard to say that the time limit should be extended because the union did not know.[125] The occurrence of the event, which gives rise to the right to file a grievance, is a condition precedent to the commencement of the running of the time limitation for filing a grievance.[126]

A party sometimes announces its intention to perform a given act, but does not culminate the act until a later date. Similarly, a party may perform an act whose adverse effect on another does not result until a later date. In such situations arbitrators have held that the "occurrence" for purposes of applying time limits is at the later date.[127] For example, where a company changed a seniority date on its records as a correction, a grievance protesting the change was held timely though not filed until 9 months later; the arbitrator stated that the basis of the grievance would be the employee's

[123]*See* Chevron U.S.A., 95 LA 393, 395 (Riker, 1990); Internal Revenue Serv., 93 LA 261, 265 (Dilts, 1989); Amana Refrigeration, 93 LA 249, 256–57 (Mikrut, Jr., 1989); Amax Coal Co., 91 LA 254 (Kilroy, 1988); Cannelton Indus., 90 LA 824, 827–28 (Stoltenberg, 1988); Cities Serv. Co., 87 LA 1209, 1212 (Taylor, 1986); Sunshine Mining Co., 72 LA 479, 483 (Flagler, 1979); Levi Strauss & Co., 69 LA 1, 5 (Goodstein, 1977); Buffalo Bd. of Educ., 68 LA 921, 923 (Dennis, 1977); Mutual Plastics Mold Corp., 48 LA 2, 8–9 (Block, 1967); Crane Co., 42 LA 781, 784 (Altieri, 1963); Dayton Econ. Drug Co., 40 LA 1182, 1183 (Geissinger, 1963); Babcock-Wilcox Co., 26 LA 501, 502–03 (Donahue, 1956); Avco Mfg. Corp., 24 LA 268, 271 (Holly, 1955); Republic Steel Corp., 24 LA 141, 143 (Platt, 1955); Patterson-Sargent Co., 23 LA 21, 23 (Willcox, 1954); Aleo Mfg. Co., 19 LA 647, 649 (Maggs, 1952); North Am. Aviation, 17 LA 715, 718 (Komaroff, 1951). *See also* Harmony, Minn., Indep. Sch. Dist. 228, 84 LA 777, 782 (Jacobowski, 1985); Dayton Tire & Rubber Co., 48 LA 83, 86 (Dworkin, 1967); Combustion Eng'g Co., 20 LA 416, 419 (McCoy, 1953). *But see* Rome Cable Corp., 87 LA 519, 521–22 (Konvitz, 1986).

[124]General Fireproofing Co., 48 LA 842, 848 (Teple, 1967). *See also* Michigan Gas Util. Co., 65 LA 368, 370 (Herman, 1975).

[125]Ekco Prods. Co., 40 LA 1339, 1341 (Duff, 1963). *See also* Oak Tree Racing Ass'n, 75 LA 1179, 1182 (Christopher, 1980) (grievant's desire to avoid "stirring things up" did not excuse late filing).

[126]Harbor Furniture Mfg. Co., 85 LA 359, 363 (Richman, 1985).

[127]*See* Uppco Inc., 93 LA 489, 494–95 (Goldstein, 1989); Rolling Acres Care Ctr., 91 LA 795, 797 (Dworkin, 1988); City of Duluth, Minn., 91 LA 238 (Gallagher, 1988); Texas Utils. Generating Co., 86 LA 1108, 1110–11 (Nicholas, Jr., 1986); Harmony, Minn., Indep. Sch. Dist., 84 LA 777, 782 (Jacobowski, 1985); Board of Educ., Geneseo Cmty. Unit Sch. Dist. 228, 75 LA 131, 133 (Berman, 1980); City of New Brunswick, N.J., 73 LA 174, 177 (Chandler, 1979); Chromalloy Div., 71 LA 1178, 1179 (Barnhart, 1978); Cities Serv. Oil Co., 70 LA 930, 934 (Caraway, 1978); General Tel. Co. of Southeast Ala., 69 LA 493, 497 (Swain, 1977); Browning-Ferris Indus. of Ohio, 68 LA 1347, 1349 (Teple, 1977); Lockheed Aircraft Corp., 55 LA 14, 16 (Krimsly, 1970); Dayton Tire & Rubber Co., 46 LA 1021, 1027 (Dworkin, 1966); Wisconsin Bridge & Iron Co., 46 LA 993, 997–99 (Solomon, 1966) (here the "occurrence" was at an intermediate point); Chattanooga Box & Lumber Co., 44 LA 373, 375 (Tatum, 1965); Union Carbide Nuclear Co., 38 LA 259, 261 (Schedler, 1962); Grayson Controls Div., 37 LA 1044, 1046 (Grant, 1961); Convair, 26 LA 622, 626 (Komaroff, 1956); Southern Cal. Edison Co., 18 LA 662, 663–64 (Warren, 1952). *Cf.* City of New Smyrna Beach, Fla., 83 LA 1086, 1090 (Alsher, 1984); Joy Mfg. Co., 44 LA 304, 307 (Sembower, 1965); North Am. Aviation, 19 LA 385, 387 (Komaroff, 1952). In *Square D Co.*, 25 LA 225, 228–29 (Prasow, 1955), the arbitrator held that an act occurred on the day it was announced, but there the union itself had clearly recognized the existence of a grievance as of that day.

frustrated attempt to exercise seniority rights based on the old date, rather than the mere change in the company's records.[128]

In this general connection, where a grievance protesting a layoff was filed 7 days after the employer signed the layoff notice, the filing was held timely although the contract placed a 5-day limit on filing grievances; it was said to be reasonable to assume that 2 days were required for the notice to reach the grievant.[129] In another case the agreement required the company to give its answer to a grievance within 10 days, but the arbitrator refused to determine the allowed period on an "hour and minute" basis where the parties had not previously applied their time limits so exactly.[130] The arbitrator in this case also stated that delivery of the company's answer to the U.S. mail was equivalent to delivery to the union.[131] In *John I. Haas, Inc.*,[132] the NLRB held that election objections are timely filed if they are postmarked no later than the day before the due date. The combined effect of these cases is that a time limit does not start to run until a party is actually informed as to the other party's position, and the response will be timely if it is thereafter deposited in the mails within the time limitations period. This is consistent with the above-noted view that doubts as to the interpretation of contractual time limits or as to whether they have been met should be resolved against disposition of grievances by forfeiture.

Under some circumstances a party may be permitted to toll the running of time limits by giving notice to the other party of a reasonable basis for delaying the filing of a grievance.[133] In addition, arbitrators occasionally will find a waiver of express and clear time limitations because of extenuating circumstances. In one case,[134] the agreement required a grievance to be filed

---

[128]Dayton Tire & Rubber Co., 46 LA 1021, 1027 (Dworkin, 1966). *See also* Butler Mfg. Co., 52 LA 633, 635–36 (Larkin, 1969).

[129]Torrington Co., 13 LA 323, 325 (Stutz, Mottram, & Sviridoff, 1949).

[130]E.W. Bliss Co., 45 LA 1000, 1002–03 (Lehoczky, 1965). *See also* Army Fin. & Accounting Ctr., 33 FLRA 889 (1989); Immigration & Naturalization Serv., 33 FLRA 885 (1989).

[131]E.W. Bliss Co., 45 LA 1000, 1003 (Lehoczky, 1965). For other cases in which delivery to the U.S. mail of a grievance or an answer to a grievance within the time-limit period was held equivalent to delivery to the addressee, see *Internal Revenue Serv.*, 93 LA 261, 265 (Dilts, 1989); *Inland Container Corp.*, 90 LA 532 (Ipavec, 1987); *Bowman Transp.*, 90 LA 347 (Duff, 1987); *B.F. Goodrich*, 84 LA 240, 243 (Nicholas, Jr., 1985); *Air Force Logistics Command*, 75 LA 597, 601 (Johannes, 1980); *Intermediate Unit I Bd. of Directors*, 73 LA 80, 83 (Duff, 1979); *Jefferson Chem. Co.*, 72 LA 892, 895 (Goodstein, 1979) (the time limit was met by mailing although company testified it did not receive the document); *Gardner Motors, Inc.*, 64 LA 428, 429 (Lightner, 1975) (same); *Huron Valley Pub. Sch.*, 63 LA 49, 50 (Watkins, 1974); *Prindle Int'l*, 61 LA 613, 616 (Heilbrun, 1973); *Greyhound Lines-West*, 61 LA 44, 51 (Block, 1973). *Cf.* Veterans Admin. Med. Ctr., 88 LA 502, 505 (Penfield, 1986); Crown Cork & Seal, 88 LA 145, 150–51 (Keefe, 1986). But in a case involving notice for wage reopening, the arbitrator held the notice must be received by the specified date, and that the "presumption of the timely delivery in due course to the addressee of a letter properly posted" was rebutted by the evidence. Covington Furniture Mfg., 71 LA 105, 108 (Murphy, 1978). *But see* Stevens Pontiac-GMC, 295 NLRB 599, 131 LRRM 1683 (1989). *See also* Department of the Army, 34 FLRA 521 (1990); National Gallery of Art, 33 FLRA 859 (1989).

[132]301 NLRB 302, 136 LRRM 1122 (1991).

[133]*See* American Smelting & Ref. Co., 29 LA 262, 265 (Ross, 1957). *See also* C. Iber & Sons, 69 LA 697, 704 (Gibson, 1977); Monogram Prods., 13 LA 782, 786 (Pierson, 1949).

[134]Sugardale Foods, 87 LA 18 (DiLauro, 1986). *See* Food Employers Council, 87 LA 514 (Kaufman, 1986) (grievance asserting typographical error in contract was timely filed although alleged error first appeared 12 years earlier, where contract contained no time limit for filing such grievance, employers had not implemented their interpretation of the disputed provision, and timeliness issue was not raised until arbitration hearing).

"within seven (7) days after the mailing by registered mail of written notice of such discharge to the Union . . . ."[135] The grievance was filed more than 6 weeks after the mailing of the notice. In holding that the grievance had been timely filed, the arbitrator found persuasive these circumstances: the grievant was off duty at the time of the discharge notice using what she believed was an appropriate leave; the grievant was suffering from an anxiety attack and being cared for at the home of a friend; the notice was mailed to the grievant's home, and, when the grievant returned to her home, she learned of the discharge notice and then immediately filed a grievance protesting her discharge.[136]

Sometimes an agreement will provide that any grievance not appealed from one step to the next within a specified time shall be considered settled on the basis of the last answer. On one occasion this type of provision was applied strictly, with the result that a grievance that, by error, had been left unappealed until the time limit had expired, was held to have been settled.[137] Similarly, agreements sometimes contain express provision for granting grievances by default if the company fails to answer or take other required action within a stated time, and these "company default" provisions also have been strictly enforced.[138] However, one arbitrator held that strict enforcement of the "default" clause did not mean that the arbitrator should automatically order the relief demanded, where granting such relief would alter or add to the agreement.[139]

However, in the absence of such an express "default" provision, the failure of the supervisor to answer within the prescribed time will not be interpreted as an admission of the grievance, because the grievant has the burden and right to carry the complaint to the next step following the lapse of

---

[135]Sugardale Foods, 87 LA 18, 20 (DiLauro, 1986).

[136]*Id.* at 21.

[137]Chrysler Corp., 1 ALAA ¶67,017 (Wolff, 1945). In several other cases, such "default" type provisions have been strictly enforced. *See* Ferro Eng'g, 90 LA 257 (Duda, Jr., 1987); Diamond Power Specialty Corp., 44 LA 878, 882–83 (Dworkin, 1964); Parke, Davis & Co., 41 LA 8, 10 (Ryder, 1963) (nor could the issue be revived by filing another grievance, based on the same incident, in the name of another employee); Republic Steel Corp., 25 LA 437, 438 (Platt, 1955). *Cf.* Allegheny Ludlum Steel Corp., 85 LA 669, 672 (Duff, 1985). Where the union on two occasions told the employer a discharge grievance was being withdrawn from the grievance procedure, it could not be reintroduced later. Associated Grocers of Colo., 74 LA 141, 143 (Finston, 1980). *See also* West Penn Handling Equip. Co., 74 LA 37, 39 (LeWinter, 1980).

[138]*See* Weyerhaeuser Co., 90 LA 870, 872 (Allen, Jr., 1988); City of Cedar Rapids, Iowa, 81 LA 149, 155–56 (Roberts, 1983); Abex Corp., 75 LA 137, 140–41 (Feldman, 1980); S.W. Shattuck Chem. Co., 69 LA 912, 916 (Culley, 1977); Rockwell Mfg. Co., 25 LA 534, 537–38 (Duff, 1955). *Cf.* Globe-Wernicke Co., 33 LA 553, 555–56 (Sanders, 1959). *But see* Delaware Dep't of Health & Soc. Servs., 87 LA 563, 567–68 (DiLauro, 1986) (the employer, who repeatedly failed to meet contractual deadlines, was ordered to adhere to time limits in processing future grievances and to schedule for fourth-step hearing all appropriate pending grievances). *See also* Electrical Workers (IBEW) Local 1842 v. Cincinnati Elec. Corp., 808 F.2d 1201, 124 LRRM 2473 (6th Cir. 1987).

[139]Wayne County Intermediate Sch. Dist., 85 LA 673, 676, 677 (Daniel, 1985).

the specified time.[140] But it has been emphasized that the supervisor should make a decision or comment on each grievance.[141]

B. Holding Hearings [LA CDI 94.57; 100.0752]

Agreements vary as to the time prescribed for holding hearings on grievances. Some agreements provide that differences are to be taken up "as soon as possible"; others simply provide that "grievances shall be first taken up by the grievant and the foreman," without specifying a time; still others provide that grievances may be adjusted with the supervisor or foreman "at the end of the working day." Reasonable prudence should be exercised in determining when to present grievances. It has been held, for instance, that when the number of employees involved in a grievance is so great that their absence from the job would interfere with production and upset morale and discipline, the shop steward has a clear duty to give management an opportunity to adjust the grievance without an interruption of work. Accordingly, a shop steward who took six or seven men off the job to discuss a grievance, without having made advance arrangements with management, was held to have been properly admonished not to do so again.[142] Similar results have been reached in other such cases where employees or their representative, in seeking to rush the hearing of their complaint, interfered with production and disregarded the need for an orderly presentation.[143]

---

[140]*See* H-N Advertising & Display Co., 87 LA 776, 779 (Kossoff, 1986); Elec. Repair Serv. Co., 69 LA 604, 608–09 (Johnston, 1977); Providence Med. Ctr., 68 LA 663, 668 (Conant, 1977); Continental Crescent Lines, 60 LA 1291, 1295 (Steele, 1973); Dewey-Portland Cement Co., 43 LA 165, 168 (Sembower, 1964); Kennecott Copper Corp., 37 LA 1103, 1104 (Emery, 1961); Stanley Aviation Corp., 26 LA 393, 394 (Seligson, 1956); Cameron Iron Works, 25 LA 295, 299 (Boles, 1955); John Deere Tractor Co., 3 LA 737, 742–43 (Updegraff, 1946). The "authority" to refer a grievance to the next step is said to rest with the grievant, not with the supervisor. Ford Motor Co., 3 LA 840, 840 (Shulman, 1946).

[141]Ford Motor Co., 3 LA 840, 841 (Shulman, 1946). *See also* Bethlehem Steel Co., 19 LA 521, 522 (Feinberg, 1952). Some agreements require management's response to be in writing. BASIC PATTERNS IN UNION CONTRACTS 34 (BNA Books 14th ed. 1995). Absent such provision, an oral response to a grievance within the contractual 5-day time limit was held to suffice and not to be invalidated by a written response after that time limit. Warren Co., 39 LA 395, 398 (Woodruff, 1962).

[142]Dwight Mfg. Co., 10 LA 786, 792 (McCoy, 1948). Suspension of a steward was found improper, where the steward was seeking to change the time for a step 1 grievance meeting that had been set without consultation with the union representative. The arbitrator held that neither party could unilaterally set the time for a grievance meeting. Southern Ind. Gas & Elec., 85 LA 716, 720 (Nathan, 1985). Where the agreement was silent on the matter, it was held that management could schedule grievance meetings after working hours and was not bound by its past practice of scheduling them during working hours. Oshkosh Truck Corp., 67 LA 103, 107–08 (Karlins, 1976). Where the agreement contained an express contractual prohibition against union activity when one of the employees was on duty, it was held that the language would not permit even a de minimis exception. General Tel. of Southwest, 86 LA 293, 295 (Ipavec, 1985). *See also* American Hoechst Corp., 68 LA 517, 521 (Purcell, 1977).

[143]*See* Arrowhead Prods., 49 LA 944, 947 (Jones, Jr., 1967); International Harvester Co., 21 LA 220, 221–22 (Platt, 1953); North Am. Aviation, 21 LA 67, 70–71 (Komaroff, 1953); Bell Aircraft Corp., 17 LA 230, 232 (Shister, 1951). *See also* Kaiser Aluminum & Chem. Corp., 90 LA 856 (Thompson, 1988); General Tel. Co. of Ind., 79 LA 225, 230–31 (Kossoff, 1982). *Cf.* Knoxville Iron Co., 70 LA 333, 335 (Beadles, 1978). In *Terry Poultry Co.*, 109 NLRB 1097, 34 LRRM 1516 (1954), an employee could be punished where he left his post to present a grievance in violation of a reasonable and nondiscriminatory plant rule. But spontaneous work

The scheduling of advanced-step hearings generally is more definite. Many plants hold regularly scheduled meetings at specified intervals to negotiate appealed grievances.[144] Such meetings are usually held weekly during working hours, but may be held monthly or at other intervals, as a matter of practice or contract provisions.[145]

Sometimes, however, these meetings are not regularly scheduled, but are made subject to "call," to be held whenever necessary. "Call" meetings may be preferred because they provide the necessary flexibility for more prompt disposition of complaints, and the number of meetings can be adjusted to the number of cases. But some parties prefer regularly scheduled meetings because of the assurance that grievances will be considered within a definite period. Moreover, regular meetings provide better opportunity for the discussion of mutual problems of policy and for the anticipation of difficulties, thus tending to reduce the number of future grievances.[146]

C. Establishment of Time Limitations
[LA CDI 93.461 et seq., 100.0733; 100.0735]

Promptness is one of the most important aspects of grievance adjustment. Failure to settle grievances with dispatch is a major cause of labor unrest. While all parties agree that promptness in the settlement of grievances leads to better labor-management relationships, opinions differ as to the best means of ensuring such promptness. Some parties believe that time limits for taking complaints to the grievance procedure, and for processing grievances through the various steps of the procedure, provide safeguards against "stalling" that might result in the accumulation of a backlog of cases and the pressing of stale claims. Others believe that the setting of specific time allowances merely limits stalling to the maximum allowable time,[147] and it sometimes operates to bar grievances that should be settled for the sake of improving the relations between parties.

---

stoppages to present grievances under the NLRA have been held protected under the facts of some cases. *See* Roseville Dodge v. NLRB, 882 F.2d 1355, 132 LRRM 2161 (8th Cir. 1989); NLRB v. Serv-Air, 401 F.2d 363, 69 LRRM 2476 (10th Cir. 1968); NLRB v. Kennametal, Inc., 182 F.2d 817, 26 LRRM 2203 (3d Cir. 1950). *See also* NLRB v. Washington Aluminum Co., 370 U.S. 9, 50 LRRM 2235 (1962). Regarding employee resistance to management's effort to terminate a grievance meeting, compare *Container Corp.*, 255 NLRB 1404, 107 LRRM 1126 (1981), with *U.S. Postal Serv. v. NLRB*, 652 F.2d 409, 107 LRRM 3249 (5th Cir. 1981). As to the right of management to specify a specific location within the plant for union representatives to interview grievants and write up their grievances, see *Walker Mfg. Co.*, 41 LA 1288, 1299 (Whelan, 1963).

[144]BASIC PATTERNS, at 35; *Grievance Procedure Under Collective Bargaining*, 63 MONTHLY LAB. REV. 175, 183 (1946).

[145]BASIC PATTERNS, at 35; Cudahy Packing Co., 7 LA 645, 646 (Fisher, 1947).

[146]*Grievance Procedure*, at 183.

[147]It has been emphasized, however, that grievance processing should not be rushed to the extent that snap judgments are prompted. Lehigh Portland Cement Co., 46 LA 132, 134–35 (Duff, 1965) (the agreement was viewed as anticipating a brief time lapse between filing time and answering time; time limits could not be shortened by employer insistence on giving immediate answers).

No set formula is available for the establishment of time limits. Rather, the special circumstances of the parties should determine, in each instance, the nature of the time-limit provisions of their agreement. The agreement may fix time limits for each step of the procedure, set an overall time limit for complete processing of a grievance, or simply forbid delay. Any of these forms might be coupled with a time limit for the initial submission of grievances. Different limits may be prescribed for the submission of different types of grievances. This was done, for instance, by a factfinding board recommendation of a 5-day limit for filing discharge and pay adjustment disputes, and a 30-day limit for all other grievances.[148]

In the final analysis, the prompt resolution of grievances depends not on the presence of contractual time limits, but on a sincere desire of the parties to settle differences.[149] However, the fact is that numerous agreements contain time limitations. Without question, such limits provide an additional element of order to the grievance procedure.[150]

8. GRIEVANCE REPRESENTATIVES [LA CDI 93.22]

A. Common Characteristics

Unless restricted by the labor agreement, both the union and the company generally are free to determine the kind and number of representatives they wish to use[151] and are likewise free to select the individuals who are to serve as their grievance representatives.[152]

---

[148]Minneapolis-Moline Power Implement Co., 2 LA 227, 241 (Van Fossen, Humphrey, & Prifrel, 1946).

[149]*See* U.S. Postal Serv., 309 NLRB 13, 141 LRRM 1193 (1992) (The Board fashioned an extraordinary remedy because of the employer's unlawful failure to process grievances within the time limits specified in the agreement. Because of the logjam that had been created, the Board, among other remedies, imposed time limits within which the employer was required to meet with the union on grievances; the employer was required to consider grievances by assigned categories and to answer unresolved grievances within certain time limits; the union was permitted, in order to expedite a large number of pending grievances, to bypass the third step and proceed directly to arbitration.).

[150]For general discussion of advantages of using time limits, see THE GRIEVANCE PROCESS 60 (Mich. St. Univ. Lab. & Indus. Rel. Ctr. 1956). Of 400 agreements included in one survey, 69% contained time limits for filing grievances in the first step, and 82% set time limits for union appeals to higher steps. BASIC PATTERNS IN UNION CONTRACTS 34, 35 (BNA Books 14th ed. 1995) (where variations in time limit provisions are also noted). Time limits also are common in federal-sector agreements. *See* A SURVEY OF NEGOTIATED GRIEVANCE PROCEDURES AND ARBITRATION IN FEDERAL POST CIVIL SERVICE REFORM ACT AGREEMENTS 35–36 (Office of Personnel Mgmt. 1980). "In the majority of agreements, failure to meet specified time limits will either advance the grievance to the next procedural step (management failure) or terminate it (union or employee failure). However, 2 percent of the agreements state that management's failure to work within the negotiated time limits would result in the Union winning the grievance." *Id.*

[151]Ford Motor Co., 1 ALAA ¶67,045 (Shulman, 1944).

[152]For the general right of each party under the NLRA to select its representatives for the purpose of collective bargaining (which of course includes grievance processing) and for some of the situations in which a party might be entitled to veto the other party's selection, see *Kudla v. NLRB*, 821 F.2d 95, 125 LRRM 2766 (2d Cir. 1987); *General Elec. Co. v. NLRB*, 412 F.2d 512, 71 LRRM 2418 (2d Cir. 1969); *NLRB v. David Buttrick Co.*, 362 F.2d 300, 62 LRRM 2241 (1st Cir. 1966); *Standard Oil Co. of Ohio v. NLRB*, 322 F.2d 40, 54 LRRM 2076 (6th Cir. 1963); *Slate Belt Apparel Contractors' Ass'n*, 274 F.2d 376, 45 LRRM 2626 (3d Cir.

Limitation of the number of representatives who may appear at various hearings or bargaining sessions is a common feature of collective bargaining agreements and is a proper subject for negotiation between the parties.[153] Sometimes the agreement will designate the participants or otherwise restrict the right of a party to select its representatives.[154]

Unions most often use "shop stewards," sometimes referred to as "committeemen." The steward represents the employee at the initial stages of the grievance procedure. The steward who performs entrusted responsibilities successfully is an asset to management as well as to represented employees. As an employee spokesman, the steward has the responsibility of policing the collective bargaining agreement and the additional responsibility of dissuading employees from pursuing complaints that are without merit.[155] In dealing with management, the steward seeks to effectuate general union policies. Union grievance committeemen usually represent employees in the intermediate stages of the grievance procedure. The grievance committee frequently has the responsibility of determining union policy in connection with grievances.

1960); *Calmat*, 281 NLRB 304, 123 LRRM 1057 (1986); *Fitzsimons Mfg. Co.*, 251 NLRB 375, 105 LRRM 1083 (1980). Under the Federal Service Labor-Management Relations Act, 5 U.S.C. §7101 et seq., the union has the right to remove a steward in response to a widespread demand from members of the bargaining unit. Government Employees (AFGE) Local 1738 v. FLRA (Veterans Admin. Med. Ctr.), 806 F.2d 1105, 124 LRRM 2014 (D.C. Cir. 1986). For arbitral recognition of this general right, see *Federal Aviation Admin.*, 71 LA 1138, 1147 (Tsukiyama, 1978); *Arizona Masonry Contractors Ass'n*, 53 LA 972, 973–74 (Hayes, 1969); *Chardon Rubber Co.*, 50 LA 634, 636 (Kabaker, 1968); *Corry-Jamestown Corp.*, 36 LA 682, 685 (Kates, 1961). Where an agreement provided for third-step grievance meetings between the employer and "an International Union Representative," the arbitrator reasoned that use of "the word 'an' rather than 'the' indicates that there is no specific individual who fulfills the role of 'International Union Representative,'" thus the International could designate the local union president as its representative at third-step meetings. St. Mary Corwin Hosp., 76 LA 1142, 1145 (Aisenberg, 1981) (past practice also supported this result).

[153]Ford Motor Co., 1 ALAA ¶67,045 (Shulman, 1944).

[154]In *Consolidation Coal Co.*, 91 LA 1011, 1013 (Stoltenberg, 1988), attendance of the supervisor of industrial and employee relations in an advisory capacity at step 2 and step 3 grievance hearings was not a violation of the agreement that barred company supervisors from participating in both step 2 and step 3 grievance hearings. In *Hamilton County Sheriff*, 91 LA 437, 439 (Modjeska, 1988), the county refused to recognize a list of union grievance representatives where they were not selected as specified in the agreement that provided for one employee per facility per shift. In *Kahala Hilton Hotel Co.*, 44 LA 453, 457 (Burr, 1965), the agreement contained an express limitation. In *Corry-Jamestown Corp.*, 36 LA 682, 685 (Kates, 1961), the agreement was interpreted to prevent the union from designating a representative to serve outside his own department. *See also* Department of Soc. Servs., State of Mich., 80 LA 521, 523–24 (Daniel, 1983). But no such restriction was found in *Federal Aviation Admin.*, 71 LA 1138, 1147 (Tsukiyama, 1978); *Chardon Rubber Co.*, 50 LA 634, 636 (Kabaker, 1968). *See also* Union Carbide Corp., 55 LA 901, 904 (Berkowitz, 1970). In *Holan Div.*, 52 LA 1078, 1081 (Stouffer, 1969), the agreement was interpreted to restrict participation by the company's attorney at a prearbitral stage of the grievance procedure.

[155]Normally, with regard to personal conduct, a union official is held to a higher standard when it involves questions of honesty, integrity, and following the rules of conduct. A union official is not immune from appropriate disciplinary action. Morton Thiokol, Inc., 93 LA 434, 444 (Allen, Jr., 1989). *See also* University of Iowa, 91 LA 466, 471 (Yarowsky, 1988); Canteen Corp., 89 LA 815 (Keefe, 1987). For related discussion, see section 3., "Attitude of Parties to the Grievance Procedure," above. Quoting an AFL-CIO statement of steward responsibilities, see *Bowater Carolina Co.*, 77 LA 336, 341 (Holley, Jr., 1981).

The management representative closest to the employees and their work is the first-line supervisor. The supervisor's effectiveness in grievance settlement is determined largely by personal capability and the amount of authority given by the employer; if the supervisor is able and has sufficient authority, better settlements as a rule will be obtained at that level than at later steps, because the supervisor often understands workplace problems better than those higher up.[156] "Foremen trained by experience, observation, and study of labor and industrial psychology are able to prevent and to rectify most of the ordinary grievances of the workers."[157] Of course, to state this is to state the ideal only. Unfortunately, in numerous plants supervisors lack authority, or fail to use it, and "pass the buck" to higher management officials.[158] Many employers, however, conduct training courses for supervisors for the purpose of enabling them better to deal with grievances and acquainting them with the applicable company policies.

Both unions and companies frequently conduct training programs for all their representatives. Such training usually attempts to familiarize the representatives with the provisions of the collective bargaining agreement and basic union or company policy. Proper training should develop a feeling of mutual respect and confidence between stewards and supervisors; one of its primary purposes should be to foster the attitude that grievances are problems to be solved, not arguments to be won. Training also increases employee understanding of the use and objectives of the grievance procedure.[159]

The conduct of labor relations at many employers is centralized in a "human resources," "personnel," "labor relations," or "industrial relations" department. Generally, it is the function of this department to unify the company's policy and promote consistency in dealings with the union. Some industrial relations departments also are responsible for grievance processing. Opinion differs as to whether this is desirable. Some commentators believe vesting this function in a staff department undercuts the authority of the supervisor and forces more grievances to the higher stages of the procedure.[160]

B. Right to Union Representation at Early Stage
[LA CDI 93.27; 100.0705]

Union representation in disputes between aggrieved employees and management has received considerable attention from the courts, the NLRB,

---

[156]*Grievance Procedure Under Collective Bargaining*, 63 MONTHLY LAB. REV. 175, 179 (1946).

[157]LAPP, HOW TO HANDLE LABOR GRIEVANCES 109–10 (1945).

[158]*Grievance Procedure*, at 179. Some reasons why the "ideal" of foreman-steward settlement often is not attained include personality clashes between foreman and steward, fear by both management and unions that such settlements may establish undesirable precedents, and fear by both foreman and the steward that they will be reversed by their superiors. THE GRIEVANCE PROCESS 57–58 (Mich. State Univ. Lab. & Indus. Rel. Ctr. 1956).

[159]These points regarding training programs are stated and discussed in *Grievance Procedure*, at 177–83. As part of a strike settlement in 1986, General Electric and the Electrical Workers (IUE) agreed to establish a joint labor-management dispute resolution education program to "improve mutual understanding" between company supervisors and union stewards. 121 LRR 228 (1986).

[160]*Grievance Procedure*, at 184.

and arbitrators. The right to union representation has been invoked to cover many areas of labor-management relations.[161]

Unions and management frequently disagree as to whether, in the interest of better relationships, employee grievances should be taken directly to the first-line supervisor or directly to the union steward and then by the steward to the supervisor. Management often holds the view that the aggrieved employee should go to the supervisor alone before going to the steward, and that the union should not enter the picture until after the first step of the grievance procedure. It is argued that better relationships are fostered if the individual employee and the supervisor discuss the grievance alone. The presence of the steward, it is thought, tends to make the grievance appear more serious than it really is. Management's right to insist on such a policy is, however, restricted by the bargaining duty imposed by the NLRA.[162]

Unions, however, often take the position that the steward should be involved in the grievance process from the start. The employee is believed to need the assistance and moral support of the steward to ensure recognition

---

[161]Such claims to union representation and adjudication under a collective bargaining agreement have not been found to create a bar against claims raised pursuant to the Fair Labor Standards Act (FLSA), 29 U.S.C. §201 et seq. (Barrentine v. Arkansas-Best Freight Sys., 450 U.S. 728, 24 WH Cases 1284 (1981)); Civil Rights Act of 1871 (McDonald v. City of West Branch, Mich., 466 U.S. 284, 115 LRRM 3646 (1984)); or statutes regulating trust funds (see Central States v. Central Transp., 472 U.S. 559, 6 EB Cases 1665 (1985); Schneider Moving & Storage Co. v. Robbins, 466 U.S. 364, 115 LRRM 3641 (1984)). Where administrative agencies have deferred certain cases to arbitration, one circuit has indicated that such deferral does not absolve the agency from explaining its reasons for accepting an arbitrator's award that contravenes agency precedent. Darr v. NLRB, 801 F.2d 1404, 123 LRRM 2548 (D.C. Cir. 1986).

[162]The NLRB has held that settlements at the first step of the grievance procedure are "adjustments" within the meaning of the NLRA §9(a) proviso and that the union must have an opportunity to be present. Bethlehem Steel Co., 89 NLRB 341, 25 LRRM 1564 (1950). The right to be present may be waived. Globe-Union, Inc., 97 NLRB 1026, 29 LRRM 1198 (1952). In *Westinghouse Electric Corp.*, 141 NLRB 733, 52 LRRM 1385 (1963), the NLRB held that the employer modified the contractual grievance procedure and thus violated the duty to bargain by inviting employees to take grievances directly to their foreman before consulting their union steward. A court disagreed, holding the employer's statement to be only a suggestion that the grievance procedure would operate more smoothly if employees discussed possible complaints with their foreman before a formal grievance arose. Westinghouse Elec. Corp. v. NLRB, 325 F.2d 126, 54 LRRM 2696 (7th Cir. 1963). In *Smith v. Arkansas State Highway Employees Local 1315*, 441 U.S. 463, 101 LRRM 2091, 2092 (1979), the public-sector employer required aggrieved employees to submit a written complaint directly to the employer and refused to consider grievances submitted by their union (which did represent its members, however, at all grievance steps subsequent to the filing of a written grievance). The Supreme Court said the fact that this "might well" be unlawful for a private employer is immaterial in deciding whether the public employer's actions violated the First Amendment of the U.S. Constitution. The Court said the First Amendment "is not a substitute for the national labor relations laws," and "does not impose any affirmative obligation on the government to listen, to respond or, in this context, to recognize the association and bargain with it." *Id.* at 464, 465. Then, in *Minnesota State Board for Community Colleges v. Knight*, 465 U.S. 271, 286–87, 115 LRRM 2785 (1984), the Supreme Court upheld a statute that required public employers to "meet and confer" only with the union on questions relating to employment but outside the scope of mandatory bargaining, the Court stating:

> The conduct challenged here is the converse of that challenged in *Smith*. There the government listened only to individual employees and not to the union. Here the government "meets and confers" with the union and not with individual employees. The applicable constitutional principles are identical to those that controlled in *Smith*.

of all of the employee's rights. Unions wish to be able to "push" grievances of employees who are too timid to approach the supervisor alone. Moreover, unions say that management benefits by the union's screening of grievances, a process that eliminates complaints that have no merit. Finally, unions feel that settlements by individuals make it possible for supervisors to play favorites and that uniform settlements can be had only if the union is present from the outset.

C. Union Representation of Employees at Investigatory Interviews [LA CDI 93.27; 100.0705]

A related matter over which unions and management have disagreed concerns union representation of employees at investigatory interviews conducted by the employer. In 1975, the Supreme Court issued its *Weingarten*[163]

---

[163]*NLRB v. J. Weingarten, Inc.*, 420 U.S. 251, 88 LRRM 2689 (1975), *rev'g* 485 F.2d 1135, 84 LRRM 2436 (5th Cir. 1973) (NLRA §8(a)(1) is violated if the employer requires the employee to submit to the interview and denies the employee's request for union representation). Simultaneously, the Court issued its decision in *Ladies' Garment Workers (ILGWU) v. Quality Manufacturing Co.*, 420 U.S. 276, 88 LRRM 2698 (1975) (discharge of an employee for refusing to submit to an investigatory interview without union representation where she reasonably feared disciplinary action is unlawful, as is the discharge of a union steward for insisting on representing the employee pursuant to her request). In *U.S. Postal Service v. NLRB*, 969 F.2d 1064, 140 LRRM 2639 (D.C. Cir. 1992), the court held that an employee of the U.S. Postal Service was entitled to consult a union steward before being interrogated concerning alleged conduct that could have resulted in discipline or criminal prosecution. In *Prudential Insurance Co. of America*, 275 NLRB 208, 119 LRRM 1073 (1985), the Board, relying on *Metropolitan Edison Co. v. NLRB*, 460 U.S. 693, 112 LRRM 3265 (1983), held that a union may waive an employee's statutory rights, including the employee's *Weingarten* right. In *Montgomery Ward & Co. v. NLRB*, 664 F.2d 1095, 109 LRRM 2005, 2007 (8th Cir. 1981), the court concluded that two employees were discharged for admitted theft rather than because they had rightfully refused to participate in an investigative interview without union representation; in refusing to uphold the NLRB's order for reinstatement and back pay, the court stated that "the employees effected their own discharge by stealing and the section 8(a)(1) violation was simply incidental to the investigation which preceded the firing." In *Greyhound Lines*, 273 NLRB 1443, 118 LRRM 1199 (1985), the Board held that an employer cannot require a union steward to remain silent during an investigatory interview that an employee believes might lead to disciplinary action. *Cf.* Continental-Indianapolis, Inc., 78 LA 409, 415–17 (House, 1982). For discussion of union representation at investigative interviews, see GORMAN, BASIC TEXT ON LABOR LAW 395–98 (1976) ("While the Supreme Court has thus determined that Section 8(a)(1) will normally guarantee the presence of the union at an investigatory interview when that is requested by the interviewed employee, it has not considered whether the union is independently entitled under Section 8(a)(5) to be informed of an interview and given an opportunity to appear, as is the case when a 'grievance' has already come into existence."); Fox, Baldovin & Fox, *The* Weingarten *Doctrine*, 40 ARB. J. No. 2, at 45 (1985); Hill, *We Only Promised You a* Weingarten, 51 OKLA. BAR ASS'N J. 1823 (1980) (collecting many post-*Weingarten* decisions of the NLRB and the lower courts); Wireman, *Union Representation at Investigatory Interviews: The Subsequent Development of* Weingarten, 28 CLEV. ST. L. REV. 127 (1979); Erickson & Smith, *The Right of Union Representation During Investigatory Interviews*, 33 ARB. J. No. 2, at 29 (1978); Craver, *The Inquisitorial Process in Private Employment*, 63 CORNELL L. REV. 1, 16–28 (1977); Nelson, *Union Representation During Investigatory Interviews*, 31 ARB. J. 181 (1976); Kurtz & Murphy, *Appendix B. Arbitration and Federal Rights Under Collective Agreements in 1974*, *in* ARBITRATION—1975, PROCEEDINGS OF THE 28TH ANNUAL MEETING OF NAA 243, 259–60 (Dennis & Somers eds., BNA Books 1976). In *Weingarten*, the Supreme Court made only a brief and inconclusive reference to the §8(a)(5) question. *See Weingarten*, 420 U.S. at 264. For the NLRB's treatment of this aspect prior to *Weingarten*, see *Erickson & Smith*.

decision on the subject. In *Weingarten*, the Supreme Court upheld the NLRB position that individual employees have the right under the NLRA to refuse to submit without union representation to an investigatory interview that the employee reasonably believes may result in disciplinary action. The Court explained that the NLRB also had "shaped the contours and limits of the statutory right," which "contours and limits" are outlined (and apparently endorsed by the Court) in the following excerpt from the Court's opinion:

> *First*, the right inheres in § 7's guarantee of the right of employees to act in concert for mutual aid and protection. . . .
>
> . . .
>
> *Second*, the right arises only in situations where the employee requests representation. In other words, the employee may forgo his guaranteed right and, if he prefers, participate in an interview unaccompanied by his union representative.
>
> *Third*, the employee's right to request representation as a condition of participation in an interview is limited to situations where the employee reasonably believes the investigation will result in disciplinary action. . . .
>
> "[The Board] would not apply the rule to such run-of-the-mill shop-floor conversations as, for example, the giving of instructions or training or needed corrections of work techniques. In such cases there cannot normally be any reasonable basis for an employee to fear that any adverse impact may result from the interview . . . ."
>
> *Fourth*, exercise of the right may not interfere with legitimate employer prerogatives. The employer has no obligation to justify his refusal to allow union representation, and despite refusal, the employer is free to carry on his inquiry without interviewing the employee, and thus leave to the employee the choice between having an interview unaccompanied by his representative, or having no interview and forgoing any benefits that might be derived from one. . . .
>
> . . .
>
> *Fifth*, . . . The employer has no duty to bargain with the Union representative at an investigatory interview. "The representative is present to assist the employee, and may attempt to clarify the facts or suggest other employees who may have knowledge of them. The employer, however, is free to insist that he is only interested, at that time, in hearing the employee's own account of the matter under investigation."[164]

The Court concluded that the Board had reached "a fair and reasoned balance upon a question within its special competence," and the Court added:

> The statutory right confirmed today is in full harmony with actual industrial practice. Many important collective-bargaining agreements have provisions that accord employees rights of union representation at investigatory interviews.

---

[164]NLRB v. J. Weingarten, Inc., 420 U.S. 251, 256, 88 LRRM 2689, 2691–92 (1975) (quoting Quality Mfg. Co., 195 NLRB 195, 199, 79 LRRM 1269, 1271 (1972), and *Board's Brief*, at 22). *See* Comment, *The Differing Nature of the* Weingarten *Right to Union Representation in the NLRB and Arbitral Forums*, 44 U. MIAMI L. REV. 467 (1989). Regarding the extent to which the employer may properly regulate the representative's participation at an investigatory interview, see also *Southwestern Bell Tel. Co. v. NLRB*, 667 F.2d 470, 109 LRRM 2602 (5th Cir. 1982); *New Jersey Bell Tel. Co.*, 308 NLRB 277, 141 LRRM 1017 (1992); *Texaco, Inc.*, 251 NLRB 633, 105 LRRM 1239, 1243 (1980) (the employer improperly conditioned a representative's right to attend by requiring that he remain silent throughout the investigatory interview). Regarding employee awareness of *Weingarten* rights, it sometimes has been contended that the employer has an obligation to apprise the employee of those rights. The NLRB rejected such a contention in *Montgomery Ward & Co.*, 269 NLRB 904, 115 LRRM 1321 (1984). *See also* Newport News Shipbuilding & Drydock Co., 78 LA 921, 926 (Garrett, 1982).

Even where such a right is not explicitly provided in the agreement a "well established current of arbitral authority" sustains the right of union representation at investigatory interviews which the employee reasonably believes may result in disciplinary action against him.[165]

Thus, in respect to instances in which the employer engages an employee in an interview or discussion that the employee reasonably believes may affect the disciplinary decision, the Board has stated that "an employee's *Weingarten* rights, with all its attendant safeguards, matures at the commencement of the interview, be it on the production floor or in a supervisor's office."[166]

The "reasonableness" of an employee's belief that discipline might result will be determined "'by objective standards under all the circumstances of the case.'"[167] There is a risk that the employee's belief may be found unreasonable. If an employee disobeys an order to meet with management in the erroneous belief that discipline may result and that he or she is entitled to union representation, discipline for insubordination may be upheld.[168]

---

[165]*Weingarten*, 420 U.S. at 267, 88 LRRM at 2695 (quoting Chevron Chem. Co., 60 LA 1066, 1071 (Merrill, 1973)). The Court cited additional arbitration decisions in accord, but also recognized that other arbitrators had held contra. Regarding arbitrability where the agreement does not expressly deal with the right, see *Humble Oil & Ref. Co. v. Industrial Workers (AIW)*, 337 F.2d 321, 57 LRRM 2112 (5th Cir. 1964).

[166]Roadway Express, 246 NLRB 1127, 1128, 103 LRRM 1050, 1052 (1979) (The Board indicated that the employer may specify the place of the interview. In this case the Board also indicated that the range of acceptable representatives should not be too narrowly drawn, the Board stating that *Weingarten* does not "state or suggest that an employee's interest can only be safeguarded by the presence of a *specific* representative sought by the employee." *Id.* at 1129, 103 LRRM at 1053) (emphasis in original). *See also* Crown Zellerbach, 239 NLRB 1124, 100 LRRM 1092 (1978); Anchortank, Inc., 239 NLRB 430, 99 LRRM 1622, 1623 (1978). For a later development concerning the requirement that activity be "concerted" in order to be protected, see *E.I. DuPont de Nemours & Co. v. NLRB*, 733 F.2d 296, 116 LRRM 2343 (3d Cir. 1984). Regarding a fair opportunity to consult with the representative before the interview, see *Pacific Tel. & Tel. Co. v. NLRB*, 711 F.2d 134, 113 LRRM 3529, 3531 (9th Cir. 1983) (the court stated that "the securing of information as to the subject matter of the interview and a pre-interview conference with a union representative" are also rights of the employee); *Climax Molybdenum Co. v. NLRB*, 584 F.2d 360, 99 LRRM 2471, 2473 (10th Cir. 1978) (the court concluded that the date of a scheduled investigatory interview left the employee adequate opportunity to consult union representatives on his own time prior to the interview, so the employer was not required to permit such consultation on company time before the interview).

[167]*Weingarten*, 420 U.S. at 257 n.5, 88 LRRM 2691 n.5 (quoting *Quality Mfg. Co.*, 195 NLRB at 198 n.3, 79 LRRM at 1271 n.3).

[168]For example, in *General Electric Co.*, 240 NLRB 479, 100 LRRM 1248, 1250 (1979), an employee was lawfully suspended for insubordination when he disobeyed an order not to leave his work station in order to consult a union steward; although faced with questions concerning his work, his foreman had told him that he would not be disciplined for faulty work, and this fact, along with other circumstances, made his belief that he might be disciplined unreasonable. In *Tastybird Food*, 88 LA 875, 878–79 (Goodstein, 1987), the arbitrator sustained the discharge of an employee for insubordination, where the employee insisted on consulting a steward before obeying his supervisor's order to transfer to a different department. The agreement provided that an employee in the grievant's classification could be moved wherever needed. *See also* Spartan Stores v. NLRB, 628 F.2d 953, 105 LRRM 2293 (6th Cir. 1980); Equitable Gas Co., 81 LA 368, 371 (Sergent, Jr., 1983); St. Regis Paper Co., 71 LA 740, 743 (Williams, 1978); Taft Broad. Co., WBRC-TV, 69 LA 307, 310 (Chaffin, 1977); Vulcan Materials Co., 68 LA 1305, 1308–09 (Marlatt, 1977).

The NLRB has continued to shape the "contours and limits of the statutory rights" established in *Weingarten*.[169] For example, the Board held that the *Weingarten* protection attached to a proceeding where the employee was being questioned by a grievance council consisting of nonsupervisory employees who had been given final authority to uphold, modify, or set aside the employer's discipline.[170] The NLRB found that *Weingarten* applied because the proceeding was investigatory in nature, and that for the purposes of grievance adjustment the council was an agent of the employer in making the final disciplinary determination.[171]

The *Weingarten* doctrine is applicable in nonunionized workplaces, as well as in unionized ones.[172] Reversing its earlier position, the Board stated that the NLRA "clearly protects the right of employees—whether unionized or not—to act in concert for mutual aid or protection."[173] It does not necessarily follow, however, that the Board will fashion a compensatory remedy for employees whose *Weingarten* rights have been violated. Where an employee who had been denied union representation at his investigatory interview was found to have been discharged for cause, the Board declined to order reinstatement with back pay and instead issued a cease-and-desist order directing the employer to refrain from its unlawful activity.[174] In another case, where the employer denied the union representative the right to speak during an investigatory interview, the Board restricted its remedy to the issuance of a cease-and-desist order although the grievant had been returned to work by an administrative law judge.[175] Arbitral selection of a remedy for a *Weingarten* violation is similarly contextually dependent.[176]

Further, evidence obtained from an employee in a meeting where *Weingarten* rights were violated may not be used against that employee in imposing discipline.[177] However, the Board has held that when no nexus ex-

---

[169]*Weingarten*, 420 U.S. at 256, 88 LRRM at 2691.

[170]Henry Ford Health Sys., 320 NLRB 1153, 1154, 152 LRRM 1033, 1033–34 (1996).

[171]*Id.* at 1154–55, 152 LRRM 1034–35.

[172]Epilepsy Found. of Northeast Ohio, 331 NLRB 676, 164 LRRM 1233 (2000).

[173]*Id.*, 164 LRRM at 1237. The Board overruled its decisions in *E.I. DuPont de Nemours & Co.*, 289 NLRB 627, 128 LRRM 1233 (1988), and *Sears, Roebuck & Co.*, 274 NLRB 230, 118 LRRM 1329 (1985), and returned to the standard in *Materials Research Corp.*, 262 NLRB 1010, 110 LRRM 1401 (1982).

[174]Taracorp Indus., 273 NLRB 221, 117 LRRM 1497 (1984) (overruling Kraft Foods, 251 NLRB 598, 105 LRRM 1233 (1980)). *But see* Lancaster Electro Plating, 93 LA 203 (Bressler, 1989) (grievant who was suspended and then discharged is entitled to back pay for the period between suspension and discharge where discharge was justified, but the employer failed to afford grievant representation prior to suspension).

[175]Greyhound Lines, 273 NLRB 1443, 118 LRRM 1199 (1985). *See also* Radisson Muehlebach Hotel, 273 NLRB 1464, 118 LRRM 1601 (1985).

[176]Maurey Mfg. Co., 95 LA 148 (Goldstein, 1990) (coworker's statement purportedly linking steward to illegal activity may not be relied on where employer disregarded worker's general question about representation and/or failed to interpret question as demand for representation); Lancaster Electro Plating, 93 LA 203 (Bressler, 1989) (grievant entitled to back pay for period between suspension and discharge where discharge was justified but employer failed to afford grievant representation prior to discharge).

[177]Frank v. Department of Transp., Federal Aviation Admin., 35 F.3d 1554, 1559–60 (Fed. Cir. 1994).

ists between an improper denial of representation and discipline imposed, the discipline stands.[178]

Additionally, *Weingarten* rights have been found not to attach to a situation where the employer has a general meeting to discuss company rules,[179] or where employees walk out of investigatory interviews after the employer legally denies them the right to union representation,[180] or where an employee, after being asked to go to the manager's office to fill out an accident report, leaves the area to get a union representative.[181] However, where a portion of the meeting consists of an investigatory interview, the Board's finding that an employee was denied *Weingarten* rights has been upheld by a court of appeals.[182]

The principles established by *Weingarten* and its progeny have been followed by arbitrators.[183] Arbitrators typically find *Weingarten* protections

---

[178]U.S. Postal Serv., 314 NLRB 227, 146 LRRM 1222 (1994). *See also* Anchorage Hilton Hotel, 102 LA 55, 58 (Landau, 1993) (absent a showing of prejudice resulting from *Weingarten* violation, it is not appropriate to overturn disciplinary action, but rather more appropriate to take the violation into account as a mitigating factor in reviewing the disciplinary penalty imposed).

[179]Northwest Eng'g Co., 265 NLRB 190, 111 LRRM 1481 (1982).

[180]Bridgeport Hosp., 265 NLRB 421, 111 LRRM 1585 (1982).

[181]Twin Coast Newspapers, 89 LA 799 (Brisco, 1987).

[182]*See* NLRB v. Southwestern Bell Tel. Co., 730 F.2d 166, 116 LRRM 2211 (5th Cir. 1984); Gulf States Mfg. v. NLRB, 704 F.2d 1390, 113 LRRM 2789, *reh'g denied*, 715 F.2d 1020, 114 LRRM 2727 (5th Cir. 1983). *See also* H.J. Heinz Co., 95 LA 82 (Ellmann, 1990).

[183]*See, e.g.,* State of Ohio, Dep't of Pub. Safety, 114 LA 1040, 1046 (Ruben, 2000); Gilmore Envelope Corp., 110 LA 1036, 1039–40 (Ross, 1998); Coca-Cola Bottling Group, 97 LA 343, 349 (Weckstein, 1991); General Dynamics Convair Div., 95 LA 500, 507 (Jones, Jr., 1990); Lancaster Electro Plating, 93 LA 203, 207 (Bressler, 1989); Pratt & Whitney Aircraft Group, 91 LA 1014, 1017 (Chandler, 1988); Bake Rite Rolls, 90 LA 1133, 1136 (DiLauro, 1988); Trailways, Inc., 88 LA 941, 946–47 (Heinsz, 1987); Equitable Gas Co., 81 LA 368, 371 (Sergent, Jr., 1983); U.S. Air Force, 80 LA 1140, 1142 (White, 1983); Continental-Indianapolis, Inc., 78 LA 409, 415–17 (House, 1982); Renaissance Ctr. P'ship, 76 LA 379, 383 (Daniel, 1981); Allied Employers, 72 LA 437, 439, 441 (Peterschmidt, 1978); St. Regis Paper Co., 71 LA 740, 743 (Williams, 1978); South Cent. Bell Tel. Co., 71 LA 174, 177 (Wolff, 1978); Vulcan Materials Co., 68 LA 1305, 1308–09 (Marlatt, 1977); Morton-Norwich Prods., 67 LA 352, 353–54 (Markowitz, 1976); Combustion Eng'g, 67 LA 349, 351 (Clarke, 1976); Clow Corp., 64 LA 668, 671–72 (Gibson, 1975). For application of *Weingarten* in the federal sector, see *Government Employees (AFGE) Local 3882 v. FLRA*, 865 F.2d 1283, 130 LRRM 2365 (D.C. Cir. 1989); *Defense Criminal Investigative Serv. v. FLRA*, 855 F.2d 93, 129 LRRM 2233 (3d Cir. 1988); *Government Employees (AFGE) Local 2544 v. FLRA (Immigration & Naturalization Serv.)*, 779 F.2d 719, 121 LRRM 2262 (D.C. Cir. 1985); *Department of Justice, Border Patrol*, 36 FLRA 41 (1990); *Department of Justice, Bureau of Prisons*, 35 FLRA 431 (1990); *Defense Mapping Agency Aerospace Ctr.*, 88 LA 651, 655–56 (Hilgert, 1986). For related considerations, see Chapter 10, section 3.A.v., "The NLRA, the Arbitrator, and the NLRB," and section 4., "Judicial Decisions." Concerning the applicability of *Weingarten* to federal-sector employment prior to enactment of the Civil Service Reform Act of 1978, codified in scattered sections of 5 U.S.C., see discussion in *Department of the Air Force*, 75 LA 994, 997 (Hart, 1980). The Civil Service Reform Act expressly provides that:

> An exclusive representative of an appropriate unit in an agency shall be given the opportunity to be represented at . . . any examination of an employee in the unit by a representative of the agency in connection with an investigation if . . . the employee reasonably believes that the examination may result in disciplinary action against the employee . . . and the employee requests representation.

5 U.S.C. §7114(a)(2). *See also* Internal Revenue Serv., 78 LA 1016, 1018, 1021 (Render, 1982). Regarding applicability of *Weingarten* to the state public sector, see *City of Edina, Minn.*, 90 LA 209, 211 (Ver Ploeg, 1987); *Birmingham-Jefferson County Transit*, 84 LA 1272, 1275 (Statham, 1985); *Anoka County, Minn.*, 84 LA 516, 519–21 (Jacobowski, 1985); *Lancaster*

implicit in the "just cause" standard contained in most collective bargaining agreements.[184] However, arbitrators will not decide *Weingarten* issues where the NLRB is involved and has not deferred to the arbitrator.[185]

Following the Board's lead, arbitrators also have found that where the contract is silent about union representation during predisciplinary investigations and interviews, an employee's right to representation may be limited to instances when the employee specifically requests union assistance.[186] However, where an employee fails to request or waives union representation, arbitrators have taken into account whether the employee might not be aware of his or her *Weingarten* rights. Thus, while employer discipline of a union president was upheld, the discipline of an employee with limited knowledge of English was mitigated.[187]

If the purpose of the meeting is only to inform the employee of disciplinary action already decided upon, *Weingarten* protection is not available. Overruling its previous position to the contrary, the NLRB held in *Baton Rouge Water Works Co.*[188] that "an employee has no Section 7 right to the presence of his union representative at a meeting with his employer held solely for the purpose of informing the employee of, and acting upon, a previously made disciplinary decision."[189]

City Sch., 81 LA 1024, 1028 (Abrams, 1983); *City of Sterling Heights*, 80 LA 825, 829 (Ellmann, 1983). *See* Tucson Unified Sch. Dist., 92 LA 544 (White, 1989); Arkansas Power & Light Co., 92 LA 144 (Weisbrod, 1989); Maui Pineapple Co., 86 LA 907, 911 (Tsukiyama, 1986) (discussion of arbitral application of *Weingarten*).

[184]Union Tank Car Co., 104 LA 699, 703 (Fullmer, 1995).

[185]Simkins Indus., 106 LA 551, 557–58 (Fullmer, 1996); Norfolk Shipbuilding & Drydock Corp., 105 LA 529, 533 (Hockenberry, 1995).

[186]Calcasieu Parish Police Jury, 86 LA 350 (Nicholas, Jr., 1985); Fry's Food Stores of Ariz., 83 LA 1248 (Weizenbaum, 1984).

[187]Indiana Convention Ctr. & Hoosier Dome, 98 LA 713 (Wolff, 1992) (employer's denial of steward's right to be present at termination interview requires that employer pay union's share of cost and expenses of arbitration proceeding); Maui Pineapple Co., 86 LA 907, 911 (Tsukiyama, 1986); Borough of Carlisle, Pa., 82 LA 1 (Woy, 1984). *See also* Stroehman Bakeries, 98 LA 873 (Sands, 1990) (just cause did not exist to discharge 17-year-old driver for alleged sexual assault on receiving clerk at customer's store, where management confronted grievant with accusation without warning or opportunity to acquire union representation).

[188]246 NLRB 995, 103 LRRM 1056 (1980).

[189]*Id.* at 997, 103 LRRM at 1058. The Board cautioned that:

[I]f the employer engages in any conduct beyond merely informing the employee of a previously made disciplinary decision, the full panoply of protections accorded the employee under *Weingarten* may be applicable. Thus, for example, were the employer to inform the employee of a disciplinary action and then seek facts or evidence in support of that action, or to attempt to have the employee admit his alleged wrongdoing or to sign a statement to that effect, or to sign statements relating to such matters as workmen's compensation, . . . the employee's right to union representation would attach. In contrast, the fact that the employer and employee thereafter engage in a conversation at the employee's behest or instigation concerning the reasons for the previously determined discipline will not, alone, convert the meeting to an interview at which the Weingarten protections apply.

Id. The Board overruled its *Certified Grocers of Cal.*, 227 NLRB 1211, 94 LRRM 1279 (1977), *enforcement denied*, 587 F.2d 449, 100 LRRM 3029 (9th Cir. 1978), decision to the extent that it was inconsistent with *Baton Rouge*, but reaffirmed the *Certified Grocers* conclusion that no longer should any distinction be drawn between "investigatory" and "disciplinary" interviews. "Thus, the full purview of protections accorded employees under *Weingarten* apply to both 'investigatory' and 'disciplinary' interviews, save only those conducted for the exclusive purpose of notifying an employee of previously determined disciplinary action." *Baton Rouge*, 246 NLRB at 997, 103 LRRM at 1058. The *Baton Rouge* exception to *Weingarten* was applied in *Allied Aviation Serv. Co. of New England*, 77 LA 455, 459 (Turkus, 1981).

In the aftermath of its *Baton Rouge* decision, the NLRB has continued to uphold the right of employers to deny union representation where the imposition of discipline already has been determined.[190]

Mirroring the NLRB holding in *Baton Rouge*, arbitrators have held that where the purpose of the meeting was to administer discipline and not to conduct an investigatory interview, employer denial of union representation did not violate the principles of *Weingarten*.[191] One arbitrator reasoned that although he would not decide the propriety of applying federal statutes, the Board's *Baton Rouge* standard led him to deny the union's *Weingarten* arguments in a case where an employee was denied union representation at a meeting where no investigation was conducted but a verbal reprimand was issued.[192] It should be noted, however, that even when an employee is working under a "last chance agreement," if discipline has not necessarily been decided upon, *Weingarten* protections apply.[193]

Weingarten does not apply during a police interview of an employee in which the employer was not allowed to participate,[194] nor does the *Weingarten* doctrine allow employees to refuse to answer an employer's questions regarding an ongoing investigation.[195] However, an employee is allowed *Weingarten* representation if asked to sign documents that could possibly damage the employee's position, where the request to sign is accompanied by threats of discipline for failure to do so.[196]

In construing the extent to which *Weingarten* applies to employer investigations, some arbitrators have limited the right to union representation to employee interviews only. As a result, there is arbitral authority for the proposition that union representation rights are not available during employer searches for physical evidence in automobiles[197] and during meetings called for the purpose of informing employees they must submit to drug screening during a physical examination.[198]

---

[190]*See* San Antonio Portland Cement Co., 277 NLRB 338, 121 LRRM 1234 (1985); Eagle Discount, 275 NLRB 1438, 120 LRRM 1047 (1985).

[191]AFG Indus., 87 LA 568 (Clarke, 1986). *See also* Fry's Food Stores of Ariz., 83 LA 1248 (Weizenbaum, 1984).

[192]*AFG Indus.*, 87 LA at 572.

[193]Trendler Metal Prods., 101 LA 749, 756 (Green, 1993). *See also* Eaglebudd Enters., 106 LA 659, 661–62 (Franckiewicz, 1996). *But compare* S&J Ranch, 103 LA 350, 361–62 (Bogue, 1994) (language in contract expressly placed burden on employer to ensure union representative was present in appropriate cases, even if the employee does not specifically make a request); Lenzing Fibers Corp., 105 LA 423, 428 (Sergent, 1995) (employees under last-chance agreements are nevertheless entitled to their "day in court").

[194]Briggs & Stratton Corp., 107 LA 1023, 1029–30 (Briggs, 1997).

[195]AT&T, 102 LA 931, 934–35 (Kanner, 1994). *Cf.* State of Ohio, Dep't of Pub. Safety, 114 LA 1040 (Ruben, 2000) (no *Weingarten* rights attached to interviews of state troopers in connection with criminal investigation of gunshot death of fugitive following high speed car chase).

[196]Ralphs Grocery Co., 101 LA 634, 638–39 (Ross, 1993).

[197]General Elec. Co., 98 LA 355 (Stutz, 1991); Shell Oil Co., 84 LA 562 (Milentz, 1985).

[198]Birmingham-Jefferson County Transit, 84 LA 1272 (Statham, 1985). *But see* General Dynamics Convair Div., 95 LA 500 (Jones, Jr., 1990) (company security investigators who reasonably believed grievant brought marijuana onto company property in her car improperly detained her and interviewed her without a union representative where memorandum concerning drug control policy required union steward "to be present for inspection" even in absence of request).

In denying an employee union representation during a performance evaluation to be conducted by a supervisor, one arbitrator held that there was as yet no grievable event.[199]

9. GRIEVANCE ADJUSTMENT BY INDIVIDUAL EMPLOYEES [LA CDI 93.305]

Much has been written concerning the individual employee's rights in grievance adjustment and arbitration, and concerning the employee's right of fair representation.[200] It is the purpose here to deal only briefly with these matters.[201]

The NLRA, as amended by the Labor Management Relations Act of 1947 (LMRA),[202] provides in Section 9(a) that the majority union shall be the "exclusive representative" of all employees in the bargaining unit, and further provides in Section 8(d) that the duty of the employer and union to bargain includes the duty to confer in good faith with respect to questions arising under the collective bargaining agreement. However, a proviso to Section 9(a) states that "any individual employee or a group of employees shall have the right at any time to present grievances to their employer and to have such grievances adjusted, without the intervention of the bargaining representative, as long as the adjustment is not inconsistent with the terms of a collective-bargaining contract or agreement then in effect," and as long as

---

[199]Anoka County, Minn., 84 LA 516, 521 (Jacobowski, 1985).

[200]*See, e.g.*, Van Wezel Stone, *A Mandatory Arbitration of Individual Employment Rights: The Yellow Dog Contract of the 1990s*, 73 DENV. U. L. REV. 1017 (1996); Ware, *Employment Arbitration and Voluntary Consent*, 25 HOFSTRA L. REV. 83 (Fall 1996).

[201]For more intense coverage, the reader is directed to the writings cited throughout the present topic. For some of the many other writings in this general area, see MALIN, INDIVIDUAL RIGHTS WITHIN THE UNION (BNA Books 1988); MCKELVEY, THE DUTY OF FAIR REPRESENTATION (1977) (a collection of articles by Aaron, Vladeck, Jones, Lipsitz, Summers, Rabin, Klein, & Donahue); GORMAN, BASIC TEXT ON LABOR LAW 695–728 (1976); Modjeska, *The Supreme Court and the Duty of Fair Representation*, 7 OHIO ST. J. ON DISP. RESOL. 1 (1991); Sherman, *The Role and Rights of the Individual in Labor Arbitration*, 15 WM. MITCHELL L. REV. 379 (1989); Jacobs, *The Duty of Fair Representation: Minorities, Dissidents and Exclusive Representation*, 59 B.U. L. REV. 857 (1979); Leffler, *Piercing the Duty of Fair Representation: The Dichotomy Between Negotiations and Grievance Handling*, 1979 U. ILL. L.F. 35 (1979); Gross & Bordoni, *Reflections on the Arbitrator's Responsibility to Provide a Full and Fair Hearing: How To Bite the Hands That Feed You*, 29 SYRACUSE L. REV. 877 (1978); Rabin, *The Impact of the Duty of Fair Representation Upon Labor Arbitration, id.* at 851; Murphy, *Due Process and Fair Representation in Grievance Handling in the Public Sector, in* ARBITRATION—1977, PROCEEDINGS OF THE 30TH ANNUAL MEETING OF NAA 121 (Dennis & Somers eds., BNA Books 1978); Ashe, *Comment, id.* at 147; Wollett, *Comment, id.* at 155; Prashker, *Comment, id.* at 161; *Discussion, id.* at 169; Summers, *The Individual Employee's Rights Under the Collective Agreement: What Constitutes Fair Representation, in* ARBITRATION—1974, PROCEEDINGS OF THE 27TH ANNUAL MEETING OF NAA 14 (Dennis & Somers eds., BNA Books 1975); Asher, *Comment, id.* at 31; Dunau, *Comment, id.* at 38; Kleeb, *Comment, id.* at 41; Katin, *Comment, id.* at 44; *Discussion, id.* at 49; Friedman, *Individual Rights in Grievance Arbitration*, 27 ARB. J. 252 (1972); FLEMING, THE LABOR ARBITRATION PROCESS 107–33 (1965); Rosen, *The Individual Worker in Grievance Arbitration: Still Another Look at the Problem*, 24 MD. L. REV. 233 (1964); Williams, *Intervention: Rights and Policies, in* LABOR ARBITRATION AND INDUSTRIAL CHANGE, PROCEEDINGS OF THE 16TH ANNUAL MEETING OF NAA 266–95 (Kahn ed., BNA Books 1963); Aaron, *Some Aspects of the Union's Duty of Fair Representation*, 22 OHIO ST. L.J. 39 (1961); Note, *Public Sector Grievance Procedures, Due Process, and the Duty of Fair Representation*, 89 HARV. L. REV. 752 (1976).

[202]29 U.S.C. §141 et seq.

"the bargaining representative has been given opportunity to be present at such adjustment." The enactment of this proviso in 1947 generated much discussion, reflecting two conflicting interpretations.

Under one interpretation (1) individual employees have a statutory right to settle their grievances directly with the employer and no agreement between the union and the employer can deprive them of this right, and (2) individual employees have a right to use the grievance and arbitration procedure without the union's assistance or over its veto.[203]

Under a second interpretation, the Section 9(a) proviso permits (as an exception to the duty to deal exclusively with the union), but does not require, the employer to adjust grievances with individual employees. Under this interpretation, the statute places a right of control in the employer, who can keep control or who can relinquish it in the collective bargaining agreement either (1) by giving individual employees a right to adjust their grievances directly with the employer, or (2) by placing the right of grievance adjustment solely in the union.[204]

Some of the uncertainty as to the scope of individual employee rights in grievance adjustment was removed by the Supreme Court's *Maddox*[205] deci-

---

[203]*See* Summers, *Individual Rights in Collective Agreements and Arbitration*, 37 N.Y.U. L. REV. 362 (1962); Lenhoff, *The Effect of Labor Arbitration Clauses Upon the Individual*, 9 ARB. J. 3, 14–16 (1954); Paul Mueller Co., 40 LA 780, 783 (Bauder, 1963); Kister Lumber Co., 37 LA 356, 358 (Volz, 1961). In *Donnelly v. United Fruit Co.*, 190 A.2d 825, 53 LRRM 2271 (N.J. 1963), the court recognized a right of individual employees to intervene, with independent representation, in arbitration proceedings between union and employer. *See also* Saginario v. Attorney Gen. of N.J., 435 A.2d 1134, 111 LRRM 2701 (N.J. 1981). For arbitration cases involving attempts of third parties or minority groups of employees to intervene in cases being processed by the union, see *Maier Brewing Co.*, 45 LA 1115, 1122–23 (Jones, 1965); *Ball Bros. Co.*, 27 LA 353, 354–55 (Sembower, 1956). *See also* Youngdahl, *Uneasy Second Thoughts on the Independent Participation by Employees in Labor Arbitration Proceedings*, 33 ARK. L. REV. 151 (1979). Related discussion is found in Chapter 7, section 3.E., "Bilateral Arbitration of Trilateral Conflicts." For a case involving a union's right to complete an arbitration instituted prior to the union's decertification, see *Trumbull Asphalt Co.*, 38 LA 1093, 1097–98 (Elson, 1962). *See also* Port of Portland, 71 LA 66, 69 (Snow, 1978).

[204]*See* Cox, *Rights Under a Labor Agreement*, 69 HARV. L. REV. 601, 621–24 (1956); Black-Clawson Co. v. Machinists Lodge 355, Dist. 137, 313 F.2d 179, 52 LRRM 2038 (2d Cir. 1962); Eastern Shore Pub. Serv. Co., 39 LA 751, 756 (Frey, 1962); General Cable Corp., 20 LA 443, 444–45 (Hays, 1953). *See also* Pabst Brewing Co., 73 LA 715, 717 (Larkin, 1979). In *North American Aviation*, 44 LA 1102, 1107–08 (Ross, 1965), the arbitrator held that a separate "employee grievance procedure" in which employees could represent themselves violated the collective bargaining agreement, stating that while NLRA §9(a) of the statute permits the employer to maintain a separate employee grievance procedure in the absence of any contrary commitment, the agreement may require (as this one did) that grievances be processed exclusively through the contract grievance procedure. In *Veterans Administration Medical Center*, 41 FLRA 1370 (1991), it was held that the agency violates §7116(a)(1) and (8) of the Federal Service Labor-Management Relations statute if it fails to allow the union an opportunity to be present during formal discussion, that is, telephone interviews of unit employees conducted by one of the agency's attorneys in preparation for a Merit Systems Protection Board hearing. In *Department of the Army, New Cumberland Army Depot*, 38 FLRA 671 (1990), it was held that employees cannot present their grievances to the employer without the union having an opportunity to be present and to participate in the meeting. The union is entitled to prior notice of the meeting so it can select its own representative. For the elements that must exist for the union's right to attach, see *Department of Justice, Bureau of Prisons*, 29 FLRA 584 (1987). *See also* City of Oak Creek, Wis., 90 LA 710 (Baron, 1988); U.S. Postal Serv., 281 NLRB 1015, 123 LRRM 1209 (1986).

[205]Republic Steel Corp. v. Maddox, 379 U.S. 650, 58 LRRM 2193 (1965).

sion in 1965 and by its *Vaca*[206] decision in 1967, though neither decision expressly discusses the Section 9(a) proviso.[207] A third decision of particular significance in regard to individual employee rights is the Court's *Hines*[208] decision of 1976.

In *Maddox*, the Supreme Court held that an employee who had not attempted to use the contractual grievance procedure to enforce his right to benefits under the collective bargaining agreement was precluded from instituting court suit against the employer for this purpose.[209] The Court explained:

> As a general rule in cases to which federal law applies, federal labor policy requires that individual employees wishing to assert contract grievances must *attempt* use of the contract grievance procedure agreed upon by employer and union as the mode of redress. If the union refuses to press or only perfunctorily presses the individual's claim, differences may arise as to the forms of redress then available. . . . But unless the contract provides otherwise, there can be no doubt that the employee must afford the union the opportunity to act on his behalf. . . . Union interest in prosecuting employee grievances is clear. Such activity complements the union's status as exclusive bargaining representative by permitting it to participate actively in the continuing administration of the contract.[210]

---

[206]Vaca v. Sipes, 386 U.S. 171, 64 LRRM 2369 (1967).

[207]Indeed, only in *Maddox* did the Court make even a passing reference expressly to the proviso. That reference is noted below.

[208]Hines v. Anchor Motor Freight, 424 U.S. 554, 91 LRRM 2481 (1976).

[209]Somewhat conversely, it was held in *Vickers Petroleum Corp.*, 73 LA 399, 400 (Miller, 1979), that the fact that a retiring employee may have a right to institute court proceedings on a pension-plan issue does not deny the right to utilize the grievance procedure to which the issue otherwise could be taken.

[210]Republic Steel Corp. v. Maddox, 379 U.S. 650, 652–53, 58 LRRM 2193, 2194 (1965) (footnotes and citations omitted) (emphasis in original). In its footnote to the first sentence of the just-quoted passage, the Court said: "The proviso of § 9(a) of the National Labor Relations Act . . . is not contra; *Black-Clawson Co. v. Machinists*, 313 F.2d 179." *Maddox*, 379 U.S. at 652 n.7. Also to be noted from *Maddox* is the Court's comment that "the federal rule would not of course preclude Maddox' court suit if the parties to the collective bargaining agreement expressly agreed that arbitration was not the exclusive remedy." *Id.* at 657–58, 58 LRRM at 2196. *See* Groves v. Ring Screw Works, 498 U.S. 168, 135 LRRM 3121 (1990) (the agreement provided for arbitration of disputes only if the parties agreed; the court ruled that the employees, who claimed they were wrongfully discharged, could sue after exhausting voluntary grievance procedures when, at the end of process, the employer decided against arbitration and the union decided not to strike). *But see* Santos v. American Broad. Co., 866 F.2d 892, 130 LRRM 2515 (6th Cir. 1989) (an employee had the right to proceed to arbitration without the union's assistance). The Supreme Court has extended its *Maddox* rule to claims of railroad employees under the Railway Labor Act, 45 U.S.C. §151 et seq., but has refused to apply it to a seaman's wage claims, to claims under Title VII of the Civil Rights Act of 1964, 42 U.S.C. §2000e et seq., or, it appears clear, to claims under the Fair Labor Standards Act. See Chapter 2, section 2.A.ii.c., "Post-*Trilogy*: Enforcement of Agreements to Arbitrate and Review of Arbitration Awards," where *Maddox* and cases on its scope of applicability are noted. In *Clayton v. Auto Workers*, 451 U.S. 679, 107 LRRM 2385 (1981), the union refused to arbitrate a discharge grievance and the time limit for arbitration expired; because the internal union appeals procedure could neither reactivate the grievance nor award complete relief (it could not order reinstatement), exhaustion of the internal union appeals procedure was not required with respect to either the employee's §301 suit against the employer on the agreement or his suit against the union for alleged breach of the duty of fair representation. In *Lingle v. Magic Chef*, 486 U.S. 399, 128 LRRM 2521 (1988), the Court held a state retaliatory discharge remedy (workers' compensation claim) was not preempted by §301 of the LMRA. In *Serrano v. Delmonico's Hotel*, 123 Lab. Cas. (CCH) ¶10,400 (S.D.N.Y. 1992), the court held that a discharged security guard, who filed an action against the employer to confirm an arbitrator's award, may have lacked standing to bring an action be-

It is now apparent that individual employees have no inherent right to independent grievance processing and arbitration with the employer. However, opportunity for independent processing may be given to employees by the employer (if it has not bargained away its right to do so), and the right to independent processing may be given to employees by the collective bargaining agreement. Of course, even apart from the two just-noted possibilities, the union does not always resist an employee's desire for independent processing even though the union may have a contractual right to do so.[211]

Many agreements do appear to give individual employees a right to present and adjust their grievances independently of the union.[212] Whether a given agreement actually does give such right is, of course, a matter of interpretation. Some tribunals find the right only if it is clearly indicated by the language of the agreement.[213]

---

cause he was not a party. The court gave the employee leave to amend his complaint to add a claim against the union for breach of its duty of fair representation. In *Food & Commercial Workers Local 7 v. Safeway Stores*, 889 F.2d 940, 132 LRRM 3090 (10th Cir. 1989), a laid-off employee whose union delayed processing her grievance was allowed to sue to enforce an arbitrator's award of back-pay damages against the union.

[211]*See, e.g.*, Maier Brewing Co., 49 LA 14, 18 (Roberts, 1967) (the union and company agreed that the contract had not been violated but where these parties nonetheless gave individual grievants full opportunity, through counsel of their own choosing, to establish otherwise). Of course, where the union is the moving party against an employee there should be no union objection to representation by counsel of the employee's own choosing. *See* Pacific Mercury Elec., 34 LA 91, 92 (Aaron, 1960). *See also* Texas Meat Packers, 42 LA 292, 293–94 (Wren, 1964). In Wirtz, *Due Process of Arbitration, in* THE ARBITRATOR AND THE PARTIES, PROCEEDINGS OF THE 11TH ANNUAL MEETING OF NAA 1, 25 (McKelvey ed., BNA Books 1958), it is said that arbitrators generally have refused to permit grievants to be represented by counsel of their own choosing rather than by the union. For instances of such refusal, see *Yale Transp.*, 41 LA 736, 737 (Kerrison, 1963); *Roadway Express*, 38 LA 1076, 1079–80 (Short, 1962). It is also said that "[a]s a general rule, the courts hold that the employee or grievant is not entitled to his or her own counsel where the contract does not provide for such representation and the employer or the union objects." Kurtz, *Appendix B. Arbitration and Federal Rights Under Collective Agreements in 1976, in* ARBITRATION—1977, PROCEEDINGS OF THE 30TH ANNUAL MEETING OF NAA 265, 283–84 (Dennis & Somers eds., BNA Books 1978) (citing cases). Regarding individual adjustment of grievances and individual choice of counsel by federal-sector employees, see Federal Service Labor-Management Relations Act, 5 U.S.C. §7114(a)(2) & (5).

[212]*See Major Collective Bargaining Agreements: Arbitration Procedures*, at 29 (U.S. Dep't Lab. Bull. No. 1425-6, 1966). For the results of union and company efforts to rectify their initial disregard of the individual grievant's contractual right to attend and participate in grievance sessions, see *Flambeau Valley Farms Coop.*, 39 LA 724, 727–29 (Anderson, 1962). With an individual employee's contractual right to file grievances may go the burden of meeting contractual time limits. Publishers' Ass'n of New York City, 39 LA 379, 382 (Schmertz, 1962). As to how arbitrators might dispose of settlements between an employer and an individual employee that conflict with the collective bargaining agreement, see *Fry's Food Stores*, 44 LA 431, 433–34 (Koven, 1965); *Bendix Corp.*, 38 LA 909, 911–12 (Schedler, 1962); *Driver-Harris Co.*, 36 LA 251 (Blumrosen, 1960).

[213]For an example of a court's reasoning process in interpreting the agreement in this regard, see *Black-Clawson Co. v. Machinists Lodge 355, Dist. 137*, 313 F.2d 179, 183, 52 LRRM 2038 (2d Cir. 1962). *Cf.* Riley Stoker Corp., 7 LA 764 (Platt, 1947). In *Mine Workers Local 12405 v. Martin Marietta Corp.*, 328 F.2d 945 (7th Cir.), *cert. denied*, 379 U.S. 880 (1964), the court interpreted the word "union" in the agreement as referring to the international, and the court held that the local union could not compel arbitration over the objection of the international.

10. Duty of Fair Representation [LA CDI 94.22; 100.020355]

The possible conflict between the union's right and obligation to represent all of the members of the bargaining unit and to determine which grievances should or will be processed up to and including arbitration, and the individual employee's right to be fairly and honestly represented, has led to a series of decisions that attempt to delineate the rights and obligations of each party.

The issues raised by grievance adjustments by individual employees must be considered in light of the doctrine that a union has a duty to represent fairly all of its members. Beginning in 1944 the Supreme Court imposed a duty of fair representation on labor unions coming within the purview of the Railway Labor Act.[214] Thus, the Court's *Steele* decision dealt with a union's attempt to discriminate against black members of the bargaining unit by the terms of a collective bargaining agreement.[215] Like *Steele*, most early "duty of fair representation" cases dealt with racial discrimination by railroad unions.[216] The duty of a labor union to fairly represent its members was extended to unions organized under the National Labor Relations Act in 1953.[217] Duty of fair representation claims are actionable in federal courts,[218] and remedies include both injunctive relief and damages.[219]

In 1962, the NLRB ruled, in *Miranda Fuel Co.*,[220] that the union's arbitrary impairment of a bargaining-unit employee's seniority status was a breach of its duty of fair representation and violated Section 8(b)(1)(A) and 8(b)(2) of the NLRA. The Board held that Section 7 of the NLRA "gives employees the right to be free from unfair or irrelevant or invidious treatment by their exclusive bargaining agent in matters affecting their employment."[221] In its 1967 *Vaca*[222] decision, the Court synthesized standards enunciated in earlier cases and recognized that the union's status as the exclusive bargaining agent was the source of its duty of fair representation:

> Under this doctrine, the exclusive agent's statutory authority to represent all members of a designated unit includes a statutory obligation to serve the interests of all members without hostility or discrimination toward any, to exercise its discretion with complete good faith and honesty, and to avoid arbitrary conduct.[223]

Vaca directly involved an employee's suit against his union in which he alleged that the union had arbitrarily and capriciously failed to take his case

---

[214]Steele v. Louisville & Nashville R.R., 323 U.S. 192, 15 LRRM 708 (1944).
[215]*Id.*
[216]*See, e.g.*, Graham v. Locomotive Firemen, 338 U.S. 232, 25 LRRM 2033 (1949); Tunstall v. Locomotive Firemen, 323 U.S. 210, 15 LRRM 715 (1944).
[217]Ford Motor Co. v. Huffman, 345 U.S. 330, 31 LRRM 2548 (1953). *See also* Syres v. Oil, Chem. & Atomic Workers Local 23, 350 U.S. 892, 37 LRRM 2068 (1955).
[218]*Graham*, 338 U.S. 232, 25 LRRM 2033.
[219]*Tunstall*, 323 U.S. 210, 15 LRRM 715.
[220]140 NLRB 181, 51 LRRM 1584 (1962), *rev'd*, 326 F.2d 172, 54 LRRM 2715 (2d Cir. 1963).
[221]*Id.* at 185.
[222]Vaca v. Sipes, 386 U.S. 171, 64 LRRM 2369 (1967).
[223]*Id.* at 177.

to arbitration. In the wide-ranging majority opinion in this case, the Supreme Court recognized that because the contractual grievance and arbitration remedies "have been devised and are often controlled by the union and the employer, they may well prove unsatisfactory or unworkable for the individual grievant."[224] Furthermore, the Court expressly rejected the notion that the individual employee has an absolute right to have a grievance taken to arbitration regardless of the provisions of the collective bargaining agreement:[225]

> Though we accept the proposition that a union may not arbitrarily ignore a meritorious grievance or process it in perfunctory fashion, we do not agree that the individual employee has an absolute right to have his grievance taken to arbitration regardless of the provisions of the applicable collective bargaining agreement. In L.M.R.A. § 203(d), . . . 29 U. S. C. § 173(d), Congress declared that "Final adjustment by a method agreed upon by the parties is . . . the desirable method for settlement of grievance disputes arising over the application or interpretation of an existing collective-bargaining agreement." In providing for a grievance and arbitration procedure which gives the union discretion to supervise the grievance machinery and to invoke arbitration, the employer and the union contemplate that each will endeavor in good faith to settle grievances short of arbitration. Through this settlement process, frivolous grievances are ended prior to the most costly and time-consuming step in the grievance procedures. Moreover, both sides are assured that similar complaints will be treated consistently, and major problem areas in the interpretation of the collective bargaining contract can be isolated and perhaps resolved. And finally, the settlement process furthers the interest of the union as statutory agent and as coauthor of the bargaining agreement in representing the employees in the enforcement of that agreement.[226]

The Court stated that an employee may seek judicial enforcement of contractual rights if the union has sole power under the agreement to invoke the higher stages of the grievance procedure, and if the employee has been prevented from exhausting the contractual remedies by the union's wrong-

---

[224]*Id.* at 185.

[225]*Id.* at 190. *See* Shores v. Peabody Coal Co., 831 F.2d 1382, 126 LRRM 2911 (7th Cir. 1987); Safran v. Steelworkers, 678 F. Supp. 1178, 130 LRRM 2349 (W.D. Pa. 1988); Anderson v. Ideal Basic Indus., 120 LRRM 2039 (E.D. Tenn. 1985), *aff'd*, 804 F.2d 950, 123 LRRM 3087 (6th Cir. 1986).

[226]*Vaca*, 386 U.S. at 191. The Court did not fear for the interests of the individual employee:

> Nor do we see substantial danger to the interests of the individual employee if his statutory agent is given the contractual power honestly and in good faith to settle grievances short of arbitration. For these reasons, we conclude that a union does not breach its duty of fair representation, and thereby open up a suit by the employee for breach of contract, merely because it settled the grievance short of arbitration.

Id. at 192. Insofar as the Railway Labor Act is concerned, the Supreme Court indicated in the *Burley* cases that, in order for a union to bind individual employees in grievance settlements before the National Railroad Adjustment Board, it must appear that the employees authorized the union in some "legally sufficient manner," which may be by custom, by union rules in the case of union members, or by the failure of an individual employee with notice of proceedings to assert his or her rights. *See* Elgin, Joliet & E. Ry. v. Burley, 327 U.S. 661, 17 LRRM 899 (1946); Elgin, Joliet & E. Ry. v. Burley, 325 U.S. 711, 16 LRRM 749 (1945). In Isaacson, *Labor Arbitration in State Courts*, 12 Arb. J. 179, 188 (1957), it was suggested that the *Burley* decisions apply only to cases under the Railway Labor Act. It may be noted that the Supreme Court did not refer to these decisions in *Vaca*.

ful refusal to process the grievance.[227] As to what is a "wrongful" refusal, the Court answered that "[a] breach of the statutory duty of fair representation occurs only when a union's conduct toward a member of the collective bargaining unit is arbitrary, discriminatory, or in bad faith."[228]

In the Court's 1976 *Hines*[229] decision, where the union had arbitrated an employee's grievance but allegedly had breached its duty of fair representation by the manner in which it processed the grievance, the Court said the question was "whether the contractual protection against relitigating an arbitral decision binds employees who assert that the process has fundamentally malfunctioned by reason of the bad-faith performance of the union."[230] The Court held that if a breach of the duty of fair representation "seriously undermines the integrity of the arbitral process," the award is not final and binding on the employee, who may sue the employer under Section 301 notwithstanding the award.[231]

In *Hines*, the Court reiterated its *Vaca* standards, including the *Vaca* reference to "arbitrary" or "perfunctory" handling of grievances as a basis for finding a breach of the union's duty (the Court also saying, however, that "this involves more than demonstrating mere errors in judgment").[232] Yet later, the Court explained that: "In particular, a union breaches its duty when its conduct is 'arbitrary, discriminatory, or in bad faith,' as, for example, when it 'arbitrarily ignore[s] a meritorious grievance or process[es] it in a perfunctory fashion.'"[233]

Finally, it is to be noted that in *Vaca* the Court indicated that an employee bringing suit against the union for alleged breach of the duty of fair representation may, and probably should, join the Section 301 action against

---

[227]Vaca v. Sipes, 386 U.S. 171, 185, 64 LRRM 2369 (1967).

[228]*Id.* at 190. In *Airline Pilots v. O'Neill*, 499 U.S. 65, 136 LRRM 2721 (1991), the Court ruled that a union violates its duty of fair representation only if its decisions are wholly arbitrary, discriminatory, in bad faith, or irrational. *See also* Goodman v. Lukens Steel Co., 482 U.S. 656, 44 FEP Cases 1 (1987) (the Court held that a union violated §1981 of the Civil Rights Act of 1871 and Title VII by failing to pursue race bias claims). *But see* Bennett v. Glass & Pottery Workers Local 66, 958 F.2d 1429, 139 LRRM 2943 (7th Cir. 1992) (a union that is guilty of "intentional misconduct" is in breach of its duty of fair representation). For other views, see 139 LRR 488 (1992).

[229]Hines v. Anchor Motor Freight, 424 U.S. 554, 91 LRRM 2481 (1976).

[230]*Id.* at 569.

[231]*Id.* at 567. For additional discussion of *Hines*, see Chapter 2, section 2.A.ii.d.(2), "De Novo Litigation of Claims Cognizable Under the Labor Management Relations Act." Regarding violation of Title VII of the Civil Rights Act of 1964 by discriminatory failure to represent an employee properly in contractual grievance proceedings, see *McDonald v. Santa Fe Trail Transp. Co.*, 427 U.S. 273, 12 FEP Cases 1577 (1976). For the right to a jury trial on a hybrid action claiming breaches of the duty of fair representation and of an LMRA §301 contract, see *Terry v. Teamsters Local 391*, 863 F.2d 334, 130 LRRM 2179 (4th Cir. 1988), *aff'd*, 494 U.S. 558, 133 LRRM 2793 (1990).

[232]*Hines*, 424 U.S. at 571. In the interim between *Vaca* and *Hines*, the Court decided *Motor Coach Employees v. Lockridge*, 403 U.S. 274, 77 LRRM 2501, 2512 (1971), which some lower courts have construed to require a showing of bad faith or hostility for a breach of the duty of fair representation.

[233]Electrical Workers (IBEW) v. Foust, 442 U.S. 42, 47, 101 LRRM 2365 (1979) (quoting Vaca v. Sipes, 386 U.S. 171, 190, 191, 64 LRRM 2369 (1967)) (punitive damages may not be assessed against a union for breach of its duty of fair representation by failing properly to pursue a grievance).

the employer in the same suit so that the employer would be liable for damages attributable to the employer's breach of the collective bargaining agreement, and the union would be liable for any increase in those damages caused by the union's refusal to process the grievance.[234] The Supreme Court in *Bowen v. U.S. Postal Service*,[235] held that the union was primarily liable for the increase in damages caused by its arbitrary refusal to process a discharge grievance to arbitration. Since then, various courts have explored the scope of the union's duty of fair representation in Section 301 breach of the duty of fair representation actions.

In decisions following *Bowen,* the courts of appeals have continued to give union representatives considerable leeway in the processing and presentation of grievances.[236] In upholding a union's decision not to proceed to arbitration in a discharge case, one court of appeals found no violation where the union based its decision on the experience of its labor attorney, the grievant's criminal conviction, the union's analysis of arbitral precedent, and other documentary evidence.[237] But, where a union failed to interview and call the one witness who could have effectively and objectively corroborated a grievant's testimony on a vital matter, the U.S. Court of Appeals for the Sixth Circuit found that the union breached its duty of fair representation.[238] In *Auto Workers v. NLRB (Ford Motor Co.)*,[239] the U.S. Court of Appeals for the District of Columbia Circuit found that the union violated the NLRA when it failed to pursue an employee's grievance based solely on the employee's status as a nonunion member. The Court found that the Board reasonably concluded that the union's "members only" policy unlawfully restrained and coerced employees under Section 7 of the NLRA.

While *Bowen* extended union liability for violations of its duty of fair representation, the Supreme Court in *DelCostello*[240] later shortened the pe-

---

[234]*Vaca*, 386 U.S. at 186–87. "Although the number of Section 301 LMRA breach of contract/breach of the duty of fair representation suits continues to swell, plaintiffs have had relatively little success in meeting the 'arbitrary, discriminatory or bad faith' conduct standard enunciated in *Vaca* . . . ." *Report of the Committee on Labor Arbitration and the Law of Collective Bargaining Agreements* 52 (American Bar Ass'n 1978). For related discussion see Chapter 2, section 2.A.ii.d.(2), "De Novo Litigation of Claims Cognizable Under the Labor Management Relations Act," where it is also indicated that in certain respects these individual suits nonetheless may be having significant impact on the arbitration process itself.

[235]459 U.S. 212, 112 LRRM 2281 (1983).

[236]Pegump v. Rockwell Int'l Corp., 109 F.3d 442, 444, 154 LRRM 2816, 2818 (8th Cir. 1997); Young v. Auto Workers-Labor Employment & Training Corp., 95 F.3d 992, 996–98, 153 LRRM 2198, 2200–02 (10th Cir. 1996); Ayala v. Union de Tronquistas de P.R. Local 901, 74 F.3d 344, 345–46, 151 LRRM 2298, 2299 (1st Cir. 1996); Conkle v. Jeong, 73 F.3d 909, 915, 151 LRRM 2065, 2067–68 (9th Cir. 1995), *cert. denied,* 519 U.S. 811 (1996); Cleveland v. Porca Co., 38 F.3d 289, 295–96, 147 LRRM 2385, 2388–89 (7th Cir. 1994); VanDerVeer v. United Parcel Serv., 25 F.3d 403, 405–06, 146 LRRM 2890, 2891–92 (6th Cir. 1994).

[237]Johnson v. U.S. Postal Serv., 756 F.2d 1461, 118 LRRM 3411, 3414 (9th Cir. 1985).

[238]Black v. Ryder/P.I.E. Nationwide, 15 F.3d 573, 585, 145 LRRM 2387, 2396–97 (6th Cir. 1994). *See also* Cruz v. Electrical Workers (IBEW) Local 3, 34 F.3d 1148, 1153–54, 147 LRRM 2176, 2181 (2d Cir. 1994) (union acted arbitrarily when it failed to conduct investigations into validity of complaints); Dutrisac v. Caterpillar Tractor Co., 749 F.2d 1270, 113 LRRM 3532 (9th Cir. 1983) (union acted arbitrarily where union failed to submit a grievance in a timely manner despite a finding that good cause for termination existed).

[239]168 F.3d 509, 160 LRRM 2955 (D.C. Cir. 1999).

[240]DelCostello v. Teamsters, 462 U.S. 151, 113 LRRM 2737 (1983).

riod of limitations for the institution of Section 301 suits to 6 months. The courts of appeals have applied the *DelCostello* limitation period to federal employees[241] and employees covered by the Railway Labor Act.[242] Where an employee brought an action claiming wrongful discharge for exercising his right to workers' compensation in violation of the collective bargaining agreement 8 months after the union informed him it would not go to arbitration, the U.S. Court of Appeals for the Eighth Circuit held that the claim was barred under either Missouri statute or *DelCostello*'s 6-month statute of limitations.[243] However, in cases where a union is charged with a violation of its duty of fair representation, and its action is unchecked by an employer's conflicting interest, the Supreme Court moved in, what may be argued, a new direction. In *Communications Workers v. Beck*[244] and *Breininger v. Sheet Metal Workers Local 6*,[245] the Court used the duty of fair representation as a vehicle to afford individual employees' private causes of action for union violations of Section 8(b)(1)(A) and 8(b)(2) of the NLRA. This approach put the case outside the exclusive jurisdiction of the NLRB.

Subsequent to *Vaca*,[246] lower courts had made differing interpretations of the *Vaca* standard and in some cases distinguished between cases involving contract administration, that is, grievance handling and arbitration, and cases involving contract negotiation. This distinction was rejected by the Supreme Court in *O'Neill*:[247]

> We doubt, moreover, that a bright line could be drawn between contract administration and contract negotiation. Industrial grievances may precipitate settlement negotiations leading to contract amendments, and some strikes and strike settlement agreements may focus entirely on questions of contract interpretation. . . . Finally, some union activities subject to the duty of fair representation fall into neither category.[248]

The *O'Neill* Court likened the duty owed by a union to its members to that of a fiduciary to its beneficiaries:

> The duty of fair representation is thus akin to the duty owed by other fiduciaries to their beneficiaries. For example, some Members of the Court have analogized the duty a union owes to the employees it represents to the duty a trustee owes to trust beneficiaries. . . . Others have likened the relationship between union and employee to that between attorney and client. . . . The fair representation duty also parallels the responsibilities of corporate officers and directors toward shareholders. Just as these fiduciaries owe their beneficiaries a duty of care as well as a duty of loyalty, a union owes employees a duty to represent them adequately as well as honestly and in good faith.[249]

---

[241]Pham v. Government Employees (AFGE) Local 916, 799 F.2d 634, 123 LRRM 2206 (10th Cir. 1986).

[242]Triplett v. Railway, Airlines & S.S. Clerks Local 308, 801 F.2d 700, 123 LRRM 2975 (4th Cir. 1986).

[243]Johnson v. Hussmann Corp., 805 F.2d 795, 123 LRRM 3074 (8th Cir. 1986).

[244]487 U.S. 735, 128 LRRM 2729 (1988) (union-security clause).

[245]493 U.S. 67, 71, 132 LRRM 3001 (1989) (hiring-hall deferral).

[246]386 U.S. 171, 64 LRRM 2369 (1967).

[247]Air Line Pilots v. O'Neill, 499 U.S. 65, 136 LRRM 2721 (1991).

[248]*Id.* at 77, 136 LRRM at 2725–26 (citations omitted).

[249]*Id.* at 75, 136 LRRM at 2724 (citations omitted).

The courts of appeals have applied *O'Neill* using the *Vaca* tripartite standard to examine the union's handling of grievances,[250] contract negotiation,[251] the administration of union-security clauses,[252] and even the implementation of an arbitral award.[253] However, one court has determined that the analysis used in *O'Neill* does not apply to the operation of a hiring hall.[254]

11. PRIVILEGES AND PROTECTION OF GRIEVANCE REPRESENTATIVES

In order to facilitate the operation of the grievance machinery, labor agreements frequently give special privileges and immunities to union grievance representatives. Subject to restraints imposed by courts and arbitrators, these contractual protections serve to ensure the union's ability to handle grievances and administer the contract. Some arbitration decisions also provide disciplinary immunity to grievance representatives for actions taken in connection with their grievance administration duties.[255]

A. Superseniority [LA CDI 117.237]

Many agreements provide superseniority for union representatives, assuring their continued employment as long as they hold office.[256] Although the underlying purpose of superseniority provisions is to promote continuity of effective union representation by experienced representatives, there is considerable arbitrable authority limiting superseniority benefits to rights and privileges clearly protected by the agreement.[257] One arbitrator has ex-

---

[250]Young v. Auto Workers-Labor Employment & Training Corp., 95 F.3d 992, 153 LRRM 2198 (10th Cir. 1996); Black v. Ryder/P.I.E. Nationwide, 15 F.3d 573, 145 LRRM 2387 (6th Cir. 1994).

[251]Griffin v. Air Line Pilots Ass'n, 32 F.3d 1079, 146 LRRM 3092 (7th Cir. 1994).

[252]Nielsen v. Machinists Local Lodge 2569, 94 F.3d 1107, 153 LRRM 2161 (7th Cir. 1996), *cert. denied*, 520 U.S. 1165 (1997); Electronic Workers (IUE) v. NLRB (Paramax Sys. Corp.), 41 F.3d 1532, 148 LRRM 2070 (D.C. Cir. 1994). *See also* California Saw & Knife Works, 320 NLRB 224, 151 LRRM 1121 (1995), *modified on other grounds*, 321 NLRB 731, 152 LRRM 1241 (1996).

[253]Nida v. Plant Prot. Ass'n Nat'l, 7 F.3d 522, 144 LRRM 2530 (6th Cir. 1993).

[254]Plumbers & Pipe Fitters Local 32 v. NLRB (Rockford Corp.), 50 F.3d 29, 33–34, 148 LRRM 2833, 2837 (D.C. Cir.), *cert. denied*, 516 U.S. 974 (1995) (finding that unions wield increased power when they are acting as employers in the operation of a hiring hall, the standard for determining whether a union acting as an employer breached its duty of fair representation should be lowered to "a high standard of fair dealing").

[255]Comparable protections may exist for employer grievance representatives. However, union fines of member-supervisors with no collective bargaining or grievance handling responsibility do not violate the NLRA. NLRB v. Sheet Metal Workers Local 104 (Simpson Sheet Metal), 64 F.3d 465, 150 LRRM 2071 (9th Cir. 1995); Sheet Metal Workers Local 33 (Cabell Sheet Metal & Roofing), 316 NLRB 504, 148 LRRM 1277 (1995).

[256]For statements by the Supreme Court and by the War Labor Board in support of such superseniority, see *U.S. Plastics Prods. Corp.*, 36 LA 808, 810–11 (Tischler, 1961). The union has a responsibility to notify the employer as to which employees hold union office with entitlement to superseniority. Rex Windows, Inc., 41 LA 606, 607 (Lehoczky, 1963). *See also* Lydall E., Inc., 85 LA 329, 335–36 (Larney, 1985); Marine Corps Logistics Base, 76 LA 1264, 1267 (Gentile, 1981).

[257]Matanuska Elec. Ass'n, 107 LA 402, 407 (Landau, 1996) (alternate shop steward not protected from layoff under contract provision that only allows for retention of one shop steward); Walker Mfg. Co., 106 LA 1075, 1080 (Dichter, 1996) (while considering the purpose of superseniority clauses, the arbitrator must look first and foremost to the provisions

plained: "Superseniority obviously is a contradiction of the basic principle of seniority . . . and should be carefully limited to the terms by which it is created. It is clearly an exception to the rule which seniority demands, that older employees in point of service are entitled to preference."[258]

Furthermore, the NLRA's decisions in *Dairylea*[259] and *Gulton*[260] have limited the reach of superseniority provisions. *Dairylea* provides that provisions that are not on their face limited to layoff and recall are presumptively invalid, and the burden of rebutting that presumption rests on the party asserting their lawfulness.[261] *Gulton* provides that officers not involved in grievance processing or other on-the-job agreement administration should not have received superseniority.[262] The presumed illegality of a superseniority clause not limited to layoff and recall may be rebutted by showing that having the same steward on the job furthers effective administration of the labor agreement.[263] Arbitrators have, however, permitted layoff of union stewards where they would have been retained in an area they did not previously represent,[264] or where they would have bumped a more senior employee from a different classification.[265]

Finally, it must be stressed that an employee ordinarily should not be deprived of normal seniority rights by virtue of service as a union representative. Thus, an employer improperly refused to award a vacant job to a union representative (who was entitled to the job by seniority and qualifications) on the ground that her necessary absences from the job to attend to union matters would result in inefficient operations. In this case the arbitrator stated that seniority provisions characteristically involve a compromise with

---

of the agreement). *See also* Amerimark Bldg. Prods., 104 LA 1066, 1070 (Klein, 1995); Masolite Concrete Prods., 103 LA 10, 15 (Keenan, 1994); USS, Div. of USX Corp., 102 LA 810, 812–13 (Petersen, 1993).

[258]American Monorail Co., 40 LA 323, 326 (Teple, 1963).

[259]Dairylea Coop., 219 NLRB 656, 89 LRRM 1737 (1975), *enforced sub nom.* NLRB v. Teamsters Local 338, 531 F.2d 1162, 91 LRRM 2929 (2d Cir. 1976).

[260]Gulton Electro-Voice, 266 NLRB 406, 112 LRRM 1361 (1983), *enforced sub nom.* Electrical Workers (IUE) Local 900 v. NLRB, 727 F.2d 1184, 115 LRRM 2760 (D.C. Cir. 1984).

[261]*Dairylea*, 219 NLRB at 658, 89 LRRM at 1738–39. For examination of many post-*Dairylea* cases, see Kaplan, *Superseniority for Union Representatives as Unfair Labor Practice*, 41 A.L.R. Fed. 309 (1979).

> [T]he cases disclose a distinction between superseniority provisions designed to achieve "continuity" and those which are not necessary to insure the effective presence of the union representative on the job, but which, rather, provide preferences for the representative as a reward for union activity, or to make such an office as that of steward more desirable, thereby assisting the union in maintaining its own organization by means of on-the-job benefits, the latter constituting an unfair labor practice.

Id. at 312. For cases upholding superseniority provisions prohibiting transfer or reassignment of union representatives out of their particular shift, department, or job assignment, see *id.* at 325–28. Legality of superseniority provisions granting union representatives a *preference* as to shifts has depended "upon the relationship of the shift to the particular duties which the union representative performs relative to insuring effective enforcement of the collective bargaining agreement." *Id.* at 328.

[262]Gulton Electro-Voice, 266 NLRB 406, 409–10, 112 LRRM 1361, 1364–65 (1983). For further examination of the post-*Gulton* cases, see Note, *New Limits on Superseniority: Ignoring the Importance of Efficient Union Operations*, 86 Colum. L. Rev. 631 (1986).

[263]Goodyear Tire & Rubber Co., 322 NLRB 1007, 154 LRRM 1119 (1997).

[264]Masolite Concrete Prods., 103 LA 10, 15 (Keenan, 1994).

[265]Walker Mfg. Co., 106 LA 1075, 1079 (Dichter, 1996).

efficiency, and that the need for competent union representatives requires that employees not be prejudiced by reason of their union position.[266]

B. Plant Access [LA CDI 93.244; 100.020313]

Many agreements give nonemployee union representatives access to the workplace for the purpose of investigating grievances.[267] Furthermore, some arbitrators have considered that such a right is implicit in a collective bargaining agreement even if not expressly given,[268] because it is essential that union representatives be given an opportunity, as management is, to examine all circumstances surrounding a grievance.[269] Thus, nonemployee union representatives, such as the union business agent, may be given reasonable access to the plant. But certain limitations must be observed. For example, one arbitrator held that the employer is entitled to know the subject of the grievance for which the union representative seeks entry to the plant.[270] Speaking of the right of entrance, the arbitrator said:

> There should be a legitimate reason for entering a specific area of the plant. It does not give the Union representative the right to roam the plant at will, and it would be a clear violation of the agreement for the Union to use this opportunity to engage in organizational activities.[271]

---

[266]American Lava Corp., 42 LA 117, 119–20 (Hon, 1964). *See also* Heil Co., 54 LA 1123, 1124 (Marshall, 1971). *Cf.* Social Sec. Admin., 69 LA 1149, 1153 (Kaplan, 1977).

[267]Of course, grievance investigation is not the only purpose for which an agreement may authorize plant access by nonemployee union representatives. For example, the broad purpose stated by one agreement was "to carry on Association business." Fort Wayne Cmty. Sch., 68 LA 1256, 1256 (Eagle, 1976).

[268]*See* Collins Radio Co., 36 LA 815, 820–22 (Rohman, 1961) (the employer was directed to grant union access to a building in which disputed duties were performed); Librascope, Inc., 30 LA 358, 363–64 (Jones, Jr., 1958). *Contra* Wheland Co., 32 LA 1004, 1006–07 (Tatum, 1959). As to a right to plant access for the purpose of investigating grievances under the NLRA, compare *Sierra Publ'g Co. dba Sacramento Union v. NLRB*, 889 F.2d 210, 132 LRRM 2961 (9th Cir. 1989), *Subbiondo & Assocs.*, 295 NLRB 132, 132 LRRM 1006 (1989), *Colonna's Shipyard*, 293 NLRB 15, 132 LRRM 1073 (1989), and *Adolph Coors Co.*, 150 NLRB 1604, 58 LRRM 1272 (1965), with *Westinghouse Elec. Corp.*, 113 NLRB 954, 36 LRRM 1416 (1955). *See also* Asarco, Inc. v. NLRB, 805 F.2d 194, 123 LRRM 2985 (6th Cir. 1986) (right of union access to accident site and report); NLRB v. National Broad. Co., 798 F.2d 75, 123 LRRM 2182 (2d Cir. 1986) (right of union access to remote broadcasting facilities to observe whether the contract was being violated); Peerless Food Prods., 236 NLRB 161, 98 LRRM 1182 (1978).

[269]For a discussion of the respective obligations of the parties in the investigation of grievances, see *Jonco Aircraft Corp.*, 20 LA 211, 212 (Merrill, 1953). For an example of the intense emotions and turmoil that may be generated by plant access disputes, see *Waycross Sportswear*, 53 LA 1061 (Marshall, 1969).

[270]Standard Motor Prods., 11 LA 1147, 1152 (Hill, 1949). In *Farah Manufacturing Co.*, 65 LA 654, 658 (Cohen, 1975), the agreement was construed to require the union to identify the specific grievance that it intended to investigate. In *Naval Air Rework Facility*, 72 LA 129, 132 (Kaufman, 1979), the arbitrator said that "bad faith should not be presumed" in considering whether a plant-access request was made "for a proper purpose."

[271]Standard Motor Prods., 11 LA 1147, 1153 (Hill, 1949). *See also* Montgomery Ward & Co., 85 LA 913, 915–16 (Caraway, 1985); Air Carrier Engine Serv., 66 LA 506, 509–11 (Albert, 1976); Bendix Aviation Corp., 39 LA 393, 394 (Cahn, 1962). As to plant access by nonemployee union organizers under the NLRA, see *Lechmere, Inc. v. NLRB*, 502 U.S. 527, 139 LRRM 2225 (1992); *NLRB v. Babcock & Wilcox Co.*, 351 U.S. 105, 38 LRRM 2001 (1956). However, an employer acts unlawfully when it attempts to remove nonemployee organizers, engaged in distributing union literature to employees, from a public area adjacent to employer's parking lot. Lechmere, Inc., 308 NLRB 1074, 141 LRRM 1159 (1992). Regarding the scope of the company's obligation to make records available to union representatives under plant access "investigation" clauses, see *North Am. Aviation*, 19 LA 385, 389–90 (Komaroff, 1952).

In the absence of contrary contract provisions, management may impose reasonable requirements governing the access of nonemployee union representatives to the plant. Thus, it has been held that management could require the union president-steward, while on leave for union business, to sign in at the plant main gate as a "visitor," but could not restrict him to talking to only one employee at a time.[272] Neither could an employer require union agents to make advance appointments for plant visits or to give advance notice as to the reason for visits where the agreement gave the right to plant access "for the purpose of ascertaining whether or not this agreement is being observed."[273]

While union access to an employer's premises for grievance investigation generally has been upheld by arbitrators, access for other nongrievance-related activities has received greater scrutiny.[274] Where a contract required union representatives to make arrangements with the company prior to entering the premises to "discuss matters of contract administration," an arbitrator ruled that the contract did not allow solicitation of membership by a nonemployee union representative.[275] However, in a case where an employer repeatedly denied the union representative access to investigate violations of the union-security clause, and on one occasion had the union representative arrested for trespassing, an arbitrator found that the employer interfered with the union's contractual right to visit the premises.[276] Although recognizing the union's obligation not to unreasonably interrupt employees during a peak business period, an arbitrator held the employer responsible for creating a confrontational situation where the circumstances called for "a spirit of cooperation and consideration."[277]

Where a contract permitted union safety officials access to the employer's premises, an arbitrator found the employer's requirement that union officials sign waivers releasing the employer from all liability was unreasonable.[278] However, because the union officials were covered by workers' compensation, and because without the waiver union officials would be granted greater rights than employee members, an arbitrator reasoned that the employer's requirement of waiver of liability for specific visits by union safety officials was reasonable.[279]

C. Special Immunity [LA CDI 118.664]

Arbitrators have been reluctant to uphold discipline of union stewards engaged in grievance representation if it interferes with the union's griev-

---

[272]Manning, Maxwell & Moore, Inc., 37 LA 475, 482–83 (Stutz, 1961).

[273]Associated Hosps. of the E. Bay, 47 LA 858, 860–61 (Koven, 1966). *Cf.* Air Carrier Engine Serv., 66 LA 506, 510 (Albert, 1976). *See also* Utah Power & Light, 88 LA 310, 313–14 (Feldman, 1986).

[274]California Pie Co., 329 NLRB 88, 162 LRRM 1390 (1999); Holyoke Water Power Co., 273 NLRB 1369, 118 LRRM 1179 (1985), *enforced*, 778 F.2d 49, 120 LRRM 3487 (1st Cir. 1985), *cert. denied*, 477 U.S. 905 (1986). *But see* NLRB v. American Nat'l Can Co., 293 NLRB 901, 131 LRRM 1153 (1989), *enforced*, 924 F.2d 518, 136 LRRM 2374 (4th Cir. 1991).

[275]Montgomery Ward & Co., 85 LA 913 (Caraway, 1985).

[276]Piper's Restaurant, 86 LA 809 (Riker, 1986).

[277]*Id.* at 810.

[278]Utah Power & Light, 88 LA 310 (Feldman, 1986).

[279]*Id.* at 314.

ance handling responsibilities or otherwise threatens to disrupt labor-management relations.[280] Many disciplinary actions are set aside or reduced because the "cause" for the discipline (often abusive language in heated exchanges with supervisors) emerged from, or was related to, union steward duties.[281] Where an employer suspended an employee acting as a union representative for using profanity during a meeting as well as causing damage to a door by slamming it, the arbitrator found the suspension without just cause because the representative had not intended to damage the door and was merely expressing his adamant opposition to the company's position.[282]

Where an employer fired a steward for alleged theft of legal pads, the arbitrator held that discharge was improper, as past practice of the parties permitted stewards to use legal pads for grievances and other union-related activities.[283] One arbitrator found the 3-day suspension of a union steward for insubordination, when he spoke back to a supervisor in a grievance scheduling dispute, violated the contract. Company representatives had unilaterally established the time the steward could file a grievance and refused the steward's request to change the meeting time.[284] Imposition of discipline, the arbitrator reasoned, restricted the steward's access to a supervisor and violated the union's access to the grievance procedure.[285]

While a steward's conduct in the course of union business is protected, the immunity is not absolute,[286] and discipline of stewards in extreme situa-

---

[280]Tennsco Corp., 107 LA 689, 693 (Nicholas, Jr., 1996) ("Decisions of Arbitrators recognize that Union Stewards, representing fellow employees in grievance meetings, are entitled to equal stature with Management and may not be subjected to disciplinary action when using 'ungentlemanly' language in the course of their representation. . . . 'The very nature of the collective bargaining process is that an employee who is designated as a Union representative must be free to discuss Union matters as though he were not a Company employee. Otherwise, an employee would be inhibited in the performance of his duties as a Union representative, by fear of discipline for the use of strong language.' . . . Undeniably, the use of 'liar' was a bad choice of words. However, I do not find that such choice of words was either egregious or malicious.") (quoting Owens-Illinois, Inc., 73 LA 663 (Witney, 1979)). See Lee C. Moore Corp., 84 LA 1166 (Duff, 1985) (discharge of local union president was sustained where he engaged in serious misconduct by making harassment "hang up" calls to plant manager while he was off duty).

[281]See Tennsco, 107 LA at 693; P.Q. Corp., 106 LA 381, 384 (Cipolla, 1996).

[282]P.Q. Corp., 106 LA at 384. For related discussions, see Seidman, Discipline of Union Officers by Public Management, 32 Arb. J. 256 (1977); Leahy, Grievances Over Union Business on Company Time and Premises, 30 Arb. J. 191 (1975).

[283]Carnation Co., 84 LA 80 (Wright, 1985). See also Charleston Naval Shipyard, 86 LA 874, 876–77 (Odom, Jr., 1986); Devon Apparel, 85 LA 645, 646–47 (Rock, 1985).

[284]Southern Ind. Gas & Elec. Co., 85 LA 716 (Nathan, 1985).

[285]Id. at 720–21.

[286]For instances in which immunity was denied for infractions pertaining to the individual's service as an employee, see Arden Farms Co., 45 LA 1124, 1130–32 (Tsukiyama, 1965); General Elec. Co., 43 LA 838, 842 (Kornblum, 1964). In General Elec. Co., 40 LA 1126, 1156–57 (Davey, 1963), the arbitrator sustained the discharge of a union officer for writing an article in the union newspaper maliciously disparaging the employer's product—the misconduct was viewed as that of an employee. In Linn v. Plant Guard Workers Local 114, 383 U.S. 53, 61 LRRM 2345 (1966), the Supreme Court held the states are not preempted from giving damages for false and defamatory statements (if made with malice) during union organizational campaigns conducted under the NLRA. Then, in Letter Carriers Branch 496 v. Austin, 418 U.S. 264, 86 LRRM 2740 (1974), the Supreme Court ruled that: (1) the Linn principles apply also where federal-sector employment is involved; (2) "malice" under Linn requires knowledge of falsity or reckless disregard of the truth; and (3) the union's characterization of nonmembers as "scabs" during an organizational campaign was not a false or

tions has been upheld even though the basis for the discipline was related to the employee's conduct as steward.[287] One arbitrator upheld the termination of a union steward who had disobeyed his supervisor's direct orders, causing $2,000 in damage to company machinery.[288] In another case, the arbitrator reinstated a terminated union steward, but without back pay or benefits, finding that the employee's record of absences warranted some discipline and that steward status does not prevent discipline for nonunion activities.[289] The suspension of a steward for refusing to remove defamatory postings critical of the company's medical insurance was affirmed.[290]

In upholding the discharge of a union steward for racial harassment of another employee, an arbitrator held that the steward's position created no immunity from plant rules against harassment.[291] Another arbitrator found a steward's comments toward a female supervisor to be beyond the level of "shop talk" and were intended to "demean and degrade." He concluded that there was just cause for the steward's termination.[292]

An employer was found to have had just cause to discharge a shop steward for insubordination when the shop steward refused to take a drug test under a policy that was properly adopted, reasonably announced, and fairly applied.[293] In another case, the reprimand issued to a union president who failed to indicate the time spent on union business on his time card was found to be proper.[294] Just cause also existed to discharge a chief steward for leaving work without permission and threatening the lives of coworkers.[295]

---

defamatory statement (thus, the state was preempted from awarding damages) because one of the generally accepted definitions of "scab" is "one who refuses to join a union." In *General Motors Corp. v. Mendicki*, 367 F.2d 66, 63 LRRM 2257 (10th Cir. 1966), accusations uttered at a *grievance hearing* were held unqualifiedly privileged and immune from liability for damages. For views of other courts on the extent of privilege carried by communications made in grievance or arbitration proceedings, see Spivey, *Libel—Privilege in Labor Grievance Matter*, 60 A.L.R.3d 1041. Regarding NLRA protection from discipline, in *Boilermakers Local Lodge D-357 (Southwestern Portland Cement Co.)*, 288 NLRB 1156, 128 LRRM 1193 (1988), the Board found that a union unlawfully coerced a member who gave his employer a witness statement for use in a potential grievance proceeding by subjecting him to internal union charges; in *Hawthorne Mazda*, 251 NLRB 313, 105 LRRM 1057 (1980), an employee was unlawfully discharged for repeated statements that members of management were either incompetent or idiots, where the statements were made during a grievance hearing in which the employee was acting as informal spokesperson for fellow employees. *See also* Crown Cent. Petroleum Corp., 177 NLRB 322, 71 LRRM 1418 (1969). But in *Hotel St. Moritz*, 251 NLRB 67, 105 LRRM 1116 (1980), a steward's conduct was "so opprobrious" that it was unprotected under the NLRA.

[287]*See* Converters Paperboard Co., 108 LA 149, 154–56 (Brodsky, 1997); Mid-West Chandelier Co., 102 LA 833 (Murphy, 1994) (union steward/bargaining committee member properly suspended for statements to employees concerning management discriminatory motive even though steward was acting in committee member capacity by informing employees of status of negotiations where there was no support for statements or evidence of anti-union animus); Overhead Door Corp., 101 LA 610, 612–13 (Cocalis, 1993).

[288]Bermuda Dunes Country Club, 104 LA 1082, 1086 (Darrow, 1995).

[289]Kasle Steel Corp., 107 LA 1006, 1009–10 (Kerner, 1996). *See also* National Linen Supply, 107 LA 4 (Ross, 1996); Sheridan Health Care Ctr., 106 LA 1125 (Draznin, 1996); Tyson Foods, 105 LA 1119 (Moore, 1996).

[290]Dalfort Corp., 85 LA 70 (White, 1985).

[291]Peninsular Steel Co., 88 LA 391 (Ipavec, 1986).

[292]Hobart Corp., 88 LA 512 (Strasshofer, 1986).

[293]Crescent Metal Prods., 91 LA 1129 (Coyne, 1989).

[294]Alofs Mfg. Co., 89 LA 5 (Daniel, 1987).

[295]International Paper Co., 89 LA 985 (O'Grady, 1987).

The termination of another steward for extorting money from employees who were hired through a hiring hall was similarly affirmed.[296]

An employee's status as a union steward (or officer) does not create a special duty that subjects the steward's actions to greater liability than those of ordinary employees. So where an employer terminated four union stewards for participating in a work stoppage over a change in plant starting time, an arbitrator held that the company's action in terminating the stewards while issuing reprimands to other employees was based on the steward's union status and could not constitute just cause.[297]

12. Pay for Time Spent Handling Grievances
[LA CDI 93.50; 100.0705]

Many employers compensate union representatives and other employees for time spent in handling grievances during working hours.[298] In some large plants it is the practice of management to pay for full-time union stewards.[299]

---

[296]OK Grocery Co., 92 LA 440 (Stoltenberg, 1989).

[297]Schnadig Corp., 85 LA 692 (Seidman, 1985).

[298]As to variations of this practice, see Basic Patterns in Union Contracts 36 (BNA Books 14th ed. 1995). A high percentage of federal-sector agreements contain some provision for paid grievance and arbitration time. See A Survey of Negotiated Grievance Procedures and Arbitration in Federal Post Civil Service Reform Act Agreements 52 (Office of Personnel Mgmt. 1980). The Civil Service Reform Act's requirement that federal agencies grant "official time" to employee representatives in negotiations was construed by the Supreme Court in Bureau of Alcohol, Tobacco & Firearms v. FLRA, 464 U.S. 89, 114 LRRM 3393 (1983). See also Patent Office Professional Ass'n v. FLRA, 872 F.2d 451, 131 LRRM 2018 (D.C. Cir. 1989); Government Employees (AFGE) Council of Locals 214 v. FLRA (Air Force Logistics Command), 798 F.2d 1525, 123 LRRM 2177 (D.C. Cir. 1986); Department of the Air Force, Sacramento Air Logistic Ctr., 26 FLRA 674 (1987).

[299]BASF Wyandotte v. Chemical Workers Local 227, 791 F.2d 1046, 122 LRRM 2750 (2d Cir. 1986) (employee union official can receive paid time off to conduct union-related business other than direct meetings with management). See also NLRB v. BASF Wyandotte Corp., 798 F.2d 849, 123 LRRM 2320 (5th Cir. 1986). Under a proviso to NLRA §8(a)(2), an employer may permit employees to confer with him or her during working hours without loss of time or pay. Under LMRA §302, employer payments to employee representatives are prohibited, with the express exception of compensation for services as an employee. Management also may pay union representatives for time spent discussing grievances with management. Several carefully reasoned arbitral opinions (some after the 1959 amendment of §302) have concluded that employer payments to union representatives for time spent in processing grievances and administering the agreement are legal, though some of these opinions recognized that a court might disagree. See John H. Davis Painting Co., 44 LA 866, 867–71 (Seibel, 1965); P.R. Mallory & Co., 36 LA 351, 364–71 (Stark, 1960); Great Lakes Pipe Co., 36 LA 291, 297–300 (Beatty, 1960); Industrial Rayon Corp., 35 LA 228, 234–35 (Dworkin, 1960); Borg-Warner Corp., 10 LA 471, 473–74 (Gregory, 1948). See also W.R. Grace & Co., 70 LA 1007, 1008 (Williams, 1978); Patterson-Sargent Co., 23 LA 21, 23 (Willcox, 1954); Standard Oil Co., 16 LA 734, 735–36 (Kelliher, 1951). In Communications Workers v. Bell Atlantic Network Services, 670 F. Supp. 416, 126 LRRM 3015 (D.D.C. 1987), the federal district court held that a collective bargaining agreement lawfully permitted employees to take unpaid leaves of absence for union business without losing fringe benefits. In Fleming Foods of Cal., 90 LA 1071 (Askin, 1988), when the employer closed the plant for 9 years, payment of accrued severance pay to an employee who had been working full time as a union official was upheld. But see Trailways Lines v. Trailways, Inc., Joint Council of Amalgamated Transit Union, 785 F.2d 101, 121 LRRM 3167 (3d Cir. 1986) (the court ruled that payments made by an employer to a pension trust fund for employees who were on leave of absence and working full time for a union were illegal). In Iron Workers Local 426 v. Bechtel Power Corp., 634 F.2d

Unions take the position that the activity of union grievance represen-tatives benefits management as much as employees. It is to the advantage of both parties if grievance representatives are very capable persons who can undertake and ably discharge responsibility. Payment for time spent in han-dling grievances is one way to secure the services of such persons. Grievance time pay also facilitates prompt settlement, thereby improving morale and plant efficiency.

But even where the agreement did not specifically require pay for time spent by employees in discussing their conduct with management prior to possible assessment of discipline, they were held entitled to pay for all time lost from work. The arbitrator reasoned that they should have been called in during nonworking time.[300] Pay for nonworking time utilized by employees on their own grievances has been denied, however.[301]

Emphasizing that the basic purpose of pay for grievance time is to com-pensate union officials who help management resolve differences with em-ployees, an arbitrator construed a contractual provision to pay grievance representatives for time lost as inapplicable to the grievant himself, and opined that "it might be very unwise to offer to pay employees for time lost while settling their own grievances."[302]

In some cases, the employer has not been required to pay union repre-sentatives for time spent at arbitration hearings in the absence of a clear and specific contractual requirement for such pay.[303] However, so definite a

---

258, 106 LRRM 2385 (6th Cir. 1981), employer contributions to an industry steward fund violated §302; the steward, with the function of overseeing employer compliance with the collective bargaining agreement, was found to be under the real control of the union, the court rejecting the union's contention that the steward was an employee of the employer and that payments to the steward represented compensation for services as an employee.

[300]Bethlehem Steel Co., 19 LA 261, 262–64 (Shipman, 1952).

[301]Allied Chem. Corp., 47 LA 686, 690 (Hilpert, 1966); Bethlehem Steel Co., 17 LA 436, 439 (Killingsworth, 1951). For reasons why an interest arbitrator refused to approve a pub-lic-sector union's request for compensated off-duty bargaining time, see City of Renton, 71 LA 271, 274–75 (Snow, 1978).

[302]American Car & Foundry Co., 2 LA 644, 645–46 (Larkin, 1945).

[303]See Youngstown Vindicator Printing Co., 88 LA 17, 20–22 (Cohen, 1986) (past practice and bargaining history considerations supported the conclusion that a contractual leave provision did not require granting unpaid leave of absence for the purpose of attending arbi-tration hearings; in accordance with past practice, the employer scheduled the employees off, thus permitting absence from work without need for any approved leave of absence or any replacement at overtime rates); Greenville Steel Car Co., 68 LA 20, 25 (May, 1977); Dow Chem. Co., 50 LA 1025, 1027 (Updegraff, 1968); Cabot Corp., 50 LA 230, 231 (Bothwell, 1967); Consolidated Indus., 43 LA 331, 332 (Bennett, 1964); Victoreen Instrument Co., 38 LA 319, 320 (Begley, 1962); Reeves Pulley Co., 36 LA 1044, 1046 (Updegraff, 1961); Magnavox Co. of Tenn., 28 LA 107, 108 (Marshall, 1957); Continental Can Co., 25 LA 700, 707–08 (Campbell, 1955); Purex Corp., 21 LA 763, 768 (Spaulding, 1953); Plastic Jewel Co., 14 LA 775, 780 (Fulda, 1950); Merrill-Stevens Dry Dock & Repair Co., 12 LA 1021, 1022 (Coogler, 1949); Allis-Chalmers Mfg. Co., 8 LA 945, 946–48 (Gorder, 1947); Copeland Refrigeration Corp., 8 LA 33, 35 (Lehoczky, 1947). See also U.S. Army Corps of Eng'rs, 86 LA 856, 858–59 (Madden, 1986) (a complaint was filed with the Equal Employment Opportunity Commis-sion (EEOC) but no grievance was filed; arbitrator held that the employer cannot be re-quired to reimburse the union for travel and per diem expenses the union paid to its repre-sentative to represent an employee in a statutory EEO complaint). In some of these cases the arbitrator noted the absence of any clearly established practice to pay for arbitration time. Although recognizing that both the employer and the public benefit from labor-management activities of union representatives, the arbitrator advocated strict construction of contrac-tual provisions relating to employer payment for the time involved:

provision for such pay has not been required in all cases.[304] Some arbitrators have held that past practice should determine whether grievance and arbitration handling time is compensable where the agreement is silent or ambiguous.[305] One arbitrator held that past practice entitled the union representatives to compensation not only for time spent on processing grievances, but also for time spent conducting general union business, even though such compensation was not expressly authorized in the contract.[306]

Under an agreement providing that union representatives shall be paid for time spent "conferring with management," time spent researching company records (relevant to grievances) in the absence of management was held to be compensable if the amount of time is "relatively slight and of an incidental nature."[307] Payment for grievance work is generally made on a

---

[T]he substitution through collective bargaining of employer-paid-for (whether in the public sector or in the private sector) time for an employee to conduct Union (labor-management) activities in place of the normal duties to which the employee has been assigned ought not to be lightly inferred . . . . In case of doubt or ambiguity in the contract language used, the doubt or ambiguity should in the view of the arbitrator militate against the interests and the side claiming that the government as an employing agency has waived the requirement that an employee perform his normal duties. It can be done, but the contract should be clear and convincing.

Social Sec. Admin., 73 LA 789, 797 (Rothman, 1979). But believing that a federal agency employer's interpretation of a provision relating to pay for representational work would "operate as a penalty against" a shop steward, with the "larger effect" being "to chill this shop steward and all others who might follow him from accepting the job," an arbitrator rejected the employer's interpretation (which could have jeopardized some of the employee's fringe benefits, such as sick leave and retirement credits), and he concluded "that an action by management which undermines union representation—where an alternative is available— was not intended in establishing collective bargaining relationships between the federal government and its employees." Marine Corps Dev. Command, 71 LA 726, 730 (Ables, 1978). The potential intensity of differences between parties in the federal public sector concerning this subject is indicated by another arbitrator's comment that a case under consideration by him "presents the latest chapter in a long-standing and unfortunately acrimonious set of disputes between the parties on the subject of the Union's right to have certain of its representatives attend grievance arbitration hearings on official time." Social Sec. Admin., 87 LA 434, 438 (Hoh, 1986). The Court of Appeals for the District of Columbia Circuit ruled that the Federal Labor Relations Authority (FLRA) improperly ordered federal agencies to pay travel and per diem expenses to their employees who are required to appear at FLRA proceedings. An FLRA regulation requiring such payments is invalid as exceeding the power conferred by §713(c) of the Federal Service Labor-Management Relations Act. Department of the Air Force v. FLRA, 877 F.2d 1036, 131 LRRM 2864 (D.C. Cir. 1989).

[304]See Board of Mental Retardation, Lucas County, 69 LA 862, 864 (Feldman, 1977); Crane Co., 62 LA 469, 471 (Smith, 1974); Buckeye Holmesville Mfg. Co., 53 LA 866, 866–67 (McIntosh, 1969); Modine Mfg. Co., 23 LA 243, 245 (Porter, 1954). Cf. Transit Union Local 1605 v. Central Contra Costa County Transit Auth., 73 F. Supp. 2d 1117 (N.D. Cal. 1999) (determining that time spent negotiating was not compensable under the Fair Labor Standards Act because not for benefit of Central Contra Costa County Transit Auth. (CCCTA) nor controlled by CCCTA).

[305]Morton Salt, 104 LA 444, 446 (Fullmer, 1995); Motor Wheel Corp., 102 LA 922, 930–31 (Chattman, 1994). See Whitman & Barnes, 46 LA 637, 639 (Smith, 1965); Celanese Polymer Co., 38 LA 49, 51 (Dunau, 1961); General Controls Co., 31 LA 240, 242–43 (Jones, Jr., 1958); Johnson Bronze Co., 22 LA 352, 357 (Dworkin, 1954); Bauer Bros. Co., 21 LA 529, 532 (Brown, 1953).

[306]Motor Wheel Corp., 102 LA 922, 930–31 (Chattman, 1994).

[307]Standard Oil Co., 16 LA 734, 735–36 (Kelliher, 1951).

straight-time basis.[308] Some agreements, however, provide that grievance representatives "shall not lose pay for time spent" in grievance meetings with management. Under such a provision, one arbitrator held that representatives had to be paid a special differential that they would have received had they not been called from work for grievance meetings, even though another provision of the agreement stated that the differential was to be paid only in case of actual performance of differential work.[309] But under a similar provision in an agreement that also provided that grievance conferences should be held during working hours, a minimum of 4-hours' pay at straight time, in accordance with call-in pay provisions, was held to be sufficient for less than 4 hours of grievance work performed after working hours, and the arbitrator rejected the union demand for payment at the overtime rate.[310]

Various control methods have been used to prevent abuse of grievance-pay practices. Some agreements limit the amount of time that may be spent in such activity;[311] others contain no specific limit, but state that a "reasonable amount" of time will be paid for.[312] Management has been held entitled to require the union representative to fill out forms giving a general account of grievance services performed and the time involved.[313] This right is said to accompany management's contractual obligation to pay for such services.[314] Use of such report forms is not considered to be espionage or interference with union activity.[315]

---

[308]*Grievance Procedure Under Collective Bargaining*, 63 Monthly Lab. Rev. 175, 184 (1946). *But see* International Harvester Co., 22 LA 196, 197–98 (Cole, 1954). As to applicability of cost-of-living adjustments to grievance time pay, see *Bethlehem Steel Co.*, 33 LA 632, 636–37 (Feinberg, 1959). *See also* Department of the Air Force, Air Force Logistics Command, 93 LA 207 (Fox, 1989); Department of the Air Force, 91 LA 757 (Howell, 1988).

[309]Bethlehem Steel Co., 10 LA 284, 287–88 (Dodd, 1948).

[310]Ford Roofing Prods. Co., 5 LA 182, 184 (Wardlaw, 1946).

[311]Similarly, the agreement may expressly limit the pay for grievance activity or limit the number of individuals who may collect grievance pay. *See Basic Patterns in Labor Arbitration Agreements*, 34 LA 931, 935 (1960). *But see* Philadelphia Naval Shipyard, 90 LA 466 (Lang, 1987) (the employer improperly suspended a shop steward, denied pay for official time spent on grievance, and denied official time off and annual leave because the steward refused to work on a different grievance).

[312]Where the agreement by implication provided pay for grievance handling but did not state any limitation, and where past practice was to pay for all time so spent, it was held that the employer could not unilaterally limit the amount of paid time but could challenge in specific instances the reasonableness of the amount of time claimed for grievance activity. Goss Co., 44 LA 824, 826–27 (Pedrick, 1964). The burden of demonstrating use of excessive time similarly was placed on the employer in *Houdaille Industries*, 73 LA 872, 874–75 (Frost, 1979) (the agreement stated no specific limit on allowable time but did prohibit abuse).

[313]*See* TRW, Inc., 50 LA 909, 914–15 (Cahn, 1968); Columbus Auto Parts Co., 36 LA 166, 169 (Seinsheimer,1961) (merely saying "union business" did not suffice); Chrysler Corp., 33 LA 112, 123 (Wolff, 1959); Bell Aircraft Corp., 11 LA 729, 730–31 (Jaffe, 1948); Ford Motor Co., 2 LA 382, 383 (Shulman, 1944). *See also* Social Sec. Admin., 90 LA 72, 74 (Gallagher, 1987) (the arbitrator held that the employer had the right to request and receive reports from the union on the time employees spent (without loss of pay) in union representational activities); Alofs Mfg. Co., 89 LA 5, 6–8 (Daniel, 1987) (written reprimand to union president was sustained where he failed to indicate on his timecard the amount of time spent on union business and failed to notify his supervisor when his absence for union business started and ended).

[314]Bell Aircraft Corp., 11 LA 729, 730–31 (Jaffe, 1948).

[315]Ford Motor Co., 2 LA 382, 383 (Shulman, 1944).

Many companies require union representatives to report to their supervisor before leaving work to handle grievances. Where an agreement provided that stewards were to be compensated for earnings lost in handling grievances, but did not spell out a procedure to be followed, an arbitrator held that management could require stewards to notify their supervisor when leaving work to handle grievances, and to clock out and in for the period of time away from the steward's work station, provided that prior notification should not be required in emergencies or if the supervisor is not readily available.[316] Another means of protecting grievance-pay practices from abuse is to provide, in the agreement, that management may inaugurate a grievance at an advanced step of the grievance procedure if abuse is believed to exist.[317] Likewise, such abuse may lead directly or indirectly to the proper warning or punishment of the grievance representative.[318]

13. WRITTEN STATEMENT OF GRIEVANCE [LA CDI 93.309; 100.0715]

Grievances typically are required to be in writing, thereby establishing a record of the grievance, and are presented at an early stage of the grievance procedure. By putting the grievance in writing, it is less likely to become distorted while being processed through the grievance procedure.[319] Additionally, written grievances without merit often are dropped.

Some commentators consider it important to have a written grievance filed at the beginning, or "first step," of the grievance procedure in view of the value of a complete written record.[320] However, many parties prefer informal oral discussion at the first step, considering written grievances to be best suited to the later steps of the procedure. These parties may oppose written presentation of grievances at the first step on the ground that it makes the procedure too inflexible and cumbersome, discourages employees

---

[316]Picker X-Ray Corp., 44 LA 463, 465–66 (Di Leone, 1965). The arbitrator also stated that the prior practice of not requiring stewards to do these things when the union business was within their own department did not preclude management from establishing reasonable procedures to guard against abuse of the right to conduct union business on company time. *Id.* at 465. In *Active Products Corp.*, 67-1 ARB ¶8261 (Seinsheimer, 1967), a plant rule requiring stewards to clock out and in was held reasonable and enforceable by discipline. In *Jenkins Bros.*, 11 LA 432, 434–35 (Donnelly, 1948), management (with some contractual basis) could require stewards to clock out and in when leaving work to process grievances, but the arbitrator stated that such action by management may be shortsighted in view of the dissatisfaction it may cause.

[317]*See* Minneapolis-Moline Power Implement Co., 2 LA 227, 241 (Van Fossen, Humphrey, & Prifrel, 1946); International Harvester Co., 1 LA 512, 521–22 (Marshall, Spencer, & Holly, 1946).

[318]*See* University of Cal., Berkeley, 94 LA 450, 454–55 (Wilcox, 1989); Reichhold Chems., 73 LA 636, 640 (Hon, 1979); Ward LaFrance Truck Corp., 69 LA 831, 838 (Levy, 1977); Dayton Malleable Iron Co., 48 LA 1345, 1348–49 (Teple, 1967); Ford Instrument Co., 39 LA 1185, 1185–86 (Cahn, 1962); Chrysler Corp., 33 LA 112, 123 (Wolff, 1959). *See also* Kaiser Aluminum & Chem. Corp., 90 LA 856, 860 (Thompson, 1988).

[319]For a related discussion, see Chapter 7, section 3.C., "Changing the Scope of the Grievance."

[320]UPDEGRAFF, ARBITRATION AND LABOR RELATIONS 138 (BNA Books 1970); UPDEGRAFF & MCCOY, ARBITRATION OF LABOR DISPUTES 53 (1946).

from voicing their complaints, and impedes prompt settlement.[321] Indeed, the more common practice in both private and public sectors is well illustrated by the federal-sector practice of utilizing oral grievances at the first step of the grievance procedure but written grievances at the second step.[322]

One interest arbitrator, recognizing that the presentation of grievances in writing is a well-established practice in industry, granted an employer's request for a provision requiring grievances carried beyond the employee's immediate superior to be presented in writing on simple forms provided by the company.[323] In this connection, a clause requiring that grievances be "filed" at the second step within a specified time was interpreted to require that grievances be stated "in writing" at that step.[324]

If the employer discusses grievances not filed in writing when required by the labor agreement, the "written grievance" requirement may be considered to have been waived.[325] Thus, one arbitrator, in placing the burden on management to raise the issue promptly, stated that if management desires to insist on strict compliance with "written grievance" requirements, it should express its disapproval of oral grievances at the time when they first become a subject of discussion between the parties. "The company's failure to raise the objection at that time constitutes a waiver of that requirement."[326] Another arbitrator ruled otherwise, however, declaring that "if there is any place in the interpretation of collective bargaining agreements where strict or technical construction is necessary it is in that which provides for the grievance machinery and procedure."[327]

---

[321]For a most interesting program by one company and union for speedy and informal handling of most complaints "at the level of the shop floor, without written grievances," see Ross, *Distressed Grievance Procedures and Their Rehabilitation, in* Labor Arbitration and Industrial Change, Proceedings of the 16th Annual Meeting of NAA 104, 128 (Kahn ed., BNA Books 1963).

[322]*See A Survey of Negotiated Grievance Procedures and Arbitration in Federal Post Civil Service Reform Act Agreements* 25–26 (Office of Personnel Mgmt. 1980) (of the 452 agreements surveyed, 90% specified oral process at the first step but all of the agreements required the grievance to be in writing at the second step).

[323]New York City Omnibus Corp., 7 LA 794, 820–21 (Cole, 1947).

[324]Jones & Laughlin Steel Corp., 16 LA 788, 789 (Cahn, 1951). *See also* Ranco, Inc., 48 LA 974, 977 (Gibson, 1967). *Cf.* John Morrell & Co., 69 LA 264, 266–67, 276 (Conway, 1977) (a writing was not required where no contractual "reference to a grievance . . . being a written instrument" was found).

[325]*See* Wisconsin Tissue Mills, 102 LA 601, 604–05 (Jacobs, 1994). *See also* Wyandot, Inc. v. Food & Commercial Workers Local 227, 205 F.3d 922, 163 LRRM 2705 (6th Cir.) (filing written grievance 12 days after deadline was untimely and barred reinstatement), *cert. denied*, 531 U.S. 820 (2000).

[326]Lapham-Hickey Co., 3 LA 327, 333 (Gilden, 1946). *See also* Royal Paper Prods., 48 LA 636, 638 (Seitz, 1966); Zirkel, *Procedural Arbitrability of Grievance Cases*, 13 J. Collective Negotiations No. 4 (1984).

[327]Firestone Tire & Rubber Co., 9 LA 518, 522 (Rader, 1948). *See also* Printing Pressmen No. 16 (Philadelphia) v. International Paper Co., 648 F.2d 900, 107 LRRM 2618, 2621 (3d Cir. 1981). For related material, see section 3.B., "Failure to Comply Strictly With Technical Requirements of the Grievance Procedure," above.

14. OBSERVANCE OF GRIEVANCE PROCEDURE

Arbitrators recognize that the grievance procedure, when adhered to, advances peaceful and constructive industrial relations, with resultant benefits to labor, management, and the public. Moreover, arbitrators realize that the success of arbitration itself may be jeopardized if the grievance procedure is not carefully followed.

Arbitration awards show that arbitrators expect the parties to pay due respect to the grievance procedure, not only by using it, but also by observing its formal requirements. Such respect is in the nature of a "condition precedent." In some cases, it is held to be a condition precedent to the assumption of jurisdiction by the arbitrator. The requirement that these conditions precedent be met is somewhat analogous to the requirement by the courts that an available administrative remedy be exhausted before the court will give relief. In other cases, it is a condition precedent to an award of requested relief. In these cases the arbitrator takes jurisdiction but, on learning of the grievant's failure to fulfill the condition precedent, denies relief, in whole or in part.

Limiting arbitral jurisdiction to cases in which the parties have made bona fide efforts to settle can be expected to result in improved handling of grievances at the lower levels. The National War Labor Board learned from experience that settlements through negotiations are encouraged when arbitrators refuse to take jurisdiction over grievance issues until the parties show that they have exhausted all chances of settlement through negotiations.[328] Arbitrators can do this unless the agreement permits direct resort to arbitration.[329] A New York court, in granting an employer's motion for a stay of arbitration, spoke of the requirement that conditions precedent be performed prior to arbitration:

> One of the preliminary steps, viz. submission to the grievance committee of the association, was omitted entirely as were other steps in connection with some of the issues tendered for arbitration. No explanation is here given for such omission or neglect. It was incumbent upon the union, under the terms of the contract, to exhaust all other methods of conciliation as provided for therein before it could invoke the remedy of arbitration. Until it complies with the conditions of the contract in respect to all the essential acts on its part to be performed or offers a reasonable and just excuse for non-performance, the union will be enjoined from proceeding with the arbitration.[330]

---

[328]Aluminum Co. of Am., 12 WAR LAB. REP. 446, 455 (1943).

[329]For instance, where the grievance procedure had not been exhausted, the dispute was held to be nonarbitrable in *Berger Steel Co.*, 46 LA 1131, 1138 (Goldberg, 1966); *Barboursville Clay Mfg. Co.*, 39 LA 760, 762–63 (Blair, 1962); *Bee Line*, 20 LA 675, 678 (Feinberg, 1953); *North Am. Aviation*, 19 LA 729, 731–33 (Komaroff, 1953). *See also* Byrd Plastics, 51 LA 79, 82–83 (Nichols, 1968); Copperweld Steel Co., 46 LA 941, 945 (Dworkin, 1966). For related discussion, see Chapter 7, section 3.C., "Changing the Scope of the Grievance."

[330]*In re* Picture Frame Workers Local 18465, 8 LA 1063, 1064 (N.Y. Sup. Ct. 1947). If federal law applies to the case, questions of procedural arbitrability (such as whether the preliminary steps of the grievance procedure have been exhausted or excused) are to be decided by the arbitrator. John Wiley & Sons v. Livingston, 376 U.S. 543, 555–59, 55 LRRM 2769 (1964). But note the situation involved in *Philadelphia Newspapers*, 68 LA 401, 405 (Jaffee, 1977). *See also* Typographical Union Local 6 (New York) v. Printers League Section of the Association of Graphic Arts, 919 F.2d 3, 135 LRRM 3012 (2d Cir. 1990). For related discussions, see Chapter 6, "Determining Arbitrability."

A. Use of Grievance Procedure Versus Self-Help [LA CDI 93.40]

Arbitrators often deny or limit requested relief, notwithstanding the merits of the original complaint, where the grievant has resorted to self-help rather than to the grievance procedure. Most arbitrators have taken the position that employees must not take matters into their own hands, but must obey orders and carry out their assignments, even when they believe those assignments are in violation of the agreement, and then turn to the grievance procedure for relief.[331]

The fact that employees acted by "advice of counsel" has been held not to provide a defense or justification for self-help.[332] So where an employee following an on-the-job back injury refused to take a drug test on the advice of his personal lawyer, when the test was mandated by a mutually agreed-upon policy that adequately protected the employee's privacy, his subsequent grievance was denied.[333]

A refusal to obey management's orders is not immunized by the fact that the employee was "caught in the middle" between company and union, though

---

[331]*See* Freeman Decorating Co., 110 LA 331, 335 (Allen, Jr., 1998); Park Mansions, 105 LA 849, 852 (Duff, 1995); Virgin Island Tel. Corp., 101 LA 273, 278 (Nicholas, Jr., 1993); Armco, Inc., 93 LA 561, 562–63 (Strongin, 1989); Lockheed Corp., 83 LA 1018, 1022 (Taylor, 1984); Freeman United Coal Mining Co., 83 LA 776, 780–81 (Creo, 1984); Department of the Air Force, 75 LA 170, 175 (Dash, Jr., 1980); Hygrade Food Prods. Corp., 74 LA 99, 105 (O'Neill, 1980); American Cyanamid Co., 74 LA 15, 17 (Friedman, 1980); General Elec. Co., 73 LA 1273, 1277 (Maroney, 1979); Prismo-William Armstrong Smith Co., 73 LA 581, 587 (Jedel, 1979); Library of Cong., 73 LA 549, 551 (Cromwell, 1979); Standard Shade Roller Div., 73 LA 86, 89 (Dawson, 1979); Vulcan Hart Corp., 72 LA 1093, 1095 (Wallace, 1979); Griffin Pipe Prods. Co., 72 LA 1033, 1035 (Doyle, 1979); Hertz Corp., 72 LA 733, 736 (Gootnick, 1979); Teleflex, Inc., 72 LA 668, 674 (Chalfie, 1979); Grocers Baking Co., 72 LA 591, 594 (Daniel, 1979); County of Genesee, 72 LA 564, 566 (Kanner, 1979); General Elec. Co., 72 LA 405, 407 (Craver, 1979); Lozier Corp., 72 LA 164, 167, 169 (Ferguson, 1979); National Sanitation Found., 71 LA 1199, 1202 (McDonald, 1978); CECO Corp., 71 LA 1148, 1150 (Caraway, 1978); Clinton Corn Processing Co., 71 LA 555, 566 (Madden, 1978); Georgia Kraft Co., 71 LA 222, 226 (Spritzer, 1978); Arnold Bakers, Inc., 70 LA 1144, 1147 (Robins, 1978); Addressograph-Multigraph Co., 70 LA 1058, 1060 (Ipavec, 1978); Hoerner Waldorf Corp., 70 LA 335, 337 (Talent, 1978); Western Union Int'l, 70 LA 285, 287 (Turkus, 1978); Kast Metals Corp., 70 LA 278, 282 (Roberts, 1978); Amax Lead Co., 70 LA 1, 3 (1978); Logan Steel Stamping, 69 LA 792, 794 (Letson, 1977); Quaker Oats Co., 69 LA 727, 731 (Hunter, 1977); Southern Bell Tel. & Tel. Co., 69 LA 582, 586 (Rimer, 1977); Montana Dep't of Agric., 69 LA 502, 506 (Beck, 1977); Bucyrus-Erie Co., 69 LA 93, 99 (Lipson, 1977); Brockway Pressed Metals, Inc., 69 LA 64, 67 (Mullaly, 1977); Midland-Ross Corp., 68 LA 1010, 1014 (Simon, 1977); Mrs. Baird's Bakeries, 68 LA 773, 778 (Fox, 1977); American Hoechst Corp., 68 LA 517, 521–26 (Purcell, 1977); B.J. Hughes, Inc., 68 LA 391, 396 (Sabo, 1977); Eaton Corp., 68 LA 291, 295–96 (Boals, 1977). In most of the preceding cases, the grievants' actions in taking matters into their own hands was a significant factor in the arbitrator's decision to deny the grievance or to grant relief in part only. However, the fact that employees may be penalized for resorting to self-help does not constitute a waiver of the union's right to arbitrate the issue that led to the self-help. Mansfield Tire & Rubber Co., 36 LA 1348, 1351 (Teple, 1961) (the propriety of a contested work assignment was held arbitrable). *See also* P.I.E. Nationwide, 295 NLRB 43, 131 LRRM 1674 (1989) (employee asserted protected right under contract); Government Employees (AFGE) Local 1857, 34 FLRA 745 (1990); Veterans Admin. Med. Ctr., 34 FLRA 666 (1990).

[332]Robertshaw-Fulton Controls Co., 36 LA 4, 9 (Hilpert, 1961). *Accord* Champion Int'l Corp., 73 LA 921, 923–24 (Rimer, Jr., 1979); San Antonio Air Logistics Ctr., 73 LA 455, 463 (LeBaron, 1979). *Cf.* Ingalls Shipbuilding Corp., 39 LA 419, 430 (Hebert, 1962).

[333]Marigold Foods, 94 LA 751, 754, 755 (Bognanno, 1990). *But see* Pepsi Cola Bottling of San Diego, 93 LA 520, 524–26 (Randall, 1989).

that circumstance may be taken into account in reviewing the level of discipline imposed.[334] But, where an initial refusal to obey was followed by obedience, some arbitrators have mitigated the penalty.[335]

An important exception to the general rule against resorting to self-help exists where obedience to orders would expose the employee to a serious health or safety hazard.[336] Some arbitrators have recognized other possible exceptions to the duty to obey orders, such as where the order commands the performance of an immoral or criminal act,[337] where the employee has a right to union representation that would be denied by obedience to the order,[338] where the order violates the rights or domain of the union itself by interfering with the union's contractual right to investigate and process grievances,[339] where an order interferes with the employee's proper use of the grievance procedure,[340] where the order commands skilled trade workers to perform work wholly unrelated to their craft,[341] or where the order "is *quite clearly*

---

[334]*See* Safeway Stores, 51 LA 413, 416–17 (Gillingham, 1967); Contra Costa Readymix, 38 LA 200, 204–05 (Koven, 1962). *See also* Philips Indus., 87 LA 1122, 1126–28 (Rezler, 1986); Boise Cascade Corp., 84 LA 886, 890 (Eisele, 1985).

[335]*See, e.g.*, Browning-Ferris Indus. of Mich., 69 LA 787, 789 (Kanner, 1977); Tubular Prods. Co., 28 LA 255, 257 (Stutz, 1957); American Sugar Ref. Co., 24 LA 66, 71 (Reynard, 1955).

[336]This exception was expressly noted by many of the arbitrators cited above as authority for the general rule. This exception is discussed in detail in Chapter 16, section 5., "Refusal to Obey Orders—The Safety and Health Exceptions," and section 6., "Employee Complaints of Specific Hazards."

[337]This possible exception was recognized but did not apply in *Temco Aircraft Corp.*, 29 LA 693, 696 (Boles, 1957). In *Univac Division*, 48 LA 619, 620–21 (Cahn, 1967), the arbitrator stated that an employee's personal moral or religious beliefs do not excuse a refusal to obey orders. *See also* Rockford Newspapers, 63 LA 251, 252 (Kelliher, 1974). *But see* Ralston Purina Co., 61 LA 14, 15 (Krislov, 1973). Exceptions to the general rule might exist as to an order that would humiliate the employee (*see* Sheller Mfg. Corp., 34 LA 689, 689 (McCoy, 1960)), or would invade some personal right that the arbitrator considers inviolable (*see* Scott Paper Co., 52 LA 57, 59 (Williams, 1969)).

[338]*See* Allied Employers, Inc., 72 LA 437, 439, 441 (Peterschmidt, 1978); Southern Cal. Edison Co., 61 LA 453, 463 (Block, 1973); Arcrods Co., 39 LA 784, 788–89 (Teple, 1962); Valley Iron Works, 33 LA 769, 771 (Anderson, 1960). For related discussion, see section 8.B., "Right to Union Representation at Early Stage," above.

[339]*See* St. Joe Paper Co., 68 LA 124, 127–28 (Klein, 1977); Telex, Inc., 35 LA 873, 880 (Kinyon, 1960); International Harvester Co., 16 LA 307, 310–11 (McCoy, 1951); Ford Motor Co., 10 LA 213, 214 (Shulman, 1948). *See also* Walker Mfg. Co., 41 LA 1288, 1297–99 (Whelan, 1963); International Salt Co., 39 LA 238, 241 (Mittenthal, 1962); Dynamic Mfrs., 36 LA 1193, 1195–96 (Maguire, 1960). *Cf.* Home Furniture Co., 50 LA 1140, 1142 (Porter, 1967); Friedrich Refrigerators, 39 LA 934, 936–37 (Williams, 1962).

[340]*See* Food Employers Council, 40 LA 1100, 1102 (McNaughton, 1963); Braniff Airways, 27 LA 892, 900 (Williams, 1957); General Teleradio, Inc., 18 LA 418, 428 (Rosenfarb, 1952). In *Nuclear Fuel Services*, 53 LA 252, 255–56 (King, 1969), another exception was found where the refusal to obey an order resulted from the company's own failure to honor the grievance procedure. In *Goodyear Atomic Corp.*, 71 LA 619, 622 (Gibson, 1978), the fact that the grievance procedure was burdened by a large backlog did not excuse the refusal to obey an order instead of turning to the grievance procedure.

[341]*See* Ironrite, Inc., 28 LA 394, 397 (Haughton, 1956); Ford Motor Co., 3 LA 782, 783 (Shulman, 1946). However, the arbitrator in *Ford Motor Co.*, 19 LA 237, 238–39 (Shulman, 1952), declared that this exception would apply in rare cases only, and this limitation was again emphasized in *Ford Motor Co.*, 30 LA 46, 55 (Platt, 1958). In *Sheller Manufacturing Corp.*, 34 LA 689, 692 (McCoy, 1960), a related exception was recognized as to orders that have no reasonable relation to the employee's job duties. *See also* Titanium Metals Corp. of Am., 55 LA 690, 693–94 (Block, 1970). Here again, however, the exception may be viewed as a narrow one. *See* Minnesota Mining & Mfg. Co., 42 LA 1, 11–12 (Solomon, 1964).

and indisputably beyond the authority of" the company.[342] The foregoing list exemplifies, but does not exhaust, the commonly recognized exceptions to the general duty to obey management's orders.[343]

Even where a fact situation brings one of the exceptions into play, the exception may be deemed to give only personal and individual immunity to the immediately affected employees.[344] Some actions that may be taken properly by individuals for individual reasons may be improper when taken as a group or concerted action to force concessions from an employer.[345] For example, where employees as a group refused to report for early morning "start up" work, the group action was held to be improper, even assuming that the work was voluntary to the extent that individual employees, for individual reasons, could refuse the work:

> Such individual right to refuse work as may be inherent in the Agreement was intended to be motivated by purely individual reasons, not by a desire to join with others to compel a solution to a problem by group action—or inaction. The settlement of grievances or other disputes during the life of the Agreement is supposed to be accomplished by means of the grievance procedure and arbitra-

---

[342]Dwight Mfg. Co., 12 LA 990, 996 (McCoy, 1949) (emphasis in original). *See also* Ross Clay Prods. Co., 43 LA 159, 163–64 (Kabaker, 1964) (permitting self-help where the employer acted directly contrary to an arbitration award that had just been issued). Some arbitrators have held that employees need not obey orders to work overtime where the contract permits them to refuse such work. *See* Stanray Corp., 48 LA 492, 497 (Sembower, 1967); National Lead Co. of Ohio, 48 LA 61, 63 (McCoy, 1966); West Penn Power Co., 27 LA 458, 461–63 (Begley, 1956); A.D. Juilliard & Co., 17 LA 606, 609–10 (Maggs, 1951). *See also* Hawaiian Airlines, 37 LA 275, 277 (Burr, 1961). *Cf.* Pratt & Whitney, Inc., 53 LA 200, 202–03 (Seitz, 1969); American Mach. & Foundry Co., 50 LA 181, 185 (Geissinger, 1968); Joy Mfg. Co., 44 LA 141, 144 (Mullins, 1965); Robertshaw-Fulton Controls Co., 36 LA 4, 8–10 (Hilpert, 1961); Southern Bell Tel. & Tel. Co., 34 LA 925, 927–28 (Wollett, 1960); United Eng'g & Foundry Co., 21 LA 145, 150 (Young, 1953); Glamorgan Pipe & Foundry Co., 15 LA 645, 651 (Fuchs, 1950). In *Green Bay Packaging*, 87 LA 1057, 1061–62 (Gundermann, 1986), the company had no contractual right to compel attendance at United Way meetings although the company was willing to pay overtime for such attendance. In *Equitable Bag Co.*, 52 LA 1234, 1237–38 (Hayes, 1969), an employee could not be punished for refusing to attend firefighting training on overtime, the arbitrator stating that an employee cannot be punished for refusing to train for a job that he or she cannot be required to perform (firefighting as distinguished from fire prevention). *Cf.* Washington Hosp. Ctr., 80 LA 601, 604–05 (Rothschild, 1983). In *Marion Power Shovel Division*, 72 LA 417, 420 (Kates, 1979), the arbitrator found an "unmistakable specific right of refusal" of temporary transfer, so an employee could not be disciplined for disobeying an order to accept one.

[343]*See* Tribune Co., 93 LA 201, 203 (Crane, 1989); Ashland Oil, 91 LA 1101, 1104–05 (Volz, 1988); EZ Communications, 91 LA 1097, 1100–01 (Talarico, 1988); Orthodox Jewish Home for Aged, 91 LA 810, 816 (Sergent, 1988); Cheltenham Nursing & Rehab. Ctr., 89 LA 361, 363–64 (DiLauro, 1987); Lucky Stores, 88 LA 841, 845–46 (Gentile, 1987); Fluor Corp., 76 LA 921, 922 (Weiss, 1981); Trans World Airlines, 72 LA 747, 749–50 (Jones, Jr., 1979); Rome Cable Communications, 70 LA 28, 33 (Dallas, 1978); United Tel. Co. of Ohio, 55 LA 862, 864–65 (Duff, 1970); Allied Maint. Co. of Ill., 55 LA 731, 743 (Sembower, 1970); Dravo-Doyle Co., 54 LA 604, 606 (Krimsly, 1971); Productol Chem. Co., 54 LA 574, 575–76 (Lennard, 1971). *See also* Hugo Neu-Proler Co., 109 LA 880 (Richman, 1997); Department of Agric., Animal & Plant Health Inspection Serv., 38 FLRA 1291 (1991).

[344]*Id.* To illustrate, employees not affected by a safety hazard would not be justified in using self-help instead of the grievance procedure. Metal Specialty Co., 43 LA 849, 853–54 (Volz, 1964).

[345]*See* Sealtest Foods, 47 LA 848, 854 (Mullin, Jr., 1966); Westinghouse Elec. Corp., 47 LA 621, 627–28 (Altrock, 1966); Joy Mfg. Co., 44 LA 141, 144 (Mullin, Jr., 1965); Metal Specialty Co., 43 LA 849, 853–54 (Volz, 1964); Ford Motor Co., 41 LA 609, 615 (Platt, 1963).

tion, not by group refusals to perform work. And if the problem is one not compassable by those procedures, it must remain to be handled in negotiations at expiration time.[346]

Union representatives should not instruct employees to disobey management's orders.[347] Indeed, many arbitrators have recognized a special responsibility on the part of union leaders to uphold the agreement and to take affirmative action to persuade employees to use the grievance procedure for matters subject thereto in lieu of taking matters into their own hands (as by refusing to obey orders or by striking in violation of a no-strike obligation).[348] However, while many arbitrators have recognized the special responsibility, they have disagreed (at least prior to the Supreme Court's 1983 *Metropolitan Edison*[349] decision) as to what discipline, if any, may be assessed against union officers for failure to fulfill that special responsibility.

---

[346]Fitchburg Paper Co., 47 LA 349, 352 (Wallen, 1966). *See also* Pratt & Whitney, 53 LA 69, 71–72 (Feinberg, 1969).

[347]*See* E.A. Norris Plumbing Co., 90 LA 462 (Christopher, 1987); Stevens Shipping & Terminal Co., 86 LA 373, 375–77 (Anderson, 1985); Mark Twain Marine Indus., 73 LA 551, 555–56 (Guenther, 1979); Wright Mach., 39 LA 1080, 1081–82 (Strong, 1962); Jos. Schlitz Brewing Co., 37 LA 76, 81–82 (Abrahams, 1961); Publishers' Ass'n of New York City, 37 LA 62, 71–74 (Abersold, 1961); Bethlehem Steel Co., 19 LA 43, 46–47 (Feinberg, 1951); Commercial Pac. Cable Co., 11 LA 219, 221–22 (Kerr, 1948); Nathan Mfg. Co., 7 LA 3, 4–7 (Scheiber, 1947); Ford Motor Co., 3 LA 779, 780 (Shulman, 1944). An exception has been recognized, however, as to "action falling primarily within the Union's domain." Ford Motor Co., 10 LA 213, 214 (Shulman, 1948). The existence of a grievance procedure, and particularly the availability of arbitration, for resolving a dispute implies a no-strike obligation even if there is no express no-strike clause in the contract (or if such a clause is too narrow to cover the dispute). *See* Teamsters Local 174 v. Lucas Flour Co., 369 U.S. 95, 49 LRRM 2717 (1962); Ingersoll-Rand Co., 51 LA 83, 88 (Teple, 1968); Trailways of New England, 46 LA 369, 371 (Wallen, 1965).

[348]*See* Weber Aircraft, 114 LA 765, 768 (Gentile, 2000); USCP-Wesco, Inc., 109 LA 225, 230 (Grabuskie, 1997); Morton Thiokol, Inc., 93 LA 434, 440–41 (Allen, Jr., 1989); Lancaster Electro Plating, 93 LA 203, 206 (Bressler, 1989); New Jersey Bell Tel. Co., 77 LA 1038, 1040–42 (Wolff, 1981); Clinton Corn Processing Co., 71 LA 555, 565 (Madden, 1978); St. Francois County, 69 LA 102, 114 (Elbert, 1977); Bucyrus-Erie Co., 69 LA 93, 101 (Lipson, 1977); Powermatic/Houdaille, Inc., 65 LA 1245, 1248 (Byars, 1975); Stevens Air Sys., 64 LA 425, 428 (Stashower, 1975); Stokely-Van Camp, Inc., 60 LA 109, 117 (Karasick, 1973); Sealright Co., 53 LA 154, 157–58 (Belcher, 1969); Acme Boot Co., 52 LA 1047, 1050 (Oppenheim, 1969); Elgin Sweeper Co., 50 LA 1029, 1032–34 (Graff, 1968); Belmont Smelting & Ref. Works, 50 LA 691, 692–94 (Turkus, 1968); Gold Bond Stamp Co. of Ga., 49 LA 27, 33 (King, 1967); United Parcel Serv., 47 LA 1100, 1100–02 (Schmertz, 1966); Lind Constr. Co., 47 LA 369, 370 (Summers, 1966); Okonite Co., 45 LA 976, 979 (Kennedy, 1965); International Shoe Co., 45 LA 81, 85 (Larkin, 1965); American Radiator & Standard Sanitary Corp., 43 LA 644, 649 (Koven, 1964); Ward Foods, Inc., 43 LA 608, 609 (Dworet, 1964); Deere & Co., 43 LA 182, 189 (Davis, 1964); Drake Mfg. Co., 41 LA 732, 735 (Markowitz, 1963); Ford Motor Co., 41 LA 609, 613–15 (Platt, 1963); Hawaiian Elec. Co., 39 LA 688, 690–91 (Burr, 1962); American Radiator & Standard Sanitary Corp., 37 LA 401, 406 (Volz, 1961); E.W. Wholesale Meat Co., 37 LA 36, 42 (Koretz, 1961); Cuneo E. Press, Inc., 36 LA 214, 215 (Crawford, 1961); Borden Chem. Co., 34 LA 325, 328 (Wallen, 1959); Vickers, Inc., 33 LA 594, 601 (Bothwell, 1959); Wesson Oil & Snowdrift Co., 29 LA 622, 623–24 (Kelliher, 1957); Aurora Gasoline Co., 29 LA 495, 497 (Howlett, 1957); Green River Steel Co., 25 LA 774, 777 (Sembower, 1955); Skenandoa Rayon Corp., 21 LA 421, 424 (Feinberg, 1953); Canadian Gen. Elec. Co., 18 LA 919, 923–24 (Laskin, 1951); International Harvester Co., 14 LA 986, 988–89 (Seward, 1950); Armour & Co., 8 LA 758, 769–70 (Gilden, 1947); Bethlehem Steel Co., 2 LA 194, 198–99 (Shipman, 1945). *Contra* Pittsburgh Standard Conduit Co., 33 LA 807, 808 (McCoy, 1959).

[349]Metropolitan Edison Co. v. NLRB, 460 U.S. 693, 112 LRRM 3265 (1983).

Arbitrators have generally agreed that union officers may be disciplined more severely than other employees where the officers have urged or led other employees to engage in misconduct under the agreement. The disputed question has been whether officers who have participated in misconduct, but not as an instigator or leader, should be more vulnerable to discipline than other offenders because of the officer's special responsibility.[350]

Under the NLRA, opinion also was divided on the latter question prior to the *Metropolitan Edison* decision. The Supreme Court decided the question in favor of union officials, although it did recognize that their statutory protection can be waived by the union. The decision teaches that under the NLRA:

- A general no-strike clause does not impose a higher duty on union officials than on other employees to prevent illicit work stoppages, and NLRA §8(a)(3) protects union officials against being disciplined more severely than other employees for like misconduct.
- This NLRA protection can be waived by the union, but any waiver of the statutory right must be "explicitly stated," or "[m]ore succinctly, the waiver must be clear and unmistakable."[351]

The Supreme Court stated in *Metropolitan Edison* that the case did "not present the question whether an employer may impose stricter penalties on union officials who take a leadership role in an unlawful strike," but the Court noted that where presented in other cases the NLRB had answered the question in the affirmative.[352]

---

[350]Examination of the cases cited in footnote 348, above, reveals that many arbitrators answered this question in the affirmative, but some disagreed. For example, an arbitrator upheld the more severe discipline of union officers, explaining that they "had the duty of setting an example for their fellow employees," and if the employees "could not be induced to return to work, the union officers should have gone back to their jobs." Stokely-Van Camp, Inc., 60 LA 109, 117 (Karasick, 1973). Illustrating the other view, however, another arbitrator stated that "a Union official bears a higher responsibility . . . [but] is entitled to the same treatment as any other employee, and cannot be signaled out." Stevens Air Sys., 64 LA 425, 428 (Stashower, 1975). For cases involving claims against the union for alleged failure to make a reasonable effort to prevent or terminate unauthorized work stoppages, see *Rust Eng'g Co.*, 75 LA 189, 196 (Eigenbrod, 1980); *National Homes Mfg. Co.*, 72 LA 1127, 1130 (Goodstein, 1979); *S.J. Groves & Sons Co.*, 52 LA 74, 78 (Scheib, 1969); *Forest City Publ'g Co.*, 50 LA 683, 689–90 (Kabaker, 1968); *Belmont Smelting & Ref. Work*, 50 LA 691, 692–94 (Turkus, 1968); *Metro E. Journal*, 47 LA 610, 613 (Kelliher, 1966); *Bradlees Family Circle Stores*, 47 LA 567, 572–74 (House, 1966); *Booth Newspapers*, 43 LA 785, 788 (Platt, 1964). In *Carbon Fuel Co. v. Mine Workers*, 444 U.S. 212, 216, 221, 102 LRRM 3017 (1979), the Supreme Court held that an international union was not liable under the LMRA for failure to use reasonable efforts to prevent or end "wildcat" strikes by local unions where it was not shown that the International was "responsible according to the common-law rule of agency." Here there was no evidence that the International had instigated, supported, ratified, or encouraged any of the work stoppages. The employer's reliance on the arbitration and "integrity" clauses of the national agreement was rejected, the bargaining history showing that the parties "purposely decided not to impose" the alleged obligation upon the International. *See also* Mine Workers v. Gibbs, 383 U.S. 715, 61 LRRM 2561 (1966).

[351]Metropolitan Edison Co. v. NLRB, 463 U.S. 693, 708, 112 LRRM 3265 (1983). *See also Arbitration and Selective Discipline of Union Officials After* Metropolitan Edison, 44 U. Miami L. Rev. 443 (1989). For more on the *Metropolitan Edison* decision, see Chapter 11, section 3.C., "Temporary or Ad Hoc Arbitrators."

[352]*Metroplitan Edison*, 463 U.S. at 699. Regarding the NLRB's view on this aspect, the Court stated:

The overall necessity for observing the grievance procedure is effectively explained in the following statement:

> Some men apparently think that, when a violation of contract seems clear, the employee may refuse to obey and thus resort to self-help rather than the grievance procedure. That is an erroneous point of view. In the first place, what appears to one party to be a clear violation may not seem so at all to the other party. Neither party can be the final judge as to whether the contract has been violated. The determination of that issue rests in collective negotiation through the grievance procedure. But, in the second place, and more important, the grievance procedure is prescribed in the contract precisely because the parties anticipated that there would be claims of violations which would require adjustment. That procedure is prescribed for all grievances, not merely for doubtful ones. Nothing in the contract even suggests the idea that only doubtful violations need be processed through the grievance procedure and that clear violations can be resisted through individual self-help. The only difference between a "clear" violation and a "doubtful" one is that the former makes a clear grievance and the latter a doubtful one. But both must be handled in the regular prescribed manner.[353]

It was observed further that:

> When a controversy arises, production cannot wait for exhaustion of the grievance procedure. While that procedure is being pursued, production must go on. And someone must have the authority to direct the manner in which it is to go on until the controversy is settled. That authority is vested in supervision. It must be vested there because the responsibility for production is also vested there; and responsibility must be accompanied by authority. It is fairly vested there because the grievance procedure is capable of adequately recompensing employees for abuse of authority by supervision.[354]

B. Company Obligation to Honor the Grievance Procedure

In a number of cases, arbitrators have emphasized management's obligation to preserve the integrity of the grievance procedure.[355] For example, in view of the obligation to utilize fully the possibilities of settlement inher-

---

The Board has held that employees who instigate or provide leadership for unprotected strikes may be subject to more severe discipline than other employees. . . . In making this factual determination the board has recognized that a remark made by a union official may have greater significance than one made by a rank-and-file member.

Id. at 699 n.6 (citations omitted). In the latter regard, see *General Shale Corp.*, 80 LA 375, 377 (Cromwell, 1983). *See also* Indiana & Mich. Elec. Co., 273 NLRB 1540, 118 LRRM 1177 (1985), *aff'd sub nom.* Electrical Workers (IBEW) Local 1392 v. NLRB, 786 F.2d 733, 121 LRRM 3259 (6th Cir. 1986).

[353]Ford Motor Co., 3 LA 779, 780–81 (Shulman, 1944). *But see* Gross & Greenfield, *Arbitral Value Judgments in Health and Safety Disputes: Management Rights Over Workers' Rights*, 34 BUFF. L. REV. 645 (1986).

[354]Ford Motor Co., 3 LA 779, 781 (Shulman, 1944). However, the "unusual health hazard or similar sacrifice" exception to the duty to obey orders was recognized. *Id.* at 782. The reasoning regarding the "work now and grieve later" concept was quoted in *Amax Lead Co.*, 70 LA 1, 3 (Norman, 1978) (the reasoning "is not new, neither is it out of date"). *See also* National Radio Co., 60 LA 78, 83 (Cox, 1973).

[355]For a very strong statement as to the obligation of both parties to observe the grievance procedure and preserve its integrity, see *Gregg & Sons*, 45 LA 981, 984–85 (Healy, 1965).

ent in the grievance procedure, an employer was held to have acted improperly in bypassing the union committee that represented certain grievants and communicating an offer of settlement directly to the grievants themselves.[356]

The company in another case was held to have an obligation to furnish information to the union, on request, as to how the company had complied with a settlement reached in the grievance procedure so the union could determine if the settlement was carried out.[357] In another situation, where an arbitrator found that management had a contractual obligation to exhaust the negotiation machinery before resorting to disciplinary action, management's failure to do so was held to be sufficient basis for reinstating discharged employees, although the discharges were otherwise justified.[358] However, absent such contractual requirement the employer need not resort to the grievance procedure before punishing an employee for misconduct.[359] In a "slowdown" case, the arbitrator condemned the company for taking "the law into its own hands" by assessing a wage cut for the slowdown instead of utilizing the "adequate grievance provisions" or other remedies available under the contract (including the right to discipline or lock out employees engaged in the slowdown).[360]

It may be noted that some agreements require maintenance of the status quo pending grievance settlement, both parties being obligated to maintain the conditions prevailing immediately prior to some stated point (such as prior to the incident or prior to filing the grievance).[361]

C. Exhaustion of Grievance Procedure as Condition Precedent for Arbitration

The critical nature of some disputes may lead the parties to stipulate that all prearbitral steps are waived, and that the dispute is to be taken directly to arbitration.[362] The agreement itself may provide for the direct

---

[356]Central Franklin Process Co., 17 LA 142, 145 (Marshall, 1951).

[357]North Am. Aviation, 17 LA 121, 124–25 (Komaroff, 1951). For related material, see section 3., "Attitude of Parties to the Grievance Procedure," above.

[358]Gloucester, Mass., Fisheries, 1 ALAA ¶67,340 (Kirsch, 1946). *See also* Sears, Roebuck & Co., 35 LA 757, 780 (Miller, 1960). In *San Angelo Packing Co.*, 52 LA 261, 263 (Sartain, 1969), an otherwise justified discharge was set aside because the employer refused to participate in meetings on the discharge grievance as required by the agreement. *See also* Printing Indus. of Wash., D.C., 52 LA 306, 309 (Daly, 1969).

[359]Falls Stamping & Welding Co., 48 LA 107, 113 (Dworkin, 1967). Nor was the employer required to use the grievance procedure instead of direct punishment by virtue of the added fact that the actions for which the employee was punished might have been done in his role as a union officer. Beckett Paper Co., 51 LA 936, 939–40 (Gibson, 1968). *Accord* Chrysler Corp., 33 LA 112, 123 (Wolff, 1959). *Contra* American Airlines, 31 LA 144, 145 (Gray, 1958).

[360]Jacobs Mfg. Co., 29 LA 512, 517–18 (Scheiber, 1957). *See also* Buchholz Mortuaries, 69 LA 623, 630 (Roberts, 1977).

[361]*See* McCall Corp., 43 LA 951, 954, 956 (Layman, 1964). Regarding the employer's obligation concerning the photographic preservation of evidence for the grievance procedure, see *Airco Alloys & Carbide*, 63 LA 395, 398–99 (Sembower, 1974).

[362]*See* Orgill Bros. & Co., 68 LA 797, 799 (Simon, 1977); Magnode Prods., 47 LA 449, 449 (Hayes, 1966); Calumet & Hecla, Inc., 25 LA 663, 664 (Smith, 1955); United Tavern, 16 LA 210, 214 (Slavney, 1951).

appeal of such disputes to arbitration, but this type of provision has been held inapplicable to ordinary employee grievances.[363]

However, a party that refuses to comply or fails to comply properly with the negotiation steps of the grievance procedure will not be permitted to prevent arbitration on the ground that the grievance procedure has not been exhausted.[364] Nor must the grievance procedure be exhausted where to do so would be "futile,"[365] or a "useless and idle gesture,"[366] or where compliance with the prearbitral grievance procedure has been rendered unrealistic or impossible by plant closure or removal.[367]

If an agreement provides only an informal type of grievance procedure, the arbitrator may not insist that the parties follow all formal preliminaries before asserting jurisdiction. One arbitrator has stated, for instance, that to give an arbitrator jurisdiction in such a case it is necessary only that the issue be one on which the parties have had some prior discussion and on which the "realistic possibilities" of settlement at the lower grievance steps have been exhausted.[368]

15. GRIEVANCE SETTLEMENTS AS BINDING PRECEDENTS
[LA CDI 93.49; 100.0785]

It is to be expected that a mutual settlement of a grievance by the parties ordinarily will be held binding on them insofar as the particular instance is involved.[369] It also seems obvious that where a grievance has been settled

---

[363]Ford Motor Co., 1 ALAA ¶67,030 (Shulman, 1944). The agreement also provided for direct appeal in *New Orleans S.S. Ass'n*, 45 LA 1099, 1101 (Oppenheim, 1965).

[364]City of Meriden, 48 LA 137, 140–41 (Summers, 1967) (involving improper compliance with lower steps). *See also* Glass Bottle Blowers v. Arkansas Glass Container Corp., 183 F. Supp. 829, 46 LRRM 2950, 35 LA 153 (E.D. Ark. 1960) (involving refusal to comply with lower steps); Brynmore Press, 8 LA 511, 512–14 (Rains, 1947) (same).

[365]Barbet Mills, Inc., 16 LA 563, 565 (Livengood, 1951). *See also In re* Roto Supply Sales Co., 28 LA 657, 658 (N.Y. Sup. Ct. 1957).

[366]*In re* Greenstone, 29 LA 161, 162 (N.Y. Sup. Ct. 1957). *See also* General Tire & Rubber Co. v. Rubber Workers, 191 F. Supp. 911, 49 LRRM 2001, 37 LA 496 (D.R.I. 1961). In *Avco Corp.*, 65 LA 1195, 1199–1200 (Taylor, 1975), the union requested a default judgment based on the employer's refusal to participate in separate step-2 hearings on each of 37 identical grievances, but the request was denied because the grievants were not unduly prejudiced by the procedure utilized by the employer, though it did not comply literally with that specified in the agreement.

[367]H.K. Porter Co., 49 LA 147, 153–54 (Cahn, 1967); Sidele Fashions, 36 LA 1364, 1369 (Dash, Jr., 1961).

[368]Reading St. Ry., 8 LA 930, 933 (Simkin, 1947).

[369]*See* Carpenters Dist. Council (Chicago) (Polk Bros.), 90 LA 745 (Hockenberry, 1988); Georgia Kraft Co., 90 LA 262 (Yancy, 1987); Sea-Land Freight Serv., 87 LA 633, 635–37 (D'Spain, 1986); E.&J. Gallo Winery, 86 LA 153, 159–61 (Wyman, 1985); Olinkraft, Inc., 73 LA 194, 195–96 (Marcus, 1979); Brown Co., 59 LA 235, 238 (Bloch, 1972); Elwell-Parker Elec. Co., 48 LA 1361, 1364 (Kates, 1967). Where necessary, a subsequent grievance may be filed on the question of the other party's compliance with the prior settlement. Lockheed Aircraft Serv. Co., 44 LA 51, 58–59 (Roberts, 1965). *See also* Dierks Paper Co., 47 LA 756, 759 (Morgan, 1966); Royal McBee Corp., 40 LA 504, 506 (Turkus, 1963). Another possible means of enforcing grievance settlements is court action under LMRA §301. *See* Teamsters Local 89 v. Riss & Co., 372 U.S. 517, 52 LRRM 2623 (1963); Meat Cutters v. M. Feder & Co., 224 F. Supp. 739 (E.D. Pa. 1963). *See also* Mine Workers Dist. 2 v. Barnes & Tucker Co., 561 F.2d 1093, 96 LRRM 2144 (3d Cir. 1977); National Steel & Shipbuilding Co., 87 LA 1008, 1010 (Alleyne, 1986). *Cf.* City of Lansing, Mich., 87 LA 808, 813–14 (Borland, 1981). Regard-

by mutual agreement of the parties, the same issue that is involved in such "settled" grievance, though appearing in the guise of another grievance, should not ordinarily be subject to arbitration at the request of only one party (or, if the issue does reach arbitration, the prior settlement should constitute a binding precedent). "It is essential to good labor-management relations . . . that grievance settlements not be disturbed in the absence of a conclusive showing of changed conditions."[370] One arbitrator would add that settlements are open to investigation on substantial charge of fraud or grievous error.[371] Another arbitrator would not consider a prior grievance settlement to be a binding precedent where "the basis for the joint disposition of the previous grievance is sufficiently clouded to preclude its automatic application" when the same issue reaches him.[372]

---

ing the NLRB's policy of deferring under certain circumstances to voluntary settlements, see *Roadway Express v. NLRB*, 647 F.2d 415, 107 LRRM 2155 (4th Cir. 1981). *See also* Hammontree v. NLRB, 925 F.2d 1486, 136 LRRM 2478 (D.C. Cir. 1991) (*en banc*); United Techs. Corp., 268 NLRB 557, 115 LRRM 1049 (1984). *See generally* Lynch, *Deferral, Waiver, and Arbitration Under the NLRA: From Status to Contract and Back Again*, 44 U. MIAMI L. REV. 237 (1989); Edwards, *Deferral to Arbitration and Waiver of the Duty to Bargain: A Possible Way Out of Everlasting Confusion at the NLRB*, 46 OHIO ST. L.J. 23 (1985).

[370]Standard Oil Co., 13 LA 799, 800 (Kelliher, 1949). *Accord* Cannelton Indus., 91 LA 744 (Volz, 1988); Swift & Co., 49 LA 82, 83 (McCoy, 1967); General Tel. Co. of the Southwest, 45 LA 300, 301 (Barnhart, 1965); International Harvester Co., 19 LA 812, 814 (Emery, 1953); Monsanto Chem. Co., 17 LA 36, 39–40 (Wallen, 1951); Tennessee Coal, Iron & R.R., 7 LA 378, 380 (Blumer, 1947). *Contra* New York Air Brake Co., 36 LA 621, 625 (Raimon, 1960) (particularly as to lower step settlements); General Am. Transp., 15 LA 672, 673 (Brandschain, 1950). *See also* General Elec. Co., 85 LA 481, 482–84 (Gibson, 1985). One arbitrator found no binding precedent in a prior settlement because "one settlement does not make for a past practice." Consolidated Aluminum Corp., 53 LA 122, 124 (Hayes, 1969). In *Vulcan Mold & Iron Co.*, 41 LA 59, 60–61 (Brecht, 1963), the arbitrator held that even where an issue has been arbitrated, the award cannot constitute a bar to the arbitration of similar issues—the earlier award would influence the subsequent arbitrator but would not bar the issue from arbitration. Regarding the latter view, see discussion in Chapter 11, section 3., "Authoritative Prior Awards."

[371]Tennessee Coal, Iron, & R.R., 7 LA 378, 380 (Blumer, 1947). No precedent will exist where it is uncertain whether any settlement was ever reached. *See* National Cash Register Co., 47 LA 248, 250–51 (Nichols, 1966). Of course, a settlement will not bind future cases if it was reached with the understanding that it not establish a precedent for any future case. *See, e.g.*, Joy Mfg. Co., 86 LA 517, 518–19 (Duff, 1986); Norris Indus., 73 LA 1129, 1132 (Roumell, Jr., 1979); Quaker Oats Co., 69 LA 727, 728 (Hunter, Jr., 1977); Alpha Cellulose Corp., 50 LA 300, 302 (Gilden, 1968). *Cf.* Mead Corp., 84 LA 875, 881 (Sergent, Jr., 1985). In an effort to encourage settlement of grievances short of arbitration, the coal industry adopted a contractual provision in 1978 placing settlements reached at the first step of the grievance procedure on a nonprecedential basis. See discussion in THE PRESIDENT'S COMMISSION ON COAL, LABOR-MANAGEMENT SEMINAR I, COLLECTIVE BARGAINING (Mar. 21, 1979), at 11–12, 26, 52 (No. 0-302-756, Gov't Printing Office 1979); THE PRESIDENT'S COMMISSION ON COAL, LABOR-MANAGEMENT SEMINAR IV, GRIEVANCE AND ARBITRATION PROCEDURES (June 20, 1979), at 23, 43, 53 (No. 0-302-759, Gov't Printing Office 1979) ("non-precedential effect of settlements or withdrawals at step one has encouraged resolution of complaints" there; the provision "is working fine at some member company mines, and at other company mines, it does not work that well").

[372]Neches Butane Prods. Co., 70 LA 1251, 1253 (Bailey, 1978). *See also* General Elec. Co., 85 LA 36, 40 (Gibson, 1985) (because all the facts involved in the other six grievances were not presented, it was impossible to ascertain if the circumstances in those instances were identical to those in the present case). In *Federal Aviation Admin.*, 68 LA 1213, 1217 (Yarowsky, 1977), settlement of a similar grievance at another location of the federal agency employer was held to "have no binding precedential effect because only the *result* of the informal grievance [settlement] is known." That arbitrator believed that "it would be necessary to analyze the totality of circumstances before one could gain a perspective" regarding the settlement; "no record was made of [the settlement] conferences and as a result they lack binding effect on a subsequent grievance arbitration." *Id.* (emphasis in original). *See also* Keystone Steel & Wire Co., 84 LA 369, 371 (Schwartz, 1985).

Aside from any effect of settlements as binding precedents, settlements may be accepted by an arbitrator as indicating the proper interpretation of ambiguous contract language. It has been observed, in this regard, that "[w]here the parties themselves settle a grievance the evidence of intent as to the meaning of a provision carries special weight."[373]

Somewhat different considerations are involved, however, where a grievance has not been mutually settled, but simply has been denied by management at some prearbitral step of the grievance procedure and, for various possible reasons such as lack of funding or available witnesses, has not been appealed further. If management's denial of a grievance is "accepted" by the union in order to provide the elements of a "settlement," an arbitrator might consider it as a binding precedent.[374] But numerous arbitrators have held that the mere failure to appeal a grievance is not per se acquiescence in the disposition of the issue on the basis of management's final answer that would bar the issue from arbitration in a subsequent case.[375] This is particularly so where withdrawal of a case from the grievance procedure is done "without prejudice,"[376] or where the withdrawing party indicates that it intends ultimately to seek an arbitral ruling on the issue.[377] To ensure against the possibility of a binding precedent, a party apparently is well advised to state some such condition in deciding not to appeal a grievance further.[378]

---

[373]Bendix-Westinghouse Auto. Air Brake Co., 23 LA 706, 710 (Mathews, 1954). *See also* Washington Hosp. v. Retail, Wholesale & Dep't Store Union, 442 F. Supp. 93, 97 LRRM 2485, 2486 (W.D. Pa. 1978); McDonnell Douglas Corp., 78 LA 401, 404 (Winton, 1982); Southern Cal. Edison Co., 61 LA 453, 459–60 (Block, 1973); Menasco Mfg. Co., 50 LA 265, 267 (Ray, 1968). But a prior settlement could not operate to amend a clear and unambiguous provision of the agreement in *Lukens Steel Co.*, 35 LA 246, 248 (Crawford, 1960). *See also* Kiowa Corp., 72 LA 96, 100–01 (McKenna, 1979). As to a matter not treated by the collective bargaining agreement, a settlement may amount to a special agreement governing future rights of the parties. *See* Peoples Gas Light & Coke Co., 39 LA 224, 225–26 (Davis, 1962).

[374]*See* U.S. Steel Corp., 21 LA 26, 30 (Garrett, 1953). *See also* Ethyl Corp., 95 LA 632, 636 (Blum, 1990); Teepak, Inc., 83 LA 205, 211 (Fish, 1984).

[375]*See* Spartek, Inc., 89 LA 594, 596–97 (Johnson, 1987); Continental Forest Indus., 75 LA 53, 55 (Anderson, 1980); Continental Oil Co., 52 LA 179, 180–81 (Merrill, 1969); Armstrong Cork Co., 49 LA 288, 289 (Stein, 1967); Kramer Trenton Co., 48 LA 314, 316 (Dash, Jr., 1966); Line Materials Indus., 46 LA 1106, 1110 (Teple, 1966); Controls for Radiation, 46 LA 578, 581–82 (Stouffer, 1966); Patterson Steel Co., 45 LA 783, 787 (Autrey, 1965); Pittsburgh Plate Glass Co., 45 LA 696, 702 (Jenkins, 1965); Cornish Wire Co., 45 LA 271, 275, 277 (Fallon, 1965); Wheland Co., 44 LA 5, 6 (Williams, 1964); Washington Metal Trades, 39 LA 1249, 1251 (Peck, 1962); National Fireworks Ordnance Corp., 23 LA 289, 291 (Smith, 1954); Union Carbide & Carbon Corp., 16 LA 811, 816 (Gilden, 1951); Tennessee Coal, Iron & R.R., 6 LA 426, 429 (Blumer & Kelly, 1945). *See also* City of Alliance, Ohio, 87 LA 921, 925–27 (Dworkin, 1986). In *Beck v. Reliance Steel Products Co.*, 860 F.2d 576, 129 LRRM 2822 (3d Cir. 1988), the court held that an agreement providing that all pending grievances shall be "dropped" does not bar arbitration of a union's claims on behalf of employees laid off before the agreement was executed. *Cf.* Parke, Davis & Co., 41 LA 8, 10 (Ryder, 1963).

[376]Ohio Steel Foundry Co., 36 LA 445, 446 (Dworkin, 1961); Greer Hydraulics, 29 LA 706, 708 (Friedman, 1957). *Cf.* Mason & Hanger Corp., 111 LA 60 (Caraway, 1998); Los Angeles Police Dep't, 89 LA 1090, 1091 (Feldman, 1987).

[377]Indiana State Teachers Ass'n, 90 LA 579, 584 (Heekin, 1988); Lion Oil Co., 25 LA 549, 552 (Reynard, 1955).

[378]*See* Kaiser Aluminum & Chem. Corp., 28 LA 439, 440 (McCoy, 1957).

Sometimes the collective bargaining agreement deals specifically with this matter. For example, under a clause providing that grievances not appealed to arbitration were "to be considered settled on the basis of the decision last made," an arbitrator refused to decide an issue that had been involved in two prior grievances that had been withdrawn:

> The present grievance appears plainly to be an attempt to reinstate the former grievances which had already been withdrawn by the Union. To permit this, in the absence of proof that the earlier withdrawal was induced by the Company through fraud, misrepresentation, intentional concealment of facts, overreaching or through mutual mistake, would encourage the relitigation of grievances after they had been disposed of by the parties in the proper exercise of their discretion. This would indeed undermine the grievance procedure and the Umpire system. Here, there is no claim or proof that the Company had anything to do with the Union's decision to withdraw the earlier grievances from the procedure and from arbitration. It was a voluntary action presumably taken with full knowledge of all the facts, and must be held binding on the Union.[379]

Other arbitrators have reached similar results.[380] One arbitrator stated that the only exception "would be a situation in which the 'new' grievance would embrace factors and changed conditions which would clearly distinguish the latter grievance from the former."[381] However, some cases have reached a contrary result on the basis that the contractual language did not clearly indicate an intention that the underlying issue as well as the individual grievance be deemed settled.[382] One arbitrator believed that the question whether the underlying issue as well as the specific grievance are both to be considered settled should be answered on a case-by-case basis.[383]

---

[379]Republic Steel Corp., 25 LA 437, 438 (1955).

[380]See New England Tel. & Tel. Co., 52 LA 869, 874–75 (Murphy, 1969); Modine Mfg. Co., 39 LA 624, 627–29 (Smith, 1962); West Penn Power Co., 31 LA 297, 299–300 (Duff, 1958); Babcock & Wilcox Co., 24 LA 541, 547–48 (Dworkin, 1955); Raycrest Mills, 15 LA 417, 419 (Myers, 1950).

[381]Babcock & Wilcox Co., 24 LA 541, 548 (Dworkin, 1955).

[382]See Continental Oil Co., 52 LA 179, 180–81 (Merrill, 1969); General Tel. Co. of the Southwest, 45 LA 300, 301–02 (Barnhart, 1965); Pittsburgh Steel Co., 25 LA 157, 162 (May, 1955).

[383]Kansas City Power & Light Co., 71 LA 381 (Elkouri, 1978). The arbitrator stated that:

> [W]here the provision does not expressly state that that the underlying issue as well as the specific grievance which the Union failed to carry forward are both to be considered settled in the Company's favor (or in the Union's favor if the Company fails to give its decision within the specified time), it would seem that the fact of such foreclosure could be determined only on a case by case basis. The answer to be reached in any given case would depend in significant part upon how thoroughly the particular prior grievance was treated in the grievance discussions and, of paramount importance, upon a clear showing that the specific nature and scope of the prior grievance are precisely the same as the specific nature and scope of the subsequent grievance which the Company is seeking to bar by the operation of the [provision].

Id. at 385. Although the required showings for a bar were not made in that case, the fact that the prior grievances were dropped by the union was relevant to the question of damages where the underlying issue was again raised. Id. at 386. In Mine Workers District 5 v. Consolidated Coal Co., 666 F.2d 806, 109 LRRM 2001, 2003–04 (3d Cir. 1981), a lower court was held to have erred in applying a prior settlement to a subsequent grievance, the prior settlement having lacked specificity and the earlier grievance having differed from the subsequent grievance. See also ITT Power Sys. Corp., 84 LA 288, 290–91 (Elkin, 1985) (a material factor present in the subsequent grievance but absent in the earlier grievance without more prevented a bar).

16. NOTICE OF INTENT TO ARBITRATE [LA CDI 94.05; 100.0752]

Collective bargaining agreements frequently provide that parties who wish to arbitrate disputes not settled by the negotiation steps of the grievance procedure must give notice of desire and intent to arbitrate within a specified period of time.[384] Arbitrators often have held that failure to give the required notice, unless waived by the other party or otherwise excused, renders the dispute nonarbitrable.[385]

Failure to meet notice requirements does not bar arbitrability where there is a reasonable excuse or the presence of other justification for the delay. In such cases, jurisdiction will be assumed and the dispute will be decided on the merits.[386] This was true where the parties in the past had

---

[384]*See Major Collective Bargaining Agreements:Arbitration Procedures* 30–31 (U.S. Dep't Labor Bull. No. 1425-6, 1966). Many agreements also state time limits on the selection of the arbitrator. *Id.* at 51–52. Where an issue is in arbitration, some agreements toll the time limits for similar grievances pending decision of the representative or "test" case. *Id.* at 70. *See also* Gonce v. Veterans Admin., 872 F.2d 995, 131 LRRM 3259 (D.C. Cir. 1989); North Shore Gas Co., 84 LA 1016, 1018–19 (Seidman, 1985). *But see* Walker v. J.C. Bradford & Co., 938 F.2d 575 (5th Cir. 1991) (a 2-year delay while the issue was being litigated was held not to constitute a waiver of the agreement to arbitrate); Home Club v. Barlow, 818 S.W.2d 192 (Tex. Ct. App. 1991); Gunn v. Veterans Admin. Med. Ctr., 892 F.2d 1036, 133 LRRM 2148 (Fed. Cir. 1990); PPG Indus., 90 LA 1033 (Edelman, O'Malley, & Martin, 1988).

[385]*See* Tomkins Indus., 114 LA 1299 (Eisenmenger, 2000); Logan Co., 90 LA 949 (High, 1988); Inland Container Corp., 90 LA 532 (Ipavec, 1987); Williams Air Force Base, 89 LA 370, 372–73 (Smith, 1987); Pettibone Corp., 75 LA 14, 16 (Donoghue, 1980); Chase Bag Co., 69 LA 85, 86 (Wolff, 1977); Burdick Corp., 68 LA 933, 937 (Mueller, 1977); Textile Paper Prods., 51 LA 384, 387–89 (Hebert, 1967); Precision Extrusions, 49 LA 338, 341–42 (Stouffer, 1967); Erwin Mills, Inc., 47 LA 606, 607 (Stark, 1966) (dispute not arbitrable where notice was mailed 1 day late as indicated by postmark); Rochester Tel. Corp., 46 LA 1185, 1188 (Feinberg, 1966) (notice must be unequivocal, a conditional notice not sufficing); Lake Shore Coach Co., 44 LA 1190, 1192 (Geissinger, 1965); Booth Broad. Co., 41 LA 97, 99–100 (Ellmann, 1962); Magma Copper Co., 39 LA 772, 776 (Keeler, 1962); Pacific Cement & Aggregates, 39 LA 668, 670 (Burr, 1962); Aluminum Indus., 36 LA 1460, 1463 (Seinsheimer, 1961); Deep Rock Oil Co., 20 LA 865, 866 (Emery, 1953); Management Servs., 20 LA 34, 34–35 (McCoy, 1953); Walter Kidde & Co., 16 LA 369, 371 (Handsaker, 1951); Autocar Co., 13 LA 266, 267–69 (Abersold, 1949); Bethlehem Steel Co., 6 LA 397, 399–403 (Levy, 1947); Bethlehem Steel Co., 5 LA 742, 744–46 (Dodd, 1946); Southwestern Greyhound Lines, 4 LA 458, 461 (Updegraff, 1946). Where the agreement did not state a time limit for proceeding to arbitration, an implied requirement that a party act within a reasonable time was found in *Cleveland Pneumatic Tool Co.*, 43 LA 869, 872–74 (Dworkin, 1964), and in *Hydraulic Press Mfg. Co.*, 39 LA 1135, 1138–39 (Dworkin, 1962).

[386]*See* Williams Air Force Base, 89 LA 370, 372–73 (Smith, 1987); Cities Serv. Co., 87 LA 1209, 1212 (Taylor, 1986); Rome Cable Corp., 87 LA 519, 522 (Konvitz, 1986); Quaker Oats Co., 86 LA 673, 675–76, 678 (Peterson, 1986); Southeast Container Corp., 69 LA 884, 885 (Seidenberg, 1977); H.K. Porter Co., 49 LA 147, 153–54 (Cahn, 1967); Karnish Instruments, 45 LA 545, 547 (Bender, 1965); Standard-Thomson Corp., 26 LA 633, 634 (Lehoczky, 1956); Whitlock Mfg. Co., 19 LA 234, 236 (Stutz, 1952); Walter Kidde & Co., 18 LA 193, 195–96 (Abruzzi, 1951); Eagle-Picher Mining & Smelting Co., 17 LA 205, 206 (Prasow, 1951); Bethlehem Steel Co., 17 LA 7, 8 (Selekman, 1951); B.F. Goodrich Co., 8 LA 883, 884 (McCoy, 1947); Manhattan Transit Co., 8 LA 844, 845 (Trotta, 1947); Bethlehem Steel Co., 7 LA 276, 278 (Simkin, 1947); Bethlehem Steel Co., 4 LA 509, 510–13 (Brandschain, 1946); International Shoe Co., 3 LA 500, 503–04 (Wardlaw, 1946). *But see* Precision Extrusions, 49 LA 338, 342 (Stouffer, 1967). In some cases, dispute centers on *when* the time limit started running. In *Newspaper Agency Corp.*, 43 LA 1233, 1235 (Platt, 1964), the contract stated a time limit for giving notice of intent to appeal from awards of local arbitrators to an appeals board (within 5 days after the award has been "rendered"); the time limit was held not to have started running until receipt of an award some 10 days after its date. For related material, see section 7., "Time Limitations," above.

mutually accepted a loose interpretation of their contractual time limits.[387] A reasonable excuse may be a good-faith mistake or difference of opinion,[388] or it may be the unavoidable absence of an essential party, so as to make the observance of time limits impracticable.[389] Furthermore, a reasonable excuse may be said to exist if it would be futile to request arbitration within the time limit.[390] In one case, a request for an extension of time was held adequate to preserve the union's right to appeal a grievance to arbitration where the delay was not unreasonable under the circumstances.[391] Finally, a request for arbitration will be timely where the union and company have ongoing conversations within the relevant period concerning the grievance.[392]

In a situation raising an equitable estoppel issue, a commitment made but later repudiated by one party was held to be a reasonable excuse for the failure of the other party to comply literally with the notice requirement.[393] Finally, the right to enforce time limits may be waived, as by signing a submission agreement to arbitrate and failing to raise the time issue until the arbitration hearing.[394]

Although arbitrators are compelled to apply contractual limitations, they may do so with apparent displeasure. Witness, for example, the following statement by an arbitrator:

> It should be frankly noted that the umpire reaches his conclusion with real regret. "A time limitation is a summary bar. Its imposition precludes application of principles of equity, of fairness, and of justice, regardless of merit. . . . " But the company in these cases has carefully refrained from any conduct which could properly be deemed a waiver of the strict procedural requirements . . . . There is nothing here to buttress the liberal interpretation which the umpire would much prefer to adopt, no peg upon which he can "hang his hat." These grievances must be choked off at this point. It is ruled that they have all been appealed too late . . . .[395]

---

[387]*See* May Dep't Stores, 84 LA 53, 56 (Morgan, 1985); Hempstead Bus Corp., 49 LA 681, 682 (Wolf, 1967); Stanray Corp., 48 LA 492, 496 (Sembower, 1967); Standard-Thomson Corp., 26 LA 633, 634 (Lehozcky, 1956). *See also* Walter Kidde & Co., 18 LA 193, 195–96 (Abruzzi, 1951). Where each party had "sinned" as to observing contractual procedural requirements, the arbitrator refused to hold the union strictly to the time limit for proceeding to arbitration. Penn Jersey Boiler & Constr. Co., 50 LA 177, 179 (Buckwalter, 1967). *See also* Air Force Logistics Command, 85 LA 1168, 1169–70 (Sergent, Jr., 1985). Arbitrators have disagreed as to whether the time limit for proceeding to arbitration is extended by continued negotiations toward settlement of the grievance. A "yes" answer was given by *National Cleaning Contractors*, 70 LA 917, 919–20 (Dworkin, 1978); *United Tel. Co. of Fla.*, 69 LA 87, 92 (Carson, Jr., 1977); *Montgomery Ward & Co.*, 49 LA 271, 272–73 (Updegraff, 1967). But it was "no" in *Lake Shore Coach*, 44 LA 1190, 1192 (Geissinger, 1965); *Booth Broad. Co.*, 41 LA 97, 99–100 (Ellmann, 1962).

[388]*See* Bethlehem Steel, 7 LA 276, 278 (Simkin, 1947); International Shoe, 3 LA 500, 503–04 (Wardlaw, 1946).

[389]Ohmer Corp., 5 LA 278, 280 (Lehoczky, 1946).

[390]Forse Corp., 39 LA 709, 716 (Dworkin, 1962); Manhattan Transit, 8 LA 844, 845 (Trotta, 1947).

[391]Carpenter Steel Co., 44 LA 1185, 1186–87 (Kerrison, 1965).

[392]Cone Mills Corp., 103 LA 745 (Byars, 1994); Granite Constr. Co., 100 LA 585 (Richman, 1993).

[393]B.F. Goodrich Co., 8 LA 883, 884 (McCoy, 1947).

[394]*See* Mount Sinai Hosp. Med. Ctr. of Chi., 73 LA 297, 299 (Dolnick, 1979); Louisiana-Pacific Corp., 68 LA 638, 643 (Kenaston, 1977); National Fireworks Ordnance Corp., 23 LA 289, 291 (Smith, 1954); Lawrence Prods. Co., 14 LA 310, 311 (Marshall, 1950). *But see* Aluminum Indus., 36 LA 1460, 1463 (Seinsheimer, 1961).

[395]Bethlehem Steel Co., 6 LA 397, 402 (Levy, 1947). *See also* North Shore Gas Co., 84 LA 1016, 1018–19 (Seidman, 1985); Textile Paper Prods., 51 LA 384, 387–89 (Hebert, 1967); Pietro Scalzitti Co., 49 LA 302, 309–10 (Sembower, 1967).

The fact that many arbitrators consider a contractual provision for notice of appeal to arbitration to be far more than a mere formality, and indeed
to be, in effect, a statute of limitations, is particularly significant in view of
the fact that questions of procedural arbitrability (including time-limit compliance) are to be decided by the arbitrator if the federal law applies to the
case.[396] Under an agreement that required written notice of intent to arbitrate, a timely oral announcement of intention was held not to be sufficient.[397]
However, a timely oral announcement of intent to arbitrate was held sufficient where the agreement did not specifically require written notice.[398] Unless the agreement expressly requires the notice to be in some particular
form or requires the use of some particular terminology, substance should
govern over form and a notice should be held sufficient if it clearly and unequivocally advises the other party within the time limit that the grievance
is being taken to arbitration.[399]

Some agreements provide that within a specified time after notice of
intent to arbitrate has been given, a joint request is to be submitted asking
that an arbitrator act on the dispute. Failure of the parties to act within the
specified time may be held to render the dispute nonarbitrable.[400] But if one
party fails to meet its obligation in some material respect, that party cannot
prevent arbitration on the ground that the other party alone referred the
case to arbitration.[401] Where the agreement states no time limit for proceed-

[396]In *John Wiley & Sons v. Livingston*, 376 U.S. 543, 555–59, 55 LRRM 2769 (1964), the
Supreme Court noted that the lower courts disagreed as to whether the court or the arbitrator should decide if "procedural" conditions to arbitration have been met. Some of the cases
cited by the Court as evidencing the conflict involved compliance with time limits. The Supreme Court held that questions of procedural arbitrability are for the arbitrator rather
than the court. *See also* Teamsters Local 765 v. Stroehmann Bros. Co., 625 F.2d 1092, 104
LRRM 3005, 3007 (3d Cir. 1980). For related discussion, see Chapter 2, "Legal Status of
Arbitration in the Private Sector," and Chapter 6, "Determining Arbitrability."
[397]Bethlehem Steel Co., 5 LA 742, 746 (Dodd, 1946). *See also* Williams Air Force Base, 89
LA 370, 372 (Smith, 1987); Joy Mfg. Co., 44 LA 469, 472 (Mittenthal, 1965).
[398]*See* Ironrite, Inc., 28 LA 398, 400 (Whiting, 1956); Lincoln Indus., 19 LA 489, 491
(Barrett, 1952). *See also* General Precision, 42 LA 589, 592 (Roberts, 1964).
[399]*See* Trumbull County, Ohio, Dep't of Human Servs., 90 LA 1267 (Curry, Jr., 1988);
City of Oregon, Ohio, 90 LA 431 (Stieber, 1988); Veterans Admin., 90 LA 350 (Wilcox, 1987);
Mount Mary Coll., 44 LA 66, 72 (Anderson, 1965); Chase Bag Co., 42 LA 153, 156 (Elkouri,
1963); Lake Mills Redi-Mix, 38 LA 307, 310 (Mueller, 1962). Of course, the notice must be
given by a party that has a contractual right to take the grievance to arbitration. Fiberboard
Paper Prods. Corp., 46 LA 59, 61–62 (Roberts, 1966).
[400]*See* Cement Asbestos Prods. Co., 70 LA 180, 182 (Cocalis, 1978); General Tel. Co. of
Ohio, 50 LA 1207, 1210–11 (Teple, 1968); John Deere Harvester Works, 10 LA 778, 781–82
(Updegraff, 1948). *Cf.* Wells Fargo Alarm Serv., 88 LA 567, 570–71 (Richman, 1986) (a wage
grievance was held arbitrable, even though the union did not submit timely demand for
arbitration, but back pay was not awarded in light of the untimely demand for arbitration);
McGraw-Edison Co., 42 LA 995, 998 (Teple, 1964). A court insisted on strict application of a
contractual notice requirement in *Detroit Coil Co. v. Machinists Lodge 82*, 100 LRRM 3138,
3140–41 (6th Cir. 1979).
[401]*See* Rust Eng'g Co., 75 LA 189, 196 (Eigenbrod, 1980); Hess Oil & Chem. Corp., 52 LA
1035, 1039–40 (Bothwell, 1969); Malone & Hyde, Inc., 5 LA 443, 445–46 (Wardlaw, 1946).
Waivers were found in *Associated Wholesale Grocers*, 73 LA 781, 786 (Roberts, 1979); *Cuyahoga
Metro. Hous. Auth.*, 70 LA 85, 88–89 (Oberdank, 1977). Arbitration was not defeated where
both parties were responsible for delay in selecting an arbitrator. American Air Filter Co., 54
LA 1251, 1253 (Dolnick, 1970). *See also* Farmland Indus., 72 LA 1302, 1305 (Heneman, Jr.,
1979). Nor was arbitration defeated where a party made a timely request to the appointing
agency but its response was delayed. Sprague Devices, 72 LA 376, 378 (Cox, 1979).

ing to the selection of an arbitrator after notice of intent to arbitrate has been given, considerable delay in selecting an arbitrator might occur without rendering the dispute nonarbitrable,[402] particularly when both parties have contributed to the delay.[403]

---

[402]*See* City of Oregon, Ohio, 90 LA 431, 433 (Stieber, 1988) (grievance arbitrable, despite 2-year delay in selecting arbitrator, where union timely informed the City of intent to arbitrate and City attorney failed to respond to union's telephone calls); Chase Bag, 42 LA 153, 155–56 (Elkouri, 1963) (notice of intent to arbitrate need be given only to the other party within the prescribed time limit, with notice to the appointing agency to be given within a reasonable time thereafter); Magma Copper Co., 40 LA 45, 48–49 (Gorsuch, 1962) (and cases cited therein). *See also* City of Maumee, Ohio, 90 LA 946, 948–49 (Graham, 1988); Social Sec. Admin., 89 LA 457, 465–67 (Feigenbaum, 1987); Immigration & Naturalization Serv., 81 LA 157, 158 (White, 1983); Keystone Consol. Indus., 71 LA 574, 578–79 (Cohen, 1978) (660-day delay in requesting arbitration panel was unreasonable); General Tel. Co. of Southeast, 69 LA 493, 497–98 (Swain, 1977) (9-month delay was reasonable where the parties met regarding the grievance during the interim); Maclin Co., 52 LA 805, 807–09 (Koven, 1969). Where timely notice of intent to arbitrate is given, a reasonable time will then be permitted for filing any necessary court action to compel arbitration. Rubber Workers Local 198 v. Interco, Inc., 415 F.2d 1208, 72 LRRM 2377 (8th Cir. 1969).

[403]*See* American Commercial Marine Servs., 102 LA 209 (Dilts, 1993); Internal Revenue Serv., 93 LA 261, 265–66 (Dilts, 1989); American Transp. Corp., 81 LA 318, 321–22 (Nelson, 1983); General Precision, 42 LA 589, 592 (Roberts, 1964); Sinclair Ref. Co., 38 LA 1251, 1254 (Gilden, 1962).

Chapter 6

Determining Arbitrability

When an existing dispute is taken to arbitration by a joint submission of the parties, there ordinarily is no problem of arbitrability because by the submission the parties identify the dispute and agree to its arbitration. A different situation may be presented, however, when one party invokes the arbitration clause of a collective bargaining agreement by a demand or notice of intent to arbitrate a dispute that has arisen during the term of the agreement. Here arbitration may be resisted by the other party on the ground that the dispute is not arbitrable.[1] It may be asserted, for instance, that the case does not involve any of the types of disputes that are covered by the

---

[1]For a careful treatment of the question of arbitrability, see GROSSMAN, THE QUESTION OF ARBITRABILITY: CHALLENGES TO THE ARBITRATOR'S JURISDICTION AND AUTHORITY (1984). For extensive categorization and discussion of specific grounds on which arbitrability might be challenged, see Smith & Jones, *The Impact of the Emerging Federal Law of Grievance Arbitration on Judges, Arbitrators, and Parties*, 52 VA. L. REV. 831, 839 (1966); Smith & Jones, *The Supreme Court and Labor Dispute Arbitration: The Emerging Federal Law*, 63 MICH. L. REV. 751, 780 (1965). For additional discussions of arbitrability issues and the roles of courts and arbitrators in the determination of arbitrability, see FAIRWEATHER'S PRACTICE AND PROCEDURE IN LABOR ARBITRATION 32–87, 116–72 (Schoonhoven ed., BNA Books 4th ed. 1999); McDermott, *Arbitrability: The Courts Versus the Arbitrator*, 23 ARB. J. 18 (1968); Pirsig, *Arbitrability and the Uniform Act*, 19 ARB. J. 154 (1964); Smith, *Arbitrators and Arbitrability*, *in* LABOR ARBITRATION AND INDUSTRIAL CHANGE, PROCEEDINGS OF THE 16TH ANNUAL MEETING OF NAA 75 (Kahn ed., BNA Books 1963); Cornfield, *Developing Standards for Determining Arbitrability*, 14 LAB. L.J. 564 (1963).

arbitration clause,[2] or that while covered by the arbitration clause the dispute is not arbitrable because some condition precedent to arbitration, such as exhaustion of the grievance procedure or timely notice of intent to arbitrate, has not been met.[3]

1. Where Arbitrability Challenges Might Be Lodged
[LA CDI 94.09; 100.0765]

Challenges to arbitrability are presented either to the arbitrator or to the courts. Where the collective bargaining agreement provides that the determination of arbitrability is vested in the arbitrator or where the parties agree to submit the question to arbitration, the arbitrator has jurisdiction over the determination. Absent collective bargaining provisions or agreement, the matter is for the courts to decide.[4] If an appointing agency is named in the arbitration clause, the challenge may be filed with it. There is no uniformity of policy of the various agencies in regard to processing cases and appointing an arbitrator where one party files a challenge to arbitrability. Some of the agencies do appoint an arbitrator in such instances, at least where a minimal showing of an arbitration clause is made, and the party protesting arbitrability is permitted to raise that issue before the arbitrator or the courts.[5]

In deciding where to lodge the challenge to arbitrability, the challenger may be influenced in varying degree by the particular language of the arbitration clause, by the state or federal law that governs the case,[6] and, possibly most important, by the challenger's general attitude toward the arbitration process. The challenger also might take a passive attitude, forcing the other party to seek enforcement of the arbitration clause by a court or arbitrator, at which stage the challenger will raise the issue of arbitrability.

2. Determination by the Courts [LA CDI 94.09; 100.0765]

Although the parties often leave arbitrability questions in the hands of the arbitrator, jurisdictional issues may be raised by a party in a court proceeding. The nature and extent of court participation may depend largely on the applicable law and the language of the arbitration clause.

---

[2]For related discussion, see Chapter 3, section 3.C., "Rights Arbitration Contract Clauses," and Chapter 22, section 2., "Interest Arbitration and Contract Clauses."

[3]See Chapter 5, "Grievances: Prelude to Arbitration," for discussion of these conditions precedent.

[4]*See* AT&T Techs. v. Communications Workers, 475 U.S. 643, 121 LRRM 3329 (1986).

[5]For discussion of the policy and procedures of the various appointing agencies (state, federal, and private) where arbitrability is questioned, see Justin, *Arbitrability and the Arbitrator's Jurisdiction, in* Management Rights and the Arbitration Process, Proceedings of the 9th Annual Meeting of NAA 1, 11–15 (McKelvey ed., BNA Books 1956). For additional discussion of American Arbitration Association and Federal Mediation and Conciliation Service policy (the rules of both agencies provide for ex parte proceedings), see *McDermott*, 23 Arb. J. at 31–33, 37. *See also Arbitrability*, 18 LA 942, 951 (1951).

[6]*See generally* Chapter 2, "Legal Status of Arbitration in the Private Sector."

The courts may become concerned with arbitrability questions in several ways:[7]

1. The party challenging arbitrability may seek a temporary injunction or "stay of arbitration" pending determination of arbitrability.
2. The party demanding arbitration may seek a court order compelling the other party to arbitrate where the applicable law upholds agreements to arbitrate future disputes; the latter party then raises the issue of arbitrability.
3. The issue of arbitrability may be considered when an award is taken to court for review or enforcement, unless the parties have clearly vested the arbitrator with exclusive and final right of determining arbitrability, or unless the right to challenge arbitrability is held by the court to have been otherwise waived under the circumstances of the case.[8]

The federal courts' function in cases where arbitrability is contested is delimited by teachings of the *Steelworkers Trilogy*.[9] Two of the *Trilogy* decisions deal with substantive arbitrability (i.e., whether the subject matter of the dispute is arbitrable).[10] In *Steelworkers v. American Manufacturing Co.*,[11] the U.S. Supreme Court stated:

> The function of the court is very limited when the parties have agreed to submit all questions of contract interpretation to the arbitrator. It is confined to ascertaining whether the party seeking arbitration is making a claim which on its face is governed by the contract. Whether the moving party is right or wrong is a question of contract interpretation for the arbitrator. In these circumstances the moving party should not be deprived of the arbitrator's judgment, when it was his judgment and all that it connotes that was bargained for.[12]

In *Steelworkers v. Warrior & Gulf Navigation Co.*,[13] the Court stated that "arbitration is a matter of contract and a party cannot be required to submit to arbitration any dispute which he has not agreed so to submit."[14] In its next sentences, however, the Court declared:

---

[7]*See* Chapter 2, "Legal Status of Arbitration in the Private Sector"; McDermott, *Arbitrability: The Courts Versus the Arbitrator,* 23 ARB. J. 18, 20 (1968); Smith & Jones, *The Supreme Court and Labor Dispute Arbitration: The Emerging Federal Law*, 63 MICH. L. REV. 751, 753 (1965); Pirsig, *Arbitrability and the Uniform Act,* 19 ARB. J. 154 (1964). *See also* Note, *Judicial Review of Labor Arbitration Awards After the* Trilogy, 53 CORNELL L. REV. 136, 139–44 (1967).

[8]Regarding waiver of right to court review of arbitrability, see section 4., "Delay in Contesting Arbitrability," below.

[9]Steelworkers v. American Mfg. Co., 363 U.S. 564, 46 LRRM 2414, 34 LA 559 (1960); Steelworkers v. Warrior & Gulf Navigation Co., 363 U.S. 574, 46 LRRM 2416, 34 LA 561 (1960); Steelworkers v. Enterprise Wheel & Car Corp., 363 U.S. 593, 46 LRRM 2423, 34 LA 569 (1960). For a summary of the significant teachings of the *Trilogy* and other Supreme Court decisions affecting arbitration, see Chapter 2, section 2.A., "Federal Law: Private Sector." Concerning the public sector, federal and state, respectively, see Chapter 20, section 4.A.i., "Role and Scope of Federal-Sector Grievance Procedure and Arbitration," and Chapter 21, section 6., "Determining Arbitrability and Compelling Arbitration."

[10]The Supreme Court ruled as to procedural arbitrability in *John Wiley & Sons v. Livingston,* 376 U.S. 543, 55 LRRM 2769 (1969), discussed in note 26, below.

[11]363 U.S. 564, 46 LRRM 2414, 34 LA 559 (1960).

[12]*Id.* at 567–68, 46 LRRM at 2415, 34 LA at 560.

[13]363 U.S. 574, 46 LRRM 2416, 34 LA 561 (1960).

Yet, to be consistent with congressional policy in favor of settlement of disputes by the parties through the machinery of arbitration, the judicial inquiry under § 301 must be strictly confined to the question whether the reluctant party did agree to arbitrate the grievance or did agree to give the arbitrator power to make the award he made. An order to arbitrate the particular grievance should not be denied unless it may be said with positive assurance that the arbitration clause is not susceptible of an interpretation that covers the asserted dispute. Doubts should be resolved in favor of coverage.[15]

In *American Manufacturing*, the Supreme Court expressly rejected the *Cutler-Hammer*[16] doctrine that a contract cannot be said to provide for arbitration "[i]f the meaning of the provision sought to be arbitrated is beyond dispute . . . ."[17] In rejecting that doctrine, the Supreme Court stated that the courts are not to weigh the merits of grievances:

> The courts, therefore, have no business weighing the merits of the grievance, considering whether there is equity in a particular claim, or determining whether there is particular language in the written instrument which will support the claim. The agreement is to submit all grievances to arbitration, not merely those which the court will deem meritorious. The processing of even frivolous claims may have therapeutic values of which those who are not a part of the plant environment may be quite unaware.[18]

A. Substantive Arbitrability [LA CDI 94.09; 100.0765]

Under federal law, the question of substantive arbitrability is for the court when asked to stay or compel arbitration, unless the arbitration clause

---

[14]*Id.* at 582.

[15]*Id.* at 1353, 46 LRRM at 2419–20, 34 LA at 564–65 (footnote omitted). The Supreme Court subsequently explained that the quoted language "established a strong presumption favoring arbitrability." Nolde Bros. v. Bakery & Confectionery Workers Local 358, 430 U.S. 243, 254, 94 LRRM 2753 (1977). The party resisting arbitration might claim that bargaining history shows the parties intended to exclude the disputed matter from arbitration. Courts of appeals disagree as to whether they should consider such evidence. Conflicting decisions on the question are collected in *Technical Eng'rs Local 13 v. General Elec. Co.*, 531 F.2d 1178, 1183 n.13, 91 LRRM 2471 (3d Cir. 1976); *Communications Workers v. Southwestern Bell Tel. Co.*, 415 F.2d 35, 40 n.10, 71 LRRM 3025 (5th Cir. 1969). For additional material concerning the presumption of arbitrability, see Chapter 2, section 2.A.ii.b., "The *Trilogy*."

[16]Machinists v. Cutler-Hammer, Inc., 271 App. Div. 917, 67 N.Y.S.2d 317, 19 LRRM 2232 (N.Y.), *aff'd*, 297 N.Y. 519, 74 N.E.2d 464, 20 LRRM 2445 (1947).

[17]*Id.* at 918, 67 N.Y.S.2d at 318. This New York doctrine has since been repudiated there by statutory amendment. N.Y.C.P.L.R. §7501 (1963). But concerning arbitrability of public-sector disputes in New York, see Chapter 21, section 6.B., "Applying the Rules and Compelling Arbitration." *But see* Metropolitan Opera Ass'n v. Chaiken, 161 A.D.2d 169, 554 N.Y.S.2d 557 (N.Y. App. Div. 1990) ("unusual" arbitration clause indicated parties intent to resurrect *Cutler-Hammer* doctrine).

[18]Steelworkers v. American Mfg. Co., 363 U.S. 564, 568, 46 LRRM 2414, 2415–16, 34 LA 559, 560–61 (footnote omitted). The Court added:

> The union claimed in this case that the company had violated a specific provision of the contract. The company took the position that it had not violated that clause. There was, therefore, a dispute between the parties as to 'the meaning, interpretation and application' of the collective bargaining agreement. Arbitration should have been ordered.

Id. at 569, 46 LRRM at 2416.

clearly specifies that the arbitrator shall make the determination.[19] However, even though the agreement does not expressly leave the determination of arbitrability to the arbitrator, and in spite of the fact that the parties have first gone to court, courts have left the initial determination to the arbitrator. This was the result, for instance, where arbitrability could not be determined without delving into the merits:

> In these circumstances we believe the matter should proceed to arbitration, where the arbitrator may determine the subsidiary facts upon which depend both the merits of the controversy and his jurisdiction to decide it. A finding of jurisdiction, unlike a finding on the merits when jurisdiction is not in question . . . will not be insulated from subsequent judicial review. . . . We believe full recognition of the role of labor arbitration requires court intervention in a case such as this only when it has become absolutely necessary, viz., on a petition to vacate or enforce the award.[20]

But in another case a district court was held to have erred in delegating to an arbitrator the determination of arbitrability.[21]

The ability of the courts to defer the question of arbitrability back to the arbitrator, where arbitrability was intertwined with the merits of the case, was apparently put to rest in *AT&T Technologies v. Communications Workers*.[22] There, the Supreme Court reaffirmed the *Steelworkers Trilogy* and other prior holdings, stating:

> The first principle gleaned from the *Trilogy* is that "arbitration is a matter of contract and a party cannot be required to submit to arbitration any dispute which he has not agreed so to submit." [Steelworkers v. Warrior & Gulf Navigation Co., 363 U.S. 574, 582, 46 LRRM 2416, 34 LA 561 (1960).] This axiom recognizes the fact that arbitrators derive their authority to resolve disputes only because the parties have agreed in advance to submit such grievances to arbitration. *Gateway Coal Co. v. Mine Workers* [Dist. 4, Local 6330], 414 U.S. 368[, 85 LRRM 2049] (1974).
>
> The second rule, which follows inexorably from the first, is that the question of arbitrability—whether a collective-bargaining agreement creates a duty for the parties to arbitrate the particular grievance—is undeniably an issue for

---

[19]The concurring opinion to *American Manufacturing* states: "Since the arbitration clause itself is part of the agreement, it might be argued that a dispute as to the meaning of that clause is for the arbitrator. But the Court rejects this position, saying that the threshold question, the meaning of the arbitration clause itself, is for the judge unless the parties clearly state to the contrary." *American Mfg.*, 363 U.S. at 571. *See also* Bakery & Confectionery Workers Local 358 v. Nolde Bros., 530 F.2d 548, 552–53, 91 LRRM 2570 (4th Cir. 1975), *aff'd*, 430 U.S. 243, 255 n.8, 94 LRRM 2753 (1977). In *Atkinson v. Sinclair Ref. Co.*, 370 U.S. 238, 241, 50 LRRM 2433 (1962), the Supreme Court stated that under its decisions "whether or not" a party is "bound to arbitrate, as well as what issues it must arbitrate, is a matter to be determined by the Court on the basis of the contract entered into by the parties."

[20]Camden Indus. Co. v. Carpenters Local 1688, 353 F.2d 178, 180, 60 LRRM 2525 (1st Cir. 1965). Subsequently this same court did stress that a court in reviewing an arbitrator's conclusion on arbitrability "must make its own independent determination" on the question. Mobil Oil Corp. v. Oil, Chem. & Atomic Workers Local 8-766, 600 F.2d 322, 101 LRRM 2721, 2723 (1st Cir. 1979). For other instances in which courts have found it difficult to consider arbitrability without penetrating the merits, see McDermott, *Arbitrability: The Courts Versus the Arbitrator*, 23 ARB. J. 18, 27–29 (1968), where it is also noted that attorneys arguing arbitrability will frequently have difficulty in doing so without delving into some aspect of the merits.

[21]Westinghouse Broadcasting Co. v. Theatrical Stage Employees Local 804, 616 F.2d 97, 103 LRRM 2798, 2799 (3d Cir. 1980).

[22]475 U.S. 643, 121 LRRM 3329 (1986).

judicial determination. Unless the parties clearly and unmistakably provide otherwise, the question of whether the parties agreed to arbitrate is to be decided by the court, not the arbitrator. *Warrior & Gulf*, . . . at 582–583.[23]

Where the arbitrator is to rule on both arbitrability and the merits, evidence and argument on the question of arbitrability will be *heard* before the presentation on the merits.

The Court expressly reaffirmed this principle in *John Wiley & Sons, Inc. v. Livingston*, 376 U.S. 543[, 55 LRRM 2769] (1964). The "threshold question" there was whether the court or an arbitrator should decide if arbitration provisions in a collective-bargaining contract survived a corporate merger so as to bind the surviving corporation. *Id.*, at 546. The Court answered that there was "no doubt" that this question was for the courts. "'Under our decisions, whether or not the company was bound to arbitrate, as well as what issues it must arbitrate, is a matter to be determined by the Court on the basis of the contract entered into by the parties.' . . . The duty to arbitrate being of contractual origin, a compulsory submission to arbitration cannot precede judicial determination that the collective bargaining agreement does in fact create such a duty." *Id.*, at 546–547 (citations omitted).

The third principle derived from our prior cases is that, in deciding whether the parties have agreed to submit a particular grievance to arbitration, a court is not to rule on the potential merits of the underlying claims. Whether "arguable" or not, indeed even if it appears to the court to be frivolous, the union's claim that the employer has violated the collective-bargaining agreement is to be decided, not by the court asked to order arbitration, but as the parties have agreed, by the arbitrator. "The courts, therefore, have no business weighing the merits of the grievance, considering whether there is equity in a particular claim, or determining whether there is particular language in the written instrument which will support the claim. The agreement is to submit all grievances to arbitration, not merely those which the court will deem meritorious." [Steelworkers v. American Mfg. Co., 363 U.S. 564, 568, 46 LRRM 2414, 34 LA 559 (1960) (footnote omitted).]

Finally, where it has been established that where the contract contains an arbitration clause, there is a presumption of arbitrability in the sense that "[a]n order to arbitrate the particular grievance should not be denied unless it may be said with positive assurance that the arbitration clause is not susceptible of an interpretation that covers the asserted dispute. Doubts should be resolved in favor of coverage."[*Warrior & Gulf*, at 582–83.] Such a presumption is particularly applicable where the clause is as broad as the one employed in this case, which provides for arbitration of "any differences arising with respect to the interpretation of this contract or the performance of any obligation hereunder . . . ." [*Id.* at 584–85.][24]

---

[23]*Id.* at 648–49.

[24]*Id.* at 643–45, 121 LRRM 3331–32. For courts applying *AT&T Techs.*, see, e.g., *Franklin Elec. Co. v. Auto Workers Local 1000*, 886 F.2d 188, 132 LRRM 2457 (8th Cir. 1989) (where party initially objects to jurisdiction of arbitrator but does not expressly reserve the question of arbitrability for judicial review and submits the matter, on the merits, to the arbitrator, it cannot later claim that the arbitrator was without authority to decide the issue); *Rockwell Int'l Corp. v. Hanford Atomic Metal Trades Council*, 851 F.2d 1208, 128 LRRM 3058 (9th Cir. 1988) (trial court was limited to issue of arbitrability because determination on the merits was within the authority of the arbitrator pursuant to the collective bargaining agreement); *Teamsters Local 70 v. Interstate Distrib. Co.*, 832 F.2d 507, 126 LRRM 3127 (9th Cir. 1987) (question of termination of collective bargaining agreement containing a very broad arbitration clause is not question of arbitrability but interpretation of termination clause and therefore arbitrable); *Morristown Daily Record v. Graphic Communications Local 8N*, 832 F.2d 31, 126 LRRM 2902 (3d Cir. 1987) (trial court can resolve question of arbitrability without encroaching on substance of the grievance); *Machinists v. Republic Airlines*, 829 F.2d 658,

B. Procedural Arbitrability [LA CDI 94.09; 100.075]

In respect to the determination of procedural arbitrability, the Supreme Court has ruled that questions of procedural arbitrability are for arbitrators to decide and not for the courts. When a court has determined that the subject matter of a dispute is arbitrable (substantive arbitrability), the arbitrator is to decide all procedural questions that grow out of the dispute and bear on its final disposition.[25] The Supreme Court stated that procedural questions, such as whether the preliminary steps of the grievance procedure have been exhausted or excused, ordinarily cannot be answered without consideration of the merits of the dispute.[26]

3. Determination by the Arbitrator [LA CDI 94.09; 100.0765]

The determination of arbitrability is often left by the parties to the arbitrator, either by the terms of the collective bargaining agreement or by agree-

---

126 LRRM 2690 (8th Cir. 1987) (court, not arbitrator, should decide whether prior grievance settlement makes new grievances on same subject nonarbitrable); *Oil, Chem. & Atomic Workers Local 4-23 v. American Petrofina Co. of Tex.*, 820 F.2d 747, 125 LRRM 3145 (5th Cir. 1987) (court referred to arbitration the issue of whether employee discharged during strike was still an employee and whether discharge was for just cause).

For arbitrators applying *AT&T Techs.*, see, e.g., *Midwesco Filter Resources*, 103 LA 859, 861 (Duff, 1994) ("no reliable indication that the Parties to the instant dispute ever mutually intended to confer upon the undersigned the legal power to make the initial jurisdictional determination as to whether the arbitration clause in their Agreement covers this dispute over an alleged oral settlement"); *City of Corpus Christi*, 99 LA 71, 72 (Marlatt, 1992) (emphasis in original) ("It necessarily follows from *AT&T Technologies* that the mere *assertion* by the employer of substantive exclusion from arbitration, no matter how frivolous such assertion may be, is sufficient to divest the arbitrator of jurisdiction and to compel the Union to take the threshold issue of arbitrability into the courts."). *Cf.* Beatrice/Hunt-Wesson Inc., 92 LA 383, 387 (Brisco, 1989) ("Conceivably, the Arbitrator could retreat and refer that decision to the courts who, presumably, would apply the principles set out above. To defer this matter, now more than a year from its inception, to a judicial proceeding would cause unnecessary expense and delay to the parties. The Arbitrator will, therefore, make his determination of substantive arbitrability, full of the knowledge that if he errs, the Courts stand ready to correct.").

For analyses of *AT&T Techs.*, see Gould, *Judicial Review Labor Arbitration Awards—Thirty Years of the* Steelworkers Trilogy*: The Aftermath of* AT&T *and* Misco, 64 N.D. L. Rev. 464 (1989); Feller, AT&T Technologies*: The Aftermath*, The Chronicle (NAA), Oct. 1987, at 3; Stanton, *The Roles of the Court and the Arbitrator in Grievance Arbitration: The Impact of* AT&T Technologies v. Communication Workers of America, 14 N. Ky. L. Rev. 153 (1987); Feller, AT&T Technologies: *Who Decides Arbitrability?*, The Chronicle (NAA), Oct. 1986, at 3.

[25]*See, e.g.*, Crone, *The Continuing Battle Over Procedural Issues: Is It a Decision for the Courts or the Arbitrator?*, 20 Mem. St. U. L. Rev. 145 (1989); Stipanovich, *Of Procedural Arbitrability: The Effects of Noncompliance With Contract Claims Procedures*, 40 S.C. L. Rev. 847 (1989).

[26]John Wiley & Sons v. Livingston, 376 U.S. 543, 557–58, 55 LRRM 2769 (1964) (the Court also noted that a different ruling would produce frequent duplication of effort by court and arbitrator, and needless delay). In *Operating Eng'rs Local 150 v. Flair Builders*, 406 U.S. 487, 80 LRRM 2441 (1972), the Supreme Court refused to narrow the scope of this ruling as to the arbitrator's jurisdiction to decide procedural questions. *See also* Iron Workers Local 539 v. Mosher Steel Co., 796 F.2d 1361, 123 LRRM 2428 (11th Cir. 1986); Denhardt v. Trailways, Inc., 767 F.2d 687, 119 LRRM 3226 (10th Cir. 1985) (case distinguishes between substantive and procedural arbitrability).

ment of the parties. There are sound reasons for this. The delay and expense of court proceedings are avoided. Moreover, the arbitrator can be expected to exercise the industrial relations expertise that the parties contemplated when they provided for arbitration.

The collective bargaining agreement itself may specifically provide that the arbitrator is to rule on questions of arbitrability as well as on the merits of the dispute.[27] This provides the surest method for parties to minimize court involvement in the arbitration process. Further, the parties by special submission or stipulation may authorize the arbitrator, either specifically or impliedly, to rule both on questions of arbitrability and on the merits of the dispute.[28] Where it is clear that the parties have authorized the arbitrator to determine arbitrability, the courts will not readily overturn the arbitrator's ruling on that issue.[29] Most significant, however, is the fact that even where the parties have not clearly authorized the arbitrator to determine arbitrability, the arbitrator often does so as an implicit part of the assignment and the parties generally accept the conclusions without resort to litigation.

Arbitrators appear generally agreed that the legitimate interests of the parties are adequately served by submitting arbitrability issues to the arbitrator.[30] Furthermore, the hundreds of substantive arbitrability issues that have been decided by arbitrators would appear to indicate general concurrence by arbitrators in the view that "an agreement to arbitrate future disputes of a specified kind vests in a duly appointed arbitrator power to deter-

---

[27]It is not uncommon for the collective bargaining agreement to provide expressly for determination of arbitrability by the arbitrator, although a few agreements specify court determination. *See A Survey of Negotiated Grievance Procedures and Arbitration in Federal Post Civil Service Reform Act Agreements* 11 (Office of Personnel Mgmt. 1980); *Major Collective Bargaining Agreements: Arbitration Procedures*, at 24–26 (U.S. Dep't Labor Bull. No. 1425-6, 1966). *See also* Laborers Dist. Council (S. Cal.) v. Berry Constr., 984 F.2d 340, 142 LRRM 2388 (9th Cir. 1993) (power to determine arbitrability may be granted to an arbitrator either explicitly or through a broad arbitration clause); LAWI/CSA Consolidators v. Teamsters Local 63, 849 F.2d 1236, 128 LRRM 2968 (9th Cir. 1988) (arbitration clause does not "clearly and unmistakably" leave arbitrability question for determination by the arbitrator); Food & Commercial Workers Locals 770, 889 & 1442 v. Lucky Stores, 806 F.2d 1385, 124 LRRM 2187 (9th Cir. 1986) (district court erred by denying union's petition to compel employer to arbitrate dispute where collective bargaining agreement provided for question of arbitrability to be decided in the first instance by the arbitrator).

[28]*See, e.g.*, Pennsylvania Power & Light Co., 86 LA 1151 (Light, 1986); Super Valu Stores, 86 LA 619 (Smith, 1985); Park-Pitt Bldg. Co., 47 LA 234 (Duff, 1966).

[29]*See, e.g.*, Orion Pictures Corp. v. Writers Guild W., 946 F.2d 722, 138 LRRM 2685 (9th Cir. 1991) (employer was precluded from raising the issue of the arbitrator's authority once both parties submitted the issue to arbitration for a decision); Vic Wertz Distrib. Co. v. Teamsters Local 1038, 898 F.2d 1136, 133 LRRM 2936, 2939 (6th Cir. 1990) (where "the parties 'clearly and unmistakably' submitted the issue of arbitrability to the arbitrator, without reservation, we will review the arbitrator's decision under the same deferential standard employed when reviewing an arbitrator's ruling on the merits"); Metal Prods. Workers Local 1645 v. Torrington Co., 358 F.2d 103, 62 LRRM 2011 (2d Cir. 1966); Steelworkers v. North Range Mining Co., 249 F. Supp. 754, 61 LRRM 2697 (D. Minn. 1966); Wiese Rambler Sales Co. v. Teamsters Local 43, 64 LRRM 2139, 47 LA 1152 (Wis. Cir. Ct. 1966).

[30]Smith, *Arbitrators and Arbitrability, in* Labor Arbitration and Industrial Change, Proceedings of the 16th Annual Meeting of NAA 75 (Kahn ed., BNA Books 1963).

mine whether a particular dispute, with respect to which one party invokes arbitration, is a dispute of that kind."[31]

An American Bar Association committee has stated that "the function of the arbitrator to decide whether or not an allegation of nonarbitrability is sound could be compared to that of a trial judge who is asked to dismiss a complaint on motion for a directed verdict or for failure to state a cause of action. This analogy indicates that a preliminary decision relating to arbitrability by the arbitrator *is an inherent part of his duty*."[32] That arbitrators are capable of self-restraint is evidenced by the committee's conclusion, based on examination of many awards, that "arbitrators generally are well aware of the limitations of their authority and scrupulously try to avoid any transgression of those limitations."[33]

The question arises whether substantive arbitrability must be determined by a court in the first instance where a party, without going to court, challenges the arbitrator's jurisdiction to determine arbitrability. In *Master Builders' Ass'n of Western Pennsylvania*,[34] the arbitrator concluded that he should not refuse to rule on arbitrability in such case:

> [An arbitrator] would be remiss in his responsibilities as an arbitrator, if he were to refuse to rule on the arbitrability of a given dispute, where the arbitration provisions are of an all inclusive nature and where one party requests that such ruling be made. Obviously, any ruling that he makes is not self-enforcing, and court action will be required for such enforcement, if either party refuses to abide by the award. Should such action take place all parties are well aware that the Courts will be the final source of determining arbitrability.[35]

With regard to procedural arbitrability, it should be recalled that even where challenge to arbitrability is first lodged in the courts, the Supreme

---

[31]Barbet Mills, Inc., 19 LA 737, 738 (Maggs, 1952). *See also* West Penn Power Co., 24 LA 741, 742 (McCoy, 1955); Metropolitan Police Dep't Labor Comm., 84 LA 595 (Edes, 1985).

[32]*Arbitrability*, 18 LA 942, 950 (1951) (emphasis added). The committee's view was relied on in *Sandia Corp.*, 40 LA 879, 886 (Gorsuch, 1963). Also note the statement of the Supreme Court in *W.R. Grace & Co. v. Rubber Workers Local 759*, 461 U.S. 757, 765, 113 LRRM 2641, 2644 (1983), as follows: "Because the authority of arbitrators is a subject of collective bargaining, just as is any other contractual provision, the scope of the arbitrator's authority is itself a question of contract interpretation that the parties have delegated to the arbitrator."

[33]*Arbitrability*, 18 LA at 951. A district court is obliged to give an arbitrator's decision as to arbitrability the same deference as is due an arbitrator's decision on the merits. Pack Concrete v. Cunningham, 866 F.2d 283, 130 LRRM 2490 (9th Cir. 1989). *Accord* Pennsylvania Power Co. v. Electrical Workers (IBEW) Local 272, 886 F.2d 46, 132 LRRM 2388 (3d Cir. 1989).

[34]45 LA 892 (McDermott, 1965).

[35]*Id.* at 896. The arbitrator cited court decisions supporting his conclusion that he need not wait for a court to rule first as to arbitrability, but other court decisions were cited to the contrary. *Id.* at 895. For other expressions on this question, see *Hertz Corp.*, 81 LA 1, 8–9 (Mittelman, 1983); *Negco Enters.*, 68 LA 633, 635–36 (Helfeld, 1976); *City of Meriden*, 48 LA 137, 139 (Summers, 1967); *Mississippi Lime Co. of Mo.*, 32 LA 1013, 1022 (Hilpert, 1959). For related discussion, see McDermott, *Arbitrability: The Courts Versus the Arbitrator*, 23 Arb. J. 18 (1968).

Court has held that questions of procedural arbitrability are for the arbitrator rather than the court.[36]

A. *Trilogy* Arbitrability Criteria and the Arbitrator
[LA CDI 94.09; 100.0765]

Several arbitrators have emphasized that when parties present to an arbitrator the question of substantive arbitrability, the arbitrator (1) should exercise individual judgment on the question, (2) should not be restricted to the criteria established for the courts by the *Trilogy*, and (3) should not decide the issue slavishly on the basis of how a court might decide it.[37] Some other arbitrators, in holding that doubts concerning arbitrability should be resolved in the affirmative, appear to have their eye on the basic *Trilogy* standard of presumptive arbitrability.[38]

May an arbitrator determine a dispute to be nonarbitrable after a court has ordered arbitration under the *Trilogy*? One arbitrator has expressed the belief that an arbitrator may do so (though he did not do so in the case before

---

[36]See section 2., "Determination by the Courts," above. *See also* Teamsters Local 744 v. Metropolitan Distrib., 763 F.2d 300, 119 LRRM 2955 (7th Cir. 1985); Teamsters Local 765 v. Stroehmann Bros., 625 F.2d 1092, 104 LRRM 3005, 3007 (3d Cir. 1980); Zirkel, *Procedural Arbitrability of Grievance Cases*, 13 J. COLLECTIVE NEGOTIATIONS No. 4, at 351 (1984).

[37]*See* Stroh Brewery Co., 85 LA 89 (Boyer, 1985); Mobil Oil Co., 43 LA 1287, 1289 (Turkus, 1965); Bell Tel. Lab., 39 LA 1191, 1203–05 (Roberts, 1962); Hughes Tool Co., 36 LA 1125, 1129 (Aaron, 1960). *See also* Western Elec. Co., 46 LA 1018, 1021 (Dugan, 1966).

[38]*See* St. Anthony Indep. Sch. Dist., 91 LA 982 (Flagler, 1988); Dallas Power & Light Co., 87 LA 415 (White, 1985); BASF Wyandotte Corp., 85 LA 602 (Nicholas, Jr., 1985); Vinton Cmty. Sch. Dist., 83 LA 632 (Madden, 1984); Governor George Ariyoshi, 77 LA 467, 470 (Tanaka, 1981); University of Dubuque, 75 LA 420, 426 (Sinicropi, 1980); Ingram Mfg. Co., 75 LA 113, 116 (Caraway, 1980); Alliance Mach. Co., 74 LA 1058, 1060 (Feldman, 1980); San Antonio Air Logistics Ctr., 73 LA 455, 456–57 (LeBaron, 1979); Veterans Admin. Hosp., 72 LA 66, 70 (Carson, 1978); Asarco, Inc., 71 LA 730, 736 (Roberts, 1978); Max Rudolph Trucking Co., 69 LA 1167, 1170 (Rule, 1977); General Tel. Co. of the Southwest, 53 LA 246, 248 (Morris, 1969); Babcock & Wilcox Co., 51 LA 741, 742 (Kates, 1968); Gulf States Util. Co., 51 LA 284, 286 (Ray, 1968); American Motors Sales Corp., 48 LA 1040, 1043 (Yagoda, 1967); Heckethorn Mfg. & Supply Co., 36 LA 380, 381 (Warns, 1960). Many arbitrators have denied that the 1960 *Trilogy* has made them more inclined to decide in favor of arbitrability. Smith, *Arbitrators and Arbitrability*, in LABOR ARBITRATION AND INDUSTRIAL CHANGE, PROCEEDINGS OF THE 16TH ANNUAL MEETING OF NAA 75 (Kahn ed., BNA Books 1963). An early study supports this denial. *See Appendix D: Report of the Research and Education Committee, National Academy of Arbitrators: The* Steelworkers' Trilogy *and the Arbitrator, id.* at 360. For an extensive survey of views of arbitrators and parties concerning the impact of *Trilogy* arbitrability teachings on arbitrators, see Smith & Jones, *The Impact of the Emerging Federal Law of Grievance Arbitration on Judges, Arbitrators, and Parties*, 52 VA. L. REV. 831, 866 (1966), where numerous decisions by arbitrators are also examined for indications as to *Trilogy* influence. Authors Smith and Jones concluded that, "The total impact upon arbitrators, although real, is difficult to evaluate fully at this time." *Id.* at 912. *See* Naval Plant Representative Office, 91 LA 964, 967 (Abrams, 1988) (stating that arbitrators, unlike courts, should not apply a "presumption of arbitrability").

him) because there may be surface indication of arbitrability to justify a court in ordering arbitration, whereas the arbitrator, after delving deeper into the case, may conclude that it was not intended to be arbitrable.[39] Court decisions go both ways on this question.[40]

B. Procedural Techniques for Ruling on Arbitrability
[LA CDI 94.09; 100.0765]

Sometimes arbitrability is the sole question before the arbitrator, but probably more often the arbitrator is called on to rule on both the preliminary issue of arbitrability and, if the dispute is found to be arbitrable, also on the merits.[41] The question remains whether the arbitrator should *rule* on arbitrability before any presentation is made on the merits, or whether the ruling on arbitrability should be reserved until the full case has been presented. One school of thought holds that a ruling on arbitrability should be made before the presentation on the merits. This view was elaborated in *Babcock & Wilcox Co.*:[42]

> The Chairman is of the opinion that when a party raises the issue of arbitrability, it is better practice to pass upon this issue at the time it is presented, and before hearing the dispute on the merits, for the reason that whenever possible parties should have the right to an interim decision or ruling on any question presented during the course of the hearing, and that this procedure is preferable to the reservation of the ruling until after the conclusion of the hearing.[43]

---

[39]Zoological Soc'y of San Diego, 50 LA 1, 7 (Jones, Jr., 1967). In *Sun Life Insurance Co.*, 87 LA 598 (Harkless, 1986), the arbitrator found the dispute nonarbitrable after the court had held the dispute to be arguably within the arbitration clause. *See also* Bunn-O-Matic Corp., 70 LA 34, 37–38 (Talent, 1977); Warrior & Gulf Navigation Co., 36 LA 695, 697 (Holly, 1961) (company contention). *Cf.* General Tel. Co. of Ohio, 70 LA 904, 908–09 (Feldman, 1978).

[40]*See Appendix B: Arbitration and Rights Under Collective Agreements: Report of Committee on Law and Legislation for 1965, in* PROBLEMS OF PROOF IN ARBITRATION, PROCEEDINGS OF THE 19TH ANNUAL MEETING OF NAA 366, 377–78 (Jones ed., BNA Books 1967); Smith & Jones, *The Supreme Court and Labor Dispute Arbitration: The Emerging Federal Law*, 63 MICH. L. REV. 751, 761 (1965). *See also* E.I. DuPont de Nemours & Co., 293 NLRB 896, 131 LRRM 1193 (1989) (the NLRB recognized the propriety of an arbitrator holding a dispute to be nonarbitrable after the Board had held it to be presumptively arbitrable).

[41]Some statistics are provided in *Substantive Aspects of Labor-Management Arbitration*, 28 LA 943, 944 (1957). *See* Steelworkers v. Fermet Reclamation, 627 F. Supp. 1213 (N.D. Ill. 1986) (employer not entitled to have a separate arbitrator to decide arbitrability and substantive issue); State of Ohio, 90 LA 1199 (Sharpe, 1988) (the arbitrator first conducted a hearing to determine arbitrability and held the dispute arbitrable; he subsequently found the dispute nonarbitrable based on the merits).

[42]22 LA 456 (Dworkin, 1954).

[43]*Id.* at 460. For other instances in which this procedure was used (sometimes by specific agreement of the parties), see *Chevron U.S.A.*, 95 LA 393, 395 (Riker, 1990); *Hughes Aircraft*, 89 LA 205, 206 (Richman, 1987); *Department of the Air Force*, 84 LA 1173, 1177 (Holley, Jr., 1985); *American Foundry & Mfg. Co.*, 83 LA 525, 526 (Newmark, 1984); *Veterans Admin. Hosp.*, 72 LA 66, 67 (Carson, 1978); *Country Belle Coop. Farmers*, 48 LA 600, 603 (Duff, 1967); *Bridgeport Brass Co.*, 45 LA 90, 91 (Bennett, McDonough, & Romano, 1965); *Stepan Chem. Co.*, 45 LA 34, 34 (Anrod, 1965); *Avco Corp.*, 43 LA 765, 766 (Kornblum, 1964); *Hydraulic Press Mfg. Co.*, 39 LA 1135, 1135 (Dworkin, 1962); *Great Lakes Pipe Line Co.*, 34 LA 617, 618 (Howard, 1959). The interim ruling as to arbitrability might be verbal, in which case it will later be restated in a written opinion that also covers the merits. *See* Dynamic Mfrs., 36 LA 635, 636 (Crane, 1960).

Under this procedure only one hearing might prove to be necessary,[44] but two hearings often are required.[45]

Another view holds that the ruling on arbitrability may be reserved until the full case has been heard:

> The arbitrator may properly reserve his ruling upon arbitrability until after he has heard evidence and argument upon the merits. A contrary rule would cause needless delay and expense, necessitating two hearings whenever the arbitrator needed time to consider the question of arbitrability. Furthermore, in many cases, it is only after a hearing on the merits has informed the arbitrator of the nature of the dispute that he is in a position to determine whether it is of the kind covered by the agreement to arbitrate.
> . . . This procedure does not, of course, preclude the party who loses from obtaining any judicial review of the arbitrator's decision to which it is entitled by law; to reassure the Company about this I explicitly ruled that its participation in the hearing upon the merits would not constitute a waiver of its objections to arbitrability.[46]

It would seem that the choice between these two procedures should be dictated by consideration of all the circumstances of the particular case. Such a flexible procedure has been used by the Connecticut State Board of Mediation:

> The Board will inform the party protesting arbitrability that it will be permitted to raise that issue at the hearing. The Board will then first hear arguments on arbitrability before it proceeds to the merits of the dispute. The Board makes clear that at the hearing both parties must be prepared to proceed on the merits after the Board has heard them on arbitrability.

---

[44]*See* Hercules Powder Co., 47 LA 336, 338–39 (Boothe, 1966). In *Lockheed Aircraft Service Co.*, 44 LA 51, 59 (Roberts, 1965), the arbitrator held the grievance to be arbitrable and remanded it to the parties, to be heard on the merits only if the parties could not resolve it.

[45]*See* Sugardale Foods, 87 LA 18 (DiLauro, 1986); Kelsey-Hayes Co., 83 LA 21 (Keefe, 1984); Cuyahoga Metro. Hous. Auth., 70 LA 86, 89 (Oberdank, 1977); Negco Enters., 68 LA 633, 634, 638 (Helfeld, 1976); Board of Educ., City of New York, 47 LA 91, 92 (Stark, 1966); International Shoe Co., 46 LA 1063, 1063 (McCoy, 1966); International Shoe Co., 45 LA 1055, 1056 (McCoy, 1966); Crowell-Collier Broad. Corp., 45 LA 635, 640 (Jones, Jr., 1965); Crowell-Collier Broad. Corp., 45 LA 633, 635 (Jones, Jr., 1965); Stepan Chem. Co., 45 LA 34, 34 (Anrod, 1965); Board of Educ., City of New York, 44 LA 1150, 1154 (Stark, 1965).

[46]Barbet Mills, Inc., 19 LA 737, 738 (Maggs, 1952). The arbitrator explained his view in greater detail in *Caledonia Mills, Inc.*, 15 LA 474, 476–77 (Maggs, 1950). For other instances in which the ruling on arbitrability was reserved until the merits had been heard (the arbitrator sometimes saying this would minimize delay and costs), see *Lutheran Senior City*, 91 LA 1308 (Duda, Jr., 1988) (parties agreed to present evidence on timeliness as well as on the merits, and the arbitrator would rule on merits only if he found the grievance to be timely filed); *North Star Steel Co.*, 87 LA 40, 42 (Miller, 1986) (ruling on arbitrability reserved until merits of case had been heard); *H. Olson Distrib.*, 85 LA 302 (Weiss, 1985) (arbitrator found it unnecessary to determine the controverted issue of arbitrability where it was readily apparent that grievance must be denied on its merits; arbitrator assumed without deciding that dispute was arbitrable); *Vogue Coach Corp.*, 72 LA 1156, 1156–57 (Gentile, 1979); *American Petrofina Oil & Refinery*, 71 LA 852, 853 (Mewhinney, 1978); *City of Detroit*, 71 LA 340, 340–41 (Munger, 1978); *Appalachian Reg'l Hosps.*, 69 LA 794, 799 (Cantor, 1977); *Velsicol Chem. Corp.*, 52 LA 1164, 1168–69 (Oppenheim, 1969); *Nicholson Cleveland Terminal Co.*, 51 LA 837, 838 (Gibson, 1968); *Karnish Instruments*, 45 LA 545, 545 (Bender, 1965); *Menasco Mfg. Co.*, 45 LA 502, 503 (Boles, 1965); *Petrolite Corp.*, 45 LA 261, 262 (Singletary, 1965); *Union Carbide Nuclear Co.*, 35 LA 499, 499 (Schedler, 1960). This approach is suggested also in *Arbitrability*, 18 LA 942, 950–51 (1951). For an instance where it was necessary to get into the merits before the arbitrability issue could be decided, see *Chesapeake & Potomac Tel. Co.*, 46 LA 321, 322 (Seward, 1965). *See also* A.S. Abell Co., 75 LA 537, 539 (Freund, 1980).

After the issue on arbitrability has been presented, "the Board will assess the circumstances then obtaining to determine if it will proceed directly to the merits."

Under its policy, the Board reserves the right either to require the parties "to go forward directly on the merits" at the same hearing or to determine that "the decision on arbitrability should be made first before proceeding on the merits.[47]

Some agreements expressly give the arbitrator the option of hearing the arbitrability issue and the merits either together or in separate proceedings.[48] Even without such contractual provision, however, the arbitrator might require a party (against its wishes) to proceed to the merits before the ruling is made on arbitrability.[49] What should an arbitrator do when a party insists, against the opposition of the other party, on a ruling as to arbitrability before proceeding to the merits? A panel discussion by the National Academy of Arbitrators indicated that some arbitrators would issue an oral ruling as to arbitrability at the hearing, while some would proceed to the merits (possibly ex parte) despite the objections of one party.[50]

Finally it may be noted that regardless of *when* the ruling on arbitrability is made, it will often be placed in the arbitrator's written decision of the case at a point prior to the discussion of the merits.[51]

---

[47]Justin, *Arbitrability and the Arbitrator's Jurisdiction, in* Management Rights and the Arbitration Process, Proceedings of the 9th Annual Meeting of NAA 1, 12 (McKelvey ed., BNA Books 1956).

[48]*Major Collective Bargaining Agreements: Arbitration Procedures* 25 (U.S. Dep't Labor Bull. No. 1425-6, 1966) (noted that most agreements specify use of the same arbitrator for determining arbitrability and merits). *See, e.g.*, E-Systems, Inc., 86 LA 441, 441 (Traynor, 1986) (contract specified, "If one of the parties considers that the matter in dispute is not an arbitral issue, the arbitrator shall first determine that question . . .").

[49]As under the policy of the Connecticut State Board, noted hereinabove, or as the arbitrator did in *Union Carbide Nuclear Co.*, 35 LA 499, 499 (Schedler, 1960). *See also* Vogue Coach, 72 LA 1156, 1156–57 (Gentile, 1979). A "special appearance" to contest arbitrability did not prevent a ruling on the merits where the submission was broad enough to include the merits. Lake Mills Redi-Mix, 38 LA 307, 312 (Mueller, 1962).

[50]*Procedural Problems in the Conduct of Arbitration Hearings: A Discussion, in* Labor Arbitration—Perspectives and Problems, Proceedings of the 17th Annual Meeting of NAA 1–2, 21–22 (Kahn ed., BNA Books 1964) (all participants indicated, however, that their choice of action might vary with the situation). *See also* Crane Carrier Co., 47 LA 339, 340 (Merrill, 1966); Burgmaster Corp., 46 LA 750, 750 (Lennard, 1966); Burgmaster Corp., 46 LA 746, 747, 749–50 (Lennard, 1965). For discussion as to proceeding ex parte, see Chapter 7, section 5.D.i., "Default Awards in Ex Parte Proceedings"; Master Builders' Ass'n of W. Pa., 45 LA 892 (McDermott, 1965). The arbitrator did proceed ex parte to the merits in *Velsicol Chemical*, 52 LA 1164, 1168–69 (Oppenheim, 1969), and issued a default award against the company, which had refused to introduce evidence or cross-examine as to the merits. In *North Clackamas School District No. 12*, 68 LA 503, 504 (Snow, 1976), the union submitted evidence on both arbitrability and merits but the employer declined to participate in the portion of the hearing relating to the merits. The arbitrator held the dispute arbitrable in an initial award and then followed a procedure involving use of briefs to obtain the positions of both parties on the merits.

[51]*See* Babcock & Wilcox Co., 22 LA 456, 460 (Dworkin, 1954); Barbet Mills, Inc., 19 LA 737, 739 (Maggs, 1952).

4. DELAY IN CONTESTING ARBITRABILITY [LA CDI 94.59; 100.0760]

The right to contest arbitrability before the arbitrator is usually held not waived merely by failing to raise the issue of arbitrability until the arbitration hearing.[52] Whether participation in an arbitration hearing on the merits constitutes a waiver of the right to court review of arbitrability may depend on the terms of an applicable statute or on the view of the particular court. No uniform rule exists as to this question.[53] As a precaution against such waiver, a participant in an arbitration hearing on the merits may expressly reserve the right to court review of arbitrability.[54] Likewise, an arbitrator who calls for evidence and argument on the merits of a dispute before ruling on a challenge to arbitrability may emphasize that "participation in the hearing upon the merits would not constitute a waiver of objections to arbitrability."[55]

---

[52]*E.g.*, Coblentz, Ohio, Sch. Dist., 93 LA 80 (Kates, 1989); Wackenhut Servs., 91 LA 1343 (Hardbeck, 1988); Super Mkt. Serv. Corp., 89 LA 538 (DiLauro, 1987) (employer should have raised issue of arbitrability of dispute at the hearing, not in post-hearing brief); Denver, Colo., Pub. Sch., 88 LA 507 (Watkins, 1987); Ajayem Lumber Midwest, 88 LA 472 (Shanker, 1987); Springfield, Ohio, Bd. of Educ., 87 LA 16 (Feldman, 1986); Pennsylvania Dep't of Corrs., 86 LA 978 (Kreitler, 1986); Vogue Coach Corp., 72 LA 1156, 1159–60 (Gentile, 1979); City of Meriden, 71 LA 699, 701 (Mallon, 1978); International Paper Co., 70 LA 71, 74 (Robertson, 1978); Nashville Bridge Co., 48 LA 44, 46 (Williams, 1967); Western Elec. Co., 46 LA 1018, 1021 (Dugan, 1966); Jack & Heintz Precision Indus., 20 LA 289, 292 (Young, 1952); Commercial Pac. Cable Co., 11 LA 219, 220 (Kerr, 1948); Phillips Petroleum Co., 7 LA 595, 598 (Rader, 1947). *Cf.* Frederick J. Dando Co., 69 LA 48, 51 (DiLeone, 1977); Tacoma, Wash., Sch. Dist. No. 10, 69 LA 34, 38 (Peterschmidt, 1977); Wedron Silica Co., 47 LA 282, 283 (Greene, 1966). As to how far into the arbitration hearing a party may wait before first contesting arbitrability, see *City of Wyandotte*, 74 LA 2, 4 (McDonald, 1980); *Apex Mach. & Tool Co.*, 45 LA 417, 421–22 (Layman, 1965); *Caterpillar Tractor Co.*, 39 LA 534, 537 (Sembower, 1962). *Cf.* Fort Frye Sch. Dist., 91 LA 1140 (Dworkin, 1988) (failure to raise timeliness argument constituted a waiver).

[53]*See, e.g.*, Machinists Lodge 1777 v. Fansteel, Inc., 900 F.2d 1005, 134 LRRM 2089 (7th Cir. 1990); Teamsters Local 764 v. J.H. Merritt & Co., 770 F.2d 40, 120 LRRM 2017 (3d Cir. 1985); Ficek v. Southern Pac. Co., 338 F.2d 655, 57 LRRM 2573 (9th Cir. 1964), *cert. denied*, 380 U.S. 988 (1965); Longshoremen (ILA) v. Hanjin Container Lines, 727 F. Supp. 818, 133 LRRM 3036 (S.D.N.Y. 1989); Humble Oil & Ref. Co. v. Teamsters Local 866, 271 F. Supp. 281, 65 LRRM 3016 (S.D.N.Y. 1967); National Cash Register Co. v. Wilson, 35 LA 646 (N.Y. Ct. App. 1960). *See also* Piggly Wiggly Operators' Warehouse v. Teamsters Local 1, 602 F.2d 134, 103 LRRM 2646, 2649 (5th Cir. 1980). For other material relevant to this question, see Chapter 2, "Legal Status of Arbitration in the Private Sector."

[54]Under many statutes this precaution would suffice. But under the New York statute it might be inadequate. *See* McNamara v. Air Freight Haulage Co., 61 LRRM 2424, 46 LA 768 (N.Y. Sup. Ct. 1966). In *George Day Construction Co. v. Carpenters Local 354*, 722 F.2d 1471, 115 LRRM 2459, 2462 (9th Cir. 1984), a suit under LMRA §301, the court explained:

> Had the employer objected to the arbitrator's authority, refused to argue the arbitrability issue before him, and proceeded to the merits of the grievance, then, clearly the arbitrability question would have been preserved for independent judicial scrutiny. The same result could be achieved by making an objection as to jurisdiction and an express reservation of the question on the record. However, where, as here, the objection is raised, the arbitrability issue is argued along with the merits, and the case is submitted to the arbitrator for decision, it becomes readily apparent that the parties have consented to allow the arbitrator to decide the entire controversy, including the question of arbitrability.

[55]Barbet Mills, 19 LA 737, 738 (Maggs, 1952). *See also* Nursing Home, 74 LA 432, 432 (Wolff, 1980); Negco Enters., 68 LA 633, 638 (Helfeld, 1976).

Chapter 7

Arbitration Procedures and Techniques

Arbitration procedures are shaped by legal requirements, the agreement of the parties, and the directions of the arbitrator.[1] If the parties have agreed to arbitrate under the rules of an administrative or appointing agency, some procedural matters will be governed by those rules.[2] In addition, the conduct of the arbitrator is generally subject to the *Code of Professional Responsibility*.[3]

---

[1]For general discussions of arbitration procedure, see Fairweather's Practice and Procedure in Labor Arbitration 12–31, 198–240, 513–638 (Schoonhoven ed., BNA Books 4th ed. 1999); The Common Law of the Workplace (St. Antoine ed., BNA Books 1998); Labor Arbitration: A Practical Guide for Advocates (Zimny, Dolson, & Barreca eds., BNA Books 1990); Brand, Labor Arbitration, The Strategy of Persuasion (1987); Hill & Sinicropi, *Improving the Arbitration Process: A Primer for Advocates*, 27 Willamette L. Rev. 463 (Summer 1991); St. Antoine, *Arbitration Procedures, in* Labor Arbitrator Development: A Handbook 55 (Barreca, Miller, & Zimny eds., BNA Books 1983); Ver Ploeg, *Labor Arbitration: The Participant's Perspective*, 43 Arb. J. No. 1, at 36 (1988); Nicolau, *Can the Labor Arbitration Process Be Simplified? If So, in What Manner and at What Expense?, in* Arbitration 1986: Current and Expanding Roles, Proceedings of the 39th Annual Meeting of NAA 69 (Gershenfeld ed., BNA Books 1987).

[2]The American Arbitration Association (AAA), Labor Arbitration Rules (Including Expedited Labor Arbitration Rules) [hereinafter AAA Rule(s)], are published at <http://www.adr.org>. The Regulations of the Federal Mediation and Conciliation Service (FMCS), 29 C.F.R. pt. 1404, are published at <http://fmcs.gov>.

[3]The Code of Professional Responsibility for Arbitrators of Labor-Management Disputes is jointly promulgated by the NAA, the AAA, and the FMCS.

    The National Academy of Arbitrators will expect its members to be governed in their professional conduct by this Code. . . . The American Arbitration Association and the Federal Mediation and Conciliation Service will apply the Code to the arbitrators on their rosters in cases handled under their respective appointment or referral procedures. Other arbitrators and administrative agencies may, of course, voluntarily adopt the Code and be governed by it.

The National Academy of Arbitrators web site is at <http://www.naarb.org>. For a historical inquiry into its development, see McKelvey, *Appendix D. Ethics Then and Now: A Comparison of Ethical Practices, in* Arbitration 1985: Law and Practice, Proceedings of the 38th Annual Meeting of NAA 283 (Gershenfeld ed., BNA Books 1986). The NAA also provides advisory opinions on ethical matters in arbitration at its web site.

1. NEED FOR A HEARING

Although in some cases the parties submit the dispute for decision entirely on the basis of stipulated facts, written briefs, and affidavits,[4] a hearing in the presence of the arbitrator is necessary in almost all cases, to give each party a full and fair opportunity to inform the arbitrator about material aspects of the dispute. Even when the parties believe that their case can properly be resolved without a hearing, the arbitrator may not always agree.[5]

2. CONTROL OF ARBITRATION PROCEEDINGS

The arbitration proceeding is under the jurisdiction and control of the arbitrator, subject to rules of procedure that may be jointly prescribed by the parties and that, in the arbitrator's estimation, allow for a full and fair hearing.[6] The arbitrator must give the parties an adequate opportunity to present their cases. At the same time, the arbitrator must be satisfied that the information necessary to decide the case is made available and that the hearing is run efficiently.[7]

---

[4]AAA Rule 33 provides: "The parties may provide, by written agreement, for the waiver of oral hearings. If the parties are unable to agree as to the procedure, the AAA shall specify a fair and equitable procedure."

[5]Where the facts were in issue but the parties wanted to submit the case without a hearing (the arbitrator being directed to investigate the facts by interviewing the affected persons), the arbitrator convinced the parties that the benefits and safeguards of a hearing were indispensable. San Juan Star, 43 LA 445, 445–46 (Helfeld, 1964).

For cases where the dispute was submitted to the arbitrator for decision without a hearing, see *Defense Mapping Agency—Aerospace Ctr.*, 88 LA 651 (Hilgert, 1986); *City of Dayton*, 88 LA 236 (Heekin, 1986); *Dep't of Health & Human Servs.*, 83 LA 883 (Edes, 1984); *United States Steel Corp.*, 59 LA 195, 196 (Garrett, 1972) (illustrating that waiver of hearing may result in a narrower ruling by the arbitrator); *Kent of Grand Rapids*, 18 LA 160, 160–61 (Platt, 1952). For a suggested procedure when parties submit their case to an arbitrator without a hearing, see KAGEL, ANATOMY OF A LABOR ARBITRATION 121–23, 171–74 (BNA Books 2d ed. 1986).

[6]*See, e.g.*, FMCS Regulations, 29 C.F.R. §§1404.8, 1404.13; CODE OF PROFESSIONAL RESPONSIBILITY §5(A)(1) & (1)(a). *See also* Mine Workers v. Marrowbone Dev. Corp., 232 F.3d 383, 165 LRRM 2769 (4th Cir. 2000) (vacating award when arbitrator did not allow union to present its full case); Laborers v. U.S. Postal Serv., 751 F.2d 834, 841, 118 LRRM 2216 (6th Cir. 1985) ("Arbitrators are not bound by formal rules of procedure and evidence, and the standard for judicial review of arbitration procedures is merely whether a party to arbitration has been denied a fundamentally fair hearing.").

[7]*Procedural Rulings During the Hearing, in* ARBITRATION 1982: CONDUCT OF THE HEARING, PROCEEDINGS OF THE 35TH ANNUAL MEETING OF NAA 138 (Stern & Dennis eds., BNA Books 1983); Smith, *The Search for Truth: I. The Search for Truth—The Whole Truth, in* TRUTH, LIE DETECTORS, AND OTHER PROBLEMS IN LABOR ARBITRATION, PROCEEDINGS OF THE 31ST ANNUAL MEETING OF NAA 40, 48–49 (Stern & Dennis eds., BNA Books 1979); Davey, *What's Right and What's Wrong With Grievance Arbitration: The Practitioners Air Their Views*, 28 ARB. J. 209, 215, 223–24 (1973); Jaffe, chair, *The Arbitration Hearing—Avoiding a Shambles, in* PROCEEDINGS OF THE 18TH ANNUAL MEETING OF NAA 75 (Jones ed., BNA Books 1965). In *Rose Con, Inc.*, 70 LA 972, 975 (Walsh, 1978), because of the inexperience of the parties in presenting their positions, the arbitrator permitted them to present their case informally, as an "open forum."

It is significant that most arbitration statutes contain little detail about the arbitration process from the time the arbitrator is selected until the award has been issued. Even where statutes address procedural questions, the parties may be permitted to waive statutory requirements. The procedural rules of administrative agencies also may be waived by the parties; if the rules are not observed,[8] they fail to object and go forward.

It is the arbitrator's job to decide questions about procedural matters that are not covered by applicable law or rules and on which the parties have not reached agreement. As the U.S. Supreme Court commented: When a court has determined that the subject matter of a dispute is arbitrable, "'procedural' questions which grow out of the dispute and bear on its final disposition should be left to the arbitrator."[9]

The arbitrator should, and ordinarily will, comply with the wishes of the parties when they agree on procedural matters.[10] Agreement may be reached at the hearing, or earlier, in the submission or in the collective bargaining agreement. Above all, however, it is the arbitrator's responsibility to assure that employers, unions, and grievants have a full and fair hearing. Occasionally, this may "require an arbitrator to assert an independence of the parties in order to fulfill arbitral obligations that transcend or even conflict with the intentions of the employer and/or union parties to the contract."[11]

---

[8]Waiver is permitted by AAA Rule 34. Under FMCS Regulations, 29 C.F.R. §1404.8, parties have the right "jointly to select any arbitrator or arbitration procedure acceptable to them."

[9]John Wiley & Sons v. Livingston, 376 U.S. 543, 557, 55 LRRM 2769 (1964). See, e.g., Steelworkers v. Ideal Cement Co. Div., 762 F.2d 837, 119 LRRM 2774 (10th Cir. 1985) (matters of procedure fall solely within discretion of the arbitrator); Government Employees (AFGE) Local 916, 34 FLRA 850 (1990) (arbitrator has broad discretion in procedural matters; no violation in refusing to allow "sufficient" time for briefs); Government Employees (NAGE) Local R4-106, 34 FLRA 134 (1990) (arbitrator's decision not to proceed with case remanded to him was within broad procedural authority that is not subject to review).

[10]See, e.g., Paperworkers v. Misco, Inc., 484 U.S. 29, 39, 126 LRRM 3113 (1987) ("The parties bargained for arbitration to settle disputes and were free to set the procedural rules for arbitration to follow if they chose."). Where arbitrators failed to follow a procedural requirement specified by the agreement, a federal court remanded the case to them for compliance with the contractual procedure. Smith v. Union Carbide Corp., 350 F.2d 258, 60 LRRM 2110 (6th Cir. 1965).

[11]Gross & Bardoni, Reflections on the Arbitrator's Responsibility to Provide a Full and Fair Hearing: How to Bite the Hand that Feeds You, 29 Syracuse L. Rev. 877, 879–80 (1978). In order to ensure a fair hearing, arbitrators have prohibited the admission of evidence when a party failed to furnish a list of proposed witnesses and exhibits sufficiently in advance of the arbitration. Simmons Indus., 101 LA 1201, 1204–05 (Stephens, 1993). Arbitrators also have prohibited the admission of an affidavit tendered by a party after the arbitration hearing. Grace Indus., 102 LA 119, 122–23 (Knott, 1993). See also Dunsford, The Presidential Address: The Adversary System in Arbitration, in Arbitration 1985: Law and Practice, Proceedings of the 38th Annual Meeting of NAA 1 (Gershenfeld ed., BNA Books 1986); Aaron, The Role of the Arbitrator in Ensuring a Fair Hearing, in Arbitration 1982: Conduct of the Hearing, Proceedings of the 35th Annual Meeting of NAA 30 (Stern & Dennis eds., BNA Books 1983).

3. Prehearing Issues

A. Initiating Arbitration [LA CDI 94.05; 100.0752]

Arbitration may be initiated by a joint submission of the parties, a demand or notice invoking a collective bargaining agreement arbitration clause, or both. A submission, sometimes called a "stipulation" or an "agreement to arbitrate," is an ad hoc arrangement used where there is no previous contractual provision on the subject. The submission, which must be signed by both parties, describes an existing dispute; it often also names the arbitrator or the method of appointing the arbitrator.[12] A submission may provide considerable detail regarding the arbitrator's authority, the procedure to be used at the hearing, and other matters that the parties wish to control.[13]

Most collective bargaining agreements provide for the arbitration of disputes about the application or interpretation of the current collective bargaining agreement. Generally, arbitration may be initiated unilaterally by serving the other party with a written demand or notice of intent to arbitrate; the other party may reply with a statement of its position, but the arbitration will proceed if it does not.[14] No submission will be required to make arbitration enforceable by the courts if the case is covered by state or federal law under which agreements to arbitrate future disputes are specifically enforceable.[15]

Collective bargaining agreements usually do not provide for the arbitration of "interest" disputes, that is, disputes over the terms of future con-

---

[12]*See, e.g.*, Challenger Caribbean Corp v. Union Gen. de Trabajadores de P.R., 903 F.2d 857, 134 LRRM 2330 (1st Cir. 1990); High Concrete Structures of N.J. v. Electrical Workers (UE) Local 166, 879 F.2d 1215, 131 LRRM 3152 (3d Cir. 1989); Carpenters Dist. Council (Greater St. Louis) v. Anderson dba Anderson Cabinets, 619 F.2d 776, 104 LRRM 2188 (8th Cir. 1980); Retail, Wholesale & Dep't Store Union, New England Joint Bd. v. Decatur & Hopkins Co., 677 F. Supp. 657, 125 LRRM 2959 (D. Mass. 1987); Glover Bottled Gas Corp./ Synergy Gas Corp., 91 LA 77 (Simons, 1987); Kraft Foods Co., 15 LA 336, 336 (Elson, 1950). In *H.K. Porter Co. v. Saw, File & Steel Prods. Workers*, 406 F.2d 643, 70 LRRM 2385 (3d Cir. 1969), a submission indicating the parties' preferences as to the arbitrator's jurisdiction in the case was upheld over the general grievance and arbitration procedures of the collective bargaining agreement. Clarity is not always achieved in the submission, and the burden may fall on the arbitrator to make the initial interpretation of an ambiguous submission in order to determine the scope of his or her jurisdiction. Eagle Rubber Co., 35 LA 256 (Dworkin, 1960).

[13]Ottley v. Schwartzberg, 819 F.2d 373 (2d Cir. 1987) (the arbitrator's authority was determined by the submission); Chemical Workers Local 566 v. Mobay Chem. Corp., 755 F.2d 1107, 118 LRRM 2859 (4th Cir. 1985) (the parties, not the arbitrator, must define the issues; the submission is the "source and limit" of the arbitrator's power; absent a formal submission agreement, the agreement to arbitrate particular issues may be implied).

[14]AAA Rule 7 provides for initiation of arbitration under an arbitration clause in a collective bargaining agreement, and AAA Rule 9 provides for initiation under a submission. The FMCS encourages parties to make joint requests, but the FMCS Regulation adds that: "In the event . . . that the request is made by only one party, the OAS will submit a panel of arbitrators. However, the issuance of a panel—pursuant to either joint or unilateral request—is nothing more than a response to a request." FMCS Regulations, 29 C.F.R. §1404.9(a).

[15]Illustrating arbitration by court order, see *Silver Lake Bd. of Educ.*, 88 LA 885 (Madden, 1986); *Bechtel Civil & Minerals*, 87 LA 153 (Beck, 1986); *B&K Invs.*, 71 LA 366, 367 (Turkus, 1978); *Amoco Oil Co.*, 70 LA 979, 981 (Britton, 1978) (an instance in which the court narrowly confined the arbitrator's jurisdiction).

tracts. An agreement to arbitrate such disputes most often is entered into after the parties have reached impasse over specific issues and the existing contract has, or is about to, expire. In such cases the parties will use one instrument only, which will contain full provision for the arbitration.[16]

B. Stating the Issue [LA CDI 97.07; 100.0710]

The grievance statement filed at the initial step of the internal dispute resolution process may define the issue or issues, especially if the statement is carefully worded or if the parties fail to agree on a statement of the issue.[17] The parties sometimes specifically agree to this use of the grievance form.[18] As the grievance is processed through the several steps of the internal procedure, the issue may be more significantly defined.[19]

Sometimes the parties agree to a statement of the issue during the course of the hearing, when the evidence places the dispute in sharper focus.[20] The arbitrator also may initiate a discussion to clarify the issue and its scope,[21] which could produce a different statement, perhaps worded by the arbitrator and accepted by the parties. In many cases, the arbitrator must clarify the issue. The parties may request it[22] or the contract may provide that if the parties do not agree on the issue, it will be determined by the arbitrator.[23] The arbitrator may incorporate the parties' separate submissions into one of

---

[16]For examples of instruments used in such instances, see *A.S. Abell Co.*, 45 LA 801, 806–07 (Cluster, Gallagher, & Kraushaar, 1965); *River Valley Tissue Mills*, 3 LA 245, 246 (Blair, 1946). *See also* Tribune Publ'g Co., 28 LA 477, 478–79 (Ross, 1957); Connecticut Power Co., 26 LA 904, 904–05 (Donnelly, Curry, & Mottram, 1956); Atlas Raincoat Mfg. Co., 25 LA 54, 55 (Davis, 1955).

[17]Bowaters S. Paper Corp., 52 LA 674, 675 (Oppenheim, 1969); Johnson Bronze Co., 34 LA 365, 365 (McDermott, 1960); New Haven Clock & Watch Co., 18 LA 203, 203 (Stutz, 1952).

[18]Borden Mfg. Co., 25 LA 629, 630 (Wettach, 1955); Lukens Steel Co., 15 LA 408, 409 (D'Andrade, 1950); Texas Gas Transmission Corp., 27 LA 413, 413 (Hebert, 1956).

[19]Heppenstall Co., 22 LA 84, 85 (Reid, 1954). For other cases in which the issue developed at the hearing replaced the grievance statement, see *City of Southfield*, 78 LA 153, 153 (Roumell, Jr., 1982); *NCR-Worldwide Serv. Parts Ctr.*, 74 LA 224, 235 (Mathews, 1980); *U.S. Postal Serv.*, 71 LA 1188, 1193–94 (Garrett, 1978); *Pennsylvania Elec. Co.*, 45 LA 630, 633 (McCoy, 1965).

[20]*See* Marblehead Lime Co., 48 LA 310, 310 (Anrod, 1966); Republic Oil Co., 15 LA 895, 895 (Klamon, 1951).

[21]Section 5.A.1.b. of the Code of Professional Responsibility states that an arbitrator may "restate the substance of issues or arguments to promote or verify understanding."

[22]*See* Immigration & Naturalization Serv., 34 FLRA 342 (1990) (when parties are unable to phrase the issue and they granted arbitrator authority to do so, the Federal Labor Relations Authority (FLRA) will accord the arbitrator wide authority to frame the issue); City of Evanston, Ill., 95 LA 679 (Dilts, 1990); Alleghany County Comm'rs, 83 LA 464 (Mayer, 1984); Anchor Hocking Glass Corp., 46 LA 1049, 1049–50 (Daugherty, 1966).

[23]Lockheed Aircraft Corp., 23 LA 815, 815–16 (Marshall, 1955). *See also* Black, Sivalls, & Bryson, 42 LA 988, 989 (Abernethy, 1964).

his or her own wording,[24] or adopt one party's wording as an accurate statement of the issue.[25]

The parties may not know precisely what the issue is at the outset of the hearing.[26] Even when they have signed a submission stating the issue, it may be ambiguous and in need of clarification.[27] If the issue stated by the parties is not broad enough to encompass the entire dispute, an arbitrator may ask the parties for additional authorization.[28] Formal pleadings are not used in arbitration but, at some point, the issue to be resolved by the arbitrator must be specifically stated. Courts generally give the same deference to an arbitrator's interpretation of the statement and scope of the issue submitted as they give to the arbitrator's interpretation of the collective bargaining agreement.[29]

C. Changing the Scope of the Grievance [LA CDI 93.07; 100.0710]

One party to the arbitration may allege that the other is attempting to change or enlarge the scope of the case by raising issues, arguments, or claims for the first time at the hearing. When this happens, arbitrators emphasize

---

[24]Butler Paper Co., 91 LA 311 (Weiss, 1988); Northrup Worldwide Aircraft Servs., 90 LA 79 (Bankston, 1987); Bechtel Civil & Minerals, 87 LA 153 (Beck, 1986); City of La Habra, 74 LA 590, 590, 593 (Gentile, 1980); International Paper Co., 72 LA 421, 423 (Howell, 1979); Temple-Eastex, 69 LA 782, 782–83 (Taylor, 1977); East Orange Bd. of Educ., 69 LA 674, 674–75 (Spencer, 1977). In some of these cases the parties expressly requested that the arbitrator frame the issue after they had been unable to agree on it. National Gypsum Co. v. Oil, Chem. & Atomic Workers, 147 F.3d 399, 158 LRRM 2853 (5th Cir. 1998) (employer impliedly consented to arbitrator's framing of issue when it proceeded with arbitration without having agreed with union on precise issue); Borden Co., 46 LA 1175, 1175 (Bellman, 1966) (the parties declined to attempt a joint statement of the issue and left it to the arbitrator). In C&D Batteries, 31 LA 272, 273, 275–76 (Jaffee, 1958) (party could not defeat the arbitration by walking out on failure to achieve a joint statement of the issue).

[25]See North County Transit Dist., 89 LA 768 (Collins, 1987); General Tel. Co. of Cal., 85 LA 476 (Collins, 1985); Pan American World Airways, 83 LA 732 (Draznin, 1984); Magma Copper Co., 51 LA 9, 10 (Abernethy, 1968); Gisholt Mach. Co., 23 LA 105, 108 (Kelliher, 1954).

[26]See Mundet Cork Corp., 18 LA 254, 255 (Reynolds, 1952).

[27]See Zia Co., 52 LA 89, 90 (Cohen, 1969) (both parties signed a reworded submission to clarify the issue); McKinney Mfg. Co., 19 LA 291, 292 (Reid, 1952) (the arbitrator had implied authority to restate the issue contained in the submission).

[28]See Southern Cal. Gas Co., 91 LA 100 (Collins, 1988) (each party proposed a statement of the issue and stipulated that the arbitrator had the authority to frame the appropriate issue); American Smelting & Ref. Co., 29 LA 262, 264 (Ross, 1957). Absent such broadened authority from the parties, the arbitrator may confine himself or herself to the narrowly stipulated issue. See Orgill Bros. & Co., 68 LA 797, 802 (Simon, 1977); Pacific Tel. & Tel. Co., 49 LA 121, 122, 125 (Roberts, 1967); John J. Nissen Baking Co., 48 LA 12, 15–16 (Fallon, 1966).

[29]National Gypsum Co. v. Oil, Chem. & Atomic Workers, 147 F.3d 399, 158 LRRM 2853 (5th Cir. 1998). Even where the agreement expressly provided that the issue "shall be mutually agreed upon," a federal court held that arbitration would not be defeated by inability of the parties to agree on a statement of the issue. Socony Vacuum Tanker Men's Ass'n v. Socony Mobil Oil Co., 369 F.2d 480, 63 LRRM 2590 (2d Cir. 1966).

substance over form to uncover the merits of the case.[30] An arbitrator might agree to hear the claims if they involve only a modified line of argument, an additional element closely related to the original issue, refinement or correction of the stated grievance, or introduction of new evidence,[31] so long as the opposing party has had a fair opportunity to prepare to meet the claims.

Arbitrators also have disallowed the presentation of issues not raised until the hearing[32] on the ground that the other party has been surprised or otherwise unfairly disadvantaged. Even a claim that the prearbitral discussions were flawed because of a misprint in the complaint was not considered by an arbitrator on the day of the hearing without substantial supportive evidence concerning the error.[33]

If one party changes its position so that the other is taken by surprise and finds it difficult or impossible to present its case adequately, the arbitrator may grant a continuance or remand the case to the parties for further negotiations.[34] If a new issue arises at arbitration, an arbitrator ordinarily will refuse to consider the new matter over the objection of the other party.[35] Where a party fails to address, at the hearing, an issue raised in the original grievance, the issue is deemed waived or abandoned and the arbitrator will not consider it.[36] Even if the collective bargaining agreement requires an employee grievance to specifically identify the provision that allegedly has been violated, arbitrators will rarely dismiss a grievance that does not mention the term or terms so long as the employer understood the nature of the dispute.[37]

Occasionally, in a case with several issues, one will remain unaddressed during the grievance process. If it arises during the hearing, the arbitrator

---

[30]*See, e.g.*, Mohawk Rubber Co., 86 LA 679 (Groshong, 1986); Hamady Bros. Food Mkt., 82 LA 81 (Silver, 1983). In overruling a party's objection to an element that was relevant to the dispute but had not been discussed by the parties prior to arbitration, one arbitrator said the objection was "based upon an unreasonably and unjustifiably limited and restrictive concept of arbitration" in labor relations. Washington Motor Transp. Ass'n, 28 LA 6, 9 (Gillingham, 1956).

[31]The general subject of new issues and evidence at the arbitration stage is treated by Fleming, The Labor Arbitration Process 144–53 (Univ. of Ill. Press 1965).

[32]National Educ. Ass'n, 86 LA 592 (Wahl, 1985); Florida Power Corp., 86 LA 59 (Bell, 1986); Federal Bureau of Prisons, 82 LA 950 (Kanzer, 1984).

[33]Commonwealth of Pa., 86 LA 978 (Kreitler, 1986).

[34]*See* Southern Minn. Sugar Coop., 90 LA 243 (Flagler, 1987); Keebler Co., 86 LA 963 (Nolan, 1986); Florida Power Corp., 86 LA 59 (Bell, 1986).

[35]*See* Stone Container Corp., 91 LA 1186 (Ross, 1988); National Labor Relations Bd., 76 LA 450, 456 (Gentile, 1981); Bethlehem Steel Corp., 50 LA 1214, 1214 (Seward, 1968); Swift & Co., 17 LA 537, 540 (Seward, 1951). *Cf.* U.S. Army Safety Ctr., 75 LA 238, 240 (Dallas, 1980); Standard Oil Co. of Cal., 54 LA 677, 680 (Koven, 1971).

[36]Texas Utils. Elec. Co., 90 LA 625 (Allen, Jr., 1988). Conversely, an employer was not allowed to add a ground for discharge at the hearing. Pittsburgh Press Club, 89 LA 826 (Stoltenberg, 1987).

[37]Kliklok Corp., 102 LA 183, 185 (Frost, 1993). Arbitration proceeded, however, where the employer "was not in fact in the dark or uninformed as to what [the] grievance was all about at the time it came to arbitration." Black, Sivalls, & Bryson, 42 LA 988, 991 (Abernethy, 1964). *But see* International Paper Co., 108 LA 758, 764–65 (Nicholas, Jr., 1997) (union prevailed on the merits but was denied consequential damages because they were not requested in the grievance as required by the collective bargaining agreement).

may remand the case so that the parties may consider and attempt to resolve the issue.[38]

D. Simultaneous Arbitration of Several Grievances
[LA CDI 93.07; 94.602; 100.0710]

There are times when one party wants to arbitrate several grievances before the same arbitrator in one proceeding and the other party objects. The question of whether grievances are to be resolved in one or separate proceedings is decided by the arbitrator.[39] Arbitration of grievances reaching arbitration at the same time can be compelled by either party unless the contract clearly and unambiguously provides otherwise.[40] Many arbitrators have expressly considered and rejected the contention that a different result is required if the term "grievance," rather than "grievances," is in the contract.[41]

Arbitration of multiple grievances has been denied where the contract provides otherwise and there is a past practice of arbitrating only one grievance at a time.[42] Circumstances may justify other exceptions to the rule, as where there are individual grievances involving widely separated plants, with separate contracts and witnesses in different locations; an inordinately large number of grievances; or grievances requiring an arbitrator with specialized knowledge.[43] Arbitration of multiple grievances may not be required if "it is clearly shown that to do so would result in confusion, prejudice or substantial detriment to either party."[44] Once an arbitrator has been selected,

---

[38]Lyondell Petrochemical Co. Div., 89 LA 95 (Caraway, 1987).

[39]Avon Prods. v. Auto Workers Local 710, 386 F.2d 651, 67 LRRM 2001 (8th Cir. 1967); Machinists Dist. 10 v. Dings Co., 36 F. Supp. 2d 857, 161 LRRM 2741 (E.D. Wis. 1999); American Can Co. v. Paperworkers Local 412, 356 F. Supp. 495, 82 LRRM 3055, 3057 (E.D. Pa. 1973) (citing other cases in accord). Cf. Oil, Chem. & Atomic Workers Local 2-477 v. Continental Oil Co., 524 F.2d 1048, 90 LRRM 3040, 3040–42 (10th Cir. 1975).

[40]See Ben Franklin Transit, 91 LA 880 (Boedecker, 1988); American Metal Climax, 53 LA 239, 244–45 (Dworkin, 1969); Continental Oil Co., 51 LA 1001, 1004–05 (Traynor, 1968); American Brake Shoe Co., 41 LA 1017, 1019–20 (Jaffe, 1963); Standard Oil Co., 32 LA 442, 444 (Fleming, 1959). But see National Distillers & Chem. Corp., 85 LA 622 (Caraway, 1985) (arbitrator had jurisdiction over only one of four grievances because contract language did not authorize consolidation of grievances).

[41]All of the arbitrators of the cases listed in the previous note were confronted with this contention and all rejected it. See also Electrical Workers (IBEW) Local 2188 v. Western Elec. Co., 661 F.2d 514, 108 LRRM 3027, 3028 (5th Cir. 1981).

[42]See Day & Zimmermann, 51 LA 215, 220 (Marshall, 1968); Remington Rand Univac, 42 LA 65, 66–67 (Lockhart, 1964); Anaconda Am. Brass Co., 39 LA 814, 819–20 (Turkus, 1962).

[43]American Brake Shoe Co., 41 LA 1017, 1019–20 (Jaffe, 1963). These exceptions have been recognized by Chamberlain Corp., 49 LA 355, 356 (Duff, 1967) (backlog of 52 cases); Harshaw Chem. Co., 44 LA 97, 101 (Seinsheimer, 1965) (nature of cases might require different arbitrators); Fairchild Engine & Airplane Corp., 7 LA 112, 112–13 (Taylor, 1947) (simultaneous arbitration of grievances under separate contracts not required).

[44]American Metal Climax, 53 LA 239, 244 (Dworkin, 1969). In Appalachian Power Co., 53 LA 1012, 1013 (Reid, 1969), the arbitrator would hear only one of four grievances where the other three had not been processed in accordance with the agreement and the employer was not prepared to go forward.

a party may not submit additional grievances without the arbitrator's consent and agreement by the other party.[45]

E. Bilateral Arbitration of Trilateral Conflicts [LA CDI 94.155]

Some grievances involve the conflicting interests of employees represented by different unions. Often, the dispute is about work assignments.[46] Resolution of such trilateral conflicts can be facilitated by consolidating the claims in one arbitration proceeding, but it is not uncommon for one of the unions to reject that proposal.[47]

In *Carey v. Westinghouse Electric Corp.*,[48] the Supreme Court required the employer to arbitrate a work assignment jurisdictional dispute on demand by only one of the unions. The Court said:

> To be sure, only one of the two unions involved in the controversy has moved the state courts to compel arbitration. So unless the other union intervenes, an adjudication of the arbiter might not put an end to the dispute. Yet the arbitration may as a practical matter end the controversy or put into movement forces that will resolve it.[49]

Where only one of two affected unions is a party to a pending arbitration proceeding, arbitrators are in disagreement as to whether the arbitrator may invite the second union to participate in the proceeding against the wishes of the union that filed the grievance.[50] The efforts of the second union to inter-

---

[45]AAA Rule 7 provides: "After the arbitrator is appointed, no new or different claim may be submitted except with the consent of the arbitrator and all other parties." *But see* Sylvania Elec. Prods., 24 LA 199, 201–05, 210 (Brecht, 1954) (under AAA Rule 7, grievances filed at the start of the arbitration hearing were accepted against the objection of one party where they added no new issue, arose from the same action as the grievance specifically identified in the demand for arbitration, and were fully anticipated in that demand).

[46]Conflicting seniority interests were involved in *American Sterilizer Co. v. Auto Workers Local 832*, 278 F. Supp. 637, 67 LRRM 2894 (W.D. Pa. 1968). *See also* Associated Brewing Co., 40 LA 680, 682–83 (Kahn, 1963) (trilateral arbitration of a seniority dispute).

[47]*See, e.g.*, Longshoremens (ILA) Local 1351 v. Sea-Land Serv., 214 F.3d 566, 164 LRRM 2525 (5th Cir. 2000) (refusing to order tripartite arbitration, due to one party's reliance on a final judgment involving only two of the parties); U.S. Postal Serv. v. Rural Letter Carriers, 959 F.2d 283 (D.C. Cir. 1992) (compelling tripartite arbitration to avoid duplication of efforts and possibility of conflicting awards); Retail, Wholesale & Dep't Store Union Local 390 v. Kroger Co., 927 F.2d 275, 136 LRRM 2776 (6th Cir. 1991); Industrial Workers (UIW) v. Kroger Co., 900 F.2d 944, 134 LRRM 2076 (6th Cir. 1990) (refusing to order tripartite arbitration when one union had no part in selecting arbitrator); Drywall Tapers & Painters of Greater N.Y. Local 1974 v. Plasterers Local 530, 889 F.2d 389, 132 LRRM 2805 (2d Cir. 1989) (injunction barring a union from performing work that arbitrator had determined to be within jurisdiction of another union was sufficiently clear to furnish a basis for a contempt order).

[48]375 U.S. 261, 55 LRRM 2042 (1964). *See also In re* Marine Eng'rs Dist. 1, Pac. Coast Dist., 723 F.2d 70, 79, 114 LRRM 3431, 3436 (D.C. Cir. 1983) ("If the Supreme Court in *Carey* was willing to *compel* arbitration even though one of the contesting unions might not be a party before the arbitrator, it was an abuse of discretion for the District Court to *enjoin* an arbitration merely because of the presence of such a risk.") (emphasis in original).

[49]*Carey*, 375 U.S. at 265. *See also* NLRB v. Plasterers & Cement Masons Local 79 (Southwestern Constr. Co.), 404 U.S. 116, 134, 78 LRRM 2897 (1971) (the employer has a right to participate in National Labor Relations Board (NLRB) proceedings to determine jurisdictional disputes under §10(k) of the National Labor Relations Act (NLRA)).

[50]Holding that the arbitrator has no authority to extend an invitation to the second union, see *General Dynamics Corp.*, 51 LA 902, 903–05 (Helbling, 1968); *Lockheed-California Co.*, 46 LA 865, 868–70 (Block, 1966); *Thorsen Mfg. Co.*, 44 LA 1049, 1052 (Koven, 1965);

vene in the pending arbitration have also produced varied results.[51] Where the union that initiated the arbitration does not oppose a trilateral proceeding, arbitrators have differed as to whether the arbitrator should compel the absent union to participate.[52]

Jurisdictional disputes may be resolved by the National Labor Relations Board (NLRB) in a proceeding under Section 10(k) of the National Labor Relations Act (NLRA)[53] with an award of the work to one of the unions.[54] "Before the Board may proceed with the determination of a dispute pursuant to Section 10(k) of the Act [NLRA], it must be satisfied that (1) there is a reasonable cause to believe that Section 8(b)(4)(D) has been violated and (2) the parties have not agreed upon a method for the voluntary adjustment of the dispute."[55]

In the special circumstances of one trilateral conflict,[56] the consolidation of pending but separate arbitration proceedings into a trilateral proceeding was required under Section 301 of the Labor Management Relations Act (LMRA).[57] Because each of the two unions had a bilateral arbitration pending with the employer, and the arbitration clause in each of the two contracts was sufficiently broad to permit the employer to submit disputes to arbitration, the employer's motion to consolidate the two proceedings was granted in order to avoid duplication of effort and the possibility of conflicting awards.[58] However, when an employer failed to seek a court order com-

---

Philco Corp., 42 LA 604, 606 (Lazarus, 1963). Other arbitrators have extended the invitation. *See* Lockheed-California Co., 49 LA 981, 985–87 (Jones, 1967); Mayfair Mkts., 42 LA 14, 21–24 (Jones, Jr., 1964). Even when only one union is before an arbitrator, the arbitrator may examine and comment on the second union's agreement with the employer and suggest how the two agreements may be reconciled. *See, e.g.,* Walter S. Johnson Bldg. Co., 75 LA 543, 547–48 (Denson, 1980).

[51]*See* Sinclair-Koppers Co., 52 LA 648, 651–52 (Leonard, 1969); Stardust Hotel, 50 LA 1186, 1188 (Jones, Jr., 1968).

[52]*Compare* E.R. Wagner Co., 43 LA 210, 211–12 (Fleming, 1964), *with* National Steel & Shipbuilding Co., 40 LA 625, 630–31 (Jones, Jr., 1963), *and* National Steel & Shipbuilding Co., 40 LA 838, 840–42 (Jones, Jr., 1963). *See also* Jones, *On Nudging and Shoving the National Steel Arbitration Into a Dubious Procedure*, 79 Harv. L. Rev. 327 (1965); Bernstein, *Nudging and Shoving All Parties to a Jurisdictional Dispute Into Arbitration: The Dubious Procedure of* National Steel, 78 Harv. L. Rev. 784 (1965). In *Borg-Warner Corp.*, 54 LA 24, 28–30 (Sembower, 1969), the arbitrator directed the complaining union to arrange with the other union a schedule for hearing the work-assignment dispute.

[53]29 U.S.C. §151 et seq.

[54]Auto Workers v. Rockwell Int'l Corp., 619 F.2d 580, 104 LRRM 2050, 2052 (6th Cir. 1980) (NLRB award controlled over a prior conflicting arbitration award and the employer was not liable for failing to comply with the award).

[55]Mine Workers Local 1269 (Ritchey Trucking), 241 NLRB 231, 232, 100 LRRM 1496, 1497 (1979). For cases dealing with conflicts between the NLRB determination and arbitration awards with regard to jurisdictional disputes between unions, see *T. Equip. Corp. v. Massachusetts Laborers' Dist. Council*, 166 F.3d 11, 160 LRRM 2257 (1st Cir. 1999); *Sea-Land Serv. v. Longshoremen (ILWU) Local 13*, 939 F.2d 866, 138 LRRM 2057 (9th Cir. 1991); *Laborers Dist. Council (N. Cal.) (W.B. Skinner, Inc.)*, 292 NLRB 1038, 130 LRRM 1259 (1989).

[56]Columbia Broad. Sys. v. American Recording & Broad. Ass'n, 414 F.2d 1326, 72 LRRM 2140 (2d Cir. 1969).

[57]29 U.S.C. §141 et seq.

[58]In *Emery Air Freight Corp. v. Teamsters Local 295,* 185 F.3d 85, 161 LRRM 2993 (2d Cir. 1999), the district court refused the employer's request for an order requiring trilateral arbitration because (1) the two union locals' arbitration procedures were incompatible, and neither local had agreed to follow the other's procedure; (2) no court intervention was necessary to "keep the peace" because both locals' agreements had no-strike clauses; and (3) it was

pelling trilateral arbitration until it became subject to conflicting arbitration awards under separate agreements with two unions, the request was too late.[59]

Under the Railway Labor Act (RLA),[60] the Supreme Court has held that when a union brings a work assignment jurisdictional dispute, the National Railroad Adjustment Board must dispose of the entire dispute by joining the other union in the proceedings and by considering the contracts and practices of both unions.[61] Arbitrators have concluded that special boards established under the 1966 amendments to the RLA similarly must act to dispose of the entire matter in jurisdictional dispute cases.[62]

F. Representatives in Arbitration

Each party has the right to be represented in arbitration proceedings by persons of its own choosing.[63] The choice of representative will vary according to the circumstances and needs of the party and the case. There will be times when the person who was the advocate during the steps of the internal grievance procedure will be chosen to present the case, but there will be occasions when other union or company representatives, or especially their counsel, will present the case. The grievant should not represent himself or herself or share that function with the union's representative.[64]

One or both of the parties may be represented by attorneys.[65] If there is a conflict between two grievants who cannot be represented by a single attorney, each of them, as well as the union, with the consent of the parties, may have separate representation in the separate arbitration of their cases,

---

possible one union local's arbitration would produce a result that did not conflict with the other local's arbitration. But in other cases the employer was not held to conflicting arbitration awards, and trilateral arbitration was ordered. Retail, Wholesale & Dep't Store Union Local 390 v. Kroger Co., 927 F.2d 275, 276, 136 LRRM 2776 (6th Cir. 1991); Machinists Local 850 v. T.I.M.E.-DC, Inc., 705 F.2d 1275, 113 LRRM 2677 (10th Cir. 1983). Trilateral arbitration has been ordered between one union and two employers. *See* Steelworkers v. Crane Co., 456 F. Supp. 385 (W.D. Pa. 1978).

[59]Louisiana-Pacific Corp. v. Electrical Workers (IBEW) Local 2294, 600 F.2d 219, 102 LRRM 2070, 2074–75 (9th Cir. 1979) (initially, the employer should have contracted with each union for tripartite arbitration of jurisdictional disputes, or should have sought a possible court order for such arbitration before arbitrating separately with either of the unions).

[60]45 U.S.C. §151 et seq.

[61]Transportation Communications Union v. Union Pac. R.R., 385 U.S. 157, 63 LRRM 2481 (1966).

[62]Western Pac. R.R., 50 LA 1013, 1015–17 (Wyckoff, 1968); Southern Pac. Co., 49 LA 1052, 1054–58 (Mann, 1967).

[63]*See also* Ogden Servs. Corp., 107 LA 696, 698–99 (Lipson, 1996) (the right of grievants to be represented by persons of their own choosing included the right to choose a union representative in arbitrating a dispute with a nonunion employer).

[64]For a convincing demonstration that this limitation should be observed, see *Western Union Int'l*, 70 LA 285, 285–86 (Turkus, 1978).

[65]Some arbitration statutes expressly state that either party has a right to be represented by an attorney and that waivers of this right are subject to limitations stated in the statute. AAA Rule 20 states: "Any party may be represented by counsel or other authorized representative." For discussions of attorney advocates in arbitration, see Garrett, *The Role of Lawyers in Arbitration, in* Arbitration and Public Policy, Proceedings of the 14th Annual Meeting of NAA 102 (Pollard ed., BNA Books 1961), *summarized in Current Problems of Arbitration*, 35 LA 963, 966 (1961); Aaron, *Some Procedural Problems in Arbitration*, 10 Vand. L. Rev. 733, 748 (1957).

even though the bargaining agreement declares the union to be the sole collective bargaining representative.[66] In some situations, the parties may agree not to use attorneys, as is the practice in some industries or in expedited arbitrations. A union ordinarily does not breach its duty of fair representation merely because it uses a union representative rather than an attorney to represent the grievant at the arbitration hearing.[67]

G. Prehearing Conferences

A prehearing conference with the arbitrator and representatives of the parties may be scheduled to decide on hearing procedures or clarify the issues to be considered.

Section 4.1.a.–b. of the Code of Professional Ethics provides:

> a. The primary purpose of prehearing discussions involving the arbitrator is to obtain agreement on procedural matters so that the hearing can proceed without unnecessary obstacles. If differences of opinion should arise during such discussions and, particularly, if such differences appear to impinge on substantive matters, the circumstances will suggest whether the matter can be resolved informally or may require a prehearing conference or, more rarely, a formal preliminary hearing. When an administrative agency handles some or all aspects of the arrangements prior to a hearing, the arbitrator will become involved only if differences of some substance arise.
>
> b. Copies of any prehearing correspondence between the arbitrator and either party must be made available to both parties.

H. Preparing Cases for Arbitration

The arbitrator's comprehension of a case depends on the evidence and arguments presented at the arbitration hearing. An advocate must understand the case in order to communicate it effectively to the arbitrator, and full understanding depends on thorough preparation.[68]

In some cases, the facts are especially important and each party will concentrate on proving, usually through testimony, but occasionally through economic and statistical data, that the facts are as that party sees them. Where the dispute is about the interpretation of a contract provision, the

---

[66]General Mills, 92 LA 969 (Dworkin, 1989).

[67]Baxter v. Paperworkers Local 7370, 140 F.3d 745, 747, 157 LRRM 2852 (8th Cir. 1998); Bruno v. Steelworkers, 983 F.2d 1065 (6th Cir. 1993); Galindo v. Stoody Co., 793 F.2d 1502, 123 LRRM 2705 (9th Cir. 1986); Valentin v. U.S. Postal Serv., 787 F.2d 748, 751, 122 LRRM 2033 (1st Cir. 1986); Camacho v. Ritz-Carlton Water Tower, 786 F.2d 242, 121 LRRM 2801 (7th Cir. 1986); Del Casal v. Eastern Airlines, 634 F.2d 295, 301, 106 LRRM 2276 (5th Cir. 1981); Walden v. Teamsters Local 71, 468 F.2d 196, 81 LRRM 2608 (4th Cir. 1972); Mullen v. Bevona, 162 LRRM 2856 (S.D.N.Y. 1999); Lettis v. U.S. Postal Serv., 39 F. Supp. 2d 181 (E.D.N.Y. 1998); Barton v. Transportation Communications Union, 25 F. Supp. 2d 790, 159 LRRM 2935 (E.D. Mich. 1998); Vance v. Lobdell-Emery Mfg. Co., 932 F. Supp. 1130, 153 LRRM 2331 (S.D. Ind. 1996); Dirring v. Lombard Bros., 619 F. Supp. 911 (D. Mass. 1989).

[68]For a practitioner's guide, see MAUET, FUNDAMENTALS OF PRE-TRIAL TECHNIQUES (Aspen 4th ed. 1999); MAUET, FUNDAMENTALS OF TRIAL ADVOCACY (Aspen 5th ed. 1999). For other discussions relating to case preparation, see BAER, WINNING IN LABOR ARBITRATION ch. 6 (1982); KAGEL, ANATOMY OF A LABOR ARBITRATION 48–65 (BNA Books 2d ed. 1986).

facts may be less important or undisputed. The following checklist offers
guidelines that may be helpful in preparing to present a case:

1. Review the history of the case.
2. Study the contract to find the clauses bearing directly or indirectly
   on the dispute. Comparing current provisions with those contained
   in prior agreements might reveal changes significant to the case.
3. Examine the instruments used to initiate the arbitration to determine the general authority of the arbitrator and the scope of the
   arbitration.
4. Talk to all persons who might be able to aid development of a full
   picture of the case, including those with different viewpoints and
   those whom the other party might use as witnesses. You will better
   understand your own case, as well as your opponent's; if you can
   anticipate your opponent's case, you can better prepare to rebut it.
5. Interview each of your witnesses to determine what they know about
   the case, make certain they understand how their testimony relates
   to the case, and cross-examine them to check their testimony and
   acquaint them with the process of cross-examination.[69]
6. Make a written summary of the expected testimony of each witness,
   to be reviewed as the witness testifies so that no important points
   are overlooked. Some advocates outline in advance the questions to
   be asked each witness.
7. Examine all records and documents that might be relevant to the
   case. Organize those you expect to use and make copies for use by
   the arbitrator, the other advocate, and the reporter if one is used. If
   necessary documents are in the exclusive possession of the other
   party, ask that they be made available before or at the hearing.

---

[69]Concerning the need for such prearbitration interviews and their general propriety
and benefits to the arbitration process, one arbitrator has stated:

   It is almost routine for [an advocate] to go to the locale of a pending arbitration a
day or two before a scheduled hearing in order to interview witnesses and plan the
details of the morrow's presentation. It is not at all unusual for that pre-hearing occasion to be the first time that the advocate has had the chance to get first-hand accounts
of witnesses, to identify possible discrepancies among their accounts, to press them as a
cross-examiner is apt to, to observe their demeanor and evaluate their credibility, to
assess the potential influence on the course of the hearing of what they have to say and
how they are apt to say it in the context of the hearing. . . .
   . . . [This is] an important part of the administration of the grievance procedure. It
is by no means unusual for cases to be settled on the day—or even the hour—before the
hearing is to convene based on the advocate's last-minute, eye-opened assessment of the
significance of these prehearing contacts.
   Of course, this otherwise proper investigative pre-hearing procedure may be converted to an improper one if the advocate or a colleague with authority somehow acts
improperly in a material way in the course of it. The parameters of legitimate inquiry
are set by the employment relationship. Job-related conduct of the employee and fellow
workers is within the area of the permissible, whereas prying into subjects of a personal
nature or concerning conduct that is not job-related is foreclosed. Nor is there any license to conduct interviews in a manner coercive or demeaning to the employee.
Pacific Southwest Airline, 70 LA 205, 213 (Jones, Jr., 1978).

8. Visit the physical premises involved in the dispute to visualize what occurred and what the dispute is about. Also, consider asking at the hearing that the arbitrator visit the site, accompanied by both parties.

9. Consider using pictorial or statistical exhibits, if they will be helpful in illustrating your point.

10. Determine past practice in comparable situations.

11. In interpretation cases, prepare a written argument to support your view as to the proper interpretation of the disputed language.

12. In "interest" or "contract writing" cases, collect and prepare economic and statistical data to aid evaluation of the facts.

13. Research the parties' prior arbitration awards and the published awards of other parties on the subject of the dispute to see how similar issues have been approached in other cases.

14. Prepare an outline of your case and discuss it with other persons in your group. You will have a better understanding of the case, strengthen it by uncovering matters that need further attention, and underscore important policy and strategy considerations. Use the outline at the hearing to organize your presentation.

I. Stipulations of Fact

An agreement on facts can expedite the hearing by reducing the number of witnesses and allowing the parties and the arbitrator to concentrate on disputed issues. The parties may come to the hearing with a fact stipulation or enter into one at the hearing.[70] The arbitrator may suggest that the parties attempt to stipulate to facts and may recess the hearing to permit the parties to determine whether they can do so.[71]

J. Withdrawing Grievances From Arbitration [LA CDI 93.53; 100.0740]

A grievance usually may be withdrawn before the hearing begins. Once the hearing has begun, it may not be withdrawn over the objection of the other party unless permitted by the arbitrator.[72] Often, the matter of with-

---

[70]*See* Magma Copper Co., 83 LA 281 (Kelliher, 1984); Central Greyhound Lines, 46 LA 1078, 1078–79 (McCoy, 1966); Burgermeister Brewing Corp., 44 LA 1028, 1029–30 (Updegraff, 1965); Associated Gen. Contractors, 38 LA 500, 502 (Kagel, 1962). Advocates should exercise care when entering into stipulations. *See, e.g.*, Pan Am World Servs., 91 LA 806, 809 (Bickner, 1988) (arbitrator did not permit employer to withdraw from a stipulation of fact).

[71]Inland Container Corp., 28 LA 312, 312 (Ferguson, 1957). Section 5.A.1.b. of the Code of Professional Responsibility states: "An arbitrator may: encourage stipulations of fact . . . ."

[72]For court decisions holding that the complainant may not withdraw from arbitration proceedings, see *Old Dutch Farms v. Milk Drivers & Dairy Employees Local 584*, 222 F. Supp. 125, 54 LRRM 2387 (E.D.N.Y. 1963). In *United Aircraft Corp. v. Machinists, Canel Lodge 700*, 77 LRRM 3167 (D. Conn. 1971), the court ordered arbitration at the employer's request, where the union had requested arbitration but then attempted to withdraw the case "without prejudice." For similar views, see also *Denver Pub. Sch.*, 88 LA 507, 510 (Watkins, 1986) (the arbitrator has authority to rule on the employer's or union's right to withdraw grievance from arbitration because he or she has authority to rule on any procedural issues raised in connection with the hearing of a grievance). In *Harry S. Truman Mem'l Veterans Hosp.*, 74 LA 1021, 1022 (Hoffmeister, 1980), the union was not permitted to withdraw its

drawal will be covered in the collective bargaining agreement. Such provisions are fairly common, generally permitting withdrawal only by mutual consent of the parties. Withdrawal may also be covered by federal or state statute.

Grievances may be withdrawn for a number of reasons. For example, a union was allowed to withdraw a grievance without prejudice before it was considered by the arbitrator because it learned that the disputed action had not taken place.[73] Another union was permitted to withdraw its grievance after the hearing where it offered to do so "with prejudice," the arbitrator considering such withdrawal to be equivalent to a decision on the merits against the withdrawing party.[74] However, an arbitrator has held that an employee's withdrawal of a grievance after a second-step meeting was res judicata and prevented an examination of the same issue later in the arbitration of a new grievance.[75]

K. Arbitrator's Charges When Case Is Canceled
[LA CDI 94.65; 100.0780]

A former general counsel of the FMCS once observed, "A real problem for arbitrators today is the cancellation of a case after he has been selected and a date for hearing set."[76] While emphasizing that efforts by the parties to settle cases "should be seriously pursued right up to the time set for the hearing," he recognized that "many cases are scheduled for arbitration with little expectation that they will actually be heard. . . . This situation, which . . . places a great burden on labor arbitrators, all of whom have scheduling problems just like we do, is recognized in our regulations."[77]

The *Code of Professional Responsibility* provides that arbitrators should establish in advance "the basis for charges, if any, for . . . postponement or cancellation of hearings by the parties and the circumstances in which such

---

grievance after it had joined the employer in selecting an arbitrator. *Procedural Problems in the Conduct of Arbitration Hearings: A Discussion, in* LABOR ARBITRATION: PERSPECTIVES AND PROBLEMS, PROCEEDINGS OF THE 17TH ANNUAL MEETING OF NAA 1, 22–23 (Kahn ed., BNA Books 1964).

[73]Princeton Worsted Mills, 25 LA 587, 588 (Hill, 1955); Hess Oil & Chem. Corp., 51 LA 445, 448 (Gould, 1968) (demand for arbitration could be resubmitted after having been withdrawn where all contractual time limits were still met and the contract did not provide for withdrawal and resubmission of grievances). *Cf.* City of New Smyrna Beach, Fla., 83 LA 1086, 1091 (Alsher, 1984).

[74]Loewenthal, Walker & Heimberg, 72 LA 578, 580 (Ables, 1979).

[75]Hawks Nest Mining Co., 92 LA 414 (Volz, 1989).

[76]Richard P. McLaughlin, *Cost, Time, Training Factors in Labor Arbitration*, 70 LRR 428, 430, (address of Apr. 8, 1969, originally entitled *Labor Arbitration Today*).

[77]*Id.* Under FMCS Arbitration Policies and Procedures, as revised in 2002, arbitrators are permitted to "charge a per diem and other predetermined fees for services, if the amount of such fees have been provided in advance to FMCS." Specific information regarding "[e]ach arbitrator's maximum per diem and other fees are set forth on a biographical sketch which is sent to the parties when panels are submitted." FMCS Regulations, 29 C.F.R. §1404.15(a). Section 1404.15(b) provides that: "In cases involving unusual amounts of time and expenses relative to the pre-hearing and post-hearing administration of a particular case, an administrative charge may be made by the arbitrator."

charges will normally be assessed or waived."[78] In many cases, the arbitrator bills the parties if the hearing is canceled after a hearing date has been set.

4. THE ARBITRATION HEARING

A. Time, Place, and Notice of Hearing [LA CDI 94.45]

There is no fixed rule for setting the date and location of an arbitration hearing.[79] The arbitrator, if available, will ordinarily meet at the time and place agreed to by the parties. If the parties cannot agree, the arbitrator or the administering agency will decide.[80] The arbitrator should always act to ensure adequate notice to the parties.[81] If one of the parties refuses to cooperate in choosing a date for the arbitration hearing after having had sufficient opportunity, the arbitrator must proceed without unnecessary delay to avoid subverting the arbitral process.[82]

The hearing room is selected by the parties or an administering agency. Frequently, some "neutral ground" such as a hotel suite is used; this may minimize interruptions that sometimes occur when the hearing is held at the plant. Other parties prefer to use a conference room at the company because this may reduce costs, will make records and witnesses more quickly available, and will require less time for any visit by the arbitrator to the site of the dispute. A conference table arrangement (with the arbitrator at the head of the table) is most satisfactory if there are not too many participants. A "courtroom" arrangement tends to be more formal, but it may be preferred if there are numerous participants. It is best if the hearing room is well lighted and ventilated.

The parties should anticipate whether special accommodations will be required for persons attending the hearing. These might include access, seating arrangements, or sign or foreign language interpreters. Unless otherwise agreed, the party requiring the accommodation arranges and pays for it.[83]

---

[78]Section 2.K.1.b.1.d. *See* Kahn, *Matter of Nomenclature: Call them "Scheduling Fees,"* AAA STUDY TIME (1990), at 6; Berkeley & Jewett, *When Arbitrators Lose Cases: The Case for a Docketing Fee*, AAA STUDY TIME No. 3, at 2 (1989).

[79]Under some arbitration statutes, the time and place for the hearing are fixed by the arbitrator, who may also be responsible for giving timely notice.

[80]For one agency's rules relating to these matters, see AAA Rules 10 and 19. For factors considered by one arbitrator in specifying the location of the hearing pursuant to request by the parties when they could not agree on location, see *Immigration & Naturalization Serv.*, 76 LA 180, 184 (Rule, 1981). Regarding insistence on the location for arbitration hearings and its relation to the duty to bargain under the NLRA, see *Indiana Bell Tel. Co.*, 252 NLRB 544, 105 LRRM 1325 (1980). The city where the hearing was to be held was the subject of arbitration when the language of the agreement was susceptible to conflicting interpretations. Highgate Pictures, 90 LA 485 (Gentile, 1988).

[81]For actions taken to assure due process to a grievant who did not receive notice of the arbitration hearing, see *Eaton Corp.*, 73 LA 403, 404–05 (Howlett, 1979).

[82]Shop 'n Save Warehouse Foods, 86 LA 1098 (Cohen, 1986).

[83]For example, AAA Rule 21 provides, "Any party wishing an interpreter shall make all arrangements directly with the interpreter and shall assume the costs of the service."

B. Attendance at Hearings

An arbitration hearing usually is not open to the public, even in the public sector, although some public-sector interest arbitration hearings are open by statute.[84] The arbitrator may require witnesses, except parties to the case, to leave the hearing room during the testimony of other witnesses,[85] so they will not be influenced by their testimony.[86] All persons having a direct interest in the case ordinarily are entitled to attend the hearing.[87] Others may attend by agreement of the parties or with permission of the arbitrator.[88] In some recent cases, absence of the grievant was not fatal to the hearing when the grievant was adequately and fairly represented by a union official.[89] In another case, where the record sustained proof of a "sensitive" issue, an arbitrator held that a witness need not appear if the witness would be subject to a humiliating cross-examination.[90]

An employer may be adversely affected if too many employees miss work to attend an arbitration hearing. In one case, employees were held entitled to "excused absences" from their jobs while attending a hearing as potential

---

[84]*But see, e.g.*, Deerfield, Wis., Cmty. Sch. Dist., 93 LA 316 (Michelstetter, 1988).

[85]*See* Northern States Power Co., 86 LA 1088 (Boyer, 1986); Douglas Aircraft Co., 28 LA 198, 203–04 (Jones, Jr., 1957). A survey of its members by the National Academy of Arbitrators (NAA) revealed that many would grant motions for exclusion of witnesses from the hearing in disciplinary cases, but few would exclude the grievant. *Procedural Problems During Hearings*, The Chronicle (NAA), Apr. 1981, at 6. In *Economy Forms Corp.*, 45 LA 430, 432 (Bauder, 1965), it was held that where the arbitration concerns discipline against several employees, all of them are entitled to hear all of the testimony. Even where the contract expressly provided for exclusion of witnesses except when testifying, the discharged employee's presence at the hearing could not be limited. International Smelting & Ref. Co., 45 LA 885, 886 (Kornblum, 1965).

[86]An arbitrator's failure to exclude witnesses as requested by a party does not render the award vulnerable, because it is for the arbitrator to determine the credibility of witnesses. *See* Transport Workers Local 234 v. Philadelphia Transp. Co., 283 F. Supp. 597, 68 LRRM 2094 (E.D. Pa. 1968). In *Anderson Concrete Corp.*, 103 LA 433, 438 (Kindig, 1994), the arbitrator's order that witnesses be sequestered required only that they be absent from the hearing room during the testimony of other witnesses.

[87]For example, AAA Rule 22 expressly provides that "[p]ersons having a direct interest in the arbitration are entitled to attend hearings."

[88]Section 2.C.1.a. of the Code of Professional Responsibility states:

    Attendance at hearings by persons not representing the parties or invited by either or both of them should be permitted only when the parties agree or when an applicable law requires or permits. Occasionally, special circumstances may require that an arbitrator rule on such matters as attendance and degree of participation of counsel selected by a grievant.

AAA Rule 22 states that "[i]t shall be discretionary with the arbitrator to determine the propriety of the attendance of any other person." For rulings on attendance questions, see *Grand Ledge Bd. of Educ.*, 76 LA 81, 85–86 (McDonald, 1980) (applicability of open meeting statute to grievance meetings conducted by school board); *Bell Helicopter Textron*, 72 LA 490, 493–94 (Moore, 1979) (attendance by the attorney of a nonemployee witness against whom grievant had filed civil suit*); Internal Revenue Serv.*, 71 LA 359, 361 (Belcher, 1978) (attendance by grievant's wife and children). In *Los Angeles Unified School District*, 76 LA 804, 808 (Christopher, 1981), a grievance was dismissed because the grievant gave information to the news media in violation of a nondisclosure agreement.

[89]Texas Utils. Mining Co., 87 LA 815 (Allen, Jr., 1986); American Inks, 87 LA 691 (DiLauro, 1986).

[90]Veterans Admin. Med. Ctr., 87 LA 405 (Yarowsky, 1986).

witnesses, but not if they attended merely as observers.[91] An unnecessary party also may properly be denied paid leave from the job to attend a hearing on an issue that involves the entire bargaining unit.[92]

C. Continuances

Arbitrators may, at their discretion, grant continuances or adjourn the hearing on their own motion or joint request of the parties,[93] or on the application of one party for good cause.[94] Failing to grant a continuance for good cause may make the proceedings vulnerable to court challenge.[95]

Not infrequently, continuances are requested because witnesses are absent. In such instances, a continuance ordinarily will be granted, though opposed by the other party, if the arbitrator is convinced that the request for a continuance was made in good faith and that the absence of the witness was not the fault of the requesting party.[96] The claim of surprise and inability to meet an unforeseen issue also may be reason to grant a continuance.[97]

After the hearing has begun, if a party requests a continuance because material witnesses or evidence are absent, an arbitrator may refuse the request except on a statement or affidavit showing that the moving party diligently tried to produce the evidence and believes it to be true, as well that the evidence can be made available and there is the probability of producing it within a reasonable time. An arbitrator may refuse to grant the request where the participants are numerous and have traveled long distances to attend the hearing or where it would otherwise be difficult to arrange a satisfactory time for reconvening the hearing. The opposing party may accept the evidentiary facts alleged in the statement or affidavit as having been proven for purposes of the case. The parties also may agree that the evidence will be submitted within a certain time, with the opposing party being given

---

[91]Monterey Coal Co., 79 LA 1107, 1111–12 (1982).

[92]Social Sec. Admin., 87 LA 434 (Hoh, 1986).

[93]"Courts typically uphold arbitrators' refusals to grant postponements in grievance and interest arbitration proceedings. The moving party must show good cause initially and prejudice ultimately, with the reviewing court deferentially construing doubts in favor of the arbitrator's judgment." Zirkel & Winebrake, *Legal Boundaries for Partiality and Misconduct of Labor Arbitrators*, 1992 Det. Coll. L. Rev. 679, 697–98 (1992) (citations omitted). *See, e.g.,* Schmidt v. Finberg, 942 F.2d, 1571 (11th Cir. 1991); Boston Celtics v. Shaw, 908 F.2d 1041 (1st Cir. 1990); Roche v. Service Employees Local 32B-32J, 755 F. Supp. 622, 140 LRRM 3056 (S.D.N.Y. 1991).

[94]AAA Rule 23 provides: "The arbitrator for good cause shown may postpone the hearing upon the request of a party or upon his or her own initiative and shall postpone when all of the parties agree thereto." The Code of Professional Responsibility does not expressly mention granting or denying continuances requested by one party.

[95]If arbitration proceedings "are to have dignity and command respect, then no party to a dispute can be allowed to decide when, where and how the hearings are to be conducted." Textile Workers v. Upholsterers, 24 LA 529, 531 (Cole, 1955). *See also* Ping v. National Educ. Ass'n, 870 F.2d 1369, 131 LRRM 2082 (7th Cir. 1989); Allendale Nursing Home v. Joint Bd. Local 1115, 377 F. Supp. 1208, 87 LRRM 2498 (S.D.N.Y. 1974); Florida Staff Org., 91 LA 1094 (Mase, 1988).

[96]*See, e.g.,* Bethlehem Steel, 17 LA 676, 677 (Shipman, 1951).

[97]Consolidation Coal Co., 92 LA 813 (Seidman, 1989); Lyondell Petrochemical Co. Div., 89 LA 95 (Caraway, 1987).

an opportunity to reply. If the agreement specifies time limits within which action must be taken, no continuance should be granted that would over-reach the deadline unless it is extended by the parties.

D. Bifurcation of Arbitrability and Merits

Where there is a question as to arbitrability, one or both of the parties may wish to wait for a ruling before proceeding on the merits. The question of whether to bifurcate the hearing is for the arbitrator to decide, unless the contract provides otherwise. It is generally more efficient to hear the case in full, because the arbitrator can still decide the question of arbitrability first.

E. Split Hearings and Interim or Partial Awards

In some cases, the arbitrator may hear and rule on some aspects of the case before others.[98] The arbitrator may also decide some issues, refer others to the parties for further negotiations, and retain jurisdiction to decide the deferred issues should negotiations fail.[99] If an arbitrator determines after the hearing that additional information is necessary in order to reach a decision, the case might be returned to the parties for additional factfinding or other action to produce the needed information.[100] In such cases, the arbitra-

---

[98]Where an alleged contract violation, if established, would have involved possible losses by numerous employees whose individual factual situations were not identical, it was agreed that a decision on the proper interpretation of the contract would be reached "before taking further testimony upon the detailed rights and possible losses of each individual employee . . . because of the length of time which seemed likely to be consumed in testimony upon the individual situations . . . ." Fruehauf Trailer Co., 19 LA 159, 160 (Spaulding, 1952). *See also* Pittsburgh Bd. of Pub. Educ., 85 LA 816 (Bolte, 1985); Publishers' Ass'n of New York City, 66-1 ARB ¶8284 (Turkus, 1966). In *American Totalisator Co.*, 74 LA 377, 388 (Gentile, 1980), a default award was issued stating that the union violated the agreement and calling for another hearing to determine damages.

[99]*See* Clow Water Sys. Corp., 93 LA 83 (Miller, 1989); Springfield, Ill., Sch. Dist. 186, 91 LA 1293 (Malin, 1988); Pacific Southwest Airlines, 88 LA 639 (Williams, 1986); Tri-State Asphalt Corp., 72 LA 102, 109 (LeWinter, 1979); National Broad. Co., 71 LA 762, 771 (Gentile, 1978); Swartz Creek, Mich., Cmty. Sch., 70 LA 1185, 1189 (Lipson, 1978); Vulcan Mold & Iron Co., 52 LA 396, 403 (Kates, 1969); Bethlehem Mines Corp., 50 LA 33, 35 (Porter, 1967); Hillbro Newspaper Printing Co., 48 LA 1304, 1305 (Jones, Jr., 1967); Goodyear Tire & Rubber Co., 44 LA 1212, 1215 (Begley, 1965); United States Steel Corp., 44 LA 168, 174–75 (Garrett, 1965); Bethlehem Steel Co., 38 LA 1166, 1170 (Valtin, 1962); Weyerhaeuser Co., 37 LA 323, 330 (Dworkin, 1961).

[100]*See* Service Employees, 91 LA 530 (Weiler, 1987); East Ohio Gas Co., 91 LA 366 (Dworkin, 1988); City of Crystal, Minn., 89 LA 531 (Bard, 1987); Times Journal Publ'g Co., 75 LA 939, 940 (Williams, 1980) (grievance held arbitrable but hearing on the merits postponed pending conclusion of related court proceeding); Max Factor & Co., 73 LA 742, 745 (Jones, Jr., 1979) (interim award directed the parties to seek a federal agency ruling on a relevant aspect of the case, the hearing being continued pending the results of that effort); Babcock & Wilcox Co., 72 LA 1073, 1075 (Mullin, Jr., 1979) (grievant to undergo psychiatric examination, and the case to be returned to arbitrator if parties cannot then agree on final disposition); United States Steel Corp., 53 LA 40, 44 (Garrett, 1969); Publishers' Ass'n of New York City, 36 LA 86, 91 (Seitz, 1960). The arbitrator may also deny the grievance without prejudice. *See* Jones & Laughlin Steel Corp., 23 LA 33, 37 (Cahn, 1954). *Cf.* AP Parts Co. v. Auto Workers, 923 F.2d 488, 136 LRRM 2288 (6th Cir. 1991) (award vacated where arbitrator remanded for negotiation an issue already negotiated).

tor may issue an interim award, and issue a supplemental or final award to dispose of the later phase.[101]

F. Transcript of Hearing

A formal written record of the hearing is not always necessary, and the taking of a transcript is the less frequent practice.[102] Whether the expense and additional time involved in use of a transcript are justified depends on the case.[103] In simple cases, the arbitrator can take adequate notes, and, in contract interpretation cases, where facts are undisputed, the arbitrator's notes and the parties' evidence and statements ordinarily make a transcript unnecessary. However, in complicated or lengthy cases, a transcript will help the parties prepare their briefs, as well as help the arbitrator study the case.[104] The transcript may be valuable in a court review of the arbitration proceedings, although less than 1 percent of private-sector awards are appealed.[105]

---

[101]*See* Westvaco, 91 LA 707 (Nolan, 1988); Highland Park, Mich., Pub. Sch., 90 LA 984 (Borland, 1985); General Tel. Co. of Cal., 77 LA 1021, 1024 (Bickner, 1981); Greyhound Lines, 53 LA 464, 470 (Lennard, 1969).

Interim or partial awards have been challenged under state law where they were not authorized by the parties. UPDEGRAFF, ARBITRATION AND LABOR RELATIONS 280–81 (BNA Books 1970). *But see* American Fed'n of Teachers Local 1147 v. Scranton Sch. Dist., 444 A.2d 1144, 113 LRRM 3296, 3300 (Pa. 1982) (nothing in the collective bargaining agreement or applicable statute prohibited the procedure that had been followed, and judicial disfavor of bifurcated proceedings was insufficient to overturn the arbitrator's decision). *See also* Public Safety Dep't, Alaska v. Public Safety Employees Ass'n, 732 P.2d 1090, 125 LRRM 2116 (Alaska 1987).

For cases under federal law, see *Public Serv. Elec. & Gas Co. v. Electrical Workers (IBEW) System Council U-2*, 703 F.2d 68, 112 LRRM 3333 (3d Cir. 1983) (where the parties agreed to hold separate hearings on the merits and the remedy; a finding against the company on the merits was not a final order nor subject to court review before the hearing had been held on the remedy); *Ladies' Garment Workers (ILGWU) Local 246 v. Evans Mfg. Co.*, 318 F.2d 528, 53 LRRM 2455, 40 LA 864 (3d Cir. 1963) (an arbitrator may issue an interim award without agreement by both parties).

[102]The FMCS reports that of the 2,669 FMCS "award cases" in the 2002 fiscal year, transcripts were taken in 931, and no transcript was taken in the remaining 1,738 cases. FMCS, *Federal Mediation and Conciliation Service Arbitration Statistics Fiscal Year 2002, available at* <http://admin.fmcs.gov/assets/files/Arbitration/2002arbstatistics/2002Averages.doc> (last modified Oct. 8, 2002). But "[m]ost [federal-sector] agreements make some provision for transcripts of the arbitration proceedings." A SURVEY OF NEGOTIATED GRIEVANCE PROCEDURES AND ARBITRATION IN FEDERAL POST CIVIL SERVICE REFORM ACT AGREEMENTS 50 (Office of Personnel Management 1980).

[103]One arbitrator said, "In almost all cases the arbitrator will not need a transcript of the hearing." Murphy, *The Ten Commandments for Advocates: How Advocates Can Improve the Labor Arbitration Process, in* ARBITRATION 1992: IMPROVING ARBITRAL AND ADVOCACY SKILLS, PROCEEDINGS OF THE 45TH ANNUAL MEETING OF NAA 253, 261 (Gruenberg ed., BNA Books 1993).

[104]In public-sector arbitration hearings, or in cases under judicial review, the transcript might become a matter of public record and subject sensitive testimony to public scrutiny.

[105]Sharpe, *Judicial Review of Labor Arbitration Awards: A View From the Bench, in* ARBITRATION 1999: QUO VADIS? THE FUTURE OF ARBITRATION AND COLLECTIVE BARGAINING, PROCEEDINGS OF THE 52D ANNUAL MEETING OF NAA 126, 141, 154–55 (Grenig & Briggs eds., BNA Books 2000).

The *Code of Professional Responsibility* and the AAA Rules set forth guidelines for the use of transcripts.[106] Ordinarily, any party is entitled to have a reporter present to record the proceedings.[107]

A party is not required to order or contribute to the cost of the transcript, but may be given access to the transcript if it is being provided to the arbitrator.[108] It is rare for disputes about transcripts to reach arbitration,

---

[106]Section 5.B. of the CODE OF PROFESSIONAL RESPONSIBILITY provides:

B. Transcripts or Recordings
1. Mutual agreement of the parties as to use or non-use of a transcript must be respected by the arbitrator.
   a. A transcript is the official record of a hearing only when both parties agree to a transcript or an applicable law or regulation so provides.
   b. An arbitrator may seek to persuade the parties to avoid use of a transcript, or to use a transcript if the nature of the case appears to require one. However, if an arbitrator intends to make appointment to a case contingent on mutual agreement to a transcript, that requirement must be made known to both parties prior to appointment.
   c. If the parties do not agree to a transcript, an arbitrator may permit one party to take a transcript at its own cost. The arbitrator may also make appropriate arrangements under which the other party may have access to a copy, if a copy is provided to the arbitrator.
   d. Without prior approval, an arbitrator may seek to use a personal tape recorder to supplement note taking. The arbitrator should not insist on such a tape recording if either or both parties object.

The AAA Rules provide:
21. Stenographic Record and Interpreters
Any party wishing a stenographic record shall make arrangements directly with a stenographer and shall notify the other parties of such arrangements in advance of the hearing. The requesting party or parties shall pay the cost of the record. If the transcript is agreed by the parties to be or, in appropriate cases, determined by the arbitrator to be the official record of the proceeding, it must be made available to the arbitrator and to the other party for inspection, at a time and place determined by the arbitrator.

[107]*See* Maremont Corp., 71 LA 333, 333–34 (Coven, 1978), (the union's objection to the presence of a reporter was overruled). In *Chicago Cartage Co. v. Teamsters Local 710*, 659 F.2d 825, 829, 108 LRRM 2567, 2569–70 (7th Cir. 1981), a hearing by a grievance committee composed only of union and company members was considered "analogous to a collective bargaining session," and a party accordingly had no right to have the hearing recorded.

[108]*See* Brown, *Pre-Hearing Processes—Old and New: I. Pre-Hearing Procedures: We Make the Process What It Is, in* ARBITRATION 1996: AT THE CROSSROADS, PROCEEDINGS OF THE 49TH ANNUAL MEETING OF NAA 94, 97 (Najita ed., BNA Books 1997); Grovner v. Georgia-Pacific Corp., 625 F.2d 1289, 105 LRRM 2706 (5th Cir. 1980) (duty of fair representation not breached where the union did not order a transcript); Electrical Workers (IUE) Local 1000 v. Markle Mfg. Co., 94 LRRM 2766 (W.D. Tex. 1975), *aff'd*, 536 F.2d 388, 94 LRRM 2781 (5th Cir. 1976).

A survey of NAA members found arbitrators to be divided on access to the transcript by a nonpaying party, where the party objected to having the transcript made: 116 arbitrators would place no restrictions or conditions on recording a transcript; 78 members would allow the transcript to be made only if the union were given access; 5 members would sustain the union's objection; 4 members would permit the company to have a transcript made for its purposes, but use their notes as the official record; 1 member would not take a case if the parties would not provide a transcript of the proceedings; and 1 member would require the union to share the cost. *Procedural Problems During Hearings*, THE CHRONICLE (NAA), Apr. 1981, at 1.

When asked directly if they would allow the Union access to the transcript, 49 members responded that they would not do so. The remaining members would permit the union to have access to the transcript, but often under some limitation; that is, only if the transcript is used in the arbitrator's office, in the offices of the Company, etc. However, 19 members would not permit the Union to use the transcript if the Company objected to the procedure.

Id.

which may indicate that parties generally reach a mutually acceptable understanding on transcript use and costs. Equal sharing of the transcript cost remains the most common practice, with each party paying for extra copies it orders. Where an employer alone requested a transcript of the proceedings, the employer bore the full cost, although the arbitrator asked for a courtesy copy and required that the copy be made available to the union if the transcript were to be the official record.[109] In some instances the collective bargaining agreement provides the method for determining which party pays for transcripts.[110]

One way to lessen expenses is to simply record the proceedings.[111] The hearing may be recorded with the understanding that if the arbitrator needs part or all of the record, it will be transcribed.[112] Some arbitrators themselves record the entire proceedings on tape, in addition to taking notes, where no official reporter was being used.[113] Arbitrators generally will allow a party to tape-record the arbitration hearing over the other party's objection in the absence of any contract provision barring the practice, where the tapes are not part of the record and duplicates are made available to the objecting party.

The transcript generally consists of the evidence and statements of the parties. Other information to be included is the names of the parties; the date, time, and place of the hearing; the name of the arbitrator or arbitrators, name of the chair of an arbitration, and the manner of designation; appearances for the parties; any stipulations of fact; and the name of the reporter. If there is a special agreement, submission, or stipulation for arbitration, it should be identified and included in the record.

The arbitrator or parties may go off the record for comment or discussion that is not material to the record, or for matters on which the advocates do not wish to be committed. After discussion, any such matter or understanding may be put in the record. Delay and errors can be avoided if parties

---

[109]Department of Agriculture, 93 LA 920, 928–29 (Seidman, 1989). *See also* Nuturn Corp., 84 LA 1058, 1060 (Seidman, 1985) (employer bore full cost of transcript when union said it would be satisfied with its own tape recording of hearing). For cases involving disputes over payment of transcript costs, see *Furry Mach.*, 89 LA 739 (Goldstein, 1987); *General Tel. Co. of Southwest*, 79 LA 102, 103 (Holman, 1982); *ITT Cont'l Baking Co.*, 75 LA 764, 770 (Flagler, 1980).

[110]*See, e.g.*, City of Joliet, Ill., 88 LA 303, 310 (Hill, 1986) (contract provided that "fee and expenses of the arbitrator and the cost of a written transcript shall be borne solely by the party against whom the arbitrator rules"); City of Reno, Nev., 87 LA 707 (Richman, 1986) (contract provided that arbitrator was to determine payment of costs of reporter and transcript).

[111]Moog Indus., 15 LA 676, 677 (Klamon, 1950). *See also* Henry Vogt Mach. Co., 49 LA 1115, 1115 (Gibson, 1968); Lockheed Aircraft Serv. Co., 44 LA 51, 52 (Roberts, 1965). Such a record probably will not be accepted by the arbitrator as an official record unless both parties agree. *See Procedural Problems in the Conduct of Arbitration Hearings: A Discussion, in* LABOR ARBITRATION: PERSEPCTIVES AND PROBLEMS, PROCEEDINGS OF THE 17TH ANNUAL MEETING OF NAA 1, 31 (Kahn ed., BNA Books 1964).

[112]American Potash & Chem. Corp., 17 LA 364, 370 (Grant, 1951).

[113]Mobil Oil Co., 46 LA 140, 140 (Hebert, 1966). Also tape-recording the proceedings, see *Kisco Co.*, 75 LA 574, 585 (Stix, 1980); *John Morrell & Co.*, 74 LA 756, 758 (Stokes, 1980); *Ward Lafrance Truck Corp.*, 69 LA 831, 834 (Levy, 1977) (arbitrator refused to make the tape recording available to either party after the union objected to the company's request for a copy); *Ormet Corp.*, 68 LA 559, 562 (Taylor, 1977).

who intend to read or quote lengthy passages at the hearing furnish extra copies for use by the reporter.

G. Hearing Procedures

i. Oaths of Arbitrator and Witnesses

An arbitrator's oath is not required at common law and can be waived by the parties even where it is required by statute.[114]

The AAA Rules reflect general practice concerning the arbitrator's oath of office and the swearing of witnesses:

> Before proceeding with the first hearing, each arbitrator may take an oath of office and, if required by law, shall do so. The arbitrator may require witnesses to testify under oath administered by any duly qualified person and, if required by law or requested by either party, shall do so.[115]

When an arbitrator takes the oath of office, he or she swears faithfully and fully to hear and examine the matters in controversy and make a just award according to the best of his or her understanding. At some appointing agencies, the oath of office is written into the instrument of appointment and is affirmed by the arbitrator by signing the instrument in accepting the case.

Where witnesses are to be placed under oath, each may be sworn individually immediately before testifying, or all persons scheduled to testify may be sworn at the start of the hearing. The arbitrator, reporter, or hearing clerk asks if the witness solemnly swears or affirms that the testimony he or she is about to give in the case is "the truth, the whole truth, and nothing but the truth." The witness, with right hand raised, answers, "I do."[116]

ii. Manner of Presentation

Civility is the standard at any arbitration hearing. Witnesses and opposing counsel should be treated with courtesy and respect. Witnesses "are not to be subjected to argumentative or demeaning conduct by counsel nor is their prior testimony to be misrepresented in cross-examination . . . [B]adgering or belittling a witness . . . is contrary to good practice. Such behavior can also lose the respect of the arbitrator."[117]

---

[114]Even without an express waiver, one will be implied by participating in the hearing without objection. Robinson v. Navajo Freight Lines, 372 P.2d 801, 38 LA 321, 49 LRRM 3048 (N.M. 1962).

[115]AAA Rule 24. The Code of Professional Responsibility does not address this matter.

[116]In *Aristocrat Travel Products*, 52 LA 314, 316–17 (Koven, 1968), an employee could be discharged for giving perjured testimony in a prior case involving the earlier discharge of the employee. For related discussion, see Tidwell, *The Effects of Perjury Committed at an Arbitration Hearing*, 38 Arb. J. No. 3, at 44 (1983).

[117]Kagel, *Practice and Procedure, in* The Common Law of the Workplace 24 (St. Antoine ed., BNA Books 1998).

iii. Order of Presenting Case

Generally speaking, the party asserting a claim presents its case first. This order is usually reversed in discipline cases, because the company has the burden of proving wrongdoing by the employee.[118] In other types of cases, such as promotion, transfer, and contracting-out, the facts may be developed in a more orderly way if the employer presents its case first, because it is in possession of the necessary information. Nevertheless, the union still has the burden of proof in these cases.[119]

Arbitrators differ on whether to allow the grievant in a discipline case to be called as a witness by the employer.[119a] Some arbitrators believe that the employer must prove its case with evidence other than the grievant's testimony. A survey by the NAA found that a large majority of the responding members would permit the company to call a union member as its first witness in the discharge case over the union's objection, and a somewhat smaller majority would permit the company to call the grievant. Most of the responding members said if they did not permit the company to call a union member as its first witness, they would allow a supervisor to testify as to what the member told him concerning the discharge incident.[120]

After the parties have presented their cases, they may present rebuttal evidence. The hearing will not be adjourned until each party has nothing further to add.[121]

---

[118]AAA Rule 26 provides:

The Arbitrator may vary the normal procedure under which the initiating party first presents its claim, but in any case shall afford full and equal opportunity to all parties for the presentation of relevant proofs.

[119]*See* Rohm & Haas Tex., 91 LA 339 (McDermott, 1988); Bethlehem Steel Corp., 91 LA 293 (McDermott, 1988). *See also* Douglas Aircraft Co., 28 LA 198, 202–03 (Jones, Jr., 1957); Armstrong Cork Co., 18 LA 651, 651 (Pigors, 1952). *But see* Latrobe Steel Co., 38 LA 729, 734 (Wood, 1962); Sealtest Dairy Prods. Co., 35 LA 205, 208–09 (Morvant, 1960).

[119a]*See* Chapter 8, section 4.G., "Use of Adverse Witnesses."

[120]*Procedural Problems During Hearings*, The Chronicle (NAA), Apr. 1981, at 1, 6. "154 members would overrule the objection and only 19 would sustain it. Another 50 members were ambivalent." *Id.* Many of those who would overrule the objection explained that "arbitration is a civil matter and either side may call as a witness anyone they please." As to the grievant, "63 members would sustain the Union's objection if the grievant were called as the first witness, 115 would overrule the objection, and 44 would rule according to the circumstances. Those who refuse to permit the grievant (or a Union member in some cases) to be called as the first witness reason, primarily, that the Company has the obligation to establish at least a *prima facie* case through its own witnesses." *Id.* Recent discussion of this issue in the NAA's "Maillist" reflects continued division among arbitrators. *Heard on the E-Street*, The Chronicle (NAA), Oct. 2002, at 14. Several arbitrators expressed discomfort with the practice but, ultimately, would allow it. One noted that "I find that the tactic is usually used by incompetent but aggressive management lawyers." *Id.* Many arbitrators have concluded that the issue turns on perception of the arbitrator's role—"whether the arbitrator sits to decide whether management acted correctly on the basis of what it knew at the time it imposed discipline, or rather to decide *de novo* the employee's guilt or innocence." *Id.*

[121]In *Harvey Aluminum v. Steelworkers*, 263 F. Supp. 488, 64 LRRM 2580 (D. Cal. 1967), an award was vacated because of the arbitrator's refusal to consider certain testimony on the grounds that it should have been presented as part of the employer's case-in-chief and was not proper rebuttal; the employer had the right to assume that the arbitrator would permit the presentation of all material evidence before closing the hearing.

iv. Opening Statements and Closing Arguments

An opening statement is a brief and general outline of what the dispute is about and what the advocate intends to prove.[122] Even if the advocate prepares a written opening statement, it should be presented orally.

Closing arguments are brief statements of the parties' arguments and the evidence they have presented to support them. The arbitrator will always permit the parties to make closing arguments, though possibly limiting the amount of time, and will sometimes request specifically that they do so. Closing arguments and post-hearing briefs sometimes serve much the same purpose. While the parties sometimes choose to use both, they more frequently choose to use one or the other.

v. Examining Witnesses [LA CDI 94.60519]

The manner in which witnesses are examined may promote or impede a party's case and will affect the character of the arbitration proceeding generally. In this regard, an excellent guide was offered:

> 19. Prove your case by your own witnesses. Do not try to establish it by evidence gleaned from people put on the stand by your opponent. They are there to oppose you, not help you.
> 20. If you cross-examine the other parties' witnesses, *make it short*. Do not unduly prolong cross-examination in attempts to get damaging admissions. The more questions you ask on cross-examination, the more opportunity you give a hostile witness to repeat the adverse testimony he came to give. Choose most carefully the inquiries you make of such parties. Make them as few as possible.
> 21. Each party has the right to ask leading questions [so worded as to suggest an answer] when cross-examining hostile witnesses. Each party should save time by asking its own witnesses leading questions, excepting at points where disputed facts are involved. Testimony on controverted matters should be brought out by questions which do not suggest the answer, if possible.[123]

It is sometimes better on direct examination to ask the witness to tell the story in his or her own way, without questioning, although this is not advisable when examining adverse witnesses.

---

[122]For more extensive comment as to what might be included in opening statements, see Mauet, Fundamentals of Trial Advocacy (Aspen 5th ed. 1999); Bornstein, *The Opening Statement in Arbitration Advocacy: An Arbitrator's Perspective*, 38 Arb. J. No. 1, at 49 (1983); Roberts & Dash, *How to Get Better Results From Labor-Management Arbitration*, 22 Arb. J. 1, 3, 8–9 (1967).

[123]Updegraff, *Preparation for Arbitration*, 22 LA 889, 890 (1954) (emphasis in original). *See also* Friedman, *Problems of Cross-Examination in Labor Arbitration*, 34 Arb. J. No. 4, at 6 (1979), *commented on by* Kaufman, *Cross-Examination*, 35 Arb. J. No. 1, at 3 (1980); Stauffer Chem. Co., 85 LA 889 (Brisco, 1985) (cross-examination of witness not mandatory).

vi. Exhibits

Some evidence may be presented and preserved in written form as exhibits. Each party may submit its own exhibits and the parties may also submit exhibits jointly.[124]

To offer an exhibit as evidence, the advocate should use a witness to identify the exhibit and demonstrate its authenticity and accuracy, in the event the other party does not accept the exhibit for what it is purported to be. An exhibit is introduced into evidence at the point in the hearing where it is relevant, and exhibits should be identified and marked as they are introduced into evidence.[125] Advocates should bring to the hearing copies of each exhibit for each party, for the arbitrator, and for the reporter.

vii. Objections to Evidence [LA CDI 94.60505; 100.0775]

Each party is entitled to object when it believes the other party is seeking to introduce improper evidence or argument at the arbitration hearing.[125a] Such objections, when based on some plausible grounds, can serve a useful function even if overruled, for the arbitrator will have been cautioned to examine the challenged evidence or argument more closely before giving it weight. A party also is entitled to object to evidence considered irrelevant, for the record should not be burdened with a mass of material having little or no bearing on the issue. Objections that are repetitious or have no plausible basis should be avoided.[126]

viii. Participation by the Arbitrator in the Hearing

Arbitrators should be informed as fully as possible about the disputes they are to resolve. Accordingly, they may participate in the hearing by asking questions and seeking information to the extent reasonably necessary.[127]

---

[124]Parties should "put as much of the evidence as possible in black and white, as simply and plainly and logically as possible," because visible evidence "is often far more persuasive than evidence which one hears and may forget." Jaffee, *Need for Exhibits in Labor Arbitration*, 15 ARB. J. 203, 205 (1960).

[125]Exhibits are identified and marked in numerical or alphabetical order of introduction. A separate series is used for each party, as well as for joint exhibits. The first exhibit submitted by the company would be identified as Company Ex. #1, the next as Company Ex. #2, and so on. The union's exhibits would be identified as Union Ex. #1, and so on.

[125a]*See* Chapter 8, section 8., "Admissibility."

[126] "Do not make captious, whimsical or unnecessary objections to testimony or arguments of the other party. Such interruptions are likely to waste time and confuse issues. The arbitrator, no doubt, will realize without having the matter expressly mentioned more than once, when he is hearing weak testimony such as hearsay and immaterial statements." Updegraff, 22 LA at 890. *See also* KAGEL, ANATOMY OF A LABOR ARBITRATION 91 (BNA Books 2d ed. 1986); Alleyne, *Delawyering Labor Arbitration*, 50 OHIO ST. L.J. 93 (1989).

[127]Section 5.A.1.b. of the CODE OF PROFESSIONAL RESPONSIBILITY states that: "An arbitrator may . . . restate the substance of issues or arguments to promote or verify understanding; question the parties' representatives or witnesses, when necessary or advisable, to obtain additional pertinent information; and request that the parties submit additional evidence, either at the hearing or by subsequent filing."

The arbitrator "should be satisfied that he knows enough to be able to decide" the case and "cannot simply sit back and judge a debate. He must seek to inform himself as fully as possible and encourage the parties to provide him with the information."[128] However, an arbitrator must not be so active as to risk "taking the case away from the parties, appearing to one side or the other as becoming counsel for their adversary."[129] Arbitrators disagree about whether it is appropriate to study the entire collective bargaining agreement so that all relevant provisions have been considered.[130] The views of 17 arbitrators who replied to the question of whether "the arbitrator is justified in making a totally independent study of the contract" were summarized by the AAA as follows:

> Most of those replying indicated either that arbitrators were not justified in doing so or that they should do so only upon request of the parties or when they have given the parties an opportunity to respond to the arbitrator's findings. Several people cited the danger that clauses may have meanings for the parties that are not apparent to an outsider. One arbitrator said, however, that in some instances he would automatically review the contract, while two others indicated that when a provision in dispute was ambiguous, they would examine the entire contract to determine the interest or intent of the parties.[131]

[128]Shulman, *Reason, Contract, and Law in Labor Relations*, 68 Harv. L. Rev. 999, 1017–18 (1955), *reprinted in* Management Rights and the Arbitration Process, Proceedings of the 9th Annual Meeting of NAA 160, 190, 191 (McKelvey ed., BNA Books 1957). An arbitrator who does not take the initiative where necessary to adequately explore relevant aspects at the hearing may later feel some regret for not having done so. *See* Halstead Metal Prods., 49 LA 325, 331 (Wagner, 1967). *See also* Brown & Gentile, *Point-Counterpoint: The Arbitrator as Activist?*, The Chronicle (NAA), Sept. 1992, at 7; Flagler, *Appendix D: Modern Shamanism and Other Folderol—The Search for Certainty, in* Arbitration 1986: Current and Expanding Roles, Proceedings of the 39th Annual Meeting of NAA 187 (Gershenfeld ed., BNA Books 1987). For examples of how an arbitrator might participate in the interrogation of a witness, see *United States Steel Corp.*, 94 LA 1109 (McDaniel, 1990); *Johnson Controls*, 84 LA 659 (Imundo, Jr., 1985); *Allied Chem. Corp.*, 49 LA 773, 778–80 (Davey, 1967); *Booth Newspapers*, 43 LA 785, 789–90 (Platt, 1964).
[129]Kagel, *Practice and Procedure, in* The Common Law of the Workplace 26 (St. Antoine ed., BNA Books 1998), adding that "[m]ost arbitrators would not take offense at counsel's pointing out that the arbitrator's questioning of a witness is premature or unnecessary, if it is, and that counsel will be getting to that subject with this witness or with another." *Id. See also* Section 5.A.1.c. of the Code of Professional Responsibility: "An arbitrator should not intrude into a party's presentation so as to prevent that party from putting forward its case fairly and adequately"; Dunsford, *The Presidential Address: The Adversary System in Arbitration, in* Arbitration 1985: Law and Practice, Proceedings of the 38th Annual Meeting of NAA 1 (Gershenfeld ed., BNA Books, 1986); Seitz, *Some Observations on the Role of an Arbitrator*, 34 Arb. J. No. 3, at 3, 6–7 (1979).
[130]*See* Butler County, Ohio, Dep't of Human Servs., 93 LA 294 (Van Pelt, 1989); Pacific Towboat & Salvage Co., 88 LA 907 (Perone, 1987); ASG Indus., 68 LA 304, 309–10 (Elkouri, 1977) (the arbitrator's evaluation may be aided significantly by examining the agreement to determine the presence or absence of express provisions relating to a relevant aspect of the case). *See also* Perma Line Corp. of Am. v. Painters Local 230, 639 F.2d 890, 106 LRRM 2483, 2486 (2d Cir. 1981). *But see* Crane, *The Use and Abuse of Arbitral Power, in* Labor Arbitration at the Quarter-Century Mark, Proceedings of the 25th Annual Meeting of NAA 66, 71–72 (Dennis & Somers eds., BNA Books 1973) (disapproving of independent studies).
[131]AAA Study Time, Apr. 1978, at 3.

ix. Site Visits

The arbitrator's understanding of the case may be improved by visiting the physical site involved in the dispute. In some types of cases, such as job evaluation, a plant tour is virtually indispensable.[132] Either the parties or the arbitrator may suggest the visit.[133]

x. Settlements at Arbitration Stage

Disputes may be settled by the parties after the grievance has reached arbitration. Some disputes are settled before the hearing takes place, and possibilities of settlement may be even stronger after the hearing has begun, because the parties sometimes see the dispute in a new light. It is not unusual for the hearing to disclose an underlying misunderstanding that may have blocked an earlier settlement or uncover new thoughts, new facts, and occasionally new areas of agreement that provide real opportunities for constructive settlements.[134]

Parties and their arbitrators should not ignore possibilities for settlement. There are several methods to facilitate negotiation. The hearing may be recessed for direct negotiations at the request of the parties or at the arbitrator's suggestion, if accepted by the parties. The hearing may be closed with the understanding that the award will be delayed pending negotiations by the parties for a specified time, with an award to be issued only if no settlement is reached. It may be agreed that the arbitrator will rule or comment on some aspects of the case in an interim decision, with unresolved matters to be decided by the arbitrator only if negotiations fail.

Whatever procedure is used, it should be undertaken only with the agreement of the parties. If they show no interest in an arbitrator's suggestion for further negotiations, the arbitrator should not attempt to force acceptance.

At any point in the arbitration process, one or both of the parties may invite the arbitrator to mediate. Whether or not the arbitrator mediates the

---

[132]For the practical significance of seeing the job in its setting, see *Amana Refrigeration*, 89 LA 751 (Bowers, 1987); *Quaker Oats Co.*, 84 LA 1085 (Newmark, 1985); *Ryland Ford*, 83 LA 195 (Jacobowski, 1984); *Quaker Oats Co.*, 69 LA 727, 731 (Hunter, Jr., 1977); *Warren Wire Co.*, 47 LA 577, 579 (Rubin, 1966); *Pearl Brewing Co.*, 42 LA 145, 148 (Bothwell, 1964); *American Steel & Wire Co.*, 16 LA 264, 266 (Forrester, 1951).

[133]Section 5.D.1.a of the Code of Professional Responsibility provides:

1. An arbitrator should comply with a request of any party that the arbitrator visit a work area pertinent to the dispute prior to, during, or after a hearing. An arbitrator may also initiate such a request.

a. Procedures for such visits should be agreed to by the parties in consultation with the arbitrator.

The arbitrator has discretionary authority to make plant visits in cases governed by AAA Rule 30. Inspection, which provides: "Whenever the arbitrator deems it necessary, he or she may make an inspection in connection with the subject matter of the dispute after written notice to the parties, who may, if they so desire, be present at such inspection."

[134]Platt, *The Chrysler-UAW Umpire System: Comment, in* The Arbitrator and the Parties, Proceedings of the 11th Annual Meeting of NAA 141, 144 (McKelvey ed., BNA Books 1958). *See* Shearer, *Reducing the Costs of Arbitration Through Increasing the Parties' Options*, 40 Arb. J. No. 2, at 74 (June 1985) (suggesting that arbitrators use procedures that give the parties an opportunity to settle at the beginning and end of the hearing).

dispute absent a contractual requirement depends on agreement of the parties and the arbitrator.[135] It has been suggested that mediation of grievances at arbitration hearings undermines the lower steps of the grievance procedure and could create the appearance of impropriety if mediation fails and the case has to be adjudicated.[136] However, the prevailing opinion was stated by Robert Coulson, a former President of the AAA:

> The arbitrator is free to suggest settlement or, in appropriate cases, to attempt to mediate. The Code of Professional Responsibility is flexible in this regard. Few labor awards are challenged because a labor arbitrator has attempted to mediate. In practice, a "bionic neutral" frequently sets the parties upon the road toward settlement.[137]

Ordinarily, the arbitrator does not participate in settlement negotiations.

5. Post-Hearing Issues

A. Post-Hearing Briefs

The use of post-hearing briefs is quite common.[138] Their purpose is to summarize and comment on evidence and present legal argument.[139] No new evidence should be included in post-hearing briefs;[140] expanded discussion and interpretation of the agreement and citation and discussion of prece-

---

[135]Section 2.F.2.a.–c. of the Code of Professional Responsibility provides that:

    a. Once arbitration has been invoked, either party normally has a right to insist that the process be continued to decision.

    b. If one party requests that the arbitrator mediate and the other party objects, the arbitrator should decline the request.

    c. An arbitrator is not precluded from suggesting mediation. To avoid the possibility of improper pressure, the arbitrator should not so suggest unless it can be discerned that both parties are likely to be receptive. In any event, the arbitrator's suggestion should not be pursued unless both parties readily agree.

See Kagel, *Mediating Grievances, in* Arbitration 1993: Arbitration and the Changing World of Work, Proceedings of the 46th Annual Meeting of NAA 76 (Gruenberg ed., BNA Books 1994); House, *Management Perspective, id.,* at 89; Ish, *Comment, id.* at 96.

[136]Smith Meter Inc., 86 LA 1009 (Creo, 1986).

[137]Coulson, *Certification and Training of Labor Arbitrators: Should Arbitrators Be Certified? Dead Horse Rides Again, in* Arbitration—1977, Proceedings of the 30th Annual Meeting of NAA 173, 182 (Dennis & Somers eds., BNA Books 1978).

[138]FMCS Fiscal Year 2002 statistics show that briefs were filed in 2,186 cases and not filed in 483 cases, a filing rate of 82%. *See* Helburn, *What Arbitrators Need From the Parties: III. The End Is Near: A Note on Effective Closure, in* Arbitration 1977: The Next Fifty Years, Proceedings of the 50th Annual Meeting of NAA 272 (Najita ed., BNA Books 1998).

[139]For discussion of the advantages and disadvantages of using briefs, see *Helburn,* NAA 50th Proceedings. For additional discussion of briefs, see Sharpe, *Advocates Must Write Effective Briefs,* 50 Disp. Resol. J. No. 1, at 63 (1995); Ray, *On Writing the Post-Hearing Arbitration Brief,* 47 Arb. J. No. 4, at 58 (Dec. 1992); Bornstein, *To Argue, To Brief, Neither or Both: Strategic Choices in Arbitration Advocacy,* 41 Arb. J. No. 1, at 77 (1986).

[140]*See* Swanton Local Sch., 93 LA 498 (Bittel, 1989); Texas Utils. Elec. Co., 90 LA 625 (Allen, Jr., 1988); St. Louis Paint Mfg. Co., 88 LA 1251 (Penfield, 1987). Matters that were first mentioned in a party's post-hearing brief and that were not related to any proofs submitted at the hearing were not considered in *Tibbetts Plumbing-Heating Co.,* 46 LA 124, 126 (Stouffer, 1966). *See also* Daniel Int'l Corp., 71 LA 903, 908 (Bernstein, 1978); American S.S. Co., 44 LA 530, 537 (Keefe, 1965).

dents and articles should be provided. Occasionally, arbitrators find it necessary to confer with the parties or call them together for additional hearing when some point of critical importance develops as a result of filing briefs. Arbitrators also have issued awards without considering post-hearing briefs.[141]

A stipulation as to the type of briefs to be submitted, if any, will be enforced by the arbitrator unless modified by mutual agreement. The *Code of Professional Responsibility* so provides, but otherwise recognizes that the arbitrator has considerable discretion concerning briefs.[142]

If there is no agreement, the arbitrator usually will accept and consider the brief of either party. A party wishing to file a post-hearing brief should give notice at the hearing; once the hearing is closed, the arbitrator may be more reluctant to accept a brief filed over the opposition of the other party.

A deadline for filing can be stipulated or set by the arbitrator. A common arrangement is for both parties to mail briefs simultaneously on a specified date to the arbitrator, who is then responsible for the exchange. Alternatively, both parties may submit their briefs to the arbitrator and to the other party.

If either party fails to submit a brief within the specified time, the arbitrator may proceed to decide the case, especially if there is no request for an extension of time.[143] The arbitrator may grant an extension for reasonable cause,[144] and many arbitrators are inclined to consider a brief even if it is submitted late.[145]

---

[141]In *Glass Bottle Blowers Local 139 v. Anchor Hocking Corp.*, 361 F. Supp. 514, 84 LRRM 3000 (W.D. Pa. 1973), an award was enforced even though it was issued before the timely filing of the union's brief, the court finding that the brief added nothing to the positions of the parties in the transcript.

[142]Section 6.A.1.a.–b. of the CODE OF PROFESSIONAL RESPONSIBILITY provides:

1. An arbitrator must comply with mutual agreements in respect to the filing or nonfiling of post hearing briefs or submissions.

a. An arbitrator may either suggest the filing of post hearing briefs or other submissions or suggest that none be filed.

b. When the parties disagree as to the need for briefs, an arbitrator may permit filing but may determine a reasonable time limitation.

2. An arbitrator must not consider a post hearing brief or submission that has not been provided to the other party.

[143]*See* Beech-Nut Packing Co., 20 LA 575, 576 (Davis, 1953); Pan Am. Ref. Corp., 15 LA 464, 465 (Klamon, 1950).

[144]*See* Needham Packing Co., 44 LA 1057, 1059 (Davey, 1965).

[145]*Procedural Problems During Hearings*, THE CHRONICLE (NAA), Apr. 1981, at 1, 7. *See* National Academy of Arbitrators Advisory Opinions, *available at* <http://www.naarb.org>. *See also* University of Cal. (Berkeley), 93 LA 450 (Wilcox, 1989) (short delay did not prejudice the union's case; therefore employer's late brief accepted). In *Sheller Manufacturing Co.*, 40 LA 890, 891 (Davey, 1963), the arbitrator rejected the union's request to consider the company brief as "null and void" where it was filed 1 day late, the arbitrator stating that briefs are only an "aid" to the arbitrator and that the union was not prejudiced by the late filing.

B. Advisory Opinions

Arbitrators are reluctant to issue advisory opinions.[146] It is premature to submit to arbitration a hypothetical question; "each case must be judged on its own merits when, and if, it arises."[147] An arbitrator may be more inclined to issue an advisory opinion if the requesting party demonstrates that it is necessary to protect the party's interests under the contract,[148] or if the arbitrator is convinced that both parties desire one.[149] Parties to a collective bargaining agreement may also provide contractually for advisory opinions.[150]

A similar situation arises when there is not enough evidence for an arbitrator to make an informed ruling on a grievance. In such a situation, one arbitrator ruled that the "issue accordingly must be left open and unresolved by the award . . . without prejudice to the rights of either Party in the event either of the Parties raises the issue in the future."[151] When neither party argued the interpretation of a particular contract provision, the arbitrator refused to dispose of the grievance on those grounds.[152]

C. Consent Awards

When parties settle their dispute during the course of arbitration, they often request that the arbitrator set forth the terms of the settlement in an award. Concerning such requests, AAA Rule 39 states that the arbitrator may "set forth the terms of the agreed settlement in an award."[153] Section 2.I.1.a. of the *Code of Professional Responsibility* provides more detail:

> 1. Prior to issuance of an award, the parties may jointly request the arbitrator to include in the award certain agreements between them, concerning some or all of the issues. If the arbitrator believes that a suggested award is proper, fair, sound, and lawful, it is consistent with professional responsibility to adopt it.

---

[146]*See* City of Marion, Ohio, 91 LA 175 (Bittel, 1988); DeBourgh Mfg. Co., 90 LA 471 (Flagler, 1987); Pacific Southwest Airlines, 70 LA 833, 834–35 (Jones, Jr., 1978); Saginaw News-Booth Newspapers, 61 LA 1205, 1212 (Platt, 1973); Trans World Air Lines, 47 LA 1127, 1130–31 (Platt, 1967); Schofield Mfg. Co., 45 LA 225, 227–29 (Duff, 1965); Grand Rapids Die Casting Co., 44 LA 827, 829 (Howlett, 1965) (no ruling on moot question); Jacob A. Braton, 64–3 ARB ¶9161 (Turkus, 1964) (no ruling on moot question); Magnavox Co., 35 LA 237, 240–41 (Dworkin, 1960). *See also* Typographical Union Local 16 (Chicago) v. Chicago Sun-Times, 860 F.2d 1420, 129 LRRM 2948 (7th Cir. 1988) (contract's arbitration clause has no provision for advisory opinions); Alpha Beta Co. v. Retail Clerks Local 428, 671 F.2d 1247, 110 LRRM 2169 (9th Cir. 1982). *Cf.* Long Island Press, 37 LA 1034, 1036–37 (Seitz, 1961).

[147]Monarch Mach. Tool Co., 27 LA 640, 642 (Ferguson, 1956).

[148]*See* Goodyear Aerospace Corp., 86 LA 584 (Fullmer, 1985); Decker Mfg. Corp., 84 LA 608 (Keefe, 1985); Tappan Co., 49 LA 922, 926–27 (Dworkin, 1967).

[149]*See* Vista Chem. Co., 92 LA 329 (Duff, 1989); Magma Copper Co., 83 LA 281 (Kelliher, 1984); Monsanto Co., 68 LA 101, 101–02 (Dworkin, 1977). However, even where both parties wanted a declaratory judgment for future cases, one arbitrator did not render one. D-V Displays Corp., 41 LA 937, 942 (Kates, 1963).

[150]Wolff, Crane, & Cole, *The Chrysler-UAW Umpire System*, *in* The Arbitrator and the Parties, Proceedings of the 11th Annual Meeting of NAA 111, 118 (McKelvey ed., BNA Books 1958).

[151]Kansas City Power & Light Co., 71 LA 381, 393 (Elkouri, 1978).

[152]AFG Indus., 87 LA 568 (Clarke, 1986).

[153]In *Chase Bag Co.*, 53 LA 612, 612 (Larson, 1969), the withdrawal of an AAA case "with prejudice" was confirmed by an award.

a. Before complying with such a request, an arbitrator must be certain that he or she understands the suggested settlement adequately in order to be able to appraise its terms. If it appears that pertinent facts or circumstances may not have been disclosed the arbitrator should take the initiative to assure that all significant aspects of the case are fully understood. To this end, the arbitrator may request additional specific information and may question witnesses at a hearing.

This also applies to the agreed case, in which the arbitrator is made aware that the company and union have a common view as to the merits of the case but want a hearing for the record, or for some other purpose such as arbitral review of their proposed solution or arbitral consideration of the different view of some individual or group.[154] Some arbitrators do not care to participate in such proceedings. Others will do so as long as they are satisfied that it will serve some useful purpose and will be just.

D. Default Awards

i. Default Awards in Ex Parte Proceedings [LA CDI 94.603]

When a party deliberately fails to appear for a hearing after due notice, the arbitrator will hear testimony and render an award based on the evidence, as if both parties had participated.[155] Some of these cases have involved state arbitration statutes providing for default awards, or collective bargaining agreements specifically providing for default awards in the event of willful or deliberate default by one of the parties, others were subject to

---

[154]*See* Gordon Wyman Co., 68 LA 997, 999–1000 (Keefe, 1977) (the employee was rescued from the consequences of the settlement between the company and the union); Eaton, *Labor Arbitration in the San Francisco Bay Area*, 48 LA 1381, 1389 (1967); *Appendix D. Survey of Arbitration in 1964, in* PROCEEDINGS OF THE 18TH ANNUAL MEETING OF NAA 243, 252 (Jones ed., BNA Books 1965); Fleming, *Due Process and Fair Procedure in Labor Arbitration, in* ARBITRATION AND PUBLIC POLICY, PROCEEDINGS OF THE 14TH ANNUAL MEETING OF NAA 69, 87–90 (Pollard ed., BNA Books 1961).

[155]"A general arbitration clause in a contract would be rendered meaningless if its implementation depended on the willingness of each party to the contract to present its case, as the party desiring no change in relationships could nullify arbitration simply by refusing to make an appearance." Velvet Textile Corp., 7 LA 685, 691 (Pope, 1947). *See* Westlake, Inc., 90 LA 1129 (Armstrong, 1988). *See also* Shore Manor, 71 LA 1238, 1241 (Katz, 1978) (default award issued against State of New Jersey); Hubbard & Johnson Lumber Co., 70 LA 526, 527–28 (Feller, 1978) (employer had commenced but refused to complete its presentation); Sunshine Convalescent Hosp., 62 LA 276, 278–79 (Lennard, 1974); Immigration & Naturalization Serv., 59 LA 119, 123 (Lennard, 1972) (default award issued against federal agency employer, whose representatives attended the hearing but only as observers). *Cf.* Vickers Inc., 39 LA 614, 621 (Prasow, 1962). *See also* Department of Veterans Affairs, 101 LA 731, 735 (Curry, Jr., 1993) (a collective bargaining agreement provided for default in favor of the grievant if the employer failed to comply with the time limits in the grievance steps and if the remedy requested was "legal and reasonable under the circumstances"; the arbitrator held that even though the employer's actions were not timely, he could not make a determination on whether the remedy requested was legal and reasonable under the circumstances without a hearing on the merits because the case dealt "with a subject matter and allegations far too important to be resolved on [a] technical procedural basis").

AAA Rule 27, Arbitration in the Absence of a Party or Representative,[156] which provides:

> Unless the law provides to the contrary, the arbitration may proceed in the absence of any party or representative who, after due notice, fails to be present or fails to obtain a postponement. An award shall not be made solely on the default of a party. The arbitrator shall require the other party to submit such evidence as may be required for the making of an award.[157]

Section 5.c.1.–2. of the *Code of Professional Responsibility* similarly specifies:

1. In determining whether to conduct an ex parte hearing, an arbitrator must consider relevant legal, contractual, and other pertinent circumstances.
2. An arbitrator must be certain, before proceeding ex parte, that the party refusing or failing to attend the hearing has been given adequate notice of the time, place, and purposes of the hearing.

ii. Enforcement of Default Awards [LA CDI 94.603]

No arbitrator or tribunal may issue a binding decision unless jurisdiction over the dispute has attached. An arbitrator may be vested with jurisdiction by agreement of the parties for a case, a group of cases, or as permanent arbitrator of stated tenure; by decree of court; or by collective bargaining agreement provisions specifying the procedures of an appointing agency.[158] If the agreement expressly requires cooperation of the parties, a court may refuse to enforce a default award.[159] It is unlikely that an otherwise proper default award will be upheld if the absent party was not given adequate notice or if other due process considerations were not satisfied.[160] If a union

---

[156]In *Thompson Fuel Service*, 42 LA 62, 62 (Kerrison, 1964), the arbitrator had no doubt that he could issue a default award where law did not provide to the contrary. But in *A.B.C. Cartage & Trucking Co.*, 42 LA 55, 58–59 (Whelan, 1963), the arbitrator refused to issue a default award where the case was not covered by AAA rules or by any statute expressly authorizing such awards.

[157]FMCS Regulations, 29 C.F.R. §1404.13 also provides for ex parte proceedings. Its rule is similar to the AAA's.

[158]Teamsters Local 745 v. Braswell Motor Freight Lines, 392 F.2d 1, 68 LRRM 2143 (5th Cir. 1968) (refusing to enforce default award where the agreement makes no provision for designating an arbitrator without participation of both parties or expressly requires cooperation); American Fed'n of Teachers Local 958 (Providence) v. McGovern, 319 A.2d 358, 363, 86 LRRM 2899 (R.I. 1974) (enforcing a default award against a public-sector employer so that the employer could not prevent an award being issued by failing to appear for the hearing).

[159]The court may find that the proper remedy of the party in default is a suit to compel arbitration. Sam Kane Packing Co. v. Meat Cutters Local 171, 477 F.2d 1128, 83 LRRM 2298 (5th Cir. 1973); Fuller v. Pepsi-Cola Bottling Co. of Lexington, Ky., 406 S.W.2d 416, 63 LRRM 2220 (Ky. 1966).

[160]*See* Bevona v. 820 Second Ave. Assocs., 27 F.3d 37, 146 LRRM 2673 (2d Cir. 1994) (default award vacated when employer did not attend hearing but collective bargaining agreement did not cover the employees of an independent contractor); Toyota of Berkeley v. Automobile Salesmen's Union Local 1095, 834 F.2d 751, 127 LRRM 2112 (9th Cir. 1987); Asbestos Workers Local 34 v. General Pipe Covering, 613 F. Supp. 858 (D. Minn. 1987). A default award was not enforced when the employer waited several hours for the proceeding to begin, had to leave for other business, and before leaving asked for the hearing to be rescheduled. Teamsters, Chicago v. Denton Cartage Co., 648 F. Supp. 1009, 124 LRRM 2627 (N.D. Ill. 1986). A default award was vacated, and reinstatement of employees replaced by members of

attempts to withdraw a grievance from arbitration on a "nonprecedent" and/ or "without prejudice" basis, the company may object and insist that the hearing proceed with or without the participation of the union.[161]

E. Reconsideration and Clarification of Award and Retention of Jurisdiction

i. The Doctrine of Functus Officio

a. Application of the Doctrine

When there is dissatisfaction with an award, or it is unclear, the parties may agree to ask the arbitrator to reconsider or clarify it. If they do not agree, the arbitrator may not have jurisdiction because of the common law doctrine of functus officio (office performed), which provides that an arbitrator's jurisdiction ends when a final award is issued.[162]

---

a different union was not enforced, because the affected employees were not covered by the collective bargaining agreement and the arbitrator accordingly had no power to adjudicate the dispute. *Bevona, supra,* 27 F.3d 37. The Ohio Court of Appeals affirmed the dismissal of a union's action for enforcement of grievances that the union argued was automatically granted because of the employer's failure to comply with various procedural requirements in the grievance process. The court held that the lower court lacked subject matter jurisdiction because the union had not proceeded to arbitration and the default award could be enforced. North Cent. Local Educ. Ass'n v. North Cent. Local Sch. Dist. Bd. of Educ., 155 LRRM 2511 (Ohio Ct. App. 1996). *But see* Department of Veteran Affairs, 101 LA 731, 735 (Curry, Jr., 1993) (the agreement conditioned default on finding that the requested remedy was "legal and reasonable under the circumstances," and the award was not enforced despite the employer's untimely response to the grievance because the subject matter was "too important to be resolved on [a] technical procedural basis").

[161]Guardian Indus. Corp., 86 LA 844 (Joseph, 1986).

[162]Mercury Oil Ref. Co. v. Oil Workers, 187 F.2d 980, 983, 16 LA 129 (10th Cir. 1951). *Accord* Colonial Penn Ins. Co. v. Omaha Indem. Co., 943 F.2d 327 (3d Cir. 1991); Food & Commercial Workers Local P-9 v. George A. Hormel & Co., 776 F.2d 1393, 120 LRRM 3283 (8th Cir. 1985); Devine v. White, 697 F.2d 421, 433, 112 LRRM 2374 (D.C. Cir. 1983) (indicating that the rule is applicable also to federal-sector arbitration); Pressmen & Platemakers Local 28 (Salt Lake) v. Newspaper Agency Corp., 485 F. Supp. 511, 104 LRRM 2326 (D. Utah 1980); Indigo Springs v. New York Hotel Trades Council, 59 LRRM 3024 (N.Y. 1965); Jannis v. Ellis, 308 P.2d 750 (Calif. Dist. Ct. App. 1957) (citing STURGES, COMMERCIAL ARBITRATIONS AND AWARDS §220). *See* Ellmann, *Functus Officio Under the Code of Professional Responsibility: The Ethics of Staying Wrong, in* ARBITRATION 1992: IMPROVING ARBITRAL AND ADVOCACY SKILLS, PROCEEDINGS OF THE 45TH ANNUAL MEETING OF NAA 190 (Gruenberg ed., BNA Books 1993); Nichols, *Labor Perspective, id.* at 210; Campbell, *Management Perspective, id.* at 204; Nolan, *Comment, id.* at 219. *Cf.* Red Star Express Lines v. Teamsters Local 170, 809 F.2d 103, 124 LRRM 2361 (1st Cir. 1987). The term "functus officio" is defined as "without further authority or legal competence because the duties and functions of the original commission have been fully accomplished." BLACK'S LAW DICTIONARY (7th ed. 1999). "The policy which lies behind this [doctrine] is an unwillingness to permit one who is not a judicial officer and who acts informally and sporadically, to re-examine a final decision which he has already rendered, because of the potential evil of outside communication and unilateral influence which might affect a new conclusion." LaVale Plaza v. R.S. Noonan, Inc., 378 F.2d 569, 572 (3d Cir. 1967). The policies and limitations of the doctrine of functus officio are discussed in Nicolau, *Should Arbitrators Retain Jurisdiction Over Awards?: I. O Functus Officio: Is it Time to Go?, in* ARBITRATION 1992: THE CHANGING WORLD OF DISPUTE RESOLUTION, PROCEEDINGS OF THE 51ST ANNUAL MEETING OF NAA 115 (Briggs & Grenig eds., BNA Books 1999); Markel, Functus Officio: *Does the Doctrine Apply in Labor Arbitration?,* 1998 J. DISP. RESOL. 53; Tepstein, *Confirming an Amended Labor Arbitration Award in Federal Court: The Problem of Functus Officio,* 8 AM. REV. INT'L ARB. 65 (1997); Dunsford, *The Case for Retention of Remedial Jurisdiction in Labor Arbitration Awards,* 31 GA. L. REV. 201 (1996); Werner & Holtzman, *Clarification of Arbitration Awards,* 3 LAB. LAW. 183 (1987); Dilts, *Award Clarification: An Ethical*

The doctrine is said to support the arbitral objective of producing quick and final settlement of disputes by ensuring that whatever decision or award the arbitrator renders will (hopefully) be the final word on the matter. In addition, the doctrine is said to deter rash or hasty decision making; if the arbitrator only gets one shot at an issue, the arbitrator will likely be more careful and deliberate in arriving at a conclusion. [162a]

However, the doctrine creates problems in practice because arbitrators, after all, are human and thus susceptible to error. [162b] They may leave loose ends dangling, they may leave problems unresolved, and they may leave resolutions vague or unclear. In particular, arbitrators may leave their final remedy unclear.

For example, the parties may dispute exactly what is meant by the arbitrator's order for the employer to make the grievant whole. Furthermore, the arbitrator may leave out important remedial components in an award of back pay to the grievant. [162c]

Moreover, as Judge Posner argued in *Excelsior Foundry*, [162d] equating an arbitrator to a judge is misleading—when a judge retires, the parties may seek reconsideration from another judge. If functus officio applies, however, the parties to an arbitration proceeding may be denied access to an equivalent forum for their subsequent issues. [162e] Instead of the judge retiring, it would be as if the courts themselves closed their doors. [162f] After the dust settles, the application of functus officio, which in most cases precludes the arbitrator from reconsidering a previous award, [162g] may lead to the very result that the parties hoped to avoid in the first place: they may have to take their dispute to court to resolve an ambiguity in an arbitral award.

Dilemma?, 33 LAB. L.J. 366 (1982); Seitz, *Problems of the Finality of Awards, or* Functus Officio *and All That, in* LABOR ARBITRATION: PERSPECTIVES AND PROBLEMS, PROCEEDINGS OF THE 17TH ANNUAL MEETING OF NAA 165 (Kahn ed., BNA Books 1964). It has been suggested that the functus officio doctrine should be discarded entirely on the ground that it is an outdated relic of the common law dating back to 1285 when King Edward of England issued an edict fining any justices who altered their records after a decision had been issued. *See* Ellmann, *Functus Officio Under the Code of Professional Responsibility: The Ethics of Staying Wrong, in* ARBITRATION 1992: IMPROVING ARBITRAL AND ADVOCACY SKILLS, PROCEEDINGS OF THE 45TH ANNUAL MEETING OF NAA 190 (Gruenberg ed., BNA Books 1993)

[162a]Indeed, despite the criticism, courts and arbitrators still regularly apply the doctrine. *See* Legion Ins. Co. v. VCW, Inc., 198 F.3d 718 (8th Cir. 1999). *See also* Northern Ind. Pub. Serv. Co., 116 LA 426, 430 (Fowler, 2001) (punctuating the award by noting, "[a]ccordingly, the arbitrator is functus officio"); Department of Commerce, Patent & Trademark Office, 2000-1 ARB ¶3382, at 5300 (Moore, 1999) (denying motion to reconsider award).

[162b]*See, e.g.,* Glass & Pottery Workers Local 182B v. Excelsior Foundry Co., 56 F.3d 844, 847, 149 LRRM 2358 (7th Cir. 1995) ("Arbitrators are no more infallible than judges. They make mistakes and overlook contingencies and leave much to implication and assumption.").

[162c]*See, e.g.,* Kennecott Utah Copper Corp. v. Becker, 186 F.3d 1261, 162 LRRM 2610 (10th Cir. 1999).

[162d]Glass & Pottery Workers Local 182B v. Excelsior Foundry Co., 56 F.3d 844, 149 LRRM 2358 (7th Cir. 1995).

[162e]*See id.* at 847.

[162f]*See id.*

[162g]Functus officio may even bar an arbitrator from rehearing a case after a federal district court has remanded the matter after having had the opportunity to confirm or vacate the award. *See* Legion Ins. Co. v. VCW, Inc., 198 F.3d 718, 720 (8th Cir. 1999).

Because of such concerns, recent case law and commentary question the strength and wisdom of functus officio in the arbitration context.[162h]

Following the Supreme Court's decisions distinguishing labor arbitration cases from commercial cases,[163] the federal courts, relying on Section 301 of the LMRA,[164] have developed principles for determining when an award may be set aside, corrected and enforced, or resubmitted to the arbitrator for clarification and interpretation.[165]

Under the federal law as developed under Section 301, the courts may return an award to the arbitrator for clarification or interpretation where it is ambiguous.[166] However, the fact that a court may have power to return an award to an arbitrator for interpretation does not necessarily mean that the arbitrator may undertake to render an interpretation independently.[167] Fur-

---

[162h]Dunsford, *The Case for Retention of Remedial Jurisdiction in Labor Arbitration Awards*, 31 GA. L. REV. 201 (1996); Smit, *Correcting Arbitral Mistakes*, 10 AM. REV. INT'L ARB. 225 (1999) (noting that an arbitrator's error can lead to extensive litigation in the courts before the case is remanded to the arbitrator for clarification); Tepstein, *Confirming an Amended Labor Arbitration Award in Federal Court: The Problem of Functus Officio*, 8 AM. REV. INT'L ARB. 65 (1997) (noting the additional litigation that may attend a dispute over the interpretation of an arbitral award). *See also* Kennecott Utah Copper Corp. v. Becker, 186 F.3d 1261, 1270–71 (10th Cir. 1999) (citing *Excelsior Foundry*, noting the state of the doctrine and reserving the question of whether the doctrine of functus officio is incorporated by federal common law); Clarendon Nat'l Ins. Co. v. TIG Reinsurance Co., 183 F.R.D. 112, 117 (S.D.N.Y. 1998) ("In cases like this one [involving a simple mistake] the functus officio doctrine may simply have outlived its usefulness.").

[163]Steelworkers v. American Mfg. Co., 363 U.S. 564, 46 LRRM 2414 (1960); Steelworkers v. Warrior & Gulf Navigation Co., 363 U.S. 574, 46 LRRM 2416 (1960); Steelworkers v. Enterprise Wheel & Car Corp., 363 U.S. 593, 46 LRRM 2423 (1960); Textile Workers v. Lincoln Mills, 353 U.S. 448, 458, 40 LRRM 2113 (1957).

[164]29 U.S.C. §185.

[165]Dunsford, 31 GA. L. REV. at 224.

[166]Bakery, Confectionery & Tobacco Workers Local 362-T v. Brown & Williamson Tobacco Corp., 971 F.2d 652, 141 LRRM 2248 (11th Cir. 1992); Transportation Communications Union v. Atchison, Topeka & Santa Fe Ry., 956 F.2d 156, 139 LRRM 2596 (7th Cir. 1992); New York Bus Tours v. Kheel, 864 F.2d 9, 130 LRRM 2277 (2d Cir. 1988); Electrical Workers (IBEW) Local 2222 v. New England Tel. & Tel. Co., 628 F.2d 644, 105 LRRM 2211, 2214–15 (1st Cir. 1980) (the parties disagreed on computation of a wrongfully discharged employee's loss of earnings, and where (1) the court cited numerous cases recognizing the power of courts to resubmit awards "to the original arbitrators for 'interpretation' or 'amplification,'" and (2) the court held that as "an issue falling directly within the scope of the parties' submission to the Arbitration Board, . . . the partly resolved matter of remedy was properly returned to the Board [by the district court] for further consideration"); Steelworkers v. W.C. Bradley Co., 551 F.2d 72, 95 LRRM 2177, 2177 (5th Cir. 1977); Electrical Workers (IBEW) Local 369 v. Olin Corp., 471 F.2d 468, 82 LRRM 2338 (6th Cir. 1972); Hanford Atomic Metal Trades Council v. General Elec. Co., 353 F.2d 302, 61 LRRM 2004, 2008 (9th Cir. 1965); Mail Handlers Local 311 v. U.S. Postal Serv., 741 F. Supp. 1267, 136 LRRM 2305 (N.D. Tex. 1990); Communications Workers v. Radio Station WUFO, Sheridan Broad. Corp., 126 LRRM 2240 (S.D.N.Y. 1987); Steelworkers v. Interpace Corp., Shenango China Div., 447 F. Supp. 387, 97 LRRM 3189, 3192 (W.D. Pa. 1978); Electrical Workers (IBEW) Local 494 v. Brewery Proprietors, 289 F. Supp. 865, 69 LRRM 2292, 2295 (E.D. Wis. 1968).

[167]In *Union Local 679 v. Richmond-Chase Corp.*, 191 Cal. App. 2d 841, 36 LA 881, 882 (Cal. Dist. Ct. App. 1961), the court under the California statute ordered a rehearing by an arbitration board to clarify its award, but the court denied that the board itself had authority to order the rehearing. A court under LMRA §301 reaffirmed the principle under prior cases that an arbitrator's powers on remand are limited to the specific matter remanded for clarification. Printing Pressmen Local 1 v. U.S. Trucking Corp., 411 F. Supp. 469, 96 LRRM 2535, 2539–40 (S.D.N.Y. 1977). In *Printing Industry of Washington, D.C.*, 40 LA 727, 728–29 (McCoy, Hall, Evans, Nolan, & Fraipont, 1963), an arbitrator stated that on rendering his award he had lost all power over the case and that the court order subsequently returning the case to him must be looked to for determining the scope of his new authority. The functus

thermore, the courts themselves refuse to return an award to the arbitrator where the court believes the disagreement over its implementation constitutes a new dispute that would require the arbitrator to pass on issues beyond the scope of the original submission—such new disputes are to be remedied by filing a new grievance under the grievance/arbitration provisions of the collective bargaining agreement.[168]

b. Exceptions to the Doctrine [LA CDI 94.63; 100.0777]

There are three widely followed judicially created exceptions to the rule of functus officio. An arbitrator may correct a mistake that is apparent on the face of the award, finish an incomplete award, and clarify an ambiguity.[169] The first exception allows an arbitrator to correct an award where

---

officio doctrine was also acknowledged by *B&I Lumber*, 81 LA 282, 283–84 (Lumbley, 1983); *Kohn Beverage Co.*, 78 LA 1156, 1157 (Abrams, 1982) (refusing to reconsider his decision on the basis of newly discovered evidence); *Expedient Servs.*, 68 LA 1082, 1084 (Dworkin, 1977); *Mrs. Baird's Bakeries*, 51 LA 919, 920–24 (Purdom, 1968); *American Maize Prods. Co.*, 37 LA 673, 674 (Sembower, 1961); *Ocoma Foods Co.*, 36 LA 979, 980 (Bothwell, 1961). *Cf.* Continental Can Co., 53 LA 619, 623 (Kates, 1969); Giant Tiger Super Stores Co., 43 LA 625, 633 (Kates, 1964); Aaxico Airlines, 47 LA 289, 316 (Platt, 1966).

[168]Paperworkers Local 675 v. Westvaco Corp., 461 F. Supp. 1022, 105 LRRM 2360, 2362 (W.D. Va. 1978); Machinists Local 1893, Dist. Lodge 80 v. Aerojet-General Corp., 263 F. Supp. 343, 65 LRRM 2421, 2423 (C.D. Cal. 1966); Mine Workers Dist. 50 v. Revere Copper & Brass, 204 F. Supp. 349, 51 LRRM 2033, 2034 (D. Md. 1962). The *Westvaco* court stated:

> [R]emand is particularly inappropriate where a collateral dispute has arisen from an award which is not self-executing. . . . These awards often impose upon the parties the need to take additional actions which, in turn, give rise to new disputes. The implementation of these awards may constitute new grievances which can be remedied only by resort to the established grievance procedure.

Westvaco, 461 F. Supp. at 1024, 105 LRRM at 2362 (citation omitted). Stating that it had such a case before it, the *Westvaco* court then classified the dispute additionally as one involving the "application" of the award as distinguished from the "interpretation" of the award:

> It is crucial to distinguish between disputes arising from the application of the award and those which concern the interpretation of an award. . . . Whereas the latter may be remanded to permit clarification of the arbitrator's decision, the former present entirely new issues upon which the arbitrator has not ruled. . . . The question of whether the Company adhered to the guidelines established by the arbitrator is a subsequent, albeit related, matter. This new dispute can be remedied only by resort to the grievance procedures contained in the collective bargaining agreement.

Id. at 1025 (citations omitted).

[169]Green v. Ameritech Corp., 200 F.3d 967, 977 (6th Cir. 2000); Hyle v. Doctor's Assoc., 198 F.3d 368, 370 (2d Cir. 1999); Office & Prof'l Employees Local 471 v. Brownsville Gen. Hosp., 186 F.3d 326, 331, 161 LRRM 3057 (3d Cir. 1999); Teamsters Local 312 v. Matlack, Inc., 118 F.3d 985, 991, 155 LRRM 2738 (3d Cir. 1997); Teamsters Local 631 v. Silver State Disposal Serv., 109 F.3d 1409, 1411, 154 LRRM 2865 (9th Cir. 1997); Teamsters Local 731 v. A.W. Zengeler Cleaners, 167 LRRM 2024 (N.D. Ill. 2001); Personnel Data Sys., Inc. v. Openplus Holdings PTY Ltd., 2001 WL 52546, 2001 U.S. Dist. LEXIS 403 (E.D. Pa. Jan. 18, 2001); Barousse v. Paper, Allied-Industrial, 165 LRRM 2507 (E.D. La. 2000); New York Hotel & Motel Trades Council v. Hotel St. George, 988 F. Supp. 770, 781, 158 LRRM 2241 (S.D.N.Y. 1998); Cadillac Uniform & Linen Supply v. Union de Tronquistas de P.R. Local 901, 920 F. Supp. 19, 21, 152 LRRM 2416 (D.P.R. 1996); Dean Foods Co. v. Steelworkers Local 5840, 911 F. Supp. 1116, 1127, 153 LRRM 2234 (N.D. Ind. 1995). For a survey of how arbitrators and federal courts deal with clarification of arbitration awards, see Holtzman, *Clarification of Arbitration Awards*, 3 LAB. LAW. 183 (Winter 1987); *McClatchy Newspapers v. Typographical Union No. 46 (Central Valley)*, 686 F.2d 731, 111 LRRM 2502 (9th Cir.), *cert. denied*, 459 U.S. 1071, 111 LRRM 3064 (1982). *See also* Kennecott Utah Copper Corp. v. Becker, 195 F.3d 1201, 162 LRRM 2641 (10th Cir. 1999) (upholding clarification of award in spite of ex parte contact), *cert denied*, 531 U.S. 1035 (2000).

One commentator notes that the "three exceptions language" was found in dicta in McClatchy Newspapers v. Typographical Union No. 46 (Cent. Valley), 686 F.2d 731, 734 n.1,

there are clerical mistakes or obvious errors of arithmetic computation, but not in cases of alleged mistakes where extraneous facts must be considered.[170] The second exception applies where the award does not adjudicate an issue that has been submitted, because, if an arbitrator has not decided an issue, it remains open for adjudication.[171] The third applies if the award, although seemingly complete, leaves doubt whether the submission has been fully executed.[172] When disputes about ambiguous awards are litigated, the cases are often remanded to the arbitrator for clarification, but not always.[173]

---

111 LRRM 2502 (9th Cir. 1982) (citing LaVale Plaza v. R.S. Noonan, Inc., 378 F.2d 569, 573 (3d Cir. 1967)). He says that the U.S. Court of Appeals for the Ninth Circuit cited *LaVale Plaza* out of context, because the court in that case was concerned with the different question of whether a court could resubmit an award to an arbitrator for clarification. Nevertheless, *McClatchy* has been cited and followed by many courts. Dunsford, *The Case for Retention of Remedial Jurisdiction in Labor Arbitration Awards*, 31 GA. L. REV. 201, 224 (1996).

[170]Teamsters Local 312 v. Matlack, 118 F.3d 985, 991, 155 LRRM 2738 (3d Cir. 1997). The NAA's Advisory Opinion No. 20 states that arbitrators are allowed to make corrections as to the identity of employees, back-pay calculations, and "other corrections of similar evident clerical mistakes or computational errors." The opinion concludes that such corrections are consistent with common and statutory law and are necessary to avoid unfair burdens on the parties and misuse of the arbitration process.

[171]Colonial Penn Ins. Co. v. Omaha Indem. Co., 943 F.2d 327, 332 (3d Cir. 1991) (a commercial arbitration case often cited by this court in its decisions in traditional labor cases).

[172]*Id.* The U.S. Court of Appeals for the Ninth Circuit compared the completion and ambiguity exceptions, finding that "[t]he completion exception to the doctrine of *functus officio* applies when an arbitration award fails to resolve an issue or 'specify the remedy in definite terms.'" Teamsters Local 631 v. Silver State Disposal Serv., 109 F.3d at 1411 (quoting Courier-Citizen Co. v. Graphic Communications Local 11, 702 F.2d 273, 279, 112 LRRM 3122 (1st Cir. 1983). The ambiguity exception, it said, applies when "'the award, although seemingly complete, leaves doubt whether the submission has been fully executed.'" *Silver State Disposal Serv., supra* (quoting *La Vale Plaza,* 378 F.2d at 572).

For another case about the completion exception, see *Matlack.* The employer believed the arbitrator would rule first on procedural questions. The arbitrator issued an award in favor of the union on both the procedural issues and the merits. After some exchange of correspondence, the arbitrator withdrew, the employer refused to comply with the award, and the union sued to enforce it. The district court vacated the award, finding it to be incomplete, because the arbitrator had not heard the merits of the case, and therefore was outside the doctrine of functus officio.

For a complex case pertaining to ambiguity, see *Office & Prof'l Employees Local 471 v. Brownsville Gen. Hosp.,* 186 F.3d 326, 161 LRRM 3057 (3d Cir. 1999). The court found that the resignation of a therapist named in a last-chance agreement created an unforeseen ambiguity in the award that should be resolved by the arbitrator. Although the arbitrator could not revisit the merits of the dispute, it said, "a remand for clarification . . . is consistent with the policy of judicial restraint that is the thrust of federal arbitral jurisprudence. . . . 'Such a remand avoids the court's misinterpretation of the award and is therefore more likely to give the parties the award for which they bargained.'" *Id.* at 332 (quoting *Colonial Penn, supra,* 943 F.2d at 334). *See also* New York Hotel & Motel Trades Council v. Hotel St. George, 988 F. Supp. 770, 158 LRRM 2241 (S.D.N.Y. 1998).

For a case about clarification, see *Cadillac Uniform & Linen Supply v. Union de Tronquistas de P.R. Local 901,* 920 F. Supp. 19, 152 LRRM 2416 (D.P.R. 1996) (where the arbitrator mistakenly ordered reinstatement without pay and then corrected it, the award was enforced because the arbitrator had only clarified his original intention by amending the award).

[173]*See, e.g.,* Machinists Local 701 v. Joe Mitchell Buick, Inc., 930 F.2d 576, 137 LRRM 2121 (7th Cir. 1991) (award enforced because of assumption that arbitrator's failure to mention offsets in the award meant that no offset was granted, not that the ruling was ambiguous). *But see* Food & Commercial Workers Local 100A v. John Hofmeister & Son, 950 F.2d 1340, 139 LRRM 2110 (7th Cir. 1991) (an arbitrator's make-whole award was found to be ambiguous where the arbitrator had not specified the period for reimbursement of back pay); Operating Eng'rs Local 841 v. Murphy Co., 82 F.3d 185, 152 LRRM 2315 (7th Cir. 1996) (award enforced despite ambiguity about damages because employer should have addressed question of damages during the hearing).

Judge Posner of the U.S. Court of Appeals for the Seventh Circuit said functus officio operates as a default rule, which the parties may agree not to abide by.[174] In the *Hotel Greystone* case,[175] the employer argued that an impartial chairman was functus officio when he reconsidered and then reopened an award, although the industry's impartial chairman had often interpreted the parties' agreement to permit reconsideration on a showing that the previous award was clearly erroneous or that there existed newly discovered evidence previously unavailable to the requesting party.[176] The court, citing *Excelsior Foundry*,[177] upheld the award, finding that "nothing in this opinion depends on the vitality of the doctrine *functus officio* because . . . the parties have chosen by agreement not to be subject to it . . . ."[178]

Both federal and state legislation provide exceptions to the doctrine of functus officio.[179] For example, the common law doctrine of functus officio has been modified by statute in some states to permit the arbitrator to modify or correct the award, to the limited extent stated in the statute, on submission by a court or on direct application to the arbitrator by one of the parties.[180]

The Uniform Arbitration Act (UAA)[181] permits an arbitrator to modify or correct an award on an evident miscalculation or discrepancy in the award,

---

[174]Glass & Pottery Workers Local 182B v. Excelsior Foundry Co., 56 F.3d 844, 846, 149 LRRM 2358 (7th Cir. 1995). *Excelsior Foundry* is a widely quoted and discussed case. A grievant was reinstated on the condition that he complete a rehabilitation program within 60 days. The award did not state who would pay for the treatment. The union received clarification but, because of the delay, the grievant could not complete the treatment program on time. The district court found that the arbitrator could not extend the deadline because of the doctrine of functus officio. The appeals court found otherwise. Judge Posner said the doctrine of functus officio "originated in the bad old days when judges were hostile to arbitration and ingenious in hamstringing it. . . . Today, riddled with exceptions, it is hanging on by its fingernails and whether it can be said to exist in labor arbitration is uncertain." *Id.* at 846 (citations omitted). Underlying the functus officio doctrine, he said, is the idea that arbitrators are considered to be "judges for a case," who resign the office after having issued an award and may not revisit it. *Id.* at 846–47. However, resignation of a judge does not deprive parties in litigation of clarification or reconsideration of a ruling since another judge will be appointed to consider the motion. By denying arbitrators the "inherent power to reconsider . . . decisions within a reasonable time," which are among "the ordinary powers of judges," he said, the utility of arbitration is reduced. *Id.* at 847. Rather than declaring functus officio dead, Judge Posner, using an exception to the rule, found that the arbitrator had interpreted his award, "allowing the union and [the grievant] to crawl through the loophole in the doctrine of functus officio for clarification or completion, as distinct from alteration, of the arbitral award." *Id.*

[175]Hotel Greystone Corp. v. New York Hotel & Motel Trades Council, AFL-CIO, 902 F. Supp. 482, 152 LRRM 2061 (S.D.N.Y. 1995).

[176]*Id.* at 484.

[177]Glass & Pottery Workers Local 182B v. Excelsior Foundry Co., 56 F.3d 844, 149 LRRM 2358 (7th Cir. 1995).

[178]*Hotel Greystone*, 902 F. Supp. at 485 n.2.

[179]For example, the Back Pay Act, 5 U.S.C. §5596, confers statutory jurisdiction on an arbitrator to consider a request for attorneys' fees when federal employees are involved. Therefore, a request for award of attorneys' fees under authority of the Back Pay Act is permissible, even if the arbitrator did not reserve jurisdiction over the case after delivery of the award. Department of the Navy, Naval Weapons Station, 113 LA 1214 (Lubic, 2000); Vandenberg Air Force Base, 106 LA 107 (Feldman, 1996).

[180]*See* Chapter 2, section 2.B.ii., "State Arbitration Statutes." For an example of a proceeding based on a motion for modification of award under state statute, see *Reserve Mining Co.*, 55 LA 648 (Sembower, 1970).

[181]7 U.L.A. §§1–25.

an imperfect form of award, or if the arbitrator "awarded on a matter not submitted" to him.[182] The UAA specifies that the application shall be made within 90 days after delivery of the award to the applicant.[183]

Clarification is also addressed in Section 6.D. of the *Code of Professional Responsibility*. It presently provides[184] that "[n]o clarification or interpretation of an award is permissible without the consent of both parties," and that under agreements that permit or require clarification or interpretation of an award, an arbitrator must afford both parties an opportunity to be heard.[185] However, it is doubtful that this section precludes arbitral retention of jurisdiction to resolve issues relating to the implementation of a remedy.[186]

---

[182]*Id.* §13. This provision is discussed by Dilts, *Award Clarification: An Ethical Dilemma?*, 33 Lab. L.J. 366 (1982). For states adopting the UAA, see Chapter 2, section 2.B.ii., "State Arbitration Statutes." The New York statute does not list "clarification" as one of the grounds, but this ground is possibly included in the intent of the statute. *See An Outline of Procedure Under the New York Arbitration Law*, 20 Arb. J. 73, 90–91 (1965).

[183]7 U.L.A. §13.

[184]The members of the NAA ratified the following amendment to Rule 6.D. on June 4, 2000, but the FMCS and the AAA have rejected it:

D. Clarification or Interpretation of Awards

1. Unless directed to do so by appropriate authority, or at the joint request of the parties, an arbitrator may not reconsider the merits of a final award or accept a motion for such reconsideration.

2. Clarification or interpretation of an award is permissible upon the request of a party.

3. The arbitrator must afford the parties an opportunity to present their respective views.

[185]Section 6.D.2.–3. *See* Pulaski County, Ark., Special Sch. Dist., 114 LA 1135, 1138 (Stoia, 2000) (stating that the arbitrator will not clarify an award he granted because "[a]ccording to the Code of Professional Responsibility for Arbitrators of Labor-Management Disputes— *No clarification or interpretation of an award is permissible without the consent of both parties*") (emphasis in original). For an understanding and analysis of Section 6.D. of the Code of Professional Responsibility, see Lumbley, *Understanding the Functus Officio Morass*, 16 LERC Monograph Series 91 (2000). For an analysis of whether functus officio applies in labor arbitration, see Markel, *Functus Officio: Does the Doctrine Apply in Labor Arbitration?*, 1998 J. Disp. Resol. 53 (1998). By memorandum of March 3, 1980, to persons on its roster of arbitrators, the FMCS reminded them of this Code provision and the FMCS stated: "The submission of a Decision removes an arbitrator from further authority for a particular matter. Absent a *joint* request, any response by an arbitrator to both parties [should] be limited to stating the function of the office ceases with the Decision submission. Even an abbreviated explanation is too much." More often any agreement to request an interpretation by the arbitrator will be reached after the need for an interpretation arises. *See* Brass-Craft Mfg. Co., 36 LA 1438, 1438 (Kahn, 1961). Sometimes the parties at that time select a different arbitrator to interpret the original arbitrator's award. *See* Newspaper Guild Local 25 (San Antonio) v. Hearst Corp., San Antonio Light Div., 481 F.2d 821, 83 LRRM 2728, 2730, 2732 (5th Cir. 1973) (the parties jointly selected a second arbitrator whose clarification award was upheld, but where the court stated as dictum that the preferable procedure is clarification by the original arbitrator). One survey indicated that labor, management, and arbitrators alike appear generally to favor giving arbitrators power to interpret their awards. Special Sch. Dist. No. L, Minneapolis Pub. Sch., 87 LA 522 (Fogelberg, 1986); Dispatch Printing Co., 70 LA 104, 105 (Kanner, 1978).

[186]One arbitrator explained the difference between the general rule that prohibits the clarification or interpretation of an award under this proviso and the exception to that rule that allows arbitrators to properly retain limited jurisdiction to address remedial questions. *See* Sears Logistics Servs., 97 LA 421 (Garrett, 1991).

One arbitrator has explained that this proviso differs significantly from the original prohibition contained in the original *Code of Ethics for Arbitrators*, the forerunner to the present *Code*, which stated in Part II, Section 5.a., that an award "should reserve no future duties to the arbitrator except by agreement of the parties."[187] The deletion of this quoted phrase, he stated, means that an arbitrator can perform "future duties" relating to remedial questions because doing so constitutes an exception to the functus officio doctrine. Arbitrators "are not really functus officio until our job is finished."[188]

Another arbitrator has conducted a similar exegesis on the history of Section 6.D.1. and reports that "nothing in the current Code makes it improper for an arbitrator to retain jurisdiction of an award for the purpose of clarifying or interpreting the remedy."[189] He points out that the NAA's Committee on Professional Responsibility and Grievances (CPRG)—which helps promulgate changes to the Code and which also helps enforce its provisions vis-à-vis its own members—has never ruled that retaining limited jurisdiction for remedial questions is unethical.[190] That is something it easily could have done given the fact that many past presidents of the NAA have supported retention of jurisdiction for remedial purposes.[191]

The Supreme Court has agreed that remedial back-pay issues should be decided by the arbitrator who has heard the case, rather than the courts, and remanded a disputed back-pay question to an arbitrator even though he had not retained jurisdiction "so that the amounts due the employees may be definitely determined by arbitration."[192] In so ruling, the Supreme Court upheld the prior decision of the U.S. Court of Appeals for the Fourth Circuit, which stated that the functus officio doctrine "should not be applied today in the settlement of employer-employee disputes."[193] Because the arbitrator in

---

[187]Rehmus, *The Code and Postaward Arbitral Discretion, in* ARBITRATION 1989: THE ARBITRATOR'S DISCRETION DURING AND AFTER THE HEARING, PROCEEDINGS OF THE 42D ANNUAL MEETING OF NAA 127, 127 (Gruenberg ed., BNA Books 1990).

[188]*Id.* at 136.

[189]Dunsford, *The Case for Retention of Remedial Jurisdiction*, 31 GA. L. REV. 201, 252 (1996).

[190]*Id.* at 244–52. *See also Appendix D. Formal Advisory Opinions, 1953–1991 (With CPRG Notes June 1996), in* THE NATIONAL ACADEMY OF ARBITRATORS: FIFTY YEARS IN THE WORLD OF WORK 371 (Gruenberg, Najita, & Nolan eds., BNA Books 1998), which lists all of the formal advisory opinions issued by CPRG and its predecessors, none of which state that retaining limited jurisdiction to resolve remedial issues is unethical.

[191]Nicolau, *O Functus Officio: Is It Time to Go?, in* ARBITRATION 1998: THE CHANGING WORLD OF DISPUTE RESOLUTION, PROCEEDINGS OF THE 51ST ANNUAL MEETING OF NAA 115, 115–16 (Briggs & Grenig eds., BNA Books 1999); Seitz, *Problems of the Finality of Awards, or Functus Officio and All That, in* LABOR ARBITRATION: PERSPECTIVES AND PROBLEMS, PROCEEDINGS OF THE 17TH ANNUAL MEETING OF NAA 165, 177 n.5 (Kahn ed., BNA Books 1964); Jones, *Talk of the Town,* THE CHRONICLE (NAA), May 1990, at 2; Dunsford, 31 GA. L. REV. at 273 n.318. Arbitrator Nicolau also has suggested that Section 6.D.1. of the CODE OF PROFESSIONAL RESPONSIBILITY be amended so that a single party can obtain clarification of an award. *See* Nicolau, NAA 51ST PROCEEDINGS, at 132–33. The NAA proposed such a change in 2000, but it was subsequently rejected by both the AAA and the FMCS who are cosignatories to the CODE OF PROFESSIONAL RESPONSIBILITY and whose agreement is needed for any CODE changes.

[192]Steelworkers v. Enterprise Wheel & Car Corp., 363 U.S. 593, 599, 46 LRRM 2423 (1960).

[193]Enterprise Wheel & Car Corp. v. Steelworkers, 269 F.2d 327, 332, 44 LRRM 2349 (4th Cir. 1959).

that case was empowered to resolve that remedial issue even though he did not retain jurisdiction, it is difficult to see how arbitrators would not have that same power in those cases where they *do* retain jurisdiction. Various courts since that time have remanded remedial questions to arbitrators.[194]

ii. Retaining Limited Jurisdiction to Resolve Remedial Issues

The arbitration process does not automatically end in those cases where a grievance has been sustained and where a remedy has been ordered. Questions over the application of a remedy can arise after an arbitration award has been issued, which is why arbitrators may decide, at their discretion, to retain limited jurisdiction to resolve any such remedial issues.[195]

---

[194]*See* Sunshine Mining Co. v. Steelworkers, 823 F.2d 1289, 124 LRRM 3198 (9th Cir. 1987); Courier-Citizen Co. v. Graphic Communications Local 11, 702 F.2d 273, 112 LRRM 3122 (1st Cir.1983). *See also* Dunsford, *The Case for Retention of Remedial Jurisdiction*, 31 GA. L. REV. 201, 236 n.176 (1996), for some of the court cases upholding the right of arbitrators to retain remedial jurisdiction. Dunsford reports that there is only one case that states that arbitrators lack the authority to retain remedial jurisdiction, *Philadelphia Newspapers v. Newspaper Guild Local 10 (Greater Phila.)*, No. Civ. A86-6192, 1987 WL 17744 (E.D. Pa. Sept. 28, 1987), which decision he finds is distinguishable.

[195]It is common for arbitrators to retain jurisdiction so that their awards are properly carried out and disagreements about the award can be resolved. *See, e.g.*, Weyerhaeuser Co. Forest Prods., 108 LA 26, 32 (Levak, 1997) (arbitrator retained jurisdiction to resolve any disagreement between the parties concerning the amount of back pay or benefits due); Dresser Indus., 103 LA 696, 700 (Redel, 1994) (arbitrator retained jurisdiction for a period of 30 days to implement his award if requested, despite union's statement that the parties could work out the remedy after arbitrator found a contract violation when the employer failed to pay first-shift maintenance employees for their 15-minute lunch period); Young's Commercial Transfer, 101 LA 993 (McCurdy, 1993) (arbitrator who retained jurisdiction to resolve disputes arising from the calculation of back pay subsequently interpreted contract to require payment of pension contributions as part of back pay); Hexcel Corp., 101 LA 700, 703 (Silver, 1993) (arbitrator retained jurisdiction in the event the parties could not agree on the calculation of amounts due to employees as the remedy for the company's improper subcontracting of work). The federal courts have confirmed the right of arbitrators to retain jurisdiction over disputes about implementation of the award, at their discretion. Air Line Pilots v. Aviation Assocs., 955 F.2d 90, 139 LRRM 2454 (1st Cir. 1992); Synergy Gas Co. v. Sasso, 853 F.2d 59, 129 LRRM 2041 (2d Cir. 1988); Hughes Aircraft Co. v. Electronic & Space Technicians Local 1553, 822 F.2d 823, 125 LRRM 3243 (9th Cir. 1987) (arbitrator properly retained jurisdiction but it did not extend to deciding merits of grievances not previously submitted to him); Pathmark Stores v. Service Employees Local 1199, 160 LRRM 2346, 2349 (S.D.N.Y. 1999) ("An arbitrator may retain jurisdiction regarding issues that arise out of the rendering of an award, and the maintenance of jurisdiction does not require the award to be vacated."); Case-Hoyt Corp. v. Graphic Communications Workers Local 503, 5 F. Supp. 2d 154, 158 LRRM 3016 (W.D.N.Y. 1998) (a union's resort to contempt charges violated the strong federal policy favoring arbitration, and the court could not investigate the merits of the dispute); Dean Foods Co. v. Steelworkers Local 5840, 911 F. Supp. 1116, 153 LRRM 2234 (N.D. Ind. 1995); Paperworkers v. Gaylord Container Corp., 755 F. Supp. 158, 136 LRRM 2570 (E.D. La. 1991); Dreis & Krump Mfg. Co v. Machinists Dist. 8, 1985 WL 3752 (N.D. Ill. Nov. 8, 1985), *aff'd*, 802 F.2d 247, 123 LRRM 2654 (7th Cir. 1986); Hilton Int'l Co. v. Union de Trabajadores de la Industria Gastronomica de P.R., 600 F. Supp. 1446, 119 LRRM 2011 (D.P.R. 1985). The parties may also agree to have an arbitrator retain jurisdiction. *See* Somerset Printing, 91 LA 1235 (Levy, 1988); East Ohio Gas Co., 91 LA 366 (Dworkin, 1988); Warehouse Distribution Ctrs., 90 LA 979 (Weiss, 1987); Manville Forest Prods. Corp., 85 LA 85 (Nolan, 1985); Lear Siegler, Inc., 75 LA 1298, 1300 (Weiss, 1980); Social Sec. Admin., 75 LA 628, 632 (House, 1980); Seattle Dep't Stores, 75 LA 6, 12 (Beck, 1980); Elliott Precision Block Co., 45 LA 929, 932 (Roberts, 1965); Five Star Hardware & Elec. Corp., 44 LA 944, 947 (Wolff, 1965); Gaslight Club, 39 LA 14, 18–19 (Benewitz, 1962). Issues that have been resolved after the award was issued have included the amount of back pay and the appropriate remedy for the contract violation. *See* Amana Refrigeration, 93 LA 258 (Mikrut, Jr., 1989);

One arbitrator maintains that "in virtually all cases of grievance arbitration where a remedy is called for, labor arbitrators ought to routinely retain jurisdiction of the award solely for the purpose of resolving any disputes among the parties regarding the meaning, application, and implementation of that remedy."[196] He adds: "The retention of power would be *sua sponte* and not dependent on the express agreement of the parties."[197] Another arbitrator goes further and adds: "an arbitrator is derelict in his duty in a discharge or seniority case if he fails to reserve jurisdiction to settle back pay or relative placement issues."[198]

Remedial issues ordinarily are not addressed until after an arbitrator sustains a grievance and orders relief:

> It is established and accepted beyond peradventure that an arbitrator can 'fashion' a remedy; but at the hearing, not only the arbitrator but, also, the advocates haven't the foggiest notion of what difficulties and problems may be encountered and what prescribing a remedy, at hearing's end, may entail. Several days may be spent in the presentation of the substantive issue of whether, indeed, in fact and law, the contract provisions had been violated.
>
> Should the parties at the hearings address themselves to such matters as the calculation of damages or a canvass of all of the things necessary to make a damaged grievant whole (such as the ascertainment of a relative seniority rights to a job, the completion of therapy for a disabled alcoholic or otherwise incapacitated employee, the exertion of efforts by the employer and the union to identify a substitute job in which a long-service employee can function, etc.), several more days of hearing would be required. It is not the arbitrator but the *parties*, who, either expressly or implicitly, recognize the fact that this would be an utter waste of time because, if the award should sustain the employer's

---

Poly Tech, 91 LA 512 (Gunderson, 1988); Plain Dealer Publ'g Co., 90 LA 1042 (Kates, 1988); Cincinnati Post & Times Star, 68 LA 129, 143 (Chalfie, 1977); Bartelt Eng'g Co., 51 LA 582, 589 (Sembower, 1968); Union-Tribune Publ'g Co., 51 LA 421, 428 (Jones, Jr., 1968); American-International Aluminum Corp., 49 LA 728, 731 (Howlett, 1967); Hadley Adhesive & Chem. Co., 49 LA 229, 231 (Erbs, 1967); Borden Ice Cream Co., 45 LA 1034, 1039 (McKelvey, 1965). Other issues include the identity of employees entitled to payments under the award. *See* Amana Refrigeration, 89 LA 751, 754 (Bowers, 1987) (identity of employees who worked on newly installed machinery and were entitled to higher pay rate); Halle Bros. Co., 42 LA 705, 709 (Kabaker, 1964) (identity of employees entitled to payment when department store closed for national day of mourning pursuant to contractual 40-hour workweek guarantee). *See also* Todd Shipyards Corp., 50 LA 645, 657 (Prasow, 1968) (retention of jurisdiction to determine remedy if parties are unable to do so within 90 days when the group grievance is for invalid compulsory retirement at age 65); Consolidated Badger Coop., 43 LA 65, 76 (Anderson, 1964) (retention of jurisdiction to determine amounts owing to bargaining-unit employees who were improperly converted from employee status to individual contractor or distributor status); Ingersoll-Rand Co., 42 LA 483, 490 (Scheiber, 1964) (retention of jurisdiction to determine damage liability to employees improperly retired at age 65).

[196]Dunsford, *The Case for Retention of Remedial Jurisdiction*, 31 GA. L. REV. 201, 204 (1996). Remarks elaborating on this subject were presented to the NAA. *See* Dunsford, *Should Arbitrators Retain Jurisdiction Over Awards?: I. On Retaining Jurisdiction, in* ARBITRATION 1998: THE CHANGING WORLD OF DISPUTE RESOLUTION, PROCEEDINGS OF THE 51ST ANNUAL MEETING OF NAA 102 (Briggs & Grenig eds., BNA Books 1999).

[197]Dunsford, 31 GA. L. REV. at 205.

[198]*Quoted in* Rehmus, *The Code and Postaward Arbitral Discretion, in* ARBITRATION 1989: THE ARBITRATOR'S DISCRETION DURING AND AFTER THE HEARING, PROCEEDINGS OF THE 42D ANNUAL MEETING OF NAA 127, 128 (Gruenberg ed., BNA Books 1990).

position, there would be no occasion at all to confront or deal with these matters.[199]

Retaining limited jurisdiction is particularly needed when a so-called "make-whole" remedy is issued in discipline cases.[200] There is an inherent tension in fashioning a remedial order that provides needed specificity to the parties regarding what must be done, while at the same time providing needed elasticity to resolve any unaddressed, remedial questions. One formula suggested for retaining jurisdiction in a discharge case where reinstatement and back pay have been awarded is phrased as follows:

> To rectify the employer's violation of the contractual just cause standard, and in order to restore the status quo ante, the employer shall immediately offer to reinstate the grievant to his/her former position and to immediately make the grievant whole by restoring his/her lost seniority and by paying to him/her a sum of money, including all benefits, that he/she would have earned from the time of his/her termination to the time of the employer's offer of reinstatement. That sum is to be reduced by any monies he/she received during the time of his/her termination that he/she would not have otherwise received but for his/her termination, and minus any monies that the grievant should have earned by way of mitigation.
>
> To resolve any questions that may arise over the interpretation or application of this award or the administration of the foregoing remedy, the arbitrator retains jurisdiction [for at least 60 days or indefinitely] solely for these limited purposes.[201]

Whether the retention of limited jurisdiction should be for a fixed or open-ended period is debatable. A fixed period tells the parties they must act expeditiously by a certain date in order to comply with the arbitrator's remedial order. The courts, though, may find that an arbitrator is required to retain jurisdiction indefinitely to resolve all remedial questions, regardless of how long that takes.[202] In addition, parties sometimes do not meet fixed deadlines. If a party objects to the arbitrator retaining jurisdiction, particularly *after* the deadline has passed, the arbitrator then must decide whether his or her retention should be extended over the objection of one of the par-

---

[199]Seitz, *Letter to the Editor: Final Comments on Retaining Jurisdiction*, STUDY TIME, Jan. 1981, 3-4, *reprinted in* Dunsford, 31 GA. L. REV. at 207–08. Seitz was one of the chief proponents for retaining jurisdiction—which he accomplished via "interim awards." *See* Seitz, *Problems of the Finality of Awards, or Functus Officio and All That, in* LABOR ARBITRATION: PERSPECTIVES AND PROBLEMS, PROCEEDINGS OF THE 17TH ANNUAL MEETING OF NAA 165 (Kahn ed., BNA Books 1964).

[200]The perils of not retaining jurisdiction can be seen in *Machinists Local 701 v. Joe Mitchell Buick, Inc.*, 930 F.2d 576, 137 LRRM 2121 (7th Cir. 1991) (per curiam) (the court ruled that an employer could not seek to offset either the grievants' alleged failure to mitigate damages or the amount of money the grievants received in unemployment compensation benefits because the arbitration award was silent on those questions; if jurisdiction were retained in that case, the arbitrator could have resolved those issues).

[201]This formula for retention of jurisdiction was developed by Arbitrator Amedeo Greco.

[202]*See* Printing Specialties Union v. Litton Fin. Serv., 181 Cal. Rptr. 6, 10 (Ct. App. 1982) (the court ruled that an arbitrator had to retain jurisdiction indefinitely and that he erred in retaining jurisdiction for a fixed period).

ties. That problem does not arise if the arbitrator's retention of jurisdiction is open-ended. However, unlimited retention of jurisdiction may remove any sense or urgency in complying with the remedy ordered. One proposed compromise recommends that the arbitrator state that he or she retains jurisdiction *"for at least"* 30 or 60 days. That provides for a timeline, while at the same time allowing the arbitrator to extend his or her retention of jurisdiction if it is necessary to do so.

Parties in all cases should indicate at the outset of the hearing whether they want the arbitrator to retain jurisdiction. Such an agreement will obviate the need to address remedial issues during the arbitration hearing and after the arbitration award has been issued.

If a party objects to the arbitrator retaining jurisdiction at the beginning of a hearing, the arbitrator can rule on the issue in the same way that he or she rules on other procedural matters. Some arbitrators routinely raise this issue themselves at the beginning of the hearing even if the parties do not do so. They maintain this issue should be addressed "up front" so that the parties can express their views and, if agreement has been obtained, avoid subsequent court challenges.

Not all arbitrators agree with this view. One arbitrator contends that if there is a question over remedy, "I view it as a separate dispute. I do not feel the parties should be compelled to come back to me, and I will allow them to go to somebody else."[203]

Some arbitrators fear that a party may try to obtain reconsideration of the merits of a grievance under the guise of having the arbitrator rule on remedial issues. That view overlooks the need to retain limited jurisdiction in those cases where there is a bona fide dispute over the remedy and where the arbitrator is in the best position to resolve it. Moreover, an arbitrator can simply rule that any such reconsideration is improper because it is beyond the scope of the arbitrator's limited retention of jurisdiction.

Other arbitrators contend that retaining jurisdiction only delays and prolongs the arbitration process. But, because it takes far greater time to resolve such issues in the courts, the real question is whether that delay is preferable to the much greater delays, and costs, experienced in the court systems.

One arbitrator states that because of *Enterprise Wheel*[204] and the other *Steelworkers Trilogy* cases,[205] the Supreme Court in effect decided to "keep the law out" of arbitration disputes by emphasizing the breadth of arbitration agreements, by making arbitration awards final and binding, and by

---

[203]Zack, *Decision-Making, in* Labor Arbitration Development: A Handbook 111, 132 (Barreca, Miller, & Zimny eds., BNA Books 1983), *quoted in* Dunsford, *The Case for Retention of Remedial Jurisdiction,* 31 Ga. L. Rev. 201, 265–66 (1996). *See also* Brand, Labor Arbitration—The Strategy of Persuasion 120 (1987); Eischen, The Arbitration Hearing: Administration, Conduct and Procedures in Labor and Employment Arbitration §1.04(4) (Boorstein & Gosline eds., 1988).

[204]Steelworkers v. Enterprise Wheel & Car Corp., 363 U.S. 593, 46 LRRM 2423 (1960).

[205]Steelworkers v. American Mfg. Co., 363 U.S. 564, 46 LRRM 2414 (1960); Steelworkers v. Warrior & Gulf Navigation Co., 363 U.S. 574, 46 LRRM 2423 (1960).

insulating the merits of disputes from court review.[206] Retaining limited jurisdiction to resolve remedial questions also serves to "keep the law out" by making sure that grievances are resolved within the parties' own system of self-governance, rather than through the courts.

6. EXPEDITED ARBITRATION PROCEDURES [LA CDI 94.33]

Where there is a large accumulation of grievances, the parties may be able to expedite arbitration procedures to their mutual satisfaction and benefit.

An expedited procedure was adopted by one union and employer to cut the costs and time involved in arbitrating a backlog of grievances. Under the expedited procedure: (1) Each party prepares a written statement of the grievance and facts, and submits a copy to the other party; (2) Each party states its thinking as to how the facts fit the contract, again with a copy to the other party; (3) Both parties seek to arrive at a joint statement, and failing that, their diverse views are submitted to the arbitrator; and (4) A hearing is held where the arbitrator asks questions and listens to statements limited to facts and opinions submitted in the aforementioned statements. No post-hearing briefs are filed and no opinion accompanies the award unless the arbitrator feels that comments are needed (an award without an opinion would not serve as a precedent under their plan but could be used "as a basis for conversation").[207] Another example is the program of the steel industry, which has provided one of the most extensive experiences with expedited arbitration.[208]

---

[206]Murphy, *The Presidential Address: The Academy at Forty, in* ARBITRATION 1987: THE ACADEMY AT FORTY, PROCEEDINGS OF THE 40TH ANNUAL MEETING OF NAA 1, 4 (Gruenberg ed., BNA Books 1988).

[207]Ingersoll-Rand Co., 42 LA 965, 966–67 (Scheiber, 1964) (Where 25 grievances were settled during preparation of joint statements and the parties were able to agree on a statement of facts in 18 of the 19 remaining cases; the arbitrator did write short opinions in most of the 19 cases. No doubt a significant factor in the success of the plan was the fact that the arbitrator had long served the parties prior to use of the expedited procedure.).

[208]*See* Fischer, *The Steelworkers Union and the Steel Companies, in* ARBITRATION OF SUBCONTRACTING AND WAGE INCENTIVE DISPUTES, PROCEEDINGS OF THE 32D ANNUAL MEETING OF NAA 198, 201 (Stern & Dennis eds., BNA Books 1980). Also discussing the steel program, see Kauffman, *The Idea of Expedited Arbitration Two Decades Later,* 46 ARB. J. No. 3, at 34 (1991); Cohen, *The Search for Innovative Procedures in Labor Arbitration,* 29 ARB. J. 104 (1974); Fischer, *Updating Arbitration, in* ARBITRATION OF INTEREST DISPUTES, PROCEEDINGS OF THE 26TH ANNUAL MEETING OF NAA 62 (Dennis & Somers eds., BNA Books 1974); St. John, *Comment, id.* at 73; Stoner, *Comment, id.* at 80; Fischer, *Comment, id.* at 86 (explaining that, in what appears to be isolation award arbitration, the arbitrators in the program "can't read each other's decisions, nor can they learn what they are," that it "becomes improper for anybody to tell what was decided in a case last week," that to some extent there is "a built-in lack of predictability," that the parties "have accepted this because that's what the system is," and that the parties "have weighed the pros and cons of that situation"); Fischer, *The Steel Industry's Expedited Arbitration: A Judgment After Two Years,* 28 ARB. J. 185 (1973). In 1973, the AAA adopted a special set of rules for expedited arbitration. For discussion and statistics concerning AAA expedited arbitration programs, see McDermott, *Evaluation of Programs Seeking to Develop Arbitrator Acceptability, in* ARBITRATION—1974, PROCEEDINGS OF THE 27TH ANNUAL MEETING OF NAA 329, 336–46 (Dennis & Somers eds., BNA Books 1975).

Some methods for expediting arbitration proceedings are included among the following possibilities enumerated by one arbitrator: (1) dry run arbitration; (2) prehearing statements; (3) avoidance of "brinkmanship" prior to actual arbitration; (4) greater use of submission agreements; (5) more effective use of factual stipulations and consequent reduced use of witnesses; (6) elimination of transcripts, except under special circumstances; (7) elimination of post-hearing briefs; (8) drastic shortening of opinions; (9) early issuance of award with brief statement of reasoning, followed later by full opinion; (10) greater use of memorandum opinions or even the equivalent of bench rulings; (11) increased use of "instant" arbitration; (12) expanded use of the hearing officer technique for routine cases under the guidance of senior arbitrators.[209]

Expedited arbitration without question does have benefits, but it has limitations and can carry significant liabilities as well.[210]

Regarding expedited arbitration in the federal sector, see A SURVEY OF NEGOTIATED GRIEVANCE PROCEDURES AND ARBITRATION IN FEDERAL POST CIVIL SERVICE REFORM ACT AGREEMENTS 41 (Office of Personnel Mgmt. 1980), reporting that: "Expedited arbitration or mini-arbitration has been adopted in 20 of the [323] agreements sampled. This device is not a substitute for, but a supplement to existing arbitration procedures."

[209]Davey, *Restructuring Grievance Arbitration Procedures: Some Modest Proposals*, 54 IOWA L. REV. 560, 565 (1969) (discussing each of these suggestions, *id.* at 566–77). For an example of "instant" arbitration, see *Pacific Maritime Ass'n*, 90 LA 578, 579 (Sutliff, 1988).

[210]For discussions relating to the benefits, limitations, and/or liabilities of expedited arbitration, in addition to the articles cited above, see Sandver, Blaine & Woyar, *Time and Cost Savings Through Expedited Arbitration Procedures*, 36 ARB. J. No. 4, at 11 (1981); Selby, *The United Mine Workers and Bituminous Coal Operators' Association, in* ARBITRATION OF SUBCONTRACTING AND WAGE INCENTIVE DISPUTES, PROCEEDINGS OF THE 32D ANNUAL MEETING OF NAA 181, 187–88 (Stern & Dennis eds., BNA Books 1980); THE PRESIDENT'S COMMISSION ON COAL, LABOR-MANAGEMENT SEMINAR III, WILDCAT STRIKES (Apr. 27, 1979), at 26–30 (Gov't Printing Office 1979, No. 0-302-758); Murray & Griffin, *Expedited Arbitration of Discharge Cases*, 31 ARB. J. 263 (1976); Miller, *Presidential Reflections, in* ARBITRATION—1975, PROCEEDINGS OF THE 28TH ANNUAL MEETING OF NAA 1 (Dennis & Somers eds., BNA Books 1976); Seitz, *Some Thoughts on the Vogue for Instant Arbitration*, 30 ARB. J. 124 (1975); Schlager, *Expedited Arbitration on the LIRR*, 30 ARB. J. 273 (1975). Arbitration proceedings are greatly expedited by court order, as in *Philadelphia Newspapers*, 68 LA 401, 402, 405 (Jaffee, 1977). Some contractual expedited arbitration procedures provide for withdrawal from the expedited process if it becomes apparent that the issues are sufficiently complex or significant to be better served by conventional arbitration. *See, e.g.*, Veterans Admin. Med. Ctr., 87 LA 1015 (Eisler, 1986).

Chapter 8

Evidence

1. EVIDENTIARY RULES

A. Strict Observance of Judicial Jury Trial Rules of Evidence Usually Not Required [LA CDI 94.60525; 94.60505; 100.0775]

Unless directed by the contract, strict observance of legal rules of evidence is not necessary in arbitration. While the parties may expressly require the arbitrator to observe legal rules of evidence, they seldom do so. In fact, they sometimes specifically provide that strict observance of such rules shall not be required.[1] Tripartite committees, set up by the National Academy of Arbitrators (NAA) to study evidence problems, agreed that the observance of rules of evidence should not be strictly required in arbitration proceedings.[2]

As stated by one federal court:

> In an arbitration the parties have submitted the matter to persons whose judgment they trust, and it is for the arbitrators to determine the weight and credibility of evidence presented to them without restrictions as to the rules of admissibility which would apply in a court of law.[3]

---

[1]*See* Goodyear Eng'g Corp., 24 LA 360, 361 (Warns, 1955).

[2]Jones, Jr., chair, *Problems of Proof in the Arbitration Process*: *Report of the West Coast Tripartite Committee, in* PROBLEMS OF PROOF IN ARBITRATION, PROCEEDINGS OF THE 19TH ANNUAL MEETING of NAA 149–50, 163 (Jones ed., BNA Books 1967) [hereinafter *West Coast Report*]; Stark & Feinberg, cochairs, *Problems of Proof in the Arbitration Process: Report of The New York Tripartite Committee, id.* at 295, 296 [hereinafter *New York Report*]. This volume contains extensive discussion, with a wide variety of viewpoints, as to the precise extent to which the various legal rules of evidence should be applied in arbitration. One committee reached a consensus on some general precepts to aid in gauging the extent of desirable resort to rules of evidence in a given case. *West Coast Report, supra,* at 163–66. Another committee summarized the basic rules of evidence used by courts and made suggestions as to their applicability in arbitration proceedings. Duff, chair, *Problems of Proof in the Arbitration Process: Report of the Pittsburgh Tripartite Committee*, NAA 19TH Proceedings, at 245, 249–60 [hereinafter *Pittsburgh Report*]. For other books dealing with various aspects of evidence in arbitration, see ZACK & BLOCH, LABOR AGREEMENT IN NEGOTIATION AND ARBITRATION 47–60 (BNA Books 2d ed. 1996); FAIRWEATHER'S PRACTICE AND PROCEDURE IN LABOR ARBITRATION 326–447 (Schoonhoven ed., BNA Books 4th ed. 1999); HILL & SINICROPI, EVIDENCE IN ARBITRATION (BNA Books 2d ed. 1987). For workshop discussions of various aspects of evidence in arbitration, see *Admissibility of Evidence, in* ARBITRATION 1982: CONDUCT OF THE HEARING, PROCEEDINGS OF THE 35TH ANNUAL MEETING OF NAA 107 (Stern & Dennis eds., BNA Books 1983); *Procedural Rulings During the Hearing, id.* at 138. *See also* Alleyne, *Delawyering Labor Arbitration*, 50 OHIO ST. L.J. 93 (1989) (proposing a simplified evidence code for labor arbitration). *But see* Andrews, *Legalism in Arbitration: II. A Management Attorney's View, in* ARBITRATION 1985: LAW AND PRACTICE, PROCEEDINGS OF THE 38TH ANNUAL MEETING OF NAA 191, 197 (Gershenfeld ed., BNA Books 1986) (asserting that "[t]he time has come for stricter adherence to evidentiary rules in labor arbitration").

[3]Instrument Workers Local 116 v. Minneapolis-Honeywell Regulator Co., 54 LRRM 2660, 2661 (E.D. Pa. 1963).

Another federal court, in reviewing an arbitration award within the court's jurisdiction under Section 301(a) of the Labor Management Relations Act (LMRA),[4] wrote "[i]t is well established that rules of evidence as applied in court proceedings do not prevail in arbitration hearings."[5] This has long been the rule under common law,[6] and is the rule under most of the state statutes that deal with the matter.[7] Where a case is covered by a state arbitration statute that is either silent or not specific on a point, the common law would ordinarily apply.[8]

In the absence of legislatively imposed limitations, courts have ruled not only that arbitrators are not bound by the "technical" exclusionary rules—in particular the rule against admission of hearsay evidence[9]—but also that they may not exclude relevant evidence because of "technical" procedural reasons.[10]

B. Evidentiary Rules Under Arbitration Statutes

The arbitration statutes typically do not inform the arbitral judgment with respect to the admissibility of proffered evidence.

The Federal Arbitration Act[11] applies to private-sector employment arbitration proceedings other than those involving contracts of employment of seamen, railroad employees, and other transportation workers.[12] The Federal Arbitration Act, however, does not deal directly with evidence admissibility issues. It authorizes the arbitrator to "summon in writing any person to attend . . . as a witness and in a proper case to bring with him . . . any book, record, document, or paper, which may be deemed material as evidence in this case."

---

[4]29 U.S.C. §151 et seq.

[5]Harvey Aluminum, Inc. v. Steelworkers, 263 F. Supp. 488, 490, 64 LRRM 2580 (C.D. Cal. 1967). As persuasive guides to this effect, the court quoted a state court decision and American Arbitration Association (AAA) Rule 28. The court recognized that the parties can require use of legal rules of evidence. *Harvey Aluminum*, 64 LRRM at 2582–83. In *Meat Cutters Local 540 v. Neuhoff Bros. Packers*, 481 F.2d 817, 820, 83 LRRM 2652 (5th Cir. 1973), the court, in upholding an arbitrator's refusal to consider the results of polygraph tests as evidence of guilt, said that "[v]iewed as a question of admissibility of evidence, the arbitrator has great flexibility and the courts should not review the legal adequacy of his evidentiary rulings."

[6]See cases cited in 6 C.J.S. 203 n.52.

[7]*See* Justin, *Arbitration: Proving Your Case*, 10 LA 955, 962–63 (1948). For example, the procedural rules of the Connecticut State Board of Mediation and Arbitration provide that "[c]onformity to legal rules of evidence shall not be necessary." Conn. Agencies Regs. §31-91-37 (1999). One of the few states that has changed the common law rule by statute is Georgia, whose arbitration statute provides that the "examination of witnesses and the admission of testimony shall be governed by the rules of the superior courts . . . ." Ga. Code Ann. §9-9-76 (Michie Supp. 2002). However, restrictive statutes such as this would be inapplicable to any case covered by LMRA §301. *See* Chapter 2, section 2.B., "State Law: Private Sector."

[8]*See* Chapter 2, section 2.B., "State Law: Private Sector."

[9]Farkas v. Receivable Fin. Corp., 806 F. Supp. 84 (E.D. Va. 1992); Petroleum Separating Co. v. Interamerican Ref. Corp., 296 F.2d 124 (2d Cir. 1961). *Cf.* Petroleum Transp. Ltd., Ionian Challenger v. Yacimientos Petroliferos Fiscales, 419 F. Supp. 1233 (S.D.N.Y. 1976).

[10]Teamsters Local 251 v. Narragansett Improvement Co., 503 F.2d 309, 87 LRRM 2279 (1st Cir. 1974).

[11]9 U.S.C. §1 et seq.

[12]Circuit City Stores, Inc. v. Adams, 532 U.S. 105, 85 FEP Cases 266 (2001).

The 1955 Uniform Arbitration Act, adopted or substantially followed in 49 states, provides that "[t]he parties are entitled to be heard, to present evidence material to the controversy and to cross-examine witnesses appearing at the hearing."[13]

However, the Revised Uniform Arbitration Act (2000) goes further and authorizes the arbitrator to "determine the admissibility, relevance, materiality and weight of any evidence."[14]

To the extent that state statutes do not conflict with the Federal Arbitration Act, they are not preempted. Of course, in any event, the parties may elect in their collective bargaining agreement to arbitrate under state law rather than under the Federal Arbitration Act.[15] Although most state laws are not instructive as to the kind of evidence that may or must be heard in an arbitration proceeding, many adopt the approach of Section 10 of the Uniform Arbitration Act, which provides for vacation of an arbitration award if the arbitrator was guilty of misconduct by "refusing to hear evidence pertinent and material to the controversy."[16]

C. Evidentiary Rules of Arbitration Agencies

The rules of arbitration agencies that the parties may be required to follow similarly commit the evidence admission-exclusion decision to the arbitrator's discretion. For example, Rule 28 of the American Arbitration Association's (AAA) Labor Arbitration Rules provides that the arbitrator is the judge of the relevancy and materiality of the evidence offered and that conformity to legal rules of evidence shall not be necessary.[17] Similarly, the

---

[13]7 U.L.A. §5. *See* Cooker, *Discovery in Labor Arbitration,* 72 MINN. L. REV. 1281 (1988); South Home v. Byrd, 102 N.C. App. 255, 401 S.E.2d 822 (1991).

[14]7 U.L.A. 15 (2000); Cold Mountain Builders v. Lewis, 746 A.2d 921 (Me. 2000) (arbitrators have broad discretion as to what evidence they will consider).

[15]Mastrobuono v. Shearson Lehman Hutton, Inc., 514 U.S. 52 (1995); Allied-Bruce Terminix Cos. v. Dobson, 513 U.S. 265 (1995).

[16]*E.g.*, KENTUCKY REV. STAT. ANN. §417.160(d) (Michie 1992); OHIO REV. CODE §2711.10(C) (West 1994); INDIANA CODE ANN. §34-57-2-13(a)(4) (Michie 1998).

[17]American Arbitration Association Labor Arbitration Rule 28 (2002) states:

The parties may offer such evidence as is relevant and material to the dispute, and shall produce such additional evidence as the arbitrator may deem necessary to an understanding and determination of the dispute. An arbitrator authorized by law to subpoena witnesses and documents may do so independently or upon the request of any party. The arbitrator shall be the judge of the relevance and materiality of the evidence offered and conformity to legal rules of evidence shall not be necessary. All evidence shall be taken in the presence of all of the arbitrators and all of the parties except where any of the parties is absent, in default or has waived the right to be present.

One arbitrator has interpreted Rule 28 to mean that arbitrators are empowered to judge the "relevancy and materiality" of the evidence only, and are not authorized to exclude items as incompetent, so that most evidence, including hearsay, is literally received unless it is of so little probative value that it can be eliminated without impairing proof of the issues. The arbitrator concluded that the Rule did not empower him to exclude hearsay as incompetent, but rather as permitting him to judge the "weight" of the evidence in his final decision. Relevancy and materiality include "weight," because an arbitrator's "duty to resolve factual disputes necessarily implies that he has to 'weigh' the evidence." Lever Bros. Co., 82 LA 164, 167 (Stix, 1983). *Cf.* Zirkel & Winebrake, *Legal Boundaries for Partiality and Misconduct of Labor Arbitrators,* 92 DET. C.L. REV. 679, 699 (1992) ("Courts grant labor arbitrators wide leeway in determining what evidence to hear and rarely vacate an award on grounds that the arbitrator improperly considered or denied evidence.").

National Railroad Adjustment Board (NRAB) rules do not require strict adherence to the rules of evidence used by judicial tribunals.[18]

The 1951 *Code of Ethics and Procedural Standards for Labor-Management Arbitration* provided that: "The arbitrator should allow a fair hearing, with full opportunity to the parties to offer all evidence which they deem reasonably material. He may, however, exclude evidence which is clearly immaterial."[19] The *Code of Professional Responsibility for Arbitrators of Labor-Management Disputes*, which was intended to supersede the *Code of Ethics*, is less restrictive than the *Code of Ethics* concerning the exclusion of evidence, stating in Section 5.A.1. only that an arbitrator "must provide a fair and adequate hearing which assures that both parties have sufficient opportunity to present their respective evidence and argument." Seemingly, it acknowledges the parties' interests in having leeway to present what they deem important.

2. Evidentiary Standards

A. The Liberal Admission of Evidence Philosophy: Use of the Nonjury Trial Evidentiary Standard

Arbitrators recognize the need to achieve a satisfactory balance between procedural efficiency and other interests:

> At the hearing the arbitrator must provide for procedural efficiency, and at the same time assure himself that he is getting all that he needs to decide the case. To be successful at this he must bear in mind simultaneously a number of complex considerations. The attorneys must be allowed to present their cases fully as they see them. Witnesses should be allowed to say what they feel is important, sometimes even when it is technically irrelevant. It is sometimes necessary to be aware of political considerations within the union or among management people involved in the case, or between union and management in the plant or industry.[20]

The net result of the flexible approach toward the admission of evidence is that, in a majority of cases, "any evidence, information, or testimony is acceptable which is pertinent to the case and which helps the arbitrator to understand and decide the problem before him."[21]

In regard to the flexible application of legal rules of evidence in arbitration proceedings, one arbitrator concluded that:

---

[18]Jones, National Railroad Adjustment Board 24 (1941). This is a finding of the Attorney General's Committee on Administrative Procedure. The NRAB's formal rules contain the general statement that the parties in their submissions "must clearly and briefly set forth all relevant, argumentative facts, including all documentary evidence submitted in exhibit form." 29 C.F.R. §301.5(d), (e).

[19]Part II, Rule 4(e).

[20]Eaton, *Labor Arbitration in the San Francisco Bay Area*, 48 LA 1381, 1391–92 (1967). *See, e.g.,* Flight Attendants (AFA) v. US Air, 960 F.2d 345, 350, 139 LRRM 2967 (3d Cir. 1992) ("The essence of the arbitral function is processing evidence to find facts and determine the grievance issues. The admissibility of evidence is for the arbitrator to decide.").

[21]Simkin & Kennedy, *Arbitration of Grievances* (U.S. Dep't of Labor, Div. of Labor Standards, Bull. No. 82) (1946), at 25.

> [Arbitrators] have established the pattern of ordered informality; performing major surgery on the legal rules of evidence and procedure but retaining the good sense of those rules; greatly simplifying but not eliminating the hearsay and parol evidence rules; taking the rules for the admissibility of evidence and remolding them into rules for weighing it; striking the fat but saving the heart of the practices of cross-examination, presumptions, burden of proof, and the like.[22]

Flexible arbitral application of formal rules of evidence is particularly justified in regard to those rules of proof that come from the criminal law. The application of these principles of proof in the field of arbitration, which deals with intra-workplace employer-employee relations, probably should not be accepted without consideration of the appropriateness of their use in the determination of rights by arbitrators under collective bargaining agreements.[23]

Arbitration, as originally conceived and practiced, supported the general rule of free admissibility of testimony and other evidence and rejected the judicial exclusionary rules of evidence in order that arbitrators be as fully informed as possible about the dispute to be resolved.

> First, the exclusionary rules were developed principally in the context of jury trials, to prevent lay jurors from being misled. . . . A second and broader consideration is how the exclusion of evidence may affect the perception of the employees and supervisors who are not familiar with legal technicalities. They want to tell the arbitrator what *they* think is important. If they are denied the opportunity to do so and are on the losing side, they will feel they were denied a fair hearing. . . .
>
> A third consideration is that the arbitrator who is asked to exclude evidence as irrelevant or immaterial is not in a very good position to make an intelligent ruling. A trial judge has the benefits of pleadings, pretrial conferences, and frequently pretrial briefs. This familiarity enables the judge to make informed rulings. . . .[24]

The inapplicability of the legal rules restricting the admission of evidence results in the parties being given a free hand to present any type of evidence thought to strengthen and clarify their case. Indeed, it has been observed that "the more serious danger is not that the arbitrator will hear too much irrelevancy, but rather that he will not hear enough of the relevant."[25]

In fact, the liberal reception of evidence is not as extreme a departure from traditional judicial practice as many persons might believe. Judges who are trying cases without a jury typically receive evidence very freely, on the

---

[22]Wirtz, *Due Process of Arbitration, in* THE ARBITRATOR AND THE PARTIES, PROCEEDINGS OF THE 11TH ANNUAL MEETING OF NAA 1, 13 (McKelvey ed., BNA Books 1958).

[23]For a similar view with extensive discussion, see Edwards, *Due Process Considerations in Labor Arbitration*, 25 ARB. J. 141 (1970).

[24]Murphy, *The Ten Commandments for Advocates: How Advocates Can Improve the Labor Arbitration Process, in* ARBITRATION 1992: IMPROVING ARBITRAL AND ADVOCACY SKILLS, PROCEEDINGS OF THE 45TH ANNUAL MEETING OF NAA 253, 263–64 (Gruenberg ed., BNA Books 1993) (emphasis in original).

[25]Shulman, *Reason, Contract, and Law in Labor Relations*, 68 HARV. L. REV. 999, 1017 (1955), *reprinted in* MANAGEMENT RIGHTS AND THE ARBITRATION PROCESS, PROCEEDINGS OF THE 9TH ANNUAL MEETING OF NAA 169 (McKelvey ed., BNA Books 1956). *See* Town of Melbourne Beach, Fla., 91 LA 280 (Frost, 1988) (citing Shulman with approval).

basis that they can determine its weight and relevancy after the entire case has been presented.[26]

B. Use of Administrative Agency Evidentiary Standards

Even more analogous to the arbitration context than the practice in nonjury trials are the evidentiary standards observed by administrative agencies. The criteria for admissibility or exclusion of evidence in federal administrative proceedings are found in the Administrative Procedure Act (APA):[27]

> Except as otherwise provided by statute, the proponent of a rule or order has the burden of proof. Any oral or documentary evidence may be received, but the agency as a matter of policy shall provide for the exclusion of irrelevant, immaterial, or unduly repetitious evidence. . . . A party is entitled to present his case or defense by oral or documentary evidence, to submit rebuttal evidence, and to conduct such cross examination as may be required for a full and true disclosure of the facts. In rule-making or determining claims for money or benefits or applications for initial licenses an agency may, when a party will not be prejudiced thereby, adopt procedures for the submission of all or part of the evidence in written form.[28]

Under the APA most, if not all, evidence is admitted, but given only such weight, if any, as the hearing officers, that is, administrative law judges (ALJs), in their discretion and judgment believe appropriate. Equally with professional arbitrators, and unlike lay jurors, ALJs are deemed to possess the training and experience necessary to properly evaluate the reliability of proffered evidence and disregard insubstantial, unreliable, or unfairly prejudicial evidence in formulating their decisions.

The theory—common to both arbitral and agency proceedings—is that

> the gate keeping function to evaluate evidence occurs when the evidence is considered in decisionmaking rather than when the evidence is admitted. Even though it arises later in the [arbitral or] administrative process than it does in jury trials, the [arbitrator's and] ALJ's duty to screen evidence for reliability, probativeness, and substantiality similarly ensures that final [arbitral and] agency decisions will be based on evidence of requisite quality and quantity.[29]

---

[26]In this regard, see comments by McDermott, *The Presidential Address—An Exercise in Dialectic: Should Arbitration Behave as Does Litigation?*, *in* DECISIONAL THINKING OF ARBITRATORS AND JUDGES, PROCEEDINGS OF THE 33D ANNUAL MEETING OF NAA 1, 13, 16–17 (Stern & Dennis eds., BNA Books 1981); Smith, *The Search for Truth: I. The Search for Truth—The Whole Truth, in* TRUTH, LIE DETECTORS, AND OTHER PROBLEMS IN LABOR ARBITRATION, PROCEEDINGS OF THE 31ST ANNUAL MEETING OF NAA 40, 50 (Stern & Dennis eds., BNA Books 1979). *See also* Roberts, *Evidence: Taking It for What It's Worth, in* PROCEEDINGS OF THE 40TH ANNUAL MEETING OF NAA 112, 118 (Gruenberg ed., BNA Books 1988) ("objections advanced at arbitration regarding a lack of materiality or relevance are entitled to a contemporaneous arbitral ruling accompanied by a statement of the grounds for admission or exclusion"). For a similar view and extensive discussion of the matter, see Hill & Westhoff, *I'll Take It for What It Is Worth—The Use of Hearsay Evidence by Labor Arbitrators: A Primer and Modest Proposal*, 1998 J. DISP. RESOL. 1 (1998).

[27]5 U.S.C. §556(d).

[28]*Id.*

[29]U.S. Steel Mining Co. v. Director, Office of Workers Compensation Programs, 187 F.3d 384, 389 (4th Cir. 1999). *See also* Johnson Controls Battery Group, 113 LA 769, 773 (Cantor, 1999).

Just as in arbitration proceedings, the "rules for admission of evidence before ALJs are . . . aimed not so much to protect the ALJ from prejudice but rather to facilitate efficiency in the process."[30]

By virtue of the APA's broad guidelines, hearsay evidence may be freely admitted.[31] Thus, the U.S. Court of Appeals for the Eleventh Circuit upheld an agency's decision to rely on an out-of-court statement of a power company representative that he had warned a contractor not to work in proximity to energized lines. The court stated that:

> Hearsay is admissible in administrative hearings and may constitute substantial evidence if found reliable and credible. *Williams v. U.S. Dep't of Transp.*, 781 F.2d 1573, 1578 n.7 (11th Cir. 1986). We have identified several factors that demonstrate hearsay's probative value and reliability for purposes of its admissibility in an administrative proceeding: whether (1) the out-of-court declarant was not biased and had no interest in the result of the case; (2) the opposing party could have obtained the information contained in the hearsay before the hearing and could have subpoenaed the declarant; (3) the information was not inconsistent on its face; and (4) the information has been recognized by courts as inherently reliable. *See U.S. Pipe & Foundry Co. v. Webb*, 595 F.2d 264, 270 (5th Cir. 1979) (citing *Richardson v. Perales*, 402 U.S. 389, 402–06, 91 S.Ct. 1420, 1428–30, 28 L.Ed.2d 842 (1971) (Footnote omitted)).[32]

The abrogation of the judicial exclusionary rules in favor of the liberal admission of evidence in administrative adjudicatory proceedings is not, however, without its critics.[33]

3. EVIDENTIARY GUIDELINES

A. Should All Evidence Be Received?

Perhaps the most extreme position—free and unrestricted reception of all evidence—was advanced as follows:

> One of the fundamental purposes of an arbitration hearing is to let people get things off their chest, regardless of the decision. The arbitration proceeding is the opportunity for a third party, an outside party, to come in and act as a sort of father confessor to the parties, to let them get rid of their troubles, get them out in the open, and have a feeling of someone hearing their troubles. Because I believe so strongly that that is one of the fundamental purposes of arbitration, I don't think you ought to use any rules of evidence. You have to make up your own mind as to what is pertinent or not in the case. Lots of times I have let people talk for five minutes, when I knew all the time that they were talking it had absolutely nothing to do with the case—just completely foreign to it. But there was a fellow testifying, either as a worker or a company representative, who had something that was important for him to get rid of. It was a good time for him to get rid of it.[34]

---

[30]*U.S. Steel Mining*, 187 F.3d at 388.

[31]J.A.M. Builders, Inc. v. Herman, 233 F.3d 1350, 19 OSH Cases 1241 (11th Cir. 2000).

[32]*Id.* at 1354.

[33]Glickman, *The Modern Hearsay Rule Should Find Administrative Law Application*, 78 NEB. L. REV. 135 (1999); Hill & Westhoff, *I'll Take It For What It's Worth—The Use of Hearsay by Labor Arbitrators: A Primer and Modest Proposal*, 1998 J. DISP. RESOL. 1 (1998).

[34]William Simkin, Conference on Training of Law Students in Labor Relations, *in* VOL. III, TRANSCRIPT OF PROCEEDINGS 636–37 (1947). The "therapeutic" approach has many adherents, but also some critics. *See Pittsburgh Report*, *supra* note 2, at 245–47. There have been

Even adherents of a more formal and structured approach to evidentiary issues frequently recognize that some excursions into extraneous matter may help the arbitrator get the background of the case or may help in understanding the viewpoints of the parties. Moreover, the relevance of evidence offered in arbitration, though it may appear at first glance not to be germane to the case, cannot always be determined accurately until the entire case has unfolded.[35] Accordingly, from a procedural standpoint arbitrators often accept evidence while reserving their response thereto until the challenged evidence can be evaluated in the light of the whole record.[36] The objection to the evidence, even if overruled, will serve to caution the arbitrator to examine the challenged evidence more closely before giving it weight.[37]

Actually, the admission of proffered evidence is much less likely to render the proceedings vulnerable to court challenge than is the exclusion of it.[38] Indeed, under many statutes an arbitrator's refusal to hear evidence may provide a ground for vacating the award.[39]

Of course, certain classes of evidence should be excluded. Confidential or privileged information acquired during contract negotiations, mediation efforts or settlement discussions, or employee assistance program counseling generally should not be admitted absent consent to disclose given by the party involved. Under certain circumstances, the source of the evidence may render it inadmissible. In the public sector, where evidence is uncovered during a police search, Fourth Amendment considerations may render it inadmissible.[40]

Whether evidence is admissible is a different question from what weight or probative value is to be given to it. For example, where a private investigator's report formed the sole basis for a termination decision, and

---

some complaints by parties about the looseness of arbitration proceedings in the matter of presentation of evidence. *See* Smith & Jones, *Management and Labor Appraisals and Criticisms of the Arbitration Process: A Report and Comments*, 62 MICH. L. REV. 1115, 1127–30 (1964).

[35]As to this, see an interesting discourse in *Procedural Problems in the Conduct of Arbitration Hearings: A Discussion, in* LABOR ARBITRATION: PERSPECTIVES AND PROBLEMS, PROCEEDINGS OF THE 17TH ANNUAL MEETING OF NAA 1, 10–11 (Kahn ed., BNA Books 1964). *See also* Smith, *The Search for Truth: I. The Search for Truth—The Whole Truth, in* TRUTH, LIE DETECTORS, AND OTHER PROBLEMS IN LABOR ARBITRATION, PROCEEDINGS OF THE 31ST ANNUAL MEETING OF NAA 49 (Stern & Dennis eds., BNA Books 1979).

[36]*See, e.g.,* American Shipbuilding Co., 69 LA 944, 947 (Ruben, 1977); San Gamo Elec. Co., 44 LA 593, 599–600 (Sembower, 1965); Capitol Airways, 40 LA 1048, 1052 (Seinsheimer, 1963); Potash Co. of Am., 16 LA 32 (Garrett, 1951).

[37]For further discussion, see Chapter 7, section 4.G.vii., "Objections to Evidence."

[38]*See* Harvey Aluminum, Inc. v. Steelworkers, 263 F. Supp. 488, 64 LRRM 2580 (C.D. Cal. 1967). *But see also* Meat Cutters Local 540 v. Neuhoff Bros. Packers, 481 F.2d 817, 820, 83 LRRM 2652 (5th Cir. 1973); Newspaper Guild Local 35 (Washington-Baltimore) v. Washington Post Co., 442 F.2d 1234, 76 LRRM 2274 (D.C. Cir. 1971).

[39]The UAA so provides. *See also* Chapter 2, "Legal Status of Arbitration in the Private Sector."

[40]Goldstein, *The Arbitrator's Responsibility to the Parties: Part II. Criminal Justice System in the Workplace, in* ARBITRATION 1990: NEW PERSPECTIVES ON OLD ISSUES, PROCEEDINGS OF THE 43D ANNUAL MEETING OF NAA 220 (Gruenberg ed., BNA Books 1991). Exclusion of evidence that is not promptly disclosed is discussed in section 3.c., "Requiring the Production of Evidence," below.

the report contained unsworn hearsay evidence and lacked corroborative testimony, it was admissible but entitled to little weight.[41]

B. What Type of Evidence Should Be Used?
[LA CDI 94.60515; 94.60521; 94.60525; 94.60529; 100.0775]

The specific evidence introduced in individual cases will vary greatly from case to case according to the question involved, the available evidence, and the burden of proof. In disputes over the setting of general wage rates, for instance, the most important type of evidence is documented statistical and economic data on such matters as prevailing practice, cost of living, ability to pay, and the like.[42]

In discharge or discipline cases, witness testimony concerning the facts that led to the disciplinary action comprises the most important evidence. Arbitrators have consistently ruled that the burden of proof in such cases rests with the employer and that the arbitrator may determine the weight and relevancy of evidence to decide the controversy.[43] However, the current status of an employee is not material in determining just cause for disciplinary action by an employer stemming from a past conflict.[44]

An employer's decision to rely solely on hearsay evidence in a case where it has the burden of proof has been deemed insufficient to sustain its case.[45] Where employees have been discharged or severely disciplined on alcohol or drug charges, the employer must produce verifiable evidence. If an employee has been tested, the employer must produce documentation of confirmed test results. If the employer refuses to give an employee a blood test, or urinalysis, despite the employee's request for one, the employer may not rely on observations of supervisory personnel for evidence.[46] If a private investigator especially hired by the employer or the employee's supervisor observes or suspects alcohol or drug use, any observable contraband should be confiscated and produced as evidence.[47] But, an arbitrator did not require the ac-

---

[41]Tarmac Va., 95 LA 813 (Gallagher, 1990). *See* Shoreline Sch. Dist., 96 LA 159 (Corbett, 1990) (discharge was upheld on hearsay testimony of children's statements regarding bus driver's lecture on abortion when corroborated by grievant's testimony). *But see* J&L Specialty Prods. Corp., 94 LA 600 (Duda, Jr., 1990) (coworker's written statement was not admissible, where there had been no opportunity to cross-examine during the grievance process and the agreement prohibited employer from calling as a witness in arbitration any employee from the plant in which the grievance arose).

[42]In one such case, "[n]o witnesses were heard but counsel for each party argued their positions and commented on the exhibits." Pensacola News-Journal, 49 LA 433, 433 (King, 1967). Documentary evidence in the form of joint exhibits was the only evidence presented in the "rights arbitration" case of *Alameda County Superintendent of Schools*, 76 LA 566, 566 (Anderson, 1981). *See also* Chapter 22, section 9., "Standards Applicable in Both Private-Sector and Public-Sector Interest Arbitration."

[43]Hilton Int'l Co. v. Union de Trabajadores de la Industria Gastronomica de P.R. Local 610, 600 F. Supp. 1446, 119 LRRM 2011 (D.P.R. 1985). See also *Meridian Med. Techs.*, 115 LA 1564 (King, Jr., 2001), and cases cited therein.

[44]Savannah Transit Auth., 86 LA 1277, 1280 (Williams, 1985).

[45]ABC Rail Prods. Corp., 110 LA 574 (Kenis, 1998) (employer did not prove just cause for the grievant's discharge, where the alleged victim of a threat from the grievant did not appear as a witness and the employer relied instead only on a statement from the alleged victim).

[46]Durion Co., 85 LA 1127, 1129–30 (Coyne, 1985).

[47]United States Borax & Chem. Corp., 84 LA 32 (Richman, 1984); Air Treads of Atlanta, 83 LA 1323 (Yancy, 1984).

tual contraband to be presented where the investigator produced as corroborating evidence daily reports of the drug activity made and filed with the investigative agency.[48]

Arbitrators have overturned disciplinary actions for alcohol or drug use if the evidentiary basis for the employer's case is incomplete. Such situations include the failure to prove the chain of custody in drug testing,[49] the lack of probable cause to require drug screening,[50] and the need to establish a nexus to the ability to perform on the job.[51]

The value of expert witness testimony in these cases was explained by an arbitrator as follows:

> Having reserved ruling on the qualifications of Union's expert witness, Dr. Russo, I now say that Dr. Russo's testimony may be deemed relevant on the issue of the propriety of Company's adherence to the NIDA [National Institute on Drug Abuse] guidelines. While Dr. Russo is not seen as an expert on challenge to Company's policy [termination for refusal to give a specimen or otherwise follow the testing procedures; termination for attempting to give an invalid specimen], his testimony is of assistance to your Arbitrator, as fact-finder, in determining whether Company's Program departs so substantially from the NIDA guidelines as to deny employees their rights of essential fairness and due process.[52]

Sometimes expert testimony is seen as essential to the employer's case. Where a medical review officer (MRO) was impersonated by a lay representative of the testing laboratory, an arbitrator found the nonperformance of his function required reversal of the discharge of a truck driver who had tested positive for marijuana use:

> As is readily apparent, the Medical Review Officer [M.R.O.] is regarded as the "lynchpin" of the drug testing process. The Medical Review Officer, who must be a licensed physician, has the obligation to review and interpret any confirmed positive test result, to examine the chain-of-custody documents and assure their regularity, to inquire into the subject's medical history and other relevant factors, to explore all alternative possibilities for the positive result after consultation with the subject and to reject any test results based upon a sample which had not been obtained or processed in accordance with the Departmental Regulations.
> The duties imposed upon an "M.R.O." in the case of a positive test result are not merely "administrative," they must be performed personally by the M.R.O. and may not be delegated. His role is designated as "essential."[53]

Responding to the employer's attempt to remedy the deficiency by having two certified MROs independently review the records and testify to the validity of the test results, the arbitrator continued:

---

[48]Georgia Pac. Corp., 85 LA 542 (King, 1985). *See also* Consumer Plastics Corp., 88 LA 208 (Garnholz, 1987).

[49]Metropolitan Transit Auth., 93 LA 1214 (Baroni, 1990).

[50]Utah Power & Light Co., 94 LA 233 (Winograd, 1990). *But see* Carlon, 99 LA 677 (Hoffman, 1992) (policy required "reliable witnesses" to establish probable cause to test); Day & Zimmermann, 94 LA 399 (Nicholas, Jr., 1990) (upholding random drug testing in an ammunition plant).

[51]See discussion in *Chicago Transit Authority*, 96 LA 1165 (Goldstein, 1991).

[52]Litton/Ingalls Shipbuilding, 97 LA 30, 35 (Nicholas, Jr., 1991).

[53]Schwebel Bakery Co., 118 LA 1028, 1038 (Ruben, 1997) (opinion explains the "gas/chromotography-mass/spectrometry" analysis).

However, none of these after-the-fact opinions satisfy the [Department of Transportation's] Regulation which expressly requires that the review must be performed "by the Medical Review Officer . . . *prior* to the transmission of the results to the employer['s] administrative officials." . . .

Rejection of such evidence does not rest on the Union's objection that the *ex post* procurement of such testimony to justify the Employer's reliance upon the deficient [laboratory] report cannot be impartial and independent. Rather, rejection is necessary in order to assure the parties obey the controlling Departmental Regulations. . . .

The parties have incorporated by reference into their Contract the Department of Transportation's drug testing Regulations, and the Arbitrator is bound to give effect to those Regulations. . . .[54]

Likewise, in the arbitration of medical and health issues, expert medical testimony or documentation is usually necessary. Where there is a conflict between doctors' opinions as to an employee's physical or mental condition, the employer may have a responsibility to obtain an impartial third opinion.[55]

In contract interpretation cases, the history of precontract negotiations and the past practice of the parties in applying the disputed provision may be of great importance. In some cases, visual or pictorial evidence is useful. The arbitrator's understanding of the dispute may be greatly improved, for instance, by visiting the physical site directly involved in the case.[56] Pictorial evidence also may be provided at the hearing room, as where photographs of employees operating machines were submitted to the arbitrator in a job-rating dispute.[57] In another case, a videotape purporting to show strike misconduct was relied upon by the arbitrator.[58] Indeed, as long as evidence "fits" and is relevant to the case, the unusual nature of the evidence should not bar its admission and consideration. Thus, in one case the sound and time recordings of the movements of a diesel locomotive were admitted to indicate the extent to which it was being utilized in a certain operation and to compare its efficiency with that of a steam locomotive.[59]

Ordinarily each party has the right to decide in what form it shall present its evidence; thus, one arbitrator refused to require a party to present its evidence through witnesses rather than through statements and exhibits.[60]

---

[54]*Id.* at 1039.

[55]*See* A.Y. McDonald Mfg. Co., 99 LA 118 (Loebach, 1992) (rejecting company doctor's opinion for failing to consider psychologist's evaluation or to relate grievant's medical condition to job requirements); Pepsi-Cola Gen. Bottlers, 98 LA 112 (Madden, 1991) (rejecting as conclusive one doctor's opinion, although no other doctor's opinion was in evidence); Kansas City Area Transp. Auth., 98 LA 57 (Cohen, 1991) (concerning evidence of depression and post-trauma stress).

[56]For full discussion, see Chapter 7, section 4.G.ix., "Site Visits."

[57]Brown & Sharpe Mfg. Co., 21 LA 461, 464–69 (Waite, 1953). *See also* Lucky Stores, 91 LA 624 (Ross, 1988) (photographs showing grievant's hair over 16-month period in dispute over compliance with hair-grooming rule); D.O. Inc. of Warren, 90 LA 1123 (Coyne, 1988) (reprimand improper for severe damage to warehouse door and wall, where employer presented no pictures of damage and union's pictures showed little or no damage); General Elec. Co., 75 LA 118, 120 (Larkin, 1980); Westinghouse Elec. Corp., 26 LA 836, 842 (Simkin, 1956).

[58]Pennzoil Co., 76 LA 587, 589 (Duff, 1981). For other uses of videotape/electronic surveillance, see *Emporium-Capwell*, 91 LA 845 (Concepcion, 1988); *A. Finkl & Sons*, 90 LA 1027 (Wolff, 1988); *Quaker Oats Co.*, 89 LA 1076 (Wright, 1987).

[59]Republic Steel Corp., 24 LA 336, 339 (Platt, 1955).

[60]Sewanee Silica Co., 47 LA 282, 283 (Greene, 1966). See section 9.D., "Unsupported Allegations," below.

Evidentiary standards utilized in awards in employer-promulgated arbitration proceedings where there is no union representation, no collective bargaining agreement, and no bargaining unit in the plant, may not be afforded precedential value.[61]

C. Requiring the Production of Evidence [LA CDI 94.60502]

Parties subject to the National Labor Relations Act (NLRA)[62] have a statutory duty, though by no means unlimited, to provide information needed by a requesting party in connection with grievance processing.[63] When this duty is not complied with, use of unfair labor practice proceedings, of course, may be available to obtain access to needed information but often would be prohibitively slow.[64] Some of the other methods that may be available for requiring the production of evidence in appropriate situations include arbitral issuance of subpoenas and direct requests by the arbitrator to the party possessing it. These other methods and certain related matters are treated below.

---

[61]Phillips 66 Co. Rail Car Maint. Ctr., 93 LA 707 (Goodstein, 1989).

[62]29 U.S.C. §151 et seq.

[63]In *NLRB v. Acme Indus. Co.*, 385 U.S. 432, 64 LRRM 2069 (1967), the U.S. Supreme Court recognized an employer obligation to provide information to the union to enable it to evaluate grievances that had been filed. The Court stated that the National Labor Relations Board's (NLRB) action in requiring the employer to provide information "was in aid of the arbitral process," which "can function properly only if the grievance procedures leading to it can sift out unmeritorious claims." *Id.* at 438. In *Machinists Dist. 10 (Square D Co.)*, 224 NLRB 111, 92 LRRM 1202, 1203 (1976), the NLRB majority wrote that, assuming, without deciding, that a union's duty to furnish information is "parallel" to that of the employer, there is "no statutory obligation on the part of either to turn over to the other evidence of an undisclosed nature that the possessor of the information believes relevant and conclusive with respect to its rights in an arbitration proceeding." For other cases relating to the scope of the duty to provide information in connection with grievance processing, see *Chesapeake & Potomac Tel. Co. v. NLRB*, 687 F.2d 633, 111 LRRM 2165 (2d Cir. 1982) (the union successfully utilized unfair labor practice proceedings to obtain information after the company had declined to comply with an arbitrator's subpoena for its production); *Communications Workers Local 1051 v. NLRB (AT&T, Long Lines Dep't)*, 644 F.2d 923, 106 LRRM 2960 (1st Cir. 1981) (the employer improperly refused to furnish the union photocopies of grievance-related documents—requiring the union to hand-copy the documents impeded the contractual grievance procedure); *Procter & Gamble Mfg. Co. v. NLRB*, 603 F.2d 1310, 102 LRRM 2128 (8th Cir. 1979) (employer improperly refused the union's request for information regarding a job evaluation plan needed by the union to evaluate two grievances alleging discriminatory job evaluation; this case is also useful for its collection of other cases dealing with various aspects of the duty to provide information); *Machinists Lodges 743 & 1746 v. United Aircraft Corp.*, 534 F.2d 422, 90 LRRM 2272, 2303 (2d Cir. 1975) (the employer could require the union to pay the cost of furnishing information where the amount of material requested was substantial). Under the facts in *U.S. Steel Corp.*, 79 LA 249, 252–53 (Neyland, 1982), the company's "assessment of a service fee for the furnishing of relevant information to the Union was improper." *See also* U.S. Postal Serv., 310 NLRB 391, 142 LRRM 1233 (1993); Teamsters Local 921 (San Francisco Printing Co.), 309 NLRB 901, 142 LRRM 1260 (1992). See *Reports on Conversations With Complaining Customer Are Not "Witness Statements" Exempt From Disclosure*, 137 LRR 363 (Sept. 21, 1991), for a general discussion of an employer's obligation to give a union information relevant to its duties as bargaining agent.

[64]Limitations of NLRB proceedings in this regard were asserted by Heinsz, Lowry, & Torzewski, *The Subpoena Power of Labor Arbitrators*, 1979 Utah L. Rev. 29, 34 (1979), as follows:

Although the *Acme* [NLRB v. Acme Indus. Co., 385 U.S. 432, 64 LRRM 2069 (1967)] holding is noteworthy for its recognition of the importance of full and reliable data prior

D. Evidence Requested by Arbitrator

In a significant sense, the absence of arbitral subpoena power is not very important, because the parties usually are willing to provide any data or evidence requested by the arbitrator either on the arbitrator's own motion or on motion of one of the parties.[65] Arbitrators do not hesitate to request the production of data or information if they have reasonable basis to believe that it will be germane to the case.[66] While the arbitrator often initiates the request for the production of evidence,[67] in other instances the arbitrator may make the request on the motion of the party that otherwise does not have access to the evidence in question.[68]

In one case, the arbitrator issued "an interim award" during the course of the hearing "directing the Company to submit certain payroll information to the Union for its use in connection with" the case.[69] Prior to the hearing in another case, an arbitration board of three neutrals issued the following order:

> Each party shall produce, at least three working days in advance of the hearing, for the use of the other party such specific documents or information in the employment history of either the challenging striker or the challenged replacement on which it expects to rely at the hearing. Further, at the demand of either party made at least five working days in advance of the hearing the

---

to invoking the arbitral process, it is of limited value due to the time-consuming procedure required to enforce its right of access to information. On the average it takes approximately one and one-half years from the time an unfair labor practice charge is filed in an NLRB regional office until the Board renders its decision. In the meantime, the arbitration is postponed while the tensions and pressures that arbitration was designed to quickly eliminate continue to build. Thus, the remedy provided by *Acme*, though useful in the proper context (e.g., collective bargaining), simply cannot meet the paramount need of the arbitral process—timely and efficient access to information. (footnotes omitted).

[65]*See, e.g.*, Clay City Pipe Co., 20 LA 538, 542 (Young, 1952). *See also* FLEMING, THE LABOR ARBITRATION PROCESS 175 (Univ. of Ill. Press 1965); Hoellering & Goetz, *Piercing the Veil: Document Discovery in Arbitration Hearings*, 47 ARB. J. 58 (1992); Tupman, *Discovery and Evidence in U.S. Arbitration: The Prevailing Views*, 44 ARB. J. 27 (1989); Cooper, *Discovery in Labor Arbitration*, 72 MINN. L. REV. 1281 (1988).

[66]*See* Chesapeake & Potomac Tel. Co. of W. Va., 21 LA 367, 369–71 (Dworkin, 1953). AAA Labor Arbitration Rule 44 provides that "the expenses of any witness or the cost of any proof produced at the direct request of the arbitrator, shall be borne equally by the parties, unless they agree otherwise, or unless the arbitrator, in the award, assesses such expenses or any part thereof against any specified party or parties."

[67]*See* E&G Eng'rs, 71 LA 441, 443 (Jones, Jr., 1978); City of Renton, 71 LA 271, 272 (Snow, 1978); Detroit Edison Co., 43 LA 193, 200 (Smith, 1964); Resistoflex Corp., 19 LA 761, 762 (Levy, 1952).

[68]*See* Ohio Dep't of Transp., 89 LA 890 (Rivera, 1987); Weyerhaeuser Co., 64 LA 869, 873 (Barnhart, 1975); Fruehauf Trailer Co., 29 LA 372, 373 (Jones, Jr., 1957); I. Hirst Enter., 24 LA 44, 47 (Justin, 1954); Chesapeake & Potomac Tel. Co. of W. Va., 21 LA 367, 369–71 (Dworkin, 1953); News Syndicate Co., 18 LA 55, 56 (Feinberg, 1952). However, one arbitrator stated it was beyond his authority to require that a transcription of the hearing be provided to the parties at a shared expense since the collective bargaining agreement between the parties did not specifically require it. Nuturn Corp., 84 LA 1058, 1060 (Seidman, 1985). *See generally* HILL & SINICROPI, EVIDENCE IN ARBITRATION 95–98 (BNA Books 2d ed. 1987).

[69]News Syndicate Co., 18 LA 55, 56 (Feinberg, 1952). Similar action by an arbitrator was upheld in *Ladies' Garment Workers (ILGWU) Local 246 v. Evans Mfg. Co.*, 318 F.2d 528, 53 LRRM 2455, 40 LA 864 (3d Cir. 1963). *See also* Highland Park Pub. Sch., 90 LA 984 (Borland, 1985).

other party shall produce such pertinent specific documents as the demanding party believes to be in the possession of the other party.[70]

In what one interest arbitration panel described as "an extraordinary case," the unions' claims for a change in the method of collecting employer contributions to fringe benefit funds were dismissed with prejudice because two locals repeatedly refused to submit documentary evidence requested by the panel. The documentary evidence was readily available to the locals and the unions did not explain their refusal.[71]

Perhaps the most practical rule to follow is that "neither the Company nor the Union should be allowed to withhold relevant and material testimony or other evidence except possibly in special circumstances . . . such as possible criminal incrimination, trade secrets and classified Defense mat-

---

[70]Yale & Towne Mfg. Co., 39 LA 1156, 1160 (Hill, Horlacher, & Seitz, 1962). *See also* Kaiser Aluminum & Chem. Corp., 87 LA 236 (Feldman, 1986); Evening News Ass'n, 68 LA 1314, 1318 (Volz, 1977). In *E&G Eng'rs*, 71 LA 441, 444–45 (Jones, Jr., 1978), the arbitrator stated that, although insufficient cause had been shown "for the issuance of an arbitral order of discovery," parties in arbitration may be "subject to arbitral discovery," in that the "obligation of disclosure to a proper degree and in proper circumstances is implicit in the contractual grievance procedure." However, it seems unlikely that wide support would exist for arbitral use of the full panoply of pretrial "discovery" procedures used by courts to enable a party to obtain information for use in preparing for trial (the term "discovery" as generally used in a technical sense in relation to court litigation concerns the acquisition of information in advance of trial as distinguished from requiring witnesses or documents first to be made available at the trial). For federal court rules relating to discovery, see 28 U.S.C. §1731 et seq., FED. R. CIV. P. 26–37. Rule 26 states the following methods of obtaining discovery: "depositions upon oral examination or written questions; written interrogatories; production of documents or things or permission to enter upon land or other property, for inspection and other purposes; physical and mental examinations; and requests for admission." Rule 45 deals with use of subpoenas to command the presence of persons or the production of "books, papers, documents or tangible things" at hearings or trials, or (as concerns discovery) at the taking of depositions. For pros and cons of arbitral use of court discovery procedures, see *West Coast Report, supra* note 2, at 170–71; Jones, Jr., chair, *Problems of Proof in the Arbitration Process: Workshop on West Coast Tripartite Committee Report, in* PROBLEMS OF PROOF IN ARBITRATION, PROCEEDINGS OF THE 19TH ANNUAL MEETING OF NAA 214, 218–27 (Jones ed., BNA Books 1967) [hereinafter *West Coast Report Workshop*]; *New York Report, supra* note 2, at 295, 304; Stark, chair, *Problems of Proof in the Arbitration Process: Workshop on New York Tripartite Committee Report*, NAA 19TH PROCEEDINGS, at 305, 333–34 [hereinafter *New York Report Workshop*]; FLEMING, THE LABOR ARBITRATION PROCESS 61–63 (Univ. of Ill. Press 1965); Sembower, *Halting the Trend Toward Technicalities in Arbitration, in* CRITICAL ISSUES IN LABOR ARBITRATION, PROCEEDINGS OF THE 10TH ANNUAL MEETING OF NAA 98, 102 (McKelvey ed., BNA Books 1957). *See also* Jonco Aircraft Corp., 20 LA 211, 212 (Merrill, 1953); North Am. Aviation, 19 LA 385, 390 (Komaroff, 1952). *But see* McFall, *The Search for Truth: Comment, in* TRUTH, LIE DETECTORS, AND OTHER PROBLEMS IN LABOR ARBITRATION, PROCEEDINGS OF THE 31ST ANNUAL MEETING OF NAA 152, 154 (Stern & Dennis eds., BNA Books 1979). Urging voluntary exchange by the parties of full information prior to the hearing, see Smith, *The Search for Truth: I. The Search for Truth—The Whole Truth, id.* at 40, 46; Zack, *Avoiding the Arbitrator: Some New Alternatives to the Conventional Grievance Procedure: Suggested New Approaches to Grievance Arbitration, in* ARBITRATION—1977, PROCEEDINGS OF THE 30TH ANNUAL MEETING OF NAA 105, 110–11 (Dennis & Somers eds., BNA Books 1978). In *Westinghouse Transport Leasing Corp.*, 69 LA 1210, 1215 (Sergent, Jr., 1977), the arbitrator considered that a party that has reason to believe that information that it lacks will be relevant at the hearing and is in the possession of the other party, should ask the latter to provide it prior to the hearing and should not be permitted to claim surprise if no request was made and the information is introduced into evidence at the hearing.

[71]Associated Gen. Contractors, 93 LA 753 (Sacks, 1989). For a review of the principle that failure to disclose documentary evidence relied on, at the earliest possible time, constitutes a denial of due process rights and requires exclusion of the evidence, see *Avis Rent-A-Car Sys.*, 99 LA 277 (DeLoach, 1992).

ters."[72] Applying the "relevant and material" qualification, arbitrators have refused to order the production of evidence for the purpose of uncovering grievances as distinguished from testing the validity of specific claims.[73]

E. Arbitrator's Subpoena Power and Discovery Authority
[LA CDI 94.60502]

It has been generally accepted that unless authorized by applicable statute or by the collective bargaining agreement, the arbitrator has no subpoena power.[74] Prior to the Supreme Court's decision in *Circuit City Stores,*

---

[72]Tectum Corp., 37 LA 807, 810 (Autrey, 1961). *See also* U.S. Borax & Chem. Corp., 93 LA 68 (Wilmoth, 1989); Safeway Stores, 89 LA 627 (Staudohar, 1987).

[73]*See* Santa Clara County, Cal., 36 LA 42, 43–44 (Wyckoff, 1961); Chrysler Corp., 22 LA 128, 138 (Wolff, 1954). *See also* Ozark Air Lines, 87 LA 1074 (Heekin, 1986); U.S. Steel Corp., 63 LA 98, 100 (Garrett, 1974).

[74]The Supreme Court construed the Federal Arbitration Act as generally applicable to private-sector employment contracts except those covering transportation employees. The Federal Arbitration Act authorizes arbitrators to issue subpoenas. However, whether the Federal Arbitration Act applies to collective bargaining agreements is still uncertain. *See* Wright v. Universal Mar. Serv. Corp., 525 U.S. 70, 159 LRRM 2769 (1998). In Heinz, *An Arbitrator's Authority to Subpoena: A Power in Need of Clarification, in* ARBITRATION 1985: LAW AND PRACTICE, PROCEEDINGS OF THE 38TH ANNUAL MEETING OF NAA 201 (Gershenfeld ed., BNA Books 1986), the arbitrator concluded that:

A review of the status of the law today concerning the power of arbitrators to issue subpoenas reveals that there is much conflict not only among those who question whether the power exists, but even among those who believe in such authority. There is also considerable disagreement as to the proper legal bases of the subpoena power. In such a situation an arbitrator issuing a subpoena on any legal ground today risks not only a reversal of his award but also potential tort liability. Such disharmony and uncertainty in the law can only weaken the arbitral process. Although §301 provides perhaps the best foundation for granting the subpoena power to labor arbitrators, it is more important that the courts clarify whether arbitrators possess the authority and, if so, on what legal grounds they might issue subpoenas. Only in this way can the parties and arbitrators involved in the arbitration process assure that they are acting within proper legal limits.

Id. at 222. *See also* Luskin & Elson, cochairs, *Problems of Proof in the Arbitration Process: Report of the Chicago Area Tripartite Committee, in* PROBLEMS OF PROOF IN ARBITRATION, PROCEEDINGS OF THE 19TH ANNUAL MEETING OF NAA 86, 99 (Jones ed., BNA Books 1967) [hereinafter *Chicago Area Report*]; Elson & Luskin, cochairs, *Problems of Proof in the Arbitration Process: Workshop on Chicago Tripartite Committee Report, id.* at 110, 140 [hereinafter *Chicago Report Workshop*]; *Pittsburgh Report, supra* note 2, at 245, 258. A report from the AAA also states:

It should also be noted that in some states there are statutes other than the arbitration statute which authorize the arbitrator to issue subpoenas. For example, Vermont's statute covering public sector labor disputes gives the arbitrator subpoena power . . . .

Arbitrator Subpoena Power, Law. Arb. Letter, Vol. 3, No. 26, at 1 (AAA 1979). However, some of the states having legislation giving arbitrators subpoena power do not *apply their statutes to labor contracts.* In the federal sector, the Civil Service Reform Act of 1978, Pub. L. No. 95-454 (codified as amended in scattered sections of 5 U.S.C.), specifies subpoena power for Federal Labor Relations Authority (FLRA) members, the FLRA General Counsel, the Federal Service Impasses Panel (FSIP), and ALJs, but it is silent regarding subpoena power for arbitrators. 5 U.S.C. §7132. Finally, it may be noted that some agreements do expressly grant the arbitrator power to call witnesses and to require production of documentary evidence. *See, e.g., Major Collective Bargaining Agreements: Arbitration Procedures* 66–67 (U.S. Dep't Labor Bull. No. 1425-6, 1966). For extensive and informative discussions of arbitral subpoena power, see Bedikian, *Use of Subpoenas in Labor Arbitration: Statutory Interpretations and Perspectives,* 1979 DET. C. L. REV. 575, strongly endorsing subpoena power for arbitrators; Heinsz, Lowry, & Torzewski, *The Subpoena Powers of Labor Arbitrators,* 1979

Inc. v. Adams,[75] there was doubt that the Federal Arbitration Act[76] applied to employment contracts. As a result of *Circuit City*, arbitration of disputes arising out of private-sector collective bargaining agreements, other than those covering transportation workers, may well be subject to the procedures of the Federal Arbitration Act.

Section 7 of the Federal Arbitration Act authorizes an arbitrator to

> summon in writing any person to attend . . . as a witness and in a proper case to bring with him . . . any book, record, document or paper which may be deemed material as evidence in the case.[77]

However, it remains unclear whether the Federal Arbitration Act applies to collective bargaining agreements.[78] In light of the uncertainty,[79] one observer pointed to LMRA Section 301 and suggested "the idea that because the arbitration process is now federal" an argument can be made that even in states that do not authorize arbitrators to issue subpoenas an arbitrator may do so.[80]

The Supreme Court in *Paperworkers v. Misco, Inc.*[80a] recognized that federal courts may look to the Federal Arbitration Act for guidance in developing federal law under Section 301 of the LMRA.[80b]

In *Television and Radio Artists v. WJBK-TV*,[80c] the U.S. Court of Appeals for the Sixth Circuit overturned a district court's dismissal of an action seeking enforcement of an arbitral subpoena against a third party, holding that the district court had erred in refusing to enforce the subpoena under Section 301 of the LMRA based on its determination that the subpoenaed information was not relevant to the proceeding.

Utah L. Rev. 29 (1979), stating that "thus far the judiciary has failed to fashion an arbitral subpoena process," and urging that it be done. *Id.* at 55. Also informative, see *Report of the Subcommittee on Labor Arbitration Procedures*, ABA Section of Labor and Employment Law Committee Reports 322–28 (1979).

[75]532 U.S. 105, 85 FEP Cases 266 (2001).

[76]9 U.S.C. §1 (1999).

[77]9 U.S.C. §7 (1999).

[78]Wright v. Universal Mar. Serv. Corp., 525 U.S. 70, 159 LRRM 2769 (1998).

[79]*See, e.g.*, Deerfield Cmty. Sch. Dist., 93 LA 316 (Michelstetter, 1988). See the results of the NAA survey, *Procedural Problems During Hearings*, The Chronicle (NAA), Apr. 1981, quoted in notes 93–94, below.

[80]Comment of T.L. Tolan, *in Chicago Report Workshop, supra* note 74, at 143–44. For more detailed suggestions along similar lines, see Heinsz, Lowry, & Torzewski, 1979 Utah L. Rev. at 48–55, who concluded that a "strong argument can be made that the proper basis of an arbitral subpoena is section 301 of the Labor Management Relations Act and the collective bargaining agreement," and that "the federal courts should establish the proper guidelines for the granting of arbitral subpoenas to assure the uniformity so necessary in labor cases," *id.* at 55; Matto, *The Applicability of State Arbitration Statutes to Proceedings Subject to LMRA Section 301*, 27 Ohio St. L.J. 692, 705–08 (1966). One court in fact did conclude that "pursuant to the authority embodied in section 301, subpoenas issued by labor arbitrators are, in appropriate circumstances, enforceable in the federal district courts"; but the court refused to enforce the subpoenas in question "until the arbitrator [was] given the opportunity to consider the relevance of the information sought and to rule on the Company's objections." Wilkes-Barre Publ'g Co. v. Newspaper Guild Local 120 (Wilkes-Barre), 559 F. Supp. 875, 113 LRRM 3409, 3414–15 (M.D. Pa. 1982). For related discussion, see Chapter 2, section 2.A.ii., "The Labor Management Relations Act."

[80a]484 U.S. 29, 40 n.9, 126 LRRM 3113 (1987).

[80b]29 U.S.C. §185.

[80c]164 F.3d 1004, 160 LRRM 2193 (6th Cir. 1999).

The Sixth Circuit held that apart from the question of whether the Federal Arbitration Act directly applies to collective bargaining agreements, guidance could be found in the statute's provisions and in court decisions concerning a district court's power to enforce subpoenas.

Although concluding that an arbitrator is authorized to issue a subpoena duces tecum to compel a third party to produce such records, either before or at the arbitration hearing, that the arbitrator deems material to the case,[80d] the court cautioned that its decision was not to be read to mean that a party to the arbitration is entitled to any discovery, and stated that it did *not* reach the question of whether an arbitrator may subpoena a third party for a discovery deposition in connection with a pending arbitration proceeding.[80e]

One arbitrator asserted that the adoption of contractual grievance and arbitration procedures carries with it an implied contractual duty to provide information in appropriate situations, and that this provides a proper basis for an arbitrator to issue a subpoena or an "arbitral discovery order."[81]

In states that have adopted or followed the approach of the 1995 UAA and apply it to labor arbitration proceedings, the subpoena authority of arbitrators is even more explicit. Section 7 provides for arbitral

> issuance of subpoenas for the attendance of witnesses and the production of . . .
> documents and other evidence . . . [and] may permit a deposition to be taken . . . of
> a witness who cannot be subpoenaed or is unable to attend the hearing . . . .[82]

The courts are divided, however, as to whether the UAA permits more comprehensive pretrial discovery.[83]

The subpoena issuance power of arbitrators is preserved and discovery authority explicitly conferred in the Revised Uniform Arbitration Act (2000) (RUAA).[84]

The RUAA addresses the issue of subpoenas and discovery in Section 17. The RUAA provides that an arbitrator may issue a subpoena for attendance of a witness and for the production of records at any hearing. The subpoena is to be served in a similar manner to subpoenas in a civil action and may be enforced in a civil action.[85] Section 17(b) provides for an arbitrator to permit a deposition of any witness to be taken for use as evidence at the hearing, including a witness that cannot be subpoenaed or is unable to

---

[80d]The court stated that the relevance of the information and the appropriateness of the subpoena should be determined in the first instance by the arbitrator. *Id*. at 1010.

[80e]The court noted, however, that at least one decision had held that an arbitrator may not compel attendance of a nonparty at a prehearing deposition, although the arbitrator could compel prehearing document production. *Id*. at 1009 n.7.

[81]*See* Bedikian, *Use of Subpoenas in Labor Arbitration: Statutory Interpretations and Perspectives*, 1979 DET. C. L. REV. 575, 598–601; Jones, *The Accretion of Federal Power in Labor Arbitration—The Example of Arbitral Discovery*, 116 U. PA. L. REV. 830, 836–38 (1960). In *E&G Eng'rs*, 71 LA 441, 445 (Jones, Jr., 1978), the arbitrator used both the term "subpoena" and the term "arbitral order of discovery" in connection with his view that an implied contractual obligation exists and supports arbitral commands for the production of information in proper circumstances.

[82]7 U.L.A. §7. *See* Cooker, *Discovery in Labor Arbitration*, 72 MINN. L. REV. 1281 (1988); South Home v. Byrd, 102 N.C. App. 255, 401 S.E.2d 822 (1991).

[83]7 U.L.A. §17 cmt. 2. (2002).

[84]The Revised Uniform Arbitration Act was designed to avoid preemption by the Federal Arbitration Act.

[85]7 U.L.A. §17(a).

attend a hearing. Section 17(c) provides for general discovery as an arbitrator determines is appropriate under the circumstances, taking into account the needs of the parties and the desirability of ensuring that the proceeding is fair, expeditious, and cost effective. The arbitrator may order a party to the arbitration proceeding to comply with discovery-related orders, issue subpoenas for attendance of a witness and for the production of records and other evidence at a discovery proceeding. Action may be taken against a non-complying party to the extent available were the controversy to have been litigated in a civil action.[85a] The RUAA incorporates those laws compelling a person under subpoena to testify, and all fees for attending judicial proceedings, depositions, and discovery proceedings apply to the arbitration as if the controversy were subject to a civil action in the state.[85b]

In comment 8 to the RUAA, the drafters stated that case law was clear that arbitrators have the power under Section 7 of the Federal Arbitration Act to issue orders such as subpoenas to nonparties whose information may be necessary for a full and fair hearing. The drafters also noted that under the Federal Arbitration Act and the Uniform Arbitration Act, courts have allowed nonparties to challenge the propriety of subpoenas and other discovery-related orders of arbitrators. Since arbitrators' orders are not self-enforcing, a nonparty may refuse to comply, and, at that point, the party seeking the information must proceed in court to enforce the arbitrator's order.[85c] The drafters note that courts have been very solicitous of the nonparty status of a third party and have scrutinized the degree to which a nonparty is required to divulge certain information that may put it at a competitive disadvantage or that is not sufficiently relevant to the arbitration proceeding.

The drafters described the intent of Section 17 as follows:

> The intent of Section 17 is to follow the present approach of courts to safeguard the rights of third parties while insuring that there is sufficient disclosure of information to provide for a full and fair hearing. Further development in this area should be left to case law because (1) it would be very difficult to draft a provision to include all the competing interests when an arbitrator issues a subpoena or discovery order against a nonparty (e.g., courts seem to give lesser weight to nonparty's claims that an issue lacks relevancy as opposed to nonparty's claims that a matter is protected by privilege); (2) state and federal administrative laws allowing subpoenas or discovery orders do not make special provisions for nonparties; and (3) the courts have protected well the interests of nonparties in arbitration cases.[85d]

[85a]*Id.* §17(d).

[85b]*Id.* §17(f).

[85c]Allied Auto. Group, Inc., 111 LA 748 (Nolan, 1998). The arbitrator noted that since the employees in question constitute transportation workers within the meaning of the Federal Arbitration Act, decisions under that statute are noncontrolling. The arbitrator went on to hold that although the board of arbitration had legal authority under Section 301 of the Labor Management Relations Act to issue subpoenas, the exercise of that right should not be a ministerial act. The arbitrator wrote: "[W]e should exercise that authority against third parties only after the party requesting a subpoena demonstrates the relevance of the testimony sought. In a case of a grievance alleging a scheme between the signatory and non-signatory to evade the law, testimony of the non-signatory's officials would be relevant once the Union has provided some independent evidence of the scheme's existence." *Id.* at 751.

[85d]7 U.L.A. §17 cmt. 8.

While the NRAB does not have the subpoena power,[86] its rules of procedure provide that the parties are charged "with the duty and responsibility of including in their original written submission all known relevant, argumentative facts and documentary evidence."[87]

Even though an arbitrator has the power to issue a subpoena duces tecum, the power need not be exercised. In one case, an arbitrator refused to require an employer to produce a written report completed by a supervisor under the theory that such documents are similar to an attorney's "work product" and are protected, absent contract language to the contrary.[88]

Where a subpoena had been issued by an arbitrator pursuant to state statute, a federal court responded as follows when asked to enforce the subpoena:

> Had the arbitrator and plaintiff's counsel utilized the enforcement procedures prescribed by the Federal Arbitration Act, . . . we would not be confronted with the hybrid question of defendant's compliance with a state subpoena. The plaintiff elected to proceed through avenues afforded by state process; it is not now within this Court's prerogative to intervene and enforce that process. Procedural niceties and technical obstructionism, however, with rare exception, should not be judicially nurtured; especially, is this true when lawful arbitration procedural remedies are already in progress. . . . This Federal Court does have concurrent enforcement jurisdiction and possesses the necessary statutory authority [citing the FAA] to enforce the procedures attendant upon the orderly consummation of this arbitration hearing. . . . Under this aegis, it will act *sua sponte* to sever the Gordian knot which created the impasse. The defendant shall produce forthwith the disputed file material for an *in camera* inspection by the arbitrator.
>
> Such a procedure will, of course, deny to the plaintiff-Union its claim of a carte blanche discovery privilege, to peruse the employer's file. Arbitration has never afforded to litigants complete freedom to delve into and explore at will, the adversary party's files under the pretense of pre-trial discovery. . . .
>
> It must be assumed that the presiding arbitrator is an experienced person well versed in evaluating the alleged claims of the employer, that some files contain classified security information involving national defense or plant security, personal health records and other similar confidential data. All of this should be screened from the file, except where the arbitrator determines it to be relevant evidence in the dispute. Even in the latter instances, proper safeguards should be ordered, such as sealing the record or limiting its access to counsel only, so that no unnecessary harm or prejudice or unnecessary embarrassment may be caused to anyone.[89]

In public-sector arbitration, an arbitrator's subpoena may be unenforceable as a matter of state law. [89a]

---

[86]JONES, NATIONAL RAILROAD ADJUSTMENT BOARD 25 (1941).

[87]29 C.F.R. §301.7(b).

[88]P.P.G. Indus., 90 LA 479, 481 (Sedwick, 1987).

[89]Machinists Local Lodge 1746 v. United Aircraft Corp., 329 F. Supp. 283, 286–87, 77 LRRM 2596 (D. Conn. 1971) (The court also upheld the arbitrator's authority to reopen the arbitration hearing in order to issue a subpoena that, by oversight, the arbitrator had failed to issue earlier in the arbitration proceedings.). *See also* Great Scott Supermarkets v. Teamsters Local 337, 363 F. Supp. 1351, 84 LRRM 2514, 2515–16 (E.D. Mich. 1973). In *Teamsters Local 757 v. Borden, Inc.*, 78 LRRM 2398 (S.D.N.Y. 1971), the court refused to enforce a subpoena obtained by a union from a state court, where an arbitrator had already taken the union's request for production of the desired books and records under advisement.

[89a]University of Mich., 114 LA 1394, 1401 n.24 (Sugerman, 2000) (grievant reinstated without back pay because although no adverse inference was drawn against grievant who

The American Arbitration Association has promulgated National Rules for the Resolution of Employment Disputes (National Rules) and Labor Arbitration Rules. In the National Rules, Rule 7 addresses discovery. This section states that the arbitrator shall have the authority to order such discovery by way of deposition, interrogatories, document production, or otherwise as the arbitrator considers necessary for a full and fair exploration of the issues in dispute, consistent with the expedited nature of arbitration. The National Rules provide in "Rule 24. Evidence" that an arbitrator may subpoena witnesses or documents upon the request of any party or may do so independently.

The Labor Arbitration Rules do not contain any rule dealing directly with discovery. Rule 28 provides that an arbitrator authorized by law to subpoena witnesses and documents may do so independently or on the request of any party.[89b]

One group expressed the view that "[e]ven assuming its legality, the use of the subpoena [duces tecum] is not to be encouraged. Demands for relevant information by either party should be honored without the formality of a subpoena."[90] However, in replying to that group and in urging that arbitrators should have subpoena power, some other commentators denied that this authority would inject undue formality into the arbitration process, and they explained that adequate safeguards against abuse of arbitral subpoena power exist by virtue of court superintendence of the exercise of that power.[91]

---

failed to provide his telephone records, which were not subject to production under Michigan law, the suspicion remained that the records in question would have proved harmful to the grievant's case).

[89b]For commentary dealing with subpoenas and discovery and arbitration, see *Subpoenas and Labor Arbitration*, 10 WORLD ARB. & MEDIATION REP. 68 (Mar. 1999); *Discovery in Arbitration*, 10-APR. BUS. L. TODAY 22 (3-4/01 Carnathan).

[90]*Pittsburgh Report, supra* note 2, at 258. The Chicago Tripartite Committee agreed. *Chicago Area Report, supra* note 74, at 99. This Committee deemed use of subpoenas justified in some situations (as where an employee is reluctant to take time off to testify) but of doubtful wisdom in others (as where an employee is required to testify against a fellow employee). *Id.* at 100.

[91]Heinsz, Lowry, & Torzewski, *The Subpoena Power of Labor Arbitrators*, 1979 UTAH L. REV. 29 (1979). The authors stated in part:

> Most courts and labor arbitrators have appropriately resisted any attempt to create an arbitral discovery process that would include interrogatories, depositions, and related procedures. Such procedures are expensive and technical. Their implementation would unduly delay the arbitration and would lessen the utility of arbitration as a prompt and inexpensive method of resolving disputes.
>
> But these are not real dangers to granting an arbitral subpoena power. . . . Empowering labor arbitrators to subpoena relevant evidence and witnesses, without adding a full scale pre-arbitration discovery process, will neither slow nor change the nature of arbitration. The grant of arbitral subpoena power will simply increase the facts available to the decision-maker.
>
> . . . A labor arbitrator . . . has the expertise to determine whether claimed information is material. Further, arbitral subpoenas are in the nature of administrative subpoenas. The subpoenas are neither self-executing nor self-enforcing, nor can an arbitrator compel compliance with a subpoena by a contempt citation or other enforcement mechanisms. If compliance is not forthcoming, the party who sought the arbitral subpoena must apply to a court for its enforcement. Similarly, the party who objects to a subpoena may apply to a court to quash it. Thus, upon proper motion by either party a court will review the matter and act as a judicial check on arbitral subpoena power to assure that only relevant evidence is being required and that the legal rights of the parties are adequately protected.

Id. at 40–42 (footnotes omitted).

Nevertheless, there is a clear indication that a variance sometimes exists between the absence of formal subpoena authority and actual arbitral practice. In fact, most arbitrators are willing to, and do, issue subpoenas.[92] This was clearly shown by an NAA survey of its members, who were asked the following question:

> You are requested by a party to issue a subpoena for the testimony of a person who is outside the parties' relationship and lives in a city distant from the hearing location. You have no information as to the substantive nature of the case. What do you do: (a) in a state which has a subpoena statute; (b) in a state which has no subpoena statute; and (c) if the request for the subpoena is under the Federal Arbitration Act?[93]

The responses revealed that "a majority of members under all three conditions will issue a subpoena without qualification or concern in regard to its enforcement."[94]

When a subpoena is to be issued, a procedure along the following lines might be utilized: The requesting party will prepare the subpoena and submit it to the arbitrator for signature; then the arbitrator or the requesting party will cause it to be served (by anyone other than a party to the case); the subpoena may thereupon be challenged as to scope, materiality, or reason-

---

[92]*See, e.g.*, Kroger Co., 115 LA 15 (Wolff, 2000) (arbitrator directed the union to provide the names of the employees who were allegedly denied rest periods, and documents pertaining to that allegation); Olin Corp., 90 LA 1206 (Fitzsimmons, 1988). *Contra* Teamsters Local 282, Case No. 13-300-426-99, 1999 WL 1066015 (Gregory, 1999) (arbitrator denied the employer access to the grievant's personal notes).

[93]*Procedural Problems During Hearings*, THE CHRONICLE (NAA), Apr. 1981, at 1, 7.

[94]*Id.* at 7. The survey also found that:

> The size of the majority declines considerably, however, if the request for a subpoena is made in a state without a statute. The concern here is whether the subpoena can be enforced. . . .
>
> There are a number of members who may ultimately issue a subpoena but only after certain steps are taken. Among these steps are: (1) insisting upon supporting arguments and/or disclosure of the reasons for requesting the subpoena before issuing the subpoena; (2) insisting that the other party be notified prior to issuing the subpoena; (3) cautioning the party requesting the subpoena as to possible liability for the expense of the witness; and (4) attempting to persuade the party to use other means to obtain the presence of the witness.

Id. at 7.

In part, the preference for establishing conditions or refusing to issue a subpoena prior to the hearing arises from a concern that the parties may be improperly requesting a subpoena and concern that the use of a subpoena may damage the arbitration process. Many of those members who do issue subpoenas upon request do so, however, with some qualms. *See also* Bedikian, *Use of Subpoenas in Labor Arbitration: Statutory Interpretations and Perspectives*, 1979 DET. C. L. REV. 575. There Arbitrator Harry H. Platt stated:

> The matter of subpoenaing witnesses or requiring the production of books and records is really a matter for the courts, unless there is a clear provision to the contrary granting such activity to an arbitrator. Although as an arbitrator, I have signed subpoenas upon request, the legality or validity is something I do not vouch for. There is no warranty, and certainly there are no contempt powers.

Id. at 594–95. Additionally, Arbitrator Robert G. Howlett stated:

> I have, on a number of occasions, issued subpoenas in private sector cases under the United States Arbitration Act. I have never had a case where the subpoena has not been obeyed. Clearly, the Act does not apply to any public sector situation. I have issued subpoenas in public sector cases—patently, without authority. However, they have always been obeyed.

Id. at 596–97.

ableness.[95] The arbitrator can weigh the interest of the parties and place restrictions on the use of materials obtained by subpoena.[96]

The party's refusal to comply with an arbitrator's subpoena allows an arbitrator to draw adverse inferences about the party's case, but does not justify granting the requesting party's motion to dismiss.[97]

F. Preservation of Evidence

Parties may have an obligation to cooperate in the preservation of evidence for use in grievance processing. Failure to take reasonable steps to preserve potentially illuminating evidence can weaken a party's position.[98] In this regard, an arbitrator ruled that where the parties fail to agree on what pictures should be taken at the scene of an accident, the scene must be "frozen"—left undisturbed—until a neutral can decide whether pictures are justified "with due regard to securing to the company full protection of any and all trade secrets concerning materials and equipment."[99]

Unconfirmed suspicion of alcohol or drug use is not grounds for discharge. If an employee is observed and suspected of an alcohol or drug violation, the contraband and/or container must be confiscated and preserved as evidence. Failure by employers to preserve items in question for inspection and use as corroborative evidence has led to the reinstatement of the grievant.[100]

---

[95]See Owens-Corning Fiberglas Corp., 86 LA 1026 (Nicholas, Jr., 1986); Automatic Elec. Co., 42 LA 1056, 1057, 1060–64 (Sembower, 1964); Schulze & Burch Biscuit Co., 42 LA 280, 281–82, 290 (Solomon, 1964). These three cases also recognize that use of subpoenas may present troublesome time problems, sometimes requiring adjournment of the hearing to a later date. In the latter regard, see also General Telephone Co. of Cal., 77 LA 1021, 1024 (Bickner, 1981), utilizing an "interim award" relative to subpoenas. See Indiana Gas Co., 109 LA 116 (Imundo, Jr., 1997) (management's failure to subpoena a witness with 3 days notice did not warrant a continuance). UAA §7 authorizes the arbitrator to issue (or cause to be issued) subpoenas and provides for court enforcement. The New York statute in addition authorizes issuance of subpoenas by the attorneys of record. N.Y. C.P.L.R. §§2308(b), 7505. In Teamsters Local 757 v. Borden, Inc., 78 LRRM 2398, 2399 (S.D.N.Y. 1971), the court observed that "[u]nder the United States Arbitration Act it is clear that only an arbitrator can issue a subpoena while under state law an attorney of record may issue a subpoena."

[96]In Minnesota Ass'n of Professional Employees, 97 LA 1107, 1112 (Ver Ploeg, 1991), the arbitrator required production of certain data subject to restrictions embodied in a protective order that the state contended was classified and private under MINN. STAT. §13.43. In Deerfield Community School District, 93 LA 316 (Michelstetter, 1988), the arbitrator issued a subpoena requiring production of data from two experts on local farm conditions to facilitate determination of their credibility where there was no evidence that the union intended to harass the witnesses, the request was not unduly burdensome, and orders limiting access to information would protect the witnesses' privacy interests. Also, failure of witnesses to testify, even when issued a subpoena, does not automatically result in a subpoena enforcement action. In Sterling Chemicals, 93 LA 953 (Taylor, 1989), the arbitrator noted the failure of several witnesses to respond to a subpoena. Nevertheless, based on the entire record, the grievance was denied.

[97]Niemand Indus., 88-1 ARB ¶8070, 3336–37 (Sergent, 1987). See generally BORNSTEIN & GOSLINE, LABOR AND EMPLOYMENT ARBITRATION §§7.01–7.05 (1989); GRENIG & ESTES, LABOR ARBITRATION ADVOCACY 36 (1989); HILL & SINICROPI, EVIDENCE IN ARBITRATION 285–90 (BNA Books 2d ed. 1987).

[98]See, e.g., Laura Scudder's, Inc., 87 LA 403 (Darrow, 1986).

[99]Airco Alloys & Carbide, 63 LA 395, 398–99 (Sembower, 1974).

[100]United States Borax & Chem. Corp., 84 LA 32 (Richman, 1984) (marijuana); Air Treads of Atlanta, 83 LA 1323 (Yancy, 1984) (suspected beer cans).

4. TYPES OF EVIDENCE

A. Right of Cross-Examination: Anonymous Witnesses and Confidential Documents

Because of the significantly prejudicial inability to cross-examine an anonymous accusing witness or defend against a secret accusatory document, arbitrators ordinarily will not accept an offer of evidence if it is conditioned on nondisclosure to the other party. Thus, for instance, disciplinary action based solely on the charge of an employee whose identity the employer was unwilling to reveal was set aside by an arbitrator who stated that no matter how meritorious the reasons for nondisclosure may be, it results in a lack of competent proof.[101] Like reasoning applies to employer reliance on allegedly confidential records not available as proof,[102] and to an employee's defense assertions supported by evidence that the union is unwilling to disclose.[103]

In certain limited situations, however, nondisclosure has not resulted in rejection of evidence. For example, one arbitrator accepted reports of professional "spotters," although the bus driver against whom the reports were used was not permitted to confront the spotters or otherwise know their identity, considering that (1) control over bus drivers is essential for the safety of the public and protection of company property, and the spotter system provides the only practical means by which supervision can exert its responsibility in the transit industry; (2) open identification of the spotters would destroy the effectiveness of the system; (3) the spotters, unlike ordinary employees, were trained observers taught to be accurate and objective, having no personal contacts with the employees and having no incentive to falsify facts; (4) the spotters' reports were prepared before the decision to discharge was made; and (5) there was no tangible basis for believing that the company was biased against the grievant.[104]

---

[101]Murray Corp. of Am., 8 LA 713, 714 (Wolff, 1947). *Accord* City of Bremerton, 97 LA 937 (Calhoun, 1991); Marin Tug & Barge, 91 LA 499 (Huffcut, 1988); Southern Cal. Gas Co., 89 LA 393 (Alleyne, 1987); Wolpin Co., 69 LA 589, 592 (Burwell, 1977); Bamberger's, 59 LA 879, 881 (Glushien, 1972); Michigan Standard Alloys, 53 LA 511, 513 (Forsythe, 1969); Pick-N-Pay Supermarkets, 52 LA 832, 834 (Haughton, 1969); Owens-Corning Fiberglas Corp., 48 LA 1089, 1091 (Doyle, 1967) (involving anonymous tip); Ames Harris Neville Co., 42 LA 803, 805 (Koven, 1964); Hooker Chem. Corp., 36 LA 857, 859 (Kates, 1961); A.C.&C. Co., 24 LA 538, 540–41 (Scheiber, 1955); Bower Roller Bearing Co., 22 LA 320, 323 (Bowles, 1954); Lockheed Aircraft Corp., 13 LA 433, 434 (Aaron, 1949). *See also* Gosline, *Witnesses in Labor Arbitration: Spotters, Informers, and the Code of Silence*, 43 ARB. J. 44 (1988); Wirtz, *Due Process of Arbitration, in* THE ARBITRATOR AND THE PARTIES, PROCEEDINGS OF THE 11TH ANNUAL MEETING OF NAA 1, 16–17 (McKelvey ed., BNA Books 1958) (discussion of "absentee evidence"). Where an accuser did confront the grievant at the arbitration hearing, failure to identify the accuser at the grievance meeting was held not to be improper. Cleaners Hangers Co., 39 LA 661, 664, 667 (Klein, 1962). *Accord* Max Factor & Co., 61 LA 886, 889–90 (Jones, Jr., 1973); Allied Maint. Co. of Ill., 55 LA 731, 735–37 (Sembower, 1970); Washburn-Purex Co., 53 LA 841, 844 (Sembower, 1969). *See also* Babcock & Wilcox Co., 75 LA 716, 720 (Johnston, 1980). *Cf.* Peachtree Doors, 91 LA 585 (Yarowsky, 1988) (employer obligated to maintain confidentiality).

[102]*West Coast Report, supra* note 2, at 204.

[103]Berg Airlectro Prods. Co., 46 LA 668, 672, 675–76 (Sembower, 1966).

[104]Los Angeles Transit Lines, 25 LA 740, 744–46 (Hildebrand, 1955). *Accord* Metropolitan Transit Auth., 88 LA 361 (Nicholas, Jr., 1987) (citing with approval Arbitrator George H. Hildebrand in *Los Angeles Transit Lines*); Shenango Valley Transit Co., 23 LA 362, 365

Another arbitrator added a very important qualification, however: "the necessity for the system would not justify its sloppy or unfair use in disciplinary procedure."[105] Thus, even where spotters were identified and testified, an arbitrator could not place strong weight on their testimony or written reports since the testimony was shaky and the reports had not been written up promptly.[106]

Some arbitrators are unreceptive to suggestions that the arbitrator interview spotters or other accusers in private,[107] and one arbitrator insists that the spotter be produced, if the spotter is to be relied upon, "even though the consequence would be to destroy his usefulness to the company."[108] Even where an accuser's identity is known to the grievant, if the accuser does not appear at the hearing to testify and be subject to cross-examination, it is still likely that the accuser's statement will be given reduced weight or will not

---

(Brecht, 1954). *See also* Twin City Rapid Transit Co., 37 LA 748, 750, 754 (Levinson, 1961); Delta Cartage Co., 29 LA 291, 292 (Oppenheim, 1957); Pennsylvania Greyhound Lines, 19 LA 210, 211 (Seward, 1952). In *Muskegon County Bd. of Comm'rs*, 71 LA 942, 948 (Allen, Jr., 1978), the discharge of grievant based on complaints received by grievant's fellow staff employees and from many clients of the county employer's drug rehabilitation program was sustained by the arbitrator, despite the hearsay and essentially anonymous character of the evidence, where (1) there was no animosity between grievant and his fellow employees, and (2) federal Department of Health, Education & Welfare (now the Department of Health & Human Services) regulations prevented disclosure of identity of the clients without their written consent. Believing the employer justified in not seeking consent for disclosure of identity because to do so could undermine the entire program, the arbitrator stated that "when one hears such complaints fed to several counsellors by many clients at different times and under different circumstances, it is logical to assume that there is substance in the accusations, and it is not the result of a mass conspiracy against an employee singled out for some unapparent reason." In *Wayne County Juvenile Court*, 68 LA 369, 370–71 (Forsythe, 1977), involving discharge of employees for alleged abusive treatment of children in custody, a child protection statute preserved the anonymity of persons reporting child abuse; the reports of such persons were admitted into evidence "to comply with the intent of" the statute. *See also* Gosline, *Witnesses in Labor Arbitration: Spotters, Informers, and the Code of Silence*, 42 Arb. J. 44 (1988).

[105]*Los Angeles Transit Lines*, 25 LA 740, 745 (Hildebrand, 1955). Another arbitrator added still another qualification: "in assessing the degree of discipline," the sworn denial of the accused should be given "the benefit of the doubt" as against the written report of the undisclosed spotter. Twin City Rapid Transit Co., 37 LA 748, 754 (Levinson, 1961).

[106]Twin City Transit, 65-2 ARB ¶8438 (Elkouri, 1965). Where the grievant is confronted with the spotter at the arbitration hearing, the spotter's testimony and report will be accepted into evidence. *See also* Dietrich Indus., 88 LA 214 (Feldman, 1986); Consumer Plastics Corp., 88 LA 208 (Garnholz, 1987); Pacific Bell, 87 LA 313 (Schubert, 1986); Specialty Paper Box Co., 51 LA 120, 126 (Nathanson, 1968); Grand Union Co., 48 LA 812, 816 (Scheiber, 1967) (also holding that delayed confrontation of the accused by the spotter is not improper, because premature confrontations impair future usefulness of spotter).

[107]*Procedural Problems in the Conduct of Arbitration Hearings: A Discussion*, in Labor Arbitration: Perspectives and Problems, Proceedings of the 17th Annual Meeting of NAA 1, 21 (Kahn ed., BNA Books 1964).

[108]*Id.* at 19. In one case a spotter was placed behind a screen where he was visible only to the arbitrator and counsel for the parties. Fleming, *Due Process and Fair Procedure in Labor Arbitration*, in Arbitration and Public Policy, Proceedings of the 14th Annual Meeting of NAA 69, 85 (Pollard ed., BNA Books 1961). Fleming also discussed confrontation cases in general. *Id.* at 82–87. Sometimes the collective bargaining agreement itself will indicate the extent to which testimony or proof by professional investigators may be used and the extent to which it must be subjected to cross-examination, as in *Bee Line*, 20 LA 675, 676 (Feinberg, 1953).

be admitted into evidence at all.[109] For example, a statement signed by numerous employees making certain factual assertions in a disciplinary case was admitted into evidence, over strenuous objections of the company, but could be given "very little weight" since most of the signers did not testify and were not subject to cross-examination.[110] However, the mere fact that a party presented its non-disciplinary case by written statements and exhibits, rather than through use of witnesses subject to cross-examination, was held not to deprive the opponent of a fair hearing where adequate opportunity to respond to the evidence did exist.[111]

In all of the above circumstances when arbitrators admit the statements, they seek to offset the effects of the lack of confrontation and cross-examination by admitting the evidence only "for what it is worth."[112]

B. Telephone Testimony

A related issue arises when one of the parties seeks to introduce non-expert witness testimony by telephone. While some arbitrators have permitted telephone testimony for basic background information or as a last resort,[113] most arbitrators view the use of telephone testimony with skepticism. Permitting a witness to testify by telephone prevents both the arbitrator, and the opposing advocate, from evaluating the witness's demeanor and thus hinders the ability to judge the witness's credibility. It also impairs a party's right to confront and to effectively cross-examine the witness.[114]

---

[109]*See* City of Pembroke Pines, Fla., 93 LA 365, 368 (Cantor, 1989) ("If the witness had appeared, the accusations made might have been proven."); Rohr Indus., 93 LA 145, 155 (Goulet, 1989) (no just cause for discharge when only evidence of wrongdoing was hearsay statements of three coworkers, only one of whom testified); Kent State Univ., 91 LA 895 (Curry, Jr., 1988); P.P.G. Indus., 90 LA 479 (Sedwick, 1987); Carnation Co., 89 LA 853 (Madden, 1987); Air Force Logistics Command, 75 LA 597, 602 (Johannes, 1980); 75 LA 155, 167 (Keenan 1980); Cleveland Cliffs Iron Co., 73 LA 1148, 1155 (Garrett, 1980); Keystone Steel & Wire Co., 72 LA 780, 783 (Elson, 1979); Apollo Merchandisers Corp., 70 LA 614, 618 (Roumell, Jr., 1978); General Tel. Co. of Ky., 69 LA 351, 354 (Bowles, 1977); Bethlehem Steel Corp., 68 LA 581, 584 (Seward, 1977); Penn Jersey Boiler & Constr. Co., 50 LA 177, 180 (Buckwalter, 1967); Rich Mfg. Co., 46 LA 154, 161 (Block, 1966). *Cf.* Baker Marine Corp., 77 LA 721, 722–23 (Marlatt, 1981); Monsanto Chem. Intermediates Co., 75 LA 592, 596 (Penfield, 1980).

[110]Rich Mfg. Co., 46 LA 154, 161 (Block, 1966). Customer accusations of employee disrespect carried less significance where the customers, though identified, were absent from the arbitration hearing. Penn Jersey Boiler & Constr. Co., 50 LA 177, 180 (Buckwalter, 1967).

[111]Sewanee Silica Co., 47 LA 282, 283 (Greene, 1966) (change in job classification).

[112]See section 4.C., "Hearsay Evidence," below.

[113]*See* Continental Carbon Co., 114 LA 1263 (Chumley, 2000) (because the human resource director was unable to attend the hearing, the arbitrator gave the union the choice of allowing the phone testimony, or postponing the hearing to a later date); Antilles Consol. Sch. Sys., 109 LA 1070 (Bressler, 1998); Immigration & Naturalization Serv., 98 LA 593 (Sweeney, 1992).

[114]In *Hillhaven Corp.*, 87 LA 360 (Corbett, 1986), the arbitrator rejected the company's request to allow telephone testimony of a key witness who was not present at the hearing because it "would result in questionable evidence." Specifically, the arbitrator held that telephone testimony "suffers from the inability to view the witness for the purpose of credibility." *Id.* at 363. *See also* St. Thomas/St. John Police Benevolent Assoc., 1994 WL 851213, at *15–16 (Kessler, 1994) ("Credibility cannot be weighed as effectively by telephone as it can be in person . . . [t]his is not merely a technical witness, or a disinterested expert testifying to a scientific conclusion . . . [s]uch a witness must not be merely heard, he must be seen as well during his testimony.").

C. Hearsay Evidence [LA CDI 94.60525]

"Hearsay" may be generically defined as "a statement, other than one made by the declarant while testifying at the hearing, offered in evidence to prove the truth of the matter asserted."[115] The definition includes assertions made outside of the arbitration tribunal offered to prove the truth of the assertions.[116]

The evidentiary value of the hearsay statement depends on the credibility of the declarant, who is, however, not subject to cross-examination and whose perception, memory, and truthfulness cannot be tested.[117] For this reason hearsay evidence is excluded from jury trials unless the hearsay falls within one of the "numerous exceptions where 'circumstantial guarantees of trustworthiness' justify departure from the general rule."[118]

Arbitrators are not in the position of lay jurors; they are expected to possess the cultivated judgment necessary to fairly determine the testimonial trustworthiness of the hearsay in question, and whether, in the absence of the ability to cross-examine the declarant, the opposing party has a fair opportunity and means to counter the testimony in an appropriate fashion.

Evidence of a hearsay character is often presented at arbitration hearings. Arbitrators will admit such evidence, but usually only after evaluating the reliability of the evidence. Where the reliability of the evidence is particularly questionable, arbitrators will exclude it.[119] If the evidence is admitted, many arbitrators qualify its reception, because of the lack of opportunity for cross-examination, by informing the parties that it is admitted only "for what it is worth."[120] One survey of labor arbitrators revealed the following responses as to whether hearsay evidence should be received:

---

[115]Fed. R. Evid. 801.

[116]McCormick on Evidence §246 (5th ed. 1999).

[117]Id. §245.

[118]Id. §253.

[119]In *Lewis Tree Service*, 114 LA 852 (Dissen, 2000), the arbitrator excluded written statements from purported witnesses obtained by management shortly before arbitration, concluding that the timing of the statements made their trustworthiness suspect. He stated, however, that hearsay should "be considered, provided some indicia of reliability can attach to the hearsay." *See, e.g.*, Lancaster, Ohio, City Bd. of Educ., 114 LA 673 (Feldman, 2000) (arbitrator did not consider testimony of mothers in a school bus driver's hearing about what their children told them, because the children themselves may not have been competent to testify).

[120]For general discussion of the hearsay rule *and its many exceptions* at law, with suggestions as to treatment of hearsay evidence in arbitration, see *Chicago Area Report, supra* note 74, at 90–91; *West Coast Report, supra* note 2, at 187–89, 212; *Pittsburgh Report, supra* note 2, at 249–50; Duff, chair, *Problems of Proof in the Arbitration Process: Workshop on Pittsburgh Tripartite Committee Report, in* Problems of Proof in Arbitration, Proceedings of the 19th Annual Meeting of NAA 263, 272–79 (Jones ed., BNA Books 1967) [hereinafter *Pittsburgh Report Workshop*]; *New York Report, supra* note 2, at 297–98. The text offers alternative definitions: "Hearsay consists of testimony given by a person who states, not what he knows of his own knowledge, but what he has heard from others." *Pittsburgh Report, supra* note 2, at 249. Another, more comprehensive definition, states: "'Hearsay evidence' is evidence of a statement that was made other than by a witness while testifying at the hearing and that is offered to prove the truth of the matter stated. A statement offered for some purpose other than to prove the fact stated by it is not hearsay." *West Coast Report, supra* note 2, at 212. *See also* Apollo Merchandisers Corp., 70 LA 614, 618 (Roumell, Jr., 1978). For two of the relatively infrequent instances in which an arbitrator sustained the objection to hearsay evidence, giving no consideration at all to it, see *Ohio Dep't of Rehab. & Correction,*

On the admission of hearsay into arbitration proceedings the consensus can be described as a collective shrug, a throwing-up of the hands, and a proclamation that it is inevitable. Many responses of both sides indicated that hearsay "has to come in," and that the arbitrator "can't keep it out." Admission of hearsay is justified to keep arbitration from becoming too cumbersome through procedural wrangling, or by the requirement that every witness who might be brought in be required to appear. It is agreed that the arbitrator must have wide latitude, and that he should let a witness with a grievance "get it out." Though the parties should feel that they have had their say in an informal manner, once admitted hearsay should be carefully weighed for its probative value. Despite the general fatalism expressed about the admission of hearsay evidence, there was still substantial opposition to its use.[121]

It is impossible to say just what the arbitrator in an individual case will consider hearsay evidence to be "worth." One arbitrator observed that "the reasons calling for the existence of a hearsay rule in common law jury actions should at least guide the judgment of the arbitrator in the evaluation of the weight, if any, to be attributed to such evidence in an arbitration proceeding."[122] In many cases very little weight is given to hearsay evidence, and it is exceedingly unlikely that an arbitrator will render a decision supported by hearsay evidence alone.[123] Further, hearsay evidence will be given

---

88 LA 1019, 1025 (Duda, Jr., 1987); Warner Robins Air Logistics Ctr., 74 LA 217, 220 (Clarke, 1980). For related discussion, see section 4.A., "Right of Cross-Examination: Anonymous Witnesses and Confidential Documents," above. See also *ABC Rail Prods. Corp.*, 110 LA 574, 580 (Kenis, 1998), discussing policy reasons for admitting hearsay in arbitration hearings, as highlighted in other decisions.

[121]Eaton, *Labor Arbitration in the San Francisco Bay Area*, 48 LA 1381, 1385 (1967). *See also* Wright, *The Use of Hearsay Evidence in Arbitration, in* ARBITRATION 1992: IMPROVING ARBITRAL AND ADVOCACY SKILLS, PROCEEDINGS OF THE 45TH ANNUAL MEETING OF NAA 289 (Gruenberg ed., BNA Books 1993). In *Walden v. Teamsters Local 71*, 468 F.2d 196, 81 LRRM 2608, 2609 (4th Cir. 1972), the court held that a union's failure to object to hearsay evidence in arbitration did not constitute a breach of its duty of fair representation, the court declaring that: "An arbitration hearing is not a court of law and need not be conducted like one. Neither lawyers nor strict adherence to judicial rules of evidence are necessary complements of industrial peace and stability—the ultimate goals of arbitration."

[122]Continental Paper Co., 16 LA 727, 728 (Lewis, 1951). The reason underlying an applicable exception to the hearsay rule was considered by an arbitrator in admitting hearsay statements as technically competent evidence without being given reduced weight. Faribault State Hosp., 68 LA 713 (Lipson, 1977). In *Faribault*, which involved res gestae declarations of a deceased employee whose discharge was the subject of the arbitration, the arbitrator stated that the "reason for the exception is the assumption that statements made contemporaneously with a crucial event, or while the declarant is excited are more likely to be true." *Id.* at 719.

[123]In the latter regard, see *San Francisco Gen. Hosp.*, 90 LA 1293, 1296 (Winograd, 1988). *See also* Sparklett Devices, 90 LA 910, 914 (Fowler, 1988); Phillips Painting Contractors, 72 LA 16, 19 (Brisco, 1978); Par Beverage Corp., 35 LA 77, 80 (Schmidt, 1960); Firestone Tire & Rubber Co., 20 LA 880, 885–86; (Gorder, 1953); Valier & Spies Milling Co., 19 LA 571, 574 (Klamon, 1952); Andrew Williams Meat Co., 8 LA 518, 522 (Cheney, 1947). *Cf.* McLouth Steel Corp., 35 LA 103, 108–09 (Siegel, 1960). In *Air France*, 71 LA 1113, 1116 (Turkus, 1978), the only evidence presented against the grievant was the record of testimony against him in a court case; the arbitrator gave such evidence "no probative value" because he "did not hear any of the witnesses whose testimony is now presented by way of the trial record, and was in no position to evaluate their credibility." In *Department of Veterans Affairs*, 110 LA 1083, 1086 (Kubie, 1998), the arbitrator sustained a grievance where "the record contain[ed] virtually no evidence as to what the Grievant said," and the Department's case "relie[d] entirely upon the kind of third-hand, double hearsay [that] jeopardizes fundamental fairness." In *Berberich Delivery Co.*, 79 LA 277, 283–84 (Kubie, 1982), a discharge for burglary was upheld on the basis of hearsay evidence where it was corroborated by evidence of grievant's flight from a law officer, by his failure to deny his involvement when questioned by his employer, and by his failure to testify in his own defense at the arbitration hearing.

little weight if contradicted by evidence that has been subjected to cross-examination.[124] In *IBP, Inc.*,[125] the arbitrator agreed "that hearsay evidence has a place in the arbitration setting, [but] it cannot outweigh otherwise apparently credible live testimony such as that given before the Arbitrator at hearing by a Grievant."[126] The weight given to hearsay evidence may depend on the source from which the testifying witness obtained the information. A pertinent observation concerning the weight of hearsay evidence was made by another arbitrator:

> [A] competent arbitrator may be depended upon substantially to discount some kinds of hearsay evidence that he has admitted over objection. He will do so selectively, however, and not on the assumption that hearsay evidence, as such, is not to be credited. If, for example, a newly appointed personnel manager, or a recently elected business agent, offers a letter to his predecessor from a third party, the arbitrator is likely to ignore the fact that the evidence is hearsay; if satisfied that the document is genuine, he will give it such weight as its relevancy dictates. On the other hand, hearsay testimony about statements allegedly made by "the boys in the shop" or by executives in the "front office," though perhaps not excluded from the record by the arbitrator, probably will have no effect on his decision.[127]

i. *Affidavits of Nonpresent Witnesses* [LA CDI 94.60519]

Affidavits are sometimes used in arbitration but are subject to the same limitations as other forms of hearsay evidence.[128] In this connection, AAA Rule 29 provides that arbitrators may receive and consider the evidence of witnesses by affidavit but should give it only such weight as they deem it entitled to after consideration of any objections made to its admission.[129] A similar approach was taken by the *Code of Ethics and Procedural Standards for Labor-Management Arbitration*, with the added qualification that the arbitrator "should afford the other side an opportunity to cross-examine the persons making the affidavits or to take their depositions or otherwise interrogate them."[130]

---

[124]*See, e.g.*, Howell Ref. Co., 27 LA 486, 492 (Hale, 1956). *See also* Tri-State Asphalt Corp., 72 LA 102, 106–07 (LeWinter, 1979); Borden Co., 20 LA 483, 484 (Rubin, 1953).

[125]112 LA 981 (Lumbley, 1999).

[126]*Id.* at 983 (internal citations omitted).

[127]Aaron, *Some Procedural Problems in Arbitration*, 10 VAND. L. REV. 733, 744 (1957).

[128]CF Motorfreight, 110 LA 186, 190 n.4 (Murphy, 1997) ("A notarized statement or affidavit normally is not given much weight in arbitrations when the individual involved is not present to testify at the arbitration hearing."); Grace Indus., 102 LA 119 (Knott, 1993) (affidavit of grievant's supervisor was not admissible, in part because the supervisor, who accused the grievant of wrongdoing, was not present at the hearing and the employer's representative offered no explanation for her absence or showing that any attempt was made to have her appear). *See, e.g.*, City of Berkeley, 88 LA 603, 605 (Staudohar, 1987); South Haven Rubber Co., 54 LA 653, 654–55 (Sembower, 1971); Borden Co., 20 LA 483, 484 (Rubin, 1953). *See also* Boise Cascade Corp., 114 LA 1379, 1384 (Crider, 2000) ("an affidavit is simply an unacceptable substitute for witness stand testimony in a case . . . where the absent witnesses are ones whose testimony is essential to prove crucial elements . . . and no real justification is offered for failing to appear and testify").

[129]*Accord* Snapper Power Equip., 89 LA 501, 505 (Weston, 1987).

[130]Part II, §4(e). The CODE OF PROFESSIONAL RESPONSIBILITY FOR ARBITRATORS OF LABOR-MANAGEMENT DISPUTES, which was intended to supersede the Code of Ethics, does not deal expressly with the use of affidavits.

D. Contemporaneous Written Notes

It has become commonplace in arbitration hearings for parties to introduce contemporaneous notes, reports, or written statements in order to refresh a witness's recollection, impeach a witness's credibility, or use as stand-alone evidence to prove or disprove certain facts.[131] Even when the author of the written material is not available to testify, arbitrators have allowed these contemporaneous notes into evidence over hearsay objections.[132] The admissibility of notes or reports made contemporaneously with the event in question has considerable support in the Federal Rules of Evidence as a hearsay exception.[133]

E. The Parol Evidence Rule [LA CDI 94.60521]

The parol evidence rule is frequently applied in arbitration cases.[134] Under the parol evidence rule, a written agreement may not be changed or modified by any oral statements or arguments made by the parties in connection with the negotiation of the agreement. A written contract consummating previous oral and written negotiations is deemed, under the rule, to embrace the entire agreement, and, if the writing is clear and unambiguous,

---

[131]*See generally* Department of the Air Force, 114 LA 1351 (Richard, 2000); Ryder Student Transp. Servs., 108 LA 743 (Franckiewicz, 1997); City Colleges of Chi., 106 LA 292 (Kohn, 1995); Westvaco Corp., 105 LA 180 (Nolan, 1995).

[132]Department of the Air Force, 114 LA 1351 (Richard, 2000) (contemporaneous counseling notes); Ryder Student Transp. Servs., 108 LA 743 (Franckiewicz, 1997) (interview notes of adolescent witnesses); Westvaco Corp., 105 LA 180 (Nolan, 1995) (contemporaneous records relied on over double and triple hearsay).

[133]FED. R. EVID. 803(5) reads as follows:

A memorandum or record concerning a matter about which a witness once had knowledge but now has insufficient recollection to enable the witness to testify fully and accurately, shown to have been made or adopted by the witness when the matter was fresh in the witness' memory and to reflect that knowledge correctly. If admitted, the memorandum or record may be read into evidence but may not itself be received as an exhibit unless offered by an adverse party.

See also MCCORMICK ON EVIDENCE §§279–281 (5th ed. 1999).

[134]Swanson Plating Co., 111 LA 373 (Harlan, 1998) (parol evidence rejected where contract clearly stated that laid-off employees get medical insurance coverage); Spartan Stores, 105 LA 549 (Kanner, 1995); Savannah Symphony Soc'y, 102 LA 575, 579 (Howell, 1994); City of Hartford, Conn., 97 LA 1016, 1018 (Freedman, 1991); Down River Forest Prods., 94 LA 141, 144–45 (Gangle, 1989); Technocast, Inc., 91 LA 164, 168 (Miller, 1988); Weil-McLain Co., 86 LA 784 (Cox, 1986); City of Depere, 86 LA 733 (Greco, 1986); Eureka Sec. Printing Co., 85 LA 1040 (DiLauro, 1985); Ferry-Morse Seed Co., 84 LA 75 (Duda, Jr., 1984). *See also* City of Evanston, Ill., 95 LA 679, 684 (Dilts, 1990); Day & Zimmerman, 91 LA 1003, 1006 (Belcher, 1988); Thomas/Sysco Food Servs., 90 LA 1036, 1039 (Wren, 1988); Ames Dep't Stores, 90 LA 452, 455 (Shanker, 1988); Northern Cal. Woodworking Mfrs. Ass'n, 79 LA 946, 947–48 (Koven, 1982); National Can Corp., 77 LA 405, 408 (Boner, 1981); Milwaukee Metro. Sewerage Dist., 76 LA 1220, 1228 (Mukamal, 1981); Klopfenstein's, 75 LA 1224, 1226 (Lumbley, 1980); Selig Mfg. Co., 71 LA 86, 89 (Foster, 1978); Niagara Plastics Co., 69 LA 1036, 1040 (Lewis, 1977); Tennessee-American Water Co., 69 LA 175, 176 (Finley, 1977); Thunderbird Hotel, 69 LA 10, 13 (Weiss, 1977); Bates Container, 68 LA 1006, 1009 (Sisk, 1977); Lord Corp., 68 LA 983, 985–86 (Cooley II, 1977); Burkhart-Randall, Textron Co., 68 LA 57, 63 (Render, 1977). The rule might be held waived if not advanced at the hearing. *See* American Can Co., 1 ALAA ¶67,165 (McCoy, 1943).

oral testimony will not be allowed to vary the contract.[135] This is said to be a rule of substantive law that, when applicable, defines the limits of a contract.[136] Sometimes the collective bargaining agreement will specifically prohibit consideration of verbal agreements that conflict with its provisions.[137]

While some might argue that arbitrators should consider any evidence showing the true intention of the parties and that this intention, as found by the arbitrator, should be given effect whether expressed by the language used or not, the often expressed contractual denial of power to the arbitrator to add to, subtract from, or modify the agreement provides special justification for the observance of the parol evidence rule.

There are exceptions to the parol evidence rule, however.[138] Thus, a collateral agreement not intended to be reduced to writing or an entirely distinct contemporaneous agreement may be held valid.[139] Moreover, an arbitrator may permit the use of parol evidence to show fraud or mutual mistake at the time of negotiations.[140] Of course, the parol evidence rule does not bar admission of evidence of precontract negotiations to aid in the interpretation of ambiguous language in the contract.[141]

It should also be remembered that the parties to a contract may amend or add to it by subsequent written agreement, as was elaborated by one arbitrator:

---

[135]RESTATEMENT (SECOND) OF CONTRACTS §§209, 210 (1981). *See also id.* App. Vol. 9, at 674–77 (1991).

[136]FARNSWORTH, CONTRACTS 465–66 (2d ed. 1990).

[137]*See* Pillsbury Mills, 14 LA 1045, 1047–48 (Kelliher, 1950).

[138]*See, e.g.*, City of Hartford, Conn., 97 LA 1016, 1018 (Freedman, 1991).

[139]Northern Ill. Mason Employers Council, 91 LA 1147, 1155 (Goldstein, 1988); Pettibone Corp., 70 LA 383, 385–86 (Gootnick, 1978); Barton Salt Co., 46 LA 503, 505 (Merrill, 1966); United Drill & Tool Corp., 28 LA 677, 680–81 (Cox, 1957); Trane Co., 23 LA 574, 580 (Spillane, 1954); Swift & Co., 8 LA 428, 429 (Gregory, 1947). *See also* Reden Corp., 50 LA 413, 416–17 (Roberts, 1968); Pennsylvania Truck Lines, 42 LA 311, 313 (Krimsly, 1964). A party alleging a contemporaneous oral agreement has the burden of proving it by clear and convincing evidence. *See* Sanilac County Rd. Comm'n, 52 LA 252, 255 (Howlett, 1969); Western Elec. Co., 46 LA 1018, 1020–21 (Dugan, 1966); B.P. John Furniture Corp., 32 LA 708, 711 (Tongue, 1959). *See also* American Motors Sales Corp., 48 LA 1040, 1044 (Yagoda, 1967). Arbitrators have held the collective bargaining agreement to be the controlling document where it conflicts with group insurance policies. *See* Chapter 9, section 3.A.x., "Insurance Policies."

[140]International Harvester Co., 17 LA 592, 594 (Forrester, 1951); Terre Haute Water Works Corp., 5 LA 747, 749 (Updegraff, 1946). *But see* Springfield Mech. Servs., 111 LA 403, 405–06 (Pratte, 1998) (rule does not apply to a writing used as evidence of a fact rather than as evidence of a contract). *See also* Chapter 10, section 9., "Waiver and Estoppel," and Chapter 18, section 3.K., "Remedies for Mistake."

[141]*See* Chapter 9, section 3.A.ii., "Precontract Negotiations and Bargaining History"; Fors Farms, 112 LA 33 (Cavanaugh, 1999); West Contra Costa, Calif., Unified Sch. Dist., 107 LA 109, 114 (Henner, 1996); Spartan Stores, 105 LA 549, 553 (Kanner, 1995); Jefferson Smurfit Corp., 102 LA 164, 166 (Duff, 1994); Saginaw Bd. of Educ., 101 LA 194, 198 (McDonald, 1993); Klein Mfg. Co., 101 LA 18, 20 (Traynor, 1993); Dayton Walther Corp., 96 LA 570, 572 (Wren, 1991) (explaining that "arbitral authority is quite liberal in allowing into evidence testimony with respect to contract negotiations, the parties' interpretation of terms in the agreement, and the like"); Pacific Bell, 93 LA 1199, 1202–03 (Freeman, 1989). In *Brigham Apparel Corp.*, 52 LA 430, 431 (Andersen, 1969), the arbitrator acted on the basis that the parol-evidence "doctrine does not preclude the admissibility of evidence designed to explain an ambiguity or to establish the meaning of terms or provisions which have a particular trade or occupational meaning."

Although the Labor Agreement is the chief instrument that guides the parties in their relationships there frequently arises an occasion when it is thought necessary or desirable to clarify, add to, or change the Agreement in some manner. This is what a side agreement does. They are very commonly used because the parties find them useful in some instances and necessary in other cases.[142]

Furthermore, on the basis of very strong proof, some arbitrators hold that a collective bargaining agreement may be deemed to have been amended by an oral agreement or subsequent practice.[143]

i.   Formal Versus Informal Records

Business records are a frequent source of proof in arbitration. Complete data taken directly from original business records ordinarily will be given more weight than estimates or informal records.[144] However, even informal records kept by the union or by the employees themselves may be given significant weight if the company has kept no formal records of the activity in question.[145]

ii.   The Best Evidence

The "Best Evidence" or "Original Document Rule" has been stated as follows:

> In proving the terms of a writing, where the terms are material, the original writing must be produced unless it is shown to be unavailable for some reason other than the serious fault of the proponent.[146]

A worthy view as to application of the "best evidence" concept in arbitration has been offered by a New York area tripartite committee:

> Best Evidence—Where objection is made to the introduction of evidence of a secondary nature on the ground that it is not the best evidence, the original document should be produced unless it is shown, for reasons satisfactory to the arbitrator, that it is not available. Reproductions of original documents shall be deemed the best evidence unless the authenticity of the purported original document is significantly in question.[147]

---

[142]Fox Mfg. Co., 47 LA 97, 101 (Marshall, 1966). See also Roadway Express, 105 LA 114, 116 (Eagle, 1995); CBS, Inc., 103 LA 596 (Christopher, 1994); Owens-Corning Fiberglas Corp., 102 LA 757 (Dworkin, 1994); ASG Indus., 70 LA 1225, 1228 (Cantor, 1978). Recognizing certain requirements for the binding effect of such subsequent agreements, see Cyclops Corp., 76 LA 76, 81 (Ipavec, 1981); General Tire & Rubber Co., 71 LA 813, 815–16 (Richman, 1978).

[143]See Chapter 12, "Custom and Past Practice."

[144]See Jonco Aircraft Corp., 22 LA 819, 823 (Merrill, 1954). See also Worcester Quality Foods, 90 LA 1305, 1308 (Rocha, Jr., 1988); Jim Walter Res., 90 LA 367 (Nicholas, Jr., 1987). Cf. Adrian Coll., 89 LA 857, 860 (Ellmann, 1987) (supervisor's diary not admissible as a business record).

[145]See Bethlehem Steel, 16 LA 926, 927–28, 931–32 (Feinberg, 1951).

[146]McCormick on Evidence §230 (West 5th ed. 1999).

[147]New York Report, supra note 2, at 299–300. Other tripartite committees expressed similar views. Chicago Area Report, supra note 74, at 92; Pittsburgh Report, supra note 2, at 252. The West Coast Committee referred to the best evidence rule at law as "a rather narrowly drawn prescription which mandates that 'no evidence other than the writing itself is admissible to prove the content of a writing.'" West Coast Report, supra note 2, at 189.

A West Coast area tripartite committee suggested that "[f]ailure, without adequate explanation, to produce a more reliable form of evidence should itself be recognized to have evidentiary weight adverse to the profferer of the lesser valued proof."[148]

F. Obtaining Information Through Coerced Employee Interviews
[LA CDI 100.5523; 118.306]

Of course, each party ordinarily should be free to interview any person who may have information relevant to a given grievance, provided the person voluntarily cooperates in the interview and the information sought is germane and appropriate to the proper preparation of the party's case. A more difficult question concerns the right of an employer to *require* employees to cooperate in the interview.

In *Cook Paint & Varnish v. NLRB*,[149] the U.S. Court of Appeals for the District of Columbia held that "[a]s part of a contractual arbitration procedure, an employer may conduct a legitimate investigatory interview in preparation for a pending arbitration," with the basic limitation that the interview "may not pry into protected union activities."[150] Quoting with approval the views of the arbitrator regarding the need for prearbitration interviews, the court refused to enforce an NLRB ruling that the employer violated the NLRA when its attorney told two employees they could be disciplined if they did not answer questions relating to a discharged coworker's grievance that was to be arbitrated. Rejecting the NLRB's apparently per se rule that an employer may never threaten an employee with discipline for refusing to cooperate in prearbitration interviews, the court said:

> The method in which disputes are resolved through a grievance-arbitration process is a contractual matter to be determined by the parties. The Board may not construct an inflexible rule that any compulsory interview conducted in preparation for a pending arbitration violates the Act.
>
> In so holding, we do not suggest that limits do not exist on the permissible scope of a legitimate pre-arbitration interview. An employer may in certain cases be forbidden from inquiring into matters that are not job-related. An employer also may be prohibited from prying into union activities, or using the interview as an excuse to discover the union strategies for arbitration.[151]

---

[148]*West Coast Report, supra* note 2, at 189. *See also* Internal Revenue Serv., 93 LA 261, 265 (Dilts, 1989) (finding grievance arbitrable where employer failed to produce "best evidence" of tardy notice, e.g., the return receipt or postmarked envelope). Also discussing application of the "best evidence" concept in arbitration, see HILL & SINICROPI, EVIDENCE IN ARBITRATION 30–31 (BNA Books 2d ed. 1987).

[149]648 F.2d 712, 106 LRRM 3016 (D.C. Cir. 1981).

[150]*Id.* at 723.

[151]*Id.* at 721–22. *See also* Department of the Air Force, 36 FLRA 748 (1990); Department of the Air Force, 35 FLRA 594 (1990). For related discussion, including the statement by the arbitrator quoted in *Cook*, see Chapter 7, section 3.H., "Preparing Cases for Arbitration."

i.　Confessions and Guilty Pleas to Criminal Charges
[LA CDI 100.552514; 118.643]

An arbitrator may ordinarily be expected to give little or no weight to a signed "confession" if the signature was obtained through inducements, compulsions, or threats.[152] One arbitrator explained:

> Such methods of obtaining confessions of guilt are patently wrong. A confession, to be valid in prosecuting a case must be statements given by the suspected person of his own free will and choice. Inducements and threats invalidate such documents as evidence.[153]

However, where the evidence showed neither "physical nor mental duress procuring the grievant's admissions of guilt, nor promises of leniency or reward in exchange for such admissions," the admissions could be used even though statements by security officers that grievant could be arrested helped induce the admissions.[154] Nor would a confession be deemed to be the product of duress or coercion merely because it was made under the pressure of circumstances.[155]

On the other hand, the mere fact that a "confession" is purely voluntary does not always endow it with validity. Thus, a confession of strike leadership was given no weight where there was no evidence surrounding the confession to indicate that the employee was in fact a "leader."[156]

---

[152]*See* Consolidation Coal Co., 99 LA 945 (Dissen, 1992); Heckett Div., 95 LA 195 (Nicholas, Jr., 1990); King Co., 89 LA 681 (Bard, 1987); Kroger Co., 71 LA 989, 991 (Heinsz, 1978); Safeway Stores, 55 LA 1195, 1202 (Jacobs, 1970); U.S. Steel Corp., 29 LA 272, 277 (Babb, 1957); Kroger Co., 12 LA 1065, 1067 (Blair, 1949). In *Thrifty Drug Stores Co.*, 50 LA 1253, 1262 (Jones, Jr., 1968), confession statements made by an employee in admitting guilt, but also implicating other employees, were regarded with skepticism; the question was "whether the statements are so tainted by compulsions created by the manner of their taking as to make it too speculative for a trier of fact . . . to give them credence as evidence against those whom they would implicate." But as to the *Thrifty Drug* decision, see comments by Edwards, *Due Process Considerations in Labor Arbitration*, 25 ARB. J. 141, 150–51 (1970). In *Casting Eng'rs*, 71 LA 949, 951–52 (Petersen, 1978), an employee's confession supported his discharge but was insufficient to incriminate other employees whom he also named in the confession. *See also* Rohr Indus., 93 LA 145, 157–58 (Goulet, 1989).

[153]Kroger Co., 12 LA 1065, 1067 (Blair, 1949).

[154]Weirton Steel Co., 50 LA 103, 104–05 (Kates, 1968). In *Weirton*, the arbitrator stated that he did "not subscribe to the doctrine that purity must always envelop those engaged in attempting to ascertain the truth, or that subterfuge or pretence is always improper in a truth-seeking endeavor." *Id*. at 105. *See also* Wisconsin Dep't of Health & Soc. Servs., 90 LA 333 (Imes, 1988); Excel Corp., 89 LA 1275 (McDermott, 1987); Newport News Shipbuilding & Drydock Co., 78 LA 921, 928 (Garrett, 1982). In *Lucky Stores*, 53 LA 1274 (Eaton, 1969), confessions were used although the employees had not been notified of any right to remain silent. The arbitrator stated that rules of the criminal law under the Constitution "do not necessarily apply in the same way to private investigations where there is no agent of the state present, which is the case here." *Id*. at 1276.

[155]Eastern Air Lines, 46 LA 549, 555 (Seidenberg, 1965). An employee's spontaneous or impromptu remark to a detective, "you got me fair and square," was admitted into evidence as "a damaging admission against interest" in the arbitration of the employee's discharge, although it had been excluded in a criminal action against the employee. Dannon Milk Prods., 76 LA 133, 137, 139 (Kramer, 1980). *See also* General Tel. Co. of Ind., 90 LA 380 (Cooper, 1987).

[156]Union Tank Car Co., 49 LA 383, 388–89 (Crawford, 1967).

An employee's plea of guilty in public criminal proceedings ordinarily can be accepted in arbitration as an indication of guilt.[157] A plea of nolo contendere also may be accepted as an indication of guilt because it operates as an admission of the facts on which the charge was based and results in the entry of a judgment of conviction.[158]

ii. *Offers of Compromise and Admissions*

Offers of compromise made in attempting to settle disputes[159] prior to their submission to arbitration are usually excluded from the record.[160] It is recognized that a party to a dispute may make an offer with the hope that a compromise can be reached and the dispute ended.[161] Even the mere introduction of such evidence may impair future attempts at dispute settlement. Thus, it has been strongly urged that offers of compromise should not be admitted into evidence.[162]

---

[157]*See* Department of the Air Force, 74 LA 949, 952 (Ward, 1980). Although a grievant testified that he had pleaded guilty to criminal charges only on advice of an attorney as "the easiest way out" and the way to obtain a suspended sentence, the arbitrator declared that "it is not possible to go behind such a plea." Northwest Airlines, 53 LA 203, 206 (Sembower, 1969). *See also* Washington Metro. Area Transit Auth., 94 LA 1172 (Garrett, 1990); West Monona, Iowa, Cmty. Sch. Dist., 93 LA 414 (Hill, Jr., 1989); Pepsi-Cola San Joaquin Bottling Co., 93 LA 58 (Lange III, 1989); Burger Iron Co., 92 LA 1100 (Dworkin, 1989); Bard Mfg. Co., 91 LA 193 (Cornelius, 1988); AMF Inc., 69 LA 987, 988 (Kleeb, 1977). In *American Airlines*, 68 LA 1245, 1247 (Harkless, 1977), a jury's "guilty" verdict was conclusive against the grievant in subsequent arbitration proceedings. *But see* King Co., 89 LA 681, 687 (Bard, 1987) ("while an arbitrator is prepared to take note of a jury's decision or a guilty plea in court, he nevertheless makes independent determinations both as to facts and applicable law"). For discussion of the preclusive effect of a guilty plea or conviction, see section 5., "Arbitral Use of the Doctrines of Res Judicata and Collateral Estoppel Following the Termination of Criminal, Civil, and Administrative Proceedings Arising Out of the Same Factual Context," below.

[158]In sustaining a discharge in *Great Scot Food Stores*, 73 LA 147, 148 (Porter, Jr., 1979), the arbitrator stated that although a "no contest" plea "is not identical with a technical conviction, the grievant by his plea, admitted to the facts." *See also* Standard Oil Co., 89 LA 1155 (Feldman, 1987); Vernors, Inc., 80 LA 596, 600 (McDonald, 1983). *But see* Akers Motor Lines, 41 LA 987, 990–91 (Woodruff, 1963). *See also* U.S. Postal Serv., 89 LA 495 (Nolan, 1987); General Tel. Co. of Cal., 87 LA 441 (Collins, 1986).

[159]For discussion of whether a conviction of a criminal offense is entitled to res judicata, issue preclusion, or collateral estoppel treatment, see section 5., "Arbitral Use of the Doctrines of Res Judicata and Collateral Estoppel Following the Termination of Criminal, Civil, and Administrative Proceedings Arising Out of the Same Factual Context," below.

[160]*See* Price-Pfister Brass Mfg. Co., 25 LA 398, 403–04 (Prasow, 1955); Stylon S. Corp., 24 LA 430, 436 (Marshall, 1955); E.I. DuPont de Nemours & Co., 14 LA 494, 497 (Cornsweet, 1950). *See also* Chapter 9, section 3.A.iv., "Compromise Offers in Grievance Settlement Negotiations."

[161]Universal Milking Mach. Co., 2 LA 399, 402 (Elson, 1946). *See also* Sterling Beef Co., 91 LA 1049, 1053 (Watkins, 1988); Akron Beacon Journal Publ'g Co., 85 LA 314, 318 (Oberdank, 1985).

[162]*Chicago Area Report, supra* note 74, at 93–94; *West Coast Report, supra* note 2, at 190; *Pittsburgh Report, supra* note 2, at 253; *Pittsburgh Report Workshop, supra* note 120, at 287–88. However, it should be noted that Rule 408 of the Federal Rules of Evidence provides in pertinent part: "Evidence of conduct or statements made in [settlement offer] or compromise negotiations is likewise not admissible. . . . This rule . . . does not require exclusion when the evidence is offered for another purpose, such as proving bias or prejudice of a witness. . . ." *See* Tribune Co. v. Purcigliotti, 1996 WL 337277 (S.D.N.Y. June 19, 1996); Kraemer v. Franklin & Marshall Coll., 909 F. Supp. 267 (E.D. Pa. 1995); Federal Deposit Ins. Corp. v. Moore, 898 P.2d 1329 (Okla. Ct. App. 1995); Gestetner Holdings, PLC v. Nashua Corp., 784 F. Supp. 78 (S.D.N.Y. 1992); Young v. U.S. Postal Serv., 1988 WL 126906 (S.D.N.Y. Nov. 23, 1988).

While admissions and statements against interest other than those made in settlement attempts may be considered by an arbitrator, the arbitrator can be expected to recognize that as a matter of law they are not conclusive.[163] However, admissions made by the grievant in the presence of union representatives during prearbitral grievance hearings may be given significant weight.[164] This is true also of grievant's admissions at the arbitration hearing itself.[165]

One arbitrator accepted, but refused to consider, testimony of outsiders to the effect that a discharged employee had admitted his guilt to them. The arbitrator urged that the testimony of outsiders, whether or not relevant, should not generally be admitted since the frequent admission of such testimony would tend to retard the growth of healthy industrial relations and would encourage the calling of character witnesses to refute or support the testimony of the outsiders, the building of technical alibis, and other legalistic practices that would prolong hearings at great expense but to no useful purpose.[166]

Admissions that have been acted on by others and those that appear in the record of prior proceedings so as to partake of the nature of judicial admissions may be held by arbitrators to be weighty evidence against the party making them.[167] Thus, where a party assumed a position in an arbitration case that was inconsistent with the position of that party in a prior arbitra-

---

[163]Harley-Davidson Co., 6 LA 395, 397 (Lappin, 1947). Regarding *grievance meeting* admissions and statements against interest other than offers of compromise, the question has been debated whether, from a policy standpoint, they should be considered by arbitrators. "Yes," stated General Electric Labor Relations Counsel Earl F. Jones, Jr., in *Letter to the Editor*, AAA STUDY TIME, Oct. 1979, noting that an earlier *Letter to the Editor* from Arbitrator Sidney L. Cahn had advocated the exclusion of such evidence. To this view Jones replied: "[U]nless the parties agree that grievance discussions are not to be brought up at hearings, the arbitrator should not impose such a prohibition"; if "a need is seen to protect the integrity of the grievance procedure by a blanket exclusion of evidence relating to offers of settlement and compromise, there is no basis for broadening the policy to apply to statements helpful in resolving questions of fact, especially in discipline cases." *Id.* at 4, 5. In rebuttal, Arbitrator Cahn explained: "The difficulty that I envision with this proposal is that once the 'door is opened' to admit testimony relating to admissions against interest or prior inconsistent statements, opposing counsel would have the evidentiary if not the legal right to introduce testimony of everything discussed by the parties during such grievance meetings." *Letters to the Editor*, AAA STUDY TIME, Jan. 1980, at 4, where a separate letter from Arbitrator Peter Seitz discouraged arbitral use against a party of statements made during grievance sessions because "acceptance of such testimony will have long-range damaging effects on the dispute-resolving system of . . . the parties." *Id.* at 3.

[164]Diebold, Inc., 48 LA 893, 900 (Bradley, 1967); *Chicago Area Report, supra* note 74, at 93, where a Chicago Area Tripartite Committee "agreed that admissions of the grievant during the grievance procedure present no problem." The Committee stated: "These certainly should be admitted in evidence. Admissions by other employees in the bargaining unit in the grievance procedure, and particularly the representatives of the union, fall into a different category. It is here the arbitrator should exercise the utmost caution." *Id.*

[165]Bethlehem Steel, 42 LA 307, 309–10 (Hughes, 1964).

[166]General Motors Corp., 2 LA 491, 497, 503 (Hotchkiss, 1938). *Cf.* Continental Paper Co., 16 LA 727, 728–29 (Lewis, 1951).

[167]*See, e.g.*, Commercial Filters Div., 91 LA 25 (Bethel, 1988); Mor-Flo Indus., Inc., 89 LA 762 (King, 1987); Herlitz, Inc., 89 LA 436 (Allen, Jr., 1987); Trew-Craft Corp., 87 LA 1113 (Kanner, 1986); North Am. Aviation, 21 LA 248, 251 (Komaroff, 1953); Goodyear Tire & Rubber Co. of Ala., 6 LA 681, 684 (McCoy, 1947). *See also* Kellogg Co., 28 LA 303, 308 (Meltzer, 1957).

tion case involving the same contract clause, the position taken in the prior case was one of the reasons for a decision against the party in the subsequent case.[168]

While the record of proceedings before a state workers' compensation commission was ruled inadmissible in a subsequent arbitration hearing as to the employee's capability of performing the job, the arbitrator nevertheless permitted statements made by the employee in the compensation proceedings to be used by the employer at the arbitration hearing for purposes of impeaching the employee as a witness.[169]

Testimony from other proceedings must be evaluated with special care and in the full setting of the prior proceeding. Moreover, one arbitrator observed that sometimes even in the same case an apparently damaging admission by a witness will have resulted from a momentary confusion, and that the arbitrator should exercise care not to overemphasize any single item of testimony, especially if it is inconsistent with other testimony of the witness and with the rest of the party's case.[170]

G. Use of Adverse Witnesses [LA CDI 94.60519]

Except for the following limitation, it appears accepted that the arbitrator should not limit the right of parties to call witnesses from the other side.[171] The common limitation on the right to call witnesses from the other side concerns management's right to call the grievant as its first witness in dis-

---

[168]Goodyear Tire & Rubber Co. of Ala., 6 LA 681, 684 (McCoy, 1947). The prior case was heard by the same arbitrator. Goodyear Tire & Rubber Co., 4 LA 231 (McCoy, 1946). *See also* Los Angeles County Dep't of Pub. Soc. Servs., 93 LA 164 (Knowlton, 1988); Apex Ready-Mix Concrete Co., 58 LA 1111, 1116 (Kates, 1972) (a term used by a party was "construed as a declaration against interest" and was given weight against the party in the same case).

[169]Vulcan Mold & Iron Co., 42 LA 734, 736–37, 739 (Sembower, 1964). In *St. Joe Minerals Corp.*, 70 LA 1110, 1114 (Roberts, 1978), admissions against interest made in unemployment compensation proceedings were similarly admissible in arbitration for impeachment purposes.

[170]General Elec. Corp., 16 LA 554, 559 (Willcox, 1951).

[171]See results of a 1981 survey by the NAA noted in Chapter 7, section 4.G.iii., "Order of Presenting Case"; *Chicago Area Report, supra* note 74, at 99; *Pittsburgh Report, supra* note 2, at 258; *New York Report Workshop, supra* note 70, at 324. However, it has been suggested that the calling of witnesses from the other side should not be encouraged. *Chicago Area Report*, at 99. As a matter of policy, some companies never call bargaining-unit members as witnesses. *West Coast Report Workshop, supra* note 70, at 233; *New York Report Workshop*, at 328. However, a party making no effort to call a person to testify might have little standing to complain that the other party failed to use the person as a witness. F.M. Stamper Co., 51 LA 533, 537 (Eaton, 1968). In *Jaeger Machine Co.*, 55 LA 850, 852 (High, 1970), inferences adverse to the union's case were created when the union refused to permit its representative to testify when the employer attempted to call him as a witness.

charge or disciplinary actions.[172] There is a division of opinion as to whether the company should have the right to call the grievant as a witness.[173]

Advocates for unions contend that an arbitrator who permits this practice is, in essence, allowing management to circumvent the rule that the employer must present its case first in matters involving discipline and discharge. The facts surrounding the employer's decision to discipline or discharge are within the employer's knowledge, and, considering the employer's advantage of access to personnel records and of initial disciplinary power, it is only equitable for the employer to present its entire case before the grievant is required to testify. This procedure is not designed to exempt the grievant from testifying, but rather is an attempt to ensure a fair hearing. Should the union attempt to close its case without calling the grievant, the arbitrator does have the authority to require the grievant's testimony, unless there are special circumstances that might involve criminal self-incrimination, trade secrets, or classified defense matters involving the grievant. Only in the rare cases in which the arbitrator requires the union to testify first should grievant's testimony precede management's testimony.[174]

Question has been raised as to whether a party calls an adverse witness at its peril; opinion differs as to how strictly such party should be held bound by the testimony of an adverse witness.[175]

---

[172]Rohm & Haas Tex., 91 LA 339, 343 (McDermott, 1988) (arbitrator refused to allow the grievant to be called as the employer's first witness in a hearing regarding a discharge for excessive absenteeism, because the employer had the burden of presenting its case and would have ample opportunity to cross-examine the grievant); City of San Antonio, Tex., 90 LA 159, 162 (Williams, 1987) (arbitrator required the employer to make a prima facie case regarding its disciplinary charges before allowing it to call the grievant as a witness and found that the criminal law restrictions against self-incrimination do not apply in labor arbitration). *See generally* BORNSTEIN & GOSLINE, LABOR AND EMPLOYMENT ARBITRATION §4.03[1][a][i][B] (1989); GRENIG & ESTES, LABOR ARBITRATION ADVOCACY 85 (1989); HILL & SINICROPI, EVIDENCE IN ARBITRATION 273–78 (BNA Books 2d ed. 1987); LEVIN & GRODY, WITNESSES IN ARBITRATION: SELECTION, PREPARATION, AND PRESENTATION 123–25 (BNA Books 1987); *Procedural Rulings During the Hearing, in* ARBITRATION 1982: CONDUCT OF THE HEARING, PROCEEDINGS OF THE 35TH ANNUAL MEETING OF NAA 138 (Stern & Dennis eds., BNA Books 1983).

[173]*See, e.g., City of San Antonio, Tex.*, 90 LA 159 (compelling grievant to testify at arbitration hearing challenging his suspension did not violate privilege against self-incrimination because arbitration is not a criminal proceeding and procedural fairness was satisfied by requiring the employer to make a prima facie case before allowing it to call grievant). See also results of a 1981 survey by the NAA noted in Chapter 7, section 4.G.iii., "Order of Presenting Case"; *West Coast Report, supra* note 2, at 201–02; *West Coast Report Workshop, supra* note 70, at 228–29; *Pittsburgh Report, supra* note 2, at 258; *New York Report, supra* note 2, at 324–25. See also panel discussion, *Procedural Problems in the Conduct of Arbitration Hearings: A Discussion, in* LABOR ARBITRATION: PERSPECTIVES AND PROBLEMS, PROCEEDINGS OF THE 17TH ANNUAL MEETING OF NAA 1, 27 (Kahn ed., BNA Books 1964). For related material, see section 4.H., "Failure of Grievant to Testify," below, and Chapter 7, section 4.G.iii., "Order of Presenting Case."

[174]*See* Aaron, *The Role of the Arbitrator in Ensuring a Fair Hearing, in* ARBITRATION 1982: CONDUCT OF THE HEARING, PROCEEDINGS OF THE 35TH ANNUAL MEETING OF NAA 30 (Stern & Dennis eds., BNA Books 1983). *But see* St. Marie's Gopher News, 93 LA 738 (Eisele, 1989) (despite strong union objection, the company was allowed to call the grievant as its first witness because this arbitrator, in his experience, had found that such allowance had not materially affected the outcome of the case).

[175]See panel discussion, *Procedural Problems*, NAA 17TH PROCEEDINGS, at 28 ("Ordinarily, a party may not impeach its own witness through his own testimony, except where he is a hostile witness or his testimony can be shown to constitute surprise."); *New York Report, supra* note 2, at 302 ("A hostile witness is one who manifests so much hostility or prejudice under examination that the party who has called him is allowed to cross-examine him, i.e.,

A related aspect is involved in the following question included in a survey of its members by the NAA:

> The testimony is clear that there is a witness in regard to an important controverted fact but, upon your inquiry, neither party intends to call that witness. What would you do?[176]

Not surprisingly, the responses indicated a division of opinion. Those members

> who hold the view that it is the obligation of the parties to present the evidence and the role of the arbitrator to decide the issue upon the facts presented will take no action. Those members who believe that a full and fair hearing depends upon the presentation of all evidence will take some action ranging from calling the witness to discussing the matter with the parties.[177]

H. Failure of Grievant to Testify

The individual grievant often is able to cast light on the dispute and ordinarily takes the witness stand. Indeed, arbitrators prefer that the grievant do so, as explained by one arbitrator: "I would like to see the grievant on the stand at some point during the proceeding, and I feel a little uncomfortable, frankly, when he is not. I don't know how many other people share that feeling."[178]

It is not unexpected that the failure of a grievant to appear and testify at the hearing of the grievance in some cases has been one of the factors leading to the arbitrator's conclusion that the grievance lacked merit.[179] How-

---

to treat him as though he had been called by the opposite party."). In *A-T-O, Inc.*, 72 LA 408, 410 (Shister, 1979), the arbitrator refused to permit the union to impugn the credibility of a company official it had called as a witness. Conversely, the testimony of an employer's official who testified pursuant to subpoena was "especially persuasive" on an arbitrator where it supported the union's case. Hempstead Pub. Sch. Bd. of Educ., 69 LA 808, 809, 811 (Gootnick, 1977).

[176]*Procedural Problems During Hearings*, The Chronicle (NAA), Apr. 1981, at 6.

[177]*Id.* at 6–7, where the following details are reported:

> Eighty-one members would not take any action whatsoever; another six would do nothing unless there was a due process question or problem, and another six members would call the witness only if it appeared that the case would turn on this testimony. Twenty members would call the witness on their own motion. Another 24 members might call the witness depending on the circumstances; that is, they would determine if there is a valid reason why the party does not wish to call the witness. The remaining members would take a variety of actions such as discussing the matter with the parties and urging that the witness be called or warning the parties that the testimony is crucial and noting what inference could be drawn by the failure of the witness to testify. However, these members would leave to the party the final decision as to whether the witness should be called.

Id. at 6.

[178]Comment by Russell Smith, *West Coast Report Workshop*, *supra* note 70, at 232. This statement was made in an NAA discussion; a poll was taken in response to this statement, revealing that a "very large majority" of those present shared his feeling. *Id.* For additional discussion of this matter, see Smith, *The Search for Truth: I. The Search for Truth—The Whole Truth*, in Truth, Lie Detectors, and Other Problems in Labor Arbitration, Proceedings of the 31st Annual Meeting of NAA 40, 54–56 (Stern & Dennis eds., BNA Books 1979), where he still expressed the belief that "grievant ought to give his version," but where he also acknowledged that "the notion that an employee ought not to have to testify when a disciplinary penalty assessed against him is being reviewed has some appeal."

[179]*See* Peachtree Doors, 91 LA 585 (Yarowsky, 1988); City of Hallandale, Fla., 91 LA 352 (Frost, 1988); Oregon Dep't of Human Justice, 90 LA 165 (Levak, 1987); Marathon Petroleum Co., 89 LA 716 (Grimes, 1987); C-E Bldg. Prods., 60 LA 506, 508 (Hall, 1973); Royal

ever, arbitrators sometimes have expressly stated that the failure of a grievant to testify creates no inference against him or her.[180] Even so, an arbitrator may pointedly note that the grievant's failure to testify has left the employer's case unrefuted.[181] The latter situation assumes, of course, that the company has adequately established its case by probative evidence.[182]

In most cases, a grievant's testimony will be beneficial to his or her case. It sometimes has happened, however, that "the chief witness against the grievant was the grievant."[183] Furthermore, if the grievant does take the witness stand, the grievant has an "obligation to testify frankly and fully."[184]

A question thus arises whether an employee may refuse to testify in arbitration by the exercise of a privilege against self-incrimination. One survey indicated that "there is a fairly clear consensus in the arbitration opinions" that the privilege against self-incrimination "established in the criminal law has no place, at least as such, in the arbitration of grievance cases (invariably discharge or disciplinary cases)."[185] In that same survey, however, an arbitrator spoke as follows: "My evaluation of a discharged employee's not testifying has depended on the circumstances. . . . I don't think one can generalize here."[186] One arbitrator proposed a set of rules whose effect would appear to give at least minimal application in arbitration to the privilege against self-incrimination.[187] Furthermore, another arbitrator urged arbi-

---

Shoe Mfg. Co., 52 LA 469, 473 (Carmichael, 1969); NRM Corp., 51 LA 177, 181 (Teple, 1968); Special Motor Freight, 48 LA 1036, 1038 (Hardy, 1967) (grievant was present but did not testify); Sealtest Foods, 41 LA 575, 576 (Turkus, 1963) (but same arbitrator viewed the grievant's silence differently in *United Parcel Service*, 45 LA 1050, 1051–52 (Turkus, 1965), because criminal charges were still pending against the grievant); Pilot Freight Carriers, 22 LA 761, 764 (Maggs, 1954); Brown Shoe Co., 16 LA 461, 465–66 (Klamon, 1951). *See also* 3M Co., 72 LA 949, 950–51 (Grabb, 1979); International Harvester Co., 23 LA 64, 65 (Cole, 1954).

[180]*See* Colgate Palmolive Co., 50 LA 504, 506 (McIntosh, 1968); National Carbide Co., 49 LA 692, 696 (Kesselman, 1967); Publishers' Ass'n of N.Y. City, 43 LA 400, 405 (Altieri, 1964); Maryland State Fair & Agric. Soc'y, 40 LA 1311, 1313 (Foster, 1962). It has been noted that there may be innocent explanations of failure to testify, as where the individual is "inarticulate, unintelligent, or easily confused." *West Coast Report, supra* note 2, at 201. Moreover, a grievant may not testify on advice of counsel because of a pending criminal proceeding. *See also* VRN Int'l, 74 LA 806, 809 (Vause, 1980). Parties sometimes stipulate that the nonappearance of the grievant shall not be prejudicial to his or her interests. *See* U.S. Rubber Co., 25 LA 417, 418 (Hall, 1955).

[181]*See* Colgate Palmolive Co., 50 LA 504, 506 (McIntosh, 1968); National Carbide Co., 49 LA 692, 696 (Kesselman, 1967); Southern Bell Tel. & Tel. Co., 26 LA 742, 745–46 (McCoy, 1956). In *Pepsi Cola Bottling Co.*, 70 LA 434, 435 (Blackmar, 1978), the grievant *did* testify regarding a transaction between himself and his supervisor, but the supervisor did not testify, so it was deemed "proper to conclude that he would not dispute the grievant's testimony" concerning the transaction. *See also* William Feather Co., 68 LA 13, 15 (Shanker, 1977).

[182]*See* Phillips Painting Contractors, 72 LA 16, 20 (Brisco, 1978).

[183]Diebold, Inc., 48 LA 893, 900 (Bradley, 1967). *See also* Capitol Mfg. Co., 46 LA 633, 636 (Gibson, 1966).

[184]Clark Grave Vault Co., 47 LA 381, 382 (McCoy, 1966). *See also* General Elec. Co., 72 LA 391, 403–04 (MacDonald, 1979).

[185]Wirtz, *Due Process of Arbitration, in* THE ARBITRATOR AND THE PARTIES, PROCEEDINGS OF THE 11TH ANNUAL MEETING OF NAA 1, 19–20 (McKelvey ed., BNA Books 1958) (where several unreported arbitration decisions are noted). *See also* Simoniz Co., 44 LA 658, 662–63 (McGury, 1964); Lockheed Aircraft Corp., 27 LA 709, 712–13 (Maggs, 1956); Brown Shoe Co., 16 LA 461, 465–66 (Klamon, 1951).

[186]Wirtz, NAA 11TH PROCEEDINGS, at 19 n.19.

[187]FLEMING, THE LABOR ARBITRATION PROCESS 185–86 (Univ. of Ill. Press 1965) (discusses the constitutional privilege against self-incrimination in some detail, *id.* at 181–85). *See* Carlson & Phillips, *Due Process Considerations in Grievance Arbitration Proceedings*, 2 HASTINGS CONST. L.Q. 519, 538–41 (1975) (discusses Fleming's proposed set of rules).

trators to give consideration to all Fifth Amendment principles, including the privilege against self-incrimination.[188] However, this view has been criticized.[189]

Employee discipline for "refusal to cooperate" has been upheld in some court and arbitration cases, even though the employee's position was based on the privilege against self-incrimination.[190] This was so, for instance, where an arbitrator upheld the discharge of an employee for refusal to be finger-printed in connection with an investigation into the theft of company products.[191] Failure of a grievant to testify, when faced with a forgery charge, allowed an arbitrator to draw the inference that the grievant had no ad-

---

[188]See Thrifty Drug Stores Co., 50 LA 1253, 1260–63 (Jones, Jr., 1968); West Coast Report, supra note 2, at 199–200. In the circumstances of one case, an arbitrator gave strong recognition to the privilege against self-incrimination. United Parcel Serv., 45 LA 1050, 1051–52 (Turkus, 1965). In Phillips Painting Contractors, 72 LA 16, 19–20 (Brisco, 1978), the arbitrator pointed out that California statutes make the privilege against self-incrimination applicable in arbitration proceedings, but that the privilege had not been properly invoked as concerned a question that posed "no real or substantial danger of incrimination." In a public-sector case, the arbitrator allowed a police officer to refuse to testify in the city's case on Fifth Amendment grounds, then allowed him to waive that right and testify once he had heard the city's case. City of Youngstown, Ohio, 107 LA 588, 590 (Skulina, 1996).

[189]Edwards, Due Process Considerations in Labor Arbitration, 25 ARB. J. 141, 151, 154–55, 157, 165 (1970). The criticized view is said to be "unrealistic in terms of providing a reasonable guide for harmonious collective bargaining between the parties." Id. at 154. The "standard of 'fairness,' which has traditionally been employed by arbitrators as the more flexible replacement for due process, seems far better suited to the composite needs of all of the parties to the tripartite collective bargaining relationship." Id. at 169. For other discussions relating to arbitral application of constitutional concepts, see Getman, What Price Employment? Arbitration, the Constitution, and Personal Freedom, in ARBITRATION—1976, PROCEEDINGS OF THE 29TH ANNUAL MEETING OF NAA 61 (Dennis & Somers eds., BNA Books 1976); Dunsford, Comment, id. at 71; Jones, Comment, id. at 85. See also Cameron Iron Works, 73 LA 878, 881 (Marlatt, 1979); Jones Dairy Farm, 72 LA 968, 971 (Maslanka, 1979).

[190]See FLEMING, THE LABOR ARBITRATION PROCESS 182–84 (Univ. of Ill. Press 1965).

[191]Colgate-Palmolive Co., 50 LA 441, 443–44 (Koven, 1968). In Foote & Davies, 88 LA 125 (Wahl, 1986), the arbitrator reduced the grievant's back-pay award because of his refusal to submit to a blood test to determine whether he was under the influence of intoxicants, because his refusal frustrated the only objective means of determination. In Exact Weight Scale Co., 50 LA 8, 8–9 (McCoy, 1967), the arbitrator held that an employee could not be discharged for refusing to say whether or not he had violated a company rule, but that back pay should be denied because the employee could have mitigated damages by answering promptly (he had finally answered "no," but not until the arbitration hearing). In Trans World Airlines, 46 LA 611, 612 (Wallen, 1965), the company was held entitled to require a hostess to demonstrate that she was not wearing a wig in connection with enforcement of regulations as to length of hair. Another arbitrator upheld a broadcasting company's right to require members of its news staff to fill out financial interests questionnaires (to prevent conflict of interest problems) against the charge that the requirement subjected the employees to self-incrimination. National Broad. Co., 53 LA 312, 318–19 (Scheiber, 1969). See also City of Bridgeport, Conn., 56 LA 52, 53–54 (Johnson, 1971). For cases involving self-incrimination arguments in connection with use of blood tests in determining sobriety, see Bi-State Dev. Agency, 72 LA 198, 205 (Newmark, 1979) (private employer would not be violating employee's constitutional rights in requiring sobriety test); Capital Area Transit Auth., 69 LA 811, 815 (Ellmann, 1977) ("profound issues of constitutional law" would be raised in requiring public authority employees to submit to sobriety test); Tennessee River Pulp & Paper Co., 68 LA 421, 426 (Simon, 1977). An employer's refusal to give a blood test requested by an employee left inadequate proof of intoxication, so reinstatement was ordered in Continental Conveyor & Equip. Co., 69 LA 1143, 1149 (Tucker, Jr., 1977). For related materials, see Chapter 17, section 10.E., "Employer Inspection of Employee Belongings," and section 15., "Union Bulletin Boards."

equate explanation of his conduct.[192] When a grievant failed to take the stand to refute any of the charges in a drug-use-related hearing, the arbitrator held that the grievant's inaction weighed against him.[193] In another case, the arbitrator held that, although the failure of the grievant to testify did not automatically create a negative inference, the failure of the grievant to call any witnesses at all in his case allowed the arbitrator to determine that the company's case was unrebutted.[194]

I. Significance of Failure to Provide Documentary Evidence or Call Available Witnesses

The significance of a refusal or failure of a party to provide data or evidence requested by an arbitrator has been addressed as follows:

> An arbitrator has no right to compel the production of documents [it might be otherwise if the arbitration is carried out under an arbitration statute] by either side. He may, however, give such weight as he deems appropriate to the failure of a party to produce documents on demand. The degree of weight to be attached to such failure will depend upon the relevancy of the documents requested to the issues at hand. If the information withheld appears to be strongly pertinent, the withholding of it may be vital in the making of a decision. If it is of doubtful relevancy and merely represents an attempt by one party to probe through the files of another on the mere chance that its position may be generally strengthened thereby, then the failure to produce such records should be disregarded.[195]

The failure of a party to call as a witness a person who is available to it and who should be in a position to contribute informed testimony may permit the arbitrator to infer that had the witness been called, the testimony

---

[192]Republic Airlines, 83 LA 127, 131 (Seidman, 1984). *See also* City of Saginaw, Mich., 108 LA 188 (Daniel, 1997) (grievant's failure to testify when discharged after his larceny conviction allowed the arbitrator to drawn an adverse inference).

[193]Marathon Petroleum Co., 89 LA 716, 720, 723 (Grimes, 1987). *See generally* BORNSTEIN & GOSLINE, LABOR AND EMPLOYMENT ARBITRATION §§7.01–7.05 (1989); GRENIG & ESTES, LABOR ARBITRATION ADVOCACY 83–84 (1989); HILL & SINICROPI, EVIDENCE IN ARBITRATION 261–68 (BNA Books 2d ed. 1987). But see also in *Department of Labor*, 98 LA 1129 (Barnett, 1992), where an adverse inference was drawn against the government because of its failure to produce the supervisor to testify that he did not engage in behavior attributed to him by the grievant.

[194]Michigan Employment Sec. Agency, 109 LA 178 (Brodsky, 1997).

[195]American Tel. & Tel. Co., 6 LA 31, 43 (Wallen, 1947). *See also* Department of Health & Human Servs., Soc. Sec. Admin., 86 LA 1205, 1211 (Kubie, 1986) ("If I learn that one party without good cause has withheld or is withholding pertinent information subject to its control from the other—or from me—I make it clear at an early stage that I will be free to assume, should it seem appropriate to do so, that the withheld, repressed or concealed information would undercut the position of the party in whose control it is."); Barnard Eng'g Co., 86 LA 523, 528 (Brisco, 1985) ("[His] deliberate and calculated refusal to comply with the subpoena, regardless of its legal effectiveness, compels the conclusion that had he brought the subpoenaed documents they would have been adverse to his position . . . ."). A Pittsburgh Tripartite Committee stated that "an arbitrator should be free to draw conclusions from an individual's failure to testify." *Pittsburgh Report, supra* note 2, at 258. Cf. statement of Arbitrator Daniel Kornblum, *in New York Report Workshop, supra* note 70, at 328–29; Chesapeake & Potomac Tel. Co. of W. Va., 21 LA 367, 371 (Dworkin, 1953). For some instances in which a party's refusal to submit requested data or evidence created an inference against the party, see *Piscataway Township Bd. of Educ.*, 74 LA 1107, 1110 (Jacobson, 1980); Vickers Petroleum Corp., 73 LA 623, 625 (Carter, 1979); Pettibone Corp., 70 LA 383, 387 (Gootnick, 1978).

adduced would have been adverse to the position of that party.[196] Where an employer failed to have the single accusing witness appear, however, the arbitrator expressed concern because of the accuser's absence and found insufficient evidence to support the employee's discharge.[197]

In cases where an employee is discharged for substance abuse, sufficient documentation of employee conduct is mandatory to meet the employer's burden of proof, whether it be confirmed medical tests or investigative reports, or actual confiscated contraband. Arbitrators will sustain grievances where the employer fails to provide verifiable evidence. One arbitrator stated that "to discharge a person for suspected but unconfirmed intoxication is to discharge unjustly."[198] Another arbitrator wrote: "[A]rbitrators do not make decisions based on 'feelings' and 'intuitions.' One man's word is not enough to convince this arbitrator that another man is lying and guilty of committing a rule violation."[199] Yet another arbitrator sustained a grievance arising out of a warning for alleged neglect of duty and noted the absence of eyewitness testimony and the reliance on circumstantial evidence that was found not to be compelling.[200]

i.   *Circumstantial Evidence* [LA CDI 94.60505]

Evidence is circumstantial when it does not directly prove the existence of a fact, but gives rise to a logical inference that such fact exists.[201] One arbitrator has given the following familiar example: "Proof that a defendant was observed standing over a victim with a smoking gun in his hand permits the inference that it was the defendant who pulled the trigger."[202] Drawing inferences and factual conclusions from circumstantial evidence has been said to be an arbitrator's stock-in-trade.[203]

---

[196]*See* Southern Cal. Permanente Med. Group, 92 LA 41, 45 (Richman, 1989); Cal-Compack Foods, 105 LA 865 (Oestreich, 1995); Mississippi Power Co., 90 LA 220 (Jewett, 1987); Downtown St. Paul Partners, 90 LA 67 (Cooper, 1987); Schlage Lock Co., 88 LA 75 (Wyman, 1986); Amoco Oil Co., 87 LA 493 (Goldstein, 1986); Shop Rite Foods, 75 LA 625, 628 (Gowan, 1980); General Elec. Co., 74 LA 578, 580–81 (Schor, 1980); Tri-State Asphalt Corp., 72 LA 102, 106–07 (LeWinter, 1979); Hempstead Pub. Sch. Bd. of Educ., 69 LA 808, 811 (Gootnick, 1977); O&A Elec. Coop., 67 LA 598, 600 (Bowles, 1976); Brass-Craft Mfg. Co., 36 LA 1177, 1184 (Kahn, 1961); Standard Oil Co., 25 LA 32, 36 (Burris, 1955). For related discussion, see section 4.H., "Failure of Grievant to Testify," above. In *Van Haaren Specialized Carriers*, 247 NLRB 1185, 103 LRRM 1361 (1980), the NLRB refused to defer to an arbitration award, because the company had failed to call as a witness an official whose testimony would be crucial to the NLRA issue.

[197]St. Charles Grain Elevator Co., 84 LA 1129, 1132 (Fox, 1985); Veterans Admin. Med. Ctr., 82 LA 25, 27 (Dallas, 1984).

[198]Durion Co., 85 LA 1127, 1129 (Coyne, 1985) (alcohol).

[199]Air Treads of Atlanta, 83 LA 1323, 1327 (Yancy, 1984) (alcohol). *See also* Advance Transp. Co., 105 LA 1089 (Briggs, 1995) (random alcohol testing); United States Borax & Chem. Corp., 84 LA 32, 35 (Richman, 1984) (drugs).

[200]Jaite Packaging Co., 90 LA 1061, 1064 (Fullmer, 1988).

[201]*See* Soule Steel Co., 85 LA 336, 343 (Richman, 1985); Amax Chem. Corp., 83 LA 635, 538 (Bell, 1984).

[202]Anchor Hocking Corp., 85 LA 783, 786 (Ruben, 1985).

[203]Dietrich Indus., 83 LA 287, 289 (Abrams, 1984).

Circumstantial evidence often is relied on by arbitrators to decide cases.[204] For instance, such evidence was dispositive in sustaining the discharge of an airline employee for making more than 20 false reservations for fictitious passengers to assure travel for his family members who could ride free on the employer's planes on a space-available basis. One arbitrator acknowledged that the evidence was wholly circumstantial, but the web of circumstances was so persuasive that a conclusion of guilt was inescapable.[205] Likewise, circumstantial evidence also has been determinative in vindicating a grievant.[206]

Circumstantial evidence may be the only evidence available in some cases, such as theft,[207] drug usage,[208] concerted work stoppages,[209] and situations where the grievant's state of mind is at issue.[210]

---

[204]*See, e.g.*, Kroger Co., 108 LA 229 (Frockt, 1997); American Nat'l Can Co., 105 LA 812 (Moore, 1995); Atlantic Southeast Airlines, 103 LA 1179 (Nolan, 1994); Exxon Co. U.S.A., 101 LA 777 (Baroni, 1993).

[205]Frontier Airlines, 82 LA 1283, 1287–88 (Watkins, 1984). Other cases where arbitrators have relied on circumstantial evidence include: Consolidation Coal Co., 99 LA 945, 950 (Dissen, 1992); Oregon Dep't of Human Justice, 90 LA 165, 171–72 (Levak, 1987); Anchor Hocking, 85 LA 783, 786–87 (Ruben, 1985); Southwestern Bell Tel., 84 LA 583, 585–86 (Penfield, 1985); Farm Stores, 81 LA 344, 347–48 (Hanes, 1983); Combustion Eng'g, 80 LA 503, 505–06 (Heinsz, 1983).

[206]*See, e.g.*, City of Berkeley, Cal., 106 LA 364, 367–68 (Pool, 1996) (library assistant absolved of taking fine money by his actions inconsistent with intent to steal); Soule Steel Co., 85 LA 336 (Richman, 1985) (grievant reinstated where circumstantial evidence indicated that coworker operated crane that fell).

[207]*See, e.g.*, Abbott-Northwestern Hosp., 94 LA 621, 629 (Berquist, 1990) (circumstantial evidence established that grievant had the opportunity to steal his employer's answering machine, the motive to do so, and the connection to the stolen property); Kansas City Area Transp. Auth., 82 LA 409, 414 (Maniscalco, 1984) (discharge upheld of bus company maintenance employee who was seen after 4:45 a.m. in bus barn with unattended buses that had coins in their fare boxes, and later observed leaving the bus barn with towel containing an object the size of a cantaloupe under his arm, and who had made a large coin deposit in the bank on an earlier occasion); Bethlehem Steel Corp., 81 LA 268, 271–72 (Sharnoff, 1983) (grievant's guilt in stealing coemployee's truck established by circumstantial evidence, including unexplained presence of grievant's fingerprints on truck's rearview mirror).

[208]*See, e.g.*, Trane Co., 96 LA 435, 437 (Reynolds, 1991); Consolidation Coal Co., 87 LA 729, 735–36 (Hoh, 1986); Maverick Tube Co., 86 LA 1, 4–5 (Miller, 1985).

[209]*See, e.g.*, Plainville Concrete Servs., 104 LA 811 (High, 1995) ("sick-out" of seven employees, and absence of eighth employee allegedly because of his inability to make appropriate babysitter arrangements, led arbitrator to conclude that employees' actions were more probably concerted); Cooper/T. Smith Stevedoring Co., 99 LA 297, 304–05 (Massey, 1992) (failure of any of two dozen longshoremen present at shape-up to sign up for work led arbitrator to conclude that a concerted work stoppage had occurred); Mann Packing Co., 83 LA 552, 555 (Concepcion, 1984) (arbitrator concluded that because the entire 28-member crew lagged behind harvesting support equipment after talking among themselves while repairs were being made to the equipment, crew members deliberately engaged in a work slowdown). *See also* Longview Fibre Co., 69 LA 1182, 1185 (Mueller, 1977); Lone Star Steel Co., 48 LA 949, 950–51 (Jenkins, 1967); General Am. Transp. Corp., 42 LA 142–43 (Pollack, 1964); Timken Roller Bearing Co., 7 LA 239, 240 (Harter, 1947); Stockham Pipe Fittings Co., 4 LA 744, 746–47 (McCoy, 1946). *But see* Veterans Admin., 85 LA 272, 278–79 (Statham, 1985) (arbitrator concluded that evidence of all four medical technologists, who comprised the entire scheduled evening shift, calling in sick, did not support presumption that technologists engaged in concerted withholding of services); Westinghouse Elec. Co., 48 LA 211, 213 (Williams, 1967) (arbitrator was not reasonably convinced that defective work by 21 grievants was a concerted effort).

[210]*See, e.g.*, Formica Corp., 104 LA 36, 40 (Silver, 1994) (whether grievant intended to create safety hazard); Yellow Freight Sys., 103 LA 388, 391 (Odom, Jr., 1994) (whether employer retaliated against employee); City of Berkeley, Cal., 94 LA 1198, 1203 (Bogue, 1990) (whether employer discriminated against grievant because of his race).

Generally speaking, circumstantial evidence is equally as probative as direct evidence.[211] It can be utilized to satisfy a party's burden of proof by inference from those circumstances proven.[212] Some arbitrators have even gone so far as to say that circumstantial evidence may be more persuasive than direct testimony in some instances. A tripartite panel reporting to the 19th Annual Meeting of NAA opined:

> Since "direct" evidence may be falsified due to the commission of perjury by witnesses, it is not necessarily more probative than circumstantial evidence. Indeed, the latter may be more reliable than so-called "direct" evidence to the degree that close reasoning by inference in a particular situation may actually weave a tighter factual web, often less subject to the diversion of doubts of credibility than is true where reliance must be had solely on the "I saw him do it" kind of direct evidence.[213]

Not infrequently, circumstantial facts have been found strong enough to overcome the effect of direct testimony to the contrary.[214]

The question, therefore, is not whether circumstantial evidence is valid, but what reasonable inferences may be drawn from the circumstances presented.[215] It is not sufficient that the circumstances give rise to mere suspicion or speculation; the circumstances must lead to inferences and factual conclusions based on a reasonable probability.[216] "If the evidence producing the chain of circumstances pointing to [guilt] is weak and inconclusive, no probability of fact may be inferred from the combined circumstances."[217] The facts offered as circumstantial evidence must afford a basis for a reasonable inference of the existence or nonexistence of the fact sought to be proved. The reasonable inference sought to be reached must be more probable and natural than any other explanation, although it is not necessary to be adequate that circumstantial evidence exclude every reasonable theory except guilt.[218] As a basic safeguard, one arbitrator has emphasized that an arbitrator in using circumstantial evidence "must exercise extreme care so that by

---

[211]See Problems of Proof in Arbitration, Proceedings of the 19th Annual Meeting of NAA (Jones ed., BNA Books 1967); Wholesale Produce Supply Co., 101 LA 1101, 1104 (Bognanno, 1993).

[212]See Michigan Milk Producers Ass'n, 114 LA 1024, 1029 (McDonald, 2000); Atlantic Southeast Airlines, 103 LA 1179, 1183 (Nolan, 1994); Lone Star Steel Co., 48 LA 949, 951 (Jenkins, 1967).

[213]West Coast Report, supra note 2, at 192. See also Federal Aviation Admin., 106 LA 38, 41 (Frost, 1996); Consolidation Coal Co., 87 LA 729, 735 (Hoh, 1986); Southwestern Bell Tel., 84 LA 583, 585–86 (Penfield, 1985); Amax Chem. Corp., 83 LA 635, 638 (Bell, 1984); Combustion Eng'g, 80 LA 503, 505 (Heinsz, 1983); Grand Union Co., 48 LA 812, 815 (Scheiber, 1967); Lone Star Steel, 48 LA 949, 950–51 (Jenkins, 1967).

[214]See, e.g., Wholesale Produce Supply Co., 101 LA 1101, 1105 (Bognanno, 1993); Anchor Hocking Corp., 85 LA 783, 787 (Ruben, 1985); Kansas City Area Transp. Auth., 82 LA 409, 414 (Maniscalco, 1984); Farm Stores, 81 LA 344, 347–48 (Hanes, 1983); Bethlehem Steel Corp., 81 LA 268, 270–72 (Sharnoff, 1983).

[215]See Farm Stores, 81 LA 344, 347 (Hanes, 1983). See also Southwestern Bell Tel., 84 LA 583, 585 (Penfield, 1985).

[216]See Dietrich Indus., 83 LA 287, 289 (Abrams, 1984); Kraft, Inc., 82 LA 360, 365 (Denson, 1984).

[217]South Penn Oil Co., 29 LA 718, 721 (Duff, 1957). See also San Gamo Elec. Co., 44 LA 593, 601–03 (Sembower, 1965); T-K Roofing Mfg. Co., 44 LA 577, 578 (Duff, 1965).

[218]See Frontier Airlines, 82 LA 1283, 1288 (Watkins, 1984); Westinghouse Elec. Co., 48 LA 211, 213 (Williams, 1967).

due deliberation and careful judgment, he may avoid making hasty or false deductions."[219]

ii. *Arbitral Notice and Presumptions* [LA CDI 94.60505]

Judges take "judicial notice" of widely known facts of commerce, industry, history, and natural science, and of ordinary meanings of words. Similarly, in arbitration many matters are assumed or accepted without discussion or citation of authority. Thus, it may be said that arbitrators also take judicial notice.[220] Not surprisingly, some arbitrators have spoken in terms of taking "arbitral" notice.[221]

Of special significance is the practice of arbitrators of taking arbitral notice of industry practice affecting some disputed matters.[222] Thus, arbitral notice has been taken of the "general understanding that tips, unless guaranteed by the employer, cannot and should not be used in making a 'wage adjustment.'"[223] Another arbitrator took arbitral notice of the fact that it is

---

[219]South Penn Oil, 29 LA 718, 721 (Duff, 1957). *See also* University of Pa., 99 LA 353, 359 (DiLauro, 1992); Maverick Tube Co., 86 LA 1, 4 (Miller, 1985); Purex Corp., 82 LA 12, 17 (Fitzsimmons, 1984).

[220]Norris Plumbing Fixtures, 104 LA 174, 177 (Richman, 1995) (that smoking is unhealthy); Motion Picture & Television Fund, 103 LA 988, 991 (Gentile, 1994) (as to the greatness of the Aztec and Mayan cultures); PMI Food Equip. Group, 103 LA 547, 557 (Imundo, Jr., 1994); Amerigas, 102 LA 1185, 1188 (Marino, 1994); George Koch Sons, 102 LA 737, 741–42 (Brunner, 1994); Wisconsin Tissue Mills, 102 LA 601, 605 (Jacobs, 1994); Bi-State Dev. Agency, 88 LA 854, 859 (Brasil, 1987); Social Sec. Admin., 69 LA 1149, 1151 (Kaplan, 1977); Alexander's Pers. Providers, 68 LA 249, 253 (Katz, 1977); Ohse Meat Prods., 48 LA 978, 980 (Roberts, 1967); Weyerhaeuser Co., 46 LA 707, 708 (Kelliher, 1966); Electric Hose & Rubber Co., 46 LA 613, 615 (Kerrison, 1966); Jaeger Mach. Co., 43 LA 901, 905 (Stouffer, 1964); Marion Power Shovel Co., 43 LA 507, 509 (Dworkin, 1964); Alderson Research Labs., 41 LA 895, 897 (Wildebush, 1963); Washington Publishers Ass'n, 39 LA 159, 160 (Cayton, 1962); Philip Carey Mfg. Co., 36 LA 65, 70 (Rock, 1960); Duluth Rests., 20 LA 658, 662–63 (Lockhart, 1953); Applied Arts Corp., 20 LA 337, 340 (Ryder, 1953); North Am. Aviation, 19 LA 10, 13 (Komaroff, 1952); Pittsburgh Steel Co., 6 LA 575, 578 (Wagner, 1947); Pittsburgh Screw & Bolt Corp., 6 LA 292, 294 (Wagner, 1947). It should also be recognized in passing that arbitrators sometimes rely on their own prior knowledge and experience. *See* Hudson Pulp & Paper Corp., 70 LA 1073, 1076 (Sobel, 1978); Social Sec. Admin., 69 LA 1149, 1151 (Kaplan, 1977); Converters Ink, 68 LA 593 (Sembower, 1977). In the last cited case, the arbitrator stated: "The Arbitrator is fully aware that no arbitrator should stray beyond the record, but the principle also is universally accepted that no arbitrator or other finder of facts has to ignore all of his prior learning and experience, for indeed it is that which the parties take into account when they compliment him with their mutual selection as arbitrator." *Id.* at 595–96. In *Eder Bros. v. Teamsters Local 1040*, 92 Lab. Cas. (CCH) ¶55,296 (Conn. 1980), it was held that arbitrators, as experts in the field under dispute, could rely on their own knowledge.

[221]Fayette County Area Vo-Tech Sch., 94 LA 894, 899 (McDowell, 1990) (arbitral notice that there is an adverse relationship between smoking and health); Trans World Airlines, 93 LA 167 (Eisler, 1989) (arbitral notice that virtually any kind of message is being used on home telephone answering devices); W-L Molding Co., 72 LA 1065, 1068 (Howlett, 1979) (took "arbitral notice that people do pound on vending machines when the product they seek to purchase . . . or their change is not returned"); Textron, Inc., 48 LA 1373, 1376 (Altrock, 1967) (that electricians were in short supply in the area at the time).

[222]Northwest Airlines, 89 LA 268, 272 (Flagler, 1987); Electric Hose & Rubber Co., 46 LA 613, 615 (Kerrison, 1966); North Am. Aviation, 19 LA 10, 13 (Komaroff, 1952); Sayles Biltmore Bleacheries, 17 LA 451, 454 (Maggs, 1951); Grocers Wholesale Outlet, 16 LA 914, 915 (Donnelly, 1951); Standard Steel Spring Co., 16 LA 317, 319 (Platt, 1951); Christ Cella's Rest., 7 LA 355, 357 (Cahn, 1947); Lionel Corp., 7 LA 121, 122 (Shipman, 1947). *See also In re* Hopkins, 13 LA 716, 717 (N.Y. Sup. Ct. 1949).

[223]Christ Cella's Rest., 7 LA 355, 357 (Cahn, 1947).

not common industrial practice to use the rate received by the highest paid experimental employees as the base rate on new jobs when production begins.[224]

Arbitrators also may use presumptions as aids in deciding issues. Presumptions, which are conceptually related to judicial notice, result in the prima facie assumption of the truth of a matter. Thus, they take the place of evidence on the part of the party in whose favor they operate, and they require the other party to produce evidence or argument to show that that which is presumed is not true.

To illustrate, one arbitrator held that in determining the right to benefits under an employee group insurance plan, a nonworking wife's dependency on her husband for support is so basic that it will be presumed in the absence of proof to the contrary.[225] Presumptions are used frequently in the interpretation of contract provisions. For instance, parties are presumed to have intended a valid contract,[226] to have intended all words used in an agreement to have effect,[227] and to have intended language to have its commonly accepted meaning.[228]

Presumptions may also be used in "interest arbitration" matters. Thus, an arbitrator, in determining the amount of wage increase necessary to offset a rise in living costs, ruled that it was "presumptively proper" to consider only the change in living costs occurring after the parties' last wage negotiation, there being a presumption that all pertinent factors were considered in previous bargaining.[229]

5. Arbitral Use of the Doctrines of Res Judicata and Collateral Estoppel Following the Termination of Criminal, Civil, and Administrative Proceedings Arising Out of the Same Factual Context [LA CDI 94.60553; 100.0783]

Arbitration cases involving the discipline or discharge of an employee, or the denial of an employee's contract violation claim, frequently follow the termination of criminal, civil, or administrative proceedings that arose out of the same factual context. In such cases, it is not uncommon for unions and

---

[224]Pittsburgh Steel Co., 6 LA 575, 578 (Wagner, 1947).

[225]Rock Hill Printing & Finishing Co., 21 LA 335, 340 (Shipman, 1953). *See also* Steel Erecting Contractors, 50 LA 1080, 1082 (Kabaker, 1968); Gallagher Co., 46 LA 882, 884 (Gross, 1966). *But see* Vision-Ease, 102 LA 116 (Mathews, 1106) (bonus for attendance was awarded even though grievant's attendance was impossible to predict and, due to employer's wrongful actions, no presumption of attendance could attach).

[226]Firestone Tire & Rubber Co., 20 LA 880, 889 (Gorder, 1953); Union Switch & Signal Co., 9 LA 702, 703 (Horvitz, 1948); Warren Foundry & Pipe Corp., 5 LA 282, 283 (Tischler, 1946).

[227]Cleveland Metroparks, 101 LA 1122, 1125 (Bittel, 1993); John Deere Tractor Co., 5 LA 631, 632 (Updegraff, 1946). *But see* Kroger Co., 107 LA 801, 805–06 (Howell, 1996) (rejected the use of a presumption to discredit testimony due to the interest of the witness in the outcome of the case).

[228]Marblehead Lime Co., 48 LA 310, 312–13 (Anrod, 1966); City of Meriden, Conn., 48 LA 137, 142 (Summers, 1967); Goodyear Tire & Rubber Co., 2 LA 367, 370–71 (McCoy, 1946).

[229]New York City Omnibus Corp., 7 LA 794, 802 (Cole, 1947).

employers to try to utilize the results of these other proceedings either to avoid a hearing altogether, or to support an argument before the arbitrator. The arbitrator then must decide what weight, if any, is to be given to the result. In making this decision the doctrines of res judicata and collateral estoppel become relevant.

The doctrine of res judicata, or "claim preclusion," is "[a]n affirmative defense barring the same parties from litigating a second lawsuit on the same claim, or any other arising from the same transaction or series of transactions and that could have been—but was not—raised in the first suit."[230] To be applicable, the doctrine requires that the following four elements be present:

1. Identity in the thing sued for in both actions;
2. Identity of the cause of action in both actions;
3. Identity of the parties to the actions;
4. Identity of the quality or capacity of the persons for or against whom the claim is made.[231]

The doctrine of collateral estoppel, or "issue preclusion," is "[a]n affirmative defense barring a party from relitigating an issue determined against that party in an earlier action, even if the second action differs significantly from the first one."[232] To be applicable, the doctrine requires that the following four elements be present:

1. The issue at stake is identical to the one involved in the prior litigation;
2. The issue has been actually litigated in the prior suit;
3. The determination of the issue in the prior litigation was a critical and necessary part of the judgment in the action; and
4. The party against whom the earlier decision is asserted had a full and fair opportunity to litigate the issue in the earlier proceeding.[233]

6. TYPES OF PROCEEDINGS

A. Criminal Proceedings [LA CDI 100.5521514; 118.643]

Disciplinary cases often come to arbitration after the employee has been subjected to criminal prosecution for the same alleged misconduct that formed the basis for the discipline. These cases may present the issue of whether the disposition of a collateral proceeding binds the arbitrator in the "just cause" inquiry.[234]

---

[230]BLACK'S LAW DICTIONARY 1312 (7th ed. 1999).
[231]Albrecht v. State, 444 So.2d 8, 12 (Fla. 1984); West v. Kawasaki Motors Mfg. Corp., 595 So.2d 92, 94 (Fla. Dist. Ct. App.), *review denied*, 604 So.2d 489 (Fla. 1992).
[232]BLACK'S LAW DICTIONARY 25 (7th ed. 1999).
[233]Baxas Howell Mobley, Inc. v. BP Oil Co., 630 So.2d 207, 209 (Fla. Dist. Ct. App. 1993).
[234]These cases are distinguishable from those in which a grievant is disciplined because of the impact the fact of conviction is alleged to have on the grievant's ability to perform his or her job. *See, e.g.*, Ashland County, Ohio, Dep't of Human Servs., 111 LA 584 (Kindig, 1998)

Arbitrators generally do not view themselves as bound by a judicial determination of guilt or innocence.[235] The reasons behind this view include (1) the purposes of the two proceedings are different,[236] (2) the burdens of proof that generally govern the two proceedings are different,[237] and (3) the determination of the existence or absence of "just cause" is to be based on the evidentiary record adduced at the arbitral hearing.[238]

However, while arbitrators are not precluded from making independent factual findings in the arbitral proceedings as to whether the same underlying conduct constituting the gravamen of the crime occurred in a manner that justified the employer's disciplinary action under the collective bargaining agreement, evidence of a conviction is typically accorded "great weight."[239] Conversely, the dismissal of criminal charges or an employee's acquittal of

---

(criminal conviction for domestic violence disqualified grievant from holding investigator position).

[235]*See, e.g.,* City of Oklahoma City, Okla., 110 LA 385 (Greer, 1998) (fire chief could consider the criminal prosecution of firefighter for drug possession, even though firefighter had pled "no contest" and was found neither guilty nor not guilty, since employers may require standard of conduct that is higher than that applied by courts in criminal cases); City of Las Vegas, Nev., Fire Dep't, 105 LA 398, 403 (Robinson, 1995) ("In labor arbitration, whether or not an employee is found guilty or is acquitted in a criminal matter should not affect the disciplinary action taken under a collective bargaining agreement.").

[236]*See, e.g.,* Bruno's Food Fair, 104 LA 306, 311 (Hart, 1995) ("[I]t must be recognized that charges brought in the courts are for the purpose of enforcing applicable laws whereas the disciplinary process applied by the employer is for the purpose of enforcing the terms of the Labor Agreement.").

[237]*See, e.g.,* AT&T, 102 LA 931, 934 (Kanner, 1994) (declining to consider evidence of grievant's being found not guilty in a criminal proceeding concerning the conduct that formed the basis for employee's discharge, because, among other things, "the evidentiary standard in a criminal proceeding is beyond a reasonable doubt which is a much higher standard than the standard of preponderance of the evidence in arbitration").

[238]*See, e.g.,* Broward County, Fla., Sheriff's Office, 112 LA 609, 619 (Hoffman, 1999) ("Although the grievant was not found guilty in the criminal courts of such a felony, it is not critical to a finding that just cause exists for the termination. . . . [T]he arbitrator is concerned with the record made at the arbitration and whether that evidence supports a just cause finding."). At least one arbitrator has rejected a union's argument that a plea agreement reducing a criminal charge against the grievant precluded him from concluding that the grievant had committed the offense for which he was discharged. All the agreement signified, explained the arbitrator, was that "the grievant's attorney in the criminal case was a good plea-bargainer." Dunlop Tire Corp., 104 LA 653, 659 (Teple, 1995).

[239]Teamsters Local 863 v. Jersey Coast Egg Producers, 773 F.2d 530, 536 (3d Cir. 1985) ("It is for the arbitrator . . . to decide whether a misdemeanor conviction supports a discharge under the terms of the collective bargaining agreement."); Dacco, Inc., 114 LA 1517 (Shieber, 2000) (grievant's arrest for assault is a factor in finding grievant engaged in misconduct for which he was discharged); Quaker Oats Co., 110 LA 816 (Crider, 1998) (grievant's past murder conviction held to be evidence of his proclivity for violence and justified the employer's refusal to reinstate the grievant while he awaited trial on an attempted murder charge); Cuyahoga County, Ohio, Sheriff's Dep't, 110 LA 307 (Richard, 1998) (criminal conviction supported discharge of correction officer for underlying misconduct); Indiana Bell Tel. Co., 99 LA 756 (Goldstein, 1992) (employee's misdemeanor conviction for patronizing a prostitute in a vacant lot while on duty, although not entitled to res judicata effect, is to be given "great weight" because of greater burden of proof); Boise Cascade Corp., 97 LA 8 (Flagler, 1991) (contempt conviction of employee for violating temporary restraining order entered to control strike-related violence constituted just cause for discharge); Washington Metro. Area Transit Auth., 94 LA 1172 (Garrett, 1990) (grievant's guilty plea to drug possession sustained discharge for violating drug policy); Snow Mountain Pine Co., 94 LA 929, 932 (Levak, 1990). *But see* Cook County, Ill., Soc. Serv. Dep't, 111 LA 417 (Doering, 1998) (arbitrator credits grievant's denial of guilt despite grievant having entered guilty plea in court).

them does not require the overturning of a disciplinary sanction based on the facts giving rise to the prosecution.[240]

B. Civil Litigation

The extent to which an antecedent judgment in a civil case will be given preclusive effect depends on the arbitrator's assessment of whether the parties, issues, and the standards and burden of proof in the judicial proceeding were identical to those involved in the arbitral proceeding. In *Minneapolis Special School District No. 1*,[241] the employer school district demoted a teacher. The union and the teacher filed a lawsuit, which was subsequently settled with compensation to the teacher. The union also grieved the demotion. The arbitrator ruled that the settlement agreement was entitled to res judicata and collateral estoppel effect, because the settlement agreement involved the same parties and the same issue of the grievant's right to reassignment.

A contrary decision was reached in *City of Oak Creek, Wisconsin*,[242] where a lawsuit filed by individual police officers against their city, alleging that the city lacked authority to declare a moratorium on hiring or the filling of vacancies, had been dismissed. The union grieved the moratorium as the violation of a contract right. The arbitrator found that there was no identity of the parties or of claims, because it was not clear whether the court had based its decision solely on external law rather than on the labor contract.

The issue of res judicata also can arise when the same substantive arbitrability issue presented to the arbitrator has been previously presented directly to a court. For example, in *County of Santa Clara, California*,[243] when the employer refused to arbitrate a grievance, the union successfully filed a court action to compel arbitration. The court ruled specifically that the grievance was substantively arbitrable and ordered the employer to proceed to arbitration. At the hearing, the employer tried again to raise the issue of substantive arbitrability, but the arbitrator ruled that the order compelling arbitration necessarily included a determination that the grievance, on its face, was substantively arbitrable, and that because the employer refused arbitration in favor of a court determination of the issue, the employer had waived its right to relitigate the issue and was bound by the court's determination.

---

[240]Service Trucking Co., 41 LA 377, 380 (Turkus, 1963) ("Although the acquittal is not conclusive, it must be given due and serious consideration."); Bruno's Food Fair, 104 LA 306 (Hart, 1995) (employer met burden of proof at arbitral hearing to sustain discharge of employee for shoplifting although found not guilty of criminal charges). *See also* Associated Grocers of Ala., 83 LA 261 (Odom, Jr., 1984) (employee's acquittal of criminal charges not given res judicata and collateral estoppel effect in arbitration of employee's discharge arising from same facts, because there was no identity of parties or issues). The same result was reached in *Muskegon Heights Police Dep't*, 88 LA 675 (Girolamo, 1987) (employer had heightened burden of proof to sustain discharge where police officer acquitted of domestic violence charge, but acquittal not given preclusive effect because of lack of identity of parties or issues). *See also* Dannon Milk Prods., 76 LA 133 (Kramer, 1980).
[241]94 LA 961 (Berquist, 1990).
[242]90 LA 710 (Baron, 1988).
[243]97 LA 635 (Chvany, 1991).

C. Administrative Agency Proceedings [LA CDI 94.553]

Arbitrators may give significant weight to the findings of an administrative agency depending on an evaluation of the comprehensiveness and fairness of the adjudicatory proceedings; however, because the statutory standards being enforced are different than the terms of the labor contract, arbitrators seldom give agency decisions preclusive effect.

i. Federal Administrative Agency Proceedings

a. Equal Employment Opportunity Commission [LA CDI 94.553]

Typically, adjudicated findings of the federal or a state employment discrimination commission do not preclude an arbitrator from deciding whether discrimination occurred under a collective bargaining agreement. Such findings are, however, considered "noteworthy" because they arise from proceedings with evidence and legal standards similar to arbitration.[244]

In *American Fuel Cell & Coated Fabrics Co.*,[245] a black female employee who had been terminated for failing to meet production standards filed a grievance alleging that her termination was the result of racial discrimination. Concurrently, the employee filed a discrimination charge against the employer with the Equal Employment Opportunity Commission (EEOC). The EEOC subsequently ruled that there was no probable cause to find racial discrimination and dismissed the charge. The employer then argued that the determination of the EEOC should be given res judicata effect. The arbitrator rejected that argument because the EEOC was interpreting federal law, while he was interpreting the language in the labor contract. Nevertheless, viewing the evidence independently, the arbitrator agreed with the findings of the EEOC and concluded that the employer's decision was not based on race. Conversely, when a discharged employee attempted to excuse his poor attendance by claiming the employer unlawfully failed to accommodate his religious convictions, the arbitrator refused to take up the claim, noting that the issue had already been considered and resolved by the state and federal agencies charged with enforcement of discrimination claims.[246]

---

[244]Cincinnati State Tech. & Cmty. Coll., 114 LA 153, 158 (Heekin, 2000) (findings by Ohio commission and Equal Employment Opportunity Commission (EEOC) on disability discrimination "noteworthy," but not collateral estoppel of issue under contract); American Fuel Cell & Coated Fabrics Co., 97 LA 1045, 1049 (Nicholas, Jr., 1991) (EEOC ruling finding no race discrimination not res judicata of issue unless collective bargaining agreement requires). *But see* City of Hialeah, Fla., 110 LA 481 (Richard, 1998) (such similarity precluded arbitrator from deciding whether a grievant was fired from her teaching job for just cause under the contract because a state agency tribunal had already come to that determination). *Cf.* International Paper Co., 112 LA 412, 422 (Chumley, 1999) (arbitrator considered EEOC ruling of "no cause" in dismissing contractual discrimination claim); KIAM, 97 LA 617 (Bard, 1991) (finding no sexual harassment where agency found a hostile work environment existed).

[245]97 LA 1045 (Nicholas, Jr., 1991).

[246]JPI Transp. Prods., 93 LA 716 (Kindig, 1989).

b. National Labor Relations Board

In *Geauga Co.*,[247] the union filed a grievance concerning the employer's termination of laid-off striking workers who had been on the recall list for 2 years. The same employees had individually filed charges with the NLRB, alleging that their termination constituted an unfair labor practice. The NLRB declined to issue a complaint and dismissed the charges for lack of probable cause. At the subsequent arbitration hearing, the employer argued that the decision of the NLRB should be given res judicata effect. The arbitrator refused because the NLRB's decision was based on federal labor law, while he was only concerned with the labor contract.[248] The arbitrator noted that the substantive issues decided by the NLRB were different and the Board's dismissal of a charge did not constitute an "adjudication."

ii. State and Local Government Administrative Agency Proceedings

In *City of Minneapolis, Minnesota*,[249] the arbitrator ruled that a decision of the City's Civil Service Commission on a job assignment complaint should not be given preclusive effect because the Commission was concerned with violation of the Civil Service rules, whereas the arbitrator was obligated to determine if the City's actions violated the labor contract.

But, in *City of Hialeah, Florida*,[250] the arbitrator held that the findings of the Florida Division of Administrative Hearings in a teacher's discharge case constituted a sufficient decision on the merits to be given both res judicata and collateral estoppel effect in the subsequent arbitration proceedings, because the parties had had an adequate opportunity to litigate the merits of the discharge, the administrative agency had resolved the disputed issues of fact, and the burdens and standards of proof were essentially the same in both proceedings. The arbitrator reached this conclusion despite the fact that Florida law provided that the employee may obtain a de novo arbitration hearing after invoking the administrative remedy. By way of dicta, the arbitrator stated that a decision in an unemployment compensation proceeding would not necessarily compel the same result, because the burden and standards of proof differ significantly from those obtaining in an arbitration proceeding.

---

[247]92 LA 54, 58 (Fullmer, 1988).

[248]*See also* Anderson-Tully Co., 88 LA 7 (Hart, 1986) (arbitrator held that no res judicata or collateral estoppel effect would be given to decision of NLRB to dismiss unfair labor practice charge, because NLRB only had jurisdiction to interpret federal labor law, not language in collective bargaining agreement). *Accord* Boardman Co., 91 LA 489 (Harr, 1988) (finding of successor liability in spite of NLRB's refusal to issue complaint against the successor); Contract Carpets, 68 LA 1022 (Finston, 1977). Similarly, in *Schuyler-Chemung-Tioga Boces*, 87 LA 372 (Schamel, 1986), the arbitrator refused to give res judicata or collateral estoppel effect to a decision of the state public employee relations board.

[249]103 LA 1103 (Jacobowski, 1995).

[250]110 LA 481 (Richard, 1998) (the arbitrator quoted from *United States v. Utah Constr. & Mining Co.*, 384 U.S. 394, 422 (1966): "[When] an administrative agency is acting in a judicial capacity and resolved disputed issues of fact properly before it which the parties have had an adequate opportunity to litigate, the courts have not hesitated to apply res judicata to enforce repose.").

iii. Unemployment Compensation Agency Hearings [LA CDI 94.553]

It has been almost universally accepted that unemployment compensation agency decisions are not given res judicata or collateral estoppel effect in subsequent arbitration proceedings.[251] However, a novel refinement of the doctrine was formulated in *Mead Corp.*[252] In that case, the union offered an unemployment compensation decision favorable to the grievant as evidence in support of its position that the employer lacked just cause to discharge the employee for sexual harassment. The employer objected, citing an Ohio law that precluded an arbitrator from giving res judicata or collateral estoppel effect to the findings or decision of that agency. Notwithstanding the statute, the arbitrator admitted the decision into evidence, reasoning that he was not precluded from considering the decision. However, the arbitrator gave no weight to the decision because it was apparent from the record that it was not based on anything resembling the comprehensive record provided during the arbitration proceeding.

7. Arbitrator Consultation of Experts

The nature of some cases makes the use of independent technicians helpful. In such cases, arbitrators sometimes request permission to bring in specialists for impartial study of the disputed matter. Thus, an arbitrator consulted an electrical engineer, in the presence of both parties, as to whether a power failure was a cause beyond the employer's control so as to relieve the employer of any obligation for call-in pay.[253] Likewise, another arbitrator was authorized to secure the services of a handwriting expert in fixing responsibility for errors in shipping orders.[254] It also has been done in the determination of proper incentive rates for new operations.[255]

In some cases in which arbitrators consulted outside sources, the arbitrator's opinion did not expressly indicate whether advance permission to do so was obtained.[256] In another case, the arbitrator's request that the parties procure the services of an outside expert (to study and express an

---

[251]Rittman Nursing Ctr., 113 LA 284 (Kelman, 1999); City of Stillwater, Okla., 103 LA 684 (Neas, 1994); Aircraft Workers Alliance, 99 LA 585 (Sharpe, 1992); Boise Cascade Corp., 90 LA 791 (Nicholas, Jr., 1988); Rust Eng'g Co., 85 LA 407 (Whyte, 1985); City of Burlington, Iowa, 82 LA 21 (Kubie, 1984); Bon Secours Hosp., 76 LA 705 (Feldesman, 1981) (arbitrator rejected employer's argument that decision by state employment security administration appeals referee denying unemployment compensation benefits to employee should be given res judicata effect on arbitration proceeding because of lack of identity of parties or subject matter). See also discussion in Chapter 10, section 5., "Administrative Rulings."

[252]113 LA 1169 (Franckiewicz, 2000).

[253]Chrysler Corp., 21 LA 573, 577 (Wolff, 1953). One group expressed the view that the arbitrator should always advise the parties when seeking expert advice and should give them opportunity to comment on the expert's opinion before reaching a decision. *Chicago Area Report*, *supra* note 74, at 108.

[254]Hiram Walker & Sons, 18 LA 447, 448 (Kelliher, 1952). *See also* Seaview Indus., 39 LA 125, 127–30 (Duncan, 1962).

[255]Container Co., 6 LA 218, 220 (Whiting, 1946). *See also* Simmons Co., 33 LA 725, 727 (Ross, 1959).

[256]*See* Paragon Bridge & Steel Co., 45 LA 833, 837–38 (Vines, 1965); Simmons Co., 33 LA 725, 727 (Ross, 1959); Pittsburgh Standard Conduit Co., 32 LA 481, 482 (Lehoczky, 1959). One arbitrator appointed an industrial engineer to make technical studies on disputed mat-

opinion as to a safety-crew size issue) was virtually an order that they do so.[257] Fairness dictates, however, that the parties be informed of the expert's report and be given an opportunity to respond to it in an appropriate fashion.

It was the union that took the initiative where it "evoked a promise from the Arbitrator that he would check with competent medical authority, as well as law enforcement officials," regarding the reliability of blood tests in determining whether a person was intoxicated or under the influence of alcohol.[258]

One arbitrator emphasized that "[w]hile an arbitrator may obtain technical assistance, he cannot delegate the decision-making authority which has been conferred upon him individually."[259]

A. Opinion Evidence by Expert Witnesses [LA CDI 94.60519]

Ordinarily, "the function of a witness is to relate what he has seen and heard, not to draw inferences from these observations or from other facts. This rule does not apply to the 'expert.' The 'expert' is allowed to draw inferences and conclusions because, in theory, his knowledge is superior to that of the person having to resolve the issue, be it judge, jury, or arbitrator."[260] Before permitting expert testimony, a foundation showing such expertise, subject to cross-examination, must be provided.[261]

Testimony of expert witnesses can be significant in the arbitration of drug cases.[262] For example, where the issue was whether the grievant actu-

---

ter; the engineer "received excellent cooperation from both parties." *Simmons*, 33 LA at 727. *See also* M&A Elec. Power Coop. v. Electrical Workers (IBEW) Local 702, 773 F. Supp. 1259, 138 LRRM 2460 (E.D. Mo. 1991) (upholding award where arbitrator, after the hearing and without knowledge of either party, consulted a crane operator instructor; arbitrator's conduct did constitute misbehavior).

[257]American Oil Co., 51 LA 484, 489 (Barnhart, 1968). In *Naval Air Rework Facility*, 73 LA 644, 644–45 (Flannagan, 1979), the arbitrator gave the union "the opportunity, if it so desired," of having tests made by an outside specialist after the union had failed to meet its burden of proof on a safety issue at an initial hearing; a specialist was utilized and his conclusions were given serious consideration by the arbitrator. *See also Naval Air Rework Facility*, 73 LA 201, 205–06 (Livengood, 1979) (a specialist similarly was utilized to examine and report as to alleged safety and health hazards).

[258]Tennessee River Pulp & Paper Co., 68 LA 421, 425 (Simon, 1977).

[259]Simmons Co., 33 LA 725, 727 (Ross, 1959). In this instance, the arbitrator received "a confidential report in full detail" from the technical assistant whom he had appointed; the arbitrator found the report "most helpful" in reaching a decision, which he emphasized was solely his own. *Id.*

[260]*Pittsburgh Report*, supra note 2, at 253. Related statements by other tripartite committees are also available. *Chicago Area Report*, supra note 74, at 94–95; *Chicago Report Workshop*, supra note 74, at 114–15; *New York Report*, supra note 2, at 298. *See, e.g.,* Kalamazoo County Rd. Comm'n, 88 LA 1049, 1054–55 (Lewis, 1987); Schlage Lock Co., 88 LA 75, 76–79 (Wyman, 1986).

[261]THE COMMON LAW OF THE WORKPLACE: THE VIEWS OF ARBITRATORS §1.57 (St. Antoine ed., BNA Books 1998).

[262]*See, e.g.,* Giant Eagle Mkts. Co., 101 LA 581 (Zobrak, 1993); Federal Aviation Admin., 93 LA 41, 47 (Allen, Jr., 1989); Bowman Transp., 90 LA 347, 349 (Duff, 1987); Metropolitan Transit Auth., 88 LA 1247, 1250 (King, 1987). In a related matter, blood-alcohol test results have been admitted for the truth of the matter without testimony from the person administering the test where the laboratory that performed the test was duly certified and independent from the employer and no issue was raised concerning chain of custody of the sample. United Parcel Serv., 101 LA 589 (Briggs, 1993); Associated Wholesale Grocers, 112 LA 1212 (Murphy, 1999).

ally signed the chain of custody certification relating to the grievant's drug test, an expert's testimony was found by the arbitrator to be "highly persuasive and credited" on the issue of the signature's authenticity.[263]

Nevertheless, the testimony of an expert is not conclusive. For example, a counselor's opinion that a grievant, who was discharged for drug activity that occurred 2 years prior to his discharge, was likely to continue in drug-related activities once released from an alternative housing facility, was outweighed by grievant's 16-months' employment with the company without indication that he continued to engage in drug activity.[264]

In addition to the admission of opinion evidence by expert witnesses that is generally admitted by courts of law, it is suggested that arbitrators in their discretion may admit any opinion testimony from knowledgeable persons if such testimony might be helpful.[265] Arbitrators have also permitted "expert" testimony from handwriting analyst experts,[266] toxicologists,[267] a psychologist/social worker,[268] and polygraph operators.[269]

B. Medical Evidence [LA CDI 94.60529]

Medical evidence is frequently offered in arbitration on issues relating to the physical fitness or qualifications of employees for some given type of work or, indeed, for any continued employment with the company.[270] Another use of medical evidence concerns verification of illness by doctors' certificates for purposes of excusing absences under an employer's attendance policy.

---

[263]Southern Cal. Rapid Transit Dist., 96 LA 20 (Gentile, 1990).

[264]Giant Eagle Mkts., 101 LA 581 (Zobrak, 1993).

[265]*New York Report, supra* note 2, at 298.

[266]Peninsular Steel Co., 88 LA 391 (Ipavec, 1986); Schlage Lock Co., 88 LA 75, 76–77 (Wyman, 1986).

[267]Vivi Color, 97 LA 850 (Strasshofer, 1991); Trailways, Inc., 88 LA 1073, 1076 (Goodman, 1987).

[268]King Soopers, 86 LA 254, 260 (Sass, 1985).

[269]Ohio Dep't of Rehab. & Corr. 88 LA 1019, 1027 (Duda, Jr., 1987). For a full discussion of the admissibility of testimony regarding polygraph tests, see section 9.C., "The Lie Detector," below.

[270]*See* Bradford White Corp., 113 LA 114 (Allen, 1999) (arbitrator relied on the expertise of medical clinic personnel to determine the ability of the grievant to perform light duty work). For related material, see Chapter 13, section 26., "Disqualifying Employees for Physical or Mental Reasons"; Chapter 14, section 7.D.x., "Employee's Physical and Psychological Fitness"; Chapter 16, section 7., "Employee Physical or Mental Conditions as a Safety Hazard." For general discussion of medical and psychiatric testimony in arbitration, see Miller, *The Use of Experts in Arbitration: I. Expert Medical Evidence: A View From the End of the Table, in* Arbitration and Social Change, Proceedings of the 22d Annual Meeting of NAA (Somers & Dennis eds., BNA Books 1970); Sears, *The Use of Experts in Arbitration: III. Observations on Psychiatric Testimony in Arbitration, id.* at 151. For other informative discussions of these or related aspects, see Hill & Sinicropi, Evidence in Arbitration 29–34 (BNA Books 2d ed. 1987); Volz, *Health and Medical Issues in Arbitration, Employee Benefit Plans, and the Doctor's Office: I. Medical and Health Issues in Labor Arbitration, in* Truth, Lie Detectors, and Other Problems in Labor Arbitration, Proceedings of the 31st Annual Meeting of NAA 156 (Stern & Dennis eds., BNA Books 1979); Wolkinson, *Arbitration and the Employment Rights of the Physically Disadvantaged*, 36 Arb. J. No. 1, at 23 (1981); Cramer, *Arbitration and Mental Illness: The Issues, the Rationale, and the Remedies*, 35 Arb. J. No. 3, at 10 (1980).

A doctor's statement that corroborated a grievant's claim of tendonitis in her arm that prevented her from lifting heavy loads reinforced the arbitrator's conclusion that grievant did not intend to be insubordinate when she refused to do work directed by her supervisor.[271]

C. Written Statements Versus Oral Testimony

While doctors sometimes testify in person, their testimony is more often offered in the form of written statements or affidavits. It is understandable that where one party's doctor testifies in person, his or her opinion may carry greater weight with the arbitrator in contrast to the other party's use of only written statements.[272] Of course, the parties may stipulate that written statements of doctors (though not subject to cross-examination) shall be given the same effect as if the doctors had testified.[273] Even without such stipulation, the arbitrator might give the statements "full weight" in the absence of other evidence minimizing their significance.[274]

D. Shall Medical Evidence Be Weighed? [LA CDI 94.60529]

Both parties often submit medical evidence concerning the grievant's physical qualifications, and it is not surprising that the opinion of the grievant's doctor and that of the employer's medical adviser do not always agree. In many cases, the arbitrator has not attempted to resolve such conflicts in medical evidence, but has been inclined to uphold the employer if it acted in good faith pursuant to good-faith medical advice from its doctor (some of these arbitrators spoke in terms of upholding the employer's action unless the doctor's advice or its application was unreasonable, capricious, or arbitrary).[275] One arbitrator, for instance, stated that the arbitrator can only decide "whether the medical determination was made in a manner and by

---

[271]Stockham Valve & Fittings, 102 LA 73 (Poole, 1993).

[272]See Lamson & Sessions Co., 43 LA 61, 64 (Kates, 1964); Westinghouse Elec. Corp., 41 LA 449, 453–54 (Stockman, 1963); Chris Craft Corp., 40 LA 229, 230–31 (Russell, 1963). Arbitrators sometimes have stressed the unsatisfactory aspects of presenting medical evidence by written statements. See American Smelting & Ref. Co., 48 LA 1187, 1190 (Leonard, 1967); George A. Hormel & Co., 43 LA 484, 487 (Boles, 1964).

[273]See Highland Park Pub. Sch., 90 LA 986, 996 (Borland, 1988); Southern Cotton Oil Co., 26 LA 353, 356 (Kelliher, 1956).

[274]See White Motor Co., 28 LA 823, 829 (Lazarus, 1957); United Parcel Serv., 101 LA 589 (Briggs, 1993) (involving the admission of blood-alcohol test results where the testing was performed by an independent laboratory); Saginaw Township Bd. of Educ., 73 LA 952, 953–54 (Roumell, Jr., 1979); Brown & Williamson Tobacco Co., 69 LA 644, 649 (Moberly, 1977) (involving use in arbitration of depositions of doctors previously taken in workers' compensation proceedings). The weight of written statements was greatly reduced by other evidence in American Iron & Machine Works Co., 19 LA 417, 420 (Merrill, 1952).

[275]See Hercules, Inc., 91 LA 521 (Nolan, 1988); Bi-State Dev. Agency, 90 LA 91, 95 (Heinsz, 1987); Valvoline Oil Co., 89 LA 209, 210 (Brisco, 1987); Trailmobile, 78 LA 499, 503 (Nelson, 1982); Port Auth. of Allegheny County, 78 LA 437, 443 (Creo, 1982); Pacific Tel. & Tel. Co., 66 LA 433, 438–39 (Barrett, 1976); Philco-Ford Corp., 62 LA 351, 353–54 (Fleischli, 1974); Mason & Hanger-Silas Mason Co., 50 LA 476, 486–87 (Guse, 1968); Hughes Aircraft Co., 49 LA 535, 539 (Doyle, 1967); W.R. Grace & Co., 47 LA 254, 256 (Cayton, 1966); American Body & Trailer, 47 LA 12, 14 (Elkouri, 1966); Carter Prods., 45 LA 724, 726 (Kerrison, 1965); Union Carbide Corp., 66-1 ARB ¶8030 (Stouffer, 1965); Lamson & Sessions Co., 43 LA 61, 64 (Kates, 1964); Gulf States Utils. Co., 41 LA 519, 523 (Autrey, 1963); Westinghouse Elec.

. . . a procedure indicating that it was fairly and reasonably made."[276] In addition, another arbitrator explained:

> The judgment of the plant physician is entitled to great weight. He is conversant with the requirements of the occupation involved and the risks inherent in such work. It is generally held that where there is a conflict in the views of qualified physicians, whose veracity there is no reason to question, the Company is entitled to rely on the views of its own medical advisers.[277]

In some cases the arbitrator has undertaken to weigh conflicting medical evidence.[278] In thus searching for a preponderance of the evidence, the arbitrator's role has been compared "to that of a lay jury which must decide between conflicting expert testimony."[279]

Corp., 41 LA 449, 453–54 (Stockman, 1963); Chris Craft Corp., 40 LA 229, 230–31 (Russell, 1963); Labor Standards Ass'n, 38 LA 1049, 1054 (May, 1962); Copper Range Co., 37 LA 581, 584 (Thompson, 1961); Maremount Auto. Prods., 37 LA 175, 176 (Kelliher, 1962) (involving psychiatric opinion); Ideal Cement Co., 33 LA 141, 145 (Quinlan, 1959); Ideal Cement Co., 31 LA 256, 259–60 (Hoel, 1958) (holding also that if the employer has the employee examined by several doctors and receives conflicting opinions, the employer may decide which opinion to follow in the absence of error or unreasonableness); Northrop Aircraft, 24 LA 732, 738 (Prasow, 1955) (quoting Swift & Co. (Gregory, 1946)); General Mills, 24 LA 290, 298 (Abernethy, 1955); International Harvester Co., 24 LA 274, 275 (Wirtz, 1955). By the same token, if a doctor selected by the employer makes findings that support an employee, the employer should not lightly disregard those findings. Thus, where an orthopedic specialist selected by the employer had given the grievant a medical clearance, the arbitrator declared that "the Company cannot make a medical judgment contrary to that formally expressed by the specialist selected by the Company itself." Bethlehem Steel Corp., 70 LA 332, 333 (Strongin, 1978). See also Hamilton County Sheriff, 90 LA 1012 (Loeb, 1988); Peterson Spring Corp., 74 LA 744, 747–48 (Keefe, 1980). Likewise, an employee under postoperative care of his personal physician has a right to rely on that doctor's opinion that he is *not yet able* to return to work. International Harvester Co., 22 LA 138, 139 (Platt, 1954). See also Sears, Roebuck & Co., 72 LA 238, 240 (Blackmar, 1979); Peabody Galion Corp., 68 LA 78, 81–82 (Draper, 1977); Cit-Con Oil Corp., 37 LA 575, 580 (McConnell, 1961).

[276]International Harvester Co., 24 LA 274, 275 (Wirtz, 1955). In *Erie Forge & Steel Corp.*, 47 LA 629, 633–34 (Mullin, Jr., 1966), the arbitrator stated that while the company doctor's opinion is normally controlling, it will not be so where that opinion or its application is arbitrary or capricious. See also Rohm & Haas Tex., 68 LA 498, 501–02 (White, 1977); Colgate-Palmolive Co., 64 LA 293, 298–300 (Traynor, 1975). In *Crane Co.*, 47 LA 227, 231–33 (Mullin, Jr., 1966), the arbitrator held that the employer should have had the employee examined again where the employer was confronted with conflicting opinions from company and employee doctors, the most recent examination (by the employee's doctor) having indicated the employee to be fit. Compare, however, *Goss Co.*, 43 LA 640, 643 (Epstein, 1964), where the employer acted on the opinion of the employee's first doctor, but the employee sought to stand on the opinion of his second doctor.

[277]Hughes Aircraft Co., 49 LA 535, 539 (Doyle, 1967). See also Weirton Steel Corp., 89 LA 201, 204 (Sherman, 1987) (giving greater weight to employer's physician, who was "familiar with the working conditions at the Power House").

[278]See East Ohio Gas Co., 91 LA 366 (Dworkin, 1988); City of Grand Rapids, Mich., 88 LA 947, 952 (Roumell, Jr., 1987); Firestone Tire & Rubber Co., 88 LA 217, 222 (Cohen, 1986); Southern Cal. Rapid Transit Dist., 87 LA 589, 593 (Christopher, 1986); St. Joe Minerals Corp., 70 LA 1110, 1114–15 (Roberts, 1978); General Mills, 69 LA 254, 262–64 (Traynor, 1977); Reynolds Metals Co., 54 LA 1041, 1044–47 (Purdom, 1971); Magnavox Co., 46 LA 719, 723–24 (Dworkin, 1966); Reynolds Metals Co., 43 LA 734, 737–38 (Boles, 1964); Geo. A. Hormel & Co., 43 LA 484, 487 (Boles, 1964); U.S. Steel Corp., 38 LA 395, 398–99 (Wallen, 1962). For instances of at least limited weighing of such evidence, see *American Smelting & Ref. Co.*, 48 LA 1187, 1191–92 (Leonard, 1967); *Great Lakes Carbon Corp.*, 48 LA 1175, 1178–79 (Roberts, 1967). See also Brown & Williamson Tobacco Co., 69 LA 644, 651–52 (Moberly, 1977).

[279]U.S. Steel Corp., 38 LA 395, 399 (Wallen, 1962). See also General Mills, 69 LA 254, 262–63 (Traynor, 1977); Reynolds Metals, 54 LA 1041, 1047 (Purdom, 1971).

Although one arbitrator apparently would to some extent weigh conflicting medical testimony, he has held that where there is "direct conflict in the medical testimony, with nothing to swing the balance preponderantly on one side or the other," the company "is entitled to rely on the views of its own medical advisers, if it has given" the grievant "fair notice and opportunity to overcome those views before reaching a final decision."[280]

E. Special Factors in Considering Medical Evidence
[LA CDI 94.60529]

Whether the arbitrator weighs the medical evidence or only assumes to decide whether the employer's determination was fairly and reasonably made, certain factors or considerations of special significance to the arbitrator may be present in the given case. For instance, a stale diagnosis may fare poorly against one that is current;[281] medical opinion based on extensive examination of the employee and observation over a period of time will carry added weight;[282] medical opinion based only on the notes of another doctor (who examined the employee) may carry limited weight;[283] the opinion of a medical specialist will usually carry added weight,[284] but will not necessarily control over the opinion of a general practitioner.[285] In some types of cases, it is imperative that the doctor direct the medical evaluation to the specific work requirements and environment of the employee's job. Where the employee's doctor failed to do this, his opinion stood up poorly against "the judgment of the Company physician and of the Company officials with their knowledge of the job to be done and the hazards involved."[286]

---

[280]Ideal Cement Co., 20 LA 480, 482 (Merrill, 1953). *See also* American Iron & Mach. Works Co., 19 LA 417, 420 (Merrill, 1952); Southern Cotton Oil Co., 26 LA 353, 356 (Kelliher, 1956).

[281]*See* North Shore Gas Co., 40 LA 37, 43–44 (Sembower, 1963). *See also* City of Southfield, Mich., 91 LA 613 (Elkin, 1988); United States Steel, 62-1 ARB ¶8223 (McDermott, 1961).

[282]*See* Pennsylvania Tire & Rubber Co. of Miss., 69-1 ARB ¶8395 (Williams, 1969). *See also* Whitaker Cable Corp., 50 LA 1152, 1155 (Allen, Jr., 1968); Alcas Cutlery Corp., 62-2 ARB ¶8369 (Guthrie, 1962). In *A.M. Castle & Co.*, 41 LA 391, 400 (1963), the arbitrator relied on "the clearest, most succinct and unequivocal opinion" from the doctor closest to the case.

[283]*See* U.S. Pipe & Foundry Co., 36 LA 481, 484 (King, 1960). *See also* City of Hartford, 69 LA 303, 305 (Mallon, McDonough, & Zuilkowski, 1977). *Cf.* Public Serv. Elec. & Gas Co., 59 LA 425, 428 (Daly, 1972).

[284]*See* Floyd Valley Packing Co., 86 LA 1246 (Hoffmeister, 1986); Marion Power Shovel Co., 66 LA 647, 654 (Teple, 1976); Great Lakes Carbon Corp., 48 LA 1175, 1178–79 (Roberts, 1967); E.W. Bliss Co., 42 LA 1042, 1044 (Cahn, 1964); U.S. Steel Corp., 38 LA 395, 399 (Wallen, 1962).

[285]*See* Gulf States Utils. Co., 44 LA 1252, 1260 (Murphy, 1965). Even the testimony of lay witnesses may be relevant and competent in reference to an employee's physical ability for work. *See* North Shore Gas, 40 LA 37, 43 (Sembower, 1963). However, a medical doctor's opinion that grievant might not "psychologically be a good employee" carried little weight with the arbitrator, who commented that the doctor was not a psychiatrist. Whitaker Cable Corp., 50 LA 1152, 1156 (Allen, Jr., 1968).

[286]Gulf States Utils. Co., 47 LA 42, 46–48 (Murphy, 1966). *See also* Lone Star Indus., 88 LA 879, 885 (Berger, 1987); American Zinc Co. of Ill., 46 LA 645, 653 (Abernethy, 1966). But an employer did not prevail where it relied solely on the lay judgment of company officials as against the opinion of the employee's "medical experts." Texlite, Inc., 48 LA 509, 512 (Ray, 1966). Also illustrating that lay opinion ordinarily will not fare as well as professional medical opinion, see *Emery Indus.*, 72 LA 956, 959 (Ipavec, 1979); *Ohio Steel Tube Co.*, 70 LA 899, 903–04 (Di Leone, 1978); *B.F. Goodrich Co.*, 69 LA 922, 926 (Klein, 1977).

F. Use of "Neutral" Doctors [LA CDI 94.60529]

Some agreements provide that if the company's doctor and the employee's doctor disagree as to the employee's physical condition, these two doctors shall jointly select a third doctor, whose findings shall be controlling.[287] This course of action also might be taken pursuant to an arbitrator's suggestion in the course of the hearing.[288] In a case where there was insufficient evidence to warrant a finding as to the grievant's physical fitness for continued employment, the arbitrator by his award specified a detailed procedure for securing impartial determination of the employee's physical condition.[289]

G. Doctor's Certification of Illness [LA CDI 94.60529]

A frequent use of medical evidence concerns written certificates from doctors stating that employees named in the certificates were examined on a stated date and were found to be ailing. Arbitrators have held that these certificates, although not conclusive, should be given significant weight in determining whether the absence from work is to be excused due to illness.[290]

---

[287]*See, e.g.,* Lucas W., 91 LA 1272 (Alleyne, 1988); Lone Star Indus., 74 LA 1049, 1050–51 (Cohen, 1980). Even where the parties in agreeing to use a third doctor do not expressly agree that such doctor's findings shall be controlling, an arbitrator understandably will give very careful consideration to those findings. *See* Bethlehem Steel Corp., 75 LA 169, 170 (Strongin, 1980); U.S. Steel Corp., 72 LA 1131, 1134–35 (Dybeck, 1979). Furthermore, where the agreement specified use of a third doctor to resolve conflicts in medical opinion, the arbitrator, in substance, insisted that such procedure be utilized as the means of resolving the medical issue. Jno. H. Swisher & Sons, 68 LA 947, 951–53 (Rutherford, 1977). For the response of other arbitrators where parties disregarded their agreement to use a third doctor for resolving medical conflicts, see *City of Cincinnati, Ohio,* 70 LA 954, 955–56 (May, 1978); *AIR Carrier Engine Serv.,* 65 LA 666, 670–71 (Naehring, 1975). In *Colgate-Palmolive Co.,* 64 LA 293, 298 (Traynor, 1975), the agreement contained no provision for resolving conflicts in medical opinion, but the arbitrator took the parties to task for resorting to arbitration without first trying to resolve the matter by using an "agreed-upon physician"; he recommended that they agree on a neutral doctor, "give him a detailed description of the duties the Grievant would be required to perform, or even let him observe the duties, then give the Grievant a full and complete examination and agree that they will abide by his decision." *See also* Brockway Glass Co., 77 LA 113, 120 (Teple, 1981).

[288]*See* Social Sec. Admin., 87 LA 1026, 1039 (Wolff, 1986) (where arbitrator ordered reinstatement if examination by physicians determined that grievant's inability to perform resulted from alcohol withdrawal; arbitrator outlined the procedure for selecting the physicians); Dayton Malleable Iron Co., 43 LA 959, 960 (Stouffer, 1964).

[289]New Tronics Corp., 46 LA 365, 368 (Kates, 1966). The procedure was: (1) the grievant shall cause herself to be examined by professionals of her own choosing; (2) the company, which had not yet had her examined, may have her examined by professionals of its choice; (3) if the above procedure produces a conflict of medical opinion, neutral medical experts are to be selected by the parties, or by the arbitrator if the parties cannot agree; (4) the neutral findings shall be controlling; (5) the expense of neutral experts shall be shared by the parties. In *Ideal Cement Co.,* 33 LA 141, 143, 145 (Quinlan, 1959), medical testimony was sharply divided but sufficient to warrant a finding as to grievant's condition; the arbitrator noted that no provision of the agreement authorized him to appoint a neutral doctor as requested by one of the parties. *See also* Dispatch Printing Co. v. Teamsters Local 284, 782 F. Supp. 1201, 142 LRRM 2163 (S.D. Ohio 1991); Pacific Bell, 91 LA 653 (Kaufman, 1988).

[290]*See* Penn Manor Sch. Dist., 73 LA 1227, 1229 (Crawford, 1979); Dayton Tire & Rubber Co., 59 LA 635, 642 (Witney, 1972); Fenwick Fashion, 42 LA 582, 584–85 (Elbert, undated); Delta Cartage Co., 29 LA 291, 292 (Oppenheim, 1957); Carolina Coach Co., 20 LA 451, 453 (Livengood, 1953); Tennessee Coal, Iron & Ry. Co., 11 LA 909, 912 (Seward, 1948); Bell Aircraft Corp., 1 LA 281, 282 (Griffin, undated). One arbitrator expressed doubt that such certificates are too reliable, especially if submitted to the employer after extensive time has elapsed. Midland-Ross Corp., 49 LA 283, 287 (Larkin, 1967).

Such certificates, however, may be impeached if shown to have been given as a favor, to have been obtained through misrepresentation, or to have been based on a mistake.[291] The right of management to *require* a doctor's certificate as proof of illness is discussed in Chapter 17.[292]

H. Evidence Obtained by Allegedly Improper Methods
[LA CDI 94.60543]

It is sometimes argued that evidence should be excluded because it was obtained through the violation of an employee's expectation of privacy or in some allegedly repugnant manner. The broad question for the arbitrator is said to be that "absent a constitutional right or a right specified in the contract, may the arbitrator reject evidence because the manner in which it has been obtained is reprehensible or distasteful to him or because it is his opinion that sound labor-management relations would be better served by such exclusion."[293] Reported arbitration decisions reveal that arbitrators differ significantly in their views as to the use of such evidence, though the inclination to accept and rely on it appears to be fairly strong.[294]

I. Search of an Employee's Person or Property [LA CDI 94.60543]

Absent a state constitution or statute providing a right of privacy in the private-sector employment context, employees have no constitutional or statutory protection against unreasonable searches and seizures. The portion of the Fifth Amendment of the U.S. Constitution that is incorporated into the "due process clause" of the Fourteenth Amendment and made applicable to the states applies only when the employer is a governmental entity.[295] While,

---

[291]*See* Detroit Water & Sewerage Dep't, 91 LA 639 (Brown, 1988); Marquette Tool & Die Co., 88 LA 1214, 1218 (Hilgert, 1987); North Island Naval Air Rework Facility, 88 LA 23, 26 (Weiss, 1986); O-Cel-O Gen. Mills, 59 LA 869, 870 (Shister, 1972); Delta Cartage, 29 LA 291, 292 (Oppenheim, 1957); Carolina Coach, 20 LA 451, 453 (Livengood, 1953); Pullman-Standard Car Mfg. Co., 2 LA 509, 513 (Courshon, 1945). *See also* Rock Island Arsenal, 76 LA 441, 445–46 (Garman, 1981) (certificate inadequate not because the signature was stamped or affixed by a nurse, but because it did not state that the doctor himself had examined the employee); True Temper Corp., 74 LA 22, 24 (Duff, 1979) (medical slip was equivocal and was not signed by the doctor himself). In discussing the company's "suggestion" that a doctor's *medical release for returning to work* was his response to grievant's economic needs and her desire to return to work rather than to her physical condition, the arbitrator reasoned that, even though the doctor was concerned about the employee's personal problems, "it is also true that his potential liability if he recommended that a patient be returned to work and that patient could not perform without re-injuring herself would logically preclude his giving such a release solely to help the patient out financially." St. Regis Paper Co., 75 LA 737, 740 (Andersen, 1980).

[292]*See* Chapter 17, section 3.B., "Sick Leave."

[293]*Chicago Area Report, supra* note 74, at 106.

[294]For additional discussion of the matters treated in the present topic, see Greenbaum, *Employee Privacy, Monitoring, and New Technology: I. Introduction, in* ARBITRATION 1988: EMERGING ISSUES FOR THE 1990S, PROCEEDINGS OF THE 41ST ANNUAL MEETING OF NAA 163 (Gruenberg ed., BNA Books 1989); *Chicago Area Report, supra* note 74, at 105–06; *Chicago Report Workshop, supra* note 74, at 129–34, 138–39; Craver, *The Inquisitorial Process in Private Employment*, 63 CORNELL L. REV. 1 (1977).

[295]For a detailed discussion of the application of statutory and constitutional protections to the arbitration process, see DISCIPLINE AND DISCHARGE IN ARBITRATION 35–57, 179–86, 411–59 (Brand ed., BNA Books 1998 & Supp. 2001).

as a general rule, arbitrators admit evidence by private employers obtained through unconsented searches so long as the employer's methods are not egregious, they have excluded evidence when the employer's conduct was considered in some way unfair or in violation of fundamental concepts of fair play.[296] Thus, for example, in one case, evidence obtained by a supervisor's search of an employee's lunch box in the employee's tool locker was admitted, where the tool locker was open to everyone in the shop and the supervisor had earlier observed the employee in a limited-access storeroom with parts not required for the equipment he was repairing. The arbitrator found that the supervisor's search was supported by reasonable cause and was not a dramatic intrusion on the employee's privacy.[297]

However, in a second case, the arbitrator disregarded evidence of cocaine and drug paraphernalia found in the grievant's vehicle, after the arbitrator concluded that the vehicle search was instituted without adequate grounds, in violation of the employer's rules. The investigator who requested the search testified that he did not know the names of any of the eight employees who allegedly informed on the grievant, causing the arbitrator to conclude there was no reasonable basis for the search.[298]

The propriety of a search may turn on the employee's expectation of privacy. In accepting evidence obtained by a locker search in *General Electric Co.*,[299] the arbitrator acted on the belief that past practice and employee expectations should determine the propriety of locker searches: "If employee lockers have not been considered private and the personal property of the employees involved, and if employees have not reasonably expected the lockers to be inviolate, then a search of an employee locker" is not improper; but a search is improper "if employees at a plant have long believed and relied

---

[296]See *Union Oil Co. of Cal.*, 99 LA 1137, 1150 (McKay, 1992), and cases cited therein. Evidence seized by government authorities, but excluded in court under the Fourth Amendment because the search was found to be illegal, has nevertheless been admitted in arbitration hearings. *See, e.g.*, Kerr-McGee Chem. Corp., 90 LA 55, 60–61 (Levin, 1987); Aldens, Inc., 61 LA 663 (Dolnick, 1973).

[297]American Welding & Mfg. Co., 89 LA 247, 252 (Dworkin, 1987). *See also* Rust Eng'g Co., 85 LA 407, 410 (Whyte, 1985) (evidence of marijuana obtained from search of zippered compartment of wallet lost by grievant was admitted, where motive of search was to obtain positive identification, not prosecution, of owner); Kraft, Inc., 82 LA 360 (Denson, 1984) (employees properly cited for insubordination for refusing to permit search of their possessions, where employer had probable cause to believe they had violated its rule against possession of drugs on company property); Orgill Bros. & Co., 66 LA 307 (Ross, 1976) (discharge sustained where employee refused to permit body search after box-shaped bulge on back of his leg was observed by guard as employee was exiting warehouse); Fruehauf Corp., 49 LA 89 (Daugherty, 1967) (grievance denied when employee refused to allow search of lunch bucket as he entered plant, where employer sought to curb problem of employees drinking on preholiday shift).

[298]Kerr-McGee Chem. Corp., 90 LA 55 (Levin, 1987). *But see* Georgia Power Co., 93 LA 846, 851 (Holley, Jr., 1989) (arbitrator concluded that employer's use of drug detection dog to search vehicles was proper when used to determine validity of supervisor's "reasonable belief" that there might be a drug problem among employees, and there was no evidence that supervisor's or his superior's actions were arbitrary, capricious, or discriminatory). *See also* Ross-Meehan Foundries, 55 LA 1078 (King, 1970) (arbitrator reduced discharge to suspension where employer did not have a "very good reason" for searching employee's lunchbox without first seeking employee's permission).

[299]72 LA 391 (MacDonald, 1979).

upon the circumstance that their lockers were considered private areas and that these could not be opened without the personal consent of the owner of the locker. . . ."[300]

i. *Surveillance of Employees* [LA CDI 94.60543]

Although not unanimous, arbitrators generally admit otherwise reliable evidence obtained by videotaped or closed-circuit television surveillance of employees.[301] When challenged, the critical issues are usually whether the employer unilaterally could install the monitoring system, or whether the employee had a reasonable expectation of privacy.[302] In one case, an arbitrator allowed into evidence videotapes of the grievant having sex with her supervisor in a hotel's banquet office. He found that the participants did not have a reasonable expectation of privacy under the circumstances. He also found that the grievant had consented at least to a limited invasion of her privacy through her voluntary participation in sex in this location.[303]

The use of cameras in work areas to monitor employees has been justified on the ground that this is a different method of fulfilling the supervisor's function of observing employees at work.[304] A videotape of physical activity engaged in by an employee outside his home was admitted into evidence against the employee who contested his discharge for falsely claiming an injury-caused inability to work.[305]

---

[300]*Id.* at 397–98. *Compare* Kawneer Co., 86 LA 297, 300–01 (Alexander, 1985) (employees who were required to purchase their own locks for their toolboxes had a higher expectation of privacy regarding their toolboxes, and an employer could search them only if it had a reasonable basis for believing there was a violation of a published rule of conduct), *with* International Nickel Co., 50 LA 65 (Shister, 1967) (visual examination of employees' lockers without permission of employees was permitted where, among other considerations, there was a past practice of the employer's opening lockers without consent).

[301]For a general discussion of surveillance, see Black, *Surveillance and the Labor Arbitration Process, in* ARBITRATION AND THE EXPANDING ROLE OF NEUTRALS, PROCEEDINGS OF THE 23D ANNUAL MEETING OF NAA 1 (Somers & Dennis eds., BNA Books 1970).

[302]*Compare* Casting Eng'rs, 76 LA 939, 941 (Petersen, 1981) (installation of videotaping equipment in time-clock area was permissible and evidence accepted against employees discharged for theft of time), Colonial Baking Co., 62 LA 586 (Elson, 1974) (employer's unilateral installation of closed-circuit television system in production areas for security purposes in high crime area, not for disciplinary purposes, was justified under management-rights clause), *and* Cooper Carton Corp., 61 LA 697 (Kelliher, 1973) (management-rights clause entitles employer to install two television cameras to enable its vice president and production manager, both of whom had heart conditions, to observe operations and jobs being run by foremen), *with* Super Mkt. Serv. Corp., 89 LA 538 (DiLauro, 1987) (employer experiencing extensive pilferage did not have right to install closed-circuit television monitoring system without giving union opportunity to bargain), *and* EICO, Inc., 44 LA 563 (Delaney, 1965) (employer violated a maintenance-of-working conditions clause by unilaterally installing a closed-circuit television system on the production floor).

[303]Wyndham Franklin Plaza Hotel, 105 LA 186 (Duff, 1995).

[304]FMC Corp., 46 LA 335, 338 (Mittenthal, 1966) (while holding that the employer did not violate the contract by installing a camera in its receiving room, the arbitrator declined to decide whether evidence obtained through its use would be admissible in a disciplinary dispute). *See also* Emporium-Capwell, 91 LA 845 (Concepcion, 1988); Cooper Carton, 61 LA 697, 698–99 (Kelliher, 1973).

[305]*See* A. Finkl & Sons Co., 90 LA 1027 (Wolff, 1988).

Evidence provided by "spotters," though sometimes found to be suspect and insufficient, generally is allowed.[306] The use of confidential "spotters" and the admissibility of their reports and testimony are discussed elsewhere in this chapter.[307]

ii. Taping of Employees' Conversations and Monitoring of Computers

Because of federal and state legislation limiting the use of telephone monitoring, there are few arbitration decisions of modern vintage on the subject.[308] In one such case, the taped conversation of a 911 communicator in which she laughed enthusiastically at the caller's racially insensitive song parody was admitted, but the grievance was sustained for other reasons.[309]

While there have been few reported decisions involving computer monitoring or monitoring of employees' e-mails, one arbitrator upheld an employer's authority to access an employee's e-mail sent over the employer's computer, even though the employee had a personal password to access his e-mails and the employer's policies did not expressly state that e-mails could be read by the employer.[310]

In another case, an arbitrator had to determine if an employee was properly disciplined for accessing a supervisor's personal computer "basket" of mail and copying a proposed disciplinary letter. Finding that under the circumstances of that case, the employee reasonably expected to have access to anything on the computer as long as it was not electronically blocked, and that the employer and supervisor had negligently failed to block access to the proposed disciplinary letter, the arbitrator set aside that portion of the discipline attributable to the employee's initially entering the supervisor's "basket" of mail. However, the arbitrator sustained the discipline of the grievant for pulling up the letter and making a copy of it without prior approval.[311]

J. Drug and Alcohol Testing [LA CDI 100.552545; 118.653]

The admissibility of evidence obtained from drug and alcohol testing is discussed in Chapter 13.[312]

---

[306]See Briggs & Stratton Corp., 107 LA 1023, 1029 (Briggs, 1997); Chivas Prods., 101 LA 546 (Kanner, 1993); U.S. Borax & Chem. Corp., 84 LA 32 (Richman, 1984).

[307]See section 4.A., "Right of Cross-Examination: Anonymous Witnesses and Confidential Documents," above.

[308]In a case arising before the enactment of federal telephone recording legislation, one arbitrator permitted use of evidence obtained against an employee by tape recorder, while another excluded such a recording, requiring the person who made the recordings to testify on a recollection basis. Compare Sun Drug Co., 31 LA 191, 194 (Marcus, 1958) (recording admitted), with Needham Packing Co., 44 LA 1057, 1059 (Davey, 1965) (recording excluded).

[309]Dane County, Wis., 97 LA 221 (Flaten, 1991). Taped conversations with undercover agents also have been used as evidence on occasion. See, e.g., Associated Grocers of Colo., 82 LA 414 (Smith, 1984).

[310]PPG Indus., 113 LA 833 (Dichter, 1999).

[311]Press Democrat Publ'g Co., 93 LA 969 (McKay, 1989).

[312]See Chapter 13, section 26.F., "Drug and Alcohol Testing." See also Discipline and Discharge in Arbitration 185 n.229, 338–39 (Brand ed., BNA Books 1998 & 2001 Supp.).

i.   *Entrapment*

The defense of entrapment is available to an accused in a criminal prosecution who can show that he was innocent of any predisposition or intent to commit a criminal act, but was induced to do so by an undercover law enforcement agent.[313] Objections that evidence should be excluded because it was improperly obtained through entrapment have not been favorably received by arbitrators.

Though not finding entrapment, one arbitrator viewed as a mitigating circumstance the fact that the grievant, who had sold marijuana to an undercover agent in the plant, did not solicit sales, but had responded to the undercover agent's request for marijuana.[314] Arbitrators also have allowed employers to use bait to catch thieves.[315]

8. ADMISSIBILITY

A. Admissibility of Improperly Obtained Documents

How should documents inexplicably obtained from the opposing party be treated when offered as evidence at an arbitration hearing? In one such case, the union was allowed to introduce internal management documents summarizing discussions with the union, but "*only* to provide background" concerning the development of the issues before the arbitrator. In accepting the documents, the arbitrator pointed out that a "highly informal relationship" existed between the parties, and that it was not "uncommon for documents prepared for internal consumption by either party to get into the hands of representatives of the other party."[316]

B. "New" Evidence at Arbitration Hearings [LA CDI 94.60549]

Evidence that has not been disclosed during the prehearing grievance steps is sometimes offered at the arbitration hearing.[317] A variety of reasons may account for the appearance of this "new evidence," for example, the parties may have a practice not to present all the evidence during the grievance procedure; the particular grievance may have been quickly advanced through the steps of the grievance procedure; or some facts are later discovered, or information has not been fully developed during the grievance procedure, or information has been withheld, intentionally or unintentionally.

---

[313]*See* Heinrich Motors, 68 LA 1224, 1228 (Hildebrand, 1977).

[314]Aeronca, Inc., 93 LA 782, 789 (Doering, 1989).

[315]*See, e.g.*, New Jersey Bell Tel. Co., 55 LA 226, 228–30 (Hill, 1970) (coins planted in pay phone); U.S. Steel Corp., 49 LA 101, 102–05 (Dybeck, 1967) (bait money placed in locker).

[316]National Steel Corp., 102 LA 1159, 1167–68 (Garrett, 1994). *But see* Press Democrat Publ'g Co., 93 LA 969 (McKay, 1989) (employee suspended for pulling up and printing proposed disciplinary letter from supervisor's computer "basket").

[317]As to how frequently surprise evidence is encountered, see Eaton, *Labor Arbitration in the San Francisco Bay Area*, 48 LA 1381, 1385 (1967).

Some of the factors involved in an arbitrator's decision to accept or reject such new evidence include whether there is an explicit contractual requirement regarding the matter, the need for consideration of all the facts relevant to the case, the need to protect the integrity of the grievance procedure, general notions of fairness, whether the newly discovered evidence is consistent with the theory of the proponent's case, and the nature of the case being arbitrated.

Any possible element of surprise in the use of new evidence is largely mitigated or eliminated by the fact that arbitrators who accept newly submitted evidence will take any reasonable steps necessary to assure the opposing party adequate opportunity to respond thereto, regardless of whether the evidence had been withheld in good or bad faith.[318] If the arbitrator deems it necessary, the case may be returned to the parties for further consideration in light of the new evidence, or the hearing may be recessed for whatever time necessary to give the surprised party the opportunity to prepare or revise its defense.[319] Such interruptions of the arbitration hearing can be avoided if parties using new evidence will submit it to the other party prior to the hearing whenever the nature of the evidence makes it reasonably foreseeable that the other party will need time to prepare a response.[320]

Unless the contract expressly provides that new evidence must be excluded, arbitrators generally favor receiving it. A survey conducted by Arbitrator W. Willard Wirtz indicated that "unless some deliberate attempt to mislead the other party is disclosed, and particularly if the 'new' evidence or argument appears substantially material, most arbitrators will be disinclined to rule the matter out of the proceedings."[321] In this regard, Arbitrator Ralph Seward explained that many prearbitral grievance meetings "are informal and deal with the surface of a problem without in any sense taking real evidence,"[322] and Arbitrator Wirtz observed that the "company, for its part, may very reasonably not have made the thorough investigation it will properly

---

[318]As to the reaction of surprised parties, "there is no evidence that they feel that the procedural steps which arbitrators have taken to protect their rights to respond to surprise materials have been less than satisfactory." Fleming, The Labor Arbitration Process 153–54 (Univ. of Ill. Press 1965). For cases where the arbitrator took steps to mitigate the element of unfairness for new or surprise evidence, see *B.F. Goodrich Co.*, 91 LA 1033 (Duff, 1988); *RB&W Corp.*, 90 LA 1057 (Traynor, 1988); *Wells Aluminum Corp.*, 86 LA 983 (Wies, 1986).

[319]See Wirtz, *Due Process of Arbitration, in* The Arbitrator and the Parties, Proceedings of the 11th Annual Meeting of NAA 1, 16 (McKelvey ed., BNA Books 1958). In *Pittsburgh Steel Co.*, 48 LA 585, 587 (Valtin, 1967), the arbitrator received the new material into evidence and gave the surprised party an election to have the case remanded or to proceed with it; the party chose to proceed.

[320]See the arbitrator's suggestions in *Jonco Aircraft Corp.*, 22 LA 819, 823 (Merrill, 1954). *See also* Smith, *The Search for Truth: I. The Search for Truth—The Whole Truth, in* Truth, Lie Detectors, and Other Problems in Labor Arbitration, Proceedings of the 31st Annual Meeting of NAA 40, 46 (Stern & Dennis eds., BNA Books 1979).

[321]Wirtz, NAA 11th Proceedings, at 15. *See also* Rose Printing Co., 88 LA 27 (Williams, 1986); Hospital Serv. Plan of N.J., 62 LA 616, 620 (Kaplan, 1974); Inland Steel Container Co., 60 LA 536, 537 (Marcus, 1973); Worthington Corp., 47 LA 1170, 1171–72 (Livengood, 1966); Central Soya Co., 46 LA 65, 70 (Kesselman, 1966); North Am. Aviation, 17 LA 183, 185–86 (Komaroff, 1951).

[322]Wirtz, NAA 11th Proceedings, at 15.

consider warranted if the union ultimately decides to take the case seriously enough to go to arbitration."[323]

A Tripartite Committee of the NAA stated:

> In some situations . . . it is the practice of the parties not to present all the evidence during the grievance procedure. In other situations the parties may recognize from the outset that a particular grievance must be arbitrated and pass quickly through the steps of [the] grievance procedure. In cases like these, evidence not disclosed prior to the hearing should be admitted. In general, evidence discovered after the grievance was processed should also be admitted. The arbitrator, however, should grant adjournments or take other measures to assure a fair hearing and to protect a party taken by surprise as to evidence concerning a material issue.[324]

The absence of any contract provision restricting acceptance of new evidence has sometimes been emphasized by arbitrators in receiving evidence presented for the first time at the arbitration hearing.[325] But even where an agreement provided that "the facts concerning the case shall be made available to both parties" at an early stage, facts acquired later could be introduced at subsequent steps of the grievance procedure or at the arbitration hearing.[326] Thus, under a contract requiring the employer to furnish all available evidence to the union "and/or" the arbitrator, the withholding of evidence until the arbitration hearing was ruled not to be improper where the union was granted 10 days to consider the evidence; sufficient time for consideration of the evidence was deemed the basic purpose of the provision.[327]

Conversely, while stating that "it is understandable that the evidence which comes out at the arbitration hearing is more detailed and more complete than that which is produced in the preliminary steps of the grievance machinery," the umpire considered that delay in presenting evidence "mitigates its relative importance."[328] Moreover, he refused to accept evidence offered by a party for the first time at the arbitration stage where the evidence was known to the party at the earlier grievance stages and would have expanded the party's claim if admitted at the arbitration stage.[329]

In cases where an employer furnished recently acquired evidence at the arbitration hearing, acceptable "new" evidence was distinguished from "surprise" evidence that prejudiced the union. Exhibits that were substantive,

---

[323]*Id.* at 5, 16. *See also* San Gamo Elec. Co., 44 LA 593, 600 (Sembower, 1965).

[324]*New York Report, supra* note 2, at 302–03. Other tripartite committees were likewise in general agreement that new evidence should be admitted into evidence and that the arbitrator should take reasonable steps to protect the other party. *Chicago Area Report, supra* note 74, at 104; *Chicago Report Workshop, supra* note 74, at 142–43; *Pittsburgh Report, supra* note 2, at 260–61.

[325]*See* North Am. Aviation, 17 LA 183, 185–86 (Komaroff, 1951); Carbon Fuel Co., 1 ALAA ¶67,327 (Moler, 1946). The above-quoted Tripartite Committee took the position that to the extent that the contract specifically requires full disclosure, new evidence should be rejected by the arbitrator. *New York Report, supra* note 2, at 302. *But see* Zinsco Elec. Prods., 64 LA 107, 109 (Caraway, 1975) (the parties in their contract expressly agreed not to withhold evidence but did not expressly state any penalty for withholding evidence or authorize its exclusion from arbitration).

[326]American Steel & Wire Co., 5 LA 193, 206–07 (Blumer, 1946).

[327]Texas Co., 7 LA 735, 739 (Carmichael, 1947).

[328]Bethlehem Steel, 21 LA 655, 656 (Feinberg, 1953).

[329]Bethlehem Steel, 18 LA 366, 367 (Feinberg, 1951).

relevant, and easily understood were admitted into evidence regardless of their surprise value.[330]

It is the intentional, calculated withholding of evidence that arbitrators criticize most severely. In this regard, the view of one umpire is no doubt shared by many arbitrators:

> [S]ound collective bargaining requires frank and candid disclosure at the earliest opportunity of all the facts known to each party. There will undoubtedly be times when facts are not discovered, and therefore not disclosed, until after the grievance has been partially processed, and problem enough is created by those instances. There is not a scintilla of justification for the withholding of information by either party from and after the time it is discovered.[331]

In one case, however, even the calculated withholding of evidence did not result in its rejection by the arbitrator where, from the outset, the attitude of the party from whom it was withheld was such as to put all prearbitral steps on an adversarial basis, "with both sides primarily pointed at an ultimate arbitration instead of mutual ascertainment of fact, compromise, or some other solution based upon general collective bargaining considerations."[332]

When the arbitration tribunal is serving essentially in an appellate capacity, there is obviously strong reason to confine the evidence to what was considered below. In this regard, the rules of the NRAB require that "all data submitted in support" of the party's position "must affirmatively show the same to have been presented to the [other party] and made a part of the particular question in dispute."[333]

C. Consideration of Post-Discipline Evidence [LA CDI 94.60549]

Some agreements require that the employer inform the employee of all grounds for discharge at the time of discharge. Under such provisions, arbitrators typically hold that only evidence bearing on the charges made at the time of discharge should be considered in determining the existence of cause.[334] Even absent such specific contractual provisions, however, arbitrators generally hold that a discharge "must stand or fall upon the reason given at the time of discharge"; the employer cannot add other reasons when the case reaches arbitration.[335]

---

[330]Wells Aluminum Corp., 86 LA 983 (Wies, 1986); Lever Bros. Co., 82 LA 164 (Stix, 1983).

[331]General Motors Umpire Decision No. F-97 (1950). The arbitrator chastised both parties for calculated withholding of evidence in *Sperry-Rand Corp.*, 46 LA 961, 966 (Seitz, 1966), and noted that such practice can be "self-defeating." Also suggesting that the practice "is likely to boomerang," see Davey, *The John Deere-UAW Permanent Arbitration System*, Critical Issues in Labor Arbitration, Proceedings of the 10th Annual Meeting of NAA 161, 170 (McKelvey ed., BNA Books 1957).

[332]Bethlehem Steel, 6 LA 617, 619 (Wyckoff, 1947).

[333]29 C.F.R. §301.5(d), (e). Also, §301.7(b) charges the parties "with the duty and responsibility of including in their original written submission all known relevant, argumentative facts and documentary evidence."

[334]Bethlehem Steel, 29 LA 635, 640–43 (Seward, 1957); Forest Hill Foundry Co., 1 LA 153, 154 (Brown, 1946).

[335]*See* Safeway, Inc., 105 LA 718, 722 (Goldberg, 1995). The arbitrator rejected after-acquired evidence, holding that the discharge "must rise or fall" based on the facts as they

Nevertheless, arbitrators have admitted "after acquired" evidence in three distinct situations: (1) as further evidence of predisciplinary misconduct, (2) as evidence of post-disciplinary conduct affecting the remedy, and (3) as evidence of disparate treatment.

D. After-Acquired Evidence

i. *After-Acquired Evidence of Predisciplinary Misconduct*

After-acquired evidence of predisciplinary misconduct has been allowed when it involved a second identical instance of the grievant's theft that resulted in his discharge.[336] After-acquired evidence of predisciplinary misconduct also has been admitted where such evidence would have been disclosed if the employer had conducted its own investigation prior to discharging the employee.[337] The post-discharge discovery of false statements on an employment application was held to be insufficient to dismiss a grievance, but it was admitted for purposes of determining an appropriate remedy.[338]

While evidence of predischarge misconduct discovered after the discharge may be considered, the existence of such misconduct must be established according to a process that allows the grievant to respond.[339] Arbitrators also may consider after-acquired favorable pre- and post-discharge conduct.[340]

---

were known at the time of the termination. West Va. Pulp & Paper Co., 10 LA 117, 118 (Guthrie, 1947). *See also* E&J Gallo Winery, 80 LA 765, 769–70 (Killion, 1983); Nickles Bakery, 73 LA 801, 802 (Letson, 1979); Gardner Denver Co., 51 LA 1019, 1022 (Ray, 1968); Unimart, 49 LA 1207, 1210 (Roberts, 1968). *Cf.* Trailways Southeastern Lines, 81 LA 365, 366 (Gibson, 1983); Wilshire Indus./Wilshire Stor-All, 71 LA 56, 58 (Mueller, 1978); Mitchell Bros. Truck Line, 48 LA 953, 956 (Peck, 1967). For decisions discussing this topic in other fora, see, e.g., *Golden Day Sch. v. NLRB*, 644 F.2d 834, 107 LRRM 2558 (9th Cir. 1979); *NLRB v. Miller Redwood Co.*, 407 F.2d 1366, 70 LRRM 2868 (9th Cir. 1969); *NRLB v. Yazoo Valley Elec. Power Ass'n*, 405 F.2d 479, 70 LRRM 2049 (5th Cir. 1968); *NLRB v. Bin-Dictator Co.*, 356 F.2d 210, 61 LRRM 2366 (6th Cir. 1966); *NLRB v. National Furniture Mfg. Co.*, 315 F.2d 280, 52 LRRM 2451 (7th Cir. 1963); *American Petrofina Co.*, 92 LA 578 (Dunn, 1989); *Potashnick Constr. Co.*, 77 LA 893 (Richardson, 1981). For additional material on this subject, see e.g., THE COMMON LAW OF THE WORKPLACE: THE VIEWS OF ARBITRATORS §6.11 (St. Antoine ed., BNA Books 1998); FAIRWEATHER'S PRACTICE AND PROCEDURE IN LABOR ARBITRATION §12.II., at 262 (Schoonhoven ed., BNA Books 4th ed. 1999); Nicolau, *The Arbitrator's Remedial Powers: I.*, in ARBITRATION 1990: NEW PERSPECTIVES ON OLD ISSUES, PROCEEDINGS OF THE 43D ANNUAL MEETING OF NAA 73 (Gruenberg ed., BNA Books 1991); Nicolau, *After-Acquired Evidence— Will the* McKennon *Decision Make a Difference*, J. DISP. RESOL. 17 (July 1995). *See also* Heritage Cable Vision, 112 LA 1 (Feller, 1999); Pullman-Standard, 47 LA 752 (McCoy, 1966).

[336]Bill Kay Chevrolet, 107 LA 302 (Wolff, 1996). *See also* AT&T, 102 LA 931, 940 (Kanner, 1994) (grievant was allowed to introduce evidence at the arbitration hearing that he did not disclose prior to his discharge).

[337]Group W Cable of Chi., 93 LA 789, 797 (Fischbach, 1989).

[338]Lenox Hill Hosp., 102 LA 1071 (Simons, 1994).

[339]Jackson Gen. Hosp., 113 LA 1040, 1046 (Sharpe, 2000).

[340]Butterkrust Bakeries, 78 LA 562, 563 (Cocalis, 1982); H.K. Porter Co., 74 LA 969, 972 (Finan, 1980); Texaco, Inc., 42 LA 408, 411 (Prasow, 1963); Spaulding Fiber Co., 21 LA 58, 58–59 (Thompson, 1953). Sometimes less leeway has been recognized for such consideration of the grievant's post-discharge actions than for consideration of new predischarge information in the grievant's favor. *See, e.g.*, Mobil Oil Corp. v. Oil, Chem. & Atomic Workers Local 8-831, 679 F.2d 299, 110 LRRM 2620, 2623–24 (3d Cir. 1982); Sharon Steel Corp., 71 LA 737, 740 (Klein, 1978).

ii.   *After-Acquired Evidence of Post-Disciplinary Conduct*

One arbitrator set forth the general rule concerning the admissibility of after-acquired evidence of post-disciplinary conduct and its exception:

> It is true that in most grievance arbitrations, the basic issue to be determined is whether management's action was proper based upon the facts known at the time the action was taken. Normally, the clock stops at that moment, and anything that occurs subsequently is irrelevant. However, there are occasions, especially in discharge cases, where events occurring after the incident giving rise to the grievance are given some weight by arbitrators.[341]

In one case, a grievant's post-discharge misconduct was allowed as evidence that he was the aggressor in the assault leading to his discharge, but was disallowed in considering the merits of his discharge and in determining an appropriate remedy.[342] In another case, although after-acquired evidence of a grievant's predischarge sexual harassment was not permitted as an additional basis to uphold his termination, after-acquired evidence of the grievant's post-disciplinary threats against his coworkers rendered reinstatement an inappropriate remedy.[343] There, the employee's failure to deny the negative post-discharge conduct was held to stand as undisputed evidence against him.[344]

The distinction drawn in some opinions is between additional grounds for discharge, which remain inadmissible, and evidence of pre- or post-discharge conduct relevant to the originally stated grounds.[345] These decisions evince a willingness to admit evidence of pre- and post-discharge conduct to support or refute the original grounds for termination, and to determine whether reinstatement is an appropriate remedy.[346] An arbitrator's expression of the rationale is instructive:

> In my view, post-discharge evidence garnered by either party can be admitted during arbitral hearing. An extreme example serves to make the point. In the event a post-discharge witness confesses to a theft charged against the grievant; or a witness recants a prior statement given to the employer thereby denoting the grievant's innocence, it flies in the face of fairness and justice to

---

[341]Texaco Inc., 42 LA 408, 411 (Prasow, 1963).

[342]Pepsi-Cola Bottling Co., 107 LA 257 (Ross, 1996).

[343]Jackson Gen. Hosp., 113 LA 1040 (Sharpe, 2000).

[344]*Id.* at 1047.

[345]*See, e.g.,* Keystone Steel & Wire Co., 114 LA 1466 (Goldstein, 2000). *But see* Pullman-Standard, 47 LA 752, 753 (McCoy, 1966) (ordinarily a discharge made for one explicit reason cannot be justified in arbitration for an entirely different reason, but this rule does not apply where the employee has fair opportunity to defend against the additional grounds and the grounds would be reason for another discharge immediately following a reinstatement by the arbitrator).

[346]Shaefer's Ambulance Serv., 104 LA 481 (Calhoun, 1995). *See also* Pepsi-Cola Bottling Co., 107 LA 257 (Ross, 1996) (evidence of post-discharge misconduct by grievant admitted to determine the method of operation used by grievant); Nabisco Brands, 80 LA 238, 242 (Madden, 1983) (considering the grievant's post-discharge misconduct to be the decisive factor against him in that it served to discredit his denial of the original dishonesty charge); Mobay Chem. Corp., 77 LA 219, 222 (Lubow, 1981); St. Johnsbury Trucking Co., 74 LA 607, 608–09 (Knowlton, 1980); Taft Broad. Co., WBRC-TV, 69 LA 307, 311 (Chaffin, 1977); Granite City Steel Co., 53 LA 909, 918 (McKenna, 1969); Perini, M-K, Leavell, 46 LA 1044, 1048 (Merrill, 1966) (additional offense at time of discharge formed "part of one connected whole"). For related matters, see section 8.B., "'New' Evidence at Arbitration Hearings," above.

simply ignore such evidence. Conversely, where, for example, the grievant was discharged for being under the influence of alcohol on the job, and subsequent to the discharge the employer discovered empty liquor bottles in his locker; or an employee is discharged for the theft of an item valued at $5.00 and subsequent to discharge it is discovered that he stole items valued at $500.00, again such evidence should be admitted at arbitral hearing.

In my opinion, it is not consequently discovered evidence but rather subsequently discovered grounds for discharge that is precluded at arbitral hearing. An employer is limited to the grounds set forth at the time of discharge. But neither the employer nor the union is precluded from offering at arbitration, evidence that is discovered post-discharge.[347]

Other arbitrators have limited their consideration of post-discharge conduct only for purposes of assessing whether the penalty should be mitigated.[348] The rationale is that post-discharge rehabilitation should be considered because "the prime purpose of industrial discipline is not to inflict punishment for wrongdoing, but to correct individual faults and behavior and to prevent further infractions."[349] Some arbitrators appear particularly willing to consider post-discharge rehabilitative treatment as a mitigating factor in determining the propriety of discharge where drug and/or alcohol addiction was involved.[350] In one case, for example, the arbitrator considered the misconduct a consequence of the employee's illness.[351] The author of that opinion observed:

> [M]ost arbitrators routinely exclude evidence of pre-discharge conduct unearthed after the discharge even if it is of the same nature as the act for which the discharge occurred. Most arbitrators also refuse to consider, as a basis for the discharge, evidence of acts occurring after the discharge.
>
> Yet, given the proper circumstances, many of us have little hesitancy in considering a "troubled" employee's attempts at rehabilitation, even though those attempts might not have begun until after the discharge. Some of us also consider less uplifting post-discharge conduct in certain circumstances, not as grounds for discharge, but when considering the proper penalty to be imposed. . . .

---

[347]AT&T, 102 LA 931, 940 (Kanner, 1994). *See also* Bill Kay Chevrolet, 107 LA 302 (Wolff, 1996).

[348]Keystone Steel & Wire, 114 LA 1466 (Goldstein, 2000); Lenox Hill Hosp., 102 LA 1071 (Simons, 1994); Emhart Corp., 69 LA 839, 841–42 (Weitzman, 1977); Columbus Show Case Co., 44 LA 507, 513–14 (Kates, 1965); Catholic Press Soc'y, 40 LA 641, 651 (Gorsuch, 1963) (post-discharge misconduct may be considered in judging the appropriateness of the penalty, just as the employee's past record may be considered); Trailways Southeastern Lines, 81 LA 365, 366 (Gibson, 1983) (predischarge misconduct of which the employer was unaware used in penalty reviews); Sunshine Specialty Co., 55 LA 1061, 1068–69 (Levin, 1970).

[349]Ashland Oil, 90 LA 681 (Volz, 1988). *See also* Keystone Steel & Wire, 114 LA 1466 (Goldstein, 2000); General Tel. Co. of Ind., 90 LA 689 (Goldstein, 1988).

[350]Keystone Steel & Wire, 114 LA 1466 (Goldstein, 2000); Vons Cos., 106 LA 740 (Darrow, 1996); USS, Div. of U.S. Steel, 104 LA 82 (Dybeck, 1994); Meijer, Inc., 103 LA 834 (Daniel, 1994); AAFES Distribution, 107 LA 290 (Marcus, 1996); Ashland Oil, 90 LA 681, 687 (Volz, 1988); Northwest Airlines, 89 LA 943 (Nicolau, 1984), *rev'd sub nom.* Northwest Airlines v. Air Line Pilots, 633 F. Supp. 779 (D.D.C. 1985), *rev'd*, 808 F.2d 76, 124 LRRM 2300 (D.C. Cir. 1987) (aff'g 89 LA 943) (reinstating airline pilot discharged for consuming alcoholic beverages within 24 hours of flight who was found to be an alcoholic and who offered post-discharge evidence of his progress in rehabilitation). *But see* Duquesne Light Co., 92 LA 907, 910–11 (Sergent, Jr., 1989).

[351]Northwest Airlines, 89 LA 943 (Nicolau, 1984). *See also* Youngstown Hosp. Ass'n, 82 LA 31 (Miller, 1983).

. . . In deciding whether or not just cause has been proven, we do have the authority to examine and weigh the underlying cause for misconduct. We have that authority because the proven alcoholic or drug addict or employee plagued with mental illness suffers from a diagnosable and treatable disease medically differentiating him from others. The fact that these diseases are treatable makes all the difference.[352]

Another arbitrator in 1995 provided an extensive review of the decisions on this topic.[353] Other arbitrators apply a balancing test, examining various factors to determine whether mitigation is appropriate in all the facts and circumstances.[354] These factors may include: (1) whether the grievant did the act under the influence of alcohol or drugs or while the grievant was an alcohol or drug abuser; (2) whether the grievant's work record was relatively clear of disciplinary action or whether prior disciplinary action resulted from alcoholism or drug abuse; (3) whether the grievant is successfully participating in an employee assistance program or similar rehabilitation program that indicates likely successful rehabilitation; and (4) whether the grievant was a long-term employee.[355] Waiting too long before seeking treatment, taking inappropriate post-termination jobs (e.g., bartending), and other behavior indicative of failure to fully confront his or her problems can work against the former employee under this approach.[356]

But, still other arbitrators view post-discharge rehabilitative efforts as irrelevant because (1) the grievant could have sought treatment or notified the employer of an illness prior to discharge, and (2) crediting a grievant's post-discharge rehabilitation effectively second-guesses the employer's decision based on facts that did not exist at the time.[357]

Where the grievant withheld evidence of drug rehabilitation until the arbitration hearing, the arbitrator applied the general rule. He reasoned:

> In the grievance report and throughout the grievance procedure the grievant denied use of drugs at the plant. Although the Company was apprised of the confinement of the grievant in a rehabilitation program, at no time prior to Arbitration hearing did the grievant seek a mitigation of the penalty based upon an acknowledgment of wrong-doing.
>
> In the opinion of the Arbitrator, in order to consider a mitigation of a discharge, those facts which potentially warrant a lesser penalty than was imposed, must be made known to the Company prior to the hearing on just and proper cause. A review of just and proper cause must be limited to the information available to the Company when it made its decision. . . .

---

[352]Nicolau, *The Arbitrator's Remedial Powers*, *in* Arbitration 1990: New Perspectives on Old Issues, Proceedings of the 43d Annual Meeting of NAA 73, 73–74, 81 (Gruenberg ed., BNA Books 1991). *See also* Philip Morris U.S.A., 99 LA 1016 (Volz, 1992) (concerning the nature of the diseases of alcoholism and drug abuse and post-discharge rehabilitation evidence); Group W Cable of Chi., 93 LA 789, 796 (Fischbach, 1989) (regarding admissibility of post-discharge evidence to permit "a more comprehensive inquiry of the Company's disciplinary decision in conjunction with the evidence proffered by the Union which tends to exculpate the grievant from a dischargeable offense").

[353]Ocean Spray Cranberries, 105 LA 148 (Dichter, 1995).

[354]Keystone Steel & Wire, 114 LA 1466 (Goldstein, 2000).

[355]*Id.* at 1471 (citing General Tel. Co. of Ind., 90 LA 689 (Goldstein, 1988)).

[356]*Id.* at 1472.

[357]*See* P.H. Glatfeler Co., 103 LA 879 (Singer, 1994); Duquesne Light Co., 92 LA 907 (Sergent, Jr., 1989).

... [Admission and rehabilitation evidence] was withheld by the grievant until his appearance at the arbitration hearing. . . . [A]lthough provided an opportunity to submit information he wished the Company to consider, the grievant declined to do so.

In order for the Arbitrator to give any consideration to the rehabilitation and admission . . . it must be apparent that this information was made known to the Company prior to its decision to proceed to arbitrate. . . . [358]

Evidence of rehabilitation from a major depressive disorder may be considered in determining the propriety and conditions of reinstatement. An arbitrator compared cases involving alcoholism and depression and found similar factors in that although alcoholism and depression may cause attendance problems, the average employee does not know or admit there is a problem until informed by a knowledgeable person. The cure usually requires professional assistance, and the employee must have a strong and persistent desire to be cured.[359]

However, there are cases where a collective bargaining agreement does not empower the arbitrator to evaluate the propriety of the penalty imposed once the grievant is found to have committed the offense with which he or she was charged. In such cases, the arbitrator may not modify the negotiated penalty regardless of evidence of post-discharge rehabilitation efforts. To do so would exceed authority granted by the agreement.

With regard to back-pay awards, employees' post-discharge conduct may be relevant in determining the amount to be awarded. Evidence of the employee's efforts to seek other employment and mitigate damages may also be considered.

iii. Post-Discharge Evidence of Disparate Treatment

Post-discharge evidence has been admitted to establish disparate treatment of a sanctioned employee. One federal court affirmed an arbitrator's finding of lack of just cause based in part on evidence of how the employer treated employees after the grievant's discharge.[360] According to the court:

Where, as here, there has been no change in the governing contract, and the time period under consideration is not unreasonably long, it is appropriate to consider an employer's post-discharge acts in determining whether that employer is treating all employees equally: evidence of an isolated act of discipline that occurred ten years prior to [grievant's] discharge would almost certainly be less probative than evidence that occurred within a year after his discharge. In fact, in some circumstances, evidence of an employer's action taken after an employee has been terminated may be the only evidence of disparate treatment.[361]

---

[358]Georgia Pac. Corp., 93 LA 754, 758 (Ipavec, 1989).

[359]Iowa-Illinois Gas & Elec. Co., 95 LA 553 (Volz, 1990).

[360]Osram Sylvania v. Teamsters Local 528, 87 F.3d 1261, 152 LRRM 2808 (11th Cir. 1996).

[361]Id. at 1265. Cf. Henkel Corp., 104 LA 494, 498–99 (Hooper, 1995) (grievance claiming disparate treatment was timely even though an event of alleged disparate treatment occurred after the grievant's discharge).

While arbitrators also have considered post-discharge evidence of disparate treatment,[362] at least one arbitrator has stated that the value of such evidence is "diminished sharply."[363]

iv. *Evidence Submitted After the Hearing* [LA CDI 94.60549]

While ordinarily no new data or evidence may be presented after the hearing in briefs or otherwise, there are exceptions.[364] Sometimes discussion at the hearing indicates the need for additional data that are not quickly available, and if the parties desire not to recess or otherwise delay the hearing, they may agree to the submission of the data to the arbitrator after the hearing has been completed. Likewise, the arbitrator either during or after the hearing may request post-hearing data or information.[365] Such post-hearing data often will be prepared jointly and submitted by the parties. If the data are individually prepared, each party ordinarily must be furnished a copy of the other party's data so that comment may be made thereon, or so that a further hearing can be requested in case of gross discrepancies.[366]

Sometimes important evidence is discovered or first becomes available after the hearing and may be considered if the opposing party has been given fair opportunity to meet it.[367] In one case, the employer was entitled to consider a grievant's earlier murder charge that came to light after the close of the hearing. The arbitrator deviated from the general rule because the grievant had refused to testify about his prior criminal misconduct and misled the union on this issue.[368]

E. Evidence to Be Heard by the Entire Board

Where there is a board of arbitration, all evidence must be taken in the presence of all of the arbitrators. Such a requirement prevails in common law arbitration,[369] in arbitration under state statutes,[370] and under AAA Rule 28.[371]

---

[362]*See* T.J. Maxx, 107 LA 78, 83 (Richman, 1996).

[363]Eagle-Picher Indus., 101 LA 473, 476 (Staudohar, 1993).

[364]See Chapter 7, section 5.A., "Posthearing Briefs."

[365]For instance, after receiving post-hearing briefs, an arbitrator requested additional data in *McInerney Spring & Wire Co.*, 20 LA 642, 643 (Smith, 1953). In *City of Renton, Wash.*, 71 LA 271, 272 (Snow, 1978), the arbitrator during the hearing requested that additional data be submitted after the hearing.

[366]*See* Northeast Airlines, 37 LA 741, 743 (Wolff, 1961); McInerney Spring & Wire Co., 20 LA 642, 643 (Smith, 1953); SIMKIN, ACCEPTABILITY AS A FACTOR IN ARBITRATION UNDER AN EXISTING AGREEMENT 59–60 (Univ. of Pa. Press 1952); UPDEGRAFF & McCOY, ARBITRATION OF LABOR DISPUTES 103 (1946). For related considerations, see section 4.A., "Right of Cross-Examination: Anonymous Witnesses and Confidential Documents," above.

[367]See discussion in HILL & SINICROPI, EVIDENCE IN ARBITRATION 318–20, 325–30 (BNA Books 2d ed. 1987).

[368]Quaker Oats Co., 110 LA 816 (Crider, 1998).

[369]Ziskind, *Labor Arbitration Under State Statutes* 3 (U.S. Dep't of Labor 1943).

[370]*Id.* at 5. While still providing that the hearing shall be conducted by all the arbitrators, statutes modeled after the UAA provide that a majority may determine any question and render a final award.

[371]*See* Szuts v. Dean Witter Rentals, 931 F.2d 830 (11th Cir. 1991) (Arbitration agreement incorporated the AAA rules and also required arbitration before a panel of at least

Case law under a state statute, for instance, holds that an agreement to arbitrate entitles the parties to the considered judgment of arbitrators based on evidence submitted in the presence of all the arbitrators, and that a party's participation at proceedings at which only three of six arbitrators were present did not constitute a waiver of the requirement that all arbitrators be present in order for their award to be binding.[372] However, where it had been agreed that the partisan members of a tripartite board of arbitration could be substituted at any time, the award was held binding although one of the arbitrators who signed it had been substituted after the hearing and had not heard the evidence.[373] Further, the deliberate refusal by a party and its representatives on a tripartite board to attend the hearing may result in the issuance of a valid default award.[374]

F. Restriction on the Scope of Cross-Examination

The arbitrator, having a paramount interest in securing all of the facts, may refuse to restrict cross-examination to matters brought out in the examination-in-chief and can be expected not to place strict limitation on the number of recross or redirect examinations. As to the first of these points, arbitral consensus appears to be that reasonably wide latitude should be permitted in cross-examination.[375] It has been suggested, however, that the cross-examiner who seeks to go beyond the direct examination area should call the witness as an adverse or hostile witness.[376] While the parties are allowed considerable latitude in cross-examining witnesses, to reveal conflicts in their testimony and to challenge credibility, arbitrators will not condone use of personal invectives against witnesses.[377]

9. WEIGHT AND CREDIBILITY OF EVIDENCE [LA CDI 94.60505]

It is within the province of the arbitrator to determine the weight, relevancy, and authenticity of evidence. The general approach of arbitrators in

---

three arbitrators. After one arbitrator was disqualified, the proceedings continued, over one party's objection, before the two remaining arbitrators. The court of appeals disapproved and remanded the case for new arbitration proceedings.).

[372]Buitoni Prods., 12 LA 667 (N.Y. Sup. Ct. 1949).

[373]West Towns Bus Co. v. Street, Elec. Ry. & Motor Coach Employees Div. 241, 168 N.E.2d 473, 35 LA 145, 148 (Ill. App. Ct. 1960).

[374]*See* Chapter 7, section 5.D.i., "Default Awards in Ex Parte Proceedings."

[375]*Chicago Area Report, supra* note 74, at 102; *Chicago Report Workshop, supra* note 74, at 147; *Pittsburgh Report, supra* note 2, at 259; *New York Report, supra* note 2, at 301. Apart from confining the subject matter of cross-examination within proper limits, a related concern is unduly protracted cross-examination. In both respects, the fact that latitude often is permitted carries a concomitant responsibility of self-restraint by the parties. In this regard, it has been urged that "[s]ince there is relatively little that an arbitrator can actually do to curtail wastefully protracted cross-examination, training advocates in that area would produce better presentations of evidence and shorter hearings." Friedman, *Problems of Cross-Examination in Labor Arbitration*, 34 ARB. J. No. 4, at 6, 11 (1979), adding that "if nothing else, nonlawyer advocates particularly could profit by reading a book like Francis Wellman's *The Art of Cross-Examination*."

[376]Brown, *Tripartite Wage Determination in Puerto Rico, in* PROBLEMS OF PROOF IN ARBITRATION, PROCEEDINGS OF THE 19TH ANNUAL MEETING OF NAA 1, 9 (Jones ed., BNA Books 1967).

[377]*See* Friden Calculating Mach. Co., 27 LA 496, 500–01 (Justin, 1956).

giving weight and credibility to evidence is effectively illustrated by a statement made by an arbitrator in reviewing the discharge of an employee. He noted that the case was illustrative of the type of situation in which the facts are to a large extent determined by the weight and credibility accorded to the testimony of the witnesses and to the documentary evidence offered by the parties. He pointed out that, in arriving at the truth in such a case, an arbitrator must consider whether conflicting statements ring true or false; that he or she will note the witnesses' demeanor while on the stand; and that the arbitrator will credit or discredit testimony according to his or her impressions of the witnesses' veracity. This arbitrator also pointed out that, in determining where the preponderance of the evidence lies with respect to any material point, the arbitrator will take into consideration whether the witness speaks from firsthand information or whether the testimony is largely based on hearsay or gossip. In summarizing, the arbitrator wrote that the duty of the arbitrator is simply to determine the truth respecting material matters in controversy, as the arbitrator believes it to be, based on a full and fair consideration of the entire evidence and after according each witness and each piece of documentary evidence the weight, if any, to which the arbitrator honestly believes it to be entitled.[378]

Another arbitrator has offered some considerations relevant in evaluating testimony:

> Any attempt to sort credible testimony from that which is not worthy of belief is very difficult for at least four basic reasons. They may be briefly stated:
>
> INTEREST. While having an interest or stake in the outcome does not disqualify a witness, it renders his testimony subject to most careful scrutiny. . . . Few witnesses will deliberately falsify but there is a common tendency to "put your best foot forward." This tendency, either consciously or subconsciously, leads many witnesses to remember and express testimony in a way favorable to the result which they hope the Hearing will produce.
>
> PERCEPTION. Frequently the initial observation is faulty or incomplete because the observer has no prior knowledge that a dispute will develop concerning what he has seen or heard and his casual sensory impression is not sharp and keen.
>
> MEMORY. The remembrance of an event weeks or months after it occurred is frequently dim and inaccurate and a witness may be confused as to facts which initially he correctly perceived. By lapse of time precise details may elude his memory.
>
> COMMUNICATION. The manner in which a witness expresses what he saw and heard may fail to communicate exactly his initial perception of the

---

[378]Andrew Williams Meat Co., 8 LA 518, 519 (Cheney, 1947). *See also* Pepsi-Cola Bottlers of Youngstown, 68 LA 792, 795 (Klein, 1977); B.J. Hughes, Inc., 68 LA 391, 395 (Sabo, 1977); Magma Copper Co., 40 LA 45, 55 (Gorsuch, 1962); Trailmobile, 28 LA 710, 715 (Coffey, 1957). "Demeanor and the spirit of responses are factors in credibility. Reliability or unreliability never lies wholly in the *words* said." Karnish Instruments, 45 LA 545, 548 (Bender, 1965). "Demeanor" was a significant factor in *Department of Labor*, 73 LA 316, 323 (Robertson, 1979); *I.E. Prods.*, 72 LA 351, 354 (Brooks, 1979); *General Elec. Co.*, 69 LA 707, 712 (Jedel, 1977). *But see* Peerless Mfg. Co., 73 LA 915, 917 (Sisk, 1979); Spartan Mills, 68 LA 1279, 1281 (Sherman, 1977) ("[T]here are suspicious looking, nervous witnesses who are clearly telling the truth and just as surely there are out-and-out liars who can look you in the eye and tell a most convincing story."); Golden Pride, 68 LA 1232, 1235 (Jaffee, 1977) (stating the belief that "the 'attitude and demeanor' of witnesses is almost always a shaky foundation on which to rest conclusions").

occurrence, so that after listening to the testimony and the cross-examination of the witnesses, the fact-finder may not have had transmitted to him a completely accurate impression of the facts, even though they were initially observed carefully and well remembered by the witness.[379]

One arbitrator cautioned that while "both sides might be subject to the unconscious influences of self-interest, personal predilection or antipathy," it is the duty of the arbitrator "to examine the testimony of each witness on its own merits."[380] This arbitrator also considered that union members are not necessarily prejudiced witnesses any more than are supervisors.[381] Another arbitrator cautioned that if grievant's testimony "is colored by bias," employees used as company witnesses also may have "a bias by reason of their employment."[382]

Widely differing versions of the facts are too frequently presented by the parties. Where the testimony is highly contradictory, it ordinarily "becomes incumbent upon the Arbitrator to sift and evaluate the testimony to the best of his ability, and reach the best conclusion he can as to the actual fact situation."[383] In some situations, however, the credibility of conflicting witnesses' testimony need not be resolved.[384] "By piecing together the parts, the broad outlines of the whole picture emerge."[385] One arbitrator observed that, in discipline cases, the truth often "lies somewhere between" the widely conflicting versions of the facts.[386] It seems clear, however, that material inconsistencies in the testimony of any witness will ordinarily detract much from the witness's credibility.[387]

---

[379]South Penn Oil Co., 29 LA 718, 720 (Duff, 1957). *See also* Parsons Contractors, 91 LA 73, 76 (Di Lauro, 1988) ("[T]here are several tests which may assist one in assessing the veracity of witnesses. This Arbitrator uses the following checklist: 1. The demeanor of the witness. . . . 2. The character of the testimony. . . . 3. The self interest of the witness. . . . "); Douglas Aircraft Co., 28 LA 198, 204–05 (Jones, Jr., 1957). *See* Pioneer Transit Mix Co., 72 LA 206, 209 (Darrow, 1979) (applying criteria from *South Penn Oil*). In *Mark VII Sales*, 75 LA 1062, 1066 (1980), the arbitrator utilized a "check list of factors" offered by California statute for consideration in evaluating testimony.

[380]Poloron Prods. of Pa., 23 LA 789, 793 (Rosenfarb, 1955).

[381]*Id.*

[382]Billingsley, Inc., 48 LA 802, 807 (Krimsly, 1967) (arbitrator added, however, that "nothing in either of these relationships to a matter in arbitration can be taken to mean there is any presumption any witness will lie").

[383]Texas Elec. Steel Casting Co., 28 LA 757, 758 (Abernethy, 1957). *See also* Weirton Steel Div., 71 LA 1082, 1083 (Kates, 1978); Stansteel Corp., 69 LA 776, 778–79 (Kaufman, 1977); Basic Magnesia, 69 LA 737, 739 (Manson, 1977); Rotor Tool Co. Div., 49 LA 210, 212 (Williams, 1967); Thermolite, Inc., 46 LA 974, 977 (Klein, 1966); Galis Mfg. Co., 46 LA 75, 80 (Wood, 1966); Murray Rubber Co., 41 LA 1327, 1329–30 (Morvant, 1963) (stating that it was his "job to unravel this maze of contradictions and extract the core of truth"). Sometimes the burden-of-proof concept becomes of critical significance when severe conflict exists in the evidence. *See* TRW, Inc., 69 LA 214, 216–17 (Burris, 1977).

[384]*See, e.g.*, Missouri Rolling Mill Corp., 88 LA 1179, 1182 (Newmark, 1987).

[385]Sampsel Time Control, 18 LA 453, 456 (Gilden, 1951). In *Borg-Warner Corp.*, 47 LA 903, 906 (Larkin, 1966), the arbitrator suggested that "[w]here the testimony of two witnesses is directly opposite, the Arbitrator must consider the surrounding circumstances to determine which story can be corroborated."

[386]Republic Aviation Corp., 17 LA 577, 579 (Cahn, 1951).

[387]*See* Robins Air Force Base, 90 LA 701, 704 (Byars, 1988) ("[e]mployers' failure to explain the inconsistencies and contradictions of their written statements renders those statements essentially worthless as evidence"); Fry's Food Stores, 71 LA 1247, 1252 (Randall, 1978) (inconsistencies in the grievant's testimony "make it highly suspect"); Hawaiian Tel.

Finally, it is recognized that testimony often may conflict even where all witnesses have testified honestly and in good faith.[388] Thus, arbitrators sometimes have explained that in resolving conflicts in testimony, "we do not mean to cast the slightest doubt on the veracity or good faith of any witness appearing before us."[389] As one arbitrator aptly observed:

> Arbitrators are not equipped with any special divining rod which enables them to know who is telling the truth and who is not where a conflict in testimony develops. They can only do what the courts have done in similar circumstances for centuries. A judgment must finally be made, and there is a possibility that that judgment when made is wrong.[390]

Co., 43 LA 1218, 1225 (Tsukiyama, 1964); Walter Butler Shipbuilders, 2 LA 633, 635–36 (Gorder, 1944). But this is not always so. In *Tampa Electric Co.*, 73 LA 98, 102 (Rimer, Jr., 1979), the arbitrator stated that much of the evidence centered "on the credibility of the grievant's explanation that he was suddenly confronted with a snake in the cab of the vehicle just before the accident," and that the company regarded the discrepancies, contradictions, and inconsistencies in the grievant's testimony to be "'tainted with deception' to exonerate the grievant from the charge made against him." The arbitrator then stated:

> We find them to reflect little more than the bewilderment and panic brought about by the sight of the snake. Rational behavior and precise recall of detail cannot be reasonably expected in these circumstances under repeated interrogations. It is one thing to find a degree of inconsistency by questioning in hindsight; it is something else to have experienced an incident such as this and retain a clear and logical recollection of what and why one did as he did. Truth is often obscured by the distraction of inconsistency.

Id. at 102–03.

[388]In *Covington Furniture Manufacturing Corp.*, 75 LA 455 (Holley, Jr., 1980), the arbitrator quoted Richard Mittenthal as follows:

> "Experience has taught [Arbitrators] that, in this kind of situation, neither [witness] may be consciously lying. When two people are involved in a highly emotional confrontation, their recollection of the facts is far from reliable. Each tends to repress whatever wrong he'd done. Each quickly recasts the event in a light most favorable to himself. As time passes [this] distorted view of the event slowly hardens. By the time the arbitration hearing is held, each [person] is absolutely certain that his account of what happened is true. Perhaps neither [person] is then telling a deliberate untruth. Their own self-interest and self-image operate to limit their capacity for reporting the truth."

Id. at 459 (quoting Mittenthal, *II. Credibility—A Will-o'-the-Wisp, in* Truth, Lie Detectors, and Other Problems in Labor Arbitration, Proceedings of the 31st Annual Meeting of NAA 61, 62 (Stern & Dennis eds., BNA Books 1979)).

An NAA panel report expressed the opinion that "the principal reason for testimonial conflicts is not the result of a reluctance to tell the truth, but is caused by marked differences in the capacity of individuals to *observe, hear, recollect,* and *communicate* external reality." Block, *Decisional Thinking—West Coast Panel Report, in* Decisional Thinking of Arbitrators and Judges, Proceedings of the 33d Annual Meeting of NAA 119, 121 (Stern & Dennis eds., BNA Books 1981). Discussing factors that affect communication in testifying, see Loftus, *Memory and Searching for the Truth: I, in* Arbitration 1987: The Academy at Forty, Proceedings of the 40th Annual Meeting of NAA 107 (Gruenberg ed., BNA Books 1988); Fraser, *The Role of Language in Arbitration,* NAA 33d Proceedings, at 23–41.

[389]Coordinating Comm. Steel Cos., 70 LA 442, 454 (Aaron, Garrett, & Seward, 1978). *See also* Basic Magnesia, 69 LA 737, 739 (Manson, 1977) (although classifying it as a "You did—I didn't" case, arbitrator concluded that "from their demeanor" the witnesses "spoke the truth as they saw it"); Hussmann Refrigerator Co., 68 LA 565, 569 (Mansfield, 1977). Conversely, an arbitrator sometimes will conclude that one witness or another necessarily testified untruthfully. Stansteel Corp., 69 LA 776, 779 (Kaufman, 1977).

[390]General Cable Co., 28 LA 97, 99 (Fleming, 1957). *See also* Federal Aviation Admin., 72 LA 761, 764–65 (Forrester, 1979). In *Overly-Hautz Co.*, 51 LA 518, 524 (Klein, 1968), the arbitrator declared: "Considering the incredibly conflicting nature of the testimony, one might feel that the parties might have decided to use a ouija board rather than an arbitrator to resolve their impasse."

A. Weighing Testimony in Discipline Cases [LA CDI 94.60515]

Special considerations are involved in weighing testimony in discharge and discipline cases. One umpire, for example, recognized that an accused employee has an incentive for denying a charge, in that the employee stands immediately to gain or lose in the case, and that normally there is no reason to suppose that a security guard, for example, would unjustifiably pick one employee out of hundreds and accuse that employee of an offense, although in particular cases the security guard may be mistaken or in some cases even malicious. This umpire declared that, "if there is no evidence of ill will toward the accused on the part of the accuser and if there are no circumstances upon which to base a conclusion that the accuser is mistaken, the conclusion that the charge is true can hardly be deemed improper."[391]

Thus, the testimony of a foreman was accepted over that of the employee whom he accused, where the foreman had many years of satisfactory service as against 7 months' service by the accused and the foreman had never discharged an employee before.[392] However, not only will the testimony of the accuser be subject to doubt and careful scrutiny if there is evidence of ill will on the accuser's part against the accused,[393] the same is true if the factual situation otherwise casts doubt on the accuser's version,[394] or if the accuser's testimony on its face is not reasonably credible.

---

[391]Ford Motor Co., 1 ALAA ¶67,274, at 67,620 (Shulman, 1954). *Accord* Cincinnati Paperboard Corp., 93 LA 505 (Dworkin, 1989); Town of Melbourne Beach, Fla., 91 LA 280 (Frost, 1988); Safeway Stores, 88 LA 1317 (Staudohar, 1987); Huron Forge & Mach. Co., 75 LA 83, 90 (Roumell, Jr., 1980); Washington Hosp. Ctr., 75 LA 32, 35 (Rothschild, 1980); General Elec. Co., 74 LA 25, 27 (Spencer, 1979); Furr's, Inc., 72 LA 960, 965 (Leeper, 1979); Georgia-Pacific Corp., 72 LA 784, 786 (Vadakin, 1979); St. Joe Minerals Corp., 70 LA 1110, 1114 (Roberts, 1978); Bucyrus-Erie Co., 70 LA 1017, 1020 (Gundermann, 1978); AMF Lawn & Garden Div., 64 LA 988, 991 (Wyman, 1975); Pennsylvania Greyhound Lines, 19 LA 210, 211 (Seward, 1952). *See also* FMC Corp., 73 LA 705, 706 (Marlatt, 1979); Combustion Eng'g, 70 LA 318, 319–20 (Jewett, 1978); Cerro Corp., 69 LA 965, 966 (Griffin, 1977); Taft Broad. Co., WBRC-TV, 69 LA 307, 309 (Chaffin, 1977); Champion Spark Plug Co., 68 LA 702, 705 (Casselman, 1977); General Elec. Co., 40 LA 1084, 1086–87 (Crawford, 1963). *Cf.* Pettibone Ohio Corp., 72 LA 1144, 1150 (Feldman, 1979); Spartan Mills, 68 LA 1279, 1281–82 (Sherman, 1977). The arbitrator in *Grand Union Co.*, 48 LA 812, 814 (Scheiber, 1967), agreed that a discharged employee has "a strong incentive for denying" guilt, but the arbitrator in *Billingsley, Inc.*, 48 LA 802, 807 (Krimsly, 1967), reminded that interest in the outcome does not raise any presumption that a discharged employee is lying. *See also* Lake Orion Cmty. Sch., 73 LA 707, 710–11 (Roumell, Jr., 1979). In *Martin Marietta Aerospace*, 80 LA 115, 118 (Raffaele, 1982), the arbitrator expressed strong disagreement with use of the principle from *Ford Motor Co.*, 1 ALAA ¶67,274 (Shulman, 1954), in arbitration.

[392]Jenkins Bros., 11 LA 432, 434 (Donnelly, 1948). *See* American Smelting & Ref. Co., 48 LA 1187, 1190 (Leonard, 1967); Texas Elec. Steel Casting Co., 28 LA 757, 758–59 (Abernethy, 1957); Trailmobile, 28 LA 710, 715 (Coffey, 1957).

[393]*See* Bethlehem Steel, 2 LA 187, 190–91 (Dodd, 1945). *See also* D.O. Inc. of Warren, 90 LA 1123, 1125 (Coyne, 1988) (the arbitrator notes also that grievant and accuser had a run-in some months previously).

[394]*See* FMC Corp., 45 LA 293, 295 (McCoy, 1965). In *Veterans Administration Medical Center*, 74 LA 830, 832 (Ludolf, 1980), the accusers were mental patients and the arbitrator stated that their testimony accordingly "must be viewed with caution" as against accused staff personnel, whose testimony "must be considered as more authentic and weighed more heavily." Also regarding the competence, weight, and evaluation of the testimony of mental patients, see Friedman, *Arbitration of Discipline for Abuse of Mental Patients*, 33 ARB. J. 16 (1978).

B. Prior Bad Acts [LA CDI 94.60515]

In some instances, arbitrators have been faced with the issue of whether a grievant's prior bad acts should be admitted into evidence to establish guilt or innocence.[395] In one such case, the employer attempted to introduce evidence of the grievant's propensity for threatening, abusive, profane, and insubordinate conduct in the past to establish the likelihood that he committed the most recent offense.[396] Although the arbitrator found the evidence "somewhat persuasive," he pointed out that the employer's lax enforcement of the grievant's past behavior played a role as well:

> Further the company's attempt to use a series of alleged prior infractions, which had never been the subject of discipline violates fundamental rules of just cause. If an employee is to be tarred with such a brush, it is obvious under this contract that he must be given such written notice of the infraction, and a chance to contest the allegation. That did not happen.[397]

Another factor that might be considered by an arbitrator in weighing testimony in discharge and discipline cases is the so-called "code" that inhibits one member of an organization and frequently one member of an unorganized working force from testifying against another.[398]

C. The Lie Detector [LA CDI 94.60529]

The Employee Polygraph Protection Act of 1988 (EPPA)[399] prohibits any employer "engaged in or affecting commerce or in the production of goods for commerce"[400] from requesting or requiring an employee to submit to a lie detector test or in any way retaliating against an employee for refusing to submit to such tests.[401]

> The term "lie detector" includes a polygraph, deceptograph, voice stress analyzer, psychological stress evaluator, or any other similar device (whether mechanical or electrical) that is used, or the results of which are used, for the purpose of rendering a diagnostic opinion regarding the honesty or dishonesty of an individual.[402]

Exempted from the EPPA's protections are federal, state, and local government employees;[403] national defense consultants and their employees;[404]

---

[395]*See generally* Wirtz, *Due Process in Arbitration, in* The Arbitrator and the Parties, Proceedings of the 11th Annual Meeting of NAA 1 (McKelvey ed., BNA Books 1998).

[396]Champion Spark Plug Co., 93 LA 1277 (Dobry, 1989).

[397]*Id.* at 1284.

[398]General Motors Corp., 2 LA 491, 502 (Hotchkiss, 1938). *See* War Mem'l Hosp., 89 LA 1166 (Borland, 1987) (union president warned against "ratting" on union sisters; note that the arbitrator was apparently convinced that both parties were guilty of witness intimidation); American Smelting & Ref. Co., 48 LA 1187, 1190 (Leonard, 1967). See also assertions by McFall, *The Search for Truth: Comment, in* Truth, Lie Detectors, and Other Problems in Labor Arbitration, Proceedings of the 31st Annual Meeting of NAA 152, 154 (Stern & Dennis eds., BNA Books 1979); *West Coast Report Workshop, supra* note 70, at 234.

[399]29 U.S.C. §§2001–2009.

[400]*Id.* §2002.

[401]*Id.*

[402]*Id.* §2001(3).

[403]*Id.* §2006(a).

[404]*Id.* §2006(b)(1)(A).

intelligence experts, consultants, and their employees;[405] and Federal Bureau of Investigation contractors.[406] There are also exemptions for private-sector employees for tests administered in connection with an ongoing investigation into theft or other economic loss to the employer's business.[407] Also exempted are employees of security and armored car services[408] and employees of manufacturers, distributors, and dispensers of controlled substances.[409]

In addition to the EPPA, a number of states and the District of Columbia also have enacted legislation restricting the use of lie detector tests as a condition of employment.[410] A number of the state statutes exclude state, county, and municipal employees, law enforcement agencies, members of fire departments, and correction department employees.[411]

In the jurisdictions that have not enacted such legislation, arbitrators consistently have reaffirmed that employers cannot take disciplinary action against employees should the employees refuse to submit to lie detector tests.[412] Moreover, the refusal of a grievant to take a lie detector test is inadmissible as a presumption of guilt.[413] An employee also is "perfectly free" to terminate a polygraph test without prejudice to himself or herself, and such termination does not establish guilt.[414]

---

[405]*Id.* §2006(b)(2)(A).
[406]*Id.* §2006(c).
[407]*Id.* §2006(d).
[408]*Id.* §2006(e).
[409]*Id.* §2006(f).
[410]*See, e.g.,* ALASKA STAT. §23.10.037 (Michie 2002); CAL. LAB. CODE §432.2 (West 1995); CONN. GEN. STAT. §31-51g (2003); DEL. CODE ANN. tit. 19, §704 (1995); D.C. CODE ANN. §36-802 (1997); HAW. REV. STAT. §378-26.5 (Michie 1999); IDAHO CODE §44-903 (Michie 2003); IOWA CODE §730.4 (1999); ME. REV. STAT. ANN. tit. 32, §7166 (West 1999); MD. LAB. & EMPL. CODE ANN. §3-702 (1999); MASS. GEN. LAWS ch. 149, §19B (1999); MICH. COMP. LAWS ANN. §37.203 (West 2001); MINN. STAT. §181.75 (2002); MONT. CODE ANN. §39-2-304 (2001); NEV. REV. STAT. ANN. §613.480 (Michie 2000); N.J. STAT. ANN. §2C:40A-1 (West 1995); OR. REV. STAT. §659.227 (2001); R.I. GEN. LAWS §28-6.1-1 (2000); VT. STAT. ANN. tit. 21, §494a (1994); VA. CODE ANN. §40.1-51.4:4 (Michie 2002); WASH. REV. CODE §49.44.120 (2002); W. VA. CODE §21-5-5b (Supp. 2003); WIS. STAT. ANN. §111.37 (West 2002). *See generally* FINKIN, PRIVACY IN EMPLOYMENT LAW pt. II (BNA Books 2d ed. 2003).
[411]*See, e.g.,* ALASKA STAT. §23.10.037 (1994) (excepting police officers and transportation department employees with police powers and working at international airports); CAL. LAB. CODE §432.2 (West 1995) (excepting employees of federal and state governments and their agencies); D.C. CODE ANN. §36-802 (1994) (excepting pre-employment, criminal, or internal disciplinary investigations conducted by metropolitan police, fire department, or department of corrections); IOWA CODE §730.4 (1994) (excepting state or political subdivisions thereof when selecting candidates for employment as police or correction officers); WIS. STAT. §111.37 (1995) (exceptions mirroring the EPPA private-sector employer exemptions).
[412]Bake Rite Rolls, 90 LA 1133, 1136 (DiLauro, 1988); Texas City Ref., 89 LA 1159, 1164 (Milentz, 1987); Glen Manor Home for the Jewish Aged, 81 LA 1178 (Katz, 1983). *But see* City of Miami, 92 LA 175, 180 (Abrams, 1989) (arbitrator held that the refusal of an employee, reasonably suspected of assault and robbery, to take the polygraph test was a valid reason for discharge because the test is a legitimate investigative tool). *See also* Orthodox Jewish Home for Aged, 91 LA 810, 815, 816 (Sergent, Jr., 1988). However, in *National Tea Co.,* 90 LA 773, 775 (Baroni, 1988), the arbitrator found that the employee's refusal to take the polygraph test justified the employer's transfer of the employee to another department, because the transfer was based on legitimate business reasons flowing from loss of confidence in the employee because of his refusal.
[413]International Minerals & Chem. Corp., 83 LA 593 (Kulkis, 1984).
[414]Mississippi Power Co., 90 LA 220, 222 (Jewett, 1987).

The results of lie detector tests are criticized because of the subjective dependency on a person's emotional state and lack of substantive authority supporting the accuracy of test results.[415] Some arbitrators reject lie detector test results on the basis that it is the arbitrator's duty as the factfinder to determine the credibility of the witnesses.[416] Even if inculpatory lie detector evidence of an accuser is admitted, the grievant's representative should be given an opportunity to cross-examine the accuser as well as the polygraph administrator.[417]

The polygraph examiner's experience and the accuracy of the test reports themselves should be subject to review[418] and his or her record of the test should be available for cross-examination at the hearing.[419]

Some arbitrators distinguish between exculpatory findings and negative results. But, even a favorable polygraph report is not admitted without voir dire or an opportunity to cross-examine the administrator.[420] Thus, where

---

[415]A.R.A. Mfg. Co., 87 LA 182 (Woolf, 1986). The arbitrator gave no weight to a polygraph examination of an employee who allegedly observed the grievant take a compressor, because the polygraph examiner failed to submit evidence of required testing experience and had not sworn to the accuracy of the report. Further, the examiner's report did not contain sufficient information for the determination of his qualifications as an expert witness, and the arbitrator had no information on the sequence or clarity of the examiner's questions or the raw data the examiner evaluated. See Bisbee Hosp. Ass'n, 79 LA 977, 986 (Weizenbaum, 1982); Buy-Low, Inc., 77 LA 380, 383–85 (Dolnick, 1981); Bunker Ramo Corp., 76 LA 857, 862–65 (Hon, 1981); Purolator Armored, 75 LA 331, 336–37 (Dolnick, 1980); Temtex Prods., 75 LA 233, 237 (Rimer, 1980); Paramount Wedding Ring Co., 71 LA 1202, 1204 (Fish, 1978); Brink's, Inc., 70 LA 909, 912 (Pinkus, 1978); Art Carved, Inc., 70 LA 869, 873–75 (Kramer, 1978) (describing how the polygraph purports to work); Bethlehem Steel, 68 LA 581, 582–83 (Seward, 1977) (the "courts have generally—indeed, almost universally—rejected polygraphic evidence unless offered with the consent of all parties concerned," and concluding that "wisdom suggests that the Impartial Umpire's office should follow this judicial approach"); Bowman Transp., 59 LA 283, 286–90 (Murphy, 1972) (stating that "until the accuracy of the state of the polygraph art is generally recognized by substantial scientific, judicial and arbitral authority, and the criteria for evaluating the polygraph technique is fully available at the arbitration hearing, . . . the arbitrator should move with great caution in this area"); National Elec. Coil Div., 46 LA 756, 761 (Gross, 1966); American Maize-Prods. Co., 45 LA 1155, 1158 (Epstein, 1965); Kwik Kafeteria, 66-1 ARB ¶8359 (Eiger, 1966); Ramsey Steel Co., 66-1 ARB ¶8310 (Carmichael, 1966); Saveway Inwood Serv. Station, 44 LA 709, 710–11 (Kornblum, 1965); Spiegel, Inc., 44 LA 405, 409 (Sembower, 1965); Sanna Dairies, 43 LA 16, 18–19 (Rice, 1964); United Mills, 63-1 ARB ¶8179 (Miller, 1963); Lag Drug Co., 63-1 ARB ¶8106 (Kelliher, 1962); National Castings Co., 41 LA 442, 442 (Walter, 1963); Illinois Bell Tel. Co., 39 LA 470, 479 (Ryder, 1962); Town & Country Food Co., 39 LA 332, 335 (Lewis, 1962); Seaview Indus., 39 LA 125, 127 (Duncan, 1962); Publishers' Ass'n of N.Y. City, 33 LA 44, 48 (Simkin, 1959). See generally Bornstein & Gosline, Labor and Employment Arbitration §5.11[4] (1989); Grenig & Estes, Labor Arbitration Advocacy 82–83 (1989); Hill & Sinicropi, Evidence in Arbitration 199–228 (BNA Books 2d ed. 1987); Flagler, Modern Shamanism and Other Folderol—The Search for Certainty, in Arbitration 1986: Current and Expanding Roles, Proceedings of the 39th Annual Meeting of NAA 187 (Gershenfeld ed., BNA Books 1987); Goldman, The Use of Polygraph Testing in a Theft Case, First Annual Labor and Employment Law Institute (1985).

[416]International Minerals & Chem. Corp., 83 LA 593 (Kulkis, 1984).

[417]Consumer Plastics Corp., 88 LA 208 (Garnholz, 1987). The arbitrator did not give any weight to a lie detector test taken by an undercover agent whose testimony concerning the employee's possession of marijuana on company property provided the sole basis of the employee's discharge, and where the union was given no opportunity to question the agent.

[418]A.R.A. Mfg., 87 LA 182, 186–87 (Woolf, 1986).

[419]Houston Lighting & Power Co., 87 LA 478 (Howell, 1986).

[420]City of Youngstown, Ohio, 107 LA 588 (Skulina, 1996).

the polygraph test-giver was not called as a witness, an arbitrator rejected the report on the grounds that the union had had no opportunity to cross-examine the administrator and, because evidence of his credentials was lacking, the administrator's statement could not qualify as expert testimony.[421]

Arbitrators have declined to give any weight to lie detector test results when the employer has relied solely on such tests in discharging an employee.[422] However, one arbitrator noted that "[a]rbitrators are not totally inhospitable to the receipt, consideration and evaluation of evidence obtained by the use of the polygraph."[423]

Arbitrators accept lie detector results only for limited purposes, noting that "such evidence has not attained scientific acceptance as a reliable and accurate means of ascertaining truth or deception."[424] Test results were accepted as corroborative of the truthful demeanor of an already credible undercover agent testifying to firsthand observations where the agent had filed daily reports with the investigative agency.[425]

In a 1979 examination and discussion of the polygraph, its degree of reliability, and court and arbitration decisions regarding its use, an arbitrator declared that "the conclusion is compelling that no matter how well qualified educationally and experientially may be the polygraphist, the results of the lie-detector tests should routinely be ruled inadmissible."[426]

An employer is not required to administer a lie detector test upon request by the grievant to assist in proving the grievant's innocence, and where independently taken by the employee it is not an error for the employer to refuse to consider such corroborative evidence.[427]

---

[421]*Id.* at 590.

[422]Avis Rent A Car Sys., 85 LA 435, 439 (Alsher, 1985).

[423]*Id.*

[424]Reynolds Metals Co., 85 LA 1046, 1052 (Taylor, 1985).

[425]Consumer Plastics Corp., 88 LA 208 (Garnholz, 1987); Georgia Pac., 85 LA 542 (King, 1985)

[426]Jones, Jr., *The Search for Truth: III. "Truth" When the Polygraph Operator Sits as Arbitrator (or Judge): The Deception of "Detection" in the "Diagnosis of Truth and Deception,"* *in* TRUTH, LIE DETECTORS, AND OTHER PROBLEMS IN LABOR ARBITRATION, PROCEEDINGS OF THE 31ST ANNUAL MEETING OF NAA 75, 151 (Stern & Dennis eds., BNA Books 1979) (also stating that in fact, with "relatively rare exceptions," arbitrators and courts do continue "to reject polygraph proof"). The article did note that, in addition to gaining acceptability with some courts and several arbitrators, the polygraph had done so with some law-review commentators and "perhaps" with the NLRB. *Id.* at 90–92. In *Bunker Ramo Corp.*, 76 LA 857, 862 (1981), the arbitrator stated concerning the polygraph that, by virtue of Jones' article and the 1977 report to the President and Congress by the Privacy Protection Study Commission, "there is now a much wider recognition of its serious deficiencies." Among other arbitrators stating reasons for questioning the use of the polygraph and for doubting the reliability of its results, see *Bethlehem Steel Corp.*, 68 LA 581, 582 (Seward, 1977); *Bowman Transp.*, 59 LA 283, 286–90 (Murphy, 1972); *B.F. Goodrich Tire Co.*, 36 LA 552, 558 (Ryder, 1961). Prior to the enactment of the EPPA, the NLRB had held that under the circumstances that existed, an employer did not violate the NLRA by disciplining employees for refusal to take polygraph tests. Shoppers Drug Mart, 226 NLRB 901, 906, 94 LRRM 1223 (1976); American Oil Co., 189 NLRB 3, 76 LRRM 1506 (1971). In *Medicenter, Mid-South Hosp.*, 221 NLRB 670, 90 LRRM 1576 (1975), an NLRB panel majority adopted without comment the ALJ's finding that polygraph testing is a mandatory subject of bargaining.

[427]City of Fort Worth, Tex., 114 LA 440 (Moore, 2000); Immigration & Naturalization Serv., 89 LA 1252, 1256 (Baroni, 1987); Texas City Ref., 89 LA 1159 (Milentz, 1987). The results of grievant's polygraph test were given no weight in the hearing on his disciplinary

D. Unsupported Allegations

Too often a party goes to arbitration with nothing but allegations to support some of its contentions or even its basic position. But allegations or assertions are not proof, and mere allegations unsupported by evidence are ordinarily given no weight by arbitrators.[428] Similarly, where neither party has provided sufficient evidence for an informed ruling on an issue or aspect of the case, the arbitrator will decline to rule upon it.[429]

Sometimes, a party will present no direct case at all, but will rely entirely upon cross-examination of the other party's witnesses or will simply contend that the other party has the burden of proof and has not proved its case. This practice has been severely criticized by arbitrators.[430]

E. Burden of Proof [LA CDI 94.60509]

It is very difficult to generalize on the application of the doctrine of "burden of proof" in the field of arbitration.[431] The burden of proof may depend on the nature of the issue, the specific contract provision, or a usage established by the parties.[432] In many cases, the arbitrator simply gets the facts and

---

suspension. The test was ordered by the grievant, it was based on limited information provided by the grievant, and it consisted of questions that reflected data that he considered important. *See also* Abbott-Northwestern Hosp., 94 LA 621 (Berquist, 1990). The employer's refusal to administer to a grievant a lie detector test as part of its investigation in a case involving theft did not render its investigation deficient. The inherent unreliability of the test and possible liability in damages due to state and federal law prohibitions rendered the employer's actions reasonable.

[428]*See* Air Force Logistics Command, 89 LA 897, 900 (Koven, 1987); Beatrice/Hunt-Wesson, Inc., 89 LA 710 (Bickner, 1987); Pacific Southwest Airlines, 74 LA 64, 68 (Rule, 1980); Bunny Bread Co., 74 LA 55, 57 (Yarowsky, 1980); City of Pontiac, Mich., 73 LA 1083, 1087 (Ellmann, 1979); N.Y. State Elec. & Gas Corp., 69 LA 865, 869 (Foltman, 1977); Bonney Forge & Foundry, 49 LA 415, 417 (Hardy, 1967); Stanley G. Flagg & Co., 47 LA 971, 973 (Crawford, 1966); Jones & Laughlin Steel Corp., 46 LA 187, 189 (Sherman, 1966) (mere surmise or speculation is not evidence); Pittsburgh Steel Co., 40 LA 487, 488 (McDermott, 1963); Armour & Co., 39 LA 1226, 1231 (Beatty, 1963); National-Standard Co., 29 LA 837, 841 (Crawford, 1957); I. Hirst Enter., 24 LA 45, 47 (Justin, 1954); Diamond Alkali Co., 16 LA 613, 615 (DiLeone, 1951); Erwin Mills, 16 LA 466, 468 (Barrett, 1950).

[429]*See, e.g.,* Northrop Corp., 88 LA 343, 346 (Rothschild, 1986); Downingtown Sch. Dist., 88 LA 59, 63 (Zirkel, 1986); Dep't of Navy, Norfolk Naval Shipyard, 70 LA 779, 786 (Margolin, 1978).

[430]*See* John Deere Waterloo Tractor Works, 20 LA 583, 584–85 (Davey, 1953); Felsway Shoe Corp., 17 LA 505, 509–10 (Justin, 1951). In *Southern Can Co.,* 68 LA 1183, 1187 (Jedel, 1977), the arbitrator voiced no objection to such reliance on cross-examination by the company. For related discussion, see Chapter 7, section 5.D.i., "Default Awards in Ex Parte Proceedings."

[431]For helpful discussions of the "burden of proof" concept at law, with comments as to its application in arbitration, see *Tenneco Oil Co.,* 44 LA 1121, 1122 (Merrill, 1965); Fleming, The Labor Arbitration Process 68–73 (Univ. of Ill. Press 1965). Fleming noted: "Part of the difficulty in talking about burden of proof is that the term means several different things and is often used without careful definition. It can mean the burden of pleading [which does not apply in arbitration], the burden of producing evidence, and the burden of persuasion. When used in the sense of burden of persuasion, it involves further questions as to the quantum of evidence, or standard of proof, which will be required to prevail in the particular case." *Id.* at 68.

[432]*See, e.g.,* Ideal Elec. Co., 93 LA 101, 108 (Strasshofer, 1989).

decides the issue without any express indication that he or she is thinking in terms of burden of proof.[433]

Arbitrators have written specifically in terms of burden of proof much more frequently in some types of cases than in other types. For instance, burden of proof considerations have been stressed fairly often in discharge and discipline cases, as well as in cases involving seniority clauses that require consideration of the fitness and ability of employees.[434] In contrast, for example, an arbitrator emphasized that "notions of burden of proof are hardly applicable to issues of interpretation."[435]

It is probable that in arbitration the burden of proof concept is usually more important in its substantive than in its procedural significance. There is, for instance, no required order of presenting evidence in arbitration cases. While the party asserting a claim usually presents its proof first, or at least a preliminary or introductory case, this practice may not be followed where the nature of the issue makes a different procedure preferable.[436]

---

[433]*See, e.g.*, Dalfort Aviation Servs., 96 LA 520 (Nicholas, Jr., 1991); Kansas City Cold Storage Corp., 94 LA 783 (Madden, 1990); Uppco, Inc., 93 LA 489 (Goldstein, 1989); Copley Press, 91 LA 1324 (Goldstein, 1988); City of Oklahoma City, 93 LA 110 (Sisk, 1989); Philips Consumer Elecs. Co., 91 LA 1040 (Nolan, 1988); Keebler Co., 91 LA 559 (Fox, Jr., 1988); City of Decatur, Ill., 89 LA 447 (Petersen, 1987).

[434]*See* Chapter 14, section 7.C., "Review of Management's Determination: Evidence and Burden of Proof"; Chapter 15, section 3.D., "Burden and Quantum of Proof." For some other types of issues in which an arbitrator has spoken specifically in terms of burden of proof, see *ARCO Pipe Line Co.*, 84 LA 907, 909 (Nicholas, Jr., 1985), which stated: "In a case such as we have here, the parties are aware that the initial burden of proof lies with Union. This is to say that the aggrieved must come forward and show that its position is supported by a preponderance of the evidence. To be sure, such proof is made quite essential when note and attention is given to the fact that Union's complaint rests on its interpretation of a given past practice." Hercules Galion Prods., 52 LA 1026, 1027 (McIntosh, 1969); Indianapolis Union Printers, 46 LA 1077, 1078 (Small, 1966); Vickers, Inc., 43 LA 1256, 1262–63 (Bothwell, 1964); Weatherhead Co., 37 LA 60, 62 (Pollock, 1961); Pittsburgh Commercial Heat Treating Co., 24 LA 715, 717 (Duff, 1955); Celotex Corp., 24 LA 369, 372–73 (Reynard, 1955); Avco Mfg. Corp., 24 LA 268, 273 (Holly, 1955); York Bus Co., 24 LA 81, 84 (Loucks, 1955); McKinney Mfg. Co., 19 LA 291, 294 (Reid, 1952); Durham Hosiery Mills, 19 LA 205, 207 (Livengood, 1952); Super-Cold Corp., 8 LA 187, 188 (Cheney, 1947); Flintkote Co., 3 LA 723, 724 (Cole, 1946). For a related discussion, see section 9.D., "Unsupported Allegations," above.

[435]Shulman, *Reason, Contract, and Law in Labor Relations*, 68 Harv. L. Rev. 999, 1018 (1955), *reprinted in* Management Rights and the Arbitration Process, Proceedings of the 9th Annual Meeting of NAA 169 (McKelvey ed., BNA Books 1956). *See also* GATX Tank Erection Corp., 74 LA 330, 332 (Holley, Jr., 1980). One arbitrator spoke vigorously against use of burden of proof concepts in arbitration (except in certain types of discharge cases), and in this regard declared: "To insist that the complaining party carries the burden of proof is manifestly absurd. Neither side has a burden of proof or disproof, but both have an obligation to cooperate in an effort to give the arbitrator as much guidance as possible." Aaron, *Some Procedural Problems in Arbitration*, 10 Vand. L. Rev. 733, 740–42 (1957). Illustrating that some arbitrators do hold the view that the complaining party generally carries the burden of proof, see *Entex, Inc.*, 73 LA 330, 333 (Fox, 1979); *Farmland Indus.*, 72 LA 1302, 1303 (Heneman, Jr., 1979); *City of Cincinnati, Ohio*, 69 LA 682, 685 (Bell, 1977). Discussing these various views, along with other aspects of burden of proof in arbitration, see Smith, *The Search for Truth: I. The Search for Truth—The Whole Truth, in* Truth, Lie Detectors, and Other Problems in Labor Arbitration, Proceedings of the 31st Annual Meeting of NAA 40, 50–54 (Stern & Dennis eds., BNA Books 1979).

[436]*See* Bethlehem Steel Corp., 91 LA 293, 296 (McDermott, 1988) (after some minor skirmishing, the arbitrator ruled that, solely as a procedural matter and in order to get the proceedings going, the company should go first with its case but that this preliminary ruling would have nothing to do with, and should not be seen as, a decision that this was a "just cause discharge matter"). For full discussion, see Chapter 7, section 4.G.iii., "Order of Presenting Case."

It may be noted that the burden of going forward with the evidence may shift during the course of the hearing; after the party having the burden of persuasion presents sufficient evidence to justify a finding in its favor on the issue, the other party has the burden of producing evidence in rebuttal.[437]

If the question of physical or mental condition arises while the employee is in active employment, the burden is ordinarily on the company to show that the employee's physical or mental ability or health is such as to justify transfer, demotion, suspension, leave, layoff, or termination. If, however, the question arises where the employee has been off work, either absent or on sick leave, the burden generally shifts to the employee to establish that his or her condition has sufficiently improved or has been restored in order to warrant reinstatement.[438]

With regard to drug- and alcohol-testing cases, the majority of arbitrators disfavor the application of the "beyond a reasonable doubt" burden of proof. However, some arbitrators have adopted the "clear and convincing"[439] standard, which is sometimes applied in cases involving an element of moral turpitude or criminal intent. Some arbitrators also require clear and convincing evidence of wrongdoing in grievances concerning sexual harassment, because such claims usually present significant credibility issues, may rely heavily on circumstantial evidence, and impair reputations.[440] Even in a case where an employee was discharged for poor work performance, one arbitrator held the standard to be clear and convincing evidence.[441]

F. Protecting Witnesses [LA CDI 94.60519]

In some situations, giving testimony in arbitration proceedings may subject the witness to varied risks of retaliation. For instance, employees and

---

[437]*See* County of Monterey, Cal., 93 LA 64 (Riker, 1989); Texas Utils. Elec. Co., 90 LA 625 (Allen, Jr., 1988); Mueller Co., 51 LA 428, 434 (Whyte, 1968); Allegheny Ludlum Steel Corp., 42 LA 343, 344 (Shipman, 1963); Reserve Mining Co., 39 LA 341, 346 (Sembower, 1962). *See also West Coast Report, supra* note 2, at 196, 211.

[438]Dana Corp., 92-1 ARB ¶8078 (Florman, 1991). *See also* General Mills, 99 LA 143 (Stallworth, 1992) (discharge set aside for failure to afford grievant opportunity to produce medical documentation that he suffered from recurring seasonal depression); South Carolina Elec. & Gas Co., 92-1 ARB ¶8081 (Haemmel, 1991) (where the employee did not wish to return from disability leave); City of Chicago, Ill., 97 LA 20 (Goldstein, 1990) (challenging employer's authority to place grievant on involuntary, unpaid medical leave to undergo recommended psycotherapy); University of Mich., 94 LA 590 (Sugerman, 1990) (relying on psychiatrist's statement to set aside resignation as "involuntary" and permit grievant to apply for disability benefits); Gerr, *Arbitration of Medical and Health Issues, in* Arbitration 1992: Improving Arbitral and Advocacy Skills, Proceedings of the 45th Annual Meeting of NAA 29 (Gruenberg ed., BNA Books 1993); Phillips, *Management Perspective, id.* at 39; D'Alba, *Labor Perspective, id.* at 52 (which also discusses testimonial privileges and confidentiality issues with regard to medical and psychiatric testimony).

[439]*See* Metropolitan Wash. Airports Auth., 111 LA 712 (Simmelkjaer, 1998) (finding that the employer's burden of proof should be "elevated to a clear and convincing standard" in drug cases); City of Kankakee, Ill., 97 LA 564 (Wolff, 1991) (applying the clear and convincing standard to alcohol abuse cases); American Steel Foundries, 94 LA 745 (Seidman, 1990) (applying clear and convincing standard for discharge cases; both that the act took place and that the employee was responsible for it).

[440]Central Mich. Univ., 99 LA 134 (McDonald, 1992); Shell Pipe Line Corp., 97 LA 957 (Baroni, 1991).

[441]Milwaukee Bd. of Sch. Directors, 110 LA 566, 572–73 (Winton, 1998).

supervisors alike may incur the displeasure of the employer as a result of their testimony. Employees may jeopardize their relations with fellow workers for testifying at the employer's request. Moreover, employees may put their own jobs at risk through their testimony. For example, employees will not be granted testimonial immunity in testifying about violation of their employer's attendance policy for which they were not cited.[442] When the need is shown, the arbitrator may seek to protect the interests of persons facing this predicament by reminding the parties of the risks involved.[443]

Witnesses may find that their privacy rights may be affected when testifying. In an interest arbitration, two witnesses who testified as experts on the financial impact of drought on local area farmers, and who were themselves farmers, were subpoenaed to provide their own federal and state income tax records relating to profit and loss from their own farming operations. The arbitrator enforced the subpoenaes subject to a protective order limiting the access of persons to the documents, closing the hearing to all but necessary persons, and not permitting the transcript of their testimony to become a public record.[444] Where witnesses fear possible intimidation by the grievant or his supporters, an arbitrator was held not to have violated the Federal Arbitration Act by keeping their identity secret until they testified.[445]

Although the arbitrator cannot ensure protection if the person does testify, there may be a firm basis for a valid grievance or unfair labor practice charge in the event of retaliation for giving testimony.[446] A union's action in fining four members for testifying in the employer's favor at an arbitration hearing violated a clause stating that "either party to this agreement shall be permitted to call employee witnesses at each step of the grievance and arbitration procedure." Furthermore, in so ruling, the arbitrator declared:

---

[442]Paxar Sys. Group, 102 LA 75 (La Manna, 1994) (the arbitrator, following NLRB precedent, found that the employer could discipline employees who revealed their own misconduct during testimony).

[443]*See* GUIDES FOR LABOR ARBITRATION 9 (Univ. of Pa. Press 1953). In *Max Factor & Co.*, 61 LA 886, 890 (Jones, Jr., 1973), the arbitrator denied the union's request for the addresses of certain witnesses against whom threats had been made. *See also* Kaiser Permanente, 77 LA 66, 71 (Draznin, 1981) (delay in revealing the identity of grievant's accuser was necessitated by concern for his safety). Further, in *Cemetery Workers & Greens Attendants Local 365 v. Woodlawn Cemetery*, 152 LRRM 2360 (S.D.N.Y. 1995), the court held that an arbitrator does not violate the Federal Arbitration Act by keeping the identity of intimidated witnesses secret until they testify.

[444]Deerfield Cmty. Sch. Dist., 93 LA 316 (Michelstetter, 1988).

[445]*Woodlawn Cemetery*, 152 LRRM 2360.

[446]*See* Berg Airlectro Prods. Co., 46 LA 668, 675–76 (Sembower, 1966); Western Insulated Wire Co., 45 LA 972, 975 (Jones, Jr., 1965). *See also* NLRB v. AA Elec. Co., 405 U.S. 2587, 79 LRRM 2587 (1972); Ebasco Servs., 181 NLRB 768, 73 LRRM 1518 (1970). In *Public Serv. Elec. & Gas Co.*, 268 NLRB 361, 115 LRRM 1006, 1007 (1983), however, the NLRB distinguished between punishing an employee for the act of giving testimony and punishing the employee for misconduct revealed by that testimony; thus, the employer could "discipline employees for their misconduct even though the misconduct was discovered as a result of their testimony at an arbitration hearing."

Even apart from such a contract provision, it would seem that any arbitration agreement would necessarily secure the right of both sides to freely call witnesses. Maturity in relations between responsible people and organizations can result in no other course of conduct.[447]

The award enjoined the union from enforcing any discipline against the four members and ordered it to revoke the fines.[448]

---

[447]N.Y. Twist Drill Mfg. Corp., 39 LA 167, 169 (Nathan, 1962).
[448]*Id.*

Chapter 9

Interpreting Contract Language

Probably no function of the labor-management arbitrator is more important than that of interpreting the collective bargaining agreement. The great bulk of arbitration cases involve disputes over "rights" under such agreements. In these cases, the agreement itself is the point of concentration, and the function of the arbitrator is to interpret and apply its provisions.

1. Disputes Over the Meaning of Contract Terms

A. Misunderstanding and the "Mutual Assent" or "Meeting of the Minds" Concept

When the parties attach conflicting meanings to an essential term of their putative contract, is there then no "meeting of the minds" so that the contract is not enforceable against an objecting party? Hardly. The voidability of a presumed contract arises only in the limited circumstances where neither party knew, or should have known, of the meaning placed on the term by the other party, or where both parties were aware of the divergence of meanings and assumed the risk that the matter would not come to issue.

The conditions under which the existence of a supposed contract can be negated were cogently reviewed by Chief Judge Posner in *Colfax Envelope Corp. v. Graphic Communications Local 458-3M (Chicago)*.[1] There, a collective bargaining agreement specified a minimum-manning requirement for printing presses as "4C 60 Press—3 Men." The designation was interpreted by the employer as referring to four-color presses 60 inches and over, by the

---

[1]20 F.3d 750, 145 LRRM 2974 (7th Cir. 1994).

union as four-color presses 60 inches and under, and by the district court as 60-inch presses only. In response to Colfax's suit under Section 301 of the Taft-Hartley Act[2] for a declaration that it had no collective bargaining agreement with the union because the parties had never agreed on an essential term—the manning requirements for Colfax's printing presses—Judge Posner remanded the matter for decision through the contractually provided arbitration process.

As Chief Judge Posner explained:

> This appeal in a suit over a collective bargaining agreement presents a fundamental issue of contract law, that of drawing the line between an ambiguous contract, requiring interpretation, and a contract that, because it cannot be said to represent the agreement of the parties at all, cannot be interpreted, can only be rescinded and the parties left to go their own ways. . . .
>
> . . .
>
> . . . Ordinarily a dispute over the meaning of a contractual term is, if the contract contains an arbitration clause, for the arbitrator to decide. But sometimes the difference between the parties goes so deep that it is impossible to say that they ever agreed—that they even *have* a contract that a court or arbitrator might interpret. In the famous though enigmatic and possibly misunderstood case of *Raffles v. Wichelhaus*, 2 H. & C. 906, 159 Eng.Rep. 375 (Ex. 1864), the parties made a contract for the delivery of a shipment of cotton from Bombay to England on the ship *Peerless*. Unbeknownst to either party, there were two ships of that name sailing from Bombay on different dates. One party thought the contract referred to one of the ships, and the other to the other. The court held that there was no contract; there had been no "meeting of the minds." . . .
>
> The premise—that a "meeting of the minds" is required for a binding contract—obviously is strained. . . . Most contract disputes arise because the parties did not foresee and provide for some contingency that has now materialized—so there was no meeting of minds on the matter at issue—yet such disputes are treated as disputes over contractual meaning, not as grounds for rescinding the contract and thus putting the parties back where they were before they signed it. So a literal meeting of the minds is not required for an enforceable contract, which is fortunate, since courts are not renowned as mind readers. Let us set the concept to one side, therefore, and ask how (else) to explain *Raffles v. Wichelhaus* and cases like it. It seems to us as it has to other courts that a contract ought to be terminable without liability and the parties thus allowed to go their own ways when there is "no sensible basis for choosing between conflicting understandings" of the contractual language, as the court said in an American *Raffles*-like case, *Oswald v. Allen*, 417 F.2d 43, 45 (2d Cir. 1969), quoting William F. Young, Jr., "Equivocation in the Making of Agreements," 64 *Colum. L. Rev.* 619, 647 (1964). In *Oswald* the misunderstanding arose because the parties did not speak the same language (literally). In *Balistreri v. Nevada Livestock Production Credit Association*, 214 Cal.App. 3d 635, 262 Cal. Rptr. 862 (1989), the parents of an aspiring farmer thought they had pledged property they owned in Sebastopol to secure a loan to their son, and indeed the lender's cover letter described the property as "your Sebastopol residence." But the actual deed of trust listed the parents' home in Petaluma as the collateral. The court held that there had been no meeting of the minds.
>
> *Raffles* and *Oswald* were cases in which neither party was blameable for the mistake; *Balistreri* a case in which both were equally blameable, the parents for having failed to read the deed of trust, the lender for having drafted a

---

[2]Labor Management Relations Act, 29 U.S.C. §185.

misleading cover letter. It is all the same. *Restatement (Second) of Contracts* §§ 20(1)(a), (b) (1981). If neither party can be assigned the greater blame for the misunderstanding, there is no nonarbitrary basis for deciding which party's understanding to enforce, so the parties are allowed to abandon the contract without liability.... These are not cases in which one party's understanding is more reasonable than the other's. Compare *Restatement, supra*, § 20(2)(b). If rescission were permitted in *that* kind of case, the enforcement of every contract would be at the mercy of a jury, which might be persuaded that one of the parties had genuinely held an idiosyncratic idea of its meaning, so that there had been, in fact, no meeting of the minds.... Intersubjectivity is not the test of an enforceable contract.

The clearest cases for rescission on the ground that there was "no meeting of the minds" (or, better, that there was a "latent ambiguity" in the sense that neither party knew that the contract was ambiguous) are ones in which an offer is garbled in transmission . . . .

. . . The difference between this case and the others is that Colfax, unlike the hapless promisors in the cases we have cited, should have realized that the contract was unclear.... But Colfax, if reasonable, could not have doubted . . . that interpretations of the kind that the union and the district judge later placed upon it would be entirely plausible. Colfax had a right to *hope* that its interpretation would prevail but it had no right to accept the [union's] . . . on the premise that either its interpretation was correct or it could walk away from the contract. "Heads I win, tails you lose," is not the spirit that animates the principle that latent ambiguity is a ground for rescission of a contract.

It is common for contracting parties to agree—that is, to *signify* agreement—to a term to which each party attaches a different meaning. It is just a gamble on a favorable interpretation by the authorized tribunal should a dispute arise. Parties often prefer a gamble in this way rather than to take the time to try to iron out all their possible disagreements, most of which may never have any consequence.

. . .

When parties agree to a patently ambiguous term, they submit to have any dispute over it resolved by interpretation. That is what courts and arbitrators are *for* in contract cases—to resolve interpretive questions founded on ambiguity. It is when parties agree to terms that reasonably appear to each of them to be unequivocal but are not, cases like that of the ship *Peerless* where the ambiguity is buried, that the possibility of rescission on grounds of mutual misunderstanding, or, the term we prefer, latent ambiguity, arises. A reasonable person in Colfax's position would have realized that its interpretation of the term "4C 609 Press—3 Men" might not coincide with that of the other party or of the tribunal to which a dispute over the meaning of the term would be submitted. It threw the dice, and lost, and that is the end of the case. It cannot gamble on a favorable interpretation and, if that fails, repudiate the contract with no liability.[3]

B. Ascertaining the Meaning of Contract Terms

The interpretation of an agreement, or a term thereof, is the ascertainment of its meaning.[4]

---

[3]*Colfax*, 20 F.3d at 751, 752–54 (emphasis in original; some citations omitted).

[4]Restatement (First) of Contracts §226 (1932); Restatement (Second) of Contracts §200 (1979). Writings that reflect the intention of the parties to express their final agreement on the subject contained therein are called "integrations." Integrations may be partial or complete, depending on whether they are intended as a complete expression only of the terms contained therein or of all terms agreed on.

The rules, standards, and principles utilized by arbitrators to interpret collective bargaining agreements and ascertain their meaning have been borrowed from the jurisprudence developed by the courts to resolve disputes over the meaning of terms contained in ordinary commercial and other nonlabor relations contracts. That jurisprudence embodies two opposing theories of interpretation.

i.   *The Objective Approach*

The so-called "objective" approach, championed by Professor Williston and reflected in the *Restatement (First) of Contracts* holds that the "meaning" of the language is that meaning that would be attached to the integration by a reasonably intelligent person acquainted with all the operative usages and knowing all the circumstances prior to and contemporaneous with the making of the integration,[5] other than oral statements by the parties of what they intended to mean.[6] Thus, the meaning the parties may themselves have attached to their language is not determinative.[7]

Indeed, the distinguished jurist Learned Hand, himself a confirmed "objectivist," commented:

> A contract has, strictly speaking, nothing to do with the personal, or individual, intent of the parties. A contract is an obligation attached by the mere force of law to certain acts of the parties, usually words, which ordinarily accompany and represent a known intent. If, however, it were proved by twenty bishops that either party, when he used the words, intended something else than the usual meaning which the law imposes upon them, he would still be held, unless there were some mutual mistake, or something else of the sort.[8]

Again, according to Judge Hand:

> It makes not the least difference whether a promisor actually intends that meaning which the law will impose upon his words. The whole House of Bishops might satisfy us that he had intended something else, and it would not make a particle of difference in his obligation . . . . Indeed, if both parties severally declared that their meaning had been other than the natural meaning, and each declaration was similar, it would be irrelevant, saving some mutual agreement between them to that effect. When the court came to assign the meaning to their words, it would disregard such declarations, because they related only to their state of mind when the contract was made, and that has nothing to do with their obligations.[9]

The objective standard, with its preference for the common meaning of words, so it is argued, promotes predictability, uniformity, and hence stability in contractual relationships and minimizes the need for extended factual inquiry into what the parties may have intended or believed.[10]

---

[5]Farnsworth, Contracts §§7.2, 7.3, at 430–31 (3d ed. 1999); Restatement (Second) of Contracts §§210(2), 215, 216 (1979).

[6]Restatement (First) of Contracts §230.

[7]Calamari & Perilllo, The Law of Contracts §3.11(a), at 151 (4th ed. 1998).

[8]Hotchkiss v. National City Bank, 200 F. 287, 293 (S.D.N.Y. 1911), *aff'd*, 201 F. 664 (2d Cir. 1912), *aff'd*, 231 U.S. 50 (1913).

[9]Eustis Mining Co. v. Beer, Sondheimer & Co., 239 F. 976, 984–85 (S.D.N.Y. 1917) (quoted in Farnsworth, Contracts §7.9, at 460 (3d ed. 1999)).

[10]Gilmore, The Death of Contract 42 (1974) (quoted in Farnsworth, §7.9, at 460); W.W.W. Assocs. v. Giancontieri, 566 N.E.2d 639, 642–43 (N.Y. 1990).

ii. The Subjective Approach

The counterpoint "subjective" analysis advanced by Professor Corbin and adopted by the *Restatement (Second) of Contracts* defines "interpretation" as the ascertainment of the meaning of an agreement or a term thereof as intended by at least one party.[11] However, the intention of a party is "the intention manifested by him rather than any different undisclosed intention."[12] Consequently, the *Restatement (Second)* formulates the answer to the question "Whose meaning prevails?" as follows:

> Where the parties have attached different meanings to an agreement or a term thereof, it is interpreted in accordance with the meaning attached by one of them if at the time the agreement was made that party did not know, or had no reason to know, of any different meaning attached by the other, and the other knew, or had reason to know the meaning attached by the first party.[13]

---

[11]RESTATEMENT (SECOND) OF CONTRACTS §§200, 220 cmt. b (1979). *See also* L&S Prods., 97 LA 282, 285 (McDonald, 1991) (function of arbitrator is to determine intent of the parties); News-Sun, 92 LA 713, 715 (Heinsz, 1989); Spokane Sch. Dist. No. 81, 92 LA 333, 335 (Smith, 1989); Bridge Terminal Transp., 92 LA 192, 195 (Gentile, 1988); Brutoco Eng'g Constr., 92 LA 33, 36 (Ross, 1988); Alpha Beta Stores, 91 LA 888, 893 (Richman, 1988); City of Davenport, Iowa, 91 LA 855, 858 (Hoh, 1988); Lockheed Space Operations Co., 91 LA 457, 462 (Richard, 1988); Container Corp. of Am., 91 LA 329, 332 (Rains, 1988); Montana Power Co., 90 LA 932, 934 (Corbett, 1987); Allied Plant Maint. Co. of Okla., 88 LA 963, 965–66 (Bankston, 1987); Silver Lake Bd. of Educ. (Shawnee County, Kan.), 88 LA 885, 888 (Madden, 1986); Pabst Brewing Co., 88 LA 656, 660 (Wyman, 1987); Magic Chef, 84 LA 15, 17 (Craver, 1984) (parties did not intend that all employees who handled fiberglass insulation be included in a certain job classification). For cases where arbitrators looked to the intent behind contract provisions in dispute in order to resolve the grievance before them, see *Brampton Woolen Co. v. Wholesale & Warehouse Workers Local* 112, 61 A.2d 796 (N.H. 1948); *Armour Food Co.*, 85 LA 640 (Thornell, 1985); *Jacksonville Shipyard*, 82 LA 90 (Galambos, 1983). For cases where arbitrators followed the usual rule that in determining the intent of the parties, inquiry is made as to what the language meant to the parties when the agreement was written, see *Grinnell Corp.*, 100 LA 78, 83 (Chumley, 1992); *Hibbing Ready Mix*, 97 LA 248, 251 (Imes, 1991); *Metro Transit Auth.*, 94 LA 349, 352 (Richard, 1990); *Dyncorp Technical Servs. Group*, 93 LA 1192, 1197 (Richman, 1990). *See also* Shop Rite Foods, 75 LA 625, 627 (Gowan, 1980); Milwaukee Bd. of Sch. Dirs., 71 LA 892, 896–97 (Winton, 1978); Parke, Davis, & Co., 13 LA 126, 131 (Platt, 1949). *Cf.* Tin Processing Corp., 20 LA 227, 231 (Boles, 1953). In *Globe Newspaper Co.*, 74 LA 1261, 1268 (Kates, 1980), the arbitrator stated that, "[t]o determine the mutual intention of the parties from the language they used, that language should be construed in the light of the purpose clearly sought to be accomplished, giving consideration to the negotiations leading to the adoption of that language." *See also* Sanyo Mfg. Corp., 109 LA 184, 191 (Howell, 1997); Autocar Co., 10 LA 61, 63 (Brecht, 1948); John Deere Harvester Works, 21 LA 139, 144 (Davey, 1953).

[12]RESTATEMENT (SECOND) OF CONTRACTS §200 cmt. 6, §212 cmt. a (1979).

[13]*Id.* §201(2). *See* Fors Farms, 112 LA 33, 40 (Cavanaugh, 1999) (union had reason to know that the employer attached a more limited meaning to the contract language); City of Reno, Nev., 111 LA 1043, 1046 (Bickner, 1998) (prior arbitration between the parties put the city on notice that the union did not share its current interpretation of the language of the agreement); Cincinnati Cordage & Paper Co., 90 LA 1144 (Duff, 1988); Delaware County Sheriff, 87 LA 1199 (Duda, Jr., 1986); Carus Corp., 71 LA 624, 629 (Kossoff, 1978); Amana Refrigeration, 68 LA 572, 573 (Calhoon, 1977); Barton Salt Co., 46 LA 503, 505 (Merrill, 1966); Deep Rock Oil Corp., 11 LA 25, 31 (Merrill, 1948); Chrysler Corp., 8 LA 452, 458 (Wolff, 1947); National Malleable & Steel Castings Co., 4 LA 110, 111 (Blair, 1946); Hershey Chocolate Corp., 1 LA 165, 167 (McCoy, 1944). *See also* WPIX, Inc., 49 LA 155, 158 (Turkus, 1967); Sarco Mfg. Co., 43 LA 263, 266 (Bender, 1964); Geneva Steel Co., 15 LA 834, 838 (Garrett, 1950). *Cf.* McCabe-Powers Body Co., 76 LA 456, 461 (McKenna, 1981) (illustrating that a party has a responsibility to be reasonably alert to what it is accepting in negotiations—the union was held bound by a dental plan that it accepted without reading and

The policy underlying this choice of meaning is that "a party that makes a contract knowing of a misunderstanding is sufficiently at fault to justify that party's being subjected to the other party's understanding."[14]

iii. Other Factors

It is important for advocates to understand that under either the "objective" or the "subjective" theory, a party's "mental processes" are irrelevant; what a party may have privately intended the words that are the subject of dispute to mean plays no role in the interpretive process if the intended meaning has not been communicated.

There are cases, of course, where the parties "gave little or no thought to the impact of their words" for a variety of reasons, such as using "a printed form that neither party prepared" or "lifting clauses from a form book." "The court will then have no choice but to look solely to a standard of reasonableness. Interpretation cannot turn on meanings that the parties attached if they attached none, but must turn on the meaning that reasonable persons in the positions of the parties would have attached if they had given the matter thought."[15]

It is possible that a word or phrase in a collective bargaining agreement is so vague or ambiguous as to be unenforceable. For example, an arbitrator declined to hold an employer in violation of a contractual requirement to register apprentice programs "where possible." The arbitrator said that the language was so vague and ambiguous that it was impossible to determine whether a violation had occurred.[16] Similarly, another arbitrator refused to grant monetary damages for a technical violation of the contract because the contract language was ambiguous and easily misunderstood.[17]

---

without being misled by the company); Webster Tobacco Co., 5 LA 164, 166 (Brandschain, 1946); Goodyear Tire & Rubber Co., 1 LA 556, 560 (McCoy, 1946). For related discussion, see Goetz, *The Law of Contracts—A Changing Legal Environment: Comment, in* TRUTH, LIE DE-TECTORS, AND OTHER PROBLEMS IN LABOR ARBITRATION, PROCEEDINGS OF THE 31ST ANNUAL MEETING OF NAA 218, 225–27 (Stern & Dennis eds., BNA Books 1979); WBAL-TV, 110 LA 614 (Fishgold, 1998) (work of "webmaster" and "webproducer" on TV station's website was within union's jurisdiction, even though collective bargaining agreement excluded work on certain equipment, where employer, but not union, knew website was in progress and did not raise issue of its intended application during bargaining).

[14]FARNSWORTH, CONTRACTS §7.9, at 462 (3d ed. 1999).

[15]*Id.* at 465–66.

[16]Toledo Edison Co., 94 LA 905, 910 (Richard, 1990).

[17]Jackson Pub. Sch., 99 LA 366, 370 (Daniel, 1992). *See also* SMG-Van Andel Arena, 111 LA 185, 192 (Brodsky, 1998); CBS, Inc., 98 LA 890, 893–94 (Christopher, 1992); GTE Prods. Corp., 85 LA 754 (Millious, 1985) (lack of contract provision expressly including or excluding layoff time from being a part of continuous service allows the company to make the determination as a managerial right); Rockwell Int'l Corp., 82 LA 42, 45 (Feldman, 1984) ("[W]here the evidence is in equipoise and where there is no clear and unambiguous language in the contract to guide the decision making involved and where prior arbitral authority does not contain any common predicate or guidelines for the findings indicated therein, the grievance must fail for lack of proof—there being no probative evidence in the file to sustain the protest as filed.").

2. Ambiguity and the Exclusion of Extrinsic Evidence

A. The "Plain Meaning" Rule [LA CDI 24.15]

A contract term is said to be ambiguous if it is susceptible of more than one meaning, that is, if "plausible contentions may be made for conflicting interpretations."[18]

Under one view, the existence of an ambiguity must be determined from the "four corners of the instrument" without resort to extrinsic evidence of any kind.[19] This is the so-called "plain meaning rule," which states that if the words are plain and clear, conveying a distinct idea, there is no occasion to resort to interpretation, and their meaning is to be derived entirely from the nature of the language used.[20]

---

[18]Armstrong Rubber Co., 17 LA 741, 744 (Gorder, 1952). *See* Kaiser Aluminum Corp. v. Matheson, 681 A.2d 392 (Del. 1996); City of St. Petersburg, Fla., 115 LA 615, 618 (Deem, 2001); Summit County, Ohio, Children Servs., 108 LA 517, 521 (Sharpe, 1997); City of Helena, 99 LA 1090, 1094 (Calhoun, 1992). *See also* Bay City, Mich., 111 LA 1124, 1128 (Allen, 1998); National Linen Serv., 110 LA 476, 479 (Frockt, 1998); Ohio Dep't of Natural Res., 90 LA 1049 (Rivera, 1988); Allis-Chalmers Corp., 71 LA 375, 378–79 (Goetz, 1978); Genova, Pa., Inc., 70 LA 1303, 1305 (Wolf, 1978). *But see* City of Independence, Mo., 111 LA 637, 642 (Neas, 1998) (even though parties may argue over language, the question is whether the arbitrator finds the language ambiguous).

[19]Calamari & Perillo, The Law of Contracts §3.10, at 148 (4th ed. 1998). *See also* Primeline Indus., 88 LA 700, 700 (Morgan, 1986).

[20]For cases in which clear and unambiguous contract language was determinative, see *Ralphs Grocery Co.*, 109 LA 33, 35–36 (Kaufman, 1997); *National Linen Serv.*, 95 LA 829, 834 (Abrams, 1990) (provisions in written agreement were binding even though union contended that written contract included terms on which the parties had not agreed); *Down River Forest Prods.*, 94 LA 141, 146–47 (Gangle, 1989); *Mott's, Inc.*, 87 LA 306, 308 (Eyraud, 1986) (citing Clean Coverall Supply Co., 47 LA 272, 277 (Witney, 1966)); *Armstrong Rubber Co.*, 87 LA 146, 149 (Bankston, 1986) (quoting Elkouri & Elkouri, How Arbitration Works 352 (BNA Books 4th ed. 1985)); *General Tel. Co. of the Southwest*, 86 LA 293, 295 (Ipavec, 1985); *Champion Int'l Corp.*, 85 LA 877, 880 (Allen, Jr., 1985); *Oak Grove Sch. Dist.*, 85 LA 653, 655 (Concepcion, 1985); *Florida Power Corp.*, 85 LA 619, 622 (Flannagan, 1985); *City of Taylor*, 84 LA 522, 524 (McDonald, 1985) (quoting *Clean Coverall*, 47 LA 272, 277 (Witney, 1966)); *Boogaart Supply Co.*, 84 LA 27, 30 (Fogelberg, 1984); *Disneyland Hotel*, 83 LA 685, 688 (Weiss, 1984); *Nekoosa Corp.*, 83 LA 676, 679–80 (Flaten, 1984); *Red Owl Stores*, 83 LA 652, 656 (Reynolds, 1984); *Western Mich. Univ.*, 82 LA 93, 97 (Kahn, 1984). In *Michigan Dep't of Soc. Servs.*, 82 LA 114, 116 (Fieger, 1983), the arbitrator expounded on the importance of this aspect of the rule, writing, "Not only is it axiomatic that the clear, unambiguous language of the agreement must be honored, but here the contract in exact terms forbids the arbitrator from ignoring 'in any way,' the specific provisions of the contract nor giving, to either party, rights which were not 'obtained in a negotiating process' . . . . Such restriction goes far beyond the simple statement that the arbitrator is bound by the language of the contract." *See also* Excel Corp. v. Food & Commerical Workers Local 431, 102 F.3d 1464, 1468, 154 LRRM 2154 (8th Cir. 1996) (finding that arbitrator ignored plain meaning of agreement, and stating that "[a]lthough an arbitrator's award is given great deference by a reviewing court, the arbitrator is not free to ignore or abandon the plain language of [the agreement], which would in effect amend or alter the agreement without authority"); Hibbing Ready Mix, 97 LA 248, 251 (Imes, 1991); Pittsburg & Midway Coal Mining Co., 87 LA 1107, 1108 (Feldman, 1986); Diamond Crystal Salt Co., 87 LA 427, 434 (Keefe, 1986); Pollock Co., 87 LA 325, 332 (Oberdank, 1986); Kroger Co., 86 LA 357, 365 (Milentz, 1986); Owens-Illinois, Inc., 86 LA 354, 357 (Darrow, 1985); Independent Sch. Dist. No. 47, 86 LA 97 (Gallagher, 1985); BASF Wyandotte Corp., 84 LA 1055, 1057 (Caraway, 1985); ARCO Pipe Line Co., 84 LA 907, 909 (Nicholas, Jr., 1985); Town of Davie, Fla., 83 LA 1153, 1157 (Kanzer, 1984); Aeronca, Inc., 82 LA 144, 146 (Finan, 1984); Magma Copper Co., 51 LA 9, 13 (Abernethy, 1968); Hadley Adhesive & Chem. Co., 49 LA 229, 230–31 (Erbs, 1967); Firestone Tire &

One arbitrator expressed a commonly held view when he stated that an arbitrator cannot "ignore clear-cut contractual language" and "may not legislate new language, since to do so would usurp the role of the labor organi-

---

Rubber Co., 29 LA 469, 473 (Hebert, 1957). In *United Grocers*, 92 LA 566, 569 (Gangle, 1989) (quoting Nolan, Labor Arbitration Law and Practice 163 (1979)), the arbitrator restated a standard for determining when an ambiguity exists:

> The test most often cited is that there is no ambiguity if the contract is so clear on the issue that the intentions of the parties can be determined using no other guide than the contract itself. This test borders on a tautology, however, for it comes perilously close to a statement that language is clear and unambiguous if it is clear on its face. Perhaps a better way of putting it would be to ask if a single, obvious and reasonable meaning appears from a reading of the language in the context of the rest of the contract. If so, that meaning is to be applied.

Accord Stewart v. KDH Deutz of Am. Corp., 980 F.2d 698, 142 LRRM 2371, 2373 (11th Cir. 1993) (ambiguities must be created by the language of the contract itself); City of Independence, Mo., 111 LA 637, 642 (Neas, 1998) (quoting Ohio Chem. & Surgical Equip. Co., 49 LA 377, 380–81 (Solomon, 1967)); Reed Tool Co., 100 LA 556, 558 (Overstreet, 1992) (if wording conveys a distinct idea, arbitrator will normally apply clear meaning); L&S Prods., 97 LA 282, 284 (McDonald, 1991); Hibbing Ready Mix, 97 LA 248, 251 (Imes, 1991); Independent Sch. Dist. 11, 97 LA 169, 173 (Gallagher, 1991); City of Flint, Mich., 97 LA 1, 6 (McDonald, 1991) (ambiguous language is language that is susceptible of different but equally plausible interpretations); Klein Tools, 90 LA 1150, 1153 (Poindexter, 1988) (contract is not ambiguous if one party negligently uses a term that does not express the meaning intended by that party, or if a party could have received a clarification of the term during negotiations). *See also* Ash Grove Cement Co., 112 LA 507, 511 (Wyman, 1999) (a party's intentions "need to have been clearly and contractually identified . . . . It is the responsibility of the architect of contract language to craft the language in a fashion that does not leave the matter in doubt"); E.M. Smith & Co., 88 LA 1124, 1126 (Dworkin, 1987) (when an apparent conflict exists between mutual intentions and the words of an agreement, it is not always appropriate for an arbitrator to give determinant force to the words and wholly ignore the meaning); Primeline Indus., 88 LA 700 (Morgan, 1986); Continental Conveyor & Equip. Co., 51 LA 1023, 1025 (McCoy, 1968); Great Atl. & Pac. Tea Co., 36 LA 391, 392 (Pollock, 1960); Moog Indus., 15 LA 676, 682 (Klamon, 1950); Minnesota Mining & Mfg. Co., 15 LA 46, 49 (Kelliher, 1950). *Cf.* Entergy/Mississippi Power & Light Co., 111 LA 507, 515 (Howell, 1998) (words given normal meaning unless there is a clear indication otherwise); Klapholz Bros., 33 LA 919, 922 (Tischler, 1959). Where the arbitration is subject to court review on matters of law, the court may apply this principle. See cases discussed in Marceau, *Are All Interpretations "Admissible"?*, 12 Arb. J. 150 (1957). Arbitrators have found that evidence of past practice is "wholly inadmissible" where language is clear and unambiguous. City of Conneaut, Ohio, 112 LA 899, 903 (Richard, 1999); U.S. Sugar Corp., 112 LA 967, 973 (Chandler, 1999); Village of Franklin Park, Ill., 109 LA 103, 109 (Witney, 1997); Metro Transit Auth., 94 LA 349, 352 (Richard, 1990). *See also* L&S Prods., 97 LA 282, 284–85 (McDonald, 1991). *But see* Koehring S. Plant, 82 LA 193, 196 (Alsher, 1984) (arbitrator found contract language unclear, justifying consideration of past practice); Alameda Unified Sch. Dist., 91 LA 60, 62 (Wilcox, 1988); Artichoke Growers Packing Co., 90 LA 120, 122 (Pool, 1987); Lithonia Lighting Div., 89 LA 781, 783 (Chandler, 1987); Kentucky Ctr. for the Performing Arts, 89 LA 344, 348 (Volz, 1987); Mentor Bd. of Educ., 89 LA 292, 294 (Sharpe, 1987); Tiger Maint. Corp., 89 LA 276, 278 (Hockenberry, 1987); Southern Ind. Gas & Elec. Co., 87 LA 1187, 1188 (Kilroy, 1986); Del Monte Corp., 86 LA 134 (Denson, 1985); Bootz Plumbing Fixtures, 84 LA 18 (Seinsheimer, 1984). *See* CFS Cont'l—L.A., 83 LA 458, 461 (Sabo, 1984) ("[T]he clear meaning and language of the Contract is subject to enforcement even though the results are harsh and may be contrary to the general expectations of one of the Parties."); Cleo Wrap, 90 LA 768 (Welch, 1988); City of Vallejo, Cal., 86 LA 1082, 1086 (Bogue, 1986); Town of N. Haven, 71 LA 983, 988 (Sacks, McDonough, & Johnson, 1978); Wyman-Gordon Co., 51 LA 561, 565 (Rauch, 1968); Palmer Square, Inc., 45 LA 530, 531 (Kerrison, 1965); Moe Levy & Sons, 4 LA 708, 711 (Platt, 1946); Carnation Co., 3 LA 229, 232 (Updegraff, 1946) (citing law cases); John Deere Tractor Co., 2 LA 469, 472 (Updegraff, 1945). *See also* International Paper Co., 90 LA 958, 960 (Levy, 1988); Holly Farms, 90 LA 509 (McDermott, 1987); San Francisco Unified Sch. Dist., 87 LA 1248, 1249 (Concepcion, 1986); Mazza Cheese Co., 84 LA 947, 949 (La Cugna, 1985). *See* Aladdin Temp-Rite LLC, 112 LA 1105 (Krislov, 1999); Earthgrains Co., 112 LA 170, 171 (Grooms, 1999); Universal Studio Tour, 93 LA 1, 3 (Gentile, 1989); Atlantic Richfield

zation and employer."[21] Even when both parties declare a provision to be ambiguous, the arbitrator may not find it so.[22]

i. Criticisms

The "plain meaning rule," although still dominant, has been uniformly criticized and rejected in the academic literature by both "objectivist" and "subjectivist" commentators, by jurists in more recent court decisions, and by a growing number of arbitrators.[23]

Co., 91 LA 835 (Nelson, 1988); Peabody-Eastern Coal Co., 90 LA 1248 (Volz, 1988); Livers Bronze Co., 89 LA 238 (Eisler, 1987); Jerome Foods, 87 LA 715 (Ver Ploeg, 1986); Commonwealth of Pa., Dep't of Corr., 86 LA 978, 981 (Kreitler, 1986); Scott Paper Co., 68 LA 838, 841 (Marcus, 1977); Lawnlite Co., 69 LA 238, 240 (Boals, 1977); Combustion Eng'g, 61 LA 1061, 1063 (Altrock, 1973); Greenlee Bros. & Co., 48 LA 938, 939–40 (Davis, 1967); Lear Siegler, Inc., 48 LA 276, 280 (Hayes, 1967); Sperry Gyroscope Co., 18 LA 916, 918 (Cole, 1952); Merrill-Stevens Drydock & Repair Co., 6 LA 838, 843 (Marshall, 1947); Blaw-Knox Co., 3 LA 753, 756 (Blair, 1946); Ingram-Richardson Mfg. Co. of Ind., 3 LA 482, 486 (Whiting, 1946). For further discussion, see Chapter 8, section 4.E., "The Parol Evidence Rule."

[21]Clean Coverall Supply Co., 47 LA 272, 277 (Witney, 1966). See also City of Bainbridge Island, Wash., 115 LA 747, 748 (Lacy, 2001); City of Tipp City, 88 LA 315, 318 (Imundo, Jr., 1987) (when language is specific and unambiguous, there is little if any room for misunderstanding what the language means and how it applies); Lorillard, Inc., 87 LA 507, 511 (Chalfie, 1986) (it is an established arbitral rule of construction that when contract language is clear and unambiguous, the intent of the parties is to be found in its clear language and not in the parties' conduct); Wolf Baking Co., 83 LA 24, 26 (Marlatt, 1984) ("No party to a Contract may evade the express terms of the Contract on the grounds that such terms are impracticable, unreasonable, or even absurd. The Contract is the Contract, and arbitrators are not free to vary its terms to achieve a more equitable or productive result . . . ."). Where evidence indicated that the contracting union could not be held responsible for the refusal of its members to cross another union's picket line, that refusal was held not covered by a contractual provision prohibiting strikes or stoppages "on the part of the Union" and lockouts "on the part of the Company." One arbitrator explained: "In such highly controversial cases, the arbitrator long ago concluded that it is best to try to interpret the words of the contract in as literal, exact, and limited a way as possible so as not to read into the contract, or inadvertently add to it, meanings which were not intended by the parties and which should not reasonably be inferred from the words used." Continental Oil Co., 69 LA 399, 404 (Wann, 1977). Cf. Mine Workers Health & Ret. Funds v. Robinson, 455 U.S. 562, 576, 109 LRRM 2865 (1982) ("[W]hen neither the collective-bargaining process nor its end product violates any command of Congress, a federal court has no authority to modify the substantive terms of a collective-bargaining contract."). See Heublein Wines, 93 LA 400 (Randall, 1988); Southern Cal. Edison Co., 90 LA 5, 7 (Moore, Castrey, & Ryan, 1987); Steelworkers Local 1010, 89 LA 380, 383 (Petersen, 1987); Community Unit Sch. Dist. No. 303 Bd. of Educ., 88 LA 1159, 1162 (Goldstein, 1987); Racine Policemen's Prof'l & Benevolent Corp., 88 LA 1038, 1045 (Baron, 1987); National Steel & Shipbuilding Co., 88 LA 834, 838 (Darrow, 1987); Thunderbird Hotel, 69 LA 10, 13 (Weiss, 1977); Hi-Ram, 68 LA 54, 55 (Daniel, 1977); American Potash & Chem. Co., 47 LA 661, 665 (Leonard, 1966); Pana Ref. Co., 47 LA 193, 194–95 (Traynor, 1966); Warwick Elecs., 46 LA 95, 98 (Daugherty, 1966); Patterson Steel Co., 45 LA 783, 786, 788 (Autrey, 1965); New York City Bd. of Educ., 44 LA 883, 887 (Scheiber, 1965); Lionel Corp., 9 LA 716, 718 (Shipman, 1948); Carnegie-Illinois Steel Corp., 5 LA 378, 382 (Blumer, 1946); Universal Milking Mach. Co., 4 LA 497, 502 (Rader, 1946); Bastian-Morley Co., 3 LA 412, 414 (Epstein, 1946); John Deere Tractor Co., 2 LA 469, 472 (Updegraff, 1945); Warner Bros. Cartoons, 2 LA 66, 67 (Peifer, 1946).

[22]E.g., Andrew Williams Meat Co., 8 LA 518, 524 (Cheney, 1947). See also Great Atl. & Pac. Tea Co., 40 LA 152, 154–55 (Scheiber, 1962).

[23]RESTATEMENT (SECOND) OF CONTRACTS §212 cmt. b (1979); WIGMORE, EVIDENCE §§2461, 2462 (Chadbourn ed., rev. ed. 1981). See FARNSWORTH, CONTRACTS, §7.10, at 467, §7.12, at 477–78 (3d ed. 1999); 11 SAMUEL WILLISTON & RICHARD A. LORD, A TREATISE ON THE LAW OF CONTRACTS §30.4, at 37–38 (4th ed. & Supp. 1999); 5 CALAMARI & PERILLO, THE LAW OF CONTRACTS §3.10, at 148–49 (4th ed. 1998); 5 CORBIN ON CONTRACTS §24.7, at 37–38 (Kniffen ed.,

It is a rare contract that needs no interpretation. It has been wisely observed that there is no "lawyer's Paradise [where] all words have a fixed, precisely ascertained meaning, . . . and where, if the writer has been careful, a lawyer having a document referred to him may sit in his chair, inspect the text, and answer all questions without raising his eyes." As Holmes cautioned "a word is not a crystal, transparent and unchanged." It is the skin of a living thought and may vary greatly in color and content according to the circumstances and the time in which it is used.[24]

The *Restatement (Second) of Contracts*, although respecting the importance of the words chosen by the parties to express their agreement, puts the matter this way:

> It is sometimes said that extrinsic evidence cannot change the plain meaning of the writing, but meaning can almost never be plain except in a context. . . . Any determination of meaning or ambiguity should only be made in the light of the relevant evidence of the situation and relations of the parties, the subject matter of the transaction, preliminary negotiations and statements made

---

rev. ed. 1998); Mark V, Inc. v. Mellekas, 114 N.M. 778, 845 P.2d 1232, 1235 (1993); Hilton Hotels Corp. v. Butch Lewis Prods., 808 P.2d 919 (Nev. 1991); Alyeska Pipeline Serv. Co. v. O'Kelley, 645 P.2d 767, 771 n.1 (Alaska 1982); Mellon Bank v. Aetna Bus. Credit, 619 F.2d 1001 (3d Cir. 1980); Pacific Gas Elec. Co. v. G.W. Thomas Drayage & Rigging Co., 69 Cal. 2d 33, 442 P.2d 641 (1968). In *Circle Steel Corp.*, 85 LA 738, 739 (Stix, 1984), the arbitrator stated that "whether a contract is ambiguous is not to be determined simply from the face of the contract (as other authorities hold), but only after taking into consideration the circumstances existing at the time the contract was adopted and the practice of the parties in applying it." The arbitrator found the intent of the parties contrary to the express language of the contract and rendered a decision based on his perception of their intent. *See also* University of Cal., 100 LA 530, 533 (Wilcox, 1992); Department of Health & Human Servs., 96 LA 1097, 1100 (Hockenberry, 1991); Pacific Bell, 93 LA 1199, 1203 (Freeman, 1989) ("in order to answer, we do not have to look to the normal, accepted rules of interpretation to construe the usage of words so they have a logical consistency within the entire document which sufficiently communicates a single clear and sensible meaning. This is because the arbitrator has paid considerable attention to the evidence presented by both sides . . . ."); Midwest Rubber Reclaiming Co., 69 LA 198, 199 (Bernstein, 1977); Carlile & Doughty, 9 LA 239, 241 (Brandschain, 1947). For discussion regarding the extent to which a showing of latent ambiguity should be permitted, see Snow, *Contract Interpretation: The Plain Meaning Rule in Labor Arbitration*, 55 FORDHAM L. REV. 681 (1987). Indeed, in the latter discussion the arbitrator agrees that there can be no such thing as a clear and unambiguous contractual provision. *Id.* at 685, 687–88, 704. Thus, he argued (1) that "the process of characterizing contractual language as 'ambiguous' or 'unambiguous' pursuant to the plain meaning rule should be discarded in favor of an approach that does not deny the relevance of extrinsic evidence to prove meanings to which a contractual provision is reasonably susceptible," and (2) that the arbitrator should consider and weigh the extrinsic evidence against the terms of the agreement to determine their relative significance in the disposition of the case. *Id.* at 705. In the following cases, the arbitrator considered past practice despite the presence of clear contract language: Brown-Forman Beverage Co., 103 LA 292 (Frockt, 1994); Weyerhaeuser Paper Co., 101 LA 457 (Byars, 1993); Ludington Area Pub. Sch., 98 LA 47 (Borland, 1991); City of Columbus, Ohio, 96 LA 32 (Mancini, 1990); Woodhaven Sch. Dist., 86 LA 215, 216 (Daniel, 1986); Rice Mem'l Hosp., 84 LA 537, 541 (Boyer, 1985); Sonoma-Marin Publ'g Co., 83 LA 512, 516 (Griffin, 1984). *See also* Pepsi-Cola Bottling Co., 97 LA 1011 (DiLauro, 1991); Mor Flo Indus., 83 LA 480 (Cocalis, 1984).

[24]FARNSWORTH, §7.8, at 454 (citing THAYER, PRELIMINARY TREATISE ON THE LAW OF EVIDENCE 428–29 (1898), and Justice Holmes's opinion in Towne v. Eisner, 245 U.S. 418, 425 (1918)) (footnotes omitted). *See also* Pacific Southwest Airlines, 73 LA 634, 635 (Jones, Jr., 1979) (illustrating that social attitudes and mores of the times may dictate an expansive interpretation of a term, where the term "regular parent-child relationship" was interpreted to include a stepdaughter); Yale & Towne Mfg. Co., 5 LA 753 (Raphael, Eddy, & Adam, 1946).

therein, usages of trade, and the course of dealing between the parties. . . . But after the transaction has been shown in all its length and breadth, the words of an integrated agreement remain the most important evidence of intention.[25]

The unanimity breaks down, however, with respect to the kinds of extrinsic evidence that may be examined in order to determine the meaning of contract language. On the one hand, the "subjectivists" would impose no limitation. Indeed, they would not even require that there be a preliminary determination of ambiguity:

> The overarching principle of contract interpretation is that the court is free to look to all the relevant circumstances surrounding the transaction. This includes the state of the world, including the state of the law at the time. It also includes all writings, oral statements, and other conduct by which the parties manifested their assent, together with any prior negotiations between them and any applicable course of dealing, course of performance or usage. The entire agreement, including all writings, should be read together in the light of all the circumstances. Since the purpose of this inquiry is to ascertain the meaning to be given to the language, there should be no requirement that language be ambigious, vague, or otherwise uncertain before the inquiry is undertaken.[26]

In keeping with this view, "all relevant extrinsic evidence is admissible on the issue of meaning, including evidence of subjective intention and what the parties said to each other with respect to a meaning."[27]

---

[25]Restatement (Second) of Contracts §212 cmt. b (1979). *See also* Food & Commercial Workers v. National Tea Co., 899 F.2d 386, 134 LRRM 2193 (5th Cir. 1990). It was proper for an airline system board of adjustment to construe seemingly unambiguous language and to consider past practice in determining the meaning of the contract. Ozark Airlines v. Air Line Pilots, 744 F.2d 1347, 117 LRRM 2562 (8th Cir. 1984). Even if a contract is superficially clear, resort to extrinsic sources is permissible if the language of the contract does not appear to express fully the intent of the parties, or if the arbitrator discerns latent ambiguity in any of its terms. In denying that a contractual provision was clear and unambiguous as one party contended, an arbitrator explained: "The law recognizes the existence of two types of ambiguities in contracts. The first type is the 'patent ambiguity,' in which language is unclear on its face—a mere reading of the contract discloses the confusion. However, there is also the category of the 'latent ambiguity,' where the language appears clear on its face but becomes unclear when an effort is made to apply it to a given situation." Midwest Rubber Reclaiming Co., 69 LA 198, 199 (Bernstein, 1977). *See, e.g.*, E.W. Scripps, 111 LA 592, 593–95 (High, 1998) (determining intent of parties from precontract negotiations); Monroe County, Ohio, Care Ctr., 109 LA 15, 18 (Richard, 1997) (determining intent from bargaining history); Michigan Milk Producers Ass'n, 95 LA 1184, 1186–87 (Kanner, 1990); Atlanta Wire Works, 93 LA 537, 540 (Williams, 1989); Bard Mfg. Co., 92 LA 616, 619 (Daniel, 1989); Lithonia Lighting Div., 89 LA 781, 783 (Chandler, 1987); Tiger Maint. Corp., 89 LA 276, 279 (Hockenberry, 1987); E.M. Smith & Co., 88 LA 1124, 1127 (Dworkin, 1987); Southwestern Elec. Power Co., 87 LA 9, 13 (Williams, 1986) (determining intent of parties from contract language, negotiations, and past practice); Los Angeles Cmty. Coll. Dist., 85 LA 988, 990 (Christopher, 1985) (determining intent of parties from contract language, position memoranda issued by employer, and past practice); Cincinnati Enquirer, 83 LA 567, 570 (Modjeska, 1984) (determining intent of parties from contract language and conduct of parties in processing grievance). In line with this philosophy, arbitrators have relied on extrinsic evidence even where the contract had a "zipper clause" stating that the collective bargaining agreement constituted the "complete agreement between the parties." Sanyo Mfg. Corp., 109 LA 184, 192 (Howell, 1997); Spartan Stores, 105 LA 549, 550 (Kanner, 1995).

[26]Farnsworth, §7.10, at 467.

[27]Calamari & Perillo, §3.12, at 153.

So, for example, one arbitrator acknowledged that "the clear language of the Hours provision of the contract, if taken by itself without relation to any other facts, would indicate that it was the intention of the negotiators . . . that the secretaries would be paid for lunch period . . . ."[28] However, despite what appeared to be clear and unambiguous language, the arbitrator looked to extrinsic evidence "to determine the true intent of the parties."[29] In light of the undisputed evidence that there was no agreement with respect to this issue, coupled with the past practice of not paying secretaries for a lunch period, the arbitrator concluded that "it was the intent of the parties that at no time would the lunch period be included."[30] Another arbitrator disregarded the clear language of a contract term providing that a "bonus" day would be earned for perfect attendance in "four three-month periods."[31] He found the parties' intent was "to reward an employee who actually works three months without absence or tardiness," and interpreted the contract to mean that, in each 3-month period during which perfect attendance was achieved by attendance on 62 successive scheduled working days, a "bonus" day would be earned.

The objectivists, however, would allow evidence of "all operative usages and knowing all of the circumstances prior to and contemporaneous with the . . . [contract]," but excluding "what the parties said to each other about meaning . . . and what the parties subjectively believed the writing meant at the time of agreement."[32]

ii. *Exceptions* [LA CDI 24.15]

Arbitrators who subscribe to the "plain meaning" doctrine nevertheless recognize an exception to this rule in the case of a mutual mistake. "A mutual mistake exists when both parties sign off [on] contract language that does not correspond with their actual agreement. In this limited circumstance, an arbitrator may reform the contract to reflect the true intent of the parties."[33]

---

[28]Maple Heights Bd. of Educ., 86 LA 338, 340 (Van Pelt, 1985). *See* Commonwealth of Pa., Bureau of Police & Safety, 87 LA 947, 949 (Hogler, 1986) (rejecting union's position that contract was clear and unambiguous and permitted no exception; although mandatory in one respect, qualified in another, therefore, subject to interpretation so as to ascertain meanings of words). *Accord* Heublein Wines, 93 LA 400, 406 (Randall, 1988); Retail Mkts. Co., 92 LA 1234, 1237 (Klein, 1989); Stroh Brewery Co., 92 LA 930, 932 (Berquist, 1989); City of Melbourne, Fla., 91 LA 1210, 1211 (Baroni, 1988); Alpha Beta Stores, 91 LA 888, 893 (Richman, 1988); Jefferson Sch., 91 LA 18, 20 (Daniel, 1988); Southern Cal. Edison Co., 90 LA 5, 7 (Moore, Castrey, & Ryan, 1987); Interbake Foods, 89 LA 1118, 1120 (Keefe, 1987); Warner Press, 89 LA 577, 579 (Brunner, 1987); Potlatch Corp., 88 LA 1184, 1186 (Corbett, 1987); Community Unit Sch. Dist. No. 303 Bd. of Educ., 88 LA 1159, 1162 (Goldstein, 1987); Inland Empire Paper Co., 88 LA 1096, 1102 (Levak, 1987); Racine Policemen's Prof'l & Benevolent Corp., 88 LA 1038, 1043 (Baron, 1987); Allied Plant Maint. Co. of Okla., 88 LA 963, 966 (Bankston, 1987); Primeline Indus., 88 LA 700, 702 (Morgan, 1986).
[29]Maple Heights Bd. of Educ., 86 LA 338, 340 (Van Pelt, 1985).
[30]*Id.* at 342.
[31]Circle Steel Corp., 85 LA 738, 740 (Stix, 1984).
[32]CALAMARI & PERILLO, §3.11, at 150–51 (footnotes omitted); RESTATEMENT (FIRST) OF CONTRACTS §§230, 231 (1932).
[33]Los Angeles County Soc. Servs. Union, 89-1 ARB ¶8189, at 3923 (Knowlton, 1988) (error in transfer agreement). *See also* Hibbing Ready Mix, 97 LA 248 (Imes, 1991) (arbitrator refused to enforce contract language that was concededly a mutual mistake of the parties); Down River Forest Prods., 94 LA 141, 145 (Gangle, 1989).

In order to nullify the clear language of the collective bargaining agreement, however, those arbitrators require that the mistake must be *mutual*. A unilateral mistake by one party does not provide a sufficient basis for contract reformation.[34]

B. The Parol Evidence Rule [LA CDI 24.108]

The "parol evidence" rule [34a] is a substantive rule of law that bars the introduction of extrinsic evidence, whether in oral, documentary, or other form, to contradict or supplement the final and complete written expression of the parties' agreement. It also bars such contradictory, but not supplementary, evidence in cases where the writing represents the final, but not the complete, expression of all the terms agreed upon, some of which may remain unwritten or contained in other writings.[35] In short, the parol evidence rule defines the subject matter of the interpretative process.[36]

The parol evidence rule does not exclude extrinsic evidence offered to interpret the terms of an agreement, at least when the language is "ambiguous,"[37] because the evidence is not directed to the determination of the content of the agreement, but rather to the meaning of the terms. Those courts and arbitrators that follow the "plain meaning rule," however, would exclude extrinsic evidence of all types to prevent the undermining of the parol evidence rule by allowing what, in effect, is an additional or contradictory term under the guise of interpretation.[38]

The critics of the plain meaning rule contend that a writing "cannot prove its own completeness and accuracy," therefore, it is not possible to determine whether the agreement is being contradicted or impermissibly augmented until the meaning of the term or terms at issue has been determined,[39] and wide latitude must be allowed for inquiry into circumstances bearing on the intention of the parties.[40] However, the meaning contended

---

[34]Pillowtex Corp., 92 LA 321, 325 (Goldstein, 1989); Cleo Wrap, 90 LA 768, 769 (Welch, 1988) (arbitrator refused to restore paragraph, mistakenly deleted by union, to the contract, where there was no fraud, deceit, or unfair labor practice on part of company); Transit Mgmt. of Southeast La., 88 LA 1055, 1058 (Baroni, 1987). *See* Cleveland Pneumatic Co., 91 LA 428, 430 (Oberdank, 1988); Jacobsen Mfg. Co., 43 LA 730, 732–33 (Anderson, 1964); Crook Paper Box Co., 27 LA 829, 831 (Compton, 1957); Patterson-Sargent Co., 23 LA 21, 24 (Willcox, 1954). *See also* Bay Meadows Racing Ass'n, 90 LA 770, 771 (Christopher, 1988); Maple Heights Bd. of Educ., 86 LA 338, 340 (Van Pelt, 1985); Diversified Maint. Co., 84 LA 894, 896 (Draznin, 1985); PPG Indus., 70 LA 1148, 1151–52 (Taylor, 1978); Deep Rock Oil Co., 20 LA 865, 867 (Emery, 1953); Goodyear Tire & Rubber Co. of Ala., 3 LA 257, 259 (McCoy, 1946). *Cf.* Peoria Malleable Castings Co., 43 LA 722, 726–27 (Sembower, 1964). For further development of this issue, see Chapter 18, section 3.K., "Remedies for Mistake."

[34a]For extended discussion of the parol evidence rule, see Chapter 8, section 4.E., "The Parol Evidence Rule."

[35]FARNSWORTH, CONTRACTS §§7.2, 7.3, at 430–31 (3d ed. 1999); RESTATEMENT (SECOND) OF CONTRACTS §§210(2), 215, 216 (1979).

[36]RESTATEMENT (SECOND) OF CONTRACTS §213.

[37]FARNSWORTH, §7.12, at 475.

[38]*See* CALAMARI & PERILLO, THE LAW OF CONTRACTS §§3.10, 3.11 (4th ed. 1998).

[39]Corbin, *The Parol Evidence Rule*, 53 YALE L.J. 603, 630 (1944).

[40]RESTATEMENT (SECOND) OF CONTRACTS §210 cmt. b (1979). Evidence of prior negotiations and contemporaneous agreements is admissible to establish whether the writing is fully, partially, or nonintegrated, and its meaning. *Id.* §214.

for "must be one to which the language of the writing, read in context, is reasonably susceptible."[41]

C. Causes of Ambiguity and Misunderstandings [LA CDI 24.15]

The language of mathematics is precise. The English language is not. Even when the greatest care is employed, ambiguity of meaning can result. Moreover, the parties or their representatives may not be skilled in draftsmanship and may employ terms in their contract that are inherently vague.[42] For example, the contract may provide that one or both parties must act on a certain matter "with reasonable promptness." Even more common is what has been called the "ambiguity of syntax" error[43] involving misplaced modifiers, inadequate punctuation, or the use of shorthand expressions.

Another source of ambiguity arises from the inclusion of inconsistent provisions in a contract or conflicting language within a particular term.[44] Still another kind of common ambiguity arises from the failure to foresee the problem that arises from the application of a term to an unexpected situation.

Most persons experienced in collective bargaining recognize the collective bargaining agreement as a comprehensive, but necessarily flexible, instrument that governs the relations between the parties. The very fact that almost all such agreements provide for the arbitration of grievances concerning agreement interpretation suggests that the parties recognize the impossibility of foreseeing and providing for every question that may arise during the life of the agreement.[45]

---

[41]*Id.* §215 cmt. b.

[42]As a drafting guide, see MARCEAU, DRAFTING A UNION CONTRACT (1965). *See also* LOUGHRAN, NEGOTIATING A LABOR CONTRACT: A MANAGEMENT HANDBOOK (BNA Books 3d ed. 2003); ZACK & BLOCH, LABOR AGREEMENT IN NEGOTIATION & ARBITRATION (BNA Books 2d ed. 1995).

[43]FARNSWORTH, CONTRACTS §7.8, at 455 (3d ed. 1999). In *National Broad. Co.*, 86 LA 586, 591–92 (Benewitz, 1986), the arbitrator applied the "golden rule" cited in FOWLER, A DICTIONARY OF MODERN ENGLISH USAGE (Gower ed., Oxford Univ. Press 2d ed. 1965), as an aid in interpreting a contract provision: "The golden rule of writing is 'that the words or numbers most nearly related should be placed in the sentence as near to one another as possible, so as to make their mutual relation clearly apparent.'" FOWLER, at 21. Similarly, the arbitrator referred to SHOSTAK, CONCISE DICTIONARY OF CURRENT AMERICAN USAGE (Washington Square Press 1968), for the proposition that "the pronoun is said to agree in gender . . . , number (*singular or plural*) and person . . . with the antecedent." *Id.* (quoted in *National Broad. Co.*, 86 LA at 592 (emphasis added)). Based on the foregoing, the arbitrator concluded:

[F]rom the placement of the words and from the number of the referential phrase, . . . the drafters of the language had chosen to limit the length of the specialized news program mentioned under condition (i) but not of the non-news television program *which is not mentioned* in condition (i).

Id. (emphasis added).

[44]Butte Water Co. v. Butte, 138 P. 195, 197 (Mont. 1914).

[45]Loew's, Inc., 10 LA 227, 232 (Aaron, 1948). Republic Steel Corporation's Director of Labor Relations, W.C. Stoner, acknowledged: "Even the most experienced negotiators cannot anticipate all the conditions and variations which can arise under a particular provision of the labor agreement, and often arbitration is the only way to fill in the gaps to arrive at a reasonable interpretation of the contract language." Stoner, *Updating Arbitration: Comment, in* ARBITRATION OF INTEREST DISPUTES, PROCEEDINGS OF THE 26TH ANNUAL MEETING OF NAA 80, 81 (Dennis & Somers eds., BNA Books 1974).

By way of illustration, the parties may have agreed on a bonus payment for "employees who have not been absent on a scheduled work day during any six month period." Is an employee on leave of absence for a month, and hence not scheduled to work, eligible for the bonus if he or she maintains perfect attendance for the 5 months after the return to work?

Finally, worthy of mention is the deliberate ambiguity caused by parties who are unable to agree on terms and, in effect, require the arbitrator to serve as an undesignated "interest" arbitrator.[46]

D. Gap-Filling and Omitted Terms

It frequently happens that there is no language in the contract applicable to a particular situation that has arisen.

> The parties to an agreement may entirely fail to foresee the situation which later arises and gives rise to a dispute; they then have no expectations with respect to that situation, and a search for their meaning with respect to it is fruitless. Or they may have expectations but fail to manifest them, either because the expectation rests on an assumption which is unconscious or only partly conscious, or because the situation seems to be unimportant or unlikely, or because discussion of it might be unpleasant or might produce delay or impasse.[47]

As one commentator points out, "[c]ourts [and arbitrators] must resolve such disputes arising from *omission* by some process other than interpretation."[48] Jurisprudence dictates that a term may be implied by application of "default rules."[49]

Under the *Restatement (Second) of Contracts* standard, when the parties "have not agreed with respect to a term which is essential to a determination of their rights and duties, a term which is reasonable in the circumstances is supplied by the courts,"[50] that is, "a term that comports with community standards of fairness and policy . . . ."[51] Most often, the standard will be "good faith" or "reasonableness under the circumstances."[52]

Under the alternative "bargaining model" standard, the term is developed based on an estimation of what the parties would have intended had they foreseen and considered the situation, subject to the constraint that it be consistent with effectuating the carrying-out of the express terms of the contract.[53]

---

[46]In *Marine Corps Development*, 71 LA 726, 728 (Ables, 1978), the parties had knowingly left a gap in a contractual provision where "the difficulty in coming to a full agreement" led them "to leave to working groups the way in which to develop the mechanics" of implementing the provision; it was those "mechanics" that ultimately brought the parties to arbitration.

[47]RESTATEMENT (SECOND) OF CONTRACTS §204 cmt. b (1979).

[48]FARNSWORTH, CONTRACTS §7.15, at 494 (3d ed. 1999) (emphasis in original).

[49]*Id.* §7.16, at 497.

[50]RESTATEMENT (SECOND) OF CONTRACTS §204.

[51]*Id.* §204 cmt. d.

[52]CALAMARI & PERILLO, THE LAW OF CONTRACTS §3.14, at 158 (4th ed. 1998); Loew's, Inc., 10 LA 227, 232 (Aaron, 1948).

[53]CALAMARI & PERILLO, §3.14, at 158–59 (citing Barco Urban Renewal Corp. v. Housing Auth., 674 F.2d 1001 (3d Cir. 1982)).

The *Common Law of the Workplace* puts forth the "arbitral jurisprudence model":

> Gap-filling procedures, now popularly known as "default rules," are used by arbitrators when evidence shows that the parties would have covered a particular subject matter if they had thought about it. The theory of default rules is that, to fill gaps, arbitrators automatically fall back on arbitral jurisprudence, unless the parties negotiated around established arbitral principles. After decades of evolution, arbitral principles are presumed to be reasonably fair and just. A party relying on an interpretation for filling a contractual gap that differs significantly from well-established arbitral jurisprudence bears the burden of proving that the parties intended to contract around a recognized gap-filler or default rule.
>
> . . . While the essence of gap-filling must be found in the parties' agreement, that essence "may include, implicitly or explicitly, an authorization for (the arbitrator) to draw upon a range of other sources, including statutory and decisional law."
>
> . . . This of course, does not mean that an arbitrator must assume the labor agreement covers every conceivable situation. Often the proper conclusion is that a silent contract has left management free to act unilaterally. In other words, an arbitrator must decide whether the agreement even has a gap and whether the parties already allocated a duty so that no gap-filling is necessary . . . .[54]

Many arbitrators have adopted the "bargaining model" approach, and, where reasonably possible, arbitrators consider what the parties would have agreed on, within the general framework of the agreement, had the matter specifically been before them.[55]

---

[54]THE COMMON LAW OF THE WORKPLACE §2.21, at 85–86 (St. Antoine ed., BNA Books 1998).

[55]*See, e.g.*, Silver Lake Bd. of Educ., Shawnee County, Kan., 88 LA 885, 888 (Madden, 1986) (held that "School Days" were days that included the minimum number of hours required for a school day in the Kansas statute, KAN. STAT. ANN. §72-1106); Oliver Rubber Co., 82 LA 38 (Daughton, 1984) (employer reasonably expected an explanation for employee absence, although not expressly called for in contractual call-in provision). *See also* Sterling Colo. Beef Co., 86 LA 866, 952 (Smith, 1986); Brooklyn Acres Mut. Homes, 84 LA 952, 955 (Abrams, 1985); Firestone Synthetic Rubber & Latex Co., 76 LA 968, 974 (Williams, 1981); Denman Rubber Mfg. Co., 72 LA 337, 339–40 (Dworkin, 1979); Honeymead Prods. Co., 69 LA 547, 550 (Hadlick, 1977); Midwest Rubber Reclaiming Co., 69 LA 198, 201 (Bernstein, 1977); Alexander's Pers. Providers, 68 LA 249, 253–54 (Katz, 1977); Hillbro Newspaper Printing Co., 48 LA 1304, 1317–18 (Jones, Jr., 1967); Wooster Sportswear Co., 46 LA 9, 11 (Dworkin, 1965); Tenneco Oil Co., 44 LA 1121, 1123 (Merrill, 1965); Rice Barton Corp., 44 LA 259, 262 (Seitz, 1964); Signal Oil & Gas Co., 43 LA 97, 101 (Block, 1964); Superior Prods. Co., 42 LA 517, 522–23 (Smith, 1964); Colonial Baking Co., 35 LA 686, 690 (Jones, Jr., 1960); Celanese Corp. of Am., 33 LA 925, 948 (Dash, Jr., 1959); Toledo Scale Co., 25 LA 94, 99 (McKelvey, 1955); American Iron & Mach. Works Co., 21 LA 129, 131 (Abernethy, 1953); Aladdin Indus., 18 LA 581, 583 (Hampton, 1952); Pacific Am. Shipowners Ass'n, 3 LA 383, 389 (Handsaker, 1946); Mueller, *The Law of Contracts—A Changing Legal Environment, in* TRUTH, LIE DETECTORS, AND OTHER PROBLEMS IN LABOR ARBITRATION, PROCEEDINGS OF THE 31ST ANNUAL MEETING OF NAA 204, 213–14 (Stern & Dennis eds., BNA Books 1979); Fleming, *Reflections on the Nature of Labor Arbitration*, 61 MICH. L. REV. 1245, 1250–52 (1963); Killingsworth, *Arbitration: Its Uses in Industrial Relations*, 21 LA 859, 861–62 (1953). Theodore J. St. Antoine stated that the arbitrator, as the parties' designated "reader" of the contract, "is their joint alter ego for the purpose of striking whatever supplementary bargain is necessary to handle the anticipated unanticipated omissions of the initial agreement." St. Antoine, *Judicial Review of Labor Arbitration Awards: A Second Look at Enterprise Wheel and Its Progeny, in* ARBITRATION—1977, PROCEEDINGS OF THE 30TH ANNUAL MEETING OF NAA 29, 30 (Dennis & Somers eds., BNA Books 1978) (also published in 75 MICH. L. REV. 1137 (1977)). Quoting this view with clear approval, see *Boise Cascade Corp. v. Steelworkers Local 7001*, 588 F.2d 127, 100 LRRM

Thus, words may be implied into an agreement with as much force and effect as if expressed therein if, from a consideration of the agreement as a whole, such inclusion by implication is called for.[56] For example, in one instance the arbitrator decided that the words "job classification" were impliedly meant to precede the phrase "hourly rates of pay."[57]

As to such situations, one survey of labor arbitration suggests:

> In such cases there is no true "intent" of the parties expressed in the agreement itself. What is asked of the arbitrator is that he conceive, or adopt from the arguments of counsel, a theory of the agreement which explains his solution to the matter not covered by the agreement, and which does no violence to the general spirit and intent which have been expressed in the agreement. The arbitrator's task might be described as having to find out what the parties would have intended had they thought to deal with the particular item under dispute, or if they had had time to deal with it. How to accomplish this procedurally becomes a cardinal task of arbitration.[58]

In one such case, the agreement expressly specified rail transport for orchestra members, no thought being given to air travel when the agreement was negotiated. When asked to decide whether the musicians could be *required* to fly on overseas trips, the arbitrator declared:

> [T]he arbitrator's responsibility here is not merely limited to searching for a mutual intent. He is not to throw up his hands and declare himself without authority to decide the case if he concludes that there is not any mutual intent on the point at issue. . . .
> This contract has the common definition of matters, which are subject to arbitration, describing them as "disputes regarding the interpretation *or application* of the provisions of this Agreement." The provisions must be *applied* to the dispute at hand, in a fair and sensible manner—the only restriction on the arbitrator is the usual admonition that his decision must not "have the effect of modifying or amending any provision of this Agreement."[59]

In holding that the members (with certain exceptions) could be required to fly, contrary to the position the union argued on a subsequent appeal, the arbitrator denied that he was "adding something" to the agreement.[60]

A similar approach was taken by another arbitrator when confronted with the question whether seniority rights would survive closure of a plant and transfer of its operations to the employer's other plant, where the multiemployer contract defined "seniority" as "length of service with the employing company in the plant involved." The arbitrator identified three possible options open to an arbitrator:

2481, 2483 (5th Cir. 1979). But for a discussion stressing that "the admonition that 'the arbitrator will not add to, subtract from, or modify this agreement' has meaning," and warning that there will be a "loss of confidence in the arbitration process" if arbitrators fail to exercise caution about filling gaps, see Adams, *Judical Review of Labor Arbitration Awards: A Second Look at* Enterprise Wheel *and Its Progeny: Comment, in* NAA 30TH PROCEEDINGS, at 52, 61.

[56]J.M. Huber, 5 LA 100, 103 (Shipman, 1946). *See also* Vickers, Inc., 15 LA 352, 356 (Platt, 1950).

[57]*J.M. Huber,* 5 LA at 103.

[58]Eaton, *Labor Arbitration in the San Francisco Bay Area,* 48 LA 1381, 1390 (1967). *See also* School City of Hobart, Ind., 109 LA 527, 532 (Goldstein, 1997); Stadiums Unlimited, 89 LA 1175, 1178–79 (Hayford, 1987); Super Valu Stores, 87 LA 453, 456–58 (Goldman, 1986).

[59]Philadelphia Orchestra Ass'n, 46 LA 513, 515 (Gill, 1966) (emphasis added).

[60]*Id.* at 517. The award withstood court challenge. Musicians Local 77 v. Philadelphia Orchestra Ass'n, 252 F. Supp. 787, 62 LRRM 2102 (E.D. Pa. 1966).

1. Give the contract language literal meaning;
2. View the contract as silent on the issue and hold the arbitrator to be without jurisdiction because resolving the question would violate the prohibition against adding to the agreement; or
3. Consider it incumbent on the arbitrator to give meaning to the term "plant" in the event of consolidation, though the present situation was not specifically contemplated in negotiations.[61]

The arbitrator chose the third approach. In doing so he stated:

> Arbitrators are constantly required and expected to give meaning to contract provisions which are unclear, in situations which were not specifically foreseen by the contract negotiators. So long as this is done by application of principles reasonably drawn from the provisions of the Agreement, and not by treating of a subject not covered at all by the Agreement, arbitral authority is not being improperly assumed.[62]

When filling gaps in the agreements between the parties, arbitrators often look to precedent established by other arbitrators.[63] However, arbitrators may refuse to fill gaps if convinced that to do so "would constitute contract-making" rather than contract interpretation or application.[64] In such cases, arbitrators often conclude that the dispute should be remanded to the parties to be resolved through negotiations because there was no mutual assent[65] and the arbitrator would be required to simply guess or legislate. In

---

[61]Superior Prods. Co., 42 LA 517, 522–23 (Smith, 1964). *See also* Trim Trends, 88 LA 1117, 1119–20 (Alexander, 1987).

[62]*Superior Prods.*, 42 LA at 523. *See also* Vindicator Printing Co., 48 LA 213, 218–19 (Smith, 1966).

[63]*See* Okonite Co., 112 LA 501 (Frockt, 1999) (sharing of filing fee); Commercial Intertech Corp., 111 LA 557 (Smith, 1998) (contracting); Central Armature Works, 111 LA 473 (Feldman, 1998) (time for filing grievance).

[64]Labor Standards Ass'n, 50 LA 1009, 1012 (Kates, 1968). *See also* Ava Foods, 87 LA 932, 936 (Hunter, 1986); Independent Sch. Dist. No. 47, 86 LA 97, 102 (Gallagher, 1985); McCreary Tire & Rubber Co., 85 LA 137, 138 (Fischer, 1985).

[65]*See* H.F. Behrhorst & Sons, 88 LA 972, 975 (Gates, 1986); Bunny Bread Co., 85 LA 1118, 1120 (Krislov, 1985); Mor Flo Indus., 83 LA 480, 482 (Cocalis, 1984); Consolidation Coal Co., 67 LA 257, 260 (Lubow, 1976); Hornell City Sch. Dist., 64 LA 1221, 1226 (Dennis, 1975); T&M Rubber Specialties Co., 54 LA 292, 297–98 (Sembower, 1971); Gulf Eng'g Co., 29 LA 188, 191 (Sweeney, 1957); Joliet City Lines, 20 LA 199, 201–02 (Garman, 1953); Eastern Stainless Steel Corp., 12 LA 709, 714 (Killingsworth, 1949); Cudahy Packing Co., 7 LA 507, 510 (Fisher, 1947); Rheem Mfg. Co., 7 LA 70, 74 (Killingsworth, 1947); Boston Sausage & Provision Co., 6 LA 667, 669 (Copelof, 1947). *See also* Snap-On Tools Corp., 75 LA 822, 824 (Cox, 1980); Georgia-Pacific Corp., 70 LA 633, 635 (Rayl, Jr., 1978); Tin Processing Corp., 20 LA 362, 363–64 (Johannes, 1953); Carlile & Doughty, 9 LA 239, 241 (Brandschain, 1947); Goodyear Tire & Rubber Co. of Ala., 1 LA 556, 560 (McCoy, 1946). *Cf.* Dayton Rubber Co., 19 LA 766, 767 (Lehoczky, 1952). The National Labor Relations Board (NLRB) has held that there was no binding agreement without a meeting of the minds. Computer Scis. Corp., 258 NLRB 641, 108 LRRM 1233, 1233 (1981); McKinzie Enters., 250 NLRB 29, 104 LRRM 1321, 1322 (1980). The "meeting of the minds" requirement was questioned by Garrett, *The Role of Lawyers in Arbitration*, *in* Arbitration and Public Policy, Proceedings of the 14th Annual Meeting of NAA 102, 121 (Pollard ed., BNA Books 1961). *See also* Consolidated Rail Corp. v. Railway Labor Executives' Ass'n, 491 U.S. 299, 317–18, 131 LRRM 2601, 2608 (1989) ("There need be no 'meeting of the minds' between the parties on the details of drug-testing methods or confidentiality standards for Conrail's current drug-testing program arguably to be justified by the parties' agreement."); Eastern Air Lines v. Air Line Pilots, 861 F.2d 1546, 1551, 130 LRRM 2284 (11th Cir. 1988) ("[T]he fact that two parties did not agree on all important terms at the time of contracting does not void the contract as a matter of course—parties can agree to dispense with agreement over the precise content of a particular substantive term.

any case, the arbitrator must give due consideration to contractual limitations on arbitral authority and avoid gap-filling that would result in a basic
addition to, subtraction from, or modification of the agreement.[66]

3. "Legislation" Versus "Interpretation"

Both the more literal, mechanical approach to agreement interpretation
and, at the other extreme, the indirect rewriting of the agreement by the
substitution of the arbitrator's views under the guise of interpretation harm
the collective bargaining process.[67] In regard to the latter danger, the U.S.
Supreme Court's *Enterprise Wheel*[68] doctrine limits the arbitrator's authority to interpret and apply the collective bargaining agreement:

> [A]n arbitrator is confined to interpretation and application of the collective
> bargaining agreement; he does not sit to dispense his own brand of industrial
> justice. He may of course look for guidance from many sources, yet his award is
> legitimate only so long as it draws its essence from the collective bargaining
> agreement. When the arbitrator's words manifest an infidelity to this obliga-
> tion, courts have no choice but to refuse enforcement of the award.[69]

Indeed, if the arbitrator's award does not "draw its essence" from the
collective bargaining agreement, it constitutes legislation rather than interpretation and will not be enforced by the courts.[70] The line between "interpretation" and "legislation," however, cannot be drawn with exactitude. One
arbitrator openly declared that, although the arbitration of a dispute must
be confined within the scope of the existing agreement, its adjudication necessitates some *legislating* to clarify and remove the uncertainties, obscuri-
ties, and ambiguities that exist in the agreement.[71] Another commentator

---

. . . [T]he provision that is 'material' is the actual agreement to postpone resolution of the
substantive term. Thus, the agreement to dispense with 'mutual assent' over a given term is
itself a product of 'mutual assent.'"). For related discussion, see Chapter 18., section 1.,
"Scope of Remedy Power," and section 1.C., "Scope of Remedy Power Limited by the Agreement"; Chapter 10, section 7., "Contract Principles."

[66]For cases in which the parties did give special authorization for the particular case, see
National Cleaning Contractors, 70 LA 917, 923 (Dworkin, 1978); *Standard Oil Co.*, 24 LA
424, 425 (Beatty, 1954); *Munising Wood Prods. Co.*, 22 LA 769, 771 (Ryder, 1954). *See also*
Bethlehem Steel Corp., 87 LA 887, 888 (Valtin, 1986).

[67]National Tube Co., 11 LA 378, 380 (Seward, 1948).

[68]Steelworkers v. Enterprise Wheel & Car Corp., 363 U.S. 593, 46 LRRM 2423 (1960).

[69]*Id.* at 597, 46 LRRM at 2425.

[70]The *Enterprise Wheel* doctrine has been recognized as limiting the arbitrator's author-
ity in *Paperworkers v. Misco, Inc.*, 484 U.S. 29, 126 LRRM 3113 (1987) (applying *Enterprise
Wheel* doctrine), and in the following arbitrations: American Petrofina Co. of Tex., 92 LA 578,
583 (Dunn, 1989); Department of Labor, 92 LA 477, 482 (Grossman, 1989); Cleveland Twist
Drill Co., 92 LA 105, 108 (Strasshofer, 1989); Geauga Co., 92 LA 54, 59 (Fullmer, 1988);
Checker Motors Co., 91 LA 1198, 1201 (Lipson, 1988); Harvard Indus., 91 LA 849, 855
(Ellmann, 1988); Rolling Acres Care Ctr., 91 LA 795, 799 (Dworkin, 1988); Arizona Bank, 91
LA 772, 774 (Fine, 1988); Polysar, Inc., 91 LA 482, 484 (Strasshofer, 1988); Glover Bottled
Gas Corp./Synergy Gas Corp., 91 LA 77, 91 (Simons, 1987); TPC Liquidation, 88 LA 696, 699
(Lumbley, 1987); Schuykill Valley Sch. Dist., 87 LA 1190, 1191 (Zirkel, 1986); Airco Carbon,
86 LA 6, 9 (Dworkin, 1986); Lithonia Lighting Co., 85 LA 627, 629 (Volz, 1985); May Dep't
Stores, 84 LA 53, 55–56 (Morgan, 1985).

[71]Borg-Warner Corp., 3 LA 423, 428–29 (Gilden, 1944). *See also* Madison Warehouse
Corp., 112 LA 300, 306 (Suardi, 1998) ("Judges and arbitrators frequently impose obliga-
tions on contracting parties that they did not believe they had undertaken."); Capitol Barg
Dry Cleaning Co., 8 LA 586, 588–89 (Rice, 1947).

has suggested that it is not only expected that something of the arbitrator's personality will "creep into the decision," but that this is quite necessary.[72] Advocating the exercise of judgment by arbitrators, one commentator pointed to what he viewed as the "inescapable truth":

> [T]he ultimate responsibility of an arbitrator in the interpretive process is to rely on his or her background of experience or expertise in the collective bargaining process, with due regard to the relationship of the given parties and their presentations so as to provide as practical and realistic an interpretation as is possible under the given agreement.[73]

Rejecting what he deemed the "myths" of contract interpretation, the commentator gave Shakespearean advice to future arbitrators: "'And this above all, to thine own self be true and it must follow as the night the day that thou canst not then be false to any man.'"[74]

Despite such "activist" attitudes, most arbitrators view the scope of their authority as limited to the extent described by another arbitrator:

> [The arbitrator's] function is not to rewrite that Agreement and certainly it is not to suggest, imply nor to inform the Parties of what changes should be effected, renegotiated or changed even if his sense of justice and fairness so dictate, or even if he believes the Agreement contains inequities. Nor can the Arbitrator allow the economic consequences of an Award [to] influence him in his ultimate decision. The Arbitrator's Award . . . must derive its essence from the Agreement, and . . . tell the Parties what they can or cannot do inside of that Agreement.[75]

A. Rules to Aid Interpretation

While the "overarching principle of contract interpretation" requires ascertainment of meaning in light of "all the relevant circumstances surrounding the transaction,"[76]

> [c]ourts start with the assumption that the parties have used the language in the way that reasonable persons ordinarily do. . . . The process of interpreta-

---

[72]Garrett, *Contract Interpretation: I. The Interpretive Process: Myths and Reality, in* ARBITRATION 1985: LAW AND PRACTICE, PROCEEDINGS OF THE 38TH ANNUAL MEETING OF NAA 121 (Gershenfeld ed., BNA Books 1986). Arbitrators, however, must give due consideration to contractual limitations on their authority. *See* Macomb County, Mich., 96 LA 130, 132 (Glazer, 1990); Potlatch Corp., 95 LA 737, 742 (Goodstein, 1990); Dalfort Aviation Servs., 94 LA 1136, 1144 (Allen, Jr., 1990); Kimstock, Inc., 94 LA 387, 389 (Gentile, 1990); Kendall Mills, 8 LA 306, 309 (Lane, 1947). *See also* Conagra, Inc., 70 LA 1296, 1299 (Levy, 1978); Janitrol Aero Div., 47 LA 667, 668 (Boehm, 1966).

[73]Garrett, NAA 38TH PROCEEDINGS, at 143.

[74]*Id.* at 148 (quoting from *Hamlet*, act I, scene iii).

[75]Lorillard, Inc., 87 LA 507, 512 (Chalfie, 1986). *See also* Dalfort Aviation Servs., 94 LA 1136, 1144 (Allen, Jr., 1990) (arbitrators are not empowered to "impose" or "create" contractual obligations that are not set forth in the agreement itself). *Accord* Sanyo Mfg. Corp., 109 LA 184, 192 (Howell, 1997). *See also* Hibbing Ready Mix, 97 LA 248, 251 (Imes, 1991); Sherwin-Williams Co., 92 LA 464, 470 (Allen, Jr., 1989) (arbitrator refused to "fill gaps" and remanded issue to negotiation, where there was no "meeting of minds," no applicable past practice, and no dictionary definition of ambiguous term); Pollock Co., 87 LA 325, 335 (Oberdank, 1986); Associated Grocers, 86 LA 895, 903 (Weizenbaum, 1985); RRS, Inc., 86 LA 664, 666 (Redel, 1985); Goodyear Aerospace Corp., 86 LA 584, 586 (Fullmer, 1985); Brooklyn Acres Mut. Homes, 84 LA 952, 955 (Abrams, 1985).

[76]FARNSWORTH, CONTRACTS §7.10, at 467 (3d ed. 1999).

tion therefore turns in good part on what the courts regards as normal habits in the use of language, habits that would be expected of reasonable persons in the circumstances of the parties. . . . Some of the assumptions that courts make as to normal habits in the use of language are so widely shared and so frequently articulated that they have come to be regarded as rules of contract interpretation. Some of these rules had been encapsulated in Latin maxims that have a special ring of authority, albeit sometimes a hollow one. None of these rules, however, has a validity beyond that of its underlying assumptions.[77]

The rules so formulated are used both in determining what meanings are reasonably possible and in choosing among possible meaning.[78] Sometimes two or more of the rules of interpretation conflict in a given case. Where this is so, the arbitrator is free to apply whichever rule seems to produce the most reasonable result.[79] Sometimes, however, a combination of two or more of the standards may be applied consistently in construing an ambiguous word or clause. The statement of Mr. Justice Holmes, that "it is not an adequate discharge of duty for courts to say: We see what you are driving at, but you have not said it, and therefore we shall go on as before,"[80] appears to express the attitude of many arbitrators who strive to determine what the parties were driving at and to effectuate their intent.

i.   Giving Words Their Normal or Technical Meaning

Arbitrators give words their ordinary and popularly accepted meaning in the absence of a variant contract definition, or extrinsic evidence indicating that they were used in a different sense or that the parties intended some special colloquial meaning.[81] Consequently, in the absence of such evi-

---

[77]*Id.* §7.11, at 469–70.

[78]Restatement (Second) of Contracts §202 (1979). Citing additional legal authorities and offering a summarized list of interpretation standards, see *Tri-County Metro. Transp. Dist. of Or.*, 68 LA 1369, 1370–71 (Tilbury, 1977); *Moran Towing & Transp. Co.*, 1 ALAA ¶67,012, at 67,015 (Kidd, 1944). This view is practiced by many arbitrators, but there have been occasional expressions of doubt. *See* Crescent Warehouse Co., 10 LA 168, 171 (Aaron, 1948). Some parties expressly provide that in reaching a decision, the arbitrator shall use the standards of interpretation used by courts. Even without such express provision, use of those standards by arbitrators is proper and often will strengthen the award. *See* Smith Steel Workers, DALU 19806 v. A.O. Smith Corp., 626 F.2d 596, 105 LRRM 2044, 2045–46 (7th Cir. 1980); Johnson Bronze Co. v. Auto Workers, 621 F.2d 81, 104 LRRM 2378, 2380 (3d Cir. 1980). Standards of construction are aids to the ascertainment of intent, not means to defeat intent. Republic Steel Corp., 5 LA 609, 614 (McCoy, 1946).

[79]*See, e.g.*, Inspiration Consol. Copper Co., 50 LA 58, 62 (Block, 1968).

[80]Johnson v. United States, 163 F. 30, 32 (1st Cir. 1908).

[81]Quadcom 9-1-1 Pub. Safety Communications Sys., 113 LA 987, 991–92 (Goldstein, 1999); City of Independence, Mo., 111 LA 637, 640 (Neas, 1998); Gerber Prods. Co., 111 LA 344, 346–48 (Knott, 1998); Kaiser Permanente, 100 LA 119, 120 (Knowlton, 1992) (finding that the term "physical disability," by its plain meaning, does not include mental illness). Other cases applying this principle include: Metro Transit Auth., 94 LA 349, 352 (Richard, 1990); Vermont Dep't of Corr., 93 LA 595, 597 (Toepfer, 1989); Prime Health, 93 LA 334, 337 (Clark, 1989); Newaygo County Rd. Comm'n, 92 LA 918, 921 (Brown, 1989); Gulf Printing Co., 92 LA 893, 895 (King, 1989) (finding that "three consecutive days" means 3 days in succession without regard to any modifier such as "work"); Rogers-Wayne Metal Prods. Co., 92 LA 882, 887 (House, 1989); West Penn Power Co., 92 LA 644, 647 (Dworkin, 1989); College Cmty. Sch. Dist., 91 LA 610, 612 (Madden, 1988); Orange Unified Sch. Dist., 91 LA 525, 527 (Collins, 1988); Montana Power Co., 90 LA 932, 933 (Corbett, 1987); Kentucky Ctr. for the Performing Arts, 89 LA 344, 348 (Volz, 1987); Mentor Bd. of Educ., 89 LA 292, 294 (Sharpe, 1987); Coca-Cola Foods, 88 LA 129, 131 (Naehring, 1986); Anaheim Union High Sch. Dist., 84 LA 101,

dence when each of the parties has a different understanding of what is intended by certain contract language, the party whose understanding is in accord with the ordinary meaning of that language is entitled to prevail.[82]

Arbitrators often apply their understanding of words or phrases in the contract without citing any authority.[83] One arbitrator determined that a provision awarding administrative leave with pay when an employee was requested or subpoenaed to appear before a court as a witness *for the People* did not apply when the employee was called to testify on behalf of a party in a general civil case.[84] In another case, the arbitrator stated that "[u]nless specifically and mutually accepted by the parties as an illness qualifying for sick leave, the definition of illness may not be expanded to include intoxication."[85]

Many arbitrators apply a "reasonable man standard" in interpreting words or phrases in collective bargaining agreements.[86] For instance, the word "may" was "reasonably" given its ordinary "permissive" meaning in the

---

104 (Chance, 1984) (finding parties intended a special colloquial meaning for "on site" file). *See also* Mesker Indus., 85 LA 921, 928 (Mikrut, 1985); Wagner Castings Co., 83 LA 507, 511 (Talent, 1984). In *L&O Growers Ass'n*, 82 LA 814 (Weiss, 1984), the company advanced an argument that lemon trees and orange trees were intended to be treated differently with regard to "wet time," that is, the time during which a worker is prevented from working by excessive moisture on the trees. The company focused on the fact that lemons rot when they are wet and oranges do not, suggesting that such knowledge was intended to be understood in the contract. The arbitrator rejected this argument, concluding that "[w]etness on orange trees is not any different than wetness on lemon trees when it comes to the question of whether 'a worker is prevented from working.' Thus, the clear meaning of the language is in accord with its reasonable and common-sense interpretation." *Id.* at 815. In *Vlasic Foods*, 74 LA 1214 (Lipson, 1980), the arbitrator drew a distinction between (1) situations in which parties allegedly have amended clear language by past practice, and (2) situations in which the parties in negotiating their agreement never intended that certain words were to carry their ordinary meaning. He concluded that in the case before him, "where the evidence is overwhelming that something other than the ordinary meaning was intended, the application of the words in said [special] sense does not manifest an infidelity to the contract but indeed carries out the agreement of the parties." *Id.* at 1217–18. *Accord* Schnadig Corp., 83 LA 1194, 1197 (Goldman, 1984); Walton Labs., 47 LA 375, 377 (Yagoda, 1966); Great Lakes Dredge & Dock Co., 5 LA 409, 410 (Kelliher, 1946). In *Emerson Electric Co.*, 84 LA 1014, 1016 (Cohen, 1985), the context did indicate to the arbitrator that the parties, in using the term "plant" to indicate the coverage of the collective bargaining agreement, meant "a production facility and not just a 'general facility'"; thus, he held that custodial or maintenance personnel who work in a facility that is solely office space and has no production activity in it are not covered by this agreement.

[82]Stuart Hall Co., 86 LA 370, 372 (Madden, 1985). *Cf.* City of Sandusky, Ohio, 98 LA 519, 523 (McDonald, 1992) (moving party has burden of proving its contract interpretation); Gulf Printing Co., 92 LA 893, 895 (King, 1989) (burden falls on party contending for a construction other than that based on ordinary meaning to prove that special circumstances exist warranting particular construction).

[83]*See, e.g.*, Summit County, Ohio, Bd. of Mental Retardation & Developmental Disabilities, 100 LA 4, 10 (Dworkin, 1992) (arbitrator applied his understanding of "reasonable grounds to believe"); Campbell Soup Co., 99 LA 1097, 1105 (Allen, Jr., 1992) (interpreting "available work"); Department of the Navy, 86 LA 92, 96 (Connors, 1985) (arbitrator applied "most common meaning" of the words "discuss" and "negotiate"); Mid-America Canning Corp., 85 LA 900, 904 (Imundo, 1985) (arbitrator applied his understanding of meaning of "one full calendar year of active employment").

[84]Michigan Dep't of Soc. Servs., 82 LA 114 (Fieger, 1983).

[85]Air Force Logistics Command, 85 LA 735, 737 (Dilts, 1985).

[86]*See, e.g.*, Allied-Signal, Inc., 99 LA 284, 286 (Brisco, 1992) (arbitrator must give ambiguous language reasonable construction); California State Univ., 86 LA 549, 555 (Koven, 1986) ("In the absence of any agreed-upon definition by the parties themselves, an arbitrator cannot formulate a definition for all times and for every situation. Instead, that term must

absence of strong evidence that a mandatory meaning was intended.[87] In another case, the word "day" or "workday" was "reasonably" interpreted as a calendar day, from midnight to midnight.[88]

a. Trade or Technical Terms

When it comes to trade or technical terms, arbitrators follow a parallel principle and interpret them in the appropriate specialized sense unless the contract defines them differently, or extrinsic evidence proves they were used otherwise. For instance, the term "union shop" was applied in the sense commonly used in labor circles instead of in a special sense (which would not have required maintenance of membership) urged by management; the arbitrator declared that if the employer did not intend or understand the meaning of the term as it is expressed in collective bargaining and industrial relations parlance, it should not have let it be used in the contract.[89] Under similar reasoning, the term "regular hourly rate" was given its generally accepted meaning in industry.[90] However, an arbitrator gave a medical term its popular meaning after he "conducted his own 'Gall[o]p Poll'" with laymen, who all agreed as to the meaning of the disputed term; he assumed, absent proof to the contrary, that the negotiators were laymen.[91]

b. Use of Dictionary Definitions

Arbitrators often have ruled that, in the absence of a showing of mutual understanding of the parties to the contrary, the usual and ordinary definition of terms as defined by a reliable dictionary should govern.[92] The use of dictionary definitions in arbitral opinions provides a neutral interpretation

---

be defined in terms of what a reasonable person would deem to be 'careful consideration' under a particular set of facts."); Container Corp. of Am., 84 LA 604, 607 (Allen, Jr., 1985) (application of the "reasonable man" interpretation of a word in the collective bargaining agreement instead of an interpretation that would stretch or torture the term). *Westvaco*, 83 LA 904, 907 (Heekin, 1984), involved the assignment of mandatory overtime "with proper notice." The arbitrator determined that the *basic implication* of the common phrase "with proper notice" was that an employee should have enough time to become reasonably prepared for such assignment.

[87]*See* Social Sec. Admin., 87 LA 1096, 1098 (Avins, 1986); Federal Stampings, 84 LA 438, 442 (Jacobowski, 1985); Social Sec. Admin., 76 LA 569, 571 (McDonald, 1981); M.H. Rhodes, Inc., 25 LA 243, 246 (Hogan, 1955); Continental Oil Co., 22 LA 880, 881 (Reynard, 1954). *Cf.* U.S. Army Forces Command, 84 LA 1093, 1097 (Alsher, 1985).

[88]*See* Liberty, Ohio, Local Bd. of Educ., 112 LA 27, 31 (Morgan, Jr., 1999); AMF W. Tool, 49 LA 718, 723 (Solomon, 1967) (and cases cited therein). In *Pratt & Lambert*, 76 LA 685, 690 (Denson, 1981), the word "month" was given its ordinary meaning of "calendar" month.

[89]Safeway Stores, 1 ALAA ¶67,096, at 67,169 (Carmichael, 1944). *See also* Columbian Carbon Co., 47 LA 1120, 1125 (Merrill, 1967) (applying a term in its technical sense). *Cf.* Northway Prods. Co., 39 LA 791, 794–95 (Sullivan, 1962). In *Southern New England Tel. Co.*, 61 LA 184, 187 (Zack, 1973), the arbitrator reasoned that the term "hired" should be viewed in its labor relations context and not in its ordinary dictionary usage.

[90]R.M.F., Inc., 50 LA 789, 790 (Sherman, 1968). *See also* Kentucky Ctr. for the Performing Arts, 89 LA 344, 348 (Volz, 1987) (giving the term "rehearsal" its industry meaning).

[91]American Synthetic Rubber Co., 50 LA 25, 30 (Kesselman, 1967) (discussing meaning of term "oral surgery").

[92]*See, e.g.*, Bureau of Engraving, 114 LA 598, 670–71 (Bard, 2000); Cardinal Foods, 90 LA 521, 525 (Dworkin, 1988); Steel Valley Sch. Dist., 84 LA 1178 (Stoltenberg, 1985); Consolidation Coal Co., 84 LA 36 (Rybolt, 1984); Department of Health, Educ. & Welfare, 72 LA 788, 794 (Hayes, 1979); Pana Ref. Co., 47 LA 193, 195 (Traynor, 1966); Capitol Mfg. Co., 46

of a word or phrase that carries the air of authority.[93] If the parties have defined a word or phrase in their agreement, however, an arbitrator should not look outside the agreement for a definition.[94] An examination of the entire agreement and its application to the subject matter under consideration may result in the interpretation of words not in the general dictionary sense, but in a mutually agreed sense.[95] In any event, dictionary definitions may be considered simply "as an aid" to the arbitrator in the search for meaning.[96] As Judge Learned Hand aptly observed: "[I]t is one of the surest in-

---

LA 633, 635–36 (Gibson, 1966); Combustion Eng'g, 46 LA 289, 292 (Murphy, 1966); Wallingford Steel Co., 29 LA 597, 603 (Cahn, 1957); International Paper Co., 23 LA 497, 500 (Hebert, 1954); Firestone Tire & Rubber Co., 20 LA 880, 888 (Gorder, 1953); National Lock Co., 18 LA 459, 461 (Luskin, 1952).

[93]Arbitrators have consulted standard dictionaries in *General Servs. Admin.*, 97 LA 1218, 1221 (Hooper, 1991); *VME Am.*, 97 LA 137, 138 (Bittel, 1991) (using *Webster's Collegiate Dictionary* to discern meaning of "consult"); *Pacific Bell*, 93 LA 1199, 1202 (Freeman, 1989); *Pepsi Cola Bottling Co. of San Diego*, 93 LA 520, 524 (Randall, 1989); *Internal Revenue Serv.*, 93 LA 261, 272 (Dilts, 1989); *Courier Journal*, 93 LA 227, 232 (Tharp, 1989); *Sam Blount Co.*, 93 LA 209, 213 (Holley, Jr., 1989); *Food Barn Stores*, 93 LA 87, 89 (Fogelberg, 1989); *Texas Util. Generating Div.*, 92 LA 1308, 1313 (McDermott, 1989); *City of Wayzata, Minn.*, 92 LA 664, 666 (Fogelberg, 1989); *Grain Processing Corp.*, 92 LA 265, 269–70 (Hilgert, 1989); *Hartman Elec. Mfg.*, 92 LA 253, 255 (Rybolt, 1989); *City of Dinuba, Cal., Elementary Sch. Dist.*, 91 LA 1397, 1399 (Rothstein, 1989); *Baltimore Sun*, 91 LA 1133, 1138 (Wahl, 1988); *Harvard Indus.*, 91 LA 849, 853 (Ellmann, 1988); *Rolling Acres Care Ctr.*, 91 LA 795, 800 (Dworkin, 1988); *College Cmty. Sch. Dist.*, 91 LA 610, 612 (Madden, 1988); *Champion Int'l Corp.*, 91 LA 245, 250–51 (Duda, Jr., 1988); *Steelworkers*, 89-1 ARB ¶8303 (Holley, 1988) (arbitrator consulted *The New Webster Encyclopedia Dictionary* and *Webster's Seventh New Collegiate Dictionary* for the meaning of "incidental"). Other decisions where arbitrators used dictionary definitions include: *West Va. Wesleyan Coll.*, 90 LA 1103, 1105 (Duff, 1988); *Cardinal Foods*, 90 LA at 526; *Crown Cork & Seal Co.*, 90 LA 329, 331–32 (Kapsch, Sr., 1987); *City of Elyria, Ohio*, 90 LA 292, 295 (Dworkin, 1987); *Naval Med. Clinic*, 90 LA 137, 143 (Rothschild, 1987); *Associated Milk Producers*, 89 LA 1186, 1191 (Wyman, 1987) (arbitrator looked to *Webster's New Collegiate Dictionary* to define "maintain" and "amendment"); *Spartan Printing Co.*, 89 LA 605, 608 (Flaten, 1987) (arbitrator looked to *Webster's New Collegiate Dictionary* to define "concurrent"); *Warner Press*, 89 LA 577, 580 (Brunner, 1987) (arbitrator looked to *Webster's New Collegiate Dictionary* and *Black's Law Dictionary* to define "possible"); *City of Cadillac, Mich.*, 88 LA 924, 926 (Huston, 1987) (arbitrator looked to *Webster's Third International Dictionary* to define "leave of absence"); *Pabst Brewing Co.*, 88 LA 656, 660 (Wyman, 1987); *Homestake Mining Co.*, 88 LA 614, 616 (Sinicropi, 1987) (arbitrator looked to the *Random House Dictionary* to define "permanent" and "temporary"); *Derby Cap Mfg. Co.*, 87 LA 1042, 1047 (Imundo, Jr., 1986) (arbitrator looked to dictionary definition of term "spouse"); *Kroger Co.*, 85 LA 1198, 1201 (St. Antoine, 1985) (arbitrator looked to *Webster's International Dictionaries* and *Black's Law Dictionary* for meaning of the phrase "and/or"); *Albright & Wilson*, 85 LA 908 (Shanker, 1985) (arbitrator looked to standard dictionary definition of "inadvertent"); *Dubuque, Iowa, Cmty. Sch. Dist.*, 85 LA 636, 638 (Dilts, 1985) (arbitrator looked to *Webster's Dictionary* to define word "comparable" as used in requirement that health insurance benefits be comparable to those in stated policy); *American Foundry & Mfg. Co.*, 83 LA 525, 528 (Newmark, 1984) (arbitrator looked to *Webster's New Collegiate Dictionary* for definition of "immediate").

[94]*See City of Duluth, Minn.*, 100 LA 309, 312 (Ver Ploeg, 1992) (although dictionary definitions were "helpful," arbitrator found that reference to other contract provision provided more guidance).

[95]*See Fran Jom, Inc.*, 75 LA 97, 99 (Siegel, 1980); *Moran Towing & Transp. Co.*, 1 ALAA ¶67,012 (Kidd, 1944).

[96]*Cincinnati Post & Times Star*, 68 LA 129, 138 (Chalfie, 1977). *See also Belknap, Inc.*, 69 LA 599, 601 (Teple, 1977); *Herbert Materials*, 69 LA 286, 289 (Roberts, 1977); *Thunderbird Hotel*, 69 LA 10, 13 (Weiss, 1977). Where the dictionary gives several definitions for the word in question, the arbitrator, of course, will select the one that is most applicable and appropriate to the subject matter of the grievance. *E.g., Area Educ. Agency 13*, 70 LA 555, 558 (Smith, 1978).

dexes of a mature and developed jurisprudence not to make a fortress out of the dictionary."[97]

Furthermore, it sometimes happens that dictionary definitions can be found to cover opposing contentions.[98] In such situations (and indeed ordinarily), it is desirable that interpretations not rest on dictionary definitions alone, but be additionally supported by other considerations, especially where the persons drafting the agreement were laymen untrained in the precise use of words.[99] Where the arbitrator is faced with "words of art" or technical terms, the use of a standard dictionary is inappropriate.[100] Instead, trade or technical terms of a particular industry may be interpreted by resort to a special dictionary for that industry,[101] and a labor relations dictionary may be used for general industrial terms.[102] In construing a term used in an employee medical benefits provision, the arbitrator found the definition contained in a medical dictionary more reliable than that contained in a general dictionary.[103]

c. *Keeping Meaning Consistent Throughout Collective Bargaining Agreement*

Whether the words are "ordinary" or of a technical nature, it is said to be "a well recognized rule of construction that a word used by the parties in one sense is to be interpreted, in the absence of countervailing reasons, as employed in the same sense throughout the writing."[104] Use of two different terms may be held to imply different meanings.[105]

---

[97]Cabell v. Markham, 148 F.2d 737, 739 (2d Cir.), *aff'd*, 326 U.S. 404 (1945). *See also* Giuseppi v. Walling, 144 F.2d 608, 624 (2d Cir. 1944) (Hand, J., concurring) ("there is no surer way to misread any document than to read it literally").

[98]*See* Atlanta Newspapers, 20 LA 809, 817 (Dworet, 1953). *See also* Federal-Mogul Corp., 61 LA 745, 749 (Cole, 1973).

[99]*See* Lavoris Co., 16 LA 173, 175 (Lockhart, 1951); International Harvester Co., 12 LA 650, 652 (McCoy, 1949); U.S. Pipe & Foundry Co., 5 LA 492, 494 (McCoy, 1946).

[100]Rival Mfg. Co., 99 LA 743, 744 (Thornell, 1992) (using *Black's Law Dictionary*); Hughes Mkts., 97 LA 912, 917 (Prayzich, 1991) (arbitrator consulted *Black's Law Dictionary* for definition of "dishonesty"); Hillel Day Sch. of Metro. Detroit, 89 LA 905, 908 (Lipson, 1987) (arbitrator looked to *Black's Law Dictionary* to define "family"); Flowers Baking Co., 89 LA 666, 670 (Rice, 1987) (arbitrator looked to *Roberts' Dictionary of Industrial Relations* to define "full-time job"); Ramsey County, St. Paul, Minn., 88 LA 1103, 1106 (Miller, 1987) (arbitrator looked to *Roberts' Dictionary of Industrial Relations* and *Black's Law Dictionary* to define "just cause"); Waverly Cmty. Unit Sch. Dist. 6, 88 LA 688, 691 (Berman, 1986) (arbitrator looked to *Roberts' Dictionary of Industrial Relations* to define "salary," "wage," and "fringe benefits"); Hartz Mountain Indianapolis Branch Warehouse, 86 LA 1137, 1138 (Seidman, 1986) (arbitrator looked to *Black's Law Dictionary* for definition of "day"); Dillon Stores Co., 84 LA 84, 88 (Woolf, 1984) (arbitrator consulted *Bouvier's Law Dictionary* for the definition of "promissory estoppel").

[101]Columbian Carbon Co., 47 LA 1120, 1125 (Merrill, 1967).

[102]Sam Blount Co., 93 LA 209 (Holley, Jr., 1989); National Can Corp., 70 LA 1268, 1269 (Boner, 1978); Wisconsin Porcelain Co., 36 LA 485, 487 (Anderson, 1961).

[103]Crown Cork & Seal Co., 90 LA 329 (Kapsch, Sr., 1987).

[104]Vickers, Inc., 15 LA 352, 356 (Platt, 1950). *See also* Gooch Foods, 93 LA 28 (Smith, 1989); California Drilling & Blasting Co., 91 LA 66, 68 (Weiss, 1988); Consolidation Coal Co., 89 LA 179, 182 (Wren, 1987); Ford Motor Co., 48 LA 1213, 1215 (Platt, 1967).

[105]*See* Ames Dep't Stores, 90 LA 452 (Shanker, 1988); Hanz Trucking, 46 LA 1057, 1062 (Anderson, 1966) (the contract used two different terms in setting up hourly pay rates for the same work performed under different circumstances). *Cf.* Borden Co., 36 LA 496, 500–01 (Morvant, 1961).

When parties have changed the language of their agreement, arbitrators presume that they intended a changed meaning.[106] By the same token, continued use of certain key terms in successive agreements justified a party's assumption that no change in meaning was intended by the other party that had failed to state otherwise in negotiations.[107]

ii.   *Precontract Negotiations and Bargaining History*
[LA CDI 24.37]

Precontract negotiations frequently offer a valuable aid in the interpretation of ambiguous provisions.[108] Where the meaning of a term is in dispute, it will be deemed, if there is no evidence to the contrary, that the parties intended it to have the same meaning as that given it during the negotiations leading up to the agreement.[109] Indeed, even evidence of

---

[106]*See* Lyondell Petrochemical Co., 89 LA 95 (Caraway, 1987); King County Fire Prot. Dist. No. 39, 86 LA 640 (Lang, 1985); Midwest Printing Co., 85 LA 615 (Ver Ploeg, 1985); Carling Brewing Co., 46 LA 715, 717 (Kates, 1966); Capital Cities Broad. Corp., 44 LA 861, 865 (Kates, 1965); Douglas Aircraft Co., 40 LA 201, 204 (Prasow, 1962); Deep Rock Oil Co., 20 LA 865, 867 (Emery, 1953). In *Lakeside Malleable Casting Co.*, 48 LA 1104, 1106 (Anderson, 1967), the deletion of an express exception was deemed a clear indication of intent to abolish the exception. *Cf.* Chromalloy Div.-Okla., 71 LA 1178, 1180 (Barnhart, 1978). Where two provisions of a contract were contradictory, the one adopted later in point of time was held controlling. National Distillers Prods. Co., 53 LA 477, 479 (Jones, Jr., 1969).

[107]Coordinating Comm. Steel Cos., 70 LA 442, 454 (Aaron, 1978). *See also* City of Baltimore, Md., 91 LA 425 (Craver, 1988); Minnesota State Bd. for Cmty. Colls., 84 LA 307 (Gallagher, 1985).

[108]FARNSWORTH, CONTRACTS §7.12 (3d ed. 1999). Arbitrators consider bargaining history and past practice as interpretive aids. Downingtown Sch. Dist., 88 LA 59, 61 (Zirkel, 1986). *See* John F. Kennedy Ctr. for the Performing Arts, 101 LA 174, 179 (Ables, 1993) ("Prior negotiations, discussions, meetings, complaints, grievances, unfair labor practice charges, disputes in arbitration or in court, leave foot-prints on what is troubling parties in a collective bargaining relationship."); Kohlenberger Eng'g Corp., 12 LA 380 (Prasow, 1949); BASF Wyandotte Corp., 77 LA 492 (Liebowitz, 1981). *See also* Lackawanna Leather, 113 LA 603, 608 (Pelofsky, 1999); Youngstown City Sch. Dist., 99 LA 169, 170 (Richard, 1992); Mentor Bd. of Educ., 89 LA 292, 294 (Sharpe, 1987); Sacramento City Unified Sch. Dist., 88 LA 113, 116 (Wilcox, 1986); Pittsburgh Brewing Co., 88 LA 95, 96 (Duff, 1986). Significantly, the types of bargaining history considered vary. *See, e.g.*, Copper & Brass Sales, 105 LA 730 (Nelson, 1995) (considering employer's statements and amended proposal); National Steel Corp., 102 LA 1159 (Garrett, 1994) (considering employer's internal memoranda); City of Columbus, Ohio, 102 LA 477 (Kindig, 1994) (considering employer's rejection of union proposal); Atascadero Unified Sch. Dist., 101 LA 673 (Bickner, 1993).

[109]Schnuck Mkts., 107 LA 739 (Cipolla, 1996); Copper & Brass Sales, 105 LA 730 (Nelson, 1995); Everfresh Beverages, 104 LA 577 (Ellmann, 1994); Rhone-Poulenc, 103 LA 1085 (Bernstein, 1994); National Steel Corp., 102 LA 1159 (Garrett, 1994); United Can Co., 102 LA 806 (Hoh, 1993); Taylorville Cmty. Unit Sch. Dist. 3, 102 LA 367 (Nathan, 1993); Atascadero Unified Sch. Dist., 101 LA 673 (Bickner, 1993); State of Ohio, 100 LA 125 (Graham, 1992); City of Roseburg, Or., 97 LA 262 (Wilkinson, 1991); Schauer Mfg. Corp., 94 LA 1116 (Dworkin, 1990); Atlanta Wire Works, 93 LA 537 (Williams, 1989); Milford Cmty. Sch. Dist., 89-1 ARB ¶8060 (Baron, 1988); E.M. Smith & Co., 88 LA 1124 (Dworkin, 1987); Downingtown Sch. Dist., 88 LA 59 (Zirkel, 1986); Pacific Southwest Airlines, 86 LA 437 (Darrow, 1985); Southern Ind. Gas & Elec. Co., 86 LA 342 (Schedler, 1985); Midwest Printing Co., 85 LA 615 (Ver Ploeg, 1985); W.E. Plechaty Co., 84 LA 571 (Duda, Jr., 1985); Ferry-Morse Seed Co., 84 LA 75 (Duda, Jr., 1984); N-Ren Corp. S., 81 LA 438 (Boyer, 1983); Maine Employment Sec. Comm'n, 74 LA 17 (Babiskin, 1980). *But see* Giant Cement Co., 103 LA 146, 147 n.1 (Nolan, 1994) (refusing to consider union negotiator's statements to members before ratification vote and evidence of informal discussions because contract contained clause that provided that the "parties' proposals and counterproposals shall not be referred to, in

subsequent negotiations may establish the prior understanding of the parties.[110]

a. *Proposed Clause Rejected or Withdrawn* [LA CDI 24.37]

If a party attempts, but fails, in contract negotiations, to include a specific provision in the agreement, arbitrators will hesitate to read such provision into the agreement through the process of interpretation.[111] In a nutshell, a party may not obtain "through arbitration what it could not acquire through negotiation."[112] One arbitrator explained that "there is a hazard" in making a specific contract demand in negotiations:

> If the provision gets caught up in a grievance, the Party who proffers the language will have to bear the burden of demonstrating in a later arbitration proceeding that its omission ought not to be given its normal significance. Normally, of course, the plain inference of the omission is that the intent to reject prevailed over the intent to include.[113]

Where a union had consistently proposed a seniority requirement for entitlement to overtime in different contract negotiations over a period of

---

any way, in arbitration"). Sometimes, however, little may actually have been said on a provision during the negotiations, and, even where it is accepted that there were discussions, there may be little evidence of what was actually said at the time. In *City of Williamsport*, 68 LA 99 (Kreitler, 1977), the absence of extensive discussion when new language was placed into the agreement was a factor leading to a narrow construction of the language. Rejecting an interpretation that would have broadly expanded prior coverage of certain medical benefits, the arbitrator stated that, if the parties had intended a broad extension of coverage, "normally there would have been discussion to such effect" during negotiations. Of course, this does not mean that arbitrators ever will lightly treat contractual language as surplusage. Thus, where words were deliberately added to a provision by the parties in the course of their negotiations, the addition of the words could not be taken to have been a meaningless gesture. Kansas City Power & Light Co., 71 LA 381 (Elkouri, 1978).

[110]Ralston Foods, 113 LA 176 (Smith, 1999); Sacramento Reg'l Transit Dist., 110 LA 855 (Bogue, 1998).

[111]*See* Columbia Hosp. for Women Med. Ctr., 113 LA 980 (Hockenberry, 1999); People's Gas Light & Coke Co., 109 LA 1133 (Bethel, 1998); Jostens Printing & Publ'g Div., 107 LA 505 (Berger, 1996); Louis Dreyfus Corp., 106 LA 260 (Berger, 1996); Lockheed Aeronautical Sys. Co., 104 LA 803 (Duff, 1995); City of Columbus, Ohio, 102 LA 477 (Kindig, 1994); Michigan State Univ., 104 LA 516 (McDonald, 1995); Bethlehem Steel Corp., 104 LA 452 (Das, 1995); Thomas/Sysco Food Servs., 90 LA 1036 (Wren, 1988); Mentor Bd. of Educ., 89 LA 292 (Sharpe, 1987); Community Unit Sch. Dist. No. 303 Bd. of Educ., 88 LA 1159 (Goldstein, 1987); City of Highland Park, Mich., 76 LA 811, 815 (McDonald, 1981); Board of Governors of Wayne State Univ., 76 LA 368, 372 (Cole, 1981); Santa Cruz City Sch. Dist., 73 LA 1264, 1269 (Heath, 1979); Library of Cong., 72 LA 691, 693 (Merrifield, 1979); Midwest Steel & Iron Works Co., 71 LA 1235, 1237 (Nutt, 1979); Heartland Educ. Agency, 71 LA 809, 812 (Nitka, 1978); Board of Water Works of Pueblo, Colo., 71 LA 637, 645, 647 (Aisenberg, 1978); Eagle-Picher Indus., 71 LA 473, 475 (Yarowsky, 1978); Ingram Mfg. Co., 70 LA 1269, 1272 (Johannes, 1978); Central Tel. Co., 70 LA 1217, 1224 (Kennedy, 1978); Indiana State Teachers Ass'n Bd. of Dirs., 70 LA 1091, 1096 (Nathan, 1978); Lohr Distrib. Co., 70 LA 925, 929 (Megley, 1978); Hewitt-Robins, 70 LA 662, 663 (Collins, 1978); Department of Air Force, 69 LA 247, 250 (Owen, 1977); W.R. Grace & Co., 68 LA 966, 969 (Oldham, 1977); Detroit News, 68 LA 51, 54 (Volz, 1977).

[112]U.S. Postal Serv. v. Postal Workers, 204 F.3d 523, 530, 163 LRRM 2577 (4th Cir. 2000).

[113]Progress-Bulletin Publ'g Co., 47 LA 1075, 1077 (Jones, Jr., Levin, Whaley, Edward, & Nevins, 1966). *See also* Hillbro Newspaper Printing Co., 48 LA 1304, 1319 (Jones, Jr., 1967).

25 years, and the company had just as consistently rejected the proposal, the arbitrator found this circumstance significant in interpreting contract language that did not specifically and clearly deal with the issue.[114] Similarly, another arbitrator concluded that the parties did not mutually intend that the bargaining unit would perform certain work exclusively, where the union's original proposal that the work could only be done by unit members was not adopted, and the parties ultimately agreed to language allowing supervisors to perform bargaining-unit work under limited conditions.[115]

However, the withdrawal or rejection during contract negotiations of a proposed clause spelling out a right has been held not to be an admission that the right would not exist without the clause, where the proponent stated at the time that it would stand firm on the position that the right existed even without the proposed clause.[116] A similar result was reached where withdrawal of a proposal was encouraged by the other party's statement that the proposal was not necessary.[117] An arbitrator explained:

> [I]t is fundamental that it is not for the Labor Arbitrator to grant a party that which it could not obtain in bargaining.
> This restriction, however, has its limitations. If, in fact, the parties were in dispute, on the proper interpretation of a contract clause and one of them unsuccessfully sought in collective bargaining to obtain clarification, it would not necessarily follow that the interpretation sought by the unsuccessful party was wrong.[118]

A party's unsuccessful attempt to obtain a clause severely restricting the other party does not compel the conclusion that a more limited restriction did not inhere in the contract.[119]

The obverse of the coin is that where a party has initially objected to a particular proposal, citing a particular reason, but the proposal is ultimately

---

[114]Stone Creek Brick Co., 83 LA 864 (Dworkin, 1984). *Contra* Hussman Corp., 84 LA 137, 141 (Roberts, 1983).

[115]Matanuska Elec. Ass'n, 111 LA 596 (Landau, 1998).

[116]*See* Courier-Citizen Co., 42 LA 269, 271 (Myers, 1964) (rejection); Washington Metal Trades, 39 LA 1249, 1252 (Peck, 1962) (withdrawal); Robertshaw-Fulton Controls Co., 21 LA 436, 439 (Wolff, 1953) (same). As to the effect of withdrawal without such assertion of right, compare *Olin Mathieson Chem. Corp.*, 50 LA 1061, 1068 (Talent, 1968), with *F.E. Myers & Bros. Co.*, 43 LA 338, 341 (Teple, 1964).

[117]Philadelphia Orchestra Ass'n, 46 LA 513, 514 (Gill, 1966). *Cf.* Fox River Paper Co., 114 LA 9 (Daniel, 1999).

[118]Hospital Serv. Plan, 47 LA 993, 993–94 (Wolff, 1966). *See also* Okonite Co., 112 LA 501 (Frockt, 1999); Crown Cork & Seal Co., 104 LA 1133 (Wolff, 1995); United Can Co., 102 LA 422 (Randall, 1993); Sanyo Mfg. Corp., 89 LA 80 (Nicholas, Jr., 1987); Food Employers Council, 87 LA 514 (Kaufman, 1986); Empire Tractor & Equip. Co., 85 LA 345 (Koven, 1985); Miller Brewing Co., 75 LA 1189, 1194 (Richman, 1980); Safeway Stores, 73 LA 976, 981 (Feller, 1979); Vickers Petroleum Corp., 73 LA 623, 626 (Carter, 1979); True Temper Corp., 70 LA 774, 776 (Di Leone, 1978); Standard Oil Co. of Cal., 69 LA 164, 168 (Anderson, 1977); Copps Distrib. Co., 54 LA 824, 828 (Krinsky, 1971); Sealtest Foods Div., 48 LA 797, 799 (Valtin, 1966); Weatherproof Co., 46 LA 53, 57 (Traynor, 1966); New York Herald Trib., 36 LA 753, 759 (Cole, 1960). One arbitrator rejected the company's contention that it merely had been seeking clarification where he found that "the Company was reaching for something radically different from a clarification; it was attempting to change the language of the provision, and was unsuccessful." Sterilon Corp., 40 LA 531, 532 (Shister, 1963). *See also* International Paper Co., 70 LA 71, 75 (Robertson, 1978).

[119]*See* National Distillers & Chem. Corp., 76 LA 286, 290 (Gibson, 1981); Hugo Neu-Proler Co., 50 LA 1270, 1272 (Bailer, 1968); Celanese Corp. of Am., 33 LA 925, 950 (Dash, Jr., 1959).

adopted, it may be interpreted as having the scope or effect feared by the objecting party. For example, in one case, an arbitrator was faced with the following circumstances: During negotiations the union president had refused to agree to the new-hire classification proposed by the company because it would permit the company to schedule the new hires for unlimited hours to the detriment of the existing employees.[120] Eventually, however, the union abandoned its refusal and accepted the new-hire provision. The very same reason that had been advanced by the union for rejecting the clause during negotiations was raised once more by the union in a grievance. Recognizing that the union was "attempting to obtain through arbitration what it could not through negotiations and a strike," the arbitrator denied the grievance.[121]

b. *Meaning Not Communicated During Negotiations* [LA CDI 24.37]

Unlike the case where a party has expressed its understanding of the meaning of a term during negotiations, an arbitrator considered a case where a party had never communicated the meaning it claimed to have attached to the term.[122] There, the union president testified that throughout the negotiations the union had refused to accede to an employer proposal allowing the company the right to take an employee off his job to make way for a partially disabled employee. The language ultimately included in the contract reflected a revised employer proposal and entirely omitted the sentence to which the union objected.[123] Although the evidence suggested that the company's senior vice president had been under the impression that the right to do so was not *lost* by the omission of the sentence, his understanding was never communicated to the union.[124] Remarking that "[the] intent manifested by the parties to each other during negotiations by their communications and their responsive proposals—rather than undisclosed understandings and impressions—is considered by the arbitrators in determining contract language,"[125] the arbitrator ruled that the contract gave the employer no right to displace senior employees. However, when terms are adopted without discussion during negotiations, an arbitrator may resort to

---

[120]Kroger Co., 86 LA 357, 364 (1986).

[121]*Id.* at 365. *See also* Columbia Hosp. for Women Med. Ctr., 113 LA 980 (Hockenberry, 1999) (party may not be permitted to secure in arbitration that which it could not secure at the bargaining table); Louis Dreyfus Corp., 106 LA 260, 263 (Berger, 1996) (parties to a collective bargaining agreement may not secure through the arbitration process that which they were unable to achieve in contract negotiations); Marriott Facilities Mgmt., 101 LA 211, 217 (Allen, Jr., 1993) (company could not obtain a provision via arbitration when the union had expressly rejected a similar provision during negotiations).

[122]Kahn's & Co., 83 LA 1225, 1229–30 (Murphy, 1984). *See also* Jefferson Smurfit Corp., 102 LA 164 (Duff, 1994) (pointing out that the union had agreed to provisions at negotiations without objecting to employer's interpretation); Ladish Co., 100 LA 690, 694 (Redel, 1992).

[123]*Kahn's*, 83 LA at 1230. The omitted language read as follows: "This may require removing an able bodied senior employee to other duties within the department or within the plant that this senior employee is capable of performing." *Id.* at 1229.

[124]*Id.* at 1230.

[125]*Id.*

an objective standard and interpret the terms in accordance with the ordinary meaning of the words used.[126]

The examination of the situation of the parties at the time of the negotiations so as to view the circumstances as the parties viewed them, and to judge the meaning of the agreement accordingly, may require more than testimonial evidence. To this end the arbitrator might request the complete details of the bargaining history.[127] Recordings and minutes of bargaining meetings provide important evidence,[128] as well as the actual text of the proposals exchanged by the parties during negotiations.[129] Thus, in one case, a union's "Negotiations Bulletin" was found to provide a "useful clue."[130]

Of course, even if no stenographic record is kept and no notes are taken relevant to negotiation history, the credible testimony of persons who attended the negotiations may be relied on.[131] However, all testimony may not

---

[126]*See, e.g.*, Costco Wholesale Corp., 114 LA 39 (Hockenberry, 2000) (where each party had its own contradictory understanding of a contract proposal but did not inform the other of its interpretation, arbitrator had to look to language to determine its meaning); Broughton Foods Co., 101 LA 286 (Jones, Jr., 1993) (noting union's silence on contested issue during negotiations); Port Jefferson Pub. Sch. Bd. of Educ., 82 LA 978, 980 (Marx, 1984) (it was successfully argued that "[t]he absence of negotiations discussion as to the word 'employee', rather than limiting the meaning, goes to make it all-inclusive"). *But see* Atascadero Unified Sch. Dist., 101 LA 673 (Bickner, 1993) (parties had no discussions focusing on restrictions on assignment of teachers' aides); Ashland County Bd. of Mental Retardation & Developmental Disabilities, 101 LA 302 (Fullmer, 1993) (bargaining history not indicative of parties' intent when subject of grievance was not discussed during negotiations). *See also* WBAL-TV, 110 LA 614 (Fishgold, 1998); Mason City, Iowa, Cmty. Sch. Dist., 109 LA 1125 (Hoh, 1997); Brooklyn Acres Mut. Homes, 84 LA 952, 955 (Abrams, 1985) (testimony regarding bargaining history did not include practical situation of what would occur in instant case where no qualified bidders applied; thus, union's testimony did not warrant a conclusion any different from that which could be achieved by a simple examination of clause).

[127]*See, e.g.*, Detroit Edison Co., 43 LA 193, 200–10 (Smith, 1964) (the parties prepared a comprehensive exhibit at arbitrator's request).

[128]*See* Southern Bag Corp., 110 LA 207 (Caraway, 1998); Schnuck Mkts., 107 LA 739 (Cipolla, 1996); Department of Def. Dependent Sch., 105 LA 211 (Feigenbaum, 1995); Daily Racing Form, 102 LA 23 (Heinsz, 1993); Atascadero Unified Sch. Dist., 101 LA 673 (Bickner, 1993); Dep't of Labor, 74 LA 977 (Shister, 1980); Brown & Williamson Tobacco Corp., 71 LA 1009 (Sickles, 1978); California Elec. Power Co., 21 LA 704 (Grant, 1953); North Am. Aviation, 19 LA 138 (Komaroff, 1952); Columbia Steel Co., 7 LA 512 (Blumer, 1947); C.G. Hussey & Co., 5 LA 446 (Blair, 1946). In *W.R. Grace & Co.*, 68 LA 966, 969 (Oldham, 1977), the union protested that the company's bargaining history exhibits were "excerpts pulled from the composite minutes, and that the documents may be self-serving"; in relying on the exhibits, the arbitrator explained that they "contain the only material in the company files bearing on the contract provision in question" and that the union had failed to submit evidence to support any inference that the exhibits were "distorted out of context" or, with regard to "the self-serving nature of the documents," to challenge their accuracy. In *Blue Cross of N. Cal.*, 73 LA 352, 357 (Barrett, 1979), "shorthand notes," backed by a witness's sworn testimony that they were "notes that he had made in an across-the-table presentation," were accepted as bargaining history evidence.

[129]Friedrich Air Conditioning Co., 112 LA 907, 908 (Halter, 1999).

[130]Los Angeles Herald Exam'r, 45 LA 860, 862 (Kadish, 1965). *See also* Gardinier, Inc., 77 LA 535, 539 (Phelan, 1981) (a "handout prepared by the Company for the Union's use in its ratification meeting" likewise provided a clue to the parties' intent).

[131]*See* Independent Sch. Dist. 282, 91 LA 982 (Flagler, 1988); City of Cheyenne, Wyo., 89 LA 133 (Allen, Jr., 1987); County of Riverside, Cal., 86 LA 903 (Gentile, 1985); Southern Ind. Gas & Elec. Co., 86 LA 342 (Schedler, 1985); Inland Container Corp., 74 LA 75, 79 (Roberts, 1980); Maine Employment Sec. Comm'n, 74 LA 17, 20 (Babiskin, 1980); City of Cincinnati, 69 LA 682, 686 (Bell, 1977); Sidney Wanzer & Sons, 46 LA 426, 428–29 (Dolnick, 1966); Lehigh Portland Cement Co., 42 LA 458, 465 (Hebert, 1964); Borden's Farm Prods., 3 LA 401, 402–03 (Burke, 1945). In *Manitowac Engineering Co.*, 69 LA 336, 338 (Yaffe, 1977), the

be given equal weight. Where one witness testifies of his own knowledge while another testifies as to what a third person told him, it is reasonable to credit the direct testimony over the hearsay to resolve a conflict.[132] Furthermore, an equivocal statement made by a party during negotiations will not establish that the party agreed to the other's position.[133]

In one case, the arbitrator concluded that where the testimony of a union witness was not supported by his own notes of the negotiations, the union was unable to sustain its contentions as to what had occurred during the negotiations.[134] Not all evidence as to what occurred in negotiations is admissible, however. If, for example, the evidence qualifies as a privileged communication it will be excluded.[135] Finally, if, prior to or during negotiations, a company announces its intention to discontinue a policy or practice that had provided a benefit, the union must secure the benefit through negotiations or be deemed to have "bargained away" the benefit.[136]

iii. *Prior Settlements* [LA CDI 93.49; 100.0785]

Sometimes light is shed on ambiguous provisions by prior settlements by the parties of grievances involving those provisions. It has been suggested, in this regard, "Where the parties themselves settle a grievance the evidence of intent as to the meaning of a provision carries special weight."[137] In effect,

---

recollection testimony was not sufficiently precise to be relied on. *See also* Hadley-Dean Glass Co., 69 LA 1057, 1061 (Stix, 1977); Union Free Sch. Dist. No. 3 Bd. of Educ., 68 LA 412, 413 (Silver, 1977) (the arbitrator could place "no reliance on such recollections [of the negotiators], beset as they are with faulty recall and self-serving statements of a conclusory nature").

[132]T.J. Maxx, 113 LA 533, 537 (Richman, 1999).

[133]Madison Warehouse Corp., 112 LA 300 (Suardi, 1998).

[134]Aladdin Temp-Rite LLC, 112 LA 1105 (Krislov, 1999). *See also* Colgate-Palmolive Co., 112 LA 1148 (Cox, 1999) (union's argument that employee is entitled to discontinued long-term disability coverage because employer knew of union's interpretation of contract language failed, where union relied on contested statement of unidentified employer witness assuring that long-term disability coverage would be continued, such assurance was not in meeting notes, without support in contract language, and contrary to medical coverage contained in booklet incorporated into contract); Hamilton County, Ohio, Sheriff, 111 LA 363 (Paolucci, 1998) (testimony of union witness, who was only one to testify about bargaining history, that he and employer representative agreed that percentage increases of insurance copayments of bargaining-unit members and nonbargaining-unit members would always match was not persuasive where no written proposal was ever made consistent with that claim); Southern Bag Corp., 110 LA 207 (Caraway, 1998).

[135]*See* Air Reduction Chem. & Carbide Co., 41 LA 24, 26 (Warns, 1963) (statements of mediators in assisting parties to reach agreement were held privileged). *Accord* Day Care Council, 55 LA 1130, 1135 (Glushien, 1970). For similar results under the National Labor Relations Act (NLRA), 29 U.S.C. §§151–169, see *NLRB v. Joseph Macaluso, Inc.*, 104 LRRM 2097 (9th Cir. 1980). *But see* National Steel Corp., 102 LA 1159, 1167–68 (Garrett, 1994) (where employer and union shared informal negotiating relationship, it was permissible for arbitrator to consider for limited purposes management's internal documents summarizing discussions with union).

[136]Union Carbide Corp., 113 LA 538, 541 (Woolf, 1999). *See also* Tecumseh Corrugated Box Co., 110 LA 458 (Feldman, 1998).

[137]Bendix-Westinghouse Auto. Air Brake Co., 23 LA 706, 710 (Mathews, 1954). *See also* International Harvester Co., 19 LA 812, 814–15 (Emery, 1953); Monsanto Chem. Co., 17 LA 36, 39 (Wallen, 1951). Cases in which arbitrators considered prior settlements in rendering their decisions include *Campbell Group*, 102 LA 1031, 1038–40 (Ferree, 1994) (company's expansion of smoking ban to outside lean-to is not reasonable when union and company

settlements may constitute binding precedents for the parties in the absence of a disclaimer of precedential value.[138] Even clearly proven oral agreements of the parties as to the application of ambiguous language may subsequently be given significant weight by an arbitrator in interpreting that language.[139] For a settlement to have binding effect in a subsequent case, however, there can be no significant differences between the grievance that gave rise to the settlement and the current grievance.[140]

Arbitrators are reluctant, however, to view the granting of a grievance as a concurrence in the union's proffered meaning of the applicable contract provision without a clear indication that the parties had concurred as to the meaning of the language in question. The same can be said of the failure to file a grievance—it must be clear that the failure to file results from the parties' agreement on the interpretation of the contract. Where there is no mutual agreement, neither the failure to file a grievance nor the settlement of a grievance prior to arbitration can constitute a precedent.[141]

Of course, arbitrators who strictly follow the "plain meaning" doctrine may disregard a past settlement that is inconsistent with the "clear language" of the agreement in subsequent cases involving that language[142] on the theory that, while prior settlements may aid an arbitrator in interpreting ambiguous contractual language, such settlements cannot alter the meaning of negotiated provisions.[143] In this vein, an arbitrator noted that "[i]t is of course, the arbitrators [sic] job to interpret the labor agreement, not write it. This is mentioned only as a factor possibly bearing on subsequent interpretations."[144]

---

earlier agreed to settlement of grievance to provide lean-to as smoking area); *Joy Techs.*, 96 LA 740, 744 (Hewitt, 1990); *Allegheny Ludlum Steel Corp.*, 85 LA 669 (Duff, 1985) (arbitrator looked to reason behind parties' prior settlement on similar issue in holding that grievance before him lacked merit); *National Distillers & Chem. Corp.*, 85 LA 622 (Caraway, 1985) (arbitrator considered employer payment of wages at overtime rates in settlement of past grievances as evidence that union's contract interpretation was proper). Arbitrators also consider past arbitration awards that have addressed the same or related language in construing collective bargaining agreements. *See, e.g.*, Gulf States Utils. Co., 102 LA 470, 475 (Massey, 1993) (noting that interpretation of transfer/promotion provision was consistent with arbitration 20 years earlier involving similar facts and contract language); Nevada Cement Co., 101 LA 725, 730 (Concepcion, 1993) (prior arbitration award's interpretation of collective bargaining agreement to include past practice that console operators work 8-hour shifts gave practice contractual status).

[138]For further discussion, see Chapter 5, section 15., "Grievance Settlements as Binding Precedents."

[139]*See* Autocar Co., 19 LA 89, 92 (Jaffee, 1952). *See also* Great Lakes Homes, 46 LA 520, 522 (Gundermann, 1966).

[140]ACS, 111 LA 566 (Kilroy, 1998).

[141]Pepsi-Cola Co., 112 LA 1034 (Block, 1999); Mason & Hanger Corp., 111 LA 60 (Caraway, 1998). *See also* Georgia-Pacific Corp., 112 LA 474 (Landau, 1999). *But cf.* Columbia Gas Transmission, 111 LA 910 (Felice, 1999) (company bound by grievance settlement where its actions demonstrated mutual agreement).

[142]International Harvester Co., 19 LA 812, 815 (Emery, 1953).

[143]Flexible Materials, 101 LA 408, 412 (Oberdank, 1993); Sterling China Co., 100 LA 697, 699–700 (Ipavec, 1992).

[144]Goodyear Aerospace Corp., 86 LA 584, 586 (Fullmer, 1985).

iv.   *Compromise Offers in Grievance Settlement Negotiations*
[LA CDI 93.49; 100.0785]

Unlike the treatment of proposals made in contract negotiations containing terms sought by a party, no consideration will be given in the interpretation of an agreement to compromise offers or to concessions offered by one party and rejected by the other during grievance settlement negotiations that precede arbitration.[145]

> [It] is clear that any offer made by either party during the course of conciliation [mediation] cannot prejudice that party's case when the case comes to arbitration. It is the very essence of conciliation that compromise proposals will go further than a party may consider itself bound to go, on a strict interpretation of its rights.[146]

v.   *Custom and Past Practice of the Parties* [LA CDI 24.351 et seq.]

One of the most important standards used by arbitrators in the interpretation of ambiguous contract language is that of the relevant custom or past practice of the parties. For extensive discussion of this standard of interpretation, see Chapter 12, section 7., "Role of Custom and Practice in Interpretation of Ambiguous Language."

vi.   *Industry Practice*

Evidence of the custom and practice of the industry in which the parties operate may shed light on the intended meaning of an ambiguous provision.[147] An even stronger guide is supplied when the same agreement has been entered into by one employer with several unions or by one union with several employers. In these situations, practice of any of the pairs of parties operat-

---

[145]*See* Cleveland Pneumatic Indus., 39 LA 20, 22 (Kates, 1962); United States Steel Corp., 26 LA 812, 824 (Garrett, 1956); Price-Pfister Brass Mfg. Co., 25 LA 398, 403–04 (Prasow, 1955); Dewey & Almy Chem. Co., 25 LA 202, 205 (Gorder, 1955); John Deere Ottumwa Works, 20 LA 737, 742 (Davey, 1953); Super-Cold Corp., 10 LA 417, 419 (O'Rourke, 1948); Fulton-Sylphon Co., 8 LA 993, 996 (Greene, 1947); Universal Milking Mach. Co., 2 LA 399, 402 (Elson, 1946). *See also* A.M. Castle & Co., 41 LA 391, 397 (Sembower, 1963). For related discussion, see Chapter 8, section 4.F.ii., "Offers of Compromise and Admissions."

[146]Fulton-Sylphon Co., 8 LA 993, 996 (Greene, 1947).

[147]*See* 5th Ave. Musical Theatre, 111 LA 820, 821 (Snow, 1998); Glasgow Sch. Dist. No. 1-1A, 92 LA 281, 284 (Corbett, 1988). *See also* Aircraft Mechanics v. Ozark Air Lines, 597 F.2d 1155, 101 LRRM 2358 (8th Cir. 1979); Flynn Firebrick Constr. Co., 98 LA 898, 901 (Wolff, 1992); Chicago & N.W. Transp. Co., 97 LA 555, 561 (Dennis, 1991); Curtis Sand & Gravel Co., 96 LA 972, 975 (Richman, 1991); ADM Milling Co., 96 LA 664, 666 (Levy, 1991); Pay Less Drug Stores, 95 LA 116, 118 (Rothstein, 1990); Sonoco Prods. Co., 95 LA 58, 62 (Heinsz, 1990); Alpha Beta Stores, 91 LA 888, 894 (Richman, 1988); Firestone Synthetic Rubber & Latex Co., 76 LA 968, 975 (Williams, 1981); Midwest Steel & Iron Works Co., 71 LA 1235, 1237 (Nutt, 1979); Latrobe Steel Co., 68 LA 953, 957 (Sherman, Jr., 1977); Pan Am. World Airways, 48 LA 513, 515–17 (Duff, 1967); John J. Nissen Baking Co., 48 LA 12, 16 (Fallon, 1966); Desert Highway Hotel Corp., 46 LA 989, 992 (Foley, undated); Pittsburgh Steel Co., 46 LA 774, 782 (McDermott, 1966); Food Employers Council, 45 LA 291, 292–93 (Roberts, 1965); Liebman Breweries, 35 LA 384, 385 (Kornblum, 1960); Highway Transp. Ass'n of Upstate N.Y., 11 LA 1081, 1082 (Hill, 1948); Connecticut River Mills, 6 LA 1017, 1022 (Wallen, 1947); Pittsburgh Screw & Bolt Corp., 6 LA 292, 293 (Wagner, 1947).

ing under the agreement may be taken as some indication of the intended meaning of the language used,[148] but the arbitrator would not be bound by such practice.[149]

Where the past practice of the parties in the plant and industry practice differ, the plant practice ordinarily will govern.[150] However, if the industry practice is well established, while the plant practice is not adequately established, the arbitrator may follow the industry practice as the better guide.[151] Custom and practice of an industry other than that in which the parties operate may be accorded little if any weight. A practice may be necessary and reasonable in one industry, but meaningless or foolish in another industry.[152] Of course, evidence of industry practice will not be given weight if it is too meager to furnish a reliable guide.[153]

vii. *Interpretation in Light of Purpose*

Judicial doctrine recorded in the *Restatement (Second) of Contracts* holds that when the principal purpose that the parties intended to be served by a provision can be ascertained, the purpose is to be given great weight in interpreting the words of the provision.[154] Arbitrators agree that an interpretation in tune with the purpose of a provision is to be favored over one that conflicts with it.[155]

---

[148]*See* Bakery, Confectionery & Tobacco Workers, 90 LA 752 (Lesnick, 1987); Stevens Shipping & Terminal Co., 86 LA 373 (Anderson, 1985); ITT-Continental Baking Co., 74 LA 92, 95 (Ross, 1980); Furr's, Inc., 71 LA 233, 237 (Finston, 1978); Durkee-Atwood Co., 70 LA 765, 766 (Grabb, 1978); Geo. A. Hormel & Co., 58 LA 852, 853–54 (Brown, 1972); Leland Airborne Prods. Div., 48 LA 1011, 1013–14 (Geissinger, 1967); Lake Mining Co., 20 LA 297, 299 (Marshall, 1953); Smith Display Serv., 17 LA 524, 526 (Sherbow, 1951); Reynolds Alloy Co., 1 ALAA ¶67,186 (McCoy, 1943). *See also* E.W. Bliss Co., 53 LA 725, 729 (McDermott, 1969); New York Shipping Ass'n, 46 LA 1112, 1115 (Turkus, 1966); National Elevator Mfg. Indus., 43 LA 277, 283–88 (Seitz, 1964); Tin Processing Corp., 20 LA 458, 459–60 (Emery, 1953). *Cf.* Ohio Steel Tube Co., 70 LA 899, 902 (Di Leone, 1978); Celanese Polymer Co., 38 LA 242, 244–45 (Wolff, 1961).

[149]Sidney Wanzer & Sons, 47 LA 708, 711 (Kamin, 1966).

[150]*See* West Foods, 76 LA 916, 919 (Alleyne, 1981); Beitzell & Co., 74 LA 884, 886 (Oldham, 1980); New York Seven Up Bottling Co., 24 LA 601, 603 (Cahn, 1955). *See also* Weston Paper & Mfg. Co., 76 LA 1273, 1275 (Bowles, 1981) (practice varied among the company's several plants, so the arbitrator considered only the practice at the plant involved in the case).

[151]York Bus Co., 24 LA 81, 84, 87–88 (Loucks, 1955); Sayles Biltmore Bleacheries, 17 LA 451, 454 (Maggs, 1951).

[152]Certain-Teed Prods. Corp., 1 LA 354, 358 (Gorder, 1946). *But cf.* CWC Textron–Golden Operations, 73 LA 15, 19 (Seinsheimer, 1979); Liquid Air, 70 LA 420, 422 (Rose, 1978); American Synthetic Rubber Corp., 46 LA 1158, 1159–60 (Dolson, 1966). *See* Carnation Co., 38 LA 270, 272 (Peck, 1962) (considering practice in the locality). For arbitral decisions employing general industry practice over a broad area as an interpretive guide, see *Grundy Elec. Coop.*, 91 LA 440 (Yarowsky, 1988); *Hamilton County, Ohio, Sheriff*, 91 LA 437 (Modjeska, 1988); *U.S. Ref. Co.*, 90 LA 123 (Curry, Jr., 1987); *Columbia Mills*, 48 LA 87, 90 (Raimon, 1966); *Southern Standard Bag Corp.*, 47 LA 26, 29 (Whyte, 1966); *Publishers Bureau of N.J.*, 45 LA 1073, 1074 (Stein, 1965). *See also* Philips Indus., 87 LA 1122 (Rezler, 1986); Courtauds, Inc., 32 LA 643, 644 (McCoy, 1959).

[153]Kaiser Found. Hosps., 102 LA 83, 84–85 (Knowlton, 1993); Lehigh Portland Cement Co., 42 LA 458, 466 (Hebert, 1964).

[154]RESTATEMENT (SECOND) OF CONTRACTS §202, cmt. d (1981).

[155]Louisiana-Pacific Corp., 86 LA 301, 304 (Michelstetter, 1986) (purpose determined from evidence of past practice and bargaining history). In *Associated Fur Manufacturers*, 85 LA 810, 811 (Kramer, 1985), the arbitrator stated that "[a] collective bargaining agreement

viii. The Contract as a Whole

The *Restatement (Second) of Contracts* comments:

Meaning is inevitably dependent on context. A word changes meaning when it becomes part of a sentence, the sentence when it becomes part of a paragraph. A longer writing similarly affects the paragraph . . . .Where the whole can be read to give significance to each part, that reading is preferred . . . .[156]

In the arbitral domain, numerous decisions have invoked this interpretive principle. One of the earliest stated:

The primary rule in construing a written instrument is to determine, not alone from a single word or phrase, but from the instrument as a whole, the true intent of the parties, and to interpret the meaning of a questioned word, or part, with regard to the connection in which it is used, the subject matter and its relation to all other parts or provisions.[157]

In the years that followed, the concept that the disputed portions "must be read in light of the entire agreement"[158] has received widespread acceptance.[159]

---

is not a painting in still life. It is a document which tries to portray a living-together relationship of two parties who are interested in 'mutual survival.'" In that context, the arbitrator commented on the interpretation urged by the union as follows: "[It would] put a wholly unnatural premium upon excessive technicality and . . . ignore the manifest intent of the [parties]." In *Globe Newspaper Co.*, 74 LA 1261, 1268 (1980), the arbitrator stated: "To determine the mutual intention of the parties from the language they used, that language should be construed in the light of the purpose clearly sought to be accomplished, giving consideration to the negotiations leading to the adoption of that language." *See also* Rentschler v. Missouri Pac. R.R., 253 N.W. 694 (Neb. 1934); Waco Int'l, 111 LA 808, 809, 812 (Talarico, 1998); Cardinal Foods, 90 LA 521, 525 (Dworkin, 1988); Public Hous. Agency, St. Paul, Minn., 87 LA 33, 34 (Gallagher, 1986); Texas Utils. Generating Co., 85 LA 814, 816 (Caraway, 1985); *Associated Fur Mfrs.*, 85 LA 810, 811 (Kramer, 1985); William M. Orr Co., 48 LA 1359, 1361 (Krimsly, 1967).

[156]RESTATEMENT (SECOND) OF CONTRACTS §202, cmt. d (1981).

[157]Riley Stoker Corp., 7 LA 764, 767 (Platt, 1947). *See also* U.S. W. Communications, 114 LA 752, 753–54 (Monat, 2000); Great Atl. & Pac. Tea Co., 70 LA 1003, 1006 (Horowitz, 1978).

[158]Hemlock Pub. Sch. Bd. of Educ., 83 LA 474, 477 (Dobry, 1984) (applying totality of contract article to find that grievant was not wrongfully denied right to teach physical education classes taught by junior employees in another building). The arbitrator in *Wells Badger Industries*, 83 LA 517, 520 (Hales, 1984), cited ELKOURI & ELKOURI, HOW ARBITRATION WORKS (BNA Books 3d ed. 1973), for the proposition that a labor agreement should be construed as a whole in order to arrive at the true intent of the parties. *See also* State Comp. Mut. Ins. Fund, 98 LA 723, 726 (Calhoun, 1992); City of Cleveland, 92 LA 1052, 1054 (Sharpe, 1989); Spokane Sch. Dist. No. 81, 92 LA 333, 335 (Smith, 1989); City of Saginaw, Mich., 92 LA 137, 141 (Ellmann, 1989); City of Melbourne, Fla., 91 LA 1210, 1212 (Baroni, 1988); Northern Ill. Mason Employers Council, 91 LA 1147, 1153 (Goldstein, 1988); Allied Plant Maint. Co. of Okla., 88 LA 963, 967 (Bankston, 1987).

[159]*E.g.*, Milton Roy Co., 77 LA 377, 379 (Dunham, 1981); Warren Molded Plastics, 76 LA 739, 743 (Abrams, 1981); Anaconda Co., 74 LA 345, 347 (Gowan, 1980); U.S. Customs Serv., 72 LA 700, 701 (Maggiolo, 1979); Sioux City Cmty. Sch. Dist., 70 LA 725, 728 (Greco, 1978); Hugo Neu-Proler Co., 69 LA 751, 756 (Richman, 1977); Lithonia Lighting Div., 69 LA 406, 410 (Rutherford, 1977); Safeway Stores, 49 LA 443, 445 (Tongue, 1967); Teeters Packing Co., 47 LA 748, 751–52 (Geissinger, 1966); Southwestern Bell Tel. Co., 47 LA 475, 477 (Erbs, 1966); Matthiessen & Hegeler Zinc Co., 47 LA 159, 161 (Krimsly, 1966); Eagle-Picher Co., 45 LA 738, 741 (Anrod, 1965); Sea-Land Serv., 40 LA 1248, 1250 (Turkus, 1963); American Zinc Co. of Ill., 29 LA 334, 339–42 (Merrill, 1957); Machlett Lab., 26 LA 117, 120 (Scheiber, 1956); Applied Arts Corp., 20 LA 337, 340 (Ryder, 1953); Hart Cotton Mills, 11 LA 992, 993 (Maggs, 1948); Terre Haute Brewing Co., 10 LA 487, 493 (Hampton, 1948); Republic Steel Corp., 5 LA 609, 613 (McCoy, 1946); Link Belt Co., 1 ALAA ¶67,315 (Gilden, 1945). Might the particular

Typical of arbitral thinking is the following:

> Sections or portions cannot be isolated from the rest of the agreement and given construction independently of the purpose and agreement of the parties as evidenced by the entire document. . . . The meaning of each paragraph and each sentence must be determined in relation to the contract as a whole.[160]

When a contract contained both a clause stating that "wages shall be paid for jury duty and/or the answer of a subpoena" and a clause providing for time off for union business without pay, an arbitrator interpreted the former in light of the latter:

> When the negotiators of this agreement indicated and stated that payment shall be made for jury duty and in answer of a subpoena, they understood, presumably, that if the answer of a subpoena was for union business and its furtherance or for personal business, that no payment of wage would be made.[161]

a. Giving Effect to All Clauses and Words

If an arbitrator finds that alternative interpretations of a clause are possible, one of which would give meaning and effect to another provision of the contract, while the other would render the other provision meaningless or ineffective, the inclination is to choose the interpretation that would give effect to all provisions.[162] In the words of one arbitrator:

---

placement or location of a word or clause possibly be given any significance? *See* Independent Sch. Dist. No. 279, 71 LA 116, 119 (Fogelberg, 1978); Boyle-Midway, 70 LA 963, 966 (Traynor, 1978). *See also* City of Oklahoma City, Okla., 93 LA 110 (Sisk, 1989); Commonwealth Aluminum Corp., 89 LA 1097 (Corbett, 1987); Waverly Cmty. Unit Sch. Dist. 6, 88 LA 688 (Berman, 1986).

[160]Great Lakes Dredge & Dock Co., 5 LA 409, 410 (Kelliher, 1946). *See also* Township of Pemberton, N.J., 114 LA 523, 529 (DiLauro, 2000); Anaconda Co., 74 LA 345, 347 (Gowan, 1980).

[161]Indiana Bell Tel. Co., 88 LA 122, 125 (Feldman, 1986). *See* Michigan Dep't of Soc. Servs., 82 LA 114 (Fieger, 1983). There, the arbitrator observed the fact that the word "People" was capitalized in the agreement, thus giving "some indication of what was meant." *Id.* at 116. However, he looked to the "language of the penultimate paragraph" for the key. In that paragraph, the drafters "conceived that a witness could appear in a role other than as a witness for the 'People,' and specifically state [sic] that when he does, he does not receive administrative leave." *Id.* Thus, the arbitrator denied the grievance seeking administrative leave to witnesses subpoenaed to testify at an appeal from the denial of unemployment benefits.

[162]*E.g.*, Fire Fighters (IAFF), 112 LA 663 (Lubic, 1999); City of Davenport, Iowa, 91 LA 855 (Hoh, 1988); George A. Hormel & Co., 91 LA 617 (Feldman, 1988); Evanite Battery Separator, 90 LA 225 (Murphy, 1987); Napolitano Constr. Co., 87 LA 950 (Fulmer, 1986); Kaiser Permanente, 76 LA 635, 638 (Richman, 1981); Government Employees (AFGE), 75 LA 1288, 1292 (Ordman, 1980); Kansas City Power & Light Co., 71 LA 381, 395 (Elkouri, 1978); West Allis-West Milwaukee Sch. Dist., 70 LA 387, 394 (Gratz, 1978); Taylor Prods. Div., 50 LA 535, 538 (Witney, 1968); City of Meriden, 48 LA 137, 140 (Summers, 1967); American Potash & Chem. Co., 47 LA 661, 665 (Leonard, 1966); Perini, M-K, Leavell, 46 LA 1044, 1047 (Merrill, 1966); Apex Mach. & Tool Co., 45 LA 417, 424–25 (Layman, 1965); Houston Publishers, 42 LA 1073, 1075 (Fraker, 1964); Eastern Airlines, 40 LA 1217, 1221 (Rohman, 1963); United Carbon Co., 39 LA 310, 314 (Hale, 1962); Firestone Tire & Rubber Co., 29 LA 469, 473 (Hebert, 1957); Alpha Cellulose Corp., 27 LA 798, 800 (Kelliher, 1956); Mathieson Chem. Corp., 12 LA 1117, 1120 (Coffey, 1949); Deep Rock Oil Corp., 11 LA 25, 30 (Merrill, 1948); Loew's, Inc., 10 LA 227, 233 (Aaron, 1948); Birmingham Post, 4 LA 310, 313 (McCoy, 1946). *Cf.* McInerney Spring & Wire Co., 9 LA 91, 94 (Platt, 1947).

It is axiomatic in contract construction that an interpretation that tends to nullify or render meaningless any part of the contract should be avoided because of the general presumption that the parties do not carefully write into a solemnly negotiated agreement words intended to have no effect.[163]

The principle extends not only to entire clauses, but also to individual words. Ordinarily, all words used in an agreement should be given effect. The fact that a word is used indicates that the parties intended it to have some meaning, and it will not be declared surplusage if a reasonable meaning can be given to it consistent with the rest of the agreement.[164] It is only when no reasonable meaning can be given to a word or clause, either from the context in which it is used or by examining the whole agreement, that it may be treated as surplusage and declared to be inoperative.[165]

ix. Company Manuals and Handbooks [LA CDI 24.111]

Company-issued booklets, manuals, and handbooks that have not been the subject of negotiations or agreed to by the union have been found by arbitrators to constitute "merely a unilateral statement by the Company and [are] not sufficient to be binding upon the Union."[166] However, policy manu-

---

[163]John Deere Tractor Co., 5 LA 631, 632 (Updegraff, 1946). *See also* Russell, Burdsall & Ward Corp., 84 LA 373 (Duff, 1985); Maritime Serv. Comm., 49 LA 557, 562–63 (Scheiber, 1967).

[164]Armstrong Rubber Co., 87 LA 146, 150 (Bankston, 1986); Beatrice Foods Co., 45 LA 540, 543 (Stouffer, 1965); Borden's Farm Prods., 3 LA 401, 402 (Burke, 1945). Other cases where this rule was applied include *Independent Sch. Dist. 11*, 97 LA 169, 173 (Gallagher, 1991); *VME Ams.*, 97 LA 137, 138 (Bittel, 1991); *Nelson Tree Serv.*, 95 LA 1143, 1147 (Loeb, 1990); *City of Melbourne, Fla.*, 91 LA 1210, 1212 (Baroni, 1988); *Alpha Beta Stores*, 91 LA 888, 894 (Richman, 1988); *Plough, Inc.*, 90 LA 1018, 1020 (Cromwell, 1988); *City of N. Las Vegas, Nev.*, 90 LA 563, 566 (Richman, 1988); *General Tel. Co. of the Southwest*, 86 LA 293, 295 (Ipavec, 1985) ("It is a rule of contract interpretation that each word and phrase of a contract is to be given meaning on the theory that if the parties to the contract had not intended to give each word and each phrase meaning, then they would have deleted such language in order to assist the eventual interpreter."); *Pittsburgh Bd. of Pub. Educ.*, 85 LA 816 (Bolte, 1985); *GTE Prods. Corp.*, 85 LA 754, 757 (Millious, 1985) ("If the parties had intended that continuous service was the same as seniority, then the language of Article 8 separately setting forth continuous service as a condition for payment would be unnecessary and redundant."); *Hamady Bros. Food Mkt.*, 82 LA 81, 84 (Silver, 1983) ("It is presumed as an essential part of any collective bargaining agreement that all terms and conditions stated therein shall be given effect reasonably.").

[165]American Shearer Mfg. Co., 6 LA 984, 985–86 (Myers, 1947). *See also* Western Employers Council, 49 LA 61, 62–63 (McNaughton, 1967).

[166]Greer Steel Co., 50 LA 340, 343 (McIntosh, 1968). *See also* City of Miamisburg, Ohio, 104 LA 228, 232–34 (Fullmer, 1995) (educational incentive provision in collective bargaining agreement controlled rather than provision concerning education reimbursement in employee handbook); Rhone-Poulenc, 103 LA 1085, 1087–88 (Bernstein, 1994) (statement in employee benefits handbook reserving right to employer to change benefits plan did not alter binding commitments made in collective bargaining agreement); Centel Bus. Sys., 95 LA 472, 478 (Allen, Jr., 1990) ("Company-created handbook cannot take precedence over labor agreement language if there is conflict."); Hughes Airwest, 71 LA 1123, 1125 (Roberts, 1978); Westinghouse Elec. Corp., 45 LA 131, 140 (Hebert, 1965). A company's interoffice memorandum was held not binding on the company where it had not been adopted as a contract between the parties by either formal amendment or past practice. Tenn Flake of Middlesboro, 55 LA 256, 258 (May, 1970). The term "manual" as used in this topic does not relate to the *Federal Personnel Manual*, which is highly relevant in federal-sector arbitration. Regarding that *Manual*, and regarding other special considerations relating to the federal sector, see Chapter 20, section 4.A.ii.c., "Governmentwide Rules or Regulations," and section 4.A.ii.d., "Nongovernmentwide Rules or Regulations."

als may have binding effect if they are within the scope of management's right to promulgate reasonable rules.[167] Unilaterally promulgated company policies that conflict with the terms of the parties' collective bargaining agreement are, of course, nonbinding.[168] A handbook, however, may aid an arbitrator in interpreting inconclusive contractual language.[169]

x.   *Insurance Policies*

Sometimes a group insurance contract entered into by the employer with an insurance carrier will conflict with or otherwise not fully carry out the terms of the collective bargaining agreement between the employer and the union. Arbitrators confronted with this type of situation frequently have concluded that the insurance contract did not constitute a part of the collective bargaining agreement, and they have held that the collective bargaining agreement must control over the insurance contract (thus, the scope of the employer's obligation to the employees has been determined by the collective bargaining agreement).[170] One arbitrator stated:

---

[167]City of Ada, Okla., 112 LA 530, 531 (Eisenmenger, 1999) (nepotism policy contained in manual binding on employees); Lane County, Or., 111 LA 481 (Downing, 1998) (even though manual was binding, employee was improperly suspended where employer failed to show conduct violated rules contained in manual); Housing Auth. of Louisville, Ky., 111 LA 121 (Heekin, 1998) (employee was properly terminated under handbook where several employees had been terminated under same provision and only one grievance was filed, which was not appealed to arbitration); Georgia-Pacific Corp., 87 LA 217 (Cohen, 1986) (policy manual distributed to all employees of the predecessor company, and given and explained to all new hires, created an enforceable contract).

[168]See, e.g., Ventura County, Cal., Cmty. Coll., 112 LA 1094, 1095 (Rule, 1999) (implementation of antinepotism policy against grievant contrary to contract and therefore violation); Simpson Paper Co., 86 LA 503 (Leach, 1985) (arbitrator required company to amend its absentee control policy so as not to conflict with terms of collective bargaining agreement).

[169]The right of an arbitrator to consider a company pamphlet and a bulletin containing company rules in interpreting the collective bargaining agreement was upheld in *Furniture Workers Local 395 v. Virco Manufacturing Corp.*, 257 F. Supp. 138 (E.D. Ark. 1966). Cf. Group Health Ass'n, 102 LA 605, 608 (Feigenbaum, 1994) (physicians laid off less than 5 weeks after notice of employer's sale of business were entitled to 5 weeks' pay, as guaranteed by closing agreement); Central Hudson Gas & Elec. Corp., 101 LA 894, 899–900 (Eischen, 1993) (utility workers who worked in another utility's territory during ice-storm emergency under mutual aid contract were entitled to wages based on special rate, which was established by company memorandum, rather than rate specified in mutual aid contract); Florida State Univ. Bd. of Regents, 99 LA 425, 427 (Goggin, 1992); Greater Cleveland Reg'l Transit Auth., 97 LA 581, 584 (Feldman, 1991); Centel Bus. Sys., 95 LA 472, 478 (Allen, Jr., 1990) (arbitrator refused to rely on handbook that was not distributed to employees until after the grievance arose, but noted that arbitrators sometimes look to handbooks that have existed long enough to establish a past practice).

[170]See Diamond Brands, 112 LA 265, 267 (Jacobowski, 1999) ("The provision and the new carrier policy for the no-fault offset does not alter nor take precedence over the contract obligation to provide the full S&A [sickness and accident] benefit. The union did not participate in writing the policy with the carrier; rather[,] it negotiated the benefit with the company."); Kansas City Cold Storage Corp., 94 LA 783 (Madden, 1990); Youngstown State Univ., 87 LA 628 (Graham, 1986); GAF Corp., 77 LA 256, 262–64 (Rezler, 1981); Nassau County Sch. Bd., 76 LA 1044, 1047 (Sweeney, 1981); Morton Norwich Prods., 75 LA 602, 607 (Wolff, 1980) (it was "the obligation of the employer to obtain an insurance contract which would provide coverage and benefits which were . . . provided for in the" collective bargaining agreement, and if the "insurance contract does not measure up to those benefits, the Company is required to make the grievant whole for the benefits contracted for by the Company and the

In innumerable arbitration and court decisions it has been held that the union-company contract always controls in these instances, and that the Company is acting as an agent of the parties to secure insurance coverage consistent with the terms of the Agreement so that the Agreement always controls and if the insurance policy is inconsistent therewith, it is subordinate. The unfortunate and regrettable result of this is that often the Company, in innocently trying to carry out its obligation[,] is stuck with liability because the insurance carrier has inserted into its policy terms which are inconsistent with the labor-management agreement which is the entire basis for the obtaining of the policy in the first instance.[171]

Thus, if the collective bargaining agreement specifically defines the benefits to be offered bargaining-unit employees, its mandate is controlling, notwithstanding conflicting provisions in the insurance policy.[172] In a case where the employer's insurance carrier refused to pay benefits because the insured did not meet its definition of "totally disabled," even though she was totally disabled under the terms of the collective bargaining agreement, the arbitrator held that the agreement's definition was controlling:

> Travelers was not a party in the negotiations of the Agreement between the parties. A definition in the policy provided by Travelers to the Company may have been inconsistent with or inadequate for the commitment the Company made to the Union. Any such problem must be resolved by Travelers and the Company. In any event, the Company must live up to its commitment to the Union.[173]

However, the terms of an insurance contract have been held binding on both the employer and the union where the contract was incorporated into

---

Union"); Minnesota Mining & Mfg. Co., 75 LA 380, 382 (Foster, 1980); Masonite Corp., 72 LA 1013, 1015 (High, 1979); S. Nordhaus Co., 71 LA 843, 846 (Johannes, 1978) (the "contract between the Company and the insurance carrier was not made a part of the collective bargaining agreement, therefore the Arbitrator may interpret and apply only the contract with the Union"); Wenning Packing Co., 71 LA 796, 798 (Roomkin, 1978) ("the employer is the purchaser of the contract with the carrier, and, as such, holds the ultimate liability for the subcontractor's performance"); Pennsylvania Tire & Rubber Co. of Miss., 71 LA 794, 796 (Williams, 1978); Dayton Press, 71 LA 134, 139–40 (Barone, 1978); Tru-Foto Co., 70 LA 660, 662 (Porter, Jr., 1978); Village of Hales Corners, 67 LA 290, 292 (Knudson, 1976); Georgia-Pacific Corp., 66 LA 352, 353–54 (Sembower, 1976); Eagle Lock Corp., 64 LA 995, 996 (Blum, Botte, & Klinski, 1975) (employee rights under the collective bargaining agreement "cannot be compromised by the non-payment of premiums by the employer and/or oversights and mistakes of the insurance company"); Armak Co., 63 LA 997, 1006–07 (Shanker, 1974); CMI Corp., 61 LA 864, 866 (Volz, 1973); Gilbert & Bennett Mfg. Co., 58 LA 815, 817 (Larkin, 1972); Ferro Corp., 56 LA 1308, 1312 (Teple, 1971); Orr Indus., 53 LA 1302, 1303–04 (Howlett, 1969); Feather-Lite Mfg. Co., 53 LA 18, 20 (Holly, 1969) (although the collective bargaining agreement provided that insurance benefits shall be determined by regulations established in the insurance contract, such regulations could not remove a benefit clearly provided by the collective bargaining agreement).

[171]Georgia-Pacific Corp., 66 LA 352, 353–54 (Sembower, 1976). But the employer sometimes benefits by the rule that the collective bargaining agreement is the controlling document. See Masonite Corp., 72 LA 1013, 1015 (High, 1979) (the employer's obligation under the collective bargaining agreement was narrower than the obligation that arguably would have existed under the insurance contract). In Smithco Engineering, 89 LA 747 (Goodstein, 1987), the arbitrator used a new approach where the employer changed insurers and the union challenged the equality of benefits under the new policy. Instead of requiring the employee to accept the lesser benefit and file a grievance to recover the difference, the arbitrator required the employer to provide the benefit under the old policy and file a grievance to recover any overpayment from the employee.

[172]East Liverpool Bd. of Educ., 94 LA 989, 992 (Bittel, 1990).

[173]Atlantic Richfield Co., 85 LA 916, 920 (Duda, Jr., 1985).

the collective bargaining agreement by reference, or where the parties were found otherwise to have agreed on the benefits or other terms of the insurance contract.[174] Some collective bargaining agreements have been interpreted to require the employer merely to maintain insurance coverage in force without assuming an obligation to assure performance by the insurance carrier.[175] Arbitrators read broadly general contract language relating to the insurance benefits to be provided employees and require an express exception or limitation if a benefit or claim potentially within the general language is to be excluded.[176]

xi. The Mention of One Thing Is the Exclusion of Another

Frequently, arbitrators apply the principle that "when parties list specific items, without any more general or inclusive term, they intend to exclude unlisted items, even though they are similar to those listed. From this assumption comes the rule *expressio unius est exclusio alterius* ('the expres-

---

[174]*See* Basin Elec. Power Coop., 91 LA 675 (MacLean, 1988); Smithco Eng'g, 89 LA 747 (Goodstein, 1987); Beecher Peck & Lewis, 74 LA 489, 493 (Lipson, 1980); TSC Indus., 71 LA 786, 789 (Archer, 1978); Rubatex Corp., 68 LA 780, 783 (Matthews, 1977); Anheuser-Busch, 68 LA 396, 400 (Cohen, 1977); General Felt Indus., 66 LA 786, 792–93 (Simon, 1976); Whirlpool Corp., 66 LA 13, 17–18 (Witney, 1976); Chrysler Corp., 42 LA 372, 374 (Strashower, 1964). *See also* Allied Plant Maint. Co. of Tenn., 90 LA 553 (Nicholas, Jr., 1988); American Hosp. Supply Corp., 73 LA 117, 123 (Chapman, 1979); Ryder Truck Rental, 69 LA 1112, 1115 (Duff, 1977). Where the employer and union are found to have agreed on the level of benefits but not on a particular policy or carrier, the employer's obligation is to provide the agreed level of benefits but not necessarily to continue use of a particular carrier. *See* Ad-Art, 78 LA 533, 535 (Randall, 1982); *American Hosp. Supply*, 73 LA at 122–23; Bearfoot Corp., 65 LA 1208, 1211 (Marshall, 1975); Houdaille Indus., 59 LA 1294, 1296 (Karlins, 1972).

[175]*See* Celotex Corp., 62 LA 752, 755 (Ray, 1974). *See also* CPG Prods. Corp., 78 LA 973, 978 (Dworkin, 1982); Dunmore Sch. Dist., 75 LA 405, 408 (Handsaker, 1980); Babcock & Wilcox Co., 63 LA 779, 781–82 (King, 1974). In this general type of situation, a dispute based on the insurance carrier's failure to pay benefits allegedly due under the insurance policy may be held nonarbitrable as not involving a dispute arising under the collective bargaining agreement. In this regard, a distinction has been recognized between (1) disputes concerning the question whether the employer has met its obligation to furnish insurance coverage (this would involve interpretation of the collective bargaining agreement), and (2) disputes concerning an insurance carrier's failure to pay benefits allegedly due under the insurance policy (this would not involve interpretation of the collective bargaining agreement unless the parties in some manner have made the policy a part of their agreement). *See* WJLA, Inc. v. Broadcast Employees, 103 LRRM 2952 (D.D.C. 1980); Georgia-Pacific Corp., 79 LA 1308, 1311 (Nicholas, Jr., 1982); Dunmore Sch. Dist., 75 LA 405, 408 (Handsaker, 1980); Dravo Corp., 67 LA 264, 265–67 (LeWinter, 1976); Louisville Cooperage Co., 63 LA 165, 167–68 (Volz, 1974); Anaconda Aluminum Co., 57 LA 479, 481–82 (Volz, 1971); Stewart-Warner Corp., 54 LA 931, 932 (Larkin, 1971); Whitehead & Kales Co., 49 LA 1128, 1131 (Ryder, 1968).

[176]*See* Letters Indus., 74 LA 569, 572–73 (Roumell, Jr., 1980); Pennsylvania Tire & Rubber Co. of Miss., 71 LA 794, 796 (Williams, 1978); Ohio Steel Tube Co., 70 LA 899, 902–03 (Di Leone, 1978); North Am. Rockwell, 62 LA 360, 363 (Sembower, 1974); Efficient Indus. Corp., 53 LA 304, 311–12 (Klein, 1969). *See also* Minnesota Mining & Mfg. Co., 75 LA 380, 381 (Foster, 1980); Pacific Southwest Airlines, 73 LA 634, 635 (Jones, Jr., 1979); Hooker Chem. Co., 70 LA 767, 771 (Traynor, 1978); Eaton Corp., 59 LA 189, 193 (Ross, 1972). *Cf.* Hormel Fine Frozen Foods, 75 LA 1129, 1138–41 (Neas, 1980); Suburban Mfg. Co., 69 LA 928, 930 (Flannagan, 1977); Crown Cork & Seal Co., 68 LA 240, 244 (Carson, Jr., 1977); Lever Bros. Co., 57 LA 572, 576–77 (Howlett, 1971). Where the collective bargaining agreement was ambiguous regarding coverage of a claim but an insurance booklet was "very clear and definitive" against it, the claim was held not covered. Barber Colman Co., 78 LA 433, 436–37 (Holley, Jr., 1982).

sion of one thing is the exclusion of another')."[177] Thus, contracts that specify certain exceptions imply that there are no other exceptions,[178] and those that expressly include some guarantees in an agreement are thought to exclude other guarantees.[179] The hazards of this rule of interpretation in some instances lead parties to use general rather than specific language,[180] or to follow a specific enumeration with the statement that the clause is not to be necessarily restricted to the things specifically listed.

xii. *The Doctrine of* Ejusdem Generis

When parties follow a list of specific items with a more general or inclusive term, it is assumed that they intend to include under the latter only items that are like the specific ones, that is, of the same general nature or class as those enumerated, unless it is shown that a broader scope was intended.[181] This principle is referred to as *ejusdem generis*—of the same kind. The principle has been invoked frequently by arbitrators.[182]

---

[177]Farnsworth, Contracts §7.11, at 470–71 (3d ed. 1990). *See* Quebecor Printing Memphis, 114 LA 421 (Robinson, 2000); Broughton Foods Co., 101 LA 286, 287 (Jones, Jr., 1993) (applying legal maxim in denying pay to hourly compensated drivers for time spent on pre- and post-trip inspections); Columbia Local Sch. Dist., 100 LA 227, 231 (Fullmer, 1992) (citing the legal maxim of *expressio unius est exclusio alterius*); Square D Co., 99 LA 879, 882 (Goodstein, 1992); Gateway Foods of Pa., 98 LA 798, 799 (Duff, 1991); Macomb County, Mich., 96 LA 130, 133 (Glazer, 1990); City of Dayton, Ohio, 88 LA 236, 238 (Heekin, 1986); City of Meriden, 87 LA 163, 165 (Davis, 1986) (statute defines funds from which contribution is to be made; limited to regular pay, longevity pay, and holiday pay; does not include assessing accumulated sick leave and vacation pay); Iowa Meat Processing Co., 84 LA 933, 935 (Madden, 1985) (prohibition attaching to interdepartmental transfer under §10 of the contract indicates no such prohibitions or conditions for intradepartmental transfer); Allegheny Intermediate Unit, 82 LA 187, 192–93 (McDowell, 1984) (separation of certain benefits to specific section of collective bargaining agreement entitled "fringe benefits" was meant to exclude other benefits from provision for fringe benefits as used in the contract). *See also* Albright & Wilson, 85 LA 908, 912 (Shanker, 1985); Aeronca, Inc., 82 LA 144 (Finan, 1984); City of Hollywood, Fla., 82 LA 48 (Manson, 1983); Hoover Universal, 77 LA 107, 112–13 (Lipson, 1981) (discussing the principle in some detail); County of Orange, Cal., 76 LA 1040, 1043 (Tamoush, 1981); Hewitt-Robins, 70 LA 662, 663 (Collins, 1978); National Lead Co., 51 LA 1266, 1268 (Malkin, 1968); WPIX, Inc., 49 LA 155, 158 (Turkus, 1967); Martin-Marietta Corp., 46 LA 430, 435 (Sembower, 1966); General Teleradio, 18 LA 418, 423 (Rosenfarb, 1952); Branch River Wool Combing Co., 16 LA 685, 688 (Copelof, 1951); A.D. Juilliard & Co., 10 LA 541, 549 (Hobbs, 1948); Terre Haute Brewing Co., 10 LA 487, 494 (Hampton, 1948); Richard R. Olmsted Co., 7 LA 81, 84 (Potter, 1947); Goodyear Tire & Rubber Co. of Ala., 3 LA 257, 259 (McCoy, 1946). *Cf.* Avco Mfg. Corp., 24 LA 268, 271 (Holly, 1955); Pilot Freight Carriers, 22 LA 761, 762 (Maggs, 1954); Ross Gear & Tool Co., 15 LA 345, 349 (Gilden, 1950). *But see* Jefferson Smurfit Corp., 102 LA 164, 166 (Duff, 1994) (recognizing the legal maxim but declining to apply it to union's contention that the naming of a specific company executive or his representative in step 3 of the grievance procedure was a limitation on the number of representatives the company could have at the grievance step meeting).

[178]*See* Western Consumers, 85 LA 143 (Koven, 1985); Columbia Gas of Pa., 83 LA 639 (Bolte, 1984); Wagner Castings Co., 83 LA 507 (Talent, 1984); St. Louis Symphony Soc'y, 70 LA 475, 479 (Roberts, 1978); A.O. Smith Corp., 47 LA 654, 661 (Dworkin, 1966); Modecraft Co., 44 LA 1045, 1049 (Jaffee, 1965).

[179]Great Atl. & Pac. Tea Co., 46 LA 372, 374 (Scheiber, 1966).

[180]Loew's, Inc., 10 LA 227, 232 (Aaron, 1948).

[181]Farnsworth, §7.11, at 471.

[182]*See* United Tech. Essex Group, 77 LA 561, 568 (House, 1981); Masonite Corp., 62 LA 558, 560 (Gibson, 1974); International Shoe Co., 46 LA 752, 755 (Hilpert, 1966); Ohio Natural Casing & Supply Co., 43 LA 888, 890–91 (Leach, 1964); Fafnir Bearing Co., 39 LA 530,

For instance, it was held that a clause providing that seniority shall govern in all cases of layoff, transfer, "or other adjustment of personnel" should not be interpreted to require allocation of overtime work on the basis of seniority.[183] The doctrine has been held inapplicable, however, where the specific words preceding the general words embrace all objects of their class because, except for this qualification, the general words that follow the specific enumeration would be meaningless.[184]

xiii. The Principle of Noscitur a Sociis

Noscitur a sociis (known by one's association) signifies that a word takes on coloration from its association with accompanying words. Thus, a term requiring arbitration prior to an employee being "disciplined, reprimanded, reduced in compensation or deprived of any professional advantage[s] does not encompass 'dismissal' because all the terms following 'disciplined' indicate a lesser, not a greater, form of discipline."[185] Many arbitrators follow this maxim in holding that contract sections in dispute must be read in the light of the other sections in the agreement to establish the intent of the parties.[186]

xiv. Exact Terms Given Greater Weight Than General Language

Unless a contrary intention appears from the contract interpreted as a whole, or from relevant extrinsic circumstances, more specific provisions

---

533 (McCoy, 1962); Sperti Faraday, Inc., 37 LA 9, 13 (Bradley, 1961); Badger Concrete Co., 35 LA 912, 914 (Mueller, 1961); American Bakeries Co., 34 LA 781, 784 (Rohman, 1960). *See also* Giant Stores, 74 LA 909, 915 (Larney, 1980); Peoria Malleable Castings Co., 43 LA 722, 728 (Sembower, 1964); Northway Prods. Co., 39 LA 791, 794 (Sullivan, 1962); General-Electro Mech. Corp., 93 LA 218, 219–20 (Stocker, 1989) (where an enumeration of matters governed by seniority was followed by the designation "etc.," the term "etc." was ambiguous and its meaning was to be determined by reference to the practice in question).

[183]Canadian Indus., 19 LA 170, 172 (Hanrahan, 1951).

[184]Ralphs Grocery Co., 112 LA 449, 452 (Gentile, 1999); St. Louis Terminal Warehouse Co., 19 LA 807, 808–09 (Treiman, 1952). *See also* Publishers' Ass'n of N.Y. City, 46 LA 388, 394 (Moskowitz, 1966).

[185]CALAMARI & PERILLO, THE LAW OF CONTRACTS §3.13, at 155 (4th ed. 1998) (citing Lakeland Cent. Sch. Dist., Shrub Oak, Bd. of Educ. v. Barni, 66 A.D.2d 340, 412 N.Y.S.2d 908, 101 LRRM 2260 (1979), *rev'd on other grounds*, 49 N.Y.2d 311, 401 N.E.2d 912, 103 LRRM 2903 (1980)).

[186]In *Eagle Point Sch. Dist.*, 100 LA 496, 507 (Wilkinson, 1992), the arbitrator interpreted "deception" as requiring aggravating circumstances because the word appeared in the context of serious offenses. *See also* Macomb County, Mich., 96 LA 130, 134 (Glazer, 1990); Firestone Tire & Rubber Co., 20 LA 880, 888 (Gorder, 1953); Deep Rock Oil Corp., 11 LA 25, 31 (Merrill, 1948); Boston Daily Newspapers, 6 LA 179, 182 (Wallen, 1946). Cases that consider context in resolving the meaning of a disputed contract section include *Washington Metro. Area Transit Auth.*, 108 LA 465, 470 (Feigenbaum, 1997) (finding that sentences should not be read in isolation but, rather, in concert with those surrounding them because they were part of the same thought); *Spartan Stores*, 105 LA 549 (Kanner, 1995); *Giant Cement Co.*, 103 LA 146, 149 (Nolan, 1994); *General Elec. Co.*, 102 LA 261, 265–66 (Sugerman, 1993); *Dresser-Rand Co.*, 100 LA 333, 335–36 (Pribble, 1992); *City of Sacramento Police Dep't*, 99 LA 527, 530 (Freeman, 1992); *Monon Corp.*, 99 LA 395 (Bittel, 1992); *Tynan Lumber Co.*, 98 LA 1103, 1106 (Pool, 1992); *B.F. Nelson Folding Cartons*, 98 LA 978, 982 (Jacobowski, 1991); *Weinstein Wholesale Meat*, 98 LA 636, 639 (Eagle, 1992); *Board of Educ., Prince George's County, Md.*, 85 LA 999, 1000 (Flannagan, 1985); *Zeigler Coal Co.*, 85 LA 971, 975 (Creo, 1985).

should restrict the meaning of a general provision.[187] The reason for this preference is explained by the *Restatement (Second) of Contracts* in this manner:

> People commonly use general language without a clear consciousness of its full scope and without awareness that an exception should be made. Attention and understanding are likely to be in better focus when language is specific or exact, and in case of conflict the specific or exact term is more likely to express the meaning of the parties with respect to the situation than the general language.[188]

For example, where a contract contained a general provision stating that the company should "continue to make reasonable provisions for the safety and health of its employees," and another provision stating that "wearing apparel and other equipment necessary properly to protect employees from injury shall be provided by the Company in accordance with practices now prevailing . . . or as such practices may be improved from time to time by the Company," it was held that the employer was not obligated to furnish rain clothes to employees because such apparel had not been furnished or required in the past. The arbitrator noted that had the general clause stood alone, he would have been required to determine whether the furnishing of rain clothes was reasonably necessary for the safety and health of the employees.[189] The exception to a general provision should, however, be kept within proper bounds.[190]

xv. Avoidance of Harsh, Absurd, or Nonsensical Results

When one interpretation of an ambiguous contract would lead to harsh, absurd, or nonsensical results, while an alternative interpretation, equally plausible, would lead to just and reasonable results, the latter interpreta-

---

[187]Square D Co., 99 LA 879, 882 (Goodstein, 1992); City of Aurora, Colo., 96 LA 1196, 1201 (Snider, 1990); Nationwide Indus. Corp., 93 LA 286, 288 (Richard, 1989); Coca-Cola Foods, 88 LA 129, 131 (Naehring, 1986); Airco Carbon, 86 LA 6, 9 (Dworkin, 1986) ("A broadly observed principle of contract interpretation, acknowledged in both courts of law and arbitration, holds that specific language prevails over general language."); Chillicothe Tel. Co., 84 LA 1, 3 (Gibson, 1984); Department of Labor, 74 LA 977, 979 (Shister, 1980); Beecher Peck & Lewis, 74 LA 489, 493 (Lipson, 1980); Bristol Steel & Iron Works, 73 LA 573, 578 (Nicholas, Jr., 1979); Paul Mueller Co., 71 LA 781, 783 (Cohen, 1978); Riverdale Plating & Heat Treating Co., 71 LA 43, 47 (Petersen, 1978); Central Tel. Co. of N. Am., 69 LA 231, 234 (Holly, 1977); Eastern Airlines, 48 LA 1005, 1010 (Seidenberg, 1967); Teeters Packing Co., 47 LA 748, 751 (Geissinger, 1966); Carling Brewing Co., 46 LA 715, 717 (Kates, 1966); Continental Oil Co., 44 LA 183, 187 (Abernethy, 1965); Caterpillar Tractor Co., 39 LA 534, 538 (Sembower, 1962); Haloid Co., 29 LA 376, 380 (McKelvey, 1957); Magnavox Co., 28 LA 554, 556 (Fleming, 1957); Tennessee Coal, Iron & R.R., 12 LA 530, 531 (McCoy, 1949); Westinghouse Elec. Corp., 12 LA 462, 469 (Wyckoff, 1949). *See also* City of Houston, Tex., 86 LA 1068, 1072 (Stephens, 1986) (where there may be a conflict between two contract provisions, the specific will govern over the general).

[188]Restatement (Second) of Contracts §203 cmt. e (1981).

[189]Tennessee Coal, Iron, & R.R., 12 LA 530, 531 (McCoy, 1949).

[190]*See* Unitog Co., 85 LA 740, 742 (Heinsz, 1985) ("when an exception is stated to a general principle, the exception should 'be strictly though, to be sure, properly construed and applied'" (citing Verniton Corp., 77 LA 349, 352 (Shipman, 1981); Fulton-Sylphon Co., 8 LA 983, 984 (Greene, 1947)).

tion will be used.[191]   Indeed, where the extreme positions taken by both parties would produce absurd results, an arbitrator may reject them and make an independent interpretation of the disputed provision.[192]

---

[191]THE COMMON LAW OF THE WORKPLACE §2.12, at 74 (St. Antoine ed., BNA Books 1998); Quadcom 9-1-1 Pub. Safety Communications Sys., 113 LA 987, 992 (Goldstein, 1999) (arbitrator followed the principle of interpretation, but determined that the employer's contention that the interpretation would be harsh and burdensome was without merit); General Elec. Co., 102 LA 261, 266 (Sugerman, 1993) (arbitrator cited general principle in ELKOURI & ELKOURI, HOW ARBITRATION WORKS 354 (BNA Books 4th ed. 1985), in adopting employee's interpretation of bumping provision in order to avoid a "harsh, absurd, or nonsensical" result); Schalmont Cent. Sch. Dist., 87 LA 151, 152 (Babiskin, 1986) (interpreting "days" for purposes of sick leave as "work days" to avoid nonsensical result). One arbitrator interpreted "work day" to mean "twenty-four hours" to avoid rendering a provision meaningless. West Penn Power Co., 92 LA 644, 648 (Dworkin, 1989). In *Portland Water District*, 87 LA 1227 (Chandler, 1986), the arbitrator interpreted the contract so as to avoid a nonsensical result in favor of a result that was just and reasonable. Similarly, the arbitrator in *Charley Bros. Co.*, 84 LA 655, 658 (Probst, 1985), stated that he was required to establish the appropriate meaning of an agreement consistent with its language that would avoid an obviously absurd result, in finding that an employer properly denied an overtime assignment to an employee who was in the middle of a 5-day suspension. In *Eagle Iron Works*, 85 LA 979, 981 (Thornell, 1985), the arbitrator sustained the grievance because the employer's interpretation of the contract's vacation entitlement provision "would have a harsh result and one not called for by the contract." *See also Square D*, 99 LA 879 (arbitrator awards have held that agreements are to be given a reasonable construction so as to avoid harsh, illogical, or absurd results); Downtown St. Paul Partners, 90 LA 67, 71 (Cooper, 1987); TPC Liquidation, 88 LA 696, 698 (Lumbley, 1987); John Morrell & Co., 76 LA 1017, 1022 (Nathan, 1981); Fort Pitt Steel Casting Div., 76 LA 909, 911 (Sembower, 1981); Amax Lead Co. of Mo., 74 LA 998, 1004 (Roberts, 1980); Marine Corps Dev., 71 LA 726, 730 (Ables, 1978); Midwest Rubber Reclaiming Co., 69 LA 198, 200 (Bernstein, 1977); Inspiration Consol. Copper Co., 50 LA 58, 62 (Block, 1968); Pan Am. World Airways, 48 LA 513, 516 (Duff, 1967); Marblehead Lime Co., 48 LA 310, 314 (Anrod, 1966); Euclid Elec. & Mfg. Co., 45 LA 641, 643 (Kates, 1965); Pennsylvania R.R., 37 LA 220, 225 (Robertson, 1961); Rockwell Spring & Axle Co., 23 LA 481, 486 (Dworkin, 1954); Vickers, Inc., 15 LA 352, 355 (Platt, 1950); Deep Rock Oil Corp., 11 LA 25, 29 (Merrill, 1948); Yale & Towne Mfg. Co., 5 LA 753, 757 (Raphael, Eddy, & Adam, 1946); Goodyear Tire & Rubber Co., 2 LA 367, 370 (McCoy, 1946); Metal & Thermit Corp., 1 LA 417, 419 (Gilden, 1946). *See also* Loveless v. Eastern Air Lines, 681 F.2d 1272, 111 LRRM 2001, 2004–07 (11th Cir. 1982); American Safety Razor Co., 90 LA 1140, 1143 (Bowers, 1988) ("To uphold such conduct flies in the face of common sense and even the literal interpretation of the contract language which the union has urged in this proceeding."); Bowman Transp., 88 LA 711, 712 (Cocalis, 1987); Western Beaver County Sch. Dist., 86 LA 1291, 1293 (Heekin, 1986); Glaser Bros./Royal Distribs., 85 LA 43, 45 (Draznin, 1985); Waukegan News-Sun, 74 LA 1063, 1065 (Edes, 1980); Washington Mack Trucks, 71 LA 412, 420 (Cushman, 1978) (read literally, the contested overtime-equalization clause "applies to any kind of work performed by members of the bargaining unit"; but in view of the new and unusual features of the off-site project that produced the overtime in question, and because the contract was entered into before there ever had been any off-site work, it was concluded that the clause "was not intended to apply to off-site work"); Lithonia Lighting Div., 69 LA 406, 408, 410 (Rutherford, 1977); Tecumseh Prods. Co., 65 LA 762, 763–64 (Seitz, 1975); Martin Co., 49 LA 255, 256 (McCoy, 1967); Sperry-Rand Corp., 46 LA 961, 963–64 (Seitz, 1966) (declaring that it "is not difficult to make an ass of the law by a too literal reading of words used by the parties in expressing their bargain"); Capitol Mfg. Co., 46 LA 598, 601 (Gibson, 1966); Food Employers Council, 45 LA 291, 292–93 (Roberts, 1965); Heckethorn Mfg. & Supply Co., 36 LA 380, 381 (Warns, 1960); Hiram Walker & Sons, 33 LA 629, 631–32 (Updegraff, 1959); Shook Bronze Co., 9 LA 656, 657 (Lehoczky, 1948). The switch to daylight savings time has produced a pair of contrasting cases in which the arbitrator's attitude toward literal application of contractual language is worthy of note. *See* Magma Copper Co., 51 LA 9, 12 (Abernethy, 1968); Anheuser-Busch, 33 LA 752, 753 (Roberts, 1959).

[192]Evening News Ass'n, 50 LA 239, 245 (Platt, 1968); D-V Displays Corp., 41 LA 937, 942 (Kates, 1963). *See also* Federal Mogul Corp., 86 LA 225 (Blinn, 1985); City of Taylor, 84 LA 522, 525 (McDonald, 1985).

Arbitral avoidance of absurd results is shown in a case where a contract provided for paid vacations for employees in the "active employ" of the company on a specified date, and the arbitrator refused to interpret the language so as to produce the "absurd" result of disqualifying employees absent on such date due to illness or any other valid reason.[193] In another case, an interpretation was rejected because it would have placed a premium on contract violations by encouraging unauthorized strikes.[194]

Another arbitrator found "arbitral surgery" justified where necessary to prevent absurd results:

> Experience teaches that contracting parties are not always absolutely precise, nor can they be expected to be, in their agreement formulations. Not infrequently, words or phrases are unthinkingly included which, if construed according to their literal meaning would produce results in opposition to the main purpose and object of a provision. This is often true when, as here, some of the language used was drafted by others in a different context and in response to other circumstances and policies. In such a case there can be no doubt as to the right of an interpreter to modify and mitigate—in effect excise—the unpremeditated, unintended language in order to prevent an absurd result and to give effect to the true intention of the parties.[195]

By comparing arbitral surgery with oral surgery, an arbitrator illustrated the absurdity of a company's policy regarding "doctor's" excuses for sick days. In that case, the company rejected an excuse from a chiropractor on the ground that a "physician's" note was required.[196] Carrying this policy out to its potential limits, the arbitrator described the "genuine predicament" of an employee experiencing the "painful symptoms of a physical condition, such as an aching, abscessed tooth . . . ."[197] Under a strict interpretation of the company's policy of accepting only a physician's note, the employee "would be compelled to go through the pro forma gesture of having a physician certify what perhaps only a dentist would truly know about his or her condition."[198]

xvi. Effect of Arbitrator's Knowledge of the Experience and Training of the Negotiators

The extent to which an arbitrator will interpret a contract according to the "plain meaning" of the words used may, to some extent, depend on the training and experience of the negotiators.[199] If the arbitrator finds that they were laymen unskilled in the precise use of words, and if the contract on its face bears evidence of a lack of precision, the arbitrator may refuse to apply

---

[193]Consolidation Coal Co., 83 LA 1158, 1159, 1161 (Duff, 1984).
[194]A.D. Juilliard & Co., 2 LA 140, 141 (Copelof, 1946).
[195]Evening News Ass'n, 50 LA 239, 245 (Platt, 1968).
[196]*Consolidation Coal*, 83 LA at 1159–60.
[197]*Id.* at 1161. *See also* ASG Indus., 68 LA 304, 310 (Elkouri, 1977); Rockwell Spring & Axle Co., 23 LA 481, 486 (Dworkin, 1954).
[198]*Consolidation Coal*, 83 LA at 1161.
[199]Earth Grains Div. (Paris), 98 LA 632, 636 (Woolf, 1992); Sonoco Prods. Co., 95 LA 58, 62 (Heinsz, 1990).

a literal meaning test.[200] Under such circumstances, the arbitrator might conclude that the writing "should be considered as a somewhat imperfect attempt to embody rules which were better understood than it was possible to express in words."[201] This approach includes resolving issues of procedural arbitrability in light of the negotiators' skill and experience,[202] as well as resolving the substantive merits of a case based on an assessment of the skill, experience, and, hence, the ability of the negotiators to articulate their intent.[203]

A less liberal approach is likely to be taken if the arbitrator knows that the negotiators for both parties were experts in drafting collective bargaining agreements,[204] or, to state it in other ways, if the arbitrator believes that the negotiators were "capable and shrewd,"[205] "sophisticated veterans" of negotiations,[206] or "experienced in labor relations matters."[207]

In applying a literal interpretation standard to a contested provision, an umpire emphasized that: "The negotiators were not tyros in the art. They were skilled hands who worked hard, intelligently, and alertly. The agreement was not negotiated in a hurry or under pressure. Careful scrutiny was given to the language after agreement was reached on the substance."[208]

Focusing on the lack of discussion over the contract terms urged by the company, an arbitrator found it difficult to believe that had such terms been discussed, the experienced union negotiator would not have objected strenuously.[209] Thus, even a silent record may reflect the intent of the parties when viewed in light of the training and experience of the negotiators.

---

[200]*See* U.S. Pipe & Foundry Co., 5 LA 492, 494 (McCoy, 1946). *See also* Sidney Wanzer & Sons, 46 LA 426, 429 (Dolnick, 1966). Similar liberal construction was utilized in interpreting a strike settlement agreement drafted by a citizens committee. Yale & Towne Mfg. Co., 39 LA 1156, 1157–58 (Hill, Horlacher, & Seitz, 1962).

[201]Moran Towing & Transp. Co., 1 ALAA ¶67,012, at 67,015 (Kidd, 1944).

[202]*See, e.g.*, City of Joliet, Ill., 112 LA 468, 473 (Perkovich, 1999) (holding grievance arbitrable even though hearing was held beyond 60-day limit specified in contract. "Thus, to conclude that the parties, represented by experienced and knowledgeable negotiators, would intend that the grievances not heard in arbitration would be dismissed is indeed harsh, nonsensical and/or absurd."); Universal Foods Corp., 82 LA 105, 108 (Belcher, 1984) (holding grievance arbitrable because parties did not provide for end to grievance process if arbitrator not timely selected. "[I]t is obvious that the negotiators were not novices, but were professionals in the most favorable connotation.").

[203]*See* Woodings-Verona Tool Works, 84 LA 68, 74 (McDermott, 1984) (arbitrator stressed skill of negotiators drafting an agreement and held that they were aware of difference in meaning between "termination" and "layoff" in providing that employees on layoff before a plant closing were not entitled to severance pay). *See also* Maple Heights Bd. of Educ., 86 LA 338, 340 (Van Pelt, 1985) ("While it is difficult for this Arbitrator to understand how parties of the caliber dealing with this contract would first, permit a typographical error to become a part of the permanent record, and second, to permit the same error to continue throughout a series of contracts, nevertheless it apparently happened.").

[204]*See* Pettibone Corp., 70 LA 383, 386 (Gootnick, 1978); Continental S. Lines, 69 LA 1077, 1079 (Marcus, 1977); U.S. Steel Corp., 69 LA 740, 749 (Garrett, 1977); Hilo Transp. & Terminal Co., 36 LA 1132, 1135 (Burr, 1961); Flintkote Co., 26 LA 526, 528 (Morvant, 1956); Pioneer Mfg. Co., 20 LA 910, 911 (Anderson, 1953); Armstrong Rubber Mfg. Co., 19 LA 683, 686 (Margulies, 1952); Kendall Mills, 8 LA 306, 308 (Lane, 1947).

[205]Carnation Co., 3 LA 229, 232 (Updegraff, 1946). *See also* John Deere Tractor Co., 2 LA 469, 472 (Updegraff, 1945).

[206]Hilo Transp. & Terminal Co., 36 LA 1132, 1135 (Burr, 1961).

[207]Earth Grains Div. (Paris), 98 LA 632, 636 (Woolf, 1992).

[208]Ford Motor Co., 1 ALAA ¶67,126, at 67,265 (Shulman, 1945).

[209]W.E. Plechaty Co., 84 LA 571, 576 (Duda, Jr., 1985).

B. Rules of Interpretation Based on Public Policy

Some principles of interpretation to ascertain contract meaning are based not so much on assumptions about the intention of the parties as derived from common experience as they are on assumptions about public policy,[210] and therefore ascertain the "legal meaning" of words independent of the meanings the parties themselves may have attached to the language.[211] Some of the more common "rules of construction" in this category are discussed below.

i.   *Interpretation in Light of the Law* [LA CDI 24.17]

Arbitrators strive to give effect to the collective bargaining agreement rather than to dismember it, and, whenever two interpretations are possible, one making the agreement valid and lawful and the other making it unlawful, the former will be chosen. The parties are presumed to have intended a valid contract.[212]

Similarly, the public interest may be a relevant factor in contract interpretation.[213] Arbitrators often construe collective bargaining agreements in light of statutes and case law,[214] and may treat applicable regulations as implied terms of the contract. In *GTE North*,[215] the issue concerned whether

---

[210]*See* Calamari & Perillo, The Law of Contracts §3.13, at 156–58 (4th ed. 1998).

[211]Farnsworth, Contracts §7.11, at 472 (3d ed. 1999).

[212]*See* Shook, Inc., 87 LA 1221, 1226 (Hayford, 1986); Mason & Hanger-Silas Mason Co., 75 LA 1038, 1040 (Shearer, 1980); Stokely-Van Camp, 71 LA 109, 112–13 (Snow, 1978); Firestone Tire & Rubber Co., 20 LA 880, 889 (Gorder, 1953); Union Switch & Signal Co., 9 LA 702, 703 (Horvitz, 1948); Warren Foundry & Pipe Corp., 5 LA 282, 283 (Tischler, 1946); Pullman Co., 2 LA 445, 452 (Shake, 1944). *See also* Bechtel Civil & Minerals, 87 LA 153 (Beck, 1986).

[213]Maritime Serv. Comm., 49 LA 557, 562 (Scheiber, 1967). *See also* Girard Coll., 71 LA 1051, 1054 (Kramer, 1978).

[214]*See, e.g.*, UNDS, 112 LA 14, 17 (Haber, 1999) (arbitrator looked to NLRB case law when asked to enforce union-security clause); Fantasy-Blanke Baer Corp., 111 LA 1057 (Marino, 1999) (application of federal law on independent contractors); Kaiser Permanente, 99 LA 490, 492 (Henner, 1992) (application of Americans with Disabilities Act (ADA), 42 U.S.C. §12101 et seq.); Host Int'l, 94 LA 492, 496 (Talarico, 1990) (application of Pennsylvania liquor control laws); City of Keokuk, Iowa, 88 LA 1129, 1132 (Murphy, 1987); Montgomery County, Md., Gov't, 86 LA 220 (Hockenberry, 1985) (application of the codes of Montgomery County, the State of Maryland, and Maryland case law in grievance involving police officers); Container Corp. of Am., 84 LA 489 (Nicholas, Jr., 1985) (NLRB and circuit court decisions examined to determine who is a "supervisor" under the NLRA); Cooper T. Smith Stevedoring Co., 84 LA 94 (Baroni, 1984) (arbitrator considered NLRB and federal case law in resolving jurisdictional dispute); San Diego Plasterers Pension Group Ins., 83 LA 662 (Weckstein, 1984) (arbitrator considered Taft-Hartley Act, Labor-Management Reporting and Disclosure (Laudrum-Griffin) Act, 29 U.S.C. §302, Employee Retirement Income Security Act (ERISA), 29 U.S.C. §1001 et seq., and case law in finding that trust instruments should not be amended to require employer or representative of employer trustees to be signatory to collective bargaining agreement with union); Clark County Sch. Dist., 75 LA 827, 829 (Rogosin, 1980); Carbon County, Pa., 73 LA 1305, 1307 (Handsaker, 1980); Flour Mills of Am., 20 LA 564, 566 (Reeves, 1952); New York Cent. R.R., 20 LA 318, 320 (Horvitz, 1953); Evans Prods. Co., 19 LA 457, 458 (Platt, 1952). For extensive discussion of use by arbitrators of substantive rules of law, see Chapter 10, "Use of Substantive Rules of Law."

[215]113 LA 665 (Brodsky, 1999). *See* Alcoa Bldg. Prods., 104 LA 364 (Cerone, 1995) (even where the contract is silent, an arbitrator has authority to address external legal issues due to the potential conflict between federal law and the agreement and the parties' stipula-

to apply the provisions of the ADA when the contract did not provide for its application. The arbitrator held that the contract incorporated the ADA by means of a general nondiscrimination clause.[216] The arbitrator may be given authority to apply the law in the contract.[217] Often, the parties themselves submit grievances in which they explicitly or implicitly require the arbitrator to apply legal provisions.[218] In some cases where the contract is silent on the issue, however, arbitrators have refused to apply statutory law in rendering their decisions,[219] at least where the contract provision in question does not require what the law prohibits, or prohibits what the law requires.

But, some arbitrators hold fast to the philosophy that the contract controls, despite potential conflict with the law:

---

tions). *See also* Perfection Bakeries, 110 LA 1043 (Stallworth, 1997); Champion Int'l Corp., 106 LA 1024 (Howell, 1996) (where the contract is silent regarding the arbitrator's legal authority to apply external law, the arbitrator can imply external law into general contract provisions).

[216]*GTE N.*, 113 LA at 671.

[217]Interstate Brands Corp., 113 LA 161, 168 (Howell, 1999) (arbitrator applied the ADA when contract stated that "[t]his agreement shall be interpreted to permit the reasonable accommodation of disabled persons as required by state and/or federal law, including the Americans With Disabilities Act (ADA)"); Citicasters Co., 110 LA 214, 217 (Kaufman, 1998) (arbitrator's authority to determine statutory refusal to bargain issue flowed from contract, which provided that contractual provisions that conflicted with NLRA shall be deemed modified to conform to it).

[218]*E.g.*, Detroit Edison Co., 96 LA 1033, 1046–47 (Lipson, 1991) (contract provision prohibiting unlawful discrimination by the company reflected parties' intent to incorporate federal and state employment law into collective bargaining agreement); Enstar Natural Gas Co., 96 LA 592, 595 (Carr, 1990) (arbitrator required to determine whether application of agreement complied with Internal Revenue Code); Union Trs., 87 LA 1237 (Wolff, 1986) (legality of employer pension fund contributions in light of NLRA, §302(c)(5)(B)); Rock County, 87 LA 1 (Larney, 1986) (application of Fair Labor Standards Act, 29 U.S.C. §201 et seq.); Lakeville Cmty. Sch., 85 LA 945 (Grinstead, 1985) (consideration of teacher tenure act in interpreting collective bargaining agreement); Litton Sys., 84 LA 688 (Bognanno, 1985) (arbitrator considered whether employer violated §§8(a)(5) and 8(d) of Taft-Hartley Act); Johnson Controls, 84 LA 659 (Imundo, Jr., 1985) (arbitration concerning application of Interstate Commerce Commission regulations); Plumbers & Steamfitters Local 131 Pension Fund, 84 LA 632 (Holden, 1985) (arbitrator considered ERISA provisions in determining whether it was proper for local union pension fund to impose an administrative fee on reciprocal payments made to National Pension Fund); Bevles Co., 82 LA 203, 207 (Monat, 1983) (arbitrator agreed that "the labor agreement does not exist in a vacuum" in holding that parties intended external law to apply to their collective bargaining agreement); Wyatt Mfg. Co., 82 LA 153 (Goodman, 1983) (arbitrator considered, inter alia, Supreme Court decisions of *First Nat'l Maint. Corp. v. NLRB*, 452 U.S. 666, 107 LRRM 2705 (1981), and *Fibreboard Paper Prods. Corp. v. NLRB*, 379 U.S. 203, 57 LRRM 2609 (1964), in considering employer's duty to bargain over partial closure of business).

[219]*See, e.g.*, Peabody Coal Co., 98 LA 882, 884 (Feldman, 1992) (arbitrators do not generally base their decisions on statutory provisions unless the contract directs the arbitrator to do so); Reyco Indus., 85 LA 1034 (Newmark, 1985) (refusal to apply law of bailment in lieu of clear language of collective bargaining agreement in determining employer's liability for employee's stolen tools); Koehring S. Plant, 82 LA 193, 196 (Alsher, 1984) (arbitrator found contract language unclear, justifying consideration of past practice and refused to observe dicta in Pennsylvania Court of Common Pleas opinion that conflicted with an express provision in collective bargaining agreement). In *City of Burlington*, 82 LA 21 (Kubie, 1984), the arbitrator declined to consider whether an unemployment compensation hearing officer's prior determination that grievant was not guilty of misconduct disqualifying him from benefits had a collateral estoppel effect on the instant grievance. The arbitrator held that the hearing officer's determination involved a more difficult standard for the employer to satisfy than the standard of "just cause."

[w]here there is clear conflict between the agreement and the law the arbitrator "should respect the agreement and ignore the law." . . . [P]arties call upon an arbitrator to construe their agreement rather than to destroy it, and that there is no reason to credit arbitrators with special expertise with respect to the law as distinguished from the agreement. Thus, arbitrators should respect "the agreement that is the source of their authority and should leave to the courts or other official tribunals the determination of whether the agreement contravenes a higher law. Otherwise, arbitrators would be deciding issues that go beyond not only the submission agreement but, also arbitral competence."[220]

Especially in the context of rising numbers of discrimination claims, the arbitrator's role may be viewed as changing. One arbitrator has suggested that, while arbitrators may not base their determination entirely on their views of an applicable statute without regard to the language of the agreement, where the rights set forth in the agreement are similar to those created by legislation, they must consider the statute.[221] Forced by these circumstances to consider the relative competence of arbitrators to judges, she concluded that arbitrators today "are not afraid to look to applicable statutory and decisional law [and] will apply it if it is relevant."[222]

One arbitrator, when dealing with a contract "subject to all existing or future applicable statutes of the Federal Government," declared the following:

> Since the Agreement requires that it comply with future laws, and such laws invalidate a provision, then it follows that in interpreting and applying the Agreement, we must find Article XVI invalid [because it undeniably violates federal statute 5 U.S.C. §7106(a)].[223]

---

[220]Jefferson-Smurfit Corp., 103 LA 1041, 1048–49 (Canestraight, 1994) (quoting Elkouri & Elkouri, How Arbitration Works 371 (BNA Books 4th ed. 1985)) (absent some right in the agreement, employers are under no obligation to accommodate an employee's disability). *See* Altoona Hosp., 102 LA 650, 652 (Jones, Jr., 1993); Franklin County Children Servs. Bd., 95 LA 1011, 1015 (Mancini, 1990) (The arbitrator's "jurisdiction is limited to an interpretation of the agreement and a determination as to whether the Agency has failed to abide by the contractual provisions. As such, the arbitration proceeding is concerned with contractual rather than statutory rights."); George A. Hormel & Co., 90 LA 1246, 1248 (Goodman, 1988) (arbitrators have no authority to interpret external law even though an arbitrator might be well acquainted with the law in question or well qualified to do so).

[221]Willig, *Arbitration of Discrimination Grievances: Arbitral and Judicial Competence Compared, in* Proceedings of the 39th Annual Meeting of NAA 101 (Gershenfeld ed., BNA Books 1987). *See, e.g.*, KIAM, 97 LA 617, 624 (Bard, 1991) (employers are obligated to promulgate sex discrimination policies that reflect state and federal laws); Fairmont Gen. Hosp., 87 LA 137, 140 (Bolte, 1986) (applying both applicable law and traditional standards of contract interpretation to hospital's unilateral adoption of mandatory retirement age).

[222]Willig, NAA 39th Proceedings, at 108. *But see* James A. Haley Veterans Hosp., 82 LA 973, 974 (Wahl, 1984). The traditional constraints still apply. In this case, the arbitrator felt himself bound by the federal case law on the issue of termination of probationary employees despite the recognition that this decision "regretfully, may deprive [the grievant] of his 'day in court' to have the merits of his termination reviewed. . . . That is beyond an arbitrator's power to remedy." *Id.* at 976. *See also* St. Louis Tel. Employees' Credit Union, 97 LA 412, 416 (Cohen, 1991) (arbitrator upheld employer's termination based on employee's violation of state law, despite lack of "just cause" as defined by the contract).

[223]Government Printing Office, 94 LA 1262, 1265 (Aronin, 1990). *See also* Independent Sch. Dist. 11, 97 LA 169, 172–73 (Gallagher, 1991).

The arbitrator asserted that this finding did not exceed his arbitral authority because it did not add to, subtract from, or modify the agreement beyond the intent of the parties.[224]

ii. Interpretation Against Party Selecting the Language

The "contra proferentem" (against the proponent) principle states that "if language supplied by one party is reasonably susceptible to two interpretations . . . the one that is less favorable to the party that supplied the language is preferred."[225] The rule promotes careful drafting of language and accurate disclosure of what the language is intended to mean by penalizing the proponent who is "at fault" for negligently drafting the text.[226] Arbitrators have applied this principle to provisions involving management rights[227] and seniority.[228]

One arbitrator resorted to the rule in a case involving a contest over a contract reopening:

> The record shows that it was the District that proposed Article 28.6. General rules of contract interpretation hold that clear language should be applied as it is written, and ambiguous language is construed against the party that proposes it. The language in Article 28.6 is clear enough on its face, but ambiguity can be said to arise as to its application because of conflict with the three-year salary agreement. If the language is deemed clear and is applied literally,

---

[224]*Government Printing Office*, 94 LA at 1265.

[225]Farnsworth, Contracts §7.11, 473 (3d ed. 1999). This rule was applied in *Crown Cork & Seal Co.*, 104 LA 1133, 1134 (Wolff, 1995) (ambiguity in work-schedule provision need not be construed against the employer because it was unclear which party drafted provision); *Georgia-Pacific Corp.*, 87 LA 217, 221 (Cohen, 1986) (citing Brown & Sharpe Mfg. Co., 11 LA 228, 233 (Healy, 1948), and concluding that because document was drafted solely by company and probationary employees were not expressly excluded therein as in other documents drafted by company, probationary employees were covered by document); *Mesker Indus.*, 85 LA 921 (Mikrut, 1985) (calculation of 3-month rolling period in absentee-control program ambiguous; arbitrator construed language against company that drafted it). *See also* Tubetech, Inc., 113 LA 1025 (Richard, 1999); San Jose/Evergreen Cmty. Coll. Dist., 111 LA 892 (Staudohar, 1998); Leo's IGA, 92 LA 337, 339 (Corbett, 1989); Silver's, Inc., 89 LA 850, 853 (McDonald, 1987); Potlatch Corp., 88 LA 1184, 1187 (Corbett, 1987). *But see* Vigo County Sch. Corp., 98 LA 988, 992 (Brookins, 1992) (the notion that ambiguous language should be construed against the drafter "is an interpretive canon of last resort which should be applied only where other interpretive efforts have failed").

[226]Potlatch Corp., 88 LA 1184 (Corbett, 1987); Independent Sch. Dist. No. 47, 86 LA 97, 103 (Gallagher, 1985); Lemoyne Coll., 73 LA 846, 850 (McKelvey, 1979); Miami Valley Ready-Mixed Concrete Ass'n, 71 LA 524, 532 (Barone, 1978); Eaton Corp., 71 LA 89, 92 (Dyke, 1978); Wurlitzer Co., 44 LA 1196, 1201 (Kahn, 1965); Borden Co., 36 LA 496, 502 (Morvant, 1961); Timken-Detroit Axle Co., 21 LA 196, 198 (Smith, 1953). *See also* Laclede Gas Co., 89 LA 398 (Mikrut, 1987); Georgia-Pacific Corp., 87 LA 188 (Gibson, 1986); John Morrell & Co., 75 LA 1119, 1128 (Bard, 1980); Zenetron, Inc., 74 LA 861, 864 (Speroff, 1980); Mechanical Prods., 73 LA 569, 573 (Shaw, 1979); County of Los Angeles, 68 LA 1132, 1138 (Richman, 1977); International Register Co., 49 LA 988, 990 (Anrod, 1967); American Synthetic Rubber Co., 47 LA 1078, 1080 (Sales, 1966); Pittsburgh Plate Glass Co., 45 LA 696, 702 (Jenkins, 1965); Central Soya Co., 41 LA 370, 372 (Small, 1962); Clinton Engines Co., 39 LA 943, 947 (Haughton, 1962); Bethlehem Supply Co., 17 LA 632, 635 (Emery, 1951); Brown & Sharpe Mfg. Co., 11 LA 228, 233 (Healy, 1948); Deep Rock Oil Corp., 11 LA 25, 32 (Merrill, 1948); Chrysler Corp., 8 LA 452, 458 (Wolff, 1947); Universal Milking Mach. Co., 2 LA 399, 403 (Elson, 1946). *Cf.* Elastic Stop Nut Corp., 48 LA 663, 667 (Scheiber, 1967).

[227]*See* Stow City Sch. Dist. Bd. of Educ., 99 LA 871, 876 (Dworkin, 1992).

[228]*See* Nelson Tree Serv., 95 LA 1143, 1146 (Loeb, 1990).

the result favors the Association's claim for reopening. If the language is judged ambiguous it can be construed against the drafter, which is the District.[229]

Because the rule is not dependent on the meaning attached by the parties, it is applied when the intention of the parties cannot be ascertained by use of the primary principles of interpretation,[230] and therefore should not be applied if there is no discovered ambiguity.[231] Moreover, where the final text of a provision differs substantially from the original proposal, and both parties approve the final draft[232] and there is no showing that the other party was misled,[233] the rule will not be applied.

iii. Duty of Good Faith and Fair Dealing

Standard contract jurisprudence holds that "[e]very contract imposes upon each party a duty of good faith and fair dealing in its performance and its enforcement."[234] The duty has both prohibitory and mandatory components. "A party may thus be under a duty not only to refrain from hindering or preventing the occurrence of conditions of the party's own duty or the performance of the other party's duty, but also to take affirmative steps to cooperate in achieving these goals."[235]

The implied covenant of "good faith and fair dealing" is similar to the principle of reason and equity, and is deemed to be an inherent part of every collective bargaining agreement.[236] Indeed, this implied covenant is sometimes referred to as the doctrine of reasonableness.[237] The obligation prevents any party to a collective bargaining agreement from doing anything that will have the effect of destroying or injuring the right of the other party to receive the fruits of the contract,[238] and it applies equally to management and labor.[239] The covenant does not arise out of agreement of the parties, but rather out of the operation of the law.[240]

The doctrine was originally created to protect employees who could be fired at will under common law,[241] and the majority of arbitration and judi-

---

[229]San Jose/Evergreen Cmty. Coll. Dist., 111 LA 892, 896 (Staudohar, 1998).

[230]See Deep Rock Oil Corp., 11 LA 25, 32 (Merrill, 1948). See also National Cash Register Co., 46 LA 317, 320 (Kates, 1966); Pennsylvania Truck Lines, 42 LA 311, 314 (Krimsly, 1964). For a suggestion of a stronger justification for using the rule where commercial rather than labor contracts are involved, see U-Brand Corp., 72 LA 1267, 1270–71 (Ruben, 1979).

[231]John Deere Tractor Co., 2 LA 469, 472 (Updegraff, 1945).

[232]Crescent Warehouse Co., 10 LA 168, 171 (Aaron, 1948).

[233]International Harvester Co., 13 LA 133, 135 (McCoy, 1949). See also Naegele Outdoor Adver. Co. of Louisville, 76 LA 1033, 1036 (Mulhall, 1981); Allis-Chalmers Corp., 71 LA 375, 381 (Goetz, 1978); Garden State Paper Co., 58 LA 912, 917 (Block, 1972).

[234]Restatement (Second) of Contracts §205 (1981).

[235]Farnsworth, Contracts §7.17, at 506 (3d ed. 1999) (footnotes omitted).

[236]Steelworkers Local 4264 v. New Park Mining Co., 273 F.2d 352, 356–57, 45 LRRM 2158 (10th Cir. 1959).

[237]Ashland Oil Co., 95 LA 339 (Volz, 1990); Arvin Indus., 88 LA 1188 (Volz, 1987).

[238]III Williston on Contracts §670; Restatement (Second) of Contracts §201; Ashland Oil Co., 95 LA 339 (Volz, 1990).

[239]Indianapolis Pub. Transp. Corp., 94 LA 1299 (Volz, 1990).

[240]Roadmaster Corp., 98 LA 847 (Christenson, 1992).

[241]Milne Employee Ass'n v. Sun Carriers, 960 F.2d 1401, 1411, 143 LRRM 2663 (9th Cir. 1991); Garibaldi v. Lucky Food Stores, 726 F.2d 1367, 1373 n.9, 1374, 1374–75 n.11, 115 LRRM 3089 (9th Cir. 1984), cert. denied, 471 U.S. 1099 (1985).

cial decisions addressing this covenant involve employee discharges. While many states allow a discharged at-will employee to use the implied covenant of good faith as a discrete cause of action for wrongful discharge, it is clear that when an employee is represented by a union that is a party to a collective bargaining agreement, Section 301 of the LMRA preempts the state law claim for breach of the implied covenant of good faith and fair dealing.[242] Unionized employees protected by a collective bargaining agreement do not have a comparable lack of job security.[243] So long as the collective bargaining agreement provides a level of security that is comparable to that provided by the implied duty of good faith and fair dealing, such as a "just cause" provision for discipline or discharge, the exclusive remedy for a claim that an employer has breached the implied covenant of good faith and fair dealing in terminating an employee is provided by Section 301.[244]

Arbitration and judicial decisions often cite the implied covenant of good faith and fair dealing in a number of other contexts, but the doctrine serves as little more than an interpretive tool to aid arbitrators and judges in their case-by-case determinations of breaches of collective bargaining agreements. Arbitrators frequently use the implied covenant of good faith and fair dealing in their discussions of subcontracting issues.[245] The same is true when the issue being arbitrated involves other aspects of reserved management rights. Essentially, the implied covenant of good faith and fair dealing serves as a springboard for a case-by-case determination of reasonableness.[246] Thus,

---

[242]Allis-Chalmers Corp. v. Lueck, 471 U.S. 202, 220, 118 LRRM 3345 (1985); Brown v. Lucky Stores, 246 F.3d 1182, 1189, 11 AD Cases 1195 (9th Cir. 2001); Garley v. Sandia Corp., 236 F.3d 1200, 17 IER Cases 224 (10th Cir. 2001); Audette v. Longshoremen (ILWU) Local 24, 195 F.3d 1107, 1112, 162 LRRM 2705 (9th Cir. 1999); Rissetto v. Plumbers & Steamfitters Local 343, 94 F.3d 597, 599, 153 LRRM 2111 (9th Cir. 1996); Schlacter-Jones v. General Tel. of Cal., 936 F.2d 435, 440, 6 IER Cases 897 (9th Cir. 1991); Cook v. Lindsay Olive Growers, 911 F.2d 233, 238–39, 7 IER Cases 1767 (9th Cir. 1990); Jackson v. Southern Cal. Gas Co., 881 F.2d 638, 644–45, 131 LRRM 3238 (9th Cir. 1989).

[243]Garibaldi v. Lucky Food Stores, 726 F.2d 1367, 1374–75 n.11, 115 LRRM 3089 (9th Cir. 1984).

[244]Young v. Anthony's Fish Grottos, 830 F.2d 993, 999, 2 IER Cases 1086 (9th Cir. 1987).

[245]See, e.g., WMHT Educ. Telecomm., 108 LA 108 (Babiskin, 1997) ("Few issues have engendered more litigation and mistrust than subcontracting and/or claimed violations with regard to the assignment of 'unit work' to 'non-unit' personnel." Id. at 110. "There are literally hundreds of reported cases involving 'subcontracting,' 'unit work' and 'employee/independent contractor' issues." Id. at 111.). See also City of Watervliet, N.Y., 116 LA 238 (Babiskin, 2001); Libbey Glass, Inc., 116 LA 182 (Ruben, 2000); City of Evansville, Ind., 112 LA 775 (Cohen, 1999); Finch, Pruyn & Co., 111 LA 1 (Babiskin, 1998); Furniture Workers Div., Case No. 97-02178-2, 1997 WL 901860 (Holley, Jr., 1997); Angelus Block Co., 100 LA 1129 (Prayzich, 1993); Bundy Corp., 100 LA 873 (Volz, 1993).

[246]United Tech. Auto., 108 LA 769 (Richard, 1997) (used the implied covenant as an interpretive tool in determining whether management had exercised its reserved rights in a reasonable manner). See also Super Valu Stores, 93 LA 931 (Eisele, 1989); Continental Fibre Drum, 86 LA 780 (Hart, 1986); Associated Grocers, 86 LA 895 (Weizenbaum, 1985); Pickands Mather & Co., 78 LA 1183 (Garrett, 1982); Uniroyal, Inc. 76 LA 1049 (Nolan, 1981). Assume that X has contracted to cut Y's lawn once every 7 days for $25 per cut. X therefore has some discretion as to when in a 7-day period he will cut Y's lawn. A first cuts the lawn on the seventh day after the contract (thus fulfilling X's obligation to cut the lawn during the first 7-day period), but then X returns on the very next (eighth) day to cut the lawn, when it is not needed. X needs to perform hardly any work and Y receives almost no benefit. If Y sued X for failure to perform the contract based on the clause that requires X to cut the lawn once every 7 days, Y would probably lose, because X has literally met that obligation. But if Y sues X based on a breach of the implied covenant of good faith and fair dealing that is inherent in

the covenant serves as the basis for the proposition that managerial discretion must be exercised reasonably[247] and discretionary management decisions will be reviewed to determine if they were arbitrary, capricious, or discriminatory.[248]

It should be noted that the implied covenant of good faith and fair dealing does not inject new obligations or duties into the labor agreement.[249] The implied covenant governs only conduct in those areas that are controlled by the agreement and does not impose a duty to act in good faith in matters outside of the agreement.[250] Consequently, while the implied covenant can serve as a basis for a claim of breach of a collective bargaining agreement, the claim must be coupled with some specific allegation of a violation of the collective bargaining agreement or the federal labor laws.[251] Some courts have noted that the doctrine cannot override express terms of an integrated written contract.[252]

iv. Fair Bargain Concept

Allied to the principle of avoiding harsh results and interpreting in an equitable manner, the "fair bargain" concept assumes that the negotiation process resulted in a fair bargain, and that "an interpretation which sacrifices a major interest of one of the parties while furthering only a marginal interest of the other should be rejected in favor of an interpretation which sacrifices marginal interests of both parties in order to protect their major concerns."[253]

---

every contract, then Y might win if it could be shown that Y had a justified expectation that X would not cut his lawn 2 days in a row. The covenant comes into play because X had some discretion as to when, in a 7-day period, X would cut the lawn and X, ostensibly, abused that discretion and acted in an unreasonable manner.

[247]Miami Beach Fraternal Order of Police, Case No. 96-19443-8, 1997 WL 910355 (Kravit, 1997).

[248]See, e.g., City of Boulder v. Public Serv. Co. of Colo., 996 P.2d 198, 204 (Colo. Ct. App. 1999) ("[T]he doctrine [i.e., the implied covenant of good faith and fair dealing] is applied only when 'one party has discretionary authority to determine certain terms of the contract such as quantity, price or time,'" quoting Amoco Oil Co. v. Ervin, 908 P.2d 493, 498 (1995)).

[249]See Foley v. Aspen Ski Lodge, 208 F.3d 225 (10th Cir. 2000) (table) (unpublished decision).

[250]E.I. DuPont de Nemours & Co. v. Martinsville Nylon Employees' Council Corp., 78 F.3d 578 (4th Cir. 1996) (unpublished decision).

[251]It is clear from a review of the judicial and arbitration decisions that a claim of breach of the implied covenant of good faith and fair dealing will not stand on its own. A party must allege that there is some cognizable violation of the collective bargaining agreement or the federal labor laws and that such a violation constituted a breach of the implied duty of good faith and fair dealing *in addition to* a violation of a specific contractual provision or statute. For example, in *Carlisle Tire & Rubber Co.*, 99 LA 893, 894 (McMillen, 1992), the union claimed that the employer, in moving its operation to a different state and closing the plant, "breached the implied covenant of good faith and fair dealing . . . *by withdrawing any severance benefits during negotiations* on the closure" of the company's operations (emphasis added). The arbitrator noted that the union did not cite to a violation of any specific provision of the collective bargaining agreement and noted that "[w]ithout the violation of a specific provision in the contract, the grievance procedure and arbitration are not called into play." *Id.* at 895. The arbitrator then noted that "the breach of contract claim is basically nonarbitrable for lack of any proper grievance." *Id.*

[252]See Lemken v. Intel Corp., 134 F.3d 382 (10th Cir. 1998) (unpublished decision); Bourgeous v. Horizon Healthcare Corp., 117 N.M. 434, 438, 872 P.2d 852, 9 IER Cases 596 (1994); Borbely v. Nationwide Mut. Ins. Co., 547 F. Supp. 959 (D.N.J. 1981).

[253]Sharon Steel Corp. v. Chase Manhattan Bank, 691 F.2d 1039, 1051 (2d Cir. 1982) (quoted in FARNSWORTH, CONTRACTS §7.11, at 473 (3d ed. 1999)).

v. *Reason and Equity*

It is widely recognized that if a contract "is clear and unambiguous it must be applied in accordance with its terms despite the equities that may be present on either side."[254] Arbitrators strive where possible to give *ambiguous* language a construction that is reasonable and equitable to both parties rather than one that would give one party an unfair and unreasonable advantage.[255] The arbitrator, it has been said, should "look at the language in the light of experience and choose that course which does the least violence to the judgment of a reasonable man."[256]

In addition to reviewing various indicia of the intentions of the parties such as past practice and even arbitral precedent, one arbitrator noted that he could not "overlook the equity aspects surrounding [the] grievance . . . which serves to guide him in making for a proper and fair interpretation of the language embodied in [the contract]."[257] Thus he considered the great financial burden on employees who had already retired if their petition for continuation of insurance coverage were denied, particularly because many would find it difficult, if not impossible, to obtain medical coverage due to their advanced age and medical condition. With that in mind, the arbitrator found "that the factor of equity buttresse[d] [his] finding that those employees who had already retired would not be affected by the [retenchment] language of the 1984 Agreement."[258] Another arbitrator, however, cautioned that "[c]lear and unambiguous contractual language may not be compromised by notions of equity."[259]

---

[254]Firestone Tire & Rubber Co., 29 LA 469, 473 (Hebert, 1957). *See also* Magma Copper Co., 51 LA 9, 13 (Abernethy, 1968); Hadley Adhesive & Chem. Co., 49 LA 229, 230–31 (Erbs, 1967).

[255]*See* Clean-A-Rama, 99 LA 370 (Concepcion, 1992) (finding that interpretation by a party that is in conformity with logical and realistic reading of contracts should prevail); Varied Prods. of Ind., 95 LA 1264, 1265 (Witney, 1990) (finding that denying holiday pay for reporting to work 2 minutes late was unreasonable interpretation of contract provision requiring employee to work an 8-hour day immediately following holiday to qualify for holiday pay); Centel Bus. Sys., 95 LA 472 (Allen, Jr., 1990) (reasoning that, where neither party's interpretation can be accommodated under contract language, arbitrator must fashion remedy as reasonably and logically as possible). *See also* A.D. Juilliard & Co., 17 LA 606 (Maggs, 1951); Pan Am. Airways, 12 LA 478 (Broadwin, 1949); Clifton Paper Bd. Co., 11 LA 1019 (Stein, 1949). For arbitrators construing ambiguous provisions in such manner as to minimize possible harm to the parties and their relationship, see *City of Joliet, Ill.*, 112 LA 468 (Perkovich, 1999); *Geuder, Paeschke, & Frey Co.*, 69 LA 871 (Wyman, 1977); *Keystone Consol. Indus.*, 68 LA 165 (Cyrol, 1977). *See also* Goetz, *The Law of Contracts—A Changing Legal Environment: Comment, in* TRUTH, LIE DETECTORS, AND OTHER PROBLEMS IN LABOR ARBITRATION, PROCEEDINGS OF THE 31ST ANNUAL MEETING OF NAA 218, 227–28 (Stern & Dennis eds., BNA Books 1979).

[256]Clifton Paper Bd. Co., 11 LA 1019, 1020 (Stein, 1949).

[257]Jim Walter Res., 87 LA 857, 862 (Nicholas, Jr., 1986).

[258]*Id. See also* Valley Hosp. Ass'n, 97 LA 661, 669 (Calhoun, 1991).

[259]Cincinnati Enquirer, 94 LA 1121, 1126 (Witney, 1990). *See* Iowa Indus. Hydraulics, 100 LA 1208, 1211 (Pelofsky, 1993); University of Ill. at Chi. Bd. of Trs., 100 LA 728, 735 (Goldstein, 1992); Public Hous. Agency, St. Paul, 87 LA 33, 38 (Gallagher, 1986); Los Angeles Unified Sch. Dist., 85 LA 905, 908 (Gentile, 1985); Hemlock Pub. Sch. Bd. of Educ., 83 LA 474, 477 (Dobry, 1984) (holding that arbitrator's "first obligation is to observe the limits of his power as articulated by the labor agreement. The parties created this arbitral forum, and the Arbitrator is duty-bound to honor the restrictions. Under this contract, his authority is narrowly defined: notions of fairness or equity are not relevant considerations."). *But see* Purity Baking Co., 95 LA 172, 175 n.12 (Gordon, 1990) ("[I]n a significant number of 'rights'

Considerations of fairness enter into the equation where the contract allows for the exercise of discretion on the part of the employer, however, the employer's actions may not be arbitrary, capricious, discriminatory, or unreasonable.[260]

"Equity" may also be a factor in the formulation of a remedy. One arbitrator apportioned a back-pay award based on the 25 percent equity he found favoring the grievant:

> In cases where the remedy can be divisible, such as back pay or seniority as compared to reinstatement or reprimand, and where the merits are somewhat split, an all-or-nothing solution does not seem to be equitable or effective. Thus, in this case, the arbitrator concludes that the balance weighs partially—approximately one quarter—in favor of [grievant].[261]

vi. Avoidance of a Forfeiture

It is a familiar maxim that the law abhors a forfeiture.[262] If an agreement is susceptible of two constructions, one of which would work a forfeiture and one of which would not, the arbitrator will be inclined to adopt the interpretation that will prevent the forfeiture.[263] One arbitrator elaborated on this principle in the context of a case involving the compensation claim of an employee under a clause requiring retroactive pay for employees unjustly discharged, where the employee had suffered no loss of earnings while off the company payroll.

---

decisions involving melding of seniority units . . . arbitrators confess to relying almost exclusively on equity considerations."); Rockwell Int'l Corp., 84 LA 496, 502 (Feldman, 1985). *See* Lorillard, Inc., 87 LA 507, 512 (Chalfie, 1986) ("[Arbitrator's] function is not to rewrite that Agreement and certainly it is not to suggest, imply nor to inform the Parties of what changes should be effected, renegotiated or changed even if his sense of justice and fairness should so dictate, or even if he believes the Agreement contains inequities."); Pollock Co., 87 LA 325, 335 (Oberdank, 1986) ("[T]he arbitrator does not sit as a Chancellor in Equity. Rather, his function is to interpret and apply the collective bargaining agreement before him.").

[260]*See* Michigan Employment Sec. Comm'n, 84 LA 473 (Fieger, 1985); Hussmann Corp., 84 LA 23 (Maniscalco, 1984); Chillicothe Tel. Co., 84 LA 1 (Gibson, 1984).

[261]Chestnut Operating Co., 82 LA 121, 123 (Zirkel, 1983). *See also* Oakland Cal. Unified Sch. Dist., 111 LA 165 (Levy, 1998) (school district required to pay only 25% of teacher's compensation from time he had been released to return to work after surgery until reinstatement after settlement of disability claim, where district contributed to delay by setting up committee that did not meet regularly and by tying accommodations to settlement, but grievant delayed proceedings by not responding promptly to proposals, by proposing revisions, and by delaying signing final agreement).

[262]In *Lithonia Lighting Co.*, 85 LA 627, 630 (Volz, 1985), the arbitrator stated that "it is a familiar principle that the law abhors a forfeiture of a valuable right, such as the termination of seniority . . . ." He applied this principle to set aside the termination of grievant's seniority under ambiguous contract language. *Accord* City of Joliet, Ill., 112 LA 468, 473 (Perkovich, 1999).

[263]*See* City of Marion, Ohio, 91 LA 175 (Bittel, 1988); Northrup Worldwide Aircraft Servs., 90 LA 79 (Bankston, 1987); Thrifty Drug Stores, 88 LA 822 (Ross, 1987); CPC Int'l, 76 LA 986, 993 (Edes, 1981); Badger Concrete Co., 35 LA 912, 914 (Mueller, 1961); Alpha Cellulose Corp., 27 LA 798, 800 (Kelliher, 1956); Mode O'Day Corp., 1 LA 490, 494 (Cheney, 1946). *See also* Lithonia Lighting, 85 LA 627 (Volz, 1985).

A party claiming a forfeiture or penalty under a written instrument has the burden of proving that such is the unmistakable intention of the parties to the document. In addition, the courts have ruled that a contract is not to be construed to provide a forfeiture or penalty unless no other construction or interpretation is reasonably possible. Since forfeitures are not favored either in law or in equity, courts are reluctant to declare and enforce forfeiture if by reasonable interpretation it can be avoided.[264]

Consequently, the clause was interpreted by the arbitrator as an indemnity (rather than a forfeiture) clause, and the grievance was denied.

On the issue of the timeliness of a grievance, in addition to the "tolling" doctrine borrowed from equity to avoid the running of the statute of limitations when there is good reason to do so, arbitrators employ the "avoidance of forfeiture" analysis to reach the same result. It has been said that, "[a]s a general statement, forfeiture of a grievance based on missed time limits should be avoided whenever possible . . . ."[265]

Another arbitrator found a grievance to be arbitrable, even though it took longer than the 60 days specified in the contract to conduct a hearing:

> More specifically, that just and more reasonable result is evidence [sic] by the second rule of contractual interpretation, that the law abhors a forfeiture. First, the party seeking the forfeiture bears the burden of proving its necessity . . . . Second, arbitrators are strongly disinclined to find the forfeiture when the issue giving rise to the possible penalty is the timeliness of the grievance. Not only is that the case in the instant matter, but the timeliness involved is not with respect to the initial filing, where the Employer might argue that there would be some harm to it if the matter were not timely raised, but rather with respect to the processing of the claim once it had been filed.[266]

Still another arbitrator noted that "[w]hile it is not for an arbitrator to rewrite a contract, if the contract is ambiguous insofar as time limitations are concerned, since the law abhors forfeitures, the ambiguity should be resolved in favor of timeliness."[267] Quoting that statement, an arbitrator interpreted a contract provision requiring the filing of a grievance within 5 days of the event to mean 5 working days,[268] and concluded that notification of the filing of a grievance 6 calendar days after the occurrence on which it was based was timely.

The potential for conflict, however, between such a rule of construction and the intention of the parties was highlighted by another arbitrator:

> This arbitrator must respectfully disagree with those arbitrators who would stretch clear language of default to the ultimate limit perceiving some obligation to avoid all forfeitures notwithstanding the parties' clear agreement. It

---

[264]Mode O'Day, 1 LA 490, 494 (Cheney, 1946) (numerous court cases are cited). *See also* City of Joliet, Ill., 112 LA 468 (Perkovich, 1999) (the party seeking the forfeiture bears the burden of proving its necessity).

[265]Safeway Stores, 95 LA 668, 673 (Goodman, 1990). *See also* City of Saginaw, Mich., 96 LA 718 (Borland, 1990); Concrete Pipe Prods. Co., 87 LA 601 (Caraway, 1986).

[266]City of Joliet, Ill., 112 LA 468, 473 (Perkovich, 1999).

[267]*In re* Clougherty Packing Co., 85 LA 1053, 1057 (Richman, 1985).

[268]Concrete Pipe Prods, 87 LA 601, 604 (Caraway, 1986).

seems appropriate to let the parties determine the extent to which defaults will be excused, and where the language chosen reflects no such intent but rather an inflexible and absolute application, then the arbitrator has no right to interfere. To resolve doubts and avoid a forfeiture is one thing; to rationalize disregard of a clear contractual mandate is another indeed.[269]

---

[269]Wayne County, Mich., Intermediate Sch. Dist., 85 LA 673, 675–76 (Daniel, 1985). *See* Akron, Ohio, City Bd. of Educ., 86 LA 164, 169 (Dworkin, 1986) ("It is broadly held that contractual forfeiture clauses must be enforced, but only if all facts necessary to trigger divestiture are adequately proven.").

Chapter 10

Use of Substantive Rules of Law

1. General Considerations

A. Applying External Law [LA CDI 94.553; 100.30]

Arbitration exists as a private alternative to the courts. As such, the rules are those drafted not by legislators, who then enact them into statutes, but by the parties themselves. They are private rules, and the party chosen to interpret and apply them—the arbitrator—is an individual who draws his or her authority from the collective bargaining agreement, or the agreement, to submit the matter to arbitration. As such, private-sector parties are free to control the degree to which the arbitrator is to consider external law, including statutes and regulations, in deciding the case.[1]

---

[1]For arbitral authority on this issue, see *San Francisco, Cal., Unified Sch. Dist.*, 114 LA 140, 140 (Riker, 2000) (grievance alleging violation of the Americans with Disabilities Act (ADA), 42 U.S.C. §12101 et seq., arbitrable because, in the collective bargaining agreement, the school district expressly retained "all rights, authorities and duties conferred upon and vested in it by [federal and California state laws]"); *Alcoa Bldg. Prods.*, 104 LA 364 (Cerone, 1995) (where the contract was silent regarding the arbitrator's authority to address external legal issues, the arbitrator applied external law based on potential conflict between federal law and the agreement and the parties' stipulation); *Multi-Clean, Inc.*, 102 LA 463 (Miller, 1993) (arbitrator lacked the authority to determine whether the employer violated the ADA where the collective bargaining agreement limited arbitrator jurisdiction to interpretation of contract terms only); *Exxon Co. U.S.A.*, 101 LA 997 (Sergent, 1993) (arbitrator lacked jurisdiction to hear a dispute arising under a last chance agreement where the grievance did not pose questions arising out of the contract but rather questioned the legality of the last chance agreement under the Fair Labor Standards Act (FLSA), 29 U.S.C. §201 et seq., and the ADA); *City of Fort Dodge, Iowa*, 93 LA 759 (Cohen, 1989) (parties' contractual references to various statutes indicated their intention to have statutory provisions apply); *Pepsi Cola Bottling Co. of San Diego*, 93 LA 520 (Randall, 1989) (arbitrator concluded that a party's use of the term "probable cause" with respect to drug testing was presumed to apply in its legal sense); *ICI Ams.*, 93 LA 408 (Gibson, 1989) (arbitrator considered whether employer violated Title VII based on a clause in the contract prohibiting discrimination in employment); *Star*

To be sure, the field of labor relations, although developed through collective bargaining and arbitration, has never been purely private. Various state and federal legislation has always existed, providing varying degrees of detailed regulation of working conditions in various industries. But the protection provided by many of these statutes was relatively sparse; arbitration provided far more comprehensive protection.

Beginning in the 1960s, however, sweeping federal employment-related legislation became more of a reality. The emergence of the Equal Pay Act of 1963,[2] Title VII of the Civil Rights Act of 1964,[3] the Occupational Safety and Health Act (OSH Act) of 1970,[4] the Employee Retirement Income Security Act (ERISA)[5] of 1974, as well as the Americans with Disabilities Act (ADA) of 1990 and the Family and Medical Leave Act (FMLA) of 1993,[6] among other statutes,[7] brought new life to the question of whether, and to what extent, arbitrators should consider external law.[8]

Tribune, 93 LA 14 (Bognanno, 1989) (arbitrator applied National Labor Relations Board (NLRB, or the Board) law based on contractual union activity nondiscrimination clause); *Alpha Beta Co.*, 92 LA 1301, 1302 (Wilmoth, 1989) (arbitrator considered federal cases concerning burden shifting procedure in discrimination grievance based on contract clause stating that neither the employer nor the union would discriminate against any individual on the basis of, among other things, age "in accordance with the provisions and requirements of state and federal laws"); *Florida Power Corp.*, 87 LA 957 (Wahl, 1986) (arbitrator considered the applicability of the FLSA based on a contract clause defining a grievance to include violation of the law "governing employer-employee relationship"). *But cf.* Cosmic Distrib., 92 LA 205 (Prayzich, 1989) (arbitrator declined to consider external law regarding wages of returning economic strikers where parties stipulated that the only issue was whether the company had violated the collective bargaining agreement); Cleveland Twist Drill Co., 92 LA 105 (Strasshofer, 1989) (arbitrator ruled that he was not empowered to consider the Age Discrimination in Employment Act (ADEA), 29 U.S.C. §621 et seq., and the National Labor Relations Act (NLRA), 29 U.S.C. §151 et seq., in ruling on grievance of retirees concerning early retirement and age discrimination claims because the collective bargaining agreement excluded early retirees, thus depriving him of jurisdiction to rule on those issues).

For federal court authority on this issue, see *AGCO Corp. v. Anglin*, 216 F.3d 589 (7th Cir. 2000) (explaining that, although arbitration agreements must not be so broadly construed as to encompass claims that were not intended to be arbitrated by the parties, a party that willingly and without objection allows an issue to be submitted to arbitration cannot later argue that the arbitrator lacked authority to decide the matter); *Richmond, Fredericksburg & Potomac R.R. v. Transportation Communications Union*, 973 F.2d 276, 141 LRRM 2115, 2117 (4th Cir. 1992) (parties define issues submitted and no statutory barrier to submitting questions involving the interpretation of statutes or case law exists); *High Concrete Structures of N.J. v. Electrical Workers (UE) Local 166*, 879 F.2d 1215, 131 LRRM 3152, 3154 (3d Cir. 1989) (terms of submission may empower arbitrator to resolve disputes that go beyond the four corners of a collective bargaining agreement); *Postal Workers v. U.S. Postal Serv.*, 789 F.2d 1, 122 LRRM 2094 (D.C. Cir. 1986) (court observed arbitrator had authority to rule on legal issues in view of contract clause requiring compliance with applicable laws); *Jones Dairy Farm v. Food & Commercial Workers Local P-1236*, 760 F.2d 173, 119 LRRM 2185, 2186 (7th Cir. 1985) (parties may have question of law resolved by an arbitrator rather than a judge).

[2]29 U.S.C. §206.

[3]42 U.S.C. §2000e et seq.

[4]29 U.S.C. §651 et seq.

[5]29 U.S.C. §1001 et seq.

[6]29 U.S.C. §2601 et seq.

[7]*E.g.*, the Fair Labor Standards Act (FLSA), 29 U.S.C. §201 et seq.; the Age Discrimination in Employment Act (ADEA), 29 U.S.C. §621 et seq.; the Rehabilitation Act of 1993, 29 U.S.C. §701 et seq.

[8]*See* Richmond, Fredericksburg & Potomac R.R. v. Transportation Communications Union, 973 F.2d 276, 141 LRRM 2115, 2117 (4th Cir. 1992) (parties define issues submitted and no statutory barrier to submitting questions involving the interpretation of statutes or case law

In agreeing to resolve disputes by arbitration, parties choose to substitute a private solution for litigation in courts of law. Because the appointment and authority of the arbitrator are under the control of the parties, they can by the submission agreement expressly regulate (but do not often do so) the extent to which the arbitrator is to consider applicable law.

The parties may expressly direct that the case be decided consistent with applicable law,[9] or they may restrict the arbitrator's authority to interpret the law.[10] Similarly, the parties can determine in the submission agreement the extent to which the decision is to be final[11] by providing, for example, that the award is to be final only with respect to limited areas, such as questions of fact,[12] or, alternatively, providing that it is to be final except in case of "gross mistake of law or fact."[13] However, unless the parties spe-

---

exists); High Concrete Structures of N.J. v. Electrical Workers (UE) Local 166, 879 F.2d 1215, 131 LRRM 3152, 3154 (3d Cir. 1989) (terms of submission may empower arbitrator to resolve disputes that go beyond the four corners of a collective bargaining agreement); Jones Dairy Farm v. Food & Commercial Workers Local P-1236, 760 F.2d 173, 119 LRRM 2185, 2186 (7th Cir. 1985) (parties may have question of law resolved by an arbitrator rather than a judge).

[9]See Dorado Beach Hotel Corp. v. Hotel & Rest. Employees Local 610, 959 F.2d 2, 140 LRRM 2067, 2069 (1st Cir. 1992) (arbitrator properly based award on Puerto Rican law when collective bargaining agreement itself, as well as parties' submissions, empowered arbitrator to resolve dispute according to law); North Adams Reg'l Hosp. v. Massachusetts Nursing Ass'n, 889 F. Supp. 507, 513 (D. Mass. 1995) (court ruled that where the parties empowered the arbitrator to determine whether the contract was violated, the arbitrator could reasonably resort to traditional rules of contract construction); Vista Chem. Co., 99 LA 994 (Baroni, 1992) (agreement expressly adopted external law regarding employee drug testing); Alaska Dep't of Admin., 96 LA 937 (Robinson, 1991) (arbitrator has authority to resolve dispute regarding compensation for state employees' voluntary overtime work where the collective bargaining agreement explicitly provided that the public policy standards contained in the FLSA would be the criteria for determining overtime eligibility); East St. Louis, Ill., Sch. Dist. No. 189, 88 LA 1120, 1123 (Canestraight, 1987) (parties agreed on "this Arbitrator to sit for hearing after the Supreme Court decision in Hudson to make a determination of the constitutionality and proper method for fair share provision in the contract"); Barnard Eng'g Co., 86 LA 523, 524 (Brisco, 1985) (agreement specified that disputes must be "interpreted pursuant to applicable NLRB and judicial principles"); Sonic Knitting Indus., 65 LA 453, 463–65 (Helfeld, 1975); A.S. Abell Co., 45 LA 801, 807 (Cluster, Gallagher, & Kraushaar, 1965); New York City, N.Y., Bd. of Educ., 44 LA 997, 1001 (Stark, 1964). Cf. Southern Cal. Gas Co., 91 LA 100, 104 (Collins, 1988) (arbitrator implied from the language of the contract that the applicable section "be applied in a manner consistent with the provision of federal law").

[10]See, e.g., Magic Chef, 88 LA 1046, 1047 (Caraway, 1987) (agreement provided that the arbitrator "shall not have the authority to interpret any state or federal law"). See also Ingalls Shipbuilding Corp., 54 LA 484, 487 (Boothe, 1971) (through their actions, parties jointly waived a contract provision otherwise prohibiting the arbitrator from interpreting any state or federal statute).

[11]See Trade & Transport v. Natural Petrol Charterers, 931 F.2d 191, 195 (2d Cir. 1991) (if parties agree that the arbitrator is to make the final decision only as to a part of the dispute, the arbitrator has the authority and responsibility to do so, and once the submitted issues have been decided, the arbitrator's authority over those questions ends); Corporate Printing Co. Inc. v. Typographical Union No. 6 (New York), 147 LRRM 2918, 2921 (S.D.N.Y. 1994) (the parties, through the submission agreement, "determine the scope of the arbitrator's authority," and when part of the dispute is submitted with the intent that the arbitrator's decision be final on the issue submitted, the "arbitrator has authority and responsibility to issue a final . . . award").

[12]See submission in Food Employers Council, 20 LA 724, 725 (Van de Water, 1953), which specifically made the award reviewable as to law by the courts.

[13]E.g., Goodyear Eng'g Corp., 24 LA 360, 362 (Warns, 1955).

cifically limit the powers of the arbitrator to any aspect of the issue submitted, it is often presumed that they intend to make the arbitrator the final judge on all questions that may arise in the disposition of the issue, including not only questions of fact but also questions of contract interpretation, rules of interpretation, and questions, if any, with respect to substantive law.[14]

B. Errors of Law [LA CDI 94.68]

Long ago the U.S. Supreme Court emphasized that arbitration awards are not generally subject to being set aside for errors of law:

> Arbitrators are judges chosen by the parties to decide the matters submitted to them, finally and without appeal. As a mode of settling disputes, it should receive every encouragement from courts of equity. If the award is within the submission, and contains the honest decision of the arbitrators, after a full and fair hearing of the parties, a court of equity will not set it aside for error, either in law or fact. A contrary course would be a substitution of the judgment of the chancellor in place of the judges chosen by the parties, and would make an award the commencement, not the end, of litigation.[15]

Similarly, in a 1953 case involving the Federal Arbitration Act,[16] the Supreme Court stated that: "In unrestricted submissions, . . . the interpretations of the law by the arbitrators in contrast to manifest disregard are not subject, in the federal courts, to judicial review for error in interpretation."[17]

---

[14]*See* Hirras v. National R.R. Passenger Corp., 10 F.3d 1142, 145 LRRM 2137, 2140 (5th Cir. 1994) (there is no statutory barrier to prevent submission of questions involving the interpretation of statute or case law); Richmond, Fredericksburg & Potomac R.R. v. Transportation Communications Union, 973 F.2d 276, 141 LRRM 2115, 2118 (4th Cir. 1992) (when parties submit an issue without limiting the sources the arbitrator may consult, the arbitrator may base the decision on any number of grounds, including statutes and case law); Marriott Host Int'l, 94 LA 862 (Rule, 1990) (parties' submission did not limit the scope of the remedy to what was provided for by the collective bargaining agreement). *But see* Sprint/Central Tel. Co.-Nev., 114 LA 633, 640 (Baroni, 2000) (arbitrator refused to accept jurisdiction over dispute as to whether contractors were employees of the company because that determination required application of Internal Revenue Service guidelines, which were beyond the "four corners" of the labor contract and, therefore, beyond the scope of the arbitrator's authority).

[15]Burchell v. Marsh, 58 U.S. 344, 17 Howard 344 (1854).

[16]9 U.S.C. §§1–14. For related discussion, see Chapter 1, section 7.B.i.d.(3), "Manifest Disregard of the Law," and Chapter 2, section 2.A.i., "The Federal Arbitration Act," section 2.A.ii.c.(6), "Awards Based on, or Inconsistent With, Statutory Law," and section 2.A.ii.c.(9), "Vacatur Because of 'Evident Partaility,' 'Misconduct,' 'Corruption,' and 'Manifest Disregard of the Law.'"

[17]Wilko v. Swan, 346 U.S. 427, 436 (1953) (citing *Burchell*). In evaluating this statement, the U.S. Court of Appeals for the Ninth Circuit stated that "manifest disregard of the law must be something beyond and different from a mere error in the law or failure on the part of the arbitrators to understand or apply the law"; a manifest disregard of the law "might be present when arbitrators understand and correctly state the law, but proceed to disregard the same." San Martine Co. de Navegacion, S.A. v. Saguenay Terminals, 293 F.2d 796, 801 (9th Cir. 1961). For subsequent reference to *Wilko* and its theme of limited judicial review of awards, see Justice Harlan's concurring opinion in *U.S. Bulk Carriers v. Arguelles*, 400 U.S. 351, 358, 76 LRRM 2161 (1971). *See also* Willemijn Houdstermaatschappij v. Standard Microsystems, 103 F.3d 9, 12 (2d Cir. 1997) (the court, recognizing that district courts may vacate arbitration awards when arbitrators are in manifest disregard of the law, defined manifest disregard as "'something beyond and different from a mere error in the law or failure on the part of the arbitrators to understand or apply the law. . . . Manifest disregard . . . may be found . . . if the arbitrator 'understood and correctly stated the law but proceeded to ignore it.'") (quoting Siegel v. Titan Indus. Corp., 779 F.2d 891, 892 (2d Cir. 1985)); Matteson

The continued vitality of the general rule that awards are not impeach-able for errors of law has been recognized by federal and state courts in both statutory and common law arbitration.[18]

---

v. Ryder Sys., 99 F.3d 108, 153 LRRM 2740 (3d Cir. 1996) (an arbitration award will be enforceable only to the extent it does not exceed the scope of the parties' submission); Prudential-Bache Sec. v. Tanner, 72 F.3d 234, 239–40 (1st Cir. 1995) ("in order to demon-strate that an arbitrator recognized and ignored applicable law under manifest disregard of loss standard of review, there must be a showing in the record, that the arbitrator knew the law and expressly disregarded it"); United Parcel Serv. v. Teamsters Local 430, 55 F.3d 138, 141, 149 LRRM 2395, 2397 (3d Cir. 1995) (where the parties' collective bargaining agree-ment provides for binding arbitration, courts are not authorized to reconsider the merits of an arbitrator's award, and "[a] contrary rule would undermine the federal policy which fa-vors settling labor disputes through arbitration"); Office & Professional Employees Local 2 v. Washington Metro. Area Transit Auth., 724 F.2d 133, 141, 115 LRRM 2210, 2217 (D.C. Cir. 1984) (where an arbitrator chose between two conflicting lines of cases on a question of law, the award withstood court challenge even though the view that the arbitrator followed was subsequently rejected by the Supreme Court in proceedings involving other parties, because the arbitrator is not required to "have the ability to predict future Supreme Court decisions").

[18]See, e.g., Richmond, Fredericksburg & Potomac R.R, 973 F.2d 276 (award enforceable where grounded on arbitrator's good-faith assessment of applicable law); Tanoma Mining Co. v. Mine Workers Local 1269, 896 F.2d 745, 133 LRRM 2574 (3d Cir. 1990); Concourse Beauty Sch. v. Polakov, 685 F. Supp. 1311 (S.D.N.Y. 1988). For cases under the Labor-Man-agement Relations Act (LMRA), 29 U.S.C. §141 et seq., see Perma-Line Corp. of Am. v. Paint-ers Local 230, 639 F.2d 890, 106 LRRM 2483 (2d Cir. 1981); Typographical Union No. 173 (Dallas) v. A.H. Belo Corp., 372 F.2d 577, 581, 583, 64 LRRM 2491 (5th Cir. 1967); Bell Aerospace Co. v. Auto Workers Local 516, 356 F. Supp. 354, 356, 82 LRRM 2970 (W.D.N.Y. 1973); Transport Workers Local 234 v. Philadelphia Transp. Co., 283 F. Supp. 597, 599, 68 LRRM 2094 (E.D. Pa. 1968); Hod Carriers Dist. Council (Northern Cal.) v. Pennsylvania Pipeline, 103 Cal. App. 3d 163, 108 LRRM 2550, 2553 (1980) (findings "on questions of law or fact by the arbitrator are final and conclusive"). Under the Federal Arbitration Act, see Raytheon Co. v. Rheem Mfg. Co., 322 F.2d 173, 182 (9th Cir. 1963). Under state common law, see Moncharsh v. Heily & Blase, 832 P.2d 899 (Cal. 1992) (arbitrator's decision not review-able even though error of law resulted in substantial injustice to a party); Guille v. Mush-room Transp. Co., 229 A.2d 903, 905, 65 LRRM 2524 (Pa. Ct. 1967). Under state statute, see Hayob v. Osborne & Stonewood, 992 S.W.2d 265 (Mo. Ct. App. 1999) (court enforced arbitra-tion award and explained that "'[m]anifest disregard for the law is not a statutory basis for vacating an award'" (quoting Stifel, Nicolaus & Co. v. Francis, 872 S.W.2d 485, 485 (Mo. App. 1994)). "Arbitrators exceed their jurisdiction only when they decide matters beyond the scope of the arbitration agreement or which clearly were not submitted to them for arbitra-tion . . . even if [the arbitrator's award is] repugnant to the laws of the state . . . ," Hayob, 992 S.W.2d at 269); In re Marine Eng'rs Dist. 2, 233 N.Y.S.2d 408, 51 LRRM 2561, 2564 (N.Y. Sup. Ct. 1962); Kesslen Bros. v. Board of Conciliation & Arbitration, 32 LA 859, 859 (Mass. 1959). For many other cases, see 6 C.J.S. Arbitration and Award §105, at 251. For general discussion as to the limited scope of review of arbitration awards in the private sector, see Chapter 2, section 2.A.ii.b., "The Trilogy," section 2.A.ii.c., "Post-Trilogy: Enforcement of Agreements to Arbitrate and Review of Arbitration Awards," section 2.B.i., "State Common Law," and section 2.B.ii., "State Arbitration Statutes" (very few of the private-sector statutes grant any right of review for mistake of law).

For a comprehensive statement of the rule that awards may not be overturned for a mistake or an error of law, see Judge Edwards' decision in Postal Workers v. U.S. Postal Service, 789 F.2d 1, 7 n.20, 122 LRRM 2094, 2098–99 n.20 (D.C. Cir. 1986). See also Upshur Coals Corp. v. Mine Workers Dist. 31, 933 F.2d 225, 229, 137 LRRM 2397 (4th Cir. 1991) (arbitration award is enforceable even if it resulted from a misinterpretation of law, faulty legal reasoning, or an erroneous conclusion, and may be reversed only when an arbitrator understands and correctly states the law, but proceeds to disregard it); Sheet Metal Workers Local 359 v. Arizona Mech. & Stainless, 863 F.2d 647, 130 LRRM 2097 (9th Cir. 1988); Stead Motors of Walnut Creek v. Machinists Lodge 1173, 843 F.2d 357, 127 LRRM 3213 (9th Cir. 1988), reh'g en banc, 886 F.2d 1200, 132 LRRM 2689 (9th Cir. 1989); Masters, Mates & Pilots v. Trinidad Corp., 803 F.2d 69, 123 LRRM 2792, 2795 (2d Cir. 1986); Aetna Cas. & Sur. Co. v. Dietrich, 803 F. Supp. 1032, 1038 (M.D. Pa. 1992) (arbitrator is final judge of both

In *Steelworkers v. Enterprise Wheel & Car Corp.*,[19] the Supreme Court appeared to substantially limit the degree to which courts could second-guess arbitration decisions. Unless the award was the product of fraud, or somehow exceeded the arbitrator's authority, or unless it failed to "draw its essence" from the labor contract, the Supreme Court told courts to refrain from reviewing the merits.[20] Yet, both the district courts and circuit courts of appeals have too often ignored that mandate, which ultimately necessitated the Supreme Court to revisit the subject in *Paperworkers v. Misco, Inc.*[21]

---

law and fact under common law and mistake of either does not require vacating the judgment).

For cases under LMRA, see *Bevles Co. v. Teamsters Local 986*, 791 F.2d 1391, 122 LRRM 2666, 2667 n.2 (9th Cir. 1986); *Ethyl Corp. v. Steelworkers Local 7441*, 768 F.2d 180, 183, 119 LRRM 3566, 3568 (7th Cir. 1985), *cert. denied*, 475 U.S. 1010 (1986) ("a court of equity will not set . . . . aside [an arbitrator's award] for error either in law or fact"); *Jones Dairy Farm v. Food & Commercial Workers Local P-1236*, 755 F.2d 583, 118 LRRM 2841, *vacated*, 760 F.2d 173, 119 LRRM 2185 (7th Cir.), *cert. denied*, 474 U.S. 845 (1985) (Judge Posner observed that a party submitting legal claims for an arbitrator to rule on cannot later be heard to complain about an erroneous legal ruling); *Television & Radio Artists v. Storer Broad. Co.*, 745 F.2d 392, 398, 117 LRRM 2553, 2557 (6th Cir. 1984) ("If an arbitration award represents a plausible interpretation of the contract based on essentially factual determinations within the context of the collective bargaining agreement, judicial inquiry should cease and the award should be enforced. This remains so notwithstanding any error in the legal conclusions based essentially upon record supported factual findings, absent a manifest disregard of the law, in situations involving a mixed fact-law determination.").

For a court to vacate an award as a manifest disregard of the law, there must be some showing in the record that the arbitrator knew the law and expressly disregarded it. Marshall v. Green Giant Co., 942 F.2d 539, 550 (8th Cir. 1991). If an arbitrator does not state the reasons for an award, a court will not vacate it as a manifest disregard of the law. J.A. Jones Constr. Co. v. Flakt, Inc., 731 F. Supp. 1061, 1064 (N.D. Ga. 1990).

[19]363 U.S. 593, 46 LRRM 2423, 34 LA 569 (1960).

[20]*Id.* at 596–99.

[21]484 U.S. 29, 126 LRRM 3113 (1987). In *Misco*, the Supreme Court set forth guidelines for nonenforcement of an arbitration award for violating public policy. The reviewing court first must examine whether the award creates "any explicit conflict with other 'laws and legal precedents' rather than [assessing] 'general considerations of supposed public interests.'" *Id.* at 43, 126 LRRM at 3119 (quoting W.R. Grace & Co. v. Rubber Workers Local 759, 461 U.S. 757, 766, 113 LRRM 2641 (1983)). The court next must determine that a violation of the public policy clearly has been shown. *See also* Newsday, Inc. v. Typographical Union No. 915 (Long Island), 915 F.2d 840, 135 LRRM 2659 (2d Cir. 1990) (arbitrator's award that reinstated an employee discharged for several instances of sexual harassment set aside; reinstatement order violated the explicit public policy against sexual harassment); Delta Airlines v. Air Line Pilots, 861 F.2d 665, 130 LRRM 2014 (11th Cir. 1988) (a well-defined and dominant public policy precluded enforcement of an arbitrator's award reinstating a pilot discharged for operating passenger aircraft while under the influence of alcohol); City of Tulsa, Okla. v. Public Employees Relations Bd., 845 P.2d 872, 879, 135 LRRM 3165, 3171 (Okla. 1990) ("City's failure to honor an unconstitutional demand cannot be the subject of a grievance requiring mandatory arbitration"); Meat Cutters Local 540 v. Great W. Food Co., 712 F.2d 122, 125, 114 LRRM 2001, 2003 (5th Cir. 1983) ("the public policy of preventing people from drinking and driving is embodied in the case law, the applicable regulations, statutory law, and pure common sense"—to enforce "an award which compels the reinstatement to driving duties of a truck driver who admittedly drank while on duty, would violate this public policy"); Postal Workers v. U.S. Postal Serv., 682 F.2d 1280, 1285, 110 LRRM 2764, 2768 (9th Cir. 1982) (an award "will not be vacated because of erroneous findings of fact or misinterpretations of law," but "the courts cannot enforce an arbitrator's award if it requires the performance of an illegal act)"; Perma-Line Corp. of Am. v. Painters Local 230, 639 F.2d 890, 895, 106 LRRM 2483, 2487 (2d Cir. 1981) ("an award may be set aside if it compels the violation of law or is contrary to a well accepted and deep rooted public policy"); World Airways v. Teamsters, 587 F.2d 800, 99 LRRM 2325, 2327–38 (9th Cir. 1978); Meat Cutters Local P-1236 v. Jones Dairy Farm, 519 F. Supp. 1362, 108 LRRM 2128, 2132–33

In *Misco*, an arbitrator reinstated an employee who operated a safety-sensitive job, notwithstanding that marijuana had been found in his car in the parking lot. The U.S. Court of Appeals for the Fifth Circuit refused to enforce the award, believing that allowing a drug user to operate that machinery would be against public policy. The Supreme Court reversed, noting that "as long as the arbitrator is even arguably construing or applying the contract and acting within the scope of his authority, that a court is convinced he committed serious error does not suffice to overturn his decision."[22]

Conceding that accepted common law doctrine prohibits the enforcement of contracts that are against public policy, the Court warned:

> [A] court's refusal to enforce an arbitrator's *interpretation* of [labor] contracts is limited to situations where the contract as interpreted would violate "some explicit public policy" that is "well defined and dominant, and is to be ascertained 'by reference to the laws and legal precedents and not from general considerations of supposed public interests.'"[23]

Inherent in the Court's warning was the recognition of the national policy favoring private arbitration as a preferred means of dispute settlement. But courts are hard-pressed to ignore arbitration decisions they think are ill advised, particularly where they result in the reinstatement of, for example, a

---

(W.D. Wis. 1981) (collecting cases invalidating awards found to conflict with public policy); Cook County Bd. of Trustees, Community Coll. Dist. 508 v. Teachers Local 1600, 386 N.E.2d 27, 100 LRRM 2723, 2727 (Ill. 1979); Goodyear Tire & Rubber Co. v. Sanford, 540 S.W.2d 478, 482–85, 92 LRRM 3492 (Tex. Civ. App. 1976) (collecting federal and state cases invalidating awards found to conflict with public policy). But in *Transit Union Division 1309 v. Aztec Bus Lines*, 654 F.2d 642, 108 LRRM 2412, 2413 (9th Cir. 1981), the court cautioned that "[p]ublic policy should not be turned into 'a facile method of substituting judicial for arbitral judgment.'" *Id.* at 644 (quoting Dunau, *Three Problems in Labor Arbitration*, 55 Va. L. Rev. 427, 446 (1969)). Similarly, in the New York public-sector case of *Port Jefferson Station Teachers Ass'n v. Brookhaven-Comsewogue Union Free School District*, 383 N.E.2d 553, 554, 99 LRRM 3438 (N.Y. Ct. App. 1978), the court declared that "[i]ncantations of 'public policy' may not be advanced to overturn every arbitration award that impairs the flexibility of management of a school district. . . . Only when the award contravenes a strong public policy, almost invariably involving an important constitutional or statutory duty or responsibility, may it be set aside." The Supreme Court is similarly restrictive, stating in *W.R. Grace & Co.*, 461 U.S. 757, 766, 113 LRRM 2641, 2645 (1983) (quoting Muschany v. United States, 324 U.S. 49, 66 (1945)), that to refuse under public policy to enforce a contract as interpreted by an arbitrator, the public policy "must be well defined and dominant, and is to be ascertained 'by reference to the laws and legal precedents and not from general considerations of supposed public interests.'" For more on the latter decision, see Chapter 14, section 2.A.iv., "Seniority Systems and the Arbitral Enforcement of Antidiscrimination Clauses Resulting in 'Reverse Discrimination' Claims." *See* Exxon Corp. v. ESSO Workers' Union, 118 F.3d 841, 846, 155 LRRM 2782 (1st Cir. 1997) (in recognizing that courts must refrain from enforcing contracts that violate public policy, the court noted that "[t]o determine whether a particular case fits within the confines of this class . . . the court must [first] review existing statutes, regulations, and judicial decisions to ascertain whether they establish a well defined and dominant public policy. . . . [If so, the court must then] determine whether the arbitral award clearly violates the discerned public policy . . ."); Electrical Workers (IBEW) Local 97 v. Niagra Mohawk Power Corp., 950 F. Supp. 1227, 1234, 156 LRRM 2372 (N.D.N.Y. 1996) (because of "federal statutes, regulations and case law that support a finding of a well-defined and dominant public policy against employment of individuals who deliberately violate nuclear safety rules . . . and given the strong public policy issues involved, the court will review findings of arbitration panel de novo").

[22]Paperworkers v. Misco, Inc., 484 U.S. 29, 38, 126 LRRM 3113 (1987).

[23]*Id.* at 43 (quoting *W.R. Grace & Co.*, 461 U.S. at 766 (emphasis in original) (quoting *Muschany*, 324 U.S. at 66)).

chemical plant supervisor who tested positive for cocaine,[24] the return to work of an alcoholic airline pilot who flew while intoxicated,[25] or the reinstatement of a postal worker who stole mail.[26] As noted by one commentator,[27] the U.S. Courts of Appeals for the Fourth,[28] Sixth,[29] Seventh,[30] Ninth,[31] Tenth,[32] and District of Columbia[33] Circuits have been more deferential to the arbitrator's awards, even where so-called public policy matters were at issue. The proper test in such instances is not whether the employee activity in such cases is at odds with public policy, but whether the *reinstatement* is offensive to public policy. Stated otherwise, if the employer could, without violating some "well defined and dominant" public policy, have reinstated the employee (and there is no question that the employer in all such circumstances retains that right), then the arbitrator, by implementing the same result, has not violated public policy. Said the commentator:

> In short, the key is whether the remedial action ordered by the arbitrator, not the triggering conduct of the employee, is contrary to public policy. . . . But the award-issuing *arbitrator* did not and his decision should stand. Indeed, recog-

---

[24]*See* Exxon v. Baton Rouge Oil & Chem. Workers, 77 F.3d 850, 151 LRRM 2737 (5th Cir. 1996).

[25]*See Delta Airlines*, 861 F.2d 665.

[26]U.S. Postal Serv. v. Letter Carriers, 847 F.2d 775, 128 LRRM 2842 (11th Cir. 1988).

[27]St. Antoine, *The Changing Role of Labor Arbitration*, 76 Ind. L.J. 83 (2001).

[28]*See, e.g.*, Westvaco Corp. v. Paperworkers, 171 F.3d 971, 976–78, 160 LRRM 2844 (4th Cir. 1999) (upholding award requiring reinstatement of employee who had harassed coworker).

[29]*See, e.g.*, Tennessee Valley Auth. v. Tennessee Valley Trades & Labor Council, 184 F.3d 510, 519–21, 161 LRRM 2844 (6th Cir. 1999) (upholding arbitrator's award for reinstatement of nuclear reactor unit operator who tested positive for marijuana); MidMichigan Reg'l Med. Ctr.–Clare v. Professional Employees Div. of Serv. Employees Local 79, 183 F.3d 497, 504–06, 161 LRRM 2853 (6th Cir. 1999) (upholding arbitrator's award for reinstatement of a nurse who negligently handled equipment during cardiac emergency); Monroe Auto Equip. Co. v. Auto Workers Local 878, 981 F.2d 261, 269, 142 LRRM 2150 (6th Cir. 1992) (upholding arbitrator's award of reinstatement for installer of automobile test equipment who violated company drug policy), *cert. denied*, 508 U.S. 931 (1993).

[30]*See, e.g.*, Chrysler Motor Corp. v. Industrial Workers (AIW), 959 F.2d 685, 686–87, 139 LRRM 2865 (7th Cir.) (upholding arbitrator's award for reinstatement of male forklift operator who had sexually harassed female coworker by grabbing her breasts), *cert. denied*, 506 U.S. 908 (1992).

[31]*See, e.g.*, Food & Commercial Workers Local 588 v. Foster Poultry Farms, 74 F.3d 169, 174–75, 151 LRRM 2013 (9th Cir. 1995) (upholding arbitrator's award that reinstated employees who had failed drug test and rescinded employer's drug-testing program, pending bargaining with the union despite state regulation mandating random drug testing); Stead Motors of Walnut Creek v. Machinists Lodge 1173, 886 F.2d 1200, 1202, 1209–17, 132 LRRM 2689 (9th Cir. 1989) (auto mechanic had repeatedly failed to tighten lug nuts on car wheels; court would vacate award on public policy grounds only if policy "specifically militates against the relief ordered by the arbitrator"), *cert. denied*, 495 U.S. 946 (1990). *But cf.* Garvey v. Roberts, 203 F.3d 580, 590–92, 163 LRRM 2449, 2456 (9th Cir. 2000) (vacating denial of baseball player's collusion claim, because arbitrator's finding "is completely inexplicable and borders on the irrational" and because arbitrator dispensed "his own brand of industrial justice").

[32]*See, e.g.*, Kennecott Utah Copper Corp. v. Becker, 195 F.3d 1201, 1205–08, 162 LRRM 2641 (10th Cir. 1999) (upholding arbitrator's award for reinstatement of employee who had tested positive for marijuana following accident); Communication Workers v. Southeastern Elec. Coop., 882 F.2d 467, 468, 132 LRRM 2381 (10th Cir. 1989) (upholding arbitrator's award for reinstatement of electric utility lineman who in isolated incident sexually harassed customer in her home).

[33]*See, e.g.*, Northwest Airlines v. Air Line Pilots, 808 F.2d 76, 77–78, 124 LRRM 2300 (D.C. Cir 1987) (upholding arbitrator's award for conditional reinstatement of alcoholic airline pilot who had flown while intoxicated).

nizing the possibility of the rehabilitation of wrongdoers is a hallmark of a humane and caring society. Despite the ominous implications of a grant of certiorari when the court of appeals did not even deign to publish its opinion, the Supreme Court should recognize the distinction and rule accordingly.[34]

The Supreme Court reaffirmed its *Misco* holding in *Eastern Associated Coal Corp. v. Mine Workers District 17*.[35] There, the Court considered the case of a mobile equipment operator found to have used marijuana on the job. Following his reinstatement by the arbitrator, the company challenged the award. The Supreme Court affirmed a decision of the U.S. Court of Appeals for the Fourth Circuit and refused to overturn the award. Citing *Misco*, the Court observed that, while there exists a strong public policy against drug use, the arbitration award itself was not contrary to any relevant policy. The Court stated:

> The award violates no specific provision of any law or regulation. It is consistent with DOT [Department of Transportation] rules requiring completion of substance-abuse treatment before returning to work . . . for it does not preclude [the employer] from assigning [the employee] to a non-safety-sensitive position until [the employee] completes the proscribed treatment program. . . .
>
> . . . Neither Congress nor the Secretary [of Transportation] has seen fit to mandate the discharge of a worker who twice tests positive for drugs. We hesitate to infer a public policy in this area that goes beyond the careful and detailed scheme Congress and the Secretary have created.
>
> We recognize that reasonable people can differ as to whether reinstatement or discharge is the more appropriate remedy here. But both the employer and Union have agreed to entrust this remedial decision to an arbitrator. We cannot find in the Act, the regulations, or any other law or legal precedent an "explicit," "well defined," "dominant" public policy to which the arbitrators decision "runs contrary."[36]

---

[34]St. Antoine, *The Changing Role of Labor Arbitration*, 76 IND. L.J. 83, 97 (2001) (footnote omitted).

[35]531 U.S. 57, 165 LRRM 2865 (2000).

[36]*Id.* at 65–67 (citing Paperworkers v. Misco, Inc., 484 U.S. 29, 43, 126 LRRM 3113 (1987); W.R. Grace & Co. v. Rubber Workers Local 759, 461 U.S 757, 766, 113 LRRM 2641 (1983)). *See* St. Mary Home v. Service Employees Dist. 1199, 116 F.3d 41, 45, 155 LRRM 2456, 2460 (2d Cir. 1997) (quoting Paperworkers v. Misco, Inc., 484 U.S. 29, 36, 126 LRRM 3113 (1987) ("[A] court's authority to refuse to enforce an arbitral award on public policy grounds is narrowly circumscribed 'to situations where the contract as interpreted would violate some explicit public policy that is well defined and dominant . . .'"); Transportation Union Local 1589 v. Suburban Transit Corp., 51 F.3d 376, 148 LRRM 2796, 2800 (3d Cir. 1995) (court upheld arbitrator's decision that employee discharge was too harsh when employer failed to demonstrate that a company policy in favor of protecting coworkers and customers from violent conduct of employees was an explicit public policy that would undermine the arbitration award; public policy argument failed); G.B. Goldman Paper Co. v. Paperworkers Local 286, 957 F. Supp. 607, 621, 154 LRRM 2489, 2494 (E.D. Pa. 1997) (the court ruled that public policy concerning workplace safety was not violated by arbitration award reinstating employee who was discharged for harassing fellow employees in violation of company rules, where arbitrator found employee's actions were not so extreme that reinstatement would violate public policy); Auto Workers Local 771 v. Micro Mfg., 895 F. Supp. 170, 150 LRRM 2362, 2364 (E.D. Mich. 1995) (arbitrator's award reinstating employee who violated an explicit and well-defined public policy was not vacated, because the arbitrator's decision itself did not violate any law or clear dictate of public policy; one seeking to vacate an arbitration award on public policy grounds must show that the award itself violates the law); Food & Commercial Workers Local 588 v. Foster Food Prods., 146 LRRM 2793, 2801–04 (E.D. Cal. 1994) (upholding arbitrator's award for reinstatement of drivers who were discharged for failing or refusing to take a drug test as not violating public policy).

Regarding federal-sector arbitration, awards are subject to challenge if they conflict with controlling laws, rules, or regulations.[37] In the state and local government sector, a number of states have expressly endorsed the rule that awards are not impeachable for errors of law, but of course both the applicability of this rule and the general relationship between external law and arbitration in the state public sector must be determined on a state-by-state basis.[38]

Even though arbitration awards are generally final insofar as the application of the agreement is concerned, surviving statutory issues and rights might render the award nonfinal and/or provide a party with additional recourse in a court of law.[39] In addition to continuing to recognize rights under the National Labor Relations Act (NLRA), Fair Labor Standards Act (FLSA), and Title VII of the Civil Rights Act, courts have refused to enforce awards that have affected rights under the Civil Rights Acts (42 U.S.C. §1983[40] and 42 U.S.C. §1981)[41] the ADEA,[42] and ERISA.[43] Despite this possible lack of enforcement and finality, arbitration remains a viable substitute for litigation even with respect to rights under most employment statutes,[44] and it is becoming more common for arbitrators to consider and apply statutes and external law in the resolution of grievances.[45]

---

[37]See Chapter 20, section 4.A.i., "Role and Scope of Federal-Sector Grievance Procedure and Arbitration," section 4.A.ii.b.,"Governmentwide Rules or Regulations," section 4.A.ii.c.,"Non-Governmentwide Rules or Regulations," and section 5., "Review of Arbitration Awards."

[38]See Chapter 21, section 4.C., "Contractual Terms Versus Statutory Law Covering Similar Matters," section 7., "Judicial Review of Arbitration Awards in State and Local Government Employment."

[39]See the discussion below in section 2.B., "U.S. Supreme Court Statements Regarding Arbitral Consideration of External Law," section 2.D., "Some Ramifications or Consequences of Arbitrator's Choice Respecting External Law." See also Chapter 2, section 2.A.ii.d., "De Novo Litigation Following Arbitration."

[40]McDonald v. City of West Branch, Mich., 466 U.S. 284, 290, 115 LRRM 3646 (1984).

[41]Wilmington v. J.I. Case Co., 793 F.2d 909, 40 FEP Cases 1833, 1839–41 (8th Cir. 1986); Rodgers v. General Motors Corp., 739 F.2d 1102, 35 FEP Cases 349, 351 (6th Cir. 1984), cert. denied, 470 U.S. 1054 (1985); Strozier v. General Motors Corp., 635 F.2d 424, 24 FEP Cases 1370, 1371–72 (5th Cir. 1981).

[42]Cooper v. Asplundh Tree Expert Co., 836 F.2d 1544, 45 FEP Cases 1386 (10th Cir. 1988); Johnson v. University of Wis.-Milwaukee, 783 F.2d 59, 39 FEP Cases 1822 (7th Cir. 1986); Cook v. Pan Am. World Airways, 771 F.2d 635, 38 FEP Cases 1344, 1348–49 (2d Cir. 1985), cert. denied, 474 U.S. 1109 (1986); Steck v. Smith Barney, Harris Upham & Co., 661 F. Supp. 543, 43 FEP Cases 1736 (D.N.J. 1987) (refusal to order arbitration on termination claim even though court found that claim was covered by arbitration clause in individual employment agreement).

[43]Burke v. Latrobe Steel, 775 F.2d 88, 6 EB Cases 2307 (3d Cir. 1985).

[44]For a good description of the evolution of the issue of arbitrating statutory employment claims and the status of this issue among the various federal circuits, see Williams v. Cigna Financial Advisors, 197 F.3d 752, 81 FEP Cases 747 (5th Cir. 1999).

[45]See, e.g., Laporte Pigments, 114 LA 1 (Marino, 2000) (arbitrator held that the ADA was not violated when the employee was terminated for absenteeism due to drug and alcohol addiction); PCC Airfoils, 113 LA 504 (Sharpe, 1999) (arbitrator discussed the purposes of the FMLA and state workers' compensation law and found that the employer's new attendance policy did not contravene those statutes); Safelite Glass Corp., 113 LA 110, 114 (Smith, Jr., 1999) (arbitrator found racial discrimination grievance arbitrable because "the Company should not be able to use any contractual provision [such as a management-rights clause] to establish a pattern and practice of racial discrimination"); Clallam County, Wash., Pub. Hosp. Dist. 1, 105 LA 609, 612 (Calhoun, 1995) (arbitrator applied the Civil Rights Act of

Keeping in mind that the extent to which arbitrators will consider any factor outside the collective bargaining agreement may depend on the degree to which the parties have restricted the arbitrators' authority with respect to the interpretation and application of the agreement, as a rule, arbitrators retain relatively wide discretion to deal with the law according to their best judgment. Clearly defined law will usually be given more consideration than unsettled and uncertain law or rules based on controversial views as to what should be the "public policy." Finally, arbitrators often do not cite legal decisions, but they do take cognizance—in essence "a quasi-judicial or arbitral notice"—of the legal principle(s) concerning the issue under consideration. In the informality of arbitration, it seems natural for arbitrators to state such principles without deeming it necessary to cite specific supporting authority.

This chapter discusses the extent to which arbitrators do in fact have recourse to substantive law and to decisions of courts and administrative agencies on questions similar to the one before the arbitrator.

The views and practices of several arbitrators will be examined to demonstrate some of the varying ways in which they utilize external law.

Given the range of views and the uncertainty as to whether arbitrators will or will not apply external law, parties may be well advised to consider the potential application of pertinent laws, legal principles, and court and administrative rulings when negotiating collective bargaining agreements and preparing cases for arbitration.

1964 in evaluating whether a company had made a sufficient effort to reasonably accommodate an employee's religious needs and practices); Schuller Int'l, 103 LA 1127, 1131–32 (Allen, 1994) ("an arbitrator is not required to interpret all the federal and state laws, but he must follow the clear written interpretations and directives from recognized authority issuing a final decision as to the application of a particular law"); City of Orange, Tex., 103 LA 1121, 1125 (Nicholas, Jr., 1994) (arbitrator used authority to consider city ordinances as well as collective bargaining agreement, since "it is well settled that the arbitrator has secondary jurisdiction to review and apply the relevant external law to any matter brought before him in an arbitration context"); Minnegasco, Inc., 103 LA 43, 46 (Bognanno, 1994) (arbitrator considered Minnesota state law in evaluating public utility company's termination of pregnant employee with lifting restriction); Rock Island Arsenal, 99 LA 1043 (Brunner, 1992) (arbitrators are increasingly considering external law in resolving disputes); Lakeland, Ohio, Cmty. Coll., 93 LA 909 (Richard, 1989) (arbitrator considered the ADEA in evaluating college's forced retirement of tenured professor); Bundy Tubing, 93 LA 905, 908 (Volz, 1989) (arbitrator ruled that it was proper to look at the provisions of federal law and their impact on the dispute between the parties, namely, whether the employee had to elect Consolidated Omnibus Budget Reconciliation Act of 1985 (COBRA) coverage to be eligible for the benefits in question); Star Tribune, 93 LA 14 (Bognanno, 1989) (arbitrator applied provisions of NLRA to discharge); Alpha Beta Co., 92 LA 1301 (Wilmoth, 1989) (ADEA and Title VII of the Civil Rights Act of 1964 law on pretext applied by arbitrator); Murphy Oil U.S.A., 92 LA 1148 (Goodman, 1989) (arbitrator applied NLRA and NLRB decisions in reaching conclusion concerning rights of economic strikers to vacation benefits); Mueller Steam Specialties, 89 LA 151 (Goetz, 1987) (an employer and union submitted to an arbitrator a dispute, pending for many years, as to whether the union had been properly certified under the NLRA). Despite the holding in *Alexander v. Gardner-Denver Co.*, 415 U.S. 36, 55–60, 7 FEP Cases 81 (1974), to the effect that an arbitration award did not bar an employee's statutory right to trial de novo on a discrimination claim under Title VII, an employer and nonrepresented employee submitted the employee's sex and national origin discrimination claims to an arbitrator who found on all issues for the defendant. Heublein, Inc., 84 LA 836 (Tait, 1985). In another case, parties to a consent decree in a civil rights suit under 42 U.S.C. §1983 agreed to submit disputes with respect to application of the decree to arbitration rather than to the court. Sheriff of Lake County, Ill., 82 LA 918 (Eagle, 1984).

2. Range of Views as to Application of "Law"

To what extent should arbitrators consider "law" in resolving private-sector[46] disputes? A spectrum of arbitral views exists on the issue, and each view commands some, if not considerable, support in arbitral practice.

This section will review the range of arbitral thinking on the subject and the pronouncements of the Supreme Court relevant to the consideration or application of external law by arbitrators. The following portion will explore the capabilities of arbitrators to address sometimes complex and often unsettled questions of external law. The remainder of the chapter explores arbitrators' application of statutory law, court decisions, administrative rulings, and fundamental principles of the common law.

A. Views of Arbitrators

Arbitrators generally accept the following three propositions. First, an arbitrator may consider all relevant factors, including relevant law, where the contractual provision at issue has been formulated loosely. Second, where a contractual provision is susceptible to two interpretations, one compatible with, and the other repugnant to, an applicable statute, the statute is a relevant consideration in interpreting the language, and arbitrators should seek to avoid an interpretation that would make the agreement invalid. Finally, where the submission makes it clear that the parties want an advisory opinion as to the law, such opinion would be within the arbitrator's role.[47]

---

[46]Arbitrators in the federal sector are required to deal with external law, and awards are subject to challenge where they conflict with controlling laws, rules, or regulations. For federal sector, see Chapter 20, section 4.A.i., "Role and Scope of Federal-Sector Grievance Procedure and Arbitration," and section 5., "Review of Arbitration Awards." The relationship between external law and arbitration in the state and local government sector must be determined on a state-by-state basis, and has in fact varied depending on the contents of the particular state arbitration statute and the views of the state's courts. See Chapter 21, section 4.C., "Contractual Terms Versus Statutory Law Covering Similar Matters." Arbitrators in state-sector cases, like private-sector arbitrators, have disagreed on the question of considering external law where neither the collective bargaining statute nor the collective bargaining agreement is definitive or unequivocal with respect to the relationship between contract terms and relevant external law.

[47]Formulated in Meltzer, *Ruminations About Ideology, Law, and Labor Arbitration, in* The Arbitrator, the NLRB, and the Courts, Proceedings of the 20th Annual Meeting of NAA 1, 15, 31 (Jones ed., BNA Books 1967). Regarding Meltzer's first point, an arbitrator may find a statute (or cases construing it) a helpful guide when an agreement is ambiguous or does not expressly adopt the statutory standards. See William Penn Sch. Dist., Pa., 99 LA 815 (Zirkel, 1992) (where a collective bargaining agreement expressly incorporates relevant state legislation, there is no doubt that the arbitrator has not only the authority but the obligation to apply the controlling statutory language and the ample line of case law that interprets and clarifies it); City of Edmond, Okla., 99 LA 510 (Woolf, 1992) (when an agreement is silent or ambiguous, an arbitrator also may consider past practice and external law); U.S. Customs Serv., 99 LA 41 (Abrams, 1992) (when parties adopt statutory language as their frame of reference, they want their contract to be read the same way as statutory language would be read); Alaska Dep't of Admin., 96 LA 937 (Robinson, 1991) (arbitrator has authority to resolve dispute regarding compensation for state employees' voluntary overtime work through consideration of federal laws when the parties explicitly provided in the collective bargaining agreement that the public policy standards contained in the FLSA would be the criteria for determining overtime eligibility); Georgia Power Co., 93 LA 846 (Holley, Jr., 1989) (employee challenged discharge after a test for drug use, which arose after a search of the grievant's car, proved to be positive; arbitrator comprehensively reviewed Fourth Amend-

ment case law and pertinent arbitrable authorities): County of Monterey, Cal., 93 LA 841 (Riker, 1989) (arbitrator applied First Amendment case law in construing issue of whether discipline of employee for communications outside normal channels was proper); Pontiac, Mich., Sch. Dist. Bd. of Educ., 93 LA 745 (Lipson, 1989) (arbitrator reinstated school maintenance man discharged for possession of marijuana because there was inadequate proof that substance was marijuana and because school district lacked sufficient basis to search an employee's locker; arbitrator made extensive analysis of constitutional provisions concerning probable cause and Fourth Amendment rights); Golden W. Broadcasters, 93 LA 691 (Jones, Jr., 1989) (arbitrator applied NLRA bargaining law); Consolidation Coal Co., 93 LA 473 (Seidman, 1989) (arbitrator necessarily had to look at law concerning sympathy strikes). Recent scholarly comment may be found in Zirkel, *The Use of External Law in Labor Arbitration: An Analysis of Arbitral Awards*, 1985 Detroit C. L. Rev. 31; Scheinholtz & Miscimarra, *The Arbitrator as Judge and Jury: Another Look at Statutory Law in Arbitration*, 40 Arb. J. 55 (1985); Meltzer, NAA 20th Proceedings, at 15, 31.

See also Van Waters & Rogers v. Teamsters, 56 F.3d 1132, 1137, 149 LRRM 2525 (9th Cir. 1995) ("an arbitrator may look 'to (the law)' for guidance so long as the decision draws its essence from the [a]greement"); Charter Communications Entm't I L.P., 114 LA 769, 779–80 (Kelly, 2000) (analyzing federal and state law while considering same sex harassment grievance); Laporte Pigments, 114 LA 1, 4–5 (Marino, 2000) (referring to the ADA); Groendyk Mfg. Co., 113 LA 656, 659–60 (West, 1999) (finding that federal regulations do not prohibit Saturday work); GTE N., 113 LA 665, 671 (Brodsky, 1999) (applying the ADA where a collective bargaining agreement contained a "conflict with law" clause and discussing the various external law theories); Conagra Frozen Foods, 113 LA 129, 131 (Baroni, 1999) (applying federal sexual harassment law); Pleasant Ridge Manor, 112 LA 517, 520 (Franckiewicz, 1999) (considering state case law when defining the arbitrator's role); International Mill Serv., 104 LA 779, 781 (Marino, 1995) (declaring without analysis that arbitrator must examine " 'external law,' specifically Title VII, definitions and standards and the concept of 'just cause' " to determine whether the company had just cause to discharge grievant, and whether grievant sexually harassed another employee); Johnson Controls World Servs., 104 LA 336, 342 (Goodstein, 1995) (interpreting the ADA to determine whether general equal opportunity clause in the contract required the company to accommodate). *But see* Union Camp Corp., 104 LA 295, 302 (Nolan, 1995) (observing that authorities on arbitral authority to award tort damages for sexual harassment would have been more helpful than the judicial authorities cited by the company); Clow Valve Co., 102 LA 286, 288 (Berger, 1994) (considering terms of the FLSA and the Iowa Workers' Compensation Law in finding that company must compensate employee for time spent in a work-related medical visit); Minnesota Dep't of Corr., 88 LA 535 (Gallagher, 1987) (considered Title VII law in construing issue); Capital Dist. Transit Sys., No. 1, 88 LA 353 (La Manna, 1986); Morton Salt Div., 88 LA 254 (Finan, 1987); Olin Corp., 86 LA 1193 (Penfield, 1986) (in construing propriety of wage set-off, arbitrator considered state statute where contract was silent).

Regarding Meltzer's second point, see *Dyno Nobel, Inc.*, 104 LA 376, 382–83 (Hilgert, 1995) (declining to uphold grievance at the risk of requiring the company to violate OSH Act); Seminole, Fla., Fire Rescue, 104 LA 222, 227–28 (Sergent, 1994) (considering company's fear of violating ERISA in interpreting collective bargaining agreement).

Regarding Arbitrator Meltzer's third point, see *Borden Chems. & Plastics*, 113 LA 1080 (Pratte, 1999) (requiring contract reformation in response to OSHA regulations); Penn Window Co., 112 LA 922, 926 (Franckiewicz, 1999) ("While there is often controversy as to whether an arbitrator should consider external law such as the NLRA, in this case, the parties agree that I should determine whether the facts give rise to a violation of the NLRA."); UNDS, 112 LA 14, 17 (Haber, 1999) (informing the parties that they should be prepared to argue external law if the same arises again); Westvaco Corp., 111 LA 887, 889 (Nicholas, Jr., 1998) (noting that the parties agreed that a sexual harassment complaint was governed by external law after the federal district court dismissed the case because the grievant had not exhausted the contractually required grievance and arbitration procedure); ATC/Vancom, 111 LA 268, 271 (Richman, 1998) (pursuing an FMLA issue and not a Title VII argument where the union wanted to address those claims and the employer desired the opposite); Perfection Bakeries, 110 LA 1043, 1047 (Stallworth, 1997) (reviewing ADA law at the prompting of both parties); Grand Haven Stamped Prods. Co., 107 LA 131, 135 (Daniel, 1996) (interpreting the FMLA when the parties relied on its interpretation in delineating their respective positions and referred to the statute in their contract); Johns Hopkins Bayview Med. Ctr., 105 LA 193, 197 (Bowers, 1995) (interpreting the ADA when the parties' agreement prohibited discrimination "to the extent provided by law"); Alcoa Bldg. Prods., 104 LA 364, 368 (Cerone, 1995) (parties consented to arbitrator interpretation of the ADA); Laidlaw Transit, 104 LA 302, 305–06 (Concepcion, 1995) (sustaining grievance based on company's failure to provide rea-

Another proposition regarding the role of external law is more controversial. One commentator urged that where there is clear conflict between the agreement and law, the arbitrator "should respect the agreement and ignore the law." He reasoned that parties call on an arbitrator to interpret their agreement rather than to destroy it, and that there is no reason to credit arbitrators with special expertise to discern the law as distinguished from the meaning of an agreement. Thus, arbitrators should respect "the agreement that is the source of their authority and should leave to the courts or other official tribunals the determination of whether the agreement contravenes a higher law. Otherwise, arbitrators would be deciding issues that go beyond not only the submission agreement but also arbitral competence."[48]

---

sonable accommodation when the union urged application of the ADA and company did not object); *Consentino's Brywood Price Chopper*, 104 LA 187, 189–90 (Thornell, 1995) (finding that the company "failed to meet its contractual and statutory obligation of reasonable accommodation" when the union claimed the company violated the contract and the ADA, each of which require reasonable accommodation for an employee with a physical handicap); *San Francisco Newspaper Agency*, 88 LA 296 (Gentile, 1986); *Fermi Nat'l Accelerator Lab.*, 88 LA 79 (Wies, 1986) (by litigating statutory issue under the NLRA, the parties implicitly asked the arbitrator to rule on it); *Florida Power Corp.*, 87 LA 957, 960 (Wahl, 1986) (contract provided for the arbitrator to pass on a legal question by defining a grievance to include an alleged violation of law "governing the employee-employer relationship" or "supervisory conduct which unlawfully . . . denies to any employee his job or any benefit arising out of his job"; thus, the arbitrator considered the contention that the grievants performed compensable work under the FLSA); *San Francisco, Cal., Unified Sch. Dist.*, 87 LA 750 (Wilcox, 1986) (labor agreement nondiscrimination clause coextensive with Title VII); *Veterans Admin. Med. Ctr.*, 83 LA 1219, 1224–25 (Rotenberg, 1984) (contract provided that all matters covered by the agreement were to be governed by applicable federal statutes; accordingly, the arbitrator was called on to construe the challenged section of the collective bargaining agreement under 5 U.S.C. §7106); *Crown Zellerbach Corp.*, 83 LA 1001 (Howell, 1984); *Palo Alto, Cal., Unified Sch. Dist.*, 83 LA 156 (Concepcion, 1984); *Farmers Union Cent. Exch.*, 82 LA 799 (Kapsch, Sr., 1984) (nondiscrimination referred to Equal Employment Opportunity Commission (EEOC) –Affirmative Action Programs duties; arbitrator applied Title VII law in ruling on grievance). In *Aro, Inc.*, 54 LA 453, 456 (Caraway, 1971), a court mandate required the arbitrator to review federal and state law to ascertain the legality of an unusual union shop agreement that was being requested; the arbitrator made an extensive review of relevant law as the basis of his ruling. *See also* Landy Packing Co., 71 LA 427, 432–33 (Flagler, 1978); Swanson-Dean Corp., 68 LA 682, 683, 685 (Jackson, 1977).

[48]*Meltzer*, NAA 20TH PROCEEDINGS, at 16–17. Another arbitrator has commented: "I don't wish to seem perverse in urging arbitrators to issue awards that may fly in the face of applicable law. But I just can't see any source of arbitral power to exercise a more extended jurisdiction unless the parties themselves have so provided." St. Antoine, *The Role of Law in Arbitration: Discussion, in* DEVELOPMENTS IN AMERICAN AND FOREIGN ARBITRATION, PROCEEDINGS OF THE 21ST ANNUAL MEETING OF NAA 75, 79 (Rehmus ed., BNA Books 1968). He explained: "[T]he arbitrator in the usual case remains just the 'reader' of the instrument before him. And if, after giving due weight to the presumption of legality, he cannot reconcile the contract and the law, he should render the award compelled by the contract." *Id.* at 82. He reiterated his views in St. Antoine, *Judicial Review of Labor Arbitration Awards: A Second Look at* Enterprise Wheel *and Its Progeny, in* ARBITRATION—1977, PROCEEDINGS OF THE 30TH ANNUAL MEETING OF NAA 29, 34–36 (Dennis & Somers eds., BNA Books 1978), where he also indicated that he had modified his view in one important respect:

It has previously been assumed, by others as well as by me, that insofar as an arbitrator's award construes a statute, it is advisory only, and the statutory question will be examined *de novo* if the award is challenged in the courts. I no longer think this is the necessary result. As between the parties themselves, I see no impediment to their agreeing to a final and binding arbitral declaration of their statutory rights and duties. Obviously, if an arbitrator's interpretation of an OSHA requirement did not adequately protect the employees, or violated some other basic public policy, a court would not be bound by it. But if the arbitrator imposed more stringent requirements, I would say the

Several arbitrators have agreed with the call to disregard external law where there is a clear conflict between the collective bargaining agreement and the law.[49]

In sharp contrast to this position, one arbitrator insisted that "[a]rbitrators, as well as judges, are subject to and bound by law, whether it be the Fourteenth Amendment to the Constitution of the United States or a city ordinance. All contracts are subject to statute and common law; and each contract includes all applicable law."[50] He also asserted that:

> There is a responsibility of arbitrators, corollary to that of the General Counsel and the NLRB, to decide, where relevant, a statutory issue, that the NLRB, consistent with its announced policy, may avoid a decision on the merits, and the statutory policy of determining issues through arbitration may be fulfilled.[51]

---

award should be enforced. The parties agreed to that result, and their agreement should be accorded the same finality as any other arbitration contract.

Whatever damage may be done to the pristine purity of labor arbitration by this increased responsibility for statutory interpretation, I consider an expanded arbitral jurisdiction inevitable. Such recent statutes as Title VII of the Civil Rights Act, the Pension Reform Act (ERISA), and OSHA are so interwoven in the fabric of collective bargaining agreements that it is simply impracticable in many cases for arbitrators to deal with contractual provisions without taking into account statutory provisions.

Id. at 36. *See also* Contracts, Metals & Welding, 110 LA 673, 680 (Klein, 1998) ("It is clear that the current status of the existing law is that an 'accommodation' of a disabled employee under the ADA cannot require 'trumping' the seniority rights of other employees."); St. Antoine, *Deferral to Arbitration and Use of External Law in Arbitration*, 10 INDUS. REL. L.J. No. 1, at 19 (1988). *See, e.g.*, City of Laredo, Tex., 91 LA 381, 385 (McDermott, 1988) (employer's argument with respect to state constitution is beyond the scope of the arbitrator's authority); Holly Farms, 90 LA 509, 514 (McDermott, 1987) ("The interpretation of that law and its application is clearly not within the purview of this arbitrator. His authority in this case relates solely to the labor agreement . . . .").

[49]Hunter Eng'g Co., 82 LA 483 (Alleyne, 1984). *See also* Roadmaster Corp. v. Laborers Local 504, 851 F.2d 886, 889, 128 LRRM 2953, 2955 (7th Cir. 1988) ("the arbitrator should restrict his consideration to the contract, even if such decision conflicts with federal statutory law"); Olin Corp., 103 LA 481, 483 (Helburn, 1994) (company was not obligated to accommodate disabled employee in a way that violated contractually granted seniority rights); U.S. Playing Card Co., 87 LA 937 (Duda, Jr., 1986); BASF Wyandotte Corp., 84 LA 1055 (Caraway, 1985); Health Care & Ret. Corp. of Am., 84 LA 919 (Cerone, 1985). In *American Sterilizer Co.*, 104 LA 921 (Dissen, 1995), the arbitrator relied on a prior arbitrator's decision that the parties' collective bargaining agreement specifically incorporated the ADA and then interpreted its application to the facts at hand. *See also* Meijer, Inc., 103 LA 834, 840 (Daniel, 1994) ("Under a contract requiring just cause for disciplinary action against an employee, rights established by law, such as ADA, must be taken into consideration in determining whether just cause exists."). *But see* Dinagraphics, Inc., 102 LA 947, 953 (Paolucci, 1994) (when collective bargaining agreement did not prohibit discrimination based on disability, the ADA was inapplicable).

[50]Howlett, *The Arbitrator and the NLRB: The Arbitrator, the NLRB, and the Courts, in* THE ARBITRATOR, AND THE NLRB, AND THE COURTS, PROCEEDINGS OF THE 20TH ANNUAL MEETING OF NAA 67, 83 (Jones ed., BNA Books 1967). *See also* Union Oil Co. of Cal., 99 LA 1137, 1148 (McKay, 1992) ("[E]xternal law cannot be ignored in reaching an arbitration decision. The parties' contract is obviously most relevant, but the contract cannot be interpreted in a vacuum. It was written in the context of the laws of the land and must, in this arbitrator's opinion, be read in that context."). *See, e.g.*, Tenneco Packaging, 112 LA 761, 768 (Kessler, 1999) ("The Labor Agreement provisions are overridden by the state and Federal acts.").

[51]Howlett, NAA 20TH PROCEEDINGS, at 78–79. He also stated the arbitrator has a duty to "probe" to determine whether a statutory issue is involved. *Id.* at 92. In 1982, the same arbitrator stated that: "In federal, state, and local government arbitration, arbitrators must consider what has been improperly called 'external law.' More than in the private sector, statutes and government regulations are *part* of the collective bargaining contracts." Howlett, *Observations on Labor Arbitration*, AAA NEWS & VIEWS No. 1, at 6 (1982). *See also* Gross, *The Labor Arbitrator's Role: Tradition and Change*, 25 ARB. J. 221 (1970).

Another arbitrator advanced the intermediate view that "although the arbitrator's award may *permit* conduct forbidden by law but sanctioned by contract, it should not *require* conduct forbidden by law even though sanctioned by contract."[52] He emphasized that arbitrators are "part of a private process for the adjudication of private rights and duties," and that they "should not be asked to assume public responsibilities and to do the work of public agencies."[53]

Another arbitrator has also vigorously advocated the view that arbitrators should not be asked to assume public responsibilities and to do the work of public agencies:

> If arbitration begins to do the business of the NLRB and the courts, interpreting legislation, effectuating national rather than private goals as a kind of subordinate tribunal of the Board, that voluntarism which is the base of its broad acceptance could be eroded and its essential objectives changed. Arbitration can be weakened by freighting it with public law questions which in our system should be decided by the courts and administrative agencies. Arbitration should

---

[52]Mittenthal, *The Role of Law in Arbitration, in* Developments in American and Foreign Arbitration, Proceedings of the 21st Annual Meeting of NAA 42, 50 (Rehmus ed., BNA Books 1968) (emphasis in original). *Cf.* Acme Foundry Co., 45 LA 1025, 1027 (Altieri, 1965).

[53]Mittenthal, NAA 21st Proceedings at 58. Asked to comment on the Mittenthal view, Arbitrators Meltzer and Howlett each reiterated their own views. *See* Meltzer, *The Role of Law in Arbitration: A Rejoinder, in* Developments in American and Foreign Arbitration, Proceedings of the 21st Annual Meeting of NAA 58 (Rehmus ed., BNA Books 1968); Howlett, *A Reprise, in id.* at 64. Still a fourth view, similar to Mittenthal's but with distinctions of consequence to some cases, was presented to the NAA at a later meeting. *See* Sovern, *When Should Arbitrators Follow Federal Law?, in* Arbitration and the Expanding Role of Neutrals, Proceedings of the 23d Annual Meeting of NAA 29 (Somers & Dennis eds., BNA Books 1970). At yet later NAA meetings the discussion continued, as did the disagreement, as to the extent to which arbitrators should concern themselves with law and public policy in resolving disputes. *See* McKelvey, *The Presidential Address: Sex and the Single Arbitrator, in* Arbitration and the Public Interest, Proceedings of the 24th Annual Meeting of NAA 1 (Somers & Dennis eds., BNA Books 1971); Wirtz, *Arbitration Is a Verb, in id.* at 30; Jones, Jr., *The Role of Arbitration in State and the National Labor Policy, id.* at 42; Morris, *Comment, in id.* at 65; Feller, *Comment, in id.* at 78. A questionnaire regarding this issue was sent to 200 Academy members. The 79 responses reflected an almost equal division in support for the two basic views. Young, *The Authority and Obligation of a Labor Arbitrator to Modify or Eliminate a Provision of a Collective Bargaining Agreement Because in His Opinion It Violates Federal Law*, 32 Ohio St. L.J. 395, 396 (1971) (including indications of how those who responded rate themselves as to knowledge of specific federal statutes). One-third of the arbitrators responding to a later survey "indicated that they believed a collective bargaining agreement must be read to include by reference all public law applicable thereto," and about two-thirds of the responding arbitrators "stated that they believed that an arbitrator has no business interpreting or applying a public statute in a contractual grievance dispute." Edwards, *Arbitration of Employment Discrimination Cases: An Empirical Study, in* Arbitration—1975, Proceedings of the 28th Annual Meeting of NAA 59, 79 (Dennis & Somers eds., BNA Books 1976) (also, "nearly one half of the responding arbitrators did indicate that an arbitrator should be free to *comment* on the relevant law if it appears to conflict with the collective bargaining agreement)" *id.* (emphasis in original)). *See, e.g.*, Textron Lycoming, 104 LA 1043, 1047 (Duff, 1995) (refusing to consider company's arguments based on statute and policy-based safety considerations when the arbitrator's authority is limited to interpreting the terms of the collective bargaining agreement). In contrast, many arbitrators have indicated that they would feel free to comment on the relevant law if it appears to conflict with the collective bargaining agreement. *See* Alcoa Bldg. Prods., 104 LA 364, 368–69 (Cerone, 1995) (the ADA compelled reasonable accommodation, but the company went too far when it violated a union member's contractual seniority rights to accommodate disabled employee); Rodeway Inn, 102 LA 1003, 1014–15 (Goldberg, 1994) (refusing to interpret contract in a manner that would be "repugnant" to the policies set forth in Title VII).

not be an initial alternative to Board adjudication; it has been (and should be) a separate system of judicature respecting *private* rights and duties resulting in final decisions—not decisions on *public* matters reviewable by the Board and deferred to if not repugnant to the Labor Act.[54]

Other arbitrators have also emphasized that they would not interpret or apply an agreement in a way that would require a party to commit an illegal act.[55] One arbitrator stated that "he cannot bring himself to render an opinion and award, which, if carried out, would result in both parties to the arbitration being guilty of unlawful conduct," and he refused to order the employer to discharge an employee as requested by the union where such discharge would place both the employer and the union in violation of the NLRA.[56] What if the statute is subject to constitutional challenge? In refus-

---

[54]Seitz, *The Limits of Arbitration*, 88 Monthly Lab. Rev. 763, 764 (1965) (emphasis in original). *See also* Lithibar Matik Inc.,112 LA 957, 965 (Sugerman, 1999) (explaining why public policy should be left to the Board); Flowers Baking Co., 89 LA 666, 671 (Rice, 1987) (refusing to analyze claim under ERISA because arbitration was not the proper forum to adjudicate issues of external federal statutory law); Pride Prof'l Servs., 88 LA 229, 232 (Gallagher, 1986) (arbitrator's authority does not include power to levy penalties created by statute); City of Bethany, Okla., 87 LA 309, 312 (Levy, 1986) (refusing to assume jurisdiction over the FLSA); Cuyahoga County, Ohio, Welfare Dep't, 76 LA 729, 731–32 (Siegel, 1981) (he would "not assume functions which belong in the courtroom or before a public agency and which are not rightfully his"); Thrifty Corp., 72 LA 898, 903 (Barrett, 1979); Cessna Aircraft Co., 72 LA 367, 369 (Laybourne, 1979) (it is "not within the authority or jurisdiction of the arbitrator to enforce laws enacted by a legislative body"); Hughes Airwest, 71 LA 1123, 1126 (Roberts, 1978) (if the employer "breaches a statutory obligation the recourse of the victimized employee must be to the appropriate agency or court"); Chicago Transit Auth., 69 LA 563, 565 (Larkin, 1977). In some instances, to ignore external law would render an arbitrator's award a nullity. In dictum, in *Foster Food Products*, 88 LA 337 (Riker, 1986), the arbitrator stated, "In fact, the employees' rights exist and are protected even if a collective bargaining agreement or company policy or practice says the opposite." *Id.* at 340.

Others have held that in some instances to ignore external law would render an arbitrator's award a nullity. *See, e.g.*, Michigan Dep't of Corr., 103 LA 37, 39 (Sugerman, 1994) ("Although plenary jurisdiction to interpret Freedom of Information Act [FOIA, 5 U.S.C. §701 et seq.] remains with the judiciary, I must examine the FOIA exemptions to the extent it is necessary to ascertain whether a contractual violation has occurred."); Raybestos Prods. Co., 102 LA 46, 54 (Kossoff, 1993) (company could override collective bargaining agreement provisions regarding smokers' rights if a statute, OSHA regulations, or binding court decision required an employer to subordinate smokers' right to nonsmokers' rights). *But see* Rock Island County, Ill., 104 LA 1127, 1133 (Witney, 1995) (rejecting union's invitation to apply provisions of the FMLA when the union agreed to more limited leave terms in the parties' collective bargaining agreement).

[55]*See* Champion Int'l Corp., 106 LA 1024, 1031 (Howell, 1996) (while the EEOC is responsible for enforcing the ADA, the arbitrator may consider the ADA in interpreting the parties' collective bargaining agreement); Alcoa Bldg. Prods., 104 LA 364, 368–69 (Cerone, 1995) (the ADA compelled reasonable accommodation, but the company went too far when it violated a union member's contractual seniority rights to accommodate disabled employee); Rodeway Inn, 102 LA 1003, 1014–15 (Goldberg, 1994) (refusing to interpret contract in a manner that would be "repugnant" to the policies set forth in Title VII); Clarion-Limestone Area Sch. Dist., 90 LA 281 (Creo, 1988); Duquesne Club, 89 LA 1302 (Talarico, 1987); Miami Valley Ready-Mixed Concrete Ass'n, 71 LA 524, 531 (Barone, 1978); California-Sample Serv. Co., 70 LA 338, 341 (Draznin, 1978); Sperry Rand Corp., 44 LA 965, 966–67 (Stein, 1965); Globe-Democrat Publ'g Co., 41 LA 65, 71–72 (Smith, 1963); Buckstaff Co., 40 LA 833, 835 (Young, 1963); International Breweries, 37 LA 638, 646–47 (Dworkin, 1961); Hillside Transit Co., 22 LA 470, 473 (Anderson, 1954); F.H. Hill Co., 8 LA 62, 65 (Abernethy, 1947).

[56]Buckstaff Co., 40 LA 833, 835 (Young, 1963). Moreover, one arbitrator stated:

I recognize, however, that the authority to decide these legal questions is vested in the Board and the courts, not in the Arbitrator. The parties have agreed that my task has been to interpret their agreement. This I have done. My only concern, with respect

ing to award a union-security provision that would be illegal under a state statute, an arbitrator touched on the question of constitutionality and explained that the validity of the statute must be assumed:

> No award of this board can give validity to any contract which contravenes the law of any state. If it is indeed true that the Kansas law is ineffective because unconstitutional, that result has not yet been authoritatively declared by a court of last resort. The act must be assumed effective until otherwise determined.[57]

In *Duraloy*,[58] the arbitrator attempted to identify the circumstances under which an arbitrator should or should not consider external law in deciding a grievance:

> First, the Agreement itself might incorporate various laws, or require or authorize an arbitrator to consider them. Second, the Agreement might forbid the arbitrator from giving any consideration to outside laws. Since the role of an arbitrator is to give effect to the Agreement, few would dispute that the arbitrator should consider external law in the first situation, and should not in the second. Likewise, where the Agreement does not contain any explicit instruction, but the parties at the hearing agree that the arbitrator should, or should not, consider the effects of outside legislation, the arbitrator ought to follow their instruction. A third situation occurs where a reference to external legislation might assist in interpreting specific provisions of an Agreement. For ex-

---

to the legal issues (aside from their relevance in the matter of contract interpretation) has been whether my award will have the effect of ordering the Company to perform an illegal act.
Globe-Democrat Publ'g Co., 41 LA 65, 75 (Smith, 1963).

[57]Kansas City Pub. Serv. Co., 8 LA 149, 159 (Updegraff, Sawyer, Gage, Zimring, & Hargus, 1957) (an "interest" arbitration). *See also* Plumbers' Union Health & Welfare Fund, 32 LA 661, 663–64 (Callaghan, 1959). If a contract adopts one of two alternatives permitted by statute, the agreement does not conflict with the statute but simply limits the parties to one of two possibilities under the law. Wilson & Co., 1 LA 368, 378 (Lohman, undated).

[58]100 LA 1166 (Franckiewicz, 1993). In *Gerland's Food Fair*, 93 LA 1285 (Helburn, 1989), the arbitrator dealt with a "classic dilemma." If he applied Taft-Hartley §302(c)(4) as interpreted and applied by the NLRB, the grievance would have to be denied. If, however, the negotiated agreement governed, the grievance would have to be sustained. The arbitrator concluded that the "general rule [was] that the arbitrator draws authority not from external sources, unless they are made part of the contract or incorporated into the parties' charge to the arbitrator, but from the labor agreement which brought the arbitration process into being." *Id.* at 1288. Following established Supreme Court doctrine and the fact that the arbitrator draws authority from the negotiated agreement, the arbitrator sustained the grievance, holding that "the award must honor and give life to the contract." *Id.* at 1289. *See also* City of Lake Worth, Fla., 101 LA 78 (Abrams, 1993) (city violated collective bargaining agreement by failing to appropriate sufficient funds for contract's third-year pay increase, despite claim that state law provided that failure of the legislature to appropriate money sufficient to fund a collective bargaining agreement did not constitute an unfair labor practice; because nothing in the parties' agreement required the arbitrator to read, interpret, or apply enacted legislation, external law did not apply and the arbitrator's job was to resolve any grievance in accordance with the collective bargaining agreement); Detroit Edison Co., 96 LA 1033 (Lipson, 1991) (expressing strong support for the principle that it is an arbitrator's role to apply the parties' contract rather than the law in resolving a dispute). *See, e.g.*, City of Flint, Mich., 104 LA 125, 126–27 (House, 1995) (contract at issue in sexual harassment case incorporated the EEOC Guidelines on Discrimination Because of Sex and the Michigan state employment discrimination statute's definition of forbidden conduct); San Francisco, Cal., Unified Sch. Dist., 104 LA 215, 217 (Bogue, 1995) (applying the federal and state disabilities laws to a case arising out of a contract that incorporated both by reference); Angus Chem. Co., 102 LA 388, 392 (Nicholas, Jr., 1994) (employee was not "disabled" as defined in the ADA when the parties had explicitly incorporated the ADA into the collective bargaining agreement).

ample, an Agreement might refer to "overtime" without defining what is intended by the term. In such a case, the arbitrator might refer to the Fair Labor Standards Act. Additionally, Agreements frequently borrow terms used elsewhere in the law, such as "bargain in good faith", or "discrimination on the basis of race, sex, religion or national origin", or "probable cause". In such cases I believe that most arbitrators, and most courts would consider it appropriate for an arbitrator to take the relevant statute into account in interpreting the meaning of the phrase in the Agreement. A fourth situation occurs where the Agreement is silent, but the arbitrator is asked to consider some statute, case or regulation and read it into the Agreement. For example, a contract might contain no provision relating to health or safety, but the arbitrator might be asked to require the employer to comply with OSHA [Occupational Safety and Health Act] regulations. The fifth situation, which might be considered the reverse of the fourth, is where the contract imposes an obligation, but one party contends that the contractual obligation would conflict with the law, and that the arbitrator should therefore decline to follow the contract as written. My view is that in the fourth and fifth situations described above, the arbitrator should consider only the agreement and not the external law. Where reference to statutes, regulations or decisions is not necessary in interpreting an agreement, the only effect of considering such external sources of law would be to amend the contract by adding or subtracting. The proper role for an arbitrator is only to interpret a contract, and not to rewrite it.[59]

---

[59]Duraloy, 100 LA 1166, 1172 (Franckiewicz, 1993). Regarding the first assertion in *Duraloy*, see *Packaging Corp. of Am.*, 114 LA 809, 812 (Nolan, 2000) (incorporating federal, state, and municipal safety laws into an agreement); *GTE N.*, 113 LA 1047, 1051–52 (Daniel, 1999) (the agreement required compliance with the ADA); *Integram-St. Louis Seating*, 113 LA 693, 697–99 (Marino, 1999) (applying the FMLA because the parties incorporated it into their agreement); *Interstate Brands Corp.*, 113 LA 161, 168 (Howell, 1999) (dismissing a grievance after applying the ADA as required by the collective bargaining agreement); *G.E. Railcar Repair Servs. Corp.*, 112 LA 632, 638 (O'Grady, 1999) (the grievant's notice was insufficient under the FMLA); *National Gypsum Co.*, 112 LA 248, 256 (Nicholas, Jr., 1999) (compliance with the FMLA); *Aerospace Ctr. Support*, 112 LA 108, 110 (Welch, 1999) (the parties granted the arbitrator jurisdiction to apply the FMLA with generic contract language that stated, "Any controversy which has not been satisfactorily adjusted under the grievance procedure and which involves: a. The discharge of an employee . . . may be submitted for settlement to an Arbitrator"); *Mason & Hanger Corp.*, 111 LA 60, 63 (Caraway, 1998) (involving shift preference conflicts caused by the ADA and seniority provisions); *Cramer, Inc.*, 110 LA 37, 42 (O'Grady, 1998) ("Increasingly, arbitrators are asked to consider matters of Federal or state law in the ever more complex world of labor-management relations."); *San Francisco, Cal., Unified Sch. Dist.*, 104 LA at 217 (applying the federal and state disabilities laws to a case arising out of a contract that incorporated both by reference); *City of Flint, Mich.*, 104 LA at 126–27 (contract at issue in sexual harassment case incorporated the EEOC Guidelines on Discrimination Because of Sex and the Michigan state employment discrimination statute's definition of forbidden conduct); *Angus Chem. Co.*, 102 LA at 392 (employee was not "disabled" as defined in the ADA when the parties had explicitly incorporated the ADA into the collective bargaining agreement). *See also* Roadway Package Sys., 112 LA 540, 545 (Richard, 1999) (a contract between a delivery service and a driver was governed by Pennsylvania law); American Sterilizer Co., 104 LA 921, 924–25 (Dissen, 1995) (relying on a prior arbitrator's decision that the parties' agreement specifically incorporated the ADA and then applying it); Meijer, Inc., 103 LA 834, 840 (Daniel, 1994) ("Under a contract requiring just cause for disciplinary action against an employee, rights established by law, such as ADA, must be taken into consideration in determining whether just cause exists."). *But see* Dinagraphics, Inc., 102 LA 947, 953 (Paolucci, 1994) (when collective bargaining agreement did not prohibit discrimination based on disability, the ADA was inapplicable).

Regarding the "third situation" in *Duraloy, Allied Healthcare Prods.*, 113 LA 992 (Marino, 2000) (considering NLRB law when interpreting a recognition clause and a memorandum of understanding); *Akzo Nobel Salt*, 113 LA 645 (Goldberg, 1999) (referring to the Worker Adjustment and Retraining Notification (WARN) Act, 29 U.S.C. §2101 et seq., for instruction while noting that it did not control); *Henkel Corp.*, 104 LA 494, 499 (Hooper, 1995) (noting

A number of other arbitrators have stated that their role is not to assume jurisdiction over areas that are the responsibility of the NLRB and the courts.[60]

In *Hunter Engineering Co.*,[61] the grievant, who was vice president of his local union, claimed that superseniority accorded him by a provision of the applicable agreement protected him from layoff. The employer argued that the provision was illegal pursuant to the NLRB's *Gulton* decision.[62] The arbitrator, while recognizing that the employer correctly interpreted the law,

---

that Title VII was useful in deciding race discrimination issue, while observing that the outcome of the case "does not depend on the particular legal construct that the arbitrator chooses to employ"); *Thermo King Corp.*, 102 LA 612, 615 (Dworkin, 1993) (recognizing that the arbitrator lacks authority to decide whether company violated the ADA, but looking to the ADA for guidance in determining whether the company-imposed penalty on the grievant was just and fair); *Multi-Clean, Inc.*, 102 LA 463, 467 (Miller, 1993) (when parties failed to define "reasonable accommodation" in the collective bargaining agreement provision addressing age and disability, the arbitrator turned to the ADA definition in interpreting the phrase's contractual meaning).

Regarding the "fourth situation," see *PPG Indus.*, 113 LA 833, 839–40 (Dichter, 1999) (considering the Electronic Communications Privacy Act, 18 U.S.C. §2701 et seq., on the union's request where the company disciplined the grievant for sending pornographic material via e-mail); *Georgia Pac. Corp.*, 112 LA 317, 321 (Caraway, 1999) (reviewing race discrimination issues raised by the union while addressing an antinepotism policy).

[60]Cosmic Distribution, 92 LA 205 (Prayzich, 1989) (arbitrator lacks authority to rule on claim that employer violated the LMRA when it demoted and reduced wages of returning economic striker where the matter was not deferred to arbitration by the NLRB in conjunction with the filing of unfair labor practice charges and where the parties stipulated that the issue was whether the company violated the collective bargaining agreement in so doing); George A. Hormel & Co., 90 LA 1246 (Goodman, 1988) (arbitrator had no authority to interpret the FLSA regarding pay for wash-up time); FMC N. Ordinance Div., 90 LA 834 (Bognanno, 1988) (arbitrator had no authority to decide unfair labor practice claim). *Cf.* Holly Farms, 90 LA 509 (McDermott, 1987) (arbitrator was without authority to decide claim under state handicap law); Antrim County, Mich., Sheriff's Dep't, 89 LA 928 (Frost, 1987); S.D. Warren Co., 89 LA 688 (Gwiazda, 1985) (arbitrator declined to consider questions of public policy and state law in considering discharge of employees found in possession of or selling drugs on company property); Flowers Baking Co., 89 LA 666 (Rice, 1987) (arbitrator had no authority to decide claim to severance pay under ERISA); Indiana Bell Tel. Co., 88 LA 401, 404 (Feldman, 1986) ("[T]his arbitrator has no jurisdiction over any NLRB defenses, that activity being the proper subject for another forum."); Florida Power Corp., 87 LA 957, 960 (Wahl, 1986) ("This Arbitrator stands with those of his colleagues, who would avoid a judicial role, such as interpreting a statute, whenever possible; that function belongs to a court. The arbitrator's normal role and the area in which he can be most helpful is to interpret and apply the Agreement which the parties have entered into."); City of Bethany, Okla., 87 LA 309, 312 (Levy, 1986) ("It is not for the arbitrator to assume, and he will not assume, jurisdiction over the Fair Labor Standards Act, as that is a federal statute, or regulation and is subject to the jurisdiction of an administrative law judge. The arbitrator will not decide whether or not the FLSA was applicable to this situation, and particularly to the work week and the exclusion of captains and assistant chiefs as to overtime."). *But compare* Bake Rite Rolls, 90 LA 1133 (DiLauro, 1988) (reinstated employee discharged for refusal to take polygraph test in violation of state law); Fleming Foods of Cal., 90 LA 1071 (Askin, 1988) (payment of severance pay to union officers on leave of absence not precluded by LMRA); Mike-Sell's Potato Chip Co., 90 LA 801 (Cohen, 1988) (arbitrator had jurisdiction to consider whether two subsidiaries were a "single employer"). *See also* Owens-Illinois, 83 LA 1265 (Cantor, 1984); Elwell-Parker Elec. Co., 82 LA 327 (Dworkin, 1984). *Compare* Andex Indus., 111 LA 615, 618 (Allen, 1998) (making no distinction between the roles of arbitrators and the courts in forming ADA policy).

[61]82 LA 403 (Alleyne, 1984).

[62]Gulton Electro-Voice, 266 NLRB 406, 112 LRRM 1361 (1983), *enforced sub nom.* Electrical Workers (IUE) Local 900 v. NLRB, 727 F.2d 1184, 115 LRRM 2760 (D.C. Cir. 1984).

chose to ignore *Gulton*, stating that: "Except when agreements provide to the contrary, the grievance-arbitration procedure is best served when arbitrators adhere to areas of conventional contract interpretation, leaving pure questions of contractual legality to those authorized by law to resolve such questions."[63]

When considering a similar issue, however, another arbitrator reached a different conclusion, reasoning that it would be a violation of the NLRA, as articulated in various NLRB opinions, to interpret the agreement to accord seniority preference to union stewards. Therefore, he refused to interpret the agreement to afford stewards any more benefits than NLRB guidelines permitted.[64]

Another arbitrator also rejected the view that every collective bargaining agreement should be deemed to embody all the relevant law.[65] But, with respect to those agreements that specifically incorporate external law, he noted that, if the parties incorporate external law into the agreement and make it clear that they want the arbitrator to interpret and apply external law, the arbitrator must do so, even though this will open up the decision to more extensive review in the courts.[66] It is clear, however, that in each case

---

[63]Hunter Eng'g, 82 LA 483, 485 (Alleyne, 1984). *See, e.g.,* Fors Farms, 112 LA 33, 36–42 (Cavanaugh, 1999) (considering the parol evidence rule and other contract law principles); 5th Ave. Musical Theatre Co., 111 LA 820, 824 (Snow, 1998) (relying on the Restatement (Second) of Contracts); Springfield Mech. Servs., 111 LA 403, 405 (Pratte, 1998) (refusing to apply the parol evidence rule to administrative forms); Boise Cascade Corp., 111 LA 231, 235–38 (Snow, 1998) (applying the maxim expressio unius est exclusio alterius). *Compare Lucas W.*, 91 LA 1272, 1272 (Alleyne, 1988), where the arbitrator held that the employer did not violate the nondiscrimination clause of the state workers' compensation act by discharging an employee for absenteeism on his return from industrial injury leave. Contractual provisions requiring the employer to comply with state and federal nondiscrimination laws warranted the consideration of external laws in that case.

[64]Ex-Cell-O Corp., 85 LA 1190 (Statham, 1985). This position, attributed to Howlett, *The Arbitrator and the NLRB: The Arbitrator, the NLRB, and the Courts, in* The Arbitrator, the NLRB, and the Courts, Proceedings of the 20th Annual Meeting of NAA 67, 83 (Jones ed., BNA Books 1967), has gained some acceptance. *See, e.g.,* U.S. Steel Corp., 89 LA 221 (Neumeier, 1987) (arbitrator recognized superseniority where there was no conflict with the NLRA); City of Toledo, Ohio, 88 LA 137 (Feldman, 1986) (affirmative action obligation incorporated into contract); Olin Corp., 86 LA 1193 (Penfield, 1986) (arbitrator construed statute on deduction from wages in ruling on grievance); City of Grand Rapids, Mich., 86 LA 819 (Frost, 1986) (according to arbitrator, contractual nondiscrimination provision is parallel to Title VII requiring analysis of grievance as if sex discrimination case in court); Saucelito Ranch, 85 LA 282 (Draznin, 1985); Columbus Nursing Home, 82 LA 1004 (Laybourne, 1984) (arbitrator construed garnishment statute in ruling on discharge); Bevles Co., 82 LA 203 (Monat, 1983). *See also* Russell Div., 114 LA 107 (Solomon, 2000) (referring to the NLRA when determining whether bargaining was required before issuing work assignments); Snap-Tite, 110 LA 512, 519 (Franckiewicz, 1998) ("In an arbitration case, the arbitrator has more flexibility than the NLRB generally accords itself to adjust the remedy to the equities of the situation.").

[65]Feller, *Relationship of the Agreement to External Law, in* Labor Arbitration Development: A Handbook 33 (Barreca, Miller, & Zimny eds., BNA Books 1983). *See also* City of Lake Worth, Fla., 101 LA 78 (Abrams, 1993) (rejecting argument that all state laws are part of the collective bargaining agreement when it does not say that in the agreement).

[66]*Feller,* at 37. *See also* William Penn Sch. Dist., 99 LA 815 (Zirkel, 1992) (when the parties' collective bargaining agreement expressly incorporates relevant state legislation, there is no doubt that the arbitrator has not only the authority, but also the obligation, to apply the controlling statutory language and the ample line of case law that interprets and clarifies it).

the question whether external law is expressly incorporated into the relevant provision of an agreement may well determine the result.[67]

The expressions of many other arbitrators fall somewhere within the spectrum of these doctrinal views.[68] However, in evaluating these expres-

---

[67]Rock Island County, Ill., 104 LA 1127, 1133 (Witney, 1995) (rejecting the union's invitation to apply provisions of the FMLA when the union agreed to more limited leave terms in the parties' collective bargaining agreement); Jefferson Smurfit Corp., 103 LA 1041, 1048 (Canestraight, 1994) (company's failure to accommodate disabled employee did not violate collective bargaining agreement when parties failed to expressly or implicitly incorporate federal disability laws into the agreement); Racine, Wis., Unified Sch. Dist., 102 LA 327, 332 (Baron, 1993) (reasoning that the parties' agreement that designated the union as the exclusive bargaining unit "with all the rights and responsibilities under the Municipal Relations Act," which included protections related to conditions of employment, extended the arbitrator's jurisdiction to consider external law); Detroit Edison Co., 96 LA 1033, 1036 (Lipson, 1991) (where contract prohibited discrimination "because of race, creed, color, national origin, sex, or age," and that clause was adopted against the background of longstanding federal and state laws against employment discrimination, it demonstrated the parties' intent to incorporate external law into their contract). There are other situations when matters external to a collective bargaining agreement may impinge upon it. For example, in *St. Louis Telephone Employees' Credit Union*, 97 LA 412 (Cohen, 1991), the grievant's termination was caused simply by the cancellation of her bond coverage. In upholding the grievant's discharge, the arbitrator noted that "this is a situation where external law must be considered" because a state law required all credit union employees to be bonded and the company had no choice short of jeopardizing its very existence but to discharge the grievant if she was not bonded. *Id.* at 416. *See also* Michigan Dep't of Transp., 104 LA 1196, 1201 (Kelman, 1995) (analyzing Title VII's provisions in rejecting the company's argument that a lesser degree of discipline would have resulted in Title VII lawsuit against the company); Host Int'l, 94 LA 492 (Talarico, 1990) (employer had the right to take corrective action to ensure compliance with state law where it prohibited anyone under 18 from serving alcohol despite a claim that the employee's job description did not contain an age limit); Food Barn Stores, 93 LA 87 (Fogelberg, 1989) (reliance on the FLSA concerning meaning of uniform); Star Tribune, 93 LA 14 (Bognanno, 1989); City of Springfield, Ill., 92 LA 1298 (Yarowsky, 1989). *Compare* McCreary Tire & Rubber Co., 85 LA 137, 140 (Fischer, 1985) ("ERISA requirements as such do not govern the issue insofar as the contractual status is involved."), *and* Los Angeles, Cal., Cmty. Coll. Dist., 87 LA 252 (Kaufman, 1986) (where agreement did not incorporate external law, external law was not applied), *with* Florida Power Corp., 87 LA 957, 960 (where agreement authorized arbitrator to pass on a legal question, external law was applied). *See generally* Zirkel, *The Use of External Law in Labor Arbitration: An Analysis of Arbitral Awards*, 1985 Detroit C. L. Rev. 31 (author examined 100 cases decided between 1972 and 1982 in light of mode of analysis and citation of legal authority, noting that external law was more evident in context out of which dispute arose than in content).

[68]*See* Chevron U.S.A., 95 LA 393 (Riker, 1990); Tamco Distrib. Co., 90 LA 1263 (Talarico, 1988); George A. Hormel & Co., 90 LA 1246 (Goodman, 1988); Defense Mapping Agency—Aerospace Ctr., 88 LA 651 (Hilgert, 1986); Eau Claire County, Wis., 76 LA 333, 334 (McCrary, 1981); City of Rochester, Mich., 76 LA 295, 298 (Lipson, 1981); T.N.S., Inc., 76 LA 278, 283–84 (Hardin, 1981); Burbank, Ill., Bd. of Educ., Sch. Dist. 220, 76 LA 158, 159 (Berman, 1981); Norwood, Ohio, Bd. of Educ., 74 LA 697, 699 (Coyle, 1980); City of Scranton, Pa., 73 LA 927, 928 (Gomberg, 1979); Reichhold Chems., 73 LA 636, 637 (Hon, 1979); Alameda-Contra Costa Transit Dist., 71 LA 889, 892 (Randall, 1978); Miami Valley Ready-Mixed Concrete Ass'n, 71 LA 524, 531 (Barone, 1978); Muskego-Norway, Wis., Sch. Dist., 71 LA 509, 512–13 (Rice II, 1978); Landy Packing Co., 71 LA 427, 432–33 (Flagler, 1978); Mechanical & Sheet Metal Contractors of Kan., 71 LA 286, 287 (Yarowsky, 1978); Stokely-Van Camp, 71 LA 109, 112–13 (Snow, 1978); Grower-Shipper Vegetable Ass'n of Cent. Cal., 70 LA 350, 353 (Ross, 1978); Union Tribune Publ'g Co., 70 LA 266, 269 (Richman, 1978); Newbury Mfg. Co., 70 LA 257, 262 (Rutherford, 1978); Schien Body & Equip. Co., 69 LA 930, 934–35 (Roberts, 1977); Lake County, Ohio, Bd. of Mental Retardation, 69 LA 869, 870 (Siegel, 1977); City of San Antonio, Tex., 69 LA 541, 545 (Caraway, 1977); New York State Dep't of Corr. Servs., 69 LA 344, 350 (Kornblum, 1977); Frederick J. Dando Co., 69 LA 48, 52 (Di Leone, 1977); United Tel. Co. of Ohio, 68 LA 887, 893 (Ipavec, 1977); Northwest Airlines, 68 LA 31, 33–34 (Bloch, 1977). *See also* Apcoa, Inc., 107 LA 705, 711 (Daniel, 1996) (recognizing applicability of the FMLA when parties incorporated the statute into their collective bargaining agreement, but commenting

sions, it should be kept in mind that external law may be considered for some purposes, but not for others, and any given arbitrator quite properly may feel justified in relying on external law in one situation while declining to do so for some other situation.[69] Consider the following comment:

> The extent to which external law should be a factor in the arbitration of a dispute between parties to a collective agreement presents a difficult and thorny question. Many who have pontificated on the subject have regretted their words when faced with the arbitration of the next case. The only thing of which it is possible to be certain is that it would not be prudent to lay down broad rules on the subject without a degree of tentativeness and caution.[70]

Turning to arbitral reliance on principles of the common law as applied to statutory provisions, while not all arbitrators will agree fully, probably most do share the view that "long and generally accepted judicial principles" can serve well in the forum of arbitration.[71] In this regard, one arbitrator commented:

> This arbitrator long has been intrigued by how parties to labor arbitration, while naturally eschewing all intentions of being "legalistic," nevertheless so often tread the same time-worn paths of the development of the great com-

---

that contract may afford *greater* benefits than the statute); Enesco Corp., 107 LA 513, 518 (Berman, 1996) (employer subject to statutory leave obligations is still bound by contractual leave promises that exceed the statutory requirement); Michigan Dep't of Corr., 104 LA 1192, 1194 (Sugerman, 1995) (assuming, without question, the authority to apply the FLSA and the Portal-to-Portal Act, 29 U.S.C. §251 et seq., to the parties' wage dispute); Indiana Mich. Power Co., 103 LA 248, 252 (Alexander, 1994) (while the arbitrator's job is to determine whether just cause existed for the discharge, the statutory and decisional law under Title VII provides guidance in evaluating actionable conduct); Reed Mfg. Co., 102 LA 1, 6 (Dworkin, 1993) (declining to broadly construe a management-rights clause in the parties' collective bargaining agreement, noting "[s]ometimes the federal labor policy proscribes protections that not even the most broadly drawn Management Rights language in a contract can supersede"). For one commentator's view, see Greenfield, *How Do Arbitrators Treat External Law?*, 45 INDUS. & LAB. REL. REV. 683 (1992). *See also* Brennan, *Arbitration in a Changing Environment, in* ARBITRATION 1991: THE CHANGING FACE OF ARBITRATION IN THEORY AND PRACTICE, PROCEEDINGS OF THE 44TH ANNUAL MEETING OF NAA 2 (Gruenberg ed., BNA Books 1991). The disagreement among arbitrators over consideration of external law also exists where state law is concerned. In a number of cases, arbitrators have decided disputes on the basis of the collective bargaining agreement rather than a state statute or regulation. *See* New Haven Bd. & Carton Co., 46 LA 1203, 1205 (Kornblum, 1966); Simmons Co., 39 LA 766, 768 (Schedler, 1962); Stanley Works, 39 LA 374, 378 (Summers, 1962). However, in other cases arbitrators have considered state statutes and regulations in deciding the grievance. *See* Weyerhaeuser Co., 54 LA 857, 858–59 (Zack, 1971); Providence, R.I., Sch. Comm., 53 LA 207, 208–10 (MacLeod, 1969); American Super Mkt., 51 LA 597, 599 (Block, 1968); Phillips Petroleum Co., 50 LA 522, 527 (Allen, Jr., 1968).

[69]For example, compare the approach of one arbitrator in *Max Factor & Co.*, 73 LA 742, 744–45 (Jones, Jr., 1979), with his approach in *Pacific Southwest Airlines*, 70 LA 833, 837 (Jones, Jr., 1978).

[70]Ellenville, N.Y., Cent. Sch. Dist., 74 LA 1221, 1222 (Seitz, 1980). As noted in section 2.C., "Capability of Arbitrators to Deal With External Law," below, the arbitrator, in 1981, reiterated his general belief that it is undesirable for arbitrators to decide statutory issues. However, the present case involved a different purpose for consideration of external law, and he did note certain external law in determining the sense of the agreement.

[71]The latter thought was expressed in *Trubitz Hardware & Electric Co.*, 32 LA 930, 935 (Scheiber, 1959), in applying a basic principle of agency law. The arbitrator also stated that "the avoidance of procedural legalism should not be accompanied by a disregard for such principles of law as have long been our guiding stars." *Id. See, e.g.*, Madison Warehouse Corp., 112 LA 300, 306 (Suardi, 1998) (considering agency authority).

mon law. Nor should this be surprising, because after all the vaunted Anglo-American common law consists of the vast heritage of experience—the accumulated customs, viewpoints, and usages of ordinary people just like ourselves.[72]

B. U.S. Supreme Court Statements Regarding Arbitral Consideration of External Law

Those who conclude that where there is clear conflict between the agreement and law, the arbitrator "should respect the agreement and ignore the law," find support in the opinion of the Supreme Court in the *Enterprise Wheel* case.[73] There, the Court commented on the appropriate treatment of the arbitrator's award in this fashion:

> It may be read as based solely upon the arbitrator's view of the requirements of enacted legislation, which would mean that he exceeded the scope of the submission. Or it may be read as embodying a construction of the agreement itself, perhaps with the arbitrator looking to "the law" for help in determining the sense of the agreement.[74]

The Court subsequently spoke specifically to the arbitrator's function where the labor agreement conflicts with external law in the course of its opinion in *Gardner-Denver*.[75] The Court wrote that an arbitrator "has no general authority to invoke public laws that conflict with the bargain between the parties," that arbitration is "a comparatively inappropriate forum for the final resolution of rights created by Title VII" of the Civil Rights Act, that the arbitrator's "task is to effectuate the intent of the parties rather than the requirements of enacted legislation," and that "[w]here the collective-bargaining agreement conflicts with Title VII, the arbitrator must follow the agreement."[76]

---

[72]Caterpillar Tractor Co., 39 LA 534, 537 (Sembower, 1962).

[73]Steelworkers v. Enterprise Wheel & Car Corp., 363 U.S. 593, 46 LRRM 2423 (1960).

[74]*Id.* at 597–98, 46 LRRM at 2425.

[75]Alexander v. Gardner-Denver Co., 415 U.S. 36, 7 FEP Cases 81 (1974).

[76]*Id.* at 53, 56, 56–57, 57, 7 FEP Cases at 87, 89. The actual holding in *Gardner-Denver* was that an employee's statutory right to trial de novo on his discrimination claim under Title VII was not foreclosed by prior submission of his claim to final arbitration (where the award was adverse to the employee) under the nondiscrimination clause of a collective bargaining agreement. For citation of many articles discussing *Gardner-Denver* and its possible impact on arbitration, see Chapter 2, section 2.A.ii.d., "De Novo Litigation Following Arbitration." In extending the *Gardner-Denver* holding to individuals who seek recovery under the FLSA following an adverse decision in arbitration proceedings arising from the same event, the Court in *Barrentine v. Arkansas-Best Freight System*, 450 U.S. 728, 24 WH Cases 1284 (1981), reiterated that an arbitrator "'has no general authority to invoke public laws that conflict with the bargain between the parties.'" *Id.* at 744 (quoting *Gardner-Denver*, 415 U.S. at 53). The Court also stated that "the arbitrator is required to effectuate the intent of the parties, rather than to enforce the statute." *Id.* at 744. As concerns conflict between agreement and statute, it is interesting to note that Congress in the Railway Labor Act (RLA), 45 U.S.C. §151 et seq., expressly provided that certain provisions of the Act are "made a part of the contract of employment between the carrier and each employee, and shall be held binding upon the parties, regardless of any other express or implied agreements between them." RLA §2, Eighth. For arbitral recognition of this requirement, see *Texas International Airlines*, 68 LA 244, 248 (Gruenberg, 1977).

However, in no sense has the Supreme Court stated that an arbitrator should not examine external law in interpreting and applying the collective bargaining agreement. Indeed, as noted above, the Court in *Enterprise Wheel* expressly recognized the propriety of "the arbitrator looking to 'the law' for help in determining the sense of the agreement."[77] Furthermore, in *Gardner-Denver*'s now famous "Footnote 21," the Court in a sense invited arbitrators to examine external law. The Supreme Court used the note to indicate the terms on which lower courts in Title VII discrimination actions "may properly accord [a prior arbitration decision] great weight." Footnote 21 states:

> We adopt no standards as to the weight to be accorded an arbitral decision, since this must be determined in the court's discretion with regard to the facts and circumstances of each case. Relevant factors include the existence of provisions in the collective-bargaining agreement that conform substantially with Title VII, the degree of procedural fairness in the arbitral forum, adequacy of the record with respect to the issue of discrimination, and the special competence of particular arbitrators. *Where an arbitral determination gives full consideration to an employee's Title VII rights*, a court may properly accord it great weight. This is especially true where the issue is solely one of fact, specifically addressed by the parties and decided by the arbitrator on the basis of an adequate record. But courts should ever be mindful that Congress, in enacting Title VII, thought it necessary to provide a judicial forum for the ultimate resolution of discriminatory employment claims. It is the duty of courts to assure the full availability of this forum.[78]

In its *Gilmer* decision,[79] moreover, the Supreme Court expressed confidence in an arbitrator's capability to resolve statutory claims. In *Gilmer*'s Footnote 5 the Court noted:

> The Court in *Alexander v. Gardner-Denver Co.*, . . . also expressed the view that arbitration was inferior to the judicial process for resolving statutory claims. . . . That "mistrust of the arbitral process", however, has been undermined by our recent arbitration decisions. "[W]e are well past the time when judicial suspicion of the desirability of arbitration and of the competence of arbitral tribunals inhibited the development of arbitration as an alternative means of dispute resolution."[80]

---

[77]*Enterprise Wheel*, 363 U.S. at 598. When the arbitrator on considering external law finds conflict between law and agreement, it is only then that the court calls for the arbitrator to disregard the law to the extent that it is contrary to the agreement.

[78]*Gardner-Denver*, 415 U.S. at 60 n.21, 7 FEP Cases at 90 (emphasis added). For additional material regarding *Gardner-Denver* and its Footnote 21, see Chapter 2, section 2.A.ii.d., "De Novo Litigation Following Arbitration." For other related discussion, see section 3.A.i., "Title VII of the Civil Rights Act," below. In its FLSA *Barrentine* decision, the Supreme Court quoted with obvious reaffirmance *Gardner-Denver*'s Footnote 21 factors relevant in a court's determination of the weight to be accorded an arbitral decision, and the Court also quoted the Footnote 21 statement that, "'Where an arbitral determination gives full consideration to an employee's [statutory] rights, a court may properly accord it great weight.'" *Barrentine*, 450 U.S. at 743 n.22) (quoting *Gardner-Denver*, 415 U.S. at 60 n.21) (bracketed word "statutory" supplied by the Court).

[79]Gilmer v. Interstate/Johnson Lane Corp., 500 U.S. 20, 55 FEP Cases 1116 (1991).

[80]*Id.* at 34 n.5 (citations omitted) (quoting Mitsubishi Motors Corp. v. Soler Chrysler-Plymouth, 473 U.S. 614, 626–27 (1985)).

The Court responded to *Gilmer*'s contention that judicial review of arbitration decisions is too limited by noting that "'such review is sufficient to ensure that arbitrators comply with the requirements of the statute'" at issue.[81] Thus, it appears that as long as an arbitrator's decision resolving a statutory claim complies with the statute's requirements, it will not be disturbed on appeal. This view is consistent with the Court's increased willingness to recognize the capability of arbitrators to deal with statutory issues.

C. Capability of Arbitrators to Deal With External Law

Some arbitrators and judges, including some members of the Supreme Court, have expressed doubt concerning abitrators' ability to address and manage external law. However, many arbitrators believe that they possess the requisite capability, and qualified observers in the field of labor law and arbitration have expressed the belief that the requisite capability is in fact possessed by many if not most arbitrators. For instance, while one arbitrator stated that he did "not regard it as desirable for arbitrators to make final and binding decisions on the meaning and application of public statutes . . . except in public sector cases where such action is wholly unavoidable," he nonetheless stated that his "own view is that most arbitrators are at least as competent and as qualified as most judges to decide employment discrimination or fair labor standards cases."[82] In the latter regard, one lecturer stated:

> [I]t is a mistake to assume that more cases will be decided right if we multiply the levels of review. Courts aren't right more often than arbitrators and the parties because they are wiser. They are "right" because they have the final say. There is no such thing as a perfect decision.[83]

As this commentator indicated, the question whether arbitrators are *capable* of deciding statutory issues and the question whether they *should* do so are two different questions.

Of course, few, if any, arbitrators or judges are or have any logical need to be walking encyclopedias of the law. Arbitrators, like judges, rely to a greater or lesser extent on current research, and on the representatives of the parties to explore and argue the relevant law. The capacity to compre-

---

[81]*Gilmer*, 500 U.S. at 32 n.4, 55 FEP Cases at 1122 n.4 (quoting Shearson/American Express v. McMahon, 482 U.S. 220, 232 (1987)).

[82]Seitz, *Render Unto Caesar (Arbitrators and Public Laws)* [Letter to the Editor], AAA Study Time, Oct. 1981. *See also* Willig, *Arbitration of Discrimination Grievances: Arbitral and Judicial Competence Compared*, in Arbitration 1986: Current and Expanding Roles, Proceedings of the 39th Annual Meeting of NAA 101 (Gershenfeld ed., BNA Books 1987); Edwards, *Advantages of Arbitration Over Litigation: Reflections of a Judge*, in Arbitration 1982: Conduct of the Hearing, Proceedings of the 35th Annual Meeting of NAA 16, 21, 27–28 (Stern & Dennis eds., BNA Books 1983). Compare the conclusions stated in the discussion of this subject by Bartlett, *Employment Discrimination and Labor Arbitrators: A Question of Competence*, 85 W. Va. L. Rev. 873, 907–09 (1983).

[83]James E. Westbrook, *The End of an Era in Arbitration: Where Can You Go if You Can't Go Home Again*, unpublished (1980).

hend and to evaluate weighty subject matter, and to apply it to the specific case, is the critical requirement, and here most arbitrators are qualified.[84]

However, in light of recent developments and resulting uncertainty in the NLRB's deferral policy, some commentators and courts[85] have questioned the efficiency of arbitration as an institution and, by implication, the capability of arbitrators to properly apply the law under the NLRA.

For example, one scholar has suggested that deferral places an "awesome responsibility" on arbitrators that dictates changes in the way such cases are handled.[86] Among other things, he recommended that arbitrators who are uncomfortable with NLRA issues should decline to handle such cases, and that a standard of review appropriate to the statutory nature of a deferred case should be adopted.[87] Suggesting that the *Enterprise Wheel*[88] standard (which draws its essence from the contract) "may no longer suffice, at least not in such simplistic form,"[89] he recommended as an alternative that, where the arbitrator applies the NLRA, the standard of review should be something akin to whether the award is "repugnant to the purpose and policies of the [NLRA]."[90]

D. Some Consequences of Arbitrator's Choice Respecting External Law

In most arbitrations, the award actually constitutes a final disposition of the disputed matter in that the award is accepted, and no subsequent arbitration, court, or administrative agency proceedings involving the disputed activity or incident have taken place. However, all arbitration awards are subject to the possibility of at least limited review by a court or administrative agency. Furthermore, because some activities or incidents involve both statutory and contractual rights, a grievant after arbitrating may be able to pursue statutory rights in other tribunals. In these instances, developments after an award is issued may be affected by the arbitrator's consideration or disregard of external law.

Arbitrators in private-sector cases are *not required* to consider external law unless to do so is clearly mandated by the submission agreement under which the arbitrator accepts and is vested with jurisdiction, or by the collective bargaining agreement itself. Arbitrators in the federal public sector do

---

[84]If an individual arbitrator is confronted with an issue beyond his or her competence, a safeguard is provided by the Code of Professional Responsibility for Arbitrators of Labor-Management Disputes mandate that: "When an arbitrator decides that a case requires specialized knowledge beyond the arbitrator's competence, the arbitrator must decline appointment, withdraw, or request technical assistance." Code §1.B.1. (2000, as amended).

[85]*See, e.g.*, Taylor v. NLRB (Ryder Truck Lines), 786 F.2d 1516, 122 LRRM 2084, 2088–89 (11th Cir. 1986); Ray, *Individual Rights and NLRB Deferral to the Arbitration Process: A Proposal*, 28 B.C. L. Rev. 1 (1986); Moses, *Deferral to Arbitration in Individual Rights Cases: A Re-examination of* Spielberg, 51 Tenn. L. Rev. 187 (1984).

[86]Morris, *NLRB Deferral to the Arbitration Process: The Arbitrator's Awesome Responsibility*, 7 Indus. Rel. L.J. 290 (1985).

[87]*Id.* at 309–10.

[88]Steelworkers v. Enterprise Wheel & Car Corp., 363 U.S. 593, 46 LRRM 2423 (1960).

[89]Morris, 7 Indus. Rel. L.J. at 310.

[90]*Id.* at 311–12.

have a responsibility by statute to consider external law. Arbitrators in the state public sector may, or may not, have a responsibility to do so, depending on the applicable state arbitration statute and agreements between the parties. Certainly many, if not most, arbitrators of cases in the private sector, and some arbitrators of cases in the state public sector, have the option of considering or of not considering external law.

Some possible post-award developments that may be affected by the arbitrator's consideration of external law, or failure to do so, are discussed below.

i. Private-Sector Cases Subject to Section 301 of the LMRA in Which the Arbitrator Does Not Consider External Law

The arbitrator may choose to consider only the collective bargaining agreement and give no consideration to external law. Here the award usually will draw its essence from the agreement and, if the award does not command the performance of an illegal act and is not contrary to some explicit and recognized public policy, it likely would withstand court review. However, there may be statutory issues growing out of the same matter. For instance, if the arbitrator did not consider any NLRA issue, the NLRB would not defer to the award. Furthermore, issues under the FLSA or Title VII of the Civil Rights Act would be subject to de novo court proceedings regardless of whether the arbitrator considered them in rendering an award adverse to the grievant.[91]

ii. Private-Sector Cases Subject to Section 301 of the LMRA in Which the Arbitrator Does Consider External Law

The arbitrator may choose to consider external law along with the collective bargaining agreement. Here, if the agreement and the external law are reasonably reconciled, with no clear conflict between them, and if the arbitrator merely looks to the law for help in determining the sense of the agreement, it is likely that the award will draw its essence from the agreement. Provided the award does not order the performance of an illegal act and is not contrary to an explicit and recognized public policy, the award likely would withstand court review. The mere fact that the arbitrator may have misconstrued the law used as an aid in determining the sense of the agreement likely would not invalidate the award in view of the generally recognized rule that awards are not impeachable for errors of law. However, if the agreement and external law do conflict, and if the award is based, to use the Supreme Court's *Enterprise Wheel* words, "solely upon the arbitrator's

---

[91]*See, e.g.*, Manitowoc Eng'g Co., 291 NLRB 915, 130 LRRM 1072 (1988) (illustrating that where an arbitrator bases the award on a contract provision that is contrary to law, the award may be displaced by NLRB or court decision). For discussions relevant to the foregoing summary, see section 1., "General Considerations," and section 2.B., "U.S. Supreme Court Statements Regarding Arbitral Consideration of External Law," above, and section 3.A.v.,"The NLRA, the Arbitrator, and the NLRB," below; Chapter 2, section 2.A.ii.c., "Post-*Trilogy*: Enforcement of Agreements to Arbitrate and Review of Arbitration Awards," and section 2.A.ii.d.,"De Novo Litigation Following Arbitration."

view of the requirements of enacted legislation, which would mean that he exceeded the scope of the submission," [92] the award would not withstand court review unless both parties authorized the arbitrator to decide the case in conformity with external law. Furthermore, there may be statutory issues growing out of the same matter and on which proceedings before other tribunals still may be possible unless foreclosed by considerations other than an arbitration award adverse to the grievant. For instance, even if the arbitrator did consider and rule against a grievant's Title VII or FLSA claim, the claim still would be subject to de novo court proceedings. The court could not "defer" to the award by accepting its results as conclusive on the statutory issue and thus deny the grievant access to the courts (as the NLRB sometimes does when an arbitrator has decided an NLRA issue). Rather, the court must hear the Title VII or FLSA issue anew and reach its own decision on the issue, though in reaching that decision the court under *Gardner-Denver*'s Footnote 21[93] or *Barrentine*'s Footnote 22[94] has discretion to accord some weight and sometimes great weight to the arbitrator's decision.[95]

iii. *Private-Sector Cases Governed by State Arbitration Law*
[LA CDI 94.08]

The possible results for private-sector cases governed by state law must be evaluated on a state-by-state basis. But it is to be expected that results reached in private-sector cases under state law generally would not vary significantly from the results suggested above under the Section 301 doctrine. Furthermore, even if the arbitration itself is not covered by Section 301, but is governed by state law, the FLSA or Title VII of the Civil Rights Act may apply to the given employment. If so, the grievant's right to court litigation of any FLSA or Title VII claims would not be foreclosed by an arbitration award adverse to the grievant, regardless of the particular state's doctrine.

iv. *Federal Public-Sector Cases* [LA CDI 100.30]

The Civil Service Reform Act[96] requires arbitrators in the federal public sector to deal with external law. Moreover, federal public-sector arbitration awards are subject to challenge where they conflict with controlling laws, rules, or regulations.[97]

---

[92]Steelworkers v. Enterprise Wheel & Car Corp., 363 U.S. 593, 597, 46 LRRM 2423, 2425 (1960).

[93]Alexander v. Gardner-Denver Co., 415 U.S. 36, 60 n.21, 7 FEP Cases 81, 90 n.21 (1974).

[94]Barrentine v. Arkansas-Best Freight Sys., 450 U.S. 728, 473 n.22, 24 WH Cases 1284, 1290 n.22 (1981).

[95]For discussion relevant to the foregoing summary, see section 1., "General Considerations," and section 2.B., "U.S. Supreme Court Statements Regarding Arbitral Consideration of External Law," above, and section 3.A.v., "The NLRA, the Arbitrator, and the NLRB," below; Chapter 2, section 2.A.ii.d., "De Novo Litigation Following Arbitration."

[96]5 U.S.C. §7101 et seq.

[97]*See* Chapter 20, section 4., "Channels for Processing Federal-Sector Grievances," and section 5., "Review of Arbitration Awards."

v. State Public-Sector Cases [LA CDI 100.30]

The relationship between external law and arbitration in the state public sector must be evaluated on a state-by-state basis and has, in fact, varied among the states.[98] It should be noted that Title VII of the Civil Rights Act applies to states and their subdivisions, [99] as does the FLSA[100] and the FMLA.[100a] Thus, here again there may be rights under these statutes that could be litigated in court and, regardless of the particular state's doctrine, would not be foreclosed by an arbitration award adverse to the grievant.

Regardless of whether a case falls within the private sector, the federal public sector, or the state public sector, the validity of an award ordinarily should not be jeopardized merely because, to use the words of the Supreme Court in the Section 301 *Enterprise Wheel* decision,[101] the arbitrator pursued a course of "looking to 'the law' for help in determining the sense of the agreement,"[102] as distinguished from the situation in which an award is "based solely upon the arbitrator's view of the requirements of enacted legislation . . . ."[103]

3. STATUTORY LAW

This section addresses arbitrator decisions that have considered and applied specific labor and employment statutes. In some instances, an arbitration agreement will refer to a specific statute as a standard or guide for determining the scope and application of rights under the agreement, and in such cases the arbitrator should consider the statute when fashioning a resolution to the grievance.[104] More often, however, agreements are silent on this issue, and arbitrators must decide the extent, if any, to which they will apply any relevant statutes. Judicial decisions involving some of these statutes are considered in the next section.

---

[98]*See* Chapter 21, section 4.C., "Contractual Terms Versus Statutory Law Covering Similar Matters," and section 7., "Judicial Review of Arbitration Awards in State and Local Government Employment."

[99]Fitzpatrick v. Bitzer, 427 U.S. 445 (1976) (holding that the Eleventh Amendment does not bar a back-pay award for violation of Title VII, because that amendment and the principle of state sovereignty that it embodies are limited by the enforcement provisions of §5 of the Fourteenth Amendment).

[100]Garcia v. San Antonio Metro. Transit Auth., 469 U.S. 528 (1985) (the Court held that the application of the overtime provisions of the FLSA to a municipality was constitutional under the Commerce Clause, U.S. CONST. art. I, §8. The Court rejected as unsound in principle and unworkable in practice a rule of state immunity from federal regulation that turned on whether a particular governmental function is "integral" or "traditional.")

[100a]Nevada Dep't of Human Res. v. Hibbs, 123 S. Ct. 1972, 8 WH Cases 2d 1221 (2003).

[101]Steelworkers v. Enterprise Wheel & Car Corp., 363 U.S. 593, 46 LRRM 2423, 2425 (1960).

[102]*Id.* at 598.

[103]*Id.* at 597.

[104]*See, e.g.*, City of Sapulpa, Okla., 90 LA 11, 12 (Goodstein, 1987) ("Agreement specifically provides that the parties' negotiated agreement is subject to the terms and provisions of the Fair Labor Standards Act . . . .").

A. Specific Federal Employment Statutes

i. Title VII of the Civil Rights Act

Arbitrators generally consider Title VII claims in arbitrations where the grievance specifically states a claim under Title VII and the collective bargaining agreement includes a nondiscrimination clause either incorporating the statutory prohibitions or referring to the statute.[105] It is common for many agreements to include nondiscrimination and anti–sexual harassment provisions.[106] Some agreements refuse to recognize discrimination claims unless they violate federal or state law, thus forcing arbitrators to consider statutes like Title VII.[107] Others contain nondiscrimination clauses that are even broader than Title VII, and prohibit discrimination or harassment based on sexual orientation.[108]

In recent cases, some arbitrators have demonstrated a willingness to consider Title VII claims even absent a specific nondiscrimination or antiharassment policy in the agreement.[109] In considering Title VII in place of a specific antiharassment policy, one arbitrator noted that, given "the strong public policy argument alone, widely established by courts and legislatures, [a disciplined] Grievant was placed on notice of the legal prohibition against sexual harassment. Whether [Grievant] was [actually] aware of the prohibi-

---

[105]*Compare* ATC/Vancom, 111 LA 268 (Richman, 1998) (arbitrator declined to consider a Title VII claim where the Title VII provision was included in the agreement and the grievance contained a Title VII claim but the union specifically disclaimed the Title VII claim at hearing; the union has the right to determine issues brought forth at arbitration and the union declined to assert Title VII), *with* ABC Rail Prods. Corp., 110 LA 574 (Kenis, 1998) (arbitrator considered that Title VII applies to same-sex sexual harassment; however, grievant's conduct did not rise to the level of sexual harassment). *See generally* Safeway, Inc., 112 LA 1050 (Silver, 1999); Gunite Corp., 111 LA 897 (Cohen, 1999); Westvaco Corp., 111 LA 887 (Nicholas, Jr., 1998).

[106]*See generally* Lockheed Martin Space Sys. Co., 114 LA 481, 481 (Gentile, 2000) (the language of nondiscrimination/antiharassment provision "is similar to the terms of up to 85 percent of [agreements] that track statutory and decisional law in the area at issue") (citing The Common Law of the Workplace 204 (St. Antoine ed., BNA Books 1998)); City of Ada, Okla., 113 LA 422 (Goodman, 1999); Safeway, Inc., 112 LA 1050 (Silver, 1999); Ralphs Grocery Co., 112 LA 120 (Prayzich, 1999); Gunite Corp., 111 LA 897 (Cohen, 1999); Westvaco Corp., 111 LA 887 (Nicholas, Jr., 1998); Baskin Robbins, 111 LA 554 (Richman, 1998); ATC/Vancom, 111 LA 429 (Prayzich, 1998); U.S. Marine Corps, 110 LA 955 (Cornelius, 1998).

[107]*See* Gorges Quik-to-Fix Foods, 113 LA 1005, 1006–07 (Crow, 1999) (although discrimination was ultimately not at issue, the collective bargaining agreement included language stating that "[alleged discrimination] shall not be considered discrimination unless the alleged discrimination also violates applicable federal or state laws").

[108]*See* Department of Veterans Affairs, 113 LA 961 (Gangle, 1999) (example of nondiscrimination clause that includes sexual orientation among its provisions).

[109]*See* Conagra Frozen Foods, 113 LA 129, 133 (Baroni, 1999) (Title VII makes sexual harassment in the workplace illegal; "federal law is binding on everyone, whether it is incorporated in Company policy or not"). *See also* Stone Container Corp., 114 LA 395, 406 (Imundo, Jr., 2000) (although arbitrator does not specifically discuss Title VII, he notes, "even if such a [sexual harassment] policy did not formally exist, common sense would dictate that employees should know that harassing one another is unacceptable behavior"); Department of Veterans Affairs, 113 LA 961, 965 (Gangle, 1999) (arbitrator considers Title VII through case law interpreting the statute; "some types of misconduct [including sexual harassment] that are considered so egregious that they are generally known to be prohibited in all workplaces").

tion . . . is not important. . . . [H]e *'should have known,'* given the widespread effect of the strong public policy against sexual harassment."[110]

In several reported cases, arbitrators have found the employer justified in discharging an employee who was creating a hostile work environment for coworkers under the legal precedents independent from the agreement, because the law requires such work environments to be maintained.[111]

One theme that seems to find support in a majority of these arbitration decisions is that the discharge of an employee causing a hostile or offensive working environment for coworkers will usually be upheld if the employee has a history of such conduct and had prior notice of the possible consequences of his or her actions.[112]

ii. Fair Labor Standards Act

In the past, arbitrators had disagreed over whether the provisions of the agreement or the provisions of the FLSA should control in the event of conflict between them.[113] One arbitrator held that where the statute is clear, the agreement must be interpreted and applied in a manner consistent with the

---

[110]Conagra Frozen Foods, 113 LA 129, 133 (Baroni, 1999) (emphasis in original).

[111]*See* Worldwide Flight Servs., 115 LA 680, 684 (Jennings, 2001) ("'Those in managerial positions have an obligation under the law of the country to ensure that the work place is free from harassment of this nature,'" (quoting Peninsular Steel Co., 88 LA 391, 395 (Ipavec, 1986)); Railey's of N.M., 115 LA 674, 680 (O'Grady, 2001) ("For the arbitrator not to recognize the right of management to maintain a harassment-free work environment . . . would be a total miscarriage of industrial justice . . . .").

[112]*See* Electric Mach. Co., 115 LA 1039 (Jacobowski, 2001) (misconduct of a sexual nature was serious, but discharge was too severe, where the employee was not previously warned of seriousness of behavior); Railey's of N.M., 115 LA 674, 679–80 (O'Grady, 2001) (employee properly discharged for calling coworkers "chinks" where he engaged in previous egregious and despicable acts toward coworkers); Commercial Printing Co., 115 LA 393 (Statham, 2000) (hostile environment created by male employee asking female employee for sex 20–30 times in one evening, but discharge reduced to over 1-year suspension, where employer had no written sexual harassment policy and never advised its employees of consequences of engaging in such conduct); Alumnitec, Inc., 114 LA 1584 (Kindig, 2000) (employer had good and sufficient cause to discharge employee for sexual harassment, even though evidence was female employee's word against grievant's, where grievant had a history of prior bad acts and sexual harassment discipline and he apologized to employee on the day of the incident after grabbing her crotch and trying to kiss her); Northwest Publ'ns, 114 LA 761 (Bognanno, 2000) (suspension without just cause for bringing full frontal-nude photograph of wife to work, where photograph was an overhead shot from a considerable distance of her swimming on back in a lagoon and was not pornographic, where employee had no previous incidents or counseling); Progressive Processing, 114 LA 725 (Paolucci, 2000) (employer had just cause to discharge employee for asking female co-workers for sexual favors in exchange for money, where employee had prior discharge for sexual harassment and criminal conviction on charge of child enticement).

[113]Arbitrators have considered the FLSA in the following cases: U.S. Navy, 112 LA 289 (Harris, Jr., 1999); City of Joliet, Ill., 88 LA 303 (Hill, 1986); Florida Power Corp., 87 LA 957 (Wahl, 1986); Rock County, Wis., 87 LA 1 (Larney, 1986). The arbitrator declined to rule on the FLSA in *City of Bethany, Okla.*, 87 LA 309, 312 (Levy, 1986). Regarding the *Barrentine v. Arkansas-Best Freight System*, 450 U.S. 728, 24 WH Cases 1284 (1981), decision and the likewise relevant *Alexander v. Gardner-Denver Co.*, 415 U.S. 36, 7 FEP Cases 81 (1974), decision, see section 2.B., "U.S. Supreme Court Statements Regarding Arbitral Consideration of External Law," above.

statute.[114] However, where a party argued that an adverse decision would conflict with the FLSA, the arbitrator declared that it was the contract language on which he must focus and rule.[115]

In light of the 1981 decision of the Supreme Court in *Barrentine v. Arkansas-Best Freight System*,[116] it is clear that an arbitrator's adverse decision on an employee's minimum wage claim will not preclude the unsuccessful employee from bringing a private cause of action under the FLSA in federal court.[117] Moreover, there is authority for the proposition that a party may be able to bring an FLSA case directly in federal court even if the claim is encompassed by the arbitration agreement.[118]

iii. Americans With Disabilities Act

Over the past decade, a number of arbitrators have had to wrestle with the ADA on the question as to what extent, if any, it should be considered in the resolution of claims of discrimination by employees alleging handicaps.[119]

---

[114]Pennsylvania Elec. Co., 47 LA 526, 527 (Stein, 1966) (rejecting the argument that "Fair Labor Standards Act questions should be resolved in another forum"). In accord as to the controlling effect of the statute, *Youngstown Sheet & Tube Co.*, 14 LA 752, 756 (Updegraff, 1950). *See also* Curtis Mathes Mfg. Co., 73 LA 103, 105 (Allen, Jr., 1979); Allied Employers, 66 LA 131, 133 (Gillingham, 1976). *Cf.* Cincinnati Gas & Elec. Co., 74 LA 1042, 1044 (Strasshofer, 1980); Brighton Elec. Steel Casting Div., 47 LA 518, 523 (Krimsly, 1966). In *Mason & Hanger-Silas Mason Co.*, 75 LA 1038, 1040 (Shearer, 1980), the FLSA rather than past practice was followed as the controlling guide for interpreting an ambiguous agreement. In *Chevron U.S.A., Inc.*, 78 LA 1241, 1248–51 (Killion, 1982), heavy reliance was placed on the federal courts' formulation of the definition of "hours worked" under the FLSA and Portal-to-Portal Act because the collective bargaining agreement at issue did not define the term itself.

[115]Hilo Transp. & Terminal Co., 33 LA 541, 543 (Burr, 1959). *Accord* City of Joliet, Ill., 88 LA 303, 309 (Hill, 1986); International Harvester Co., 17 LA 29, 30 (Seward, 1951); California Cotton Mills Co., 16 LA 335, 337 (Marshall, 1951). *See also* Hubbard & Johnson Lumber Co., 70 LA 526, 528–29 (Feller, 1978). A number of arbitrators have considered the question whether an increase in the minimum wage under the FLSA may be relied on by the employer toward fulfilling its obligation to grant a periodic wage increase specified by the agreement. *See e.g.*, Brigham Apparel Corp., 52 LA 430, 433–35 (Andersen, 1969); Curtis Mathes Co., 52 LA 145, 147–48 (Merrill, 1968); Volupte Co., 48 LA 816, 818 (Gershenfeld, 1967); Movie Star of Ellisville, 42 LA 250, 251 (Owen, 1964).

[116]450 U.S. 728, 24 WH Cases 1284 (1981).

[117]*Id.* at 743.

[118]Albertson's, Inc. v. Food & Commercial Workers, 157 F.3d 758, 159 LRRM 2452 (9th Cir. 1998).

[119]*See* GTE N., 113 LA 665, 672 (Brodsky, 1999) (where collective bargaining agreement contains a nondiscrimination clause and a "conflict with law" provision, the ADA will be considered in a discharged employee's grievance, and, "[f]urthermore, compliance with the ADA can also be viewed in the case at hand as a component of 'just cause'"); Johns Hopkins Bayview Med. Ctr., 105 LA 193, 197–98 (Bowers, 1995) (employer violated ADA by failing to provide a reasonable accommodation to employees who were injured on the job); Alcoa Bldg. Prods., 104 LA 364, 368 (Cerone, 1995) (where the collective bargaining agreement is silent regarding the arbitrator's authority to address external legal issues, the arbitrator found "both the potential conflict between federal law and the agreement, as well as parties' stipulations allow [arbitrator] to apply external law," such as the ADA); Jefferson Smurfit Corp., 103 LA 1041, 1048–49 (Canestraight, 1994) (arbitrator ruled that "absent any source of arbitral power to exercise jurisdiction in the area's external law by providing so in the collective bargaining agreement, it is not within arbitrator's jurisdiction to apply either the Rehabilitation Act of 1993 [29 U.S.C. §701 et seq.] or the Americans with Disabilities Act of 1990"); Meijer, Inc., 103 LA 834, 840 (Daniel, 1994) (arbitrator ruled "under collective bargaining contract requiring just cause for disciplinary action against employee, rights established by law, such as ADA must be taken into consideration determining whether just cause exists");

A general, nonspecific arbitration requirement in a collective bargaining agreement does not compel an employee to submit a discrimination claim cognizable under the ADA to an arbitrator rather than filing a lawsuit in federal court.[120] However, once a claim is submitted to an arbitrator, the provisions of the ADA, as judicially interpreted, certainly may be looked to for guidance and applied by the arbitrator to the extent relevant.

The ADA generally obligates the employer to reasonably accommodate a qualified individual with a disability unless that accommodation creates an undue hardship. Therefore, an issue frequently raised in arbitration is the degree to which the rights of an employee with a disability can be limited by a term of a collective bargaining agreement such as a seniority provision.[121] Although the ADA contains no language expressly protecting seniority systems, the Supreme Court has held that, in the absence of special circumstances, it will ordinarily be unreasonable in the "run of cases" to assign a qualified disabled employee to a position governed by a seniority system in violation of established seniority rules that would assign the position to a more senior employee.[122] Job modification and job transfer issues, which arise under a collective bargaining agreement, invariably require application of the ADA's "reasonable accommodation" analysis.[123] As in the case of other

---

Merrimack County Dep't of Corr., 102 LA 1096, 1098 (McCausland, 1994) (arbitrator ruled when the employer imposed job qualifications the employee could not meet; terminating the employee who did not satisfy the requirements of a qualified individual with a disability did not violate the ADA). *But see* Thermo King Corp., 102 LA 612, 615–16 (Dworkin, 1993) (in determining whether an employer's actions in discharging an alleged disabled employee were discriminatory, the arbitrator, who was empowered to decide whether the discharge was just and fair in making this determination, looked to the ADA for guidance); Angus Chem. Co., 102 LA 388, 392–93 (Nicholas, Jr., 1994) (arbitrator analyzed the meaning of "qualified individual with a disability" under the ADA); Clark County, Ohio, Sheriff's Dep't, 102 LA 193, 197 (Kindig, 1994) (arbitrator relied on ADA to rule that county improperly tried to make an "accommodation" and violated contract); Stone Container Corp., 101 LA 943 (Feldman, 1993) (agreement did not permit examination of external law, but finding of contractual violation was consistent with the ADA); Altoona Hosp., 102 LA 650, 652 (Jones, Jr., 1993) (where the union contends the employer violated the ADA, the arbitrator ruled interpretation of the ADA is "a function of the appropriate agency or commission, and ultimately the courts, not the arbitrator," where the collective bargaining agreement does not permit the arbitrator to consider the ADA).

[120]Wright v. Universal Maritime Serv. Corp., 525 U.S. 70, 159 LRRM 2769 (1998). In *Wright,* the Supreme Court left open the issue whether a very specific and explicit arbitration clause negotiated by a union could preclude an employee from bringing an ADA statutory claim in a federal court. *Id.* at 79.

[121]Mason & Hanger Corp., 111 LA 60 (Caraway, 1998) (employer violated collective bargaining agreement when it allowed a disabled employee with less seniority to work the day shift as an accommodation); Alcoa Bldg. Prods., 104 LA 364, 369 (Cerone, 1995) (arbitrator found that the "Company went too far in attempting to comply with ADA"); Clark County, Ohio, Sheriff's Dep't, 102 LA 193 (Kindig, 1994) (employer violated seniority provisions in the contract by placing a disabled employee into a first-shift position as a reasonable accommodation under the ADA because there was no attempt to discuss the transfer with the union).

[122]U.S. Airways v. Barnett, 535 U.S. 391 (2002) (disabled employee bears the burden of proving special circumstances that make creating an exception to the seniority rule reasonable; such "special circumstances" might include showing that the employer has frequently exercised permitted discretions to change the seniority system in past so as to reduce employees' expectations that system will be followed).

[123]San Francisco, Cal., Unified Sch. Dist., 114 LA 140 (Riker, 2000) (finding no requirement, either in the collective bargaining agreement or the ADA, to accommodate a disabled employee who cannot perform the essential functions of the job); Los Angeles, Cal., Cmty. Coll. Dist., 112 LA 733 (Kaufman, 1999) (arbitrator held that the transfer of a teacher to a

employment regulatory statutes, conflicts between the terms of the legislation and provisions of the agreement will present challenges to the arbitral process.[124]

iv. Family and Medical Leave Act

The FMLA[125] has most often been encountered in labor arbitration in disciplinary cases involving attendance and leave of absence issues. Among other entitlements, the FMLA requires an employer to provide up to 12 weeks of unpaid but protected leave, annually, for an employee's own "serious health condition" or to care for an immediate family member with a "serious health condition."[126] In the majority of cases involving the FMLA, arbitrators rely on the provisions of the FMLA and the Department of Labor (DOL) regulations without regard to whether the collective bargaining agreement says anything about the FMLA.[127] Arbitrators also look to the statute for

---

position at a closer community college would be a reasonable accommodation under the ADA); Andex Indus., 111 LA 615 (Allen, 1998) (arbitrator decided that the ADA does not require an employer to grant an alcoholic employee unrestricted time off as a reasonable accommodation); Rheem Mfg. Co., 108 LA 193 (Woolf, 1997) (arbitrator found no violation of the collective bargaining agreement or the ADA when a disabled employee was reassigned to a lower position because he could not perform the essential functions of the former job); Champion Int'l Corp., 106 LA 1024 (Howell, 1996) (arbitrator analyzed issues relating to return to work from disability leave under the collective bargaining agreement and the ADA; held that the employer is obligated to attempt to find a reasonable accommodation for an employee); Johns Hopkins Bayview Med. Ctr., 105 LA 193, 197–98 (Bowers, 1995) (arbitrator found the employer had failed to provide a reasonable accommodation to employees who were injured on the job, thus finding the employer violated the ADA); Johnson Controls World Servs., 104 LA 336 (Goodstein, 1995) (no violation of the ADA reasonable accommodation obligation); Multi-Clean, Inc., 102 LA 463 (Miller, 1993) (arbitrator looked to the ADA to define reasonable accommodation in termination of an employee with medical restrictions).

[124]For analyses of the ADA in the context of collective bargaining, see Schoen, *Does the ADA Make Exceptions in a Unionized Workplace? The Conflict Between the Reassignment Provision of the ADA and Collectively Bargained Seniority Systems*, 82 MINN. L. REV. 1391 (1998); Stahlhut, *Playing the Trump Card: May an Employer Refuse to Reasonably Accommodate Under the ADA by Claiming a Collective Bargaining Obligation?*, 9 LAB. LAW. 71 (Winter, 1993); Stewart, *The Impact of the Americans with Disabilities Act on Collective Bargaining Agreements*, ABA Section of Labor and Employment Law, 1993 Mid-Winter Meeting; Smith, *Accommodating the Americans with Disabilities Act to Collective Bargaining Obligations Under the NLRA*, 18 EMPLOYEE REL. L.J. No. 2, at 273, 274 (Autumn, 1992).

[125]29 U.S.C. §2601 et seq., with Department of Labor (DOL) regulations at 29 C.F.R. §825 et seq.

[126]29 U.S.C. §2612(a)(1)(C) & (D).

[127]*See* Budget Rent-A-Car Sys., 115 LA 1745 (Suardi, 2001) (employee was a "qualified employee" for purposes of the FMLA, but employee's medical certification provided to his employer to prove the alleged need to care for a seriously ill child did not qualify under the FMLA or its regulations); Integram-St. Louis Seating, 113 LA 693 (Marino, 1999) (employer had just cause to discharge employee, where employee did not submit request for leave or proper certification of serious health condition and employee's unexcused absence was allegedly for a doctor's visit long planned for his mother); Tenneco Packaging, 112 LA 761 (Kessler, 1999) (termination of employee for absence to care for her son set aside, where employer did not post state FMLA notice or allow employee to substitute vacation days for unpaid leave per statute); GE Railcar, 112 LA 632 (O'Grady, 1999) (grievant did not provide adequate notice of his need to take FMLA leave, nor did his medical condition rise to level of a "serious health condition" under the FMLA); System Sensor, 111 LA 1186 (Cohen, 1999) (employer did not violate collective bargaining agreement in discharging employee whose FMLA leave entitlement had expired, particularly where the employee had been absent on FMLA and other leave for 50% of her short career); Apcoa, Inc., 107 LA 705, 711 (Daniel, 1996) (arbitra-

guidance in attendance cases, even if not citing specific provisions of the FMLA.[128]

A minority of arbitrators have refused to rely on the statute or refer to the FMLA in their decisions, based either on a lack of "authority" in the contract to do so or on contract language more restrictive than the FMLA entitlements.[129]

In deciding discipline cases with FMLA leave issues, arbitrators apply the same common labor arbitration principles as applied in other types of discipline cases.[130]

Arbitrators have generally been in agreement with the courts in finding that an employer may rely on the certification from an employee's health care provider in making a decision whether leave qualifies as FMLA leave. In *GE Railcar*,[131] the employee was found not to have a serious health condition, based in part on the employee's medical documentation stating he was able to return to work, and also stating that his doctor did not find him unable to perform his job duties because of his high blood pressure or his laryngitis.[132]

---

tor has jurisdiction and authority over issues regarding the FMLA, where the parties, by agreement, incorporate into the contract the terms of the FMLA); Enesco Corp., 107 LA 513, 518 (Berman, 1996) (company's denial of leave to an employee under FMLA's 1-year employment requirement, where the employee had not been employed for over a year, was an error because the labor contract itself provided otherwise); General Mills, Inc., 107 LA 472, 475–76 (Feldman, 1996) (arbitrator interpreted the leave requirement under FMLA to determine whether employer had properly discharged employee who had already used all his leave under the FMLA); Grand Haven Stamped Prods. Co., 107 LA 131, 135–37 (Daniel, 1996) (an employer could not require employees who needed FMLA leave to care for family members to exhaust their vacation benefits, even though the FMLA provides an employer may require such, where the collective bargaining agreement provided otherwise and the choice of such in the contract was rejected by both parties after the FMLA's enactment); Morgan Foods, Inc., 106 LA 833, 836 (Goldman, 1996) (upheld employer's decision to dismiss employee, interpreting that the FMLA "does not require that a leave of absence be granted simply because an employee wishes to be with an ill family member").

[128]*See* Career Sys. Dev. Corp., 113 LA 920, 923 (Pool, 1999) (employees improperly disciplined for excused, and even paid, absences, were "exercising their contractual rights much the same as if they would exercise their statutory rights if taking leave under the Family and Medical Leave Act").

[129]*See* GAF Bldg. Materials Corp., 114 LA 1528 (Goodman, 2000) (arbitrator was not authorized by collective bargaining contract to determine whether employer violated any statute, including the FMLA, when he disciplined employee who had record of absenteeism, where contract provides that in certain alleged contract violations there may also be recourse to administrative agency and makes unenforceable any contract provision in conflict with any applicable state or federal law). *See also* PCC Airfoils, 113 LA 504 (Sharpe, 1999) (company's new attendance policy's requirement that doctor sign medical certification was reasonable—without considering the FMLA's broader definition of "health care provider" that would allow certification by an attending nurse); Rock Island County, Ill., 104 LA 1127 (Whitney, 1995) (rejecting union's invitation to apply provisions of the FMLA when the union agreed to more limited leave terms in the parties' collective bargaining agreement).

[130]*See* Koppers Indus., 115 LA 152 (Jenks, 2000) (employee properly discharged for filing false FMLA form, stating he was unable to do any work, while at same time working a second job); BF Goodrich, 111 LA 602 (Paolucci, 1998) (employee's unreasonable and inaccurate, but honestly held belief, that she had been granted FMLA leave to care for son, was a "mitigating factor" requiring her reinstatement to employment without back pay).

[131]112 LA 632 (O'Grady, 1999)

[132]*See* Stoops v. One Call Communications, 141 F.3d 309, 4 WH Cases 2d 779 (7th Cir. 1998) (employer could rely on "negative certification"—that condition of employee was not a serious health condition—in denying employee's subsequent request for FMLA leave). *See*

In recent court decisions, several portions of the DOL regulations have been found to be invalid where the regulation states that an employee is to retain his or her full 12-week entitlement to annual FMLA leave, in spite of taking FMLA-qualifying time off work; where the employer fails to properly designate the time off as FMLA leave, or fails to give proper notice to the employee of its FMLA designation, or fails to give correct notice whether the employee is even eligible for FMLA leave.[133] In these cases, the courts have found that the regulations "add requirements and grant entitlements beyond those of the statute."[134]

v. The NLRA, the Arbitrator, and the NLRB [LA CDI 94.553]

a. Disputes Involving Both Statutory Construction and Contract Interpretation Issues

Where a dispute involves both statutory construction or application issues under the NLRA, and interpretation issues under the collective bargaining agreement, dual jurisdiction exists in the NLRB and the arbitrator. This dual jurisdiction, as reflected by decisions of the Supreme Court, was summarized as follows:

> (1) the availability of arbitration does not preclude Board exercise of jurisdiction over unfair labor practices, (2) the availability of a Board remedy does not bar arbitration, and (3) the Board has discretion to refuse to exercise its jurisdiction when in its judgment federal policy would best be served by leaving the parties to contract remedies.[135]

---

also Frazier v. Iowa Beef Processors, 200 F.3d 1190, 5 WH Cases 2d 1445 (8th Cir. 2000) (dismissal of FMLA claim affirmed, where employee's medical records were "completely devoid of any evidence that his shoulder injury was of such severity as to make him unable to perform his job").

[133]*See* Woodford v. Community Action of Greene County, 268 F.3d 51, 7 WH Cases 2d 906 (2d Cir. 2001) (regulation at 29 C.F.R. §825.110(d) is invalid, where it would allow an otherwise ineligible employee to be covered by the FMLA, if employer notice to employee incorrectly stated employee had requisite 1,250 hours). *Accord* Brungart v. BellSouth Telecommunications, 231 F.3d 791, 796–97, 6 WH Cases 2d 737 (11th Cir. 2000); Dormeyer v. Comerica Bank-Ill., 223 F.3d 579, 582, 6 WH Cases 2d 435 (7th Cir. 2000). *See also* Ragsdale v. Wolverine Worldwide, 218 F.3d 933, 6 WH Cases 2d 298 (8th Cir. 2000) (the regulation at 29 C.F.R. §825.208(c) was invalid, where employee would retain entire 12 weeks of FMLA entitlement if employer fails to designate FMLA time off work as such; citing McGregor v. Autozone, Inc. 180 F.3d 1305, 5 WH Cases 2d 737 (11th Cir. 1999)).

[134]*See McGregor*, 180 F.3d at 1308; Dormeyer v. Comerica Bank-Ill., 223 F.3d 579, 582, 6 WH Cases 2d 298 (7th Cir. 2000) (the regulation tries to "change the Act" because it makes employees eligible for FMLA leave who are ineligible under the FMLA).

[135]Brown, *The National Labor Policy, the NLRB, and Arbitration, in* Developments in American and Foreign Arbitration, Proceedings of the 21st Annual Meeting of NAA 83, 84 (Rehmus ed., BNA Books 1968). Relevant decisions include: NLRB v. Strong Roofing & Insulating Co., 393 U.S. 357, 70 LRRM 2100 (1969); NLRB v. Acme Indus. Co., 385 U.S. 432, 64 LRRM 2069 (1967); NLRB v. C&C Plywood Corp., 385 U.S. 421, 64 LRRM 2065 (1967); Carey v. Westinghouse Elec. Corp., 375 U.S. 261, 55 LRRM 2042 (1964); Smith v. Evening News Ass'n, 371 U.S. 195, 51 LRRM 2646 (1962); Woodlawn Cemetery v. Cemetery Workers Local 365, 930 F.2d 154, 136 LRRM 2982 (2d Cir. 1991); Hutter Constr. Co. v. Operating Eng'rs Local 139, 862 F.2d 641, 129 LRRM 3034 (7th Cir. 1988); Cliftex Corp. v. Clothing & Textile Workers Local 377, 625 F. Supp. 903 (D. Mass. 1986). See also discussion in *Painters Dist. Council 48 (Orange Belt) v. Maloney Specialties*, 639 F.2d 487, 106 LRRM 2183 (9th Cir. 1980).

In its *Carey*[136] decision (involving a jurisdictional dispute between two unions and an employer), the Supreme Court held that an arbitrator could act, but should the Board disagree with the arbitrator its ruling would take precedence. As the Court stated: "The superior authority of the Board may be invoked at any time. Meanwhile the therapy of arbitration is brought to bear in a complicated and troubled area."[137]

Arbitrators themselves have long considered that they are not prevented from acting on contract issues merely because the dispute may also involve statutory issues that can be taken to the NLRB.[138] Similarly, the fact that the NLRB had dismissed unfair labor practice charges has not deterred arbitrators from subsequently taking jurisdiction over contract issues involved in the dispute.[139] However, in a dispute involving both statutory and contract issues, a decision reached by the NLRB on the statutory issue may serve to nullify a subsequent arbitral award of damages based entirely on contract violations if the award is found to "clash" with the NLRB decision.[140]

---

[136]Carey v. Westinghouse Elec. Corp., 375 U.S. 261, 272, 55 LRRM 2042 (1964). *See also* Eichleay Corp. v. Iron Workers, 944 F.2d 1047, 137 LRRM 2781 (3d Cir. 1991); NLRB v. Yellow Freight Sys., 930 F.2d 316, 137 LRRM 2045 (3d Cir. 1991); Nelson v. Electrical Workers (IBEW) Local 46, 899 F.2d 1557, 134 LRRM 2118 (9th Cir. 1990); A. Dariano & Sons v. Painters Dist. Council 33, 869 F.2d 514, 130 LRRM 2890 (9th Cir. 1989).

[137]*Carey*, 375 U.S. at 272.

[138]*See* Gaylord Container Corp., 93 LA 465 (Abrams, 1989); Sam Brown Co., 89 LA 645 (Newmark, 1987); Magic Chef, 88 LA 1046 (Caraway, 1987); Beaumont Concrete Co., 76 LA 228, 229 (Gentile, 1981); Sav-On Drugs, 73 LA 1313, 1317 (Gentile, 1979); Redfield Co., 69 LA 1024, 1030 (Aisenberg, 1977); Negco Enters., 68 LA 633, 635 (Helfeld, 1976); Burgmaster Corp., 46 LA 746, 747–49 (Lennard, 1965); Cooper Thermometer Co., 45 LA 1182, 1183 (Johnson, 1966) (unfair labor practice charge involves breach of law whereas grievance involves breach of the agreement); General Am. Transp. Corp., 42 LA 1308, 1310–11 (Rohman, 1964); Sears, Roebuck & Co., 35 LA 757, 783 (Miller, 1960) (filing of unfair labor practice charges does not constitute an election of remedies or waiver of rights under the agreement asserted in grievance filed at same time); Houdaille Indus., 35 LA 455, 457 (Schmidt, 1960); Marlin Rockwell Corp., 22 LA 651, 652 (Stutz, Mottram, & Curry, 1954); Harbor Furniture Mfg. Co., 22 LA 201, 207 (Kaplan, 1954); Panhandle E. Pipe Line Co., 19 LA 609, 611–12 (Updegraff, Klamon, & Raymond, 1952). In *National Radio Co.*, 60 LA 78, 81, 84 (Cox, 1973), the arbitrator suspended arbitration pending completion of NLRB proceedings, but 2 years later the NLRB deferred to arbitration; he then considered the statutory issue and found no unfair labor practice.

[139]*See* Trane Co., 89 LA 1112 (McIntosh, 1987); Anderson-Tully Co., 88 LA 7 (Hart, 1986); Meridian Woodworking Co., 87 LA 645 (Howell, 1986); Dan's Mkt., 72 LA 706, 710 (Harter, 1979); Courtaulds N. Am., 51 LA 309, 310 (McCoy, 1968); Lone Star Gas Co., 42 LA 345, 346 (Schedler, 1964); Weyerhaeuser Co., 37 LA 308, 312 (Sembower, 1961); International Harvester Co., 24 LA 332, 335 (Cole, 1955). *Cf.* Pratt & Whitney Aircraft Group, 91 LA 1014 (Chandler, 1988) (one of two grounds for refusing to hear the issue was NLRB dismissal of charges).

[140]*See* T. Equip. Corp. v. Massachusetts Laborers' Dist. Council, 166 F.3d 11, 160 LRRM 2257 (1st Cir. 1999). This was a railroad station construction case where the collective bargaining agreement provided that the job of "stripping" would be done jointly by members of the Carpenters' and Laborers' unions. The Carpenters later complained that they should do all the stripping. The Laborers countered that they should do at least 50% of the stripping according to the agreement. When the Laborers were prevented from stripping they filed a contractual grievance against the employers alleging breach of the agreement. Arbitration was requested and scheduled on November 14, 1995. On November 9, 1995, the Carpenters threatened that if the Carpenters were removed from the stripping work they would be pulled from the site and the union would no longer refer Carpenters to the employers. The employers filed an unfair labor practice charge with the NLRB against the Carpenters' union under 29 U.S.C. §160(k) (also known as a §10(k) hearing) alleging that the Carpenters had threatened to strike because of the stripping dispute. The arbitration hearing was postponed pend-

(1) Arbitrator Consideration of NLRA Issues[141]

When an arbitrator takes jurisdiction of a dispute that involves issues under both the agreement and the NLRA, the question may arise as to whether the arbitrator should be confined primarily to the agreement and leave statutory issues to the NLRB.

Although an arbitrator may look to numerous sources for guidance, the arbitrator's decisional authority is limited to contractual issues; the arbitrator does not have the inherent authority to decide issues concerning compliance with the NLRA.[142] "If an arbitral decision is based 'solely upon the arbitrator's view of the requirements of enacted legislation,' rather than on an interpretation of the collective-bargaining agreement, the arbitrator has 'exceeded the scope of the submission,' and the award will not be enforced" by a court of law.[143] Thus, the parties and the arbitrator should always be cognizant of the scope of the authority vested in the arbitrator.

In many cases, arbitrators have considered NLRA issues (often with an express finding that there has or has not been conduct of a type that would violate the NLRA),[144] or they have at least considered the NLRA and NLRB

---

ing a Board decision. The Board found that the Carpenters were better equipped to strip and awarded the job of stripping to the Carpenters. Subsequently, at the arbitration hearing, the arbitrator reasoned that he had jurisdiction to hear the case because the arbitration arose under the parties' collective bargaining agreement and concerned rights and obligations under the contract. The arbitrator found that the agreement, which provided that Laborers and Carpenters were to share the work of stripping, was clearly violated when the employers assigned all the stripping work to the Carpenters. The arbitrator reasoned that an award of money damages based on contract violations did not conflict with the NLRB's award of work based on the §10(k) proceeding. Thus, damages in the form of lost wages and benefits were awarded to the Laborers. The U.S. Court of Appeals for the First Circuit affirmed the district court's grant of the employer's motion to vacate the arbitration award. The appellate court rejected the distinction between "'seeking the work and seeking payment for the work'" and concluded that the NLRB §10(k) decision clashed with the arbitration award. *T. Equip. Corp.*, 166 F.3d at 19 (quoting Roofers Local 30 v. NLRB, 1 F.3d 1419, 1427 (3d Cir. 1993). The court further noted that "'[s]hould the Board disagree with the arbiter, . . . the Board's ruling would of course, take precedence; and if the employer's action had been in accord with that ruling, it would not be liable for damages . . . .'" *T. Equip. Corp.*, 166 F.3d at 19 (quoting *Carey*, 375 U.S. at 272).

[141]See also discussion in Chapter 2, section 2.A.ii.c.(2), "Concurrent Arbitral and NLRB Jurisdiction."

[142]*See* Alexander v. Gardner-Denver Co., 415 U.S. 36, 53–54, 7 FEP Cases 81 (1974); Steelworkers v. Enterprise Wheel & Car Corp., 363 U.S. 593, 597, 46 LRRM 2423 (1960); Lincoln Brass Works, 102 LA 872, 877 (Haskew, 1994); American Crystal Sugar Co., 99 LA 699, 704–05 (Jacobowski, 1992); Hannaford Bros. Co., 93 LA 721, 725–26 (Chandler, 1989).

[143]*Gardner-Denver*, 415 U.S. at 53–54 (quoting *Enterprise Wheel*, 363 U.S. at 597), *cited in* Roadmaster Corp. v. Laborers Local 504, 851 F.2d 886, 888–89, 128 LRRM 2449 (7th Cir. 1988). *Accord* Granite Constr. Co., 101 LA 297, 300 (Richman, 1993) ("Were the Arbitrator to base a finding on an alleged violation of the Act, the Arbitrator would be exceeding his jurisdiction, since the Arbitrator interprets contracts, not statutes.") (citing *Gardner-Denver*, 415 U.S. 36); Duraloy, 100 LA 1166, 1172 (Franckiewicz, 1993) ("The courts seem to agree that the arbitrator has no business writing obligations into or out of an agreement on the basis of the requirements of external law.").

[144]This is also true with other statutes. *See, e.g.,* Laporte Pigments, 114 LA 1 (Marino, 2000) (in a case involving both statutory and contract issues, the arbitrator made a threshold decision that the employer did not violate the ADA in discharging an employee).

doctrine in deciding contractual issues.[145] Particularly where the NLRB has deferred to arbitration, many arbitrators have addressed the statutory issue and have expressed a conclusion on it.[146] Arbitrators appear to be particu-

---

[145]Most of the cases cited in footnotes 146 and 147, *infra*, are applicable here. *See also* Material Serv. Corp., 94 LA 37 (Cox, 1989); TCI Gen. Contractor, 93 LA 281 (Christenson, 1989); Pittston, Pa., Area Sch. Dist., 93 LA 117 (Zirkel, 1989); Crowley Constructors, 91 LA 32 (Draznin, 1988); Allied Prods. Co., 90 LA 651 (Baroni, 1988); General Elec. Co., 90 LA 96 (Kilroy, 1987); Westwood Prods., 77 LA 396, 398 (Peterschmidt, 1981); Solar Excavating Co., 77 LA 32, 37 (Hearne, 1981); Central Ill. Pub. Serv. Co., 76 LA 300, 307 (Kossoff, 1981); Department of the Air Force, 75 LA 1011, 1013–14 (Gibson, 1980); Reyco Indus., 75 LA 689, 694 (Talent, 1980); Huron Forge & Mach. Co., 75 LA 83, 91–96 (Roumell, Jr., 1980); Aztec Plumbing Corp., 74 LA 633, 637–39 (Ross, 1980); Brockway Glass Co., 74 LA 601, 604 (Kreimer, 1980); Pierce Co., 74 LA 214, 215–16 (Fitch, 1980); Holland Plastics, 74 LA 69, 73 (Belcher, 1980); Markle Mfg. Co., 73 LA 1292, 1296 (Williams, 1980); Owens-Illinois, Inc., 73 LA 663, 669 (Witney, 1979) ("the Arbitrator must be mindful of the policies established by" the NLRB, because it "may reverse an arbitrator's decision should it be repugnant to its construction and application of" the NLRA); Portec Paragon Div., 72 LA 804, 806–07 (Ellmann, 1979); Dan's Mkt., 72 LA 706, 711 (Harter, 1979); South Cent. Bell Tel. Co., 72 LA 333, 336–37 (Morris, 1979); Eaton Corp., 71 LA 89, 92–93 (Dyke, 1978); San Francisco Elec. Contractors Ass'n, 68 LA 1288, 1293–94 (Koven, 1977); J.L. Clark Mfg. Co., 68 LA 448, 453 (Fields, 1977); Ozark Border Elec. Coop., 67 LA 438, 441 (Maniscalco, 1976); Pacific Tel. & Tel. Co., 67 LA 45, 50 (Barsamian, 1976). Where the NLRB has already made findings on an issue, an arbitrator will likely honor those findings. *See* General Tire & Rubber Co., 71 LA 579, 581 (Barnhart, 1978); Burgmaster Corp., 46 LA 746, 747–49 (Aisenberg, 1977); Middle States Tel. Co., 44 LA 580, 584–85 (Larkin, 1965). *Cf.* Contract Carpets, 68 LA 1022, 1032 (Finston, 1977); Continental Oil Co., 68-1 ARB ¶8175 (Hebert, 1967). In *Ernst Steel Corp.*, 217 NLRB 1069, 1069 n.1, 89 LRRM 1233, 1233 (1975), the NLRB stated that issues concerning compliance with a previous NLRB reinstatement order constituted "a matter clearly inappropriate for determination by an arbitrator." In *A.S. Abell Co.*, 75 LA 537, 539 (Freund, 1980), a grievance was held nonarbitrable where it was found to involve the interpretation of an NLRB order rather than the collective bargaining agreement.

[146]*See* Star Tribune, 93 LA 14 (Bognanno, 1989); Ryan-Walsh Stevedoring Co., 89 LA 831 (Baroni, 1987); Twin Coast Newspapers, 89 LA 799 (Brisco, 1987); Super Mkt. Serv. Corp., 89 LA 538 (DiLauro, 1987); Fermi Nat'l Accelerator Lab., 88 LA 79 (Wies, 1986); Servomation Corp., 77 LA 545, 546, 552 (Lieberman, 1981); Brinks, Inc., 76 LA 1120, 1124–25 (Rothman, 1981); Kenton Mfg. Co., 76 LA 817, 819, 821 (Hannan, 1981); Georgia Power Co., 76 LA 761, 769–70 (Foster, 1981); Century Boat Co., 76 LA 699, 700, 705 (Keefe, 1981); Adams Bus. Forms, 76 LA 516, 517, 520 (Eisler, 1981); C.F. Indus., 76 LA 499, 500, 504 (Bognanno, 1981); Keebler Co., 75 LA 975, 981–84 (Morris, 1980); Roanoke Iron & Bridge Works, 75 LA 917, 920 (Boetticher, 1980); ITT Cont'l Baking Co., 75 LA 764, 765, 770 (Flagler, 1980); VRN Int'l, 75 LA 243, 245, 249 (Vadakin, 1980); George Banta Co., 74 LA 388, 395–96 (Goldberg, 1980) (stating a conclusion on the statutory bargaining issue that the NLRB had deferred, but refusing to consider a statutory issue that had not been deferred to arbitration); Nichols Constr. Corp., 73 LA 1252, 1254, 1256 (Marlatt, 1979); Campbell Truck Co., 73 LA 1036, 1037, 1040 (Ross, 1979); Sterling Regal, Inc., 72 LA 1186, 1188–89 (Kaplan, 1979); Messenger Corp., 72 LA 865, 872–73 (Brooks, 1979); Anheuser-Busch, 72 LA 594, 596 (Seidman, 1979) (stating that the parties asked him to consider the NLRA charges "and apply the applicable federal law thereto in accordance with the usual practice under a *Collyer* referral"); International Paper Co., 72 LA 421, 430–31 (Howell, 1979) (stating that the NLRB having deferred, it was his "responsibility" to make a determination on the NLRA charge); Coca Cola Bottling Co., 72 LA 73, 77, 81 (Mikulina, 1979); Houston Publishers Ass'n, 71 LA 667, 670, 673–74 (Traynor, 1978); General Tel. Co. of Pa., 71 LA 488, 489, 493 (Ipavec, 1978); Universal City Studios, 71 LA 325, 326, 329 (Roberts, 1978); United Tel. Co. of the Carolinas, 71 LA 244, 248 (Foster, 1978); Charles Chips Distrib. Co., 68 LA 1139, 1146 (Dyke, 1977). In some of the above cases, the arbitrator indicated either that both parties had expressly authorized arbitral consideration of the statutory issue or that one party had opposed it, but in the other cases the arbitrator offered no comment on this aspect. Obviously, in all of the cases the arbitrator believed that jurisdiction did exist to address the statutory issue. For a good illustration that an arbitrator's ordinary jurisdiction to resolve disputes over the interpretation and application of the collective bargaining agreement may reasonably be found to cover issues identical to discrimination or bargaining-duty issues that the NLRB has deferred to arbitration, see the reasoned analysis in *National Radio Co.*, 60 LA

larly disposed to look to the NLRA and to consider NLRB doctrine when confronted with bargaining-unit and union-security questions under the agreement.[147] Representational issues present a difficult question for arbitrators because it is unclear whether such an issue is a question for the arbitrator to decide or for the NLRB.[148]

While it may be noted that in its *Raley's*[149] decision the NLRB appeared to adopt a policy of honoring arbitration awards in representation disputes

---

[78], 81–85 (Cox, 1973). Another example is provided in *Keebler Co.*, 75 LA 975 (Morris, 1980), where the arbitrator found he had jurisdiction over a bargaining-duty issue, but he cautioned that NLRB deferral "cannot vest the Arbitrator with any authority which he does not have under the collective agreement," *id.* at 981, and where he recalled the Supreme Court's *Gardner-Denver* statement that arbitrators have "'no general authority to invoke public laws that conflict with the bargain between the parties.'" *Id.* (quoting Alexander v. Gardner-Denver Co., 415 U.S. 36, 53, 7 FEP Cases 81 (1974)). However, even where the NLRB has deferred to arbitration, some arbitrators have found the issue involved to be nonarbitrable. *See* T.N.S., Inc., 76 LA 278, 283–84 (Hardin, 1981); Pacific Southwest Airlines, 70 LA 833, 837 (Jones, Jr., 1978) (even though the company had concurred in the union's statement of the issue as being whether the company violated the agreement and/or federal labor statutes, the arbitrator ruled on the contract issue but stated that a violation of the NLRA "is a matter for the NLRB to determine," because the agreement did not "vest the Arbitrator with the responsibility so to determine"); Western Mass. Elec. Co., 65 LA 816, 820–25 (Summers, 1975) (even under a broad arbitration clause, the arbitrator argued forcefully for a presumption against arbitrability of alleged NLRA violations, which presumption "can be rebutted by a showing that [the parties] considered and consciously agreed that arbitration was preferable to Board procedures for deciding the particular category of cases").

[147]*See* Baltimore Sun, 91 LA 1133, 1138 (Wahl, 1988); Northwest Publ'ns, 91 LA 1089, 1091 (Miller, 1988); McKesson Chem. Co., 78 LA 283, 286–87 (Kossoff, 1982); Jewel Cos., 76 LA 1197, 1199–1200 (McCurdy, 1981); American Baking Co., 75 LA 1074, 1075 (Seldin, 1980); Aztec Plumbing Corp., 74 LA 633, 637–39 (Ross, 1980); Bon Secours Hosp., 73 LA 751, 754 (Matthews, 1979); Times Journal Publ'g Co., 72 LA 971, 974 (Williams, 1979); Kraemer, Edward, & Sons, 72 LA 684, 688–89 (Martin, 1979); Esco Corp., 72 LA 628, 630 (Maslanka, 1979); St. Francis Hosp., 72 LA 370, 372–73 (Grossman, 1979); Shore Manor, 71 LA 1238, 1242 (Katz, 1978); Landy Packing Co., 71 LA 427, 435–36 (Flagler, 1978); Schnadig Corp., 71 LA 228, 230–31 (Marcus, 1978); Nibco of Dayton, 70 LA 230, 232–33 (Gibson, 1978); Anthony Forest Prods. Co., 70 LA 58, 64, 66–67 (Williams, 1978); Scharlin, Daniel & Assocs., 69 LA 394, 399 (Lucas, 1977); Beyerl Chevrolet, 68 LA 343, 344–45 (Bolte, 1977); Washington Metro. Area Transit Auth., 61 LA 1259, 1271–74 (Porter, 1973). However, as explained in footnote 213, below, the NLRB has taken the position that "questions of representation, accretion, and appropriate unit" are matters "for decision of the Board rather than an arbitrator." Recognizing NLRB decisions in this regard, bargaining-unit accretion issues were held nonarbitrable in *Alcolac, Inc.*, 75 LA 110, 112–13 (Chernick, 1980); *White Motor Corp.*, 64 LA 1028, 1032–34 (Perry, 1975). *But see* Kahler Corp., 97 LA 895 (Imes, 1991); Manhattan Eye, Ear, & Throat Hosp., 80 LA 82, 85–86 (Kaplan, 1982).

[148]St. Mary's Med. Ctr., 322 NLRB 954, 154 LRRM 1099 (1997); Marion Power Shovel, 230 NLRB 576, 95 LRRM 1339 (1977); Commonwealth Gas Co., 218 NLRB 857, 858, 89 LRRM 1613 (1975). For a discussion of the history of NLRB deferral to arbitration decisions in representation cases, see *Swift Cleaning & Laundry*, 106 LA 954, 958–60 (Nelson, 1995).

[149]Raley's, Inc., 143 NLRB 256, 53 LRRM 1347 (1963). *See also* Teamsters Local 776 v. NLRB (Rite Aid Corp.), 973 F.2d 230, 141 LRRM 2176 (3d Cir. 1992); Teamsters Local 682 v. Bussen Quarries, 849 F.2d 1123, 129 LRRM 2287 (8th Cir. 1988); Ortiz Funeral Home Corp., 250 NLRB 730, 105 LRRM 1094, 1095 (1980) (refusing to defer to an arbitration award and citing several NLRB decisions including *Marion Power Shovel Co.*, 230 NLRB 576, 95 LRRM 1339 (1977)). In *Marion Power Shovel Co.*, the prearbitral deferral was refused, the Board stating: "The determination of questions of representation, accretion, and appropriate unit do[es] not depend upon contract interpretation but involve[s] the application of statutory policy, standards, and criteria. These are matters for decision of the Board rather than an arbitrator." *Id.* at 577–78, 95 LRRM at 1341–42. In *Hershey Foods Corp.*, 208 NLRB 452, 457, 85 LRRM 1312 (1974), the Board stated that its *Raley's* decision must be deemed superseded where it is inconsistent with certain later cases. *See* Teamsters Local 748 v. Haig Berberian, Inc., 623 F.2d 77, 105 LRRM 2172 (9th Cir. 1980) (holding that the court lacked jurisdiction to review the NLRB's refusal in a representation case to defer to an arbitration award).

under certain conditions, under subsequent decisions it appears unlikely that the NLRB will defer to arbitration in representation cases (either by prearbitral deferral or by honoring an award). In one case, an arbitrator noted that the Board would defer to arbitration certain representation issues such as those that involve a few employees or a department, or where the representation question "turns solely on an interpretation of the parties' contract."[150]

Thus, both arbitrators and courts allow arbitration to proceed unless the dispute is "'so primarily representational'" that it falls within the Board's sole jurisdiction.[151]

(2) Arbitrator Refusal to Consider NLRA Issues

In some cases arbitrators have refused to consider NLRA issues (or have disclaimed authority to do so) or to consider the NLRA and NLRB doctrine in deciding contractual issues.[152] Even where the parties had provided, in sub-

---

[150]*See* Manitowac Eng'g Co., 114 LA 749, 751–52 (Vernon, 2000) (grievance was ultimately dismissed on a finding that the issue in the case did not rest primarily on the nature of the agreement and was so representational as to fall within the Board's sole jurisdiction). For a well-written opinion on the extent of an arbitrator's jurisdiction in representation cases, see *ATC/Vancom of Nev. P'ship*, 110 LA 626 (King, Jr., 1998) (noting that if an agreement allows arbitration of contractual disputes that may affect representational issues, the concurrent jurisdiction of the NLRB will not deprive parties of their bargain).

[151]Food & Commercial Workers Local 400 v. Shoppers Food Warehouse Corp., 35 F.3d 958, 961, 147 LRRM 2321, 2323 (4th Cir. 1994) (quoting Clothing & Textile Workers v. Facetglas, Inc., 845 F.2d 1250, 1252, 128 LRRM 2252, 2254 (4th Cir. 1988)). *See also* Minn-Dak Farmers Coop. Employees Org. v. Minn-Dak Farmers Coop., 3 F.3d 1199, 1201, 144 LRRM 2214, 2216 (8th Cir. 1993); Textile Processors Local 1 v. D.O. Summers Cleaners & Shirt Laundry Co., 954 F. Supp. 153, 155, 154 LRRM 2574, 2576 (N.D. Ohio 1997); Road Sprinkler Fitters Local 699 v. Grinnell Fire Prot. Sys. Co., 155 LRRM 2184, 2187 (E.D. Pa. 1997); Swift Cleaning & Laundry, 106 LA 954, 960 (Nelson, 1995).

[152]*See* Columbia Hosp. for Women Med. Ctr., 113 LA 980, 986 (Hockenberry, 1999). *See also* Pilgrim's Pride Corp., 110 LA 764, 766–97 (Goodstein, 1998); Phelps Dodge Copper Prods. Co., 94 LA 393 (Blum, 1990); Gerland's Food Fair, 93 LA 1285 (Helburn, 1989) (when an NLRB finding did not resolve the dispute, the arbitrator looked to the collective bargaining agreement to determine whether the employer was precluded from forming a new business organization and assigning work to newly hired nonunion employees); Butler Paper Co., 91 LA 311 (Weiss, 1988); Chevron Chem. Co., 78 LA 1235, 1240 (Taylor, 1982); Baker Marine Corp., 77 LA 721, 724 (Marlatt, 1981); T.N.S., Inc., 76 LA 278, 283–84 (Hardin, 1981); Beaumont Concrete Co., 76 LA 228, 229, 232 (Gentile, 1981); Keen Mountain, Va., Constr. Co., 76 LA 89, 94 (Cantor, 1980); Klopfenstein's, 75 LA 1224, 1226 (Lumbley, 1980); Beecher Peck & Lewis, 74 LA 489, 492 (Lipson, 1980); Singer Co., 71 LA 204, 214 (Kossoff, 1978); Pacific Southwest Airlines, 70 LA 833, 837 (Jones, Jr., 1978); Grower-Shipper Vegetable Ass'n of Cent. Cal., 70 LA 350, 352–53 (Ross, 1978); Central Tel. Co. of Va., 68 LA 957, 961 (Whyte, 1977); American Bakeries Co., 68 LA 414, 416 (Schatzki, 1977); Doces Sixth Ave., 68 LA 386, 391 (Beck, 1977); Western Mass. Elec. Co., 65 LA 816, 822–24 (Summers, 1975). Some years ago, a survey of 2,300 cases administered by the American Arbitration Association revealed 338 with issues that also fell within the NLRB's scope of activities, but in only 54 of the latter cases did the arbitrator in some manner acknowledge NLRB policies. Waks, *The "Dual Jurisdiction" Problem in Labor Arbitration: A Research Report*, 23 ARB. J. 201, 205–07, 226 (1968). Some arbitrators consider themselves without authority to interpret federal labor law and precedent absent deferral of an unfair labor practice charge by the NLRB. Norfolk, Va., Shipbuilding & Drydock Corp., 105 LA 529 (Hockenberry, 1995). Other arbitrators will use the deferral doctrine as a means to justify consideration of violations of the NLRA even though no charge has been filed. *See, e.g.*, Lithibar Matik, 109 LA 446 (Hodgson, 1997); Mid-West Chandelier, Co., 102 LA 833 (Murphy, 1994). The reasoning behind the decision to consider the NLRA absent a charge appears to arise from the conclusion that a party could have filed an NLRB charge, and it is common practice to do so. *Lithibar Matik*, 109 LA at 453–54.

mitting discharge grievances to arbitration, that the arbitrators "shall consider the standards of strike misconduct as contained in adjudications under the National Labor Relations Act," the arbitrators declared that while the word "shall" required them to give decisions under the NLRA "considerable weight," it did not require them "to follow any of such decisions blindly."[153]

Particularly concerning allegations of refusal to bargain, many arbitrators have taken the view that their function is to interpret and apply the agreement rather than to enforce affirmative duties under the statute, and they have refused to decide whether the statutory duty to bargain had been violated.[154]

Arbitrators need not, however, forsake the NLRA and Board precedent in their entirety. An arbitrator may consider the NLRA and Board precedent as evidence relevant to the resolution of the contractual dispute where the NLRA or Board precedent informs the dispute at issue.[155] Generally, however, arbitrators whose decisions consider Board precedent clarify that they are not bound by it and may even eventually decide the issue contrary to such precedent.[156] For example, in both *Lincoln Brass Works,*[157] and *Wyandot, Inc.,*[158] the arbitrators were faced with disputes over the employers' unilat-

---

[153]Southern Bell Tel. & Tel. Co., 25 LA 85, 86–87 (Alexander, McCoy, Schedler, & Whiting, 1955).

[154]*See* Columbia Hosp. for Women Med. Ctr., 113 LA 980, 986 (Hockenberry, 1999); Pilgrim's Pride Corp., 110 LA 764, 766–67 (Goodstein, 1998); Colwell Gen., Inc., 104 LA 1036, 1042 (Brunner, 1995); American Crystal Sugar Co., 99 LA 699 (Jacobowski, 1992); Stone Container Corp., 95 LA 729, 734–35 (Nolan, 1990); Phelps Dodge Copper Prods. Co., 94 LA 393, 397–98 (Blum, 1990); Wyandot Inc., 92 LA 457, 461 (Imundo, Jr., 1989); Beecher Peck & Lewis, 74 LA 489, 492 (Lipson, 1980); Singer Co., 71 LA 204, 214 (Kossoff, 1978); Pacific Southwest Airlines, 70 LA 833, 837 (Jones, Jr., 1978); American Bakeries Co., 68 LA 414, 416 (Schatzki, 1977); Doces Sixth Ave., 68 LA 386, 391 (Beck, 1977); Western Mass. Elec. Co., 65 LA 816, 822–24 (Summers, 1975); Libby, McNeill & Libby, 54 LA 1295, 1297–98 (Marshall, 1971); Pittsburgh Brewing Co., 53 LA 470, 474–77 (McDermott, 1969); Hess Oil & Chem. Corp., 51 LA 752, 758–59 (Gould, 1968); Butler Mfg. Co., 50 LA 109, 111 (Larkin, 1968); Humiston-Keeling Co., 48 LA 1257, 1258–59 (Malinowski, 1967); Hillbro Newspaper Printing Co., 46 LA 310, 315 (Darragh, 1965); John W. Hobbs Corp., 45 LA 651, 652–54 (Hilpert, 1965); C. Finkbeiner, Inc., 44 LA 1109, 1114–15 (Roberts, 1965); Red Star Yeast & Prods. Co., 43 LA 267, 269 (Kelliher, 1964); Detroit Edison Co., 43 LA 193, 209–10 (Smith, 1964); Bendix Corp., 41 LA 905, 908 (Warns, 1963); Washington Aluminum Co., 41 LA 314, 315 (Seidenberg, 1963); Penick & Ford, Ltd., 38 LA 869, 877 (Graff, 1962); Mallinckrodt Chem. Works, 38 LA 267, 268–70 (Hilpert, 1961); California & Hawaiian Sugar Ref. Corp., 35 LA 695, 697 (Ross, 1960); Magnavox Co., 35 LA 237, 241 (Dworkin, 1960). *See also* Phoenix Newspapers v. Teamsters Local 752, 989 F.2d 1077, 1079 n.1, 142 LRRM 2819 (9th Cir. 1993) (citing Challenger Caribbean Corp. v. Union Gen. de Trabajadores de P.R., 903 F.2d 857, 865–66 (1st Cir. 1990)); Lincoln Brass Works, 102 LA 872, 877 (Haskew, 1994); Stauffer Chem. Co., 80 LA 782, 784 (Cohen, 1983); Total Petroleum, 78 LA 729, 731 (Roberts, 1982); Keebler Co., 75 LA 975, 981–82 (Morris, 1980). For related discussion, see Chapter 13, section 2.A.i., "The Duty to Bargain: Right of Unilateral Action."

[155]*See* Steelworkers v. Enterprise Wheel & Car Corp., 363 U.S. 593, 597, 462 LRRM 2423 (1960); Lincoln Brass Works, 102 LA 872, 877 (Haskew, 1994); American Crystal Sugar Co., 99 LA 699, 704–05 (Jacobowski, 1992); Hannaford Bros. Co., 93 LA 721, 725–26 (Chandler, 1989). *Cf.* Phelps Dodge Copper Prods. Co., 94 LA 393, 399 (Blum, 1990) (arbitrator noted that reasons why the Board considers drug testing to be a mandatory bargaining topic are "similar" to reasons why an employer violated the contract by going beyond its management prerogatives in instituting drug testing).

[156]*See Lincoln Brass Works,* 102 LA at 877; *American Crystal Sugar Co.,* 99 LA at 704.

[157]102 LA 872, 874–75 (Haskew, 1994).

[158]92 LA 457, 457 (Imundo, Jr., 1989).

eral changes in workplace smoking policies. In each case, the Board had *Collyerized*[159] the union's Section 8(a)(5) charge, which alleged that the unilateral change constituted a failure to bargain in good faith.[160] The unions then cited Board cases holding that an employer's unilateral change in smoking rules violates Section 8(a)(5).[161] The arbitrators, however, each concluded that they did not have the authority to decide the unfair labor practice allegations[162] and therefore declined to follow the cited Board precedent. Instead, the arbitrators decided the grievances on the basis of the contract language, which they concluded allowed the employers to change the smoking rules without bargaining.[163]

Other arbitrators imply, sub silentio, that they do not have the authority to rule on unfair labor practice allegations. Other than briefly mentioning that unfair labor practice charges have been deferred by the Board, these awards contain no discussion or resolution of the specific unfair labor practice charges,[164] even where one party asks the arbitrator to decide unfair labor practice issues.[165] In most reported cases, however, where the NLRB had deferred an NLRA bargaining duty issue to arbitration, arbitrators considered and expressed a conclusion on it.[166] However, the conclusion of the arbitrator must not be in conflict with the Board's interpretation of the statute. For example, in an action to vacate an award following a Board deferral to arbitration, the U.S. Court of Appeals for the Ninth Circuit refused to enforce the arbitrator's remedial finding because it was based on an improper interpretation of the NLRA. In that failure-to-bargain case, the arbitrator

---

[159]Collyer Insulated Wire, 192 NLRB 837, 77 LRRM 1931 (1971).

[160]*Lincoln Brass Works*, 102 LA at 874–75; *Wyandot*, 92 LA at 461.

[161]*Lincoln Brass Works*, 102 LA at 875–76; *Wyandot*, 92 LA at 457.

[162]*Lincoln Brass Works*, 102 LA at 877; *Wyandot*, 92 LA at 461.

[163]*Lincoln Brass Works*, 102 LA at 875–78; *Wyandot*, 92 LA at 463–64.

[164]Lincoln Foodservices Prods., 114 LA 1745, 1746–53 (Imundo, Jr., 2000); Occidental Chem. Corp., 114 LA 1660, 1662–64 (Brunner, 2000); Bureau of Engraving, 113 LA 396, 397–402 (Fogelberg, 1999); Aerospace Cmty. Credit Union, 112 LA 58, 60–69 (Kelly, 1999); Freeman Decorating Co., 108 LA 887, 888–92 (Baroni, 1997); Mid-Continent Bottlers, 95 LA 1003, 1004–06 (1990) (Reynolds, 1990).

[165]Aerospace Cmty. Credit Union, 112 LA 58, 61 (Kelly, 1999).

[166]*See, e.g.,* Qwest Communications, 115 LA 1537, 1538, 1545 (Staudohar, 2001); Arizona Portland Cement Co., 115 LA 1279, 1282–85 (Grabuskie, 2001); Hollister Inc., 115 LA 856, 858–61 (Cohen, 2001); Continental Carbon Co., 114 LA 1263, 1267–68, 1270–74 (Chumley, 2000); Coca-Cola Bottling Co., 114 LA 1153, 1153–57 (Bernstein, 2000); Johnson-Tombigbee Mfg. Co., 113 LA 1015, 1015–16 (Howell, 2000); United Parcel Serv., 113 LA 225, 226–31 (Allen, Jr., 1999); Butler Restoration, 109 LA 614, 615–22 (Kanner, 1997); National Linen Supply, 107 LA 4, 5–9 (Ross, 1996); United Cent. Tel. Co., 104 LA 246, 250 (Baroni, 1995) (although arbitrator states that the NLRA's duty to bargain was incorporated into the contract, the contractual provisions recounted in the award include no such incorporation); Mid-West Chandelier Co., 102 LA 833, 835–36 (Murphy, 1994); PQ Corp., 101 LA 694, 700 (Pratte, 1993). *See also* Dayton Newspapers, 91 LA 201, 210 (Kindig, 1988); Michigan Bell Tel. Co., 90 LA 1186 (Howlett, 1988); Exxon Co., U.S.A., 89 LA 979 (Baroni, 1987); Servomation Corp., 77 LA 545, 546, 552 (Lieberman, 1981); Kenton Mfg. Co., 76 LA 817, 819, 821 (Hannan, 1981); Adams Bus. Forms, 76 LA 516, 517, 520 (Eisler, 1981); Keebler Co., 75 LA 975, 981–84 (Morris, 1980); George Banta Co., 74 LA 388, 395–96 (Goldberg, 1980); Campbell Truck Co., 73 LA 1036, 1040 (Ross, 1979); Anheuser-Busch, 72 LA 594, 596–98 (Seidman, 1979); International Paper Co., 72 LA 421, 430–31 (Howell, 1979); Houston Publishers Ass'n, 71 LA 667, 670, 673–74 (Traynor, 1978); General Tel. Co. of Pa., 71 LA 488, 489, 493 (Ipavec, 1978); Universal City Studios, 71 LA 325, 326, 329 (Roberts, 1978); United Tel. Co. of the Carolinas, 71 LA 244, 248 (Foster, 1978).

had imposed an affirmative obligation to agree rather than an obligation to bargain in good faith.[167] Duty-to-bargain issues may be so closely related to contractual issues that an arbitral decision based strictly on an interpretation of the contract might necessarily decide the statutory issue. In a deferral case where a nurses' association alleged that the hospital's unilateral action to eliminate matching contributions to the nurses' retirement plan constituted a breach of its duty to bargain, the arbitrator noted that one reason given by the NLRB for deferring the case was that the dispute could be resolved by deciding whether or not there had been a contract violation. The arbitrator found that the hospital had repeatedly advised the association that it would not bargain over matters addressed in the contract and that contractual language did not support an argument that the hospital had to bargain changes in retirement plan contributions.[168]

b. NLRB Policy on Deferral to Arbitration

The Board may decline to exercise its jurisdiction and thus accommodate the arbitration process both before and after the arbitration and issuance of an award. While the Supreme Court has held that the Board "'is not precluded from adjudicating unfair labor practice charges even though they might have been the subject of an arbitration proceeding and award,'"[169] the Court also has held that the Board may decline to exercise its authority to decide an unfair labor practice allegation where doing so would further an aim of the NLRA.[170]

Prearbitration, the Board or one of its regional directors may "defer" resolution of an unfair labor practice charge[171] (and in some situations the General Counsel's complaint[172]) in situations where the parties have agreed to arbitrate related contractual claims, the resolution of which may make it unnecessary for the Board to resolve the unfair labor practice allegations. In "deferring," the Board is not granting authority to the arbitrator to decide the unfair labor practice allegation, but requiring that the party filing the charge "exhaust available grievance procedures before pursuing an unfair labor practice charge."[173] Thus, while courts, arbitrators, and the Board may occasionally use the phrase "deferring the charge to arbitration," the phrase

---

[167]Phoenix Newspapers v. Teamsters Local 752, 989 F.2d 1077, 142 LRRM 2819 (9th Cir. 1993).

[168]See Columbia Hosp. for Women Med. Ctr., 113 LA 980 (Hockenberry, 1999). But see Independent Lift Truck Builders v. NAACO Materials Handlers Group, 202 F.3d 965, 163 LRRM 2321 (7th Cir. 2000) (in similar unilateral action case employer must arbitrate if the collective bargaining agreement so requires).

[169]Carey v. Westinghouse Elec. Corp., 375 U.S. 261, 271, 55 LRRM 2042 (1964) (quoting International Harvester Co., 138 NLRB 923, 925–26, 51 LRRM 1155 (1962)). See 29 U.S.C. §160(a).

[170]Carey, 375 U.S. at 271.

[171]See Dennison Nat'l Co., 296 NLRB 169, 169, 132 LRRM 1076 (1989); Badger Meter, 272 NLRB 824, 824, 117 LRRM 1358 (1984).

[172]See Tri-Pak Mach., 325 NLRB 671, 671, 158 LRRM 1049 (1998); Dame & Sons Constr. Co., 292 NLRB 1044, 1044, 130 LRRM 1226 (1989).

[173]See Plumbers & Pipe Fitters Local 520 v. NLRB (UE&C-Catalytic), 955 F.2d 744, 752, 139 LRRM 2457 (D.C. Cir.), cert. denied, 506 U.S. 817 (1992).

should not be understood as conveying any authority to the arbitrator to decide the unfair labor practice allegations. The Board, or one of the Board's regional directors,[174] is merely delaying processing the charge[175] to conserve the Board's resources and give arbitration a chance to resolve the dispute.

Board policy on deferral to arbitration has been neither consistent nor always clearly defined, and the matter has been controversial both within and outside the NLRB.[176] Regarding this issue, a former NLRB General Counsel stated that:

> There are simply not enough hours in the day to recount all the legal arguments that have been made about how much or how little deference to arbitration is required by the NLRA. And there is no need to, because the statute compels no conclusion, one way or the other. Rather, there is plenty of room in the act to argue for or against deferral. One either believes that private means of dispute resolution should be emphasized and encouraged, even where unfair labor practices may be involved, or that the NLRB's obligation to enforce the NLRA comes first.[177]

In *Collyer Insulated Wire*,[178] the Board articulated the basic test for deciding which charges to defer. The current formulation of the *Collyer* test states that deferral is appropriate where: (1) the underlying dispute arises

---

[174]*See* Utility Workers Local 246 v. NLRB (Southern Cal. Edison Co.), 39 F.3d 1210, 1212, 147 LRRM 2860 (D.C. Cir. 1994).

[175]*See* NLRB v. Roswil, Inc., 55 F.3d 382, 386–87, 149 LRRM 2332 (8th Cir. 1995); *Utility Workers*, 39 F.3d at 1212; Graphic Arts Local 97B v. Haddon Craftsmen, 796 F.2d 692, 695, 123 LRRM 2697 (3d Cir. 1986).

[176]For discussions of NLRB policy and cases in reference to deferring to arbitration where no award has yet been issued, and also in reference to honoring awards that have been issued, see The Developing Labor Law ch. 18 (Hardin & Higgins, Jr., eds., BNA Books 4th ed. 2001); Gorman, Basic Text on Labor Law 751–65 (1976); Lynch, *Deferral, Waiver, and Arbitration Under the NLRA: From Status to Contract and Back Again*, 44 U. Miami L. Rev. 237 (1989); Greenfield, *The NLRB's Deferral to Arbitration Before and After* Olin: *An Empirical Analysis*, 42 Indus. & Lab. Rel. Rev. 34 (1988); Comment, *Distinguishing Arbitration and Private Settlement in NLRB Deferral Policy*, 44 U. Miami L. Rev. 341 (1989); Comment, *Further Convolutions in a Convoluted Policy*: Olin, Taylor, *and NLRB Deferral to Arbitral Decisions*, 82 Nw. U. L. Rev. 443 (1988); Alleyne, *Courts, Arbitrators, and the NLRB: The Nature of the Deferral Beast, in* Decisional Thinking of Arbitrators and Judges, Proceedings of the 33d Annual Meeting of NAA 240 (Stern & Dennis eds., BNA Books 1981); Gregorich, *The NLRB and Deferral to Awards of Arbitration Panels*, 38 Wash. & Lee L. Rev. 124 (1981); Irving, Jr., *Arbitration and the National Labor Relations Board*, 35 Arb. J. No. 1, at 5 (1980); Edwards, *Labor Arbitration at the Crossroads: The "Common Law of the Shop" v. External Law*, 32 Arb. J. 65, 71–76 (1977); Teple, *Deferral to Arbitration: Implications of NLRB Policy*, 29 Arb. J. 65 (1974); Nash, Wilder, & Banov, *The Development of the* Collyer *Deferral Doctrine*, 27 Vand. L. Rev. 23 (1974); Getman, Collyer Insulated Wire: *A Case of Misplaced Modesty*, 49 Ind. L.J. 57 (1973); Isaacson & Zifchak, *Agency Deferral to Private Arbitration of Employment Disputes*, 73 Colum. L. Rev. 1383 (1973); Brown, *The National Labor Policy, the NLRB, and Arbitration, in* Developments in American and Foreign Arbitration, Proceedings of the 21st Annual Meeting of NAA 83 (Rehmus ed., BNA Books 1968); Ordman, *The Arbitrator and the NLRB: I. Arbitration and the NLRB—A Second Look, in* The Arbitrator, the NLRB, and the Courts, Proceedings of the 20th Annual Meeting of NAA 47 (Jones ed., BNA Books 1967); Cushman, *Arbitration and the Duty to Bargain*, 1967 Wis. L. Rev. 612 (1967); McCulloch, *The Arbitration Issue in NLRB Decisions*, 19 Arb. J. 134 (1964).

[177]Irving, Jr., 35 Arb. J. No. 1, at 5, 6 (it was also predicted, *id.* at 9, that "the future will see the Board placing more, not less, reliance on arbitrators for the very practical reason that the Board will find it more profitable to channel its scarce resources in other directions").

[178]192 NLRB 837, 842, 77 LRRM 1931 (1971).

from "the confines" of a long and productive collective bargaining relationship, (2) there is no allegation of enmity on the part of the employer toward the employee's "exercise of protected rights," (3) the parties are willing to arbitrate the underlying dispute, (4) the arbitration agreement covers the dispute, and (5) the unfair labor practice centers on the collective bargaining agreement.[179] While the Board requires that both parties must have agreed to arbitrate contractual disputes, it has never required that the parties or the contract's arbitration clause empower the arbitrator to "decide" the unfair labor practice allegations.[180] The Board's rationale for "*Collyerizing*" the charge or complaint is that "arbitral interpretation of the *contract*" (*not* arbitral interpretation of the *Act)* may "resolve both the unfair labor practice issue and the contract interpretation issue."[181] This kind of deferral is known as *Collyer* or "pre-arbitration deferral."

However, the Board generally will not defer to arbitration cases where deferral would force a party to file a grievance twice to resolve an ultimate issue. For example, where a union alleged that the employer violated Section 8(a)(1) and (5) of the NLRA by failing and refusing to provide the union with pricing information for certain products necessary for the union's performance of its representative duties, the NLRB found that deferral was inappropriate because the dispute resolution might depend on the requested information. As such, the union would be forced into a two-stage proceeding, one to decide a definitional issue, and then a second to decide the union's entitlement to confidential information and whether the agreement was violated. The Board stated that it "'has generally refused to defer issues that would result in a two-tiered system requiring a union to file a grievance to obtain information potentially relevant to its processing of a second underlying grievance.'"[182] Also, where statutory and contractual issues are very much intertwined it is unlikely that the Board will defer the contract issue to arbitration, especially if the statutory issue is not properly deferrable. The NLRB has stated that in such cases established Board policy disfavors bifurcation due to the "inefficiency and overlap that may occur from the consideration of certain issues by an arbitrator and others by the Board."[183]

---

[179]*See* Tri-Pak Mach., 325 NLRB 671, 672, 158 LRRM 1049 (1998) (citing United Techs. Corp., 268 NLRB 557, 558, 115 LRRM 1049 (1984)).

[180]*See* Bay Shipbuilding Corp., 251 NLRB 809, 809–10, 105 LRRM 1376 (1980) (Board defers charge even though employer's stipulation of issues for arbitrator did not include question regarding whether the NLRA was violated). *Cf.* McKenzie Eng'g Co., 326 NLRB 473, 477 n.3, 161 LRRM 1342 (1998) (employer did not agree to arbitrate dispute, where it asserted that *contractual dispute* was not covered by contract), *enforcement granted*, 182 F.3d 622 (8th Cir. 1999); U.S. Postal Serv., 324 NLRB 794, 794, 156 LRRM 1229 (1997) (same); Columbus Foundries, 229 NLRB 34, 36–37, 95 LRRM 1090 (1977) (same).

[181]*See* Collyer Insulated Wire, 192 NLRB 837, 841–42, 77 LRRM 1931 (1971) (emphasis added).

[182]Earthgrains Baking Cos., Inc., 327 NLRB 605, 611, 166 LRRM 1238 (1999) (quoting American Nat'l Can Co., 293 NLRB 901, 903, 131 LRRM 1153 (1989); citing General Dynamics Corp., 268 NLRB 1432, 1432 n.2, 115 LRRM 1199 (1984)).

[183]Avery Dennison, 330 NLRB 389, 390, 163 LRRM 1033 (1999). *See* N.D. Peters & Co., 327 NLRB 922, 167 LRRM 1335 (1999) (one reason the Board refused to defer to arbitration was that there was merit in the claim of employer animosity to the employee's exercise of protected rights).

In its *Adams Dairy*[184] decision, the NLRB recognized that statutory re-fusal-to-bargain issues might not fall within the scope of an arbitrator's au-thority. In holding that a union's failure to resort to arbitration did not war-rant dismissal of a refusal-to-bargain complaint under the NLRA, the Board explained:

> The contract subjects to its arbitration procedures only such disputes as concern "the interpretation or application of the terms of this Agreement." But in the instant case, the precise union claim, which is the subject of the com-plaint before us, does not relate to the meaning of any established term or condition of the contract, or to any asserted misapplication thereof by Respon-dent. It is directed instead at Respondent's denial to it of a statutory right guaranteed by §8(d) of the Act [NLRA], namely, the right to be notified and consulted in advance, and to be given an opportunity to bargain, about sub-stantial changes in the working conditions of unit employees in respects *not covered by the contract.* As the particular dispute between the Union and Re-spondent now before us thus involves basically a disagreement over statutory rather than contractual obligations, the disposition of the controversy is quite clearly within the competency of the Board, and not of an arbitrator who would be without authority to grant the Union the particular redress it seeks and for which we provide below in our remedial order.[185]

In the *Schlitz*[186] case, the NLRB did defer to arbitration by refusing to exercise its jurisdiction where (1) the collective bargaining agreement pro-vided for arbitration; (2) the union was challenging a unilateral action by the employer that was not patently erroneous or designed to undermine the union, but rather was based on a substantial claim of contractual privilege; and (3) it appeared that arbitration would resolve both the contract inter-pretation issue and the intertwined unfair labor practice issue in a manner compatible with the purposes of the NLRA.

In 1971, the latter case was reaffirmed in the "strikingly similar" *Collyer*[187] case, in which the NLRB adopted a policy of deferring to arbitra-tion in unilateral action cases where such conditions are met, but the Board in deferring to arbitration expressly retained jurisdiction over the dispute "for the purpose of entertaining an appropriate and timely motion for fur-ther consideration upon a proper showing that either (a) the dispute has not, with reasonable promptness after the issuance of this decision, either been resolved by amicable settlement in the grievance procedure or submitted promptly to arbitration, or (b) the grievance or arbitration procedures have not been fair and regular or have reached a result which is repugnant to the [NLRA]."[188]

---

[184]Adams Dairy Co., 147 NLRB 1410, 56 LRRM 1321 (1964).

[185]*Id.* at 1415.

[186]Jos. Schlitz Brewing Co., 175 NLRB 141, 70 LRRM 1472 (1969). *But see* Wire Prods. Mfg. Corp., 329 NLRB 155, 163, 165 LRRM 1014 (1999) (the collective bargaining agree-ment provided for arbitration, and issues could have been contractually resolvable but the Board refused to defer to arbitration at the employer's request because the employer's uni-lateral actions served to undermine the collective bargaining process and evidenced contin-ued "enmity toward the principles of collective bargaining").

[187]Collyer Insulated Wire, 192 NLRB 837, 841, 843, 77 LRRM 1931, 1936, 1938 (1971) (two members dissented to the deferral to arbitration and the majority opinion reviewed the history of the Board's accommodation to the arbitration process).

[188]*Id.* at 843, 77 LRRM at 1938.

The NLRB extended its *Collyer* deferral policy to discrimination cases in 1972 but again restricted it to unilateral action cases in 1977.[189] The NLRB did continue its *Dubo*[190] policy under which the Board defers discrimination cases if the charging party is processing the same matter through arbitration either voluntarily or by court order.

Then in 1984 the NLRB once again changed course. Satisfied that the *Collyer* doctrine had "worked well because it was premised on sound legal and pragmatic considerations," and that it "deserves to be resurrected and infused with renewed life," the Board indicated that it would henceforth defer not only unilateral action cases, but also cases alleging violation of the interference, restraint, or coercion, and discrimination provisions of the NLRA.[191]

The Board has also adopted a post-deferral arbitration policy. Post-arbitration deferral arises when a party files an unfair labor charge (or seeks to reassert a *Collyerized* charge) after the arbitrator has ruled on a related contractual dispute. The seminal Board decision on post-arbitral deferral is *Spielberg Manufacturing Co.*[192] Under *Spielberg*, the Board refrains from deciding an unfair labor practice allegation if the parties have previously arbitrated a contractual dispute that essentially resolved the factual basis for the unfair labor practice charge.[193] But after long adhering to a policy of not deferring to the award unless the unfair labor practice issue before the Board was passed on by the arbitrator,[194] the Board also in 1984 announced that it "would find that an arbitrator has adequately considered the unfair labor practice if":[195]

1. The arbitration proceedings were fair and regular.[196]
2. All parties have agreed to be bound by the arbitration.[197]

---

[189]General Am. Transp. Corp., 228 NLRB 808, 94 LRRM 1483 (1977); National Radio Co., 198 NLRB 527, 80 LRRM 1718 (1972).

[190]Dubo Mfg. Corp., 142 NLRB 431, 53 LRRM 1070 (1963). The scope of the *Dubo* policy is explained by Nash, Wilder, & Banov, *The Development of the* Collyer *Deferral Doctrine*, 27 VAND. L. REV. 23, 71–72 (1974). For an explanation that the *Dubo* policy remained intact, see Irving, Jr., *Arbitration and the National Labor Relations Board*, 35 ARB. J. No. 1, at 5 (1980).

[191]United Techs. Corp., 268 NLRB 557, 115 LRRM 1049, 1051 (1984). *See also* Hammontree v. NLRB, 925 F.2d 1486, 136 LRRM 2478 (D.C. Cir. 1991) (deferring decision on discrimination claim pending exhaustion of grievance arbitration procedures).

[192]112 NLRB 1080, 36 LRRM 1152 (1955).

[193]*See id.*

[194]*See* Suburban Motor Freight, 247 NLRB 146, 103 LRRM 1113 (1980); Raytheon Co., 140 NLRB 883, 52 LRRM 1129 (1963). Sometimes arbitrators expressly indicate that they have not undertaken to pass upon NLRA issues. *See* Pacific Southwest Airlines, 70 LA 833, 837 (Jones, Jr., 1978); Evening News Ass'n, 50 LA 239, 248 (Platt, 1968); Butler Mfg. Co., 50 LA 109, 111 (Larkin, 1968); Paragon Bridge & Steel Co., 44 LA 361, 372 (Casselman, 1965); Douglas & Lomason Co., 23 LA 812, 814 (Bowles, 1954).

[195]Olin Corp., 268 NLRB 573, 574, 115 LRRM 1056, 1058 (1984).

[196]*See* Nationsway Transp. Serv., 327 NLRB 1033, 164 LRRM 1339 (1999) (the Board refused to defer to an arbitrator's award because the interests of both the employer and the union were adverse to that of the employee and as such the proceedings were not fair and regular).

[197]Note that an arbitral award may be honored even though the Board finds there exists a "substantial issue" as to whether the remedy is repugnant to the NLRA. *See* Laborers Local 294 (Associated Gen. Contractors of Cal.), 331 NLRB 259, 164 LRRM 1169 (2000).

3. The decision of the arbitrator was not "clearly repugnant to the purposes and policies of the [NLRA]."[198]
4. "[T]he contractual issue [considered by the arbitrator] is factually parallel to the unfair labor practice issue."[199]
5. "The arbitrator was presented generally with the facts relevant to resolving the unfair labor practice."[200]

The NLRB decision no longer requires an arbitrator to expressly consider a violation of the NLRA in reaching a decision to sustain a deferral.[201] The arbitrator need only address the contractual issue that is factually parallel to the unfair labor practice charge.[202]

Following the issuance of an arbitration decision, the NLRB can review that decision and its associated proceedings, and reinvoke its process to prosecute the underlying unfair labor practice.[203] If the arbitral decision is compatible with the policies and purposes of the NLRA, then the Board will dismiss the charge.[204] However, if the decision is not compatible with those policies and purposes, the Board will prosecute the charge and the underlying dispute, which the arbitrator presumably was charged to decide, will continue unresolved.[205] The risk that an arbitration decision will not fully and

---

[198]Olin Corp., 268 NLRB 573, 574, 115 LRRM 1056 (1984).

[199]*Id.*

[200]*Id.* (The Board also stated (1) that it no longer would be required that the award "be totally consistent with Board precedent," *id.* at 574; (2) that the award will be honored unless it "is 'palpably wrong,' i.e., unless the arbitrator's decision is not susceptible to an interpretation consistent with the Act," *id.* (quoting International Harvester Co., 138 NLRB 923, 929, 51 LRRM 1155 (1962); and (3) that "the party seeking to have the Board ignore the determination of an arbitrator has the burden of affirmatively demonstrating the defects in the arbitral process or award," *id.*). *See also* Hertz Corp., 326 NLRB 1097, 160 LRRM 1083 (1998); Hallmor Inc., 327 NLRB 292, 160 LRRM 1083 (1998) (when a party has reneged on its agreement under *Collyer* not to raise a timeliness issue before the arbitrator when such an agreement is necessary to secure deferral of the unfair labor practice case to arbitration, the party forfeits any right to obtain the Board's deferral to the resulting arbitration award).

[201]*See, e.g.,* Laborers Local 294 (Associated Gen. Contractors of Cal.), 331 NLRB 259, 164 LRRM 1169 (2000) (deferring to an arbitrator's award, because the contractual violation considered by the arbitrator was based on the same theory as that presented in the unfair labor practice complaint); Hertz Corp., 326 NLRB 1097, 160 LRRM 1083 (1998) (although the arbitrator did not apply the explicit standards under the NLRA, the charge should be deferred to the arbitration award); Specialized Distribution Mgmt., Inc., 318 NLRB 158, 150 LRRM 1239 (1995) (deferring to the arbitration award even though the arbitrator did not explicitly discuss the unfair labor practice issue); Derr & Gruenewald Constr. Co., 315 NLRB 266, 147 LRRM 1153 (1994) (deferral to an award was appropriate even though the union did not present the arbitral panel with the details of the employee's activities protected under the NLRA). *See also* Servair, Inc. v. NLRB, 726 F.2d 1435, 1440–41 (9th Cir. 1984); Motor Convoy, Inc., 303 NLRB 135, 137 LRRM 1169 (1991); Teledyne Indus., 300 NLRB 780, 135 LRRM 1293 (1991); Garland Coal & Mining Co., 276 NLRB 963, 964, 120 LRRM 1159 (1985).

[202]*See* Equitable Gas Co. v. NLRB, 966 F.2d 861, 867, 140 LRRM 2521 (4th Cir. 1992); Bakery, Confectionary & Tobacco Workers Local 25 v. NLRB (Pet, Inc.), 730 F.2d 812, 815, 115 LRRM 3390 (D.C. Cir. 1984); *Laborers Local 294,* 331 NLRB 259.

[203]United Techs Corp., 268 NLRB 557, 560, 115 LRRM 1049 (1984); Spielberg Mfg Co., 112 NLRB 1080, 1082, 36 LRRM 1152 (1955).

[204]*See, e.g., Spielberg Mfg Co.,* 112 NLRB at 1082.

[205]*See, e.g.,* Mobil Oil Exploration & Producing, U.S., 325 NLRB 176, 156 LRRM 1273 (1997), *enf'd,* 200 F.2d 230, 163 LRRM 2387 (5th Cir. 1999); Cirker's Moving & Storage Co., 313 NLRB 1318, 146 LRRM 1171 (1994); United Cable Television Corp., 299 NLRB 138, 135 LRRM 1033 (1990); Barton Brands, 298 NLRB 976, 135 LRRM 1022 (1990); Cone Mills Corp., 298 NLRB 661, 134 LRRM 1105 (1990).

finally resolve the dispute before the arbitrator is of considerable concern, as it contravenes the purpose of the grievance and arbitration provision of a collective bargaining agreement itself.[206]

While the Board may have softened the requirement that an arbitrator specifically address violations of the NLRA that are deferred to the arbitration, arbitrators generally continue to consider the statute in deciding such grievances. Indeed, even those who may be loath to consider external law in interpreting a collective bargaining agreement recognize the need to ensure that their decisions are not contrary to the policies and purposes of the statute, and thus ensure that their decisions are in fact final and binding on the parties.

The Board's *Olin Corp.*[207] decision increased the propensity for an arbitrator's decision to be the final and binding result in cases involving violations of the NLRA deferred to arbitration because it created a presumption that the arbitration proceedings and decision comport with the policies and purposes of the NLRA. The Board shifted the burden of proof that the arbitration decision did not meet the five-part test to the party seeking to have the NLRB refuse to defer to the award and reinstate processing of the charge.[208] Previously the burden was with the party seeking to sustain the deferral;[209] however, now the party seeking to have the NLRB reject deferral must "affirmatively demonstrat[e] the defects in the arbitral process or award."[210]

Arbitrators have continued to accept and act on their authority to decide disputes involving both alleged unfair labor practices and violations of collective bargaining agreements,[211] and have approved the dual arbitral-Board jurisdiction over disputes involving issues historically within the Board's jurisdiction.[212] While recognizing the broad discretion in the NLRB to defer to arbitration, courts have nonetheless reviewed NLRB decisions in unfair labor practice cases for possible abuse of that discretion.[213]

---

[206]One arbitrator wrote that "[t]he Arbitrator's function and the end goal of an arbitration clause is to resolve contractual disputes in a final and binding manner." Manitowac Eng'g Co., 114 LA 749, 752 (Vernon, 2000). Where the NLRB might "assert jurisdiction and ultimately have the last word," the arbitrator's decision would not be final and binding. *Id.*

[207]Olin Corp., 268 NLRB 573, 574, 115 LRRM 1056 (1984). *Accord* New Orleans Cold Storage & Warehouse Co. v. NLRB, 201 F.2d 592, 597, 163 LRRM 2330 (5th Cir. 2000).

[208]*Id.*

[209]The NLRB's creation of this presumption directly overruled *Suburban Motor Freight*, 247 NLRB 146, 103 LRRM 1113 (1980), which placed the burden of demonstrating that the proceedings met the requirements under *Spielberg Mfg. Co.*, 112 NLRB 1080, 36 LRRM 1152 (1955), on the party seeking to have the NLRB defer to the arbitral award. *Suburban Motor Freight*, 247 NLRB 146.

[210]*Olin Corp.*, 268 NLRB at 574.

[211]Swift Cleaning & Laundry, 106 LA 954, 960 (Nelson, 1995).

[212]Bricklayers Local 9 v. Carlton, Inc., 850 F. Supp. 498, 502 (S.D. W. Va. 1994).

[213]First, note that the Supreme Court inferentially approved the NLRB's *Collyer* policy in William E. Arnold Co. v. Carpenters Dist. Council, 417 U.S. 12, 16, 86 LRRM 2212 (1974). *See also* NLRB v. City Disposal Sys., 465 U.S. 822, 838, 115 LRRM 3193 (1984). Many lower court decisions have dealt directly with NLRB deferral in unfair labor practice cases. Those that are cited below collect additional decisions, discuss the changing policy of the Board on deferral, and serve to illustrate some of the possible results in court review of NLRB deferral actions. On prearbitral deferral, see *NLRB v. Yellow Freight Sys.*, 930 F.2d 316, 137 LRRM 2045 (3d Cir. 1991); *NLRB v. Northeast Okla. City Mfg. Co.*, 631 F.2d 609, 105 LRRM 2618 (10th Cir. 1980) (the Board did not abuse its discretion in refusing to defer to arbitration);

B. Other Federal Statutes

The provisions of the OSH Act have often been considered in the disposition of safety and health issues by arbitrators.[214]

Arbitrators have increasingly interpreted and applied the Worker Adjustment and Retraining Notification (WARN) Act of 1993 [214a] in the context of plant closures and or mass layoffs.[215]

One arbitrator explained, "[i]n any conflict between a collective bargaining agreement and the law with reference to the rights of a returning veteran, it has repeatedly been held that the law must prevail."[216]

On a similar note, another arbitrator held that regulations under the National Security Act[217] were, as a matter of public policy, superimposed on the collective bargaining agreement when the employer entered into a "security agreement" with the Department of Defense, and that the regulations

---

Wheeling-Pittsburgh Steel Corp. v. NLRB, 618 F.2d 1009, 104 LRRM 2054 (3d Cir. 1980) (upholding the Board's failure to defer to arbitration). On deferral to awards, see *Equitable Gas Co. v. NLRB*, 966 F.2d 861, 140 LRRM 2521 (4th Cir. 1992) (the Board should have deferred to the arbitrator's award); *NLRB v. Aces Mech. Corp.*, 837 F.2d 570, 127 LRRM 2513 (2d Cir. 1988); *Distillery Workers Local 2 v. NLRB (Charmer Indus.)*, 664 F.2d 318, 107 LRRM 3137 (2d Cir. 1981) (the Board abused its discretion in refusing to defer to an award); *Ad Art v. NLRB*, 645 F.2d 669, 106 LRRM 2010 (9th Cir. 1980) (upholding the Board did not abuse its discretion in refusing to defer to an award); *Bloom v. NLRB*, 603 F.2d 1015, 102 LRRM 2082 (D.C. Cir. 1979) (the Board's deferral to an award); *Stephenson v. NLRB*, 550 F.2d 535, 94 LRRM 3224 (9th Cir. 1977) (the Board abused its discretion in deferring to an award). *See also* New Orleans Cold Storage & Warehouse Co. v. NLRB, 201 F.3d 592, 163 LRRM 2330 (5th Cir. 2000) (the Board did not abuse its discretion in refusing to defer to an award because the unfair labor practice issue before the Board was not considered by the arbitrator as required by the fourth prong of the *Spielberg* test); Mobil Exploration & Producing U.S. v. NLRB, 200 F.3d 230, 163 LRRM 2387 (5th Cir. 1999) (the Board did not abuse its discretion in refusing to defer to an arbitral award).

[214]Cases applying the OSH Act and related regulations: Packaging Corp. of Am., 114 LA 809 (Nolan, 2000); Borden Chems. & Plastics, 113 LA 1080 (Pratte, 1999); Cajun Elec. Power Coop., 111 LA 769 (O'Grady, 1998). *See also* Chapter 16, section 2.C., "OSH Act Considerations."

[214a]29 U.S.C. §2101 et seq.

[215]For cases applying WARN and related regulations, see *Akzo Nobel Salt*, 113 LA 645 (Goldberg, 1999); *A.I.M. Corp.*, 111 LA 463 (Florman, 1998).

[216]International Harvester Co., 22 LA 583, 585 (Cole, 1954). *Accord* Clarion-Limestone, Pa., Area Sch. Dist., 90 LA 281, 286 (Creo, 1988); Capital Dist. Transit Sys., No. 1, 88 LA 353, 356 (La Manna, 1986); Independent's Serv. Co., 75 LA 696, 697, 699 (Blackmar, 1980); Kaiser Aluminum & Chem. Corp., 46 LA 624, 633 (Hebert, 1966); Hancock Steel Co., 23 LA 44, 47 (Parker, 1954). For other cases in which arbitrators took note of the statutory rights of veterans, see *Vie de France Corp.*, 74 LA 449, 454, 457 (Margolin, 1980); *Granite City Steel Co.*, 54 LA 1055, 1058–59 (Bothwell, 1971); *Dayton Tire & Rubber Co.*, 46 LA 1021, 1025–26 (Dworkin, 1966); *Goodyear Tire & Rubber Co.*, 41 LA 716, 717 (McCoy, 1963); Hemp & Co., 37 LA 1009, 1013 (Updegraff, 1962); *American News Co.*, 23 LA 113, 119–24 (Justin, 1954). *But see* Mittenthal, *The Role of Law in Arbitration*, *in* DEVELOPMENTS IN AMERICAN AND FOREIGN ARBITRATION, PROCEEDINGS OF THE 21ST ANNUAL MEETING OF NAA 42, 47, 51–55 (Rehmus ed., BNA Books 1968); Meltzer, *The Role of Law in Arbitration: A Rejoinder*, *id.* at 58, 59–60. For summary and analysis of court decisions on veterans' reemployment rights, see *U.S. Steel Corp.*, 51 LA 1253, 1255–56 (Garrett, 1968); *U.S. Steel Corp.*, 51 LA 1244, 1248–49 (Garrett, 1968). *See also* U.S. Steel Corp., 56 LA 312, 314–15 (Wolff, 1971). Later decisions of interest regarding veterans' employment rights include *Monroe v. Standard Oil Co.*, 452 U.S. 549, 107 LRRM 2633 (1981); *Coffy v. Republic Steel Corp.*, 447 U.S. 191 (1980); *Personnel Adm'r of Mass. v. Feeney*, 442 U.S. 256 (1979).

[217]50 U.S.C. §401 et seq.

took precedence over any provisions of the collective bargaining agreement that might have conflicted with them.[218]

In times of wage stabilization, arbitrators have taken steps to avoid transgression on wage stabilization legislation.[219] In one case, an overtime claim was rejected because its allowance would have resulted in a clear violation of the Wage Stabilization Act.[220] However, another arbitrator emphasized that while wage stabilization regulations should be considered in determining wage adjustments, the influence of wage stabilization on an arbitrator's decision should vary "in direct ratio to the certainty, clarity and stage of its evolution."[221]

4. JUDICIAL DECISIONS

A. Arbitral Adherence to Judicial Precedent [LA CDI 94.553]

Court decisions can influence an arbitrator's decision. An arbitrator's willingness to follow judicial precedent will depend largely on which court or courts rendered the decisions, and the unanimity or conflict of decisions on the issue presented in arbitration.

Most arbitrators will follow decisions of courts of last resort that are on the point. When the Supreme Court, in particular,[222] or the highest tribunal

---

[218]Wisconsin Tel. Co., 26 LA 792, 806 (Whelan, 1956). As to limitations on statutory regulation of employment in national defense facilities, see *United States v. Robel*, 389 U.S. 258 (1967), involving the Subversive Activities Control Act, 50 U.S.C. §§783, 796, 797.

[219]*See* City of Cheboygan, Mich., 57 LA 1090, 1091 (Keefe, 1971); Durso & Geelan Co., 17 LA 748, 750–51 (Donnelly, Curry, & Clark, 1951); Los Angeles Standard Rubber, 17 LA 353, 354, 361 (Warren, 1951); Felt Cos., 16 LA 881, 882 (Lesser, 1951); Frederick Loeser & Co., 16 LA 399, 404 (Justin, 1951). *See also* Consolidated Shipbuilding Corp., 19 LA 303, 306 (Rose, 1952). For related discussion, see Chapter 22, section 9.N.ii., "Governmental Wage Stabilization."

[220]Monsanto Chem. Co., 1 ALAA ¶67,089 (Copelof, 1944). *See also* Macy's N.Y., 57 LA 1115, 1118 (Stark, 1971). In *Clarkstown, N.Y., Cent. Sch. Dist. No. 1, Bd. of Educ.*, 58 LA 191, 193 (Markowitz, 1972), the arbitrator refused to rule as to the validity of an increase under wage stabilization, having concluded that the question must be decided by the stabilization agency.

[221]Merchants Bank of N.Y., 16 LA 901, 904 (Rosenfarb, 1951).

[222]*See* UNICCO Serv. Co., 2000 WL 1139488 (Neas, 2000) (relying on *Fibreboard Paper Prods. v. NLRB*, 379 U.S. 206, 57 LRRM 2609 (1964), for the scope of the duty to bargain); Department of Veterans Affairs, 114 LA 1665 (Benedetto, 2000) (citing the *Steelworkers Trilogy* (Steelworkers v. American Mfg. Co., 363 U.S. 564, 46 LRRM 2414 (1960); Steelworkers v. Warrior & Gulf Navigation Co., 363 U.S. 574, 46 LRRM 2416 (1960); Steelworkers v. Enterprise Wheel & Car Corp., 363 U.S. 593, 46 LRRM 2423 (1960)) for deciding arbitrability); Hurley Med. Ctr., 2000 WL 1508178 (Sperka, 2000) (relying on *Daubert v. Merrill Dow Pharm.*, 509 U.S. 579 (1993), in analyzing the standards for the admissibility of scientific evidence); Teamsters Local 767, 113 LA 1106 (Allen, Jr., 2000) (relying on *Finnigan v. Leu*, 456 U.S. 431, 110 LRRM 2321 (1982), in determining whether an appointed union business agent can be discharged from his or her position by a new union president); City of Columbus, Ohio, Attorney's Office, Case No. 99-17, 1999 WL 1491628 (Chattman, 1999) (the arbitrator looked to decisions from the Supreme Court in determining whether a disciplined police officer's search was a "reasonable search"); Baton Rouge Sheet Metal Workers Pension Plan, Case No. 98-09428, 1998 WL 1033434 (Nicholas, Jr., 1998) (relying on *Firestone Tire & Rubber Co. v. Burch*, 489 U.S. 101, 10 EB Cases 1873 (1989), in determining whether a trustee's decision was arbitrary and capricious).

of the state in which the parties operate has ruled on an issue, arbitrators normally will tailor their awards to fit within the parameters set forth in the judicial holding.[223]

The willingness of arbitrators to accept the mandates of courts of last resort has been particularly evident in cases involving sexual harassment and discrimination, as well as those implicating reasonable accommodation issues under the ADA and comparable state statutes.[224] In cases involving claims of discrimination, arbitrators will look to both case law and the extensive guidelines published by the EEOC.[225]

Where the Supreme Court has rendered a decision on a point in question, arbitrators are particularly apt to follow the ruling.[226] For instance, where a national trucking company established a nonunion division, and the union grieved the diversion of work to that division, the arbitrator used the *Steelworkers Trilogy*,[227] *Buffalo Forge*,[228] and a Michigan Supreme Court decision[229] to find the dispute regarding arbitration with the nonsignatory employer to be arbitrable.[230]

Of course, seemingly applicable rulings issued by the Supreme Court or other tribunals must be analyzed to determine whether they are really distinguishable from the case at hand. For example, in a dispute over whether time spent submitting to a drug test constituted compensable hours worked, the arbitrator ruled that he was not bound to accept the Supreme Court's

---

[223]*See* Hughes Aircraft Co., 107 LA 157 (Richman, 1996); Columbus Metro. Hous. Auth., 103 LA 104 (Fullmer, 1994) (citing Paperworkers v. Misco, Inc., 484 U.S. 29, 126 LRRM 3113 (1987), for assistance in resolving after-acquired evidence issue); Curtis Sand & Gravel, 108 LA 64 (Richman, 1997) (arbitrability of postcontract discharge); Concordia Foods, 102 LA 990 (Bernstein, 1994); Chicago Transit Auth., 96 LA 1165, 1172 (Goldstein, 1991); City of Decatur, Ill., 89 LA 447, 451 (Petersen, 1987); County of Ramsey, Minn., 89 LA 10, 13 (Gallagher, 1987); City of Cincinnati, Ohio, 75 LA 1261, 1264–65 (Seifer, 1980); City of Scranton, Pa., 74 LA 514, 518 (Avins, 1980); National Homes Mfg. Co., 72 LA 1127, 1129 (Goodstein, 1979); Schneier's Finer Foods, 72 LA 881, 885–87 (Belkin, 1979); Dentler-Facs, 69 LA 368, 375 (Williams, 1977); J. Schoeneman, 69 LA 325, 328 (Oppenheimer, 1977); City of Warren, Mich., 68 LA 1195, 1197 (Rehmus, 1977).

[224]Lockheed Martin Space Sys. Co., 114 LA 481 (Gentile, 2000) (adopting the standards from *Meritor Savings Bank v. Vinson*, 477 U.S. 57, 40 FEP Cases 1822 (1986), and its progeny, for standards on whether sexual harassment exists). See additional ADA cases cited in footnotes 119 and 123, above.

[225]San Francisco, Cal., Unified Sch. Dist., 104 LA 215 (Bogue, 1995).

[226]Great W. Carpet Cushion Co., 95 LA 1057 (Weiss, 1990) (employer ordered to comply with union-security clause of collective bargaining agreement (distinguishing NLRB v. General Motors, 373 U.S. 734, 53 LRRM 2313 (1963), *and* Communications Workers v. Beck, 487 U.S. 735, 128 LRRM 2729 (1988)); Snow Mountain Pine Co., 94 LA 929 (Levak, 1990) (picket line misconduct and arbitrability of grievance arising under interim agreement); E-Systems, 86 LA 441 (Traynor, 1986) (grievances ruled not arbitrable because retiree-grievants were not employees within the meaning of the NLRA) (citing Allied Chem. & Alkali Workers Local 1 v. Pittsburgh Plate Glass Mfg. Co., 404 U.S. 157, 78 LRRM 2974 (1971)); Municipality of Anchorage, Alaska, 82 LA 256 (Hauck, 1983); Wyatt Mfg. Co., 82 LA 153 (Goodman, 1983).

[227]Steelworkers v. American Mfg. Co., 363 U.S. 564, 46 LRRM 2414 (1960); Steelworkers v. Warrior & Gulf Navigation Co., 363 U.S. 574, 46 LRRM 2416 (1960); Steelworkers v. Enterprise Wheel & Car Corp., 363 U.S. 593, 46 LRRM 2423 (1960).

[228]Buffalo Forge Co. v. Steelworkers, 428 U.S. 397, 92 LRRM 3032 (1976).

[229]Kaleva-Norman-Dickson Sch. Dist. No. 6 v. Kaleva-Norman-Dickson Sch. Teachers' Ass'n, 393 Mich. 583, 227 N.W.2d 500, 89 LRRM 2078 (1975).

[230]Complete Auto Transit, 96 LA 745 (Ellmann, 1990).

definition of "work." Rather, he noted that, although the Court established that definition under the FLSA, the arbitrator's duty was to interpret the term as used in the collective bargaining agreement, not under the FLSA.[231] Likewise, in analyzing whether a public employer's decision to test promoted, transferred, and demoted employees for drugs violated the parties' collective bargaining agreement, the arbitrator held that a decision of the California Supreme Court upholding the constitutionality of such testing did not constitute binding precedent on the issue.[232] The arbitrator noted that the grievance raised an issue of contract interpretation, not constitutionality, and therefore the Court's ruling was not instructive on the question.

Arbitrators also have shown a willingness to follow well-reasoned lower court decisions. One arbitrator considered a federal circuit's interpretation of the word "may" in a discharge clause binding.[233] The arbitrator concluded that a provision stating the employer "may" discharge an employee where contractual preconditions are met did not also require the employer, pursuant to the law of that circuit, to meet an implicit "just cause" standard.

As part of what may be seen as a growing trend, two arbitrators relied on state court decisions to find that employee handbooks issued by the employer were part of a labor contract.[234]

B. Arbitral Disagreement With Judicial Decisions

In some instances, however, arbitrators disagree with the decisions handed down by courts and refuse to follow them.[235] Thus, where one arbitrator believed that an opinion by a federal district court was contrary to accepted rules of statutory construction, he declared that he was not bound by the construction because it was not a decision of a court of last resort.[236]

---

[231]Beaver Local Sch. Dist. Bd. of Educ., Case No. 97-25809, 1998 WL 1110777 (Ruben, 1998). *See* County of L.A., 68 LA 1132, 1136–37 (Richman, 1977) (illustrating that even where the Supreme Court has spoken on a matter, an arbitrator will exercise care to determine the real import of the decision and the limits of its application). *See also* Swanson-Dean Corp., 68 LA 682, 685–86 (Jackson, 1977); West Allis-West Milwaukee, Wis., Joint City Sch. Dist. No. 1, 68 LA 644, 648–49 (Yaffe, 1977); Negco Enters., 68 LA 633, 636–38 (Helfeld, 1976).

[232]Clark County, Las Vegas, Nev., 114 LA 1608 (Silver, 2000).

[233]Kimberly-Clark Corp., 82 LA 1090 (Keenan, 1984).

[234]Ohio Power Co., 94 LA 463 (Strasshofer, 1990); Georgia-Pacific Corp., 87 LA 217 (Cohen, 1986).

[235]City of Columbus, Ohio, Attorney's Office, 1999 WL 1491628 (Chattman, 1999) (arbitrator not bound by criminal conviction); City of Sterling Heights, Mich., 89 LA 723 (Keefe, 1987) (finding a policeman had raped the victim, in spite of contrary jury verdict in criminal trial); Stark County Eng'r, 88 LA 497 (Kates, 1986); Reynolds Metals Co., 85 LA 1046 (Taylor, 1985); Allegheny, Pa., Intermediate Unit, 82 LA 187 (McDowell, 1984) (rejecting dicta of court).

[236]Dow Chem. Co., 1 LA 70, 74–75 (Whiting, 1945). *See also* North Bay Reg'l Ctr., 89 LA 1181, 1182 (Concepcion, 1987) (arbitrator refused to be bound by lower court decisions on agency fees under the NLRA, because the Supreme Court had not yet decided the issue); Ogden Air Logistics Ctr., 75 LA 936, 938 (Smedley, 1980); Fort Wayne State Hosp. & Training Ctr., 70 LA 253, 255–56 (Witney, 1978); American Oil Co., 7 LA 487, 490–91 (Edelman, 1961); Journal Publ'g Co., 22 LA 108, 110 (Seering, Wykoff, Abramson, Knight, & Rodbury, 1954).

In a unique ruling, the U.S. Court of Appeals for the Fifth Circuit remanded a case to the arbitrator to allow him to consider the public policy question of reinstating a drug user.[237] After the Fifth Circuit's decision, but before the remand hearing with the arbitrator, the Supreme Court reversed a similar decision of the court in *Misco*.[238] The arbitrator on remand determined that the Supreme Court's decision on the issue was controlling and that "the instructions of the Fifth Circuit have been severely and substantially limited" by the Supreme Court's subsequent decision.[239]

Other arbitrators have refused to follow court precedents and have declared that there are no "binding" precedents in arbitration.[240] However, another arbitrator held, "It would be unseemly for a mere arbitrator to flout the jurisprudence of the United States Court of Appeals because he did not believe that its decision exercising jurisdiction over him was based on sound legal thinking."[241]

Arbitrators are less likely to honor a lower court decision where there appears to be a conflict among the circuits on the issue. Thus, where two federal district courts had ruled one way and two others had ruled otherwise, an arbitrator declared that the parties were without the benefit of an authoritative judicial decision, and he decided the issue without reliance on any of the precedents.[242]

C. Use of Judicial Decisions for Guidance

Although arbitrators may not feel constrained to follow court decisions, they may still seek guidance from these decisions.[243] The arbitrator in *De-*

---

[237]Oil, Chem., & Atomic Workers Local 4-228 v. Union Oil Co. of Cal., 818 F.2d 437, 125 LRRM 2630 (5th Cir. 1987).

[238]Paperworkers v. Misco., Inc., 484 U.S. 29, 126 LRRM 3113 (1987).

[239]Union Oil Co. of Cal., 92 LA 777, 790 (Nicholas, Jr., 1989).

[240]Bradford White Corp., 113 LA 114 (Allen, 1999); Southern Extract Co., 59 LA 697 (Goodman, 1972).

[241]Veterans Affairs Dep't, 95 LA 253, 257 (Avins, 1990).

[242]Bell Aircraft Corp., 2 LA 22, 24 (Sharkey, 1946). Regarding conflicting court decisions, see also *Redfield Co.*, 69 LA 1024, 1027 (Aisenberg, 1977); *Ozark Smelting & Mining Div.*, 46 LA 697, 698–99 (Schedler, 1966); *McCord Corp.*, 40 LA 173, 177 (Willingham, 1962); *Sivyer Steel Casting Co.*, 39 LA 449, 454–55 (Howlett, 1962); *Pet Milk Co.*, 21 LA 180, 181 (Sanders, 1953).

[243]Washington Metro. Area Transit Auth., 94 LA 1172 (Garrett, 1990) (guilty plea for possession necessitates sustaining discharge for violating drug policy; potential for expungement does not change finding); Pepsi Cola Bottling Co. of San Diego, 93 LA 520, 524–25 (Randall, 1989) ("[t]he decisions of the courts which define 'probable cause' are . . . controlling in the interpretation of the" collective bargaining agreement that used the term); Teledyne Monarch Rubber, 89 LA 565 (Shanker, 1987) (excellent discussion of the relocating and transfer of work issue and its relation to NLRB and court decisions stemming from *Auto Workers v. NLRB (Illinois Coil Spring Co., Milwaukee Spring Div.)*, 765 F.2d 175, 119 LRRM 2801 (D.C. Cir. 1985)); Hughes Aircraft Co., 89 LA 205 (Richman, 1987) (substantial use of court decisions to determine principle of "equitable tolling" in an otherwise untimely grievance); Misco, Inc., 89 LA 137 (Fox, 1983) (relying in part on the failure of the prosecutor to prosecute an employee for possession of marijuana and award of compensation by unemployment bureau to sustain grievance protesting discharge—decision underlying the 1987 Supreme Court case, *Paperworkers v. Misco, Inc.*, 484 U.S. 29, 126 LRRM 3113 (1987)); Hopeman Bros., 88 LA 373 (Rothschild, 1986); Capital Dist. Transit Sys., No. 1, 88 LA 353 (La Manna, 1986); Sea-Land Freight Serv., 87 LA 633 (D'Spain, 1986); Hillhaven Corp., 87 LA 360 (Corbett, 1986) (successor obligations regarding past practices); Georgia-Pacific Corp., 87 LA 217

troit Edison Co.,[244] a case involving the validity of a physical ability test for promotion as applied to female employees, found no violation of the collective bargaining agreement after extensively analyzing external law. Although not bound by the external law, the arbitrator was impelled to examine federal and state law because the nondiscrimination clause read, "Neither the Company nor the Union will in violation of any state or federal law, discriminate . . . ."[245]

Many arbitrators similarly will seek guidance from decisions in the disposition of contract issues, even though they may not necessarily feel obligated to adhere to particular court decisions.[246] However, when called on to decide cases relating to traditional labor law issues, such as whether a successor employer is bound by a contract entered into with the predecessor, arbitrators have almost universally relied on court and NLRB decisions.[247] This is also true in cases involving sexual harassment[248] and other forms of

---

(Cohen, 1986) (handbook as implied contract); Burnside-Graham Ready Mix, 86 LA 972 (Wren, 1986) (successor problem in merger situation); Federal Wholesale Co., 86 LA 945 (Cohen, 1985); Firestone Tire, 83 LA 12 (Lipson, 1984) (employee versus independent contractor); Eastern Non-Ferrous Foundry, 82 LA 524 (DiLauro, 1984); Old Dominion Wood Preserves, 82 LA 437 (Foster, 1984); Ethyl Imco Corp., 82 LA 290 (Yarowsky, 1983); Bevles Co., 82 LA 203 (Monat, 1983); Southern Cal. Rapid Transit Dist., 82 LA 126 (Draznin, 1983); U.S. Gov't Printing Office, 82 LA 57 (Feldesman, 1983).

[244]96 LA 1033 (Lipson, 1991) (this case also demonstrates the excellent use of expert testimony in arbitration).

[245]*Id.* at 1036.

[246]*See* Avnet, Inc., 107 LA 921 (Kadue, 1996) (nonunion arbitration—employment at will and emotional distress issues); Baltimore Sun Co., 107 LA 892 (Liebowitz, 1996) (current drug use under the ADA); Greene County, Ohio, Sheriff's Dep't, 107 LA 865 (Felice, 1996) (definition of "negligence"); Bethlehem Steel Corp., 105 LA 1175 (Das, 1996) (ERISA issues on pension eligibility); Lyondell Petrochemical Co., 104 LA 108 (Baroni, 1995) (use of court cases to decide breach of duty of fair representation grievance); Coca-Cola Bottling Co. of Mich., 104 LA 97 (McDonald, 1994) (use of federal court decisions for guidance in resolving credibility); Michigan Dep't of Corr., 103 LA 37 (Sugerman, 1994); Martin-Brower Co., 102 LA 673 (Dilts, 1994) (FLSA decisions relied on to determine whether drug testing under Department of Transportation (DOT) regulations is compensable); Taylorville, Ill., Cmty. Unit Sch. Dist. 3, 102 LA 367 (Nathan, 1993); Dyncorp Wallops Flight Facility, 101 LA 1033 (Jones, 1993) (extensive use of external law and agency decisions to determine the validity of a request to discharge a nonjoining employee in a right-to-work state where the facility was under the Department of Defense); Young's Commercial Transfer, 101 LA 993 (McCurdy, 1993) (use of state arbitration law to determine that arbitrator had the right to retain jurisdiction for application of remedy); Hendrickson Turner Co., 101 LA 919 (Dworkin, 1993) (U.S. Court of Appeals for the Third Circuit decisions relied on in interpreting last-chance agreement grievance); Exxon Co. U.S.A., 101 LA 777 (Baroni, 1993) (case law used to determine due process rights for searches); Helix Elec., 101 LA 649, 651 (Kaufman, 1993) (federal law examined to determine availability of punitive damages); Kolar Buick, 101 LA 29 (Miller, 1993) (promissory estoppel criteria). *See also* Indiana State Reformatory, 91 LA 1068 (Baroni, 1988); Armstrong Cork Co., 73 LA 1144, 1145 (Eyraud, 1979); Continental Conveyor & Equip. Co., 69 LA 1143, 1147–48 (Tucker, Jr., 1977); Bethlehem Steel Corp., 68 LA 581, 582–83 (Seward, 1977); John Deere Plow Works, 47 LA 414, 419 (Sembower, 1966); Pension Fund Trs., Theatrical Stage Employees Local 161, 47 LA 393, 395 (McMahon, 1966); Burnham Corp., 46 LA 1129, 1130–31 (Feinberg, 1966).

[247]Tandem Props., 92 LA 325 (Koven, 1989); Mike-Sell's Potato Chip Co., 90 LA 801 (Cohen, 1988); Hillhaven Corp., 87 LA 360 (Corbett, 1986); Burnside-Graham Ready Mix, 86 LA 972 (Wren, 1986).

[248]*See* Hughes Family Mkts., 107 LA 331 (Prayzich, 1996); T.J. Maxx, 107 LA 78 (Richman, 1996); International Mill Serv., 104 LA 779 (Marino, 1995); Rodeway Inn, 102 LA 1003 (Goldberg, 1994) (use of court decisions to determine protection to complainant of sexual harassment where complainant allegedly made slanderous remarks about owner); Renton, Wash., Sch. Dist., 102 LA 854 (Wilkinson, 1994); American Protective Servs., 102 LA 161

discrimination.[249] Of course, the parties may always authorize the arbitrator to apply external law to the resolution of their problem, as was done in a construction industry case involving alleged subcontracting.[250]

Arbitrators in public-sector arbitrations, whether municipal, state, or federal, tend to rely more heavily on court cases for authority, or at least for guidance.[251]

Generally, arbitrators who are asked to interpret collective bargaining agreements that incorporate (implicitly or explicitly) state law standards will rely on state court decisions.[252] Where a union claimed that a company violated the duty of good faith and fair dealing alleged by the union to be part of every contract, the arbitrator found after analysis of case law that the principle had not been adopted by West Virginia, but also found that if it had, the company had not violated it.[253]

(Gentile, 1994) (used Supreme Court and U.S. Court of Appeals for the Second Circuit cases and EEOC regulations in deciding case of discharge for sexual harassment by (not of) a female employee); General Dynamics, 100 LA 180 (Francis, 1992); Fry's Food Stores of Ariz., 99 LA 1161 (Hogler, 1992) (homosexual harassment a violation of Tucson ordinance). For a careful analysis of public policy against harassment, see *Stroehmann Bakeries v. Teamsters Local 776*, 969 F.2d 1436, 140 LRRM 2625 (3d Cir. 1992) (used to deny mitigation); *Newsday, Inc. v. Typographical Union Local 915 (Long Island)*, 915 F.2d 840, 135 LRRM 2659 (2d Cir. 1990); *KIAM*, 97 LA 617 (Bard, 1991) (no just cause for discharge for sexual harassment, although finding that a hostile environment existed); *Kalamazoo Label Co.*, 95 LA 1042 (Ellmann, 1990); *Western Lake Superior Sanitary Dist.*, 94 LA 289 (Boyer, Jr., 1990); *Kraft, Sealtest Foods Huntington Div.*, 89 LA 27 (Goldstein, 1987); IBP, Inc., 89 LA 41 (Eisler, 1987).

[249]See Goodyear Tire & Rubber Co., 107 LA 193 (Sergent, 1996) (religious accommodation); Clallam County, Wash., Pub. Hosp. Dist. 1, 105 LA 609 (Calhoun, 1995) (same); Boise Cascade Corp., 105 LA 223 (Michelstetter, 1995) (ADA issues); Minnegasco, Inc., 103 LA 43 (Bognanno, 1994) (pregnancy accommodation); MSI Servs., 102 LA 727 (Madden, 1994) (placement in bargaining unit); Thermo King Corp., 102 LA 612 (Dworkin, 1993) (use of the ADA for guidance on claimed "handicap" drug problem); Multi-Clean, Inc., 102 LA 463 (Miller, 1993) (reasonable accommodation requirements under ADA); Angus Chem. Co., 102 LA 388 (Nicholas, Jr., 1994) (ADA case determining whether employee was "otherwise qualified"); Municipality of Anchorage, Alaska, 101 LA 1127 (Carr, 1994) (ADA and arbitrability of statutory claim); City of Dearborn Heights, Mich., 101 LA 809 (Kanner, 1993) (attempt to reconcile ADA reasonable accommodation requirements with binding past practice of job assignments; scholarly opinion); Vicksburg, Mich., Cmty. Sch., 101 LA 771 (Daniel, 1993) (religious belief accommodation); Michigan Dep't of Pub. Health, 101 LA 713 (Kanner, 1993) (use of case law to find reverse discrimination); Public Serv. Co. of Colo., 99 LA 1081, 1087–90 (Goodman, 1992) (excellent analysis of seniority versus affirmative action); Cleveland Twist Drill Co., 92 LA 105 (Strasshofer, 1989).

[250]Blount, Inc., 96 LA 451 (Christopher, 1991).

[251]North County Transit Dist., 89 LA 768, 771 (Collins, 1987) (right to order drug test); City of Dearborn, Mich., 89 LA 766 (Ellmann, 1987) (duty to negotiate and waiver of right); Williams Air Force Base, 89 LA 671 (Smith, 1987) (award of attorney fees to union); City of Chi. Dep't of Police, 89 LA 631 (Goldstein, 1987) (legal defense in civil lawsuit); Michigan Dep't of Transp., 89 LA 551 (Borland, 1987) (grant of continuance; excellent discussion of relative considerations); Social Sec. Admin., 89 LA 457 (Feigenbaum, 1987) (laches defense); City of Decatur, Ill., 89 LA 447 (Petersen, 1987) (no beard rule); Clover Park Sch. Dist., Tacoma, Wash., 89 LA 76 (Boedecker, 1987) (right to cross-examine complainant in sexual harassment); County of Ramsey, Minn., 89 LA 10 (Gallagher, 1987) (cost of defense for civil action in sexual harassment case).

[252]See Steel Valley Sch. Dist., Munhall, Pa., 2000 WL 1481885 (Parkinson, 2000); Jackson-Milton Educators' Ass'n, Case No. 99-0129-05866-6, 2000 WL 367149 (D'Eletto, 1999).

[253]Weirton Steel Corp., 89 LA 201 (Sherman, 1987). *But see* Geauga Co., 92 LA 54 (Fullmer, 1988). *See also* Complete Auto Transit, 96 LA 745 (Ellmann, 1990); Press Democrat Publ'g Co., 93 LA 969 (McKay, 1989).

5. Administrative Rulings

As they do with court decisions, arbitrators often rely on administrative rulings, but do not necessarily consider them controlling.[254] The weight to be given by arbitrators to rulings of administrative and executive agencies of the government is determined by a variety of factors, the most important of which is the authority of the agency making the ruling. The weight accorded administrative rulings also may be affected by the extent to which the identity of the issues put before the administrative body matches those in the grievance.[255]

One arbitrator expressed an interesting view regarding the weight to be given to administrative interpretive rulings in considering an interpretation of the Selective Service Act[256] made by the Director of Selective Service:

> The interpretation of an administrative agency is entitled to weight, but it is not decisive especially when it is a newly formulated one and one not long in effect, one on which the actions of men have not been based over a long period of time. In this instance, the opinion of the Director is one man's opinion entitled to respect. It may be persuasive, but it is not controlling. It has not the authority of law. It has not the power to change the provisions of a statute or a contract.[257]

The arbitrator thereupon declared that the interpretation of the director had raised doubts in the minds of honest men and he refused to rely on it.

---

[254]General Refractories Co., 99 LA 311 (Richard, 1992) (no res judicata for industrial commission finding of improper receipt of workers' compensation benefits, in discharge arbitration for same offense); Gerland's Food Fair, 93 LA 1285 (Helburn, 1989); Geauga Co., 92 LA 54 (Fullmer, 1988) (NLRB's refusal to issue a complaint where employer failed to reinstate certain strikers is not res judicata as to grievance by union on same issue); Boardman Co., 91 LA 489 (Harr, 1988) (finding successor liability despite the NLRB's refusal to issue a complaint against the successor); Sam Brown Co., 89 LA 645 (Newmark, 1987) (employer violated the agreement by not requiring a sole employee to join union, finding contrary NLRB cases to be inapposite); City of Crystal, Minn., 89 LA 531 (Bard, 1987) (EEOC guidelines in police pregnancy-maternity leave); Barnard Eng'g Co., 86 LA 523 (Brisco, 1985) (NLRB decisions used for guidance in determining alter-ego work diversion). *But see* United Elec. Supply Co., 82 LA 921 (Madden, 1984) (considered EEOC Guidelines as a general standard in discharge for sexual harassment).

[255]City of Hialeah, Fla., 110 LA 481 (Richard, 1998) (arbitrator has the authority and discretion to determine whether issues are precluded by a prior hearing of an administrative body based on the same principles embodied in res judicata and collateral estoppel); Weyerhaeuser Co., 92 LA 361 (Woolf, 1989) (arbitrator is not bound by stare decisis).

[256]50 U.S.C. §451 et seq.

[257]Bell Aircraft Corp., 2 LA 22, 24 (Sharkey, 1946). *See also* Northern States Power Co., 87 LA 1077, 1079 (Fogelberg, 1986); Archer-Daniels-Midland Co., 26 LA 561, 564 (Lindquist, 1955). In *Millinocket, Maine, Sch. Comm.*, 65 LA 805 (Purcell, 1975), the arbitrator declared:

> Whatever might be the leanings of the Equal Employment Opportunity Commission regarding the pregnancy-sick leave question, they are not binding upon this or any other arbitrator. The interpretative bulletins of such governmental agencies do not constitute law. Such opinions are transitory, and subject to sudden and frequent changes due to the tendency of governmental agencies towards the broadest kind of presumption and authority. Their reach is always greater than their grasp in the belief that the courts are always there to correct any excesses in which they might indulge themselves. In any event, it is not the function of such agencies *nor even of the courts*, to interpret the collective bargaining agreement. That is the peculiar authority of the arbitrator.

Id. at 810 (emphasis in original).

In another case, however, the arbitrator did rely on a prior opinion letter issued by the Minnesota Department of Teaching in deciding whether the grievant fell within the job classification of site administrator or of building principal under the Minnesota Code.[258]

Rules and regulations issued by government agencies and executive departments implementing and applying their statutory authority tend to be given significant weight.[259]

Arbitrators usually look to NLRB precedent where a union official is disciplined. In one case, where a union committee member made improper and false statements about a supervisor/translator that caused great damage to labor management relations during negotiations, the arbitrator upheld the 2-week suspension, relying on NLRB decisions.[260] Obviously, in cases *"Collyerized"* by the NLRB, to properly rule on the alleged unfair labor practices, arbitrators are compelled to address and decide these issues within the guidelines developed by over 50 years of decisional authority of the Board.[261] However, the fact that grievable conduct also may be an unfair labor practice does not deter arbitrators from ruling on whether such conduct breaches the collective bargaining agreement.[262] In a case where a witness for the union testified that he had violated the attendance policy without being given absenteeism points, but thereafter was assessed because of his testimony, the arbitrator relied on *Public Service Electric & Gas Co.*[263] for authority to disallow the requested immunity.[264]

---

[258]Independent Sch. Dist. No. 2142, St. Louis County Sch., Minn., 114 LA 452 (Daly, 2000).

[259]Teamsters Local 767, 113 LA 1106, 1109 (Allen, Jr., 2000) ("Arbitrators often have to incorporate the language of other documents—state laws, federal laws, army regulations, EEOC regulations, etc.—in order to derive a full explanation for the resolution of a grievance."); Abbott-Northwestern Hosp., 95 LA 258 (Miller, 1989) (NLRB rulings relied on to find employer's unilateral changes breached collective bargaining agreement); Food Barn Stores, 93 LA 87, 91 (Fogelberg, 1989) ("Normally, arbitrators are most reluctant to interpret contract language in a manner which might be inconsistent with applicable external law or governmental regulations."); Kaiser Permanente Med. Care Program, 89 LA 841, 845 (Alleyne, 1987) (NLRB award of interest on back-pay claims found to be persuasive for similar remedy in private sector); Hartford Provision Co., 89 LA 590 (Sacks, 1987) (no violation of union security by refusal of company to put son and nephew of owner into union, based on NLRB criteria); U.S. Steel Corp., 89 LA 221 (Neumeier, 1987) ("super seniority" of local union president); Witco Chem. Corp., 89 LA 349 (Rothstein, 1987) (duty to notify union of unit changes, and remedy); Mueller Steam Specialties, 89 LA 151 (Goetz, 1987) (by settlement agreement of parties, arbitrator decided NLRB refusal-to-bargain charges based on objections to election); Florida Power Corp., 87 LA 957 (Wahl, 1986) (use of Department of Labor Interpretative Bulletin in resolving "mealtime pay" dispute).

[260]Mid-West Chandelier Co., 102 LA 833 (Murphy, 1994). *See also* EWI, Inc., 108 LA 50 (Brookins, 1997); Tennsco Corp., 107 LA 689 (Nicholas, Jr., 1996).

[261]Johnston-Tombigbee Mfg. Co., 113 LA 1015 (Howell, 2000) (noting that the arbitration award met the requirements of NLRB deferral); Columbia Hosp. for Women Med. Ctr., 113 LA 980 (Hockenberry, 1999) (discussing the scope of his arbitral authority in a Collyerized case). *See also* Twin Coast Newspapers, 89 LA 799 (Brisco, 1987); Joe Wheeler Elec. Membership Coop., 89 LA 51 (Yancy, 1987). *But see* American Crystal Sugar Co., 99 LA 699, 704 (Jacobowski, 1992) (where there was no specific joint submission for an NLRB-type determination, even though deferred by the NLRB, the arbitrator refused to make one, and "leaves to the NLRB the its own appropriate determinations").

[262]Anaconda Cmty. Hosp. & Nursing Home of Anaconda, 114 LA 132 (Pool, 2000); Scrupples, Inc., 111 LA 1209 (Evans, 1999); WJA Realty, 104 LA 1157 (Haemmel, 1995); Complete Auto Transit, 96 LA 745 (Ellmann, 1990).

[263]267 NLRB 361, 115 LRRM 1006 (1983).

[264]Paxar Sys. Group, 102 LA 75 (La Manna, 1994).

Where an employer refused a union's requests during the grievance procedure for the evidence the employer relied on to support a discharge for dishonesty, the arbitrator held that the employer could not introduce the denied documents into evidence over the union's objections in light of NLRB and Supreme Court decisions holding that such refusal constituted an unlawful refusal to bargain.[265]

However, in a discharge case involving acquired immunodeficiency syndrome (AIDS), the guidelines of the Centers for Disease Control (CDC) were given no weight where they were at odds with a state statute defining a communicable disease. The arbitrator found the employer's written policy concerning AIDS was both reasonable and in accord with the state statute, although contrary to the CDC policy guidelines.[266]

On occasion arbitrators will refuse to adjudicate disputes cognizable by an administrative agency. For example, an arbitrator declined jurisdiction when called on to determine how several collective bargaining agreement wage classifications should be applied to the employer under the new state minimum wage law, deferring instead to the state labor commissioner.[267]

In a construction industry case, the arbitrator declined to rule on the applicability of a contract to the employer, holding that it was within the exclusive jurisdiction of the NLRB because the issue was representational.[268] This decision seems to conflict with *Carey v. Westinghouse Electric Corp.*,[269] where the Supreme Court held, "However the dispute be considered—whether one involving work assignment or one concerning representation—we see no barrier to use of the arbitration procedure."[270] One arbitrator declined to rule on the applicability of an agreement to a separate facility of a dry cleaning establishment, relying on more recent NLRB cases to conclude that it was for the Board to decide such accretion issues.[271]

In an unusual ruling, an arbitrator found that a company's unilaterally adopted drug-testing program, to the extent it complied with DOT regulations, was valid, but that its provisions that exceeded the regulations were not valid, because they violated the Section 8(a)(5) (refusal to bargain in good faith) provision of the LMRA.[272]

Arbitrators continue to give very little weight to the decisions and rulings of state unemployment compensation commissions.[273] The hearings tend

---

[265]Avis Rent-A-Car Sys., 99 LA 277 (DeLoach, 1992).

[266]Nursing Home, 88 LA 681 (Sedwick, 1987).

[267]Alpha Beta Co., 94 LA 477 (Gentile, 1989).

[268]Leviton Constr. Co., 95 LA 386 (Murphy, 1990). *But see* Kahler Corp., 97 NLRB 895 (Imes, 1991) (despite NLRB finding of no accretion, the arbitrator held there was a contract violation by assigning bargaining-unit work to new division).

[269]375 U.S. 261, 55 LRRM 2042 (1964).

[270]*Id.* at 272.

[271]Swift Cleaning & Laundry, 106 LA 954 (Nelson, 1995).

[272]Amerigas, 102 LA 1185 (Marino, 1994).

[273]Rittman Nursing & Rehab. Ctr., 113 LA 284 (Kelman, 1999) (award of unemployment benefits does not establish that grievant was innocent of work-related misconduct). *See also* IPC Corinth Div., 111 LA 973 (Nicholas, Jr., 1998); Westin Hotel, 90 LA 1194, 1197 (Dobry, 1988); Boise Cascade Corp., 90 LA 791, 795 (Nicholas, Jr., 1988); General Tire Co., 90 LA 373, 374 (Groshong, 1987); Eastern Airlines, 90 LA 272, 276 (Jedel, 1987); Pacific Towboat & Salvage Co., 88 LA 907, 909 (Perone, 1987); Rust Eng'g Co., 85 LA 407 (Whyte, 1985); City of Burlington, Iowa, 82 LA 21 (Kubie, 1984); Bon Secours Hosp., 76 LA 705, 709–10 (Feldesman,

to be perfunctory and lack a fully developed record. Often, the employer will not contest the employee's application at all, or present little in the way of testimonial evidence. Similarly, the employee may attempt to support his or her claim without counsel or witnesses.

Workers' compensation proceedings are treated in like manner; thus, where an employer disregarded the seniority provisions of a contract to accommodate the Ohio Industrial Commission's desire to return an injured worker to useful employment, an arbitrator found the contract provisions controlling.[274]

The rulings of state and federal agencies charged with enforcement of antidiscrimination laws are treated with greater respect. When a discharged employee attempted to excuse his poor attendance by claiming the employer unlawfully failed to accommodate his religious convictions, the arbitrator refused to consider the defense, because these agencies had found in favor of the employer on that issue, albeit by refusing to issue a complaint.[275]

6. Agency Principles

A. Responsibility for Acts of Agent [LA CDI 94.22]

Arbitrators place strong reliance on the generally recognized principles of agency. The rule that parties are held responsible for the tortious acts committed by their agents within the scope of their employment is well recognized.[276] For instance, an employer was required to compensate an em-

---

1981); New York Wire Mills Corp., 76 LA 232, 239 (LeWinter, 1981); ITT Cont'l Baking Co., 75 LA 764, 768–69 (Flagler, 1980); Owens-Illinois, 73 LA 663, 666 (Witney, 1979); Messenger Corp., 72 LA 865, 873 (Brooks, 1979); Foodland Supermarket, 71 LA 1224, 1231 (Gilson, 1978); Kasch, Kurz, Inc., 68 LA 677, 681 (Imundo, Jr., 1977). *But see* Misco, Inc., 89 LA 137 (Fox, 1983). In *Yellow Cab Co.*, 44 LA 445, 446 (Jones, Jr., 1965), the arbitrator pointed out that the procedures, functions, and issues in the state unemployment compensation agency and arbitration proceedings are different, and he stated that there is "no functional incongruity" in contradictory decisions from the two proceedings. In *Union Fork & Hoe Co.*, 68 LA 432, 439 (Ipavec, 1977), a decision by the Ohio Bureau of Employment Services carried little weight with the arbitrator, and neither did a decision by the Indiana State Employees' Appeal Commission in *Fort Wayne State Hospital & Training Center*, 70 LA 253, 255 (Witney, 1978).

[274]Container Corp. of Am., 88 LA 708 (Graham, 1987).

[275]JPI Transp. Prods., 93 LA 716 (Kindig, 1989).

[276]*See* Army & Air Force Exch. Serv., 113 LA 641 (Allen, Jr., 1999) (union violated the contract and past practice by allowing its authorized spokesperson for day-to-day issues to be located 150 miles from the company's headquarters); Avis Rent-A-Car Sys., 107 LA 197 (Shanker, 1996) (written extension of probationary period for less time than allowed by the collective bargaining agreement held binding on company); Labrae Local Sch. Dist., Braceville & Warren Township, Ohio,101 LA 246 (Sharpe, 1993) (school district bound by agent's agreement to pay employees' benefits); Stockton, Cal., Unified Sch. Dist., 89 LA 754 (Gallagher, 1987) (supervisor work assignment binding, even if the assignment had been "specifically forbidden"). *But see* Hanna Mining Co., 82 LA 1219 (Garrett, 1984) (the employer was not bound by erroneous statement of a supervisor, where the employer was acting in fiduciary capacity); Bethlehem Steel, 26 LA 646, 647 (Seward, 1956). *See also* Downtown St. Paul Partners, 90 LA 67, 70 (Cooper, 1987). For cases dealing with the possibility that one may be the "alter ego" of another so as to impose responsibilities toward third parties on that basis, see *Columbia Gas Transmission*, 112 LA 916, 918 (Tharp, 1999); *St. Louis Symphony Soc'y*, 106 LA 158, 163 (Fowler, 1996); *Dutko Wall Sys.*, 89 LA 1215, 1219 (Weisinger, 1987); *Ryan-Walsh Stevedoring Co.*, 89 LA 831, 833 (Baroni, 1987); *Frantz Klodt & Son*, 87 LA 831, 835 (Ver Ploeg, 1986); *Ecoscience, Inc.*, 81 LA 132, 139–40 (Gentile, 1983); *R.E. Walsh Contract-*

ployee for lost earnings attributable to the erroneous diagnosis by the employer's doctor of the employee's condition.[277]

A principal may be held responsible for the act of its agent within the scope of the agent's general authority even though the principal has not specifically authorized the act in question; it is enough if the principal empowered the agent to represent it in the general area within which the agent acted.[278] On this basis, arbitrators have held employers responsible for or bound by various actions of supervisors.[279] Of course, the employer will not be bound by an act of a supervisor or other management representative if no basis exists to establish authority for the act.[280] Thus, an employer was held

---

ing Co., 79 LA 1312, 1313–16 (Jones, Jr., 1982); *Mobil Oil Corp.*, 63 LA 263, 265 (Sinclitico, 1974); *Hanz Trucking*, 46 LA 1057, 1060 (Anderson, 1966); *Beckering Constr. Co.*, 43 LA 514, 518–19, 524–25 (Howlett, 1964). In *Sterling Regal*, 69 LA 513, 537 (Kaplan, 1977), the arbitrator, in placing responsibility for certain incidents on an international union as principal, declared that any discussion of the authority of its local union was irrelevant because the international "not only devised the game plan, acted as coach and called the signals from the bench, but also ran with the ball on every play."

[277]Chris-Craft Corp., 27 LA 404, 406–07 (Bothwell, 1956); Centrifugal Foundry Co., 26 LA 370, 373 (Bowles, 1956); Instant Milk Co., 24 LA 756, 758–59 (Anderson, 1955). *See also* Dwyer Instruments, 74 LA 668 (Greco, 1980) (disapproving unnecessary and sole reliance on the company doctor's opinion of grievant's medical condition and ability to work). In *Pickands Mather & Co.*, 74 LA 1, 2 (Kahn, 1980), the negligence of an employee in grading a company road was imputed to the employer, who then became liable under the agreement for damage resulting to another employee's car. *Cf.* Donaldson Mining Co., 89 LA 188, 191 (Zobrak, 1987).

[278]Sunset Line & Twine Co., 79 NLRB 1487, 1509 (1948) (citing the Restatement of Agency). *See also* Penske Truck Leasing, 110 LA 833 (Bumpass, 1998) (the company violated the contract through the actions of its agent, although the supervisor who terminated the grievant without proper procedures had acted outside the scope of his actual authority); General Motors Corp., 92 LA 624 (Kahn, 1988) (settlement of a local grievance by a shift supervisor and local union cannot contravene master national agreement that is clearly contrary); Jefferson Sch., 91 LA 18 (Daniel, 1988) (collective bargaining agreement provided for modification only by school board and union, so board not bound by agreement signed only by assistant superintendent and union); Agrico Chem. Co., 86 LA 799 (Eyraud, 1985) (agent had no authority to bind employer to lifetime contract).

[279]*See* Penske Truck Leasing, 110 LA 833, 837 (Bumpass, 1998); Howard P. Foley Co., 73 LA 280, 283 (Smith, 1979); Daniel Int'l Corp., 71 LA 903, 908 (Bernstein, 1978); Metro Contract Servs., 68 LA 1048, 1053 (Moore, 1977); Koehring Co., 54 LA 1010, 1018 (Cantor, 1970); U.S. Pipe & Foundry Co., 54 LA 820, 823–24 (Jones, Jr., 1971); Northern Ohio Tel. Co., 48 LA 773, 775 (Kates, 1966); Syart Concrete Constr., 37 LA 958, 960 (McNaughton, 1961). *See also* Flat River Glass Co., 76 LA 946, 952 (Newmark, 1981); Faribo Turkeys, 37 LA 1108, 1111 (Graff, 1961). *Cf.* Hughes Aircraft Co., 48 LA 1123, 1124 (Beatty, 1967); Tactair Fluid Controls Corp., 41 LA 252, 255 (Horlacher, 1962). In *Rust Engineering Co.*, 77 LA 488, 490 (Williams, 1981), responsibility was traced to a union, where certain actions of its steward in connection with illicit picketing were found to be within the steward's "scope of authority."

[280]*See* City of Midwest City, Okla., 109 LA 1112 (Baroni, 1998) (city not bound by mistake of fact made by personnel technicians who did not have authority to pay out public funds); City of Tarpon Springs, Fla., 107 LA 230 (Deem, 1996) (deputy chief did not have authority to issue suspension; no double jeopardy where the penalty was subsequently increased); Container Corp. of Am., 104 LA 263 (Baroni, 1995) (employee relations manager had no authority to make a side deal with the grievant for a job position outside of the grievant's seniority structure); City of Tacoma, Wash., 103 LA 950 (Bradburn, 1994) (city's attorney did not have authority to determine which city officials were necessary to grant approval of grievance settlement with union). *See also* City of Anaheim, Cal., 91 LA 579, 583 (Bickner, 1988); Homestake Mining Co., 90 LA 720, 722 (Fogelberg, 1987); Consolidated Packaging Corp., 73 LA 962, 964 (Herman, 1979) (a "foreman has no authority to bind his employer to make payments which are not required by" the agreement); City of New Haven, Conn., 73 LA 928, 932 (Stewart, 1979); Interharvest, Inc., 68 LA 1326, 1328 (Griffin, 1977); Crouse-Hinds Co., 48 LA 606, 608 (Kates, 1967); Simmons Co., 25 LA 426, 429 (Daugherty, 1955). *Cf.* ITT-

not bound by an agreement reached between the plant superintendent and the union committee, where both the committee and the superintendent knew that it was subject to the approval—never received—of company officials.[281]

In the construction industry, association-wide bargaining is the rule, but the authority of the bargaining agent to speak for all members may be at issue. In one California case, the arbitrator found that where four contractors were still members of the association at the time of a reopener, they were bound by the contract, even though they had not authorized the negotiator to act on their behalf. To accomplish their desired goal, the four had to timely withdraw their membership, not just their authority.[282] Similarly, a union that authorized its vice president to settle a grievance was held bound by the settlement even though it was rejected by the union membership when submitted for their approval.[283] Commitments made by past union officials also have bound their successors.[284] Moreover, an oral agreement between the company and a union president was held binding though it involved deviation from the seniority provisions of the collective bargaining agreement because the president had made numerous such agreements in the past without objection from the union.[285]

Phillips Drill Div., 69 LA 437, 439 (Kuhn, 1977) (employer was bound by foreman's interpretation of the agreement, where the interpretation was not clearly erroneous and grievant had relied on it); Operating Eng'rs Local 132, 68 LA 254, 256 (Wagner, 1977). The mere fact that a person undertakes to act for another or claims authority to do so is not sufficient, without more, to establish agency. See Hatfield Wire & Cable Div., 73 LA 680, 683 (Aisenberg, 1979) (the union president "was not authorized to speak on behalf of" the company when he "took it upon himself to go to the gate and not let the employees in the plant" after a fire had occurred); American Shipbuilding Co., 69 LA 944, 957–58 (Ruben, 1977).

[281]Kempsmith Mach. Co., 5 LA 520, 530 (Marshall, 1946). Cf. Landy of Wis., 70 LA 839, 841 (Lee, 1978). If a company representative is found to have had authority to commit the company to a settlement, the company will be bound. General Tel. Co. of Ill., 49 LA 493, 499 (Kesselman, 1967). See generally Klopfenstein's, 75 LA 1224 (Lumbley, 1980) (company not bound by precontract terms discussed by union and company negotiators that never received company approval, where they knew such approval was required).

[282]Kendall Cotton Mills, 24 LA 684, 687–88 (Dworet, 1955). See also Glass Container Mfrs., 49 LA 974, 979–80 (Dworkin, 1967); Mattel, Inc., 41 LA 1345, 1347 (McNaughton, 1964); General Insulated Wire Works, 38 LA 522, 523 (Wallen, 1961); American Can Co., 37 LA 465, 465 (Rock, 1961). See Mason & Hanger-Silas Mason Co., 45 LA 727, 729, 731 (Williams, 1965); Eimco Corp., 41 LA 1184, 1188–89 (Dykstra, 1963); Delta Petroleum Co., 41 LA 288, 292–93 (Morvant, 1963); Bendix-Westinghouse Auto. Air Brake Co., 39 LA 327, 332 (Kates, 1962); Bethlehem Steel Co., 30 LA 967, 969 (Valtin, 1958); Jarecki Mach. & Tool Co., 12 LA 161, 164 (Platt, 1949). See also Monarch Mach. Tool Co., 74 LA 854, 856 (Gibson, 1980); Avco Corp., 40 LA 1042, 1047 (Dworkin, 1963); General Insulated Wire Works, Inc., 38 LA 522, 523 (Wallen, 1961); W.E. Caldwell Co., 28 LA 434, 436 (Kesselman, 1957).

[283]Kendall Cotton Mills, 24 LA 684, 687–88 (Dworet, 1955). See also Glass Container Mfrs., 49 LA 974, 979–80 (Dworkin, 1967); Mattel, Inc., 41 LA 1345, 1347 (McNaughton, 1964); General Insulated Wire Works, Inc., 38 LA 522, 523 (Wallen, 1961); American Can Co., 37 LA 465, 465 (Rock, 1961).

[284]See Master Builders' Ass'n, 48 LA 865, 867 (Kates, 1967); Borden Co., 33 LA 302, 305–06 (Morvant, 1959); General Aniline & Film Corp., 25 LA 50, 53 (Shister, 1955).

[285]Lockheed Aircraft Corp., 23 LA 815, 820–21 (Marshall, 1955). See also Health Care & Ret. Corp., 99 LA 916 (Hockenberry, 1992) (finding that the union negotiator had apparent authority to settle); Balls Super Food Store, 90 LA 1008, 1011 (Madden, 1988); Quaker State Oil Ref. Corp., 88 LA 585, 587 (Duff, 1986); Airline Paper Stock Co., 45 LA 146, 149–50 (Wepstein, 1965); Samuel M. Gertman Co., 45 LA 30, 33 (Kennedy, 1965). The union president's waiver of a contractual prohibition against plant removal did not bind the employees in Douwe Egberts Superior Co., 78 LA 1131, 1137 (Ellmann, 1982).

The same agency principles apply to employees. Where an employee was discharged after he told an undercover agent the name of a fellow employee from whom the agent could purchase drugs, the arbitrator found that hearsay could not establish an agency relationship between the employee and the seller.[286]

B. Subsequent Ratification of Agent's Action

Even where no agency authority exists at the time of an act, it may be supplied retroactively by subsequent ratification. Ratification may be express, but it also may be implied by silence after knowledge of the unauthorized act,[287] or by actual operation under an unauthorized agreement.[288]

Arbitrators have strictly required a showing of authorization or ratification by the union membership of any action of a union committee that changes the terms of the collective agreement. "To hold otherwise would mean that a local Union committee meeting with management could dissipate the contractual benefits of its membership without its approval."[289] For this reason, a union field representative cannot change collective bargaining agreements unless such authority is clearly vested in the representative by the union membership.[290] Similarly, a shop steward has no authority to bind the union by an agreement altering or creating an exception to the collective bargaining agreement, or the authority to waive strict performance of the agree-

---

[286]Southern Cal. Permanente Med. Group, 92 LA 41 (Richman, 1989).

[287]Pacific Am. Shipowners Ass'n, 10 LA 736, 746 (Miller, 1948). *See also* Jefferson Sch., 91 LA 18, 20 (Daniel, 1988); Shop Rite Foods, 67 LA 159, 162–63 (Weiss, 1976); Samuel M. Gertman Co., 45 LA 30, 33 (Kennedy, 1965); United Drill & Tool Corp., 28 LA 677, 690 (Cox, 1957).

[288]Safeway Stores, 95 LA 668 (Goodman, 1990) (acceptance by implementation of agreement before signing). *See* Lafe Pharmacy, 1 ALAA ¶67,469 (Singer, 1946). *See also* Dynair Servs., 91 LA 1261, 1264 (D'Spain, 1988); American Bakeries, 66 LA 962, 964 (Williams, 1976); Fox Mfg. Co., 47 LA 97, 101 (Marshall, 1966).

[289]Flintkote Co., 9 LA 976, 977 (Naggi, 1948). In accord with the general proposition, see *Pineridge Coal Co.*, 110 LA 933, 935 (Feldman, 1998); *Allegheny Cemetery*, 72 LA 1220, 1222–23 (Dean, Jr., 1979); *Duquesne Brewing Co.*, 50 LA 845, 850 (Altrock, 1968); *Sohio Chem. Co.*, 44 LA 624, 628–29 (Witney, 1965); *Convair*, 34 LA 860, 861 (Schedler, 1960); *Curtis Screw Co.*, 23 LA 89, 91 (Thompson, 1954); *Jarecki Mach. & Tool Co.*, 12 LA 161, 164 (Platt, 1949); *McLouth Steel Corp.*, 11 LA 805, 808 (Platt, 1948); *Russell Mfg. Co.*, 10 LA 55, 55 (Donnelly, Curry, & Clark, 1948). *See also* General Foods Corp., 71 LA 969, 973–75 (Witney, 1978); Sargent-Fletcher Co., 49 LA 76, 80–81 (Lennard, 1967). *Cf.* Hayes Int'l Corp., 79 LA 999, 1005–06 (Valtin, 1982); Midwest Mfg. Corp., 29 LA 848, 852–54 (Anrod, 1957); American Suppliers, 28 LA 424, 427–28 (Warns, 1957). In *Eagle Mfg. Co.*, 51 LA 970, 979 (Lugar, 1968), it was held, somewhat in converse, that a majority of the employees could not excuse employer action contrary to the collective bargaining agreement, where the employer's action was not approved by the union as the contracting party. *See also* Colt Indus. Operating Corp., 73 LA 1087, 1091 (Belshaw, 1979). For related discussion, see Chapter 5, section 9., "Grievance Adjustment by Individual Employees."

[290]Rubber Workers Local 670 v. Rubber Workers, 822 F.2d 613, 125 LRRM 2969 (6th Cir. 1987); McLouth Steel Corp., 11 LA 805, 808 (Platt, 1948). But for the opposite side of that coin, see *Mohawk Rubber Co.*, 93 LA 777 (Aronin, 1989) (grievance committee's settlement binding on union membership that voted to override settlement and go to arbitration, where contract permits settlement by committee and contains no provision to allow settlement to be overturned).

ment.[291] However, where a bargaining committee had full understanding of the negotiated agreement, a Spanish-speaking unit was held bound by its ratification vote against a claim of "mistake" because of lack of understanding by the unit.[292]

C. Authority to Bind a Party [LA CDI 24.06]

An arbitrator will hold a party bound by the act of its agent, though unauthorized, if the party is found to have clothed the agent with "apparent" or "ostensible" authority to act.[293] For instance, a company was so bound where it held out an employers association as its agent by permitting one of its officers to sit on the association's bargaining committee without disclosing an intent not to be bound by the agreement being negotiated on behalf of the association's members.[294] A union was held bound by actions of its officer where the officer, with the union's knowledge, appeared to be speaking for the union and the union failed to openly disavow that action.[295]

Where a grievant's personal lawyer advised him to refuse a drug test, his insubordination discharge was upheld in arbitration. The arbitrator de-

---

[291]Valley Metal Prods. Co., 25 LA 83, 84 (Ryder, 1955); Pacific Mills, 2 LA 545, 548 (McCoy, 1946). *See also* Janitorial Serv., 33 LA 902, 909 (Whelan, 1959). For example, in *Freeman Decorating Co.*, 108 LA 887 (Baroni, 1997), the arbitrator held that the work stoppage caused by the steward was a clear violation of the collective bargaining agreement, not merely a result of the steward's right to perform confrontational duties as a union representative.

[292]Pillowtex Corp., 92 LA 321 (Goldstein, 1989).

[293]*See* Triton Coll., 107 LA 796, 798 (Greco, 1996); Charley Bros., 76 LA 854, 856 (Talarico, 1981); Mason & Hanger-Silas Mason Co., 69 LA 329, 332–33 (Goodstein, 1977); Town of Waterford, Conn., 68 LA 735, 737 (Sacks, 1977); Aro Corp., 54 LA 1265, 1267–68 (Sembower, 1971); Mac Coal Co., 52 LA 1125, 1128–30 (Krimsly, 1969); Gill Studios, 52 LA 506, 509 (Madden, 1969); Foster Grading Co., 52 LA 197, 199–200 (Jarvis, 1968); Glass Container Mfrs., 49 LA 974, 979–80 (Dworkin, 1967); Hillbro Newspaper Printing Co., 48 LA 1166, 1170–71 (Roberts, 1967); Michigan Gas & Elec. Co., 45 LA 85, 88–89 (Fallon, 1965); Midwest Mfg. Corp., 29 LA 848, 852–54 (Anrod, 1957); United Drill & Tool Corp., 28 LA 677, 690 (Cox, 1957); Lockheed Aircraft Corp., 23 LA 815, 820–21 (Marshall, 1955); Allen Beam Co., 16 LA 584, 585 (Myers, 1951). In *Western Condensing Co.*, 37 LA 912, 915 (Mueller, 1962), an employee was held bound by the actions of his wife under this concept. In *Maier Brewing Co.*, 45 LA 1115, 1123 (Jones, 1965), an employer was not permitted to challenge or "probe behind" the apparent authority, on which the employer could rely, of union representatives to enter into a collective bargaining agreement.

Apparent authority arises when, as a result of some manifestation or holding out by the principal, the third person reasonably believes the agent is authorized. Roadway Express, 105 LA 114 (Eagle, 1995) (company reasonably relied on the union officer's apparent authority as secretary-treasurer to orally modify written provision in the collective bargaining agreement); Service Health Care & Ret. Corp., 99 LA 916 (Hockenberry, 1992) (deciding that the company relied on apparent authority of union representative to negotiate on behalf of grievant); Todd-Pacific Shipyards, 86 LA 171 (Draznin, 1985) (company attorney handled first and second steps of the grievance and agreed there would be no suspension; later suspension by vice president held invalid; union must be able to rely on word given in grievance meeting). *Cf.* Nature's Best, 110 LA 365 (Gentile, 1998) (upholding employer's decision to refuse to recognize the apparent authority of an employee as shop steward until it received formal notification of employee's status from the union.

[294]Pope & Talbot, 1 ALAA ¶67,157, at 67,321 (Cheney, 1942). *See also* Maier Brewing Co., 49 LA 14, 19 (Roberts, 1967); Judy Bond, Inc., 38 LA 1171, 1172 (Mintzer, 1962).

[295]Railway Carmen v. Railroad Trainmen, 44 LA 540, 543 (Wallen, 1965). *See also* Plymouth Locomotive Works, 90 LA 474, 478 (Bressler, 1988); Arvin Indus., 77 LA 14, 18 (Yarowsky, 1981). *Cf.* Tennessee-American Water Co., 69 LA 175, 176 (Finley, 1977).

clared that the lawyer's advice was destructive of the collective bargaining process and conflicted with the exclusivity of the union's representational rights.[296]

D. Imputation of Knowledge

Arbitrators have applied the rule that knowledge of an agent is imputed to the principal. Knowledge held by a union regarding the existence and nature of a grievance settlement may be charged to the employee affected, and the employer relieved from making good any loss suffered by the employee as a result of the union's failure to notify him or her of the settlement.[297]

Knowledge held by a management representative may be imputed to the employer,[298] and that of a union agent may be charged to the union.[299] In some cases, however, arbitrators have pointed to the limited authority of the agent and have refused to impute the agent's knowledge to the principal.[300]

As to imputing knowledge of the individual employee to the union, one arbitrator has taken the view that knowledge of individual union members concerning the employer's policy and practices under the agreement "cannot be without more charged to the Union, for members of a Union are not necessarily agents of the Union."[301] But another arbitrator has declared that as to knowledge of company policy, "the knowledge of the employee must be the knowledge of the Union."[302]

---

[296]Marigold Foods, 94 LA 751 (Bognanno, 1990).

[297]Ford Motor Co., 1 LA 409, 410 (Shulman, 1945). *See also* Alameda Unified Sch. Dist., 91 LA 60, 62 (Wilcox, 1988); Interbake Foods, 89 LA 1118, 1121 (Keefe, 1987); Dayton Malleable Iron Co., 27 LA 179, 182 (Warns, 1956). *But see* Outdoor Sports Indus., 77 LA 880, 882–83 (Aisenberg, 1981). In *Newspaper Agency Corp.*, 43 LA 1233, 1235 (Platt, 1964), notice to union representatives who resided at points distant (in different states) from the local union and who were not known to be authorized to receive the notice (copies of the arbitration decision), was not notice to the local union. In *Safelite Glass Corp.*, 113 LA 110 (Smith, Jr., 1999), the arbitrator found that a minority employee's grievance challenging his starting pay as being lower than that of white employees was timely, even though union knew of wages for a month but did not notify grievant until he passed his probationary period.

[298]*See* Struck Constr. Co., 74 LA 369, 373 (Sergent, Jr., 1980); Metro Contract Servs., 68 LA 1048, 1053 (Moore, 1977); Misco Precision Casting Co., 40 LA 87, 90 (Dworkin, 1962).

[299]Anheuser-Busch, 33 LA 752, 753 (Roberts, 1959); Boys & Men's Shop, 8 LA 214, 217–18 (Rosenfarb, 1947).

[300]*See* Amoco Tex. Ref. Co., 71 LA 344, 348 (Gowan, Jr., 1978); Hawthorn-Mellody Farms, 52 LA 557, 560 (Kates, 1969); Wyandotte Chems. Corp., 36 LA 1169, 1172 (Hilpert, 1961). *Cf.* William Feather Co., 68 LA 13, 19 (Shanker, 1977).

[301]Boys & Men's Shop, 8 LA 214, 218 (Rosenfarb, 1947). As to union responsibility for employee actions in breach of the no-strike clause, see *National Homes Manufacturing Co.*, 72 LA 1127, 1130 (Goodstein, 1979) (the union "is responsible for the actions of its members, at least until it has made a good faith effort to get the members to honor their Contract"). *See also* General Am. Transp. Corp., 42 LA 142, 144 (Pollack, 1964). *But see* Booth Newspapers, 43 LA 785, 790 (Platt, 1964).

[302]Chattanooga Box & Lumber Co., 44 LA 373, 376 (Tatum, 1965). *Accord* Sinclair Mfg. Co., 49 LA 310, 313–14 (Nichols, 1967) (imputing to the union an employee's knowledge that the agreement was being violated). *See also* Summit County, Ohio, Children Servs., 108 LA 517, 522 (Sharpe, 1997). In *Tri-State Engineering Co.*, 69 LA 980, 984 (Brown, 1977), the arbitrator stated that company policy regarding proof of illness must be "communicated to all employees," and that an "informal discussion with the plant shop committee cannot be said to be proper notice."

E. Agent's Right to Indemnification [LA CDI 24.906]

As to the principal's obligation to indemnify its agents, an arbitrator resorted to basic principles of agency law to determine whether an employee was entitled to be indemnified by his employer for monetary loss the employee suffered in defending legal actions against him growing out of certain things he did allegedly in the employer's interest.[303]

7. CONTRACT PRINCIPLES [LA CDI 24.101; 24.105; 24.40]

Arbitrators are expected to recognize the fundamental principles of contract law,[304] including the concepts of offer and acceptance,[305] need for consideration,[306] and anticipatory repudiation (breach).[307] In addition, arbitrators are expected to recognize the obligation to perform the contract despite the existence of hardships.[308]

---

[303]Trubitz Hardware & Elec. Co., 32 LA 930, 934–35 (Scheiber, 1959). *See also* City of Chi., 91 LA 393 (Meyers, 1988) (requiring city to provide police officer with representation in civil suit alleging that police officer beat the plaintiff).

[304]*See* Aurora, Ohio, City Sch. Dist. Bd. of Educ., 108 LA 69 (Sharpe, 1997) (applying principles of construction regarding general versus specific contract language); Greenteam of San Jose, Cal., 103 LA 705 (McCurdy, 1994) (applying general contract principles to successors); City of Detroit, Mich., 102 LA 440 (Lipson, 1994) (parol evidence rule examined to determine validity of oral "side bar" agreement); International Paper Co., 101 LA 278 (Duff, 1993) (defining doctrine of "nunc pro tunc" to find provision of contract to be retroactive); Nelson Tree Serv., 95 LA 1143, 1146 (Loeb, 1990) (ambiguous contract language most strongly construed against party who drafted it). *See also* Western Piece Dyers & Finishers, 95 LA 644, 646 (Goldstein, 1990). *See generally* Chapter 9, "Intepreting Contract Language."

[305]*See* Westwood Prods., 77 LA 396, 399 (Peterschmidt, 1981); Laclede Steel Co., 54 LA 647, 648 (Kelliher, 1971); Plumbing-Heating & Piping Employers Council of N.C., 54 LA 478, 482–83 (Eaton, 1971); General Cable Corp., 20 LA 406, 408 (Hays, 1953). *See also* Penn Window Co., 112 LA 922, 928 (Franckiewicz, 1999); Schulze & Burch Biscuit Co., 42 LA 280, 288 (Solomon, 1964).

[306]*See* Dixie-Portland Flour Mills, 46 LA 838, 840 (Hon, 1966); United Drill & Tool Corp., 28 LA 677, 685–86 (Cox, 1957). For a discussion of the application in arbitration of this and various other principles of contract law, see Mueller, *The Law of Contracts—A Changing Legal Environment, in* TRUTH, LIE DETECTORS, AND OTHER PROBLEMS IN LABOR ARBITRATION, PROCEEDINGS OF THE 31ST ANNUAL MEETING OF NAA 204 (Stern & Dennis eds., BNA Books 1979); Goetz, *Comment, in id.* at 218; Meiners, *Comment, in id.* at 229.

[307]*See* Metro E. Journal, 47 LA 610, 612 (Kelliher, 1966). *See generally* Central Ohio Transit Auth., 113 LA 1134, 1141 (Imundo, Jr., 2000) (error of giving written attendance warning did not serve to repudiate existing last chance agreement); Western Mich. Univ., 111 LA 534, 539 (Daniel, 1998) (failure by employer to take any special steps to enable an employee's performance of contract not a repudiation).

[308]Michigan Dep't of Transp., 112 LA 1179 (Allen, 1999); Waller Bros. Stone Co., 108 LA 609 (Weatherspoon, 1997). *See* Abbott-Northwestern Hosp., 95 LA 258 (Miller, 1989) (hospital violated contract by unilaterally enhancing benefits despite continuing shortage of nurses); Airco Carbon, 86 LA 6, 9 (Dworkin, 1986) ("No arbitrator is empowered to relieve a party of a bad bargain or to improve an existing contract."); Cascade Corp., 82 LA 313 (Bressler, 1984). *See also* Seng Co., 51 LA 928, 931–32 (Sembower, 1968) (in accord as to hardship and also noting that only in extreme cases will impossibility of performance be accepted as an excuse for not performing a contract). Regarding impossibility of performance, see also *Powermatic Houdaille*, 72 LA 1293, 1296 (Flannagan, 1979) (time was extended where it was impossible to perform within time specified by agreement); *Gimbel Bros.*, 69 LA 847, 851 (Lubow, 1977) (contractual obligation would be modified only as justified by impossibility of performance); *C. Iber & Sons*, 69 LA 697, 703 (Gibson, 1977) (employer failed to act timely in claiming impossibility of performance); *North Clackamas, Or., Sch. Dist. No. 12*, 68 LA 503, 506–07 (Snow, 1977). Regarding federal-sector agreements, see *Federal Aviation*

Arbitrators have also applied the principle that there can be no binding contract without a meeting of the minds.[309] Where arbitrators find that there has been no meeting of the minds on a matter, they may recommend further negotiations by the parties,[310] unless they construe their authority to be broad enough to empower them to decide the dispute on the merits.[311] Generally, the intent of a written agreement is that it will not go into effect unless signed by the parties.[312]

Admin., 68 LA 375, 378–79 (Moore, 1977). The Supreme Court recognized impossibility as a possible defense to breach of contract but rejected economic necessity as a defense in *W.R. Grace & Co. v. Rubber Workers Local 759*, 461 U.S 757, 767–68 n.10, 768–69 n.12, 113 LRRM 2641, 2645 n.10, 2646 n.12 (1983). This case is discussed generally in Chapter 14, section 2.A.iv., "Seniority Systems and the Arbitral Enforcement of Antidiscrimination Clauses Resulting in 'Reverse Discrimination' Claims."

[309]*See* Union Foundry Co., 113 LA 63 (Baroni, 1999) (arbitrator refused to impose prior agreement just because there was no meeting of the minds on the instant agreement); Potomac Edison Co. (Allegheny Power), 110 LA 420 (Talarico, 1997) (finding no meeting of the minds regarding alleged past practice, and, thus, no agreement based on past practice); Q.C., Inc., 106 LA 987 (McGury, 1996) (settlement of prior discharge grievance was not a last-chance agreement unless both parties agree that it is so); Sunnyside Coal Co., 104 LA 886 (Sharpe, 1995) (where parties disagreed as to the incorporation of external law, refuting employer's implication of external law that would have nullified salary provisions and even the existence of the contract itself); City of Lake Worth, Fla., 101 LA 78 (Abrams, 1993) (finding a valid agreement based on the objective evidence of a national successor agreement and local interim agreement). *See also* T.J. Maxx, 105 LA 470 (Richman, 1995); Globe Ticket & Label Co., 105 LA 62 (McCurdy, 1995); Kroger Grocery & Meats, 104 LA 422 (Duff, 1995); Mead Corp., 104 LA 161 (Krislov, 1995); Flint Ink Corp., 98 LA 474, 478 (Fogelberg, 1991); Methodist Hosp., 94 LA 616, 620 (Bognanno, 1990); Detroit Water & Sewerage Dep't, 91 LA 639, 646 (Brown, 1988); Plumbers & Pipefitters Pension Plan Local 520, 87 LA 1177 (Everitt, 1986); Columbia Pictures Indus., 87 LA 772, 775 (Gentile, 1986); Sea-Land Freight Serv., 87 LA 633 (D'Spain, 1986); Pollock Co., 87 LA 325, 333 (Oberdank, 1986); Bunny Bread Co., 85 LA 1118 (Krislov, 1985); Immigration & Naturalization Serv., 78 LA 842, 847 (Kaplan, 1982); Bethlehem Steel Corp., 76 LA 308, 311 (Sharnoff, 1981); Snap-On Tools Corp., 75 LA 822, 824 (Cox, 1980); Georgia-Pacific Corp., 70 LA 633, 635 (Rayl, Jr., 1978); Kellogg Co., 68 LA 1110, 1121–22 (Bowles, 1977); Burkhart-Randall Co., 68 LA 57, 62 (Render, 1977); Consolidation Coal Co., 67 LA 257, 260 (Lubow, 1976); Chemetron Corp., 58 LA 1084, 1087 (Garman, 1972); T&M Rubber Specialties Co., 54 LA 292, 297–98 (Sembower, 1971); Allegheny Ludlum Steel Corp., 46 LA 885, 886 (Shipman, 1965); Tin Processing Corp., 20 LA 362, 363 (Johannes, 1953); Joliet City Lines, 20 LA 199, 201–02 (Garman, 1953); Carlile & Doughty, 9 LA 239, 241 (Brandschain, 1947); Roman Dress Co., 8 LA 475, 478 (Copelof, 1947); Goodyear Tire & Rubber Co. of Ala., 1 LA 556, 560 (McCoy, 1946). The NLRB held that there was no binding agreement without a meeting of the minds in *Computer Scis. Corp.*, 258 NLRB 641, 108 LRRM 1233, 1233 (1981); *McKinzie Enters.*, 250 NLRB 29, 104 LRRM 1321, 1322 (1980). The meeting of the minds requirement is questioned in Garrett, *The Role of Lawyers in Arbitration, in* ARBITRATION AND PUBLIC POLICY, PROCEEDINGS OF THE 14TH ANNUAL MEETING OF NAA 102, 121 (Pollard ed., BNA Books 1961). Fraud in the inducement of a contract was the basis for voiding it in *Hasting Mfg. Co.*, 49 LA 297, 299–300 (Howlett, 1967), but the fact that a contractual promise was given under coercive circumstances did not excuse its performance in *City of New Haven*, 50 LA 661, 663 (Summers, 1968).

[310]*See, e.g.*, T&M Rubber Specialties Co., 54 LA 292, 297–98 (Sembower, 1971); Tin Processing Corp., 20 LA 362, 364 (Johannes, 1953); Carlile & Doughty, 9 LA 239, 241 (Brandschain, 1947); Roman Dress Co., 8 LA 475, 478 (Copelof, 1947). *See also* Chemineer, Inc., 76 LA 697, 699 (Strasshofer, 1981).

[311]*See* Standard Oil Co., 24 LA 424, 425 (Beatty, 1954); Munising Wood Prods. Co., 22 LA 769, 771 (Ryder, 1954); Capitol Barg Dry Cleaning Co., 8 LA 586, 589 (Rice, 1947); American Woolen Co., 6 LA 286, 288 (Wallen, 1946). For related discussion and other cases, see Chapter 9, section 3., "'Legislation' Versus 'Interpretation'"; Chapter 18, section 1.C., "Scope of Remedy Power Limited by the Agreement."

[312]*See* Williams Furnace Co., 107 LA 215 (Monat, 1996) (no agreement found where proposed written settlement agreement of oral settlement of grievance is rejected; parties contemplated written settlement). *See also* Family Food Park, 86 LA 1184 (Petersen, 1986). *Cf.* Safeway Stores, 95 LA 668 (Goodman, 1990).

Promises made by one party that are not supported by consideration from the other usually are not enforceable, so where an employer, on the day prior to a ratification meeting, repudiated a promise to pay for attendance at the meeting, the arbitrator found the repudiation to be effective and no obligation to pay was found to exist.[313] However, one arbitrator utilized the promissory estoppel theory in a case where an employer's chief executive officer promised in a letter to the bargaining unit 30 new jobs if the agreement was ratified, but later attempted to transfer work that would have eliminated the jobs.[314] The arbitrator ordered the company to return sufficient work to keep 30 employees employed for the duration of the agreement.[315] Other documents may be incorporated into a labor agreement by reference.[316] In a case where a handbook and a contract frequently contained identical language, the arbitrator found the handbook to be incorporated by reference into the contract.[317]

Generally, arbitrators follow the common law principle that parties to a contract should administer its provisions in good faith, but obviously are entitled to fully exercise rights confided to them by specific contract language.[318] For example, where a city unexpectedly lost revenue relied on to provide contract police service to other communities, impossibility of performance was not a defense to a claim for back pay for laid-off policemen until they found other suitable employment.[319] Where a new contract was silent on the calculation of retroactive pay, a side oral agreement was found not to violate the parol evidence rule or a "zipper clause," but was a proper stand-alone agreement supported by adequate consideration.[320]

In one of the few reported decisions involving a nonunion employer, an arbitrator held that a memorandum of understanding, prepared unilaterally by the employer without input by the employees, was binding on the employer as well as the employees.[321] Where the employer's brief attempted to define "insubordination" and cited arbitration cases in union settings, the arbitrator, in a broad, sweeping statement (which may be justifiably open to

---

[313]Litton Precision Gear, 107 LA 52 (Goldstein, 1996).

[314]Kuhlman Elec. Corp., 106 LA 429 (Duda, Jr., 1996).

[315]*Id.*

[316]Rittman Nursing & Rehab. Ctr., 113 LA 284 (Kelman, 1999) (handbook incorporated by reference); Pennsylvania Power Co., 113 LA 217 (Duff, 1999) (memorandum of agreement incorporated by reference and used to decide whether violation occurred).

[317]Gavin Sch. Dist. No. 37, Ill., 98 LA 417 (Stallworth, 1991) (school board policies not included in collective bargaining agreement, which includes benefits provided in School Code of Illinois and other laws and regulations); Centel Bus. Sys., 95 LA 472, 478 (Allen, Jr., 1990) (employer-promulgated insurance handbook not in existence for appreciable period of time prior to grievance cannot be incorporated into collective bargaining agreement); Hayssen Mfg. Co., 82 LA 500 (Flaten, 1984). *But see* General Tel. Co. of Cal., 89 LA 867 (Collins, 1987) ("Supervisor's Guide to Successful Labor Relations" issued by the company to supervisors not binding on the company absent contractual provision to that effect).

[318]Geauga Co., 92 LA 54 (Fullmer, 1988) (company was accused of manipulating overtime and recall—but within the terms of the agreement—so as to terminate the seniority of employees on layoff more than 24 months).

[319]City of Evansdale, Iowa, 92 LA 688, 691 (Miller, 1989).

[320]City of Hartford, Conn., 97 LA 1016 (Freedman, 1991). *See also* CCair, Inc., 106 LA 56 (Nolan, 1995) (oral modification of agreement under the RLA).

some criticism), held, "[N]or will this arbitrator look to any such awards for any guidance or understanding, based upon the experience of others in unlike situations under dissimilar conditions."[322]

8. Unjust Enrichment

The principle of unjust enrichment holds that "one shall not unjustly enrich himself at the expense of another."[323] One arbitrator elaborated:

> The general principle of unjust enrichment is that one person should not be permitted to enrich himself unjustly at the expense of another, but the party so enriched should be required to make restitution for property or benefits received, where it is just and equitable, and where such action involves no violation or frustration of the law.[324]

This doctrine has been applied in some arbitration cases.[325]

The "unjustly at the expense of another" element is not always present when a person receives an apparent "windfall." Thus, in the absence of a contractual provision to the contrary, an arbitrator upheld the right of a family to double insurance coverage because separate insurance programs furnished by their separate employers covered both spouses. The double family benefit was a legitimate result of the family's double employment.[326] In some cases, it may well be considered improper for an individual to secure double benefits, as where an employee secured unemployment compensa-

---

[321]Phillips 66 Co. Rail Car Maint. Ctr., 93 LA 707 (Goodstein, 1989).

[322]*Id.* at 712.

[323]Bouvier's Law Dictionary 3376 (8th ed. 1984).

[324]Cyclops Corp., 51 LA 613, 616 (Marshall, 1968) (reliance on the doctrine "must be supported by clear and convincing evidence," which did not exist in this case). Where the employer has an obligation to recover public money paid erroneously, deduction will be allowed. City of Midwest City, Okla., 109 LA 1112 (Baroni, 1998).

[325]KSTW-TV, 111 LA 94 (Lundberg, 1998) (seller must pay employees severance at asset sale where the contract tied severance pay to longevity). *See also* Village Meats, 91 LA 1023, 1026 (Shanker, 1988); Aeolian Corp., 72 LA 1178, 1180 (Eyraud, Jr., 1979); General Tire & Rubber Co., 71 LA 813, 816 (Richman, 1978); Cudahy Packing Co., 51 LA 822, 835 (Somers, 1968); Memphis Publ'g Co., 48 LA 931, 933 (Cantor, 1967). In *American Maize Products Co.*, 37 LA 673, 675 (Sembower, 1961), the employer was required to pay an employee under the "quantum meruit" principle for the value of services performed by the employee, where the employer knew of it and did nothing to halt the work. *See also* Stockton, Cal., Unified Sch. Dist., 89 LA 754, 759 (Gallagher, 1987). *Cf.* McDonnell Douglas Helicopter Co., 93 LA 429, 433 (Cloke, 1989); City of Chi., 91 LA 1077, 1078 (Cox, 1988).

[326]Hawthorn-Mellody Farms, 52 LA 557, 560–61 (Kates, 1969). *Accord* Safeway Stores, 114 LA 1551 (DiFalco, 2000); Meadow Gold Dairies, 110 LA 865 (Bognanno, 1998); Potlatch Forests, 51 LA 589, 592 (Williams, 1968); Associated Gen. Contractors of Am. (Akron, Ohio, Chapter), 67–1 ARB ¶8390 (Nichols, 1967); Goodyear Atomic Corp., 66–2 ARB ¶8567 (Seinsheimer, 1966). *Cf.* McDonnell Aircraft Corp., 68–1 ARB ¶6210 (Bothwell, 1967); Massachusetts Leather Mfrs. Ass'n, 41 LA 1321, 1322 (Wallen, 1962). For cases in which a "coordination of benefits" provision was present so as to prevent double benefits, see *C.H. Stuart & Co.*, 54 LA 335, 337 (Shister, 1971); *George L. Mesker Steel Corp.*, 47 LA 1142, 1149 (Klamon, 1967); *Babcock & Wilcox Co.*, 39 LA 136, 138 (Uible, 1962); *Minnesota Mining & Mfg. Co.*, 38 LA 245, 248 (Graff, 1962). For cases involving the scope of coverage where both spouses are employed by the same company, see *Union Welding Co.*, 49 LA 612, 612 (Blistein, 1967); *Minnesota Mining & Mfg. Co.*, 32 LA 843, 847 (Thompson, 1959).

tion covering a period for which he also received workers' compensation.[327] Similarly, an employer was not entitled to retain a windfall, even though the result was a double payment to the employee.[328]

The principle of unjust enrichment will not be applied in the absence of fraud, duress, mistake,[329] or other inequitable condition. So it was that an employer, although enriched by an employee's handiwork, was held not to have been unjustly enriched.[330]

Arbitrators have used the principle of unjust enrichment to deny back pay to a reinstated employee in a discharge case.[331] Compensation for overtime hours not worked was denied on similar grounds, there being no evidence the employer had not acted in good faith in reducing hours of "overtime shifts."[332]

9. WAIVER AND ESTOPPEL

Frequently, one party to a collective bargaining agreement will charge that the other party has waived or is estopped from asserting a right under the agreement.[333] Arbitrators generally do not appear to be concerned with all of the legal distinctions between the term "waiver" and the term "estoppel," but they have often applied the underlying principle to reach a "fair and just" result.[334]

---

[327]National Union Elec. Corp., 77 LA 815, 818–19 (Traynor, 1981). Also denying entitlement to double benefits, see *Supervalu, Inc.*, 114 LA 677 (Greco, 2000) (employee to repay unemployment and employer to give back pay for that period of time); *Bethlehem Steel Corp.*, 73 LA 264, 266 (Strongin, 1979); *Louisiana-Pacific Corp.*, 68 LA 638, 643–44 (Kenaston, 1977); *Consolidated Aluminum Corp.*, 62 LA 480, 481 (Williams, 1974).

[328]LB&B Assocs., 114 LA 865 (Harris, Jr., 2000). Generally, however, the concept of double compensation of the same benefit to an employee is so unusual as to require clear and unequivocal contract language. AirTran Airways, 114 LA 897 (Sergent, 2000) (denying windfall to employees). The concept of a windfall is not appropriately applied to pay for attendance at a disciplinary meeting that presumably benefited the employer as well as the employee, who attended on his day off. County of St. Clair, Ill., Sheriff's Dep't, 114 LA 1557 (Goldstein, 2000).

[329]Mistake, alone, will not serve to support an adjustment, where one party relied on the mistaken enrichment to ratify the agreement. San Jose/Evergreen, Cal., Cmty. Coll. Dist., 111 LA 892 (Staudohar, 1998) (mutual mistake in including a wage reopener was relied on by employees in ratifying the contract and thus was upheld).

[330]In *City of Conneaut, Ohio*, 112 LA 899, 903 (Richard, 1999), the arbitrator recognized, "A deal is a deal," and found the union estopped from asserting that supervisors who "assist" briefly are "working." *See also* Dunn Coal & Dock Co., 110 LA 798 (Feldman, 1998) (resignation by employee waived right to grieve termination); Amherst Coal Co., 84 LA 1181, 1184 (Wren, 1985).

[331]Smurfit Recycling Co., 103 LA 243, 248 (Richman, 1994). The purpose for deducting interim earnings from a back-pay award is to make whole without double-dipping. Quaker Oats Co., 110 LA 204 (Moreland IV, 1998).

[332]Ohio Edison Co., 102 LA 717, 726 (Sergent, 1994). *See also* University Med. Ctr., 114 LA 28 (Bogue, 2000) (award of overtime pay is too speculative).

[333]For related discussion, see Chapter 5, section 5.C., "Waiver of Procedural Requirements and Substantive Rights."

[334]Simeus Foods Int'l, 114 LA 436 (Moreland IV, 2000) (no waiver, mutual delay); Archer Daniels Midland Co., 111 LA 518 (Pratte, 1998) (same); Ryder Truck Rental, 96 LA 1080, 1084 (Gibson, 1991). For an excellent discussion of the differences among waiver, estoppel, laches, and past practice, see *City of Great Falls, Mont.*, 88 LA 396, 399–400 (McCurdy, 1986). *See also* Health Care & Ret. Corp., 99 LA 916, 917–20 (Hockenberry, 1992) (detrimental reliance); Arch of W. Va., 97 LA 479, 482–83 (Tranen, 1991) (rendering performance

A. Estoppel [LA CDI 24.78]

"Estoppel" or "equitable estoppel" is a "defensive doctrine preventing one party from taking unfair advantage of another when, through false languge or conduct, the person to be estopped has induced another person to act in a certain way, with the result that the other person has been injured in some way."[335] The scope of estoppel claims in arbitration cases continues to grow.[336]

---

impossible); Dalfort Aviation Servs., 96 LA 520, 523–524 (Nicholas, Jr., 1991) (doctrine of essential fairness); General Mills, 95 LA 1060, 1062–63 (Klein, 1990) (forfeiture); Purity Baking Co., 95 LA 172, 177–78 (Gordon, 1990) (reliance on expectancy); NorStat, Inc., 94 LA 676, 680 (Bittel, 1990) (expectation of predictability); Jenison, Mich., Pub. Sch., 94 LA 545, 554–55 (Roumell, Jr., 1990) (detrimental reliance); Westvaco Corp., 94 LA 165, 167 (Duff, 1990) (forfeiture); City of Paducah, Ky., 94 LA 154, 156–57 (Daniel, 1990) (same); City of Pontiac, 94 LA 14, 16 (Daniel, 1989) (same); Connecticut State Bd. of Educ., 93 LA 1033, 1037 (Sacks, 1989) (same); Atlanta Wire Works, 93 LA 537, 543 (Williams, 1989) (lured into false sense of security); Rolling Acres Care Ctr., 91 LA 795, 799–800 (Dworkin, 1988); Michigan Bell Tel. Co., 90 LA 1186 (Howlett, 1988); Big V Supermarkets, 90 LA 848, 850 (Goldsmith, 1987); Fleming Foods of Mo., 89 LA 1292 (Yarowsky, 1987); Lennox Indus., 89 LA 1065 (Gibson, 1987); City of Dearborn, Mich., 89 LA 766 (Ellmann, 1987); Waller Bros. Stone Co., 89 LA 600, 603 (Graham, 1987); U.S. Steel Corp., 89 LA 300 (Dybeck, 1987); Reyco Indus., 81 LA 1133 (Rohlik, 1983); W-L Molding Co., 76 LA 190, 194 (Beitner, 1981); Riley Gear Corp., 69 LA 1186, 1188 (Goodman, 1977); Michigan Gas & Elec. Co., 45 LA 85, 90 (Fallon, 1965); Jaeger Mach. Co., 43 LA 901, 906 (Stouffer, 1964); Jones & Laughlin Steel Corp., 22 LA 270, 272–73 (Cahn, 1954) (where union elects to treat job as "new" for one purpose, it is "new" for all purposes); Staley Milling Co., 21 LA 300, 306 (Klamon, 1953); General Cable Corp., 20 LA 406, 408 (Hays, 1953); National Malleable & Steel Castings Co., 4 LA 110, 111–12 (Blair, 1946).

[335] Black's Law Dictionary 571 (7th ed. 1999). "Equitable estoppel" is distinguishable from "promisory estoppel," which is defined as the doctrine that "a promise made without consideration may nevertheless be enforced to prevent injustice if the promisor should have reasonably expected the promisee to rely on the promise and if the promisee did actually rely on the promise to his or her detriment." *Id.*

[336] *See* Central Hudson Gas & Elec. Corp., 101 LA 894, 898–99 (Eischen, 1993); Ralphs Grocery Co., 94 LA 880, 885 (Kaufman, 1990). Cases pro and con involving claims of "equitable" estoppel include: Mead Prods., 114 LA 1753 (Nathan, 2000) (where parties agreed on effects of ADA in bumping rights in limited instance, union was estopped from bringing just that limited issue to arbitration but was not estopped either from challenging the effects of the narrow agreement or from overbroad application by the employer to other employees when an employee complained); Michigan Milk Producers Ass'n, 114 LA 1652 (Allen, 2000) (pay shortage owed to date of constructive discovery); Township of Copley, Ohio, 114 LA 1189 (Shanker, 2000) (employer estopped from refusing to process grievances where official gave employees wrong date of filing); City of Claremore, Okla., 114 LA 936 (Crider, 2000) (employer cannot vest authority in fire chief and then deny he can bind city in labor matters); Chicago Sch. Reform Bd. of Trs., 114 LA 932 (Cohen, 2000) (estopped by silence); Palm Beach, Fla., County Sch. Bd., 114 LA 780 (Richard, 2000) (action excused, where other party failed to provide critical information to permit the action); United Int'l Investigative Serv., 114 LA 620 (Maxwell, 2000) (estoppel by silence); USS, Div. of USX Corp., 112 LA 227 (Das, 1998) (union is equitably estopped from using delay of grievance to prevent employer from taking on a project); S. Rosenthal & Co., 111 LA 1148 (Talarico, 1998) (erroneously given benefit may be withdrawn where employee experienced no detrimental reliance); Westvaco Corp., 111 LA 887 (Nicholas, Jr., 1998) (union failed to perfect second prong of grievance at many turns); University of Minn., 111 LA 774 (Daly, 1998) (diminution of award equitable); State of Iowa, 111 LA 262 (Kohn, 1998) (grievance denied despite misstatement by employer representative at Step 3 of grievance); Wilmette, Ill., Sch. Dist. 39, 111 LA 15 (Wolff, 1998) (estopped by silence); Goodman Beverage Co., 108 LA 37, 42 (Morgan, Jr., 1997) (employer was precluded from canceling the vacation of an employee who had paid for reservations in advance when there was no contractual provision authorizing the employer to alter vacation schedule); Johnson Controls World Servs., 108 LA 191, 192 (Specht, 1996) (on equitable grounds short of full estoppel, union was prohibited from challenging layoff and work guar-

The following cases are illustrative. During contract negotiations, a company that gave an oral assurance that it would limit the number of employees the company would reclassify in order to induce the union to agree on a contract and end a strike was held estopped and bound to observe the assurance, because the union had changed its position to its detriment in reliance on the assurance.[337]

---

antee actions by employer that union had helped implement); International Paper Co., 101 LA 278, 281 (Duff, 1993) (estoppel against company denied, there being no proof of detrimental reliance by the employees); General Refractories Co., 99 LA 311 (Richard, 1992); Indianapolis Water Co., 96 LA 530, 534 (Heekin, 1990); Williams Natural Gas Co., 93 LA 223, 227 (White, 1989). One arbitrator found no estoppel by what the union told the employees before ratification. Quadcom 9-1-1 Pub. Safety Communications Sys., 113 LA 987 (Goldstein, 1999).

Claims of "promissory" estoppel cases include: Kolar Buick, 101 LA 29, 32 (Miller, 1993); Red Wing Shoe Co., 98 LA 329, 333 (Jacobowski, 1992); Fairview Southdale Hosp., 96 LA 1129, 1136 (Flagler, 1991); Watauga Indus., 95 LA 613, 616 (Kilroy, 1990); Peoria, Ill., Sch. Dist. 150, 95 LA 329, 337 (Draznin, 1990); Willamette Indus., 94 LA 555, 559 (Perone, 1990); Central States, Southeast & Southwest Areas Health & Welfare Fund, 91 LA 701, 704 (McAlpin, 1988) (employer bound by commitment made during negotiations); Jim Walter Res., 87 LA 857, 862 (Nicholas, Jr., 1986) (representation to retirees at exit interview that they had insurance for life); Armco, Inc., 86 LA 928, 929 (Seidman, 1985) (medical treatment undertaken in reliance on personnel department official's assurance of plan coverage; theory of promissory estoppel prevents company from denying coverage that was otherwise properly denied). See also Consolidation Coal Co., 99 LA 945, 949 (Dissen, 1992) (promissory estoppel for misleading grievant in employer's investigation requires that grievant's admission be excised, but there is other evidence of his sleeping on the job); McCorkle Mach. Shop, 97 LA 774, 776 (Kilroy, 1991) (employer estopped from discharge of employee who was led to believe in discussion of incident that no disciplinary action would result); Chambers & Owen, 96 LA 152, 154–55 (Redel, 1991) (employer bound by representation to union concerning insurance benefits). But see Michigan Dep't of Soc. Servs., 87 LA 398, 403 (Frost, 1986) (no detrimental reliance where no dental treatment was undertaken in reliance on insurance coverage); Keebler Co., 86 LA 963, 966–67 (Nolan, 1986) (denying estoppel where no substantial and detrimental reliance shown). See also City of Santa Cruz, Cal., 107 LA 1053, 1056 (Staudohar, 1996) (employer was not estopped from enforcing employee residency requirement); Triton Coll., 107 LA 796, 797–800 (Greco, 1996) (employer estopped on theory of detrimental reliance to deny agreement granting employee time to reconsider and retract resignation); Kansas City, Mo., Fire Dep't, 107 LA 519, 523–26 (Berger, 1996) (employer estopped from contending condition of settlement agreement in discipline case had not been met); Ogden Fairmount, Inc., 105 LA 492, 499 (O'Grady, 1995) (union estopped from challenging hiring practice adopted at its behest and from which it had benefited for more than a year); WorldSource Coil Coating, 102 LA 17, 22–23 (Florman, 1993) (employer was not estopped from denying bumping qualifications of employees despite earlier instances where bumps were permitted and despite presumption of qualification); Army & Air Force Exch. Serv., 101 LA 1173, 1176 (Marlatt, 1993) (federal agency estopped from claiming cost of preparing grievance on matter that was already moot); City of Novi, Mich., 101 LA 1028, 1030 (Brown, 1993) (union not estopped to challenge new leave policy when applied even though it had not done so when the policy was promulgated); Indiana Gas Co., 88 LA 666, 669 (Seidman, 1987); City of Depere, 86 LA 733, 734 (Greco, 1986); Pennsylvania Bureau of Labor Relations, 77 LA 438, 442–43 (Dunn, 1981); City of San Jose, Cal., Fire Dep't, 76 LA 732, 735 (Concepcion, 1981); Monarch Mach. Tool Co., 74 LA 854, 856 (Gibson, 1980); Pacific Tel. & Tel. Co., 73 LA 448, 455 (Marcus, 1979); Ohio State Univ., 69 LA 1004, 1011 (Bell, 1977); Town of Waterford, Conn., 68 LA 735, 737 (Sacks, 1977); Continental Distilling Sales Co., 52 LA 1138, 1141 (Sembower, 1969) (issue was decided on the basis of estoppel); Fox Mfg. Co., 47 LA 97, 101–02 (Marshall, 1966) (there was an express waiver of certain rights for the future).

[337]International Harvester Co., 17 LA 101, 103 (McCoy, 1951). See also Gross Mfg. Corp., 68 LA 1248, 1252 (Ruben, 1977); Master Builders' Ass'n, 48 LA 865, 867 (Kates, 1967); Collins Radio Co., 36 LA 15, 17 (Schedler, 1961); International Harvester Co., 18 LA 306, 307 (Forrester, 1952). But see County of Wayne, 71 LA 864, 868–69 (Roumell, Jr., 1978); County of Santa Clara, Cal., 71 LA 751, 754 (Barsamian, 1978); Bartelt Eng'g Co., 51 LA 582, 588 (Sembower, 1968); Hoover Chem. Prods. Div., 48 LA 373, 376–77 (Keefe, 1967); Del E. Webb Corp., 48 LA 164, 166–67 (Koven, 1967); Dixie-Portland Flour Mills, 46 LA 838, 840–41 (Hon, 1966).

However, where, based on an assumed settlement the union did not sign, a company had reinstated a discharged worker who had been off work for 1 day, the union was not estopped from proceeding with the grievance for the day's pay, because no fully executed settlement existed.[338]

Public employers, under proper circumstances, and where equity would require, also may be bound by the doctrine of equitable estoppel when they act as employers and engage in the collective bargaining process.[339]

B. Waiver[340] [LA CDI 24.78]

"Waiver" is defined as the voluntary relinquishment or abandonment—expressed or implied—of a legal right and requires that the party alleged to have waived a right must have had both knowledge of the existing right and the intention of foregoing it.[341]

There can be no waiver of a contract right without knowledge that the right is being abridged.[342]

Especially common in arbitration is that species of waiver known in law as "acquiescence."[343] This term denotes a waiver that arises by tacit consent or by failure of a person for an unreasonable length of time to act on rights of which the person has full knowledge.[344] While arbitrators generally hold that acquiescence by one party to violations of an express rule by the other party precludes action about past transactions,[345] they do not consider that acqui-

---

[338]Buckeye Steel Casting Co., 92 LA 630 (Fullmer, 1989).

[339]City of Reno, Nev., 87 LA 707, 713 (Richman, 1986).

[340]See also Chapter 5, section 5.C., "Waiver of Procedural Requirements and Substantive Rights," and section 7.A.iv., "Waiver of Time Limits."

[341]BLACK'S LAW DICTIONARY (7th ed. 1999).

[342]University Med. Ctr., 114 LA 28 (Bogue, 2000); City of Miami, 89 LA 86, 90 (Abrams, 1987).

[343]The "acquiescence" of a fire chief in paying annual clothing allowances in the past to firefighters retiring before the allowance due date was not a mistake but a continuation of a long, mutually accepted practice. City of Elyria, Ohio, 106 LA 268, 271 (Fullmer, 1996). The union acquiesced in past practice application of attendance policy where it failed to grieve practice and a prior warning on same issue. Alkar Div., 111 LA 944 (Dichter, 1998); Colonial Baking Co., 32 LA 193, 199 (Piercey, 1959) (acquiescence in failure to pay contractual overtime premium); Pacific Am. Shipowners Ass'n, 10 LA 736, 746 (Miller, 1948).

[344]One arbitrator distinguished acquiescence (ratification by mere silence) from estoppel (binding a party by its words or actions) and concluded that ratification by "mere silence" is not favored. FMC Corp., 114 LA 1771 (Suardi, 2000). Nine years of subcontracting while the union stood by waived the right to grieve. Consolidation Coal Co., 111 LA 587 (Jenks, 1998). Another arbitrator decided evidence presented was not sufficient to prove the union had full knowledge of the facts and had "acquiesced" in a practice used by the employer to fill vacancies during layoff periods; hence, the union had not waived its right to grieve the matter. General Tel. Co. of Cal., 106 LA 1043, 1048 (Grabuskie, 1996). An arbitrator recognized that a union's failure to bring a prior grievance may be based on various factors and is not, necessarily, acquiescence. Lackawanna Leather, 113 LA 603 (Pelofsky, 1999). For a "tacit acquiescence" case involving the absence of contract language despite the presence of a "zipper clause," see City of Frederick, Okla., 106 LA 298, 303 (Neas, 1996).

[345]Coos-Curry Elec. Coop., 111 LA 47 (Calhoun, 1998) (failure to enforce rule against alcohol precluded enforcement in this case, where employer knew of prior transgressions and failed to act); Peabody Coal Co., 82 LA 1251, 1258 (Roberts, 1984); Port Drum Co., 82 LA 942, 944 (Holman, 1984); Servicecare, Inc., 82 LA 590, 592–93 (Talarico, 1984). But even where a contract permits the union to challenge a work rule, the union does not waive that right by waiting for application of the rule before filing a grievance. Mayflower Vehicle Sys., 114 LA 1249 (Franckiewicz, 2000).

escence precludes application of the rule to future conduct.[346] Arbitrators may consider the failure to act on a right given by a contract, as well as other

---

[346]A company that apparently had acquiesced in a long-past practice of nonenforcement of an "early quit" rule advised the union of its intent to enforce the rule and posted notice accordingly, thus repudiating acquiescence and past practice. No waiver was found where the employer's variation in practice was slight. Conoco, Inc., 114 LA 921 (Florman, 2000); Globe Indus., 110 LA 379 (Imundo, Jr., 1998) (no waiver despite union acquiescence in past). It was held that the company had not waived its rulemaking rights and did not have to reach mutual agreement with the union to enforce this rule. Michigan Hanger Co., 106 LA 377, 380 (Smith, 1996).

A number of decisions have addressed the issue of waiver caused by not objecting to or grieving action at an earlier opportunity. For example, a union was deemed not to have waived the right to grieve a new tipping policy for some employees even though a similar policy had been in effect for others without objection for several years. ITT Sheraton/Sheraton Bal Harbour Resort, 102 LA 903, 908–09 (Hoffman, 1994). A union was held not to have waived its right to challenge a new layoff point system by waiting until it was used by the employer. Wilson Trophy Co., 104 LA 529, 532 (Suardi, 1995). *See also Mayflower Vehicle Sys.*, 114 LA 1249; Excel Corp., 106 LA 1069, 1071–72 (Thornell, 1996) (a health care cost containment change made unilaterally by the employer, where several earlier changes had not been grieved); New Orleans S.S. Ass'n, 105 LA 79, 85 (Nicholas, Jr., 1995) (a random testing drug policy where 20 other employees had been tested earlier without protest). In *Clorox Co.*, 103 LA 932, 939 (Franckiewicz, 1994), it was held that the right to grieve a work standard was not waived by dropping earlier grievances, where the purpose of dropping those grievances could not be determined. Likewise, failure to challenge a subsequent breach does not negate a union's ability to bring the case at hand. U.S. Sugar Corp., 112 LA 967 (Chandler, 1999).

A claim of waiver under a "zipper-clause" was denied in *City of Cleveland, Ohio*, 106 LA 195, 201 (Cohen, 1995). For a discussion of the view of the NLRB on zipper-clause waivers, see *Southern Bag Corp.*, 108 LA 348, 352–54 (Overstreet, 1997). *See also* Shelby, Ohio, City Sch. Dist., 112 LA 97 (Goldberg, 1999); California Neon Prods., 91 LA 485, 489 (Kaufman, 1988); Crown, Cork & Seal, 88 LA 145, 149 (Keefe, 1986); Fire Dep't, County of L.A., Cal., 76 LA 572, 575 (Rule, 1981); Furnitureland, 76 LA 71, 75 (Ruben, 1981); Neville Chem. Co., 73 LA 405, 409 (Richman, 1979); County of Orange, 70 LA 1172, 1174 (Dennis, 1978); Cooper Bessemer Corp., 50 LA 829, 831–32 (Howlett, 1968); Sinclair Mfg. Co., 49 LA 310, 313 (Nichols, 1967); Anaconda Aluminum Co., 48 LA 219, 222–23 (Allen, 1967); Coakley Bros. Co., 47 LA 356, 362–63 (Anderson, 1966); Courier-Citizen Co., 42 LA 269, 272 (Myers, 1964); Bethlehem Steel Co., 36 LA 162, 164 (Seward, 1961); Higgins, Inc., 24 LA 750, 752 (Morvant, 1955); Texas-New Mexico Pipe Line Co., 17 LA 90, 91–92 (Emery, 1951); Durham Hosiery Mills, 12 LA 311, 316 (Maggs, 1949); Merrill-Stevens Dry Dock & Repair Co., 10 LA 562, 563 (Douglas, 1948); International Harvester Co., 9 LA 484, 490–91 (Courshon, 1947); Chrysler Corp., 5 LA 333, 336 (Wolff, 1946); Goodyear Tire & Rubber Co., 4 LA 231, 233 (McCoy, 1946). For other cases reflecting these principles, see materials on continuing violations and on negligent delay in filing grievances in Chapter 5, section 7., "Time Limitations."

An employer that failed to repudiate a prior memorandum of agreement during bargaining waived any right to argue that the subsequent contract negated it. Weyerhaeuser Co., 114 LA 1477 (Neas, 2000). *See also* KSTW-TV, 111 LA 94 (Lundberg, 1998) (prior grievance raised and abandoned does not constitute waiver of enforcement of rights by union); Powdertech Corp., 110 LA 880 (Doering, 1998) (employer retains right to assign overtime in absence of volunteers); Port of Seattle, 110 LA 753 (Skratek, 1998) (union's allowing a supervisor to perform unit work in a time of personnel shortage does not waive the right to challenge assignment of unit work in the future); Glidden Co., 96 LA 195, 196–97 (Levy, 1990); Del Monte Corp., 86 LA 134, 138 (Denson, 1985) (requiring union notice to company if union intends to enforce a right that it had failed for some time to enforce); Houston Publisher's Ass'n, 83 LA 767, 775 (Milentz, 1984); City of Gainesville, Fla., 82 LA 825, 829 (Hall, 1984); L&O Growers Ass'n, 82 LA 814, 816 (Weiss, 1984).

Where unauthorized work stoppages were a direct violation of the contract, the fact that the employer "sat on its rights" was not a waiver but rather an exercise of its right to manage operations and direct the workforce, and enforcement of the attendance policy was upheld. Cannelton Indus., 111 LA 913 (Harlan, 1998). There is no acquiescence where a business agent of one union fails to assert rights belonging to another local. Allegro Carting, 111 LA 152 (Henner, 1998).

evidence, to establish the intent of the parties in agreeing to general language, such as a broad management-rights clause.[347]

Questions of timeliness in the pursuit of grievance and arbitration procedures continue to be a major source of arbitral decisions on waiver issues. The failure to act on a timely basis has been held to be a waiver.[348] However, there are a number of cases rejecting claims of waiver.[349] An employer may

---

[347]Tecumseh, Mich., Bd. of Educ., 82 LA 609, 613 (Daniel, 1984). For a comprehensive discussion on the effect of broad management-rights clauses in the face of a change in work rules, see *Russell Div.*, 114 LA 107 (Solomon, 2000). Past practice has been given varying effect. *See* Atlantic City Showboat, 113 LA 530 (Zirkel, 1999) (in absence of a zipper clause or strong management-rights clause regarding a right to change work assignments, union correctly relied on past practice of assignment of work in resisting a change). *Contra* Earthgrains Co., 112 LA 170 (Grooms, Jr., 1999) (no contract violation with unilateral changes in employees' work schedules directly controverting years of past practice); Finch, Pruyn & Co., 111 LA 1 (Babiskin, 1998) (employer retains right to change job classes even with zipper clause). Noncompliance is not a waiver of clear contract language. Montour, Pa., Sch. Dist., 114 LA 1150 (Duff, 2000).

[348]Federal Bureau of Prisons, Sheridan, Or., 114 LA 1126 (Gangle, 2000) (continuing violation discussed and distinguished); City of Solon, Ohio, 114 LA 321 (Oberdank, 2000) (effect of amending grievance); Delta Beverage Group, 114 LA 284 (Chandler, 2000) (timeliness of grievance); Chicago Transit Auth., 113 LA 912 (Wolff, 1999) (person reviewing evidence); City of Anadarko, Okla., 113 LA 559 (Baroni, 1999) (timeliness of grievance); Village of Bourbannais, Ill., 113 LA 332 (Traynor, 1999) (arbitrability); Montgomery County, Ohio, Children's Servs. Bd., 112 LA 974 (Paolucci, 1999) (appropriateness of grievance); Salem City, Ohio, Sch., 112 LA 929 (Richard, 1999) (timeliness and presentation to proper person); Safeway Stores, 112 LA 562 (Snow, 1999) (timeliness); Raytheon Sys. Co., 111 LA 1002 (Prayzich, 1999) (same); Independent Sch. Dist. 23, Frazee, Minn., 110 LA 1117 (Daly, 1998) (employer failed to meet three-part test to allow theory of continuing violation); Georgia-Pacific Corp., 110 LA 269 (Oestreich, 1998) (timeliness of grievance); Monroe Mfg., 107 LA 877, 879 (Stephens, 1996) (advancing grievance to next step in procedure); District of Columbia Pub. Sch., 105 LA 1037, 1038 (Johnson, 1995) (adding subject at arbitration step); Schuykill Metals Corp., 102 LA 253, 254 (O'Grady, 1994) (right to arbitrate); Summit County, Ohio, Eng'rs Office, 101 LA 368, 372 (Morgan, Jr., 1993) (filing of grievance).

[349]Sprint/Central Tel. Co.-Nev., 114 LA 633 (Baroni, 2000) (time limits unclear); Simeus Foods Int'l, 114 LA 436 (Moreland IV, 2000) (timeliness of answer); UNICCO Serv. Co., 114 LA 345 (Kohler, 2000) (settlement); Interstate Brands Corp., 114 LA 334 (Paolucci, 2000) (continuing violation); Housing Auth. of Louisville, 112 LA 839 (Krislov, 1999) (right to grieve lack of annual review not forfeited); Montana Power Co., 112 LA 818 (Henner, 1999) (timeliness); Georgia-Pacific Corp., 112 LA 474 (Landau, 1999) (employer's missing deadlines will not waive defense); City of Joliet, Ill., 112 LA 468 (Perkovich, 1999) (grievance not arbitrated within 60 days is not forfeited); Willow Run, Mich., Cmty. Sch., 112 LA 115 (Brodsky, 1999) (timeliness of grievance); Danis-Shook Joint Venture No. 25, 111 LA 1095 (Klein, 1999) (mutual noncompliance); Lyondell-Citgo Ref. Co., 111 LA 1033 (Halter, 1999) (sequence of arbitrations was not a past practice); Rainbo Baking Co., 111 LA 948 (Grabuskie, 1999) (timeliness evidence "murky"); Johnstown Wire Techs., 111 LA 216 (Franckiewicz, 1998) (employer failure to follow procedures); Los Angeles Cmty. Coll. Dist., 110 LA 13 (Gentile, 1998) (parallel grievance preserved union's rights); Township of Redford, Mich., 109 LA 1136 (Mackraz, 1998) (mutual informal discussions); Michigan Capital Med. Ctr., 106 LA 893, 895–96 (Mackraz, 1996) (lack of knowledge of work schedules of employees subject to bumping); Department of Veterans Affairs Med. Ctr., 103 LA 74, 77–79 (Gentile, 1994) (joint waiver by implied consent); Jim Walter Res., 101 LA 385, 387–88 (Feldman, 1993) (a joint waiver). There are also cases in which a claim of waiver through untimeliness was rejected, but the claiming party won on the merits. Stevens County, Minn., 105 LA 500, 505 (Jacobowski, 1995) (step requirements); Department of the Air Force, 102 LA 525, 530 (Cipolla, 1994) (filing of grievance); City of Richmond, Cal., 102 LA 373, 375–76 (Riker, 1994) (arbitrability of subject). An employer is not required to raise defenses early in the grievance procedure, because the union has the burden of proving a contract violation. Sheriff of Cook County, Ill., 110 LA 777 (Wolff, 1998). *See also* Indiana Hosp., 110 LA 693 (Dean, Jr., 1998) (failure to raise defense early is too harsh in new bargaining relationship).

not stipulate to arbitrability and then raise timeliness,[350] and a denial based on timeliness may be defeated where the merits are discussed later without expressly preserving the timeliness challenge,[351] or where the parties agreed to hold a grievance in abeyance pending bargaining.[352] However, processing a grievance does not waive a timeliness argument, where the objection is expressly preserved.[353]

In many cases, a claim of procedural waiver has been denied because the claim was first advanced at arbitration or at an advanced grievance step.[354] As one arbitrator recognized:

> Parties often evolve their own system for dealing with grievances, at variance with the literal terms of their collective bargaining agreement. Of course, parties are free to modify or waive the requirements of their agreement. Once such a change has evolved, either party may still insist that the literal requirements of the agreement be followed. But if it decides to so insist, it must give advance warning to the other party of its intent to demand strict adherence to the terms of agreement, lest the other party be "sandbagged" by its reliance on the assumption that the actual practice, rather than the literal terms, would continue in effect.[355]

---

[350]Simeus Foods Int'l, 114 LA 436 (Moreland IV, 2000); Georgia-Pacific Corp., 112 LA 474 (Landau, 1999); Aerospace Cmty. Credit Union, 112 LA 58 (Kelly, 1999); Mission Foods, 111 LA 501 (Snider, 1998).

[351]Whayne Supply Co., 111 LA 940 (Imundo, Jr., 1998).

[352]Union Camp Corp., 110 LA 820 (Nicholas, Jr., 1998).

[353]Island County, Wash., 113 LA 104 (Stuteville, 1999) (a waiver of grievance timeliness is generally an amendment to the parties' contract and should be in writing).

[354]Town of Ossining, N.Y., 114 LA 1761 (Henner, 2000) (post-hearing brief too late to raise timeliness of grievance); O'Bleness Mem'l Hosp., 114 LA 1601 (Fullmer, 2000) (employer's noncompliance with informal first step); Richland County, Ohio, Dep't of Human Servs., 114 LA 1416 (Brodsky, 2000) (failure to sign grievance); City of Centralia, Wash., 114 LA 929 (Smith, 2000) (timeliness of grievance); Corn Prods. Int'l, 114 LA 415 (Petersen, 2000) (untimely discipline); Tubetech, Inc., 113 LA 1025 (Richard, 1999) (matters of procedural arbitrability must be raised at first opportunity or are waived); Columbia Gas Transmission Corp., 112 LA 571 (Sergent, 1999) (employer not decisionmaker); Crestline, Ohio, Exempted Village Sch., 111 LA 114 (Goldberg, 1998) (continuing grievance); Southern Cal. Gas Co., 110 LA 1029 (Kaufman, 1998) (timeliness of filing); International Paper, 110 LA 250 (Paolucci, 1998) (timeliness of grievance); City of Roswell, N.M., 109 LA 1153 (Wyman, 1998) (failure to sign grievance); Antilles Consol. Sch. Sys., Fort Buchanan, P.R., 109 LA 1070 (Bressler, 1998) (timeliness of grievance); Georgia Pac. Corp., 107 LA 182 (Cocalis, 1996) (timeliness of grievance); Lake, Ohio, Local Bd. of Educ., 108 LA 236, 241 (Fullmer, 1997) (election of remedies); City of Fairbanks, Alaska, 105 LA 903, 912 (Landau, 1995) (existence of prior pending grievance on same subject without objection); Licking County, Ohio, Sheriff's Office, 105 LA 824, 828–29 (Paolucci, 1995) (use of grievance forms); Stevens County, Minn., 105 LA 500, 505 (Jacobowski, 1995) (step requirements); Stone Container Corp., 105 LA 385, 389 (Berquist, 1995) (timeliness of grievance); Defense Logistics Agency, 104 LA 439, 442 (Gentile, 1995) (notification requirements); Masolite Concrete Prods., 103 LA 10, 14 (Keenan, 1994) (demand for arbitration); City of Sterling Heights, Mich., 102 LA 1067, 1070 (Daniel, 1994) (arbitrability); Sorg Paper Co., 102 LA 289, 290 (Cohen, 1993) (late filing of grievances).

Occasionally, an issue raised for the first time at hearing is allowed. City of Claremore, Okla., 114 LA 936 (Crider, 2000) (union permitted to present evidence of past practice where employer was neither surprised nor prejudiced).

[355]City of Akron, 111 LA 705, 708 (Franckiewicz, 1998). Withdrawal of a waiver of timeliness must be specific and unambiguous. Highland County, Ohio, Sheriff's Dep't, 114 LA 204 (Keenan, 1999) (notice of intent to arbitrate, above, was not sufficient to withdraw).

It also has been held that the similar doctrine of laches—unreasonable delay by one party that may prejudice another—did not bar a claim by a retiring public employee for sick leave credit earned 20 years earlier while he was employed by other public entities.[356] Rather, laches may apply to overcome specific contract language where procedural timelines are not followed.[357]

Many arbitrators view a change in contract language as a waiver of past practice.[358] A prior election of remedies has also been considered as a waiver of arbitration.[359] In another "waiver-theory" case, an arbitrator found that an individual grievant could not waive a pay provision under the contract.[360] In *Gencorp Automotive*,[361] the arbitrator decided that a "last-chance" agree-

---

[356]Union-Scioto Local Bd. of Educ., Chillicothe, Ohio, 106 LA 337, 334 (Dworkin, 1996). An employer is not estopped from discharging an employee who intentionally lied on the application form, even after many years. United Parcel Serv., 112 LA 813 (Peterson, 1999).

[357]George E. Failing Co., 114 LA 1686 (Harr, 2000) (union failed to preserve arbitrability when it delayed arbitration request). Laches is defined in BLACK'S LAW DICTIONARY 879 (7th ed. 1999) as an "equitable doctrine by which a court denies relief to a claimant who has unreasonably delayed or been negligent in asserting the claim, when that delay or negligence has prejudiced the party against whom relief is sought."
Cases where the doctrine of laches was used to bar recovery by grievant or action by a party include: *North Coast Container Corp.*, 114 LA 795 (Franckiewicz, 2000); *City of Erie, Pa., School Dist.*, 113 LA 516 (Miles, 1999); *Custom Cartage Servs. Div.*, 111 LA 353 (Wolff, 1998); *General Refractories Co.*, 99 LA 311 (Richard, 1992); *Southwest Airlines Co.*, 93 LA 543 (Fox, Jr., 1989); *City of Buffalo, N.Y.*, 93 LA 5 (Pohl, 1989); where use of time was reasonable: *Federal Bureau of Prisons*, 114 LA 475 (Cohen, 2000); *City of Minneapolis, Minn., Library Bd.*, 94 LA 369 (Gallagher, 1989); *Gaylord Container Corp.*, 93 LA 465 (Abrams, 1989); *Internal Revenue Serv.*, 93 LA 261 (Dilts, 1989); and where 6-year-old complaint was a "continuing violation": *City of Edmond, Okla.*, 99 LA 510 (Woolf, 1992).

[358]Ash Grove Cement Co., 112 LA 507 (Wyman, 1999) (despite lack of intent to do so, union waived past practice argument when it agreed to new seniority language).

[359]City of Riviera Beach, Fla., 114 LA 833 (Wolfson, 2000) (election of remedies by union of litigating unfair labor practice charge before state labor board waived right to arbitrate; arbitrator was empowered to rule on issue of arbitrability; grievants were estopped from pursuing grievance); Central Pa. Inst. of Tech. Joint Operating Comm., 114 LA 513 (D'Eletto, 2000) (some parts of grievance were fully adjudicated previously and some were allowed); C. Iber & Sons, 69 LA 697, 704 (Gibson, 1977) (use of NLRB and federal courts did not deprive arbitrator of jurisdiction for some aspects of dispute); Aeronca, Inc., 68 LA 461, 468 (Kindig, 1977) (grievant bound by prior election of remedy); Pepsi-Cola Bottling Co., 50 LA 574, 591 (Klamon, 1968) (electing not to cross picket line forfeited benefits that would have accrued if employees had worked); Allegheny Ludlum Steel Corp., 33 LA 669, 674–75 (Seward, 1959) (no election of remedies where issues presented to workers' compensation board and arbitration were completely different); Chrysler Corp., 6 LA 369, 372 (Wolff, 1947) (unaware that qualifying dates for vacation changed while he was in the Army, the grievant who elected 90-day leave under GI Bill rather than establishing a sooner rehire date was credited nonetheless, because by operation of Selective Service Act he was rendered an employee on furlough during the war and not a new employee). Where the contract calls for tolling pending an alternative resolution, the employer is estopped from raising timeliness to defeat the grievance. Department of the Army, 111 LA 737 (Henner, 1998). Refusal to accept severance pay in the mistaken belief that they were laid off with recall rights did not create the remedy they preferred or affect the employees' entitlement to severance pay after the correct contract interpretation was ascertained. McGean-Rohco, 93 LA 9, 14 (Strasshofer, 1989).

[360]County of St. Clair, Ill., Sheriff's Dep't, 114 LA 1557 (Goldstein, 2000).

[361]104 LA 113, 117–18 (Malin, 1995). *See also* Fort James Corp., 113 LA 742 (Brown, 1999) (employer failed to assert that last-chance agreement waived recourse by the union until arbitration; arbitrator upheld terms of last-chance agreement, where union acknowledged it was valid and enforceable, and denied grievance).

ment did not waive the contractual right to grieve and arbitrate discharge of the employee for "just cause." Nor did a verbal agreement between the company and the union to fill permanent jobs without posting bids waive the right of an employee to a proper layoff notice.[362]

Acceptance by the union of modification of a discharge to a suspension during grievance proceedings did not waive the union's right to continue processing the grievance under the contract, particularly where the employer later offered further modification,[363] but acceptance of enhanced severance pay packages by employees on layoff waived their reinstatement rights even though they had been laid off in violation of the contract.[364] So long as the union raises a general concept in processing the grievance, it may not be deemed to have waived a more specific argument of the same nature.[365]

One arbitrator blurred the line between the concepts of waiver and estoppel by holding "that failure to enforce a right under a contract does not usually constitute a waiver unless the other party is prejudiced, damaged, or injured by the fact it was misled. In other words, there must be serious detrimental reliance before there can be an estoppel."[366] Most arbitrators do not require such a showing of prejudice but do require strict minimum standards such as, "clear evidence will be required";[367] "only one with authority

---

[362]Wisconsin Power & Light Co., 105 LA 22, 26 (Imes, 1995).

[363]Greater Cleveland Reg'l Transit Auth., 103 LA 270, 275 (Feldman, 1994).

[364]United Cent. Tel. Co. of Tex., 104 LA 246, 251 (Baroni, 1995).

[365]Consolidated Drum Reconditioning, 108 LA 523 (Richman, 1997) (union allowed to argue that probationary period was satisfied in successor employer situation, where the union did raise the issue that employees were not "new").

[366]SNE Corp., 82 LA 731, 734 (Flaten, 1984) (requiring serious reliance for estoppel). *See also* UNNICO Serv. Co., 113 LA 432 (Marcus, 1999) (quitting without notice and reaffirming the next day let the company down sufficiently to permit denial of revocation); Northrop Grumman Technical Servs., 112 LA 498 (Crider, 1999) (detrimental reliance theory rejected in safety-sensitive situation where grievant's duty superseded misinformation provided); Roadway Express, 109 LA 1064 (Nathan, 1997) (employee was not permitted to rescind her resignation, where other employees relied to their detriment on the resignation by applying for job posting); Dresser Indus., 96 LA 1063, 1068 (Nicholas, Jr., 1991); Fedders Air Conditioning, U.S.A., 95 LA 449, 451, 452 (Cooper, 1990); Superior Meat Co., 94 LA 1087, 1080 (Ross, 1990). Union did not waive right to grieve change in health insurance plan where it had been misled: Watauga Indus., 99 LA 829, 833 (Byars, 1992); Chambers & Owen, 96 LA 152, 154–55 (Redel, 1991); Allis-Chalmers Mfg. Co., 8 LA 945, 947 (Gorder, 1947). *See also* Bendix Corp., 76 LA 493, 498–99 (Cantor, 1981); George Ellis Co., 68 LA 261, 265–66 (Sacks, 1977); Bell Aircraft Corp., 24 LA 324, 327 (Somers, 1955).

[367]Huron County, Mich., Bd. of Comm'rs & Sheriff, 114 LA 487 (Sugerman, 2000) (clear waiver, where contract stated insurance issues could not be grieved); 5th Ave. Musical Theatre Co., 111 LA 820 (Snow, 1998) (no bargaining waiver by union absent clear intent by management in bargaining); Fina Oil & Chem. Co., 111 LA 107, 112 (Bankston, 1998) (applied "'consciously yielded or clearly and unmistakably waived'" standard in bargaining context finding no waiver by union) (quoting Unit Drop Forge Div., 171 NLRB 600, 601, 68 LRRM 1129, 1131 (1968), which quoted Rockwell-Standard Corp., 166 NLRB 124, 132, 65 LRRM 1601 (1967), which quoted Press Co., 121 NLRB 976, 978, 42 LRRM 1493 (1958)); University of Ill. at Chi., Bd. of Trs., 100 LA 728 (Goldstein, 1992) (no implied estoppel, where there is an express contractual preclusion of grievance and no express waiver); Universal Foods Corp., 91 LA 607, 609 (Wahl, 1988); Farrell Lines, 86 LA 36, 39–40 (Hockenberry, 1986) (clear and unmistakable); Mosaic Tile Co., 13 LA 949, 950 (Cornsweet, 1950). Evidence to prove acquiescence or waiver must be clear and unmistakable: Weinstein Wholesale Meat, 98 LA 636, 639 (Eagle, 1992); Shawnee County Sheriff's Dep't, 97 LA 919 (Berger, 1991); City of Roseburg, Or., 97 LA 262, 265 (Wilkinson, 1991); or clear and unequivocal: Uppco, Inc., 93 LA 489, 494 (Goldstein, 1989); Brookfield-La Grange Park Dist. 95 Bd. of Educ., Cook County, Ill., 93 LA 353, 359 (Nathan, 1989). *See* Pretty Prods., 96 LA 169, 172

to waive provisions of an agreement may do so";[368] or "the waiver of one right or provision, standing alone, will not be held to constitute the waiver of another."[369]

(Bittel, 1990) (requiring clear and convincing evidence of waiver). For distinction between waiver and zipper clause, see *Walgreen Co.*, 85 LA 1195, 1198 (Wies, 1985); *U.S. Dep't of Health & Human Servs.*, 83 LA 883, 888 (Edes, 1984); *Firestone Tire*, 83 LA 12, 15–16 (Lipson, 1984). As to whether statutory bargaining rights are waived by zipper clause, see also *Midwest Dental Prods. Corp.*, 94 LA 467, 471 (Wies, 1990); *Kansas City, Kan.*, 94 LA 191, 195–198 (Berger, 1989).

[368]Republic Steel Corp., 5 LA 609, 618 (McCoy, 1946); Pacific Mills, 2 LA 545, 548 (McCoy, 1946). See also Chapter 5, section 5.C., "Waiver of Procedural Requirements and Substantive Rights."

[369]Brown Univ., 113 LA 485 (Alleyne, 1999); Ogden Food Travel Servs., 90 LA 134, 135 (Cocalis, 1987); Minnesota Dep't of Natural Res., 87 LA 265, 272 (Bard, 1986); Union Carbide Corp., 46 LA 195, 198 (Cahn, 1966); Stearms Coal & Lumber Co., 1 LA 274, 276 (Dwyer, 1946).

Chapter 11

Precedential Value of Arbitral Awards

1. The Publication of Awards

The reporting and publication of labor arbitration awards has been said to make available a means of lessening the economic and social cost of industrial disputes.[1] Arbitrators possess a mass of solid, practical experience in the field of labor relations, and the benefit of their experience is conveyed through their published awards to representatives of both labor and management.[2]

While serving with the Federal Mediation and Conciliation Service (FMCS) as Director of its Office of Arbitration Services, L. Lawrence Schultz itemized the following "values" of published arbitration awards:

> (1) They constitute a key portion of the current news that makes up the collective bargaining arena. (2) They serve as guidelines for the parties in their continuing relationship and provide information for them to use in resolving their grievances prior to arbitration. (3) They fashion the industrial common law of the shop, which is repeatedly referred to by the highest court of the land. (4) They provide arbitrators with an indication of where others are going in similar situations. And (5) they furnish a complete or partial response to a question he frequently hears—Who is this arbitrator?[3]

In addition, reported awards have been said to be "live tools, to be used in shaping and applying the collective bargaining agreement."[4]

A. General Caliber of Arbitration Decisions: Importance of Prior/Published Awards

While emphasizing the importance of independent thinking by arbitrators, an arbitrator concluded that the reasoning used and principles enunciated by outstanding arbitrators have had a decidedly positive effect on the general caliber of arbitration decisions.[5] Another noted, "it is obvious that in arbitration as in other fields, respect must be paid to accumulated wisdom and experience."[6] A third arbitrator commented, "published awards are not binding on another arbitrator, but the thinking of experienced men is often

---

[1]Statement of John W. Taylor, *Reporting of Labor Arbitration: Pro and Con*, 1 Arb. J. (N.S.) 420 (1946). Publication of awards is strongly favored by unions, management, and arbitrators alike, according to statistics in Warren & Bernstein, *A Profile of Labor Arbitration*, 16 LA 970, 983 (1951). Publication of awards is a means of ensuring accountability of arbitrators.

It is important to remember, however, that the total of all published awards is only a small percentage of those rendered. Jones & Smith, *Management and Labor Appraisals and Criticism of the Arbitration Process: A Report With Comments*, 62 Mich. L. Rev. 1115, 1152 (1964). See section 1.B., "Criticism of Published Awards," below, for an enunciation of the view that there are drawbacks to publishing arbitration awards.

[2]Statement of Theodore Kheel, *Reporting of Labor Arbitration: Pro and Con*, 1 Arb. J. (N.S.) 424 (1946).

[3]*The Publication of Arbitration Awards*, in Arbitration—1975, Proceedings of the 28th Annual Meeting of NAA 208, 209 (Dennis & Somers eds., BNA Books 1976). Publication of awards also makes them widely available as teaching materials.

[4]Justin, *Arbitration: Precedent Value of Reported Awards*, 21 LRRM 8, 8 (1947).

[5]Day & Zimmermann, 51 LA 215, 219 (Marshall, 1968).

[6]Cochran Foil Co., 26 LA 155, 157 (Warns, Jr., 1956).

helpful to him."[7] One arbitrator, in turn, stated that prior awards "may be referred to for advice and for statements of the prevailing rule and standards."[8]

In the same vein, an arbitrator wrote:

> As to arbitral decisions rendered under other contracts between parties not related to those in the case at hand, usefulness depends upon similarity of the terms and of the situations to which they are to be applied. They must be weighed and appraised, not only in respect to these characteristics, but also with regard to the soundness of the principles upon which they proceed. Certainly, an arbitrator may be aided in formulating his own conclusions by knowledge of how other men have solved similar problems. He ought not to arrogate as his own special virtues the wisdom and justice essential to sound decision. In at least two instances in recent months I have found by investigation that a strong current of arbitral decision had overborne my first impression of the implications of particular language. To yield to this "common sense of most," especially as, on examination, the reasoning on which it was based carried plausibility, was neither to evade my responsibility nor to sacrifice my intellectual integrity. Contrariwise, it reduced discriminatory application of similar provisions. It enabled me to make use of the wisdom of others at work in the same field.[9]

Numerous other arbitrators have made similar statements,[10] recognizing the undoubted wisdom of seeking to profit from experience.

Prior awards can be of use to parties engaged in the negotiation of collective bargaining agreements. Knowledge of how specific clauses have been interpreted by arbitrators will help negotiators avoid pitfalls in the drafting of agreement language, and this service is one of the important reasons for writing fully reasoned opinions.[11]

Published awards on a matter also provide the setting for evaluating related cases. The settlement of disputes by the parties themselves before reaching arbitration significantly contributes to industrial stability. The fact that the parties can review published awards on the issue involved that are indicative of the likely outcome if the matter were to go to arbitration[12] fosters the settlement process.

---

[7]S.H. Kress & Co., 25 LA 77, 79 (Ross, 1955). *See also* Huntington Alloys, 73 LA 1050, 1053 (Shanker, 1979); Armour Agric. Chem. Co., 47 LA 513, 517 (Larkin, 1966).

[8]National Lead Co., 28 LA 470, 474 (Roberts, Stony, London, Miller, & Davenport, 1957).

[9]Merrill, *A Labor Arbitrator Views His Work*, 10 VAND. L. REV. 789, 797–98 (1957).

[10]*E.g.*, Texas Air Nat'l Guard, 115 LA 249, 252 (Moore, 2000); Terex/American Crane Corp., 114 LA 47, 50 (Nolan, 1999); Goodyear Tire & Rubber Co., 98 LA 1196, 1197 (Florman, 1992); Atlantic Richfield Co., 69 LA 484, 487 (Sisk, 1977); Aro, Inc., 47 LA 1065, 1072 (Whyte, 1966); Maui Pineapple Co., 47 LA 1051, 1053 (Tsukiyama, 1966); Gremar Mfg. Co., 46 LA 215, 218 (Teele, 1965); Greer Limestone Co., 40 LA 343, 348 (Lugar, 1963); Marathon Elec. Mfg. Corp., 29 LA 518, 523 (Thompson, 1957); Western Gear Corp. of Tex., 26 LA 84, 87 (Boles, 1956); Philadelphia Transp. Co., 25 LA 379, 381–82 (Scheiber, 1955); Cooper-Bessemer Corp., 25 LA 146, 149 (Reid, 1955); Safe Bus Co., 21 LA 456, 460 (Livengood, 1953); Great Lakes Carbon Corp., 19 LA 797, 799 (Wettach, 1953); Coca-Cola Bottling Works Co., 19 LA 432, 434 (Schmidt, 1952).

[11]Crane Carrier Co., 47 LA 339, 341 (Merrill, 1966); Deep Rock Oil Corp., 11 LA 25, 26 (Merrill, 1948).

[12]*See* Pratt & Whitney Co., 28 LA 668, 672 (Dunlop, 1957).

A practical need for the reasoned opinions of prior awards was made clear in the report of an Emergency Board created under the Railway Labor Act.[13] The Emergency Board found that the principal cause of the large number of undisposed claims before the First Division of the National Railroad Adjustment Board was that the First Division did not write fully reasoned opinions or encourage such opinions by referees assigned to it. The result was the accumulation of a vast number of awards of no precedential value and of no assistance in the application of the rules interpreted by the awards.[14]

B. Criticism of Published Awards

The reporting of awards to make them available for guidance in other cases is not without its critics. It has been pointed out that the publication of awards leads to a greater reliance on precedent, and that one of the great advantages of arbitration—its high degree of informality—is lost should the arbitration tribunal be bound by precedent. "Precedent," as used in this chapter, means *the force that is given to prior decisions.*

One of the strongest statements against giving precedential force to awards was made by Leo Cherne:

> The effects of publishing domestic arbitration awards are inevitable and inevitably undesirable. The fact of publication itself creates the atmosphere of precedent. The arbitrators in each subsequent dispute are submitted to the continuous and frequently unconscious pressure to conform. A bad award—and there are such in both the courtroom and the arbitration tribunal—will have the effect of stimulating other bad ones; a good one, by the weight of precedent, may be applied where the subtleties of fact should urge a different award.[15]

Opponents of the publication of awards because of their use as precedents borrow from the criticism directed at the doctrine of precedent in law, that is, the binding force of prior decisions ties the present to the past in such a degree as to stultify progress, and the observance of precedent becomes an end in itself, with the result that justice sometimes is superseded by consistency. In their view, the arbitrator should search for a rule of reason that will render justice and at the same time permit the parties to continue "living together"; the desirable rule is determined in part by the character of the disputants—by their economic position, their strength or weakness, their importance to the community, the history of their past relation-

---

[13]45 U.S.C. §151 et seq.

[14]Report to the President by the Emergency Board created July 18, 1947 (report dated July 30, 1947). At the time, in contrast to the First Division, the Second, Third, and Fourth Divisions did prepare fully reasoned opinions. Sometimes arguments before a referee sitting with one of these divisions would consist largely of debates about the meaning and applicability of particular precedents. *See* Miller, *The Railroad Adjustment Board*, 3 ARB. J. (N.S.) 181 (1948); Garrison, *The National Railroad Adjustment Board: A Unique Administrative Agency*, 46 YALE L.J. 567, 581–82 (1937). *See also* Daughterty, Whiting, & Guthrie, *Arbitration by the National Railroad Adjustment Board, in* ARBITRATION TODAY, PROCEEDINGS OF THE 8TH ANNUAL MEETING OF NAA 93–127 (McKelvey ed., BNA Books 1955).

[15]Cherne, *Should Arbitration Awards Be Published?*,1 ARB. J. (N.S.) 75 (1946). For other arguments against use of awards as precedent, see McPherson, *Should Labor Arbitrators Play Follow-the-Leader?*, 4 ARB. J. (N.S.) 163 (1949).

ships, and their objectives in taking their present stand. These factors require each case to be decided on its own and have to explain why two arbitrators dealing with different parties but similar facts will arrive at seemingly conflicting decisions.[16]

Despite this criticism, it appears that most employers and unions acknowledge that arbitration awards constitute an expanding body of labor-management rules. Parties frequently cite and discuss the prior awards of other parties.[17] Even where collective bargaining agreements expressly provide that no decision establishes a precedent for other cases, actual practice under such provisions may disclose that the parties themselves apply prior decisions to later disputes involving the same point.[18] Recognition that "the body of recorded decisional precedent in arbitration proceedings is constantly growing" led a dissenting partisan member of a tripartite board to issue an opinion recording his views in order "to guide those who may have occasion in the future to refer to the decision and award as a precedent."[19]

C. Who Decides to Publish?

The decision as to whether an award should be submitted for publication is not, however, the prerogative of the arbitrator. At least in the private sector, arbitration awards are the property of the parties. As one arbitrator noted:

> The award and opinion are the arbitrator's work product, but not the arbitrator's property. They "belong" to the parties in the arbitration proceeding and must be treated as confidential unless a statute requires or the parties jointly agree to publication.[20]

---

[16]See Levenstein, *Reporting of Labor Arbitration: Pro and Con*, 1 ARB. J. (N.S.) 420, 426 (1946).

[17]See, e.g., Goodyear Tire & Rubber Co., 115 LA 216 (Stallworth, 2000); King Soopers Inc., 115 LA 207, 212 (Watkins, 2000); Snohomish County, Wash., Pub. Util. Dist. 1, 115 LA 1 (Levak, 2000); White Consol. Indus., 114 LA 1031 (Nicholas, Jr., 2000); ITT, 75 LA 729, 730 (Howlett, 1980); Sandusky Dressed Beef Co., 69 LA 766, 767–68 (Strasshofer, 1977); Philips Indus., 69 LA 712, 717 (Kindig, 1977); Hygrade Food Prods. Corp., 69 LA 414, 416–18 (Harter, 1977); Kankakee Elec. Steel Co., 53 LA 178, 181–83 (Sembower, 1969); Dow Chem. Co., 22 LA 336, 341–45 (Klamon, 1954). For many other such instances, the reader need merely scan volumes of reported awards.

One survey indicated there is considerable support, particularly from the management side, for the proposition that arbitrators should make greater use of precedent in deciding cases. Jones & Smith, *Management and Labor Appraisals and Criticisms of the Arbitration Process: A Report With Comments*, 62 MICH. L. REV. 1115, 1150 (1964). Union acceptance of precedent is illustrated by the fact that precedents often are used in arbitration under the AFL-CIO internal disputes plan. *See, e.g.*, Retail Clerks, 43 LA 255, 257 (Cole, 1964); Shipbuilding Workers, 43 LA 249, 252 (Cole, 1964).

[18]See Rosenblatt, *The Impartial Machinery of the Coat and Suit Industry*, 3 ARB. J. 224, 226 (1939).

[19]Journal Publ'g Co., 22 LA 108, 113 (Seering, Wykoff, Abramson, Knight, & Rodbury, 1954).

[20]Eischen, *The Arbitration Hearing: Administration, Conduct and Procedures, in* LABOR AND EMPLOYMENT ARBITRATION 1–58 (Bornstein, Gosline, & Greenbaum eds., LEXIS Publ'g 2001).

The private nature of arbitration and the obligation of an arbitrator not to publish or comment publicly on an award without the consent of the parties are emphasized by the *Code of Professional Responsibility for Arbitrators of Labor-Management Disputes (Code of Professional Responsibility)*.[21]

D. Attitude of Arbitrators Toward Other Published Opinions

Of great practical significance is the attitude of arbitrators themselves toward the published opinions of others. An extensive survey of labor arbitration disclosed that 77 percent of the 238 responding arbitrators believed that prior published decisions under *other* contracts should be given "some weight."[22] In this regard, the *Code of Professional Responsibility* recognizes that arbitrators may exercise independent discretion concerning the precedential effect given to prior published opinions unless the parties have indicated mutual agreement to the contrary.[23]

---

[21]Arbitrator Dennis R. Nolan explained:

Parties seldom [submit awards for publication], so that puts the burden on arbitrators.

The Code of Professional Responsibility formerly required the arbitrator to obtain the parties' express approval before submitting any award for publication. When arbitrators raised the issue before issuing the award, parties sometimes felt pressured to agree. Rather than offend the parties, many arbitrators simply decided not to submit awards for publication. Asking for permission after the award proved time consuming and frustrating, because many parties with no objection just did not bother to reply.

To deal with this dilemma, the National Academy of Arbitrators proposed amending the Code to allow a simpler process. The other sponsors of the Code, the AAA [American Arbitration Association] and FMCS, quickly agreed. Current § 2.C.1.c. allows an arbitrator to state when issuing the award that failure to answer the inquiry within 30 days "will be considered an implied consent to publish."

LABOR AND EMPLOYMENT ARBITRATION IN A NUTSHELL 268–69 (West Group 1998).

Another arbitrator has pointed out:

Some arbitrators believe that the proceeding is private to the parties involved, so that they are free to have the decision published, if they wish, without the arbitrator's involvement. These arbitrators will not seek permission for publication.

Kagel, *Practice and Procedure, in* THE COMMON LAW OF THE WORKPLACE: THE VIEWS OF ARBITRATORS §106 (St. Antoine ed., BNA Books 1998).

[22]Warren & Bernstein, *A Profile of Labor Arbitration*, 16 LA 970, 982 (1951). For citation of many cases where published opinions under other contracts did have some persuasive influence on the arbitrator, see section 4., "Persuasive Prior Awards," below.

[23]The *Code of Professional Responsibility* provides:

G. Reliance by an Arbitrator on Other Arbitration Awards or on Independent Research

1. An arbitrator must assume full personal responsibility for the decision in each case decided.

a. The extent, if any, to which an arbitrator properly may rely on precedent, on guidance of other awards, or on independent research is dependent primarily on the policies of the parties on these matters, as expressed in the contract, or other agreement, or at the hearing.

b. When the mutual desires of the parties are not known or when the parties express differing opinions or policies, the arbitrator may exercise discretion as to these matters, consistent with acceptance of full personal responsibility for the award.

CODE OF PROFESSIONAL RESPONSIBILITY FOR ARBITRATORS OF LABOR-MANAGEMENT DISPUTES §2(G) (as amended 2001). For relevant court cases, see section 3.C., "Temporary or Ad Hoc Arbitrators," below. Particularly in expedited arbitration, the parties may place some or even severe limitations on the use of precedents and/or on the precedential force of the expedited awards themselves. *See* Chapter 7, section 6., "Expediting the Arbitration Machinery"; Dresser Indus., 72 LA 138, 141–42 (Laybourne, 1979).

Arbitrators take divergent views on the extent to which they should independently research published awards for guidance. Many arbitrators take the approach that they should not look beyond the arguments of the parties. Other arbitrators, however, sometimes are unwilling to rely solely on the parties for making precedents available, and they search for relevant awards on their own.[24] Where one party has cited arbitral awards to support its position, some arbitrators may allow the other party time to consider them and respond.[25] Where neither party has referred to published opinions on an issue, some arbitrators occasionally invite both parties to submit any they consider relevant.[26] But one arbitrator cautioned against the mechanical resort to citations as a substitute for a well-developed theory of the case: "My strong impression is that time might be used more productively working with the case at hand rather than looking for supporting awards."[27]

While it might be expected that persons trained in law would be more inclined to cite published opinions as precedents for their decisions, nonattorneys appear to be just as fond of relying on the awards of others. It has been noted "that laymen in a judicial position are quite as eager as lawyers in pursuing, and quite as contentious in dissecting, the available precedents . . . ."[28]

Accepting, then, that arbitrators and the parties rely on published awards, inquiry is directed to the quantum of force to be given such awards. In seeking an answer, it is helpful by way of analogy to consider the precedential effect accorded judicial decisions.

2. The Judicial Doctrine of Precedent

A. Civil Law Versus Common Law

The precedential use of labor arbitration awards finds its own precedent in both the civil and common law. In theory, the continental civil law system differs from the Anglo-American system of common law by its official nonacceptance of the doctrine of precedent. Scholars have pointed out, however, that this supposed difference between the common law and civil law systems is more apparent than real, because the civil law courts do not ignore precedents to the extent that their general theories might indicate, while our own courts do not follow precedents as slavishly as many of their utterances would suggest. In all of the civil law countries, the binding force of precedents is

---

[24]*See* United States Geological Survey, 115 LA 276 (Hoffman, 2000); Lucent Techs., 115 LA 301 (Caraway, 2001); Carbon County, Pa., 73 LA 1305, 1307 (Handsaker, 1980); Prismo-William Armstrong Smith Co., 73 LA 581, 584–85 (Jedel, 1979); Wiregrass Elec. Coop., 69 LA 1245, 1246 (Ferguson, 1977); Max Rudolph Trucking Co., 69 LA 1167, 1171 (Rule, 1977); Federal-Mogul Corp., 69 LA 919, 921 (Morgan, Jr., 1977); National Serv. Indus., 69 LA 406, 410 (Rutherford, 1977); General Tel. Co. of Ky., 69 LA 351, 352 (Bowles, 1977).

[25]*See, e.g.*, Simmons Co., 15 LA 921, 922 (Elson, 1950).

[26]*See, e.g.*, A.D. Julliard & Co., 15 LA 934, 938 (Maggs, 1951).

[27]Helburn, *What Arbitrators Need From the Parties: III. The End Is Near: A Note on Effective Closure, in* Arbitration 1997: The Next Fifty Years, Proceedings of the 50th Annual Meeting of NAA 272, 275 (Najita ed., BNA Books 1998).

[28]Garrison, *The National Railroad Adjustment Board: A Unique Administrative Agency*, 46 Yale L.J. 567, 583 (1937).

recognized in one situation, termed a "settled course of decision." Thus, although a single prior decision is not regarded as binding, a settled course of decisions on an issue is regarded as controlling.[29]

i. English Doctrine of Precedent

The doctrine of precedent under the common law system does not operate as inexorably as many persons assume. Sir John William Salmond, in his influential work, *Salmond on Jurisprudence*, analyzed the English doctrine of precedent.[30] He divided decisions into two classes, authoritative and persuasive. These were said to differ in the kind of influence exercised by each on the future course of the administration of justice.

The authoritative precedent was defined as one that judges must follow whether they approve of it or not; the persuasive precedent was defined as one that judges are under no obligation to follow, but which is to be taken into consideration and given such weight as its intrinsic merit seems to demand.

Salmond specified as authoritative the decisions of the superior courts of justice in England.[31] A large body of decisions was designated as persuasive, including (1) foreign judgments, and more especially those of American courts; (2) decisions of superior courts in other parts of the British Commonwealth of Nations; (3) judgments of the Privy Council when sitting as the final court of appeal from other members and parts of the Commonwealth; and (4) judicial dicta. Thus, even in England, where the rule of stare decisis was developed, a vast number of decisions has persuasive force only.[32]

ii. U.S. Doctrine of Stare Decisis

In the United States, the degree of control to be allowed a prior decision varies with the particular case. A renowned scholar, Robert Von Moschzisker, after acknowledging that the doctrine of stare decisis is based on the premise that certainty in law is more important than correct legal principles,[33] made the following statement:

> If the rule demanded absolute rigid adherence to precedents (as in the English House of Lords), then there might be good ground for the persistence among the uninformed of the erroneous idea just referred to, but the proper American conception comprehends *stare decisis* as a flexible doctrine, under which the degree of control to be allowed a prior judicial determination depends largely on the nature of the question at issue, the circumstances attend-

---

[29]Shartel & Wolff, *Civil Justice in Germany*, 42 MICH. L. REV. 863, 866–67 (1944). *See also* LLOYD, INTRODUCTION TO JURISPRUDENCE 366–72 (2d ed. 1965); BODENHEIMER, JURISPRUDENCE 290–91 (Harvard Univ. Press 1962).

[30]SALMOND ON JURISPRUDENCE §53 (Williams ed., 11th ed. 1957).

[31]Salmond also divided authoritative precedents into two kinds, absolute and conditional. Absolute decisions must be followed without question, however unreasonable or erroneous they may be considered to be. Conversely, courts possess a certain limited power to disregard decisions having merely conditional authority. *Id.*

[32]For explanations as to why this should be so, see CROSS, PRECEDENT IN ENGLISH LAW 12–14 (Oxford Univ. Press 1961).

ing its decision, and, perhaps, somewhat on the attitude of individual participating judges.[34]

He also spoke of the situation in which a departure should be made from precedent:

> Therefore, except in the classes of cases which demand strict adherence to precedent, when a court is faced with an ancient decision, rendered under conditions of society radically different from those of today, and when it is sought to have this ancient decision control present-day conditions even though the attending facts in the two controversies be alike, still there is nothing in the doctrine of *stare decisis* to prevent a departure from the earlier decision and (in the absence of a legislative enactment covering the matter) the restatement of the governing rule there laid down, or acted on, to meet the change in the life of the people to serve whose best interests it was originally invoked.[35]

An accurate statement of the American doctrine of stare decisis is contained in Daniel H. Chamberlain's classic treatise:

> A deliberate or solemn decision of a court or judge, made after argument on a question of law fairly arising in a case, and necessary to its determination, is an authority, or binding precedent, in the same court or in other courts of equal or lower rank, in subsequent cases, where "the very point" is again in controversy; but the degree of authority belonging to such precedent depends, of necessity, on its agreement with the spirit of the times or the judgment of subsequent tribunals upon its correctness as a statement of the existing, or actual law, and the compulsion or exigency of the doctrine is, in the last analysis, moral and intellectual, rather than arbitrary or inflexible.[36]

As another scholar observed, precedents are not self-effectuating; rather, they control only to the extent that they are accepted as binding by judges in later cases, and varying force is attached to different kinds of precedents.[37]

The distinction between decisions with authoritative force and decisions with persuasive force is recognized in labor arbitration.

3. AUTHORITATIVE PRIOR AWARDS [LA CDI 94.554; 100.0783]

Prior labor arbitration awards that interpreted the existing terms of a contract between the same parties are not binding in exactly the same sense

---

[33]Literally, "that which has been decided," and referring to a principle controlling of subsequent decisions.

[34]Von Moschzisker, *Stare Decisis in Courts of Last Resort*, 37 HARV. L. REV. 409, 414 (1924).

[35]*Id.* at 418.

[36]CHAMBERLAIN, THE DOCTRINE OF STARE DECISIS 19 (1885). *See also* Grenig, *Stare Decisis, Res Judicata, and Collateral Estoppel and Labor Arbitration*, 38 LAB. L.J. 195 (Apr. 1987); Catlett, *The Development of the Doctrine of Stare Decisis and the Extent to Which It Should Be Applied*, 21 WASH. L. REV. 159 (1946).

[37]SHARTEL, OUR LEGAL SYSTEM AND HOW IT OPERATES 418–19 (Univ. of Mich. 1951). Professor Shartel indicated the several respects in which the variation in weight of precedents is apparent: (1) As regards the place and court in which the precedent is cited—a decision of the supreme court of state X has a different weight when cited in state X than when cited in state Y; (2) as regards the character of the judicial statement—a unanimous opinion will have more weight than a divided opinion; (3) as regards the scope of acceptance of the view— one supported by general authority will be more forceful; (4) as regards age and confirmation in later cases; and (5) as regards the subject matter involved in the previous decision.

that authoritative legal decisions are, yet they may have a force that can be fairly characterized as authoritative. This is true of arbitration awards rendered both by permanent umpires and by temporary or ad hoc arbitrators.

A. Final and Binding Decisions

Some collective bargaining agreements contain a provision making the arbitrator's decision final and binding on the particular dispute before him or her. In interpreting such a provision, which read "[t]he arbitrator's decision shall be final and shall govern only the dispute before him," an arbitrator explained that:

> The primary purpose of such a provision is to recognize the binding effect of an arbitrator's award in resolving the dispute immediately before him, but it also has a larger implication. It must be assumed that the parties are interested in achieving the same result in similar cases and establishing a consistent body of arbitral interpretation of the same provisions of the contract under similar facts.[38]

This view is referred to as the "contractual approach."[39]

Although some arbitrators take the position that they are retained to exercise independent judgment and need not necessarily follow a prior award,[40] others hold that prior decisions are deemed incorporated into the labor agreement,[41] particularly when the provision previously so interpreted has been carried forward intact into a successor agreement.

One arbitrator argues that although both finality and consistency should be sought as integral to the parties' continuing relationship,[42] mechanical application of a stare decisis/res judicata/collateral estoppel policy should be

---

[38]Peabody Coal Co., 89 LA 885, 887 (Volz, 1987). *See also* Bruce Hardwood Floors, 113 LA 687, 692 (O'Grady, 1999).

[39]Heinsz, *Grieve It Again: Of Stare Decisis, Res Judicata and Collateral Estoppel in Labor Arbitration*, 38 B.C. L. Rev. 275 (1997). "As in most arbitral situations, the first rule is to follow the intent of the parties . . . . Some agreements specifically state that prior decisions are binding; others state just the opposite." *Id.* at 286. For an arbitrator "to refuse to follow contractual dictates concerning the binding nature of previous awards would cause the decision to be void because it would not be based on the 'essence' of the contract as required by *Enterprise Wheel* [*Steelworkers v. Enterprise Wheel & Car Corp.*, 363 U.S. 593, 46 LRRM 2423 (1960)]." *Id.* at 288.

[40]*Id.* at 291–93. One arbitrator noted that an arbitrator should not reach a contrary result to a prior award on the same set of facts on the same contract language unless he finds that the prior award contained material errors of fact or reached a clearly wrong interpretation of contract terms. Naval Air Rework Facility, 86 LA 1129, 1132 (Hewitt, 1986).

[41]Heinsz, 38 B.C. L. Rev. at 288–91.

[42]*Id.* at 300.

avoided.[43] Instead, arbitrators should consider a number of factors when faced with relevant prior decisions,[44] including prior inconsistent ones.[45]

Any well-reasoned and well-written prior arbitration opinion has persuasive qualities where it is "on point" with the subject matter of a current grievance; however, to be given preclusive effect it must be between the same parties, must invoke the same fact situation, must pertain to the same contractual provisions, must be supported by the same evidence, and must concern an interpretation of the specific agreement before the arbitrator.[46] Consequently, where a new incident gives rise to the same issue that is covered by a prior award, the new incident may be taken to arbitration, but, in the

---

[43]*See also* Valtin, *Other People's Messes: The Arbitrator as Cleanup Hitter: Comment, in* Arbitration 1994: Controversy and Continuity, Proceedings of the 47th Annual Meeting of NAA 271 (Gruenberg ed., BNA Books 1994).

    I doubt that any of us is a member of absolute loyalty to either the incorporation camp or the independent judgment camp—at least not to the point of announcing to the parties upon the beginning of the hearing, "It's all over—I'm an incorporator," or "You may as well proceed as if the prior decision didn't exist—it is of no moment to me." Rather, we will be found in the one camp or the other, and interchangeably, depending on the totality of the particular record before us and what we think needs to be done about it.

    The fact that we come out as an incorporator does not mean we have foregone making a judgment. It merely means we have made the judgment that, in this instance and by all involved in it, the prior decision should stand. I understand why the other school has the name of the independent judgment school. But it must not be taken to connote the lack of independent judgment where an arbitrator comes out as an incorporator.

    The result in any of these cases may be characterized as a victory of the one school over the other. But, as a matter of our responsibility, it does not matter how we come out. Either way, as long as we have given earnest consideration to all that is before us, there is compliance with the Code's canon for assuming "full responsibility for the decision in each case decided."

[44]These factors include fact considerations, party identity, the requirements of the Code of Professional Responsibility, deference to prior decisions (also referred to by Heinsz as the "principle of constraint" (Heinsz, 38 B.C. L. Rev. at 293, 297)), and the parties' contractual expectations. *Id.* at 294–97.

[45]Heinsz points out that prior inconsistent awards present an altogether different situation:

    When an arbitrator is faced with prior, inconsistent interpretations, each of which is reasonable, the rationale for the incorporation theory wanes because the parties have achieved neither consistency nor finality. Certainly the parties do not intend to incorporate into their collective bargaining agreement clauses which cancel each other out. By calling in the third arbitrator, they have indicated that they have been unable to resolve the matter either in negotiations or through the grievance process. In this situation [Arbitrator Edward] Krinsky decided that "it would seem best that this arbitrator do what the parties have asked him to do in their stipulation of the issue; namely to review the merits of the issue and make an award." (Escanaba Paper Co., FMCS No. 79K/22108, at 6–7.) Applying the independent judgment theory is a sensible approach in this circumstance. While the third arbitrator may be influenced by the soundness of the reasoning of *A* or *B*, who were faced with the same issue between the same parties, this effect is more like the persuasiveness of precedent rather than the principle of constraint.

Id. at 299.

[46]GAF Bldg. Materials Corp., 112 LA 871, 876 (Marcus, 1999) (following precedent on reinstatement concerning employee testing positive for alcohol use; "[o]nce an arbitrator decides an issue within the realm of reason, the disappointed party's remedy is not to present the same issue to a different arbitrator, but to seek resolution by changing the policy under authority set forth in the management rights clause, or when negotiating renewal of the labor agreement."). *See also* Trailways Lines v. Trailways Joint Council, 807 F.2d 1416, 124 LRRM 2217 (8th Cir. 1986).

absence of materially changed circumstances, it may be controlled by the prior award.[47]

The policy behind giving binding effect to a prior arbitration award and its limitations has been expressed in these terms:

> The parties have agreed in the instant Contract that when a dispute thereunder is submitted to arbitration the decision "shall be final and binding upon all parties."
>
> But, an arbitration award is not conclusive only with respect to the outcome of a particular grievance. Rather, it is also dispositive of the underlying issue presented by the grievance. The consequence is that a decision on the validity of a particular interpretation or application of a Contract term has continuing effect.
>
> Were the parties free to repeatedly submit the same issue to arbitral resolution, "shopping" for a different result, the "common rule" of the work place would be destroyed. Contract terms are expected to be applied uniformly to all similarly situated employees. A provision cannot be allowed to mean one thing for one employee and something else for another employee. If that situation were to prevail, the collective bargain made for employees in the unit would break down and be replaced, in effect, by a series of individual bargains. Irrational discriminations, where similarly situated employees are treated dissimilarly, would then become the rule in a universe of chaos.
>
> Accordingly, regardless of the decision an arbitrator might be inclined to render, were a dispute brought to him as a matter of first impression, he is bound to defer to the opinion of a prior arbitrator upon the same issue.
>
> This principle of arbitral *"res judicata,"* however, is not without its limitations.
>
> Preclusive effect may be given to a prior award only where the issues are identical and the subsequent dispute cannot be distinguished from the one earlier ruled upon.
>
> Thus, the second arbitrator must first be satisfied that the issue he is required to decide is identical to that presented in the previous case. Next, assuming he has made that determination, the arbitrator must ascertain whether there have been any changes in the circumstances or conditions material to the original holding which would make inappropriate continued adherence to the earlier ruling.
>
> If there are none, he must then define the nature and extent of the ruling made in the earlier arbitration and properly apply it to the facts of grievance before him.
>
> Finally, the Arbitrator is obliged to inquire whether or not any extraordinary and compelling reasons exist why the initial decision should not be followed, as, for example, where it is shown that perpetuation of the ruling would produce more harm than its abandonment.[48]

When the destiny of a party's claim is governed by a prior award, the claim may be said to be precluded under res judicata concepts, or the decision thereon controlled by stare decisis concepts, or a fact essential to the decision controlled by collateral estoppel concepts. But, regardless of whether the arbitrator speaks in terms of stare decisis, res judicata, or collateral es-

---

[47]For example, see *Albertson's, Inc.*, 114 LA 1768, 1770–71 (Watkins, 2000) (citing Elkouri & Elkouri: How Arbitration Works 609–10 (Volz & Groggin eds., BNA Books 5th ed. 1997)).
[48]Burnham Corp., 88 LA 931, 934–35 (Ruben, 1987).

toppel, the prior award will have been the primary factor in the disposition of the present claim.[49]

B. Permanent Umpires [LA CDI 94.554; 100.0783]

As noted in the previous section, when a prior grievance that has resulted in an arbitration award cannot be distinguished factually or otherwise from a subsequent grievance, it should be deemed authoritative and, hence, controlling of the outcome, unless the second arbitrator is convinced that the first award was manifestly erroneous and that adhering to its holding for the remainder of the contract term would do more harm than holding to the contrary.

The concept of a "collective bargain" implies that the terms and conditions of employment will be uniform for all similarly situated employees in the bargaining unit, creating what is often referred to as the "common rule of the shop." The terms of a contract should not mean one thing to one employee and something else to another.

If an award on a particular contract interpretation issue is final and binding only with respect to the individual grievant, there need never be "finality," and the terms and conditions of employment under which each

---

[49]*See, e.g.,* Bofors-Lakeway, 72 LA 159, 161–63 (Kelman, 1979) (makes reference to both res judicata and stare decisis). See also *Allen v. McCurry*, 449 U.S. 90, 94 (1980), for the U.S. Supreme Court definition of res judicata: "Under res judicata, a final judgment on the merits of an action precludes the parties or their privies from relitigating issues that were *or could have been* raised in that action" (emphasis added). The "essential elements" of res judicata "are generally stated to be (1) a final judgment on the merits in an earlier suit, (2) an identity of the cause of action in both the earlier and the later suit, and (3) an identity of the parties or their privies in the two suits." Nash County Bd. of Educ. v. Biltmore Co., 1980–81 Trade Cases ¶63,715, at 77,816 (4th Cir. 1981) (stating also that "collateral estoppel is generally regarded as merely a 'branch' or 'other prong' of res judicata," *id.* at 77,819). In one sense, collateral estoppel is broader than res judicata in that "[u]nder collateral estoppel once a court has decided an issue of fact or law necessary to its judgment, that decision may preclude litigation of the issue in a suit *on a different cause of action* involving a party to the first case." *Allen,* 494 U.S. at 94 (emphasis added) (the Court referred to the "related" doctrines of res judicata and collateral estoppel). In another sense, collateral estoppel is narrower than res judicata in that collateral estoppel "extends only to questions 'distinctly put in issue and directly determined' in" the prior action. Emich Motors Corp. v. General Motors Corp., 340 U.S. 558, 569 (1951) (quoting Frank v. Magnum, 237 U.S 309, 334 (1915)). For a detailed arbitral analysis of the judicial doctrines of stare decisis, res judicata, and collateral estoppel, see *Timken Roller Bearing Co.,* 32 LA 595, 597–99 (Boehm, 1958). On stare decisis and res judicata, see Block, *Decisional Thinking—West Coast Panel Report, in* DECISIONAL THINKING OF ARBITRATORS AND JUDGES, PROCEEDINGS OF THE 33D ANNUAL MEETING OF NAA 119, 143 (Stern & Dennis eds., BNA Books 1981). The issuance of an arbitration award generally bars any subsequent court or arbitration action on the merits of the same event. *See* Chapter 2, section 2.A.ii.d., "De Novo Litigation Following Arbitration"; Todd Shipyards Corp. v. Marine & Shipbuilding Workers Local 15, 242 F. Supp. 606, 59 LRRM 2613 (D.N.J. 1965); Hi-Torc Motor Corp., 40 LA 929, 930–31 (Kerrison, 1963); Hall v. Sperry Gyroscope Co., 21 LA 758, 762 (N.Y. 1954). It was not considered a res judicata situation, however, where the subsequent proceedings involved a different issue: Arch of W. Va., 90 LA 1220, 1222 (Volz, 1988); Engelhard Indus., 82 LA 680 (Nicholas, Jr., 1984); Arch of Ill., 82 LA 625 (Hewitt, 1984); Ralston Purina Co., 75 LA 1163, 1166–67 (Shanker, 1980); Town of W. Orange, N.J., 70 LA 581, 582–83 (Dennis, 1978); Aristocrat Travel Prods., 52 LA 314, 315 (Koven, 1968)); a different party: Dallas Morning News, 45 LA 413, 416 (Johannes, 1965); or a similar issue but a different incident: Vulcan Mold & Iron Co., 41 LA 59, 60–61 (Brecht, 1963).

employee works would depend on the fortuity of the predilection of each succeeding arbitrator appointed to deal repetitively with the recurrent issue. Prior awards typically have such "authoritative" force in arbitrations conducted by permanent umpires or chairs. In this regard, one umpire offered the following thought: "Where a reasonably clear precedent can be found in prior Umpire decisions, the considerations in favor of following that precedent are very strong indeed, in the absence of relevant changes in contract language or a showing that the precedent decision or decisions were erroneous."[50]

Another umpire, who served for many years as umpire for the Ford Motor Company and the United Automobile Workers, spoke of precedent in the permanent umpire systems as follows:

> [I]n this system a form of precedent and stare decisis is inevitable and desirable. I am not referring to the use in one enterprise, say United States Steel, of awards made by another arbitrator in another enterprise, say General Motors . . . .
>
> But the precedent of which I am now speaking refers to the successive decisions within the same enterprise. Even in the absence of arbitration, the parties themselves seek to establish a form of stare decisis or precedent for their own guidance—by statements of policy, instructions, manuals of procedure, and the like. This is but a means of avoiding the pain of rethinking every recurring case from scratch, of securing uniformity of action. . . .
>
> When the parties submit to arbitration in the system of which I speak, they seek not merely resolution of the particular stalemate, but guidance for the future, at least for similar cases. They could hardly have a high opinion of the arbitrator's mind if it were a constantly changing mind. Adherence to prior decisions, except when departure is adequately explained, is one sign that the determinations are based on reason and are not merely random judgments.[51]

In the hosiery industry, it was explained at one point that prior awards had become a part of the "common law" of the industry: "The Impartial Chairman will hesitate, therefore, to write any decision contrary to the precedents already established."[52] In that industry, the principles enunciated in the de-

---

[50]Goodyear Tire & Rubber Co., 36 LA 1023, 1025 (Killingsworth, 1961). In this instance, however, the umpire could not find a clear guide from prior umpire decisions. The authoritative force of prior umpire decisions is illustrated by *Bethlehem Steel Co.*, 43 LA 228, 232 (Crawford, 1964). For illustrations as to how basic principles established by prior umpire decisions are utilized, see *Bethlehem Steel Corp.*, 70 LA 162, 163–64 (Strongin, 1978); *Courtaulds N. Am.*, 47 LA 609, 609 (McCoy, 1966); *United States Steel Corp.*, 46 LA 414, 416 (Florey, 1966). Of course, a prior umpire decision is not an authoritative precedent for a distinguishable case. *See* Bethlehem Steel Corp., 47 LA 270, 272 (Gill & Seward, 1966).

[51]Shulman, *Reason, Contract, and Law in Labor Relations*, 68 Harv. L. Rev. 999, 1020 (1955), *reprinted in* Management Rights and the Arbitration Process, Proceedings of the 9th Annual Meeting of NAA 169, 193–94 (McKelvey ed., BNA Books 1956). For more on the important role of precedent in umpireships, see Killingsworth, *Arbitration: Its Uses in Industrial Relations*, 21 LA 859, 861–63 (1953); Reilly, *Arbitration's Impact on Bargaining*, 16 LA 987, 990–91 (1951); Davey, *The John Deere-UAW Permanent Arbitration System, in* Critical Issues in Labor Arbitration, Proceedings of the 10th Annual Meeting of NAA 161, 174 (McKelvey ed., BNA Books 1957); Wolff, Crane, & Cole, *The Chrysler-UAW Umpire System, in* The Arbitrator and the Parties, Proceedings of the 11th Annual Meeting of NAA 111, 115, 128 (McKelvey ed., BNA Books 1958).

[52]Kennedy, Effective Labor Arbitration 63 (1948). "In fact each decision becomes a part of the National Labor Agreement which provides 'all decisions and rulings of the Impartial Chairman . . . not in conflict with the terms of this Agreement are hereby adopted and shall be binding upon the parties hereto.'" *Id.* at 62.

cisions, not the identity of the impartial chairman, were said to be all-important; the fact that the person serving as the impartial chairman changed from time to time did not lead to the voiding of past decisions.[53]

Full opinion decisions of the Arbitration Review Board that existed under the National Bituminous Coal Wage Agreement continue to have precedential effect on cases to which they apply, even though the Arbitration Review Board itself has been abolished.[54] However, the decisions of a former chairperson are entitled to no greater weight than those of other coal industry arbitrators.[55]

One permanent board of arbitration was called on to render an opinion as to the binding effect of decisions made at grievance meetings and at arbitration hearings. After defining a "grievance" as a particular complaint and an "issue" as the general contractual question that it raised, the board took the following position:

> (1) A grievance which has been settled in grievance meetings or in arbitration or which has not been appropriately appealed if the proposed settlement has not been accepted, remains settled. This grievance cannot be reinstituted.
> (2) An issue that is settled by the parties in grievance meetings remains settled. Such a settlement, if accepted by both parties, is equivalent to a separate, local agreement. [*Editor's note:* For full discussion of the precedential effect of grievance settlements, see Chapter 5, section 15., "Grievance Settlements as Binding Procedents."]
> (3) Either party may bring an issue to this Board (by the appropriate procedure) even though the party has not appealed the decision on a grievance incorporating the issue. While the given grievance may not be reinstated, another grievance may be processed to the Board in order that the party may secure a final ruling on the issue.
> (4) A grievance even though generally similar to a grievance which has been settled may be processed if it raises an issue which is [in any way] different from an issue that has been settled.
> (5) An issue which has been ruled on by an umpire prior to the constitution of this Board remains settled unless the ruling is in conflict with the ruling of other umpires entrusted with the same issue. In such a situation, either party is entitled to a ruling from this Board (by following the procedure prescribed in the Agreement) which will dissipate the conflicting arbitration decisions. Further, if the ruling by the umpire is not clear, either party is privileged to process a grievance to this Board so as to secure a clear ruling on the issue.

---

[53]Full-Fashioned Hosiery Indus., 2 ALAA ¶67,542 (Dash, Jr., 1946). Somewhat similar to national labor-management arrangements as concerns precedential force of decisions, umpire decisions rendered under the AFL-CIO Internal Disputes Plan have been researched for precedential use: "While it is clear that each complaint made under this plan must rise or fall on its own facts and merits[,] it is also clear that there should be some uniformity in the interpretation of" the Plan. Steelworkers, 51 LA 1080, 1084 (Kleeb, 1968). *See also* Farrell Lines, 73 LA 64, 67 (Steuer, 1979); Laborers, 71 LA 858, 860 (Kleeb, 1978).

[54]Cannelton Indus., 90 LA 705, 708–09 (Stoltenberg, 1988) (res judicata applied where company failed to show previous award was "clearly an instance of bad judgment; was made without the benefit of some important and relevant facts; was based on a substantial error of law or fact or conflicts with a Board decision. . . . A subsequent arbitrator is not to substitute his [own] judgment for that of the prior arbitrator simply because he might have ruled differently in deciding the dispute"). *See also* Arch on the Green, 89 LA 892 (Seidman, 1987); North River Energy Co., 88 LA 447 (Witney, 1987).

[55]Freeman United Coal Mining Co., 87 LA 665, 667–68 (Clarke, 1986).

Also, if the ruling of the umpire on an issue appears not to be in line with the rulings of this Board, a grievance dealing with that issue may be processed to this Board. Rulings by this Board on issues have precedence over the rulings made by other umpires. Issues ruled on by this Board shall remain settled and no grievance clearly confined to such issues may be processed to this Board.[56]

A Bethlehem Steel Company umpire stated that "though he does not consider that he is necessarily bound by the decisions of prior umpires, he does believe that a heavy burden of persuasion rests on the party who urges that such prior decisions should be reversed."[57] When this heavy burden is met and a later umpire is convinced that a prior decision is erroneous, it will be reversed.[58] He also noted that while the "dictum statements" of other Bethlehem system umpires "are entitled to respect," no presumption of correctness attaches to them.[59] Of course, the distinction between what is dictum and what is part of a holding is sometimes open to interpretation.

Finally, it should be pointed out that umpires are quite capable of reversing their own prior rulings.[60]

C. Temporary or Ad Hoc Arbitrators [LA CDI 94.554; 100.0783]

Prior awards issued by temporary arbitrators, also known as ad hoc arbitrators, also may have authoritative force. Their awards interpreting a collective bargaining agreement usually become binding parts of the agreement and will be followed by arbitrators thereafter.[61] Accordingly, an arbi-

---

[56]Tennessee Coal, Iron & R.R., 6 LA 426, 429 (Blumer & Kelly, 1945). Because it was decided that the issue presently involved had been ruled on previously, the grievance was denied. *See also* American Steel & Wire Co., 11 LA 945, 945 (Seward, 1948).

[57]Bethlehem Cornwall Corp., 25 LA 894, 897 (Seward, 1956). For more of that umpire's views, see *Bethlehem Steel Co.*, 20 LA 87, 90–91 (Seward, 1953). *See also* Pittsburgh Steel Co., 46 LA 774, 775–76 (McDermott, 1966); Bethlehem Steel Co., 41 LA 587, 590 (Crawford, 1963).

[58]Bethlehem Steel Co., 24 LA 379, 380–81 (recommended decision by Alexander, approved by Seward, 1955). Where there was a much more complete presentation of evidence before a subsequent umpire, he modified a prior umpire ruling. United States Steel Corp., 48 LA 1149, 1158–59 (McDermott, 1967).

[59]Bethlehem Steel Co., 28 LA 351, 352 (Seward, 1957).

[60]*See* International Harvester Co., 21 LA 214, 215 (Cole, 1953).

[61]*See* Ideal Elec. Co., 92 LA 1192, 1198–99 (Duda, Jr., 1989); Todd Pac. Shipyards Corp., 91 LA 30, 31–32 (Alleyne, 1988); Logan Co., 90 LA 949, 951 (High, 1988); Howard Paper Mills, 87 LA 863, 866 (Dworkin, 1986); Fire Fighters (IAFF), 86 LA 1201, 1203 (Alleyne, 1986); Consolidation Coal Co., 82 LA 889, 891–92 (Abrams, 1984); Hoosier Energy Rural Elec. Coop., 80 LA 1146, 1148 (Seidman, 1983); Webster Cent. Sch. Dist., 80 LA 1138, 1139–40 (Brand, 1983); Department of the Interior, 78 LA 620, 624 (Levak, 1982); City of Milwaukee, Wis., 78 LA 89, 98 (Yaffe, 1982); Pacific Tel. & Tel. Co., 77 LA 1088, 1096 (Brown, 1981); Pacific Southwest Airlines, 76 LA 197, 200 (Ross, 1981); Safeway Stores, 75 LA 798, 800 (Madden, 1980); Armstrong World Indus., 75 LA 720, 721–22 (Johnston, 1980); Pillsbury Co., 75 LA 523, 529 (Fitch, 1980); Detroit Edison Co., 73 LA 565, 568–69 (Lipson, 1979); Cook County, Ill., Bd. of Educ., 73 LA 310, 314–15 (Hill, 1979); Bofors-Lakeway, 72 LA 159, 161–63 (Kelman, 1979); Marley Cooling Tower Co., 71 LA 306, 313 (Sergent, Jr., 1978); General Tel. Co. of Ohio, 70 LA 240, 244–45 (Ellmann, 1978); Shurtleff & Andrews, 68 LA 439, 441 (Dobranski, 1977); Tennessee River Pulp & Paper Co., 68 LA 421, 431 (Simon, 1977). For the opposing view, see *Hotpoint Co.*, 23 LA 562, 567 (Baab, 1954); *General Elec. Co.*, 9 LA 757, 763 (Wallen, 1948). But the arbitrator did hold prior awards binding in *Allegheny Ludlum Steel Corp.*, 43 LA 1041, 1042–43 (Wallen, 1964), and in *Gorton-Pew Fisheries Co.*, 16 LA 365, 368 (Wallen, 1951). *Gar Wood Indus.*, 22 LA 605, 606 (Ryder, 1954), would give such awards "serious and weighty consideration though not binding [effect]." *See*

trator declared that where a "prior decision involves the interpretation of the identical contract provision, between the same company and union, every principle of common sense, policy, and labor relations demands that it stand until the parties annul it by a newly worded contract provision."[62] Building on this principle, the arbitrator expressed the view that where identical contractual provisions are adopted by joint negotiations of a union with a number of competing companies, an award construing the provision should be given great weight in like cases involving any of the companies.[63] Another arbitrator agreed that an arbitration decision involving a different plant of the employer and a different local union should be given great weight where

---

also Texaco, Inc., 75 LA 76, 81 (LeBaron, 1980). It appears clear from court decisions that an arbitrator is not *required* to follow a prior award construing the same agreement. *See* Connecticut Light & Power Co. v. Electrical Workers (IBEW) Local 420, 718 F.2d 14, 114 LRRM 2770, 2775 (2d Cir. 1983); New Orleans S.S. Ass'n v. Longshoremen (ILA) Local 1218, 626 F.2d 455, 105 LRRM 2539, 2548 (5th Cir. 1980) (stating that the question whether an "award can be given an effect akin to res judicata or stare decisis with regard to future disputes that may arise between the parties" is a proper question for the arbitrator if the parties do not agree otherwise); Westinghouse Elevators of P.R. v. S.I.U. de P.R., 583 F.2d 1184, 99 LRRM 2651, 2653 (1st Cir. 1978); Riverboat Casino dba Holiday Casino v. Local Joint Executive Bd. of Las Vegas, 578 F.2d 250, 99 LRRM 2374, 2375 (9th Cir. 1978); Little Six Corp. v. Mine Workers Local 8332, 701 F. Supp. 26, 112 LRRM 2922 (4th Cir. 1983) (holding it is for the arbitrator to determine the preclusive effect of a prior award). *See also* Fournelle v. NLRB, 670 F.2d 331, 343 n.22, 109 LRRM 2441, 2450 n.22 (D.C. Cir. 1982). In *W.R. Grace & Co. v. Rubber Workers Local 759*, 461 U.S. 757, 113 LRRM 2641, 2644 (1983), the arbitration clause in the collective bargaining agreement limited the authority of arbitrators to the interpretation and application of the "express" provisions of the agreement, and the finality clause specified that the decision of an arbitrator "within his jurisdiction and authority as specified in this Agreement shall be final and binding . . . ." *Id.* at 763 n.5. Under these provisions, an arbitrator concluded that a prior arbitrator had acted outside his jurisdiction and that this deprived the prior award of precedential force under the agreement. As to this the Supreme Court stated:

[The arbitrator's] initial conclusion that he was not bound by the [prior] decision was based on his interpretation of the bargaining agreement's provisions defining the arbitrator's jurisdiction and his perceived obligation to give a prior award a preclusive effect. . . . Because the authority of arbitrators is a subject of collective bargaining, just as is any other contractual provision, the scope of the arbitrator's authority is itself a question of contract interpretation that the parties have delegated to the arbitrator. [The arbitrator's] conclusions that [the prior arbitrator] acted outside his jurisdiction and that this deprived the [prior] award of precedential force under the contract draw their "essence" from the provisions of the collective-bargaining agreement. Regardless of what our view might be of the correctness of [the arbitrator's] contractual interpretation, the Company and the Union bargained for that interpretation. A federal court may not second-guess it.

Id. at 765, 113 LRRM at 2644. By use of the phrase "*his perceived* obligation to give a prior award a preclusive effect" (emphasis added), the Court does not appear to be expressing any view of its own concerning the precedential force of a prior award. Rather, by the total quoted statement the Court was indicating merely that the arbitrator was authorized to reach conclusions, that his conclusions did draw their essence from the agreement, and that a court accordingly may not substitute its own views and conclusions.

[62]Pan Am. Ref. Corp., 2 ALAA ¶67,937, at 69,464 (McCoy, 1948). *See also* Southeastern Pa. Transp. Auth., 100 LA 767, 773 (Goulet, 1992); Regional Transit Auth., 94 LA 489, 491–92 (Fullmer, 1990); Macomb County Rd. Comm'n, 94 LA 139, 141 (Coyle, 1989).

[63]American-St. Gobain Corp., 39 LA 306, 306 (McCoy, 1962). *See also* Shurtleff & Andrews, 68 LA 439, 441 (Dobranski, 1977). One arbitrator considered that prior awards involving identical contractual language between locals of the same union and divisions of the same company should be given "great, but not controlling, weight." Reynolds Mining Corp., 33 LA 25, 28 (Bauder, 1959). *But see* Atlantic Gummed Paper Corp., 35 LA 680, 681 (Rubin, 1960).

the contract language was identical and where the union's primary negotiator at both plants was the same person.[64]

The persuasive force of a prior award was held to be particularly strong where the contract language was not changed after the award, and it had been followed in contract administration.[65] For a second arbitrator to change a prior decision that the parties have not seen fit to change, in the absence of a substantial change in the facts of the case or in the pertinent language of the contract, encourages repetitive arbitrations of the same issue and allows problems to remain unresolved to the detriment of the relations between the parties.[66]

One arbitrator urged that a proper regard for the arbitration process and for stability in collective bargaining relations requires acceptance by an arbitrator, even though not technically binding, of any interpretation of the parties' contractual relations rendered by a previous arbitrator, if on point and if based on the same agreement.[67]

It seems obvious that the binding force of any award ordinarily should not continue after the provision on which the award is based is materially changed or is eliminated entirely from the parties' agreement.[68] However, if the agreement is renegotiated without materially changing a provision that has been interpreted by an arbitrator, the parties may be held to have adopted the award as a part of the contract.[69] Indeed, the binding force of an award may even be strengthened by such renegotiation without change.[70] In this regard, an arbitrator explained:

---

[64]Cone Mills Corp., 86 LA 992 (Nolan, 1986).

[65]Freeman United Coal Mine Co., 84 LA 1302 (Feldman, 1985). See also Port Drum Co., 82 LA 942 (Holman, 1984).

[66]See Florida Power Corp., 87 LA 957, 960 (Wahl, 1986). In the following cases, prior decisions were not followed: no renegotiation of agreement, Weyerhaeuser Co., 92 LA 361 (Woolf, 1989); facts were not asserted, Fairmont Gen. Hosp., 91 LA 930 (Hunter, Jr., 1988); and facts changed, North Suburban Mass Transit Dist., 90 LA 809 (Meyers, 1988). Similarly, in Federal Wholesale Co., 92 LA 271 (Richard, 1989), a prior decision barring subcontracting was not followed where the previous arbitrator recognized but did not factually find "a special business need" that was found by the second arbitrator.

[67]O&S Bearing Co., 12 LA 132, 135 (Smith, 1949) (prior award was not followed, however, because it involved a temporary special agreement rather than the agreement before the arbitrator). Accord Lehigh Portland Cement Co., 46 LA 132, 137 (Duff, 1965); Mobil Oil Co., 46 LA 140, 146 (Hebert, 1966); Brewers Bd. of Trade, 38 LA 679, 680 (Turkus, 1962).

[68]PPG Indus., 113 LA 833 (Dichter, 1999). See also Teledyne Amco, 76 LA 932, 934 (Raymond, 1981); Mead Corp., 43 LA 661, 662–64 (Dunau, 1964); Bethlehem Steel Co., 41 LA 624, 626 (Porter, 1963). An award may cease to be binding even before the contract expires if the parties follow a practice inconsistent with the award. Waterfront Employers Ass'n of the Pac. Coast, 2 ALAA ¶67,949 (Miller, 1948).

[69]See Todd Shipyards Corp., 69 LA 27, 28 (Jones, Jr., 1977); Taylor Stone Co., 50 LA 208, 212 (Stouffer, 1967); Owens-Illinois Glass Co., 43 LA 715, 721 (Dworkin, 1964); Avco Corp., 64–1 ARB ¶8292 (Marshall, 1963); United States Indus. Chems. Co., 41 LA 348, 351 (Geissinger, 1963); Lukens Steel Co., 37 LA 711, 715 (Crawford, 1961); Stewart-Warner Corp., 33 LA 816, 819 (Uible, 1960); Federal Bearings Co., 22 LA 721, 725–27 (Justin, 1954); Union Elec. of Mo., 16 LA 816, 818 (Kelliher, 1951); Gorton-Pew Fisheries Co., 16 LA 365, 368 (Wallen, 1951); International Harvester Co., 16 LA 217, 218–19 (McCoy, 1951). See also Aerojet-General Corp., 37 LA 853, 856–57 (Killion, 1961); Crown Upholstering Co., 18 LA 777, 779–80 (Kaplan, 1952). Contra Corn Prods. Co., 50 LA 1093, 1095–96 (Kamin, 1968).

[70]See Hoosier Energy Rural Elec. Coop., 80 LA 1146, 1147–48 (Seidman, 1983); Todd Shipyards Corp., 69 LA 27, 28 (Jones, Jr., 1977); Butler Mfg. Co., 42 LA 304, 306–07 (Johnston, 1964); Federal Bearings Co., 22 LA 721, 725–27 (Justin, 1954) (while he apparently was otherwise inclined to give an award involving the same parties only "a 'persuasive' force

[T]he arbitration process would hardly survive the erosion of confidence in its effectiveness were second-thought arbitrators freely to set aside first-impression arbitral awards so that awards would lose their acceptability as being final and binding. It is not surprising, therefore, that it is unusual, indeed rare, for a later arbitrator to find the earlier award not final and binding. Even so, however, there do arise circumstances in which the occasion seems compelling to the later arbitrator to disregard or modify the earlier award. After all, it is the integrity and intelligence of each arbitrator that are commissioned by the disputants who jointly select each to make his or her own appraisal and decision. . . .

But this dilemma for the second arbitrator largely if not wholly disappears once the agreement has expired after issuance of the prior award. For upon its expiration the opportunity exists in negotiations to alter, amend or modify any arbitral interpretation deemed to have warped or otherwise sufficiently mutilated the intent of the earlier draftsmen as to warrant that effort by the disadvantaged party. Of course, such an effort has its costs too and they may militate against undertaking it. But that is a decision for the bargainer to make in terms of its own priorities in the overall bargaining relationship. That the earlier award remains untouched by later negotiations, or even demonstrably unmentioned in them, in no wise signifies that a cost-benefit appraisal has not been made, however crude or casual it may have been.

So an arbitrator who is summoned to office by the parties in the course of a subsequent term of their agreement, and is importuned by one of them to overturn that earlier award, should feel considerably relieved of any concern for possible error having done violence to the intent of the parties by the earlier arbitrator. That latter's award has now had the ultimate review of subsequent collective bargaining negotiations and has survived the test for whatever reason.[71]

---

which compels consideration," still, where the parties did not disturb the award in renegotiating their agreement, he found "no basis or warrant to disturb it"); Gorton-Pew Fisheries Co., 16 LA 365, 368 (Wallen, 1951). *See also* B.F. Goodrich Chem. Co., 73 LA 603, 604–05 (Tharp, 1979); Holland Suco Color Co., 43 LA 1022, 1024 (Geissinger, 1964).

[71]Todd Shipyards Corp., 69 LA 27, 28 (Jones, Jr., 1977). *See also* Block, *Decisional Thinking—West Coast Panel Report*, in DECISIONAL THINKING OF ARBITRATORS AND JUDGES, PROCEEDINGS OF THE 33D ANNUAL MEETING OF NAA 119, 143 (Stern & Dennis eds., BNA Books 1981). It seems likely that, for purposes other than establishing a waiver of statutory rights, an arbitrator properly may hold that an award is still binding under a subsequent agreement on the basis of a less demanding showing than the "clear and unmistakable" showing required by the U.S. Supreme Court for an award to qualify as an "explicit" waiver of National Labor Relations Act (NLRA), 29 U.S.C. §151 et seq., protection. In this regard, in *Metropolitan Edison Co. v. NLRB*, 460 U.S. 693, 112 LRRM 3265 (1983), the Court held:

(1) A general no-strike clause did not impose a higher duty upon union officials than upon other employees to prevent illicit work stoppages, and NLRA § 8(a)(3) protected union officials against being disciplined more severely than other employees for like misconduct.

(2) This NLRA protection can be waived by the union, but any waiver of the statutory right must be "explicitly stated," or "[m]ore succinctly, the waiver must be clear and unmistakable."

Id. at 708, 112 LRRM at 3271.

(3) While two arbitration decisions under the parties' prior agreement had imposed a higher duty on union officials, this did not "establish a pattern of decisions clear enough to convert the union's silence into binding waiver," and this was especially so in light of the collective agreement provision making arbitration decisions binding "for the term of *this* agreement."

Id. at 709, 112 LRRM at 3272 (emphasis in original).

The employer had argued that "the union's failure to change the relevant contractual language in the face of two prior arbitration decisions constitutes an implicit contractual waiver." *Id.* at 708, 1123 LRRM at 3271. To this the Court replied:

A number of arbitrators have identified the circumstances under which, and the reasons why, a prior award need not be followed. One arbitrator observed that while "it is only fair and reasonable to expect an arbitrator's decision to apply to subsequent cases of the same nature," and that "the refusal to apply the arbitrator's decision to similar cases leaves unsolved and unsettled the general problem covered by the decision," nevertheless, the refusal to apply an award to cases of the same nature is justified where it is shown that any one of the following conditions obtains: (1) the previous decision clearly was an instance of bad judgment, (2) the decision was made without the benefit of some important and relevant facts or considerations, or (3) new conditions have arisen questioning the reasonableness of the continued application of the decision.[72]

Other arbitrators have agreed that an arbitrator is justified in refusing to follow an award considered to be clearly erroneous,[73] or one whose continued application is rendered questionable by changed conditions.[74] In the opin-

---

[W]e do not doubt that prior arbitration decisions may be relevant—both to other arbitrators and to the Board—in interpreting bargaining agreements. But to waive a statutory right the [union official's higher] duty must be established clearly and unmistakably. Where prior arbitration decisions have been inconsistent, sporadic, or ambiguous, there would be little basis for determining that the parties intended to incorporate them in subsequent agreements.

Id. at 708–09, 112 LRRM at 3271–72 (footnote omitted). The Court also stated:

An arbitration decision may be relevant to establishing waiver of this statutory right when the arbitrator has stated that the bargaining agreement itself clearly and unmistakably imposes an explicit duty on union officials to end unlawful work stoppages. Absent such a statement, the arbitration decision would not demonstrate that the union specifically intended to waive the statutory protection otherwise afforded its officials. In this case, however, the two arbitration decisions did not purport to determine the parties' specific intent.

Id. at 709 n.13, 112 LRRM at 3271 n.13. Cf. *Fournelle v. NLRB*, 670 F.2d 331, 109 LRRM 2441, 2450 (D.C. Cir. 1982), in which the court pointed to certain distinctions between the facts there and those in the *Metropolitan Edison* case.

[72]Inland Steel Co., 1 ALAA ¶67,121, at 67,248 (Blumer, 1944). *See also* Waterfront Employers Ass'n of the Pac. Coast, 7 LA 757, 758 (Kerr, 1947), where the arbitrator added obvious and substantial errors of fact or law and the lack of fair and full hearing as justification for refusal to apply the prior award, but he placed the burden of proof on the party alleging any of these grounds.

[73]*See* City of Detroit, 68 LA 848, 853 (Roumell, Jr., 1977); Coleman Co., 52 LA 357, 359 (Carter, 1969); American Cyanamid Co., 49 LA 314, 319 (Waldron, 1967); Mississippi Lime Co. of Mo., 32 LA 1013, 1017 (Hilpert, 1959); American Steel Foundries, 19 LA 779, 787 (Klamon, 1952); North Am. Aviation Inc., 15 LA 626, 630–31 (Komaroff, 1950). *See also* discussion in Connecticut Light & Power Co. v. Electrical Workers (IBEW) Local 420, 718 F.2d 14, 114 LRRM 2770 (2d Cir. 1983).

[74]*See* Packaging Corp. of Am., 102 LA 1099 (Odom, Jr., 1994) (Twenty years after a 1973 arbitration award that required management "to continue to furnish nurses on all shifts, and weekends," *id.* at 1101, the company discontinued such staffing because the number of employees served had been reduced by more than one-half and it had instituted a program to train and equip employees to provide emergency medical response. Denying the union's grievance, the arbitrator found that "replacing old ways of doing things with new methods . . . [was] adequate to serve the safety needs of the Bargaining Unit personnel," and concluded that "[a]lthough the logic of . . . [the prior] award has survived, new methods and changing conditions require a different result," *id.* at 1102); Braun Baking Co., 43 LA 433, 439–40 (May, 1964); Armstrong Cork Co., 34 LA 890, 894 (Morvant, 1960). In *National Broad. Co.*, 71 LA 762, 769 (Gentile, 1978), the master agreement provided that an arbitrator shall not consider any issue that had been the subject of a previous arbitration, "except upon a showing of . . . new evidence, change of condition, or circumstances."

ion of one arbitrator, a party is not ordinarily justified in seeking an award contrary to a prior decision by submitting (in a different case but with the same issue) additional evidence to a subsequent arbitrator;[75] but in several cases the presentation of additional evidence or clarification of previously presented evidence has produced a contrary award by the subsequent arbitrator.[76]

An arbitrator understandably may feel less firmly bound by another arbitrator's award if it is not accompanied by a reasoned opinion,[77] and dictum statements of a prior ad hoc arbitrator may carry little or no weight.[78]

Frequently, when prior awards are cited by a party as being authoritative, the arbitrator will avoid giving preclusive effect by distinguishing them.[79] Often the differences will be clear, but there are cases where the drawing of a distinction can prove to be troublesome. For instance, in one case the company cited an award rendered two years earlier in a case involving the same company but a different union. The arbitrator wrote that the similarity of the two cases made the prior award germane; moreover, the issue was not one of peculiar relevancy to a particular bargaining unit. But then he stated that, while the prior decision carried weight in appraising the merits of the present case, its mere existence did not foreclose him from reaching a different conclusion. Reconciling the apparent philosophical inconsistency, he went on to explain that there was no adequate opinion in the earlier award, and that it was on a slightly different issue.

> Placing the Company in the position of having two arbitrators make different rulings on the same question is repugnant to all parties; the very dignity of arbitration is endangered, and, on the surface, it would appear that arbitra-

---

[75]Douglas Aircraft Co., 49 LA 744, 748, 752 (Kotin, 1967) (arbitrator also indicated that this may be justified where production of the evidence was foreclosed by circumstances beyond the control of the party).

[76]*See* Universal City Studios, 78 LA 79, 88 (Rothschild, 1982); National Distillers Prods. Co., 53 LA 477, 480 (Jones, Jr., 1969); United States Steel Corp., 48 LA 1149, 1158–59 (McDermott, 1967); Westinghouse Elec. Corp., 45 LA 889, 891–92 (Cayton, undated); Wheland Co., 38 LA 1199, 1207 (Murphy, 1962).

[77]See *Weyerhaeuser Co.*, 92 LA 361, 364 (Woolf, 1989), in which the arbitrator pointed out the need to write fully reasoned opinions if prior awards are to be persuasive on subsequent arbitrators, noting that the lack of discussion in the prior decision regarding the interpretation of the language of the labor agreement prevented her from "evaluating the reasonableness, soundness and validity of that decision" and resulted in her declining to follow the prior award. *See also* General Dynamics Corp., 53 LA 424, 427 (Roberts, 1969); John J. Nissen Baking Co., 48 LA 12, 17 (Fallon, 1966).

[78]*See* Blaw-Knox Co., 50 LA 1086, 1088 (Meltzer, 1968).

[79]*See* Racine Unified Sch. Dist., 100 LA 1020, 1024–25 (McAlpin, 1993); Emerson Elec. Co., 78 LA 339, 341 (Stonehouse, 1982); Burdick Corp., 76 LA 611, 619 (Petrie, 1981); Naval Ordnance Station, 74 LA 1055, 1057 (Fitch, 1980); West Mifflin Area Sch. Dist., 74 LA 627, 629 (Hays, 1980); United States Steel Corp., 70 LA 1131, 1135 (Dunsford, 1978); Chicago Bridge & Iron Co., 70 LA 584, 586 (Harrison, 1978); Town of W. Orange, N.J., 70 LA 581, 584 (Dennis, 1978); Consolidated Aluminum Corp., 70 LA 538, 543 (Murphy, 1978); Kast Metals Corp., 70 LA 278, 283 (Roberts, 1978); American Shipbuilding Co., 69 LA 944, 953 (Ruben, 1977); International Paper Co., 69 LA 857, 861 (Taylor, 1977); Belknap, Inc., 69 LA 599, 601 (Teple, 1977); Federal Aviation Admin., 68 LA 375, 377 (Moore, 1977).

tion is dangerously subjective. Therefore, it is only after sincere and prolonged deliberation that the undersigned makes the following [contrary] ruling.[80]

Of course, the parties are free in any case to confirm, limit, or eliminate entirely the precedential value of a forthcoming award.[81]

There may be times, however, when an arbitrator wants to limit the precedential effect of an award, for example, when the parties have signaled their acceptance of a particular disposition limited to the one case. The arbitrator may include a statement to that effect, such as the one made by this arbitrator: "The Arbitrator finds and emphasizes that his Award applies solely to the instant case, and his decision shall not be used in any way as a binding precedent on either of the parties concerning the question of overtime assignments or other matters."[82]

4. Persuasive Prior Awards

A. Degree of Persuasive Force

While prior awards between the parties may have authoritative force, awards involving the same issue but issued under contracts between other parties are considered to have persuasive force only.[83] Nothing is settled by

---

[80]Brown & Sharpe Mfg. Co., 7 LA 134, 138–39 (Healy, 1947). For possible courses of action available to a third arbitrator when confronted with the conflicting decisions of two prior arbitrators, see *Minnesota Mining & Mfg. Co.*, 75 LA 534, 536 (Haemmel, 1980); *Minnesota Mining & Mfg. Co.*, 75 LA 380, 384 (Foster, 1980); *Coleman Co.*, 55 LA 510, 513 (Wann, 1970); *Mallinckrodt Chem. Works*, 50 LA 933, 935 (Goldberg, 1968); *New York City Bd. of Educ.*, 45 LA 43, 44 (Rock, 1965). In *Graphic Arts Local 97-B v. Haddon Craftsmen*, 489 F. Supp. 1088, 1096–98 (M.D. Pa. 1979), the court refused to set aside either of two conflicting awards where each drew its essence from the agreement. In *Connecticut Light & Power Co. v. Electrical Workers (IBEW) Local 420*, 718 F.2d 14, 20, 114 LRRM 2770 (2d Cir. 1983), the court set aside one of two conflicting awards even though each drew its essence from the agreement, but it stressed that special circumstances required its action, and it recognized that generally "inconsistency with another award is not enough by itself to justify vacating an award."

[81]*See, e.g.,* Motor Car Dealers Ass'n of Kansas City, 49 LA 55, 56 (Beatty, 1967) (award to govern the disposition of pending like grievances); Superior Prods. Co., 42 LA 517, 523 (Smith, 1964) (award not to bind other parties to master agreement); Milwaukee Cartage Exch. & Wis. Motor Carrier, 19 LA 106, 106 (Anderson, 1952) (award to govern future like grievances). Such a stipulation itself required interpretation in *Howard P. Foley Co.*, 73 LA 1205, 1206–07 (Smith, 1979). Only a small percentage of collective bargaining agreements contain any provision as to the precedential effect of awards. *See Basic Patterns in Labor Arbitration Agreements*, 34 LA 931, 940 (1960). *See, e.g.,* Article 15.5.C.3.f. in Agreement Between United States Postal Service and American Postal Workers Union, AFL-CIO, 2000–2003, *available at* <http://www.apwu.org/departments/ir/irframe.htm>. Sometimes the arbitrator will specify that the award is not to have authoritative precedential force. *See* Thrifty Corp., 72 LA 898, 905 (Barrett, 1979); Vindicator Printing Co., 48 LA 213, 219 (Smith, 1966); Pittsburgh Plate Glass Co., 36 LA 21, 22 (Lehoczky, 1960).

[82]Fashion Shoe Prods., 84 LA 325, 331 (Hilgert, 1985).

[83]Salmond defined the persuasive precedent as one that depends for its influence on its own merits and on that alone. Salmond on Jurisprudence §53 (Williams ed., 11th ed. 1957). Salmond also included judicial dicta with the persuasive precedents. Thus, it might be said that dicta in prior awards differ from decisions in prior awards primarily in regard to the degree of force exerted by each.

saying that such prior awards do or do not have the force of precedent. Rather, it is essential that one recognize that the precedential force of prior awards is always a question of degree.

There are many cases where, in varying degree, the arbitrator was persuaded by prior awards. In some of these cases, the arbitrator spoke in terms of finding "support" in prior awards, but, regardless of the terminology, the effect is the same—the arbitrator relied on or otherwise made use of prior awards.[84]

It is easy for an arbitrator to be persuaded by, or to rely on, a prior award that is in near agreement with the arbitrator's own views. Moreover, most thoughtfully prepared awards rely on principles that will command respect by reason of their logic and the fair result that they yield under the facts. Such awards can be characterized as "objectively reasonable." That is, they reflect what a "reasonably prudent person" would decide under the given circumstances. In particular, the considered judgment of any widely known and respected arbitrator cannot be ignored or dismissed lightly.[85]

---

[84]*See, e.g.,* Lucent Techs., 115 LA 228 (Caraway, 2000); Wisconsin Dep't of Health & Soc. Servs., 91 LA 596, 598 (Flaten, 1988); Kinlock Coal Co., 71 LA 1232, 1235 (Clarke, 1979); Ogden Newspapers, 71 LA 1208, 1210 (Fisher II, 1978); Dayton Press, 71 LA 1034, 1038 (Barone, 1978); Muskegon County Bd. of Comm'rs, 71 LA 942, 947 (Allen, Jr., 1978); Livonia Pub. Sch., 71 LA 937, 941 (Kanner, 1978); Kellogg Co., 71 LA 494, 497 (Hon, 1978); Standard Packaging Corp., 71 LA 445, 449 (Fogelberg, 1978); Bethlehem Steel Corp., 71 LA 420, 425 (Seward, 1978); General Elec. Co., 71 LA 164, 169 (Maroney, 1978); Park Poultry, 71 LA 1, 5 (Cohen, 1978); Ingram Mfg. Co., 70 LA 1269, 1272 (Johannes, 1978); Central Tel. Co., 70 LA 1217, 1223 (Kennedy, 1978); Minnesota Mining & Mfg. Co., 70 LA 1078, 1083 (Boyer, Jr., 1978); NCR, 70 LA 756, 759 (Gundermann, 1978); Mountain States Tel. & Tel. Co., 70 LA 729, 741 (Goodman, 1978); Pickwick Int'l, 70 LA 676, 679 (Ross, 1978); FMC Corp., 70 LA 574, 575 (Nigro, 1978); Chevron Oil Co., 70 LA 572, 573 (Davis, 1978); American Steel, 70 LA 494, 496 (Beck, 1978); Butler Mfg. Co., 70 LA 426, 427 (Welch, 1978); Playboy Club of Century City, 70 LA 304, 308 (Herman, 1978); H.D. Lee Co., 70 LA 245, 247–49 (Ferguson, 1978); Teledyne Indus. Diecast, 70 LA 185, 186 (Cox, 1978); Mammoth Plastics, 70 LA 182, 185 (Tharp, 1978); Mid-America Dairymen, 70 LA 116, 120 (Fitzsimmons, 1978); Evans Prods. Co., 70 LA 89, 92 (Baum, 1978); Anthony Forest Prods. Co., 70 LA 58, 65 (Williams, 1978); Houdaille Indus., 69 LA 1080, 1083 (Hunter, Jr., 1977); Tri-State Eng'g Co., 69 LA 980, 983 (Brown, 1977); Schien Body & Equip. Co., 69 LA 930, 939 (Roberts, 1977); Suburban Mfg. Co., 69 LA 928, 930 (Flannagan, 1977); B.F. Goodrich Co., 69 LA 922, 927 (Klein, 1977); East Orange Bd. of Educ., 69 LA 674, 676 (Spencer, 1977); Control Data Corp., 69 LA 665, 669 (Hatcher, 1977); Transit Mgmt. of Fla., 69 LA 609, 611 (Kanzer, 1977); Belknap, Inc., 69 LA 599, 603 (Teple, 1977); Superior Dairy, 69 LA 594, 598 (Abrams, 1977); Pacific Tel. & Tel. Co., 69 LA 469, 475 (Marcus, 1977); Acme Elec. Corp., 69 LA 176, 179 (Croft, 1977); Noll Mfg. Co., 69 LA 170, 175 (Ward, 1977). Regarding possible effects of citing precedents in arbitration, cf. Jennings & Martin, *The Role of Prior Arbitration Awards in Arbitral Decisions*, 29 LAB. L.J. 95, 100–06 (1978); Harris, *The Use of Precedent in Labor Arbitration*, 32 ARB. J. 26 (1977).

[85]*See* Texas Air Nat'l Guard, 115 LA 249, 252 (Moore, 2000) ("In every decade since 1944 this standard of interpreting CBAs [collective bargaining agreements] and upholding discipline when an employee refuses to perform work when ordered to do so has been followed by experienced and nationally recognized arbitrators."). *See also* Terex/American Crane Corp., 114 LA 47, 50 (Nolan, 1999) ("One of America's greatest arbitrators, Yale Law School Dean Harry Shulman, explained the distinction [that not every practice is binding] many years ago . . . .") Basler Elec. Co., 47 LA 870, 873 (Stix, 1966); Martin Aircraft Tool Co., 25 LA 181, 185 (Spaulding, 1955); Continental Oil Co., 22 LA 880, 882–83 (Reynard, 1954); Firestone Tire & Rubber Co., 20 LA 880, 888 (Gorder, 1953); Allied Chem. & Dye Corp., 18 LA 315, 319 (Fulda, 1949); Aviation Maint. Corp., 8 LA 261, 272 (Aaron, 1947); Bethlehem Steel Co., 6 LA 397, 402 (Levy, 1947).

The attitude of one eminent arbitrator, the late David A. Wolff (the Chrysler Umpire), when considering the award of another eminent arbitrator, the late Harry Shulman (the Ford Umpire), is instructive:

> The Chairman realizes that, despite the great similarity of contract provisions and their apparent common origin and despite the fact of similarity of parties, location and type of business, there are distinctions which exist and must be observed. The parties are not the same parties. Their practices are not identical. Even their application of the considered contract provisions has varied. Further, while Dr. Shulman and the Chairman both act as umpires they were not selected, nor do they act for, the same parties. The parties making the selections undoubtedly had in mind the known general thinking of each at the time of selections and made the selections on an individual basis. On the other hand, points of similarity may not be disregarded. In addition the Chairman has high regard for Dr. Shulman's sincerity, clarity of thought, and reasoning processes. The Chairman does not propose to unthinkingly adopt Dr. Shulman's determination in another case as his own in the instant case. However, to the extent to which he believes it here applicable, he makes use of it with appreciation.[86]

In any event, it would seem that whenever either party cites an award, the arbitrator should not ignore it. Respect for the citing party and the integrity of the arbitral process require the arbitrator to consider all the contentions of a party.[87] One arbitrator believed that fair consideration of a prior award relied on by one of the parties to be so important that he reconvened the hearing for that purpose.[88]

---

[86]Chrysler Appeal Bd. Case No. 573 (Wolff, 1948).

[87]Even where the parties agreed that their arbitrator was not *bound* by precedents, an arbitrator considers those cited by the parties. *See* Bates Container, 68 LA 1006, 1009 (Sisk, 1977); Meyer's Bakery of Little Rock, 38 LA 1135, 1140 (Hon, 1962). Sometimes the bulk of an opinion will be devoted to the discussion of precedents cited by the parties and researched by the arbitrator. *See* Watkins Trucking, 48 LA 1101, 1102–04 (Klein, 1967). In *Bethlehem Steel Co.*, 43 LA 79, 83 (Valtin, 1964), the arbitrator stated he had extensively reviewed the precedents cited by the parties, "because he thinks that it is important to make clear what effect is being given them in deciding the present case." In contrast, see the comments of Dean (and arbitrator) Charles Rehmus:

> There are some very acceptable and respected arbitrators whose opinions read as if they were written by the Supreme Court. They are filled with footnotes and citations—of law, of NAA [National Academy of Arbitrators] papers, and most commonly, cases by other arbitrators. They analyze others' opinions. These are busy arbitrators, but ones who clearly feel comfortable with a style in which their opinions are salted and peppered with footnotes and citations.
>
> Yet I can point out other equally acceptable arbitrators who almost never cite another arbitrator's opinion or award. I rarely cite other arbitrators' opinions and awards, even if the parties cited them to me in their briefs or gave me copies of them at the hearing. I read them. I go to the library and look them up. But my experience is that seldom are they on all squares with the issue before me. They arose from different facts under another contract with different language. There is little point in going into a detailed explanation of why this or the other case cited by one of the parties is not persuasive in my decision. Unless it is a prior award received by these parties and under the same collective bargaining agreement, I rarely bother to cite or distinguish another case.

Writing the Opinion, in ARBITRATION IN PRACTICE 220 (Zack ed., ILR Press 1984).

[88]Boston Daily Newspapers, 6 LA 179, 183–86 (Wallen, 1946). *See also* S.W. Shattuck Chem. Co., 69 LA 912, 915 (Culley, 1977). In *Warehouse Employees Local 169 v. Acme Mkts.*, 473 F. Supp. 709, 105 LRRM 3206 (E.D. Pa. 1979), an award was not vacated merely because the arbitrator refused to reopen the hearing to consider an award in another case.

While precedential use of awards occurs primarily in rights arbitration, such use is by no means unknown in interest arbitration. Prior awards are considered frequently in interest cases.[89] In some circumstances, a prior interest award may have special persuasive significance to other parties "similarly facing the same inquiry."[90]

In all civil law countries, as noted above, the binding force of "a settled course of decision" is recognized. An analogous concept has developed in labor arbitration. Where there is a settled course of arbitral decision on a point, the principle stated in the decisions is often very persuasive, or at least affords highly comforting support for a later ruling.[91] It is unlikely that any such course of decision will be based on faulty reasoning. In this sense, it can be correctly said that "it is not the long line of previous decisions that is determinative," but "the validity of the reasoning behind the principle."[92]

Finally, in the event of court review, an award may more likely be sustained if supported by prior awards.[93]

B. Arbitrator Disagreement With Prior Awards

By no means are arbitrators always swayed by cited awards, even awards that are reasonably on point. Arbitrators are alert to factual and contract-language distinctions between cases.[94] Moreover, when arbitrators cannot agree with the conclusions of cited opinions, they do not hesitate to say so.[95]

---

[89]For example, in *Patriot News Co.*, 15 LA 871, 874 (Egan, 1950), the arbitrator spoke of studying "dozens of arbitration decisions."

[90]Union R.R., 20 LA 219, 224 (Gilden, 1953).

[91]*See* Gulf Oil Co.–U.S., 78 LA 8, 14 (Leeper, 1981); Los Angeles Fire Dep't, 76 LA 572, 575 (Rule, 1981); Pet Inc., 76 LA 32, 40 (Goldstein, 1980); Traverse City Iron Works, 76 LA 21, 26 (Heinsz, 1980); Oscar Mayer & Co., 75 LA 555, 559 (Eischen, 1980); Norris Indus., 73 LA 1129, 1132 (Roumell, Jr., 1979); Kraemer, Edward, & Sons, 72 LA 684, 687–88 (Martin, 1979); ITT Auto. Elec. Prods. Div., 70 LA 830, 832 (Hon, 1978); H.D. Lee Co., 70 LA 245, 249 (Ferguson, 1978); Atlantic Richfield Co., 69 LA 484, 487 (Sisk, 1977); Morton Salt Co., 69 LA 388, 393 (Walter, 1977); Angelus Sanitary Can Mach. Co., 68 LA 973, 975 (Ashe, 1977); Teledyne Still-Man Mfg., 68 LA 188, 191 (Jewett, 1977); I-T-E Imperial Corp., 68 LA 1, 6 (Johnson, 1977). In *Koehring Division*, 46 LA 827, 829 (King, 1966), the arbitrator stated that parties should take notice as to how given provisions generally have been interpreted by arbitrators, and that if a party desires some other meaning, it should negotiate that other meaning into the contract by clear language.

[92]Bachmann Uxbridge Worsted Corp., 23 LA 596, 602 (Hogan, 1954).

[93]*See* Bakery & Confectionery Workers Local 458 v. Hall Baking Co., 69 N.E.2d 111, 115, 19 LRRM 2285 (Mass. 1946).

[94]*See* FabriSteel Mfg. Co., 115 LA 321 (Brodsky, 2000); Styberg Eng'g Co., 77 LA 780, 783 (Petrie, 1981); Marion Power Shovel Co., 72 LA 417, 421 (Kates, 1979); Stein, Inc., 71 LA 124, 128–29 (Klein, 1978) (distinguishing certain cases cited by one party, and following cases cited by the other party); Van Dyne-Grotty, 70 LA 1288, 1289 (Lewis, 1978); Admiral Mach. Co., 70 LA 575, 578 (Laybourne, 1978); Veterans Admin. Hosp., 70 LA 491, 494 (Snow, 1978); Economy Bushing Co., 70 LA 290, 294 (Krinsky, 1978) (distinguishing his own prior decision); International Paper Co., 70 LA 71, 75 (Robertson, 1978); Mooney-Kiefer-Stewart, Inc., 69 LA 477, 483 (Render, 1977); Rountree Transp. Co., 68 LA 1359, 1362 (Saracino, 1977); Bates Container, 68 LA 1006, 1009 (Sisk, 1977); Hubbell Metals, 68 LA 762, 765 (Marcus, 1977). In *SCM Corp.*, 52 LA 457, 461–63 (Edgett, 1969), the arbitrator distinguished precedents cited by a party and supplied other precedents to "buttress" his finding.

[95]*See* Social Sec. Admin., 91 LA 927, 929–30 (Kaplan, 1988); Metromedia, Inc., 77 LA 424, 427 (Brisco, 1981); Northwestern Bell Tel. Co., 75 LA 148, 152 (Karlins, 1980); Heaven Hill Distilleries, 74 LA 42, 46 (Beckman, 1980); Kennecott Copper Corp., 69 LA 52, 58 (Platt, 1977); Hess Oil & Chem. Corp., 52 LA 1035, 1043 (Bothwell, 1969); American Air Filter Co.,

It also is possible that prior decisions, though sound for their day, will be considered to be out of step with changed times. Alterations in public attitudes, often crystallized by federal and state legislation and regulation, may cause arbitrators to re-examine the premises and hence the continued vitality of earlier awards. For example, in reviewing the discharge of an employee for the alleged sexual harassment of three female employees during a company-sponsored sales conference held at a hotel, an arbitrator refused to follow several decisions reached a decade earlier in which similar and even more egregious episodes of sexual harassment had been found not to constitute just cause for discharge. He opined that the prior decisions were "not in keeping with current arbitral thinking on the subject. . . . [B]oth societal and judicial views on the seriousness of sexual harassment have undergone dramatic change between then and now."[96]

When confronted with conflicting prior awards, an arbitrator may reject those that are unconvincing or that fail to set forth with clarity the rationale behind them. Clearly reasoned opinions may be accepted with the statement that the "reasoning applies with persuasive force to the instant case."[97] Where there are clear lines of arbitral precedent going each way on an issue, arbitrators will use their best judgment as to which line should be applied to the case under consideration.[98]

Sometimes an arbitrator will dismiss cited awards with the statement that, after careful examination, nothing has been found to alter the arbitrator's thinking on the matter.[99] An arbitrator also might acknowledge cited awards, but give no indication as to their persuasive force.[100]

---

47 LA 129, 140 (Hilpert, 1966); Patterson Steel Co., 45 LA 783, 787 (Autrey, 1965); Union News Co., 43 LA 602, 604 (Altieri, 1964); Dynamic Mfrs., 36 LA 635, 639 (Crane, 1960); Management Servs., 20 LA 34, 36 (McCoy, 1953); Mundet Cork Corp., 16 LA 964, 966 (Handsaker, 1951); Consolidated Chem. Indus., 6 LA 714, 716 (Whitton, 1947).

[96]Superior Coffee & Foods, 103 LA 609, 613 (Alleyne, 1994). See also Phelps Dodge Morenci, 114 LA 819 (Brisco, 2000); American Elec. Power, 114 LA 506 (Hewitt, 2000); ConAgra Frozen Foods, 113 LA 129 (Baroni, 1999); Southern Airways, 47 LA 1135, 1141 (Wallen, 1966).

[97]Consolidated Chem. Indus., 6 LA 714, 716–17 (Whitton, 1947). See also Terex/American Crane Corp., 114 LA 47 (Nolan, 1999); American Metaseal Co., 70 LA 295, 297–98 (Kanner, 1978); Riverside Paper Corp. of Appleton, 52 LA 1218, 1220 (Bellman, 1969); Consolidated Aluminum Corp., 51 LA 1129, 1133 (Bothwell, 1968); Sargent-Fletcher Co., 49 LA 76, 77 (Lennard, 1967); Line Materials Indus., 46 LA 1106, 1110 (Teple, 1966); Maui Pineapple Co., 46 LA 849, 851 (Tsukiyama, 1966); R.H. Macy & Co., 46 LA 692, 696 (Yagoda, 1966); Douglas Aircraft Co., 19 LA 854, 855–56 (Merrill, 1953).

[98]See Missouri Pub. Serv. Co., 77 LA 973, 977 (Maniscalco, 1981); Lloyd Ketcham Oldsmobile, 77 LA 953, 959 (Hilgert, 1981); Milwaukee Transp. Serv., 77 LA 807, 813 (Jones, Jr., 1981); Fruehauf Corp., 48 LA 1069, 1073 (Stieber, 1967); Packaging Corp. of Am., 40 LA 544, 547 (Beatty, 1963); Quaker Oats Co., 35 LA 535, 541 (Valtin, 1960). In Omaha Cold Storage Terminal, 48 LA 24, 26, 32 (Doyle, 1967), the arbitrator decided contra to his view in an earlier case with other parties, now having been persuaded by a later line of cases that he considered to be better reasoned.

[99]See Wolf Creek Nuclear Operating Corp., 115 LA 641, 645 (Berger, 2001); St. Regis Paper Co., 46 LA 967, 970 (Stieber, 1966); General Tel. Co. of Cal., 44 LA 691, 694 (Prasow, 1965); Andrew Williams Meat Co., 8 LA 518, 525 (Cheney, 1947).

[100]See Anaconda Wire & Cable Co., 10 LA 20, 24 (Scheiber, 1948); Lebanon Steel Foundry, 6 LA 633, 634 (Brandschain, 1947).

Because arbitrators recognize that use of their awards may be sought in similar cases, they sometimes caution against the precedential use of a particular award, especially if there are features peculiar to that case that make the award inappropriate as a guide for any other case.[101] Moreover, care should be taken when choosing prior published awards for citation, because the citing of prior published awards can be abused. As has been pointed out, many published decisions are written by relatively inexperienced arbitrators, while the vast body of arbitration decisions by the most experienced arbitrators have never been published. "If there is a 'body of arbitral law' it may be likened to an iceberg, of which only the tip is perceptible . . . ."[102]

5. PRECEDENT AND THE EVOLUTION OF SUBSTANTIVE PRINCIPLES

The controversy over the use of awards as precedents is accompanied by a related controversy regarding development of substantive principles through arbitration. Substantive principles are the Siamese twins of precedent.[103] No arbitrator can serve long without becoming aware of the existence of certain more or less generally recognized principles. The question is "not *whether* principles are being evolved, but *what* they are and *how far* they should carry."[104] As to "how far" substantive principles should carry, it is obvious that no principle should be applied automatically without careful thought and thorough consideration.[105] Because many awards are never published, however, it is difficult to determine precisely the extent to which substantive principles are being developed and applied.[106] Frequently, where an

---

[101]*See* International Smelting & Ref. Co., 45 LA 885, 889 (Kornblum, 1965); Bethlehem Steel Co., 29 LA 322, 324 (Seitz, 1957); Ideal Cement Co., 20 LA 465, 467 (Ralston, 1953); Naumkeag Steam Cotton Co., 19 LA 430, 431 (Wolff, 1952); Walla Walla Canning Co., 6 LA 323, 326 (Prasow, 1947). *See also* Eltra Corp., 76 LA 62, 68 (Raymond, 1981).

[102]Seitz, *The Citation of Authority and Precedent in Arbitration (Its Use and Abuse)*, 38 ARB. J. No. 4, at 60 (1983).

[103]"The appearance of precedent in labor arbitration probably results less from a conscious effort to develop a case law, and more from general recognition of the validity of certain principles for the treatment of similar cases." Holman, *The Back-Pay Issue in Arbitration*, II I.L. RES. No. 1, at 6–8 (1955).

[104]Petshek, *Discussion of Principles Emerging From Grievance Arbitration*, 1953 PROCEEDINGS OF IRRA 154, 156 (1953) (emphasis in original).

[105]*See* Electro Metallurgical Co., 22 LA 684, 686 (Shister, 1954).

[106]For factors that various publishers consider in deciding which awards to publish (of those that are available for publication), see Cole, *How Representative Are Published Decisions?: Part I, in* ARBITRATION 1984: ABSENTEEISM, RECENT LAW, PANELS, AND PUBLISHED DECISIONS, PROCEEDINGS OF THE 37TH ANNUAL MEETING OF NAA 170 (Gershenfeld ed., BNA Books 1985); *The Publication of Arbitration Awards, in* ARBITRATION—1975, PROCEEDINGS OF THE 28TH ANNUAL MEETING OF NAA 208, 210–13 (Dennis & Somers eds., BNA Books 1976). *See also* Stewart, *Memo From the Executive Editor*, 36 LA vii–viii (1962), in which users of *Labor Arbitration Reports* also are assured that they "can rely on the long experience and mature judgment of BNA's [the Bureau of National Affairs, Inc.] editorial staff to provide full coverage of significant new decisions." It is important to remember, however, that the total of all published awards is only a small percentage of those rendered. Jones & Smith, *Management and Labor Appraisals and Criticisms of the Arbitration Process: A Report With Comments*, 62 MICH. L. REV. 1115, 1152 (1964).

arbitrator might be inclined to consider precedent, there simply is no reported case similar to the one under consideration.[107]

While many of the awards that are published, presumably in full, have little utility as guides for other parties, some decisions, "due to the logic of their problem-solving persuasiveness, are potential candidates for wide application beyond the parties."[108] As one observer begrudgingly admitted, "From the published awards, it is evident that standards have been turned by the lathe of arbitration for a wide range of problems."[109]

A. Abuse of the Term "Principle"

The term "principle" is "abused when it is employed as a synonym for *binding* precedent,"[110] rather than as a widely recognized and followed precept. "Principles" typically arise from a settled course of arbitral decisions on a point. But, a guiding principle might be revealed through a single well-reasoned decision, which becomes the "leading case" on the point.[111] Likewise, arbitrators sometimes discern substantive principles through a process that might be called "negative inference." For instance, in one case the arbitrator stated that he had been "unable to find any authority among the thousands of arbitration decisions" for a holding that a certain type of con-

---

[107]*See* Immigration & Naturalization Serv., 76 LA 180, 184 (Rule, 1981); Mobil Oil Corp., 76 LA 3, 5 (Allen, Jr., 1981); Brinks, Inc., 73 LA 162, 163 (Hannan, 1979); Container Corp. of Am., 73 LA 51, 55 (Hathaway, 1979); Denman Rubber Mfg. Co., 72 LA 337, 340 (Dworkin, 1979); Public Serv. Co. of N.M., 70 LA 788, 791 (Springfield, 1978); Indiana Bell Tel. Co., 70 LA 669, 671 (Edes, 1978); Liquid Air, 70 LA 420, 421 (Rose, 1978); Scharlin, Daniel & Assocs., 69 LA 394, 398 (Lucas, 1977).

[108]Petshek, at 157.

[109]Manson, *Substantive Principles Emerging From Grievance Arbitration: Some Observations, in* 1953 PROCEEDINGS OF IRRA 136, 137 (1953).

A president of the National Academy of Arbitrators (NAA) stated it as follows:

The greatest accomplishment [of the arbitration process], in my estimation, has been the development of a quite substantial and functional industrial jurisprudence. To some extent, we have drawn upon and adapted legal doctrines from the larger society; but to a much greater extent, we have evolved doctrines carefully tailored to the particular circumstances of American industrial relations. Our raw material has been millions of hours of testimony and argument from the contesting parties themselves. We have winnowed and sifted, accepted and rejected, and then reconsidered and modified. We have sat at the center of one of the greatest free markets for ideas that our nation, or any nation, has ever seen. From the competition of ideas has gradually developed a substantial body of principles that is generally accepted not only by arbitrators but by labor and management.

Killingsworth, *Twenty-Five Years of Labor Arbitration—And the Future, in* LABOR ARBITRATION AT THE QUARTER-CENTURY MARK, PROCEEDINGS OF THE 25TH ANNUAL MEETING OF NAA 11, 18 (Dennis & Somers eds., BNA Books 1973). Compare the statement of another NAA president in Barrett, *The Presidential Address: The Common Law of the Shop, in* INTEREST ARBITRATION DISPUTES, PROCEEDINGS OF THE 26TH ANNUAL MEETING OF NAA 95, 97 (Dennis & Somers eds., BNA Books 1974).

[110]Manson, 1953 PROCEEDINGS OF IRRA, at 147 (emphasis added).

[111]*See* Texas Air Nat'l Guard, 115 LA 249, 252 (Moore, 2000) (recognizing the leading-case status of Arbitrator Harry Shulman's decision in *Ford Motor Co.*, 3 LA 779 (Shulman, 1944)); Grand Sheet Metal Prods. Co., 17 LA 388, 390 (Kelliher, 1951) (noting the leading-case status of a decision in *Supermatic Prods.*, 14 LA 139 (Bernstein, 1950)).

duct by an employee constitutes a punishable offense.[112] In another case, the arbitrator upheld a company's actions in training employees for duties outside their assigned classification, where a study of arbitration decisions revealed no suggested limitation on the right of management to do so.[113]

In actual practice, it is not at all uncommon for an arbitrator to preface the assertion of an established rule or principle with some statement such as "the chief concern to arbitrators is," "it has become a well-accepted principle," or "it is a general rule that," or "the consensus is," or "the weight of authority is." In doing this, arbitrators frequently cite other decisions,[114] but just as frequently they cite few or no specific cases to support their assertion that the principle does in fact exist.[115] Possibly the true significance of such statements lies in the fact that the arbitrator was willing to accept arbitration awards as a source of fundamental substantive principles.

---

[112]United States Pipe & Foundry Co., 20 LA 513, 516 (McCoy, 1953). *See also* George Ellis Co., 68 LA 261, 269 (Sacks, 1977); Goodyear Atomic Corp., 45 LA 671, 680 (Teple, 1965); Petroleum Chems., 37 LA 42, 49 (Hebert, 1961); Pacific Intermountain Express Co., 23 LA 440, 446 (Howard, 1954); Russell Creamery Co., 21 LA 293, 298 (Cheit, 1953); Beaunit Mills, 20 LA 784, 787 (Williams, 1953).

[113]Goodyear Atomic Corp., 45 LA 671, 680 (Teple, 1965).

[114]*See, e.g.*, Georgia-Pacific Corp., 115 LA 799, 804 (Pratte, 2001) (citing ELKOURI & ELKOURI: HOW ARBITRATION WORKS 439–40 (Volz & Goggin eds., BNA Books 5th ed. 1997); Los Angeles County Fire Dep't, 76 LA 572, 575 (Rule, 1981); Oscar Mayer & Co., 75 LA 555, 559 (Eischen, 1980); General Elec. Co., 74 LA 578, 579 (Schor, 1980); Lithonia Lighting Co., 74 LA 30, 32 (Rimer, 1980); Norris Indus., 73 LA 1129, 1132 (Roumell, Jr., 1979); Indiana State Teachers Ass'n Bd. of Directors., 70 LA 1091, 1095 (Nathan, 1978); Evans Prods. Co., 70 LA 89, 92 (Baum, 1978); Social Sec. Admin., 69 LA 1239, 1242 (Kaye, 1977); Sandusky Dressed Beef Co., 69 LA 766, 770 (Strasshofer, 1977); Badger Coal Co., 69 LA 756, 758 (Wren, 1977); Electrical Repair Serv. Co., 69 LA 604, 607 (Johnston, Jr., 1977); Arco-Polymers, 69 LA 379, 386 (Milentz, 1977); New York State Dep't of Corr. Servs., 69 LA 344, 349 (Kornblum, 1977); City of Hartford, 69 LA 303, 306 (Mallon, McDonovan, & Zuilkowski, 1977); Vertex Sys., 68 LA 1099, 1101 (Marcus, 1977); Bremer County Highway Dep't, 68 LA 628, 632 (Yarowsky, 1977).

[115]*See, e.g.*, DCI, Inc., 115 LA 693, 699 (Daly, 2001); Pratt & Lambert, 76 LA 685, 690 (Denson, 1981); General Felt Indus., 74 LA 972, 975 (Carnes, 1979); Crepaco, Inc., 74 LA 437, 439 (Hutchison, 1980); Lithonia Lighting Co., 74 LA 30, 32 (Rimer, 1980); Commonwealth of Pa., 73 LA 556, 561 (Gerhart, 1979); Fabsteel Co., 72 LA 1214, 1216 (Bothwell, 1979); Henry B. Gilpin Co., 72 LA 981, 986 (Stone, 1979); Area Educ. Agency 12, 72 LA 916, 927 (Sembower, 1979); Teleflex, 72 LA 668, 673 (Chalfie, 1979); A-T-O, Inc., 72 LA 408, 410 (Shister, 1979); Lozier Corp., 72 LA 164, 167 (Ferguson, 1979); Nugent Sand Co., 71 LA 585, 586 (Kanner, 1978); Bethel Sch. Dist. No. 403, 71 LA 314, 319 (Beck, 1978); General Elec. Co., 70 LA 1174, 1176 (Abrams, 1978); Fitas, Mahoning County Eng'r, 70 LA 895, 897 (Cohen, 1978); FMC Corp., 70 LA 574, 575 (Nigro, 1978); Veterans Admin. Reg'l Office, 70 LA 514, 517 (Denson, 1978); Brunswick Corp., 70 LA 413, 416 (Murphy, 1978); City of Los Angeles, Cal., 70 LA 308, 318 (Christopher, 1978); Inland Container Corp., 70 LA 199, 200 (Schroeder, 1978); Quadraflex, 69 LA 1123, 1128 (Griffin, 1977); Menasco Mfg. Co., 69 LA 759, 762 (Bergeson, 1977); Ore-Ida Foods, 69 LA 375, 377 (Curry, Jr., 1977); Taft Broad. Co., WBRC-TV, 69 LA 307, 309 (Chaffin, 1977); Baltimore News Am., 68 LA 1054, 1056 (Seidenberg, 1977); San Francisco Unified Sch. Dist., 68 LA 767, 769 (Oestreich, 1977); Union Camp Corp., 68 LA 708, 712 (Morgan, Jr., 1977); International Shoe Co., 68 LA 444, 447 (Roberts, 1977); North Star Steel Co., 68 LA 114, 123 (Hadlick, 1977); Dura Corp., 68 LA 94, 98 (Cabe, 1977); William Feather Co., 68 LA 13, 19 (Shanker, 1977). However, if the parties themselves allege the existence of an established principle, they should be prepared to prove it. *See* Potter & Brumfield, Inc., 27 LA 812, 814 (Fisher, 1956); Princeton Worsted Mills, 25 LA 587, 591 (Hill, 1955).

6. JUDICIAL TREATMENT OF PRECEDENTIAL VALUE OF ARBITRATION AWARDS

Court challenges to arbitration awards that follow or reject one or more prior awards may be presented in a variety of forms, such as petitions to compel arbitration, to enjoin arbitration proceedings, to confirm awards, and to vacate awards.

A. General Rule: Preclusive Effect of First Award up to Second Arbitrator

Courts have asserted that the "black letter" law, as enunciated by the Supreme Court in *W.R. Grace & Co. v. Rubber Workers Local 759*,[116] is that arbitral awards are not entitled to the same precedential effect as judicial decisions, nor are they considered to be conclusive or binding in subsequent arbitration cases involving the same contract language but different incidents or grievances.[117] "Whether an award has a binding precedential effect on a future dispute is a subject for arbitration,"[118] at least absent express

---

[116]461 U.S. 757, 113 LRRM 2641 (1983).

[117]El Dorado Technical Servs. v. Union Gen. de Trabajadores de P.R., 961 F.2d 317, 140 LRRM 2314, 2317–18 (1st Cir. 1992) (petition to vacate subsequent award where court noted that both awards were "plausible" reading of same contract language). *See also* Laborers Local 504 v. Roadmaster Corp., 916 F.2d 1161, 135 LRRM 2831 (7th Cir. 1990) (motion to compel; attorneys' fees awarded to union).

[118]*See* Mine Workers Dist. 17 v. Island Creek Coal Co., 179 F.3d 133, 161 LRRM 2463 (4th Cir. 1999); ANR Advance Transp. Co. v. Teamsters Local 710, 153 F.3d 774, 159 LRRM 2082 (7th Cir. 1998). The arbitration decisions were not vacated despite decisions in earlier arbitrations; the courts stated that the issues and rationale of the earlier decisions were unclear or were based on different facts even if the prior decision arose out of the same general fact situation. *See also* National Elevator Indus. v. Elevator Constructors, 647 F. Supp. 976, 125 LRRM 2169, 2170 (S.D. Tex. 1986) (motion for injunction to enjoin arbitration claiming subsequent arbitration barred by prior arbitration and prior judicial decision confirming it; further, denial of *Boys Markets v. Retail Clerks Local 770*, 398 U.S. 235, 74 LRRM 2257 (1970), injunction not preclusive as not a decision on the merits).

Vacating an arbitration award did not preclude a second proceeding on issues raised in the first case where the arbitrator, in making the vacated award, specifically left open questions without deciding them. The court found that the "parties . . . contemplated further proceedings" as made plain by the arbitrator's decision. John Morrell & Co. v. Food & Commercial Workers Local 304A, 992 F.2d 205, 207, 143 LRRM 2211, 2213 (8th Cir. 1993). *See also* Operating Eng'rs Local 370 v. Morrison-Knudsen Co., 786 F.2d 1356, 122 LRRM 2558 (9th Cir. 1986) (where the issue is arguably arbitrable, the collateral estoppel effects, if any, of prior litigation settlement is for the arbitrator to decide); Postal Workers (Pittsburgh Metro Area) v. U.S. Postal Serv., 463 F. Supp. 54, 105 LRRM 2415 (W.D. Pa. 1978) (no enforcement of local settlements as final and binding awards absent agreement language), *aff'd*, 609 F.2d 503, 105 LRRM 2798 (3d Cir. 1979), *cert. denied*, 445 U.S. 950 (1980).

The extent to which a prior decision, in this case by a joint union-management board, is the final decision is a procedural question to be determined by arbitration, "unless the intended preclusive effect of a procedural provision and the fact of the breach are both so plain that no rational mind could hurdle the barrier." Longshoremen (ILA) Local 333, United Marine Div. v. McAllister Bros., 671 F. Supp. 309, 313, 127 LRRM 2117, 2121 (S.D.N.Y. 1987) (motion to stay arbitration and cross-motion to compel) (citing Rochester Tel. Corp. v. Communications Workers, 340 F.2d 237, 58 LRRM 2223 (2d Cir. 1965)).

There have been cases where a second arbitration award was upheld that held differently from the first award, where both awards were by the same arbitrator and where different evidence was presented in the second case. *See, e.g.*, Hotel & Rest. Employees Local 54 v. Adamar, Inc., 682 F. Supp. 795, 126 LRRM 3029 (D.N.J. 1987). In *Action Distrib. Co. v.*

language in the first award[119] or in the terms of the collective bargaining agreement itself.[120] The extent to which an arbitrator is bound by the decision of a predecessor "can be determined only by reference to the agreement as a whole,"[121] and, where the agreement is silent, the "arbitrator may decline to follow arbitral precedent when his judgment is that earlier decisions are erroneous."[122]

Courts nonetheless entertain challenges to arbitral awards that are claimed to be inconsistent with a binding prior award, with the cited vice being that the award fails to draw its essence from the agreement.[123] A reviewing court is less likely to vacate the award on that ground if the arbitra-

---

Teamsters Local 1038, 977 F.2d 1021, 141 LRRM 2606 (6th Cir. 1992), the court, although citing the *Steelworkers Trilogy* (*Steelworkers v. American Mfg. Co.*, 363 U.S. 564, 46 LRRM 2414 (1960); *Steelworkers v. Warrior & Gulf Navigation Co.*, 363 U.S. 574, 46 LRRM 2416 (1960); *Steelworkers v. Enterprise Wheel & Car Corp.*, 363 U.S. 593, 46 LRRM 2423 (1960)), discussed the issues in terms of traditional "claims preclusion" language. The court determined that its definition of "claim preclusion" was inapplicable to a petition to vacate a second award because underlying facts had not occurred, in this case the solicitation of new hires, at the time of the first decision and the bases for the second decision were different. "These are clearly different issues, and the resolution of the one did not bar the resolution of the other." *Action Distrib.*, 977 F.2d at 1026, 141 LRRM at 2610.

[119]*See* Oil, Chem., & Atomic Workers Local 4-16000 v. Ethyl Corp., 644 F.2d 1044, 107 LRRM 2417 (5th Cir. 1981) (arbitration decision that employer is to desist from like violations will be enforced against prospective employer actions provided the company actions do not materially differ from prior condemned conduct, allocating burdens to be carried by respective parties to so show; If conduct does materially differ, new case is to be decided in arbitration); National Elevator Indus. v. Elevator Constructors, 647 F. Supp. 976, 125 LRRM 2169 (S.D. Tex. 1986) (arbitration decision describing application of nationwide agreement to a particular geographic area must be limited to its specific terms; court will not expand to apply nationwide); Paperworkers Local 1206 v. Georgia-Pacific Corp., 798 F.2d 172, 123 LRRM 2345, 2345 (6th Cir. 1986) (Union suit that company had "[w]illfully failed and refused to carry out the terms" of first award; 30 grievances filed since first award was issued. Whether award has prospective application is for an arbitrator to decide, where court found that first award did not purport to decide any issue but that presented and did not mention prospective application and where the pending second case had important factual differences, thereby distinguishing *Ethyl Corp.*, above; *Electrical Workers (UE) v. Honeywell, Inc.*, 522 F.2d 1221, 90 LRRM 2193 (7th Cir. 1975) (court denied injunctive and other relief when union claimed that four past arbitration awards should be made applicable to 100 pending grievances when court found that union did not seek to aggregate the pending grievances into a single arbitration, which the court stated could be done (citing ELKOURI & ELKOURI, HOW ARBITRATION WORKS (BNA Books 2d ed. 1960)), where union had not sought the relief requested of the court from an arbitrator, nor had the union alleged that the factual bases of the past awards were substantially identical to the pending grievances. See *Ethyl Corp.*, 644 F.2d at 1053–55, 107 LRRM at 2424–26, for critique of this decision).

[120]S.E.L. Maduro (Fla.) v. Longshoremen (ILA) Local 1416, 765 F.2d 1057, 120 LRRM 2036 (11th Cir. 1985); South Carolina Stevedores Ass'n v. Longshoremen (ILA) Local 1422, 765 F.2d 422, 119 LRRM 3112 (4th Cir. 1985) (in both cases, master agreement prevailed over local agreements).

[121]Hotel Ass'n of Washington, D.C. v. Hotel & Rest. Employees Local 25, 963 F.2d 388, 390, 140 LRRM 2185, 2186 (D.C. Cir. 1992) (petition to vacate second award).

[122]*Id.* (quoting Fournelle v. NLRB, 670 F.2d 331, 344 n.22, 109 LRRM 2441, 2450 n.22 (D.C. Cir. 1982)). The court distinguished its own decision in *Chambers v. Teamsters Local 639*, 578 F.2d 375, 97 LRRM 2823 (D.C. Cir. 1978), which enforced a first decision as final on its own interpretation of the facts and agreement after a second decision overturned the first decision where the union took a different position vis-à-vis the same grievants who in the second grievance were trying to enforce the first decision.

[123]*See, e.g.,* American Nat'l Can Co. v. Steelworkers Local 3628, 120 F.3d 886, 155 LRRM 2905 (8th Cir. 1997) (affirming district court's enforcement of award in which arbitrator declined to give preclusive effect to prior award).

tor has in the challenged award adequately distinguished the prior award.[124] Courts also may seek to reconcile the claimed inconsistencies so as to avoid overstepping their limited role in reviewing what is intended to be a final and binding award.[125]

A contractual clause that an arbitration award is "final and binding" is, by itself, insufficient to "unequivocally import the principle of precedent into arbitral decision making" to establish that a subsequent arbitrator's decision, which rejected an earlier one interpreting the same contract provision under similar facts, did not draw its essence from the agreement.[126]

B. Exceptions and Variations

There have been, however, exceptions to, and variations from, the judicial doctrine that the precedential value of a prior award between the parties is to be determined by the subsequent arbitrator.

i. Inconsistent Decisions

In an alternative holding, one court, notwithstanding its recognition that "an arbitrator generally has the power to determine whether a prior award is to be given preclusive effect," asserted that courts "have also recognized that the doctrine of res judicata may apply to arbitrations with strict factual identities."[127]

---

[124]*Id.* (distinguishing Trailways Lines v. Trailways, Inc. Joint Council, 807 F.2d 1416, 124 LRRM 2217 (8th Cir. 1986) (affirming vacation of award that failed to afford preclusive effect to prior award, where arbitrator did not seriously consider the potential preclusive effect of the prior award, despite the apparent identity of material facts).

[125]Thus, in *Sheet Metal Workers Local 359 v. Madison Indus. of Ariz.*, 84 F.3d 1186, 152 LRRM 2505 (9th Cir. 1996), the U.S. Court of Appeals for the Ninth Circuit resolved a dispute concerning the enforceability of an interest-arbitration award that overturned a prior inconsistent grievance arbitration award by giving it prospective effect only. In that case, several months after a grievance arbitration award had held that work given to production employees belonged to building trades employees who had been improperly laid off, the collective bargaining agreement expired and an interest-arbitration award allocated the contested work to production workers in the new contract. In denying the employer's contention that the earlier arbitration award should be set aside as a result of the interest arbitration, the Ninth Circuit held that the later award resolved only the "parties' dispute about the allocation of work between production and building trades workers for the purposes of a *new* contract," *id.* at 1192 (emphasis in original), and "the reasonableness of [the] . . . interpretation of the old contract was not affected by the [subsequent] decision . . . ." *Id.*

[126]*See* Independent Lift Truck Builders v. NACCO Materials Handling Group, 202 F.3d 965, 163 LRRM 2321 (7th Cir. 2000) (disputes concerning the construction of the agreement, including the finality provision regarding arbitration is for the arbitrator rather than the court). *See also* Hotel Ass'n of Washington, D.C. v. Hotel & Rest. Employees Local 25, 963 F.2d 388, 390, 140 LRRM 2185, 2187 (D.C. Cir. 1992). *Accord* Transit Mix Concrete Corp. v. Teamsters Local 282, 809 F.2d 963, 125 LRRM 3192 (2d Cir. 1987) (petition to enjoin second arbitration denied; arbitration clause makes arbitrable any dispute concerning interpretation or application of agreement).

[127]*Trailways Lines*, 807 F.2d at 1425, 124 LRRM at 2223 (citing Electrical Workers (UE) v. Honeywell, Inc., 522 F.2d 1221, 90 LRRM 2193 (7th Cir. 1975), and Chemical Workers Local 189 v. Purex Corp., 427 F. Supp. 338, 95 LRRM 2271 (D. Neb. 1977), *aff'd per curiam*, 566 F.2d 48, 96 LRRM 3371 (8th Cir. 1977)) (prior interpretation by arbitrator that is dictum not binding on the parties to preclude second arbitration). The court stated that "although not the basis for our decision," it had grave concerns with the second arbitrator's treatment of the first award. *Trailways Lines*, 807 F.2d at 1425. It further pointed out that the second arbitrator, whose decision it vacated for imposing his own brand of industrial

However, when past arbitration decisions were divided over whether an employee's offense had to be listed among enumerated "sins" in order to justify peremptory discharge, another court vacated as "implausible" an arbitrator's decision upholding a discharge where the grievant had not been given timely prior warning, and the employee's offense was not included in the catalog of "cardinal sins," which, when committed, could result in summary discharge. Concluding that the absence of consistency prevented the establishment of a clear-cut law of the shop that could be deemed to have amended the contract, the court stated:

> The result might be different in a case in which the CBA [collective bargaining agreement] says one thing, and the law of the shop as established by prior arbitration decisions says something different. In that situation, despite the bargained-for language in the CBA, the parties might nonetheless have an understanding different from that expressed in the agreement.[128]

The court's decision is subject to valid criticism because it failed to examine the history of negotiations, consider the dates of the prior awards in relationship to the effective date of the subject agreement, determine whether any of the prior awards had been brought to the attention of the arbitrator whose award was subject to challenge, and consider whether any of the prior awards upholding discharges for nonenumerated offenses had explained why the contrary awards setting aside such discharges were inapplicable. Instead, the court implicitly found that all awards in accord with the arbitrator's decision sub judice necessarily had to be likewise "implausible."

ii. Contradictory Conclusions

Sometimes arbitration awards addressing the same factual issue and interpreting the identical language in collective bargaining agreements between an employer and two or more unions reach contradictory conclusions. One approach has been to enforce both awards notwithstanding the effect on the employer.[129] A second approach, when the remedies are in such conflict that both cannot be carried out, is to enforce neither award but to order the parties to participate in tripartite arbitration before a new arbitrator.[130]

---

justice, failed to give any reason for not following the prior decision except that the latter expressed a "minority view" about banning beards. *Id.* at 1419. "If an arbitrator does not accord any precedential effect to a prior award in a case like this, or at least explain the reasons for refusing to do so, it is questionable when, if ever, a 'final and binding' determination will evolve from the arbitration process." *Id.* at 1425–26. The court cited ELKOURI & ELKOURI, HOW ARBITRATION WORKS 428 (BNA Books 4th ed. 1985) for statements about the precedential effects of prior awards. *Trailways*, 807 F.2d at 1425–26, 124 LRRM at 2224.

[128]Hawaii Teamsters Local 996 v. United Parcel Serv., 229 F.3d 847, 852, 165 LRRM 2200 (9th Cir. 2000).

[129]Louisiana-Pacific Corp. v. Electrical Workers (IBEW) Local 2294, 600 F.2d 219, 102 LRRM 2070 (9th Cir. 1979).

[130]Retail, Wholesale, & Dep't Store Union Local 390 v. Kroger Co., 927 F.2d 275, 136 LRRM 2776 (6th Cir. 1991). *But see* Longshoremen (ILA) Local 1351 v. Sea-Land Serv., 214 F.3d 566, 164 LRRM 2525 (5th Cir. 2000) (court refused to uphold an order for and a subsequent tripartite arbitration award where the initial award had been confirmed by a New York federal district court, relying on a case that was not a labor dispute, that had held tripartite arbitration cannot be ordered without all three parties consenting in writing).

iii. Effect of Prior Judicial Proceeding [LA CDI 94.553]

Issue or claim preclusive effect may be accorded to a prior arbitration award that has been upheld by a court decision. For example, in *Longshoremen (ILA) Local 1351 v. Sea-Land Service*,[131] the court held that an arbitrator's award that had been affirmed by a federal district court precluded another district court from ordering the appellant to rearbitrate the same dispute in a tripartite arbitration with another interested party.[132]

Likewise, a divided U.S. Court of Appeals for the Eighth Circuit panel found that a jury decision concerning liability for a strike in violation of a no-strike clause precluded enforcement of a contrary arbitration award.[133] The court stressed that the appellant had properly relied on the final judgment of the federal district court.[134]

As contrasted with jury verdicts and final judgments, arbitrators need not defer to interim judicial interpretations of the very contracts that arbitrators are hired to interpret. In a decision significant for its analysis of the "meeting of the minds" doctrine,[135] the U.S. Court of Appeals for the Seventh Circuit upheld a district court judge's grant of a union's counterclaim to compel arbitration, but asserted that the judge's conclusion that "the disputed term unequivocally bears the meaning that she assigned to it . . . does not bind the arbitrator."[136] The company had accepted a multi-employer collective bargaining agreement that contained an ambiguous minimum-manning requirement. When the employer brought suit for rescission under Section 301 of the Taft-Hartley Act[137] on the ground that there was "no meeting of the minds," the district court judge not only decided that a binding contract had been formed, but also purported to resolve the ambiguity. Chief Judge Posner wrote that not only was the arbitrator free to interpret the contractual provision

---

[131]214 F.3d 566, 572, 164 LRRM 2525 (5th Cir. 2000).

[132]*Id.* at 572–73 (citing, inter alia, Universal Am. Barge Corp. v. J-Chem, Inc., 946 F.2d 1131, 1135 (5th Cir. 1981) (collateral estoppel applicable to arbitration proceedings)).

[133]*Id.* at 572.

[134]John Morrell & Co. v. Food & Commercial Workers Local 304A, 913 F.2d 544, 135 LRRM 2233 (8th Cir. 1990). The court found the arbitrator was not authorized to determine the same issue decided by the jury because neither party had submitted evidence on the issue and thus the arbitrator exceeded his authority. Nonetheless, the court cited several cases as authority for its position that judicial issue and claim preclusion may bar enforcement of arbitration awards. *Id.*, 135 LRRM at 2246 (citing Miller Brewing Co. v. Ft. Worth Distrib. Co., 781 F.2d 494, 501 (5th Cir. 1986) (nonlabor arbitration waived by prior judicial action dismissed for want of prosecution and prior dismissal res judicata under Texas law of claims that could have been raised in initial case)); Telephone Workers Local 827 (N.J.) v. New Jersey Bell Tel. Co., 584 F.2d 31, 18 FEP Cases 298 (3d Cir. 1978) (arbitration an improper collateral attack by a class member bound by a consent decree); Burmah Oil Tankers v. Trisun Tankers, 687 F. Supp. 897, 899 (S.D.N.Y. 1988) (prior confirmed nonlabor arbitration award precludes new claim arising out of same ship charter that could have been but was not raised in first case under terms of charter agreement); Hudson-Berlind v. Teamsters Local 807, 597 F. Supp. 1282, 119 LRRM 3599 (E.D.N.Y. 1984) (prior National Labor Relations Board determination).

[135]Colfax Envelope v. Chicago Graphic Communications Local 458-3M, 20 F.3d 750, 145 LRRM 2974 (7th Cir. 1994).

[136]*Id.* at 755.

[137]29 U.S.C. §185.

differently from the district court, but "[i]t will therefore be open to . . . [the employer] to argue to the arbitrator that, under a proper interpretation of the contract, there really was no meeting of the minds over the manning requirements and therefore that the contract should be rescinded after all."[138]

A contrary result was reached by the U.S. Court of Appeals for the Sixth Circuit in reviewing an arbitrator's conclusion, based on the evidentiary record before him, that there was no enforceable agreement to arbitrate despite a district court's prior contrary determination.[139] The district court had vacated the arbitration award on the ground that the issue of arbitrability had not been submitted to the arbitrator and that his reexamination of the issue was barred by the doctrine of res judicata. The court noted that resolution of a dispute over whether a valid agreement to arbitrate exists is traditionally reserved to the courts, and that the arbitrator had not indicated any reason why the district court's prior judgment was not a bar to his consideration of the issue: "Arbitrators are not free to ignore the preclusive effect of prior judgments under the doctrines of *res judicata* and *collateral estoppel,* although they generally are entitled to determine in the first instance whether . . . the prior judicial determination [is entitled to] preclusive effect."[140]

There are occasions, however, when it is a court, and not an arbitrator, that is guilty of exceeding its authority, and a subsequent arbitration award trumps a prior judicial judgment. In 1992, an employer was successful in vacating an arbitration award that had set aside the peremptory discharge of an employee for insubordination for failure to accord the employee "institutional due process."[141] The contract provided that employees were subject to discharge for "just cause," but also included a section that listed reasons, including "insubordination" and "sleeping on duty," for which employees could be immediately discharged. The district court said that the arbitrator had exceeded her authority because once the employer had determined that an employee had been insubordinate, it could discharge that employee without observing any further procedural safeguards. A year later, the employer similarly discharged an employee for "sleeping on the job," and another arbitrator reduced the penalty to a suspension on the ground that the employer had failed to consider mitigating circumstances. The district court again vacated the award, but this time the court of appeals stepped in and reversed,[142] holding that the arbitrator could reasonably read the contractual provisions as requiring consideration of appropriate mitigating circumstances. Because the arbitrator had arguably construed and applied the agreement, he fulfilled the precise task that the parties had bargained for him to do; the appellate court therefore held that both the district court's decision sub judice and its 1992 judgment were in error.

In another case, the U.S. Court of Appeals for the Seventh Circuit was faced with the situation where three employer-favored arbitration decisions

---

[138]*Colfax*, 20 F.3d at 755, 145 LRRM at 2978.

[139]Aircraft Braking Sys. Corp. v. Auto Workers Local 856, 97 F.3d 155, 153 LRRM 2402 (6th Cir. 1996), *cert. denied*, 519 U.S. 1143 (1997).

[140]*Id.* at 159, 153 LRRM at 2406.

[141]Southern Council of Indus. Workers v. Bruce Hardwood Floors, 784 F. Supp. 1345, 139 LRRM 2775 (N.D. Tenn. 1992).

[142]Bruce Hardwood Floors v. Southern Council of Indus. Workers, 8 F.3d 1104, 144 LRRM 2622 (6th Cir. 1993).

had preceded, and three more had followed, an intervening award that favored the union on the common issue of whether the employer's staffing practices, designed to minimize overtime, violated the contract.[143] The fourth arbitrator had not been informed of the three prior decisions. The district court enforced the fourth award, and then, in a later proceeding, also confirmed the other six. The Seventh Circuit, again speaking through Judge Posner, held that most arbitrators would give preclusive effect to the first arbitration award "provided that the usual conditions of res judicata were fulfilled."[144] On the separate question whether the initial district court judgment enforcing the fourth arbitral award should have been given res judicata effect in the second set of proceedings, the court held that "the res judicata effect of a judicial decision merely confirming an arbitral award is extremely limited. All it amounts to is a determination that there is no basis for upending *that* award; the effect on subsequent awards must be left to the arbitrators who make them."[145]

iv. *NLRB's General Rule* [LA CDI 94.553]

Despite its policy of deferral to arbitration in appropriate contexts,[146] the NLRB adheres to its general rule that "if the Government was not a party to prior private litigation, it is not barred from litigating an issue involving enforcement of Federal law which the private plaintiff has litigated unsuccessfully."[147] This principle is based on policy considerations related to the Board's congressionally imposed duty to address federal labor law issues that affect interstate commerce.[148] Thus, the Board, as a public agency asserting public rights, should not be collaterally estopped by the resolution of private claims asserted by private parties.[149] In so deciding, the Board cited court decisions supporting this principle[150] and one criticizing it.[151] Despite the general rule, however, under at least some circumstances, the Board has

---

[143]Consolidation Coal Co. v. Mine Workers Dist. 12, 213 F.3d 404, 164 LRRM 2321 (7th Cir. 2000).

[144]*Id.* at 407, 164 LRRM at 2323.

[145]*Id.* at 408–09, 164 LRRM at 2324 (emphasis in original).

[146]See *Collyer Insulated Wire*, 192 NLRB 837, 77 LRRM 1931 (1971) (NLRB defers processing of unfair labor practice cases in order to give the grievance-arbitration process an opportunity to resolve parallel disputes, yet retains jurisdiction to review the award to make sure that statutory rights have been adequately safeguarded), discussed generally in Chapter 10, section 3.A.v.b., "NLRB Policy on Deferral to Arbitration."

[147]Field Bridge Assocs., 306 NLRB 322, 140 LRRM 1012 (1992) (citing Allbritton Communications, 271 NLRB 201, 202 n.4, 116 LRRM 1428 (1984) (and sources cited), enf'd, 766 F.2d 812, 119 LRRM 3290 (3d Cir. 1985)).

[148]*Id.*

[149]*Id.* at 322–23.

[150]Peninsula Shipbuilders' Ass'n v. NLRB, 663 F.2d 488, 492, 108 LRRM 2400 (4th Cir. 1981); NLRB v. Huttig Sash & Door Co., 377 F.2d 964, 970, 65 LRRM 2431 (8th Cir. 1967); Typographical Union No. 17 (New Orleans) v. NLRB (E.P. Rivas, Inc.), 368 F.2d 755, 767, 63 LRRM 2467 (5th Cir. 1966).

[151]NLRB v. Donna-Lee Sportswear Co., 836 F.2d 31, 127 LRRM 2209 (1st Cir. 1987).

accorded res judicata effect to an arbitrator's determination that had been confirmed by a state civil court order.[152]

v.   *Arbitral Awards and Enforcement of Federal Statutory Rights*
[LA CDI 94.553]

Arbitral awards may not be given res judicata or issue preclusive effect in subsequent litigation to enforce federal statutory rights.[153] Following the Supreme Court's decision in *McDonald v. City of West Branch, Michigan*,[154] the U.S. Court of Appeals for the Second Circuit vacated the judgment of a federal district court that had dismissed a retaliatory discharge suit under 42 U.S.C. Section 1983, on res judicata grounds,[155] relying on arbitral denial of a grievance alleging that there had been no contractual just cause for her termination. The Second Circuit held that "no federal statute or judicially fashioned rule 'permits a federal court to accord res judicata or collateral estoppel effect to an unappealed arbitration award in a case brought under 42 U.S.C. Section 1983.'"[156] The articulated basis for this rule was fourfold: first, that the "complex legal analysis" involved in such cases is outside an arbitrator's expertise; second, that the arbitrator's authority is limited by the collective bargaining agreement; third, that there may be tensions between the individual's interest and the union's interest in the arbitration of the discharge; and fourth, that "arbitral fact-finding is not equivalent to judicial fact-finding."[157]

---

[152]*See* R.E. Dietz Co., 311 NLRB 1259, 145 LRRM 1025 (1993) (Board finds arbitrator's award regarding payments owed to union employees after an unfair labor practice to be an adjudication with res judicata effect because the award was confirmed by a civil court).

[153]For related discussion, see Chapter 2, section 8., "The Expanding Role of Arbitration in the Resolution of Statutory Employment Claims Under Collective Bargaining Agreements."

[154]466 U.S. 284, 115 LRRM 3646 (1984).

[155]Williams v. Perry, 229 F.3d 1136, 2000 U.S. App. LEXIS 25382 at *3–4 (2d Cir. 2000) (unpublished).

[156]*Id.* at *6 (quoting Dean Witter Reynolds, Inc. v. Byrd, 470 U.S. 213, 222 (1985)).

[157]*Id.* at *5.

Chapter 12

Custom and Past Practice

Unquestionably, the custom and past practice of the parties constitute one of the most significant evidentiary considerations in labor-management arbitration. Proof of custom and past practice may be introduced for any of the following major purposes: (1) to provide the basis of rules governing matters not included in the written contract; (2) to indicate the proper interpretation of contract language; or (3) to support allegations that the "clear language" of the written contract has been amended by mutual agreement to express the intention of the parties to make their written language consistent with what they regularly do in practice in the administration of their labor agreement.

This chapter discusses the use of custom and past practice for each of these purposes.[1]

---

[1]For other discussions of custom and practice, see Mittenthal, *Arbitration Classics: Part II. The Ever-Present Past, in* ARBITRATION 1994: CONTROVERSY AND CONTINUITY, PROCEEDINGS OF THE 47TH ANNUAL MEETING OF NAA 184 (Gruenberg ed., BNA Books 1994). The paper was

1. Custom and Practice as a Term of the Contract

Under certain circumstances, custom and past practice may be held enforceable through arbitration as being, in essence, a part of the parties' "whole" agreement. Some of the general statements of arbitrators in this regard may be noted:

It is generally accepted that certain, but not all, clear and long standing practices can establish conditions of employment as binding as any written provision of the agreement.[2]

In cases where the contract is completely silent with respect to a given activity, the presence of a well established practice, accepted or condoned by both parties, may constitute in effect, an unwritten principle on how a certain type of situation should be treated.[3]

A union-management contract is far more than words on paper. It is also all the oral understandings, interpretations and mutually acceptable habits of action which have grown up around it over the course of time. Stable and peaceful relations between the parties depend upon the development of a mutually satisfactory superstructure of understanding which gives operating significance and practicality to the purely legal wording of the written contract. Peaceful relations depend, further, upon both parties faithfully living up to their mutual commitments as embodied not only in the actual contract itself but also in the modes of action which have become an integral part of it.[4]

[I]t is well recognized that the contractual relationship between the parties normally consists of more than the written word. Day-to-day practices mutually accepted by the parties may attain the status of contractual rights and duties, particularly where they are not at variance with any written provision negotiated into the contract by the parties and where they are of long standing and were not changed during contract negotiations.[5]

Custom can, under some unusual circumstances, form an implied term of a contract. Where the Company has always done a certain thing, and the matter is so well understood and taken for granted that it may be said that the Contract was entered into upon the assumption that that customary action would continue to be taken, such customary action may be an implied term.[6]

In the light of the [arbitration] decisions, . . . it seems to me that the current of opinion has set strongly in favor of the position that existing practices, in respect to major conditions of employment, are to be regarded as included within a collective bargaining contract, negotiated after the practice has become established and not repudiated or limited by it. This also seems to me the reasonable view, since the negotiators work within the frame of existent practice and must be taken to be conscious of it.[7]

---

presented at the National Academy of Arbitrator's (NAA's) Continuing Education Conference in Pittsburgh, October 30, 1993. *See also* Broida, A Guide to Federal Labor Relations Authority Law & Practice ch. 6 (16th ed. 2003); Stanley, *Unambiguous Collective Bargaining Agreement Language Controls Unless Past Practice Is So Widely Acknowledged and Mutually Accepted That It Amends Contract*, 74 U. Det. Mercy L. Rev. 389 (1997); McLaughlin, *Custom and Past Practice in Labor Arbitration*, 18 Arb. J. 205 (1963).

[2] Arbitrator Dallas L. Jones, in *Alpena Gen. Hosp.*, 50 LA 48, 51 (Jones, 1967).

[3] Arbitrator Thomas J. McDermott, in *Texas Util. Generating Div.*, 92 LA 1308, 1312 (McDermott, 1989).

[4] Arbitrator Arthur T. Jacobs, in *Coca-Cola Bottling Co.*, 9 LA 197, 198 (Jacobs, 1947).

[5] Arbitrator Marlin M. Volz, in *Metal Specialty Co.*, 39 LA 1265, 1269 (Volz, 1962).

[6] Arbitrator Whitley P. McCoy, in *Esso Standard Oil Co.*, 16 LA 73, 74 (McCoy, Reber, & Daniel, 1951). In *Beaunit Fibers*, 49 LA 423, 424 (McCoy, 1967), the arbitrator emphasized the "under some circumstances" words of limitation.

[7] Arbitrator Maurice H. Merrill, in *Phillips Petroleum Co.*, 24 LA 191, 194–95 (Merrill, 1955).

Many other arbitrators,[8] and the U.S. Supreme Court,[9] have expressed similar thoughts.

Even in the nonunion setting, a past practice was held in one case to constitute a condition of employment.[10] There, the employer had a noncontractual handbook that pledged to treat employees fairly. The arbitrator held that "fairness" required the employer to take into account the way other employees in similar circumstances had been treated in the past.[11] So, where employees who had completed a year-long training program had always been promoted, the employer was found to have made an implicit commitment to new trainees to continue the process, and, if the company did not plan to promote them, it had a responsibility to inform the trainees at the outset.[12]

More, however, is required in the decision of specific cases than a consideration of general thoughts. The particular facts, the relevant bargaining history, the relationship between the parties, and the subject matter of the practice or custom and its treatment (if any) in the collective bargaining agreement are the commonly controlling factors.

2. EVIDENCE REQUIRED TO ESTABLISH A BINDING PAST PRACTICE [LA CDI 24.351]

When it is asserted that a past practice constitutes an implied term of a contract, strong proof of its existence ordinarily will be required.[13] Indeed,

---

[8]*See* Kobelco Stewart Bolling Inc., 108 LA 1093, 1096–97 (Curry, Jr., 1997); Albertson's, Inc., 106 LA 897, 900 (Kaufman, 1996); GTE Hawaiian Tel. Co., 98 LA 832, 834–35 (Najita, 1991); Michigan Dep't of State Police, 97 LA 721, 722 (Kanner, 1991); Dahlstrom Mfg. Co., 97 LA 314, 318 (Duda, Jr., 1991); Greyhound Food Mgmt., 95 LA 820, 824 (Staudohar, 1990); Dixie Mach. Welding & Metal Works, 88 LA 734, 736–37 (Baroni, 1987); Hudson Pulp & Paper Corp., 53 LA 845, 848 (Mills, 1969); Bangor Punta Operations, 48 LA 1275, 1276 (Kates, 1967); Association of Shower Door Indus., 47 LA 353, 355 (Koven, 1966); Formica Corp., 44 LA 467, 468 (Schmidt, 1965); Keystone Lighting Corp., 43 LA 145, 148 (Horlacher, 1964); Fruehauf Trailer Co., 29 LA 372, 375 (Jones, Jr., 1957); Morris P. Kirk & Son, 27 LA 6, 10 (Prasow, 1956); E.W. Bliss Co., 24 LA 614, 618–19 (Dworkin, 1955); Northland Greyhound Lines, 23 LA 277, 280 (Levinson, 1954); Firestone Tire & Rubber Co., 20 LA 880, 883 (Gorder, 1953); B.F. Goodrich Chem. Co., 20 LA 818, 823 (Hale, 1953); International Harvester Co., 20 LA 276, 280 (Wirtz, 1953); Sioux City Battery Co., 20 LA 243, 244 (Updegraff, 1953); General Aniline & Film Corp., 19 LA 628, 629 (Talbott, 1952); Republic Steel Corp., 17 LA 105, 108 (Marshall, 1951); John Morrell & Co., 17 LA 81, 85 (Gilden, 1951); American Seating Co., 16 LA 115, 117 (Whiting, 1951); Mt. Carmel Pub. Util. Co., 16 LA 59, 62 (Hampton, 1951).

[9]In *Steelworkers v. Warrior & Gulf Navigation Co.*, 363 U.S. 574, 46 LRRM 2416 (1960), the Court stated:

The labor arbitrator's source of law is not confined to the express provisions of the contract, as the industrial common law—the practices of the industry and the shop—is equally a part of the collective bargaining agreement although not expressed in it.

Id. at 582, 46 LRRM at 2419.

[10]Indiana Mich. Power Co., 107 LA 1037 (Render, 1997).

[11]*Id.* at 1042.

[12]*Id.*

[13]*E.g.*, GTE Hawaiian Tel. Co., 98 LA 832, 834–35 (Najita, 1991); Michigan Dep't of State Police, 97 LA 721, 722 (Kanner, 1991) ("It is well settled that a condition of employment which arises through long-standing past practice is binding upon the parties."); Dahlstrom Mfg. Co., 97 LA 314, 318 (Duda, Jr., 1991) ("Even in the absence of an agreement on the matter by the Parties a past practice may be binding if, as stated by Arbitrator Richard Mittenthal, 'it is shown to be the understood and accepted way of doing things over an extended period of time.'"); Greyhound Food Mgmt., 95 LA 820, 824 (Staudohar, 1990); Dixie Mach. Welding & Metal Works, 88 LA 734 (Baroni, 1987). Of course, parties may expressly incorporate past practices as a part of their collective bargaining agreement by reference, and thus plainly render them enforceable through arbitration. Alabama By-Products Corp., 83 LA 1270 (Clarke, 1984). The party alleging the existence of a binding practice has the burden of establishing it. *See* Ringgold, Pa., Sch. Dist., 75 LA 1216, 1219 (Duff, 1980); Kelsey-Hayes Co., 74 LA 50, 53 (Heinsz, 1980); Columbian Carbon Co., 48 LA 919, 922 (Ray, 1967).

many arbitrators have recognized that, "In the absence of a written agreement, 'past practice', to be binding on both Parties, must be (1) unequivocal; (2) clearly enunciated and acted upon; (3) readily ascertainable over a reasonable period of time as a fixed, and established practice accepted by both Parties."[14]

Another commonly used formulation requires "clarity, consistency, and acceptability."[15] The term "clarity" embraces the element of uniformity.[16] The term "consistency" involves the element of repetition,[17] and "acceptability"

---

[14]Celanese Corp. of Am., 24 LA 168, 172 (Justin, 1954). These criteria, or similar ones, have been articulated and accepted in *Lake Erie Screw Corp.*, 108 LA 15, 19 (Feldman, 1997); *Grand Haven Stamped Prods. Co.*, 107 LA 131, 137 (Daniel, 1996); *Kansas City Power & Light Co.*, 105 LA 518, 523 (Berger, 1995); *Crescent Metal Prods.*, 104 LA 724, 726 (Cohen, 1994); *City of York, Pa.*, 103 LA 1111, 1115 (DiLauro, 1994); *Curved Glass Distribs.*, 102 LA 33, 36 (Eischen, 1993); *Fry's Food & Drug of Ariz.*, 101 LA 1179, 1181 (Oberstein, 1993); *Consolidation Coal Co.*, 99 LA 163, 167 (Roberts, 1992); *North Slope Borough Sch. Dist.*, 98 LA 697, 699–700 (Corbett, 1992); *Tennessee Valley Auth.*, 97 LA 73, 80 (Bankston, 1991); *Toledo Edison Co.*, 96 LA 908, 915 (Bressler, 1991); *Aurora Casket Co.*, 96 LA 855, 858 (Gibson, 1991); *Lawrence Paper Co.*, 96 LA 297, 302 (Berger, 1991); *Pierce Co.*, 95 LA 1029, 1031 (Wolff, 1990); *Town of Henrietta, N.Y.*, 95 LA 373, 378 (Pohl, 1990); *Topps Chewing Gum*, 94 LA 356, 359 (DiLauro, 1990); *Texas Util. Generating Div.*, 92 LA 1308, 1312 (McDermott, 1989); *Wyman-Gordon Co.*, 91 LA 225, 230 (Cyrol, 1988); *City of Marion, Ohio*, 91 LA 175, 179 (Bittel, 1988); *Dixie Mach. Welding & Metal Works*, 88 LA 734, 734 (Baroni, 1987); *Super Valu Stores*, 87 LA 453 (Goldman, 1986); *Farrell Lines*, 86 LA 36, 39 (Hockenberry, 1986); *Packaging Corp. of Am.*, 85 LA 700, 705 (Ruben, 1985); *Belleville Shoe Mfg. Co.*, 84 LA 337, 341 (Pratte, 1985); *Fashion Shoe Prods.*, 84 LA 325, 329–30 (Hilgert, 1985); *Washington Metro. Airport Police Branch*, 84 LA 203, 208 (Kaplan, 1985); *Emerson Elec. Co.*, 83 LA 895, 897 (Fitzsimmons, 1984); *Ethyl Corp.*, 83 LA 602, 604 (White, 1984); *Charleston Naval Shipyard*, 82 LA 476 (Groshong, 1984). For other statements of criteria for a binding practice, see *Transportation Enters.*, 75 LA 1226, 1230 (Johnson, 1980); *Logemann Bros. Co.*, 75 LA 615, 621–22 (Bard, 1980); *Charles H. Johnston's Sons Co.*, 75 LA 337, 341 (Chapman, 1980); *Veterans Admin.*, 72 LA 57, 61–62 (Goodman, 1978); *Minnesota Gas Co.*, 71 LA 544, 549 (Bognanno, 1978); *County Line Cheese Co.*, 69 LA 1088, 1092 (Leahy, 1977); *Control Data Corp.*, 69 LA 665, 670 (Hatcher, 1977); *Borough of Rutherford*, 68 LA 229, 231 (Beckerman, 1977). In *Sperry Rand Corp.*, 54 LA 48, 52 (Volz, 1971), the arbitrator stated that: "Leniency by individual supervisors must be distinguished from mutual agreement or acquiescence by the contracting parties in a consistent course of repetitive action." *See also* Hanna Mining Co., 73 LA 949, 951 (Kahn, 1979). Where national policy of a federal agency employer governed a matter, local departure from that policy could not result in a binding practice. Dep't of Justice, Immigration & Naturalization Serv., 77 LA 638, 643 (Weckstein, 1981) (higher management had been unaware of the local departure). Also concerning certain limitations on the binding quality of past practice in the federal sector, see *Utah Army Nat'l Guard*, 74 LA 770, 774–75 (Wiggins, 1980); *U.S. Army*, 70 LA 360, 364–65 (Griffin, 1978).

[15]Harbison-Walker Refractories, 114 LA 1302, 1305 (Smith, 2000); Crescent Metal Prods., 104 LA 724, 726 (Cohen, 1994); General Mills, 101 LA 953, 958 (Wolff, 1993). *See* H. Meyer Dairy Co., 105 LA 583, 587 (Sugerman, 1995).

[16]*See H. Meyer Dairy Co.*, 105 LA at 587.

[17]Monroe County Intermediate Sch. Dist., 105 LA 565, 567 (Brodsky, 1995) ("[A] practice can be established if, when one circumstance occurs, it is consistently treated in a certain way. The occurrence need not be daily or weekly, or even yearly, but when it happens, a given response to that occurrence always follows."); Weyerhauser Co., 105 LA 273, 276 (Nathan, 1995) ("A 'practice' as that concept is understood in labor relations refers to a pattern of conduct which appears with such frequency that the parties understand that it is the accepted way of doing something."); Brown-Forman Beverage Co., 103 LA 292, 294 (Frockt, 1994) ("[T]he general principle is that a practice exists when a certain result has been utilized in repetitive and identical circumstances."). A practice that is at best "checkered" does not exhibit the requisite repetitiveness to constitute a binding past practice. *See* Consolidation Coal Co., 104 LA 751, 756 (Franckiewicz, 1995). Mere habit or happenstance does not rise to the requisite level of frequency to create a binding practice. *See* Consolidation Coal Co., 106 LA 328, 332 (Franckiewicz, 1996). Moreover, one or two occurrences normally do not constitute a past practice. *See* Harbison-Walker Refractories, 114 LA 1302, 1305 (Smith, 2000); Nature's Best, 107 LA 769, 772 (Darrow, 1996) (holding that one-time payment of wage differential does not create past practice); *Weyerhauser Co.*, 105 LA at 276 (holding that a past practice is not created by one prior experience); Globe Ticket & Label Co., 105 LA 62, 66 (McCurdy, 1995) (holding that one occurrence does not create a practice); Stevens County, 104 LA 928, 932 (Daly, 1995) (holding that two occurrences within 4 months does not establish a past practice).

speaks to "mutuality" in the custom or practice.[18] However, the mutual acceptance may be tacit—an implied mutual agreement arising by inference from the circumstances.[19] While another factor sometimes considered is whether the activity was instituted by bilateral action or only by the action of one party,[20] the lack of bilateral involvement should not necessarily be given controlling weight.[21]

3. MUTUALITY [LA CDI 24.20]

It has been noted that, where a custom or practice has been enforced, the element of "mutuality" usually has been supplied by implication—that is, there has been "implied mutual agreement." In this regard, existing employee benefits usually affect all or at least sizable groups of employees, and thus are likely to be in the thoughts of union and company negotiators. It reasonably may be assumed, therefore, that the parties in shaping bargaining demands for wages and other employee benefits do so with silent recognition of the existing unwritten benefits and favorable working conditions.

It may be less plausible to assume that bargaining demands are shaped with any comparable silent thought, and hence "implied agreement," as to continuation of practices regarding methods of operation and direction of the workforce—matters falling within the fundamental areas of basic management responsibility.

---

[18]Michigan Hanger Co., 106 LA 377, 380 (Smith, 1996); Service Employees Local 415, 101 LA 483, 486 (Concepcion, 1993).

[19]See T.J. Maxx, 105 LA 470, 474 (Richman, 1995) ("'A proposal submitted in negotiations to change a past practice which is then withdrawn, may be evidence of the abandonment of an attempt to change the past practice.'" (Dixie Container Corp., 47 LA 1072, 1077 [Jaffee, 1966]). 'Silence in the face of a statement of position during negotiations can give rise to a contractual obligation under the doctrine of acceptance by silence.' (Las Vegas Joint Executive Bd. v. Riverboat Casino, 817 F.2d 524, 125 LRRM 2942 (9th Cir. 1987)."); Dixie Mach. Welding & Metal Works, 88 LA 734, 737 (Baroni, 1987); U.S. Indus. Chems. Co., 76 LA 620, 623 (Levy, 1981); Mead Corp., 45 LA 881, 884 (Wood, 1965); Bonanza Air Lines, 44 LA 698, 700 (Jones, Jr., 1965); Formica Corp., 44 LA 467, 468 (Schmidt, 1965); Continental Baking Co., 20 LA 309, 311 (Updegraff, 1953). Awareness of a practice is to be presumed from its long-established and widespread nature. Bethlehem Steel, 33 LA 374, 376 (Valtin, 1959). But see Boulevard Distillers & Importers, 94 LA 657, 660–61 (Heekin, 1990). A few arbitrators require that the consent be specifically acknowledged orally or in writing. National Unif. Serv., 104 LA 901, 907 (Klein, 1995); Atlantic Southeast Airlines, 102 LA 656, 659 (Feigenbaum, 1994); Fry's Food & Drug of Ariz., 101 LA 1179, 1181 (Oberstein, 1993). For a discussion of what a party should do to avoid being bound by a practice commenced by the other party, see Donaldson Co., 20 LA 826, 830–31 (Louisell, 1953).

[20]See Illinois Power Co., 93 LA 611, 614 (Westbrook, 1989); Country Lane Foods, 88 LA 599, 602 (Strasshofer, 1986); Montgomery Ward & Co., 85 LA 913, 915 (Caraway, 1985); International Paper Co., 85 LA 790, 791–92 (Garnholz, 1985); Department of Def., Dependent Sch., 71 LA 1031, 1033 (Lubic, 1978); Beaunit Fibers, 49 LA 423, 424 (McCoy, 1967); Hillbro Newspaper Printing Co., 48 LA 1166, 1168 (Roberts, 1967); League of N.Y. Theatres, 47 LA 75, 78 (Turkus, 1966); Glamorgan Pipe & Foundry Co., 46 LA 1007, 1008 (Dugan, 1966); Michigan Consol. Gas Co., 42 LA 385, 388 (Howlett, 1964); Columbus Auto Parts Co., 36 LA 166, 170 (Seinsheimer, 1961); International Harvester Co., 20 LA 276, 280 (Wirtz, 1953); General Cable Corp., 17 LA 780, 783 (Cahn, 1952). See also Mittenthal, Past Practice and the Administration of Collective Bargaining Agreements, in ARBITRATIION AND PUBLIC POLICY, PROCEEDINGS OF THE 14TH ANNUAL MEETING OF NAA 30, 33 (Pollard ed., BNA Books 1961).

[21]See Sterling Furniture Mfrs., 46 LA 705, 706 (Hanlon, 1966); Union Asbestos & Rubber Co., 39 LA 72, 75 (Volz, 1962) (holding a practice as to employee benefits to be binding though unilaterally instituted by the employer). In contrast, in some of the decisions cited elsewhere in this chapter, certain methods of operations unilaterally instituted by management, in the exercise of discretion in the performance of management functions, were held not to constitute binding practices. Thus, the critical consideration may be the subject matter of the practice rather than whether it was established by unilateral or bilateral action.

Management freedom of action in these latter matters may be essential for efficient and progressive operation of the enterprise, and thus serves the long-run interests of all employees.[22]

Many arbitrators recognize the "employee benefit"/"basic management function" dichotomy in determining whether a practice has binding effect.[23] In effect, this analysis of the custom and practice issue may be said to give employees the "benefit of the doubt" as to certain matters, and management the benefit of the doubt as to others.

4. THE SCOPE OF PAST PRACTICE

Even when a practice is found to be binding on the parties, questions may arise as to its scope. In this general regard, it appears reasonable that the underlying circumstances must be considered to give a practice its true dimensions: "A practice is no broader than the circumstances out of which it has arisen, although its scope can always be enlarged in the day-to-day administration of the agreement."[24]

---

[22]Illustrating that good-faith changes by management in methods of operation or in the direction of the workforce may be upheld notwithstanding express recognition that the change would result in a loss of wages or benefits by some employees, see *Fairview Southdale Hosp.*, 96 LA 1129, 1135 (Flagler, 1991); *Hilliard Corp.*, 75 LA 548, 550 (Konvitz, 1980); *Safeway Stores*, 73 LA 207, 215 (Goodman, 1979); *Browning-Ferris Indus. of Ohio*, 68 LA 1347, 1351–52 (Teple, 1977); *George Wiedemann Brewing Co.*, 54 LA 52, 55–56 (Volz, 1971); *Kroger Co.*, 52 LA 440, 443, 445 (Doyle, 1968) (stating that the "fact that the Company's basic motive is economy is not evidence of bad faith"); *St. Regis Paper Co.*, 51 LA 1102, 1107–08 (Solomon, 1968); *Shell Oil Co.*, 44 LA 1219, 1223 (Turkus, 1965). However, where one arbitrator found that the "only reason" for a change in work assignments was to avoid payment of overtime, which by 20-year practice had been a "substantial segment" of employee paychecks, he decided against the employer on the basis that "the economic benefit to the employees outweighs the Company's interest in changing its method of operation." Liquid Air, 73 LA 1200, 1203–05 (Weiss, 1979) (in regard to other past practice cases, "often the result can be explained by a weighing of the gravity of the Company's interest in making the change against the gravity of the employees' interest in retaining the traditional practice"). In the latter regard, an arbitrator denied a grievance in *Anheuser-Busch*, 72 LA 594, 597 (Seidman, 1979), where he found that the employer's action in lowering the temperature in the beer storage area "was dictated by marketing conditions"; the change did not adversely affect the health or safety of employees, but "it inconvenienced the employees in requiring them to purchase extra clothing and to work in a less desirable environment"; the change "assured their continued employment during a period that usually resulted in layoffs"; and "[o]n the whole it therefore had a beneficial rather than a deleterious effect on their economy."

[23]In some cases, the arbitrators have spoken expressly in terms of this distinction between employee benefits and basic management functions. *See* Fairview Southdale Hosp., 96 LA 1129, 1135 (Flagler, 1991); Social Sec. Admin., 79 LA 449, 457–59 (Mittleman, 1982); Servomation Corp., 77 LA 545, 551 (Lieberman, 1981); Saginaw Mining Co., 76 LA 911, 914 (Ruben, 1981); Le Blond Mach. Tool, 76 LA 827, 833–34 (Keenan, 1981); State of Alaska, 74 LA 459, 466–67 (Hauck, 1979); ITT-Continental Baking Co., 74 LA 92, 95 (Ross, 1980); Union Oil Co. of Cal., 73 LA 892, 895–96 (Goldberg, 1979); Kiowa Corp., 73 LA 391, 395 (Maniscalco, 1979); George Wiedemann Brewing Co., 54 LA 52, 55–56 (Volz, 1971); Studebaker Corp., 51 LA 813, 818–19 (Witney, 1968); Ingalls Shipbuilding Corp., 49 LA 654, 657–58 (Eyraud, 1967); Bangor Punta Operations, 48 LA 1275, 1276 (Kates, 1967); Sinclair Ref. Co., 66–1 ARB ¶8039, at 3129 (Warns, 1965); Standard Bag Corp., 45 LA 1149, 1151 (Summers, 1965); Torrington Co., 45 LA 353, 355 (Kennedy, 1965); Shell Oil Co., 44 LA 1219, 1223–24 (Turkus, 1965); Dayton Precision Corp., 44 LA 1217, 1218 (Kates, 1965); Celotex Corp., 43 LA 395, 399–400 (Ray, 1964); Tenneco Oil Co., 42 LA 833, 835–37 (Rubin, 1964); Honolulu Gas Co., 41 LA 1115, 1116–17 (Tsukiyama, 1963); Harnischfeger Corp., 40 LA 1329, 1331–32 (Anrod, 1963); Borden Co., 39 LA 1020, 1023 (Morvant, 1962); Union Asbestos & Rubber Co., 39 LA 72–75 (Volz, 1962).

[24]*Mittenthal*, NAA 14TH PROCEEDINGS, at 32–33. *See also* McCreary Tire & Rubber Co., 72 LA 1279, 1284 (Rollo, 1979); CF Chems., 69 LA 217, 221 (Bode, 1977).

5. What Matters May Be the Subject of a Binding Past Practice

Examination of many reported decisions suggests that there are no unanimously accepted standards for determining what matters may be the subject of binding practice. However, certain considerations have been stressed.

A. Major Condition of Employment [LA CDI 24.111; 24.351 et seq.]

In determining whether a practice may be treated as an implied term of the agreement, one arbitrator suggested that it is binding if it concerns a "working condition," but may be unilaterally discontinued if it involves a "gratuity."[25] Another arbitrator, however, doubted the validity of this test and suggested that perhaps the best test, though admittedly inexact, is that the usage, to achieve contractual status, must concern a "major condition of employment."[26]

This approach was championed by Archibald Cox and John T. Dunlop, who urged: "A collective bargaining agreement should be deemed, unless a contrary intention is manifest, to carry forward for its term the major terms and conditions of employment, not covered by the agreement, which pre-

---

[25]Fawick Airflex Co., 11 LA 666, 668–69 (Cornsweet, 1948). For practices upheld as benefits, see *GTE Hawaiian Tel. Co.*, 98 LA 832, 838 (Najita, 1991) (no evidence that taxi service eliminated by employer was merely gratuity); *Reliance Elec. Co.*, 90 LA 641, 645 (Wolff, 1988) (company nurse was benefit and working condition). Where past practice was not upheld as benefit, see *Kroger Co.*, 99 LA 905, 907 (Wahl, 1992) (giving of pizza parties, pen and pencil sets, and gifts of value for good attendance, longevity, or safe driving constituted "commonplace practice" of providing production incentives and was not a past practice); *Shawnee County, Kan., Sheriff's Dep't*, 97 LA 919, 924 (Berger, 1991) ("There is some indication in arbitration decisions that enforceability is more frequently found where the practice involves a matter central to working conditions, as opposed to a mere gratuity."); *Dahlstrom Mfg. Co.*, 97 LA 314, 319 (Duda, Jr., 1991) (giving gifts such as pizza parties, donuts, and gift certificates at sole discretion of company did not constitute binding past practice); *Hennepin County, Minn.*, 96 LA 685, 687 (Scoville, 1991) (employee wellness program was "purely gratuitous benefit"); *City of Anaheim, Cal.*, 91 LA 579, 583 (Bickner, 1988) (administrative procedures that convey incidental advantages are not binding); *Scott Paper Co.*, 82 LA 755, 757 (Caraway, 1984); *Ohio Precision Castings*, 82 LA 117, 120 (Murphy, 1983). The theory in these cases seems to be not that a "gratuity" is de minimis, but that an unnecessary, commonplace, or mutually beneficial practice does not imply an intent to be bound. Thus, in *State of Minn., Dep't of Labor & Indus.*, 83 LA 621, 625 (Gallagher, 1984), the arbitrator stated: "An agreement to be bound is not implied . . . where the practice is not controversial or when . . . it benefits both parties."

[26]Phillips Petroleum Co., 24 LA 191, 194 (Merrill, 1955). *See also* Northeast Ohio Reg'l Sewer Dist., 100 LA 742, 747 (Johnson, 1992) (shift-trading practice constituted term or condition of employment); Dierberg's Mkt., 99 LA 521, 527 (O'Grady, 1992) (30-year past practice of including retirees in referrals to fill extra hours); City of Detroit, Dep't of Transp., 99 LA 326, 328 (Kanner, 1992) (parking space considered condition of employment); Russell Coal, Inc., 98 LA 1107, 1111 (Nigro, 1992) (practice of assigning only end-loader operators on idle days); Food Gallery, 98 LA 707, 709 (Duff, 1992) (practice of offering senior part-time employees extra hours); ARCO Marine, 96 LA 319, 324 (Brisco, 1990) (practice of imposing 30-day suspension plus warning on first offenders of drug and alcohol policy); Amoco Performance Prods., 95 LA 1081, 1084 (Florman, 1990) (practice of keeping wage rate equal for all crafts); United Exposition Serv. Co., 95 LA 951, 960 (Allen, Jr., 1990) (practice of making additional labor requests through union hiring hall); Purity Baking Co., 95 LA 172, 178 (Gordon, 1990) (11-year practice of using date of hire as seniority date); Basler Elec. Co., 94 LA 888, 893 (Canestraight, 1990) (binding practice where employer's long history of permitting smoking established term or condition of employment); Ferndale Sch. Dist., 88 LA 468, 471 (Stoltenberg, 1987); Airco Carbon, 86 LA 6, 11 (Dworkin, 1986) (management could not unilaterally amend erroneous incentive pay standard in use for 30 years); Clinchfield Coal Co., 85 LA 382, 385 (Rybolt, 1985) (employees have right to rely on practice they believe in effect); Hoover Co., 85 LA 41, 42 (Shanker, 1985) ("past practice . . . set the context and understanding within which the employees operated"); Rola, 84 LA 998, 1000 (Baroni, 1985) (unfair to change practice without contract negotiations); Johnson Controls, 84 LA 553, 559–61 (Dworkin, 1985) (employer bound by practice of providing pay for missed overtime

vailed when the agreement was executed."[27] However, the "major condition of employment" test leaves many questions unanswered. From whose standpoint is something "major"? Where is the line to be drawn? Cox and Dunlop characterized as major such things as "basic wages, seniority, and pensions," but they apparently were willing to exclude such matters as job content, workloads, and incentive systems.[28]

B. Methods of Operation or Direction of the Workforce
[LA CDI 24.351 et seq.]

The line between practices that are binding and those that are not may well be drawn on the basis of whether the matter involves methods of operation or direction of the workforce, or whether it involves a "benefit" of peculiar personal value to the employees (though also involving the employer's purse).[29]

Arbitrators are often hesitant to permit unwritten past practice or methods of doing things to restrict the exercise of traditional and recognized functions of management. As Arbitrator Whitley P. McCoy wrote:

> But caution must be exercised in reading into contracts implied terms, lest arbitrators start re-making the contracts which the parties have themselves made. The mere failure of the Company, over a long period of time, to exercise a legitimate function of management, is not a surrender of the right to start exercising such right. If a Company had never, in 15 years and under 15 contracts, disciplined an employee for tardiness, could it thereby be contended that the Company could not decide to institute a reasonable system of penalties for tardiness? Mere non-use of a right does not entail a loss of it.[30]

---

rather than make-up opportunity); City of Detroit, 84 LA 301, 305–07 (Roumell, Jr., 1985) (employer bound by practice of posting promotional opportunities); Saginaw Mining Co., 82 LA 735, 738 (Feldman, 1984) (employer bound by practice of providing employees monthly printout of excused absences).

[27]Cox & Dunlop, *The Duty to Bargain Collectively During the Term of an Existing Agreement*, 63 Harv. L. Rev. 1097, 1116–17 (1950).

[28]*Id.* at 1118. When the source of the past practice is found in an employee handbook, arbitrators have disagreed as to its binding nature. *See* Indiana Mich. Power Co., 107 LA 1037, 1041 (Render, 1997) ("[P]ast practice can serve the parties well even when operating under a non contractual handbook."); City of Miamisburg, Ohio, 104 LA 228, 233 (Fullmer, 1995) ("[T]he arbitrator knows of no basis upon which the Employer can be held required [sic] to conform to a past practice in a non-contractual handbook benefit.").

[29]*See* Consolidation Coal Co., 106 LA 328, 335 (Franckiewicz, 1996) (practice of granting shift preference by seniority had "meaningful personal value" compared with "relatively minor" impact on management's ability to direct the workforce); Consolidation Coal Co., 105 LA 1110, 1115 (Talarico, 1995) (admitted practice of paying 4-hour minimum for call-back work did not impinge on management's right to direct the workforce); Sheboygan County, Wis., 105 LA 605, 608 (Dichter, 1995) (county may not unilaterally change practice of allowing compensatory time to be used for sick time); H. Meyer Dairy Co., 105 LA 583, 587 (Sugerman, 1995); Central Aluminum Co., 103 LA 190, 197 (Imundo, Jr., 1994); St. Louis Post-Dispatch, 99 LA 976, 987 (Mikrut, Jr., 1992) (employer improperly capped reimbursement of Medicare premiums in violation of 25-year practice); Fruehauf Trailer Corp., 97 LA 1023, 1026 (Kahn, 1991) (employer improperly discontinued 2-year practice of allowing employees to clock out 5 minutes prior to end of shift in order to wash up); Allen Dairy Prods. Co., 97 LA 988, 992 (Hoh, 1991) (personal leave practice); Toledo Edison Co., 96 LA 908, 916 (Bressler, 1991) (overtime pay for lunch period); Weyerhaeuser Co., 95 LA 834, 836 (Allen, Jr., 1990) ("past practice . . . generally held binding where it involves a benefit of peculiarly personal value to the employees"—paid lunch period); City of Miami, 89 LA 86, 89 (Abrams, 1987) (work schedule is job benefit). *Compare* City of Alliance, Ohio, 98 LA 603, 605 (Hewitt, 1992) (firefighters' past use of room for TV "does not possess the status and is not of the peculiar value to the employees that would permit it to stand against legitimate business use of the City's facility"). *But see* Fairview Southdale Hosp., 96 LA 1129, 1134–36 (Flagler, 1991) (elimination of 25-year practice of providing free parking for employees).

[30]Esso Standard Oil Co., 16 LA 73, 74 (McCoy, Reber, & Daniel, 1951). Citing this case with clear approval, see *Greif Bros. Corp.*, 114 LA 554, 561 (Kenis, 2000); *Groendyk Mfg. Co.*,

One of the most cogent and provocative published statements regarding the binding force of custom was that of Umpire Harry Shulman, in a case involving operating methods and direction of the workforce (assignment of work), wherein he urged that past practice not be "enshrined without carefully thought out and articulated limitations":

> A practice, whether or not fully stated in writing, may be the result of an agreement or mutual understanding. And in some industries there are contractual provisions requiring the continuance of unnamed practices in existence at the execution of the collective agreement. . . . A practice thus based on mutual agreement may be subject to change only by mutual agreement. Its binding quality is due, however, not to the fact that it is past practice but rather to the agreement in which it is based.
>
> But there are other practices which are not the result of joint determination at all. They may be mere happenstance, that is, methods that developed without design or deliberation. Or they may be choices by Management in the exercise of managerial discretion as to the convenient methods at the time. In such cases there is no thought of obligation or commitment for the future. Such practices are merely present ways, not prescribed ways, of doing things. The relevant item of significance is not the nature of the particular method but the managerial freedom with respect to it. Being the product of managerial determination in its permitted discretion such practices are, in the absence of contractual provision to the contrary, subject to change in the same discretion. The law and the policy of collective bargaining may well require that the employer inform the Union and that he be ready to discuss the matter with it on request. But there is no requirement of mutual agreement as a condition precedent to a change of practice of this character.
>
> A contrary holding would place past practice on a par with written agreement and create the anomaly that, while the parties expend great energy and time in negotiating the details of the Agreement, they unknowingly and unintentionally commit themselves to unstated and perhaps more important matters which in the future may be found to have been past practice. The contrary holding would also raise other questions very difficult to answer. For example, what is properly a subject of a practice? Would the long time use of a wheel barrow become a practice not to be changed by the substitution of four-wheeled buggies drawn by a tow tractor? Or would the long time use of single drill presses be a practice prohibiting the introduction of multiple drill presses? Such restraints on technological change are alien to the automobile industry. Yet such might be the restraints, if past practice were enshrined without carefully thought out and articulated limitations.[31]

113 LA 656, 660 (West, 1999); *Shawnee County, Kan., Sheriff's Dep't*, 97 LA 919, 926 n.16 (Berger, 1991); *Gates Rubber Co.*, 96 LA 445, 448 (Sergent, 1991); *General Mills*, 95 LA 1060, 1063 (Klein, 1990); *A.P. Green Indus.*, 94 LA 73, 78 (Garnholz, 1990); *Red River Army Depot*, 80 LA 267, 269 (Mewhinney, 1983); *W.E. Plechaty Co.*, 78 LA 404, 408 (Abrams, 1982); *Pennwalt Corp.*, 77 LA 626, 632 (Erbs, 1981); *Midland Brick & Tile Co.*, 74 LA 537, 542 (Roberts, 1980); *Town of Niagara, N.Y.*, 74 LA 312, 315 (Babiskin, 1980); *Safeway Stores*, 73 LA 207, 212 (Goodman, 1979); *Anheuser-Busch*, 68 LA 396, 399 (Cohen, 1977); *Colt Indus.*, 52 LA 493, 496 (Turkus, 1969); *Celotex Corp.*, 43 LA 395, 399 (Ray, 1964). Agreeing that mere nonuse of a right does not entail its loss, see *Qwest Communications*, 115 LA 1418 (Reeves, 2001); *City of Auburn, Me., Police Dep't*, 78 LA 537, 540 (Chandler, 1982).

[31]*Ford Motor Co.*, 19 LA 237, 241–42 (Shulman, 1952). Citing this Shulman statement with clear approval, see *New Era Cap Co.*, 114 LA 90, 99 (Eischen, 2000); *Terex/American Crane Corp.*, 114 LA 47, 50 (Nolan, 1999); *Potomac Edison Co. (Allegheny Power)*, 110 LA 420, 424 (Talarico, 1997); *GTE Hawaiian Tel. Co.*, 98 LA 832, 835 (Najita, 1991); *Material Serv. Corp.*, 98 LA 152, 164–65 (Fischbach, 1991); *Anchor Hocking Corp.*, 80 LA 1267, 1273 (Abrams, 1983); *Flint & Walling*, 79 LA 430, 432 (Guenther, 1982); *Total Petroleum*, 78 LA 729, 736 (Roberts, 1982); *May Dep't Stores*, 76 LA 254, 256 (Hannan, 1981); *Price Bros. Co.*, 76 LA 10, 12 (Shanker, 1980); *Hilliard Corp.*, 75 LA 548, 550 (Konvitz, 1980); *Safeway Stores*, 73 LA 207, 212 (Goodman, 1979); *Vindicator Printing Co.*, 72 LA 229, 233 (Teple, 1979); *American Petrofina Oil & Refinery*, 71 LA 852, 855 (Mewhinney, 1978); *California Portland Cement Co.*, 70 LA 81, 84 (Anderson, 1978); *Anheuser-Busch*, 68 LA 396, 400 (Cohen, 1977);

The viewpoints of McCoy and Shulman have been followed by numerous other arbitrators[32] who have recognized wide authority in management to control methods of operation and to direct the workforce, including the right without penalty to make changes if these do not violate some right of the employees granted by the written contract. If a given change, or the method of putting it into effect, does result in the violation of some contractual right of identified employees, then the arbitrator can be expected to award compensation to the employees for the loss sustained, even if the arbitrator does not take the further step of ordering management to revert to the prior practice.

Numerous cases involving the authority of management to control methods of operation and to direct the workforce are collected in Chapter 13, under topic headings such as section 5., "Control of Operation Methods," section 8., "Control of Quality Standards", section 9., "Job and Classification Control," section 11., "Determination of Size of Crews," and section 13., "Scheduling Work." Here, however, a few specific examples are noted. In some cases, past practice has not operated to prevent management from changing work schedules,[33] reassigning work,[34] determining the number of workers needed

---

International Tel. & Tel. Corp., 54 LA 869, 871 (Updegraff, 1971); *St. Regis Paper Co.*, 51 LA 1102, 1107 (Solomon, 1968); *Ingalls Shipbuilding Corp.*, 49 LA 654, 658 (Eyraud, 1967); *Glamorgan Pipe & Foundry Co.*, 46 LA 1007, 1008 (Dugan, 1966); *FMC Corp.*, 46 LA 335, 337 (Mittenthal, 1966); *Shell Oil Co.*, 44 LA 1219, 1222 (Turkus, 1965); *Celotex Corp.*, 43 LA 395, 399 (Ray, 1964); *Ingersoll-Rand Co.*, 42 LA 965, 970–71 (Scheiber, 1964); *Wyandotte Chems. Corp.*, 39 LA 65, 67 (Mittenthal, 1962); *International Minerals & Chem. Corp.*, 37 LA 528, 531 (Donaldson, 1961). For additional discussion of this subject, see Shulman, *Reason, Contract, and Law in Labor Relations*, 68 Harv. L. Rev. 999, 1011–13 (1955), *reprinted in* Management Rights and the Arbitration Process, Proceedings of the 9th Annual Meeting of NAA 169, 184–88 (McKelvey ed., BNA Books 1956).

[32]See cases cited in notes 30 and 31, above. *See also* Groendyk Mfg. Co., 113 LA 656 660 (West, 1999); Atlanta Newspapers, 77 LA 876, 880 (Gibson, 1981); Zimmer Mfg. Corp., 75 LA 16, 18 (Kiok, 1980); Hopwood Foods, 73 LA 418, 421 (Leahy, 1979); Scott Paper Co., 72 LA 1115, 1123 (Simon, 1979); Detroit News, 68 LA 51, 53 (Volz, 1977); Continental Can Co., 53 LA 809, 810 (Cahn, 1969); Hillbro Newspaper Printing Co., 48 LA 1166, 1168 (Roberts, 1967); League of N.Y. Theatres, 47 LA 75, 78 (Turkus, 1966); Standard Bag Corp., 45 LA 1149, 1151 (Summers, 1965); Pure Oil Co., 45 LA 557, 557–58 (Updegraff, 1965); Michigan Consol. Gas Co., 42 LA 385, 388 (Howlett, 1964). *But see* Campbell Plastics Corp., 51 LA 705, 706 (Cahn, 1968).

[33]*See* Albemarle Corp., 115 LA 1601, 1607 (Goodman, 2001); Washoe County, Nev., Sch. Dist., 113 LA 1053, 1059–60 (Hoh, 1999); Toledo, Wash., Sch. Dist. 237, 113 LA 652, 655 (Snow, 1999); Earthgrains Co., 112 LA 170, 174 (Grooms, Jr., 1999); Wortz Co., 99 LA 809, 811 (McKee, 1992); Shrewsbury Coal Co., 98 LA 108, 111–12 (Volz, 1991); City of Norton, Ohio, 97 LA 1090, 1094 (Nelson, 1991); Hopwood Foods, 73 LA 418, 421 (Leahy, 1979); Detroit News, 68 LA 51, 53 (Volz, 1977); St. Regis Paper Co., 51 LA 1102, 1110 (Solomon, 1968); Universal Foods Corp., 44 LA 226, 233 (Hebert, 1965); Calumet & Hecla, 42 LA 25, 30 (Howlett, 1963); Honolulu Gas Co., 41 LA 1115, 1116–17 (Tsukiyama, 1963); Federal Rice Drug Co., 27 LA 123, 125 (Reid, 1956); Parke, Davis & Co., 24 LA 496, 499–500 (Ryder, 1955); Esso Standard Oil, 16 LA 73, 74–75 (McCoy, Reber, & Daniel, 1951). *See also* Belcor, Inc., 77 LA 23, 26–27 (McKay, 1981). *Cf.* Cannon Elec. Co., 39 LA 93, 95–96 (Meyers, 1962).

[34]*See* Allied Signal, 113 LA 124, 126 (Thornell, 1999); State of Mont., Dep't of Justice, 111 LA 257, 262 (Prayzich, 1998); Material Serv. Corp., 98 LA 152, 164 (Fischbach, 1991); Potlatch Corp., 79 LA 272, 275–76 (O'Connell, 1982); City of Rogers City, 77 LA 393, 395 (Daniel, 1981); Safeway Stores, 73 LA 207, 215 (Goodman, 1979); General Time Corp., 70 LA 855, 859 (Kossoff, 1978); FMC Corp., 70 LA 110, 113 (Shister, 1978); Central Soya Co., 68 LA 864, 866–67 (Cox, 1977); Ceco Corp., 49 LA 234, 236–37 (Daugherty, 1967); Tennessee River Pulp & Paper Co., 45 LA 201, 206 (Kesselman, 1965); Shell Oil Co., 44 LA 1219, 1224 (Turkus, 1965); Olin Mathieson Chem. Corp., 43 LA 1064, 1066 (Larkin, 1964); Wyandotte Chems., 39 LA 65, 67–68 (Ray, 1964); Gas Serv. Co., 35 LA 637, 640 (Beatty, 1960); National Gypsum Co., 35 LA 353, 356 (Abernethy, 1960); H.H. Robertson Co., 22 LA 701, 703 (Blair, 1954); Ford Motor Co., 19 LA 237, 240–42 (Shulman, 1952). *Cf.* Canteen Corp., 71 LA 48, 54 (Buchanan, 1978); R. Wallace & Sons Mfg. Co., 23 LA 776, 778–79 (Myers, 1954).

on a job,[35] adding or eliminating job duties within reasonable limits,[36] eliminating a job,[37] discontinuing a particular line of business services or activity,[38] not filling a temporary vacancy,[39] discontinuing the maintenance of collateral information on seniority lists,[40] changing the method of using work-progress timecards,[41] using a formal instead of an informal method of determining skill and ability of employees,[42] rotating certain employees between two operating units to familiarize them with both operations,[43] changing the payday to Friday in order to reduce Friday absenteeism,[44] determining the frequency of holding safety meetings,[45] or making other changes in the methods of operation or in the direction of the workforce.[46]

Obviously, a past practice that supports management's actions in such matters has been cited as an additional reason for upholding management.[47]

In permitting unilateral change by management, arbitrators sometimes have pointed out that the matter may be subject to negotiations if requested by the union; but, if any such negotiations fail to produce agreement, management may exercise its unilateral judgment in making or continuing the change.[48]

---

[35]See International Salt Co., 42 LA 1188, 1190–91 (Mittenthal, 1964); Standard Oil Co., 30 LA 115, 117 (Updegraff, 1958); National Container Corp., 29 LA 687, 692–93 (Marshall, 1957); American Zinc Co., 18 LA 827, 830–31 (Updegraff, 1952). See also Jumer's Castle Lodge, 69 LA 315, 319–20 (Wright, 1977).

[36]See Memphis Publ'g Co., 110 LA 438, 443 (Grooms, Jr., 1998); United States Steel Corp., 54 LA 155, 158 (McDaniel, 1971); Overmyer Mould Co., 43 LA 1006, 1009–10 (Kelliher, 1964); Pan-Am S. Corp., 25 LA 611, 613–14 (Reynard, 1955); Dow Chem. Co., 22 LA 336, 342–43, 351 (Klamon, 1954); St. Joseph Lead Co., 20 LA 890, 891 (Updegraff, 1953); Globe-Union, Inc., 18 LA 320, 322–23 (Updegraff, 1951). Cf. City of Southgate, 67 LA 368, 371 (Ellmann, 1976).

[37]See Alabama Educ. Ass'n, 113 LA 493, 499 (Singer, Jr., 1999); Potter & Brumfield, Inc., 29 LA 324, 326–28 (Warns, Jr., 1957); Cochran Foil Co., 26 LA 155, 160 (Warns, Jr., 1956); Cannon Elec. Co., 19 LA 283, 286–87 (Warren, 1952).

[38]Detroit Edison Co., 43 LA 193, 209 (Smith, 1964).

[39]Celotex Corp., 43 LA 395, 399–400 (Ray, 1964).

[40]International Harvester Co., 22 LA 191, 192 (Platt, 1954).

[41]W.O. Larson Foundry Co., 42 LA 1286, 1292 (Kates, 1964).

[42]Lockheed Aircraft Corp., 25 LA 748, 751–52 (Williams, 1956). See also Columbia Steel Co., 15 LA 840, 841–42 (Garrett, 1950).

[43]Mathieson Chem. Corp., 18 LA 620, 624–25 (Smith, 1952). But as to the frequency of shift rotation, see Carnation Co., 34 LA 345, 349–50 (Marshall, 1960).

[44]Glamorgan Pipe & Foundry Co., 46 LA 1007, 1008 (Dugan, 1966).

[45]Ingalls Shipbuilding Corp., 49 LA 654, 657–58 (Eyraud, 1967).

[46]See Peabody Coal Co., 99 LA 390, 393 (Feldman, 1992) (vacation pay prorated to retiring workers); GTE-North, 97 LA 506, 509 (Pelofsky, 1991) (assignment of overtime); Gates Rubber Co., 96 LA 445, 448 (Sergent, 1991) (scheduling 3-week rather than 2-week vacation shutdown); Southern Clay, 92 LA 731, 734–35 (Odom, Jr., 1989); Le Blond Mach. Tool, 76 LA 827, 833–34 (Keenan, 1981); Koppers Co., 73 LA 837, 840 (Morgan, 1979); TRW, Inc., 72 LA 1047, 1050 (Whyte, 1979); City of Joliet, Ill., 70 LA 938, 940 (Eagle, 1978); Kast Metals Corp., 70 LA 278, 281–82 (Roberts, 1978); Oshkosh Truck Corp., 67 LA 103, 107 (Karlins, 1976).

[47]See Alabama Educ. Ass'n, 113 LA 493, 499 (Singer, Jr., 1999); City of Bay City, Mich., 111 LA 1124, 1128 (Allen, 1998); CBI Servs., 98 LA 1111, 1114–16 (Cohen, 1992); Masterbilt Prods. Corp., 97 LA 1042, 1044–45 (Daniel, 1991); ADM Milling Co., 96 LA 664, 665–66 (Levy, 1991); A.O. Smith Corp., 95 LA 69, 73 (Fullmer, 1990); State of Alaska, 73 LA 990, 991–92 (Hauck, 1979); Central State Univ., 54 LA 1159, 1162 (Snyder, 1971); E.I. duPont de Nemours & Co., 39 LA 496, 500 (Holly, 1962); Pan-Am S. Corp., 25 LA 611, 613–14 (Reynard, 1955); American Seating Co., 16 LA 115, 117 (Whiting, 1951). See also Macmillan Bloedel Containers, 68 LA 510, 513 (Berger, 1977); National Rejectors, 48 LA 941, 949 (McKenna, 1967).

[48]See Anheuser-Busch, 72 LA 594, 596–97 (Seidman, 1979); Bethlehem Steel Corp., 69 LA 1100, 1101 (Sharnoff, 1977); United States Pipe & Foundry Co., 28 LA 467, 467–68 (Hepburn, 1957); Lockheed Aircraft Corp., 25 LA 748, 751–52 (Williams, 1956); Blackhawk Mfg. Co., 7 LA 943, 945 (Updegraff, 1947); New York Car Wheel Co., 7 LA 183, 187 (Whiting, 1947). It also has been suggested that, even concerning changes that management may not be strictly required to discuss, discussion may be "the better practice." Bethlehem Steel, 16 LA 68, 70 (Feinberg, 1950). See also Chamberlain & Kuhn, Collective Bargaining 135–36 (2d ed. 1965); Chamberlain, Management's Reserved Rights: Discussion, in Management Rights and the Arbitration Process, Proceedings of the 9th Annual Meeting of NAA 138, 145–47 (McKelvey ed., BNA Books 1956).

C. Practice Involving a Benefit of Personal Value to Employees
[LA CDI 24.351 et seq.]

In contrast to the freedom of management to make changes in the exercise of basic management functions, arbitrators often have ruled an established custom or practice to be binding where it involved a "benefit" of peculiar personal value to the employees. These cases generally do not involve methods of operation or control of the workforce. Thus, management was not permitted to discontinue (or, in some cases, to change) the following "benefits" or "working conditions": work schedules,[49] wash-up periods,[50] lunch period arrangements,[51] paid work breaks,[52] free coffee or free meals,[53] utilities at discount or nominal charge,[54] bonuses,[55] various other monetary benefits or allowances,[56] maternity leaves of absence,[57] notice to union before discharge for dishonesty is implemented,[58] and special rights for senior employees.[59] This catalog is by no means exhaustive.[60]

---

[49]*See* Pulaski County, Ark., Special Sch. Dist., 114 LA 1135, 1138 (Stoia, 2000); City of Claremore, Okla., 114 LA 936, 939 (Crider, 2000); J.C.&N. Maint., 111 LA 902, 905 (Statham, 1998).

[50]*See* Fruehauf Trailer Corp., 97 LA 1023, 1026 (Kahn, 1991); Ruralist Press, 51 LA 549, 551 (Holly, 1968); Anaconda Aluminum Co., 45 LA 277, 279 (Duff, 1965); Harnischfeger Corp., 40 LA 1329, 1331–32 (Anrod, 1963); Goodyear Tire & Rubber Co., 35 LA 929, 930–31 (Killingsworth, 1960); International Harvester Co., 20 LA 276, 280 (Wirtz, 1953); John Deere Waterloo Tractor Works, 18 LA 276, 278 (Davey, 1952). *Cf.* Allied Chem. Corp., 49 LA 773, 783–84 (Davey, 1967).

[51]*See* Coca-Cola Bottling Co. of N. Ohio, 110 LA 1164, 1174 (McDonald, 1998); Toledo Edison Co., 96 LA 908, 916 (Bressler, 1991); Weyerhaeuser Co., 95 LA 834, 836 (Allen, Jr., 1990); Minnesota Gas Co., 71 LA 544, 550 (Bognanno, 1978); Sherwin-Williams Co., 51 LA 490, 493–94 (Kates, 1968); Lancaster Glass Corp., 40 LA 13, 17 (Teple, 1963); Darling & Co., 39 LA 964, 974–75 (Klamon, 1962); Elberta Crate & Box Co., 32 LA 228, 233 (Murphy, 1959); Dayton Steel Foundry Co., 30 LA 35, 38 (Wagner, 1958); E.W. Bliss Co., 24 LA 614, 619 (Dworkin, 1955); West Pittston Iron Works, 3 LA 137, 138 (McCoy, 1944). *Cf.* Zimmer Mfg. Corp., 75 LA 16, 18 (Kiok, 1980); Continental Can Co., 54 LA 311, 314 (Marshall, 1971); United Fuel Gas Co., 33 LA 137, 138–39 (McIntosh, 1959).

[52]*See* Formica Corp., 44 LA 467, 468 (Schmidt, 1965); Ingalls Iron Works Co., 32 LA 960, 961 (Reid, 1959).

[53]*See* Board of Pub. Utils., 76 LA 446, 450 (Grether, 1981); Farmland Indus., 72 LA 1302, 1307 (Heneman, Jr., 1979); Greater L.A. Zoo Ass'n, 60 LA 838, 842 (Christopher, 1973); Alpena Gen. Hosp., 50 LA 48, 51–52 (Jones, 1967); Lutheran Med. Hosp., 44 LA 107, 110 (Wolf, 1965); Beech-Nut Life Savers, 39 LA 1188, 1191 (Handsaker, 1962); Cushman Sons, 37 LA 381, 383 (Scheiber, 1961). Regarding restaurant meals versus TV dinners or box lunches, see *Ideal Basic Indus.*, 73 LA 107, 110 (Jones, 1979); Southern Ind. Gas & Elec. Co., 62 LA 96, 101–02 (Dolson, 1974).

[54]Central Ill. Pub. Serv. Co., 42 LA 1133, 1149–50 (Willingham, 1964); Phillips Petroleum Co., 24 LA 191, 195 (Merrill, 1955).

[55]See Chapter 13, section 24., "Bonuses," where cases permitting the discontinuance of bonuses are also cited.

[56]*See* Silver Bell Mining LLC, 112 LA 1175, 1178 (Peck, 1999) (travel time); St. Louis Post-Dispatch, 99 LA 976, 987 (Mikrut, Jr., 1992) (company improperly capped reimbursement of Medicare premiums); State of Alaska, 74 LA 459, 467–68 (Hauck, 1979) (low-rental housing); United Salt Corp., 72 LA 534, 536 (Porter, 1979) (right to work on employee's birthday falling on a holiday and thus earn double pay); Sunshine Mining Co., 72 LA 479, 485 (Flagler, 1979) (receipt of 25 shares of stock after 25 years of service); South Cent. Bell Tel. Co., 72 LA 333, 336 (Morris, 1979) (commercial driver's license paid for by employer); Tri-State Asphalt Corp., 72 LA 102, 107 (LeWinter, 1979) (paid insurance premiums during layoff); Glasgow Elec. Co., 70 LA 470, 475 (Ross, 1978) (payment of employee's salary during workers' compensation waiting period); American Shipbuilding Co., 69 LA 944, 955–56 (Ruben, 1977) (holiday pay); Lennox Indus., 68 LA 855, 858 (Burns, 1977) (paid committee time).

[57]Northland Greyhound Lines, 23 LA 277, 280 (Levinson, 1954).

[58]Coca-Cola Bottling Co., 9 LA 197, 198 (Jacobs, 1947).

[59]International Minerals & Chems. Corp., 36 LA 92, 95 (Sanders, 1960); Fruehauf Trailer Co., 29 LA 372, 375 (Jones, Jr., 1957).

[60]*See* Fina Oil & Chem. Co., 111 LA 107, 111–12 (Bankston, 1998) (mandatory use of pagers); Allen Dairy Prods. Co., 97 LA 988, 992 (Hoh, 1991) (personal leave practice); City of

In some cases, however, management has been allowed to discontinue or reduce customary employee benefits because the employer, in giving the benefit, had emphasized that it was to be a gratuity only and not a part of the wage structure, or because a change of circumstances or necessity justified the change.[61]

6. REGULATION, MODIFICATION, OR TERMINATION OF PRACTICE AS IMPLIED TERM OF CONTRACT [LA CDI 24.351 et seq.]

In a number of cases, arbitrators have held a given practice to be binding on management, but, at the same time, have upheld the right of management to regulate and police it against abuse.[62] For example, where management imposed a limitation on to how often employees could take breaks to use the company vending machine, an arbitrator upheld the limitation with the following explanation:

> [I]nherent in every practice is the principle that it is not to be abused and that, if it is, reasonable corrective action may be taken. It can not be inferred that the other party has accepted or acquiesced in the excesses constituting the abuse so as to make them binding. The employees, no less than management, are under a duty to act reasonably. Both must cooperate and meet the other halfway in following sound industrial practices which will enable the plant to be operated efficiently for the ultimate benefit of the men as well as the Company.[63]

Even if a practice of providing an employee benefit is held to be binding, the administrative arrangements by which the company has provided the

---

Miami, 89 LA 86, 89 (Abrams, 1987) (work schedule a job benefit); Weston Paper & Mfg. Co., 76 LA 1273, 1277–78 (Bowles, 1981) (time off for union executive board meetings); Eau Claire County, 76 LA 333, 335 (McCrary, 1981) (assistance in starting car in cold weather); Lozier Corp., 74 LA 475, 481 (Murphy, 1980) (use of chewing tobacco); City of New Brunswick, N.J., 73 LA 174, 177 (Chandler, 1979) (employee option as to form of compensation for overtime); General Mills Fun Group, 72 LA 1285, 1289–90 (Martin, 1979) (use of progressive discipline); FWD Corp., 71 LA 929, 931 (Lynch, 1978) (use of personal coffeepots and radios on company premises); Bureau of Nat'l Affairs, 68 LA 1000, 1005–06 (Fields, 1977) (holiday on Inauguration Day); Potomac Elec. Power Co., 66 LA 399, 403 (Seidenberg, 1976) (paid leave immediately prior to retirement).

[61]See Fairview Southdale Hosp., 96 LA 1129, 1134 (Flagler, 1991); Social Sec. Admin., 70 LA 699, 706–07 (Atleson, 1978); Anheuser-Busch, 68 LA 396, 401 (Cohen, 1977); Proform, Inc., 67 LA 493, 496 (Render, 1976); Falstaff Brewing Corp., 53 LA 405, 409 (Teple, 1969); Hillbro Newspaper Printing Co., 48 LA 1166, 1168 (Roberts, 1967); Morningstar-Paisley, Inc., 42 LA 765, 766 (Stein, 1964); Mallinckrodt Chem. Works, 38 LA 267, 268–69 (Hilpert, 1961); Bowman Dairy Co., 37 LA 635, 637–38 (Volz, 1961); U.S. Steel Corp., 36 LA 220, 222 (McDermott, 1961); Crompton & Knowles Corp., 34 LA 59, 62 (Fallon, 1959); Western Greyhound Lines, 33 LA 157, 161–64 (Kleinsorge, 1959); Ingalls Iron Works Co., 32 LA 960, 960 (Reid, 1959); Rockwell-Standard Corp., 30 LA 593, 595–98 (Schmidt, 1958); Pennsylvania R.R., 26 LA 749, 750–51 (Lynch, 1956); Robertshaw-Fulton Controls Co., 24 LA 745, 747–48 (Morris, 1955); Donaldson Co., 20 LA 826, 829–31 (Louisell, 1953); New York Trap Rock Co., 19 LA 421, 422 (Giardino, 1952); Drug Prods. Co., 10 LA 804, 805 (Naggi, 1948).

[62]See Mechanical Prods., 91 LA 977, 980–82 (Roumell, Jr., 1988) (abuse of unlimited vending machine use); Department of the Navy, Norfolk Naval Shipyard, 75 LA 847, 849 (McCandless, 1980); Lozier Corp., 74 LA 475, 481 (Murphy, 1980); Wallace Murray Corp., 72 LA 470, 475 (Abrams, 1979); Glasgow Elec. Co., 70 LA 470, 475 (Ross, 1978); Dover Corp., 69 LA 779, 782 (Edes, 1977); United States Steel Corp., 50 LA 974, 976 (Miller, 1968); Bangor Punta Operations, 48 LA 1275, 1276 (Kates, 1967); Dayton Precision Corp., 44 LA 1217, 1218 (Kates, 1965); Formica Corp., 44 LA 467, 468 (Schmidt, 1965); Tenneco Oil Co., 42 LA 833, 835–37 (Rubin, 1964); Eastern Airlines, 40 LA 1217, 1221 (Rohman, 1963); Metal Specialty Co., 39 LA 1265, 1269 (Volz, 1962); Dover Corp., 33 LA 860, 861–62 (McIntosh, 1959). Abuse of a practice was one of the factors justifying the termination of the practice by the employer in Kentile Floors, 55 LA 808, 813 (Cyrol, 1970). See also Lawson-United Feldspar & Mineral Co., 189 NLRB 350, 76 LRRM 1588 (1971).

[63]Metal Specialty Co., 39 LA 1265, 1269 (Volz, 1962). See also Mechanical Prods., 91 LA 977, 981 (Roumell, Jr., 1988) (citing Metal Specialty Co.).

benefit may be subject to change at the prerogative of management.[64] For example, in two cases, management was permitted to provide substitute parking facilities for employees when the established benefit (parking near the work site) and legitimate management interests came into conflict.[65] Public safety also has been held to justify a change from past practice.[66]

Arbitrators have recognized that an otherwise binding practice may be modified or eliminated where the underlying basis for the practice has changed.[67] This principle was articulated by one arbitrator as follows: "It must be stated as a general proposition that, absent language in a collective bargaining agreement expressly or impliedly to the contrary, once the conditions on which a past practice has been based are changed or eliminated, the practice may no longer be given effect."[68] Thus, a 25-year practice of allowing painters 10 minutes overtime to clean their brushes could be discontinued unilaterally by management when it eliminated the congestion problem that had been the underlying reason for the practice.[69]

---

[64]Bethlehem Steel Corp., 50 LA 202, 205 (Strongin, 1968) (the company could relocate the place of giving medical services by closing a branch dispensary and centralizing all services in one dispensary). For other indications of management control over arrangements in providing employee benefits, see *Reliance Elec. Co.*, 55 LA 294, 301–02 (Walter, 1970) (company could reposition vending machines and require employees to use only certain ones); *United States Steel Corp.*, 48 LA 55, 57 (Florey, 1966) (practice required company to make food service available, but company could decide "how," providing the arrangement was reasonable).

[65]Jervis B. Webb Co. of Ga., 52 LA 1314, 1315 (Holly, 1969); Beaunit Fibers, 49 LA 423, 424–25 (McCoy, 1967). *See also* City of Detroit Dep't of Transp., 99 LA 326, 329–31 (Kanner, 1992) (employer properly ordered union members to use new parking lot rather than smaller, more congested lot). Exceptions to the requirements of past practice may be justified by special circumstances. *See* Sterling Brewers, 53 LA 1078, 1087 (Witney, 1969) (the arbitrator refused to give "slavish adherence" to past practice under the circumstances).

[66]City of Reno, Nev., 93 LA 220, 222–23 (Winograd, 1989).

[67]*See* Goodyear Tire & Rubber Co., 107 LA 193, 196 (Sergent, 1996) (holding that circumstances surrounding the practice of being exempt from overtime draft for Sunday work had changed, because Sunday work had become part of the regular workweek); United Ref. Co., 105 LA 411, 415 (Harlan, 1995) (stating that the conditions underlying the practice of starting mediation sessions at 2:00 p.m. had changed significantly when the frequency of sessions increased dramatically); Lockheed Aeronautical Sys. Co., 104 LA 840, 844 (Hewitt, 1995) (a change in attitudes regarding smoking was a change in underlying circumstances giving rise to the practice of permitting smoking); Reed Mfg. Co., 102 LA 1, 6 (Dworkin, 1993) ("[O]nce the support disappears, so does the binding quality of the practice."). *But see* Cross Oil & Ref. of Ark., 104 LA 757, 763 (Gordon, 1995) (citing Johns-Mansville Sales Corp. v. Machinists Local Lodge 1609, 621 F.2d 756, 104 LRRM 2895 (5th Cir. 1980), and stating that individual health hazards to smokers themselves are beyond the company's legitimate business interests, and limited smoking practices continue even in asbestos factories where medical reasons against smoking seem compelling). *See also* Independent Sch. Dist. 197, 97 LA 364, 367 (Fogelberg, 1991) ("Arbitral theory holds that a past practice is legitimized by the underlying conditions upon which it is based. Once these conditions change, the practice is not necessarily binding any longer."); Precision Stainless, 99 LA 1113, 1116 (Yarowsky, 1992) (practice of allowing employees to work earlier shift in order to avoid heat became unnecessary where conditions changed when plant was moved to new building); State of Minn., 99 LA 187, 189 (Bognanno, 1992) (unauthorized entry into supervisor's office constituted invasion of privacy where past practice of routinely entering office for files ended when files were relocated); City of Alliance, Ohio, 98 LA 603, 605 (Hewitt, 1992) ("When conditions upon which the practice was established have changed, the practice may be modified provided it is for legitimate business reasons."); Pierce Co., 95 LA 1029, 1032 (Wolff, 1990) ("Binding past practices, absent a change in the conditions out of which they arose, ordinarily cannot be changed unilaterally."); Greyhound Food Mgmt., 95 LA 820, 824 (Staudohar, 1990) (overtime distribution); News-Sun, 91 LA 1324, 1331 (Goldstein, 1988); E.G.&G. Fla., 85 LA 585, 594 (Richard, 1985); General Tire & Rubber Co., 83 LA 811, 813 (Feldman, 1984); Miners Clinic, 83 LA 445, 448 (Probst, 1984); Butler County Mushroom Farm, 82 LA 170, 171 (Jones, Jr., 1984).

[68]Gulf Oil Co., 34 LA 99, 100 (Cahn, 1959).

[69]Newport News Shipbuilding & Drydock Co., 48 LA 1239, 1242–43 (Crawford, 1967).

Even absent any such change in the underlying basis of a practice, an impressive line of arbitral thought holds that a practice that is not subject to unilateral termination during the term of the collective bargaining agreement is subject to termination at the end of said term by giving due notice of intent not to carry the practice over to the next agreement; after being so notified, the other party must have the practice written into the agreement to prevent its discontinuance.[70] One arbitrator explained:

> Consider first a practice which is, apart from any basis in the agreement, an enforceable condition of employment on the theory that the agreement subsumes the continuance of existing conditions. Such a practice cannot be unilaterally changed during the life of the agreement. For, . . . if a practice is not discussed during negotiations most of us are likely to infer that the agreement was executed on the assumption that the practice would remain in effect.
>
> The inference is based largely on the parties' acquiescence in the practice. If either side should, during the negotiation of a later agreement, object to the continuance of this practice, it could not be inferred from the signing of a new agreement that the parties intended the practice to remain in force. Without their acquiescence, the practice would no longer be a binding condition of employment. In face of a timely repudiation of a practice by one party, the other must have the practice written into the agreement if it is to continue to be binding.[71]

---

[70]*See* Grand Haven Stamped Prods. Co., 107 LA 131, 137 (Daniel, 1996); Albertson's, Inc., 106 LA 897, 900 (Kaufman, 1996); Penn Emblem Co., 101 LA 884, 886 (Byars, 1993); St. Paul Indep. Sch. Dist. No. 625, 95 LA 1236, 1241 (Gallagher, 1990); National Tea Co., 94 LA 730, 733 (Baroni, 1990) (past practices do not continue ad infinitum, but may be repudiated by either party through timely and proper notification of intent to take such action before or during negotiations); Consolidation Coal Co., 82 LA 889, 891–93 (Abrams, 1984); Standard Oil Co., 79 LA 1333, 1336 (Feldman, 1982); State of Alaska, 74 LA 459, 467 (Hauck, 1979); Department of Def., Dependent Sch., 71 LA 1031, 1033 (Lubic, 1978); Weyerhaeuser Co., 71 LA 61, 63 (Rauch, 1978); Alpena Gen. Hosp., 50 LA 48, 51 (Jones, 1967); Meltzer, *Ruminations About Ideology, Law, and Labor Arbitration, in* THE ARBITRATOR, THE NLRB, AND THE COURTS, PROCEEDINGS OF THE 20TH ANNUAL MEETING OF NAA 1, 35–36 (Jones ed., BNA Books 1967); Mittenthal, *Past Practice and the Administration of Collective Bargaining Agreements, in* ARBITRATION AND PUBLIC POLICY, PROCEEDINGS OF THE 14TH ANNUAL MEETING OF NAA 30, 56–57 (Pollard ed., BNA Books 1961). *But see* United States Borax & Chem. Corp., 48 LA 641, 643–47 (Bernstein, 1967). For National Labor Relations Board (NLRB) decisions not requiring mutual assent for the discontinuance of a practice after giving due notice of intent not to carry it over to the next agreement, see *City Hosp. of E. Liverpool, Ohio*, 234 NLRB 58, 97 LRRM 1125, 1126 (1978) (union had notice of proposed changes and failed to make a timely request for bargaining); *Lee Deane Prods.*, 181 NLRB 1047, 74 LRRM 1025 (1970) (there was extensive bargaining before management discontinued the practice). In *Aeronca, Inc.*, 253 NLRB 261, 105 LRRM 1541, 1544 (1980), the NLRB said that "an employer is not required to forgo needed changes, but it must first notify and bargain with the Union." On review, the U.S. Court of Appeals for the Fourth Circuit held that the NLRB had not been warranted in finding that the employer violated the Labor Management Relations Act when it discontinued its past practice of giving Christmas turkeys, the court finding that bargaining on the matter had been waived. Aeronca, Inc. v. NLRB, 650 F.2d 501, 107 LRRM 2687 (4th Cir. 1981). *See also* Torrington Co. v. Metal Prods. Workers Local 1645, 362 F.2d 677, 62 LRRM 2495 (2d Cir. 1966). There may or may not be a statutory duty to bargain on the discontinuance of a practice. *Compare* Benchmark Indus., 270 NLRB 22, 116 LRRM 1032 (1984), *and* Peerless Food Prods., 236 NLRB 161, 98 LRRM 1182 (1978), *with* NLRB v. Pepsi-Cola Distrib. Co. of Knoxville, Tenn., 646 F.2d 1173, 107 LRRM 2252 (6th Cir. 1981), *and* Beacon Journal Publ'g Co., 164 NLRB 734, 65 LRRM 1126 (1967). On the question of whether it is an arbitrator's function to decide whether any statutory duty to bargain has been violated, see Chapter 10, section 3.A.v., "The NLRA, the Arbitrator, and the NLRB." For general discussion of the duty to bargain, see Chapter 13, section 2.A.i., "The Duty to Bargain: Right of Unilateral Action," and section 2.A.ii., "Duration of Limitation on Unilateral Action: Contract Limitation Versus Statutory Duty to Bargain."

[71]Mittenthal, NAA 14TH PROCEEDINGS, at 56. In contrast, repudiation of a practice that gives meaning to ambiguous language in the written agreement would not be significant— the effect of this kind of practice can be terminated only by rewriting the language. *Id.* Similarly, a practice could not be unilaterally terminated where such action would defeat rights under a newly adopted contract provision that was premised on the practice. Kroger Co., 36 LA 129, 130–31 (Updegraff, 1960).

Similarly, the binding status of the practice may be found to have ended through the give and take of bargaining.[72] Arbitrators generally are unwilling to grant to any party by way of a past practice a demand that the party was unable to obtain at the bargaining table.[73] The termination of a practice also may be based on its gradual discontinuance over a period of time.[74]

However, where an employer continued to reimburse for stolen tools even though an earlier letter of agreement providing for such reimbursement had been nullified by the current contract, an arbitrator held that the continuing reimbursement amounted to an amendment to the contract.[75]

Where successor employers are involved, circumstances may[76] or may not[77] imply an intent to be bound by the practices of a predecessor.

7. Contract Clauses Regarding Custom

The status of unwritten practices or customs may be dealt with specifically in the written agreement by the addition of a well-constructed "zipper clause," which commonly takes the form of either an acknowledgment that

---

[72]See Marley Cooling Tower Co., 110 LA 1171, 1177 (Berger, 1998); Bayer, Inc., 105 LA 100, 102 (Duff, 1995); Daniels Co., 102 LA 1064, 1067 (Franckiewicz, 1994); Thrifty Corp., 85 LA 780, 782–83 (Gentile, 1985); Laclede Steel Co., 54 LA 647, 648 (Kelliher, 1971); Westlake Moving & Storage, 50 LA 125, 127–28 (Roberts, 1968); Milwaukee Spring Co., 39 LA 1270, 1273 (Gundermann, 1962). See also Memphis Light, Gas, & Water Div., 69 LA 687, 696 (Simon, 1977) (a practice could be terminated by management "in view of the fact that the vehicle upon which past practice was based was done away with by the parties in hard-nosed negotiations at the insistence of the Union"); National Can Corp., 45 LA 470, 475 (Stouffer, 1965). Cf. Ferro Corp., 70 LA 369, 375 (Cohen, 1978) (new contract clause did not terminate a practice by inference where the proponent of the clause failed to state in negotiations that a collateral effect would be discontinuance of the practice). However, the binding effect of a practice may be confirmed as a result of negotiations. See Leeds & Northrup Co. v. NLRB, 391 F.2d 874, 67 LRRM 2793 (3d Cir. 1968) (the union had reduced its demands because management withdrew its proposal to modify a practice). See also Doss Aviation, 107 LA 39, 49 (Ferree, 1996) (stating that a past practice cannot be voided by language mistakenly inserted into a subsequent contract).

[73]See Grand Haven Stamped Prods., 107 LA 131, 136–37 (Daniel, 1996); HS Auto., 105 LA 681, 686 (Klein, 1995); Dean Foods Vegetable Co., 105 LA 377, 380 (Dichter, 1995); Lockheed Aeronautical Sys. Co., 104 LA 803, 805–06 (Duff, 1995).

[74]See Bethlehem Steel, 37 LA 956, 958 (Seward, 1961). But a practice will not be deemed to have been changed or eliminated merely by a single unprotected departure from the practice. Bethlehem Steel Corp., 48 LA 1205, 1208 (Seward, 1967).

[75]Southern Clay, 92 LA 731 (Odom, Jr., 1989).

[76]See Printpack, Inc., 112 LA 1115, 1117 (Crider, 1999) (noting successor employer's having negotiated a new contract and discussed subject of the past practice in negotiations).

[77]See McGrath Motors, 97 LA 714, 720 (Wolff, 1991) (rejecting union's assertion that a disputed bonus paid by predecessor employer constituted a "past practice" where successor agreed to maintain benefits); Crane Plumbing, 95 LA 942, 950 (Bell, 1990) (successor employer bound to continue predecessor's 20-year past practice of providing "well baby" care for newborn dependents of its employees and their spouses); Aurora/Hydromatic Pumps, 95 LA 276, 281–82 (Dworkin, 1990) (successor employer bound by union's grievance settlement with predecessor where employer assumed predecessor's past practices); National Roll Co., 95 LA 863, 866 (Hewitt, 1990) (employer not bound by predecessor employer's 3-year past practice of vacation payment to retirees); Friedland Indus., 94 LA 816, 820 (Daniel, 1990) (union not bound by past practice regarding use of temporary employees to perform bargaining-unit work where practice developed under predecessor employer); Williams-Russell & Johnson, 91 LA 1215, 1217 (Byars, 1989) (employer practice of paying contributions to employee individual retirement accounts for leave hours as well as work hours upheld, despite contract language requiring contributions only for each hour worked, where practice had been applied by predecessor and was adopted and applied consistently by employer, survived challenge during contract negotiations, and was unchallenged in subsequent talks); Family Food Park, 86 LA 1184, 1188 (Petersen, 1986).

the written contract constitutes the parties' entire agreement[78] and is a waiver of the right to bargain about other conditions,[79] or a specific affirmation that management rights are not limited by prior practices.[80]

If the contract language is explicit, the binding effect of customs or practices may be eliminated. Thus, even where a practice of providing employees with a "bonus" was the product of negotiations between company and union and had existed for several years, but had not been written into the contract, an arbitrator held that it could be unilaterally discontinued by the employer because the written contract provided:

> This contract represents complete collective bargaining and full agreement by the parties in respect to rates of pay, wages, hours of employment or other conditions of employment which shall prevail during the term hereof and any matters or subjects not herein covered have been satisfactorily adjusted, compromised or waived by the parties for the life of this agreement.[81]

But a clause, stating only that "this contract expresses the entire agreement between the parties," was held by another arbitrator to eliminate automatically only those practices that conflicted with the contract's terms, because practices, the arbitrator said, are not necessarily matters for agreement.[82]

A contract adding the further condition that it "cancels all previous Agreements, both written and oral" to the provision that the document "constitutes the entire Agreement between the parties" was still found to be ineffective to cancel past practices. The arbitrator declared that the provision had "no magical dissolving effect upon practices or customs which are continued in fact unabated and which span successive contract periods."[83]

Of course, zipper clauses do not negate practices that are relied on for the purpose of casting light on ambiguous contract language.[84]

---

[78]In *George E. Failing Co.*, 93 LA 598, 602 (Fox, Jr., 1989), the arbitrator held that the following agreement precluded the company from relying on past practice:

It is understood and agreed that this Agreement will replace and supersede any and all previous agreements and that it shall be firm on all points covered herein. No amendments, modifications, change or interpretive alteration shall be effective unless it is executed in writing, dated and signed by the individuals who have executed this Agreement, or their successors.

[79]NLRB v. Southern Materials Co., 447 F.2d 15, 77 LRRM 2814 (4th Cir. 1971); Exxon Research & Eng'g Co., 317 NLRB 675, 150 LRRM 1308 (1995). To meet the standard of "clear and unmistakable waiver" in the absence of specific contract language, it must be shown that the matter waived was fully discussed and explored, and that the waiving party consciously yielded its rights. Trojan, Yacht Div., 319 NLRB 741, 150 LRRM 1321 (1995).

[80]Hayssen Mfg. Co., 82 LA 500 (Flaten, 1984); Hesco Indus., 81 LA 649 (Chapman, 1983).

[81]Bassick Co., 26 LA 627, 630 (Kheel, 1956). *See also* Grand Haven Stamped Prods. Co., 107 LA 131, 137 (Daniel, 1996); Hubbell Indus. Controls, 100 LA 350, 354 (Talarico, 1992); Midwest Dental Prods. Corp., 94 LA 467, 472 (Wies, 1990); Augsburg Coll., 91 LA 1166, 1173 (Gallagher, 1988); Dura Corp., 68 LA 94, 98 (Cabe, 1977); Lone Star Brewing Co., 53 LA 1317, 1319–20 (Autrey, 1969); Oxford Paper Co., 44 LA 630, 634 (Dworkin, 1965); Micro Precision Gear & Mach. Corp., 42 LA 165, 168 (Klein, 1964); Magnavox Co., 36 LA 160, 162 (Larkin, 1960); Illinois Brick Co., 21 LA 398, 400 (Edes, 1953).

[82]American Seating Co., 16 LA 115, 116–17 (Whiting, 1951). *See also* Wallace Murray Corp., 72 LA 470, 474–75 (Abrams, 1979); Falstaff Brewing Corp., 53 LA 405, 407 (Teple, 1969); Elberta Crate & Box Co., 32 LA 228, 233 (Murphy, 1959). *Cf.* Zanesville Transformer Plant, 53 LA 1024, 1027 (Lewis, 1969).

[83]Fruehauf Trailer Co., 29 LA 372, 374, 375 (Jones, Jr., 1957). *See also* Haveg Indus., 52 LA 1146, 1150 (Kates, 1969); Chesapeake & Potomac Tel. Co., 50 LA 417, 421 (Duff, 1968). *Cf.* New York Trap Rock Co., 19 LA 421, 423 (Giardino, 1952). *But see* School City of Hobart, 86 LA 557, 563 (Alexander, 1985) (clear meaning of zipper clause not overcome by continuation of benefit practice during first year of 3-year agreement).

[84]*See* Becton, Dickinson & Co., 54 LA 686, 688 (Nichols, 1971); Kelsey-Hayes Co., 37 LA 375, 376–77 (Gill, 1961).

The counterparts for zipper clauses are clauses designed to ensure continuance of some or all of the established practices or local working conditions.[85] Of course, under such clauses the question often arises as to which practices or local working conditions are to be preserved.[86] Where a letter of agreement on local practices specifically listed certain practices to be continued, an arbitrator ruled that the omission of other practices from the list did not imply that the other practices could be eliminated unilaterally; rather, the effect of the list was to eliminate the need for proof as to the existence of the practices listed. Other usages were not annulled without explicit language supporting their termination.[87] In a contrary decision, where other parties similarly listed certain practices to be continued, another arbitrator upheld the employer's unilateral termination of an unlisted practice.[88]

General "catch-all" provisions, designed to freeze general working conditions, have been held to be ineffective to nullify an express provision of the contract.[89] Thus, such a clause was held not to require the employer to continue a customary paid holiday—the day before Christmas—because the contract specifically listed paid holidays and Christmas Eve was not on the list. In another decision, a generalized "custom preservation" clause was held inappropriate to "expand and broaden an already specific provision."[90] Such clauses also have been interpreted as limited to employee benefits and incapable of restricting basic management functions, absent clear indication of such intent.[91]

Another type of custom or practice-recognition clause may provide that if the employer attempts to change or eliminate an established practice, it shall, on challenge through the grievance and arbitration procedure, bear the burden of "justifying" its action.[92] But another such clause states that a

---

[85]For a variety of such clauses, see *Russell Coal Inc.*, 98 LA 1107, 1110–11 (Nigro, 1992); *City of Greenfield*, 77 LA 8, 8–9 (Yaffe, 1981); *Hoboken, N.J., Bd. of Educ.*, 75 LA 988, 991 (Silver, 1980); *City of Hanford*, 72 LA 639, 643 (Mullennix, 1979); *North Clackamas Sch. Dist. No. 12*, 68 LA 503, 506 (Snow, 1977); *Singer Co.*, 52 LA 176, 177 (Cahn, 1968); *Marathon County Farmers Union Coop.*, 48 LA 206, 209 (Lee, 1967); *Colorado Fuel & Iron Corp.*, 47 LA 1131, 1133, 1135 (Prasow, 1966); *Republic Steel Corp.*, 40 LA 73, 75 (Stashower, 1963). For clauses ensuring that existing minimum standards will not be lowered, see *Stokely-Van Camp*, 74 LA 691, 694 (Stern, 1980); *Interroyal Corp.*, 68 LA 75, 76 (Belshaw, 1977); *Produce, Inc.*, 50 LA 453, 454 (Keefe, 1968); *Jacob Ruppert*, 35 LA 503, 504 (Turkus, 1960). For a Board of Inquiry report as to the history of the steel industry "local working conditions" clause, and as to union and employer contentions regarding the effect of the clause on progress, see *Steel Indus.*, 33 LA 236, 239–40 (Taylor, 1959). In two cases, public-sector interest arbitrators were reluctant to bind public employers by maintenance-of-practice clauses that would impair management's efforts to achieve efficient and high quality operations. Oscoda Area Sch. Bd. of Educ., 55 LA 568, 573 (Bloch, 1970); Arlington Educ. Ass'n, 54 LA 492, 495–96 (Zack, 1971).

[86]*See* City of Greenfield, 77 LA 8, 10 (Yaffe, 1981); City of Waterbury, 52 LA 963, 964 (Stutz, 1969); United States Steel Corp., 40 LA 1201, 1202 (Florey, 1963) ("guideposts" for resolving the question under the steel industry clause are quoted); Bethlehem Steel Co., 35 LA 755, 756 (Valtin, 1960).

[87]Bakelite Co., 29 LA 555, 558–59 (Updegraff, 1957). *Cf.* Sargent Indus., 52 LA 1273, 1275–76 (Lennard, 1969).

[88]Latrobe Die Casting Co., 69 LA 678, 678–79 (Altrock, 1977).

[89]Valley Dolomite Corp., 11 LA 98, 100 (McCoy, 1948). *See also* Bethlehem Steel Co., 45 LA 778, 779 (Seward, 1965); Penn Dye & Finishing Co., 41 LA 193, 199 (Abersold, 1962).

[90]Machlett Lab., 26 LA 117, 120 (Scheiber, 1956).

[91]Borden Co., 39 LA 1020, 1023 (Morvant, 1962).

[92]*See* Bethlehem Steel, 29 LA 418 (Stark, 1957); Bethlehem Pac. Coast Steel Corp., 17 LA 382 (Miller, 1951). *See also* City of Tampa, Fla., 74 LA 1169, 1173–74 (Wahl, 1980) (practices made subject to change if not done "in an arbitrary or capricious manner"); U.S. Postal Serv., 71 LA 1188, 1195–96 (Garrett, 1978); Haddon Craftsmen, 23 LA 210, 212 (Gill, 1954). A similar result might be reached even without a specific contract clause. *See* John Deere Waterloo Tractor Works, 18 LA 276, 278 (Davey, 1952).

past practice should not be considered to control or to prohibit change if the practice contributes to inefficient or uneconomical operations.[93]

8. ROLE OF CUSTOM AND PRACTICE IN INTERPRETATION OF AMBIGUOUS LANGUAGE [LA CDI 24.15]

The custom or past practice of the parties is the most widely used standard to interpret ambiguous and unclear contract language. It is easy to understand why, as the parties' intent is most often manifested in their actions. Accordingly, when faced with ambiguous language, most arbitrators rely exclusively on the parties' manifestation of intent as shown through past practice and custom. Indeed, use of past practice to give meaning to ambiguous contract language is so common that no citation of arbitral authority is necessary.[94]

The general attitude of arbitrators is illustrated by one arbitrator, who, in noting that the parties had operated under a provision for nearly 3 years before requesting an arbitrator to interpret it, stated that he had a context of practices, usages, and rule-of-thumb interpretations by which the parties themselves had gradually given substance to the disputed term.[95] Nonetheless, in another case the arbitrator cautioned that, "[i]n interpreting a collective agreement probably nothing is more capable of constructive use or susceptible to serious abuse as appeals to custom and practice."[96]

Where practice has established a meaning for language contained in past contracts and continued by the parties in a new agreement, the language will be presumed to have the meaning given it by that practice.[97] Thus, as one arbitrator commented:

> There would have to be very strong and compelling reasons for an arbitrator to change the practice by which a contract provision has been interpreted in

---

[93]Mead Corp., 42 LA 643, 646 (Hawley, 1964).

[94]For court decisions upholding the authority of arbitrators to consider past practice in interpreting collective agreements, see *Smith Steel Workers, DALU 19806 v. A.O. Smith Corp.*, 626 F.2d 596, 105 LRRM 2044 (7th Cir. 1980); *Boise Cascade Corp. v. Steelworkers Local 7001*, 588 F.2d 127, 100 LRRM 2481 (5th Cir. 1979); *Auto Workers Locals 932, 1147, 107, 337 v. White Motor Corp.*, 505 F.2d 1193, 87 LRRM 2707 (8th Cir. 1974); *Electronic Workers (IUE) Local 689 v. Hewitt Soap Co.*, 65 F. Supp. 2d 717, 162 LRRM 2342 (S.D. Ohio 1999).

[95]Eastern Stainless Steel Corp., 12 LA 709, 713 (Killingsworth, 1949). *See also* E.J. Brach Corp., 1999 WL 638105, at 21 (Wolff, 1999) ("[a]n established past practice becomes part of the written Agreement under clear principles of labor contract construction").

[96]Standard Bag Corp., 45 LA 1149, 1151 (Summers, 1965). *See also* Fairbanks, Ohio, Local Bd. of Educ., 112 LA 996 (Stewart, 1999).

[97]*See* Barrett Paving Materials, 78 LA 819, 822 (Murphy, 1982); ITT-Continental Baking Co., 77 LA 1045, 1048 (Richman, 1981); Michigan Adjutant Gen., 77 LA 203, 206–07 (Lipson, 1981); Community Mental Health Ctr. of Linn County, 76 LA 1236, 1240 (Mueller, 1981); Mason & Hanger-Silas Mason Co., 75 LA 106, 109 (Johannes, 1980); Western Kraft Paper Group, 74 LA 13, 15 (Allen, Jr., 1980); Polaris Indus., 72 LA 1104, 1106 (Kapsch, Sr., 1979); Norfolk Naval Shipyard, 72 LA 364, 366 (Moran, 1979); City of Meriden, 71 LA 699, 701 (Mallon, 1978); Lohr Distrib. Co., 70 LA 925, 928 (Megley, 1978); Coordinating Comm. Steel Cos., 70 LA 442, 454 (Aaron, 1978) (although management asserted that a new agreement dealt with "a totally new concept," the arbitrators held that, absent specific declaration by management to the contrary in negotiations, the union was justified in assuming that certain key terms used in the new agreement would carry the meaning given those same terms in previous agreements by unvarying practice of the parties); Sheboygan County, 70 LA 92, 96 (Gratz, 1978); East Orange Bd. of Educ., 69 LA 674, 677 (Spencer, 1977). In *Genova Pa., Inc.*, 70 LA 1303, 1305 (Wolf, 1978), precontract practice was given significant weight in resolving an ambiguity in the parties' initial contract.

a plant over a period of several years and several contracts. There would have to be a clear and unambiguous direction in the language used to effect such a change.[98]

The weight to be accorded past practice as an interpretative guide may vary greatly from case to case. In this regard, the degree of mutuality is an important factor. Unilateral interpretations might not bind the other party.[99] However, continued failure of one party to object to the other party's interpretation is sometimes held to constitute acceptance of such interpretation so as, in effect, to make it mutual.[100] Even when there is no direct evidence that one party was aware of the practice, mutuality may be inferred. While arbitrators sometimes refuse to charge a party with knowledge of what is going on in the plant,[101] claims of lack of knowledge often carry relatively little weight and a party may be "assumed" to know what is transpiring,[102] or that the party "knew or should have reasonably known" of the asserted practice.[103] Even successor unions sometimes are charged with knowledge of prac-

---

[98]Webster Tobacco Co., 5 LA 164, 166 (Brandschain, 1946). *See also* Duquesne Brewing Co. of Pittsburgh, 54 LA 1146, 1149 (Krimsly, 1971). However, prior practice may be "an unsafe guide" after contract provisions have been changed. Huebsch Originators, 47 LA 635, 639 (Merrill, 1966). *See also* Riback Supply Co., 74 LA 1030, 1032 (Heinsz, 1980); Sheboygan County, 70 LA 92, 97 (Gratz, 1978); ITT Nesbitt, 63 LA 400, 403 (Simon, 1974); Anheuser-Busch, 53 LA 584, 585 (Bothwell, 1969) (holding past practice to be superseded by the adoption of new contract language that is clear and unambiguous).

[99]*See* Letters Indus., 74 LA 569, 570 (Roumell, Jr., 1980); Hughes Aircraft Co., 47 LA 916, 920–21 (Roberts, 1966) (verbal protest each time company did the act, and grievance was ultimately filed after protests were disregarded); Grand Rapids Die Casting Co., 44 LA 954, 956 (Howlett, 1965) (union lacked knowledge of company's method of payment, so no showing of mutuality); New Jersey Bell Tel. Co., 43 LA 651, 660 (Altieri, 1964); Columbian Carbon Co., 27 LA 762, 766–67 (Hebert, 1956); Hotpoint Co., 23 LA 562, 569 (Baab, 1954); Weaver Mfg. Co., 11 LA 825, 826 (Updegraff, 1948); Richard Olmsted Co., 7 LA 81, 84 (Potter, 1947). *See also* Tecumseh Prods. Co., 54 LA 381, 387 (Sullivan, 1971).

[100]*See* Fairbanks, Ohio, Local Bd. of Educ., 112 LA 996 (Stewart, 1999) (union tacitly accepted employer's interpretation of contract language by failing to raise earlier challenge to practice); Dillon Stores Co., 84 LA 84, 87 (Woolf, 1984); H.D. Lee Co., 76 LA 1261, 1264 (Dallas, 1981); Dayton Press, 76 LA 1253, 1256 (Seinsheimer, 1981); Eltra Corp., 76 LA 62, 68 (Raymond, 1981); Sacramento Reg'l Transit Dist., 69 LA 763, 766 (Ashe, 1977); C.H. Stuart & Co., 54 LA 335, 338–39 (Shister, 1971); Hess Oil & Chem. Corp., 53 LA 941, 944 (Boothe, 1969); United Gas Distribution Co., 53 LA 234, 239 (Marshall, 1969) (union reluctantly went along with management's action for a time, then negotiated briefly on it without reaching agreement, then failed to pursue the matter for several years thereafter); Trabon Eng'g Corp., 49 LA 220, 223–24 (Teple, 1967); Chattanooga Box & Lumber Co., 44 LA 373, 376 (Tatum, 1965); Mansfield Tire & Rubber Co., 44 LA 326, 334 (Layman, 1965) (arbitrator spoke of "tacit recognition" of the practice); Morgan Eng'g Co., 33 LA 46, 51 (Teple, 1959); Willys Motor, 22 LA 289, 291 (Allen, 1954); Pennsylvania Greyhound Lines, 4 LA 584, 586 (Kirsh, 1946); Procter & Gamble Mfg. Co., 1 LA 313, 316 (Prasow, Mitchell, & Daugherty, 1945). *Cf.* Paul Mueller Co., 71 LA 781, 783 (Cohen, 1978); St. Louis Symphony Soc'y, 70 LA 475, 480 (Roberts, 1978) (stating that "acquiescence in a practice on a few occasions when its application is immaterial to claimed rights of the party hardly suggest[s] assent to be bound by the practice under circumstances where it would prejudice claimed rights."); Irving Air Chute Co., 53 LA 13, 16–17 (Jones, Jr., 1969) (complex method of pay required considerable period of time for various facets to manifest themselves to the employees); Mountain States Tel. & Tel. Co., 47 LA 739, 742 (Peck, 1966) (failure to protest trifling matters could not be the basis of a practice).

[101]*See* GAF Corp., 77 LA 256, 264–65 (Rezler, 1981); Burdick Corp., 76 LA 611, 618–19 (Petrie, 1981); Globe-Union, Inc., 69 LA 565, 568 (Fitch, 1977); Hekman Furniture Co., 39 LA 1148, 1152 (Cole, 1963); Raybestos Manhattan, 36 LA 958, 960 (Scheiber, 1961); Weber Aircraft Corp., 24 LA 821, 826–27 (Jones, Jr., 1955).

[102]Baer Bros., 16 LA 822, 824 (Donnelly, 1951). *See also* U.S. Indus. Chems. Co., 76 LA 620, 622–23 (Levy, 1981). Polaris Indus., 72 LA 1104, 1106 (Kapsch, Sr., 1979); MacMillan Bloedel Containers, 68 LA 510, 513 (Berger, 1977); Chattanooga Box & Lumber, 44 LA 373, 376 (Tatum, 1965) (stating that as to prior practice "the knowledge of the employee must be the knowledge of the Union").

[103]Owens-Corning Fiberglas Corp., 19 LA 57, 63 (Justin, 1952). *See also* Wagner Elec. Corp., 76 LA 773, 780 (Roberts, 1981); Associated Univs., 73 LA 188, 190 (Wolf, 1979); Alpha

tice under the same contract language as administered by the company and the predecessor union.[104] Similarly, an employer who takes over a unionized operation without negotiating a new, albeit identical, contract could be bound by existing past practice.[105]

Arbitrators, however, normally will consider only the past practice of the parties at issue, and not the past practice of other parties, in interpreting the same or similar contract language. Accordingly, one arbitrator noted that the fact that other employers of a multiemployer agreement had used certain pay practices in the past was insufficient to serve as binding past practice for all other members of the multiemployer agreement, as the "mutual understanding" requirement of past practice standard was not present.[106]

As has been noted, to establish a binding past practice as an implied term of the contract, "the way of operating must be so frequent and regular and repetitious so as to establish a mutual understanding that the way of operating will continue in the future."[107] Put somewhat differently, "the practice must be of sufficient generality and duration to imply acceptance of it as an authentic construction of the contract."[108] Accordingly, a "single incident" has been held insufficient to establish a "practice."[109]

In contrast, for purposes of interpreting ambiguous language, relatively few past instances have been required to establish a binding practice.[110] This

---

Beta Co., 70 LA 436, 439 (Rule, 1978); Bonanza Airlines, 44 LA 698, 700 (Jones, Jr., 1965); Pittsburgh Press Co., 42 LA 1277, 1280 (McDermott, 1964); Deroe & Reynolds, 22 LA 608, 609 (Porter, 1954).

[104]Wagner Elec. Corp., 21 LA 524, 527 (Brown, 1953). See also Bonanza Airlines, 44 LA 698, 700 (Jones, Jr., 1965); White House Milk Co., 29 LA 45, 49–50 (Anderson, 1957). The successor union's actual knowledge of a practice and its failure to negotiate a change in contract language is still a stronger basis for holding it bound by the practice. See National Cash Register Co., 50 LA 1242, 1246 (Wolff, 1968). See also Sioux City Brewing Co., 20 LA 243, 247 (Updegraff, 1953). Cf. Infant Socks, 51 LA 400, 404 (Moberly, 1968). Successor employers were held bound by their predecessor's practice in Tri-State Asphalt Corp., 72 LA 102, 105–07 (LeWinter, 1979); Darling & Co., 68 LA 917, 920 (Martin, 1977).

[105]Yale Hoists, 113 LA 1101 (Nicholas, Jr., 1999).

[106]General Contractors of St. Louis/Bloomsdale Excavating Co., 2001 WL 845886 (Suardi, 2001).

[107]PPG Indus., 110 LA 968, 969 (Felice, 1998).

[108]Sheller Mfg. Corp., 10 LA 617, 620 (Mathews, 1948). See also Grand Rapids Gravel Co., 115 LA 120 (McDonald, 2000) (15-month health care coverage for the medication Viagra® created binding past practice); Penreco, 113 LA 811 (Goodman, 1999) (14-year practice binding on parties); City of Detroit Dep't of Transp., 99 LA 326, 328 (Kanner, 1992) (4-year practice); GTE Hawaiian Tel. Co., 98 LA 832, 834–38 (Najita, 1991) (50-year practice); Chicago Vitreous Corp., 45 LA 494, 495 (Daugherty, 1965); Tennessee River Pulp & Paper Co., 45 LA 201, 206 (Kesselman, 1965); Procter & Gamble Mfg. Co., 45 LA 26, 29 (Feinberg, 1965); Columbian Carbon Co., 27 LA 762, 766–67 (Hebert, 1956). For a discussion of the standards of effectiveness to which practices are generally held, see Raytheon Serv. Co., 94 LA 27, 28 (Hart, 1989) (where contract is silent, employer need not follow alleged past practice when evidence is insufficient to establish practice); Dobbelaere, Leahy, & Reardon, The Effect of Past Practice on the Arbitration of Labor Disputes, 40 ARB. J. No. 4, at 27 (1985).

[109]Wichita Eagle & Beacon Publ'g Co., 113 LA 29 (Yehle, 1999) (one-time occurrence many years prior to current conduct insufficient to create a binding past practice); National Ass'n for the Advancement of Colored People, 73 LA 372, 377 (Goldsmith, 1979); AMF W. Tool, 49 LA 718, 725 (Solomon, 1967); Kurtz Bros., 43 LA 678, 681 (Duff, 1964); Ottawa River Paper Co., 22 LA 835, 837 (Smith, 1954). See also Dayton Press, 71 LA 1034, 1038 (Barone, 1978); Michigan Maple Block Co., 70 LA 935, 936 (Keefe, 1978); United States Steel Corp., 53 LA 1215, 1216 (Dybeck, 1969). Two incidents did not suffice in York Bus Co., 24 LA 81, 87 (Loucks, 1955). See also Veterans Admin. Ctr., 69 LA 800, 803 (Doyle, 1977).

[110]See Jenison Pub. Sch. Dist., 81 LA 105, 114–15 (Roumell, Jr., 1983); Patterson-Kelley Co., 54 LA 593, 596 (Mullin, Jr., 1971); Kennecott Copper Corp., 34 LA 763, 771 (Kadish, 1960); North Am. Cement Corp., 28 LA 414, 417 (Callaghan, 1957). See also GATX Tank Erection Corp., 74 LA 330, 332 (Holley, Jr., 1980); Honeymead Prods. Co., 74 LA 248, 252 (Fogelberg, 1980).

is especially so when the incidents giving rise to the issue rarely occur.[111] However, it is obvious that an asserted past practice provides no guide where the evidence regarding its nature and duration is "highly contradictory."[112] Where such conflict exists, the arbitrator will be inclined to rely entirely on other standards of interpretation. Conversely, where the parties handle issues on an ad hoc basis, depending on the circumstances of the case, at least one arbitrator has ruled that the parties have created an established past practice of determining issues on a case-by-case basis.[113]

To be given interpretative weight, past practice need not be absolutely uniform. Arbitrators have held the "predominant pattern of practice" to be controlling even though there had been scattered exceptions to the "clearly established pattern."[114] So it is that once established, the binding effect of a past practice generally will not be nullified by such isolated inconsistent actions, absent some manifestation by the parties to permanently discontinue or alter the practice.[115] In this connection, several arbitrators have noted that errors committed by lower ranked administrative employees, even when intentionally done, do not alter an established practice or create a new one.[116] The scope of a practice, however, is confined to the specific situation out of which it arose and does not control the outcome of even a similar, but factually distinguishable, issue. "A practice implies the consistent handling of repetitive and like situations. An arbitrator has no more authority to extend a practice beyond its limits than he has to amend or add to the written contract."[117]

---

[111]Keego Harbor, Mich., Police Dep't, 114 LA 859, 863 (Roumell, Jr., 2000); Kennecott Copper Corp., 34 LA 763, 771 (Kadish, 1960) (even a single incident that was "fully parallel" to the situation before the arbitrator sufficed where parallel situations would not likely arise often).

[112]Reliance Steel Prods. Co., 24 LA 30, 32 (Lehoczky, 1954). *See also* Monsanto Research Corp., 70 LA 530, 533 (Gibson, 1978); United States Steel Corp., 68 LA 1094, 1096 (Rimer, Jr., 1977); National Lead Co., 48 LA 1161, 1165 (Gould, 1967); Corhart Refractories Co., 47 LA 648, 649 (McCoy, 1966) (practice could not be established by mere general statement without reference to names or dates); Tenneco Oil Co., 44 LA 1121, 1127 (Merrill, 1965); Texas-U.S. Chem. Co., 27 LA 793, 795 (Reynard, 1956).

[113]E.J. Brach Corp., 1999 WL 638105 (Wolff, 1999).

[114]Curtis Cos., 29 LA 434, 439 (Yoder, 1957). *See also* Todd Shipyards Corp., 50 LA 645, 657 (Prasow, 1968); Shell Chem. Co., 47 LA 1178, 1181 (Rohman, 1967); United States Steel Corp., 42 LA 1172, 1179 (McDermott, 1964).

[115]FabriSteel Mfg. Co., 115 LA 321 (Brodsky, 2000) (past practice will not be altered by a single contrary settlement of a grievance); Universal Coops., 110 LA 935 (Cohen, 1998) (previous practice of not paying stewards for time spent during contract negotiations was not changed by mistaken contrary practice).

[116]Liberty, Ohio, Local Bd. of Educ., 112 LA 27, 32 (Morgan, Jr., 1999) (two isolated instances of alleged past practice insufficient to alter 25-year contrary practice). *See, e.g.,* State of Alaska, 114 LA 1304 (Gaba, 2000) (past practice of a party's agent cannot bind that party, unless the agent is acting at the party's direction); Universal Coops., 110 LA 935, 940–41 (Cohen, 1998) (foreman's incorrect belief that stewards were entitled to pay while on negotiating committee was insufficient to change consistent past practice). Erroneous administrative procedure by one department, though carried on for 10 years, did not bind the company as a practice where no rational basis for the procedure was shown. U.S. Indus. Chems. Co., 47 LA 651, 654 (McGury, 1966). *See also* Crown Zellerbach Gaylord, 76 LA 603, 606 (Mewhinney, 1981) (mistake by a payroll clerk "does not in itself constitute a binding past practice"); Pacific Northwest Bell Tel. Co., 71 LA 504, 508 (Harter, 1978) (isolated mistakes by employer clerks or even officials do not create established practices, but "when an official is responsible for a policy to be followed four or five years . . . his action can not be dismissed as an isolated one that sheds no light on company policy"); Shell Oil Co., 71 LA 449, 452 (Mewhinney, 1978).

[117]General Refractories Co., 54 LA 1180, 1182 (Volz, 1971). *See also* United Vintners, 75 LA 275, 279 (Barsamian, 1980); Grand Valley Coop., 74 LA 326, 329 (Daniel, 1980); Washington Star Communications, 70 LA 1189, 1193 (Gamser, 1978); United Aircraft Prods., 69 LA 1103, 1107 (Chapman, 1977); Cook United, 53 LA 266, 269 (Klein, 1969); Ohio Power Co., 45 LA 1039, 1045 (Leach, 1965).

9. Custom and Practice at Variance With Clear Contract Language

While custom and past practice are used very frequently to establish the intent of contract provisions that are susceptible to differing interpretations, arbitrators who follow the "plain meaning" principle of contract interpretation[118] will refuse to consider evidence of a past practice that is inconsistent with a provision that is "clear and unambiguous" on its face.

> Plain and unambiguous words are undisputed facts. The conduct of Parties may be used to fix a meaning to words and phrases of uncertain meaning. Prior acts cannot be used to change the explicit terms of a contract. An arbitrator's function is not to rewrite the Parties' contract. His function is limited to finding out what the Parties intended under a particular clause. The intent of the Parties is to be found in the words which they, themselves, employed to express their intent. When the language used is clear and explicit, the arbitrator is constrained to give effect to the thought expressed by the words used.[119]

Many arbitrators and federal courts have expressed similar views.[120]

The clear language of the contract has been enforced even where the arbitrator believed that, on the basis of equity, past practice should have governed:

> In the opinion of the Impartial Tribunal[,] the practice would not have grown up in the first place and would not have been tolerated by the parties if the situation did not justify it. The sudden refusal of the union to continue with a practice that has apparently proved satisfactory for many years, thus precipitating the present dispute, may well be severely criticized as an unreasonable stand not necessary to

---

[118]*See* Chapter 9, section 2., "Ambiguity and the Exclusion of Extrinsic Evidence."

[119]Phelps Dodge Copper Prods. Corp., 16 LA 229, 233 (Justin, 1951). *See also* Hoteles Condado Beach v. Union de Tranquistas de P.R. Local 901, 763 F.2d 34, 119 LRRM 2659 (1st Cir. 1985); Peabody Coal Co., 99 LA 390, 392 (Feldman, 1992); Hertz Corp., 98 LA 258, 262 (Cushman, 1991); Gates Rubber Co., 96 LA 445, 447 (Sergent, 1991); National Roll Co., 95 LA 863, 866 (Hewitt, 1990); Cincinnati Enquirer, 94 LA 1121, 1127 (Witney, 1990); East Liverpool, Ohio, Bd. of Educ., 94 LA 989, 992 (Bittel, 1990); George E. Failing Co., 93 LA 598, 602 (Fox, Jr., 1989); Heublein Wines, 93 LA 400, 406 (Randall, 1988); Prime Health, 93 LA 334, 339 (Clark, 1989); Landmark Hotel Corp., 93 LA 180, 184 (Draznin, 1989); Texas Util. Generating Div., 92 LA 1308, 1313 (McDermott, 1989); Warner Cable of Akron, 91 LA 48, 52 (Bittel, 1988); Hayward Unified Sch. Dist., 89 LA 14, 16 (Concepcion, 1987); Toledo Area Reg'l Transit Auth., 87 LA 192 (Duda, Jr., 1986); May Dep't Stores, 84 LA 53 (Morgan, 1985); Dole Can Plant, 83 LA 253 (Tsukiyama, 1984); City of Gainesville, Fla., 82 LA 825 (Hall, 1984); Consolidation Coal Co., 82 LA 819 (Feldman, 1984); Associated Wholesale Grocers, 81 LA 1126 (O'Reilly, 1983); Veterans Admin., 81 LA 946 (Dunn, 1983).

[120]*See* Lackawanna Leather, 113 LA 603, 608 (Pelofsky, 1999) ("When . . . the language of the agreement is clear and unambiguous the Arbitrator must give effect to that language without resort to evidence of the parties' negotiations or to evidence of the parties' conduct."); BASF Wyandotte Corp., 84 LA 1055, 1057–58 (Caraway, 1985) ("Where a conflict exists between the clear and unambiguous language of the contract and a long standing past practice, the Arbitrator is required to follow the language of the contract. . . . While the Arbitrator recognizes that it is difficult to accept the overturn of a fifteen (15) year past practice, the Arbitrator is required to do so in light of the clear and certain language . . . ."); Tide Water Oil Co., 17 LA 829, 833 (Wyckoff, 1952) (Established practice "is a useful means of ascertaining intention in case of ambiguity or indefiniteness; but no matter how well established a practice may be, it is unavailing to modify a clear promise."). *See also* City of Meriden, 87 LA 163 (Davis, 1986); Bureau of Engraving, 80 LA 623, 625 (Reynolds, 1983); Amax Coal Co., 77 LA 1058, 1063 (Witney, 1981); Styberg Eng'g Co., 77 LA 780, 784 (Petrie, 1981); Grain Processing Corp., 75 LA 1254, 1261 (Stix, 1980); Master Builders' Ass'n of W. Pa., 74 LA 1072, 1076 (McDermott, 1980); City of Allentown, Pa., 73 LA 924, 926 (Handsaker, 1979); Halle Indus., 72 LA 993, 995 (Dolnick, 1979); Truesdell GMC Truck, 72 LA 380, 382 (Heinsz, 1979); Veterans Admin., 72 LA 57, 62 (Goodman, 1978); Intalco Aluminum Co., 70 LA 1229, 1231 (Peterschmidt, 1978); Fred Meyer Inc., 70 LA 608, 613 (Sinclitico, 1978); Exxon Chem. Co., 68 LA 362, 367 (Bailey, 1977). *But see* Louisiana-Pacific Corp., 79 LA 658, 664 (Eaton, 1982). *See also* Anheuser-Busch, Inc. v. Teamsters Local 744, 280 F.3d 1133, 169 LRRM 2513 (7th

protect any substantial right of the workers. . . . If it were at all possible the decision should be that the position of the workers is in violation of the contract.[121]

Thus, if a past practice, although in existence for several years, arose from an obviously mistaken view of a contractual obligation, it need not be allowed to continue.[122] A related rule is that a party's failure to file grievances or to protest past violations of a clear contract rule does not bar that party, after notice to the violator, from insisting on compliance with the clear contract requirement in future cases.[123]

Past practice dealing with employee discipline, if viewed as "an exercise of managerial discretion," may be altered under the authority of a management-rights clause, provided the employer gives prior notice of the change.[124]

Some decisions have supported the contrary view that the parties' "'day-to-day actions [, when they] run counter to the plain meaning of the contract's words, evidence[ ] an intent to substitute that which they actually do for that which they said in writing they would do.'"[125] Similarly, past practice might indicate an exception to the general application of a contract clause.[126]

When is contractual language "clear and unambiguous"? In most cases, this determination will be relatively easy to make. However, there are cases where a latent ambiguity may appear when there is an attempt to apply the language to a particular situation.

In explaining a "latent ambiguity" and the necessity for considering past practice in interpreting the disputed term, one arbitrator has stated:

> The arbitrator will declare an agreement to be clear and unambiguous where he is able to determine its meaning without any other guide than a knowledge of the simple facts on which, from the nature of the language, in general,

---

Cir. 2002) (clear contract terms cannot be modified by past practice); Electronic Workers (IUE) Local 791 v. Hurd Corp., 7 Fed. Appx. 319, 335, 2001 WL 210578, 2001 U.S. App. LEXIS 3062 (6th Cir. 2001) (unpublished) (it is well settled that an "arbitrator may not consider past practice when the terms of the contract are clear . . . 'past practice or custom should not be used to interpret or give meaning to a provision or clause of the collective bargaining agreement.'" (quoting Beacon Journal Publ'g Co. v. Akron Newspaper Guild Local 7, 114 F.3d 596, 601, 155 LRRM 2482 (6th Cir. 1997)).

[121]Chicago Ass'n of Dress Mfrs., 1 ALAA ¶67,234, at 67,521 (Hodes, 1945). *But see* Transit Union Local 1498 v. Jefferson Partners, 229 F.3d 1198, 165 LRRM 2596 (8th Cir. 2000) (approving arbitrator's use of "fairness" to fashion remedy for contract violation).

[122]City of Palo Alto, Cal., 107 LA 494, 498–99 (Riker, 1996) (although for 25 years the city had paid employees on inactive military leave, the unambiguous language of the memorandum of agreement between the parties, based on state law, required only that employees be paid for active duty leave; therefore, the "unambiguous and clear language [of the agreement was] controlling"). *See also* Hogan, *Past Practice and the Administration of Collective Bargaining Agreements: Discussion, in* ARBITRATION AND PUBLIC POLICY, PROCEEDINGS OF THE 14TH ANNUAL MEETING OF NAA 63 (Pollard ed., BNA Books 1961) (questioning "mutual acceptance" element if there had been no "meeting of the minds").

[123]*See* Rock County, Wis., 80 LA 1217, 1220 (Briggs, 1983); Master Builders' Ass'n of W. Pa., 74 LA 1072, 1076 (McDermott, 1980); C&S Wholesale Grocers, 71 LA 676, 679 (Charm, 1978); Intalco Aluminum Co., 70 LA 1229, 1231 (Peterschmidt, 1978); Servomation Corp., 68 LA 1294, 1300 (Perry, 1977). For discussion of related points, see Chapter 10, section 9., "Waiver and Estoppel."

[124]Tecumseh Prods. Co., 107 LA 371, 378 (Keenan, 1996) (employer's notice that employees could be discharged for a first offense of fighting on company premises negated past practice of giving a 2-week suspension for fighting).

[125]City of Palo Alto, Cal., 107 LA, 494, 498 (Riker, 1996) (quoting Wallen, *The Silent Contract vs. Express Provisions: The Arbitration of Local Working Conditions, in* COLLECTIVE BARGAINING AND THE ARBITRATOR'S ROLE, PROCEEDINGS OF THE 15TH ANNUAL MEETING OF NAA 117 (Kahn ed., BNA Books 1962)).

[126]Standard Brands, 25 LA 851, 853 (Justin, 1955). *See also* Bee Cee Mfg. Co., 77 LA 402, 404–05 (Roberts, 1981).

its meaning depends. Where, however, the simple facts allow both sides to advance plausible contentions for conflicting interpretations, the Arbitrator will declare the language to be unenforceable, and will make reference to pre-contract bargaining history, past practice and other applicable rules of construction in order to arrive at the true meaning of the disputed provision.[127]

10. PAST PRACTICE AS EVIDENCING AN AMENDMENT OF THE CONTRACT

Of course, the parties to a contract may amend it by a subsequent agreement. This result was produced, for instance, by a special "interpretation agreement" of the parties.[128] While one arbitrator emphasized that evidence of past practice "is wholly inadmissible where the contract language is plain and unambiguous,"[129] he also recognized that, on the basis of very strong proof, it may establish that the parties had agreed to amend the provision:

> While, to be sure, parties to a contract may modify it by a later *agreement*, the existence of which is to be deduced from their course of conduct, the conduct relied upon to show such modification must be unequivocal and the terms of modification must be definite, certain, and intentional.[130]

To similar effect, another arbitrator noted that where contract language is clear, the "[e]xistence of a [binding] past practice may be established where it is shown to be the understood and accepted way of doing things over an extended period of time. Mutuality of the parties must be shown."[131] Likewise, an arbitrator declared that a party contending that clear language has been modified must "show the assent of the other party and the minds of the parties . . . to have met on a definite modification."[132] Other arbitrators have required convincing proof that the practice reflected mutual agreement to amend the contract.[133]

---

[127]Keego Harbor, Mich., Police Dep't, 114 LA 859, 863 (Roumell, Jr., 2000) (quoting Inland Empire Paper Co., 88 LA 1096, 1102 (Levak, 1987)).

[128]Borg-Warner Corp., 29 LA 629, 633–34 (Marshall, 1957). *See also* Fox Mfg. Co., 47 LA 97, 101 (Marshall, 1966) (contract amended by subsequent side agreement); Olin Mathieson Chem. Corp., 40 LA 575, 575–76 (Summers, 1963).

[129]Penberthy Injector Co., 15 LA 713, 715 (Platt, 1950).

[130]Gibson Refrigerator Co., 17 LA 313, 318 (Platt, 1951) (emphasis added). *See also* Hondaille-Hershey Corp., 22 LA 65, 68 (Platt, 1954). *Compare* Vlasic Foods, 74 LA 1214, 1217–18 (Lipson, 1980) ("it [is] poor policy to allow a 'practice' to modify a clear contractual undertaking of parties," *id.* at 1218, but the arbitrator did permit use of practice to establish that the parties never intended contractual language to be given its ordinary meaning). *See also* City of New Haven, Conn., 100 LA 22, 23 (Freedman, 1992). *See generally* HILL & SINICROPI, MANAGEMENT RIGHTS: A LEGAL AND ARBITRAL ANALYSIS 20, 49–53 (BNA Books 1986).

[131]Reed Tool Co., 115 LA 1057, 1061 (Bankston, 2001).

[132]Merrill-Stevens Dry Dock & Repair Co., 10 LA 562, 563 (Douglas, 1948).

[133]Bethlehem Steel, 13 LA 556, 560 (Killingsworth, 1949) (positive acceptance or endorsement of the practice by the parties must be shown). *See also* Hercules Prods., 81 LA 191, 193 (Goodman, 1983) (finding that "the parties by their actions effectively modified the written agreement"); Total Petroleum, 78 LA 729, 737 (Roberts, 1982); Rockwell Int'l, 71 LA 1055, 1057 (Rimer, Jr., 1978); Houston Elecs. Corp., 70 LA 887, 890 (Felice, 1978); Hi-Ram, 68 LA 54, 56 (Daniel, 1977); Evening News Ass'n, 54 LA 716, 719–20 (Mittenthal, 1971); National Carloading Corp., 48 LA 1355, 1357 (Daugherty, 1967); Hospital Serv. Plan, 47 LA 993, 994 (Wolff, 1966); Spreckels Sugar Co., 47 LA 720, 722–23 (Updegraff, 1966); New Jersey Tel. Co., 47 LA 495, 500–01 (Koretz, 1966); Pana Ref. Co., 47 LA 193, 195–96 (Traynor, 1966); Mobil Oil Co., 46 LA 140, 151 (Hebert, 1966); Marathon City Brewing Co., 45 LA 453, 458 (McCormick, 1965); Cornish Wire Co., 45 LA 271, 276–77 (Fallon, 1965); Wheland Co., 44 LA 5, 6–7 (Williams, 1964); Great Lakes Carbon Corp., 43 LA 1173, 1176 (Anrod, 1964); Frisch & Co., 42 LA 421, 424–25 (Yagoda, 1964); National Lead Co., 28 LA 470, 474 (Roberts, Stony, London, Miller, & Davenport, 1957); Bird & Son, 27 LA 605, 607 (Hoban, 1956); Texas-New Mexico Pipe Line Co., 17 LA 90, 91 (Emery, 1951). But long, unchallenged practice was deemed sufficient by *Metropolitan Coach Lines*, 27 LA 376, 383 (Lennard, 1956); *Charles*

Some courts have enforced awards that give effect to a practice that is contrary to unambiguous language. "[A]n arbitrator's award that appears contrary to the express terms of the agreement may nevertheless be valid if it is premised upon reliable evidence of the parties' intent."[134]

11. Past Practice as a "Gap-Filling" Remedy

Arbitrators have sometimes recognized that contract language may cover a matter generally but fails to cover all of its aspects—that is, "gaps" sometimes exist. It has been recognized that established practice may be used, not to set aside contract language, but to fill in the contract's gaps.[135]

Rights or benefits that are defined generally, or that do not specify the consequences of a violation, may be given specific application by reference to past practice.[136] For example, where a contract gave a union steward the right to a "reasonable time to attend to necessary union business," the practice of permitting the steward to conduct a card check on company time was sustained.[137] Where a contract granted paid leave for emergencies, the practice of not having treated snow days as emergencies controlled.[138] Typical of the "gap-filling" uses of past practice are those cases in which an arbitrator must choose between alternative possible remedies, such as whether to award back pay or make-up work.[139]

Bruning Co., 25 LA 826, 827 (Gifford, 1955); *Smith Display Serv.*, 17 LA 524, 526 (Sherbow, 1951). *See also* White Mfg. Co., 74 LA 1191, 1195 (LeBaron, 1980); Pitman-Moore Div., 49 LA 709, 714–18 (Seinsheimer, 1967); American Saint Gobain Corp., 46 LA 920, 923 (Duff, 1966). The mere fact that an arbitrator adheres to past practice as against literal language of the agreement does not mean that the award does not draw its essence from the agreement. *See* H.K. Porter Co. v. Saw, File & Steel Prods. Workers No. 22254, 333 F.2d 596, 56 LRRM 2534 (3d Cir. 1964); Teamsters Local 249 v. Potter-McCune Co., 412 F. Supp. 8, 92 LRRM 2701 (W.D. Pa. 1976).

[134]Electrical Workers (IBEW) Local 199 v. United Tel. Co. of Fla., 738 F.2d 1564, 1568, 117 LRRM 2094, 2097 (11th Cir. 1984). *Contra* Machinists Dist. 72 v. Teter Tool & Die Co., 630 F. Supp. 732, 121 LRRM 3270, 3273 (N.D. Ind. 1986) (award drawing its essence not from language of contract but from bargaining history not enforced).

[135]*See* EG&G Fla., 93 LA 897, 901–02 (Lane, 1989); J.I. Case Co., 93 LA 107, 109 (Kates, 1989); Monarch Rubber Co., 44 LA 246, 250 (McCoy, 1965); National Lead Co., 28 LA 470, 474 (Roberts, Stony, London, Miller, & Davenport, 1957); Allen Mfg. Co., 25 LA 216, 225 (Hogan, 1955); Texas-New Mexico Pipe Line Co., 17 LA 90, 91 (Emery, 1951); Bethlehem Steel Co., 17 LA 65, 67 (Killingsworth, 1951). *See also* Pacific Southwest Airlines, 71 LA 1136, 1138 (Greer, 1978). Where the contract is silent on an issue, past practice may be considered. *See* J.I. Case Co., 93 LA 107, 109 (Kates, 1989); EG&G Fla., 93 LA 897, 901–02 (Lane, 1989); Greyhound Food Mgmt., 95 LA 820, 824 (Staudohar, 1990).

[136]*E.g.*, Kent State Univ., 91 LA 895, 904 (Curry, Jr., 1988); Central Brass Mfg. Co., 91 LA 386, 391 (Dworkin, 1988); Wyman-Gordon Co., 91 LA 225, 229–30 (Cyrol, 1988); City of Sweet Home, Or., 89 LA 255, 257 (Runkel, 1987).

[137]S.F.C. Bldg. Corp., 88 LA 706 (Canestraight, 1987).

[138]City of Beloit, Wis., Sch. Dist. Bd. of Educ., 82 LA 177 (Greco, 1984).

[139]Johnson Controls, 84 LA 553, 559–61 (Dworkin, 1985).

Chapter 13

Management Rights

1. Views Regarding Management Rights

A. Management View [LA CDI 2.01; 100.03]

Under the common law, owners of business establishments possess certain freedoms of action, incident to their legal status, that are commonly called management rights or management prerogatives. The word "right" has been defined by Webster to mean "power, privilege, or immunity vested in one (as by authority or social custom . . . or . . . by the law[)] . . . ."[1] Webster has defined the word "prerogative" to mean the "right attached to an office or rank to exercise a special privilege or function; . . . an official hereditary right . . . that may be asserted without question and for which there is in theory no responsibility or accountability as to the fact and manner of its exercise . . . ."[2]

Two management spokesmen, noting that the term "management prerogative" is as distasteful to union representatives as the term "closed shop" is to many management representatives, denied that management prerogative refers to a divine right to manage. These spokesmen would define the term as referring to "those rights, or that authority, which management must have in order successfully to carry out its function of managing the enterprise."[3]

Management spokesmen generally adhere to the position that "residual" or "reserved" powers are in management. These spokesmen declare that under the common law an employer, as property owner, may operate a business in any chosen manner, except where common law rights have been limited by

---

[1] Webster's Third New International Dictionary of the English Language 1955 (Gove ed., 1993).

[2] *Id.* at 1791.

[3] Hill & Hook, Management at the Bargaining Table 56 (1945). *See also* Phelps, *Management's Reserved Rights: An Industry View, in* Management Rights and the Arbitration Process, Proceedings of the 9th Annual Meeting of NAA 102 (McKelvey ed., BNA Books 1956).

constitutional legislation or by collective bargaining agreements.[4] Management takes the position that it need not look to the collective bargaining agreement to determine what rights it has reserved to itself, but should look to the agreement only to determine what rights it has ceded away or agreed to share with employees. Thus, one management spokesman defined "the doctrine of reserved rights" as "the simple and understandable view that management, which must have the right to manage, has reserved its right to manage unless it has limited its right by some specific provision of the labor agreement."[5]

B. Labor View

As might be expected, labor spokesmen deny that the rights of management are so broad. For instance, while serving as General Counsel of the United Steelworkers of America, Arthur Goldberg expressed that union's view of the reserved rights concept:

> This concept is not only distasteful; it is based on extreme over-simplification of history. It overlooks the degree to which collective bargaining modifies workers' rights—the right to cease work, the right to press a point without regard to any set of rules or guides, the right to improvise concepts of fairness on the basis of the necessities of the moment without commitment to the future. How could management obtain employee acceptance of job evaluation without the union's modification of the inherent right of workers to press wage complaints on whatever ground appears suitable at the moment. No—this wresting away process is not all one way by any means.
> . . .
> What then are management's reserved rights? These are usually rights reserved in the agreement subject to the substantive clauses of the agreement. Some of these rights relate to subjects excluded from the collective bargaining area by custom, by law, or by express provision. When a contract says that management has the exclusive right to manage the business, it obviously refers to the countless questions which arise and are not covered by wages, hours, and working conditions, such as determination of products, equipment, materials, prices, etc.
> Not only does management have the general right to manage the business, but many agreements provide that management has the exclusive right to direct working forces and usually to lay off, recall, discharge, hire, etc.

---

[4]*See* FAIRWEATHER'S PRACTICE AND PROCEDURE IN LABOR ARBITRATION 299–301 (Schoonhoven ed., BNA Books 4th ed. 1999). "The residual rights—often called 'management rights'—construction principle is the simple view that management had all rights necessary to manage the plant . . . and that unless management limited its managerial rights by a specific term of the agreement, those rights did not evaporate and hence are still retained by management after the labor agreement is signed." *Id.* at 299. *See* HILL & SINICROPI, MANAGEMENT RIGHTS: A LEGAL AND ARBITRAL ANALYSIS 6 (BNA Books 1986); STORY, ARBITRATION AS A PART OF THE COLLECTIVE BARGAINING AGREEMENT 9 (1948). *See also* Bowers, *Management Decision Making and the Waiver of Statutory Bargaining Obligations: An Employer Perspective*, 21 U. TOL. L. REV. 861 (Summer 1990).

[5]Fairweather, *American and Foreign Grievance Systems: I. A Comparison of British and American Grievance Handling, in* DEVELOPMENTS IN AMERICAN AND FOREIGN ARBITRATION, PROCEEDINGS OF THE 21ST ANNUAL MEETING OF NAA 1, 15 (Rehmus ed., BNA Books 1968). *See also* PRASOW & PETERS, ARBITRATION AND COLLECTIVE BARGAINING: CONFLICT RESOLUTION IN LABOR RELATIONS 33 (2d ed. 1983) ("[M]anagement does not look to the collective agreement to ascertain its rights; it looks to the agreement to find out which and how many of its rights and powers it has conceded outright and agreed to share with the union").

The right to direct, where it involves wages, hours, or working conditions, is a procedural right. It does not imply some right over and above labor's right. It is a recognition of the fact that somebody must be boss; somebody has to run the plant. People can't be wandering around at loose ends, each deciding what to do next. Management decides what the employee is to do. However, this right to direct or to initiate action does not imply a second-class role for the union. The union has the right to pursue its role of representing the interest of the employee with the same stature accorded it as accorded management. To assure order, there is a clear procedural line drawn: the company directs and the union grieves when it objects. To make this desirable division of function workable, it is essential that arbitrators not give greater weight to the directing force than the objecting force.[6]

In the past, some attempt has been made to draw a line separating matters of interest to the union from those of sole concern to management. Such an attempt was made at the President's Labor-Management Conference in 1945, but without success. There, management members of the Committee on Management's Right to Manage did agree on a specific classification of management functions. The labor members, however, were unable to accept any such clear-cut classification. They submitted a separate report explaining their position:

> The extensive exploratory discussions of the committee have brought forth the wide variety of traditions, customs, and practices that have grown out of relationships between unions and management in various industries over a long period of time.
> Because of the complexities of these relationships, the labor members of the committee think it unwise to specify and classify the functions and responsibilities of management. Because of the insistence by management for such specification, the committee was unable to agree upon a joint report. To do so might well restrict the flexibility so necessary to efficient operation.
> It would be extremely unwise to build a fence around the rights and responsibilities of management on the one hand and the unions on the other. The experience of many years shows that with the growth of mutual understanding the responsibilities of one of the parties today may well become the joint responsibility of both parties tomorrow.
> We cannot have one sharply delimited area designated as management prerogatives and another equally sharply defined area of union prerogatives without either side constantly attempting to invade the forbidden territory, thus creating much unnecessary strife.[7]

Objective observers appear to share, in part at least, the views expressed by the labor members of the Committee.[8] "Collective bargaining is too dynamic to permit drawing a statutory line between management's prerogatives and the areas of joint responsibility."[9]

---

[6]Goldberg, *Management's Reserved Rights: A Labor View, in* Management Rights and the Arbitration Process, Proceedings of the 9th Annual Meeting of NAA 118, 122–23 (McKelvey ed., BNA Books 1956).

[7]*The President's National Labor-Management Conference, Nov. 5–30, 1945*, at 57–61 (U.S. Dep't of Labor, Div. of Labor Standards, Bull. No. 77, 1946).

[8]*See* Chamberlain, The Union Challenge to Management Control 156–57 (1948). *See also* Ewing, Do It My Way or You're Fired: Employee Rights and the Changing Role of Management Prerogatives (1983).

[9]Cox & Dunlop, *Regulation of Collective Bargaining by the National Labor Relations Board*, 63 Harv. L. Rev. 389, 430 (1950).

The scope of such "implied" management rights remains the subject of frequent controversy.[10]

Various conclusions have at different times been reached by neutral commentators concerning how far unions may desire or be inclined to push into management areas:

> Some unions appear constantly to seek a larger share in the governance of the industry while others believe that they should avoid responsibility for the conduct of the business.[11]

> There is no consciousness of invading managerial prerogatives. By the same token there is no area of management which most [unions] would hesitate to put on "next year's list" if they felt the interests of the union were involved.[12]

> In the daily shop work of job assignments, skill classification, production standards, and maintenance of discipline, union officers show little desire to join in managing and in initiating action; they prefer to retain their freedom to protest management's decisions and to stay out of the cross-fire of criticism and avoid the wounding resentments of their own members.
> Unions have not pushed massively and inexorably into vital policy areas. They have pushed when they could and when it was in their clear interest to do so, advancing when management was careless or weak and retreating when management aggressively resisted them. When unions do enlarge their powers, it is almost always in those areas where they have long been established: wages, hours, and conditions of employment.[13]

C. Arbitrator's View

i. Residual/Reserved Rights

In any study of arbitration, the view taken by arbitrators in regard to management rights is of great interest and importance. Many arbitrators have expressly recognized that the residual powers are in management.[14]

---

[10]Zebco Corp., 104 LA 613 (Cohen, 1995); Owens-Illinois, Inc., 102 LA 1196 (Feldman, 1994); Reed Mfg. Co., 102 LA 1 (Dworkin, 1993); A.E. Piston Prods. Co., 101 LA 98 (Fogelberg, 1993); American Crystal Sugar Co., 99 LA 699 (Jacobowski, 1992). *See also* Trap Rock Indus., 982 F.2d 884, 142 LRRM 2300 (3d Cir. 1992); Container Corp. of Am., 91 LA 329 (Rains, 1988) (employer had inherent right to eliminate job classifications).

[11]Cox & Dunlop, 63 Harv. L. Rev. at 431. In 1980, United Automobile Workers President Douglas Fraser won election to the board of directors of Chrysler Corporation, becoming "the first U.S. labor leader to participate in management of a company with which his union bargains." LRR (BNA), May 19, 1980.

[12]Chamberlain, The Union Challenge to Management Control 157 (1948).

[13]Chamberlain & Kuhn, Collective Bargaining 92 (1965).

[14]ABTCO, Inc., 104 LA 551 (Kanner, 1995); Akron Brass Co., 101 LA 289 (Shanker, 1993) (employer had right to prohibit smoking in lunchrooms because it is conforming to a widespread industrial pattern). *See* American Crystal Sugar Co., 99 LA 699, 703–04 (Jacobowski, 1992) (certain matters are within the inherent or natural rights of management in its affairs); Potomac Edison Co., 96 LA 1012, 1014 (Talarico, 1991) (it is well established that management has the fundamental right to establish reasonable work rules); Minnesota Mining, 81 LA 338, 341 (Boyer, 1983); Unit Parts Co., 80 LA 1180, 1183 (Nelson, 1983); Pioneer Holding Co. of Minn., 79 LA 292, 296 (Gallagher, 1982); Gulf Oil Co.—U.S., 78 LA 8, 11 (Leeper, 1981); Excelsior Truck Leasing, 77 LA 1224, 1227 (Mullaly, 1981); Lloyd Ketcham Oldsmobile, 77 LA 953, 957–58 (Hilgert, 1981); United Parcel Serv., 77 LA 940, 943 (Dean, 1981); Sequoia Rock Co., 76 LA 114, 116 (Lennard, 1981); Babcock & Wilcox Co., 75 LA 716, 718 (Johnston, 1980); Rollins Envtl. Servs., 75 LA 655, 658 (Mann, 1980); Dwyer

No doubt, the likelihood that arbitrators will have occasion to refer to the residual rights doctrine is greatly reduced by the extensive practice of parties expressly to include a management-rights clause in their collective bargaining agreement. Nonetheless, even where the agreement does contain such a clause, the arbitrator still may recognize the residual rights doctrine.[15]

To illustrate the variations in arbitral statements recognizing the "residual" or "reserved" rights doctrine, we may note the following arbitrator comments:

> It is a well recognized arbitral principle that the Collective Bargaining Agreement imposes limitations on the employer's otherwise unfettered right to manage the enterprise. Except as expressly restricted by the Agreement, the employer retains the right of management. This is known as the Reserved Rights Doctrine; it lies at the foundation of modern arbitration practice.[16]

> Collective bargaining agreements, generally, are devised to establish and grant certain rights to employees, which rights they would not otherwise have under common law. It is also a normal and well recognized principle in the interpretation of such Agreements that the rights of management are limited and curtailed only to the degree to which it has yielded specified rights. The

---

Instruments, 75 LA 498, 502 (Van Pelt, 1980); Town of Niagara, N.Y., 74 LA 312, 314 (Babiskin, 1980); Southern Gage Co., 74 LA 296, 298 (Herrick, 1980); ITT-Continental Baking Co., 74 LA 92, 95 (Ross, 1980); ITT Continental Baking Co., 72 LA 1234, 1236 (Hunter, Jr., 1979) (where the agreement contains "no reference to managerial prerogatives," it "must be assumed the general labor relations principle of the right of the employer to operate his business enterprise at his discretion applies unless limited or restricted by" the agreement); National Homes Mfg. Co., 72 LA 1127, 1129 (Goodstein, 1979); Olympia Brewing Co., 72 LA 20, 30 (Madden, 1978); Texas Utils. Generating Co., 71 LA 1205, 1208 (Mewhinney, 1979); Vacaville Unified Sch. Dist., 71 LA 1026, 1028 (Brisco, 1978); Tri-State Transit Auth., 71 LA 716, 719 (Bolte, 1978); Menasco Mfg. Co., 71 LA 696, 697–98 (Gowan, Jr., 1978); Albertson's, Inc., 71 LA 632, 634 (Ross, 1978); St. Louis Symphony Soc'y, 70 LA 475, 481–82 (Roberts, 1978); B.F. Goodrich Chem. Div., 70 LA 326, 329 (Oppenheim, 1978); Tennessee-American Water Co., 69 LA 175, 176 (Finley, 1977); Browning-Ferris Indus. of Ohio, 68 LA 1347, 1351–52 (Teple, 1977); Department of Health, Educ., & Welfare, 68 LA 1178, 1179 (Schuman, 1977); Union Camp Corp., 68 LA 708, 712 (Morgan, Jr., 1977); Doces Sixth Ave., 68 LA 386, 389, 391 (Beck, 1977); Detroit News, 68 LA 51, 52 (Volz, 1977). *See also* Valmont Elec., 102 LA 439 (Hoffmeister, 1994) (employer had reason to discharge employees rather than just lay them off following closing of employer's business); Stone Container Corp., 101 LA 720 (Helburn, 1993); Phillips 66 Co., 101 LA 1146 (Sherman, 1993); Kelly Air Force Base, 98 LA 773 (O'Grady, 1992); Pearl Brewing Co., 98 LA 449 (Nicholas, Jr., 1992); Lockheed Aeronautical Sys. Co., 98 LA 87 (Caraway, 1991); Oklahoma Pub. Serv. Co., 97 LA 951 (Overstreet, 1991); Detroit Edison Co., 96 LA 1033 (Lipson, 1991).

[15]City of Columbus, Ohio, 105 LA 481 (Ferree, 1995); Leggett & Platt, 104 LA 1048 (Statham, 1995); Freeman Decorating Co., 102 LA 149 (Baroni, 1994); Johnson Controls, 101 LA 964 (Cohen, 1993); Montgomery Ward & Co., 98 LA 597 (Nicholas, Jr., 1992); Wall Tube & Metal Prods. Co., 77 LA 857, 858, 860 (Eyraud, 1981); Teledyne Amco, 76 LA 932, 934 (Raymond, 1981); Government Employees (AFGE), 75 LA 1288, 1291–92 (Ordman, 1980); Associated Wholesale Grocers, 73 LA 781, 787 (Roberts, 1979); Safeway Stores, 73 LA 207, 209–10 (Goodman, 1979); Department of Health, Educ. & Welfare, 72 LA 788, 791, 793 (Hayes, 1979); Teleflex, Inc., 72 LA 668, 673 (Chalfie, 1979); Champion Bldg. Prods., 70 LA 1196, 1197 (Grooms, Jr., 1978); Fred Meyer, Inc., 70 LA 608, 611 (Sinclitico, 1978); Taft Broad. Co. of Pa., 68 LA 1379, 1381 (Lubow, 1977); Clipper Int'l Corp., 68 LA 1202, 1205 (Brown, 1977); Johns-Manville Sales Corp., 68 LA 989, 991 (Hays, 1977).

[16]Arbitrator C. Chester Brisco, in *Vacaville Unified Sch. Dist.*, 71 LA 1026, 1028 (Brisco, 1978) (footnote omitted). Another concise statement is in *Cleveland Newspaper Publishers Association*, 51 LA 1174, 1181 (Dworkin, 1969), as follows: "It is axiomatic that an employer retains all managerial rights not expressly forbidden by statutory law in the absence of a collective bargaining agreement. When a collective bargaining agreement is entered into, these managerial rights are given up only to the extent evidenced in the agreement."

right of Management to operate its business and control the working force may be specifically reserved in a labor agreement. However, even in the absence of such a specific reservations clause, as is the case here, those rights are inherent and are nevertheless reserved and maintained by it and its decisions with respect to the operations of the business and the direction of the working forces may not be denied, rejected, or curtailed unless the same are in clear violation of the terms of the contract, or may be clearly implied, or are so clearly arbitrary or capricious as to reflect an intent to derogate the relationship.[17]

[T]he underlying premise of collective bargaining agreements is that management retains all rights of a common law employer which are not bargained away or limited by the collective bargaining agreement. The parties commenced their negotiations from a position where management enjoys all rights of a common law employer. That is, it is free to set the conditions of employment in any manner it desires without any limitation, except those imposed by law. The employee's options are to either accept or reject employment upon those terms. In collective bargaining the employees withhold or threaten to withhold acceptance of employment unless the conditions of employment are modified in the respects successfully bargained for. Where the collective bargaining agreement does not modify or limit management's prerogatives, management retains the prerogatives of a common law employer. The significance of the silence of a collective bargaining agreement upon a subject matter is that management retains its common law rights toward that subject matter which it has not bargained away. The Union argument presupposes the Employer must have contract authority to take a particular action. In fact, the converse is true, and the Union must show that a particular act of management was contrary to contractual limitations placed upon management or obligations imposed upon management by the contract.[18]

There has been some limited judicial recognition and approval of the residual rights doctrine in Labor-Management Relations Act (LMRA)[19] cases.[20] The Supreme Court also seemed to have endorsed the doctrine in the *Warrior & Gulf*[21] case, but the significance of the Court's comments is not clear. One arbitrator suggested that the *Warrior & Gulf* decision "would appear to give full weight to the reserved rights doctrine" but with the additional condition that such rights are likewise subject to the willingness of employees to work under the particular unilaterally imposed conditions.[22]

---

[17]Arbitrator Lewis E. Solomon, in *Fairway Foods*, 44 LA 161, 164 (Solomon, 1965). *See also* Conwed Corp., 55 LA 997, 1001–02 (Solomon, 1970).

[18]Arbitrator Raymond R. Roberts, in *St. Louis Symphony Soc'y*, 70 LA 475, 481–82 (Roberts, 1978). *See also* Beacon Journal Publ'g Co., 55 LA 329, 335 (Larkin, 1970); National Lead Co., 43 LA 1025, 1027–28 (Larkin, Scott, & Moon, 1964).

[19]29 U.S.C. §141 et seq.

[20]United States Steel Corp. v. Nichols, 229 F.2d 396, 399–400, 37 LRRM 2420 (6th Cir.), *cert. denied*, 351 U.S. 950 (1956). The *Nichols* view as to residual rights was quoted with approval in *Gunther v. San Diego & Ariz. E. Ry.*, 198 F. Supp. 402, 47 LRRM 2887 (S.D. Cal. 1961), *rev'd on other grounds*, 382 U.S. 257, 60 LRRM 2496 (1965). For arbitral reference to the *Nichols* case, see *Beatrice Foods*, 55 LA 933, 935–37, 943 (Young, 1970); *Cleveland Newspaper Publishers Ass'n*, 51 LA 1174, 1181 (Dworkin, 1969); *Herman Nelson Div.*, 50 LA 1177, 1181 (Sembower, 1968); *Gran Columbiana*, 42 LA 559, 560–62 (Altieri, 1964); *Hercules Powder Co.*, 37 LA 771, 775–76 (Jones, 1961); *Hale Bros. Stores*, 32 LA 713, 717–18 (Ross, 1959).

[21]Steelworkers v. Warrior & Gulf Navigation Co., 363 U.S. 574, 584, 34 LA 561, 565, 46 LRRM 2416 (1960).

[22]International Smelting & Ref. Co., 54 LA 657, 660 (Cahn, 1971).

Another arbitrator suggested that the decision in effect rejects the "pristine" or "original" reserved rights doctrine.[23]

However, some of the National Labor Relations Board (NLRB, or the Board) concepts and policies respecting the bargaining duty are at odds with the residual rights doctrine as applied by many arbitrators, and can produce results different from those reached in arbitration.[24]

ii. Inherent Rights

In a number of cases, arbitrators have concluded that they have the power to identify "inherent rights" of the employer.[25]

The traditional management view is that management "has reserved its right to manage unless it has limited its right by some *specific* provision of the labor agreement."[26] In many cases, arbitrators have in fact spoken in terms of a specific contractual provision (containing either an express or implied limitation) as being necessary in order to limit management's rights. In other cases, some arbitrators (at least as to some types of issues, such as subcontracting) have taken the view that limitations on management rights are not necessarily restricted to those contained in some specific provision of the agreement but may exist as "implied obligations" or "implied limitations" under some general provision of the agreement, such as the recognition clause, seniority provisions, or wage provisions.[27]

It has also been observed that, in practice, arbitrators may tend to modify the residual rights theory by imposing a standard of reasonableness as an implied term of the agreement.[28] Certainly, many arbitrators are reluctant to uphold arbitrary, capricious, or bad-faith managerial actions that adversely affect bargaining-unit employees. Even where the agreement expressly states a right in management, expressly gives it discretion as to a matter, or ex-

---

[23]Killingsworth, *The Presidential Address: Management Rights Revisited, in* Arbitration and Social Change, Proceedings of the 22d Annual Meeting of NAA 1, 7–10 (Somers & Dennis eds., BNA Books 1970).

[24]The Board's decisions are detailed in section 2.A.i., "The Duty to Bargain: Right of Unilateral Action," below.

[25]Lenzing Fibers Corp., 103 LA 531 (Nicholas, Jr., 1994); Forms Mfrs., 103 LA 29 (Mikrut, Jr., 1994); Quaker Oats Co., 91 LA 271 (Schwartz, 1988).

[26]Fairweather, *American and Foreign Grievance Systems: I.A. Comparison of British and American Grievance Handling, in* Developments in American and Foreign Arbitration, Procedings of the 21st Meeting of NAA 1, 15 (Rehmus ed., BNA Books 1968) (emphasis added).

[27]For example, see section 15., "Right to Subcontract," below. *See also* Bethlehem Steel, 30 LA 678, 682–83 (Seward, 1958). The term "implied obligations" has sometimes been given a meaning much more restrictive on management than the term "implied limitations." *See* Wiggins, The Arbitration of Industrial Engineering Disputes 73–74 (BNA Books 1970).

[28]Kentucky Ctr. for the Arts, 104 LA 971 (Ghiz, 1995); Hyatt Cherry Hill, 103 LA 99 (DiLauro, 1994); Potomac Edison Co., 96 LA 1012 (Talarico, 1991); East Ohio Gas Co., 91 LA 366 (Dworkin, 1988). *See* Robert E. McKee, Inc., 39 LA 411, 413–14 (Oppenheim, 1962). See also section 15., "Right to Subcontract," below. In *Johnson Bronze Co. v. Auto Workers*, 621 F.2d 81, 82, 104 LRRM 2378, 2380 (3d Cir. 1980), the court stated that an arbitrator had "imposed a reasonableness requirement onto" management's decision and could properly do so.

pressly makes it the "sole judge" of a matter, management's action must not be arbitrary, capricious, or taken in bad faith.[29]

iii. *Past Practice* [LA CDI 24.351 et seq.]

It is also to be remembered that numerous arbitrators have accepted the view that under some circumstances unwritten practices and industrial custom, as to some matters, should be held binding on both parties as being in essence a part of their "whole" agreement. Thus, past practice and industry custom is another possible source of the definition of, or a limitation on, management rights.[30]

However, a divergent past practice may be rejected in favor of an express management right.[31]

2. LIMITATIONS ON MANAGEMENT RIGHTS

In recent decades, there has been progressive invasion of once unchallenged areas of exclusive managerial decision. Many matters that were once regarded as the "rights" or "prerogatives" of management have ceased to be so characterized. Inroads into management areas have been made by legislation, collective bargaining, and arbitration.

A. Inroads Made by Legislation

Beginning in the last decade of the nineteenth century, and continuing thereafter, the enactment of state and federal legislation has restricted, to some extent, the right of management to offer employment on its own terms. Restrictions are found in laws relating to minimum wages and maximum hours, child labor, health and safety, workers' compensation, unemployment insurance, "yellow-dog" contracts, fair employment practices, and the like. Such congressional legislation as the Sherman Antitrust Act,[32] the Clayton

---

[29]*See* Williams Pipe Line Co., 70 LA 664, 666 (Barnhart, 1978); Anaheim Union High Sch. Dist., 70 LA 645, 647–48 (Grenig, 1978); Dow Jones & Co., 70 LA 375, 379 (Kornblum, 1978); Colson Co., 54 LA 896, 900 (Roberts, 1971); Yale Univ., 53 LA 482, 486 (Sandler, 1969); Denver Publ'g Co., 52 LA 552, 556 (Gorsuch, 1969); Federal Paper Bd. Co., 51 LA 49, 53 (Krimsly, 1968); Gulf Oil Corp., 36 LA 1353, 1355–56 (Merrill, 1961). Where an agreement expressly retained residual rights for management, an arbitrator cautioned that, "Management's actions in exercising its reserved powers must not be arbitrary, capricious, or taken in bad faith." Reichhold Chems., 73 LA 636, 640 (Hon, 1979).

[30]Conoco, Inc., 104 LA 1057 (Neigh, 1995) (management-rights clause did not dissolve past practice and customs that had existed for several years); Southern Cal. Edison Co., 104 LA 1072 (Concepcion, 1995); Crescent Metal Prods., 104 LA 724 (Cohen, 1994). *See also* Masterbilt Prods. Corp., 97 LA 1042 (Daniel, 1991) (practice of not converting temporary workers to full-time status after 60 days was an 8-year practice and therefore upheld). For full discussion, see Chapter 12, section 1., "Custom and Practice as a Term of the Contract."

[31]City of Marion, Ohio, 91 LA 175 (Bittel, 1988) (prior assignment of inspectors exclusively to day shift did not create a binding past practice, and seniority clause was upheld).

[32]15 U.S.C. §1 et seq.

Act,[33] the Robinson-Patman Act,[34] and the Securities Exchange Act,[35] each in its own way, has incrementally, if indirectly, drained the reservoir of management rights. More direct federal restriction on management rights came about through the Railway Labor Act of 1926 (RLA),[36] the National Labor Relations Act of 1935 (NLRA),[37] the LMRA, the Labor-Management Reporting and Disclosure Act of 1959,[38] and the Civil Rights Act of 1964.[39] In recent years, Congress has continued to place limitations on management rights by enacting legislation designed to protect employees. Examples of such legislation are the the Equal Pay Act of 1963,[40] the Age Discrimination in Employment Act of 1967,[41] the Occupational Safety and Health Act of 1970,[42] the Worker Adjustment and Retraining Notification (WARN) Act of 1988,[43] the Drug-Free Workplace Act of 1988,[44] the Employee Polygraph Protection Act of 1988,[45] the Americans with Disabilities Act of 1990 (ADA),[46] and the Family and Medical Leave Act of 1993.[47]

Employers also should take note of the Uniformed Services Employment and Reemployment Rights Act (1994)[48] and of amendments to the Fair Labor Standards Act.[49]

Of course, any discussion of these statutes necessarily involves consideration of court and NLRB decisions construing that legislation, as is apparent in the following subtopic.

i. The Duty to Bargain: Right of Unilateral Action

a. Mandatory Subjects of Bargaining [LA CDI 100.021505]

The labor relations acts, by legitimizing and endorsing collective bargaining, set the stage for overall restriction of management rights through the provisions of collective bargaining agreements. The original NLRA placed on employers a legally enforceable or "mandatory" duty to bargain with duly authorized employee representatives on subjects falling within the terms "rates of pay, wages, hours of employment, or other conditions of employ-

---

[33]15 U.S.C. §12 et seq.
[34]15 U.S.C. §§13a, 13b, 21a.
[35]15 U.S.C. §78a et seq.
[36]45 U.S.C. §151 et seq.
[37]29 U.S.C. §151 et seq.
[38]29 U.S.C. §401 et seq.
[39]42 U.S.C. §2000e et seq.
[40]29 U.S.C. §206.
[41]29 U.S.C. §621 et seq.
[42]29 U.S.C. §651 et seq.
[43]29 U.S.C. §2101 et seq.
[44]41 U.S.C. §701 et seq.
[45]19 U.S.C. §2001 et seq.
[46]42 U.S.C. §12101 et seq.
[47]26 U.S.C. §2601 et seq.
[48]38 U.S.C. §§4301 et seq.
[49]29 U.S.C. §201 et seq.

ment."[50] The same obligation is continued, and made applicable to unions, in the NLRA as amended by the LMRA.

It is well settled that unilateral decisions made by an employer during the course of a collective bargaining relationship concerning matters that are mandatory subjects of bargaining are regarded as per se refusals to bargain.[51]

Cases decided by the NLRB or the courts have held that, in addition to wages and hours, the area of mandatory bargaining may cover such subjects as holiday and vacation pay,[52] subcontracting,[53] discharges,[54] workloads and work standards,[55] bonuses,[56] pensions,[57] profit sharing,[58] insurance benefits,[59] change of insurance plan administrator,[60] merit increases,[61] union shop,[62] checkoff of union dues,[63] hiring hall,[64] work schedules,[65] plant rules,[66] rest periods,[67] placing existing practices in the contract,[68] management

---

[50]For the concept of mandatory, permissible, and unlawful subjects of bargaining, see *NLRB v. Borg-Warner Corp.*, 356 U.S. 342, 42 LRRM 2034 (1958). For articles containing discussion of duty to bargain and unilateral action, see Woolters & Langdon, *The Duty to Bargain Over Business Decisions: The* Dubuque *Case*, 43 Lab. L.J. 579 (1992); Crough, *The Viability of Distinguishing Between Mandatory and Permissive Subjects of Bargaining in a Cooperative Setting: In Search of Industrial Peace*, 41 Vand. L. Rev. 557 (1988); Brittain & Heshizer, *Management Decision Bargaining: The Interplay of Law and Politics*, 38 Lab. L.J. 220 (1987); Ellmore, *Subcontracting: Mandatory or Permissive Subject of Bargaining?*, 36 Lab. L.J. 773 (1985); George, *To Bargain or Not to Bargain: A New Chapter in Work Relocation Decisions*, 69 Minn. L. Rev. 667 (1985); Susser, *NLRB Restricts Mandatory Bargaining Over Managerial Changes*, 35 Lab. L.J. 415 (1984); Note, *Section 8(d) of the NLRA and the Duty to Decision-Bargain Over Work Relocation: Some Observations on Management Rights After* Milwaukee Spring II, 36 Syracuse L. Rev. 1055 (1985).

[51]ICH Corp., 2000 NLRB LEXIS 550, 2000 WL 3366 4359 (Aug. 23, 2000); Carpenters Local 1031, 321 NLRB 30, 152 LRRM 1049 (1996).

[52]Union Mfg. Co., 76 NLRB 322, 21 LRRM 1187 (1948); Singer Mfg. Co., 24 NLRB 444, 6 LRRM 405 (1940), *enforced*, 119 F.2d 131, 8 LRRM 740 (7th Cir. 1941).

[53]Fibreboard Paper Prods. Corp. v. NLRB, 379 U.S. 203, 57 LRRM 2609 (1964). For some limits as to the duty, see *Westinghouse Elec. Corp.*, 150 NLRB 1574, 58 LRRM 1257 (1965).

[54]NLRB v. Hoosier Veneer Co., 120 F.2d 574, 8 LRRM 723 (7th Cir. 1941).

[55]Woodside Cotton Mills Co., 21 NLRB 42, 6 LRRM 68 (1940).

[56]NLRB v. Niles-Bement-Pond Co., 199 F.2d 713, 31 LRRM 2057 (2d Cir. 1952).

[57]Inland Steel Co., 77 NLRB 1, 21 LRRM 1310 (1948), *enforced*, 170 F.2d 247, 22 LRRM 2506 (7th Cir. 1948), *cert. denied*, 336 U.S. 960 (1949).

[58]NLRB v. Black-Clawson Co., 210 F.2d 523, 33 LRRM 2567 (6th Cir. 1954).

[59]W.W. Cross & Co. v. NLRB, 174 F.2d 875, 24 LRRM 2068 (1st Cir. 1949); R.E.C. Corp., 296 NLRB 1293, 132 LRRM 1268 (1989); Advertiser's Mfg. Co., 294 NLRB 740, 132 LRRM 1024 (1989).

[60]Keystone Consol. Indus., 237 NLRB 763, 99 LRRM 1036 (1978).

[61]J.H. Allison & Co., 70 NLRB 377, 18 LRRM 1369 (1946), *enforced*, 165 F.2d 766, 21 LRRM 2238 (6th Cir.), *cert. denied*, 335 U.S. 814 (1948).

[62]NLRB v. Andrew Jergens Co., 175 F.2d 130, 24 LRRM 2096 (9th Cir. 1949). The amended NLRA bans closed shops and restricts other forms of union security.

[63]United States Gypsum Co., 94 NLRB 112, 28 LRRM 1015, *amended*, 97 NLRB 889, 29 LRRM 1171 (1951).

[64]NLRB v. Associated Gen. Contractors (Houston Chapter), 349 F.2d 449, 59 LRRM 3013 (5th Cir. 1965).

[65]Hallam & Boggs Truck & Implement Co., 95 NLRB 1443, 28 LRRM 1457 (1951), *enforced*, 198 F.2d 751, 30 LRRM 2602 (10th Cir. 1952); Wilson & Co., 19 NLRB 900, 5 LRRM 560 (1940), *enforced*, 115 F.2d 759, 7 LRRM 575 (8th Cir. 1940).

[66]Timken Roller Bearing Co., 70 NLRB 500, 18 LRRM 1370 (1946), *enforcement denied on other grounds*, 161 F.2d 949, 20 LRRM 2204 (6th Cir. 1947).

[67]National Grinding Wheel Co., 75 NLRB 905, 21 LRRM 1095 (1948).

[68]Union Carbide & Carbon Corp. (Niagara Falls, N.Y.), 100 NLRB 689, 30 LRRM 1338 (1952), *amended without affecting this point*, 105 NLRB 441, 32 LRRM 1276 (1953).

rights,[69] "zipper" clauses,[70] "most favored nations" clauses giving the employer equality in terms negotiated by the union with the employer's competitors,[71] incentive pay plans,[72] in-plant cafeteria and vending machine food and beverage prices and services,[73] company-owned houses,[74] stock purchase plans,[75] employee discounts,[76] paid coffee break,[77] accumulation of seniority while employee is in a supervisory status,[78] no-strike clauses,[79] production work by supervisors,[80] installation of new machinery,[81] transfer of employees to a new location,[82] and pay to employees while serving on a union negotiating committee.[83]

Other additions to the list of mandatory subjects of bargaining that have evolved as a result of litigation include employee safety;[84] termination of union privileges;[85] employer's payments to the union trust fund;[86] use of a recreation fund;[87] disbursement of state funds allocated to increase wages and benefits;[88] costs of arbitration hearing transcripts;[89] allocation of severance and vacation pay following closure of a plant;[90] layoff decisions with

---

[69]NLRB v. American Nat'l Ins. Co., 343 U.S. 395, 30 LRRM 2147 (1952).
[70]NLRB v. Tomco Communications, 567 F.2d 871, 97 LRRM 2660, 2664 (9th Cir. 1978).
[71]Dolly Madison Indus., 182 NLRB 1037, 74 LRRM 1230 (1970).
[72]NLRB v. East Tex. Steel Castings Co., 211 F.2d 813, 33 LRRM 2793 (5th Cir. 1954).
[73]Ford Motor Co. v. NLRB, 441 U.S. 488, 498, 101 LRRM 2222 (1979) (the establishment of in-plant food prices is not among those managerial decisions "which lie at the core of entrepreneurial control").
[74]NLRB v. Lehigh Portland Cement Co., 205 F.2d 832, 32 LRRM 2463 (4th Cir. 1953). *Cf.* NLRB v. Bemis Bros. Bag Co., 206 F.2d 33, 32 LRRM 2535 (5th Cir. 1953).
[75]NLRB v. Richfield Oil Corp., 231 F.2d 717, 37 LRRM 2327 (D.C. Cir. 1956).
[76]Central Ill. Pub. Serv. Co., 139 NLRB 1407, 51 LRRM 1508 (1962), *enforced*, 324 F.2d 916, 54 LRRM 2586 (7th Cir. 1963).
[77]Fleming Mfg. Co., 119 NLRB 452, 41 LRRM 1115 (1957). *See also* Pepsi-Cola Bottling Co. of Fayetteville, 330 NLRB 900, 903, 170 LRRM 1322 (2000) (regarding lunch and break periods).
[78]Mobil Oil Co., 147 NLRB 337, 56 LRRM 1215 (1964).
[79]Shell Oil Co., 77 NLRB 1306, 22 LRRM 1158 (1948).
[80]Regal Cinemas, 1999 NLRB LEXIS 233, at *22, 1999 WL 33452970 (Apr. 12, 1999); Globe-Union, Inc., 97 NLRB 1026, 29 LRRM 1198 (1952).
[81]Renton News Record, 136 NLRB 1294, 49 LRRM 1972 (1962).
[82]Cooper Thermometer Co. v. NLRB, 376 F.2d 684, 65 LRRM 2113 (2d Cir. 1967).
[83]Axelson, Inc., 234 NLRB 414, 97 LRRM 1234 (1978).
[84]Asarco, Inc. v. NLRB, 805 F.2d 194, 123 LRRM 2985 (6th Cir. 1986); Oil, Chem. & Atomic Workers Local 5-114 v. NLRB (Colgate-Palmolive Co.), 711 F.2d 348, 113 LRRM 3163 (D.C. Cir. 1983).
[85]NLRB v. BASF Wyandotte Corp., 798 F.2d 849, 123 LRRM 2320, 2322 (5th Cir. 1986) (unilateral termination of use of office, phone, and copy machine formerly extended to union president).
[86]Southwestern Steel & Supply v. NLRB, 806 F.2d 1111, 123 LRRM 3290 (D.C. Cir. 1986), *overruled in part by* Staunton Fuel & Material, 1998 LEXIS 967, at *131, 1998 WL 1976898 (Dec. 17, 1998), without affecting this point; American Commercial Lines, 291 NLRB 1066, 131 LRRM 1561 (1988) (same).
[87]Getty Ref. & Mktg. Co., 279 NLRB 924, 122 LRRM 1150, 1151 (1986).
[88]Sheltering Pines Convalescent Hosp., 255 NLRB 1195, 107 LRRM 1145 (1981).
[89]Communications Workers (Chesapeake & Potomac Tel. Co.), 280 NLRB 78, 124 LRRM 1009 (1986).
[90]Armour & Co., 280 NLRB 824, 123 LRRM 1266 (1986).

limited exceptions;[91] Christmas bonuses;[92] profit-sharing benefits;[93] drug and alcohol testing of current employees;[94] implementation of a drug- and alcohol-testing policy;[95] change in paid lunch policy;[96] the number of members on a union grievance committee;[97] banned use of all personal radios;[98] elimination of shift work;[99] implementation of a light duty program;[100] use of a mandatory, rotating leave-without-pay roster to reduce staffing;[101] replacement of economic strikers by permanent subcontract;[102] change of driver dispatch procedure;[103] implementation of a smoking ban;[104] removal of guns from security guards;[105] production incentive bonuses;[106] on-call procedures;[107] amendments to pension plans to comport with Internal Revenue Code requirements for tax-exempt status;[108] the number of hours worked in and out of the office;[109] restricting telephone use to emergencies only;[110] placing new, restrictive conditions on conversations among employees;[111] requiring route salesmen to account for their product on a nightly rather than a weekly basis;[112] change in starting time;[113] new attendance policy;[114] and providing free parking to employees.[115]

---

[91]Carpenters Local 1031, 321 NLRB 30, 152 LRRM 1049 (1996) (overruling the Board's earlier holding in *Mike O'Connor Chevrolet-Buick-GMC Co.*, 209 NLRB 701, 85 LRRM 1419 (1974), *enforcement denied on other grounds*, 512 F.2d 684, 88 LRRM 3121 (8th Cir. 1975) (a change in terms or conditions of employment that affected only one employee did not constitute a violation of §8(a)(5) of the NLRA)).

[92]Freedom WLNE-TV, 278 NLRB 1293, 122 LRRM 1214 (1986).

[93]*Id.*

[94]Star Trib., 295 NLRB 543, 131 LRRM 1404 (1989); Johnson-Bateman Co., 295 NLRB 180, 131 LRRM 1393 (1989) (pre-employment drug and alcohol testing is not a mandatory subject of bargaining). *See also* RCA Corp., 296 NLRB 1175, 132 LRRM 1348 (1989); United Cable Television Corp. of Conn., 296 NLRB 163, 132 LRRM 1058 (1989).

[95]Delta Tube & Fabricating Corp., 323 NLRB 153, 155 LRRM 1129 (1997).

[96]Van Dorn Mach. Co., 286 NLRB 1233, 128 LRRM 1265 (1987).

[97]Southwestern Portland Cement Co., 289 NLRB 1264, 131 LRRM 1063 (1987).

[98]Murphy Oil U.S.A., 286 NLRB 1039, 127 LRRM 1111 (1987). *But cf.* J.R. Simplot Co., 238 NLRB 374, 99 LRRM 1684 (1978).

[99]Fast Food Merchandisers, 291 NLRB 897, 131 LRRM 1436 (1988). *See also* Metropolitan Teletronics Corp., 279 NLRB 957, 122 LRRM 1107, *enforced*, 819 F.2d 1130, 127 LRRM 2048 (2d Cir. 1987).

[100]Jones Dairy Farm, 295 NLRB 113, 131 LRRM 1497 (1989). *See also* Southern Cal. Edison Co., 284 NLRB 1205, 126 LRRM 1324 (1987).

[101]Rocky Mountain Hosp., 289 NLRB 1370, 130 LRRM 1493 (1988).

[102]Land Air Delivery v. NLRB, 862 F.2d 354, 130 LRRM 2118 (D.C. Cir. 1988), *cert. denied*, 493 U.S. 810 (1989).

[103]Teamsters Local 171 v. NLRB (A.G. Boone Co.), 863 F.2d 946, 130 LRRM 2033 (D.C. Cir. 1988), *cert. denied*, 490 U.S. 1065 (1989).

[104]W-I Forest Prods., 304 NLRB 957, 138 LRRM 1089 (1991).

[105]Northside Ctr. for Child Dev., 310 NLRB 165, 142 LRRM 1153 (1993).

[106]Sartorius, Inc., 323 NLRB 1275, 158 LRRM 1060 (1997).

[107]United Parcel Serv., 323 NLRB 593, 157 LRRM 1111 (1997).

[108]Trojan Yacht Div., 319 NLRB 741, 150 LRRM 1321 (1995).

[109]Watsonville Newspapers, LLC, 327 NLRB 957, 160 LRRM 1248 (1999).

[110]Pepsi-Cola Bottling Co. of Fayetteville, Inc., 330 NLRB 900, 903, 170 LRRM 1322 (2000).

[111]*Id.*

[112]*Id.*

[113]*Id.* at 904.

[114]Ryder/Ate, Inc., 331 NLRB 889 (2000); Dorsey Trailers, 327 NLRB 835, 165 LRRM 1392 (1999).

[115]Anderson Enters., 329 NLRB 760, 765, 166 LRRM 1123 (1999).

b. Expanding Subjects of Mandatory Bargaining

The above enumeration of mandatory bargaining subjects is not exhaustive. Nor is it final. Subjects that have been directly held to fall within or without the area of mandatory bargaining might be held otherwise by future decisions. In general, the tendency has been to expand the area. For instance, the NLRB has moved significantly in holding economic decisions of management to be mandatory subjects of bargaining if job security or working conditions are affected.[116] However, the NLRB has held that there remains no duty to bargain over a managerial decision that would otherwise be a mandatory bargaining subject if there are "compelling economic considerations" underlying the decision,[117] or if the decision is not "a material, substantial, and significant one affecting the terms and conditions of employment of bargaining unit employees."[118]

In some instances, the NLRB has encountered stiff court of appeals resistance, particularly as to economic decisions to move or terminate all or part of the business.[119] In its *Darlington*[120] decision under the NLRA, the Supreme Court did not reach the question as to whether an employer must bargain on a purely economic decision to terminate part, as distinguished from all, of its business. That question was finally reached in 1981 by the Court in its *First National Maintenance*[121] decision, where the Court con-

---

[116]*See* Dixie Ohio Express Co., 167 NLRB 573, 66 LRRM 1092 (1967); Town & Country Mfg. Co., 136 NLRB 1022, 1027, 49 LRRM 1918 (1962). The NLRB had previously long held that the employer, absent any anti-union motive, was not required to bargain over economic decisions to make technological improvements, to relocate operations, to subcontract, and the like, although there was a duty to bargain about the effects of such decisions on the employees.

[117]Mike O'Connor Chevrolet-Buick-GMC Co., 209 NLRB 701, 703, 85 LRRM 1419 (1974), *enforcement denied on other grounds*, 512 F.2d 684, 88 LRRM 3121 (8th Cir. 1975). *See also* Bundy Corp., 292 NLRB 671, 131 LRRM 1645 (1989); Van Dorn Mach. Co., 286 NLRB 1233, 128 LRRM 1265 (1987).

[118]United Tech. Corp., 278 NLRB 306, 308, 121 LRRM 1156 (1986) (unilateral implementation of a health care Correct-A-Bill plan).

[119]NLRB v. International Harvester Co., 618 F.2d 85, 104 LRRM 3098 (9th Cir. 1980); NLRB v. Acme Indus. Prods., 439 F.2d 40, 76 LRRM 2697 (6th Cir. 1971); Morrison Cafeterias Consol. v. NLRB, 431 F.2d 254, 74 LRRM 3048 (8th Cir. 1970); NLRB v. Drapery Mfg. Co., 425 F.2d 1026, 74 LRRM 2055 (8th Cir. 1970); NLRB v. Transmarine Navigation Corp., 380 F.2d 933, 65 LRRM 2861 (9th Cir. 1967); NLRB v. Royal Plating & Polishing Co., 350 F.2d 191, 60 LRRM 2033 (3d Cir. 1965). However, in these cases the court did recognize a duty to bargain about the effects of the employer's decision on the employees.

[120]Textile Workers v. Darlington Mfg. Co., 380 U.S. 263, 275, 58 LRRM 2657 (1965) (an employer has the absolute right to terminate its entire business for any reason it chooses, including anti-union bias, but termination of part of a multienterprise business will violate the NLRA if the employer is motivated by a purpose to "chill" unionism in the remaining parts of the business and if the employer reasonably can foresee that the partial closing will have that effect). In a case under the RLA, a union threatened to strike to force a railroad to amend the collective bargaining agreement to require mutual consent in order to abolish existing jobs (the railroad had received public utility commission approval to close certain stations that were little used and wasteful); the Supreme Court held that the union's demand was "not unlawful" under the RLA and that the Norris-LaGuardia Anti-Injunction Act, 29 U.S.C. §101 et seq., prevented an injunction against the strike. Railroad Telegraphers v. Chicago & North W. Ry., 362 U.S. 330, 340, 45 LRRM 3104 (1960).

[121]First Nat'l Maint. Corp. v. NLRB, 452 U.S. 666, 107 LRRM 2705 (1981) (rejecting both the NLRB conclusion that the employer had an obligation to bargain on the economic decision itself, and the court of appeals conclusion that the employer presumptively had such obligation).

cluded "that the harm likely to be done to an employer's need to operate freely in deciding whether to shut down part of its business purely for economic reasons outweighs the incremental benefit that might be gained through the union's participation in making the decision."[122] But the Court went on to state "that the decision itself is *not* part of §8(d)'s 'terms and conditions' . . . over which Congress has mandated bargaining."[123]

Although the Supreme Court stated in *First National Maintenance* that "we of course intimate no view as to other types of management decisions, such as plant relocations, sales, other kinds of subcontracting, automation, etc., which are to be considered on their particular facts,"[124] the Supreme Court did make the following statement of obvious relevance in the judging of future cases involving the duty to bargain in reference to such other types of purely economic decisions by the NLRB and the courts:

> Management must be free from the constraints of the bargaining process to the extent essential for the running of a profitable business. It also must have some degree of certainty beforehand as to when it may proceed to reach decisions without fear of later evaluations labeling its conduct an unfair labor practice. Congress did not explicitly state what issues of mutual concern to union and management it intended to exclude from mandatory bargaining. Nonetheless, in view of an employer's need for unencumbered decisionmaking, bargaining over management decisions that have a substantial impact on the continued availability of employment should be required only if the benefit, for labor-management relations and the collective bargaining process, outweighs the burden placed on the conduct of the business.[125]

---

[122]*Id.* at 686.

[123]*Id.* (emphasis added).

[124]*Id.* at 686 n.22. For different views of NLRB members as to what is the critical factor in determining whether these other types of management decisions are subject to mandatory bargaining, see *Otis Elevator Co.*, 269 NLRB 891, 891, 115 LRRM 1281 (1984), (the Board reconsidered its earlier decision against an employer "in light of the Supreme Court's opinion in *First National Maintenance*" and held that the employer lawfully refused to bargain over its decision to consolidate and transfer bargaining-unit work from one facility to another).

[125]*First Nat'l Maint.*, 452 U.S. at 678–79. This statement was a part of the Court's preliminary discussion of the duty to bargain on management decisions, after which discussion the Court turned "to the specific issue at hand: an economically motivated decision to shut down part of a business." *Id.* at 680. In its preliminary discussion the Court also stated that "Congress had no expectation that the elected union representative would become an equal partner in the running of the business enterprise in which the union's members are employed." *Id.* at 676. Relevant to the determination of any bargaining obligation, the Court categorized management decisions:

> Some management decisions, such as choice of advertising and promotion, product type and design, and financing arrangements, have only an indirect and attenuated impact on the employment relationship. . . . Other management decisions, such as the order of succession of layoffs and recalls, production quotas, and work rules, are almost exclusively "an aspect of the relationship" between employer and employee. . . . The present case concerns a third type of management decision, one that had a direct impact on employment, since jobs were inexorably eliminated by the termination, but had as its focus only the economic profitability of [the operations being shut down]. . . .

Id. at 676–77 (citations omitted). In discussing the specific issue of "an economically motivated decision to shut down part of a business," the Court stated:

> There is an important difference . . . between permitted bargaining and mandated bargaining. Labeling this type of decision mandatory could afford a union a powerful tool for achieving delay, a power that might be used to thwart management's intentions in a manner unrelated to any feasible solution the union might propose.

c. "Shifting Burden" Analysis

Following the Supreme Court's *First National Maintenance* decision, the NLRB held in *Otis Elevator*[126] that "decisions which affect the scope, direction, or nature of the business" are excluded from section 8(d) of the NLRA. However, the NLRB later overruled *Otis Elevator*, in part, in *Dubuque Packing Co.*,[127] by establishing a "shifting burden" analysis for determining whether relocation is a mandatory subject of bargaining.

Section 8(d) of the NLRA as amended by the LMRA provides, in part, that

> to bargain collectively is the performance of the mutual obligation of the employer and the representative of the employees to meet at reasonable times and confer in good faith with respect to wages, hours, and other terms and conditions of employment, or the negotiation of an agreement, or any question arising thereunder and the execution of a written contract incorporating any agreement reached if requested by either party, but such obligation does not compel either party to agree to a proposal or require the making of a concession . . . .[128]

In general, the duty is to bargain on request.[129]

d. "Zipper" Clauses[129a]

Section 8(d) of the NLRA also provides that there is no duty to bargain about proposals to make changes in the collective bargaining agreement that would take effect during its term.

Employers' claims that a union has "waived" its right to demand negotiations over changes in the terms and conditions of employment that are not specifically addressed in the collective bargaining agreement are subject to strict scrutiny. To establish a waiver of the statutory right to negotiate over mandatory subjects of collective bargaining, there must be a clear and unmistakable relinquishment of that right.[130] Management-rights language

---

Id. at 683. Finally, while the employer was not required to bargain on the economic decision itself, the Court stated that the union must be given an opportunity to bargain over the effects of the decision, and that "bargaining over the effects of a decision must be conducted in a meaningful manner and at a meaningful time, and the Board may impose sanctions to insure its adequacy." *Id.* at 681–82.

[126]Otis Elevator Co., 269 NLRB 891, 893, 115 LRRM 1281, 1283, *corrected*, 269 NLRB 891, 116 LRRM 1075 (1984).

[127]Food & Commercial Workers Local 150-A (Dubuque Packing Co.), 303 NLRB 386, 391, 137 LRRM 1185 (1991), *enforced in relevant part*, 1 F.3d 24, 143 LRRM 3001 (D.C. Cir. 1993).

[128]As to the general nature of the duty to bargain, see *NLRB v. Insurance Agents (Prudential Ins. Co.)*, 361 U.S. 477, 45 LRRM 2704 (1960).

[129]*See* NLRB v. Sands Mfg. Co., 306 U.S. 332, 4 LRRM 530 (1939); NLRB v. Columbian Enameling & Stamping Co., 306 U.S. 292, 299, 4 LRRM 524 (1939). Where a union did not object or request bargaining after being notified by management of anticipated changes, the employer did not violate the bargaining duty by making the changes unilaterally. NLRB v. Humble Oil & Ref. Co., 161 NLRB 714, 63 LRRM 1357 (1966). *See also* NLRB v. Island Typographers, 705 F.2d 44, 113 LRRM 2207 (2d Cir. 1983); United States Contractors, 257 NLRB 1180, 108 LRRM 1048 (1981); City Hosp. of E. Liverpool, Ohio, 234 NLRB 58, 97 LRRM 1125 (1978).

[129a]For related discussion of arbitral treatment of "zipper clauses," see Chapter 12, section 7., "Contract Clauses Regarding Custom."

[130]Trojan Yacht Div., 319 NLRB 741, 150 LRRM 1321 (1995); Exxon Research & Eng'g Co., 317 NLRB 675 (1995).

that merely reserves to the employer the authority to create and enforce reasonable rules does not rise to the level of a clear and unmistakable waiver.[131] Even a union's acquiescence in previous unilateral changes does not operate as a permanent waiver of its rights to bargain over the changes.[132]

In the *Jacobs*[133] case, the NLRB held, and the U.S. Court of Appeals for the Second Circuit affirmed, that "those bargainable issues which have never been discussed by the parties, and which are in no way treated in the contract, remain matters which both the union and the employer are obliged to discuss at any time."[134] The Board emphasized, however:

> In so holding, we emphasize that under this rule, no less than in any other circumstance, the duty to bargain implies only an obligation to *discuss* the matter in question in good faith with a sincere purpose of reaching some agreement. It does not require that either side agree, or make concessions. And if the parties originally desire to avoid later discussion with respect to matters not specifically covered in the terms of an executed contract, they need only so specify in the terms of the contract itself. Nothing in our construction of §8(d) precludes such an agreement, entered into in good faith, from foreclosing future discussion of matters not contained in the agreement.[135]

It thus appeared from the *Jacobs* case that any duty to bargain during the term of the agreement could be avoided by use of general waiver or so-called "zipper clauses" stating that the right to bargain on matters not covered by the agreement is waived or stating that the collective bargaining agreement constitutes the complete agreement of the parties. However, the NLRB (with considerable court support) narrowly construes such clauses so as to give them very limited effect. For instance, in holding a general waiver or zipper clause insufficient to constitute a waiver of the union's right to demand bargaining on a change in the method of handling operations in the employer's shipping room when the employer had refused to discuss the change, but had referred the union to the grievance and arbitration procedure, the Board stated that a "union's statutory right to be notified and consulted concerning any substantial change in employment may be waived by contract, but such waiver must be expressed in clear and unmistakable terms, and will not lightly be inferred."[136] Furthermore, the Board reiterated that even where a waiver clause is stated in sweeping terms, it must appear from an evaluation of the negotiations that the particular matter in issue was fully discussed or consciously explored and that the union consciously yielded or clearly and

---

[131]Southern Cal. Edison Co., 310 NLRB 1229, 143 LRRM 1073 (1993). *See also* Paul Mueller Co., 332 NLRB 312, 170 LRRM 1303, 1305 (2000) (the NLRB did not address the Administrative Law Judge's determination that a management-rights provision did not provide "the required clear and unmistakable waiver of the Union's right to bargain" on the transfer of work to another plant, but upheld the ruling, holding that such a waiver is normally linked to the duration of the bargaining contract, which had expired).

[132]Delta Tube & Fabricating Corp., 323 NLRB 153, 155 LRRM 1129 (1997); Owens-Brockway Plastic Prods., 311 NLRB 519, 143 LRRM 1304 (1993).

[133]Jacobs Mfg. Co., 94 NLRB 1214, 28 LRRM 1162 (1951), *aff'd*, 196 F.2d 680, 30 LRRM 2098 (2d Cir. 1952).

[134]*Id.* at 1219.

[135]*Id.*

[136]Eaton, Yale, & Towne, 171 NLRB 600, 601, 68 LRRM 1129, 1131 (1968) (footnote omitted).

unmistakably waived its interest in the matter.[137] The NLRB subsequently continued to recognize these requirements,[138] although it has not always applied the criteria rigidly.[139] In at least one type of midterm bargaining situation the NLRB endorsed the "literal" application of zipper clauses.[140]

---

[137]*See also* CBS Corp., 326 NLRB 861, 861, 160 LRRM 1021 (1998) (a zipper clause "privileged the Union's refusal to discuss subcontracting" during the term of the contract, because the clause "zipped up" bargaining over discussed matters, and subcontracting had been discussed in negotiations); *Eaton, Yale, & Towne*, 171 NLRB at 601.

[138]In *Rockwell International Corp.*, 260 NLRB 1346, 1347, 109 LRRM 1366, 1367 (1982) (footnote omitted), the Board rejected the administrative law judge's (ALJ's) finding that a zipper clause waived the union's right to bargain over the cost of coffee at the plant, the Board reiterating that: the duty to bargain "continues during the existence of a bargaining agreement concerning any mandatory subject of bargaining which has not been specifically covered in the contract and regarding which the union has not clearly and unmistakably waived its right to bargain," and where "an employer relies on a purported waiver to establish its freedom unilaterally to change terms and conditions of employment not contained in the contract, the matter at issue must have been fully discussed and consciously explored during negotiations and the union must have consciously yielded or clearly and unmistakably waived its interest in the matter." For other cases illustrating the Board's reluctance to find a waiver even though the agreement contains a zipper clause, and indicating a reviewing court's response in the given case, see *Aeronca, Inc.*, 253 NLRB 261, 105 LRRM 1541 (1980), *enforcement denied*, 650 F.2d 501, 107 LRRM 2687 (4th Cir. 1981); *Pepsi-Cola Distrib. Co. of Knoxville, Tenn.*, 241 NLRB 869, 100 LRRM 1626 (1979), *enforced*, 646 F.2d 1173, 107 LRRM 2252 (6th Cir. 1981); *Auto Crane Co.*, 214 NLRB 780, 88 LRRM 1143 (1974), *enforcement denied*, 536 F.2d 310, 92 LRRM 2363 (10th Cir. 1976).

[139]In *Radioear Corp.*, 199 NLRB 1161, 81 LRRM 1402, 1403 (1972), an NLRB majority stated that in some situations the rule of "clear and unequivocal" waiver should not be rigidly applied but rather that a variety of factors may be considered, such as the precise wording of the zipper clause, bargaining history, and past practice. In this case, the Board ultimately found a waiver on considering the particular circumstances along with the existence of a zipper clause. Radioear Corp., 214 NLRB 362, 87 LRRM 1330 (1974). *See also* Columbus & S. Ohio Elec. Co., 270 NLRB 686, 116 LRRM 1148 (1984); Bancroft-Whitney Co., 214 NLRB 57, 87 LRRM 1266 (1974).

[140]Shortly after issuing its 1982 *Rockwell*, 260 NLRB 1346, decision, the NLRB, in *GTE Automatic Electric*, 261 NLRB 1491, 1491, 110 LRRM 1193 (1982), "decided to reconsider the issue of whether a wrap-up (or zipper) clause, by itself, constitutes a waiver of the Union's right to bargain during the term of the contract concerning matters not specifically covered by the contract." The zipper clause in that case expressly waived the right to bargain "with respect to any subject or matter referred to, or covered in" the agreement, and also "with respect to any subject or matter not specifically referred to or covered by" the agreement. *Id.* The Board concluded that the zipper clause waived midterm bargaining over the implementation of a savings and investment plan for nonunion employees, "because the implementation of the plan benefiting the nonunion employees does not constitute a unilateral change of existing working conditions and because the bargaining history is completely silent on the matter in issue." *Id.* The Board stated that by permitting the employer "to invoke the zipper clause as a shield against the Union's midterm demand for bargaining over a new benefit, and by giving literal effect to the parties' waiver of their bargaining rights, industrial peace and collective-bargaining stability will be promoted." *Id.* at 1491–92 (footnote omitted). One member dissented, and the majority cautioned that:

> Our holding does not disturb cases involving (1) a party's waiver or lack of waiver of its right to bargain over specific matters during a contract term because of the negotiating history and surrounding circumstances . . . ; (2) a party engaging in deceptive conduct during negotiations, so that there is no conscious or knowing waiver of rights . . . ; or (3) an employer unilaterally changing the employees' existing working conditions, then using the zipper clause as a "sword" to justify its refusal to discuss the unilateral changes made to the status quo . . . .

Id. at 1492 n.3 (citations omitted).

e. Unilateral Action When Agreement Has Not Been Reached

The duty to bargain in good faith does not mean that agreement must be reached.[141] Where bargaining to an impasse fails to produce agreement on a matter, management is privileged to take unilateral action consistent with its proposals in bargaining.[142] However, unilateral action by an employer on matters "which are in fact under discussion" has been viewed by the Supreme Court as obstructing bargaining as much as "a flat refusal" to bargain and has been held (absent excusing or justifying circumstances) to be a violation of the bargaining duty.[143] Moreover, under NLRB doctrine, the employer generally must bargain before changing wages or terms and conditions of employment established by a collective bargaining agreement even though the agreement has expired.[144]

---

[141]The NLRB is without power to compel a company or a union to agree to any substantive contractual provision of a collective bargaining agreement. NLRB v. Burns Int'l Sec. Servs., 406 U.S. 272, 80 LRRM 2225 (1972); H.K. Porter Co. v. NLRB, 397 U.S. 99, 73 LRRM 2561 (1970). In *Locomotive Engineers v. Baltimore & Ohio Railroad*, 372 U.S. 284, 289, 52 LRRM 2524 (1963) (quoting Terminal R.R. Ass'n of St. Louis v. Railroad Trainmen, 318 U.S. 1, 6 (1943)), the Supreme Court reiterated that the RLA "'does not undertake governmental regulation of wages, hours, or working conditions.'"

[142]In *NLRB v. Crompton-Highland Mills*, 337 U.S. 217, 225, 24 LRRM 2088 (1949), after a bargaining impasse had been reached but before negotiations had been completely terminated, the employer unilaterally granted a wage increase substantially greater than had been proposed in bargaining; the Supreme Court concluded that "under the circumstances" this was an unfair labor practice, but the Court indicated that it would have been proper for the employer to unilaterally grant the increase it proposed but which had been rejected by the union in bargaining. For other cases recognizing the employer's right to institute proposals after bargaining has failed, see *Burns Int'l Sec. Servs.*, 406 U.S. at 294–95, 80 LRRM at 2234; *Newspaper Printing Corp. v. NLRB*, 692 F.2d 615, 111 LRRM 2824, 2828 (6th Cir. 1982) (the employer was upheld in changing work assignments after bargaining to impasse, the court expressly stating that "[f]ollowing good faith bargaining to impasse on a mandatory subject, an employer may unilaterally change terms and conditions of employment"); *University of Chicago v. NLRB*, 514 F.2d 942, 89 LRRM 2113 (7th Cir. 1975) (upholding unilateral action taken during the term of the agreement after having bargained to impasse); *Television & Radio Artists (Taft Broad. Co.) v. NLRB*, 395 F.2d 622, 67 LRRM 3032 (D.C. Cir. 1968); *NLRB v. U.S. Sonics Corp.*, 312 F.2d 610, 615, 52 LRRM 2360 (1st Cir. 1963); *Times Herald Printing Co.*, 221 NLRB 225, 90 LRRM 1626, 1629–30 (1975). Explaining the necessity for this rule, see Schatzki, *The Employer's Unilateral Act—A Per Se Violation—Sometimes*, 44 Tex. L. Rev. 470, 495–96 (1966); Durbin & Gooch, *Unilateral Action as a Legitimate Economic Weapon: Power Bargaining by the Employer Upon Expiration of the Collective Bargaining Agreement*, 37 N.Y.U. L. Rev. 666, 673 (1962). In *Allied Chem. & Alkali Workers Local 1 v. Pittsburgh Plate Glass Co.*, 404 U.S. 157, 188 78 LRRM 2974 (1971), the Supreme Court held that benefits for retired workers are only a "permissive" and not a "mandatory" subject of bargaining, and that "a unilateral mid-term modification of a permissive term such as retirees' benefits does not" violate the NLRA duty to bargain.

[143]NLRB v. Katz, 369 U.S. 736, 50 LRRM 2177 (1962). For interpretations giving a limited scope to this decision, see Fairweather, *The "Fibreboard" Decision and Subcontracting*, 19 Arb. J. 76, 77 (1964); Durbin & Gooch, 37 N.Y.U. L. Rev. at 699–702. Business needs may privilege unilateral action, consistent with offers rejected by the union, although no impasse has been reached. NLRB v. Bradley Washfountain Co., 192 F.2d 144, 29 LRRM 2064 (7th Cir. 1951); Raleigh Water Heater Mfg. Co., 136 NLRB 76, 49 LRRM 1708 (1962).

[144]*See* NLRB v. Burns Int'l Sec. Servs., 406 U.S. 272, 292–93, 80 LRRM 2225, 2233 (1972). In *Clear Pine Mouldings v. NLRB*, 632 F.2d 721, 729, 105 LRRM 2132, 2137 (9th Cir. 1980), the court, in upholding an NLRB decision, stated that "[a]s long as the bargaining obligation is not extinguished, the company has a continuing duty to bargain without instituting unilateral benefit changes, even after expiration of the prior agreement." *See also* Charles Righello Co., 78 LA 777, 779–80 (Koven, 1982). Thus, even if a mandatory matter of bargaining is not under discussion and the agreement has expired, unilateral action generally is permitted under NLRB doctrine only after the matter has been placed on the bargaining table and an impasse in bargaining has been reached (or after notice of intended action

f. Arbitration Clauses Versus Duty to Bargain

The significance of collective bargaining agreement arbitration clauses (and awards issued thereunder) in relation to the legal duty to bargain has been considered in the courts and by the NLRB. One view is illustrated by the U.S. Court of Appeals for the Sixth Circuit decision in the *Timken*[145] case. Here the union charged the employer with an illegal refusal to bargain on the subject of subcontracting. The employer claimed the right to subcontract under the management-rights clause of the agreement. In holding that the employer's action was not a refusal to bargain, the court said that the dispute "was a dispute as to the interpretation of the management clause, and the contract specifically provided that such disputes were to be settled within the grievance procedures and, if they failed, by arbitration."[146] Thus, the court held that the company could lawfully insist on the use of the grievance procedure and ultimately on arbitration to determine whether the management-rights clause was broad enough in scope to include subcontracting. Concerning this decision, two professors explained that it "implies that [the company] could lawfully stand on a favorable arbitration award until the expiration of the contract."[147] Furthermore, they expressed the conclusion

---

is given and the other party fails to request bargaining). The rationale offered by an arbitrator is that: "The natural assumption of both parties, when work continues beyond the expiration date of an agreement, is that those provisions of the expired agreement not in issue in the negotiations will continue to govern." He added that the expiration date of a collective agreement, "unlike that of a commercial contract, does not indicate an intention of the parties that the rules contained in the agreement will terminate at that time but merely that, until the specified date, neither party will use its economic power to compel changes in the rules." Feller, *The Law & Arbitration*, The Chronicle (NAA), Sept. 1980, at 1, 3. However, an employer can make unilateral changes in wages, hours, and working conditions after the expiration of an agreement where the employer has "a reasonably based good faith doubt of the union's majority status." Pride Ref. v. NLRB, 555 F.2d 453, 459, 95 LRRM 2958, 2963 (5th Cir. 1977). *Accord* Beacon Upholstery Co., 226 NLRB 1360, 1367–68, 94 LRRM 1334 (1976). Under the RLA, the Supreme Court has held that the obligation of both parties in major disputes where the RLA's status quo provisions have been invoked "is to preserve and maintain unchanged those actual, objective working conditions and practices, broadly conceived, which were in effect prior to the time the pending dispute arose and which are involved in or related to that dispute," whether or not those conditions are covered in an existing collective agreement; the Court held that a railroad accordingly was precluded from making certain outlying assignments at places in which there previously had been none. Detroit & Toledo Shore Line R.R. v. Transportation Union, 396 U.S. 142, 153, 72 LRRM 2838, 2842 (1969) (the Court did not reach the duty to bargain issue). In *World Airways*, 54 LA 101, 105–07 (Roberts, 1971), the arbitrator considered the *Shore Line* decision inapplicable, where the employer claimed contractual right for the contested action and the dispute thus involved contract interpretation rather than a major dispute under the RLA. *See also* Transportation Union v. Georgia R.R., 452 F.2d 226, 78 LRRM 3073 (5th Cir. 1971). As to permitted unilateral action under the RLA after bargaining has been exhausted, see *Baltimore & Ohio R.R.*, 372 U.S. 284 (employer may put its bargaining proposals as to crews into effect); *Railway & S.S. Clerks v. Florida E. Coast Ry.*, 382 U.S. 1008, 62 LRRM 2177 (1966) (within limits employer may make unilateral changes beyond its bargaining proposals).

[145]Timken Roller Bearing Co. v. NLRB, 161 F.2d 949, 20 LRRM 2204 (6th Cir. 1947), *denying enforcement to* 70 NLRB 500, 18 LRRM 1370 (1946). *See also* Square D Co. v. NLRB, 332 F.2d 360, 56 LRRM 2147 (9th Cir. 1964).

[146]*Timken*, 161 F.2d at 955.

[147]Cox & Dunlop, *Regulation of Collective Bargaining by the National Labor Relations Board*, 63 Harv. L. Rev. 389, 424 (1950).

that any duty to bargain during the term of the agreement can be channeled into a grievance and arbitration procedure:

> During the term of a collective bargaining agreement, an offer to follow the contract grievance procedure satisfies any duty to bargain collectively with respect to a matter to which the contract grievance procedure may apply. A refusal either to follow the contract procedure or to discuss the issue at large is a violation of Sections 8(a)(5) and 8(b)(3) [of the NLRA].[148]

In regard to subcontracting, the NLRB has stated that if the employer's decision to subcontract (or to reorganize, consolidate, or relocate) turned on a reduction of labor costs, it would be a subject of mandatory bargaining,[149] but if it turned on a "fundamental change in the scope and direction of the enterprise," the company would not be required to bargain.[150]

Under one pre-*Collyer*[151] line of NLRB decisions, the duty to bargain could be so channeled,[152] but another pre-*Collyer* line of NLRB decisions held that unilateral action by an employer could justify NLRB action on refusal-to-bargain charges despite provision in the agreement for arbitration.[153] The

---

[148]Cox & Dunlop, *The Duty to Bargain Collectively During the Term of an Existing Agreement*, 63 HARV. L. REV. 1097, 1101 (1950) (emphasis omitted). *See also* National Radio Co., 60 LA 78, 82, 85 (Cox, 1973). *Compare* Keebler Co., 75 LA 975, 982–84 (Morris, 1980). Where the situation does point toward the use of arbitration, the union may have some possibility of obtaining a court injunction to maintain the status quo pending arbitration of its dispute over unilateral changes by management. *See* Texaco Indep. Union v. Texaco, Inc., 452 F. Supp. 1097, 98 LRRM 2128 (W.D. Pa. 1978) (collecting other cases on the matter).

[149]*See, e.g.*, Illinois Coil Spring Co. (II), 268 NLRB 601, 115 LRRM 1065 (1984), *aff'd sub nom.* Auto Workers v. NLRB, 765 F.2d 175, 119 LRRM 2801 (D.C. Cir. 1985). *See also* Stockell, *The Scope of Mandatory Bargaining: A Critique and a Proposal*, 40 INDUS. & LAB. REL. REV. 19–34 (Oct. 1986).

[150]Otis Elevator Co., 269 NLRB 891, 893, 115 LRRM 1281, 1283, *corrected*, 269 NLRB 891, 116 LRRM 1075 (1984). *See, e.g.*, Inland Steel Container Co., 275 NLRB 929, 119 LRRM 1293 (1985).

[151]Collyer Insulated Wire, 192 NLRB 837, 77 LRRM 1931 (1971).

[152]*See, e.g.*, McDonnell Aircraft Corp., 109 NLRB 930, 935, 34 LRRM 1472 (1954) (the employer had satisfied the bargaining duty by willingness to arbitrate a grievance over unilateral action). For other cases in this line of decisions, see *Bemis Bros. Bag Co.*, 143 NLRB 1311, 53 LRRM 1489 (1963); *Hercules Motor Corp.*, 136 NLRB 1648, 50 LRRM 1021 (1962); *National Dairy Prods. Corp.*, 126 NLRB 434, 45 LRRM 1332 (1960).

[153]*See, e.g.*, Eaton, Yale, & Towne, 171 NLRB 600, 68 LRRM 1129 (1968); Adams Dairy Co., 147 NLRB 1410, 56 LRRM 1321 (1964); Beacon Piece Dyeing & Finishing Co., 121 NLRB 953, 42 LRRM 1489 (1958); John W. Bolton & Sons, 91 NLRB 989, 26 LRRM 1598 (1950). For discussion of both lines of cases, see Peck, *Accommodation and Conflict Among Tribunals, in* SOUTHWEST LEGAL FOUNDATION 15TH ANN. INST. ON LABOR LAW 138–42 (1969). In *NLRB v. C&C Plywood Corp.*, 385 U.S. 421, 64 LRRM 2065 (1967), the agreement contained a wage scale to be effective upon signing of the agreement, "with wages closed for the term of" the agreement. *Id.* at 423 n.3, 64 LRRM at 2066 n.3. However, the agreement gave the employer the right "to pay a premium rate over and above the contractual classified wage rate to reward any particular employee for some special fitness, skill, aptitude or the like." *Id.* at 423. Soon after signing the agreement, the employer announced that all members of certain crews would be paid a premium if their crews met certain production standards. The NLRB denied that the agreement gave the employer the right to do this and held the unilateral change in contractual pay rates was a violation of the bargaining duty. The U.S. Court of Appeals for the Ninth Circuit reasoned that the agreement "arguably" allowed the employer's act and divested the NLRB of jurisdiction over the union's unfair labor practice charge. The Supreme Court upheld the Board's jurisdiction to interpret the agreement in order to determine whether the employer had violated any duty to bargain. In so holding, the Court noted that the agreement did not contain an arbitration clause. In *NLRB v. Huttig Sash & Door Co.*, 377 F.2d 964, 968–69, 65 LRRM 2431 (8th Cir. 1967), even though the agreement did contain an arbitration clause, the court relied on *C&C Plywood* in upholding

Collyer decision is an important step in changing Board jurisprudence toward directing midterm refusal-to-bargain claims to arbitration as allegations of breaches of contracts.[154] But it is in any event *only* a step in that direction.

g. *Arbitrators' Views Versus the Board's View*

The NLRB's tendency is (1) to hold economic decisions of management (not merely the effects of the decision but the making of the decision itself) to be matters of mandatory bargaining if job security or working conditions are affected, and (2) to construe waiver or zipper clauses narrowly, giving them very limited effect. These tendencies are at odds with the interpretations of general management-rights clauses and observance of the residual rights doctrine indulged in by many arbitrators. Also, as mentioned earlier, the Board may take jurisdiction in unilateral action cases despite the presence of an arbitration clause (or even after an award has been issued). As a former general counsel of the NLRB explained in comparing the approach taken by many arbitrators with that of the Board:

> In evaluating contractual provisions urged as a defense to unfair labor practice charges involving unilateral action, many arbitrators differ from the Board in their approach.
>
> The Board's evaluation of the circumstances in which the claim of privileged unilateral action is made usually involves considerations other than the interpretation of a single specific contract provision. Frequently, the claim of privilege is predicated, at least in part, on the presence of a generalized management prerogative clause, the absence of any express contractual prohibition of the particular action taken, or the union's failure to obtain a specific prohibition during negotiations. The Board has developed statutory principles for evaluating these general circumstances. For example, the Board with court approval has held that a waiver of statutory rights must be clear and unmistakable; waiver will not be found merely because a contract is silent on a subject protected by the [NLRA], or because the contract contains a general management prerogative clause, or because the union in contract negotiations failed to obtain contractual protection for its statutory rights.

NLRB jurisdiction to find a bargaining duty violation in the unilateral reduction of wages. That dual jurisdiction technically does exist in the NLRB (to enforce the statute) and the arbitrator (to interpret and apply the agreement) appears clear. *See* Chapter 10, section 3.A.v., "The NLRA, the Arbitrator, and the NLRB."

[154]The aforementioned argument finds some support in cases such as *Roy Robinson Chevrolet*, 228 NLRB 828, 828, 94 LRRM 1474, 1475 (1977), where an NLRB majority, in deferring to arbitration prior to issuance of any award, stated that "if the arbitrators should decide that the contract terms did give the Employer" the right to take the challenged unilateral action, "then the Employer's conduct would also perforce have been lawful under the Act." However, this support for the argument is obviously weakened by the Board's retention of jurisdiction for use if the arbitrators "reach a result which is repugnant to the Act." *Id.* at 831, 94 LRRM at 1477. Illustrating NLRB refusal to defer to awards considered to be repugnant to its bargaining duty doctrine, see *Alfred M. Lewis, Inc.*, 229 NLRB 757, 95 LRRM 1216 (1977). The argument is additionally weakened by cases such as *Radioear Corp.*, 214 NLRB 362, 87 LRRM 1330 (1974) (the NLRB, after having deferred to arbitration prior to issuance of an award, ultimately refused to defer to the arbitrator's award because he had refused to rule on the statutory bargaining issue along with his express ruling that the employer's unilateral action had not violated the collective bargaining agreement). Upon considering the *Radioear* case *on the merits*, the Board itself found a waiver of bargaining and thus no statutory violation. For discussion of NLRB deferral policy, see Chapter 10, section 3.A.v., "The NLRA, the Arbitrator, and the NLRB."

Many arbitrators, since they are concerned solely with whether there has been a breach of contract, consider it improper for arbitrators to apply the statutory principles developed by the Board or to apply them differently than the Board does. Some arbitrators apply the so-called "residual rights" theory where management takes unilateral action, holding that management is free to act unless the collective bargaining agreement expressly prohibits the challenged conduct. . . .

. . .

. . . In short, in a unilateral-action case, a reference to an arbitrator for a decision of the contract question may well either be a futile gesture or lead to a result in conflict with the policies of the [NLRA].[155]

In turn, an arbitrator stated that a bargaining duty claim that he had been asked to consider was "one which an arbitrator would tend to view from a perspective quite different from that of the Board":

The Union's claim here is not substantive but procedural—that the Company took action which it was ultimately entitled to take, but it did so without first notifying and bargaining with the Union. From an arbitrator's perspective, the Company's procedure followed the customary sequence—the Company took an action it believed it was entitled to take, the Union filed a grievance, and the parties then discussed whether the Company could or should take that action. This is the procedure through which almost all cases reach arbitration and is taken so much for granted that the wording of most grievance provisions, like the one here, presuppose that the employer will first act and the union will then grieve. To be sure employers frequently discuss matters with the union before taking action to minimize problems and promote good labor relations, but from [the] perspective of the arbitrator there would normally be no implied obligation on the employer to do so.

The perspective of the Board is quite different. The Board apparently starts from the base line proposition that an employer can make no changes in wages, hours or working conditions without first bargaining with the union to impasse. This duty to bargain before acting continues substantially unchanged after the parties have made a collective agreement, and even broad management rights clauses and "zipper" clauses may not be sufficient to relieve the employer of this obligation unless the particular term or condition of employment which the employer seeks to change is specifically described as being within the employers' unilateral control. The Board's perspective is so different that an arbitrator may fail to appreciate the Board's view and sympathetically apply it. Nor will the arbitrator find much helpful guidance in the Board's decisions. The Board does not explain why, after the parties have constructed a grievance procedure to order their relationship, the employer's willingness to bargain through the grievance procedure after taking action is not sufficient to fulfill his statutory obligation to bargain in good faith.[156]

---

[155]Ordman, *The Arbitrator and the NLRB: I. Arbitration and the NLRB—A Second Look,* in THE ARBITRATOR, THE NRLB, AND THE COURTS, PROCEEDINGS OF THE 20TH ANNUAL MEETING OF NAA 47, 64–65, 66 (Jones ed., BNA Books 1967) (footnotes omitted). The conclusion was that "[t]he exercise of Board discretion to defer to arbitration must be determined on a case-by-case basis." *Id.* at 67. For discussion and cases reflecting the Board's practice as to deferring to arbitration (both before and after an award has been rendered), see Chapter 10, section 3.A.v., "The NLRA, the Arbitrator, and the NLRB."

[156]Western Mass. Elec. Co., 65 LA 816, 823–24 (Summers, 1975) (footnotes omitted). *See also* SUMMERS, WELLINGTON & HYDE, LABOR LAW CASES AND MATERIALS 750, 867–68 (2d ed. 1982).

From the standpoint of an arbitrator *who is limited by the common prohibition that the arbitrator not add to, subtract from, or modify the agreement*, the following categories or possibilities appear most likely when action taken by an employer in the management of the enterprise is challenged by an arbitrable grievance:[157]

1. The arbitrator may find that the action is prohibited (1) expressly or impliedly by some specific provision of the agreement, or (2) by an "implied limitation" or "implied obligation" under some general provision of the agreement, such as the recognition clause, or (3) by the arbitrary, capricious, or bad faith character of the action, or (4) by some binding past practice deemed a part of the "whole" agreement.[158]
2. The arbitrator may find that management expressly or impliedly has an affirmative right to take the action under the management-rights clause or some other provision in the agreement, or under some past practice.
3. The arbitrator may find that the action is neither expressly nor impliedly covered by any part of the agreement or by any binding practice, but is an action taken in the good-faith management of the enterprise.

No doubt many arbitrators, and certainly those who adhere to the residual rights doctrine, would deny the grievance unless the arbitrator finds that one of the possibilities under category 1 properly applies under the facts.[159]

In contrast to the aforementioned possibilities, the essence of NLRB doctrine is "that the contract does not permit unilateral action *without prior discussion* unless the employer's right to take such action is clearly and unmistakably spelled out in the contract."[160] However, while the NLRB continues to adhere to the principle that a waiver of a mandatory subject of bar-

---

[157]For a different method of classifying cases, and from a somewhat different standpoint, see SIMKIN & FIDANDIS, MEDIATION AND THE DYNAMICS OF COLLECTIVE BARGAINING 179–84 (BNA Books 2d ed. 1986).

[158]For discussion, see section 1., "Views Regarding Management Rights," above.

[159]In this general regard, many arbitrators have taken the view that their function is to interpret and apply the agreement rather than to enforce affirmative duties under the NLRA, and they have refused to decide whether any statutory duty to bargain has been violated. It is also to be noted, however, that where the NLRB had expressly deferred an NLRA bargaining duty issue to arbitration, many arbitrators have considered and expressed a conclusion on it. *See* Chapter 10, section 3.A.v., "The NLRA, the Arbitrator, and the NLRB."

[160]Mittenthal, *I. The Role of Law in Arbitration*, *in* DEVELOPMENTS IN AMERICAN AND FOREIGN ARBITRATION, PROCEEDINGS OF THE 21ST ANNUAL MEETING OF NAA 42, 56–57 (Rehmus ed., BNA Books 1968) (emphasis in original). As noted above in this subtopic, the "clear and unmistakable" rule subsequently has not always been applied rigidly by the NLRB. As also noted above, in section 2.A.i.d., "'Zipper' Clauses," generally under NLRB doctrine the employer also must bargain before changing wages or terms and conditions of employment established by a collective bargaining agreement, even though the agreement has expired.

gaining must be established by "clear and convincing" evidence, courts have both questioned[161] and imposed limitations[162] on the doctrine.

As to the possibility of narrowing the area of conflict between arbitrators and the NLRB, one arbitrator suggested that the evolution of basic principles that command general acceptance "is more likely to be achieved by Board movement toward arbitration concepts than the other way around."[163]

ii. *Duration of Limitation on Unilateral Action: Contract Limitation Versus Statutory Duty to Bargain*

Where an arbitrator finds that management *is* contractually bound as to a matter, either by the parties' written collective bargaining agreement or by virtue of a binding past practice as part of their "whole" agreement, management generally will remain bound at least until the end of the term of the collective bargaining agreement.[164] When that point is reached, management, of course, may make proposals with the thought of altering or terminating the contractual limitation on management's freedom to act. If bargaining reaches an impasse (or if bargaining has been waived by the union), management then will be privileged to put its proposal into effect unilaterally.

However, where an arbitrator finds that management is *not* contractually bound as to a matter, either by the parties' written collective bargaining agreement or by virtue of any binding past practice, management is restricted from acting on the matter only if there is a statutory duty to bargain on it. And if a duty to bargain does in fact exist, management, not being contractually bound, may open the matter for bargaining even before the end of the term of the collective bargaining agreement. Furthermore, after bargaining to an impasse (or if bargaining has been waived by the union), management

---

[161]Chicago Trib. v. NLRB, 974 F.2d 933, 976, 141 LRRM 2209 (7th Cir. 1992) ("[W]e wonder what the exact force of the 'clear and unmistakable' principle can be when the parties have an express written contract and the issue is what it means or whether the principle makes sense now that the Supreme Court has held that even a waiver of previous constitutional rights need not be proved by clear and convincing evidence.").

[162]Electrical Workers (IBEW) Local 47 v. NLRB (California Edison Co.), 927 F.2d 635, 641, 137 LRRM 2723 (D.C. Cir. 1991) ("[W]here the contract fully defines the parties' rights as to what would otherwise be a mandatory subject of bargaining, it is incorrect to say that the union has 'waived' its statutory right to bargain; rather, the contract will control and the 'clear and unmistakable' intent standard is irrelevant."). *Accord Chicago Trib.*, 974 F.2d at 937.

[163]Mittenthal, NAA 21ST PROCEEDINGS, at 58. Were arbitrators to make decisions consistent with "Board law," it "would mean the rejection of a method of contract construction which [arbitrators] have helped to develop over the past 25 years and which the parties have accepted by and large. . . . On the other hand, if arbitrators continue on the present course, the division between the arbitrator and the Board is likely to widen." *Id.* at 57. For general discussion of arbitral adherence to legal doctrine, see Chapter 10, section 2., "Range of Views as to Application of 'Law.'"

[164]Regarding past practice, see Chapter 12, section 6., "Regulation, Modification, or Termination of Practice as Implied Term of Contract."

then will be privileged to put its proposal into effect notwithstanding that the term of the collective bargaining agreement may not have expired.[165]

It is thus apparent that a statutory bargaining duty limitation on management's freedom to act may be of shorter duration than a contractual limitation on that freedom.[166]

B. Inroads Through Collective Bargaining

Collective bargaining is said to be "the very mechanism by which organized workers may achieve control and exercise it jointly with management"; and again, "[t]he primary mechanism by which unions may share managerial authority in the corporation is collective bargaining, including both contract negotiations and grievance procedures, supported by the power of the strike."[167]

Restrictions made by collective bargaining agreements on management rights are not always confined to the area of wages, hours, and conditions of employment. In fact, it is conceivable that such restrictions might invade the entire field of management functions. There is nothing to prevent weaker employers from bargaining, and making concessions, with respect to practically any matter in the area of management functions concerning which stronger unions may wish to have a voice.

Management has been cautioned that the invasion of its rights through collective bargaining may be more far-reaching than appears on the surface, and that its rights often are given away unwittingly:

> *Economist Sumner H. Slichter:* In actual bargaining, the working rules of trade unions are built up gradually one or two at a time. This leads to an atomistic consideration of their effects, which may cause their effects as a whole to be overlooked.[168]

> *Attorney Robert Abelow:* Rights are often given away—not taken away. Employers frequently negotiate away their responsibilities by accepting proposals which at the time seem innocuous or not immediately harmful. Being mainly concerned with the immediate problems at hand, employers are prone to make concessions on proposals, the effect of which they do not foresee, or if they do, seem too far off to worry about.[169]

---

[165]*See, e.g.,* Pet, Inc., 264 NLRB 1288, 1290, 111 LRRM 1495, 1498 (1982) (footnote omitted) (the NLRB deferred to an arbitration award, where the arbitrator had determined that "work rules are separate from the collective-bargaining agreement and can be changed (either tightened or relaxed) midterm after the required bargaining as long as the rules as changed do not conflict with the collective-bargaining agreement)"; University of Chi. v. NLRB, 514 F.2d 942, 89 LRRM 2113, 2117 (7th Cir. 1975) (the court upheld the employer's unilateral transfer of work after bargaining to impasse during the term of the agreement). The NLRB expressly agreed with the latter decision and reached a similar result in *Illinois Coil Spring Co.* (II), 268 NLRB 601, 115 LRRM 1065, 1067 (1984), *aff'd sub nom.* Auto Workers v. NLRB, 765 F.2d 175, 119 LRRM 2801 (D.C. Cir. 1985).

[166]*See also* Superior Dairy, 68 LA 976, 980 (Chattman, 1976).

[167]Chamberlain, The Union Challenge to Management Control 105 (1948).

[168]Slichter, Union Policies and Industrial Management 578 (1941).

[169]Abelow, *The Challenge to Management's Rights, in* Symposium on Labor Relations Law 260, 263 (Slovenko ed., 1961).

Where frontal attacks on management rights have not met with success, union negotiators have developed flanking maneuvers that have been more effective. The success of such maneuvers is said to be attributable to the fact that they are methods of approach that appear on the surface to be reasonable and that their encroachment on management rights often is not perceived until too late. These indirect methods of invasion are considered to include (1) mutual-consent clauses, (2) joint committees of labor and management, (3) clauses for the application of strict length-of-service seniority, and (4) unlimited arbitration clauses.[170]

C. Inroads Through Arbitration

Some commentators have expressed the belief that arbitration is a device by which a union may broaden its authority within an industrial enterprise.[171] It is said that management rights may be lost through the use of "wide open" arbitration clauses under which the arbitrator is given authority to decide questions raised by the union concerning any matter, whether within or without the scope of the collective bargaining agreement. Moreover, warning is given that management rights also may be lost through "the creation of contract ambiguities due to inept use of the English language, which enable an arbitrator to interpret a clause in a manner not intended by the employer."[172] One writer added, however, that management rights may be protected as well through the arbitration provisions of an agreement.[173]

When an "interest" dispute over the terms of a prospective agreement is submitted to arbitration, there is some substitution of the judgment of the arbitrator for that of the parties. "To the extent that his decision finds in favor of the union, whether in whole or in part, he becomes the instrument by which union power has been extended."[174]

Management representatives have recommended the use of certain "protective" clauses in arbitration provisions that are designed to prevent the invasion of management rights. Protective clauses have become a widely used method of preventing arbitrators from "interpreting away" management rights.[175] In addition to limiting an arbitrator's consideration to the literal

---

[170]Dunn, Management Rights in Labor Relations 111–12 (1946); Hill & Hook, Management at the Bargaining Table 61 (1945). *See also Abelow*, at 263.

[171]Dunn, at 131; Hill & Hook, at 111–12; *Abelow*, at 266–68. *See also* Chamberlain, at 107. However, it has been pointed out that union rights also may be lost through arbitration. Cooper, *Comments, in* Symposium on Labor Relations Law 285, 287.

[172]Story, Arbitration as a Part of the Collective Bargaining Agreement 4 (1948).

[173]*Id.* at 1.

[174]Chamberlain, The Union Challenge to Management Controls 107 (1948). For one arbitration board's explanation for the surrender of management rights (and also of the union's right to test its contentions by a show of economic strength) in interest arbitration, see *Pan Am. Airways*, 5 LA 590, 595 (Cahn, 1946).

[175]Of 400 bargaining agreements analyzed in one survey, 82% placed some type of restriction on the arbitrator. Of those, 92% contained a general restriction prohibiting the arbitrator from adding to, subtracting from, or in any way altering contract language. Basic Patterns in Union Contracts 38 (BNA Books 14th ed. 1995).

text of the agreement, many clauses may expressly restrict the arbitrator's authority to the precise issues submitted for resolution.[176] The following clauses have been suggested as examples:

> The sole and only function of the arbitrator shall be to decide if there was or was not a violation of an express provision or provisions of the agreement, and in the performance of such function he shall apply the law of the state in which the agreement was executed.[177]

> Provided, however, that if such a grievance is carried to arbitration, the Arbitrator shall not substitute his judgment for that of Management and shall reverse the decision of Management only if he finds that it has acted arbitrarily and without reason, or for the purpose of escaping or defeating any of the other articles of this Agreement.[178]

> [The arbitrator] (a) shall have no power to change, detract from, substitute his judgment for, or add to the provisions of this agreement.[179]

3. MANAGEMENT-RIGHTS CLAUSES

While management representatives have sometimes disagreed in the past regarding the advisability of having a management-rights clause, such provisions now appear to be widely favored by management.[180]

---

[176]*See, e.g.,* Oak Hills, Ohio, Local Sch., 108 LA 171, 173 (Oberdank, 1997); Shawnee Local Bd. of Educ., 104 LA 682, 684 (Weisheit, 1995) ("The arbitrator shall expressly confine himself/herself to the precise issue(s) submitted for arbitration and shall have no authority to determine any other issue(s) not so submitted.").

[177]Lamfrom, *Comments, in* SYMPOSIUM ON LABOR RELATIONS LAW 283, 284 (Slovenko ed., 1961). For a similar suggestion, see STORY, ARBITRATION AS A PART OF THE COLLECTIVE BARGAINING AGREEMENT 10 (1948). *See also* Van Der Vaart Brick & Bldg. Supply Co., 72 LA 663, 664 (McCrary, 1979). In *Worcester County Teachers' Association,* 54 LA 796, 806 (Seidenberg, 1971), the arbitrator recommended adoption of an arbitration clause prohibiting the arbitrator from adding to, subtracting from, or altering the terms of the agreement, and also providing: "Neither shall the Arbitrator have the power to alter or modify any policy of the School Board or action of the Superintendent of Schools, not clearly inconsistent with the terms of the Agreement."

[178]Clifton, *Management Functions, in* N.Y.U. 1ST ANNUAL CONFERENCE ON LABOR 89, 97 (1948). A similar clause was involved in *DeLaval Separator Co.,* 18 LA 900, 901–03 (Finnegan, 1952).

[179]Metal Container Corp., 83 LA 564, 566 (Naehring, 1984). *See, e.g.,* Ohio Power Co., 98 LA 700, 703 (Heekin, 1991) (arbitrator shall not add to, detract from, or modify any part of the employee handbook or any supplement thereto); Western Steel Group, 94 LA 1177, 1181 (Bittel, 1990) (arbitrator's award shall be based solely on an interpretation of the written terms of the agreement as to the issue involved); Kimstock, Inc., 94 LA 387, 389 (Gentile, 1990) (arbitrator shall have no power to make any award that would modify, waive, amend, or change the provisions of the labor agreement).

[180]Of 400 agreements analyzed in a survey, 80% contained a management-rights clause. BASIC PATTERNS IN UNION CONTRACTS 38 (BNA Books 14th ed. 1995). For a collection of views as to use of management-rights clauses, see *Cummins Diesel Sales Corp.,* 34 LA 636, 641 (Gorsuch, 1960). Of 1,536 agreements analyzed in one study, 931 contained management-rights clauses. *Characteristics of Major Collective Bargaining Agreements, January 1, 1978,* at 21 (U.S. Dep't Labor Bull. No. 2065, 1980). As a mandatory subject of bargaining, employers may insist that the agreement contain a management-rights clause. NLRB v. American Nat'l Ins. Co., 343 U.S. 395, 30 LRRM 2147 (1952).

Although management-rights clauses are common, there is no consensus as to their form or content.[181] Many management-rights clauses contain a "saving clause," a clause indicating that management retains all rights not modified by the contract or that the enumerated rights in a detailed clause are not necessarily all-inclusive.[182] Such clauses may, in fact, strengthen the employer's position before the arbitrator.[183]

The clause may provide simply that "all normal prerogatives of management shall be retained by the Company except as specifically limited or abridged by the provisions of this agreement."[184] Clauses with much more detail as to management's rights are illustrated by the following provision stating specific powers to be exercised by management:

> Section 1. It is expressly agreed that all rights which ordinarily vest in and are exercised by employers such as COMPANY, except such as are clearly relinquished herein by COMPANY, are reserved to and shall continue to vest in COMPANY. This shall include, this enumeration being merely by way of illustration and not by way of limitation, the right to:
> (a) Manage the plant and direct the working forces, including the right to hire and to suspend, discipline or discharge employees for proper cause.
> (b) Transfer employees from one department and/or classification to another.
> (c) Lay off or relieve employees from duty because of lack of work or for other legitimate reasons.
> (d) Promote and/or transfer employees to positions and classifications not covered by this agreement, it being understood employees in the bargaining unit cannot be forced to take a position outside the bargaining unit.
> (e) Make such operating changes as are deemed necessary by it for the efficient and economical operation of the plant, including the right to change

---

[181]For examples of detailed clauses, see *Kiro, Inc.*, 317 NLRB 1325, 151 LRRM 1268, 1269 (1995) (television network); *Reckitt & Colman Inc.*, 108 LA 726, 727 (Thornell, 1997); *Summit County, Ohio, Children Servs.*, 108 LA 517, 517–18 (Sharpe, 1997) (county agency); *Summit County, Ohio, Childrens Servs.*, 108 LA 459, 461 (Smith, 1997) (same); *Phelps Dodge Magnet Wire Co.*, 108 LA 21 (Curry, Jr., 1996); *American Drug Stores*, 107 LA 985 (Richman, 1996); *Ottawa Truck*, 107 LA 844, 845 (Murphy, 1996); *American Red Cross Blood Servs.*, 106 LA 224, 225 (Grooms, Jr., 1996) (charitable organization); *Central Mich. Univ.*, 102 LA 787, 789 (House, 1994) (university); *I.T.T. Rayonier*, 101 LA 865, 868 (Lane, 1993). For an example of statute detailing rights for public employers, see *Butte Sch. Dist. 1*, 108 LA 265, 266 (Prayzich, 1997) (considering effect of Mont. Code Ann. §39-31-303 (1995)).

[182]Of 400 contracts in a survey, 44% contained a savings clause. BASIC PATTERNS IN UNION CONTRACTS 79 (BNA Books 14th ed. 1995). For examples, see *Integrated Distribution Sys.*, 108 LA 737 (Neas, 1997) (all decisions on matters or subjects not defined by agreement are reserved to employer); *Arcata Graphics Distribution Corp.*, 102 LA 961 (Hart, 1994) (nothing in the agreement shall be construed or interpreted as denying or limiting rights of company to exercise all customary and usual rights of management); *Gulf States Utils. Co.*, 102 LA 470, 471 (Massey, 1993) (rights are not all-inclusive but indicate types of matters where rights shall belong to or are inherent to management); *I.T.T. Rayonier*, 101 LA 865, 868 (Lane, 1993) (enumerated rights not exclusive).

[183]St. Louis Coca-Cola Bottling Co., 105 LA 356, 360 (O'Grady, 1995) (finding savings clause "controlling" when it authorized company "to exercise rights not specifically set forth in the Agreement upon which the parties negotiated or had the opportunity to negotiate whether or not such rights have been exercised by the Company in the past").

[184]K&T Steel Corp., 52 LA 497, 500 (Simon, 1969). *See also* Winnebago County, Sheriff's Dep't, 53 LA 1305, 1305, 1307 (Gundermann, 1969). The clause in *Unit Rig & Equipment Co.*, 78 LA 788, 790 (Sisk, 1982), states: "The Company retains the exclusive right to manage the business. All the rights, powers, functions, and authority of the Company which are not abridged by the specific provisions of this Agreement are retained by the Company."

the normal work-week, the number of hours normally worked during the work-week, the length of the normal workday, the hours of work, the beginning and ending time of each shift or assignment, and the number of shifts to be operated.

(f) Transfer persons from positions and classifications not covered by this agreement to positions and/or classifications covered hereby.

(g) Maintain discipline and efficiency.

(h) Hire, promote, demote, transfer, discharge or discipline all levels of supervision or other persons not covered by this agreement.

(i) Determine the type of products to be manufactured, the location of work within the plant, the schedules of production, the schedules of work within work periods, and the methods, processes, and means of manufacture and the conduct of other plant operations.[185]

The simpler clauses were once favored because of their clear-cut statement of the rule that the employer has all the proprietary rights of management except as restricted by the terms of the agreement.[186] However, as one reaction to the 1960 *Steelworkers Trilogy*,[187] many management representatives now prefer a much more extensive and detailed clause to specify as fully as possible the matters over which management retains full discretion.[188] Indeed, one management spokesman urged that the desirability of a strong and detailed management-rights clause is now "redoubled" as serving a dual purpose: "One is statutory—protection against the [NLRB] and its duty-to-bargain philosophy—and the other contractual—protection against the invasion of the management area through arbitration."[189]

No doubt, a management-rights clause may strengthen the employer's position before an arbitrator.[190] It is also clear that during the term of a

---

[185]Agreement between Southern Aircraft Corp. and International Union of United Autoworkers, Aircraft & Agricultural Implement Workers of Am. *See also* Washington County, Or., 78 LA 1081, 1084 (Tilbury, 1982) (county employer); T.N.S., Inc., 76 LA 278, 280 (Hardin, 1981); Van Der Vaart Brick & Bldg. Supply Co., 72 LA 663, 664 (McCrary, 1979); Jackson Pub. Sch., 71 LA 177, 180 (Keefe, 1978) (public school employer); Mid-America Dairymen, 70 LA 116, 118 (Fitzsimmons, 1978); Ohio State Univ., 69 LA 1004, 1004 (Bell, 1977) (university employer); City of Hartford, 69 LA 303, 303 (Mallon, McDonough, & Zuilkowski, 1977) (municipal employer); Yoder Bros., 69 LA 115, 117 (Ipavec, 1977). Management-rights clauses in federal-sector agreements often amount to an incorporation into the agreement of management-rights provisions of the Civil Service Reform Act. *See* ACTION, 78 LA 740, 740 (Phelan, 1982); Department of the Army, 77 LA 918, 919 (Heliker, 1981); Department of Justice, Immigration & Naturalization Serv., 77 LA 638, 639 (Weckstein, 1981).

[186]*See* STORY, ARBITRATION AS A PART OF THE BARGAINING AGREEMENT 11 (1948); DUNN, MANAGEMENT RIGHTS IN LABOR RELATIONS 109 (1946).

[187]Steelworkers v. American Mfg. Co., 363 U.S. 564, 46 LRRM 2414 (1960); Steelworkers v. Warrior & Gulf Navigation Co., 363 U.S. 574, 46 LRRM 2416 (1960); Steelworkers v. Enterprise Wheel & Car Corp., 363 U.S. 593, 46 LRRM 2423 (1960).

[188]Smith & Jones, *The Impact of the Emerging Federal Law of Grievance Arbitration on Judges, Arbitrators, and Parties*, 52 VA. L. REV. 831, 897–902 (1966) (detailed clauses favored by management representatives are quoted). For an agreement using *both* the simpler "residual rights" clause and the detailed clause, see *Almaden Vineyards*, 56 LA 425, 426 (Kagel, 1971). *See also* Wall Tube & Metal Prods. Co., 77 LA 857, 857 (Eyraud, 1981); Teledyne Amco, 76 LA 932, 932–33 (Raymond, 1981).

[189]O'Connell, *Erosion of Management Rights*, 1969 LAB. REL. Y.B. 345, 350, 353 (BNA Books 1970).

[190]*See, e.g.*, City of Rochester, Mich., 76 LA 295, 298–99 (Lipson, 1981); Control Data Corp., 69 LA 665, 670 (Hatcher, 1977); Superior Dairy, 69 LA 594, 598 (Abrams, 1977); Superior Dairy, 68 LA 976, 982 (Chattman, 1976); National Cash Register Co., 46 LA 317, 320 (Kates, 1966). In *A. Hoen & Co.*, 64 LA 197, 199, 204 (Feldesman, 1975), the company claimed residual rights, but the arbitrator gave "some significance" to the union's assertion that "the lack of a management rights clause in the collective agreement is a telling blow" to the company's case.

collective bargaining agreement that contains a broad and detailed management-rights clause, the employer may not be required to bargain about some changes on which, in the absence of such clause, it might otherwise be compelled to bargain.[191] Another significant purpose of such clauses is to aid union officials in explaining to the membership what the agreement does and does not give them.[192]

4. Impact of Arbitration on Management Rights

The extensive use of labor-management arbitration has resulted in the evolution of a private, ever-developing system of industrial jurisprudence. Included within the growing body of industrial rulings are many involving management-rights issues. While legal principles, as well as court and administrative board decisions, loom in the background, relatively wide discretion generally is left to arbitrators in the private sector to deal with the law according to their best judgment.[193] It should be recognized, therefore, that arbitral case law is in itself a separate and distinct institution. It also should be recognized that the industrial jurisprudence of arbitrators will not always be in absolute harmony with the course of decisions under the NLRA.[194]

The primary objective of the remainder of this chapter will be to consider the effective scope of management rights as evidenced and outlined by arbitration awards.

5. Control of Operation Methods

In general, arbitrators have recognized broad authority in management (absent clear limitations in the agreement) to determine methods of operation.[195] It has been said that, unless restricted by contract, management has

---

[191]See Consolidated Foods Corp., 183 NLRB 832, 74 LRRM 1374 (1970); Cello-Foil Prods., 178 NLRB 676, 72 LRRM 1196 (1969); LeRoy Mach. Co., 147 NLRB 1431, 56 LRRM 1369 (1964); Borden Co., 10 NLRB 802, 35 LRRM 1133 (1954). As to management's right to insist on a clause ensuring it the right to take unilateral action on matters not specifically covered by the agreement, see Long Lake Lumber Co., 182 NLRB 435, 74 LRRM 1116 (1970) (insistence on such a clause was not an unlawful refusal to bargain).

[192]See Phelps, Management's Reserved Rights: An Industry View, in Management Rights and the Arbitration Process, Proceedings of the 9th Annual Meeting of NAA 102, 113–14 (McKelvey ed., BNA Books 1956).

[193]For extensive discussion, see Chapter 10, section 1., "General Considerations," and section 2., "Range of Views as to Application of 'Law,'" where comment is made also in reference to arbitrators in the public sector.

[194]See section 2.A.i.g., "Arbitrators' Views Versus the Board's View," above; Chapter 10, section 3.A.v., "The NLRA, the Arbitrator, and the NLRB."

[195]See American Crystal Sugar Co., 99 LA 699, 703 (Jacobowski, 1992); Container Corp. of Am., 91 LA 329, 331 (Rains, 1988); Potlatch Corp., 79 LA 272, 276 (O'Connell, 1982); Pillsbury Co., 75 LA 523, 529, 531 (Fitch, 1980); Zimmer Mfg. Corp., 75 LA 16, 17 (Kiok, 1980); ITT-Continental Baking Co., 74 LA 92, 95 (Ross, 1980); General Tel. Co. of Southeast (Ala.), 69 LA 493, 498–99, 501 (Swain, 1977); Colson Co., 54 LA 896, 900 (Roberts, 1971); FMC Corp., 54 LA 807, 814 (Whyte, 1971); Shell Oil Co., 44 LA 1219, 1223 (Turkus, 1965); Corn Prods. Co., 42 LA 173, 175 (Kamin, 1964); Rockwell-Standard Corp., 41 LA 1087, 1090 (Markowitz, 1963); Modern Bakeries, 39 LA 939, 940–41 (Koven, 1962); New York Air Brake Co., 36 LA 621, 626 (Raimon, 1960); Carlyle Tile Co., 29 LA 787, 792 (Dworkin, 1958); Bernheim Distilling Co., 28 LA 441, 444–45 (Kesselman, 1957); Monsanto Chem. Co., 27 LA

the right "to determine what is to be produced, when it is to be produced, and how it is to be produced."[196] Again, unless restricted by the agreement, management has the right to determine what work shall be done;[197] to determine what kinds of services and business activity to engage in;[198] and to determine the techniques, tools, and equipment by which work on its behalf shall be performed.[199]

Management must have some discretion as to the method of carrying on its operations. It "should not be put in a straight jacket."[200] Because a primary function of management is to operate on the most efficient basis,[201] it may, at its discretion, eliminate individual jobs as well as entire job classifications.[202] Barring restrictive contractual language, a job may be eliminated

---

736, 742–43 (Roberts, 1956); Dow Chem. Co., 22 LA 336, 351 (Klamon, 1954); Goodyear Tire & Rubber Co. of Ala., 6 LA 681, 687 (McCoy, 1947). *See also* City of Albert Lea, Minn., 79 LA 1151, 1154 (Gallagher, 1982); Charter Int'l Oil Co., 71 LA 1072, 1076 (Taylor, 1978); City of Toledo, 70 LA 216, 220 (Heinsz, 1978); Nebraska Consol. Mills Co., 40 LA 700, 705–06 (Davey, 1963); Schlitz Brewing Co., 30 LA 147, 149 (Fleming, 1958). For related discussion, see Chapter 12, section 1., "Custom and Practice as a Term of the Contract"; Stein, *Management Rights and Productivity*, 32 Arb. J. 270 (1977). Contract clauses requiring management to discuss or give notice of operational changes have been narrowly construed so as not to impose an undue limitation on management. *See* Red Star Yeast & Prods. Co., 43 LA 267, 268–69 (Kelliher, 1964); Detroit Edison Co., 43 LA 193, 206–07 (Smith, 1964); Diamond Crystal Salt Co., 41 LA 510, 512 (Uible, 1963); Taylor-Wharton Co., 40 LA 114, 117–18 (Jaffee, 1962). *Cf.* Star Mfg. Co., 68 LA 147, 150–51 (Hall, 1977) (imposing a notice requirement where the contract was silent).

[196]Torrington Co., 1 LA 35, 42 (Courshon, 1945). *See* International Paper Co., 108 LA 1207, 1210 (Hart, 1997); Georgia-Pacific Corp., 107 LA 872, 876 (Neigh, 1996); Arizona Chem. Co., 107 LA 836, 842–43 (Grooms, Jr., 1996); Houston Lighting & Power Co., 106 LA 1188, 1194 (Johnson, 1996). *See also* Dyncorp, 101 LA 1193, 1196 (Richman, 1993) (grievance not arbitrable); General Tel. Co. of Southeast (Ala.), 69 LA 493, 501 (Swain, 1977); Colson Co., 54 LA 896, 900 (Roberts, 1971); Colonial Bakery Co., 22 LA 163, 165 (Bauder, 1953).

[197]Pacific Mills, 9 LA 236, 238 (McCoy, 1947); Gulf Oil Corp., 3 LA 798, 800 (Carmichael, 1946).

[198]Detroit Edison Co., 43 LA 193, 209 (Smith, 1964) (also holding that a past practice of engaging in a particular line of activity of itself provides no contractual assurance that it will be continued). *See also* First Nat'l Maint. Corp. v. NLRB, 452 U.S. 666, 680–86, 107 LRRM 2705 (1981) (discussed in section 2.A.i.b., "Expanding Subjects of Mandatory Bargaining," above).

[199]Corn Prods. Co., 42 LA 173, 175 (Kamin, 1964). *See also* Lockheed-Georgia Co., 73 LA 1007, 1011 (Crane, 1979); Scott Paper Co., 72 LA 1115, 1121–23 (Simon, 1979); Bell Helicopter Co., 44 LA 682, 686 (Rohman, 1965).

[200]Shell Oil Co., 44 LA 1219, 1223 (Turkus, 1965); Thompson Mahogany Co., 5 LA 397, 399 (Brandschain, 1946).

[201]*See* State of Alaska, 73 LA 990, 991 (Hauck, 1979); Safeway Stores, 73 LA 207, 209 (Goodman, 1979); Champion Int'l Corp., 72 LA 1204, 1209 (Larrabee, 1979); General Tel. Co. of Southeast (Ala.), 69 LA 493, 501 (Swain, 1977); Central Soya Co., 68 LA 864, 866 (Cox, 1977); Kimberly-Clark Corp., 54 LA 250, 252 (Larkin, 1971); Shell Oil Co., 44 LA 1219, 1223 (Turkus, 1965); McGough Bakeries Corp., 36 LA 1388, 1392 (Eyraud, 1961); Dover Corp., 33 LA 860, 861 (McIntosh, 1959); Carlyle Tile Co., 29 LA 787, 792 (Dworkin, 1958); National Container Corp., 29 LA 687, 692 (Marshall, 1957); Bernheim Distilling Co., 28 LA 441, 445 (Kesselman, 1957); Avon Prods., 26 LA 422, 426–27 (Ridge, 1956); W.L. Douglas Shoe Co., 10 LA 261, 265 (Myers, 1948).

[202]International Paper Co., 108 LA 1207 (Hart, 1997) (company was allowed to eliminate a job classification and demote the workers); Illinois Cement Co., 108 LA 667 (Kossoff, 1997) (cement manufacturer facility eliminated former console helper A, B, and C classifications when each of these positions was renamed and given additional duties, making them new classifications); Hyatt Cherry Hill, 103 LA 99 (DiLauro, 1994) (the company, following a management-rights clause, eliminated a cashier's classification and position and then required the food servers to complete these duties without a pay raise); I.T.T. Rayonier, 101 LA

when most of the tasks previously fulfilled by this position "have been reduced to the point where the remaining tasks can be performed logically, efficiently and safely by other employees."[203]

Even in instances where such operational changes result in the discontinuance of the union, arbitrators agree that management retains its right to make such changes as long as the act itself is not wrongful.[204] "In the operation of any plant, management has a fixed obligation to see that unnecessary costs are dispensed with and that production programs are changed to meet changing production demands. This is an inherent right . . . ."[205]

However, though management's unilateral determination of the methods of operations will prevail in many situations, bargaining is usually required before changes in working conditions are allowed.[206]

The determination of the line of demarcation between "operation methods" and "working conditions" does not lend itself to any easy, mechanistic formula. In one case, the arbitrator noted the difficulty that such determina-

---

865 (Lane, 1993) (15 of 20 positions were eliminated in the company's attempt to become more competitive by way of a profit improvement program). Duquesne Light Co., 90 LA 758 (Duff, 1988) (senior field service representative classification properly eliminated, where contract recognized employer's right to relieve employees from duty for lack of work); Downtown St. Paul Partners, 90 LA 67 (Cooper, 1987) (management-rights clause permitted employer to close hotel restaurants and bar and lay off employees); Flowers Baking Co. of W. Va., 89 LA 113 (Flannagan, 1987) (checker-loader classification properly eliminated, where contract gave employer right to "cease any job").

[203]International Paper Co., 108 LA 1207, 1211 (Hart, 1997).

[204]Zebco Corp., 104 LA 613 (Cohen, 1995) (a company in need of additional space moved its packaging operation and most of the union employees to a new location but required the employees to be nonunionized); Union Carbide Agric. Prods. Co., 84 LA 788 (Seinsheimer, 1985). *Cf.* Witco Chem. Corp., 89 LA 349 (Rothstein, 1987) (employer violated contract by failing to notify union of decision to contract truck-driving duties and eliminate job classification).

[205]Youngstown Sheet & Tube Co., 4 LA 514, 517 (Miller, 1946). *See also* Pillsbury Co., 75 LA 523, 529 (Fitch, 1980); City of Hamtramck, 71 LA 822, 827 (Roumell, Jr., 1978) (stating that the municipal employer in question "could have been charged with incompetency if it had not taken steps to modernize its procedures"); Dominion Elec. Co., 20 LA 749, 750 (Gross, 1953); Union Starch & Ref. Co., 15 LA 782, 789 (Klamon, 1950). However, where the agreement expressly prohibited the employer from using spray equipment without written consent of the union, the arbitrator enforced the restriction even though such equipment would have been more efficient for the particular job. Claremont Painting & Decorating Co., 46 LA 894, 895–96 (Kerrison, 1966).

[206]Macy's, 108 LA 489 (Gregory, 1997) (company was allowed to determine method of operations regarding the implementation of two separate shifts but was not allowed to unilaterally change the working conditions by issuing and requiring workers to wear certain clothing); Georgia-Pacific Corp., 108 LA 90 (Frost, 1996) (company was not allowed unilaterally to change working conditions regarding its absenteeism program); Regional Transp. Dist., Denver, Colo., 107 LA 813 (Finston, 1996) (company was properly determining methods of operation when it implemented mechanic work teams); Klamath Falls, Or., Fire Dist. 1, 106 LA 789 (Buchanan, 1996) (company was not allowed to adopt working conditions unilaterally, requiring firefighters to take physical fitness test); Alcan-Toyo Am., 102 LA 566 (Draznin, 1993) (company was not allowed to make changes unilaterally in working conditions regarding policy of absenteeism and tardiness). *But see* Consolidation Coal Co., 105 LA 1110 (Talarico, 1995) (company was not allowed to change unilaterally its past practice of paying workers for a minimum of 4 hours' overtime when they called employees in to work for times other than those in their regular schedule); Sheboygan County, Wis., 105 LA 605 (Dichter, 1995) (company was not allowed to change unilaterally past practice of using compensatory time for sick leave); Arch of Ill., 104 LA 1102 (Cohen, 1995) (company was not allowed to change unilaterally its starting times on work shifts); Conoco, Inc., 104 LA 1057 (Neigh, 1995) (company was not allowed to determine method of operation in regard to scheduling replacement workers when an agreement with the union predetermined this process).

tion may entail. There the agreement of the parties recognized the exclusive right of management to determine methods of operation, but it also restricted the right of management to change working conditions by requiring negotiations with the union before such changes could be made. The employer changed the operations of some employees from a noncontinuous to a continuous basis in the interest of plant efficiency, with the result that the employees were ordered to work through a period previously allowed for washing up. The arbitrator ruled that the order requiring the employees to work through the wash-up period was proper as an incidental result of the employer's good-faith exercise of the exclusive right to determine methods of operation. He stated the general considerations involved:

> The distinction between a change in working conditions, which by the terms of the contract must be the subject of negotiation prior to its institution, and a change in methods of operation, which by the terms of the contract is a sole function of management, is not easy to define or even to make clear by example. Abolition or sharp curtailment of an existing practice concerning rest time, wash-up time, paid lunch period, furnishing of shower baths and lockers, matters pertaining to sanitation, safety and health, or such like matter are clearly changes in working conditions. On the other hand, a change from the use of pot heaters to McNeill presses or from noncontinuous to continuous operation is just as clearly a change primarily in methods of operation. The latter changes usually cause, with respect to the individuals affected, some change of their working habits, but they are primarily and essentially changes in methods, not in conditions, and as such are exclusively a management function, subject only to the right of affected employees to resort to the grievance procedure to correct abuses or hardships such as decreased earnings or stretchout. Of course a change that was merely in form one of method, used as a pretext to institute a change of working conditions, would not be justifiable.[207]

The right of management to determine the types of machinery and equipment to be used and to determine the processes of manufacture may be stated specifically in the agreement.[208] This right also might be ruled to be included in a clause reserving the right of general management of the plant to the employer.[209] Even if such right is not specified in the agreement, numerous

---

[207]Goodyear Tire & Rubber Co. of Ala., 6 LA 681, 687 (McCoy, 1947). Dealing with the line between "operation methods" and "working conditions," see also City of Albert Lea, Minn., 79 LA 1151, 1154 (Gallagher, 1982); National Distillers Prods. Co., 77 LA 217, 219 (Curry, 1981); Department of Labor, Mine Health & Safety Admin., 75 LA 369, 374–76 (Cantor, 1980) (federal agency employer); Susquehana Corp., 55 LA 1306, 1308–09 (Kabaker, 1970); Concord Provision Co., 44 LA 1134, 1137–38 (Stouffer, 1965); Hawthorne-Mellody Farms, 40 LA 300, 303–04 (Kovenock, 1963); Modern Bakeries, 39 LA 939, 940–41 (Koven, 1962); Carlyle Tile Co., 29 LA 787, 792–93 (Dworkin, 1958); National Container Corp., 29 LA 687, 692–93 (Marshall, 1957); Bernheim Distilling Co., 28 LA 441, 444 (Kesselman, 1957); Monsanto Chem. Co., 27 LA 736, 742–43 (Roberts, 1956); St. Joseph Lead Co., 20 LA 890, 891 (Updegraff, 1953); EMGE Packing Co., 15 LA 603, 607–08 (Hampton, 1948).

[208]Associated Shoe Indus. of Southeastern Mass., 10 LA 535, 537–39 (Myers, 1948).

[209]City of N. Olmsted, Ohio, 106 LA 865 (Miller, 1996) (because of the general management-rights clause, the city was not required to invest in new computer equipment to continue direct deposits when the bank unilaterally discontinued its manual direct deposit system). See the following cases as examples of this principle applied in various operational contents: Schnuck Mkts., 101 LA 401, 407 (Hilgert, 1993); French Paper Co., 106 LA 737, 739 (House, 1996) ("The Management's Rights clause of the Agreement gives to management the right to promulgate rules and regulations so long as they are not inconsistent or in conflict with the provisions of this Agreement."); St. Louis Coca-Cola Bottling Co., 105 LA 356, 360 (O'Grady, 1995) (management-rights clause implicitly authorized employer to imple-

cases expressly or inferentially recognize that it can be exercised as a residual management power except as it has been restricted by the agreement.[210]

As a corollary, it follows that the employer has the right to have the employees operate improved machines and perform changed operation methods in good faith up to the level of their productive capacity.[211] Employees may be inclined to resist technological change, for workers who have spent years in a skilled trade are reluctant to risk its disappearance. "The need of the manufacturer to improve production methods is matched by the concern of the employees that they may be thrown out on the streets."[212]

In this general regard, it has been observed that:

> Whenever a job is abolished, a machine discontinued, or work in a department is discontinued, men lose jobs and their seniority rights to jobs are affected. But this involves no wrong of itself; it is merely one of the forms of injury or damage flowing from an act. The primary question is whether the act was wrongful. If it was not, then no question can properly arise as to damage.[213]

---

ment modified light duty program, where assignments were outside the bargaining unit); Frito-Lay, 93 LA 48, 57–58 (Creo, 1989) (employer properly introduced handheld computers as improvement to company's sales system, and such change did not trigger duty to bargain over effects of such change, where management-rights clause provided employer the right to "improve sales methods, operations or conditions," *id.* at 50); Foote & Davies/Mid-America Webpress, 88 LA 1285, 1287–88 (Cohen, 1987). *See also* National Park Serv., 72 LA 314, 322 (Pritzker, 1979); College of Osteopathic Med. & Surgery, 70 LA 1140, 1143–44 (Nitka, 1978); New York Air Brake Co., 36 LA 621, 626 (Raimon, 1960); Champion Lampworks, 11 LA 703, 705–06 (Healy, 1948); W.L. Douglas Shoe Co., 10 LA 261, 264–65 (Myers, 1948).

[210]*See* Frito-Lay, 93 LA 48, 57–58 (Creo, 1989); ITT-Continental Baking Co., 74 LA 92, 95–96 (Ross, 1980); Babcock & Wilcox Co., 45 LA 897, 902 (Dworkin, 1965); Oxford Paper Co., 45 LA 609, 610–11 (Cahn, 1965); Rockwell-Standard Corp., 41 LA 1087, 1090 (Markowitz, 1963); Castle & Cooke Terminals, 40 LA 62, 63 (Kagel, 1962); Modern Bakeries, 39 LA 939, 940–41 (Koven, 1962); McGough Bakeries Corp., 36 LA 1388, 1392 (Eyraud, 1961); California & Hawaiian Sugar Ref. Corp., 35 LA 695, 697–98 (Ross, 1960); Standard Oil Co., 30 LA 115, 117 (Updegraff, 1958); Phillips Petroleum Co., 26 LA 1, 3 (Beatty, 1956); A.C.L. Haase Co., 17 LA 472, 475 (Townsend, 1951); Blackhawk Mfg. Co., 7 LA 943, 945 (Updegraff, 1947). Even where the agreement expressly imposed some requirement or limitation on management in regard to automation or technological changes, the provisions were narrowly interpreted to apply only to sweeping and fundamental changes. L.A. Herald Exam'r, 45 LA 860, 861–62 (Kadish, 1965); Mackay Radio & Tel. Co., 42 LA 612, 617–19 (Koven, 1964).

[211]Associated Shoe Indus. of Southeastern Mass., 10 LA 535, 539 (Myers, 1948). *See also* Potlatch Corp., 79 LA 272, 276 (O'Connell, 1982); Mueller Co., 52 LA 162, 164 (Porter, 1968); Sperry Rand, 45 LA 996, 998 (Lehoczky, 1965); Quaker Oats Co., 41 LA 1147, 1150 (Tatum, 1963); McGraw-Edison Co., 38 LA 644, 646 (Whiting, 1962); A.O. Smith Corp., 34 LA 165, 169 (Stouffer, 1959); Hershey Chocolate Corp., 17 LA 268, 270 (Brecht, 1951). In *San Antonio Air Logistics Ctr.*, 73 LA 455, 463 (LeBaron, 1979), the union improperly encouraged employees not to cooperate in an employer survey being conducted to improve production. *See also* San Antonio Air Logistic Ctr., 73 LA 1074, 1079–81 (Caraway, 1979).

[212]Associated Shoe Indus. of Southeastern Mass., 10 LA 535, 538 (Myers, 1948).

[213]Allegheny Ludlum Steel Corp., 20 LA 455, 457 (McCoy, 1953). *See also* Arkansas Educ. Ass'n, 94 LA 1190, 1196–97 (Allen, Jr., 1990); Container Corp. of Am., 91 LA 329, 331 (Rains, 1988); Almaden Vineyards, 56 LA 425, 429 (Kagel, 1971); California & Hawaiian Sugar Ref. Corp., 35 LA 695, 697–98 (Ross, 1960); Schlitz Brewing Co., 30 LA 147, 149 (Fleming, 1958); AVCO Mfg. Corp., 28 LA 135, 136–37 (Updegraff, 1957); Monsanto Chem. Co., 27 LA 736, 742–44 (Roberts, 1956); Phillips Petroleum Co., 26 LA 1, 3 (Beatty, 1956). However, in *Premier Albums of New Jersey*, 41 LA 945, 946–47 (Mazur, 1963), it was held that, while the employer had the right to introduce new machinery, no worker could be terminated due to the change.

It also has been suggested that the exercise of this management function serves to protect the interests of the employees as well as of the employer, for if the employer is permitted to operate new machinery, "his competitive position will be enhanced, improving his chance to win new business and thereby to provide greater employment."[214]

6. Wage Adjustments Following Changes in Operation Methods
[LA CDI 114.308; 114.93]

Changes in operation methods, which are largely left within the discretion of management, often necessitate adjustments in wage rates. While the employer has wide discretion in determining operation methods, the determination of wage rates for new or changed processes is closely restricted.

The right initially to determine the job rate for a new or altered job may be given to management by the agreement. The following clause is illustrative:

> [R]ates on all new or changed operations shall be temporarily established by the employer . . . . If a grievance arises therefrom, the price shall be negotiated . . . . If unable to agree the matter shall be arbitrated in accordance with this contract.[215]

Where a change in the manner of operations is negligible, the employer is not required to negotiate a piece rate change with the union, even though the contract requires the employer to set the wage scale temporarily and to notify the union in the event of any new or experimental operation.[216] If the agreement does not give the employer the right initially to set the new rate, an arbitrator may require the employer to bargain before setting a rate.[217]

---

[214]Associated Shoe Indus. of Southeastern Mass., 10 LA 535, 539 (Myers, 1948).

[215]*Id.* at 537. *See also* Sperry Corp., 80 LA 166, 167 (Taylor, 1983); Alumax Aluminum Mill Prods., 69 LA 168, 169 (Cerone, 1977); Borg-Warner Plumbing Prods. Div., 63 LA 384, 385 (Seinsheimer, 1974); Diamond Power Specialty Corp., 46 LA 295, 296 (Duff, 1966); Pittsburgh Plate Glass Co., 32 LA 957, 958–59 (Lehoczky, Fisher, & Myers, 1959) (interest arbitrators ordered use of a similar clause); Veeder-Root, Inc., 21 LA 387, 389–90 (Shipman, 1953); John Morrell & Co., 9 LA 931, 937 (Gilden, 1948). Absent a specific provision for arbitration of rates of changed jobs, some arbitrators have denied their authority to set the rate. *See* Laclede Gas Co., 49 LA 1270, 1274 (Erbs, 1967); Groveton Papers Co., 41 LA 1169, 1174–76 (Gregory, 1963). But a different conclusion was reached in *Virginia-Carolina Chemical Corp.*, 23 LA 228, 233–34 (Marshall, 1954). For other cases dealing with the arbitrator's authority to set the rate on changed jobs, see *Penn-Dixie Cement Corp.*, 47 LA 601, 605–06 (Shister, 1966); *U.S. Slicing Mach. Co.*, 41 LA 1076, 1081–82 (Willingham, 1963).

[216]Jack T. Baillie Co., 84 LA 285 (Concepcion, 1985) (change in manner of loading haul trucks by eliminating manual handling and allowing all handling to be done by forklift, where handling by loaders merely requires insertion of sticks and making higher stacks, cartons are no longer burned, and rhythm of loading is extended).

[217]Copco Steel & Eng'g Co., 6 LA 156, 164 (Platt, Herman, & Lavery, 1947). *See also* Virginia-Carolina Chem. Corp., 23 LA 228, 233 (Marshall, 1954); Crossett Lumber Co., 14 LA 544, 546 (Carmichael, 1950); Wetter Numbering Mach. Co., 13 LA 177, 180 (Justin, 1949). *But see* Peerless Wire Goods Co., 49 LA 202, 204 (Lewis, 1967) (management's right to create new jobs carries with it the right to set a new rate for the job if the job is not the same as existing classifications); Metal Textile Corp., 24 LA 726, 728 (Sizelove, 1955); Union Starch & Ref. Co., 15 LA 782, 791 (Klamon, 1950). *See also* A.D. Juilliard & Co., 14 LA 802, 805 (Gregory, 1950) (past practice strongly influenced the result reached).

Even where an agreement provided that existing rates should be continued without change, management was not precluded from establishing new piece rates after introducing new equipment that materially changed job duties. One arbitrator reasoned that the requirement that rates be continued was based on the assumption that equipment and methods would remain the same and, because that assumption was not borne out by subsequent events, the requirement did not apply.[218]

Many disputes concerning rates for new or changed operating methods involve questions of arbitrability.[219] Arbitrators have recognized certain principles or standards to be considered in determining rates for new or changed operations when the contract is silent on the subject. These principles are discussed below because of their obvious practical importance.[220]

A. Hourly Rated Employees [LA CDI 114.308]

The rule generally applied in the case of employees who work for hourly rather than incentive rates is that an increase in hourly rates should accompany any *material* increase in the workload.[221] Where the matter was not specifically covered by the contract, for instance, an arbitrator ruled that when a change is made in job content, the job should be restudied to determine whether the original workload has been changed sufficiently to necessitate an adjustment in the wage rate. He stated that it does not follow that simply because work has been added to a job there necessarily must be an increase in pay. Although presumptively an increase in work duties warrants an increase in compensation, the entitlement to an increase in pay "depends upon whether the workload was too light and the increase does not make it too heavy or whether the workload was proper and the increase is material and makes it too heavy."[222]

Another arbitrator appeared unwilling to give so much weight to the factor of a previously light workload, where the agreement provided that consideration should be given to the adjustment of rates when the workload is materially increased. He ruled that such a provision does not permit the

---

[218]A.C.L. Haase Co., 17 LA 472, 477–79 (Townsend, 1951).

[219]In some cases, such disputes have been held nonarbitrable. *See* Addressograph-Multigraph Corp., 46 LA 1189, 1194 (Teple, 1966); United States Steel Co., 44 LA 774, 777 (McDermott, 1965); Dura Corp., 36 LA 329, 330 (Warns, 1960).

[220]For related material, see section 7., "Production Standards, Time Studies, and Job Evaluation," below.

[221]Arizona Chem. Co., 107 LA 836, 844 (Grooms, Jr., 1996); Integrated Health Servs. of Greater Pittsburgh, 107 LA 384, 392 (Dean, Jr., 1996); North Pittsburgh Tel. Co., 101 LA 931, 942–43 (Garrett, 1993). *See* Kraft, Inc., 86 LA 882 (Sabghir, 1986). For related material, see section 11., "Determination of Size of Crews," below.

[222]Goodyear Tire & Rubber Co. of Ala., 6 LA 924, 925 (McCoy, 1947). *See also* American La France, 71 LA 141, 142 (Waite, 1978); Virginia Folding Box Co., 51 LA 1051, 1054–55 (Marshall, 1968); Socony Mobil Oil Co., 44 LA 992, 995–96 (Shister, 1965); Dow Chem. Co., 40 LA 966, 969–70 (Prasow, 1963); United States Ceramic Tile Co., 35 LA 113, 116–17 (Seinsheimer, 1960); National Container Corp., 29 LA 687, 692–93 (Marshall, 1957); Bethlehem Steel Co., 28 LA 530, 531–32 (Valtin, 1957). For factors that an arbitrator considered in applying a contractual requirement that employees do "a reasonable day's work," see *Arketex Ceramic Corp.*, 42 LA 125, 130–31 (Seinsheimer, 1964).

employer to discount entirely a material increase in the workload on the ground that the previous workload was too light, but that this is one of the factors that, without having a decisive effect, may be taken into consideration as limiting the increase to be granted.[223] A slight increase in workload does not call for a higher rate.[224]

An increase in productivity is not necessarily viewed as an increase in workload. Thus, arbitrators may require a grievant to show "how much of the increased productivity . . . may be attributed to the machine itself and how much to the crew" before determining whether increased compensation is merited.[225] Often these decisions reflect an arbitrator's interpretation of what constitutes "substantial changes" or "significant changes."[226]

Thus, changing to new machines that produce more but that require less skill and effort does not constitute such change in the workload as to require revision of rates.[227] Where, however, a new machine or operation involves more than a slight increase in duties, skill, responsibility, or hazards, rate revision may be required.[228] In one case, a wage increase was ordered for operators of a new machine even though it was easier to operate than any other equipment in the plant, the arbitrator stating that the operator "is responsible for operating a more sophisticated—and expensive—piece of machinery which at least has the potential for significantly greater profits than other machines and he should share in the expected increase in productivity."[229]

---

[223]Continental Can Co., 5 LA 247, 250 (Updegraff, 1946).

[224]*See* Continental Grain Co., 80 LA 1106, 1108 (Edes, 1983); Mead Corp., 41 LA 1038, 1041 (Strong, 1963); United States Ceramic Tile Co., 35 LA 113, 116–17 (Seinsheimer, 1960); Pan Am. Ref. Corp., 4 LA 773, 775 (Abernethy, 1946). *See also* Minnesota Mining & Mfg. Co., 80 LA 1078, 1081–82 (Miller, 1983) (the contract dealt expressly with the matter). As to what might be considered more than slight, see *Central Screw Co.*, 13 LA 220, 222 (Kelliher, 1949); *Cranston Print Works Co.*, 5 LA 115, 118 (Copelof, 1946).

[225]Menasha Corp., 108 LA 308, 311 (Ellmann, 1997). *See also* Mead Prods., 104 LA 730 (Borland, 1994) (arbitrator found there was no significant change; thus employees were not entitled to an increase in wages when a warehouse computer information system was installed).

[226]Cooper Indus., 104 LA 383 (Imundo, Jr., 1995) (arbitrator determined that installing a new computer system in the shipping department was a substantial change and should be accompanied by a wage increase).

[227]Central Screw Co., 11 LA 108, 111 (Edes, 1948); E.F. Houghton & Co., 4 LA 716, 717–18 (Cahn, 1946). *See also* Sperry Corp., 80 LA 166, 170–71 (Taylor, 1983) (by management's introduction of computer terminals, the employees in question "were merely exposed to a new tool which permitted them to perform their work easier and more accurately"); Alumax Aluminum Mill Prods., 69 LA 168, 170 (Cerone, 1977); Johnson Bronze Co., 32 LA 216, 220 (Wood, 1959); Consolidated Chem. Indus., 13 LA 223, 225 (White, 1949).

[228]*See* Bean, Morris, & Co., 54 LA 418, 420 (McIntosh, 1971); Marhoeffer Packing Co., 48 LA 577, 578 (Hertz, 1967); Warren Wire Co., 47 LA 577, 579–80 (Rubin, 1966); Jessup Farms, 45 LA 964, 967 (Roberts, 1965); Premier Albums of N.J., 41 LA 945, 947 (Mazur, 1963); National Cash Register Co., 40 LA 565, 568–69 (Prasow, 1963); Line Materials Indus., 38 LA 584, 585 (Lehoczky, 1961); Weyerhaeuser Co., 37 LA 323, 330 (Dworkin, 1961).

[229]Printing Indus. of Metro Wash., D.C., 71 LA 838, 842 (Ables, 1978) (the amount of increase was limited, however, in recognition of "the impact of such increase in wages on the existing relationship between wages and other equipment"). *Compare* Marsh Stencil Mach. Co., 33 LA 1, 4–5 (Klamon, 1959) (less skill was required on new machines and hourly rated employees claimed the benefit of increased productivity).

B. Incentive Employees [LA CDI 114.394]

A study by the U.S. Department of Labor on incentive wage plans explained:

> An incentive wage plan is a method of wage payment by which workers receive extra pay for extra production. In establishing wage incentive plans, consideration must be given to (1) the base rate for the job; (2) the amount of work required to earn the base rate; and (3) the relationship between extra work above the base and extra pay for the extra performance.[230]

Another study by the same agency stated that most incentive plans fall within one of two basic types: a piecework plan or some type of standard-hour plan.[231] The study noted, however, that "[m]any agreements do not clearly indicate whether the applicable system is piecework or a form of standard-hour plan."[232]

---

[230]*Incentive Wage Provisions; Time Studies and Standards of Production* 1 (U.S. Dep't of Labor, Bureau of Labor Statistics, Bull. No. 908-3, 1948). For an explanation of several different types of incentives used in industry (productivity incentive, continuity of operation incentive, quality incentive), see *Keystone Steel & Wire Co.*, 55 LA 41, 50 (McKenna, 1970). In *Weatherhead Co.*, 55 LA 837, 840 (Fish, 1970), the arbitrator listed reasons that might justify management in placing a ceiling on incentive production. For cases dealing with union access to incentive system data and records, see *Tappan Co.*, 49 LA 922, 928 (Dworkin, 1967); *Hydril Co.*, 37 LA 279, 282 (Lehoczky, 1961). For labor, management, and neutral views on arbitration of incentive disputes, see Fairweather, *Arbitration of Disputes Involving Incentive Problems: An Industry View*, in Critical Issues in Labor Arbitration, Proceedings of the 10th Annual Meeting of NAA 61 (McKelvey ed., BNA Books 1957); Gomberg, *Arbitration of Disputes Involving Incentive Problems: A Labor View*, in *id.* at 85; Haughton, *Discussion*, in *id.* at 94. For other general discussions, see Rubin, *Arbitration of Wage Incentives: Three Perspectives: I. The Arbitration of Incentive Issues*, in Arbitration of Subcontracting and Wage Incentive Disutes, Proceedings of the 32d Annual Meeting of NAA 92 (Stern & Dennis eds., BNA Books 1980); Gomberg, *III. The Present Status of Arbitration Under Wage Incentive Payment Plans*, in *id.* at 116; Unterberger, *The Arbitration of Wage Incentive Cases*, 23 Arb. J. 236 (1968); Davis, *Incentive Problems, (Workshop No. 2)*, in Management Rights and the Arbitration Process, Proceedings of the 9th Annual Meeting of NAA 50 (McKelvey ed., BNA Books 1956); Morrison, *Arbitration of Wage Incentives*, 11 Arb. J. (n.s.) 199 (1956); Waite, *Problems in the Arbitration of Wage Incentives*, in Arbitration Today, Proceedings of the 8th Annual Meeting of NAA 25 (McKelvey ed., BNA Books 1955); Seybold, *Discussion*, in *id.* at 35; Unterberger, *Discussion*, in *id.* at 40.

[231]*Major Collective Bargaining Agreements: Wage-Incentive, Production Standard, and Time-Study Provisions* (U.S. Dep't of Labor, Bureau of Labor Statistics Bull. No. 1425–18, 1979), at 3. "Piecework, the simplest system, pays the individual a set 'price' per unit of output. A minimum or base rate usually is set, and employees producing below or at the base rate receive the minimum; faster workers receive more." *Id.* A standard-hour plan "is usually based on time, rather than money, per unit or output. The standard, often expressed as 100 percent, refers to the amount of work of specified quality which an average experienced employee can produce in an hour, working at normal performance with proper allowances for rest, personal needs, and minor delays. Under most standard-hour plans, employees are credited with additional earnings for production exceeding the standard." *Id.*

[232]*Id.* The study also explained that incentive systems "are best suited to work that is repetitive, readily measurable, and performed at a pace subject to control by the worker or group"; that group incentives are most appropriate where a number of employees work together on a task and an individual's work cannot be separately measured; that the incentive concept always has been somewhat controversial; that some employers reject incentive plans as too difficult and costly to administer, or as creating friction among employees; that some unions claim, among other criticisms, that incentive plans "are divisive, undermine group solidarity, create undesirable competition among employees, and contribute to excessive stress and fatigue"; but that incentive systems can be successful under collective bargaining, as "is evident from the large number of such plans that have continued over many years." *Id.* at 1, 4.

In reviewing the rates of incentive employees, arbitrators sometimes apply a "maintenance of prior earnings" standard. This standard cannot be applied, however, where the contract expressly recognizes that the employer, at its discretion, may find it necessary or desirable from time to time to establish new incentive rates or adjust existing incentive rates because of certain conditions.[233]

Another standard, much less concrete, requires the maintenance of the ratio of earnings to effort expended.[234] Under the "ratio of earnings to effort" standard, no change in incentive rates is in order unless there is a change in the amount of incentive effort required per unit of incentive production.[235] Application of this standard means that employees receive increased earnings on that part of increased production that is is caused by increased work effort, and that management receives the benefit from that part of increased production that is caused by mechanical improvements.[236]

Reduction of incentive rates has been allowed where the introduction of new machinery has resulted in increased production without requiring an increase in effort.[237] Moreover, reduction of incentive rates has been ordered where employees controlled production on new machines at a very low level.[238]

---

[233]Timken Co., 85 LA 377 (Morgan, 1985). *See also* USX, Div. of USX Corp., 90 LA 1279 (Garrett, 1988) (employer properly paid incentive employee at standard hourly rate for time spent taking audiology test at employer's direction).

[234]This standard was used by *Wheeling Steel Corp.*, 37 LA 669, 670 (Shipman, 1961); *Dayton Steel Foundry Co.*, 22 LA 450, 452 (Lehoczky, 1954); *Anaconda Wire & Cable Co.*, 10 LA 20, 23–24 (Scheiber, 1948); *American Steel & Wire Co.*, 8 LA 846, 849 (Blumer, 1947); *Wilson Steel & Wire Co.*, 6 LA 579, 582 (Hampton, 1947); *Container Co.*, 6 LA 218, 219–20 (Whiting, 1946); *La Follette Shirt Co.*, 4 LA 482, 483 (Dwyer, 1946). *See also* A.O. Smith Corp., 79 LA 889, 893–94 (Briggs, 1982). As a preamble to his discussion of incentive issues, an arbitrator stated:

I should emphasize the basic theme that the so-called incentive issues arise from pay-for-production systems of compensation. The employer and the union have established this relationship of work and pay by negotiation and practice; it is the function of the arbitrator to decide the issues to confirm and continue the accepted ratio.

Rubin, NAA 32D Proceedings, at 92 (he also stated that the "paucity" of published incentive cases "should not be misunderstood . . . to be the true picture of the number of such issues arbitrated in this country," *id.* at 93).

[235]American Steel & Wire Co., 8 LA 846, 849 (Blumer, 1947).

[236]Carnegie-Illinois Steel Corp., 5 LA 712, 720 (Blumer, 1946) (explained that the change in incentive effort is not necessarily the same as the change in work required for the operation). *See also* Allegheny Ludlum Steel Corp., 28 LA 129, 131 (McCoy, 1957); Veeder-Root, Inc., 21 LA 387, 390 (Shipman, 1953).

[237]Jenkins Bros., 11 LA 432, 435 (Donnelly, 1948); Reliance Mfg. Co., 3 LA 677, 679 (Whiting, 1946). *Cf.* Bethlehem Steel Co., 17 LA 650, 653–54 (Shipman, 1951). For the imposition of a time limit (within a "reasonable time") for changing incentive rates in response to changes in production methods, see *Worthington Corp.*, 34 LA 497, 503 (Crawford, 1959) (management waited too long to change the rate (producing lower earnings)). *See also* Victor Balata Textile & Belting Co., 70 LA 1154, 1156 (Dunn, 1978). *But see* Borg-Warner Plumbing Prods. Div., 63 LA 384, 386 (Seinsheimer, 1974). For an illustration that the incentive premium can lose its appeal to employees, see *Jenkins Bros.*, 33 LA 275, 277 (Donnelly, 1959).

[238]Associated Shoe Indus. of Southeastern Mass., 10 LA 535, 538–39 (Myers, 1948). *See also* Wolverine Shoe & Tanning Corp., 15 LA 195, 196–97 (Platt, 1950). Concerning the pace at which employees should work when paid on a group incentive basis, see *Pittsburgh Plate Glass Co.*, 36 LA 21, 22 (Lehoczky, 1960).

It can be expected that no adjustment in incentive rates will be required as long as the change in the workload is slight.[239]

7. PRODUCTION STANDARDS, TIME STUDIES, AND JOB EVALUATION

A. Production Standards [LA CDI 118.27]

Whether wages are computed on a time or incentive basis, there is usually some formal or informal determination of the output expected of employees on each operation. This expected production is commonly called the work load or production standard and represents the amount of work required or expected to be done in a given time by the average, qualified operator under normal conditions . . . . [240]

Where an agreement contains no express provisions on the subject, many cases have held that management has the right to set reasonable production standards and to enforce them through discipline.[241] In other cases, this gen-

---

[239]Jack T. Baillie Co., 84 LA 285 (Concepcion, 1985) (change in manner of loading haul trucks by eliminating manual handling and allowing all handling to be done by forklift); Schlueter Mfg. Co., 10 LA 295, 296–97 (Hilpert, 1948) (it was ruled, however, that the overall effect of a succession of minor additions to an operation could be considered); Goodyear Tire & Rubber Co. of Ala., 5 LA 30, 35 (McCoy, 1946). Some agreements expressly provide for change in incentive rates when there is a "substantial" change in operations. For cases involving the application of such provisions, see *Allegheny Ludlum Steel Corp.*, 28 LA 129 (McCoy, 1957); *Veeder-Root, Inc.*, 21 LA 387 (Shipman, 1953); *Jones & Laughlin Steel Corp.*, 21 LA 84 (Cahn, 1953); *Allegheny Ludlum Steel Corp.*, 20 LA 455 (McCoy, 1953); *Pacific Hard Rubber Co.*, 18 LA 375 (Warren, 1952).

[240]*Incentive Wage Provisions; Time Studies and Standards of Production* 37 (U.S. Dep't of Labor, Bureau of Labor Statistics, Bull. No. 908-3, 1948). A "production standard is the level of production which may be reasonably expected from an average worker, or a group of workers, when working to normal capacity on specified jobs, or job classifications, with due consideration for quality of workmanship, an efficient method of operation, and the continued health and safety of the worker." *Major Collective Bargaining Agreements: Wage-Incentive, Production-Standard, and Time-Study Provisions* 22 (U.S. Dep't of Labor, Bureau of Labor Statistics, Bull. No. 1425-18, 1979). To be suitable for a production standard: "the work performed must be repetitive and capable of being done uniformly by all workers involved in the task," the "job content must remain constant from one measuring period to the next," and the "method of operation and the goods produced must be capable of being objectively and accurately measured." *Id.* Of 1,438 agreements surveyed, 23% contained production-standard provisions and "virtually all" of these "allow union input to the establishment of the standard or a procedure through which an appeal may be made." *Id.*

[241]Ingalls Shipbuilding, 101 LA 683 (Koenig, Jr., 1993) (employee discharged, where company required employee to meet rigorous standards). *See* Grand Union Co., 80 LA 588, 589, 591 (Ray, 1983) (having previously upheld the company's right "to unilaterally institute production standards," in the present challenge to a standard the arbitrator stated that the "burden of proving that the standard is unreasonable rests upon the Union" and has not been met); Amerdyne E., 71 LA 263, 265–66 (Seinsheimer, 1978); Eaton Corp., 69 LA 71, 73, 75 (Kasper, 1977) (the company had "no formal production standards," but grievant had notice "about the numerical rate of production" that the company reasonably expected); Great Atl. & Pac. Tea Co., 68 LA 485, 488 (Seidenberg, 1977); Industrial Wire Prods., 50 LA 917, 921 (McCoy, 1968); Whirlwind, Inc., 50 LA 888, 894–95 (Solomon, 1968); Industrial Wire Prods., 50 LA 136, 140 (McCoy, 1968); Buddy L Corp., 49 LA 581, 583 (McIntosh, 1967); Pacific Outdoor Advertising Co., 46 LA 1196, 1199–2000 (Roberts, 1966); Universal Foods Corp., 44 LA 393, 394–95 (Gilden, 1965); Adams Tooling, 43 LA 1155, 1157–58 (Willingham, 1965); W.O. Larson Foundry Co., 42 LA 1286, 1291–92 (Kates, 1964); Package Mach. Co., 38 LA 894, 896 (Altieri, 1962); United States Ceramic Tile Co., 37 LA 758, 759–60 (McIntosh, 1961); Whitewater Elecs., 36 LA 1442, 1444–45 (Mueller, 1961) (discharge was reversed on contract procedural grounds); Mosler Lock Co., 33 LA 913, 915 (Schmidt, 1959); National Lead Co. of Ohio, 32 LA 865, 867 (Schedler, 1959); Olin Mathieson Chem. Corp., 32 LA 317,

eral right of management was expressly or impliedly recognized, but the discipline for failure to meet a production standard did not stand because the standard was unreasonable or because the discipline was unjust for some other reason.[242] However, it is essential that workers be given adequate notice of the production standard before disciplinary action is taken.[243]

If the collective bargaining agreement gives management the exclusive right to manage the plant and direct the employees, the employer has the right to order an employee to increase the speed of a machine that could yield an output approximately at the ceiling for incentive earnings.[244] Arbitrators do agree that management has the right to enforce reasonable production standards through discipline.[245]

B. Time Studies [LA CDI 114.398]

The purpose of a time study is to measure the work of an operation. "Each element of the operation is studied and a determination is made of the

---

321 (Bradley, 1959); Harbison-Walker Refractories Co., 32 LA 122, 124 (Williams, 1959); Menasco Mfg. Co., 31 LA 33, 37 (Prasow, 1958); Johnson Serv. Co., 30 LA 1048, 1049–50 (Eckhardt, 1958); Menasco Mfg. Co., 30 LA 264, 266 (Neff, 1958). *See also* Cardinal Health, 108 LA 1039 (LaRocco, 1997) (company was allowed to continue using a one-in-a-thousand error production rate and to discipline those with notice of the standard who continually failed to meet it); Hertz Corp., 103 LA 65 (Poole, 1994) (company was allowed to implement a new production standard system and to discipline those who failed to perform acceptably). *Cf.* Union Carbide Corp., 70 LA 201, 203–04 (Jones, Jr., 1978). For cases upholding discharge of incentive employees who consistently failed to produce enough to earn the federal minimum wage, see *Florsheim Shoe Co.*, 74 LA 705, 709 (Roberts, 1980); *Williams Mfg. Co.*, 54 LA 737, 744 (Bradley, 1971). In *Wallace-Murray Corp.*, 55 LA 372, 375–76 (Kabaker, 1970), the arbitrator explained that incentive workers may not be performing satisfactorily even though they may be earning their guaranteed minimum hourly wage, the guarantee being intended merely to protect them against complete loss of earnings due to some outside cause, such as a mechanical breakdown. Somewhat akin to the application of production standards, see *City of Toledo*, 70 LA 216 (Heinsz, 1978) (involving low productivity in issuance of traffic citations, where municipal employer had ordered increased citations in an effort to reduce traffic fatalities); *Cosmos Broad. of La.*, WDSU-TV, 68 LA 1332 (Taylor, 1977) (involving discharge of a TV weather reporter who had a low popularity rating).

[242]*See* Birmingham Ornamental Iron Co., 79 LA 582, 584 (Crane, 1982); Jno. H. Swisher & Son, 77 LA 409, 415 (Steele, 1981); Magnetics, Inc., 51 LA 1280, 1283–84 (Krimsly, 1969) (production standard was "fraught with statistical distortions"); Kelly-Springfield Tire Co., 42 LA 1162, 1166 (McCoy, 1964) (employer may not set production standard on individual employee basis but must set it for the job involved); Rockwell Mfg. Co., 40 LA 866, 872–74 (Teple, 1963); Lanier Uniform Rental Serv., 39 LA 130, 133–34 (Murphy, 1962); Midwest Mfg. Corp., 38 LA 896, 902 (Davis, 1962) (failure to meet new production standard was due to lack of practice rather than alleged slowdown); John Wood Co., 35 LA 584, 586–87 (Ruckel, 1960) (discipline for failure to make standard must be related to consistency with which employee falls below standard); Wertheimer Bag Co., 33 LA 694, 698–700 (Maggs, 1959); International Shoe Co., 33 LA 203, 204–05 (McCoy, 1959) (constantly changing standard was unfair and unreliable). *See also* Dearborn Brass Co., 66 LA 602, 604 (Sinicropi, 1976).

[243]Cummins Cumberland, 106 LA 993 (Heekin, 1996) (arbitrator did not allow the company to discipline an employee for failing to meet the production standard when it did not provide proof that notice was posted or transmitted to the employees after a new policy was implemented).

[244]Weston Paper, 85 LA 454 (Cyrol, 1985).

[245]Laidlaw Waste Sys., 90 LA 570 (Clifford, 1987) (employer properly discharged 9-year employee for failure to meet production requirements). *But see* Featherlite Trailers of Iowa, 90 LA 761 (Schwartz, 1987) (manufacturing company improperly discharged assembly-line employee, where company failed to define work standards).

time required for its performance by a normal experienced operator working with normal effort and without undue fatigue."[246] One arbitrator explained:

> [I]n conjunction with job evaluation (which determines relative base rates) it actually evaluates each incentive job in like terms and makes the ideal of "equal pay for equal work" possible. When properly carried out, all jobs in the plant pay relatively equally well, and an expenditure of extra effort or skill applied to any job pays off equally well.[247]

It is common practice to determine production standards through time studies, and where the contract specifically states that any bona fide change in the methods, machines, tools, fixtures, materials, design, quality, specifications, or other conditions that affect work content requires a new time study, the employer has no right to revise its 30-year-old method of calculating incentive pay unilaterally.[248] The union, however, has the right to make independent time studies in connection with the prosecution of an incentive pay grievance.[249]

Companies may be restricted by contract from unilaterally conducting these studies and implementing changes to incentive programs without permitting the union to participate in the process.[250] Some contracts prohibit an arbitrator from establishing or modifying incentive rates. Nonetheless, arbitrators have held that they may still determine whether the process for establishing the rates is equitable.[251]

If the parties do not object, arbitrators may use time studies to review rates after operation changes.[252] Arbitrators also may order or sustain the use of time studies in rate-setting where such studies have been used by the parties for this purpose in the past.[253]

---

[246]Ford Motor Co., 12 LA 949, 951 (Shulman, 1949). *See also* Timken Roller Bearing Co., 51 LA 101, 105 (Dworkin, 1968).

[247]Timken Roller Bearing Co., 6 LA 979, 983 (Lehoczky, 1947) (also noting that use of time study in setting new rates may be favored over comparison with rates for similar operations because the establishment of new rates on the basis of existing rates tends to perpetuate existing intraplant inequities). But, under the concept of "red circle" rates, which may be used for a variety of bona fide reasons, there is at least a temporary departure from the job evaluation objective of relative equality. For explanation and discussion of red circle rates, see *John Morrell & Co.*, 76 LA 1017, 1021–22 (Nathan, 1981); *Airtherm Prods.*, 72 LA 87, 88–89 (Sisk, 1979) (stating that a red circle rate "is assigned to an individual employee and as such it is considered a personal rate as distinguished from the established rate set forth in the rate schedules"); *Memphis Light, Gas, & Water Div.*, 69 LA 687, 692–93 (Simon, 1977).

[248]Airco Carbon, 86 LA 6 (Dworkin, 1986).

[249]Fafnir Bearing Co. v. NLRB, 362 F.2d 716, 62 LRRM 2415 (2d Cir. 1966); Armstrong Cork Co., 41 LA 1053, 1056–58 (Shister, 1963). As to the use of company-paid union time study personnel, see *Pittsburgh Plate Glass Co.*, 34 LA 908, 910–11 (Lehoczky, 1960).

[250]Permold Corp., 101 LA 390 (DiLeone, 1993) (after acquiring a better saw, the company was not allowed to implement a new production standard unilaterally because the operation was considered to have been changed). *But see* Lawrence Paper Co., 107 LA 730 (Murphy, 1996) (company reserved the right to contractually modify, amend, or adjust previously established standards on significant changes but was obligated to notify the union, which could then pursue a grievance).

[251]*Lawrence Paper Co.*, 107 LA at 735.

[252]*See* Simmons Co., 33 LA 725, 727 (Ross, 1959); Container Co., 6 LA 218, 220 (Whiting, 1946).

[253]*See* Armstrong Tire Co., 95 LA 1050, 1052 (Kindig, 1990); Timken Roller Bearing Co., 6 LA 979, 983–84 (Lehoczky, 1947); National Malleable & Steel Castings Co., 4 LA 189, 194 (Gilden, 1946). *Cf.* Schlueter Mfg. Co., 10 LA 295, 296 (Hilpert, 1948).

C. Job Evaluation [LA CDI 114.303]

"Job evaluation" is not only used in determining relative base rates, but, as stated by one authority, "[j]ob evaluation attempts to determine the worth of each job in relationship to the worth of all other jobs."[254]

A widely used method of job evaluation is the "point" method, under which, in general:

1. Factors are selected (and defined or described) that are common to the range of jobs to be rated (e.g., learning time, skill, responsibility, judgment decision, physical demand, working conditions, and the like).
2. Different grades or degrees are specified (and defined or described) for each factor (e.g., Grade A, Grade B, and so on) to be used, to indicate the extent to which the factor exists in the given job.
3. A point value is assigned to each grade or degree of each factor (e.g., Responsibility Factor Grade C may be assigned 45 points).
4. The job evaluator selects the grade or degree of each factor that most nearly describes the requirements for the job as indicated by the evidence.
5. The total point value of the job is then obtained by simple addition.

To illustrate, if it is concluded that Skill Factor Grade A (10 points), Responsibility Factor Grade D (65 points), Judgment Decision Factor Grade B (25 points), and Working Conditions Factor Grade B (20 points) apply to the job, the total point value of the job will be 120 points. A job thus evaluated at 120 points will, by a previously set scale, carry a specified wage rate.[255] When a job evaluation is involved, an arbitrator's task under this system is to determine the applicable grade for each factor on the basis of the evidence and, typically, personal observations during a plant visit. The parties may then determine the total point value of the job and the rate or labor grade that that point value calls for under their agreement.

A basic function of job evaluation is determining the true requirements of the job. One arbitrator observed:

> One of the major blocks to the bilateral settlement of job evaluation disputes is rooted in the fact that the parties concerned do not have a common basis for their discussions. In this case, for example, the grievant is strongly

---

[254]Lanham, Job Evaluation 3 (1955). Job evaluation "involves several major phases such as securing and analyzing facts about jobs, writing up these facts into descriptions of the jobs, studying these descriptions and evaluating the jobs according to some rating method, and then pricing the jobs in relation to the evaluation." *Id.* at 5. For other writing on job evaluation, see Zack & Bloch, Labor Agreement in Negotiation and Arbitration 302 (BNA Books 2d ed. 1995); Wiggins, The Arbitration of Industrial Engineering Disputes 91 (BNA Books 1970); Johnson, Boise, & Pratt, Job Evaluation (1946); Unterberger, *Automation and Job Evaluation Techniques, in* Arbitration and Industrial Change, Proceedings of the 16th Annual Meeting of NAA 238 (Kahn ed., BNA Books 1963); Unterberger, *Arbitration of Job Evaluation Cases*, 17 Arb. J. 219 (1962); Murphy, *Job Classification Arbitrations Under Bethlehem Steel Agreements*, 16 Arb. J. 8 (1961).

[255]For extensive discussion of the point method, see Lanham, at 73–74; the Lanham study also discusses several other generally accepted methods. For citation of arbitration cases revealing a variety of job evaluation plans, see Wiggins, at 103. *See also* Sherwin Williams Co., 80 LA 649, 651–52 (Wolff, 1983) (the job evaluation plan utilized 11 factors).

influenced by what he knows he brings to the job while the Company insists that only those characteristics listed in the job's description and only to the degree that they are detailed, are of value. In actual application, neither position is wholly correct; many of the grievant's abilities are not required to the degree he thinks they are and conversely, the availability of certain "extra" ability, over and above what the job description calls for, is frequently essential. The job's description, after all, represents a theoretical analysis of what the job has been planned to require and not necessarily what it actually requires. This statement cuts both ways. Your arbitrator knows of many jobs whose descriptions call for degrees of knowledge and skills which the specific occupant could *never* produce nor will he ever be required to produce them.[256]

The arbitrator also emphasized that it is the job, not the person or machine, that is being evaluated:

Again, two different jobs performed on the same make and model machine tool by the same operator in the same type of department may still carry different wage rates, all because it is the specific job that is being evaluated and not the man or the machine as such. The same lathe, for example, could be utilized for work which could range in value through perhaps five labor grades, from rough turning through the most intricate precision work. For this basic reason, one cannot accept unsupported examples from other plants as "evidence" of specific job—or factor—values.[257]

8. CONTROL OF QUALITY STANDARDS

Management has been held to have the right at all times to exercise control over the standards of quality of its products because "a lowering in the degree of quality under a competitive market may have serious and disastrous results."[258] Thus, it has been ruled that management had the right to determine what work was faulty, and whether it should be reworked or scrapped, where the determination was made by people well qualified and experienced in all departments, and the employer's policy resolved all doubts in favor of the employees.[259] In another case, where management was upheld in slowing the pace of processing hides through vats, the arbitrator declared that "the Company has the right to maintain quality within its operation and no incentive pace can be justified which does not produce quality product."[260]

The "competitive market" was stressed by another arbitrator sustaining the demotion of an employee for faulty work:

In managing the Plant and directing the working forces Management has the right and the duty to insure the highest quality standards so that its product

---

[256]Victor Mfg. & Gasket Co., 48 LA 957, 958 (Lehoczky, 1967) (emphasis in original).

[257]*Id.* at 959. *See also* McGill Mfg. Co., 67 LA 1094, 1097–98 (Petersen, 1976) (the arbitrator (1) reiterated the "caveat that the function of job evaluation is to rate the job and not the man," and (2) placed the burden of proof on the union to show by "tangible and convincing evidence" that management's judgment in job evaluation was incorrect and should be reversed by the arbitrator).

[258]Torrington Co., 1 LA 20, 26 (Courshon, 1945).

[259]*Id.* As to management's right to establish and enforce a quality control program, see *Patent Button Co.*, 43 LA 1208, 1211–14 (King, 1965).

[260]Howes Leather Co., 71 LA 606, 609 (Hewitt, 1978).

can be sold in a competitive market with the resultant benefits to the employer and employees, each of whom has a stake in the success of the enterprise. How this quality-control is to be attained is also the responsibility of Management.

. . . We are aware that most industries are becoming more competitive as their respective sales forces contest for a place in the market. Unless quality standards are maintained and unless a Company is in a position where it can provide a high quality product it cannot successfully exist in a competitive economy. Failure to achieve quality in a product not only reduces the benefit to the ultimate consumer but also places the Company in jeopardy with, at least potentially, a resultant disadvantage to itself and to its employees. In not a few industries the competition in quality of final product is as important as price competition.[261]

The company may have a legitimate concern not only with respect to the sale of its product, but also with regard to its reputation and the safety of persons who use its product. In this connection, the grievance of an employee who was discharged for faulty work was denied by an arbitrator, who stated:

In such situations the manufacturing concern must be in a position to protect its reputation and the quality of its product. A company's failure to do so would redound to the detriment of all persons connected with the enterprise— owners, management and employees.[262]

He stated further:

The Company necessarily is concerned with the production of good castings and the safety of persons who use its products. If faulty castings are produced by the . . . Company it will not only lose customers but property may be damaged and persons who come in contact with equipment in which its castings are placed may be injured, or even death may result.[263]

Management has the right to formulate and enforce reasonable rules for protecting the quality of its products.[264] Pursuant to such rules, it may, in appropriate circumstances, discharge or discipline employees who fail to meet quality standards.[265]

In upholding the decision of a shipyard company to discharge an employee for unsatisfactory work, one arbitrator declared: "Producing an acceptable Naval or Commercial vessel is what the shipyard business is all about. The quality of the welding must pass rigorous testing, or the shipyard cannot remain in business."[266]

---

[261]American Radiator & Standard Sanitary Corp., 29 LA 167, 170 (Duff, 1957). Similarly, another arbitrator sustained the demotion of an employee, where management's action was based on an "honest desire to improve efficiency and the quality of the Company's product." Firestone Tire & Rubber Co., 33 LA 206, 208 (McCoy, 1959).

[262]Valley Steel Casting Co., 22 LA 520, 525 (Howlett, 1954).

[263]Id. at 526. See also Macomber, Inc., 39 LA 719, 723 (Teple, 1962); Lockheed Aircraft Corp., 31 LA 1036, 1037 (McIntosh, 1958). But in Lockheed Aircraft Corp., 35 LA 684, 685 (Grant, 1960), discharge was commuted to layoff despite serious faulty work, the arbitrator determining that the company must share the responsibility for the failure to inspect the work properly.

[264]Kellogg Co., 55 LA 84, 88 (Shearer, 1970) (management had a rule regulating the length of hair and sideburns to protect its products from hair contamination).

[265]Id. See also Patent Button Co., 43 LA 1208, 1214 (King, 1965).

[266]Cardinal Health, 108 LA 1039 (LaRocco, 1997) (production standard of 1 error per 1,000 lines filled was reasonable; Champion Dairypak, 105 LA 462 (Allen, Jr., 1995) (employee discharged for neglect of duties); S&J Ranch, 103 LA 350 (Bogue, 1994) (employee discharged for poor quality of work); Southwestern Bell Tel. Co., 102 LA 531 (Nolan, 1994) (employee discharged for tone and manner complaints).

Management also has the right to institute an inspection and testing program. As declared by an arbitrator:

> Management obviously is free to inspect products and to make sure that quality standards are being met. Inspection is a recognized and commonly followed part of practically every manufacturing process. Equally well-established is the rule that the work of any employee—craft or otherwise—is at all times subject to scrutiny and critical examination.[267]

While management has wide freedom to control quality standards, the fairness of penalties imposed for faulty work may be closely scrutinized by arbitrators.[268]

9. Job and Classification Control

Cases involving the right of management to establish, eliminate, or combine jobs or job classifications, to assign duties and tasks, and to transfer duties between jobs or between job classifications defy neat categorization. This difficulty springs in part from the fact that the words "job" and "classification" at times are used synonymously and at other times are intended to carry different meanings.[269] The problem is compounded because different terminology may be utilized in the decisions of cases involving similar issues (the arbitrator's choice of terminology often conforms to that used by the parties in presenting the given case), or conversely because different meanings may be intended even though similar terminology is used. The failure of arbitrators to define clearly the terminology that they use in their opinions makes it virtually impossible to arrange the cases into clearly defined compartments. The frequent borderline situations have produced many shadings of arbitral opinion touching on otherwise basic issues.

---

[267]Bethlehem Steel, 32 LA 541, 542 (Valtin & Seward, 1959). In *U.S. Pipe & Foundry Co.*, 79 LA 936, 940 (Galambos, 1982), the arbitrator stated that: "Supervision entails quality control. There is no way a foreman could be expected to supervise those who are assigned to his supervision without exerting a control over the quality of their work."

[268]*See* American Forest Prods. Corp., 44 LA 20, 22–23 (Lucas, 1965); Patent Button Co., 43 LA 1208, 1212–14 (King, 1965); Riverside Book Bindery, 38 LA 586, 592–93 (McKelvey, 1962); Evinrude Motors Co., 36 LA 1302, 1304 (Marshall, 1961); Ohio Steel Foundry Co., 36 LA 491, 495 (Dworkin, 1961); Lockheed Aircraft Corp., 35 LA 684, 685 (Grant, 1960); American Radiator & Standard Sanitary Corp., 29 LA 167, 169–70 (Duff, 1957); Carr, Adams, & Collier Co., 27 LA 656, 659–62 (Graff, 1956); Valley Steel Casting Co., 22 LA 520, 524–27 (Howlett, 1954); Florence Stove Co., 19 LA 650, 652 (Noel, 1952).

[269]For example:

> There is no question that the word "job" may have a different meaning from the word "classification." Two men may have the same classification, for example, "painter", but one may have the job of keeping certain rooms painted while the other has the job of keeping certain equipment painted. On the other hand, the two words are sometimes used synonymously. The question is in what sense did the parties use the word [in their agreement].

Fulton-Sylphon Co., 2 LA 116, 117–18 (McCoy, 1946). *See also* Olin Mathieson Chem. Corp., 50 LA 1061, 1066–67 (Talent, 1968); Humble Oil & Ref. Co., 49 LA 445, 450 (Hebert, 1967); Columbian Carbon Co., 27 LA 762, 764–65 (Hebert, 1956); Golden Belt Mfg. Co., 20 LA 19, 21 (Livengood, 1953); Goodyear Tire & Rubber Co., 1 LA 121, 124 (McCoy, 1945).

For these reasons there is a close relationship between (and frequent overlapping of) the materials in the subtopics that make up the remainder of this topic.[270]

A. Establishing, Eliminating, and Combining Jobs and Classifications [LA CDI 114.304; 117.334]

The right of management to establish new jobs or job classifications is sometimes specifically stated in the agreement, along with some provision for union challenge of management's actions via the grievance procedure and arbitration.[271] The right also has been recognized as being vested in management except as restricted by the agreement, and it likewise might be included within the scope of a general management-rights clause.[272]

The creation of new jobs outside the bargaining unit as a result of new functions undertaken by an employer also has been upheld as a manage-

---

[270]For other important related material, see Chapter 12, section 1., "Custom and Practice as a Term of the Contract."

[271]See, e.g., Titan Wheel Int'l, 97 LA 514, 520 (Smith, 1991); Day & Zimmerman, 91 LA 1003, 1006 (Belcher, 1988); Pan Am World Servs., 84 LA 1161, 1166 (Bowers, 1985); Arco Oil & Gas Co., 84 LA 235, 238–40 (Baroni, 1985); T.N.S., Inc., 76 LA 278, 281 (Hardin, 1981); Alumax Aluminum Mill Prods., 69 LA 168, 169 (Cerone, 1977).

[272]Meijer Inc., 114 LA 1048 (Fullmer, 2000) (past practice did not limit employer's right to revise job classifications); Greif Bros. Corp., 114 LA 554 (Kenis, 2000) (employer not contractually bound to maintain classifications in agreement); Fox River Paper Co., 114 LA 9 (Daniel, 1999) (classification eliminated for justifiable business reason); Johnston-Tombigbee Mfg. Co., 113 LA 1015 (Howell, 2000) (elimination of lead person classification valid where there had been a reduction in workforce and restructuring of operations); U.S. Pipe & Foundry Co., 113 LA 943 (Owens, 1999) (job classifications in agreement did not contain language insulating them from elimination); International Paper Co., 112 LA 412 (Chumley, 1999) (combination of jobs valid where combination did not substantially change duties of existing jobs); King County, Wash., 111 LA 312 (Snow, 1998) (noting arbitrators have long recognized that management retains authority over job classifications absent some contractual restriction); Illinois Cement Co., 108 LA 667 (Kossoff, 1997) (employer did not violate contract when it combined operator classification with helper classifications); Lake Erie Screw Corp., 108 LA 15 (Feldman, 1997) (employer did not have right to unilaterally create training position); Houston Lighting & Power Co., 106 LA 1188 (Johnson, 1996) (employer did not violate contract where agreement contains no "work peculiar" clause basing job assignment on classifications); Marmon/Keystone Corp., 106 LA 519 (Franckiewicz, 1996) (combined job treated as newly created position); Port Everglades Auth., 104 LA 65 (Wahl, 1995) (elimination of job not improper where employer may determine the size and composition of its working force); Hyatt Cherry Hill, 103 LA 99 (DiLauro, 1994) (same). See Steel Parts Corp., 93 LA 623 (Stoia, 1989) (employer had right to establish job classifications); Day & Zimmerman, 91 LA 1003, 1006 (Belcher, 1988); Arco Oil & Gas Co., 84 LA 235, 238–40 (Baroni, 1985) (employer had right to change classification where contract language was broad); Hercules Engines, 50 LA 997, 999–1000 (Laybourne, 1968); Vertol Div., 50 LA 624, 631–32 (Buckwalter, 1968) (here the contract did restrict the right); American Sugar Co., 46 LA 91, 94 (Ray, 1966); Hercules Powder Co., 45 LA 448, 450 (Shafer, 1965); Independent Lock Co. of Ala., 36 LA 1392, 1394 (Murphy, 1961); Axelson Mfg. Co., 30 LA 444, 448 (Prasow, 1958); Wyandotte Chem. Corp., 17 LA 697, 700–01 (Platt, 1952); St. Clair Rubber Co., 16 LA 955, 957 (Bowles, 1951); Irvington Varnish & Insulator Co., 8 LA 1041, 1042–43 (Reynolds, 1947). See also Phillips Petroleum Co., 66 LA 941, 942, 944 (Stephens, 1976). Contra as to job classifications (requiring bargaining before their establishment), Armstrong Rubber Co., 18 LA 90, 92 (Donnelly, 1952); General Motors Corp., 7 LA 368, 371 (Griffin, 1947). In some cases the question arises as to what constitutes a "new job." For the answer given in one case, see Allegheny Ludlum Steel Corp., 32 LA 446, 451–52 (Platt & Mittenthal, 1949). See also Wisconsin Dep't of Health & Soc. Servs., 69 LA 842, 846–47 (Sinicropi, 1977); Gulf States Paper Corp., 63 LA 1007, 1010–11 (Bryan, Jr., 1974).

ment prerogative.[273] Under an agreement stating that rates "for any new classifications will be negotiated," management not only had the right but was held to have an implied duty to establish a new classification when the company introduced a new and substantially different machine.[274] Where job classifications are specifically enumerated in the agreement, and especially if the system appears intended to be exclusive, management may not be permitted to establish new classifications unilaterally,[275] but, as noted hereinbelow, many arbitrators have rejected the view that jobs or classifications are frozen by the mere fact that they are mentioned in the agreement.[276]

Arbitrators often have recognized the right of management, unless restricted by the agreement, to eliminate jobs (and where a few duties remain to reallocate them) where improved methods or other production justification exists and management otherwise acts in good faith.[277]

In upholding this right of management to eliminate jobs or classifications, one arbitrator offered the following evaluation:

> The impact of a changing technology upon the work force has posed problems to both management and labor not easy of solution. That this issue has been a persistent and vexing one over the years is indicated by the significant number of arbitration proceedings on this subject dating back to the earliest reported decisions. A review of these decisions reveals that they fall into two

---

[273]Appalachian Reg'l Healthcare, 103 LA 297 (Duff, 1994) (employer did not violate the collective bargaining agreement when it created an in-house bill collector group, rather than hiring an outsider, because the members of the billing clerks bargaining unit had separate and distinct duties from those of the new collectors unit).

[274]Lockheed-Georgia Co., 48 LA 518, 519, 521 (King, 1967).

[275]See Eagle Nest Co., 100 LA 706 (Feldman, 1993) (employer violated contract when it combined classifications); Superior Tube Co., 96 LA 619 (DiLauro, 1990) (employer improperly established new classifications); Pan Am World Servs., 84 LA 1161, 1166 (Bowers, 1985) (reclassification of position violated contract); Menasha Corp., 84 LA 989, 992 (Duff, 1985) (where there is no substantial change in job content, unilateral reclassification is not permitted).

[276]See Container Corp. of Am., 91 LA 329 (Rains, 1988) (wage provision requiring parties' consent to change "hourly rates and job classifications" schedules did not restrict management's right to eliminate job classifications); United States Steel Corp., 85 LA 1026 (Petersen, 1985); Engelhard Indus., 82 LA 680 (Nicholas, Jr., 1984).

[277]Cleveland Elec. Illuminating Co., 105 LA 817 (Franckiewicz, 1995) (employer did not violate collective bargaining agreement when it eliminated jobs, following redesign of internal mail delivery system to achieve greater efficiency); Hyatt Cherry Hill, 103 LA 99 (DiLauro, 1994) (employer, in financial difficulty, did not violate the contract when it eliminated cashier classification and added those duties to food servers without increasing salary, to maintain efficiency of the employees and reallocate their responsibilities in accordance with their abilities); Dresser Indus., 96 LA 1063 (Nicholas, Jr., 1991); Reynolds Metal Co., 95 LA 1243 (Holley, Jr., 1990); Courier Journal, 93 LA 227 (Tharp, 1989) (employer properly placed new video display terminals in advertising department and transferred work to that department); Day & Zimmerman, 91 LA 1003 (Belcher, 1988); Flowers Baking Co. of W. Va., 89 LA 113 (Flannagan, 1987); Morton Thiokol, Inc., 86 LA 1102 (Ipavec, 1986); Bethlehem Steel Corp., 86 LA 880 (Henle, 1986); Union Carbide Agric. Prods. Co., 84 LA 788, 791 (Seinsheimer, 1985); Quaker Oats Co., 84 LA 390 (Edelman, 1985); Formosa Plastics Corp., 83 LA 792 (Taylor, 1984); United States Steel Corp., 82 LA 534 (Jones, Jr., 1984); Roadmaster Corp., 82 LA 225 (Granack, 1983) (employer had right to redesignate job as nonunit position where job bore little resemblance to old position). See Container Corp. of Am., 91 LA 329, 332 (Rains, 1988); Mead Corp., 84 LA 875, 879–81 (Sergent, Jr., 1985); Glenmore Distilleries Co., 80 LA 1043, 1045–46 (McIntosh, 1983); Cerro Gordo Care Facility, 80 LA 11, 13 (Loihl, 1982); Wall Tube & Metal Prods. Co., 77 LA 857, 859–60 (Eyraud, 1981); Illinois-American Water Co., 77 LA 284, 287 (Ross, 1981); Gulf-Western Indus., 62 LA 1132, 1134 (Hutcheson, 1974). For related discussion, see section 16., "Assigning Work Out of the Bargaining Unit," below.

fairly distinct categories which seem noteworthy here: (1) One line of cases emphasizes that where a Collective Bargaining agreement sets forth a comprehensive rate structure, the wage rate established for each classification evidences an agreement between the parties as to the wage rate, as well as the classification; these cases then go on to provide that, in general, the terms of this bargained for exchange may not be unilaterally altered. To the extent that some of these decisions regard the classification structure as being unalterably frozen during the life of the Agreement, they do not represent the weight of arbitration authority. (2) A second group of cases holds that the existence in the Agreement of a negotiated rate structure does not guarantee that the classifications will remain unchanged during the term of the Agreement. The reason advanced for this interpretation is that economic necessity in a competitive market makes it essential that management have the degree of flexibility necessary to adapt the work force to changed conditions. Where arbitrators have upheld management's right to eliminate jobs or classifications and reallocate residual job duties, they have stressed that such changes must be made in good faith, based upon factors such as a change in operations, technological improvements, substantially diminished production requirements, established past practice, etc. It is this second line of cases which appears to reflect the present weight of authority on this issue.[278]

Many arbitrators have spoken in terms of combining jobs or job classifications and have often held that management has the right, where not restricted by the agreement, to combine jobs or job classifications in determining methods of operation.[279] Arbitrators also have held that management has the right, unless restricted by the agreement, to combine jobs or classifications where there is insufficient work in one (or in each) of them for a normal day's work and where excessive workloads do not result from the combination.[280] Likewise, in the absence of contractual restriction, manage-

---

[278]American Cement Corp., 48 LA 72, 76 (Block, 1967). *See also* Western Kraft Paper Group, 76 LA 1129, 1131 (Curry, 1981); Freeport Kaolin Co., 72 LA 738, 739–41 (Vadakin, 1979); Knights of Columbus, 67 LA 334, 337–38 (Holden, Jr., 1976); Yale Univ., 65 LA 435, 437 (Seitz, 1975); Mead Corp., 64 LA 421, 424–25 (Ferguson, 1975); Kraftco Corp., 61 LA 517, 521–23 (Kaplan, 1973); Ethyl Corp., 57 LA 869, 872 (Sembower, 1971); Omaha Cold Storage Terminal, 48 LA 24, 25–32 (Doyle, 1967); Georgia-Pacific Corp., 40 LA 769, 772–74 (Leflar, 1963).

[279]*See* United States Steel Corp., 85 LA 1026 (Petersen, 1985) (employer did not violate contract by combining jobs that were both position-rated jobs in same seniority unit); Cigna Healthplans of Cal., 84 LA 422, 427 (Rothschild, 1985); Hennepin Paper Co., 83 LA 214 (Gallagher, 1984); Amoco Oil Co., 65 LA 577, 581 (Cohen, 1975); Pie-Pacific Intermountain Express, 61 LA 357, 358–59 (Warns, 1973). *See also* Howmet Corp., 63 LA 179, 182 (Forsythe, 1974) (merger of classifications in connection with prohibition against sex discrimination). *But see* Carborundum Co., 41 LA 997, 999 (McIntosh, 1963) (clause freezing classifications was strictly enforced); Shenango, Inc., 41 LA 285, 286–87 (Crawford, 1963) (where contract provided for craft jobs and training programs, management could not combine jobs in such a way as to virtually eliminate the craft system); Continental Oil Co., 39 LA 1058, 1059, 1063–64 (Coffey, 1962).

[280]*See* Container Corp. of Am., 91 LA 329, 331 (Rains, 1988); Oberdorfer Foundries, 66 LA 1069, 1071 (Rill, 1976); United States Steel Corp., 47 LA 1092, 1093 (Florey, 1966); United States Steel Corp., 40 LA 305, 306 (Duff, 1963); Bernheim Distilling Co., 28 LA 441, 443–45 (Kesselman, 1957); Fletcher-Enamel Co., 27 LA 466, 467–68 (Somers, 1956); Central Fibre Prod. Co., 18 LA 216, 217–18 (Kelliher, 1952). *See also* Lukens Steel Co., 37 LA 711, 714–15 (Crawford, 1961); Dayton Malleable Iron Co., 17 LA 666, 668 (Hampton, 1951); American Zinc Co., 16 LA 252, 255–56 (Gilden, 1951); Union Starch & Ref. Co., 15 LA 782, 789–90 (Klamon, 1950). *Cf.* United Wallpaper, 25 LA 188, 190–91 (Sembower, 1955).

ment has been permitted to abolish two job classifications and establish a new classification following technological change in equipment[281] or following a change in products.[282]

B. Interjob and Interclassification Transfer of Duties
[LA CDI 117.334]

Short of eliminating or combining jobs or job classifications, some of the duties of one job or classification sometimes are transferred to another job or classification.[283] At this point, however, the matter is considered primarily (but not exclusively) from the standpoint of the effect of the transfer on workers in the "giving" job or classification.[284]

In a variety of situations the interclassification transfer of work has been upheld where no restriction was found in the agreement (in some instances, the employer's right of action was reinforced by a general management-rights clause).[285] For example, under a contract giving management the right to

---

[281]*See* International Paper Co., 43 LA 1137, 1142 (Marshall, 1964); International Paper Co., 43 LA 1118, 1123–24 (Marshall, 1964); Libby, McNeill, & Libby, 37 LA 466, 467–68 (Cobb, 1961); Mansfield Tire & Rubber Co., 35 LA 434, 436 (Uible, 1960); Great Lakes Carbon Corp., 19 LA 797, 799 (Wettach, 1953). *See also* Leavenworth Times, 71 LA 396, 404 (Bothwell, 1978); Continental Oil Co., 71 LA 185, 190–91 (Towers, 1978) (management had the right to merge departments following equipment change); Triangle Conduit & Cable Corp., 36 LA 1097, 1100 (Blair, 1961); Simoniz Co., 32 LA 115, 116–17 (Fleming, 1959); West Va. Pulp & Paper Co., 15 LA 754, 761 (Copelof, 1950).

[282]Square D Co., 46 LA 39, 43 (Larkin, 1966); Hewitt-Robins, Inc., 30 LA 81, 83–86 (Kates, 1958).

[283]The right of management to require workers in the "receiving" job or classification to perform the work is discussed in section 9.D., "Assignment of Duties and Tasks," below.

[284]Fort James Corp. 113 LA 1089 (Giblin, 2000) (employer has right to reassign employees where contract has no language that restricts it); Johnston-Tom Bigbee Mfg Corp., 113 LA 1015 (Howell, 2000) (employer must show "good cause" to reassign bargaining-unit work); Atlantic City Showboat, 113 LA 530 (Zirkel, 1999) (employer violated contract by reassigning employees contrary to past practice); Alabama Educ. Ass'n, 113 LA 493 (Singer, 1999) (employer did not violate contract, where it has past practice of redistributing duties); GTE-Florida, 112 LA 919 (Frost, 1999) (employer did not violate contract, where reassigning work was caused by technological change); International Paper Co., 112 LA 412 (Chumley, 1999) (employer allowed to eliminate position and spread duties to other jobs); Koch Nitrogen Co., 111 LA 449 (Howell, 1998) (employer has right to combine classifications, where there is insufficient work); Ajax-Superior Plant, 111 LA 155 (Skulina, 1998) (employer violated contract when it eliminated classification by subcontracting part of the classification's job duties and reassigning rest); Finch, Pruyn & Co., 111 LA 1 (Babiskin, 1998) (employer has right to eliminate classification and to reassign job duties); PPG Indus., Inc., 110 LA 966 (Felice, 1998) (employer had right to reassign duties due to introduction of new machinery); Indspec Chem. Corp., 109 LA 161 (Fagan, 1997) (reassignment violated past practice); Washington Teachers Union, 108 LA 821 (Bernhardt, 1997) (employer violated contract when it reclassified secretary, where job duties did not change); I.T.T. Rayonier, 101 LA 865 (Lane, 1993) (transfer of work not improper, where positions were hybrid classification). For important related discussion, see section 15., "Right to Subcontract," and section 16., "Assigning Work Out of the Bargaining Unit," below.

[285]Greif Bros. Corp., 114 LA 554 (Kenis, 2000) (employer did not violate contract when it reassigned duties of eliminated position to newly created position, where contract expressly contemplates changes in job contents and the creation of new jobs when changing conditions and circumstances so require); International Paper Co., 112 LA 412 (Chumley, 1999) (transfer of duties to other positions did not substantially change duties of existing jobs where computers handled statistical calculations that were main function of job); SBS Transit, 112 LA 263, 265 (Graham, 1999) (reclassifying full-time position as part-time position was reasonable, where employer acted in response to business problems); Washington, D.C., Teachers Local 6, 108 LA 821 (Bernhardt, 1997) (employer violated contract when it reclassified

manage the work and direct the workforce and containing no provision expressly prohibiting unilateral changes in job content, one arbitrator held that management could remove from the "oiler's" job the relatively minor tasks of lubricating and cleaning cranes and assign these duties to cranemen, even though these duties were mentioned in the oiler's job description and not in the cranemen's. He added that the union could request reevaluation of the cranemen's job if it believed that the added duties justified a higher rate, but it could not prevent management from making the changes in job content.[286]

Under another contract reserving to the company the right to "manage the plant and direct the working force" and stating that "the usual and customary rights of the employer remain unimpaired," the arbitrator upheld the transfer of certain unskilled and semiskilled work from one classification to another. He explained:

> In part the union relied upon a contention that since the agreement between the parties includes a list of job classifications with the hourly wage rates agreed for the same that none of the duties of any job classification so listed may be essentially changed since this would indirectly at least alter the compensation for work in the designated classification.
>
> The company asserts the position that in the absence of negotiated job descriptions it is within the usual rights, powers and privileges of management to assign duties to one classification and subsequently when efficiency and economy seem to require the same, to take such job duties from a classification which has been discharging them and assign such duties to another classification.
>
> In this connection it must be observed that innumerable unskilled and semi-skilled duties are commonly found in industrial plants to be within the scopes of duties of several job classifications. It is normally regarded as within the prerogatives of management to transfer unskilled or semi-skilled duties which do not characterize or fall within the scope of characteristically high skilled jobs, to one or another group of skilled, semi-skilled or unskilled workers from time to time as convenience and economy within the plant appeared to make it desirable. This is all within the commonly recognized scope of managerial authority and normally under management clauses is recognized to be proper.
> . . .

---

secretary, where job duties did not change); I.T.T. Rayonier, 101 LA 865 (Lane, 1993) (transfer of work not improper where positions were hybrid classification). *See* Schmidt Baking Co., 99 LA 717 (Wahl, 1992) (driver retained after plant closure was properly assigned a route formerly assigned to drivers at a different plant); St. Louis Post-Dispatch, 93 LA 548 (Heinsz, 1989) (reassignment to another bargaining unit permitted, where task was not referred to in jurisdiction clause and was not significant); Iowa-Illinois Gas & Elec. Co., 91 LA 1181 (Volz, 1988) (employer properly transferred work from bargaining-unit electricians to salaried electronic technicians, where electricians' job description did not specifically cover disputed work); Allied Prods. Co., 90 LA 651 (Baroni, 1988) (employer properly told maintenance-department repairmen to use forklift instead of assigning duties to equipment operator, where broad management-rights clause gave employer exclusive right to determine assignments); Century Plaza Hotel, 83 LA 1314 (Kaufman, 1984); Stokely-Van Camp, 83 LA 838 (Nicholas, Jr., 1984); Columbus Jack Corp., 83 LA 797 (Duda, Jr., 1984). The temporary transfer of work (such as on holidays) merely to effect a savings in labor costs was found improper in *Lockheed Aircraft Corp.*, 55 LA 964, 969 (Atwood, 1970); *Aluminum Indus.*, 33 LA 14, 18–19 (Seinsheimer, 1959); *Courtaulds, Inc.*, 32 LA 848, 849–50 (McCoy, 1959). *But see* Lea Indus., 75 LA 1070, 1073 (Foster, 1980); Mead Corp., 61 LA 797, 801 (Marcus, 1973).

[286]National Supply Co., 26 LA 666, 668 (Aaron, Albright, & Clayton, 1956) (the transfer in no way impaired job security).

. . . There can be no doubt that normally in industry generally, the assignment and reassignment of unskilled and semi-skilled duties such as those here involved would be entirely and exclusively within the discretion of management in the absence of a clear, express agreement otherwise.[287]

An arbitrator recognized an "inherent right of management" to take a job that initially or originally may have required a considerable degree of skill and then establish a production line in which this fairly complex job becomes essentially routine and repetitive.[288] In that case, management was permitted to remove the assignment of certain work from skilled workers, who claimed a "proprietary interest" in the work after it had become simplified, and to assign it exclusively to employees in a lower classification. To hold otherwise, he declared, would deny the company the right to operate with the greatest degree of skill and efficiency. He noted that nothing in the contract prevented the company "from using lesser grades of skill on a job if higher grades of skill are wholly unnecessary to perform such jobs."[289]

Where workers in one classification suffer layoff or other adverse consequences as a result of management's transfer of substantial work from their classification to another, arbitrators have sometimes deemed such transfer a violation of the workers' seniority rights where the transfer was not justified by emergency or other such reason.[290] But some arbitrators are unwilling to interpret a seniority clause as a guarantee that the job or classification will remain unchanged. For instance, in upholding the right of management to transfer work from one classification to another where not expressly restricted by the agreement, an arbitrator reasoned:

Seniority protects and secures an employee's rights in relation to the rights of other employees in his seniority group; it does not protect him in relation to the existence of the job itself. By the use of an objective measure, length of service, the rights of one employee are balanced against the other employees' rights.

The rights inherent in seniority do not themselves guarantee the continued existence of the job, or that it shall be maintained without change in content. Seniority can only stand as a bar to changes in job content if the contract so expressly provides, or if it can be shown that the changes are motivated on the part of management by a desire to evade the seniority clause. . . .

While it is certainly true that changes in job content of a classification may adversely affect the job opportunities of the employees involved by reducing the amount of work available to them, the problem is still essentially one of jurisdiction, rather than of seniority. The majority view of arbitrators appears to be that management has the right, if exercised in good faith, to transfer

---

[287]Pure Oil Co., 45 LA 557, 558 (Updegraff, 1965).

[288]McConnell Aircraft Corp., 21 LA 424, 427–28 (Klamon, Sonnemann, & Connors, 1953).

[289]Id. See also General Dynamics Corp., 74 LA 1225, 1228–29 (Brisco, 1980); Modern Bakeries, 39 LA 939, 940–41 (Koven, 1962); Marsh Stencil Mach. Co., 33 LA 1, 4–5 (Klamon, 1959).

[290]See Cleveland Pneumatic Tool Co., 34 LA 743, 750–51 (Dworkin, 1960) (the possibility of future harm sufficed); Enterprise Wheel & Car Corp., 23 LA 196, 199–202 (Livengood, 1954); Robertshaw-Fulton Controls Co., 15 LA 147, 150–51 (Gregory, 1949); Chrysler Corp., 14 LA 163, 164–65 (Ebeling, 1950). See also McDonnell Aircraft Corp., 32 LA 870, 872–73 (Klamon, 1959).

duties from one classification to another, and to change, eliminate, or establish new classifications, unless the agreement specifically restricts this right.[291]

But, speaking in terms of the right of management to transfer work from one seniority unit to another, as opposed to the transfer of work within a seniority unit, some arbitrators hold that management may not do so even though there is no express prohibition in the agreement.[292] Other arbitrators permit management to transfer work from one seniority unit to another where there is no specific restriction in the agreement and the transfer is made in good faith in the interest of efficiency.[293]

On a related issue, an arbitrator held that employees in the original seniority unit need not be offered an opportunity to follow work to a new location unless the work transferred constituted the essence of the jobs in question.[294]

C. Jurisdictional Disputes [LA CDI 7.15]

A jurisdictional dispute has been defined as either a controversy concerning whether particular work must be performed by workers in one bargaining unit as opposed to workers in another bargaining unit, or a controversy over which union should represent employees performing particular work.[295] Most frequently, the issue involves the determination of which group of workers has the exclusive right to perform certain work or to fill particular jobs.[296] One commentator has described the significance of work jurisdiction controversies to labor organizations in these terms:[297]

---

[291]Reynolds Metals Co., 25 LA 44, 48–49 (Prasow, 1955). *See also* Safeway Stores, 73 LA 207, 215 (Goodman, 1979); Kimberly-Clark Corp., 40 LA 259, 262 (Hon, 1963); E.I. DuPont de Nemours & Co., 39 LA 496, 499–500 (Holly, 1962); American Sugar Ref. Co., 38 LA 714, 717 (Quinlan, 1961); Fabricon Prods., 35 LA 63, 66 (Prasow, 1960); Lockheed Aircraft Corp., 33 LA 357, 359–60 (Warns, 1959) (also suggesting that jobs "tailor-made" to the company's requirements are more subject to unilateral change than traditional craft jobs); Reynolds Mining Corp., 33 LA 25, 28–29 (Bauder, 1959); Bakelite Co., 29 LA 555, 557 (Updegraff, 1957); Goodyear Tire & Rubber Co., 28 LA 374, 376–77 (Thompson, 1957); Ludowici-Celadon Co., 25 LA 897, 899 (Uible, 1955); Wyandotte Chem. Corp., 17 LA 697, 700–01 (Platt, 1952).

[292]Lukens Steel Co., 15 LA 408, 411–12 (D'Andrade, 1950). In general accord, though applying a de minimis exception, *United States Steel Corp.*, 35 LA 832, 835 (Shipman, 1960). *See also* Kelly-Springfield Tire Co., 72 LA 742, 746 (LeWinter, 1979); O'Keefe & Merritt Co., 63 LA 202, 206–07 (Sullivan, 1974); D. Schreiber Cheese Co., 44 LA 873, 877 (Anderson, 1965); Allegheny Ludlum Steel Corp., 40 LA 742, 749–53 (Seitz, 1963); R. Wallace & Sons Mfg. Co., 23 LA 776, 778–79 (Myers, 1954). *Cf.* Taft Broad. Co. of Pa., 68 LA 1379, 1382 (Lubow, 1977).

[293]Douglas & Lomason Co., 23 LA 691, 695 (Bowles, 1954). *Accord* FMC Corp., 70 LA 110, 113 (Shister, 1978); General Cable Co., 40 LA 865, 865–66 (Cahn, 1963); Blaw-Knox Co., 33 LA 828, 829–30 (Kelliher, 1959). *See also* Anchor Hocking Corp., 80 LA 1267, 1274–75 (Abrams, 1983); Allegheny Ludlum Steel Corp., 66 LA 596, 597 (Dybeck, 1976); Ceco Corp., 49 LA 234, 236–37 (Daugherty, 1967); United States Steel Co., 36 LA 273, 276, 280 (Crawford, 1960); United States Steel Corp., 35 LA 541, 543 (Garrett, 1960); Fabricon Prods., 35 LA 63, 66 (Prasow, 1960); Bethlehem Supply Co., 25 LA 366, 368 (Springfield & Seward, 1955).

[294]Bethlehem Steel Corp., 86 LA 880 (Henle, 1986).

[295]Carey v. Westinghouse Elec. Corp., 375 U.S. 261, 263, 55 LRRM 2042 (1964).

[296]General Elec. Corp., 16 LA 554 (Wilcox, 1951).

[297]Boilermakers, 106 LA 49 (Bankston, 1996).

Few concepts have been so significant in the historical development of the American labor movement as that of jurisdiction. Traditionally, jurisdiction has been as important to a union as territory has been to a nation; it constitutes the job boundary line within which or the work territory over which the union has "sovereign" rights. As long as other unions recognize and respect its jurisdiction, a union possesses a monopoly of organizing and administering the work and workers defined by that jurisdiction. It has posted "no poaching" signs over certain kinds of work or clusters of jobs, and other unions have observed its exclusive rights. If another union contests its job boundaries and invades its work territory by organizing workers of the given characteristics, it is as though a nation had invaded the territory of a neighboring state. Jurisdictional conflict ensues.[298]

The jurisdictional fight always encompasses one or more labor unions, and the employer may prefer to assign the work to members of one union to the exclusion of all other employees or have the discretion to assign the work to any employee regardless of the bargaining units. Sometimes, the employer simply wants to be told who can perform the work without any risk of fomenting a grievance from other workers.

i. Allocation of Responsibility for Settling Jurisdictional Disputes Between the NLRB and the Arbitral Forum [LA CDI 7.15; 94.553]

Even though the NLRB has jurisdiction to decide employee representation issues,[299] a jurisdictional dispute can be resolved under the grievance-arbitration procedure of a collective bargaining contract.

The NLRB's jurisdiction arises under Section 8(b)(4)(D) of the LMRA, making it an unfair labor practice for a union to engage in a strike to force an employer "to assign particular work to employees in a particular labor organization . . . ."[300] The Supreme Court, in *Carey v. Westinghouse Electric Corp.*,[301] held that arbitrating a jurisdictional dispute is not contrary to the administrative regulatory scheme because a union contesting the employer's assignment of work should not have to force the controversy to a work stoppage to obtain a remedy.[302] The Court further suggested that the persuasive weight of the arbitration opinion might be great enough to cause the NLRB to defer to the arbitration award.[303]

---

[298]*Id.* at 53 (quoting CHAMBERLAIN, THE LABOR SECTOR 94–95 (1965)).

[299]*Carey*, 375 U.S. at 271–72.

[300]29 U.S.C. §158 (b)(4)(D).

[301]375 U.S. 261, 55 LRRM 2042 (1964).

[302]*Id.* at 264. In *Carey*, the employer refused to arbitrate a grievance, brought by the union representing production employees, alleging that the company violated the collective bargaining agreement by assigning certain work to technical employees represented by another union. The Court disagreed with the employer's contention that the NLRB had exclusive jurisdiction over the dispute.

[303]*Id.* Two commentators observed that *Carey* simply extended the principle that federal preemption is inapplicable to the enforcement of collective bargaining agreements. Smith & Jones, *The Supreme Court and Labor Dispute Arbitration: The Emerging Federal Law*, 63 MICH L. REV. 751, 770 (1965).

But, under the provisions of which contract should the arbitration be held? When a union grieves an employer's decision to assign work to members of another union and the arbitration is held under the auspices of the grieving union's contract, the union whose members are performing the disputed work may not participate in the arbitration and that union's agreement may not be properly before the arbitrator. If the grieving union prevails and the employer reassigns the work, the employer may have to defend a grievance brought by the union representing the employees who lost the work. In the worst-case scenario, two unions could separately and successfully grieve and arbitrate under their respective agreements. The employer then is confronted with conflicting arbitration decisions ordering it to exclusively assign the work to members of both unions.[304] The Court, in *Carey*, acknowledged this dilemma, stating that when the union to which the work was assigned declines to intervene, the arbitration decision may not fully and finally resolve the dispute because the nonparticipating union would not be bound by the arbitrator's holding.[305] Despite this dilemma, the Court concluded that the arbitrator still has jurisdiction to decide the substance of the work jurisdictional dispute between and among the participating parties.[306] Because the arbitrator's award may adversely affect a nonparticipating party,[307] it is obviously preferable to convene a trilateral (or multilateral) arbitration.[308] In a dispute where each of five unions sought to have the disputed work exclusively assigned to its members, the district court ordered an arbitration proceeding that bound all five unions.[309] In the railroad industry, an arbitration tribunal is required by the RLA to notify another craft union and permit the union to participate in the arbitration when one union is claiming work that members of the other craft perform.[310]

Since *Carey*, arbitrators have decided jurisdictional disputes based on the grievance brought by the union asserting a right to perform the disputed work, even though the union whose members are performing the disputed work chooses not to participate in the arbitration.[311]

ii. Factors Utilized to Resolve Jurisdictional Disputes [LA CDI 7.15]

When deciding if a union involved in a jurisdictional dispute had committed an unfair labor practice under Section 8(b)(4)(D), the NLRB originally concentrated its analysis on its own certification findings and the terms of the collective bargaining agreement. However, the Supreme Court held

---

[304]The International Brotherhood of Teamsters and the International Association of Machinists and Aerospace Workers successfully prosecuted grievances over the assignment of aircraft cleaning work so that an airline was presented with orders that it exclusively assign the work to Teamsters and exclusively assign the work to Machinists. A district court ordered all three parties (employer, Teamsters, and Machinists) to arbitrate the dispute, *de novo*, in a trilateral arbitration proceeding. Braniff Airways, 79 LA 383 (Sisk, 1982).

[305]Carey v. Westinghouse Elec. Corp., 375 U.S. 261, 265, 55 LRRM 2042 (1964).

[306]*Id.*

[307]Smith & Jones, 63 Mich L. Rev., at 772.

[308]*Id.* at 774.

[309]Union Camp Corp., 61 LA 1305 (Foster, 1974).

[310]45 U.S.C. §§151, 153 First (j).

[311]CF Motor Freight, 110 LA 186 (Murphy, 1997); National Steel & Shipbuilding Co., 56 LA 353 (Block, 1971).

that the NLRB analysis was too narrow and directed the NLRB to consider other criteria, such as past practice and industry customs, to determine which of two or more employee groups had the right to perform the disputed work.[312] In response, the NLRB formulated the following seven factors that were to be considered on a case-by-case basis in the adjudication of jurisdictional disputes:[313]

1. the skills and work involved;
2. NLRB certifications;
3. company and industry past practices;
4. agreements between unions and agreements between employers and unions;
5. awards of arbitrators, joint boards, and the AFL-CIO in similar or identical cases;
6. the assignment of work made by the employer; and
7. the efficient and safe operation of the employer's business.[314]

The list of factors is nonexclusive, and the weight to be given any of them depends on the record made in each case.

The U.S. Court of Appeals for the Second Circuit agreed with the NLRB that jurisdictional disputes are best decided on a case-by-case basis, but suggested that the NLRB give precedential weight to past decisions in order to impart more predictability into its adjudications.[315]

iii. *Disputes Resolved Under the AFL-CIO Constitution*
[LA CDI 7.051]

As part of its antiraiding prohibition, Article XX of the AFL-CIO Constitution establishes an internal disputes plan to resolve disputes when two or more affiliated unions seek the exclusive right to perform the same work. Article XX provides that each union shall respect the "established work relationship" of every other affiliated union and defines an "established work relationship" as work that members of a union customarily have performed.[316]

---

[312]NLRB v. Radio & Television Broad. Eng'rs (Columbia Broad. Sys.), 364 U.S. 573, 47 LRRM 2332 (1961).

[313]Machinists Lodge 1743 (J.A. Jones Constr. Co.), 135 NLRB 1402, 49 LRRM 1684 (1962). The NLRB announced that it would not promulgate any rules for making jurisdictional awards. It would use the factors on a case-by-case basis.

[314]*Id.* The NLRB relied heavily on the fifth factor, following the precedential rulings by the AFL-CIO that had adjudged that the operation of electric cranes in factories belonged to electricians, rather than machinists.

[315]NLRB v. Teamsters Local 584 (Hertz Corp.), 535 F.2d 205, 92 LRRM 2486 (2d Cir. 1976).

[316]AFL-CIO CONST. art. XX, §3 reads:

(a) Each affiliate shall respect the established work relationship of every other affiliate. For purposes of this Article, an "established work relationship" shall be deemed to exist as to any work of the kind that the members of an organization have customarily performed at a particular plant or worksite, whether their employer is the plant operator, a contractor, or other employer. No affiliate shall by agreement or collusion with any employer or by the exercise of economic pressure seek to obtain work for its members as to which an established work relationship exists with any other affiliate, except with the consent of such affiliate.

(b) This section shall not be applicable to work in the railroad industry.

Section 3 specifically forbids a union from colluding with an employer or invoking economic pressure to obtain work for its members that is subject to such an established work relationship with another affiliated union.[317] Section 20 provides that the plan is "the sole and exclusive method for settlement and determination" of such disputes, and an affiliated union is barred from pursuing a judicial remedy.[318] Finally, Section 2 prohibits an affiliated union from attempting to represent employees with whom "an established collective bargaining relationship exists with any other affiliate."[319]

Arbitrators have applied the Article XX standard. Thus, in one case, custodians at a building had been represented by the Service Employees International Union (SEIU) for many years. Another employer obtained the building maintenance contract and, in accordance with its collective bargaining agreement, recognized the Laborers' International Union of North America (LIUNA) as the representative of the building custodians. The arbitrator found that the evidence of a successorship (rather than accretion) was strong because the nature and location of the work and most of the workforce remained the same. He therefore concluded that the custodial work at the building must continue to be recognized as a separate, viable bargaining unit, and LIUNA had breached Article XX, Section 2 of the AFL-CIO Constitution.[320]

Many arbitrations under Article XX, Section 3 turn on the existence or lack of an established work relationship. The kind of work that members of a union historically and customarily have performed gives rise to an established work relationship.[321] The nature of the work, rather than the tools used to perform the work, generally is considered more significant in determining which group of workers customarily performed certain work. Thus, it was held by one arbitrator that even though carpenters had operated a machine to cut plastic for 6 years, they did not have a right to operate the machine when the employer expanded the tool's use to cut metal, because boilermakers had historically performed metal-cutting tasks.[322]

In another case, the demarcation of work in a mega-grocery store between employees represented by the Bakery, Confectionery, and Tobacco Workers International Union and retail clerks represented by the United Food and Commercial Workers (UFCW) was set by analyzing the usual skills and duties of each group. When the grocery store closed a scratch-type baking operation and inaugurated a bake-off (sales) operation, the Bakery Workers sought to represent individuals in the bake-off system. The arbitrator found that clerks historically performed bake-off tasks in grocery stores, while bakers historically performed scratch-type bakery functions in grocery stores, and therefore awarded the work to the clerks.[323] In a similarly reasoned opin-

---

[317]*Id.*

[318]*Id.* §20.

[319]*Id.* §2.

[320]Service Employees, 103 LA 799 (Lesnick, 1994).

[321]Machinists Lodge 1862, 55 LA 1174 (Kleeb, 1970) (Boilermakers violated article XX, §3 by threatening to strike to obtain the right to operate furnaces when employees represented by the Machinists had customarily operated plant furnaces).

[322]Boilermakers, 106 LA 49 (Bankston, 1996).

[323]Bakery, Confectionary & Tobacco Workers, 90 LA 752 (Lesnick, 1987).

ion, another arbitrator held that a baking operation that integrates bakery production with bakery goods sales can also accrete to the UFCW-represented clerks.[324]

When the employer introduces technological innovations or a new method of performing work, two unions may argue over the assignment of the work, especially when the new system results in the elimination of duties for the members of one or both unions. When, in one case, a newspaper implemented a new photoengraving and platemaking process (the Grace Letterflex system) and assigned the work to photoengravers represented by the Graphic Arts International Union (GAIU), the International Printing and Graphic Communications Union alleged that the Grace Letterflex system should have been assigned to its stereotypers. The arbitrator held that the work was customarily performed by photoengravers, albeit not by the new methodology. The arbitrator relied on the GAIU collective bargaining agreement that contained language that the photoengraving processes and new photoengraving systems, however evolved, constitute work that must be assigned to photoengravers.[325]

When, in another case, television stations started using videotape, an arbitrator had to decide whether editing videotape was work belonging to technicians represented by the International Brotherhood of Electrical Workers (IBEW) or employees represented by the International Alliance of Theatrical Stage Employees, Moving Picture Technicians, Arts, and Allied Crafts (IATSE). The latter claimed the work, arguing that videotape editing was a substitute for motion picture film work, which work was expressly mentioned in the IATSE agreement. The arbitrator held that videotape was a development of magnetic sound and picture tape, the editing of which had been historically handled by IBEW technicians.[326] The same arbitrator had previously ruled that film-editing work accrued to IATSE members when IATSE had an established work relationship with regard to technicians and editing employees who performed such editing work at affiliated companies.[327]

iv. Jurisdictional Disputes Between Crafts [LA CDI 7.15]

As one arbitrator observed: "The issue in a representation case continues to be: who should be represented by whom? The issue in a jurisdictional dispute case is: who should do a particular job? . . . [and] nothing in a representation case can answer the question of the meaning of the Contract . . . ."[328] Another arbitrator similarly declared that, while the boundaries of the bargaining unit fix voting rights, they do not presumptively determine a craft's

---

[324]Food & Commercial Workers, 90 LA 660 (Lesnick, 1987). The NLRB ruled that the bakery department where baked goods were produced and sold was a separate bargaining unit from the rest of the grocery store. The UFCW prevailed in a representation election. The losing Bakery, Confectionery & Tobacco Workers Union sought to represent the baking department employees through the article XX procedures.

[325]International Printing & Graphics Communications Union, 64 LA 897 (Cole, 1974).

[326]Theatrical Stage Employees, 65 LA 333 (Kleeb, 1975) (the arbitrator noted that IATSE waited 6 years before bringing the claim that its members have a right to edit videotape).

[327]Theatrical Stage Employees, 56 LA 148 (Kleeb, 1970).

[328]General Elec. Corp., 16 LA 554, 558 (Wilcox, 1951).

jurisdiction over work.[329] Because representation is not dispositive concerning who performs the work, the language of the agreement and any past practice thereunder must be looked to in order to resolve the dispute.

The language in the collective bargaining agreements (and/or agreements among unions) is the starting point for resolving craft jurisdictional disputes.

Where an agreement specifically refers to the work issue, arbitrators find this factor to be controlling. For example, when an Internation Union of Operating Engineer's agreement specifically alluded to the disputed work, and the scope clause in the International Brotherhood of Teamsters's agreement did not mention it, the company was held to have improperly assigned the work to members of the Teamsters.[330]

In another case, the International Association of Machinists and Aerospace Workers (IAM) alleged that the company violated its agreement by assigning employees represented by the IBEW to operate a new tool to clean, install, and replace quartz lamps, and to polish quartz lamp protector shields. The tool and dye workers, represented by the IAM, had used the new tool in its experimental stage, but the electrical workers were permanently assigned the tool. The arbitrator found no violation, because the IBEW classification of work rule specifically described the type of work in dispute and so the company had ultimately assigned the work to the correct craft.[331]

Arbitrators concur that if the agreement language is unclear, ambiguous, or silent, then a past practice controls the outcome of the dispute. So under a general scope clause in a railroad collective bargaining agreement, a union must establish that its members had exclusively performed the disputed work in the past to successfully claim the work.[332] In another case, the arbitrator found that a clear past practice that revealed that electricians, rather than plumbers, invariably performed the particular pipework in question "trumped" the vaguely drafted "scope clause" in the contract.[333]

Conversely, when the evidence evinced a blurred line between journeymen's work (employees represented by the IAM) and helpers' work (employees represented by the International Union of Mine, Mill, and Smelters Workers), the arbitrator concluded that the IAM failed to offer sufficient proof of a past practice showing that journeymen had previously performed the work to the exclusion of helpers.[334]

In the absence of clear provisions in the agreement or a well-entrenched past practice, arbitrators consider a variety of other factors to resolve craft jurisdictional disputes. To illustrate, at a construction site, the IBEW and

---

[329]International Minerals & Chem. Corp., 16 LA 372 (Abernathy, 1951).

[330]Cooper T. Smith Stevedoring Co., 84 LA 94 (Baroni, 1984) (although the agreement covered the disputed work, the arbitrator also commented that a past practice manifested that Operating Engineers had traditionally performed the work). *But see* Inspiration Consol. Copper Co., 85 LA 1147 (Rothschild, 1985) (the company's need for more efficient operations justified a deviation from the past practice of assigning the disputed work).

[331]McDonnell Douglas Corp., 85 LA 848 (Gibson, 1985).

[332]Machinists, National Railroad Arbitration Board (NRAB) Award No. 12783 (Fletcher, 1994). However, a positions and work scope rule that gives railroad craft workers a right to the work once the work is assigned to the craft will take precedence, even if other employees have performed the work in the past. Railway Clerks, NRAB Award No. 149 (LaRocco, 1988).

[333]General Elec. Corp., 166 LA 554 (Wilcox, 1951).

[334]U.S. Potash, 12 LA 534 (Abernathy, 1949).

Operating Engineers disagreed about which workers could operate cable installation machinery. The arbitrator divided the work between the two crafts based on the type of work traditionally performed by each craft.[335]

In the absence of other considerations, a management-rights clause may give the employer the prerogative to assign the disputed work to either craft,[336] and a "strong" management-rights clause may permit the employer to change work assignments despite a drastic adverse affect on the bargaining unit losing the work. In one case, for economic reasons, the company removed railroad tracks and began using trucks to haul ore that previously had been transported by train. The company assigned the new truck-driving jobs to employees represented by the Mine, Mill, and Smelters Workers, precipitating the layoff of about 80 percent of the employees in the bargaining unit represented by the Brotherhood of Railroad Trainmen. The arbitrator concluded that, because the scope clause in the Trainmen's agreement referred only to railroad jobs such as engineers, firemen, and hostlers, the unusually strong management-rights clause vested the company with the discretion to assign the truck-driving duties to employees other than trainmen.[337]

"Safety" and "efficiency" may be deemed dispositive factors. When the IAM claimed that work, consisting of the inspection of mechanical devices, currently performed by Teamsters, must be assigned to IAM-represented employees, the arbitrator found that efficient operations, and most importantly, safety in plant operations, justified assigning the disputed work to machinists.[338]

Other criteria resorted to in order to adjudicate craft jurisdictional disputes include whether the disputed work involved a skill central to the traditional skills of the members of the grieving union, whether the company had an intent or motive to denigrate contractual rights, whether the employees represented by the grieving union suffered any economic loss, and whether the work assignment was permanent or brief in duration.[339]

Of course, precedent may be found dispositive. Thus, when the Brotherhood of Maintenance of Way Employees grieved that the work of cutting and removing brush and trees along the railroad's right of way had been assigned improperly to signalmen represented by the Brotherhood of Railroad Signalmen, the arbitration board followed prior arbitration decisions that had held that brush cutting generally belongs to maintenance of way employees unless the brush or trees interfere with signal lines, in which case the work belongs to signalmen.[340] Presumably, if either union had been dissatisfied with these arbitral precedents, the union could have pressed for specific language in the negotiations for the next collective bargaining agreement to cover the disputed work.

---

[335]Operating Eng'rs, 36 LA 1285 (Goldberg, 1961) (Operating Engineers operated machinery to dig trenches for cable; Electrical Workers operated machinery that actually handled the cable).

[336]Continental Oil Corp., 32 LA 668 (Hoel, 1959).

[337]Kennecott Copper Corp., 41 LA 651 (Gorsuch, 1963).

[338]CF Motor Freight, 110 LA 186 (Murphy, 1997).

[339]National Steel & Shipbuilding Co., 56 LA 353 (Block, 1971).

[340]Maintenance of Way Employes, NRAB Award No. 35529 (Benn, 2001) (the company also contended that it assigned the disputed work to signalmen due to an emergency, but the arbitration board found that no genuine emergency occurred).

Where the contract unequivocally provides that an arbitrator cannot decide a jurisdictional dispute, the arbitrator must dismiss a union's grievance alleging that its members are entitled to perform the disputed work.[341]

In the railroads, the shopcraft unions are parties to a special agreement requiring the leaders of the unions to attempt to resolve a jurisdictional dispute before any union brings a grievance, and a failure to comply with this procedure warrants dismissal of any union's grievance over work assignments.[342]

v. Jurisdictional Disputes Between Industrial Unions [LA CDI 7.15]

The collective bargaining agreements governing employees performing unskilled or semiskilled work usually do not contain precise descriptions of covered work, and so the past practice is said to be the most important factor in resolving jurisdictional disputes.

For example, in one case, an arbitrator decided that an employer had breached its agreement with the Allied Industrial Workers of America when the company assigned the work of shuttling trailers between the storage area and the driveway lot to transportation drivers represented by the Teamsters because the evidence showed that, in the past, plant workers had performed shuttle service.[343] In another case, an employer had always utilized a helper from another bargaining unit to assist garbage truck operators in loading trash. The uninterrupted past practice necessitated assigning the loading work to the helper even after the employer purchased a new dumpster truck.[344]

However, where a union expressly agreed to relinquish certain elements of a work process that its members traditionally had performed (in exchange for job security terms), the union could not later claim that the entire work process belonged to employees represented by that union.[345]

The location where work traditionally had been performed or the geographical layout of the employer's operation can determine the outcome of a jurisdictional dispute. In one case, employees represented by the IAM historically had operated forklifts and other devices to move materials within the company's warehouse. When the company opened a new warehouse in a separate building, a dispute developed between the IAM and the truck drivers (members of the Teamsters) over who had a right to haul materials between the two warehouses. The arbitrator characterized the two warehouses as a single, integrated storage system so that transporting materials between

---

[341]Walt Disney Prods., 66 LA 1060 (Gentile, 1976). Presumably, a contract term depriving any arbitrator of jurisdiction compels the grieving union to utilize the AFL-CIO internal disputes plan.

[342]Sheet Metal Workers, NRAB Award No. 11070 (Briggs, 1986); Railway Carmen/TCU, NRAB Award No. 12232 (Simon, 1992).

[343]Fruehauf Trailer Co., 40 LA 360 (Childs, 1963). See also Braniff Airways, 79 LA 383 (Sisk, 1982) (the past practice delineated a difference between aircraft cleaning work and tidying-up duties).

[344]Radio Corp. of Am., 43 LA 762 (Dunau, 1964).

[345]Albany Int'l Engineered Fabrics, 102 LA 1127 (Briggs, 1994).

the two buildings was akin to moving materials within a warehouse, which meant the work belonged to the IAM-represented employees.[346]

In another warehouse case, a brewery constructed a new loading dock, precipitating a dispute between the Teamsters and the Brewery Workers over which union's members would operate forklifts on the dock. The Brewery Workers had previously performed loading work inside the plant. Inasmuch as the new loading dock was outside the plant, the Teamsters union was found to have the stronger claim to the work because their members had always performed tasks outside the plant, although not this particular task.[347]

vi. Jurisdictional Disputes Between Craft Unions and Industrial Unions [LA CDI 7.15]

Arbitrators look first to the provisions of the collective bargaining agreements entered into with the employer by each of the contesting unions to determine jurisdictional disputes. For example, when the IAM collective bargaining agreement expressly provided that all production and maintenance work was within the exclusive province of production employees[348] but the employer assigned production work requiring little skill to perform to craft workers represented by the IBEW, the arbitrator decided that the production workers held the sole right to perform the disputed work.

Similarly, when a hotel assigned housekeeping employees represented by the Hotel Employees and Restaurant Employees International Union to operate a name-tag imprinting machine that an engineer or apprentice represented by the Operating Engineers had operated for several years (although employees other than engineers had initially operated the machine), the arbitrator held that the broad management-rights clause gave the hotel the right to make a good faith transfer of the work assignment, and further that operating the name-tag imprinter was not craft work because the housekeeping employees were able to learn how to operate the machine very quickly.[349]

One arbitrator observed, in an early jurisdictional controversy between the Longshoremen's Union and the Waterfront Employees Association over checking lumber, that when neither of the union's collective bargaining agreements referred to the disputed work, the past practice controls. There the past practice gave the employer the flexibility of assigning the checking work to either group.[350]

---

[346]Olin Corp., 67 LA 465 (Brown, 1976).

[347]Theodore Hamm Brewing Co., 34 LA 698 (Kinyon, 1960) (the employer remained neutral, wanting only to know which group of workers had a right to perform the work; the arbitrator also relied on the so-called "Chicago Agreement" drawing the work jurisdictional line at the brewery building; all inside work went to the Brewery Workers and all outside work went to the Teamsters).

[348]Westinghouse Elec. Corp., 12 LA 462 (Wyckoff, 1949).

[349]Century Plaza Hotel, 83 LA 1314 (Kaufman, 1984) (the hotel transferred the work because making name tags was a low priority in the engineering department resulting in delays in producing tags; the task became the top priority for the housekeeping employees).

[350]Waterfront Employers of the Pac. Coast & Portland, 6 LA 565 (Kerr, 1947).

Work that is normally classified as industrial work can be incidental to the duties of craft employees. In one case, the employer assigned carpenters to drive a truck about 500 yards from the carpentry shop to a greenhouse, take measurements at the greenhouse, return to the shop via truck, collect necessary materials, and drive the truck back to the greenhouse with materials to weatherproof the greenhouse. The arbitrator rejected the Teamsters' claim that the truck-driving work belonged to its members by ruling that driving the truck and hauling the materials were incidental to the customary duties of carpenters.[351]

Sometimes a change in circumstances can justify the transfer of work from one bargaining unit to another. For many years, an employee dubbed "the fire marshal" in the Pipefitters' bargaining unit inspected fire extinguishers during the day shift. Apparently, there was not a fire marshal position on the second or third shifts. The advent of new workplace safety regulations mandated by the OSH Act led the company to assign production workers, represented by the Insulation Production Workers Union, to ascertain if fire extinguishers were operable during the second and third shifts. If they discovered an inoperable extinguisher, they brought the unit to the fire marshal's station for repair. The arbitrator decided that the work of determining whether or not a fire extinguisher was operable required no skill or experience, did not result in the loss of the fire marshal's position, and did not infringe on the traditional skills of pipefitters.[352]

Other circumstances such as the introduction of automated equipment, which renders obsolete the necessity of having a specialized skill to perform the work, can justify the transfer of work from a craft unit to a unit of semi-skilled employees.[353]

vii. Public-Sector Jurisdictional Disputes in the Public Sector
[LA CDI 7.15; 100.020301]

There are few reported decisions involving work jurisdictional disputes among public employee unions or between a public-sector and a private-sector union in a governmental workplace.[354] In a work assignment dispute between school custodians and school electricians, the SEIU and IBEW resolved the controversy via the AFL-CIO internal disputes plan.[355] However, the same criteria considered in private-sector cases are likely to be relied on by arbitrators when deciding jurisdictional disputes in public employment.

---

[351]ACS, 111 LA 566 (Kilroy, 1998) (the arbitrator also noted that the Teamsters had never before complained when the carpenters drove trucks during the course of their normal duties).
[352]Owens-Corning Fiberglas Corp., 61 LA 448 (Doyle, 1973).
[353]Des Moines Register, 115 LA 894 (Wolff, 2001).
[354]Jurisdictional disputes at public building construction sites involve private-sector employees.
[355]Service Employees Local 208 (Hammond, Ind., Sch. Sys.), 55 LA 28 (Kleeb, 1970).

D. Assignment of Duties and Tasks

i. *Management Discretion* [LA CDI 100.08; 117.331]

In general, management is permitted to exercise much more discretion in assigning individual duties and tasks to workers than it is permitted in assigning workers to regular jobs. While the assignment of workers to regular jobs often requires the observance of contractual "seniority" and "fitness and ability" considerations,[356] collective bargaining agreements much less frequently contain direct restrictions on the right of management to assign duties and tasks to workers.[357] Thus, in the latter regard, arbitrators have held that, unless the agreement provides otherwise, employees are not en-

---

[356]*See* Allied Healthcare Prods., 113 LA 992 (Marino, 2000) (maintenance employees not entitled to do work done by engineers); Allied Signal, 113 LA 124 (Thornell, 1999) (employee not entitled to specific work, where job description is ambiguous and past practice conflicting); Matanuska Elec. Ass'n, 111 LA 596 (Landau, 1998) (job descriptions did not establish exclusive right to perform function); Peabody Coal Co., 111 LA 308 (West, 1998) (employer did not violate contract, by eliminating job and giving duties to driver); AGCO Corp., 111 LA 296 (Stallworth, 1998) (employer did not violate contract where it assigned overtime to checker not inspector); Kokomo Gas & Fuel Co., 108 LA 1056 (Imundo, Jr., 1997) (employer did not violate contract when supervisor performed work, where work did not displace employee regularly assigned to do the job); MidAmerican Energy Co., 108 LA 1003 (Jacobowski, 1997) (employer did not violate contract when it assigned work to mechanics even though technicians had traditionally done that work where contract obligates both parties to efficiency); Quanex Corp., 108 LA 841 (House, 1997) (employer violated contract, where it left job vacant in three-person operation); Greif Bros. Corp., 108 LA 818 (Harlan, 1997) (employer violated contract when it allowed supervisor to perform bargaining-unit work); Farmland Indus., 108 LA 363 (Pelofsky, 1997) (contract did not limit employer's right to assign trained personnel outside the department); Butte, Mont., Sch. Dist. No. 1, 108 LA 265 (Prayzich, 1997) (contract not violated by reassignment to less favorable job); Rheem Mfg. Co., 108 LA 193 (Woolf, 1997) (reassignment to lower grade job upheld); ITT Higbie Baylok, 108 LA 178 (Duda, Jr., 1997) (employer did not violate contract, where it required operators rather than setup employees to set up line where there were no written job descriptions); Northwest Ind. Symphony Soc'y, 106 LA 185 (Nathan, 1996) (management has right to determine job content, where it has right to determine nature of activities); City of Orange, Tex., 103 LA 1121 (Nicholas, Jr., 1994) (duties improperly assigned, where the contract states working conditions to remain unchanged); Albertson's, Inc., 103 LA 793 (Peck, 1994) (arbitrator not to determine classification, where contract provides that employer will judge qualifications); Servicemaster Co., 103 LA 411 (McGury, 1994) (restructuring proper where contract has no limitation on work performed); North Pittsburgh Tel. Co., 101 LA 931 (Garrett, 1993) (substantial change of duties improper); White-New Idea Farm Equip. Co., 101 LA 461 (High, 1993) (unit work properly assigned to management employees as result of technological change); Caterpillar, Inc., 101 LA 372 (Daniel, 1993) (duty improperly assigned to nonunit employee); Youngstown Hosp. Ass'n, 88 LA 251 (DiLeone, 1986). *See also* Chapter 14, "Seniority."

[357]*See* Frito-Lay, 93 LA 48, 54 (Creo, 1989) (employer properly introduced hand-held computers to be used by driver-salesmen, where contract reserved to management the right to "improve sales methods, operations or conditions"); Ralston Purina Co., 85 LA 1 (Cohen, 1985) (no contract violation, where employees are assigned to do two jobs simultaneously); Otis Elevator Co., 84 LA 1260, 1264 (Heinsz, 1985) (employer upheld in not assigning employee to do overtime work); Associated Elec. Coop., 84 LA 1020, 1025 (Penfield, 1985); Litton Sys., 84 LA 273, 276–77 (Marcus, 1985) (no contract violation, where assignments to employees outside department do not result in loss of work opportunities to department personnel); Lake Erie Screw Corp., 84 LA 175 (Dworkin, 1985); Stokely-Van Camp, 83 LA 838 (Nicholas, Jr., 1984).

titled to exercise their seniority to select the duties or machines that they particularly prefer within their classification.[358]

In one case, an arbitrator, speaking of hourly rated employees, observed that "it is assumed throughout industry that the employer has the general right to make reasonable changes from time to time in the job duties of every individual. The employer may decrease or increase the duties as long as the total work load remains in reasonable bounds."[359] This broad right of management in the assignment of duties and tasks is evidenced by numerous other arbitration cases, in some of which the right was reinforced by a general management-rights clause.[360]

Certainly, where jobs are classified by titles (if formally classified at all) but the parties have not negotiated a detailed description of job content, management will be permitted wide authority to assign any work that is of the same general type as, or is reasonably related to, or is incidental to, the regular duties of the job.[361] However, a change in job duties by adding work

---

[358]*See* Michigan Consol. Gas Co., 42 LA 385, 388 (Howlett, 1964); Day & Zimmerman, 41 LA 502, 506 (Burris, 1963); Republic Steel Corp., 37 LA 591, 593 (Stashower, 1961); Rockwell Register Corp., 36 LA 1160, 1162–63 (Bowles, 1961); Gas Serv. Co., 35 LA 637, 639–40 (Beatty, 1960); Allegheny Ludlum Steel Corp., 26 LA 546, 548 (Montgomery, 1956); Yale & Towne Mfg. Co., 24 LA 160, 162 (Sanders, 1955). *See also* Baldwin-Whitehall Sch. Dist., 73 LA 1123, 1126 (Stoltenberg, 1979).

[359]St. Joseph Lead Co., 20 LA 890, 891 (Updegraff, 1953).

[360]Alabama Educ. Ass'n, 113 LA 493 (Singer, Jr., 1999) (management had right to reassign and redistribute duties); Allied Signal, 113 LA 124 (Thornell, 1999) (job description allowed assignment of operating the automatic wire bonder machine to employees in a different classification); GTE-Florida, 112 LA 919 (Frost, 1999) (management may make changes in assignments when substantial changes in the technological or manufacturing process have been made); Tendercare, Inc., 111 LA 1192 (Borland, 1998) (change in assignments valid, where past practice of rotation did not limit management's contractual right to schedule employees); Raynor Mfg. Co., 93 LA 774 (Edelman, 1989) (new tasks added to job do not justify upgrading of classification, where new tasks require higher skill level but not significant percentage of time); Friction Div. Prods., 92 LA 225 (Dorsey, 1988) (janitor-custodians who removed bags from dust collectors were not temporarily performing a higher rated job because removal of bags was a minor function); Associated Elec. Coop., 84 LA 1020 (Penfield, 1985); Magic Chef, 84 LA 15 (Craver, 1984) (employer had right to assign new duties without reclassifying position). See also cases cited in note 356, above. Regarding the duty of employees to do the work assigned to them and to utilize the grievance procedure rather than self-help if they think an assignment is improper, see Chapter 5, section 14.A., "Use of Grievance Procedure Versus Self-Help."

[361]*See* Gas Serv. Co., 70 LA 569, 571 (Goetz, 1978); Humble Oil & Ref. Co., 49 LA 445, 450–51 (Hebert, 1967); United States Steel Corp., 49 LA 86, 89 (Dybeck, 1967) ("maintenance of local conditions" provision does not limit the level of work load); Champion Papers, 49 LA 33, 38 (Whyte, 1967); Penn-Dixie Cement Corp., 48 LA 52, 54 (Duff, 1966); Overmyer Mould Co., 43 LA 1006, 1009–10 (Kelliher, 1964); Olin Mathieson Chem. Corp., 40 LA 257, 259 (Oppenheim, 1963); International Minerals & Chem. Corp., 37 LA 528, 531 (Donaldson, 1961); Evans Prods. Co., 29 LA 677, 679 (Ryder, 1957); Goodyear Tire & Rubber Co., 28 LA 374, 376 (Thompson, 1957); Ludowici-Celadon Co., 25 LA 897, 899 (Uible, 1955); Pan-Am S. Corp., 25 LA 611, 613 (Reynard, 1955); Peter Roselle & Sons, 25 LA 422, 424 (Berkowitz, 1955); Reynolds Metals Co., 25 LA 44, 48–49 (Prasow, 1955); Douglas & Lomason Co., 23 LA 691, 695 (Bowles, 1954); H.H. Robertson Co., 22 LA 701, 703 (Blair, 1954); United States Steel Corp., 22 LA 157, 161 (Hawley, 1953); Wheland Co., 20 LA 803, 806 (Dworet, 1953); Republic Steel Corp., 20 LA 800, 802 (Marshall, 1953); Ford Motor Co., 19 LA 237, 238–42 (Shulman, 1952); Librascope, Inc., 18 LA 462, 468 (Gaffey, 1952); Standard Oil Co., 17 LA 408, 409 (Gilden, 1951); Metalwash Mach. Co., 16 LA 505, 507 (Lesser, 1951); Diemolding Corp., 2 LA 274, 276–77 (Kharas, 1946). In some of these cases the agreement contained a management-rights clause; in others it did not. In *Federal Aviation Admin.*, 68 LA 1213, 1216–17 (Yarowsky, 1977), the arbitrator refused to interpret in a "restrictive and limited fashion" a new provision that prohibited air traffic controllers from being assigned to duties

that is not related to the regular duties may be held improper.[362] Even where an agreement expressly recognized a right of management to reassign duties across classification lines, the arbitrator cautioned management that a limitation was necessarily implied under the standard of reasonableness—duties must be compatible with the classification to which they are transferred.[363] Nonetheless, where the need is sufficiently strong, employees may be assigned duties or tasks that are foreign to their regular job.[364]

ii. Limitations [LA CDI 117.342]

A significant limitation on the right of management to assign work to skilled tradesmen (as opposed to production workers) was recognized in two decisions by an umpire who refused to permit the assignment of work to one trade that characteristically was performed by a different trade.[365] Some years later, another umpire "reaffirmed" these decisions, but in doing so he pointed out important exceptions:

> (a) Umpire Opinions A-223 and A-278 are reaffirmed. It is ruled that a skilled tradesman may not be required to do work wholly different from and unrelated to the central skill of his trade. If such bald assignment is attempted because of a shortage of work in his trade or a desire to get the other work done, he may refuse it and take a layoff instead.
> (b) In emergencies, the Company may make assignments across trade lines.
> (c) In cases where the capabilities of tradesmen overlap, work which is within the scope of two or more trades may be assigned to any of the trades within whose normal and proper scope it falls. In determining whether a task falls within the normal scope of more than one trade, due regard must be had for accepted standards in the trades generally and for clearly established in-plant assignment practices which are based on agreement or mutual understanding or which are characterized by acquiescence for a long time, with

---

not having a reasonable relationship to their primary function; he upheld the assignment of the task of changing and filing tapes, stating that it would be economically wasteful to call a technician to change the tapes, the controllers previously had shared the task with supervisors, and, unlike certain other tasks formerly performed by controllers (such as cutting grass around the tower, keeping time and attendance records, and conducting public tours around the facility), this task was not "far removed from the essential function of traffic controllers."

[362]American Zinc Co., 18 LA 827, 830–31 (Updegraff, 1952). See also City of Southgate, 67 LA 368, 371 (Ellmann, 1976); American Oil Co., 55 LA 1182, 1183 (Dorsey, 1970); Central State Univ., 54 LA 1159, 1162–63 (Snyder, 1971). Where an agreement excluded supervisors from the bargaining unit, supervisory duties could not be assigned to unit employees. Arkla Chem. Corp., 54 LA 62, 64–65 (Prewett, 1971). The right to assign workers to tasks outside the plant has sometimes been arbitrated, but such assignment was held improper in Schick, Inc., 2 LA 552, 553 (Stone, 1945), but held proper in Southland Oil Co., 53 LA 1308, 1310 (Williams, 1969); Morris Paper Mills, 20 LA 653, 656–57 (Anrod, 1953) (on the basis of practice).

[363]Vickers, Inc., 47 LA 716, 719 (Keefe, 1966). See also Social Sec. Admin., 69 LA 251, 253 (Haber, 1977).

[364]See Oshkosh Truck Corp., 72 LA 909, 913–14 (Kossoff, 1979); Goodyear Atomic Corp., 45 LA 671, 680 (Teple, 1965) (all employees were required to handle emergency equipment); Glen Rock Lumber & Supply Co., 38 LA 904, 906 (Turkus, 1962) (the task of walking the company watchdog could fall on any employee, except the union steward).

[365]Ford Motor Co., 3 LA 782, 783 (Shulman, 1946). In Ford Motor Co., 19 LA 237, 238–39 (Shulman, 1952), the umpire repeated the restriction but emphasized that it was to be narrowly applied. In Champion Papers, 49 LA 33, 38 (Whyte, 1967), the multicraft assignment of work to craft workers was upheld.

the consequences that the parties may be assumed to have agreed with reference to them and for their continuance.

(d) Relatively minor tasks which are complementary to a principal job but which do not require a long period of reasonably continuous work and which are within the capabilities of the principal tradesman on the job and can be performed by him with safety, are incidental work which can properly be assigned to the principal tradesman.[366]

Another set of "standards to determine whether management validly exercised its right to assign . . . challenged work . . . in keeping with the principle of craft integrity" was offered by an arbitrator:

1) Skilled tradesmen should not be required to do work wholly different from and unrelated to the central skill of their trades;

2) Intent must not be to destroy jobs or deny any other contract rights and the assignment made must be in good faith and be reasonably related to the efficient operation of the plant;

3) Greater latitude should be given where there is no economic loss to the employees—no layoffs or denial of overtime work opportunities;

4) Assignments which are occasional and of short duration rather than permanent should be viewed with greater liberality as reasonable exercises of management prerogatives in overlapping areas of work; and

5) Borderline work assignments which will be made only when members of classifications, for whom work is central rather than peripheral, are not available should be given more leeway than when permanent reassignments of duties are made.
    . . . .

Obviously, there is no craft whose work, tools, and skills are absolutely independent of all other crafts. Principles of craft jurisdiction must be applied with common sense and some flexibility. Judgments may be based upon:

1) the type of tools required
2) nature of the materials being worked on
3) character of the training required
4) level of skill involved
5) generally accepted elements of the trade . . . .

No one of these by itself is necessarily controlling. One can only judge on the basis of all the relevant facts, whether a job requires the special skills of a particular trade.[367]

iii. Unskilled Work Assigned to Skilled Workers [LA CDI 117.342]

Regarding the assignment of unskilled work to skilled workers, an arbitrator commented:

---

[366]Ford Motor Co., 30 LA 46, 55 (Platt, 1958). The exception stated in paragraph (d) was applied in *Amoco Oil Co.*, 70 LA 485, 490–91 (Rezler, 1978); *Shell Oil Co.*, 44 LA 1219, 1223–24 (Turkus, 1965); *Shell Oil Co.*, 44 LA 989, 990–91 (Updegraff, 1965). In *Kaiser Aluminum & Chem. Corp.*, 44 LA 449, 452 (Rohman, 1965), the arbitrator explained: "A modern development coincidental with automation is the fostering of combination skills. No longer will an individual skilled in that one craft perform work solely of that craft. True, his primary duties will be confined to that craft but, in addition, he will also perform the work of other crafts which are incidental to the necessary completion of that task."

[367]Tennessee River Pulp & Paper Co., 45 LA 201, 205 (Kesselman, 1965). These standards were quoted and followed in *General Dynamics Corp.*, 74 LA 1225, 1229 (Brisco, 1980); *National Steel & Shipbuilding Co.*, 56 LA 353, 356 (Block, 1971).

While workers in skilled classifications obviously should not be required to do a large amount of unskilled work, some measure of this is a part of every job. The most practical restraint on the amount of unskilled work that a company will assign to highly skilled workers is the cost involved. Few employers would feel that they could afford to have highly paid hourly employees spend very much of their time doing chores which could be performed by unskilled laborers.[368]

In another case, an additional reason was recognized for assigning some associated greasing and lubricating duties to skilled repairmen—they are more likely to spot trouble than other employees with less skill.[369]

In the absence of contractual restrictions on the right of management to assign new duties or reallocate old duties as reasonably required by technological changes, management may be permitted considerable leeway to do so.[370]

iv. Detailed Job Descriptions

Even when there are detailed job descriptions, one arbitrator has held that they do not prohibit minor changes in job content, noting that any ban on such changes must be stated in the agreement "in unmistakable language," and that the "purpose of job evaluation and job descriptions is to provide for equitable wage rates, not to provide a control over job content."[371] But the existence of detailed job descriptions, especially if negotiated, may deprive management of the right to make substantial changes in job duties.[372] One arbitrator went a step further, holding that even where there is no written

---

[368]Lockheed Aircraft Serv., 21 LA 292, 293 (Warren, 1953) (upholding the assignment of cleanup work to craftsmen for a short time every few weeks despite the fact that their job descriptions did not mention such work). *See also* Hubinger Co., 83 LA 1211 (Jacobowski, 1984); St. Regis Corp., 82 LA 1244 (Coyne, 1984). *But see* Anderson City Lines, 36 LA 531, 536 (Willingham, 1960). In *Mosaic Tile Co.*, 21 LA 278, 282–83 (Young, 1953), cleanup work could not be required of incentive workers, who were distinguished from hourly rated workers on the basis that additional duties do not reduce the earnings of the latter.

[369]United States Steel, 40 LA 414, 414 (Florey, 1963).

[370]Perfection Bakeries, 97 LA 741 (Cabe, 1991) (management had fundamental right to determine what duties employees would perform); Akron Gen. Med. Ctr., 94 LA 1183 (Dworkin, 1990); Courier Journal, 93 LA 227 (Tharp, 1989); Bethlehem Steel Corp., 85 LA 681 (Lilly, 1985); Stokely-Van Camp, 83 LA 838 (Nicholas, Jr., 1984). *But see* Kelly-Springfield Tire Co., 72 LA 742, 746 (LeWinter, 1979); Nebraska Consol. Mills Co., 22 LA 785, 788–90 (Doyle, 1954); National Tile & Mfg. Co., 12 LA 631, 634 (Hampton, 1949). For related discussion, see section 11., "Determination of Size of Crews," below.

[371]United States Steel Corp., 26 LA 325, 326 (Holly, 1956). *See also* Hobet Mining, 85 LA 1077, 1080 (Henle, 1985); Avco Corp., 71 LA 59, 61 (Hon, 1978); Indiana Reformatory, 70 LA 620, 625 (Witney, 1978) (the contested assignment was "reasonably related to the essence of the duties and the fundamental characteristics of" the detailed job description); Valley Mould & Iron Co., 53 LA 1130, 1131 (Cahn, 1969) ("job description cannot be considered as an agreement in and of itself as to how the job will be performed in the future or that it will continue to be performed without change"). *But see* Allied Plant Maint. Co. of Okla., 88 LA 963, 966–67 (Bankston, 1987).

[372]*See Allied Plant Maint. Co. of Okla.*, 88 LA 963 (employer improperly directed maintenance mechanics to clean machinery because the contract clearly allocated the task of cleaning the plant to janitors); Cadillac Gage Co., 87 LA 853 (Pelt, 1986) (employer violated contract and was ordered to pay wages for one-half hour of unit work to union when manufacturing manager sorted bolts); United States Steel Corp., 82 LA 910 (Shore, 1984).

job description, management may not make a substantial change in the traditional job content of classified occupations during the life of the contract.[373] However, in subsequently upholding the right of management to eliminate a contract classification and assign its duties to another classification, that arbitrator acted "on the premise that a freezing of classifications by implication would unduly restrict and hamper the Company in making decisions that would improve the economy and productivity of the plant."[374]

v. *Assignment of Work Within or Outside of Job Classification*
[LA CDI 117.345]

Many cases have spoken in terms of job classifications, and arbitrators remain divided on the issue of the assignment of work outside an employee's classification.[375] In one such case, an arbitrator upheld the right of management to assign an employee small amounts of work outside his classification, observing that work jurisdictional lines can be very crippling to efficient operations and should not be read into an agreement by inference.[376] While recognizing that management may require employees to perform duties outside their classification for temporary periods, another arbitrator held that management may not require the performance of such duties as a regular and continuing part of their jobs.[377]

It is not unusual, of course, to find duties and tasks that may properly fall within two or more separate job classifications. In regard to this phenomenon an arbitrator wrote:

---

[373]Nebraska Consol. Mills Co., 22 LA 785, 789–90 (Doyle, 1954). *See also* New Eng. Tel. & Tel. Co., 44 LA 1264, 1270–71, 1273 (Rubin, 1965); Concord Provision Co., 44 LA 1134, 1138 (Stouffer, 1965); New York Tel. Co., 18 LA 853, 854 (Wolff, 1952); Bell Tel. Co. of Pa., 45 LA 234, 238 (Wolff, 1965) (there was a special agreement).

[374]Omaha Cold Storage Terminal, 48 LA 24, 31 (Doyle, 1967). For related discussion, see section 9.A., "Establishing, Eliminating, and Combining Jobs and Classifications," above.

[375]*Compare* Stokely-Van Camp, 83 LA 838 (Nicholas, Jr., 1984) (employer's right to assign work outside classification upheld), *with* Amax Coal Co., 82 LA 846 (Witney, 1984) (employer precluded from assigning work outside classification). *See also* Lockheed Aeronautical Sys. Co., 98 LA 87 (Caraway, 1991) (company did not violate contract by assigning non-bargaining-unit employee to operate facsimile machine, where machines were tool of general usage, parties never intended job descriptions to grant exclusive jurisdiction to unit, and management reserved the right to assign tasks for most economical and efficient performance); Youngstown Hosp. Ass'n, 88 LA 251 (DiLeone, 1986) (after layoff, remaining work properly assigned to a non-bargaining-unit employee).

[376]Phillips Petroleum Co., 29 LA 226, 228 (Beatty, 1957). *See also* Union Oil Co. of Cal., 73 LA 892, 895 (Goldberg, 1979); Orrville Prods., 72 LA 816, 818–19 (Dworkin, 1979); Avco Corp., 71 LA 59, 61 (Hon, 1978); Kimberly-Clark Corp., 54 LA 250, 252 (Larkin, 1971); Pittsburgh-Des Moines Steel Co., 48 LA 364, 370–72 (Solomon, 1967); Dierks Paper Co., 47 LA 756, 760 (Morgan, 1966); United States Steel Corp., 46 LA 602, 604–05 (Williams, 1966); Gulf States Utils. Co., 43 LA 491, 497 (Hebert, 1964); Reliance Elec. & Eng'g Co., 41 LA 1045, 1049–50 (Klein, 1963); Cook Paint & Varnish Co., 40 LA 733, 735 (Beatty, 1963); Goodyear Tire & Rubber Co., 28 LA 374, 376–77 (Thompson, 1957); Ludowici-Celadon Co., 25 LA 897, 899 (Uible, 1955); Reynolds Metals Co., 25 LA 44, 48–49 (Prasow, 1955); Curtiss-Wright Corp., 22 LA 831, 833 (Wallen, 1953). *But see* Day & Zimmermann, 54 LA 1080, 1083 (Caraway, 1971); Virginia-Carolina Chem. Corp., 42 LA 336, 338–39 (Volz, 1964); American Mach. & Foundry Co., 41 LA 815, 818–19 (Teple, 1963); ALCO Prods., 32 LA 873, 879–82 (Hale, 1959); Jones & Laughlin Steel Corp., 32 LA 221, 221–22 (Cahn, 1959).

[377]Linde Air Prods. Co., 20 LA 861, 864 (Shister, Green, & Boyd, 1953). *See also* Amax Coal Co., 83 LA 1029, 1032 (Kilroy, 1984); Jenkins Bros., 20 LA 586, 588 (Donnelly, 1953); Dayton Malleable Iron Co., 17 LA 666, 668 (Hampton, 1951); Bethlehem Steel, 16 LA 926, 928–30 (Feinberg, 1951); Bethlehem Steel Co., 8 LA 113, 115–16 (Simkin, 1947).

[M]anagement may assign tasks which involve minor and occasional variation from job descriptions to employees in different classifications when what is required falls within the skills and other factors which are common to the several classifications. The arbitrator believes that this principle is well established except where there are specific contract provisions otherwise.[378]

In reaching this conclusion, the arbitrator spoke at length of the natural overlapping of duties between classifications:

It is understandable that in the interests of job security, unions press for inviolability of job classifications. Certainly, practices which permitted more or less discriminate transfer of duties from one classification to another, or the assignment of tasks now to one classification and now to another, would lead to anxieties about the kind and amount of work that might be available to particular employees at different times.

However, the reality is that there is much overlapping in jobs and their classifications. It would take an almost completely rationalized industry to provide for each worker absolutely distinct jobs. In highly specialized production work, operations are split off from general operations, and there may in consequence be an approach to fairly exclusive jobs one from another. However, in maintenance work duties are by the nature of the needs necessarily more general.

It is reassuring to be able to place things in neat categories. Is aspirin a drug and therefore to be sold only under a physician's prescription? How about the new tranquilizers? Is there a sharp line between intelligence and stupidity, or a gradually changing quality ranging from genius to idiot?[379]

When work falls within the job descriptions of two or more crafts or classifications, or is by nature a borderline or overlapping duty of two or more crafts or classifications, or if it has been performed by two or more crafts or classifications in the past, management has been permitted considerable leeway in assigning the work and ordinarily has not been limited to assigning it exclusively to one of the crafts or classifications.[380] However,

---

[378]Goodyear Tire & Rubber Co., 28 LA 374, 377 (Thompson, 1957).

[379]Id. at 376.

[380]See Morton Salt Div., 88 LA 254, 257 (Finan, 1987) (no violation where engineers were assigned to paint equipment as incidental to housekeeping functions); Youngstown Hosp. Ass'n, 88 LA 251, 253 (DiLeone, 1986). But see Amax Coal Co., 82 LA 846, 848–51 (Witney, 1984) (classification provisions were violated, where grievant was assigned out of classification while employee of different classification performed primary duty expressed in job title of grievant's classification); Southwest Forest Indus., 81 LA 421, 422–24 (Bickner, 1983); Interlake, Inc., 78 LA 239, 240–41 (Porter, 1982); Abbott Northwestern Hosp., 75 LA 1238, 1239–40 (Heneman, 1980); General Dynamics Corp., 74 LA 1225, 1229 (Brisco, 1980); Allied Chem. Corp., 73 LA 1041, 1042 (Yatsko, 1979); Manistee Forge Corp., 73 LA 1011, 1014 (Frost, 1979); Safeway Stores, 73 LA 207, 211, 215 (Goodman, 1979); Ford Aerospace Communications Corp., 72 LA 1209, 1213–14 (Gilson, 1979); Singer Co., 71 LA 204, 214 (Kossoff, 1978); Aeronca, Inc., 70 LA 1243, 1245 (Morgan, Jr., 1978); Mid-Penn Tel. Corp., 70 LA 644, 645 (Altrock, 1978); Food Fair Stores, 64 LA 1069, 1071–72 (Fields, 1975); United States Steel Corp., 62 LA 762, 763 (Beilstein, 1974); National Steel & Shipbuilding Co., 56 LA 353, 356 (Block, 1971); Portland Co., 51 LA 411, 413 (Wren, 1968); Jos. Schlitz Brewing Co., 51 LA 41, 44–45 (Bothwell, 1968) ("[I]n dealing with the problem of work jurisdiction where there are several crafts in a plant, the arbitrator cannot ignore the language contained in other craft union agreements with the Company, or practice in the past in administering the language."); Ingalls Shipbuilding Corp., 50 LA 1001, 1003 (Eyraud, 1968); Bethlehem Steel Corp., 50 LA 1214, 1216 (Seward, 1968); Kaiser Steel Corp., 50 LA 361, 366 (Block, 1968). As to claiming a particular share of work over which there is overlapping craft jurisdiction, see United States Steel Corp., 54 LA 184, 187–88 (Garrett, 1971). In Rayonier, Inc., 36 LA 883, 888 (Christon, 1961), procedures were suggested for harmonious operations

where work of an overlapping nature had long been assigned to one craft, the mere whim or caprice of management was not a reasonable basis for diverting the work to another craft.[381] Furthermore, work that was the "jugular vein" of one craft and not de minimis could not be assigned to another craft.[382]

Management generally has been held to have considerable discretion in unusual situations to make temporary or emergency assignments of tasks across job or classification lines. For instance, one arbitrator ruled that in case of emergency or breakdown it is reasonable for an employer to require maintenance employees with certain occupational titles to assist employees with other occupational titles:

> Many years of experience have proven to me that a plant maintenance crew is somewhat similar to the crew of a ship or a football team. Each member has a designated position or title and spends most of his team time attending to the duties and tasks associated with his designated position. However, when an emergency arises, they all respond as a crew and assist in getting the ship back on an even keel, weathering the storm, or, as in the case of the football team, advancing the ball to the opposing team's goal line.[383]

What the arbitrator said in regard to maintenance employees would appear to apply to plant employees generally. For instance, an employer was upheld in assigning an emergency job that arose on a nonworkday to the only two employees scheduled to work on that day, despite the fact that the work did not fall within the duties of their job classifications. The arbitrator stated that management should have the right to meet unusual situations in this manner unless restricted from doing so by the agreement.[384]

Finally, it should be remembered that while management often has wide authority to assign duties and tasks to employees, they in turn may challenge the fairness of the rate paid for the job after its change.[385] Moreover,

---

where the company had contracts with each of four unions, each contract reserving work within the union's jurisdiction to its members.

[381]Dow Chem. Co., 32 LA 587, 592 (Gorsuch, 1964).

[382]Shell Chem. Co., 47 LA 1178, 1180–81 (Rohman, 1967).

[383]Youngstown Sheet & Tube Co., 4 LA 514, 520 (Miller, 1946).

[384]Thompson Mahogany Co., 5 LA 397, 399 (Brandschain, 1946). For other cases permitting such temporary and/or emergency assignments, see *Warner Press*, 89 LA 577, 580 (Brunner, 1987) (contract that required that temporarily transferred employees be returned to regular jobs "as soon as possible" meant "as soon as practicable"; therefore, employer had right to keep employees on transfer assignment for the remainder of the shift); *Standard Register Co.*, 83 LA 1068, 1071–72 (Abrams, 1984); *Dow Corning Corp.*, 83 LA 1049, 1052 (Seidman, 1984); *Amax Coal Co.*, 83 LA 1029, 1033 (Kilroy, 1984); *Tecumseh Prods. Co.*, 82 LA 738, 741–42 (Cabe, 1984); *Midland-Ross Corp.*, 77 LA 714, 716 (Weiss, 1981); *Champion Int'l Corp.*, 72 LA 1204, 1209 (Larrabee, 1979); *Olin Corp.*, 65 LA 968, 974–75 (Mikrut, 1975); *Wellsville Fire Brick Co.*, 62 LA 205, 208 (Belcher, 1974); *Phillips Petroleum Co.*, 61 LA 1147, 1149 (Mewhinney, 1973).

[385]Menasha Corp., 108 LA 308 (Ellmann, 1997) (no right to wage increase, where no substantial change in workload or job content); Cleveland Elec. Illuminating Co., 108 LA 120 (Franckiewicz, 1997) (meter readers entitled to higher pay for reading commercial and industrial meters); Arizona Chem. Co., 107 LA 836 (Grooms, Jr., 1996) (operators given supervisors' duties entitled to wage increase); Integrated Health Servs. of Greater Pittsburgh, 107 LA 384 (Dean, Jr., 1996) (addition of similar duties and unrelated duties entitle employee to pay increase); Mead Prods., 104 LA 730 (Borland, 1994) (employees were not entitled to a wage increase, where employer did not change duties and functions within the job classifications but only method of completion); Cooper Indus., 104 LA 383 (Imundo, Jr., 1995) (sub-

employees temporarily performing work that is rated higher than their regular work may be entitled to the higher rate for performing the higher rated work.[386]

10. Hiring of Employees

Except as restricted by statute or the collective bargaining agreement, management retains the unqualified right to hire or not to hire. Particularly significant statutory restrictions are (1) those against discrimination on the basis of unionism under the National Labor Relations Act and the Railway Labor Act;[387] (2) the Age Discrimination in Employment Act of 1967 (ADEA);[388] (3) the Civil Rights Act of 1964 prohibiting discrimina-

---

stantial change in job requires new rate); Schnadig Corp., 101 LA 1166 (Duff, 1993) (employees entitled to higher rate under temporary transfer). *See* Streater Div., 93 LA 122, 124 (Bognanno, 1989); Amana Refrigeration, 89 LA 751, 753–54 (Bowers, 1987); Brass Prods. Co., 85 LA 465, 467–68 (Lipson, 1985); Western Gear Corp., 78 LA 1263, 1265, 1267 (Draznin, 1982); Amoco Oil Co., 65 LA 577, 581 (Cohen, 1975); Ohio & W. Pa. Dock Co., 39 LA 1065, 1073 (Dworkin, 1962); United States Metals Ref. Co., 26 LA 822, 823–24 (Cahn, 1961); Dow Chem. Co., 22 LA 336, 351 (Klamon, 1954). For full discussion, see section 6., "Wage Adjustments Following Changes in Operation Methods," above.

[386]*See also* Florida Power Corp., 85 LA 619, 621–22 (Flannagan, 1985); Engelhard Indus., 82 LA 680, 683 (Nicholas, Jr., 1984); Vendo Co., 65 LA 1267, 1270 (Madden, 1975); Caldwell Foundry & B Mach. Co., 65 LA 773, 775 (Styles, 1975); General Servs. Admin., 63 LA 487, 499 (Lippman, 1974); International Shoe Co., 35 LA 265, 268 (Larkin, 1960); Diamond State Tel. Co., 32 LA 200, 212–15 (Seward, Lindell, Jr., McNeil, Feiler, & Carroll, 1959); Phelps Dodge Corp., 25 LA 64, 65–66 (Kelliher, 1955); Power Equip. Co., 16 LA 215, 216 (Platt, 1951); American Bemberg Co., 11 LA 145, 147 (Hepburn, 1948); Benjamin Elec. Mfg. Co., 8 LA 389, 393–94 (Elson, 1947). *See also* Inland Steel Corp., 263 NLRB 1091, 111 LRRM 1193 (1982). *Cf.* O'Neal Steel, 47 LA 796, 798 (Steele, 1966); Kroger Co., 35 LA 480, 482–83 (Howlett, 1960); B.F. Goodrich Co., 8 LA 883, 890–91 (McCoy, 1947). In view of the overlap of duties among different classifications, guides (garnered from reported arbitration decisions) have been offered for determining whether an employee is performing work of a higher classification. *See* Alaska Dep't of Transp. & Pub. Facilities, 78 LA 999, 1005–06 (Tilbury, 1982); Hanna Mining Co., 73 LA 123, 125–26 (Axon, 1979).

[387]Strengthening the prohibitions against considering an applicant's union activity or affinity in hiring decisions, the Supreme Court has held that employers cannot refuse to hire applicants who are seeking employment for the sole purpose of organizing the work force (a practice generally known as "salting"). NLRB v. Town & Country Elec., 516 U.S. 85, 150 LRRM 2897 (1995). *See, e.g.,* Phelps Dodge Corp. v. NLRB, 313 U.S. 177, 8 LRRM 439 (1941) (upholding the NLRB's power to require an employer to hire applicants who had been rejected because of their union affiliation even though they had obtained substantially equivalent employment elsewhere).

[388]29 U.S.C. §621 et seq. Also of interest is Exec. Order No. 11,246, which establishes affirmative action obligations with regard to hiring and other terms and conditions of employment on the part of federal government contractors. These obligations extend the prohibition on discriminatory employment practices to an applicant's or employee's gender or minority status. Those companies that are covered by these various affirmative action obligations should take note that the U.S. Department of Labor's Office of Federal Contract Compliance Programs (OFCCP) (the department responsible for overseeing the hiring and employment practices of those companies that are government contractors, or that are recipients of federal financial assistance) has issued regulations governing a federal contractor's obligations to implement affirmative action plans, which expand the preexisting obligations in several respects. 29 C.F.R. §§1641.1–1641.8. Another statute of interest is the Rehabilitation Act of 1973, 29 U.S.C. §701 et seq., under which employers who enter into certain procurement contracts with federal agencies must adopt affirmative action plans for employment and advancement of qualified handicapped individuals. *See* Volz, *Health and Medical Issues in Arbitration, Employee Benefit Plans, and the Doctor's Ofice: I. Medical and Health Issues in Labor Arbitration, in* Truth, Lie Detectors, and Other Problems in Labor Arbitra-

tion because of race, color, religion, sex, or national origin;[389] and (4) the ADA.[390]

Contractual restrictions on the right to hire exist most often in seniority or union security provisions.[391]

A. Arbitral Recognition of Management's Rights

Arbitral recognition of management's basic right to control hiring is illustrated in the following lines of cases:

- Company rules against hiring spouses or other relatives of present employees have been upheld;[392]
- Management's right to hire has been said to include the right to set pre-employment standards and to implement them by requiring applicants to give accurate information as to their work and medical history and their record as law-abiding citizens;[393]

TION, PROCEEDINGS OF THE 31ST ANNUAL MEETING OF NAA 156, 184–86 (Stern & Dennis eds., BNA Books 1979). *See also* Segal, *II. Employee Benefit Plans in Arbitration of Health and Medical Issues, id.* at 187, 201. Programs or activities receiving federal financial assistance are prohibited by the ADEA from discriminating (including employment discrimination) against qualified handicapped individuals. *See* Consolidated Rail Corp. v. Darrone, 465 U.S. 624, 34 FEP Cases 79 (1984).

[389]*See, e.g.,* Phillips v. Martin Marietta Corp., 400 U.S. 542, 3 FEP Cases 40 (1971) (the Civil Rights Act does not permit one hiring policy for women with preschool-age children and another for men with such children). In *Furnco Construction Corp. v. Waters,* 438 U.S. 567, 577–78, 17 FEP Cases 1062 (1978), the Supreme Court stated that the Civil Rights Act prohibits the employer "from having as a goal a workforce selected by any proscribed discriminatory practice, but it does not impose a duty to adopt a hiring procedure that maximizes hiring of minority employees." In *Texas Department of Community Affairs v. Burdine,* 450 U.S. 248, 259, 25 FEP Cases 113 (1981), the Court stated than an employer is not required "to hire the minority or female applicant whenever that person's objective qualifications" are equal to those of a white male applicant.

[390]Consistent with the the ADA's prohibition against discriminating against employees on the basis of handicap, pre-employment inquiries into an applicant's medical history are prohibited—such inquiries being permitted only following an offer of employment and pursuant to a post-offer medical examination. 42 U.S.C. §12112(d). Drug tests, however, are not considered a "medical examination" covered by such prohibition. 42 U.S.C. § 12114(d). The provisions of the ADA are generally parallel, but not necessarily identical, to the provisions of the Rehabilitation Act of 1973. 42 U.S.C. §12101 et seq. The ADA prohibits discrimination against qualified individuals with disabilities in regard to job application procedures, and the hiring, advancement, or discharge of employees. See Chapter 16, "Safety and Health," for further discussion.

[391]See section 10.B., "Seniority Provisions," and section 10.C., "Union-Security Clauses," below.

[392]*See also* Georgia Pac. Corp., 112 LA 317 (Caraway, 1999) (employer did not discriminate when it made an exception to its antinepotism policy for two white applicants, after declining to make an exception for several black applicants: applying Title VII standards for establishing racial discrimination, held that the white applicants had special skills required for the positions they were applying for, while the black applicants did not possess the job skills and qualifications required for the positions for which they applied, and two of these applicants also did not satisfy the collective bargaining agreement's procedural requirements for referral; employer's decisions were based on legitimate business reasons and not unlawful discriminatory motives). *See* American Mach. & Foundry Co., 68 LA 1309, 1314 (Novak, 1977); Robertshaw Controls Co., 55 LA 283, 286 (Block, 1970); Midland-Ross Corp., 55 LA 258, 260 (McNaughton, 1970); Studebaker Corp., 49 LA 105, 109–10 (Davey, 1967); Hughes Aircraft Co., 48 LA 1123, 1124 (Beatty, 1967); Euclid Elec. & Mfg. Co., 45 LA 641, 643 (Kates, 1965).

[393]*See* Noranda Aluminum, 94 LA 690 (Pratte, 1990) (discharge upheld where 2-year employee failed to disclose during application process acute heat exhaustion 7 years earlier); Salt River Project Agric. Improvement & Power Dist., 91 LA 1193 (Ross, 1988) (grievant

- The employer may hire additional employees even though this may mean less overtime or other reduced opportunities for existing employees;[394]
- The employer may not be required to hire any new employee to fill a vacancy where the employer had no bids for the position from its employees and there was no contractual requirement for maintaining a specified number of employees within the classification.[395]

B. Seniority Provisions [LA CDI 119.121]

Management's ability to hire may be restricted by the seniority provisions of the collective bargaining agreement. For example, an employer may be required to recall qualified laid-off employees before hiring new employees.[396] Similarly, seniority provisions may be violated if a position is filled with a new employee rather than a current employee with the most seniority,[397] unless management can show that current employees lack the ability to perform in such a position.[398]

In a situation where the company conceded that its right to hire was qualified by the seniority clause, it was nevertheless permitted to hire an already qualified person to fill a job opening because none of its present employees could perform the job without intensive training.[399] Similarly, other arbitrators have recognized management's right to hire a new employee where

---

failed to list drug-dealing conviction on "felony questionnaire" with original application for employment); Mor-Flo Indus., 89 LA 762 (King, 1987) (employee was properly discharged for intentionally withholding information concerning lower-back injuries during preemployment interview); Laclede Gas Co., 86 LA 480 (Mikrut, 1986); Morton Thiokol, 85 LA 834 (Williams, 1985); Owens-Illinois, 83 LA 1265 (Cantor, 1984). *See also* Inland Steel Corp., 263 NLRB 1091, 111 LRRM 1193 (1982). It should be noted, however, that caution must be exercised when making hiring decisions based on an individual's prior criminal record: the Equal Employment Opportunity Commission's (EEOC's) guidelines provide that a hiring policy involving prior criminal record may not take arrest records into account and may only take into consideration convictions that are "job related," with reference to the particular job applied for. In addition, statutes in several states regulate the extent to which arrest or conviction records may be lawfully considered in making hiring decisions.

[394]*See* Alexander Water Co., 45 LA 1165, 1166 (McCoy, 1965); Buxbaum Co., 42 LA 1293, 1295–96 (Geissinger, 1964); Phillips Chem. Co., 38 LA 1152, 1154 (Larson, 1962); Dow Chem. Co., 33 LA 685, 692 (Hale, 1959). *See also* Jumer's Castle Lodge, 69 LA 315, 318, 320 (Wright, 1977).

[395]Connecticut Coke Co., 28 LA 360, 361–62 (Stutz & Mottram, dissent by Curry, 1957). For related material, see section 11., "Determination of Size of Crews," and section 12., "Vacancies," below.

[396]*See* Diamond Power Specialty Co., 83 LA 1277 (Kindig, 1984) (dictum). *Cf.* Singer Co., 86 LA 917 (Wahl, 1986) (employer violated contract by failing to promote grievants while they were on layoff).

[397]*See* Oberlin Coll., 93 LA 289 (Fullmer, 1989) (employer violated contract by improperly awarding library position to an applicant from outside the bargaining unit instead of to library assistant, where previous arbitrator had ruled that vacancy must be given to internal applicant provided one was qualified); Chillicothe Tel. Co., 84 LA 1 (Gibson, 1984); Potomac Elec. Power Co., 82 LA 352 (Everitt, 1984).

[398]*See* Illinois Cereal Mills, 88 LA 350 (Petersen, 1986); Emery Mining Corp., 85 LA 1211 (Feldman, 1985); National-Standard Co., 85 LA 190 (Duda, Jr., 1985); Monsanto Co., 85 LA 73 (Madden, 1985); Brooklyn Acres Mut. Homes, 84 LA 952 (Abrams, 1985); Lockheed-Georgia Co., 84 LA 701 (Daly, 1985); Dakota Elec. Ass'n, 84 LA 114 (Boyer, 1985); St. Paul Dispatch & Pioneer Press, 82 LA 1273 (Ver Ploeg, 1984); Rohm & Haas Tex., 82 LA 271 (Taylor, 1984).

[399]Wagner Elec. Corp., 20 LA 768, 775 (Klamon, 1953).

it had no qualified employee for the job,[400] or where other reasonable justification existed for the action.[401] In one case, the employer was held to have been justified in filling a vacancy by hiring a new employee where the only employees who were qualified to perform the job were on strike and a posting of the vacancy for bids "would have been an idle gesture."[402]

C. Union-Security Clauses [LA CDI 8.01 et seq.; 100.020303]

The employer's discretion in hiring may be restricted by a union-security clause, such as a "maintenance-of-membership" provision, to the extent that any such clause is enforceable under applicable state and federal statutes. Where the union-security provision is lawful, arbitrators appear to frown on hiring practices that circumvent the provision.[403] For instance, one employer was ordered to discharge again an employee who had been previously employed as a production worker and discharged pursuant to a maintenance-of-membership provision, but subsequently rehired as an assistant foreman. The arbitrator declared that the rehiring of the worker under these circumstances was a cause of dissension and violated the intent of the maintenance-of-membership provision.[404]

Under contracts providing for union referrals in hiring but containing the requirement that referrals be satisfactory to management, arbitrators have allowed employers considerable discretion in rejecting union-referred candidates.[405] But the employer must exercise good faith in reaching its de-

---

[400]See note 398, above. For a contract giving management broad authority to hire persons needed because of their special training, ability, or experience, see *Jefferson City Cabinet Co.*, 35 LA 117, 123 (Marshall, 1960).

[401]*See* Otis Elevator Co., 5 LA 173, 174 (Davey, 1944). An employer that had been unable to fill certain jobs due to a tight labor market was upheld in offering a higher than contractual starting wage rate to new hires who already possessed certain experience or training. Bowmar Instrument Corp., 62 LA 955, 958 (Volz, 1974). For other cases in which management was challenged for hiring at a higher than contractual starting wage rate, see *County of Orange*, 70 LA 1172, 1174 (Dennis, 1978); *Denton Sleeping Garment Mills*, 60 LA 453, 457–58 (Kallenbach, 1973).

[402]Allied Chem. & Dye Corp., 16 LA 28, 29 (McCoy, 1951). For legal doctrine concerning management's right to hire and retain workers hired during economic strikes, see *NLRB v. Fleetwood Trailer Co.*, 389 U.S. 375, 66 LRRM 2737 (1967); *NLRB v. Mackay Radio & Tel. Co.*, 304 U.S. 333, 2 LRRM 610 (1938). *See also* Laidlaw Corp., 171 NLRB 1366, 68 LRRM 1252 (1968). For arbitration decisions, see *Plough, Inc.*, 55 LA 109 (Merrill, 1970); *Unarco Indus.*, 53 LA 784 (Gorsuch, 1969); *Robertshaw Controls Co.*, 42 LA 823 (Turkus, 1964); *Yale & Towne Mfg. Co.*, 39 LA 1156 (Hill, Horlacher, & Seitz, 1962); *Dynamic Mfrs.*, 36 LA 635 (Crane, 1960); *Wilson & Co.*, 34 LA 125 (Weinstein, 1960); *Bird & Son, Inc.*, 33 LA 777 (Loucks, 1959).

[403]*See* Loew's, Inc., 10 LA 227, 232–33 (Aaron, 1948); Briskin Mfg. Co., 1 LA 331, 333 (Updegraff, 1946); Merrill-Stevens Co., 1 LA 15, 19–20 (Fabinski, 1944).

[404]*Merrill-Stevens Co.*, 1 LA at 19–20.

[405]*See* Barnard & Burk, Inc., 74 LA 550, 557–58 (Taylor, 1980); Reynolds Elec. & Eng'g Co., 52 LA 327, 332 (Latimer, 1969); Borden's Farm Prods., 8 LA 593, 595 (Feinberg, 1947); Good Humor Corp., 3 LA 367, 369 (Reynolds, 1946). *See also* Johns-Manville Sales Corp., 68 LA 989, 991 (Hays, 1977); Pan Am. S.S. Co., 18 LA 764, 766 (Bennett, 1952) (interest dispute); Building Owners & Managers Ass'n, 5 LA 38, 40 (Wyckoff, 1946) (same). In *Consolidated Papers*, 71 LA 595, 598 (Mueller, 1978), the arbitrator reminded that "in the absence of a contractual hiring hall arrangement . . . the matter of determining who to hire into employment is generally recognized as solely a management prerogative." Also regarding management's determination of *who* to hire where there was no hiring hall or other such limitation, see *Sears, Roebuck & Co.*, 78 LA 900, 903 (Flannagan, 1982); *Houston Publishers Ass'n*, 71 LA 667, 671–72 (Traynor, 1978).

cision.[406] It also has been held that an employer who had agreed to fill its staffing needs from candidates referred by the hiring hall had discretion in making its selection, but it could not secure employees through direct hire in the absence of a contract provision reserving the right to do so.[407]

11. DETERMINATION OF SIZE OF CREWS [LA CDI 117.3351]

Many grievances have involved the right of management to determine the number of employees to be utilized in a given operation.[408] Crew-size determinations may be of a more or less permanent nature,[409] as, for example, where a new operation or new equipment is installed or where management eliminates a job to accommodate reduced production needs and market changes, or such determinations may affect a given crew only temporarily, as where the company does not fill a crew member's position during a brief absence.

It has been held that management has the right unilaterally to determine the size of crews necessary for operation of the plant, either under a general management-rights clause[410] or as a matter of management preroga-

[406]Matson Navigation Co., 29 LA 209, 213 (Cobb, 1957). *See also* Newark Newspaper Publishers' Ass'n, 43 LA 245, 246 (Schmertz, 1963).

[407]Union Painting Contractors Ass'n, 42 LA 902, 908–09 (Seligson, 1964). *See also* Evening News Ass'n, 50 LA 239, 245 (Platt, 1968). *But see* Johnson County Asphalt, 66 LA 403, 408 (Traynor, 1976) (the union failed to refer workers through the hiring hall); Todd Shipyards Corp., 65 LA 1019, 1023 (Koven, 1975) (an affirmative action plan was a factor). The use of hiring halls is legal under the NLRA if not used as an instrument of discrimination on the basis of unionism. Teamsters Local 357 v. NLRB (Los Angeles-Seattle Motor Express), 365 U.S. 667, 47 LRRM 2906 (1961). By virtue of federal preemption, hiring-hall discrimination that violates or arguably violates the NLRA may not be remedied by a state court award of damages. Farmer v. Carpenters Local 25 430 U.S. 290, 94 LRRM 2759 (1977). In *General Building Contractors Association v. Pennsylvania*, 458 U.S. 375, 29 FEP Cases 139 (1982), an employer who had no right to control the union was not liable for its violation of Title VII of the Civil Rights Act by racially discriminatory operation of a hiring hall.

[408]It also may be noted that one of the most critical interest disputes of many years involved crews in the railroad industry. *See* Railroads, 41 LA 673 (Aaron, Healy, & Seward, 1963). *See also* Bethlehem Steel Corp., 92 LA 553 (Witt, 1988) (employer improperly reduced crew size); Dinagraphics, Inc., 92 LA 453 (Heekin, 1989) (employer did not violate contract by unilaterally assigning a crew of three employees, rather than a crew of four, to operate press). *Compare* Kroger Co., 86 LA 357, 368 (Milentz, 1986), *with* Hubinger Co., 83 LA 1211 (Jacobowski, 1984).

[409]Cooper/T. Smith Stevedoring Co., 99 LA 297 (Massey, 1992). *But see* Idaho Statesman, 98 LA 753 (Corbett, 1992) (employer did not violate contract, where contract contained no mandatory manning requirement).

[410]*See* Brooklyn Union Gas Co., 47 LA 425, 427 (Wolf, 1966); Mead Corp., 46 LA 70, 71 (King, 1966); Plimpton Press, 40 LA 720, 726 (Sembower, 1963); Pittsburgh Steel Co., 40 LA 67, 70 (McDermott, 1963); Johnson Bronze Co., 34 LA 365, 367 (McDermott, 1960); Electro Metallurgical Co., 28 LA 252, 254 (Marshall, 1957); Youngstown Sheet & Tube Co., 12 LA 865, 869 (Updegraff, 1949).

tive,[411] so long as no other provision of the agreement is violated by the employer's determination.[412]

Union challenges to management action in determining the size of crews have presented arbitrators with a variety of issues for their consideration. The union may argue that a contract's manning provision limits the company's right of action, or it may charge the violation of a clause not specifically related to crew size, such as the recognition, seniority, or layoff clause, or a clause concerned with filling vacancies.[413] Additionally, the union may urge safety or health considerations, or question the reasonableness of the increased burden on remaining crew members.[414] The arbitrator may be called on to wrestle with issues arising from technological or process changes, or changes in operation methods and procedures that result in idle time for employees affected by such changes. New economic and production needs also may give rise to challenges when they displace workers.[415]

---

[411]*See* American Red Cross, 103 LA 580, 585 (Garrett, 1994) (employer did not violate collective bargaining agreement when it evaluated manpower needs and decreased number of employees at blood donor sites); WCI Steel, 103 LA 114 (Duda, Jr., 1994) (employer did not violate collective bargaining agreement when it decreased the number of boiler operator positions from two to one); Leavenworth Times, 71 LA 396, 405 (Bothwell, 1978); West Flagler Assocs., 61 LA 1253, 1258 (Greene, 1973); Pittsburgh & Conneaut Dock Co., 55 LA 19, 22 (Teple, 1970); Mobil Oil Co., 46 LA 140, 151 (Hebert, 1966); International Salt Co., 42 LA 1188, 1191 (Mittenthal, 1964); Meyer's Bakery of Little Rock, 38 LA 1135, 1139 (Hon, 1962); National Container Corp., 29 LA 687, 692–93 (Marshall, 1957); Pacific Am. Shipowners Ass'n, 10 LA 736, 745 (Miller, 1948). *See also* Centric Corp., 70 LA 817, 825–26 (Richardson, 1978); Standard Oil Co., 30 LA 115, 117 (Updegraff, 1958). The National War Labor Board recognized this to be a management function. American Smelting & Ref. Co., 21 War Lab. Rep. 163 (1945).

[412]Quanex Corp., 108 LA 841 (House, 1997) (employer violated collective bargaining agreement when it unilaterally decreased crew size from three to two people by not filling a vacancy; the contract and past practice mandated union negotiation over job duties, rates of pay, and job combinations). *See* Mead Corp., 46 LA 70, 72 (King, 1966); KXTV, 33 LA 421, 423 (Ross, 1959); Mobil Oil Co., 61-4 ARB ¶8069 (Willingham, 1961). Some arbitrators would require management's action in reducing the size of a crew to "meet the test of reasonableness." Continental Can Co., 35 LA 602, 607 (McKelvey, 1960). *See also* Falstaff Brewing Corp., 63–1 ARB ¶8199 (Hoffman, 1963); Penn-Dixie Cement Corp., 33 LA 442, 445 (Reid, 1959).

[413]*See* Quanex Corp., 108 LA 841 (House, 1997); Keystone Steel & Wire Co., 45 LA 648, 650 (Daugherty, 1965); International Salt Co., 42 LA 1188, 1190 (Mittenthal, 1964); Plymouth Oil Co., 36 LA 919, 921 (Hale, 1961); Standard Oil Co., 36 LA 245, 248 (Stouffer, 1960); Reynolds Mining Corp., 33 LA 25, 27 (Bauder, 1959); Carlyle Tile Co., 29 LA 787, 789 (Dworkin, 1958); Connecticut Coke Co., 28 LA 360, 361 (Stutz & Mottram, dissent by Curry, 1957); Bethlehem-Sparrows Point Shipyard, 19 LA 523, 525 (Feinberg, 1952); Pathe Labs., 19 LA 487, 488 (Wolff, 1952). For related material, see section 5., "Control of Operation Methods," and section 9., "Job and Classification Control," above; section 12., "Vacancies," and section 19., "Layoff of Employees," below; Chapter 14, "Seniority."

[414]Pennsylvania Steel Tech., 105 LA 189 (Kahn, 1995) (decreasing the number of strand operators from two to one did not create a substantial risk to health and safety because other workers, although not in the immediate vicinity, were near to help if there was an accident; the arbitrator found that risks present were not created as a result of or attributable to reduction in crew size). *See* Keebler Co., 86 LA 963 (Nolan, 1986). *Cf.* City of Laredo, Tex., 91 LA 381 (McDermott, 1988) (city did not violate contractual health and safety provision when it reduced crews from four firefighters to three); Western Fuel Oil Co., 89 LA 772 (Kaufman, 1987) (employer's reduction in staffing did not violate the contract or jeopardize employees' health and safety).

[415]In *Pittsburgh Plate Glass Co.*, 36 LA 21, 22–23 (Lehoczky, Fisher, & Myers, 1960), and *Pittsburgh Plate Glass Co.*, 33 LA 614, 617–19 (Lehoczky, Fisher, & Myers, 1959), the arbitrators developed general principles as a guide in determining specific manpower proposals.

A. Does a Crew in Fact Exist?

The preliminary question may arise as to whether a group of employees actually constitute a "crew." Commenting in regard to the parties' local working conditions clause, an arbitrator noted that the mere fact that a certain number of employees perform a given operation for a number of years does not necessarily establish a local working condition governing crew size. He continued, "It is the *relationship* between this course of conduct, and some *given set of underlying circumstances* which is important in determining whether there has been a recurring response which has evolved as the normal and accepted reaction in dealing with the problem."[416]

In holding that an employer had acted within its rights under a management-rights clause when it eliminated two maintenance employees, the arbitrator stated that employees are not a "crew" simply because employment has been stable for a long period of time and thus manning requirements have remained the same. He further observed:

> Most arbitrators hold to the position that a crew for purposes of local working conditions exists where the employees making up the work force have a relationship that is interdependent to each other. This would mean that, when one member is removed or absent, the remaining workers are required to assume an increased amount of work, or there is a significant change in the type of work they are required to perform. In other words, there must be a relationship between the repetitive nature of the work and the interdependence of members to each other.[417]

Another arbitrator cautioned that "[t]he problem of *crew* sizes must be differentiated from the size of a work force in a particular department or other sub-division of the plant which usually fluctuates in size, depending on many circumstances."[418]

In summary, then, to demonstrate the existence of a crew in the absence of a contractual definition, it must be shown that (1) an established course of conduct has existed (2) with respect to the assignment of a specific number of employees (3) who have performed in an interdependent manner (4) a particular type of work (5) under a given set of circumstances (6) for a significant period of time.

In the absence of a "local working conditions" clause, it has been suggested that an even stronger showing as to the existence of a crew would be required.[419]

The remaining topics discussed below involve established crews.

---

[416]United States Steel Corp., 33 LA 394, 404 (Garrett, 1959) (emphasis added).

[417]Pittsburgh Steel Co., 40 LA 67, 68–69 (McDermott, 1963). *See also* United States Steel Corp., 66 LA 543, 547 (Klaus, 1976); Pittsburgh Steel Co., 47 LA 317, 319 (Sherman, 1966); Pittsburgh Steel Co., 46 LA 733, 734 (McDermott, 1966); Jones & Laughlin Steel Corp., 39 LA 151, 153 (Duff, 1962). *Cf.* United States Steel Corp., 40 LA 903, 907–08 (Crawford, 1963); Bethlehem Steel Co., 39 LA 921, 925 (Porter, 1962).

[418]Jones & Laughlin Steel Corp., 39 LA 151, 153 (Duff, 1962) (emphasis in original).

[419]*See* Platt, *The Silent Contract vs. Express Provisions: The Arbitration of Local Working Conditions: Discussion, in* COLLECTIVE BARGAINING AND THE ARBITRATOR'S RULE, PROCEEDINGS OF THE 15TH ANNUAL MEETING OF NAA 140, 147 (Kahn ed., BNA Books 1962).

B. Limiting Contract Provisions

Of course, a particular crew size may be fixed by a specific contract provision stating the number of employees in the crew, with the result that management likely would be denied the right to eliminate a member of that crew. This was an arbitrator's ruling when new equipment was installed that, absent the clause specifying the crew size, might have justified the reduction.[420]

Somewhat less specifically, a clause may call for "adequate help,"[421] "adequate manpower,"[422] or a "sufficient number" of employees.[423] Or the contract may require the employer to schedule the "normal number" of employees,[424] the "standard force,"[425] or the "full crew."[426]

Management's right to determine crew size may be restricted by a contract clause requiring joint determination with the union following any significant change in equipment or method of operation.[427] The right of management to reduce the size of a crew also may be limited by a clause, such as is prevalent in the steel industry contracts, that requires maintenance of established local working conditions unless the underlying basis for the condition has changed.[428] However, the mere existence of a local working conditions clause or one calling for adequate help does not necessarily freeze the number of employees in a crew, because many factors, discussed hereinbelow, singly or in combination, nevertheless may justify a change in the size of the crew. Arbitrators considering such contract clauses often have been

---

[420]Barton Salt Co., 46 LA 503, 505 (Merrill, 1966); Edition Bookbinders of N.Y., 42 LA 1167, 1171 (Altieri, 1964). In both cases the contract was specific as to certain crew complements but not as to others. *See also* Cincinnati Post & Times Star, 68 LA 129, 141 (Chalfie, 1977) (a layoff that would not have resulted "but for" the introduction of new equipment violated a provision requiring that any reduction in force resulting from automation be accomplished by attrition rather than layoff, and this was so regardless of the need to reduce the workforce because of economic problems); Weston Biscuit Co., 21 LA 653, 654 (Flink, 1953).

[421]Schlitz Brewing Co., 30 LA 147, 148 (Fleming, 1958); Pabst Brewing Co., 29 LA 617, 621 (Fleming, 1957).

[422]Lone Star Brewing Co., 50 LA 458 (Hebert, 1968); Pearl Brewing Co., 42 LA 145, 147 (Bothwell, 1964).

[423]American Pipe & Constr. Co., 43 LA 1126, 1134 (Ladar, 1964).

[424]Gulf Oil Corp., 42 LA 294, 297 (Rehmus, 1964); Sherwin-Williams Co., 25 LA 879, 881 (Kelliher, 1956).

[425]Keystone Steel & Wire Co., 45 LA 648, 650 (Daugherty, 1965).

[426]Plymouth Oil Co., 36 LA 919, 922 (Hale, 1961); Continental Can Co., 35 LA 602, 603 (McKelvey, 1960).

[427]*E.g.*, Memphis Publ'g Co., 50 LA 186, 190 (Duff, 1967).

[428]*See* WCI Steel, 103 LA 114 (Duda, Jr., 1994); United States Steel Corp., 33 LA 394, 397–404 (Garrett, 1959). *See also* Pickands Mather & Co., 75 LA 229, 232–33 (Beilstein, 1980); United States Steel Co., 43 LA 1048, 1050 (Florey, 1964); United States Steel, 40 LA 984, 986 (Crawford, 1963); American Chain & Cable Co., 39 LA 432, 434 (McDermott, 1962). Some contracts are silent as to past practices, while other contracts contain local working conditions clauses. On the question of whether there is a significant difference in results reached by arbitrators under these two types of contracts, see Wallen, *The Silent Contract vs. Express Provisions: The Arbitration of Local Working Conditions, in* COLLECTIVE BARGAINING AND THE ARBITRATOR'S ROLE, PROCEEDINGS OF THE 15TH ANNUAL MEETING OF NAA 117 (Kahn ed., BNA Books 1962); Bailer, *Discussion, id.* at 137; Platt, *Discussion, id.* at 140.

confronted with changes in operations[429] or technology, or questions of employee safety, and their findings that a proper crew had or had not been provided has been based on the evidence presented in the given case. Under a local working conditions clause, an arbitrator held that substantial cumulative changes in warehouse and shipping procedures justified the reduction in crew size; even though instituted over a period of years, the changes were considered to be "part and parcel of the same improvement pattern."[430]

Even if a contract provision mandates a minimum number of employees to man a crew, if the employer, in good faith after making a reasonable effort, cannot find enough qualified employees to fill the positions, the employer is not required to hire or promote underqualified individuals to fill out the complement.[431]

C. Technological and Process Changes

Arbitrators are in general agreement that where substantial changes in technology or manufacturing processes have been made, management has the right to make changes in the size of the crew, unless restricted by the agreement.[432] This is true even where the contract contains a local working conditions clause, for it is reasoned that the changes in technology or processes cause a change in the basis for the existence of such condition.[433] Of course, the changes must be substantial enough to result in a material re-

---

[429]USS, Div. of USX Corp., 110 LA 837 (St. Antoine, 1998) (where the minimum manning language setting forth the circumstances under which trucking crew levels could be changed was ambiguous, the arbitrator required the parties to establish clarifying criteria).

[430]United States Steel Corp., 41 LA 56, 58–59 (Altrock, 1963). *See also* Cities Serv. Oil Co., 42 LA 479, 482 (Hawley, 1964).

[431]Savannah Symphony Soc'y, 102 LA 575 (Howell, 1994) (employer did not violate the collective bargaining agreement when only 26 of 35 slots were filled, because employer made reasonable effort to find qualified individuals; it was in the middle of the performing season, and employer was not required to fill all 35 positions).

[432]WCI Steel, 103 LA 114 (Duda, Jr., 1994) (employer did not violate collective bargaining agreement with the introduction of caster slabs to strip mill, to increase efficiency; employer thus required only one operator rather than two for occasional fine tuning on some of the coils); James River Corp., 102 LA 893, 896 (Jones, 1994) (arbitrator upheld the elimination of jobs as result of new computer technology; management has the right to improve productivity of operations to enable company to compete effectively in global economy). *See* Ladish Co., 100 LA 690, 693–94 (Redel, 1992); James B. Beam Distilling Co., 96 LA 844, 848 (Florman, 1990); Container Corp. of Am., 91 LA 329, 331 (Rains, 1988); Union Carbide Agric. Prods. Co., 84 LA 788, 791 (Seinsheimer, 1985); Grinnell Coll., 83 LA 39, 43 (Nathan, 1984); Dravo Corp., 76 LA 903, 908 (Duff, 1981); Continental Oil Co., 71 LA 185, 190 (Towers, 1978); Lone Star Brewing Co., 50 LA 458, 461 (Hebert, 1968); Edition Bookbinders of N.Y., 42 LA 1167, 1171 (Altieri, 1964); Cities Serv. Oil Co., 42 LA 479, 482 (Hawley, 1964); Flagstaff Brewing Corp., 63-1 ARB ¶8199 (Hoffman, 1963); Oliver Tyrone Corp., 63-1 ARB ¶8092 (Joseph, 1962). *See also* Printing Indus. of Metro Wash., D.C., 71 LA 838, 841–42 (Ables, 1978).

[433]*See* Bethlehem Steel Corp., 77 LA 372, 374 (Seward, 1981); National Distillers & Chem. Corp., 67 LA 759, 762–63 (Chapman, 1976) (acquisition of new equipment changed the underlying basis for the team concept asserted by the union, and, in any event, the union's "team concept" did not qualify as a "condition" but rather fell within management's right to direct the workforce). *See also* National Steel Corp., 77 LA 1042, 1045 (Seinsheimer, 1981).

duction in the employees' workload in order to justify the reduction in crew size.[434]

Moreover, there must be a "reasonable causal relationship" between the changes and the reduction in the crew, not only in the substance of the change, but also in the span of time between the change in equipment or process and the change in crew size.[435] Thus, where a series of changes was completed and the employer did not act to reduce the crew size until 10 years later, the arbitrator refused to uphold the reduction.[436] However, even though there was a substantial span of time between the first of several changes and the reduction in crew size, management was upheld where it acted with "reasonable dispatch following the last of several related changes which rounded out the total picture of altered circumstances affecting the jobs in question."[437] The arbitrator stated that the changes "are not properly considered as individual and isolated changes but must be viewed in their cumulative effect."[438]

D. Changes in Type of Operations, Methods, and Procedures

Substantial changes in the type of operations or in the method of operations[439] have been considered as factors in justifying management's reduction of the size of crews. Thus, under a contract providing for "the normal number of men . . . required for the then existing conditions," an employer was upheld when it eliminated a helper from a crew because a modernization program had made substantial changes in the type of operation and had substantially reduced the quantity of work to be performed by such helper. The work that remained did "not appear . . . to burden unduly" the remaining crew members.[440]

Under a local working conditions clause, an arbitrator held that substantial cumulative changes in warehouse and shipping procedures justified

---

[434]*See* United States Steel Corp., 51 LA 1303, 1306 (Garrett, 1968); Birmingham News Co., 49 LA 1018, 1026 (Platt, 1967); United States Steel Co., 43 LA 1048, 1050 (Florey, 1964); Braun Baking Co., 43 LA 433, 440 (May, 1964); American Chain & Cable Co., 39 LA 432, 435 (McDermott, 1962). *See also* Keystone Steel & Wire Co., 55 LA 41, 53–54 (McKenna, 1970).

[435]*See* United States Steel Corp., 40 LA 984, 987–88 (Crawford, 1963). *See also* Kaiser Steel Corp., 44 LA 353, 357–58 (Bernstein, 1965).

[436]United States Steel Corp., 40 LA 984, 987–88 (Crawford, 1963).

[437]United States Steel Corp., 41 LA 468, 479 (McDermott, 1963). *See also* Mobil Oil Co., 46 LA 140, 148–49 (Hebert, 1966); Continental Can Co., 35 LA 602, 607 (McKelvey, 1960); United States Steel Corp., 34 LA 556, 558 (Sherman, 1960).

[438]United States Steel Corp., 41 LA 468, 480 (McDermott, 1963).

[439]As to changes in the type of operations, see *Pittsburgh Steel Co.*, 43 LA 770, 772 (McDermott, 1964); *Cities Serv. Oil Co.*, 42 LA 479, 482 (Hawley, 1964); *Gulf Oil Corp.*, 42 LA 294, 297 (Rehmus, 1964). As to changes in the method of operations, see *Castle & Cooke Terminals*, 76 LA 1099, 1104 (Gilson, 1981); *Mead Corp.*, 64–3 ARB ¶9169 (Fallon, 1964); *Bethlehem Steel*, 36 LA 162, 163 (Seward, 1961); *Midwest Carbide Corp.*, 35 LA 618, 620–21 (Brown, 1960).

[440]Gulf Oil Corp., 42 LA 294, 297 (Rehmus, 1964). *See also* Dinagraphics, Inc., 92 LA 453 (Heekin, 1989); Container Corp. of Am., 91 LA 329 (Rains, 1988) (employer properly eliminated three bargaining-unit positions during modernization, where action was necessary to improve efficiency of operations); Mead Corp., 84 LA 875, 879–80 (Sergent, Jr., 1985); Engelhard Indus., 82 LA 680, 683 (Nicholas, Jr., 1984).

the reduction in crew size; even though instituted over a period of years, the changes were considered to be "part and parcel of the same improvement pattern."[441]

Absent an explicit contractual prohibition, management's right to eliminate positions and reassign remaining duties when methods of operation have been changed also has been upheld.[442] However, a permanent reassignment may be subject to contractual seniority provisions.[443] The elimination of positions, previously required by a 40-year-old arbitration decision, was upheld as a management right when the fundamental operations of the company changed to obviate the need for the now redundant positions.[444]

E. Market Changes

One arbitrator considered market changes an important factor, along with improved and new equipment and procedures, in upholding management's right to reduce the size of crews.[445] Similarly, in the absence of a contractual requirement to maintain crew sizes, where changes occurred in customers' buying habits as well as in methods of operation that in turn substantially reduced the amount of work available to the employees involved, it was held that the company had the right to reduce the crew size.[446]

F. Production Needs and Reduced Operations

When operations are reduced in order to adapt to production needs, arbitrators appear to be in general agreement that management may reduce

---

[441]United States Steel Corp., 41 LA 56, 58–59 (Altrock, 1963). *See also* Cities Serv. Oil Co., 42 LA 479, 482 (Hawley, 1964).

[442]*See* Fort James Corp., 113 LA 1089 (Giblin, 2000) (where redesign of mill operations required changes in preventive maintenance and repair methods, the employer did not violate the collective bargaining agreement by eliminating the project crew and transferring crew members to maintenance crews, as the crew members' work did not change, there was no effect on crew seniority, and the employer had previously made similar changes in maintenance crew size); James B. Beam Distilling Co., 96 LA 844 (Florman, 1990) (distillery filler operator position properly eliminated and remaining duties transferred following automation of line, where only 10% of duties remained following automation); Container Corp. of Am., 91 LA 329 (Rains, 1988) (employer properly eliminated three bargaining-unit positions during modernization, where action was necessary to improve efficiency of operations); Flowers Baking Co. of W. Va., 89 LA 113 (Flannagan, 1987); Mead Corp., 84 LA 875, 879–80 (Sergent, Jr., 1985); Union Carbide Agric. Prods. Co., 84 LA 788 (Seinsheimer, 1985); Engelhard Indus., 82 LA 680, 683 (Nicholas, Jr., 1984).

[443]Pennsylvania Power Co., 113 LA 217 (Duff, 1999) (while an employer, under a "temporary assignments" clause, may form a crew of bargaining-unit employees to be temporarily reassigned to certain work, it violates the collective bargaining agreement if the work is in the nature of a permanent reassignment and is not assigned on the basis of seniority).

[444]Packaging Corp. of Am., 102 LA 1099 (Odom, Jr., 1994) (employer did not violate the contract when it eliminated plant nurses for the second and third weekend shifts, because the nature of the operation had become less dangerous and the company trained employees on different shifts in emergency medical care to substitute for these nurses; the employer was entitled to seek new and more efficient methods to serve the same needs).

[445]*See* Cities Serv. Oil Co., 42 LA 479, 482 (Hawley, 1964). With regard to fiscal crises as a cause for crew reductions by public-sector employers, see *City of Yonkers, Fire Dep't*, 66 LA 318, 321 (Zack, 1976); City of N.Y., Fire Dep't, 66 LA 261, 265–66 (Schmertz, 1976).

[446]Mead Corp., 64–3 ARB ¶9169 (Fallon, 1964).

the size of crews so long as such action is not barred by the contract, does not create a safety hazard, and there is no evidence of bad faith.[447] Thus, when a certain operation had been discontinued, it was held that management had the right to eliminate a job pertaining to the operation and assign the relatively few remaining duties of the job to another crew member.[448]

G. Workload and Idle Time

Unions frequently challenge a company's action on the basis that a reduced crew results in an excessive workload for the remaining crew members. However, working conditions may be changed significantly by technological or process improvements, by reducing or discontinuing certain operations, or by changes in methods and procedures, and the like. When such factors have resulted in a substantial amount of idle time for the employees in a crew, arbitrators have held that a company properly may reduce the crew and reallocate whatever duties remain to other employees in the crew.[449] In most of such cases, the arbitrator has found that the remaining work allocated to the other crew members did not excessively increase their workload.[450]

If there is a finding that the elimination of a job from the crew has increased the workload of the remaining crew members, some adjustment in their rate of pay may be ordered. Under such circumstances, one arbitrator held that there was an "increase in job content" that triggered a contract provision allowing for the negotiation of an adjustment in wage rate.[451] In another situation, where the company was not permitted under the contract to operate with a crew member absent but nevertheless required three mem-

---

[447]See Formosa Plastics Corp., 83 LA 792, 796 (Taylor, 1984); United States Steel Corp., 82 LA 534, 537 (Jones, Jr., 1984); International Salt Co., 42 LA 1188, 1190–91 (Mittenthal, 1964); Pittsburgh Steel Co., 40 LA 487, 489 (McDermott, 1963); Bethlehem Steel Co., 37 LA 83, 84 (Seward, 1961); Bethlehem Steel, 36 LA 217, 218 (Valtin, 1961); Bethlehem Steel Co., 34 LA 584, 585 (Seward, 1960); Republic Steel Corp., 31 LA 217, 218 (Platt, 1958). But see Georgetown Steel Corp., 84 LA 549, 552 (Schroeder, 1985) (arbitrator sustained reduction of crew on weekdays when use of foremen to do bargaining-unit work was de minimis, but found violation of clause prohibiting supervisors from doing unit work, when crew reduction on weekends resulted from foremen being assigned more than de minimis amount of unit work).

[448]Pittsburgh Steel Co., 40 LA 70, 72 (McDermott, 1962). The arbitrator made no finding regarding the question of excessive workload on the remaining crew. See also James B. Beam Distilling Co., 96 LA 844 (Florman, 1990); Brunswick Pulp & Paper Co., 91 LA 307 (Taylor, 1988) (nondisciplinary terminations upheld, where employer showed terminations were caused by attrition, seasonal reduction in relief requirements, and new equipment).

[449]Pittsburgh Steel Co., 40 LA 70, 72 (McDermott, 1962); Reynolds Mining Corp., 33 LA 25, 28 (Bauder, 1959). See also Foster Wheeler Corp., 64–1 ARB ¶8103 (Shister, 1963).

[450]See Lone Star Brewing Co., 50 LA 458, 461 (Hebert, 1968); Pittsburgh Steel Co., 46 LA 733, 734 (McDermott, 1966); Pearl Brewing Co., 42 LA 145, 147–48 (Bothwell, 1964); Gulf Oil Corp., 42 LA 294, 297 (Rehmus, 1964); Mead Corp., 64–3 ARB ¶9169 (Fallon, 1964); Johnson Bronze Co., 34 LA 365, 367 (McDermott, 1960); National Container Corp., 29 LA 687, 692 (Marshall, 1957). One arbitrator found that in fact the workload of the remaining crew was less than it had been before the crew was reduced due to reduced operations and improved methods. Midwest Carbide Corp., 35 LA 618, 621 (Brown, 1960).

[451]Mobil Oil Co., 61–4 ARB ¶8069 (Willingham, 1961). See also Buffalo Forge Co., 97 LA 947 (Fullmer, 1991); American Welding & Mfg. Co., 91 LA 1054 (Kates, 1988); Amana Refrigeration, 89 LA 751 (Bowers, 1987); Englehard Indus., 82 LA 680 (Nicholas, Jr., 1984).

bers of a four-man crew to perform all the tasks of the crew, the arbitrator directed the company to pay each of those three members an additional sum equivalent to one-third of the regular wages the fourth crew member earned, as compensation for the additional work duties performed while he was absent.[452]

In some instances, however, an alleged reduction in crew size may be nothing more than an attempt to reclassify an existing job. One arbitrator found a contract violation where an employer ostensibly eliminated evening and Saturday telephone operator jobs by reclassifying the incumbents as console attendants and reducing their wages. The employer relied on a reduction in the workload caused by implementation of a new telephone system, but the arbitrator concluded that although the level of work was less intense due to the new system, the essential duties of the job remained unchanged. Thus, the position was not, in fact, eliminated.[453]

H. Use of Supervisors or "General Help" [LA CDI 117.339]

The fact that the company assigns supervisors or "general help" to perform work that would have been done by the eliminated crew member may be pertinent in determining whether a reduction in the crew was in fact justified. The weight to be accorded such a factor would depend on the amount and frequency of work performed by personnel outside the crew in question. Thus, where foremen or general help have not given inordinate assistance to those remaining in the reduced crew, arbitrators have held that this factor would not be determinative of the decision in the case.[454] However, where the union proved that foremen were persistently performing the work that would have been done by the eliminated crew member, the arbitrator considered that the company by such action tacitly recognized that the crew was short-handed.[455] The introduction of new technology may justify reduc-

---

[452]Southwest Steel Corp., 38 LA 344, 346–47 (Duff, 1962). *See also* Pittsburgh Steel Co., 66–1 ARB ¶8286 (McDermott, 1966).

[453]Grinnell Coll., 83 LA 39, 43 (Nathan, 1984). However, the arbitrator did find that the employer was justified in eliminating the day-shift operator's job and assigning day-shift telephone work to a nonunit employee because the nature of the work itself on day shift had changed.

[454]*See* Dresser Indus., 96 LA 1063 (Nicholas, Jr., 1991) (employer did not violate contract by eliminating dispatcher position and transferring remaining duties, where majority of dispatcher's duties were taken over by computer and remainder were de minimis and had been performed by supervisors prior to computerization); Kelsey Mem'l Hosp., 88 LA 406 (Pincus, 1986) (employer did not violate contract by reducing employee's hours and later laying him off, despite union's belief that this action resulted from supervisors' performance of bargaining-unit work); Georgetown Steel Corp., 84 LA 549, 551–52 (Schroeder, 1985) (elimination of weigh-clerk position on weekdays, when foreman's performance of those duties was de minimis, was justified, but foreman's performance of weigh-clerk tasks on weekends was not de minimis and elimination of that job on weekends violated the contract); Formosa Plastics Corp., 83 LA 792, 797 (Taylor, 1984) (elimination of field-time clerk job was held justified where foreman workload did not significantly increase by assuming remaining field-time clerk duties); United States Steel Corp., 82 LA 534, 537 (Jones, Jr., 1984) (elimination of spare parts attendant and reassignment of duties to craftsmen held justified).

[455]United States Steel Corp., 61–2 ARB ¶8527 (Garrett, 1961). *See also* Keystone Steel & Wire Co., 45 LA 648, 650–51 (Daugherty, 1965).

tion of crew size and reassignment of job responsibilities to nonunit employees.[456]

I. Safety or Health Hazard

Management's right to determine the size of work crews frequently has been challenged on the ground that a reduction in the size of the crew has resulted in a safety or health hazard to the remaining employees. This argument has been advanced in the wake of, among other things, technological changes,[457] introduction of safety equipment and procedures,[458] changes in operations and methods,[459] changes in production needs and reduced operations,[460] and the introduction of new production procedures.[461] However, by far the preponderance of cases involving such changes has held either that there was no sufficient showing of a safety hazard or that there was no increase in the normal and inherent hazard of the job.[462]

It should be observed that in many jobs there are certain normal and inherent risks that cannot be avoided if the jobs are to be performed at all. Thus, in crew safety cases it must be determined (1) whether a safety hazard actually exists; and (2) if so, whether it is an abnormal safety hazard. Of

---

[456]Tone Bros., 114 LA 547 (Jay, 1999) (where new computerized inventory management system substantially eliminated expeditors' job functions and altered the nature of their work, so that most of the remaining duties were the same as those of supervisors, the employer did not violate the collective bargaining agreement by reducing expeditor positions and creating nonunit position of wave planner).

[457]See Gulf Power Co., 92 LA 991, 994 (Baroni, 1989); Bethlehem Steel Corp., 77 LA 372, 374 (Seward, 1981); U.S. Air Force, 74 LA 820, 822 (Gershenfeld, 1980); Pearl Brewing Co., 42 LA 145, 147–48 (Bothwell, 1964); United States Steel Corp., 41 LA 432, 434–35 (Duff, 1963); United States Steel Corp., 41 LA 300, 301–02 (Duff, 1963); Wyandotte Chems. Corp., 41 LA 230, 236 (Howlett, 1963); Penn-Dixie Cement Corp., 34 LA 442, 445 (Reid, 1959); United States Steel Corp., 34 LA 127, 135–36 (Garrett, 1960).

[458]See Virginia Elec. & Power Co., 102 LA 445 (Aronin, 1993); Dravo Corp., 76 LA 903, 907 (Duff, 1981); Jones & Laughlin Steel Corp., 43 LA 583, 587 (Duff, 1964); Pickands-Mather & Co., 43 LA 427, 429 (Lehoczky, 1964); Reserve Mining Co., 39 LA 341, 346–47 (Sembower, 1962); Union Carbide Metals Co., 37 LA 501, 503 (Murphy, 1961).

[459]See Newport Steel Corp., 78 LA 1229, 1233 (Murphy, 1982); Castle & Cooke Terminals, 76 LA 1099, 1104 (Gilson, 1981); Pickands-Mather & Co., 43 LA 427, 429 (Lehoczky, 1964); United States Steel Corp., 41 LA 432, 434–35 (Duff, 1964); Wyandotte Chems. Corp., 41 LA 230, 236 (Howlett, 1963); Penn-Dixie Cement Co., 33 LA 442, 445 (Reid, 1959).

[460]See Airport Auth. of Washoe County, 86 LA 237, 243 (Christopher, 1985); Bethlehem Steel Corp., 69 LA 162, 162 (Sharnoff, 1977); International Salt Co., 42 LA 1188, 1191 (Mittenthal, 1964); Bethlehem Steel Co., 37 LA 83, 84 (Seward, 1961); Bethlehem Steel, 36 LA 217, 218 (Valtin, 1961); Republic Steel Corp., 31 LA 217, 218–19 (Platt, 1958).

[461]United States Steel Corp., 41 LA 300, 301–02 (Duff, 1963).

[462]See cases cited in notes 457–461, above. In only two of these cases was an increased hazard found: Bethlehem Steel Corp., 69 LA 162, 163 (Sharnoff, 1977); Jones & Laughlin Steel Corp., 43 LA 583, 587 (Duff, 1964). See also American Pipe & Constr. Co., 43 LA 1126, 1134–35 (Ladar, 1964). But see Ball Metal Food Container, 113 LA 446 (Heekin, 1999) (employer removal of ink room attendant from plant color room, without ensuring that there was another employee within sight, created a safety hazard due to noisy conditions at the plant making communications difficult in the event of injury and violated collective bargaining agreement); New York State Elec. & Gas Corp., 111 LA 339 (Lurie, 1998) (employer violated the collective bargaining agreement by putting employee's safety at risk when it used a one-person crew to both operate the bucket truck and perform street light maintenance, where the "operating instructions" and safety regulations required use of a two-person maintenance crew).

course, such determinations must be made on the basis of the facts in each case. A crew safety dispute may include the question of whether an additional employee would eliminate the alleged safety hazard, or the question of possible increased hazard to an employee left working alone when all the other crew members are eliminated. In a case involving the former issue, an arbitrator required the return of an employee to the crew when he found that a genuine safety hazard existed despite the installation of electronic safety devices and other automatic equipment. He held the innovations were not adequate to "insure an equivalent amount of protection which would be furnished if a vigilant employee was also on duty."[463] However, conditions may be such that the presence of an additional experienced employee would still not eliminate the alleged hazard.[464]

In instances where the company has eliminated the crew save for one employee, arbitrators appear to be in general agreement that working alone is not a "hazard per se."[465] In such a case, where the remaining employee had instructions to request additional help if he felt it necessary, the arbitrator found it significant that no such requests had been made.[466] Arguments that such instructions place an "unreasonable psychological or physical burden" on the employee have been rejected.[467]

Two other aspects of crew size issues may be mentioned briefly here. These relate to (1) the obligation of management to provide reasonably safe working conditions; and (2) the obligation of an employee to stay on the job unless a real safety or health hazard exists, and, conversely, the employee's right to be relieved of duty pending correction of abnormally hazardous conditions.[468] In this connection it has been held that management has the right

---

[463]Jones & Laughlin Steel Corp., 43 LA 583, 587 (Duff, 1964). *See also* Gulf Power Co., 92 LA 991, 994 (Baroni, 1989); American Pipe & Constr. Co., 43 LA 1126, 1134–35 (Ladar, 1964). In *United States Steel Corp.*, 54 LA 317, 320 (Garrett, 1971), an apprentice could not be substituted for one of the two regular men on a crew, the practice being to use two journeymen for safety reasons and there being no change in conditions to affect the need for two journeymen. *See also* Bethlehem Steel Corp., 69 LA 162, 163–64 (Sharnoff, 1977) (the hazard involved in the operation left "little or no margin for error").

[464]Bethlehem Steel Corp., 36 LA 217, 219 (Valtin, 1961). *See also* Brooklyn Union Gas Co., 47 LA 425, 429 (Wolf, 1966); United States Steel Corp., 41 LA 432, 434–35 (Duff, 1963). In *Newport Steel Corp.*, 78 LA 1229, 1234 (Murphy, 1982), the arbitrator concluded that (1) obstruction of the engineer's line of vision was "an inherent safety risk which cannot be avoided if locomotive engines are to be used" for certain purposes in the employer's operations, and (2) the risk could "be managed by steps other than adding an additional person on the crew operating each locomotive engine." Conditioned on use of alternative measures, including installation and maintenance of equipment for direct radio communication between crew members, use of an additional crew member was not required. *See also* Bethlehem Steel Corp., 66 LA 77, 79 (Reel, 1976). In *Lever Bros. Co.*, 64 LA 503, 507 (Block, 1975) (emphasis in original), the arbitrator concluded that adding another crew member would not substantially reduce possible risks, and he stated that "it is not reasonable to ask a Company to increase their operating costs, and ultimately the price of their products to the public, in order to achieve a *minimal hypothetical* reduction in *possible* risk to a few employees."

[465]Pickands-Mather & Co., 43 LA 427, 429 (Lehoczky, 1964). *See also* Western Fuel Oil Co., 89 LA 772, 775–76 (Kaufman, 1987); U.S. Air Force, 74 LA 820, 824 (Gershenfeld, 1980); International Salt Co., 42 LA 1188, 1192 (Mittenthal, 1964); United States Steel Corp., 41 LA 300, 301–02 (Duff, 1963); Bethlehem Steel, 36 LA 217, 219 (Valtin, 1961).

[466]Pearl Brewing Co., 42 LA 145, 148 (Bothwell, 1964).

[467]Brooklyn Union Gas Co., 47 LA 425, 428 (Wolf, 1966).

[468]For discussion on these points, see Chapter 5, section 14.A., "Use of Grievance Procedure Versus Self-Help," and Chapter 16, "Safety and Health."

to direct a crew to work under conditions of extreme heat and humidity if there is a compelling public necessity for the work to be performed.[469]

12. VACANCIES [LA CDI 119.121]

It is generally recognized that, in the absence of a contract provision limiting management's rights to fill vacancies, such as, for example, a clear requirement to maintain a certain number of employees on a particular job, it is management's right to determine whether a vacancy exists and whether and when it should be filled.[470] But where duties associated with the vacancy are reassigned and continue to be performed by employees in other jobs, arbitrators will examine whether the employer has intentionally avoided contractually required job posting and bidding procedures.[471]

Contractual provisions dealing with the posting of vacancies, but not specifically requiring management to fill them, have been narrowly construed. Thus, when a provision for the posting of "permanent vacancies" was said not to be applicable when a company decided that there was no need to replace a promoted employee, the arbitrator ruled that no vacancy existed.[472]

---

[469]Virginia Elec. & Power Co., 102 LA 445 (Aronin, 1993) (employer did not violate collective bargaining agreement by requiring workers to work in extreme heat and humidity when the work was necessary at that specific time and employer had taken all necessary precautionary steps to prevent damage to workers' health).

[470]See also Pennsylvania Power Co., 94 LA 902 (Duff, 1990); Bethlehem Steel Corp., 90 LA 577 (Oldham, 1987) (change in working conditions was sufficient to allow temporary vacancies in toolroom attendant position to remain unfilled); Morton Thiokol, Inc., 86 LA 1102, 1106 (Ipavec, 1986); Rock Island Ref. Corp., 86 LA 173, 176 (Morgan, 1985); Quaker Oats Co., 84 LA 390, 392 (Edelman, 1985); Consolidation Coal Co., 84 LA 36, 39 (Rybolt, 1984) (employer not required to fill vacancies where conditions fluctuated and vacancies were deemed not permanent); NN Metal Stamping, 83 LA 801, 804 (Abrams, 1984); Miners Clinic, 83 LA 445, 448 (Probst, 1984); Paxall, Inc., 82 LA 708, 712 (Gallagher, 1984). But see Lone Star Steel Co., 29 LA 13, 16–17 (Davey, 1957) (the contract made it mandatory to fill vacancies). For related discussion, see section 11., "Determination of Size of Crews," above.

[471]See Homestake Mining Co., 88 LA 614 (Sinicropi, 1987) (employer violated contract by assigning employee to load-dispatcher duties on relief basis without posting position as permanent vacancy and paying him applicable rate); North River Energy Co., 85 LA 449, 452 (Witney, 1985) (company manipulated job duties and failed to post jobs "for sole purpose of avoiding" duty to post); Jim Walter Res., 85 LA 290, 293 (Feldman, 1985) (fact that employee has been on "temporary assignment" for 1.5 years indicated there was a permanent vacancy that had to be filled). For similar reasoning, see dictum in Quaker Oats Co., 84 LA 390, 392 (Edelman, 1985) (even though the company has a right to leave position vacant, there may be a violation if job duties are reassigned to others, resulting in undue burden or other indications that there remains need for vacated position).

[472]Sherwin-Williams Co., 49 LA 74, 75 (Ray, 1967). See also Germain's, Inc., 82 LA 1022, 1023–24 (Pollard, 1984); Gulf-Western Indus., 62 LA 1132, 1134 (Hutcheson, 1974); Rheem Mfg. Co., 46 LA 1027, 1029–30 (Block, 1966); Burger Iron Co., 40 LA 819, 821 (Seinsheimer, 1963). In Philips ECG, 79 LA 123, 126–27 (Shister, 1982), the agreement provided that "[a]ll vacancies in jobs covered by the agreement will be posted by the Company," id. at 124, but the arbitrator stated that all that this "dictates is the posting and filling procedure, if the attending facts and circumstances warrant the posting and filling of the vacancy." Id. at 126 (emphasis added). In holding that the employer had a right not to post a job that was vacated by the incumbent's retirement and to transfer the remaining duties to other classifications in an effort to make operations more efficient, the arbitrator cautioned that there "must be— as there was here—a compelling reasonable and good faith basis for the Company's abstention from filling a vacancy . . . ." Id. at 127–28.

Under another contract requiring posting of vacancies and giving preference in filling the vacancies to senior employees in their given classification, the arbitrator held that neither the posting, seniority, nor classification provisions implied any restriction on management's right to determine if a vacancy existed and, if so, whether to fill it.[473] But, where insufficient work existed to justify filling the job of an employee who had retired, management was not required to post the job and could assign the excess duties occasioned by the retirement to another employee, subject only to the possibility that the job of the latter employee would be subject to reevaluation.[474]

Even when a job has been posted for bid, there is no guarantee that a vacancy exists and will be filled.[475] Thus, in a case where the successful bidder was allowed to withdraw his bid and return to his original job, an arbitrator denied the grievance of another employee, who, in turn, bid on the first employee's job after it had been posted for bid.[476]

Arbitrators also have been reluctant to find that management's discretion in filling vacancies is restricted by an asserted past practice, such as a custom of posting vacancies. However, one arbitrator ruled that when the union and the company have a past practice of negotiating job classifications, work duties, pay rates, and job combinations, management may not unilaterally refuse to fill a vacancy.[477] One arbitrator held that management's prerogative to decide whether or when to fill a vacancy derives from the general management right to direct the workforce and may not be infringed on by past practice, at least in the absence of proof that prior postings did not reflect management determinations that production needs warranted filling of the vacancies.[478]

With respect to temporary vacancies occasioned by absences occurring because of illness, vacations, and the like, management has the right, unless clearly restricted by the agreement, to fill them.[479]

---

[473]Fairway Foods, 44 LA 161, 164–68 (Solomon, 1965). The mere fact that a job classification has been dormant for a lengthy period does not mean that it has been abolished. See Ohio Chem. & Surgical Equip. Co., 40 LA 481, 485 (Sembower, 1963).

[474]Link-Belt Co., 36 LA 825, 827 (Crawford, 1961). See also Colson Co., 54 LA 896, 900–01 (Roberts, 1971).

[475]See Computing & Software, 61 LA 261, 267 (Shieber, 1973); R.C. Can Co., 52 LA 894, 897–98 (Kesselman, 1969); McCall Corp., 43 LA 951, 956 (Layman, 1964). See also U.S. R.R. Ret. Bd., 71 LA 498, 503 (Sembower, 1978).

[476]R.C. Can Co., 52 LA 894, 897–98 (Kesselman, 1969) (a prior agreement existed, however, that would produce a different result if a successful bidder already had commenced work on his new job).

[477]Quanex Corp., 108 LA 841 (House, 1997) (employer violated the contract when it did not fill vacancy on the crew; the parties had negotiated every job classification and rate of pay in the past and for the current contract).

[478]See National Elec. Benefit Fund, 87 LA 914, 920–21 (Lubic, 1986).

[479]See Amax Chem. Corp., 81 LA 1122, 1124–25 (Nelson, 1983); Mobay Chem. Corp., 64 LA 259, 260 (Tharp, 1975); Pittsburgh & Conneaut Dock Co., 55 LA 19, 22 (Teple, 1970); Celotex Corp., 43 LA 395, 399–400 (Ray, 1964); Great Atl. & Pac. Tea Co., 41 LA 492, 496 (Roberts, 1963); Phillips Chem. Co., 38 LA 1152, 1154 (Larson, 1962); American Gilsonite Co., 36 LA 266, 267–68 (Seligson, 1960); Standard Oil Co., 36 LA 245, 249–50 (Stouffer, 1960); National Zinc Co., 29 LA 467, 468 (Abernethy, 1957); United States Rubber Co., 28 LA 538, 541–42 (Hebert, 1957); Electro Metallurgical Co., 28 LA 252, 254 (Marshall, 1957); United States Steel Corp., 22 LA 157, 159 (Hawley, 1953); Reynolds Metals Co., 16 LA 352, 356 (Klamon, 1951). In *Minnesota Mining & Mfg. Co.*, 73 LA 378, 380 (Stern, 1979), management was upheld in filling a temporary vacancy by overtime rather than by recalling an

Contract provisions stating that temporary vacancies "will" or "shall" be filled by a stated procedure have been construed merely to specify the procedure to be used *if* management decides to fill a vacancy.[480]

13. Scheduling Work [LA CDI 100.47; 115.250]

Collective bargaining agreements may deal expressly with the scheduling of work. For example, the agreement may fix or regulate shifts,[481] define the workweek,[482] provide that scheduling is an exclusive function of management,[483] or, in some respect, limit the employer's right to schedule work.[484] The agreement also may be interpreted as impliedly restricting management's rights in the scheduling of work. For example, in one case nonspecific contract language was interpreted as precluding management from instituting 7-day continuous shift operations.[485]

Most arbitrators have recognized that, except as restricted by the agreement, the right to schedule work remains in management.[486] Much of the

---

employee from layoff; the arbitrator pointed out that the utilized procedure was not specifically prohibited by the agreement, that the union had failed to establish its allegation of employer purpose to avoid holiday pay, and that "[s]table employment and the avoidance of temporary callbacks is usually regarded as a sound practice." The fact that management may have elected to fill temporary vacancies in the past does not bind it to do so in the future. *See* Celotex Corp., 43 LA 395, 399–400 (Ray, 1964); Great Atl. & Pac. Tea Co., 41 LA 492, 496 (Roberts, 1963).

[480]*See* United States Rubber Co., 28 LA 538, 541 (Hebert, 1957); Great Lakes Pipe Line Co., 25 LA 885, 888 (Roberts, 1955); United States Steel Corp., 22 LA 157, 159 (Hawley, 1959). The posting of schedules and scheduling of employees does not guarantee the number of employees who are to work and require replacements for sick employees. Standard Oil Co., 36 LA 245, 249–50 (Stouffer, 1960).

[481]*See, e.g.,* Curtiss-Wright Corp., 36 LA 629, 629–30 (Crawford, 1960).

[482]*See, e.g.,* H. Meyer Dairy Co., 108 LA 765 (West, 1997) (employer violated collective bargaining agreement when it reduced the number of days in a workweek from 4 to 3 when the contract allowed for discretion between 4 and 5 days); Willamette Indus., 107 LA 897 (Howell, 1996) (employer violated collective bargaining agreement when it unilaterally changed the workweek from a 4-day/10-hours-per-day week to a 5-day/8-hours-per-day week without consulting the union as required by the contract); Bethlehem Steel Corp., 92 LA 430 (Sharnoff, 1989); Norfolk Naval Shipyard, 54 LA 588, 589 (Cushman, 1971).

[483]*See, e.g.,* Tribune-Star Publ'g Co., 95 LA 210 (Witney, 1990); Celanese Corp. of Am., 30 LA 797, 798 (Jaffee, 1958).

[484]*See, e.g.,* Ambridge Borough, 73 LA 810, 812 (Dean, 1979); Taylor Stone Co., 29 LA 236, 237 (Dworkin, 1957).

[485]Morse Chain Co., 43 LA 557, 560–61 (Cahn, 1964).

[486]American Greetings Corp., 107 LA 1209 (West, 1996) (employer did not violate the contract when it did not grant overtime work to maintenance employees who had no training on equipment, despite practice of granting overtime when equipment is being installed, serviced, or modified). *See* Fort Dodge Labs., 87 LA 1290, 1293 (Smith, 1986) (reference in contract to "regularly scheduled" workweek meant employer could not set schedule with different starting times on different days of the week); Bowen Enters., 87 LA 548, 552 (Hannan, 1986) (contract requiring part-time employees to be scheduled maximum number of hours for which they are available means senior part-time employees must be scheduled up to 32-hour maximum before junior part-timers receive any hours over the contractual minimum of 17); Kroger Co., 86 LA 357, 361 (Milentz, 1986) (employer's scheduling practice violated contract clause saying two employees would not be scheduled where one could be scheduled to do the work); H. Meyer Dairy Co., 84 LA 131, 134 (Ghiz, 1985) (employer violated contract by not providing required notice prior to schedule change); Schnadig Corp., 83 LA 1194, 1197 (Goldman, 1984) (contract prohibited unilateral changes in starting or quitting time); Red Owl Stores, 83 LA 652, 656 (Reynolds, 1984) (contract required at least one employee to be on duty at all times). *But see* Broekhuizen Produce Co., 82 LA 221, 224 (Roumell, Jr., 1984) ("maintenance-of-standards" clause that makes reference to hours of work nevertheless does not establish a guarantee of hours).

following material deals with the application of this rule, providing some guidance as to the scope of management's rights—and limitations thereon—in this area.

A. Shifts and Workweek [LA CDI 115.301 et seq.]

Management has been permitted to suspend operations temporarily, eliminate double-time work, change the number of shifts, and change the number of days to be worked. Thus, where nothing in the agreement clearly guaranteed any particular amount of work each week, and the agreement did not otherwise restrict management's right to suspend operations, management could determine whether work should go forward and its decision to close down on a given day was upheld because it acted for a valid reason and not arbitrarily.[487] The elimination of Sunday (double-time) work was upheld even though such work had been scheduled regularly for many years. In that that case the arbitrator stated: "While the agreement contains no 'management rights' clause, the scheduling of work is a normal and customary function of management which would not ordinarily be deemed limited or waived except by some express provision of the agreement."[488]

Similarly, where the contract contained no express limitation on work scheduling, management was permitted to change from a schedule of two 6-hour shifts, 6 days a week, to a schedule of one 8-hour shift, 5 days a week. The arbitrator held that the change was not barred either by the contract's reference to 6-hour shifts (which he said did not crystallize the workweek but merely provided the framework for overtime computation), or by the provision on preservation of "present practices and policies."[489] Management's right to change from a 5-day work schedule to a 6-day schedule also has been upheld.[490]

---

[487]*See* TRW, Inc., 48 LA 1365, 1367–68 (Kabaker, 1967) (closing on the day before Christmas and the day before New Year's because of reduced orders); Deere & Co., 45 LA 388, 396–98 (Solomon, 1965) (closing to give holiday to nonunit employees though this meant unit employees did not work); Henry Pratt Co., 42 LA 51, 53 (Davidson, 1963); Alsco, Inc., 41 LA 970, 972–74 (Kabaker, 1963) (shortage of materials justified sending certain employees home); American Zinc Co., 36 LA 1031, 1034 (Klamon, 1961); Foster Wheeler Corp., 35 LA 788, 790–92 (Stark, 1960).

[488]New Jersey Brewers' Ass'n, 33 LA 320, 322 (Hill, 1959).

[489]Kimberly-Clark Corp., 42 LA 982, 986–88 (Sembower, 1964) (the change was discussed with the union prior to being instituted). For a case similarly permitting management to change from a 6-day work schedule to a 5-day schedule, see *St. Regis Paper Co.*, 51 LA 1102, 1107–08 (Solomon, 1968) (there was no express restriction and the contract contained a general management-rights clause; the arbitrator distinguished several other cases in which past actions of the parties made out a joint understanding as to scheduling). A "maintenance-of-standards" clause was held not to prevent management from changing from a 48-hour workweek to a 40-hour workweek in *Borden Co.*, 39 LA 1020, 1023–24 (Morvant, 1962). Long-established differences in a company's summer and winter schedules did constitute a binding "local working condition" under the agreement in *Bethlehem Cornwall Corp.*, 31 LA 793, 795–96 (Valtin, 1958). *See also* Carpenter Funds Admin. Office of N. Cal., 72 LA 410, 413 (Maloney, 1979).

[490]Goodyear Tire & Rubber Co., 32 LA 77, 80 (Shister, 1958); Screw Mach. Prods. Co., 3 WAR LAB. REP. 553, 556 (1942) (the decision was signed by the public, labor, and management members of the panel). In *Belcor, Inc.*, 77 LA 23, 26–27 (McKay, 1981), a work schedule change from 5 days on and 2 days off to 7 days on and 3 or 4 days off, in order to distribute the burden of working weekends, was upheld.

In validating such changes arbitrators have spoken of management's right "to schedule the work with a view to optimum efficiency,"[491] and have expressed the view that limitations on the right "ought not be lightly inferred."[492] The mere fact that traditionally a workweek had consisted of 5 consecutive days has been held not to have given employees a vested interest in the continuation of the schedule.[493] So, under agreements containing a general management-rights clause, but otherwise silent on the particular subject, management was deemed to have the authority to establish staggered work schedules,[494] to change from fixed to rotating shifts,[495] and to add an extra shift to permit 7-day operations.[496] However, while recognizing management's right to establish work schedules except as restricted by the agreement, one arbitrator ruled that management was not privileged to schedule shifts in such a way as to deprive employees of certain rest periods to which they were entitled under the contract.[497] Neither could a company change from fixed to rotating shifts where the change would impair the contractual right of senior employees to their preferred shift and days off.[498]

---

[491]Kimberly-Clark Corp., 42 LA 982, 986 (Sembower, 1964).

[492]St. Regis Paper Co., 51 LA 1102, 1107 (Solomon, 1968).

[493]Calumet & Hecla, 42 LA 25, 28–31 (Howlett, 1963) (the employer changed from scheduling Monday through Friday and began scheduling employees for 5 days during the week as required by operational needs); Columbia Steel Co., 7 LA 881, 883 (Blumer, 1947). *See also* Georgia-Pacific Corp., 77 LA 1156, 1158–59 (Mewhinney, 1981) (upholding a schedule change that no longer assured some employees of having 2 consecutive days off).

[494]Ingram-Richardson Mfg. Co. of Ind., 3 LA 482, 485 (Whiting, 1946). For other cases construing the contract as not requiring the workweek to be composed of 5 consecutive days and thus permitting "staggered" or "split" work schedules, see *Pacific Tel. & Tel. Co.*, 49 LA 1000, 1002–04 (Koven, 1967); *Magnode Prods.*, 47 LA 449, 452 (Hayes, 1966); *International Minerals & Chem. Co.*, 13 LA 192, 199 (Schedler, 1949); *Columbia Steel Co.*, 7 LA 881, 883 (Blumer, 1947). *See also* Celanese Corp. of Am., 30 LA 797, 799–803 (Jaffee, 1958); Sinclair Ref. Co., 15 LA 142, 146–47 (Abrahams, 1950).

[495]Morris P. Kirk & Son, 27 LA 6, 10 (Prasow, 1956); General Cable Corp., 15 LA 910, 912 (Kaplan, 1950) (there was no management-rights clause). *See also* Washington County, Or., 78 LA 1081, 1091 (Tilbury, 1982). For a case dealing with arbitrability, where the agreement contained no provision relating expressly to management's action in changing from fixed to rotating shifts, see *Iowa Beef Processors v. Meat Cutters*, 627 F.2d 853, 105 LRRM 2149, 2152 (8th Cir. 1980). In *Carnation Co.*, 34 LA 345, 349–50 (Marshall, 1960), management was bound by past practice as to the frequency of shift rotation.

[496]Minnesota Mining & Mfg. Co., 15 LA 46, 49 (Kelliher, 1950). For other cases permitting the adding of shifts, see *Associated Wholesale Grocers*, 73 LA 781, 787 (Roberts, 1979) ("the Arbitrator cannot find a limitation upon the Company's right to establish new, different, or additional shifts from time to time as its requirements dictate"); Baltimore News Am., 68 LA 1054, 1056 (Seidenberg, 1977) (pointing out that the employer established the new shift for bona fide business reasons, the arbitrator stated that the "weight of arbitral authority is that the institution, or modification of existing shifts, absent a specific contractual prohibition against it, is an appropriate exercise of managerial judgment"); Detroit News, 68 LA 51, 53 (Volz, 1977); Latrobe Steel Co., 34 LA 34, 36 (McCoy, 1960). Where an agreement established three specific regular shifts and contained a general management-rights clause, operational requirements were held to justify management's establishment of an "oddball" shift for one employee different from the shifts specified in the agreement. Scott Paper Co., 48 LA 591, 593 (Williams, 1967).

[497]Wilson & Co., 1 LA 342, 347 (Lohman, 1946). *See also* Bakelite Co., 29 LA 555, 559 (Updegraff, 1957) (a change in scheduled lunch periods).

[498]Reynolds Metals Co., 35 LA 800, 802–03 (Ross, 1961). Other contractual rights of employees have likewise been protected against invasion by managerial scheduling actions. *See* United States Borax & Chem. Corp., 50 LA 304, 306 (McNaughton, 1968); Uddo & Taormina, 45 LA 72, 74 (Howard, 1965).

Nor could an employer unilaterally change the hours of work and rates of pay, because changes in duration of shifts impinge directly on the union's right to bargain over rates of pay, wages, hours of work, and other conditions of employment.[499]

One arbitrator was asked to decide whether, in the absence of a contractual provision, an employer had the right to reschedule hours of work for operations at night and, if so, on what basis of compensation. The arbitrator concluded that there was no question as to the company's right to assign employees to night work, but that it must pay a night-work differential that had been paid in the past.[500] Another arbitrator upheld management's right to schedule Sunday work where not prohibited by the agreement; the reasonableness of management's action was tested from the point of view of the needs of the business rather than the convenience of the employees.[501]

When an agreement is silent as to the commencement and end of a workweek, the employer may change the day on which the workweek begins if the change is not made arbitrarily.[502] Again, where the contract contains no express restriction on the employer's right to determine the starting time for work shifts, the employer has been permitted unilaterally to change the starting and stopping time.[503] Even where an agreement specifies the shift start-

---

[499]JM Mfg. Co., 84 LA 679 (Sisk, 1985).

[500]Everett Dyers & Cleaners, 11 LA 462, 466 (Myers, 1948). In *FMC Corp.*, 50 LA 261, 263 (Koven, 1968), management could change an employee from an evening schedule to a daytime schedule, where the change was for sound business reasons and where management had changed schedules in the past.

[501]Drake Bakeries, 38 LA 751, 753–54 (Wolf, 1962). *See also* Stanley Works, 39 LA 374, 378 (Summers, 1962). For related discussion, see Chapter 17, section 6., "Non-Safety-Related Accommodation of Employee Religious Beliefs." The Vietnam Era Veterans' Readjustment Assistance Act of 1974, 38 U.S.C. §3696 et seq., does not require employers to make work schedule accommodations for employee-reservists not made for other employees. Monroe v. Standard Oil Co., 452 U.S. 549, 107 LRRM 2633 (1981). *See also* Roosevelt Hosp., 78 LA 877, 880 (Kramer, 1982) (contract provision giving employees the right to two out of five weekends off was not violated by employer's action in scheduling an employee's weekends off to coincide with her reservist obligations).

[502]Schulze's Bakery, 5 LA 255, 257 (Wardlaw, 1946) (the arbitrator also pointed out that the change was made in conformance with industry practice in the area). *See also* Arctic Utils., 75 LA 653, 654–55 (Colbert, 1980) (employer could utilize a Wednesday through Wednesday schedule even though the agreement specified a Monday-through-Sunday workweek for overtime payment purposes); Stepan Chem. Co., 65 LA 636, 637 (Rezler, 1975); Bethlehem Steel Co., 33 LA 324, 326 (Valtin, 1959). A provision requiring union consent for changing the day on which the workweek begins was strictly enforced in *Redi-Gas Service*, 48 LA 197, 198 (Olson, 1967).

[503]*See* Grand Rapids Die Casting Co., 44 LA 954, 955 (Howlett, 1965); Lone Star Gas Co., 42 LA 345, 346–48 (Schedler, 1964); Honolulu Gas Co., 41 LA 1115, 1116–17 (Tsukiyama, 1963); United States Steel Corp., 41 LA 1050, 1052–53 (Mittenthal, 1963); Robertshaw-Fulton Controls Co., 36 LA 1035, 1036–37 (Warns, 1960) (contractual requirement to "consult" with union as to change in starting time did not require union consent for a change); U.S. Pipe & Foundry Co., 28 LA 467, 467–68 (Hepburn, 1957); Federal Rice Drug Co., 27 LA 123, 125 (Reid, 1956). *See also* Miami Inspiration Hosp., 68 LA 898, 900 (Aisenberg, 1977); Corn Prods. Co., 50 LA 741, 743 (Kates, 1968); Ideal Corrugated Box Co., 46 LA 129, 131–32 (Hayes, 1965). The agreement itself may be construed to give management the unilateral right to make the change. *See* Morris Bean & Co., 49 LA 661, 663 (McIntosh, 1967); Hugo Bosca Co., 49 LA 659, 660–61 (McIntosh, 1967). It also may be construed to deny such right. *See* Cannon Elec. Co., 39 LA 93, 96 (Meyers, 1962); Purity Stores, 38 LA 803, 807–08 (Koven, 1962).

ing times, management may be justified in requiring certain employees to report early in order to perform essential preshift "start-up" work.[504]

Under agreements that expressly define a "normal" or "regular" work-week, management often has been permitted considerable leeway in making adjustments in the workweek as needed for efficient operations.[505] For ex-ample, although an agreement specified a normal workweek of Monday through Friday, special production needs justified the scheduling of one employee to a Tuesday through Saturday workweek.[506] By the same token, under another agreement that provided for a regular workweek of 5 days, management was entitled to schedule a 4-day workweek during a period of reduced production. The arbitrator in that case stated that the provision for a regular workweek was designed to regularize employment and furnish norms from which overtime premiums could be calculated, and not to guar-antee employment for all or any group of employees for any specific number of hours per day or days per week.[507] However, one arbitrator found such a restriction in a contractual reference to a "regularly scheduled" workweek. The contract there recited that the workweek would be "five consecutive or regularly scheduled days of eight hours each."[508] The arbitrator interpreted this language as prohibiting management from establishing a variable daily starting time because such a schedule was not regular within the meaning of the contract.[509]

However, even where an agreement specifically disclaimed a work guar-antee and expressly reserved the right to management to adjust work sched-ules to meet operating requirements, an arbitrator concluded that another contractual provision establishing normal workday, workweek, and shift hours was violated when the schedule was modified during Christmas and New Year's weeks. The employer was held not to have a right to change the

---

[504]Fitchburg Paper Co., 47 LA 349, 351–52 (Wallen, 1966); American Brake Shoe Co., 33 LA 344, 347–48 (Gilden, 1959). *See also* McDonnell Aircraft Corp., 21 LA 91, 97 (Klamon, 1953). *But see* Howe Scale Co., 24 LA 565, 566 (Myers, 1955).

[505]*See* Coca-Cola Foods, 88 LA 129, 132 (Naehring, 1986); Family Food Park, 86 LA 1184, 1187–88 (Petersen, 1986); FMC Corp., 85 LA 18, 21 (Karlins, 1985); Arnold Bakers, 70 LA 1144, 1147 (Robins, 1978); Monsanto Research Corp., 70 LA 530, 532–33 (Gibson, 1978); Stacy Mfg. Co., 50 LA 1211, 1213 (Daugherty, 1968) (shut down for 1 day on three separate occasions); Link-Belt Co., 48 LA 570, 572 (Cayton, 1966); Universal Foods Corp., 44 LA 226, 229–30, 233 (Hebert, 1965); Stanley Works, 39 LA 374, 377 (Summers, 1962) (although the contract spoke of a normal Monday through Friday workweek, management could use 7-day continuous-shift schedules for certain operations); Triangle Conduit & Cable Co., 33 LA 610, 613 (Gamser, 1959); Menasco Mfg. Co., 30 LA 465, 469–70 (Boles, 1958); Pittsburgh Screw & Bolt Corp., 29 LA 615, 617 (Kelliher, 1957); Parke, Davis & Co., 24 LA 496, 500 (Ryder, 1955). *See also* Georgia-Pacific Corp., 71 LA 1256, 1259 (Howell, 1978).

[506]Universal Foods Corp., 44 LA 226, 229–30, 233 (Hebert, 1965).

[507]Triangle Conduit & Cable Co., 33 LA 610, 613 (Gamser, 1959) (the layoff provisions were not violated). Very clear language is required for a guaranteed wage. New York Herald Tribune, 36 LA 753, 761 (Cole, 1960). *See also* Southwest Forest Indus., 80 LA 553, 557–58 (Traynor, 1983); North Am. Rayon Corp., 78 LA 880, 883 (Whyte, 1982); Oscar Mayer & Co., 75 LA 555, 558 (Eischen, 1980); Tri-State Transit Auth., 71 LA 716, 718–19 (Bolte, 1978). *Cf.* Anchor Hocking Corp., 81 LA 502, 507–09 (Abrams, 1983).

[508]Fort Dodge Labs., 87 LA 1290, 1293 (Smith, 1986).

[509]*Id. See also* Bethlehem Steel Corp., 92 LA 430 (Sharnoff, 1989) (employer violated contract by unilaterally changing work schedule from "normal" 8-hour/day, 5-day week to 12-hour/day, 3-day week).

schedule arbitrarily. In reaching this decision the arbitrator explained that the employee "adjusts his life" to the "normal routine," and that the employer had not provided satisfactory evidence that a change from the normal work schedule was necessary.[510]

In the absence of an explicit contract provision, there is a division of arbitral authority on the right of management to reduce the workweek in lieu of making layoffs.[511] Thus, one arbitration board held that management had the right to reduce hours of work in the absence of anything in the agreement restricting such right. There, the contract defined the normal workweek as 5 days of 8 hours each, and set forth the procedure for layoffs in case of a reduction in work. The arbitration board held that the employer was not prohibited from reducing hours per day to 7 in lieu of making layoffs. The arbitration board declared that the clauses defining the normal workday and normal workweek were standard clauses serving ostensibly as a basis for the calculation of overtime, that the working of the hours specified was not made mandatory, and that the agreement said nothing in regard to the necessity of making layoffs in lieu of reducing hours of work.[512]

A contrary result was reached by another arbitration board, which held that an employer who reduced the workweek of some employees from 5 to 4 days was required to apply the "layoff" provisions of the agreement in doing so. The agreement provided for a basic workweek of 5 days and made seniority govern in case of layoff.[513] A similar result was reached in another case

---

[510]Aro, Inc., 34 LA 254, 259 (Tatum, 1960). For other cases in which deviation from the normal or regular schedule was held improper, see *General Precision*, 42 LA 589, 593 (Roberts, 1964); *Traylor Eng'g & Mfg. Div.*, 36 LA 687, 689–90 (Crawford, 1961) (employer could not expand workweek to continuous shift where contract spoke of normal workweek of 40 hours); *Crossett Lumber Co.*, 28 LA 20, 33 (Carmichael, 1956); *Mississippi Aluminum Corp.*, 27 LA 625, 627 (Reynard, 1956); *Armstrong Rubber Co.*, 17 LA 463, 465–66 (Donnelly, Mottram, & Curry, 1951). *See also* Armstrong Cork Co., 65 LA 582, 587–88 (Yagoda, 1975).

[511]Some arbitrators have emphasized their conclusion that each case on this issue must turn on its own facts and contractual provisions. *See* Ampco-Pittsburgh Corp., 80 LA 472, 477 (Briggs, 1982); A. Hoen & Co., 64 LA 197, 199 (Feldesman, 1975); Patent Button Co. of Tenn., 37 LA 877, 882 (Stouffer, 1961); Cook Mach. Co., 35 LA 845, 848 (Boles, 1960); Motch & Merryweather Mach. Co., 32 LA 492, 496 (Kates, 1959).

[512]Geuder, Paeschke, & Frey Co., 12 LA 1163, 1164–65 (Blumer, Marshall, & Friedrich, 1949). *See also* Ampco-Pittsburgh Corp., 80 LA 472, 476–78 (Briggs, 1982) (stating certain limitations on the right); Rochester Monotype Composition Co., 77 LA 474, 477 (Miller, 1981) ("no language limits the Company's freedom to decide on a reduction in the work week instead of a layoff," rather, two provisions in the agreement "reinforce one another and provide that absolute right"); O'Neal Steel, 66 LA 118, 127 (Grooms, Jr., 1976); Rex Chainbelt, 52 LA 852, 855–57 (Murphy, 1969); Patent Button Co. of Tenn., 37 LA 877, 881–83 (Stouffer, 1961); Blaw-Knox Co., 32 LA 746, 748 (Cahn, 1959); Dayton Steel Foundry Co., 30 LA 938, 947 (Witney, 1958); Supermatic Prods. Corp., 25 LA 794, 797–99 (Prasow, 1956); Nolte Brass Foundry Co., 24 LA 874, 876–77 (Ebeling, 1955); Wausau Iron Works, 22 LA 473, 475 (Slavney, 1954); Great Lakes Pipe Line Co., 18 LA 801, 807 (Piper, 1952); American Agric. Chem. Co., 18 LA 625, 627 (Dash, Jr., 1952).

[513]United Smelting & Aluminum Co., 13 LA 684, 685–86 (Donnelly & Sviridoff, Mottram dissenting, 1949). *See also* Cooper Airmotive, 77 LA 901, 903–04 (Dunn, 1981); City of Highland Park, 76 LA 811, 815 (McDonald, 1981); Board of Governors, Wayne State Univ., 76 LA 368, 372 (Cole, 1981); Arkansas-Missouri Power Co., 74 LA 1254, 1260 (McKenna, 1980); Fitas, Mahoning County Eng'r, 70 LA 895, 898 (Cohen, 1978) (the agreement provided that its terms "in all instances shall be subject to and subservient to local budgetary requirements," but the arbitrator rejected the county's contention that this permitted reduction in the workweek in lieu of layoff by seniority where a budget deficit existed); G.C. Murphy Co.,

where a provision defining the "basic working week" as 40 hours was held violated by a reduction of the workweek for the purpose of sharing the work. The arbitrator opined that seniority must be honored by the use of layoffs; but he cautioned that the 40-hour provision did not guarantee individual employees 40 hours of work and did not limit management's right to reduce the workweek when necessary for reasons of plant efficiency or product quality.[514]

B. Work Schedule Changes to Avoid Overtime [LA CDI 115.307]

Management may be denied the right to make temporary changes in the work schedule where the purpose of doing so is to avoid contractual overtime payments. Even under a contract providing that nothing therein should "be interpreted as interfering in any way with the Company's right to alter, re-arrange or change, extend, limit or curtail its operations . . . whatever may be the effect upon employment, when, in its sole judgment and discretion, it may deem it advisable to do all or any of said things."[515] An employer was denied the right to change the work schedule for one week because the arbitrator found the sole reason for doing so was to avoid incurring overtime.[516] In the absence of limiting contract language, other arbitrators have permitted management to change work schedules to avoid the payment of overtime, holding that the company is not obligated to provide overtime work.[517]

---

68 LA 1072, 1075 (Sembower, 1977); A. Hoen & Co., 64 LA 197, 199, 203–04 (Feldesman, 1975); Aro Corp., 55 LA 859, 861 (Hertz, 1970); Ruberoid Co., 40 LA 460, 464 (Hughes, 1963); Morris Mach. Works, 40 LA 456, 459–60 (Williams, 1963); Cook Mach. Co., 35 LA 845, 848–49 (Boles, 1960); Motch & Merryweather Mach. Co., 32 LA 492, 500–01 (Kates, 1959); Goodman Mfg. Co., 25 LA 308, 312 (Larkin, 1955); Valley Metal Prods. Co., 25 LA 83, 84 (Ryder, 1955); Preferred Utils. Mfg. Co., 24 LA 846, 848 (Donnelly, 1955); International Harvester Co., 24 LA 311, 313 (Cole, 1955); John Deere Des Moines Works, 24 LA 88, 91–92 (Davey, 1955); Republic Steel Corp., 14 LA 1031, 1039 (Selekman, 1950). In one such case, the arbitrator rejected the employer's contention that "layoffs believed at their inception to be but of brief duration are not layoffs but are matters of scheduling work." Bethlehem Steel, 5 LA 578, 588 (Brandschain, 1946). In *Wilshire Mfg. Jewelers*, 49 LA 1079, 1082 (Jones, Jr., 1967), a contractual provision on work sharing was construed to *require* management to reduce hours of employees instead of laying off or discharging some of the employees for lack of work.

[514]Motch & Merryweather Mach. Co., 32 LA 492, 497–98, 500–01 (Kates, 1959).

[515]Kennecott Copper Corp., 6 LA 820, 822 (Kleinsorge, 1947).

[516]*Id.* For other awards denying management the right in question, see *United Carbon Co.*, 39 LA 310, 314–15 (Hale, 1962); *Marathon S. Corp.*, 35 LA 249, 254 (Maggs, 1960); *United States Potash Co.*, 21 LA 416, 419 (Beatty, 1953); *Gibson Refrigerator Co.*, 17 LA 313, 315 (Platt, 1951); *Inland Steel Co.*, 12 LA 624, 627 (Gilden, 1949); *Carnegie-Illinois Steel Corp.*, 5 LA 402, 406 (Blumer, 1946); *Hudson County Bus. Owners' Ass'n*, 5 LA 69, 71 (Trotta, 1946). *But see* Tribune-Star Publ'g Co., 95 LA 210 (Witney, 1990); Fedders-U.S.A., 92 LA 418 (Cohen, 1989) (employer had the right under the contract to change the starting time from 7:00 a.m. to 6:00 a.m. and to stop paying overtime to employees who were called prior to 7:00 a.m.); Western Airlines, 85 LA 311, 314 (Brisco, 1985).

[517]*See* Seamless Rubber Co., 27 LA 92, 93 (Stutz & Williams, Curry dissenting, 1956); Chrysler Corp., 21 LA 210, 214 (Wolff, 1953); United States Potters Ass'n, 19 LA 213, 214–15 (Uible, 1952). *See also* Clipper Int'l Corp., 68 LA 1202, 1205–06 (Brown, 1977); Long Beach Naval Shipyard, 62 LA 769, 771 (Jones, Jr., 1974); Industrial Rayon Corp., 36 LA 233, 238 (Dworkin, 1960); American Bakeries Co., 34 LA 781, 784 (Rohman, 1960); Olin Mathieson Chem. Corp., 24 LA 619, 622 (Warns, 1955); Phillips Pipe Line Co., 20 LA 432, 433 (Coffey, 1953); National Tube Co., 16 LA 517, 525 (Sturges, 1951). For related discussion, see section 14.B., "Equalization of Overtime," below.

Still other arbitrators have held that where the change is made prior to the commencement of the workweek,[518] or is made with a full week's notice,[519] management's purpose is irrelevant.

Finally, it may be noted that the "right" of management to schedule work has been held to carry with it the "duty" to do so. One arbitrator ruled that an employer who abdicates such right by permitting employees to determine their own overtime schedules must be held partly responsible for any trouble caused by such schedules.[520]

C. Changes in Work Schedule Due to Emergency [LA CDI 115.251; 115.252]

Arbitrators appear to be generally inclined to allow management a great deal of flexibility in making unscheduled and emergency changes in the work schedule if made in good faith and for reasonable cause.[521] Even where the agreement in some respect limits management's right to make changes in the work schedule or imposes some obligation on management in doing so, the limitation or obligation may be held inapplicable if there is an emergency, an act of God, or a condition beyond the company's control.[522] An employer may temporarily reassign employees to work in a different depart-

---

[518]National Zinc Co., 4 LA 768, 772 (Wardlaw, 1946). *See also* Stauffer Chem. Co., 44 LA 961, 964 (Autrey, 1965); United Carbon Co., 39 LA 310, 315 (Hale, 1962).

[519]Wilson & Co., 7 LA 601, 602 (Lohman, 1947).

[520]Fulton Glass Co., 10 LA 75, 78 (Hampton, 1948).

[521]*See* West Bend Co., 94 LA 4, 6 (Baron, 1989); FMC-Ordnance Div., 84 LA 163, 168 (Wyman, 1985); Weil-McLain, 81 LA 941, 942–43 (Cox, 1983); Tri-State Transit Auth., 71 LA 716, 719 (Bolte, 1978); Ingalls Iron Works Co., 70 LA 982, 983–84 (MacLafferty, 1978); County Line Cheese Co., 69 LA 1088, 1092–93 (Leahy, 1977); Atlantic Foundry Co., 63 LA 73, 75–76 (Ipavec, 1974); Otto B. Inc., 62 LA 1221, 1226 (Eriksen, 1974); New York Herald Trib., 36 LA 753, 757–58 (Cole, 1960); United Eng'g & Foundry Co., 31 LA 93, 95 (Reid, 1958); Bloomer Bros. Co., 28 LA 494, 503 (Thompson, 1957); Montreal Mining Co., 26 LA 43, 46–47 (Graff, 1956); Gibson Refrigerator Co., 17 LA 313, 315 (Platt, 1951); Pan Am. Airways, 13 LA 326, 327–28 (Reynolds, 1949); American Can Co., 10 LA 579, 581 (Stein, 1948); Sealed Power Corp., 7 LA 485, 489 (Platt, 1947).

[522]*See* Schuff Steel Co., 94 LA 1248, 1251 (Thompson, 1990); Cerro Metal Prods., 94 LA 124, 126–27 (Lubow, 1990); West Bend Co., 94 LA 4, 6 (Baron, 1989); United Parcel Serv., 74 LA 191, 194 (Gershenfeld, 1980); San Francisco Theatre Owners Ass'n, 51 LA 1151, 1153 (Koven, 1969) (provision requiring notice of layoff applies to normal layoff situations, not to abnormal situation of suspension of operations due to strike); Borden, Inc., 51 LA 1069, 1071 (Moran, 1968) (riot justified shutdown though riot was not one of the express contractual exceptions to notice of layoff requirement); Lockheed-Georgia Co., 51 LA 720, 721 (Cantor, 1968) (contract stated no exception to reporting pay but one was implied for civil disorders); Electronics Communications, 51 LA 692, 695–96 (Madden, 1968) ("act of God" was only express exception to reporting pay provision but civil disorders justified shutdown); Supermatic Prods. Corp., 25 LA 794, 797–99 (Prasow, 1956); Inland Steel Co., 16 LA 277, 279 (Cornsweet, 1950). *But see* C. Schmidt Co., 69 LA 80, 83 (Albrechta, 1977); Kroger Co., 32 LA 112, 114 (Emerson, 1959) (provision for notice of schedule change stated no exception for strike and none would be implied). In *Airborne Freight Corp.*, 74 LA 1037, 1040 (Darrow, 1980), the agreement expressly guaranteed 40 hours of work "for the scheduled work week," and the arbitrator refused to imply any exception based on acts of God or conditions beyond the control of management. *Cf.* Gimbel Bros., 69 LA 847, 851 (Lubow, 1977). For some general definitions, see section 13.E., "Emergencies," section 13.G., "Acts of God," and section 13.H., "Condition Beyond the Control of Management," below.

ment, classification, or shift, or on overtime if required by an unanticipated business necessity.[523]

D. Reporting Pay [LA CDI 114.720 et seq.]

The right to make some unscheduled changes in the work schedule is implicit in the agreement itself if the agreement contains a provision for "reporting pay," as a great number of agreements do. The import is that management has the right to make such changes, but the right is accompanied by an obligation to make the contractually specified payment to employees.[524] Moreover, many reporting pay clauses state express exceptions even as to the obligation to pay if the employees are not used because of an emergency or condition beyond the control of management. Thus, in the bulk of the cases the right to make the unscheduled change in work hours has not been questioned, the dispute centering rather on the company's obligation for reporting pay where employees reported for work but were not used.

In one early case, an arbitrator ruled that a clause giving management the exclusive right to schedule working hours permitted it to make temporary changes in the work schedule without consulting the union. There, the arbitrator held that the employer was not obligated to pay employees for a half-hour waiting period on a day when they were scheduled to work at 10 a.m. but were unable to begin work until 10:30 a.m. The call-in pay clause was held not to cover the situation because the employees actually worked and received pay for more hours than were guaranteed by the clause. In sustaining the right of the employer to make temporary changes in the work schedule, the arbitrator said:

> This is the usual "management prerogative" type of clause [speaking of the clause giving the employer the right to schedule working hours]. Experience shows that this clause is inserted in the contract at the instance of management to make clear that it has freedom to do certain things without having to consult with the union. So, in this case, the Company retained the exclusive right to schedule working hours, without consultation with the union. In the opinion of the arbiter the clause cannot fairly be read to mean in addition that the Company, once it has set the working hours, must pay for hours not worked unless failure to work was for reasons beyond the Company's control.[525]

Under an agreement containing a minimum pay guarantee of 4 hours for employees who report to work and are not put to work and also for employees who, after having been put to work, are laid off before completing 4 hours of work, but providing that the guarantee should not apply in case of strike, breakdown of equipment, or act of God, an arbitrator held that the employer's decision to send employees home when the machine to which they were assigned broke down, rather than to provide them with other work, represented the exercise of a management prerogative that the union was

---

[523]Wagner Castings Co., 103 LA 156 (Talent, 1994) (employer did not violate collective bargaining agreement when workers from another classification were required to complete a last-minute order made for the company's largest client).

[524]See also Bethlehem Steel, 33 LA 285, 291 (Stark, 1959).

[525]Libby, McNeill & Libby, 11 LA 872, 874 (Fleming, 1948).

not entitled to challenge in the absence of a contractual requirement that the employer provide alternative work. As to the wisdom of the employer's decision, he said:

> However, in most instances, it might be much wiser from both the point of view of economy of operation and employee morale if a determined effort were made to find other work in these situations, particularly if it is true that preceding foremen used to concern themselves more with this problem. As the union points out, the men suffer the inconvenience and expense of coming to work, packing lunch, and paying for transportation so that management should make every effort to find work for the men to do wherever possible. Still, this is entirely a matter of management policy and not something that management would have to do because of any contract obligation.[526]

Many times unscheduled changes in work have been made as a direct or indirect result of weather conditions. For instance, under an agreement giving management exclusive authority to schedule production and determine shifts,[527] and under an agreement giving it the right to direct and assign the workforce,[528] management was not required to pay employees for scheduled hours not worked when, because of severe weather, employees were dismissed early to permit them to reach their homes safely—despite the fact that sufficient work was available. In other cases, weather conditions have been found to present an emergency, an act of God, or a condition beyond the control of management so as to justify unscheduled changes in work or (where it was the issue) to relieve management of any reporting pay or other such obligation.[529] But a different fact situation may result in a different conclusion.[530]

One arbitrator held that, "The decision as to the suitability of weather conditions for certain types of work must be made by Management; this de-

---

[526]Bethlehem Steel, 4 LA 450, 454–55 (Brandschain, 1946). *See also* FMC-Ordnance Div., 84 LA 163, 166–69 (Wyman, 1985); Terre Haute Water Works Corp., 5 LA 747, 749 (Updegraff, 1946).

[527]Sealed Power Corp., 7 LA 485, 489 (Platt, 1947).

[528]Pan Am. Airways, 13 LA 326, 327–28 (Reynolds, 1949).

[529]*See, e.g.,* Whirlpool Corp., 86 LA 969, 970–72 (High, 1987); Sawbrook Steel Castings Co., 85 LA 763, 768 (Witney, 1985); United Parcel Serv., 74 LA 191, 194 (Gershenfeld, 1980); Bunny Bread Co., 74 LA 55, 57 (Yarowsky, 1980) (the agreement contained an express guarantee of 40 hours, but "when the plant cannot be operated for a limited time because of conditions beyond the control of the employer, performance of the contract according to its strict terms is excused"); Babcock & Wilcox Co., 71 LA 283, 285 (Shister, 1978) (insufficient gas for production due to extremely cold weather); Textron, Inc., 70 LA 656, 660 (Grabb, 1978) (the weather "kept 30% of the employees at home" and the union "did not seriously nor effectively question that the assembly line could not function with 30% of the employees absent"); Bangor Prods. Corp., 63 LA 213, 215 (McLeod, 1974); Anaconda Aluminum Co., 46 LA 1123, 1125–29 (Stouffer, 1966) (in snowstorm it sufficed that impossibility of orderly and efficient operations could be reasonably anticipated); H. Willett, Inc., 38 LA 655, 657 (Cabe, 1962) (plant too cold because gas company could not supply enough fuel); United States Steel Co., 36 LA 991, 993 (Platt, 1961); Bethlehem Steel, 33 LA 285, 291 (Stark, 1959); American Can Co., 10 LA 579, 581 (Stein, 1948).

[530]*See, e.g.,* Georgia-Pacific Corp., 86 LA 1244, 1246 (Chandler, 1986) (failure to give advance notice required by contract); Compco Corp., 85 LA 725, 729–30 (Martin, 1985); Missouri Valley, 82 LA 1018, 1020 (Yaney, 1984) (radio station that employer relied on to broadcast notice not to report in failed to do so). *But see* West Bend Co., 94 LA 4 (Baron, 1989) (reporting pay properly denied employees who came in to work on basis of erroneous radio announcement stating plant had resumed operation after power outage, even though employer had told employees to listen to radio to learn when they should report).

cision should be made on the basis of its best judgment in the light of the immediate circumstances and must be respected provided there is no abuse by Management of its authority.'"[531] Nonetheless, weather conditions were held not to constitute an emergency so as to relieve management of a reporting-pay obligation where the employer's fears of much absenteeism (and thus of inefficient operations) because of a snowstorm proved to be unfounded, and the arbitrator determined that the storm was not severe enough to create an emergency.[532] Management, however, can require employees either to report during severe weather conditions or incur absence points, but its policy must be applied equitably. In one case, an employer was held to have violated the contract when it provided transportation during a snowstorm for some employees but penalized for their absences those who were not offered a ride.[533]

Bomb threats and actual or threatened riots or civil disturbances have been deemed conditions beyond the control of management, thus employers have not been required to give reporting pay or otherwise to compensate employees for time lost when management canceled scheduled work in view of the circumstances.[534] However, if under the facts the employees reasonably can be viewed as having been held on standby under the employer's control while a bomb search was conducted, they likely will be held entitled to pay for the time involved.[535]

E. Emergencies [LA CDI 114.721]

Managerial freedom to act may be expanded and managerial obligations may be narrowed if management's performance is affected by an emergency, an act of God, or a condition beyond the control of management. The collec-

---

[531]Bethlehem Steel Co., 27 LA 482, 485 (Feinberg, 1956) (quoting Bethlehem Steel Co., Dec. 5-5 (Stowe)).

[532]Schuller Int'l, 107 LA 1109 (Hockenberry, 1996).

[533]Westinghouse Elec. Corp., 51 LA 298, 300–01 (Altrock, 1968). See also National Homes Corp., 71 LA 1106, 1108 (Dobranski, 1978). For cases in which excessive absenteeism (making operations impracticable) was held not to be a condition beyond management's control under the facts, see Chrysler Corp., 51 LA 1089, 1092 (Alexander, 1968); Ohio Natural Casing & Supply Co., 43 LA 888, 890–91 (Leach, 1964). But in Dresser Industries, 71 LA 1007, 1009 (Kreimer, 1978), there was an "unanticipated shortage of available manpower" when employees "necessary to effectuate production" failed to report for work, and this constituted a condition beyond the control of management.

[534]See Oklahoma Chromalloy Am. Corp., 62 LA 463, 465 (Erbs, 1974); Chicago Bridge & Iron Co., 58 LA 355, 356 (Strongin, 1972); Goodyear Tire & Rubber Co., 55 LA 1119, 1120 (Sartain, 1970); General Cable Corp., 54 LA 696, 697 (Updegraff, 1971); Koppers Co., 54 LA 408, 411 (Duff, 1971); American Standard, 52 LA 736, 740 (Feller, 1969); Borden, Inc., 51 LA 1069, 1071 (Moran, 1968); Lockheed-Georgia Co., 51 LA 720, 721 (Cantor, 1968); Electronics Communications, 51 LA 692, 695–96 (Madden, 1968). See also Plumbers & Pipe Fitters Local 198 v. Nichols Constr. Corp., 502 F. Supp. 465 (M.D. La. 1980). In Pennsylvania State University, 67 LA 33, 35 (Stonehouse, Jr., 1976), the campus was closed for 1 day in order to avoid potential hazards arising from a rock concert being held in the vicinity, and it was held that the rock concert constituted an "unforeseen circumstance" within the meaning of that term in the agreement as an exception to the required 2-week notice of layoff.

[535]See Dresser Indus., 72 LA 1232, 1234 (Warns, 1979); Pickwick Int'l, 70 LA 676, 679 (Ross, 1978); McQuay-Perfex, Inc., 69 LA 511, 513 (Nitka, 1977).

tive bargaining agreement may expressly provide exceptions for these situations or an arbitrator may hold such exceptions to be inherent and necessarily implied.

Whether any of these situations is actually involved must be decided on a case-by-case, fact-intensive basis. Emphasizing the individualized nature of emergencies, one arbitrator refused to generalize on the subject, considering it not to be within the arbitrator's province to prescribe a comprehensive definition of an "emergency."[536] Nonetheless, some arbitrators have offered definitions or guides that may be of use. They are noted in the present topic subject to the foregoing caveat.

One arbitrator defined the term "emergency" as "an unforeseen combination of circumstances which calls for immediate action," and he added that there is no emergency where the situation permits the exercise of discretion.[537] In determining whether a breakdown of equipment constituted an emergency and, if so, whether it was such an emergency as would justify a departure from contractual procedures for distribution of overtime, an arbitrator expressed the following viewpoint:

> Does Management have the power to meet emergencies in an exceptional manner?
>
> Common sense and the entire pattern of American industrial experience make it necessary to acknowledge that emergencies do develop as a result of factors beyond the control of even the best of Managements and that a Company should not be penalized for taking steps to cope with such unforeseen developments even if it necessitates failure to observe all provisions of the contract. However, there are limits and standards which must be observed:
>   1) Management must not be directly responsible for the emergency
>   2) The emergency must involve a situation which threatens to impair operations materially
>   3) The emergency must be of limited time duration
>   4) Any violation or suspension of contractual agreements must be unavoidable and limited only to the duration of the emergency
>
> . . .
>
> The breakdown of one of the production lines in the acid plant on June 12 did pose what could broadly be called an emergency because it created a situation which called for quick action. However, the Arbitrator feels that a distinction must be made between: 1) those emergencies which can and should be met within the provisions of the Agreement because the dangers to production etc. are minimal, and 2) those which are so exceptional and so dangerous to the

---

[536]Coleman Co., 49 LA 431, 432 (Lazar, 1967).

[537]Canadian Porcelain Co., 41 LA 417, 418 (Hanrahan, 1963). For other statements or guides as to what is an emergency, see *Missouri Power & Light Co.*, 80 LA 297, 301 (Westbrook, 1982); *Ambridge Borough*, 73 LA 810, 813 (Dean, 1979); *Lennox Indus.*, 70 LA 417, 419 (Seifer, 1978) ("emergency" is acceptably defined as "a sudden, generally unexpected occurrence or set of circumstances demanding immediate action"); *Wadsworth, Ohio, City Bd. of Educ.*, 68 LA 418, 420 (Siegel, 1977); *Gallaher Drug Co.*, 42 LA 1181, 1183 (Suagee, 1964); *General Elec. Co.*, 40 LA 513, 521 (Killion, 1962); *Mrs. Fay's Pies*, 37 LA 811, 817–18 (Koven, undated). Where an *employee* relies on an alleged emergency, the number of employees affected sometimes may be a relevant consideration. *See also* Social Sec. Admin., 74 LA 1117, 1120–21 (Garman, 1980) (construing Federal Personnel Manual provisions); Social Sec. Admin., 72 LA 951, 954–56 (Hildebrand, 1979) (the agreement required consideration of the individual employee's situation).

operations of a plant that measures going beyond the Agreement must be taken to cope with the problems.[538]

A company's slumping sales and rapidly declining reputation in the market area because of quality problems was considered to be a legitimate emergency so as to authorize the performance of quality assurance tests in order to protect the quality of the product.[539]

If an emergency does arise, the determination of the membership of a work crew affected by the emergency lies within management's sound discretion, and management may select employees junior in service for overtime opportunities occasioned by the emergency if the more senior employees are not capable of handling the situation.[540]

Pursuant to an agreement providing for notice except in emergencies when employees are to be laid off because of a reduction in force, it was held that a strike by some of the employees constituted an emergency.[541] An emergency was also found to have existed when a deliberate slowdown by the employees resulted in an accumulation of stock in one department, making continued production impossible.[542] Although a contract stated that employees were to be given 1 week's advance notice in case of "arbitrary layoff," and contained no exception for "emergencies," the employer was not required to

---

[538]Virginia-Carolina Chem. Co., 42 LA 237, 240 (Kesselman, 1964). In *NER-Worldwide Service Parts Center*, 74 LA 224, 234–35 (Matthews, 1980), the arbitrator concluded that "while an emergency may have existed overall," *id.* at 234, its impact did not reach the "particular situation" involved in the grievance and thus the emergency could not justify the course of action being challenged by the grievance.

[539]Coca-Cola St. Louis & Soft Drink Co., 89-2 ARB ¶8326 (Marino, 1989).

[540]Central Pa. Water Supply Co., 101 LA 873 (Talarico, 1993) (when a large water main broke, the employer had the right to choose employees able to fix the problem most capably; however, the employer must have a reason for choosing a junior employee over a senior employee and cannot make arbitrary decisions; the employer did not violate seniority-overtime provisions when faced with an emergency and the senior employee did not perform well in high pressure situations).

[541]American Airlines, 27 LA 448, 450 (Wolff, 1956); Owens-Corning Fiberglas Corp., 23 LA 603, 605–06 (Uible, 1954). Strikes were held to create emergencies or conditions beyond management's control in *Professional Golf Co.*, 51 LA 312, 319–20 (Hebert, 1968) (strike threat); *Woods Indus.*, 49 LA 194, 195–96 (Gorsuch, 1967) (unforeseen strike at supplier plant); *Great Atl. & Pac. Tea Co.*, 33 LA 502, 506 (Seitz, 1959). A plant shutdown when some of the company's employees struck did not violate the no-lockout provision in the agreement of other employees. Bell Aerospace Corp., 54 LA 745, 749 (Seitz, 1971). *Cf.* Consolidated Freightways Corp. of Del., 51 LA 603, 605–06 (Wyckoff, 1968). A consumer boycott of meat confronted the employer with a severe drop in sales and qualified as an "emergency" permitting a work schedule change in *Thriftimart, Inc.*, 61 LA 992, 994 (Irwin, Jr., 1973).

[542]Lone Star Steel Co., 28 LA 465, 466 (McCoy, 1957). Where a slowdown by some employees made operations impossible, a no-lockout clause was not violated when innocent employees were sent home. United States Steel Corp., 42 LA 97, 100–01 (Garrett, 1963). For cases involving the shutdown of operations (with consequent reporting pay claims) when some employees began drinking prematurely before a holiday, see *Lawnlite Co.*, 66 LA 1122, 1124 (King, 1976); *Chase Bag Co.*, 60 LA 544, 546 (Emery, 1973).

give advance notice of layoff when a shipment of materials failed to arrive on time. The arbitrator concluded that the situation was an emergency.[543]

F. Giving Notice of Work Schedule Changes in Emergencies

It is to be noted that, even where a change in the work schedule is fully justified, the question still may be presented as to whether the agreement or the circumstances impose a duty on the employer to notify the employees of the change, or at least to make a reasonable effort to give notice. If such a duty does exist, the question may remain as to whether the effort to give notice was a reasonable one when management failed to reach some employees who accordingly reported for work.[544] In one case, after recognizing that a severe snowstorm can be regarded as an act of God and that "management has the right to decide when to operate or not operate the plant, in the light of weather conditions and the general capability of employees to get to work,"[545] the arbitrator stated:

> However, when management makes the decision not to operate the plant on a certain shift, its contractual exemption from reporting pay must be construed in a reasonable way—subject to a rule of reason. If management holds off its decision whether to operate a shift or not until a time that is so close to the actual shift starting time that all employees cannot be expected to get the word before they leave home, it is only fair that those relatively few employees in the circumstances of this case who reported for work in good faith believing that they were required to do so, should receive the reporting pay called for in the collective agreement.[546]

---

[543]Lavoris Co., 16 LA 173, 175 (Lockhart, 1951). For other cases in which cancellation of operations was justified because of unexpected shortage of materials, parts, or merchandise, see *Van de Kamp's*, 77 LA 611, 617 (Sabo, 1981); *Lennox Indus.*, 70 LA 417, 419 (Seifer, 1978); *Tecumseh Prods. Co.*, 61 LA 274, 278 (Krinsky, 1973); *Alsco, Inc.*, 41 LA 970, 972–74 (Kabaker, 1963). *Cf.* Sims Cab, 74 LA 844, 846 (Millious, 1980). An interest arbitrator recommended that the new agreement provide that no notice be required in emergencies. National Airlines, 16 LA 532, 534 (Payne, 1951).

[544]For some cases dealing with these aspects, see *Material Service Corp.*, 99 LA 789, 791–92 (Petersen, 1992); West Bend Co., 94 LA 4, 6–7 (Baron, 1989); Georgia-Pacific Corp., 86 LA 1244, 1245–46 (Chandler, 1986); Sawbrook Steel Castings Co., 85 LA 763, 768 (Witney, 1985); Compco Corp., 85 LA 725, 729–30 (Martin, 1985); Missouri Valley, 82 LA 1018, 1020 (Yaney, 1984); Gould Pumps, 71 LA 551, 554 (Dean, Jr., 1978); Ingalls Iron Works Co., 70 LA 982, 984 (MacLafferty, 1978); Textron, Inc., 70 LA 656, 660 (Grabb, 1978) (under the facts, notice on the day in question was not possible and notice on the prior evening would have been "imprudent" because there are "simply too many winter storm watches which do not develop into crippling storms such as the one in question"); Monsanto Research Corp., 70 LA 530, 533–34 (Gibson, 1978); R.J. Tower Corp., 67 LA 1029, 1031 (Stieber, 1976); Muskegon Piston Ring Co., 55 LA 685, 689 (Heilbrun, 1970); Niagara Mach. & Tool Works, 55 LA 396, 402 (Young, 1970); Koppers Co., 54 LA 408, 410 (Duff, 1971); Maremont Corp., 52 LA 705, 707 (Larkin, 1969); F.&M. Schaefer Brewing Co., 51 LA 276, 278 (Roberts, 1968); Chase Bag Co., 44 LA 748, 752 (Klein, 1965); Deere & Co., 43 LA 300, 302 (Davis, 1964); Package Mach. Co., 41 LA 47, 51 (Altieri, 1963).

[545]Environmental Elements Corp., 72 LA 1059, 1061 (Merrifield, 1979).

[546]*Id.* (each case of this type "must be judged on the basis of the particular circumstances"). This also appears true of cases in which employees arrive at the plant and find it closed at their regular starting time, they leave promptly assuming that operations have been canceled, the plant is opened shortly thereafter, and the employees then request reporting pay. *See* Fruehauf Corp., 73 LA 627 (Thompson, 1979); Wisconsin Wood Prods. Co., 1 LA 435 (Updegraff, 1946).

Many cases have considered the adequacy of radio announcements as a method of giving notice. Management's effort to notify employees of schedule changes by radio announcements was deemed adequate under the circumstances of some cases,[547] but not adequate in other cases.[548]

G. Acts of God [LA CDI 114.721]

An "act of God" was defined by an arbitrator as "an act, event or occurrence which is due exclusively to an extraordinary natural force free of human interference and which could not have been prevented by the exercise of reasonable care and foresight."[549] Another arbitrator noted in a case involving the temporary closing of an office, because of an epidemic, that "the proper focus is not whether the catastrophe or disaster is controllable by one degree or the other by human beings; but, whether the circumstances are so out of control that the facilities are required to be closed."[550]

H. Condition Beyond the Control of Management [LA CDI 114.721]

A "condition beyond the control of management" was briefly defined by an arbitrator as "a condition which could not be reasonably expected and prepared for by the Company."[551] A more detailed definition was given by another arbitrator:

> Considered in context "cause beyond the control of the management" cannot mean all causes over which, regardless of reason, the Company exercises no control. Rather, and at most, it must mean either a cause not falling within the general area of the Company's responsibilities or, if falling within this area,

---

[547]*See* Murphy Miller, Inc., 49 LA 929, 931–32 (Volz, 1967) (employees knew that this method would be used); Armstrong Cork Co., 49 LA 856, 861–63 (Yagoda, 1967); Westinghouse Elec. Corp., 38 LA 1064, 1067–68 (Warns, 1962) (there were many employees to be notified and this method had been used previously). In *Kiowa Corp.*, 72 LA 96, 101 (McKenna, 1979), the company was upheld in using the radio to call employees back to work following the end of a strike.

[548]*See* National Homes Corp., 71 LA 1106, 1108 (Dobranski, 1978); Gould Pumps, 71 LA 551, 554 (Dean, Jr., 1978); Bunker Hill Co., 51 LA 873, 874–75 (Luckerath, 1968) (normal method was telephone call or visit to employee's home); Westinghouse Elec. Corp., 51 LA 298, 302 (Altrock, 1968) (radio announcement 2 hours before shift start); Shulton, Inc., 43 LA 919, 932 (Wildebush, 1964) (radio would not suffice where other methods were specified by the contract); General Dynamics Corp., 40 LA 1157, 1160–61 (Hoban, 1963).

[549]United States Steel Co., 36 LA 991, 993 (Platt, 1961). This definition was applied in *Bethlehem Steel Corp.*, 71 LA 817, 819 (Sharnoff, 1978) (the union unsuccessfully contended that the 1977 "Johnstown flood" could have been prevented by the exercise of reasonable care and foresight by the Johnstown community and thus should not be classified as an act of God). In *National Homes Corp.*, 71 LA 1106, 1108 (Dobranski, 1978), the arbitrator offered a definition of the term "natural calamity" used in the agreement involved there.

[550]Erie County, Ohio, Bd. of Mental Retardation & Developmental Disabilities, 111 LA 1121 (Goldberg, 1999) (an influenza breakout that "hit almost everyone" was considered an "act of God").

[551]Gould Nat'l Batteries, 42 LA 609, 611 (Linn, 1964). *See also* Ralston Purina Co., 71 LA 519, 524 (Andrews, 1978). For distinctions between the terms "act of God" and "condition beyond the control of management," see *Miller Printing Mach. Co.*, 64 LA 141, 145 (McDermott, 1975). *See also* Blairsville Mfg. Co., 72 LA 845, 847 (Robins, 1979).

a cause which could not be anticipated or, if anticipated, could not have been guarded against at all or except by unreasonably burdensome or unrealistic measures. However, if a cause does fall within this area and could have been anticipated and reasonably guarded against, failure to provide such necessary safeguards, either unintentionally or as a calculated risk, would not place the cause beyond the control of the management.[552]

A power failure was held not to be beyond the control of management where the company had known of the potential danger and did not take steps to correct it.[553] Machine or equipment breakdowns have similarly been held not to be beyond the control of management in some cases,[554] but have been held otherwise under the circumstances of other cases.[555]

I. Holidays [LA CDI 115.71]

One arbitrator held that when a holiday work schedule has been established, management cannot change its collective mind and cancel the shift without paying employees at the overtime rate for the holiday that they would have otherwise worked.[556]

14. OVERTIME [LA CDI 100.4805; 115.501 et seq.]

Among the numerous overtime issues that have arisen, those that appear to have been arbitrated most frequently concern (1) management's right to require employees to work overtime, (2) management's contractual obligation to equalize overtime opportunities among the employees, and (3) the determination of a proper remedy where management has violated an employee's contractual right to overtime. These three basic issues are discussed below.

---

[552]Chrysler Corp., 21 LA 573, 579 (Wolff, 1953).

[553]See also Mead Corp., 54 LA 1218, 1219 (Porter, Jr., 1971). In other cases, however, power failures have been found to be beyond management's control. See E.W. Bliss Co., 55 LA 522, 525 (Geissinger, 1970); Erie Artisan Corp., 51 LA 850, 852 (Strasshofer, Jr., 1968) (trouble could not be anticipated); Package Mach. Co., 41 LA 47, 51 (Altieri, 1963). In *General Electric Co.*, 70 LA 330, 331 (Altrock, 1978), a shortage of natural gas making production impossible was held to constitute a "power failure" within the meaning of the agreement, notwithstanding the union's contention that the parties had never considered gas to be power. "The fact that the Union, at least, was not thinking about gas when the contract was negotiated is of interest, but many things happen to us that cannot be foreseen; otherwise, life would be a total bore." *Id.* at 331. See also Heiner's Bakery, 68 LA 986, 988 (Wagner, 1977). Regarding management's obligation where it detained employees longer than was reasonably necessary to investigate a power outage, see *La Favorite Rubber Mfg. Co.*, 74 LA 513, 514 (Brent, 1980).

[554]See A.O. Smith Corp., 51 LA 1183, 1194 (Sullivan, 1968) (trouble was foreseeable); Bunker Hill Co., 51 LA 873, 875 (Luckerath, 1968) (failure to make reasonable inspection). *See also* Rubatex Corp., 52 LA 1270, 1272 (Powers, 1969).

[555]See Chase Bag Co., 44 LA 748, 751–52 (Klein, 1965); Mrs. Fay's Pies, 37 LA 811, 818 (Koven, undated); Gould-Nat'l Batteries, 36 LA 654, 657 (Anderson, 1961).

[556]Fairbanks N. Star Borough, 103 LA 614 (Landau, 1994) (employer violated the contract when it unilaterally canceled holiday work and did not pay shift workers overtime for the holiday or straight pay for the day that it was closed; the cancellation was unprecedented and not attributable to an emergency, an act of God, or circumstances beyond the company's control).

A. Right to Require Overtime [LA CDI 115.305]

Although the right of management to require employees to work over-time has been stated in various ways, the essence of most decisions is that, where the agreement is silent on the subject, management has the right to make reasonable demands for overtime work from employees.[557] Thus, in the absence of contract prohibition, overtime may be required if it is of "reasonable duration, commensurate with employee health, safety and endurance, and the direction is issued under reasonable circumstances."[558] However, management must be willing to accept reasonable excuses advanced by an employee who declines the overtime assignment.[559] Several arbitrators

---

[557]Ironton Iron, 105 LA 257 (High, 1995) (company had scheduled mandatory overtime to compensate for production delays under a management-rights clause allowing this authority; the right to schedule overtime was limited only by the reasonableness of the amount); Ohio Edison Co., 102 LA 717 (Sergent, 1994) (company change in scheduling overtime shift from 8 to 7.5 hours to avoid having to provide a break for a second meal was unreasonable). *See* Auburn, Me., Police Dep't, 78 LA 537, 540 (Chandler, 1982); Pennwalt Corp., 77 LA 626, 632 (Erbs, 1981); National Hose Co., 73 LA 1048, 1049 (Robins, 1979); Halsey W. Taylor Co., 55 LA 1185, 1186–87 (Gibson, 1970); Stokely-Van Camp, 54 LA 773, 779 (Witney, 1971); Roberts Brass Mfg. Co., 53 LA 703, 705–06 (Volz, 1969); American Mach. & Foundry Co., 50 LA 181, 184–85 (Geissinger, 1968); American Body & Equip. Co., 49 LA 1172, 1175–76 (Bothwell, 1967); Dodge Mfg. Corp., 49 LA 429, 431 (Epstein, 1967); A.O. Smith Corp., 67–1 ARB ¶8115 (Howlett, 1967); Sangamo Elec. Co., 48 LA 1327, 1329–30 (Dammers, undated); Van Dorn Co., 48 LA 925, 928 (Kabaker, 1967); Link-Belt Co., 48 LA 570, 571–72 (Cayton, 1966); Fruehauf Corp., 46 LA 15, 20–21 (Dworkin, 1966). *See also* County of Cambria, Pa., 70 LA 625, 628 (Duff, 1978) (in upholding mandatory overtime, the arbitrator suggested that public-sector employees have a particularly strong obligation to work overtime in emergency situations of the type involved there, but he expressed no view as to "whether an employee may refuse overtime under non-emergency situations").

[558]Texas Co., 14 LA 146, 149 (Gilden, 1949). *See also* Quaker Oats Co., 84 LA 1085, 1090 (Newmark, 1985) (not reasonable due to safety hazard); Halsey W. Taylor Co., 55 LA 1185, 1186–87 (Gibson, 1970); American Body & Equip. Co., 49 LA 1172, 1175 (Bothwell, 1967); Van Dorn Co., 48 LA 925, 928 (Kabaker, 1967); Fruehauf Corp., 46 LA 15, 20 (Dworkin, 1966); Eagle-Picher Co., 45 LA 738, 740 (Anrod, 1965).

[559]American Body & Equip. Co., 49 LA 1172, 1175–76 (Bothwell, 1967). *See also* Lear Seating Corp., 98 LA 194, 196 (Ellmann, 1991); Hugo Neu-Proler Co., 69 LA 751, 756 (Richman, 1977); Hygrade Food Prods. Corp., 69 LA 414, 418 (Harter, 1977); Halsey W. Taylor Co., 55 LA 1185, 1187 (Gibson, 1970); Roberts Brass Mfg. Co., 53 LA 703, 705–06 (Volz, 1969); A.O. Smith Corp., 67–1 ARB ¶8115 (Howlett, 1967); American Mach. & Foundry Co., 50 LA 181, 184–85 (Geissinger, 1968); Eagle-Picher Co., 45 LA 738, 741 (Anrod, 1965); Westinghouse Elec. Corp., 39 LA 299, 302 (Barrett, 1962); Vulcan Mold & Iron Co., 39 LA 292, 298 (Brecht, 1962); International Salt Co., 35 LA 306, 312–13 (Bradley, 1960); Bell Aircraft Corp., 25 LA 755, 758 (Kharas, 1955); Wagner Malleable Iron Co., 24 LA 526, 528 (Fleming, 1955); Merrill Stevens Dry Dock & Repair Co., 21 LA 513, 515 (Douglas, 1953). Even with a reasonable excuse, an employee who is unable to work any overtime for a prolonged period (as distinguished from refusing a particular overtime assignment) may risk involuntary leave of absence. *See* Ionia Gen. Tire, 75 LA 324, 327–30 (Roumell, Jr., 1980). *See also* Kimberly-Clark Corp., 80 LA 945, 949 (Weiss, 1983). In Fruehauf Corp., 46 LA 15, 21 (Dworkin, 1966), flimsy excuses of personal inconvenience did not suffice to justify the refusal to work overtime. In *Westinghouse Elec. Corp.*, 47 LA 621, 628 (Altrock, 1966), the arbitrator stated that, "in an atmosphere of concerted action, individual excuses should be subjected to particular scrutiny." *Accord* Westinghouse Elec. Corp., 51 LA 472, 476 (Edes, 1968); Michigan Seamless Tube Co., 48 LA 1077, 1081 (Keefe, 1967). For the NLRB's view that a concerted refusal to work overtime is a strike, see *Electrical Workers (IUE) Local 742 (Randall Bearings, Inc.)*, 213 NLRB 824, 87 LRRM 1272 (1974); *Meat Cutters Local P-575 (Iowa Beef Packers)*, 188 NLRB 5, 76 LRRM 1273 (1971). Often under the facts, such refusal to work overtime will be unprotected conduct under the NLRA as a partial strike or as a breach of a no-strike clause. *See* NLRB v. Graphic Communications Local 13-B (Western Publ'g Co.), 682 F.2d 304, 110 LRRM 2984, 2987 (2d Cir. 1982); Excavation-Construction Co. v. NLRB, 660 F.2d 1015, 108

have suggested that the employer must give reasonable notice in advance of the overtime detail,[560] but the adequacy of notice may be viewed merely as one of the relevant considerations in determining the adequacy of any excuse offered for not working the overtime.

Even apart from the frequent recognition of the right to require overtime work as an inherent or residual right of management, arbitrators have often found implied contractual support for the existence of the right in provisions recognizing management's right to direct the workforces, to schedule work, and to distribute overtime.[561] In contrast, arbitrators have been reluctant to find any implied contractual prohibition of the right. It has been held, for instance, that the fact that an agreement specifies a "normal" workday as one of a certain number of hours, or a "normal" workweek as one of a certain number of days, does not prohibit management from requiring employees to work overtime because the word "normal" implies occasional resort to "abnormal."[562] This is said to be especially so where the agreement provides for time and one-half for hours over a certain number a week, since the latter provision "clearly recognizes an obligation on the company to pay for overtime, and surely by implication, that workers are obliged to work reasonably necessary overtime unless specifically excused."[563] Similarly, a provision stating that "employees refusing overtime will be charged with such overtime for purposes of equalization" was not interpreted as barring compulsory over-

---

LRRM 2561, 2564–65 (4th Cir. 1981); Poppin Fresh Pies, 256 NLRB 233, 107 LRRM 1201 (1981). See also discussion of NLRA doctrine in *Central Ill. Pub. Serv. Co.*, 76 LA 300, 305–06 (Kossoff, 1981); *Huron Forge & Mach. Co.*, 75 LA 83, 94–95 (Roumell, Jr., 1980).

[560]*See* Roberts Brass Mfg. Co., 53 LA 703, 705 (Volz, 1969); A.O. Smith Corp., 67–1 ARB ¶8115 (Howlett, 1967); Eagle-Picher Co., 45 LA at 741; Sunbeam Elec. (P.R.) Co., 41 LA 834, 842 (Helfeld, 1963); Vulcan Mold & Iron Co., 39 LA 292, 298 (Brecht, 1962).

[561]*See* McConway & Torley Corp., 55 LA 31, 32 (Cohen, 1970); Colt Indus., 52 LA 493, 496 (Turkus, 1969); Michigan Seamless Tube Co., 48 LA 1077, 1081 (Keefe, 1967); Link-Belt Co., 48 LA 570, 572 (Cayton, 1966); Fruehauf Corp., 46 LA 15, 21 (Dworkin, 1966); Eagle-Picher Co., 45 LA 738, 740 (Anrod, 1965); Lockheed Missiles & Space Co., 41 LA 868, 869 (Roberts, 1963); Lockheed-Georgia Co., 40 LA 407, 409–10 (Oppenheim, 1963); Wright Mach., 39 LA 1080, 1082 (Strong, 1962); International Salt Co., 35 LA 306, 311 (Bradley, 1960). *See also* Newspaper Guild (Washington-Baltimore) v. Bureau of Nat'l Affairs, 97 LRRM 3068 (D.D.C. 1978).

[562]Carnegie-Illinois Steel Corp., 12 LA 810, 811 (Seward, 1949). *Accord* Seilon, Inc., 51 LA 261, 263 (Volz, 1968); Link-Belt Co., 48 LA 570, 572 (Cayton, 1966); Fruehauf Corp., 46 LA 15, 20–21 (Dworkin, 1966); Jones & Laughlin Steel Corp., 29 LA 708, 709–10 (Cahn, 1957). *Cf.* Central Tel. Co. of Va., 69 LA 1133, 1138 (Daly, 1977). However, management could not require overtime, where an agreement definitely established the length of the work week by providing that the "eight (8) hour day and forty (40) hour week . . . shall be in effect without revision, during the term of this contract." Connecticut River Mills, 6 LA 1017, 1019 (Wallen, 1947). *See also* Baker & Taylor Co., 1 ALAA ¶67,318 (Honvitz, 1944). In *Midcon Fabricators*, 68 LA 1264, 1272 (Dugan, 1977), it was held unreasonable to require an employee to work 1 hour overtime on a regular daily basis, especially since "such a regular 9 hour work day schedule is in derogation of" a contract provision "calling for" an 8-hour day. *See also* General Tel. Co. of Cal., 79 LA 399, 402–03 (Christopher, 1982).

[563]Nebraska Consol. Mills Co., 13 LA 211, 214 (Copelof, 1949). *Accord* Coca-Cola Foods, 88 LA 129, 131–32 (Naehring, 1986); Pennwalt Corp., 77 LA 626, 631 (Erbs, 1981); Eagle-Picher Co., 45 LA 738, 740–41 (Anrod, 1965); International Salt Co., 35 LA 306, 311 (Bradley, 1960); McDonnell Aircraft Corp., 21 LA 91, 94 (Klamon, 1953). *Contra* A.D. Juilliard & Co., 17 LA 606, 608–09 (Maggs, 1951); National Elec. Coil Co., 1 LA 468, 470 (Lehoczky, 1945).

time, but deemed merely to provide a guide for management in administering overtime.[564]

Furthermore, neither the fact that the employer may have been lenient in exercising the right to require overtime work, nor the fact that overtime has been voluntary in the past, precludes management's right to mandate overtime where the volunteer approach fails to supply the number of workers needed.[565] Finally, a contract provision requiring advance notice for voluntary overtime has been held not to limit management's right to require mandatory overtime or require management to give advance notice.[566]

An agreement may specifically or by implication provide that the employee has the option of declining overtime.[567] Under such a provision it has been held that the employee must ask to be excused if he or she does not intend to work overtime.[568] Where employees did properly exercise their option not to work overtime, management could not force them to do so by calling the assignment a work order to be "obeyed now and grieved later."[569]

Sometimes the agreement will contain a provision specifically giving management the right to require overtime work.[570] Even so, the right of the employer to discipline an employee for refusing to work overtime may depend on the facts of the case and the existence of extenuating circumstances. Thus, an umpire stated that, while "an employee's refusal to work overtime may be a breach of duty for which he may properly be disciplined, his refusal may be justified and, if justified, is not ground for disciplinary penalty."[571] It should also be noted that employees' refusal to work overtime in protest

---

[564]Roberts Brass Mfg. Co., 53 LA 703, 705 (Volz, 1969). *See also* American Mach. & Foundry Co., 50 LA 181, 183–84 (Geissinger, 1968); Eagle-Picher Co., 45 LA 738, 741 (Anrod, 1965).

[565]*See* Pennwalt Corp., 77 LA 626, 632 (Erbs, 1981); Dresser Indus., 65 LA 313, 316 (Bell, 1975); Roberts Brass Mfg. Co., 53 LA 703, 706 (Volz, 1969); Colt Indus., 52 LA 493, 496 (Turkus, 1969); Champion Bait Co., 51 LA 287, 288 (Carpenter, 1968); American Body & Equip. Co., 49 LA 1172, 1176 (Bothwell, 1967); Michigan Seamless Tube Co., 48 LA 1077, 1081 (Keefe, 1967); Van Dorn Co., 48 LA 925, 928 (Kabaker, 1967); Link-Belt Co., 48 LA 570, 571–72 (Cayton, 1966); Fruehauf Corp., 46 LA 15, 21 (Dworkin, 1966); Eagle-Picher Co., 45 LA 738, 742 (Anrod, 1965); Wright Mach., 39 LA 1080, 1082 (Strong, 1962). But past practice was held controlling in *Edwards Motor Transit Co.*, 29 LA 482, 484–85 (Rock, 1957); *Dortch Stove Works*, 9 LA 374, 374–75 (McCoy, 1948).

[566]Chromalloy Am. Corp., 83 LA 80, 85 (Taylor, 1984).

[567]Keystone Steel & Wire, 94 LA 423, 424 (Goldstein, 1990); Lear, Inc., 28 LA 242, 245–46 (Bradley, 1957); West Penn Power Co., 27 LA 458, 462 (Begley, 1956).

[568]Lear, Inc., 28 LA 242 (Bradley, 1957).

[569]West Penn Power Co., 27 LA 458 (Begley, 1956).

[570]*See* Ionia Gen. Tire, 75 LA 324, 326 (Roumell, Jr., 1980); National Folding Box Co., 13 LA 269, 272 (Copelof, 1949); Ford Motor Co., 11 LA 1158, 1160 (Shulman, 1948); Deere & Co., 11 LA 561, 565 (Updegraff, 1948); International Shoe Co., 2 LA 201, 202 (Klamon, 1946).

[571]Ford Motor Co., 11 LA 1158, 1160 (Shulman, 1948). *See also* Pullman Trailmobile, 74 LA 967, 969 (Ekstrom, 1980). In the *Ford Motor* case, it was found that the employee's refusal was justified because the order for overtime work was made shortly before quitting time, and the reason for the refusal was that the employee would miss his usual ride and the use of public transportation would require additional time far out of proportion to the overtime he was asked to work. In *Cyclops Corp.*, 78 LA 1067, 1069 (Marlatt, 1982), the arbitrator stated that "for transportation problems to justify a refusal to work [overtime], there would have to be evidence that the employee would be exposed to some genuine hardship or danger."

against an employer's unilateral schedule change is a protected concerted activity under the NLRA.[572]

B. Equalization of Overtime [LA CDI 117.3271]

By no means are employees always compelled to work overtime. To the contrary, many employees "prize the opportunity" to work overtime:

> Many employees prize the opportunity to add to their income by working overtime. Indeed the possibility of earning such extra income has come to be regarded as a vital ingredient of the whole employment package and is often featured as such in company recruitment advertisements. Hence the demand for equitable distribution of overtime work assignments.[573]

Where the agreement does not contain a provision guaranteeing overtime to employees, management not only has the right to determine whether work shall be performed on an overtime basis,[574] it also has the right to allocate the overtime.[575]

Many agreements do deal with the allocation of overtime. Some leave management little or no discretion in the matter. For example, where the agreement provided that "overtime shall be distributed proportionately among all qualified employees" within a given work group, it was held that day-to-day equalization of overtime was called for.[576] More often, the agreement will contain a modified equalization provision calling for equalization of overtime among the employees within the specified equalization unit or group "as far as practicable," or "as equally as possible," or the like. Such provisions have generally been held to allow management reasonable flexibility in the interest of efficient operations and have been interpreted to permit equalization over a reasonable period of time.[577] In this latter regard, it has

---

[572]NLRB v. Mike Yurosek & Sons, 53 F.3d 261, 149 LRRM 2094 (9th Cir. 1995).

[573]American Enka Corp., 52 LA 882, 884 (Pigors, 1969).

[574]Continental Can Co., 53 LA 809, 810 (Cahn, 1969). See also City of Rogers City, 77 LA 393, 395 (Daniel, 1981); Neches Butane Prods. Co., 70 LA 1251, 1254–55 (Bailey, 1978); Massachusetts Inst. of Tech., 56 LA 751, 752 (Zack, 1971); Shenango Valley Water Co., 53 LA 741, 746 (McDermott, 1969); Mead Corp., 46 LA 459, 471 (Klamon, 1966); Richardson Co., 45 LA 451, 453 (Lanna, 1965); Standard Oil Co., 61–3 ARB ¶8812 (Emerson, 1961). In Liquid Air, 73 LA 1200, 1203–05 (Weiss, 1979), certain overtime by 20-year practice had been a "substantial segment" of employee paychecks and was held not subject to unilateral discontinuance by the employer. See also Union Camp Corp., 79 LA 415, 416 (Crane, 1982); Alabama Metal Indus. Corp., 66 LA 1065, 1066 (King, 1976). For related discussion, see section 13., "Scheduling Work," above; Chapter 12, section 1., "Custom and Practice as Part of the Contract."

[575]Graham Bros., 16 LA 83, 85 (Cheney, 1951) (citing Bethlehem Steel Co., 11 WAR LAB. REP. 190 (1943)). See also Washington Mack Trucks, 71 LA 412, 419 (Cushman, 1978); Philadelphia Naval Shipyard, 69 LA 1093, 1096 (Comey, 1977); Container Corp. of Am., 51 LA 1146, 1147–48 (Morris, 1968); Mead Corp., 46 LA 641, 643 (Hilpert, 1966); Robertshaw-Fulton Controls Co., 20 LA 212, 216 (Marshall, 1953).

[576]Mason & Hanger-Silas Mason Co., 36 LA 425, 434–35 (Hale, 1961). Also requiring daily equalization or otherwise leaving little flexibility in the distribution of overtime, see Reynolds Metal Co., 66–3 ARB ¶8950 (Listerhill, 1965); United States Indus. Chems. Co., 33 LA 335, 338–39 (Sullivan, 1959); Standard Oil Co., 28 LA 100, 101–02 (Doyle, 1957).

[577]See Lithonia Lighting, 89 LA 781, 783–86 (Chandler, 1987); Kaiser Aluminum & Chem. Corp., 54 LA 613, 617–18 (Bothwell, 1971); McCall Corp., 49 LA 933, 939 (Stouffer, 1967); Reflector Hardware Corp., 49 LA 886, 888 (Kelliher, 1967); Dallas Power Co., 49 LA 360, 362–64 (Ray, 1967); Duquesne Light Co., 48 LA 848, 851 (Shister, 1967); Hawaiian Airlines,

been stated that under an "as equally as possible" provision "no employee has a pre-emptory right to overtime on any particular day that it is available."[578] Under a similar provision, one arbitrator said:

> The decision as to what is as "equitable a basis as possible" rests with Management, subject to the Union's right to grieve that it was equitably possible for the Company to have given the assignment to employees other than those selected. In so doing the Union has the burden of proving that the Company deliberately or unreasonably bypassed the employee with the lower amount of overtime.[579]

But another arbitrator held that "the burden falls on the employer to justify its action" if an employee who already has more overtime than other employees is afforded the next overtime opportunity.[580] In a situation where it was apparent that overtime had been awarded unequally under a modified equalization provision, the arbitrator held that the employer had an obligation not to further skew the overtime accounts before taking steps to equalize the distribution of overtime.[581]

Regardless of where the ultimate burden of proof is held to fall, it is clear that management must remain alert to the underlying objective of equalization provisions. Thus, an arbitrator cautioned that, while the need for flexibility should be recognized, also to be taken into account is "the rule that the general aim of the agreement is for overtime to be equalized, albeit qualified by the Company's doing so with some latitude, and that this imposes a duty upon the Company to meet an appropriate test of diligence under the particular circumstances of each instance."[582]

---

47 LA 781, 784–85 (Tsukiyama, 1966); United States Borax & Chem. Corp., 46 LA 385, 386 (Guild, 1966); Anaconda Aluminum Co., 68-1 ARB ¶8266 (Cugna, 1968); American Enka Corp., 68-1 ARB ¶8091 (Hardy, 1967) (past practice refuted the union's contention for day-to-day equalization); Standard Ultramaine 64–1 ARB ¶8303 (Seinsheimer, 1963); Singer Co., 42 LA 830, 831 (Cahn, 1964); Hercules Powder Co., 40 LA 526, 529 (McCoy, 1963); Cargill, Inc., 39 LA 929, 930 (Williams, 1962). *See also* Portec Inc., 73 LA 56, 58–59 (Jason, 1979). *But see* United States Indus. Chems. Co., 33 LA 335, 338–39 (Sullivan, 1959).

[578]Sundstrand Corp., 66–2 ARB ¶8700, at 5422 (Kelliher, 1966). *Accord* Duquesne Light Co., 48 LA 848, 851 (Shister, 1967). *See also* Reflector Hardware Corp., 49 LA 886, 888 (Kelliher, 1967).

[579]McCall Corp., 49 LA 933, 939 (Stouffer, 1967). *Accord* Standard Ultramarine & Color Co., 64–1 ARB ¶8303 (Seinsheimer, 1963).

[580]Vendo Co., 53 LA 494, 497 (Myers, 1969) (the agreement provided that "every effort will be made to distribute overtime equally"). *Accord* Menasco Mfg. Co., 69 LA 759, 761 (Bergeson, 1977).

[581]Del Monte Corp., 86 LA 134 (Denson, 1985). *See also* Lockheed Space Operations Co., 91 LA 457 (Richard, 1988) (employer contractually required to equalize overtime may not deny overtime requests of newly certified operators in favor of more experienced operators).

[582]Pittsburgh Plate Glass Co., 32 LA 622, 624 (Sembower, Kimmell, & D'Orazio, 1958). *See also* Albright & Wilson, 85 LA 908, 912 (Shanker, 1985); Colt Indus. Operating Corp., 73 LA 1087, 1089, 1091 (Belshaw, 1979); Portec Inc., 73 LA 56, 59 (Jason, 1979). For some guidelines that have been offered for the equalization of overtime, see *McCall Corp.*, 49 LA 933, 939–41 (Stouffer, 1967); *Singer Mfg. Co.*, 35 LA 526, 529 (Cahn, 1960). As to the scope of management's obligation to notify employees of available overtime, see *Inland Container Corp.*, 74 LA 110, 114–15 (Boals, 1980); *Martin-Brower Co.*, 67 LA 778, 779 (Fields, 1976); *Borg Warner Corp.*, 55 LA 474, 476–77 (Sembower, 1970); *Greif Bros. Corp.*, 55 LA 384, 385 (Markowitz, 1970); *Ameteklamb Elec.*, 55 LA 353, 356 (Geissinger, 1970). As concerns mandatory overtime and the individual's right of privacy, the question has arisen whether the union may contractually obligate employees to answer their home telephone for possible calls from the employer. *See* Tennessee River Pulp & Paper Co., 60 LA 627, 632–33 (Murphy, 1973) (giving an affirmative answer under the facts). *See also* City of Albert Lea, Minn., 79 LA 1151, 1154 (Gallagher, 1982).

Arbitrators have recognized various considerations that may be relevant in judging whether management has administered the overtime equalization provision in a reasonable manner. Among others, these include such factors as ability to do the required work,[583] safety and plant protection,[584] and reasonably assured availability.[585] Arbitrators have disagreed as to whether cost is a relevant consideration.[586]

15. RIGHT TO SUBCONTRACT

A. Scope of the Right [LA CDI 117.380]

The right of management to subcontract, in the absence of specific contract restriction, has been the subject of numerous arbitration cases.[587] The basic and difficult problem is that of maintaining a proper balance between the employer's legitimate interest in efficient operation and effectuating economies, on the one hand, and the union's legitimate interest in protecting

---

[583]*See* R.E. Phelon Co., 77 LA 128, 132–33 (Clark, 1981); Myers Drum Co., 55 LA 1048, 1052 (Koven, 1970); Continental Can Co., 51 LA 1086, 1089 (Merrill, 1968). *See also* Washington Mack Trucks, 71 LA 412, 419 (Cushman, 1978). But management cannot insist that ability, if adequate, be as great as that of the employee who normally performs the work. Paragon Bridge & Steel Co., 48 LA 995, 1000 (Gross, 1967).

[584]Airco Alloys & Carbide Co., 51 LA 156, 160–61 (Kesselman, 1968).

[585]*See* Texas Utils. Generating Co., 71 LA 1062, 1064 (Marcus, 1978); Quaker State Oil Ref. Corp., 56 LA 848, 851 (Waldron, 1971); Eaton, Yale & Towne, 54 LA 950, 953 (France, 1971). *Cf.* Buchholz Mortuaries, 69 LA 623, 627 (Roberts, 1977); Goodyear Aerospace Corp., 52 LA 1098, 1100 (Lehoczky, 1969).

[586]Holding it a relevant factor: United States Borax & Chem. Corp., 46 LA 385, 386 (Guild, 1966); Reynolds Metal Co., 68–1 ARB ¶8148 (Bladek, 1968); Robertshaw-Fulton Controls Co., 22 LA 144, 147 (Livengood, 1953). Holding it not relevant: Southern Can Co., 68 LA 1183, 1190 (Jedel, 1977); U.S. Borax & Chem. Corp., 54 LA 387, 392 (Levin, 1971); American Enka Corp., 52 LA 882, 885 (Pigors, 1969); Continental Can Co., 51 LA 1086, 1088 (Merrill, 1968); Union Carbide & Carbon Corp., 16 LA 811, 816 (Gilden, 1951).

[587]The arbitrability of subcontracting disputes also has been the subject of arbitration decisions, many of which are collected in *Celanese Corp. of Am.*, 33 LA 925, 936–48 (Dash, Jr., 1959). *See* United States Steel Corp., 77 LA 190, 194 (Dybeck, 1981); Olympia Brewing Co., 72 LA 20, 27 (Madden, 1978). For Supreme Court doctrine as to arbitrability, see *Steelworkers v. Warrior & Gulf Navigation Co.*, 363 U.S. 574, 46 LRRM 2416 (1960). For a general discussion of arbitrability, see Chapter 6, "Determining Arbitrability." Many arbitration cases involve the interpretation and application of contract provisions expressly dealing with subcontracting. Arbitrators also have treated the question of whether clauses denying management the right to assign work of unit employees to employees outside the unit prohibit the subcontracting of such work to persons not in the employ of the company at all. *See* National Distillers & Chem. Corp., 76 LA 286, 290–91 (Gibson, 1981); Mid-America Dairymen, 70 LA 116, 120 (Fitzsimmons, 1978); Mobil Chem. Co., 51 LA 363, 371 (Witney, 1968); Stix, Baer, & Fuller Co., 27 LA 57, 73 (Klamon, 1956); Cannon Elec. Co., 26 LA 870, 873 (Aaron, 1956); Deroe & Reynolds, 22 LA 608, 608–09 (Porter, 1954); Yale & Towne Mfg. Co., 19 LA 882, 883 (Cahn, 1953); International Harvester, 12 LA 707, 709 (McCoy, 1949). *See also* Ralston Purina Co., 78 LA 35, 38 (Harrison, 1982) (contractual prohibition against supervisors performing unit work did not apply where the supervisor actually performed the contested work as an independent contractor). For an extensive discussion of subcontracting disputes, see Sinicropi, *Revisiting an Old Battle Ground: The Subcontracting Dispute, in* ARBITRATION OF SUBCONTRACTING AND WAGE INCENTIVE DISPUTES, PROCEEDINGS OF THE 32D ANNUAL MEETING OF NAA 125 (Stern & Dennis eds., BNA Books 1980) (citing several other articles on the subject).

the job security of its members and the stability of the bargaining unit, on the other.[588]

Arbitrators generally have held that management has the right, if exercised in good faith, to subcontract work to independent contractors (the work thus to be done by nonemployees of the employer) unless the agreement specifically restricts the right.[589] The reasoning of these arbitrators is reflected in the following statement:

> It is true, of course, that job security, and an opportunity to perform available work, is of concern to a union and that the letting of work to outsiders by an employer may in some instances be said to be a derogation of the basic purposes of their collective bargaining agreement. Nevertheless, it is also true that where the subject has assumed importance in the relations between the parties a provision is generally inserted in the agreement defining their respective rights. It has almost been universally recognized that in the absence of such a provision an employer may, under his customary right to conduct his business efficiently, let work to outside contractors if such letting is done in good faith and without deliberate intent to injure his employees.[590]

Where the agreement does not deal specifically with subcontracting, most of the later cases fall into one of four categories: (1) a "management-right" clause supplies the necessary authority to subcontract;[591] (2) management can subcontract if it does so reasonably and in good faith;[592] (3) the recogni-

---

[588]*See* U.S. Pipe & Foundry Co., 113 LA 943 (Owens, 1999) (subcontracting based on legitimate business purposes and bargaining unit); Westvaco Corp., 112 LA 1083, 1085 (Duff, 1999) (long-range interests of the bargaining unit in economic survival and competitiveness of employer outweigh immediate impact of layoffs); USS, Div. of USX, 112 LA 227 (Das, 1998); Angelus Block Co., 100 LA 1129, 1134–35 (Prayzich, 1993); American Standard, 52 LA 190, 192 (Hon, 1969); Kaiser Aluminum & Chem. Corp., 43 LA 307, 313 (Hebert, 1964); Temco Aircraft Corp., 27 LA 233, 235 (Larson, 1956); General Metals Corp., 25 LA 118, 120 (Lennard, 1955); Stockholders Publ'g Co., 16 LA 644, 648 (Aaron, 1951).

[589]*See* Olin Mathieson Chem. Corp., 52 LA 670, 672 (Bladek, 1969); Stoneware, Inc., 49 LA 471, 473 (Stouffer, 1967); Mead Corp., 46 LA 459, 468–70 (Klamon, 1966); Richmond Baking Co., 30 LA 493, 495–96 (Warns, 1957); Waller Bros. Stone Co., 27 LA 704, 709 (Dworkin, 1956); Carbide & Carbon Chems. Co., 26 LA 74, 78 (Marshall, 1956); *See* National Sugar Ref. Co., 13 LA 991, 1001 (Feinberg, 1949); International Harvester, 12 LA 707, 709 (McCoy, 1949); Ohmer Corp., 11 LA 197, 199 (Kelliher, 1948); Swift & Co., 10 LA 842, 843 (Healy, 1948); Babcock Printing Press Co., 10 LA 396, 405–06 (Hill, 1948); Amos Keag Mills, Inc., 8 LA 990, 992 (Copelof, 1947). In *Singer Co.*, 71 LA 204, 208–11 (Kossoff, 1978), the arbitrator surveyed court decisions on subcontracting as an alleged violation of the agreement (as distinguished from any possible violation of a statutory duty to bargain), where the agreement does not expressly prohibit subcontracting, and concluded that: "Most courts who have considered the issue have held that where a contract contains no express prohibition of subcontracting there is no violation where an employer replaces employees covered by the contract by giving out the work to an independent contractor." *Id.* at 208.

[590]National Sugar Ref. Co., 13 LA 991, 1001 (Feinberg, 1949). For a more recent case adopting this view, see *Custom Indus. USA*, 115 LA 1625 (Pratte, 2001) ("It has long been recognized that *in the absence* of a specific prohibition against a 'transfer, allocation, or assignment of work out of the bargaining unit,' the Company may have such a right under the typical management rights clause") (emphasis in original) (citing Stewart-Warner Corp., 22 LA 547, 551 (Burns, 1954)).

[591]GES Exposition Servs., 108 LA 385 (Levy, 1997).

[592]For holdings that the recognition, seniority, wage, and other such clauses do not restrict management's right to subcontract and basing the award on factors pointing to the reasonableness and good-faith test, see *Libbey Glass*, 116 LA 182 (Ruben, 2000) (recognition clause of collective bargaining agreement does not bar employer from subcontracting work of packaging glassware into cartons according to customer specifications, because clause may indicate that bargaining unit owns the job but not that it owns the work); *Westvaco Corp.*,

tion, seniority, wage, and other such clauses of the agreement limit management's right to subcontract, and certain standards of reasonableness and good faith are applied in determining whether these clauses have been violated;[593] and (4) the employer's business interest must be balanced against

---

112 LA 1083 (Duff, 1999); *USS, Div. of USX*, 112 LA 227 (Das, 1998); *East Cleveland, Ohio, Bd. of Educ.*, 111 LA 879 (Adamson, 1998); *Olin Corp.*, 109 LA 919 (O'Grady, 1997); *Joseph Horne Co.*, 78 LA 262, 267 (Ipavec, 1982); *Olympia Brewing Co.*, 72 LA 20, 28–30 (Madden, 1978); *Hess Oil & Chem. Corp.*, 51 LA 752, 757 (Gould, 1968*); Samuel Bingham Co.*, 51 LA 575, 577 (Emery, 1968); *Upson Co.*, 49 LA 805, 809 (Shister, 1967); *International Tel. & Tel. Corp.*, 47 LA 325, 327 (Abrahams, 1966); *Linde Co.*, 43 LA 554, 557 (Murphy, 1964); *Duquesne Light Co.*, 40 LA 444, 447 (McCoy, 1963); *Allis-Chalmers Mfg. Co.*, 39 LA 1213, 1218 (Smith, 1962); *Sinclair Ref. Co.*, 38 LA 718, 721–22 (Larkin, 1962*); Olin Mathieson Chem. Corp.*, 36 LA 1147, 1151–52 (McDermott, 1961); *Black-Clawson Co.*, 34 LA 215, 220 (Teple, 1960); *American Airlines*, 29 LA 594, 594–95 (Wolff, 1957); *Hershey Chocolate Corp.*, 28 LA 491, 493–94 (Wallen, 1957); *Kollsman Instrument Corp.*, 28 LA 270, 273 (Kornblum, 1957); *Hearst Consol. Publ'ns*, 26 LA 723, 725 (Gray, 1956); *Carbide & Carbon Chems. Co.*, 24 LA 158, 159–60 (Kelliher, 1955); *Dalmo Victor Co.*, 24 LA 33, 34–37 (Kagel, 1954); *Phillips Pipe Line Co.*, 20 LA 432, 433–34 (Coffey, 1953); *Tungsten Mining Corp.*, 19 LA 503, 506 (Maggs, 1952); *Librascope, Inc.*, 19 LA 219, 220 (Grant, 1952).

[593]General Am. Door Co., 115 LA 1697 (Marino, 2001) (an employer would normally be prohibited from subcontracting: (1) unless it acts in good faith, (2) unless it acts in conformity with past practices, (3) unless it acts reasonably, (4) unless the act deprives only a few employees of employment, (5) unless the act was dictated by business requirements, (6) if the act is barred by the recognition clause, (7) if the act is barred by seniority provisions, or (8) if the act violates the spirit of the agreement); East Cleveland, Ohio, Bd. of Educ., 111 LA 879 (Adamson, 1998) (board of education did not violate contract when it subcontracted alternative school's operation, where contract's recognition clause, provided that union is exclusive bargaining representative of group of employees set forth in clause, but did not reflect mandate as to subcontracting); Port of Seattle, Wash., 110 LA 753 (Skratek, 1998) (agency violated the agreement when it subcontracted research and development work, even though there was no restriction against contracting-out in agreement, because employer's ability to contract out work is limited by recognition clause, a union-security clause, and other provisions in the agreement that confer benefits on employees); Olin Corp., 109 LA 919 (O'Grady, 1997) (employer's subcontracting of janitorial work did not violate union-security provision in the contract, where the clause stated that one of the considerations for granting union security was that it would lead to higher levels of efficiency and productivity, and transfer of janitorial work, which is marginal to the primary work of the unit, must be viewed as permitting "higher level of efficiency"). For cases holding that such clauses do limit management, but listing standards pointing to the test of good faith and reasonableness, see City of Detroit, 79 LA 1273, 1277–78 (Mittenthal, 1982); Campbell Truck Co., 73 LA 1036, 1039 (Ross, 1979); Inland Tool & Mfg., 71 LA 120, 123–24 (Lipson, 1978); American Air Filter Co., 54 LA 1251, 1255 (Dolnick, 1971); Trane Co., 49 LA 585, 587–88 (Somers, 1967); Riegel Paper Corp., 36 LA 714, 716 (Williams, 1961); Temco Aircraft Corp., 27 LA 233, 235 (Larson, 1956); General Metals Corp., 25 LA 118, 120 (Lennard, 1955); A.D. Juilliard Co., 21 LA 713, 724–25 (Hogan, 1953). For cases not listing standards, but recognizing a general test of reasonableness and good faith, see Dutch Maid Bakery, 52 LA 588, 592 (King, 1969); KUP Sutherland Paper Co., 40 LA 737, 740 (Kadish, 1963); St. Regis Paper Co., 30 LA 379, 380 (Hill, 1958); Texas Gas Transmission Corp., 27 LA 413, 419 (Hebert, 1956); Cannon Elec. Co., 26 LA 870, 873 (Aaron, 1956); Koppers Co., 22 LA 124, 128 (Reid, 1954); National Tube Co., 17 LA 790, 792–94 (Garrett, 1951). For instances in which the arbitrator found a strict limitation in such clauses, see Continental Tenn. Lines, 72 LA 619, 620–21 (Cocalis, 1979); Twin City Milk Producers, 42 LA 1121, 1122 (Gundermann, 1964). One arbitrator who had found that the recognition, seniority, and wage clauses restrict subcontracting went on to state:

> After a thoughtful consideration of this question the Arbitrator concludes that the Recognition Clause when considered together with the Wage Clause, the Seniority Clauses, and other clauses establishing standards for covered jobs and employees limits the Company's right to subcontract during the term of the Contract. The Contract sets forth standards of wages and working conditions applicable to those employees and those jobs covered by the Recognition Clause. When the contract was signed the employees in the mending room were on the covered jobs, and the Contract contemplated that work nor-

the impact on the bargaining unit.[594] It appears obvious, however, that the end result ordinarily would be the same regardless of which of these approaches is taken.[595]

In the final analysis, the thinking of many arbitrators is probably reflected in the following statement:

> In the absence of contractual language relating to contracting out of work, the general arbitration rule is that management has the right to contract out work as long as the action is performed in good faith, it represents a reasonable business decision, it does not result in subversion of the labor agreement, and it does not have the effect of seriously weakening the bargaining unit or important parts of it. This general right to contract out may be expanded or restricted by specific contractual language.[596]

B. Standards for Evaluating Propriety of Subcontracting
[LA CDI 117.380 et seq.]

As set forth in the preceding section, where the labor agreement is silent about subcontracting, one important factor considered by arbitrators under the "balancing" test is the effect of subcontracting on the bargaining unit or unit employees. Where subcontracting has little or no effect on the unit or its members, it is likely to be upheld by an arbitrator.[597] Where subcontracting

---

mally performed by them would continue to be so performed as long as the work was available. To allow the Company, after signing an agreement covering standards of wages and conditions for mending room jobs and employees, to lay off the employees and transfer the work to employees not covered by the agreed standards would subvert the Contract and destroy the meaning of the collective bargaining relation.
A.D. Juilliard Co., 21 LA 713, 724 (Hogan, 1953).

[594]Gaylord Container Corp., 106 LA 461 (Baroni, 1996) (subcontracting rights depend on the balancing of an employer's legitimate interest in efficiency and the union's legitimate interest in job security).

[595]For court approval of arbitral use of a "reasonableness" or "balancing" test in determining the permissibility of subcontracting, where the contract is silent or ambiguous on the right to subcontract, see Sears, Roebuck & Co. v. Teamsters Local 243, 683 F.2d 154, 110 LRRM 3175 (6th Cir. 1982) (however, the court found that an arbitrator had improperly used such a test to overrule subcontracting, where the employer had a clear right under an express contract provision).

[596]Shenango Valley Water Co., 53 LA 741, 744–45 (McDermott, 1969). See Hughes Electron Dynamics, 115 LA 473 (Richman, 2001); Pemco Aeroplex, 109 LA 385 (Lunie, 1997); Blue Diamond Coal Co., 78 LA 702, 704 (Davies, 1982); Exxon Co., U.S.A., 78 LA 144, 147 (Light, 1981); Uniroyal, Inc., 76 LA 1049, 1052 (Nolan, 1981); Transit Auth. of River City, 74 LA 616, 619 (Chapman, 1980); Kenworth Truck Co., 73 LA 947, 949 (Doyle, 1979); Central Ohio Transit Auth., 71 LA 9, 15 (Handsaker, 1978). See also Mead Corp., 75 LA 665, 666–67 (Gross, 1980); ILSCO Corp., 74 LA 659, 662 (Ipavec, 1980); Campbell Truck Co., 73 LA 1036, 1039 (Ross, 1979); Cives Steel Co., 72 LA 800, 803 (Atleson, 1979); West Va. Armature Co., 68 LA 316, 320 (Hunter, Jr., 1977). For arbitrators emphasizing that each subcontracting case must be decided on its own, see Schluderberg & Kurdle Co., 53 LA 819, 823 (Seidenberg, 1969); Trane Co., 49 LA 585, 587 (Somers, 1967); W.S. Dickey Clay Mfg. Co., 46 LA 444, 447 (Kates, 1966). If subcontracting is found to have been proper, the union might be found to have violated the no-strike clause by refusing to handle subcontracted material. See Pittsburgh Brewing Co., 53 LA 470, 475 (McDermott, 1969); Dalmo Victor Co., 24 LA 33, 37–38 (Kagel, 1954).

[597]See International Paper, 117 LA 21 (Frockt, 2002) (where employer was not obligated to create overtime opportunities and employees were not deprived of work opportunities as a result of subcontracting, there was no violation of the collective bargaining agreement); Libbey Glass, 116 LA 182 (Ruben, 2000) (employer did not violate the collective bargaining agree-

is used either to replace current employees or in lieu of recalling employees on layoff, it is less likely to be upheld.[598] A second factor—the employer's justification for subcontracting work—also is an important factor. Arbitrators are more likely to uphold the contracting out of work where it is justified by sound business reasons.[599]

---

ment when it subcontracted work normally done by the bargaining unit, where employees did not experience a reduction in work); U.S. Pipe & Foundry Co., 114 LA 426 (Nicholas, Jr., 2000) (employer did not violate the collective bargaining agreement by contracting out work normally performed by the bargaining unit due to excessive amounts of absenteeism, where there were no bargaining-unit employees on layoff); Crown Cent. Petroleum Corp., 97 LA 64 (Nicholas, Jr., 1991) (employer who has reserved the right to subcontract off-shift work may do so where no employees are demoted or laid off, even if availability of overtime and shift-differential pay for unit employees is reduced); Ideal Elec. Co., 93 LA 101 (Strasshofer, 1989) (employer properly subcontracted company mail delivery where no truck drivers had recall rights, duties required only half-hour per day, no employees on layoff, and no layoff resulted); Certainteed Corp., 88 LA 995 (Nicholas, Jr., 1987) (that employees were fully employed and unavailable is one factor favoring propriety of subcontracting); M.A. Hanna Co., 88 LA 185 (Petersen, 1986) (subcontract proper where unit welders were unfamiliar with contractor's special processing methods and procedures); Ohio Valley Fed. Credit Union, 82 LA 805 (Duda, Jr., 1984) (subcontract of new membership recruitment work justified, where credit union needed rapid increase in membership to meet expansion needs).

[598]See Weyerhaeuser Paper Co., 117 LA 1758 (Neas, 2002) (subcontracting clause violated by purchases of precast product, where employees had been assigned to cut product); American Crystal Sugar, 116 LA 916 (Jacobowski, 2002) (language of the collective bargaining agreement, which provided that all work that fell within the experience and qualifications of the bargaining-unit employees was to be performed by bargaining-unit employees, inherently precluded subcontracting, and employer violated the collective bargaining agreement when it subcontracted work typically done by the bargaining unit when there were employees on layoff); Honeywell Fed. Mfg. & Techs., 116 LA 626 (King, 2001) (an employer is entitled to much greater latitude regarding a subcontracting decision when it does not concern a bargaining unit with employees on layoff, because when no employees are on layoff, no one has been deprived of the "fruits of the contract"); Eaton Corp., 114 LA 1691 (Lalka, 2000) (subcontracting, when not limited by contractual language, is not a right to be exercised with unfettered abandon, because inherent in every collective bargaining agreement is job security for bargaining-unit members; outsourcing that has as its central purpose nothing more than transferring work customarily performed by bargaining-unit members to non-bargaining-unit members must be presumed to be an attack on the bargaining unit; to permit such an attack would render the collective bargaining process an exercise in futility, with hard won labor agreements being circumvented by outsourcing); Bethlehem Steel Corp., 97 LA 614, 616 (Das, 1991) (employer violated agreement by subcontracting carpenters' work, where carpenters were available but on suspension); MSB Mfg. Co., 92 LA 841 (Bankston, 1989) (employer violated labor agreement by subcontracting delivery where 4 of 13 unit positions were lost and average earnings of remaining unit members decreased); Trane Co., 89 LA 1112 (McIntosh, 1987) (contracting out for janitorial services improper where 186 unit employees were laid off); North Star Steel Co., 87 LA 40 (Miller, 1986) (subcontracting improper where six unit employees were laid off and available). But see Alofs Mfg. Co., 98 LA 92, 98 (Daniel, 1991) (agreement not violated when company does not return subcontracted work to plant in order to recall laid-off employees where layoffs were caused by recession, not subcontracting).

[599]See Hughes Electron Dynamics, 115 LA 473 (Richman, 2001) (where decision to contract is merely one of convenience and there is no showing of a compelling business reason, subcontracting is in violation of the collective bargaining agreement); GTE N., 98 LA 617, 619 (Ray, 1992) (company properly assigned work to contractor where work was unscheduled and had to be done immediately, technician assigned to job was unable to do it, and contractor had requisite expertise); Collis, Inc., 95 LA 1078, 1081 (Duff, 1990) (subcontracting proper where employer faced with excess work load reasonably concluded that employees had ample work, wanted no more, and union made inadequate effort to secure overtime when offered); Federal Wholesale Co., 92 LA 271 (Richard, 1989) (severely financially distressed employer justified in subcontracting work to obtain substantial operational savings); Champion Int'l Corp., 91 LA 245 (Duda, Jr., 1988) (subcontracting proper in face of general contractual prohibition excepting "where necessary to help finish a job," where bargaining

A canvass of arbitral decisions reveals that a more complete list of the factors examined in determining the propriety of subcontracting under the balancing test would include the following:

1. *Past practice.* Whether the company has subcontracted work in the past.[600]
2. *Justification.* Whether subcontracting is done for reasons such as economy,[601] maintenance of secondary sources for production and

---

unit could supply 200–300 man-hours, and subcontractor used over 900 man-hours to finish job); M.A. Hanna Co., 88 LA 185 (Petersen, 1986) (subcontracting proper where unit welders were unfamiliar with special processing methods and procedures); Ohio Valley Fed. Credit Union, 82 LA 805 (Duda, Jr., 1984) (subcontracting proper to fill special need for member recruitment).

[600]For cases in which past practice was one of the factors considered, see *Besser Co.*, 117 LA 1413 (Elkin, 2002) (there was no past practice of subcontracting, where other instances of subcontracting did not violate the collective bargaining agreement and the most recent attempt to subcontract did; the agreement must be silent or ambiguous before past practice may be referenced); *Illinois-American Water Co.*, 117 LA 647 (Suardi, 2002) (cleaning of a new facility was not deemed exclusively bargaining-unit work based on past practice, where the janitorial work done by employees at the old facility was often either lackluster or not done at all); *Honeywell Fed. Mfg. & Techs.*, 116 LA 626 (King, 2001) (employer did not violate the collective bargaining agreement when using a subcontractor to supply safety goggles when it had done the same for safety shoes for the previous 5 years without complaint from the union); *Genex Ltd.*, 99 LA 559, 565–66 (Bard, 1992); *Vincent Metals Div.*, 98 LA 1152, 1157 (Berquist, 1991); *Harvard Indus.*, 98 LA 1100, 1102–03 (Kindig, 1992); *Honeywell, Inc.*, 86 LA 667, 672–73 (Eagle, 1986); *Ready Mixed Concrete Corp.*, 81 LA 1047, 1049 (Jones, 1983); *Delta Ref. Co.*, 78 LA 710, 715 (Boals, 1982); *Exxon Co., U.S.A.*, 78 LA 144, 147 (Light, 1981); *Ralston Purina Co.*, 78 LA 35, 38 (Harrison, 1982); *H-N Adver. & Display Co.*, 77 LA 1096, 1101 (Cyrol, 1981); *Latrobe Steel Co.*, 76 LA 670, 673 (Sherman, 1981); *Hobart Mfg. Co.*, 73 LA 29, 31 (Turkus, 1979); *Cives Steel Co.*, 72 LA 800, 803, 804 (Atleson, 1979); *S. Rosenthal Co.*, 64 LA 101, 102 (Seidman, 1975). Subcontracting was permitted as to perishables, largely on the basis of long past practice, even where the contract expressly prohibited subcontracting without negotiations. Safeway Stores, 51 LA 1093, 1094–95 (Koven, 1969). For another past practice exception to an express contract limitation, see *Grocers Dairy Co.*, 69 LA 7, 10 (Keefe, 1977). For full discussion of custom and practice generally, see Chapter 12, "Custom and Past Practice."

[601]For cases in which economy was considered along with other factors in upholding subcontracting, see *Nexitra, LLC*, 116 LA 1780, 1785 (Gregory, 2002) (employer that lost $345 million in 3 years had sufficient business reason to subcontract work, despite the fact that it may have resulted in the layoff of employees in the bargaining unit: "The Employer, however, was overwhelmed in a collapsing sector of a recessionary economy; the situation the Employer faced, and continues to face, is anything but static. Business as had been usual would have guaranteed business disaster."); *Libbey Glass*, 116 LA 182, 187 (Ruben, 2000) (collective bargaining agreement that provided that "the employer must be in a competitive position, which means it must produce efficiently and at cost consistent with fair labor standards," was not violated when employer subcontracted out work typically done by the bargaining unit, where the subcontractor's costs were less and the focus was on keeping costs down to retain a customer's business); *Collis, Inc.*, 95 LA 1078, 1081 (Duff, 1990); *Gaylord Container Corp.*, 93 LA 465, 469 (Abrams, 1989); *Burger Iron Co.*, 78 LA 57, 59 (Van Pelt, 1982); *Rinker Materials Corp.*, 76 LA 1174, 1178 (Vause, 1981); *Transit Auth. of River City*, 74 LA 616, 620 (Chapman, 1980); *Central Ohio Transit Auth.*, 71 LA 9, 17 (Handsaker, 1978) (employer, as a public body, "has an obligation to operate as efficiently as possible in the interest of the taxpayer"); *Hadley-Dean Glass Co.*, 69 LA 1057, 1066, 1071 (Stix, 1977) (in upholding the subcontracting, the arbitrator stated that it related to "an important element of cost bearing on the Company's ability to be competitive on a particular job which was up for bids"). For cases in which the economy factor was outweighed by other considerations, see *U.S. Plywood-Champion Papers*, 51 LA 997, 1001 (Volz, 1968); *West Virginia Pulp & Paper Co.*, 51 LA 842, 846 (Seinsheimer, 1968). Some arbitrators have stressed that economy in the form of lower labor costs gives little or no support to management's action. *See* Uniroyal, Inc., 76 LA 1049, 1053–54 (Nolan, 1981); National Distillers & Chem. Corp., 76 LA 286, 291 (Gibson, 1981); U.S. Plywood-Champion Papers, 51 LA 997, 1001 (Volz, 1968); Hess Oil & Chem. Corp., 51 LA 752, 758 (Gould, 1968).

manpower aid,[602] augmenting the regular workforce,[603] plant security measures,[604] safety reasons,[605] emergencies,[606] or other sound business reasons.[607]

3. *Effect on the union or bargaining unit.* Whether subcontracting is being used as a method of discriminating against the union and/or whether it substantially prejudices the status and integrity of the bargaining unit.[608]

4. *Effect on unit employees.* Whether members of the bargaining unit are discriminated against,[609] displaced,[610] deprived of jobs previously

---

[602]Peabody Coal Co., 82 LA 1251 (Roberts, 1984); Dalmo Victor Co., 24 LA 33, 37 (Kagel, 1954). *See also* KUP Sutherland Paper Co., 40 LA 737, 741 (Kadish, 1963).

[603]Midwest Coca-Cola Bottling, 116 LA 1153 (Bognanno, 2002) (clause in collective bargaining agreeement stating that the employer may subcontract in an "overflow situation" meant that the employer could subcontract work when it expected that the work was in excess of available capacity; however, the employer failed to meet its burden of proving excess work); Vincent Metals Div., 98 LA 1152 (Berquist, 1991); Phillips Pipe Line Co., 20 LA 432, 433 (Coffey, 1953); Carborundum Co., 20 LA 60, 61 (Cummins, 1952).

[604]*See* Singer Co., 71 LA 204, 213–14 (Kossoff, 1978); Superior Dairy, 68 LA 976, 981 (Chattman, 1976); Keene Corp., 63 LA 798, 800 (Ludolf, 1974); A.D. Juilliard & Co., 22 LA 266, 270 (Kelly, 1954). *Cf.* Lorraine Mfg. Co., 22 LA 390, 391 (Horovitz, 1954).

[605]Gaylord Container Corp., 93 LA 465 (Abrams, 1989).

[606]GTE N., 98 LA 617 (Ray, 1992).

[607]*See* International Paper, 117 LA 21 (Frockt, 2002) (where subcontractor's process of cleaning off machinery was more effective than that of the bargaining unit, thus lessening the potential for the machinery catching fire, employer was justified in subcontracting work); Illinois-American Water Co., 117 LA 647 (Suardi, 2002) (the presence of dignitaries and visitors in a new facility is a legitimate business reason to insist on a higher quality of janitorial work and, consequently, to subcontract work); Gaylord Container Corp., 93 LA 465, 469 (Abrams, 1989); Peabody Coal Co., 82 LA 1251, 1253 (Roberts, 1984); Kenworth Truck Co., 73 LA 947, 949 (Doyle, 1979) (reason was to improve product quality); Olympia Brewing Co., 72 LA 20, 28–29 (Madden, 1978); City of Hamtramck, 71 LA 822, 827 (Roumell, Jr., 1978); West Va. Armature Co., 68 LA 316, 321 (Hunter, Jr., 1977); Upson Co., 49 LA 805, 806–07 (Shister, 1967); Pennsalt Chems. Corp., 46 LA 1166, 1169–70 (Kesselman, 1966); KUP Sutherland Paper Co., 40 LA 737, 741 (Kadish, 1963); Allis-Chalmers Mfg. Co., 39 LA 1213, 1219 (Smith, 1962); Sinclair Ref. Co., 38 LA 718, 722 (Larkin, 1962); Bethlehem Steel, 30 LA 678, 683 (Seward, 1958); Babcock Printing Press Co., 10 LA 396, 405 (Hill, 1948).

[608]*See* Illinois-American Water Co., 117 LA 647 (Suardi, 2002) (the employer did not act with the intent to undermine the integrity of the bargaining unit, to retaliate against union members, or to achieve illicit ends when it subcontracted cleaning work after moving to a new facility; the new facility created new and more extensive janitorial demands and, because the bargaining unit was unable to sufficiently clean the old facility, the employer's decision to subcontract work was warranted); Honeywell Fed. Mfg. & Techs., 116 LA 626, 632 (King, 2001) (an employer's "ability to subcontract work arises when the Company is attempting to serve legitimate business needs rather than merely saving labor costs or otherwise harming the Union"); Associated Univs., 95 LA 1139, 1141 (Ilivicky, 1990); Golden W. Broads., 93 LA 691, 698 (Jones, Jr., 1989); Kansas City Power & Light Co., 78 LA 1124, 1127 (Madden, 1982); Delta Ref. Co., 78 LA 710, 715–16 (Boals, 1982); Blue Diamond Coal Co., 78 LA 702, 705 (Davies, 1982); Rinker Materials Corp., 76 LA 1174, 1178 (Vause, 1981); Mead Corp., 75 LA 665, 667 (Gross, 1980); Transit Auth. of River City, 74 LA 616, 620 (Chapman, 1980); Campbell Truck Co., 73 LA 1036, 1039 (Ross, 1979); Singer Co., 71 LA 204, 213 (Kossoff, 1978); Superior Dairy, 68 LA 976, 982 (Chattman, 1976); Buhr Mach. Tool Corp., 61 LA 333, 339 (Sembower, 1973).

[609]*See* Chamberlain Mfg. Corp., 54 LA 1135, 1139 (Slade, 1971); Olin Mathieson Chem. Corp., 52 LA 670, 672 (Bladek, 1969); Texas Gas Transmission Corp., 27 LA 413, 420 (Hebert, 1956); Hercules Powder Co., 21 LA 330, 334 (Williams, 1953); Appalachian Elec. Coop., 19 LA 815, 818 (Holly, 1953).

[610]*See* Hughes Electron Dynamics, 115 LA 473 (Richman, 2001) (employer violated the collective bargaining agreement, where, for the sake of convenience, it subcontracted work done by three truck drivers, which resulted in the removal of the drivers from their current

available to them,[611] or are laid off[612] by reason of the subcontract. Subcontracting may be justified by other considerations even where layoffs will result.[613] Moreover, arbitrators have considered whether layoffs could be anticipated, saying that subcontracting is to be judged by foresight rather than hindsight.[614] Another factor in judging subcontracting is whether unit employees lose regular or overtime earnings,[615] but loss of overtime often has not been a weighty factor where the agreement did not contain any overtime guarantee.[616]

    5. *Type of work involved.* Whether it is work that is normally done by unit employees,[617] or work that is frequently the subject of subcon-

---

positions and their placement in another department); Pickands Mather & Co., 78 LA 1183, 1189 (Garrett, 1982); Transit Auth. of River City, 74 LA 616, 620 (Chapman, 1980); West Virginia Pulp & Paper Co., 51 LA 842, 847 (Seinsheimer, 1968); Videotape Prods. of N.Y., 51 LA 600, 601 (Turkus, 1968); El Mundo, Inc., 50 LA 69, 72–73 (Wolff, 1967); Trane Co., 49 LA 585, 588 (Somers, 1967) (there was displacement but it was de minimis); Sealtest Foods Div., 48 LA 797, 801–02 (Valtin, 1966).

[611]*See* Southwestern Bell Tel. Co., 117 LA 654 (Fowler, 2002) (subcontracting out 67% of an employee's work resulted in a constructive layoff, as the employee was transferred to another position 35 miles away from his home and the employer and, consequently, was in violation of collective bargaining agreeement that barred subcontracting if it caused layoff); Angelus Block Co., 100 LA 1129, 1135 (Prayzich, 1993); USS, Div. of USX Corp., 97 LA 650, 651–52 (Petersen, 1991); MSB Mfg. Co., 92 LA 841, 844–46 (Bankston, 1989); Manville Forest Prods. Corp., 85 LA 85, 89–90 (Nolan, 1985); Drummond Coal Co., 82 LA 473, 475 (Nicholas, Jr., 1984); City of Hamtramck, 71 LA 822, 826 (Roumell, Jr., 1978); Mid-America Dairymen, 70 LA 116, 121 (Fitzsimmons, 1978).

[612]*See* Angelus Block Co., 100 LA 1129, 1135 (Prayzich, 1993); Central Ohio Transit Auth., 71 LA 9, 16 (Handsaker, 1978); American Air Filter Co., 54 LA 1251, 1256 (Dolnick, 1971).

[613]*See* Olympia Brewing Co., 72 LA 20, 29–30 (Madden, 1978); Dutch Maid Bakery, 52 LA 588, 592–93 (King, 1969).

[614]*See* Illinois-American Water Co., 117 LA 647 (Suardi, 2002) (determination of whether subcontracting has resulted in layoffs can only be made if evidence that the layoff actually occurred is provided; evidence regarding the mere possibility of layoffs is not enough); Marquette Mfg. Co., 51 LA 230, 234 (Mullin, Jr., 1968); Columbus Auto Parts Co., 36 LA 1079, 1081 (Alexander, 1961).

[615]*See* International Paper, 117 LA 21 (Frockt, 2002) (where employees were not deprived of work opportunities as a result of subcontracting, there was no violation of the collective bargaining agreement); West Va. Pulp & Paper Co., 51 LA 842, 847 (Seinsheimer, 1968); El Mundo, Inc., 50 LA 69, 72 (Wolff, 1967); Pennsalt Chems. Corp., 46 LA 1166, 1170 (Kesselman, 1966); Koppers Co., 22 LA 124, 126–27 (Reid, 1954).

[616]*See* Crown Cent. Petroleum Corp., 97 LA 64, 66 (Nicholas, Jr., 1991); Cives Steel Co., 72 LA 800, 803 (Atleson, 1979); Southern Ohio Coal Co., 70 LA 891, 895 (Ipavec, 1978) (under contract permitting subcontracting if employer does not have "available" employees, employer could subcontract where employees could be available only through overtime work); Weyerhaeuser Co., 68 LA 7, 12 (Petrie, 1977). *But see* Alabama Metal Indus. Corp., 66 LA 1065, 1066 (King, 1976) (by virtue of years of past practice, the overtime work in question had become an implied term of the contract); Ashland Chem. Co., 64 LA 1244, 1247 (Carmichael, 1975) (awarding employees overtime compensation for improperly subcontracted work "inasmuch as they were fully occupied and would have had to do the disputed work on overtime").

[617]*See* Southwestern Bell Tel. Co. 117 LA 654 (Fowler, 2002); Illinois-American Water Co., 117 LA 647 (Suardi, 2002); Harvard Indus., 98 LA 1100, 1103 (Kindig, 1992); Joseph Horne Co., 78 LA 262, 266–67 (Ipavec, 1982); Rinker Materials Corp., 76 LA 1174, 1178 (Vause, 1981); Olin Mathieson Chem. Corp., 52 LA 901, 903 (Amis, 1969); Air Reduction Co., 52 LA 40, 43–44 (Shister, 1969); West Va. Pulp & Paper Co., 51 LA 842, 847 (Seinsheimer, 1968). Even where this factor is in the union's favor, it may be outweighed by other considerations in the company's favor. *See* Schluderberg & Kurdle Co., 53 LA 819, 823 (Seidenberg, 1969); Upson Co., 49 LA 805, 807 (Shister, 1967).

tracting in the particular industry,[618] or work that is of a "marginal" or "incidental" nature.[619]

6. *Availability of properly qualified employees.* Whether the skills possessed by available members of the bargaining unit are sufficient to perform the work.[620]

7. *Availability of equipment and facilities.* Whether necessary equipment and facilities are presently available or can be purchased economically.[621]

8. *Regularity of subcontracting.* Whether the particular work is frequently or only intermittently subcontracted.[622] In one case, the arbitrator pointed out that the subcontracting had not been so regular

---

[618]*See* Schluderberg & Kurdle Co., 53 LA 819, 824 (Seidenberg, 1969); El Mundo, Inc., 50 LA 69, 72 (Wolff, 1967); Sealtest Foods Div., 48 LA 797, 802 (Valtin, 1966).

[619]*See* American Air Filter Co., 54 LA 1251, 1256 (Dolnick, 1971); Schluderberg & Kurdle Co., 53 LA 819, 824 (Seidenberg, 1969). *See also* Central Ohio Transit Auth., 71 LA 9, 17 (Handsaker, 1978).

[620]*See* Southwestern Bell Tel. Co., 117 LA 654 (Fowler, 2002); United States Steel Corp., 117 LA 118 (Petersen, 2002); Nexitra, LLC, 116 LA 1780 (Gregory, 2002) (subcontracting warehouse work instead of reinstating laid-off employees was not a violation of the collective bargaining agreement, where the employees were not qualified to perform the necessary works); American Crystal Sugar, 116 LA 916 (Jacobowski, 2002) (language in the collective bargaining agreement, which provided that all work that fell within the experience and qualifications of the bargaining-unit employees was to be perfomed by the bargaining unit, inherently precluded subcontracting); USS, Div. of USX, 115 LA 70 (Bethel, 2000) (employer violated the collective bargaining agreement when it subcontracted all repair work, parts of which could be performed by employees in the bargaining unit that had both the skills and the equipment to do so); James River Corp., 100 LA 387, 392 (Massey, 1992); GTE N., 98 LA 617, 619 (Ray, 1992); Bethlehem Steel Corp., 97 LA 614, 616 (Das, 1991); Inland-Rome, Inc., 93 LA 666, 673 (Williams, 1989); M.A. Hanna Co., 88 LA 185, 186–87 (Petersen, 1986); Rebel Coal Co., 79 LA 535, 538 (Wren, 1982); Delta Ref. Co., 78 LA 710, 715 (Boals, 1982); Hubinger Co., 75 LA 742, 746 (Sinicropi, 1980); FMC Corp., 75 LA 485, 492 (LeWinter, 1980).

[621]*See* Illinois-American Water Co., 117 LA 647 (Suardi, 2002) (employer's unwillingness to purchase the equipment necessary to allow the bargaining unit to perform the necessary cleaning duties and to utilize instead the subcontractor's services and equipment was reasonable); Slater Steels, 116 LA 1244 (Kilroy, 2002) (employer's decision not to purchase new equipment that would cost between $500,000 and $906,000, and to subcontract the work that required the use of the equipment instead, was not arbitrary or capricious); Collis Corp., 95 LA 89, 91 (Hewitt, 1990); Gaylord Container Corp., 93 LA 465, 469 (Abrams, 1989); Consolidation Coal Co., 84 LA 1037, 1040–41 (Duda, Jr., 1985); Chase Barlow Lumber Co., 76 LA 336, 339 (Beckman, 1981); Scott Paper Co., 72 LA 1115, 1124–26 (Simon, 1979); City of Hamtramck, 71 LA 822, 827–28 (Roumell, Jr., 1978).

[622]*See* Slater Steels, 116 LA 1244, 1248 (Kilroy, 2002) (the stainless steel manufacturer had contracted out the production of large rolls since the 1960s, which contributed to the arbitrator's decision in favor of the employer); Honeywell Fed. Mfg. & Techs., 116 LA 626 (King, 2001) (although company previously provided prescription safety glass to its employees at its own expense, the decision to subcontract safety glasses services did not violate terms of the collective bargaining agreement, partly because safety shoe services had already been contracted out 5 years earlier, without opposition from the union); Lau Indus., 114 LA 462, 466 (Imundo, Jr., 2000) (employer did not violate terms of the collective bargaining agreement where the type of work at issue (landscaping) was routinely shared with outside contractors); Texas Gas Transmission Corp., 27 LA 413, 419 (Hebert, 1956) (first time the job had been necessary); Temco Aircraft Corp., 27 LA 233, 236 (Larson, 1956); General Metals Corp., 25 LA 118, 121 (Lennard, 1955) (subcontracted work was to be done continuously, not intermittently).

in amount or type of work that additional places could have been made available to permanent employees within the bargaining unit.[623]

9. *Duration of subcontracted work.* Whether the work is subcontracted for a temporary or limited period,[624] or for a permanent or indefinite period.[625] Even where it is permanent, however, the harm may be outweighed by the justifications for the subcontracting.[626]

10. *Unusual circumstances involved.* Whether the action is necessitated by an emergency, some urgent need, or a time limit for getting the work done.[627] Also, the subcontracting may be justified because a "special job" is involved,[628] or because it is necessitated by a strike or other such situation.[629]

11. *History of negotiations on the right to subcontract.* Whether management's right to subcontract has been the subject of contract

---

[623]Temco Aircraft Corp., 27 LA 233, 236 (Larson, 1956).

[624]*See* GTE Hawaiian Tel. Co., 94 LA 711, 718 (Gilson, 1990); Delta Ref. Co., 78 LA 710, 715 (Boals, 1982) (the "work was of a 'one-shot' nature"); Rinker Materials Corp., 76 LA 1174, 1178 (Vause, 1981); Hubinger Co., 75 LA 742, 746 (Sinicropi, 1980); City of Hamtramck, 71 LA 822, 828 (Roumell, Jr., 1978); Samuel Bingham Co., 51 LA 575, 577 (Emery, 1968); Pennsalt Chems. Corp., 46 LA 1166, 1170 (Kesselman, 1966); KUP Sutherland Paper Co., 40 LA 737, 741 (Kadish, 1963) (subcontracting was episodic and temporary).

[625]*See* American Crystal Sugar Co., 116 LA 916, 919 (Jacobowski, 2002) (despite the fact that the employer regularly subcontracted short-term specialty work in the past, the arbitrator reasoned that the employer violated the contract when it subcontracted a more permanent type job (mud-trucking work)); West Virginia Pulp & Paper Co., 51 LA 842, 847–48 (Seinsheimer, 1968); Sealtest Foods Div., 48 LA 797, 801 (Valtin, 1966); W.S. Dickey Clay Mfg. Co., 46 LA 444, 447–48 (Kates, 1966); General Metals Corp., 25 LA 118, 121 (Lennard, 1955).

[626]*See* Singer Co., 71 LA 204, 211–14 (Kossoff, 1978); Superior Dairy, 68 LA 976, 981–82 (Chattman, 1976); Keene Corp., 63 LA 798, 800 (Ludolf, 1974); Schluderberg & Kurdle Co., 53 LA 819, 823–24 (Seidenberg, 1969).

[627]*See* Illinois-American Water Co., 117 LA 647, 653 (Suardi, 2002) (employer's decision to subcontract janitorial work at its new facility was reasonable because of the presence of dignitaries and other visitors at facility); Eaton Corp., 114 LA 1691, 1695 (Lalka, 2000) (subcontracting to meet customer demands was reasonable, especially because employer was faced with capacity constraints, evidenced by the fact that it had hired 10 new employees who worked overtime and no one was laid off at the time of the subcontracting); GTE N., 98 LA 617, 619 (Ray, 1992); Multiplex Co., 78 LA 1221, 1225 (O'Reilly, 1982); ILSCO Corp., 74 LA 659, 662–63 (Ipavec, 1980); Chevron U.S.A., 74 LA 269, 272 (Estes, 1980); Chemed Corp., 73 LA 734, 737 (Gibson, 1979); Phillips Stamping Co., 53 LA 670, 675 (Nichols, 1969); Dutch Maid Bakery, 52 LA 588, 593 (King, 1969); Continental Copper & Steel Indus., 51 LA 435, 439 (Wagner, 1968); Linde Co., 43 LA 554, 556 (Murphy, 1964); Allis-Chalmers Mfg. Co., 39 LA 1213, 1220 (Smith, 1962); Central Soya Co., 36 LA 1173, 1176 (Sembower, 1961); Joseph S. Finch & Co., 29 LA 609, 612 (Duff, 1957); General Metals Corp., 25 LA 118, 121 (Lennard, 1955); A.D. Juilliard & Co., 22 LA 266, 270 (Kelly, 1954).

[628]*See* Lau Indus., 114 LA 462, 466-67 (Imundo, Jr., 2000) (the large commercial lawn mower required to landscape the grounds was a specialized tool, further reinforcing the employer's right to subcontract the work); Texas Gas Transmission Corp., 27 LA 413, 419 (Hebert, 1956). *See also* M.A. Hanna Co., 88 LA 185 (Petersen, 1986).

[629]*See* Kennecott Copper Corp., 36 LA 510, 512 (Updegraff, 1960); Owens-Corning Fiberglas Corp., 23 LA 603, 605–06 (Uible, 1954); Cone Finishing Co., 16 LA 829, 831 (Maggs, 1951).

negotiations.[630] Arbitrators have pointed to the union's unsuccessful attempt to negotiate a restriction on subcontracting.[631] However, it has been emphasized that while this factor may support giving management considerable latitude in subcontracting, it cannot imply that there is no restriction at all, for parties may try to solidify or expand existing rights through bargaining.[632]

Another possible standard bears comment. In some cases, an ostensible standard for disapproving subcontracting is the fact of performance of the work on the company's premises. However, review of such cases indicates that the arbitrator was primarily concerned about employee layoff, displacement, or the like; thus, the "premises" standard may be of minimal significance.[633]

It should be borne in mind, however, that an employer's decision to subcontract may violate not only the contract, but also federal labor law. The NLRB reviews an employer's decision to subcontract to determine whether it is "inherently destructive" of the employees' "Section 7"[634] rights.

In *International Paper Co.*,[635] the employer, during negotiations, permanently subcontracted bargaining unit work during a lawful lockout of employees. Applying the inherently destructive doctrine, the Board held that the decision to permanently subcontract the work violated Section 8(a)(3) of the NLRA. The Board noted that not only did employees lose their jobs, but also those employees returning from the strike to perform nonsubcontracting work would have to work side by side with the "independent contractor" employees. Under these circumstances, the employer's decision seemed to render impotent the employees' right to resist the employer's bargaining proposals. In rendering this decision, the Board issued the following guiding principles for future application of the inherently destructive doctrine:

---

[630]Bargaining history may, for instance, indicate the intended limits of permissible subcontracting. *E.g.*, Nexitra, LLC, 116 LA 1780 (Gregory, 2002); Honeywell Fed. Mfg. & Techs., 116 LA 626 (King, 2001); Great Atl. & Pac. Tea Co., 54 LA 1189, 1191–92 (Britton, 1971). As to failure to object when put on notice of management's subcontracting intentions, see *Continental Oil Co.*, 52 LA 532, 537 (Abernethy, 1969).

[631]*See* Exxon Co., U.S.A., 78 LA 144, 147 (Light, 1981); Burger Iron Co., 78 LA 57, 59 (Van Pelt, 1982); Shenango Valley Water Co., 53 LA 741, 746 (McDermott, 1969); Olin Mathieson Chem. Corp., 52 LA 670, 672 (Bladek, 1969); El Mundo, Inc., 50 LA 69, 70–71 (Wolff, 1967); Hughes Aircraft Co., 45 LA 184, 188–89 (Guse, 1965); American Airlines, 27 LA 174, 177–79 (Wolff, 1956); Stix, Baer & Fuller Co., 27 LA 57, 71–74 (Klamon, 1956); Parke, Davis & Co., 26 LA 438, 453–54 (Haughton, 1956); Hertner Elec. Co., 25 LA 281, 289 (Kates, 1955).

[632]Allis-Chalmers Mfg. Co., 39 LA 1213, 1218 (Smith, 1962).

[633]For cases mentioning the "premises" aspect, see *Bendix Corp.*, 41 LA 905, 907 (Warns, 1963); *Hearst Consol. Publ'ns*, 26 LA 723, 725–26 (Gray, 1956); *New Haven Gas Co.*, 24 LA 882, 884 (Stutz, 1955); *Weber Aircraft Corp.*, 24 LA 821, 827–28 (Jones, Jr., 1955); *Magnolia Petroleum Co.*, 21 LA 267, 269–73 (Larson, 1953). *See also* International Paper Co., 72 LA 421, 430 (Howell, 1979).

[634]29 U.S.C. §157.

[635]319 NLRB 1253, 151 LRRM 1033 (1995), *enforcement denied*, 115 F.3d 1045, 155 LRRM 2641 (D.C. Cir. 1997) (although court applied the "inherently destructive" doctrine, it held that it was not satisfied here bcause actions of employer were not "inherently destructive").

1. "[T]he severity of harm to employees' . . . rights caused by the employer['s] conduct must be determined," and such determination should include "the severity of harm suffered by the employees for exercising their rights as well as the severity of the impact on the statutory right being exercised."[636]
2. Conduct of temporary duration that seeks to put pressure on union members to accept particular management proposals must be distinguished from conduct that has "'far reaching effects which would hinder future bargaining'"[637] or "'creates visible and continuing obstacles to the future exercise of employee rights.'"[638]
3. "[A] distinction [also] must be drawn between an employer's 'hostility to the process of collective bargaining' and its simple intention to support its bargaining position as to [employee] compensation and other matters."[639]
4. "[C]onduct may be inherently destructive of employee rights if it "discourages collective bargaining in the sense of making it seem a futile exercise in the eyes of employees.'"[640]

More recently, in applying *International Paper*, the Board in *Fairfield Tower Condominium Ass'n*[641] held that an employer that permanently subcontracted work after a bargaining unit went on strike violated Section 8(a)(5) of the NLRA, as such acts qualify as unlawful discouragement of lawful strike activity. The Board stated:

> By exercising their statutory right to strike, the porters suffered the ultimate in industrial capital punishment—permanent loss of employment. . . . [N]othing could be more destructive of employee rights or send a more effective message about the dangers and ultimate futility of engaging in lawful concerted activity in furtherance of collective bargaining.[642]

C. Notice of Intent to Subcontract; Duty to Bargain [LA CDI 117.386]

The collective bargaining agreement may require notice of intent to subcontract.[643] When the contract is silent as to subcontracting, sufficient prior

---

[636]*Id.* at 1269.

[637]*Id.* (quoting Portland Williamette Co. v. NLRB, 534 F.2d 1331, 1334, 92 LRRM 2113 (9th Cir. 1976)).

[638]*Id.* (quoting Inter-Collegiate Press v. NLRB, 486 F.2d 837, 845, 84 LRRM 2562 (8th Cir. 1973)).

[639]*Id.* (quoting American Ship Bldg. Co. v. NLRB, 380 U.S. 300, 309, 58 LRRM 2672 (1965)).

[640]*Id.* at 1270 (quoting Esmark, Inc. v. NLRB, 887 F.2d 739, 749, 132 LRRM 2710 (7th Cir. 1989), quoting in turn Boilermakers Local 88 v. NLRB (National Gypsum Co.), 848 F.2d 756, 764 (D.C. Cir. 1988)).

[641]2002 WL 31174515, 2002 NLRB Lexis 447 (Sept. 24, 2002).

[642]*Id.* at *11.

[643]*See* Inland-Rome, Inc., 93 LA 666, 673 (Williams, 1989); Philip A. Hunt Chem. Corp., 70 LA 1182, 1184 (Malkin, 1978); Rock Island Ref. Corp., 70 LA 322, 324–25 (High, 1978); Mid-America Dairymen, 70 LA 116, 120 (Fitzsimmons, 1978); United States Steel Corp., 54 LA 1207, 1209 (Duff, 1971); Bethlehem Steel Corp., 53 LA 993, 996 (Strongin, 1969) (failure to give notice did not prejudice union in this instance); Milprint, Inc., 46 LA 724, 727–29 (Graff, 1966). A contractual notice requirement was not violated by failure to give notice in an emergency. Jos. Schlitz Brewing Co., 51 LA 41, 46 (Bothwell, 1968). *Cf.* Kaiser Found. Hosps., 61 LA 1008, 1013–14 (Jacobs, 1973).

notification for meaningful discussions to occur generally should be given,[644] although some arbitrators have held that no notice is required.[645]

Notice requirements may be narrowly interpreted. Thus, under a contract stating that when work is contracted-out the company will promptly notify the union "of the reason for contracting it out," advance notice of intent to subcontract was not required.[646] Nor did the company violate the contractual notice requirement by failing to notify the union where the employer did not have qualified employees or the necessary equipment, and the subcontracting of work was not expected to become routine.[647] However, in another case the parties had a mutual understanding that under their collective bargaining agreement the company would give notice and discuss its subcontracting plans with the union before entering into subcontracting arrangements. When this understanding was violated, an arbitrator devised a special remedy designed to return the parties as nearly as possible to the status quo ante and to deter future violations of the notice and discussion requirement.[648]

Apart from any contractual requirement for notice and discussion, the Supreme Court's *Fibreboard*[649] decision holds that in certain circumstances the employer has a duty to bargain about subcontracting under the NLRA. In this decision the Court said:

> We are . . . not expanding the scope of mandatory bargaining to hold, as we do now, that the type of "contracting out" involved in this case—the replacement of employees in the existing bargaining unit with those of an independent contractor to do the same work under similar conditions of employment—is a statutory subject of collective bargaining under § 8(d). Our decision need not and does not encompass other forms of "contracting out" or "subcontracting" which arise daily in our complex economy.[650]

---

[644]*See* Riverton Corp., 109 LA 97 (Feigenbaum, 1997); United Techs., 105 LA 1214 (McGury, 1995); Pittsburgh Brewing Co., 53 LA 470, 477 (McDermott, 1969). *See also* Delta Ref. Co., 78 LA 710, 716 (Boals, 1982); Inland Tool & Mfg., 71 LA 120, 124 (Lipson, 1978).

[645]*See* Olgebay Norton Taconite Co., 107 LA 1153 (Neumeier, 1997) (employer did not violate agreement, even though it did not give notice to union before sending main frame to subcontractor for inspection and machine work, where nothing in agreement requires employer to provide union with contracting-out notice before sending piece of equipment to subcontractor for inspection); Haveg Indus., 52 LA 1146, 1151 (Kates, 1969).

[646]Electric Autolite Co., 35 LA 415, 420 (Willcox, 1960) (emphasizing that the contract used the word "when" rather than "before").

[647]M.A. Hanna Co., 88 LA 185 (Petersen, 1986). *But see* Jackson Pub. Sch., 99 LA 366, 370 (Daniel, 1992) (school required to give notice despite contract provision stating that subcontracting that does not require layoffs or prevent recalls does not require notice).

[648]*See* AK Steel Corp., 105 LA 869 (Strongin, 1995) (employer must pay all affected employees for hours a contractor spent rebuilding a steel mold as a remedy for the employer's failure to give the union timely notice of contracting-out as required by the agreement, even though it was not clear from the record whether the unit employees were capable of performing the work); Milprint, Inc., 51 LA 748, 750–51 (Somers, 1968). *See also* Rock Island Ref. Corp., 70 LA 322, 324–25 (High, 1978).

[649]Fibreboard Paper Prods. Corp. v. NLRB, 379 U.S. 203, 57 LRRM 2609 (1964).

[650]*Id.* at 215, 57 LRRM at 2613–14 (footnote omitted). In *Westinghouse Electric Corp.*, 150 NLRB 1574, 58 LRRM 1257 (1965), the NLRB held that: (1) the company did not violate the NLRA by failing to consult the union about each of thousands of annual subcontracting decisions, where the subcontracting was motivated solely by economic considerations; (2) it comported with traditional methods by which the company conducted its operations; (3) it did not vary significantly in kind or degree from subcontracting of work under established

In evaluating the scope of *Fibreboard*, one arbitrator spoke of the Supreme Court's "cautious approach toward recognizing unilateral subcontracting as a mandatory subject for bargaining,"[651] another reminded that the Court "limited the decision to the facts in the case,"[652] and a third arbitrator concluded that the decision does not apply where the agreement contains a subcontracting clause.[653]

The *Fibreboard* decision was followed by the NLRB for a number of years. Then, in *Otis Elevator Co.*,[654] the Board held that an employer's decision to subcontract is a mandatory subject of bargaining if it turns on labor costs rather than on a change in the nature or direction of the enterprise.[655] Following the Supreme Court's approach in *First National Maintenance Corp. v. NLRB*,[656] where the Court held that the employer had no duty to bargain

---

practice; (4) it had no demonstrable adverse effect on employees in the bargaining unit; and (5) the union had an opportunity to bargain about subcontracting practices at general negotiating meetings. But the Board said that bargaining would be required if the subcontracting involved a departure from previously established operating practices, effected a change in conditions of employment, or resulted in a significant impairment of job tenure, employment security, or reasonably anticipated work opportunities for those in the bargaining unit. In *Union Carbide Corp.*, 178 NLRB 504, 72 LRRM 1150 (1969), the Board considered the elimination of job classifications to be merely one factor to be considered, and this factor in this instance was outweighed by other considerations. In *Hayes-Albion Corp.*, 190 NLRB 146, 77 LRRM 1052 (1971), the layoff of one employee was similarly just one of several factors to be considered, and it was outweighed by other considerations. The NLRB's *Westinghouse* standards were accepted and applied by the court in *Equitable Gas Co. v. NLRB*, 637 F.2d 980, 106 LRRM 2201 (3d Cir. 1981) (however, the court, on applying the standards, rejected the Board's finding that there was a duty to bargain over the subcontracting in question). In instances where a duty to bargain does exist, the following statement becomes relevant as concerns the scope of the employer's obligation: "[U]nless transfers are specifically prohibited by the bargaining agreement, an employer is free to transfer work out of the bargaining unit if: (1) the employer complies with [*Fibreboard*] by bargaining in good faith to impasse; and (2) the employer is not motivated by anti-union animus . . . ." University of Chicago v. NLRB, 514 F.2d 942, 949, 89 LRRM 2113, 2117 (7th Cir. 1975), *quoted with approval in* Newspaper Printing Corp. v. NLRB, 692 F.2d 615, 622, 111 LRRM 2824, 2830 (6th Cir. 1982).

[651]Hess Oil & Chem. Corp., 51 LA 752, 759 (Gould, 1968).

[652]Peet Packing Co., 55 LA 1288, 1296 (Howlett, 1970). *See also* Delta Ref. Co., 78 LA 710, 716 (Boals, 1982).

[653]Hughes Aircraft Co., 45 LA 184, 189–90 (Guse, 1965). For other cases in which the arbitrator commented as to the *Fibreboard* decision or considered its applicability to the dispute before him, see *Quinn Concrete Co.*, 79 LA 843, 847 (Murphy, 1982); *Campbell Truck Co.*, 73 LA 1036, 1040 (Ross, 1979); *Superior Dairy*, 68 LA 976, 979–80 (Chattman, 1976); *Mead Johnson Terminal Corp.*, 54 LA 886, 894–95 (Witney, 1971); *Pittsburgh Brewing Co.*, 53 LA 470, 474, 477 (McDermott, 1969); *Anaconda Aluminum Co.*, 48 LA 409, 411 (Volz, 1967); *Fraser-Nelson Ship Bldg.*, 45 LA 177, 181 (Gundermann, 1965); *Purex Corp.*, 45 LA 174, 175–76 (Guild, 1965).

[654]269 NLRB 891, 115 LRRM 1281 (1984).

[655]*Id.* at 893 n.5, 115 LRRM at 1283 n.5.

[656]452 U.S. 666, 107 LRRM 2705 (1981). The issue decided in *First Nat'l Maintenance* was whether an employer could terminate part of the business without bargaining with the union. The Supreme Court said the employer had no duty to bargain in this instance. For a more extensive discussion of the duty to bargain, see section 2.A.i., "The Duty to Bargain: Right of Unilateral Action," and section 2.A.ii., "Duration of Limitation on Unilateral Action: Contract Limitation Versus Statutory Duty to Bargain," above. Included there is some reference to the *First National Maintenance* decision, in which the Supreme Court commented regarding *Fibreboard* (*First Nat'l Maint.*, 452 U.S. at 678, 107 LRRM at 2710), and which sometimes may be relevant in determining the existence of a duty to bargain on subcontracting. Compare the different tests devised by Board members in *Otis Elevator Co.*, with the new test devised by the Board in *Dubuque Packing Co.*, 303 NLRB 386, 391, 137 LRRM 1185 (1991). For cases, see Chapter 10, section 3.A.v., "The NLRA, the Arbitrator, and the NLRB."

over a partial termination of a business, the Board noted that the same analysis also applied to subcontracting decisions. The *Otis Elevator* decision was affirmed by the U.S. Court of Appeals for the Fifth Circuit in *Steelworkers Local 2179 v. NLRB (Inland Steel Container Co.).*[657]

In *Mid-State Ready Mix*,[658] the Board again examined the issue of subcontracting and the duty to bargain. Without abandoning the test developed in *Otis Elevator*, the Board held that the duty to bargain arises any time the subcontracting merely involves replacing current employees with contract employees doing the same work at the same facility, regardless of whether the decision was based on labor costs.[659] If, however, the decision to subcontract was attributable to a change in the scope and direction of the business, then the obligation does not attach.[660]

16. ASSIGNING WORK OUT OF THE BARGAINING UNIT

A. Determining Whether the Assignment Is Permissible
[LA CDI 117.340]

Arbitrators are divided on the question of whether, in the absence of contract provisions to the contrary, management has the right to assign bargaining-unit work to employees outside the unit. Many of the cases have involved the assignment of such work to supervisory employees; others involved the assignment to salaried workers or nonunit production or maintenance employees. In holding that management has such right, some arbitrators have emphasized the absence of a specific restriction in the contract. For example, in one case, the arbitrator stated:

> A careful examination of the contract fails to reveal any provision that specifically prohibits the Company from making a bona fide transfer, allocation or assignment of work out of the bargaining unit—which is the issue posed in this particular case. In the absence of a specific prohibition or limitation to the contrary it must be assumed that these are reserved and retained powers of management . . . .[661]

---

[657]822 F.2d 559, 125 LRRM 3313 (5th Cir. 1987). For Board decisions following the same approach, see *Garwood-Detroit Truck Equip.*, 274 NLRB 113, 118 LRRM 1417 (1985) (decision to subcontract mounting and service work not a mandatory subject of bargaining because the decision was a significant change in business operations); UOP, Inc., 272 NLRB 999, 117 LRRM 1429 (1984); Fraser Shipyards, 272 NLRB 496, 117 LRRM 1328 (1984).

[658]307 NLRB 809, 140 LRRM 1137 (1992).

[659]*Id.*, 140 LRRM at 1138.

[660]Power, Inc., 311 NLRB 599, 145 LRRM 1198 (1993).

[661]Stewart-Warner Corp., 22 LA 547, 551 (Burns, 1954). For other cases in which the arbitrator stressed the absence of any clear contractual prohibition (in some of the cases the arbitrator also relied on a management-rights clause), see *Associated Univs.*, 95 LA 1139, 1140 (Ilivicky, 1990); *Collis Corp.*, 95 LA 89, 91–92 (Hewitt, 1990); *SIPCO, Inc.*, 93 LA 1225, 1230–32 (Slade, 1990); *Superior Dairy*, 69 LA 594, 598 (Abrams, 1977); *Daniel Scharlin & Assocs.*, 69 LA 394, 398 (Lucas, 1977); *National Automatic Tool Co.*, 54 LA 692, 696 (Kates, 1971); *Olin Mathieson Chem. Co.*, 42 LA 1025, 1040–41 (Klamon, 1964); *Sperry Gyroscope Co.*, 42 LA 31, 39 (Yagoda, 1963); *Sinclair Ref. Co.*, 38 LA 718, 722 (Larkin, 1962); *Mt. Carmel Pub. Util. Co.*, 16 LA 59, 65 (Hampton, 1951); *Bassick Co.*, 13 LA 135, 136 (Lane, 1949); *Goetz Ice Co.*, 7 LA 412, 413–14 (Cheney, 1947). *See also* Kroger Co., 52 LA 440, 443–45 (Doyle, 1968); C. Finkbeiner, Inc., 44 LA 1109, 1113–14 (Roberts, 1965). *But see* Angelus Block Co., 100 LA 1129, 1133–36 (Prayzich, 1993) (when the contract is silent on the subject of subcontracting, absence of prohibiting language is not, in itself, controlling).

Other arbitrators, in the absence of a specific contract restriction, have relied on one or more of the following considerations to uphold management's action:[662]

1. The quantity of work or the effect on the bargaining unit is minor or de minimis in nature.[663]
2. The work is supervisory or managerial in nature.[664]
3. The work assignment is a temporary one for a special purpose or need.[665]
4. The work is not covered by the contract.[666]
5. The work is experimental.[667]
6. Under past practice, the work has been performed exclusively by bargaining-unit employees.[668]
7. The transfer was caused by a reorganization or change in work methodology or processes.[669]

---

[662]In *Cleveland Electric Illuminating Co.*, 105 LA 817, 823 (Franckiewicz, Stevers, & Boyle, 1995), for example, the panel identified the following relevant factors: (1) whether in the past work had been performed exclusively by bargaining-unit employees; (2) whether layoffs, displacement from jobs, or loss of pay to employees resulted from transfer of work; (3) "the effect on the bargaining unit"; (4) the amount of work involved"; (5) the legitimacy of the company's reasons for making the change"; (6) whether a change had occurred in the type of work being performed; (7) "whether the change was in response to changes in the economic climate"; and (8) whether the transfer of work was caused by a reorganization or change in work methodology or processes. The panel concluded that the determination of whether a transfer of work was permissible should be made on a case-by-case basis. Because the work at issue had been primarily a nonunit function in the past, and because the transfer of work occurred during a company reorganization, the panel concluded that there was no violation of the agreement.

[663]*See* WCI Components, 95 LA 11, 16 (Byars, 1990); ARMCO, Inc., 92 LA 703, 704 (Strongin, 1989); New Jersey Tpk. Auth., 72 LA 905, 908 (Chandler, 1979); Superior Dairy, 69 LA 594, 598 (Abrams, 1977); Daniel Scharlin & Assocs., 69 LA 394, 398 (Lucas, 1977).

[664]*See* Excelsior Truck Leasing, 77 LA 1224, 1227 (Mullaly, 1981); Evergreen Indus., 76 LA 535, 537, 539 (Beck, 1981); International Nickel Co., 50 LA 107, 109 (Calhoon, 1968). In *Daniel Scharlin & Assocs.*, 69 LA 394, 398–99 (Lucas, 1977), the "confidential" nature of the work was a significant factor in the decision for the employer.

[665]*See* M.A. Hanna Co., 88 LA 185, 188 (Petersen, 1986); Valentine & Cos., 13 LA 456, 459 (Fulda, 1949); Pan Am. Airways, 13 LA 390, 390–91 (Kerr, 1949); Lukens Steel Co., 12 LA 584, 585 (D'Andrade, 1949).

[666]*See* Cosmos Broad. Corp., 92 LA 1076, 1080 (Daniel, 1989); Peoria Water Co., 80 LA 478, 483 (Fitzsimmons, 1983); Lake City Elks Lodge 1800, 72 LA 643, 648 (Neill, 1979); National Automatic Tool Co., 54 LA 692, 695–96 (Kates, 1971).

[667]*See* Farmland Indus., 96 LA 815, 822 (Murphy, 1991); United States Steel Corp., 52 LA 880, 882 (Dybeck, 1969). For some definitions and views as to what constitutes "experimental" work in this regard, see *Addison Prods. Co.*, 74 LA 1145, 1149, 1153–54 (Stephens, 1980).

[668]*See* Flint & Walling, 79 LA 430, 433 (Guenther, 1982); Evergreen Indus., 76 LA 535, 539 (Beck, 1981); Teledyne Monarch Rubber, 75 LA 963, 966 (Feldman, 1980); Lake City Elks Lodge 1800, 72 LA 643, 649 (Neill, 1979); Superior Dairy, 69 LA 594, 598 (Abrams, 1977).

[669]Tower Auto. Prods., 114 LA 626 (Nathan, 2000) (nature of the work changed, where different skills were required for the manufacturing process and these new skills were outside the normal experience and training of the bargaining-unit employees); Allied Signal, 113 LA 124 (Thornell, 1999) (assignment of operating new machine was properly moved to another classification, where the employee's skills were a better fit); GTE-Florida, 112 LA 919 (Frost, 1999) (in absence of contract restriction, management may make changes in assignments when substantial changes in technology or manufacturing processes have been made). *But see* Owens Ill., Inc., 111 LA 1135 (Feldman, 1999) (purchase of new equipment did not allow employer to deprive bargaining unit of work).

8. There is a change in the character of the work.[670]

9. Automation or a technological change involved.[671]

10. An emergency is involved.[672]

11. Some other special situation or need is involved.[673]

Other arbitrators have ruled against the right of management to assign work out of the bargaining unit, on the ground that it is not included within

---

[670]Tower Auto. Prods., 114 LA 626 (Nathan 2000); Tone Bros., 114 LA 547 (Jay, 1999) (work as altered was no longer exclusively bargaining-unit work); GTE-Florida, 112 LA 919 (Frost, 1999) (in the absence of a contract restriction, management may make changes in assignments when substantial changes in technology or manufacturing processes have been made). *But see* Owens Ill., Inc., 111 LA 1135 (Feldman, 1999) (purchase of new equipment did not allow employer to deprive bargaining unit of work); WBAL-TV, 110 LA 614 (Fishgold, 1998) (technological advances in broadcasting were within the union's jurisdiction, where the parties expressly contemplated that the union's jurisdiction was not limited to technology that was present at the time the contract was drafted). *See* Lake City Elks Lodge 1800, 72 LA 643, 649 (Neill, 1979); National Automatic Tool Co., 54 LA 692, 695–96 (Kates, 1971); Bridgeport Brass Co., 30 LA 282, 288 (Stutz, 1958); Celotex Corp., 24 LA 369, 374 (Reynard, 1955).

[671]Removal of accounting, payroll, billing, time keeping, and other clerical work from the bargaining unit on establishment of centralized electronic data processing programs has been upheld in numerous cases. In one such case, the arbitrator stated that "utilization of computer technology and centralization of data processing have become very common in American business practice." Safeway Stores, 42 LA 353, 358 (Ross, 1964). *See also* Ethyl Corp., 50 LA 322, 334–37 (Dworkin, 1968); United States Steel Corp., 45 LA 555, 556 (Altrock, 1965); McCall Corp., 44 LA 201, 208–10 (Dworkin, 1965); Curtiss-Wright Corp., 43 LA 5, 8 (Seitz, 1964); National Dairy Prods. Corp., 41 LA 506, 509 (Altieri, 1963); United States Steel Corp., 37 LA 302, 305 (Garrett, 1961); Bethlehem Steel Co., 35 LA 72, 73 (Feinberg, 1960); Van Norman Mach. Co., 28 LA 791, 796–97 (Pigors, 1957). *Cf.* Ohio Brass Co., 68 LA 492, 498 (Leach, 1977); Ford Motor Co., 41 LA 124, 126–29 (Platt, 1963); Illinois Bell Tel., 62–3 ARB ¶8944 (Gilden, 1962); Rockwell-Standard Corp., 39 LA 24, 27 (Anderson, 1962). Centralization of design engineering work was upheld in *United States Steel Corp.*, 44 LA 1224, 1228 (Florey, 1965), as was centralization of reproduction and stationery operations in *Phillips Chemical Co.*, 39 LA 82, 84–85 (Larson, 1962). For other cases involving work claims in connection with centralized control systems, see *Joseph Horne Co.*, 78 LA 262, 266–67 (Ipavec, 1982); *Caterpillar Tractor Co.*, 73 LA 945, 947 (Cox, 1979); *General Dynamics Corp.*, 69 LA 136, 140 (Rule, 1977). Computer monitoring and control of production machines near the production situs may be a significantly different matter. *See* Bethlehem Steel, 46 LA 730, 732 (Seward, 1966) (upholding the union); Alan Wood Steel Co., 35 LA 157, 159 (Valtin, 1960) (same). *Cf.* Williams Pipe Line Co., 80 LA 338, 342–43 (Ross, 1983); Great Lakes Carbon Corp., 48 LA 746, 750 (Block, 1967); Blaw-Knox Co., 66–2 ARB ¶8430 (Cahn, 1966); Goodyear Tire & Rubber Co., 35 LA 917, 919–19 (Killingsworth, 1961) (past practice and de minimis were factors in favor of the company); Monsanto Chem. Co., 27 LA 736, 743 (Roberts, 1956). Regarding technological change, see also *Bell Tel. Co. of Pa.*, 75 LA 750, 760–61 (Garrett, 1980). In *Hamm Brewing Co.*, 28 LA 46, 49 (Lockhart, 1956), the new machine did not change the job, but only made it more efficient.

[672]*See* GTE N., 98 LA 617, 618–19 (Ray, 1992); National Cash Register Co., 46 LA 782, 789 (Begley, 1966); Intermountain Chem. Co., 26 LA 58, 61 (Kadish, 1956). *See also* American Bemberg, 19 LA 372, 374 (McCoy, 1952).

[673]*See* Gaylord Container Corp., 93 LA 465, 469–70 (Abrams, 1989) (employer did not own proper equipment); Unit Parts Co., 80 LA 1180, 1184 (Nelson, 1983) (economic necessity); National Cash Register Co., 48 LA 400, 401–02 (Updegraff, 1967) (unit employees were absent); Great Lakes Pipe Line Co., 27 LA 748, 754 (Merrill, 1956) (need for supervisor's presence); National Supply Co., 27 LA 332, 334–35 (Aaron, 1956) (plant security problem); Kennecott Copper Corp., 25 LA 263, 266 (Aaron, 1955) (safety problem); Corn Prods. Ref. Co., 20 LA 690, 703 (Klamon, 1953) (minor preparations for reopening plant after shutdown due to strike).

the scope of general management-rights clauses.[674] Similarly, arbitrators have so ruled on the basis that the recognition,[675] seniority,[676] or job security clause[677] is violated by such action; or that the job, being listed in the contract, is a part of the contract, and its reassignment outside the bargaining unit violates the contract.[678]

The reasoning underlying this view was elaborated by one arbitrator:

> Job security is an inherent element of the labor contract, a part of its very being. If wages is the heart of the labor agreement, job security may be considered its soul. Those eligible to share in the degree of job security the contract affords are those to whom the contract applies. . . .
>
> The transfer of work customarily performed by employees in the bargaining unit must therefore be regarded as an attack on the job security of the employees whom the agreement covers and therefore on one of the contract's basic purposes.[679]

Some arbitrators take an intermediate position, agreeing that the recognition, seniority,[680] and other such contract clauses do evidence an intention to restrict the performance of unit work to unit employees, but at the same time not considering such provisions to create an absolute restriction. Arbitrators in this camp recognize that the assignment of such work outside the bargaining unit may be proper where there is "good cause,"[681] where it is de minimis,[682] where the work is supervisory in nature,[683] or where there is

---

[674]*See* American Bakeries Co., 46 LA 769, 772 (Hon, 1966); Bethlehem Steel, 17 LA 295, 299 (Selekman, 1951); West Va. Pulp & Paper Co., 12 LA 1074, 1080 (Copelof, 1949); Kraft Foods Corp., 10 LA 254, 256–57 (Coffey, 1948); New Britain Mach. Co., 8 LA 720, 722–23 (Wallen, Knauss, & Kosinki, 1947).

[675]*See* Holland Plastics, 74 LA 69, 75 (Belcher, 1980); KIRO-TV, 51 LA 1221, 1223 (Peck, 1968); Virginia Elec. & Power Co., 48 LA 305, 309 (Porter, 1966); Kroger Co., 33 LA 188, 193 (Howlett, 1959); Hamm Brewing Co., 28 LA 46, 48–49 (Lockhart, 1956); Sangamo Elec. Co., 27 LA 631, 633 (Kelliher, 1956); Bethlehem Steel Co., 21 LA 283, 284 (Feinberg, 1952); Lear, Inc., 20 LA 681, 683–84 (Boyce, 1953); Kay Mfg. Corp., 13 LA 545, 550 (Komaroff, 1949).

[676]*See* Holland Plastics, 74 LA 69, 75 (Belcher, 1980); Clover Creamery Co., 50 LA 613, 614 (Jaffee, 1968); Sangamo Elec. Co., 27 LA 631, 633 (Kelliher, 1956); American Bemberg, 19 LA 372, 374 (McCoy, 1952); Corn Prods. Ref. Co., 18 LA 346, 351 (Gilden, 1952); Bethlehem Steel Co., 16 LA 111, 113 (Killingsworth, 1951)*;* West Virginia Pulp & Paper Co., 12 LA 1074, 1080 (Copelof, 1949); New Britain Mach. Co., 8 LA 720, 722–23 (Wallen, Knauss, & Kosinki, 1947).

[677]*See* Hamm Brewing Co., 28 LA 46, 48–49 (Lockhart, 1956). *See also* American Oil Co., 40 LA 466, 468–69 (Dykstra, 1963).

[678]*See* American Bakeries Co., 46 LA 769, 772 (Hon, 1966); Olin Mathieson Chem. Corp., 41 LA 1348, 1350 (Oppenheim, 1964); Continental Oil Co., 22 LA 880, 882 (Reynard, 1954); Wheeling Steel Corp., 21 LA 35, 40–41 (Shipman, 1953); Cooperative Mills, 20 LA 603, 604 (Lehoczky, 1953). In some cases the work was supervisory in nature, but this did not privilege the assignment. *See* Resistoflex Corp., 19 LA 761, 763 (Levy, 1952); Bethlehem Steel, 17 LA 295, 300 (Selekman, 1951); Owl Drug Co., 10 LA 498, 502 (Pollard, 1948).

[679]New Britain Mach. Co., 8 LA 720, 722 (Wallen, Knauss, & Kosinki, 1947).

[680]MSB Mfg. Co., 92 LA 841 (Bankston, 1989).

[681]Cotton Bros. Baking Co., 51 LA 220, 223–24 (Hebert, 1968); Great Lakes Pipe Line Co., 27 LA 748, 753 (Merrill, 1956).

[682]Costco Wholesale Corp., 114 LA 39 (Hockenberry, 2000) (no evidence indicating hourly position had been replaced); Consumer Prods. Co., 112 LA 550 (Jenks, 1999) (manager performing bargaining-unit work did not displace bargaining-unit employee). *See* Ideal Elec. Co., 93 LA 101, 103–04 (Strasshofer, 1989); Crown Zellerbach Corp., 52 LA 1183, 1186 (Roberts, 1969); Joseph S. Finch & Co., 41 LA 883, 883–84 (Crawford, 1963); American Bemberg, 19 LA 372, 374 (McCoy, 1952).

[683]*See* Buckeye Cellulose Corp., 76 LA 889, 893 (Ipavec, 1981) (reclaiming supervisory duties); Pacific Motor Trucking Co., 75 LA 941, 943 (Ward, 1980) (confidential material was

an emergency or some other justification,[684] but may be improper if layoffs and displacements from jobs result[685] or employees suffer loss of pay. [686]

A related view as to the proper approach for judging the assignment of bargaining-unit work to persons outside the unit was offered in *Chrysler Corp.*[687] In that case, the agreement recognized management's right "to manage its plants and offices and direct its affairs and working forces."[688] The

---

involved); Lilly Indus. Coatings, 73 LA 594, 598–99 (Epstein, 1979); Conwed Corp., 55 LA 997, 1002–05 (Solomon, 1970); Atlantic Richfield Co., 53 LA 958, 959–60 (Duff, 1969) (de minimis); Crown Zellerbach Corp. 52 LA 1183, 1186 (Roberts, 1969); Alfred M. Lewis, Inc., 50 LA 553, 555 (Meiners, 1968) (supervisors did work of unit employees who refused to cross picket line); National Elec. Contractors Ass'n, 48 LA 1180, 1183–84 (Lucas, 1967); Interchemical Corp., 48 LA 124, 132 (Yagoda, 1967); Diamond Nat'l Corp., 46 LA 1030, 1034 (Gross, 1966) (supervisors did the work during vacation shutdown, as in the past); Hughes Aircraft Co., 44 LA 727, 730 (Guse, 1965); Paragon Bridge & Steel Co., 44 LA 361, 371–72 (Casselman, 1965); Geigy Chem. Co., 40 LA 806, 809–10 (Hebert, 1963); Peoples Gas Light & Coke Co., 39 LA 224, 229 (Davis, 1962); Texas Gas Corp., 36 LA 1141, 1146–47 (Ray, 1961); Acheson Dispersed Pigments Co., 36 LA 578, 584 (Hale, 1960); Marion Power Shovel Co., 36 LA 416, 419 (Teple, 1960); Goodyear Tire & Rubber Co., 35 LA 917, 919 (Killingsworth, 1961); Kroger Co., 33 LA 188, 193 (Howlett, 1959); Marinette Paper Co., 30 LA 43, 45 (Clements, 1958); White Motor Co., 26 LA 399, 400 (Crawford, 1956) (de minimis); Moraine Paper Co., 24 LA 696, 699 (Fulda, 1955); Cannon Elec. Co., 19 LA 283, 286–87 (Warren, 1952); Celotex Corp., 16 LA 321, 323–24 (Ralston, 1951); Metal & Thermit Corp., 1 LA 417, 419 (Gilden, 1946). *See also* American Saint Gobain Corp., 46 LA 920, 924 (Duff, 1966) (quality-testing purposes).

[684]Okonite Co., 112 LA 1060 (Abrams, 1999) (emergency exception applied where no bargaining-unit employees had volunteered to work overtime). *See* KIRO-TV, 51 LA 1221, 1223 (Peck, 1968); Olin Mathieson Chem. Corp., 41 LA 1348, 1350 (Oppenheim, 1964); American Bemberg, 19 LA 372, 374 (McCoy, 1952). *But see* Citicasters Co., WKRC-TV, 114 LA 1367 (Lewis, 2000) (no emergency where employer knew in advance that computer needed upgrade and specifically planned ahead and scheduled installation time); Michigan Dep't of Transp., 112 LA 1179 (Allen, 1999) (no emergency where employer created lack of skill in bargaining unit by not training replacement or deferring promotion until replacement was trained).

[685]*See* Owens Ill., Inc., 111 LA 1135 (Feldman, 1999) (purchase of new equipment did not allow employer to deprive bargaining unit of work). *See also* Cleveland Elec. Illuminating Co., 105 LA 817 (Franckiewicz, 1995).

[686]*See also* Atlantic City Showboat, 113 LA 530, 531 (Zirkel, 1999) (employer's past practice of assigning room servers to gambling area limited the employer's contractually unrestricted right to assign work according to "the requirements of business and according to skill and efficiency"); Okonite Co., 112 LA 1060, 1060 (Abrams, 1999) (employer was not required to force bargaining-unit employees to work overtime, where there was a past practice of assigning such work on a volunteer basis); City of Conneaut, Ohio, 112 LA 899 (Richard, 1999) (union estopped from asserting in the future that the city violated an agreement prohibiting supervisors from performing bargaining-unit work when employees are available, where the union had a past practice of allowing supervisors to do incidental bargaining-unit work that assisted employees); Matanuska Elec. Ass'n, 111 LA 596 (Landau, 1998) (past practice before bargaining unit formed also considered); ACS, 111 LA 566 (Kilroy, 1998) (past practice of allowing carpenters to perform truck driving in the course of their duties during regular time hours extended to driving during overtime hours as well). *But see* Tendercare, Inc., 111 LA 1192 (Borland, 1998) (past practice of rotation did not modify employer's contractually "unfettered right" to assign and transfer employees and to direct and schedule workforce); Sears, Roebuck & Co., 111 LA 378 (Franckiewicz, 1998) (past practice inapplicable, where previous incident occurred under a different and more restrictive contractual provision regarding work preservation); Marley Cooling Tower Co., 110 LA 1171 (Berger, 1998) (past practice preceding new agreement inapplicable, where the parties negotiated a dramatic change in management's right to assign overtime); Department of Veterans Affairs, 110 LA 611 (Smith, Jr., 1998) (past practice could not limit management's absolute right to assign work where it was not listed as an exception to this right in the agreement).

[687]36 LA 1018 (Smith, 1961).

[688]*Id.* at 1022.

arbitrator stated that, "This 'right', which obviously exists even though the Agreement does not so provide, must be balanced against the interests and rights which the Union and bargaining unit employees have under the [recognition, seniority, and wage clauses of the] Agreement."[689] He explained:

> In the opinion of the Umpire, this is not a case of "absolutes" one way or the other. Rather, it is a case of an appropriate balancing of the legitimate interests of management, the bargaining unit employees, and their union representative. The managerial interest in efficient allocation of work should not have to stop at the boundaries of a defined bargaining unit. On the other hand, the decision to allocate work to employees outside the bargaining unit should be one made in the honest exercise of business judgment, and not arbitrarily, capriciously, or in bad faith.[690]

Other arbitrators have used a similar "balancing of interests" approach,[691] and considered the effect on the bargaining unit.[692] Thus, in *Cleveland Electric Illuminating Co.*,[693] for example, the panel concluded that the determination of whether a transfer of work was permissible should be made on a case-by-case basis. Because the work at issue had been primarily a nonunit function in the past, and because the transfer of work occurred during a company reorganization, the panel concluded that there was no violation of the agreement.[694]

Sometimes the agreement will specifically prohibit management from assigning work of unit employees to nonunit employees. Where such prohibition exists, absent some justifying circumstance, arbitrators generally hold that such action is not permitted under the contract.[695] However, arbitrators

---

[689]*Id.*

[690]*Id.*

[691]*See* Bon Secours Hosp., 73 LA 751, 755 (Matthews, 1979) (the work transfer was a "reasonable and necessary response to changing technology" and was done "without animus towards the Union"); Jackson Pub. Sch., 71 LA 177, 180–81 (Keefe, 1978) (school employer was motivated by economy and efficiency, not by prejudice toward the bargaining unit); Reactive Metals, 46 LA 978, 981–82 (Gibson, 1966); Safeway Stores, 42 LA 353, 357 (Ross, 1964). *See also* Bell Tel. Co. of Pa., 75 LA 750, 760–61 (Garrett, 1980) (discerning "common basic principles reflected in" the opinions of other arbitrators who had served the same parties in this type of case).

[692]*See also* ACS, 111 LA 566, 568 (Kilroy, 1998) (overtime driving was incidental in nature). *But see* Matanuska Elec. Ass'n, 111 LA 596 (Landau, 1998) (supervisor's work was not de minimis where his time sheets for previous 2 years showed 10 hours of service work on projects and supervisor's work on another project was longer than 30 minutes).

[693]105 LA 817 (Franckiewicz, 1995).

[694]*Id.*

[695]*See* Bethlehem Steel Corp., 97 LA 614, 615–16 (Das, 1991); Roberts & Schaefer Co., 72 LA 624, 626 (Cantor, 1979); Dow Corning Corp., 70 LA 959, 963 (Thomson, 1978); Beyerl Chevrolet, 68 LA 343, 346 (Bolte, 1977); Woodman's Food Mkts., 64 LA 938, 940 (Knudson, 1975); United States Steel Corp., 62 LA 743, 748 (Fisfis, 1974); United States Steel Corp., 55 LA 160, 169–70 (McDermott, 1970); Minnesota Mining & Mfg. Co., 49 LA 474, 478–79 (Solomon, 1967); West Va. Pulp & Paper Co., 48 LA 657, 662 (Rubin, 1966); Precision Gears & Prods., 28 LA 70, 71–72 (Gamser, 1957); Tri City Grocery Co., 27 LA 692, 696 (Klamon, 1956); Bell Aircraft Corp., 26 LA 397, 398–99 (Emery, 1955); International Harvester Co., 24 LA 332, 333 (Cole, 1955); Carey Salt Co., 17 LA 669, 670 (Ralston, 1951); Merrill Stevens Dry Dock & Repair Co., 17 LA 516, 520 (Hawley, 1951); Continental Can Co., 16 LA 162, 165 (Gilden, 1951); United Aircraft Prods., 10 LA 143, 147 (Wardlaw, 1948). *See* Florida Power Corp., 76 LA 963, 965 (Amis, 1981); Marathon Oil Co., 70 LA 518, 522 (Helburn, 1978); Stauffer Chem. Co., 44 LA 188, 191–92 (Seinsheimer, 1965); Tin Processing Corp., 28 LA 321, 323 (Hawley, 1957); General Anline & Film Corp., 27 LA 144, 147 (Davis, 1956); Miller & Hart, Inc., 21 LA 657, 658 (Kelliher, 1953); Rock Hill Printing & Finishing Co., 19 LA 467,

sometimes have interpreted the prohibitory clause narrowly, to apply only to the category of nonunit employees specifically stated in the clause, or only to assignments at certain locations.[696] Of course, the disputed work in fact may be held not to be bargaining-unit work or not to be exclusively so within the meaning of the restrictive clause.[697]

Where the unambiguous language of a contract provided only that a company could subcontract maintenance work, the company was found entitled to subcontract other types of work, including production work.[698] Conversely, where a collective bargaining agreement did not restrict the company from having outside vendors stock soda but was ambiguous regarding whether the company could use these vendors to stock private-label soda

---

469–71 (Jaffee, 1952); Continental Paper Co., 18 LA 476, 477–78 (Handsaker, 1952); Adolf Coors Co., 18 LA 156, 158–60 (King, 1952). The language of the prohibitory clause may imply that there is to be no de minimis exception. *See* Ideal Cement Co., 52 LA 49, 50 (Williams, 1969); Wheland Co., 34 LA 904, 907 (Tatum, 1960).

[696]*See* SIPCO, Inc., 93 LA 1225, 1230–32 (Slade, 1990) (new section specialized in new processing work not previously done in plant); Ferranti-Packard Elec., 55 LA 1157, 1158–59 (Weatherill, 1970) (the clause expressly restricted the performance of unit work by supervisors or salaried employees, but no restriction was stated as to such work by any other category of nonunit employees); Hercules Inc., 54 LA 517, 521 (Wolff, 1971); Minnesota Mining & Mfg. Co., 50 LA 1165, 1169–70 (Lewis, undated) (the clause did not apply to other locations); Crown Cork & Seal Co., 43 LA 1264, 1265, 1268 (Woodruff, 1964). *See also* Spartan Stores, 79 LA 30, 33 (Daniel, 1982); Consolidated Aluminum Corp., 70 LA 538, 541 (Murphy, 1978).

[697]*See* Louisville Cement Co., 79 LA 584, 587 (Archer, 1982); Western Kraft Paper Group, 74 LA 13, 15 (Allen, 1980); American Cyanamid Co., 73 LA 529, 531 (Weisenfeld, 1979); National Steel Corp., 70 LA 777, 779 (Kelliher, 1978); Consolidated Aluminum Corp., 70 LA 538, 540 (Murphy, 1978); California Portland Cement Co., 70 LA 81, 84–85 (Anderson, 1978) (operation of new equipment was properly assigned to employees outside the bargaining unit who historically had performed the function now accomplished by use of the new equipment, and unit employees by performing that function more recently on a temporary and de minimis basis did not establish a binding practice in their behalf); Robertshaw Controls Co., 69 LA 826, 828 (Hitchcock, 1977) (occasional counting of parts by nonunit auditors to verify inventory counts made by unit employees constituted a work element of both jobs); Sloan Valve Co., 68 LA 479, 480 (Cohen, 1977); United States Steel Corp., 54 LA 118, 121–23 (Garrett, 1971); Worthington Corp., 46 LA 1065, 1070 (Dworkin, 1966) (the clause did not apply to radically different work although the end result remained essentially the same); National Lead Co. of Ohio, 28 LA 349, 350 (Schedler, 1957); Walker Mfg. Co., 28 LA 288, 293 (Luskin, 1957). In several of the foregoing cases, supervisors had also performed the work and the arbitrator concluded that the bargaining unit did not have exclusive right to it. In *Kansas City Power & Light Co.*, 71 LA 381, 386–87 (Elkouri, 1978), the parties in 1971 had negotiated a job description for computer programmers, and the collective bargaining agreement specifically prohibited the assignment of bargaining-unit work to supervisors or employees outside the unit. The arbitrator concluded that "it would be equally untenable" to hold either, at one extreme, that the programmers were restricted to the programming they were doing on the machines that were in use when the job description was negotiated, or, at the other extreme, that the programmers had the exclusive right to *all* computer programming notwithstanding significant changes that had evolved in data processing technology since the job description was negotiated. The arbitrator further concluded that "in the absence of job description language pertaining expressly and unequivocally to the particular piece of work being examined, the question whether the given work should be deemed included under the job description and, if so, whether the work is the exclusive domain of" the bargaining-unit employees, must be determined by considering various relevant factors (some of which were outlined by the arbitrator). *Id.* at 387.

[698]Lockheed Aeronautical Sys. Co., 104 LA 803 (Duff, 1995). Similarly, where the contract gave a company the right to abolish or create new jobs, the company did not violate the agreement when it eliminated a janitorial position and hired an outside contractor to perform the work. James River Corp., 104 LA 475 (Bittel, 1995).

from the company's own warehouse, the arbitrator looked to extrinsic evidence to aid in interpreting the contract.[699] Because products from the company's warehouse had not been stocked previously by outside vendors, and because evidence from both the company negotiator and the company president supported the contention that the provision was intended to include only outside products, the arbitrator found that the company had violated the contract.

Job classifications in a collective bargaining agreement may or may not freeze the classification structure during the life of the contract, thereby precluding the company from reassigning work.[700] One arbitrator, following what he believed was the more modern view, concluded that "the rights of [the] management clause prevailed over the classification clause, particularly in the light of economic necessity which demands increased efficiency in job assignments and in operations generally."[701] In cognate decisions adopting this line of reasoning, other arbitrators have held that where a contract does not expressly prohibit the elimination of jobs or reassignment of work, a company generally can eliminate jobs, combine positions, and reassign work.[702] Other arbitrators, however, look to see whether the job descriptions included in the contract were negotiated by the parties.[703]

B. Plant Removals [LA CDI 117.42]

In connection with the foregoing discussion of the assignment of work out of the bargaining unit, the related subject of partial or complete plant removal is briefly noted here. Many of the cases involved collective bargaining agreements containing express clauses on the subject. These express clauses vary widely, ranging from absolute prohibition of removals to a mere requirement that advance notice be given.[704] However, there are numerous

---

[699]Schnuck Mkts., 107 LA 739 (Cipolla, 1996).

[700]Department of the Air Force, 110 LA 1107 (Coyne, 1998) (assignment did not violate agreement, where position description did not entitle only unit employees to overtime work). *But see* Consumer Prods. Co., 112 LA 550 (Jenks, 1999) (ambiguous job description and conflicting past practices created doubt as to whether assigned work was within the bargaining unit).

[701]James River Corp., 102 LA 893, 896 (Jones, 1994).

[702]International Paper Co., 108 LA 1207 (Hart, 1997) (employer properly eliminated technician position, where certain job duties were transferred to employees at a different location and a computerized information system reduced some of the technician's former duties); Illinois Cement Co., 108 LA 667 (Kossoff, 1997) (employer within its rights to combine job classifications as part of effort to cross-train employees and increase efficiency).

[703]Allied Signal, 113 LA 124 (Thornell, 1999) (employer violated agreement, where it did not make operating engineers the lead craft maintaining environmental control equipment as required by their negotiated job description); Matanuska Elec. Ass'n, 111 LA 596 (Landau, 1998) (job descriptions did not give unit exclusive jurisdiction to all design engineering work, where descriptions were not negotiated and nothing in them indicated exclusive jurisdiction).

[704]*See* Sears Logistics Servs., 95 LA 229, 230–31 (Garrett, 1990); Greif & Co., 78 LA 825, 831–34 (Seibel, 1982); California Metal Trades, 69 LA 1075, 1076 (Boner, 1977); Federal-Mogul Corp., 61 LA 745, 749 (Cole, 1973); California Metal Trades Ass'n, 60 LA 56, 58–59 (Kenaston, 1973); Union Tank Car Co., 55 LA 170, 178–79 (Platt, 1970); Owens-Illinois, Inc., 53 LA 1219, 1220 (Reid, 1969); Hoover Chem. Prods. Div., 48 LA 373, 378 (Keefe, 1967); Emerson-Pryne Co., 45 LA 1104, 1108 (Reid, 1966); Empire Textile Corp., 44 LA 979, 988 (Scheiber, 1965); Sidele Fashions, 36 LA 1364, 1384–86 (Dash, Jr., 1961); Address-O-Mat, 36 LA 1074, 1076–77 (Wolff, 1961); Meilman, 34 LA 771, 774–76 (Gray, 1960); Centra Leather Goods Corp., 25 LA 804, 806–07 (Kheel, 1956); Horowitz, 8 LA 1001, 1004–05 (Brower, 1947).

cases in which a removal was challenged in the absence of an express contract provision restricting plant removals.[705]

---

[705]*See* Dayton Walther Corp., 96 LA 570, 572–73 (Wren, 1991); Continental Tel. Sys., 80 LA 1355, 1357–58 (Wren, 1983); Pabst Brewing Co., 78 LA 772, 775–76 (Wolff, 1982); Leeds-Dixon Lab., 74 LA 407, 410–12 (Kramer, 1980); Food Fair Stores, 71 LA 873, 874 (Hardy, 1978); Inland Tool & Mfg., 71 LA 120, 123–24 (Lipson, 1978); E-Lite Co., 66 LA 800, 802 (Kronish, 1976); Air Carrier Engine Serv., 65 LA 1028, 1034 (Kanzer, 1975); Sealtest Dairy, 65 LA 858, 860 (LeMay, 1975); Robertshaw Controls Co., 62 LA 194, 196 (Shister, 1974); Ex-Cell-O Corp., 60 LA 1094, 1099–1100 (Sembower, 1973); Jos. Schlitz Brewing Co., 58 LA 653, 657–62 (Lande, 1972); Linde Co., 40 LA 1073, 1078–79 (Murphy, 1963); Sivyer Steel Casting Co., 39 LA 449, 458–59 (Howlett, 1962); Johns Manville Fiber Glass, 38 LA 621, 622–23 (McIntosh, 1961); United Packers, 38 LA 619, 620 (Kelliher, 1962); John B. Stetson Co., 28 LA 514, 517–18 (McGoldrick, 1957). For cases involving the applicability to plant removals of contractual clauses restricting subcontracting, see *Douwe Egberts Superior Co.*, 78 LA 1131, 1137 (Ellmann, 1982); *Lever Bros. Co.*, 65 LA 1299, 1302–04 (Edes, 1975); *Metal Textile Corp.*, 42 LA 107, 110–11 (Rubin, 1964); *Selb Mfg. Co.*, 37 LA 834, 842–43 (Klamon, 1961). The agreement did not contain an express provision on plant removal in *Illinois Coil Spring Co. (I),* 265 NLRB 206, 210, 111 LRRM 1486, 1490 (1982) (footnote omitted), but under the facts the NLRB held that the employer,

> even though it bargained with the Union about its [economic] decision to relocate and is willing to bargain about the effects of its decision, by deciding, without the consent of the Union, to transfer its assembly operations and to lay off unit employees at its Milwaukee facility during the term of its collective-bargaining agreement in order to obtain relief from the labor costs imposed by that agreement, acted in derogation of its bargaining obligation under Section 8(d), and hence violated Section 8(a)(1), (3), and (5) of the Act.

However, the NLRB overruled this decision and the line of NLRB decisions on which it was based in *Illinois Coil Spring Co. (II),* 268 NLRB 601, 602, 115 LRRM 1065, 1067 (1984), where the Board stated that although the parties no doubt could draft a work-preservation clause, it "is not for the Board . . . to create an implied work-preservation clause in every American labor agreement based on wage and benefits or recognition provisions." *Id.* at 602 (footnote omitted). The Board concluded that "neither wage and benefits provisions nor the recognition clause . . . preserves bargaining unit work at the Milwaukee facility for the duration of the contract," *id.*, and that "no other term contained in the contract restricts Respondent's decision-making regarding relocation." *Id.* In *Dubuque Packing Co.,* 303 NLRB 386, 137 LRRM 1185 (1991), the NLRB set forth a new standard by which to judge whether an employer has an obligation to bargain over its decision to relocate work to a new plant. Under the test formulated in *Dubuque,* the general counsel has the initial burden of establishing a prima facie case that the decision is a mandatory subject of bargaining by meeting a two-part test. First, the general counsel must establish that the decision involved a relocation of unit work. Second, the general counsel must establish that this relocation of unit work was unaccompanied by a basic change in the nature of the employer's operation. If the general counsel satisfies this two-part test, the burden then shifts to the employer to rebut the general counsel's prima facie case by establishing any one of the following: (1) the work performed at the new location varies significantly from the work performed at the former plant, or (2) the work performed at the former plant is to be discontinued entirely and not moved to the new location, or (3) the employer's decision involves a change in the scope and direction of the enterprise. Even if the employer is unable to rebut the general counsel's prima facie case, it still may show that the decision to relocate was a nonmandatory subject of bargaining by proffering one of two affirmative defenses. The employer can establish an affirmative defense by showing either of the following by a preponderance of the evidence: (1) that labor costs (direct and/or indirect) were not a factor in the decision; or (2) that even if labor costs were a factor in the decision, the union could not have offered labor cost concessions that could have changed the employer's decision to relocate. There may or may not be a duty to bargain on a given management decision to transfer bargaining-unit work from one location to another. *See* Power, Inc., 311 NLRB 599, 145 LRRM 1198 (1993); Otis Elevator Co., 269 NLRB 891, 115 LRRM 1281 (1984). See also section 2.A.i., "The Duty to Bargain: Right of Unilateral Action," and section 15., "Right to Subcontract," above.

17. Workplace Rules

A. Management's Unilateral Right to Establish Work Rules
[LA CDI 100.15; 118.25]

It is well established in arbitration that management has the fundamental right to establish unilaterally reasonable plant or workplace rules not inconsistent with law or the collective bargaining agreement.[706] Thus, when the agreement is silent on the subject, management has the right to formulate and enforce plant rules as an ordinary and proper means of maintaining discipline and efficiency and of directing the activities of the workforce.[707]

This unilateral right of management to establish plant rules also exists under various types of management-rights clauses.[708] Even where an agree-

---

[706]*See* Branch County, Mich., Rd. Comm'n, 114 LA 1697, 1704 (Allen, 2000); Eaton Corp., 114 LA 1007, 1015 (Hodgson, 2000); Philips Indus., Inc., 87 LA 1122, 1124–28 (Rezler, 1986); Packaging Corp. of Am., 86 LA 753, 757–58 (Smith, 1986); Walgreen Co., 85 LA 1195, 1197–98 (Weis, 1985); Mister A's Rest., 80 LA 1104, 1105 (Christopher, 1983); Niagara Mohawk Power Corp., 74 LA 58, 62 (Markowitz, 1980); Northwest Airlines, 68 LA 31, 34 (Bloch, 1977); People's Gas Light & Coke Co., 73 LA 357, 361 (Gundermann, 1979); Social Sec. Admin., 71 LA 963, 967 (Ables, 1978); Kerotest Mfg. Corp., 71 LA 744, 748 (Blue, 1978); Macmillian Boledel Containers, 70 LA 667, 669 (Doering, 1978); Robertshaw Controls Co., 69 LA 77, 79 (Duff, 1977). In *Industrial Finishing Co.*, 40 LA 670 (Daugherty, 1963), the arbitrator stated that:

> A union sometimes implies that a company's rules have little or no force or effect because same were not agreed to by the union. It is a settled rule of arbitration that a company has the right unilaterally to issue and enforce rules that (1) do not conflict with any provision of the parties' agreement or of law and (2) are reasonably related to the safe, orderly, and efficient operation of the company's business.

Id. at 671. But in *Keebler Co.*, 75 LA 975, 982–84 (Morris, 1980), the arbitrator held (1) that the recognition clause in the collective bargaining agreement "'should be equated to the statutory duty to bargain,'" *id.* at 982 (quoting South Cent. Bell Tel. Co., 72 LA 333, 336 (Morris, 1979)); (2) that the particular plant rules at issue in the case were mandatory subjects of bargaining under the NLRA; and (3) that the employer's unilateral action in respect to the rules "would constitute a violation of the duty to bargain" under the NLRA and "did constitute a violation of [the recognition clause] of the collective bargaining agreement for the same reason." *Keebler Co.*, 75 LA at 984. *See also* Rohr Indus., 79 LA 900, 904 (Richman, 1982). Regarding the nature of the recognition clause, cf. *Newspaper Printing Corp. v. NLRB*, 692 F.2d 615, 111 LRRM 2824 (6th Cir. 1982); *Illinois Coil Spring Co. (II)*, 265 NLRB 206, 111 LRRM 1486, 1490 (1982), discussed in section 16.B., "Plant Removals," above. For general discussion of plant rules and their enforcement, see Daykin, *Arbitration of Work Rules Disputes*, 18 Arb. J. 36 (1963); Stessin, *Management Prerogatives and Plant Rule Violations*, 14 Arb. J. 3 (1959). For a general discussion of management's right to implement rules, see Hill & Sinicropi, Management Rights: A Legal and Arbitral Analysis 65 (BNA Books 1986).

[707]Federal Mach. & Welder Co., 5 LA 60, 69 (Whiting, 1946). *Accord* Citgo Petroleum Corp., 112 LA 594, 597 (Nicholas, Jr., 1999); General Foods Corp., 91 LA 1251, 1254–56 (Goldstein, 1988); Mechanical Prods. Inc., 91 LA 977, 980–82 (Roumell, Jr., 1988); Phillips Indus., 87 LA 1122, 1124–28 (Rezler, 1986); Peabody Coal Co., 79 LA 433, 435 (Mittelman, 1982); Le Blonde Mach. Tool, 76 LA 827, 832 (Keenan, 1981); Western Indus., Inc., 53 LA 878, 883 (Solomon, 1969).

[708]*See* Conoco Inc., 113 LA 637, 640 (Allen, Jr., 1999) (even if the agreement does not contain a management-rights clause, the employer may still promulgate new work rules unilaterally); Overhead Door Co., 70 LA 1299, 1301 (Dworkin, 1978); Kast Metal Corp., 70 LA 278, 281 (Roberts, 1978); Missouri Research Labs., 55 LA 197, 208 (Erbs, 1970); Borg-Warner Corp., 47 LA 691, 697 (Bradley, 1966); Cumberland Chem. Co., 46 LA 356, 357 (Dahl, 1966); Sylvania Elec. Prods., 32 LA 1025, 1027 (Wallen, 1958); Columbus Coated Fabrics

ment required management to discuss plant rules with the union before being put into effect, one arbitrator observed:

> The purpose of the discussion is to ascertain whether the rule itself contains any loopholes, or whether its enforcement will give rise to unexpected problems. After a discussion, the company, at its option, may put the rule into effect, even though union approval is not obtained.[709]

If an agreement vests in management the right "to establish reasonable rules for the management of the plant and to maintain discipline among its employees," the rules so established must be considered a part of the agreement, and a clause prohibiting the arbitrator from adding to the terms of the agreement does not preclude the arbitrator from considering established plant rules in determining whether an employee had been properly disciplined. On arbitrator stated:

> As a practical matter, it is not possible to embody in a collective bargaining contract a complete code of plant rules. Such a code would make the contract too long and cumbersome. It would introduce into collective bargaining new sources of delay and dispute. It would prevent the necessary adjustments and modifications of rules between periods of negotiation.[710]

B. Challenging the Rules

The right to promulgate work rules is not unlimited.[711] After plant rules are promulgated, they may be challenged through the grievance procedure on the ground that they violate particular provisions of the agreement or that they are unfair, unreasonable, arbitrary, or discriminatory.[712] This right

---

Corp., 26 LA 638, 640 (Stouffer, 1956); Bell Aircraft Corp., 20 LA 448, 450–51 (Shister, 1953); Electric Storage Battery Co., 16 LA 118, 120 (Baab, 1951); International Harvester Co., 12 LA 73, 74–75 (McCoy, 1949); John Morrell & Co., 9 LA 931, 934 (Gilden, 1948); Joy Mfg. Co., 6 LA 430, 432 (Healy, 1946).

[709]Borg-Warner Corp., 16 LA 446, 453 (Gilden, 1951). *See also* Flowserve Corp., 111 LA 813 (Jennings, 1998) (company violated the agreement when it failed to consult with the union before issuing a new plant rule, as required by the agreement); McGraw Edison Co., 76 LA 249, 251 (Sergent, Jr., 1981); Capital Area Transit Auth., 69 LA 811, 815 (Ellmann, 1977) (a plant rule promulgated without giving the union prior notice and opportunity for discussion as required by the agreement was not an acceptable basis for disciplinary action). *Cf.* United States Steel Corp., 48 LA 1149, 1157 (McDermott, 1967); Weatherproof Co., 46 LA 53, 58–59 (Traynor, 1966); Farmbest, Inc., 44 LA 609, 612 (Karlins, 1965).

[710]American Zinc Co. of Ill., 20 LA 527, 530 (Merrill, 1953).

[711]Mayflower Vehicle Sys., 114 LA 1249, 1256 (Franckiewicz, 2000) ("[T]he Employer's discretion in establishing work rules is large, [but] it is not unlimited. Any rule that contradicted explicit or implicit mandates of the collective bargaining agreement could not be a reasonable rule."); Flowserve Corp., 111 LA 813, 819 (Jennings, 1998) (past practices may limit the issurance of new work rules).

[712]*See* Conoco Inc., 113 LA 637, 640 (Allen, Jr., 1998); Ideal Elec. Co., 98 LA 410, 415 (Heekin, 1991); Milwaukee Transp. Serv., 77 LA 807, 814 (Jones, Jr., 1981); Bucyrus-Erie Co., 69 LA 970, 974 (Fleischli, 1977); Schein Body & Equip. Co., Inc., 69 LA 930, 935–36 (Roberts, 1977) (an implied limitation on the company's express contractual right to establish plant rules is that they must not be unreasonable, as well as not "arbitrary, capricious, or discriminatory"); Electric Repair Serv. Co., 67 LA 173, 178 (Towers, 1976); Anaconda Aluminum Co., 51 LA 281, 283 (Dolson, 1968); Hartman Elec. Mfg. Co., 48 LA 681, 687 (Dyke, 1967); Trans World Airlines, 47 LA 1127, 1129–30 (Platt, 1967); ARO, Inc., 47 LA 1065, 1069 (Whyte, 1966); Cannon Elec. Co., 46 LA 481, 483–84 (Kotin, 1965); All States Trailer Co., 44 LA 104, 105 (Leflar, 1965); American Standard, 30 LA 231, 235 (Thompson, 1958); Lukens

to challenge applies even when the agreement expressly gives management the right to establish plant rules.[713] Indeed, management's general right to promulgate plant rules unilaterally usually is not contested; the challenge is directed rather to the content or particular application of some specific rule.[714]

Although rules promulgated unilaterally by the employer are subject to the grievance procedure, and a union need not delay its challenge until employees have been disciplined for failing to comply with them,[715] a union does not waive its right to contest a work rule if it waits until the rule has been applied or enforced.[716]

C. Management-Promulgated Work Rules and the Statutory Duty to Bargain

Unilaterally issued work rules may cover matters that the NLRA indicates would be subject to the mandatory duty to bargain.[717] On demand, management must bargain with respect to such rules that affect conditions of employment, and the filing of a grievance challenging a rule might be

---

Steel Co., 29 LA 731, 733 (Crawford, 1957); Detroit Gasket & Mfg. Co., 27 LA 717, 720–22 (Crane, 1956); Maccabees, 27 LA 99, 104–05 (Smith, 1956); Ideal Cement Co., 13 LA 943, 945 (Donaldson, 1950); Pullman-Standard Car Mfg. Co., 2 LA 509, 514 (Courshon, 1945).

[713]*See* Ore-Ida Foods, 69 LA 375, 377 (Curry, 1977); Central Tel. Co. of N. Am., 69 LA 231, 234 (Holly, 1977); Central Tel. Co. of Va., 68 LA 957, 961–62 (Whyte, 1977); Capital Mfg. Co., 48 LA 243, 248 (Klein, 1967).

[714]*See, e.g,* Sprague Devices, 79 LA 543, 546 (Mulhall, 1982); Public Serv. Co. of N.M., 78 LA 883, 885 (Harr, 1982); Union Tank Car Co., 77 LA 249, 255 (Taylor, 1981); Schmidt Cabinet Co., 75 LA 397, 399 (Berns, 1980); Maryland Specialty Wire, 74 LA 983, 985 (Buchanan, 1980); Allied Chem. Corp., 74 LA 412, 416 (Eischen, 1980); Big Star No. 35, 73 LA 850, 853–54 (Murphy, 1979); Cagle's Poultry & Egg Co., 73 LA 34, 37–38 (Roberts, 1979); Hoover Co., 72 LA 297, 299–301 (Feldman, 1979). For instances in which the union unsuccessfully attempted to impose a bargaining obligation even though the agreement expressly authorized management to make plant rules, see *Gerstenslager Co.*, 114 LA 1290, 1293 (Lalka, 2000) (a rule application can be challenged in the grievance process to "redress the injustice"); Hoover Co. 77 LA 1287, 1289 (Strasshofer, 1982); Lima Register Co., 76 LA 935, 937 (Heinsz, 1981).

[715]Allen Dairy Prods. Co., 97 LA 988, 991 (Hoh, 1991); Altec Corp., 71 LA 1064, 1066 (Hays, 1978); Bucyrus-Erie Co., 69 LA 970, 974 (Fleischli, 1977); Northwest Airlines, 68 LA 31, 33 (Bloch, 1977); Linde Co., 34 LA 1, 6 (Schmidt, 1959) ("Employees should not be forced to run the risk of disciplinary penalty by refusing obedience in order to determine whether a regulation is a proper exercise of management's prerogatives."). But in *Pacific Southwest Airlines*, 70 LA 833 (Jones, Jr., 1978), the arbitrator rejected the union's request for a ruling as to the reasonableness of a new absenteeism plan unilaterally adopted by management. Being unwilling to rule "in the abstract and without evidence of specific applications," he explained that "the reasonableness or unreasonableness of a promulgated absenteeism policy—or most any kind of detailed written policy, for that matter—cannot realistically be determined until those charged with its implementation have had a chance to translate its abstract expressions into specific applications." *Id.* at 834–35. *See also* Aluminum Co. of Am. v. Auto Workers, 630 F.2d 1340, 105 LRRM 2390 (9th Cir. 1980) (the court held a similar grievance request to be nonarbitrable).

[716]*See* Mayflower Vehicle Sys., 114 LA 1249, 1256 (Franckiewicz, 2000).

[717]29 U.S.C. §159(a) defines mandatory subjects of bargaining as "rates of pay, wages, hours of employment, or other conditions of employment," and 29 U.S.C. §158(d) defines mandatory subjects as "wages, hours, and other terms and conditions of employment."

considered by an arbitrator "as a demand to negotiate on the subject."[718] Even where an agreement gave management a general right to make and modify rules "for purposes of discipline and efficiency," arbitrators have held that "after they have once become a subject of mutual agreements, very specific bargaining and agreement are required to make their modification again exclusively a matter of company decisions and announcements."[719] Although a rule affects conditions of employment, such as one establishing an absentee and tardiness program, a union may lose its right to bargain over the substance of the program if previously it has refused to bargain over work guidelines.[720]

Parties seeking arbitral resolution may have other conflict resolution tools at their disposal—state statutory causes of action or the federal statutory right conferred by the NLRA to file charges of unfair labor practices for violating the duty[721] to *negotiate*[722] (rather than just arbitrate[723]) over mandatory subjects of collective bargaining.[724]

---

[718]Federal Mach. & Welder Co., 5 LA 60, 68–69 (Whiting, 1946); Borg-Warner Corp., 3 LA 423, 433–34 (Gliden, 1944). In *Pet, Inc.*, 264 NLRB 1288, 1290, 111 LRRM 1495, 1498 (1982) (footnote omitted), the NLRB deferred to an arbitration award, where the arbitrator had determined that "work rules are separate from the collective-bargaining agreement and can be changed (either tightened or relaxed) midterm after the required bargaining as long as the rules as changed do not conflict with the collective-bargaining agreement." *See also* Lima Register Co., 76 LA 935, 937 (Heinsz, 1981). For related discussion, see section 2.A.i., "The Duty to Bargain: Right of Unilateral Action," and section 2.A.ii., "Duration of Limitation on Unilateral Action: Contract Limitation Versus Statutory Duty to Bargain," above.

[719]Ampco Metal, Inc., 3 LA 374, 378–79 (Updegraff, 1946). *See* Consolidated Papers, 66 LA 1256, 1260–61 (Gundermann, 1976); Southern Extract Co., Inc., 59 LA 697, 698–99 (Goodman, 1972); R. Herschel Mfg., Inc., 47 LA 20, 25 (Stembower, 1966); Buffalo-Springfield Roller Co., 5 LA 391, 396 (Hampton, 1946). *See also* Protec Inc., 72 LA 804, 807 (Ellmann, 1979). Even as to negotiated rules, however, where the term of the agreement has expired, management may put its proposals into effect unilaterally after having bargained on them to an impasse.

[720]Litton Sys., 84 LA 688, 692–93 (Bognanno, 1985).

[721]29 U.S.C. §158(a)(5) (management's duty), and 29 U.S.C. §158(b)(3) (union's duty).

[722]*But see* Good Samaritan Hosp., 335 NLRB No. 73, 172 LRRM 1234 (2001) (employer's unilateral implementation of new work rules regarding a mandatory subject of bargaining did not violate 29 U.S.C. §158(a)(5) where the union clearly and unmistakably waived its right to bargain).

[723]The U.S. Court of Appeals for the Ninth Circuit stated:

An essential aspect of the Union's role in collective bargaining is its right to be consulted by the employer about mandatory subjects of bargaining and to make comments, objections, or suggestions to the employer before action is taken. This is a practical method to insure the stability of industrial relations. . . . It would wholly undercut the duty to bargain if the employer were allowed to act with reference to a mandatory bargaining subject and then simply defend its actions in a later arbitration hearing.

Alfred M. Lewis, Inc., v. NLRB, 587 F.2d 403, 408, 99 LRRM 2841 (9th Cir. 1978), *enf'g* 229 NLRB 757, 95 LRRM 1216 (1977).

[724]The Supreme Court has described mandatory subjects of bargaining as such matters that are "plainly germane to the 'working environment' and not among those 'managerial decisions which lie at the core of entrepreneurial control.'" Ford Motor Co. v. NLRB, 441 U.S. 488, 498, 101 LRRM 2222 (1979) (quoting Fibreboard Paper Prods. Corp. v. NLRB, 379 U.S. 203, 222–23, 57 LRRM 2609 (1964) (Stewart J., concurring)). For a recent example of the Board's process in analyzing whether a unilateral management action implicates a mandatory subject of bargaining, see *Colgate-Palmolive Co.*, 323 NLRB 515, 155 LRRM 1034 (1997) (videotaping employees is a mandatory subject).

The parties' decision to forego,[725] or at least delay,[726] statutory prosecution of a cause of action, or their federal right to negotiate,[727] may be motivated by a desire to avoid lengthy, time-consuming, and costly litigation, or a desire to avoid creating an unduly antagonistic labor relationship. Thus, arbitral decisions discussing the validity of work rules each contain a subtext supporting the essential positive values of arbitration itself. Each of these cases is itself, then, a statement of parties' belief in the benefits of the informal adjudication of disputes by arbitration rather than by a governmental agency[728] that does not have as one of its core concerns the future continued positive relations between these parties or speedy, inexpensive resolution of conflicts, but rather the vindication of statutory rights Congress commanded that it impose.[729]

Arbitral decisions reflect recognition of the state and federal regulatory precedents,[730] but do not consider these decisive on the contract issues in-

---

[725]Under federal labor law, an employer can, but need not, require the union to first prosecute any claim that management's actions violate the labor contract in the arbitration forum before invoking state or certain federal judicial forums. Republic Steel Corp. v. Maddox, 379 U.S. 650, 652–53, 58 LRRM 2193 (1965), reaff'd in Lingle v. Norge Div. of Magic Chef, 486 U.S. 399, 406, 128 LRRM 2521 (1988). See also Steelworkers v. Rawson, 495 U.S. 362, 368, 134 LRRM 2153 (1990); Allis Chalmers Corp. v. Lueck, 471 U.S. 202, 118 LRRM 3345 (1985) (federal subject matter preemption).

[726]The NLRB will defer refusal to bargain unfair labor practice charges at the request of either party after the parties first use their arbitration machinery, subject to possible later Board review of the ultimate award, where (1) there is a stable collective bargaining relationship, (2) there is final and binding dispute-solving machinery available and the combination of past and present alleged misconduct does not appear to be of such character as to render the use of the machinery unpromising or futile, (3) the parties are willing to arbitrate and show their willingness by agreeing to waive any procedural defects that may be raised, and (4) the Board can easily conclude that the underlying dispute before it centers on the interpretation or application of the collective bargaining contract itself, in contrast to an issue that involves an interpretation of statutory rights or protections of the NLRA. Collyer Insulated Wire, 192 NLRB 837, 77 LRRM 1931 (1971). However, the Board will become reinvolved in a dispute it previously deferred to arbitration when a party shows noncompliance with an arbitral award. New Assocs. dba Hospitality Care Ctr., 310 NLRB 1209, 1209–10 (1993).

[727]See Atlas Tack Corp., 226 NLRB 222, 93 LRRM 1236 (1976), enf'd, 559 F.2d 1201, 96 LRRM 2660 (1st Cir. 1977), for a useful discussion of when Board deferral is not required. For example, the Board will step in and find an employer violates the NLRA where, even though the collective bargaining agreement contains a grievance mechanism, the employer totally disregards the contract and unilaterally promulgates and enforces policies regarding absenteeism, reporting for work or tardiness, and stopping along travel routes, without prior notice to the union and affording the union an opportunity to bargain about these mandatory subjects of collective bargaining, unless the union clearly and unmistakably waives its right to bargain about the rules at issue. A&M Trucking, 314 NLRB 991, 147 LRRM 1097 (1994), supplemented, 318 NLRB 438, 150 LRRM 1046 (1995).

[728]See NLRB Statements of Procedure §§101.8,-.10, and -.12. Unfair labor practice complaints are filed with a regional director of the Board and prosecuted by its general counsel, not by the party charging the violation. E.J. Clemente Contracting Corp., 335 NLRB No. 98 (2001). Also, note that the rules of evidence are followed in these hearings, and the Board's processes provide for further appeals to review legal as well as factual error—another component typically absent from the arbitral process. NLRA, 29 U.S.C. §§151, 160.

[729]29 U.S.C. §153.

[730]For example, state statutes may define certain compensation as "wages" or specify wage-deduction procedures, while federal statutes may declare the right to request and obtain certain information, and the right to be notified of and negotiate concerning pending changes in work rules.

volved.[731] A decision that purports to apply only "the law" strays from both the arbitrator's expertise (the common law of the shop[732]) as well as away from the arbitrator's authority (the contract itself[733]). At that point, the arbitrator's decision could be too distant from the legitimate source of power that gives arbitral decisions strength to prevent an unhappy party from collaterally attacking the result in court, thus voiding the very benefits that attracted the parties to arbitration in the first place—informal, cost-effective, quick resolution of a singular dispute.[734]

Key to the contractual fulcrum on which these decisions rest is the principle that the party alleging a contract violation bears the burden of proof. Thus, an arbitrator held that a newly issued work rule on a mandatory subject of bargaining was valid where the employer had reserved the right to issue the work rule, and the union did not carry its burden to show what portion of the contract was violated.[735] Conversely, where the company unilaterally changed the negotiated break time policy, and the union introduced evidence that the change violated an explicit term of the contract, the grievance was upheld.[736]

D. Reasonableness of the Rules [LA CDI 118.25]

Arbitrators recognize that contracts are interstitial documents that cannot possibly foresee and cover all possible future scenarios.[737] Hence, arbi-

---

[731]"If an arbitral decision is based 'solely upon the arbitrator's view of the requirements of enacted legislation,' rather than on an interpretation of the collective-bargaining agreement, the arbitrator has 'exceeded the scope of the submission,' and the award will not be enforced. . . . Thus the arbitrator has authority to resolve only questions of contractual rights . . . ." Alexander v. Gardner-Denver Co., 415 U.S. 36, 53–54, 7 FEP Cases 81, 87 (1974) (quoting Steelworkers v. Enterprise Wheel & Car Corp., 363 U.S. 593, 597, 46 LRRM 2423 (1960)).

[732]See the Steelworkers Trilogy: Steelworkers v. American Mfg. Co., 363 U.S. 564, 46 LRRM 2414 (1960); Steelworkers v. Warrior & Gulf Navigation Co., 363 U.S. 574, 46 LRRM 2416 (1960); Steelworkers v. Enterprise Wheel & Car Corp., 363 U.S. 593, 46 LRRM 2423 (1960).

[733]The arbitrator's "source of authority is the collective-bargaining agreement . . . . The arbitrator, however, has no general authority to invoke public laws that conflict with the bargain between the parties . . . ." Gardner-Denver, 415 U.S. at 53 (citing Enterprise Wheel & Car, 363 U.S. at 597).

[734]"Not all disputes between an employee and his employer are suited for binding resolution in accordance with the procedures established by collective bargaining. While courts should defer to an arbitral decision where the employee's claim is based on rights arising out of the collective-bargaining agreement, different considerations apply where the employee's claim is based on rights arising out of a statute designed to provide minimum substantive guarantees to individual workers." Barrentine v. Arkansas-Best Freight Sys., 450 U.S. 728, 737, 24 WH Cases 1284 (1981). See also Hines v. Anchor Motor Freight, 424 U.S. 554, 562–63, 91 LRRM 2481 (1976); Gateway Coal Co. v. Mine Workers Dist. 4, Local 6330, 414 U.S. 368, 377–80, 85 LRRM 2049 (1974); Contra Costa Legal Assistance Workers v. Contra Costa Legal Servs. Found., 878 F.2d 329, 330, 131 LRRM 2934 (9th Cir. 1989); Roadmaster Corp. v. Laborers Local 504, 851 F.2d 886, 888, 128 LRRM 2449 (7th Cir. 1988).

[735]Motor Appliance Corp., 106 LA 484 (Suardi, 1996).

[736]Basler Elec. Co., 94 LA 888 (Canestraight, 1990).

[737]Industrial Finishing Co., 40 LA 670 (Daugherty, 1963) (management has the right to flesh out bare-bones contractual provisions, where the rule is reasonable, related to health and safety, and does not conflict with any specific contractual provision).

trators typically recognize the implicitly retained[738] or contractually enumerated management right to promulgate workplace rules. But, management's right to issue rules is limited to what is "reasonable."[739]

The test of reasonableness of a plant rule "is whether or not the rule is reasonably related to a legitimate objective of management,"[740] and is clearly stated so that employees can appreciate its import.[741]

The assessment of the reasonableness of a rule under this standard required consideration of such matters as the adequacy of the notice of the adoption or amendment of the rule,[742] the number of employees who are affected either adversely or positively and the degree of inconvenience or benefit,[743] the health or safety purpose or other justification of the rule,[744] whether the rule "shadows" existing federal rules,[745] or whether it imposes an idiosyncratic personal preference.[746]

Plant rules not only must be reasonable in their content but also in their application.[747] Thus, a rule requiring the wearing of safety glasses in the

---

[738]Quaker State Corp. 92 LA 898 (Talarico, 1989).

[739]"Reasonable" means "sensible." Intertec Sys. LLC, 114 LA 1785 (Skulina, 2000) (fact that the rules can be applied overbroadly does not make them "unreasonable," but rather makes them grist for a future arbitration over the particular application/incident); Quaker State Corp., 92 LA 898 (Talarico, 1989) ("reasonable" means related to the legitimate interest of management and not an undue burden on employees).

[740]Robertshaw Controls Co., 55 LA 283, 286 (Block, 1970). *See also* Plasti-Line Inc., 114 LA 1240, 1249 (Mancini, 2000); Allen Dairy Prods. Co., 97 LA 988, 991 (Hoh, 1991); Mechanical Prods., 91 LA 977, 981 (Roumell, Jr., 1988); General Tel. Co. of Cal., 77 LA 1052, 1055 (Schuster, 1981); Lloyd Ketcham Oldsmobile, 77 LA 953, 958–59 (Hilgert, 1981); Stroh Die Casting Co., 72 LA 1250, 1253 (Kerkman, 1979); Sun-Maid Raisin Growers of Cal., 72 LA 133, 135 (Weiss, 1979).

[741]*See* Hoover Co., 77 LA 1287, 1290 (Strasshofer, 1982) ("a reasonable rule must be one which the employees can understand and comply with"); Chemetco, 71 LA 457, 459 (Gibson, 1978); Randle-Eastern Ambulance Serv., 65 LA 394, 398–99 (Sherman, 1975); Bamberger's, 60 LA 960, 964 (Trotter, 1973).

[742]ARO, Inc, 47 LA 1065 (Whyte, 1966).

[743]Macy's, 108 LA 489 (Gregory, 1997) (dress code); Wyandot Inc., 92 LA 457 (Imundo, Jr., 1989).

[744]*But see* Lincoln Brass Works (employer's unilateral ban on smoking without first furnishing health and safety committee information on the basis of the changed rule is invalid, but will remain in force because it meets many reasonableness tests, but any discipline imposed under it is overturned and the employer is ordered to present all pertinent information to the committee and modify the rule under an agreed procedure).

[745]Mississippi Power & Light Co., 92 LA 1161 (Taylor, 1989).

[746]*But see* Albertson's, Inc., 102 LA 641 (Darrow, 1994) (management's unilateral change in policy to require drivers to have conservative hairstyle without beards is valid, because management needs right to establish appearance codes consistent with its chosen public image, which will change over time, and policy affects only the employees who have public contact); Reed Mfg. Co., 102 LA 1 (Dworkin, 1993) (management's unilateral change in rules banning negative T-shirt messages is valid, where employer changed marketing strategy to invite potential clients into previously closed factory and negative T-shirt messages were over 10 years old, but policy was overly broad and invalid so far as it bars messages that will be covered during customer tours, or are union insignia protected under the NLRA); B.F. Goodrich Co., 90 LA 1297 (McIntosh, 1988) (marketing strategy is peculiar management right). *Accord* Fairmont-Zarda Dairy, 106 LA 583 (Rohlik, 1995) (unilaterally issued no-beard rule not reasonable, where it applies to employees the public does not see).

[747]*See* Allied Chem. Corp., 74 LA 412, 416 (Eischen, 1980); Niagara Mohawk Power Corp., 74 LA 58, 64 (Markowitz, 1980); Cagle's Poultry & Egg Co., 73 LA 34, 43–45 (Roberts, 1979); Park Poultry, 71 LA 1, 6 (Cohen, 1978); Ore-Ida Foods, 69 LA 375, 378 (Curry, 1977); Gates

plant could not be applied during lunch periods where the risk of injury was remote.[748]

E. Changing the Rules

Management is permitted to change workplace rules that are not restricted by the agreement[749] or by established past practice[750] in order to meet changed circumstances. But, once such a policy has been subject to negotiations, it becomes a term of the parties' contract, and subsequent unilateral changes may violate the contract.[751] In any case, it has been emphasized that "sound industrial relations policy dictates that abrupt changes in the rules should be accompanied by a gradual educational process."[752]

Rubber Co., 68 LA 1273, 1277–78 (Eckhardt, 1977). In upholding an employer's unilaterally established absenteeism policy, the arbitrator stated:

> If a plan is fair on its face and its operation in the concrete cases at hand produces just results, and other common tests of reasonableness are satisfied, a plan ought not to be declared invalid based on the mere existence of some remote probability that it could operate perversely in the indefinite future under hypothetical circumstances which have not as yet materialized.

Robertshaw Controls Co., 69 LA 77, 79 (Duff, 1977), *quoted with approval in* Union Tank Car Co., 77 LA 249, 256 (Taylor, 1981).

[748]Bauer Bros. Co., 48 LA 461, 463 (Kates, 1967). It has been held that management's right to supervise employees does not extend to their personal lives after they leave the plant. Pioneer Gen-E-Motors Corp., 3 LA 487, 488 (Blair, 1946). For related material, see Chapter 15, section 3.A.i., "Off-Duty Misconduct Away From Employer's Premises." However, it also has been held that the employees' personal lives may be governed by plant rules where the conduct or situation in question affects plant operations. *See* F.E. Myers & Bros. Co., 43 LA 338, 340 (Teple, 1964); Cummins Diesel Sales Corp., 34 LA 636, 641–42 (Gorsuch, 1960); Ford Motor Co., 28 LA 583, 585–86 (Platt, 1957); Lockheed Aircraft Corp., 28 LA 411, 413–14 (Willingham, 1957); Metropolis Metal Spinning & Stamping Co., 28 LA 328, 330 (Friedman, 1956); American Monorail Co., 27 LA 540, 542 (Kates, 1956); Mechanical Handling Sys., Inc., 26 LA 401, 402–04 (Keller, 1956); Modern Coach Corp., 24 LA 810, 812–13 (Holden, 1955); International Harvester Co., 21 LA 709, 710 (Cole, 1953).

[749]*See* American Steel Foundries, 99 LA 765, 769 (Rimmel, 1992); Hoover Co., 95 LA 419, 423–24 (Lipson, 1990); B.F. Goodrich Co., 90 LA 1297, 1301–02 (McIntosh, 1988); Sanyo Mfg. Corp., 85 LA 207, 209–10 (Kelliher, 1985); Litton Sys., 84 LA 688, 692–93 (Bognanno, 1985); Trojan Luggage Co., 81 LA 409, 412–13 (Lane, 1983); Public Serv. Co. of N.M., 78 LA 883, 885 (Harr, 1982); Stroh Die Casting Co., 72 LA 1250, 1253 (Kerkman, 1979); Kast Metal Corp., 70 LA 278, 281 (Roberts, 1978) (among "the rights contemplated in management's prerogative to direct the working force is management's right to promulgate reasonable rules and regulations governing the conduct of employees, [and] the right to modify, amend, and change those rules and regulations from time to time to respond to changing conditions and requirements of the business"); Ore-Ida Foods, 69 LA 375, 377 (Curry, 1977); Butler Mfg. Co., 50 LA 109, 111 (Larkin, 1968); Florence Stove Co., 19 LA 650, 651 (Noel, 1952).

[750]*See* Anaconda Aluminum, 51 LA 281, 283 (Dolson, 1968); Standard Oil Co., 11 LA 689, 690 (Updegraff, 1948). *See also* Mechanical Prods., 91 LA 977, 981 (Roumell, Jr., 1988); Clinchfield Coal Co., 85 LA 382, 385–86 (Rybolt, 1985). For related discussion, see Chapter 12, section 1., "Custom and Practice as a Term of the Contract."

[751]Tyson Foods, 92 LA 1121 (Goodstein, 1989).

[752]Maccabees, 27 LA 99, 105 (Smith, 1956); Joy Mfg. Co., 6 LA 430, 434 (Healy, 1946). *See also* S.S. White Dental Mfg. Co., 48 LA 1337, 1338 (Turkus, 1967).

F. Subject Matter of Workplace Rules

i. Rules Governing Attendance

Management has the right to establish unilaterally reasonable rules governing attendance.[753] However, attendance policies that disregard all excuses, including personal or sick days to which employees are contractually entitled, or that treat all categories of absence as carrying equal weight, have been struck down as unreasonable.[754]

Arbitrators may find unilateral rule changes that "substantially" alter attendance policies to be violations of the contract.[755] Thus, despite

---

[753]*See* Hughes Aircraft Co., 105 LA 1019 (Richman, 1995); Chanute Mfg. Co., 101 LA 765 (Berger, 1993) (grievance contesting the reasonableness of an employer's revision of its attendance policy held to be arbitrable and subject to implied requirement of reasonableness despite the reservation of management's right to issue rules regulating absenteeism); Kansas Power & Light Co., 87 LA 867 (Belcher, 1986) (company cannot unilaterally, and surreptitiously, abandon its no-fault attendance policy in favor of fault-based system without notice—which is both a statutory and arbitral imperative—to the union). *See also* General Foods Corp., 91 LA 1251, 1256 (Goldstein, 1988) (unilateral adoption of attendance policy upheld); B.F. Goodrich Co., 90 LA 1297 (McIntosh, 1988) (arbitrator saves unilaterally issued rule by superimposing just cause standard onto it, where the contract reserves management right and subject matter is not "peculiar benefit," but instead regards plant efficiency and market competition); Dial Corp., 90 LA 729, 734 (Hilgert, 1988) (no duty to bargain over disciplinary rules); Robertshaw Controls Co., 69 LA 77, 79 (Duff, 1977). For a general discussion of management's right to implement rules, see Hill & Sinicropi, Management Rights: A Legal and Arbitral Analysis 65 (BNA Books 1986). *See* Conoco Inc., 113 LA 637, 639–40 (Allen, 1999); PCC Airfoils, 113 LA 504, 512 (Sharpe, 1999) (the absenteeism policy was reasonable and did not violate public policy); Crown Cork & Seal Co., 112 LA 749 (Cohen, 1999) (unilaterally implemented absenteeism policy is valid, especially where the union had an opportunity to review and oversee the modification); City of Bangor, Me., 111 LA 175, 178 (Alleyne, 1998). *But see* Dry Storage Corp 113 LA 264, (Singer, 1999) (a company could not unilaterally impose a new attendance policy, where the previous policy was considered part of the agreement).

[754]Supervalu, Inc., 116 LA 361 (Dean, Jr., 2001) (rejecting employer's attempt to unilaterally change absenteeism policy, where employer previously had surrendered the right to make unilateral changes in settlement agreements regarding unfair labor practice charges); Darling Store Fixtures, 108 LA 183, 187–88 (Allen, Jr., 1997) (discharge for excessive absenteeism violated contract, where most of employee's absences normally would have been excused, employee did not receive last-chance letter, grievant's disciplinary record had been cleared, and management appeared to make questionable disciplinary assessments in attempt to set employee up for discharge); Mead Containerboard, 105 LA 1068, 1070 (Goodman, 1995) (upholding absenteeism policy as reasonable, where it adequately defined terms "habitual tardiness or chronic absenteeism"); Simpson Indus., 104 LA 568, 574 (Bressler, 1995) (upholding right of the company to institute new absenteeism policy unilaterally under an agreement that only required the company to submit new rules to the union beforehand, which the company did); Chanute Mfg. Co., 101 LA 765, 771 (Berger, 1993) (rejecting company's elimination of rolling period for removing stale absences as unreasonable, but upholding new limits on personal day-off policy to entire day units as reasonable); St. Joseph Mercy Hosp., 87 LA 529, 533 (Daniel, 1986).

[755]Georgia-Pacific Corp., 108 LA 90 (Frost, 1996) (unilateral change in absenteeism policy to require doctor's excuse is substantial change and requires bargaining). A "substantial" change may just be another label for an "unreasonable" change. *See* Akron Bldg. Components, 92 LA 68 (Roumell, Jr., 1988) (contracts contain both substantive and procedural rights regarding plant rules; management's rights are "substantive" and include right to issue "reasonable" rules, while union's right is the "procedural" right to notice and an opportunity to be heard). *Cf.* Pepsi-Cola General Bottlers, 92 LA 1272 (Madden, 1989) (unilateral change in company policy to deduct shortages from employee collection accounts was held to have violated the contractual wage rate).

management's right to promulgate reasonable rules, an employer's unilaterally issued absenteeism and tardiness rules were found to be improper because they established a point system that fundamentally altered the employment relationship, and thus represented a major change in working conditions that should have been subject to negotiations with the union.[756]

A number of employers have adopted no-fault attendance policies, which provide for discipline and discharge because of excessive absenteeism regardless of the reasons for the absences. Such policies are considered legitimate when implemented to improve and control the attendance of employees, especially where there has been excessive absenteeism.[757]

A no-fault attendance policy allows an employer to terminate an employee automatically once they have been on leave or absent for a predetermined number of days. The typical no-fault policy involves the accumulation of "points," "incidents," "occurrences," or "occasions" for absences, which results in a progressive disciplinary action. Many arbitrators find that no-fault attendance policies are reasonable, but there is disagreement among arbitrators as to whether the just cause standard applies to discipline issued under the policy. Some arbitrators have concluded that such policies must conform to "just cause" provisions in a collective bargaining agreement[758] and, in particular, allow for the taking into account of mitigating circumstances.

A number of arbitrators have concluded that the just cause standard and provisions of a no-fault attendance policy are in conflict and cannot operate together.[759] Two commentators have expressed this view in the following terms: "All that is left is a hollow mechanical function, a mere reading of the plan's listed penalty for a numbered 'absence occurrence.' Thus, the plan seems inconsistent with the just cause standard."[760]

Other arbitrators affirm the applicability to no-fault attendance policies of the just cause elements of notice, evenhanded treatment, and consideration of mitigating circumstances.[761]

---

[756]Alcan-Toyo Am., 102 LA 566 (Draznin, 1993); Hertz Corp., 102 LA 481 (Frost, 1993) (unilaterally issued attendance policy is invalid, where the contract unambiguously states that a warning shall have no force or effect after 6 months).

[757]See Tenneco Packaging Burlington Container Plant, 112 LA 761, 767 (Kessler, 1999) (the no-fault attendance policy did not violate the Family and Medical Leave Act); National Gypsum Co., 112 LA 248, 253 (Nicholas, Jr., 1999); ATC/Vancom, 111 LA 268, 272 (Richman, 1998) (no-fault attendance policies were reasonable).

[758]See All Am. Gourmet Co., 88 LA 1241, 1245–47 (Zobrak, 1987) (the discharge of a grievant was improper, because the no-fault plan was not administered with proper safeguards to ensure consistent application). See also National Gypsum Co., 112 LA 248, 256 (Nicholas, Jr., 1999) (no-fault policies must provide for progressive discipline); Cooper Indus., 94 LA 830, 834 (Yarowsky, 1990) (citing a study that found that in 93.1% of the cases where the employer failed to conduct an impartial investigation into the reasons for the employee's absences, the grievant was returned to work).

[759]See Kirk & Blum Mfg. Co., 112 LA 327, 331 (Duff, 1999); General Tires, 93 LA 771, 773 (Groshong, 1989).

[760]Block & Mittenthal, Arbitration and the Absent Employee: Absenteeism, in Arbitration 1984: Absenteeism, Recent Law, Panels, and Published Decisions, Proceedings of the 37th Annual Meeting of NAA 77 (Gershenfeld ed., BNA Books 1985).

[761]Lockheed Martin Aeronautics Co., 114 LA 1015, 1023 (Howell, 2000) (the just cause requirement and a no-fault attendance policy are compatible); Interlake Material Handling Div., 113 LA 1120, 1126 (Lalka, 2000) (the policy was valid but inconsistent in its application); Cutler Hammer/Eaton Corp., 113 LA 409, 413–14 (Hoh, 1999).

ii. *Rules Governing Smoking* [LA CDI 124.70]

Arbitrators increasingly have been called on to assess the validity of plant rules that restrict or ban smoking on company property and the discipline imposed on employees who flout the rules.[762] Arbitrators have upheld grievances over the application of "no-smoking" policies[763] that establish a per se rule that a violation of a smoking policy automatically results in discharge.[764]

The reasonableness of a work rule prohibiting smoking also may depend on whether the policy prohibits smoking only in work areas, or whether it restricts smoking outside work areas such as the parking lot or the employee's personal car.[765] If the policy is not overly restrictive[766] and applies equally to all similarly situated employees, arbitrators have held that the policy is reasonable.[767]

Unreasonableness was found in one case where an employee admittedly walked off his shift without permission to smoke a cigarette in a nonrestricted area. The employee was discharged under the company's conduct rules that authorized the discharge penalty for the first offense of smoking in an unauthorized place or at an unauthorized time. The arbitrator concluded that violation of the rule did not per se establish "good cause" for termination. Instead, the arbitrator considered that although the break was taken at an unauthorized time, the grievant did not smoke in a restricted area and hence did not threaten either the health or the safety of coworkers, such threats being the stated reasons behind the rule. Moreover, he noted that the pen-

---

[762]IPC Corinth Div., 111 LA 973, 979 (Nicholas, Jr., 1998); Koch Ref. Co., 99 LA 733, 737 (Cohen, 1992); Cereal Food Processors, 96 LA 1179, 1183 (Madden, 1991); Witco Corp., 96 LA 499, 506 (Nelson, 1991); Hoover Co., 95 LA 419, 422 (Lipson, 1990); Wyandot Inc., 92 LA 457, 464 (Imundo, Jr., 1989); Central Tel. Co. of Nev., 92 LA 390, 397 (Leventhal, 1989); Honeywell, 92 LA 181, 186 (Lennard, 1989); Acorn Bldg. Components, 92 LA 68, 75–76 (Roumell, Jr., 1988); J.R. Simplot Co., 91 LA 375, 379–80 (McCurdy, 1988); Worthington Foods, 89 LA 1069, 1080 (McIntosh, 1987); Lennox Indus., 89 LA 1065, 1068 (Gibson, 1987). For cases overturning particular smoking restrictions as overly broad or unreasonable, see *VME Ams.*, 97 LA 137, 140 (Bittel, 1991) (smoking prohibited on company premises, including parking lots and grounds); *Curwood, Inc.*, 96 LA 506, 512 (O'Grady, 1991) (unilateral implementation of rule prohibiting smoking in all areas of plant); *Tokheim Corp.*, 96 LA 122, 125 (Cox, 1990) (policy prohibiting use of tobacco products on company premises, including parking lot and vehicles unreasonable); *Flxible Corp.*, 95 LA 1163, 1168 (Wallace-Curry, 1990) (company failed to establish legitimate business objective for unilateral implementation of no-smoking policy). For related discussion see Chapter 16., section 3.C., "No-Smoking Policies."

[763]Fairchild Indus. Prods., 115 LA 361, 364 (Nolan 2000); Barnstead-Thermolyne Corp., 107 LA 645, 654 (Pelofsky, 1996); Hobart Corp., 103 LA 547, 557 (Imundo, Jr., 1994); Lincoln Brass Works, 102 LA 872, 879 (Haskew, 1994).

[764]Barnstead-Thermolyne Corp., 107 LA 645, 654 (Pelofsky, 1996) (discharge was without just cause).

[765]VME Ams., 97 LA 137, 140 (Bittel, 1991) ("[t]otal ban against smoking on 'Company premises' is unreasonable and invalid insofar as it includes "'adjacent areas such as grounds and parking lots'").

[766]Tomkins Indus., 112 LA 281 (Rimmel, 1998).

[767]Timkin Co., 108 LA 422, 426 (Kindig, 1996) (the company's revised smoking rule was reasonable where there was adequate notice and it treated all employees equally, including visitors and vendors). *See also* Tomkins Indus., 112 LA 281, 285 (Rimmel, 1998) (mere fact that salaried workers may have more designated smoking areas, because of their varied work assignments, is insufficient, without more, to find a violation of the contract).

alty for leaving one's job without permission was only a corrective interview for the first offense, and that the grievant had 14 years of service with a good performance record. Finding that the discharge was without just cause, the arbitrator instead imposed a 6-month disciplinary suspension without pay.[768]

A total smoking ban on an employer's premises is valid if necessary to further a legitimate management objective. For example, an employer's goal of fostering better health among its employees and reducing various costs associated with employees' use of tobacco products has been held to be a legitimate management objective.[769] One arbitrator-approved employer's policy statement articulating the reasons for its nonsmoking rule read:

> [T]o conform to overall corporate policy; to provide a healthy, safe, comfortable environment for all employees, not just for those who smoke; to respond to customer comments on unsightly butts and housekeeping problems which go to perceptions of quality; to reduce absenteeism, low productivity and health care costs associated with smoking; to promote negotiated Wellness Program . . . .[770]

iii. *Drug and Alcohol Policies* [LA CDI 100.552545; 118.653]

Arbitrators are frequently called on to assess the extent to which companies can establish and enforce drug and alcohol policies.[771] Arbitrators have upheld upheld employers' unilateral issuance of drug testing policies where there is reasonable suspicion that employees are in possession of illegal drugs or have used illegal drugs on the employer's premises.[772] However, some arbitrators have declined to uphold disciplinary measures for violations of mandatory random drug-testing policies in private-sector employment[773] in the absence of special safety considerations[774] or federal or state regulations. In denying enforcement of these policies, arbitrators have raised concern that such policies place the burden on the employee to prove his or her innocence, and not on the employer to prove there was reasonable suspicion to test an employee for drug or alcohol use on the job, or for being under

---

[768]Barnstead-Thermolyne Corp., 107 LA 645 (Pelofsky, 1996).

[769]Plasti-Line, Inc., 114 LA 1240, 1249 (Mancini, 2000). *See also* Fairchild Indus. Prods., 115 LA 361 (Nolan, 2000) (other legitimate objectives could include protecting the health of present employees, preventing loss of customers, and facilitating the hiring and retention of employees); J.R. Simplot Co., 91 LA 375, 381 (McCurdy, 1988).

[770]ITT Higbie Baylock, 105 LA 1084, 1088 (Florman, 1996) (policy was reasonable and advanced management objectives).

[771]Branch County, Mich., Rd. Comm'n, 114 LA 1697 (Allen, 2000) (drug policy was fair and reasonable); GAF Bldg. Materials Corp., 112 LA 871, 874–76 (Marcus, 1999). For related discussion, see Chapter 16, section 2.A., "Alcohol and/or Drug Use and Testing."

[772]Fitzpatrick Co., 108 LA 686, 690 (Briggs, 1997).

[773]Ohio Star Forge Co., 110 LA 705, 706–07 (Gibson, 1998); Bayer Corp., 108 LA 316, 320 (Zobrak, 1997).

[774]MII Inc., 115 LA 1461, 1466–67 (Brodsky, 2001); Ohio Star Forge Co., 110 LA 705, 707 (Gibson, 1998).

the influence of drugs or alcohol while at work.[775] Many contracts provide an opportunity for employees to undergo substance abuse counseling or treatment and become rehabilitated.

In *Bayer Corp.*,[776] for example, the agreement provided that any drug and alcohol program would attempt to achieve an "optimum level of rehabilitation consistent with overall safety and efficient operations."[777] An employee whose job performance was otherwise deemed satisfactory was discharged after he had failed his second drug test. Following his first positive test, the employee was required to undergo only 1 hour of counseling. After his second positive test, he was required to undergo an additional 2 hours of counseling. Although recognizing that an employee's failure of two drug tests would ordinarily call for the discharge penalty, the arbitrator concluded that a total of 3 hours of counseling did not constitute the required optimum level of rehabilitation. Accordingly, he ruled that on successful completion of a comprehensive rehabilitation program, the grievant was to be returned to his former job, but without back pay or benefits.

An employer may unilaterally change its substance abuse policy to comply with federal standards.[778]

iv. Rules Relating to Health and Safety

Management may establish and enforce workplace rules unilaterally to ensure the health and safety of employees or others.[779] However, these rules must not conflict with the collective bargaining agreement.[780] Because of the

---

[775]Seneca Wire Mfg. Co., 113 LA 886, 891 (Lalka, 1999); Exxon Pipeline Co., 109 LA 951, 956–57 (Abercrombe, 1997). *See* Day & Zimmermann, 94 LA 399, 406 (Nicholas, Jr., 1990) (munition plant); Utah Power & Light Co., 94 LA 233 (Winograd, 1990) (company cannot unilaterally issue a drug-testing policy that intruded into employees' private lives); Dow Chem. Co., 91 LA 1385, 1389 (Baroni, 1989) (chemical plant); Arkansas Power & Light Co., 88 LA 1065, 1068 (Weisbrod, 1987) (nuclear power plant). An employer's unilateral additions to a substance abuse policy, beyond the random testing mandated by federal law, were held invalid in *AmeriGas*, 102 LA 1185 (Marino, 1994). As a result, the arbitrator fashioned a remedy with some statutory-sounding provisions: employer must raise challenged provisions in current contract negotiations with the union because this is a mandatory subject to bargaining and there is no evidence that the union waived its right to negotiate the provisions in question. *Id.* at 1187. *See also* Phelps Dodge Copper Prods. Co., 94 LA 393 (Blum, 1990) (invasive drug-testing program invalid because it was "arbitrary and capricious").

[776]108 LA 316 (Zobrak, 1997).

[777]*Id.* at 320.

[778]Gerstenslager Co., 114 LA 1290, 1293 (Lalka, 2000).

[779]*See* Ash Grove Cement Co., 117 LA 1511, 1516 (Jenks, 2002) ("The workplace violence procedures implemented by the Company are reflective of the Company's responsibility to protect the health and safety of all its employees and are justified as reasonable in light of violence within its corporate system and throughout workplaces nationally."); Ashland Oil, 97 LA 226, 231–32 (Volz, 1991); United Tel. Co. of Fla., 78 LA 865, 869–70 (Clarke, 1982); Chemetco, 71 LA 457, 459–60 (Gibson, 1978); J.R. Simplot Co., 68 LA 912, 915 (Conant, 1977); Nu-Ply Corp., 50 LA 985, 986 (Hnatiuk, 1968). For additional cases and related discussion, see Chapter 16, section 2., "Management Rights and Obligations in Safety and Health Matters."

[780]Packaging Corp. of Am., 114 LA 809, 813 (Nolan, 2000) (the new safety shoe policy issued by management was inconsistent with the agreement and not required by OSHA regulations).

potential for serious injury, violations of health and safety rules may result in immediate termination.[781]

Zero tolerance safety rules, including those prohibiting workplace violence,[782] that mandate suspension or discharge of an offending employee have been upheld as reasonable.[783] Even though an employer has been lax in the enforcement of health and safety rules, or has been inconsistent in their application, arbitrators have held that the employer is not necessarily barred from enforcing the rules in the future.[784]

As with all other classes of plant rules, an employer may unilaterally amend and modify health and safety rules so long as the changes satisfy the "reasonableness" standard.[785]

v.   *Rules Relating to Off-Duty Conduct*

Employers may issue work rules that penalize off-duty conduct of their employees that reflects adversely on the employer, impairs relations with the public and customers, or creates friction within the workforce.[786]

These rules generally have been upheld by arbitrators, so long as the employer demonstrates the connection between the off-duty misconduct and the actual or potential "damage to [the] company's . . . reputation and problems of interrelationship with other employees at work."[787] A different conclusion may be reached where a work rule regarding off-duty conduct does

---

[781]Union Tank Car Co., 110 LA 1123 (Lalka, 1998) (other employees may be at risk while employee is going through steps of progressive discipline). See related discussion in Chapter 16, section 3.A., "Issuance of Safety and Health Rules."

[782]Mason Hanger Corp., 111 LA 469, 473 (Baroni, 1998) (upholding zero tolerance policy); Golden State Foods Corp., 108 LA 705, 708 (Gentile, 1997) (upholding discharge for workplace violence based on grabbing of coworker, where 6 weeks prior to the incident, employer had distributed and implemented zero tolerance policy for actual or threatened violence); Packaging Corp. of Am., 106 LA 122, 125 (Nicholas, Jr., 1996) (upholding grievance by employee who violated weapons policy, where company failed to consult union first, as required under agreement; arbitrator nonetheless stated that he believed company policy was valid).

[783]*See* Smurfit Stone Container Div., 114 LA 562 (Marino, 2000) (an employer may implement and enforce safety rules such as a zero tolerance policy).

[784]Rock-Tenn Co., 110 LA 1109, 1114 (Bard, 1998) (an employer is not forever barred from enforcing rules, where the evidence fails to show the employer had abandoned the safety rules).

[785]Flowserve Corp., 111 LA 813, 819 (Jennings, 1998).

[786]Intertec Sys. LLC, 114 LA 1785, 1786 (Skulina, 2000) (upholding company rule that prohibited off-duty conduct that put the company in "bad light in the community"); Pleasantview Fire Prot. Dist., 113 LA 388, 393 (Goldstein, 1999) (the arbitrator outlined the three principles arbitrators consider in determining whether rules or policies regarding employees' conduct are reasonable: (1) whether adequate notice has been given to the employees of the rules or policies before they are enforced, (2) whether the rules or policies are reasonably related to the legitimate objectives of management, and (3) whether the rules or policies are enforced in a nondiscriminatory manner). For related discussion, see Chapter 15, section 3.A.i., "Off-Duty Misconduct Away From Employer's Premises," and section 3.A.ii, "Off-Duty Misconduct on Company Premises."

[787]City of New Hope, Minn., 89 LA 427, 430 (Bard, 1987). *Cf.* Western Mich. Univ., 115 LA 628, 632–33 (Daniel, 2000) (the employee's drug misconduct off campus was reasonably connected to his employment).

not appear to have any demonstrable relationship to the employer's business or operations.[788]

vi. *Other Rules Governing Employee Conduct*

Employer-promulgated sexual harassment policies,[789] confidential information protection programs,[790] and employee dress codes,[791] among others,[792] have been contested by unions. The outcomes tend to be highly fact-specific.

G. Posting of Rules

The decision as to whether plant rules are to be posted is a part of the managerial function, and the posting of rules ordinarily is not a condition precedent to management's right to discipline employees for the violation of them.[793] However, except where the nature of the prohibited activity is such

---

[788]Department of Corr. Servs., 114 LA 1533, 1537–38 (Simmelkjaer, 1997). For an earlier discussion of this topic, see Hill, Jr. & Kahn, *Discipline and Discharge for Off-Duty Misconduct: What Are the Arbitral Standards?*, *in* ARBITRATION 1986: CURRENT AND EXPANDING ROLES, PROCEEDINGS OF THE 39TH ANNUAL MEETING OF NAA 121 (Gershenfeld ed., BNA Books 1987); Chicago Pneumatic Tool Co., 38 LA 891, 893 (Duff, 1961).

[789]American Mail-Well Envelope, 105 LA 1209, 1213–14 (Paull, 1995) (upholding sexual harassment policy, but sustaining grievant's claim that 3-day suspension was not justified); ABTCO, Inc., 104 LA 551, 554–55 (Kanner, 1995) (male employee properly discharged, under last-chance agreement, for sexually offensive conduct against female employee). See related discussion in Chapter 17, section 7., "Protection Against Sexual Harassment."

[790]Southwestern Bell Tel. Co., 107 LA 928, 937 (Nolan, 1996) (upholding discharge of two telephone company salesclerks for personal use of confidential information in violation of known rule prohibiting such use); US W. Communications, 107 LA 791, 796 (Yehle, 1996) (discharge of 25-year employee by telephone company for first violation of code of conduct that prohibited personal use of company information upheld where policy was unambiguous and communicated to employees.

[791]Intertec Sys., 114 LA 1785, 1785 (Skulina, 2000) (upholding company rule that prohibited the "[w]earing of apparel with remarks or pictures which are disrespectful"); Macy's, 108 LA 489, 495 (Gregory, 1997) (company violated agreement when it unilaterally instituted mandatory dress code, where clothing requirement was mandatory subject of bargaining between parties); Fairmont-Zarda Dairy, 106 LA 583, 591 (Rohlik, 1995) (sustaining grievance based on no-beard policy, where no uniform industry ban existed, no government regulations supported ban, no intracompany problem existed, no showing was made that beard cover was unavailable as alternative, and long hair and mustaches were permitted); Motion Picture & Television Fund, 103 LA 988, 922 (Gentile, 1994) (upholding company's right to prohibit operator/receptionist from wearing nose jewelry); Albertson's, Inc., 102 LA 641, 645 (Darrow, 1994) (upholding policy requiring conservative hairstyles, given discretion afforded to company, company's desire to protect public image, fact that employees not covered by policy had no public contact, and existence of longstanding practice). For related discussion, see Chapter 17, section 5., "Personal Appearance: Hair and Clothes."

[792]Meridian Med. Techs., 115 LA 1564, 1568 (King, 2001) (refusal to comply with work orders).

[793]Eastern Air Lines, 44 LA 459, 461 (Murphy, 1965) (there is no one way of either establishing or publicizing a rule); Patterson Steel Co., 37 LA 862, 864 (Merrill, 1961); Ross Gear & Tool Co., 35 LA 293, 296 (Schmidt, 1960); Bethlehem Steel Co., 7 LA 334, 335 (Killingsworth, 1946); Watt Car & Wheel Co., 4 LA 67, 69 (Blair, 1946). *See also* Beverage Concepts, 114 LA 340 (Cannavo, 1999) (upholding policy even though it had not been promulgated or published where the company had consistently followed a particular practice); Temperature Control, 59 LA 1226, 1230 (Cowan, 1972); Ohio Power Co. 50 LA 501, 504 (Teple, 1967) (plant rules need not be in writing); Pacific Northwest Bell, 48 LA 498, 501–02 (Lowell, 1967).

that employees should know it is improper,[794] rules must be communicated effectively to employees in some manner.[795]

Thus, in the absence of posted rules, management bears the burden of proving that employees knew, or should have known, of the policy before it can be enforced.[796] Further, if the rules are not posted, management's decision to discipline an employee for a violation may be vulnerable to attack on the ground of discrimination.[797] Especially when management chooses to fix discharge as the appropriate penalty for a violation of a rule, no doubt should be left in the minds of the employees as to the existence and nature of the rule and the consequences for its violation.[798]

18. SENIORITY [LA CDI 117.201]

Management's right of action is very often restricted by requirements of seniority recognition. Chapter 14, "Seniority," is devoted to discussion of seniority concepts and to an examination of the standards utilized by arbitrators in evaluating management actions in the setting of seniority requirements.

19. LAYOFF OF EMPLOYEES

A. Principal Issues Involved [LA CDI 100.68; 117.101 et seq.]

In the absence of contractual restriction, it is the right of management to determine the number of employees to be used at any given time and to lay off employees in excess of that number, giving any required recognition to seniority.[799] Recognition of seniority is the most significant type of restric-

---

[794]*See* Ashland Oil & Ref. Co., 28 LA 874, 877–78 (Badley, 1957); Omar Inc., 26 LA 641, 642 (Beatty, 1956); Keystone Box Co., 18 LA 336, 339 (Harkins, 1952). *Cf.* International Paper Co., 52 LA 1266, 1269 (Jenkins, 1969); Koopers Co., 69 LA 613, 614 (Harkless, 1977). *See also* Overhead Door Co. of Ky, 70 LA 1299, 1301 (Dworkin, 1978).

[795]*See* Saint Gobain Norpro,116 LA 960, 965, 967 (Fullmer, 2001); Bright-O Inc., 54 LA 498, 500 (Mullin, Jr., 1970); Ohio Power Co., 50 LA 501, 504 (Teple, 1967); Great Atl. & Pac. Tea Co., 48 LA 910, 914 (Keefe, 1967); Abex Corp., 47 LA 441, 442–43 (Kates, 1966) (an employer "takes an unnecessary risk of enforcement in failing to put all its shop rules in written form"); Eastern Air Lines, 44 LA 459, 461 (Murphy, 1965); Lester Eng'g Co., 43 LA 1268, 1273 (Klein, 1965); Lawrence Bros., 28 LA 83, 87 (Davis, 1957); D.M. Watkins Co., 14 LA 787, 790 (Healy, 1950). *See also* Donaldson Mining Co., 91 LA 471, 475–76 (Zobrak, 1988); Kessler Coals, 69 LA 630, 636, 639 (Dyke, 1977).

[796]Clinchfield Coal Co., 85 LA 382, 385–86 (Rybolt, 1985); Stauffer Chem. Co., 83 LA 332, 335–36 (Blum, 1984); Great Atl. & Pac. Tea Co., 48 LA 910, 914 (Keefe, 1967); Lawrence Bros., 28 LA 83, 87 (Davis, 1957); D.M. Watkins Co., 14 LA 787, 790 (Healy, 1950).

[797]Bethlehem Steel Co., 7 LA 334, 335 (Killingsworth, 1946); Watt Car & Wheel Co., 4 LA 67, 69 (Blair, 1946).

[798]Menasha Corp., 90 LA 427, 430 (Clark, 1987); Gamble Bros., 68 LA 72, 74 (Krislov, 1977). *Cf.* Pacific Northwest Bell Tel. Co., 48 LA 498, 501–02 (Lovell, 1967); Hayes Indus., 44 LA 820, 822–23 (Teple, 1965); Joy Mfg. Co., 6 LA 430, 434 (Healy, 1946). *See also* Donaldson Mining Co., 91 LA 471, 475–76 (Zobrak, 1988).

[799]*See* Dyncorp Tech. Servs., 116 LA 1156, 1160–61 (Goodman, 2001); Baker Coll., 112 LA 720, 724–25 (Daniel, 1998); Koch Nitrogen Co., 111 LA 449, 453–56 (Howell, 1998); Supervalu, Inc., 109 LA 423, 426–27 (Watkins, 1997); Birmingham Sash & Door Co., 106 LA 180, 110 (Bain, 1996); City of Pontiac, Mich., 73 LA 1083, 1086–87 (Ellmann, 1979); Na-

tion placed by many agreements on the layoff right.[800] Clauses requiring advance notice for layoff in order to permit employees to plan ahead are not uncommon, and often are readily agreed to by employers because they also prefer to plan ahead.[801]

Further, in the case of plant closings, the federal Worker Adjustment and Retraining Notification (WARN) Act[802] requires companies that employ more than 100 employees to provide 60-day notice for reasonably foreseeable shutdowns.

The meaning of the term "layoff," and allegations that employees have been laid off in fact, even if not in name or form, are frequent issues in arbitration.[803] Arbitrators have ruled that the term "layoff" must be interpreted

---

tional Biscuit Co., 55 LA 312, 324 (Blair, 1970); Combustion Eng'g, 46 LA 289, 291 (Murphy, 1966); Bethlehem-Sparrows Point Shipyard, 19 LA 523, 525 (Feinberg, 1952); Pathe Labs., 19 LA 487, 488 (Wolff, 1952); Portable Prods. Corp., 10 LA 883, 885 (Feinberg, 1948). *See also* CBS, Inc., 74 LA 1209, 1212–14 (Turkus, 1980); Nashua Corp., 64 LA 256, 258 (Edes, 1975); Westinghouse Elec. Corp., 47 LA 941, 946–47 (Hebert, 1966); American Thread Co., 39 LA 268, 269 (McCoy, 1962); Art Metal Constr. Co., 36 LA 458, 462 (Reid, 1961); O'Rourke Baking Co., 24 LA 770, 774 (Nagle, 1955). Where the contract listed four reasons for layoffs, management could lay off only for those reasons. City of Milwaukee, 55 LA 926, 931–32 (Sembower, 1970). For discussion of the rights of laid-off employees, see *Durnan & Good Co.*, 78 LA 34, 35 (Florey, 1982); *Great Atl. & Pac. Tea Co.*, 74 LA 422, 427–28 (Dean, 1980); *National Tea Co.*, 59 LA 1193, 1197 (Joseph, 1972); *American Thread Co.*, 39 LA 268, 269 (McCoy, 1962); *Border Queen*, 35 LA 560, 563–64 (Brown, 1960); *United States Steel Corp.*, 25 LA 443, 449–51 (Whelan, 1955). For related discussion, see Chapter 14, section 7., "Use of Seniority and Ability Provisions and Layoffs."

[800]Olin Corp., 83 LA 346 (Wolff, 1984); Wayne Pump Co., 35 LA 623, 625 (Horlacher, 1960). For the renunciation of an employer's system of weighing seniority, in which an employee of 1 year of service was awarded two points, while an employee of 18 years of service was awarded only four points, see *Legal Aid Found. of Los Angeles*, 105 LA 694, 699–701 (Feller, 1995). For the application of a clause providing for layoff by seniority but authorizing exceptions for special skills, see *Trane Co.*, 44 LA 212, 216 (Markowitz, 1965). For the application of a clause providing that an employer may consider seniority, ability, qualifications, and physical fitness, see *Standard Havens*, 92 LA 926 (Madden, 1989). For the application of a still less strict requirement of seniority recognition, see *Government Employees (AFGE)*, 76 LA 473, 478 (Oldham, 1981) (the agreement required seniority recognition in layoff and recall, "except where such reduction and recall would cause injury to AFGE operations").

[801]*See* International Playing Card & Label Co., 116 LA 717 (Hoffman, 2001) (upholding a clause providing employees with reporting pay unless they are notified prior to end of preceding shift); Mobil Chem. Co., 50 LA 80, 81–82 (Kesselman, 1968) (interpreting a clause to permit very few exceptions to the notice requirement). For related discussion, see section 13.C., "Changes in Work Schedule," above. For a clause interpreted to permit very few exceptions to the notice requirement, see *Mobil Chem. Co.*, 50 LA 80, 81–82 (Kesselman, 1968). In *Oregon Steel Mills*, 66 LA 79, 81 (Hedges, 1976), the agreement required "a 30-day prior notice before" layoff. The arbitrator stressed that the notice must be clear and specific: "It means that the employee is entitled to be put on notice of the date that he is to be laid off 30 days before that date. It does not mean that he is merely entitled to be put on notice that at some indefinite date in the future, more than thirty days following the notice he will be laid off." *Id.*

[802]29 U.S.C. §2101 et seq. For a discussion on what constitutes "reasonably foreseeable" under the WARN Act, see *A.I.M. Corp.*, 111 LA 463, 466–67 (Florman, 1998).

[803]*See* Hugo Neu-Proler Co., 109 LA 880, 884–86 (Richman, 1997) (declaring a layoff is a decrease in workforce); District Concrete Co., 74 LA 719, 721–22 (Ordman, 1980); Great Atl. & Pac. Tea Co., 74 LA 422, 427–28 (Dean, 1980) (in drawing a distinction between "permanent layoff" and "immediate discharge," the arbitrator stated that a "layoff is essentially a preservation of some benefits of employment notwithstanding the employee's separation from active employment"); T&S Coal Co., 73 LA 882, 884–85 (Leahy, 1979); Reyco Indus., 73 LA 833, 836 (Bothwell, 1979) (dealing with the "question whether an unrecalled employee at the conclusion of a strike becomes a laid off employee"); American Motors Corp., 72 LA 1160,

to include any suspension from employment arising out of a reduction in the workforce, and that the scheduling of employees not to work or the use of the term "not scheduled" by management does not make the occurrence any less a layoff.[804] One arbitrator defined "layoff," in the context of a particular clause, as an "actual severance from the Company's payroll, and a break in continuous service."[805]

B. Downgrading

Downgrading is often tied to layoffs. It has been held that downgrading "is such an intimate concomitant of layoff" that layoff seniority provisions must be applied in downgrading.[806] Some contracts contain provisions permitting employees to accept layoff in lieu of downgrading.[807] Where a contract was silent regarding the right of employees to choose layoff rather than downgrading, one arbitrator held that they are deemed to have such right if downgrading involves a significant reduction in pay.[808]

1164 (Ipavec, 1979) (the term "permanent layoff" connotes a layoff "which is considered lasting or intended to last indefinitely . . . and . . . for a relatively long period of time"); California Metal Trades, 69 LA 1075, 1077 (Boner, 1977); Mahoney Plastics Corp., 69 LA 1017, 1022 (King, 1977); J.R. Simplot Co., 68 LA 1167, 1169 (Flagler, 1977) (collecting several definitions of "layoff"); Steelcraft Mfg. Co., 68 LA 925, 927 (Gibson, 1977); Teledyne Electro Finishing, 68 LA 36, 39–40 (Cole, 1977); Polar Ware Co., 65 LA 1, 3, 5 (Mueller, 1975) (shutdown as a layoff); California Brewers Ass'n, 57 LA 742, 750–51 (Block, 1971); Spiegel, Inc., 55 LA 981, 985–86 (Cohen, 1970); Borden, Inc., 51 LA 1069, 1071 (Moran, 1968); Combustion Eng'g, 46 LA 289, 292–93 (Murphy, 1966); Menasco Mfg. Co., 45 LA 502, 505, 508 (Boles, 1965); Faultless Rubber Co., 40 LA 1067, 1069 (Teple, 1963); Weber Showcase & Fixture Co., 27 LA 40, 45 (Prasow, 1956); Continental Can Co., 26 LA 924, 929–30 (Campbell, 1956); Continental Can Co., 23 LA 137, 141 (Platt, 1954); Stewart-Warner Corp., 22 LA 695, 696–98 (McCormick, 1954); American Metal Prods. Co., 22 LA 181, 183 (Marshall, 1954); American Mfg. Co., 19 LA 231, 232–33 (Emery, 1952); Great Lakes Pipe Line Co., 18 LA 801, 808 (Piper, 1952); Bethlehem Steel, 16 LA 71, 72 (Feinberg, 1950). In *Radio Station WFDF*, 79 LA 424, 426–27 (Ellmann, 1982), the arbitrator found that the grievant had not been laid off but rather had been terminated (and thus was entitled to contractual severance pay), because there was no "reasonable expectancy of employment in the near future."

[804]*See* USS, Div. of USX Corp., 113 LA 939, 941–42 (Das, 1999) (calling an employer's order to take a vacation for 10 days a "layoff"); Exide Corp., 98 LA 626, 628 (Daly, 1992) (shutting down all shifts for 3 days constitutes layoff, not "short work week"); Charles H. Johnston's Sons Co., 75 LA 337, 340–41 (Chapman, 1980); Bethlehem Steel Co., 14 LA 191, 195 (Feinberg, 1950); United Smelting & Aluminum Co., 13 LA 684, 686 (Donnelly & Sviridoff, Mottram dissenting, 1949); Bethlehem Steel, 5 LA 578, 587 (Brandschain, 1946). *Cf.* Alabama Asphaltic Limestone Co., 48 LA 767, 768 (Williams, 1967). *But see* BASF Corp., 116 LA 1676, 177–78 (Crider, 2002) (maintaining an employer's right to schedule vacation time without having to invoke layoff provisions); Kroger Co., 114 LA 1139, 1142 (Murphy, 2000) (upholding employer's right to reduce hours if employee refused to transfer).

[805]Bethlehem Steel, 16 LA 71, 72 (Feinberg, 1950). *See also* Continental Can Co., 26 LA 924, 929 (Campbell, 1956).

[806]Kenworth Motor Truck Corp., 8 LA 867, 869 (Seering, 1947). *See also* Ford Motor Co., Opinions of the Umpire, Opinion A-30 (1943). But this result was not reached where downgrading was not tied to layoffs. Lockheed Aircraft Corp., 10 LA 222, 226 (Aaron, 1948). *See also* Boeing Co., 101 LA 240, 243–45 (Staudohar, 1993); Bethlehem Steel Corp., 77 LA 396, 396 (Strongin, 1981); Adams Bus. Forms, 76 LA 516, 520 (Eisler, 1981); Ohio Seamless Tube Co., 1 LA 298, 300–01 (Mathews, 1946).

[807]*See* Tappan Co., 40 LA 149, 150 (Dworkin, 1962); Carbide & Carbon Chems. Co., 20 LA 205, 206 (Shister, 1953).

[808]Caterpillar Tractor Co., 23 LA 313, 315–16 (Fleming, 1954). *See also* United Eng'g & Foundry Co., 47 LA 164, 169–70 (McCoy, 1966); Bethlehem Steel Co., 15 LA 698, 703 (Shipman, 1950). *Cf.* United States Steel Corp., 31 LA 988, 991–92 (Garrett, 1959).

However, it has been held that if an employee who had the right to bump into a lower paying classification chooses to take the layoff instead, he or she loses the right to grieve over any potential difference in wages that would have resulted from the downgrade.[809]

C. Temporary/Emergency Layoffs [LA CDI 117.1138]

Numerous cases have arisen involving the observance of seniority in temporary layoffs. Contracts sometimes expressly allow management to disregard seniority in making temporary layoffs.[810] Such agreements generally indicate the maximum period that may be considered temporary, varying in different contracts from a specified number of hours up to as many as 30 days.[811]

In cases where the agreement contains no specific exception from the requirement of observing seniority in making "temporary" or "emergency" layoffs, arbitrators have disagreed as to the right of management to disregard seniority in making such layoffs.[812] Some of these cases can be recon-

---

[809]See Meyer on Main, 101 LA 1070, 1073 (Cipolla, 1993).

[810]E.g., Cytec Fiberite, 116 LA 568, 571 (Bickner, 2001); Union Camp Corp., 95 LA 1054, 1055 (Strasshofer, 1990); Sam Blount Co., 93 LA 209, 211 (Holley, Jr., 1989); Thombert, Inc., 91 LA 1275, 1275 (Yarowsky, 1988); Wagner Elec. Corp., 76 LA 773, 774 (Roberts, 1981); Lennox Indus., 70 LA 417, 417 (Seifer, 1978); Tecumseh Prods. Co., 65 LA 471, 473 (Solomon, 1975); Marsh Stencil Mach. Co., 33 LA 1, 4 (Klamon, 1959); Bloomer Bros. Co., 28 LA 494, 497 (Thompson, 1957); John Deere Des Moines Works, 24 LA 88, 89 (Davey, 1955); General Cable Corp., 15 LA 910, 913 (Kaplan, 1950); Thomasville Chair Co., 8 LA 792, 794 (Waynick, 1947); Ford Motor Co., 1 LA 544, 545 (Shulman, 1945). In Barler Metal Products, 38 LA 1, 4–5 (Sembower, 1962), it was held that the "temporary" character of a layoff is determined in advance, rather than retrospectively.

[811]See cases cited in note 810, above; Anaconda Am. Brass Co., 43 LA 1092, 1093–94 (Feinberg, 1964); International Harvester Co., 18 LA 785, 786 (Cornsweet, 1952); Chrysler Corp., 12 LA 826, 828 (Ebeling, 1949). Even where the contract fixes a maximum period, a series of temporary layoffs without observing seniority has sometimes been permitted. See Anaconda Aluminum Co., 43 LA 775, 777–79 (Volz, 1964); Alliance Mfg. Co., 37 LA 177, 180 (Kates, 1961). Cf. Tecumseh Prods. Co., 65 LA 457, 476 (Solomon, 1975). An interesting situation was presented under a contract that required observance of seniority only in case of layoffs for "indefinite" periods. There the employer was permitted to provide 1 week's work for all employees and then to lay off all employees for 1 week, rather than to lay off junior employees indefinitely, the arbitration board ruling that the layoffs were for definite, temporary periods. Whitlock Mfg. Co., 13 LA 253, 254 (Stutz, Mottram, & Curry, 1949).

[812]Cases requiring observance of seniority: Johnston-Tombigbee Mfg. Co., 113 LA 1015, 1023 (Howell, 2000); Eureka Sec. Printing Co., 85 LA 1040, 1046 (DiLauro, 1985); Macomb County Rd. Comm'n, 82 LA 721, 724–25 (Roumell, Jr., 1984); Hyster Co., 66 LA 522, 529–31 (Kossoff, 1976); Nashua Corp., 64 LA 256, 258 (Edes, 1975); Hauserman, 63 LA 409, 412 (LeVerde, 1974); Yale & Towne Mfg. Co., 40 LA 1115, 1118–20 (Tatum, 1963); General Elec. Co., 40 LA 513, 520–21 (Killion, 1962); Wheland Co., 38 LA 1199, 1202 (Murphy, 1962); Greer Limestone Co., 35 LA 299, 303 (Lugar, 1960); Ross Clay Prods. Co., 30 LA 441, 443 (Duff, 1958); North Range Mining Co., 29 LA 724, 726–27 (Howlett, 1957); Continental Can Co., 23 LA 137, 141 (Platt, 1954); Curtis Screw Co., 23 LA 89, 92 (Thompson, 1954); Stewart-Warner Corp., 22 LA 695, 698 (McCormick, 1954); American Metal Prods. Co., 22 LA 181, 184 (Marshall, 1954); Ansonia Wire & Cable Co., 21 LA 400, 401 (Stutz, 1953); Fruehauf Trailer Co., 19 LA 159, 163–64 (Spaulding, 1952); Bethlehem Steel Co., 14 LA 413, 416 (Feinberg, 1950); Quaker Oats Co., 13 LA 529, 531 (Gorder, 1949); F.C. Russell Co., 12 LA 893, 895 (Uible, 1949); Merrill-Stevens Dry Dock & Repair Co., 10 LA 88, 91 (McCoy, 1948); Bethlehem Steel, 5 LA 578, 587–88 (Brandschain, 1946); General Mach. Corp., 5 LA 24, 25 (Whiting, 1946); Link-Belt Co., 1 LA 530, 537 (Gilden, 1946). Cases not requiring the observance of seniority: St. Vincent Mercy Med. Ctr., 117 LA 785, 791–92 (Imundo, Jr., 2002);

ciled on the basis of differing contract language, including contractual requirements for notice of layoff,[813] or by distinguishing between "temporary" and "emergency" layoffs.[814]

Issues concerning "temporary" or "emergency" layoffs may be approached "in the light of the well known fact that the common purpose of seniority layoff provisions is to give protection as between classes of employees on the assumption that some of them may properly be suspended under conditions of lack of work, and not to guarantee work."[815] One arbitrator construed the contract in question as being broadly applicable to temporary as well as permanent suspensions of work (those where there is no immediate prospective need of the services involved), but not as requiring the employer to follow seniority "when the emergency is such that, due to time limitations, it would be either impossible or unreasonably burdensome to give effect to these rules."[815a]

D. Reducing the Workweek [LA CDI 117.323]

The question sometimes arises regarding management's right to reduce the workweek of all its employees in lieu of laying off junior employees. In the absence of a specific contract provision covering this issue, arbitrators have ruled both ways.[816]

Union Camp Corp., 95 LA 1054, 1056 (Strasshofer, 1990); Bristol Steel & Iron Works, 73 LA 573, 577 (Nicholas, Jr., 1979); New Orleans Bd. of Trade, 52 LA 368, 372 (Caraway, 1969) (past practice supported employer); Lehigh Portland Cement Co., 37 LA 778, 784 (Klamon, 1961); American Iron & Mach. Works Co., 32 LA 345, 350–51 (Abernethy, 1959); International Paper Co., 23 LA 497, 500 (Hebert, 1954); United States Steel Corp., 21 LA 71, 74–75 (Garrett, 1953); Todd Shipyards Corp., 20 LA 345, 347–48 (Prasow, 1953); Lake Mining Co., 20 LA 297, 299 (Marshall, 1953); National Tube Co., 18 LA 517, 518 (Morgan, 1952); American Iron & Mach. Works Co., 18 LA 285, 289 (Horton, 1952); Lavoris Co., 16 LA 173, 175 (Lockhart, 1951); Shell Oil Co., 14 LA 681, 685 (Bauder, 1950); Bethlehem Steel Co., 14 LA 191, 196 (Feinberg, 1950); American Can Co., 10 LA 579, 581 (Stein, 1948); Riverton Lime & Stone Co., 8 LA 506, 509 (Dwyer, 1947); International Harvester Co., 8 LA 129, 134 (Elson, 1947). *See also* Cherry Growers, 24 LA 232, 237–38 (Howlett, 1955); Veeder-Root, Inc., 15 LA 192, 194 (Healy, 1950). Observance of seniority in emergency recalls was not required in *Hayes Mfg. Corp.*, 14 LA 970, 976 (Platt, 1950); *Firestone Tire & Rubber Co.*, 14 LA 552, 562 (Platt, 1950). *See also* Federal Bearings Co., 48 LA 179, 181 (Turkus, 1966). *Cf.* Robbins & Myers, Inc., 22 LA 875, 880 (Dworkin, 1954).

[813]*See* Johnson Controls World Serv., 108 LA 191 (Specht, 1996) (because the union was consulted prior to a furlough of government employees before a government shutdown, and the union had not reserved any claims relating to the furlough, the arbitrator held that the union was equitably estopped from later pursuing grievances based on alleged loss of work). *See also* General Dynamics, 101 LA 187, 192–93 (Richman, 1993) (employer was required to consult and receive approval from the union before laying off a missile mechanic union steward, thus providing notice of a layoff).

[814]In at least one instance, however, opposite results were reached within the same month by two different arbitrators applying the same contractual provision to similar fact situations. *See* International Harvester Co., 9 LA 399, 401 (Hays, 1947); International Harvester Co., 8 LA 129, 134 (Elson, 1947).

[815]Dow Chem. Co., 12 LA 763, 767 (Smith, 1949).

[815a]*Id. See also* Union Camp Corp., 95 LA 1054, 1056 (Strasshofer, 1990); Machinists Silvergate Dist. Lodge 50, 73 LA 1127, 1128–29 (Zimring, 1979); Kaiser Steel Co., 48 LA 1199, 1201 (Roberts, 1967).

[816]This is discussed and cases are cited in section 13., "Scheduling Work," above.

Arbitrators continue to interpret the term "layoff" broadly to include any reduction in the normal workweek that results in loss of work. An arbitrator has held, in such an instance, that a contract that requires available hours be distributed on the basis of seniority prohibits an employer from reducing the hours or shifts of senior employees in order to avoid laying off junior employees.[817]

E. Other Factors Affecting Layoffs [LA CDI 117.1133]

If the contract provides that seniority governs only "where ability, skill and qualifications are equal," an employer can consider factors such as absenteeism and disciplinary status in determining whether to lay off an employee out of seniority order.[818] However, a company was held to have violated the contract by laying off a senior employee who had received only one point less on evaluations than a retained junior employee and, accordingly, was judged to be "substantially" equally qualified in experience, skill, and efficiency.[819]

An employer may not seek to accommodate handicapped employees at the expense of seniority rights. It has been held that an employer violated a collective bargaining contract when it assigned an employee to the swing shift in order to accommodate a disabled employee.[820]

F. Bumping [LA CDI 117.1135; 117.125]

Layoffs often give rise to "bumping" issues. Arbitrators have emphasized that, absent any contract provision permitting it, senior employees have no right to bump junior employees merely because the senior employee wants

---

[817]Yaffee Printing Co., 101 LA 1019 (Pelofsky, 1993). The contract provided that the last employee hired would be the first laid off; the company reduced the workweek for all employees when sales declined by closing the plant on Fridays and staggering work assignments pro rata. The arbitrator concluded that the contract did not guarantee work for all employees but required that the available hours be distributed on the basis of seniority. Accordingly, the company was directed to make whole the senior employees who were improperly laid off (or had their normal workweek reduced).

[818]Houston Lighting & Power Co., 102 LA 582 (Nicholas, Jr., 1994). See White Consol. Indus., 114 LA 1031, 1038–40 (Nicholas, Jr., 2000) (senior employee was laid off after 35 years because he could no longer perform efficiently); St. Clare Hosp., 112 LA 602, 605–08 (Cavanaugh, 1998) (company properly reduced the junior employee's hours even though he possessed certification at the time of the layoff and the hospital had waived the certification for the senior employee because both employees were still considered relatively equal); Entergy/Mississippi Power & Light Co., 111 LA 507, 516–17 (Howell, 1998) (employer did not violate collective bargaining agreement when it laid off senior employee who had difficulties performing basic mechanic's work); H&K Dallas, 108 LA 600 (Moore, 1997) (company properly laid off two senior employees, where one of junior employees retained had demonstrably greater skills and abilities and the other employee was in a different classification). See also Lawrence Berkeley Nat'l Lab., 108 LA 376 (Silver, 1996) (employer did not violate contract or discriminate against black employee by laying him off, where at least 30% of his job duties were eliminated, many of the remaining duties were assigned to a number of employees other than the white employee who allegedly received favorable treatment, and the remaining evidence, including statistical evidence, did not support the grievant's position).

[819]Matanuska Elec. Ass'n, 107 LA 402 (Landau, 1996).

[820]Mason & Hanger Corp., 111 LA 60, 63–64 (Caraway, 1998).

the job of the junior employee—no layoff being involved.[821] However, in the absence of any contract prohibition, "it is almost universally recognized that senior employees, under a plant-wide seniority system, have the right to bump junior employees from their jobs in order to avoid their own layoff, provided they can perform the work of the juniors."[822] The right to bump in short-term temporary layoff situations may be considerably more limited.[823] If full-time and part-time employees are combined on a seniority roster, and the bumping provision makes no distinction between them, the least senior employee, either full time or part time, would be the first to be bumped.[824]

In a case where a contract contained a provision giving senior employees the right to bump junior employees in a layoff situation, but specified that ability and experience, along with seniority, would be determining factors in making layoff decisions, the employer properly disallowed senior employees without training to bump junior apprentices who had completed a 27–30 month apprenticeship.[825] However, where a contract required only

---

[821]*See* Super Save IGA, 74 LA 1218, 1220 (Nolan, 1980); H.K. Porter Co., 48 LA 579, 581–82 (Volz, 1967); Kiely & Mueller, 39 LA 670, 671 (Turkus, 1962); Potlatch Forests, 39 LA 494, 495 (Williams, 1962). *See also* Copps Distrib. Co., 54 LA 824, 827–28 (Krinsky, 1971); National Gypsum Co., 64–1 ARB ¶8255 (Carmichael, 1963). The purpose of "bumping" is explained and it is distinguished from "transfer" in *Borden Ice Cream Co.*, 37 LA 140, 141–42 (Markowitz, 1961).

[822]Darin & Armstrong, 13 LA 843, 847 (Platt, 1950). *See also* Jackson County, Ohio, Sheriff's Office, 116 LA 1753, 1759 (Kindig, 2002); Lackawanna Leather, 113 LA 603, 610 (Pelofsky, 1999); Matanuska Elec. Ass'n, 107 LA 402, 407–08 (Landau, 1996); Lockheed Space Operations Co., 91 LA 457, 462–65 (Richard, 1988); Metalloy Corp., 91 LA 221, 223–25 (Daniel, 1988); Amoco Oil Co., 67 LA 14, 21–22 (Hellman, 1976); General Elec. Co., 43 LA 499, 504 (Altieri, 1964); American Bosch Arma Corp., 42 LA 403, 404, 407 (Kornblum, 1964); Borden Ice Cream Co., 37 LA 140, 141 (Markowitz, 1961); Warren Petroleum Corp., 26 LA 532, 535–36 (Larson, 1956); McLouth Steel Corp., 22 LA 883, 885 (Parker, 1954); E.I. duPont de Nemours & Co., 14 LA 494, 498 (Cornsweet, 1950); Rhode Island Tool Co., 11 LA 827, 831 (Healy, 1948). The present ability requirement is obviously important. *See* Latrobe Constr. Co., 114 LA 311, 314 (Duff, 2000); Creasey Co., 71 LA 789, 790 (Modjeska, 1978); Corn Prods. Co., 50 LA 1093, 1099 (Kamin, 1968); U.S. Indus. Chems. Co., 41 LA 348, 351–52 (Geissinger, 1963); Chromcraft Corp., 35 LA 128, 132 (Klamon, 1960). Although the senior employee is not entitled to training, a reasonable trial period to demonstrate his or her present ability has sometimes been required in bumping situations. *See* Miami Sys. Corp., 99 LA 506, 509–10 (Curry, Jr., 1992); Island Creek Coal Co., 96 LA 1069, 1074–75 (Roberts, 1991); Shore Metal Prods. Co., 24 LA 437, 442 (Prasow, 1955); Rome Grader Corp., 22 LA 167, 170 (McKelvey, 1953); United States Slicing Mach. Co., 22 LA 53, 55 (Kelliher, 1954); Nickles Bakery, 17 LA 486, 487 (Randle, 1951). *See also* Nestle Co., 74 LA 89, 91 (Craver, 1980). *Cf.* Sheldahl, Inc., 78 LA 706, 710 (Rotenberg, 1982); American Lava Corp., 24 LA 517, 518 (Tatum, 1955); Victor G. Bloede Co., 23 LA 779, 781 (McCoy, 1955). Employees *already* on layoff were denied bumping rights in *North Am. Mfg. Co.*, 65 LA 617, 620 (Bourne, 1975); *American Thread Co.*, 39 LA 268, 269 (McCoy, 1962). *Cf.* Wagner Elec. Corp., 76 LA 773, 776, 781 (Roberts, 1981). An arbitrator upheld an agreement that guaranteed seniority rights would not take a backseat to financial considerations. *See* Yale Hoists, 113 LA 1101, 1105–06 (Nicholas, Jr., 1999). For related discussion, see Chapter 14, section 7., "Use of Senority and Ability Provisions and Layoffs."

[823]*See* Lackawanna Leather, 113 LA 603, 608–10 (Pelofsky, 1999); United Screw & Bolt Corp., 42 LA 669, 671 (Kates, 1964); Robertshaw Fulton Controls Co., 30 LA 962, 963 (Blair, 1958); American Smelting & Ref. Co., 15 LA 172, 179 (Fuchs, 1950). *Cf.* International Minerals & Chem. Corp., 22 LA 306, 310 (Seibel, 1954).

[824]Cabell Huntington Hosp., 115 LA 833, 836 (Tharp, 2001).

[825]Murphy Oil U.S.A., 86 LA 54 (Allen, Jr., 1985). *See also* Dentsply Int'l, 85 LA 24, 28–29 (Murphy, 1985); Chromalloy-Sturm Mach. Co., 84 LA 1001, 1006 (Imundo, Jr., 1985); Brooklyn Acres Mut. Homes, 84 LA 952, 955–56 (Abrams, 1985); Container Corp. of Am., 84 LA 604, 608 (Allen, Jr., 1985); Cascade Corp., 82 LA 313, 326 (Bressler, 1984). *But see* Joy

that a senior employee be "qualified" for the position sought in order to bump a junior employee, the arbitrator held it was improper to deny the senior employee's bumping rights on the basis of a safety policy promulgated unilaterally by the employer.[826]

A company's contractual right to select group leaders gives it the right to deny bumping rights to more senior group leaders, because group leaders are chosen for the specific mix of work group and supervisor involved.[827]

Where the position sought is outside the bargaining unit, the principle does not necessarily apply and arbitrators have upheld the denial of bumping right.[828] By the same token, where there was work to be done in a classification whose members were on layoff status, an employer was prohibited from bringing in employees from another classification instead of recalling the in-classification employees from layoff.[829]

Mfg., 82 LA 1205, 1208 (Schedler, 1984) (because words "experienced" or "qualified" did not appear in layoff or recall provisions, experienced employee could be laid off by the employer and replaced with a senior employee without experience). *See also* Teepak, Inc., 83 LA 205, 211 (Fish, 1984) (employer may place a limit on the number of employees who may bump into a particular classification within a certain time period so as to avoid having too many untrained employees in any one classification). For cases regarding a senior employee's entitlement to a reasonable trial period to demonstrate present ability, see *United States Steel Corp.*, 82 LA 655, 657 (Knapp, 1984); Culligan USA, 82 LA 213, 215 (Tamoush, 1984). *But see* Macomb County Rd. Comm'n, 82 LA 721, 724 (Roumell, Jr., 1984) (senior employee with questionable qualifications is not entitled to trial period in layoff situation, but is entitled to reasonable break-in period). *See also* General Battery Corp., 82 LA 751, 754 (Schedler, 1984). For a case supporting management's right to require testing to determine a senior employee's qualifications for a position to which the employee wishes to bump, see *International Salt Co.*, 91 LA 710 (Shieber, 1988). *See also* Northrop Grumman Corp., 107 LA 850 (Nicholas, Jr., 1996) (company properly denied senior employee bumping rights where contract provided that senior employee had to possess substantially equal ability, skill, and efficiency, and company determined that he did not meet these criteria); Phillips Pipeline Co., 105 LA 1132 (Goodman, 1996) (employee properly disqualified after bumping, where he could not learn new job skills within required 1-month period); Coca-Cola Bottling Co. of Mich., 104 LA 97 (McDonald, 1994) (employer again laid off two employees properly when they could not demonstrate ability to perform necessary tasks within 20 working days, as required under the contract); Anderson Concrete Corp., 103 LA 433 (Kindig, 1994) (company properly denied bumping rights where senior employee never held sought-after position, he was at best minimally qualified for position, there was no contractual requirement that he be given a tryout period, and company had consistently conditioned bumping rights on fitness and ability qualifications).

[826]Lockheed Space Operations Co., 91 LA 457 (Richard, 1988).

[827]Donaldson Co., 114 LA 302 (Scoville, 2000).

[828]*See also* Robinson Fiddler's Green Mfg. Co., 115 LA 1523, 1526 (Fullmer, 2001); Grey Eagle Distribs., 107 LA 673 (Pratte, 1996) (company properly laid off senior employee and allowed junior employee to do light-duty work, which was not always performed by classified employees and was not, therefore, deemed to be bargaining-unit work); ALSCO, 106 LA 1146 (Rybolt, 1996) (employer properly brought junior employee back from layoff where return was not to specific job opening but in downsizing situation where junior employee was being brought back to do whatever work was necessary); WorldSource Coil Coating, 102 LA 17 (Florman, 1993).

[829]Associated Univs., 105 LA 1041 (Liebowitz, 1995). *See also* Dubovsky & Sons, 108 LA 19 (Marx, 1996) (employer violated the contract by laying off three employees while temporary vacation employees continued to work). *But see* Johnston-Tombigbee Mfg. Co., 113 LA 1015, 1023 (Howell, 2000) (arbitrator held senior employees may displace junior employees in lowest pay grade, because all laid-off senior employees were lead persons, and there should be no question about their skill and ability to perform in lowest pay grade); AGCO Corp., 111 LA 296, 302–03 (Stallworth, 1998) (employee is allowed to perform de minimis work outside classification).

Arbitrators recognize a company's prerogative to deny bumping rights to senior employees who fail to meet contractually specified fitness and ability qualifications,[830] or who fail to demonstrate that they can become qualified to perform the work within a contractually specified period of time.[831]

Even in cases where management seeks to transfer employees it may be required to consider ability and seniority, and the right to transfer employees is not considered absolute.[832] Bumping may be subject to a "waiting period." Thus, an employer was justified in laying off a senior driver for 1 day for lack of work and refusing to allow him to bump a junior employee, where the weight of the contractual reduction-in-force language favored a waiting period before bumping rights could be asserted.[833]

But in one case where the language of an agreement did not permit bumping during layoffs of fewer than 5 consecutive workdays, but the past practice had allowed bumping during layoffs of any length, the company was found to have improperly laid off senior employees during a short-term layoff without allowing them to exercise bumping rights.[834]

While it is generally accepted that an employee facing layoff may exercise the bumping right laterally or downward, that is, to a job equal to his or her own or a lower classification, some arbitrators have allowed "upward" bumping. Where arbitrators have denied the right of an employee to bump into a higher-rated classification, they have based their decisions on one or more of the following reasons:

1. A layoff may not be used as a means of achieving a promotion. The rationale of these cases seems to be that a promotion can be sought only when a vacancy exists; promotions must be governed by the promotion clause of the collective bargaining agreement; and because

---

[830]*See* Kaiser Fluid Techs., 114 LA 262, 267, 267–68 (Hoffman, 2000) (employer properly prohibited a senior employee from bumping a junior employee, where the senior employee had not run the equipment in 15 years); Northrop Grunman Corp., 107 LA 850 (Nicholas, Jr., 1996) (company properly denied senior employee bumping rights, where contract provided that senior employee had to possess substantially equal ability, skill, and efficiency, and company determined that he did not meet these criteria); Anderson Concrete Corp., 103 LA 433 (Kindig, 1994).

[831]*See* Twin Cities Pub. Television, 117 LA 97, 98–99 (Daly, 2002) (employer did not violate a contract when it laid off floor director instead of allowing her to bump junior design specialist, where the position requires different skills and educational backgrounds); City of Selah, Wash., 114 LA 980, 982–83 (Latsch, 2000) (arbitrator held city did not violate the collective bargaining agreement when it laid off utility worker, who had seniority over retained employee, where senior employee was not qualified, and city did not have time to allow her to learn to fulfill the duties); ACCO U.S.A., 112 LA 101, 102–04 (Gross, 1998) (senior employee could not bump an employee if he could not show he was able to perform the job); Phillips Pipeline Co., 105 LA 1132 (Goodman, 1996); Coca-Cola Bottling Co. of Mich., 104 LA 97 (McDonald, 1994).

[832]City of Omaha, 83 LA 411 (Cohen, 1984).

[833]United Parcel Servs., 90 LA 670 (Statham, 1988).

[834]Central Aluminum Co., 103 LA 190 (Imundo, Jr., 1994). *But see* Hewitt Soap Co., 107 LA 763 (Fullmer, 1996) (company properly declined to lay off 3 probationary employees in addition to 21 employees with seniority, where contract did not require that probationary employees be laid off along with employees with seniority and none of senior employees attempted to exercise bumping rights to bump probationary employees).

upward bumping would result in a promotion in violation of the promotion requirements of the contract, it cannot be permitted.[835]
2. A showing was made that past practice prohibits upward bumping, or there was no showing of past practice allowing it.[836]
3. The history of contract negotiations indicates an intent to preclude upward bumping.[837]
4. While the contract would permit upward bumping, it does not require that it be permitted, and in the absence of a showing of practice by the parties, the arbitrator cannot sustain a claim to upward bumping.[838]

Arbitrators who have permitted upward bumping have done so on the basis of one or more of the following reasons:

1. The contract does not specifically prohibit it.[839]
2. The layoff provisions of the agreement are broad.[840]
3. Upward bumping does not conflict with the promotion provisions of the agreement.[841]
4. Past practice of the parties either supports or does not prohibit upward bumping.[842]

---

[835]*See* Saginaw Rd. Comm'n, 76 LA 899, 902–03 (McDonald, 1981); Toronto Gen. Hosp., 71 LA 295, 300 (Brown, 1978); Schott's Bakery, 38 LA 430, 433–34 (McSwain, 1962); Warren Petroleum Corp., 26 LA 532, 536 (Larson, 1956); U.S. Rubber Co., 25 LA 417, 420–21 (Hall, 1955); Bethlehem Steel, 24 LA 261, 266–67 (Seward, 1955); Poloron Prods. of Pa., 23 LA 789, 795–96 (Rosenfarb, 1955); Link-Belt Co., 22 LA 736, 737 (Horvitz, 1954); International Harvester Co., 15 LA 891, 892 (Seward, 1950); National Gypsum Co., 14 LA 938, 941 (Abernethy, 1950). *See also* Superior Sch. Dist., 72 LA 719, 723 (Pieroni, 1979); Ford Motor Co., 3 LA 863, 865 (Shulman, 1946).

[836]*See* Buchmin Indus., 84 LA 1069, 1072 (Rothschild, 1985); Bethlehem Steel, 30 LA 815, 819 (Seward, 1958); Armco Steel Corp., 30 LA 1, 8 (Hebert, 1958); Duriron Co., 23 LA 220, 222 (Warns, Jr., 1954). In *Empire-Reeves Steel Corp.*, 44 LA 653, 657 (Nichols, 1965), past practice permitted upward bumping but only on a limited basis—this controlled the decision.

[837]*See* Bethlehem Steel, 24 LA 261, 266–67 (Seward, 1955).

[838]*See* Bethlehem Steel, 30 LA 815, 819 (Seward, 1958). Where a contract was "highly permissive" as to upward bumping, the arbitrator said that criteria of "productivity, tensions and morale" should be applied in determining whether to permit it in any particular layoff. C.E. Howard Corp., 38 LA 128, 129–30 (Pollard, 1961).

[839]*See* Whirlpool Corp., 62 LA 192, 194 (Jacobowski, 1974); McNamar Boiler & Tank Co., 30 LA 886, 892 (Burris, 1958); Borg-Warner Corp., 29 LA 629, 633–34 (Marshall, 1957); International Harvester Co., 21 LA 214, 216 (Cole, 1953); Indian Sales Corp., 20 LA 394, 396 (Low, 1953). *Cf.* International Harvester Co., 15 LA 891, 892 (Seward, 1950). In *Bethlehem Steel*, 16 LA 478, 483 (Shipman, 1951), the arbitrator recognized that downward bumping is the general rule, but he held that there should be some exceptions. In *Air Reduction Sales Co.*, 34 LA 294, 296 (Hawley, 1960), the arbitrator said that to deny upward bumping in layoff would seriously restrict departmental seniority rights and might lead to substitution of classification seniority for the broader departmental seniority specified by the contract.

[840]*See* Greater Louisville Indus., 44 LA 694, 697 (Volz, 1965); McNamar Boiler & Tank Co., 30 LA 886, 892 (Burris, 1958); Indian Sales Corp., 20 LA 394, 396 (Low, 1953); International Harvester, 14 LA 502, 503–04 (Seward, 1950).

[841]*See* Aetna Paper Co., 29 LA 439, 441–42 (Warns, 1957). *See also* Chrysler Corp., 12 LA 738, 740 (Ebeling, 1949).

[842]*See* International Harvester Co., 21 LA 214, 216 (Cole, 1953). *See also* Diamond Int'l Corp., 81 LA 797, 801–03 (Rocha, Jr., 1983); Whirlpool Corp., 62 LA 192, 194 (Jacobowski, 1974); Greater Louisville Indus., 44 LA 694, 697 (Volz, 1965).

It has been held, however, that senior employees have an obligation to notify management of their desire to exercise bumping privileges,[843] whereupon management has a duty to disclose the jobs that may be bumped into and to inform junior employees of their layoff under the seniority provisions of the agreement.[844] In recalls, management has been held to have the duty of taking the initiative in ascertaining from employees whether they are available for jobs to which their seniority entitles them.[845]

An employer properly refused to allow a senior employee to bump a partially disabled junior employee who held a modified job. The arbitrator noted that the modified job assignment was available to the employee only as long as the disability continued, and the modified job assignment did not become a regular job.[846]

A contractual requirement that disqualifies an employee from bumping into a position she was not physically able to perform does not violate the ADA, an arbitrator held, because the provision also could disqualify nondisabled employees who lacked the physical ability to do a particular job.[847]

20. PROMOTION AND/OR TRANSFER OF EMPLOYEES

A. Promotion of Employees

i.　Definition [LA CDI 119.02]

The term "promotion" usually connotes an upward movement to a better job or a higher rating in the same job. However, some parties or arbitrators have used the term less specifically, with the result that there has been some

---

[843]See General Am. Transp., 15 LA 672, 676 (Brandschain, 1950); Union Elec. Steel Corp., 13 LA 464, 467 (Blair, 1949). See also Sims Cab, 74 LA 844, 847 (Millious, 1980); Business Forms, 65 LA 1031, 1034 (McDermott, 1975); Westinghouse Elec. Corp., 43 LA 178, 180–81 (Stein, 1964). But see Harding Glass Co., 34 LA 297, 300 (Warns, 1960); Star Watch Case Co., 33 LA 524, 527–28 (Howlett, 1959) (involving union representatives with superseniority).

[844]Archer Daniels Midland Co., 111 LA 518, 524–25 (Pratte, 1998) (employee did not lose right to bump even though he did not make such a request until 1 day before the arbitration hearing because the employer did not inform him of this right); Union Elec. Steel Corp., 13 LA 464, 467 (Blair, 1949). See also Westinghouse Elec. Corp., 43 LA 178, 180–81 (Stein, 1964); Sperti Faraday, 37 LA 9, 11–13 (Bradley, 1961). Some arbitrators require the employee to specify the job into which he or she desires to bump. See Weber Showcase & Fixture Co., 27 LA 40, 48 (Prasow, 1956); Link-Belt Co., 6 LA 803, 813 (Gilden, 1947).

[845]Thor Corp., 13 LA 319, 323 (Baab, 1949). See also Central Armature Works, 111 LA 473, 476–77 (Feldman, 1998) (recall rights of laid-off employees cannot surpass time worked).

[846]Keystone Steel & Wire, 93 LA 1188 (Goldman, 1989).

[847]Mead Prods., 114 LA 1753 (Nathan, 2000).

overlapping and intermingling of the terms "promotion" and "transfer." The mixed nature of some employee job movements also should be kept in mind: promotions often involve transfers, transfers may involve promotions, but not all promotions involve transfers, and certainly not all transfers involve promotions.

In concluding that the term "promotion" generally indicates movement to a higher job classification, one arbitrator referred to industrial practice, the practice of the particular parties, and the following definitions contained in a dictionary of labor terms:

PROMOTION. Transfer of an employee to a higher job classification.

TRANSFER. Shift of an employee from one job to another within a Company. A *lateral transfer* is a change in an employee's job within a department, to another machine or to very similar duties. [848]

Agreeing that the term "promotion" refers to upward movement, another arbitrator stated that the term generally appears "in a context of collective bargaining agreements connoting an upward movement to a higher occupational classification requiring superior skills or greater effort and to which, for such reasons, a higher minimum wage scale is attached."[849] He also noted that the term is "never associated with an outward or lateral movement of employees, to the operation of different machines, or the performances of different work drawing identical wage rates."[850] It also has been held that a lateral or downward movement could not be considered a promotion "even though such a movement may lead to higher pay, a job more to the liking of the worker, and higher ultimate maximum pay."[851]

Another arbitrator held that a hotel properly refused to allow an assistant chief engineer to bid downward to a journeyman engineer position after it determined that it could not lose his expertise. The arbitrator, noting that there was no past practice permitting bids to lower-rated jobs, pointed out

---

[848]Pittsburgh Plate Glass Co., 30 LA 981, 982 (Kelliher, 1958) (quoting the CCH DICTIONARY OF LABOR TERMS). In another case, an arbitrator found that the terms "promotion" and "transfer" had been defined by the contract. United States Steel, 21 LA 707, 708 (Kelliher, 1953).

[849]Bunker Hill & Sullivan Mining & Concentrating Co., 8 LA 1010, 1011 (Cheney, 1947).

[850]*Id.* at 1011 (permitting an employee to select the job, machine, or place of work "would in effect be confiding the management of the business, and the direction of the working forces to employees to no small degree," *id.*).

[851]Rochester Tel. Co., 26 LA 231, 238, 234–35 (Thompson, 1956) (past practice was a factor in the decision). For other cases considering that lateral or downward movements are not promotions, see *Puget Sound Tug & Barge Co.*, 77 LA 831, 836 (Lumbley, 1981) (there was no upward movement requiring superior skills or greater effort for the work assignment in question, nor was a promotion indicated merely by the higher wage paid for the inconvenience of working at that location); *Patterson-Kelley Co.*, 54 LA 593, 595–96 (Mullin, Jr., 1971) (the contract expressly spoke of the right to bid on "higher rated" jobs); *Mansfield Tire & Rubber Co.*, 40 LA 1212, 1214–15 (Kates, 1963) (the contract provided that employees shall be "promoted" to fill vacancies, and the arbitrator said that "in the absence of extraordinary conditions surrounding the opening for which a lateral or downward bid is made, such a bid . . . generally does not involve a 'promotion'"); *Bethlehem Steel Co.*, 30 LA 550, 551 (Seward, 1958); *Superior Paper Prods. Co.*, 26 LA 849, 852 (Reid, 1956); *Blaw Knox Co.*, 23 LA 159, 162 (Reid, 1954); *Gisholt Mach. Co.*, 23 LA 105, 107 (Kelliher, 1954); *Bethlehem Steel Co.*, 12 LA 588, 591 (Selekman, 1949).

that the union's claim that "promotion may be defined as any job an employee desires regardless of the reason" was so broad as to destroy the meaning of the word promotion.[852]

ii. Seniority [LA CDI 119.121]

Where an agreement provided that "[p]romotions to all vacancies" will be made on the basis of seniority and ability, however, an arbitrator followed the view that movement to a job with clearly better working conditions or from which advancement opportunities are or may be better may be viewed as a promotion even though the job does not pay more.[853] Moreover, if the agreement provides for recognition of seniority in the filling of vacancies, but does not use language that is reasonably clear in linking or limiting job vacancies and bidding procedures to promotion or advancement, the arbitrator may hold that employees are entitled to exercise their seniority for lateral or downward movement.[854]

Management's general right to control promotions, except as limited by the collective bargaining agreement, was elaborated on by one arbitrator as follows:

> When there is no contract provision at all limiting the Company's rights in selecting men for promotion, the Company's rights, of course, are unlimited. If the only contract restriction is one against discrimination for Union activity, then that is the only restriction. In other words, absent a contract right in favor of the employees, or a contract restriction on a company, the latter may ignore

---

[852]Disneyland Hotel, 83 LA 685, 688 (Weiss, 1984). *See also* Forms Mfrs., 103 LA 29 (Mikrut, Jr., 1994).

[853]Indiana Chair Co., 34 LA 856, 857–58 (Russell, 1960). *See also* Fansteel Metallurgical Corp., 36 LA 570, 572 (Marshall, 1960); International Paper Co., 33 LA 719, 721 (Hawley, 1959); Continental Paper Co., 24 LA 723, 724 (Pfaus, 1955); Medart Co., 18 LA 701, 711–12 (Klamon, 1952). Past practice supported the claimed right to lateral movement in *Picker X-Ray Corp.*, 42 LA 179, 181–82 (Nichols, 1964). Seniority may not be disregarded by calling a promotion a merit increase. Bestwall Gypsum Co., 43 LA 475, 481 (Marshall, 1964).

[854]For such holdings, see *Diversitech Gen.*, 90 LA 562, 563 (DiLeone, 1988) (fact that company had past practice of disallowing bids to lower classifications could not overcome unambiguous language of contract and evidence showing union had never concurred with company's policy); *Bowater Lumber Co.*, 77 LA 421, 423–24 (Ferguson, 1981); *Continental Conveyor & Equip. Co.*, 55 LA 270, 272–74 (Hayes, 1970) (employee must have a reasonable motive rather than "whim or fancy" for the move); *Kellogg Co.*, 55 LA 89, 91 (King, 1970); *Steel Prods. Eng'g Co.*, 47 LA 952, 954–55 (Altrock, 1966) (fact that senior employee was needed more in present job could not defeat his right to fill vacancy by transfer); *Glamorgan Pipe & Foundry Co.*, 44 LA 10, 11–12 (Crawford, 1965); *Southern Bakeries Co.*, 41 LA 329, 331 (Marshall, 1963); *Yardley Plastics Co.*, 40 LA 1305, 1307–08 (McIntosh, 1963); *Howard Indus.*, 38 LA 371, 373 (Slavney, 1962); *Personal Prods. Corp.*, 36 LA 785, 785–86 (Cahn, 1961). *But see* Lakewood Bd. of Educ., 90 LA 375, 376–77 (Graham, 1987); Caterpillar Tractor Co., 52 LA 733, 735–36 (Doyle, 1969) (contract construed to permit company to fill vacancies by lateral transfer but not to require it—clear language would be required to give employees a right of lateral transfer by seniority); Nashville Bridge Co., 48 LA 573, 575–76 (McPherson, 1967) (an express provision would be required to give employees an unqualified right to exercise seniority for downward movement); Bethlehem Steel Co., 44 LA 457, 458 (Gill, 1965) (absent a local practice permitting it, employee could not exercise seniority for lateral or downward movement); Pittsburgh Plate Glass Co., 44 LA 7, 8–9 (Woodruff, 1965); Continental Paper Co., 24 LA 723, 723–24 (Pfaus, 1955). In *Tenn-Tex Alloy & Chem. Corp.*, 43 LA 152, 157–59 (Hebert, 1964), the term "any open job" was narrowed in scope by past practice.

not only seniority but also even skill, ability, and physical fitness. The employees must obtain benefits at the bargaining table, not from arbitrators. Arbitrators are bound by the contract under which they are arbitrating.[855]

The right of management to promote employees, however, is frequently qualified by seniority provisions.

The general ruling is that, consistent with the terms of the agreement, management can consider skill, ability, and experience along with seniority in making promotions.[856] In *International Paper Co.*,[857] for example, the arbitrator upheld the employer's decision to adopt a "team concept" for one of its production lines instead of the traditional organization. The arbitrator concluded that the broad language of the agreement, which gave management the right to "reduce, alter, combine, transfer, assign or cease any job, department, or service,"[858] allowed the company to implement the team concept without consulting or bargaining with the union.

In *Conoco, Inc.*,[859] an employer was held to have properly denied an otherwise qualified employee promotion to a crane operator position where, after a psychological evaluation called into question his fitness for this stressful position, the employee declined to undergo further examination.[860] However, where an employer relied on a test that did not accurately reflect relative qualifications for promotion, and the employer did not take into account the grievant's successful performance history, the arbitrator ruled that the unsuccessful senior bidder was entitled to the promotion.[861] Similarly, where the tests administered by an employer in making promotion decisions were not directly related to the qualifications required for the job in question, the arbitrator ruled that the company could not deny promotions to employees based on the test results.[862]

---

[855]New Britain Mach. Co., 45 LA 993, 995–96 (McCoy, 1965). *See also* Department of Health, Educ., & Welfare, 68 LA 1178, 1179 (Schuman, 1977); Detroit Gasket & Mfg. Co., 50 LA 455, 457–58 (Jones, Jr., 1968); Caterpillar Tractor Co., 46 LA 562, 565 (Kates, 1966); Micro Precision Gear & Mach. Corp., 42 LA 165, 167–68 (Klein, 1964); Taft-Pierce Mfg. Co., 20 LA 835, 836 (Bailer, 1953); Parke Davis & Co., 17 LA 568, 569 (Beneduce, 1951). *Cf.* Lear Siegler, Inc., 75 LA 1298, 1299 (Weiss, 1980); Niagara County Cmty. Coll., 73 LA 90, 95 (Denson, 1979). In *Sun Oil Co.*, 52 LA 463, 468–69 (Abernethy, 1969), management could select a junior employee for temporary promotion to a supervisory job expressly excluded from the agreement. *See also* Brighton Corp., 68 LA 837, 838 (High, 1977).

[856]Ardco, 108 LA 326 (Wolff, 1997); Lehigh Portland Cement Co., 105 LA 860 (Baroni, 1995); Spontex, Inc., 105 LA 254 (Modjeska, 1995); Nordson Corp., 104 LA 1206 (Franckiewicz, 1995); Lafarge Corp., 104 LA 592 (Hoffmeister, 1995); Bowater, Inc., 103 LA 1000 (Nolan, 1994).

[857]107 LA 1042 (Hooper, 1996).

[858]*Id.* at 1048.

[859]102 LA 417 (Goodstein, 1994).

[860]*See also* Lion, Inc., 109 LA 19 (Kaplan, 1997) (company did not violate agreement when it required each applicant for warehouse position to have commercial driver's license, even though this arguably discriminated against older employees, where contract did not contain nondiscrimination clause and union failed to make out claim of discrimination); Hughes Aircraft Co., 107 LA 596 (Richman, 1996) (employer reasonably declined to permit employee to take promotion test where she had weight-lifting restrictions that precluded her from performing all normal job duties of that classification and vocational rehabilitation plan was based on permanent inability to perform lifting tasks of type required).

[861]Kansas City Power & Light Co., 104 LA 857 (Berger, 1995).

[862]GTE Tel. Operations, 103 LA 1205 (Duff, 1994).

The general problems encountered in the operation of "seniority" and "fitness and ability" clauses discussed in Chapter 14, "Seniority," apply here. There are, in addition, some other considerations that should be noted.

Temporary assignments to better jobs, such as may be made while incumbents are on vacation, may be held not to be promotions and thus not to require the application of contract seniority provisions governing promotions.[863] To require the recognition of seniority in such cases, it has been said, would impose a handicap and serious detriment to management in its direction of the workforce.[864] Moreover, it has been held that management may compel designated employees to accept temporary promotion against their will.[865]

In a case involving an alleged breach of the duty of fair representation, it was held that a union was blameless when it refused to pursue a grievance on behalf of an employee who attempted to decline a promotion.[866] The arbitrator ruled that because the contract allowed only the two most senior employees to "freeze" in their present positions rather than be promoted, the grievant, a less senior employee, was properly required to accept the promotion notwithstanding his reluctance to do so.

Management has not been permitted unilaterally to change qualifications customarily required for a job if the change would impair the right of senior employees to be promoted in accordance with the contract's promo-

---

[863]*See* Ex-Cell-O Corp., 85 LA 1190, 1194–95 (Statham, 1985); Container Corp. of Am., 84 LA 489, 493–96 (Nicholas, Jr., 1985); Copper Cities Mining Co., 24 LA 421, 423 (Prasow, 1955); Lukens Steel Co., 18 LA 932, 933 (D'Andrade, 1952); Castle Dome Copper Co., 17 LA 644, 646–47 (Prasow, 1951); Lukens Steel Co., 12 LA 584, 585 (D'Andrade, 1949); Wilson & Co., 5 LA 695, 696 (Lohman, 1946). *See also* Georgia Power Co., 72 LA 340, 344–46 (Chandler, 1979); La Favorite Rubber Mfg. Co., 70 LA 1048, 1050 (Collins, 1978); Westinghouse Elec. Corp., 45 LA 889, 890–91 (Cayton, undated); Vickers, Inc., 44 LA 274, 279–80 (Oppenheim, 1965); Cit-Con Oil Corp., 33 LA 348, 350–51 (Hebert, 1959); Shell Oil Co., 20 LA 202, 204 (Grant, 1953). *But see* Homestake Mining Co., 88 LA 614, 615–16 (Sinicropi, 1987); Bethlehem Steel Corp., 47 LA 549, 551 (Seward, 1966); West Va. Pulp & Paper Co., 20 LA 385, 393 (Copelof, 1953). For cases concerned with the application of "fitness and ability" requirements of seniority provisions in temporary promotions, see *WITCO Chem. Co.*, 38 LA 108, 110–11 (Daugherty, 1961); *Great Atl. & Pac. Tea Co.*, 28 LA 733, 734–35 (Emery, 1957); *Lockheed Aircraft Serv.*, 21 LA 228, 231 (Warren, 1953).

[864]Wilson & Co., 5 LA 695, 696 (Lohman, 1946).

[865]*See* Tastybird Foods, 88 LA 875, 877–79 (Goodstein, 1987); Elastic Stop Nut Corp., 27 LA 877, 879–80 (Justin, 1956); Michigan Seamless Tube Co., 24 LA 132, 135–36 (Ryder, 1955); Phillips Oil Co., 18 LA 798, 801 (Howard, 1952). *See also* Jones & Laughlin Steel Co., 16 LA 767, 769 (Cahn, 1951). *But see* Electric Metallurgical Co., 20 LA 281, 282 (McCoy, 1953); Pittsburgh Plate Glass Co., 8 LA 317, 323 (Blair, 1947). In *Bethlehem Steel*, 37 LA 1099, 1102–03 (Valtin, 1962), the arbitrator concluded that employees could be required to accept temporary promotion but not permanent promotion. For cases holding that management could require senior employees to accept permanent promotion, see *American Cyanamid Co.*, 75 LA 346, 352–53 (May, 1980); *Warner & Swasey Co.*, 43 LA 1011, 1015–17 (Seinsheimer, 1964); *Gisholt Mach. Co.*, 23 LA 105, 108–09 (Kelliher, 1954). In *Ethan Allen, Inc.*, 78 LA 343, 346 (Kasper, 1982), the agreement provided that employees "desiring consideration for a vacancy shall sign their names" at a specified place, and "the right to bid for a vacancy necessarily entails the right to not bid, unless . . . there is language to limit the exercise of that contractual right."

[866]Lyondell Petrochemical Co., 104 LA 108 (Baroni, 1995).

tion clause.[867] Management also may not hold a successful bidder on the old job beyond a reasonable time to train his or her replacement.[868]

B. Transfer of Employees

i. Management's Right to Transfer [LA CDI 100.08; 120.01]

The general rule regarding the right of management to transfer employees was stated by one arbitrator as follows: "Unless restricted by agreement, law, custom, practice, or estoppel, management has the right to effect transfers as a necessary element in the operation of its business."[869] The arbitrator also considered the right to transfer to be included within the right to direct the workforce.[870]

Some agreements explicitly recognize management's right to transfer. While such agreements sometimes make the transfer right subject to other terms of the agreement, it appears that arbitrators generally require any restriction on the right to be clearly stated.[871] However, management's right to transfer will be restricted to the extent that a limitation is necessary to preserve contractual rights of employees.[872] Thus, for instance, an employer could not require employees to transfer to service outside the unit covered by the collective bargaining agreement, for they otherwise might be stripped of

---

[867]*See* Kuhlman Elec. Co., 26 LA 885, 890–91 (Howlett, 1956); Bridgeport Gas Co., 26 LA 289, 291 (Stutz, 1956); Pennsylvania Salt Mfg. Co., 14 LA 12, 16 (Frohlich, 1949). *See also* Corn Prods. Ref. Co., 20 LA 142, 146–47 (Gilden, 1953).

[868]Columbus Bolt & Forging Co., 35 LA 215, 220 (Stouffer, 1960).

[869]Chrysler Corp., 6 LA 276, 281 (Wolff, 1947). *See also* City of Marion, 91 LA 175, 179–81 (Bittel, 1988); Midland Brick & Tile Co., 77 LA 49, 55 (Newmark, 1981); Dwyer Instruments, 75 LA 498, 503 (Van Pelt, 1980); Doces Sixth Ave., 68 LA 386, 389–90 (Beck, 1977); Sanilac County Rd. Comm'n, 52 LA 252, 254–55 (Howlett, 1969); Henry Vogt Mach. Co., 49 LA 1115, 1117 (Gibson, 1968); Lamb Elec., 46 LA 450, 454–55 (Klein, 1966); Sandia Corp., 40 LA 879, 888 (Gorsuch, 1963); ARO, Inc., 39 LA 1074, 1078–79 (Murphy, 1962); Diamond Portland Cement Co., 35 LA 162, 167 (Teple, 1960); Phillips Petroleum Co., 34 LA 179, 180 (Doyle, 1960); McCord Corp., 30 LA 290, 292 (Sembower, 1958); Bethlehem Steel, 28 LA 437, 438 (Seward, 1957); Blaw Knox Co., 23 LA 159, 162 (Reid, 1954); Gisholt Mach. Co., 23 LA 105, 107 (Kelliher, 1954); General Baking Co., 14 LA 83, 86 (Feinberg, 1950); Acme Boot Mfg. Co., 9 LA 442, 443 (Hepburn, 1948).

[870]Chrysler Corp., 6 LA 276, 281 (Wolff, 1947). *See also* Bruno's, Inc., 81 LA 382, 383 (Foster, 1983); Gas Serv. Co., 33 LA 219, 223 (Stockton, 1959); Lewisburg Chair Co., 24 LA 399, 400 (Donnelly, 1955); Gisholt Mach. Co., 23 LA 105, 107 (Kelliher, 1954).

[871]*See* Adams Bus. Forms, 76 LA 516, 519 (Eisler, 1981); Giant Stores, 74 LA 909, 910, 915 (Larney, 1980); Giant Tiger Super Stores Co., 45 LA 206, 209–10 (Williams, 1965); Kollmorgen Corp., 44 LA 111, 113–14 (Fallon, 1965); Combustion Eng'g, 42 LA 911, 915 (Dunlop, 1964); J-M Poultry Packing Co., 36 LA 1433, 1437 (Morvant, 1961); Borden Mfg. Co., 25 LA 629, 634 (Wettach, 1955); Bradley Lumber Co. of Ark., 23 LA 456, 459 (Singletary, 1954); National Co., 23 LA 67, 75 (Copelof, 1954); Curtiss-Wright Corp., 11 LA 139, 142–43 (Uible, 1948); Ingalls Iron Works Co., 8 LA 26, 29 (Wagner, 1947).

[872]*See* Corte Constr. Co., 48 LA 463, 470–75 (Lugar, 1967); Bethlehem Steel Co., 42 LA 809, 814 (Hughes, 1964); McGraw-Edison Co., 40 LA 961, 964–65 (Stouffer, 1963). In *Sohio Chem. Co.*, 44 LA 624, 628 (Witney, 1965), permitting two employees to trade positions was held to violate the intent, if not the letter, of contractual provisions for job bidding; the arbitrator added that the employer could not have ordered the trade. *See also* City of Mt. Pleasant, Mich., Sch. Dist. 76 LA 1062, 1065–66 (Brooks, 1981).

rights under the agreement and be required to work under conditions over which they have no control.[873]

A transfer may be effected when the employer requires employees to rotate among jobs within their classification,[874] move from one shift to another,[875] move from one job to another in a different classification in the same job class,[876] move to a new machine on the same job,[877] or move to a new location for the same job.[878]

In the absence of a contract provision to the contrary, it has been held that the employer's right to transfer workers is not conditioned on the willingness of the workers to be transferred,[879] and that the employer has the right to determine whether a transfer is temporary or permanent.[880] Moreover, management has been held to have the right and duty to transfer an employee if his or her presence in a given occupation creates some undue hazard for the employee or others.[881] Various other justifications similarly have been accepted by arbitrators in upholding transfers required by management.[882] However, the right to transfer as a form of discipline is seldom allowed.[883]

---

[873]Corte Constr. Co., 48 LA 463, 470–75 (Lugar, 1967) (citing other cases in support of the arbitrator's conclusions). *See also* J.L. Clark Mfg. Co., 68 LA 448, 453 (Fields, 1977).

[874]Simmons Co., 25 LA 194, 198 (Elson, 1955). *Cf.* Olin Mathieson Chem. Corp., 50 LA 1061, 1066 (Talent, 1968).

[875]Midland Rubber Co., 18 LA 590, 595 (Cheney, 1952). *See also* Wash/Clipper Corp., 69–2 ARB ¶8610 (Graff, 1969). Employees have no right to exercise their seniority for shift preference unless the right clearly exists under a contract provision or past practice. *See* Midland Brick & Tile Co., 77 LA 49, 54–55 (Newmark, 1981); Dwyer Instruments, 75 LA 498, 502, 504 (Van Pelt, 1980); Dorsey Trailers, 49 LA 527, 529 (Pointer, 1967); Darling & Co., 44 LA 718, 719 (Doyle, 1965); Meramac Mining Co., 38 LA 103, 104 (Updegraff, 1962); International Minerals & Chems. Corp., 36 LA 92, 94–95 (Sanders, 1960) (past practice was shown); Kuhlman Elec. Co., 19 LA 199, 200 (Platt, 1952).

[876]Bethlehem Steel, 28 LA 437, 437–38 (Seward, 1957).

[877]Gisholt Mach. Co., 23 LA 105, 107 (Kelliher, 1954). *See also* Republic Steel Corp., 37 LA 591, 593 (Stashower, 1961).

[878]Phillips Petroleum Co., 34 LA 179, 180 (Doyle, 1960).

[879]*See* City of Marion, 91 LA 175, 179 (Bittel, 1988); Tastybird Foods, 88 LA 875, 879 (Goodstein, 1987); Doces Sixth Ave., 68 LA 386, 389–90 (Beck, 1977); ARO, Inc., 39 LA 1074, 1078–79 (Murphy, 1962); Diamond Portland Cement Co., 35 LA 162, 167 (Teple, 1960); Bethlehem Steel, 28 LA 437, 438 (Seward, 1957); Lewisburg Chair Co., 24 LA 399, 400 (Donnelly, 1955). *See also* National Ass'n for the Advancement of Colored People, 73 LA 372, 375–76 (Goldsmith, 1979); Wurlitzer Co., 44 LA 1196, 1201 (Kahn, 1965).

[880]Jones & Laughlin Steel Corp., 23 LA 33, 36 (Cahn, 1954). For some possible tests for distinguishing between permanent and temporary transfer, see *Continental Can Co.*, 37 LA 386, 388–89 (Sembower, 1961).

[881]International Shoe Co., 14 LA 253, 255 (Wallen, 1950). *See also* Bethlehem Steel Corp., 64 LA 380, 381 (Strongin, 1975); Mason & Hanger-Silas Mason Co., 50 LA 476, 487 (Guse, 1968); Sinclair Research, 49 LA 649, 651 (Teple, 1967); McLouth Steel Corp., 35 LA 103, 105, 109 (Siegel, 1960). *Cf.* McDonnell Co., 48 LA 533, 538–39 (Coles, 1967).

[882]*See* Northern States Power Co., 79 LA 203, 207 (Flagler, 1982); Madison Metro. Sch. Dist., 69 LA 1138, 1142 (Weisberger, 1977) (personality clash); Van Huffell Tube Corp., 49 LA 346, 350–51 (Teple, 1967) (personality clash between employee and foreman); Southwestern Bell Tel. Co., 45 LA 229, 233 (Williams, 1965) (incompetence); Brown Shoe Co., 40 LA 1025, 1027 (Holly, 1963) (need for more direct supervision of indifferent employees). But the justification for involuntary transfer was not accepted in *Laurel Highlands Sch. Dist.*, 76 LA 562, 565 (Talarico, 1981); *Mississippi Power & Light Co.*, 38 LA 838, 846–47 (Wissner, 1962).

[883]*See* Parkside Manor, 53 LA 410, 413 (Belcher, 1969); City of Stamford, 49 LA 1061, 1062 (Johnson, 1967); Consolidated Foods Corp., 47 LA 1162, 1163–64 (Kelliher, 1967); Connecticut Chem. Research Corp., 30 LA 505, 506 (Stutz, 1958); Allegheny Ludlum Steel Corp.,

ii. Disabled Employees [LA CDI 120.03]

One recurrent problem is whether an employee with a disability that prevents him or her from performing his in-classification job may or must be transferred to another classification, the duties of which the employee is able to perform. In *Minnegasco, Inc.*,[884] the arbitrator considered whether a company that had placed a disabled employee on a leave of absence because it determined it could not reasonably accommodate her in her present position should have transferred her temporarily to another classification out of contract-mandated seniority order instead. Although the union agreed to waive the contractual transfer restriction, the company declined to do so. The arbitrator ruled that the company had properly excluded the grievant from her present position on the basis of her disability, and that it had no obligation under external law to waive the bargained-for contract provisions governing temporary transfers.

In *Alcoa Building Products*,[885] the employer did attempt to accommodate a disabled employee who was certified as able to return to work with limitations on lifting, by displacing a successful bidder from a job that did not require heavy lifting. Relying on pertinent EEOC guidelines, the arbitrator ruled that the company had no duty under the ADA, and no right under the collective bargaining agreement, to rescind the promotion awarded to the successful bidder.

The issue in *Dinagraphics, Inc.*[886] was whether an employer could disqualify an employee from his electrician position and permanently transfer him to an inspector position because he suffered from arthritic gout, which prevented him from performing his electrician duties satisfactorily. The arbitrator concluded that because the contract was silent on the issue, the employer, as a matter of inherent prerogative, had the right to transfer an employee who could not perform the job for which he was being paid, and the employee was not entitled to retain his former position under the ADA.

iii. Seniority [LA CDI 120.10]

Sometimes a transfer is made for the purpose of training an employee to operate another type of equipment. In *Arcata Graphics Distributing Corp.*,[887] the arbitrator considered whether, in the absence of a contractual provision, an employer can temporarily transfer a senior employee from his preferred shift in order to train him on a different machine. The contract provided that

---

26 LA 546, 549 (Montgomery, 1956); Mosaic Tile Co., 16 LA 922, 926 (Stashower, 1951). *See also* Area Educ. Agency 12, 72 LA 916, 927 (Sembower, 1979). *Cf.* Bruno's, Inc., 81 LA 382, 383 (Foster, 1983).

[884]103 LA 43 (Bognanno, 1994).

[885]104 LA 364 (Cerone, 1995). *See also* Ralphs Grocery Co., 109 LA 33 (Kaufman, 1997) (company violated contract by permitting employees at one facility to bid on interim jobs at another facility, where agreement permitted multifacility bidding only on annual basis).

[886]102 LA 947 (Paolucci, 1994). For related discussion, see Chapter 10, section 3.A.iii, "Americans With Disabilities Act."

[887]102 LA 961 (Hart, 1994).

the employer was required to cross-train employees but was silent on whether seniority affected training assignments. Since the machine in question was not being operated on the grievant's regular shift, and the grievant was promptly returned to his preferred shift following the training, the arbitrator concluded that the company's action was reasonable and taken in good faith, and so denied the grievance.

Seniority, moreover, does not control transfers to fill newly created positions where the contract requires only that seniority be followed when a vacancy occurs in an existing job.[888]

iv. Pay Rate [LA CDI 120.201 et seq.]

Sometimes employees who have been temporarily transferred to another, more highly rated position do not perform all the duties of the new position. In cases where the temporary transferee does not perform the "core functions" of the new position, the transferee has been held not to be entitled to the higher rate.[889] However, where the employee is transferred to a new position (e.g., a setup person), but assigned responsibilities consistent with those of a higher-rated job (e.g., a "leadman"), the company is required to pay the wage rate of the higher classification.[890]

21. DEMOTION OF EMPLOYEES

A. Management's Right to Demote [LA CDI 100.70; 119.801 et seq.]

The collective bargaining agreement may specifically recognize management's right to demote employees, or the right may be held to be included with a general management-rights clause such as, for example, one giving management the right to select, assign, and direct the workforce and to promote and transfer employees.[891] The right may be held to remain in management, except as restricted by the agreement, as a residual power.[892] In many cases, the arbitrator does not expressly state any particular source of the right to demote, but merely upholds management's decision if it has acted on some reasonable basis in making a demotion.[893]

---

[888]Flat River Glass Co., 102 LA 842 (Maniscalco, 1994).

[889]Escalade Sports, 108 LA 781 (Witney, 1997); Ottawa Truck, 107 LA 844 (Murphy, 1996).

[890]Capitol Mfg. Co., 102 LA 865 (Duda, Jr., 1994).

[891]Drug Prods. Co., 10 LA 804, 805 (Naggi, 1948). See also Southern Ind. Gas & Elec. Co., 100 LA 160, 162 (Euker, 1992); Delphi Body Works, 83 LA 276, 278 (Roomkin, 1984); Roper Corp., 78 LA 1160, 1163 (Jaffe, 1982); General Elec. Co., 71 LA 479, 480, 487 (Bridgewater, 1978); Weyerhaeuser Co., 51 LA 192, 195 (Whyte, 1968); Lehigh Portland Cement Co., 66–3 ARB ¶9060 (Duff, 1966); Hart's Food Stores, 43 LA 934, 934, 938 (France, 1964).

[892]See E.I. DuPont de Nemours & Co., 17 LA 580, 585 (Cornsweet, 1951). See also Alpha Portland Cement Co., 71 LA 659, 666 (Leeper, 1978); Weyerhaeuser Co., 51 LA 192, 195 (Whyte, 1968); WLEU Broad. Co., 7 LA 150, 152 (Whiting, 1947).

[893]See, e.g., Midland-Ross Corp., 76 LA 1161, 1163–64 (Falcone, 1981); Southwestern Bell Tel. Co., 55 LA 1025, 1027–29 (Seinsheimer, 1970); Montgomery Ward & Co., 48 LA 429, 437 (Gorsuch, 1967); Ideal Cement Co., 45 LA 793, 796 (King, 1965).

The right to demote, however, has been held to be subject to the limitation that it may not be exercised in an arbitrary, capricious, or discriminatory manner.[894]

B. Management's Right to Demote Contracted Away
[LA CDI 100.70; 119.801 et seq.]

The right to demote sometimes has been found to have been contracted away. Such was the case, for instance, under a clause providing that wage rates fixed by the contract should be continued during the term of the contract, because the contractual wage rates were established on the basis of specific individuals.[895] A clause requiring promotions to be made on the basis of ability and seniority was interpreted to require the same for demotions on the ground that otherwise the promotion clause would be meaningless as employees could be demoted immediately after promotion.[896] Management also was denied the right to demote under an agreement that was silent with respect to demotion, but that provided permanent job status for employees surviving a trial period on the job. The employer was required to lay off employees in slack periods rather than to demote.[897]

C. Disciplinary Demotions [LA CDI 100.5509; 118.02]

Some arbitrators have held that management may not use demotion as a form of discipline unless the agreement specifically so provides, because such action would violate the contract seniority rights of the employees.[898] It

---

[894]*See* Safeway Stores, 73 LA 497, 504 (Goodman, 1979); Alpha Portland Cement Co., 71 LA 659, 666 (Leeper, 1978); Batesville Mfg. Co., 55 LA 261, 268–70 (Roberts, 1970); Weyerhaeuser Co., 51 LA 192, 195 (Whyte, 1968); Koppers Co., 49 LA 663, 665 (Malkin, 1967); Machine Prods. Co., 26 LA 245, 248 (Hawley, 1956); General Refractories Co., 24 LA 470, 483 (Hale, 1955); Bell Aircraft Corp., 19 LA 671, 673 (Shister, 1952).

[895]National Vulcanized Fibre Co., 3 LA 259, 263 (Kaplan, 1946). *See also* Western Air Lines, 9 LA 419, 421 (Aaron, 1948).

[896]Raytheon Mfg. Co., 15 LA 291, 295 (Healy, 1950). *See also* Gold Circle Disc. Foods, 67 LA 1315, 1316 (McIntosh, 1976); Batesville Mfg. Co., 55 LA 261, 267–70 (Roberts, 1970); General Refractories Co., 24 LA 470, 483 (Hale, 1955). *Cf.* Bell Aircraft Corp., 19 LA 671, 673 (Shister, 1952).

[897]Merrill-Stevens Dry Dock & Repair Co., 10 LA 88, 90 (McCoy, 1948). *See also* Armstrong Bros. Tool Co., 65 LA 258, 260 (Daugherty, 1975) ("[H]owever unreasonable in general it might seem to deny to management its traditional right to demote or permanently transfer an employee for proper cause, the Arbitrator is compelled to hold that under the language of this particular Agreement agreed to by both Parties, this particular Company's management did not possess said right . . . .").

[898]Gaylord Container Corp., 107 LA 1139 (Allen, Jr., 1997). *See* Thompson Bros. Boat Mfg. Co., 55 LA 69, 72–73 (Moberly, 1970); Duquesne Light Co., 48 LA 1108, 1111 (McDermott, 1967) (also noting the view that disciplinary demotion may be viewed as an indeterminate sentence that has no terminal point and may go far beyond the extent of the penalty warranted by the infraction committed); Allied Tube & Conduit Corp., 48 LA 454, 456 (Kelliher, 1967); National Carbide Co., 47 LA 154, 157–58 (Kesselman, 1966); Albert F. Goetze, Inc., 47 LA 67, 73 (Rosen, 1966); H.K. Porter Co., 46 LA 1098, 1105 (Dworkin, 1966); American Steel & Wire Co., 6 LA 379, 382 (Blumer, 1946). *See also* Blaw-Knox Co., 33 LA 108, 110 (Reid, 1959); Machine Prods. Co., 26 LA 245, 247–48 (Hawley, 1956). *Cf.* Firestone Tire & Rubber Co., 74 LA 565, 567–68 (Whyte, 1980); Wagner Castings Co., 74 LA 80, 86–87 (Talent, 1980); Diamond Nat'l Corp., 39 LA 1143, 1147 (Altieri, 1963). Arbitrators have reached different conclusions as to whether disciplinary demotion is permitted under a clause giving the right to "demote" for "cause." *See* Lukens Steel Co., 42 LA 252, 254 (Crawford, 1963) (not permitting it); Macomber, Inc., 37 LA 1061, 1063–64 (Updegraff, 1961) (permitting it).

was held in one case, for instance, that management did not have the right to use temporary demotion as a means of discipline for negligence in job performance (as opposed to lack of ability to perform the job), where such discipline was not provided for specifically by the agreement and where the demoted employee's position was temporarily filled by a junior employee in contravention of the seniority clause. The arbitrator said:

> The company's right to discipline flows from the general managerial prerogatives recognized in the management clause. In accordance with established legal construction, the exercise of such general prerogatives is limited by the specific clauses in the labor agreement. Thus, management in exercising its general prerogatives lacks the contractual right to abridge designated contractual privileges of the employees covered by the agreement unless specific provision is made for [such] . . . .[899]

Management also has been denied the right to discipline an employee by demotion where the contract gave the employer the right to discipline employees by various specified means that did not include demotion, on the theory of expressio unius est exclusio alterius.[900] Management likewise has not been overruled in demoting an employee for occasional carelessness or failure to obey instructions. The arbitrator distinguished between a lack of ability and temporary poor performance, but recognizing that some form of discipline should be imposed in such a case.[901]

Disciplinary demotions of two security guards were set aside by an arbitrator as violating the contract that stated that disciplinary actions shall include (from the least to most severe) written warning, suspension, and termination. Pointing out that inclusion of specific items, as a general rule, means nonlisted items are excluded, the arbitrator went on to state that upholding of demotions would constitute an impermissive addition to the contract.[902]

However, management has been held justified in using demotion as a form of discipline where the employee's refusal to obey a work order was typical of his uncooperative attitude, and the contract did not set out any

---

[899]American Steel & Wire Co., 6 LA 379, 382 (Blumer, 1946).

[900]*See* Reynolds Alloys Co., 2 LA 554, 555 (McCoy, 1943). *See also* Allied Tube & Conduit Co., 48 LA 454, 456 (Kelliher, 1967); H.K. Porter Co., 46 LA 1098, 1105 (Dworkin, 1966); International Harvester, 14 LA 882, 883 (McCoy, 1950). *But see* Southwest Petro-Chem, 92 LA 492, 495–96 (Berger, 1988) (while the company was foreclosed from demoting employee for disciplinary action under the contract, if the employee's misconduct would have warranted termination, the company could have exercised leniency by allowing the employee to return at a lower grade level). See also Chapter 9, section 3.A.xi., "The Mention of One Thing Is the Exclusion of Another."

[901]Republic Steel Corp., 25 LA 733, 735 (Platt, 1955). *See also* American Nat'l Can Co., 95 LA 873, 877–80 (Borland, 1990); Cook Paint & Varnish Co., 70 LA 195, 197–98 (Keefe, 1978) (quoting a textbook discussion of distinctions between "careless work" and "incompetence"); Thompson Bros. Boat Mfg. Co., 55 LA 69, 73 (Moberly, 1970); Bethlehem Steel Co., 28 LA 330, 332 (Valtin, 1957). In *Greater Cleveland Regional Transit Authority*, 71 LA 27, 28 (Young, 1978), applicable Merit System Rules permitted discharge or discipline for acts of "misfeasance, malfeasance, or nonfeasance," but also expressly permitted disciplinary demotion rather than discharge where the offending employee "is considered worthy of a trial in a lower grade."

[902]Mason & Hanger-Silas Mason Co., 96 LA 1150, 1159 (Anthony, 1991).

particular methods of discipline.[903] In addition, the demotion of the employee was affirmed where it was deemed necessary as a safety measure.[904]

One arbitrator expressed the view that demotion *for a fixed period* should be available to management as a disciplinary measure whenever the employee would be subject to disciplinary suspension:

> Although I am aware that some arbitrators have expressed the opinion that demotion is an inappropriate disciplinary response, I cannot accept this view. If an employer can suspend an employee for disciplinary reasons, it logically follows that the employer has the right to suspend such an employee from his regular job and place him in a lower rated job for disciplinary reasons. Indeed, . . . the collective agreement in this matter specifically provides that the employer may relieve an employee from duty "for other legitimate reasons." However that may be, a disciplinary demotion, like a suspension, should be for a definite period of time if it is to be corrective discipline rather than mere punishment.[905]

Finally, it has been emphasized that if demotion is used as discipline, the contract's procedural requirements for discipline must be met.[906]

D. Nondisciplinary Demotions: Lack of Qualifications
[LA CDI 119.805]

In considering an agreement that was silent on the matter of demotion for lack of qualifications, an umpire stated that it may be assumed that, in the interest of achieving optimum performance, management may make periodic or sporadic appraisals of its employees and demote those whose performance falls below standard. Elaborating, he said:

> We may assume further that the obligation to perform satisfactorily is a continuous condition of the maintenance of the better job and that an employee's performance, though once adequate, may fall below standard and merit demotion, either because his own performance has deteriorated or, though it has not deteriorated, because the standard in his occupation has been raised by the greater ability of those around him. Such a demotion would be an instance of

---

[903]Lewers & Cooke, 30 LA 542, 545 (Cobb, 1958). *See also* Asplundh Tree Expert Co., 84 LA 1207, 1211–15 (Smith, 1985) (grievant's entire record, especially his hostile attitude toward employer, justified demotion); Eastern Airlines, 46 LA 1034, 1038–39 (Yagoda, 1966); Diamond Nat'l Corp., 39 LA 1143, 1147 (Altieri, 1963); Copeland Refrigeration Corp., 8 LA 923, 924 (Lehoczky, 1947) (the arbitrator did not speak of "discipline" but the demotion was clearly disciplinary).

[904]*See* Iowa Power, 97 LA 1029, 1031–32 (Thornell, 1991); Archer, Daniels, Midland Processing Co., 91 LA 9, 14 (Cerone, 1988); Santiam S. Corp., 68 LA 46, 50–51 (Mann, Jr., 1977); Bethlehem Steel Corp., 64 LA 380, 381 (Strongin, 1975); United Parcel Serv., 61 LA 765, 768 (Steele, 1973); Paperworkers Local 86, 61 LA 617, 621 (Somers, 1973) (permitting temporary demotion, possibly to become permanent); Braniff Airways, 29 LA 487, 488–89 (Yeager, 1957); Connecticut Power Co., 18 LA 457, 458–59 (Donnelly & Mottram, Curry dissenting, 1952). *See also* Denison Mines, 68 LA 613, 617–18 (O'Shea, 1977); Northwest Natural Gas Co., 36 LA 1038, 1041 (Tongue, 1961); Carnegie-Illinois Steel Corp., 17 LA 328, 329 (Morgan, 1951).

[905]Libby, McNeill & Libby of Can., 74 LA 991, 998 (O'Shea, 1980).

[906]Alexander's Mkts., 51 LA 165, 168, 170 (Levin, 1968). *See also* Firestone Tire & Rubber Co., 74 LA 565, 568 (Whyte, 1980).

the Company's continuing interest in the satisfactory performance of each of its jobs.[907]

Following that reasoning, arbitrators continue to uphold nondisciplinary demotions where an employee is found to lack the qualifications for the job,[908] or if an employee's performance on a new job fails to meet management's standards.[909]

In downgrading for lack of qualifications shortly after an employee begins performing a different job, management may be required to show by substantial proof that the employee is not qualified and cannot qualify for the job within a reasonable time.[910] Where an employee has occupied a job

---

[907]Ford Motor Co., Opinions of the Umpire, Opinion A-30, at 1 (1943). In *Wheatland Tube Co.*, 66 LA 247, 248 (Feldman, 1976), the arbitrator stated the general proposition as follows: "The Company must maintain its competitive place in the market. If the Company was forced to keep incompetent personnel, there would be no jobs for anyone. Management is charged with the efficient operation of the facility. One of the elements of maintaining that efficiency is to remove inefficient personnel." Also permitting demotion for incompetence or lack of qualifications: Delphi Body Works, 83 LA 276, 278 (Roomkin, 1984); Safeway Stores, 73 LA 497, 505–06 (Goodman, 1979); Southwestern Bell Tel. Co., 55 LA 1025, 1028–29 (Seinsheimer, 1970); Beatrice Foods, 54 LA 998, 1007 (McKenna, 1971) (employee found unqualified at the end of a trial period on a new job has no right to continue in the new job, but, pusuant to contract authorization, must be returned to former job); Weyerhaeuser Co., 51 LA 192, 195 (Whyte, 1968); Duquesne Light Co., 48 LA 1108, 1111–12 (McDermott, 1967); Montgomery Ward & Co., 48 LA 429, 437 (Gorsuch, 1967); Lehigh Portland Cement Co., 66–3 ARB ¶9060 (Duff, 1966); Union Oil Co. of Cal., 47 LA 1001, 1009 (Block, 1966); Ideal Cement Co., 45 LA 793, 796 (King, 1965); H.K. Porter Co., 44 LA 1180, 1181 (McCoy, 1965); Huffman Mfg. Co., 38 LA 882, 886–87 (Stouffer, 1962); Curtiss-Wright Corp., 9 LA 77, 80 (Uible, 1947); Warren City Mfg. Co., 7 LA 202, 225 (Abernethy, 1947). *See also* Witherup Fabrication & Erection Co., 74 LA 906, 909 (May, 1980); St. Regis Paper Co., 74 LA 896, 901 (Harter, 1980) ("outlasting" the probationary period "does not mean that an employee has a job for life regardless whether he is competent"; the discharge of an employee who had refused the employer's offer of a less demanding job was upheld); Columbus Dispatch Printing Co., 47 LA 1015, 1017 (Platt, 1966); Owl Drug Co., 10 LA 498, 508 (Pollard, 1948) (demotion for incompetence permitted under contract permitting demotion for "cause").
   As between demotion or discharge of unqualified employees, an arbitrator may consider demotion to be the solution that gives fair consideration to the legitimate interests of both management and the employee. *See* Northwest Airlines, 53 LA 357, 360 (Sembower, 1969) (involving formerly qualified employees whose abilities had deteriorated); Hawaiian Tel. Co., 44 LA 218, 222–23 (Tsukiyama, 1965) (same); Times Publ'g Co., 40 LA 1054, 1060 (Dworkin, 1963) (same). For a like view where the employee does not perform satisfactorily after promotion, see *Public Library of Youngstown & Mahoning County*, 73 LA 20, 27–28 (Klein, 1979); *Alden's Shopper's World*, 46 LA 539, 543–44 (Kamin, 1966); *Convair Div.*, 34 LA 860, 863 (Schedler, 1960). *Cf.* United Centrifugal Pumps, 77 LA 60, 65–66 (Griffin, 1981). For the related discussion of failure to meet production standards, see section 7., "Production Standards, Time Studies, and Job Evaluation," above. For other related discussion, see section 26., "Disqualifying Employees for Physical or Mental Reasons," below.
   [908]Cabell Huntington Hosp., 105 LA 980 (Bethel, 1995) (demotion upheld where employee failed to achieve national certification even though the certification was only an employer-mandated, not a state-mandated, requirement).
   [909]NATCO L.P., 102 LA 771 (Marcus, 1994) (inability to get along with other supervisors and inability to manage valid reasons to demote newly appointed supervisor).
   [910]United Aircraft Prods., 10 LA 143, 146 (Wardlaw, 1948). *See also* Batesville Mfg. Co., 55 LA 261, 269–70 (Roberts, 1970); Flintkote Co., 51 LA 1300, 1302–03 (Nicholas, Jr., 1968); Braniff Airways, 38 LA 861, 864–65 (Shister, 1962); Applied Arts Corp., 35 LA 545, 548 (Howlett, 1960). *Cf.* McGraw-Edison Co., 79 LA 1006, 1010–11 (Kubie, 1982); General Elec. Co., 71 LA 479, 487–88 (Bridgewater, 1978) ("the Union did not sustain its burden of proving that the Grievant did not, in fact, receive a full break-in," or "its burden of proving that the removal [of Grievant from the] classification for inability was inappropriate").

for a long period of time, it has been held that management must show that the employee is no longer able or willing to perform the job duties.[911] However, the mere fact that an employee has been retained in a job for a number of years does not necessarily warrant a finding by the arbitrator that the employee was qualified for it.[912]

A lack of qualifications has been found by an arbitrator, and demotion therefore considered justified, for example, where a truck driver's operator's license was revoked,[913] the employee was unable to perform the job duties satisfactorily,[914] the employee was physically or psychologically unable to perform the job duties or was unable to perform them safely,[915] and a leadman displayed racial prejudice in a plant employing many black workers.[916] In the latter instance, the arbitrator said that the employee's prejudice "made it clear he could no longer do an effective job as leadman."[917] One arbitrator,

---

[911]Dewey & Almy Chem. Co., 25 LA 316, 322 (Somers, 1955). *See also* Archer, Daniels, Midland Processing Co., 91 LA 9, 12–13 (Cerone, 1988); Foodland Supermarket, 87 LA 92, 96–99 (Ling, 1986); Alpha Portland Cement Co., 71 LA 659, 666 (Leeper, 1978); Thompson Bros. Boat Mfg. Co., 55 LA 69, 73 (Moberly, 1970); United States Steel Corp., 48 LA 67, 68–69 (McDermott, 1966); General Refractories Co., 24 LA 470, 484 (Hale, 1955); North Am. Aviation, 17 LA 784, 789 (Komaroff, 1952). For cases dealing with the necessity for warning the employee that his or her work is poor, see *Alpha Portland Cement Co.*, 71 LA 659, 666 (Leeper, 1978); *Beatrice Foods*, 54 LA 998, 1008–09 (McKenna, 1971); *Standard Oil Co.*, 25 LA 32, 36 (Burris, 1955); *Hiram Walker & Sons*, 18 LA 447, 449 (Kelliher, 1952); *North Am. Aviation*, 17 LA 784, 789 (Komaroff, 1952).

[912]E.I. DuPont de Nemours & Co., 17 LA 580, 586–87 (Cornsweet, 1951). *See also* J.R. Simplot Co., 53 LA 1181, 1192 (Simon, 1969); U.S. Borax & Chem. Corp., 36 LA 970, 973–74 (Keeler, 1961); American Radiator & Standard Sanitary Corp., 29 LA 167, 170 (Duff, 1957).

[913]Virginia-Carolina Chem. Corp., 18 LA 892, 895 (Hepburn, 1952). In *J.A. McMahon Co.*, 44 LA 1274, 1277–79 (Dworkin, 1964), an employee's physical condition made him uninsurable and this was a "legitimate" reason for placing him on layoff status under the contract.

[914]*See* Penn Traffic Bi-Lo Mkts., 91 LA 1087, 1088–89 (Duff, 1988); Kinlock Coal Co., 71 LA 1232, 1235 (Clarke, 1979); Titanium Metals Corp., 49 LA 1144, 1147 (Block, 1967); Koppers Co., 49 LA 663, 665 (Malkin, 1967); Hart's Food Stores, 43 LA 934, 938 (France, 1964); Pittsburgh Metallurgical Co., 41 LA 40, 46 (Willingham, 1963) (employee could not do all elements of job due to fear of heights); American Radiator & Standard Sanitary Corp., 29 LA 167, 170 (Duff, 1957); Chance Vought Aircraft Corp., 27 LA 682, 684 (Wolff, 1956); Machine Prods. Co., 26 LA 245, 248 (Hawley, 1956); Robertshaw-Fulton Controls Co., 24 LA 745, 746 (Morris, 1955); E.I. DuPont de Nemours & Co., 17 LA 580, 586–87 (Cornsweet, 1951). *See also* Midland-Ross Corp., 76 LA 1161, 1163–64 (Falcone, 1981).

[915]*See* Crucible, Inc., 80 LA 28, 28 (Strongin, 1982) (management "is not required to keep on the job an employee who cannot perform 100 percent of it"); Roper Corp., 78 LA 1160, 1163 (Jaffe, 1982); J.R. Simplot Co., 53 LA 1181, 1192 (Simon, 1969); Youngstown Sheet & Tube Co., 47 LA 146, 150 (Killingsworth, 1966); Gulf States Utils. Co., 44 LA 1252, 1263 (Murphy, 1965); Bethlehem Steel Co., 42 LA 137, 138 (Porter, 1964); Gulf States Utils. Co., 41 LA 519, 523 (Autrey, 1963); United States Steel Corp., 41 LA 112, 116–17 (Tripp, 1963); Republic Steel Corp., 38 LA 105, 107 (Ryder, 1962); U.S. Borax & Chem. Corp., 36 LA 970, 973–74 (Keeler, 1961); Jersey Cent. Power & Light Co., 7 LA 560, 563–64 (Copelof, 1947). *See also* Southern Bell Tel. & Tel. Co., 55 LA 1206, 1214 (Davey, 1970) (demotion upheld though failure to take required training course was due to employee's nervous condition). *Cf.* Eastern Shore Pub. Serv. Co., 39 LA 107, 110–13 (Horlacher, 1962) (demotion based primarily on workers' compensation medical reports and award). In *Simoniz Co.*, 54 LA 172, 174–75 (Talent, 1971), an employee claimed (unsuccessfully) a contractual right to demotion on the basis of his alleged physical condition.

[916]North Am. Aviation, 20 LA 789 (Komaroff, 1953). In *Pacific Gas & Electric Co.*, 48 LA 264, 266 (Koven, 1966), a service man who made improper advances to a female customer could be demoted from his public-contact job.

[917]North Am. Aviation, 20 LA 789, 794 (Komaroff, 1953).

however, refused to permit the company to demote an employee for lack of qualifications where the company was aware of the employee's shortcomings at the time of his promotion but promoted him in spite of them. The promotion was not made on a trial basis, and the employee's work was no worse after the promotion than it had been before.[918]

Disciplinary demotions for poor performance may be reviewed under general standards of "reasonableness," rather than the traditional "just cause" criteria. Accordingly, any disciplinary demotion must be supported with proof that the employee was performing poorly and had been warned of the poor performance.[919]

Contracts that authorize a demotion penalty may provide that it may be imposed only consistent with just cause principles.[920]

E. Seniority

The role of seniority in determining whether employees can voluntarily demote themselves into a lower job classification is unclear. Some arbitrators hold that seniority may be used by employees to voluntarily demote themselves into a lower job.[921] Others have held that the right to voluntarily demote oneself into a lower job is not an inherent incident of seniority but must be expressly provided for in the contract.[922]

22. DISCIPLINE AND DISCHARGE

The right of management to discipline or discharge employees has been dealt with extensively by arbitrators and is a subject to which a separate chapter is devoted in this book. For discussion of discharge and discipline the reader is directed to Chapter 15., "Discipline and Discharge."

For discussion of nondisciplinary termination of employees, see section 25., "Compulsory Retirement" and section 26., "Disqualifying Employees for Physical or Mental Reasons," below.

23. MERIT INCREASES [LA CDI 114.483]

Merit rating is concerned not with what an employee does but with how the employee does it. Thus, it may be immaterial that some employees re-

---

[918]Bethlehem Steel, 18 LA 368, 369 (Feinberg, 1951). *See also* National Coop. Ref. Ass'n, 37 LA 973, 975 (Emery, 1961). For cases dealing with how long a period management may be permitted to determine the fitness of an employee who has been promoted, see *Kimco Auto Prods.*, 49 LA 669, 672 (Owen, 1967); *Smith Scott Co.*, 48 LA 270, 272 (Burns, 1966).

[919]GES Exposition Servs., 108 LA 311 (Levy, 1997); Regional Transp. Dist., 104 LA 1201 (Yehle, 1995); Stein Printing Co., 101 LA 553 (Byars, 1993).

[920]Avis Rent a Car Shuttlers, 105 LA 1057 (Wahl, 1995) (just cause principles allowed employer to temporarily, but not permanently, demote employee who had engaged in sexually offensive behavior).

[921]Tetra Pak, 108 LA 470 (Fowler, 1997).

[922]Alltel Fla., 101 LA 799 (Thornell, 1993).

ceive a higher rate than others doing the same work.[923] Furthermore, in determining eligibility for merit increases, there is no presumption of progress or improvement due solely to the passage of time.[924]

The collective bargaining agreement may make specific provision for merit increases.[925] In this regard, one arbitrator observed:

> It is well established that merit increases are an appropriate subject for collective bargaining, and bargaining thereon frequently results in contractual provisions establishing objective standards for merit increases or fixing a regular review period or making such increases subject to review or negotiation by the union, or other types of such provisions.[926]

Another arbitrator held that, where the contract specifically allows management to make discretionary "overscale payments," management may grant individual employees a merit increase without bargaining with the union.[927]

Where a collective bargaining agreement specified minimum wage rates for classifications and provided for a 10-cent-per-hour premium over the rates shown "for an employee in any of such classifications who achieves and applies a high degree of proficiency in all phases of his work, as determined by the Employer," the arbitrator held that this specific provision for rewarding meritorious service implied that it was the only means of giving individual merit increases without negotiations.[928] The arbitrator also expressed the view that, absent a clause expressly giving management such right, management cannot unilaterally give individual increases under any agreement that contains a wage schedule.[929] However, other arbitrators have upheld

---

[923]CIT Mental Health Servs., 89 LA 442 (Graham, 1987); Bethlehem Steel, 21 LA 614, 616 (Feinberg, 1953); International Harvester Co., 14 LA 77, 79 (Seward, 1948). For arguments against permitting merit increases, see *American Bakeries Co.*, 68 LA 414, 417 (Schatzki, 1977). On the question whether merit increases may terminate when the employee transfers to a different job, see *Whittaker Corp.*, 63 LA 193, 196 (Rybolt, 1974) (past practice controlled the result).

[924]Ralph C. Coxhead Corp., 21 LA 480, 483 (Cahn, 1953). In *Koehring Co.*, 65 LA 638, 640 (Coyne, 1975), the arbitrator stressed that, "A 'merit' pay raise means just that. It is something awarded a person for meritorious service. It is not a right to which one is entitled by virtue of his presence on the payroll." In contrast, in considering a "longevity related" compensation system in *Morris, Bean & Co.*, 69 LA 615 (Ruben, 1977), the arbitrator stated:

> [T]he Company argues that longevity related compensation systems intrinsically presuppose that an employee will continue regularly working at his job increasing in skill and experience over time and thereby becoming more valuable to his employer. This view is reinforced where . . . the parties provide that employees must work a specified percentage of the available working time in order to qualify for the periodic wage increases.

Id. at 620. *See also* Beloit Corp., 64 LA 547, 548 (Cox, 1975). *Cf.* Medalist Indus., 57 LA 503, 509 (Solomon, 1971).

[925]Davis Co., 41 LA 932, 933 (Holly, 1963) (the arbitrator emphasized that the word "merit" implies increases, not decreases, in pay under a clause authorizing management to fix wages of individual employees "on a basis of merit").

[926]Sommers & Adams Co., 6 LA 283, 285 (Whiting, 1947).

[927]Anderson Wood Prods. Co., 104 LA 1017 (Cocalis, 1995).

[928]J. Gruman Steel Co., 54 LA 521, 522, 524–25 (Somers, 1971). *See also* Valve Corp. of Am., 48 LA 869, 871–72 (Johnson, 1967).

[929]J. Gruman Steel Co., 54 LA 521, 525 (Somers, 1971). *See also* Morris, Bean & Co., 69 LA 615, 621 (Ruben, 1977); Frito-Lay, 42 LA 426, 428–29 (Lee, 1964). Even where a unilateral right of management to give merit increases on an individual basis is conceded, this does not include the right to give a blanket increase to a group of employees. Atlanta Newspapers, 43 LA 758, 759–60 (King, 1964). As to group increases, see also *Champion Parts*

such increases where the contract provided only for "minimum rates of pay" and contained no restrictions on management's right to pay higher rates.[930]

However, in another case, the arbitrator rejected a union contention that merit increases were no longer a matter of unilateral determination by management (as they had been by past practice) after minimum and maximum salary ranges were written into the collective bargaining agreement. The arbitrator explained:

> It should be noted that the subject of merit increases has long been an appropriate subject for collective bargaining. Therefore, a Union is within its rights when it seeks to negotiate contractual provisions that will eliminate an existing merit wage increase program, modify it, or that will establish contractual procedures for the operation of any such program. However, if the Union fails to negotiate such contractual provisions, it is not within the power of an arbitrator, absent mutual permission of the parties, either to abolish an existing merit increase system or to write procedures into the contract as to how such system will be administered.
>
> . . .
>
> . . . [W]hat the Union negotiated into the 1968 contract was a set of rate ranges to apply to salaried workers in the bargaining unit. Nothing was agreed to that relates to how individual employees would move from the bottom job rate in his class to the upper limit. In the absence of any such contractual language, and in view of the past practice that has prevailed at this plant, this determination still remains a function of management. In such circumstances the conclusions of management with respect to the granting of specific merit increases are not generally subject to successful challenge in arbitration unless it can be shown in individual cases that management acted unfairly, arbitrarily, discriminatorily, or completely unreasonabl[y]. This has long been the generally-held principle in arbitration. Thus, the negotiation of the rate ranges did not, as the Union contends, eliminate the merit increase system. The very presence of a rate range requires either that the maximum rate be achieved through a prescribed procedure, usually referred to as automatic progression, or in the absence of joint agreement on such procedure, the movement from bottom to top remains subject to the evaluation of management.
>
> There is no right in the existing agreement for the Union to insist that the Company negotiate individual merit increase cases. The most that can be required is that, given the requirement in Paragraph 2 of the intent to establish a harmonious relationship, the Company has the obligation to discuss cases with the Union and to explain the Company position. It does not have to secure Union agreement, and it retains the right to make the final determination. As long as that determination was not arbitrary, unfair, discriminatory or very unreasonable it is not subject to being overruled.[931]

Rebuilders, 73 LA 599, 602 (Carson, 1979); *International Harvester Co.*, 65 LA 178, 181 (Caraway, 1975); *Elkhart Brass Mfg. Co.*, 62 LA 1036, 1039–40 (Thomson, 1974). In *NLRB v. C&C Plywood*, 385 U.S. 421, 64 LRRM 2065 (1967), the contract expressly recognized management's right to give individual merit increases but this did not include the right to give group increases. The case concerned the duty to bargain under the NLRA. For further discussion, see section 2.A.i., "The Duty to Bargain: Right of Unilateral Action," above.

[930]Coffeyville Flour Mill, 100 LA 561 (Hendrix, 1992); CIT Mental Health Servs., 89 LA 442 (Graham, 1987).

[931]H.K. Porter Co., 55 LA 593, 595–96 (McDermott, 1970). In *Means Stamping Co.*, 46 LA 324, 326 (Cole, 1966), the contract stated maximum and minimum rates for classifications and it was held that management could not give merit increases that would result in rates above the specified maximum.

Many other arbitrators have similarly recognized that where the collective bargaining agreement contains no provision regarding the granting of merit increases, or where it makes provision for merit increases without stating by whom the initial determination is to be made, the determination of when individual employees should be given merit increases still remains the function of management.[932] However, one arbitrator has observed that when merit increases are not permitted under the contract but wage differentials based on "special aptitude or competitive situations" are, special aptitude increases must be made on a case-by-case basis, and that the process may not be used as a guise for merit increases.[933]

Where management has the right to make the determination regardless of the source of the right, it appears clear that its conclusions in regard to merit increases are not generally subject to successful challenge in arbitration unless unfair, arbitrary, or discriminatory,[934] or unless the decision is based on a misconception of existing facts or insufficient evidence.[935] In this general connection, an arbitrator stated:

> [M]erit is difficult to prove and the parties themselves, through daily observation of the employee, have usually gained greater knowledge of the employee's abilities and efficiency than the Umpire can ever have. In the absence of de-

---

[932]*See* Washington Aluminum Co., 41 LA 314, 315 (Seidenberg, 1963); United Eng'g & Foundry Co., 40 LA 143, 145–46 (Wood, 1963); Bethlehem Steel, 21 LA 614, 616 (Feinberg, 1953); Parke Davis & Co., 17 LA 568, 569–70 (Beneduce, 1951); National Lock Co., 15 LA 180, 181–82 (Luskin, 1950); Union Starch & Ref. Co., 15 LA 4, 12 (Townsend, 1950); Consolidated Vultee Aircraft Corp., 10 LA 678, 680 (Updegraff, 1948); Warren City Mfg. Co., 7 LA 202, 217 (Abernethy, 1947); Sommers & Adams Co., 6 LA 283, 285 (Whiting, 1947); Atlas Imperial Diesel Engine Co., 3 LA 1, 3 (Gorder, 1946). *See also* C.F. Mueller Co., 75 LA 135, 137 (Light, 1980); VS Evansville State Hosp., 74 LA 1090, 1093, 1095 (Deitsch, 1980); City of Danville, Ill., 70 LA 403, 408 (Fish, 1978); Taylor-Winfield Corp., 45 LA 153, 155–56 (Kates, 1965); H.J. Scheirich Co., 40 LA 411, 413 (Porter, 1963); Wetter Numbering Mach. Co., 14 LA 96, 102 (Cahn, 1950). This right may be held to be included within a general management-rights clause (*see* Pet Frozen Foods Div., 73 LA 181, 194 (Erbs, 1979); McInerney Spring & Wire Co., 9 LA 91, 94–95 (Platt, 1947)), or it may be given specifically to management by the agreement (*see* Bethlehem Steel, 26 LA 824, 826 (Seward, 1956); Supermatic Prods. Corp., 14 LA 139, 142 (Bernstein, 1950)).

[933]Meuer, Inc., 1998 WL 1033311 (Daniel, 1998).

[934]*See* Pet Frozen Foods Div., 73 LA 181, 184 (Erbs, 1979); Veterans Admin. Reg'l Office, 70 LA 514, 517–18 (Denson, 1978); Social Sec. Admin., 69 LA 1239, 1242 (Kaye, 1977); Wisconsin Dep't of Indus., Labor, & Human Relations, 64 LA 663, 667–68 (Marshall, 1975); Kansas City Power & Light Co., 60 LA 852, 856–57 (Allen, Jr., 1973); Koppers Co., 50 LA 296, 298 (Cayton, 1968); Crouse-Hinds Co., 48 LA 606, 608 (Kates, 1967); Cerro Copper & Brass Co., 47 LA 126, 128 (Altrock, 1966); Union Metal Mfg. Co., 40 LA 452, 454–56 (Stouffer, 1962); United Eng'g & Foundry Co., 40 LA 143, 146 (Wood, 1963); Burger Iron Co., 39 LA 799, 800 (McIntosh, 1962); Bethlehem Steel, 21 LA 614, 616 (Feinberg, 1953); Ralph C. Coxhead Corp., 21 LA 480, 482–83 (Cahn, 1953) (criteria used by management was considered in evaluating eligibility for merit increases); Supermatic Prods. Corp., 14 LA 139, 143 (Bernstein, 1950); Consolidated Vultee Aircraft Co., 10 LA 678, 680 (Updegraff, 1948); McInerney Spring & Wire Co., 9 LA 91, 95–96 (Platt, 1947); Warren City Mfg. Co., 7 LA 202, 217 (Abernethy, 1947).

[935]Bethlehem Steel Co., 21 LA 614, 616 (Feinberg, 1953); Atlas Imperial Diesel Engine Co., 3 LA 1, 4 (Gorder, 1946). In *Dahlstrom Mfg. Corp.*, 39 LA 90, 92 (Duff, 1961), the contract expressly required management to state its reason for refusing a merit increase; the arbitrator said that this "strongly implies that Management's reason must not be arbitrary, capricious or discriminatory. When challenged in Arbitration, the Company should show that its reason is based on evidence and standards that are reasonable, demonstrable and objective." *See also* Wisconsin Dep't of Indus., Labor, & Human Relations, 64 LA 663, 668 (Marshall, 1975).

tailed proof, a third party is generally not in a position to determine whether an employee has demonstrated increased efficiency or whether the quality of his work has improved. It is recognized that that determination can best be made by the employee's supervisor, who is closest to the employee in these matters.[936]

Where discipline is taken into consideration by management in making performance evaluations, an employer was held to have rightfully denied a merit increase to an employee who was suspended for sexual harassment.[937] Under certain circumstances, management may be required to review employee merit ratings at reasonable intervals. This was the result under an agreement that, in providing for merit increases, gave management the right to make initial determinations but required management to be "fair,"[938] and it also was the result under another agreement that permitted the company to determine merit increases subject only to the restriction that the determination not be arbitrary or capricious.[939] Of course, as noted above, the contract may specifically provide for periodic review of each employee's rate and record.[940]

24. Bonuses [LA CDI 114.45]

The question of the right of management, in the absence of contractual limitation, unilaterally to eliminate or alter bonus practices remains unsettled.[941]

In cases where the facts indicated that the bonus had become an integral part of the wage structure, thus constituting a deferred wage payment, arbitrators have held that management may not eliminate or alter bonus plans unilaterally, despite the fact that bonuses were not mentioned in the contract.[942] The presence of several or all of the following types of evidence

---

[936]Bethlehem Steel Co., 21 LA 614, 616 (Feinberg, 1953). *See also* Veterans Admin. Reg'l Office, 70 LA 514, 517–18 (Denson, 1978); Dahlstrom Mfg. Corp., 39 LA 90, 92 (Duff, 1961) ("Management's discretion must be heavily relied upon because no other rule is practicable."); Ralph C. Coxhead Corp., 21 LA 480, 483 (Cahn, 1953); Pacific Airmotive Corp., 16 LA 508, 509 (Warren, 1951); Supermatic Prods. Corp., 14 LA 139, 143 (Bernstein, 1950).

[937]Consolidated Edison Co. of N.Y., 113 LA 342 (Jensen, 1999).

[938]International Harvester Co., 13 LA 809, 812 (Seward, 1949).

[939]Bethlehem Steel, 26 LA 824, 826 (Seward, 1956).

[940]*See* Domore Office Furniture, 58 LA 817, 818 (Ray, 1972); Pacific Airmotive Corp., 16 LA 508, 508–09 (Warren, 1951). For related discussion, see Chapter 14, section 7.D.v., "Merit Rating Plans." *See also* University Med. Ctr., 114 LA 28 (Bogue, 2000) (a wrongfully discharged employee was not entitled to a back-pay award of merit pay for the period covering his discharge, because there was no evidence that the employee met performance standards that would qualify him for a merit increase; however, the company was required to evaluate the employee during the 6-month period following his reinstatement, in order to ascertain whether he qualified for a post-reinstatement merit increase).

[941]For important related materials, see Chapter 12, section 1., "Custom and Practice as a Term of the Contract."

[942]*See* H. Phillips Co., 69 LA 1250, 1254 (Lee, 1977); Advance Die Casting Co., 65 LA 810, 815 (Gundermann, 1975); Sioux Tools, 64 LA 571, 575 (Fitzsimmons, 1975); American Air Compressor Corp., 62 LA 637, 639 (Kerrison, 1974); Stepan Chem. Co., 45 LA 34, 37–38 (Anrod, 1965); Tonawanda Publ'g Co., 43 LA 892, 894–96 (Seitz, 1964); Keystone Lighting

would tend to indicate that a bonus has become an integral part of wages: long usage; treatment by the company of bonus payments as relevant considerations during contract negotiations, in wage calculations (such as vacation pay), or in hiring; failure of the company to make it clear that the bonus was a gift or gratuity; stability and predictability of the amount of the bonus; relating the bonus to work performed by the employee; and payment of the bonus in such a way as to create an expectation by the employees at the end of the year.[943]

However, in cases where the facts indicated that the bonus was a gratuity given at the discretion of management and not paid as part of wages, management was permitted to alter or eliminate the bonus plan unilaterally in the absence of contractual restriction.[944] The presence of several or all of the following types of evidence would tend to indicate that the bonus is a

---

Corp., 43 LA 145, 149–51 (Horlacher, 1964); City Towel Serv., 42 LA 415, 416 (Ellmann, 1964); Metal Hose & Tubing Co., 41 LA 182, 184 (Berkowitz, 1963); Budd Co., 36 LA 1335, 1340 (Crawford, 1961); Pennsylvania Forge Co., 34 LA 732, 739–40 (Crawford, 1960); Nazareth Mills, 22 LA 808, 818–19 (Dash, Jr., 1954); Felsway Shoe Corp., 17 LA 505, 509–10 (Justin, 1951); Libby, McNeil & Libby, 5 LA 564, 571 (Prasow, 1946); Pullman-Standard Car Mfg. Co., 2 LA 509, 514 (Courshon, 1945); General Television & Radio Corp., 2 LA 483, 490 (McCoy, 1942). *See also* Monument Mills, 29 LA 400, 404 (Stutz, 1957) (involving contract clauses providing for payment of bonuses to employees); Pierce Governor Co., 25 LA 165, 170 (Sullivan, 1955) (same); Minnesota Min. & Mfg. Co., 15 LA 618, 622 (Lehoczky, 1950) (same). In *Continental Carbon Co.*, 114 LA 1263 (Chumley, 2000), the arbitrator found that a unilateral decision by management, without notice to the union, to cease paying a Christmas bonus that was not mentioned in the contract but which had been paid for 14 consecutive years, was an unfair labor practice under the NLRA and, implicitly, the union contract as well. Significantly, the new owners of the company continued the practice for 3 years after their acquisition, before unilaterally discontinuing it. The arbitrator posited that this was a perfect example of how to violate every rule of "managerial etiquette" in dealing with employees. The company was required to reinstate the Christmas bonus by the arbitrator. The case is an excellent illustration of the interplay between arbitration and the federal labor law on contract issues.

[943]See cases cited in note 942, above. Maintenance of benefits clauses have had some weight in some cases (*see* American Petrofina Co., 65–2 ARB ¶8464 (Emery, 1965); City Towel Serv., 42 LA 415, 416 (Ellmann, 1964); Metal Hose & Tubing Co., 41 LA 182, 184 (Berkowitz, 1963)), but not in others (*see* Great Atl. & Pac. Tea Co., 62 LA 209, 211 (Duff, 1974); Morningstar-Paisley, Inc., 42 LA 765, 766 (Stein, 1964); Telemetal Prods., 33 LA 139, 140 (Singer, 1959); American Lava Corp., 32 LA 395, 399–400 (Klamon, 1959)), depending on other supporting evidence.

[944]See Vulcan Iron Works, 79 LA 334, 336 (Williams, 1982); Proform, Inc., 67 LA 493, 496 (Render, 1976); Great Atl. & Pac. Tea Co., 62 LA 209, 211–12 (Duff, 1974); Beacon Journal Publ'g Co., 55 LA 329, 335–36 (Larkin, 1970); F.M. Stamper Co., 51 LA 533, 536–37 (Eaton, 1968); Indianapolis Union Printers, 46 LA 1077, 1078 (Small, 1966); Knomark, Inc., 46 LA 472, 472–73 (Singer, 1966); Morningstar-Paisley, Inc., 42 LA 765, 766 (Stein, 1964); Mid-State Steel, 42 LA 417, 419–20 (Russell, 1964); Midwest Dental Mfg. Co., 42 LA 331, 332–33 (Kelliher, 1964); White Baking Co., 38 LA 216, 217 (McIntosh, 1962); South Penn Oil Co., 34 LA 586, 592 (Duff, 1960); Telemetal Prods., 33 LA 139, 140 (Singer, 1959); American Lava Corp., 32 LA 395, 399–401 (Klamon, 1959); Rockwell Standard Corp., 32 LA 388, 392–93 (Duff, 1959); Bassick Co., 26 LA 627, 628–30 (Kheel, 1956); Cortland Baking Co., 25 LA 853, 855–56 (Kharas, 1955); National Distillers Prods. Corp., 24 LA 500, 506 (Delehanty, 1953); Andrew Williams Meat Co., 8 LA 518, 526 (Cheney, 1947); Renart Sportswear Corp., 6 LA 654 (Cahn, 1947). Under particular contract clauses providing for a bonus, a bonus may nevertheless be considered a gratuity. *See* General Controls Co., 10 LA 341, 344 (Cheney, 1948); Bastian-Morley Co., 3 LA 412, 418 (Epstein, 1946). In *T&M Rubber Specialties Co.*, 54 LA 292, 296–98 (Sembower, 1971), the arbitrator concluded that the bonus was not a gratuity but that he could not make an award in favor of the employees, because the amount for payment as bonuses had been determined by the board of directors in the past depending on "success of year"; he directed the parties to bargain on the matter.

gift: annual consideration and vote by the board of directors as to whether, when, and how much to pay; distribution of bonus checks separately from paychecks; variation in amount or nature of the bonus; payment to all employees without having previously announced a bonus plan; and statements posted by the company that bonus payments are discretionary and union acquiescence in some way to such statements.[945]

The right to a quality-based bonus does not follow employees who transfer to a new department even though these employees are producing a product similar to the type produced in the old department.[946] Furthermore, where a contract provides that bonuses are paid to those employees "actively at work," employees receiving sickness/accident benefits or workers' compensation benefits are not entitled to the bonuses.[947]

25. COMPULSORY RETIREMENT [LA CDI 116.43]

In the earlier cases on compulsory retirement on reaching a certain age, arbitrators often stated as a general principle that in the absence of specific contractual restriction, management had the right to establish compulsory retirement plans unilaterally. In some of these cases, the arbitrator expressly denied that compulsory retirement would violate the seniority or discharge provisions of the agreement.[948] However, in upholding compulsory retirement, these arbitrators usually emphasized the fact that the plan under consideration was longstanding; that it had been established and administered without objection from the union; and that it had been administered without arbitrariness, discrimination, or caprice.[949] However, where the collective

---

[945]See cases cited in note 944, above. *But see* Madison Warehouse Corp., 112 LA 300 (Suardi, 1998) (a contract that contained an express provision governing the payment of bonuses stated that they be paid on a corporatewide basis; arbitrator held that an equivocal statement by a union representative in response to a company representative's suggestion that certain employees' bonus calculations were going to be based on the performance of their plant alone (he purportedly said that the company's suggestion "made sense") was not sufficient to alter the historical "systemwide" way that the bonuses were calculated under the contract).

[946]Pretty Prods., 103 LA 1107 (Kindig, 1994).

[947]USS, Div. of USX Corp., 106 LA 193 (Neyland, 1995).

[948]*See* Todd Shipyards Corp., 27 LA 153, 156 (Prasow, 1956); General Aniline & Film Corp., 25 LA 50, 52–53 (Shister, 1955); Pan Am. Airways, 13 LA 326, 328–29 (Reynolds, 1949); Swift & Co., 9 LA 560, 561 (Gregory, 1946); American Salt Corp., 9 LA 124, 126 (Gorsuch, 1947); General Am. Transp. Corp., 7 LA 773, 778 (Ridge, 1947); Metals Disintegrating Co., 4 LA 601, 603–04 (Kirsh, 1946).

[949]See the cases cited in note 948, above. For cases in which the arbitrator emphasized these facts while not stating the aforementioned principle, see *H.D. Lee Co.*, 70 LA 245, 249–50 (Ferguson, 1978); *Pittsburgh-Des Moines Steel Co.*, 66 LA 1207, 1210–11 (Caraway, 1976); *Todd Shipyards Corp.*, 50 LA 645, 657 (Prasow, 1968); *Montgomery Ward & Co.*, 46 LA 302, 305 (Gilden, 1966); *Northwest Airlines*, 29 LA 541, 543–45 (Schedler, 1957); *Sandia Corp.*, 27 LA 669, 671 (Schedler, 1956); *Hercules Powder Co.*, 23 LA 214, 216–17 (Shipman, 1954); *International Minerals & Chem. Corp.*, 22 LA 732, 735–36 (Gilden, 1954); *Afro-American Co. of Balt.*, 17 LA 587, 589 (McConnell, 1951); *Ohio Steel Foundry Co.*, 14 LA 490, 491–92 (Lehoczky, 1950). In *United States Steel Corp. v. Nichols*, 229 F.2d 396, 399–400, 37 LRRM 2420 (6th Cir.), *cert. denied*, 351 U.S. 950 (1956), the company had a reasonable and nondiscriminatory policy of compulsory retirement going back some years. Then the parties bargained on the question of dealing expressly with the subject in the collective bargaining agreement. The court held that their failure to reach agreement did not deprive management of the right to compel an employee to retire under its policy and that the employer did

bargaining agreement likewise was silent as to compulsory retirement but where there was no established policy of compulsory retirement that had been accepted in practice by both parties, many arbitrators held that compulsory retirement violated the seniority, discharge, or discrimination provisions of the agreement.[950]

The previous existence of an established plan of compulsory retirement became even more significant on enactment of the ADEA. In the Supreme Court's *United Air Lines v. McMann*[951] decision in 1977, the ADEA was construed as still permitting compulsory retirement of persons covered by the ADEA (ages 40 through 64) *provided* the employer acted pursuant to a bona fide retirement plan that was in existence before passage of the ADEA.

However, Congress, by 1978 amendments to the ADEA, both (1) expanded the range of protected ages to 40 through 69,[952] and (2) expressly provided

---

not violate the collective bargaining agreement in doing so (the employee had alleged violation of the "proper cause" for discharge provision). For related discussion, see section 2.A.i., "The Duty to Bargain: Right of Unilateral Action," above. The *Nichols* case was discussed in *H.D. Lee Co.*, 70 LA 245, 248 (Ferguson, 1978); *Pittsburgh-Des Moines Steel Co.*, 66 LA 1207, 1210 (Caraway, 1976); *Beatrice Foods*, 55 LA 933, 935–37, 943 (Young, 1970); *Herman Nelson Div.*, 50 LA 1177, 1181 (Sembower, 1968); *Gran Columbiana*, 42 LA 559, 560–62 (Altieri, 1964); *Quick Mfg.*, 39 LA 1003, 1007–08 (Teple, 1962); *Hercules Powder Co.*, 37 LA 771, 775–76 (Jones, 1961); *Hale Bros. Stores*, 32 LA 713, 717–18 (Ross, 1959).

[950]*See* Putnam Hosp. Ctr., 87 LA 985, 989 (Altieri, 1986) (violated antidiscrimination provision of labor contract); Simpson Bldg. Supply, 73 LA 59, 62–63 (Chiesa, 1979) (the union did not have and could not be charged with knowledge of the employer's policy of compulsory retirement); Chicago Zoological Soc'y, 61 LA 387, 388 (Kelliher, 1973); Honeggers' & Co., 56 LA 251, 253–55 (Anrod, 1971); Beatrice Foods, 55 LA 933, 942–43 (Young, 1970); Cummins Power, 51 LA 909, 913–15 (Gorsuch, 1968); Consolidated Packaging Corp., 51 LA 46, 48–49 (Moore, 1968); Herman Nelson Div., 50 LA 1177, 1180–82 (Sembower, 1968) (contract was not silent but was ambiguous as to compulsory retirement); H.K. Porter Co., 49 LA 224, 227–28 (Block, 1967); Armour Agric. Chem. Co., 47 LA 513, 516–18 (Larkin, 1966) (past practice of compulsory retirement was not adequately shown, but even if shown the arbitrator stated it would violate seniority provisions of contract); Gran Columbiana, 42 LA 559, 561–62 (Altieri, 1964); Ingersoll-Rand Co., 42 LA 483, 489–90 (Scheiber, 1964) (most recent practice was not to compel retirement); Quick Mfg., 39 LA 1003, 1007–10 (Teple, 1962); Hercules Powder Co., 37 LA 771, 775–77 (Jones, 1961); Hunter Eng'g Co., 37 LA 350, 355 (Granoff, 1961); Western Air Lines, 33 LA 84, 87–88 (Schedler, 1959); Gordon Foods, 32 LA 1022, 1025 (Hepburn, 1959); Hale Bros. Stores, 32 LA 713, 717–19 (Ross, 1959); S.H. Kress & Co., 25 LA 77, 79–82 (Ross, 1955); Bloomfield Tool Corp. & Kidde Mfg. Co., 9 LA 921, 924–26 (Justin, 1948). Notwithstanding the significance that many arbitration cases have placed on the existence or absence of a longstanding and applied compulsory retirement policy in determining whether to uphold compulsory retirement, some cases have upheld management's unilateral institution of compulsory retirement (where the agreement did not expressly restrict the right) even though there was no established practice for it. *See, e.g.,* Packaging Corp. of Am., 40 LA 544, 546–47 (Beatty, 1963). *See also* Cook & Brown Lime Co., 50 LA 597, 600 (Rice, 1968); Brickle's Inc., 45 LA 500, 500–02 (Bell, undated).

[951]434 U.S 192, 195, 203, 16 FEP Cases 146 (1977) (the Court relied on §4(f)(2), and stated that it found "nothing to indicate Congress intended wholesale invalidation of retirement plans instituted in good faith before" passage of the ADEA).

[952]29 U.S.C. §631, which, however, also states an exception applicable to certain high-level executives who are not protected beyond age 64; subsection (d) of 29 U.S.C. §631 also originally stated an exception applicable to tenured college professors, but was repealed in 1993. See discussion below at note 955 and related text. The ADEA protects federal employees in general even at age 70 and above (see 29 U.S.C. §§631, 633a), but some must retire at a stated age, as in the case of air traffic controllers at age 56 and firefighters and law enforcement officers at age 55 (see 5 U.S.C. §8335). The Foreign Service Act of 1946 (the updated Foreign Service Act of 1980 is codified at 22 U.S.C. §3901 et seq.) requires persons covered by the Foreign Service retirement system to retire at age 60, a requirement upheld as to constitutionality in *Vance v. Bradley*, 449 U.S. 93, 19 FEP Cases 1 (1979). Employees of

that "no . . . plan shall require or permit the involuntary retirement of any individual . . . because of the age of such individual."[953]

In 1986, Congress further amended the ADEA by removing the 70-year age limitation applicable to employees protected under it.[954] With limited exceptions, for example, for persons in "a bona fide executive or a high policymaking position," compulsory retirement of employees 65 or older is prohibited.[955] In 1990, Congress amended the ADEA by enacting the Older Workers Benefit Protection Act.[956a] In 1993, Congress again amended the ADEA, this time by repealing a section that permitted institutions of higher learning to force professors over the age of 70 serving under a contract of unlimited tenure to retire.[956]

26. Disqualifying Employees for Physical or Mental Reasons[957]
[LA CDI 100.552565; 118.655]

A. Management Rights [LA CDI 100.552565; 118.655]

There are numerous reported arbitration decisions concerning managerial action in disqualifying employees for physical or mental reasons. While

---

state and local governments are covered by the ADEA, and the Supreme Court upheld the constitutionality of that coverage in *EEOC v. Wyoming*, 460 U.S. 26, 31 FEP Cases 74 (1983).

[953]29 U.S.C. § 623(f)(2), the amended ADEA §4(f)(2). Congress did specify a grace period within which compulsory retirement because of age would not be covered by the express prohibition in certain circumstances, the grace period to end by January 1, 1980. The January 1, 1980, termination of grace period came "three months too late to help Grievant escape his mandatory retirement at age sixty-five" in *Reynolds Metals Co.*, 74 LA 1121, 1123 (Welch, 1980). Sometimes protection beyond that accorded by the ADEA will be available from another source. For example, in *Magee-Women's Hosp.*, 62 LA 987, 990 (Joseph, 1974), a contractual prohibition against discrimination "on account of . . . age" was held equally applicable to all employees and not merely a parallel protection of employees covered by the ADEA; thus, the employer could not involuntarily retire an employee who was too old to be protected by the ADEA. In *Pepsi-Cola Bottlers*, 80 LA 752, 756 (Lieberman, 1983), it was concluded that the agreement's nondiscrimination clause was intended merely to make the agreement conform to federal law and did not bar compulsory retirement at age 70, but compulsory retirement nonetheless was barred by a pension plan that was made a part of the agreement and contemplated voluntary retirement only. Also, state law may protect against compulsory retirement because of age and place no age limit on the protection. *See, e.g.*, Alta Bates Hosp., 74 LA 278, 279–80 (Barsamian, 1980). In any event, an involuntarily retired employee may be required at least to "commence" proceedings under state law before going to federal court under the ADEA. *See* Oscar Mayer & Co. v. Evans, 441 U.S. 750, 19 FEP Cases 1167 (1979); Curto v. Sears, Roebuck & Co., 552 F. Supp. 891, 30 FEP Cases 1196, 1200–03 (N.D. Ill. 1982).

[954]29 U.S.C. §631(a).

[955]*Id.* §631(c). *See* Fairmont Gen. Hosp., 87 LA 137 (Bolte, 1986) (employer could not enforce mandatory retirement at age 70, where labor contract did not provide for mandatory retirement age; ADEA held inapplicable because the employee was 70 years of age and was not protected by the ADEA as it existed at that time). *See also* Putnam Hosp. Ctr., 87 LA 985, 989 (Altieri, 1986) (employer improperly discharged employee on her 70th birthday in violation of antidiscrimination provision of labor contract).

[956]29 U.S.C. §631(d) (repealed by Pub. L. No. 99-592, §6(b)).

[956a]Pub. L. No. 101-433, codified as amended at 29 U.S.C. §§623, 626, and 630.

[957]The material contained in this topic constitutes only a portion of the treatment of the subject. For other aspects, see Chapter 8, section 7.B., "Medical Evidence," and Chapter 16, section 7., "Employee Physical or Mental Condition as a Safety Hazard."

the disqualification often results in termination, it also may result in layoff, leave of absence, or a refusal to permit the employee to return to work following an accident or medical leave.

Management's right to terminate employees whose physical condition renders them unable or unfit to perform their job has been repeatedly affirmed,[958] as has been the termination of employees because of mental unfitness (psychiatric problems or mental illness) for work.[959] Termination because the employee's physical or mental condition rendered continued employment unduly hazardous to the employee or to others has been frequently upheld.[960]

---

[958]*See* Meier Metal Servicenters, 100 LA 816 (Morgan, Jr., 1993); Metropolitan Sports Facilities Comm'n, 92 LA 959 (Bognanno, 1989); Lucas W., Inc., 91 LA 1272 (Alleyne, 1988) (employer properly discharged employee who refused to do spray painting even though employer assigned work where employee did not have to lift arms above shoulders per doctor's orders); Mercy Convalescent Ctr., 90 LA 405 (O'Grady, 1988) (nursing home properly discharged employee suffering from conjunctivitis); Florida Power Corp., 87 LA 1213, 1220–21 (Singer, 1986); Phillip Morris, U.S.A., 87 LA 975, 977 (Flannagan, 1986); Papercraft Corp., 85 LA 962, 966 (Hales, 1985); Missouri Minerals Processing, 85 LA 939, 945 (Talent, 1985); National-Standard Co., 85 LA 401, 403 (Butler, 1985); Bethlehem Mines Corp., 84 LA 484, 488 (Hewitt, 1985); Porritts & Spencer, 83 LA 1165, 1168 (Byars, 1984); United States Steel Corp., 82 LA 913, 916 (Tripp, 1984). *See also* Agrico Chem. Co., 86 LA 799, 805 (Eyraud, 1985) (employer properly removed employee from light duty and placed him on involuntary medical leave); Mead Corp., 86 LA 201, 206 (Ipavec, 1985) (employee who accidentally inhaled chlorine gas and missed 2 years of work was properly denied vacancy in pulp mill job where employee still suffered symptoms and job required working with chlorine); Transportation Mgmt. of Tenn., 82 LA 671, 676 (Nicholas, Jr., 1984) (employer properly disqualified employee from position as commercial bus driver following heart attack). For related discussion, see section 21., "Demotion of Employees," above; Volz, *Health and Medical Issues in Arbitration, Employee Benefit Plans, and the Doctor's Office: I. Medical and Health Issues in Labor Arbitration*, in TRUTH, LIE DETECTORS, AND OTHER PROBLEMS IN LABOR ARBITRATION, PROCEEDINGS OF THE 31ST ANNUAL MEETING OF NAA 156 (Stern & Dennis eds., BNA Books 1979).

[959]Port of Tacoma, 96 LA 361 (Latsch, 1991); Safeway Stores, 94 LA 851 (Staudohar, 1990); East Ohio Gas Co., 91 LA 366 (Dworkin, 1988) (acute anxiety depression); Danly Mach. Corp., 87 LA 883, 886 (Cox, 1986) (multiple phobias); Savannah Transit Auth., 86 LA 1277, 1279–80 (Williams, 1985) (medication and emotional problems following death of spouse); Amoco Oil Co., 86 LA 929, 932 (Holman, 1985) (fear of fire and explosion). *But see* Pacific Bell, 91 LA 653 (Kaufman, 1988) (company failed to obtain current medical evidence on whether employee's diabetes was under control before discharging); Tenneco Oil Co., 83 LA 1099, 1104 (King, 1984) (company failed to prove that discharge was for just cause where employee's psychiatrist recommended 1-month absence from work). For cases in which mental illness was asserted as a mitigating factor in discharge for misconduct, see Algoma Steel Corp., 73 LA 1256, 1259 (O'Shea, 1979); *Allis-Chalmers Corp.*, 73 LA 1230, 1233–34 (Goetz, 1979); *Associated Press*, 49 LA 564, 568 (Sugerman, 1967); *Cities Serv. Ref. Corp.*, 39 LA 604, 606 (Coffey, 1962). For general discussions of these and related aspects, see Greenbaum, *The "Disciplinatrator," the "Arbichiatrist," and the "Social Psychotrator"—An Inquiry Into How Arbitrators Deal With a Grievant's Personal Problems and the Extent to Which They Affect the Award*, 37 ARB. J. No. 4, at 51 (1982); Cramer, *Arbitration and Mental Illness: The Issues, the Rationale, and the Remedies*, 35 ARB. J. No. 3, at 10 (1980).

[960]Sacramento Mun. Util., 91 LA 1073 (Concepcion, 1988); Union Oil Co. of Cal., 87 LA 612, 615 (Nicholas, Jr., 1986) (employee would be endangering his health by climbing to heights above 6 feet after cerebral hemorrhage and surgery); Peabody Coal Co., 84 LA 511, 515 (Duda, Jr., 1985) (large abdominal hernia a potential hazard to employee if reemployed); Spang & Co., 84 LA 342, 346 (Joseph, 1985) (return to heavy lifting duties would create high risk to employee with back problems); Chapter 16, section 7., "Employee Physical or Mental Condition as a Safety Hazard." *See also* National Rolling Mills, 84 LA 1144, 1150 (DiLauro, 1985); Owens-Illinois, 83 LA 1265, 1269 (Cantor, 1984); Mobile Video Servs., 83 LA 1009, 1012 (Hockenberry, 1984).

However, there are many cases in which the arbitrator required management to return an employee to work where the evidence indicated that the employee was not so affected or disabled as to be unable to perform the job satisfactorily or safely,[961] or medical evidence indicated that the employee had regained sufficient capacity to perform job duties at an average standard.[962] A similar result has been reached where the employee's condition had existed for a long period of time, during which the employee had performed satisfactorily and safely.[963] In one case, management could not terminate an employee who was physically handicapped when hired 17 years earlier, whose condition was not deteriorating, and who, though a slow worker, had not received any complaint from supervision as to his work.[964]

B. Americans With Disabilities Act [LA CDI 94.553; 100.30]

The ADA[965] creates new issues for employers and arbitrators. Under the ADA, employers are obligated to reasonably accommodate[966] a qualified in-

---

[961]Farm Fresh Catfish Co., 91 LA 721 (Nicholas, Jr., 1988) (dismissal for safety reasons improper, where based on single fainting incident on production floor); Metropolitan Sports Facilities Comm'n, 90 LA 868 (Bognanno, 1988) (improper to discharge maintenance worker who had performed job on limited basis for 5 years); Morgan Adhesives Co., 87 LA 1039, 1041–42 (Abrams, 1986) (reinstatement without back pay, where alcoholic employee had good work record and was pursuing medical and psychological treatment); Sperry Corp. Aerospace & Marine Group, 86 LA 520, 523 (Byars, 1986) (contract did not allow employer discretion to deny leave of absence based on employee's ability to work); Gase Baking Co., 86 LA 206, 211 (Block, 1985) (employer improperly denied employee's request to bump into position because of pulmonary problem, where that problem had caused employee to miss only 1 day of work over period of several years); Youngstown Hosp. Ass'n, 82 LA 31, 35 (Miller, 1983) (discharge disproportionate discipline for absenteeism; alcoholism as mitigating circumstance). See also Alton Packaging Corp., 83 LA 1318, 1322–23 (Talent, 1984); SCM Corp., 83 LA 1186, 1188 (Speroff, 1984); Manufacturing Co., 82 LA 614, 619 (Ray, 1984).

[962]Payless Stores, 95 LA 1 (Yarowsky, 1990).

[963]See True Temper Corp., 87 LA 1284 (Nicholas, Jr., 1986); Kaiser Steel Corp., 68 LA 192, 196 (Christopher, 1977); Magnavox Co., 46 LA 719, 723–24 (Dworkin, 1966); American Optical Co., 42 LA 818, 821–22 (Teple, 1964); United Gas Improvement Co., 40 LA 799, 804–05 (Lande, 1963). See also Dan-Van Rubber, 68 LA 217, 220 (Rothschild, 1977).

[964]American Optical Co., 42 LA 818, 821–22 (Telple, 1964).

[965]For recent analysis of the ADA in the context of collective bargaining, see Stewart, *The Impact of the Americans With Disabilities Act on Collective Bargaining Agreements* (presented at ABA Section of Labor & Employment Law, 1993 Mid-Winter Meeting); Stahlhut, *Playing the Trump Card: May an Employer Refuse to Reasonably Accommodate Under the ADA by Claiming a Collective Bargaining Obligation?*, 9 LAB. LAW. 71 (1993); Smith, *Accommodating the Americans With Disabilities Act to Collective Bargaining Obligations Under the NLRA*, 18 EMPLOYEE REL. L.J. 273 (Autumn 1992). For related discussion, see Chapter 10, section 3.A.iii., "Americans With Disabilities Act."

[966]42 U.S.C. §12111(9). A reasonable accommodation will vary with the circumstances but may include the following: making existing facilities readily accessible and usable, job restructuring, modifying work schedules, reassigning to a vacant position, acquiring/modifying equipment, modifying training materials/examinations/policies, and providing readers/interpreters. An employee's or applicant's need for such accommodations cannot be the basis for the employment decision.

dividual with a disability[967] unless such accommodation creates an undue hardship.[968]

Along these lines, a significant issue is the degree to which the rights of an employee with a disability are limited by the collective bargaining agreement. Another issue is how to apply the ADA in instances where the agreement specifically covers disabled employees but fails to specify what type of accommodations the employer must make. In one case, where the contract required an employer to place an employee who was incapacitated for regular work due to nonwork injury in "any work he can do," the arbitrator held that the term must be interpreted in harmony with the ADA's requirement that the employer make "reasonable accommodations" for employees with physical limitations.[969]

As the ADA has been developed further through litigation and interpretation by the courts and the EEOC, arbitral resolution of disability cases has undergone a sea change. Increasingly, arbitral decisions are informed by ADA case law, the statute's implementing regulations, EEOC guidelines, and parallel state laws.[970]

Arbitrators have repeatedly held that employers must reasonably accommodate employees who have physical or mental impairments, and have looked to the ADA for guidance.[971] The right to a reasonable accommodation has been found not only where the collective bargaining agreement expressly incorporates the ADA, or includes a nondiscrimination clause covering dis-

---

[967]*Id.* § 12111(8). A qualified person with a disability is an employee who satisfies the prerequisites of the position and is able to perform the essential functions of the job, with or without reasonable accommodations. A person with a disability is a person having any physical or mental impairment that substantially limits one or more of an individual's major life activities or if the person has a record of an impairment or is regarded as having an impairment (42 U.S.C. §12102(2)). A major life activity is defined as caring for oneself, performing manual tasks, walking, seeing, hearing, speaking, learning, breathing, working (29 C.F.R. §1630, 2(I)).

[968]42 U.S.C. §12111(10). An accommodation that would impose an "undue hardship" on the operation of the business is one requiring "significant difficulty or expense" and that does not include either a direct threat to safety or adjustments primarily for the personal benefit of the employee or applicant.

[969]Cleveland Elec. Illuminating Co., 100 LA 1039, 1043–45 (Lipson, 1993).

[970]Flamingo Hilton-Laughlin, 108 LA 545, 554–57 (Weckstein, 1997) (in determining whether employee was "disabled" and whether employer was required to restructure job as a reasonable accommodation, the arbitrator looked to the ADA's statutory language, regulations, and case law); Boise Cascade Corp., 105 LA 223, 229–32 (Michelstetter, 1995) (in determining employee's obligation to disclose physical impairment during medical examination, the arbitrator interpreted the ADA, regulations, case law, and the Minnesota Human Rights Act §363 and interpretive case law).

[971]Davis Wire Corp., 114 LA 1345, 1350 (Olson, Jr., 2000) (employer arbitrarily disqualified employee when it failed to seek clarification of employee's doctor's medical release and failed to provide a reasonable accommodation of a stool for employee to use occasionally, where doing so was reasonable). Courts also have had to consider the impact of collective bargaining agreement arbitration provisions on disability discrimination claims. *E.g.*, Maher v. New Jersey Transit Rail Operations, 125 N.J. 455, 539 A.2d 750, 59 FEP Cases 807 (1991) (plaintiff's failure to arbitrate his state law disability discrimination claim warranted dismissal).

ability,[972] but also under a general "just cause" provision.[973] In one case, where the union had invoked the ADA and the employer raised defenses available under the Act, the arbitrator applied the ADA because the contract contained a nondiscrimination clause and a conflict of law provision.[974]

Under contracts that specifically incorporate the protections provided by the ADA, arbitrators have held, in accord with the ADA, that the employer is required to offer a reasonable accommodation to qualified employees who would otherwise be unfit to perform their currently assigned duties.[975] Consistent with ADA precedent, however, arbitrators also have held that employers are not precluded from terminating a physically or mentally disabled employee where a proposed accommodation is refused or where the employee, with or without a reasonable accommodation, is not qualified to do the job.[976] Moreover, an employee's status as an alcoholic has not been found to excuse the employee's poor attendance or failure to satisfactorily meet performance standards, as long as the employee had not first requested an accommodation for such a condition.[977] The ADA contains specific language permitting employers to discipline employees whose performance problems result from alcohol or drug use on the same basis as other employees.[977a] At least one arbitrator has ruled, however, that under the ADA, a mentally impaired employee who obtained post-termination treatment, rendering the chance of relapse or recurrence negligible, was entitled to reinstatement.[978]

In the context of accommodation, at least one arbitrator has ruled that the employee was not a qualified individual with a disability because his restrictions against climbing and long periods of standing did not substantially limit major life activities.[979] Further, the employer had attempted to accommodate the employee by offering to reassign him to other jobs.[980] The

---

[972]Flamingo Hilton-Laughlin, 108 LA 545 (Weckstein, 1997) (reasonable accommodation required by nondiscrimination clause that explicitly incorporated ADA); Continental Cement Co., 107 LA 829 (Hilgert, 1996); AAFES Distribution, 107 LA 290 (Marcus, 1996); Boise Cascade Corp., 105 LA 223 (Michelstetter, 1995); Multi-Clean, Inc., 102 LA 463 (Miller, 1993).

[973]National Linen Supply, 107 LA 4 (Ross, 1996) (employer's ability to reasonably accommodate employee's condition incorporated into just-cause standard); Beckett Paper Co., 106 LA 1135 (Goggin, 1996) (same).

[974]GTE N., 113 LA 665, 672 (Brodsky, 1999).

[975]Davis Wire Corp., 114 LA 1345, 1350 (Olson, Jr., 2000); Multi-Clean, Inc., 102 LA 463 (Miller, 1993) (employer must ascertain whether a reasonable accommodation could be made to provide grievant with employment).

[976]Flamingo Hilton-Laughlin, 108 LA 545, 554 (Weckstein, 1997) (employer did not violate collective bargaining agreement by discharging employee, after employee refused to accept a new position offered as a reasonable accommodation, in light of the fact that such refusal rendered the employee ineligible as a "qualified individual with a disability" under the EEOC guidelines).

[977]Continental Cement Co., 107 LA 829 (Hilgert, 1996) (although alcoholism is a statutory disability under the ADA, employees must meet attendance and other work-performance obligations).

[977a]42 U.S.C. §12114(c)(4).

[978]AAFES Distribution, 107 LA 290 (Marcus, 1996) (employee who suffered from schizophrenic disorder was discharged without just cause despite obscene and abusive language, bizarre behavior, and unexcused absences, where her post-discharge treatment greatly reduced the chance of a relapse).

[979]GTE N., 113 LA 665, 672 (Brodsky, 1999).

[980]Id.

employee's refusal to accept reassignment and insistence on the employer creating a "special job" for him was considered unreasonable and such action was not required under the ADA because "the ADA does not require: 'creating a new job, moving another employee, promoting the disabled employee, or violating another employee's rights under a collective bargaining agreement.'"[981]

Arbitrators have also addressed physical and mental qualifications under collective bargaining agreements that neither expressly prohibit discrimination against disabled employees nor incorporate the ADA. For example, just-cause discharges have been upheld where, despite the employer's provision of the requested reasonable accommodation, the employees could not perform the essential functions of their jobs.[982] This requirement (i.e., that disabled employees be able to perform, with or without a reasonable accommodation, the essential functions of their positions) is included in the express language of the ADA.

The ADA provides that where an employee poses a direct threat to the health or safety of others that cannot be eliminated with reasonable accommodation, the employee is not qualified to perform his essential job functions.[983] In one case, the summary discharge of an employee with a psychiatric disorder that triggered outbursts against coworkers was upheld because the misconduct was so egregious that it rendered the employee unfit to work.[984] Discharges of employees addicted to alcohol or illegal drugs have been upheld where the employees were deemed medically unfit because of their failure to comply with a rehabilitation program.[985]

---

[981]*Id.* at 673 (quoting Cassidy v. Detroit Edison Co., 138 F.3d 629, 634 (6th Cir. 1998)). *See also* Sherwin-Williams Co., 113 LA 1184, 1191 (Statham, 2000) (applying the ADA, employer failed to demonstrate it could not accommodate the employee by reassigning her to another job without undue hardship, especially where company had past practice of accommodating employees); Mason & Hanger Corp., 111 LA 60, 63–64 (Caraway, 1998) (displacing one employee to accommodate a disabled employee violated collective bargaining agreement because accommodations should not "trump seniority rights of other employees," *id.* at 64); Henkel Corp., 110 LA 1121, 1126 (West, 1998) (employee's heart condition was not a disability, but even if it were, requiring accommodation would violate seniority obligations under the collective bargaining agreement and may impose undue hardship on employer); Contracts, Metals & Welding, 110 LA 673, 680 (Klein, 1998) ("'The ADA does not require that an employer provide the best accommodation possible to a disabled employee. . . . Nor is an employer required to accommodate a disabled employee in exactly the way he or she requests,'" quoting Eckles v. Consolidated Rail Corp., 890 F. Supp. 1391, 1399, 4 AD Cases 1134, 1140 (S.D. Ind. 1995)).

[982]National Linen Supply, 107 LA 4 (Ross, 1996) (employer is not obligated to retain an employee who is so disabled that he cannot consistently perform his job); Beckett Paper Co., 106 LA 1135 (Goggin, 1996) (employee could not be accommodated, nor did post-discharge treatment warrant reinstatement, where doctor found employee so disabled as to be unable to perform the essential functions of his job).

[983]Interstate Brands Corp., 113 LA 161, 168 (Howell, 1999) (discharge was consistent with ADA and the contract, where employee refused to take appropriate prescribed medication and his behavior was a safety threat).

[984]Rohm & Haas Tex., 104 LA 974 (Koenig, Jr., 1995) (a discharged employee who suffered from bipolar disorder was not disparately treated, where other employees had been discharged for directly threatening coworkers, even though future outbursts could be controlled by medication).

[985]Andex Indus., 111 LA 615, 619 (Allen, 1998) (ADA and applicable state law do not require employer to allow employee with alcoholism unrestricted time off of job as it is not a reasonable accommodation); Westinghouse Hanford Co., 101 LA 46 (Nelson, 1993) (employer's conclusion that an employee was medically unfit because of the employee's failure to follow

On March 25, 1997, the EEOC issued its *Guidance on Psychiatric Disabilities and the Americans with Disabilities Act*[986] (*Guidelines*). The *Guidelines* take an expansive view of mental disabilities, which are defined largely in terms of the disorders set forth in the *Diagnostic Statistical Manual*, and discuss some of the unique accommodation issues raised in the context of such disabilities.

On July 25, 2000, the EEOC issued a new enforcement guidance entitled *Disability-Related Inquiries and Medical Examinations of Employees Under the Americans with Disabilities Act (ADA).*[987] These guidelines, which are not enforceable regulations, state that if an employee requests a reasonable accommodation, the employer cannot send the employee to the company doctor to confirm the need for the accommodation. Instead, the company must get a medical confirmation from the employee's health care provider. Only if that information is inadequate can the company send the employee to a company doctor. These new guidelines will undoubtedly be cited by employees and relied on by arbitrators when such circumstances arise.[988]

The Supreme Court further clarified several major aspects of the ADA in three decisions in 1999. In *Sutton v. United Air Lines*,[989] the Court held that a person's alleged disability must be determined in its mitigated or corrected state, that is, whether an impairment substantially limits a major life activity (the threshold inquiry in any ADA case) requires examining the actual and present impairments. If the individual remains substantially limited in a major life activity notwithstanding the use of a corrective device or medications, then the ADA would still apply to the person.

In *Murphy v. United Parcel Service*,[990] the Court further elaborated on its holding in *Sutton*, but with more specific focus on when a person is "regarded as disabled," or when the company mistakenly believes the impairment is substantial when it is not. As in *Sutton*, the analysis of whether an employee is "regarded as disabled" also includes an assessment of the employee's condition in its mitigated state.

In *Albertsons, Inc. v. Kirkingburg*,[991] the Court held that even the corrective measures a person's own body may take to compensate for an impairment must be taken into consideration when assessing a disability. The Court further emphasized that a disability must be evaluated on a case-by-case basis.

---

an alcohol rehabilitation program was not unreasonable). The ADA expressly provides that a "qualified individual with a disability" does not include employees who currently are engaging in illegal drug use. 42 U.S.C. §12114(a).

[986]ADA Manual (BNA) §70:1281 et seq.

[987]8 FEP Manual (BNA) §405:7701 (2000). In addition to the two EEOC enforcement guidances mentioned in this chapter, the EEOC has issued numerous other enforcement guidance and accompanying question-and-answer materials related to the ADA. They can be found in several places, including the EEOC's website, Volume 8 of BNA's Fair Employment Practices (FEP) Manual, or in Volume 3 of BNA's EEOC Compliance Manual.

[988]The new guidelines can be reviewed on the EEOC's website at <http://www.eeoc.gov>.

[989]527 U.S. 471, 9 AD Cases 673 (1999).

[990]527 U.S. 516, 9 AD Cases 691 (1999).

[991]527 U.S. 555, 9 AD Cases 694 (1999).

Sutton, *Murphy*, and *Albertsons* are significant cases that must be included in any assessment of an alleged disability. The issues they raise further deepen the analysis of how the ADA applies to the workplace.

When interpreting collective bargaining agreements, arbitrators have also applied the provisions of the FMLA.[992] The FMLA has been applied even when the labor contract does not expressly incorporate the statute.[993]

The FMLA requires covered employers to provide eligible employees with 12 weeks' unpaid leave during a 12-month period for their serious health conditions. On conclusion of the FMLA leave, the employer must reinstate the employee to his or her original job, or, if that is unavailable, to an equivalent position. An employer's duty to provide eligible employees with FMLA leave is in addition to, not a substitution for, the employer's obligation to reasonably accommodate the employee pursuant to the ADA. Thus, an employee who becomes "disabled" (as defined by the ADA) may be entitled to 12 weeks of FMLA leave as well as additional leave to reasonably accommodate his or her ailment. If a company has another leave of absence policy, the existence of FMLA leave cannot, by itself, be the basis for limiting any other leave of absence provided in the collective bargaining agreement.[994]

C. Significance of Workers' Compensation Disabilities and Costs
[LA CDI 116.44]

The mere fact that an employee has been awarded workers' compensation previously for permanent partial disability (or has received compensation under settlement of a claim) does not per se establish an inability or unfitness for employment so as to justify management's refusal to use the employee.[995] In one case, an employee had asserted and affirmed in a settle-

---

[992]*See* Apcoa, Inc., 107 LA 705 (Daniel, 1996) (employer impermissibly discharged employee, where employer failed to notify employee that leave was designated as FMLA leave). For related discussion in Chapter 10, section 3.A.iv. "Family and Medical Leave Act."

[993]*See* Big River Zinc Corp., 108 LA 692 (Draznin, 1997) (employer properly discharged employee who did not return from FMLA leave at the time he was supposed to report to work and who did not provide a timely response to a request for information regarding his medical status).

[994]City of Englewood, Ohio, 113 LA 624, 627 (Kohler, 1999).

[995]*See* A.Y. McDonald Mfg. Co., 99 LA 118, 123–24 (Loebach, 1992) (company failed to conduct current medical and emotional status assessment prior to discharging grievant); Peabody Galion Div., 78 LA 1205, 1214–15 (Williams, 1982); Kaiser Steel Corp., 68 LA 192, 195 (Christopher, 1977) (compensation agency's finding of 69% permanent disability was not proof of actual inability to perform work); Zellerbach Paper Co., 68 LA 69, 71 (Stashower, 1977); Habuda Coal & Supply Co., 53 LA 334, 337 (Teple, 1969); Goodyear Tire & Rubber Co., 52 LA 55, 56 (Ray, 1968); Universal Carloading & Distrib. Co., 51 LA 137, 140 (Somers, 1968) (arbitrator should take notice of agency's 33% disability finding, but it is not conclusive as to right to return to work); Whitaker Cable Corp., 50 LA 1152, 1155 (Allen, Jr., 1968) (10% disability); Texas Lime Co., 49 LA 403, 404–05 (Emery, 1967) (50% disability); Specification Steel Corp., 47 LA 812, 815 (Roberts, 1966); Page Dairy Co., 42 LA 1051, 1055–56 (Kiroff, 1964) (50% disability); Vulcan Mold & Iron Co., 42 LA 734, 736–37, 739 (Sembower, 1964); Shahmoon Indus., 42 LA 392, 398–99 (Blumrosen, 1963); Carhart Refractories Co., 39 LA 138, 141–42 (Volz, 1962) (35% disability); Lockheed Aircraft Serv., 37 LA 729, 731–32 (Roberts, 1961); Dietrich Bros., 36 LA 797, 803 (Jaffee, 1961); Spector Freight Sys., 34 LA 149, 152 (Cayton, 1960); Rock Hill Printing & Finishing Co., 19 LA 189, 191 (Jaffee, 1952). *But see* Goss Co., 43 LA 640, 643 (Epstein, 1964); Bethlehem Steel Co., 39 LA 600, 602–03 (Crawford, 1962); Dayton-Portsmouth Foundry Co., 34 LA 204, 206–07 (Stouffer, 1960).

ment agreement that "my injuries are serious, disabling and permanent in nature," and that such "permanent disability does seriously affect my ability to perform the type of work for which I am otherwise qualified."[996] The arbitrator declared that this was not conclusive as to the employee's physical status 3 months later and that the employer improperly refused to permit him to return to work where the employer offered no other evidence to establish the employee's inability to work and where the employee's physician certified to his physical capacity to perform the job.[997]

Moreover, where an employee was otherwise able and fit to perform the job, some arbitrators have not permitted the employer to deny the right to continued employment merely because it could impose workers' compensation liability on the employer in the future or could increase its insurance rates.[998] Nor can an employer, under a contractual provision allowing termination of an employee on sick leave, discharge an employee who is on sick leave for an occupational disease covered by workers' compensation.[999] However, other arbitrators have indicated that these potential liabilities are relevant though not conclusive considerations in reference to the right to continued employment.[1000]

An employer may require an employee to return to work after a physician determines, in connection with the employee's application for workers' compensation benefits, that the employee is not disabled.[1001] Typically, state laws include antiretaliation provisions in their workers' compensation statutes that may be implicated where an employer's treatment of an employee receiving such benefits differs from its handling of employees on other types

---

[996]Goodyear Tire & Rubber Co., 52 LA 55, 56 (Ray, 1968).

[997]Id.

[998]See Expert Dairy Serv., 45 LA 217, 221 (Kuvin, 1965); Weather Lead Co., 42 LA 513, 517 (Kabaker, 1964); Barth Smelting & Ref. Co., 42 LA 374, 376 (Berkowitz, 1964).

[999]Lithonia Lighting Co., 85 LA 627, 631 (Volz, 1985).

[1000]See T. Marzetti Co., 91 LA 154, 157–58 (Sharpe, 1988) (discharge of employee for accruing excessive absence points upheld, despite union claim that inclusion of absences attributable to industrial injuries violates public policy); Mead Paper, 91 LA 52, 56–57 (Curry, Jr., 1988) (proper to discharge employee with 59 work-related accidents as "unsuited for industrial work"); Hillsboro Glass Co., 88 LA 107, 113 (Traynor, 1986) (upholding management decision to deny job bid to employee awarded 12.5% permanent partial disability); Roadway Express, 87 LA 465, 472 (Chapman, 1986) (company permitted to present evidence of excessive workers' compensation claims); E.&J. Gallo Winery, 86 LA 153, 161 (Wyman, 1985) (upholding termination of employee who accepted vocational rehabilitation and monetary settlement for industrial injury); Papercraft Corp., 85 LA 962, 966 (Hales, 1985) (discharge proper when employees receiving workers' compensation are unable to perform job duties); Port Auth. of Allegheny County, 78 LA 437, 443 (Creo, 1982); McCreary Tire & Rubber Co., 72 LA 1279, 1285 (Rollo, 1979); Purex Corp., 60 LA 933, 938 (Doyle, 1973); McGill Mfg. Co., 58 LA 1120, 1122 (Davis, 1972); Universal Carloading & Distrib. Co., 51 LA 137, 143 (Somers, 1968); Arketex Ceramic Corp., 50 LA 1171, 1176 (Seinsheimer, 1967) (management has right "to protect itself"); Dayton-Portsmouth Foundry Co., 34 LA 204, 208 (Stouffer, 1960). See also Rust Eng'g Co., 76 LA 263, 266–67 (Dallas, 1980); Neville Chem. Co., 74 LA 814, 819 (Parkinson, 1980); Atlas Metal Parts Co., 67 LA 1230, 1235 (Kossoff, 1976).

[1001]City of Santa Cruz, Cal., 104 LA 660 (Pool, 1995) (although employee produced a physician's statement in support of her contention that she was disabled, city had just cause to discharge firefighter for willful failure to return to work after a psychiatric examination conducted to determine eligibility for workers' compensation benefits concluded that the employee was not disabled).

of leave.[1002] In one more recent case, the arbitrator held the company violated the collective bargaining agreement where it set as a condition of an employee's return to work the requirement that he drop his workers' compensation claim.[1003]

D. Excessive Absences Due to Illness [LA CDI 118.6366]

All reasonable management readily excuses occasional absences due to illness. However, management may properly seek to guard against false claims of illness.[1004] Moreover, it may feel impelled to terminate employees whose genuinely poor health condition requires excessive absences.

The right to terminate employees for excessive absences, even where they are caused by illness, is generally recognized by arbitrators. However, no simple rule exists for determining whether absences are in fact "excessive."[1005] In this regard, one arbitrator explained:

> At some point the employer must be able to terminate the services of an employee who is unable to work more than part time, for whatever reason. Efficiency and the ability to compete can hardly be maintained if employees cannot

---

[1002]*See* Jefferson Smurfit Corp., 103 LA 1041 (Canestraight, 1994) (employer did not terminate employee in violation of Missouri law in retaliation for her filing a workers' compensation claim, where the employee was not discharged until 7 months after company officials and employee last discussed claim).

[1003]Curry Transfer & Storage Co., 112 LA 866 (Harlan, 1999).

[1004]For discussion of the steps available to management for this purpose, see Chapter 17, section 3.B., "Sick Leave."

[1005]*See* Mallinckrodt, Inc., 95 LA 966, 970 (Hilgert, 1990); Philip Morris U.S.A., 94 LA 41, 44–45 (Dolson, 1989); Goodyear Tire & Rubber Co., 88 LA 745, 747–49 (Dworkin, 1987); Phillip Morris, U.S.A., 87 LA 975, 977 (Flannagan, 1986); Pepsi-Cola Bottlers of Akron, 87 LA 83, 87–88 (Morgan, 1986); General Metal & Heat Treating, 80 LA 7, 10–11 (Wolk, 1982); Arizona Portland Cement Co., 79 LA 128, 132 (Weizenbaum, 1982); Mueller Co., 78 LA 673, 680–82 (Richardson, 1982) (upholding discharge following progressive discipline for excessive absences, some of which were due to illness); Monsanto Co., 76 LA 509, 513 (Thompson, 1981); Hawaii Transfer Co., 74 LA 531, 532 (Tsukiyama, 1980) ("[A]n excessive absentee record covering an extended period of employment, even though attributable to genuine and medically verified illnesses or for other non-fault reasons, provide a sufficient basis to terminate the employment relation."); Butler Mfg. Co., 70 LA 426, 427 (Welch, 1978); Pacific Maritime Ass'n, 70 LA 422, 425 (Hoffman, 1978); Quadraflex, 69 LA 1123, 1128 (Griffin, 1977); Atlantic Richfield Co., 69 LA 484, 492–93 (Sisk, 1977) (holding also that the employee was not subject to progressive discipline, *id.* at 490–91); Scott & Fetzer Co., 69 LA 18, 20–23 (Chattman, 1977); South Cent. Bell Tel. Co., 65 LA 482, 486–87 (Stouffer, 1975); Coca-Cola Bottling Co. of Youngstown, 65 LA 357, 358–59 (Oberdank, 1975); Husky Oil Co., 65 LA 47, 58 (Richardson, 1975) (upholding discharge for excessive absences caused by short-term illnesses over a 6-year period, where the employee did not cooperate or improve his attendance after warning); Kimberly-Clark Corp., 62 LA 1119, 1121–22 (Shieber, 1974); Pennsylvania Tire & Rubber Co. of Miss., 59 LA 1078, 1082–83 (Simon, 1972); Cleveland Trencher Co., 48 LA 615, 618 (Teple, 1967); United States Plywood Corp., 46 LA 436, 439–40 (Anderson, 1966) (the employee could not be denied insurance or pension benefits, there being no misconduct); Keystone Steel & Wire Co., 43 LA 703, 714 (Klamon, 1964); Kurtz Bros., 43 LA 678, 680–82 (Duff, 1964) (the contract provided that employees "shall not lose their seniority rights" when off due to illness, but the arbitrator said that this did not require that sick leave be extended beyond a reasonable time). In one case, the arbitrator purported to deny that there is a "right" to terminate an employee for excessive absences due to illness, but nonetheless in substance he did recognize it as an ultimate right (the contract expressly requiring corrective discipline) by his refusal to bar management "from seeking to apply discipline to combat serious, repetitive absenteeism by individual employees, even though absences on sick leave or approved leave without pay may be involved." U.S. Postal Serv., 73 LA 1174, 1181 (Garrett, 1979).

be depended upon to report for work with reasonable regularity. Other arbitrators have so found, and this Arbitrator has upheld terminations in several appropriate cases involving frequent and extended absences due to illness.[1006]

In a similar vein, another arbitrator explained:

> Illness, injury, or other incapacitation by forces beyond the control of the employee are mitigating circumstances, excuse reasonable periods of absence, and are important factors in determining whether absences are excessive. However, if an employee has demonstrated over a long period of time an inability due to chronic bad health or proneness to injury to maintain an acceptable attendance record, an employer is justified in terminating the relationship, particularly where it has sought through counseling and warnings to obtain an improvement in attendance.[1007]

Examination of the cases cited in this subtopic makes it readily apparent that there is no fixed or generally accepted rule as to when the "excessive" absence point is reached[1008]—the particular facts and circumstances of the given case often will be considered along with the number of absences, the amount of time involved, and the prospects as to future absences.[1009] Moreover, an arbitrator may require considerable tolerance on the part of management where the equities in favor of the employee are strong.[1010]

In one case, the arbitrator recognized the general right of management to terminate employees for excessive absences due to illness, but he stated

---

[1006]Cleveland Trencher Co., 48 LA 615, 618 (Teple, 1967). *See also* Celanese Corp. of Am., 9 LA 143, 145 (McCoy, 1947).

[1007]Louisville Water Co., 77 LA 1049, 1052 (Volz, 1981) (however, reinstatement was ordered—but without back pay—because the employee "may well have been lulled into a false sense of job security"). *See also* Growmark, Inc., 100 LA 785, 788–89 (Ver Ploeg, 1993); Weber Aircraft, 100 LA 417, 423–24 (Jennings, 1992); Philip Morris U.S.A., 99 LA 1016, 1019–20 (Volz, 1992) (concept that illness excuses absences applies to alcoholism if facts establish it has reached stage at which it may properly be considered a disease); Snap-On Tools, 98 LA 905, 908–10 (Stallworth, 1992).

[1008]*But see* Interlake Material Handling Div., 113 LA 1120, 1123 (Lalka, 2000) (no fault attendance policy upheld, where it "1) provide[s] for a specific number of absences before imposing discipline, 2) provide[s] for progressive discipline, 3) permit[s] certain types of absences . . . , and 4) permit[s] employees to periodically cleanse their attendance records . . . ."). Ultimately, as the arbitrator stated in this case, an attendance policy is judged reasonable from its content and application. *Id.* at 1123.

[1009]Ordinarily, neither the number of absences nor any other single factor will be conclusive in determining whether an employee's absenteeism may reasonably be deemed "excessive," where illness is involved. *See, e.g.,* Northrop Corp., 91 LA 231, 233–34 (Weiss, 1988); Safeway Stores, 79 LA 742, 744, 746 (MacLean, 1982); Burns Int'l Sec. Servs., 78 LA 1163, 1165 (Kelliher, 1982) (discharge under an absenteeism policy that applied automatic penalties was overruled because management had not considered excusing occasional absences due to illness and had not considered the potential for regular attendance in the future, but the arbitrator did state that "the Greivant must be warned that if he accepts reinstatement he can be terminated even for justifiable illnesses if they become excessive"); Safeway Stores, 75 LA 430, 437–39 (Winograd, 1980); Kimberly-Clark Corp., 62 LA 1119, 1122 (Shieber, 1974) ("in order to sustain the discharge of an employee for excessive absences due to illness or injury," it must be shown both "that the employee has a high rate of absences" and "that the employee will probably be unable to return to work as a dependable employee in the future"); Laclede Gas Co., 58 LA 881, 885–86 (Erbs, 1972).

[1010]*See, e.g.,* Weber Aircraft, 100 LA 417, 423–24 (Jennings, 1992); Northrop Corp., 91 LA 231, 232–34 (Weiss, 1988); East Ohio Gas Co., 78 LA 71, 73 (Michelstetter, 1982); Safeway Stores, 75 LA 430, 438 (Winograd, 1980); County of Monroe, 72 LA 541, 543 (Markowitz, 1979); Trans World Airlines, 44 LA 280, 282–83 (Gilden, 1965).

that the right "cannot be exercised capriciously or with disregard for the employee's seniority and stake in maturing fringe benefits."[1011] He also noted a distinction between "intermittent" absences and "extended" absences, pointing out that an extended absence imposes a lesser burden on management because it permits "continuous coverage of the vacancy without taxing the employer with constant uncertainty over the filling of the opening."[1012]

Discharges for absenteeism also implicate the ADA. In one case, the arbitrator held that the employer did not violate the ADA when it discharged the employee for absenteeism.[1013] The employee, who failed to notify the company of his drug and alcohol addiction until after his discharge, was not entitled to any preferential treatment: "[P]ublic policy is not furthered if employees may insulate themselves from the consequences of misbehavior or misconduct by suddenly enrolling in a rehabilitation clinic to avoid discipline."[1014] Moreover, it is well settled that an employee who is deemed excessively absent is not an otherwise qualified individual with a disability.[1015]

Discharges for absenteeism may implicate the FMLA as well. In one case, the arbitrator concluded that discharge for excessive absenteeism does not violate the FMLA where the employee's claimed medical condition of a respiratory infection was not a serious health condition under the FMLA.[1016] However, it is important to keep in mind that the FMLA does cover both work-related and non-work-related serious health conditions, and at least one arbitrator held that the employer cannot count absences related to such conditions when the employee otherwise qualifies for an FMLA leave of absence.[1017]

Finally, it may be noted that grievances challenging management's adoption of absentee control plans and/or challenging the application of such plans in specific instances have frequently reached arbitration.[1018]

[1011]Great Atl. & Pac. Tea Co., 48 LA 910, 912–13 (Keefe, 1967). *See also* Safeway Stores, 75 LA 430, 438 (Winograd, 1980); Scott & Fetzer Co., 69 LA 18, 23 (Chattman, 1977); Caterpillar Tractor Co., 67 LA 203, 209 (Wolff, 1976); Union Carbide Chems. Co., 35 LA 469, 477 (Hale, 1960); Rock Hill Printing & Finishing Co., 14 LA 153, 155 (Soule, 1949).

[1012]Great Atl. & Pac. Tea Co., 48 LA 910, 913 (Keefe, 1967).

[1013]Laporte Pigments, 114 LA 1, 4–5 (Marino, 2000).

[1014]*Id.* at 5.

[1015]Andex Indus., 111 LA 615, 619 (Allen, 1998).

[1016]ATC/Vancom, 111 LA 268, 272–73 (Richman, 1998).

[1017]Ohio Valley Coal Co., 110 LA 859, 864 (West, 1998).

[1018]*See* Webster Elec. Co., 83 LA 141, 146–47 (Kindig, 1984); Saginaw Mining Co., 81 LA 672, 673–74 (Feldman, 1983); Cosmair, Inc., 80 LA 22, 25 (Kerrison, 1982); Giant Foods, 79 LA 916, 920 (Seibel, 1982) (upholding management's absenteeism plan involving use of progressive discipline, and in doing so the arbitrator recognized that "discharge on a non-disciplinary basis may be appropriate, even for absences due to legitimate illness"); Carnation Co., 79 LA 679, 680–81 (de Grasse, 1982); Peabody Coal Co., 79 LA 433, 435–36 (Mittelman, 1982); Amoco Chems. Corp., 79 LA 89, 94–95 (Byars, 1982); C&P Tel. Co., 78 LA 15, 16 (Sanders, 1982); Mor-Flo Indus., 77 LA 889, 893 (Nigro, 1981) ("the Company has the management right unilaterally to adopt an absenteeism policy," but the collective bargaining agreement "grants the employees certain rights with which the absenteeism policy cannot conflict"); New Castle State Hosp., 77 LA 585, 590–93 (Deitsch, 1981) ("Termination of an employee whose poor health precludes regular work attendance is understandable, reasonable, and justifiable, given the need of an enterprise to efficiently accomplish its objectives," *id.* at 590, but management's new policy on absenteeism was subject to challenge, being neither clear nor consistently administered); Kennecott Copper Corp., 77 LA 505, 512–16 (Richardson, 1981); Union Tank Car Co., 77 LA 249, 255–56 (Taylor, 1981) (management's "no fault" point system for controlling absenteeism was upheld, because the arbitrator could

E. Right to Require Physical Examination
[LA CDI 100.552565; 118.655]

Management's good-faith right to require job applicants to submit to a physical examination is so basic that it rarely has been an issue in arbitration.[1019] The utility of physical examinations obviously is not ended once the applicant has been hired and has commenced service with the employer— situations arise to warrant physical examinations during the employment relationship.

It is clear from reported arbitration decisions that management has the right, unless restricted by the agreement, to require employees to have physical examinations where the right is reasonably exercised under proper circumstances, such as where an employee desires to return to work following an accident or sick leave, or following extended layoff, or where an employee has bid on a job requiring greater physical effort.[1020] However, it has been

---

not "set aside what appears to be a reasonable work rule on the grounds that it might be unreasonably applied in the future," and when "the unfortunate accumulator of assigned points is discharged or some other discipline is imposed, the justice of such a penalty can only be determined on the merits of that particular case," *id.* at 256); Le Blond Mach. Tool, 76 LA 827, 832 (Keenan, 1981); General Elec. Co., 74 LA 847, 850–53 (Abrams, 1980) ("Merely because the Company has followed its own unilaterally established disciplinary system does not necessarily mean that a resulting discharge was for 'just cause,'" *id.* at 851); Union Carbide Corp., 74 LA 681, 683, 687 (Bowers, 1980); Morton-Norwich Prods., 74 LA 202, 205 (Nitka, 1980); Sweco, Inc., 73 LA 684, 687 (Hardbeck, 1979); Portec Paragon Div., 72 LA 804, 807 (Ellmann, 1979) (management violated past practice by changing its absenteeism plan); Sun-Maid Raisin Growers of Cal., 72 LA 133, 135 (Weiss, 1979); Kerotest Mfg. Corp., 71 LA 744, 749 (Blue, 1978); Georgia Pac. Corp., 71 LA 195, 196, 199 (Imundo, Jr., 1978); Park Poultry, 71 LA 1, 5–6 (Cohen, 1978); Pacific Southwest Airlines, 70 LA 833, 834–36 (Jones, Jr., 1978); Robertshaw Controls Co., 69 LA 77, 79–80 (Duff, 1977); Celanese Piping Sys., 66 LA 674, 676 (McIntosh, 1976). For related discussion, see Scott & Taylor, *An Analysis of Absenteeism Cases Taken to Arbitration: 1975–1981*, 38 Arb. J. No. 3, at 61 (1983).

[1019]In *Conveyor Co.*, 38 LA 1141, 1143 (Roberts, 1962), the arbitrator emphasized the "inherent right" to require a physical examination of job applicants, but in that case there was strong evidence that the contract was intended to prohibit exercise of the right.

[1020]*See* City of Tampa, Fla., 113 LA 296, 299–300 (Deem, 1999) (company requirement that any employee returning from a leave of absence for longer than 6 months must undergo a physical examination, including a drug test, was not arbitrary or capricious but a "proper right of management." However, because the employee was required to submit to a physical examination after he had returned to work, and had not been notified that he would have to submit to a physical examination and drug test to be reinstated, the grievance was granted). *See also* USS, Div. of USX Corp., 96 LA 567, 570 (Petersen, 1990); Mason & Hanger-Silas Mason Co., 92 LA 131, 133–34 (McKee, 1989); Pacific Towboat & Salvage Co., 89 LA 287, 288–89 (Perone, 1987); ITT Cont'l Baking Co., 84 LA 41, 46–48 (Traynor, 1984); Caterpillar Tractor Co., 83 LA 226, 229–30 (Smith, 1984); Library of Cong., 78 LA 784, 786–87 (Rothschild, 1982); Williams Pipe Line Co., 78 LA 617, 619–20 (Moore, 1982) (dealing also with the scope of permitted use of information obtained in the course of the examination); National Steel Corp., 76 LA 103, 107–08 (Roberts, 1981) ("The Company's requirement that the examination be administered by the Company physician rather than another is not unreasonable," *id.* at 108); Atlas Metal Parts Co., 67 LA 1230, 1235–36 (Kossoff, 1976); Pittsburgh Plate Glass Co., 52 LA 985, 986–87 (Duff, 1969); Aetna Bearing Co., 50 LA 351, 352 (Kelliher, 1968); Southern Conn. Gas Co., 48 LA 1357, 1358 (Johnson, 1967); Automatic Canteen Co., 47 LA 1, 6 (Keefe, 1966); Chatfield Paper Corp., 46 LA 530, 532 (McIntosh, 1966); Graphic Arts Ass'n of St. Louis, 45 LA 39, 42 (Bothwell, 1965); E.W. Bliss Co., 43 LA 217, 223–24 (Klein, 1964) (in view of safety considerations, diabetic could be required to submit to weekly medical examination at his own expense); Reynolds Metals Co., 42 LA 161, 164 (Phelps, 1964); North Shore Gas Co., 40 LA 37, 42–43 (Sembower, 1963); McDonnell Aircraft Corp., 37 LA 960, 966 (Klamon, 1961); Keeney Mfg. Co., 37 LA 456, 458 (Donnelly, 1961); Gravely Tractors, 32 LA 686, 689 (Stouffer, 1958); Fulton Glass Co., 31 LA 824, 826 (Boles, 1958);

emphasized that "this right is not an absolute one exercisable at the whim" of management, and that it "cannot be arbitrarily insisted upon without reasonable grounds."[1021]

The right of management to require preemployment examinations for disabled individuals has been limited by the ADA. As a result of the passing of the ADA, covered employers are prohibited from conducting a medical examination of a disabled job applicant prior to making a job offer unless an inquiry can be made into the ability of the applicant to perform essential job-related functions. At the post-employment stage, a covered employer is prohibited from requiring a medical examination unless such an examination is shown to be job-related and consistent with business necessity.

Under contracts containing a disability nondiscrimination clause, it has been held that an employer may conduct a physical examination to ascertain an employee's functional fitness to return to work.[1022] Although arbitrators have generally deemed the ADA and the FMLA incorporated into contractual nondiscrimination clauses, there is no such consensus about incorporating statutory or regulatory standards for requiring physical examinations.[1023] The ADA's interpretive regulations permit employers to "require a medical examination (and/or inquiry) of an employee that is job-related and consistent with business necessity."[1024] Moreover, under the FMLA an employer

---

Chris-Craft Corp., 27 LA 404, 406 (Bothwell, 1956) (could require physical examination in recall); Doehler-Jarvis Corp., 12 LA 896, 897–98 (Stashower, 1949). *See also* Sterling Brewers, 53 LA 1078, 1086 (Witney, 1969) (under past practice employees had returned to work on the basis of their own doctor's certifications, but this did not make demand for physical examination by the company-designated doctor improper, where justified by the circumstances). The fact that the contract states certain ailments or situations for which a physical examination may be required does not deprive management of the right to require one in other proper circumstances. *See* Inspiration Consol. Copper Co., 50 LA 58, 62 (Block, 1968); Minnesota Mining & Mfg. Co., 42 LA 1, 8–11 (Solomon, 1964). *Cf.* Buckeye Forging Co., 42 LA 1151, 1156–58 (Klein, 1964). In *Western Airlines*, 74 LA 923, 925–26 (Richman, 1980), an employee who agreed to release his medical records for examination only by the company physician could not be required to release them for examination by other company personnel as a precondition for returning to work after medical leave of absence.

[1021]Conchemco, Inc., 55 LA 54, 57 (Ray, 1970) (reasonable grounds were not found). Also not finding reasonable grounds, see *Southern Champion Tray Co.*, 92 LA 677, 679 (Williams, 1988); *Department of the Army*, 91 LA 137, 152–54 (Huffcut, 1988); *MGM Grand Hotel*, 65 LA 261, 264 (Koven, 1975); *Jamestown Tel. Corp.*, 61 LA 121, 123–24 (France, 1973); *Standard-Knapp Div.*, 50 LA 833, 835 (Cahn, 1968); *Borg-Warner Corp.*, 37 LA 378, 379 (Dworet, 1961) (could not require all employees absent 2 weeks for whatever reason to submit to physical examination); *Caterpillar Tractor Co.*, 36 LA 104, 105–06 (Daugherty, 1961) (reasonable grounds did not exist for requiring psychiatric examination). An employer's use of physical examinations ordinarily would not violate Title VII of the Civil Rights Act, 42 U.S.C. §2000e. *See, e.g.*, Warren v. Veterans Hosp., 382 F. Supp. 303, 10 FEP Cases 1169, 1172 (E.D. Pa. 1974). However, in some cases a violation has been indicated, such as where the physical examination was purposely utilized to further the employer's discriminatory practices. *See* EEOC Decision 71-1332, 3 FEP Cases 489 (1971); EEOC Decision 70-134, 2 FEP Cases 237 (1969). *See generally* Hill & Sinicropi, *Medical Screening, in* Management Rights: A Legal and Arbitral Analysis 165 (BNA Books 1986).

[1022]Cessna Aircraft Co., 104 LA 985 (Thornell, 1995) (employer had the right to require an employee who had been on a leave of absence because of a workplace injury to take a physical examination in order to ascertain the employee's ability to perform the job, but the employer is nevertheless required to accommodate any existing disability).

[1023]*See id.*

[1024]29 C.F.R. §1630.14(c).

may have a uniformly applied policy or practice that requires all similarly situated employees who take leave for a serious health condition to obtain and present certification from the employee's health care provider that the employee is able to resume work.[1025]

Further, under contracts that do not expressly prohibit disability discrimination, arbitrators have held that an employee has the right to be paid for time spent taking a physical examination,[1026] and that employers may not indiscriminately or inconsistently require physical or psychological examinations.[1027]

F. Drug and Alcohol Testing [LA CDI 124.60]

As national concern about the effects of drug and alcohol abuse in the workplace has increased, employers have with increasing frequency adopted methods to detect and control the problem. Among the measures are random and "reasonable suspicion"–based programs to test employees for use of drugs or alcohol. As a result, arbitrators are being required to resolve challenges to implementation of such programs and the discipline resulting from positive test results.[1027a]

The NLRB has held that drug and alcohol testing of incumbent employees is a mandatory subject of bargaining and that, absent a "clear and unmistakable waiver" of the union's bargaining rights, an employer must bargain with the union prior to implementing a testing policy.[1028] Arbitrators have reached differing conclusions concerning whether contract language or other circumstances support a management right unilaterally to establish testing policies. In some circumstances, arbitrators have upheld unilateral implementation of testing policies because of contract language preserving the right of management to enforce reasonable rules or safety requirements.[1029] However, some arbitrators have refused to recognize a right to

---

[1025]Id. §825.310(a).

[1026]City of Washington, Ohio, 108 LA 892 (Wren, 1997) (requiring an employee to submit to a physical examination is tantamount to ordering him to perform work, and therefore the employee is entitled to a premium for time spent in taking a physical examination).

[1027]City of Monmouth, Ill., 105 LA 724 (Wolff, 1995) (city was not permitted to require employee on leave for shoulder injury to submit to psychological examination or drug test prior to employee's return to work).

[1027a]See related discussion in Chapter 14, section 7.D.xiv., "Drug Abuse as a Factor."

[1028]Johnson-Bateman Co., 295 NLRB 180, 131 LRRM 1393 (1989). A dispute arising from the unilateral modification of an existing physical examination requirement covering incumbent railway employees is a "minor dispute" under the RLA, subject to compulsory and binding adjustment-board arbitration. Consolidated Rail Corp. v. Railway Labor Executives' Ass'n, 491 U.S. 299, 131 LRRM 2601 (1989). See also Penn Window Co., 112 LA 922, 927 (Franckiewicz, 1999) (the company was required to notify the union and on request to bargain about implementing a drug-testing program, even though the company already had rules prohibiting employees from reporting to work "under the influence of drugs").

[1029]See Dow Chem. Co., 91 LA 1385 (Baroni, 1989); Texas Utils. Elec. Co., 90 LA 625 (Allen, Jr., 1988); B.F. Shaw Co., 90 LA 497 (Talarico, 1988); Fleming Foods of Mo., 89 LA 1292 (Yarowsky, 1987); Ashland Oil, 89 LA 795 (Flannagan, 1987); Albuquerque Publ'g Co., 89 LA 333 (Fogelberg, 1987).

adopt such policies unilaterally, even where the contract reserves management's right to adopt reasonable work rules.[1030]

Even where management has the right to adopt a drug- or alcohol-testing policy, specific provisions of the policy are sometimes struck down as unreasonable,[1031] or because the policy has not been applied consistently to all employees.[1032] In some cases, discipline has been overturned when it was determined that there was not a reasonable basis to require testing,[1033] or where a reasonable explanation existed for the employee's positive test result.[1034] Thus, requiring testing on return from layoff was found improper where the contract called for requiring a physical if there was reasonable cause to question fitness for work.[1035] Similarly, an anonymous telephone call was held an insufficient basis to require testing, because the arbitrator believed a drug test to be "too intrusive an invasion of privacy to be supported on the basis of an anonymous call."[1036] Nevertheless, an employee's

---

[1030]*See* Seneca Wire & Mfg. Co., 113 LA 886 (Lalka, 1999) (no reasonable grounds existed for unilateral implementation of random drug testing where a substance abuse problem did not exist at the company and the principal reason for such testing was to obtain lower premiums on workers' compensation insurance); Omnisource Corp., 113 LA 862 (Loeb, 1999) (balancing right of employee's privacy with employer's right to manage its business, arbitrator found that no reasonable cause existed to implement drug-testing policy where, based on facts, company's work environment would not outweigh right of privacy of employee and no evidence existed of past drug use); Wheatland Farms, 96 LA 596 (Nelson, 1991); Utah Power & Light Co., 94 LA 233 (Winograd, 1990); Material Serv. Corp., 94 LA 37 (Cox, 1989); Boston Edison Co., 92 LA 374 (Nicolau, 1988); Philips Indus., 90 LA 222 (DiLeone, 1988); Laidlaw Transit, 89 LA 1001 (Allen, 1987) (alcohol and drug policy not within the scope of a contractual provision authorizing employer to issue reasonable work rules).

[1031]Stone Container Corp., 95 LA 729 (Nolan, 1990); Stone Container Corp., 91 LA 1186 (Ross, 1988) (policy of testing all employees involved in industrial accidents and calling for automatic suspension pending receipt of test results deemed unreasonable); Sharples Coal Corp., 91 LA 1065 (Stoltenberg, 1988) (policy calling for observed urination in some circumstances deemed unreasonable); Vulcan Materials Co., 90 LA 1161 (Caraway, 1988) (policy imposing random testing held to violate contract provision prohibiting discipline without just cause); Maple Meadow Mining, 90 LA 873 (Phelan, 1988) (rule permitting discipline for off-duty misconduct having no impact on the job is overly broad); Young Insulation Group of Memphis, 90 LA 341 (Boals, 1987) (rule mandating discharge solely on the basis of test results showing more than 10 ng/ml of metabolite of marijuana in urine sample deemed unreasonable). *See also* Elkouri & Elkouri, Resolving Drug Issues (BNA Books 1993); Denenberg & Denenberg, Alcohol and Other Drugs: Issues in Arbitration (BNA Books 1991); Denenberg & Denenberg, *Employee Drug Testing and the Arbitrator: What Are the Issues*, 42 Arb. J. No. 2, at 19 (1987).

[1032]Biolab, Inc., 114 LA 279, 284 (Brodsky, 2000).

[1033]*See* Havens Steel Co., 100 LA 1190 (Thornell, 1993); Westinghouse Elec. Corp., 99 LA 201 (Allen, Jr., 1992); Jim Walters Res. No. 7 Mine, 95 LA 1037 (Roberts, 1990); Utah Power & Light Co., 94 LA 233 (Winograd, 1990); Material Serv. Corp., 94 LA 37 (Cox, 1989); Tribune Co., 93 LA 201 (Crane, 1989).

[1034]Nature's Best, 114 LA 217, 221–22 (Grabuskie, 1999) (no just cause for discharge, where employee was forthright in his explanation of taking pain medications and work rules did not require termination for positive drug test). *But see* North Star Steel, 114 LA 234, 241–42 (Eisenmenger, 1999) (employees were provided with adequate notice that termination could result if a drug-test sample was tampered with, even though policy did not specifically state tampering was grounds for discharge, where policy statement includes that accurate testing is part of the policy, that all employees are expected to comply with the policy, and failure to comply can lead to discipline, up to and including discharge).

[1035]ITT Barton Instruments Co., 89 LA 1196 (Draznin, 1987). *See also* Stanadyne, 91 LA 993 (Fullmer, 1988).

[1036]Southern Cal. Gas Co., 89 LA 393, 398 (Alleyne, 1987). *But see* Georgia Power Co., 92 LA 1033 (Abrams, 1989).

request for rehabilitation after being asked to take a drug test, but before the test is actually taken, does not have to be honored because such a request "carries the presumption that the request for rehabilitation is not sincere."[1037]

Though drug tests are not considered medical examinations under the ADA, tests to determine how much, if any, alcohol an individual has consumed are considered medical examinations and are not statutorily exempt.[1038] Although not governed by the ADA, the implementation of drug tests is a mandatory subject of bargaining under the NLRA, and arbitrators continue to invalidate drug-testing programs that are unreasonable in their implementation or administration.[1039] Conversely, employers' disciplinary actions based on a drug-testing policy will be upheld where the policy is reasonable in both design and implementation.[1040]

Where the testing policy has not been consistently applied, employees who have been terminated for refusing to take a drug test have been reinstated with back pay.[1041]

27. SELECTION AND CONTROL OF SUPERVISORS [LA CDI 102.03]

Arbitrators have recognized that it is the function and responsibility of management to run the business and to produce profits. It is generally accepted as incident to management's right to control operations that management must be permitted to select and control supervisory personnel without union interference.[1042] In the words of one arbitrator:

[1037]Biolab, Inc., 114 LA 279, 284 (Brodsky, 2000) (the company's post-accident testing policy will be followed, where it was consistently enforced and no evidence exists that the employee was treated differently).

[1038]*EEOC Guidance on Pre-Employment Disability-Related Inquiries and Medical Examinations Under the ADA*, ADA MANUAL (BNA) §70:1103 et seq.

[1039]Pioneer Flour Mills, 101 LA 816 (Bankston, 1993) (where employer's requirement that employee submit to drug test is not based on reasonable suspicion, employee's right to privacy prevails).

[1040]Integrated Distribution Sys., 108 LA 737, 740 (Neas, 1997) (policy permitting employer to test an employee "any time . . . an employee is involved in an accident" is reasonable and employer is not obligated to give the employee the right to talk to the union representative where the policy does not extend such a right); Jefferson Smurfit Corp., 106 LA 306 (Goldstein, 1996) (drug-testing policy's differentiation between major and minor injuries with regard to mandatory testing was reasonable); Atlas Processing Co., 106 LA 172 (Baroni, 1996) (employer reasonably unilaterally implemented random drug-testing program after just-cause program failed); Wooster, Ohio, City Bd. of Educ., 102 LA 535 (High, 1993) (employer reasonably scheduled off-duty testing of employees to accommodate individuals with scheduling problems, where collective bargaining agreement did not restrict time of testing).

[1041]Munster Steel Co., 108 LA 597 (Cerone, 1997) (employer unlawfully discriminated against employee by requiring employee to submit to drug test on the day of an in-plant injury, where on other occasions employees were permitted to be tested at a later date).

[1042]For cases illustrating management's broad control and discretion as to supervisory personnel, see *Kelly Air Force Base*, 98 LA 773, 774–76 (O'Grady, 1992); *City of Key West Util. Bd.*, 78 LA 39, 41–42 (Weston, 1982); *Dravo Corp.*, 75 LA 1042, 1044 (Hannan, 1980); *Stayton Canning Co.*, 75 LA 2, 6 (Axon, 1980); *Department of Hous. & Urban Dev.*, 69 LA 67, 70–71 (Foster, 1977) (in concluding that the collective bargaining agreement promotion provisions did "not cover the staffing of supervisory positions which are outside the bargaining unit," the arbitrator stated that, "Since contractual control over out-of-unit promotions is rare in the realm of labor relations," he "must insist on explicit evidence" that the federal

> It is a fundamental principle of American industry that the selection and retention of foremen or other supervisory personnel is the sole prerogative of management . . . . There is no doubt that the union may not, as a matter of right, demand the dismissal or demotion of a foreman and that such a demand is not a proper subject matter for a grievance.[1043]

Thus, an arbitrator held that, unless the agreement expressly permits, or the employer waives the jurisdiction issue and submits the dispute on the merits, a demand by the union for discipline or discharge of a supervisory employee ordinarily is not arbitrable, and that even where the arbitrator can exercise jurisdiction in such disputes, it should be done sparingly and

---

agency employer had knowingly agreed to such control); *Ozark Elec. Coop.*, 51 LA 1113, 1115 (Bothwell, 1968) (can pay management personnel on any basis employer desires); *Litton Sys.*, 51 LA 296, 297–98 (Williams, 1968); *Electrographic Corp.*, 51 LA 197, 199–200 (Sembower, 1968) (employer has right to determine how many persons are to be made supervisors); *Socony Mobil Oil Co.*, 44 LA 992, 993 (Shister, 1965); *Eastern Air Lines*, 44 LA 145, 147–48 (Seidenberg, 1964) (selection of supervisors is not governed by seniority or other contract provisions); *Houston Chronicle*, 43 LA 9, 11 (Oppenheim, 1964); *Kimberly-Clark Corp.*, 42 LA 79, 82 (Hawley, 1963) (need not consider seniority in filling temporary vacancy in foreman position); *Thiokol Chem. Corp.*, 27 LA 432, 436–37 (Williams, 1956) ("Supervisors hold their positions at the will of the company except where the company has specifically yielded its power," *id.* at 437); *Duquesne Light Co.*, 11 LA 1023, 1031 (Whiting, 1948). The NLRA expressly excludes supervisors from the definition of "employee" and also bars the states from compelling employers to accord bargaining rights to supervisors. *See* Beasley v. Food Fair of N.C., 416 U.S. 653, 86 LRRM 2196 (1974). *See also* Safeway Stores, 73 LA 497, 502–03 (Goodman, 1979) (quoting the NLRA §2(11) definition of "supervisor"); J.L. Clark Mfg. Co., 68 LA 448, 453 (Fields, 1977); Bendix Corp., 49 LA 1154, 1155 (Updegraff, 1967); H.W. Gossard Co., 38 LA 301, 305–06 (Purdom, 1962). Thus, supervisors are subject to management's unilateral right of control except as management voluntarily limits that right by contract. By decisional law, "managerial employees" and certain "confidential" employees are likewise excluded from NLRA coverage. Regarding managerial employees, see *NLRB v. Yeshiva Univ.*, 444 U.S. 672, 103 LRRM 2526 (1980); *NLRB v. Textron, Inc.*, 416 U.S. 267, 85 LRRM 2945 (1974) (excluded "managerial employees" include not merely those in positions susceptible to conflicts of interest in labor relations, but also those who formulate and effectuate management policies). Under the facts in *Curtis Noll Corp.*, 218 NLRB 1447, 89 LRRM 1417 (1975), certain management trainees were held to be managerial employees not protected by the NLRA, even though as trainees they perform solely nondiscretionary rank-and-file work. Regarding "confidential" employees, see *NLRB v. Hendricks County Rural Elec. Membership Corp.*, 454 U.S. 1170, 108 LRRM 3105 (1981) (upholding the NLRB's practice of excluding from bargaining units only those "confidential" employees who assist and act in a confidential capacity to persons engaged in the formulation and effectuation of management policies in the field of labor relations). As concerns the RLA, that statute does not expressly exclude supervisors from its coverage, and, pointing somewhat in the other direction, its rather indefinite definition of the term "employee" refers at one point to "employee or subordinate official" as falling within the term. *See* RLA §1, Fifth; 45 U.S.C. §151, Fifth. In *Lum v. China Airlines*, 413 F. Supp. 613, 92 LRRM 2451 (D. Haw. 1976), the court pointed out that persons may be covered by the RLA although they have some supervisory duties. In *Frontier Airlines*, 8 NMB No. 99 (1981), noted by the National Mediation Board (NMB) in its 47 ANN REP. 22 (1981), certain foremen who had authority to discipline and evaluate employees, handle and resolve grievances, and participate in budgetary matters and commit carrier resources, were held to be "management officials" not covered by the RLA. Considering the RLA's full definition of "employee" along with cases such as those just noted, it is apparent that the level of a person's authority and the extent to which the person is subject to supervision and direction in the rendition of services are basic factors in determining whether the person is an employee or subordinate official, covered by the RLA, or is a management official subject to unilateral control by the carrier.

    [1043]King Powder Co., 1 LA 215, 216 (Whiting, 1944). This also was the view of the War Labor Board. Stanoland Oil & Gas, 20 WAR LAB. REP. 211 (1944).

only on very clear grounds.[1044] Many other arbitrators have agreed with this view, either by holding the union's demand to be nonarbitrable,[1045] or by holding that the arbitrator has no authority to order management to punish supervisory personnel.[1046]

However, while recognizing management's control over supervisors as a general right, the arbitrator explained in another case that, "in very extreme cases, where a foreman's conduct is beyond the limits of lawfulness or decency, making for an intolerable condition which management itself could not with decency condone, it may become arbitrable," or where there is "a menace to the life and health of the employees while at their work," an arbitrable issue may be presented.[1047] In still another case, the arbitrator required an employer to remove from the department a foreman who, on many occasions, had used profanity in the presence of female employees and had addressed obscene remarks to them. In requiring the removal, he said that "management has, by contract (seniority clauses, etc.), given the employees rights to their jobs under decent working conditions."[1048]

[1044]Electro Metallurgical Co., 19 LA 8, 8–10 (McCoy, 1952). For one arbitrator's cautious approach to the imposition of sanctions, even where an express contractual directive regarding the conduct of supervisors had been violated, see *U.S. Customs Serv.*, 78 LA 945, 951 (Pastore, 1982).

[1045]*See* Merico, Inc., 67 LA 284, 287 (Archer, 1976); U.S. Comm'n on Civil Rights, 67 LA 271, 277–78 (Sisk, 1976); Western Indus., 53 LA 878, 884–86 (Solomon, 1969); Reserve Mining Co., 49 LA 752, 757–60 (Sembower, 1967); Penn Ventilator Co., 27 LA 806, 810 (Brecht, 1956); Mosaic Tile Co., 13 LA 949, 950 (Cornsweet, 1950); Bethlehem Steel Co., 5 LA 684, 686 (Selekman, 1946); Wright Aeronautical Corp., 1 LA 75, 78–79 (Smith, 1943). *See also* Griffin Pipe Prods. Co., 72 LA 1033, 1034 (Doyle, 1979); American Body & Equip. Co., 45 LA 707, 710–12 (Coffey, 1965). In *San Juan Star*, 43 LA 445, 445–46 (Helfeld, 1964), the employer did agree to arbitrate the alleged misconduct of two supervisors, and the submission agreement specified that they would be discharged if the charges were established (they were not established).

[1046]Union Camp Corp., 104 LA 295 (Nolan, 1995) (arbitrator did not have authority to require the employer to discipline a supervisor who sexually harassed subordinates or to require supervisor to apologize, although arbitrator was empowered to require the employer to take necessary measure to ensure that supervisor did not commit such harassment in the future). *See* San Antonio Packing Co., 68 LA 893, 897 (Bailey, 1977); Marinette Gen. Hosp., 67 LA 785, 788 (Schoenfeld, 1976); Defense Supply Agency, 50 LA 221, 225–26 (Geissinger, 1968); Allied Chem. Corp., 47 LA 686, 690–91 (Hilpert, 1966); Sangamo Elec. Co., 15 LA 32, 35 (Klamon, 1950) (only in "very rare and unusual circumstances" should the demand be sustained); Branch River Wool Combing Co., 10 LA 237, 240 (Copelof, 1948); Ford Motor Co., 1 ALAA ¶67,011 (Shulman, 1945); King Powder Co., 1 LA 215, 216 (Whiting, 1944). *Cf.* Barber-Greene Co., 39 LA 870, 874–75 (Elson, 1962) (the arbitrator ordered the company to "formalize" the reprimand that the company itself had given a supervisor for violating the agreement).

[1047]Goodyear Tire & Rubber Co. of Ala., 5 LA 30, 34 (McCoy, 1946).

[1048]Continental Can Co., 1 LA 65, 68 (McCoy, 1945). For other cases involving alleged abusive language by foremen, see *United States Steel Corp.*, 50 LA 976, 977–78 (Florey, 1968); *National Steel & Shipbuilding Co.*, 40 LA 125, 127 (McNaughton, 1963); *Penn Ventilator Co.*, 27 LA 806, 809–11 (Brecht, 1956). In *Veterans Admin.*, 75 LA 733, 735 (Hyman, 1980), a regulation requiring "employees to live up to common standards of acceptable work behavior" was held by the arbitrator to "apply with perhaps special force to supervisory employees in their dealing with subordinates," and because the evidence established "a pattern of harassment of the Grievant by his supervisor," the arbitrator "directed" the federal agency employer "to admonish the [supervisor] to exert special efforts to avoid any repetition of similar behavior in the future . . . ."

Furthermore, even where management may not be required to discipline supervisors, it will be required to compensate employees injured by their wrongful acts.[1049] An umpire, for instance, ruled that "to the extent that a foreman or other representative of managerial authority takes action detrimental to an employee and in violation of the parties' contract, the grievance procedure is properly invoked to provide appropriate redress."[1050] He added, however, that "what is called for is protection of the employees within their contractual rights as distinguished from mere punishment of the Company's supervisory or other managerial representatives," and that, while punishment of a supervisor may be the only feasible way to stop improper treatment of employees, the umpire can only direct that such improper conduct be stopped, and "how the result is to be achieved is . . . a matter normally left to the Company."[1051]

In another case, an arbitrator held a grievance demanding the removal of a foreman not to be arbitrable, but he gave the union 10 days to submit an amended grievance requesting an available and appropriate arbitrable remedy.[1052]

Accompanying the right of management to control supervisors is the function and responsibility to inform them fully as to their rights, authorities, and duties. It has been held that management must compensate employees for any loss suffered as a result of its failure to instruct and train its foremen fully.[1053]

Management's right to discipline or discharge supervisors may be limited by contract.[1054] In one case, an arbitrator summarized management's broad right of control over supervisors under the NLRA, but he also pointed out that an employer voluntarily may become committed to contractual limitations on that right of control "by choosing to include . . . supervisory personnel in the bargaining unit, and by failing to provide in any manner that

---

[1049]Profile Cotton Mills, 2 LA 537, 538–39 (McCoy, 1942). *See also* Penn Ventilator Co., 27 LA 806, 810–11 (Brecht, 1956); Mosaic Tile Co., 13 LA 949, 950 (Cornsweet, 1950); King Powder Co., 1 LA 215, 216 (Whiting, 1944); Wright Aeronautical Corp., 1 LA 75, 78 (Smith, 1943).

[1050]Ford Motor Co., 1 ALAA ¶67,011, at 67,012 (Shulman, 1945).

[1051]*See also* San Antonio Packing Co., 68 LA 893, 897 (Bailey, 1977); Armstrong Cork Co., 38 LA 781, 784 (Jensen, 1962) (union is entitled to assurances against future misconduct by supervisor but no right to a public apology from him); General Cable Corp., 35 LA 381, 383 (Dworet, 1960).

[1052]Reserve Mining Co., 49 LA 752, 757–60 (Sembower, 1967) (any amended grievance would be returned to a lower step of the grievance procedure for de novo proceedings from that point).

[1053]Standard Oil Co., 11 LA 689, 691 (Updegraff, 1948).

[1054]Even the captain of a ship was protected by a just-cause requirement, where he was covered by the collective bargaining agreement. Cargo & Tankship Mgmt. Corp., 38 LA 602, 612 (Gellhorn, 1962). By the agreement, management may accept other limitations on its rights as to supervisors. *See, e.g.,* Southwest Airmotive Co., 41 LA 353, 358 (Elliott, 1963). Where employees are temporarily transferred to supervisory positions, they may remain covered by the agreement for various purposes. *See* Bethlehem Steel, 39 LA 1101, 1103–04 (Seward, 1963).

they be afforded less protection, . . . [and thereby it will be considered to have] waived its right to treat these employees differently."[1055]

Where bargaining-unit employees acquire rights under the contract and later become supervisors, their discharge presents an arbitrable issue insofar as the union claims a right under the collective bargaining agreement for the individual to return to the bargaining unit. The claimed right has been upheld in some cases but denied in other cases.[1056]

Awards vary on the question of whether management has a right, in the absence of a specific contractual provision on the matter, to place former bargaining unit employees back into the unit on the basis of seniority accumulated during work in the unit or with accumulated seniority for time spent in supervisory service.[1057]

[1055]Safeway Stores, 73 LA 497, 503 (Goodman, 1979). For NLRA limitation on a *union's* right to discipline supervisor-members whom the employer has permitted to join, see *American Broad. Cos. v. Writers Guild of Am. W.*, 437 U.S. 411, 98 LRRM 2705 (1978) (a critical consideration being whether discipline imposed by the union may adversely affect the supervisor's performance of collective bargaining grievance-adjustment tasks and thereby unlawfully coerce or restrain the employer). For the application of contracts that require supervisors to be union members but which limit the union's right to discipline them, see *Journal Co.*, 43 LA 1073, 1075–83 (Smith, 1964); *Dallas Morning News*, 40 LA 619, 621–24 (Rohman, 1963). *See also* California Horse Racing Indus., 79 LA 654, 658 (Gentile, 1982).

[1056]*See* American Metaseal Co., 70 LA 295, 300 (Kanner, 1978); White Pidgeon Paper Co., 68 LA 177, 180, 183 (Coyle, 1977); Greyhound Lines-West, 61 LA 1139, 1141–42 (Kelliher, 1973); Royal Indus., 60 LA 572, 575 (Davey, 1973); Rodman Indus., 59 LA 101, 104–06 (Fleischli, 1972); Cedar Rapids Eng'g Co., 58 LA 374, 378, 381 (Epstein, 1972); Datron Sys., 57 LA 645, 651, 656 (Peters, 1971); Fred Reuping Leather Co., 57 LA 58, 60–61 (Somers, 1971); Gould, Inc., 56 LA 712, 720 (Schurke, 1971); Chromalloy Am. Corp., 54 LA 965, 972–73, 981 (Elliott, 1971); Gibson Refrigerator, 50 LA 1052, 1056 (Keefe, 1968); Babcock & Wilcox Co., 48 LA 1234, 1236–39 (Gibson, 1967); Georgia Marble Co., 40 LA 193, 198 (Marshall, 1963); American Zinc Co. of Ill., 29 LA 334, 336 (Merrill, 1957); F.H. Noble & Co., 28 LA 641, 642–43 (Baab, 1957); Thiokol Chem. Corp., 27 LA 432, 436–37 (Williams, 1956); Pryne & Co., 26 LA 919, 920–21 (Duff, 1956); Sangamo Elec. Co., 25 LA 452, 455 (Anrod, 1955); Tin Processing Corp., 16 LA 48, 50 (Emery, 1951). In *J.J. Clark Mfg. Co.*, 68 LA 448, 452–53 (Fields, 1977), it was held that the "privilege of the Employer to select an employee [for supervisory service outside the bargaining unit] without regard to seniority or other qualifications does not imply acceptance is mandatory." *Id.* at 452. The arbitrator declared that the "authority to compel an employee to work outside the unit in a supervisory capacity has such serious potential consequences that it may not be implied . . . ." *See also* Cedar Coal Co., 75 LA 224, 227–28 (Wren, 1980) (employee could not be required to accept a responsibility similar to that exercised by the foreman as "a member of the management team," *id.* at 227).

[1057]For discussion and cases on this issue, see Chapter 14, section 3.D., "Service Outside the Seniority Unit."

Chapter 14

Seniority

1. RECOGNITION OF SENIORITY

One of the most significant limitations on the exercise of managerial discretion is the requirement that employee seniority be recognized in job assignment, promotions, layoffs, and other personnel actions. Indeed, the effect of seniority recognition is dramatic from the standpoint of employer, union, and employee alike, because "every seniority provision reduces, to a greater or lesser degree, the employer's control over the work force and compels the union to participate to a corresponding degree in the administration of the system of employment preferences which pits the interests of each worker against those of all the others."[1]

---

[1]Aaron, *Reflections on the Legal Nature and Enforceability of Seniority Rights*, 75 HARV. L. REV. 1532, 1534–35 (1962).

A. Definition of Seniority [LA CDI 117.201]

In the absence of a definition of the term in the collective bargaining agreement, seniority "is commonly understood to mean the length of service with the employer or in some division of the enterprise."[2] Functionally, seniority "means that . . . [employees] retain their jobs according to the length of service with their employer and that . . . [employees] are promoted to better jobs on the same basis."[3] Put somewhat differently, "the chief purpose of a seniority plan is to promote maximum security [for] workers with the longest continuous service."[4]

It should be kept in mind that "seniority is a relationship between employees in the same seniority unit, rather than a relationship between jobs."[5] As stated by one arbitrator:

> Seniority protects and secures an employee's rights in relation to the rights of other employees in his seniority group; it does not protect him in relation to the existence of the job itself. By the use of an objective measure, length of service, the rights of one employee are balanced against other employees' rights.[6]

Because of the conflict created within the workforce by a seniority system, one court permitted intervention by nongrieving employees in an arbitration involving seniority rights of other employees in the same seniority unit, observing that in such a controversy "for every person whose seniority is advanced, someone will be adversely affected by such advancement."[7]

---

[2]Curtiss-Wright Corp., 11 LA 139, 142 (Uible, 1948). *See also* Shop Rite Foods, 79 LA 1081, 1083 (Carter, 1982); Industrial Rayon Corp., 24 LA 73, 76 (Dworkin, 1955); Armstrong Cork Co., 23 LA 366, 367 (Williams, 1954). Sometimes seniority is linked to a particular classification by custom or practice.

[3]LAPP, HOW TO HANDLE PROBLEMS OF SENIORITY 1 (1946). *See also* Industrial Rayon Corp., 24 LA 73, 76 (Dworkin, 1955).

[4]Darin & Armstrong, 13 LA 843, 845 (Platt, 1950). *See also* Armstrong Cork Co., 23 LA 366, 367 (Williams, 1954); McFeely Brick Co., 22 LA 379, 381 (Reid, 1954); International Harvester Co., 21 LA 231, 232 (Cole, 1953). "In the broadest sense, the set of rights that make up 'seniority' may be separated into two distinct categories: (1) the rights of an employee relative to other employees in competitive situations, as in layoffs, promotions, transfers, and choice of shifts or vacation periods, and (2) the rights of the employee to benefits, usually financial, that increase automatically with length of service." *Major Collective Bargaining Agreements: Administration of Seniority* 1 (U.S. Dep't of Labor Bull. No. 1425-14, 1972). For U.S. Supreme Court discussion of seniority and seniority systems, see *American Tobacco Co. v. Patterson*, 456 U.S. 63, 76, 28 FEP Cases 713 (1982) ("'Seniority provisions are of 'overriding importance' in collective bargaining.'") (quoting Humphrey v. Moore, 375 U.S. 335, 346, 55 LRRM 2031 (1964)); *California Brewers Ass'n v. Bryant*, 444 U.S. 598, 610–11, 22 FEP Cases 1 (1980); *Franks v. Bowman Transp. Co.*, 424 U.S. 747, 766, 12 FEP Cases 549 (1976) (speaking of competitive status seniority and recognizing that "[s]eniority systems and the entitlements conferred by credits earned thereunder are of vast and increasing importance in the economic employment system of this Nation").

[5]Axelson Mfg. Co., 30 LA 444, 448 (Prasow, 1958).

[6]*Id. See also* Shop Rite Foods, 79 LA 1081, 1083 (Carter, 1982); General Elec. Co., 54 LA 350, 352 (Cahn, 1971); International Tel. & Tel. Corp., 47 LA 325, 326–27 (Abrahams, 1966).

[7]Iroquois Beverage Corp., 27 LA 906, 907 (N.Y. Sup. Ct. 1955). In *Belanger v. Matteson*, 346 A.2d 124, 91 LRRM 2003 (R.I. 1975), a union was held to have breached its duty of fair representation when it argued for the application of strict seniority in the arbitration of grievances of senior employees who had been denied promotion under a clause making seniority controlling only if the qualifications of competing employees are equal, because the union had failed to give proper consideration to the qualifications of junior applicants. A court panel's like finding under similar facts was not endorsed by a majority of the full court

B. Competing Interests

Seniority issues in arbitration arise out of the attempt by the parties to promote their respective interests. In this regard, one professor balanced the interests of management against those of the employees and analyzed the "costs" of seniority to both management and employees:

> To be sure, the full utilization of seniors cannot be achieved without costs. When seniors "get the breaks," the more ambitious and capable of the junior men may feel frustrated. Moreover, a management that likes to see a clear line of promotability from within the work force does not welcome the inflexibility that sometimes comes from giving preference to older, perhaps less adaptable workers. But these costs were measured when the contract was made. The parties presumably concluded that the price was worth paying. From the standpoint of the men, they must have concluded that the deferment of youthful hope was offset by the assurance of fair opportunity for veteran employees. From the standpoint of management, they must have concluded that an occasional personal rigidity was offset by the enhanced loyalty and stability that are encouraged by an effective seniority clause.[8]

An arbitrator added the union as an interested party, aside from its representation of the employees:

> Traditionally, a union considers seniority both as a useful organizing tool and as a basic objective in collective bargaining negotiations. It is, therefore, utilized in evoking what is often considered a latent, if unexpressed, need of workers; and, it is also employed to demonstrate the value of concerted activities as opposed to the results workers can expect from trying to "go it alone" in dealing with management.[9]

In the latter regard, another arbitrator underscored a special concern of workers:

> A major reason why unorganized workers decide to elect a union as their representative is to insulate their job tenure from the adverse effects of the preferential treatment of favored workers in cases of workforce reduction and work opportunities or the retaliatory decisions of supervisors whom they might offend.
> The seniority system has obvious imperfections when compared to an ideally efficient method for determining whom to retain or dismiss in a workforce reduction. To the extent that it is enforced, however, seniority does militate against personal retaliation or preference . . . .[10]

In an arbitration case involving not only contract interpretation but also some "interest" aspects, the arbitrator further analyzed the struggle in rela-

---

on rehearing in *Smith v. Hussmann Refrigerator Co.*, 619 F.2d 1229, 103 LRRM 2321 (8th Cir. 1980), but a majority did find a breach of the duty of fair representation in some other respects, for instance, in failure to notify certain affected employees of an arbitration hearing or to invite them to attend, and in agreeing to resubmit an arbitration award for clarification without notifying employees to whom the award was favorable. For an analysis of the *Hussmann* decision, in which a divided court produced four opinions, see DeHaven, *Fair Representation in the Arbitration of Grievances—The Eighth Circuit Adds Another Straw*, 47 Tenn. L. Rev. 631 (1980).

[8]Universal Atlas Cement Co., 17 LA 755, 757 (Gellhorn, 1951). *See also* Cessna Aircraft Co., 80 LA 257, 262 (Cantor, 1983) (reminding that management, too, benefits from seniority recognition).

[9]Schedler, *Arbitration of Seniority Questions*, 28 LA 954, 954 (1957).

[10]Overly Mfg. Co. of Cal., 68 LA 1343, 1345–46 (Jones, Jr., 1977).

tion to the application of seniority in the extreme situation. He first considered the objectives of the parties: the union striving for greater security in tenure for certain workers and the company trying to avoid a "burdensome seniority system carried to the extreme of shuffling men in the course of a day's work."[11] The objectives of both parties, he believed, were proper. The arbitrator noted that the company was offering the union a job-standing list that would provide for promotion, reduction in force, and overtime in accordance with strict seniority, but not for such short periods as a day's work. In refusing to award the seniority arrangement requested by the union, he stated:

> I must agree with the company that carrying seniority to the extreme requested by the union would make for a wasteful, cumbersome and uneconomical method of operation. It has in it an element of "made work" (the few minutes or hours that would be necessary in making the shifts in personnel). It can hardly be denied anymore that made work is economically unsound. If carried to the extreme it would make for much work and little production. Efficiency of operations is something to be desired in every business[;] it enures to the benefit of all including the public, and an enterprise that cannot operate as efficiently as its competition will suffer the consequences.[12]

C. Source of Seniority "Rights"

Even prior to the advent of collective bargaining agreements, employers generally gave job preference to their older employees, not as any binding obligation but as a matter of equity, so long as they could do the required work.[13] However, seniority benefits exist as "rights" only to the extent made so by contract.[14] As stated by an arbitrator:

---

[11]Standard Oil Co., 24 LA 424, 426 (Beatty, 1954).

[12]*Id.* at 427.

[13]Lapp, How to Handle Problems of Seniority 2–3 (1946).

[14]*See* McDonnell Douglas Astronautics Co., 80 LA 1016, 1018 (Roberts, 1983); Madison Furniture Indus., 79 LA 265, 267 (Howell, 1982); Washington County, Or., 78 LA 1081, 1086 (Tilbury, 1982); Sheldahl, Inc., 78 LA 706, 709 (Rotenberg, 1982); Reyco Indus., 75 LA 689, 694 (Talent, 1980); Ionia, Mich., Pub. Sch. Bd. of Educ., 75 LA 297, 301 (Lipson, 1980); Taft Broad. Co. of Pa., 68 LA 1379, 1381 (Lubow, 1977); Browning-Ferris Indus. of Ohio, 68 LA 1347, 1352 (Teple, 1977); Allen Elec. & Equip. Co., 54 LA 828, 829 (Geissinger, 1971); General Elec. Co., 54 LA 350, 352 (Cahn, 1971); Aerojet-General Corp., 49 LA 1073, 1076 (Killion, 1967); National Cash Register Co., 48 LA 743, 744 (Volz, 1967); Otis Elevator Co., 48 LA 621, 624 (Roberts, 1966); Heckett Co., 48 LA 184, 185 (Williams, 1966); New Britain Mach. Co., 45 LA 993, 995–96 (McCoy, 1965); Bergen Mach. & Tool Co., 44 LA 301, 303 (Buckwalter, 1965); Columbia Broad. Sys., 37 LA 330, 332 (Scheiber, 1961); Celotex Corp., 37 LA 240, 244 (Mitchell, 1961); Petroleum Haulers, 35 LA 378, 380 (Luskin, 1960); Allianceware Inc., 35 LA 74, 76 (Kabaker, 1960); Timken Roller Bearing Co., 32 LA 595, 600–01 (Boehm, 1958); Mathews Conveyer Co., 30 LA 221, 222 (Cahn, 1958); Industrial Rayon Corp., 24 LA 73, 76 (Dworkin, 1955); Tide Water Associated Oil Co., 21 LA 604, 607 (Shipman, Fillhower, & Pelowitz, 1953). *See also* Lowdon Co., 54 LA 555, 558 (Larson, 1971); Atlas Processing Co., 46 LA 860, 864 (Oppenheim, 1966); Superior Prods. Co., 42 LA 517, 524 (Smith, 1964). For court recognition of this rule, see *Aeronautical Indus. Dist. Lodge 727 v. Campbell*, 337 U.S. 521, 24 LRRM 2173 (1949); *Trailmobile v. Whirls*, 331 U.S. 40, 19 LRRM 2531 (1947). Seniority benefits sometimes may exist by virtue of statute, as in the case of veterans' employment rights under federal legislation. Regarding the latter, see Chapter 10, section 3.B., "Other Federal Statutes."

> [W]hatever seniority rights employees have exist only by virtue of the collective bargaining agreement that is in existence between the union and the employer. Such seniority rights depend wholly upon the contract. They arise out of the contract. Before a collective bargaining contract is in existence, there are no seniority rights.
>
> Therefore, until we have a contract, the employer has the right, which he has always exercised, to shift workers around and promote and demote them. The very purpose of collective bargaining was to constrict such rights of management and, reciprocally, to gain for the workers job-security rights based upon seniority and to insure such rights contractually. Thus, we start with the situation, before the existence of a contract, where the employer has all rights in connection with promotions and transfers and need pay no heed to seniority of the workers, and the workers have no rights to promotions or transfers because of length of service.
>
> How does this situation change when a collective bargaining agreement is in existence? It changes to the extent that these rights are given up by the employer and given to the workers under the terms of the contract. Therefore, whatever the employer has yielded in his absolute time-established rights of hiring, firing, promoting, and demoting and whatever the workers have gained in the way of seniority rights with respect to these matters must be measured entirely by the contract.[15]

Thus, an employee who was laid off prior to the effective date of the first contract between the employer and the union was not entitled to any seniority rights or any other rights provided by the contract. Only employees of the company who were in its employ on or after the effective date of the contract were entitled to invoke the provisions of the agreement.[16]

Seniority rights do not necessarily remain fixed and static; they may be modified in subsequent agreements, with the current agreement governing. For instance, in ruling that the seniority rights of a returning veteran (who did not qualify for reemployment rights under federal legislation) were governed by the contract in effect at the time of his return, rather than the contract in effect at the time he entered the armed forces, the arbitrator stated:

> Seniority rights under a collective agreement are entirely the products of the Agreement. Their characteristics and their effects are determined solely by the Agreement. In the absence of special provisions to the contrary, the collective Agreement creates rights and binds parties only for the term of the Agreement. Nothing in . . . [any of the parties'] Agreements indicates a purpose to single out seniority rights for individual employees and give them a vested effectiveness beyond the period of the Agreement and beyond the power of the parties to modify by later Agreements. Modification of prior seniority provisions in subsequent Agreements is a fairly common feature of collective bargaining. And while it is true that such modifications commonly result in the increase of seniority rights of some employees, they also necessarily result in some decrease or change in the seniority rights of other employees.[17]

---

[15]Alan Wood Steel Co., 4 LA 52, 54 (Brandschain, Zwissler, & Irwin, 1946). *See also* Malone & Hyde, Inc., 43 LA 347, 348 (Rubin, 1964); Richmond Fireproof Door Co., 35 LA 682, 683 (McIntosh, 1960); Curtiss-Wright Corp., 11 LA 139, 143 (Uible, 1948).

[16]Acme Galvanizing Co., 19 LA 575, 577 (Gooding, 1952). *See also* Reyco Indus., 75 LA 689, 694–95 (Talent, 1980); County of Wayne, 71 LA 864, 867–69 (Roumell, Jr., 1978); Kansas City Power & Light Co., 52 LA 1087, 1097–98 (Klamon, 1969). Cf. *Timken Co.*, 79 LA 142, 146–47 (Morgan, 1982), and *Evening Sentinel*, 62 LA 1059, 1060 (Purcell, 1974), where employees with contractual seniority suffered layoff while apprentices worked.

[17]Ford Motor Co., 23 LA 296, 297 (Shulman, 1954). *See also* Wyoming Pub. Sch., 77 LA 295, 298 (Kotch, 1981). The Supreme Court recognized that unions and employers, acting in

In renegotiating the seniority provisions of a collective bargaining agreement, the union's bargaining discretion is limited by its status as the exclusive bargaining representative for all its members,[18] which gives rise to its duty of fair representation to each.[19] In addition, the freedom of bargaining representatives and employers as well may be judicially constrained should the doctrine of estoppel be found applicable.[20]

While seniority rights may be modified during the course of negotiations between the parties, they also may be subject to unilateral modification, when warranted, by a change in conditions or circumstances.[21] Thus, the U.S. Court of Appeals for the Seventh Circuit upheld the finding of an arbitrator that a company did not violate its collective bargaining agreement by unilaterally changing its seniority system after 30 years from a dual chapel seniority system, which maintained different lists for day and night operations, to a companywide seniority system.[22] The court agreed with the arbitrator's reasoning that

> even though the dual chapel seniority system was an established past practice, such practices can be changed either by a clause to the contrary in a collective bargaining agreement or unilaterally by either party when the conditions upon which the practice was based are substantially changed or eliminated.[23]

Collective bargaining agreements generally provide for the recognition of seniority in many aspects of the employment relationship. In addition to promotions and layoffs, seniority may govern rehiring, shift preference, transfers, vacations, days off, and overtime work. Indeed, consideration of seniority looms so importantly that it has been said that "one of the principal purposes for entering into a collective bargaining agreement is usually to secure for the employees the prized right of seniority . . . ."[24]

---

good faith, may modify seniority rights provided for in a collective bargaining agreement. *See* Ford Motor Co. v. Huffman, 345 U.S. 330, 31 LRRM 2548 (1953). For other authority, see *Hass v. Darigold Dairy Prods. Co.*, 751 F.2d 1096, 1099, 118 LRRM 2530, 2532 (9th Cir. 1985); *Cooper v. General Motors Corp.*, 651 F.2d 249, 107 LRRM 3161, 3163 (5th Cir. 1981); *Annotation*, 90 A.L.R. 2d 1003, 1004–06 (1963); Kramer, *Seniority and Ability, in* MANAGEMENT RIGHTS AND THE ARBITRATION PROCESS, PROCEEDINGS OF THE 9TH ANNUAL MEETING OF NAA 41, 41–42 (McKelvey ed., BNA Books 1956). Of course, company and union representatives must be duly authorized in order to validly alter seniority rights. Toledo Edison Co., 79 LA 895, 900 (Kates, 1982).

[18]*Darigold Dairy Prods. Co.*, 751 F.2d at 1099.

[19]*Id.*

[20]*Id. See also* Bob's Big Boy Family Rests. v. NLRB, 625 F.2d 850, 853–54, 104 LRRM 3169 (9th Cir. 1980); Terones v. Pacific States Steel Corp., 526 F. Supp. 1350, 1356 (N.D. Cal. 1981).

[21]*See* Printing Pressmen No. 7 (Chicago Web) v. Chicago Newspaper Publishers Ass'n, 772 F.2d 384, 120 LRRM 2511 (7th Cir. 1985). *See also* Rohm & Haas Tex., 93 LA 137 (Allen, Jr., 1989) (notwithstanding provision in collective bargaining agreement that the most junior employees be selected for involuntary temporary assignments, employer properly assigned unwilling senior bargaining unit employee to workers' committee, where employer's proposal requiring employees to attend meetings that are reasonably related to the performance of duties was added to subsequent agreement); Kroger Co., 92 LA 346 (Pratte, 1989) (past practice of using companywide seniority eliminated in contract negotiations). *But see* Exxon Shipping Co., 89 LA 731 (Katz, 1987) (employer violated agreement when it unilaterally changed basis for seniority).

[22]*Chicago Newspaper Publishers Ass'n*, 772 F.2d at 386, 120 LRRM at 2512.

[23]*Id.*

[24]Cournoyer v. American Television Co., 28 LA 483, 485 (Minn. 1957).

2. Interaction of Seniority Systems With Federal Statutes

A. Civil Rights Act [LA CDI 94.553]

In considering the materials in this section on seniority systems and the antidiscrimination provisions of the Civil Rights Act of 1964,[25] it should be noted that the Civil Rights Act can be violated even without discriminatory intent. For example, impermissible independent discrimination may result from reliance on tests unrelated to job duties or from requiring other than bona fide occupational qualifications.

i. Discrimination Resulting From the Operation of a Bona Fide Seniority System

The Supreme Court has declared that the "unmistakable purpose" of Section 703(h) of the Civil Rights Act of 1964 "'was to make clear that the routine application of a bona fide seniority system would not be unlawful under Title. VII.'"[26] Section 703(h) provides:

> Notwithstanding any other provision of this subchapter [Title VII], it shall not be an unlawful employment practice for an employer to apply different standards of compensation, or different terms, conditions, or privileges of employment pursuant to a bona fide seniority or merit system . . . provided that such differences are not the result of an intention to discriminate because of race, color, religion, sex, or national origin . . . .

To qualify as a "bona fide" seniority system under the Civil Rights Act, the system must be established and administered without discriminatory intent. In a case in which an employee had insufficient seniority to avoid working on Saturdays to accommodate his religious beliefs, the Supreme Court ruled that "absent a discriminatory purpose, the operation of a seniority system cannot be an unlawful employment practice even if the system has some discriminatory consequences."[27]

---

[25]42 U.S.C. §2000e et seq.

[26]Trans World Airlines v. Hardison, 432 U.S. 63, 82, 14 FEP Cases 1697, 1705 (1977) (quoting Teamsters v. United States (T.I.M.E., Inc.), 431 U.S. 324, 352, 14 FEP Cases 1514 (1977)).

[27]Id. Compare the Court's statement on bona fide seniority systems and age discrimination under the Age Discrimination in Employment Act (ADEA), 29 U.S.C. §621 et seq., in Trans World Airlines v. Thurston, 469 U.S. 111, 122, 36 FEP Cases 977 (1985). See also Lorance v. AT&T Techs., 490 U.S. 1656, 49 FEP Cases 1656 (1989); California Brewers Ass'n v. Bryant, 444 U.S. 598, 610–11, 22 FEP Cases 1 (1980); Altman v. AT&T Techs., 870 F.2d 386, 49 FEP Cases 400 (7th Cir. 1989); Gantlin v. West Virginia Pulp & Paper Co., 734 F.2d 980, 34 FEP Cases 1316 (4th Cir. 1984); Calloway v. Westinghouse Elec. Corp., 642 F. Supp. 663, 41 FEP Cases 1715 (M.D. Ga. 1986). See JPI Transp. Prods., 93 LA 716 (Kindig, 1989) (upholding discharge of employee who refused to work on Saturday, his Sabbath, in face of rotation, seniority-based weekend overtime distribution system); Department of Corr. Servs., 92 LA 1059 (Babiskin, 1989) (although employer could not violate contractual or seniority rights of other employees by granting shift changes or more favorable vacation leave, it could have accommodated employee's religious beliefs by granting unpaid leave for observation of Sabbath). Cf. Mitchell v. Jefferson County Bd. of Educ., 936 F.2d 539, 56 FEP Cases 644 (11th Cir. 1991) (not bona fide seniority system); Pennsylvania v. Operating Eng'rs Local 542, 770 F.2d 1068, 38 FEP Cases 673 (3d Cir. 1985) (seniority system not bona fide because union hiring hall referral system was vehicle for intentional discrimination), cert. denied,

However, the U. S. Court of Appeals for the Ninth Circuit has held that "the existence of a neutral seniority system does not relieve the employer of its duty to reasonably accommodate the religious beliefs of its employees, so long as the accommodation can be accomplished without disruption of the seniority system and without more than a *de minimis* cost to the employer."[28]

ii. Discrimination Intended to Be Achieved by a Seniority System

If the seniority system is established or administered with an intent to discriminate against minorities, it does not qualify as "bona fide" under the Civil Rights Act.[29]

iii. Discrimination That Is Perpetuated by a Bona Fide Seniority System

So long as a seniority system is established and administered without discriminatory intent, it will not violate the Civil Rights Act even if consideration of seniority in promotions perpetuates the effects of prior independent discrimination. In one case a district court found that, although the seniority system had and continued to have the inevitable effect of perpetuating disparities and disadvantages associated with race, the plaintiff minority employees had no basis for relief, because neither the union nor the company had been motivated by racial considerations in establishing the seniority system.[30]

While Section 703(h) provides immunity for the "operation" or "routine application" of a bona fide seniority system, that section does not prevent unlawful independent discrimination from having some impact on the bona fide seniority system itself. In the latter regard, it is clear that where unlawful discrimination against a person has occurred after July 2, 1965, the effective date of Title VII, the courts, on a timely charge, may remedy it by relief

---

474 U.S. 1060 (1986). For extensive discussion of the Civil Rights Act and bona fide seniority systems, see LINDEMANN & GROSSMAN, EMPLOYMENT DISCRIMINATION LAW 54–66 (BNA Books 3d ed. 1996).

[28]Balint v. Carson City, Nev., 180 F.3d 1047, 1054, 79 FEP Cases 1750 (9th Cir. 1999) (plaintiff's job application with county sheriff's department was rejected on the basis that her assertion that she could not work on her religion's Saturday Sabbath was "incompatible" with the sheriff's seniority shift-bidding system; the court held that summary judgment in favor of the sheriff was improper where genuine issues of material fact existed as to whether voluntary shift trades and/or shift splitting would reasonably accommondate plaintiff without undue hardship to the sheriff and without violating the established seniority system).

[29]Pennsylvania v. Operating Eng'rs Local 542, 770 F.2d 1068, 38 FEP Cases 673 (3d Cir. 1985).

[30]Goodman v. Lukens Steel Co., 580 F. Supp. 1114, 39 FEP Cases 617 (E.D. Pa. 1984), *modified on other grounds*, 777 F.2d 113, 39 FEP Cases 658 (3d Cir. 1986), *aff'd*, 482 U.S. 656, 44 FEP Cases 1 (1987). The district court found that the company's unit seniority system was adopted because it represented the standard practice throughout the steel industry and was assumed to be best suited to operating efficiency. Furthermore, the court noted that, even if the seniority system had been established for the express purpose of perpetuating racial disparities, a shift to a different seniority system would have been unlikely to provide any net benefit to black employees, then or in the future. *See also* Salinas v. Roadway Express, 735 F.2d 1574, 35 FEP Cases 533 (5th Cir. 1984) (the court held that a dual seniority system for road and city drivers does not violate Title VII, although it may perpetuate pre–Civil Rights Act discrimination).

adequate to achieve the "make-whole" purposes of the Civil Rights Act, and that such relief may include an award of retroactive or "constructive" seniority that may date back to the initial discrimination. Thus, an employee may be placed on the seniority list in the position that would have resulted had the discrimination never occurred.[31] To the extent that a victim does receive such "constructive" seniority, the post–Civil Rights Act discrimination, having thus been remedied, will not be perpetuated by a bona fide seniority system.

Challenges to a seniority system may be filed under Title VII of the Civil Rights Act either "when the system is adopted, when an individual becomes subject to the seniority system, or when a person aggrieved is injured by the application of the seniority system or provision of the system."[32]

As concerns discrimination occurring prior to the effective date of Title VII, often referred to in Supreme Court decisions as "pre-Act" discrimination, the Supreme Court has held that persons "who suffered only pre-Act discrimination are not entitled to relief, and no person may be given retroactive seniority to a date earlier than the effective date of the Act."[33] The Court made clear "that an otherwise neutral, legitimate seniority system does not become unlawful under Title VII simply because it may perpetuate pre-Act discrimination," for "Congress did not intend to make it illegal for employees with vested seniority rights to continue to exercise those rights, even at the expense of pre-Act discriminatees."[34] However, the immunity given to bona

---

[31]Sheet Metal Workers Local 28 v. EEOC, 478 U.S. 421, 445, 41 FEP Cases 107 (1986); Teamsters v. United States (T.I.M.E.-DC, Inc.), 431 U.S. 324, 14 FEP Cases 1514 (1977); Franks v. Bowman Transp. Co., 424 U.S. 747, 12 FEP Cases 549 (1976). In *Franks*, the Supreme Court held that the §703(h) exemption of bona fide seniority systems was not intended to "restrict relief otherwise appropriate once an illegal discriminatory practice occurring after the effective date of the Act is proved," *Franks*, 424 U.S. at 762, and the Court stated that a remedy "slotting the victim in that position in the seniority system that would have been his," *id*. at 765, and that there have been no discrimination "ordinarily . . . will be necessary to achieve the 'make-whole' purposes of the Act." *Id*. at 766. Subsequently in *Teamsters*, the Court stated that "after the victims have been identified and their rightful place determined, the District Court will . . . be faced with the delicate task of adjusting the remedial interests of discriminatees and the legitimate expectations of other employees innocent of any wrongdoing." *Teamsters*, 431 U.S. at 372. The Court explained further that "when immediate implementation of an equitable remedy threatens to impinge upon the expectations of innocent parties, the courts must 'look to the practical realities and necessities inescapably involved in reconciling competing interests,' in order to determine the 'special blend of what is necessary, what is fair, and what is workable.'" *Id*. at 375 (quoting Lemon v. Kurtzman, 411 U.S. 192, 200–01 (1973)). *Cf.* Fire Fighters (IAFF) Local 1784 v. Stotts, 467 U.S. 561, 34 FEP Cases 1702 (1984) (lower court erred in overriding seniority system absent finding either that system was not bona fide or that such remedy was necessary to make whole a proven victim of unlawful discrimination). *See also* 42 U.S.C. §2000e-2(j) (precluding a court from awarding relief simply to create a balanced workforce).

[32]42 U.S.C. §2000e-5(e)(2). This provision was added to Title VII by Section 112 of the Civil Rights Act of 1991, Pub. L. No. 102-166, 105 Stat. 1088 (1991), and nullifies the Supreme Court's holding in *Lorance v. AT&T Technologies*, 490 U.S. 1656, 49 FEP Cases 1656 (1989), that the limitations period under Title VII for a seniority system that is facially nondiscriminatory and nondiscriminatorily applied but allegedly adopted for discriminatory reasons begins to run at the time of adoption. *See also* Loftis, *The Civil Rights Act of 1991's Answer to* Lorance v. AT&T Technologies, Inc., 7 B.Y.U. J. Pub. L. 185 (Spring 1993). *Cf.* Barrow v. New Orleans S.S. Ass'n, 932 F.2d 473, 56 FEP Cases 156 (5th Cir. 1991) (applying *Lorance* in an ADEA case decided prior to the passage of the 1991 Civil Rights Act).

[33]Teamsters v. United States (T.I.M.E.-DC, Inc.), 431 U.S. 324, 356–57, 14 FEP Cases 1514 (1977).

[34]*Id*. at 354. *See also* Ameritech Benefit Plan Comm. v. Communication Workers, 220 F.3d 814, 823, 83 FEP Cases 794 (7th Cir. 2000) (no violation of Title VII where employer's

fide seniority systems is an exception. Generally, business policies or practices that are neutral on their face and in their intent, but the effect of which nonetheless is to discriminate or perpetuate discrimination against a protected class, prima facie violate the Civil Rights Act.[35]

As construed by the Supreme Court, Section 703(h) immunizes (1) the perpetuation of pre–Civil Rights Act discrimination by a bona fide seniority system, and (2) post–Civil Rights Act discrimination resulting from the operation of a bona fide seniority system. But where an employee has been independently and illegally discriminated against, Section 703(h) does not limit a court's authority to remedy the discrimination by adequate relief that may include an award of "constructive" seniority to "slot" the victim into his or her rightful place ahead of other employees on a bona fide system's seniority list.[36]

iv. Seniority Systems and Arbitral Enforcement of Antidiscrimination Clauses Resulting in "Reverse Discrimination" Claims [LA CDI 106.25; 107.30]

While illegal post–Civil Rights Act discrimination may be remedied through court action, many grievants allege discrimination because of race, sex, religion, or the like through the arbitration process. Many such cases[37] note that many, but not all, arbitrators subsequent to the Supreme Court's *Gardner-Denver*[38] decision have considered Title VII doctrine in dealing with

---

bona fide seniority system had the effect of discriminating against women who had taken pregnancy or maternity leave prior to the effective date of Title VII). Furthermore, post–Civil Rights Act discrimination not timely charged is the legal equivalent of pre–Civil Rights Act discrimination; thus, its effects also may be lawfully perpetuated by a bona fide seniority system. United Air Lines v. Evans, 431 U.S. 553, 14 FEP Cases 1510 (1977). In the latter regard, the requirement for filing a timely charge is subject to waiver, estoppel, and equitable tolling. Zipes v. Trans World Airlines, 455 U.S. 385, 28 FEP Cases 1 (1982). The Supreme Court has held that §703(h) protects a seniority system, regardless of whether the seniority system itself was adopted before or after the effective date of the Civil Rights Act. American Tobacco Co. v. Patterson, 456 U.S. 63, 76, 28 FEP Cases 713 (1982). The Supreme Court has indicated that, within limits, significant freedom must be afforded employers and unions to create "differing" seniority systems. California Brewers Ass'n v. Bryant, 444 U.S. 598, 610–11, 22 FEP Cases 1 (1980). Finally, the Supreme Court has found that, under §703(h), "a showing of disparate impact is insufficient to invalidate a seniority system," *Pullman-Standard Div. v. Swint*, 456 U.S. 273, 277, 28 FEP Cases 1073 (1982), and reiterated that "'absent a discriminatory purpose, the operation of a seniority system cannot be an unlawful employment practice even if the system has some discriminatory consequences.'" *Id.* (quoting *Hardison*, 432 U.S. at 82). Challenges to a seniority system under Title VII will require a trial on the issue of discriminatory intent, which the Supreme Court has found to be "a pure question of fact." *Pullman-Standard Div.*, 456 U.S. at 287.

[35]Teamsters v. United States (T.I.M.E.-DC, Inc.), 431 U.S. 324, 353, 14 FEP Cases 1514 (1977).

[36]In other words, the operation of a bona fide seniority system cannot be the basis of a charge of illegal discrimination; but the seniority system itself can be affected or compromised to the limited extent that constructive seniority is awarded by a court to remedy illegal discrimination that resulted totally apart from the operation of the seniority system. Stated more concisely, a bona fide seniority system cannot be penalized or compromised as a result of something it did, but it can be compromised to some extent as a result of something that it did not do.

[37]The cases are included in the Chapter 10, section 3.A.i., "Title VII of the Civil Rights Act."

[38]Alexander v. Gardner-Denver Co., 415 U.S. 36, 7 FEP Cases 81 (1974).

discrimination issues. A factor in some of the cited cases was the existence of collective bargaining agreement clauses stating that the parties would comply with antidiscrimination law, or expressly voiding any part of the agreement to the extent that it conflicts with federal or state law, or simply prohibiting discrimination on the basis of a protected class. This section considers, however, only arbitration cases in which grievants had alleged a violation of their contractual seniority rights by the employer in favoring, rather than discriminating against, other persons as members of a minority group. These are so-called "reverse discrimination" cases. In such cases, the employer may or may not have acted with the belief that such action was legally required; but, regardless of motivation, a clash with collective bargaining agreement rights may result.

It is apparent that bona fide seniority systems on the whole have legitimate standing even vis-à-vis Title VII of the Civil Rights Act. It is also apparent that where illegal post–Civil Rights Act discrimination does occur, the operation of a bona fide seniority system may be reconciled with rights under the Civil Rights Act by an award of "constructive" seniority or other relief from a court. In some cases, an arbitrator also may be able fully or partially to reconcile the operation of a collective bargaining agreement seniority system with rights under the Civil Rights Act; but in order for the arbitrator to do so by an award enforceable under federal law, the award must draw its essence from the collective bargaining agreement and must not order the performance of an unlawful act or one that would violate an established public policy. Such an award would be justified where the collective bargaining agreement contains a clause expressly voiding any part of the agreement found to conflict with the Civil Rights Act. Even absent an express provision of this sort, the interpretative process, sometimes aided by bargaining history or past practice, may produce an enforceable award achieving in whole or in part the needed reconciliation of collective bargaining agreement and statute. In some cases, an arbitrator will find no basis within the arbitrator's authority for achieving the needed reconciliation and will issue an award based on the arbitrator's understanding of the collective bargaining agreement alone. Here again, to be enforceable the award must draw its essence from the agreement and must not order the performance of an unlawful act or one that would violate a recognized public policy.

Where an employer, with the agreement or approval of the union, has entered into a conciliation agreement or affirmative action plan on behalf of some minority group, arbitrators likely will honor the conciliation agreement or affirmative action plan when it conflicts with the collective bargaining agreement.[39]

---

[39]City of Toledo, Ohio, 88 LA 137 (Feldman, 1986) (the terms of a settlement stipulation resolving a race discrimination suit in which the union was a party and providing for specific promotion ratios, overrode the provisions of a collective bargaining agreement that was allegedly violated when a black employee was promoted in accordance with the settlement of the lawsuit); Washtenaw County, 87 LA 364 (Roumell, Jr., 1986); Hayes Int'l Corp., 79 LA 999 (Valtin, 1982) (the conciliation agreement in question had been forced on the employer "by the government," *id.* at 1002, and the union through its officers "extended a cooperative hand and thereby gave its approval for the use of the program," *id.* at 1006); Flint Bd. of Educ., 77 LA 244, 246–48 (Daniel, 1981) (the "union by various actions . . . did enter into an

However, where the employer enters into a conciliation agreement or affirmative action plan without obtaining the union's consent, an arbitrator may give priority to conflicting provisions of a collective bargaining agreement.[40]

In cases decided prior to the Supreme Court's 1983 *W.R. Grace*[41] decision, many arbitrators gave priority to the collective bargaining agreement seniority provisions in that situation.[42] However, because of the specific facts involved, the decisions of other arbitrators who gave priority to the conciliation agreement or affirmative action plan were not necessarily in conflict.

---

agreement with the employer to permit application of affirmative action concepts in the selection of candidates" for apprenticeship, and that "implicit in this is the agreement to accept modification of strict seniority," *id.* at 248). *See also* Douglas County, Glide Sch. Dist. No. 12, 79 LA 1138, 1145 (Lehleitner, 1982); International Paper Co., 68 LA 155, 159 (Taylor, 1977). In *Steelworkers v. Weber*, 443 U.S. 193, 20 FEP Cases 1 (1979), only 1.83% of the skilled craft workers in the plant were black, even though the workforce in the local community was approximately 39% black. This imbalance resulted because the employer lawfully had previously hired trained outsiders with prior craft experience; the Supreme Court took judicial notice that blacks long had been excluded from craft unions, and that, accordingly, few had craft experience. The employer and the union voluntarily adopted an affirmative action plan for on-the-job craft training, reserving half of the training slots for blacks. Although some blacks accepted for training had less seniority than whites who were excluded, the Supreme Court upheld the plan when challenged under Title VII. The Court pointed out that the plan's purposes mirrored those of the Title VII, the plan did not unnecessarily trammel the interests of white employees (none was discharged and half of the trainees would be white), and the plan was a temporary measure to eliminate a manifest racial imbalance in traditionally segregated job categories. The Court emphasized that its decision dealt only with private, voluntary plans, and was not concerned "with what Title VII requires or with what a court might order to remedy a past proven violation of the Act." *Id.* at 200. In the latter regard, we have noted above how courts may provide relief for victims of illegal discrimination. However, in *Fire Fighters (IAFF) Local 1784 v. Stotts*, 467 U.S. 561, 34 FEP Cases 1702 (1984), a decision dealing directly with court authority rather than with what private parties may do independently of a court order, the Supreme Court held that bona fide seniority systems may not be altered by a court for the benefit of persons who themselves were not the victims of illegal discrimination. Stating that the legislative history of Title VII "made clear that a court was not authorized to give preferential treatment to non-victims," the Court quoted that legislative history's statement that "[u]nder title VII, not even a court, much less the [Equal Employment Opportunity] Commission, could order racial quotas or the hiring, reinstatement, admission to membership or payment of back pay for anyone who is not discriminated against in violation of this title." *Id.* at 581–82. The Supreme Court concluded that the district court, by an affirmative action consent decree, had improperly required white employees to be laid off or demoted when an otherwise applicable and bona fide seniority system would have called for the layoff of black employees who had less seniority and who had not been victims of illegal discrimination.

[40]Public Serv. Co. of Colo., 99 LA 1081 (Goodman, 1992).

[41]W.R. Grace & Co. v. Rubber Workers Local 759, 461 U.S. 757, 113 LRRM 2641 (1983).

[42]For cases in which the arbitrator gave priority to the collective bargaining agreement, see *City of Detroit, Dep't of Police*, 78 LA 486, 492 (Kahn, 1982); *Southwestern Elec. Power Co.*, 77 LA 553, 558, 561 (Bothwell, 1981); *Struck Constr. Co.*, 74 LA 369, 372–73 (Sergent, Jr., 1980); *City of Detroit, Mich.*, 73 LA 717, 722 (Daniel, 1979); *Jefferson Chem. Co.*, 72 LA 892, 896 (Goodstein, 1979) (holding that the collective bargaining agreement was controlling over an affirmative action plan, but that selection of a qualified minority member did not violate an unqualified grievant's rights under the seniority and ability clause of the agreement); *USM Corp.*, 69 LA 1051, 1056–57 (Gregory, 1977). *See also* Orchids Paper Prods. Concel, 76 LA 101, 103 (Ross, 1980); Hollander & Co., 64 LA 816, 819–21 (Edelman, 1975). For cases in which the arbitrator gave priority to the conciliation agreement or affirmative action plan, see *International Paper Co.*, 69 LA 857, 861 (Taylor, 1977); *Copolymer Rubber & Chem. Corp.*, 64 LA 310, 312, 314 (Dunn, 1975); *Bethlehem Steel Corp.*, 63 LA 63, 64–65 (Strongin, 1974). *See also* County of Santa Clara, 71 LA 290, 294–95 (Koven, 1978); ASG Indus., 62 LA 849, 852–54 (Foster, 1974); Day & Zimmermann, 60 LA 495, 499–500 (Marcus, 1973). For the various and sometimes divergent actions of arbitrators where a court consent

Curiously, even where two arbitration decisions reached different conclusions on the same issue under the same agreement, courts have upheld the validity of both decisions provided that each drew its essence from the agreement.[43]

In the *W.R. Grace* case, the employer, without union agreement or approval, entered into an Equal Employment Opportunity Commission (EEOC) conciliation agreement containing seniority provisions that conflicted with those of the collective bargaining agreement. The employer then obtained a federal district court order declaring that the conciliation agreement took precedence over the collective bargaining agreement. While the order was still in effect, the employer laid off some male employees contrary to their seniority rights under the collective bargaining agreement, adhering instead to the EEOC conciliation agreement. Although the male employees were reinstated after reversal of the district court's order that had given priority to the EEOC agreement, their grievances for back pay remained unsettled and were carried to arbitration. The first grievance to reach arbitration was heard and denied by the arbitrator who, as stated by the Supreme Court, "concluded that although the grievant was entitled to an award under the collective bargaining agreement, it would be inequitable to penalize the Company for conduct that complied with an outstanding court order."[44] The next grievance to reach arbitration was heard and sustained by another arbitrator, who strictly applied the seniority provisions of the collective bargaining agreement, found a violation, and awarded back pay. The first arbitration award was not taken to court. The second award was. The district court concluded that public policy prevented enforcement of the second award, but the U.S. Court of Appeals for the Fifth Circuit disagreed.[45]

A unanimous Supreme Court held that the lower court had properly granted enforcement of the second award of back pay.[46] In so deciding, the Supreme Court provided useful guidance for the resolution of future cases:

1. Regarding modification of the collective bargaining agreement by the conciliation agreement, the court of appeals had held that, because the seniority system was not motivated by a discriminatory purpose, it was lawful and could not be modified without the union's consent. The Supreme Court agreed and explained:

---

decree had been entered against the employer or against both the employer and the union, see *Bethlehem Steel Corp.*, 75 LA 353 (Sharnoff, 1980); *United States Steel Corp.*, 70 LA 1235, 1241–42 (Garrett, 1978); *United States Steel Corp.*, 66 LA 663 (Das, 1976); *Mountain States Tel. & Tel. Co.*, 64 LA 316 (Platt, 1975); *Stardust Hotel*, 61 LA 942 (Jones, Jr., 1973); *Virginia Elec. & Power Co.*, 61 LA 844 (Murphy, 1973). For additional discussion of arbitrators and Title VII, see Chapter 10, section 3.A.i., "Title VII of the Civil Rights Act."

[43]*See*, *e.g.*, Graphic Arts Local 97-B v. Haddon Craftsmen, 489 F. Supp. 1088, 1096–98 (M.D. Pa. 1979) (the court refused to set aside either of two conflicting awards where each drew its essence from the agreement).

[44]*W.R. Grace*, 461 U.S. at 762, 113 LRRM at 2643.

[45]W.R. Grace & Co. v. Rubber Workers Local 759, 652 F.2d 1248, 107 LRRM 3251 (5th Cir. 1981).

[46]W.R. Grace & Co. v. Rubber Workers Local 759, 461 U.S. 757, 771, 113 LRRM 2641, 2647 (1983).

In this case, although the Company and the Commission [EEOC] agreed to nullify the collective-bargaining agreement's seniority provisions, the conciliation process did not include the Union. Absent a judicial determination, the Commission, not to mention the Company, cannot alter the collective-bargaining agreement without the Union's consent. . . . Permitting such a result would undermine the federal labor policy that parties to a collective-bargaining agreement must have reasonable assurance that their contract will be honored.[47]

2. The Supreme Court ruled that the court of appeals "was correct" in enforcing the award, which drew its essence from the collective bargaining agreement, for

[u]nder well-established standards for the review of labor arbitration awards, a federal court may not overrule an arbitrator's decision simply because the court believes its own interpretation of the contract would be the better one. . . . Unless the [arbitrator's] decision does not 'dra[w] its essence from the collective bargaining agreement,' . . . a court is bound to enforce the award and is not entitled to review the merits of the . . . dispute. . . . even when the basis for the arbitrator's decision may be ambiguous.[48]

3. Turning to the district court's refusal to enforce the arbitration award on public policy grounds, the Supreme Court agreed that a court may not enforce a collective bargaining agreement that is contrary to public policy. However, the Supreme Court noted the limitation that such a public policy "must be well defined and dominant, and is to be ascertained 'by reference to the laws and legal precedents and not from general considerations of supposed public interests.'"[49]

---

[47]*Id.* (citations omitted) (the Court also explained in detail why it believed that enforcement of the arbitration award in this case would encourage rather than discourage participation by both the employer and the union in "conciliation and true voluntary compliance with federal employment discrimination law," *id.*). *See also* United States v. City of Chicago, 870 F.2d 1256, 50 FEP Cases 682 (7th Cir. 1989) (equitable decrees are not to be made without consideration of the interests of third parties who may be affected); EEOC v. Safeway Stores, 714 F.2d 567, 32 FEP Cases 1465 (5th Cir. 1983), *cert. denied*, 467 U.S. 1204 (1984).

[48]*W.R. Grace*, 461 U.S. at 764, 113 LRRM at 2644 (citing Steelworkers v. Enterprise Wheel & Car Corp., 363 U.S. 593, 46 LRRM 2423 (1960)). The Court explained that the award drew its essence from the collective bargaining agreement in that the second arbitrator (1) interpreted provisions of the agreement as not requiring him to follow the prior award on the same issue; (2) interpreted the agreement as providing "no good-faith defense to claims of violation of the seniority provisions," *W.R. Grace*, 461 U.S. at 765; and (3) "In effect . . . interpreted the collective-bargaining agreement to allocate to the Company the losses caused by the Company's decision to follow the District Court order that proved to be erroneous." *Id.* at 767, 113 LRRM at 2644–45. The Court also stated that "although conceivably we could reach a different result were we to interpret the contract ourselves, we cannot say that the award does not draw its essence from the collective bargaining agreement." *Id.* at 765–66 (footnote omitted). For related discussion concerning the refusal to follow the prior award, see Chapter 11, section 3.B., "Temporary or Ad Hoc Arbitrators," where the *W.R. Grace* decision is examined.

[49]*W.R. Grace*, 461 U.S. at 766, 113 LRRM at 2645 (quoting Muschany v. United States, 324 U.S. 49, 66 (1945)).

Considering the question of obedience to court orders, the Supreme Court stated:

> It is beyond question that obedience to judicial orders is an important public policy. An injunction issued by a court acting within its jurisdiction must be obeyed until the injunction is vacated or withdrawn. . . . A contract provision the performance of which has been enjoined is unenforceable. . . . Here, however, enforcement of the collective-bargaining agreement as interpreted by [the second arbitrator] does not compromise this public policy.
>
>   . . .
>
> Even assuming that the District Court's order was a mandatory injunction, nothing in the collective bargaining agreement as interpreted by [the arbitrator] required the Company to violate that order. [The arbitrator's] award neither mandated layoffs nor required that layoffs be conducted according to the collective-bargaining agreement. The award simply held, retrospectively, that the employees were entitled to damages for the prior breach of the seniority provisions.[50]

By no means does the *W.R. Grace* decision answer all of the important questions in this complex area. The Supreme Court expressly cautioned, for instance, that it was not deciding "whether some public policy would be violated by an arbitral award for a breach of seniority provisions ultimately found to be illegal," and neither was the Court deciding "whether such an award could be enforced in the face of a valid judicial alteration of seniority provisions . . . to provide relief to discriminatees under Title VII or other law."[51]

---

[50]*Id.* at 766–67, 768–69, 113 LRRM at 2645, 2646 (citations and footnotes omitted). The Court continued:

> In this case, the Company actually complied with the District Court's order, and nothing we say here causes us to believe that it would disobey the order if presented with the same dilemma in the future. Enforcement of [the arbitrator's] award will not create intolerable incentives to disobey court orders. Courts have sufficient contempt powers to protect their injunctions, even if the injunctions are issued erroneously. . . . In addition to contempt sanctions, the Company here was faced with possible Title VII liability if it departed from the conciliation agreement in conducting its layoffs. . . .
>   Nor is placing the Company in this position with respect to the court order so unfair as to violate public policy. Obeying injunctions often is a costly affair. Because of the Company's alleged prior discrimination against women, some readjustments and consequent losses were bound to occur. The issue is whether the Company or the Union members should bear the burden of those losses. As interpreted by [the arbitrator], the collective-bargaining agreement placed this unavoidable burden on the Company. By entering into the conflicting conciliation agreement, by seeking a court order to excuse it from performing the collective-bargaining agreement, and by subsequently acting on its mistaken interpretation of its contractual obligations, the Company attempted to shift the loss to its male employees, who shared no responsibility for the sex discrimination. The Company voluntarily assumed its obligations under the collective-bargaining agreement and the arbitrators' interpretations of it. No public policy is violated by holding the Company to those obligations, which bar the Company's attempted reallocation of the burden.

Id. at 769–70, 113 LRRM at 2646–47 (citation and footnote omitted). The Court also stated that "while it may have been economic misfortune for the Company to postpone or forgo its layoff plans," *id.* at 768 n.12, 113 LRRM at 2646 n.12, it could have avoided liability under either agreement by doing so; prior to conducting the layoffs, the company could have requested a stay from the district court to permit it to follow the collective bargaining agreement pending review by a higher court. The Court also noted that compensatory damages for breach of contract may be available even when specific performance of the contract would violate public policy, and that increased cost of performance does not constitute "impossibility" serving as a defense to breach of contract claims. *Id.* at 768 n.13, 113 LRRM at 2646 n.13.

[51]*Id.* at 767 n.9, 113 LRRM at 2645 n.9 (citation omitted). Thus, the second award possibly would not have been enforceable if the collective bargaining agreement seniority system

The possibility exists that, under the *W.R. Grace* facts, an award in the company's favor could be issued that would be valid as drawing its essence from the collective bargaining agreement.[52] The Supreme Court itself appears to have identified two different possible bases on which an arbitrator could have given priority to the conciliation agreement over the collective bargaining agreement: the "legality" clause and impossibility of performance.[53]

In the *W.R. Grace* decision, the Supreme Court again sent a message to the lower courts by forcefully reaffirming that when the parties have selected an arbitrator to interpret their agreement, it is the arbitrator's interpretation that they bargained for. The courts must honor the award if its essence is drawn from the agreement, even though a court could reach, and may prefer, a different interpretation. To be upheld, however, the award must not order the performance of an unlawful act or one that would violate an established public policy.

---

in fact had been invalid, as the district court erroneously believed when it gave priority to the conciliation agreement. Likewise, *if* the district court had identified victims of sex discrimination and had determined their "rightful place," and then had awarded constructive seniority after having performed the "delicate task" of adjusting their remedial interests and the legitimate expectations of male employees, and *if* the arbitrator had refused *then* to credit that constructive seniority, the second award may not have been enforceable.

[52]It is possible, too, that the first arbitration award would have been upheld had the union challenged it in court. The validity of that award was not directly litigated and the Supreme Court stated that its validity was not relevant to the issue before the Court, which concerned "[o]nly the enforceability of the [second arbitration] award." *Id.* at 765 n.7, 113 LRRM at 2644 n.7.

[53]First, in upholding the second award, the Supreme Court stated: "although conceivably we could reach a different result were we to interpret the contract ourselves, we cannot say that the award does not draw its essence from the collective bargaining agreement." *Id.* at 765–66 (footnote omitted). In stating that the Court itself conceivably could reach a different result from the second arbitrator, the Court pointed to the "legality" clause in the collective agreement. *Id.* at 765 n.8, 113 LRRM at 2645 n.8. The clause states:

> In the event that any provision of this Agreement is found to be in conflict with any State or Federal Laws now existing or hereinafter enacted, it is agreed that such laws shall supersede the conflicting provisions without affecting the remainder of these provisions.

Id. This "legality" clause is equally a part of the collective bargaining agreement, and it is equally subject to interpretation by the arbitrator. Although the second arbitrator obviously did not interpret the clause as requiring priority for the conciliation agreement, different interpretations of the clause may reasonably be reached. The clause could be given an interpretation with controlling weight in the company's favor. A second possibility for an award in the company's favor within the essence of the collective bargaining agreement is to utilize impossibility of performance as a defense to the breach of the collective bargaining agreement seniority provisions. In this regard, in a footnote the Supreme Court stated:

> Although [the second arbitrator] could have considered the District Court order to cause impossibility of performance and thus to be a defense to the Company's breach, he did not do so. Impossibility is a doctrine of contract interpretation. . . . For the reasons stated in the text [i.e., because of the limitations on court review of arbitration awards], we cannot revise [the second arbitrator's] implicit rejection of the impossibility defense. Even if we were to review the issue *de novo*, moreover, it is far from clear that the defense is available to the Company, whose own actions created the condition of impossibility.

Id. at 768 n.10 (citations omitted). The Court appears to be saying that an arbitrator could utilize the impossibility defense to hold for the company, although a court, as distinguished from an arbitrator, may be more limited in doing so under the facts. In any event, the Supreme Court hardly was rejecting the defense for the second arbitrator's use had he been disposed to apply it.

B. Age Discrimination in Employment Act [LA CDI 106.25]

The exemption in Section 703(h) of the Civil Rights Act of 1964 immunizing the noninvidiously discriminatory "routine application" of a bona fide seniority system has been extended beyond Title VII to both the ADEA[54] and the Americans with Disabilities Act (ADA).[55]

Thus, a school district's refusal to hire an older teacher because her salary position, based on a collectively bargained, experience-driven wage schedule, would have been "too high" did not violate the ADEA.[56] The salary schedule was viewed as a seniority system that was established for a nondiscriminatory purpose. Consequently, it was not violative of the ADEA despite the disparate effect on older teachers seeking employment with the district.

In determining whether a seniority system is discriminatory, courts have applied the burden-shifting analysis used for disparate treatment claims under Title VII.[57] In an arbitration case in which a union claimed that a discharge was racially motivated and violative of the antidiscrimination provision of the collective bargaining agreement, the arbitrator was faced with the "burden of proof" question in determining whether the evidence should be considered under the Title VII standard or the traditional "just cause" requirement.[58] The arbitrator concluded that, under either line of analysis, the employer must establish that it had a valid and genuine reason for taking the challenged employment action.

---

[54]29 U.S.C. §623(f)(2). *See* Hiatt v. Union Pac. R.R. 65 F.3d 838, 150 LRRM 2265 (10th Cir. 1995) (no violation of ADEA where the railroad had a longstanding policy of not carrying over brakemen's seniority on promotion to conductor; fact that older brakemen were disadvantaged by mandatory promotions to conductor were irrelevant so long as seniority policy was applied uniformly), *cert. denied*, 516 U.S. 1115 (1996).

[55]42 U.S.C. §12112(b)(5)(A). *See* Eckles v. Consolidated Rail Corp., 94 F.3d 1041, 1047, 155 LRRM 2653 (7th Cir. 1996) (the ADA does not require an employer to offer an employee an accommodation that would require the "otherwise valid seniority rights of other employees to be trumped"), *cert. denied*, 520 U.S. 1146 (1997) . This case will be discussed further in section 2.C., "Americans With Disabilities Act," below.

[56]EEOC v. Newport Mesa Unified Sch. Dist., 893 F. Supp. 927, 68 FEP Cases 657 (C.D. Cal. 1995).

[57]Aka v. Washington Hosp. Ctr., 156 F.3d 1284, 1288–90, 159 LRRM 2467 (D.C. Cir. 1998) (summary judgment in favor of employer reversed on disparate treatment and ADA claims on basis that issue of intentional discrimination is one for the jury, and there were genuine issues of material fact relative to whether the employee could have been reassigned to an available "vacant" position for which he was qualified and whether that would not have resulted in an undue hardship to the employer); Dodd v. Runyon, 114 F.3d 726, 74 FEP Cases 738 (8th Cir. 1997) (employee's motion for summary judgment denied, where factual issue existed as to whether seniority system was administered in a discriminatory fashion); Bailey v. Norfolk & W. Ry., 527 S.E.2d 516, 540, 164 LRRM 2010 (W. Va. 1999) (court used similar burden-shifting analysis under state antidiscrimination statute to uphold jury verdict finding that employer had placed plaintiffs at the bottom of the conductor seniority list by creating separate seniority systems for brakemen and conductors, with an impermissible age motivation); Crump v. Chicago Hous. Auth., No. 97 C 2135, 1998 WL 164869, at *5, 1998 U.S. Dist. LEXIS 4654, at *14 (E.D. Ill. 1998) (employer's motion for summary judgment granted, where the use of a "birthday rule" to determine the order of layoffs among employees with the same seniority date "was not used as a shield to hide discrimination").

[58]Henkel Corp., 104 LA 494 (Hooper, 1995).

C. Americans With Disabilities Act [LA CDI 106.25]

The ADA makes it unlawful for a covered employer not to make reasonable accommodations to the known physical or mental limitations of an otherwise qualified individual with a disability, unless such covered employer can demonstrate that the accommodation would impose an undue hardship on the operation of its business.[59] An employer may face the dilemma that a reasonable accommodation of an otherwise qualified individual with a disability violates the contractual seniority rights of bargaining unit employees.[60] Contractual seniority obligations may support an employer's contention that accommodation would impose an undue hardship.[61] One legal commentator and arbitrator summed up the interplay between seniority systems and the duty to accommodate as follows:

> It is important to recognize that both seniority systems and the duty to accommodate are designed to enhance the employment opportunities of workers. Seniority operates directly, by making length of service a factor in who receives work. Anti-discrimination legislation operates indirectly, by ensuring that certain factors do not determine who gets the work. Since both systems involve competition between workers, some will see their employment opportunities expanded and others will not.[62]

Courts also have recognized the importance of protecting collectively bargained seniority rights from unwarranted intrusion.[63] In regard to judicial intrusion in the area of seniority rights, the U.S. Court of Appeals for the Eighth Circuit stated:

> We believe that these rights are entitled to protection regardless of whether a plaintiff seeks a reasonable accommodation or claims the seniority system has

---

[59]42 U.S.C. §12112(b)(5)(A). *See also* 29 C.F.R. §1630.9.

[60]*See* Ogden Allied Plant Maint. Co. of Okla., 101 LA 467, 470 (Harr, 1993) (arbitrator held that he had no contractual jurisdiction to determine the company's obligations under the ADA to accommodate an employee's physical work restrictions, since Congress mandated the ADA be enforced by the EEOC). *Cf.* Roadmaster Corp., 98 LA 847, 851 (Christenson, 1992) (legislation does not, by itself, create contractual obligations); Ohio Civil Serv. Employees, 97 LA 942, 946 (Brunner, 1991) (arbitrator found he had the contractual authority to determine whether a contract provision was preempted by a conflicting federal tax regulation).

[61]*See* 42 U.S.C. §12112(b)(5)(A); 29 C.F.R. §1630.15(d), app. (terms of the collective bargaining agreement may be relevant to determine undue hardship if a particular accommodation would be unduly disruptive to employer's other employees or to the functioning of its business). For a further discussion of the ADA's impact on contractual seniority rights, see generally Rottenberg, *The Americans with Disabilities Act: Erosion of Collective Rights?*, 14 BERKELEY J. EMP. LAB. L. 179 (Summer 1993); *NLRB: Memorandum on Collective Bargaining*, 23 AD MANUAL (BNA) 70:1019 (1993); Frankel, *The Impact of the Americans With Disabilities Act of 1990 on Collective Bargaining Agreements*, 22 SW. U. L. REV. 257 (Autumn 1992); *NLRB: Memorandum on Collective Bargaining and ADA*, 8 AD MANUAL (BNA) 70:1031 (1992). *See also* Chapter 10, section 3., "Statutory Law."

[62]Joachim, *Seniority Rights and the Duty to Accommodate*, 24 QUEENS L.J. 131, 151 (1998).

[63]Boersig v. Electrical Workers (IBEW) Local 1439, 219 F.3d 816, 822–23, 164 LRRM 2794 (8th Cir. 2000) (a seniority system is not a "selection criterion" under 42 U.S.C. §12212(b)(6), and the appellant failed to establish that the employer designed the seniority system in order to discriminate against disabled employees; the ADA does not require the employer to renegotiate a bona fide seniority system to avoid "screening out" an employee who may not be able to attain a certain level of seniority for promotion purposes due to a disablity).

a disparate impact on disabled employees. In either case, the plaintiff invites the court to disrupt a carefully negotiated agreement between union and employer at the expense of other union employees who hold legitimate expectations of advancement based on the governing CBA [collective bargaining agreement]. This sort of judicial intrusion into labor relations is unwarranted unless an employee can show that a seniority system was designed to discriminate against the disabled.[64]

The Supreme Court has held that, in the absence of special circumstances, it ordinarily will be unreasonable in the "run of cases" to assign a qualified disabled employee to a position governed by a seniority system in violation of established seniority rules that would assign the position to a more senior employee.[65]

Arbitrators continue to be called on to resolve the conflicts between the "reasonable accommodations" that must be afforded employees with a disability and the terms of the collective bargaining agreement.[66] The conflict most often emerges when the employer grants a request for a shift change, transfer, or reassignment of duties for an employee who does not otherwise possess the requisite seniority.[67]

Consistent with the Supreme Court's *U.S. Airways* decision, lower courts agree that the ADA is not an "affirmative action" statute requiring employers to put in place measures before an employee with a disability makes known to the employer the need for an accommodation.[68] Once an employee makes the need for accommodation known, however, the employer must determine what accommodations it can make without "undue burden" that will

---

[64]*Boersig*, 219 F.3d at 822.

[65]U.S. Airways v. Barnett, 535 U.S. 391 (2002) (disabled employee bears burden of providing special circumstances that make creating an exception to the seniority rule reasonable; such "special circumstances" might include showing that the employer has frequently exercised permitted discretions to change the seniority system in the past so as to reduce employer expectations that system will be followed).

[66]Contracts, Metals, & Welding, 110 LA 673 (Klein, 1998) (employer's accommodation of disabled employee by placing the employee on the "first shift" instead of a more senior employee who attempted to exercise his shift preference seniority rights under the collective bargaining agreement was improper, because the ADA does not require that disabled workers be given an accommodation that sacrifices the collectively bargained seniority rights of other employees); City of Dearborn Heights, Mich., 101 LA 809 (Kanner, 1993) (employer properly transferred police lieutenant from the night shift because of his diabetic condition, even though he did not have such a contractual right, where no other reasonable accommodation could be made); Mason & Hanger Corp., 111 LA 60 (Caraway, 1998) (employer violated collective bargaining contract when it assigned an employee to the "swing shift" in order to allow a disabled employee with less seniority to work the day shift as an accommodation; accommodations may not trump the seniority rights of other employees); Henkel Corp./Chems. Group, 110 LA 1121 (West, 1998) (an arbitrator should consider "the spirit and letter" of the ADA when making a just cause determination involving a disabled employee; discharge of employee with heart condition was justified when job out of which she transferred previously was eliminated, where she could no longer perform the job to which she was transferred, and locating other light duty work or allowing her to remain in her current position would violate the seniority rights of other employees).

[67]Daly-Rooney, *Reconciling Conflicts Between the Americans With Disabilities Act and the National Labor Relations Act to Accommodate People With Disabilities*, 6 DePaul Bus. L.J. 387, 392 (1994); Contracts, Metals, & Welding, 110 LA 673 (Klein, 1998); Mason & Hanger Corp., 111 LA 60 (Caraway, 1998).

[68]O'Melvery, *The Americans With Disabilities Act and Collective Bargaining Agreements: Reasonable Accommodation or Irreconcilable Conflicts?*, 82 Ky. L.J. 219 (1994) (setting aside certain jobs for persons with disabilities not required).

enable it to place the employee in an available appropriate position for which the employee is qualified.[69] Thus, the U.S. Court of Appeals for the District of Columbia Circuit has held that this affirmative obligation on the part of an employer "means something more than treating a disabled employee like any other job applicant," but according a disabled employee preferential treatment for purposes of promotion, reassignment, or other forms of accommodation is permissible and consistent with the goals and purposes of the ADA, so long as collectively bargained seniority rights of other employees are not violated.[70]

Arbitrators who have considered the ADA in reaching "reasonable accommodation" decisions under collective bargaining contracts rely on contract provisions that call for the supremacy of any laws or governmental regulations,[71] antidiscrimination clauses,[72] or express agreements between the parties[73] to justify recourse to external law.

In *Eckles v. Consolidated Rail Corp.*,[74] the U.S. Court of Appeals for the Seventh Circuit held that not only did the ADA not require an employer to provide an accommodation to a disabled employee that would violate the collectively bargained seniority rights of other employees, but unless the employee demonstrates that he or she is qualified to perform the essential functions of any available job offered, accommodation is not required.[75]

Courts have generally held that an accommodation that contravenes collectively bargained seniority rights of other employees is "per se unreasonable,"[76] or unreasonable "as a matter of law."[77]

---

[69]San Francisco Unified Sch. Dist., 104 LA 215 (Bogue, 1995).

[70]Aka v. Washington Hosp. Ctr., 156 F.3d 1284, 1304–05, 159 LRRM 2467 (D.C. Cir. 1998) (ADA's reasonable accommodation requirement treats disabled and nondisabled employees differently in numerous respects, including the accommodations of "job restructuring," "part-time or modified work schedules," and the "provision of qualified readers or interpreters").

[71]Champion Int'l Corp., 106 LA 1024 (Howell, 1996) (contract provided that its terms were superseded by applicable laws or regulations); City of Dearborn Heights, Mich., 101 LA 809 (Kanner, 1993) (agreement stated that contract language could be declared invalid by operation of law); Contracts, Metals, & Welding, 110 LA 673 (Klein, 1998).

[72]San Francisco Unified Sch. Dist., 104 LA 215 (Bogue, 1995) (ADA standards utilized in case of teacher with multiple sclerosis, where agreement prohibited discrimination on the basis of "handicapped condition"); Contracts, Metals, & Welding, 110 LA 673 (Klein, 1998); Mason & Hanger Corp., 111 LA 60 (Caraway, 1998).

[73]Alcoa Bldg. Prods., 104 LA 364 (Cerone, 1995) (stipulation of parties).

[74]94 F.3d 1041, 155 LRRM 2653 (7th Cir. 1996), *cert. denied*, 520 U.S. 1146 (1997).

[75]*See* Schmidt v. Genessee County Road Comm'n, 1996 U.S. Dist. LEXIS 17727 (E.D. Mich. 1996); Massey v. Scrivner, Inc., 901 F. Supp. 1546, 150 LRRM 2629 (W.D. Okla. 1994).

[76]Willis v. Pacific Maritime Ass'n, 162 F.3d 561, 568, 160 LRRM 2053 (9th Cir. 1998) (the court rejected a "balancing test" that would make the existence of a seniority system only "a factor that must be weighed" in deciding whether an accommodation is reasonable).

[77]*Id. See also* Fluty v. JH Rudolph & Co., 215 F.3d 1329, 2000 U.S. App. LEXIS 8732, at *4 (7th Cir. 2000) (unpublished opinion) (the employer was not required to accommodate the employee by assigning him to drive a pick-up truck rather than a triaxle truck, where a separate seniority list existed for the pick-up truck driver position on which the employee would have insufficient seniority for the assignment; the ADA does not require an employer "to abrogate seniority rules in order to accommodate an employee's disability."); Davis v. Florida Power & Light Co., 205 F.3d 1301, 1306–07, 10 AD Cases 492 (11th Cir. 2000) (employer was not required to accommodate employee by agreeing employee would not be required to work any overtime where employee's job involved mandatory overtime and employee had insufficient seniority under the collective bargaining agreement to be subject to only voluntary overtime; "an accommodation that contravenes the seniority rights of other

Arbitrators have anticipated the Supreme Court's decision, concluding that the ADA does not require the bumping of more senior employees or the creation of a job in order to provide a reasonable accommodation.[78] It is unclear, however, whether the Supreme Court's holding would be extended to a situation where a nonunion employer refused to provide an accommodation that would violate the employer's unilaterally promulgated seniority system that was subject to change at the employer's discretion.[79]

An issue often faced by employers is whether to transfer a disabled employee to a vacant position as an accommodation when the employee is no longer able to perform the essential functions of his or her current job. Several courts have held that the term "vacant" has a special meaning for purposes of making accommodations required by the ADA. For example, a position will be considered vacant if the employee can demonstrate that it is currently occupied by a more junior employee whom he or she is entitled to "bump" under the terms of a collective bargaining agreement.[80] The ADA alone does not entitle an employee to bump a less senior employee as an accommodation in the absence of a provision in the collective bargaining agreement conferring this right.[81] In addition, the employee must be capable of performing the essential duties of the position to which he or she seeks to

---

employees under a collective bargaining agreement is unreasonable as a matter of law"), *cert. denied*, 531 U.S. 927 (2000); Lujan v. Pacific Maritime Ass'n, 165 F.3d 738, 743 (9th Cir. 1999) (employee was entitled to longshore jobs that he was capable of performing only if an accommodation did not interfere with a bona fide seniority system); Feliciano v. Rhode Island, 160 F.3d 780, 787, 8 AD Cases 1520 (1st Cir. 1998); Aldrich v. Boeing Co., 146 F.3d 1265, 1272, 8 AD Cases 424 (10th Cir. 1998) (transfer to any of the positions preferred by employee as reasonable accommodations would violate the seniority provisions of the collective bargaining agreement), *cert. denied*, 526 U.S. 1144 (1999); Cassidy v. Detroit Edison Co., 138 F.3d 629, 634, 8 AD Cases 326 (6th Cir. 1998); Crawley v. Runyon, No. 96-6862, 1998 WL 355529, at *8, 1998 U.S. Dist. LEXIS 9603, at *28 (E.D. Pa. June 30, 1998) (U.S. Postal Service was not required to promote employee to a higher level to accommodate employee's disability when employee only qualified for the lowest level seniority position); Kralik v. Durbin, 130 F.3d 76, 83, 7 AD Cases 1040 (3d Cir. 1997); Foreman v. Babcock & Wilcox, 117 F.3d 800, 810, 7 AD Cases 331 (5th Cir. 1997), *cert. denied*, 522 U.S. 1115 (1998).

[78]Alcoa Bldg. Prods., 104 LA 364 (Cerone, 1995) (company violated agreement when it removed a more senior employee in favor of a disabled employee); Olin Corp., 103 LA 481 (Helburn, 1994) (employer not obligated to accommodate the needs of a disabled worker in a manner that interferes with the rights of a more senior employee). *But see* Mead Prods., 114 LA 1753 (Nathan, 2000) (ADA does not require disabled employee to bump more senior employee because reasonable accommodation cannot be at the cost of rights of nondisabled employees); Mason & Hanger Corp., 111 LA 60 (Caraway, 1998); Contracts, Metals, & Welding, 110 LA 673 (Klein, 1998); City of Dearborn Heights, Mich., 101 LA 809 (Kanner, 1993) (reassignment of a disabled employee to a shift occupied by a more senior employee viewed as job restructuring and not bumping).

[79]McGlothlen & Savine, *Individual Rights and Reasonable Accommodations Under the Americans With Disabilities Act*: Eckles v. Consolidated Rail Corp.: *Reconciling the ADA With Collective Bargaining Agreements: Is This the Correct Approach?*, 46 DePaul L. Rev. 1043 (1997).

[80]Whitfield v. Pathmark Stores, No. 96-246, 1999 WL 301649, at *6, 1999 U.S. Dist. LEXIS 7096, at *23–24 (D. Del. Apr. 29, 1999) (if the collective bargaining agreement permits the bumping of more junior employees and such junior employees occupy the positions at issue, then the positions will be "vacant" for purposes of determining the employer's obligation to provide reasonable accommodation).

[81]Pond v. Michelin N. Am., 183 F.3d 592, 596, 9 AD Cases 795 (7th Cir. 1999) (employees with a contractual right to bump less senior employees have a less compelling need for an ADA remedy than those who do not possess such a right).

be assigned, with or without reasonable accommodation, before the position may be considered vacant for purposes of accommodation under the ADA.[82]

3. SENIORITY DETERMINATIONS

A. Seniority Rights and Seniority Units

Seniority rights attach only to a specific group or unit. Seniority units are defined by the collective bargaining agreement either specifically or by interpretation. They may be multiplant,[83] departmental,[84] or limited to an occupational group or classification.[85] For example, where a contract called for promotions on the basis of departmental seniority, provided the senior employee was qualified, the employer was not required to make promotions on the basis of plantwide seniority where all bidders for the job were from outside the department in which the vacancy existed.[86] In another case, where several bargaining units in the plant each had separate agreements with the employer, employees laid off from one unit were not permitted to exercise their seniority to bump employees in another unit. One arbitrator stated that because the contracts did not expressly provide otherwise, there was a presumption that layoffs and promotions "are to be made on an intra-bargaining unit basis, with the employee's seniority or length of service computed on his service within the bargaining unit and applied only among employees therein."[87]

However, the seniority dates of employees who transfer from one unit to another may be calculated differently for different purposes. For instance, in one case the original hire date of an employee transferred to another plant was used to calculate his benefits, but the date he began to work in the bargaining unit in the new plant was the date for calculating his seniority for other purposes.[88]

Although seniority often is both acquired and exercised in one unit, the contract may provide (or be so interpreted) that seniority is acquired in one unit and exercised in another. For example, a contract provision stating sim-

---

[82]Crawley v. Runyon, No. 96-6862, 1998 U.S. Dist LEXIS 3555529, at *28 (E.D. Pa. June 30, 1998).

[83]Cone Mills Corp., 103 LA 745 (Byars, 1994) (employee who completed 3-month probationary period at one of employer's plants and was subsequently transferred to another plant may not be discharged as probationary employee).

[84]Safeway Stores, 107 LA 448 (Snider, 1996) (defining departments for shift preference); Stone Container Corp., 101 LA 720 (Helburn, 1993) (employer did not violate contract when it assigned less senior employees to non-bargaining-unit work); Norwalk Furniture Corp., 100 LA 1051 (Dworkin, 1993) (contract limited exercise of employees' bargaining rights to their own department).

[85]Lear Corp., 108 LA 592 (Goldberg, 1997) (separate seniority system for restricted duty employees upheld); Duraloy Div., 100 LA 1166 (Franckiewicz, 1993) (employees may have seniority in multiple departments).

[86]Charles Bruning Co., 25 LA 826, 827–29 (Gifford, 1955). *See also* Nickles Bakery, 17 LA 486, 488 (Randle, 1951).

[87]Tide Water Associated Oil Co., 21 LA 604, 607 (Shipman, Fillhower, & Pelowitz, 1953). *See also* General Elec. Co., 54 LA 350, 352 (Cahn, 1971); De Laval Separator Co., 46 LA 1053, 1056 (Shipman, 1966).

[88]ARCO Chem., 102 LA 1051 (Massey, 1994).

ply that the employer shall operate "on a departmental and plantwide seniority basis" was construed (in the light of past practice and the history of
contract negotiations) to mean that seniority was to be exercised on a departmental basis, but measured by length of service in the plant.[89] Similarly,
seniority rights may be based on different units with respect to the various
aspects of the employment relationship. For instance, a contract may provide that departmental seniority shall govern with respect to layoff and recall, while providing for plant seniority to be exercised in bumping.[90]

B. Seniority Standing [LA CDI 117.231]

The seniority standing of an employee is his or her position on the "preference" or seniority list in relation to other employees in the seniority unit.
An employee's seniority standing may be problematic where, among other
situations, another employee in the same seniority unit began to work on the
same day but at a different hour, or had the same hiring date but began to
work on a different day. Arbitrators seem reluctant to draw too fine a line in
such situations. For example, in interpreting a collective bargaining agreement providing that an employee's continuous length of service should be
computed from the date he or she first began to work, an arbitrator held that
the seniority standing of two employees who commenced work on the same
day, though on different shifts, was the same. The arbitrator stated that
"[t]he legal as well as the popular meaning of the word 'date' imports the
day, month and year without reference to the hour."[91] Another arbitrator
further observed that it would be impractical and inconsistent with existing
industrial practice to ascertain length of service in units of less than 1 day.[92]

The contract may be explicit as to the order of seniority. For instance, it
may provide not only that seniority is to be computed from the first day
worked,[93] but also that new employees are to be registered numerically as
they check in on the first day worked with their seniority standing to be in
the same order as their names appear on the register. Under such a provision, where two employees were hired on the same day, it was held that
(barring any discrimination in the assignment of shifts) the one who "clocked
in" on the first shift had more seniority than the other who commenced work
on the same day but on the second shift.[94]

Under another contract defining seniority as continuous length of service, but containing no clause specifying a starting point from which length

---

[89]McFeely Brick Co., 22 LA 379, 382 (Reid, 1954). *See also* Township of Independence,
Mich., 74 LA 594, 599–600 (Brown, 1980); Alside, Inc., 25 LA 338, 340–41 (Kates, 1955).

[90]Harsco Corp., 30 LA 326, 327–28 (Koretz, 1957). *See also* De Laval Separator Co., 46 LA
1053, 1056 (Shipman, 1966); Kaiser Aluminum & Chem. Corp., 35 LA 692, 694–95 (McCoy,
1960); International Paper Co., 9 LA 279, 281 (Logan, 1957).

[91]Bethlehem Steel, 26 LA 567, 567 (Seward, 1956).

[92]Standard Oil Co., 3 LA 758, 759 (Whiting, 1946). *Cf.* P.M. Northwest Co., 42 LA 961,
963–64 (Lyons, 1964).

[93]Mode O'Day Co., 85 LA 297 (Thornell, 1985) (seniority begins to accumulate on the date
and hour on which the employee begins work).

[94]Robertshaw-Fulton Controls Co., 22 LA 273, 274 (Williams, 1954). *See also* Armstrong
Rubber Co., 74 LA 301, 302–03 (Williams, 1980).

of service should be computed, it was held that where one employee started to work a day before another, the former had the greater seniority because he had the longer service record, even though both were hired on the same day.[95] Where the seniority of employees was found to be equal, management was upheld in breaking the "tie" by considering the ability of the employees.[96]

i. Determining Length of Service

Ordinarily, seniority is based on length of service, although the collective bargaining agreement may provide for exceptions such as "superseniority" for union officers and stewards,[97] denial of seniority for probationary employees,[98] loss of seniority in whole or in part under specified circumstances,[99] and similar bases.[100] Because seniority, length of service, and their concomitant rights are creatures of contract, it is necessary always to look first to the contract in determining length of service and the seniority standing of employees.

While seniority often will accrue during a probationary period,[101] seniority also may begin to accumulate before a worker actually becomes a permanent employee. For instance, a worker supplied by a temporary agency may accumulate seniority during his or her temporary status when the worker is later hired as a permanent employee.[102] Some contracts, however, expressly provide that part-time employees do not accrue seniority.[103]

Collective bargaining agreements may specifically provide that employees do not lose their seniority during absences because of illness or injury.[104]

---

[95]National Biscuit Aware, 4 ALAA ¶68,530.1 (Donnelly, 1950).

[96]*See* St. Louis Sch. Dist., 90 LA 542, 544–45 (Miller, 1988); U.S. Plywood-Champion Papers, 50 LA 507, 516 (Howlett, 1968); Central Ill. Light Co., 38 LA 1058, 1060–61 (Kahn, 1962); Columbia Broad. Sys., 37 LA 330, 334 (Scheiber, 1961). In *McCall Corp.*, 49 LA 183, 186 (McIntosh, 1967), the contract specified that ties should be resolved by a joint committee of the parties; the arbitrator specified a "toss of a coin" if the committee should disagree.

[97]For discussion of superseniority, see Chapter 5, section 11.A., "Superseniority." *See also* NLRB v. Joy Techs., 990 F.2d 104, 142 LRRM 2865 (3d Cir. 1993) (a labor contract's superseniority clause that permits union committeepersons and stewards to invoke superseniority for purposes beyond layoff and recall is "presumptively invalid"); AmeriMark Bldg. Prods., 104 LA 1066 (Klein, 1995) (superseniority exercisable only with respect to order of layoff and not order of recall); USS, Div. of USX Corp., 102 LA 810 (Petersen, 1993); USS, Div. of USX Corp., 100 LA 414 (Neyland, 1992); Curtis Sand & Gravel Co., 96 LA 972 (Richman, 1991); Lockheed Aeronautical Sys. Co., 94 LA 137 (Byars, 1990).

[98]*See, e.g.*, Carbone of Am. Indus., 100 LA 720 (Dean, Jr., 1992); Borden Chem. Co., 32 LA 697, 700 (Prasow, 1959).

[99]See section 6., "Contractual Provisions for Loss of Seniority," below.

[100]For recognition of a potentially broad leeway in the parties to specify seniority or preference rights on bases other than length of service, see *U.S. Borax & Chem. Corp.*, 41 LA 1200, 1202 (Leonard, 1963).

[101]Cone Mills Corp., 103 LA 745 (Byars, 1994).

[102]Metz Baking Co., 100 LA 671 (Bard, 1993). *But see* Alltel Pa., 108 LA 872 (Oberdank, 1997) (where contract denies contractual rights to temporary employees, regular employees are not entitled to seniority credit for time served as temporary employees).

[103]Pace Fox Valley Div., 101 LA 912 (Kohn, 1993).

[104]Bethlehem Steel Corp., 100 LA 466 (Kahn, 1992) (employee did not lose seniority during absence for work-related injury); Waterous Co., 100 LA 278 (Reynolds, 1993) (contract provision stating specifically that seniority shall not be lost because of injury or illness). See also section 6., "Contractual Provisions for Loss of Seniority," below.

Some arbitrators have held that if the contract fails to state expressly that seniority does not accumulate during layoff, seniority continues to accrue.[105] Similarly, in the absence of a contrary provision in a collective bargaining agreement, employees who transfer to a new plant may retain their seniority status and may not be required to complete a new probationary period.[106]

C. Seniority Lists [LA CDI 117.232]

In the absence of a contractual provision requiring the posting of seniority lists, the employer may be held to be under an implied obligation to make proper and reasonable disclosure, on demand by an aggrieved employee or the union, of the seniority standing of the claimant and that of other employees in that seniority unit. In this regard, one arbitrator stated:

> An employee—and the union as his representative—clearly has a right to be informed of the seniority date and length of continuous service credited to him on the Company's records. By the same token, since most seniority issues involve a comparison of the relative rights of two or more employees, the employee—and the union as his representative—has a right to know the seniority dates and length of continuous service credited to the other employees in the seniority unit applicable to him at any given time. The only accurate source of such information is obviously the Company. It has the records. It is initiating the various transfers, promotions, demotions, "bumps," layoffs, recalls, etc. which are daily causing changes in those records. The information, practically obtainable from the employees themselves, could never be as accurate, up-to-date or complete as that which the Company can make available. Indeed, some employees might have an interest in concealing information as to their own seniority standing in an effort to protect themselves from being bumped.[107]

The collective bargaining agreement may specifically provide for the posting of seniority lists.[108] It also may make provision for challenging the seniority list, often within some stated time limit, and the failure of an employee to make a timely protest concerning a seniority date may be deemed a waiver of the employee's right to challenge.[109] Even without a fixed time limit, a waiver may be based on a failure to protest within a reasonable time after the employee knows, or should have known, that the date is incorrect.[110]

---

[105]Ryder Truck Rental, 95 LA 1106 (Suardi, 1990); Eagle Iron Works, 92 LA 1306 (Bognanno, 1989). *Cf.* Deschutes County, Or., 104 LA 18 (Downing, 1994) (arbitrator determined that seniority may not accumulate during layoff).

[106]Cone Mills Corp., 103 LA 745 (Byars, 1994).

[107]Bethlehem Steel Co., 24 LA 699, 702 (Seward, 1955). *See also* Mallory-Sharon Metals Corp., 33 LA 60, 66 (Dworkin, 1959); Republic Steel Corp., 18 LA 907, 909 (Platt, 1952).

[108]*See also* Firestone Synthetic Rubber & Latex Co., 85 LA 489 (Marcus, 1985).

[109]*See* Burns Int'l Sec. Servs., 101 LA 441, 444 (McCausland, 1993); Weirton Steel Div., 63 LA 750, 751 (Kates, 1974); Canton Provision Co., 53 LA 216, 220–21 (Shanker, 1969) (also dealing with management's right to correct the list); Ben Franklin Ref. Co., 41 LA 438, 440–41 (Merrill, 1963); Northeast Airlines, 37 LA 741, 744 (Wolff, 1961); Jones & Laughlin Steel Corp., 30 LA 432, 433–34 (Cahn, 1958); Republic Steel Corp., 24 LA 286, 287 (Platt, 1955); Pickett Cotton Mills, 17 LA 405, 405–06 (Soule, 1951). Employees may challenge incorrect lists at once, not being required to wait until the employee has been adversely treated by the actual application of an erroneous list. Long Beach Oil Dev. Co., 41 LA 583, 586 (Block, 1963).

[110]*See* Texstar Auto. Group, 81 LA 278, 282 (Smith, 1983); Universal Printing Co., 67 LA 456, 460 (Kubie, 1976); Linde Co., 32 LA 568, 570 (Duff, 1959). Under the circumstances, in

However, some arbitrators have been reluctant to cut off an employee's right to challenge an erroneous seniority date.[111] Moreover, even though an employee does not challenge the posted seniority date for several years, an employer may be estopped from refusing to change an admittedly incorrect date where it has consistently treated the employee in accordance with the correct date and not the posted one.[112]

D. Service Outside the Seniority Unit [LA CDI 117.2434]

The length of service credited to an employee and his or her seniority standing may be affected by service outside the seniority unit. The employee may lose or retain previously earned seniority,[113] or continue to accumulate seniority, depending on the wording of the collective bargaining agreement. A collective bargaining agreement may provide that an employee transferred out of the seniority unit to an exempt job continues to accumulate seniority[114] or retains seniority already earned.[115] In cases where there is no specific contract provision governing the seniority rights of employees transferred out of the seniority unit, awards have reflected a diversity of views. For example, it has been held variously that in such a situation the employee (1) retained seniority previously earned,[116] (2) could not continue to

---

General Plywood Corp., 36 LA 633, 634 (Porter, 1961), the employee could not reasonably be charged with knowledge of the error. *See also* Outdoor Sports Indus., 77 LA 880, 882–83 (Aisenberg, 1981).

[111]*See* Sadler Bros. Trucking & Leasing Co., 99 LA 1205 (Nicholas, Jr., 1992); B.F. Nelson Folding Cartons, 98 LA 978 (Jacobowski, 1991); Kelsey-Hayes Co., 85 LA 774 (Thomson, 1985).

[112]Republic Steel Corp., 25 LA 434, 435 (Platt, 1955).

[113]*See* ARCO Chem., 102 LA 1051 (Massey, 1994) (date employee began to work in new plant and bargaining unit, rather than total time with the company, is used for determining seniority rights but not for determining continuous service-related benefits such as pension and vacation entitlements and salary rate accrued pursuant to commitments made by employer to employee prior to his joining bargaining unit).

[114]Babcock & Wilcox Co., 79 LA 1022, 1026–27 (McDermott, 1982) (certain employees could continue to accumulate seniority for some purposes); Lockheed Missiles & Space Co., 55 LA 875 (Greene, 1970); Henney Motor Co., 35 LA 932 (Markowitz, 1960); Muskegon Piston Ring Co., 29 LA 220 (Piercey, 1957); Sterilon Corp., 27 LA 229 (McKelvey, 1956); Sangamo Elec. Co., 25 LA 452 (Anrod, 1955); Belle City Malleable Iron Co., 24 LA 60 (Kelliher, 1955); L.A. Young Spring & Wire Corp., 23 LA 400 (Platt, 1954). *But see* City of Kansas City, Kan., Water Pollution Control Div., 100 LA 534 (Berger, 1993) (former unit members promoted to supervisors had no right to use previously accumulated unit seniority to bid into barganing-unit positions).

[115]Abex Corp., 80 LA 490, 494–95 (Cohen, 1983) (the contract provided that an employee transferred to a salaried position "shall cease to accumulate seniority," but it did not state that the employee would lose any seniority already earned); Aloha Airlines, 77 LA 1171, 1178–79 (Tsukiyama, 1981); White Pidgeon Paper Co., 68 LA 177, 179, 182 (Coyle, 1977); Reynolds Metals Co., 55 LA 1011 (Brandschain, 1970); Lear Siegler, 52 LA 383 (Bradley, 1969); U.S. Borax & Chem. Corp., 41 LA 1200 (Leonard, 1963); Celotex Corp., 37 LA 240 (Mitchell, 1961); Mathews Conveyer Co., 30 LA 221 (Cahn, 1958); American Enka Corp., 26 LA 195 (Dworet, 1956) (could retain seniority up to 1 year); Linde Air Prods. Co., 26 LA 67 (Trotta, 1955).

[116]*See* United Tel. Co. of the W., 99 LA 620, 623 (Gordon, 1992) (when contract is silent, seniority should not be forfeited without substantial reason); Great Lakes Diesel Co., 75 LA 1077, 1079–80 (Di Leone, 1980) (seniority would not be lost by virtue of a provision, calling for loss of seniority on promotion to supervisor, adopted *after* the individual left the bargaining unit for a supervisory position); International Paper Co., 70 LA 1246, 1249 (Taylor, 1978); Fruehauf Corp., 54 LA 1093, 1095 (Marshall, 1971); Chromalloy Am. Corp., 54 LA 965, 972–

accumulate seniority while outside the unit,[117] (3) continued to accumulate seniority during temporary promotion out of the unit,[118] (4) continued to accumulate seniority while working outside the unit for an extended period,[119] and (5) forfeited all seniority because the employee in effect had quit voluntarily.[120] In some of the cases cited in the above categories, the results were influenced by past practice.

Seniority obtained in the bargaining unit may be retained on transfer to an exempt position[121] or reinstated after a layoff.[122] Similarly, seniority may be retained by separate agreement.[123]

A contract specifically may allow an employee to work in a second position for a certain period of time without losing his or her seniority in the first position.[124] In one case, where the employee worked outside the bargaining

---

73, 981 (Elliott, 1971); Ohio Power Co., 45 LA 1039, 1044–45 (Leach, 1965); Signal Oil & Gas Co., 43 LA 97, 100–01 (Block, 1964); Pannier Corp., 41 LA 1228, 1230–31 (McDermott, 1964); Alpha Portland Cement Co., 40 LA 495, 498–99 (Feinberg, 1962); Diamond Nat'l Corp., 36 LA 1245, 1249 (Schmidt, 1961); Hooker Chem. Corp., 36 LA 857, 858 (Kates, 1961); Champion Rivet Co., 32 LA 892, 893 (Begley, 1950); F.H. Noble & Co., 28 LA 641, 645 (Baab, 1957); Pacific Intermountain Express Co., 23 LA 440, 446 (Howard, 1954); Munising Wood Prods. Co., 22 LA 769, 771–73 (Ryder, 1954); Torrington Co., 22 LA 704, 705–06 (Myers, 1954); Singer Mfg. Co., 22 LA 492, 495 (Cahn, 1954); Wico Elec. Co., 14 LA 916, 918 (Healy, 1949); Illinois Malleable Iron Co., 14 LA 537, 540 (Lohman, 1950).

[117]See United Tel. Co. of the W., 99 LA 620, 623–24 (Gordon, 1992); Clarkston Cmty. Sch., 79 LA 48, 49–50, 53–54 (Kanner, 1982); Signal Oil & Gas Co., 43 LA 97, 100–01 (Block, 1964); Diamond Nat'l Corp., 36 LA 1245, 1249 (Schmidt, 1961); Singer Mfg. Co., 29 LA 828, 830 (Cahn, 1958); Singer Mfg. Co., 22 LA 13, 17 (Cahn, 1954); Republic Steel Corp., 17 LA 105, 108 (Marshall, 1951).

[118]See Fruehauf Corp., 53 LA 1143, 1145–46 (Caraway, 1969); National Cash Register Co., 48 LA 743, 744–46 (Volz, 1967); Goodyear Atomic Corp., 45 LA 671, 674 (Teple, 1965); McLouth Steel Corp., 28 LA 315, 317 (Haughton, 1957). See also Andrews Steel Co., 4 LA 21, 24 (Hotchkiss, 1942).

[119]See United States Steel Corp., 42 LA 1172, 1177–79 (McDermott, 1964); Borg-Warner Corp., 36 LA 691, 694 (Mishne, 1961); United States Steel Corp., 28 LA 740, 743 (Garrett, 1957); Chesapeake & Potomac Tel. Co., 25 LA 595, 596–97 (Byrnes, 1955); Tide Water Associated Oil Co., 21 LA 682, 685 (Shipman, 1953); Allied Chem & Dye Corp., 18 LA 315, 317 (Fulda, 1949); Geneva Steel Co., 15 LA 834, 836 (Garrett, 1950); Libbey, McNeill & Libbey, 14 LA 482, 486 (Roberts, 1950); Swift & Co., 8 LA 51, 52 (Gregory, 1947); Hoke, Inc., 3 LA 748, 752 (Reynolds, 1946). See also Standard Oil Co., 34 LA 285, 290 (Anrod, 1959); Applied Arts Corp., 23 LA 338, 340 (Smith, 1954). Cf. United States Steel Corp., 48 LA 872, 883 (Garrett, undated).

[120]See City of Kansas City, Kansas Water Pollution Control Div., 100 LA 534, 540 (Berger, 1993); Sterilon Corp., 40 LA 531, 532 (Shister, 1963); Grand Sheet Metal Prods. Co., 27 LA 30, 35 (Kotin, 1956); Ford Motor Co., 26 LA 898, 899–901 (Platt, 1956). See also American Oil Co., 44 LA 802, 806–07 (Gorsuch, 1965); Monfort Packing Co., 40 LA 388, 391–92 (Gorsuch, 1963); Republic Steel Corp., 17 LA 105, 108 (Marshall, 1951). Acceptance of a supervisory position at another of the company's plants, which had a different bargaining unit, resulted in loss of all seniority. Colorado Fuel & Iron Corp., 47 LA 1131, 1135 (Prasow, 1966).

[121]See Union Carbide Corp., 91 LA 181 (King, 1988) (employee promoted to supervisory position initially retained seniority, but lost it on transfer to another plant).

[122]Bethlehem Steel Corp., 92 LA 1283 (Valtin, 1989) (employee's seniority was reinstated after employee agreed to repay severance pay).

[123]Simpson Timber Co., 90 LA 1273 (LaRocco, 1988) (employer entered into oral agreement to allow employee to go on layoff status and continue to accumulate seniority in return for employee's promise never to attempt to return to work with employer); Concessions Int'l, 90 LA 1252 (Boedecker, 1988) (employees who transferred from existing enterprise at airport to minority business that "negotiated access" to airport complex kept full seniority rights they had with original employer, because original employer's contract bound minority business).

[124]Gaylord Container Corp., 102 LA 1206 (Hooper, 1994).

unit 1 day beyond the time permitted under the contract to retain seniority, the arbitrator nevertheless refused to allow the forfeiture of the accrued seniority. Despite the expiration of the period, the arbitrator reasoned that the employee should not be penalized because he had timely made a good-faith effort to inquire about returning to his original position.[125]

Arbitrators generally hold that employees cannot be credited with seniority for any service performed prior to entry into the bargaining unit.[126] However, seniority credit for preunit service has been upheld where the agreement referred to seniority in terms of length of continuous service with the company.[127] An employee may be credited with seniority for service performed outside the bargaining unit if other employees previously had been so credited and failure to do so would be discriminatory.[128] An employee's service performed before entering the bargaining unit may be considered for seniority-based benefits if not for seniority list standing.[129]

4. Extension of Seniority Rights to Different Plant or Successor Employer

Where employees acquire seniority rights under a collective bargaining agreement by performing service at a given plant for a given employer, and the plant is relocated or closed down, the employees may assert a right to extend or transfer their seniority to another plant of their employer. Similarly, where a business is sold or absorbed by merger, employees of the former business may assert a right to continue their seniority in the employ of the successor employer.

---

[125]Champion Int'l Corp., 108 LA 104 (Statham, 1997).

[126]Alleghany County Comm'rs, 83 LA 464 (Mayer, 1984) (management improperly credited employees with time worked in nonunit jobs at employer's landfill operation before work was assigned to outside contractor and employees were transferred to unit jobs in road department).

[127]See Cone Mills Corp., 103 LA 745, 746 (Byars, 1994); Caterpillar Tractor Co., 80 LA 625, 627–28 (Sisk, 1983); Paramount Die Casting Co., 38 LA 741, 744 (Alexander, 1962); Pacific Chem. & Fertilizer Co., 38 LA 188, 190–92 (Cobb, 1962); Standard Oil Co., 34 LA 285, 290 (Anrod, 1959); General Metals Corp., 26 LA 256, 258 (Guild, 1956). But see Clarkston Cmty. Sch., 79 LA 48, 55–56 (Kanner, 1982); Tide Water Associated Oil Co., 21 LA 682, 685 (Shipman, 1953). In Jenison Public School District, 81 LA 105, 116 (Roumell, Jr., 1983), seniority credit for preunit service was upheld on the basis of past practice. For a case concerning seniority credit for employees who worked during a strike that occurred following expiration of the collective bargaining agreement, see Flint Osteopathic Hosp., 81 LA 427, 430–31 (Borland, 1983) (also discusses cases concerning the accrual of seniority by employees while on strike).

[128]FRP Co., 90 LA 1106 (Statham, 1988) (arbitrator upheld award of seniority earned outside bargaining unit to black employee where white employee had previously received same treatment and to do otherwise would have constituted prima facie case of race discrimination).

[129]ARCO Chem., 102 LA 1051 (Massey, 1994) (date employee began to work in new plant and bargaining unit, rather than total time with company, is used to determine seniority rights but not to determine continuous service-related benefits such as pension and vacation entitlements and salary rate).

A. Closing or Relocation of Plant [LA CDI 117.232]

While the collective bargaining agreement or some special agreement may expressly provide for the transfer of seniority rights to other locations,[130] in the absence of such express provision, numerous arbitrators have interpreted the collective bargaining agreement as conferring seniority rights only at the plant location where service was performed. Thus, seniority rights do not survive the closing or removal of the plant.[131]

In the widely repudiated and ultimately overruled U.S. Court of Appeals for the Second Circuit decision in *Zdanok v. Glidden Co.*,[132] the court had held that seniority rights survived the expiration of a collective bargaining agreement and the relocation of the plant. In overruling its *Glidden* decision, the Second Circuit explained:

> We are persuaded that the reasoning of the majority opinion in the *Glidden* case was erroneous and that erroneous reasoning led to an incorrect result. For example, the basic proposition of the opinion, that seniority is a vested right, finds no support in authority, in logic or in the socio-economic setting of labor-management relations. Seniority is wholly a creation of the collective agreement and does not exist apart from that agreement. The incidents of seniority can be freely altered or amended by modification of the collective agreement. Ford Motor Co. v. Huffman, 345 U.S. 330, 73 S. Ct. 681, [31 LRRM 2548,] 97 L. Ed. 1048 (1953). In giving seniority a conceptual status apart from the provisions of the collective agreement and the intentions of the parties, the *Glidden* opinion seriously misconceived the nature of the employment relationship and dealt "a blow to labor-management relations."[133]

If a collective agreement does not provide for companywide seniority or integration of seniority lists, and a plant-closing agreement specifically states that such employees will be covered by all of the contract's "new hire" provisions, an employer may properly treat employees from the closed plant as "new hires" when they are transferred to another plant.[134]

---

[130]*See* C.K. Williams Co., 12 LA 987, 988 (Kerr, 1949). *See also* Federal-Mogul Corp., 61 LA 745, 749 (Cole, 1973) (contract specified preferential hiring rights at new location).

[131]*See* International Shoe Co., 46 LA 1063, 1065 (McCoy, 1966); Marsh Wall Prods., 45 LA 551, 552–54 (Kagel, 1965); Empire Textile Corp., 44 LA 979, 984–86 (Scheiber, 1965); Paragon Bridge & Steel Co., 44 LA 361, 369 (Casselman, 1965); S.B. Penick & Co., 43 LA 798, 803–04 (Turkus, 1964); Lagomarcino-Grupe Co., 43 LA 453, 459 (Davey, 1964); Sivyer Steel Casting Co., 39 LA 449, 454–56 (Howlett, 1962); United Packers, 38 LA 619, 620 (Kelliher, 1962); H.H. Robertson Co., 37 LA 928, 932 (Duff, 1962). *See also* Babcock & Wilcox Co., 80 LA 212, 218 (Klein, 1982); Humiston-Keeling Co., 48 LA 1257, 1260–61 (Malinowski, 1967) (economic closing of plant does not violate contract seniority or recognition clauses); Phillips Chem. Co., 39 LA 82, 84–85 (Larson, 1962). *Cf.* T&S Coal Co., 73 LA 882, 885 (Leahy, 1979); Superior Prods. Co., 42 LA 517, 523–24 (Smith, 1964).

[132]288 F.2d 99, 47 LRRM 2865 (2d Cir. 1961).

[133]Auto Workers Local 1251 v. Robertshaw Controls Co., 405 F.2d 29, 33, 68 LRRM 2671 (2d Cir. 1968) (the court cited several articles that had been written in criticism of the *Glidden* decision). Also rejecting the contention that seniority rights are "vested rights" that cannot be cut off or defeated by a relocation of the plant, see *Charland v. Borg-Warner Corp.*, 407 F.2d 1062, 70 LRRM 2705 (6th Cir. 1969); *Oddie v. Ross Gear & Tool Co.*, 305 F.2d 143, 50 LRRM 2763 (6th Cir. 1962). In *Cooper v. General Motors Corp.*, 651 F.2d 249, 250–51, 107 LRRM 3161, 3163 (5th Cir. 1981), the court cited *Robertshaw Controls* with approval and reiterated its own prior statement that "'collective bargaining agreements do not create a permanent status, give an indefinite tenure, or extend rights created and arising under the contract, beyond its life, when it has been terminated in accordance with its provisions . . . .'" (quoting Railway Employees Sys. Fed'n 59 v. Louisiana & Ark. Ry., 119 F.2d F.2d 509, 515, 8 LRRM 1038 (5th Cir.), *cert. denied*, 314 U.S. 656 (1941)).

[134]Safeway Stores, 87 LA 606 (Gentile, 1986).

B. Merger or Sale of Company [LA CDI 117.232]

In its 1964 *John Wiley & Sons v. Livingston*[135] decision, the Supreme Court upheld the arbitrability of grievances concerning the survival of the seniority and other rights of employees under the National Labor Relations Act (NLRA)[136] following their employer's disappearance by merger and the expiration of their collective bargaining agreement, where there was a "substantial continuity of identity in the business enterprise" before and after the merger.

After *Wiley*, the question remained as to whether not only the arbitration clause, but also substantive provisions of the predecessor's agreement, must be honored by the successor employer. In its 1972 *Burns International Security Services*[137] decision, the Supreme Court, while cautioning that its resolution of the issues "turns to a great extent on the precise facts involved here," held that a successor employer was required to bargain with the union that had represented its predecessor's employees, but that the National Labor Relations Board (NLRB, or the Board) had improperly ordered the successor to honor the predecessor's collective bargaining agreement. In holding that the successor was not bound by the predecessor's agreement, the Supreme Court observed:

> In many cases, of course, successor employers will find it advantageous not only to recognize and bargain with the union but also to observe the preexisting contract rather than to face uncertainty and turmoil. Also, in a variety of circumstances involving a merger, stock acquisition, reorganization, or assets purchase, the Board might properly find as a matter of fact that the successor had assumed the obligations under the old contract. . . . Such a duty does not, however, ensue as a matter of law from the mere fact that an employer is doing the same work in the same place with the same employees as his predecessor, as the Board had recognized until its decision in the instant case.[138]

In *Burns*, the Supreme Court distinguished its *Wiley* decision on the basis that *Wiley* "arose in the context of a § 301 suit to compel arbitration," whereas *Burns* arose "in the context of an unfair labor practice proceeding" before the NLRB.[139] However, this distinction was expressly rejected by the Supreme Court in its 1974 *Howard Johnson*[140] decision, in which the Court held that where there was "no substantial continuity of identity in the workforce hired by [the buyer] with that of the [seller], and no express or

---

[135]376 U.S. 543, 551, 55 LRRM 2769 (1964). For the arbitrator's ultimate ruling as to the extent to which the predecessor's contract was binding on the successor in *Wiley* and, in particular, the extent to which seniority rights of the predecessor's employees survived the merger, see *Interscience Encyclopedia*, 55 LA 210, 218–21, 225 (Roberts, 1970).

[136]29 U.S.C. §151 et seq.

[137]NLRB v. Burns Int'l Sec. Servs., 406 U.S. 272, 274, 80 LRRM 2225 (1972).

[138]*Id.* at 291 (citation omitted). In *Golden State Bottling Co. v. NLRB*, 414 U.S. 168, 84 LRRM 2839 (1973), the Supreme Court held that a successor purchasing a business with knowledge that the seller had unlawfully discharged an employee could be required by the NLRB to reinstate him with back pay, but the Court cautioned that "We in no way qualify the *Burns*' holdings . . . ." *Id.* at 183.

[139]*Burns*, 406 U.S. at 285.

[140]Howard Johnson Co. v. Hotel & Rest. Employees, Detroit Local Joint Executive Bd., 417 U.S. 249, 264, 86 LRRM 2449 (1974). Although the Court discounted or rejected the aforementioned distinction, the Court stated that: "We find it unnecessary, however, to decide in the circumstances of this case whether there is any irreconcilable conflict between *Wiley* and *Burns*." *Id.* at 256.

implied assumption of the agreement to arbitrate," the buyer was not required "to arbitrate the extent of its obligations to" the former employees of the seller. Although *Howard Johnson*, like *Wiley*, arose in the context of a Section 301 suit to compel arbitration, the Supreme Court believed that "the fundamental policies outlined in *Burns*," rather than *Wiley*, controlled the disposition of the case.[141]

Thus, it is apparent that even as to the arbitration clause itself, the scope of *Wiley* has been limited.[142] In the latter regard:

> It is clear that the Court has cut back on its broad pronouncements in *Wiley*, in the interest of unfettered transfer and development of capital and human resources in business transfers. In *Howard Johnson*, it ignored the "successors and assigns" provision in the [seller's] labor contract as a possible base for arbitral relief against the successor Howard Johnson; it emphasized the technical form which the transfer of assets took; and it gave no weight to the fact that the [seller's] employees retained by Howard Johnson continued to use the same skills performing the same jobs under the same working conditions as before.[143]

In its *Fall River Dyeing & Finishing Corp. v. NLRB*[144] decision, the Supreme Court reaffirmed its *Burns* rationale[145] and upheld a Board order re-

---

[141]*Id.* at 255.

[142]In *Howard Johnson*, the Supreme Court distinguished *Wiley* on the basis that: (1) *Wiley* involved a merger rather than only a sale of assets, and while "ordinarily there is no basis for distinguishing among mergers, consolidations, or purchases of assets in the analysis of successorship problems," *Howard Johnson*, 417 U.S. at 257, the existence in *Wiley* of a state statute making the surviving corporation in a merger liable for the obligations of the disappearing corporation, and the lack of any remedy against the former employer in *Wiley*, provided the basis in *Wiley* for distinguishing the different types of successorship transactions; (2) "Even more important, in *Wiley* the surviving corporation hired *all* of the employees of the disappearing corporation," *Howard Johnson*, 417 U.S. at 258 (emphasis in original), whereas in *Howard Johnson* the buyer "hired only nine of the 53 former," employees of the seller *id.* at 260,—the "continuity of identity in the business enterprise necessarily includes . . . a substantial continuity in the identity of the work force across the change in ownership." *Id.* at 263. The Court also reiterated that in successor employer cases "the employees of the terminating employer have no legal right to continued employment with the new employer," *id.* at 264, provided, of course, that the successor does not "discriminate in hiring or retention of employees on the basis of union membership or activity." *Id.* at 262 n.8. *See also* Vantage Petroleum Corp., 247 NLRB 1492, 103 LRRM 1408 (1980).

[143]Gorman, Basic Text on Labor Law 583 (1976). For other discussions of the *Wiley*, *Burns*, and *Howard Johnson* decisions, see Krupman & Kaplan, *The Stock Purchaser After Burns: Must He Buy the Union Contract?*, 31 Lab. L.J. 328 (1980); Henry, *Is There Arbitration After Burns?: The Resurrection of John Wiley & Sons*, 31 Vand. L. Rev. 249 (1978); Severson & Willcoxon, *Successorship Under Howard Johnson: Short Order Justice for Employees*, 64 Cal. L. Rev. 795 (1976); Barksdale, *Successor Liability Under the National Labor Relations Act and Title VII*, 54 Tex. L. Rev. 707 (1976).

[144]482 U.S. 27, 125 LRRM 2441 (1987). For further information on merger and successorship, see Goldstein, *Protecting Employee Rights in Successorship*, 44 Lab. L.J. 18 (1993); Seltzer, *Rights and Liabilities of Successor Corporation: Patent Licenses, Leases, and Collective Bargaining Agreements*, 22 Creighton L. Rev. 815 (1989); Chatfield-Taylor, *Successorship and the Obligation to Bargain: Clarifying the Steps Toward a Highly Subjective Analysis*, 27 Washburn L.J. 685 (1988); Mace, *The Supreme Court's Labor Law Successorship Doctrine After* Fall River Dyeing, 39 Lab. L.J. 102 (1988); Fasman & Fischer, *Labor Relations Consequences of Mergers and Acquisitions*, 13 Employee Rel. L.J. 4 (Summer 1987); Silverstein, *The Fate of Workers in Successor Firms: Does Law Tame the Market?*, 8 Indus. Rel. L.J. 153 (1986); *Sweeping up the Divestiture's Debris: Application of the Successor Employer Doctrine to Ma Bell and Her Relatives*, 37 Fed. Com. L.J. 455 (1985); Bernstein & Cooper, *Labor Law Consequences of the Sale of a Unionized Business*, 36 Lab. L.J. 327 (1985); *Successorship Doctrine: A Hybrid Approach Threatens to Extend the Doctrine When the Union Strikes Out*, 28 St. Louis U. L.J. 263 (1984); Miller & Lindsay, *Mergers & Acquisitions: Labor Relations Considerations*, 9 Employee Rel. L.J. 427 (Winter, 1983–84).

[145]NLRB v. Burns Int'l Sec. Servs., 406 U.S. 272, 80 LRRM 2225 (1972).

quiring the successor employer to bargain with the union that had represented its predecessor's employees. The Court explained that continuity of the bargaining relationship is of particular importance to the employees when a business is sold and the plans of the new employer are unclear:

[D]uring this unsettling transition period, the union needs the presumptions of majority status to which it is entitled to safeguard its members' rights and to develop a relationship with the successor.[146]

.... [Without that presumption], an employer could use a successor enterprise as a way of getting rid of a labor contract and of exploiting the employees' hesitant attitude towards the union to eliminate its continuing presence.[147]

The Court endorsed the agency's finding of "substantial continuity," even though there was a 7-month hiatus between the demise of the predecessor employer and the start-up of the new firm. Although the employer was not bound by the predecessor's contract with the union, it had "an obligation to bargain with that union so long as the new employer is, in fact, a successor of the old employer, and the majority of its employees were employed by its predecessor."[148]

Successorship, and issues related to successorship, continue to confront arbitrators. Arbitrators are called upon to decide (1) whether the successor company has any obligation under the predecessor's collective bargaining agreement,[149] (2) whether the predecessor has an obligation to require its successor to assume the predecessor's collective bargaining agreement as a condition of the transfer of the business,[150] and (3) whether a predecessor or

---

[146]*Fall River*, 482 U.S. at 39, 125 LRRM at 2446.

[147]*Id.* at 40, 125 LRRM at 2446.

[148]*Id.* at 41, 125 LRRM at 2447.

[149]For cases holding that the successor did *not* have obligations under the predecessor's agreement, see *Nevada Ready Mix*, 93 LA 1232, 1235 (Horowitz, 1989); *Arch of Ill.*, 89 LA 654 (Fullmer, 1987) (successor was not liable for paying pro rata vacation pay to employee injured on job; successor was not bound by predecessor's contract, past practice, or custom); *Family Food Park*, 86 LA 1184 (Petersen, 1986) (predecessor's past practice of assigning hours of work on the basis of seniority was not carried over when successor purchased the business and hired its predecessor's former employees); *Servicecare, Inc.*, 82 LA 590, 592–93 (Talarico, 1984) (the successor was not liable to pay an employee for accrued sick leave, even though the successor hired all the former employees of the predecessor and agreed to "take over" the contract between the union and the predecessor; arbitrator's decision is based on the fact that the successor specifically denied responsibility for accrued benefits prior to agreeing to adhere to the terms and conditions of its predecessor's contract). For cases holding that the successor had obligations under the predecessor's agreement, see *Peabody Coal Co.*, 92 LA 1086 (Stoltenberg, 1989) (ordering successor to continue predecessor's past practice of payment of matching death benefit for non-mine-related deaths); *Arch of W. Va.*, 90 LA 891 (Stoltenberg, 1988) (ordering successor to continue predecessor's practice of paying employees on weekly basis, rather than biweekly; successor was bound by terms of a national agreement, local agreement, and past practice); *Burnside-Graham Ready Mix*, 86 LA 972 (1986) (ordering a joint venture established by the merger of two companies to dovetail the two companies' seniority lists, using length-of-service method, because the joint venture as an entity succeeded to the contract rights and obligations of two companies).

[150]*See* Marley-Wylain Co., 88 LA 978 (Jacobowski, 1987) (employer violated collective bargaining agreement, which was made binding on successors and assigns, where it failed to require buyer's assumption of agreement); Wyatt Mfg. Co., 82 LA 153, 162–63 (Goodman, 1983) (the predecessor was not obligated to require its successor to assume the predecessor's contract, because the contract did not contain an express provision requiring the predecessor to secure from the successor a commitment to be bound by the contract, and there was no bargaining history to indicate an intent to at least imply such an obligation).

successor has a severance pay obligation to employees of the predecessor who were employed by the successor.[151]

Whether the surviving corporation is obligated to honor the entire collective bargaining agreement of the merged entity, one or more of its provisions, or a past practice thereunder are factual issues for the arbitrator to determine according to whether there was an express or implied assumption agreement.[152]

5. MERGER OF SENIORITY LISTS [LA CDI 117.232]

The merger of separate companies, or the consolidation of plants or departments with separate seniority lists, gives rise to the problem of determining precisely how to make a composite of employees of both operations. An extensive study of this problem is in a report to the National Academy of Arbitrators.[153] The reader is directed to that excellent summary for its in-depth consideration of methods of merging seniority lists. The present treatment will merely note the methods, identified and analyzed in that report, of making a composite seniority list for purposes of layoff, rehire, promotion, transfer, and the like.[154] Those methods are:

1. *The surviving-group principle.* Here, when one company purchases or acquires another company, the employees of the purchasing or acquiring company receive seniority preference over the employees of the purchased or acquired company. The seniority lists are merged by adding the names of the employees of the acquired company, in

---

[151]Where the predecessor was not obligated for severance pay, see *Pillsbury Co.*, 100 LA 436, 440–42 (Stallworth, 1993); *TGS Tech.*, 99 LA 988, 990–94 (Miller, 1992); *N-Ren Corp. S.*, 81 LA 438, 443 (Boyer, 1983); *Washington Star Communications*, 70 LA 1193, 1195 (Gamser, 1978); *American Petrofina*, 63 LA 1300, 1305–07 (Marlatt, 1974). Where the predecessor was obligated for severance pay, see *Ala Moana Volkswagen*, 91 LA 1331, 1334 (Tsukiyama, 1988); *Allied Chem. Corp.*, 81 LA 514, 518 (Epstein, 1983); *Stauffer Publ'ns*, 68 LA 1037, 1040 (Madden, 1977); *Ward Foods*, 61 LA 1032, 1041–42 (Dash, Jr., 1973).

[152]St. Louis Symphony Soc'y, 106 LA 158 (Fowler, 1996) (after music school merged with symphony orchestra, union that represented orchestra had jurisdiction over dispute at music school).

[153]Kennedy, *Merging Seniority Lists, in* LABOR ARBITRATION AND INDUSTRIAL CHANGE, PROCEEDINGS OF THE 16TH ANNUAL MEETING OF NAA 1 (Kahn ed., BNA Books 1963).

[154]It was also noted in the report that seniority rights may be divided into two distinct types. One type, termed "benefit seniority," is concerned with benefits such as vacations or retirement pay and usually depends solely on length of service. The other type, termed "competitive-status seniority," is concerned with such matters as layoff or promotion and is not necessarily based solely on length of service. Where the distinction between the two types of seniority is applied, it is necessary to have a seniority list for benefits and another for competitive status; this can result in discrepancies between the two types of rights. *Id.* at 2, 29. *See also* Burnside-Graham Ready Mix, 86 LA 972, 977–78 (Wren, 1986) (for discussion of four different bases for merging seniority lists); Theatrical Stage Employees Local 640 Seniority Roster, 53 LA 1253, 1258–59 (Spelfogel, 1969); Country Belle Coop. Farmers, 48 LA 600, 603–06 (Duff, 1967) (employees of an acquired company were permitted to keep all their benefit seniority but only one half of their competitive-status seniority—a separate list for each type of seniority was specified by the arbitrator); City of Green Bay, 44 LA 311, 314 (Anderson, 1965).

their seniority order, to the bottom of the list of the acquiring company.[155]

2. *The length-of-service principle*. Under this methodology, a combined seniority list is prepared by placing employees on the new list in the order of their length of service, regardless of which company or plant the employee worked for prior to the merger or consolidation. All employees are thus treated as if they had always been employed by the same company or plant.[156]

3. *The follow-the-work principle*. In this scenario, when companies merge or when plants or departments within a company are consolidated, the employees are given the opportunity to follow their work (if it still can be adequately identified) with the seniority rights to such work protected by continuation of the separate seniority lists. If the work becomes merged or its identity is otherwise lost, the seniority lists may be integrated into a single list on a ratio basis representing the amount of work brought to the consolidation by each group of employees.[157]

4. *The absolute-rank principle*. In this version, employees are placed on the merged seniority list on the basis of the rank they held on their respective prior lists. Thus, the two employees who were first on the two original lists are given the first two places on the merged list (the employee with the longer service gets the first place and the other employee gets the second); the two employees who were second on the two original lists are given the third and fourth places on the merged list; and so on. The ratio-rank principle, noted below, is much more popular than the absolute-rank principle, because the ratio-rank

---

[155]For an instance in which this method, sometimes called "endtailing," was used either exclusively or in combination with another method, see *Thomas v. Bakery, Confectionery, & Tobacco Workers Local 433*, 982 F.2d 1215, 142 LRRM 2168 (8th Cir. 1992). *See also* Carbone of Am. Indus., 100 LA 720, 726–28 (Dean, Jr., 1992); Nevada Ready Mix, 93 LA 1232, 1235–36 (Horowitz, 1989); Carling Nat'l Breweries, 71 LA 476, 478–79 (Harkless, 1978) (union position and comments); Mooney-Kiefer-Stewart, 69 LA 477, 482 (Render, 1977) (this method was required by contract); Theatrical Stage Employees Local 640 Seniority Roster, 53 LA 1253, 1258–59 (Spelfogel, 1969); Armco Steel Corp., 36 LA 981, 988–89 (Platt, 1961) (the group A list was placed near the bottom of the group B list, with the group A list being integrated only with group B employees who were on layoff).

[156]For instances in which this method was used either exclusively or in combination with another method, see *Rakestraw v. United Airlines*, 981 F.2d 1524, 142 LRRM 2054 (7th Cir. 1992), *reh'g denied*, 989 F.2d 944, 142 LRRM 3006 (7th Cir. 1993), *cert. denied sub nom.* Hammond v. Air Line Pilots, 510 U.S. 861 (1992), and 510 U.S. 906 (1993). *See also* Jack Cooper Transp. Co., 97 LA 804, 805 (Thornell, 1991); Burnside-Graham Ready Mix, 86 LA 972, 977–78 (Wren, 1986); Theatrical Stage Employees Local 640 Seniority Roster, 53 LA 1253, 1258–59 (Spelfogel, 1969); Air W. Airlines, 51 LA 717, 718–19 (Rohman, 1968); Union Spring & Mfg. Co., 46 LA 589, 598 (Wagner, 1966); Manhattan Transit Co., 45 LA 1018, 1019, 1021 (Kerrison, 1966); City of Green Bay, 44 LA 311, 315–16 (Anderson, 1965); Associated Brewing Co., 40 LA 680, 685–86 (Kahn, 1963); Western Pa. Motor Carriers Ass'n, 31 LA 976, 979 (Di Leone, 1958) (lists "dovetailed" by length of service); Moore Bus. Forms, 24 LA 793, 801–03 (Somers, 1955).

[157]This was done in *Sonotone Corp.*, 42 LA 359, 364 (Wolf, 1964), where a group of employees who brought only 70% as much work to the consolidation as another group were credited with 70% of their length of prior service and the resultant figure determined their place on a merged (length-of-service variety) seniority list. *See also* Country Belle Coop. Farmers, 48 LA 600, 603–06 (Duff, 1967).

method gives due consideration to the rank factor without producing the serious distortions that can occur under the absolute-rank method, as where the groups to be merged are of different size.[158]

5. *The ratio-rank principle.* Under this approach, integration of seniority lists may be accomplished by establishing a ratio from the number of employees in each of the groups to be merged and assigning the places on the new seniority list according to this ratio. Thus, if seniority list A has 200 employees and seniority list B has only 100 employees, the ratio is two to one. Therefore, of the first three places on the new seniority list, two are allocated to the first two employees on the A list and one is allocated to the first employee on the B list (as among the three employees, length of service may be used to determine which employee gets each of the first three places); then places 4, 5, and 6 on the new list are allocated to the third and fourth employees on the A list and to the second employee on the B list; and so on, until all the A and B employees are placed on the new list.[159]

Arbitrators may be called on not only to determine which method or combination of methods should be used in the given case, but also whether a method agreed to by the parties is fair and should be approved.[160]

Any one of the above methods, particularly the length-of-service method, may possibly be selected for exclusive use in a case.[161] However, it is not unusual for methods to be used in combination.[162] For instance, in merging two pilot seniority lists following the merger of airlines, one-third weight was given to the ratio-rank principle and two-thirds weight was given to the length-of-service principle; the arbitrator thus considered (1) length of service, and (2) the ratio of pilots in one airline to pilots in the other, but with length of service having greater weight.[163]

---

[158]In *Moore Business Forms*, 24 LA 793, 801–03 (Somers, 1955), the "rank" factor was used in combination with length of service, equal weight being given to (1) overall length of service, and (2) the employees' relative positions on the separate plant lists.

[159]This method was used, or approved of, in combination with other methods in *Delta Air Lines*, 72 LA 458, 466–69 (Platt, 1979); *Pan Am. World Airways*, 19 LA 14, 20–22 (Cole, Martin, & Saul, 1952).

[160]*See, e.g.*, Ralphs Grocery Co., 109 LA 33 (Kaufman, 1997) (no remedy awarded because union had "selectively enforced" the agreement).

[161]*See, e.g.*, Jack Cooper Transp. Co., 97 LA 804, 805 (Thornell, 1991); Burnside-Graham Ready Mix, 86 LA 972, 977–78 (Wren, 1986); City of Green Bay, 44 LA 311, 315–16 (Anderson, 1965). Length of service is given at least some weight in most cases. In *AMAX Coal Co.*, 104 LA 790 (Stoltenberg, 1995), length of service was determined to be the proper method of combining serniority lists, where two unions who represented employees at one mine were combined.

[162]*See, e.g.*, Purity Baking Co., 95 LA 172, 177–78 (Gordon, 1990); Sonotone Corp., 42 LA 359, 364 (Wolf, 1964); Armco Steel Corp., 36 LA 981, 988–89 (Platt, 1961); Moore Bus. Forms, 24 LA 793, 801–03 (Somers, 1955); Pan Am. World Airways, 19 LA 14, 20–22 (Cole, Martin, & Saul, 1952).

[163]Pan Am. World Airways, 19 LA 14, 20–22 (Cole, Martin, & Saul, 1952).

6. CONTRACTUAL PROVISIONS FOR LOSS OF SENIORITY
[LA CDI 117.2431 ET SEQ.]

Contractual provisions for loss of seniority in designated situations are not uncommon. For example, the agreement may call for loss of seniority in the event of unexcused absence for a specified period,[164] in the event the employee resigns,[165] or if an employee on leave works for another employer during the leave without the original employer's consent.[166] In some instances, the agreement will expressly indicate that loss of seniority due to unexcused absences shall also constitute a termination of the employment relationship.[167] Termination of employment without such express provision has been upheld in some cases as a concomitant of the loss of seniority,[168] but not always.[169]

Arbitrators have enforced contractual provisions that provide for the loss of seniority in the event of layoff for a certain period of time,[170] or in the event of any lengthy absence from work resulting from illness or injury.[171] However, a laid-off employee, who successfully bid to a new department from which he was subsequently laid off, was held to have maintained seniority in his original department, even though he ignored a recall notice to the new

---

[164]*See* E.B. Eddy Paper, 94 LA 325, 327 (Borland, 1990); Maremont Corp., 79 LA 1012, 1013 (Devino, 1982); ITT Gen. Controls, 76 LA 1258, 1260 (Bickner, 1981); McInerney Spring & Wire Co., 72 LA 1262, 1263 (Roumell, Jr., 1979); Brush Beryllium Co., 55 LA 709, 715 (Dworkin, 1970); Murdock Mach. & Eng'g Co., 49 LA 613, 614–15 (Rohman, 1967); National Rose Co., 43 LA 1066, 1069–70 (Autrey, 1964).

[165]*See* Marble Cliff Block & Builders Supply, 98 LA 280, 285–86 (Heekin, 1991); Clarkston Cmty. Sch., 79 LA 48, 52 (Kanner, 1982); Simmons Co., 49 LA 950, 952 (Teple, 1967); Tuttle Press Co., 49 LA 490, 492–93 (Seitz, 1967). In *Reden Corp.*, 50 LA 413, 416–17 (Roberts, 1968), the arbitrator enforced a strike settlement agreement under which the accumulation of seniority by strikers was tolled during the period of the strike.

[166]B.F. Nelson Folding Cartons, 98 LA 978 (Jacobowski, 1991) (in spite of a provision that seniority was lost by accepting other employment during leave, the company properly reinstated the seniority of an employee who violated that provision, where the employee informed his employer of his intent to work for another employer, work was slow, and he was a valuable employee).

[167]*See* Maremont Corp., 79 LA 1012, 1013 (Devino, 1982); ITT Gen. Controls, 76 LA 1258, 1260 (Bickner, 1981); Murdock Mach. & Eng'g Co., 49 LA 613, 614–15 (Rohman, 1967); Midland-Ross Corp., 49 LA 283, 283 (Larkin, 1967).

[168]*See* FMC Corp., 74 LA 1185, 1187 (Doering, 1980); Crown Cork & Seal Co., 72 LA 613, 615–16 (Daly, 1979); Boyle-Midway, 70 LA 963, 966 (Traynor, 1978); Teledyne Indus. Diecast, 70 LA 185, 186 (Cox, 1978); Sperry Rand Corp., 60 LA 793, 794–95 (Dugan, 1973); O-Cel-O Gen. Mills, 59 LA 869, 871 (Shister, 1972); A.O. Smith Corp., 47 LA 443, 446–48 (Stouffer, 1966); Buckeye Forging Co., 42 LA 1151, 1161–62 (Klein, 1964); Astatic Corp., 39 LA 414, 415–16 (Klein, 1962); Bassick Co., 38 LA 278, 279–82 (Seitz, 1962). *See also* United States Steel Corp., 78 LA 1065, 1067 (Beilstein, 1982); Rheem Mfg. Co., 72 LA 1217, 1218, 1220 (Barron, 1979). See also Chapter 15, section 3.B., "Effect of Criminal Proceedings Against the Employee," citing cases permitting or not permitting discharge of employees for absence from work due to jail confinement.

[169]*See* Cooper Indus., 78 LA 850, 855–56 (Aisenberg, 1982); Quick Mfg., 43 LA 54, 60–61 (Teple, 1964). *See also* Defoe Shipbuilding Co., 49 LA 206, 209 (Walsh, 1967).

[170]*See* Fleming Foods of Tex., 84 LA 376, 377–78 (Stephens, 1985); Boogaart Supply Co., 84 LA 27, 30 (Fogelberg, 1984).

[171]*See* Davies Can Co., 103 LA 877, 878 (Strasshofer, Jr., 1994); Porritts & Spencer, 83 LA 1165, 1168 (Byars, 1984); Trojon Luggage Co., 81 LA 366, 368 (Cromwell, 1983). In *Lithonia Lighting Co.*, 85 LA 627, 631 (Volz, 1985), the arbitrator held that absence due to a work-related injury did not constitute "sick leave." Therefore, the employee was entitled to keep seniority under the agreement, which terminated seniority after 3 years of sick leave.

department.[172] Similarly, an employee who, while serving in the National Guard, was granted an extended leave of absence by his employer to work for a different employer in a job related to his National Guard duties, was permitted to accumulate seniority during the leave period.[173]

In another case, an arbitrator ruled that a provision terminating seniority when an employee severs service from a company did not deprive the employee, who had received full retirement benefits, of his continued seniority with the company.[174] However, if a leave of absence has been improperly obtained, it may be considered a resignation, and the employee required to return to work as a new hire without seniority.[175]

7. Use of Seniority and Ability Provisions and Layoffs
[LA CDI 119.121; 119.1121; 117.1132; 117.1133]

There are two basic types of seniority provisions. The more rigid type requires the recognition of strict seniority—that is, the employer must give preference to the employee with the longest continuous service without regard to any other considerations.[176] The principal thesis underlying this approach is that, as between a junior person of superior qualities and a senior person of inferior qualities, the social claim of the latter should override both the needs of the business and the interest of the public in its efficient operation.[177] The more usual provision, however, is written so as to serve the basic aims of seniority, while recognizing other factors, especially the relative "fitness and ability" of the employees, in determining preferences in employment.[178] Such factors may include skill, ability, aptitude, competence, efficiency, training, physical fitness, judgment, experience, initiative, and leadership. In regard to this "modified seniority," one arbitrator stated:

---

[172]Pacific Southwest Airlines, 88 LA 639 (Williams, 1986). *See also* Bethlehem Steel Corp., 100 LA 466 (Kahn, 1992) (employee did not lose seniority during absence for work-related injury); Waterous Co., 100 LA 278 (Reynolds, 1993) (contract provision stating specifically that seniority shall not be lost because of injury or illness).

[173]Great Lakes Carbon Corp., 88 LA 644 (Singer, 1987) (employee could not reclaim former job by bumping because, by accepting private employment, he had violated contractual provision prohibiting gainful employment during a leave).

[174]World Airways, 83 LA 401, 405 (Concepcion, 1984) (pilot, who had reached mandatory age of retirement, 60, and who had retired while on medical leave of absence, was entitled to use seniority to downgrade to second officer position, having been certified as fit to return to duty, under contract stating that when leaves are granted because of sickness or injury, crewmember shall retain and continue to accrue seniority until able to return to duty).

[175]Rose Printing Co., 88 LA 27 (Williams, 1986).

[176]*See* Sunnyside Coal Co., 104 LA 886, 886–87 (Sharpe, 1995); Hughes Aircraft Co., 101 LA 415, 420 (Prayzich, 1993); Stacor Corp., 99 LA 263, 264 (Mayer, 1992); United Exposition Serv. Co., 95 LA 951, 952 (Allen, Jr., 1990); Overly Mfg. Co. of Cal., 68 LA 1343, 1345 (Jones, Jr., 1977); Thiokol Corp., 65 LA 1265, 1266 (Williams, 1975); Dana Corp., 27 LA 203, 204 (Mittenthal, 1956). In *Branch Motor Express Co.*, 39 LA 795, 795 (Crawford, 1962), the agreement specified strict seniority except where special training or experience was required, the exception to become effective only by special agreement of the parties.

[177]*See* Clifton, *Management Functions, in* N.Y.U. First Ann. Conf. on Labor 89, 97 (1948).

[178]*See* Darin & Armstrong, 13 LA 843, 845 (Platt, 1950). Some contracts provide for strict seniority for layoffs while calling for consideration of seniority and ability for promotions. *See* J. Weingarten, 42 LA 619, 622 (Rohman, 1964). In *New Britain Mach. Co.*, 45 LA 993,

　　Generally speaking, such modified seniority is acceptable to most unions and employers because it acknowledges the fact that wide difference in ability and capacity to perform the work required exists between employees in a plant and that such differences are a logical and legitimate consideration in determining preference in employment, especially in making promotions and demotions as well as in the reduction of forces.[179]

The contract may allow the employer to disregard seniority in cases of demonstrated need. For example, one contract allowed the employer to recall junior employees where specific employees' services were "temporarily required under certain circumstances." The employer did not violate the contract when it recalled more junior employees because of their special training that the more senior employees did not possess.[180] A contract also may allow an employer to recall salaried employees rather than more senior bargaining-unit workers to bargaining-unit positions.[181] Even in the absence of such exemptions, arbitrators have ruled that emergency situations or other unusual circumstances may excuse an employer from following the contract's seniority provisions.[182]

In deciding the meaning and application of ambiguous seniority provisions, arbitrators favor interpretations affirming the use of seniority over rejecting the use of seniority, especially where the work opportunities are limited.[183]

A. Modified Seniority Clauses

Modified seniority clauses fall into one of three basic categories: "relative ability" clauses, "sufficient ability" clauses, and "hybrid" clauses.

i.　Relative Ability Clauses [LA CDI 119.1221]

The first category contains those clauses that provide in essence that the senior employee shall be given preference if he or she possesses fitness and ability equal to that of junior employees.[184] This type of clause might be termed a "relative ability" clause, because here comparisons between quali-

---

994–95 (McCoy, 1965), the contract merely stated that the employer "will give consideration to seniority"; the arbitrator said this only required good-faith consideration of seniority and did not prevent consideration also of ability or physical fitness, or of the employer's own interest in efficient and profitable operations.

[179]Darin & Armstrong, 13 LA 843, 845–46 (Platt, 1950). *See also* Atlas Powder Co., 30 LA 674, 676 (Frey, 1958).

[180]Day & Zimmermann, 95 LA 467 (Edelman, 1990). *See also* ALSCO Div., 106 LA 1146 (Rybolt, 1996); ConAgra, Inc., 106 LA 784 (Suardi, 1996); Eagle Iron Works, 103 LA 903 (Murphy, 1994).

[181]Carbone of Am. Indus., 100 LA 720 (Dean, Jr., 1992).

[182]ARMCO, Inc., 94 LA 1245 (Eisler, 1990). *See also* Flexible Corp., 94 LA 158 (Modjeska, 1990).

[183]Dyncorp Technical Servs. Group, 93 LA 1192 (Richman, 1990).

[184]*See, e.g.*, Houston Lighting & Power Co., 103 LA 179, 188 (Fox, Jr., 1993); Type House + Duragraph, 102 LA 225, 226 (Miller, 1993); Marshalltown Area Cmty. Hosp., 76 LA 978, 979 (Smith, 1981); Cincinnati Bd. of Educ., 72 LA 524, 525 (Ipavec, 1979); University of Cal., L.A., 66 LA 342, 344 (Greer, 1976); Joseph T. Ryerson. & Son, 56 LA 1206, 1207 (Caraway, 1971); Cummins Engine Co., 56 LA 399, 401 (Larkin, 1971); Scott & Fetzer Co., 56 LA 6, 7 (Stouffer, 1971); Georgia Kraft Co., 55 LA 104, 105 (Williams, 1970); Lukens Steel Co., 46 LA 1005, 1006 (Rock, 1966); Interlake Steel Corp., 46 LA 23, 24 (Luskin, 1965); Realist, Inc., 45

fications of employees bidding for the job are necessary and proper,[185] and seniority becomes a determining factor only if the qualifications of the bidders are equal.[186]

The wording of these relative ability clauses varies. The contract may provide that seniority shall govern unless there is a marked difference in ability, or unless a junior employee has greater ability. Some clauses provide that seniority shall govern if ability (or other qualifying factors such as physical fitness, competence, etc.) is "relatively equal," or "substantially equal," or, simply, "equal." "Relatively" equal ability does not mean "exactly" equal ability.[187] Even the term "equal" does not mean exact equality, but only substantial equality.[188] Thus, whether the term used is "equal" or "relatively equal" or "substantially equal," it would appear that only an approximate or near equality of competing employees, rather than a precise equality, should be necessary in order to bring the seniority factor into play.[189] For example, an arbitrator allowed a senior employee subject to lay off to bump "upwards" into a position that had been awarded to a more qualified junior employee, where the senior employee had the "present ability to perform the work."[190] Conversely, where a junior employee is substantially superior in ability that employee may be given preference over a senior employee.[191] When a com-

---

LA 444, 444 (Keeler, 1965); Atlas Powder Co., 30 LA 674, 675 (Frey, 1958); American Smelting & Ref. Co., 29 LA 262, 265 (Ross, 1957); M.A. Hanna Co., 25 LA 480, 481 (Marshall, 1955); Stauffer Chem. Co., 23 LA 322, 323 (Reid, 1954); Pittsburgh Steel Co., 21 LA 565, 566 (Brecht, 1953).

[185]Alabama Power Co., 18 LA 24, 25 (McCoy, 1952). Relative ability is to be determined in reference to the particular job in question, not in reference to overall ability. *See also* Walgreen Co., 93 LA 482 (Baroni, 1989) (attendance records may be considered when determining qualifications); New Jersey Tel. Co., 47 LA 495, 500 (Koretz, 1966); Yuba Heat Transfer Corp., 38 LA 471, 474–75 (Autrey, 1962).

[186]*See* Carnation Pet Foods, 89 LA 1288, 1290–91 (Berger, 1987); Marshalltown Area Cmty. Hosp., 76 LA 978, 982–83 (Smith, 1981); Roanoke Iron & Bridge Works, 68 LA 1019, 1021 (Merrifield, 1977); San Francisco News-Call Bulletin, 34 LA 271, 273 (Ross, 1960); Atlas Powder Co., 30 LA 674, 677 (Frey, 1958); Pittsburgh Steel Co., 21 LA 565, 568 (Brecht, 1953); Alabama Power Co., 18 LA 24, 25 (McCoy, 1952). *But see* Weather Shield Mfg., 96 LA 338, 342–45 (Wyman, 1990).

[187]*See* Bethlehem Steel Co., 23 LA 532, 534 (Seward, 1954).

[188]*See* Poloron Prods. of Pa., 23 LA 789, 792 (Rosenfarb, 1955); Combustion Eng'g Co., 20 LA 416, 419 (McCoy, 1953). *See also* Rainier Port Cold Storage, 79 LA 441, 448 (Armstrong, 1982); Del Monte Corp., 76 LA 852, 853 (Kelliher, 1981); San Francisco News-Call Bulletin, 34 LA 271, 273 (Ross, 1960); Kuhlman Elec. Co., 26 LA 885, 889 (Howlett, 1956). *Cf.* Acme Steel Co., 9 LA 432, 435 (Gregory, 1947).

[189]*See* Republic Steel Corp., 1 LA 244, 247 (Platt, 1945). *See also* Rainier Port Cold Storage, 79 LA 441, 448 (Armstrong, 1982); New York State Elec. & Gas Co., 75 LA 1024, 1027, 1033 (Atleson, 1980); City of Traverse City, 72 LA 1061, 1064 (Roumell, Jr., 1979); Bristol Steel & Iron Works, 47 LA 263, 265 (Volz, 1966) (junior employee "need not be head-and-shoulders better, but his greater ability should be clearly discernible to outweigh the factor of seniority"); Interlake Steel Corp., 46 LA 23, 26–27 (Luskin, 1965) (junior employee loses unless there is a definite, distinct, substantial, and significant difference as to ability in employee's favor); San Francisco News-Call Bulletin, 34 LA 271, 273 (Ross, 1960) ("if the junior employee is preferred, he should be 'head and shoulders' above the senior"). *But see* Cincinnati Bd. of Educ., 72 LA 524, 527 (Ipavec, 1979) (stating that "only where the margin is diminutive shall seniority determine").

[190]Metalloy Corp., 91 LA 221, 224–25 (Daniel, 1988).

[191]*See* Weather Shield Mfg., 96 LA 338, 342–45 (Wyman, 1990); Illinois Dep'ts of Pers. & Corr., 72 LA 941, 949 (Rezler, 1979); Erie Mining Co., 49 LA 390, 395 (Dworkin, 1967); Bristol Steel & Iron Works, 47 LA at 265; Interlake Steel Corp., 46 LA 23, 28 (Luskin, 1965); Bethlehem Steel, 29 LA 710, 712 (Seward, 1957); Quaker Shipyard & Mach. Co., 19 LA 883, 888 (Frey, 1952); Mutual Tel. Co., 19 LA 270, 278–79 (Roberts, 1952).

pany is promoting an employee to a supervisory position, the employer may give greater preference to "fitness and ability" than to seniority.[192]

ii. Sufficient Ability Clauses [LA CDI 119.1221]

The second basic type of modified seniority clause provides in general that the senior employee will be given preference if he or she possesses sufficient ability to perform the job.[193] Minimum qualifications are enough under these sufficient ability clauses.[194] This type of clause may state that preference will be given to the senior qualified bidder, or to the senior employee, provided he or she is qualified or has the "necessary" ability for the job. Under this type of provision, "it is necessary to determine only whether the employee with greater seniority can in fact do the job."[195] Comparisons between applicants are unnecessary and improper, and "the job must be given to the senior bidder if he is competent, regardless of how much more competent some other bidder may be."[196] Thus, the senior qualified employee will be entitled to preference even though a junior employee possesses greater skill and ability.[197]

Under such a sufficient ability clause, an arbitrator upheld the seniority rights of laid-off employees to apply for and receive promotions to more highly paid vacant positions even though the posted notice of job openings specified it was not a recall notice. There, the grieving senior employees met the minimum qualification requirements and were entitled to "bump" the junior coworkers who had been selected.[198]

---

[192]Sebastiani Vineyards, 85 LA 371, 375 (Rothstein, 1985).

[193]See, e.g., Miami Sys. Corp., 99 LA 506, 507–08 (Curry, Jr., 1992); Arch of Ill., 94 LA 376, 378 (Fullmer, 1990); American Sawmill Mach. Co., 79 LA 106, 107 (Harrison, 1982); Chromalloy Am. Corp., 62 LA 84, 86 (Fox, Jr., 1974); Honeywell, Inc., 61 LA 1021, 1021 (Doppelt, 1973); Virginia Chems., 56 LA 920, 921 (Flannagan, 1971); Whirlpool Corp., 56 LA 40, 41 (Johannes, 1971).

[194]Central Franklin Process Co., 19 LA 32, 34 (Marshall, 1952). See also Atlantic Spring Mfg. Co., 79 LA 1147, 1150–51 (Schwartz, 1982); American Sawmill Mach. Co., 79 LA 106, 108–09 (Harrison, 1982). In Kingsberry Homes Corp., 53 LA 1345, 1347 (Rauch, 1969), the arbitrator stated that the term "if qualified" must be construed "to mean that the senior employee must have a background of such training, experience, or demonstrated aptitude and physical makeup, as to give a reasonable person cause to believe that this person can be expected to perform the job competently within a reasonable time."

[195]See National Industri Transformers, 96 LA 670, 672 (Cantor, 1991); Peabody Coal Co., 87 LA 758, 760 (Volz, 1985); Illinois Bronze Paint Co., 71 LA 850, 852 (Garman, 1978); City of New York, City Sch. Dist., Bd. of Educ., 68 LA 271, 276 (Nicolau, 1977); Republic Steel Corp., 1 LA 244, 247 (Platt, 1945). See also St. Mary's Kraft Corp., 40 LA 364, 366 (Duncan, 1963).

[196]Alabama Power Co., 18 LA 24, 25 (McCoy, 1952). See also DynAir Fueling of Nev., 102 LA 230 (Mikrut, Jr., 1993); Safeway Stores, 80 LA 1328, 1331 (Fogel, 1983); Atlantic Spring Mfg. Co., 79 LA 1147, 1150–51 (Schwartz, 1982); American Sawmill Mach. Co., 79 LA 106, 108–09 (Harrison, 1982); Miami Valley Paper Co., 78 LA 383, 385 (Kates, 1982); Corporation of Borough of Scarborough, 72 LA 1167, 1170 (Brown, 1979); National Distillers Co., 49 LA 918, 920 (Volz, 1967).

[197]Central Franklin Process Co., 19 LA 32, 34 (Marshall, 1952). See also Warner Cable of Akron, 91 LA 48, 51 (Bittel, 1988); Southern Minn. Sugar Coop., 90 LA 243, 246 (Flagler, 1987); American Sawmill Mach. Co., 79 LA 106, 108–09 (Harrison, 1982); Hughes Aircraft Co., 43 LA 1248, 1251–52 (Block, 1965).

[198]Singer Co., 86 LA 917 (Wahl, 1986).

iii. Hybrid Clauses [LA CDI 119.1221]

The third basic type of modified seniority provision, which may be called a "hybrid" clause, requires consideration and comparison in the first instance of both seniority and relative ability.[199] The hybrid clause ordinarily is worded in such general terms as "seniority and qualifications shall govern," or "due consideration shall be given to length of service, aptitude, and ability," and the like, without indicating the relative weight to be accorded these factors.[200] Arbitrators, however, require that fair and reasonable consideration be given to both seniority and relative ability, although the weight that may be accorded to each may vary from case to case.

It seems clear that under hybrid clauses the relative difference in seniority and ability of competing employees must be compared and weighed. Thus, in comparing two or more qualified employees, where the difference in length of service is relatively insignificant and there is a relatively significant difference in ability, the ability factor should be given greater weight; but where there is a relatively substantial difference in seniority and relatively little difference in abilities, length of service should be given greater weight. To illustrate, one arbitrator, giving effect to both factors under a hybrid clause, held that a much better qualified junior employee should be given preference over a senior employee who could perform the job, because there was relatively little difference in length of service, thus making relative ability the determinative factor.[201] Similarly, in interpreting another hybrid seniority clause, an arbitrator upheld the right of the employer to choose the junior employee for a promotion where the difference in length of service was relatively insignificant, the difference in abilities was substantial, and the position was one of the most critical and highest-skilled jobs in the bargaining unit.[202] However, a senior employee whose qualifications were only slightly less than those of a junior employee, but whose seniority was much greater, was given preference over the better qualified junior employee.[203]

---

[199]*See* Elkhart Cmty. Sch., 78 LA 64, 65–67 (Rifkin, 1981); Burkart-Randall, 72 LA 752, 757 (Cyrol, 1979); National Coop. Refinery Ass'n, 64 LA 1104, 1109 (Edes, 1975); Plainview-Old Bethpage Cent. Sch. Dist., 62 LA 333, 334, 337 (Cahn, 1974); British Overseas Airways Corp., 61 LA 768, 769 (Turkus, 1973); Reliance Universal, 50 LA 990, 991, 994 (Dolson, 1968); Reliance Universal, 50 LA 397, 399–400 (Alexander, 1968); Hearst Publ'g Co., 38 LA 374, 374–75 (Knowlton, 1961); Southwestern Bell Tel. Co., 30 LA 862, 870 (Davis, 1958); International Harvester Co., 21 LA 183, 185 (Cole, 1953); Inland Steel Co., 16 LA 280, 283, 285 (Cornsweet, 1951); Pennsylvania Salt Mfg. Co., 14 LA 12, 15 (Frolich, 1949); International Harvester Co., 11 LA 1190, 1192 (Wolff, 1948); Callite Tungsten Corp., 11 LA 743, 744–45 (Feinberg, 1948). *See also* Midland-Ross Corp., 48 LA 983, 988–89 (McCoy, 1967); Trans World Airlines, 45 LA 267, 268 (Beatty, 1965).

[200]In *Reliance Universal*, 50 LA 397, 399–400 (Alexander, 1968), the arbitrator held that where the contract listed seniority, ability, and experience as factors to be considered in promotions, the importance of any factor was not to be determined by the order in which it was listed. *Accord* Reliance Universal, 50 LA at 992. *Cf.* Independent Sch. Dist. No. 279, 71 LA 116, 119 (Fogelberg, 1978).

[201]Callite Tungsten Corp., 11 LA 743, 744–45 (Feinberg, 1948).

[202]Trident NGL, 101 LA 353 (Allen, Jr., 1993).

[203]*See* International Harvester Co., 21 LA 183, 185 (Cole, 1953); International Harvester Co., 11 LA 1190, 1192 (Wolff, 1948). *See also* Executive Jet Aviation, 91 LA 601, 604 (Kindig, 1988); Elkhart Cmty. Sch., 78 LA 64, 66–67 (Rifkin, 1981); Plainview-Old Bethpage Cent. Sch. Dist., 62 LA 333, 337–38 (Cahn, 1974); British Overseas Airways Corp., 61 LA 768, 769–70 (Turkus, 1973) (9 months difference in seniority "outweighed the imperceptibly slight

B. Determination of Fitness and Ability [LA CDI 119.1221]

Provisions for modified seniority, designed both to give recognition to management's right and responsibility to manage the enterprise and to protect senior employees, raise some of the most troublesome questions confronting arbitrators. Unions tend to emphasize seniority over merit and ability, while management tends to emphasize supervision's judgment of merit and ability over seniority.[204]

Arbitrators have frequently held that, where the agreement provides that "fitness and ability" factors are to be considered along with seniority under one of the modified seniority clauses, but is silent as to how and by whom the qualification determination is to be made, management is entitled to make the initial determination, subject to challenge by the union on the ground that management's decision was unreasonable under the facts, or otherwise capricious, arbitrary, or discriminatory.[205] This right to determine ability may be held by management either as a residual management right or as a necessary adjunct to the right to manage the plant and direct the workforce.[206]

---

and subtle differential in qualifications"); Southwest Airmotive Co., 41 LA 353, 359 (Elliott, 1963); Katz & Klein Optical Co., 34 LA 472, 475 (Ross, 1960).

[204]Ford Motor Co., 2 LA 374, 375 (Shuman, 1945).

[205]See American Sawmill Mach. Co., 79 LA 106, 108 (Harrison, 1982); Public Serv. Co. of Colo., 77 LA 313, 320 (Watkins, 1981); Veterans Admin. Ctr., 75 LA 910, 911 (Tillem, 1980); Rotek Inc., 73 LA 937, 940–41 (Rybolt, 1979); Illinois Dept's of Pers. & Corr., 72 LA 941, 945 (Rezler, 1979) (management is entitled to make the initial determination and the union may challenge its "appropriateness"); Cincinnati Bd. of Educ., 72 LA 524, 528 (Ipavec, 1979); Screw Conveyor Corp., 72 LA 434, 437 (Howell, 1979); Whirlpool Corp., 56 LA 40, 42–43 (Johannes, 1971); Scott & Fetzer Co., 56 LA 6, 10 (Stouffer, 1971); American Welding & Mfg. Co., 52 LA 889, 894 (Stouffer, 1969); American Cyanamid Co., 52 LA 247, 252 (Cahn, 1969) (union need not show that company action was arbitrary, capricious, or in bad faith, it sufficing to show that company made an incorrect factual determination); Containers, Inc., 49 LA 589, 594 (Anderson, 1967); Erie Mining Co., 49 LA 390, 394 (Dworkin, 1967); Atlas Processing Co., 46 LA 860, 863 (Oppenheim, 1966); Shenango Furnace Co., 46 LA 203, 208 (Klein, 1966); International Nickel Co., 45 LA 743, 747 (Kates, 1965); Southern Ohio Fabricators, 44 LA 283, 285 (Schmidt, 1965); Christy Vault Co., 42 LA 1093, 1096 (Koven, 1964); Great W. Sugar Co., 41 LA 528, 532 (Seligson, 1963); American Sugar Co., 38 LA 132, 143 (Rohman, 1961); Higgins, Inc., 37 LA 801, 805 (Hale, 1961); Bemis Bros. Bag Co., 37 LA 29, 34 (Maggs, 1961); San Francisco News-Call Bulletin, 34 LA 271, 275 (Ross, 1960) (review not limited to arbitrary or capricious action—company decision may be made in good faith but still be unreasonable). In some cases arbitrators have spoken in terms of management's decision being subject to challenge on the ground that it is "clearly wrong," or the like. See Trans World Airlines, 40 LA 697, 699–700 (Beatty, 1963); Kaiser Aluminum & Chem. Corp., 35 LA 866, 869 (Caraway, 1960); Weber Showcase & Fixture Co., 27 LA 40, 49 (Prasow, 1956); Merrill-Stevens Drydock & Repair Co., 6 LA 838, 841 (Marshall, 1947). In still other cases, particularly earlier cases, the arbitrator limited review of management's decision to the narrower ground of arbitrary, capricious, bad faith, or discriminatory action. See American Sugar Co., 46 LA 91, 94 (Ray, 1966); Gisholt Mach. Co., 23 LA 105, 109 (Kelliher, 1954); Washington Metal Trades, 23 LA 38, 39 (Carmody, 1954); Copco Steel & Eng'g Co., 22 LA 258, 260 (Parker, 1954); Coca-Cola Bottling Co., 18 LA 757, 758–59 (Murphy, 1952); Merrill Stevens Dry Dock & Repair Co., 17 LA 516, 518–19 (Hawley, 1951); Hercules Powder Co., 10 LA 624, 626 (Reynolds, 1948); Combustion Eng'g Co., 9 LA 515, 517 (Ingle, 1948); Crown Cotton Mills, 7 LA 526, 527 (Greene, 1947).

[206]See American Welding & Mfg. Co., 52 LA 889, 894 (Stouffer, 1969); Trans World Airlines, 40 LA 697, 699–700 (Beatty, 1963); American Sugar Co., 38 LA 132, 143 (Rohman, 1961); Higgins, Inc., 37 LA 801, 805 (Hale, 1961); Petro-Tex Chem. Corp., 34 LA 788, 792 (Britton, 1960); National Seal Co., 29 LA 29, 36 (Dworkin, 1957); Lockheed Aircraft Corp., 25 LA 748, 751 (Williams, 1956); Stauffer Chem. Co., 23 LA 322, 326 (Reid, 1954); Gisholt Mach. Co., 20 LA 137, 141 (Baab, 1953); Chrysler Corp., 14 LA 163, 167 (Ebeling, 1950); Hercules Powder Co., 10 LA 624, 626 (Reynolds, 1948).

A collective bargaining agreement containing a modified seniority clause may specifically provide that the employer shall be the judge of the qualifying factors, sometimes also providing for challenge of management's decision by the union through the grievance procedure.[207] Here, too, arbitrators may hold that management's determination is similarly subject to challenge.[208] Furthermore, even where the contract makes the employer the sole judge, arbitrators have held that management's action is subject to review and correction on the same grounds.[209]

C. Review of Management's Determination: Evidence and Burden of Proof [LA CDI 94.60509]

In many cases involving issues of seniority and ability, the arbitrator in reviewing management's determination does not address the issue of burden of proof, but simply considers all the evidence and arguments of the parties to reach a decision on whether the company's determination should be upheld.[210] Some arbitrators, however, will place the burden of proof on one party or the other.[211]

---

[207]*See, e.g.*, North Country Dodge, 77 LA 391, 392 (Craver, 1981); Mountain States Tel. & Tel. Co., 70 LA 729, 730 (Goodman, 1978); Mack Trucks, 55 LA 813, 816 (Larson, 1970); American Forest Prods. Corp., 53 LA 549, 549 (Koven, 1969); Fruehauf Trailer Co., 30 LA 803, 804 (Meltzer, 1958); Bemis Bros. Bag Co., 26 LA 773, 774 (Disman, 1956); International Paper Co., 19 LA 402, 403 (Ralston, Jr., 1952).

[208]*See* North Country Dodge, 77 LA 391, 392–93 (Craver, 1981); Mountain States Tel. & Tel. Co., 70 LA 729, 741 (Goodman, 1978). *See also* Teamsters Local 120 v. Sears, Roebuck & Co., 535 F.2d 1072, 92 LRRM 2980, 2982 (8th Cir. 1976). In *Inmont Corp.*, 76 LA 1127, 1129 (Westbrook, 1981), the agreement provided for recall from layoff on the basis of seniority, but provided also that employees recalled must be able to "perform the available work in the opinion of the Employer under normal direction." The arbitrator concluded that the "use of the words 'in the opinion of the Employer' rather clearly indicates the vesting of a larger measure of discretion in the Company than in the typical collective bargaining agreement," that it was "reasonable to imply a good faith limitation on this discretion from . . . the recognition clause," but that a "good faith test would not impose a reasonableness limitation on the company's discretion." *Id. See also* CPC Int'l, 76 LA 1230, 1231 (Bothwell, 1981); Carolina Concrete Pipe Co., 76 LA 626, 632 (Foster, 1981) (recognizing only an "arbitrariness or capriciousness" limitation on management's contractual right "to consider and determine the qualifications and abilities" of employees on layoff).

[209]*See* Lancaster Sch. Dist., 72 LA 693, 695 (Raymond, 1979); Plessey Precision Metals, 64 LA 266, 270 (Rule, 1975); Computing & Software, 61 LA 261, 264 (Shieber, 1973); American Forest Prods. Corp., 53 LA 549, 549 (Koven, 1969); Leonetti Furniture Mfg. Co., 52 LA 476, 479 (Peterschmidt, 1969); United Fuel Gas Co., 45 LA 307, 313–14 (Lugar, 1965); Heckethorn Mfg. & Supply Co., 36 LA 380, 381, 384 (Warns, 1960); Fruehauf Trailer Co., 30 LA 803, 807 (Meltzer, 1958); Bemis Bros. Bag Co., 26 LA 773, 778–79 (Disman, 1956); International Paper Co., 19 LA 402, 405 (Ralston, Jr., 1952); Alabama Power Co., 18 LA 24, 27 (McCoy, 1952); American Air Filter Co., 6 LA 786, 788 (Wardlaw, 1947). *Cf.* George B. Matthews & Sons, 3 LA 313, 317 (Carmichael, 1946).

[210]*See, e.g.*, Illinois Dep'ts of Pers. & Corr., 72 LA 941, 949 (Rezler, 1979); Whirlpool Corp., 56 LA 40, 42–43 (Johannes, 1971); Mack Trucks, 55 LA 813, 816–17 (Larson, 1970); Reliance Universal, 50 LA 397, 399–400 (Alexander, 1968); Bestwall Gypsum Co., 43 LA 475, 483–84 (Marshall, 1964); Mission Mfg. Co., 30 LA 365, 367–74 (Boles, 1958); American Smelting & Ref. Co., 29 LA 262, 265–67 (Ross, 1957); Weber Showcase & Fixture Co., 27 LA 40, 49 (Prasow, 1956).

[211]*See, e.g.*, Rainier Port Cold Storage, 79 LA 441, 447 (Armstrong, 1982); Super Save IGA, 74 LA 1218, 1220 (Nolan, 1980); Lamson & Sessions Co., 74 LA 1023, 1024 (Carmichael, 1980); Croatian Fraternal Union of Am., 68 LA 607, 608 (Reid, 1977); Lockheed Aircraft Corp., 56 LA 733, 737 (Coburn, 1971); Scott & Fetzer Co., 56 LA 6, 10 (Stouffer, 1971); Realist, Inc., 45 LA 444, 446 (Keeler, 1965). The contract itself may place the burden of proof on one of the parties. *See, e.g.*, Inland Steel Co., 16 LA 280, 283 (Cornsweet, 1951).

Arbitrators follow different approaches to the burden of proof question in cases involving managerial action taken under relative ability clauses.[212] In some cases, such clauses have been interpreted as placing little restriction on the employer's discretion, thereby, in effect, placing the burden of proof on the employee. Under this approach, when the union challenges management's determination it must sustain the burden of proving discrimination, caprice, arbitrariness, or bad faith on the part of the employer in evaluating abilities.[213]

In other cases, such clauses have been interpreted as strictly limiting the managerial judgment, and, in effect, placing the burden of proof on the employer. Under this approach, the employer, when bypassing senior employees, must be prepared to show, by specific and understandable evidence that relates to the capacity to perform the job in question, that the junior employee is the abler.[214]

---

[212]See discussion of relative ability clauses in section 7.A.i., "Relative Ability Clauses," above. There are various shadings of opinion within the basic approaches regarding the burden and quantum of proof. In this connection, see Howard, *The Role of the Arbitrator in the Determination of Ability*, 12 ARB. J. 14–27 (1957). In *Teamsters Local 120 v. Sears, Roebuck & Co.*, 535 F.2d 1072, 1075, 92 LRRM 2980, 2982 (8th Cir. 1976), the arbitrator's authority to specify the standard of proof to be required under a relative ability clause was upheld where neither the contract language nor the bargaining history expressly prohibited the arbitrator from doing so.

[213]See Lehigh Portland Cement Co., 105 LA 860, 864 (Baroni, 1995); Wapato, Wash., Sch. Dist., 91 LA 1156, 1159–62 (Gaunt, 1988); Feco Engineered Sys., 90 LA 1282, 1285 (Miller, 1988); Zenith Elecs. Corp., 90 LA 1020, 1025–26 (Hilgert, 1988); Carnation Pet Foods Div., 89 LA 1288, 1290–91 (Berger, 1987); Mountain States Tel. & Tel. Co., 77 LA 1229, 1234, 1236 (Hogler, 1981); Super Save IGA, 74 LA 1218, 1220–21 (Nolan, 1980); Croatian Fraternal Union of Am., 68 LA 607, 608 (Reid, 1977); Lockheed Aircraft Corp., 56 LA 733, 737 (Coburn, 1971); Scott & Fetzer Co., 56 LA 6, 10 (Stouffer, 1971); American Sugar Co., 46 LA 91, 94 (Ray, 1966); Combustion Eng'g Co., 9 LA 515, 517 (Ingle, 1948); Merrill-Stevens Drydock & Repair Co., 6 LA 838, 841 (Marshall, 1947). *See also* Lamson & Sessions Co., 74 LA 1023, 1024 (Carmichael, 1980); NLRB, Region 17, 68 LA 279, 286 (Sinicropi, 1977); Paauhau Sugar Co., 55 LA 477, 481 (Tsukiyama, 1970); Lockheed-Georgia Co., 42 LA 1301, 1306 (Flannagan, 1964); Monsanto Research Corp., 39 LA 735, 740 (Dworkin, 1962); Northwestern Bell Tel. Co., 19 LA 47, 49 (Doyle, 1952). In some cases, while the arbitrator did not speak in terms of burden of proof, he or she noted that there was no evidence that the company had acted arbitrarily or in bad faith. *See, e.g.*, Bestwall Gypsum Co., 43 LA 475, 484 (Marshall, 1964); Bemis Bros. Bag Co., 26 LA 773, 779 (Disman, 1956); Douglas Aircraft Co., 25 LA 600, 604 (Jones, Jr., 1955); Pittsburgh Steel Co., 21 LA 565, 568–69 (Brecht, 1953); Chrysler Corp., 17 LA 898, 903–04 (Wolff, 1952); Merrill Stevens Dry Dock & Repair Co., 17 LA 516, 519 (Hawley, 1951); Eagle-Picher Mining & Smelting Co., 17 LA 205, 211–12 (Prasow, 1951); John Deere Tractor Co., 16 LA 790, 792 (Levinson, 1951); Hercules Powder Co., 10 LA 624, 626 (Reynolds, 1948). *See also* Washington County, Or., 78 LA 1081, 1091–92 (Tilbury, 1982). *But see* Wolf Creek Nuclear Operating Corp., 111 LA 801, 806–07 (Erbs, 1998) (employer must show "based upon the known information, that its selection process to determine relative ability was not arbitrary and capricious; that it was not established or utilized in a biased or prejudicial manner; and that the information relied upon is factual").

[214]For cases in which the arbitrator required this or a similar showing by the employer, or in which the burden of proof was otherwise clearly placed on management, see St. Clare Hosp., 112 LA 602, 606 (Cavanaugh, 1998) ("[S]eniority is one of the hallmarks of the unionized workplace . . . . Consequently . . . seniority . . . should take a back seat only where there is clear contractual language supporting it and a compelling difference in demonstrated skills and abilities favoring the junior employee (as measured by the standards contained in the parties' agreement).");*Entergy/Mississippi Power & Light Co.*, 111 LA 507, 515–17 (Howell, 1998); *Lockheed Martin Sys. Support & Training Servs.*, 111 LA 442, 448–49 (Finston, 1998); *Union Carbide Corp.*, 97 LA 771, 772–73 (Helburn, 1991); *Weather Shield Mfg.*, 96 LA 338, 342–45 (Wyman, 1990); *Bell Helicopter Textron*, 93 LA 233, 238 (Morris, 1989); *United States Steel Corp.*, 73 LA 508, 512 (Kahn, 1979); *City of Traverse City*, 72 LA 1061, 1064 (Roumell, Jr., 1979); *Screw Conveyor Corp.*, 72 LA 434, 437 (Howell, 1979) (stating that, when chal-

In still other relative ability cases, an even heavier burden is, in effect, placed on the employer, and the employer is required, when challenged, not only to show greater ability in the junior employee to whom it has given preference, but also to show the absence of discrimination and arbitrariness and the presence of good faith.[215]

Some arbitrators utilize a burden-shifting approach, requiring the union to make an initial showing that the employee is qualified to perform the job in question. If the union meets its burden, the employer must then establish (e.g., through "clear and convincing evidence") that the junior employee has materially better qualifications.[216]

In cases involving sufficient ability clauses,[217] arbitrators have placed the burden on the employer to show that the bypassed senior employee is not competent to do the job, and the fact that a junior employee is more competent than the senior employee is irrelevant.[218]

Apart from this required showing by the employer under such clauses, if the union specifically alleges discrimination or abuse of discretion, it may be

---

lenged, the employer must show, and had done so here, that "standards for comparison of applicants' qualifications were established in good faith," that they "were applied fairly and impartially," and that the "decision that junior applicant was substantially better qualified was not clearly unreasonable"); *Lockheed Aircraft Corp.*, 55 LA 325, 328 (Tive, 1970); *Standard Oil Co. of Cal.*, 54 LA 298, 301 (Beeson, 1971); *International Harvester Co.*, 54 LA 264, 268–269 (Sullivan, 1971).

[215]*See* Atlas Powder Co., 30 LA 674, 677 (Frey, 1958); Illinois Bell Tel. Co., 14 LA 1021, 1026 (Kelliher, 1950). *See also* Ralph M. Parsons Co., 69 LA 290, 293 (Rule, 1977); Allied Chem. & Dye Corp., 29 LA 394, 397 (Reid, 1957); Flexonics Corp., 24 LA 869, 873 (Klamon, 1955).

[216]Thus, in *Inkster, Mich., Bd. of Educ.*, 112 LA 522, 526 (Allen, 1998), the arbitrator determined that: "In disputes involving seniority versus ability, there is considerable arbitral authority indicating the Union bears the initial burden of proof in establishing the senior employee has the necessary job qualifications. If the Union offers clear and convincing evidence the senior employee is equally qualified, then the burden of proof shifts to management to offer clear and convincing evidence a junior employee has better qualifications." *See also* Marshalltown Area Cmty. Hosp., 76 LA 978, 983 (Smith, 1981) (discussing shifting burden of proof). *Cf.* Houston Lighting & Power Co., 103 LA 179, 185–86 (Fox, Jr., 1993) (both the union and the employer were required to present whatever evidence they could in support of their respective positions, and each party had the "burden of the affirmative" on particular aspects within the development of the case; the burden of proof was on the employer to disclose a legitimate reason for bypassing the senior employee, and the union had to produce sufficient evidence that the evaluation process was unreasonable or discriminatory).

[217]See discussion on "sufficient ability" clauses in section 7.A.ii., "Sufficient Ability Clauses," above.

[218]Pittsburgh Plate Glass Co., 8 LA 317, 329 (Blair, 1947). *See also* Executive Jet Aviation, 91 LA 601, 604 (Kindig, 1988); Warner Cable of Akron, 91 LA 48, 51–52 (Bittel, 1988); Sweetheart Cup Corp., 80 LA 289, 292 (Kelliher, 1982); Royster Co., 55 LA 432, 434 (Amis, 1970); General Elec. Co., 43 LA 499, 506 (Altieri, 1964); American Oil Co., 38 LA 906, 908 (Dykstra, 1962); Higgins, Inc., 37 LA 801, 806 (Hale, 1961); California Spray-Chem. Corp., 25 LA 681, 684 (Galenson, 1955); Bell Aircraft Corp., 25 LA 618, 623 (Shister, 1955); Corn Prods. Ref. Co., 25 LA 130, 142 (Hale, 1955); Pacific Gas & Elec. Co., 23 LA 556, 558 (Ross, 1954); Rome Grader Corp., 22 LA 167, 170 (McKelvey, 1953); Standard Oil Co., 16 LA 586, 587 (Pollard, 1951). *Cf.* Government Employees (AFGE), 113 LA 998, 1004–05 (Paull, 1999) (because senior bidder should receive promotion if minimally qualified, management is required to show by competent evidence that the senior bidder is not entitled to the position); Langendorf Baking Co. of Seattle, 76 LA 540, 542–44 (Lumbley, 1981); Missouri Utils. Co., 68 LA 379, 385 (Erbs, 1977); E.F. Hauserman Co., 39 LA 609, 612–13 (Dworkin, 1962); Wallingford Steel Co., 29 LA 597, 598 (Cahn, 1957).

required to prove such allegations by clear and convincing evidence.[219] The union has also been held to have the burden of proof where there is an established past practice allowing the employer the freedom to select employees for particular positions. So, in one case, a practice existed of permitting the employer to choose group leaders on the basis of ability to lead, guide, and instruct, rather than on seniority.[220]

When a hybrid clause is involved,[221] arbitrators appear to place the burden on the employer to show why the ability factor was given greater weight than the seniority factor in bypassing the senior employee.[222]

But, if strict seniority is involved, that is, if the agreement requires the observance of seniority but contains no fitness and ability qualifications, the burden is clearly on the employer to justify a failure to give preference to the senior employee. For example, under a strict seniority clause, an employer passing over a senior but handicapped employee would have the burden of proving that the senior employee was not qualified for the work or that the performance of the work would harm the senior employee.[223]

Finally, it should be emphasized that the approach taken by any arbitrator as to which party has the burden of proof will depend in great measure on the terms of the contract and the facts of the case—in one case under one contract in one set of circumstances an arbitrator may decide the issue simply by examining the facts without referring to burden of proof, while in another case under another contract in another set of circumstances the same arbitrator may place the burden of proof on one party or the other.[224] However, whether or not the arbitrator speaks in terms of burden of proof, in most cases when management's determination is challenged, both parties are expected to produce whatever evidence they can in support of their respective contentions, and the arbitrator decides whether management's determination should be upheld as being reasonably supported by the evidence and as not having been influenced by improper elements.

---

[219]*See* Sylvania Elec. Prods., 24 LA 703, 705 (Shister, 1955); Washington Metal Trades, 23 LA 38, 39 (Carmody, 1954); Crown Cotton Mills, 7 LA 526, 527 (Greene, 1947). *See also* Public Serv. Co. of Colo., 77 LA 313, 318–20 (Watkins, 1981).

[220]E-Systems, 84 LA 194 (Steele, 1985). *See also* Carlton Coll., 113 LA 786, 792–93 (Daly, 2000) (union did not show senior employee was qualified by preponderance of evidence); Oil-Dri Prod. Co., 89 LA 1035, 1036 (Rice, 1987) (union has burden to prove beyond preponderance of evidence that employer violated sufficient ability clause).

[221]See discussion on "hybrid" clauses in section 7.A.iii., "Hybrid Clauses," above.

[222]Elkhart Cmty. Sch., 78 LA 64, 66 (Rifkin, 1981); Southwestern Bell Tel. Co., 30 LA 862, 871 (Davis, 1958). Also, in *International Harvester Co.*, 21 LA 183, 185 (Cole, 1953), the employer was held not to have given sufficient weight to the much greater seniority of the senior employee. *See also* Plainview-Old Bethpage Cent. Sch. Dist., 62 LA 333, 337 (Cahn, 1974); Dewey-Portland Cement Co., 43 LA 165, 169–70 (Sembower, 1964). *Cf.* Reliance Universal, 50 LA 397, 399–400 (Alexander, 1968). In *Callite Tungsten Corp.*, 11 LA 743, 744 (Feinberg, 1948), the employer was upheld where there was little difference in seniority and much difference in ability. *See also* Burkart-Randall Co., 72 LA 752, 757 (Cyrol, 1979).

[223]Chrysler Corp., 5 LA 333, 336 (Wolff, 1946). *Cf.* Croatian Fraternal Union of Am., 68 LA 607, 607–08 (Reid, 1977).

[224]*See, e.g.*, Flexonics Corp., 24 LA 869, 873 (Klamon, 1955); International Harvester Co., 20 LA 460, 462 (Platt, 1953); Dixie Cup Co., 19 LA 639, 646 (Klamon, 1952); Darin & Armstrong, 13 LA 843, 846 (Platt, 1950); International Harvester Co., 11 LA 1190, 1192 (Wolff, 1948); Chrysler Corp., 5 LA 333, 336 (Wolff, 1946).

D. Factors Considered in Determining Fitness and Ability
[LA CDI 119.1221]

The determination of ability is by no means susceptible to any set formula applicable to any and all circumstances.[225] The precise factors or criteria applicable in one set of circumstances involving one contract may not be proper or sufficient in another situation under another contract. Nevertheless, reported arbitration awards show that, in the absence of a contract provision designating the method to be used or the factors to be considered in determining ability, management has been permitted broad discretion to determine ability so long as the method used is fair and nondiscriminatory.[226] Thus, employers properly have employed written or oral performance or aptitude tests and trial periods on the job. They also properly have relied on merit rating plans and opinions of supervision. Likewise, they properly have considered production, attendance, or disciplinary records and the relative education, experience, and physical fitness of the candidates.

Technical qualifications for a job are clearly pertinent to management's consideration of an employee's "fitness and ability." Some of the factors discussed herein, such as the use of tests, technical training, and experience, are geared to the technical requirements of a job. However, arbitrators generally have permitted or required management to consider other factors as well. For example one arbitrator pointed out:

> To limit consideration to the one factor of technical knowledge of the job, would appear to be unduly restrictive. . . . [T]he Company could properly consider additional factors in deciding who was qualified for the particular job. . . . The criteria used by the Company [education, ability to express himself, alertness, attendance record, flexibility and ability to learn new duties] do not appear unreasonable or arbitrary, as related to the job . . . in this case. They seem to be appropriate and relevant factors for qualification of a man for the duties and responsibilities of this job.[227]

Another arbitrator went further and imposed a duty on management to consider other matters in addition to technical knowledge:

> In its assessment of comparative abilities, the Company has the right and the duty to prepare, record, and examine tangible and objective (in so far as possible) evidence concerning such matters as, for example: innate capacity;

---

[225]Arbitrators generally recognize that "[r]arely if ever will two or more individuals have identical ability, aptitudes, skills, personalities, and energy levels." Inkster, Mich., Bd. of Educ., 112 LA 522, 527 (Allen, 1998). *See also* Screw Conveyor Corp., 72 LA 434, 437 (Howell, 1979) ("Human beings are different and cannot be inspected and measured as finished products from the assembly line."). The import of the inexactitude of comparison depends on the parties' contract.

[226]*See* International Salt Co., 91 LA 710, 711 (Shieber, 1988); Celotex Corp., 53 LA 746, 755 (Dworkin, 1969); Containers, Inc., 49 LA 589, 592 (Anderson, 1967); Trans World Airlines, 45 LA 267, 268 (Beatty, 1965); Caradco, Inc., 35 LA 169, 172 (Graff, 1960); Kaiser Aluminum & Chem. Corp., 33 LA 951, 952 (McCoy, 1959); Lockheed Aircraft Corp., 25 LA 748, 751 (Williams, 1956); Bendix Aviation Corp., 19 LA 257, 260 (Bailer, 1952); Stauffer Chem. Co., 8 LA 278, 280 (Blair, 1947). *See also* Screw Conveyor Corp., 72 LA 434, 437 (Howell, 1979).

[227]John Deere Tractor Co., 16 LA 790, 792 (Levinson, 1951). *See also* Leach Mfg. Co., 82 LA 235 (Harrison, 1984) (employee's need for supervision is a relative factor in determining lack of qualifications).

prior job experience and performance; attendance, health, and related factors; tests, if available, such as those to indicate the likelihood of successful performance in the new position.[228]

In any event, the factors considered must be consistent with the collective bargaining agreement and relate directly to job requirements and the employee's ability to meet those requirements.[229] It is clear that the more objective factors have greater acceptability, and the more that such factors are properly considered by management in a given situation, the stronger the case for the decision.

The factors most commonly utilized are discussed in detail below. No particular significance is attached to the order in which they appear, and it should be noted that factors other than those considered here may also be pertinent to any given case.[230]

i.   Use of Tests

a.   General Support for Testing [LA CDI 119.128]

Even in the absence of a specific contract provision, management has been held entitled to give reasonable and appropriate written,[231] oral,[232] performance,[233] aptitude,[234] and physical abilities tests, relevant to job perfor-

---

[228]Southwestern Bell Tel. Co., 30 LA 862, 871 (Davis, 1958). *See also* Siemens Energy & Automation, 91 LA 598, 600–01 (Goggin, 1988); State of Minn., 91 LA 68, 71–72 (Bognanno, 1988); Mergenthaler Linotype Co., 20 LA 468, 474–75 (Justin, 1953).

[229] *See* Public Serv. Co. of Colo., 77 LA 313, 318–19 (Watkins, 1981).

[230]For example, in addition to other factors used, the necessity of personal interviews with job applicants has been considered. *See* South Cent. Bell Tel. Co., 52 LA 1104, 1111–12 (Platt, 1969); Semling-Menke Co., 46 LA 523, 525 (Graff, 1966). In *California State Univ.*, 71 LA 647, 652 (Staudohar, 1978), the following factors indicated merit in connection with promotion to full professor: "teaching effectiveness, academic honors and awards, publications, professional activities, and service to the campus and community."

[231]*See* Hobet Mining, 99 LA 1187 (Roberts, 1992); Union Carbide Corp., 96 LA 976 (Nicholas, Jr., 1991) (employer has authority to unilaterally adopt a more objective framework for evaluating employees such as a test measuring 12 criteria); James River Corp., 93 LA 874 (Allen, Jr., 1989) (test that was fair, valid, relevant, and administered unbiasedly could be used by employer); Dakota Elec. Ass'n, 84 LA 114 (Boyer, 1985). *But see* Hussmann Refrigerator Co., 62 LA 554, 555–58 (Yarowsky, 1974). Regarding the right of management to use written tests as an aid in training and instructing employees, see *Union Camp Corp.*, 73 LA 67, 70–71 (Heinsz, 1979).

[232]*See* State of Minn., 91 LA at 71–72; Osseo, Minn., Indep. Sch. Dist. No. 279, 71 LA 116, 118 (Fogelberg, 1978); Joy Mfg. Co., 70 LA 4, 12, 14–15 (Mathews, 1978); I-T-E Imperial Corp., 68 LA 1, 4–6 (Johnson, 1977); Hammarlund Mfg. Co., 19 LA 653, 655 (Bailer, 1952). However, oral testing as applied to mechanical skills might not, standing alone, provide a reliable guide because an employee may have skill in performing a mechanical job but lack the ability to communicate the knowledge when questioned orally, and vice versa. Collins Radio Co., 39 LA 436, 440 (Rohman, 1962).

[233]*See* Lovejoy, Inc., 74 LA 811, 813–14 (Herman, 1980); General Elec. Co., 72 LA 1307, 1310 (Marcus, 1979); Osseo, Minn., Indep. Sch. Dist. No. 279, 71 LA 116, 118 (Fogelberg, 1978); United States Steel Corp., 53 LA 777, 779–80 (McDaniel, 1969); Dayton Steel Foundry Co., 38 LA 63, 67–68 (Bradley, 1962); Phillips Petroleum Co., 29 LA 246, 248–49 (Singletary, 1957); Bendix Aviation Corp., 19 LA 257, 260 (Bailer, 1952).

[234]*See* Safeway Stores, 80 LA 1328, 1332–33 (Fogel, 1983); Illinois Bell Tel. Co., 76 LA 432, 436 (Erbs, 1981); Northwestern Bell Tel. Co., 75 LA 148, 148 (Karlins, 1980); Union Camp Corp., 68 LA 708, 711–12 (Morgan, Jr., 1977) (the union contended that the company was "bound by past practice since they had not used mechanical aptitude tests up until the time which gave rise to the grievances," but the arbitrator disagreed, stating that the com-

mance,[235] as an aid in determining the ability of competing employees. Moreover, recognizing the company's authority to institute and utilize tests, one arbitrator held that "the company is vested with continuing authority to change its testing methods and procedures in accordance with the exercise of sound judgment."[236] Another arbitrator held that an asserted "negative" past practice of not testing for a specific job will not preclude testing for new jobs that are technologically advanced.[237]

Many arbitrators look with favor on the use of valid and reliable tests in appropriate situations. As one arbitrator noted: "The employment of tests, fairly and objectively administered, would appear to be desirable, and in the interests of the employees, the company, and the union. A sound testing procedure should serve to allay any suspicion among competing employees as to favoritism or discrimination in awarding jobs."[238] Another arbitrator declared that use of tests constitutes an "effort to apply some objective measure of qualifications, rather than to leave the determination to the general judgment and subjective reactions of supervision."[239] Still another arbitrator wrote: "In the absence of proof of bias, prejudice, discrimination or injustice, the reasonable exercise of judgment as to ability is helped rather than hindered by the tests in question"—but he cautioned that his remarks were not to be taken as "open approval for tests of any kind under any circumstances."[240]

---

pany previously had been "determining ability and the institution of the test is simply another method of measuring ability"); Robertshaw Controls Co., 67 LA 678, 682 (Wagner, 1976); Menasha Corp., 64 LA 307, 319 (Kabaker, 1975); American Oil Co., 50 LA 1227, 1231–32 (Simon, 1968); New Jersey Bell Tel. Co., 49 LA 735, 737 (Uible, 1967); United Carbon Co., 49 LA 465, 467 (Bennett, 1967); Scott Paper Co., 47 LA 552, 553 (Wolff, 1966); Equitable Gas Co., 46 LA 81, 91 (Wagner, 1965) (citing many cases, id. at 87–90); Perfect Circle Corp., 43 LA 817, 822 (Dworkin, 1964); Armstrong Cork Co., 42 LA 349, 351–52 (Handsaker, 1964); Atlas Powder Co., 30 LA 674, 677 (Frey, 1958). Management was held entitled to use aptitude tests to select applicants for training for newly created jobs in Celanese Piping Sys., 64 LA 462, 465–66 (Fitch, 1975); Equitable Gas Co., 46 LA 81, 85 (Wagner, 1976); Bethlehem Steel Co., 44 LA 967, 969 (Porter, 1967), even where the contract provided that the senior employee shall be given a trial period on the job, see Pretty Prods., 43 LA 779, 783 (Nichols, 1964). For cases discussing the propriety of aptitude tests for specific jobs, see Central Soya Co., 41 LA 1027, 1031–32 (Tatum, 1963); Caradco, Inc., 35 LA 169, 171–74 (Graff, 1960); Acme-Newport Steel Co., 31 LA 1002, 1005 (Schmidt, 1959). As for the use of written tests as an aid to determine the aptitude of employees for other jobs in the line of progression, see Eastern Stainless Steel Co., 56 LA 503, 505–06 (Strongin, 1971); New Jersey Bell Tel. Co., 47 LA 495, 500 (Koretz, 1966); Latrobe Steel Co., 34 LA 37, 38 (McCoy, 1960). On the question whether an employee should be permitted to take an aptitude test again after having previously failed it, see Dayton-Walther Corp., 65 LA 529, 532 (Laybourne, 1975).

[235]Detroit Edison Co., 96 LA 1033 (Lipson, 1991).

[236]Celotex Corp., 53 LA 746, 756 (Dworkin, 1969). See also Sterling Drug, 79 LA 1255, 1259 (Gibson, 1982) (employer could change test where its continued use would result in a violation of the Civil Rights Act by company and union). But also as to making changes, see Star Mfg. Co., 79 LA 868, 875–76 (Hilgert, 1982); Hooker Chem. Co., 61 LA 421, 426–28 (Simon, 1973). In Bethlehem Steel Corp., 48 LA 1205, 1208–09 (Seward, 1967), a "local working conditions" clause precluded management from adding a second entirely different test in addition to the one that could be used under past practice, but management was not precluded from revising the original test.

[237]Fox River Paper Co., 96 LA 17 (Stern, 1990).

[238]Mead Containers, 35 LA 349, 352 (Dworkin, 1960). See also Peabody Coal Co., 83 LA 1080, 1083 (Seidman, 1984); Celotex Corp., 53 LA 746, 755 (Dworkin, 1969).

[239]International Harvester Co., 21 LA 183, 184 (Cole, 1953). See also Goodyear Tire & Rubber Co., 66–2 ARB ¶8652 (Lehoczky, 1966); Ball Bros. Co., 27 LA 353, 357 (Sembower, 1956) (approving the use of tests but finding the administration of them improper); M.A. Hann Co., 25 LA 480, 484–85 (Marshall, 1955).

[240]Stauffer Chem. Co., 23 LA 322, 326 (Reid, 1954).

b. Four Requirements That Tests Must Meet

Arbitrators generally hold that tests used in determining ability must be (1) specifically related to the requirements of the job, (2) fair and reasonable, (3) administered in good faith and without discrimination, and (4) properly evaluated. In some awards, the arbitrator may find it necessary to discuss all of the above requirements, or the arbitrator will simply affirm that all four of the requirements have been met.[241] In other awards, the arbitrator may discuss one or more of the requirements, implying that the rest of the requirements have been met.

(1) Related to Job Requirements

With respect to the first requirement, it has been held that the test must be related to the skill and knowledge required in the job.[242] For example, a

---

[241]One arbitrator thoroughly examined the testing procedure and the application of its results, noting that management employed a specialist to design and evaluate the tests, that the tests were related to the skills and qualifications required in the job, that a trained administrator and test examiners gave the tests, and that it was standard procedure to offer each employee an opportunity to take the tests twice as an extra precaution against error. *See* Glass Containers Mfrs. Inst., 47 LA 217, 223 (Dworkin, 1966). For some instances in which the arbitrator expressly affirmed that all four general requirements had been met, see *Star Mfg. Co.*, 79 LA 868, 877 (Hilgert, 1982), (briefly discusses some of the requirements); *General Elec. Co.*, 72 LA 1307, 1310 (Marcus, 1979) (same).

[242]*See* Dunlop Tire Corp., 111 LA 578, 581 (Heinsz, 1998); Lehigh Portland Cement Co., 105 LA 860, 863–64 (Baroni, 1995); GTE Tel. Operations, 103 LA 1205, 1207 (Duff, 1994); State of Minn., 91 LA 68, 71–72 (Bognanno, 1988); Feco Engineered Sys., 90 LA 1282, 1285 (Miller, 1988) (test not sufficiently related to specific job to prove ability or inability of grievant to perform work); Safeway Stores, 80 LA 1328, 1336 (Fogel, 1983); Consolidated Coal Co., 77 LA 785, 791 (Ruben, 1981); United States Steel Corp., 70 LA 1235, 1242 (Garrett, 1978) (tests not prepared on the basis of the specific requirements of any given trade or craft job were not "job related" within meaning of the agreement, which covered many separate trade or craft jobs with widely different skills and ability); International Steel Co., 64 LA 1093, 1096 (Witney, 1975); Gulf States Utils. Co., 62 LA 1061, 1073–74 (Williams, 1974); Butler Mfg. Co., 52 LA 633, 638 (Larkin, 1969) (citing other cases on the point that a general aptitude test having no relation to the job in question may not be used as a proper guide for denying a senior employee a promotion); International Tel. & Tel. Corp., 49 LA 1068, 1073 (Barnhart, 1967); Martin Co., 46 LA 1116, 1123 (Gorsuch, 1966); Equitable Gas Co., 46 LA 81, 91 (Wagner, 1965); Mead Containers, 35 LA 349, 353 (Dworkin, 1960); Latrobe Steel Co., 34 LA 37, 38–39 (McCoy, 1960). In *Griggs v. Duke Power Co.*, 401 U.S. 424, 436, 3 FEP Cases 175 (1971), the Supreme Court stated: "Nothing in the [Civil Rights] Act precludes the use of testing or measuring procedures" so long as the tests used "measure the person for the job and not the person in the abstract." In *Albemarle Paper Co. v. Moody*, 422 U.S. 405, 431, 10 FEP Cases 1181 (1975), the Supreme Court reiterated its *Griggs* holding that the Civil Rights Act forbids the use of employment tests that are discriminatory in effect unless the employer meets the burden of showing that any given requirement has a manifest relation to the employment in question. The Court added:

This burden arises, of course, only after the complaining party or class has made out a *prima facie* case of discrimination, *i.e.*, has shown that the tests in question select applicants for hire or promotion in a racial pattern significantly different from that of the pool of applicants. If an employer does then meet the burden of proving that its tests are "job-related," it remains open to the complaining party to show that other tests or selection devices, without a similarly undesirable racial effect, would also serve the employer's legitimate interest in "efficient and trustworthy workmanship." Such a showing would be evidence that the employer was using its tests merely as a "pretext" for discrimination.

Id. at 425 (quoting McDonnell Douglas Corp. v. Green, 411 U.S. 792, 801, 5 FEP Cases 965 (1973)). For other Supreme Court decisions relating to testing and civil rights, see *Connecticut v. Teal*, 457 U.S. 440, 29 FEP Cases 1 (1982); *County of Los Angeles v. Davis*, 440 U.S. 625, 19 FEP Cases 282 (1979) (recognizing liability under Title VII for discrimination suf-

written test given to ascertain clerical and arithmetical ability required on the job is a proper aid in determining ability,[243] as is a test requiring performance of duties identical with those actually performed on the job.[244] The employer may not change the requirements of the job through the test,[245] nor may it include general abstract questions not based on the type of problems that would actually arise on the job.[246]

A test once used as only one of several factors in determining fitness and ability may not become the sole or primary criterion, nor may the qualifying score be changed without prior notice to senior bidders.[247]

(2) Fair and Reasonable [LA CDI 119.128]

A test will probably be considered fair and reasonable if, among other possible characteristics, it covers all relevant factors,[248] the questions are not unduly difficult,[249] and it is given under proper (though not necessarily ideal) conditions.[250] Frequently, the arbitrator will simply state or imply that the test in question has been examined and found to be fair and reasonable.[251]

---

fered by employees barred from promotion through use of a non-job-related test, even if it was not intended to discriminate and although the "bottom line" result of the promotional process was an appropriate racial balance; the Court pointed to a provision of Title VII the principal focus of which is the protection of the individual employee rather than protection of the minority group as a whole); *Washington v. Davis*, 426 U.S. 229, 12 FEP Cases 1415 (1976). In 1979 the EEOC, Office of Personnel Management (OPM), and certain other enforcement agencies for equal employment opportunity issued Uniform Guidelines on Employee Selection Procedures, applicable to most public and private employers. 29 C.F.R. §1607. For some arbitral note or discussion of legal rules regarding testing and civil rights, see *Sterling Drug*, 79 LA 1255, 1258 (Gibson, 1982); *Northwestern Bell Tel. Co.*, 75 LA 148, 152 (Karlins, 1980); *Joy Mfg. Co.*, 70 LA 4, 16–17 (Mathews, 1978); *Gulf States Utils. Co.*, 62 LA at 1070–72, 1076. For related discussion, see Chapter 10, section 3.A.i., "Title VII of the Civil Rights Act."

[243]*See* United States Steel Corp., 46 LA 414, 416 (Florey, 1966); Wallingford Steel Co., 29 LA 597, 599 (Cahn, 1957).

[244]*See* United States Steel Corp., 53 LA 777, 779–80 (McDaniel, 1969); Dayton Steel Foundry Co., 38 LA 63, 67–68 (Bradley, 1962); Bendix Aviation Corp., 19 LA 257, 260 (Bailer, 1952).

[245]*See* Kuhlman Elec. Co., 26 LA 885, 890–91 (Howlett, 1956).

[246]*See* Consolidated Coal Co., 77 LA 785, 791 (Ruben, 1981); Mosler Safe Co., 56 LA 328, 331 (Kates, 1971); Butler Mfg. Co., 52 LA 633, 638 (Larkin, 1969); Latrobe Steel Co., 34 LA 37, 38–39 (McCoy, 1960).

[247]Zenith Elecs. Corp., 90 LA 1020 (Hilgert, 1988).

[248]*See* Mead Paper Chilpaco Mill, 113 LA 203, 207 (Sharpe, 1999) (emphasis in original) ("[T]he Union's burden is to show that the use of the test in these circumstances was *unreasonable* rather than the perhaps lesser burden of showing that it was not the *most reasonable* method.") (emphasis in original); Campbell Soup Co., 113 LA 21, 24–25 (Allen, Jr., 1999); James River Corp., 93 LA 874, 878 (Allen, Jr., 1989); Bendix Aviation Corp., 19 LA 257, 260 (Bailer, 1952).

[249]*See* Hammarlund Mfg. Co., 19 LA 653, 655 (Bailer, 1952). Where a test was passed by most of the employees who took it, an arbitrator stated that this "would certainly negate the claim that the test is unfair." I-T-E Imperial Corp., 68 LA 1, 6 (Johnson, 1977).

[250]*See* Hammarlund Mfg. Co., 19 LA 653, 655 (Bailer, 1952) (the fact that conditions under which the test was given were not ideal was not sufficient to make the test unfair or unreasonable).

[251]*See* Entergy/Mississippi Power & Light Co., 111 LA 507, 516–17 (Howell, 1998); State of Minn., 91 LA 68, 71–72 (Bognanno, 1988); Osseo, Minn., Indep. Sch. Dist. No. 279, 71 LA 116, 118 (Fogelberg, 1978); New Jersey Bell Tel. Co., 49 LA 735, 737 (Uible, 1967); Martin Co., 46 LA 1116, 1123 (Gorsuch, 1966); Wallingford Steel Co., 29 LA 597, 599 (Cahn, 1957); American Smelting & Ref. Co., 29 LA 262, 265 (Ross, 1957); Stauffer Chem. Co., 23 LA 322, 325 (Reid, 1954); Youngstown Sheet & Tube Co., 18 LA 413, 414 (Lehoczky, 1952). In *Patterson Steel Co.*, 66–3 ARB ¶8949, at 6309 (Logan, 1966), the arbitrator found the test "ill con-

(3) Administered in Good Faith and Without Discrimination
[LA CDI 119.128]

The test must be fairly administered and graded and uniformly applied.[252] Not only must the test be given to all applicants for the job,[253] but the company may not give a junior employee an unfair advantage by temporarily assigning the employee to the job shortly before the test is to be given, thus enabling the employee to learn the practical operation of the machine that is part of the test.[254] A test may be considered questionable if it is so "critical" that it goes beyond determining the type and amount of ability required for the job and selects only the exact number of applicants needed to fill the vacancies.[255] Moreover, where the test is not adopted for uniform application but is devised and given after the promotion has been made or the vacancy filled in an admitted effort to "reinforce" the company's position, it is entitled to little if any weight because there is too much chance of the test being slanted.[256] In some cases, arbitrators add the further requirement that the test results be made available to the union or to the examinees.[257]

(4) Properly Evaluated [LA CDI 119.128]

The test must be properly evaluated in the light of the contract provisions relating to seniority and job requirements, and it must not be used in a

---

ceived, inexcusably unfair, and flagrantly discriminatory" where it dealt with matters far more complex than would ever be encountered on the job.

[252]See South Cent. Bell Tel. Co., 52 LA 1104, 1109 (Platt, 1969). See also James River Corp., 93 LA 874, 878 (Allen, Jr., 1999); Clark County, Nev., 63 LA 1169, 1179–80 (Lucas, 1974); Gulf States Utils. Co., 62 LA 1061, 1075 (Williams, 1974).

[253]See Bethlehem Steel, 29 LA 710, 711 (Seward, 1957). See also I-T-E Imperial Corp., 68 LA 1, 7 (Johnson, 1977); Advanced Structures, 37 LA 49, 52 (Roberts, 1961); Wallingford Steel Co., 29 LA 597, 599 (Cahn, 1957); American Smelting & Ref. Co., 29 LA 262, 265 (Ross, 1957); Sylvania Elec. Prods, 24 LA 703, 705 (Shister, 1955); Stauffer Chem. Co., 23 LA 322, 325 (Reid, 1954). Cf. Community Health Care Ctr. Plan, 66 LA 1329, 1331 (McCone & LeMay, Daniels dissenting, 1976).

[254]See Joseph T. Ryerson & Son, 56 LA 1206, 1209 (Caraway, 1971).

[255]See Ball Bros. Co., 27 LA 353, 357 (Sembower, 1956).

[256]International Nickel Co., 36 LA 343, 349–50 (Teple, 1960). Under the relative ability clause, management was nonetheless upheld in selecting the junior employee because he had greater experience on the job and thus was better qualified.

[257]See General Elec. Co., 72 LA 1307, 1310 (Marcus, 1979); American Oil Co., 50 LA 1227, 1233 (Simon, 1968); Erie Mining Co., 49 LA 465, 468 (Bennett, 1967); Scott Paper Co., 47 LA 552, 553 (Wolff, 1966); Equitable Gas Co., 46 LA 81, 91 (Wagner, 1965); Latrobe Steel Co., 34 LA 37, 39 (McCoy, 1960). See also Caradco, Inc., 35 LA 169, 174 (Graff, 1960). Contract language and its bargaining history led the arbitrator to conclude that management was not required to supply information regarding the point scores of successful applicants for promotions to any other applicants in Social Sec. Admin., 69 LA 1012, 1016–17 (Ford, 1977). One arbitrator would require that the union "be a party to the giving of the tests, the evaluation of the results, and probably to the selection of the tests to be given." Central Soya Co., 41 LA 1027, 1031–32 (Tatum, 1963). See also Fansteel Metallurgical Corp., 36 LA 570, 573 (Marshall, 1960). In Detroit Edison Co. v. NLRB, 440 U.S. 301, 100 LRRM 2728 (1979), the Supreme Court held (1) that the NLRB had improperly ordered the employer to supply to the union, rather than only to a neutral as offered by the employer, the actual question and answer sheets involved in the employer's psychological aptitude test; and (2) that the employer was not required to disclose to the union, without written consent from individual employees, the test scores linked with the employee names; the Court underscored the employer's strong interest in test secrecy and in confidentiality of scores, and noted the absence of a showing that the employer's interest was fabricated to frustrate the union in the discharge of its responsibilities.

manner inconsistent with the contract.[258] In this regard, where a contract contains a sufficient ability clause, a test may not be used to determine relative ability.[259]

c. Consideration of Other Factors in Addition to the Test [LA CDI 119.121]

Arbitrators usually take the view that while the test may be used as an aid in judging ability or as a verification of ability, the employer may not base its determination of ability solely on the results of a test, but must consider other factors and other evidence.[260] This was the opinion of one arbitrator:

> While arbitrators . . . generally permit the discreet use of testing, they strongly disfavor utilizing tests as the sole means of determining ability to perform work, much preferring that test results be considered as only one factor in making the determination. . . . It is apparent that this ability can be demonstrated through past experience, training, and education as well as achieving a passing performance on a test.[261]

It has been held that employees may be required to take a test, even though there is no provision in the agreement therefor.[262] Many arbitrators have ruled that management not only can require bidders to take a test designed to determine ability for the job, but also that it is justified in disqualifying any who refuse to take the test.[263] Thus, it has been emphasized:

---

[258]See Inkster, Mich., Bd. of Educ., 112 LA 522, 529 (Allen, 1998) ("[M]anagement appears to have placed too much emphasis on the ranking of applicants, without sufficient consideration to the equality of qualifications."); Allegheny Ludlum Steel Corp., 66–3 ARB ¶9071 (Crawford, 1966); American Smelting & Ref. Co., 29 LA 262, 265 (Ross, 1957).

[259]See Ohio Edison Co., 46 LA 801, 805 (Alexander, 1966); R.D. Werner Co., 45 LA 21, 25 (Kates, 1965); American Meter Co., 41 LA 856, 860 (Di Leone, 1963); Ball Bros. Co., 27 LA 353, 357 (Sembower, 1956).

[260]See Joseph T. Ryerson & Son, 56 LA 1206, 1209 (Caraway, 1971); Vulcan Materials Co., 54 LA 460, 466 (Block, 1971); National Distillers Co., 49 LA 918, 921 (Volz, 1967); New Jersey Bell Tel. Co., 49 LA 589, 593–94 (Anderson, 1967); Erie Mining Co., 49 LA 465, 467 (Bennett, 1967); Scott Paper Co., 47 LA 552, 553 (Wolff, 1966); Southern Standard Bag Corp., 66–1 ARB ¶8306 (Strong, 1966); Trans World Airlines, 45 LA 267, 268–69 (Beatty, 1965); R.D. Werner Co., 45 LA 21, 25 (Kates, 1965); Avco Mfg. Corp., 34 LA 71, 75 (Gill, 1959); Atlas Powder Co., 30 LA 674, 677 (Frey, 1958); Bethlehem Steel, 29 LA 710, 712 (Seward, 1957); Wallingford Steel Co., 29 LA 597, 599 (Cahn, 1957); National Seal Co., 29 LA 29, 36 (Dworkin, 1957); Kuhlman Elec. Co., 26 LA 885, 890–92 (Howlett, 1956); Stauffer Chem. Co., 23 LA 322, 325 (Reid, 1954); E.I. Du Pont de Nemours & Co., 18 LA 413, 414 (Lehoczky, 1952). But for some situations in which a test was permitted as the sole factor, see Star Mfg. Co., 79 LA 868, 875, 877 (Hilgert, 1982); Illinois Bell Tel. Co., 76 LA 432, 434, 436 (Erbs, 1981); Northwestern Bell Tel. Co., 75 LA 148, 151–52 (Karlins, 1980). One arbitrator stated that "a determination of how much weight should be given test results, along with other relevant factors, is a matter of judgment," and "when such judgment is exercised honestly and upon due consideration, it is not arbitrary action" even though there may be "room for two opinions." South Cent. Bell Tel. Co., 52 LA 1104, 1110–11 (Platt, 1969).

[261]Peabody Coal Co., 87 LA 758, 762 (1985). See also Watkins, Inc., 93 LA 660 (Hoh, 1989); Feco Engineered Sys., 90 LA 1282 (Miller, 1988).

[262]Equitable Gas Co., 46 LA 81, 91 (Wagner, 1965).

[263]See Dunlop Tire Corp., 111 LA 578, 582 (Heinsz, 1998); Union Camp Corp., 68 LA 708, 710, 712 (Morgan, Jr., 1977); Celotex Corp., 53 LA 746, 757 (Dworkin, 1969); City Prods. Corp., 51 LA 99, 99–100 (Johnson, 1968); Doughboy Indus., 66–3 ARB ¶8933 (Anderson, 1966); Link-Bell Co., 44 LA 720, 721–22 (McIntosh, 1965); E.W. Bliss Co., 64–3 ARB ¶9258 (McCoy, 1964) (employees' refusal meant that they "voluntarily passed up the opportunity to get the job"); Advanced Structures, 37 LA 49, 52–53 (Roberts, 1961); Mead Containers, 35 LA 349, 353 (Dworkin, 1960); Caradco, Inc., 35 LA 169, 174 (Graff, 1960); Bethlehem Steel, 29

[T]he . . . Company has the right to require job bidders to take written tests, as well as other job related tests, to determine their qualifications, subject to disqualification if they refuse. The bidder cannot reserve to himself the right to determine which tests he will take and which ones he will refuse. He must comply with this requirement. If the test is not a reasonable one, or is not fairly administered, or if unwarranted conclusions are drawn from the results, the appropriate remedy is through the grievance procedure.[264]

In two instances, however, arbitrators apparently considered the equities of the case at hand and held that, although the company could disqualify a bidder who had refused to take a test on the erroneous advice of the union, the bidder should be given another opportunity to take the test.[265]

ii. *Experience* [LA CDI 119.1221]

Experience is distinguishable from both seniority and productivity. It is the extent to which an employee has engaged in a particular job, type of job, or occupation. While the term "ability" does not necessarily imply prior experience on the particular job, experience is ordinarily considered a tangible, objective factor to be taken into consideration in determining fitness and ability.[266] Indeed, management sometimes has been reprimanded by an arbitrator for failing to take into consideration the experience of a bypassed senior employee.[267]

Arbitrators agree that experience is an important factor in determining fitness and ability. One arbitrator stated: "Experience usually is, and should be, one of the most important factors in determining ability."[268] Another arbitrator noted that, "[o]ther things being equal, the man who has had some experience on a job can become a competent employee in the classification faster than the man who has had no such experience,"[269] and still another

---

LA 710, 711–12 (Seward, 1957). In some of these cases, the arbitrator found on the evidence that the grievant was not qualified for the job. *Cf.* American Meter Co., 41 LA 856, 861–62 (Di Leone, 1963).

[264]Vulcan Materials Co., 54 LA 460, 466–67 (Block, 1971) (citations omitted). The arbitrator also considered the fact that the grievants had inadequacies in their ability to perform the job in question.

[265]Celotex Corp., 53 LA 746, 757 (Dworkin, 1969); Standard Oil Co., 11 LA 810, 811 (Updegraff, 1948).

[266]*See* TU Elec., 97 LA 1177, 1182 (Bailey, 1991); State of Minn., 91 LA 68, 77–78 (Bognanno, 1988); Lockheed-Georgia Co., 74 LA 1077, 1084 (Jenkins, 1980); Hawkeye Chem. Co., 74 LA 902, 906 (Heinsz, 1980); General Box Co., 48 LA 530, 531–32 (Williams, 1967) (cautioning, however, that experience must not be accorded such "overriding value" as to negate the seniority provision of the parties' agreement); Shore Metal Prods. Co., 24 LA 437, 441 (Prasow, 1955); Thor Corp., 14 LA 512, 515 (Baab, 1950). *See also* Celanese Polymer Co., 39 LA 270, 275 (Dunau, 1962).

[267]*See* Pittsburgh Annealing Box Co., 74 LA 266, 268 (Stoltenberg, 1980); Carrier Air Conditioning Co., 54 LA 434, 435–36 (Owen, 1971); International Nickel Co., 45 LA 743, 749 (Kates, 1965); International Harvester Co., 21 LA 214, 217–18 (Cole, 1953). Concerning the obligation of bidders to offer information concerning their experience, and of the employer to seek information concerning the experience of competing bidders, compare the views stated in *United States Steel Corp.*, 74 LA 788, 792 (Witt, 1980) and *Mountain States Tel. & Tel. Co.*, 70 LA 729, 742 (Goodman, 1978).

[268]International Nickel Co., 36 LA 343, 349 (Teple, 1960).

[269]Kuhlman Elec. Co., 26 LA 885, 891 (Howlett, 1956). *See also* Illinois Dep'ts of Pers. & Corr., 72 LA 941, 947 (Rezler, 1979); Reliance Universal, 50 LA 397, 400 (Alexander, 1968).

arbitrator expressed the opinion that it is "reasonable to adopt the criterion of actual experience to determine skill and ability."[270]

However, one arbitrator stated that "experience is not the sole criterion in forming a judgment of ability."[271] Another arbitrator went further in asserting that "experience [is not] in itself a factor in determining fitness and ability save and except to the extent that experience may tend to increase one's skill and ability."[272]

Experience was discounted as a factor in the application of a relative ability clause when the employer properly promoted a junior employee based on "superior" performance in an interview.[273]

In any event, all arbitrators will give some consideration to experience where it is relevant to the job requirements. It may be one of several factors used, or a major factor, or the sole or determining factor. Work experience on the job in question or on a related job evidences an employee's ability to perform the job;[274] experience on the particular job is given greater weight than experience on a related job.[275]

The weight that the arbitrator gives to experience in any particular case may depend in large measure on the contract or on the emphasis placed on this factor by the parties and on the evidence, or lack of evidence, concerning other factors relevant to the determination of fitness and ability.[276] Thus, where a contract required a job assignment to be offered to the "next senior technician with ability," and there was no evidence that the senior techni-

---

[270]Thor Corp., 14 LA 512, 515 (Baab, 1950).

[271]Seagrave Corp., 16 LA 410, 412 (Lehoczky, 1951). See also General Box Co., 48 LA 530, 531–32 (Williams, 1967); Sohio Chem. Co., 40 LA 590, 597 (Kates, 1963).

[272]Tin Processing Corp., 17 LA 193, 198 (Smith, 1951). In Iroquois Gas Corp., 39 LA 161, 162–63 (O'Rourke, 1962), present ability to perform the particular job was a factor in favor of the junior employee, where the senior employee admitted that he knew nothing about the particular job.

[273]Kroger Co., 89 LA 1307 (Byars, 1987).

[274]See Sweetheart Cup Corp., 80 LA 289, 292 (Kelliher, 1982); Whirlpool Corp., 56 LA 40, 42–43 (Johannes, 1971); Scott & Fetzer Co., 56 LA 6, 9–10 (Stouffer, 1971); Paauhau Sugar Co., 55 LA 477, 479–80 (Tsukiyama, 1970); Smart & Final Iris Co., 51 LA 896, 898–99 (Block, 1968); De Kalb-Ogle Tel. Co., 50 LA 445, 449 (Sembower, 1968); Reliance Universal, 50 LA 397, 400 (Alexander, 1968); Crown Cotton Mills, 29 LA 870, 874 (Griffin, 1957); Shore Metal Prods. Co., 24 LA 437, 441 (Prasow, 1955). Management properly may consider related work experience off the job, e.g., training courses taken off the job and work experience in a like occupation for another employer. See De Kalb-Ogle Tel. Co., 50 LA 445, 449 (Sembower, 1968); Dempster Bros., Inc., 48 LA 777, 778 (Cantor, 1967); Heckethorn Mfg. & Supply Co., 36 LA 380, 382 (Warns, 1960).

[275]See Illinois Dep'ts of Pers. & Corr., 72 LA 941, 947 (Rezler, 1979); Lockheed Aircraft Corp., 56 LA 733, 737 (Coburn, 1971); Paauhau Sugar Co., 55 LA 477, 479–80 (Tsukiyama, 1970) (the junior employee's experience and knowledge that were relevant and related to the job constituted the "material difference" required by contract in the qualifications of applicants, justifying his promotion over the senior employee who lacked such experience and knowledge); Duriron Co., 21 LA 392, 397 (Warns, Jr., 1953); Mutual Tel. Co., 19 LA 270, 279 (Roberts, 1952).

[276]For various treatments of experience, see Iowa Bd. of Regents, Iowa State Univ., 114 LA 11, 15–16 (Kessler, 1999); Mack Trucks, 55 LA 813, 816 (Larson, 1970); Reliance Universal, 50 LA 397, 400 (Alexander, 1968); United States Steel Corp., 49 LA 1160, 1171 (McDermott, 1967); U.S. Indus., 44 LA 1193, 1195 (Singletary, 1965); General Elec. Co., 43 LA 499, 504–05 (Altieri, 1964); Celanese Polymer Co., 39 LA 270, 273–75 (Dunau, 1962); Temco Aircraft Co., 28 LA 72, 75–76 (Boles, Jr., 1957); Kuhlman Elec. Co., 26 LA 885, 891 (Howlett, 1956); Seagrave Corp., 16 LA 410, 412 (Lehoczky, 1951).

cian did not have the ability to perform the work, his lack of experience was not considered.[277]

Naturally, if experience is not important to the job, little or no weight will be attached to this factor.[278] However, experience in the work may be a basic requirement for the job, thereby justifying management in giving preference to an experienced junior employee over a senior who lacks experience.[279] Moreover, the employer may be justified in giving preference to a junior employee where the junior employee has substantially greater experience than the senior employee,[280] or where the experience of the junior employee is identical with, or is more closely related to, the work involved than the experience of the senior employee,[281] or where the job requires extensive training and experience that the junior employee has but that the senior employee lacks.[282]

If other factors are equal, arbitrators sometimes have held that the senior employee who has had some experience should be given a trial or break-in period,[283] even though the junior employee selected by the company has had somewhat more experience.[284]

---

[277]Executive Jet Aviation, 91 LA 601 (Kindig, 1988).

[278]See ICI Ams., 71 LA 587, 589 (Raffaele, 1978); Mountain States Tel. & Tel. Co., 70 LA 729, 742–43 (Goodman, 1978); Cummins Engine Co., 56 LA 399, 402–03 (Larkin, 1971); Acme-Newport Steel Co., 31 LA 1002, 1005–06 (Schmidt, 1959); Temco Aircraft Co., 28 LA 72, 75–76 (Boles, Jr., 1957).

[279]See Lockheed Aircraft Corp., 56 LA 733, 737 (Coburn, 1971); De Kalb-Ogle Tel. Co., 50 LA 445, 449–50 (Sembower, 1968); E.I. DuPont de Nemours & Co., 18 LA 536, 538 (Cahn, 1952). For some kinds of jobs, such as those requiring qualities of leadership, actual experience is given special weight. See Brookhaven Nat'l Lab., 54 LA 447, 447–48 (Wolff, 1971); De Kalb-Ogle Tel. Co., 50 LA 445, 449–50 (Sembower, 1968).

[280]See Edwin Shaw Hosp., 95 LA 206, 210 (Bittel, 1990); Roanoke Iron & Bridge Works, 68 LA 1019, 1021 (Merrifield, 1977); Scott & Fetzer Co., 56 LA 6, 9–10 (Stouffer, 1971); FMC Corp., 47 LA 823, 826–27 (Roberts, 1966); Interlake Steel Corp., 46 LA 23, 27–28 (Luskin, 1965); Bemis Bros. Bag Co., 37 LA 29, 35 (Maggs, 1961); Pittsburgh Steel Co., 21 LA 565, 568–69 (Brecht, 1953); Standard Forgings Corp., 15 LA 636, 638 (Gilden, 1950); Copco Steel & Eng'g Co., 12 LA 6, 7 (Platt, 1949). The fact that the junior employee's experience is more recent as well as more substantial is entitled to weight. See Dayton Steel Foundry Co., 38 LA 63, 68–69 (Bradley, 1962); International Nickel Co., 36 LA 343, 349 (Teple, 1960).

[281]See WFMJ Television, 75 LA 400, 404–05 (Ipavec, 1980); Cheney-Bigelo Wire Works, 50 LA 1249, 1252 (Kennedy, 1968); Reliance Universal, 50 LA 990, 994–95 (Dolson, 1968); Stewart-Warner Corp., 50 LA 283, 286–87 (Stouffer, 1968); Colonial Baking Co., 34 LA 356, 358–59 (Murphy, 1960); Nicholson File Co., 34 LA 46, 49 (Warns, Jr., 1959); Illinois Bell Tel. Co., 30 LA 237, 239–278 (Fleming, 1958); Pittsburgh Steel Co., 21 LA 565, 568–69 (Brecht, 1953); Duriron Co., 21 LA 392, 397 (Warns, Jr., 1953). In Lockheed-Georgia Co., 49 LA 603, 605 (Di Leone, 1967), management's reliance on experience was not upheld because the experience of the junior employee was found to bear little resemblance to the job requirements, and the junior and senior employees were found to be otherwise substantially equal in ability.

[282]See Bell Helicopter Textron, 93 LA 233, 238 (Morris, 1989); Bethlehem Steel Corp., 48 LA 190, 191–92 (Gill, 1967); Atlas Processing Co., 46 LA 860, 863 (Oppenheim, 1966); Douglas Aircraft Co., 25 LA 600, 604 (Jones, Jr., 1955); Shore Metal Prods. Co., 24 LA 437, 441–42 (Prasow, 1955). But see Executive Jet Aviation, 91 LA 601, 604–05 (Kindig, 1988).

[283]See Cobak Tool Mfg. Co., 30 LA 279, 282 (Klamon, 1958); Nickes Bakery, 17 LA 486, 487 (Randle, 1951); West Va. Pulp & Paper Co., 16 LA 359, 365 (Copelof, 1951) (contractual provision for a trial period); Goodyear Decatur Mills, 12 LA 682, 685 (McCoy, 1949).

[284]See General Box Co., 48 LA 530, 532 (Williams, 1967) (contractual provision for a training period); Poloron Prods. of Pa., 23 LA 789, 793–94 (Rosenfarb, 1955) (contractual provision for a trial period); Tin Processing Corp., 17 LA 193, 198 (Smith, 1951); Seagrave Corp., 16 LA 410, 412 (Lehoczky, 1951).

Where the promotion is to be temporary, arbitrators tend to emphasize present fitness and ability and, hence, give greater weight to experience.[285]

iii. Training or Trial or Break-In Period on the Job

a. Use of Trial Period to Demonstrate Ability [LA CDI 119.129]

Agreements sometimes provide for a trial or break-in period on the job to determine ability, and issues in connection with the interpretation and application of such provisions are frequently arbitrated.[286] In the absence of a contractual provision, the question whether management must give the senior employee a trial period often arises.[287] Obviously, the ability, or inability, to perform a job may be demonstrated by a trial or break-in period.[288] As stated by one arbitrator: "The best evidence as to whether an employee can do a job is to give him a fair trial on it."[289] Another arbitrator elaborated on the point: "The purpose of a trial period is to afford an employee the opportunity to demonstrate that he has the ability for the job in question or can with some familiarization therewith achieve the necessary skills within a reasonable period of time to perform the job in an acceptable manner."[290]

There appears to be a close relationship between the use of tests or other criteria and a trial period on the job. Some arbitrators have expressed the view that the employer should grant the senior employee a trial period on the job, but not training, to demonstrate ability if the test results[291] or other

---

[285]See Great Atl. & Pac. Tea Co., 28 LA 733, 735 (Emery, 1957); Pacific Mills, 23 LA 623, 628 (Marshall, 1954); Lockheed Aircraft Serv., 21 LA 228, 231 (Warren, 1953). See also Union Carbide Corp., 79 LA 878, 883 (Leach, 1982).

[286]See, e.g., Singer Co., 66 LA 1310, 1313 (Darrow, 1976); Emerson Elec. Co., 54 LA 683, 684 (Williams, 1971); Delta Match Corp., 53 LA 1282, 1283 (Marshall, 1969); Trans World Airlines, 45 LA 267, 267 (Beatty, 1965); National Seal Co., 29 LA 29, 31 (Dworkin, 1957); Warren Petroleum Corp., 25 LA 661, 662 (Singletary, 1955); Virginia-Carolina Chem. Corp., 24 LA 461, 463 (Seibel, 1955); Seeger Refrigerator Co., 16 LA 525, 526 (Lockhart, 1951); West Va. Pulp & Paper Co., 16 LA 359, 361 (Copelof, 1951); Lone Star Gas Co., 9 LA 956, 960 (Potter, 1948); Inland Steel Co., 2 LA 655, 657 (Gilden, 1945). In contrast, some agreements expressly require an employee to be "immediately qualified" without training or assistance. See Kaiser Fluid Techs., 114 LA 262, 267–68 (Hoffman, 2000).

[287]Past practice may be involved. See Dearborn Fabricating & Eng'g Co., 64 LA 271, 275 (Kallenbach, 1975); Chromalloy Am. Corp., 62 LA 84, 89 (Fox, Jr., 1974); Virginia Chems., 56 LA 920, 922, 923–24 (Flannagan, 1971); Nickes Bakery, 17 LA 486, 487 (Randle, 1951); Southern Cal. Edison Co., 15 LA 162, 167 (Aaron, 1950); Columbia Steel Co., 13 LA 666, 670 (Whitton, 1949).

[288]Greenville Steel Car Co., 85 LA 75 (Abrams, 1985) (employee bumping into a job is entitled to break-in instructions).

[289]Dayton Power & Light Co., 28 LA 624, 626 (Warns, Jr., 1957). See also I-T-E Imperial Corp., 55 LA 1284, 1287 (White, 1970).

[290]American Welding & Mfg. Co., 52 LA 889, 893 (Stouffer, 1969). For discussion of various aspects of trial periods, see Howard, Seniority Rights and Trial Periods, 15 Arb. J. 51 (1960).

[291]See American Red Cross, 114 LA 823, 827 (Ellmann, 2000); Zinc Corp. of Am., 101 LA 643, 646 (Nicholas, Jr., 1993); Peabody Coal Co., 83 LA 1080, 1082 (Seidman, 1984); Consolidated Coal Co., 77 LA 785, 791–92 (Ruben, 1981); General Controls Co., 33 LA 213, 217–18 (Thompson, 1959); Linde Air Prods. Co., 25 LA 369, 372 (Shister, 1955). See also Monsanto Research Corp., 39 LA 735, 739 (Dworkin, 1962); National Seal Co., 29 LA 29, 37 (Dworkin, 1957) (the contract provision for a trial period was considered as protecting the employer's interests). Some awards appear to have treated a trial on the job as something in the nature of a performance test. See I-T-E Imperial Corp., 55 LA 1284, 1287 (White, 1970); Coca-Cola Bottling Co., 18 LA 757, 760 (Murphy, 1952). In Judson Steel Corp., 76 LA 825, 827 (Griffin,

criteria used have been inconclusive in determining the ability of the senior bidder.[292]

Thus, arbitrators generally are inclined to find that if there is a reasonable doubt as to the ability of the senior employee, and if the trial would cause no serious inconvenience, a trial period should usually be granted, but such an opportunity is not required in all cases.[293] There is a similar general agreement that the trial period should be short,[294] but adequate.[295]

b. Length of Trial Period [LA CDI 119.129]

While employers also recognize that the length of the trial period must be adequate, they oppose an unlimited or extended period to determine the fitness of an employee.[296] Most trial periods will last 30 days or less, but some can involve a longer period when required by the circumstances. For

---

1981), the arbitrator held that the senior bidder was not entitled to a trial period even though he passed a qualification test, because the test was only one factor in determining qualifications and the employer could reasonably make "a decision on qualifications based on any other information available to it." *See also* Semling-Menke Co., 62 LA 1184, 1188 (Bilder, 1974) (construing a trial period clause).

[292]*See* I-T-E Imperial Corp., 55 LA 1284, 1287–88 (White, 1970); Southwest Airmotive Co., 41 LA 353, 359 (Elliott, 1963); Collins Radio Co., 39 LA 436, 441 (Rohman, 1962); Rome Grader Corp., 22 LA 167, 170 (McKelvey, 1953). The same approach has been taken in cases that involved contract provisions for a trial period on the job. *See* Mosler Safe Co., 56 LA 328, 331 (Kates, 1971); White Motor Co., 28 LA 823, 828 (Lazarus, 1957); International Harvester Co., 21 LA 231, 234 (Cole, 1953). In *City of Traverse City*, 72 LA 1061, 1065 (Roumell, Jr., 1979), the agreement specified a 6-month probationary period in any promotion, and the arbitrator spoke of it as a "trial period" that should have been given to the senior bidder because there was "really little question that [he] can do the work."

[293]*See* Cessna Aircraft Co., 80 LA 257, 263–64 (Cantor, 1983); Lear Siegler, 75 LA 1001, 1005 (Nathanson, 1980); I-T-E Imperial Corp., 55 LA 1284, 1288 (White, 1970); Northwest Airlines, 46 LA 238, 242 (Elkouri, 1966); Vulcan Mold & Iron Co., 29 LA 743, 746–47 (Reid, 1957); Linde Air Prods. Co., 25 LA 369, 372 (Shister, 1955); Shore Metal Prods. Co., 24 LA 437, 442 (Prasow, 1955); Rome Grader Corp., 22 LA 167, 170 (McKelvey, 1953); Ford Motor Co., 2 LA 374, 376 (Shuman, 1945). *Cf.* Curtis Cos., 29 LA 50, 52 (Updegraff, 1957); Coca-Cola Bottling Co., 18 LA 757, 760 (Murphy, 1952). In some cases involving a bumping situation, arbitrators have held that the senior employee is required to have the "present ability" to perform the work and that he or she is not entitled to a trial or break-in period or a training period (some arbitrators citing the specific language of the bumping clause as requiring present ability, others emphasizing the absence of a provision for a trial, break-in, or training period). *See* Dresser Indus., 76 LA 428, 432 (Chapman, 1981); Greater Louisville Indus., 44 LA 694, 697 (Volz, 1965); Empire-Reeves Steel Corp., 44 LA 653, 656–57 (Nichols, 1965); Singer Co., 44 LA 24, 24–25 (Cahn, 1965); E.F. Hauserman Co., 39 LA 609, 612–13 (Dworkin, 1962) (citing many cases); Victor G. Bloede Co., 23 LA 779, 781 (McCoy, 1955); Illinois Malleable Iron Co., 16 LA 909, 911–12 (Updegraff, 1951). *Cf.* Collins Radio Co., 39 LA 436, 441 (Rohman, 1962) (the senior had previous experience in the work).

[294]*See* American Oil Co., 53 LA 160, 162 (Williams, 1969); Shore Metal Prods Co., 24 LA 437, 442 (Prasow, 1955); Bethlehem Steel, 23 LA 532, 533–34 (Seward, 1954); Rudiger-Lang Co., 11 LA 567, 568 (Kerr, 1948). In American Oil Co., 53 LA 160, 162 (Williams, 1969), it was held that the "sufficient" ability clause "does not contemplate that the senior employee's fitness and ability be sufficient to perform the job at peak efficiency from the first hour on it, but contemplates a reasonable familiarization (but no training) period on the new job."

[295]*See* Batesville Mfg. Co., 55 LA 261, 269–70 (Roberts, 1970); Allison Steel Mfg. Co., 53 LA 101, 111 (Jones, Jr., 1969) (inadequate supervisory assistance and alleged racial bias); Decor Corp., 44 LA 389, 392 (Kates, 1965); Rome Grader Corp., 22 LA 167, 170–71 (McKelvey, 1953); Goodyear Decatur Mills, 17 LA 324, 326 (Copelof, 1951). *See also* Raytheon Co., 113 LA 1060, 1064–65 (Richman, 1999); Maremont Corp., 71 LA 333, 337 (Coven, 1978).

[296]Smith Scott Co., 48 LA 270, 272 (Burns, 1966).

example, it has been held that while a 9-month trial period is ordinarily too long, it was not excessive where the employee for 7 months of that time was taking a training course that management expected would improve his performance.[297] In another case, it was found that although the employer is entitled to a reasonable trial period, 11 months was unreasonable where the employee had received an automatic pay increase 6 months after his promotion.[298] By way of further illustration, an arbitrator concluded that management could remove a senior employee after a 5-month trial period where he had had four separate opportunities for merit increases, but had received only one. He had consistently been warned about his work and given low ratings during the trial period.[299]

The contract may specify the amount of time for the trial or it may require only "a reasonable qualifying period." In a case involving the latter language, the arbitrator said that no particular number of hours or days must be provided; "[a]ll that is required under this contract is that a long enough period be allowed to demonstrate to management, viewing the employee's performance impartially and reasonably and in good faith, that he can or cannot fulfill the requirements of the job."[300] Another arbitrator denied a grievant entitlement to an extended trial period. Under a clause that awarded the job to "the senior employee in the plant who bid on the job and who within a reasonable period of time could be expected to prove, to the company's satisfaction, that he is qualified to do the job," an arbitrator opined that the definition of "a reasonable period of time" was within the company's discretion, even though the grievant was only given a trial period of less than 1 hour.[301]

Where a contract was silent on an extension of the training period, one arbitrator held that a company may properly extend a training period to allow the bidder additional time to qualify.[302]

c. Circumstances When a Trial Period Is Not Required

If the senior employee is obviously unfit or unqualified, as in a situation where the employee does not possess the high degree of skill for a particular vacancy that can be acquired only after a long period of training, management is not required to offer a trial period and may prefer a junior employee

---

[297]Koppers Co., 49 LA 663, 665 (Malkin, 1967) (upholding management's removal of the employee because he failed to qualify).

[298]Smith Scott Co., 48 LA 270, 272 (Burns, 1966) (new hires were given a short qualifying period of a week or two).

[299]Shenango Furnace Co., 46 LA 203, 209–10 (Klein, 1966) (the "lengthy trial period tends to negate the probability of any bad faith or prejudice" on management's part).

[300]Decor Corp., 44 LA 389, 392 (Kates, 1965). In *Seeger Refrigerator Co.*, 16 LA 525, 531 (Lockhart, 1951), interpreting similar language, a minimum of 3 months was considered necessary because of the circumstances of the case and the nature of the work.

[301]Oil-Dri Prod. Co., 89 LA 1035, 1036 (Rice, 1987).

[302]*See* Wyman-Gordon Co., 91 LA 225 (Cyrol, 1988).

or new hire who already possesses such skills.[303] Even if there is a contract provision calling for a trial period, it need not be extended to a patently unqualified senior employee.[304]

It should also be evident that no trial on the job is required where the contract makes seniority controlling only if ability is substantially equal and past service of competing applicants shows the junior to possess qualifications considerably superior to those of the senior candidate.[305]

d. Training Period Distinguished From Trial Period [LA CDI 119.129]

As a corollary proposition, it has been held that if management has granted a trial as required by the agreement, it need not continue the trial for the full period specified if the candidate has clearly demonstrated inability to perform the job. As stated by one arbitrator:

> When it becomes obvious that an employee is not going to be able to acquire the necessary skills to qualify for the job or by his attitude makes it clear that he is not going to become proficient and fails to exhibit any progress, then the employer is not obligated to continue the trial period.[306]

To rule otherwise would blur the distinction between a "trial" and a "training period." As pointed out by another arbitrator:

---

[303]See Roper Corp., 74 LA 962, 963 (Sherman, 1980); Textron, 73 LA 1290, 1291 (Hales, 1980); United States Steel Corp., 64 LA 639, 641 (Grant, 1975); Vulcan Materials Co., 54 LA 460, 466–67 (Block, 1971) (no "reasonable expectation of success on the job"); Delta Match Corp., 53 LA 1282, 1287 (Marshall, 1969); Cheney-Bigelo Wire Works, 50 LA 1249, 1252 (Kennedy, 1968) (lack of qualification shown by employee's past employment record); R.D. Werner Co., 45 LA 21, 25 (Kates, 1965); Linde Co., 39 LA 538, 541 (Wyckoff, 1962); Purex Corp., 39 LA 336, 340 (Miller, 1962); American Oil Co., 38 LA 906, 909 (Dykstra, 1962) (unsatisfactory work in jobs requiring less skill than job in question); Rome Grader Corp., 22 LA 167, 170 (McKelvey, 1953). See also Iowa Bd. of Regents, Iowa State Univ., 114 LA 11, 16 (Kessler, 1999); Campbell Soup Co., 113 LA 21, 25 (Allen, Jr., 1999) ("One must be 'qualified' at the time the bid is assessed, not at some unknown future date following some unpredictable amount of training and experience. Obviously, any employee in a new job will require a limited amount of time to become fully familiar with his/her job duties and responsibilities. However, that is merely 'familiarization' as opposed to being basically 'qualified' to perform the functions."); Public Serv. Co. of Colo., 77 LA 313, 316, 319 (Watkins, 1981); American Cyanamid Co., 52 LA 247, 249–51 (Cahn, 1969); American Bosch Arma Corp., 40 LA 403, 407 (Kornblum, 1963); Shamrock Oil & Gas Corp., 39 LA 1117, 1118–19 (Coffey, 1962); Colonial Baking Co., 34 LA 356, 359 (Murphy, 1960); Linde Air Prods Co., 25 LA 369, 372 (Shister, 1955); Shore Metal Prods. Co., 24 LA 437, 442 (Prasow, 1955).

[304]See Dwyer Prods. Corp., 48 LA 1031, 1035 (Larkin, 1967); Allied Chem. Corp., 47 LA 554, 557, 558–59 (Daugherty, 1966); U.S. Indus., 44 LA 1193, 1195 (Singletary, 1965); Monsanto Research Corp., 39 LA 735, 739 (Dworkin, 1962); Day & Zimmerman, 36 LA 145, 148 (Merrill, 1960); Kilgore Inc., 35 LA 391, 396 (Dworkin, 1960); White Motor Co., 28 LA 823, 828 (Lazarus, 1957); International Harvester Co., 24 LA 79, 80 (Platt, 1955); International Harvester Co., 21 LA 231, 234 (Cole, 1953).

[305]Semling-Menke Co., 46 LA 523, 526–27 (Graff, 1966).

[306]American Welding & Mfg. Co., 52 LA 889, 893 (Stouffer, 1969). See also Abex Corp., 71 LA 1171, 1176 (Cohen, 1978) (agreeing that the specified trial period need not be exhausted where it becomes apparent that the employee is unqualified for the job, but stating that "such an exception . . . becomes operative only where the Grievant is given a reasonable time or adequate help or directions to qualify for the job," which was not done); ICI U.S., 65 LA 869, 874–75 (Lynch, 1975); Diehl Mfg. Co., 36 LA 1266, 1269 (Kornblum, 1961). In the latter case, the arbitrator quoted from Howard, Seniority Rights and Trial Periods, 15 ARB. J. 51, 59 (1960), recognizing the "right of management to cancel the trial wherever the job candidate demonstrates his incompetence." Cf. Timex Corp., 63 LA 758, 763–64 (Gruenberg, 1974).

The purpose of a trial period is to determine whether an employee who possesses the basic qualifications can satisfactorily do a job which she does not regularly perform. It is assumed that she will not have to be trained in all aspects of the job; for a trial period is not a training period, but simply an opportunity to demonstrate ability to do the job. A trial period, in effect, is a lengthened familiarization or orientation period in which the employee is acquainted with the nature and techniques of the job. It presupposes that the employee will be given instruction and assistance and that she will not simply be turned loose to "sink or swim." But, it also assumes that she brings with her to the trial period by virtue of prior experience or education considerable knowledge, background, and skill for performing the duties of the new position. She still needs instruction in the peculiar requirements, procedures, equipment, and techniques of the job; but an intensive on-the-job training program, such as would be appropriate for a novice, is not contemplated.[307]

A number of arbitrators have agreed that while circumstances of a given case may require that an employer provide a trial or break-in period on the job, ordinarily there would be no obligation, unless the contract provides otherwise, to provide training for a senior employee to enable him or her to achieve the fitness and ability called for by the contract.[308] If a senior employee would require such extensive training (in order to qualify for a job) as to make it unreasonable under the contract to expect the employer to provide it, the employer is justified in giving preference to a junior employee who is already fully qualified.[309]

However, where the contract recognizes seniority as a factor, management may not afford training opportunities to junior employees while arbitrarily denying them to senior employees and then proceed to promote or

---

[307]Reynolds Metals Co., 66 LA 1276, 1280 (Volz, 1976).

[308]See Robertshaw Controls Co., 67 LA 678, 682 (Wagner, 1976); Mountain States Tel. & Tel. Co., 66 LA 1299, 1301–02 (Rentfro, 1976); Reynolds Metals Co., 66 LA 1276, 1280 (Volz, 1976); Federal Paper Bd. Co., 51 LA 49, 51–52 (Krimsly, 1968) (some instruction, but no training, should be given on new machine); HITCO, 47 LA 726, 734 (Prasow, 1966); Atlas Processing Co., 46 LA 860, 863 (Oppenheim, 1966); Greater Louisville Indus., 44 LA 694, 697 (Volz, 1965); Advanced Structures, 37 LA 49, 53 (Roberts, 1961); Diehl Mfg. Co., 36 LA 1266, 1270 (Kornblum, 1961); Day & Zimmerman, 36 LA 145, 148 (Merrill, 1960); Great Atl. & Pac. Tea Co., 28 LA 733, 735 (Emery, 1957); Wagner Elec. Corp., 20 LA 768, 774 (Klamon, 1953); Seagrave Corp., 16 LA 410, 412 (Lehoczky, 1951); Crown Cotton Mills, 7 LA 526, 527 (Greene, 1947). See also Western Cutlery Co., 80 LA 1367, 1372 (Wiggins, 1983); Westvaco Corp., 80 LA 118, 120 (Ipavec, 1982). Cf. Thiokol Corp., 65 LA 1265, 1267 (Williams, 1975). The agreement may provide for training as in Chicago Bridge & Iron Co., 74 LA 581, 583–84 (Sembower, 1980); Royster Co., 55 LA 432, 433 (Amis, 1970); Reichhold Chems., 49 LA 953, 954 (Williams, 1967); General Box Co., 48 LA 530, 532 (Williams, 1967). In New York State Electric & Gas Corp., 69 LA 865, 869 (Foltman, 1977), it was held under a relative ability clause that the employer properly awarded a vacancy to an employee whose qualifications were superior to those of the senior bidder, the contractual provision for training being construed to apply only "after a job award has been made in light of particular individual deficiencies or gaps." For some cases concerning the allegedly premature termination of training, see Allied Chem. Corp., 75 LA 1101, 1105 (Fox, 1980); United States Steel Corp., 66 LA 1198, 1201 (Powell, Jr., 1976); U.S. Playing Card Co., 65 LA 1070, 1073 (Leonard, 1975); Department of Army, 63 LA 924, 927 (Ferguson, 1974).

[309]See International Nickel Co., 36 LA 343, 351 (Teple, 1960); United States Pipe & Foundry Co., 30 LA 598, 599 (Murphy, 1958); Rome Grader Corp., 22 LA 167, 170 (McKelvey, 1953); Illinois Malleable Iron Co., 16 LA 909, 911–12 (Updegraff, 1951). The need for training would seem to indicate a lack of skill and ability. Poloron Prods. of Pa., 23 LA 789, 792 (Rosenfarb, 1955). See also Glidden Co., 34 LA 265, 268 (Griffin, 1960).

retain junior applicants on the basis of such training.[310] Such action not only may constitute impermissible discrimination, but also improper nullification of the seniority clause."[311] In a pair of cases, arbitrators held that training and experience received by junior employees in violation of the contracts could not be credited to the juniors in considering relative ability. In one of the cases, the contract expressly provided that management would assist senior employees to become qualified for promotion by assigning them to temporary vacancies for training purposes,[312] and, in the other, the contract expressly precluded temporary assignments exceeding 30 days.[313]

This is not to say that management may not select junior employees for training under any circumstances. Management was entitled to give training to junior employees where the senior employee was on sick leave,[314] but was not required to make special arrangements for senior employees to take only portions of a training course.[315]

Furthermore, in the absence of a contract provision dealing with training, management possesses a reasonable freedom of discretion in selecting employees for training, particularly in connection with new types of activities, but such selection must not be arbitrary or discriminatory or in conflict with the seniority provisions of the contract.[316]

Finally, if the employer has had a policy or practice of providing training for employees desiring to take it, employees who have not taken such training may not be automatically disqualified.[317] That is, the employer may not rely on training so provided as a "conclusive determinant of relative abil-

---

[310]See Gould Navcom Sys. Div., 79 LA 1193, 1196 (Rothschild, 1982); Library of Cong., 79 LA 158, 162–63 (Mullin, 1982); Sandvik Steel, 29 LA 747, 749 (Kerrison, 1957); Crown Cotton Mills, 28 LA 56, 59 (Williams, 1957); Poloron Prods. of Pa., 23 LA 789, 793 (Rosenfarb, 1955); Campbell Soup Co., 19 LA 1, 4 (Waite, 1952); United States Rubber Co., 18 LA 834, 835 (McCoy, 1952). See also Blue Diamond Mining, 80 LA 448, 452–53 (Leach, 1983); Emerson Elec. Co., 54 LA 683, 686 (Williams, 1971); Interlake Steel Corp., 46 LA 23, 27 (Luskin, 1965); Purolator Prods., 25 LA 60, 63 (Reynolds, 1955). Cf. Waste King Corp., 54 LA 1247, 1250–51 (Block, 1971) (involving a past practice of training employees in one of two areas but not in both); Great Atl. & Pac. Tea Co., 28 LA 733, 736 (Emery, 1957). Regarding the right of minority group members to equal access to training that could lead to future promotion, see discussion in Safeway Stores, 75 LA 387, 392–93 (Allen, Jr., 1980).

[311]Sandvik Steel, 29 LA 747, 749 (Kerrison, 1957). See also Gould Navcom Sys. Div., 79 LA 1193, 1196 (Rothschild, 1982); Emerson Elec. Co., 54 LA 683, 686 (Williams, 1971); Interlake Steel Corp., 46 LA 27; Poloron Prods. of Pa., 23 LA 789, 793 (Rosenbarb, 1955).

[312]United States Steel Corp., 36 LA 1083, 1087–88 (Crawford, 1961).

[313]Kroger Co., 34 LA 414, 418 (Emerson, 1959).

[314]U.S. Plywood Corp., 49 LA 726, 728 (Amis, 1967). See also William Powell Co., 63 LA 341, 344 (High, 1974).

[315]Bethlehem Steel Corp., 48 LA 1, 2 (Gill, 1966) (the seniors resisted taking the entire course because it would have required them to work temporarily in a lower classification).

[316]See Purolator Prods., 25 LA 60, 63 (Reynolds, 1955). See also Illinois Dep'ts of Pers. & Corr., 72 LA 941, 947 (Rezler, 1979). In Vulcan Materials Co., 49 LA 577, 579–80 (Duff, 1967), it was held that tests used for selecting trainees must be appropriate to ascertain the aptitude of bidders to become trainees. In John Strange Paper Co., 43 LA 1184, 1187 (Larkin, 1965), management was permitted to use a test for screening employees to be given a period of on-the-job training (even though for several years it had given each senior employee a chance at such training) so long as the system of selection was fair, uniform, and nondiscriminatory.

[317]United States Steel Corp., 22 LA 188, 190 (Garrett, 1953). See also Whirlpool Corp., 49 LA 529, 533–34 (Sembower, 1967).

ity," but must affirmatively show that the employees selected are actually better qualified.[318] In one case, the junior employee who took the training was better qualified as a result of the training and experience than the senior employees who had refused such training, and the junior therefore was entitled under the contractual relative ability clause to the promotion.[319] The fact that the senior employee in that case had not taken advantage of the training offered by the company was considered a factor against him when he was disqualified at the end of a trial period.[320]

iv. *Opinion of Supervision* [LA CDI 119.121]

While the opinion of supervisors regarding the ability of employees is considered important and is entitled at least to some consideration, absent substantial factual support it will not be deemed conclusive.[321] However, when supervisory opinion is substantiated by objective, tangible evidence, it can serve as the basis for management's assessment of the relative ability of employees.[322] Such objective evidence may include factors discussed elsewhere in this topic, such as test results, production records, periodic merit ratings, and other documentary material, as well as evidence of prior experience and results of trial periods.

The importance of supervisory opinion was noted by one arbitrator:

---

[318]United States Steel Corp., 22 LA 188, 190 (Garrett, 1953).

[319]Patapsco & Back Rivers R.R., 43 LA 51, 53–54 (Seitz, 1964). *See also* Allied Prods. Corp., 69 LA 311, 314 (Rimer, Jr., 1977); Kaiser Steel Corp., 42 LA 1109, 1113 (Bernstein, 1964) (layoff of senior employees who lacked the training that the junior employees had).

[320]*See* American Oil Co., 50 LA 1227, 1233 (Simon, 1968); National Lead Co., 48 LA 405, 408 (Wissner, 1967).

[321]*See* Entergy/Mississippi Power & Light Co., 111 LA 507, 514–15 (Howell, 1998); Helm, Inc., 92 LA 1295, 1297–98 (Feldman, 1989); Farm Fresh Catfish Co., 91 LA 721, 725 (Nicholas, Jr., 1988); Hearst Corp., 80 LA 361, 363 (Boetticher, 1983); City of Traverse City, 72 LA 1061, 1064 (Roumell, Jr., 1979); Douglas Aircraft Co. of Can., 72 LA 727, 732 (Brown, 1979); I-T-E Imperial Corp., 55 LA 1284, 1288 (White, 1970); Batesville Mfg. Co., 55 LA 261, 269 (Roberts, 1970); International Harvester Co., 20 LA 460, 462 (Platt, 1953); Public Serv. Elec. & Gas Co., 12 LA 317, 322 (Hays, 1949).

[322]*See* Cross & Trecker Co., 85 LA 721, 727 (Chalfie, 1985); Georgia Power Co., 75 LA 181, 189 (Hunter, 1980); Cincinnati Bd. of Educ., 72 LA 524, 528 (Ipavec, 1979) (in upholding the employer's transfer of a senior teacher while retaining a junior teacher under a relative ability clause, the arbitrator stated that the school principal "was adequately able . . . to substantiate the reasons for his decision . . . using objective factors," and that, "[u]nless there is a showing that the evaluation was arbitrary or unreasonable, the assessment of skill made by a supervisor or administrator in a position to make such a determination should be given considerable weight and should not be reversed by the arbitrator"); Standard Oil Co. of Cal., 54 LA 298, 301–02 (Beeson, 1971); American Welding & Mfg. Co., 52 LA 889, 893 (Stouffer, 1969); Shenango Furnace Co., 46 LA 203, 210 (Klein, 1966); Penn Controls, 45 LA 129, 130–31 (Larkin, 1965) (supervisory opinion given great weight in this case, which involved job of group leader); Givaudan Corp., 64–3 ARB ¶9087 (Feinberg, 1964); Lockheed Aircraft Serv. Co., 40 LA 1225, 1227 (Tsukiyama, 1963); Linde Co., 39 LA 538, 541 (Wyckoff, 1962); Campbell Soup Co., 19 LA 1, 4 (Waite, 1952). *See also* International Paper Co., 19 LA 402, 405 (Ralston, Jr., 1952); North Am. Aviation, 11 LA 312, 315 (Grant, 1948). For cases illustrating the important role of supervisory opinion concerning employee qualifications for promotion in the federal sector, see *Veterans Admin. Med. Ctr.*, 75 LA 910, 911 (Tillem, 1980); *Internal Revenue Serv.*, 71 LA 359, 365 (Belcher, 1978); *General Counsel of Nat'l Labor Relations Bd.*, 70 LA 859, 865 (Koven, 1978); *National Labor Relations Bd.*, 68 LA 279, 286–87, 289 (Sinicropi, 1977) (stressing, however, that "supervisory opinions without factual support will not be deemed conclusive by this arbitrator").

Considerable weight should be given to bona fide conclusions of supervisors when supported by factual evidence. In the first place, a supervisor is responsible for the efficient performance of his unit and has a legitimate concern that the employees be properly assigned to achieve this objective. In the second place, he has a deeper and more intimate acquaintance with the men under his charge than an arbitrator is able to acquire in a brief hearing.[323]

But, another arbitrator emphasized the necessity for supporting evidence:

A supervisor's testimony that he honestly believes one employee to be superior to another with respect to the promotion is certainly a factor to be considered. It is not, however, either conclusive or sufficient. The supervisor must be prepared to state the basis for his belief and to support it, not by repeated assertions but by specific and understandable evidence.[324]

Management's decision to bypass a senior employee was upheld when it reflected a composite of the opinions of several supervisors who had observed or supervised the employee's work and had formed their opinions on the basis of a variety of incidents in the senior's employment record.[325] Similarly, a negative supervisory opinion supported by evidence of an employee's inadequate performance during a trial period was found dispositive.[326]

In another case, the opinion of management was found controlling where company officers, including the president, were in almost daily contact over many years with the employees, and thus were thoroughly familiar with their abilities as well as the processes and equipment relevant to the job.[327]

Supervisory opinion has been found persuasive where several levels of supervision, familiar with the work performance of the competing bidders and with the requirements of the job being bid upon, reached a unanimous decision,[328] but not where the supervisors consulted had little or no opportunity to observe the employees they were rating and were not familiar with the requirements of the bid-on job.[329] Likewise, little, if any, weight should

---

[323]Pacific Gas & Elec. Co., 23 LA 556, 558 (Ross, 1954), *cited with approval in* Paauhau Sugar Co., 55 LA 477, 480 (Tsukiyama, 1970) (emphasizing the importance of "first line supervisorial participation" in the selection process); American Welding & Mfg. Co., 52 LA 889, 893 (Stouffer, 1969). *See also* Georgia Power Co., 75 LA 181, 189 (Hunter, 1980); San Francisco Newspaper Publishers Ass'n, 41 LA 148, 151–52, 154 (Burns, 1963); Standard Oil Co., 25 LA 32, 36 (Burris, 1955); International Harvester Co., 21 LA 214, 218 (Cole, 1953). The above view was reaffirmed in *San Francisco News-Call Bulletin*, 34 LA 271, 273–74 (Ross, 1960) ("But it does not follow that a clearly mistaken decision should be left undisturbed merely because it has not been shown to be arbitrary, discriminatory, etc.").

[324]Ford Motor Co., 2 LA 374, 376 (Shulman, 1945), *cited with approval in* City of Traverse City, 72 LA at 1064; Batesville Mfg. Co., 55 LA at 269; International Nickel Co., 45 LA 743, 748 (Kates, 1965).

[325]*See* Northwestern Bell Tel. Co., 19 LA 47, 50–51 (Doyle, 1952). *See also* Okeelanta Corp., 88 LA 420 (Richard, 1986); Cross & Trecker Co., 85 LA 721, 727 (Chalfie, 1985); Eagle-Picher Mining & Smelting Co., 17 LA 205, 211 (Prasow, 1951).

[326]*See* American Welding & Mfg. Co., 52 LA 889, 893 (Stouffer, 1969); Shenango Furnace Co., 46 LA 203, 210 (Klein, 1966); Givaudan Corp., 64–3 ARB ¶9087 (Feinberg, 1964).

[327]*See* Pittsburgh Standard Conduit Co., 32 LA 481, 482–83 (Lehoczky, 1959) (the finding was based on other factors also, including the use of a test).

[328]*See* Paauhau Sugar Co., 55 LA 477, 480 (Tsukiyama, 1970); Brookhaven Nat'l Lab., 54 LA 447, 448 (Wolff, 1971); Standard Oil Co. of Cal., 54 LA 298, 301–02 (Beeson, 1971); Penn Controls, 45 LA 129, 130–31 (Larkin, 1965).

[329]*See* Lear Siegler, 75 LA 1001, 1004–05 (Nathanson, 1980); Royster Co., 55 LA 432, 434 (Amis, 1970); Ohio Edison Co., 46 LA 801, 805 (Alexander, 1966). In *Rainier Port Cold Storage*, 79 LA 441, 448 (Armstrong, 1982), a significant factor in the arbitrator's finding that

be accorded supervisory opinion where management relied on such opinion concerning one of the bidders while not consulting supervisors of another bidder at all.[330]

v.   *Merit Rating Plans* [LA CDI 119.1221]

Merit rating plans (or performance reviews) involve essentially a documentation, usually periodically made, of supervisory opinion concerning various aspects of the "fitness and ability" of employees. A merit rating plan may include such factors as quantity and quality of work, knowledge of the job, ability to learn, initiative, acceptance of responsibility, ability to direct others, safety habits and accident record, attitude toward fellow employees and management, attendance, and personal characteristics such as moral character, physical condition, and appearance.[331] Other factors may include the quality of pertinent experience and training, special conditions of the job, and achievements that have earned incentive awards or other special recognition.[332]

Arbitrators look on merit rating plans as an aid in judging fitness and ability. However, while considering performance ratings an important aid, one arbitrator cautioned against placing exclusive reliance on them:

---

the grievant's layoff was arbitrary and capricious was the fact that officials who made the decision to lay him off instead of a junior employee failed to consult the foreman who was best qualified to give a supervisory opinion regarding grievant's ability. In choosing between two nurses bidding to fill a vacancy in *Marshalltown Area Cmty. Hosp.*, 76 LA 978, 984–85 (Smith, 1981), the promoting supervisor "talked to other hospital personnel to obtain additional information about each of the applicants," and talked with four surgeons "to obtain their input regarding the applicants." The arbitrator found that this process produced no substantive information concerning the knowledge, skills, or abilities of either candidate, and, in concluding that the senior applicant should have been awarded the vacancy, he declared that "the selection procedure could be judged more of a popularity contest than a logical attempt to identify applicants' abilities and qualifications." *Id.* at 985.

[330]*See* Northwest Airlines, 46 LA 238, 241–42 (Elkouri, 1966); International Nickel Co., 45 LA 743, 748 (Kates, 1965).

[331]*See* Western Automatic Mach. Screw Co., 9 LA 606, 608 (Lehoczky, 1948). For other discussion of merit rating plans, see Holley, *Performance Ratings in Arbitration*, 32 Arb. J. 8 (1977). In *Electrical Distribs.*, 64 LA 608, 609 (Burr, 1975), a joint union-management committee for evaluation of job performance had difficulty making an evaluation and could not agree on criteria by which to do so. A survey of collective bargaining agreements in the federal sector revealed that most contained merit promotion plans; about one-fourth of the agreements surveyed specified criteria to be used in rating employees for merit promotion purposes, very few specified consideration of seniority as a factor, and none provided "for union participation in the actual decision, itself." *A Survey of Merit Promotion Provisions in Federal Post Civil Service Reform Act Agreements* 1, 11, 32–33 (OPM 1980). For related discussion, see Ferris, *Remedies in Federal Sector Promotion Grievances*, 34 Arb. J. 37 (1979). In *Department of Health & Human Servs.*, 81 LA 980, 981–82 (Cluster, 1983), the arbitrator observed that the Civil Service Reform Act of 1978 mandates the establishment of performance appraisal systems and that OPM had issued regulations requiring individual federal agencies to establish their system by October 1, 1981; he outlined the features of the performance appraisal system involved in the grievance before him.

[332]*See* Department of Interior, 53 LA 657, 659 (Koven, 1969). For yet other factors, see *San Antonio Air Logistics Ctr.*, 74 LA 486, 487 (Coffey, 1979). Many of the factors noted above are discussed as separate criteria in other subtopics of this chapter. For an illustration that management may be more restricted in evaluating employee performance where factors are specified in the collective bargaining agreement, see *Internal Revenue Serv.*, 64 LA 486, 495–97 (McBrearty, 1975).

The word "fitness" is not synonymous with "merit;" it means the quality of being suitable to the performance of the regular duties of the job, and includes the employee's habits, industry, energy, ambition, tact, disposition, discretion, knowledge of the duties of the job, physical strength, and related attributes. It means suitability. The word "ability" means the possession of those qualities of mind, physical strength, and related job attainments which are sufficient, under the usual conditions of the job, to satisfactorily perform the basic and usual duties and tasks of the job. The Company placed too much weight on its past evaluations of the Grievant's job performance. While these performance ratings are important and serve to assist in the employer's evaluation of an employee, they are not all-inclusive.[333]

Merit or performance ratings have been a factor considered by arbitrators in upholding management's determination of ability under both a relative ability clause[334] and a sufficient ability clause.[335] However, one employee evaluation system was considered to be suspect in that "well meaning as it was intended to be, [it] tended to match the traits of each bidder against the others," thus resulting in a comparison of bidders that was not permitted under the sufficient ability clause.[336]

An arbitrator's acceptance or rejection of a merit rating plan as a criterion for measuring ability depends on whether the factors used in the plan and the weights attached to them are consistent with the collective bargaining agreement and the requirements of the job in question.[337] Thus, under a contract providing that seniority should govern where "ability, skill, and efficiency" are substantially equal, management's institution of a performance review plan was upheld because the plan did no more than document on a regular basis supervisory opinion concerning the ability, skill, and efficiency of employees. There, the arbitrator stated that management could use any method, written or unwritten, to determine the relative ability of employees "so long as that method is not unfair, arbitrary, or based on improper or irrelevant premises."[338]

---

[333]American Oil Co., 53 LA 160, 161 (Williams, 1969) (involving a sufficient ability clause). *Compare* U.S. Customs Serv., 72 LA 700, 701 (Maggiolo, 1979) (upholding the federal agency employer's denial of grievant's transfer request where his present and previous supervisors had denied him in-grade increases on the ground that he had not performed his duties at an "acceptable level of competency," the arbitrator reasoning that the employer could reasonably "assume that if the grievant was unable to perform his present GS-12 duties at an acceptable level in his present position, he would not be able to perform GS-12 duties in any branch to which he might be assigned").

[334]*See* Bristol Steel & Iron Works, 47 LA 263, 265 (Volz, 1966); Lockheed Aircraft Serv. Co., 40 LA 1225, 1227–28 (Tsukiyama, 1963); North Am. Aviation, 11 LA 312, 315 (Grant, 1948); Inland Steel Co., 4 LA 657, 666–67 (Gilden, 1946).

[335]Jeffrey Mfg. Co., 29 LA 300, 302 (Seinsheimer, 1957).

[336]Ohio Edison Co., 46 LA 801, 805 (Alexander, 1966).

[337]*See* U.S. Tobacco Co., 89 LA 611, 615 (Clarke, 1987); Plymouth Cordage Co., 27 LA 816, 819 (Hogan, 1956) (improper weight given to certain factors); Merrill Stevens Dry Dock & Repair Co., 17 LA 516, 519 (Hawley, 1951); North Am. Aviation, 11 LA 312, 315 (Grant, 1948).

[338]Lockheed Aircraft Corp., 25 LA 748, 750–51 (Williams, 1956) (union agreed that the company could determine relative ability of employees, but objected to the regular documentation of such determination). *Accord* Lockheed Aircraft Serv. Co., 40 LA 1225, 1227–28 (Tsukiyama, 1963). For a statement of management's residual rights regarding performance evaluation, see *Department of Health, Educ. & Welfare*, 72 LA 788, 791–93 (Hayes, 1979). In *Acme Steel Co.*, 9 LA 432, 436–37 (Gegory, 1947), the arbitrator stated that a merit rating plan is preferable to placing "the judgment in the hands of the foremen on an ad hoc basis,

Under another relative ability provision, the arbitrator held that some of the factors in the merit rating plan used by the company had no bearing on an employee's "ability to do the work," and, when these were discounted, the employees involved were found to possess the requisite ability.[339]

One other use of merit rating that has been the cause of grievances concerns management's right to place and retain evaluation reports in the employee's personnel file for future use, and the right of the employee and the union to be apprised of their use and to see such reports before any action is taken based on the reports that adversely affects the employee.[340]

vi. *Educational Background* [LA CDI 119.124]

Technical training acquired through attendance at trade schools, or at training programs sponsored by the company, union, or other credible sources,

---

with no systematic check on their whims and fancies from top management." For an illustration of capricious evaluations by an employee's immediate supervisor, see *Federal Aviation Admin.*, 64 LA 289, 291 (Amis, 1975). But actions of top management also may trigger improper ratings. In *San Antonio Air Logistics Ctr.*, 74 LA 486, 488–89 (Coffey, 1979), a federal agency employer reviewed overall ratings within the employer's facility and, concluding that they were too high, directed supervisors to "bring them into line if they could"; pursuant to this the grievant's supervisor rated her lower than before even though her performance had not dropped, leading the arbitrator (1) to conclude that she "did not receive a fair and just supervisory appraisal based on her job performance," and (2) to order that a new supervisory appraisal be made for the period in question. Another illustration is provided by *State of Wis.*, 64 LA 663, 667–68 (Marshall, 1975), where the arbitrator found that a management official had made "little or no use" of the customary evaluation criteria (based on which the grievant's immediate superior considered him to be deserving of a merit increase), and had withheld merit increases "not so much for failure of an individual to perform 'meritorious service' as for a disciplinary device or a substitute for the exercise of appropriate managerial action." *See also* Pennsylvania Army & Air Nat'l Guard, 72 LA 666, 668 (Mussmann, 1979); Kent State Univ., 59 LA 1007, 1014 (Kindig, 1972).

[339]Western Automatic Mach. Screw Co., 9 LA 606, 608–09 (Lehoczky, 1948). *Accord* American Oil Co., 53 LA 160, 162 (Williams, 1969) (under a sufficient ability clause). In *Merrill Stevens Dry Dock & Repair Co.*, 17 LA 516, 518–19 (Hawley, 1951), most of the factors were accepted but the company was "urged" to remove imprecise factors from its merit rating plan. Of course, even where a given factor is accepted, an arbitrator can be expected to require that its actual application be substantiated in a specific and understandable manner. National Labor Relations Bd., 68 LA 279, 289 (Sinicropi, 1977).

[340]*See* Peters Township Sch. Dist., 76 LA 68, 71 (Hannan, 1981) (ordering removal of derogatory material placed in employee's file without giving her an opportunity to review it as required by agreement); Bureau of Census, 75 LA 1194, 1200–01 (Mittleman, 1980) (dealing with alleged injury due to retention of erroneous appraisal of qualifications in grievant's file, and construing the Privacy Act of 1974, 5 U.S.C. §552a, in connection with the claim); Naval Avionics Ctr., 70 LA 967, 968–69 (Atwood, 1978) (construing the Privacy Act of 1974 and concluding that it does not prohibit the making of records but rather that Congress was concerned with access by individuals to and the improper disclosure of information pertaining to themselves and maintained by federal agencies); City of Cincinnati, 69 LA 682, 686–87 (Bell, 1977); Tacoma Sch. Dist. No. 10, 69 LA 34, 38–39 (Peterschmidt, 1977); National Cash Register Co., 48 LA 421, 424–25 (Gilden, 1967); Ohio Power Co., 48 LA 299, 304 (Leach, 1967) (where the employer feared that the report was a disciplinary device in the nature of a warning); Cincinnati Enquirer, 44 LA 200, 201 (Gusweiler, 1965) (upholding management's right to make an efficiency survey, but finding improper the forms used); McEvoy Co., 42 LA 41, 45–47 (Morvant, 1964). *See also* Mobilization for Youth, 49 LA 1124, 1126–27 (Wolff, 1967) (a report was orally imparted to supervision, was neither discussed with the employee nor made a part of her personnel record, yet was used to bar advancement). For a court decision upholding an arbitrator's power to order the removal of an unfair performance evaluation from the employee's file, see *Unit B, Kittery Teachers Ass'n v. Kittery Sch. Comm.*, 413 A.2d 534 (Me. 1980).

obviously is highly pertinent to the determination of fitness and ability so long as such training relates to the requirements of the job in question.[341] Thus, where the nature of a job required at least one course in accounting that the grievant had not taken, the company was held justified in selecting a qualified new hire.[342] However, where a junior employee's technical training was not related to the job requirements, the employer was held to have violated the contractual seniority provisions by awarding the job to him because the senior employee otherwise possessed substantially equal ability.[343] The same result was reached in another case even though the junior employee's technical training had potential value for jobs higher in the line of progression; the arbitrator emphasized that an employee's qualifications "must be measured a job at a time."[344]

An employee's formal educational background, that is, high school and college education as opposed to technical training, may also be a factor in the assessment of fitness and ability if it is pertinent to the job requirements.[345] This factor was determinative in one case where an arbitrator upheld the award of a position to a junior employee with a college education rather than to a senior employee whose experience was not closely related to the position in question.[346] But where a senior employee had 9 years of job-related experience, the employer could not select a newly hired employee with a 4-year college degree.[347]

Arbitrators seem to have taken several (not necessarily inconsistent) approaches in considering the extent to which formal education can be taken into consideration where the contract does not specify any education requirement for given jobs. It has been variously held that (1) management may require a high school education where the job was complex and carried with it automatic progressions through several classifications involving additional responsibilities,[348] (2) the formal educational background of the employee

---

[341]*See* Caldwell v. Norfolk S. Ry., 175 F.3d 1013 (4th Cir. 1999) (unpublished table decision) (a senior employee who had no training on a "skill differential" machine and who failed to obtain the requisite training on the machine on his own time, as required by the collective bargaining agreement, cannot establish a prima facie case of discriminatory failure to promote).

[342]Roosevelt Univ., 56 LA 604, 607 (Larkin, 1971). *See also* Ohio Power Co., 94 LA 463, 466 (Strasshofer, 1990); Hudson Pulp & Paper Corp., 70 LA 1073, 1076 (Sobel, 1978) (employer's requirement of 1 year training for job of computer operator held "entirely reasonable"); A.O. Smith Co., 69 LA 156, 157 (Young, 1977); United States Steel Corp., 51 LA 264, 266 (Smith, 1968).

[343]Pennsylvania Power & Light Co., 57 LA 146, 148–49 (Howard, 1971). As to the need of supervisory testimony to correlate technical training with the job requirements, see *Laupahoehoe Sugar Co.*, 38 LA 404, 412–13 (Tsukiyama, 1961).

[344]Georgia Kraft Co., 47 LA 829, 830 (Williams, 1966). *See also* Realist, Inc., 45 LA 444, 446 (Keeler, 1965). Progression was not automatic in these cases.

[345]In *Griggs v. Duke Power Co.*, 401 U.S. 424, 3 FEP Cases 175 (1971), it was held that the employer violated Title VII of the Civil Rights Act of 1964 by requiring a high school education or the passing of a standardized general intelligence test as a condition of employment in or transfer to jobs where it was not shown that such requirements were job-related and where the requirements operated to discriminate against blacks.

[346]Atlantic Richfield Co., 83 LA 960 (Allen, Jr., 1984).

[347]Stearns County, Minn., 90 LA 1181 (Kapsch, Sr., 1988).

[348]Philip Carey Mfg. Co., 30 LA 659, 661 (Warns, Jr., 1958). A different result obtained in *West Va. Pulp & Paper Co.*, 16 LA 359, 365 (Copelof, 1951), where progression was not automatic. For other cases upholding the requirement of a high school education, see *Industrial*

may be considered along with other factors,[349] (3) the employer may not automatically disqualify an employee for want of a formal education but may consider formal education in evaluating the employee's training and experience,[350] and (4) the employer may not deny a promotion to senior employees solely on the basis that they lacked a high school education or its equivalent.[351]

In the last regard, an arbitrator wrote that while a company may establish minimum qualifications for a job, it may not create "exclusionary 'barriers'" that prevent employees from competing for a given vacancy. He went on to state, "[t]hough a high school diploma (or equivalent certificate) is some evidence of basic ability to perform a given job, the lack of such 'credentials' cannot, in itself, be deemed to establish, conclusively, the opposite."[352]

The question of ability to read and write in English has arisen in several cases. Where such ability is necessary to the proper performance of the job, management may properly disqualify the employee who lacks such ability. For example, in one case, management's disqualification of senior bidders was upheld because they could not read and write well enough in English to interpret the repair manual and parts list and to make requisitions, all of

---

Garment Mfg. Co., 74 LA 1248, 1253 (Griffin, 1980) (concluding that employer did not violate either the collective bargaining agreement or the Civil Rights Act by adding the requirement of a high school education or its equivalent for vacancies in the shipping department, there being need to reduce errors and the employer's evidence indicating that high school graduates in that department perform better than their nongraduate counterparts); *Ball Bros. Co.*, 46 LA 1153, 1156–57 (Kates, 1966); *International Minerals & Chem. Corp.*, 22 LA 446, 449–50 (Seibel, 1954).

[349]*See* Bristol Steel & Iron Works, 47 LA 263, 265 (Volz, 1966); Armstrong Cork Co., 42 LA 349, 351 (Handsaker, 1964); Iroquois Gas Corp., 39 LA 161, 163 (O'Rourke, 1962); Kuhlman Elec. Co., 26 LA 885, 890 (Howlett, 1956). *See also* Illinois Dep'ts of Pers. & Corr., 72 LA 941, 949 (Rezler, 1979); Jefferson Chem. Co., 72 LA 892, 897 (Goodstein, 1979); Airco Welding Prods., 67 LA 453, 456 (Ables, 1976); Dempster Bros., 48 LA 777, 778 (Cantor, 1967); Gisholt Mach. Co., 20 LA 137, 142 (Baab, 1953). In *Lockheed-Georgia Co.*, 49 LA 603, 605 (Di Leone, 1967), it was found that the superior education of the senior bidder balanced the experience of the junior so that their overall abilities were substantially equal, entitling the former to the promotion under the relative ability clause.

[350]*See* Union Oil Co., 17 LA 62, 64–65 (Wyckoff, 1951). *See also* United States Steel Corp., 55 LA 659, 662 (McDaniel, 1970); National Coop. Refinery Ass'n, 44 LA 92, 94 (Brown, 1964).

[351]*See* Bridgeport Gas Co., 26 LA 289, 291 (Stutz, 1956). *See also* Corporation of Borough of Scarborough, 72 LA 1167, 1170–71 (Brown, 1979) (although the employer reasonably required a 10th grade education or its approved equivalent for a job, the "approved equivalent" alternative was applied too rigidly in denying the job to the senior bidder who would have completed the 10th grade equivalent course in time for an award of the job had the course instructors not extended it on their own for another 3 months); Sewanee Silica Co., 38 LA 91, 92 (Dworet, 1961). In a case where the "really serious issue" was the senior employee's age, the arbitrator disposed of the education factor by finding that the "lack of a formal high school education should not constitute a bar to his being considered" for the job. *See* CIBA Pharm. Co., 41 LA 14, 17 (Berkowitz, 1963).

[352]United States Steel Corp., 55 LA 659, 662 (McDaniel, 1970). *See also* Realist, Inc., 45 LA 444, 447 (Keeler, 1965); National Coop. Refinery Ass'n, 44 LA 92, 95 (Brown, 1964); Alan Wood Steel Co., 37 LA 14, 14–15 (Gill, 1961) (the company's concern that the removal of the educational requirement would burden it unreasonably with the giving of trial periods to unqualified employees was considered unfounded due to its testing program). In *United States Steel Corp.*, 42 LA 245, 247 (Altrock, 1964), only minimal weight was given to the fact that the junior employee's schooling was from an "accredited" school, while the senior employee's was not, and because other factors indicated that they were relatively equal in ability, the senior was entitled to the job. *Cf.* University of Dubuque, 75 LA 420, 421, 426–27 (Sinicropi, 1980).

which were essential components of the job.[353] However, in another case, communication difficulties were not considered sufficient to outweigh the job applicant's meritorious service and his ability to do the basic work of the job. Even though he had a heavy foreign accent and could read English only slowly, he could read blueprints and had effectively trained a new man on the job.[354]

vii. *Production Records* [LA CDI 119.1221]

An employee's production record is objective evidence of his or her ability and may be relied on in determining fitness and ability.[355] One arbitrator asserted that ability "is most assuredly tied up with productivity" and that productivity must be measured in terms of both quality and quantity of work.[356] Another arbitrator contended that "output reflects not only effort, but know-how, skill and general capability, and is generally regarded as a proper item to be considered in measuring ability."[357]

Production records may be the sole factor considered where there is a substantial difference in the productivity of competing employees. Thus, management's determination of relative ability based solely on productivity was upheld in one case where the grievant's production was considerably below that of other workers,[358] and in another case where there was a 17 percent difference between the senior and the junior employee's production earnings.[359] Management's reliance in part on production records has likewise been upheld where the employee consistently failed to make the minimum wage under an incentive system or where the employee's production record was consistently below the standard.[360]

---

[353]Vulcan Materials Co., 54 LA 460, 466 (Block, 1971). *See also* Gorges Quik-to-Fix Foods, 113 LA 1005, 1015 (Crow, 1999); Farm Pac Kitchens, 51 LA 31, 34 (Goodstein, 1968); Lockheed Aircraft Serv., 32 LA 289, 292–93 (Phelps, 1959). In *Texas Utils. Generating Co.*, 71 LA 1205, 1207–08 (Mewhinney, 1979), the arbitrator concluded from the evidence "that the Grievant, a high school graduate, was given a high school diploma . . . without having acquired the minimum verbal and quantitative skills necessary in order to function satisfactorily in an industrial environment."

[354]Lanson & Sessions Co., 50 LA 959, 960–61 (Dahl, 1968). *See also* Gallmeyer & Livingston Co., 20 LA 899, 901–03 (Ryder, 1953).

[355]Regarding the type of data necessary in presenting production records as evidence of fitness and ability, see *Jonco Aircraft Corp.*, 22 LA 819, 823 (Merrill, 1954). The term "work records" may or may not be broader than "production records." For cases in which the work records or production records of competing employees were a factor, see *Ebasco Constructors*, 100 LA 176, 178 (Richman, 1992); *Autodynamics, Inc.*, 99 LA 705, 707–09 (Kanner, 1992); *Leach Mfg. Co.*, 79 LA 1251, 1255 (Byars, 1982); *North Country Dodge*, 77 LA 391, 393 (Craver, 1981); *International Tel. & Tel. Corp.*, 49 LA 1160, 1170–72 (McDermott, 1967); *Dempster Bros.*, 48 LA 777, 781 (Cantor, 1967); *Allied Chem. Corp.*, 47 LA 554, 558–59 (Daugherty, 1966); *Sandia Corp.*, 31 LA 338, 340–41 (Hayes, 1958); *Pittsburgh Steel Co.*, 21 LA 565, 568 (Brecht, 1953); *Eagle-Picher Mining & Smelting Co.*, 17 LA 205, 211 (Prasow, 1951). For a statement regarding the significance of performance records, see *James N. Travirca Gen. Contracting Co.*, 56 LA 1083, 1084 (Logan, 1971).

[356]Universal Mfg. Co., 13 LA 238, 241 (Spencer, 1949).

[357]Worth Steel Co., 12 LA 931, 934 (Bell, 1949).

[358]Byer-Rolnick Corp., 45 LA 868, 872 (Ray, 1965); Universal Mfg. Co., 13 LA 238, 241 (Spencer, 1949). *See also* United States Steel Corp., 68 LA 1282, 1284 (Beilstein, 1977).

[359]Worth Steel Co., 12 LA 931, 934 (Bell, 1949).

[360]*See* North Country Dodge, 77 LA 391, 393 (Craver, 1981); Imperial Reading Corp., 52 LA 568, 570 (Kesselman, 1969); Leach Co., 51 LA 382, 383–84 (Hazelwood, 1968); United

Where there is only a minor difference in the productivity of employees, reliance on productivity alone for the determination of relative ability is unlikely to be approved.[361] Moreover, determination of ability may not be based on speculation as to the relative future productivity of competing employees.[362]

viii. Attendance Records [LA CDI 119.1225]

Attendance records may be considered at least as one of the factors used in determining fitness and ability, and in some instances it may be the sole or controlling factor. In a number of cases, an employee's attendance record has been considered as relevant and objective evidence in assessing ability and qualifications.[363] Conversely, poor attendance has been held to be a valid reason to deny a more senior employee a promotion where the contract permitted the employer to give consideration to ability.[364] A poor attendance record can be the sole or controlling factor where the job involved is critical to operations, or otherwise requires a high degree of responsibility.[365] Thus, under a contract containing a relative ability clause, the promotion of a junior over a senior employee on the basis of their relative attendance records was upheld because the records showed a "striking" difference in favor of the junior candidate and the job required a high degree of responsibility.[366] In that case, the arbitrator stated:

> It is well established as a principle that Management has the right to expect and require regular attendance on the job. While it is true that Management has in this instance been extremely negligent in enforcing this right, its negligence does not bar it from applying the right in the case of a promotion. . . .

States Time Corp., 23 LA 379, 383 (Abernethy, 1954); Dixie Cup Co., 19 LA 639, 646 (Klamon, 1952); Goodyear Clearwater Mills, 11 LA 419, 425–26 (McCoy, 1948). *See also* International Paper Co., 33 LA 719, 721 (Hawley, 1959).

[361]United States Steel Corp., 22 LA 80, 81 (Garrett, 1953).

[362]Wurlitzer Co., 41 LA 792, 795 (Duff, 1963).

[363]*See* Aurora Bd.of Educ., Case No. 97-23534, 1998 WL 1033296 (Fullmer, 1998); Illinois Dep'ts of Pers. & Corr., 72 LA 941, 946–48 (Rezler, 1979); I-T-E Imperial Corp., 55 LA 1284, 1287 (White, 1970) (the arbitrator exercised an "equitable power" in taking into consideration the attendance factor); U.S. Plywood Corp., 49 LA 726, 728 (Amis, 1967); Northwest Airlines, 46 LA 238, 241 (Elkouri, 1966) (but promotion may not be denied as punishment for tardiness); Southern Ohio Fabricators 44 LA 283, 285 (Schmidt, 1965); Southwestern Bell Tel. Co., 30 LA 862, 871 (Davis, 1958). *Cf.* St. Mary's Kraft Corp., 40 LA 364, 366 (Duncan, 1963); Central Screw Co., 11 LA 108, 109 (Edes, 1948) (the parties agreed at the hearing that "ability and skill" do not encompass absenteeism). In *Lockheed Aircraft Serv. Co.*, 40 LA 1225, 1228 (Tsukiyama, 1963), the company was upheld in its determination that the junior employee's superior qualities of leadership (a requirement of the job) outweighed the much better attendance record of the senior employee.

[364]United Can Co., 102 LA 422 (Randall, 1993).

[365]*See* Michigan Plastics Prods. Co., 100 LA 1025, 1026–27 (Kanner, 1993); Dresser-Rand Co., 100 LA 333, 338–39 (Pribble, 1992); Vehicle Processors, 99 LA 581, 583–84 (Darrow, 1992); Walgreen Co., 93 LA 482, 484 (Baroni, 1989); Holland-Suco Color Co., 52 LA 1074, 1077–78 (Kates, 1969); Metal Forge Co., 51 LA 857, 858–59 (McCoy, 1968) (stating, however, that ordinarily management cannot deny promotions solely on the basis of a poor attendance record); Emhart Mfg. Co., 43 LA 946, 950 (Turkus, 1964); Rogers Bros. Corp., 16 LA 382, 383 (Blair, 1951); Imperial Lighting Prods. Co., 8 LA 877, 879 (Blair, 1947). *See also* Pierce Governor Co., 75 LA 1282, 1285 (Petersen, 1980).

[366]Rogers Bros. Corp., 16 LA 382, 383 (Blair, 1951). *Accord* Metal Forge Co., 51 LA 857, 858–59 (McCoy, 1968).

The action of Management in invoking this right at this time is not arbitrary. True, Management could not discipline . . . [grievant] by layoffs or dismissals for an action which they have condoned over a period of time without prior notice or warning. But the right to discipline and the right of Management to choose between candidates for promotion are distinguishable. . . . Management has the right to invoke the attendance records of two employees contending for a promotion because to do otherwise would condone and even approve a record of irregular attendance at work.[367]

The same result was reached in determining whether an employee was qualified even when the employee's numerous absences were attributable to bona fide illness.[368]

However, in another instance an arbitrator held that an employer had improperly disqualified two employees for promotion under a relative ability clause by considering their use of unscheduled annual leave. Even though the employer had considered sick leave in promotion decisions under such a clause, there had been no notice that use of unscheduled annual leave would have negative consequences. [369]

However, some arbitrators have held that an employee's attendance record is not a factor to be used in determining ability or qualifications. They reason that nothing in the contract permits management to use this factor to pass over a senior employee who otherwise meets the contractual requirements, and, further, that if an employee has been excessively absent, his absenteeism is a matter for the disciplinary process and should have been dealt with at the time the offenses occurred.[370]

In cases involving excused absences for the conduct of union business, it has been held that such absences should not operate as a bar to giving the senior employee preference. However, these decisions appear to have been based in part on other factors such as past practice,[371] or on the senior employee meeting conditions such as satisfactory performance of the job during a trial period[372] or regular attendance in the future.[373] These latter decisions recognize the right of management to take corrective steps should the employee not perform in an acceptable manner.

---

[367]Rogers Bros. Corp., 16 LA 382, 383 (Blair, 1951). *Accord Emhart Mfg. Co.*, 43 LA at 950 (under a sufficient ability clause).

[368]*See* Taft-Peirce Mfg. Co., 20 LA 835, 836 (Bailer, 1953); John Deere Tractor Co., 16 LA 790, 792 (Levinson, 1951); Goodyear Clearwater Mills, 11 LA 419, 425–26 (McCoy, 1948). *Cf.* Indiana Bell Tel. Co., 9 LA 444, 447 (Kelliher, 1948).

[369]Letter Carriers Health Benefit Plan, 92 LA 295 (Hockenberry, Jr., 1989).

[370]*See* Welsh Plastics, 71 LA 80, 82 (Kahn, 1978); American Shipbuilding Co., 69 LA 234, 238 (Morgan, Jr., 1977); Dearborn Fabricating & Eng'g Co., 64 LA 271, 275 (Kallenbach, 1975); St. Mary's Kraft Corp., 40 LA 364, 366 (Duncan, 1963); Waller Bros. Stone Co., 34 LA 852, 854–55 (Dworkin, 1960); Cleveland-Cliffs Iron Co., 24 LA 599, 600 (Kelliher, 1955). *See also* Florida Power Corp., 81 LA 51, 54–55 (Kanzer, 1983); Magnode Corp., 78 LA 192, 195–97 (Storey, 1982); United States Steel Corp., 67 LA 901, 914 (Freund, 1976).

[371]*See* American Lava Corp., 42 LA 117, 120 (Hon, 1964); Douglas Aircraft Co., 23 LA 786, 788 (Warren, 1955).

[372]*See* Marlin-Rockwell Corp., 17 LA 254, 256 (Shister, 1951).

[373]*See* Goodyear Decatur Mills, 12 LA 682, 685 (McCoy, 1949).

ix. *Disciplinary Record* [LA CDI 119.1225]

If an employee's disciplinary record contains information on offenses that reflect on fitness and ability for a given job, such record may be given some consideration.[374] For example, where an employee's disciplinary record of infractions demonstrated a lack of maturity, reliability, and a sense of responsibility, management was entitled to infer that he lacked the ability, merit, and capacity required by the contract.[375] Certainly, an employer may properly consider the prior negative on-the-job performance of a senior employee who had caused property damage and abused equipment.[376] Even where the employee had not been disciplined for offenses in the past, one arbitrator upheld the right of management to consider the conduct as a ground for denying promotion:

> When the requirements of the job . . . clearly call for maturity, reliability and a sense of responsibility in addition to technical skill or expertness, it would be less than logical to deny or preclude any consideration at all to offenses directly related thereto simply because such offenses through laxity or forbearance lost vitality as a basis for subsequent disciplinary action.[377]

However, other arbitrators have held that if alleged offenses are not made the subject of discipline at the time they are committed, management may not be permitted to rely on them later in assessing employee abilities and qualifications.[378] Furthermore, a single offense for which the worker has been disciplined may not be sufficient to compel the conclusion of incompetence,[379] and an employer may not automatically disqualify a candidate on the basis of a disciplinary action without considering the nature of the action and its relation to the work to be performed.[380]

The collective bargaining agreement may provide specifically or in effect that the personnel records of the employees be considered by management in determining ability. Under such an agreement, personnel records showing that four written reprimands were issued to the senior employee in connection with his work were considered by the arbitrator to justify management's decision to promote the junior employee.[381]

---

[374]*See* Browning-Ferris Indus., Case No., 98-10762, 1998 WL 1036134 (Kilroy, 1998).

[375]Dewey & Almy Chem. Co., 25 LA 316, 318–19 (Somers, 1955). *See also* Del Monte Corp., 76 LA 852, 853 (Kelliher, 1981); Illinois Dep'ts of Pers. & Corr., 72 LA 941, 946–48 (Rezler, 1979); Scioto Beverage Co., 50 LA 17, 20 (Stouffer, 1967); Emhart Mfg. Co., 43 LA 946, 949 (Turkus, 1964); Dixie Cup Co., 19 LA 639, 646–47 (Klamon, 1952).

[376]Crown Zellerbach Corp., 84 LA 277 (Allen, Jr., 1985).

[377]Emhart Mfg. Co., 43 LA 946, 949 (Turkus, 1964). *See also* Whirlpool Corp., 68 LA 357, 361 (Mann, Jr., 1977).

[378]*See* Joffe Bros., 73 LA 965, 967 (Rothschild, 1979); Be-Rite Delivery Serv., 54 LA 151, 155 (Carlson, 1971); Cleveland-Cliffs Iron Co., 24 LA 599, 600 (Kelliher, 1955); Bethlehem Steel, 19 LA 186, 188 (Killingsworth, 1952).

[379]*See* Copco Steel & Eng'g Co., 13 LA 586, 591 (Platt, 1949). *See also* Thompson Bros. Boat Mfg. Co., 55 LA 69, 73 (Moberly, 1970) ("inability does *not* mean temporary misconduct or improper work attitudes which more properly should be treated by corrective action").

[380]Roseville Cmty. Hosp., 92 LA 421 (Concepcion, 1989).

[381]Inland Steel Co., 16 LA 280, 284 (Cornsweet, 1951).

x.　*Employee's Physical and Psychological Fitness*
[LA CDI 119.125; 119.128]

Many contracts specifically include physical fitness as a requirement for job preference.[382] However, even where the contract does not contain the physical ability requirement, it has been said that the term "ability" includes physical (and mental) ability.[383] Health records showing an employee's physical condition have been considered as "tangible and objective" evidence of fitness and ability,[384] but "old" records as to an employee's physical condition ordinarily may not be relied on when more recent medical evidence is available.[385]

In the absence of a contractual prohibition, management has been held entitled to require employees to take physical examinations, but the right must be exercised properly and not arbitrarily, capriciously, or unreasonably.[386] Management could require such examinations to determine the physical fitness or ability of the employee to perform the work, for instance, before reinstatement or promotion of an ailing employee in a job requiring weight-lifting activities,[387] or before transfer or promotion of an employee to a job demanding greater physical effort,[388] or when there is serious doubt as to the employee's ability to perform the work safely because of some physical condition or characteristic.[389]

It would seem to be a corollary to this right that it is the duty of the employer to protect the health of its employees despite their willingness to perform heavier duties. In this regard, one arbitrator stated:

---

[382]*See, e.g.*, Hercules Inc., 61 LA 621, 624 (Murphy, 1973); Celanese Fibers Co., 51 LA 1143, 1144 (Altrock, 1969); Illinois Bell Tel. Co., 30 LA 237, 238 (Fleming, 1958); Pacific Gas & Elec. Co., 23 LA 556, 557 (Ross, 1954); Nickles Bakery, 17 LA 486, 487 (Randle, 1951).

[383]*See* J.R. Simplot Co., 53 LA 1181, 1193 (Simon, 1969); Pittsburgh Plate Glass Corp., 37 LA 1047, 1050 (Siciliano, 1962); Fairbanks Co., 32 LA 772, 774 (Jenson, 1959); Doehler-Jarvis Corp., 12 LA 896, 897 (Stashower, 1949). The terms "fitness" and "qualified" also include physical and mental fitness or ability. *See* Reichhold Chems., 49 LA 952, 955 (Williams, 1967); Kilgore Inc., 35 LA 391, 394 (Dworkin, 1960); Lockheed Aircraft Corp., 34 LA 67, 70 (Tatum, 1959). *Cf.* National Dairy Prods. Corp., 34 LA 426, 427 (Cahn, 1960) (involving past practice).

[384]*See* Southwestern Bell Tel. Co., 30 LA 862, 871 (Davis, 1958). *See also* Allegheny Ludlum Steel Corp., 42 LA 343, 344 (Shipman, 1963).

[385]*See* National Lead Co., 42 LA 176, 178 (Seidenberg, 1964); North Shore Gas Co., 40 LA 37, 44 (Sembower, 1963).

[386]*See* NSS Enters., 114 LA 1458 (West, 2000); Graphic Arts Ass'n of St. Louis, 45 LA 39, 42 (Bothwell, 1965); National Coop. Refinery Ass'n, 44 LA 92, 95 (Brown, 1964); Reynolds Metals Co., 42 LA 161, 164 (Phelps, 1964); North Shore Gas Co., 40 LA 37, 42–43 (Sembower, 1963). For related discussion, see Chapter 13, section 26.E., "Right to Require Physical Examination."

[387]*See* Southern Conn. Gas Co., 48 LA 1357, 1358 (Johnson, 1967); Fulton Glass Co., 31 LA 824, 826 (Boles, 1958). *See also* Chris-Kraft Corp., 27 LA 404, 406 (Bothwell, 1956) (involving recall).

[388]*See* Union Camp Corp., 68 LA 708, 709, 712 (Morgan, Jr., 1977); Fairbanks Co., 32 LA 772, 774–76 (Jenson, 1959); Doehler-Jarvis Corp., 12 LA 896, 897–98 (Stashower, 1949).

[389]*See* NSS Enters., 114 LA 1458, 1458 (West, 2000); Chatfield Paper Corp., 46 LA 530, 532 (McIntosh, 1966); National Coop. Refinery Ass'n, 44 LA 92, 95 (Brown, 1964); E.W. Bliss Co., 43 LA 217, 224 (Klein, 1964) (periodic examinations upheld); Reynolds Metals Co., 42 LA 161, 164 (Phelps, 1964); McDonnell Aircraft Corp., 37 LA 960, 966 (Klamon, 1961).

Indeed, the Company might incur a legal liability for failure to exercise due care and reasonable judgment to protect the health of operating employees. The ability to perform a job cannot be disassociated from the health hazards involved to male as well as female employees and action the Company takes in this regard is definitely within the inherent rights of Management to operate the plant safely and efficiently.[390]

When the question of physical fitness for a particular job arises, management may place primary emphasis on the physical disability of the by-passed employee to fill the job, while placing secondary emphasis on another employee's greater physical ability.[391] Thus, it has been held that if certain work contributes to or would cause a recurrence of an employee's ill health, the employee cannot justifiably claim physical fitness for that work.[392] Similarly, a physical defect or limitation that impairs an employee's physical fitness for a particular job has been held to render that employee ineligible for the job.[393] Like results were reached where the employee's physical condition

---

[390]Mengel Co., 18 LA 392, 399 (Klamon, Hannah, & Connolly, 1952). *See also* Southern Conn. Gas Co., 48 LA 1357, 1358 (Johnson, 1967) (the company, in requiring a physical examination, argued that "it had a responsibility to all employees to give them jobs which would not prove harmful to them"); Page Dairy Co., 42 LA 1051, 1056 (Kiroff, 1964) (the company's refusal to reinstate an employee was not justified by a mere "feeling" that he might hurt himself).

[391]*See* Geauga Plastics Co., 55 LA 975, 980–81 (May, 1970) (the employee suffered incapacitating injuries in an automobile accident after being promoted); Delta Match Corp., 53 LA 1282, 1287 (Marshall, 1969) (the company was not required to give a trial period to an employee who lacked the necessary physical coordination and dexterity); Celanese Fibers Co., 51 LA 1143, 1144 (Altrock, 1969) (physical ability means present, not prospective, ability); Bethlehem Steel Co., 5 LA 578, 581 (Brandschain, 1946). In *Simoniz Co.*, 54 LA 172, 174–75 (Talent, 1971), the company was upheld in denying an employee's request for demotion to his old job on the ground of physical inability to perform his new job; in so holding, the arbitrator stated that under the agreement such a request "would be left to management's prerogative to decide."

[392]*See* Ormet Corp., 97 LA 15, 19 (Bowers, 1991); Carter Prods., 45 LA 724, 726 (Kerrison, 1965); Catts Co., 42 LA 775, 780–81 (Singletary, 1964); Kilgore Inc., 35 LA 391, 395 (Dworkin, 1960); Taft-Peirce Mfg. Co., 20 LA 835, 836 (Bailer, 1953); Universal Mfg. Co., 13 LA 238, 241 (Spencer, 1949). *Cf.* National Gypsum Co., 23 LA 800, 803 (Trotta, 1954) (there was no conclusive evidence that the new job would aggravate grievant's condition).

[393]*See* USS, Div. of USX Corp., 98 LA 117, 117–18 (Neumeier, 1991); Quincy Paper Box Co., 79 LA 419, 420, 422 (Blackmar, 1982); State of Mont., 76 LA 202, 204 (Kleinsorge, 1981); Cessna Aircraft Co., 72 LA 367, 369 (Laybourne, 1979); Owens-Corning Fiberglas Corp., 51 LA 27, 28 (Jaffee, 1968) (speech impediment justified rejection for group leader job); Gulf States Utils. Co., 44 LA 1252, 1263 (Murphy, 1965) (epileptic not qualified for hazardous work); Sinclair Ref. Co., 42 LA 376, 385 (Willingham, 1964); Lockheed Aircraft Corp., 34 LA 67, 70–71 (Tatum, 1959); Corn Prods. Ref. Co., 27 LA 680, 682 (Updegraff, 1956). It has been emphasized that each case must be decided on its own facts. *See* Consolidated Gas Supply Corp., 51 LA 152, 155–56 (Altrock, 1968). For a summary of "the fundamental requirements for the successful incorporation of disabled people into a company's work force," see *J.R. Simplot Co.*, 53 LA 1181, 1188–89 (Simon, 1969), emphasizing that handicapped workers must be properly placed and stating: "The same standards should be used in evaluating a handicapped person's ability and/or qualifications as related to the job under consideration." The company was held justified in demoting a partially blind employee from a job operating mobile equipment when it became aware of his visual problems. *Id.* at 1192. For similar statements regarding handicapped persons, see *Glass Containers Mfrs. Inst.*, 66–3 ARB ¶8999 (Dworkin, 1966). Under the Rehabilitation Act of 1973, employers who enter into certain procurement contracts with the federal government must adopt affirmative action plans for employment and advancement of qualified handicapped individuals. 29 U.S.C. §§790, 793. Also, programs or activities receiving federal financial assistance are prohibited by the Rehabilitation Act from discriminating (including employment discrimination) against qualified handicapped individuals. *See* Consolidated Rail Corp. v. Darrone, 465 U.S. 624, 34 FEP

constituted a hazard to himself, to other employees, or to the plant and equipment.[394] However, neither the fact that the senior employee weighed less than the junior[395] nor the fact that the senior worker was older[396] has been considered proof that the senior person was less able to fulfill the physical requirements of the job. Furthermore, even under a relative ability clause that expressly included physical fitness as a factor, a senior employee suffering from hypertension was held entitled to fill a vacancy for which he was physically fit. In that case, the arbitrator stated that "the junior man might have been a superior physical specimen in every sense of the word to [grievant], but there was no showing that such outstanding physical fitness was required for the job" in question.[397] In another case, an arbitrator held that an employer improperly denied the request of a physically impaired employee who had missed only 1 day of work, and whose ability to perform the work had been confirmed by a neutral physician's report.[398]

Obesity has sometimes been advanced as a reason for refusal to reinstate an employee following a layoff or medical leave, or for refusal to promote a senior employee. Where excess weight or attending physical problems affected the employee's physical fitness for the work, arbitrators have upheld management in denying the employee that work.[399] However, where obesity has not adversely affected the employee's job performance in the past, management has not been permitted to deny the employee the job.[400]

In jobs where psychological requirements are important, an employee's fitness in this regard may also be examined. Thus, with respect to a job entailing "psychological strain and stress," one arbitrator stated:

> And, however intangible these psychological requirements may be, they are not to be minimized. . . . Indeed, just as the Umpire must be convinced that [grievant] does have the requisite experience and ability to do the job, so must

---

Cases 79 (1984). Under the ADA, covered employees are required to make reasonable accommodations for the known physical or mental disabilities of an otherwise qualified individual unless such accommodation would impose an undue hardship on the employer. See section 2.C., "Americans With Disabilities Act," above.

[394]Allegheny Ludlum Steel Corp., 42 LA 343, 344–45 (Shipman, 1963). *See also* United States Steel Corp., 82 LA 913 (Dybeck, 1984) (employee's eye injury resulted in little or no depth perception and job required great accuracy of judgment of speed and direction of molten metal); General Steel Indus., 77 LA 773, 775 (Seinsheimer, 1981). For related discussions, see Chapter 16, "Safety and Health."

[395]*See* Seagrave Corp., 16 LA 410, 412 (Lehoczky, 1951).

[396]*See* Combustion Eng'g Co., 20 LA 416, 419 (McCoy, 1953).

[397]Hercules Inc., 61 LA 621, 626 (Murphy, 1973).

[398]Gase Baking Co., 86 LA 206 (Block, 1985) (employee with emphysema wanted to bump into a janitorial position that would have exposed him to more heat, humidity, and flour dust).

[399]*See* Mutual Plastics Mold Corp., 48 LA 2, 9 (Block, 1967) (accompanying factors of dizziness, hand tremors, and marked nervousness posed a safety threat); Lamson & Sessions Co., 43 LA 61, 64 (Kates, 1964); Pittsburgh Plate Glass Corp., 37 LA 1047, 1050 (Siciliano, 1962). In *Keeney Mfg. Co.*, 37 LA 456, 458 (Donnelly, 1961), conflict of opinion between the company's doctor and the grievant's doctor resulted in a ruling requiring an examination by a neutral doctor.

[400]*See* Southwest Forest Indus., 79 LA 1100, 1103 (Cohen, 1982); Mutual Plastics Mold Corp., 48 LA 2, 9–10 (Block, 1967); Magnavox Co., 46 LA 719, 724 (Dworkin, 1966); Ford Motor Co., 8 LA 1015, 1016–17 (Shulman, 1947).

he be equally convinced that the psychological requirements thereof can also be fully met by him.[401]

An employee's temperament may disqualify him or her for a responsible job. An employee's nervousness and excitability in moments of emergency were considered grounds for rejecting his bid.[402] Where an employee was placed on medical leave after he admitted having a psychological condition that prevented his performing assigned duties, the employer justifiably refused to reinstate him until he obtained a full medical release stating that he could return to work with or without restrictions.[403] Furthermore, management's refusal to recall an employee in accordance with seniority was upheld where his mental condition prevented him from performing even the simplest duties without an abnormal amount of supervision.[404]

xi. Gender as a Factor [LA CDI 107.30]

In cases involving questions of discrimination on the basis of gender, arbitrators have held that management is obligated to determine fitness and ability in relation to the particular job based on the capabilities of the individual employee and not on stereotyped ideas of employees' capabilities as a group.[405] It follows that management may not refuse consideration of an employee solely on the basis of gender. Thus, it has been held that the employer discriminated on the basis of gender when it denied contested work to a senior female employee who was found to be qualified for the work not only on the basis of training, experience, and technical knowledge, but also physically.[406] In some instances where there has been doubt concerning the physical ability of the female employee to do the work, arbitrators have ordered a trial period.[407]

---

[401]Bethlehem Steel, 18 LA 683, 684–85 (Shipman, 1952) (management failed to prove to the arbitrator's satisfaction that the senior employee had exhibited anxiety and fear in connection with his work). In *Titanium Metals Corp.*, 49 LA 1144, 1146 (Block, 1967), an employee's fear of heights justified disqualifying him from a job requiring high crane duties after completing a trial period.

[402]*See* Pacific Gas & Elec. Co., 23 LA 556, 558–59 (Ross, 1954). *Cf.* Seeger Refrigerator Co., 16 LA 525, 528–31 (Lockhart, 1951).

[403]Danly Mach. Corp., 87 LA 883 (Cox, undated).

[404]*See* White Motor Co., 28 LA 823, 828–29 (Lazarus, 1957).

[405]*See, e.g.*, Gross Distrib., 55 LA 756, 760 (Allman, 1970); Missouri Pac. R.R., 55 LA 193, 195 (Sembower, 1970); Hough Mfg. Corp., 51 LA 785, 790 (Mueller, 1968); W.M. Chace Co., 48 LA 231, 234, 236–37 (Ellmann, 1966); International Paper Co., 47 LA 896, 898 (Williams, 1966). *See also* Portage Area Sch. Dist., 1999 WL 704989 (Duff, 1999); Pet Inc., 76 LA 32, 36, 42–43 (Goldstein, 1980).

[406]*See* Youngstown Hosp. Ass'n, 79 LA 324, 326–27 (Duff, 1982); Glass Containers Corp., 57 LA 997, 999 (Dworkin, 1971); American Air Filter Co., 57 LA 549, 552–53 (Dolson, 1971); Galesburg, Ill., Cmty. Unit Sch. Dist. 205, 55 LA 895, 896–97 (Seitz, 1970); Avco Corp., 54 LA 165, 166 (Turkus, 1971); Hough Mfg. Corp., 51 LA 785, 789–92 (Mueller, 1968); Buco Prods., 48 LA 17, 19 (Forsythe, 1966); Quaker Oats Co., 42 LA 433, 439 (Petree, 1964); United States Steel Corp., 36 LA 1082, 1087–88 (Crawford, 1961). In *Gross Distrib.*, 55 LA 756, 759–61 (Allman, 1970), it was found that the company violated the contract when it retained a junior male employee without attempting to determine the senior female employee's physical ability to do the work in question.

[407]*See* I-T-E Imperial Corp., 55 LA 1284, 1286–88 (White, 1970); Creative Indus., 49 LA 140, 144 (Gershenfeld, 1967) (male employees given trial period on "delicate" work); W.M. Chace Co., 48 LA 231, 234, 236 (Ellmann, 1966); Northwest Airlines, 46 LA 238, 242 (Elkouri,

Of course, discrimination in favor of female employees has likewise been held improper. Some examples include assigning preferential work locations to junior female employees instead of to senior males,[408] giving preferential treatment by not assigning the heavy duties of a female employee's job to the female employee,[409] and recalling a junior female employee from layoff instead of the senior male for work as a cafeteria helper.[410] However, an arbitrator held that a junior female employee may be awarded a cleanup job over a senior male bidder where sex is a bona fide occupational qualification, and the senior male bidder does not have the qualifications required by conventionally accepted standards.[411]

Conversely, management has been upheld in giving preference to junior male employees over senior female employees where there was adequate justification in the requirements or circumstances of the job or in the qualifications of the individual involved. Such justification has been found in the physical requirements of the job (e.g., heavy weight lifting, physical prowess, overtime hours),[412] in standards of morality or propriety,[413] and in the

---

1966); Dewey-Portland Cement Co., 43 LA 165, 170 (Sembower, 1964). In *Paterson Parchment Co.*, 47 LA 260, 262 (Buckwalter, 1966), a training period was ordered where the contract provided for such in bumping.

[408]Cincinnati Reds, 56 LA 748, 750 (Kates, 1971).

[409]Sterling Faucet Co., 54 LA 340, 342–43 (Duff, 1971). *Cf.* Crown Zellerbach Corp., 79 LA 170, 172 (Bernhardt, 1982).

[410]Allied Chem. Corp., 35 LA 268, 270 (Valtin, 1960) (two employees were relatively equal in ability and "the notion that the male animal suffers from natural handicaps to perform kitchen duties" was rejected). *See also* Orchids Paper Prods. Concel, 76 LA 101, 102 (Ross, 1980); Creative Indus., 49 LA 140, 144 (Gershenfeld, 1967).

[411]Airco Carbon, 86 LA 25 (Stoltenberg, 1985).

[412]*See* Missouri Pac. R.R., 55 LA 193, 195 (Sembower, 1970); Canton Provision Co., 52 LA 942, 944–45 (Altrock, 1969); Super Valu Stores, 52 LA 112, 114–15 (Davis, 1968); Electric Cord Sets, 51 LA 418, 420 (Kates, 1968); Capital Mfg. Co., 50 LA 669, 671–72 (Dworkin, 1968); Pitman-Moore Div., 49 LA 709, 714–18 (Seinsheimer, 1967) (an employee must be able to do *all* the job); General Fireproofing Co., 48 LA 819, 823–24 (Teple, 1967); Robertshaw Controls Co., 48 LA 101, 106 (Shister, 1967); Lockheed-Georgia Co., 46 LA 931, 934–35 (Steele, 1966); Apex Mach. & Tool Co., 45 LA 417, 423 (Layman, 1965); Dewey-Portland Cement Co., 43 LA 165, 169 (Sembower, 1964); Minute Maid Co., 40 LA 920, 923 (Goodman, 1963); Advanced Structures, 39 LA 1094, 1097 (Roberts, 1963); Art Metal Constr. Co., 36 LA 458, 462 (Reid, 1961) (grievance sustained in theory but denied in fact because there was no work the female employees could perform); Electrical Eng'g & Mfg. Corp., 35 LA 657, 661 (Roberts, 1960); National Gypsum Co., 34 LA 41, 45 (Hebert, 1959). *See also* Pennzoil, 78 LA 1070, 1071 (Stonehouse, 1982). In *Sperry-Rand Corp.*, 46 LA 961, 964–65 (Seitz, 1966), it was held that the company could require female employees to take physical examinations although males were not required to do so, because the jobs in question required physical exertion that "may well be beyond the capacity of some women or dangerous to some." For an illustration of the problems that may be created by totally eliminating sex distinctions in the filling of jobs, see *Eagle Mfg. Co.*, 51 LA 970, 972–73, 983 (Lugar, 1968). *See also* Standard Brands, 59 LA 596, 598 (Dolnick, 1972).

[413]*See* Airco, 70 LA 760, 761 (France, 1978); City of Erie, Pa., Bd. of Educ. Sch. Dist., 70 LA 567, 569 (Duff, 1978) (school employer could bypass male physical education instructor and select female instructor, where the physical education program required the instructor to be physically present in the girls' locker room to observe emotional and other problems of students while changing clothes); FMC Corp., 70 LA 110, 112 (Shister, 1978); Corn Prods. Co. Int'l, 54 LA 303, 305–06 (Gross, 1971) (female properly was denied job of janitress in men's room); Bureau of Prisons, 52 LA 624, 631–32 (Marshall, 1969) (female teacher properly was denied position with Bureau of Prisons); Hercules Powder Co., 45 LA 448, 449–50 (Shafer, 1965) (male properly was denied job of janitress in women's restroom). *See also* Long Beach Naval Shipyard, 75 LA 63, 66 (Gentile, 1980); Brown County Mental Health Ctr., 68 LA 1363, 1365 (Lee, 1977). *Cf.* Frito-Lay, Inc., 54 LA 1142, 1144–46 (Bernstein, 1971); United States Steel Corp., 36 LA 1082, 1083 (Crawford, 1961).

female employee's lack of training, experience, or technical knowledge.[414] In such cases, it is the justifying factor, and not the gender of the individual that disqualifies the employee.

When friction between employees of different gender makes it impossible for them to work together, companies may transfer the junior employee from his or her classification or shift. However, an employer was found to have violated the contract when it followed this procedure and removed a female employee from her classification and shift because she had complained of sexual harassment by a male coworker.[415]

In many of the cases cited in this subtopic, the arbitrators referred to Title VII of the Civil Rights Act of 1964 or to state antidiscrimination laws. In some of the earlier cases, the arbitrator referred to state protective laws for women, but the dearth of recent arbitration decisions suggests that they no longer constitute a significant factor in arbitration. Title VII prohibits discrimination in employment based on sex, in addition to race, color, religion, and national origin. However, the Civil Rights Act provides that "it shall not be an unlawful employment practice for an employer to hire and employ employees . . . on the basis of . . . religion, sex, or national origin in those certain instances where religion, sex, or national origin is a bona fide occupational qualification reasonably necessary to the normal operation of that particular business or enterprise . . . ."[416]

---

[414]*See* Continental Tel. Co. of Cal., 57 LA 929, 930 (Jones, Jr., 1971); Kingsberry Homes Corp., 53 LA 1345, 1346–48 (Rauch, 1969) (although the female employee probably had the physical strength and stamina for the job); Pipe Fitters Local 205, 47 LA 836, 840 (Merrill, 1966); Lockheed-Georgia Co., 43 LA 289, 293–94 (Hawley, 1964) (to rearrange duties so that female employee could handle the job would result in discrimination in favor of female employees against male employees).

[415]Champion Int'l Corp., 105 LA 429 (Fullmer, 1995).

[416]Section 703(e). Another statute that may have relevance in this area is the Equal Pay Act of 1963, 29 U.S.C. §§201, 206, which amended the Fair Labor Standards Act, 29 U.S.C. §201 et seq. For related discussion, see section 2.A., "Civil Rights Act," above; Chapter 10, section 3.A.i., "Title VII of the Civil Rights Act." For some relevant Supreme Court decisions, see *Arizona Governing Comm. v. Norris*, 463 U.S. 1073, 32 FEP Cases 233 (1983) (paying a woman lower monthly retirement benefits than a man who made the same contributions violates Title VII (just as does requiring a woman to pay larger contributions to obtain the same benefits), and use of sex-segregated mortality tables to calculate retirement benefits violates Title VII whether or not the tables reflect an accurate prediction of longevity of women as a class); *Personnel Adm'r of Mass. v. Feeney*, 442 U.S. 256, 19 FEP Cases 1377 (1979) (a statute requiring veterans to be ranked above all other candidates for state civil service positions does not deny equal protection to women); *Dothard v. Rawlinson*, 433 U.S. 321, 15 FEP Cases 10 (1977) (height and weight qualifications for employment, which had a disproportionate impact on women applicants, were impermissible under Title VII as being based on stereotyped characterizations of the sexes and not bona fide occupational qualifications (but the refusal to employ female guards for some positions in certain maximum security male penitentiaries was upheld)); *Corning Glass Works v. Brennan*, 417 U.S. 188, 21 WH Cases 767 (1974) (an illegal discrimination had been improperly perpetuated by retention of a "red circle" rate for males who had been paid a higher rate on the night shift than was paid females on the day shift at a time when state law prohibited the employment of women at night); *Phillips v. Martin Marietta Corp.*, 400 U.S. 542, 3 FEP Cases 40 (1971) (Title VII does not permit one hiring policy for women with preschool-age children and another policy for men with such children, unless it is established to be a bona fide occupational qualification reasonably necessary to the normal operation of the particular business or enterprise). For related discussion, see Employment Discrimination Law ch. 12 (Lindemann & Grossman eds., BNA Books 3d ed. 1996); Wrong, *Arbitrators, the Law, and Women's Job Bids*, 33 Lab. L.J. 798 (1982); Rosenberg, *Sex Discrimination and the Labor Arbitration Process*, 30 Lab. L.J. 102 (1979).

Prior to the Civil Rights Act, some arbitrators felt bound by the particular agreement or the parties' past practice, which provided for separate classifications and separate seniority lists for male and female employees.[417] In one case arising after the Civil Rights Act, where separate lines of progression were maintained in such a way as to provide male employees with experience on higher-rated jobs through temporary assignments, the arbitrator directed the employer and the union (which had countenanced the practice) to negotiate integration of the lines.[418]

Subsequent to the Civil Rights Act, many parties incorporated antidiscrimination language into their agreements. In finding a violation of such a contract, an arbitrator emphasized that "[m]ale and female employees have equal claim to any work opportunity, subject only to their being eligible and qualified."[419] Under a contract containing a clause obligating the parties to "fully comply with applicable laws and regulations regarding discrimination," it was held that the clause was violated by a scheduling plan adopted without intent to discriminate but that did have the "disparate impact" of laying off female employees while hiring males. In this case, the arbitrator pointed to Supreme Court decisions recognizing that the Civil Rights Act may be violated if the practice producing the unintentional disparate impact cannot be justified by business necessity. The employer in the arbitration proceeding failed to establish business necessity and its bona fide occupation qualification claim.[420]

xii. *Personal Characteristics of Employee* [LA CDI 119.1221]

Personal characteristics of an employee may be considered if they relate directly to an ability to meet job requirements. For example, management was allowed to take into consideration the fact that an employee had been guilty in the past of certain "injudicious conduct and conversation"—evincing an interest in the cult of nudism—because the job involved not only technical knowledge but also public relations. In that case, an arbitrator stated:

> [Grievant's] interest in nudism so expressed itself as to create in management's mind a reasonable doubt as to this employee's discretion and customer-acceptance on the service job for which he bid. It should be made clear that such reaction has no necessary relation to the employee's beliefs or personal ideas. It relates directly to the question of what the job requires and a worker's ability

---

[417]*See* Owens-Illinois Glass Co., 43 LA 715, 720–21 (Dworkin, 1964); Northern Engraving & Mfg. Co., 43 LA 460, 462–63 (Eckhardt, 1964); Mead Corp., 43 LA 391, 394 (Halley, 1964) (employer's procedure also had been upheld in three prior awards under the contract); Mead Corp., 42 LA 224, 227–28 (Marshall, 1963); Container Stapling Corp., 42 LA 182, 184 (Talent, 1964); Minute Maid Co., 40 LA 920, 923 (Goodman, 1963).

[418]South Pittsburgh Water Co., 56 LA 1242, 1244–45 (Altrock, 1971).

[419]Glass Containers Corp., 57 LA 997, 999 (Dworkin, 1971).

[420]A.J. Bayless Mkts., 79 LA 703, 715–17 (Finston, 1982) (also noted that under §703(h) of the Civil Rights Act, discriminatory intent is required in order for discrimination produced by operation of bona fide seniority systems to become illegal, but the arbitrator inferred that the present dispute did not involve the seniority system). For a summary statement concerning employment practices that have disparate impact, see *Teamsters v. United States (T.I.M.E.-DC, Inc.)*, 431 U.S. 324, 335 n.15, 14 FEP Cases 1514 (1977).

to meet these requirements. A decision as to this is management's right and prerogative.[421]

An employee's attitude may be an important issue, depending on the nature of the job. In determining whether an employee is qualified for a job, supervision may evaluate the employee's attitude, including his or her "conscientious application, care for materials, concern for others in a group and response to instruction."[422] In one case, a senior employee's poor attitude was sufficient cause to award a job in a landfill to a junior employee. The landfill was a heavily regulated environment, and the position thus required solid interpersonal skills and the ability to follow orders.[423] In another case, an employee's attitude toward the job and spirit of cooperation were held to be subsumed within the term in the word "qualifications" as used in the contractual seniority provisions. The senior employee's uncooperative attitude was properly considered in denying promotion to a better job.[424] In a similar case management was again upheld in giving preference to junior employees over senior employees where, although the senior employee had the experience and aptitude for the job, he lacked the important requisites of a mature and dedicated attitude,[425] or "interest, effort and basic . . . knowledge" of the job.[426]

---

[421]Gisholt Mach. Co., 20 LA 137, 141 (Baab, 1953). See also U.S. Plywood Corp., 49 LA 726, 728 (Amis, 1967) (involving in part the "personal conduct" of an employee); Coca-Cola Bottling Co., 18 LA 757, 760 (Murphy, 1952) (involving a "special class of clients"); Standard Oil Co., 16 LA 586, 587–88 (Pollard, 1951) (the company failing to prove inability to perform the "human relations" part of a job). In Eagle-Picher Mining & Smelting Co., 8 LA 108, 111 (Potter, 1947), the filing of a suit by an employee against his employer was held not to affect his qualifications, the word "qualifications" being said to relate to physical fitness and ability rather than to "moral" qualifications.

[422]Amerace Corp., 52 LA 59, 61 (Maxwell, 1969) (the company did not discriminate against an employee when it disqualified him, on the basis of attitude, for a job vacancy to which he had been assigned for training). For other cases in which an employee's negative attitude was a factor against the employee, see Stayton Canning Co., 75 LA 2, 6 (Axon, 1980); Midwest Tanning Co., 69 LA 803, 805 (Rauch, 1977); American Welding & Mfg. Co., 52 LA 889, 893–94 (Stouffer, 1969) (the employee displayed an attitude of unwillingness to learn, rejecting instruction). In Dewey & Almy Chem. Co., 25 LA 316, 318–19 (Somers, 1955), the arbitrator stated: "A promotion represents a public recognition of an employee's ability, merit and capacity to do a higher-paid job. It would be destructive of morale to give such recognition to an employee who has shown lack of concern for his work and for his fellow employees."

[423]Browning-Ferris Indus., Case No. 98-10762, 1998 WL 1036134 (Kilroy, 1998).

[424]Norwich Pharmacal Co., 30 LA 740, 742–43 (Willcox, 1958). See also Christy Vault Co., 42 LA 1093, 1096 (Koven, 1964); Great W. Sugar Co., 41 LA 528, 534 (Seligson, 1963) (management could place strong weight on the factors of cooperation and ability to get along with others).

[425]Leach Co., 51 LA 382, 383 (Hazelwood, 1968). See also Charleston Naval Shipyard, 80 LA 708, 712 (Dallas, 1983) (at the job interview the unsuccessful senior applicant had an "indifferent, hostile, and lackadaisical" attitude toward the job); City of Dayton, Ohio, 78 LA 1114, 1119 (Daniel, 1982) (finding that the grievant was seeking the "position simply to transfer out of his current assignment," where he was having difficulty "in getting along with his superior"); Georgia Power Co., 75 LA 181, 188 (Hunter, 1980); Lovejoy, Inc., 74 LA 811, 814 (Herman, 1980) (the grievant "had not displayed the responsibility on the job which the Company had the right to expect"); Boise Cascade Corp., 73 LA 1215, 1217 (Babiskin, 1979) (a factor against grievant was his unwillingness to "pull his share of the load").

[426]United States Steel Corp., 51 LA 264, 266 (Smith, 1968). See also Kaiser Found. Health Plan, 94 LA 266 (Kaufman, 1990). But see Electronics & Space Corp., 98 LA 460 (Harrison, 1991) (fact that employee was contentious, abrasive, and did not get along with supervisor was not valid criteria for promotion decision).

However, one arbitrator held that an employee's alleged "surly and un-cooperative" attitude could justify denying a promotion only if it were shown that efforts had been made, without success, to correct his attitude, and that the attitude detracted seriously from the employee's ability to perform the job.[427] Another arbitrator found that an employer's failure to award a posted job to the only bidder because the employee was "hyper" and did not work safely violated the contract. The arbitrator questioned the meaning and validity of the term "hyper," and ruled that, because the employer had failed to show the grievant was not capable or qualified, the grievant must be afforded an on-the-job opportunity.[428]

Special requirements of the job may call for particular attributes other than technical knowledge. For example, the job may require qualities of leadership,[429] initiative,[430] the capacity for independent judgment or self-reliance,[431] the ability to get along with others,[432] the ability to deal with a "special class" of customers,[433] or availability for emergency work.[434]

---

[427]Bethlehem Steel, 19 LA 186, 188 (Killingsworth, 1952). *See also* Helm, Inc., 92 LA 1295 (Feldman, 1989) (employer improperly denied senior employee's job bid because of alleged negative attitude, poor performance, and untrustworthiness, where allegations were unsupported generalities and employee was never counseled or warned about substandard conduct). In *Pittsburgh Annealing Box Co.*, 74 LA 266, 268 (Stoltenberg, 1980), the grievant had been reprimanded for spending time away from his work area and for talking too much, but the arbitrator stated that if these offenses occurred in such a manner as to impair job performance, "they should have been dealt with when they occurred," and that because "they were not matters of discipline, beyond an occasional verbal warning, they cannot now be relied upon as evidence of" lack of ability to perform the work). *See also* Ralph M. Parsons Co., 69 LA 290, 293 (Rule, 1977). In *Carpenters Dist. Council San Diego County*, 76 LA 513, 515–16 (Kaufman, 1981), the arbitrator drew a distinction between considering attitude as a factor in promotion, where the employee is being rewarded, and in layoff; attitude could not be a factor in layoff where the grievants had never been disciplined or otherwise put on notice that their attitude problems might cost them their jobs.

[428]Carling Nat'l Breweries, 83 LA 385 (Lewis, 1984).

[429]*See* Solar Turbines Int'l, 76 LA 1010, 1012–13 (Rule, 1981); Rajay Indus., 74 LA 181, 184 (Gentile, 1980); Brookhaven Nat'l Lab., 54 LA 447, 448 (Wolff, 1971); Standard Oil Co. of Cal., 54 LA 298, 302 (Beeson, 1971); Dempster Bros., 48 LA 777, 780 (Cantor, 1967); Penn Controls, 45 LA 129, 130–31 (Larkin, 1965); Great W. Sugar Co., 41 LA 528, 534 (Seligson, 1963).

[430]*See* Standard Oil Co. of Cal., 54 LA 298, 302 (Beeson, 1971); Smart & Final Iris Co., 51 LA 896, 898–99 (Block, 1968); Dempster Bros., Inc., 48 LA 777, 780 (Cantor, 1967); Semling-Menke Co., 46 LA 523, 527 (Graff, 1966); Dixie Cup Co., 19 LA 639, 647 (Klamon, 1952). In *Penn Controls*, 45 LA 129, 130–31 (Larkin, 1965), where the job of leadman required qualities of leadership and initiative, the senior employee had demonstrated initiative in developing his own business outside of work; but it was held that "the Company has every right first to look to the factors of initiative, efficiency and leadership qualities displayed on the jobs within the plant," and the junior employee was "ahead of" the senior employee in this respect.

[431]*See* A&E Plasti Pak Co., 76 LA 142, 144 (Modjeska, 1980); Brookhaven Nat'l Lab., 54 LA 447, 448 (Wolff, 1971); Standard Oil Co. of Cal., 54 LA 298, 302 (Beeson, 1971); Southern Ohio Fabricators, 44 LA 283, 285–86 (Schmidt, 1965); Dixie Cup Co., 19 LA 639, 647 (Klamon, 1952).

[432]*See* Smart & Final Iris Co., 51 LA 896, 898–99 (Block, 1968); U.S. Plywood Corp., 49 LA 726, 728 (Amis, 1967); Armstrong Rubber Co., 45 LA 1028, 1030 (McCoy, 1966) (the senior employee was argumentative and the job required a person with an "equable, tactful disposition"); Southern Ohio Fabricators, 44 LA 283, 285–86 (Schmidt, 1965); Christy Vault Co., 42 LA 1093, 1096 (Koven, 1964); Great W. Sugar Co., 41 LA 528, 534 (Seligson, 1963).

[433]*See* Coca-Cola Bottling Co., 18 LA 757, 759–60 (Murphy, 1952).

[434]*See* Alabama Power Co., 19 LA 393, 396 (Hawley, 1952) (the grievant lived some distance from town and had no telephone).

xiii. Age as a Factor [LA CDI 119.1223]

The conflict between the interests of management and the interests of the employees over the use of age as a factor in awarding employment opportunities is evident from the following statement by an arbitrator in a decision holding that an employee's age may not be used as an automatic disqualification for a particular job:

> It is not unreasonable that Management should hesitate to invest great amounts of time and money in an apprentice, who because of age will be unable to offer many years service as a new craftsman. Some "rule of reason" then properly should be followed. But clearly, to favor youth above "seniority" is to do violence to benefits traditionally provided longer service employees. And, it surely is unreasonable . . . to assume that all persons above a given calendar age are lacking in basic ability or physical fitness for a particular job, and that persons below that age level do possess such qualifications. Such an arbitrary classification, at the very least, fails to give due weight to the fact that people "age" at radically different rates, both physically and mentally. Moreover, it appears that, historically, seniority and age have been correlative concepts, generally, to determine employee rights under the . . . Agreement.
> . . . The point is that . . . age, per se, reasonably may not be established as a proper basis for barring further consideration of other relevant qualifying factors in the selection of employees to fill apprenticeship or other vacancies . . . .[435]

The age of an older applicant or, in some cases, of a younger applicant may not be viewed as a necessarily negative consideration without a showing that the applicant's age had adversely affected physical or mental ability in such a way as to render the applicant incapable of meeting the job requirements—but in such event it would be lack of ability, and not age per se, that constitutes the bar.[436] Such was the ruling in an early case where the job required continuous close attention and a great deal of visual inspection. There, the arbitrator upheld the employer's determination that a 73-year-old employee did not have the necessary qualifications.[437]

In one case where the agreement prohibited age discrimination, the union contended that such discrimination "must be presumed" because "on this and previous occasions, the job in question was awarded to persons junior to the grievant." However, the arbitrator stated that the union had "the burden of proving that the grievant was the victim of age discrimination," but "did not meet its burden of making a prima facie case," and that he had been

---

[435]United States Steel Corp., 55 LA 659, 662–63 (McDaniel, 1970).

[436]*See* United States Steel Corp., 57 LA 237, 251–52 (McDermott, 1971); United States Steel Corp., 55 LA 659 (McDaniel, 1970); Scott Paper Co., 49 LA 45, 46–47 (Hogan, 1967) ("Age may or may not affect ability critically, depending on the man and the job."). None of the above cases made reference to the ADEA. In *William Volker & Co.*, 60 LA 349 (Block, 1973), an otherwise qualified bidder for a truck driver vacancy was disqualified by the employer because he was under the age of 21, making insurance coverage available only at a higher premium rate. In sustaining the grievance, the arbitrator considered the increased cost of insurance to be unrelated to the job's requirements, and he stated that, while the grievant "falls into a broad statistical category (those under 21) that may involve a higher risk," this factor, "*in itself*, does not prove the Grievant less qualified because it relies upon a sweeping generalization, rather than on an evaluation of his qualifications." *Id*. at 353 (emphasis in original).

[437]Emmons Looms Harness Co., 11 LA 409, 411 (Meyers, 1948).

passed over for other, legitimate reasons.[438]

Youth can be a proper consideration and an advantage in the competition for promotions when it is associated with knowledge of the latest techniques for performing the job. Where a collective bargaining agreement did not provide for promotion by seniority, an arbitrator found that the employer did not act in an arbitrary, capricious, or discriminatory manner when it selected the least senior bidder. The arbitrator concluded that the junior employee was more knowledgeable about the latest requirements and techniques of the position.[439]

Under the ADEA of 1967, as amended in 1987, which in general protects "individuals who are at least 40 years of age," it is unlawful for an employer:

> (1) to fail or refuse to hire or to discharge any individual or otherwise discriminate against any individual with respect to his compensation, terms, conditions, or privileges of employment, because of such individual's age; (2) to limit, segregate, or classify his employees in any way which would deprive or tend to deprive any individual of employment opportunities or otherwise adversely affect his status as an employee, because of such individual's age; or (3) to reduce the wage rate of any employee in order to comply with this Act.[440]

One arbitrator, after considering the ADEA, upheld the company's maximum age limit of 32 for entering a training program, stating:

> There was no illegal application of age limits which resulted in the grievant's rejection. Federal protection against age discrimination does not extend to persons under the age of 40. Furthermore, an age maximum for entry into a training program of extended duration is a reasonable qualification and is so recognized in the administration of apprenticeship programs generally.[441]

Even prior to the ADEA, in the absence of any age limitation in the contract and of any showing that the age of the employee detracted from the ability to perform the job, arbitrators appeared reluctant to permit management to rely on age as a justification for passing over a senior employee who otherwise met the job qualifications in favor of a junior employee.[442]

Several decisions have held that an employer is arbitrary in barring an

---

[438]Charleston Naval Shipyard, 80 LA 708, 712 (Dallas, 1983). *See also* American Standard, 53 LA 1157, 1159–60 (Purdom, 1969). In *United States Int'l Trade Comm'n*, 78 LA 1, 3–4 (Jones, Jr., 1981), the "evidence as a whole" negated the charge of age discrimination. For extensive discussion of what is required in order to establish a violation of the ADEA, see Player, *Proof of Disparate Treatment Under the Age Discrimination in Employment Act: Variations on a Title VII Theme*, 17 Ga. L. Rev. 621 (1983).

[439]Johnson Controls, 101 LA 964 (Cohen, 1993).

[440]29 U.S.C. §§623, 631. Pub. L. No. 99-592, §2(c)(1) directed that the age limitation of "but less than 70 years of age" be deleted (1986). The coverage and scope of the ADEA is discussed in Chapter 13, section 25., "Compulsory Retirement." For related discussion, see section 2.B., "Age Discrimination in Employment Act," above.

[441]Aro, Inc., 52 LA 372, 375 (Kesselman, 1969).

[442]*See* CIBA Pharm. Co., 41 LA 14, 18 (Berkowitz, 1963) (a 56-year-old employee should be given a physical examination to determine if he is fit for the job); North Shore Gas Co., 31 LA 994, 999–1000 (Anrod, 1958) (age limit of 30 was arbitrary and unreasonable as was barring a 34-year-old employee solely because of age); Corn Prods. Ref. Co., 20 LA 142, 147 (Gilden, 1953) (35-year-age limit was not justified for the job in question—the real test is physical ability and qualifications).

employee from an apprenticeship or a training vacancy solely because of age.[443] But other decisions have concluded that the company could set a reasonable age limit for apprenticeships or training programs.[444]

xiv. *Drug Abuse as a Factor* [LA CDI 119.1225]

Several cases have held that mandatory universal drug testing of applicants for a promotion or transfer is unreasonable because it does not necessarily relate to an employee's fitness for present duty but rather is testing for off-duty drug use and is therefore an invasion of privacy.[445] Thus, an employer was found to have improperly required laid-off employees to submit to drug screening as a condition for recall and to have violated the contract by refusing to reinstate three who tested positive for marijuana. The arbitrator reasoned that layoff status does not, by itself, create reasonable cause to test, and, in any event, the asserted practice of drug testing all recalled employees had not been applied uniformly.[446]

xv. *Interview Results* [LA CDI 119.1221]

Interview results, while not always determinative, may have a bearing on fitness and ability if they are fair and related to the job performance. Therefore, an employer may, under a relative ability clause, properly select a junior employee with a few months' experience over a senior employee with several years of experience on the basis of superior performance during an interview.[447]

An employer's promotion of a junior employee was upheld, even though the labor agreement listed job performance as a criterion of relative ability, because two interviewers rated the grieving senior employee less qualified than the junior employee in 8 out of 10 comparative categories.[448] Moreover,

---

[443]*See* American Smelting Ref. Co., 28 LA 557, 558–59 (Ross, 1957) (48-year-old employee was entitled to the job if equal in ability); Goodyear Tire & Rubber Co., 28 LA 374, 378–79 (Thompson, 1957) (absolute limit excluding employees over 40 from bidding was arbitrary and unreasonable); California Elec. Co., 19 LA 508, 512–14 (Kaplan, 1952) (company's denial of 38-year-old senior's bid on ground that he was too old was improper). *See also* Central Screw Co., 11 LA 108, 109 (Edes, 1948) (the senior employee was younger).

[444]*See* Pittsburgh Steel Co., 47 LA 88, 90–91 (McDermott, 1966) (age limit of 35 upheld); Western Air Lines, 34 LA 756, 759–60 (Wyckoff, 1960) (airline could set an age limit of 60 for training on new and faster aircraft); Sutherland Paper Co., 25 LA 716, 721 (Kallenbach, 1955) (age limit of 35 was not unreasonable). *See also* Libby, McNeill, & Libby, 37 LA 553, 558–61 (Tsukiyama, 1961). While agreeing that a proper age limit would not be unreasonable, an arbitrator found that 30 was too low, Ball Bros. Co., 46 LA 1153, 1157 (Kates, 1966), another arbitrator found that 50 was too low, National Coop. Refinery Ass'n, 44 LA 92, 95 (Brown, 1966). In *Ozark Smelting & Mining Div.*, 46 LA 697, 698–99 (Schedler, 1966), where the contract stated that a "beginning trainee shall not be over 40," the age limit was liberally construed to mean that an employee is not "over 40" until the day before his 41st birthday, the arbitrator noting conflicting court decisions on the general subject of age.

[445]Boston Edison Co., 92 LA 374 (Nicolau, 1988).

[446]ITT Barton Instruments Co., 89 LA 1196 (Draznin, 1987). For related discussion, see Chapter 13, section 17.F.iii., "Drug and Alcohol Policies," and section 26.F., "Drug and Alcohol Testing," and Chapter 16, section 2.A., "Alcohol and/or Drug Use and Testing."

[447]Kroger Co., 89 LA 1307 (Byars, 1987).

where a junior employee and the grievant had the same technical skills, but the junior employee's answers to interview questions revealed an aptitude for handling the supervisory responsibilities of the job, the company was found to have been justified in awarding the job to the junior employee.[449]

An interview, however, must be validly structured and fairly conducted. If the evaluation is deemed to be too subjective, or the questions put to the candidates too far removed from the nature of the duties required, the results may not be relied on.[450] It is questionable whether a company may utilize the interview as the sole criterion for awarding the job.[451]

---

[448]Redlands, Cal., Unified Sch. Dist., 91 LA 657 (Bickner, 1988). *See also* State of Minn., 91 LA 68 (Bognanno, 1988).

[449]Northstar Print Group, 2000 WL 1670571 (Vernon, 2000).

[450]Cook County, 1998 WL 1036133 (Briggs, 1998); Stearns County, Minn., 90 LA 1181 (Kapsch, Sr., 1988).

[451]American Red Cross, 114 LA 823 (Ellmann, 2000) (company acted arbitrarily and capriciously in not factoring employee's excellent work history with company against nervousness in interview).

Chapter 15

Discipline and Discharge

1. Introduction

Discharge or disciplinary penalties assessed by management constitute a significant percentage of the cases that reach arbitration. This chapter explores many of the concepts and standards that have been applied by arbitrators in cases of this nature.[1]

---

[1]For books on discharge and discipline, see Discipline and Discharge in Arbitration (Brand ed., BNA Books 1998 & Supp. 2001); Koven & Smith, Just Cause: The Seven Tests (BNA Books 2d ed., revised by Farwell 1992); Redecker, Employee Discipline: Policies and Practices (BNA Books 1989); Ewing, Do It My Way or You're Fired: Employee Rights and the Changing Role of Management Prerogatives (1983); Coulson, The Termination Handbook (1981); Zack & Bloch, The Arbitration of Discipline Cases: Concepts and Questions (1979); Stessin, Employee Discipline (BNA Books 1960). See also books and articles cited in Labor Arbitration: An Annotated Bibliography 48–49, 115-33 (Coleman & Haynes eds., 1994). For other discussions, see Labor and Employment Arbitration chs. 14–22 (Bornstein, Gosline, & Greenbaum eds., 2d ed. 2001); Common Law of the Workplace: The Views of Arbitrators chs. 5–6 (St. Antoine ed., BNA Books 1998); Fabiano, *The Meaning of Just Cause for Termination When an Employer Alleges Misconduct and the Employee Denies It*, 44 Hastings L.J. 399 (1993); Freed & Polsby, *Just Cause for Termination Rules and Economic Efficiency*, 38 Emory L.J. 1097 (1989); Sherman, *The Role and Rights of the Individual in Labor Arbitration*, 15 Wm. Mitchell L. Rev. 379 (1989); Heinsz, *Judicial Review of Labor Arbitration Awards: The* Enterprise Wheel *Goes Around and Around*, 52 Mo. L. Rev. 243 (1987); Knight, *The Impact of Arbitration on the Administration of Disciplinary Policies*, 39 Arb. J. No. 1, at 43 (1984); Nelson, *Insubordination: Arbitral 'Law' in the Reconciliation of Conflicting Employer/Employee Interests*, 35 Lab. L.J. 112 (1984); Malinowski, *An Empirical Analysis of Discharge Cases and the Work History of Employees Reinstated by Labor Arbitrators*, 36 Arb. J. No. 1, at 31 (1981); Saxton, *The Discipline and Discharge Case: Two Devil's Advocates on What Arbi-*

2. MANAGEMENT RIGHT TO DISCIPLINE [LA CDI 118.02]

A. The Employment-at-Will Doctrine[2]

i. The Doctrine

The employment-at-will doctrine, simply stated, means that any employment relationship that is not in writing and is intended to last for an indefinite period of time may be terminated by either party, at any time, for any reason or for no reason at all.[3] This doctrine was developed in the late 1800s by American courts and remained in effect without modification or exceptions until the mid-1930s, when the U.S. Supreme Court, in *Jones & Laughlin Steel*,[4] upheld provisions in the National Labor Relations Act (NLRA)[5] forbidding an employer from firing an employee for engaging in union activity.

In the absence of a collective bargaining agreement, most arbitrators have recognized the employment-at-will principle, concluding that the only restrictions on management's right to discipline and discharge employees

---

trators Are Doing Wrong: I. A Management Advocate's View, in ARBITRATION OF SUBCONTRACTING AND WAGE INCENTIVE DISPUTES, PROCEEDINGS OF THE 32D ANNUAL MEETING OF NAA 63 (Stern & Dennis eds., BNA Books 1980); Miller, *II. A Union Advocate's View, id.* at 75; Fallon, *Comment, id.* at 82; Jones, *Ramifications of Back-Pay Awards in Suspension and Discharge Cases: I. Ramifications of Back-Pay Awards in Discharge Cases*, in ARBITRATION AND SOCIAL CHANGES, PROCEEDINGS OF THE 22D ANNUAL MEETING OF NAA 163 (Somers & Dennis eds., BNA Books 1970); Fisher, *II. Ramifications of Back Pay in Suspension and Discharge Cases, id.* at 175.

[2]For more complete information on the employment-at-will doctrine, see GOGGIN & GROSSE, EMPLOYMENT AT WILL, FEDERAL PRACTICE MANUAL ch. 21.16 (1986); Morris, *Exploding Myths: An Empirical and Economic Reassessment of the Rise of Employment at Will*, 59 Mo. L. REV. 679 (1994); Pennington, *Comment, The Public Policy Exception to the Employment-at-Will Doctrine*, 68 TULANE L. REV. 1583 (1994); Michaels, *At-Will Employment—Change Past Due*, 57 JUL INTER-ALIA 7 (Nev. Bar Rev. 1992); DeNegris, *The Public Policy Exception: The Need to Reform Florida's at-Will Employment Doctrine After* Jarvinen v. HCA Allied Clinical Laboratories *and* Bellamy v. Halcomb, 16 NOVA L. REV. 1079 (1992); Summers, *The Contract of Employment and the Rights of Individual Employees: Fair Representation and Employment at Will*, 52 FORDHAM L. REV. 1082 (1984).

[3]Wilder v. Cody County Chamber of Commerce, 868 P.2d 211, 217, 9 IER Cases 225 (Wyo. 1994).

[4]NLRB v. Jones & Laughlin Steel Corp., 301 U.S. 1, 1 LRRM 703 (1937). In 1908, the Supreme Court struck down provisions of the Railway Labor Act, 45 U.S.C. §151 et seq., that made discrimination for membership in a labor organization a crime:

> [I]t is not within the functions of government—at least, in the absence of contract between the parties—to compel any person, in the course of his business and against his will, to accept or retain the personal services of another, or to compel any person, against his will, to perform personal services for another. The right of a person to sell his labor upon such terms as he deems proper is, in its essence, the same as the right of the purchaser of labor to prescribe the conditions upon which he will accept such labor from the person offering to sell it. So the right of the employee to quit the service of the employer, for whatever reason, is the same as the right of the employer, for whatever reason, to dispense with the services of such employee. . . . Of course, if the parties by contract fixed the period of service, and prescribed the conditions upon which the contract may be terminated, such contract would control the rights of the parties as between themselves, and for any violation of those provisions the party wronged would have his appropriate civil action.

Adair v. United States, 208 U.S. 161, 174–75 (1908).

[5]29 U.S.C. §151 et seq.

not hired for a definite term are those contained in federal and state labor relations acts or other laws dealing with various forms of discrimination.[6] However, at least one arbitrator has held that management does not have an unrestricted right to discharge at its own discretion, even where no bargaining relationship exists, because "the fair and generally accepted understanding of employer-employee relations is that there are obligations on the part of both parties," and that an "obligation of the employer is that an employee shall not be dismissed without cause."[7]

ii. Exceptions to the Doctrine[8]

Numerous exceptions to the employment-at-will doctrine, both judicially and legislatively created, have developed since the *Jones & Laughlin Steel*[9] decision. Among these are exceptions based on public policy, an implied contract of employment, and promissory estoppel.

---

[6]*See* Burris Chem., 50 LA 547, 548 (Williams, 1968); Brickle's, Inc., 45 LA 500, 501 (Bell, undated); United Brick & Tile Co., 39 LA 53, 57 (Updegraff, 1962); Columbian Carbon Co., 8 LA 634, 637–38 (Potter, 1947); Fruehauf Trailer Co., 4 LA 399, 403 (Whiting, 1946); Submarine Signal Co., 4 LA 56, 64 (Babb, 1946). *See also* Cone Mills Corp., 25 LA 772, 773 (Wettach, 1956); American Iron & Mach. Works Co., 19 LA 417, 419 (Merrill, 1952); Charles Eneu Johnson Co., 17 LA 125, 129 (Coffey, 1950); Goodyear Clearwater Mills, 8 LA 66, 67 (McCoy, 1947). *Cf.* United Food Mgmt. Servs., 41 LA 76, 78–82 (Blumrosen, 1963). As to statutory restrictions on management, see Levy, *The Role of Law in the United States and England in Protecting the Worker From Discharge and Discrimination*, 18 Int'l & Comp. L.Q. 558 (1969). Recognizing that the initiation of discipline is within the province of management, arbitrators have disclaimed the existence of arbitral authority to order the discharge or discipline of an employee. *See* City of Sandusky, Ohio, 73 LA 1236, 1240 (Keefe, 1979); General Elec. Co., 39 LA 897, 906 (Hilpert, 1962); High Standard Mfg. Corp., 38 LA 509, 515 (Dash, Jr., 1961). *Cf.* Profile Cotton Mills, 2 LA 537, 538–39 (McCoy, 1942).

[7]Daily World Publ'g Co., 3 LA 815, 817 (Rogers, 1946). During negotiations but prior to adoption of their first agreement, the parties agreed to arbitrate the dispute in question. In *Government Services*, 40 LA 84, 85 (Schedler, 1963), there was no collective bargaining agreement, but in agreeing to arbitrate a discharge, the employer was deemed to have accepted a "just cause" standard for the arbitral review. As to the latter point, see *National Lawyers Club*, 52 LA 547, 551–52 (Seidenberg, 1969); *Requarth Lumber Co.*, 43 LA 76, 77–78 (McIntosh, 1964). Public employees often have statutory protection. Federal employees, for instance, may be removed "only for such cause as will promote the efficiency of the service." 5 U.S.C. §7513(a). *See also* Social Sec. Admin., 80 LA 725, 728 (Lubic, 1983); Internal Revenue Serv., 77 LA 19, 20 (Edes, 1981). For a summary of the elaborate remedial system available to ensure fair and due process treatment of federal employees, see *Bush v. Lucas*, 462 U.S. 367, 381–90 (1983).

[8]For a fuller discussion of the erosion of the employment-at-will doctrine, see Holloway & Leech, Employment Termination: Rights and Remedies (2d ed. 1993); Gerhart & Crane, *Wrongful Dismissal: Arbitration and the Law*, 48 Arb. J. 56 (1993); Lillard, *Fifty Jurisdictions in Search of a Standard: The Covenant of Good Faith and Fair Dealing in the Employment Context*, 57 Mo. L. Rev. 1233 (1992); Cavico, *Employment at Will and Public Policy*, 25 Akron L. Rev. 497 (1992); Krueger, *The Evolution of Unjust-Dismissal Legislation in the United States*, 44 Indus. & Lab. Rel. Rev. 644 (1991); Peck, *Penetrating Doctrinal Camouflage: Understanding the Development of the Law of Wrongful Discharge*, 66 Wash. L. Rev. 719 (1991); Partee, *Reversing the Presumption of Employment at Will*, 44 Vand. L. Rev. 689 (1991); Grodin, *Past, Present and Future in Wrongful Termination Law*, 6 Lab. Law. 97 (1990); Peck, *Unjust Discharges From Employment: A Necessary Change in the Law*, 40 Ohio St. L.J. 1 (1979).

[9]NLRB v. Jones & Laughlin Steel Corp., 301 U.S. 1, 1 LRRM 703 (1937).

a. Public Policy

The "public policy" exception protects from discharge those employees who refuse to do any act that is contrary to recognized and established public policy or who acted in accordance with such a policy.[10]

b. Implied Contract of Employment [LA CDI 24.108; 24.111]

The "implied contract of employment" exception relies on provisions in employee handbooks and manuals to establish tenure or limit the proper reasons for discharge.[11] The courts have clearly stated that an employee's

---

[10]*See, e.g.*, Insignia Residential Corp. v. Ashton, 755 A.2d 1080 (Md. 2000) (wrongful discharge suit would be recognized, where employee was wrongfully terminated because she refused to submit to quid pro quo sexual harassment that would have amounted to prostitution); Gorce v. Foster, 880 P.2d 902 (Wash. 1994) (wrongful discharge action will lie against an employer for firing an employee because of the employee's refusal to dismiss a negligence action against a customer of the employer); Ortega v. IBP, Inc., 874 P.2d 1188, 10 IER Cases 855 (Kan. 1994) (where employee had not yet filed a workers' compensation claim, the employer is prohibited from firing an employee who is absent from work for a work-related injury and who might file a workers' compensation claim); City of Green Forest v. Morse, 873 S.W.2d 155, 9 IER Cases 625 (Ark. 1994) (Arkansas law recognizes at least four exceptions to the at-will doctrine: (1) cases in which the employee is discharged for refusing to violate a criminal statute, (2) cases in which the employee is discharged for exercising a statutory right, (3) cases in which the employee is discharged for complying with a statutory duty, and (4) cases in which the employee is discharged for violation of the general public policy of the state); Anderson v. Standard Register Co., 857 S.W.2d 555, 556 (Tenn. 1994) ("The cause of action for retaliatory discharge defines the balance point between the employment-at-will doctrine and rights granted employees under well-defined public policy."); Caldor v. Bowden, 625 A.2d 959 (Md. 1993) (public-policy exception protects at-will employee fired for seeking redress against coworker for sexual harassment culminating in assault and battery and/or filing a workers' compensation claim); Adams v. George W. Cochran & Co., 597 A.2d 28, 6 IER Cases 1392 (D.C. 1991) (employee may sue employer for wrongful discharge based on employee's refusal to violate statute or municipal regulation); Smith-Pfeffer v. Superintendent, Walter E. Fernald State Sch., 404 Mass. 145, 533 N.E.2d 1368, 4 IER Cases 289 (1989) (Massachusetts courts permit redress for at-will employees terminated for asserting a legally guaranteed right, e.g., filing workers' compensation claims; for doing what the law requires, e.g., serving on a jury; or for refusing to do that which the law forbids, e.g., committing perjury); Palmer v. Brown, 752 P.2d 685 (Kan. 1988) (tort of retaliatory discharge recognized to protect whistleblower).

[11]Duldulao v. St. Mary of Nazareth Hosp. Ctr., 115 Ill. 2d 482, 505 N.E.2d 314, 318, 1 IER Cases 1428 (1987). *See also* Hamersky v. Nicholson Supply Co., 517 N.W.2d 382, 385 (Neb. 1994) (an employee's at-will status can be modified by contractual terms that may be created by employee handbooks and oral representations); Hillie v. Mutual of Omaha Ins. Co., 512 N.W.2d 358, 361 (Neb. 1994) (an employee's at-will status can be modified by contractual terms that may be created by employee handbooks and oral representations); Mitchell v. Zilog, Inc., 874 P.2d 520, 523, 9 IER Cases 905 (Idaho 1994) (the presumption of an at-will employment relationship can be rebutted when the parties intend that an employee handbook or manual will constitute an element of an employee contract); Jacques v. Akzo Int'l Salt, 619 A.2d 748, 753 (Pa. Super. 1993) (an employee handbook only forms the basis of an implied contract if the employee shows that the employer affirmatively intended that it do so); Woolley v. Hoffmann-LaRoche, Inc., 99 N.J. 284, 491 A.2d 1257, 1258, 1 IER Cases 995 (1985) (absent a clear and prominent disclaimer, an implied promise contained in an employment manual that an employee will be fired only for cause may be enforceable against an employer, even when the employment is for an indefinite term and would otherwise be terminable at will); Toussaint v. Blue Cross & Blue Shield of Mich., 408 Mich. 579, 292 N.W.2d 880, 115 LRRM 4708 (1980) (a jury could find for the employee based on legitimate expectations grounded in the employer's written policy statements set forth in the manual of personnel policies). *See also* Georgia-Pacific Corp., 87 LA 217, 220 (Cohen, 1986) (noncollective bargaining context).

subjective belief that he or she could not be discharged without just cause is insufficient to alter the at-will nature of his employment.[12] Moreover, where the handbooks and/or manuals contain appropriate disclaimers of contractual intent, courts also have been reluctant to imply a just cause provision.[13] Further, courts have held that handbook provisions that put employees on notice that they may be subject to layoffs and termination in case of a reduction in force do not imply that employees may be laid off on other than a seniority basis.[14]

c. Promissory Estoppel

The "promissory estoppel" exception is similar to the implied contract exception. Under the doctrine of promissory estoppel, "[a] promise which the promisor should reasonably expect to induce action or forbearance on the part of the promisee or a third person and which does induce such action or forbearance is binding if injustice can be avoided only by enforcement of the promise."[15] Promissory estoppel acts as a substitute for consideration in a contract.[16] Courts often apply this doctrine as a means of preventing employers from refusing to honor a promise that an employee reasonably has relied on.[17]

---

[12]Boone v. Frontier Ref., 987 P.2d 681 (Wyo. 1999) (statements made as part of a performance appraisal may create an implied contract for continued employment; however, such a contract is formed only if the statements clearly show the employer's intent to create an employment relationship, where the employee may be discharged only for cause).

[13]See, e.g., Schur v. Storage Tech. Corp., 878 P.2d 51, 52 (Colo. Ct. App. 1994) (language in employee handbook that "the information contained in this handbook does not constitute an express or implied contract of employment"); Mitchell v. Zilog, Inc., 874 P.2d 520, 523, 9 IER Cases 905 (Idaho 1994); Hillie v. Mutual of Omaha Ins. Co., 512 N.W.2d 358, 361 (Neb. 1994) (an employee's at-will status can be modified by contractual terms that may be created by employee handbooks and oral representations); Rood v. General Dynamics Corp., 444 Mich. 107, 507 N.W.2d 591, 599, 9 IER Cases 1155 (1993); Smith v. Union Labor Life Ins. Co., 620 A.2d 265, 8 IER Cases 434 (D.C. 1993).

[14]McIlravy v. Kerr-McGee Corp., 74 F.3d 1017 (10th Cir. 1996). See also Herbst v. System One Info. Mgmt., LLC, 31 F. Supp. 2d 1025 (N.D. Ohio 1998) (provisions in employee handbook addressing layoffs were not considered a specific promise of job security altering the at-will nature of the employment relationship, where the provisions were vague statements that management would redeploy laid-off workers whenever possible and that they would be treated with fairness and due regard).

[15]Restatement (Second) of Contracts §90 (1999).

[16]Vancheri v. GNLV Corp., 777 P.2d 366, 369, 4 IER Cases 922, 923 (Nev. 1989) ("The doctrine of promissory estoppel . . . is intended as a substitute for consideration . . . ."). See also Goggin & Grosse, Employment at Will, Federal Practice Manual §1475.31 (1986).

[17]See Shaw v. Housing Auth. of City of Walla Walla, 880 P.2d 1006, 1009 (Wash. Ct. App. 1994) ("Promissory estoppel requires five elements: (1) a promise (2) which the promisor should reasonably expect will cause the promisee to change position and (3) which actually causes the promisee to change position (4) in justifiable reliance on the promise, so that (5) injustice can be avoided only by enforcement of the promise. . . . When an employer makes promises of specific treatment in specific situations and the employee is induced by those promises to remain on the job and not seek other employment, the promises likewise become 'enforceable components of the employment relationship.'" (citations omitted; quoting Thompson v. St. Regis Paper Co., 102 Wash. 2d 219, 230, 685 P.2d 1081, 116 LRRM 3142 (1984)). Accord Simard v. Resolution Trust Corp., 639 A.2d 540 (D.C. 1994); Barnell v. Taubman Co., 203 Mich. App. 110, 512 N.W.2d 13, 66 FEP Cases 281 (1994); Tersigni v. General Tire, 91 Ohio. App. 3d 757, 633 N.E.2d 1140, 10 IER Cases 379 (1994).

However, the courts are cautious in finding employment tenure based on promises relating to fringe benefits or incentive packages.[18]

d. Statutory Protections [LA CDI 94.553; 100.30]

In addition to the above judicially created exceptions, a number of federal[19] and state[20] statutes now afford employees protection from discharge based on discriminatory practices by the employer and from discharge in relation to protected actions such as whistleblowing, that is, bringing to the attention of management or the public information about improper activities or illegal actions,[21] or filing workers' compensation claims.[22]

Federal law now prohibits the use of polygraph or lie detector tests in employment situations,[23] and a number of states have also prohibited the

---

[18]Chrvala v. Borden, Inc., 14 F. Supp. 2d (S.D. Ohio 1998) (employer's promises in letter offering financial incentives for executives who continued to stay and satisfactorily perform their jobs until the sale of the business did not support promissory estoppel claim, where employees were terminated for failure to adequately perform their job duties). *See, e.g.*, Bear v. Volunteers of Am. Wyo., 964 P.2d 1245 (Wyo. 1998) (employer's recognition of former employee's accomplishments with increased salary did not amount to additional consideration creating permanent employment, where there was no language clearly stating the employer's intent to promise job security).

[19]*See, e.g.*, Civil Rights Act of 1964, Title VII, 42 U.S.C. §2000e; Americans with Disabilities Act (ADA), 42 U.S.C. §12101 et seq.; Age Discrimination in Employment Act, 29 U.S.C. §§621–634.

[20]Anderson v. Standard Register Co., 857 S.W.2d 555, 8 IER Cases 1106 (Tenn. 1993) (by statute an employer cannot discharge employees because of race, religion, sex, age, physical condition, or mental condition, because they report workplace safety violations, because they miss work to perform jury duty, or because they refuse to participate in or be silent about illegal activities at the workplace). *See, e.g.*, KY. REV. STAT. ANN. §344.280 (Michie 1997) (illegal to retaliate or discriminate in any way against a person because that person has opposed a practice under Chapter 344 of the Kentucky Civil Rights Act); KY. REV. STAT. ANN. §342.197 (Michie 1997) (unlawful to harass, coerce, discharge, or discriminate in any way for filing workers' compensation claim).

[21]Protection against unjust discharge has been extended in a number of jurisdictions to "whistleblowers," Civil Service Reform Act of 1978, 5 U.S.C. §2301(b)(9): Alabama (safety violations), Alaska (public employers only), Arizona (public employers only), Arkansas (public employers only), California, Colorado (public employers and those under contract to a state agency), Connecticut, Delaware (public employers, nursing home employers only), District of Columbia (public employers only), Florida, Georgia (public employers only), Hawaii, Idaho (public employers only), Illinois, Indiana (public employers and those under public contract), Iowa (public employers only), Kansas (public employers only), Kentucky (public employers only), Louisiana , Maine, Maryland (protects employees in executive branch of state government), Massachusetts (public employers only), Michigan, Minnesota, Mississippi, Missouri (public employers only), Montana, Nebraska, Nevada (public employers only), New Hampshire, New Jersey, New York, North Carolina, North Dakota, Ohio, Oklahoma, Oregon (public employees only), Pennsylvania (public employers only), Rhode Island, South Carolina (certain public employers only), South Dakota, Tennessee, Texas (public employers only), Utah (public employers only), Washington (public employers only), West Virginia (public employers only), Wisconsin (applies to employees of health care facilities only), and Wyoming (public employers only). For a typical application of such a statute, see *Rosen v. Transx Ltd.*, 816 F. Supp. 1364, 143 LRRM 2142 (D. Minn. 1993).

[22]KY. REV. STAT. ANN. §342.197 (Michie 1997) (unlawful to harass, coerce, discharge, or discriminate in any way for filing workers' compensation claim).

[23]Employee Polygraph Protection Act, Pub. L. No. 100–347 (1988), 29 U.S.C. §2001 et seq.

use of such tests as a condition of hiring or continued employment.[24] One such statute is Montana's Wrongful Discharge Act.[25] It makes a discharge wrongful if:

   (a) it was in retaliation for the employee's refusal to violate public policy or for reporting a violation of public policy;
   (b) the discharge was not for good cause and the employee had completed the employer's probationary period of employment; or
   (c) the employer violated the express provisions of its own written personnel policy.[26]

Remedies for violations under the Montana Act are limited to lost wages for 4 years offset by the amount the employee earned or reasonably should have earned since the discharge.[27] Punitive damages are recoverable on a clear and convincing showing of actual fraud or malice.[28]

B. Discipline Pursuant to a Collective Bargaining Agreement

i. Collective Bargaining Agreement Without a Just Cause Provision [LA CDI 118.01]

Many arbitrators would imply a just cause limitation in any collective agreement.[29] For instance, one arbitrator held that "a 'just cause' limitation on discharge is 'implied' in any labor agreement."[30] The reasoning is that

---

[24]Alaska, California, Connecticut, Delaware, District of Columbia, Hawaii, Idaho, Iowa, Maine, Maryland, Massachusetts, Michigan, Minnesota, Montana, Nebraska, Nevada, New Jersey, New York, Oregon, Pennsylvania, Rhode Island, Vermont, Virginia, Washington, West Virginia, and Wisconsin. For an exhaustive listing of federal and state legislation in this area, see Finkin, Privacy in Employment Law (BNA Books 2d ed. 2003). In some cases, persons subjected to, and already affected by, polygraph examinations have received punitive damages in addition to compensatory damages. See, e.g., Moniodis v. Cook, 64 Md. App. 1, 494 A.2d 212, 218, 1 IER Cases 441 (1985).

[25]Mont. Code Ann. §§39-2-901 to 905 (2001).

[26]Id. §39-2-904.

[27]Id. §39-2-905.

[28]Id.

[29]See Herlitz, Inc., 89 LA 436, 441–42 (Allen, Jr., 1987); Pfizer, Inc., 79 LA 1225, 1233–34 (Newmark, 1982); Fort Wayne Cmty. Sch., 78 LA 928, 935–36 (Deitsch, 1982); Dayton Pepsi Cola Bottling Co., 75 LA 154, 158–59 (Keenan, 1980); Huron Forge & Mach. Co., 75 LA 83, 88 (Roumell, Jr., 1980); Velsicol Chem. Corp., 52 LA 1164, 1166–67 (Oppenheim, 1969); Peerless Laundry Co., 51 LA 331, 331–33 (Eaton, 1968); Anderson Hickey Co., 50 LA 1217, 1219 (Volz, 1968); New Hotel Showboat, 48 LA 240, 241–42 (Jones, 1967); Napa Hawaiian Warehouse, 42 LA 490, 493 (Tsukiyama, 1963); Continental Air Transp., 38 LA 778, 780 (Eiger, 1962); B.F. Goodrich Tire Co., 36 LA 552, 556 (Ryder, 1961); Pacific Tel. & Tel. Co., 36 LA 503, 505 (Ross, 1960); Cameron Iron Works, 25 LA 295, 300–01 (Boles, 1955); Pilot Freight Carriers, 22 LA 761, 763 (Maggs, 1954); Atwater Mfg. Co., 13 LA 747, 749 (Donnelly, 1949). See also Sundstrand Corp., 46 LA 356, 357 (Dahl, 1966); John A. Volpe Constr. Co., 45 LA 532, 533–34 (Fallon, 1965); Higgins Indus., 25 LA 439, 440–41 (Hebert, 1955). Also, a general just cause limitation may be found to be implied from some particular provision in the agreement. See Corn Belt Elec. Coop., 79 LA 1045, 1049 (O'Grady, 1982); RLC & Son Trucking, 70 LA 600, 602 (Harkless, 1978); National Lawyers Club, 52 LA 547, 551–52 (Seidenberg, 1969); R. Munroe & Sons Mfg. Corp., 48 LA 1209, 1212 (Sherman, 1967); Perini, M-K, Leavell, 46 LA 1044, 1046–47 (Merrill, 1966); Higgins, Inc., 24 LA 453, 455–56 (Morvant, 1955).

[30]Herlitz, Inc., 89 LA 436, 441 (Allen, Jr., 1987).

"[i]f management can terminate at any time for any reason, such as one finds in the 'employment-at-will' situation, then the seniority provision and all other 'work protection' clauses of the labor agreement are meaningless."[31] "[T]he prevailing view is that to alter this implied requirement of just cause, the parties must in fact so specify in their written agreement."[32]

However, some arbitrators have held to the contrary, concluding that, where a collective bargaining agreement exists but contains no express limitation on the employer's right to discharge and discipline employees, an employer may discharge for any reason it chooses.[33] Thus, where an agreement expressly recognized the right to discharge and contained no express limitation on that right, one arbitrator was unwilling to read a just cause limitation into the agreement.[34] Another arbitrator determined that the unusual language employed by the parties and their bargaining history implied that they had rejected a just cause standard.[35]

ii. *Collective Bargaining Agreement With a Just Cause Provision*
[LA CDI 118.01]

Most collective bargaining agreements do, in fact, require cause or just cause for discharge or discipline.[36] One arbitrator discussed the general significance of these terms:

---

[31]*Id. See also* Atwater Mfg. Co., 13 LA 747, 749 (Donnelly, 1949) (quoting at length from a similar view expressed in *Coca-Cola Bottling Co. of Boston* (Wallen, unpublished), *Atwater*, 13 LA at 750–51).

[32]Binswanger Glass Co., 92 LA 1153, 1155 (Nicholas, Jr., 1989) ("[T]here is a plethora of cases in which arbitrators have implied a just cause provision in the absence of such a provision with the written language of the collective bargaining agreement . . . to which the parties have set their hands. Indeed, one of the major doctrines of the 'Trilogy' [Steelworkers v. American Mfg. Co., 363 U.S. 564, 46 LRRM 2414 (1960); Steelworkers v. Warrior & Gulf Navigation Co., 363 U.S. 574, 46 LRRM 2416 (1960); Steelworkers v. Enterprise Wheel & Car Corp., 363 U.S. 593, 46 LRRM 2423 (1960)] is that the modern day Labor-Management contract encompassing an arbitration clause is to be viewed not simply as an orderly process for resolving employer-employee conflicts, but as a 'quid pro quo.'").

[33]*See* Bohlinger v. National Cash Register Co., 18 LA 595 (N.Y. Sup. Ct. 1952) (and cases cited therein). *See also* Alyeska Pipeline Serv. Co., 76 LA 172, 174 (Eaton, 1981); Los Angeles Dodgers, 58 LA 489, 491 (Jones, Jr., 1972).

[34]Hillyer Deutsch Edwards, 19 LA 663, 664 (Emery, 1952). *See also* M.M. Sundt Constr. Co., 81 LA 432, 438 (Zechar, 1983); American Oil & Supply Co., 36 LA 331, 332 (Berkowitz, 1960); Cameron Iron Works, 24 LA 680, 683–84 (Warren, 1955); Okenite Co., 22 LA 756, 759–60 (Krivonos, 1954). *Cf.* Electrical Workers (IBEW) Local 441, 46 LA 831, 832 (Jones, Jr., 1966); Helipot Corp., 19 LA 615, 619–21 (Warren, 1952). For a contract limiting challenges of discharge action to "bad-faith" discharges, see *Pacific Tel. & Tel. Co.*, 45 LA 655, 656 (Somers, 1965). In *Reynolds Electrical & Engineering Co.*, 72 LA 1012, 1013 (Jones, Jr., 1979), a discharge grievance was held not to be arbitrable because the agreement gave management "the absolute right to . . . discharge . . . employees at its discretion." In the case of *In the Round Dinner Playhouse*, 55 LA 118, 128 (Kamin, 1970), the arbitrator took "arbitral notice" that any requirement of "just cause" for termination "is virtually unknown in the theatrical world." In *Boscobel Board of Education*, 55 LA 58, 60–61 (Wilberg, 1970), the "interests" arbitrator recommended a discharge and discipline clause less restrictive on management than the usual just cause clause.

[35]Los Angeles Dodgers, 58 LA 489, 491 (Jones, Jr., 1972).

[36]BASIC PATTERNS IN UNION CONTRACTS 7 (BNA Books 14th ed. 1995) ("'Cause' or 'just cause' is stated as a reason for discharge in 92 percent of agreements studied—95 percent in manufacturing and 88 percent in non-manufacturing."); Abrams & Nolan, *Toward a Theory of "Just Cause" in Employee Discipline Cases*, 1985 DUKE L.J. 594, 594 n.1 (1985) (citing 2 Collective Bargaining: Negotiations and Contracts (BNA) §40:1 (1983) (94% of collective bargaining agreements contain a just cause or "cause" provision)).

[I]t is common to include the right to suspend and discharge for "just cause," "justifiable cause," "proper cause," "obvious cause," or quite commonly simply for "cause." There is no significant difference between these various phrases. These exclude discharge for mere whim or caprice. They are, obviously, intended to include those things for which employees have traditionally been fired. They include the traditional causes of discharge in the particular trade or industry, the practices which develop in the day-to-day relations of management and labor and most recently they include the decisions of courts and arbitrators. They represent a growing body of "common law" that may be regarded either as the latest development of the law of "master and servant" or, perhaps, more properly as part of a new body of common law of "Management and labor under collective bargaining agreements." They constitute the duties owed by employees to management and, in their correlative aspect, are part of the rights of management. They include such duties as honesty, punctuality, sobriety, or, conversely, the right to discharge for theft, repeated absence or lateness, destruction of company property, brawling and the like. Where they are not expressed in posted rules, they may very well be implied, provided they are applied in a uniform, non-discriminatory manner.[37]

Some agreements enumerate specific grounds for discharge or discipline.[38] Where an agreement specifies certain types of misconduct for which employees may be disciplined, the employer may also impose discipline for other types of misconduct, if the specified offenses are merely illustrative and not exclusive.[39] Similarly, the listing of certain offenses in written

---

[37]Worthington Corp., 24 LA 1, 6–7 (McGoldrick, Sutton, & Tribble, 1955). For arbitration decisions finding no significant difference between these terms, see *Georgia-Pacific Corp.*, 87 LA 217, 221 (Cohen, 1986); *Huntington Alloys*, 74 LA 176, 179 (Katz, 1980); *Huntington Alloys*, 73 LA 1050, 1055 (Shanker, 1979); *Link-Belt Co.*, 44 LA 1208, 1211 (Buckwalter, 1965); *RCA Communications*, 29 LA 567, 571 (Harris, 1957). For other statements defining "cause" or "just cause," see *City of Portland, Bureau of Police*, 77 LA 820, 826 (Axon, 1981) (the "just cause test mandates that the punishment assessed be reasonable in light of all the circumstances"); *Hiram Walker & Sons*, 75 LA 899, 900 (Belshaw, 1980) (equating the term "just cause" with "the now-common expression, 'fair shake'"); *Beatrice Foods Co.*, 74 LA 1008, 1011 (Gradwohl, 1980) ("proper cause" means that management "must have a reasonable basis for its actions and follow fair procedures"); *MGM Grand Hotel*, 68 LA 1284, 1286 (Weiss, 1977); *Schneider's Modern Bakery*, 44 LA 574, 576 (Hon, 1965); *Employing Lithographer Ass'n of Detroit*, 21 LA 671, 672 (Parker, 1953); *Lincoln Indus.*, 19 LA 489, 493 (Barrett, 1952). As to the purposes of industrial discipline, see *Denver Pub. Sch.*, 73 LA 918, 920 (Meiners, 1979); *Eastern Air Lines*, 46 LA 1034, 1039 (Yagoda, 1966); *Spartan Stores*, 33 LA 40, 41 (Howlett, 1959).

[38]In *Meat Cutters Local 540 v. Neuhoff Bros. Packers*, 481 F.2d 817, 83 LRRM 2652, 2654 (5th Cir. 1973), the agreement authorized discharge for "proper cause" but did not specify individual grounds for discharge; in these circumstances, what constitutes proper cause was held to be a question for the arbitrator and not for the court. Courts often have held otherwise, however, where the collective bargaining agreement expressly states specific causes for discharge. See section 3.E.ii., "Express Contractual Authority of Arbitrator to Modify Penalties or Withdrawal of Such Authority," below.

[39]*See* New York Cent. R.R., 44 LA 552, 553 (Wyckoff, 1965); Brewer Drydock Co., 43 LA 689, 693–94 (Altieri, 1964); Kraft Foods Co., 9 LA 397, 398 (Updegraff, 1947); Reynolds Metal Co., 7 LA 752, 755 (Carmichael, 1947). *See also* City of Havre, Mont., 100 LA 866, 872 (Levak, 1992); Western Auto Supply Co., 71 LA 710, 716 (Ross, 1978); Gladieux Food Servs., 70 LA 544, 547 (Lewis, 1978); Alliance Mach. Co., 48 LA 457, 462–63 (Dworkin, 1967). But the listing of some grounds was held to exclude others in *Pacific Press*, 26 LA 339, 344 (Hildebrand, 1956). *See also* Hudson Rest. Co., 15 LA 616, 618 (Handsaker, 1950). In *Chicago Pneumatic Tool Co.*, 38 LA 891, 892 (Duff, 1961), the contract specified the right to

plant rules does not necessarily exclude other offenses as grounds for punishment.[40]

Arbitrators have held that a contract giving the right to discharge for cause and making no reference to other forms of discipline does not deprive management of the right to impose forms of discipline less severe than discharge,[41] because discharge may be too severe a penalty for an offense under the circumstances of the case.[42]

Asserting that discharge "inevitably casts a shadow on a worker's character and reputation," one arbitrator would not permit a discharge for lack of work under a just cause standard, stating that layoff is the proper action in such cases.[43] Other arbitrators have held that "discharge" is limited to cases of employee fault.[44] Excessive absenteeism may constitute such fault. A number of employers have adopted no-fault attendance policies, which provide for discipline and discharge due to excessive absenteeism, regardless of the reasons for lack of attendance. However, many arbitrators have concluded that such policies must be reasonable and otherwise conform to just cause provisions in collective bargaining agreements.[45]

---

discharge "for proper cause as agreed to by the parties," but this did not require management to obtain union agreement as to all causes. For a case involving a clause providing that no employee could be discharged "without the consent of the union," see *Crawford Clothes*, 19 LA 475, 476–79 (Kramer, 1952).

[40]*See* National Union Elec. Corp., 77 LA 815, 818 (Traynor, 1981); Emery Indus., 72 LA 110, 112 (Gentile, 1979); Koppers Co., 69 LA 613, 614 (Harkless, 1977); Gamble Bros., 68 LA 72, 74 (Krislov, 1977); Abex Corp., 64 LA 721, 725–26 (Rybolt, 1975) (failure to list an offense did not prevent discipline but did limit the scope of permitted penalty); Mount Whitney Lumber Co., 48 LA 147, 151 (Mullennix, 1967); Farmbest, Inc., 44 LA 609, 612 (Karlins, 1965). *See also* Borg-Warner Corp., 78 LA 985, 994 (Neas, 1982); 3M Co., 70 LA 587, 589 (Mueller, 1978); Champion Spark Plug Co., 68 LA 702, 705 (Casselman, 1977).

[41]*See* Sequoia Rock Co., 76 LA 114, 115–17 (Lennard, 1981); Albertson's, Inc., 71 LA 632, 637 (Ross, 1978); Whirlwind, Inc., 50 LA 888, 896 (Solomon, 1968); Northwest Publ'ns, 43 LA 1197, 1199–1202 (Sembower, 1964); Denver Post, 41 LA 33, 37–38 (Sears, 1963); A.S. Abell Co., 39 LA 859, 860–61 (Strong, 1962); Pacific Tel. & Tel. Co., 36 LA 503, 504 (Ross, 1960); Portland Gas & Coke Co., 23 LA 711, 713–14 (Kleinsorge, 1954); E.I. DuPont de Nemours & Co., 17 LA 580, 585 (Cornsweet, 1951); Auto-Lite Battery Corp., 3 LA 122, 125 (Copelof, 1946). But in some situations a different result has been reached. *See* Reynolds Elec. & Eng'g Co., 50 LA 760, 763–66 (Abernethy, 1968); National Lead Co., 39 LA 1231, 1235 (Sembower, 1962); Branch River Wool Combing Co., 18 LA 34, 38 (Copelof, 1952); Sylvania Elec. Prods. Co., 14 LA 16, 23–24 (Sugerman, 1950).

[42]*See* Lakeside Jubilee Foods, 95 LA 358, 365 (Berquist, 1990). See also section 3.F., "Factors in Evaluating Penalties," below.

[43]American Republics Corp., 18 LA 248, 253 (Hale, 1952). *See also* Motor Wheel Corp., 103 LA 671, 676 (Witney, 1994) (noting the use of the word "termination" as a euphemism for discharge, which is the ultimate discipline of an employee).

[44]*See* Vulcan Corp., 28 LA 633, 637 (Howlett, 1957); Bachmann Uxbridge Worsted Corp., 23 LA 596, 602 (Hogan, 1954); A.D. Juillard & Co., 22 LA 266, 268 (Kelly, 1954). *See also* Corley Distrib. Co., 68 LA 513, 516 (Ipavec, 1977). In *Perfection Bakeries*, 110 LA 1043, 1047 (Stallworth, 1997), and *Revere Copper & Brass*, 45 LA 254, 255 (McCoy, 1965), the terms "nondisciplinary" termination or discharge were suggested for termination not due to fault.

[45]*See* General Tire, 93 LA 771 (Groshong, 1989) (noting that most arbitrators agree that no-fault attendance policies and just cause provisions cannot be administered together). *See also* Harmon House Convalescent Ctr., 109 LA 477, 479 (Felice, 1997) (citing John Morrell & Co., 9 LA 931 (Gilden, 1948), for the proposition that "[r]ules unilaterally established by the Company providing for suspension and discharge of employees, who accumulate a specific number of absences regardless of the circumstances[,] are invalid because they conflict with contract clauses permitting discharge only for cause and providing for submission of disputes to arbitration"); Cooper Indus., 94 LA 830, 834 (Yarowsky, 1990) (citing a study which found that in 93.1% of the cases where the employer failed to conduct an impartial investiga-

iii. *Probationary Employees* [LA CDI 118.02]

Where an agreement provides that new employees are not to have seniority rights until completion of a probationary period, and is otherwise
silent as to management rights with respect to them, probationary employees may be discharged for any reason not otherwise unlawful.[46] In one case,
where the provisions of a collective bargaining agreement mentioned probationary employees, but were unclear as to whether the employees were included under a just cause clause, the arbitrator held that "the weight of arbitral authority supports the proposition that Management has broad, if not
almost unlimited, discretion where probationary employees are concerned."[47]
Some arbitrators, however, have set aside the discharge of a probationary
employee if management's action was "arbitrary, capricious, or discriminatory"; thus, "the question in such a case goes to the good faith of the Company, not to the merits of its conclusion."[48] A few arbitrators have gone further and required a showing of fairness or even just cause.[49]

Typically, seniority accrues from the date of hire, and most probationary periods are for a period of 30 to 90 days. But, if the employee has worked

---

tion into the reasons for the employee's absences, the grievant was returned to work); All
Am. Gourmet Co., 88 LA 1241, 1245–47 (Zobrak, 1987) (finding that the discharge of a grievant was improper because the no-fault plan was not administered with proper safeguards to
ensure consistent application).

[46]Joy Mfg. Co., 6 LA 430, 436 (Healy, 1946); Flintkote Co., 3 LA 770, 771 (Cole, 1946). *See
also* Stone, Labor-Management Contracts at Work 261 (1961); City of Danbury, Conn., 96
LA 1117, 1118 (Pittocco, 1991); Mode O'Day Co., 85 LA 297, 298–99 (Thornell, 1985); Murphy
Oil USA, 83 LA 935, 938 (Bognanno, 1984); Fred Sanders & Co., 42 LA 187, 188–89 (Miller,
1964); Luckenbach S.S., 6 LA 98, 102 (Kerr, 1946) ("interests" arbitration).

[47]Bridgestone (U.S.A.), 88 LA 1314, 1316 (Nicholas, Jr., 1987) (grievance based on discharge of probationary employee is not arbitrable, despite contract provision entitling a probationary employee to "union representation under the grievance procedure," because, in the
absence of seniority status, a probationary employee had no standing to bring a grievance to
arbitration).

[48]Ex-Cell-O Corp., 21 LA 659, 665 (Smith, 1953), *quoted in* County of Haw., 87 LA 349,
354 (Brown, 1985). *See also* Giant Food, 77 LA 1276, 1281 (Seibel, 1981); San Jose Mercury
News, 48 LA 143, 145 (Burns, 1966); Bergen Mach. & Tool Co., 44 LA 301, 304 (Buckwalter,
1965); Pullman-Standard, 40 LA 757, 762–63 (Sembower, 1963); Standard Oil Co. of Cal., 38
LA 350, 351–52 (Ross, 1962); North Am. Aviation, 19 LA 565, 569 (Komaroff, 1952). *See also*
Mosaic Tile Co., 9 LA 625, 630–31 (Cornsweet, 1948).

[49]*See* Phoenix Transit Sys., 70 LA 395, 397 (Hayes, 1978) (applying a "test of fairness
and reasonableness"); Phillips Petroleum Co., 34 LA 633, 635 (Donaldson, 1960) (pointing
out that the contract did not reserve to management the unrestricted right to discharge
probationary employees and that it did specify accumulation of seniority from the date of
hire, the arbitrator required just cause for their discharge); Seamless Rubber Co., 28 LA 456,
458 (Stutz, 1957) (although employees had no seniority rights until after a probationary
period, just cause was required for discharge of probationary employees). However, regarding termination of probationary employees in federal employment, see *Veterans Admin. Med.
Ctr.*, 81 LA 325, 327–30 (Gentile, 1983); *Veterans Admin. Med. Ctr.*, 81 LA 286, 287–88
(Bailey, 1983) (relying on a U.S. Court of Appeals decision in holding that the federal-agency
employer was not required to show just cause for the discharge of the grievant as a probationary employee); *U.S. Naval Ordnance Station*, 68 LA 90, 92, 94 (Krislov, 1977) (the arbitrator agreed with management's view that the Federal Personnel Manual yardstick for
measuring cause differs depending on whether a probationary employee is involved). *Cf.*
Department of Labor, 80 LA 250, 253, 255–57 (Dworkin, 1983). *See also* Pacific Power &
Light Co., 89 LA 283 (Sinicropi, 1987) (where no standard of proof was set forth in the contract, probationary employees were entitled to same rights as other employees).

outside the bargaining unit, however long the period, it may not be counted in determining seniority. So, where an employee worked for more than 15 years as a clerical worker outside the bargaining unit, was laid off, and then recalled to a job within the unit represented by the union, the employee was determined to be a probationary employee.[50]

Once an employee has served the probationary period, however, that employee is protected from termination without just cause. Consequently, in a situation where an individual whom the employer mistakenly thought was a probationary employee was mailed a termination letter 3 days after the probationary period ended, the employee was found to have been wrongfully discharged.[51]

If an agreement contains a just cause requirement for discharge, but makes no reference to any probationary period for new employees, the new employees are deemed to be included within the just cause requirement.[52] However, an early decision concluded that while a probationary period should not be read into a contract silent on mangerial rights with respect to a new employee, management may have greater latitude in determining just cause for discharge.[53]

Of course, the collective bargaining agreement may deal expressly with the discharge of probationary employees, for example, by requiring cause[54] or by affirmatively not requiring it.[55] In the latter situation, problems may arise concerning the exact limits of the probationary period.[56]

Sometimes a contract provison is unclear as to how the probationary period is to be calculated. One arbitrator decided that a county employer did not violate a contract stating that new employees were on probation for the

---

[50]Bethlehem Steel Corp., 91 LA 293 (McDermott, 1988). *See also* Weyerhaeuser Co., 93 LA 1056, 1057–58 (Bankston, 1989) (despite 6 months' experience with company while contracted through a temporary service, the employee, when hired, was probationary).

[51]Avis Rent-A-Car Sys., 107 LA 197 (Shanker, 1996).

[52]Osborn & Ulland, 68 LA 1146, 1150 (Beck, 1977); Mac Coal Co., 52 LA 1125, 1127 (Krimsly, 1969).

[53]Park Sherman Co., 2 LA 199, 200 (Lapp, 1946).

[54]In *Ford Motor Co.*, 48 LA 1213, 1214–15 (Platt, 1967), the agreement required cause for discharge after the first 30 days of the 3-month period required for an employee to acquire seniority; the arbitrator held the cause required after 30 days to be no different from the cause required for discharge of employees after expiration of the aforementioned 3-month period. The arbitrator noted that under previous agreements, probationary employees had been subject to discharge for any reason other than discrimination. The discrimination exception had been construed to include reasons of race, union activity, personal feeling, or sex. Ford Motor Co., 6 LA 853, 854 (Shulman, 1946).

[55]See A.S. Abell Co., 49 LA 264, 265–66 (Kennedy, 1967) (it was held, however, that to be free of the cause requirement, the discharge ordinarily must be effected and communicated to the employee within the probationary period). *Accord* Clow Corp., 78 LA 1077, 1079 (Smith, 1982). In *Pan American World Airways*, 50 LA 722, 724 (Galenson, 1968), the contract gave management the right to discharge probationary employees "at its option," but this did not necessarily mean that the union could be totally disregarded in the matter.

[56]See, e.g., Morton-Norwich Prods., 69 LA 550, 554 (Ipavec, 1977) (employee could not be terminated without just cause after having been granted a leave of absence that would extend beyond the probationary period); Red Jacket Mfg. Co., 69 LA 211, 213 (Erbs, 1977); Ford Motor Co., 48 LA 1213, 1216 (Platt, 1967); Crane Carrier Co., 47 LA 339, 340–41 (Merrill, 1966) (probationary period not extended by strike); Bergen Mach. & Tool Co., 44 LA 301, 303 (Buckwalter, 1965) (period was 30 working days rather than 30 calendar days where contract was not specific on the question).

HOW ARBITRATION WORKS

Ch. 15.2.C.

first 90 days worked, when the county discharged an employee who had worked 83 days, although she had been paid for 90 days, inclusive of sick leave and holidays.[57] The arbitrator concluded that days worked meant days on which the employee was physically at work.

In another public employer case, where the length of the probationary period was not specified, the arbitrator concluded that the administrative rules of the city would govern.[58]

C. Discharge Versus Resignation [LA CDI 118.07]

When an employee voluntarily resigns, concepts associated with discharge are not generally applicable. Thus, where employees evidenced clear intent to resign and sever the employment relationship, arbitrators have refused to treat the matter as a discharge.[59] Moreover, where the facts and circumstances are such as to lead management reasonably to conclude that

---

[57]Lapeer County, Mich., 108 LA 1086 (Sugerman, 1997). *See also* State Coll. Borough, Pa., 110 LA 718 (Franckiewicz, 1998) (employer need not establish that it had just cause to discharge a probationary police officer although the provision on just cause did not state that a probationary period applied or set forth the length of such a period where the just cause standard was inapplicable, where a provision on vacation benefits mentioned a probationary period and implied that new employees must complete it); City of Stockton, Cal., 108 LA 1201 (Brand, 1996) (grievant was not a probationary employee when discharged although the city's Civil Service Commission failed to classify him in a permanent status when it met 4 days after the grievant completed his 18-month probationary period and 2 days after he was placed on administrative leave, where the city charter stated that an appointment was considered completed when the probationary period ended); Consolidated Drum Reconditioning, 108 LA 523 (Richman, 1997) (despite predecessor employer's payment of employee's accrued wages and other benefits, the employee was not a new employee on probation where the agreement with successor had a progressive wage scale based on time in service that put holdover employees at levels they had earned when they left the predecessor).

[58]Avon Lake, Ohio, 95 LA 16 (Feldman, 1990).

[59]*See* State of Ohio, 96 LA 469, 471–72 (Rivera, 1991); Summit Finishing Co., 86 LA 1160, 1164 (Archer, 1986); Southern Cal. Edison Co., 86 LA 888, 890–91 (Gardner, 1985) (employee wrote resignation letter with supervisor's help 11 hours after being in accident in company car); General Tel. Co. of Ill., 86 LA 726, 730–31 (Carver, 1985) (retirement constituted effective resignation); Erie Metro. Transit Auth., 86 LA 316, 324 (Creo, 1985) (valid even though submitted to foreman with no authority to hire or fire); F.B.M. Distillery Co., 59 LA 871, 873 (Brown, 1972); Concord Fabrics, 57 LA 1200, 1206–08 (Turkus, 1971); Guerin Special Motor Freight, 48 LA 1036, 1040 (Hardy, 1967); Yale & Towne Mfg. Co., 41 LA 913, 917 (Russell, 1963); Kansas Grain Co., 29 LA 242, 245 (Doyle, 1957); Joerns Bros. Furniture Co., 20 LA 715, 717–18 (Anderson, 1953); International Shoe Co., 20 LA 618, 619–21 (Kelliher, 1953). *See also* Manchester Plastics, 110 LA 169 (Knott, 1997) (employee who did not respond within 10 days to a letter stating conditions to remain employed did not quit when he did not respond within 10 days, where he reasonably believed that he had 10 days from receipt of letter and that his response was timely made); International Paper Co., 108 LA 758 (Nicholas, Jr., 1997) (employee who was injured at work did not quit his job even though he did not attend work for 2 weeks, where he had a broken arm in a cast and could not safely drive, and he had a good employment record); Goodman Beverage Co., 108 LA 37 (Morgan, Jr., 1997) (employee who did not cut short his vacation as requested by the company did not quit his job, where, before he left on vacation, he told the employer that he was not sure he could get a refund from the hotel, and while on vacation he called the company to notify it that he could not get the refund but that he would report at the regular, scheduled time); Hickory Vinyl Corp., 105 LA 572 (Hayford, 1995) (employee who left plant without permission did not quit, where he told his supervisor that he was ill and he did not say that he was quitting his job); Stone Container Corp., 105 LA 385 (Berquist, 1995) (employee who walked off the job due to threats from his coworker did not quit but was constructively discharged, where the supervisor knew of the situation because the grievant reported it and management failed to respond). *But see* Kodiak Elec. Ass'n, 104 LA 1112 (Peck, 1995) (employee who

intent to resign exists, the matter may be treated as a resignation even though the individual never actually expresses an intention to resign.[60]

However, if an intent to resign is not adequately evidenced or if a statement of an intention to resign is involuntary or coerced, the alleged resignation will be treated as discharge for purposes of arbitral review.[61] In a case dealing with drug testing, an arbitrator deemed that an employee's resignation to avoid such testing was voluntary,[62] but ordered reinstatement because the drug tests were not administered consistent with company rules.[63] When a resignation is coerced,[64] termination occurs because an employee refuses to comply with management's request to engage in conduct not re-

---

resigned in part due to a long suspension imposed absent proper investigation by management did effectively quit his job, where management did not plan or use the matter that prompted the suspension in order to cause the employee to resign).

[60]*See* Stewart-Warner Corp., 53 LA 1103, 1107 (High, 1969); Queen City Mfg. Co., 50 LA 46, 48 (Stouffer, 1968) (employee did tell other employees she was quitting); Hanlon & Wilson Co., 49 LA 540, 544 (Scheib, 1967); Reliable Packaging, 48 LA 227, 228 (Davis, 1967); PG Publ'g, 47 LA 115, 118–19 (Duff, 1966); Studebaker Corp., 45 LA 599, 603 (Davey, 1965); Armco Steel Corps., 30 LA 224, 225 (Kelliher, 1958); Celanese Corp. of Am., 26 LA 786, 788 (Jaffee, 1956); Ring's End Fuel Co., 25 LA 608, 610–11 (Donnelly, 1955); Campbell Soup Co., 17 LA 808, 809–10 (Lewis, 1951); Dravo Corp., 15 LA 282, 290 (Crawford, 1950). *See also* Airtel, Inc., 97 LA 297, 306–10 (Prayzich, 1991). *Cf.* Acme Elec. Corp., 69 LA 176, 179–80 (Croft, 1977); Metal & Thermit Corp., 18 LA 576, 580 (Gilden, 1952); Miller & Hart, Inc., 15 LA 300, 303–04 (Kelliher, 1950); Simplicity Pattern Co., 14 LA 462, 465–66 (Platt, 1950).

[61]*See* Lakeside Jubilee Foods, 95 LA 807, 812 (Berquist, 1990); Walgreen Co., 88 LA 1265, 1268–69 (Marcus, 1987) (no intent to quit where grievant was off work with job-related injury); Louisiana Pac. Graphics, 88 LA 597, 599 (LaCugna, 1986); City of Kan. City, Mo., 87 LA 616, 618–19 (Madden, 1986) (fire marshal constructively discharged disabled firefighter after assigning him to foot patrol); Whiteway Mfg. Co., 86 LA 144, 147 (Cloke, 1986) (employee walked off the job to control anger); Armco Composites, 79 LA 1157, 1163 (House, 1982); Zell Bros., 78 LA 1012, 1015 (Mayer, 1982); Skaggs Supercenters, 73 LA 544, 546 (Cohen, 1979); Pepsi Cola Bottling Co. of Miami, 70 LA 434, 435 (Blackmar, 1978); I.U.D.S.-Midwest, 68 LA 962, 965 (Cox, 1977) (concluding that "because of the limitation on the employee's right to representation, and the limited time grievant had to reflect prior to making his decision to resign," it was not "an effective voluntary quit"); Wer Indus. Corp., 55 LA 604, 607 (Rose, 1970); Harvard Mfg. Co., 51 LA 1098, 1102 (Kates, 1968); Southern Cal. Edison Co., 51 LA 869, 871 (McNaughton, 1968); Illinois Bell Tel. Co., 48 LA 273, 276 (Dolnick, 1967); Shenango, Inc., 46 LA 985, 988 (McDermott, 1966); Kraft Foods, 45 LA 1153, 1154 (Cahn, 1966); Requarth Lumber Co., 43 LA 76, 78 (McIntosh, 1964); Lukens Steel Co., 42 LA 849, 849 (Crawford, 1964); Louisville Pub. Warehouse Co., 29 LA 128, 131–32 (Kesselman, 1957); San Francisco Newspaper Publishers Ass'n, 27 LA 11, 15–18 (Miller, 1956); McDonnell Aircraft Corp., 26 LA 48, 51–52 (Klamon, 1956); Bessemer Mfg. Co., 20 LA 868, 870 (Brower, 1953); U.S. Rubber Co., 6 LA 557, 559–60 (Healy, 1946).

[62]*See* C&A Wallcoverings, 100 LA 485, 488 (McMillen, 1993); Coca-Cola Bottling Group, 97 LA 343, 347–50 (Weckstein, 1991).

[63]Texas Utils. Generating Co., 82 LA 6 (Edes, 1983). *See also* Whiteway Mfg. Co., 86 LA 144 (Cloke, 1986); Fordham Univ., 85 LA 293, 295 (Irsay, 1985) ("[A] voluntary quit is a right exclusively reserved to an employee based on his or her actions. The critical factors to be considered in any effort to distinguish between voluntary quit and discharge are the circumstances surrounding the disputed action and intent on the part of the employee involved"). *See also* Armstrong Air Conditioning, 99 LA 533, 537–40 (Harlan, 1992) (discharge reduced to suspension because drug testing was prompted by impairment due to effects of an unknown diabetic condition); Federal Mogul Corp., 86 LA 225 (Blinn, 1985) (mitigating factors considered despite a contract provision deeming certain action to constitute a voluntary quit). *Compare* Bruce Hardwood Floors, 92 LA 259 (King, 1989) (employee determined to have voluntarily quit when he left job site, even though he was persuaded by his supervisor, in the parking lot, to return and work remainder of shift, because supervisor lacked authority to rehire the employee).

[64]MacMillan Bloedel Containers, 92 LA 592 (Nicholas, Jr., 1989) (where employees were given choice of resignation or summary discharge, resignations were viewed as constructive discharges).

quired under the contract.[65] Such terminations are viewed as discharges rather than voluntary resignations.

Sometimes in situations in which an employee has in fact submitted a resignation, the employee subsequently has attempted to withdraw it. The attempted withdrawal has been upheld in some cases[66] but not in others.[67] Arbitrators appear to consider it significant if management relied on the employee's resignation and expended effort to fill the position.[68]

3. Arbitral Principles in Discipline and Discharge Cases

A. Off-Duty Misconduct[69]

i. Off-Duty Misconduct Away From Employer's Premises
[LA CDI 100.552510; 118.634]

The right of management to discharge an employee for conduct away from the plant depends on the effect of that conduct on plant operations.[70] In this regard, an arbitrator explained in one case:

---

[65]Continental White Cap, 90 LA 1119 (Staudohar, 1988) (refusal to sign company warning against continued absenteeism was not tantamount to resignation, where signature was not required under agreement or company rules).

[66]See Moss Supermarket, 99 LA 408, 411–12 (Grupp, 1992) (company was not inconvenienced or prejudiced by withdrawal attempt); State of Minn. Pollution Control Agency, 97 LA 389, 392 (Daly, 1991) (state employer did not accept resignation offer or detrimentally rely on it); United Tel. Co. of Tex., 93 LA 1047, 1049 (Shieber, 1989) (grievant acted in a timely manner to make withdrawal of oral resignation, where irrational behavior was due to chemical imbalance because he failed to take blood pressure medicine); International Mill Serv., 88 LA 118, 121–22 (McAlpin, 1986); Renaissance Ctr. P'ship, 76 LA 379, 383 (Daniel, 1981); Muter Co., 47 LA 332, 336 (Di Leone, 1966) (notice to quit in the future is not necessarily irrevocable); Davis Cabinet Co., 45 LA 1030, 1033 (Tatum, 1965) (employee's tender of resignation is an offer that can be withdrawn prior to its acceptance); Vickers Inc., 41 LA 918, 920–21 (Seitz, 1963); Ingalls Shipbuilding Corp., 38 LA 84, 88–89 (Hebert, 1961); American Bakeries Co., 34 LA 360, 364–65 (Sembower, 1960); Consumers Union of the U.S., 22 LA 238, 238–39 (Gray, 1953). See also E.C. Jones, Inc., 53 LA 1100, 1103 (Bell, 1969) (employee punched out but changed his mind within an hour).

[67]See Safeway Stores, 79 LA 176, 178 (Winograd, 1982); H.H. Robertson Co., 50 LA 637, 640 (Kabaker, 1968) (employee signed "quit form" and company accepted it); ITT Cannon Elec., 47 LA 454, 457 (Roberts, 1966) (employee could not withdraw written resignation that had been processed by the company); Transcon Lines, 40 LA 469, 472 (Marshall, 1963) (employer had right to choose whether to accept or reject retraction of resignation); Borden Co., 38 LA 425, 429 (Morvant, 1962) (resignation is effective even without acceptance and employer is not required to permit withdrawal); Addressograph-Multigraph Corp., 29 LA 700, 703–04 (Dworkin, 1957); Ford Motor Co., 7 LA 330, 333 (Babcock, 1947); Strauss Fasteners, 3 LA 239, 241 (Kaplan, 1946).

[68]See Roadway Express, 109 LA 1064 (Nathan, 1997) (employer's refusal to reinstate the employee did not violate the contract, where she attempted to rescind her resignation, arguing that management did not evidence acceptance of her resignation, although the employer had posted and filled the job). But see Municipality of Anchorage, Alaska, 108 LA 1184 (Landau, 1997) (employer's refusal to reinstate the employee, where she withdrew her resignation after determining that her retirement incentive program was not going to be performed, her request was made 10 days before the resignation was complete, and the city had neither hired nor pursued a replacement to fill the position).

[69]See also Discipline and Discharge in Arbitration ch. 9 (Brand ed., BNA Books 1998 & Supp. 2001).

[70]For a general discussion of this subject, see Marmo, Public Employees: On-the-Job Discipline for Off-the-Job Behavior, 40 Arb. J. No. 2, at 2 (1985); Sussman, Work Discipline Versus Private Life: An Analysis of Arbitration Cases, 10 I.L.R. Res. 3 (1964). For related material, see Chapter 13, section 17., "Workplace Rules."

The Arbitrator finds no basis in the contract or in American industrial practice to justify a discharge for misconduct away from the place of work unless:

1) behavior harms Company's reputation or product . . . ;

2) behavior renders employee unable to perform his duties or appear at work, in which case the discharge would be based on inefficiency or excessive absenteeism . . . ;

3) behavior leads to refusal, reluctance or inability of other employees to work with him . . . .[71]

A fourth justification was identified by another arbitrator: "'where the off-duty conduct undermines the ability of the Employer to direct the work force.'"[72]

One arbitrator also spoke of the extent to which management may consider conduct away from the plant as the basis for discharge:

While it is true that the employer does not [by virtue of the employment relationship] become the guardian of the employee's every personal action and does not exercise parental control, it is equally true that in those areas having to do with the employer's business, the employer has the right to terminate the relationship if the employee's wrongful actions injuriously affect the business.[73]

The connection between the off-duty misconduct and the injurious effect on the business must be reasonable and discernible and not merely speculative.[74]

---

[71]W.E. Caldwell Co., 28 LA 434, 436–37 (Kesselman, 1957), *quoted in* City of New Hope, Minn., 89 LA 427, 430 (Bard, 1987); City of Shawnee, Okla., 91 LA 93, 97 (Allen, Jr., 1988). For other general statements, see *County of Orange*, 90 LA 117, 118 (Brisco, 1987) (citing another source); *U.S. Postal Serv.*, 89 LA 495, 498 (Nolan, 1987); *Marshall Brass Co.*, 78 LA 806, 808 (Keefe, 1982) (quoting another source); *City of Wilkes-Barre, Pa.*, 74 LA 33, 35 (Dunn, 1980) (commenting in regard to public-sector employees); *Movielab*, 50 LA 632, 633 (McMahon, 1968); *Great Atl. & Pac. Tea Co.*, 45 LA 495, 497 (Livengood, undated). In *Eastern Air Lines*, 45 LA 932, 936–39 (Ables, 1965), the arbitrator suggested guidelines and procedures for the parties to utilize in disputes involving off-duty misconduct. Somewhat different or additional considerations may be involved in regard to off-duty conduct of public employees. See state-sector decisions in *Polk County, Iowa*, 80 LA 639, 642 (Madden, 1983); *St. Clair County*, 80 LA 516, 519 (Roumell, Jr., 1983); *Cuyahoga County, Ohio, Welfare Dep't*, 76 LA 729, 731 (Siegel, 1981); City of Wilkes-Barre, Pa., 74 LA 33, 35 (Dunn, 1980). See federal-sector decisions in *Social Sec. Admin.*, 80 LA 725, 728–29 (Lubic, 1983); *Internal Revenue Serv.*, 77 LA 19, 21–23 (Edes, 1981); *U.S. Postal Serv.*, 72 LA 522, 523–24 (Krimsly, 1979).

[72]Procter & Gamble, 114 LA 1185, 1187 (Allen, Jr., 2000) (quoting Hughes Air Corp., 73 LA 148, 157 (Barsamian, 1979); citing Stark County Sheriff, 88 LA 65, 71 (Richard, 1986)).

[73]Inland Container Corp., 28 LA 312, 314 (Ferguson, 1957), *quoted in* City of New Hope, Minn., 89 LA 427, 430 (Bard, 1987); Elyria Bd. of Educ., 86 LA 921, 923 (Cohen, 1985).

[74]Allied Supermarkets, 41 LA 713, 714–15 (Mittenthal, 1963) (reversing discharge for second instance of "unwed motherhood"); Handy & Harman Ref. Div., 106 LA 1049, 1052–54 (McCausland, 1996) (security guard accused of domestic violence); Brockway Pressed Metals, 98 LA 1211, 1213–15 (Mayer, 1992) (failed to present any evidence of effect on company); Virginia Elec., 87 LA 1261, 1263 (Jewett, 1986) (requiring clear and convincing evidence of adverse effect on the business); U.S. Postal Serv., 72 LA 522, 524 (Krimsly, 1979); Vulcan Materials Co., 56 LA 469, 473 (Shearer, 1971). *See also* Movielab, 50 LA 632, 633 (McMahon, 1968) (the employer introduced no evidence to show adverse effect on the business as a result of the employee's being convicted (but placed on probation) on narcotics charges). *But see* Arco-Polymers, 69 LA 379, 387 (Milentz, 1977); Wheaton Indus., 64 LA 826, 828 (Kerrison, 1975) (stating that "the seriousness of the drug problem generally and the need for a company to strive to prevent drug abuse amongst its employees does warrant a finding that a company has the right to act immediately to protect its own interests and the interests of its employees from the possibility that an individual charged with possession of drugs for the purpose of sale for profit will engage in such activity on company property and with fellow employees"). In *Armco Steel Corp.*, 43 LA 977, 981 (Kates, 1964), the effect on the employer of the employee's morals conviction was uncertain and the employee had long years of service. Conditional reinstatement was ordered, with the employer permitted to discharge the employee if adverse effect within the plant or adverse outside reactions against the employer developed as a result of the conviction.

They must be such as could logically be expected to cause some harm to the employer's affairs. Each case must be judged on its own merits.[75]

There are many cases in which discharges for conduct away from the employer's place of business were held to be improper because the requirement of adverse effect on the business was not met.[76] In cases where the employee's conduct away from the worksite was found to be related to his or her employment, or was found to have an actual or reasonably foreseeable adverse effect on the business, then often discharge (or in some instances a lesser penalty) was found to be justified.[77] In one case, the arbitrator noted

---

[75]Inland Container Corp., 28 LA 312, 314 (Ferguson, 1957), *quoted in* City of New Hope, Minn., 89 LA 427, 430 (Bard, 1987); Elyria Bd. of Educ., 86 LA 921, 923 (Cohen, 1985).

[76]In addition to cases in the preceding footnotes, see *ATC/Vancom of Cal. LP*, 111 LA 244, 248 (McKay, 1998) (bus driver disciplined for off-duty driving under the influence conviction); *Iowa Pub. Serv. Co.*, 95 LA 319, 322–26 (Murphy, 1990) (assault of ex-wife and others); *Mobil Oil Corp.*, 95 LA 162, 168–69 (Allen, Jr., 1990) (minimal involvement in manufacture of drugs, where charges were dropped because of cooperation with the police); *Lockheed Aeronautical Sys. Co.*, 92 LA 669, 672 (Jewett, 1989) (misdemeanor possession of marijuana); *Fairmont Gen. Hosp.*, 91 LA 930, 934 (Hunter, Jr., 1988) (shoplifting by nurse); *City of Shawnee, Okla.*, 91 LA 93, 97 (Allen, Jr., 1988) (pleading nolo contendere to felony charge of second-degree manslaughter); *County of Orange*, 90 LA 117, 118–20 (Brisco, 1987) (physical assault of wife by sheriff's deputy); *John Morrell & Co.*, 90 LA 38, 40 (Concepcion, 1987) (possession of cocaine); City of New Hope, Minn., 89 LA 427, 430 (Bard, 1987) (drunk at employee picnic at city park); *Warner-Lambert Co.*, 89 LA 265, 268 (Sloane, 1987) (possession of handgun and small amount of cocaine); *City of Muskegon Heights, Mich., Police Dep't*, 88 LA 675, 679 (Girolamo, 1987) (physical abuse of girlfriend by police officer); Virginia Elec., 87 LA 1261, 1263–64 (Jewett, 1986) (use and possession of marijuana); *Vulcan Asphalt Ref. Co.*, 78 LA 1311, 1313 (Welch, 1982) (selling marijuana); *Ralphs Grocery Co.*, 77 LA 867, 871 (Kaufman, 1981) (homosexual conduct); *U.S. Steel Supply Div.*, 73 LA 1042, 1044 (Noble, 1979) (vehicle damage); *Valley Bell Dairy Co.*, 71 LA 1004, 1006 (Hunter, Jr., 1978) (firing gun); *Indian Head, Inc.*, 71 LA 82, 85 (Rimer, Jr., 1978) (possession of marijuana); *Honeywell, Inc.*, 68 LA 346, 350 (Goldstein, 1977) (fighting); *Operating Eng'rs Local 132*, 68 LA 254, 256 (Wagner, 1977) ("affair" with fellow employee); *Bazor Express*, 46 LA 307, 309 (Duff, 1966) ("romantic exploits at hotel" had no bearing on job as truck driver); *Central Ill. Pub. Serv. Co.*, 44 LA 133, 140 (Young, 1965) (filing bankruptcy); *Babcock & Wilcox Co.*, 43 LA 242, 244 (Duff, 1964) (contributing to delinquency of minor); United States Steel Corp., 41 LA 460, 463–64 (Altrock, 1963) (morals offense); *Linde Co.*, 37 LA 1040, 1043 (Wyckoff, 1962) (narcotics conviction); *Westinghouse Elec. Corp.*, 35 LA 315, 322–23 (Hill, 1960) (invoking Fifth Amendment in congressional investigation).

[77]*See* CSX Hotels, 93 LA 1037, 1041 (Zobrak, 1989) (theft where job required trustworthiness); City of Okmulgee, Okla., 91 LA 259, 261 (Harr, 1988) (employment at recreational center that sold beer and featured topless dancers in prohibition of city work rules); Lanter Co., 87 LA 1300, 1302 (Thornell, 1986) (convicted of distributing cocaine); New York Dep't of Corr. Servs., 87 LA 165, 166–67 (Babiskin, 1986) ("snorting" cocaine in parking lot of night club by corrections officers); Elyria Bd. of Educ., 86 LA 921, 923–27 (Cohen, 1985) (misdemeanor drug offense by high school counselor); New York State Dep't of Corr., 86 LA 793, 797 (La Manna, 1985) (correction officer smoking marijuana with three teenagers); Marshall Brass Co., 78 LA 806, 809 (Keefe, 1982) (verbal abuse of plant manager at company picnic); Gould, Inc., 76 LA 1187, 1191 (Boyer, 1981); Personnel Review Bd., N.Y. City Health & Hosps. Corp., 76 LA 387, 389–90 (Simons, 1981) (possession and sale of cocaine); Hilton Hawaiian Village, 76 LA 347, 350 (Tanaka, 1981) (theft); Safeway Stores, 74 LA 1293, 1296 (Doyle, 1980) (burglary); Central Soya Co., 74 LA 1084, 1090 (Cantor, 1980) (threatening foreman); NCR, 70 LA 756, 759 (Gundermann, 1978) (vandalizing supervisor's home); Maimonides Inst., 69 LA 876, 879 (Benewitz, 1977) (shooting incident); Electronic Memories & Magnetics Corp., 69 LA 507, 509 (Sembower, 1977) (parking in "no-parking zone" near plant); Arco-Polymers, 69 LA 379, 387 (Milentz, 1977) (possession of heroin); American Airlines, 68 LA 1245, 1247 (Harkless, 1977) (shoplifting); Inspiration Consol. Copper Co., 60 LA 173, 177–78 (Gentile, 1973) (possession of stolen property); A.B. Chance Co., 57 LA 725, 730 (Florey, 1971); Lone Star Gas Co., 56 LA 1221, 1226–27 (Johannes, 1971) (incest); Northwest Airlines, 53 LA 203, 205–06 (Sembower, 1969) (indecent practices, i.e., photographing nude males); NRM Corp., 51 LA 177, 180–81 (Teple, 1968); Rhodia, Inc., 49 LA 941, 943 (Wolf,

that certain conduct was "so obviously wrong that employees must know that they cannot retain their jobs if they do those things."[78]

Even if the away-from-the-plant misconduct involves the possession or use of drugs, the effect on the employer's business must be established.[79] However, where such conduct involves drug dealing or selling, one arbitrator determined that the nexus between the conduct and the employer's business was automatically established.[80]

It continues to be the rule that off-duty/off-premises altercations, verbal abuse, or threatening behavior toward a coworker or a supervisor may provide a sufficient nexus to the workplace to justify discharge[81] or discipline.[82]

1967); Green River Steel Co., 49 LA 117, 120–21 (Chalfie, 1967) (intoxication); Baltimore Transit Co., 47 LA 62, 66 (Duff, 1966) (Ku Klux Klan Acting Grand Dragon); Albritton Eng'g Corp., 46 LA 857, 859–60 (Hughes, 1966) (knife assault); Sundstrand Corp., 46 LA 346, 348–49 (Larkin, 1966) (fight); Eastern Air Lines, 45 LA 932, 936–39 (Ables, 1965); Great Atl. & Pac. Tea Co., 45 LA 495, 497 (Livengood, undated) (bootlegging); Menzie Dairy Co., 45 LA 283, 290–91 (Mullin, 1965); Robertshaw Controls Co., 64–2 ARB ¶8748 (Duff, 1964) (sexual perversion); Gas Serv. Co., 39 LA 1025, 1028–29 (Granoff, 1962) (employee with sordid private life, whose work required him to enter customers' homes); H.J. Scheirich Co., 39 LA 245, 248–49 (Volz, 1962); Owens-Illinois Glass Co., 38 LA 1003, 1005 (Duncan, 1962) (widespread publicity from bootlegging arrest and grand larceny conviction, reflecting adversely on coworkers and employer); Chicago Pneumatic Tool Co., 38 LA 891, 893 (Duff, 1961) (drug addiction). Similarly, in the following cases, disciplinary suspensions were upheld: Genesee County, Mich., 90 LA 48, 53–54 (House, 1987) (2-week suspension appropriate for county jail employee guilty of shoplifting); O.B. Williams Co., 87 LA 534, 535–36 (Krebs, 1986) (5-day suspension appropriate for fighting with coworker on sidewalk adjacent to business).

[78]Westvaco Corp., 95 LA 169, 172 (Abrams, 1990) (suspension of grievant pending resolution of criminal charge of beating and holding woman captive in his house was upheld, despite no posted rule allowing for suspension for off-duty misconduct).

[79]Lockheed Aeronautical Sys. Co., 92 LA 669 (Jewett, 1989) (off-duty/off-premises sale of marijuana must have nexus to conduct on job to constitute just cause for discharge; employee reinstated); Bard Mfg. Co., 91 LA 193 (Cornelius, 1988) (absent showing of adverse impact on company workplace and failure of company to investigate, felony conviction not per se basis for discharge); Pennwalt Corp., 89 LA 585 (Kanner, 1987) (discharge of employee based on off-duty/off-premises use of cocaine that caused 3 days' absence from work not justified where employee had acknowledged drug problem and sought treatment 1 year prior and otherwise had good work record); Warner-Lambert Co., 89 LA 265 (Sloane, 1987) (employer lacked just cause to discharge employee arrested for possessing handgun and cocaine, where no adverse impact demonstrated on business); Pacific Bell, 87 LA 313 (Schubert, 1986) (right to discharge for off-duty misconduct is not automatic and conviction for off-duty possession of cocaine does not demonstrate employee used drugs on job so as to furnish basis for discharge for just cause). For cases upholding dismissal of employee, see USAir, Inc., 91 LA 6, 9 (Ables, 1988) (off-duty/off-premises purchase of narcotics by airline flight attendant, followed by arrest while in uniform, provided grounds for discharge where nexus to company operations was provided by criminal prosecutor, who informed company of arrest and expressed his concern, because "I fly USAir"); American Brass Co., 89 LA 1193 (Ahern, 1987) (employee's off-duty/off-premises arrest for possession of cocaine supported inference of intent to bring illegal drugs onto company property, that he had done so previously, and was, therefore, in violation of published company policy against bringing drugs to work); Wayne State Univ., 87 LA 953 (Lipson, 1986) (discharge for off-duty drug use proper where employee's job required considerable contact with community and his off-duty drug use clearly had impact on workplace).

[80]Briggs & Stratton Corp., 107 LA 1023, 1028–30 (Briggs, 1997) (employer had just cause to discharge employee selling drugs on company premises); Trane Co., 96 LA 435, 438 (Reynolds, 1991). But see W.R. Grace & Co., 93 LA 1210, 1212 (Odom, 1989) (off-duty/off-premises conduct involving the illegal use and sales of drugs is not per se justification for a worker's discharge).

[81]Keebler Co., 92 LA 871 (Roumell, Jr., 1989) (arbitrator modified discharge based on seniority and good work record). See also General Dynamics, 100 LA 180, 182–83 (Francis, 1992).

[82]Wisconsin Power & Light Co., 99 LA 493, 495–96 (Imes, 1992) (employee sent supervisor pornographic materials).

ii. Off-Duty Misconduct on Company Premises
[LA CDI 100.552510; 118.634]

It appears clear that off-duty employees have a general obligation to observe plant rules while on company premises. They may be subject to discipline for their misconduct, even though the misconduct (which often will adversely affect employee morale, discipline, or other legitimate company interests) occurs while they are off duty and in a nonworking area of the plant, such as the company cafeteria or parking lot.[83] Indeed, another arbitrator upheld the discharge of an employee for violation of a company rule that forbade "bringing, possession or use of intoxicants or controlled or illegal drugs on company property," even though the employee, who was charged with possession of drugs with the intent to sell, was arrested across the street from the plant by the police shortly before his shift was to begin.[84]

Management's right to discipline off-duty employees for misconduct on company premises is not always upheld. One arbitrator refused to sustain the discharge of an employee where the altercation took place at a company picnic on the company farm and was related to company-furnished intoxicants and poor supervision by the company.[85] Similarly, an employer could not discharge an off-duty employee for drug possession where the employee's presence on company property was unrelated to his employment.[86] In yet another case, the arbitrator held that the employer could not discharge an employee who was arrested on premises for possession of marijuana when there was no company rule prohibiting possession and no evidence that the employee had actually used the marijuana while on company premises.[87]

iii. Off-Duty Misconduct Prior to Employment
[LA CDI 100.552510; 118.634]

An employer was permitted to discharge an employee after discovering that the employee had been arrested and convicted for criminal conduct that

---

[83]*See* Hess Oil V.I. Corp., 93 LA 580, 582–84 (Chandler, 1989); B. Green Co., 65 LA 1233, 1236 (Cushman, 1975); Safeway Stores, 65 LA 1177, 1182 (Smith, 1975); Wisconsin State Dep't of Health & Soc. Servs., 63 LA 36, 42–44 (Gratz, 1974); International Harvester Co., 50 LA 766, 767–68 (Doyle, 1968); Brown & Williamson Tobacco Corp., 50 LA 403, 407 (Willingham, 1968); Frolic Footwear, 49 LA 1253, 1257 (Larkin, 1967); Pittsburgh Plate Glass Co., 49 LA 370, 374–75 (Dworkin, 1967); Convair Div., 48 LA 1099, 1100–01 (Block, 1967); Lone Star Brewing Co., 45 LA 817, 818, 821 (Merrill, 1965) (altercation at union meeting on company premises). *See also* Container Prods., 95 LA 1129, 1132–35 (Suardi, 1990) (included situation where the employee was "passed out" in company parking lot when the employee had been conditionally reinstated on continued participation in alcoholism treatment). *Cf.* Williams Bros. Mkts., 64 LA 528, 530 (Coombs, 1975); Beckley Mfg. Corp., 48 LA 695, 696–97 (Duff, 1966).

[84]American Brass Co., 89 LA 1193, 1194 (Ahern, 1987).

[85]AFG Indus., 87 LA 1160 (Clarke, 1986). *See also* Kalamazoo County Rd. Comm'n, 88 LA 1049 (Lewis, 1987) (discipline of employees who each drank two beers during unpaid lunch was improper, even though company rule prohibited drinking on company time, because unpaid lunch period was not considered to be company time).

[86]Texas Utils. Generating Co., 82 LA 6 (Edes, 1983).

[87]Greyhound Exhibit Group, 89 LA 925 (McIntosh, 1987).

occurred prior to employment. The arbitrator found that discharge was appropriate because the conduct involved dishonesty and the company would not have hired the employee had it known of the conduct.[88]

B. Effect of Criminal Proceedings Against the Employee

Where an employee, while on the job, engages in conduct that leads to an arrest, management has been permitted to take action against the employee without waiting for a court determination of guilt. The general rule followed by arbitrators is that an employer has just cause to suspend an employee for off-duty conduct that leads to an arrest, and to convert the suspension to discharge following the employee's conviction, where the employer has made its own good-faith investigation into the alleged misconduct, the charge gives rise to a legitimate concern for the safety of employees or property, and the employer determines that the misconduct disqualifies the employee from directly rendering his or her services, impairs his or her usefulness to the employer, or is likely to have an adverse effect on the employer's business.[89]

In several cases, arbitrators have set aside the suspension of an employee pending the disposition of criminal charges arising from off-duty conduct, because the misconduct was found not to be directly tied to the workplace[90] or to have otherwise adversely affected the employer.[91]

---

[88]Alpha Beta Co., 91 LA 1225 (Wilmoth, 1988). *See also* College of St. Scholastica, 96 LA 244, 254–55 (Berquist, 1991) (upholding dismissal of employee for prior criminal record of sexual abuse discovered after the employee was charged with committing domestic abuse; however, the arbitrator noted that had the employer been a manufacturer rather than a female-dominated college, the outcome might have been different). See also section 3.B., "Effect of Criminal Proceedings Against the Employee," below.

[89]*See* Jersey Shore Steel Co., 100 LA 489 (Goulet, 1992) (just cause existed to discharge 14-year employee following arrest and guilty plea to charge of off-duty delivery and possession of marijuana); Lanter Co., 87 LA 1300 (Thornell, 1986) (just cause existed to suspend and later discharge employee charged with and convicted of distributing drugs, where employer made good-faith investigation). *See also* Occidental Chem. Corp., 97 LA 585 (Duff, 1991) (just cause to suspend and then discharge chemical plant employee arrested and convicted of off-duty arson, where employee worked with flammable and explosive chemicals and employer reasonably believed he might commit incendiary acts at other buildings; employer had duty to maintain safe workplace, and grievant would be unavailable for work due to 3–9-year prison sentence); Johnson & Johnson Patient Care, 95 LA 409 (Allen, Jr., 1990) (suspension without back pay proper based on indictment for off-duty possession of marijuana and undercover agent's report of grievant's further off-duty involvement with illegal drugs, where charges could have adverse effect on workplace, and employer reinstated grievant immediately upon dismissal of charges); Westvaco Corp., 95 LA 169, 172 (Abrams, 1990) (grievant properly suspended pending resolution of charge of assault with intent to commit murder where alleged misconduct—beating and holding a woman captive in his house—was a major scandal in small town, allegations reasonably caused employer concern for employee safety, possible disruption of operations, and potential negative effect on customers, where employer conducted an independent investigation before issuing suspension). *Cf.* Alpha Beta Co., 91 LA 1225 (Wilmoth, 1988) (summary discharge after arrest for grand theft was not supported in absence of company investigation; proper discipline pending outcome of criminal charges would be suspension; discharge allowed to stand for other reasons).

[90]Babcock & Wilcox Co., 102 LA 104 (Nicholas, Jr., 1994).

[91]U.S. Foodservice, 114 LA 1675 (Chandler, 2000) (although grievant had killed a person in a fight during hockey practice, penalty of indefinite suspension was vacated because grievant did not present a threat to coworkers or company); Startran, Inc., 104 LA 641 (Baroni, 1995); Southern Nuclear Operating Co., 102 LA 97 (Abrams, 1993).

In cases where an employee is charged with a crime allegedly committed away from company premises, the type of situation in which management may have a right to suspend the employee pending court determination of guilt was summarized as follows:

> But whether we consider this type of action [i.e., suspension pending court determination of guilt] as disciplinary or not, and notwithstanding the presumption of innocence in a criminal proceeding, the employer must have the right to protect his business from the adverse effects flowing from public accusation and arrest for serious crime, supported by a judicial finding of probable cause in a preliminary hearing, when the nature of the charge with its attendant publicity reasonably gives rise to legitimate fear for the safety of other employees or of property, or of substantial adverse effects upon the business.[92]

The arbitrator concluded in that case that the violent nature of the criminal offenses with which the employee was charged (first degree burglary and assault with intent to rape) could reasonably create feelings of danger and fear among fellow employees and supervisors, so as to interfere with the proper operation of the business and to justify the suspension pending court determination of guilt.[93]

The suspensions and subsequent discharges of employees who are ultimately found guilty of criminal charges are typically upheld when the illegal conduct relates to, and adversely affects, the employer's business.[94]

In some cases, the question before the arbitrator has concerned the employer's action in discharging or disciplining an employee after the criminal charges against the employee have been dismissed,[95] or for absence from

---

[92]Pearl Brewing Co., 48 LA 379, 390 (Howard, 1967) (arbitrator reached his conclusions after studying numerous arbitration decisions).

[93]For other cases upholding suspension pending court decision, see *Allegan Gen. Hosp.*, 99 LA 818, 820–21 (Lewis, 1992); *Westvaco Corp.*, 95 LA 169, 171–72 (Abrams, 1990); *Group W. Cable*, 80 LA 205, 211 (Chandler, 1983) (upholding the "indeterminate suspension" of grievant only "insofar as it does not become one of 'unreasonable' length"); *Safeway Stores*, 78 LA 597, 602–03 (Phelan, 1982); *Ampco Pittsburgh Corp.*, 75 LA 363, 365–66 (Seinsheimer, 1980); *Michigan Power Co.*, 68 LA 183, 186–87 (Rayl, Jr., 1977) (suspension was proper only from the time when charges were filed until they were dismissed); *Lone Star Gas Co.*, 56 LA 1221, 1226–27 (Johannes, 1971); *McDonnell Douglas Corp.*, 50 LA 274, 277 (Lennard, 1968); *City of Bridgeport*, 48 LA 186, 187 (Johnson, 1967); *Tibbetts Plumbing-Heating Co.*, 46 LA 124, 126–27 (Stouffer, 1966); *Great Atl. & Pac. Tea Co.*, 45 LA 498, 499–500 (Livengood, undated); *Great Atl. & Pac. Tea Co.*, 45 LA 495, 497–98 (Livengood, undated). For cases in which the suspension was held improper, see *Mason & Hanger-Silas Mason Co.*, 66 LA 187, 188–89 (Giles, 1976); *County of Allegheny, Pa.*, 66 LA 185, 187 (Stonehouse, Jr., 1976); *A.S. Abell Co.*, 39 LA 859, 862 (Strong, 1962). *See also* City of Mason, 73 LA 464, 475, 477 (Ellmann, 1979).

[94]Dunlop Tire Corp., 104 LA 653 (Teple, 1995) (employer had just cause to discharge employee who pleaded guilty to possessing drugs on company property); Ernst Enters., 103 LA 782 (Doering, 1994) (employer had just cause to discharge driver whose guilty plea to charge of driving under the influence of alcohol resulted in the suspension of his driver's license and resulting inability to perform assigned duties); Leestown Co., 102 LA 979 (Sergent, 1994) (discharge was not too severe for employee determined by an unemployment appeals referee to have fraudulently obtained unemployment benefits from the employer).

[95]Georgia-Pacific Corp., 99 LA 361 (Allen, Jr., 1992) (employee on indefinite suspension lasting 11 months received 60 days of back pay, where prior arbitration award upheld indefinite suspension but added that grievant would not necessarily be barred from back pay if he was acquitted or criminal charges were dismissed, where prosecutor refused to prosecute the charges of illegal drug offenses, and where grievant was concededly a productive employee, there was no hint that he was a drug user or pusher, the charges involved off-duty activities unrelated to the workplace, and the employee asserted that he had "learned a lesson"); Mobil

work due to jail confinement. In such cases, while collateral estoppel and related doctrines may not apply because of differences in the burden of proof, management nevertheless often has been upheld, but this has not always been the result.[96]

C. Types of Penalities Imposed by Management

The type of penalty assessed for wrongdoing usually is either temporary suspension or discharge.[97] Temporary suspension, or "disciplinary layoff" as it is sometimes called,[98] results in loss of pay (and sometimes seniority) for the period of suspension, and mars the employee's record. When an arbitrator reinstates a discharged employee without back pay the end result is not unlike suspension.

Warnings are, in a sense, a lesser type of discipline,[99] and, as noted in section 3.F.x., "Warnings," below, they are an important factor in evaluating discipline for subsequent offenses.

The right of management to use other types of penalties has met with arbitral disapproval.[100] This is true, for instance, in regard to the disciplin-

---

Oil Corp., 95 LA 162 (Allen, Jr., 1990) (discharge of employee arrested for manufacture of drugs in his home reduced to suspension, where the employer was not identified in the news accounts of the incident, no coworkers expressed reluctance to work with the grievant, his disciplinary record was nearly spotless, and he technically did not violate company rule requiring discharge for felony "conviction" in that charges were dismissed following cooperation with police).

[96]For a collection of cases permitting or not permitting discharge or discipline of employees for absences due to jail confinement, see *Capitol Mfg. Co.*, 48 LA 243, 248–49 (Klein, 1967). For some later cases, see *L.F. Widmann, Inc.* 99 LA 1173, 1175 (Dunn, Sr., 1992); *Ralphs-Pugh Co.*, 79 LA 6, 9–10 (McKay, 1982) (discussing factors considered by other arbitrators in such cases); *Boeing Servs. Int'l*, 75 LA 967, 968 (Kramer, 1980); *General Portland, Inc.*, 73 LA 1000, 1003 (Leeper, 1979); *McInerney Spring & Wire Co.*, 72 LA 1262, 1265 (Roumell, Jr., 1979) (stating that his study of prior decisions indicated that the "reason a discharge is proper in such cases is not because of the crime the employee has committed but rather it is simply that through the employee's own actions, he has made it impossible to fulfill his obligation to report to work"; but, reversing the discharge in the present case, the arbitrator stated that, by refusing to sign a work release program contract, it was "the Company and not the employee who . . . made it impossible for him to work"); *Crown Cork & Seal Co.*, 72 LA 613, 615–16 (Daly, 1979); *Bethlehem Steel Corp.*, 72 LA 210, 211 (Sharnoff, 1979); *Owens-Illinois*, 71 LA 1095, 1098 (Foster, 1978).

[97]Indefinite suspension has been deemed equivalent to discharge. See Art Carved, 70 LA 869, 875 (Kramer, 1978); Penn-Dixie Cement Corp., 29 LA 451, 455 (Brecht, 1957); Harriet Cotton Mills, 27 LA 523, 527 (Barrett, 1956).

[98]See Koppers Co., 11 LA 334, 335 (McCoy, 1948).

[99]See Federal Labor Union v. American Can Co., 21 LA 518 (N.J. Super. Ct. 1953). See also Bethel Sch. Dist. No. 403, 71 LA 314, 320 (Beck, 1978); Elgin Instrument Co., 37 LA 1064, 1068 (Roberts, 1961); Donaldson Co., 20 LA 826, 831 (Louisell, 1953); Fairbanks Co., 20 LA 36, 38 (Sanders, 1951). Cf. Dayton Malleable Iron Co., 48 LA 1345, 1349 (Teple, 1967). In *Columbus Board of Education*, 73 LA 382, 384 (Perry, 1979), a school official, having noticed that a female employee was wearing pants, spoke to her privately and asked if she understood the dress code requirements; concluding that this did not constitute discipline, the arbitrator explained that the official "did not tell her that her behavior was improper and did not threaten or predict a penalty for any alleged violation."

[100]L.F. Widmann Inc., 99 LA 1173 (Dunn, Sr., 1992) (just cause did not exist to keep truck driver arrested for off-duty driving under the influence on indefinite suspension after driving privileges reinstated); United States Steel Corp., 98 LA 251 (Petersen, 1991) (demotion from auto mechanic to track labor position improper for involvement in four on-the-job accidents over 10-month period); Man Roland, Inc., 97 LA 175 (Speroff, 1991) (demotion of 428-pound employee from journeyman machinist to janitor classification on recovery and

ary use of demotion or downgrading or transfers,[101] withholding monetary benefits (without actual suspension),[102] requiring employees to present a medical certificate before returning to work after allegedly being sick,[103] and forcing public apologies.[104] One arbitrator sustained the grievance of an employee demoted for failure to satisfactorily perform the duties of a position to which she had been promoted as a disciplinary action taken without just cause because the employer did not make a serious effort to train the employee in the new position.[105] Another arbitrator reinstated a discharged employee who was the victim of a coworker's threatening behavior.[106] In a limited number of situations, however, arbitrators have upheld the right of employers to transfer[107] and even demote[108] employees for workplace misconduct.

The increase of violence in the workplace has led employers to expressly prohibit employees from bringing firearms into the workplace. Arbitrators

---

return from fifth major job-related injury was improper); Mason & Hanger-Silas Mason Co., 96 LA 1150 (Anthony, 1991) (disciplinary demotions of two security guards for improper performance of duties set aside, where outside scope of discipline permitted by contract); American Nat'l Can Co., 95 LA 873 (Borland, 1990) (disqualification from furnace operator classification improper, even though employee conduct caused major product loss and interruption of operations, where discipline amounted to an "indeterminate sentence"). In some cases, however, arbitrators themselves have utilized various other penalties or remedies in upsetting managerial actions in discharge and discipline cases. See section 4., "Scope of Arbitral Remedies in Discipline and Discharge Cases."

[101]See Chapter 13, section 20., "Promotion and/or Transfer of Employees."

[102]See City of Cincinnati, Ohio, 80 LA 748, 751 (Klein, 1983); Missouri Power & Light Co., 80 LA 297, 301 (Westbrook, 1982); City of Boca Raton, Fla., 75 LA 706, 710 (Davidson, 1980); Southeastern Elec. Coop., 70 LA 1138, 1140 (Johannes, 1978); Celotex Corp., 36 LA 517, 521–22 (Dworkin, 1961); Armstrong Tire & Rubber Co., 18 LA 544, 550 (Ralston, 1952); Liberty Plating Co., 9 LA 505, 508 (Fearing, 1947). Cf. Lackawanna Leather Co., 55 LA 1309, 1312 (Scheiber, 1970). As to the denial of overtime work as punishment, compare American Standard, 53 LA 414, 415–17 (Belkin, 1969), with Greif Bros. Corp., 55 LA 384, 386 (Markowitz, 1970).

[103]See Continental Moss-Gordin Gin Co., 46 LA 1071, 1073 (Williams, 1966).

[104]See Reynolds Metals Co., 22 LA 528, 534 (Klamon, 1954). But see Four Wheel Drive Auto Co., 20 LA 823, 826 (Rauch, 1953); Crawford Clothes, 19 LA 475, 481–82 (Kramer, 1952).

[105]Klauser Corp., 102 LA 381, 383 (McCurdy, 1994).

[106]Atlas Roofing Co., 114 LA 1679, 1682 (Abrams, 2000).

[107]Memphis Light, Gas & Water Div., 100 LA 291 (Caraway, 1993) (reassignment of employee to noncustomer contact position following third customer complaint of sexual harassment proper); L.F. Widmann Inc., 99 LA 1173, 1175 (Dunn, Sr., 1992) (employer properly transferred truck driver to warehouse position following arrest for driving under the influence); Host Int'l, 94 LA 492 (Talarico, 1990) (employer properly transferred minor busboy to other facilities, where employee called acting manager "nigger" and employer discovered minor was improperly serving alcohol); National Tea Co., 90 LA 773 (Baroni, 1988) (company was justified in transferring employees who had refused to take polygraph tests concerning inventory shrinkage, despite the union's contention that this action was improper discipline under the collective bargaining agreement).

[108]Southern Ind. Gas & Elec. Co., 100 LA 160 (Euker, 1992) (employer properly demoted lineman to position of meter reader following involvement in several motor vehicle accidents); Iowa Power, 97 LA 1029 (Thornell, 1991) (demotion of working foreman to meter reader was proper, where his failure to check "potential" of 13,000 volt power line caused explosion, injury to himself, damage to company property, and interruption of power to customers); Southwest Petro-Chem, 92 LA 492 (Berger, 1988) (employer allowed to impose discipline of demotion instead of discharge when the employee's conduct merited termination).

have generally enforced such prohibitions[109] Arbitrators also have sustained the discharge of employees who were violent or who threatened violence in the workplace.[110]

Where drug or alcohol use is suspected, arbitrators have continued to limit the right of the employer to subject employees to drug testing[111] or searches.[112] However, employers have been permitted to subject employees to drug testing where the contract permits it and the employer has established the necessary "reasonable cause" or "reasonable suspicion" to warrant the test.[113] Moreover, a number of arbitrators have begun to allow random,

---

[109]Caterpillar, Inc., 114 LA 1143 (Daniel, 2000); San Diego Trolley, 112 LA 323 (Prayzich, 1999); Sandusky Cabinets, 112 LA 373 (Morgan, Jr., 1999).

[110]Champion Int'l Co., 115 LA 27 (Weston, 2000) (employee discharged for writing graffiti threatening coworker); Southwest Airlines, 114 LA 1797 (Jennings, 2000) (employee told coworkers he might go "postal"); Michigan Milk Producers Ass'n, 114 LA 1024 (McDonald, 2000); USS, Div. of USX Corp., 114 LA 948, 52 (Das, 2000) (employee discharged for chilling statements about what to do to two fellow workers with whom he had long running feud); Georgia Pac. Corp., 113 LA 679 (Jennings, 1999); B.W. Provisions, 113 LA 527 (Gentile, 1999) (employee hit his wife, who was also an employee in the workplace); Rohm & Hass Tex., 113 LA 119 (Woolf, 1999).

[111]Stone Container Corp., 95 LA 729 (Nolan, 1990) (substance abuse testing policy is unreasonable to the extent that it requires testing of all employees involved in accidents that result in personal injury, regardless of whether there is reasonable suspicion of substance abuse); Utah Power & Light Co., 94 LA 233 (Winograd, 1990) (just cause did not exist to discharge grievant for refusing to submit to drug test, where grievant's mere exhaustion of all sick leave and alleged failure to follow proper procedure in requesting day off does not provide necessary probable cause for requiring test); Tribune Co., 93 LA 201 (Crane, 1989) (an on-the-job accident alone was not sufficient to justify imposition of a drug test requiring just cause); Boston Edison Co., 92 LA 374 (Nicolau, 1988) (company not allowed to use drug testing where it failed to prove any need for test, test did not determine employee's fitness to perform, and company had other means of obtaining its objective); Young Insulation Group of Memphis, 90 LA 341 (Boals, 1987) (drug testing without probable cause improper where no relationship to job performance is proved).

[112]BellSouth Telecomms., 114 LA 1779 (Hooper, 2000) (drug found in possession of grievant by police in presence of management employee); Vista Chem. Co., 92 LA 329, 332 (Duff, 1989) (clause allowing employer to search employees' clothing for drugs should be limited to situations where employer has "reasonable suspicion" and where search is confined to "extent necessary to insure the safe and productive conduct" of business). See related discussion in Chapter 16, section 2.A., "Alcohol and/or Drug Use and Testing"; Chapter 19, section 4., "Privacy, Search and Seizure Protection, and Compulsory Drug and Alcohol Testing"; and Chapter 21, section 2.C.ii, "Illicit Drug Use and Possession," and section 2.C.iii., "Non-Drug-Related Off-Duty Criminal Offenses."

[113]Carlon, 99 LA 677 (Hoffman, 1992) (manager's observation of employee and coworker holding lighter and trying to light something close to their mouths in remote and hidden area outside plant provided reasonable suspicion to order drug test); Armstrong Air Conditioning, 99 LA 533 (Harlan, 1992) (reasonable cause existed to request drug test, where forklift operator was observed swerving forklift, driving erratically, and acting uncharacteristically nervous and fidgety); Borg Warner Auto. Diversified Transmission Prods. Corp., 99 LA 209 (Bethel, 1992) (legitimate cause to order grievants to submit to drug test based on informant's allegations of marijuana use, where grievants were found in secluded area and smell of burning marijuana became stronger as supervisors approached area); Coca-Cola Bottling Group, 97 LA 343 (Weckstein, 1991) (employer had reasonable cause to require delivery driver to submit to drug/alcohol screen where coworker reported him driving erratically, supervisors and coworkers observed other typical physical signs of drug/alcohol use, and driver acknowledged accuracy of driving report).

mandatory drug testing where the employee's job involves safety or health concerns.[114]

The Americans with Disabilities Act (ADA) allows employers to hold drug users or alcoholics to the same standards as other employees. Current users of illegal drugs are excluded from the ADA definition of a qualified individual with a disability. Generally, employees who fail to perform their job responsibilities can be disciplined or discharged, even if the failure to perfrom is due to alcohol or drug addiction. [115]

In order to avoid liability under Title VII of the Civil Rights Act, employers must investigate complaints of sexual harassment and must take appropriate action before the harassment becomes severe or pervasive.[116]

D. Burden and Quantum of Proof [LA CDI 94.60509]

There are two "proof" issues in the arbitration of discipline and discharge cases. The first involves proof of wrongdoing; the second, assuming that guilt of wrongdoing is established and that the arbitrator is empowered to modify penalties, concerns the question of whether the punishment assessed by management should be upheld or modified.[117] The present topic deals with proof of wrongdoing.[118]

---

[114]Day & Zimmermann, 94 LA 399 (Nicholas, Jr., 1990) (random drug testing of employees at ammunition plant permitted, where employees under the influence of drugs could subject themselves and many coworkers and visitors to serious or fatal injuries). *See also* Texas City Ref., 89 LA 1159 (Milentz, 1987); Ashland Oil, 89 LA 795 (Flannagan, 1987); Marathon Petroleum Co., 89 LA 716 (Grimes, 1987); Albuquerque Publ'g Co., 89 LA 333 (Fogelberg, 1987).

[115]Laporte Pigments, 114 LA 1 (Marino, 2000) (discharge for absenteeism upheld, despite the fact that the employee was addicted to alcohol and drugs). For related discussion, see Chapter 10, section 3.A.iii., "Americans With Disabilities Act"; and Chapter 14, section 2.C., "Americans With Disabilities Act."

[116]Commercial Printing Co., 115 LA 393 (Statham, 2000) (discharge penalty reduced to layoff because company had no written policy and never conducted training on sexual harassment); Alumnitec, Inc., 114 LA 1584, 1584–88 (Kindig, 2000) (arbitrator agreed that harassment on the basis of sex is a pernicious and intolerable form of misconduct, and clearly warrants severe discipline). *See also* Charter Communications Entm't I L.P., 114 LA 769 (Kelly, 2000) (sexual harassment of gay employee); Progressive Processing, 114 LA 725 (Paolucci, 2000) (offering female coworker money for sex); American Elec. Power, 114 LA 501 (Hewitt, 2000) (utility lineman discharged for making sexual advances to female customer); PPG Indus., 113 LA 833 (Dichter, 1999) (sending pornographic e-mails via employer's computer resulted in 9-month suspension without pay); Conagra Frozen Foods, 113 LA 129 (Baroni, 1999) (grievant discharged for continually created hostile climate by pervasive unwanted attention); Safeway, Inc., 112 LA 1050 (Silver, 1999) (grievant discharged for telling sexual jokes to a 16-year-old girl); Ralphs Grocery Co., 112 LA 120 (Prayzich, 1999) (grievant discharged for unwelcome kisses). See related discussion in Chapter 10, section 3.A.i., "Title VII of the Civil Rights Act"; Chapter 14, section 2.A., "Civil Rights Act"; and Chapter 17, section 7., "Protection Against Sexual Harassment."

[117]*See* Lone Star Pennsuco, 80 LA 875, 878 (Kanzer, 1983); Combustion Eng'g, 80 LA 503, 506 (Heinsz, 1983); Hilo Coast Processing Co., 74 LA 236, 239 (Tanaka, 1980); Ingersoll Prods. Div., 49 LA 882, 886 (Larkin, 1967); Pacific Northwest Bell Tel. Co., 48 LA 498, 500 (Lovell, 1967); Linear, Inc., 48 LA 319, 319–20 (Frey, 1966); American Nat'l Ins. Co., 44 LA 522, 526 (Doyle, 1965); Barcalo Mfg. Co., 28 LA 65, 67 (Levy, 1956); Monsanto Chem. Co., 27 LA 400, 404 (Reynard, 1956); Tubular Prods. Co., 26 LA 913, 913–14 (Donnelly, 1956); Valley Steel Casting Co., 22 LA 520, 524 (Howlett, 1954); Carolina Coach Co., 20 LA 451, 455 (Livengood, 1953); New Haven Clock & Watch Co., 17 LA 701, 702 (Stutz, 1952).

[118]The second proof issue—whether the punishment assessed by management should be upheld or modified—is treated in section 3.E., "Review of Penalties Imposed by Management," below.

i. Burden of Proof [LA CDI 94.60509]

The burden of proof is generally held to be on the employer to prove guilt of wrongdoing, and probably always so where the agreement requires just cause for discipline.[119] Even where the agreement is silent as to whether just cause is required for discipline and discharge decisions, arbitrators generally place the burden of proof on the employer to demonstrate just cause for such decisions.[120] Where the action of the employer is found to be nondisciplinary, the burden is often placed on the union to show that the contract was violated. After finding that a termination of employment was actually a layoff rather than a discharge, one arbitrator placed the burden of proof on the union to show that the employer violated the contract.[121] In another case, after determining that a demotion was nondisciplinary, the arbitrator held that it became the union's burden to prove a contract violation.[122]

ii. Quantum of Proof[123]

a. Proof in Ordinary Discipline Cases [LA CDI 94.60509]

The quantum of proof required to support a decision to discipline or discharge an employee is unsettled. Arbitrators have primarily imposed one of three standards, listed below from the least to the greatest burden:

1. Preponderance of the evidence;[124]

---

[119]Included among the many cases in which the arbitrators have held that the burden is on management to prove wrongdoing are: State of Iowa, Dep't of Gen. Servs., 79 LA 852, 855 (Mikrut, 1982); Rohr Indus., 78 LA 978, 982 (Sabo, 1982); Dobbs Houses, 78 LA 749, 752 (Tucker, 1982); Washington Post, 77 LA 978, 984 (Ordman, 1981); Trailways Tenn. Lines, 77 LA 210, 213 (Thompson, 1981); Mark VII Sales, 75 LA 1062, 1067 (O'Connell, 1980); General Elec. Co., 74 LA 737, 741 (Jedel, 1980); McDonnell Douglas Astronautics Co., 74 LA 726, 728 (Hardy, 1980); Cleveland-Cliffs Iron Co., 73 LA 1148, 1155 (Garrett, 1980); Mount Sinai Hosp. Med. Ctr. of Chi., 73 LA 297, 300 (Dolnick, 1979); Capital Dist. Transp. Auth., 72 LA 1313, 1316 (Cutler, 1979); Pettibone Ohio Corp., 72 LA 1144, 1149 (Feldman, 1979); Kaiser Steel Stamped Prods., 72 LA 774, 775 (Rose, 1979); Western Auto Supply Co., 71 LA 710, 714 (Ross, 1978); Libby, McNeill & Libby, 70 LA 1028, 1036 (Keltner, 1978); Brockway Pressed Metals, 69 LA 64, 67 (Mullaly, 1977). But the employee has the burden of proving the validity of the defense or excuse that the employee asserts in justification of his or her conduct. *See* Mississippi Lime Co., 29 LA 559, 561 (Updegraff, 1957). *See also* Cleveland Cliffs Iron Co., 51 LA 174, 177 (Dunne, 1967); George D. Ellis & Sons, 27 LA 562, 564–65 (Jaffee, 1956).

[120]*See* Indiana Convention Ctr. & Hoosier Dome, 98 LA 713 (Wolff, 1992); Cleveland Constr., 96 LA 354 (Dworkin, 1990); Sterling Chems., 93 LA 953 (Taylor, 1989).

[121]Kaiser Fluid Tech., 114 LA 262 (Hoffman, 2000).

[122]Archer Daniels Midland Co., 111 LA 518 (Pratte, 1998)

[123]*See also* DISCIPLINE AND DISCHARGE IN ARBITRATION 335 (Brand ed., BNA Books 1998 & Supp. 2001).

[124]*See* Rittman Nursing & Rehab. Ctr., 113 LA 284 (Kelman, 1999) (employer was required only to prove by a preponderance of the evidence that discharged nurse's aide shop steward engaged in a work stoppage despite the career-damaging consequences of such a discharge); Wholesale Produce Supply Co., 101 LA 1101 (Bognanno, 1993) (company need only prove by a preponderance of evidence that it properly discharged employee for dishonesty, because labor arbitration is not a criminal court of law and reliance on standard of beyond a reasonable doubt is inappropriate); General Elec. Co., 74 LA 25, 29 (Spencer, 1979); Hoover Universal, 73 LA 868, 871 (Gibson, 1979); Midland-Ross Corp., 52 LA 959, 962 (Erbs, 1969); Duriron Co., 49 LA 39, 39–40 (McIntosh, 1967); Du Mont Lab., 44 LA 1143, 1148

2. Clear and convincing evidence;[125]
3. Evidence beyond a reasonable doubt.[126]

Concerning the quantum of required proof, most arbitrators apply the "preponderance of the evidence" standard to ordinary discipline and discharge cases. However, in cases involving criminal conduct or stigmatizing behav-

---

(Wildebush, 1965); Barcalo Mfg. Co., 28 LA 65, 67 (Levy, 1956); Howell Ref. Co., 27 LA 486, 491 (Hale, 1956); F.J. Kress Box Co., 24 LA 401, 405 (Pollack, 1955); Southern Pac. Co., 21 LA 471, 472 (Osborne, 1953); Campbell, Wyant & Cannon Foundry Co., 1 LA 254, 262–63 (Platt, 1945). In *State University of New York*, 74 LA 299, 300 (Babiskin, 1980), the collective bargaining agreement expressly placed the burden of proof on the employer in all disciplinary proceedings and specified that: "Such burden of proof, even in serious matters which might constitute a crime shall be preponderance of the evidence on the record and shall in no case be proof beyond a reasonable doubt." By statute, a federal agency's action in disciplinary matters may be sustained on review by the Merit Systems Protection Board (MSPB) only if the agency's decision "is supported by a preponderance of the evidence." 5 U.S.C. §7701(c)(1)(B). Where a discharge for illegal sexual activity with a minor child was taken to arbitration rather than to the MSPB, the arbitrator cited the latter statute when he also utilized the "preponderance of evidence test." Social Sec. Admin., 80 LA 725, 728 (Lubic, 1983).

[125]Michigan Milk Producers Ass'n, 114 LA 1024 (McDonald, 2000) (quantum of proof in discharge case of employee accused of threatening a fellow employee is clear and convincing evidence); Professional Med Team, 111 LA 457 (Daniel, 1998) (clear and convincing evidence for discharge cases in general); Conagra Frozen Foods, 113 LA 129 (Baroni, 1999) (the arbitrator only required clear and convincing evidence in a sexual harassment case); Contempo Colours, 112 LA 356 (Daniel, 1998) (clear and convincing evidence for employee discharged for allegedly stealing a plate); American Safety Razor Co., 110 LA 737 (Hockenberry, 1998) (in a case of discharge for sexual harassment, the arbitrator rejected "beyond a reasonable doubt standard" as inappropriate in an arbitral forum); Vista Chem. Co., 104 LA 818 (Nicholas, Jr., 1995) (employer must prove by clear and convincing evidence that employee was justly discharged for sexual harassment, and arbitrator should impose strict scrutiny approach to charges of sexual harassment because of the stigmatizing effect of such charges); Carrier Corp., 103 LA 891 (Lipson, 1994) (employer's burden of proof in defending its discharge of employee for selling drugs is clear and convincing evidence whether or not the grievant is charged with committing a crime); J.R. Simplot Co., 103 LA 865 (Tilbury, 1994) (standard of proof for discharge for acts of industrial sabotage should be clear and convincing evidence, which is something more than mere preponderance and means that the trier of fact must find more than a slight tilt on the scale of justice); Litton/Ingalls Shipbuilding, 97 LA 30 (Nicholas, Jr., 1991) (clear and convincing standard); Rohr Indus., 93 LA 145 (Goulet, 1989) (same); MacMillan Bloedel Containers, 92 LA 592 (Nicholas, Jr., 1989) (same); Southern Cal. Permanente Med. Group, 92 LA 41 (Richman, 1989) (same). See Vernors, Inc., 80 LA 596, 599 (McDonald, 1983); Alvey, Inc., 74 LA 835, 838 (Roberts, 1980); Kennecott Copper Corp., 73 LA 1066, 1068 (Mewhinney, 1979); General Tel. Co. of Cal., 73 LA 531, 533 (Richman, 1979) ("[t]he standard to be applied in a case such as this [possession and use of marijuana while on the job] should be the clear and convincing evidence standard: Less than beyond a reasonable doubt but more than the ordinary prima facie case and preponderance test."); Kaiser Steel Stamped Prods., 72 LA 774, 775 (Rose, 1979); City of Cleveland, Ohio, 71 LA 1041, 1043 (Siegel, 1978); Borg-Warner Corp., 27 LA 148, 150 (Dworkin, 1956); Aviation Maint. Corp., 8 LA 261, 268 (Aaron, 1947).

[126]Jefferson County Sheriff's Office, Steubenville, Ohio, 114 LA 1508 (Klein, 2000) (employer required to prove beyond a reasonable doubt that corrections officer was guilty of sexual misconduct with female inmates because case involves potential crime and moral turpitude); Yellow Freight Sys., 103 LA 731 (Stix, 1994) (employer that discharges employee for theft must provide evidence to sustain charge beyond a reasonable doubt); Jim Walters Res. No. 7 Mine, 95 LA 1037 (Roberts, 1990) (employer must prove beyond a reasonable doubt that specimen strictly controlled at all times); S.D. Warren Co., 89 LA 688 (Gwiazda, 1985), *rev'd for other reasons sub nom.* S.D. Warren Co. v. Paperworkers Local 1069, 845 F.2d 3, 128 LRRM 2175 (1st Cir.) (beyond a reasonable doubt standard), *cert. denied*, 488 U.S. 992 (1988). *See also* Greyhound Food Mgmt., 89 LA 1138, 1141 (Grinstead, 1987) ("Attempting to steal orange juice valued at 58 cents involves moral turpitude and requires standard of proof beyond a reasonable doubt.").

ior, many arbitrators apply a higher burden of proof, typically a "clear and convincing evidence" standard, with some arbitrators imposing the "beyond a reasonable doubt" standard. But, even in cases of criminal behavior or socially stigmatizing conduct, some arbitrators require only a "preponderance of the evidence."

One arbitrator observed: "In general, arbitrators probably have used the 'preponderance of the evidence' rule or some similar standard in deciding fact issues before them, including issues presented by ordinary discipline and discharge cases."[127] But the arbitrator also noted that a higher degree of proof frequently is required where the alleged misconduct is "of a kind recognized and punished by the criminal law," and he concluded:

> [I]t seems reasonable and proper to hold that alleged misconduct of a kind which carries the stigma of general social disapproval as well as disapproval under accepted canons of plant discipline should be clearly and convincingly established by the evidence. Reasonable doubts raised by the proofs should be resolved in favor of the accused. This may mean that the employer will at times be required, for want of sufficient proof, to withhold or rescind disciplinary action which in fact is fully deserved, but this kind of result is inherent in any civilized system of justice.[128]

Concerning the quantum of proof to be imposed in a case involving theft, an arbitrator stated:

> I agree with the Union that a discharge for theft has such catastrophic economic and social consequences to the accused that it should not be sustained unless supported by the overwhelming weight of evidence. Proof beyond any reasonable doubt, even in cases of this type, may sometimes be too strict a standard to impose on an employer; but the accused must always be given the benefit of substantial doubts.[129]

Another arbitrator in such a case stated the requirement to be that "the arbitrator must be completely convinced that the employee was guilty."[130] One arbitrator suggested that, regardless of which "verbal formulas for the requisite degree of proof" arbitrators may profess to require, the fact is that "most of us 'consciously or unconsciously' require the highest degree of proof in discharge cases where the involved employee action . . . also constitutes a crime."[131] Generally, three factors are considered in determining the standard of proof necessary, though none alone seems to be determinative. Specifically, arbitrators consider whether the employee's conduct constituted criminal behavior, whether it involved moral turpitude or social stigma, and whether the sanction imposed was discharge or some lesser discipline. In cases of potentially unlawful conduct, the greater weight of authority favors

[127]Kroger Co., 25 LA 906, 908 (Smith, 1955).
[128]*Id.*
[129]Armour-Dial, 76 LA 96, 99 (Aaron, 1980).
[130]Columbia Presbyterian Hosp., 79 LA 24, 27 (Spencer, 1982).
[131]American Air Filter Co., 64 LA 404, 406–07 (Hilpert, 1975). *See also* Todd Pac. Shipyards Corp., 72 LA 1022, 1024 (Brisco, 1979); Getman, *What Price Employment? Arbitration, the Constitution, and Personal Freedom, in* ARBITRATION—1976, PROCEEDINGS OF THE 29TH ANNUAL MEETING OF NAA 61, 96 (Dennis & Somers eds., BNA Books 1976).

"clear and convincing evidence"[132] or "preponderance of the evidence,"[133] as opposed to "beyond a reasonable doubt."

An arbitrator may require a high degree of proof in one discharge case and at the same time recognize that a lesser degree may be required in others.[134] Similarly, where the proof was not strong enough to support discharge, some arbitrators have nonetheless found it strong enough to justify a lesser penalty.[135]

b. Proof in Group Discipline Cases [LA CDI 94.60509; 118.01]

In a "slowdown" case, the evidence was not specific as to the work performance of each individual, but the employer was upheld in disciplining all crew members who were on the crew for the full period of the slowdown. The arbitrator stated that, "[w]hile not every situation would or should lend itself to implicating several employees in slowdown activities, such implications seem justified where [as in the present case] the group involved is small and the focus of delay represents a team effort."[136] Likewise, group discipline of the six members on a boning crew was upheld where each individual denied any responsibility for the bad work that the crew had done but where each individual also refused to testify against any other member of the crew.[137]

---

[132]Duke Univ., 100 LA 316 (Hooper, 1993) (employer must meet clear and convincing evidence standard, but not beyond a reasonable doubt standard, to show just cause for discharge of supervisor accused of sexual harassment); Central Mich. Univ., 99 LA 134 (McDonald, 1992) (same); Indiana Convention Ctr. & Hoosier Dome, 98 LA 713 (Wolff, 1992) (employer must meet clear and convincing evidence standard to show just cause for discharge of employee who assaulted and threatened to kill supervisor); City of Kankakee, Ill., 97 LA 564 (Wolff, 1991) (employer must meet clear and convincing evidence standard to show just cause for discharge of employee for driving snowplow while under the influence of alcohol); Maurey Mfg. Co., 95 LA 148 (Goldstein, 1990) (employer must meet clear and convincing evidence standard to show just cause for discharge of employee for running an illegal, in-house game of chance).

[133]Coca-Cola Bottling Midwest, 97 LA 166 (Daly, 1991) (discharge improper for theft where employer could not even show intent to steal by a preponderance of the evidence).

[134]See Proto Tool Co., 46 LA 486, 489 (Roberts, 1966); Catler-Magner Co., 38 LA 1157, 1159 (Graff, 1961); United States Steel Corp., 29 LA 272, 277 (Babb, 1957); Cannon Elec. Co., 28 LA 879, 882–83 (Jones, Jr., 1957); Howell Ref. Co., 27 LA 486, 491 (Hale, 1956); American Smelting & Ref. Co., 7 LA 147, 149–50 (Wagner, 1947).

[135]See National Bedding & Furniture Indus., 48 LA 891, 893 (Hon, 1967); American Airlines, 47 LA 890, 896 (Sembower, 1966); Deere & Co., 45 LA 844, 845–47 (Davis, 1965); Braniff Airways, 44 LA 417, 421 (Rohman, 1965).

[136]Kennecott Copper Corp., 41 LA 1339, 1344 (Dykstra, 1963). See also Toshiba Am., 78 LA 612, 616 (Flannagan, 1982). In City of Elmira, New York, City School District, 54 LA 569, 570–71 (Markowitz, 1971), the arbitrator applied the New York "Taylor Law" under which public employees absent during a strike were presumed to be strikers and had the "burden of proof" of rebutting the presumption by showing that the absence was not related to the strike. For a similar result apart from statute, see Lone Star Steel Co., 48 LA 949, 951 (Jenkins, 1967). Cf. Briggs Mfg. Co., 74 LA 877, 880–81 (Welch, 1980).

[137]Marhoefer Packing Co., 54 LA 649, 652–53 (Sembower, 1971). In Koppers Co., 76 LA 175, 177 (Amis, 1981), the arbitrator stated: "It may be assumed that not all the grievants were directly involved" in the equipment sabotage. "On the other hand, by their silence those members [of the crew] not directly involved are guilty of conspiring to obstruct the Company investigation of the matter, and they, too, deserve a penalty." Cf. Arizona Aluminum Co., 78 LA 766, 770–71 (Sass, 1982); Oshkosh Truck Corp., 72 LA 909, 912 (Kossoff, 1979) (citing other cases supporting the arbitrator's conclusion that an employee may not be disciplined where the employer has shown neither that the employee was an actual participant in the misconduct nor that the employee knew the identity of the actual participants). In Babcock & Wilcox Co., 59 LA 72, 75–76 (Nicholas, Jr., 1972), the work "gang" located nearest to

Conversely, some arbitrators have indicated rather clearly that they consider group discipline to be improper in the absence of evidence establishing the guilt of all.[138]

In the case of an illegal strike, arbitrators will generally require the employer to base discipline on proof of each individual employee's involvement and degree of participation in the group activity. However, the fact that an employer is not able to identify each employee participating in the strike will not prevent the employer from taking reasonable disciplinary action against those employees whom it proves actually did participate.[139] Likewise, where a single company investigation of several employees resulted in their simultaneous discharge or discipline, grievances by different individuals involving different circumstances could not be lumped together and treated as one.[140]

E. Review of Penalties Imposed by Management[141]

i. Judicial Recognition of Arbitral Discretion

Court decisions recognize broad arbitral discretion to review the reasonableness of the penalty imposed by the employer in relation to the employee's wrongful conduct.[142] These decisions rely on the Supreme Court's statement

---

firecracker incidents in the plant could be suspended without pay in view of safety considerations, but more than mere circumstantial evidence would be required in order to place a disciplinary action in an employee's work record. Group discipline for failure to meet production standards was held not to be guilt by association and was upheld in *Whirlwind, Inc.*, 50 LA 888, 897 (Solomon, 1968), and in *Buddy L Corp.*, 49 LA 581, 583–84 (McIntosh, 1967).

[138]*See* Joerns Healthcare, 94 LA 17, 19–21 (Kessler, 1989); Westinghouse Elec. Co., 48 LA 211, 213 (Williams, 1967); Quick Mfg., 45 LA 53, 55–57 (Gross, 1965); Evinrude Motors Co., 36 LA 1302, 1303 (Marshall, 1961).

[139]*See* Walgreen Co., 100 LA 468 (Shieber, 1992); Super Valu Stores, 86 LA 622 (Smith, 1986); Detroit Edison Co., 82 LA 226 (Jones, 1983). *But see* Mann Packing Co., 83 LA 552 (Concepcion, 1984).

[140]Mason & Hanger-Silas Mason Co., 96 LA 1150 (Anthony, 1991); S.D. Warren Co., 189 LA 688 (Gwiazda, 1985), *rev'd for other reasons sub nom.* S.D. Warren Co. v. Paperworkers Local 1069, 845 F.2d 3, 128 LRRM 2175 (1st Cir.) (however, arbitrator applied the same standard of proof for each grievant), *cert. denied*, 488 U.S. 992 (1988).

[141]DISCIPLINE AND DISCHARGE IN ARBITRATION 389–91 (Brand ed., BNA Books 1998 & Supp. 2001).

[142]*See* Food & Commercial Workers Local 7 v. King Soopers, 222 F.3d 1223, 164 LRRM 2970 (10th Cir. 2000); Association of Western Pulp & Paper Workers Local 78 v. Rexam Graphic, 221 F.3d 1085, 165 LRRM 2137 (9th Cir. 2000); Hill v. Staten Island Zoological Soc'y, 147 F.3d 209, 158 LRRM 2709 (2d Cir. 1998); VAW of Am. v. Steelworkers, 53 F. Supp. 2d 187, 162 LRRM 2302 (N.D.N.Y. 1999); Teamsters Local 330 v. Elgin Eby-Brown Co., 670 F. Supp. 1393, 127 LRRM 2950 (N.D. Ill. 1987); Industrial Mut. Ass'n v. Amalgamated Workers Local 383, 725 F.2d 406, 115 LRRM 2503, 2507 (6th Cir. 1984); Lynchburg Foundry Co. Div. v. Steelworkers Local 2556, 404 F. 2d 259, 261, 69 LRRM 2878 (4th Cir. 1968); Auto Workers Local 1492 v. Fruehauf Trailer Corp., 153 LRRM 2821 (N.D. Ill. 1996); Teamsters Local 968 v. Sysco Food Servs., 838 F.2d 794, 127 LRRM 2925 (5th Cir. 1988); GSX Corp. of Mo. v. Teamsters Local 610, 658 F. Supp. 124, 127 LRRM 2391 (E.D. Mo. 1987); Hilton Int'l Co. v. Union de Trabajadores de la Industria Gastronomica de P.R., 600 F. Supp. 1446, 119 LRRM 2011 (D.P.R. 1985). *But cf.* Contico Int'l v. Leather Goods Workers Local 160, 738 F. Supp. 1262, 135 LRRM 2091, 2095–96 (E.D. Mo. 1990) (without citing *Paperworkers v. Misco, Inc.*, 484 U.S. 29, 126 LRRM 3113 (1987), the court found the arbitrator had exceeded his authority in setting aside the employer's discharge of employee for sleeping during work hours; the arbitrator altered, added to, and modified the terms of the collective bargaining agreement

in *Paperworkers v. Misco, Inc.*[143] that the arbitrator is to bring his informed judgment to bear in order to reach a fair solution of a problem, especially when it comes to formulating remedies.[144] In *Misco*, the arbitrator based his finding that there was not just cause for a discharge on his consideration of seven criteria, including the reasonableness of the employer's position, the relation of the degree of discipline to the nature of the offense, and the employee's past record.[145] The Court noted that "courts are not authorized to reconsider the merits of an award even though the parties may allege that the award rests on errors of fact or on misinterpretation of the contract."[146] The Court further stated:

> Normally, an arbitrator is authorized to disagree with the sanction imposed for employee misconduct. In *Enterprise Wheel [Steelworkers v. Enterprise Wheel & Car Corp.*, 363 U.S. 593, 46 LRRM 2423 (1960)], for example, the arbitrator reduced the discipline from discharge to a 10-day suspension. . . . [T]hough the arbitrator's decision must draw its essence from the agreement, he "is to bring his informed judgment to bear in order to reach a fair solution of a problem. *This is especially true when it comes to formulating remedies.*" 363 U.S. at 597 (emphasis added). The parties, of course, may limit the discretion of the arbitrator in this respect; and it may be, as the Company argues, that under the contract involved here, it was within the unreviewable discretion of management to discharge an employee once a violation of Rule II.1 [listing causes for discharge] was found. But the parties stipulated that the issue before the arbitrator was whether there was "just" cause for the discharge, and the arbitrator, in the course of his opinion, cryptically observed that Rule II.1 merely listed causes for discharge and did not expressly provide for immediate discharge. Before disposing of the case on the ground that Rule II.1 had been violated and discharge was therefore proper, the proper course would have been [to] remand to the arbitrator for a definitive construction of the contract in this respect.[147]

Of course, as *Misco* recognized, the parties may limit the discretion of the arbitrator to modify the discipline imposed by the employer by employing express language to that effect in the collective bargaining agreement.[148]

---

by interpreting ambiguous contract that provided automatic termination for violation of work rules which covered sleeping on the job by applying "arbitrary, discriminatory and capricious" standard in interpreting "discharge for cause" and by allowing for balancing of equities in finding automatic discharge was excessive penalty due to employer's contribution to employee's misconduct).

[143]484 U.S. 29, 41, 126 LRRM 3113 (1987).

[144]The Court stated that if additional facts were to be found, the arbitrator should find them in the course of any further effort the company might have made to discharge the employee for having had marijuana in his car on company premises. Had the arbitrator found that the employee had possessed drugs on the property, yet imposed discipline short of discharge because he found as a factual matter that the employee could be trusted not to use them on the job, the court of appeals could not upset the award because of its own view that public policy about plant safety was threatened. *Id.* at 42, 126 LRRM at 3120. Thus, the Court recognized the arbitrator's authority to modify the discipline even if he found a violation of the rule.

[145]*Id.* at 34 n.5, 126 LRRM at 3115 n.5.

[146]*Id.* at 36, 126 LRRM at 3116.

[147]*Id.* at 41–42, 126 LRRM at 3118.

[148]Several of these courts have cited, as an example of language providing such a limitation, an arbitration clause providing:

> The Union recognizes the right of the Company to make and enforce Rules and Regulations and that violation thereof may be just cause for discipline or discharge of employees. The only question which may be the subject of a "grievance" is whether or not the disciplined employee did or did not engage in the specific conduct . . . .

Teamsters Local 968 v. Sysco Food Servs., 838 F.2d 794, 796, 127 LRRM 2025 (5th Cir. 1988).

Consequently, courts will not hesitate to set aside an arbitrator's decision when the language of the collective bargaining agreement prohibits the arbitrator from fashioning remedies once just cause for an employer's action is found.[149]

In *Misco*, the Supreme Court also held that a reviewing court may vacate an arbitrator's decision when it contravenes a basic tenet of public policy that is "'well defined and dominant,'"[150] and ascertained under statutory law and legal precedents and not from general considerations of perceived public interest. Specifically, a court's task in reviewing a labor arbitrator's award for possible violations of public policy is limited to "determining whether the award, itself, as contrasted with the reasoning underlying the award, creates an explicit conflict with other laws and legal precedents and thus clearly violates an identifiable public policy."[151] An arbitrator's award will be vacated as conflicting with public policy only if a clear nexus exists between enforcement of the award and violation of public policy,[152] and public policy is to be narrowly construed in determining whether an arbitral award conflicts with it.[153] However, courts are showing an increasing hostil-

---

[149]Container Prods. v. Steelworkers, 873 F.2d 818, 131 LRRM 2623 (5th Cir. 1989); Georgia-Pacific Corp. v. Paperworkers Local 27, 864 F.2d 940, 130 LRRM 2208 (1st Cir. 1988); S.D. Warren v. Paperworkers, 846 F.2d 827, 128 LRRM 2432 (1st Cir. 1988); S.D. Warren v. Paperworkers, 845 F.2d 3, 128 LRRM 2175 (1st Cir. 1988); Tootsie Roll Indus. v. Bakery, Confectionery, & Tobacco Workers Local 1, 832 F.2d 81, 126 LRRM 2700 (7th Cir. 1987); Dobbs, Inc. v. Teamsters Local 614, 813 F.2d 85, 124 LRRM 2827 (6th Cir. 1987) (the court, applying the plain-meaning rule, found that the arbitrator exceeded his authority by ordering reinstatement with back pay when the contract plainly and unambiguously recognized employer's right to discharge employees for proper cause); Pennsylvania v. Independent State Stores Union, 553 A.2d 948, 130 LRRM 2780 (Pa. 1989).

[150]Paperworkers v. Misco, Inc., 484 U.S. 29, 43, 126 LRRM 3113 (1987) (quoting W.R. Grace & Co. v. Rubber Workers Local 759, 461 U.S. 757, 766, 113 LRRM 2641 (1983) (quoting, in turn, Muschany v. United States, 324 U.S. 49, 66 (1945))). *See also* Vetter, *Enforceability of Awards: I. Public Policy Post-*Misco, *in* Arbitration 1988: Emerging Issues for the 1990s, Proceedings of the 41st Annual Meeting of NAA 75 (Gruenberg ed., BNA Books 1989); Gottesman, *II. A Union Viewpoint, id.* at 88; Gould, *Judicial Review of Legal Arbitration of Awards—30 Years of the* Steelworkers Trilogy. *The Aftermath of* AT&T *and* Misco, 64 Notre Dame L. Rev. 463 (1989); Wayland, Stephens, & Franklin, Misco: *Its Impact on Arbitration Awards*, 39 Lab. L.J. 813 (1988).

[151]Electrical Workers (IBEW) Local 97 v. Niagara Mohawk Power Corp., 143 F.3d 704, 719, 158 LRRM 2198 (2d Cir. 1998).

[152]Exxon Shipping Co. v. Exxon Seamen's Union, 993 F.2d 357, 143 LRRM 2312 (3d Cir. 1993) (arbitration award reinstating helmsman discharged on basis of positive test for marijuana administered after ship ran aground violates public policy); Delta Airlines v. Air Line Pilots, 861 F.2d 665, 130 LRRM 2014 (11th Cir. 1988) (discharge of airline pilot who operated aircraft while intoxicated consistent with public policy in favor of airline safety); Iowa Elec. Light & Power Co. v. Electrical Workers (IBEW) Local 204, 834 F.2d 1424, 127 LRRM 2049 (8th Cir. 1987) (public policy favoring strict observance of federally mandated safety regulations at nuclear power site); Russell Mem'l Hosp. Ass'n v. Steelworkers, 720 F. Supp. 583, 132 LRRM 2642 (E.D. Mich. 1989) (court recognized public policy in ensuring safe and competent nursing care by vacating arbitrator's order reinstating nurse discharged for negligence).

[153]Electrical Workers (IBEW) Local 97 v. Niagara Mohawk Power Co., 143 F.3d 704, 722, 158 LRRM 2198 (2d Cir. 1998) (conditional reinstatement of employee who adulterated a drug test and had tested positive for the drug did not violate public policy because applicable regulations do not address adulteration and require only minimal response for first failure of drug test); Stead Motors of Walnut Creek v. Machinists Lodge 1173, 886 F.2d 1200, 132 LRRM 2689 (9th Cir. 1989) (state's general interest in safe motor vehicles did not form well-defined and dominant public policy necessary to bar reinstatement of negligent mechanic), *cert. denied*, 495 U.S. 946 (1990); Communications Workers v. Southeastern Elec. Coop. of

ity toward arbitration decisions that fail to recognize the seriousness of drug and alcohol abuse.[154]

In *Eastern Associated Coal Corp. v. Mine Workers District 17*,[155] the Supreme Court rejected the employer's challenge to an arbitrator's award that conditionally reinstated an employee who had twice tested positive for marijuana. The arbitrator found that the employee's 17 years of service, along with personal problems that led to his drug use, were suffcient mitigating factors to conclude that there was not just cause for discharge. The Court found that the award did not violate any specific provision of any public law or regulation, as no law or regulation prohibited the reinstatement of an employee who has failed two random drug tests. The Court also noted that the parties had "granted to the arbitrator the authority to interpret the meaning of their contract's language, including such words as 'just cause.'"[156]

For a general discussion of judicial review and vacatur of arbitration awards, see Chapter 1, section 7.B.i.d., "Scope of Judicial Review: Vacation of Award"; and Chapter 2, section 2.A.ii.c., "Post-*Triology*: Enforcement of Agreements to Arbitrate and Review of Arbitration Awards."

ii. Express Contractual Authority of Arbitrator to Modify Penalties or Withdrawal of Such Authority [LA CDI 100.559565; 118.03]

Collective bargaining agreements or submission agreements may give the arbitrator express authority to modify penalties found to be improper or too severe.[157] As noted in the previous section, some agreements expressly

---

Durant, Okla., 882 F.2d 467, 132 LRRM 2381 (10th Cir. 1989) (public policy did not preclude enforcement of arbitration award reinstating 19-year employee who sexually assaulted co-worker at home); U.S. Postal Serv. v. Letter Carriers, 839 F.2d 146, 127 LRRM 2593 (3d Cir.), *writ dismissed*, 485 U.S. 680 (1988) (no adequate public policy in favor of protecting coworkers and customers from employee's violent conduct).

[154]Gulf Coast Indus. Workers v. Exxon Co. USA, 991 F.2d 244, 143 LRRM 2375 (5th Cir. 1993) (reinstatement of oil refinery employee offends the Drug-Free Workplace Act of 1988, 41 U.S.C. §701 et seq., the ADA, Texas statutes, federal regulations, and numerous judicial decisions).

[155]531 U.S. 57, 165 LRRM 2865 (2000).

[156]*Id.* at 61.

[157]*See, e.g.,* Sundstrand Corp., 46 LA 346, 349 (Larkin, 1966). The parties clothed the arbitrator with this power at the hearing in *Dayton Malleable Iron Co.*, 17 LA 666, 666 (Hampton, 1951). In *Ken Meyer Meats*, 107 LA 1017 (Sergent, 1996), the arbitrator stated that he had authority to determine whether discharge was appropriate because by stipulating that the issue to be decided was whether there was just cause for discharge and, if not, what was the appropriate remedy, the parties had agreed that the arbitrator had full authority to address all aspects of just cause, including the appropriateness of the remedy, despite the following contractual language:

> The Company shall have the absolute right to discipline or discharge for just cause any employee for violation of any provision of this Agreement or of any reasonable rule or regulation of the Company . . . . Grievances concerning such discipline or discharge shall be limited only to the issue of whether or not any such employee discharged or disciplined engaged in the activity prohibited by this Agreement or by the Company's reasonable rules and regulation incorporated herein.

Id. at 1019.

limit the arbitrator's authority to modify penalties.[158] Under such agreements, arbitrators sometimes have sustained a discharge where they probably would have reduced the penalty but for the limitation on their authority;[159] in other instances, the denial of arbitral authority to modify penalties has resulted in the reinstatement of employees with no penalty at all, even though the employee was guilty of misconduct justifying some punishment.[160]

In one case, a party expressed serious doubt as to the wisdom of placing "the arbitrator in a position of making a 'black or white' decision,"[161] and it is not surprising that arbitrators have sometimes considered that any restriction on their authority to modify penalties must be clearly and unequivocally stated and have narrowly construed contractual provisions purporting to restrict that authority.[162] One arbitrator, for example, found that the just cause standard ("that is, action tempered by reason") governed the discharge of an employee for violating work rules that expressly provided that their violation would be considered just cause for discharge. The arbitrator reasoned that the work rules were incorporated into the agreement and that, by using "cause," "proper cause," and "just cause" in referring to discharge for rule violations, the language could not be deemed to be restrictive or be interpreted to narrow the scope of review to a unilateral decision by the company.[163]

---

[158]In *Champion Dairypak*, 105 LA 462, 462 (Allen, Jr., 1995), the arbitrator declined to substitute a lesser penalty for a termination decision he determined to be for just cause, because there was no evidence of arbitrary or bad-faith action by the company and the contract provided that the arbitrator "cannot substitute his judgment for that of Management's and can reverse the Company only if he finds the discharge or disciplinary action not supported by evidence, or the Company's action arbitrary or in bad faith."

[159]*See* Bridgford Frozen-Rite Foods, 91 LA 681, 685 (McKee, 1988); Inland Container Corp., 91 LA 544, 548–49 (Howell, 1988) (last-chance agreement); Kimco Auto Prods., 74 LA 481, 486 (Flannagan, 1980); Cleveland Alloy Castings, 69 LA 1108, 1111 (Strasshofer, 1977); Lucky Stores, 53 LA 1274, 1278 (Eaton, 1969); Allied Paper Co., 52 LA 957, 958 (Williams, 1969); Pride Packing Co., 48 LA 1092, 1093–94 (Jones, Jr., 1967); Luce Press Clipping Bureau, 40 LA 686, 688–89 (Granoff, 1963); Lunkenheimer Co., 39 LA 580, 584 (Seinsheimer, 1962). In *Hayes International Corp.*, 81 LA 99, 103–04 (Van Wart, 1983), the arbitrator concluded that he lacked authority to disturb the discharge penalty assessed for conduct that violated the requirements of a "last chance" agreement that had been signed by the employer, the union, and the employee. *See also* McDonnell Douglas Corp., 79 LA 34, 36 (Blum, 1982).

[160]*See* Welch Foods, 73 LA 908, 910–11 (Gootnick, 1979); Badger Concrete Co., 47 LA 899, 902 (Bellman, 1966); Shenango, Inc., 46 LA 985, 989 (McDermott, 1966); RCA Truck Lines, 43 LA 940, 945–46 (King, 1964).

[161]Luce Press Clipping Bureau, 40 LA 686, 688 n.6 (Granoff, 1963). Arbitral power to modify penalties was generally supported by labor and management representatives in a survey conducted by one commentator. *See* Eaton, *Labor Arbitration in the San Francisco Bay Area*, 48 LA 1381, 1386–87 (1967).

[162]*See* Central Ill. Pub. Serv. Co., 76 LA 300, 308 (Kossoff, 1981); Andrews Furniture Indus., 50 LA 600, 603 (Volz, 1968); Marion Power Shovel Co., 45 LA 580, 584 (Gilbert, 1965); Davis Fire Brick Co., 36 LA 124, 128 (Dworkin, 1960). *See also* Amoco Oil Co. v. Oil, Chem., & Atomic Workers Local 7-1, 548 F.2d 1288, 94 LRRM 2518, 2521, 2524–25 (7th Cir. 1977). For discussion of other court cases on this aspect, see Fogel, *Court Review of Discharge Arbitration Awards*, 37 ARB. J. No. 2, at 22, 32 (1982). Even a clear restriction on the arbitrator's authority was stated to be inapplicable under the circumstances in *Consolidated Paper Co.*, 33 LA 840, 846–47 (Kahn, 1959).

[163]Norfolk Shipbuilding & Drydock Corp. (NORSHIPCO), 105 LA 529, 534–35 (Hockenberry, 1995).

iii. *No Express Contractual Authority Concerning Modification of Penalties* [LA CDI 100.559565; 118.03]

Even absent express contractual authority, some arbitrators have found agreements to give them authority to modify penalties by implication.[164] Where the agreement fails to deal with the matter, the right of the arbitrator to change or modify penalties found to be improper or too severe may be deemed to be inherent in the arbitrator's power to decide the sufficiency of cause. One arbitrator elaborated:

> In many disciplinary cases, the reasonableness of the penalty imposed on an employee rather than the existence of proper cause for disciplining him is the question an arbitrator must decide. This is not so under contracts or submission agreements which expressly prohibit an arbitrator from modifying or reducing a penalty if he finds that disciplinary action was justified, but most current labor agreements do not contain such limiting clause. In disciplinary cases generally, therefore, most arbitrators exercise the right to change or modify a penalty if it is found to be improper or too severe, under all the circumstances of the situation. This right is deemed to be inherent in the arbitrator's power to discipline and in his authority to finally settle and adjust the dispute before him.[165]

Thus, some arbitrators rely on the "proportionality" element of a contractual requirement of just cause for discipline to modify penalties.[166] In *Clow Water Systems Co.*,[167] the arbitrator stated:

> Without notable exception, arbitrators emphasize the word "just" in the term [just cause], compelling employers to tailor discipline to the individual and not only to the misconduct. They see "just cause" as job-security language that requires penalties to be corrective rather than punitive. Under such interpretation, the ultimate question in a discharge dispute is not whether the miscon-

---

[164]*See* McInerney Spring & Wire Co., 21 LA 80, 82 (Smith, 1953).

[165]Platt, *The Arbitration Process in the Settlement of Labor Disputes*, 31 J. Am. Jud. Soc'y 54, 58 (1947). As to inherent authority to modify penalties, see also: Washington Hosp. Ctr., 75 LA 32, 35 (Rothschild, 1980); Continental Pac. Lines, 54 LA 1231, 1246 (Feller, 1970); Permatex Co., 54 LA 546, 550 (Goetz, 1971); Kaiser Sand & Gravel, 49 LA 190, 193 (Koven, 1967); Sanitary Bag & Burlap Co., 47 LA 327, 330 (Autrey, 1966); American Synthetic Rubber Corp., 46 LA 1161, 1165 (Dolson, 1966); Forest City Foundries Co., 44 LA 644, 646 (Strasshofer, 1965); Merchants Fast Motor Lines, 41 LA 1020, 1023 (Wren, 1963); Trumbull Asphalt Co. of Del., 41 LA 631, 636 (Sembower, 1953); Todd Shipyards Corp., 36 LA 333, 341–42 (Williams, 1961); Barcalo Mfg. Co., 28 LA 65, 69 (Levy, 1956); Weyerhaeuser Timber Co., 25 LA 634, 637–38 (Wyckoff, 1955); Higgins Indus., Inc., 25 LA 439, 442 (Hebert, 1955); E.I. DuPont de Nemours & Co., 9 LA 345, 348 (Hepburn, 1947). Indeed, the fact that most arbitrators do modify penalties found to be excessive evidences their general belief that modification authority exists. For an informative collection and discussion of court decisions concerning arbitral authority to modify penalties, see *Fogel*, 37 Arb. J. No. 2, at 32. Some of Fogel's examples are: Electrical Workers (IBEW) Local 53 v. Sho-Me Power Corp., 715 F.2d 1322, 114 LRRM 2177, 2179–80 (8th Cir. 1983); Machinists Dist. 50, Local Lodge 389 v. San Diego Marine Constr. Corp., 620 F.2d 736, 104 LRRM 2613, 2614 (9th Cir. 1980); Mine Workers Dist. 50 v. Bowman Transp., 421 F.2d 934, 936, 73 LRRM 2317 (5th Cir. 1970).

[166]In *Mason & Hanger Corp.*, 109 LA 957, 964–65 (Jennings, 1998), the arbitrator cited and relied on this reasoning, further stating: "In disciplinary matters, a penalty that is markedly too harsh for the offense is unreasonable and an abuse of managerial discretion. A penalty that flows from an incomplete analysis of both the misconduct and the individual employee is arbitrary." *Id.* at 965.

[167]102 LA 377 (Dworkin, 1994).

duct warranted the penalty, but whether the aggrieved employee deserved the penalty for committing the misconduct.[168]

Absent express limitations on their authority to modify penalties, two general views historically have been held by arbitrators. One view is that an arbitrator may not modify a penalty absent arbitrary, capricious, or discriminatory reasons, and the other view is that an arbitrator may do so if the penalty does not meet a reasonable person test. The first view evolved in a line of decisions following reasoning expressed in *Stockham Pipe Fittings Co.*:[169]

---

[168]*Id.* at 378.

[169]1 LA 160 (McCoy, 1945) (the submission specifically empowered the arbitrator to determine "what disposition" should be made of the dispute). Similarly, another arbitrator held that "the arbitrator should not substitute his judgment for that of management unless he finds that the penalty is excessive, unreasonable, or that management has abused its discretion." Franz Food Prods., 28 LA 543, 548 (Bothwell, 1957). For some of the many arbitrators expressly approving the McCoy statement in *Stockham Pipe Fittings*, see: Dyncorp, 114 LA 458, 462 (Kilroy, 2000); Oak Forest Hosp. of Cook County, 114 LA 115, 120 (Wolff, 2000); Watts Health Care Found., 112 LA 780, 782 (Cloke, 1999); G.E. Railcar Repair Servs. Corp., 112 LA 632, 635 (O'Grady, 1999); Knoll, Inc., 112 LA 438, 442 (Borland, 1998); Cuyahoga County, Ohio, Sheriff's Dep't, 110 LA 307, 307–11 (Richard, 1998); Greene County, Ohio, Sheriff's Dep't, 107 LA 865 (Felice, 1996); Airfoil Forging Textron, 106 LA 945 (Klein, 1996); City of Stillwater, Okla., 103 LA 684, 691 (Neas, 1994); Wheatland Farms, 102 LA 1175, 1178 (Woolf, 1994); Clow Water Sys. Co., 102 LA 377 (Dworkin, 1994); Indiana Bell Tel. Co., 99 LA 756 (Goldstein, 1992) (*but see* Schulze & Burch Biscuit Co., 100 LA 948, 955 (Goldstein, 1993) ("The Arbitrator is not unmindful that the initial determination of the penalty for misconduct is properly a function of Management. . . . However, inherent in the power to review is the authority to exercise the right to change or modify a penalty so that it is consonant with all proofs adduced, especially, as here, where an essential element of the case [intent to defraud] has not been proved by the Company, based on my determination." (citation omitted)); Sheriff of Broward County, Fla., 98 LA 219, 222 (Frost, 1991); McCorkle Mach. Shop, 97 LA 774, 776 (Kilroy, 1991); Interstate Brands, 97 LA 675, 677 (Ellmann, 1991); Gulf States Paper Corp., 97 LA 60, 61 (Welch, 1991); ARCO Marine, 96 LA 319, 324 (Brisco, 1990); American Transp. Corp., 81 LA 318, 324 (Nelson, 1983); Van Chevrolet, 80 LA 1298, 1301 (Madden, 1983); South Cent. Bell Tel. Co., 80 LA 891, 892 (Nicholas, Jr., 1983); Greyhound Lines, 79 LA 422, 424 (Larkin, 1982); Borg-Warner Corp., 78 LA 985, 998 (Neas, 1982); Rohr Indus., 78 LA 978, 983–84 (Sabo, 1982); Meredith Corp., 78 LA 859, 863–64 (Talent, 1982) (observing that the *Stockham Pipe Fitting* view "has been followed by a substantial and respectable segment of the arbitral community"); Dobbs Houses, 78 LA 749, 753 (Tucker, 1982). *See also* West Penn Handling Equip. Co., 74 LA 37, 41–42 (LeWinter, 1980); Atlantic Richfield Co., 69 LA 484, 487 (Sisk, 1977); Trans World Airlines, 41 LA 142, 144 (Beatty, 1963) ("[A]n arbitration clause is not an abdication by management of its duties in regard to discipline and discharge and does not grant to the arbitrator authority to redetermine the whole matter by his own standards as if he were making the original decision."); S.A. Shenk & Co., 26 LA 395, 397 (Stouffer, 1956); Phillips Petroleum Co., 25 LA 568, 571 (Kadish, 1955); Corn Prods. Ref. Co., 21 LA 105, 107 (Gilden, 1953); Brink's Inc., 19 LA 724, 727 (Reid, 1953); National Lead Co., 13 LA 28, 30 (Prasow, 1949). In *Central Illinois Public Service Co.*, 105 LA 372 (Cohen, 1995), the arbitrator stated:

> By and large, an arbitrator should not disturb a disciplinary penalty where the arbitrator's view differs somewhat from that of management. That amounts to second guessing management. If the arbitrator believes that discipline rendered was so excessive as to be arbitrary and capricious, then the arbitrator is able to alter it. For instance, in this situation, if I believed that a 30-day suspension is unwarranted, but a 27-day suspension is warranted, I would make no change.

Id. at 377. In *Frito-Lay*, 105 LA 1139 (Murphy, 1995), the arbitrator stated that he agreed with *Stockham Pipe Fittings*, but found that in the instant case the 3-day suspension penalty assessed by the company was too severe based on the circumstances, and the progressive discipline system depended on what was fair, proper, and appropriate under the circumstances. *Id.* at 1145 n.6. He further stated, "Generally, it is recognized that arbitrators have authority to adjust the penalty unless the agreement clearly states to the contrary." *Id.*

Where an employee has violated a rule or engaged in conduct meriting disciplinary action, it is primarily the function of management to decide upon the proper penalty. If management acts in good faith upon a fair investigation and fixes a penalty not inconsistent with that imposed in other like cases, an arbitrator should not disturb it.... The only circumstances under which a penalty imposed by management can be rightfully set aside by an arbitrator are those where discrimination, unfairness, or capricious and arbitrary action are proved—in other words, where there has been abuse of discretion.[170]

The second, less restricted view of the arbitrator's authority in reviewing discipline assessed under agreements requiring cause has followed the reasoning set forth in *Riley Stoker Corp.*:[171]

It is ordinarily the function of an Arbitrator in interpreting a contract provision which requires "sufficient cause" as a condition precedent to discharge not only to determine whether the employee involved is guilty of wrong-doing and, if so, to confirm the employer's right to discipline where its exercise is essential to the objective of efficiency, but also to safeguard the interests of the discharged employee by making reasonably sure that the causes for discharge were just and equitable and such as would appeal to reasonable and fair-minded persons as warranting discharge.[172]

Arbitrators in other cases have expressed similar views.[173] One arbitrator cited the following passage from *The Common Law of the Workplace* for her authority to reduce the disciplinary penalty imposed on an employee:

§10.23. Arbitral Authority to Reduce Discipline
In the absence of a contractually specified penalty or [a] clear limitation on arbitral discretion, both arbitrators and courts agree that the arbitrator may reduce the penalty imposed by management. *Most arbitrators will change a penalty if, given the facts of the case, including the grievant's seniority and work record, it is clearly out of line with generally accepted standards of discipline.* When the parties have contractually removed the arbitrator's power to change the penalty, however, arbitrators must respect this limitation.[174]

---

[170]Stockham Pipe Fittings Co., 1 LA 160, 162 (McCoy, 1945).
[171]7 LA 764 (Platt, 1947).
[172]*Id.* at 767.
[173]*See* Schulze & Burch Biscuit Co., 100 LA 948, 955 (Goldstein, 1993); Greif Bros. Corp., 81 LA 385, 386 (Frank, 1983); Pacific Tel. & Tel. Co., 73 LA 1185, 1192 (Gerber, 1979); Monfort Packing Co., 66 LA 286, 293 (Goodman, 1976); U.S. Pipe & Foundry Co., 48 LA 1349, 1353 (Coffey, 1967); Thermolite, Inc., 46 LA 974, 977 (Klein, 1966); Great Atl. & Pac. Tea Co., 45 LA 968, 970–71 (Volz, 1965); American Nat'l Ins. Co., 44 LA 522, 526–27 (Doyle, 1965); Mississippi Valley Gas Co., 41 LA 745, 750 (Hebert, 1963) (denying that the arbitrator is merely to determine whether management's action was capricious or arbitrary and declaring that he or she has a responsibility to determine whether the punishment fits the crime); Great Atl. & Pac. Tea Co., 39 LA 823, 825 (Turkus, 1962); American Radiator & Standard Sanitary Corp., 37 LA 85, 90 (Teple, 1961); Our Own Bakeries, 36 LA 537, 539 (Thompson, 1960). In *Capital Packing Co.*, 36 LA 101 (Seligson, 1961), the arbitrator stated that "a discharge case in arbitration is a hearing in equity, permitting of a flexibility and assessment of mitigating circumstances and factors not available under the more rigorous common law rules." *Id.* at 102.
[174]Wayne State Univ., 111 LA 986, 994 (Brodsky, 1998) (quoting The Common Law of the Workplace: The Views of Arbitrators 349 (St. Antoine ed., BNA Books 1998) (emphasis added by arbitrator)). The employee had been discharged for saying to his supervisor, "If I bring a 44-Magnum, can I go to sleep then?," and adding that he had "hollow-point bullets." *Wayne State Univ.*, 111 LA at 987. The arbitrator reduced the penalty to suspension where the words were threatening, were spoken within earshot of other employees, and tended to undermine supervisory authority, but the supervisor did not feel threatened because the employee had 18 years of discipline-free service, no recognized past history of violent behavior,

In *Yellow Freight System*,[175] the arbitrator stated:

> McCoy's approach [in *Stockham Pipe Fittings Co.*, 1 LA 160 (McCoy, 1945)] would apply only when the arbitrator finds that the evidence sustains the employer's charge as to the offense alleged. Moreover, although some arbitrators, following McCoy's lead, tend not to disturb the employer's choice of discipline, once the offense has been proved, it has been my practice, as it is of a majority of arbitrators, to consider whether the employer had "just cause" for the particular disciplinary measure imposed.[176]

In *Caro Center*,[177] after setting forth the positions in *Stockham Pipe Fittings* and *Riley Stoker*,[178] the arbitrator stated:

> Given the myriad of situations and the volume of cases where such penalties have been expunged, modified, or sustained, one fact is clear. Each case can be differentiated by its particular facts so as to justify the Arbitrator's conclusion. In my opinion, the bottom line followed by the majority of Arbitrators is that, where the discipline/discharge appears unreasonable in the light of all the facts, the Arbitrator has the authority to modify or vacate it. But I am also of the view that management's decision should not lightly be upset if within broad parameters of reasonableness.[179]

It often is posited that arbitrators should not interfere with discipline assessed by management if the collective bargaining agreement permits management to exercise judgment in this regard. However, such a "rule" apparently is followed more in the breach. One arbitrator offered a cogent rationale for this apparent anomaly:

> Three answers to this line of argument seem appropriate. The first is that Arbitrators very frequently do step in and upset the decisions of Management. The second is that if arbitrators could not do so, the arbitration would be of little import, since the judgment of management would in so many cases constitute the final verdict. Finally, the more careful statement of the principle would probably run to the effect that where the contract uses such terms as discharge for "cause" or for "good cause" or for "justifiable cause" an arbitrator will not lightly upset a decision reached by competent careful management which acts in the full light of all the facts, and without any evidence of bias, haste or lack of emotional balance. Even under these conditions, if the decision is such as to shock the sense of justice of ordinary reasonable men, we suspect that arbitrators have a duty to interfere.[180]

---

had shown unwavering remorse for his actions, and circumstances surrounding the threat tended to diminish its severity, including specific words spoken to the supervisor after spending part of the previous night protecting his sister from her violent husband, and the supervisor did not act threatened and accepted the employee's apology on the day of the threat.

[175]103 LA 731 (Stix, 1994).

[176]*Id.* at 736.

[177]104 LA 1092 (Kanner, 1995).

[178]*Id.* at 1094–95. He also cited the following statement of an arbitrator:

> The usual understanding is that an arbitrator who finds that a discharge was excessive punishment for misconduct may determine that some lesser punishment was justified and issue an award in accordance with that determination. . . . I think rather that I am obliged to make a judgment . . . of the employees' records, the nature of their offense and any extenuating circumstances that may exist.

Id. (quoting Continental Pac. Lines, 54 LA 1231, 1246 (Feller, 1970)).

[179]*Id.* at 1095.

[180]Fruehauf Trailer Co., 16 LA 666, 670 (Spaulding, 1951).

The principle that arbitrators can and should mitigate the discipline imposed on an employee that, when reasonably and objectively viewed, is unjust may be further refined:

> One caveat is in order to the above principle. While Arbitrators are willing to mitigate penalties where they are not prohibited by the agreement, they usually do so and should do so only where the mitigation involves a major rather than a minor change. For example, . . . a reduction of a two week suspension to a one week suspension is a minor change. Thus, even when their power to mitigate a penalty is unencumbered, arbitrators are loathe to substitute their judgment for that of management unless the degree of mitigation is a major and consequential change.[181]

Another arbitrator prefaced his quotation from the *Fruehauf* decision with this comment:

> The Arbitrator *does have* a right to alter a penalty, as [one] Arbitrator wrote:
>
> > [A]n arbitrator usually applies the equity concept in a discipline case so as to include the power to appraise penalties in terms of the fitness and fairness for the particular offense, since the extent of the penalty is logically reviewed as related to the action for which the employee is held responsible. . . . Thus, management rights, implied or expressed in an agreement, are qualified and reviewable by the need to be reasonable and fair, rather than arbitrary and capricious.[182]

Finally, it should be recognized that even arbitrators who do not lightly interfere with management's decisions in discharge and discipline matters may not fail to act firmly when management's decisions are found to be unjust or unreasonable under all the circumstances.[183] In federal sector arbitration, it has been held that "an arbitrator hearing a case under the CSRA [Civil Service Reform Act] *must* consider issues of mitigation unless the parties' contract lawfully provides otherwise."[184]

---

[181]Westinghouse Elec. Corp., 91 LA 685, 689 (Talarico, 1988)

[182]Smurfit Stone Container Div., 114 LA 562, 570 (Marino, 2000) (quoting Myers, *Concepts of Industrial Discipline, in* Management Rights and the Arbitration Process, Proceedings of the 9th Annual Meeting of NAA 59, 67 (McKelvey ed., BNA Books 1956) (emphasis in original) (the arbitrator also makes a virtually identical observation to that in *Westinghouse Electric* regarding the caveat concerning changing penalties, 114 LA at 570 n.9)).

[183]Many arbitrators are likely to agree with the following statement:

> The arbitrator must be fully cognizant that he is taking into his hands the Employer's personnel policies. The arbitrator does not live with the parties, he has not actually experienced the problems management may have which might require strong disciplinary measures. . . . At the same time, while he must use great restraint, an arbitrator must do essential justice and take the actions necessary to achieve it.

Werner-Continental, 72 LA 1, 10 (LeWinter, 1978).

The arbitrator in *Werner-Continental* quoted both *Stockham Pipe Fittings* and *Riley Stoker* without stating a preference for the view of either. He found discharge excessive on the facts and, in reducing the penalty to suspension, he stated that "the arbitrator must sustain a suspension of such length that would not shock his conscience whether he would have suspended for that period or not." *Werner-Continental*, 72 LA at 11. In *Associated Wholesale Grocers*, 112 LA 1212, 1216 (Murphy, 1999), the arbitrator cited both the *Franz Food Prods.*, 28 LA 543 (Bothwell, 1957), and *Riley Stoker* views, concluding that the employer's decision to discharge an employee could not be sustained under either standard in that case.

[184]Government Employees (AFGE) Local 2578 v. General Servs. Admin., 711 F.2d 261, 265 (D.C. Cir. 1983) (emphasis added).

iv. Mitigation Versus Leniency [LA CDI 100.559565; 118.03]

Mitigation by an arbitrator of a penalty found to be too severe should not be confused with the exercise of leniency (or clemency). The distinction between these actions was emphasized by one arbitrator when he recognized the power of arbitrators to modify penalties found on the basis of mitigating circumstances to be too severe for the offense, but at the same time declared that arbitrators have no authority to grant clemency where the penalty assessed by management is not found to be too severe.[185]

The fact that an arbitrator considers that he or she has no power of leniency or clemency, and, accordingly, that management's disciplinary action must be sustained where just cause is found, does not prevent the *recommendation* of leniency when the arbitrator personally feels that it should be considered by management.[186] Implicit in such recommendations is silent recognition by arbitrators that powers of leniency or clemency reside in management.[187]

In certain cases, the arbitrator, in upholding the penalty assessed by management, either (1) explained in detail why the arbitrator nonetheless urged the use of leniency by management,[188] or (2) explained in detail why

---

[185]Chattanooga Box & Lumber Co., 10 LA 260, 261 (McCoy, Forman, & Frazier, 1948). *See also* Ohio State Highway Patrol, 94 LA 58, 64 (Bittel, 1990); Mead Corp., 79 LA 464, 467–68 (Williams, 1982); Certainteed Corp., 78 LA 1290, 1294 (Madden, 1982); Steiger Tractor, 72 LA 175, 179 (O'Connell, 1979); Agrico Chem. Co., 70 LA 20, 27 (Hebert, 1978); Wheeling-Pittsburgh Steel Corp., 69 LA 1192, 1195 (Chockley, Jr., 1977); Indiana Harbor Belt R.R., 53 LA 990, 991–92 (Dolnick, 1969); Kroger Co., 50 LA 1194, 1198 (Abernethy, 1968); Moore's Seafood Prods., 50 LA 83, 90 (Daugherty, 1968); Arkla Air Conditioning Co., 45 LA 156, 159–60 (Larkin, 1965); Bethlehem Steel, 42 LA 307, 310 (Hughes, 1964). *But see* AMF Inc., 69 LA 987, 989 (Kleeb, 1977); Singer Co., 44 LA 1043, 1044 (Cahn, 1965). In *Hiram Walker & Sons*, 75 LA 899, 900–01 (Belshaw, 1980), the arbitrator questioned whether any valid distinction exists between arbitral power to modify penalties found to be too severe and arbitral exercise of leniency.

[186]*See* Bridgford Frozen-Rite Foods, 91 LA 681, 685 (McKee, 1988); Super-Valu Stores, 74 LA 939, 945 (Evenson, 1980); Southern Ind. Gas & Elec. Co., 74 LA 509, 513 (Paradise, 1980); FMC Corp., 70 LA 574, 575 (Nigro, 1978); McDonnell Douglas Corp., 51 LA 1076, 1080 (Bothwell, 1968); A.O. Smith Corp., 47 LA 443, 448 (Stouffer, 1966); West Va. Pulp & Paper Co., 42 LA 1251, 1255 (Abersold, 1964); Consolidated Badger Coop., 36 LA 965, 969 (Mueller, 1961); Carl Fischer, Inc., 24 LA 674, 675–76 (Rosenfarb, 1955); Bauer Bros., 23 LA 696, 702 (Dworkin, 1954); Chesapeake & Ohio R.R., 22 LA 620, 623 (Miller, 1954); United Hosiery Mills Corp., 22 LA 573, 576 (Marshall, 1954); Valley Steel Casting Co., 22 LA 520, 527 (Howlett, 1954); International Harvester Co., 21 LA 444, 446 (Kelliher, 1953); International Harvester Co., 17 LA 334, 335 (Seward, 1951).

[187]Arbitrators also have expressly recognized this power in management. *See* Super-Valu Stores, 74 LA 939, 945 (Evenson, 1980); Indiana Harbor Belt R.R., 53 LA 990, 991–92 (Dolnick, 1969); Anaconda Aluminum Co., 48 LA 182, 183 (Luckerath, 1966); West Va. Pulp & Paper Co., 45 LA 515, 517 (Daugherty, 1965); Bethlehem Steel, 42 LA 307, 310 (Hughes, 1964); Davison Chem. Co., 36 LA 1092, 1096 (Abernethy, 1961); International Harvester Co., 12 LA 1190, 1192 (McCoy, 1949); John Deere Tractor Co., 9 LA 73, 77 (Gorder, 1947).

[188]In upholding all but one of the many discharges that resulted from a prohibited work stoppage in *Clinton Corn Processing Co.*, 71 LA 555 (Madden, 1978), the arbitrator stated:

I agree with the Union that the Company has established its point many times over and to the extent any further suffering can be ameliorated by leniency it should be done. This is particularly true in the light of the fact that some facts became apparent to the Company for the first time in the hearing. To fear to approach negotiations on this subject from this point forward for fear of weakening its position will certainly be counter productive [sic] as an employer can enjoy the long run effects of good labor relations only when employees can be assured that its judgments are fair and just. Too much severity

the arbitrator did understand management's determination not to risk a less severe penalty.[189]

F. Factors in Evaluating Penalties

The more prominent of the factors relevant in the review or evaluation of penalties assessed by management for misconduct of employees are considered briefly below.

i. Nature of the Offense: Summary Discharge Versus Corrective Discipline

It is said to be "axiomatic that the degree of penalty should be in keeping with the seriousness of the offense."[190] In this regard, an arbitrator explained:

> Offenses are of two general classes: (1) those extremely serious offenses such as stealing, striking a foreman, persistent refusal to obey a legitimate order, etc., which usually justify summary discharge without the necessity of prior warnings or attempts at corrective discipline; (2) those less serious infractions of plant rules or of proper conduct such as tardiness, absence without permission, careless workmanship, insolence, etc., which call not for discharge for the first offense (and usually not even for the second or third offense) but for some milder penalty aimed at correction.[191]

---

in the matter of assessing discipline, even though legal, may not be in the best interest of the harmonious relations which make best for an efficient work force. The Union's point that more harmonious and fruitful Company-Union relations would result from greater leniency is well taken. But leniency is not within the arbitrator's province . . . . *Id.* at 571. *See also* Baker Marine Corp., 77 LA 721, 725 (Marlatt, 1981) (upholding discharge and stating that the "employer may properly consider whether more lenient discipline may serve the desired purpose of correction so that the employment relationship may be salvaged"); Steiger Tractor, 72 LA 175, 178–79 (O'Connell, 1979) (stating that the "granting of leniency in individual situations cannot act to prevent the invocation of the proscribed penalty if management finds this the desirable course of action," and that while the arbitrator must uphold the discipline in the present case and "is unable to substitute his judgment for that of management," it would appear "that as an internal personnel problem, some degree of leniency might have been considered").

[189]*See* Brooks Foundry, 75 LA 642, 644 (Daniel, 1980), where the arbitrator stated:

This employee is so highly thought of by the company that it would not be surprising that the company would have, if it could, moderated the discipline[,] but it is clear to this arbitrator that the company feels so strongly the necessity of maintaining a firm rule and consistent enforcement that it did so even when such was contrary to its own interests. It would be improper for this arbitrator where a violation has been found and where, particularly the employee has attempted to cover up the facts, to disregard the judgment of the company in assessing the penalty. The company knows its business and its operations and the manner in which it must deal with its employees. This arbitrator cannot deny that a firm and absolute approach to penalties in such cases may very well discourage numerous other instances by other employees in the future. For this reason it would be inappropriate to disturb the penalty selected in this case.

[190]Capital Airlines, 25 LA 13, 16 (Stowe, 1955).

[191]Huntington Chair Corp., 24 LA 490, 491 (McCoy, 1955). *See also* St. Joe Minerals Corp., 70 LA 1110, 1117 (Roberts, 1978).

In cases of extremely serious offenses, arbitrators recognize the need to enforce the discharge penalty.[192] Summary discharge in lieu of corrective discipline of the employee is deemed appropriate for very serious offenses. The definition of a disqualifying "serious offense" remains elastic. Sleeping on duty, for example, at least where the act is intentional and the employee attempts to avoid detection, usually warrants termination even though it is the employee's first offense.[193] Summary discharge was deemed appropriate for an employee driver who failed to report an accident, even though it was the only time he had been disciplined. The arbitrator determined that, although "failure to report an accident," standing alone, would not likely merit discharge, the employee's failure to report the accident, coupled with his bizarre behavior and his failure to take medicine prescribed for a psychiatric condition, warranted discharge.[194]

In one case, summary discharge was deemed appropriate for a single act of negligent work performance. In that case, a service technician did not perform a crucial pressure test required by the employer's protocol and thus failed to find a gas leak in the customer's heater connector.[195] Because of the risk of explosion and fire to which the customer was exposed by the oversight, the arbitrator found the negligent discharge of the employment responsibilities justified the employee's immediate discharge. In another case,

---

[192]*See, e.g.*, Valspar Corp., 113 LA 1111 (Hayford, 1999) (just cause existed for discharge of employee who repeatedly and routinely abandoned his work station for long periods of time, hid in supervisor's office, turned off the lights, and slept); San Diego Trolley, 112 LA 323 (Prayzich, 1999) (employer had just cause to discharge employee who had a loaded gun in his locker, even though it was the first violation of a rule prohibiting possession of weapons on premises); Essroc Materials, 99 LA 664, 668 (Murphy, 1992) (just cause existed for discharge of employee for second violation of substance abuse policy); Burger Iron Co., 92 LA 1100, 1105 (Dworkin, 1989) (discharge for using or selling drugs on company property upheld because it was an illegal activity); OK Grocery Co., 92 LA 440, 444 (Stoltenberg, 1989) (extorting money from fellow employees constituted just cause); Eastern Airlines, 90 LA 272, 275 (Jedel, 1987) (unauthorized use of in-house computerized communication system to send messages disparaging of management, discrediting company, or objectionable to others constituted just cause); Safeway Stores, 89 LA 627, 629 (Staudohar, 1987) (suspension upheld for negligently selling alcohol to minors); American Welding & Mfg. Co., 89 LA 247, 252 (Dworkin, 1987) (theft); Consumer Plastics Corp., 88 LA 208, 211–14 (Garnholz, 1987); Furr's, Inc., 88 LA 175, 178 (Blum, 1986); Goodyear Aerospace Corp., 86 LA 403 (Fullmer, 1985).

[193]VOCA Corp., 105 LA 368 (Rybolt, 1995).

[194]Interstate Brands Corp., 113 LA 161 (Howell, 1999). For other cases recognizing the propriety of summary discharge for serious offenses, see San Diego Trolley, 112 LA 323 (Prayzich, 1999); Pioneer Flour Mills, 109 LA 1016 (Crider, 1998); Cajun Elec. Power Coop, 108 LA 641 (Howell, 1997); South Cent. Bell Tel. Co., 80 LA 891, 893 (Nicholas, Jr., 1983); Central Soya Co., 74 LA 1084, 1090 (Cantor, 1980) (threatening a foreman); Alaska Sales & Serv. Co., 73 LA 164, 166 (Axon, 1979) (disloyalty to employer by using contacts and information obtained on the job "to turn a personal profit at their employer's expense"); Liberal Mkt., 71 LA 148, 151 (Laybourne, 1978) (extorting $20 as condition for allowing truck to be unloaded); Factory Servs., 70 LA 1088, 1091 (Fitch, 1978) (false statements concerning safety maliciously made to regulatory agency); Hayes-Albion Corp., 70 LA 696, 699 (Glendon, 1978); United States Steel Corp., 70 LA 146, 149 (Powell, Jr., 1978) (striking a foreman); Stansteel Corp., 69 LA 776, 779 (Kaufman, 1977) (possession of marijuana and giving it to fellow employee at work); National Can Corp., 68 LA 351, 352 (Turkus, 1977) ("openly defiant and egregiously insubordinate" conduct). In some of these cases, the arbitrator expressly stated that summary discharge was permissible even though the employee had long seniority with a good record.

[195]BHP Petroleum/Gasco, 102 LA 321 (Najita, 1994).

the arbitrator determined just cause existed for summary discharge of an employee for making racial slurs, where several employees had complained of the racial comments and the employee had ignored previous warnings regarding his offensive language.[196] In yet another case, the arbitrator determined that fighting on company premises is generally recognized as inherently improper and need not be expressly and specifically proscribed by management to warrant severe discipline, including summary discharge.[197]

In the less serious cases, arbitrators are very likely to change or modify an employer's discipline if such discipline is too harsh for the offense committed.[198] In those cases, discipline may be considered to be excessive "if it is disproportionate to the degree of the offense, if it is out of step with the principles of progressive discipline, if it is punitive rather than corrective, or if mitigating circumstances were ignored."[199] Arbitrators, thus, often modify disciplinary penalties imposed by management when there are mitigating circumstances that lead the arbitrator to conclude that the penalty is too severe or that the employer lacks, or has failed to follow, progressive discipline procedures.[200]

Moreover, arbitrators are likely to set aside or reduce penalties when the employee had not previously been reprimanded and warned that his or her conduct would trigger the discipline. Thus, demotion of an employee for absenteeism was found to be inappropriate where, although the employer had warned the employee that his absenteeism was a problem, the employer had failed to inform him that he could be demoted if his attendance did not improve.[201] Even when the misconduct is of a serious nature, the employee must not be lulled into believing that he or she will not be subject to sanction. Thus, the discharge of an employee for insubordination was set aside

---

[196]Eagle Snacks, 103 LA 741 (Baroni, 1994). *See also* Fry's Food Stores of Ariz., 99 LA 1161 (Hogler, 1992) (summary discharge of employee who made disparaging comment to homosexual coworker upheld because of serious nature of offense).

[197]CHAC, Inc., 114 LA 173 (Berman, 2000).

[198]*See, e.g.*, Clow Water Sys. Co., 102 LA 377, 380 (Dworkin, 1994). In *Clow*, the arbitrator explained that, when a penalty is deemed improper or too severe, the arbitrator may exercise his or her rights to change or modify the penalty as an inherent part of the arbitrator's power to finally settle the matter at hand.

[199]Discipline and Discharge in Arbitration 85 (Brand ed., BNA Books 1998 & Supp. 2001).

[200]*See* Nature's Best, 114 LA 217 (Grabuskie, 1999); Stratosphere Tower & Casino, 114 LA 188 (Bickner, 1999); Eaton Corp., 112 LA 705 (Gregory, 1999); Simmons Co., 112 LA 164 (Riker, 1999); Martin-Brower Co., 111 LA 929 (Felice, 1998); Little Rock, Ark., Sch. Dist. Bd. of Dirs., 110 LA 1114 (Bankston, 1998); Kimberly-Clark Corp., 107 LA 554 (Byars, 1996); Duke Univ., 100 LA 316 (Hooper, 1993); Memphis Light, Gas & Water Div., 100 LA 291 (Caraway, 1993); General Dynamics, 100 LA 180 (Francis, 1992); Valentec/Kisco-Olivette, 100 LA 71 (Fowler, 1992); Carl Bolander & Sons Co., 100 LA 1 (Reynolds, 1992); TRW, Inc., 99 LA 1216 (Fullmer, 1992); Consolidation Coal Co., 99 LA 945 (Dissen, 1992); Davidson Transit Mgmt., 99 LA 924 (Hart, 1992); Cyprus Bagdad Copper Corp., 99 LA 841 (White, 1992); MacMillan Bloedel Containers, 92 LA 592, 601 (Nicholas, Jr., 1989); Warren Assemblies, 92 LA 521, 523–24 (Roumell, Jr., 1989); Grinnell Corp., 92 LA 124, 126 (Kilroy, 1989); Lockheed Aircraft Serv. Co., 90 LA 297, 298 (Kaufman, 1987); Furry Mach., 89 LA 739, 743–44 (Goldstein, 1987); Pennwalt Corp., 89 LA 585, 586–87 (Kanner, 1987); Whiteway Mfg. Co., 86 LA 144, 146 (Cloke, 1986).

[201]Gaylord Container Corp., 107 LA 1138 (Allen, Jr., 1997).

because the employee had been insubordinate in the past without being subject to any discipline.[202]

Most awards where penalties are modified involve a combination of mitigating circumstances. One study that examined the trends in arbitration awards involving discharge cases found that the prior work record of the grievant was the most commonly cited factor given consideration by arbitrators, with another frequently cited consideration being the motivation or reasoning behind management's action.[203]

ii. Due Process and Procedural Requirements[204]
[LA CDI 100.5501 et seq.; 118.301]

Discharge and disciplinary action by management has been reversed where the action was found to violate basic notions of fairness or due process. Borrowing from the constitutional imperative of due process operative in the governmental employment context, arbitrators have fashioned an "industrial due process doctrine." To satisfy industrial due process, an employee must be given an adequate opportunity to present his or her side of the case before being discharged by the employer. If the employee has not been given such an opportunity, arbitrators will often refuse to sustain the discharge or discipline assessed against the employee. The primary reason arbitrators have included certain basic due process rights within the concept of just cause is to help the parties prevent the imposition of discipline where there is little or no evidence on which to base a just cause discharge.[205] Thus, consideration of industrial due process as a component of just cause is an integral part of the just cause analysis for many arbitrators.[206]

---

[202]Tenneco Packaging Corp., 106 LA 606 (Franckiewicz, 1996).

[203]Jennings, Sheffield, & Wolter, *The Arbitration of Discharge Cases: A Fourth Year Perspective*, 38 LAB. L.J. 33, 41 (1987).

[204]DISCIPLINE AND DISCHARGE IN ARBITRATION 37–57 (Brand ed., BNA Books 1998 & Supp. 2001). Mackenzie, *Is Procedural Due Process an Element of Just Cause or a Separate Issue With Distinct Remedies?: I. An Introduction to the Topic*, in ARBITRATION 2002: WORKPLACE ARBITRATION: A PROCESS IN EVOLUTION, PROCEEDINGS OF THE 55TH ANNUAL MEETING OF NAA 49 (Coleman ed., BNA Books 2002); Clarke, *II. To What Extent Do and Should the Seven Tests Guide Arbitrators or the Parties?*, *id.* at 51; Gross, *III. Substantive Due Process: The Standards for Judgment Must Also Be Fair*, *id.* at 58; Beck, *IV. Procedural Due Process, Just Cause, and the Due Process Protocol*, *id.* at 63.

[205]Lincoln Lutheran of Racine, Wis., 113 LA 72 (Kessler, 1999)

[206]*Id.* (grievant discharged for using abusive and profane language was reinstated because she never told her side of the story before she was discharged); Gerstenslager Co., 111 LA 238 (Lalka, 1998) (employee's due process rights were violated when she was denied the opportunity to have the union steward present on receipt of her separation notice, she was not given a predisciplinary interview, and she was never able to tell her side of the story); Gemala Trailer Corp., 108 LA 565 (Nicholas, Jr., 1997) (employees who were discharged for shaking a vending machine to get the produce for which they had paid were denied due process, because the employer did not question them during the investigation and relied only on the judgment and direction of the human resources manager); Boulder Yellow Cab, 102 LA 848 (Watkins, 1993) (cab company violated the due process rights of seven drivers who were discharged solely because its insurance carrier determined that their driving records made them uninsurable—the company failed to explore several other insurance options that might have enabled grievants to keep their jobs and grievants were never warned that their driving records could put their jobs in jeopardy); Arkansas Power & Light Co., 92 LA 144, 149–50 (Weisbrod, 1989) (grievant reinstated because employer violated employee's due pro-

In one case, an employee's discharge for pulling a knife on a coworker was set aside where the subject employee had never been interviewed. Fairness dictated that the employee be given the opportunity to tell his side of the story.[207]

In a case where management failed to give an employee an opportunity to be heard, an arbitrator refused to sustain the employee's discharge, pointing out:

> A just cause proviso, standing alone, demands that certain minimal essentials of due process be observed. One at least of those minimum essentials is that the accused have an opportunity, before sentence is carried out, to be heard in his own defense . . . .
> It is the *process*, not the *result*, which is at issue.[208]

In another discharge case, management failed to give the employee the opportunity to question his accuser at the arbitral hearing. In reinstating the employee, the arbitrator noted:

> [I]t is improper for the Company to rely upon the written statement of an employee without presenting his personal testimony, if his presence is requested by the union and if the party relying upon his written statement has the power to have him appear at the hearing.[209]

Arbitrators will, in many cases, refuse to uphold management's action, where it failed to fulfill some procedural requirement specified by the agreement.[210] If, however, an arbitrator feels the company has complied with the spirit of the procedural requirement, and the employee was not adversely affected by management's failure to comply, the company's action may be deemed sufficient.[211] Arbitrators have, in a few cases, refused to disturb

---

cess rights by denying him union representation during investigatory interview); Adrian Coll., 89 LA 857, 861 (Ellmann, 1987) (employer failed to make fair investigation); King Co., 89 LA 681, 685 (Bard, 1987) (discharges overturned because employees not advised of their Fifth Amendment Miranda rights); DeVry Inst. of Tech., 87 LA 1149, 1157 (Berman, 1986); Kaiser Aluminum & Chem. Corp., 87 LA 236, 243–44 (Feldman, 1986); Hogler, *Just Cause, Judicial Review, and Industrial Justice: An Arbitral Critique,* 40 Lab. L.J. 281 (1989); McPherson, *The Evolving Concept of Just Cause: Carroll R. Daugherty and the Requirement of Disciplinary Due Process,* 38 Lab. L.J. 387, 390 (1987). *But see* Beatrice/Hunt-Wesson, 89 LA 710, 715–16 (Bickner, 1987) (employer's failure to hear grievant's explanation prior to suspension did not violate industrial due process, where grievant had ample opportunity to explain his position at first grievance meeting).

[207]CR/PL P'ship (Crane Plumbing), 107 LA 1084 (Fullmer, 1996).

[208]McCartney's Inc., 84 LA 799, 804 (Nelson, 1985) (emphasis in original).

[209]Marion Power Shovel Div., 82 LA 1014, 1016 (Kates, 1984). *But see* Snapper Power Equip. Div., 89 LA 501, 505–06 (Weston, 1987).

[210]Mariott Servs. Corp., 109 LA 689 (Kaufman, 1997); Kroger Co., 108 LA 417 (Baroni, 1997); Carol Mgmt. Co., 97 LA 503 (Freedman, 1991); Polysar, Inc., 91 LA 482, 484 (Strasshofer, 1988); Warehouse Distribution Ctrs., 90 LA 979, 983 (Weiss, 1987); Adrian Coll., 89 LA 857, 861 (Ellmann, 1987); Gold Kist, 89 LA 66, 70 (Byars, 1987); Kidde, Inc., 86 LA 681, 682 (Dunn, 1985).

[211]Western Textile Prods., 107 LA 539 (Cohen, 1996); S&J Ranch, 103 LA 350 (Bogue, 1994) (compliance with the spirit of the procedural requirements in an agreement is sufficient unless the employee can prove he was adversely affected by the failure of the employer to follow procedural requirements exactly); Union Oil Co. of Cal., 91 LA 1206, 1208 (Klein, 1988) (to overturn employer's action on procedural grounds, proof must exist that grievant was denied fair consideration of the case due to procedural error; discipline sustained, but employer ordered to pay union's arbitration costs because union was forced to arbitrate because of procedural defect); Roadmaster Corp., 89 LA 126, 129 (Doering, 1987); Intermountain Rural Elec. Ass'n, 86 LA 540, 543 (Watkins, 1985); Shamrock Indus., 84 LA 1203, 1206–07 (Reynolds, 1985).

management's decision even though the company failed to comply with even the spirit of the requirement.[212]

Industrial due process also requires management to conduct a reasonable inquiry or investigation before assessing punishment.[213] Where neither the grievant nor his union was allowed to confront those accusing the grievant of wrongdoing at any time prior to the arbitration, the arbitrator determined that the grievant was prevented from preparing to fairly meet the charges and was denied industrial due process:

> Procedural fairness requires an employer to conduct a full and fair investigation of the circumstances surrounding an employee's conduct and to provide an opportunity for him to offer denials, explanations, or justifications that are relevant before the employer makes its final decision, before its position becomes polarized.[214]

In contrast, due process requirements were found to have been met in a case in which the employer had failed to post a rule warning that dishonesty might lead to discharge. The arbitrator recognized:

> While fair warning is essential to any disciplinary code, some rules of the workplace are so obvious that no employee can claim ignorance of them or of their consequences. The clearest example is theft. Every employee knows that stealing from an employer is completely unacceptable even if the employer has not posted a rule to that effect.[215]

iii.　Last-Chance Agreements[216] [LA CDI 118.815]

Last-chance agreements are intended to benefit the employee by allowing a final opportunity to correct conduct and to benefit the employer by allowing it to avoid the trouble and expense of discharging and replacing the employee.[217] One arbitrator described such agreements as

> an agreement outside of the collective bargaining agreement that is strictly construed and enforced. It can be viewed as a modification of the master collec-

---

[212]Metro Pittsburgh Pub. Broad., 89 LA 934, 936 (Talarico, 1987) (failure to provide contractually required 2-week notice did not invalidate discharge of probationary employee); Safeway Stores, 89 LA 627, 630 (Staudohar, 1987); Amax Coal Co., 85 LA 225, 228 (Kilroy, 1985) (there was no prejudice to either grievant or union); Bogalusa Cmty. Med. Ctr., 84 LA 978, 982 (Nicholas, Jr., 1985); Spang & Co., 84 LA 342, 346 (Joseph, 1985) (where grievant's suspension was for medical rather than disciplinary reasons); Phoenix Prods. Co., 82 LA 172, 174 (Imes, 1983) (decided under particular facts of case).

[213]Southern Frozen Foods, 107 LA 1030 (Giblin, 1996). See also Westvaco Corp., 105 LA 180 (Nolan, 1995) (recognizing that minimal investigation satisfies due process requirements); Alumax Extrusions, 99 LA 932 (Green, 1992); Lamar Constr. Co., 98 LA 500 (Kanner, 1992); Mason & Hanger-Silas Mason Co., 96 LA 1150 (Anthony, 1991).

[214]Shaefer's Ambulance Serv., 104 LA 481, 486 (Calhoun, 1995).

[215]Westvaco Corp., 105 LA 180, 185 (Nolan, 1995). See section 3.F.ix., "Knowledge of Rules," below.

[216]Discipline and Discharge in Arbitration 403–06 (Brand ed., BNA Books 1998 & Supp. 2001).

[217]USS, Div. of USX Corp., 114 LA 44, 46–47 (St. Antoine, 1999) (encouraging employer use on case-by-case basis of last-chance agreements without precedential effect to avoid a "past practice" claim is of benefit to employees involved, because last-chance agreements allow them to retain their jobs); Appalachian Reg'l Healthcare, 112 LA 884 (Murphy, 1999) (there is a strong public policy in favor of the enforcement of last-chance agreements); Porcelain Metals Corp., 73 LA 1133, 1138 (Roberts, 1979).

tive bargaining agreement in their application to special employees, where the Employer gives valuable consideration by giving up a contended right to discharge an employee and the employee in exchange forfeits for that limited period negotiated rights (except for those spelled out in the [last-chance agreement]) in order to demonstrate to the Employer that he or she merits retention rather than discharge.[218]

Elements of an enforceable last-chance agreement may include the presence of competent union counsel for the employee when negotiating the agreement, consideration from the employer (usually, this consists of the employer foregoing its right to terminate the employee for the recent misconduct), a standard of fairness demonstrated by the designation of a specific time period during which the employee will be subject to the agreement's terms,[219] and a clear statement of what action will result in termination.[220] Written agreements, signed by the employer and the employee or the union, are preferred.[221] These agreements are being used more frequently by employers and arbitrators to allow employees with serious discipline problems, particularly in the areas of drug and alcohol abuse, to continue their employment, provided they satisfy certain defined conditions.[222] Employers some-

---

[218]Ingersoll-Dresser Pump Co., 114 LA 297, 301 (Bickner, 1999). See also Weyerhaeuser Co., 109 LA 573, 576 (Murphy, 1997) (last-chance agreement is modification of collective bargaining agreement with respect to subject employee); International Paper Co., 109 LA 472 (Terrill, 1997) (analyzing the differing views regarding the extent to which a last-chance agreement modifies a collective bargaining agreement).

[219]Central Ohio Transit Auth., 113 LA 1134 (Imundo, Jr., 2000) (implying "reasonable time" for duration of agreement). Compare A. Schulman, Inc., 105 LA 1076, 1080 (Duda, Jr., 1996) (permanent nature of last-chance agreement was knowingly assented to by the parties). See also University of Mich., 96 LA 688, 689 (Sugerman, 1991) (the last-chance agreement is in effect for the employee's entire tenure with the employer, because arbitrators must strictly adhere to the terms of last-chance agreements and must refrain from setting a term for the last-chance agreement when the parties could have, but did not, set such a term).

[220]Ingersoll-Dresser Pump Co., 114 LA 297, 301 (Bickner, 1999). See also Louisville Water Co., 114 LA 583, 589 (Lalka, 2000); Fort James Corp., 113 LA 742 (Brown, 1999) (last-chance agreements must be enforced if they are fairly negotiated and not of unreasonable duration); Cross Oil Ref. Co., 111 LA 1013 (Bumpass, 1999) (agreement providing that employee would be discharged for future "incidents" too vague). Some arbitrators will only construe last-chance agreements as such when the document clearly states that it is a "last chance agreement." In International Paper, the parties called the document a "last chance warning." International Paper Co., 109 LA 472 (Terrill, 1997) (the distinction between "agreement" and "warning" is important, because an agreement is mutually negotiated, while a warning connotes a one-party action). See also Q.C. Inc., 106 LA 987, 992 (McGury, 1996) (settlement agreement reinstating employee does not state that it is a "last chance agreement," so it will not be considered a last-chance agreement). Because the document did not have a defined term of existence, and the parties' collective bargaining agreement stated that written warnings were effective for one year, the discharge for the employee's violation of the "last chance warning" was set aside, because the violation occurred more than 1 year after the effective date of the last-chance warning. International Paper, 109 LA at 477.

[221]See, e.g., Appalachian Reg'l Healthcare, 112 LA 884 (Murphy, 1999); Minnegasco, Inc., 110 LA 1077 (Jacobowski, 1998). Cf. Eaton Cutler-Hammer Corp., 110 LA 467, 470 (Franckiewicz, 1998); Appalachian Reg'l Healthcare, 112 LA 884, 887 (Murphy, 1999) (parties may sign a last-chance agreement to settle an actual or threatened discharge in the absence of a grievance).

[222]See, e.g., Biolab, Inc., 114 LA 279 (Brodsky, 2000); USS, Div. of USX Corp., 113 LA 712 (Petersen, 1999); USS, 111 LA 385 (St. Antoine, 1999); Eaton Cutler-Hammer Corp., 110 LA 467 (Franckiewicz, 1998); Baltimore Specialty Steels Corp., 95 LA 1191 (Strongin, 1990); Wacker Silicones Corp., 95 LA 784 (Hodgson, 1990); Butler Mfg. Co., 93 LA 441 (Dworkin, 1989); Southern Cal. Permanente Med. Group, 92 LA 41, 46 (Richman, 1989); S.E. Rykoff & Co., 90 LA 233, 237 (Angelo, 1987); TRW, Inc., 90 LA 31, 35 (Graham, 1987).

times expressly include last-chance provisions in their disciplinary pro-grams,[223] while arbitrators sometimes impose last-chance agreements in mitigation of discharge, whether or not the employer's disciplinary program provides for such a step.[224]

After determining that the last-chance agreement is enforceable, the arbitrator's role usually is limited to determining whether the employee, or in some cases, the employer, violated the terms of the agreement.[225] When considering whether there is just cause for discharge under such agreements, arbitrators do not apply the same due process considerations or procedural protections as under a normal discharge or disciplinary matter.[226] According to one arbitrator:

> Arbitrators encourage such progressive programs of salvage and rehabilitation by strict enforcement of such "last chance agreements" in accordance with the terms which the parties, including the employee, have been willing to accept. However harsh or strict such terms and even though the arbitrator might well regard such conditions as unfair, that cannot be his concern.[227]

Such agreements do, however, have some limitations, and neither the union nor the employee may, by the terms of the agreement, be deprived of access to the grievance and arbitration procedure.[228] Nevertheless, last-chance agreements should not ordinarily be construed as entitling the employee to a progressive discipline scheme provided under a collective bargaining agreement.[229]

Last-chance agreements also place responsibilities, such as the duty to give notice, on employers. Failure of the employer to enforce the terms of a last-chance agreement may lull the employee into a false sense of security. He or she may believe that the employer has "acquiesced" to the employee's

---

[223]*See, e.g.*, Integrated Metal Tech., 112 LA 676 (Stallworth, 1999); City of Las Vegas Hous. Auth., 112 LA 259 (Monat, 1999).

[224]Anchor Hocking Glass Co., 114 LA 1334, 1337 (Hewitt, 2000) (grievant required to sign last-chance agreement containing provision that the only arbitrable issue concerning an alleged violation of the last-chance agreement is whether the events or actions occurred, and that the last-chance agreement is without prejudice or precedent). *See, e.g.*, Department of Veterans Affairs, 114 LA 733 (Moore, 2000); Borden Italian Foods Co., 113 LA 13 (Marino, 1999); Glacier County, Mont., Sch. Dist. 15, 112 LA 700 (Prayzich, 1999).

[225]Ingersoll-Dresser Pump Co., 114 LA 297 (Bickner, 1999); Minnegasco, Inc., 110 LA 1077 (Jacobowski, 1998).

[226]Eaton Cutler-Hammer Corp., 110 LA 467, 470–71 (Franckiewicz, 1998) (a last-chance agreement typically defines what "just cause" will mean for the particular employee involved); Hugo Bosca Co., 109 LA 533 (Franckiewicz, 1997); Sorg Paper Co., 89 LA 1237, 1241 (Dworkin, 1987). *Contra* International Paper Co., 109 LA 472, 476–77 (Terrill, 1997) (last-chance agreement cannot waive any term of collective bargaining agreement, including "just cause" provision).

[227]Kaydon Corp., 89 LA 377, 379 (Daniel, 1987). *See also* Napco, Inc., 111 LA 77 (Franckiewicz, 1998).

[228]Cross Oil Ref. Co., 111 LA 1013, 1023–24 (Bumpass, 1999) (last-chance agreement cannot remove employee from the collective bargaining agreement provision that permits arbitration); Minnegasco Inc., 110 LA 1077 (Jacobowski, 1998); Kaydon Corp., 89 LA 377, 379 (Daniel, 1987). *See also* Monterey Coal Co., 96 LA 457 (Feldman, 1990). *But see* Lenzing Fibers Corp., 105 LA 423 (Sergent, 1995). Hendrickson Turner Co., 101 LA 919 (Dworkin, 1993); Gaylord Container Corp., 97 LA 382 (Goodman, 1991). *See also* Gencorp Auto., 104 LA 113 (Malin, 1995) (the collective bargaining agreement, not the last-chance agreement, controls the arbitrator's jurisdiction); City of Stillwater, Okla., 103 LA 684 (Neas, 1994).

[229]*See, e.g.*, Eaton Cutler-Hammer Corp., 110 LA 467 (Franckiewicz, 1998).

subsequent misconduct and that it is not subject to being used against him or her, or that the employer has waived its right to discharge the employee for violating the agreement.[230] Similar problems may arise where the employer deviates from the agreement's express provisions, such as by waiving strict enforcement of a drug-testing policy.[231]

Some arbitrators hold that a last-chance clause cannot waive the just cause requirement of a collective bargaining agreement.[232] Others have upheld agreements dispensing with the just cause requirement.[233] According to at least one arbitrator, such rights must be expressly waived.[234] Arbitrators sometimes mitigate termination to a lesser punishment where, for example, the agreement allows for disciplinary measures "up to and including termination."[235]

Employers should, of course, negotiate last-chance agreements with the union, not with individual employees, in order to avoid running afoul of the NLRA. Offering an employee a last-chance agreement, without first notifying the union, may be considered "a *per se* violation of the Act."[236] In some cases, arbitrators have ruled that individual employees "are powerless to enter into such agreements without the consent of the Union."[237] However, some arbitrators have upheld the validity of such agreements, even though unsigned by a union representative, if the employee did not exercise his right to representation by the union[238] or the employer offered the employee representation by the union but the employee declined.[239] Conversely, arbitrators have upheld the validity of last-chance agreements where the employer and the union sign, even if the employee does not sign.[240] In at least one instance, an arbitrator has held a last-chance agreement valid even though neither the union nor the employee signed it but both were aware of the terms and tacitly consented to them.[241]

Most arbitrators uphold discharges where the last-chance agreement clearly and unambiguously defines the conditions of employment and the

---

[230]Standard Prods. Co., 112 LA 76 (Brodsky, 1999)

[231]*See, e.g.*, USS, 111 LA 539 (Petersen, 1998).

[232]*See, e.g.*, Central Ohio Transit Auth., 113 LA 1134 (Imundo, Jr., 2000).

[233]*See, e.g.*, Vons Co., 114 LA 659 (Grabuskie, 2000); Merchants Fast Motor Lines, 99 LA 180, 183 (Marlatt, 1992). *See also* Butler Mfg. Co., 93 LA 441 (Dworkin, 1989).

[234]GTE of Fla., 108 LA 1115, 1119 (Cohen, 1997) (ruling that last-chance agreements that are silent as to, and do not expressly waive, just cause standards do not relieve the employer from the burden of proving just cause).

[235]*See, e.g.*, Makino, Inc., 114 LA 1110, 1111 (Donnelly, 2000).

[236]James Hardie Gypsum, 111 LA 210, 215 (Olson, Jr., 1998).

[237]Merchants Fast Motor Lines, 99 LA 180, 183 (Marlatt, 1992).

[238]Exxon Co., U.S.A., 101 LA 997, 1003 (Sergent, 1993).

[239]Tosco Ref. Co., 112 LA 306, 311 n.3 (Bogue, 1999). *Compare* Boise Cascade Corp., 114 LA 1379, 1382–83 (Crider, 2000) (imposition of last-chance agreement on employee without union representation renders last-chance agreement invalid).

[240]Southwest Ohio Reg'l Transit Auth., 109 LA 310, 314 (Murphy, 1997) (although a "close issue," last-chance agreement is valid even though the union did not sign it but did negotiate it); Pacific Rim Packaging Corp., 97 LA 457, 460 (Fields, 1991).

[241]Western Textile Prods., 107 LA 539, 547 (Cohen, 1996).

grounds for immediate termination.[242] Not every provision, however, must be clearly defined.[243] Arbitrators may overturn discharges under last-chance agreements where they are persuaded that enforcing the agreement would be unfair under the circumstances.[244]

However, the role of an arbitrator in an arbitration concerning an alleged violation of a valid last-chance agreement is generally limited to determining whether the employee's actions or conduct constituted a violation of the last-chance agreement.[245] Most arbitrators will not review the underlying actions or conduct of the employee to determine whether such actions or conduct should have led to the last-chance agreement, but at least one arbitrator has determined that this is within the arbitrator's authority.[246] If the actions or conduct by the employee is found to violate the last-chance agreement, a majority of arbitrators will enforce the penalty agreed to by the parties in the last-chance agreement, usually discharge.[247]

Despite the controversy over whether enforcement is fair, last-chance agreements are "universally considered to be voluntary" and noncoercive in the ordinary sense.[248]

When an arbitrator invalidates a last-chance agreement, the issue arises whether, because the consideration for the employee's reinstatement has been withdrawn, the status quo ante has been restored so that the discharge has been reinstated, and, because of the lapse of time, pursuit of the grievance-arbitration process may be foreclosed.

---

[242]See, e.g., Central Ohio Transit Auth., 113 LA 1134 (Imundo, Jr., 2000); A. Schulman, Inc., 105 LA 1076 (Duda, Jr., 1996); Bethlehem Structural Prods. Corp., 105 LA 205 (Witt, 1995); FDL Foods, 104 LA 1079 (Flaten, 1995); Philip Morris U.S.A., 104 LA 948 (Florman, 1995); Borg-Warner Diversified Transmission Prods. Corp., 101 LA 1014 (Malin, 1993). Cf. Packaging Corp. of Am., 105 LA 898 (Weisheit, 1995) (last-chance agreement that was too broad in scope was unenforceable).

[243]See, e.g., Central Ohio Transit, 113 LA 1134, 1141 (Imundo, Jr., 2000) (provisions of agreement, which neither clearly defined "attendance difficulties" nor included a durational limit, took precedence over attendance policy because the union failed to propose better terms).

[244]See, e.g., Penske Truck Leasing, 110 LA 833 (Bumpass, 1998) (employee reinstated where employer failed to follow termination notice); LTV Steel Mining Co., 110 LA 283 (Doepken, 1997) (employee's discharge set aside because his failure to comply with the terms of the last-chance agreement may have been due to medication errors by the employee's doctors); USS, Div. of USX Corp., 108 LA 897, 899 (Petersen, 1997) (arbitrator reinstated employee terminated for violating last-chance agreement because there was no evidence that the employee, who accidentally injured his hand at home and thereby failed to report to work, "intentionally made himself unavailable for work" in violation of the agreement); Drummond Co., 106 LA 250 (Sergent, 1996).

[245]Ingersoll-Dresser Pump Co., 114 LA 297, 301 (Bickner, 1999).

[246]Boise Cascade Corp., 114 LA 1379, 1382 (Crider, 2000).

[247]Hugo Bosca Co., 109 LA 533, 539 (Franckiewicz, 1997) (despite arbitrator's criticism of discharge penalty for the facts of the case, the last-chance agreement removes the arbitrator's discretion to modify the penalty); ABTCO Inc., 104 LA 551, 552–53 (Kanner, 1995). Compare Makino Inc., 114 LA 1110 (Donnelly, 2000) (penalty of discharge is excessive, despite last-chance agreement that allows termination for violation of the last-chance agreement).

[248]Louisville Water Co., 114 LA 583, 589 (Lalka, 2000).

iv. Weingarten *Violations* [LA CDI 93.27; 100.0705]

Decisions of the National Labor Relations Board (NLRB, or the Board) are particularly instructive in cases involving refusals to allow union representation at investigatory meetings in violation of the Board's *Weingarten*[249] rulings. In 1984, the Board held that a "cease-and-desist" order, rather than reinstatement, is the appropriate remedy where an employee's *Weingarten* rights are violated, but the employee is suspended or discharged for cause.[250] The Board considers discipline "for cause," within the meaning of Section 10(c) of the NLRA, "if it is imposed for some reason other than an employee's protected concerted activities."[251] "Cause," as used in Section 10(c), should not be confused with "just cause," as that term is used by arbitrators. "Cause, in the context of Sec. 10(c), effectively means the absence of a prohibited reason."[252]

The Board has further ruled that reinstatement is an appropriate remedy for a *Weingarten* violation "if, but only if, an employee is discharged or disciplined for asserting the right to representation."[253] Even if the employee was discharged on the basis of information obtained in violation of his or her *Weingarten* rights, the Board holds that reinstatement is not an appropriate remedy, because the discharge is considered "for cause" despite the violation.[254]

In another case, the Board let stand an administrative law judge's (ALJ) findings regarding the issues of notice and waiver of *Weingarten* rights.[255] The employee, who had reasonable cause to believe that his participation in an investigatory meeting with management would lead to disciplinary action being taken against him, requested that the bargaining unit's sole union steward be allowed to attend the meeting. Because the union steward was not at work and could not be contacted, another union member, a former union steward, attended the meeting at the employee's request. The meeting led to the employee's discharge. The ALJ found that the employer had violated the employee's *Weingarten* rights by failing, after learning that the union steward was unavailable, to notify the employee that the interview

---

[249]NLRB v. J. Weingarten, Inc., 420 U.S. 251, 88 LRRM 2689 (1975). A *Weingarten* violation occurs where an employee requests, but is denied, union representation in a meeting or investigatory interview with management that the employee reasonably believes may lead to disciplinary action against himself or herself. *Weingarten* rights are discussed in greater detail in Chapter 5, section 8.C., "Union Representation of Employees at Investigatory Interviews." *See also* Chapter 19, section 3.B., "Due Process and the Right to Union Representation During an Investigatory Interview."

[250]Taracorp Indus., 273 NLRB 221, 223, 117 LRRM 1497, 1499 (1984).

[251]Southwestern Bell Tel. Co., 273 NLRB 663, 663 n.3, 118 LRRM 1087, 1088 n.3 (1984).

[252]Taracorp Indus., 273 NLRB 221, 222 n.8, 117 LRRM 1497, 1499 n.8 (1984).

[253]*Id.* at 223 n.12, 117 LRRM at 1499 n.12.

[254]Greyhound Lines, 273 NLRB 1443, 118 LRRM 1199 (1985). *See also* Fischel, *Self, Others and Section 7: Mutualism and Protected Activities Under the National Labor Relations Act,* 89 COLUM. L. REV. 789 (1989); Orkin & Schmoyer, Weingarten: *Rights, Remedies, and the Arbitration Process,* 40 LAB. L.J. 594–602 (1989); Procopio, *A* Weingarten *Update,* 37 LAB. L.J. 340, 346–47 (1986); Hogler, Taracorp *and Remedies for* Weingarten *Violations: The Evolution of Industrial Due Process,* 37 LAB L.J. 403 (1986).

[255]Williams Pipeline Co., 315 NLRB 1, 147 LRRM 1168 (1994).

would not proceed unless the employee was willing to proceed without union representation. The employee's consent to proceed with the former steward present neither transformed the former steward into a union representative nor waived the employee's right to proper union representation.

Another Board case involved an employer who had a somewhat unconventional approach to disciplinary matters.[256] The employer would initially determine the appropriate discipline for the alleged misconduct and then refer the matter to an investigatory council to determine whether sufficient facts existed to support the disciplinary measures. The employer denied employees' requests for union representation at investigatory council hearings. The Board held that the denial of representation violated the employees' *Weingarten* rights because the council's review made the employer's disciplinary actions final and binding.

Arbitrators tend to be more flexible than the Board in selecting remedies to correct procedural violations and, despite the Board's clearly contrary approach, often order reinstatement, rather than other forms of relief, for violations of employees' *Weingarten* rights where the disciplinary action is not related to concerted activities.[257] In making such determinations, many arbitrators place on the employer the initial burden of advising the employee of the nature and purpose of the meeting, so that the employee is sufficiently informed as to whether he or she may or should exercise the right to union representation.[258] Once the employer meets this burden, the burden shifts to the employee to request union representation. Accordingly, arbitrators typically find that an employee's *Weingarten* rights were not violated if he or she failed to request union representation in an investigatory meeting that he or she had reasonable cause to believe would lead to disciplinary action against him or her.[259]

A disciplinary action may not automatically be overturned if an employee has not been prejudiced by a violation of his or her *Weingarten* rights.[260] Such a violation may, however, be a factor in determining whether to mitigate a discharge to a lesser form of discipline.[261]

In one case, for example, an arbitrator found that a written reprimand, rather than discharge, was the appropriate penalty for destruction of company property where the employee was denied union representation.[262] An-

---

[256]Henry Ford Health Sys., 320 NLRB 1153, 152 LRRM 1033 (1996).

[257]Hill & Sinicropi, Remedies in Arbitration 245–64 (BNA Books 2d ed. 1991); Fleming, The Labor Arbitration Process 139–40 (Univ. of Ill. Press 1967).

[258]County of Cook, Ill., 105 LA 974 (Wolff, 1995); Anchorage Hilton Hotel, 102 LA 55 (Landau, 1993).

[259]District of Columbia, Dep't of Corr., 105 LA 843 (Rogers, 1996); Benjamin Logan Bd. of Educ., 105 LA 1168 (Fullmer, 1995).

[260]Bi-State Dev. Agency, 105 LA 319 (Bailey, 1995) (the violation must prejudice the employee before the disciplinary actions should be overturned).

[261]Anchorage Hilton Hotel, 102 LA 55 (Landau, 1993).

[262]Transitank Car Corp., 84 LA 1112, 1114 (Sartain, 1985). *See also* Goshen Rubber, Inc., 99 LA 770 (Briggs, 1992) (just cause did not exist to discharge employee for alcohol-related incident when employee was not offered union representation); Arkansas Power & Light Co., 92 LA 144, 149 (Weisbrod, 1989); Southern Cal. Gas Co., 89 LA 393, 397 (Alleyne, 1987) (discharge overturned, where employer improperly failed to provide union representation at interview that resulted in a decision to test the employee for drug use after the employee requested such test).

other arbitrator ordered reinstatement of an employee who was discharged for theft, after finding that the employee was not given the opportunity to have a union representative present when confronted by an alleged eyewitness.[263] In contrast, another arbitrator refused to set aside the last-chance discharge of an employee found sleeping on the job, despite the fact that the employee was denied his *Weingarten* right to union representation.[264] The employer was, however, required to give the employee 1 month's pay because of the *Weingarten* violation.[265]

Employees are not entitled to union representation at all meetings with management, and "[e]very conversation on the floor of the plant between a supervisor and an employee does not require Union representation."[266] In a case where three state troopers were interviewed in connection with a criminal investigation of a high-speed car chase involving the "use of force" and, ultimately, the gunshot-wound death of the fleeing suspect, the troopers were informed that they were not the subjects of an administrative investigation as set forth in Article 18 of the contract, and that no complaint or allegation of misconduct had been made against them as would trigger such a proceeding. The troopers grieved, claiming violation of Ohio's counterpart *Weingarten* rulings. The arbitrator denied the grievances, holding:

> Of course, the Division is not privileged to conduct what is in reality a proceeding looking towards the possible disciplinary action of the Trooper being interviewed merely by labelling the process a "Criminal Investigation" rather than an "Administrative Investigation." But, in the present case the evidence does not disclose any such breach of good faith on the part of the Division. Should, in any such purported Criminal Investigation, a Trooper be interviewed and questions put to him which appear designed to elicit information which might be inculpatory and subject the Trooper to potential disciplinary action, the Trooper would at that point clearly be entitled to place on the record his contention that the examiner had crossed over the line and converted the Criminal Investigation into a precursor of an Administrative Investigation and properly renew his demand for Union representation.[267]

Employees who are informed that they are not the subjects of the investigation, and that no complaint or allegation of misconduct had been made against them, should not reasonably fear discipline.[268] An employee's mere concern about possible exposure to subsequent discipline does not necessarily warrant representation where the investigation is a straightforward request for information, and the questions do not concern the propriety or impropriety of the employee's actions or inaction.[269] Counseling sessions are

---

[263]Bake Rite Rolls, 90 LA 1133 (DiLauro, 1988). *But see* General Elec. Co., 98 LA 355 (Stutz, 1991) (discharge upheld, where employee voluntarily submitted to search of car trunk despite lack of union representation).

[264]Maui Pineapple Co., 86 LA 907 (Tsukiyama, 1986).

[265]*Id.*

[266]Heinz, U.S.A., 113 LA 500, 503 (Grupp, 1999)

[267]Ohio Dep't of Pub. Safety, 114 LA 1040, 1047–1048 (Ruben, 2000).

[268]*Id.*

[269]*Id.* (upholding an employee's suspension for insubordination, where she wrongfully refused, based on the absence of representation, her supervisors' repeated requests that she participate in a factfinding meeting; she reasonably should not have feared that discipline would result from the meeting, because the supervisors were investigating a sexual harassment claim of which she was not the subject).

another example of proceedings wherein *Weingarten* does not entitle employees to union representation because they are not "investigatory."[270]

A 1997 arbitration decision examined the role of the union representative in investigatory meetings.[271] Relying on 5 U.S.C. §7114(a)(2)(B),[272] which embodies the *Weingarten* principles, the arbitrator held that a union's representational rights must not interfere with or compromise the integrity of an employer's reasonable examination. The arbitrator upheld disciplinary measures levied against a union representative who had interfered with the employer's legitimate attempt to ascertain whether an employee was under the influence of alcohol. The union representative had provided chewing gum to the suspected employee to mask the odor of alcohol and had physically restrained the employee from participating in the employer's examination.

Another arbitrator determined that *Weingarten* does not give an employee the right to rely on a union steward's advice that he or she not answer questions during an interview.[273] The arbitrator concluded that the employee had no Fifth Amendment right to refuse to answer the employer's questions pertaining to the subject matter of a pending criminal trial, because the Fifth Amendment protects citizens only against incriminating questioning by the government, not by private employers.

v. *Consideration of Post-Discharge Misconduct or Charges and Post-Discharge Discovery of Predischarge Misconduct*

Some agreements require that the employer inform the employee of all grounds for discharge at the time of discharge. Under such provisions, arbitrators typically hold that only evidence bearing on the charges made at the time of discharge should be considered in determining the existence of cause.[274] Even absent such specific contractual provisions, however, arbitrators generally hold that discharge "must stand or fall upon the reason given at the time of discharge"; the employer cannot add other reasons when the case reaches arbitration.[275] Thus, if no discipline has been imposed for prior offenses, and the employer discharges an employee on inadequate grounds, a

---

[270]City of Independence, Mo., 113 LA 83, 89 (Hilgert, 1999).

[271]Corpus Christi Army Depot, 108 LA 1006 (Halter, 1997).

[272]This provision is among the labor-management and employee relations provisions within the Government Organization and Employees Act, 5 U.S.C. §101-8913 et seq.

[273]AT&T, 102 LA 931 (Kanner, 1994).

[274]Bethlehem Steel, 29 LA 635, 640–43 (Seward, 1957); Forest Hill Foundry Co., 1 LA 153, 154 (Brown, 1946).

[275]West Va. Pulp & Paper Co., 10 LA 117, 118 (Guthrie, 1947). *See also* E.&J. Gallo Winery, 80 LA 765, 769–70 (Killion, 1983); Nickles Bakery, 73 LA 801, 802 (Letson, 1979); Gardner Denver Co., 51 LA 1019, 1022 (Ray, 1968); Unimart, 49 LA 1207, 1210 (Roberts, 1968). *Cf.* Trailways Southeastern Lines, 81 LA 365, 366 (Gibson, 1983); Wilshire Indus./Wilshire Stor-All, 71 LA 56, 58 (Mueller, 1978); Mitchell Bros. Truck Line, 48 LA 953, 956 (Peck, 1967). For decisions discussing this topic in other fora, see, e.g.: Golden Day Sch. v. NLRB, 644 F.2d 834, 107 LRRM 2558 (9th Cir. 1979); NLRB v. Miller Redwood Co., 407 F.2d 1366, 70 LRRM 2868 (9th Cir. 1969); NRLB v. Yazoo Valley Elec. Power Ass'n, 405 F.2d 479, 70 LRRM 2049 (5th Cir. 1968); NLRB v. Bin-Dictator Co., 356 F.2d 210, 61 LRRM 2366 (6th Cir. 1966); NLRB v. National Furniture Mfg. Co., 315 F.2d 280, 52 LRRM 2451 (7th Cir. 1963); American Petrofina Co. of Tex., 92 LA 578 (Dunn, 1989); Potashnick Constr. Co., 77 LA 893 (Richardson, 1981). For additional material on this subject, see, e.g., FAIRWEATHER'S PRACTICE AND PROCEDURE IN LABOR ARBITRATION 362–67 (Schoonhoven ed., BNA Books 4th ed.

subsequent valid charge cannot save the employer's unsupported discharge.[276]

More recently, arbitrators have drawn a distinction between additional *grounds* for discharge, which remain inadmissible, and *evidence* of pre- or post-discharge conduct relevant to the originally stated grounds.[277] These decisions evince a willingness to admit evidence of pre- and post-discharge conduct not only to support or refute the original grounds for termination, but also for determining whether reinstatement is an appropriate remedy.[278] One arbitrator's expression of the rationale behind this development is instructive:

> In my view, post discharge evidence garnered by either party can be admitted at arbitral hearing. An extreme example serves to make the point. In the event a post discharge witness confesses to a theft charged against the grievant; or witness recants a prior statement given to the employer thereby denoting the grievant's innocence, it flies in the face of fairness and justice to simply ignore such evidence. Conversely, where, for example, the grievant was discharged for being under the influence of alcohol on the job and subsequent to discharge the employer discovered empty liquor bottles in his locker; or an employee is discharged for theft of an item valued at $5.00 and subsequent to discharge it is discovered that he stole items valued at $500.00, again such evidence should be admitted at arbitral hearing.
>
> In my opinion, it is not subsequently discovered evidence but rather subsequently discovered grounds for discharge that is precluded at arbitral hearing. An employer is limited to the grounds set forth at the time of discharge. But neither the employer nor the union is precluded from offering at arbitration evidence which has been discovered post discharge.[279]

Some arbitrators have qualified their consideration of evidence of post-discharge misconduct by stating that such evidence could not be used to jus-

---

1999); The Common Law of the Workplace: The Views of Arbitrators §6.11 (St. Antoine ed., BNA Books 1998); Nicolau, *After-Acquired Evidence—Will the* McKennon *Decision Make a Difference,* 50 J. Disp. Resol. 17 (July 1995); Nicolau, *The Arbitrator's Remedial Powers: Part I, in* Arbitration 1990: New Perspectives on Old Issues, Proceedings of the 43d Annual Meeting of NAA 73 (Gruenberg ed., BNA Books 1991). *See also* Heritage Cable Vision of San Jose, Cal., 112 LA 1 (Feller, 1999); Pullman Standard, 47 LA 752 (McCoy, 1966).

[276]*See* Rexam Graphics, 111 LA 1176 (Gangle, 1998). See extended discussion in Chapter 8, section 8.D.i., "After-Acquired Evidence of Predisciplinary Misconduct," and section 8.D.ii., "After-Acquired Evidence of Post-Disciplinary Conduct."

[277]*See, e.g.,* Keystone Steel & Wire Co., 114 LA 1466 (Goldstein, 2000).

[278]Shaefer's Ambulance Serv., 104 LA 481 (Calhoun, 1995). *See also* Pepsi-Cola Bottling Co., 107 LA 257 (Ross, 1996) (evidence of post-discharge misconduct by grievant admitted to determine the method of operation used by grievant); Nabisco Brands, 80 LA 238, 242 (Madden, 1983) (considering the grievant's post-discharge misconduct to be the decisive factor against him in that it served to discredit his denial of the original dishonesty charge); Mobay Chem. Corp., 77 LA 219, 222 (Lubow, 1981); St. Johnsbury Trucking Co., 74 LA 607, 608–09 (Knowlton, 1980); Taft Broad. Co., 69 LA 307, 311 (Chaffin, 1977); Granite City Steel Co., 53 LA 909, 918 (McKenna, 1969); Pullman-Standard, 47 LA 752, 753 (McCoy, 1966) (ordinarily a discharge made for one explicit reason cannot be justified in arbitration for an entirely different reason, but this rule does not apply where the employee has fair opportunity to defend against the additional grounds and the grounds would be reason for another discharge immediately following a reinstatement by the arbitrator); Perini, M-K, Leavell, 46 LA 1044, 1048 (Merrill, 1966) (additional offense at time of discharge formed "part of one connected whole"). For discussions of related matters, see Chapter 8, section 8.B., "'New' Evidence at Arbitration Hearings," and section 8.D., "After-Acquired Evidence."

[279]AT&T, 102 LA 931, 940 (Kanner, 1994). *See also* Bill Kay Chevrolet, 107 LA 302 (Wolff, 1996).

tify the discharge but could be used in determining whether, or to what the extent, the penalty should be mitigated.[280] Similarly, there is a line of cases in which a company's evidence was held inadequate to establish the offense for which the employee was disciplined, but adequate to establish a lesser offense for which an appropriate penalty (either as assessed by the employer or as mitigated by the arbitrator) was warranted.[281] While evidence of pre-discharge misconduct discovered after the discharge may be considered, the existence of such misconduct must be established according to a process that allows the grievant to respond to it.[282] Arbitrators also may consider an employee's favorable pre- and post-discharge conduct.[283]

Some arbitrators appear particularly willing to consider post-discharge rehabilitative treatment as a mitigating factor in determining the propriety of discharge where drug and/or alcohol addiction was involved.[284] In one case, for example, the arbitrator considered the misconduct a consequence of the employee's illness.[285] Another arbitrator provided an extensive review of the decisions on this topic.[286]

---

[280]Keystone Steel & Wire Co., 114 LA 1466 (Goldstein, 2000); Emhart Corp., 69 LA 839, 841–42 (Weitzman, 1977); Columbus Show Case Co., 44 LA 507, 513–14 (Kates, 1965); Catholic Press Soc'y, 40 LA 641, 651 (Gorsuch, 1963) (post-discharge misconduct may be considered in judging the appropriateness of the penalty, just as the employee's past record may be considered). For an example of making such qualified use of predischarge misconduct of which the employer was unaware, see *Trailways Southeastern Lines*, 81 LA 365, 366 (Gibson, 1983); *Sunshine Specialty Co.*, 55 LA 1061, 1068–69 (Levin, 1970).

[281]*See, e.g.*, Progressive Transp., 80 LA 546, 547 (Wilmoth, 1983); Reiter Foods, 77 LA 526, 530 (Hanes, 1981); Globe Weis, 76 LA 194, 197 (Davies, 1981); Kennecott Copper Corp., 73 LA 1066, 1068–69 (Mewhinney, 1979); Todd Pac. Shipyards Corp., 72 LA 1022, 1025–26 (Brisco, 1979); Kaiser Steel Stamped Prods., 72 LA 774, 775 (Rose, 1979); Madison Hotel, 69 LA 411, 413 (Bernhardt, 1977); Monarch Mach. Tool Co., 51 LA 391, 396 (Sembower, 1968) (insufficient evidence to support the charged offense but back pay was withheld because grievant at the investigation did not make forthright denial of charge but fostered suspicion against himself); Titus Mfg. Corp., 50 LA 133, 136 (Hughes, 1968); Templet Mfg. Co., 36 LA 839, 841 (Feinberg, 1961) (similar result where grievant failed to cooperate at the investigation). *But see* Faygo Beverage, 73 LA 912, 914 (Coyle, 1979).

[282]Jackson Gen. Hosp., 113 LA 1040, 1046 (Sharpe, 2000).

[283]Butterkrust Bakeries, 78 LA 562, 563 (Cocalis, 1982); H.K. Porter Co., 74 LA 969, 972 (Finan, 1980); Texaco, Inc., 42 LA 408, 411 (Prasow, 1963); Spaulding Fiber Co., 21 LA 58, 58–59 (Thompson, 1953). Sometimes less leeway has been afforded for such consideration of the grievant's post-discharge actions than for consideration of new predischarge information in the grievant's favor. *See, e.g.*, Mobil Oil Corp. v. Oil, Chem., & Atomic Workers Local 8-831, 679 F.2d 299, 110 LRRM 2620, 2623–24 (3d Cir. 1982); Sharon Steel Corp., 71 LA 737, 740 (Klein, 1978).

[284]Keystone Steel & Wire Co., 114 LA 1466 (Goldstein, 2000); AAFES Distribution, 107 LA 290 (Marcus, 1996); Vons Co., 106 LA 740 (Darrow, 1996); USS, Div. of USX Corp., 104 LA 82 (Dybeck, 1994); Meijer, Inc., 103 LA 834 (Daniel, 1994); Ashland Petroleum Co. Div., 90 LA 681, 687 (Volz, 1988); Northwest Airlines, 89 LA 943 (Nicolau, 1984), *aff'd sub nom.* Northwest Airlines v. Air Line Pilots, 808 F.2d 76, 124 LRRM 2300 (D.C. Cir. 1987) (reinstating airline pilot discharged for consuming alcoholic beverages within 24 hours of flight who was found to be an alcoholic and who offered post-discharge evidence of his progress in rehabilitation), *cert. denied*, 486 U.S. 1014 (1988). *But see* Duquesne Light Co., 92 LA 907, 910–11 (Sergent, Jr., 1989).

[285]Northwest Airlines, 89 LA 943 (Nicolau, 1984). *See also* Youngstown Hosp. Ass'n, 82 LA 31, 35 (Miller, 1983).

[286]Ocean Spray Cranberries, 105 LA 148 (Dichter, 1995).

Some arbitrators apply a balancing test, examining various factors to determine whether mitigation is appropriate under all the facts and circumstances.[287] These factors may include: (1) whether the grievant did the act under the influence of alcohol or drugs or while the grievant was an alcohol or drug abuser; (2) whether the grievant's work record was relatively clear of disciplinary action or whether prior disciplinary action resulted from alcoholism or drug abuse; (3) whether the grievant is successfully participating in an employee assistance program or similar rehabilitation program that indicates likely successful rehabilitation; and (4) whether the grievant was a long-term employee.[288] Waiting too long before seeking treatment, taking inappropriate post-termination jobs (e.g., bartending), and other behavior indicative of failure to fully confront his or her problems can work against the former employee under this approach.[289]

An employee's failure to deny negative post-discharge conduct permits allegations thereof to stand as undisputed evidence against him or her.[290] Arbitrators often regard aggressive post-discharge behavior as rendering an offending employee unfit for further employment.[291]

vi. Double Jeopardy [LA CDI 118.41]

Once discipline for a given offense is imposed and accepted, it cannot thereafter be increased, nor may another punishment be imposed, lest the employee be unfairly subjected to "double jeopardy."[292] The same is true where the employee does not accept the original penalty.[293] The double jeopardy doctrine also prohibits employers from attempting to impose multiple punishments for what is essentially a single act.[294] The arbitral concept of "double jeopardy" has been explained as follows:

---

[287]Keystone Steel & Wire Co., 114 LA 1466 (Goldstein, 2000).

[288]Id. at 1471.

[289]Id. at 1472.

[290]Jackson Gen. Hosp., 113 LA 1040, 1047 (Sharpe, 2000).

[291]Id.

[292]See, e.g., City of Kenosha, Wis., 76 LA 758, 760 (McCrary, 1981); Hub City Jobbing Co., 43 LA 907, 910 (Gundermann, 1964); Hi-Life Packing Co., 41 LA 1083, 1085–86 (Sembower, 1963); Misco Precision Casting Co., 40 LA 87, 90 (Dworkin, 1962); Durham Hosiery Mills, 24 LA 356, 358 (Livengood, 1955); International Harvester Co., 16 LA 616, 616–17 (McCoy, 1951). Cf. Acme Eng'g & Mfg. Corp., 81 LA 564, 567–68 (Schedler, 1983) (holding that the same incident involved two "misconducts," for which two separate penalties were proper). For other situations in which the double jeopardy concept was applied, see Federal Compress & Warehouse Co., 80 LA 1091, 1096 (Boals, 1983); City of Ontario, Or., 72 LA 1089, 1092 (Conant, 1979); United States Steel Corp., 55 LA 447, 449 (Simons, 1970) (employee who was discharged and then reinstated after full investigation could not then be discharged again for the same incident); Great Atl. & Pac. Tea Co., 48 LA 910, 914 (Keefe, 1967); Michigan Seamless Tube Co., 24 LA 132, 134 (Ryder, 1955). But see Kisco Co., 56 LA 623, 636 (Whitney, 1971) (holding that any right to assert the double jeopardy rule was waived where the employee had agreed to suspension and last-chance agreement, then breached the agreement).

[293]United Parcel Serv., 51 LA 462, 463 (Turkus, 1968); R. Munroe & Sons Mfg. Corp., 40 LA 1300, 1302–03 (Duff, 1963). Cf. General Servs. Admin., 75 LA 1158, 1162 (Lubic, 1980).

[294]Crown Cork & Seal Co., 111 LA 83, 87 (Harris, Jr., 1998); Lear Corp., 110 LA 885, 895 (Imundo, Jr., 1998) (double jeopardy prohibits punishment for lesser included offense).

"The key to this arbitral [double jeopardy] doctrine is not the Constitution but rather fundamental fairness, as guaranteed by the contractual requirement of 'just cause' for discipline. Thus when an employee has suffered a suspension for an offense it would be unfair . . . to fire him before he has committed a second offense."[295]

Some arbitrators apply the double jeopardy doctrine when management unduly delays the assignment or enforcement of discipline. One arbitrator did so on the ground that "it is a denial of procedural due process and just cause to hold a charge over an employee's head indefinitely and to revive it whenever corroborating or substantiating evidence might eventually surface."[296] Conversely, another arbitrator held that an employer did not waive its right to impose discipline by failing to act for more than 6 months, because the employer was participating in a police investigation and had agreed to take no action against its employees until the police completed their work.[297] In a somewhat unusual case, a successor employer, by agreeing to maintain the predecessor company's collective bargaining agreement while negotiating its own agreement with the union, was held to have "inherited" the discipline the predecessor imposed on an employee.[298] The successor employer violated the double jeopardy doctrine by revoking its offer of employment to an employee whom the predecessor had suspended and who had served his suspension.

Double jeopardy does not occur when an employer suspends an employee while conducting an investigation that ultimately leads to the employee's discharge. As one arbitrator noted, "[w]hile an employee cannot be twice punished for the same offense, it is permissible for an employee to be suspended pending investigation for possible termination."[299] The result is the same whether the employee is suspended with or without pay. The theory is that the suspension allows both the employer and the employee time to consider their options. One arbitrator concluded, "[e]mployers should . . . provide a cooling off period" by suspending the employee pending a full investigation."[300] Where, however, the employer suspends the employee, conducts its investigation, imposes what appears to be a "final" punishment, and then imposes additional punishment, double jeopardy exists.[301] Likewise, an employer cannot issue a disciplinary "warning" and later, after deciding more serious punishment would have been preferable (because, for example, the employer fears a third party's lawsuit related to the employee's misconduct), impose a harsher punishment.[302]

---

[295]United Int'l Investigative Serv., 114 LA 620, 626 (Maxwell, 2000) (quoting U.S. Postal Serv., 87-2 ARB ¶18490, at 5952 (Nolan, 1987)).

[296]DeVry Inst. of Tech., 87 LA 1149, 1157 (Berman, 1986).

[297]Zenith Elecs., 90 LA 881, 884–85 (Patterson, 1987). See also GTE Cal., 99 LA 196, 199 (Richman, 1992) (undercover investigation resulted in 3-month delay in imposing discipline).

[298]United Int'l Investigative Serv., 114 LA 620 (Maxwell, 2000).

[299]City of Virginia, Minn., 108 LA 59, 63 (Daly, 1997). See also Government of V.I., 103 LA 1055 (Kessler, 1994).

[300]Northwest Publ'ns, 104 LA 91, 96 (Bognanno, 1994).

[301]Laidlaw Transit Servs., 114 LA 612, 619 (Imundo, Jr., 2000).

[302]Vertrans Elevator Co., 112 LA 790, 794 (Silver, 1999); Metropolitan Tulsa Transit Auth., Tulsa, Okla., 112 LA 146, 152 (Jennings, 1999).

The double jeopardy doctrine does not apply where the discipline is imposed with the understanding that it may not be final. In one example of this principle, an arbitrator upheld the discharge of several employees for fighting, where the employer had first suspended them pending investigation and had issued a memorandum informing them that further incidents would result in their discharge.[303] The arbitrator rejected the union's double jeopardy claim because the memo did not constitute discipline and the grievants did not perceive it as such. Another arbitrator, however, held that the double jeopardy doctrine applied where the employer suspended an employee for 10 days while criminal charges were pending against him and then, when he was convicted, sought to discharge him.[304] Overturning the discharge, the arbitrator held that the employer had imposed the suspension with full knowledge of the facts, including the employee's admission of guilt.

The fact that an employee has paid a fine or served a jail sentence for acts committed in connection with his or her employment does not preclude consideration of those acts in determining whether the employer had just cause for disciplining the employee, despite any claim that such discipline constitutes double jeopardy.[305] Likewise, an employee's acquittal of criminal charges related to an incident for which he or she was disciplined does not preclude an arbitrator from upholding an employer's disciplinary action where the evidence persuades the arbitrator of the employee's guilt or misconduct.[306] In a similar vein, an employee who was terminated for failing to pass a drug screen and then, after being reinstated under a settlement agreement, was bypassed for promotion for the same reason was not subjected to double jeopardy.[307] It may, however, be unfair to deny advancement indefinitely to an employee who has already been disciplined.[308]

---

[303]Montgomery Ward & Co., 84 LA 905, 906 (Wilcox, 1985). *See also* Joerns Healthcare, 92 LA 694, 696–97 (Kessler, 1989). *But see* City of Chillicothe, Ohio, 96 LA 657 (DiLeone, 1991).

[304]Transit Mgmt. of Southeast La., 95 LA 74, 80–81 (Allen, Jr., 1990). *See also* McLain Grocery Co., 90 LA 435 (Oberdank, 1988) (discharge not allowed where two of three warnings were for substandard performance occurring in the same week).

[305]*See, e.g.*, Westinghouse Elec. Corp., 26 LA 836, 846 (Simkin, 1956) (the arbitrator also stated, however, that he could consider the previous punishment in determining the severity of the penalty assessed). For cases agreeing that the employer may punish the employee, even if the latter has been punished under the criminal law, see, e.g., *Department of the Air Force*, 74 LA 949, 951–52 (Ward, 1980); *Cooper Hosp.*, 45 LA 366, 374 (Scheiber, 1965); *Jenkins Bros.*, 45 LA 350, 351 (Stutz, 1965); *Westinghouse Elec. Corp.*, 40 LA 1169, 1173 (Schmidt, 1963); *Consolidated Badger Coop.*, 36 LA 965, 968–69 (Mueller, 1961). *See also* Sawbrook Steel Castings Co., 50 LA 725, 732 (Seinsheimer, 1968). *But see* City of Wilkes-Barre, Pa., 74 LA 33, 36 (Dunn, 1980).

[306]*See, e.g.*, City of Pontiac, Mich., 77 LA 765, 767 (Ott, 1981); Personnel Review Bd. of N.Y. City Health & Hosps. Corp., 76 LA 387, 391 (Simons, 1981); Dannon Milk Prods., 76 LA 133, 140 (Kramer, 1980); New York State Dep't of Corr. Servs., 69 LA 344, 349 (Kornblum, 1977); United Parcel Serv., 67 LA 861, 866–67 (Lubow, 1976); Chrysler Corp., 53 LA 1279, 1282 (Alexander, 1969); Allied Chem. Corp., 50 LA 616, 620 (Turkus, 1968); Flinkote Co., 49 LA 810, 814–15 (Block, 1967); Philadelphia Transp. Co., 49 LA 606, 608 (Gershenfeld, undated) (the arbitration hearing must be de novo, but the court acquittal may be introduced into evidence in support of the employee). *Cf.* American Meat Packing Co., 79 LA 1327, 1333 (Malinowski, 1982); Norfolk Naval Shipyard, 72 LA 149, 153 (Florey, 1979); General Elec. Co., 45 LA 490, 493 (Gomberg, 1965).

[307]City of Corpus Christi, Tex., 113 LA 329, 331 (Allen, Jr., 1999).

[308]City of Oakland, Cal., 112 LA 392, 399 (Silver, 1999).

Arbitrators may consider an employee's prior disciplinary offenses in determining the propriety of the penalty assessed for a later offense.[309] The double jeopardy principle does not apply, provided the later discipline is not "based *solely* on past violations for which discipline had already been imposed."[310] Double jeopardy protection also is not triggered when back pay is withheld from a reinstated employee where it is discovered that he or she concealed interim earnings.[311]

vii. Grievant's Past Record

Some consideration generally is given to the past record of any disciplined or discharged employee. An offense may be mitigated by a good past record and it may be aggravated by a poor one. Indeed, the employee's past record often is a major factor in the determination of the proper penalty for the offense. In many cases, arbitrators have reduced penalties in consideration of the employee's long, good past record.[312] In turn, an arbitrator's refusal to interfere with a penalty may be based in part on the employee's poor past record.[313] In one case, the arbitrator held that, although neither the

---

[309]*See, e.g.*, Noble Constr. & Maint. Co., 71 LA 1077, 1081 (Rule, 1978); Packaging Corp. of Am., 51 LA 127, 134 (Davey, 1968); American Airlines, 46 LA 737, 740–41 (Sembower, 1966); Bethlehem Steel Co., 41 LA 890, 892 (Porter, 1963); F.J. Kress Box Co., 24 LA 401, 407 (Pollack, 1955); Douglas Aircraft Co., 20 LA 331, 334 (Bernstein, 1953). Prior offenses are often considered in evaluating the propriety of penalties; see section 3.F.vii., "Grievant's Past Record," below.

[310]National Graphics, 112 LA 941, 948 (Pratte, 1999) (emphasis in original).

[311]Lithibar Matik, Inc., 112 LA 957, 965 (Sugerman, 1999).

[312]*E.g.*, Foods & Commercial Workers Local 7 v. King Soopers, Inc., 222 F.3d 1223, 164 LRRM 2970 (10th Cir. 2000); Silverstream Nursing Home, Case No. 14 300 00378 00 E, 2000 WL 1481892 (DiLauro, 2000); Oldmans Township Bd. of Educ., No. AR-99-640, 2000 WL 1481889 (DiLauro, 2000); USS, Div. of USX Corp., Case No. USS-39,788, 1999 WL 1074563 (Petersen, 1999); City of Southfield, Case No. 98-350, 1999 WL 908627 (McDonald, 1999); Wayne State Univ., 111 LA 986 (Brodsky, 1998); Western Res., Case No. 98-04004-9808, 1998 WL 1110785 (O'Grady, 1998); Mason & Hanger Corp., 109 LA 957 (Jennings, 1998); Pfizer, Inc., 79 LA 1225, 1236 (Newmark, 1982); Stylemaster, Inc., 79 LA 76, 78–79 (Winton, 1982); Pinkerton's of Fla., 78 LA 956, 961 (Goodman, 1982); Commonwealth of Pa., 73 LA 556, 561 (Gerhart, 1979); Ryder Truck Rental, 72 LA 824, 828 (Cohen, 1979); Sunweld Fitting Co., 72 LA 544, 558 (Hawkins, 1979); Kast Metals Corp., 70 LA 278, 284 (Roberts, 1978); City of Boulder, Colo., 69 LA 1173, 1178 (Yarowsky, 1977); Shenango, Inc., 67 LA 869, 869–70 (Cahn, 1976); Charleston Naval Shipyard, 54 LA 145, 151 (Kesselman, 1971); Ingersoll-Rand Co., 50 LA 487, 495 (Scheiber, 1968); Lockheed-California Co., 47 LA 937, 940 (Levin, 1966); Marathon Rubber Prods. Co., 46 LA 297, 302 (Lee, 1966); Clinton Engines Corp., 35 LA 428, 430 (Young, 1960); Pan Am. World Airways Sys., 33 LA 257, 259 (Seitz, 1959); Reed Roller Bit Co., 29 LA 604, 608 (Hebert, 1957); Pratt & Whitney Co., 28 LA 668, 672 (Dunlop, 1957); Ironrite, Inc., 28 LA 394, 398 (Haughton, 1956); Niagara Frontier Transit Sys., 26 LA 575, 577 (Thompson, 1957). *Cf.* Illinois Power Co., Case No. 98-15339, 1999 WL 33104849 (Vernon, 1999) (arbitrator limited to finding of just cause without consideration of employment record, where parties had already agreed on penalty if just cause was found).

[313]*E.g.*, Procter & Gamble Co., 114 LA 1185 (Allen, Jr., 2000); Aeronca, Inc., 112 LA 1063 (Duda, Jr., 1999); Baker Support Servs., Case No. 98-03384, 1999 WL 555915 (Harris, Jr., 1999); Hayes Int'l Corp., 80 LA 1313, 1320 (Traynor, 1983); St. Regis Paper Co., 74 LA 1281, 1284 (Kaufman, 1980); Douglas Aircraft Co. of Can., 70 LA 41, 49 (O'Shea, 1978); Midland-Ross Corp., 68 LA 1010, 1015 (Simon, 1977); Prophet Foods Co., 55 LA 288, 290 (Howlett, 1970); Sterling Drug, 53 LA 933, 939 (Teple, 1969); McDonnell Douglas Corp., 51 LA 1076, 1080 (Bothwell, 1968); American Cyanamid Co., 51 LA 181, 183 (Stouffer, 1968); American Airlines, 47 LA 266, 270 (Dworkin, 1966); Ekco Housewares Co., 46 LA 246, 248 (Wallen, 1965); Federal Chem. Co., 44 LA 193, 194 (Davis, 1965); Harnischfeger Corp., 43 LA 753, 756 (Gilden, 1964); Bethlehem Steel Co., 41 LA 890, 892 (Porter, 1963); Bird & Son, 30 LA 948, 950 (Sembower, 1958); Capital Airlines, 27 LA 358, 361 (Guthrie, 1956).

incident at the time of discharge nor any other single incident cited by the employer was sufficient to warrant discharge, the general pattern of the employee's unsatisfactory conduct and performance, as established by a series of incidents over an extended period, was preponderant evidence justifying discharge.[314] Other arbitrators have reached the same conclusion in similar "last-straw" situations.[315] Additionally, in one case, an arbitrator reduced the penalty, but used the employee's discipline history to impose a "last-chance provision" on the employee's reinstatement.[316]

However, there are limitations on the consideration of past offenses. For instance, an arbitrator must not rely on an unblemished employment history to reduce a penalty after finding just cause for termination when the collective bargaining agreement empowers the employer to determine the penalty.[317] One arbitrator held that although the employee's past record could not be admitted to support the employer's decision, it could be admitted to impeach the employee's claim that he was a good employee.[318] A distinction should be made between rule infractions that have been proven and mere past "charges." While an employer may have the right to post notations al-

---

[314]Electronic Corp. of Am., 3 LA 217, 218–20 (Kaplan, 1946).

[315]*See* City of Burton, Case No. 54 390 0025098, 1999 WL 555866 (Allen, 1999); Maple Creek Mining, Case No. 98598004, 1999 WL 454659 (Nicholas, Jr., 1999); Pioneer Flour Mills, 109 LA 1016 (Crider, 1998); Apcoa, Inc., 81 LA 449, 452 (Hewitt, 1983); Turco Mfg. Co., 74 LA 889, 895 (Penfield, 1980); Dura Corp., 72 LA 765, 768 (Herrick, 1979); Noble Constr. & Maint. Co., 71 LA 1077, 1081 (Rule, 1978); General Elec. Co., 70 LA 1168, 1171 (Spencer, 1978); Aggregates & Concrete Ass'n of N. Cal., Inc., 69 LA 439, 456, 459 (Griffin, 1977); National Council of Jewish Women, 57 LA 980, 992 (Scheiber, 1971); Prophet Foods Co., 55 LA 288, 290 (Howlett, 1970); Thiokol Chem. Corp., 52 LA 1254, 1257–58 (Williams, 1969); Singer Co., 52 LA 448, 450, 451 (Koven, 1969); American Motors Corp., 51 LA 945, 950 (Dunne, 1968); Honeywell Inc., 48 LA 1201, 1202, 1204 (McNaughton, 1967); Ebinger Baking Co., 47 LA 948, 951 (Singer, 1966); American Airlines, 46 LA 737, 739 (Sembower, 1966); Arden Farms Co., 45 LA 1124, 1129, 1133 (Tsukiyama, 1965); Bethlehem Steel Co., 45 LA 612, 614 (Seward, 1965); Ampex Corp., 44 LA 412, 415–16 (Koven, 1965); Great Atl. & Pac. Tea Co., 41 LA 887, 888 (Cahn, 1963); Lone Star Cement Corp., 39 LA 652, 653–54 (Oppenheim, 1962); Rowe Mfg. Co., 36 LA 639, 640, 643 (Turkus, 1961); International Shoe Co., 32 LA 485, 486 (Hepburn, 1959); National Fireworks Ordnance Corp., 20 LA 274, 275 (Roberts, 1953). *Cf.* Union Carbide Corp., 78 LA 603, 611–12 (Teple, 1982); Olin Mathieson Corp., 49 LA 573, 577 (Belshaw, 1967); Ohio Crankshaft Co., 48 LA 558, 562 (Teple, 1967); Northwestern Bell Tel. Co., 37 LA 605, 616–19 (Davey, 1961); Abbott Linen Supply Co., 35 LA 12, 14 (Schmidt, 1960); Aluminum Co. of Am., 8 LA 234, 245 (Pollard, 1945). Where there was no present offense, discharge was reversed in *Wisconsin Aluminum Foundry Co.*, Case No. 99-14977, 2000 WL 1139499 (Vernon, 2000); *Ogden Food Serv. Corp.*, 75 LA 805, 808 (Kelman, 1980); *Henry B. Gilpin Co.*, 72 LA 981, 986 (Stone, 1979); *Overhead Door Co. of Ky.*, 70 LA 1299, 1303 (Dworkin, 1978); *Northern Ind. Pub. Serv. Co.*, 69 LA 201, 210 (Sembower, 1977); *Revere Copper & Brass*, 45 LA 254, 255 (McCoy, 1965); *Metropolitan Transit Auth.*, 39 LA 855, 858 (Fallon, undated); *Magnavox Co.*, 29 LA 305, 311 (Dworkin, 1957). *Cf.* Union Oil Co. of Cal., 77 LA 428, 432 (Winton, 1981); Douglas Aircraft Co. of Can., 70 LA 41, 44–45 (O'Shea, 1978).

[316]*See* City of Melbourne, Case No. 98-00353, 1998 WL 1048334 (Cohen, 1998). *See also* Broughton Foods Co., Case No. 98-01898, 1998 WL 1033486 (Hewitt, 1998).

[317]*See* Boston Med. Ctr. v. Service Employees Local 285, 113 F. Supp. 2d 169, 165 LRRM 2392 (D. Mass. 2000) (arbitrator could not modify penalty when power to sentence is vested in the employer once just cause is found pursuant to the collective bargaining agreement). *See also* Ormet Primary Aluminum Corp., Case No. Gr. #734, 1999 WL 555893 (Parkinson, 1999).

[318]*See* ATC/Vancom of Cal. LP, 111 LA 244 (McKay, 1998).

leging rule infractions on employee records, the failure of the employer to notify employees of alleged infractions at the time of occurrence precludes the employer from using the notations to support disciplinary action at a later date, because employees should not be required to disprove stale charges.[319] Nor would an arbitrator consider past rule infractions for which the employee was in no way reprimanded,[320] or past warnings that had not been put in such form as to make them subject to a grievance.[321] If the collective bargaining agreement provides, however, that previous charges may be considered unless they have been found to be without merit, the arbitrator can consider the charge as part of the grievant's past record.[322]

If an employee is given notice of adverse record entries and does not file a grievance where able to do so, an arbitrator may subsequently accept the entries on their face without considering their merits.[323]

---

[319]Consolidated Vultee Aircraft Corp., 10 LA 907, 909 (Dwyer, 1948). *See also* Patton Sparkle Mkt., 75 LA 1092, 1095–96 (Cohen, 1980); Goodyear Aerospace Corp., 51 LA 540, 545 (Lehoczky, 1968); Basler Elec. Co., 49 LA 1100, 1109 (Sembower, 1968); Wood County Tel. Co., 46 LA 175, 180 (Lee, 1966); Rich Mfg. Co., 46 LA 154, 159 (Block, 1966); Carnation Co., 42 LA 568, 570–71 (Miller, 1964) ("Past incidents, for which no formal disciplinary action was taken and no official records maintained, and which cannot at a later date be adequately investigated, cannot be accepted" to support discharge); Harshaw Chem. Co., 32 LA 86, 88 (Belkin, 1959); A.C.&C. Co., 24 LA 538, 541 (Scheiber, 1955). *Cf.* Continental Airlines, 78 LA 313, 318–19 (Jones, Jr., 1982).

[320]Western Air Lines, 37 LA 130, 133 (Wyckoff, 1961). *See also* Boyce Mach. Corp., 48 LA 251, 255 (Oppenheim, 1967).

[321]Duval Corp., 43 LA 102, 106 (Meyers, 1964). The recording of warnings given to employees has been held to be a form of discipline that may require proper cause. Federal Labor Union v. American Can Co., 21 LA 518 (N.J. Super. Ct. 1953). *See also* Timex Corp., 54 LA 1185, 1187 (Seitz, 1971); Donaldson Co., 20 LA 826, 831 (Louisell, 1953).

[322]Louisville Water Co., 114 LA 583 (Lalka, 2000).

[323]*See* General Elec. Co., 70 LA 1174, 1175–76 (Abrams, 1978); McDonnell Douglas Corp., 51 LA 1076, 1080 (Bothwell, 1968); United Eng'g & Foundry Co., 50 LA 1118, 1121 (Stouffer, 1968). *Cf.* Overhead Door Co. of Ky., 70 LA 1299, 1302 (Dworkin, 1978); Weston Instruments, 50 LA 1127, 1129–31 (Gould, 1968). In *Purex Corp.*, 38 LA 313, 316–17 (Edelman, 1962), the employee had not been given written notice of the entries on his record but did know of them and it was company policy that employees were invited to inspect their personnel records. While the arbitrator stated that the company should use written notices, he refused to "rule that its records are so secret that they cannot be used to establish an employee's past conduct." *Id.* at 317. In proper cases, arbitrators have ordered the removal of matter from an employee's personnel file or have permitted matter to remain, with the understanding that it not be used against the employee in the future. *See* Malo Inc., 81 LA 497, 502 (Roberts, 1983); Social Sec. Admin., 68 LA 160, 163 (Kaye, 1977); Fawn Eng'g Corp., 54 LA 839, 844 (Sembower, 1971); U.S. Plywood-Champion Papers, 50 LA 115, 125 (Jenkins, 1968); Ohio Power Co., 48 LA 299, 304 (Leach, 1967); New York Bd. of Educ., 47 LA 91, 94–96 (Stark, 1966); Duval Corp., 43 LA 102, 106 (Meyers, 1964); Pullman, Inc., 41 LA 315, 317 (Stouffer, 1963). However, where three employees claimed to be ill rather than participants in a "sick-out," the arbitrator stated that he was ruling in their favor "on the basis of the weight of the evidence rather than on a firm conviction that he knows the actual facts," and for this reason his award expressly provided: "The records of these proceedings may be retained, or referred to, in the personnel record of each grievant so that the records will be available for consideration in the event any one of these grievants is involved in absenteeism in the future at a time when concerted job action of an illegal nature occurs, such as a 'sick-out.'" Federal Aviation Admin., 72 LA 761, 765 (Forrester, 1979). *See also* City of Cincinnati, Ohio, 69 LA 682, 686 (Bell, 1977).

Collective bargaining agreements sometimes limit consideration of an employee's record to a specified period.[324] Where a letter of intent that became part of the contract specified that records of disciplinary action in an employee's personnel file should be removed 2 years after issuance, provided there was no intervening disciplinary action, the arbitrator found that, because he could not consider these prior records, the present record of disciplinary action was not sufficient to justify discharge.[325] Another arbitrator held that an employee's absenteeism record prior to a previous arbitration of his earlier discharge could not be considered in determining the propriety of the second discharge, because the first arbitrator had "wiped the . . . slate clean."[326] In a similar case, however, an arbitrator permitted an employer to consider an employee's 20-year work record, despite a provision in the parties' bargaining agreement that discipline was "wiped-clean" after 1 year. The employer considered the employee's entire work history to determine the existence of mitigating circumstances that would justify leniency.[327] Conversely, when an agreement expressly restricts an arbitrator from considering mitigating factors in discharge situations, courts will not hesitate in setting aside arbitral decisions to the contrary.[328]

The need for some time limitation in the consideration of past offenses may also be recognized even where the agreement does not expressly impose one. Thus, an arbitrator while emphasizing the need to consider and weigh a grievant's past record, observed:

> In general we should say that in discharge cases the past conduct of the employee in question is of concern to the arbitrator called upon to review Management's disciplinary action. If the employee has an excellent record in the Company's service, the Union is sure to emphasize this. No arbitrator can fail to take note of a good record, the absence of prior warning notice, and other factors which may pertain to the employee's fitness to be continued on his job.
>
> By the same token, if an employee's past performance has been one of increasing disregard of his responsibilities to his job and to the employer who is paying him, no arbitrator can rightly sweep this sort of evidence under the rug and confine himself to technical evidence pertaining to a particular incident on a particular day. To do so would not add to the cause of good industrial relations. It might do irreparable harm to the arbitration process.

---

[324]*See, e.g.*, Borden Italian Foods Co., 113 LA 13 (Marino, 1999) (arbitrator abided by agreement between parties stating that the arbitrator could not consider disciplinary evidence more that 12 months old); Browning-Ferris Indus. of Mich., 69 LA 787, 789 (Kanner, 1977); United States Steel Corp., 53 LA 124, 126 (Dybeck, 1969) (employer was obviously penalized for submitting evidence in violation of such provision); Ingersoll-Rand Co., 50 LA 487, 495 (Scheiber, 1968) (such provision did not prevent consideration of *good* record prior to the limitations period); Schreiber Trucking Co., 48 LA 833, 834–35 (Kates, 1968) (such provision was narrowly construed); Arcrods Plant, 47 LA 994, 999 (Bradley, 1966); San Diego Elec. Ry. Co., 10 LA 119, 128 (Aaron, 1948). As to a provision forbidding the "pyramiding" of penalties, see *Sybron Corp.*, 52 LA 1263, 1266 (Shister, 1969).

[325]Calgon Carbon Corp., 88 LA 347, 349 (Tharp, 1987). *See also* Bethlehem Steel Corp., 92 LA 857, 860 (Witt & Valtin, 1988); Southern Cal. Permanente Med. Group, 92 LA 41, 45 (Richman, 1989); City of Rochester, N.Y., 82 LA 217, 220 (Lawson, 1984).

[326]American Brass Co., 88 LA 161, 167 (Fullmer, 1986).

[327]Babcock & Wilcox Co., 90 LA 606, 610–11 (Ruben, 1987).

[328]Georgia-Pacific Corp. v. Paperworkers Local 27, 864 F.2d 940, 130 LRRM 2208 (1st Cir. 1988); Pennsylvania v. Independent State Stores Union, 553 A.2d 948, 130 LRRM 2780 (Pa. 1989).

However, this does not mean that we are to consider everything that is introduced as having equal weight and significance. We sympathize with the position often taken by unions that there should be some limitation on how far back in the record one should be permitted to go in the matter of digging up old scores. Such historic incidents should be close enough in their relation to the problem involved in the immediate case to warrant consideration.[329]

Also emphasizing the need to consider an employee's past record, and rejecting a union request for a contractual clause to prohibit the employer or any arbitrator "from considering any previous warning notices and/or disciplinary actions which were issued more than 12 months prior to consideration of new disciplinary action," one arbitrator offered this opinion:

> As an experienced arbitrator, the undersigned feels that the proposal here made could seriously hamper the City's efforts to develop and maintain a workforce which is cooperative, dependable, and loyal to management and other employees. In an arbitration case, the Union always refers to the length of service of the Grievant as a factor deserving mercy. But if the arbitrator is not free to consider the entire record of an employee, he is unable to distinguish between a 10-year employee with a nearly perfect record and another 10-year employee with a very black record of violations and disciplines, holding onto his job only because the City and Arbitrator are barred from considering the constant repetitions of violations.[330]

Evidence of past acts showing a course of conduct has sometimes been considered relevant in some types of cases as indicating a likelihood that the employee committed the specific act with which he or she was charged.[331] Past conduct also can be used to show that the employee is not the kind to flagrantly violate work rules.[332]

Employees who have a past record of discipline may be given a harsher disciplinary penalty than first-time offenders. Thus, an employer's imposition of more severe discipline on employees with prior disciplinary records than on employees without a disciplinary history, although both groups were

---

[329]Borg-Warner Corp., 22 LA 589, 596 (Larkin, 1954). Also regarding "digging up" past matters, see *Universal Dishwashing Mach. Co.*, 17 LA 737, 740 (Reynolds, 1952). In *Consolidated Foods Corp.*, 43 LA 1143, 1148–50 (Klein, 1964), reduced weight was given to discipline assessed before the union came to the plant. But in rejecting the union's contention that the employee's record prior to establishment of the bargaining unit should not be considered in *Central Blood Bank of Pittsburgh*, 69 LA 1031, 1036 (Amis, 1977), the arbitrator stated that the employee's "employment record will be considered and it will be given what weight it deserves"; and, in fact, that record was a significant factor in the decision.

[330]City of Quincy, Ill., 81 LA 352, 359 (Block, 1982).

[331]*See* Procter & Gamble Co., 114 LA 1185 (Allen, Jr., 2000) (relying on grievant's past threats to find he could have "made good" on the charged threats); Colonial Sugars Co., 41 LA 1061, 1062 (Sweeney, 1963); National Malleable & Steel Casting Co., 12 LA 262, 264–65 (Pedrick, 1949); Lake Shore Tire & Rubber Co., 3 LA 455 (Gorder, 1946); Mueller Brass Co., 3 LA 285 (Wolf, 1946). *See also* Pacific Gas & Elec. Co., 48 LA 264, 267 (Koven, undated). *But see* Brach & Brock Confections Co., Case No. 98-133, 1999 WL 33103149 (Berman, 1999); General Tel. Co. of Ky., 69 LA 351, 356 (Bowles, 1977); Chrysler Corp., 46 LA 184, 186 (Alexander, 1966); Bird & Son, 30 LA 948, 950 (Sembower, 1958). For discussion, see FLEMING, THE LABOR ARBITRATION PROCESS 168–70 (Univ. of Ill. Press 1967); Wirtz; *Due Process of Arbitration*, *in* THE ARBITRATOR AND THE PARTIES, PROCEEDINGS OF THE 11TH ANNUAL MEETING OF NAA 1, 20–21 (McKelvey ed., BNA Books 1958) (noting that caution obviously should be exercised in using evidence of past acts for this purpose).

[332]Coca-Cola Enters., 94 LA 652, 656 (Prayzich, 1990).

active participants in an improper work stoppage, was upheld: "Certainly, the past disciplinary history of any particular grievant is a factor in determining or evaluating the appropriateness of a penalty. Any offense may be ameliorated by the lack of previous discipline, just as an offense may be exacerbated by a poor record."[333]

In determining whether a discharge will withstand review, arbitrators appear to consider the nature of the prior discipline as well as the seriousness of the employee's earlier offenses. Where an employee had been given a 1-day suspension for an earlier offense and had never received a long-term disciplinary suspension, the arbitrator held: "The lack of any long disciplinary layoff in [the employee's] record indicates that this discharge was premature."[334] It has also been held that if a long-term employee has not been disciplined in some time, and any deficiencies in the employee's early years of employment appear to have been corrected, an employer may not consider prior instances of discipline in order to justify a decision to discharge the employee.[335]

viii. Length of Service With Company

Long service with the company, particularly if unblemished, is a definite factor in favor of the employee whose discharge is reviewed through arbitration.[336] Arbitrators have recognized that the loss of seniority may work

---

[333]Public Util. Dist. 1 of Clark County, 103 LA 1066, 1074 (Paull, 1994).
[334]Tri-County Beverage Co., 107 LA 577, 581 (House, 1996).
[335]Webcraft Games, 107 LA 560 (Ellmann, 1996).
[336]Elkhart County, Ind., Gov't, 112 LA 936 (Cohen, 1999) (14 years of service where 13 were without discipline); Weyerhaeuser Paper Co., Case No. 98-11140, 1999 WL 555867 (Eisenmenger, 1999) (employer placed too much emphasis on consistency of discipline without considering length of employment); Wayne State Univ., 111 LA 986 (Brodsky, 1998) (18 years of discipline-free service was a mitigating factor); USS, Div. of USX Corp., 111 LA 52 (Neyland, 1998); Mason & Hanger Corp., 109 LA 957 (Jennings, 1998); Penn Traffic, Case No. 98-05835, 1998 WL 1041392 (Imundo, Jr., 1998); Smurfit Recycling Co., 103 LA 243 (Richman, 1994); Canteen Corp., 99 LA 649, 654–55 (Allen, Jr., 1992) (22-year "blemish-free" disciplinary record); Ball-Incon Glass Packaging Corp., 98 LA 1, 4–5 (Volz, 1991); Ohio Dep't of Youth Servs., 97 LA 734, 738 (Bittel, 1991); Rohm & Haas Tex., 92 LA 850, 856 (Allen, Jr., 1989) (14-year employee with good record reinstated where operational errors were attributed to new job classification); S.E. Rykoff & Co., 90 LA 233, 235 (Angelo, 1987) (15-year work record without prior discipline); Climate Control/McQuay, 89 LA 1062, 1064 (Cromwell, 1987) (long service was only mitigating factor); Weyerhaeuser Co., 88 LA 270 (Kapsch, 1987); Consolidation Coal Co., 85 LA 506, 511 (Hoh, 1985) (17-year employee reinstated with 20-day suspension); Victory Mkts., 84 LA 354, 357 (Sabghir, 1985) (14-year employee discharged for incompetence reinstated without back pay to lower level position because of his length of service); Potomac Elec. Power Co., 83 LA 449, 453 (Kaplan, 1984) (unblemished 21-year record of service a mitigating factor); Fisher Foods, 82 LA 505, 512 (Abrams, 1984) (discharged employee with 11 years of seniority and no prior discipline reinstated without back pay); Southwest Detroit Hosp., 82 LA 491, 492 (Ellmann, 1984) (discharge converted to 2-month suspension for 9-year employee who was considered a "relatively long term employee"); City of Burlington, Iowa, 82 LA 21, 24 (Kubie, 1984) (discharge of employee with "over thirteen years apparently blameless service" reduced to 5-day suspension). But see Nabisco Lifesavers Co., Case No. 99-06447-8, 2000 WL 1139491 (Brodsky, 2000) (holding that length of service weighs more heavily in favor of mitigation in conjunction with a previously "clean" disciplinary record, but not when employee's long service record shows a tarnished disciplinary record). See also USS, Div. of USX Corp., Case No. USS-41,257, 2000 WL 1508197 (Bethel, 2000) (grievant's discharge for alcohol consumption on company property sustained despite grievant's length of service); Willow Run Mich., Cmty.

great hardship on the employee,[337] and that it is not conducive to the improvement of relations between other workers and management.[338] Some arbitrators, however, find that whether length of service can serve as a mitigating factor depends on the type of misconduct at issue. One arbitrator stated: "It is well-established, that except for certain egregious misconduct, such as dishonesty, or other violations involving moral turpitude, . . . length of service is a proper consideration when assessing the appropriateness of the penalty of discharge."[339]

In a case in which the employee had been discharged for sleeping on the job, the arbitrator wrote:

> The company must give some credence to seniority. It is not my intent to . . . lay out the rule that seniority should govern. However, seniority is an extremely important facet of the makeup of an employee. It shows loyalty, it shows recognized ability, it shows efficiency and it is even recognized in the contract in the determining of [bid] classifications.[340]

Taking a contrary view, another arbitrator found just cause existed for discharge of a union steward with 32 years of service for violating a rule prohibiting sexual harassment. The employer had a practice of discharging both employees and management personnel found to have violated the rule, and the steward's long service and unblemished record did not excuse his conduct.[341] In a similar case, one arbitrator rejected the union's argument that consideration should be given to an employee's 23 years of service when the employee had been discharged for harassing female employees. He reasoned:

Sch., 112 LA 115 (Brodsky, 1999); Bell Fed. Credit Union, Case No. 98-15649, 1999 WL 705017 (Neas, 1999) (grievant's 18-year tenure, standing alone, was insufficient to modify penalty); CF Motor Transp., 103 LA 303 (Johnson, 1994); Safeway Stores, 84 LA 910, 915 (Staudohar, 1985) (discharge for dishonesty upheld even though grievants were long-term employees).

[337]See R.J. Tower Corp., 68 LA 1160, 1166 (Roumell, Jr., 1977); New Tronics Corp., 46 LA 365, 368 (Kates, 1966); Western Insulated Wire Co., 45 LA 972, 974–75 (Jones, Jr., 1965); Kelly-Springfield Tire Co., 37 LA 704, 706 (McCoy, 1961); Certain-Teed Prods. Corp., 24 LA 606, 609 (Simkin, 1955); Bethlehem Steel Co., 2 LA 194, 195–96 (Shipman, 1945).

[338]Argonne Worsted Co., 4 LA 81, 83 (Copelof, 1946). Nonetheless, even long service with the company will not save the job if other factors strongly justify discharge. See Nashville Gas Co., 79 LA 802, 807 (Odom, 1982); Harmony Dairy Co., 51 LA 745, 747 (Krimsly, 1968); Westinghouse Elec. Corp., 47 LA 104, 105–06 (Porter, 1966). Furthermore, in one case the arbitrator stated that better performance reasonably could have been expected of the grievant as a long-service employee, and thus that "this factor weighs against the Grievant as well as for him." Hayes-Albion Corp., 70 LA 696, 698 (Glendon, 1978). See also Walker County Med. Ctr. Co., 77 LA 1125, 1127 (Johnson, 1981). Cf. Pittsburg & Midway Coal Mining Co., 113 LA 611 (D'Eletto, 1999) (company should have considered grievant's work history).

[339]Glacier County, Mont., Sch. Dist. 15, 112 LA 700, 704 (Prayzich, 1999) (footnote omitted).

[340]Arch of Ill., 107 LA 178, 181 (Feldman, 1995).

[341]Schlage Lock Co., 88 LA 75 (Wyman, 1986). See also Indiana Bell Tel. Co., 99 LA 756, 762 (Goldstein, 1992); Can-Tex Indus., 90 LA 1230, 1231 (Shearer, 1988) (discharge of 21-year employee with good record upheld, where employee sexually harassed coworker despite warning); Babcock & Wilcox Co., 90 LA 606, 610 (Ruben, 1987) (despite 20-year service record, arbitrator sustained discharge for poor workmanship); Standard Oil Co., 89 LA 1155, 1158 (Feldman, 1987) (arbitrator upheld discharge of long-term employee who pleaded guilty to drug trafficking).

Although it is difficult to articulate a precise rule, long service is properly taken into account as a mitigating factor for minor misconduct. Seniority is not a mitigating factor when determining discipline appropriate for intentional major misconduct that directly and repeatedly violates a written prohibition, particularly when the miscreant has been instructed to cease and desist.[342]

A grievant's 22 years of service did not save him from discharge for absenteeism. The arbitrator wrote:

> Even long seniority counts for only so much. It buys extra consideration, it merits the benefit of any reasonable doubts, and it obliges an employer to view the employee's record as a whole rather than treating events in isolation. Nevertheless, even senior employees have to come to work regularly.[343]

The length of employment also can be a factor in deciding the applicable burden of proof. In one case, an arbitrator applied the clear and convincing standard after considering the employee's 15-year work history.[344]

In one case, the fact that a long-service employee was nearing eligibility for retirement was an additional factor in support of reinstatement,[345] but in another case the arbitrator refused to give weight to the fact of approaching retirement.[346]

The fact that an employee has had only a short period of employment prior to being disciplined is sometimes cited as a reason for refusing to mitigate a disciplinary penalty.[347]

ix. *Knowledge of Rules*   [LA CDI 100.15; 118.25; 118.656]

One of the two most commonly recognized principles in the arbitration of discipline cases is that there must be reasonable rules or standards, consistently applied and enforced and widely disseminated.[348]

Concerning notice of rules, one arbitrator stated: "An employee can hardly be expected to abide by the 'rules of the game' if the employer has not communicated those rules, and it is unrealistic to think that, after the fact, an arbitrator will uphold a penalty for conduct that an employee did not know was prohibited."[349] Additionally, another arbitrator stated: "Just cause requires that employees be informed of a rule, infraction of which may result in suspension or discharge, unless conduct is so clearly wrong that specific

---

[342]International Extrusion Corp., 106 LA 371, 374 (Brisco, 1996).

[343]Carolina Tel. & Tel. Co., 97 LA 653, 655 (Nolan, 1991).

[344]Milwaukee Bd. of Sch. Dirs., 110 LA 566 (Winton, 1998).

[345]Brown & Bigelow Co., 44 LA 237, 241 (Graff, 1964).

[346]American Welding & Mfg. Co., 47 LA 457, 463 (Dworkin, 1966).

[347]National Starch & Chem. Co., Case No. 990308-07735-7, 1999 WL 1995376 (Hilgert, 1999); Truck Transp. Case No. 97-23412, 1998 WL 686608 (Talent, 1998); Container Corp. of Am., 100 LA 568, 570 (Byars, 1993); Bell Helicopter Textron, 98 LA 201, 205 (Nicholas, Jr., 1991); Thorn Apple Valley, 98 LA 183, 188 (Kanner, 1991); Yankee Screw Prods., 95 LA 909, 916 (Kanner, 1990); Alpha Beta Co., 93 LA 995, 1000 (Prayzich, 1989); Kellogg Co., 93 LA 884, 893 (Clarke, 1989).

[348]*Arbitration Awards in Discharge Cases*, 28 LA 930, 931–32 (1957) (over 1,000 discharge cases examined).

[349]McQuay Int'l, Case No. 99-06558, 1999 WL 908632, at 27 (Howell, 1999).

reference is not necessary."[350] This principle is illustrated by a case where 10 air traffic controllers were disciplined for taking extended breaks in their cars of up to 4 hours and 45 minutes during their regular work hours. The employer had no rules regarding either the length of breaks or where they could be taken. In fact, there was strong evidence that the supervisors were aware of the practice and had condoned it. As a result, the arbitrator set aside the discipline imposed on all 10 employees.[351]

An employee must receive clear notice of both what the employer expects as well as the range of penalties that may be imposed for failing to meet the employer's expectations.[352] For example, where an employee was not properly put on notice that not meeting production standards could lead to discipline, the employer did not have just cause to issue a warning to the employee who failed his production quota standards.[353] However, one arbitrator upheld a discharge for violation of a new work rule that prohibited assault of another employee, despite the claim of the sanctioned employee that he had not been informed, where the collective bargaining agreement stated that employees would be conclusively presumed to have knowledge of the rules posted on the bulletin board.[354]

---

[350]Lockheed Aircraft Corp., 28 LA 829, 831 (Hepburn, 1957). *See also McQuay Int'l*, 1999 WL 908632; Federal Aviation Admin., 99 LA 929 (Corbett, 1992); Bayshore Concrete Prods. Co., 92 LA 311, 316 (Hart, 1989); Fairmont Gen. Hosp., 91 LA 930, 932 (Hunter, Jr., 1988); Donaldson Mining Co., 91 LA 471, 476 (Zobrak, 1988) (verbal policy, unwritten and unpublished, simply does not rise to the level of policy that can bind employees; company cannot demand compliance with policy that has not been communicated to affected employees, nor can employees be disciplined for violating policy they do not know exists); Menasha Corp., 90 LA 427, 430 (Clark, 1987); Foote & Davies, 88 LA 125, 127–28 (Wahl, 1986); Warner Jewelry Case Co., 87 LA 160 (Atleson, 1986) (notice and warning that violation of company work rule is grounds for discharge must be made clear to employee in order to sustain discharge); Canteen Corp., 86 LA 378, 383 (Hilgert, 1986) ("This arbitrator has always maintained that company management must be held to a high standard of basic considerations and conduct (which many arbitrators have used) in order to interpret or apply a just cause provision in a labor agreement. One of the most fundamental considerations of all is whether or not an employee is under clear notice that the behavior which was expected (or not acceptable) would lead to a certain type of penalty."); Stauffer Chem. Co., 83 LA 332, 336 (Blum, 1984); Carborundum Co., 71 LA 802, 805 (Millious, 1978) (employer "is under an obligation to properly notify all affected employees, not just Union officials"); Bethel Sch. Dist. No. 403, 71 LA 314, 320 (Beck, 1978); McCray Corp. Div., 48 LA 395, 399–400 (Witney, 1967); Stella D'Oro Biscuit Co., 48 LA 349, 350 (Cahn, 1967); Northwest Publ'ns, 48 LA 120, 123 (Neville, 1966); Chris-Craft Corp., 45 LA 117, 119 (Autrey, 1965); Wade Mfg. Co., 21 LA 676, 679 (Maggs, 1953); Koolvent Metal Awning Co., 21 LA 322, 325 (Reid, 1953); U.S. Spring & Bumper Co., 5 LA 109, 111 (Prasow, 1946). For related material, see Chapter 13, section 17.G., "Posting of Rules." In *Phillips Petroleum Co.*, 47 LA 372, 374 (Caraway, 1966), the company was required to establish that the employee had actual knowledge of the rule he was charged with violating. In *Metromedia, Inc.*, 46 LA 161, 165–67 (Dworkin, 1965), employees could be disciplined for refusing to sign a statement acknowledging receipt of a certain plant rule.

[351]Federal Aviation Admin., 99 LA 929 (Corbett, 1992).

[352]Customized Transp., 102 LA 1179 (Stallworth, 1994). *See also* Jamison Door Co., Case No. 98-02803, 1999 WL 269724 (Sergent, 1999).

[353]Cummins Cumberland, 106 LA 993 (Heekin, 1996). *See also* Consolidated Drum Reconditioning, 108 LA 523 (Richman, 1997) (employee's poor productivity did not justify discharge where he did not receive warning notices for poor productivity). *But see* University Med. Ctr., Case No. 980627-15606A, 1999 WL 1797340 (Bogue, 1999) (employers need not explicitly warn of every possible action that may warrant discipline, especially failure to perform work in a safe manner, or in compliance with established industry regulations and standards).

[354]Champion Int'l Corp., 111 LA 100 (Duda, Jr., 1998).

The "prior notice" requirement also applies to a company's drug policy. The discharge of an employee for having marijuana in his car was set aside where the car was searched on the same day that the union was notified of the company's adoption of a drug policy banning possession of drugs in automobiles on company property, and the policy was mailed to employees.[355] Similarly, the termination of an employee who failed a drug test was overturned because he had not been informed that the drug policy had been changed to allow immediate discharge.[356]

In contrast, where the conduct was clearly wrong, it has been held that employees need not be notified of rules. For example, employers need not have a rule against threatening others with loaded firearms, for "common sense alone would dictate that a weapon such as a loaded firearm would not be permitted on the premises of any employer except in the possession of a duly authorized plant protection man."[357]

x. Warnings [LA CDI 100.5503; 118.303]

Evidence of whether warnings of improper conduct, even if no penalty was posted, were given prior to discharge or other discipline is relevant in determining whether the subsequent sanctions were justified.[358] A proper warning advises the offender that future conduct of a similar nature will result in specific disciplinary action. In determining whether more severe discipline is appropriate, arbitrators make a comparison between the offenses to determine whether the warning received as a result of the first offense adequately notified the employee that he or she should not have engaged in the conduct for which the more severe discipline was imposed. In order to provide an adequate warning, the first offense does not have to be identical to the subsequent one, but the two offenses must be comparable. In one case,

---

[355]Anheuser-Busch, Inc., 107 LA 1183 (Weckstein, 1996).

[356]Pacific Offshore Pipeline Co., 106 LA 690 (Kaufman, 1996).

[357]Brown & Williamson Tobacco Corp., 50 LA 403, 412 (Willingham, 1968). *See also* San Diego Trolley, Inc., 112 LA 323 (Prayzich, 1999) (employee's discharge for carrying gun on employer's premises upheld, despite fact that employee did not know of rule; the rule is so basic and essential that it is implied); University of Cal., San Diego, 78 LA 1032, 1037 (Ross, 1982); Packaging Corp. of Am., 76 LA 643, 648 (High, 1981) (formal rule not required in order to make sleeping on the job an offense); Southern Ind. Gas & Elec. Co., 74 LA 509, 511 (Paradise, 1980); Overhead Door Co. of Ky., 70 LA 1299, 1301 (Dworkin, 1978); Philco Corp., 45 LA 437, 441 (Keeler, 1956) ("a Company does not have to establish that it had, or that it had communicated specific rules for certain well-recognized proven offenses such as drunkenness, theft, or insubordination"); Ross Gear & Tool Co., 35 LA 293, 296 (Schmidt, 1960). *But see* Board of Wayne County Comm'rs, 68 LA 369, 374–75 (Forsythe, 1977).

[358]Warnings are not necessary if the contract provides otherwise. *See* Auto Truck Transp. Corp., Case No. 990602-12081-3, 2000 WL 367143 (Baroni, 2000). Warnings ordinarily need not be in writing unless required to be so by contract. *See* Glenn L. Martin Co., 6 LA 500, 507 (Brecht, 1947). *See also* Bridgestone Firestone, Case No. 97-12191, 1998 WL 1041367 (Nolan, 1998); Bonded Scale & Mach. Co., 72 LA 520, 522 (Modjeska, 1979). *Cf.* Mead Co., 80 LA 713, 716–17 (Milentz, 1983). Where the contract does require warnings to be written, the requirement may be firmly enforced. *See* Northern Cal. Grocers Ass'n, 53 LA 85, 87–88 (Eaton, 1969); Scripto, Inc., 46 LA 1041, 1044 (Cantor, 1966). In *Covington Furniture Mfg. Corp.*, 75 LA 455, 456, 461–62 (Holley, Jr., 1980), the agreement specified that "[w]arning notices and reprimands shall be given to the employee in writing," but written warning was held not to be required for the "serious matter" of insubordination.

an arbitrator concluded that a warning for throwing water on a customer was not sufficiently comparable to playing a prank on a fellow employee to warrant more severe discipline for the second offense.[359]

Where an employee continues prohibited conduct after having been warned, the fact that there had been a prior warning stands against the employee.[360] When an employee had been warned repeatedly about leaving his place of duty, his discharge was upheld even though progressive discipline had not been used; the arbitrator said that the warnings had apprised the employee of the seriousness of his misconduct and that there was no reason to believe that "one more chance" would improve his conduct.[361] Failure to give prior warnings may be one of the reasons for the refusal by an arbitrator to sustain disciplinary action (particularly discharge).[362] As pointed out earlier, however, arbitrators have emphasized that no warning is required where the offense is serious and legally and morally wrong.[363] In one case noted above, however, prior notice of the company's drug policy was required before discharging an employee for marijuana found in his car parked on company property.[364]

---

[359]Maryland Jockey Club of Balt. City, 99 LA 1025, 1028 (Farwell, 1992).

[360]*See* City of Duluth, Minn., 113 LA 1153 (Neigh, 2000); Ward's Bldg. Maint., 111 LA 1088 (Bogue, 1998); Plain Dealer Publ'g Co., 99 LA 969, 976 (Fullmer, 1992); Food Barn Stores, 92 LA 1199, 1203 (Belcher, 1989); Hughes Aircraft Co., 92 LA 634, 636–37 (Richman, 1989); Service Am. Corp., 92 LA 241, 245–46 (Murphy, 1988); Goodyear Tire & Rubber Co., 92 LA 91, 96 (Dworkin, 1988); Jim Walter Res., 90 LA 367, 369 (Nicholas, Jr., 1987); General Tel. Co. of Cal., 89 LA 867, 870–72 (Collins, 1987) (discussing decisions of other arbitrators); Pittsburgh Press Club, 89 LA 826, 830 (Stoltenberg, 1987); Augusta Newsprint Co., 89 LA 725, 726 (King, 1987); Texas City Ref., 83 LA 923, 926 (King, 1984) (arbitrator stated general rule that it is absolutely essential for employees to know what is required of them, but found that grievant did have adequate notice and thus the discipline was proper).

[361]Potash Co. of Am., 40 LA 582, 585–86 (Abernethy, 1963). *See also* National Steel Corp., Case No. 668-98-11, 1999 WL 1712112 (O'Grady, 1999); Thatcher & Sons, 76 LA 1278, 1280 (Nutt, 1981). *But see* Greer Limestone Co., 40 LA 343, 349 (Lugar, 1963) (repeated warnings, followed by repeated noncompliance without discipline, were said to have lulled the employee into believing the warnings were not serious).

[362]*See* Albertson's, 111 LA 630 (Eisenmenger, 1998); GTE Cal., 99 LA 196 (Richman, 1992); Binswanger Glass Co., 92 LA 1153, 1156 (Nicholas, Jr., 1989); Georgia-Pacific Corp., 89 LA 1080, 1082 (Nicholas, Jr., 1987); Sanford Corp., 89 LA 968, 972 (Wies, 1987) (discharge of employee who refused to take drug test reduced, because employer failed to warn of grave consequences of disobedience); Adrian Coll., 89 LA 857, 861 (Ellmann, 1987); Peoples' Gas Light & Coke Co., 89 LA 786, 794 (Smith, 1987); Food Mktg. Corp., 88 LA 98, 102–03 (Doering, 1986); Bumper Works, 87 LA 586, 588 (Schwartz, 1986); Federal Mogul Corp., 86 LA 225, 231 (Blinn, 1985); General Tel. Co. of Cal., 86 LA 138, 141 (Maxwell, 1985); Empire Tractor & Equip. Co., 85 LA 345, 351 (Koven, 1985). In *Standard Shade Roller Division*, 73 LA 86, 90 (Dawson, 1979), warning was given but the arbitrator concluded (1) that insufficient time elapsed between the warning and discharge to have given the employee "opportunity for sober reflection," and (2) that the warning "was given too casually to qualify as a formal warning." Regarding the time element, see also *Gill Studios*, 78 LA 915, 919 (Goetz, 1982); regarding the "casual" quality, see also *Papercraft Inc.*, 80 LA 13, 15 (Anderson, 1982); *Rome Cable Communications*, 70 LA 28, 32–33 (Dallas, 1978).

[363]Ward's Bldg. Maint., 111 LA 1088 (Bogue, 1998) (the principle of progressive discipline does not always require discipline before discharge if the discharge is for serious misconduct and violations of known work rules or safety standards such as insubordination, fighting on the job, and theft); Kroger Co., 50 LA 1194, 1198 (Abernethy, 1968); Glenn L. Martin Co., 27 LA 768, 772–73 (Jaffee, 1956).

[364]Anheuser-Busch, Inc., 107 LA 1183 (Weckstein, 1996).

xi. Lax Enforcement of Rules [LA CDI 100.15; 100.33; 118.656; 118.67]

Arbitrators have not hesitated to disturb penalties where the employer over a period of time has condoned the violation of the rule in the past. Lax enforcement of rules may lead employees reasonably to believe that the conduct in question is tolerated by management.[365] Even where the employee has engaged in conduct that is obviously improper, such as threatening a supervisor, the fact that management had failed to impose discipline in the past can be a signal that unacceptable behavior will not be penalized.[366] Of course, the employer must have known of the prior violations by employees in order to be held to have waived the right to punish an employee who is detected.[367] Another qualification is illustrated by an arbitrator's holding that past condonation of the taking of small quantities of scrap metal did not immunize the attempted theft of large quantities.[368]

Although previously having been lax in enforcing rules of conduct, an employer can turn to strict enforcement after giving clear notice of the intent to do so.[369] In one case, the company had a history of lax enforcement of its rule requiring employees to wear safety glasses. Several months prior to

---

[365]See Great Plains Bag Corp., 83 LA 1281, 1285 (Laybourne, 1984); Fraser Shipyards, 78 LA 129, 137 (Greco, 1982); Lockheed Corp., 75 LA 1081, 1086 (Kaufman, 1980); Werner-Continental, 72 LA 1, 10–11 (LeWinter, 1978); Stevens Shipping & Terminal Co., 70 LA 1066, 1072 (Hall, 1978); McCormick & Baxter Creosoting Co., 55 LA 1274, 1277 (Jacobs, 1970); Coleman Co., 54 LA 281, 286 (Springfield, 1971); Chicago Mastic Co., 53 LA 428, 429–30 (Kelliher, 1969); Triple E Corp., 52 LA 1296, 1300 (Sembower, 1969); Rotor Tool Co. Div., 49 LA 210, 212 (Williams, 1967); Milwaukee & Suburban Transp. Corp., 48 LA 98, 100–01 (Somers, 1967); Scripto, Inc., 46 LA 1041, 1043 (Cantor, 1966); Gallagher Co., 46 LA 882, 884 (Gross, 1966); Harshaw Chem. Co., 46 LA 248, 251 (Volz, 1966); Rochester Tel. Corp., 45 LA 538, 540 (Duff, 1965); AIC Corp., 45 LA 517, 521 (Larkin, 1965); Misco Precision Casting Co., 40 LA 87, 90 (Dworkin, 1962). But see American Hoist & Derrick Co., 53 LA 45, 55–56 (Stouffer, 1969). In Great Atlantic & Pacific Tea Co., 77 LA 278, 283 (Seidenberg, 1981), employees had the impression that supervisors had been violating with impunity a rule against eating company merchandise, the employees not having been informed that the rule did not apply to supervisors; this appearance of laxity toward supervisors with respect to the rule led the arbitrator to reduce to suspension the discharge penalty that had been assessed against an employee for violating the rule.

[366]Champion Spark Plug Co., 93 LA 1277, 1284 (Dobry, 1989).

[367]See Southern Cal. Edison Co., 89 LA 1129, 1136 (Collins, 1987) (neither lax enforcement of a rule prohibiting false subsistence-reimbursement requests nor possible violations of the rule by several employees constitutes condonation of theft or "negative notice" sufficient to make the rule unenforceable, where there is no evidence that the company knowingly honored false receipts and claims); USM Corp., 71 LA 954, 959 (Richman, 1978); Liberal Mkt., 71 LA 148, 151 (Laybourne, 1978); Decar Plastics Corp., 44 LA 921, 923 (Greenwald, 1965). But where supervisors or other management representatives knew of rule violations in the past, their knowledge was imputed to the employer in Eberle Tanning Co., 71 LA 302, 306 (Sloane, 1978) (here the management representatives either knew or under the facts should have known of the past rule violations); Metro Contract Servs., 68 LA 1048, 1053 (Moore, 1977); Misco Precision Casting Co., 40 LA 87, 90 (Dworkin, 1962). For related discussion, see Chapter 10, section 6., "Agency Principles."

[368]United States Steel Corp., 48 LA 1114, 1118 (Mittenthal, 1967). In Hilo Coast Processing Co., 74 LA 236, 240 (1980), the arbitrator stated that the grievant's offense was so serious that "it would be unreasonable for any employee to believe" it to be one of "those types of acts which would ever be condoned by management."

[369]See Macmillan Bloedel Containers, 70 LA 667, 669 (Doering, 1978); Hartman Elec. Mfg. Co., 48 LA 681, 683 (Dyke, 1967); Fairbanks Morse, 47 LA 224, 226 (Fisher, 1966).

the discharge of grievant for not wearing the glasses, the company began a campaign to impress on employees the importance of following the safety glass rules. The discharge was upheld.[370] But, in another case, an employee discharged for smoking marijuana was reinstated because his behavior had been condoned by the employee's supervisor, who had smoked marijuana in the presence of the employee. The arbitrator stated:

> Employees are entitled to clear notice that rules will be enforced. Where, however, rules are not enforced but violations thereof are accepted by management, employees are lulled into believing that such rules are not serious. In effect, employees are "sand bagged" into violating the rules and then are unfairly punished for a violation.[371]

Another illustration of the prior warning requirement was seen in an arbitration that arose after an employer gave notice that it intended to enforce rules prohibiting nonconsensual physical touchings that had previously gone unenforced. Despite the fact that similarly situated employees had been treated more leniently in the past,[372] the employer was held to have had just cause to discharge an employee who grabbed another employee offensively. The discharge was justified because the employer had distributed a "zero tolerance" of violence policy prohibiting this kind of behavior 6 weeks before the incident.[373]

The arbitration of a case involving discharge for violation of a rule constitutes clear notice to the employees for the future that the particular type of misconduct is deemed by the employer to be a dischargeable offense.[374]

xii. Unequal or Discriminatory Treatment [LA CDI 100.33; 118.67]

It generally is accepted that enforcement of rules and assessment of discipline must be exercised in a consistent manner; all employees who engage in the same type of misconduct must be treated essentially the same, unless a reasonable basis exists for variations in the assessment of punishment (such as different degrees of fault, or mitigating or aggravating circumstances

---

[370]Carrier Corp., 110 LA 1064 (Ipavec, 1998).

[371]Chivas Prods., 101 LA 546, 550 (Kanner, 1993).

[372]Occasionally, the defense of lax enforcement is coupled with the defense of discriminatory treatment. Whirlpool Corp., 00-2 ARB ¶3634 (Jennings, 2000); Clarion Sintered Metals, 110 LA 770 (Cohen, 1998); Giant Eagle Mkts. Co., 108 LA 828 (Duff, 1997); Georgia-Pacific Corp., 108 LA 43 (Nicholas, Jr., 1997); USS, Div. of USX Corp., 106 LA 708 (Neyland, 1996).

[373]Golden States Foods Corp., 108 LA 705 (Gentile, 1997).

[374]Universal Match Corp., 42 LA 184, 186 (Coffey, 1963). In *Grand Rapids Die Casting Corp.*, 63 LA 995, 996 (Keefe, 1974), the arbitrator concluded that for the purpose of establishing order out of chaos in the plant, his award would order (1) that the employer must clear all employee records of all disciplinary entries prior to the date of his award, and (2) that thereafter the employees shall have a responsibility to obey the employer's plant rules and the employer shall have a responsibility to actively enforce them. Regarding management's responsibility to maintain order, see also *FS Servs.*, 73 LA 610, 614 (Cyrol, 1979).

affecting some but not all of the employees).[375] Applying this general rule, one decision recognized: "[T]here must be reasonable rules and standards of conduct which are consistently applied and enforced in a non-discriminatory fashion. It is also generally accepted that enforcement of rules and assessment of discipline must be exercised in a consistent manner; thus all employees who engage in the same type of misconduct must be treated essentially the same."[376]

In this regard, one arbitrator declared: "Absolute consistency in the handling of rule violations is, of course, an impossibility, but that fact should not excuse random and completely inconsistent disciplinary practices."[377]

Where a reasonable basis for variations in penalties does exist, variations will be permitted notwithstanding the charge of disparate treatment.[378] Discrimination is an affirmative defense and, therefore, the union generally has the burden of proving that the employer improperly discriminated against an employee.[379] Thus, "[i]n order to prove disparate treatment, a union must confirm the existence of both parts of the equation. It is not enough that an

---

[375]Commercial Warehouse Co., 100 LA 247, 251 (Woolf, 1992) (discharge of employee who reported for work under the influence of alcohol not upheld when evidence showed that other employees engaging in same conduct had not been disciplined); JPI Plumbing Prods., 97 LA 386, 388–89 (Kilroy, 1991); Hamilton County, Ohio, Sheriff's Dep't, 96 LA 331, 337–38 (Klein, 1990); Peabody Coal Co., 92 LA 658, 660 (Hewitt, 1989); MacMillan Bloedel Containers, 92 LA 592 (Nicholas, Jr., 1989); Worcester Quality Foods, 90 LA 1305, 1309–10 (Rocha, Jr., 1988); Beth Energy Mines, 90 LA 1111, 1114 (Feldman, 1988); Marion Gen. Hosp., 90 LA 735, 739 (Curry, Jr., 1988); Kable Printing Co., 89 LA 314, 319 (Mikrut, 1987); Joe Wheeler Elec. Membership Coop., 89 LA 51, 57 (Yancy, 1987); Navistar Int'l Corp., 88 LA 179, 182 (Archer, 1986); Nuodex, Inc., 87 LA 256 (Millious, 1986); General Bag Corp., 86 LA 739, 741 (Klein, 1985); Stedman Mach. Co., 85 LA 631, 635 (Keenan, 1985); Solar Turbines, 85 LA 525, 529 (Kaufman, 1985); Apex Int'l Alloys, 82 LA 747, 751 (Wright, 1984); ACF Indus., 82 LA 459, 463 (Maniscalco, 1984).

[376]Munster Steel Co., 108 LA 597, 600 (Cerone, 1997).

[377]Aaron, *The Uses of the Past in Arbitration, in* Arbitration Today, Proceedings of the 8th Annual Meeting of NAA 1, 10 (McKelvey ed., BNA Books 1955). *See also* Allied Aviation Fueling Co., 48 LA 1286, 1290 (Sisk, 1967); Westinghouse Elec. Corp., 26 LA 836, 844 (Simkin, 1956).

[378]Ramsey County, Minn., Sheriff's Dep't, 100 LA 208, 212 (Gallagher, 1992) (3-day suspension proper for deputy involved in automobile accident when penalty is assessed based on degree of fault); Fry's Food Stores of Ariz., 99 LA 1161, 1168 (Hogler, 1992) (discharge for sexual harassment upheld even though other employees charged with sexual harassment were only suspended or demoted); Chanute Mfg. Co., 99 LA 20, 22 (Levy, 1992); S.B. Thomas, 92 LA 1055, 1057–58 (Chandler, 1989) (prohibition against disparate treatment only requires like treatment under like circumstances; these circumstances include nature of offense, degree of fault, and mitigating or aggravating circumstances); P.D.I., Inc., 91 LA 21, 24–25 (Dworkin, 1988); Southern Ind. Gas & Elec. Co., 90 LA 1311, 1314 (Dilts, 1988) (finding different penalties for same offense was justified because employees had different disciplinary records); Nottawa Gardens Corp., 90 LA 24, 27 (Bendixsen, 1987); Northwest Airlines, 89 LA 943, 953 (Nicolau, 1984) (different treatment is not necessarily disparate treatment; arbitrators have long held that circumstances must be considered and that a wide range of factors—length of service, prior work record, degree of culpability—can properly be taken into account; indeed, if those factors are not taken into account and "equal" treatment is imposed, that in itself might be disparate); Central Ohio Transit Auth., 88 LA 628, 632 (Seinsheimer, 1987); Potomac Elec. Power Co., 88 LA 290, 295 (Feigenbaum, 1986); Eastern Airlines, 88 LA 223, 226–27 (Dworkin, 1986); Inter-Pack Corp., 87 LA 1232, 1236 (Brown, 1986); Dresser Indus., 86 LA 1307, 1311 (Taylor, 1986); Phoenix Prods. Co., 82 LA 172, 174 (Imes, 1983). *See also* Excel Corp., 89 LA 1275, 1280 (McDermott, 1987).

[379]State of Ohio, 99 LA 1169, 1173 (Rivera, 1992); Shell Pipe Line Corp., 97 LA 957, 961 (Baroni, 1991).

employee was treated differently than others; it must also be established that the circumstances surrounding his/her offense were substantively like those of individuals who received more moderate penalties."[380]

Where the union does prove that rules and regulations have not been consistently applied and enforced in a nondiscriminatory manner, arbitrators will refuse to sustain a discharge or will reduce a disciplinary penalty.[381] However, arbitrators will uphold variations in punishments among employees if a reasonable basis exists that justifies such differences. In one case, the employer was held to have had just cause to discharge an employee who had coordinated and served as leader in a "sickout" that violated the labor contract.[382] The arbitrator reasoned that the instigator could be punished more harshly with discharge, even though other employees received only warnings.

That variations in penalties assessed do not necessarily mean that management's action has been improper or discriminatory was persuasively elaborated by one arbitrator:

> The term "discrimination" connotes a distinction in treatment, especially an unfair distinction. The prohibition against discrimination requires like treatment under like circumstances. In the case of offenses the circumstances include the nature of the offense, the degree of fault and the mitigating and aggravating factors. There is no discrimination, or no departure from the consistent or uniform treatment of employees, merely because of variations in discipline reasonably appropriate to the variations in circumstances. Two employees may refuse a work assignment. For one it is his first offense, there being no prior warning or misconduct standing against his record. The other has been warned and disciplined for the very same offense on numerous occasions. It cannot be seriously contended that discrimination results if identical penalties are not meted out.[383]

Particularly in cases involving illicit strikes or slowdowns, management may vary discipline on the basis of the degree of fault and is not required to assess uniform punishment against all participants. By the same token, management may punish those who bear greater fault while not punishing other participants at all.[384] Nor is management prohibited from punishing

---

[380]Genie Co., 97 LA 542, 549 (Dworkin, 1991).

[381]Gemala Trailer Corp., 108 LA 565 (Nicholas, Jr., 1997); Schuller Int'l, 107 LA 1109 (Hockenberry, 1996); Mead Chilpaco Mill, 106 LA 1066 (Feldman, 1996); Geauga County, 106 LA 280 (DiLeone, 1996).

[382]Lockheed Martin Missiles & Space, 108 LA 482 (Gentile, 1997).

[383]Alan Wood Steel Co., 21 LA 843, 849 (Short, 1954). Regarding the arbitrator's reference in *Alan Wood Steel Co.* to "variations in discipline reasonably appropriate to the variations in circumstances," *id.*, see also *Pepsi Cola Bottling Co. of Canton, Ohio*, 78 LA 516, 527 (Keenan, 1982) ("an essentially proportionate relationship must be maintained").

[384]*See* Continental Can Co., 86 LA 11, 15–16 (Hunter, 1985); Schnadig Corp., 85 LA 692 (Seidman, 1985); Price Bros. Co., 74 LA 748, 751–52 (Laybourne, 1980); Quanex, 73 LA 9, 12 (McDonald, 1979); Clinton Corn Processing Co., 71 LA 555, 559, 565–66 (Madden, 1978); Raskin Packing Co., 56 LA 880, 882 (Murphy, 1971); Anchor Hocking Corp., 56 LA 340, 348 (McDermott, 1971); MacMillan Bloedel Prods., 55 LA 667, 670 (Holly, 1970); Acme Boot Co., 52 LA 1047, 1049–50 (Oppenheim, 1969); Avco Corp., 51 LA 1228, 1235 (Turkus, 1968); Martinsburg Mills, 48 LA 1224, 1227 (Altrock, 1967); Kaiser Steel Corp., 48 LA 855, 860–61 (Roberts, 1966); Permali, Inc., 48 LA 257, 261–63 (Krimsly, 1967) (employer can classify degrees of participation and punish different employees on that basis); American Air Filter Co., 47 LA 129, 137 (Hilpert, 1966); Charles Mundt & Sons, 46 LA 982, 984 (Malkin, 1966); Greenville Steel Car Co., 46 LA 120, 124 (Duff, 1965); Philips Indus., 45 LA 943, 952–54

the known leaders of a stoppage or those employees detected in overt activities in connection with the stoppage merely because the company is unable to identify other participants who may have been equally guilty.[385]

Arbitrators have emphasized that in illicit strike or slowdown situations the company need not deprive itself of the services of all participants but may use selective discipline on the basis of relative fault.[386] One arbitrator commented: "[I]t is unreasonable to require a Company to discharge all the workers participating in a slowdown and thereby lose its experienced work force when selective disciplinary action against one or more key leaders of the slowdown will restore production."[387]

Where all employees on a given shift refused to perform certain work, it was held that management was not required to punish all equally if doing so would impair production. In permitting management to order individual employees to perform the work and to send them home for refusing, the arbitrator explained:

> It is my opinion that management is not under an obligation to apply equal punishment to all transgressors, if to do so would cause injury to the operations. Discrimination may be validly charged only when there is either (a) a

---

(Stouffer, 1965) (employer may select certain strikers for discipline if basis for selection is reasonable); Hussman Refrig. Co., 45 LA 585, 589–90 (Autrey, 1965); Barbetta Rest., 42 LA 951, 953 (Wolff, 1964); General Am. Transp. Corp., 42 LA 142, 143–44 (Pollack, 1964) (employer may discharge strike leaders and need not prove extent of leadership); Drake Mfg. Co., 41 LA 732, 735–36 (Markowitz, 1963); Pettibone Mulliken Corp., 41 LA 110, 112 (Kelliher, 1963); H.O. Canfield Co. of Va., 40 LA 1209, 1211 (Schedler, 1963); Union Tank Car Co., 38 LA 1144, 1148–49 (Davey, 1962); Okonite Co., 37 LA 977, 980 (Pigors, 1961); American Radiator & Standard Sanitary Corp., 37 LA 401, 406 (Volz, 1961); Kaye-Tex Mfg. Co., 36 LA 660, 663–64 (Horlacher, 1960) (union declined to identify the strike leaders and employer used fairest method available in selecting employees for discipline); Alside, Inc., 33 LA 194, 198 (Teple, 1959) (employer not permitted to "pick and choose" but could single out for punishment those who had lead roles); Calumet & Hecla, 25 LA 663, 674 (Smith, 1955); Alan Wood Steel Co., 21 LA 843, 849–50 (Short, 1954); Inland Steel Co., 19 LA 601, 602 (Updegraff, 1952); Gardner-Denver Co., 15 LA 829, 830 (Morrissey, 1951); International Harvester Co., 13 LA 610, 613 (Wirtz, 1949). Many arbitrators, including some of those in the cases just cited, have recognized that union leaders have a special responsibility to promote use of the grievance procedure in lieu of self-help. For discussion of this special responsibility, along with discussion of the important question whether failure to fulfill the responsibility is a proper basis for discipline or for variations in discipline (both under the collective bargaining agreement as viewed by arbitrators and under the NLRA), see Chapter 5, section 14.A., "Use of the Grievance Procedure Versus Self-Help."

[385]See Ingersoll-Rand Co., 50 LA 487, 494 (Scheiber, 1968) (it is inevitable that some of the guilty "get away with it"); United States Steel Corp., 50 LA 472, 475–76 (Garrett, 1968); Union Tank Car Co., 49 LA 383, 388 (Crawford, 1967); Mack Trucks, 41 LA 1240, 1244 (Wallen, 1964).

[386]See Avco Corp., 51 LA 1228, 1235 (Turkus, 1968); Charles Mundt & Sons, 46 LA 982, 984 (Malkin, 1966); Philips Indus., 45 LA 943, 953 (Stouffer, 1965); Kaye-Tex Mfg. Co., 36 LA 660, 663 (Horlacher, 1960) (to require a uniform penalty against all strikers would make a nullity of the no-strike clause). Also, as a means of protecting itself, management is permitted to stagger suspensions, for it cannot be expected to suspend all guilty employees for the same period and thus make a shutdown of operations the price for taking disciplinary action. United States Steel, 40 LA 598, 600 (Seitz, 1963); Bethlehem Steel, 39 LA 686, 688 (Valtin, 1962).

[387]American Radiator & Standard Sanitary Corp., 37 LA 401, 406 (Volz, 1961). Even where the agreement provided that disciplinary action taken against employees for an illicit strike "shall be applied with equality and impartiality to all employees," management could punish those who had greater part in the strike although not punishing all participants. Drake Mfg. Co., 41 LA 732, 735–36 (Markowitz, 1963).

demonstrated inconsistency of posture towards the violations and the violators (such as is present when management tolerates, condones or ignores a series of misacts by some and then punishes others for committing the same improprieties); or (b) when the Employer is responding to an improper ulterior motive or animus, using the alleged wrongdoing as a pretext or subterfuge.[388]

Finally, it may be noted that arbitrators themselves have sometimes reduced the penalties of some employees, where management had assessed uniform discipline against all participants but where the arbitrator found different degrees of fault.[389] In one such case, the arbitrator stated that "equality of penalties does not represent equal justice," where management assessed identical penalties against the victim as well as the aggressor in a fight.[390]

xiii. Charges of Anti-Union Discrimination
[LA CDI 100.0203113; 118.6527; 118.6609; 118.664]

A charge that an employee has been discriminatorily penalized because of union activities cannot rest on mere "surmise, inference or conjecture."[391] Arbitrators require clear proof to sustain such charges.[392] However, one arbi-

---

[388]Interchemical Corp., 48 LA 124, 131 (Yagoda, 1967). *Cf.* American Radiator & Standard Sanitary Corp., 37 LA 593, 598–99 (McCoy, 1961). In *United States Steel Corp.*, 49 LA 1236, 1241–42 (McDermott, 1968), management could punish those employees who engaged in a slowdown after formal warning had been given, while not punishing violators prior to the warning; the arbitrator explained that management was engaged in a rational plan to halt the slowdown. In *Midland Ross Corp.*, 65 LA 1151, 1154 (Dallas, 1975), the employer's imposition of a more severe penalty for succeeding incidents involving a dangerous form of horseplay was held justified as a means of stopping the activity.

[389]*See* United States Steel Corp., 51 LA 546, 548 (Garrett, 1968); Hooker Chem. Corp., 36 LA 857, 859–60 (Kates, 1961); Yardley Plastics Co., 36 LA 280, 285–86 (McIntosh, 1960).

[390]United States Steel Corp., 51 LA 546, 548 (Garrett, 1968). In upholding the different penalties assessed by management against fight participants, one arbitrator commented: "The wisdom of a rule calling for identical penalties to all employees involved in a fight, without regard to culpability, is certainly open to question." Kaiser Steel Corp., 48 LA 1118, 1120 (Block, 1967).

[391]New York Racing Ass'n, 43 LA 129, 135 (Scheiber, 1964). *See also* Midwest Body, 73 LA 651, 654 (Guenther, 1979); Excel Mfg. Corp., 49 LA 509, 511 (Willingham, 1967).

[392]*See* American Transp. Corp., 81 LA 318, 324 (Nelson, 1983) (stating that to support a charge of anti-union discrimination, "there must be evidence and/or powerful inferences reasonably drawn from the evidence"); Thunderbird Inn, 77 LA 849, 852 (Armstrong, 1981) (stating that a charge of anti-union discrimination "requires clear proof," and that such proof existed in the statement of grievant's supervisor that he was mad because grievant went to the union, and that he intended to harass grievant "right out of here"); Solar Excavating Co., 77 LA 32, 37 (Hearne, 1981) (the charge of anti-union discrimination "was based on unsupported hearsay"); Steiger Tractor, 72 LA 175, 179 (O'Connell, 1979) (mere "coincidence" of discipline and assumption of union office, "standing alone," is insufficient to establish anti-union discrimination); C-E Glass, 71 LA 977, 978, 980 (Comey, 1978); National Broad. Co., 71 LA 762, 769 (Gentile, 1978); Atlas Metal Parts Co., 67 LA 1230, 1233–34 (Kossoff, 1976); Byron Jackson, Inc., 49 LA 731, 735 (Kotin, 1967) (sharp conflicts in negotiations and a strike do not by themselves constitute prima facie evidence of subsequent discrimination in treatment of union leader); Great Atl. & Pac. Tea Co., 45 LA 495, 498 (Livengood, undated) (that grievant was an active union member is not enough to make out a case of anti-union discrimination); Dixie Belle Mills, Inc., 43 LA 1070, 1072 (Dworet, 1965); Standard Oil Co. of Cal., 43 LA 529, 537 (McNaughton, 1964); Caterpillar Tractor Co., 42 LA 710, 712 (Davis, 1964); Trans World Airlines, 39 LA 1131, 1134 (Gilden, 1962); Rexall Chem. Co., 38 LA 705, 708 (Berkowitz, 1962); Firestone Tire & Rubber Co., 33 LA 206, 207 (McCoy, 1959); Washington Metal Trades, 23 LA 38, 39 (Carmody, 1954); Wade Mfg. Co., 21 LA 676, 678 (Maggs, 1953); Atlantic Broad. Co., 20 LA 7, 9 (Bailer, 1953); Northwestern Bell Tel. Co., 19 LA 111,

trator cautioned that arbitrators have an obligation to examine the evidence with special care where anti-union animus may be involved:

> Whenever an employee who holds a high union office is discharged, there is always raised the question of a real possibility that the discharge is discriminatory or undertaken in bad faith, that the Company is ridding itself of a zealous unionist under the guise of "just cause" discharge. In these cases, the arbitrator is obliged to make a thorough search and examination of the entire record to ascertain and satisfy himself that Management has not violated the collective bargaining agreement in this manner.[393]

The imposition of discipline on an employee who is a union officer or active in union matters, without a showing of animosity or open hostility, is held to be insufficient to sustain a defense that the penalty was discriminatorily[394] imposed in retaliation for the employee's representative status or conduct. But, when the behavior of a union official exceeds the limits of workplace propriety, even when the charged action itself appears to have been in furtherance of legitimate union leadership interest or action, discipline—including discharge—has been sustained.[395] However, one arbitrator has held that a union officer's belligerent behavior which caused damage to company property is not sanctionable absent a showing of "wrongful intent."[396]

xiv. Management Also at Fault

Where an employee is guilty of wrongdoing, but management (ordinarily the supervisor) is also at fault in some respect in connection with the employee's conduct, the arbitrator may be persuaded to reduce or set aside

---

122 (Doyle, 1952); Mack Mfg. Corp., 2 LA 520, 521 (Scarborough, 1944); Perkins Oil Co., 1 LA 447, 448–49 (McCoy, 1946). Cf. Pattern Assocs., 79 LA 1035, 1040 (Lipson, 1982); Sun Furniture Co., 73 LA 335, 341–42 (Ruben, 1979); City of W. Palm Beach, Fla., 69 LA 1157, 1158–59 (Remington, 1977); In the Round Dinner Playhouse, 55 LA 118, 129 (Kamin, 1970); Hoague-Sprague Corp., 48 LA 19, 23 (Wallen, 1967); Safeway Stores, 44 LA 889, 895 (Block, 1965). In all of these cases, the arbitrator found either that antiunion animus caused or that it contributed to management's action against the employee. In the latter regard it may be noted that in NLRB v. Transportation Mgmt. Corp., 462 U.S. 393, 399–405, 113 LRRM 2857 (1983), the Supreme Court upheld, as an "at least permissible" construction of the NLRA, the NLRB's 1980 Wright Line, 251 NLRB 1083, 105 LRRM 1169 (1980), rule for cases involving "mixed motives." Under this rule, the NLRB General Counsel has the burden of proving that protected conduct was "a substantial or motivating factor" in the discharge; if this burden is met, the discharge will be held to violate the NLRA unless the employer proves as an affirmative defense that the employee would have been discharged for other (valid) reasons even if the protected conduct had not been involved.

[393]Arden Farms Co., 45 LA 1124, 1130 (Tsukiyama, 1965) (where the charge of antiunion motivation was found to be without substance). See also Hoague-Sprague Corp., 48 LA 19, 23 (Wallen, 1967).

[394]Preferred Transp., 108 LA 636, 639 (Gentile, 1997); Folsom Return to Custody, 101 LA 837 (Staudohar, 1993).

[395]Converters Paperboard Co., 108 LA 149 (Brodsky, 1997); Stone Container Corp., 106 LA 475, 478–80 (Gentile, 1996). On safety matters, see Rebar Eng'g, 105 LA 662, 666 (Riker, 1995); Dye Golf Servs., 104 LA 449, 451 (Darrow, 1995).

[396]PQ Corp., 106 LA 381, 383–84 (Cipolla, 1996).

the penalty assessed by management.[397] However, the mere fact that a supervisor was not entirely without fault in an incident was held not to excuse or justify physical assault by an employee, so the employee's discharge was sustained.[398]

"Management-also-at-fault" cases can be examined by looking at the categories of alleged fault. These include, among others, claiming procedural or process faults,[399] assertions that management had prior knowledge or had given prior approval,[400] charges that management was guilty of mistakes,[401] and allegations that management had provided inadequate training.[402]

Where an employee had been disciplined for assaulting a supervisor, the supervisor's behavior could be considered in mitigation of the offense. Thus, when a young employee with no history of violence, who had just returned to work after having been hospitalized for a mental condition, assaulted his supervisor, he was reinstated without back pay, in part because the abusive supervisor had taunted the employee.[403] Similarly, where an employee was found to be "constructively insubordinate" in leaving work without permission because she feared that she might lose her temper and assault her supervisor because of his hostile tone and manner of direction, her discharge was held to be without just cause.[404] Consideration of management's procedural error caused an arbitrator to reinstate with "half back pay" a probationary employee for failure to report a criminal conviction to his employer.[405]

The defense in disciplinary cases that management was at fault may also involve issues of "toleration" or "disparate treatment." The discharges of two male employees who cornered another male employee in a dark room, forcibly lowered his pants, restrained him, and threatened sexual assault were set aside because company supervisors had been involved in or had observed similar but less aggressive acts of male-on-male sexual harassment without taking disciplinary action.[406]

---

[397]*See* Social Sec. Admin., 81 LA 1051, 1054 (Muessig, 1983); Central Ill. Pub. Serv. Co., 76 LA 300, 307–08 (Kossoff, 1981); U.S. Immigration & Naturalization Serv., 75 LA 747, 750 (Maloney, 1980); New York Air Brake Co., 74 LA 875, 877 (McDonnell, 1980); Washington Hosp. Ctr., 73 LA 535, 538 (Seidenberg, 1979); Monte Mart, 71 LA 70, 73 (Randall, 1978); General Tire & Rubber Co., 69 LA 1084, 1088 (Nicholas, Jr., 1977); Little Forest Med. Ctr., 69 LA 671, 673–74 (Smoot, 1977); Palm Desert Greens Ass'n, 69 LA 191, 192–93 (Draznin, 1977); Franklin Textiles, 68 LA 223, 225 (Kornblum, 1977). *But see* Pioneer Finishing Co., 52 LA 1019, 1022 (Schmidt, Jr., 1969).

[398]Gerber Prods. Co., 46 LA 956, 959 (Howlett, 1966).

[399]Gemala Trailer Corp., 108 LA 565 (Nicholas, Jr., 1997); Foremost Corrugated Co., 106 LA 1106 (Braufman, 1996); ATE Mgmt. & Serv. Co., 104 LA 348 (Goodman, 1994).

[400]Southern Frozen Foods, 107 LA 1030 (Giblin, 1996); Ball-Foster Glass Container Co., 106 LA 1209 (Howell, 1996).

[401]Union Carbide Corp., 110 LA 667 (Caraway, 1998); HDS Servs., 107 LA 27 (Hodgson, 1996).

[402]Peoples Natural Gas, 105 LA 37 (Murphy, 1995).

[403]Bethlehem Structural Prods. Corp., 106 LA 452, 455–56 (Witt, 1995).

[404]HDS Servs., 107 LA 27, 29–30 (Hodgson, 1996).

[405]Avis Rent-A-Car Sys., 107 LA 197, 200–202 (Shanker, 1996).

[406]Coca-Cola Bottling Co. of N. Ohio, 106 LA 776, 777, 782 (Borland, 1996). See also section 3.F.xi., "Lax Enforcement of Rules," and section 3.F.xii., "Unequal or Discriminatory Treatment," above.

If an employee's errant behavior is the result of a mental or physical problem that the employer knew or should have known about, arbitrators also tend to consider the condition a mitigating factor.[407]

The discharge of an employee who sat down on a conveyor and cursed when suspended for the safety offense was set aside because the employee had earlier complained to the employer about back pain. The arbitrator explained that it is "common medical knowledge that physical pain causes tempers to become short and people to lose some control."[408] Similarly, a technician who signed certain laboratory forms without completing the necessary tests was reinstated by an arbitrator who attributed the technician's "mental lapse" to a "stressful emotional situation" caused by his employer's denying him leave to be with his seriously ill wife.[409]

---

[407]Bethlehem Structural Prods. Corp., 106 LA 452, 455–56 (Witt, 1995).
[408]Gaylord Container Corp., 107 LA 431, 435 (Henner, 1996).
[409]Dial Corp., 107 LA 879, 882 (Robinson, 1997).

Chapter 16

Safety and Health

1. Introduction

Safety and health issues are prominent as employers and employees seek to assure workplace well-being. Indeed, disputes involving workplace safety and health often take precedence over all other conflicts between employers and employees or their unions. Such disputes may involve conditions carrying the risk of serious injury, or even death, and cause production to be halted.

In resolving these disputes, arbitrators consistently recognize the employer's right and obligation to promulgate and enforce reasonable workplace safety and health rules, and the necessity for employees to abide by these rules. However, legitimate concerns over potential hazards in the performance of job duties may even excuse employees from complying with arbitration's "work now–grieve later" maxim. In such situations, arbitrators must determine whether the employees' subjective, good-faith belief of danger is sufficient to have justified their action, or whether the employees must have been in real danger based on objective evidence existing at the time of the employees' refusal to work. Arbitrators' decisionmaking also is informed by federal and state laws and regulations setting safety and health standards. Such standards now provide protection against dangerous chemicals and processes and from secondhand smoke, workplace violence, and even from employees whose disabilities prevent them from working without endangering themselves or others.

2. Management Rights and Obligations in Safety and Health Matters

Many collective bargaining agreements contain safety and health provisions that specify that management will exert reasonable efforts to protect the safety and health of its employees.[1] In analyzing such provisions, arbitrators rule that management is not required to eliminate all known possible hazards or to utilize all possible safety and health precautions.[2] Even

---

[1]*See* Fairmont Gen. Hosp., 91 LA 930 (Hunter, 1988); King Co., 89 LA 681 (Bard, 1987); U.S. Plywood Corp., 88 LA 275 (Mathews, 1986); Zenith Elec. Corp., 88 LA 157 (Doering, 1986); Seven-Up of Ind., 87 LA 1273 (Murphy, 1986); Potter Elec. Signal Co., 75 LA 50 (Madden, 1980); Ogden Air Logistics Ctr., 73 LA 1100 (Hayes, 1979); Social Sec. Admin., 73 LA 267 (Eaton, 1979); Colt Indus., 71 LA 22 (Rutherford, 1978).

[2]*See* United States Steel Corp., 88 LA 240 (Petersen, 1986); Brooklyn Union Gas Co., 47 LA 425 (Wolf, 1966); Union Carbide Metals Co., 37 LA 501 (Murphy, 1961); Erie Mining Co., 36 LA 902 (Dworkin, 1961).

when the collective bargaining agreement is silent on this subject, arbitrators often hold that management has a right to promulgate reasonable rules and regulations to ensure the safety and health of its employees and to enforce those rules and regulations through disciplinary sanctions.[3]

As to the imposition and choice of sanctions, arbitrators frequently give employers significant latitude in disciplining employees who, for one reason or the other, have jeopardized workplace safety. For example, an employee was found to be properly subject to discipline for violating a company rule requiring employees to read flashpoints on tags before welding on tank cars, even though no fatalities or injuries had resulted from the employee's failure to read a flashpoint.[4]

A. Alcohol and/or Drug Use and Testing [LA CDI 118.653; 100.552545]

In recent years, concern about increasing drug use has led public and private employers to institute drug-testing programs.[5] Studies estimate that 8.3 million American workers are drug users[6] and cost their employers over $100 billion each year.[7] In response, Congress adopted the Omnibus Transportation Employee Testing Act of 1991,[8] which provides for drug and alcohol testing of employees in safety-sensitive positions in the transportation industry, and the Drug-Free Workplace Act of 1998,[9] which requires employers to publish a statement notifying employees that use or possession of a controlled substance is strictly prohibited in the workplace.

However, the National Labor Relations Board has held that drug and alcohol testing of incumbent employees is a mandatory subject of collective bargaining and that, absent a "clear and unmistakable waiver" of the union's bargaining rights, an employer must bargain with the union prior to implementing a testing policy.[10]

Nevertheless, arbitrators frequently are called upon to rule on the fairness of terminations pursuant to unilaterally implemented drug-testing poli-

---

[3]*See* Stone Container Corp., 91 LA 1186 (Ross, 1988); Chemetco, 71 LA 457 (Gibson, 1978); J.R. Simplot Co., 68 LA 912 (Conant, 1977); Nu-Ply Corp., 50 LA 985 (Hnatiuk, 1968); Lone Star Steel Co., 48 LA 1094 (Jenkins, 1967); Cit-Con Oil Corp., 30 LA 252 (Logan, 1958); Braniff Airways, 29 LA 487 (Yeager, 1957); Reserve Mining Co., 29 LA 367 (Kelliher, 1957); Higgins, Inc., 24 LA 453 (Morvant, 1955); Sylvania Elec. Prods., 24 LA 199 (Brecht, 1954); Pennsylvania Greyhound Lines, 19 LA 210 (Seward, 1952); Pennsylvania Greyhound Lines, 18 LA 671 (Short, 1952); Bethlehem Steel Co., 10 LA 113 (Shipman, 1948).

[4]Union Tank Car Co., 110 LA 1128 (Lalka, 1998).

[5]One survey found that drug testing is the primary form of workplace medical testing and is practiced by 67% of major U.S. firms (down from a high of 81% in 1996). Of those employers conducting drug tests, over 46% use the test results to retain or dismiss employees. AMERICAN MANAGEMENT ASSOCIATION, 2001 SURVEY ON WORKPLACE TESTING (2001).

[6] U.S. DEPT. OF HEALTH AND HUMAN SERVICES, NATIONAL HOUSEHOLD SURVEY ON DRUG ABUSE (1998).

[7]Jane Easter Bahls, *Drugs in the Workplace*, 43 H.R. MAG. 80 (1998).

[8]49 U.S.C. §31306. The law reaffirms the substance of the drug-testing regulations previously promulgated by the Department of Transportation and expands the requirements to cover testing for alcohol as well as drug use.

[9]41 U.S.C. §§701–707. Disciplinary measures and a drug-free awareness program are to be implemented as well. Failure to comply with the Drug-Free Workplace Act prevents the employer from contracting any property or services to any federal agency.

[10]Johnson-Bateman Co., 295 NLRB 180, 131 LRRM 1393 (1989). *But see* Elizabeth Tenorio, Note, *The Public Policy Exception: A Narrow Exception to Judicial Review or an Independent Means of Avoiding Arbitration?*, 1997 J. DISP. RESOL. 173 (1997).

cies.[11] Arbitrators reverse employees' terminations where the employers make critical errors in administering drug tests. For example, an arbitrator found that an employee was discharged without just cause for allegedly failing a drug test where the "chain of custody" of the employee's specimen was not maintained to preserve the integrity of the analysis.[12] Similarly, an employee who had failed a random drug test was reinstated because he was not informed that he had the right to request an independent laboratory analysis of the split sample taken from the specimen.[13]

i. *Random Testing* [LA CDI 100.552545; 118.653; 124.60]

Many employers use a "probable cause" standard for testing employees, selecting only those whose behavior or appearance suggests the use of drugs. However, some employers choose to test employees randomly. These employers argue that random testing is the only effective deterrent to drug impairment on the job, because there are not always outward manifestations of drug use and because employees who are casual users, facing the odds of being selected for a random test, are likely to think twice about using drugs or quitting their employment and thereby ridding an employer of a potentially dangerous employee. Not surprisingly, random testing is the most controversial of all the methods for testing employees for drugs.

Courts have upheld random drug testing by public employers only where the employee is in a safety-sensitive position or a public-integrity-sensitive job.[14] In reaching this result, courts have balanced the employer's need for a drug-free workplace against the individual's right to privacy and right to be free from unwarranted intrusions. Unless a public employer can demonstrate

---

[11]The number of employers who attempt to vacate arbitral reinstatements of employees discharged for drug abuse on public policy grounds will likely diminish sharply as a result of the decision by the Supreme Court in *Eastern Associated Coal Corp. v. United Mine Workers*, 531 U.S. 57, 165 LRRM 2865 (2000), where the Court upheld an arbitrator's reinstatement of an employee truck driver who had twice tested positive for marijuana. The issue before the Court was whether considerations of public policy required the lower courts to refuse to enforce that arbitration award. In affirming the arbitrator's reinstatement order, the Court held that an arbitral award could be vacated on a public policy basis only if it violated an "explicit, well-defined, and dominant" public policy. The Court went on to state that such public policy must come from law and legal precedent and not from general considerations of supposed public interests.

[12]Eagle Energy, 110 LA 257 (Feldman, 1998).

[13]Coca Cola Bottling Co., 110 LA 8 (Nadelbach, 1998). *See also* Ohio Star Forge Co., 110 LA 705 (Gibson, 1998) (random drug-testing provision of drug and alcohol policy, which provides for discharge if an employee tests positive twice, violates contractual bar against discipline without proper cause or reasonable suspicion).

[14]The Supreme Court has decided two cases dealing with random or suspicionless drug testing by governmental employers. *See* Treasury Employees v. Von Raab, 489 U.S. 656, 4 IER Cases 246 (1989) (permitting drug testing for state employees for positions that require direct involvement in drug interdiction or the carrying of weapons); Skinner v. Railway Labor Executives' Ass'n, 489 U.S. 602, 130 LRRM 2857 (1989) (upholding suspicionless drug testing of train crew members involved in accidents). These cases stand for the proposition that before random or suspicionless drug testing of current public employees can be carried out by employers, there must be some showing of "special needs" justifying the testing. *See, e.g.*, Bluestein v. Skinner, 908 F.2d 451, 5 IER Cases 887 (9th Cir. 1990) (airline industry personnel); Taylor v. O'Grady, 888 F.2d 1189, 1199, 4 IER Cases 1569 (7th Cir. 1989) (correctional officers in regular contact with inmates); Government Employees (AFGE) v. Skinner,

a compelling reason, random drug testing constitutes an unlawful "search and seizure" in violation of the Fourth Amendment.

While under Fourth Amendment analysis there must be individualized suspicion to drug-test employees in nonsafety positions, the strictures of the Fourth Amendment do not apply to private employers. A number of states, in recognition of the limits of constitutional protection, have extended the reasoning of Fourth Amendment jurisprudence to the private sector.[15]

In the private sector, arbitrators confronted with unilaterally adopted random drug-testing policies generally are not concerned with the issue of whether the unilateral implementation of the policy constituted an unfair labor practice,[16] but rather are concerned with whether it is reasonable under all the circumstances.[17] Generally, arbitrators have refused to uphold the termination of an employee pursuant to a unilaterally adopted randomly

---

885 F.2d 884, 893, 4 IER Cases 1153 (D.C. Cir. 1989) (various transportation workers), *cert. denied*, 495 U.S. 923 (1990); Federal Employees (NFFE) v. Cheney, 884 F.2d 603, 615, 4 IER Cases 1164 (D.C. Cir. 1989) (Army civilian guards), *cert. denied*, 493 U.S. 1056 (1990); Thomson v. Marsh, 884 F.2d 113, 1154 IER Cases 1248, 4 IER Cases 1445 (4th Cir. 1989) (per curiam) (civilian workers in Army chemical weapons plant); Harmon v. Thornburgh, 878 F.2d 484, 496, 4 IER Cases 1001 (D.C. Cir. 1989) (Justice Department employees with clearance for top-secret information), *cert. denied sub nom.* Bell v. Thornburgh, 493 U.S. 1056 (1990); Guiney v. Roache, 873 F.2d 1557, 1558, 4 IER Cases 637 (1st Cir.) (per curiam) (police officers carrying firearms or engaged in drug interdiction efforts), *cert. denied*, 493 U.S. 963 (1989); Rushton v. Nebraska Pub. Power Dist., 844 F.2d 562, 567, 3 IER Cases 257, 3 IER Cases 768 (8th Cir. 1988) (nuclear power plant engineers); Transport Workers' Union v. Southeastern Pa. Transp. Auth., 884 F.2d 709, 713, 132 LRRM 2331 (3d Cir. 1988) (mass transit workers). In *Knox County Education Association v. Knox County Board of Education*, 158 F.3d 361, 14 IER Cases 609 (6th Cir. 1998), *cert. denied*, 528 U.S. 812 (1999), school teachers were deemed to hold safety sensitive positions. *But see* Ruben, *The Top Ten Judicial Decisions Affecting Labor Relations in Public Education During the Decade of the 1990s: The Verdict of Quiescent Years*, 30 J.L. & EDUC. 247, 258–62 (2001) (criticizing the *Knox* decision).

[15]*See, e.g.*, CONN. GEN. STAT. §31-51x (West 2001) (allowing random drug testing of employees only if (1) such test is authorized under federal law, and (2) the employee serves in an occupation that has been designated as a high-risk or safety-sensitive occupation); IOWA CODE §730.5 (limiting random drug testing to safety-sensitive employees in the private sector). For further analysis of legislative responses to employer drug testing, see Hurd, *States Addressing Drug Testing Issues in 1999: Part I, Employment Testing*, L. & POL'Y REP., July 1999, at 110; Hurd, *States Addressing Drug Testing Issues in 1999: Part II, Employment Testing*, L. & POL'Y REP., Aug. 1999, at 118. In addition to legislative action, courts have restricted random testing to only those private employees in safety-sensitive positions. *See, e.g.*, Webster v. Motorola, 637 N.E.2d 203, 9 IER Cases 1527 (Mass. 1994) (discussing Massachusetts' statutory right to privacy and limiting random drug testing to safety-sensitive positions); Hennessey v. Coastal Eagle Point Oil Co., 609 A.2d 11, 7 IER Cases 1057 (N.J. 1992) (suggesting random drug testing is only permissible for safety-sensitive employees); Twigg v. Hercules Co., 406 S.E.2d 52, 6 IER Cases 819 (W. Va. 1990) (striking down employer's random drug-testing policy on right to privacy grounds). *But see* Gilmore v. Enogex, Inc., 878 P.2d 360, 9 IER Cases 1295 (Okla. 1994) (permitting random drug testing and reasoning that employers have a legitimate interest in a drug-free workplace); Roe v. Quality Transp. Servs., 838 P.2d 128, 7 IER Cases 1479 (Wash. 1992) (finding that, absent specific legislation, no general public policy prevents private employer from conducting random drug tests). For a general overview of legislative and judicial responses to random drug testing by private employers, see Wefing, *Employer Drug Testing: Disparate Judicial and Legislative Responses*, 63 ALB. L. REV. 799 (2000).

[16]Phelps Dodge Copper Prods. Co., 94 LA 393 (Blum, 1990) (stating in reference to a unilaterally adopted drug-testing policy that "the question before me is not whether or not there is an unfair labor practice involved here but whether or not the action taken by management could be justified by the agreement and past practice").

[17]*See* Armstrong Air Conditioning, 99 LA 533 (Harlan, 1992) (employer had reasonable cause to request drug tests to ensure the safety of its employees); Vista Chem. Co., 99 LA 994

conducted drug test unless the employer can establish a compelling reason for conducting random tests.[18] Some arbitrators reviewing private sector drug-testing policies have found random drug testing unreasonable because suspicionless drug testing improperly shifts the burden to the employee to prove his or her innocence rather than resting the burden with the employer to prove guilt.[19] Other arbitrators emphasize that, because drug testing is an intrusion of privacy, there must be a balancing of interests weighing the employer's need for testing against employees' privacy interests.

In *Dow Chemical Co.*,[20] the arbitrator opined that a drug test's reasonableness depends on two factors: (1) the nature of the industry and work environment, and (2) evidence of an existing drug problem that is serious and pervasive. There the arbitrator held that the random drug-testing program in a petrochemical plant was reasonable because of the propensity for serious accidents, and widespread drug use in the plant was established because 30 percent of workers in the machine shop had admitted to drug use or had tested positive for drugs.

(Baroni, 1992) (employer had authority to request employees to submit to drug test where there was "reasonable suspicion" of drug use); Borg Warner Auto. Diversified Transmission Prods. Corp., 99 LA 209 (Bethel, 1992) (employees were alleged to have used drugs on company property); Eaton Cutler-Hammer Corp., 110 LA 467 (Franckiewicz, 1998) (employee who failed drug test properly discharged although other employees who had tested positive for controlled substances were not discharged); Bally's Park Place Hotel/Casino, 110 LA 1200, 1203 (Herzog, 1998) (employer had just cause to discharge employee for alcohol use, where coworker saw the employee "take a shot of something," a doctor found "alcohol intoxication," and a test administered to the employee indicated that the employee had a blood alcohol content level of 0.28). *But see* Stone Container Corp., 91 LA 1186 (Ross, 1988) (mandatory drug testing of employees involved in "any" industrial accident resulting in injury was overly broad and unreasonable). For commentary on all aspects of drug-testing issues in arbitration, see Discipline and Discharge in Arbitration (Brand ed., BNA Books 1998 & Supp. 2001); Denenberg & Denenberg, Alcohol and Other Drugs: Issues in Arbitration (BNA Books 1991) (discussing legal and policy issues related to alcohol and drug use, abuse, and testing in the workplace); Elkouri & Elkouri, Resolving Drug Issues (BNA Books 1993).

[18]*See, e.g.*, Seneca Wire & Mfg. Co., 113 LA 886 (Lalka, 1999); Omnisource Corp., 113 LA 862 (Loeb, 1999); Atlas Processing Co., 106 LA 172 (Baroni, 1996); Dow Chem. Co., 91 LA 1385 (Baroni, 1989).

[19]*See, e.g.*, Ohio Star Forge Co., 110 LA 705 (Gibson, 1998); Wheatland Farms, Inc., 96 LA 596 (Nelson, 1991); Vulcan Materials Co., 90 LA 1161 (Caraway, 1988).

[20]91 LA 1385 (Baroni, 1989) (arbitrator also noted that once it has been established that random testing is necessary, the accuracy and uniformity of the results should be taken into account). In *Dow Chemical Co.*, the arbitrator also discussed the degree to which the subject policy had been discussed in bargaining and the method for conducting the tests. That the company did in fact engage in bargaining over the subject of random testing before implementation supported the finding that the policy was a reasonable one. *Id.* at 1390. In addition, because the company had presented evidence that "state-of-the-art" testing procedures and facilities would be used, the arbitrator was convinced the testing would be accurate and uniform. *Id.* at 1390–91. *See also* Atlas Processing Co., 106 LA 172 (Baroni, 1996) (arbitrator found that random drug and alcohol testing was reasonable where 18 of 184 employees had documented substance abuse problems and had been involved in 22 incidents in a 15-year period; employer reasonably concluded that their reasonable-cause policy was not working).

While not often mentioned, some arbitrators do look to whether the employer has established a nexus between the ingestion of drugs and impairment of the employee at work. In *Ohio Star Forge Co.*, 110 LA 705 (Gibson, 1998), the arbitrator stated that the methodology of random testing is made more complex by the fact that an employee may ingest a proscribed drug and test positive several days, or even weeks, later. In such circumstances, a random test produces little or no proof of job impairment. See also *Vulcan Materials Co.*, 90 LA 1161 (Caraway, 1988); *Day & Zimmermann, Inc.*, 88 LA 1001 (Heinsz, 1987), and the numerous cited cases in both public and private sectors finding random testing impermissible.

However, in *Seneca Wire & Manufacturing Co.*[21] the arbitrator found a lack of evidence that a random drug-testing program was warranted where the employer's work (drawing steel into wire for use in production of springs) was not a hazard to the community or to the employees beyond what would normally be expected in an industrial operation. The arbitrator stated that while employers in industries requiring the performance of work that is hazardous to the employees themselves or the surrounding community are generally given more latitude in implementing random drug testing, employers in nonhazardous industries must show some indicia of drug abuse among their employees serious enough that the problem could not be combated with a less intrusive means than random drug testing.[22]

The arbitrator noted that early arbitration decisions had held that even with the high degree of danger involved, there must be evidence of drug use or drug-related problems.[23] However, later decisions have focused first on the hazardous nature of the work and whether employees under the influence of drugs would subject themselves and others to serious or fatal injury.[24] The arbitrator contrasted the conditions at Seneca Wire with employers in other cases in which the employer had provided sufficient evidence justifying the implementation of a random drug-testing policy.

Seneca Wire's working conditions did not involve the type of ultra-hazardous activity that would alone justify a random drug-testing policy, nor was there evidence of a substance abuse problem—in nearly 20 years there had been only 14 instances of employees being treated for or suspected of drug or alcohol problems.[25]

Other arbitrators emphasize the reason the employer implemented the random testing policy. In *Omnisource Corp.*,[26] the arbitrator found that a metal recycling facility did not have reasonable cause to implement a random drug-testing policy. The company had acquired a new facility at which random testing of all employees was the standard policy, while in all of its other facilities the policy was to test employees only for cause and after an injury. The company informed the union that it would adopt the new policy in all its plants and, despite heated objections from the union, implemented the policy. The arbitrator stated that the company had the right to promulgate reasonable rules and regulations that it believed were necessary to the efficient operation of its business; however, the events that led to the implementation of the random drug-testing policy undercut the company's claim that it needed the policy for safety reasons. The arbitrator noted that in the

---

[21]113 LA 886 (Lalka, 1999).

[22]*Id.* However, the arbitrator in *Churchill Downs, Inc.*, 98-1 ARB ¶5139 (Sergent, 1997), found that a unilaterally implemented random drug-testing policy was valid where there was no hazardous activity involved, and that the employer had established reasonable grounds for the policy of testing pari-mutel clerks because of the large amounts of money involved and the need to ensure public confidence in the operation of the horse-betting business.

[23]Day & Zimmerman, Inc., 88 LA 1001 (Heinsz, 1987).

[24]Day & Zimmerman, Inc., 94 LA 399 (Nicholas, Jr., 1990).

[25]The arbitrator also found that the company's substance abuse policy that set a limit of .04% blood alcohol content or below was reasonable, even though state law permitted operation of a motor vehicle up to .08%, because operation of an ordinary motor vehicle is not related to the operation of an employer's vehicles or machinery.

[26]113 LA 862 (Loeb, 1999).

6-year period under the company's old policy, not a single employee had been tested for cause and, of the 40 employees tested following an accident, only one had tested positive for drugs. In addition, the company provided no convincing evidence of any urgent safety-related need for the testing. Finally, the arbitrator found that the policy was unreasonable, because a positive drug test resulted in an automatic discharge and the employer failed to provide a connection between drug-test results and impairment of job performance.

Because arbitrators generally uphold as reasonable random drug testing of safety-sensitive employees, what is and is not a safety-sensitive position often is raised in arbitration. In *Los Angeles County Metropolitan Transit Authority*,[27] the arbitrator found that a track supervisor/inspector should not have been terminated for failing a random drug test because he was not in a "safety-sensitive" position. The employer conducted random drug tests of employees in accordance with its drug and alcohol policy, which had been adopted pursuant to federal Department of Transportation (DOT) requirements. The employee's job involved inspecting and repairing heavy and light rail transit tracks. The Transit Authority's policy listed specific categories of safety-sensitive activity, including operating a revenue service vehicle, controlling dispatch or movement of revenue service vehicles or equipment, and carrying a firearm for security purposes. Because the grievant, who was assigned to track inspection and repair, was not engaged in any of these activities, he was improperly categorized as a safety-sensitive employee, even though his job was related to the safe operation of mass-transit service. The arbitrator noted that the DOT regulations clearly applied only to employees who actually performed safety-sensitive functions.[28]

ii. "Zero-Tolerance" Policies

Under a "zero-tolerance" drug policy,[29] an employee who tests positive, whether pursuant to a random or suspicion-based testing policy, will be ter-

---

[27]114 LA 70 (Hoh, 1999).

[28]Not all arbitrators completely agree with this reasoning. In *Vogel Disposal Co.*, 108 LA 1121 (Hewitt, 1997), the arbitrator denied the grievance of an employee truck driver who was assigned light-duty tasks due to an on-the-job injury and was no longer driving a truck. The arbitrator stated that because the employee's salary and benefits were based on his position as a truck driver, he was in a safety-sensitive position even though he no longer actually performed any safety-sensitive duties. Similarly, in *South Florida University*, 24 LAIS 2022 (Abrams, 1997), an engineer had volunteered to obtain a commercial drivers license (CDL), even though his job did not require driving of any kind and the only purpose for obtaining the license was to please a supervisor who said that "it would look good across the street [with the university administration]." He was terminated after testing positive for marijuana. He had tried, unsuccessfully, to be relieved of the "requirement" of holding the CDL. The arbitrator upheld the termination, finding that the university had the right to administer the test because federal regulations mandated that those *holding* a CDL were subject to random drug testing. That the engineer never had any use for or need to utilize the CDL was not relevant.

[29]It is important to note that even if a company is subject to federal laws or regulations, federal law and regulation in this area do not mandate termination for positive drug tests. For example, the Drug-Free Workplace Act of 1988 requires an employer either to "take appropriate personnel action against such employees up to and including termination . . . or require such employee to satisfactorily participate in a drug abuse assistance or rehabilita-

minated.[30] Unilaterally implemented so-called zero-tolerance policies are problematic not only because they may involve some of the issues related to random drug testing (e.g., employer must show need), but also because the notion of terminating an employee for "flunking" a drug test runs counter to the well-established doctrine of "just cause" embedded in labor agreements and applied by labor arbitrators.[31] One essential element of the just cause standard is that the employee must have knowledge of the rule allegedly violated and the disciplinary consequences of a violation.[32]

Arbitrators scrutinize zero-tolerance policies with particular care because these policies may fail to take into account all the information that is normally relevant to the termination of an employee. Thus, the arbitrator in *Kimberly-Clark Corp.*[33] refused to uphold the termination of an employee with an uncontroverted "26-year record [that was] immaculate,"[34] who was terminated pursuant to a zero-tolerance policy. The arbitrator found that the employee's long and distinguished work record should have been given serious consideration in the context of the discipline decision.[35] The arbitrator emphasized that a "just cause" decision is not limited to determining if the employee violated a rule: consideration of the employee's work history,[36]

---

tion program . . . ." 41 U.S.C. §703(1). The Omnibus Transportation Employee Testing Act of 1991 and DOT's implementing regulations mandate the suspension, but not the termination, of drivers who have driven a commercial motor vehicle while under the influence of drugs. 49 U.S.C. §31310(b)(1)(A).

[30]The arbitrator in *Kimberly-Clark Corp.*, 107 LA 554 (Byars, 1996), held that a policy in which the employer can make exceptions for particular types of substance abuse offenses (e.g., terminating employees for bringing drugs or alcohol to work but applying progressive discipline in cases where the employee reports for work under the influence) is not a zero-tolerance policy.

[31]*See* Vulcan Materials Co., 90 LA 1161 (Caraway, 1988) (random drug testing improper because suspicionless drug testing of employees forces the employee to give evidence against himself when there is no evidence of wrongdoing, and this contradicts the customary rule of discipline that an employee is presumed to be innocent of the particular offense until proven guilty).

[32]In *Advance Transportation Co.*, 105 LA 1089 (Briggs, 1995), the company had the obligation to ensure that the employee knew he could be terminated for not submitting immediately to a drug and alcohol screen. The arbitrator found that the company failed to meet that obligation and was thus unjustified in terminating the employee because he reported later than required for a random drug test.

[33]107 LA 554 (Byars, 1996).

[34]*Id.* at 559.

[35]The arbitrator stated:

Taking the supreme penalty against an employee without due consideration for a long unblemished record goes to the very heart of "just cause." Although there are offenses sufficiently egregious that discharge would be upheld regardless of the employee's history, the infraction in this case, possession of a misdemeanor amount of marijuana on Company premises, does not justify discharge for a long-service employee with an exemplary record. Moreover, an employee's awareness of the rule and the penalty associated with it does not justify discharge regardless of the circumstances.

Id. at 560.

[36]Long service, especially when unblemished, often is given significant weight by arbitrators. In a landmark arbitration decision that was appealed to, and affirmed by, the Supreme Court in 1987, *Misco, Inc.*, 89 LA 137 (Fox, 1987), the arbitrator found that the employer lacked just cause to discharge an employee who was sitting in the back seat of a coworker's car in the employer's parking lot when police found a lit marijuana cigarette. The grievant in that case was on probation for poor work performance at the time of his arrest for possession of marijuana.

consistency of the application of the rule, as well as other factors come into play in most discipline cases.[37]

In circumstances where the company is subject to extensive government regulation (beyond common DOT regulations), zero-tolerance policies have been upheld. For example, in *Argosy Gaming Co.*,[38] the arbitrator upheld the termination of an employee under such a policy (despite the employee's exemplary work record). The employer randomly tested employees for drug or alcohol use and maintained a strict zero-tolerance drug policy. The company introduced extensive testimony indicating that it functioned in an environment (riverboat casino gambling) carefully controlled by federal and state laws. In particular, from the inception of gaming in Illinois, the state had mandated that all employees of gaming operations be, in the words of the company, "squeaky clean."[39] In addition, the casino was subject to Coast Guard regulations, which required random drug testing of certain personnel.[40] Nine employees had tested positive for alcohol or illegal drugs since the policy's inception, and all had been discharged.

The arbitrator noted that circumstances in the case were unique primarily because the employer appeared to have been required by law to administer the zero-tolerance policy. Under these exceptional circumstances, the arbitrator found that the employer had the right to discharge the employee on a first drug use offense.[41]

---

[37]*See, e.g.*, Bruce Hardwood Floors, 108 LA 115 (Allen, Jr., 1997) (An employee who was terminated pursuant to a zero-tolerance policy after testing positive due to accidental ingestion of wife's tranquilizer was terminated without just cause, because the employee presented credible evidence that the ingestion of the pill was accidental, the employee had an uncontroverted long and distinguished career, and the employee had never tested positive at any other time. However, while the arbitrator believed termination was too harsh, no backpay was awarded.).

[38]110 LA 540 (Fowler, 1998).

[39]The company also was required to do background checks. The Illinois Gaming Board has determined that employees with such prior history of crimes or moral turpitude are either not to be hired or are to be terminated once such history or problem is identified. All company employees had to be fingerprinted annually to verify that no arrests or convictions had occurred during the year.

[40]46 C.F.R. §16.230 (2003). Federal law required that the employer test those employees who "are specifically assigned the duties of warning, mustering, assembling, assisting, or controlling the movement of passengers during emergencies." 46 C.F.R. §16.230(3) (2003). Under Coast Guard regulations, an employee who fails a chemical drug test for dangerous drugs "must be denied employment as a crewmember or must be removed from duties which directly affect the safe operation of the vessel as soon as possible." 46 C.F.R. §16.201(c) (2003).

[41]Other cases finding reasonable an employer's termination of an employee on a first offense include: *Kroger Co.*, 108 LA 229 (Frocht, 1997) (mechanic employee properly discharged for running marijuana operation out of home); *Bruce Hardwood Floors*, 108 LA 115 (Allen, Jr., 1997) (employee not properly discharged for accidental ingestion of tranquilizers, but would be if intentional ingestion); *Dravo Lime Co.*, 105 LA 54 (Imundo, Jr., 1995) (mining employee properly discharged for positive random drug test for marijuana); *Mason & Hangar-Silas Mason Co.*, 103 LA 371 (Cipolla, 1994) (nuclear weapons plant employee properly discharged for positive random drug test); *Ingalls Shipbuilding*, 99 LA 783 (Shieber, 1992) (electrician properly discharged for positive random drug test for marijuana); *Marathon Petroleum Co.*, 93 LA 1082 (Marlatt, 1989) (employee properly discharged where loaded handgun and half-empty bottles of alcohol found in employee's car in company parking lot); *Excel Corp.*, 89 LA 1275 (McDermott, 1987) (meatpacking employee properly discharged after signing confession that he had smoked marijuana and drunk beer in company parking lot); *Duquesne Light Co.*, 92 LA 907 (Sergent, Jr., 1989) (electrical employee properly discharged for positive random drug test for cocaine and marijuana); *US Air, Inc.*, 91 LA 6 (Ables, 1988) (flight attendant properly discharged for conviction of off-duty misdemeanor of

B. Other Safety Violations [LA CDI 118.659; 100.552575]

An employer's ability to discipline employees committing infractions of safety rules is not limited, however, to employees who violate alcohol and/or drug policies. For example, an arbitrator held that an employer had just cause to discharge an employee for repeatedly failing to observe a rule requiring employees to wear safety glasses.[42] The arbitrator noted that "the Company has a duty to protect the eye sight of all of its employees" and that the requirement that all employees entering the plant wear the specified glasses was an appropriate precaution to minimize the risk of injury.[43] In another case, an arbitrator found that an employee was properly terminated for a first violation of a safety rule. There, the violation created a situation so potentially hazardous as to excuse the company's failure to follow progressive discipline.[44]

Management's obligation to maintain a safe work environment does not require the provision of ideal conditions. "Less safe" was not considered "unsafe" where the employer laid off 39 resident-care workers in a mental health facility, but took other measures to ensure the safety of employees despite the reduced availability of assistance.[45] In another case, management was not required to provide a two-way communications system for teachers who felt endangered by increased gang activity, where adult hall monitors and off-duty police were hired and a telephone was installed to give teachers access to administrative offices and outside help.[46]

The nature and extent of employer obligations to protect employees against the danger from the presence of asbestos in the workplace have given rise to a number of decisions. In one case, an employer attempted to shield itself from liability by claiming that the union had failed to prove the level of exposure to asbestos. Because the employer had controlled the testing and blocked union access to the information, the arbitrator refused to allow the employer to benefit from its own default.[47] In another case, the employer was required to offer environmental differential pay to employees even though the level of exposure to asbestos at work was one-half of the standard set by the Occupational Safety and Health Administration (OSHA).[48] However, where a city removed friable (loose) asbestos pipe insulation, but there was no evidence of how long the condition had existed, or whether the grieving

---

drug possession); *Northwest Airlines*, 89 LA 621 (Flagler, 1987) (airline attendant properly discharged for alcohol consumption at "layover" stop).

[42]Carrier Corp., 110 LA 1064 (Ipavec, 1998) (three times in 1 week the employee had violated the rule requiring employees to wear safety glasses).

[43]*Id.* at 1067.

[44]Union Tank Car Co., 110 LA 1128 (Lalka, 1998) (upholding discharge of employee who failed to comply with safety rule requiring him to read flashpoints of substances in railroad tank cars before welding on the cars, because the violation of the rule placed all employees at risk of death or serious harm). *Cf.* Beckett Paper Co., 110 LA 425 (Heekin, 1998) (supervisor did not arbitrarily bar an employee, who had suffered an injury, from working for 2 days when the employee could not use one of his hands, thereby affecting his ability to safely operate machinery).

[45]Michigan Dep't of Mental Health, 101 LA 325 (McDonald, 1993).

[46]Racine, Wis., Sch. Dist., 108 LA 391 (Imes, 1996).

[47]Department of the Navy, 102 LA 294 (Draznin, 1993).

[48]Veterans Admin., 99 LA 229 (Duff, 1992).

firefighters had actually suffered exposure, the city was not required to maintain the firefighters' names in a special medical file or to notify them that they might have been exposed to the asbestos.[49]

When medical evidence reveals that an employee's continuance in his or her present job puts the employee at risk, management has the right to transfer the employee to a light-duty job over the employee's objections, because the employer has the legal duty to protect the health and safety of all its employees.[50] Further, despite language in the contract limiting subcontracting, management also may subcontract work that would be unsafe for its workers to perform with the equipment the employer has.[51]

C. OSH Act Considerations [LA CDI 124.70; 100.552531]

The federal Occupational Safety and Health Act of 1970 (OSH Act)[52] mandates employers to comply with specific safety and health standards and, under its "general duty" provisions, requires employers to furnish a place of employment free of hazards likely to cause death or serious physical harm to employees. The OSH Act empowers the Secretary of Labor, through OSHA, to promulgate standards that are "reasonably necessary or appropriate to provide safe or healthful employment and places of employment." The OSH Act provides for enforcement by means of:

- inspections and investigations of work facilities;
- citations by the Secretary of Labor against employers for safety and health violations (such citations order abatement of the violation and propose a penalty assessment);
- injunction proceedings to remedy imminently dangerous conditions;
- civil penalties assessed by the Occupational Safety and Health Review Commission;
- criminal penalties for certain violations; and
- employer opportunity to contest citations or proposed penalties before the Review Commission and the courts. [53]

---

[49]City of Chi., Ill., 99 LA 343 (Cox, 1992).
[50]ITT Auto., 105 LA 11 (Shanker, 1995).
[51]Basin Coop. Servs., 105 LA 1070 (Cohen, 1996).
[52]29 U.S.C. §651 et seq.
[53]Id. In Industrial Union Department v. American Petroleum Institute, 448 U.S. 607 (1980), the U.S. Supreme Court concluded that the Act "was intended to require the elimination, as far as feasible, of significant risks of harm," id. at 646, that "Congress was concerned, not with absolute safety, but with the elimination of significant harm," id. at 646, and that "the Act empowers the Secretary to promulgate health and safety standards only where a significant risk of harm exists," id. at 652. For more on the OSH Act, see Nothsetei, The Law of Occupational Safety and Health (1981); The Job Safety and Health Act of 1970 (BNA Books 1971); Gellens, Resolving Industrial Safety Disputes: To Arbitrate or Not to Arbitrate, 34 Lab. L.J. 149 (1983); Wolfson, Arbitration and OSHA, 38 Arb. J. No. 3, at 12 (1983); Britton, Courts, Arbitrators, and OSHA Problems: An Overview, Proceedings of the 33d Annual Meeting of NAA 260 (Stern & Dennis eds., BNA Books 1981); Schwartz, Comment, id. at 276; Alesia, Practice Before the United States Occupational Safety and Health Review Commission, 86 Case & Comment 34 (1981). The Federal Coal Mine Health and Safety Act of 1969, 30 U.S.C. §801 et seq., prescribes mandatory health and safety standards for the protection of coal miners and requires the Secretary of the Interior to conduct continuing surveillance of mines to detect imminently dangerous conditions, and violations of the mandatory standards, procedures being specified for abating the dangerous conditions, and violations of

Critics charge that the existence of an "antiregulatory" political environment, hostile to enforcement of the OSH Act, has significantly hindered its effectiveness.[54] Nevertheless, the OSH Act continues to have significant impact in the arbitration of safety and health issues. It has been used, for example, to support protested employer action that had been prompted directly or indirectly by a current or past OSHA citation.[55] Even where the employer had not been cited for an OSHA violation, an arbitrator upheld contested employer action taken for the purpose of meeting OSHA standards.[56]

Increasingly, employers cite the requirements of the OSH Act's "general duty" clause to support the implementation and enforcement of zero-tolerance policies against workplace violence. For example, an arbitrator referred to OSHA requirements, among other safety considerations, in upholding the employer's zero-tolerance policy:

---

standards. A summary of the Federal Coal Mine Health and Safety Act and its procedures is provided in *National Coal Operator's Ass'n v. Kleppe*, 423 U.S. 388, 391–92 (1976). *See also* Kleppe v. Delta Mining, 423 U.S. 403 (1976). Under Exec. Order No. 12,196, issued by President Carter in 1980, federal agencies "generally must: (1) comply with the same safety and health standards followed by private industry; (2) abate hazards promptly or develop abatement plans; (3) agree not to take any action against an employee for reporting accidents or participating in agency safety programs."

[54]Gross, *The Kenneth M. Piper Lecture: The Broken Promises of the National Labor Relations Act and the Occupational Safety and Health Act: Conflicting Values and Conceptions of Right and Justice*, 73 CHI.-KENT L. REV. 35 (1998).

[55]*See* Pabst Brewing Co., 88 LA 656 (Wyman, 1987) (the employer was upheld in conducting hearing tests of employees pursuant to a consent order between OSHA and the employer, and employees who came to work one-half hour early for the test were not entitled to overtime); Monsanto Co., 77 LA 495, 497–98 (Robertson, 1981) (safety rule was upheld, where the union's evidence did not establish that the employer's action in adopting and applying the rule was arbitrary or capricious and where the employer had been fined by OSHA several years earlier; the arbitrator found that "it is not unreasonable for this Company to seek to avoid any potential questioning of its safety procedures by OSHA so as not to have to litigate questionable practices."); Hater Indus., 73 LA 1025, 1027 (Ipavec, 1979); Gra-Iron Foundry Corp., 72 LA 702, 703 (Carter, 1979); Eberle Tanning Co., 71 LA 302, 305 (Sloane, 1978); Ingram Mfg. Co., 70 LA 1269, 1271–72 (Johannes, 1978); J.R. Simplot Co., 68 LA 912, 913, 916 (Conant, 1977); Baggett Transp. Co., 68 LA 82, 84 (Crane, 1977); Anaconda Aluminum Co., 64 LA 24, 27 (Larkin, 1975); Ingalls Iron Works Co., 61 LA 1154, 1155 (Griffin, 1973); Champion Int'l Corp., 61 LA 400, 408 (Chalfie, 1973) (OSHA citations with costly penalties for failure to meet time limitations on compliance "created unusual circumstances which gave rise to abnormal rather than normal operating conditions" within the meaning of the agreement). *See also* Lear Siegler, Inc. 76 LA 579, 580–81 (Kaufman, 1981); Phoenix Dye Works Co., 59 LA 912, 918–19 (Dyke, 1972). *Cf.* International Minerals & Chem. Corp., 78 LA 682, 684–85 (Jones, Jr., 1982); Allied Chem. Corp., 72 LA 795, 800 (Eischen, 1979). In *Mrs. Baird's Bakeries*, 68 LA 773, 777–78 (Fox, 1977), the arbitrator responded as follows to a union assertion that the employer's action was not required by OSHA: "Regulations set forth by OSHA are minimum standards that an employer must meet. These regulations, or standards, do not say that an employer cannot use greater safety standards than those specified . . . ." *Id.* at 77. *See also* Quaker Oats Co., 69 LA 727, 731 (Hunter, 1977). However, in *Allied Chemical Corp.*, 74 LA 412, 416–17 (Eischen, 1980), the arbitrator refused to uphold a safety rule that he found to be unreasonable, notwithstanding that a factor in its adoption was the employer's "understandable desire to avoid further legal difficulties with OSHA"; the arbitrator believed that "upon careful analysis," the OSHA citation against the employer could not "be deemed a mandate for" the employer's action. *See also* York Water Co., 60 LA 90, 92–93 (Tripp, 1973).

[56]*See* St. Joe Minerals Corp., 76 LA 421, 424 (Newmark, 1981); Anderson Elec. Connectors, 75 LA 214, 215–16 (Hardin, 1980); Bethlehem Steel Corp., 74 LA 921, 921–22 (Fishgold, 1980); Niagara Mohawk Power Corp., 74 LA 58, 62 (Markowitz, 1980); Naval Air Rework Facility, 73 LA 644 (Flannagan, 1979); Naval Air Rework Facility, 73 LA 201, 205–06 (Livengood, 1979); Phoenix Forging Co., 71 LA 879, 879–80, 882 (Dash, Jr., 1978); Mobil Chem. Co., 71 LA 535, 535–37 (May, 1978); Schmeller Aluminum Foundry Co., 70 LA 596,

The Occupational Safety and Health Administration formally recognizes the health and safety risks associated with workplace violence. According to OSHA, workplace violence is increasing at an alarming rate. . . . Employers may be cited by OSHA, under its *"General Duty" Clause*, for not providing a safe and healthful work environment, if the employer does not take *feasible steps* to prevent or abate a recognized violence hazard.[57]

OSHA demonstrated its concern over workplace violence by issuing federal advisory guidelines for preventing violent acts in the health care and social services industries.[58] Employers also may have a responsibility under the OSH Act to take feasible measures to ensure the safety of victims of domestic violence and their coworkers, if it is foreseeable that the abuser would threaten or harm the victim at work.[59]

An employer's reliance on OSHA regulations to defend against a claimed contract violation is sometimes misplaced. One arbitrator rejected an employer's argument raising OSHA regulations as a defense to a grievance that the employer had awarded an overtime opportunity out of classification in violation of the contract, noting:

It seems to this Arbitrator that where grievant was qualified and contractually entitled to the overtime, it could have been offered to him with appropriate equipment as it was to the laborer, and the OSHA regulations would have been complied with. While the Company's concern for the safety of its employees is laudatory, it cannot violate the contract, particularly where not to do so would not violate government regulations.[60]

Another arbitrator ruled that an employer did not have the right to insist that employees sign a document attesting that they had been trained to handle certain hazardous chemicals when the employees had a good-faith doubt that the training met OSHA requirements. However, he emphasized that, under such circumstances, employees should sign under protest and then grieve.[61]

---

599 (Dyke, 1978); Haveg Indus., 68 LA 841, 844 (McKone, 1977) (in addition to other evidence negating grievant's claim that a health hazard existed, "OSHA has frequently inspected the full range of manufacturing operations at the plant and made no citations with respect to" the operation in question); Robertshaw Controls Co., 62 LA 511, 511–13 (Gentile, 1974); Owens-Corning Fiberglas Corp., 61 LA 448, 448–49 (Doyle, 1973); Babcock & Wilcox Co., 59 LA 72, 74–75 (Nicholas, Jr., 1972). *See also* Sherwin Williams Co., 80 LA 649, 657 (Wolff, 1983).

[57]Mason Hanger Corp., 111 LA 469, 472 (Baroni, 1998) (emphasis in original). *See also* Eaton Corp., 114 LA 1007 (Hodgson, 2000).

[58]*See* DEPARTMENT OF LABOR OCCUPATIONAL SAFETY & HEALTH ADMIN., GUIDELINES FOR PREVENTING WORKPLACE VIOLENCE FOR HEATH CARE AND SOCIAL SERVICES WORKERS (1996).

[59]Comment, *Employer Liability for Domestic Violence in the Workplace: Are Employers Walking a Tightrope Without a Safety Net?*, 31 TEX. TECH L. REV. 139 (2000); Perin, *Employers May Have to Pay When Domestic Violence Goes to Work*, 18 REV. LITIG. 365 (Spring 1999); Robertson, *Addressing Domestic Violence in the Workplace: An Employer's Responsibility*, 16 LAW & INEQ. 633 (Summer 1998). See further discussion in section 3., "Safety and Health Rules," below.

[60]A.E. Staley Mfg. Co., 86 LA 627, 632 (Traynor, 1986). *See also* Packaging Corp. of Am., 114 LA 809 (Nolan, 2000) (employer violated contract by requiring that all employees wear safety shoes; employer misinterpreted OSHA's regulations as mandating safety shoes); Flowserve Corp., 111 LA 813 (Jennings, 1998); Mission Foods, 111 LA 501 (Snider, 1998) (employer's rule requiring that all maintenance, sanitation, and head operator employees be clean-shaven to ensure proper respirator fit found to be overly broad and unnecessary in attempt to comply with OSHA rule concerning facial hair and wearing respirators); Hercules Inc., 99 LA 803 (Sergent, 1992).

[61]James B. Beam Distilling Co., 90 LA 740, 743–44 (Ruben, 1988).

3. SAFETY AND HEALTH RULES

A. Issuance of Safety and Health Rules
[LA CDI 100.15; 118.656; 118.659; 124.70; 100.552575]

Arbitrators consistently uphold an employer's right to issue safety and health rules that comply with certain fundamental principles of labor-management relations. Thus, in common with other employer-promulgated regulations, a safety and health rule must bear a reasonable relationship to its purpose[62] and must be reasonable in application as well as in content.[63] As might be expected, safety rules prohibiting weapons, firearms, or explosives in the workplace are upheld routinely.[64]

The validity of less obviously appropriate safety rules depends on such factors as their relationship to job duties and work location and the consistency of their application.[65] The consistency requirement was not violated when all employees were prohibited from smoking in any area not designated as a smoking area,[66] or by smoking restrictions on bargaining-unit members even though salaried employees' work assignments allowed them more flexibility in going to smoking areas. Similarly, a rule requiring employees working in hazardous areas to wear "hard hats" and safety glasses was held to have been applied reasonably and nondiscriminatorily although employees who worked in an enclosure that protected them from the hazards were exempted.[67]

To enforce safety and health rules, employers must have adequately communicated the rules. However, prior notice to an employee is not required where the employee's acts involve inherent dangers or workplace violence.[68]

---

[62]A rule requiring employees to read flashpoints on tags before welding on tank cars is reasonable, even though none of the injuries that resulted in implementation of policy involved the same fact pattern. Union Tank Car Co., 110 LA 1128 (Lalka, 1998). See Cook County, Ill., Dist. 201 Bd. of Educ., 89 LA 521, 526–30 (Witney, 1987); Babcock & Wilcox, 73 LA 443, 445–47 (Strasshofer, 1979); National Airlines, 42 LA 1206, 1208 (Black, 1964); Bethlehem Steel Co., 41 LA 211, 211–12 (Barrett, 1963) (cited and followed in Bethlehem Mines Corp., 48 LA 765, 765–66 (Strongin, 1967)); United States Steel Corp., 62–1 ARB ¶8051 (McDermott, 1961). See also Southern Airways, 47 LA 1135, 1141 (Wallen, 1966). A safety rule is not unreasonable merely because its benefits are minor. United States Steel Corp., 40 LA 205, 207 (Florey, 1963).

[63]Smurfit Stone Container Div., 114 LA 562 (Marino, 2000) (the zero-tolerance policy regarding safety rules was reasonable); Bordon Italian Foods, 113 LA 13 (Marino, 1999). See also Jefferson Smurfit Corp., 114 LA 358 (Kaufman, 2000); Georgia Pac. Corp., 113 LA 679 (Jennings, 1999); B.W. Provisions, 113 LA 527 (Gentile, 1999); Bauer Bros. Co., 48 LA 861, 863 (Kates, 1967); Bethlehem Mines Corp., 48 LA 765, 767 (Strongin, 1967); National Airlines, 42 LA 1206, 1208 (Black, 1964); Bethlehem Steel Co., 41 LA 211, 213 (Barrett, 1963); United States Steel Corp., 39 LA 1140, 1142 (Seitz, 1962).

[64]Sandusky Cabinets, 112 LA 373 (Morgan, Jr., 1999).

[65]Smurfit Stone Container Div., 114 LA 562 (Marino, 2000); Minnegasco Inc., 110 LA 1077 (Jacobowski, 1998).

[66]Tomkins Indus., 112 LA 281 (Rimmel, 1998).

[67]Bethlehem Steel Co., 41 LA 213, 214 (Barrett, 1963). See also Union Tank Car Co., 110 LA 1128 (Lalka, 1998); Carrier Corp., 110 LA 1064 (Ipavec, 1998).

[68]Mayflower Vehicle Sys., 114 LA 1249 (Franckiewicz, 2000) (oral communication was sufficient); IPC Corinth Div., 111 LA 973 (Nicholas, Jr., 1998) (posting and distribution of rule through memoranda was an acceptable means of notifying employees); International Paper Co., 109 LA 472 (Terrill, 1997) (discharge upheld, where employer notified employee, but failed to adequately inform "all employees" about the policy); Snap-On Tools Corp., 104 LA 180 (Cipolla, 1995).

Of course, nonobservant employees who believe a regulation to be invalid should ordinarily file a grievance instead of resorting to self-help.[69]

B. Employee Violations [LA CDI 118.659; 100.552575]

An employee's violation of a safety rule may result in suspension, demotion,[70] or discharge, depending on the seriousness of the violation, the number of violations, and the specific provisions of a progressive discipline policy.[71] The severity of the sanction may depend on an employee's prior record. For example, where two employees had violated the same safety rules in cutting steel, but received suspensions of differing lengths—one for 3 days and the other for 7 days—an arbitrator found the disparity to be justified because the employee who was suspended for 7 days had violated another safety rule earlier in the year.[72]

Arbitrators have upheld discharges of employees who have persistently disobeyed safety regulations despite having received progressive discipline, and even for a first-time violation of a safety rule requiring strict compliance if the offense is deemed sufficiently serious.[73] This "strict compliance" rationale is particularly appropriate where the company's operations are inher-

---

[69]*See* Granite Constr. Co., 114 LA 1115 (Riker, 2000); Union Tank Car Co., 110 LA 1128 (Lalka, 1998); Eastern Air Lines, 44 LA 459, 462 (Murphy, 1965); Day & Zimmermann, Inc., 44 LA 385, 388–89 (Boles, 1965); National Lead Co., 36 LA 898, 901 (Bothwell, 1961); Allby Asphalt & Ref. Co., 34 LA 83, 85 (Daugherty, 1960).

[70]United States Borax & Chem. Corp., 36 LA 970, 972–73 (Keeler, 1961). *See* GES Exposition Servs., 108 LA 311 (Levy, 1997) (arbitrator did not uphold employee's demotion for violating employer's nonsmoking policy, among other violations, where another employee engaged in the same behavior without reprimand).

[71]*See* Union Tank Car Co., 110 LA 1128 (Lalka, 1998); Minnegasco Inc., 110 LA 1077 (Jacobowski, 1998); Carrier Corp., 110 LA 1064 (Ipavec, 1998). Discharge was too severe for an employee who was responsible for an incident in which a block fell off a cable he was operating, where there was no safety device provided by the employer. Union Carbide Corp., 110 LA 667 (Caraway, 1998).

[72]Rock-Tenn Co., 110 LA 1109 (Bard, 1998). *See* Mayflower Vehicle Sys., 114 LA 1249 (Franckiewicz, 2000); Smurfit Stone Container Div., 114 LA 562 (Marino, 2000); Jefferson Smurfit Corp., 114 LA 358 (Kaufman, 2000); Gra-Iron Foundry Corp., 72 LA 702, 702–03 (Carter, 1979); Eberle Tanning Co., 71 LA 302, 305 (Sloane, 1978); American Potash & Chem. Corp., 64–1 ARB ¶8356 (Miller, 1963); Sinclair Ref. Co., 64–1 ARB ¶8018 (Stouffer, 1963); United States Steel Corp., 63–2 ARB ¶8675 (Duff, 1963). A penalty of discharge was reduced to disciplinary suspension due to mitigating circumstances in *Goodyear Tire & Rubber Co.*, 45 LA 772, 775 (Rohman, 1965); *Marble Prods. Co.*, 40 LA 247, 254 (Marshall, 1963); *National Lead Co.*, 36 LA 898, 901 (Bothwell, 1961).

[73]Discharge followed progressive discipline in *Phelps Dodge Morenci*, 113 LA 440 (Brisco, 1999); *American Potash & Chem. Corp.*, 64–1 ARB ¶8356 (Miller, 1963). Discharge was upheld in the following cases without any indication that progressive discipline had been utilized: *Union Tank Car Co.*, 110 LA 1128 (Lalka, 1998) (employee discharged for first-time violation, where "safety rule creates situation so potentially hazardous as to preclude requirement of progressive discipline"); *National Gypsum Co.*, 78 LA 226–27 (Klaiber, 1982) (union stressed that progressive discipline had not been used); *Thatcher & Sons*, 76 LA 1278, 1280 (Nutt, 1981) (expressly holding that progressive discipline was not required); *Amoco Oil Co.*, 64 LA 511, 513–14 (Brown, 1975); *Gold Kist*, 62 LA 139, 145 (Rutherford, 1974) (discharge for first safety violation was upheld "based upon the severity of the safety hazard created").

ently hazardous.[74] In some cases, arbitrators have found management to be in violation of the contract because of failure to follow safety rules.[75]

C. No-Smoking Policies [LA CDI 124.70]

The number of cases challenging "no-smoking" policies has increased significantly, but arbitrators regularly uphold restrictions on employee use of tobacco in the workplace as an appropriate means to protect the health of fellow employees and company property.[76] Smoking may be prohibited both inside and outside the plant.[77] Management's right to implement smoking restrictions derives from its rulemaking authority and its duty to provide a safe and healthy work environment. So long as the limitation or outright ban is not unreasonable, arbitrary, or capricious, it will be upheld.[78] One arbitrator held that a company's premiseswide ban on tobacco use was not unreasonable, but rather served a legitimate management objective,[79] and did not violate a contractual "preservation-of-privileges" clause.[80] As the arbitrator explained, the company had clearly retained its managerial right to change the rules affecting employees' smoking privileges at the plant.[81]

Arbitrators, however, have held that where the parties' collective bargaining agreement provides that smoking is permitted in designated areas, management may not unilaterally ban smoking in all areas.[82] Thus, a company's unilateral implementation of a comprehensive no-smoking policy was held to have violated its collective bargaining agreement because it ended a practice of allowing employees to use outside smoking areas.[83] In that in-

---

[74]*See* Foster Wheeler Envtl. Corp., 114 LA 1081 (Calhoun, 2000); Kodiak Elec. Ass'n, 104 LA 1112 (Peck, 1995); Eastern Air Lines, 44 LA 459, 462 (Murphy, 1965); Solar Chem. Corp., 62–2 ARB ¶8651 (Taft, 1962) (insurance may have been a factor); Allby Asphalt & Ref. Co., 34 LA 83, 85 (Daugherty, 1960); General Elec. Co., 31 LA 386, 388–89 (Sutermeister, 1958).

[75]Carborundum Abrasives, 114 LA 990 (Feldman, 2000) (a company was issued a citation for failing to provide an employee with a hard hat); Noranda Aluminum, 78 LA 1331, 1333 (Kubie, 1982) (employer permitted supervisors, who are subject to same risks as line employees, to ignore safety rules that line employees must observe); Immigration & Naturalization Serv., 75 LA 849, 853 (Goodstein, 1980) (contractual requirement for rotation of duty was violated by federal agency employer's order); U.S. Army Communications Command Headquarters, 72 LA 44, 47 (Leventhal, 1979).

[76]*See* Plasti-Line, Inc., 114 LA 1240 (Mancini, 2000); Ultra-Met Co., 114 LA 1201 (Bell, 2000); Mutual Mfg. & Supply Co., 109 LA 570 (High, 1997).

[77]Bayer Corp., 110 LA 924 (Miles, 1998); Norris Plumbing Fixtures, 104 LA 174 (Richman, 1995).

[78]Plasti-Line, Inc., 114 LA 1240 (Mancini, 2000) (employer's premiseswide ban on tobacco use is not unreasonable, where it fosters better health among its employees); Timkin Co., 108 LA 422 (Kindig, 1996); Akron Brass Co., 101 LA 289 (Shanker, 1993).

[79]Plasti-Line, Inc., 114 LA 1240 (Mancini, 2000).

[80]*Id.* at 1249.

[81]*Id.*

[82]Tomkins Indus., 112 LA 281 (Rimmel, 1998); Bayer Corp., 110 LA 924 (Miles, 1998); Hobart Corp., 103 LA 1089 (Millious, 1994); PMI Food Equip. Group, 103 LA 547 (Imundo, Jr., 1994) (discusses difference between a policy and a rule, where contract states that new rules are subject to negotiation); Campbell Group, 102 LA 1031 (Ferree, 1994) (settlement of grievance providing for outside lean-to for smoking became part of the contract after it survived contract negotiations); Raybestos Prods. Co., 102 LA 46 (Kossoff, 1993) (specific language on permitted smoking areas given more weight than general language regarding employer's agreement to protect health and safety).

[83]Cross Oil & Ref., 104 LA 757, 761 (Gordon, 1995) (provision incorporating "any privilege or benefit" embraces more than "past practice").

stance, the arbitrator did apply a preservation-of-privileges provision, which stated that any privilege enjoyed by employees and not mentioned in the agreement would be incorporated into the agreement. The arbitrator concluded that the parties' bargaining history reflected that smoking was a privilege afforded employees.[84] In contrast, other arbitrators have held that even if the right to smoke is a recognized past practice, the practice cannot prevail where the conditions that gave rise to it no longer exist, and management is under no contractual obligation to expend money to modify its plant or equipment to accommodate smokers.[85] One arbitrator noted that as information about the health risks associated with smoking have become widely disseminated, public and employer attitudes toward allowing smoking in the workplace have changed correspondingly.[86]

D. Workplace Violence [LA CDI 118.640; 100.552510]

In recent years the issue of workplace violence also has come to the forefront of public and employer concerns.[87] Increased violence in the workplace has prompted employers to implement specific policies to protect workers from both physical harm and threats of physical harm. A sensitivity to the disturbing accounts of workplace violence certainly has contributed to the view that an employer's obligation to provide a safe working environment requires (1) zero tolerance for violence policies, and (2) the discipline or removal of employees who threaten or engage in violence.[88] In *Golden States Foods Corp.*,[89] an employer was found to have had just cause to discharge an employee who grabbed a fellow employee, when, just 6 weeks before the incident, the employer had implemented a zero-tolerance "Anti-Violence Policy." As another arbitrator recognized:

> Violence in the workplace is a serious concern to employers. The law requires that when an employer receives information of threats [of violence], the employer must respond. . . . Receiving such information directly or by way of hearsay is irrelevant. An employer must act on such information.[90]

---

[84]*Id.*

[85]Cummins Engine Co., 104 LA 522 (Goldman, 1995) (management has no obligation to preserve opportunity to engage in unhealthy behavior on company premises). *See also* Plasti-Line, Inc., 114 LA 1240 (Mancini, 2000); Akron Brass Co., 101 LA 289 (Shanker, 1993) (management need not incur costs to accommodate smokers).

[86]Tomkins Indus., 112 LA 281 (Rimmel, 1998) (accumulative evidence on smoking's ill effects on workers' health and productivity, documentation of cost effects of tobacco use on business and industry, and changes in attitudes about smoking have fueled efforts to impose and enforce nonsmoking regulations in the workplace); Lockheed Aeronautical Sys. Co., 104 LA 840 (Hewitt, 1995). See further discussion in section 6., "Employee Complaints of Specific Hazards," below.

[87]Procter & Gamble, 114 LA 1185 (Allen, Jr., 2000).

[88]USS, Div. of USX Corp., 114 LA 948 (Das, 2000); Steel Warehouse Co., 114 LA 498 (Cox, 1999); Georgia Pac. Corp., 113 LA 679 (Jennings, 1999); B.W. Provisions, 113 LA 527 (Gentile, 1999); Rohm & Hass Tex., 113 LA 119 (Woolf, 1999); Champion Int'l Corp., 111 LA 100 (Duda, Jr., 1998); Quaker Oats Co., 110 LA 816 (Crider, 1998); National Castings, 109 LA 974 (Gordinier, 1997); Aircraft Braking Sys., 109 LA 52 (Strasshofer, 1997); Hackett Brass Foundry, 107 LA 1199 (Allen, 1996); Trane Co., 106 LA 1018 (Kindig, 1996); Mason & Hanger-Silas Mason Co., 106 LA 636 (Moore, 1996); Thermo King Corp., 106 LA 481 (McGury, 1996); Advance Circuits, 106 LA 353 (Daly, 1996); Central Ill. Pub. Serv. Co., 105 LA 372 (Cohen, 1995); Randolph Air Force Base, 102 LA 358 (Woolf, 1993).

[89]108 LA 705 (Gentile, 1997).

[90]Advance Circuits, 106 LA 353, 355 (Daly, 1996).

In adopting such a zero-tolerance policy for actual or threatened violence, one company cited guidelines from the California Department of Industrial Relations' Division of Occupational Safety and Health.[91] These guidelines state that "[s]ome mental health professionals believe the belligerent, intimidating or threatening behavior by an employee or supervisor is an early warning sign of an individual's propensity to commit a physical assault in the future."[92]

Pursuant to such a policy, employees who make threats of physical violence in many cases are subject to the same discipline (i.e., discharge) as for actual workplace assaults.[93] Arbitrators increasingly are requiring employers to take seriously an employee's threats of physical harm.[94] In one case, the arbitrator held that the company had an obligation to remove an angry employee who made provocative remarks about the murder of employees at the post office and about getting a shotgun from home.[95] In yet another case, the employer was found to have violated its safe work environment obligation under its collective bargaining agreement when supervisors failed to stop or take action against an employee who threatened another employee with physical harm and emotional, social, and psychological distress.[96] However, some arbitrators, while upholding the discharge penalty for fighting, find acceptable a discipline of less than discharge where only oral arguments but no physical violence occurred.[97] Arbitrators also sometimes mitigate discharges where the employee's action was not intended to be "violent" or was out of character and the employee expresses regret.[98]

E. Dangerous Conditions [LA CDI 118.659; 100.552575]

Where an act is inherently dangerous, an employer does not have to prohibit employees specifically from engaging in it before taking disciplinary measures. For example, employees do not have to be told at a safety meeting that rolling under a railroad car on the track is unsafe. An employee may be disciplined for doing so without having been given prior warning.[99]

In workplaces with contaminated air, OSHA regulations require the use of respirators. Company regulations prohibiting employees who must wear respirators from having beards have been upheld.[100] Another arbitrator substantially upheld a rule that respirator users must be clean-shaven or must buy their own respirators that would permit a proper seal over a beard.[101]

---

[91]California Dep't of Industrial Relations, Division of Occupational Safety & Health, *Guidelines for Workplace Security* (1995).

[92]Golden States Foods Corp., 108 LA 705, 707 (Gentile, 1997).

[93]*Id. See also* Butler Restoration Inc., 109 LA 614 (Kanner, 1997); Levi Strauss & Co., 109 LA 255 (Eisenmenger, 1997). *But see* Marriott Educ. Servs., 112 LA 998 (Franckiewicz, 1999) (fighting should not always result in automatic discharge).

[94]Eaton Corp., 114 LA 1007 (Hodgson, 2000).

[95]Trane Co., 106 LA 1018 (Kindig, 1996) (grievant's angry remarks, together with two other serious charges, were considered just cause to discharge).

[96]Randolph Air Force Base, 102 LA 358 (Woolf, 1993).

[97]Mason & Hanger Corp., 109 LA 957 (Jennings, 1998).

[98]R.R. Donnelly Printing, 114 LA 5 (Bognanno, 1999).

[99]Snap-On Tools Corp., 104 LA 180 (Cipolla, 1995).

[100]Mission Foods, 111 LA 501 (Snider, 1998); Dyno Nobel, 104 LA 376 (Hilgert, 1995). *See also* Arizona Opera Co., 105 LA 1126 (Wyman, 1996).

[101]Mississippi Power & Light Co., 92 LA 1161 (Taylor, 1989). *See also* Dyno Nobel, 104 LA 376 (Hilgert, 1995).

But one arbitrator invalidated a rule requiring a medical evaluation for respirator users because the joint health and safety committee had not passed on the rule, and the OSHA standard on which the employer relied was not mandatory.[102]

Citing management's right to direct the workforce in a safe and productive manner, an arbitrator upheld a rule restricting the playing of radios in a power plant.[103] However, another arbitrator modified a company rule banning radio use, instead allowing, with certain restrictions, the use of radios with earphones.[104] Safety rules not only may require observance of certain procedures and practices by employees, but they also may impose a duty on employees to refrain from working under potentially unsafe conditions.[105]

4. Employee Obligations in Safety and Health Matters
[LA CDI 124.70; 100.552575]

Employees have a correlative duty to cooperate in maintaining a safe and healthy work environment. This duty may be imposed by contract, usually in the form of an agreement to cooperate in promoting safety;[106] by a state safety code;[107] or by OSHA. It also may be imposed directly on employees by safety rules promulgated under management's reserved rulemaking authority.[108] In addition, employees have inherent obligations to protect themselves and promote workplace safety.[109] An employee's obligation to comply with safety rules may carry with it the responsibility to bear or share the cost of safety apparel required by such rules.[110]

An employee who failed to comply with a rule requiring him to report promptly any injury suffered on the job was held to have been properly discharged. The arbitrator noted that employer rules requiring prompt reporting of on-the-job injuries are reasonably related to the orderly and safe op-

---

[102]Sohio Oil Co., 92 LA 201 (Strasshofer, 1988).

[103]Southern Ind. Gas & Elec. Co., 88 LA 132 (Franke, 1986).

[104]Creative Prods., 89 LA 777 (McDonald, 1987).

[105]See Porcelain Metals Corp., 73 LA 1133, 1139 (Roberts, 1979); Gold Kist, 62 LA 139, 143, 145 (Rutherford, 1974); FMC Corp., 45 LA 293, 295 (McCoy, 1965); Reserve Mining Co., 38 LA 443, 449 (Sembower, 1962); Rome Kraft Co., 61–3 ARB ¶8792 (Hawley, 1961).

[106]See ASARCO, Inc. v. NLRB, 805 F.2d 194, 123 LRRM 2985 (6th Cir. 1986). See also Eastern Coal Corp., 89 LA 759, 759–60 (Hewitt, 1987); Monarch Mach. Tool Co., 54 LA 1084, 1086–87 (Seinsheimer, 1971); Airco Alloys & Carbide Co., 51 LA 156 (Kesselman, 1968); U.S. Plywood-Champion Papers, 50 LA 115, 118 (Jenkins, 1968); Lone Star Steel Co., 48 LA 1094, 1094–95 (Jenkins, 1967).

[107]See United States Borax & Chem. Corp., 36 LA 970, 973 (Keeler, 1961).

[108]See U.S. Plywood-Champion Papers, 50 LA 115, 121 (Jenkins, 1968); Rome Kraft Co., 61–3 ARB ¶8792 (Hawley, 1961).

[109]See General Elec. Co., 31 LA 386, 389 (Sutermeister, 1958). As a corollary, employees should not be penalized for protesting hazards. Reserve Mining Co., 55 LA 648, 652 (Sembower, 1970). Cf. Globe-Union, Inc., 75 LA 682, 688–89 (Schedler, 1980). See also Leckelt v. Board of Comm'rs, 909 F.2d 820, 53 FEP Cases 1136 (5th Cir. 1990) (firing of a male homosexual nurse, who refused to turn over his HIV test results, held not to be an unlawful handicap discrimination, where the hospital had a substantial and compelling interest in protecting patients and employees from spread of communicable diseases).

[110]See Superior Plating, 109 LA 144 (Neigh, 1997) (employer could limit amount it would pay for safety glasses and require employees to pay extra costs for special frames or lens upgrades). See also Sky-Top Sunroofs, 89 LA 547 (Newmark, 1987) (employer could require

eration of its business. They are designed to facilitate immediate aid to an injured worker, to establish a record of the injury in order to investigate, detect, and remedy any hazardous condition, and to furnish notice to appropriate officials charged with responsibility for determining whether the injuries are compensable.[111]

5. REFUSAL TO OBEY ORDERS—THE SAFETY AND HEALTH EXCEPTIONS

A. Safety and Health Exception to the Obey Now–Grieve Later Doctrine [LA CDI 118.659; 118.6521; 100.552540; 100.552575]

It is a well-established principle that employees (1) must obey management's orders and carry out their job assignments, even if such assignments are believed to violate the agreement; and (2) then turn to the grievance procedure for relief.[112] An exception to this "obey now–grieve later" doctrine exists where obedience would involve an unusual or abnormal safety or health hazard.[113] But this exception has been held inapplicable where the hazard is inherent in the employee's job.[114] Moreover, when the exception is invoked, the employee must show that a safety or health hazard was the real

---

employees to pay 50% of the cost of one pair of safety shoes up to a $25 maximum); Nekoosa Corp., 83 LA 676, 680 (Flaten, 1984) (employer improperly placed limit on amount allowed for purchase of safety shoes, where contract required employer to pay the cost without limitation, but due to abuse of the program, employer may inspect such shoes to determine if they are appropriate); Hater Indus., 73 LA 1025, 1027–28 (Ipavec, 1979) (employees rather than employer had the obligation to pay for safety shoes required by OSHA, because the agreement did not specifically impose such obligation on the employer, the employer was supported by bargaining history, and the employer was "not bound to purchase safety shoes for employees by a past practice of supplying employees with safety equipment such as glasses, aprons and gloves"); Ingram Mfg. Co., 70 LA 1269, 1272 (Johannes, 1978) (contract language and bargaining history supported employer); Potash Co. of Am., 70 LA 194, 194–95 (Harr, 1978); Mobil Oil Corp., 69 LA 828, 830–31 (Ray, 1977) ("the question of who pays for safety shoes is to be resolved . . . at the bargaining table," and both past practice and bargaining history supported the employer as to this item of apparel); Hugo Neu-Proler Co., 69 LA 751, 754–55 (Richman, 1977); Baggett Transp. Co., 68 LA 82, 84 (Crane, 1977); Alabama By-Prods. Corp., 61 LA 1286, 1289 (Eyraud, 1972).

[111]Pioneer Flour Mills, 107 LA 379 (Bankston, 1996) (employee also had dismal employment record and had been given notice that further rule violations could subject him to discharge).

[112]See Chapter 5, section 14.A., "Use of Grievance Procedure Versus Self-Help."

[113]See Leland Oil Mill, 91 LA 905, 907 (Nicholas, Jr., 1988); West Penn Power Co., 89 LA 1227, 1230–32 (Hogler, 1987); Gillette Co., 79 LA 953, 961–62 (Bard, 1982); T&J Indus., 79 LA 697, 702 (Clark, 1982); Jacksonville Shipyards, 79 LA 587, 590 (McCollister, 1982); Entenmann's Bakery of Fla., 77 LA 1080, 1084 (Ness, 1981); McLung-Logan Equip. Co., 71 LA 513, 515 (Wahl, 1978); Sperry Rand Corp., 51 LA 709, 711 (Rohman, 1968); U.S. Plywood-Champion Papers, 50 LA 115, 123–24 (Jenkins, 1968); Dodge Mfg. Corp., 49 LA 429, 429–30 (Epstein, 1967); Hercules, Inc., 48 LA 788, 793–95 (Hopson, 1967); Alliance Mach. Co., 48 LA 457, 461 (Dworkin, 1967).

[114]See United Dairymen of Ariz., Case No. 97-26632 CSR2, 1998 WL 1041368 (Oberstein, 1998); Consolidated Edison Co. of N.Y., 71 LA 238, 240, 243 (Kelly, 1978); Tenneco Chems., 48 LA 1082, 1084 (House, 1967); Alliance Mach. Co., 48 LA 457, 461 (Dworkin, 1967); Duval Corp., 43 LA 102, 105 (Meyers, 1964); Bethlehem Steel Co., 41 LA 1323, 1326 (Porter, 1963); Heckett Eng'g Co., 38 LA 375, 378 (Anrod, 1962); American Radiator & Standard Sanitary Corp., 26 LA 915, 917 (Duff, 1956). Cf. Goodyear Tire & Rubber Co., 45 LA 772, 775 (Rohman, 1965); American Fork & Hoe Co., 5 LA 300, 302–04 (Gilden, 1945).

reason for the refusal,[115] and that the alleged hazard existed at the time of the employee's refusal.[116]

The exception may apply as well where the employee asserts that to perform as ordered would jeopardize the safety of others.[117] However, even assuming that there is a safety hazard sufficient to justify an employee's refusal to perform the work assigned, this right of refusal applies only to the employee assigned to do the work; other employees not assigned the work (and not affected by the unsafe condition) would not be justified in resorting to self-help (such as walking off the job) instead of using the grievance procedures.[118]

A contract clause may expressly deal with the right of an employee to refuse to work in abnormally hazardous conditions. Such a clause may give the employee the right, after reporting the alleged hazard to the supervisor, to file a grievance at an advanced step for preferred handling, or to be relieved of the job and, at management's discretion, to be assigned to another available position.[119]

The recognized "safety and health exception" to the obey now–grieve later doctrine also has been held applicable where the hazard arises from the employee's own medical condition rather than from the working conditions.[120] Several arbitrators have set aside or mitigated discipline of an allegedly insubordinate employee, where the employee's ability to perform the task as directed by the employer was compromised by medical restrictions or conditions of which the employer was aware.[121]

B. The Range of Arbitral Reasoning
[LA CDI 118.659; 118.6521; 100.552540; 100.552575]

When an employee refuses to obey orders or to perform assignments because of alleged safety or health hazards, and has been disciplined because management concluded that no unusual hazard exists, arbitrators must determine whether the employee's refusal is justified.[122] The arbitral search

---

[115]See Tenneco Chems., 48 LA 1082, 1084–85 (House, 1967); Goodrich-Gulf Chems., 48 LA 963, 965 (Rohman, 1967); Alliance Mach. Co., 48 LA 457, 461 (Dworkin, 1967); Interchemical Corp., 48 LA 124, 131 (Yagoda, 1967); Sealtest Foods, 47 LA 848, 854 (Mullin, 1966). See also Cyclops Corp., 107 LA 631 (Stanton, 1996); Colletti Trucking, 105 LA 507 (White, 1995); Dye Golf Servs., 104 LA 449 (Darrow, 1995); National Maint. & Repair, 101 LA 1115 (Fowler, 1993).

[116]City of Los Angeles, Cal., 111 LA 406 (Daly, 1998).

[117]A.M. Castle & Co., 41 LA 666, 670 (Sembower, 1963).

[118]Rittman Nursing Ctr., 113 LA 284 (Kelman, 1999); Metal Specialty Co., 43 LA 849, 853–54 (Volz, 1964) (citing and quoting from Ford Motor Co., 41 LA 608, 615 (Platt, 1963)).

[119]See, e.g., Bethlehem Steel Corp., 49 LA 1203 (Strongin, 1968); Lone Star Steel Co., 48 LA 1094, 1094–95 (Jenkins, 1967); Erie Mining Co., 46 LA 43, 50 (Dworkin, 1965); U.S. Steel Corp., 45 LA 426, 428 (Garrett, 1965); Jones & Laughlin Steel Corp., 43 LA 583, 585 (Duff, 1964). See also CF Motor Transp., 103 LA 303 (Johnson, 1994) (contract required that a reasonable person would have believed the equipment was unsafe under the circumstances confronting the employee); Halstead & Mitchell, 74 LA 946, 946–47 (Odom, Jr., 1980).

[120]Pittsburg & Midway Coal Mining Co., 106 LA 624 (Alexander, 1996).

[121]Minnesota Mining & Mfg., 112 LA 1055 (Bankston, 1999); Health Plus, 110 LA 618 (Duff, 1998); Lerio Corp., Case No. 98-16869, 1998 WL 1093475 (Grooms, 1998).

[122]By definition, a "hazard" is "potential," and determining when the "potential" is sufficient to justify an employee in refusing to obey an order depends on the facts.

for a definitive evaluative standard has proven elusive. Arbitration decisions are couched in such language as: an "employee's reasonable belief" that unusual danger is involved is enough;[123] the employee "sincerely and genuinely" feared for his life;[124] the "employee's good faith belief of the existence of a hazard does not suffice," but the "hazard must be demonstrated to exist";[125] the employee erroneously but "actually entertained" the fear of danger to his life;[126] if the employee "is sincere in his belief of danger" and "makes a 'reasonable' appraisal of the potential hazards, he is protected in his decision not to act, regardless of whether later on, in fact, it should be established that no hazard existed";[127] the "standard to be applied is not the cowardice or bravery of anyone";[128] "although their fears were based on misconceptions, they were nonetheless real";[129] the employee must obey the order unless there is a "real and imminent danger to life and limb";[130] the fact that a fellow employee is an unsafe driver was "ample reason" for grievant's fears and therefore there existed "valid and reasonable grounds for refusing the assignment";[131] considering the grievants' inadequate training and experience, "the work assignment constituted *for them* an abnormal hazard";[132] although there were some conditions "which required correction and attention in order to maintain the required standards of safety," nevertheless "there were no imminently dangerous conditions which presented a hazard to their safety and health so as to justify them in refusing to work";[133] although the em-

---

[123]Hercules, Inc., 48 LA 788, 794–95 (Hopson, 1967). *See also* Beverly Enters., 100 LA 522, 529 (Berquist, 1993).

[124]Lone Star Steel Co., 48 LA 1094, 1097 (Jenkins, 1967). *See also* Leland Oil Mill, 91 LA 905, 907 (Nicholas, Jr., 1988); Beth Energy Mines, 87 LA 577, 581 (Hewitt, 1986); Indianapolis Power & Light Co., 87 LA 559, 562 (Kates, 1986); Minnesota Mining & Mfg. Co., 85 LA 1179, 1182 (White, 1985); Imperial Foods, 69 LA 320, 324 (Crawford, 1977).

[125]Wilcolator Co., 44 LA 847, 852 (Altieri, 1964). *See also* National Maint. & Repair, 101 LA 1115 (Fowler, 1993) (noting the lack of any objective criteria to substantiate the alleged safety concerns); Knauf Fiber Glass GmbH, 101 LA 823 (Ipavec, 1993) (employee failed to establish there was an actual risk of personal injury); Northern Automatic Elec. Foundry, 90 LA 620, 624 (Poindexter, 1987) (arbitrator found no safety hazard or, if it existed, it was corrected before employee left); Amoco Oil Co., 87 LA 889, 894 (Schwartz, 1986) (dismissal upheld; no unusual or abnormal safety hazard existed when right safety equipment was supplied); Consolidated Edison Co. of N.Y., 71 LA 238, 241 (Kelly, 1978); Haveg Indus., 68 LA 841, 845 (McKone, 1977) ("When . . . a claim of health hazard has been made, the one expecting the benefit of that defense must accept the burden of establishing it.").

[126]Allied Chem. Corp., 47 LA 686, 688 (Hilpert, 1966).

[127]A.M. Castle Co., 41 LA 666, 671 (Sembower, 1963). *Cf.* Dodge Mfg. Corp., 49 LA 429, 429–31 (Epstein, 1967).

[128]Goodyear Tire & Rubber Co., 45 LA 772, 775 (Rohman, 1965).

[129]New York Shipbuilding Co., 39 LA 1186, 1188 (Crawford, 1963). *See also* Halstead Metal Prods., 49 LA 325, 330 (Wagner, 1967).

[130]Pennsylvania R.R., 45 LA 522, 522–23 (Seidenberg, 1965). *See also* Elliott Co., 70 LA 1013, 1016 (Lubow, 1978); Consolidated Edison Co., 61 LA 607, 609 (Turkus, 1973) (unless imminent danger to life or limb is satisfactorily demonstrated at the arbitration hearing, an "honest belief and fear of imminent bodily harm" does not immunize the employee from discipline, although it may be a mitigating factor relevant "to the quantum of the disciplinary penalty").

[131]U.S. Plywood-Champion Papers, 50 LA 115, 123–24 (Jenkins, 1968).

[132]Bethlehem Steel Corp., 49 LA 1203, 1206 (Strongin, 1968) (emphasis added). *See also* Imperial Foods, 69 LA 320, 323–24 (Crawford, 1977).

[133]International Salt Co., 40 LA 1285, 1291–92 (Dworkin, 1963). *See also* Northern Automatic Elec. Foundry, 90 LA 620, 624 (Poindexter, 1987); Roemer Indus., 86 LA 232, 234 (Duff, 1986).

HOW ARBITRATION WORKS Ch. 16.5.C.

ployee "honestly believed" that there would be unnecessary danger if he complied with the work order, "it was not so clearly and evidently unsafe" that he could disobey after failing to protest through the grievance procedure;[134] the hazards were "neither so compelling nor the opportunities for their correction so hopeless as to require nothing less than an abandonment of the grievance procedure";[135] grievant was "entirely sincere" in questioning the safety of the crew, but his concern was not "well founded";[136] there must be "a reasonable basis" for the allegation that the assignment is dangerous and "at least *prima facie* evidence" that the work is unsafe, but the evidence should be "more than a mere presumption";[137] a refusal is justifiable only if the situation, viewed by a "reasonable prudent person," can be considered an imminent danger;[138] despite a personnel manual that permitted delay in performance of an assignment if the "employee believes" its performance "cannot be carried out without unreasonably endangering his health or safety," "the belief of the employee must be a reasonable one and have a rational basis, . . . [it] cannot be fanciful or contrary to all known fact."[139]

Thus, the spectrum of arbitral reasoning appears to range from the purely subjective test of what the particular employee "honestly" or "sincerely" believed as to the presence of a hazard, to the "cold facts" approach of requiring a showing of actual hazard with a "real and imminent" danger to life and limb.

Arbitrators also disagree on which party bears the burden of proof to establish the safety and health exception. Some arbitrators hold that the employer "bears the burden of proving that the grievant's concerns were not reasonable."[140] Other arbitrators conclude that the employee must prove "reasonable grounds" for believing a job will be abnormally and immediately dangerous.[141]

C. The "Reasonable Person" Approach
[LA CDI 118.659; 118.6521; 100.552540; 100.552575]

In deciding cases in which employees refuse to obey orders allegedly because of the risk of injury, arbitrators often consider the mental state of the employee at the time the employee allegedly feared for his or her safety or health, but do not focus on whether the perceived danger actually existed.[142] Nevertheless, most arbitrators do require that the employee's fear be "reasonable." In applying this "reasonable person" approach, arbitrators usually attempt to ascertain whether the facts and circumstances known to

---

[134]Duval Corp., 43 LA 102, 105 (Meyers, 1964).
[135]New York Tel. Co., 42 LA 1217, 1223 (Stockman, 1964).
[136]W.P. Fuller & Co., 30 LA 545, 547 (Cobb, 1959).
[137]Marble Prods. Co., 40 LA 247, 253 (Marshall, 1963).
[138]Georgia-Pacific Corp., 106 LA 27, 32 (Kahn, 1995).
[139]Customs Serv., 68 LA 297, 301–02 (Nicolau, 1977). *See also* U.S. Steel Corp., 69 LA 39, 42–43 (Dunsford, 1977).
[140]Peoples Natural Gas Co., 107 LA 882 (Zobrak, 1996).
[141]City of Los Angeles, Cal., 111 LA 406 (Daly, 1998); Coors Brewing Co., Case No. 97-21396, 1998 WL 686614 (Nicholas, Jr., 1998); Pittsburg & Midway Coal Mining Co., 106 LA 624 (Alexander, 1996); CF Motor Transp., 103 LA 303 (Johnson, 1994).
[142]Bargar Metal Fabricating Co., 110 LA 119, 123 (Oberdank, 1998).

the employee at the time of the refusal to work would have caused a reasonable person to fear for his or her safety or health.[143] This view was summarized by one arbitrator as follows:

> The principle . . . is that an employee may refuse to carry out a particular work assignment if, at the time he is given the work assignment, he reasonably believes that by carrying out such work assignment he will endanger his safety or health. In such an instance the employee has the duty, not only of stating that he believes there is a risk to his safety or health, and the reason for believing so, but he also has the burden, if called upon, of showing by appropriate evidence that he had a reasonable basis for his belief. In the case of dispute, as is the case here, the question to be decided is not whether he actually would have suffered injury but whether he had a reasonable basis for believing so.[144]

D. Must Employees Explain Their Refusal to Perform an Assigned Task? [LA CDI 118.659; 118.6521; 100.552540; 100.552575]

Ordinarily, employees in refusal-to-obey cases express their fear of danger, and thus no question is presented as to whether the burden is on management to elicit, or on employees to express, the reasons for refusing to perform an assigned task. The question has arisen in a few cases, however. In the passage quoted above, the arbitrator appears to place the burden on employees to state not only their fears, but also their reasons for being fearful, and to be prepared to substantiate their statements with evidence.[145]

Other arbitrators would be more demanding of the employer in some circumstances. Thus, where an employee requested additional help for an assigned task but did not articulate his safety fears, the arbitrator took the approach that it did "not seem unreasonable" to impose a slightly higher standard on the company to ask an uncommunicative employee why he refused to work, once such refusal was evident.[146] However, another arbitrator thought that the failure of management to ask employees for an explanation did not "excuse them forever from making one."[147] At least one arbitrator has

---

[143]One arbitrator has applied a slightly different standard in an insubordination case, applying an "unreasonable refusal" standard in place of the "reasonable person" standard. Instead of analyzing whether the employee was reasonable in his safety concerns, the arbitrator concentrated on whether the company could demonstrate that the employee's refusal to perform the requested work was unreasonable. Peoples Natural Gas Co., 107 LA 882, 885 (Zobrak, 1996). Another arbitrator has required "good faith" on the part of the employee who refuses to work for safety reasons. The good-faith requirement appears to be somewhat akin to the reasonable person approach. Georgia-Pacific Corp., 106 LA 27, 32 (Kahn, 1995).

[144]Laclede Gas Co., 39 LA 833, 839 (Bothwell, 1962). See Bargar Metal Fabricating Co., 110 LA 119, 123 (Oberdank, 1998); Pittsburg & Midway Coal Mining Co., 106 LA 624, 630 (Alexander, 1996); Minnesota Mining & Mfg. Co., 85 LA 1179, 1182–83 (White, 1985); Jacksonville Shipyards, 79 LA 587, 590 (McCollister, 1982); United Parcel Serv., 78 LA 836, 840–41 (McAllister, 1982); Entenmann's Bakery of Fla., 77 LA 1080, 1084 (Ness, 1981); Fulton Seafood Indus., 74 LA 620, 623 (Volz, 1980); Hayes-Albion Corp., 73 LA 819, 824–25 (Foster, 1979).

[145]Laclede Gas Co., 39 LA 833, 839 (Bothwell, 1962). Accord Georgia-Pacific Corp., 106 LA 27, 32 (Kahn, 1995); Leland Oil Mill, 91 LA 905, 907 (Nicholas, Jr., 1988); Northern Automatic Elec. Foundry, 90 LA 620, 625 (Poindexter, 1987); American Radiator & Standard Sanitary Corp., 41 LA 755, 759 (Stouffer, 1963).

[146]Hercules, Inc., 48 LA 788, 795 (Hopson, 1967). But see Eaton, Yale & Towne, 50 LA 517, 521 (Levy, 1968) (the employee did not express his fears and the company did not inquire; held that insubordination justified the suspension).

[147]A.M. Castle & Co., 41 LA 666, 671 (Sembower, 1963).

held that an employee's delay in explaining his refusal to carry out orders on the grounds of safety may be strong evidence that the employee was not justified in his refusal.[148]

The burden to explain or clarify also may shift from employee to employer as a situation develops. For instance, where the company work rules provided that employees should go to their supervisor if they believed a task would require them to violate a safety rule, an arbitrator concluded that once an employee questioned the safety of an assignment, it became the supervisor's responsibility to initiate discussion and to give such advice and explanation as might be required.[149]

E. The Statutory Picture: LMRA §502, OSH Act, NLRA §7, and the STAA [LA CDI 94.553; 100.30]

i. Section 502 of the Labor Management Relations Act
[LA CDI 94.553; 100.30]

Section 502 of the Labor Management Relations Act (LMRA) provides that "the quitting of labor by an employee or employees in good faith because of abnormally dangerous conditions for work at the place of employment of such employee or employees [shall not] be deemed a strike . . . ."[150]

In its 1974 *Gateway Coal*[151] decision, involving the enjoinability of a strike rather than any question of employee discipline, the U.S. Supreme Court held both that the arbitration clause in a collective bargaining agreement was broad enough to cover safety disputes and that it gave "rise to an implied no-strike obligation." The Supreme Court then went on to state that Section 502 "provides a limited exception to an express or implied no-strike obligation," but that "a union seeking to justify a contractually prohibited work stoppage under § 502 must present 'ascertainable, objective evidence supporting its conclusion that an abnormally dangerous condition for work exists.'"[152]

In *TNS Inc.*,[153] the National Labor Relations Board (NLRB, or the Board) found that employees who manufactured radioactive depleted uranium metal products did not objectively believe they were threatened with abnormally dangerous working conditions. Relying on *Gateway Coal*, the Board held that employees must either reasonably believe "(1) that inherently dangerous conditions in the subject workplace had changed significantly for the worse . . . *or* (2) that the cumulative effects of exposure to [radioactive and/or toxic] substances had reached the point at which any further exposure would pose

---

[148]Bi-State Dev. Agency, 108 LA 166, 171 (Bailey, 1997).

[149]Rome Kraft Co., 61–3 ARB ¶8792 (Hawley, 1961).

[150]29 U.S.C. §143.

[151]Gateway Coal Co. v. Mine Workers, 414 U.S. 368, 374–83, 85 LRRM 2049 (1974).

[152]*Id.* at 385, 386–87. The Supreme Court rejected the U.S. Court of Appeals for the Third Circuit's view that "an honest belief, no matter how unjustified, in the existence of 'abnormally dangerous conditions for work' necessarily invokes the protection of § 502." *Id.* at 386. The Court stated that "[i]f the courts require no objective evidence that such conditions actually obtain, they face a wholly speculative inquiry into the motives of the workers." *Id.*

[153]309 NLRB 1348, 142 LRRM 1046 (1992) (*TNS I*).

an unacceptable risk of future injury . . . ."[154] On appeal, the U.S. Court of Appeals for the District of Columbia Circuit remanded the case to the NLRB to clarify its interpretation of Section 502, because only two of the four Board members had held that the employees had to show either a significant change for the worse in their working conditions, or that the cumulative effect of their exposure to depleted uranium had reached the point where further exposure would pose an unacceptable risk.[155] Because of the lack of majority support for the standard applied, the circuit court directed the Board to articulate a majority-supported standard applying Section 502 to employees exposed to low-level radiation.[156]

On remand,[157] the NLRB panel decided not to adopt either test set forth in *TNS I*. Instead, the Board stated that where employees stop working because of alleged cumulative, slow-acting dangers to their health and safety, they are protected under Section 502 of the LMRA only if: (1) they believed in good faith that their working conditions were abnormally dangerous; (2) their belief was a contributing cause of the work stoppage; (3) their belief was supported by ascertainable, objective evidence; and (4) the perceived danger posed an immediate threat of harm to employee health or safety.[158] Under this standard, the NLRB found that the employees, who stopped working when the collective bargaining agreement expired, had engaged in a protected work stoppage.[159] The Board, in a split-panel decision, concluded that the employees' concerns about abnormally dangerous conditions were *a* cause of their work stoppage, that they were not economic strikers, and that the company committed an unfair labor practice when it hired permanent replacements.[160] The U.S. Court of Appeals for the Sixth Circuit affirmed the NLRB's four-part standard, but concluded that there was no substantial evidence on the record considered as a whole to support the Board's finding that the "objective evidence supported the employees' belief that their workplace has become too dangerous to work in."[161] However, rather than remanding

---

[154]*Id.* at 1357–58 (emphasis in original). The Board's opinion was based on considerable evidence, but especially influenced by the employees' failure to consult with the state radiation safety enforcement agency before the walkout. *See id.* at 1359.

[155]Oil, Chem., & Atomic Workers v. NLRB (TNS Inc.), 46 F.3d 82, 84, 148 LRRM 2461 (D.C. Cir. 1995). A third Board member criticized that standard but concurred in the result because working conditions were not the "sole cause" of the walkout. *Id.* The court of appeals found that this criticism was "hopelessly shortsighted" and would lead to "absurd" and "ridiculous" results. *Id.* at 92.

[156]*Id.* at 92–93 (citing Food & Commercial Workers Local 150-A v. NLRB (Dubuque Packing Co.), 880 F.2d 1422, 1436–37, 132 LRRM 2104 (D.C. Cir. 1989)).

[157]TNS, Inc., 329 NLRB 602, 603 n.7, 166 LRRM 1018 (1999) (*TNS II*) (the plurality's two-pronged standard in *TNS I* "place[d] an unreasonably heavy burden on employees to substantiate their good-faith belief that working conditions [were] abnormally dangerous").

[158]*Id.* at 605.

[159]*Id.* at 606 (rejecting explicitly the dissenting member's opinion that protection under §502 should only result when it is shown that the employee health and safety concerns were the "proximate cause" of the work stoppage).

[160]*TNS II*, 329 NLRB 602, 610–11, 166 LRRM 1018 (1999), *order vacated*, 296 F.3d 384, 170 LRRM 2474 (6th Cir. 2002). The NLRB found that the company violated §8(a)(1) and (3) of the NLRA because it failed to reinstate the employees when they offered to return to work almost 9 months after initiating the work stoppage, as well as §8(a)(5) for withdrawing recognition from the union and refusing to bargain with it following a decertification petition the company received from a majority of the replacement employees it hired. *Id.* at 602.

[161]TNS Inc. v. NLRB, 296 F.3d 384, 170 LRRM 2474 (6th Cir. 2002).

the case for further consideration, the court vacated the Board's decision because of the Board's "inexcusable delay" (18 years) in reaching the subject decision and the potential prejudice to the employer from any back pay and reinstatement order.[162]

ii. The Occupational Safety and Health Act [LA CDI 94.553; 100.30]

In 1980, the Supreme Court handed down its *Whirlpool*[163] decision upholding a regulation issued under the OSH Act, which provided in substance that it "is the right of an employee to choose not to perform his assigned task because of a reasonable apprehension of death or serious injury coupled with a reasonable belief that no less drastic alternative is available."[164] The Court ruled that the regulation "does not conflict with the general pattern of federal labor legislation in the area of occupational safety and health," because both the National Labor Relations Act (NLRA)[165] and the LMRA give "workers a right, under certain circumstances, to walk off their jobs when faced with hazardous conditions."[166]

Since *Whirlpool*, the federal courts have continued to protect the rights of employees who refused to perform work when their refusal is based on a "reasonable apprehension of death or serious injury coupled with a reasonable belief that no less drastic alternative is available."[167] In a case decided by the U.S. Court of Appeals for the Tenth Circuit,[168] an employee who worked as a cement finisher refused to go up in a gondola because of repeated problems with the gondola and scaffolding and the employer's failure to repair the machinery. The court affirmed the trial court's finding that the employee had a "reasonable and good faith belief . . . that the gondola was both defective and hazardous and that riding in it would present an imminent risk of serious bodily injury or death."[169]

---

[162]*Id.* at 404, 170 LRRM at 2490.

[163]Whirlpool Corp. v. Marshall, 445 U.S. 1, 8 OSH Cases 1001 (1980) (upholding 29 C.F.R. §1977.12(b)(2)).

[164]*Id.* at 3–4. Under the specific language of the regulation, "an employer would not ordinarily be in violation of [the OSH Act] by taking action to discipline an employee for refusing to perform normal job activities because of alleged safety or health hazards." *Id.* at 4 n.3 (quoting 29 C.F.R. §1977.12(b)(1)). However, discipline could violate the OSH Act "[i]f the employee, with no reasonable alternative, refuses in good faith to expose himself to the dangerous condition," and the condition is "of such a nature that a reasonable person, under the circumstances then confronting the employee, would conclude that there is a real danger of death or serious injury and that there is insufficient time due to the urgency of the situation, to eliminate the danger through resort to regular statutory enforcement channels." *Id.* at 4 n.3 (quoting §1977.12(b)(2)). The Court cautioned that "any employee who acts in reliance on the regulation runs the risk of discharge or reprimand in the event a court subsequently finds that he acted unreasonably or in bad faith." *Id.* at 21.

[165]29 U.S.C. §151 et seq.

[166]*Whirlpool*, 445 U.S. at 17 n.29. Under §7 of the NLRA, "employees have a protected right to strike over safety issues." *Id.* (citing NLRB v. Washington Aluminum Co., 370 U.S. 9, 50 LRRM 2235 (1962)). Moreover, the effect of §502 of the LMRA "is to create an exception to a no-strike obligation in a collective-bargaining agreement." *Id.* (citing Gateway Coal Co. v. Mine Workers, 414 U.S. 368, 385, 85 LRRM 2049 (1974)).

[167]*Id.* at 3–4.

[168]Donovan v. Hahner, Foreman & Harness, 736 F.2d 1421–22, 11 OSH Cases 1977 (10th Cir. 1984).

[169]*Id.* at 1428–29.

iii. Section 7 of the National Labor Relations Act
[LA CDI 94.553; 100.30]

Section 7 of the NLRA gives employees the right to engage in "concerted activities for the purpose of collective bargaining or other mutual aid or protection."[170] If employees are subject to a collective bargaining agreement, their objection to unsafe working conditions may be considered as "concerted activity" under the NLRB's *Interboro*[171] doctrine, but may not necessarily be protected under Section 7 of the NLRA.[172] In *City Disposal Systems*,[173] the collective bargaining agreement expressly provided that the employer "shall not require employees to take out . . . any vehicle that is not in safe operating condition[,]" and it "shall not be a violation of this Agreement where employees refuse to operate such equipment unless such refusal is unjustified."[174] Because the employee "reasonably and honestly invoked his right to avoid driving unsafe trucks, his action was concerted[,]" but the Supreme Court stated further that it "may be that the collective bargaining agreement prohibits an employee from refusing to drive a truck that he reasonably believes to be unsafe, but that is, in fact, perfectly safe. If so, [the employee's] action was concerted but unprotected."[175]

---

[170]29 U.S.C. §157.

[171]Interboro Contractors, 157 NLRB 1295, 61 LRRM 1537 (1966), *enf'd*, 388 F.2d 495, 67 LRRM 2083 (2d Cir. 1967).

[172]*See* NLRB v. City Disposal Sys., 465 U.S. 822, 837–41, 115 LRRM 3193 (1984). The Court warned:

> The fact that an activity is concerted . . . does not necessarily mean that an employee can engage in the activity with impunity. An employee may engage in concerted activity in such an abusive manner that he loses the protection of §7. . . . Furthermore, if an employer does not wish to tolerate certain methods by which employees invoke their collectively bargained rights, he is free to negotiate a provision in his collective-bargaining agreement that limits the availability of such methods.

Id. at 837 (citations omitted) (mentioning no-strike provisions as one possible type of limitation).

[173]NLRB v. City Disposal Sys., 465 U.S. 822, 115 LRRM 3193 (1984).

[174]*Id.* at 824–25. The employee had been discharged for refusing to drive an allegedly unsafe truck, and the Court noted the NLRB's rationale that an individual employee's assertion of a contractual right is an extension of the concerted action that produced the agreement and affects the rights of all employees covered by the agreement. *Id.* at 824–26. In upholding the *Interboro* doctrine, the Supreme Court stated:

> As long as the employee's statement or action is based on a reasonable and honest belief that he is being, or has been, asked to perform a task that he is not required to perform under his collective bargaining agreement, and the statement or action is reasonably directed toward the enforcement of a collectively bargained right, there is no justification for overturning the Board's judgment that the employee is engaged in concerted activity, just as he would have been had he filed a formal grievance.

Id. at 837. It should be noted that shortly before the Supreme Court issued its *City Disposal System* decision, the NLRB itself had held in *Meyers Industries*, 268 NLRB 493, 497, 115 LRRM 1025, 1029 (1984) (*Meyers I*), that in order for action by an individual employee to qualify as "concerted," the action must "be engaged in with or on the authority of other employees, and not solely by and on behalf of the employee himself." However, in so holding, the NLRB distinguished its *Interboro* doctrine, concluding that it applies to action taken by an employee attempting to enforce an existing collective bargaining agreement, not to situations, as in *Meyers I*, where "there is no bargaining agreement, much less any attempt to enforce one." *Id.* at 496.

[175]*City Disposal Sys.*, 465 U.S. at 841. The Supreme Court pointed out that the only issue before it, and the only issue considered by the NLRB or the U.S. Court of Appeals for the

Since the *City Disposal Systems* decision, the NLRB has considered several cases where employees have refused to perform work because of alleged unsafe conditions. Where an employee seeks to invoke a contractual right by refusing to perform work believed, in good faith, to be unsafe, the employee is engaged in protected concerted activity, and, according to the Board, any discipline for refusal to perform the work violates Section 7 of the NLRA and any strike over safety issues is protected.[176] Similarly, where an employee complains to a safety committee established pursuant to the terms of a collective bargaining agreement,[177] or raises safety-related questions during employee meetings either on the employee's own behalf,[178] or as a designated spokesperson for other employees,[179] the invocation of the contractual right to so complain or inquire, in the Board's view, provides protection under the NLRA.[180]

The NLRB standards developed and applied to adjudicate safety issues that are raised in good faith by individual employees pursuant to labor agreements have not fared well in the courts. For example, in one case, the U.S. Court of Appeals for the Second Circuit reversed the NLRB's finding that the employer did not discriminate against an employee when it refused to rehire him in the mistaken belief that he had filed a complaint with OSHA.[181] The court remanded the case to the NLRB for reevaluation under its *Meyers I* standard,[182] wherein the board held that to qualify as "concerted activity," the employee's action must "be engaged in with or on the authority of other employees, and not solely by and on behalf of the employee himself."[183] On remand, the NLRB found that a lone employee's assertion of a statutory employment right was not concerted activity, because it was too remotely

---

Sixth Circuit, was whether the employee's action was "concerted," not whether it was unprotected. *Id.* The Supreme Court remanded the case to determine whether the employee's refusal to drive an allegedly unsafe truck "was unprotected, even if concerted." *Id.* In *Irvin H. Whitehouse & Sons Co. v. NLRB*, 659 F.2d 830, 108 LRRM 2578, 2582 (7th Cir. 1981), the U.S. Court of Appeals for the Seventh Circuit held that an arbitration provision created an implied no-strike obligation as to safety issues and permitted the discharge of two employees who quit work to protest allegedly unsafe conditions. The Board found, in another case, that an employee's refusal to perform a hazardous operation where he was aware, prior to taking the job, that the job was inherently dangerous was not protected. *See* Daniel Constr. Co., 264 NLRB 770, 770–71, 111 LRRM 1321, 1321 (1982).

[176]*See* Magic Finishing Co., 323 NLRB 234, 154 LRRM 1230 (1997); California Oilfield Maint., 311 NLRB 1079, 145 LRRM 1239 (1993).

[177]*See* Union Elec. Co., 275 NLRB 389, 119 LRRM 1160 (1985).

[178]*See* Talsol Corp., 317 NLRB 290, 151 LRRM 1097 (1995).

[179]*See* Grimmway Farms, 315 NLRB 1276, 148 LRRM 1247 (1995).

[180]*See* Wabash Alloys, 282 NLRB 391, 124 LRRM 1393 (1986). *See also* Bechtel Power Corp., 277 NLRB 882, 120 LRRM 1291 (1985) (employee's good-faith complaint about noxious fumes was protected activity). For additional analysis on this topic, see Cicero, TNS, Inc.—*The National Labor Relations Board's Failed Vision of Worker Self-Help to Escape Longterm Health Threats from Workplace Carcinogens and Toxins*, 24 STETSON L. REV. 19 (1992); Estlund, *What Do Workers Want? Employee Interests, Public Interests and Freedom of Expression Under the National Labor Relations Act*, 140 U. PA. L. REV. 920, 970–74 (1992); Stephens & Clay, *Protected Concerted Activity Under the NLRA: Current Interpretation of Its Definition*, 42 LAB. L.J. 640 (1991).

[181]Ewing v. NLRB, 732 F.2d 1117, 116 LRRM 2050 (2d Cir. 1984) (*Ewing I*) (declining to enforce the Board's decision in *Herbert F. Darling, Inc.*, 267 NLRB 476, 114 LRRM 1048 (1983) (*Darling I*)).

[182]Meyers Indus., 268 NLRB 493, 115 LRRM 1025 (1984) (*Meyers I*).

[183]*Id.* at 497, 115 LRRM at 1029 (footnote omitted).

related to any collective acts.[184] The employee appealed this ruling as well, which resulted in a second remand by the Second Circuit in *Ewing II*,[185] based on the absence of a definitive agency decision.

Rejecting the Second Circuit's suggested contrary approach, the NLRB adhered to the *Meyers*[186] standard.[187] The employee again appealed in *Ewing III*,[188] but the Second Circuit affirmed the *Meyers II* ruling, concluding albeit somewhat reluctantly that it constituted a reasonable interpretation of the NLRA.[189] As a result, at least one court of appeals has refused to rule that a purely unilateral safety complaint may be concerted activity protected by Section 7 of the NLRA.[190]

As set forth previously, OSHA requires the apprehension of a reasonable person under the circumstances, and Section 502 of the LMRA requires "ascertainable, objective evidence," both statutes thus obliging employees to satisfy objective standards. In contrast, in the absence of a collective bargaining agreement prohibiting an employee from refusing to work because of an alleged safety hazard, and assuming that such a refusal would qualify as a protected concerted action, the NLRB appears to interpret Section 7 of the NLRA as incorporating "the subjective test," it thus sufficing that the particular employee acted in a good-faith belief of danger in order to be protected against punishment by the employer.[191]

---

[184]Herbert F. Darling, Inc., 273 NLRB 346, 118 LRRM 1060 (1984) (*Darling II*).

[185]Ewing v. NLRB, 768 F.2d 51, 55–56, 119 LRRM 3273 (2d Cir. 1985) (*Ewing II*) (suggesting that it would be reasonable for the NLRB to hold that individual invocation of a statutory right was sufficiently related to group action to warrant protection under the NLRA).

[186]Meyers Indus., 281 NLRB 882, 123 LRRM 1137 (1986) (*Meyers II*), enf'd sub nom. Prill v. NLRB, 835 F.2d 1481, 127 LRRM 2415 (D.C. Cir. 1987) (*Prill II*). The Board decided *Meyers II* while considering *Ewing II* on remand from the Second Circuit. *See* Ewing v. NLRB, 861 F.2d 353, 357, 129 LRRM 2853 (2d Cir. 1988) (*Ewing III*).

[187]*See* Herbert F. Darling, Inc., 287 NLRB 1356, 127 LRRM 1241 (1988) (*Darling III*).

[188]Ewing v. NLRB, 861 F.2d 353, 129 LRRM 2853 (2d Cir. 1988) (*Ewing III*).

[189]*Id.* at 357–59 (agreeing with the U.S. Court of Appeals for the District of Columbia Circuit's holding in *Prill II*, 835 F.2d at 1483–85).

[190]LaBuhn v. Bulkmatic Transp. Co., 865 F.2d 119, 123, 130 LRRM 2301 (7th Cir. 1988) (state law claim of retaliation for complaining about unsafe working conditions is not preempted by §301 of the LMRA pursuant to *Lingle v. Magic Chef*, 486 U.S. 399, 128 LRRM 2521 (1988)). *See also* Beta Steel Corp. v. NLRB, 210 F.3d 374, 2000 U.S. App. LEXIS 4112, at *11–*14 (7th Cir. Mar. 14, 2000) (unpublished), enf'g 326 NLRB 1267, 160 LRRM 1176 (1998) (employee who served as safety committee chair engaged in protected concerted activity when he cosigned a safety complaint and submitted it to the company regarding a safety issue about which he had complained earlier).

[191]For an illustrative case in which the subjective test was used or arguably used, see *Tamara Foods*, 258 NLRB 1307, 108 LRRM 1218 (1981), enf'd, 692 F.2d 1171, 111 LRRM 3003 (8th Cir. 1982), where the NLRB stated that:

Inquiry into the objective reasonableness of employees' concerted activity is neither necessary nor proper in determining whether that activity is protected. . . . Whether the protested working condition was actually as objectionable as the employees believed it to be . . . is irrelevant to whether their concerted activity is protected by the Act.

Id. at 1308. The Board stated that the fact that the employees were not represented by a union or covered by a collective bargaining agreement containing a no-strike clause was of "particular significance." *Id.* The Board also reasoned that the employer's compliance with OSHA's regulations did not negate rights of employees under §7 of the NLRA. *Id.* at 1308–09. *See* NLRB v. Modern Carpet Indus., 611 F.2d 811, 103 LRRM 2167, 2169 (10th Cir. 1979), enf'g 236 NLRB 1014, 98 LRRM 1426 (1978) (court upheld the NLRB's reinstatement order, finding that the employees believed in good faith that working with radioactive lead was dangerous and, therefore, their refusal to work was protected by §7). *See also* Union Elec. Co., 275 NLRB 389, 119 LRRM 1160 (1985). For other discussions of OSHA, §502 and/

iv. The Surface Transportation Assistance Act
[LA CDI 94.553; 100.30]

The debate over the extent to which employees are protected for refusing to work because of fear of injury has reached the circuit courts in a number of cases arising under the Surface Transportation Assistance Act of 1982 (STAA).[192] The issue presented there is under what circumstances a driver may refuse to operate a motor vehicle. In one case, a driver refused to operate an oil truck because he sometimes would have to stand in the street to unwind the delivery hose and pass it beneath the truck.[193] Because the driver offered nothing more than a subjective fear of imminent physical danger, the court ruled that his refusal to operate the truck was not protected by the STAA.[194] However, another driver's refusal to drive a tractor trailer hauling a 20-ton load was found to be protected, because objective evidence supported the driver's belief that the tractor lacked power to haul the load at a safe speed on an interstate highway.[195] In still another case, the U.S. Court of Appeals for the Fourth Circuit ruled that a driver who stopped for a nap after having been awake for 19.5 hours was entitled to STAA protection.[196]

F. Compatibility of Arbitration Award With Employee Statutory Rights [LA CDI 94.553; 100.30]

In most cases of a claimed violation of employees' contractual health and safety rights, an arbitration award will not be deemed inconsistent with the employees' statutory rights unless the arbitration award holds employees to a stricter or higher standard than the statute imposes. As the previous discussion has shown, arbitrators at one end of the spectrum excuse employees from observing the obey now–grieve later rule if they meet the purely subjective test of what the particular employee believed, while arbitrators at

---

or §7 standards, see George, *Divided We Stand: Concerted Activity and the Maturing NLRA,* 56 Geo. Wash. L. Rev. 509 (1988); Karcher, *The Supreme Court Takes One Step Forward and the NLRB Takes One Step Backward: Redefining Constructive Concerted Activities,* 38 Vand. L. Rev. 1295 (1985); Smith, *Arbitrating Safety Grievances: Contract or Congress?,* 33 Lab. L.J. 238 (1982); Drapkin & Davis, *Health and Safety Provisions in Union Contracts: Power or Liability?,* 65 Minn. L. Rev. 635 (1981); McDonough, *Safety in the Workplace: Employee Remedies and Union Liability,* 13 Creighton L. Rev. 955 (1980); Summa, *Criteria for Health and Safety Arbitration,* 26 Lab. L.J. 368 (1975); Comment, *Individual Action as Concerted Activities Under Section 7 of the National Labor Relations Act: The Nonunion Context,* 54 Tenn. L. Rev. 59 (1986); Note, *Refusals of Hazardous Work Assignments: A Proposal for a Uniform Standard,* 81 Colum. L. Rev. 544, 569 (1981) (proposing that other labor law standards "should be modified to conform to the standard established in the OSHA regulation," which "most clearly resolves the conflicting interests of employees and employers").

[192]49 U.S.C. app. §§2301–2305.

[193]Castle Coal & Oil Co. v. Reich, 55 F.3d 41 (2d Cir. 1995).

[194]*Id.* at 45.

[195]Yellow Freight Sys. v. Reich, 38 F.3d 76 (2d Cir. 1994). Two drivers had noticed the same problem, even though a later inspection failed to disclose any defect, and a mechanic drove the tractor over the same highway at an acceptable speed. *Id.* at 78–79. The U.S. Court of Appeals for the Second Circuit rejected the employer's claim that there must be objective proof that a truck is actually unsafe, and concluded the STAA protects a driver whose fears are objectively reasonable at the time of the refusal. *Id.* at 81–83.

[196]Yellow Freight Sys. v. Reich, 8 F.3d 980, 8 IER Cases 1706 (4th Cir. 1993) (employee's claim of fatigue was supported by other drivers, who told him he was weaving).

the other end require employees to meet the objective test of what a reasonable person would have believed under the particular circumstances. Thus, an arbitrator who applies the objective test parallels the statutory standard under the OSH Act and Section 502 of LMRA, while an arbitrator who applies a subjective test under a collective bargaining agreement grants employees rights beyond those accorded by these statutes.

However, because a "good-faith" subjective test appears to be the standard applied by the NLRB in certain NLRA Section 7 cases, an arbitrator's use of the more rigorous objective test in reaching a decision adverse to the safety risk claim of an employee refusing a work assignment may be held incompatible with NLRA Section 7 unless the employee action otherwise constitutes unprotected conduct, while arbitration awards based on whether employees who refuse to work because of safety concerns held a "good faith belief" that the job assigned is unsafe, regardless of whether the employee turns out to have been correct, will be consistent with NLRA Section 7 decisions.[197]

Many arbitrators, however, continue to apply an objective "reasonable person similarly situated" test.[198] Some arbitrators even go so far as to require an employee to show that there was in fact a health or safety risk involved.[199] In *Wheeling-Pittsburg Steel Corp. v. NLRB*,[200] the U.S. Court of Appeals for the Sixth Circuit sustained the NLRB's refusal to defer to an arbitration award pursuant to its *Spielberg* doctrine.[201] The arbitration award had upheld an employee's discharge for refusal to operate a crane despite the employee's good-faith belief that the crane was unsafe. The Board ordered the employee reinstated, finding that he had a reasonable good-faith belief that he was in danger because rusted and missing mounting bolts had caused the crane to sway. When the employer sought a review of the NLRB's decision, the Sixth Circuit held that the arbitration award had failed to consider corroborating witnesses and was based on inaccurate factual findings. Conversely, the NLRB had heard additional evidence supporting the reasonableness of the employee's belief that had not been presented to the arbitrator.

---

[197]*See* USS, Div. of USX Corp., 114 LA 948 (Das, 2000) (the employee's discharge must be upheld because the employee did not have a good-faith belief that the operation of a forklift was unsafe, given his prior statements that he would never operate a forklift again due to discipline he received in 1992).

[198]City of Los Angeles, Cal., 111 LA 406 (Daly, 1998) (listing the various approaches taken by arbitrators, but following the "reasonable person" standard). Numerous other arbitrators have applied the "reasonable person" standard. *See* Indianapolis Power & Light Co., 87 LA 559 (Kates, 1986); Jacksonville Shipyards, Inc., 79 LA 587, 590 (McCollister, 1982); United Parcel Serv., 78 LA 836, 840–41 (McAllister, 1982); Entenmann's Bakery of Fla., 77 LA 1080, 1084 (Ness, 1981); Fulton Seafood Indus., 74 LA 620, 623 (Volz, 1980); Hayes-Albion Corp., 73 LA 819, 824–25 (Foster, 1979).

[199]For instance, in some cases, an arbitrator may determine that the employee has a good-faith belief, but still uphold the discipline. *See* United States Pipe & Foundry Co., 84 LA 770 (Singer, Jr., 1985) (upholding discipline of an employee who had a good-faith fear that the work was dangerous, but the company established that under the circumstances the conditions were reasonable and safe and of a commonplace type at foundries).

[200]821 F.2d 342, 125 LRRM 2824 (6th Cir. 1987).

[201]Spielberg Mfg. Co., 112 NLRB 1080, 36 LRRM 1152 (1955).

Even where arbitration awards are not incompatible with statutory standards, divergent outcomes may still emerge. This is demonstrated by the varying results in cases where an employee's physical condition was the basis for a refusal to work. At least one arbitrator held that an employee's physical condition cannot provide a basis for refusing to work where there was nothing abnormal and immediately dangerous about the working conditions.[202] In contrast, another arbitrator held that the physical condition of a driver who stopped for a nap because he was unduly fatigued constituted grounds for mitigating disciplinary sanction. The U.S. Court of Appeals for the Fourth Circuit later decided that the sanction violated the STAA.[203] Yet, in another case, an employee's termination for refusal to make deliveries based on a subjective fear of serious injury had been upheld in arbitration, and by an administrative law judge who agreed with the arbitrator that the refusal to make deliveries was not protected by the STAA. The Secretary of Labor refused to accept the ruling, but his order was set aside by the U.S. Court of Appeals for the Second Circuit.[204]

6. Employee Complaints of Specific Hazards
[LA CDI 124.70; 100.552575]

Under both the subjective good-faith belief and the objective reasonable belief standards in determining whether an employee is justified in refusing to perform an assigned task, arbitrators consider the evidence concerning the existence of a hazardous condition. For example, the discipline of an employee who refused to operate a crane near power lines as a lightning storm approached was set aside because the employee's good-faith belief in the danger was supported by the fact that all other work sites nearby had shut down construction that day.[205] In another case, the discipline of an employee who refused to operate a forklift, allegedly because of safety concerns, was sustained because the employee's assertion of a good-faith belief was undermined by evidence that he had previously been disciplined for the unsafe operation of a forklift and had stated that he would never operate a forklift again.[206]

The factual issues for arbitral resolution include whether employees are merely complaining of discomfort,[207] whether the complaint of hazardous

---

[202]Pittsburg & Midway Coal Mining Co., 106 LA 624 (Alexander, 1996) (employee refused to clean grease from equipment because of a gash on the employee's hand that was just beginning to heal). *But see* Beverage Concepts, 114 LA 340 (Cannavo, Jr., 1999) (upholding the employer's rule that employees may not work consecutive shifts for overtime, because of fatigue due to long hours and hot temperatures).

[203]Yellow v. Freight Sys. v. Reich, 8 F.3d 980, 8 IER Cases 1706 (4th Cir. 1993).

[204]Castle Coal & Oil Co. v. Reich, 55 F.3d 41 (2d Cir. 1995).

[205]Granite Constr. Co., 114 LA 1115 (Riker, 2000).

[206]USS, Div. of USX Corp., 114 LA 948 (Das, 2000). *See also* Bargar Metal Fabricating Co., 110 LA 119 (Oberdank, 1998) (upholding discharge of employee for insubordination, because employee did not have a reasonable belief that operation of the crane was unsafe).

[207]*See* City of Lake Worth, Fla., 97 LA 240, 243–44 (Kanzer, 1991); Allied Health Care Prods., 94 LA 178, 183–84 (Cipolla, 1990) (mere discomfort is insufficient to meet employee's burden for refusing to work); Lancaster Electro Plating, 93 LA 203, 205–07 (Bressler, 1989). *But see* Naval Air Test Ctr., 79 LA 231, 235–36 (Jones, 1982) (employer did not meet its contractual obligations, because it provided a temperature setting that caused some employees discomfort).

condition is inherent in their job,[208] and whether they communicated their concerns to their supervisor regarding the alleged safety or health risks.[209]

A. Air Quality [LA CDI 124.70; 100.552575]

One of the most commonly cited employee health and safety concerns is the air quality of their work environment. Employees have complained about the health risks associated with too much dust in the air,[210] excessive fumes,[211] and airborne asbestos.[212] Air temperature was the reason behind other grievances and refusals to work. Employees have claimed that the air temperature of the plant was too cold,[213] too warm,[214] or changed too rapidly from too cold to too warm.[215] Still other employees have refused to work because they alleged their work stations were too drafty.[216] Employees have even contended that the air was unsafe because someone was alleged to have been infected with the AIDS virus.[217]

Perhaps some of the most controversial air quality complaints relate to tobacco smoke. While some employees complain that secondhand tobacco smoke creates a health hazard giving them a right to refuse to work,[218] other

[208]Fernald Atomic Trades, 99-2 ARB ¶3161 (Adamson, 1999) (upholding discharge of employee for safety complaints, where employee's motive was to avoid working in hazardous condition).

[209]Georgia-Pacific Corp., 106 LA 27 (Kahn, 1995) (upholding suspension of employee for refusing to work, claiming it was unsafe but failing to inform the supervisor of why the employee believed it to be unsafe).

[210]Clarksburg Casket Co., 113 LA 449, 455–56 (Hewitt, 1999) (employee refused to operate a moulder sander after having filed three grievances about poor ventilation causing too much dust).

[211]Koch Ref. Co., 99 LA 733, 736–37 (Cohen, 1992) (upholding an employer smoking ban because of dangerous fumes in the work area); Michigan State Dep't of Soc. Servs., 81 LA 390, 392 (Coyle, 1983) (employees complained of ammonia fumes); Fruehauf Trailer Co., 48 LA 1291, 1295–96 (Kallenbach, 1967) (discipline of employee upheld where fumes caused only minor discomfort); Allied Chems. & Dye Corp., 31 LA 699, 701 (McIntosh, 1958) (employees complained of ammonia gas). For related discussion, see Mills, *The Energy Crisis and Labor Relations*, 35 ARB. J. No. 4, at 3 (1980).

[212]Hoboken, N.J., Bd. of Educ., 75 LA 988, 990 (Silver, 1980) (employees complained of exposure to an asbestos-covered wall); Naval Air Rework Facility, 73 LA 644 (Flannagan, 1979) (employees complained of exposure to airborne asbestos).

[213]Naval Air Test Ctr., 79 LA 231, 235–36 (Jones, 1982) (involving federal guideline on temperatures that are between 65 and 68 degrees Fahrenheit); Muter Co., 47 LA 332, 335 (DiLeone, 1966) (employees had a right to refuse to work when employer failed to provide adequate heat); Berger Steel Co., 46 LA 1131, 1135 (Goldberg, 1966) (same); American Saint Gobain Corp., 46 LA 920, 922 (Duff, 1966) (same); Alderson Research Labs., 41 LA 895, 898 (Wildebush, 1963) (same). *See also* Wood Conversion Co., 41 LA 1144, 1146 (Jaffee, 1963) (employee refused to work outside during extreme cold weather).

[214]Wilcolator Co., 44 LA 847, 852 (Altieri, 1964) (complaining that the ventilation was poor, causing the temperature to be too high).

[215]Social Sec. Admin., 73 LA 267, 267–68, 271 (Eaton, 1979) (employees complained that the temperature varied too greatly between being too cold and being too hot).

[216]Allied Health Care Prods., 94 LA 178, 183–84 (Cipolla, 1990) (employee complained that combination of perspiration and air conditioner draft caused a health hazard); Singer Co., 48 LA 1343, 1343–44 (Cahn, 1967) (employer is not liable for employee's lost time caused by a cold due to a draft at employee's work station); Muter Co., 47 LA 332, 335 (DiLeone, 1966) (employer held liable for lost time because draft caused working conditions to be too cold).

[217]Veterans Admin. Med. Ctr., 94 LA 169 (Murphy, 1990).

[218]Koch Ref. Co., 99 LA 733, 736–37 (Cohen, 1992) (upholding smoking ban because of employee complaints that fumes in the area caused a potential safety and health hazard); United Tel. Co. of Fla., 78 LA 865, 867 (Clarke, 1982) (restrictions on smoking in the cafete-

employees grieve the implementation of work rules restricting smoking at work.[219] Although recent government findings support the conclusion that secondhand smoke is unhealthy,[220] arbitrators remain divided over whether the health risks justify employer bans on smoking.[221]

Arbitrators may reject unilateral across-the-board bans on smoking as violative of contractual "maintenance of privileges" provisions,[222] but generally uphold reasonable smoking restrictions on the basis of legitimate concerns for the health of employees.[223] There is similar disagreement as to whether smoking policies are a mandatory subject of bargaining.[224]

---

ria upheld, because study showed poor ventilation); Litton Indus., 75 LA 308, 312 (Grabb, 1980) (restrictions on where employees could smoke were reasonable, because other employees complained of health risks associated with secondhand smoke).

[219]Springfield Underground, 114 LA 65 (Pratte, 2000) (upholding a unilaterally imposed work rule restricting smoking to employees' breaks and lunch periods).

[220]See Environmental Protection Agency, Respiratory Health Effects of Passive Smoking: Lung Cancer and Other Disorders (Dec. 1992); Department of Health & Human Services, The Health Consequences of Involuntary Smoking: A Report of the Surgeon General (1986).

[221]Employer work rules prohibiting or restricting smoking were upheld under the circumstances set forth in Witco Corp., 96 LA 499, 505–06 (Nelson, 1991); United Tel. Co. of Fla., 78 LA 865, 870 (Clarke, 1982); Litton Indus., 75 LA 308, 312 (Grabb, 1980). Similar rules, however, were found unreasonable under the circumstances set forth in PMI Food Equip. Group, 103 LA 547 (Imundo, Jr., 1994) (company could not unilaterally adopt indoor smoking ban, despite undisputed evidence that ban was adopted out of desire to protect nonsmokers and based on evidence of harmful effects of smoking); Campbell Group, 102 LA 1031 (Ferree, 1994); Union Sanitary Dist. 79 LA 193, 195–96 (Koven, 1982); Schien Body & Equip. Co., 69 LA 930, 932, 937–39 (Roberts, 1977); ARO Corp., 66 LA 928, 930 (Lubow, 1976).

[222]See, e.g., Cross Oil & Ref. of Ark., 104 LA 757 (Gordon, 1995) (smoking ban adopted under health and safety clause did not override broad contract clause promising no changes in employee privileges); Raybestos Prods. Co., 102 LA 46 (Kossoff, 1993) (company could not unilaterally adopt no-smoking policy, where it knew of dangers of passive smoke and still agreed to longstanding smoking provision in contract negotiations). But see Plasti-Line, Inc., 114 LA 1240 (Mancini, 2000) (upholding a unilaterally imposed smoking ban because employees did not have a guaranteed privilege to smoke); Lockheed Aeronautical Sys. Co., 104 LA 840 (Hewitt, 1995) (conditions underlying past practice have changed sufficiently to justify no-smoking policy, because of concerns over liability for secondhand smoke, the obligation to provide a safe and healthy workplace, and public perception); Norris Plumbing Fixtures, 104 LA 174 (Richman, 1995) (upholding adoption of policy that totally banned smoking because of risk to employees); Lincoln Brass Works, 102 LA 872 (Haskew, 1994) (management-rights clause allows rulemaking to protect safety of employees subsequent to the Environmental Protection Agency's designation of dangers of secondhand smoke).

[223]Springfield Underground, 114 LA 65 (Pratte, 2000) (upholding a unilaterally imposed work rule restricting smoking to employees' breaks and lunch periods); United Tel. Co. of Fla., 78 LA 865, 870 (Clarke, 1982) (upholding restriction on smoking in cafeteria). For court cases recognizing that employers who do not take reasonable steps to protect employees from tobacco smoke in the workplace may be liable for breach of the common law duty to provide a safe place to work, see McCarthy v. Washington Dep't of Soc. Health Serv., 730 P.2d 681 (Wash. Ct. App. 1986); Smith v. Western Elec. Co., 643 S.W.2d 10, 13 (Mo. Ct. App. 1982); Shrimp v. New Jersey Bell Tel. Co., 368 A.2d 408, 410, 413–16 (N.J. Super. Ct. 1976). For further discussions, see also Reitze & Carof, The Legal Control of Indoor Air Pollution, 25 B.C. Envtl. Aff. L. Rev. 247 (1998); Reynolds, Extinguishing Brushfires: Legal Limits on the Smoking of Tobacco, 53 U. Cin. L. Rev. 435 (1984); Cochran, The Worker's Right to a Smoke-Free Workplace, 19 U. Dayton L. Rev. 275 (1984).

[224]Compare Department of Health & Human Servs. v. Federal Labor Relations Auth., 920 F.2d 45, 135 LRRM 3124 (D.C. Cir. 1990); Plasti-Line, Inc., 114 LA 1240 (Mancini, 2000); W-I Forest Prods. Co., 304 NLRB 957, 138 LRRM 1089 (1991), with Internal Revenue Serv. v. Federal Labor Relations Auth., 901 F.2d 1130, 134 LRRM 2134 (D.C. Cir. 1990); Worthington Foods, 89 LA 1069 (McIntosh, 1987); and Lennox Indus., 89 LA 1065 (Gibson, 1987).

B. Employee Job Performance Capability [LA CDI 124.70; 100.552575]

Another significant workplace safety concern is employees' fear that their own inability, or that of a coworker, to perform a job places them at risk. In one case, where a fatigued employee was discharged for refusing to work overtime, the arbitrator reduced the discipline to a suspension. The arbitrator found that while the employee had an obligation to communicate legitimate health concerns to the foreman, the employer also had an obligation not to force overtime on employees who were physically unable to perform the job.[225]

The same reasoning led to the allowance of the grievance filed by another disciplined employee who had refused to work inside a column because of asthma and claustrophobia.[226] Tasks that normally would not create problems for employees who are trained and experienced, arbitrators recognize, could be unsafe and pose an undue hazard for an untrained or inexperienced employee.[227] Where a coworker's driving record raised serious doubts about his ability to operate a vehicle safely, an employee was justified in refusing to ride with him.[228] Related to anxieties about job performance capabilities is the frequently expressed complaint that a reduction in staffing levels created unsafe working conditions.[229]

C. Equipment [LA CDI 124.70; 100.552575]

Still other safety allegations concern the equipment that employees are required to operate. Among the claims are that computer display terminals caused eyestrain,[230] that the excessive noise of machinery created health problems,[231] and that the movement of a slidegate was unsafe.[232] When legitimate complaints are made about defective equipment, arbitrators reject employer arguments that the equipment has been operated for a period of time without incident,[233] and that the employee only has to use the equipment a limited number of times.[234]

---

[225]Kaiser Aluminum & Chem. Corp., 92 LA 367 (Corbett, 1989). *But see* Ermanco Inc., 101 LA 269 (Ellmann, 1993) (upholding the discharge of an employee for refusing to attend a meeting because the employee was suffering from diarrhea).

[226]USS, Div. of USX Corp., 109 LA 321 (St. Antoine, 1997).

[227]Bethlehem Steel Corp., 49 LA 1203, 1206 (Strongin, 1968). *But see* Kroger Bakery, 110 LA 635 (Baroni, 1998) (upholding discharge of an employee who refused to perform work because employee felt unqualified).

[228]U.S. Plywood-Champion Papers, 50 LA 115, 123–24 (Jenkins, 1968). *Cf.* Lucky Stores, 101 LA 135 (Christopher, 1993) (employee discharged for refusing to work with a coworker due to personal problems between the two employees).

[229]Chicago Steel & Tin Plate, 97-1 ARB ¶3192 (Cox, 1996).

[230]Social Sec. Admin., 97 LA 809 (Bernhardt, 1991).

[231]Gallis Mfg. Co., 46 LA 75, 79 (Wood, 1966).

[232]Bethlehem Steel Corp., 97 LA 1010, 1010–11 (Das, 1991).

[233]A.M. Castle & Co., 41 LA 666, 670 (Sembower, 1963) ("[A]ny insurance actuarian will state that a hazard which persists long enough has an ever-increasing curve of expectation as to whether a loss will occur.").

[234]Ogden Air Logistics Ctr., 73 LA 1100, 1103–04 (Hayes, 1979).

D. Job Sites [LA CDI 124.70; 100.552575]

Even the location of job sites has been the subject of safety concerns. Some employees charged that their personal safety was endangered because they had to work in urban areas.[235] Other employees refused to cross a picket line of another union because of fear of harm.[236] Still other employees refused to work because of a racial situation that caused them to be afraid of physical violence.[237]

7. Employee Physical or Mental Condition as a Safety Hazard [LA CDI 118.655; 100.552565]

With the passage of the Americans with Disabilities Act (ADA),[238] employers have had to balance their obligation to accommodate a disabled employee[239] with their countervailing obligation to provide a safe and healthy workplace for all employees, including the employee with a disability. Under the ADA[240] and analogous antidiscrimination provisions of collective bargaining agreements,[241] an employee's physical or mental condition may be considered a safety hazard to himself or herself and to others. Employers are under an obligation to reasonably accommodate an employee with a disability,[242] but not if such accommodation would create a safety hazard.[243] For example, in *Interstate Brands Corp.*,[244] the arbitrator upheld the discharge

---

[235]New York Tel. Co., 50 LA 21, 23–24 (McFadden, 1968) (prescribing protection to be afforded to employees assigned to work in designated urban areas in which they reasonably feared they were in personal danger of criminal or physical attack). *See also* Peoples Natural Gas Co., 107 LA 882 (Zobrak, 1996) (sustaining grievance of employee who was suspended for refusing to work at an apartment complex, where employee had reasonable cause to fear for safety).

[236]Gulf Coast Motor Lines, 49 LA 261, 261–63 (Williams, 1967) (employee's refusal to work was unjustified unless based on a "reasonable fear of violence"). *See also* Phillips Pipe Line Co., 54 LA 1019, 1024 (Davey, 1970) (the contractual safety clause did not cover safety off the job and, therefore, did not apply to a picket-line situation).

[237]City of Buffalo, N.Y., Bd. of Educ., 60 LA 357, 365 (McKelvey, 1973).

[238]42 U.S.C. §12101 et seq.

[239]"One aim of the ADA is to make the workplace more accessible for the disabled by requiring employers to make 'reasonable accommodations' to help the disabled perform the duties demanded for a specific job." Interstate Brands Corp., 113 LA 161, 168 (Howell, 1999).

[240]42 U.S.C. §12113.

[241]Alcoa Bldg. Prods., 104 LA 364 (Cerone, 1995) (arbitrator applied external law—ADA— where potential conflict existed between federal law and contract). Some arbitrators have refused to apply the ADA where it is not specifically incorporated into the collective bargaining agreement. Shell Oil Co., 109 LA 965 (Baroni, 1998).

[242]Sherwin-Williams Co., 113 LA 1184 (Statham, 2000); City of Akron, 111 LA 705 (Franckiewicz, 1998); Wayne County, N.Y., 110 LA 1156 (Babiskin, 1998); Henkel Corp., 110 LA 1121 (West, 1998); USS, Div. of USX Corp., 109 LA 321 (St. Antoine, 1997).

[243]Johnson Am. Corp., 114 LA 577 (D'Eletto, 2000); Beverage Concepts, 114 LA 340 (Cannavo, Jr., 1999) (upholding the employer's rule that employees may not work consecutive shifts for overtime, because of fatigue due to long hours and hot temperatures); Interstate Brands Corp., 113 LA 161 (Howell, 1999); Rheem Mfg. Co., 108 LA 193 (Woolf, 1997); Quantum Chem. Corp., 107 LA 343 (Hooper, 1996); National Linen Supply, 107 LA 4 (Ross, 1996); Beckett Paper Co., 106 LA 1135 (Goggin, 1996); Champion Int'l Corp., 106 LA 1024 (Howell, 1996); ITT Auto., 105 LA 11 (Shanker, 1995); Cessna Aircraft Co., 104 LA 985 (Thornell, 1995).

[244]113 LA 161 (Howell, 1999).

of a driver with psychiatric problems who had refused to continue to take his prescribed medication.

Whether physical and mental conditions pose a safety hazard must be determined on an individual basis. Arbitrators rely on medical evidence and on evidence concerning workplace conditions and job requirements in determining whether the employee's physical or mental condition creates the risk of injury. But employers are not permitted to assume that certain physical or mental conditions automatically constitute safety hazards.

Arbitrators have been sympathetic to discharged employees suffering from mental conditions. In one case, the arbitrator converted the discharge of a mentally ill employee, who made threatening comments to a company secretary, to a suspension without pay and ordered the employee to be placed on a 1-year medical leave.[245] In another case, an arbitrator ordered that an employee suffering from depression, who had been discharged for poor performance, be reinstated and granted a medical leave of absence, even though the employee never requested a leave. The arbitrator found it significant that the depression kept the victim from being aware of the need to apply for leave.[246] Similarly, when a 17-year employee, who had resigned while she was on leave for a short-term mental disability, filed a grievance beyond the time limitation, the employer was ordered to hear it.[247] Arbitrators have also shown sensitivity to the plight of employees who refused to perform work assignments because of legitimate physical or mental limitations. Thus, an employee diagnosed as suffering from asthma and claustrophobia was found not to have been insubordinate when he refused to do cleaning work inside a column.[248]

The ADA specifically excludes from coverage individuals who *currently* use illegal drugs. It is not surprising, therefore, that a plethora of decisions uphold discharges for illicit drug use and alcohol abuse and sustain the validity of rules requiring employees to undergo drug screening, particularly in safety-sensitive industries.[249]

A. Management Action: Transfer, Demotion, Layoff, Leave of Absence, or Termination [LA CDI 118.655; 117.1133; 119.802; 120.03]

The prevailing view is that management has the right and responsibility to take corrective action when an employee has a physical or mental disability that endangers the employee's own safety or that of others. Depending on the nature and extent of an employee's disability, the employee may

---

[245]Owens-Brockway Prods., 109 LA 655 (Bailey, 1997).

[246]Mine Workers Dist. 6, 110 LA 84 (Ruben, 1997). *See also* Cross Oil Ref. Co., 111 LA 1013 (Bumpass, 1999); Exxon Co., 110 LA 534 (Allen, 1998); LTV Steel Mining Co., 110 LA 283 (Doepken, 1997).

[247]Pacific Bell, 107 LA 686 (Levy, 1996).

[248]USS, Div. of USX Corp., 109 LA 321 (St. Antoine, 1997). *See also* Weirton Steel Corp., 89 LA 201 (Sherman, Jr., 1987).

[249]Biolab Inc., 114 LA 279 (Brodsky, 2000); North Star Steel, 114 LA 234 (Eisenmenger, 1999); Laporte Pigments, 114 LA 1 (Marino, 2000); Tosco Ref. Co., 112 LA 306 (Bogue, 1999); ATC/Vancom of Cal., 111 LA 244 (McKay, 1998). For a discussion of drug and alcohol testing, see section 2.A., "Alcohol and/or Drug Use and Testing," above.

be subject to transfer, demotion, layoff, leave of absence, or termination.[250] An employer may place an ailing employee on medical leave of absence if the action is justified by safety considerations. In one such case,[251] an arbitrator rejected the view that the only relevant consideration is whether the employee can give a fair day's work on the assigned job:

> Management has a right to look further than a "fair day's work." It has a right and an obligation to look to the physical well-being of its employees and the condition of the firm's physical plant. The true test is whether it appears to management that the employee can *safely* give a fair day's work on the job assigned to him without endangering either his own health or safety, the health and safety of his fellow employees, or the physical plant of the Company.[252]

Such decisions, however, must be consistent with the employer's obligations under the ADA to provide disabled employees with a reasonable accommodation. A much-contested issue is whether an employer can demonstrate undue hardship when a reasonable accommodation, such as a transfer, would cause the employer to violate a collective bargaining agreement. The majority view among the federal courts has been that seniority provisions under a collective bargaining agreement trump ADA rights. This view seems to be the approach arbitrators will take when faced with the issue. For example, an arbitrator interpreted federal case law and held that an employer violated its collective bargaining agreement when, as an accommodation, it rejected the preference of a senior employee and assigned a disabled employee, junior in seniority, to work the day shift.[253]

B. Protecting the Employee [LA CDI 117.123]

Arbitrators recognize that employee safety may be a controlling consideration in ruling on an employee's request for reinstatement to a former position. Requests for reinstatement have been denied even when the employees may have been willing to accept the risk to their own health and safety.[254]

---

[250]See cases cited in notes 251–261, below. An important aspect of physical or mental disability cases is the evidence adduced at the hearing. In this regard, see Chapter 8, section 7.B., "Medical Evidence." For other related discussion, see Chapter 13, section 26., "Disqualifying Employees for Physical or Mental Reasons."

[251]Auer Register Co., 62 LA 235 (Perry, 1974).

[252]Id. at 238–39. Also upholding compulsory medical leave for safety reasons, see *L.P. Transp. & Ampropane Transp.*, 79 LA 110, 116–17 (Wray, 1982); *Hughes Aircraft Co.*, 49 LA 535, 539–40 (Doyle, 1967). For cases holding that medical leave rather than discharge should have been utilized, see *City of Chi., Ill.*, 96 LA 876, 883–86 (Goldstein, 1990); *Payless Stores*, 95 LA 1, 4–7 (Yarowsky, 1990); *Bucklers, Inc.*, 90 LA 937, 937–39 (Braufman, 1987); *U.C. Agric. Prods. Co.*, 89 LA 432, 435–36 (Anderson, 1987); *Nursing Home*, 88 LA 681, 681–82 (Sedwick, 1987); *Appleton Elec. Co.*, 76 LA 167, 169 (Roomkin, 1981); *B.F. Goodrich Co.*, 69 LA 922, 928 (Klein, 1977) (employer had the right and obligation to sever mentally ill employee "from active employment," but the proper means of accomplishing the severance was a medical leave of absence rather than discharge for the employee's unprovoked assault upon another employee).

[253]Mason Hanger Corp., 111 LA 60 (Caraway, 1998).

[254]See Joy Mfg. Co., 73 LA 1269 (Abrams, 1980); U.S. Steel Corp., 68 LA 785 (Rakas, 1975); Pepsi Cola Gen. Bottlers, 48 LA 649 (Luskin, 1966); American Zinc Co., 46 LA 645 (Abernethy, 1966); Hughes Aircraft Co., 41 LA 535 (Block, 1963); Stauffer Chem. Co., 40 LA 18 (Hale, 1963). In *Warner & Swazey Co.*, 53 LA 643–45 (High, 1969), for example, the arbitrator upheld an employer's refusal to permit an employee to come to work with a splint on his finger because the condition created a safety hazard to the employee. *See also* Metro Atlanta Transit Auth., 79 LA 357, 362 (Aronin, 1982); United States Steel Corp., 70 LA 171, 172–73 (Garrett, 1977).

One arbitrator refused to require a company to reinstate an employee who suffered from a major depressive disorder, because the company had an "inherent duty to make certain that its employees are fully capable of performing their jobs without risk of harm either to themselves or to their fellow employees."[255] Concern about the employee's impaired mental state led the arbitrator to conclude that the company would not be able to ensure her safety and the safety of her coworkers if she returned to her position in a refinery.[256]

Another arbitrator refused to require the reinstatement of an employee with a serious back injury to a position that required lifting, because such reinstatement would have created the risk of further injury to the employee. The arbitrator rejected the employee's discrimination claim based on his assertion that his back injury constituted a "handicap," because the employee could not have been returned safely to work.[257]

In a third case, an arbitrator upheld a company's decision to deny reemployment to an employee who had been out of work for 2 years because of a serious lung injury caused by exposure to chlorine gas. Examination of the medical evidence revealed that the employee still suffered from a pulmonary problem and that the working conditions could have again exposed the employee to chlorine gas, thereby potentially worsening her condition.[258]

In an analogous context, arbitrators have upheld employers' decisions to suspend employees who could not safely perform their jobs. Thus, an arbitrator denied the grievance of an employee who was temporarily suspended from performing his job duties after he injured his right arm and thumb. The employer had determined that there was an unacceptable risk that he would harm himself in attempting to perform a job that involved pushing and pulling large rolls of paper.[259]

In contrast to these decisions, other arbitrators have granted reinstatement despite the risk to the employee's health or life, on the ground that they lacked authority under the contract to prevent the reinstatement, or that the employer had no right to decide for the employee whether the employee might risk shortening his or her life by returning to the job.[260]

---

[255]Lyondell-Citgo Ref. Co., 109 LA 24, 28 (Nicholas, Jr., 1997).

[256]Id. See also Hilltop Basic Res., 101 LA 861 (Krislov, 1993); Lone Star Indus., 88 LA 879 (Berger, 1987) (upholding transfer of cement truck driver to different position when he had suffered three epileptic seizures within 1½ years of sustaining a brain injury).

[257]Griffin Pipe Prods. Co., 87 LA 283 (Yarowsky, 1986).

[258]Mead Corp., 86 LA 201 (Ipavec, 1985). See also Illinois Cement Co., 99 LA 481 (Koenig, Jr., 1992); Peabody Coal Co., 84 LA 511 (Duda, Jr., 1985) (employee with large abdominal hernia had a physical impairment that made him a hazard to himself).

[259]Beckett Paper Co., 110 LA 425 (Heekin, 1998). See also Boeing Co., 106 LA 650 (Thornell, 1995) (upholding company's suspension of a diabetic truck driver on the ground that he posed a risk of harm to himself and others when he had abandoned his diet and could have gone into a diabetic coma while driving).

[260]Arketex Ceramic Corp., 50 LA 1171, 1175–76 (Seinsheimer, 1967) (the company could properly discharge the employee, afflicted with silicosis, and rehire him in a nonunit job in order to protect itself from increased insurance premiums); Interwoven Stocking Co., 39 LA 918, 920–21 (Valtin, 1962) (evidence did not support a finding that termination of employee, who had suffered four heart attacks, was necessarily in the best interests of the company, and that, under the contract, neither the arbitrator nor the company could decide for the employee whether he should risk shortening his life by returning to work). See also Lever Bros. Co., 66 LA 211, 215 (Bernstein, 1976).

Some arbitrators have carved out a middle ground between these two positions. In one case, for example, an arbitrator found that an employee who had an arm injury had to be given at least a trial period at her old job to determine whether she could perform its duties. The company had a practice of providing such "trial" periods, and the medical evidence did not establish that the employee risked injury to herself if she returned to her job.[261]

---

[261]Firestone Tire & Rubber Co., 88 LA 217 (Cohen, 1986). *See also* City of Brook Park, Ohio, 98 LA 758 (Nelson, 1992); Man Roland Inc., 97 LA 175 (Speroff, 1991); Excel Corp., 95 LA 1069 (Shearer, 1990).

Chapter 17

Employee Rights and Benefits

0.1 Scope of Employee Rights and Benefits

Over the years, the give and take between management and the unions
has resulted in the establishment of employee rights and benefits such as
paid vacations and paid holidays that now are incorporated into the agreement or enshrined in a well-established practice. But other rights that may
be asserted by employees are more personal in nature and are either less
firmly established or not recognized at all in labor-management relations.

These asserted personal rights often are brought to issue by grievances filed when management enforces a new plant rule, such as one dealing with personal appearance, or when management disciplines an employee for refusing to obey a new management directive issued pursuant to its contractual scheduling right, such as requiring Sunday work, or when management is perceived as having violated or abandoned an established practice. These employee rights relate more to "employee rights not so intimately connected with the production process," as opposed to those rights related to the "the area of traditional and conventional management discretion"[1] concerning operations and production.

1. VACATIONS [LA CDI 100.5203; 116.151]

Employees have no inherent right to vacations; rather, vacation rights arise out of the contract.[2] Employees, of course, are interested in vacations not only for the rest and relaxation derived from such periods away from work, but also for the pay received.

The company also has an interest, aside from immediate production needs, in employee vacations. Thus, as stated by an arbitrator:

> Vacations are for the mutual benefit of employees and employers. The employee who returns to work after a period of rest and relaxation and who has had some free time with his family and to tend to personal affairs is a more valuable man to his employer. . . . A vacation is also one of the economic attractions which a Company offers to its employees to remain on the payroll or to become employees. While a vacation may be regarded as earned or deferred compensation, it may also be considered as an investment by the Company in promoting the longevity of service of its employees and a more productive working force.[3]

Arbitrators have recognized the twofold nature of the vacation benefit: time off from work, and pay.[4] The significance of the "time off" aspect of vacations was illustrated in an unusual context. An employee who was discharged while on vacation received an arbitral award of reinstatement with back pay. When the employer sought to reduce the back pay by the amount earned by the employee at another company during the vacation, the arbitrator disallowed the offset, reasoning that "[a]n individual's vacation belongs to that

---

[1]Eastern Air Lines, 44 LA 1034, 1040 (Yagoda, 1965).

[2]*See* Peterbilt Motors Co., 66 LA 160, 161 (Williams, 1976); S.C. Indus., 65 LA 745, 747 (Williams, 1975); Golay & Co., 59 LA 1245, 1247 (Volz, 1972); Dover Corp., 48 LA 965, 968 (Volz, 1966); Modecraft Co., 44 LA 1045, 1049 (Jaffee, 1965). The myriad issues relating to vacation benefits are analyzed in Abrams & Nolan, *The Common Law of the Labor Agreement: Vacations*, 5 INDUS. REL. L.J. 603 (1983).

[3]Dover Corp., 48 LA 965, 969 (Volz, 1966). Similar language was used in *Blue Box Co.*, 61 LA 754, 755 (Gibson, 1973). *See also* Ajax Rolled Ring Co., 71 LA 460, 461 (Daniel, 1978) (noting the increasing importance of time off with or without pay because of "economic security, social and family commitments and . . . personal items of lifestyle that frequently put money in second place to doing one's own thing").

[4]*See* E.K. Wood Prods. Co., 105 LA 1153, 1155 (Dobry, 1995); Ava Foods, 87 LA 932, 934 (Hunter, 1986) (dictum).

individual and if one chooses to work at a different job during that time, rather than relaxing, that is the prerogative of the individual."[5]

The duality of the benefit has surfaced in grievances asserting an employee's claim to vacation without pay after having received vacation pay while on layoff. One arbitrator concluded that it was implicit in the contract language that once a laid-off employee had been paid vacation pay, the employee had taken the vacation for which pay was received.[6] The arbitrator found that the past practice of the parties dictated the denial of additional time off without pay after the employee returned to work. However, a second arbitrator noted that employees who received vacation pay while on layoff were unable even to visit friends and relatives during their layoff because of the reporting requirements for unemployment compensation eligibility. He found the past practice of the parties supported additional time off without pay after the employees returned to work.[7]

In a third decision, employees were held to be entitled to vacation pay when the employer ceased its operations prior to the employees' anniversary dates of employment, despite the fact that the contract provided that vacation pay was to be issued on an employee's anniversary date. Because the agreement contained other language that permitted the taking of earned vacation prior to an employee's anniversary date, the arbitrator ruled that employees who met the work requirements for vacation were entitled to their full vacation pay.[8]

In determining whether time served on National Guard duty should count toward vesting of vacation benefits, the contract, and not federal law, will be dispositive. A disappointed reservist who had met all other contract requirements for vacation except the number of days worked the previous year contended that he would have satisfied the minimum requirement but for the compulsory guard duty. The union argued that the Veterans' Benefits Act[9] required that the reservist be given vacation credit for the guard duty time. The Act provides that National Guard personnel with military training obligations lasting less than 3 months must be granted a leave of absence for the period required to carry out their training and that they must be returned to work with the seniority status and pay that they would have had if not absent for duty.

The arbitrator found the U.S. Supreme Court's decision in *Monroe v. Standard Oil Co.*[10] controlling. There the Court explicitly found that the Act "does not entitle a reservist to benefits that are conditioned upon work requirements demanding actual performance on the job."[11] Because in the

---

[5]Park 'N Fly, 108 LA 611, 612 (Marino, 1997).
[6]Koehring S. Plant, 82 LA 193, 196 (Alsher, 1984).
[7]Hess Oil V.I. Corp., 87 LA 1109 (Eyraud, 1986).
[8]Canteen Corp., 101 LA 925 (Borland, 1993).
[9]Veterans' Benefits Act, *as amended*, 38 U.S.C. §7604.
[10]452 U.S. 549, 107 LRRM 2633 (1981).
[11]*Id.* at 553 n.7.

present case vacations were based on work requirements and not remaining-in-continuous-service status, the company was justified in denying vacation to the guardsman-employee because he had not been at work the requisite number of days.[12]

The extent of vacation entitlements typically varies with length of service. Part-time or temporary service prior to an employee's becoming a full-time or "regular" employee may not be credited toward vacation entitlements unless the contract so provides.[13]

When an employee transfers to another of the company's plants, a question may arise as to whether seniority for vacation entitlements is based on the total length of employer service or only service at the plant. For example, a contract provided that vacation could be taken after one year of continuous service, but the agreement defined "company seniority" as the length of an employee's continuous service beginning with the date on which the employee began to work for a particular plant. When an employee with 5-years' seniority was transferred to another plant, the question arose as to whether she properly was permitted to schedule her vacation within her first year at the new plant. Citing the employee's ambiguous status under the collective bargaining agreement and the absence of any language specifically denying the employee her accrued benefits, the arbitrator determined that the employee was eligible for vacation because at no time was there a break in service.[14]

A. Scheduling Vacations [LA CDI 100.5203; 116.152]

From the employee's standpoint, the right to take a vacation "at a time personally selected is a valuable right,"[15] but it is a right that is limited by considerations of business needs. It is said that "one of the prerogatives of management [is] to schedule vacations at such time as best meets the needs of the business," and that "in doing so the employer will very often and perhaps wherever possible also try to do his utmost to meet the wishes of employees."[16] One arbitrator elaborated:

> Absent specific contract language, it is generally understood in industrial relations practice that a vacation is an earned equity and is generally to be taken in terms of the employee's preference, subject to the exigencies of the

---

[12]Concordia Foods, 102 LA 990 (Bernstein, 1994).

[13]E.K. Wood Prods. Co., 105 LA 1153 (Dobry, 1995) (employees' service on a part-time basis was not counted toward vacation pay, where the contract granted vacation to "regular employees" and part-timers had not been considered regular employees); Fremont Hotel & Casino, 102 LA 220 (Randall, 1993) (service prior to becoming a regular employee was not counted, where ambiguous contract language was defined by past practice to that effect).

[14]ARCO Chem., 102 LA 1051 (Massey, 1994).

[15]Welch Grape Juice Co., 48 LA 1018, 1021 (Altrock, 1967). See National Linen Serv., 110 LA 476, 479 (Frockt, 1998). The length of permitted vacation may be affected by the time when it is taken. See R.D. Werner Co., 55 LA 303, 305 (Kates, 1970) (increased vacation benefits under a new contract were not retroactive where the new contract did not expressly provide for retroactivity for employees who had already taken their vacation for the year).

[16]Sinclair Ref. Co., 12 LA 183, 189 (Klamon, 1949). This inherent right was reiterated (as dictum) in Heil Packing Co., 36 LA 454, 458 (Klamon, Freise, Sarhage, Faust, & Wrape, 1961). See also Tenneco Chems., 51 LA 699, 701 (Williams, 1968).

Company's production and maintenance requirements. Where the contract is silent on the specific policy or procedure to be followed, it must be assumed that the employee will request his vacation at a time suitable to his own preferences and that his preferences will be honored to the degree that Company requirements will permit. However, where the contract is silent, it must also be assumed that managerial discretion is greater than in those cases where contract language puts the burden on management to show need for the employee to take his vacation at a particular time, or not to take vacation at a particular time.[17]

Unfortunately, many labor agreements do not unambiguously resolve the potential conflicts between employer and employee preferences for vacation scheduling.[18] In one case, an employer who, in order to cut costs, sought to preclude employees from taking their vacation during any week in which a holiday fell on a weekday was held to have violated the labor agreement. The employer could restrict the scheduling of vacation only in those limited situations where operations would otherwise be impaired.[19]

Vacation provisions in collective bargaining agreements generally provide that seniority will prevail in vacation selection and scheduling.[20] The procedure for scheduling vacations usually is determined by contractual provisions or past practice. Where an ambiguity exists in the contract concerning the basis for calculating seniority for scheduling vacations, the past practice of the parties may determine the outcome.[21] For example, an arbitrator found that the employer improperly implemented a rule requiring 72 hours' notice and approval of a vacation request. Although the agreement gave the employer the right to schedule vacations, an established past practice continued over three contract terms had permitted employees to call in requests for vacation commencing on the same day or to make post-absence vacation requests for time already taken.[22] But where a contract gave the company the right to "determine when each employee may take his vacation," this "clear language" governed notwithstanding the existence of an inconsistent past practice, and an employer's refusal to allow one-day vacations unless notice was received in advance of the day was upheld.[23]

"Clear contract language" also may inure to the benefit of the employee. When an employer claimed that "past practice" supported its position that it could limit its drivers' vacations to the summer, when milk was not delivered to schools,[24] an arbitrator ruled that the contract clearly provided for nonsummer vacation periods, and this unambiguous language controlled.

---

[17]Hubinger Co., 29 LA 459, 461 (Davey, Wolf, & Ullrich, 1957).

[18]See Lewis County, Wash., 107 LA 321, 323–24 (Stuteville, 1996) (agreement not violated when employee's vacation scheduling request was denied, even though no other employee was scheduled for same vacation period; contract providing that no more than one employee may be on vacation at the same time set only a maximum limitation, not a minimum guarantee).

[19]National Linen Serv., 110 LA 476 (Frockt, 1998).

[20]See CGM Contractors, 93 LA 1159 (Duda, Jr., 1989); Wellslee Coca-Cola Bottling Co., 86 LA 1164 (Spilker, 1986); Commonwealth of Pa., 86 LA 1229 (Zirkel, 1985).

[21]Mercy Hosp. of Altoona, Pa., 94 LA 51, 52 (Jones, Jr., 1989).

[22]E.G.&G. Vactec, 89 LA 1108 (Miller, 1987). See also Keystone Coal Mining Co., 98 LA 1080 (Coyne, 1992).

[23]Sanderson Plumbing Prods., 106 LA 535 (Howell, 1996).

[24]Meyer Bros. Dairy, 107 LA 481 (Scoville, 1996).

In still another case, a rule requiring that employees submit vacation requests 48 hours in advance was invalidated because the labor agreement provided only that "[v]acations will be taken at such times of the year as not to interfere with the efficient scheduling of operations in the plant."[25] Moreover, an arbitrator found that changes in the contract provisions related to vacation cannot be applied retroactively, even where other changes had been applied in the past on a retroactive basis.[26] But, following the "obey now, grieve later" principle, an arbitrator upheld a discharge for insubordination where an employee defied a direct order not to take a vacation at the time requested by the employee.[27]

i. In Accordance With Operational Needs [LA CDI 100.5203; 116.152]

Whether management is given the right to schedule vacation by the agreement or possesses it as a residual power, the needs of the business and the maintenance of production are important considerations in its exercise.[28] For instance, under an agreement permitting employees to select their vacation dates whenever practicable, management was permitted to schedule vacations at such times as would not interfere with its operations or increase its costs.[29] Similarly, under a clause providing that "the vacation period shall be selected by the employees by departments in the order of their seniority," but where the contract also reserved exclusively to management the "disposition and number of the working forces," an arbitrator concluded that the vacation desires of the employees should be honored to the extent that this would not unreasonably interfere with orderly plant operations.[30]

However, the employer has the "burden to substantiate denial of vacation requests as being reasonable in light of business needs."[31] Thus, under a

---

[25]Stone Container Corp., 108 LA 917, 920 (Bain, 1997).

[26]Boulevard Distillers & Importers, 94 LA 657 (Heekin, 1990).

[27]Wilton Corp., 85 LA 667 (Smedley, 1985).

[28]See Town of Woodbridge, Conn., 70 LA 149, 150 (Pittocco, 1978); United Tel. Co. of Northwest, 64 LA 906, 911 (Hedges, 1975); Houdaille Indus., 61 LA 958, 961 (Rill, 1973); General Cable Corp., 48 LA 1000, 1004 (Kelliher, 1967). For cases dealing with the special problems involved in scheduling extended vacations, see Combustion Eng'g, 61 LA 1061, 1063 (Altrock, 1973); United States Steel Corp., 53 LA 264, 265–66 (McDaniel, 1969); Bethlehem Steel Corp., 46 LA 702, 704 (Strongin, 1966); ARMCO Steel Corp., 45 LA 120, 124–25 (Kates, 1965); Reynolds Metals Co., 44 LA 475, 478–79 (Tongue, 1965); United States Steel Corp., 44 LA 906, 909–10 (McDermott, 1965); United States Steel Corp., 43 LA 790, 795–97 (Garrett, 1964) (listing seven factors to be considered in scheduling extended vacations); Pittsburgh Steel Co., 42 LA 1002, 1007–08 (McDermott, 1964).

[29]Sinclair Ref. Co., 12 LA 183, 190 (Klamon, 1949). See also Schnuck's Baking Co., 73 LA 813, 815–16 (Erbs, 1979); Vulcan Materials Co., 73 LA 687, 690 (Taylor, 1979); ARO, Inc., 30 LA 225, 229 (Livengood, 1958); Toledo Scale Co., 25 LA 94, 98 (McKelvey, 1955); National Tube Co., 19 LA 330, 331 (Garrett, 1952). Cf. Tin Processing Corp., 17 LA 461, 462 (Emery, 1951).

[30]Carling Brewing Co., 46 LA 715, 717–18 (Kates, 1966). Cf. Town of Hamburg, N.Y., 73 LA 906, 908 (Denson, 1979). The employee must submit a request by the stated contract date in order for vacation preference to be given "consideration." MacMillan Bloedel, 65 LA 1252, 1254–55 (King, 1975).

[31]Stanwich Indus., 90 LA 895, 898 (Roumell, Jr., 1988). See also Town of Trumbull, Conn., 99 LA 173 (Cain, 1992); Westvaco Envelope Div., 94 LA 309, 317 (Dworkin, 1990) (where employer must determine whether granting a vacation schedule request would "significantly undermine production needs"); Southern Cal. Permanente Med. Group, 90 LA 900 (Kaufman, 1988); Reynolds Metals Co., 44 LA 475, 477 (Tongue, 1965) (citing many cases).

contract providing "[v]acations will, so far as possible, be granted at times most desired by employees," and reserving to the company "the final right to allot vacation periods . . . in order to insure the orderly operation of the plants," it was held that the grievant had been improperly denied his choice of vacation time since another qualified employee was available, and hence there would have been no interference with the "orderly operation of the plants."[32] But, under a similar contract clause, the employer's denial of the right to take vacations during summer months was deemed proper because business forecasts indicated that work would be at its "peak."[33]

Arbitrators have ruled against employers that unwarrantably prohibit the taking of vacations during specified times. For example, under a contract providing that "[p]reference of vacation shall be granted to employees according to seniority on dates requested *when in the judgment of the Employer such date will not impair operations*,"[34] the company implemented a policy of not scheduling vacations during holiday weeks. The arbitrator noted that "[i]f the company wanted sole discretion, without being required to provide justification, to determine whether vacations would be permitted during holiday weeks, then it should have negotiated unambiguous language to that effect."[34A]

A similar result was reached when an employer attempted to use shift seniority for vacation picks under a contract providing that seniority was measured by the length of service with the employer, and that an employee's preference for vacation time off, considered in order of seniority, was to be accommodated "whenever possible." The arbitrator reasoned that "whenever possible" was to be understood in the context of "operational needs," and the company's general right to designate each employee's vacation period did not override the specific contractual seniority provisions.[35]

Although the collective bargaining agreements under consideration in two cases reserved discretion to the employers in scheduling vacations, the employers' blanket prohibitions of vacations during certain times of the year were rejected, because there was no evidence that complete bans were operationally required.[36] In a third case, however, an employer was permitted to schedule a vacation shutdown despite the fact that it had not "endeavored," in accordance with the contract, to allow vacations at the time requested by the employees, because the vacations had been scheduled when

---

[32]United States Steel Corp., 53 LA 222, 224 (McDermott, 1969). *See also* New York Shipbuilding Corp., 43 LA 854, 855–56 (Crawford, 1964). But it has been held that management is not required to recall laid-off employees in order to accommodate vacation preferences. Bethlehem Steel, 39 LA 673, 675 (Gill, 1962).

[33]Westinghouse Elec. Corp., 40 LA 972, 974 (Cahn, 1963). *See also* B.B.D. Transp. Co., 66 LA 64, 65 (Manos, Sr., 1976).

[34]National Linen Serv., 110 LA 476, 479 (Frockt, 1998) (emphasis in original).

[34A]*Id.*

[35]Baltimore Sun Co., 103 LA 363, 370 (Cushman, 1994).

[36]Multimedia of Ohio, 87 LA 927 (Kindig, 1986); Supreme Life Ins. Co. of Am., 85 LA 997 (Cox, 1985).

production and maintenance projects were at low levels, and rescheduling vacations to other times as requested by the employees would have resulted in layoffs.[37]

Under an employee preference clause, one arbitrator ruled that management could not reserve certain weeks exclusively for foremen's vacations, because the presence of such a preference clause in the contract "obligates the Company to give priority to employees' preferences over the foremen's choices where the two conflict, so long as there is no problem about the 'orderly and efficient operation of the plant.'"[38] In another case, a 1-week vacation shutdown was the practice, but the grievant was entitled by contract to a second week of vacation. The contract was silent on vacation scheduling, the parties had no established practice, and the company had no policy for scheduling a second week. In light of these circumstances, the arbitrator stated that the vacation clause according the grievant 2 weeks could not be "frustrated by arbitrary and unreasonable denial of employee preferences," and that the grievant's preference for his second week of vacation should be granted unless an "adequate reason relating to the operational and production needs of the Company" could be shown.[39]

In instances where operational needs have been established, arbitrators have permitted management to limit the number of employees who could be on vacation at the same time.[40] But, under a "use it or lose it" policy, where an employer had reduced the complement of operators who could be on vacation at any one time too late for an employee to reschedule his remaining vacation for that year, the employer was required to restore the vacation time.[41] Another arbitrator, rejecting both the company's limit and the union's demand for no limit, formulated a procedure for determining in a flexible manner the number of employees to be on vacation at a given time.[42]

Another contract provided that "[v]acation and personal leave schedules must be arranged so as not to interfere with the regular and efficient conduct of the business of the company," and that "[v]acation selection will be granted on a seniority [length of continuous on-the-job service] basis by departments, so far as possible preference as to dates being given in the order of length of such service."[43] In the past, if, after an employee's vacation

[37]Deere & Co., 82 LA 1299 (Cox, 1984). See also Bethlehem Steel Corp., 85 LA 1130 (Sharnoff, 1985).

[38]Air Reduction Chem. & Carbide Co., 42 LA 1192, 1195 (Kesselman, 1964). See Armstrong Cork Co., 37 LA 21, 23 (Williams, 1961) (strong contract language giving management the right to designate vacation time).

[39]National Lock Co., 48 LA 588, 590–91 (Volz, 1967).

[40]See Laclede Steel Co., 54 LA 506, 507–08 (Kelliher, 1971) (management could schedule vacations on an equal basis over the full year and thus eliminate the "summer bulge" of vacations); United States Steel Corp., 46 LA 887, 890 (Gilden, 1966); Reynolds Metals Co., 44 LA 475, 476–77 (Tongue, 1965) (the company's limit was raised by the arbitrator); Bethlehem Steel Co., 36 LA 584, 585–86 (Seward, 1961).

[41]Owens-Corning Fiberglas Corp., 82 LA 1156 (Mikrut, 1984). Cf. City of Lancaster, Ohio, 87 LA 105 (Duda, Jr., 1986); Commonwealth of Pa., 86 LA 1229 (Zirkel, 1985); City of Pittsburgh, Pa., 84 LA 467 (Ipavec, 1985); Saginaw Mining Co., 83 LA 310 (Feldman, 1984).

[42]Carling Brewing Co., 46 LA 715, 717–18 (Kates, 1966). See also Mansfield Tire & Rubber Co., 32 LA 762, 766–67 (Shaw, 1959) (the arbitrator was requested to and did formulate a procedure to be followed in scheduling vacations).

[43]Schmidt Baking Co., 104 LA 574, 575 (Wahl, 1995).

selection had been approved, the employee was transferred to another department, the company would hire a part-timer to fill in. The company issued a statement, challenged by the union, that henceforth transferred employees would only be permitted to take vacation time still open in the new department. The arbitrator found the question was resolved not by the contract but by the prior practice in deciding that already selected vacations would transfer with the employees.

What happens when "operational needs" require the recall of an employee who has already started his vacation? Finding itself unexpectedly short of drivers, a beverage distributor ordered the grievant to cut short his preapproved vacation by 1 week. The employee had in the past rescheduled vacations when requested by the company. However, in this case the driver had already paid for an out-of-state vacation and could return early only upon payment of substantial additional airfare. He informed the company that he would return to work as originally scheduled after his 2-week vacation. The company considered the failure to return a voluntary resignation and terminated his employment. The arbitrator disagreed, holding that the company was equitably estopped because it had unilaterally changed the scheduled vacation that it had previously approved and upon which the employee had relied in booking his travel. The prior episodes of employee acquiescence were not precedential, because in those instances the driver had not planned out-of-state trips.[44]

ii. *During Layoffs and Shutdowns*
[LA CDI 100.5203; 116.152; 116.1554]

Historically, some correlation between vacations and what otherwise would be layoffs has been deemed not only permissible but also desirable.[45] Another arbitrator followed this dictum and permitted the scheduling of vacations to coincide with temporary shutdowns,[46] pursuant to an agreement giving management the right to schedule vacations.

There are limitations, however. For instance, where an agreement gave management the right to schedule vacations subject to the requirement that "due consideration" be given to employees' wishes, the umpire, distinguishing between temporary and indefinite layoffs, ruled that management could not require employees to take their vacations during a period of indefinite layoff where to do so would destroy the substantive features of a vacation. He reasoned:

---

[44]Goodman Beverage Co., 108 LA 37, 42 (Morgan, Jr., 1997).

[45]Ford Motor Co., 3 LA 829, 831 (Shulman, 1946).

[46]Sefton Fibre Can Co., 12 LA 101, 105 (Townsend, 1948). *See also* Deere & Co., 82 LA 1299, 1301 (Cox, 1984); General Cable Corp., 52 LA 257, 259 (Feller, 1968); Tenneco Chems., 51 LA 699, 700–01 (Williams, 1968) (involving a vacation clause giving management strong rights in the final allocation of vacation periods); Reynolds Metals Co., 39 LA 659, 660–61 (Williams, 1962); General Elec. Co., 39 LA 149, 150–51 (Whitton, 1962) (emphasizing the necessity of showing production requirements); Sylvania Elec. Prod., 37 LA 458, 464 (Jaffee, 1961); ARO, Inc., 30 LA 225, 231 (Livengood, 1958). *Cf.* Continental Can Co., 35 LA 836, 840 (Miller, 1960). In *Wyman-Gordon Co.*, 51 LA 561, 565 (Rauch, 1968), past practice strongly supported the 2-week vacation shutdown.

A vacation is a period of rest between periods of work. A layoff is a period of anxiety and hardship between periods of work. The tremendous difference lies in the assurance of the vacationer that he will return to work at the end of his vacation and the equal assurance of the employee on layoff that he does not know when he will return to work. The basic difference, with its financial, emotional, and psychological implications, is not obliterated by a form of words or by the receipt of income for a part of the indefinite period of layoff.[47]

Other arbitrators have held that where the contract provides that the employer is to consider the requests of individual employees for particular vacation times, the company may not order a vacation shutdown, since scheduling such a vacation would fail to take into account the desires of individual employees as required by contract.[48]

However, under "clear, precise, unequivocal" contract language simply stating that "[v]acations are to be granted as designated by the Management of the Company," with no reservations, restrictions, or limitations in favor of employee desires, it was held that the company had the right to designate a 2-week vacation shutdown.[49] Similarly, an arbitrator held that an employer properly scheduled a 3-week vacation shutdown despite its 20-year practice of closing for 2 weeks, where contract language specifically granted the employer the right to set the vacation period. The arbitrator ruled that past practice did not negate the employer's express contractual right to schedule a different shutdown period.[50] In another case, where the contract granted employees preference as to vacation dates, but reserved to management the "final right to allot vacation periods and to change such allotments" and (with the required notice) to schedule regular vacations during a shutdown period in lieu of previously scheduled vacations, management's right to schedule two separate vacation shutdowns during the year was affirmed.[51]

---

[47]Ford Motor Co., 3 LA 829, 831 (Shulman, 1946). *Cf.* Westinghouse Elec. Corp., 45 LA 131, 140 (Hebert, 1965). As to scheduling vacations for employees who are already on layoff, see *United States Steel Corp.*, 36 LA 603, 615–16 (Garrett, 1961). In *Kentile Floors*, 55 LA 808, 812–13 (Cyrol, 1970), the employees had started applying for unemployment compensation during plant shutdown periods, thus adding to costs; the arbitrator upheld management's right to schedule vacations during plant shutdown. *Cf.* S.C. Indus., 65 LA 745, 747–48 (Williams, 1975).

[48]*See* Welch Grape Juice Co., 48 LA 1018, 1021 (Altrock, 1967) (opinion reinforced by past practice); Koppers Co., 42 LA 1321, 1325–26 (Nichols, 1964); Vanadium Corp. of Am., 38 LA 389, 392–95 (Sembower, 1962) (distinguishing *Ford Motor Co.*); General Foods Corp., 35 LA 921, 923–24 (Manson, 1960); Quaker Oats Co., 35 LA 535, 538–39 (Valtin, 1960); Alan Wood Steel Co., 33 LA 772, 774 (Valtin, 1960); Fairbanks, Morse & Co., 32 LA 913, 916–17 (Eckhardt, 1959); Chrysler Corp., 32 LA 776, 781 (Wolff, 1959); Bethlehem Steel Co., 30 LA 992, 994 (Seward, 1958); Sherwin-Williams Co., 18 LA 934, 935 (Kelliher, 1952). *See also* Harlo Prods. Corp., 59 LA 613, 616–21 (Howlett, 1972) (discussing many cases). *Cf.* Union Camp Corp., 81 LA 254, 258 (Taylor, 1983); Tin Processing Corp., 15 LA 568, 572–73 (Smith, 1950). *But see* U.S. Indus. Chems. Co., 39 LA 1108, 1111 (Williams, 1963); Rockwell-Standard Corp., 34 LA 693, 697–98 (Schmidt, 1960); National Tube Co., 19 LA 330, 331 (Garrett, 1952).

[49]Wisconsin Bridge & Iron Co., 46 LA 993, 1004–05 (Solomon, 1966). A like result was reached in *Vogt Manufacturing Corp.*, 44 LA 488, 489–90 (Sarachan, 1965), where the contract had no provision as to scheduling vacations.

[50]Gates Rubber Co., 96 LA 445 (Sergent, 1991).

[51]United States Steel Corp., 59 LA 195, 196 (Garrett, 1972). *Cf.* Interstate Printers & Publishers, 54 LA 501, 503 (Larkin, 1971) (the contract specified a shutdown for a "two-week period during the summer").

Although for more than 20 years a plant had never experienced a vacation shutdown, the employer was entitled to impose one since the agreement unambiguously gave the employer the right to "designate any periods of time during the year for the shutting down of plant operations, for the taking of vacation."[52] The arbitrator explained that "[e]ven twenty years of a consistently applied past practice cannot serve to nullify the clear and unambiguous language of the Agreement."[53]

A vacation shutdown does not necessarily exclude the performance of all work in the plant. Thus, where the contract permitted a 2-week vacation shutdown, it was held that the shutdown need not be "total" but that the employer could work employees on essential maintenance, limited receiving and shipping, and limited clerical payroll functions.[54] But an employer's selection of a junior electrician to work through a vacation shutdown period was deemed improper since it was not in accordance with the past practice of selecting employees to work through this period on the basis of seniority in classification.[55]

iii. Fixed by Contract

Where the agreement fixes the period for taking vacations, the employer cannot designate any additional vacation period.[56] Thus, where a labor agreement referred to two 6-month vacation scheduling periods, summer and winter, an arbitrator held that the employer in a seasonal business could not, when challenged, limit employee vacations to the summer off-season, as it had done in the past.[57]

Employees have in certain situations been confined to the fixed vacation period. Thus, under a contract that entitled employees with a year's service to a paid vacation, an employee who completed his year's service after the end of the vacation period fixed by contract was required to wait until the following vacation season to take his vacation.[58]

---

[52]Willamette Indus., 106 LA 1113 (Stoltenberg, 1996).

[53]*Id.* at 1115.

[54]General Cable Corp., 48 LA 1000, 1004 (Kelliher, 1967). *See also* United States Steel Corp., 69 LA 719, 721 (Edwards, 1977) (union argued unsuccessfully that retention of a junior employee to service other operations violated seniority provisions of the agreement).

[55]Alabama By-Products Corp., 83 LA 1270 (Clarke, 1984). *Cf.* H.D. Hudson Mfg. Co., 84 LA 1141 (Gallagher, 1985) (employer had right to allow production workers with only 1 or 2 weeks of vacation who had returned to work to continue working in third week of shutdown period, rather than recall senior workers who were scheduled for 2-week vacation and leave of absence during third week).

[56]Cone Mills, 29 LA 346, 350 (McCoy, 1957). *Cf.* General Am. Transp., 15 LA 481, 484 (Kelliher, 1950). Nor may the employer provide vacation pay to laid-off employees prior to the contractually agreed vacation period, in view of the practical impact of such action on the employees' entitlement to unemployment compensation, supplemental unemployment benefits, and vacations within the agreed period as required by contract. *See* United States Steel Corp., 36 LA 113, 116 (Garrett, 1961). *See also* Mead Paper, 70 LA 186, 190 (McIntosh, 1978); A.E. Moore Co., 62 LA 149, 154–55 (Greco, 1974).

[57]Meyer Bros. Dairy, 107 LA 481 (Scoville, 1996).

[58]Kent of Grand Rapids, Inc., 18 LA 160, 162–63 (Platt, 1952); General Cable Corp., 18 LA 44, 45–46 (Cahn, 1952). *See also* Victor Metal Prods. Corp., 66 LA 333, 336–37 (Ray, 1976). For a "split vacation" case, see *Riverdale Plating & Heat Treating Co.*, 71 LA 43, 46–47 (Petersen, 1978).

Finally, the contract may state specific requirements for the posting of vacation schedules. Strictly interpreting such a contract, one arbitrator held improper a notice posted 2 days after the deadline date and reached the "equitable" solution of setting the vacation period to be the same as in prior years.[59]

iv. Remedy for Improperly Forced Vacations

While forced vacations are not always improper,[60] the question sometimes arises as to what remedy can be applied by the arbitrator when the company has improperly scheduled and "forced" vacations. Fashioning a remedy when vacation scheduling grievances prove meritorious can sometimes be a daunting task. In one case, although the arbitrator found that the employer had improperly restricted vacations to a minimum of 1 week at a time, the arbitrator declined to permit the employee unilaterally to select his remaining vacation days, the remedy sought by the union. Instead, only prospective relief was granted, and the employer was directed to abide by the contract in the future.[61] In other grievances, however, that may be the very relief the union requests.[62]

One arbitrator awarded "damages" by requiring the company to give the grievants another week's vacation with pay;[63] another refused to duplicate vacation pay but awarded another week's vacation.[64] Another arbitrator, finding that he could not "assign a monetary value to grievants' mental discomfort," refused to grant additional pay in view of the company's good-faith belief that the agreement permitted its action (which apparently had been unchallenged by the union in previous years), but he warned that the company was now on notice and could in the future be required to give the aggrieved employee "either a further vacation on the proper dates or pay-in-lieu thereof."[65]

---

[59]Interstate Indus., 46 LA 879, 881 (Howlett, 1966).

[60]*See, e.g.*, Bethlehem Steel Corp., 81 LA 1272, 1274 (Gentry, 1983) (extended vacation period a consequence of employee's low seniority ranking); Social Sec. Admin., 68 LA 160, 162–63 (Kaye, 1977) (where employees returned late from a coffee break, the Social Security Administration's action of charging the time against annual leave (vacation) was nondisciplinary and permissible under a contract permitting enforced leave when an employee is not "ready, willing and able to work"); International Paper Co., 65 LA 572, 576–77 (Moore, 1975); Indiana Army Ammunition Plant, 64 LA 1021, 1027–28 (Render, 1975) (involving U.S. Army civilian employees).

[61]Borough of Doylestown, Pa., 109 LA 1080 (DiLauro, 1997).

[62]*See* National Linen Serv., 110 LA 476 (Frockt, 1998).

[63]Scovil Mfg. Co., 31 LA 646, 651 (Jaffee, 1958). *See also* Bethlehem Steel, 37 LA 821, 824 (Valtin, 1961); Philip Carey Mfg. Co., 37 LA 134, 139 (Gill, 1961) (also involving unemployment benefits); United States Steel Corp. 33 LA 82, 84 (Garrett, 1959).

[64]Chrysler Corp., 32 LA 776, 781 (Wolff, 1959). *See also* Harlo Prods. Corp., 59 LA 613, 621 (Howlett, 1972); Vanadium Corp. of Am., 38 LA 389, 395 (Sembower, 1962); Baldwin-Lima-Hamilton Corp., 31 LA 37, 41 (Fleming, 1958).

[65]Bethlehem Steel, 31 LA 857, 858 (Seward, 1958). *See also* ACF Indus., 39 LA 1051, 1057 (Williams, 1962); Alan Wood Steel Co., 33 LA 772, 775 (Valtin, 1960).

B. Calculation of Vacation Pay [LA CDI 100.45; 100.5203; 116.1711]

Questions often arise regarding the proper calculation of vacation pay, such as whether vacation pay includes an overtime compensation component. One arbitrator held that it did not on the basis of the bargaining history for the current contract. The employer's past practice had been not to include overtime in vacation pay, and although the issue had arisen during negotiations, no change was made in the contract language.[66]

C. Vacation Benefits: Deferred Wages or "Refresher"
[LA CDI 100.45; 100.5205; 116.1711]

Originally a vacation was a gratuity "awarded" to faithful employees for past services and to "refresh" them for future service. As the collective bargaining process evolved, vacations and vacation benefits, while still providing rest and relaxation, have become part of the total economic package.

Whether the parties intended vacation benefits to serve as deferred wages or as a refresher for the employee can arise in grievances regarding carryover or forfeiture of unused vacation from one year to the next. While acknowledging that accumulated vacation pay is a form of deferred earnings and that in some jurisdictions employees are entitled by statute to compensation for accumulated but unused vacation time on termination of employment, an arbitrator noted that the parties may provide for a maximum vacation pay accumulation and require employees to "use it or lose it." The precise issue before this arbitrator was whether accrued vacation benefits were capped at 520 hours or at 520 hours plus the number of hours accumulated in the previous year, under a contract that provided "[v]acation may be carried forward with a maximum of five hundred twenty (520) hours . . . throughout the year." The arbitrator held that the 520-hour limit was a "rolling" maximum.[67]

Vacation provisions often are included in the wage section of the agreement.[68] In recognition of the industrial-relations fact that the parties themselves have bargained for and made vacation benefits a part of the agreement, most arbitrators consider such benefits to be deferred wages that vest in the employee.

The status of vacation benefits must be ascertained by examination of the contract and its bargaining history.[69] In this connection, the Supreme Court has noted that generally the presence of a work requirement in the

---

[66]Hydro Conduit Corp., 105 LA 964 (Kaufman, 1995).

[67]City of Duncan, Okla., 106 LA 398 (Cipolla, 1996).

[68]See, e.g., Infant Socks, 51 LA 400, 402 (Moberly, 1968).

[69]For discussion of various aspects of these and other related concepts and/or collections of cases, see Shieldalloy Corp., 81 LA 489, 492–93 (Talmadge, 1983); Reichhold Chems., 66 LA 745, 749 (Jackson, 1976); A.C. Krebs Co., 64 LA 791, 792–94 (White, Jr., 1975); Modernfold Indus., 60 LA 1200, 1201 (Warns, 1973); Phalo Corp., 52 LA 837, 839–40 (Murphy, 1969); Infant Socks, 51 LA 400, 402–03 (Moberly, 1968); Skag-Way Dep't Stores, 51 LA 349, 350–51 (Doyle, 1968); Telescope Folding Furniture Co., 49 LA 837, 838–39 (Cox, 1967); Dover Corp., 48 LA 965, 968–69 (Volz, 1966); Pittsburgh Steel Co., 43 LA 860, 862 (McDermott, 1964); Clinton Corn Processing Co., 41 LA 513, 514 (Larkin, 1963); Todd Shipyards Corp., 38 LA 737, 739 (Cheney, 1962); Border Queen, Inc., 35 LA 560, 565 (Brown, 1960); Jules L. Simon Co., 34 LA 170, 172 (Volz, 1959); Wamsutta Mills, Inc., 34 LA 158, 163–65 (Hogan, 1959);

contract is strong evidence that the vacation benefit was intended as a form of deferred compensation for work actually performed.[70]

Even though vacation rights may vest in the employee, entitlement to such rights is not absolute but may require compliance with conditions of the agreement, such as a minimum length of service (for example, requiring 52 full weeks of employment)[71] or being on the payroll as of a particular date.[72]

The question of the vesting of vacation rights has been raised in situations of plant closure or sale of the business,[73] voluntary quit or retirement by the employee,[74] or death of the employee.[75] In any of these cases, where

---

Penn-Dixie Cement Corp., 33 LA 316, 318 (Reid, 1959); *Brooklyn Eagle Inc.*, 32 LA 156, 168–69 (Wirtz, 1959); Feinberg, *Do Contract Rights Vest?*, *in* LABOR ARBITRATION AND INDUSTRIAL CHANGE, PROCEEDINGS OF THE 16TH ANNUAL MEETING OF NAA 194 (Kahn ed., BNA Books 1963).

[70]Foster v. Dravo Corp., 420 U.S. 92, 100–01, 89 LRRM 2988 (1975). The Court concluded that since the returning veteran had not met the work requirement in the agreement, §9 of the Military Selective Service Act did not guarantee him full vacation benefits for the year in question.

[71]Southwest Airlines Co., 93 LA 543, 546 (Fox, Jr., 1989); Great Atl. & Pac. Tea Co., 43 LA 1, 2 (Turkus, 1964). *See also* International Paper Co., 67 LA 1265, 1267 (Owen, 1976); W.T. Sistrunk Co., 67 LA 641, 643 (Beckman, 1976); Infant Socks, 51 LA 400, 403 (Moberly, 1968); Cricket Shop of Cedarhurst, 49 LA 895, 897 (Singer, 1967); Telescope Folding Furniture Co., 49 LA 837, 838 (Cox, 1967); Purex Corp., 39 LA 489, 491 (Doyle, 1962); Todd Shipyards, 38 LA 737, 739–40 (Cheney, 1962); Border Queen, 35 LA 560, 565 (Brown, 1960); San Bruno Sportservice, 33 LA 837, 840 (Ross, 1959).

[72]*See* York Wall Paper Co., 69 LA 431, 434 (Gershenfeld, 1977); Roper Corp., 61 LA 342, 346–47 (Bradley, 1973); Barg & Foster, 53 LA 692, 692–93 (Seitz, 1969). *See also* Rex Chainbelt Inc., 49 LA 646, 648 (Gilden, 1967); Greenlee Bros. & Co., 48 LA 938, 940 (Davis, 1967); Olin Mathieson Chem. Corp., 42 LA 1332, 1334 (Turkus, 1964); Purex Corp., 39 LA 489, 491 (Doyle, 1962); Brookford Mills, 28 LA 838, 841 (Jaffee, 1957) (because of the plant closure, employees' failure to be at work on the eligibility date was not attributable to them). For examples of cases viewing the "eligibility date" simply as a "cut-off date" for computing vacation pay and not as condition precedent for entitlement to vacation benefits, see *Phalo Corp.*, 52 LA 837, 840 (Murphy, 1969); *Infant Socks*, 51 LA 400, 403 (Moberly, 1968); *Telescope Folding Furniture Co.*, 49 LA 837, 838 (Cox, 1967); *Ekco Prods. Co.*, 38 LA 912, 915 (Markowitz, 1962); *Border Queen*, 35 LA 560, 565 (Brown, 1960); *Wamsutta Mills*, 34 LA 158, 163 (Hogan, 1959).

[73]In these cases, arbitrators speak in terms of vacation rights as deferred earnings that have vested in the employee; in some instances, they point out that vacation pay is by contract based on the employee's earnings. *See* Apex Ready-Mix Concrete Co., 58 LA 1111, 1116–17 (Kates, 1972); Infant Socks, 51 LA 400, 403 (Moberly, 1968); Skag-Way Dep't Stores, 51 LA 349, 350 (Doyle, 1968); National Plumbing Fixture Corp., 49 LA 421, 422 (Reid, 1967); Ekco Prods. Co., 38 LA 912, 915 (Markowitz, 1962); Border Queen, 35 LA 560, 564–65 (Brown, 1960); Wamsutta Mills, 34 LA 158, 163–65 (Hogan, 1959); Brooklyn Eagle, 32 LA 156, 168–69 (Wirtz, 1959). For discussion of the "successor employer" doctrine (NLRB and court cases) as applied to vacation rights, see *A.B.A. Diesel Parts & Serv. Co.*, 62 LA 660, 663–67 (Harter, Jr., 1974). *See also* Zenetron, Inc., 74 LA 861, 863–64 (Speroff, 1980); Bird Int'l Corp., 70 LA 1157, 1158 (Wahl, 1978); National Heat & Power Corp., 61 LA 26, 28–31 (Turkus, 1973). For related discussion, see Chapter 14, section 4.B., "Merger or Sale of Company."

[74]Where the contractual requirements prior to quitting or retirement have been met, the employee is entitled to vacation benefits. *See* Burdick Corp., 76 LA 611, 616–19 (Petrie, 1981); Rexall Drug Co., 63 LA 965, 968 (Hellman, 1974); Phalo Corp., 52 LA 837, 839–41 (Murphy, 1969); Telescope Folding Furniture Co., 49 LA 837, 838–39 (Cox, 1967); Holmes Elec. Protective Co., 42 LA 1209, 1211–13 (Altieri, 1964). But where the contractual requirements have not been met, such as employment on a particular date, the employee is not entitled to vacation pay. *See* York Wall Paper Co., 69 LA 431, 433–34 (Gershenfeld, 1977); Westvaco, 67 LA 128, 130 (Lieberman, 1976); Modernfold Indus., 60 LA 1200, 1202–03 (Warns, 1973); Barg & Foster, 53 LA 692, 692–93 (Seitz, 1969); Rex Chainbelt, Inc., 49 LA 646, 648 (Gilden, 1967); Purex Corp., 39 LA 489, 491 (Doyle, 1962). *See also* Ekco Prods. Co., 54 LA 66, 68 (Kabaker, 1971); Dover Corp., 48 LA 965, 969 (Volz, 1966).

[75]Where the employee has met contractual requirements before death, there is no forfeiture of vacation benefits. *See* Burnham Corp., 46 LA 1129, 1130–31 (Feinberg, 1966); Pittsburgh Steel Co., 43 LA 860, 862–63 (McDermott, 1964); Clinton Corn Processing Co., 41 LA

the vacation has been fully earned and the employee has fully met all the conditions required by the contract, arbitrators are in general agreement that vacation benefits must be held to have vested in the employee. But where such conditions have not been met, the employee has been denied vacation benefits.[76]

Some agreements have "use or lose" provisions in which the employee must utilize the accrued vacation within a specified period. Failure to do so will result in a loss of any unused vacation time.[77]

D. Strikes and Vacation Benefits [LA CDI 100.5203; 116.1554]

In the absence of contract language requiring a different result, arbitrators are disinclined to permit employees to benefit by the accrual of vacation credits during time spent on strike, since vacation benefits as deferred wages are part of the pay received for *working* for the company. As one arbitrator stated:

> The employer does not reward employees for being absent on strike, but if the Union's position is upheld in this case, the employers will be required to accord these employees vacation pay for time they did not work. The employers here feel aggrieved for being asked, in effect, to subsidize the strike.[78]

The effect of strikes on vacation credits is rarely treated in the contract[79] and is seldom directly covered in the strike settlement agreement. Unions have argued that the denial of vacation credits violates strike settlement agreements that require that no penalty be assessed against anyone participating in the strike. Arbitrators, however, have held that the denial of vacation credits where the contract relates such credits to time worked is not to

---

513, 515 (Larkin, 1963); United States Steel Corp., 40 LA 1308, 1310–11 (McDermott, 1963); Jones & Laughlin Steel Corp., 38 LA 479, 481 (Crane, 1962). The result was different where strict contract language required employment on an entitlement date. *See* Wagner Elec. Corp., 54 LA 232, 235–36 (Erbs, 1971); Greenlee Bros., 48 LA 938, 940 (Davis, 1967); Bethlehem Steel Corp., 47 LA 258, 259–60 (Seward, 1966); Olin Mathieson Chem. Corp., 42 LA 1332, 1333–34 (Turkus, 1964). *Cf.* American Meter Co., 44 LA 126, 127 (Kreimer, 1965).

[76]See notes 74 and 75, *supra.* For cases involving pro rata vacation pay, see *Providence Med. Ctr.*, 68 LA 663, 668 (Conant, 1977) (voluntary quit); *Verson Allsteel Press Co.*, 67 LA 735, 740–41 (LeBaron, 1976) (company made voluntary adjusted vacation payments to laid-off employees); *A.C. Krebs Co.*, 64 LA 791, 792–94 (White, Jr., 1975) (employee not eligible for pro rata vacation pay due to illness); *Wire Sales Co.*, 62 LA 185, 187–88 (Cox, 1974) (voluntary quit); *Golay & Co.*, 59 LA 1245, 1249 (Volz, 1972) (retirement).

[77]City of Danbury, Conn., 96 LA 1010, 1011–12 (Orlando, 1991).

[78]Motor Car Dealers Ass'n of Kansas City, 49 LA 55, 57 (Beatty, 1967), *cited with approval in* Unarco Indus., 53 LA 784, 791 (Gorsuch, 1969). *See also* Reichhold Chems., 66 LA 745, 749 (Jackson, 1976). Where it was established to the arbitrator's satisfaction that under past practice vacation credits had been given in all prior strike situations, full vacation time was allowed in *Mobil Oil Co.*, 42 LA 102, 105–06 (Forsythe, 1963), and upheld in *Oil, Chem. & Atomic Workers Local 7-644 v. Mobil Oil Co.*, 350 F.2d 708, 45 LA 512, 59 LRRM 2938 (7th Cir. 1965). *See also* Metro St. Louis Bargaining Ass'n, 79 LA 1294, 1300–01 (Nitka, 1982). Past practice may also deny vacation credits. *See* Continental Oil Co., 70 LA 636, 639–40 (Gottlieb, 1978); Kroger Co., 42 LA 247, 249 (Larkin, 1964); San Bruno Sportservice, 33 LA 837, 839 (Ross, 1959).

[79]*See* Evening News Ass'n, 53 LA 170, 176 (Casselman, 1969).

be considered a penalty but is simply an application of the vacation provisions of the contract.[80]

The reluctance of arbitrators to credit strike time for vacation benefits in these cases was explained as follows:

> It would seem anomalous that the parties, had they specifically considered the matter, would have intended that working time lost because of direct participation in a strike would be credited as service time whereas [the contract provides that] time lost on authorized leave of absence was not to be credited.[81]

Other cases have involved contracts basing vacation time on some qualifying phrase such as "hours worked" or "time worked,"[82] "years of service,"[83] "continuous service,"[84] "employment" by the company,[85] being "in the employ" of the company,[86] or "scheduled working days."[87] These phrases have been interpreted as requiring the actual rendition of services for vacation eligibility, and as excluding time spent on strike. Thus, a distinction must be made between the bare retention of employment status and the actual performance of services that fulfill the eligibility requirements.[88]

E. Retirement and Vacation Benefits [LA CDI 100.5203; 116.1557]

Issues regarding the vesting of vacation rights also arise in the context of retirement by an employee. Whether the employee has complied with contractual requirements prior to retiring is usually dispositive of whether there is entitlement to vacation benefits.[89] A past practice of providing retirees with full vacation benefits will not overcome clear and unambiguous contract language limiting retirees' vacation entitlements.[90] In some cases, arbitrators

---

[80]*See* Lord Mfg. Co., 47 LA 319, 322 (Kates, 1966); Kroger Co., 42 LA 247, 249 (Larkin, 1964); Vickers, Inc., 27 LA 251, 255 (Smith, 1956). *But see* Barrett Transp., 52 LA 169, 171 (Koven, 1969) (strike settlement agreement provided for "retroactivity" of fringe benefits). The company's formula for loss of vacation credits due to strike may be "even-handed," but its application may result in impermissible inequities. *See* Continental Oil Co., 70 LA 636, 640 (Gottlieb, 1978).

[81]Vindicator Printing Co., 48 LA 213, 219 (Smith, 1966).

[82]Givaudan Corp., 68 LA 337, 342 (Brent, 1977); Modecraft Co., 38 LA 1236, 1239 (Dall, 1961).

[83]Reichhold Chems., 66 LA 745, 749 (Jackson, 1976); Great Atl. & Pac. Tea Co., 43 LA 1, 2 (Turkus, 1964).

[84]Ohio Power Co., 63 LA 1235, 1240–41 (Chockley, Jr., 1974); Evening News Ass'n, 53 LA 170, 175 (Casselman, 1969). *Cf.* Mallet & Co., 34 LA 428, 431 (Wood, 1960).

[85]Union Carbide Corp., 49 LA 1180, 1181 (Cahn, 1967); Vickers, Inc., 27 LA 251, 254–55 (Smith, 1956).

[86]San Bruno Sportservice, 33 LA 837, 838–39 (Ross, 1959).

[87]Lord Mfg. Co., 47 LA 319, 321 (Kates, 1966). *See also* Hawaii Dep't of Educ., 62 LA 415, 418–20 (Kanbara, 1974). *Cf.* Ford Motor Co., 33 LA 638, 639–40 (Platt, 1959).

[88]*See* San Bruno Sportservice, 33 LA 837, 838 (Ross, 1959) (citing and quoting Safeway Stores, 22 LA 466, 469 (Hildebrand, 1954)); Vickers, Inc., 27 LA 251, 254–55 (Smith, 1956).

[89]Heekin Can, 98 LA 809 (Kossoff, 1992).

[90]Peabody Coal Co., 99 LA 390 (Feldman, 1992) (past practice of providing retirees with full vacation benefits is not binding where contract clearly provides that retirees' vacation benefits will be prorated if retirement occurs during the accrual period). *See also* National Roll Co., 95 LA 863 (Hewitt, 1990) (under agreement to pay retirees 13 weeks' vacation pay, employer properly deducted amounts paid to employees for vacation taken in year they retired).

have upheld a requirement by an employer that employees must use all vacation time earned in a prior year before retirement or lose the benefit.[91]

One of the most frequent sources of dispute is the maximum amount of unused vacation that can be cashed out upon retirement. When a labor agreement provided that an employee was entitled to accumulate up to 320 hours of vacation but could not carry over vacation time "for more than two (2) years,"[92] the employer argued that this provision was subject to its past practice of limiting vacation carryovers to 240 hours. The arbitrator determined that the former 240-hour carryover limit was actually a function of the maximum vacation allowance in prior contracts and concluded that the specific language of the present contract controlled the issue. The grievant was awarded a full vacation cash-out upon his retirement.[93]

F. Layoffs and Vacation Benefits [LA CDI 100.5203; 116.1554; 116.155]

The reasoning of the retirement cases has been applied in layoff cases. Thus, where employees have met eligibility requirements and their vacations have been earned prior to layoff, they have been held to be entitled to vacation benefits in full if fully earned,[94] or on a pro rata basis if partially earned,[95] the rationale again being that vacation pay is in the nature of additional wages. However, where the laid-off employees were found not to have met the contract's eligibility requirements, they were held not entitled to any vacation benefits.[96]

In addition to the "continuous employment" reference, one contract provided that an employee must work 60 percent or more of the total working days in a 12-month period to qualify for vacation pay. The arbitrator concluded that to interpret the "continuous employment" language to permit the employer to deduct periods of layoff would be a "redundancy."[97]

Where full-time employees had accepted part-time work instead of a layoff, the arbitrator ruled that they were entitled to earn vacation credit despite contract language to the contrary. The governing contract provided

---

[91]Municipality of Penn Hills, 96 LA 163 (Duff, 1990).

[92]Cuyahoga, Ohio, Cmty. Coll., 109 LA 268, 269 (Klein, 1997).

[93]Id. at 273.

[94]See Allied Corp., 80 LA 680, 684 (Cohen, 1983); Stackpole Carbon Co., 68 LA 67, 68 (Cooley II, 1977); Peerless Laundries, 40 LA 129, 131–35 (Lugar, 1963) (citing and discussing many cases); Penn-Dixie Cement Corp., 33 LA 316, 318–19 (Reid, 1959); Fairbanks, Morse & Co., 32 LA 278, 282–83 (Howlett, 1959) (relying in part on principles of equity).

[95]See Keene Corp., 61 LA 468, 472–73 (Barone, 1973); Todd Shipyards Corp., 38 LA 737, 739–40 (Cheney, 1962); Jules L. Simon Co., 34 LA 170, 172 (Volz, 1959) (citing cases); R.C. Williams & Co., 33 LA 428, 431 (Knowlton, 1959) (permanent layoff). See also Great Atl. & Pac. Tea Co., 43 LA 1, 2 (Turkus, 1964).

[96]See General Tire & Rubber Co., 79 LA 340, 344 (Wolff, 1982); Verson Allsteel Press Co., 67 LA 735, 740–41 (LeBaron, 1976) (but the company voluntarily made adjusted vacation payments to laid-off employees); Frye Copysystems, 65 LA 1249, 1250–52 (Yarowsky, 1975) (citing and relying upon Foster v. Dravo Corp., 420 U.S. 92, 89 LRRM 2988 (1975)); Robinett Mfg. Co., 64 LA 641, 642 (King, 1975); Penn-Dixie Cement Corp., 39 LA 1240, 1241–42 (McCoy, 1962); Todd Shipyards Corp., 38 LA 737, 740 (Cheney, 1962); International Paper Co., 35 LA 717, 720–21 (Caraway, 1960); Ohringer Home Furniture Co., 33 LA 477, 481–82 (Pollack, 1959) (permanent layoff).

[97]Iowa Mold Tooling Co., 82 LA 469, 472 (Slade, 1984).

that part-time employees were not eligible to accrue vacation credit. However, the arbitrator held that since laid-off, full-time employees continued to earn credits, it would be inequitable to deny the benefit of vacation to those who elected to continue working.[98]

Is the time an employee spends on layoff status to be included in the calculation of his vacation entitlements? Where a contract provided for a vacation accrual rate based upon time worked by an employee following the employee's anniversary date, an employer was held not to be entitled to adjust the employee's anniversary date by excluding the months during which the employee was on layoff status. The arbitrator held that an employee not in pay status in any given month did not earn vacation pay in that month, but that nothing in the contract suggested that layoffs could affect an employee's anniversary date. To the contrary, the contract expressly recognized that an employee's anniversary date could occur while an employee was on a leave of absence and hence not in pay status.[99]

In another case, although a contract provision allowed for the proration of vacation benefits for employees who voluntarily or involuntarily terminated their service with the employer, an arbitrator held that an employer was not entitled to prorate the vacation benefits of employees who had been laid off for more than 1 year. The arbitrator found that a layoff with a right of recall was not the equivalent of a termination, and the past practice of the employer had been to pay full vacation benefits to employees who had been laid off.[100]

G. Sick Leave and Vacation Benefits
[LA CDI 100.5203; 100.5206; 116.1711; 116.2501]

A continuing issue in arbitration cases is whether vacation credits are earned during time spent on sick leave. The resolution of this issue depends on specific contract language.

Where the sick leave and vacation benefits arose under different contract provisions and were separate and distinct, it was held that the employee should receive both vacation pay and sick pay.[101] Similarly, under a contract providing for both vacation and sickness benefits, employees who were on sick leave when the employer closed the plant for a vacation period were held entitled to receive their sickness benefits and to select a different time for their vacations.[102]

---

[98]Super Valu Stores, 93 LA 931 (Eisele, 1989).

[99]McDonnell Douglas Aerospace W., 104 LA 252 (Rothstein, 1995). *See also* Iowa Mold Tooling Co., 82 LA 469 (Slade, 1984); Eagle Iron Works, 85 LA 979 (Thornell, 1985). *But see* GTE Prods. Corp., 85 LA 754 (Millious, 1985) (time an employee is on involuntary layoff not included within "continuous service"); Keystone Bakery, 82 LA 405 (Bolte, 1984) (to same effect).

[100]Fabick Mach. Co., 104 LA 555 (Suardi, 1995).

[101]Airco, 62 LA 1056, 1058 (Eyraud, Jr., 1974); International Paper Co., 37 LA 1026, 1028–29 (Bothwell, 1962). *But see* Auer Register Co., 62 LA 235, 240 (Perry, 1974) (no contract provision for medical leave of absence).

[102]*See* Barber-Ellis of Can., 64 LA 993, 995 (Brown, 1975); Toledo Scale Co., 25 LA 94, 99–100 (McKelvey, 1955); Derby Gas & Elec. Co., 21 LA 745, 745 (Donnelly, Mannino, & Mottram, 1953). *Cf.* Kentucky Utils. Co., 64 LA 737, 739–40 (Cantor, 1975).

The earning of vacation credits during time spent on sick leave is another matter, however. It has been held that an employee who was on paid sick leave for a month was not entitled to vacation credits for the sick leave period, since vacation pay is earned by service; the "test should not be merely whether an employee is receiving payments from the employer," because all payments are "not necessarily 'pay' for the purpose of earning or accruing" vacation credits.[103]

Where the governing contract contained a "use or lose" vacation policy, and the employee's workers' compensation injury prevented him from returning to work before the mandated vacation cut-off date, the arbitrator held that the employer properly denied vacation pay. The arbitrator ruled that the employee's right to vacation pay failed to vest since he never actually took a vacation.[104] However, where a contract did not preclude simultaneous receipt of vacation benefits and payments under a disability plan, an employee was entitled to compensation for a vacation scheduled prior to his disability.[105]

A related issue considered in other cases is whether a discharged employee, subsequently reinstated through arbitration, receives vacation pay for the interval he or she is off from work. Where an employee was reinstated with back pay, he was awarded vacation pay for the hours he would have worked but for the discharge.[106] Where an employee was reinstated without back pay, he was denied vacation pay.[107]

H. Maternity Leave and Vacation Benefits
[LA CDI 100.5203; 116.1711; 116.207]

It has been held that time spent on maternity leave is not to be included in computing vacation pay since such leave is directed to job security and is not intended to extend to vacation eligibility.[108]

---

[103]San Francisco Newspaper Publishers Ass'n, 46 LA 260, 262–64 (Burns, 1965). *See also* West Haven, Conn., Bd. of Educ., 96 LA 624, 628 (Porter, 1991); Northwestern Gen. Hosp., 82 LA 697, 700 (Adams, 1984); Modecraft Co., 44 LA 1045, 1049 (Jaffee, 1965); Kroger Co., 37 LA 126, 129 (Reid, 1961). *But see* Oakland Tribune, 99 LA 709, 712 (Cohn, 1992) (workers' compensation claimant who had settled her claim did not waive her right to earned vacation credits "for those shifts she would have been scheduled had not the injury prevented employment"); Grundy Elec. Coop., 91 LA 440, 442 (Yarowsky, 1988) (sick leave should be taken into account for vacation purposes, because agreement based vacation entitlement on "employment," not on "work performed").

[104]Iowa-Illinois Gas & Elec. Co., 96 LA 725 (Erbs, 1991).

[105]United Parcel Serv., 97 LA 104 (Talarico, 1991).

[106]Cowlitz Redi-Mix, 85 LA 745 (Boedecker, 1985).

[107]Parker White Metal Co., 86 LA 512 (Ipavec, 1985); Carling-National Breweries, 84 LA 503 (Van Wart, 1985).

[108]American Enka Corp., 48 LA 989, 992 (Pigors, 1966). *See also* Nivison-Weiskopf Co., 58 LA 159, 161 (Mullin, Jr., 1972); Clean Coverall Supply Co., 47 LA 272, 277 (Witney, 1966); Milwaukee Spring Co., 39 LA 1270, 1273 (Gundermann, 1962). *Cf.* Franklin Mfg. Co., 58 LA 1338, 1340 (Davis, 1972) (ambiguous contract language and past practice resulted in a different award); American Mach. & Foundry Co., 38 LA 1085, 1088 (Geissinger, 1962) (same). For related discussion, see section 3.C., "Maternity or Maternity-Related Leave," below.

I. Industrial Injury Leave and Vacation Benefits

Are employees placed on contractually compensable, "full pay" industrial injury leave entitled to credit toward sick leave and vacation entitlements as well as to the receipt of holiday pay? The answer depends on the contract provisions. Thus, under a sheriff department's contract stating that "all employees shall" receive these benefits, but specifically denying benefits to employees on uncompensated leave of absence, an arbitrator held that entitlement to the benefits required nothing more than status as an employee. His interpretation was supported by the perceived purpose of the injury leave—to provide employees full protection against loss—and the fact that contracts between the union and other sheriff departments expressly conditioned the benefit entitlements upon being in active work status.[109]

J. Family and Medical Leave Act Eligibility and Vacation Benefits
[LA CDI 94.553; 100.30; 100.5203; 100.5205; 116.151; 116.202; 116.5205]

The Family and Medical Leave Act of 1993 (FMLA)[110] provides that either the employer or the employee may elect to use vested vacation time to cover an otherwise unpaid FMLA leave of absence.[111] A Department of Labor regulation, however, specifically states that if the collective bargaining agreement so provides, the choice belongs solely to the employee.[112]

Thus, an employer's insistence that an employee use his vacation entitlements to cover absences for which an FMLA leave would have been available was found to violate a contract that gave employees the right to choose their vacations subject to the employer's "staffing needs."[113] The evidence failed to establish that staffing needs were adversely affected by this employee's choosing to save his vacation entitlement.[114]

2. HOLIDAYS [LA CDI 100.5204; 116.101]

Collective bargaining agreements customarily provide for pay for named holidays not worked,[115] but one contract provision stated that an employer was required to allow "time off for all legal holidays with pay" including, in

---

[109]Trumbull County, Ohio, Sheriff's Dep't, 105 LA 545 (Nelson, 1995).

[110]29 U.S.C. §2611 et seq.

[111]Id. §2612(d)(2)(A).

[112]29 C.F.R. §825.700(a). See also Union Hosp., 108 LA 966, 971 (Chattman, 1997) ("so long as the FMLA provisions in question do not preempt or invalidate the portion of the collective bargaining agreement [CBA] at issue, an arbitrator must always adhere to the clear and unambiguous language of the CBA").

[113]Union Hosp., 108 LA 966, 973 (Chattman, 1997).

[114]Id. Accord Grand Haven Stamped Prods. Co., 107 LA 131 (Daniel, 1996).

[115]For a checklist of various aspects of holiday pay that may be covered in the contract, see ROTHSCHILD, MERRIFIELD, & EDWARDS, COLLECTIVE BARGAINING AND LABOR ARBITRATION 690–91 (2d ed. 1979). Additional discussion of holidays is provided by Abrams & Nolan, Resolving Holiday Pay Disputes in Labor Arbitration, 33 CASE W. RES. L. REV. 380 (1983). A distinction has been drawn between governmentally designated "legal holidays" and "observed holidays" for holiday pay purposes under private industry contracts. See Stein, Inc., 71 LA 124, 127 (Klein, 1978).

addition to the holidays enumerated in the agreement, "any other holiday which may hereafter be declared a general holiday by the President of the United Sates or by an act of Congress." An arbitrator held that the employer was obliged to recognize as a "legal holiday" the "National Day of Mourning" for former President Nixon, which had been declared by presidential proclamation. In the absence of any evidence of relevant bargaining history, the arbitrator relied on the dictionary definition of the term "legal holiday," the practice of other employees who had similar contract language in their agreements, and the fact that this employer had followed the leave practices of the federal government in the past, all of which supported the treatment of the National Day of Mourning as a holiday.[116]

The primary purpose of holiday pay provisions is to insure the employee against the possible loss in earnings when he or she does not work because of a holiday occurring during the workweek.[117] Some contracts explicitly or by clear implication also include pay for holidays that fall on days when the employee would not have been scheduled to work, such as a regular day off or Saturday.[118]

Where contract language provided that two holidays were to be celebrated on the same day, arbitrators have reached conflicting decisions. The two contracts in question were in force during 1989, and each provided that if any holiday fell on a Sunday, it would be celebrated on the following Monday. In 1989 Christmas Eve and New Year's Eve, both recognized holidays, fell on Sunday. The next day was also a recognized holiday, Christmas Day and New Year's Day. All employees who worked on the following Tuesday were paid at the straight-time rate under the contracts. One arbitrator held that there was no contractual basis for requiring holiday pay on the two Tuesdays and no language covering the situation where holidays were to be celebrated on the same day. Accordingly, employees were not entitled to premium pay.[119] The other arbitrator held that the parties' intent from the contract was that if a holiday fell on a Sunday it was to be celebrated on an alternative day. To hold that two holidays were required to be celebrated on

---

[116]Sheet Metal Workers' Nat'l Pension Fund, 103 LA 764 (Kaplan, 1994).

[117]Anaconda Aluminum Co., 48 LA 219, 223 (Allen, Jr., 1967). *See also* Motch & Merryweather Mach. Co., 51 LA 724, 728 (Dworkin, 1968); American Airlines, 39 LA 500, 503 (Hill, 1962); Hemp & Co., 37 LA 1009, 1010 (Updegraff, 1962); Ohringer Home Furniture Co., 33 LA 477, 483 (Pollack, 1959); Inland Steel Co., 20 LA 323, 324 (Updegraff, 1953). For a discussion of the history of holiday pay provisions, see *General Cable Corp.*, 37 LA 934, 940 (Killion, 1961); *Carson Elec. Co.*, 24 LA 667, 670–72 (Howard, 1955) (also giving examples of types of clauses as well as discussion of work requirements). In *R. Herschel Mfg. Co.*, 35 LA 826, 827 (Ruckel, 1960), the contract stated that the purpose of holiday pay is that no employee shall be deprived "of income he would have been able to earn."

[118]*See* Leewall Sportswear Co., 53 LA 1165, 1166 (Dworkin, 1969); Cleveland Transit Sys., 45 LA 905, 907 (Kates, 1965) (an "interest" arbitration); International Paper Co., 43 LA 676, 677 (Goldstein, 1964); Courier-Citizen Co., 42 LA 269, 272 (Myers, 1964); Pittsburgh-Des Moines Steel Co., 40 LA 577, 581 (Koven, 1963). *Cf.* Milwaukee Linen Supply Co., 23 LA 392, 394 (Anderson, 1954); Premium Beverages, 22 LA 806, 807 (Seligson, 1954); Cannon Elec. Co., 21 LA 120, 122 (Jones, Jr., 1953); Hanson & Whitney Co., 21 LA 59, 60 (Stutz, 1953). For a case involving the right of the company to *require* employees to work on a holiday, see *Georgia-Pacific Corp.*, 59 LA 417, 418–20 (Hilpert, 1972).

[119]Nekoosa Packaging Corp., 96 LA 442 (Clarke, 1990).

the same day would mock the purpose of an alternative day when a recognized holiday falls on a Sunday. Accordingly, the employees were awarded premium pay for work on Tuesday, December 26.[120]

An employer is not obligated to pay holiday pay to employees for holidays that occur after their termination as a result of a plant closing. Terminated employees lose all rights under the contract other than those specifically granted to such employees.[121]

In another plant-closing situation, employees were held entitled to personal holiday pay where the contract provided the holiday should be taken when mutually agreed upon by the employee and the company. But employees were not entitled to birthday holiday pay since the contract provided that such holiday was to be taken on the Monday following a birthday, and, therefore, the right had not vested at the time of the closing of the business.[122]

A. Work Requirements [LA CDI 100.5204; 116.1033]

When the contract does provide for holiday pay, the pay is considered a "fringe benefit" earned by the employee. However, while it is recognized as an earned benefit, holiday pay may be conditioned upon the employee's compliance with contractually stated work requirements.

Many employers discourage the "stretching" of holidays by requiring employees to work their shifts that immediately precede and follow a holiday as a precondition to receiving holiday pay. The employee may be required to work "specified shifts at agreed time proximate to" the holiday.[123] Thus, contracts commonly require both a stipulated minimum period of service and work on designated days surrounding the holiday in order for the employee to be eligible for holiday pay. In the latter regard, the contract may require the employee to work *his or her* last scheduled day before and *his or her* first scheduled day after the holiday,[124] the last *regularly* scheduled day before and the first *regularly* scheduled day after the holiday,[125] the last *sched-*

---

[120]Inland Container Corp., 96 LA 1023 (Duff, 1991).

[121]Container Gen. Corp., 85 LA 159 (McDermott, 1985). *See also* City of Brooklyn, Ohio, 85 LA 799 (Graham, 1985).

[122]Mahoning Sparkle Mkts., 91 LA 1366 (Sharpe, 1988).

[123]Kennecott Copper Corp., 36 LA 507, 510 (Updegraff, 1960). *See also* Watkins Trucking, 48 LA 1101, 1102 (Klein, 1967); Amron Corp., 47 LA 582, 583 (Kelliher, 1966); Celotex Corp., 36 LA 517, 521 (Dworkin, 1961); Klapholz Bros., 33 LA 919, 921 (Tischler, 1959) (and cases cited); American Lava Corp., 24 LA 517, 520 (Tatum, 1955). By far the greatest number of holiday pay arbitration cases concerned the various aspects of eligibility for such pay—compliance with work requirements, part-day absence or tardiness before or after a holiday, and the effect on eligibility of layoff, leave, vacation, or strike.

[124]*See* Duff-Norton Co., 72 LA 607, 609 (Carson, Jr., 1979); Hubbell Metals, 67 LA 638, 639 (Schaffer, 1976); National Distillers Prods. Co., 53 LA 477, 478 (Jones, Jr., 1969); Douglas & Lomason Co., 52 LA 745, 746 (Keefe, 1969); Allison Steel Mfg. Co., 48 LA 1281, 1283 (Roberts, 1967).

[125]*See* Timken Co., 75 LA 801, 804–05 (Morgan, 1980) (absence for religious reasons was not a specified exception to the work requirements clause); Matlock Truck Body & Trailer Corp., 70 LA 1273, 1274 (Warns, 1978); Belknap, Inc., 69 LA 599, 603–04 (Teple, 1977); Westvaco, 67 LA 128, 130 (Lieberman, 1976) (retired employee); A.O. Smith Corp., 51 LA 1309, 1309 (Davis, 1968); Columbiana Pump Co., 51 LA 481, 482 (Teple, 1968); Watkins Trucking, 48 LA at 1101 (Klein, 1967).

uled workday before and the first *scheduled* workday after the holiday,[126] the day before *and* the day after the holiday,[127] the day before *or* the day after the holiday,[128] the *scheduled full* workday of the plant before and after the holiday,[129] or a specified number of workdays during the period before and after the holiday.[130] A significant consequence of such work requirements clauses is that the "failure of an employee to comply with . . . [them] as a condition precedent to holiday pay operates to disqualify him from receiving such benefit."[131]

The precise language used in the particular contract applied to the facts of a given case ordinarily determines whether holiday pay should be awarded. Where the contract required employees to work the last "scheduled" workday before and the first "scheduled" workday after the holiday, it was held that Saturday overtime falls within the "scheduled workday" clause as used in the contract, and employees who refused to work as scheduled on Saturday were not entitled to holiday pay.[132]

One arbitrator distinguished the term "regular workday," which appeared in the holiday pay provision under consideration, from the term "scheduled workday," and held that employees who worked their regular workdays of Friday and Tuesday surrounding Labor Day were eligible for holiday pay even though they were scheduled for overtime on Saturday before the holiday but did not work the assignment.[133] Similarly, in interpreting a contract requirement that an employee must work "his next workday" in order to be eligible for holiday pay,[134] an arbitrator held that the reference was to the individual's work schedule, not the plant's operating schedule.[135]

---

[126]*See* Amron Corp., 47 LA 582, 583 (Kelliher, 1966); Hanger-Silas Mason Co., 41 LA 83, 84 (Larson, 1963); Galloway Co., 33 LA 890, 891 (Anderson, 1960). The contract may make a distinction between "scheduled" and "regularly scheduled" work. *See* Corhart Refractories Co., 47 LA 648, 649 (McCoy, 1966).

[127]*See* Columbus Show Case Co., 57 LA 167, 167 (Hertz, 1971); Acro Wire, Inc., 44 LA 910, 910 (Belsky, 1965); Peerless Mfg. Co., 38 LA 746, 747 (Larson, 1962); Pierson-Hollowell Co., 28 LA 693, 693 (McIntosh, 1957).

[128]*See* Lima Elec. Co., 71 LA 74, 75 (Kabaker, 1978); Young Spring & Wire Co., 41 LA 991, 993 (Hunter, 1963).

[129]*See* Price-Pfister Brass Mfg. Co., 25 LA 398, 400 (Prasow, 1955).

[130]*See* Allis-Chalmers Corp., 72 LA 840, 844 (Goetz, 1979); Anaconda Aluminum Co., 48 LA 219, 220 (Allen, Jr., 1967) ("actually works during the payroll week in which the holiday falls"); Bradlees Family Circle Stores, 47 LA 567, 568 (House, 1966) (3 scheduled workdays out of 5 scheduled workdays before and after the holiday); Kennecott Copper Corp., 36 LA 507, 508 (Updegraff, 1960) (a minimum of two shifts during the workweek in which the holiday occurs).

[131]Motch & Merryweather Mach. Co., 51 LA 724, 730 (Dworkin, 1968). *See also* ASG Indus., 66 LA 416, 419 (Foster, 1976).

[132]Youngstown Steel Door Co., 46 LA 323, 324 (Marshall, 1966). *See also* L. Gordon & Son, 67 LA 1287, 1289 (Mallet-Prevost, 1976); Goodyear Tire & Rubber Co., 44 LA 1212, 1214–15 (Begley, 1965); Peerless Mfg. Co., 38 LA 746, 748–49 (Larson, 1962); Greif Bros. Cooperage Corp., 35 LA 389, 390 (Crane, 1960).

[133]A.O. Smith Corp., 47 LA 654, 660–61 (Dworkin, 1966). *See also* Corhart Refractories Co., 47 LA 648, 649 (McCoy, 1966); Amron Corp., 47 LA 582, 584 (Kelliher, 1966); Hinde & Dauch Paper Co., 22 LA 505, 508 (McCormick, 1954). *See also* A.O. Smith Corp., 51 LA 1309, 1310 (Davis, 1968).

[134]CWC Kalamazoo, 105 LA 555, 559 (Roumell, Jr., 1995).

[135]*Id.* at 560.

Because the purpose of "surrounding days" work requirements is, as noted, to prevent employees from "stretching" holidays[136] and to assure a full work force on the day before and the day after a holiday,[137] contractual exceptions to the "surrounding days" work requirements have been interpreted narrowly.[138] But, under certain circumstances, an employee may be deemed eligible for holiday pay even if he or she fails to work the days surrounding a holiday. In one case, the collective bargaining agreement required employees to work the last scheduled workday before and the first scheduled workday after a holiday to qualify for holiday pay.[139] A "scheduled workday" was defined in the contract as follows:

> The scheduled workday *of the employee* as used herein is the workday *designated by the Company* before and after such holiday, *and* on which the employee is *directed by the Company* to appear *and* on which the employee works the *hours required by the Company*.[140]

The arbitrator held that a scheduled workday under the parties' agreement was not only the one designated by the company, but also the one the employee was directed by the company to work. In this case, the employee had been permitted by the company to leave the plant and go to a physician following a work-related injury. The arbitrator found that the reasonable implication was that the employee had not been directed to appear for work until released by his physician and, therefore, holiday pay was awarded.

In cases where an employee's absence on a required workday before or after the holiday is "excused," arbitrators are divided as to whether the employee qualifies for holiday pay. In one such case, where the employee had

---

[136]See Artichoke Indus., 81 LA 196, 197–98 (Koven, 1983); Sunstar Foods, 73 LA 777, 780 (Mueller, 1979); Lima Elec. Co., 71 LA 74, 76 (Kabaker, 1978); St. Louis Grain Corp., 70 LA 814, 816 (Erbs, 1978); Tennessee Dickel Distilling Co., 69 LA 189, 190 (Cantor, 1977); Anaconda Am. Brass Co., 53 LA 1206, 1209 (Hill, 1969); Princeton Co., 49 LA 468, 470 (Seinsheimer, 1967); Watkins Trucking, 48 LA 1101, 1102 (Klein, 1967); Zion Indus., 41 LA 414, 415 (Larkin, 1963); Alwin Mfg. Co., 38 LA 632, 634 (Sembower, 1962); National Rejectors, 28 LA 390, 393 (Cheit, 1957); John Deere Planter Works, 26 LA 322, 324 (Davey, 1956); Crucible Steel Co., 21 LA 686, 689 (Simkin, 1953); Inland Steel Co., 20 LA 323, 324 (Updegraff, 1953). *See also* General Cable Corp., 37 LA 934, 942 (Killion, 1961) (discussing the initial (historical) function and the present-day function of the work requirement clauses in the parties' former and present contracts).

[137]See Van Dyne-Grotty, 70 LA 1288, 1289 (Lewis, 1978); Regal Ware, 65 LA 795, 796 (Griffith, Jr., 1975); Interpace Corp., 58 LA 1122, 1123–24 (Meiners, 1972); Gregory Galvanizing & Metal Processing, 46 LA 102, 105 (Kates, 1966); American Brake Shoe Co., 40 LA 673, 675 (Reid, 1963); General Elec. Co., 32 LA 769, 771 (Kleinsorge, 1959); National Rejectors, Inc., 28 LA 390, 393 (Cheit, 1957).

[138]See Quebecor Printing Memphis, 114 LA 421 (Robinson, 2000); City of Mattoon, Ill., 105 LA 44 (Bailey, 1995); Thomas Sysco Food Servs., 97 LA 483, 485 (Katz, 1991); Union Foundry Co., 95 LA 380, 383 (Odom, Jr., 1990); Matlock Truck Body & Trailer Corp., 70 LA 1273, 1274–75 (Warns, 1978); St. Louis Grain Corp., 70 LA 814, 816 (Erbs, 1978); Tennessee Dickel Distilling Co., 69 LA 189, 190 (Cantor, 1977).

[139]Penthouse Furniture, 81 LA 494 (Roberts, 1983). *See also* Pennwalt Corp., 88 LA 769 (McDonald, 1987) (vacation merely changes employee's last scheduled shift before and first scheduled shift after holiday).

[140]Penthouse Furniture, 81 LA 494, 496 (Roberts, 1983) (emphasis added). *See also* Atlanta Wire Works, 93 LA 537 (Williams, 1989). *But see* Hospital Linen Serv. Facility, 92 LA 228 (Stoltenberg, 1989).

actually worked on the holiday, an arbitrator held that taking sick leave on a required preholiday or post-holiday workday did not deprive the employee of holiday pay because his absence was not offensive to the purpose of such provisions—namely, to prevent employees from "extending" holidays—and the contract excused compliance if the absence was for a bona fide reason.[141] Similarly, another arbitrator held that taking sick leave on a required workday did not defeat eligibility for holiday pay even though the absent employee did not produce a doctor's note to support his claim of illness, where neither the contract nor past practice required such verification.[142] In several other cases, however, arbitrators have held that even excused absences on a required workday do not entitle the employee to holiday pay.[143]

B. Part-Day Absence or Tardiness on Surrounding Day
[LA CDI 100.5204; 116.1034]

Contracts requiring the employee to work the surrounding days in order to qualify for holiday pay ordinarily are interpreted as requiring full days of work, so that a part-day absence[144] or tardiness[145] may serve to defeat an employee's right to such pay. However, if the part-day absence[146] or tardi-

---

[141]Willamette Indus., 107 LA 1213 (Kaufman, 1997).

[142]Bureau of Engraving, 106 LA 315 (Bard, 1996).

[143]Hewitt Soap Co., 112 LA 641 (Bell, 1999) (employee who was excused for union business on the day before a holiday was denied holiday pay because union leave day was not expressly recognized by the contract); LTV Steel Mining Co., 107 LA 1094 (Doepken, 1996) (employee who was not at work because of surgery on the day after a holiday, but was on medical leave and had failed to work any other day during pay period; contract required employee to have worked or have been on vacation during holiday pay period); CWC Kalamazoo, 105 LA 555 (Roumell, Jr., 1995) (employee took vacation day on day after a holiday and then called in sick on the next regularly scheduled workday, but did not provide medical documentation); Curved Glass Distribs., 102 LA 33 (Eischen, 1993).

[144]See Morton Salt, 91 LA 345, 349–51 (Hoffmeister, 1988) (where employee who was 9 minutes late on day following holiday was properly denied holiday pay as he failed to either call in or explain reason for being late); Long-Airdox Co., 69 LA 1129, 1131–32 (Griffith, 1977) (permission to attend union meeting was not an "excused absence"); Interpace Corp., 58 LA 1122, 1123–24 (Meiners, 1972) (unexcused absence of ill employee who left work early on day after holiday); Douglas & Lomason Co., 52 LA 745, 749 (Keefe, 1969) ("excused" pass obtained by deception); Motch & Merryweather Mach. Co., 51 LA 724, 729–30 (Dworkin, 1968) (unexcused absence after lunch period); Hercules Powder Co., 43 LA 885, 887 (Koven, 1964) (employee had a legitimate excuse but refused to state more than "personal reasons"); American Brake Shoe Co., 40 LA 673, 675 (Reid, 1963) (wildcat strike); Jefferson City Cabinet Co., 35 LA 117, 120 (Marshall, 1960) (union meeting was a form of strike). For cases where the employee left early without permission, see Princeton Co., 49 LA 468, 470 (Seinsheimer, 1967); Tension Envelope Corp., 46 LA 712, 713–14 (Bauder, 1966); Marsh Instrument Co., 34 LA 478, 478–79 (Kelliher, 1960); General Elec. Co., 32 LA 769, 771 (Kleinsorge, 1959). In C.G. Conn, 66 LA 195, 196 (Davis, 1976), properly scheduled "overtime became a part of the full scheduled work shift within the meaning" of the contract, so that employees who left at the end of their regular 8-hour preholiday shift "became ineligible for holiday pay."

[145]See Hospital Linen Serv. Facility, 92 LA 228, 230 (Stoltenberg, 1989) (employee who was sent home for lack of "light duty" after injuring self and getting treatment at hospital was not entitled to holiday pay); Van Dyne-Grotty, 70 LA 1288, 1289 (Lewis, 1978); Michigan Maple Block Co., 70 LA 935, 936 (Keefe, 1978); Crucible Steel Co., 21 LA 686, 690 (Simkin, 1953); Morgan Bros. Laundry, 14 LA 201, 203 (Fulda, 1950).

[146]For cases where permission was granted to leave early, see National-Standard Co., 73 LA 414, 417–18 (Thomson, 1979) (but other employees were not excused); American Shipbuilding Co., 69 LA 944, 957–59 (Ruben, 1977) (many cases cited at 954–55); Outboard Ma-

ness[147] is contractually or otherwise excused, holiday pay may be awarded. The theory behind the "excused" cases is that the reason for the work requirement is to prevent "stretching" the holiday, and since the employees in these cases demonstrated that they did not try to stretch the holiday, they are entitled to holiday pay.[148] A similar rationale has been applied where the work time missed was minimal, even though the contract required "full" workdays before and after the holiday;[149] the contrary result was reached if the tardiness was substantial.[150]

---

rine Corp., 54 LA 112, 116–17 (Kesselman, 1971); *Etched Metal Co.*, 53 LA 431, 432 (Kabaker, 1969); *Wagner Awning Co.*, 48 LA 321, 322 (Nichols, 1966); *Alwin Mfg. Co.*, 38 LA 632, 635 (Sembower, 1962). For other situations, see *ITT-Phillips Drill Div.*, 69 LA 437, 438–39 (Kuhn, 1977) (employee, given permission to visit doctor, returned to finish her shift); *Standard Bag Corp.*, 45 LA 1149, 1151–52 (Summers, 1965) (20-year practice of short shift on the day before Thanksgiving); *Acro Wire*, 44 LA 910, 911 (Belsky, 1965) (contractual exception for illness); *Patterson Steel Co.*, 38 LA 400, 403 (Autrey, 1962) (permission granted 10 days in advance); *National Rejectors*, 28 LA 390, 393 (Cheit, 1957) (employee left early on the day after the holiday in response to a subpoena); *John Deere Planter Works*, 26 LA 322, 323 (Davey, 1956) (contractual exception for illness); *Connecticut Valley Mfg. Co.*, 23 LA 476, 481 (Copelof, 1954) (employee had to take his father to the hospital). In one case, an arbitrator held that, under the contract language and past practice, the company was justified in paying proportional holiday pay on the basis of the number of hours actually worked on the surrounding days. Trabon Eng'g Corp., 49 LA 220, 222–23 (Teple, 1967) (also citing many cases).

[147]*See* Electrical Repair Serv. Co., 69 LA 604, 606–07 (Johnston, Jr., 1977) (company upheld when it excused employees who were late because of weather conditions but denied holiday pay to employee who did not appear for work at all); Zion Indus., 41 LA 414, 415–16 (Larkin, 1963) (one employee had car trouble and was an hour late; another missed her usual ride, walked to work, and was 26 minutes late; the arbitrator said that these employees did not extend the holiday); National Rejectors, 28 LA 390, 393 (Cheit, 1957) (carpool driver did not appear and employee took a bus); Lake City Malleable, Inc., 25 LA 753, 754–55 (Hayes, 1956) (employee was 36 minutes late on the day after the holiday); Connecticut Valley Mfg. Co., 23 LA 476, 481 (Copelof, 1954) (employee's husband was ill and needed to be given medicine on time). One arbitrator set out guidelines to aid the parties in future cases involving tardiness before and after a holiday. Crucible Steel Co., 21 LA 686, 691 (Simkin, 1953).

[148]*See* Zion Indus., 41 LA 414, 415 (Larkin, 1963); Alwin Mfg. Co., 38 LA 632, 634–35 (Sembower, 1962); National Rejectors, 28 LA 390, 393 (Cheit, 1957); Morgan Bros. Laundry, 14 LA 201, 204 (Fulda, 1950). *See also* Artichoke Indus., 81 LA 196, 197–98 (Koven, 1983) (full-day excused absence did not constitute "deliberate" stretching of holiday). But absence before a holiday for "personal reasons" (*see* Houdaille Indus., 55 LA 1098, 1101 (McDermott, 1970)) and a part-day absence for "illness" (National-Standard Co., 73 LA 414, 418 (Thomson, 1979)), both without adequate explanation, have been held insufficient reasons to qualify for holiday pay.

[149]Jostens Printing & Publ'g Div., 107 LA 505 (Berger, 1996) (1½ hours late); National Unif. Serv., 104 LA 901 (Klein, 1995) (employees reported between 30 and 42 minutes late); Greensburg Presbyterian Seniorcare, 102 LA 506 (Jones, Jr., 1993). *See also* Vertex Sys., 68 LA 1099, 1101 (Marcus, 1977) (employee was only 3 minutes late because of an ice storm and company previously had made some exceptions to "the rigid rule" by excusing employees). *But see* Hospital Linen Serv. Facility, 92 LA 228 (Stoltenberg, 1989) (employee was 9 minutes late on the day following the holiday and failed to either call in or explain why he was late when he arrived; the company was upheld in denying holiday pay); Van Dyne-Grotty, 70 LA 1288, 1289 (Lewis, 1978) (employee was 1.3 hours late, missing a "substantial portion" of the scheduled half day prior to a holiday; the company was upheld in denying holiday pay). *Cf.* Columbus Show Case Co., 57 LA 167, 168 (Hertz, 1971) (holding that the contract language "worked the day" before and after the holiday could just as reasonably mean "worked *on* the day" as "worked the *full* day") (emphasis in original).

[150]National Unif. Serv., 104 LA 901 (Klein, 1995) (employee 6 hours and 55 minutes late on the day before a holiday). *But see* Monarch Tile, 101 LA 585 (Hooper, 1993) (employee who worked only 3 hours on the day after a holiday held entitled to holiday pay, where the contract merely provided that the employee "report" for work on the employee's next regularly scheduled workday).

C. Holidays Falling During Layoff [LA CDI 100.5204; 116.1035]

The primary purpose of holiday pay is to protect the earnings of the employee when a holiday occurs on a day on which he or she otherwise would have worked. Since an employee on layoff status is not working and would have no earnings, there is no entitlement to holiday pay in the absence of a contract provision extending such benefits to laid-off employees.[151]

A threshold question may be the status of laid-off employees. In one case, the company argued that the grievants failed to achieve a "fundamental standing" for holiday pay since they were not in "active status" on the date of the holiday; it was held, however, that the word "employee" as used in the holiday pay eligibility provisions of the contract "must be given its literal meaning to include both employees actively at work and inactive employees on layoff who retain seniority status."[152]

Many grievances of this type also raise issues under the language of the "work requirements" and "excused absence" clauses of the holiday pay provision. The "excused absence" clause may excuse employees from complying with work requirements in the event of specified circumstances such as illness, and, sometimes, for "other valid excuse." Thus, in some cases where the contract did not provide for holiday pay for laid-off employees, the arbitrator, basing his opinion on the excused absence clause[153] or on the work requirements clause[154] of the holiday pay provision, reasoned that the em-

---

[151]*See* Hemp & Co., 37 LA 1009, 1010 (Updegraff, 1962). *See also* Weinman Pump Mfg. Co., 44 LA 481, 484–87 (Leach, 1965) (discussing many awards); Young Spring & Wire Corp., 41 LA 991, 993–94 (Hunter, 1963); Great Atl. & Pac. Tea Co., 40 LA 152, 154–55 (Scheiber, 1962); Ohringer Home Furniture Co., 33 LA 477, 483 (Pollack, 1959); Lunkenheimer Co., 27 LA 507, 510 (Dworkin, 1956); National Metal Spinners Ass'n, 25 LA 341, 343 (Shapiro, 1954); Masonite Corp., 23 LA 49, 51 (Ralston, 1954). *Cf.* Kramer Trenton Co., 75 LA 651, 653 (Tener, 1980) (involving broad holiday pay provisions with no qualifying factors for eligibility); Standard Lime & Stone Co., 22 LA 601, 604 (Dworkin, 1954) (same).

[152]Allis-Chalmers Corp., 72 LA 840, 844–45 (Goetz, 1979) (awarding holiday pay to one group of employees who met the contractual requirement of working in the week containing a holiday and to another group who met the "substitute" requirement of a "letter of understanding" regarding a multiple holiday week).

[153]Layoff was considered an excused absence in *Ultrametl Mfg. Co.*, 42 LA 111, 116 (Kates, 1964) (discussing many cases pro and con); *Klapholz Bros.*, 33 LA 919, 923 (Tischler, 1959) (citing many cases on various aspects of holiday pay); *Inland Steel Co.*, 20 LA 323, 324–25 (Updegraff, 1953).

[154]For cases in which the employee was found to have complied with the contract requiring work on *his* scheduled workday before and after the holiday, see *Muter Co.*, 37 LA 103, 106 (Wood, 1961); *Continental-Emsco Co.*, 31 LA 449, 451 (Prasow, 1958); *Bianchi & Co.*, 28 LA 1, 4 (Parkman, 1957); *American Lava Corp.*, 24 LA 517, 519–20 (Tatum, 1955). A like result obtained where the plant was closed for short periods surrounding the holidays and the contract required work on *the* scheduled day before and after the holidays in question. George Otto Broiler Co., 37 LA 57, 60 (Garmon, 1961). *See also* All Steel, 96 LA 1218, 1220 (Duff, 1991); R.A. Cullinan & Son, 85 LA 162, 164–66 (Newmark, 1985); Teledyne Wirz, 77 LA 691, 692 (Rossman, 1981); Reilly Tar & Chem. Corp., 66 LA 835, 836 (Blackmar, 1976). In *Premiere Corp.*, 67 LA 376, 380–81 (Fieger, 1976), bad faith was found in laying off the employees precipitously on the day before Thanksgiving and pay was awarded for that holiday; but recognizing a 90-day "reasonable time" rule as applicable, the arbitrator denied holiday pay to employees in layoff for 5 to 7 months, even though the employee may have worked "his" scheduled workday before and after the holidays included in the layoff period. In *R. Herschel Mfg. Co.*, 35 LA 826, 829 (Ruckel, 1960), the arbitrator would have had "no hesitancy in finding for the Union" on the basis of the scheduled workday clause but for another clause stating that the purpose of the holiday pay provision was that no employee should be deprived of income he or she would have been able to earn; employees in layoff did not lose the opportunity to work as a result of the holiday.

ployee had met the basic conditions of the contract and consequently qualified for holiday pay. In some of these cases, the arbitrator noted the additional fact that the layoff was of a "reasonably" short duration before and after the holiday. In one case, it was held that a layoff was not the type of "absence" specified in the contract as would disqualify an employee from the benefit of a personal holiday, since the word absence denotes circumstances over which the employee has control, when in fact the employer controls layoffs.[155] However, in other cases arbitrators rejected the argument that a layoff constituted an excused absence and refused to award holiday pay.[156] Likewise, laid-off employees were held to be disqualified from receiving holiday pay because they failed to meet the work requirements.[157]

Arbitrators award holiday pay if the facts indicate that the layoff was made in bad faith or was contrived as a means of avoiding the payment of holiday pay.[158] Of course, the contract may specifically deny holiday pay to employees in layoff status,[159] or it may specifically provide for such pay for employees in layoff status within a specified time of the holiday.[160]

Where the layoff occurred after an employer declared bankruptcy, another company bought the bankrupt's assets and called back the laid-off employees. The employees subsequently grieved the new employer's refusal to provide holiday pay. The arbitrator concluded that since the holiday had

---

[155]Louisiana-Pacific Corp., 86 LA 301 (Michelstetter, 1986).

[156]See Baggett Transp. Co., 71 LA 609, 611–12 (Marcus, 1978) (citing Great Atl. & Pac. Tea Co., 40 LA 152, 155–56 (Scheiber, 1962) (discussing many cases at 154–58)); Ohringer Home Furniture Co., 33 LA 477, 483 (Pollack, 1959) ("To say that being laid off is to be excused by the company from the necessity of meeting the conditions precedent is preposterous."); Price-Pfister Brass Mfg. Co., 25 LA 398, 403 (Prasow, 1955); J. Sklar Mfg. Co., 22 LA 18, 19–20 (Cahn, 1954).

[157]See Amelco Corp., 72 LA 528, 530 (Tanaka, 1979); Weinman Pump Mfg. Co., 44 LA 481, 487 (Leach, 1965) (discussing many cases at 484–86); Hemp & Co., 37 LA 1009, 1010 (Updegraff, 1962) (past practice also involved); Lamson & Sessions Co., 37 LA 273, 274–75 (Williams, 1961) (same); Ohringer Home Furniture Co., 33 LA 477, 482–83 (Pollack, 1959); Price-Pfister Brass Mfg. Co., 25 LA 398, 402–03 (Prasow, 1955); Masonite Corp., 23 LA 49, 51 (Ralston, 1954) (same). In all these cases, the contract required the employee to work on *the* scheduled workdays surrounding the holiday.

[158]See Premiere Corp., 67 LA 376, 380–81 (Fieger, 1976); Bradlees Family Circle Stores, 47 LA 567, 571 (House, 1966); Young Spring & Wire Corp., 41 LA 991, 994 (Hunter, 1963); Lamson & Sessions Co., 37 LA 273, 274 (Williams, 1961); Bianchi & Co., 28 LA 1, 4–5 (Parkman, 1957); National Metal Spinners Ass'n, 25 LA 341, 343 (Shapiro, 1954).

[159]See Flintkote Co., 26 LA 526, 527 (Morvant, 1956); Price-Pfister Brass Mfg. Co., 25 LA 398, 400 (Prasow, 1955).

[160]See Norris Indus., 73 LA 1129, 1130 (Roumell, Jr., 1979); Floodwood Indus., 70 LA 1200, 1201 (Boyer, Jr., 1978); GAF Corp., 70 LA 79, 79 (Bailey, 1978); Consolidated Aluminum Corp., 66 LA 938, 940 (Mann, Jr., 1976); California Brewers Ass'n, 57 LA 742, 746 (Block, 1971) (involving also a conflict between the "mandates of" the holiday pay provisions and an act of God clause); National Distillers Prods. Co., 53 LA 477, 478 (Jones, Jr., 1969); Infant Socks, 51 LA 400, 405 (Moberly, 1968); Shipley Wholesale Drug Co., 48 LA 915, 917 (Kates, 1967); Clark Grave Vault Co., 47 LA 86, 87 (McCoy, 1966); Lehigh Portland Cement Co., 46 LA 132, 135 (Duff, 1965); Aetna Bearing Co., 44 LA 817, 817 (Luskin, 1965); Continental-Emsco Co., 31 LA 449, 449 (Prasow, 1958); Rheem Mfg. Co., 29 LA 173, 175 (Ross, 1957); Lunkenheimer Co., 27 LA 507, 508 (Dworkin, 1956); L.A. Young Spring & Wire Corp., 23 LA 400, 401 (Platt, 1954). In *Norris Indus.*, 73 LA 1129, 1131–32 (Roumell, Jr., 1979), the decision rested on the issue of whether the effective date of the layoff was the last day the employees worked or the first day they were off work (citing arbitration and court cases in support of the latter). *See also* ITT, 75 LA 729, 731–32 (Howlett, 1980) (discussing many cases).

occurred prior to the call-back, the employees were not entitled to the compensation.[161]

D. Vacation or Leave and Holiday Pay [LA CDI 100.5204; 116.1036]

If the contract specifically provides for holiday pay in addition to vacation pay when the holiday happens to occur during an employee's vacation period, that holiday pay must be allowed.[162] This is so even though the employee reported back to work a day or more late after his vacation,[163] or was guilty of an unexcused absence prior to the vacation period,[164] and even though the contract contained surrounding days work requirements. In the latter regard, the rationale used by arbitrators is that such requirements are intended to meet the employer's staffing problems when a holiday occurs during a regular workweek and have no application when a holiday occurs during a vacation week.[165]

However, under a contract providing for holiday pay for holidays falling during a vacation period, an arbitrator ruled that employees who took one approved vacation day on the day after the holiday and were sick on the next day were not entitled to holiday pay. The "vacation period" was interpreted to mean more than an isolated vacation day.[166]

An employer who, in order to cut costs, sought to preclude employees from taking their vacation during any week in which a holiday fell on a weekday was held to have violated the labor agreement. The employer could restrict the scheduling of vacation only in those limited situations where operations would otherwise be impaired.[167]

A vacation shutdown clause may affect the employees' entitlement to holiday pay, as it did in a case where the contract also stated that the intent of the holiday pay clause was to pay wages for holidays not worked to employees "who are scheduled to work on the day on which the holiday falls." The employer there scheduled a vacation shutdown during the week in which a holiday fell, and the arbitrator refused to award holiday pay, resting his decision "squarely on the restrictive terms of the contract."[168] In another situ-

---

[161]Clark Bar Am., 106 LA 856 (Paolucci, 1996).

[162]Brooks Foods, 45 LA 249, 251 (Larkin, 1965) (holiday pay was awarded to employees who had elected to take their vacations during a layoff period, because they satisfied contractual requirements for such pay).

[163]See Ford Motor Co., 41 LA 621, 624 (Ill. Cir. Ct. 1963); Northwestern Steel & Wire Co., 39 LA 104, 105–06 (Sembower, 1962); Fort Smith Structural Steel Co., 36 LA 204, 206–07 (Autrey, 1960). See also Olin-Mathieson Chem. Corp., 24 LA 116, 120–21 (Reynard, 1955).

[164]See Bethlehem Steel, 27 LA 801, 802 (Seward, 1956); Miami Copper Co., 16 LA 191, 193 (Prasow, 1951) (arbitrator believed that the employee is "subject to appropriate disciplinary penalty for his unexcused absence").

[165]See Ford Motor Co., 41 LA 621, 623 (Ill. Cir. Ct. 1963); Northwestern Steel & Wire Co., 39 LA 104, 105–06 (Sembower, 1962); Fort Smith Structural Steel Co., 36 LA 204, 207 (Autrey, 1960); Miami Copper Co., 16 LA 191, 193 (Prasow, 1951).

[166]CWC Kalamazoo, 105 LA 555 (Roumell, Jr., 1995).

[167]National Linen Serv., 110 LA 476 (Frockt, 1998).

[168]Geeco, Inc., 29 LA 658, 662 (Walsh, 1957). See also Curtiss Candy Co., 64 LA 538, 539 (Epstein, 1975); Sefton Fibre Can Co., 12 LA 101, 104–06 (Townsend, 1948); Regal Ware, 65 LA 795, 796–97 (Griffith, Jr., 1975) (delaying holiday pay because of past practice).

ation, concerned with pay in lieu of vacation, the arbitrator held that an employee on leave of absence who received pay in lieu of vacation could not also receive holiday pay for a holiday occurring during the leave, because "a payment in lieu of vacation does not cover any particular time."[169]

The holiday pay issue also is complicated when both layoff and vacation are involved at the same time. Under a contract provision granting holiday pay to employees on vacation in the payroll period during which the holiday occurs, one arbitrator resolved the problem by ruling that a laid-off employee is entitled to pay for a holiday falling within his or her scheduled vacation period if the vacation is scheduled prior to the layoff or if the employee is on layoff at the time the vacation is scheduled but returns to work and remains at work until the scheduled vacation is taken; an employee who is not working at the time the vacation is scheduled or prior to the time the vacation occurs is not eligible for pay for a holiday occurring within the vacation period.[170] Another arbitrator, taking the view that vacation pay benefits are deferred earnings, ruled that employees, who were on lay-off status but eligible for vacation during the scheduled vacation shutdown, had met the basic holiday pay eligibility requirement that the "individual employee received any earnings from the Company during the pay period in which the holiday in question falls."[171]

The contract may be unclear regarding payment for holidays falling during a leave of absence. If this is the case, the determination of eligibility for holiday pay may turn on such contract provisions as the surrounding days work requirements,[172] or other requirements such as being a "regular" employee, working during the pay period in which the holiday occurs,[173] or the justifiable absence clause.[174]

In the absence of a specific contract provision for pay for holidays occurring during sick leave or other leaves of absence, arbitrators have been reluctant to award such pay.[175] Even where the contract does provide for holi-

---

[169]TRW Metals Div., 48 LA 414, 416 (Laybourne, 1967). Still another facet of holiday pay was presented in a "productivity leave" issue decided by *Washington Publishers Ass'n*, 65 LA 285, 286–87 (Ables, 1975).

[170]United States Steel Corp., 36 LA 603, 616 (Garrett, 1961). *See also* Pittsburgh Brewing Co., 88 LA 95, 97–98 (Duff, 1986); Meyer Prods., 84 LA 767, 769–70 (Laybourne, 1985); United States Steel Corp., 36 LA 385, 388 (Garrett, 1960); Firestone Tire & Rubber Co., 14 LA 552, 560 (Platt, 1950). Under contract language identical to that in *United States Steel Corp.*, 36 LA 603 (Garrett, 1961), an arbitrator held that the contract applied to employees on sick leave as well as layoff even though the holiday pay provision was "couched in layoff language." Bethlehem Steel, 41 LA 624, 627 (Porter, 1963).

[171]Lectromelt Corp., 58 LA 463, 467–68 (McDermott, 1972). *See also* Aladdin Indus., 18 LA 581, 583–84 (Hampton, 1952).

[172]*See* Mattel, Inc., 23 LA 383, 387 (Warren, 1954).

[173]*See* Femco, Inc., 50 LA 1146, 1148 (McDermott, 1968); Republic Steel Corp., 21 LA 317, 319–20 (Shipman, 1953).

[174]*See* Price Bros. Co., 60 LA 990, 992–93 (Gibson, 1973); Wooster Sportswear Co., 46 LA 9, 10 (Dworkin, 1965). In *Lithonia Lighting Co.*, 74 LA 30, 32–33 (Rimer, 1980), an employee, absent on the day after a holiday because of an ill stepchild, had a "valid excuse" within the meaning of the holiday pay provision.

[175]*See* Capital Dist. Transp. Dist., 88 LA 353 (La Manna, 1986) (employee receiving full pay during military leave not entitled to holiday pay, but credited for 1 additional day of military leave time); Femco, Inc., 50 LA 1146, 1148 (McDermott, 1968) (where the contract provided holiday pay for the "regular" employee, defined as "one having worked in the pay period in which the holiday falls," the arbitrator said that this provision excluded from holi-

day pay for employees on leave, it has been interpreted strictly. For example, a provision for holiday pay for an employee on sick leave "if his absence due to sickness begins no earlier than the second workday preceding or begins no later than the first work day following the holiday" was applied to deny holiday pay to an employee whose sick leave began earlier than the second workday preceding the holiday.[176] But where a contract provided that employees in excused absences should be paid for holidays, and a disability income benefits plan failed to list receipt of holiday pay as precluding payment of disability benefits, an employer improperly denied payment of benefits to an employee during the time it paid him holiday pay.[177]

If the contract contains no explicit provision on sick leave and holiday pay, the issue may involve the "justifiable excuse" exception to the surrounding days work requirements clause. For instance, where the contract provided that an employee would be ineligible for holiday pay if absent on either of the surrounding days "unless such absence is for justifiable cause," the arbitrator held that "an employee on sick leave must be regarded as excused from work or absent for 'just cause,'" thus qualifying for holiday pay.[178] However, although the contract was silent on the matter, the arbitrator held further that it would be "practical and reasonable" and not in conflict with any of the terms of the agreement to "imply a limitation that an employee on sick leave would be entitled to not more than two paid holidays occurring

---

day pay eligibility employees like the grievant who were on extended leaves of absence). In *San Francisco Newspaper Publishers Ass'n*, 46 LA 260, 265 (Burns, 1965), the arbitrator held that if the parties had intended to provide holiday pay for employees on sick leave, they could have done so just as they provided pay for holidays occurring during regular days off or vacations. *See also* Levitan Fruit Co., 64 LA 762, 764–65 (McGilligan, 1975); Columbia Records, 32 LA 336, 340 (Prasow, 1959) (involving past practice).

[176]*See* Columbus & S. Ohio Elec. Co., 45 LA 1021, 1023 (Schmidt, 1965). *See also* Atlas Elec. Fittings Co., 71 LA 1067, 1068 (Woy, 1978); Chardon Rubber Co., 71 LA 1039, 1040 (Gibson, 1978); Weil-McLain Co., 64 LA 625, 627 (Hadlick, 1975) (doctor's certificate required); P.V.O. Int'l, 63 LA 982, 986 (Maniscalco, 1974); Rheem Mfg. Co., 62 LA 837, 841–42 (Hilgert, 1974); Alside, Inc., 42 LA 75, 76–77 (Teple, 1964); Republic Steel Corp., 21 LA 317, 320 (Shipman, 1953); Continental Can Co., Inc., 15 LA 204, 207 (Aaron, 1950). For cases in which the sickness exception contained no restrictive language, see *Riverside Mfg. Indus.*, 69 LA 1195, 1200 (Lipson, 1977); *United States Steel Corp.*, 67 LA 97, 100 (Dunsford, 1976); *Thermoid W. Co.*, 29 LA 424, 426–27 (Kadish, 1957); *Bakers Negotiating Comm.*, 24 LA 694, 695 (Sherman, 1955).

[177]Bolens Corp., 83 LA 1286 (Wyman, 1984).

[178]Wooster Sportswear Co., 46 LA 9, 10 (Dworkin, 1965). *See also* Ideal Basic Indus., 68 LA 928, 930 (Eckhardt, 1977) (involving disability leave of absence); Hubbell Metals, 67 LA 638, 640 (Schaffer, 1976); L'anse Creuse Pub. Sch., 63 LA 544, 545–48 (Roumell, Jr., 1974) (citing many cases); Prat-Daniel Corp., 24 LA 815, 817 (Donnelly, Curry, & Mottram, 1955); Crown Upholstering Co., 18 LA 777, 779–80 (Kaplan, 1952). *Cf.* Breece Plywood, Inc., 32 LA 516, 521–22 (Warns, 1959). Nor did the employer's obligation to make sick leave payments to the union's welfare fund limit his obligation regarding holiday pay, because the contract expressly provided that the welfare payments shall not be deemed "wages due to the workers." *See* Wooster Sportswear Co., 46 LA 9, 11 (Dworkin, 1965). Regarding receipt of both workers' compensation and holiday pay, see *Penthouse Furniture*, 81 LA 494, 495 (Roberts, 1983), ("whether or not Grievant received workman's compensation for the holiday in question is irrelevant to whether or not Grievant was entitled to holiday pay under the contract"). In *Printing Industry of New York*, 44 LA 124, 125 (Kornblum, 1965), it was held that payment of sick leave pay did not necessarily preclude the requirement of proof of illness to qualify for holiday pay.

during a three month period of sick leave, providing the employee returns to work upon cessation of her illness."[179]

An established practice of denying holiday pay to employees on sick leave may lead the arbitrator to deny such pay.[180] Conversely, a past practice, or prior settlements reached by the parties, may require holiday pay to employees on sick leave.[181]

E. Holidays on Nonworkdays [LA CDI 100.5204; 116.1037]

Arbitrators disagree whether employees should receive pay for holidays falling on a nonworkday Saturday, where the contract designated certain paid holidays without distinguishing between holidays falling within or outside the regular workweek. On one hand, many arbitrators have held that employees are entitled to pay for holidays that fall on Saturdays even though the regular workweek is Monday through Friday.[182] They base their rulings on "the clear, plain and explicit" language of the contract that is "not limited or restricted by any qualifying provision."[183]

On the other hand, many other arbitrators who have denied pay for holidays falling on nonworkday Saturdays have held that while the contract language is unrestricted, it is ambiguous in that it does not contain an express provision that holiday pay should be granted regardless of the day upon which the holiday falls.[184] Some of these arbitrators felt compelled to turn to the "conduct of the parties" or their past practice that gave meaning

---

[179]Wooster Sportswear Co., 46 LA 9, 11 (Dworkin, 1965).

[180]See Goodyear Tire & Rubber Co., 38 LA 1061, 1064 (Elkouri, 1962); Breece Plywood, 32 LA 516, 521–22 (Warns, 1959); Columbia Records, 32 LA 336, 340 (Prasow, 1959). For cases involving past practice regarding eligibility for holiday pay when the employee is receiving disability pay, see Standard Oil Co., 26 LA 206, 208 (Beatty, 1956); Atlantic Ref. Co., 25 LA 100, 104 (Boles, 1955). But see Atlanta Wire Works, 93 LA 537 (Williams, 1989) (employee eligible for holiday pay, even though he failed to present doctor's excuse for sick leave taken during last regularly scheduled shift before holiday due to company's inconsistent application of requirement in past).

[181]See Caravelle Boat Co., 62 LA 1025, 1026–27 (Brown, 1974); American Smelting & Ref. Co., 44 LA 1010, 1014–15 (Koven, 1965); Atlantic Gummed Paper Corp., 35 LA 680, 681 (Rubin, 1960).

[182]See International Paper Co., 43 LA 676, 677–78 (Goldstein, 1964); Courier-Citizen Co., 42 LA 269, 272 (Myers, 1964); Woodward Wight & Co., 33 LA 494, 496 (Caraway, 1959); Carson Elec. Co., 24 LA 667, 670–71 (Howard, 1955); O'Brien Suburban Press, Inc., 21 LA 325, 326 (Donnelly, Curry, & Mottram, 1953); Pioneer Mfg. Co., 20 LA 910, 911 (Anderson, 1953); Lou Lenoff Furs Co., 20 LA 734, 737 (Gaffey, 1953); Kraft Foods Co., 12 LA 43, 45 (Phillips, 1949); E.B. Badger & Sons, Co., 7 LA 824, 826 (Albert, 1947). In two of these cases, the arbitrators awarded holiday pay despite a consistent past practice of not paying for Saturday holidays. See Courier-Citizen Co., 42 LA 269, 272 (Myers, 1964); O'Brien Suburban Press, 21 LA 325, 326 (Donnelly, Curry, & Mottram, 1953).

[183]International Paper Co., 43 LA 676, 677 (Goldstein, 1964).

[184]See Premium Beverages, 22 LA 806, 807 (Seligson, 1954); H.D. Lee Co., 21 LA 98, 101–04 (Cheit, 1953); Coca-Cola Bottling Co., 18 LA 74, 75–76 (Grant, 1951); International Harvester Co., 13 LA 983, 984–85 (Seward, 1949); M. Augenblick & Brother, 12 LA 417, 418 (Trotta, 1949); M.E. Stern & Co., 11 LA 635, 636–38 (Rosenfarb, 1947); G.W. Carnrick Co., 8 LA 334, 336–37 (Feinberg, 1947); Standard Grocery Co., 7 LA 745, 746 (Wallen, 1947); Standard Brands, 7 LA 663, 664–65 (Scheiber, 1947). See also Heil Co., 11 LA 970, 970–71 (Stein, 1948).

to the contract, and, finding a previously unchallenged practice of not paying for Saturday holidays, these arbitrators refused to grant such pay.[185]

The contract may specifically exclude Saturday holidays that are not
workdays from the holiday pay clause;[186] or it may specifically include holidays that fall on nonworkday Saturdays;[187] or the contract may contain a
qualifying clause granting pay for named holidays provided they fall on regularly scheduled workdays.[188] In the latter event, no holiday pay ordinarily
would be allowed for holidays occurring outside the regular workweek,[189] nor
would the employees under such a contract be entitled to have the Friday
preceding a Saturday holiday considered as a paid holiday.[190]

One contract stated that employees would be paid for holidays that did
not fall on a Saturday. At the time, the plant operated on the traditional
Monday through Friday, five-day workweek. Subsequently, the employer
changed to a nontraditional workweek. An arbitrator directed the company
to consider the Good Friday holiday as a day worked for purposes of computing weekly overtime for employees who were not scheduled to work on Fridays.[191]

F. Strikes and Holiday Pay [LA CDI 100.5204; 116.1039]

Arbitrators generally have been reluctant to award pay to employees for
holidays occurring while they are on strike unless the contract provides otherwise.[192] Thus, in a number of cases where work was available and sched-

---

[185]*See* Coca-Cola Bottling Co., 18 LA 74, 75–76 (Grant, 1951); M. Augenblick & Brother,
12 LA 417, 418 (Trotta, 1949); M.E. Stern & Co., 11 LA 635, 637–38 (Rosenfarb, 1947); G.W.
Carnrick Co., 8 LA 334, 336–37 (Feinberg, 1947).

[186]*See* American Can Co., 33 LA 809, 809 (Bothwell, 1959); Western Union Tel. Co., 20
LA 756, 756 (Shipman, 1953).

[187]*See* Leewall Sportswear Co., 53 LA 1165, 1166 (Dworkin, 1969); Foster Wheeler Corp.,
35 LA 788, 789 (Stark, 1960). For cases involving holiday "bumping," see *Dayton Press*, 71
LA 1034, 1037–38 (Barone, 1978) (discussing other cases); *Gulfport Shipbuilding Corp.*, 71
LA 599, 601 (Scanlon, 1978); *Stein, Inc.*, 71 LA 124, 128–29 (Klein, 1978); *Imperial Reading
Corp.*, 69 LA 806, 807 (Jones, 1977); *Hoerner Waldorf Corp.*, 61 LA 58, 61–64 (Murphy, 1973);
Indiana Moulding & Frame Co., 60 LA 737, 738 (Cohen, 1973); *Federal Paper Bd. Co.*, 59 LA
581, 582 (Altrock, 1972); *Stone Container Corp.*, 58 LA 973, 975–76 (Allen, Jr., 1972); *Greater
St. Louis Steel Plate Fabricators Ass'n*, 58 LA 123, 124 (Stix, 1972); *Anaconda Aluminum
Co.*, 66–1 ARB ¶8320 (McIntosh, 1966).

[188]*See* Printing Indus. of Washington, D.C., 42 LA 843, 844 (Clayton, 1964); Milwaukee
Linen Supply Co., 23 LA 392, 393 (Anderson, 1954); Cannon Elec. Co., 21 LA 120, 120 (Jones,
Jr., 1953); Hanson & Whitney Co., 21 LA 59, 59 (Stutz, Mottram, & Mannino, 1953); Hart
Top Mfg. Co., 18 LA 356, 357 (Pigors, 1952); Minnesota Mining & Mfg. Co., 12 LA 165, 165
(Gooding, 1949).

[189]*See* cases cited in note 188, *supra*. In *Vulcan-Mold & Iron Co.*, 21 LA 7, 8–9 (Kelliher,
1953), the employer was required to pay for a Saturday holiday despite the contract, where
there was a past practice of regularly scheduling Saturday work.

[190]Printing Indus. of Washington, D.C., 42 LA 843, 844 (Clayton, 1964). *See also* Leewall
Sportswear Co., 53 LA 1165, 1169 (Dworkin, 1969).

[191]Friskies Petcare Prods., 110 LA 20 (Thornell, 1998).

[192]*See* Anaconda Am. Brass Co., 53 LA 1206, 1209 (Hill, 1969); Mastermade Furniture
Corp., 50 LA 921, 924 (Wolff, 1968); St. Regis Paper Co., 46 LA 967, 970 (Stieber, 1966);
Gregory Galvanizing & Metal Processing, 46 LA 102, 104–05 (Kates, 1966); E.J. Lavino &
Co., 43 LA 213, 214 (Crawford, 1964); Mobil Oil Co., 42 LA 102, 107 (Forsythe, 1963); Alside,
Inc., 42 LA 75, 78–79 (Teple, 1964); American Brake Shoe Co., 40 LA 673, 675 (Reid, 1963);
Davis Eng'g Corp., 24 LA 560, 562–63 (Trotta, 1955). But where the contract has no sur-
rounding days work requirements, the result may be different. Hellenic Lines, 38 LA 339,
341–43 (Yagoda, 1962).

uled during a strike, and the contract contained a surrounding days work requirements clause, it was held that employees on strike were not entitled to pay for holidays falling during the strike period.[193] The result is ordinarily the same for holidays falling during a strike occurring in a hiatus period between contracts.[194] The rulings of the arbitrators are based on the lack of compliance with the contractual conditions for entitlement[195] or, in a hiatus period strike, on the reasoning that the right to holiday pay is a creature of contract and such right does not exist when there is no contract.[196]

Moreover, where the strike had been settled but not all the employees had been recalled when the holiday occurred, the contractual eligibility requirements were held to apply to disqualify those who had not yet returned to work.[197] In this regard, one arbitrator has stated that, despite the original purpose of the surrounding days work requirements "to encourage full staffing of the plant before and after a holiday and to prevent stretching of holiday periods," nevertheless, "when a contract states in absolute terms that holiday pay will be allowed only if" such requirements are met, it would be adding to the contract to disregard such requirements.[198]

---

[193]See Consolidation Coal Co., 93 LA 473, 475 (Seidman, 1989) (employee provided timely notice of intent not to take birthday holiday, and then he and fellow employees engaged in work stoppage period that began on last day prior to holiday and continued after); Dahlgren's, Inc., 92 LA 571 (Clifford, 1989) (striking employees failed to return on day before holiday because they were waiting for local union's ratification of strike settlement); Union Carbide Corp., 65 LA 189, 192 (May, 1975) (holiday fell during vacation that was encompassed by strike period); Mead Corp., 57 LA 1217, 1219–20 (Seinsheimer, 1971) (wildcat strike); Gregory Galvanizing & Metal Processing, 46 LA 102, 104–05 (Kates, 1966); Alside, Inc., 42 LA 75, 78–79 (Teple, 1964); American Brake Shoe Co., 40 LA 673, 675 (Reid, 1963) (same); Jefferson City Cabinet Co., 35 LA 117, 120 (Marshall, 1960) (same). See also Westmoreland Coal Co., 62 LA 681, 683 (Goldberg, 1974) (work stoppage for alleged safety reasons); Kroger Co., 25 LA 841, 844 (Klamon, 1956). Cf. Food Mach. Corp., 52 LA 512, 514–15 (Keefe, 1969); A.O. Smith Corp., 51 LA 1309, 1310 (Davis, 1968).

[194]See Alliance Mach. Co., 74 LA 1058, 1060 (Feldman, 1980); Peavey Co., 43 LA 539, 545 (Traynor, 1964); Chatham Elecs., 37 LA 3, 4 (Kerrison, 1961); Kennecott Copper Corp., 36 LA 507, 510 (Updegraff, 1960); Publishers' Ass'n of N.Y. City, 33 LA 681, 682–83 (Seitz, 1959); Dixie Fire Brick Co., 30 LA 671, 674 (Hepburn, 1958); Davis Eng'g Corp., 24 LA 560, 562–63 (Trotta, 1955). See also American Export Lines, 36 LA 1276, 1278 (Sugarman, 1961). But see Universal-Cyclops Steel Corp., 36 LA 1237, 1240–41 (Crawford, 1961) (strike settlement agreement extended the old contract).

[195]See St. Regis Paper Co., 62 LA 785, 788 (Rutledge, 1974); Gregory Galvanizing & Metal Processing, 46 LA 102, 105 (Kates, 1966); Alside, Inc., 42 LA 75, 78–79 (Teple, 1964); American Brake Shoe Co., 40 LA 673, 675 (Reid, 1963); Chatham Elecs., 37 LA 3, 4 (Kerrison, 1961); Jefferson City Cabinet Co., 35 LA 117, 120 (Marshall, 1960); Intermountain Operators League, 26 LA 149, 152 (Kadish, 1956); McKinney Mfg. Co., 19 LA 73, 75 (Brecht, 1952). In Packaging Corp. of Am., 62 LA 1214, 1216 (Gibson, 1974), the arbitrator held that, although the strike settlement agreement "reinstated" provisions of the expired contract, employees had failed to satisfy the surrounding days work requirements because they were on strike.

[196]See Ideal Elec. Co., 97 LA 730, 734 (Kindig, 1991); Alliance Mach. Co., 74 LA 1058, 1060 (Feldman, 1980); Wallace-Murray Corp., 71 LA 877, 879 (Gibson, 1978); Peavey Co., 43 LA 539, 545 (Traynor, 1964); Alside, Inc., 42 LA 75, 78 (Teple, 1964); Chatham Elecs., 37 LA 3, 4 (Kerrison, 1961); Publishers' Ass'n of New York City, 33 LA 681, 682–83 (Seitz, 1959).

[197]See Houston Chronicle Publ'g Co., 70 LA 190, 193–94 (Taylor, 1978); Gregory Galvanizing & Metal Processing, 46 LA 102, 105 (Kates, 1966); Kennecott Copper Corp., 36 LA 507, 509–10 (Updegraff, 1960); Kroger Co., 25 LA 841, 844 (Klamon, 1956).

[198]Gregory Galvanizing & Metal Processing, 46 LA 102, 105 (Kates, 1966), where the arbitrator also emphasized that this holding stood whether the last scheduled workday was "one day or three days or one week or two weeks or other period before the holiday." In this case it was the day the strike began, which was 2 weeks before the holiday.

Where agreements contain a holiday pay clause providing pay for employees on layoff within a certain period of time surrounding the holiday, unions have argued that employees awaiting recall after a strike has ended are entitled to pay under such clause. Arbitrators have ruled both ways on the issue of whether such employees are "laid-off" within the meaning of the contract. Thus, where the contract stated that an otherwise eligible employee who is "laid-off for lack of work" will be eligible for holiday pay "if his layoff begins or ends during the holiday week," one arbitrator ruled that employees who, after the strike ended, were idle while waiting to be recalled "were not laid off for 'lack of work' nor had the Company laid them off in the first instance," but their idle time resulted from the strike; they were not eligible for holiday pay for a holiday occurring during the waiting period.[199] However, under a contract clause providing that "employees on layoff two weeks prior to the holiday or two weeks after the holiday shall" be eligible for holiday pay, another arbitrator held that the term "layoff" was broad enough to include employees waiting to be called back to work after a strike; the employees therefore were held entitled to pay for the Labor Day holiday since the strike had ended on August 31.[200]

In the case of employees laid off because operations were suspended due to another union's strike, it has been held that no holiday pay was due where the contract did not provide for such pay for holidays falling within a layoff period.[201] Moreover, where the contract excused employees from complying with the surrounding days work requirements for certain named reasons or "similar good cause," it was held that employees did not qualify for the "similar good cause" excuse when they did not work the day before a holiday because an illegal strike by other employees had forced the employer to shut down the plant.[202] However, where one employee managed to report to work but was told that no work was available, and other employees were unable to enter the plant because of picket lines of employees on unauthorized strike, they were held eligible for holiday pay. The arbitrator said that "whether grievants were stopped at the gate or actually got into the plant, they did all

[199]E.J. Lavino & Co., 43 LA 213, 214 (Crawford, 1964). *See also* Intermountain Operators League, 26 LA 149, 151–53 (Kadish, 1956); Kroger Co., 25 LA 841, 844 (Klamon, 1956). In *Mobil Oil Co.*, 42 LA 102, 107 (Forsythe, 1963), a past practice of not granting holiday pay to employees awaiting recall was held controlling.

[200]St. Regis Paper Co., 46 LA 967, 969–70 (Stieber, 1966) (arbitrator took note of the surrounding days work requirements but found that the exception in the clause noted above applied to the employees in the instant case). *See also* Everbrite Elec. Sign Co., 62 LA 455, 459 (Michelstetter, 1974); Torrington Co., 12 LA 211, 212 (Camp, 1949).

[201]*See* Publishers' Ass'n of New York City, 40 LA 140, 142 (Turkus, 1963); American Airlines, 39 LA 500, 503–04 (Hill, 1962); Pan Am. World Airways, 36 LA 1232, 1235 (Wolff, 1961). In *Rockwell Manufacturing Co.*, 33 LA 77, 79–80 (Scheiber, 1959), an established practice of not providing holiday pay to laid-off employees was held controlling. Where the contract had no eligibility requirements for holiday pay, the arbitrator held that the company had an absolute obligation to pay without regard to the company's operations. *See* R.K. Baking Corp., 61 LA 1216, 1217 (Turkus, 1973); Kansas City Bakery Employers Council, 25 LA 91, 93–94 (Walsh, 1958).

[202]Phoenix Steel Corp., 44 LA 927, 928 (Crawford, 1965). *See also* Schlage Lock Co., 30 LA 105, 107–09 (Ross, 1958) (majority of arbitral decisions decline holiday pay under such circumstances, with citation of cases on both sides of the question at 108–09); Stockton Auto. Ass'n, 25 LA 687, 689–91 (Whitton, 1955).

that reasonably could have been required of them and thus their failing to work was because of a 'similar good cause.' "[203]

When employees voluntarily honor the picket line of another union, holiday pay has been denied. One arbitrator commented that "when employees voluntarily absent themselves from work in order to honor the picket line of fellow employees from another union, loss of holiday pay, like loss of wages, is part of the price which they must pay for choosing that course of action."[204]

G. Loss of Holiday Pay as Penalty for Misconduct

It generally is held that it is improper for the employer to deny holiday pay to an employee as punishment for misconduct or for violation of plant rules if the employee is otherwise eligible for the benefit.[205] However, if the employee by misconduct or by violation of plant rules fails to comply with the work requirements of the contract, the employee is disqualified for holiday pay. This was the ruling in a case in which the employees by their wildcat strike on the day before a holiday failed to comply with the surrounding days work requirements clause and thus did not qualify for holiday pay.[206]

H. Other Holiday Issues

Other holiday issues that have been arbitrated include the right of the employer to determine the day to be observed as the holiday named in the

---

[203]United States Steel Corp., 46 LA 473, 477 (McDermott, 1966). *See also* United States Steel Corp., 45 LA 509, 511 (Altrock, 1965); Detroit Steel Corp., 36 LA 99, 100 (Shipman, 1960); Kroger Co., 32 LA 30, 32–33 (McIntosh, 1959); Bethlehem Steel Co., 23 LA 141, 143 (Seward, 1954). In all these cases the employees reported for work and were sent home or were notified not to report for work because of a strike by other employees; the contract in the *Bethlehem Steel* case had a "similar good cause" exception, while the contracts in the other two cases contained language to the effect that an employee's absence with company approval or permission was an exception to the work requirements clause.

[204]Lucky Stores, 57 LA 149, 153 (Eaton, 1971) (discussing other cases at 151–52). *See also* Cities Serv. Oil Co., 70 LA 930, 934–35 (Caraway, 1978); Pearl Brewing Co., 68 LA 221, 221–22 (White, 1977); Kansas City Bakery Employers' Labor Council, 54 LA 754, 756–57 (Bauder, 1971).

[205]*See* Dillingham Mfg. Co., 91 LA 816, 819 (Nicholas, Jr., 1988); Fruehauf Corp., 54 LA 947, 950 (Tripp, 1971); Motch & Merryweather Mach. Co., 51 LA 724, 728 (Dworkin, 1968); Celotex Corp., 36 LA 517, 520–22 (Dworkin, 1961); American Brake Shoe Co., 40 LA 673, 674 (Reid, 1963); Northwestern Steel & Wire Co., 39 LA 104, 106–07 (Sembower, 1962); Galloway Co., 33 LA 890, 892 (Anderson, 1960); National Lead Co. of Ohio, 32 LA 865, 867–68 (Schedler, 1959); Standard Steel Spring Co., 16 LA 317, 319 (Platt, 1951); Parke, Davis & Co., 13 LA 126, 131–32 (Platt, 1949). *Cf.* Continental Can Co., 31 LA 558, 560–61 (Schmidt, 1958) (contract contained language justifying denial of holiday pay as a disciplinary action); McInerney Spring & Wire Co., 11 LA 1195, 1198–99 (Smith, 1948).

[206]American Brake Shoe Co., 40 LA 673, 675 (Reid, 1963). *See also* George E. Failing Co., 93 LA 598 (Fox, 1989); A. Finkl & Sons Co., 71 LA 321, 322 (Belshaw, 1978) (employee, because of misconduct on the job, was sent home early on the day after a holiday); L. Gordon & Son, 67 LA 1287, 1290 (Mallet-Prevost, 1976) (employee was absent on his scheduled (overtime) Saturday shift before a holiday because he was "fed up" with job irritations); Motch & Merryweather Mach. Co., 51 LA 724, 730 (Dworkin, 1968). *Cf.* Marmon Group, 73 LA 607, 609–10 (Marshall, 1979) (a new contract "guaranteed pay" for named holidays).

contract;[207] issues relating to employee birthday holidays;[208] the question of straight time or overtime pay for unworked holidays;[209] the question of premium pay for working on a holiday;[210] the basis for computation of holiday pay;[211] the issue of holiday pay entitlement when the employee is receiving workers' compensation;[212] issues involving probationary employees;[213] the question of whether continuous service was broken by layoff, thus making employees ineligible for a floating holiday;[214] whether an employer is required under the contract to grant an employee a floating holiday regardless of the company's anticipated heavy workload;[215] whether an employer is required to pay striking employees a floating holiday when the parties had failed to reach a successor collective bargaining agreement, the employer locked out the employees, and the union was later decertified after the employer had hired permanent replacements;[216] and the proper remedy when an employer does not timely revoke its notice of canceling work on a designated floating holiday.[217] Finally, issues concerning changes in the scheduling of employees to work or not work a scheduled holiday[218] or changes in the shift starting time to avoid holiday pay[219] frequently are considered.

---

[207]*See* Retail Mkts. Co., 92 LA 1234, 1246 (Klein, 1989); A-T-O, Inc., 72 LA 408, 410 (Shister, 1979) (practice of observing Memorial Day on last Monday in May); Omar Bakeries, 70 LA 1283, 1285 (Drotning, 1978); Yoder Bros., 69 LA 115, 119–23 (Ipavec, 1977) (past practice controlled); South Jersey Port Corp., 66 LA 192, 193 (Kelly, 1976); Kurz & Root Co., 59 LA 730, 732 (Gratz, 1972); Hess Oil & Chem. Corp., 51 LA 445, 448–49 (Gould, 1968); Michigan Gas & Elec. Co., 45 LA 85, 88–90 (Fallon, 1965). *See also* Control Data Corp., 69 LA 665, 669–70 (Hatcher, 1977) (a "floating" holiday issue).

[208]*See* Consolidation Coal Co., 93 LA 473, 475–76 (Seidman, 1989); Thomas Truck & Caster Co., 74 LA 1276 (Cohen, 1980); United Salt Corp., 72 LA 534 (Porter, 1979); Alabama By-Products Corp., 68 LA 992 (Grooms, Jr., 1977); Windsor Power House Coal Co., 68 LA 835 (Perry, 1977); North Am. Coal Corp., 67 LA 723 (Dworkin, 1976); American Smelting & Ref. Co., 65 LA 1217 (Bardwell, 1975); Hammermill Paper Co., 57 LA 177 (Greene, 1971).

[209]*See* Evanite Battery Separator, 90 LA 225, 227–28 (Murphy, 1987); Cascade Steel Rolling Mills, 74 LA 199 (Lovell, 1980); Price's Dairies, 73 LA 547 (Shearer, 1979) (commission employees); ConAgra, Inc., 70 LA 1296 (Levy, 1978) (Saturday holiday "pushed back" to Friday); Land O'Lakes, 70 LA 653 (Hadlick, 1978); Hoerner Waldorf Corp., 61 LA 58 (Murphy, 1973); Reynolds Metals Co., 56 LA 1239 (Kleinsorge, 1971); Reynolds Metals Co., 56 LA 1033 (Carson, Jr., 1971); Burton-Dixie Corp., 56 LA 652 (McKenna, 1971); Georgia-Pacific Corp., 55 LA 992 (Farinholt, Jr., 1970).

[210]*See* Anaconda Co., 74 LA 345 (Gowan, 1980); Continental Copper & Steel Indus., 73 LA 342 (Lubow, 1979); General Tire & Rubber Co., 71 LA 813 (Richman, 1978); C&S Wholesale Grocers, 71 LA 676 (Charm, 1978); Theodore Mayer & Bros., 62 LA 540 (McIntosh, 1974); Rudy Mfg. Co., 57 LA 140 (Dunne, 1971).

[211]*See* Carbon County, Pa., 73 LA 1305 (Handsaker, 1980) (shift differential); City of New York, N.Y., 73 LA 172 (Glushien, 1979); United States Steel Corp., 66 LA 1183 (Fox, Jr., 1976); Bertrand Prods., 66 LA 586 (Daniel, 1976).

[212]Stone Container Corp., 105 LA 537 (Allen, Jr., 1995). *See* Walworth County, 71 LA 1118, 1122 (Gundermann, 1978); Thomas Indus., 61 LA 627, 630 (Dallas, 1973).

[213]Seven-Up Bottling Co., 108 LA 587 (Staudohar, 1997). *See* Brown & Williamson Tobacco Co., 62 LA 1211 (Brown, 1974); Airtherm Prods., 67 LA 666 (Neas, 1976); Interstate United Corp., 60 LA 128 (Sloane, 1973).

[214]Ryder Truck Rental, 95 LA 1106 (Suardi, 1990).

[215]Bard Mfg. Co., 100 LA 516 (House, 1992).

[216]McCreary Tire & Rubber Co., 93 LA 1052 (Stoltenberg, 1989).

[217]Kimberly-Clark Corp., 97 LA 1099 (Stix, 1991).

[218]BASF Corp., 116 LA 1676 (Crider, 2002) (employer did not violate the contract when it scheduled employees off on a holiday, where employer retained the right under the contract to change the work schedule).

[219]PQ Corp., 117 LA 1034 (Erbs, 2002) (employer was permitted to change the starting time for holiday pay to 12:00 midnight on day of the holiday from 11:00 p.m. on day before the holiday, where no express prohibition existed in the contract); Wichita Eagle & Beacon

3. LEAVES

A. Leaves of Absence [LA CDI 100.5201; 116.201]

"Ordinarily, in industrial relations parlance 'leave,' when 'granted,' connotes absence from work without the imposition of penalties that might otherwise be suffered for failing to report . . . when scheduled for work."[220] A leave of absence "perpetuates the employment relationship during the absence of an employee while relieving that employee of the responsibility to be present and to perform."[221]

It has been held that except as restricted by the agreement, the granting or denial of leaves of absence is a prerogative of management, and the judgment of management will not be disturbed so long as the action taken is not unreasonable or discriminatory.[222] In some cases, past practice and custom concerning leaves of absence have determined whether management's action should be upheld.[223] Where leaves of absence were provided for in the contract, with the right reserved to the company to judge the cause for the

---

Publ'g Co., 113 LA 29 (Yehle, 1999) (new shift beginning at 2:00 p.m. was not entitled to the holiday night shift premium normally paid for work performed from 7:00 p.m. to 7:00 a.m. on the eve of the holiday); Electrical Contractor's Ass'n Chicago, Ill., 102 LA 660 (Wolff, 1994) (shift workers who began shift at 11:30 p.m. on holiday were only entitled to holiday premium for ½ hour worked, because a holiday was not defined in the contract and it therefore must be given normally understood meaning, i.e., a 24-hour period from midnight to midnight).

[220]Publishers' Ass'n of New York City, 32 LA 513, 515 (Seitz, 1959). *See also* Menasco Mfg. Co., 71 LA 696, 698 (Gowan, Jr., 1978) (a distinction is drawn, based on contract language, between "leave of absence" and "excused absence").

[221]City of Sunrise, Fla., 94 LA 80, 85 (Richard, 1990).

[222]*See* Davenport, Iowa, Osteopathic Hosp., 79 LA 973, 977 (Slade, 1982); Nashville Gas Co., 79 LA 802, 805 (Odom, 1982); Carolina Concrete Pipe Co., 76 LA 626, 631–32 (Foster, 1981); Menasco Mfg. Co., 71 LA 696, 697–98 (Gowan, Jr., 1978); Hillbro Newspaper Printing Co., 48 LA 1166, 1167–68 (Roberts, 1967); Magnavox Co., 45 LA 667, 670 (Dworkin, 1965); Farrel Corp., 43 LA 670, 673 (Fallon, 1964); I. Lewis Cigar Mfg. Co., 12 LA 661, 662 (Waite, 1949); Union Oil Co., 3 LA 108, 110 (Wardlaw, 1946). *See also* Kansas City Area Transp. Auth., 71 LA 674, 676 (Dugan, 1978); Fairbanks, Morse & Co., 21 LA 502, 511 (Elson, 1953); Campbell Soup Co., 19 LA 604, 607 (Tyree, 1952); North Am. Aviation, 15 LA 928, 933 (Aaron, 1951). *Cf.* Allied Roll Builders, 72 LA 609, 613 (Leahy, 1979). An implied limitation on management was found in contract provisions in *Joyce-Cridland Co.*, 35 LA 133, 136–37 (Schmidt, 1960).

[223]*See* Westinghouse Elec. Corp., 45 LA 621, 627–28 (Hebert, 1965); Chattanooga Box & Lumber Co., 44 LA 373, 376 (Tatum, 1965); Goodyear Tire & Rubber Co., 38 LA 1061, 1063–64 (Elkouri, 1962); Northland Greyhound Lines, 23 LA 277, 280 (Levinson, 1954); Texas Co., 19 LA 709, 710 (McCraw, 1952); 18 LA 528, 531 (Lesser). *See also* Singer Co., 52 LA 176, 177 (Cahn, 1968). For a case involving an attempted but unsuccessful discontinuance of a past practice regarding leaves of absence, see *Hillbro Newspaper Printing Co.*, 48 LA 1166, 1167–68 (Roberts, 1967). In *Saydel, Iowa, Consolidated School District*, 76 LA 673, 676 (Nathan, 1981), past practice supported a broad construction of a "business leave" provision, significantly reducing management's right to deny leave requests. But in *Columbia Gas of West Virginia*, 77 LA 990, 993–94 (Beilstein, 1981), an alleged practice of another corporate entity, who was a signatory to the contract, to pay employees absent from work due to an act of God was held not binding because the companies had separate corporate structures. For related discussion, see Chapter 12, section 1., "Custom and Practice as a Term of the Contract."

requested leave, the "arbitrary or discriminatory" test was applied by the arbitrator in determining whether leave had been properly denied.[224]

Similarly, despite an attendance policy stating that "[e]mployees who are absent for any reason in excess of six months" would be terminated, an arbitrator set aside the discharge of a warehouse employee who had been absent for more than 6 months on workers' compensation. The arbitrator noted that the policy had not always been strictly enforced and inferred that the company considered "fairness" as an element in its enforcement decisions. Fairness here required granting the grievant a leave of absence because there was no proof that the employee, if he had been released by his physician for return to work, would be unable to perform his duties.[225]

An employee is not automatically entitled to a leave of absence. This right or privilege exists by virtue of a provision in the collective bargaining agreement or a leave plan unilaterally instituted by management or by reason of past practice. For example, one arbitrator held that although the contract provided for sick leave of absence, the leave was not available to the grievant because he had not complied with the contractual requirement for the submission of a written request.[226] Another arbitrator, noting that "[t]he contract language should not be construed or applied so as to defeat its substantive purpose, namely, to make provision for necessary sick leave," held not only that the contract did not require that sick leave requests be granted automatically even though the employee presents a statement from a doctor that sick leave is necessary, but also that the company could "evaluate the factual basis of a sick leave request" and deny the request if it is frivolous and not supported by the facts.[227]

Although a leave of absence is usually considered to be a benefit for and initiated by an employee, at times a leave is involuntary and is imposed by management. For example, an arbitrator upheld the decision of a police department to place an investigator on involuntary unpaid medical leave so that the investigator could undergo psychotherapy recommended in a psychological evaluation.[228]

The Family and Medical Leave Act (FMLA)[229] enacted in 1993 requires both public-sector and private-sector employers to provide unpaid family and

---

[224]Hudson Pulp & Paper Co., 35 LA 581, 583 (Hill, 1960) (denial of leave (requested for the purpose of serving a jail sentence) was not improper). *See also* Alameda County, Cal., Superintendent of Sch., 76 LA 566, 568 (Anderson, 1981) (unqualified contract language gave complete discretion to the employer); Durant, Iowa, Cmty. Sch. Dist., 74 LA 934, 937–39 (Nathan, 1980) (the quota established by the employer was held "arbitrary on its face"). *Cf.* Carlisle, Iowa, Cmty. Sch. Dist., 77 LA 701, 704 (Yarowsky, 1981).

[225]Magnolia Mktg. Co., 107 LA 102 (Chumley, 1996).

[226]Doering's Super Valu, 47 LA 364, 368–69 (Lee, 1966). *Cf.* Cleveland Trencher Co., 48 LA 615, 618 (Teple, 1967) (the contract provided for 6 months' sick leave as a matter of right without formal application or approval).

[227]Magnavox Co., 45 LA 667, 669–70 (Dworkin, 1965). *See also* Hormel Fine Frozen Foods, 75 LA 1129, 1141 (Neas, 1980).

[228]City of Chicago, Ill., 96 LA 876, 883–87 (Goldstein, 1990).

[229]29 U.S.C. §§2601–2654. The FMLA requires both public- and private-sector employers to provide unpaid family and medical leaves. *Id.* §2611(4)(A). In enacting the FMLA, Congress intended, among other things, "to balance the demands of the workplace with the needs of families, to promote the stability and economic security of families, and to promote national interests in preserving family integrity" in a way that "accommodates the legitimate interests of employers." *Id.* §2601(b).

medical leave if they employ at least 50 employees.[230] The provisions of the FMLA apply equally to both male and female employees.[231] In many instances, the FMLA requires more extensive leaves than those contained in collective bargaining agreements.

B. Sick Leave [LA CDI 100.5206; 116.2501 et seq.]

Provision for sick leave may be negotiated into the contract,[232] or a sick leave plan or policy may be instituted unilaterally by management.[233] In any

---

The FMLA covers employers that have at least 50 employees for each working day during each of 20 or more calendar workweeks in the current or preceding calendar year and applies equally to male and female employees. *Id.* §2611(4)(A). An employee is excluded from eligibility under the FMLA if employed at a work site at which there are fewer than 50 employees or if, where the employer has more than one work site, the employer employs fewer than 50 employees within a 75-mile radius of the place of employment. *Id.* §2611(2)(B)(ii). However, certain key employees are not entitled to the FMLA's full protection. An employer may refuse to restore to work a salaried worker who is among the highest paid 10% of the organization's workers within a 75-mile radius of their place of employment. *Id.* §2614(b). This refusal to restore a job can occur only if restoration would cause substantial and grievous economic injury to the operations of the employer.

The FMLA provides that eligible employees may take a total of 12 weeks of unpaid leave during any 12-month period for one or more of the following reasons: the birth and/or care of a child; the placement of a child with the employee for adoption or foster care; the care of a spouse, son, daughter, or parent with a serious health condition; or a serious health condition that makes the employee unable to perform the functions of his or her position. *Id.* §2612(a).

The key provision of the FMLA prohibits employers from penalizing employees for taking leave. Employees returning from leave must be restored to the same positions they held before the leave or to similar positions with equivalent pay or benefits. *Id.* §2614. In addition, employers must continue to offer group health coverage to employees on leave without reducing the employer's contribution to premiums.

Employers are not obligated to pay employees who take leave under the FMLA. However, an employee may choose, or the employer may require the employee, to substitute paid vacation time, personal leave, or family or sick leave for any part of the 12-week period. *Id.* §2612(d)(2).

The FMLA is administered by the Department of Labor in accordance with the procedures applicable under the Fair Labor Standards Act. An aggrieved individual may file a charge with the Labor Department or institute a civil action for monetary and injunctive relief in state or federal court. Such actions must be brought within 2 years of the date of the last event constituting the alleged violation or, in the case of a willful violation, within 3 years. Damages may include an amount equal to lost wages, salary, and employment benefits, or, if an employee has not lost wages or benefits, an amount equal to 12 weeks' wages. *Id.* §2617. There is also a provision for the imposition of interest, equitable relief, liquidated damages, and reasonable attorneys' fees. *See* Guevara, *Family and Medical Leave Act of 1993: An Overview of the Law and Regulations (Part I)*, 37 RES GESTAE 214 (1993); Guevara, *Family and Medical Leave Act of 1993: An Overview of the Law and Regulations (Part II)*, 37 RES GESTAE 256 (1993); Fraser, *An Overview of the Family and Medical Leave Act*, 70 U. DET. MERCY L. REV. 691 (1993); Webb, Mitzner, & Klimaszewski, *Family and Medical Leave Act of 1993*, 22 COLO. LAW. 1851 (1993).

[230]29 U.S.C. §2611(4)(A)(i).

[231]*Id.* §2611(3).

[232]*See* Birmingham-Jefferson County Transit Auth., 78 LA 221, 223 (Shaffer, 1982); Illinois Dep't of Transp. & Pers., 76 LA 875, 876 (Witney, 1981); Scott Air Force Base, Ill., 76 LA 46, 47–48 (Fitzsimmons, 1980); Dubuque, Iowa, Cmty. Sch. Dist., 75 LA 862, 864 (Smith, 1980); Arkansas-Missouri Power Co., 74 LA 1254, 1255 (McKenna, 1980); Magnavox Co., 45 LA 667, 668 (Dworkin, 1965).

[233]*See* Socony Mobil Oil Co., 45 LA 1062, 1063 (Kadish, 1965); Block Drug Co., 58 LA 1198, 1200 (Trotta, 1972). In *J.H. Day Co.*, 62 LA 909, 912–13 (Paradise, 1974), the company was held bound by a long-standing "practice of paying for time spent on off-premises doctor's visits for the treatment of job-related injuries."

event, management has a legitimate concern in preventing abuse of sick leave claims, and in so doing it may formulate reasonable rules for the documentation of illness,[234] prescribe forms to be filled out by the employee and the employee's doctor,[235] or develop a system for the policing of a sick benefits plan[236] so long as it is not arbitrary, discriminatory, or unreasonable.[237]

A labor organization employer refused a field staff member's request for sick leave to undergo nonemergency surgery because his services were then needed for the conduct of a membership drive. Although the contract did not expressly require management approval before accrued sick leave could be utilized, an arbitrator denied the ensuing grievance, reasoning that management had retained the right to control the use of sick leave so long as it did not act "arbitrarily, discriminatorily or capriciously." An employee, the arbitrator continued, is not free to set his own schedule, and where the surgery could be rescheduled to a time when the employee could be better spared from the performance of his duties, the employer acted reasonably in refusing the request.[238]

---

[234]See Hormel Fine Frozen Foods, 75 LA 1129, 1141 (Neas, 1980); Tri-State Eng'g Co., 69 LA 980, 983–84 (Brown, 1977); Union-Tribune Publ'g Co., 63 LA 1093, 1096 (Greer, 1974); Federal Servs., 41 LA 1063, 1064 (Williams, 1963); General Baking Co., 40 LA 386, 388 (Corsi, 1963). See also Memphis Publ'g Co., 48 LA 554, 557–58 (Oppenheim, 1967).

[235]See Willoughby-Eastlake City Sch. Dist. Bd. of Educ., 75 LA 21, 25 (Ipavec, 1980); Ohio Edison Co., 52 LA 593, 596 (Marshall, 1969); Booth Newspapers, 41 LA 1133, 1135 (Ryder, 1963); Cities Serv. Petroleum Co., 38 LA 419, 422 (McGury, 1961).

[236]See Socony Mobil Oil Co., 45 LA 1062, 1065 (Kadish, 1965). For some cases involving abuse of sick leave and the various means used by employers to combat abuse, see Barbers Point Fed. Credit Union, 76 LA 624, 625 (Boken, 1981); Scott Air Force Base, Ill., 76 LA 46, 53–54 (Fitzsimmons, 1980); Veterans Admin., 75 LA 623, 624–25 (Sherman, 1980); United States Gov't Printing Office, 72 LA 125, 126 (Ables, 1979); Farmland Foods, 67 LA 606, 608 (Hutcheson, 1976) (contract restriction); Laclede Gas Co., 63 LA 928, 930 (Edelman, 1974).

[237]The reasonableness test was applied in National Airlines, 43 LA 1169, 1171 (Black, Jr., 1964), where the arbitrator held that even though the contract permitted the company to require a physician's certificate to confirm a sick claim, it could do so only when it has reasonable doubts as to the employee's sick claim. See also Kansas City Area Transp. Auth., 76 LA 1267, 1272 (Eisler, 1981) (stating that the "rule of reasonableness must be applied to the facts of each case" and that management "has the right to curb and correct abuses of sick leave when they are found to exist"); Altec Corp., 71 LA 1064, 1066 (Hays, 1978); Ore-Ida Foods, 69 LA 375, 378 (Curry, Jr., 1977) (common sense and reasonableness must be applied); Cities Serv. Oil Co., 62 LA 77, 82 (Taylor, 1974). Where the company's right to require a medical certificate had been the subject of bargaining in the past and had been negotiated out of the agreement, the arbitrator nevertheless ruled that "[i]f the Company has reasonable grounds for believing any employee is abusing sick leave the Company has the right to request proof of illness." Galloway Co., 49 LA 240, 242–43 (Gundermann, 1967).

[238]Indiana State Teachers Ass'n, 104 LA 737 (Paolucci, 1995). See also Land-O-Sun Dairies, 105 LA 740 (Draznin, 1995) (employee who refused mandatory overtime on ground of illness properly discharged under company policy that treated such refusal as a "voluntary quit," since employee's claim of illness was not timely communicated to employer or supported with sufficient information to allow employer to determine whether to grant grievant an exception).

Documentation may be required under suspicious circumstances,[239] such as absence before a vacation[240] or mass absences on a holiday.[241] Moreover, it has been stated that "where there is a claim under suspicious circumstances . . . the documentation required may be more exacting than otherwise might be the case."[242]

Contract provisions vary as to documentation requirements. The contract may, as in one case, specify detailed requirements for sick leave, such as a written application on a specified form, submission of a medical certificate showing date of disability, physician's personal attendance or treatment, nature of illness or injury, date of first treatment, date physician predicts employee will be able to resume work, and examination of the employee by a physician selected by the company.[243] Contracts may, of course, be less demanding, requiring merely that notice be by "registered mail, telegram, telephone, or in person within 5 days of the last day worked," but even such notice would be waived if it was "impossible to notify the Company."[244]

Where documentation is required, failure to submit any medical certification can result in loss of sick leave pay, especially if abuse of such leave is suspected. In one case, the arbitrator found that the school board properly

---

[239]See Bon Secours Hosp., 76 LA 705, 711–14 (Feldesman, 1981) (company upheld in requiring "personal" notice of illness even though such notice was not required by contract, company rules, or past practice): Barbers Point Fed. Credit Union, 76 LA 624, 625 (Boken, 1981); Rock Island Arsenal, 76 LA 441, 445–46 (Garman, 1981); American Hoechst Corp., 73 LA 1235, 1236 (Caraway, 1979); Laclede Gas Co., 63 LA 928, 930 (Edelman, 1974); Wackenhut Servs., 54 LA 1107, 1109 (Zimring, 1971). A "sick-out" was involved in *Federal Aviation Admin.*, 72 LA 761, 764–65 (Forrester, 1979), but three grievants "presented the stronger proof" that they were actually ill; the award was based on "the weight of the evidence rather than on a firm conviction" regarding the actual facts. In another "sick-out" case, disciplinary action was upheld where abuse of sick leave provisions was found. City of Hartford, Conn., 67 LA 1107, 1108–09 (Mallon, 1976).

[240]See Marion Power Shovel Co., 43 LA 507, 509–10 (Dworkin, 1964) (the contract did not require medical proof when absence due to illness did not exceed 3 days and the past practice of the company had been to accept an oral statement by the employee, but the employee "acted improperly in refusing to cooperate" by providing management with information that he had to verify his illness; the arbitrator held that grievant was properly disciplined for his refusal to cooperate).

[241]See City of Detroit, 68 LA 848, 852–54 (Roumell, Jr., Somero, & Watroba, 1977); Republic Steel Corp., 28 LA 897, 899 (Platt, 1957). Cf. Bethlehem Steel, 42 LA 851, 852 (Hill, 1964) (although grievant's explanation of an absence was open to "suspicion, if not downright disbelief," the company could not condition payment for a holiday on the employee's proving his preholiday claim of illness at home since there was no practice at the plant of making an employee prove that he had been absent for medical reasons).

[242]Cities Serv. Oil Co., 62 LA 77, 82 (Taylor, 1974). *See also* Lloyd Noland Found., 74 LA 1236, 1243 (Griffin, 1980). The requirement of documentation must be reasonable even though "circumstances were suspect." Kansas City Area Transp. Auth., 76 LA 1267, 1272 (Eisler, 1981).

[243]Birmingham-Jefferson County Transit Auth., 78 LA 221, 223–24 (Shaeffer, 1982). In federal-sector employment, the statutes and agency regulations are relevant along with the contract in the resolution of sick leave issues. *See* Scott Air Force Base, Ill., 76 LA 46, 47–48, 54 (Fitzsimmons, 1980).

[244]Eaton Corp., 67 LA 1065, 1066 (Cantor, 1976). *See also* United States Steel Corp., 64 LA 540, 541 (Beilstein, 1975).

reprimanded a teacher and withheld 1 day's pay because she failed to submit medical certification in support of a sick leave claim for a Friday absence when she had had 17 sick leave absences on Mondays, Fridays, and days before or after holidays during 2 school years.[245]

Arbitrators have recognized that medical documentation of illness provided by employees is often inadequate:

> The arbitrator agrees that, as here, often medical certification provided by an ill or injured employee leaves much to be desired. All too often, very informal prescription pad notes, sometimes stamped or signed by a nurse, are offered as proof. On the other hand, it must be remembered that extensive medical reports are expensive for an employee to obtain and time consuming for a physician. It is general practice that, unless there is some serious dispute, these forms will be used and accepted.[246]

However, a doctor's letter consisting of three sentences that did not specify an employee's illness was considered insufficient proof to substantiate sick leave for an extended period of time.[247]

Sometimes, specific contractual restrictions placed on the use of sick leave will control. For example, some contracts will not provide sick leave for an illness that is the result of an employee's misconduct. In one case, an employer properly denied sick pay to an admitted cocaine addict who underwent a 30-day hospitalization program where the agreement exempted from coverage any illness resulting from misconduct.[248] In contrast, another arbitrator awarded sick leave pay for 2 months to a grievant who had voluntarily spent 2 months at an inpatient drug and alcohol rehabilitation program. Even though the collective bargaining agreement prohibited use of sick leave when sickness was due to "use of drugs or other controlled substances," the arbitrator noted that sickness was not defined and that many similarly situated employees were granted sick leave allowance.[249]

In the absence of a formal procedure set up by the contract or by company rules, what kind of proof of illness must the employee offer and what kind of proof can the company demand? In one case, the parties had an informal practice of many years whereby the employees ordinarily would tell their foreman whether the absence was due to "sickness," and the foreman accepted the explanation if there was no reason to doubt its truthfulness. The parties had no desire to change this practice or to introduce any new rigid requirements. However, the arbitrator said that the practice does not mean that the company may never ask for proof of "sickness," and provided the following guidelines:

> In most cases, it would suffice for the employee to provide an explanation in sufficient detail to enable the supervisor to make a judgment as to whether sick leave is justified.

---

[245]Pallisades, Ill., Cmty. Consol. Sch. Dist. No. 180, 93 LA 1218, 1221–24 (Wies, 1989).

[246]Toledo, Ohio, Dist. Bd. of Health, 92 LA 1262, 1266 (Daniel, 1989).

[247]Internal Revenue Serv., 85 LA 212 (Shieber, 1985).

[248]Kansas City Cold Storage Corp., 94 LA 783, 785–87 (Madden, 1990). *See also* New Brighton, Pa., Area Sch. Dist., 84 LA 350 (Duff, 1985) (failed to meet criteria established in contract for use of sick leave).

[249]Dalfort Aviation Servs., 96 LA 520, 523–24 (Nicholas, Jr., 1991).

Some cases require more, but the proof need not be in any particular form, nor must it be the strongest and best proof possible. Verification could be in the following forms:

(a) A doctor's letter would be appropriate but should not be an absolute requirement since there may be illness without the attention of a doctor;

(b) A druggist's prescription might be adequate; or

(c) A written statement from the employee's wife, neighbor, or fellow worker might suffice.

The nature of the proof must ultimately depend upon the facts and circumstances of each case.[250]

The calculation of sick leave entitlements in terms of either hours or days usually presents no problem so long as the workday is standardized. However, when some employees regularly worked four 10-hour shifts, and the contract provided for a maximum accrual of 22 days of sick leave, the employees grieved the company's allowance of a maximum accrual of 176 hours instead of 220 hours. The arbitrator found that the contract contemplated 8-hour work days, and the prior practice was consistent with the company's calculation of sick leave.[251]

Can an employee be involuntarily placed on unpaid medical leave of absence by his employer? One arbitrator answered "yes" in a case where the company temporarily placed an employee on medical leave because, according to his physician, his medication made him sensitive to heat above 75 degrees, and the plant temperature was in the 90–95 degree range. The contract gave the company the right to relieve employees from duty for legitimate reasons. The arbitrator concluded that the company had acted reasonably, in light of the danger to the employee, in not permitting the grievant to continue working.[252]

In another case, an arbitrator found that the employer acted properly within the contractual provision in placing a teacher on sick leave after she was examined by a psychiatrist who made recommendations against her returning to teaching responsibilities.[253] In still another case, a school board unilaterally adopted a "Highly Contagious Diseases Policy" permitting it to place employees on compulsory sick or health leave upon determination that they posed a serious threat to the health and welfare of others. Recognizing that arbitrators have consistently upheld an employer's right to place an employee on leave of absence for health or medical reasons in order to ensure the safety of the employees or other personnel or to maintain efficiency of operations, one arbitrator nevertheless found that the leave policy involved

---

[250]*Republic Steel Corp.*, 28 LA 897, 899 (Platt, 1957) (a "mass absences" case), cited with the recommendation that the parties follow these guidelines in *Laclede Gas Co.*, 63 LA 928, 930 (Edelman, 1974). This approach, using the kinds of proof suggested in *Republic Steel Corp.*, was taken by the company in another "mass absences" case. Phoenix Steel Corp., 51 LA 357, 357 (Cahn, 1968). *Cf.* Bridgeport Gas Co., 31 LA 253, 255–56 (Stutz, 1958).

[251]Huntleigh Transp. Servs., 101 LA 784 (Marino, 1993).

[252]Siemens Energy & Automation, 108 LA 537 (Neas, 1997).

[253]BOCES, First Supervisory Dist.—Erie County, N.Y., 82 LA 1269, 1272 (Sabghir, 1984). *See also* County of Becker, Minn., 93 LA 673 (Neigh, 1989); ITT Higbie Mfg. Co., 85 LA 859 (Shanker, 1985).

in this instance violated the contract because it was directed at AIDS, which disease had not been demonstrated to affect a teacher's ability to perform teaching duties or to constitute a danger to others.[254]

Some sick leave plans require a waiting period, that is, days without pay, before sick leave pay becomes available. In one case, the agreement provided the "wait period" would not apply in situations involving an absence due to the same authenticated illness or injury of prolonged duration that required periodic treatment.[255] An employee who missed work on three different occasions due to back problems was found to come within this exception to the wait period. "Requiring periodic treatment" was interpreted by the arbitrator to include an illness that requires treatment as the need occurs. Another arbitrator held that after a waiting-day requirement was met, an employer must pay sick leave benefits even though this resulted in paying the employee for hours in excess of the 40-hour guaranteed workweek.[256] Nothing in the contract language tied payment of the sick leave benefit to the guaranteed workweek pay provision.

In considering the responsibility of a successor employer for sick leave that accrued under the term of employment with a predecessor, the arbitrator found that, under the particular facts of the case, the successor employer had made clear to the union that it would not be responsible for vacation benefits earned and accrued prior to the change in ownership.[257] The union acquiesced to this position by failing to take any action, and the specific issue of accrued sick leave did not arise until some time later. Nevertheless, the arbitrator found that the issues of sick leave and vacation are "reasonably identical" and that the successor employer was not liable for the previously accrued sick leave.

Other issues involving sick leave that have been arbitrated include whether an absence should be charged to sick leave or other leave;[258] whether sick leave benefits accumulate during a strike or layoff or when an employee is on workers' compensation;[259] whether employees may use sick leave during a strike, picketing, or a layoff;[260] whether employees may use sick leave

---

[254]Cook County, Ill., Bd. of Educ., 89 LA 521, 527–28 (Witney, 1987).

[255]Monsanto Indus. Chems., 85 LA 113 (Grinstead, 1985).

[256]Certified Grocers of Cal., 85 LA 414 (Sabo, 1985).

[257]Servicecare, Inc., 82 LA 590, 592–93 (Talarico, 1984). *See also* Ashland Petroleum, 90 LA 681 (Volz, 1988); City of Crystal, Minn., 89 LA 531, 537 (Bard, 1987).

[258]*See* Lithonia Lighting Co., 85 LA 627, 630 (Volz, 1985) (where 15-year employee had been on leave for a compensable occupational disease, arbitrator held employer improperly terminated seniority under contract provision providing for such termination after employee on sick leave for 3 years, since employee was not on sick leave but was absent; arbitrator pointed out that "a forfeiture clause to terminate the seniority of a long-term employee must be clear and unambiguous"); Dubuque, Iowa, Cmty. Sch. Dist., 75 LA 862, 868 (Smith, 1980); Naval Ordnance Station, 62 LA 610, 614–16 (Cabe, 1974). See also section 3.C., "Maternity or Maternity-Related Leave," below.

[259]*See* Universal Carloading & Distrib. Co., 73 LA 899, 900–01 (Rubin, 1979) (layoff); Metro Media, 72 LA 776, 778–80 (Rule, 1979) (honoring picket line); Walworth County, 71 LA 1118, 1122 (Gundermann, 1978) (workers' compensation).

[260]*See* Brinks, Inc., 78 LA 1056, 1059 (Penfield, 1982) (layoff); Hormel Fine Frozen Foods, 75 LA 1129, 1135–44 (Neas, 1980) (same); Commonwealth of Pa., 73 LA 981, 984–85 (Kanes, 1979) (strike); Givaudan Corp., 68 LA 337, 341–42 (Brent, 1977) (same); County of Santa Clara, 65 LA 992, 995–96 (Koven, 1975) (same); City of Flint, Mich., 58 LA 1376, 1378–79 (Stamm, 1972) (picketing); Reliance Universal, 57 LA 337, 339–40 (Sembower, 1971) (strike). For views of the NLRB at the time regarding the effect of strike and picketing on sick benefits, see *Emerson Elec. Co.*, 246 NLRB 1143, 103 LRRM 1073 (1979).

to tend to an ill family member;[261] whether employees are entitled to receive payment for unused accumulated sick leave upon retirement, termination, or voluntary quit;[262] whether use of sick leave is restricted to employees who are hospitalized or just under a doctor's care;[263] whether "sickness" includes injury;[264] and whether seniority accumulates during sick leave.[265] Awards in such cases depend variously upon explicit contract language, interpretation of the contract by the arbitrator, past practice, or bargaining history, or some combination of these factors.

C. Maternity or Maternity-Related Leave [LA CDI 100.5211; 116.207]

Prior to 1973, when the Equal Employment Opportunity Commission issued pregnancy leave guidelines under Title VII of the Civil Rights Act, arbitration decisions generally recognized a right to maternity or maternity-related leave only to the extent that such right was provided for by the collective agreement or existed by past practice.[266] During the period from the 1973 adoption of EEOC pregnancy leave guidelines until their use was side-tracked by the Supreme Court's 1976 decision in *General Electric Co. v. Gilbert*,[267] diverse approaches were pursued by arbitrators concerning consideration of statutory law in resolving pregnancy disability issues involved in

---

[261]*See* Detroit Lakes, Minn., Educ. Ass'n, 83 LA 66, 68–69 (Gallagher, 1984); Michigan Gas Utils. Co., 73 LA 885, 887 (Coyle, 1979); Vindicator Printing Co., 72 LA 229, 233–34 (Teple, 1979); Wiregrass Elec. Coop., 69 LA 1245, 1246–47 (Ferguson, 1977); Federal Aviation Admin., 64 LA 45, 48–50 (Jenkins, 1975); Aeronautical Radio, 59 LA 1114, 1115–16 (Griffin, 1972); City of Norwalk, Conn., 57 LA 1242, 1243–44 (Purcell, 1971).

[262]For retirement cases, see *Millersburg Area, Pa., Sch. Dist.*, 82 LA 970, 972–73 (Mayer, 1984); *Girard Coll.*, 71 LA 1051, 1053–54 (Kramer, 1978); *Republic Supply Co. of Cal.*, 58 LA 623, 626–27 (Block, 1972). For termination cases, see *City of San Antonio, Tex.*, 69 LA 541, 544–46 (Caraway, 1977); *ARA Food Servs.*, 65 LA 373, 375–76 (McKone, 1975). For voluntary quit cases, see *City of Mentor, Ohio*, 99 LA 85 (Minni, 1992); *Viking Int'l Airlines*, 85 LA 422 (Flagler, 1985).

[263]Sunrise Med., 86 LA 798 (Redel, 1985).

[264]Maryland Cork Co., 95 LA 399 (Cluster, 1990).

[265]City of Crystal, Minn., 89 LA 531, 537 (Bard, 1987).

[266]The broad scope that sometimes may be given to the term "maternity leave" is illustrated by the case in which a female employee who adopted a 3-month-old girl was held entitled to leave under a contractual "maternity leaves" provision; the arbitrator noted that the agreement did not restrict "maternity" to pregnancy or, as did another agreement, to "childbirth leave," and he declared that "no such distinction can be made that a mother adopting an infant is any less a mother or parent who requires a maternity leave than a natural mother." Ambridge Borough, Beaver County, Pa., 81 LA 915, 917 (Stoltenberg, 1983). *See also* Office & Prof'l Employees Local 2, 71 LA 93, 95–96 (Seidenberg, 1978). *But see* Chromalloy Am. Corp., 64 LA 1132, 1134 (Gruenberg, 1975) (maternity leave did not include leave for child care); South Bend Cmty. Sch. Corp., 64 LA 531, 532–33 (Belshaw, 1975) (same). *See also* Ankeny, Iowa, Cmty. Sch. Dist., 77 LA 860, 861 (Nathan, 1981) (The grievant "was pregnant with her first child. She applied for a year of parental leave pursuant to . . . the parties' Agreement. Parental leave, which differs from sick leave due to pregnancy (i.e., maternity leave), is intended to permit a new parent to spend full time with a newborn child"). In *West Side Credit Union*, 77 LA 622, 626 (Ellmann, 1981), the dispute resulted because the agreement used (without adequately distinguishing or indicating the extent of overlap in the terms) "parental and/or infant care leave," "maternity leave," and "sick leave," all terms used in reference to employees who become pregnant.

[267]429 U.S. 125, 13 FEP Cases 1657 (1976).

maternity leave cases.[268] In its *General Electric* decision, the Supreme Court held that the employer's disability benefits plan did not violate Title VII because of its failure to cover pregnancy-related disabilities, absent any indication that the exclusion of pregnancy disability benefits was a pretext for discriminating against women. The Court wrote that "gender-based discrimination does not result simply because an employer's disability-benefits plan is less than all-inclusive."[269]

However, the Pregnancy Discrimination Act of 1978 (PDA) amended Title VII of the Civil Rights Act to expressly prohibit discrimination "because of or on the basis of pregnancy, childbirth, or related medical conditions."[270] The Equal Employment Opportunity Commission then issued updated guidelines in 1979, providing in part that:

---

[268]Different schools of thought and the arbitration decisions reflecting them during this period are discussed by Wolkinson & Liberson, *The Arbitration of Sex Discrimination Grievances*, 37 Arb. J. No. 2, at 35, 41–42 (1982), where it is explained that "when resolving grievances over the denial of benefits for pregnancy-related illness or disabilities," some arbitrators relied on saving clauses (making the agreement subject to statutory law and regulations) to justify use of EEOC guidelines as an implied part of the agreement; at least one arbitrator believed that EEOC guidelines must be applied even without such a saving clause; some arbitrators rejected the concept that EEOC guidelines may be referred to when adjudicating contractual disputes. For related discussion, see Chapter 10, section 2., "Range of Views as to Application of 'Law,'" and section 3.A.i., "Title VII of the Civil Rights Act."

[269]429 U.S. at 138–39. In so holding, the Supreme Court pointed to its decision in *Geduldig v. Aiello*, 417 U.S. 484, 8 FEP Cases 97 (1974), where a state's exclusion of pregnancy from disability insurance coverage did not violate the Fourteenth Amendment. However, in *Cleveland Board of Education v. LaFleur*, 414 U.S. 632, 643–48, 6 FEP Cases 1253 (1974), the Supreme Court held invalid under the Fourteenth Amendment public school rules requiring pregnant school teachers to take maternity leave 5 months before the expected birth of their child, the Court reasoning that arbitrary cut-off dates had no valid relationship to the state's interest in preserving continuity of teaching and amounted to a conclusive presumption that every pregnant teacher who has reached such date of pregnancy is physically incapable of continuing, even when the medical evidence as to an individual woman's physical status might be wholly to the contrary. During the period between issuance of the Supreme Court's *General Electric* decision and enactment of the Pregnancy Discrimination Act of 1978, some arbitrators, "relying on saving clauses, continued to require employers to extend maternity benefits to pregnant women where there was in effect state legislation requiring pregnancy to be viewed as a disability," but some other arbitrators relied on *General Electric* "to rule that pregnancy was not a compensable illness unless there was evidence that the contractual provisions on sick pay, leave, and disability had been specifically intended to cover pregnancy." Wolkinson & Liberson, 37 Arb. J. at 42.

[270]42 U.S.C. §2000e(k), which is §701(k) of the Civil Rights Act. This section, which became effective October 31, 1978 (except that it became effective 180 days later as to any fringe benefit program or fund that was in effect on October 31, 1978), states in part:

> (k) The terms "because of sex" or "on the basis of sex" include, but are not limited to, because of or on the basis of pregnancy, childbirth, or related medical conditions; and women affected by pregnancy, childbirth, or related medical conditions shall be treated the same for all employment-related purposes . . . as other persons not so affected but similar in their ability or inability to work . . . .

In *Newport News Shipbuilding & Dry Dock Co. v. EEOC*, 462 U.S. 669, 684, 32 FEP Cases 1 (1983), the Supreme Court stated: "The Pregnancy Discrimination Act has now made clear that, for all Title VII purposes, discrimination based on a woman's pregnancy is, on its face, discrimination because of her sex." The actual holding in this case was that a health insurance plan that provided female employees benefits for pregnancy-related conditions to the same extent as for other medical conditions, but that provided less extensive pregnancy benefits for spouses of male employees, discriminated "against male employees because of *their* sex"; the Court held the plan "unlawful, because the protection it affords to married male employees is less comprehensive than the protection it affords to married female employees." *Id.* at 676.

Written or unwritten employment policies and practices involving matters such as the commencement and duration of leave, the availability of extensions, the accrual of seniority and other benefits and privileges, reinstatement, and payment under any health or disability insurance or sick leave plan, formal or informal, shall be applied to disability due to pregnancy, childbirth or related medical conditions on the same terms and conditions as they are applied to other disabilities.[271]

The termination of a temporarily disabled employee pursuant to an employment policy under which insufficient or no leave is available violates the Act if it has a disparate impact on employees of one sex and is not justified by business necessity.[272]

In *California Federal Savings & Loan Ass'n v. Guerra*,[273] the Supreme Court held that the PDA does not prohibit preferential treatment for pregnancy. The Court upheld a California statute that requires employers to provide female employees an unpaid pregnancy disability leave of up to 4 months and to reinstate these employees when they return to work. The Court found that the California statute, which provided women with a benefit not applicable to men, does not conflict with Title VII of the Civil Rights Act, as amended by the PDA. The Court reasoned that the legislative history of the PDA shows that the amendment was intended to be "'a floor beneath which pregnancy disability benefits may not drop—not a ceiling above which they may not rise.'"[274] The PDA was designed to eliminate discrimination against pregnant women, not to prohibit preferential treatment.

In some arbitration cases that were decided after the 1978 amendment became effective and in which there was an issue concerning maternity or maternity-related leave, the arbitrator expressly considered the PDA, or, in some instances, an antidiscrimination statute of the state. The state statute's requirements were inspected so as to satisfy the arbitrator that the award was compatible with the federal statute.[275] Often in these cases the question

---

[271] 29 C.F.R. §1604.10(b).

[272] The discharge of a pregnant, unmarried employee was held to violate Title VII in *Jacobs v. Martin Sweets Co.*, 550 F.2d 364, 14 FEP Cases 687, 691–92 (6th Cir. 1977). Regarding "business necessity," in *Harriss v. Pan Am. World Airways*, 649 F.2d 670, 674–75, 24 FEP Cases 947, 949–51 (9th Cir. 1980), an airline's policy of requiring a pregnant stewardess to take maternity leave immediately upon learning of her pregnancy was held justified both as a business necessity and as a bona fide occupational qualification (BFOQ), the court explaining when each of the two defenses becomes applicable.

[273] 479 U.S. 272, 42 FEP Cases 1073 (1987). The maternity leave issue has been the focus of legislation among the several states. *See, e.g.*, 2A Tenn. Code Ann. 4-21-408 (Lexis 1998).

[274] 479 U.S. at 280, 42 FEP Cases at 1079 (quoting California Fed. Sav. & Loan Ass'n v. Guerra, 758 F.2d 390, 396, 37 FEP Cases 849, 852 (9th Cir. 1985)).

[275] *See* Cheektowaga, N.Y., Cent. Sch. Bd. of Educ., 80 LA 225, 229 (Shister, 1982) (employee was not entitled to use sick leave bank to cover post-delivery care of her child under contract allowing use of bank if employee is incapacitated by severe sickness or injury); Hormel Fine Frozen Foods, 75 LA 1129, 1136–37, 1144 (Neas, 1980) (noting that the agreement "was obviously revised in order to comply with the Pregnancy Discrimination Act," the arbitrator stated that the Act requires that an employer with a sick benefit plan must treat an employee with a pregnancy-related disability the same as an employee with any other type of disability; the arbitrator found "no evidence the Company has in any manner violated the Act," and found also that neither the agreement nor past practice had been violated by denial of disability benefits for pregnancy-related partial disability that occurred during layoff); Northern Ind. Pub. Serv. Co., 74 LA 1288, 1290–93 (Cabe, 1980) (relying on EEOC guidelines, the arbitrator held that an employee who already was on unpaid pregnancy leave on the effective date of the PDA became entitled to paid sick leave from that date, notwith-

of compliance with the statute is specifically raised by a party; or the agreement may contain some provision such as a savings or legality clause requiring observance of statutory law; or the employer had taken some step reflecting an intention to comply with the requirements of the PDA. In other maternity or maternity-related leave cases decided after the 1978 amendment became effective, however, the arbitrators looked only to the agreement and any past practice, and made no mention of the PDA or any state statute in their decisions.[276]

---

standing the employer's contention that the employee had become an inactive employee when she obtained pregnancy leave under the agreement and that inactive employees had not been considered eligible for sick leave benefits); Northern Ind. Pub. Serv. Co., 74 LA 604, 606–07 (Kossoff, 1980) (here the situation and the arbitrator's view are similar to those just noted in the preceding citation, except that this arbitrator deferred final decision pending submission by the employee of medical verification of disability); Tinker Air Force Base, Okla., 72 LA 358, 359 (Davis, 1979) (contract providing for advance sick leave "for serious disability or illness" did not require advance sick leave for normal pregnancy; while pregnancy can bring about serious disability and illness, in this instance "it did not and most times it doesn't"; nor did the amended Civil Rights Act require the employer to grant the grievant's application for advance sick leave "to take care of impending pregnancy," finding that the employee's application was not denied "because of sex, pregnancy or childbirth," the grievant having been "treated like all other women who experience normal childbirth"); Red Jacket Cent. Sch. Dist., 71 LA 1219, 1221, 1223 (Drotning, 1979) (although not mentioning the federal statute, the arbitrator stated that "employment policies which treat pregnancy and childbirth differently than other physical disabilities [are] prohibited by" the New York statute, concluding that under both the statute and the employer's past practice of allowing female teachers to use up accumulated sick leave before using unpaid leave for childbearing and child-rearing purposes, the employer improperly required grievant to elect between paid sick leave and unpaid leave rather than to permit her to utilize a combination of the two); Sweet Home, N.Y., Cent. Sch. Dist., 71 LA 1102, 1106 (Shister, 1978) (this case involves the same New York statute and a contract issue and ruling similar to those just noted in prior decision, except that the facts in this decision did not involve past practice but did involve an express contract clause requiring conformance with legal requirements); Chromalloy Div.-Okla., 71 LA 1178, 1179–80 (Barnhart, 1978) (until the EEOC pregnancy leave guidelines were issued in 1973, the collective bargaining agreement expressly excluded pregnancy disability from entitlement to sickness and accident benefits, but the express exclusion was deleted in response to the EEOC guidelines; the arbitrator construed the agreement not to require sickness benefits during the period between the Supreme Court's *General Electric* decision and the effective date of the PDA, because the employer had made it clear that the employer's willingness to delete the express exclusion of pregnancy disability "arose from obedience to the law rather than from an obligation stemming from negotiation with the Union").

[276]*See* Northern Ind. Pub. Serv. Co., 80 LA 41, 44–45 (Winton, 1982) (where contract provided that leave not exceeding 30 days for "any valid reason" other than sickness or injury "shall" be granted to employees, grievant was entitled to leave to nurse her new baby since the word "valid" had been liberally interpreted under past practice); Caterpillar Tractor Co., 79 LA 1070, 1074–75 (Cyrol, 1982) (employee who had had two previous miscarriages was entitled to sickness disability benefits for period that physician certified that she was pregnant and should not do any work that involved lifting, pulling, pushing, or straining of any kind); Ankeny, Iowa, Cmty. Sch. Dist., 77 LA 860, 861, 863–64 (Nathan, 1981) (where contract provided that "parental leave shall be without salary and shall be granted for a period not to exceed one year," the parties' intent being to permit a new parent to spend full time with a newborn child, the employer improperly denied a request for 1 year of parental leave for such purpose, the employer had failed to give individual and objective consideration to the grievant's request and the denial actually had resulted from the employer's general dissatisfaction with long leaves of absence); West Side Credit Union, 77 LA 622, 626 (Ellmann, 1981) (the dispute concerned the possible total number of months of leave that employees who become pregnant are entitled to under contract clauses that were poorly drafted and that spoke of "prenatal and/or infant care leave," "sick leave," and "the maternity leave," all in reference to such employees, the dispute was resolved by a decision that the arbitrator felt was a "reasonable and reasoned interpretation of the contract"); Greensburg Salem Sch. Dist., 76 LA 241, 244 (Hannan, 1981) (past practice controlled the disposition of an issue concerning continuation of insurance coverage during unpaid maternity leave that commenced after paid sick leave had expired).

The Family and Medical Leave Act (FMLA) expressly states that it does not modify or affect any federal or state antidiscrimination legislation, including the PDA.[277] The provisions of these two laws are compatible. Under the FMLA, as under the PDA, an employee's leave for pregnancy, childbirth, or related medical conditions is treated similarly to an employee's leave for other temporary, serious health conditions. Under the FMLA, leave because of pregnancy and childbirth must be treated the same as other serious health conditions that make employees unable to work. Thus, if an employer permits substitution of paid leave for leave taken for other serious medical conditions, employees disabled by pregnancy and childbirth must also be able to substitute paid leave to the same extent as others with serious health conditions.

Relying on the collective bargaining agreement and the FMLA, an arbitrator concluded that discharging an employee at or about the time she requested a pregnancy leave violated both the FMLA and the agreement.[278] The employee had some 10 days prior to her discharge verbally advised her supervisor and the payroll clerk of her desire for a pregnancy leave. The arbitrator ruled that the request triggered a duty on the part of the company to conduct an investigation to determine whether such a leave was appropriate under the FMLA. However, the company conducted no investigation but instead discharged the employee for violation of its 3-day "no-report" rule, an event occurring after her request for leave.[279]

The same result was reached by another arbitrator who reinstated a female employee after she had been similarly terminated for failing to meet a 3-day call-in requirement.[280] The employer had refused to grant the employee the FMLA leave she sought, claiming that the worker was not eligible for the maternity leave because she had not been on the payroll a full year. The arbitrator found no 1-year requirement in the labor contract[281] and concluded that the employee was entitled to the leave, which, if granted, would not have required the employee to call in every 3 days.

Can an employee be placed on maternity leave against her wishes? An arbitrator found a public utility employer could place a pregnant employee on leave when her job as a mechanic required her regularly to lift objects heavier than the 30-pound limit recommended by her physician. The company rejected two alternatives proposed by the union. The first, requiring coworkers to lift heavier items, was found to be unreasonably disruptive. The second, allowing the pregnant employee to transfer to an available cafeteria position, was held to violate a contractual provision that forbade discrimination in transfers based on disability or sex. Although the union agreed to waive this provision, the company did not, since it was planning to subcontract the operation. The arbitrator held that "a bilateral agreement requires bilateral waiver."[282]

---

[277]29 U.S.C. §2651.
[278]Pace Indus., 109 LA 1 (Gordinier, 1997).
[279]*Id.* at 3.
[280]Enesco Corp., 107 LA 513 (Berman, 1996).
[281]*Id.* at 518–19.
[282]Minnegasco, Inc., 103 LA 43 (Bognanno, 1994).

D. Leave for Union Business [LA CDI 100.5218; 116.205]

Although requests for union leave can be made only by a small fraction of the workforce, they produce a disproportionate percentage of the grievances filed over employers' leave restrictions or denials. In one case, significant for its requirement that the employer prove a leave denial to be reasonable, an employer's reasons for denying unpaid leave to a local union president so that he could participate in the union's "Lobby [Congress] Week" was held to be insufficient.[283] The focus of Lobby Week was the potential reorganization of two districts of the U.S. Army Corps of Engineers, a subject that qualified as "of mutual concern" to the parties. The Corps asserted that it had denied the request because an "emergency weather situation" had developed, requiring the union president's services. The president did not possess any essential skill necessary to meet the emergency that management described.[284] In fact, hundreds of other employees were granted leave during the emergency. The arbitrator found that the request had actually been denied because management did not like the views on the issue that the president would express before Congress.[285]

In another case, a union's request that its president be given one-half day released time for union business was denied despite the union's especially large membership.[286] The union failed to present sufficient evidence that its business could not be administered unless the union president was granted free time during the workday.[287]

Contract provisions for leaves of absence for union business vary greatly, and whether such leave should be granted depends not only on the particular contract clause but also on the specific circumstances of each case.[288] While

---

[283]U.S. Army Corps of Eng'rs, 104 LA 30 (Baroni, 1995).
[284]*Id.* at 34.
[285]*Id.*
[286]Wooster City, Ohio, Bd. of Educ., 108 LA 502 (Feldman, 1997).
[287]*Id.* at 505.
[288]*See* C&D Batteries, 32 LA 589, 594 (Jaffee, 1959) (criteria were discussed in regard to granting leave for union business). For other discussions that may serve to provide criteria, see *Department of the Army*, 80 LA 201, 204–05 (Cloke, 1982*); Metropolitan Utils. Dist. of Omaha, Neb.*, 78 LA 969, 972–73 (Thornell, 1982) (upheld the employer's right to place a union officer on unpaid leave of absence without the consent of the union, where absence from work on union business for nearly one-half of work time was found to "seriously interfere with" the individual's "ability to perform his job with the employer"); *National Broad. Co.*, 76 LA 648, 652 (Gentile, 1981); *Diecast Corp.*, 75 LA 66, 73–76 (Howlett, 1980); *Hyde Park Foundry & Mach. Co.*, 71 LA 349, 354 (McDermott, 1978); *Hurd Millwork Corp.*, 58 LA 253, 254 (Hazelwood, 1972). As to a second leave at the end of a first leave where the contract provides for "leave of absence for six months" for union business, see *Wallingford Steel Co.*, 54 LA 1130, 1133–34 (Sherman, Jr., 1971). Where an agreement expressly specified the duration of leaves of absence, it was held that the grant or denial of "leaves for a shorter period of time [than specified in the agreement] lies within the discretion of the Company." Minnesota Mining & Mfg. Co., 55 LA 539, 542 (Karlins, 1970). *See also* Menasco Mfg. Co., 71 LA 696, 698 (Gowan, Jr., 1978). In *Davis Cabinet Co.*, 80 LA 1055, 1057–58 (Williams, 1983), the agreement provided that a leave of absence "will" be granted to employees elected to union office; under this provision, the employer was required to grant a leave to a laid-off employee who was elected to union office 7 days before she otherwise would have lost her seniority because of continuous layoff for 12 months, notwithstanding the employer's contention that her sole reason for requesting the leave was to extend her recall and seniority rights. The employee's apparent expectation here was that the employer-employee relationship would continue by virtue of the leave of absence and that valuable contractual rights

internal affairs of the union and union "secrets" need not be divulged, the employer is entitled to enough information regarding the nature of the union business involved and the probable duration of the absence to permit an intelligent choice whether to grant or deny leave.[289]

One arbitrator set aside a unilaterally adopted policy statement that placed undue limitations on the contractually provided right to be away from work for union business. However, he observed that the term "union activities" is not unlimited and that arbitrators must determine whether, under the facts and circumstances of each case, "the nature of the particular activity is an appropriate basis for absence."[290] He continued:

> [A]rbitrators apply the twin concepts of reasonableness and undue burden as limitations upon requests for leaves of absence for Union activities. . . . What these two concepts essentially mean, when construed together with [an article requiring] regularity of attendance, is that if the activity in question reasonably can be done on off-duty time without encroaching on work hours, it should be done then. In such case the need of the Company for his or her services exceeds the need to be absent from work which, boiled down, is what 'undue burden' means. Replacing an absent employee ordinarily places a burden upon management and added expense whenever overtime is involved. The concept of reasonableness requires accommodation by both sides.[291]

Another arbitrator noted that, in determining which activities constitute official union business, arbitrators generally give "wide latitude to the unions," and suggested the following classification:

> Generally, official union business falls within two broad areas: the first area includes those activities performed by the union as the bargaining representatives for the employees; a second and broader area includes those activities which the union performs on behalf of itself as an entity. The latter activities include such things as organizing (Walker Manufacturing, 42 LA 632 [, 636 (Anderson, 1964)]), political activity (Consolidation Coal Co., 84 LA 1042 [(Feldman, 1985)]), and bargaining in another plant (Hurd Millwork, 58 LA 523 [(Hazelwood, 1972)]).[292]

When a contract limited leaves of absence to 2 years but did not so restrict leaves for union business, an arbitrator refused to imply a similar limitation

---

accordingly would be retained. For other cases illustrating the possibility that important consequences may result from continued employer-employee relationship during leave of absence for union business, see *Dravo Corp.*, 68 LA 618, 624–25 (McDermott, 1977) (upholding discharge of union president for leading illicit work stoppage while on leave as full-time union officer receiving pay from union); *Western Textile Prods. Co.*, 64 LA 709, 718–20 (Dworkin, 1975) (holding that for purposes of determining pension benefits, the employee could include as credited years of service with the employer his 22-year leave of absence while serving as union officer; the arbitrator stated that the "concept of 'leave of absence' implies that some form of employee-employer relationship continues in effect").

[289]*See* Gulf Oil Co., 78 LA 8, 14 (Leeper, 1981); Home Furniture Co., 50 LA 1140, 1144 (Porter, 1967); Walker Mfg. Co., 42 LA 632, 636 (Anderson, 1964); Telex, Inc., 35 LA 873, 881 (Kinyon, 1960); C&D Batteries, 32 LA 589, 593–94 (Jaffee, 1959); Carter Carburetor Corp., 11 LA 569, 572 (Hilpert, 1948). *See also* Ward Lafrance Truck Corp., 69 LA 831, 838 (Levy, 1977); United Eng'g Co., 64 LA 1274, 1278 (Rule, 1975).

[290]Sharples Coal Co., 91 LA 1317, 1322 (Volz, 1988) (citing Consolidation Burning Star No. 5 Mine, No. 84-12-85-12, at 17 (Hahn, unpublished)).

[291]*Id.*

[292]Hillshire Farm Co., 88 LA 1148, 1153 (Gundermann, 1987). *See also* City of San Antonio, Tex., 92 LA 76 (McDermott, 1989); Texas Utils. Generating Co., 86 LA 1108 (Nicholas, Jr., 1986).

and allowed a union officer to maintain his seniority and employment relationship indefinitely.[293]

Not all requests for union leave or released time have been so successful in arbitration. Thus, a union was held to have violated the collective bargaining agreement when a local president used official time to attend a district caucus where she was unexpectedly seated as a voting delegate.[294] The contract allowed the use of official time only for joint labor/management committee activities, not for internal union business.[295] The arbitrator, however, found that there was no "willful abuse of official time" because the local president did not originally intend to get involved in internal union business, and did not think she would be seated as a delegate and be eligible to vote.[296]

While many arbitrators have held that leave for "union business" does not encompass union political activity,[297] one arbitrator stated that the "modern labor law of this country" requires a different conclusion, namely that "union activities . . . do not mean some, those that are liked, those that involve non-political activity, but rather it means *all* union activity."[298] Another arbitrator, in determining that participation in school board election activities constituted "normal business activity," similarly observed:

> In the public sector, political activity is interwoven with bargaining activity as public employee unions seek to influence the legislative bodies which control their fate at the bargaining table. Whether one views this as proper or wise, it is undeniably part of normal union business in the public sector.[299]

Under some contracts, arbitrators have approved the action of management in granting leave for union business on a conditional basis,[300] and in others, past practice of the parties and industry practice have influenced or

---

[293]Panhandle E. Pipe Line Co., 103 LA 996 (Allen, Jr., 1994).

[294]Army & Air Force Exch. Serv., 108 LA 618 (Baroni, 1997).

[295]*Id.* at 621.

[296]*Id.* at 622.

[297]*See* Husky Oil Co., 37 LA 249, 251–52 (Simpson, 1961); Anchor Duck Mills, 5 LA 428, 430 (Hepburn, 1946). *Cf.* Le Roi Mfg. Co., 8 LA 350, 354 (Updegraff, 1947). Regarding picketing as "union business," in *Jackson, Michigan, Public Schools*, 64 LA 1089 (Keefe, 1975), the employer was not obligated to pay teachers for time spent picketing another school under a contract entitling union delegates to up to 25 days' pay per year for "union business." The arbitrator declared it to be "incontrovertibly clear that payment by any Management to its Employees for engaging in strike-activities elsewhere, even though involving another Employer, is incompatible with Management's natural philosophy and repugnant to its material interests, inasmuch as proliferation of such arrangements could eventually result in a paid-for stranger-pickets closing down the home activity of the original Employer." *Id.* at 1092. *See also* National Broad. Co., 76 LA 648, 652 (Gentile, 1981).

[298]Consolidation Coal Co., 84 LA 1042, 1044 (Feldman, 1985) (emphasis in original).

[299]Orange Unified Sch. Dist., Orange County, Cal., 91 LA 525, 529 (Collins, 1988) (holding also that attendance at arraignment of school board members and officials on charges of misappropriation of public funds and willful misconduct was within union's "normal business activities" since indictment related to district's financial condition and ability to pay employees).

[300]*See* Husky Oil Co., 37 LA 249, 252 (Simpson, 1961); U.S. Indus. Chems. Co., 36 LA 400, 404 (Teple, 1961). *Cf.* Blaw-Knox Co., 41 LA 739, 743–44 (Klein, 1963); Manning, Maxwell & Moore, 37 LA 475, 483 (Stutz, 1961).

determined the arbitrator's decision.[301] Under a consistently observed master labor agreement provision requiring an employee to obtain supervisory approval to discuss union matters during duty hours, an arbitrator found that an unsanctioned meeting between a national union representative and a bargaining unit member during work time to discuss a grievance violated the agreement.[302] Even in the absence of such a provision, the arbitrator continued, management could reasonably prohibit employees on duty from coming and going at will to meet one another.[303] The union was ordered to seek approval in the future for the release of employees during their shifts.[304]

Turning to public-sector labor relations, a county did not violate a collective bargaining agreement by denying a request for a 35-day union leave so that an employee could attend union training sessions. Such a leave, the arbitrator decided, need not be granted in the absence of an express contractual mandate or a binding past practice.[305] The contract provided that union leave "may," rather than "shall," be granted. The county had at one time granted such leave to two employees, but this was insufficient to establish the requisite past practice.[306]

When a steward leaves his work station to attend to a union function without supervisory authorization, he may be subject to discipline. Under a collective bargaining agreement that allowed stewards a reasonable time to handle employee problems after first notifying a supervisor, an employer was found to have had good cause to discharge a shop steward who left his work area to report on an alleged altercation without giving such notice.[307] The steward, the arbitrator noted, had had disciplinary problems in the past.

Whether a union officer must be paid for time spent on union business is determined by the contract. Thus, on the basis of the collective bargaining agreement, an arbitrator decided that a local union president was entitled to pay for time spent at a Step III grievance meeting but not entitled to pay for time spent at a predischarge meeting.[308] Since the company had for many years made payment to successive local union presidents for their attendance at Step III meetings, this "practice" informed the otherwise silent text. However, because the agreement specified pay only for settling "grievances," meetings concerned only with a potential discharge were not within the scope of the provision.[309]

---

[301]*See* Weston Paper & Mfg. Co., 76 LA 1273, 1276–78 (Bowles, 1981); Diecast Corp., 75 LA 66, 75 (Howlett, 1980); Houston Elecs. Corp., 70 LA 887, 889–91 (Felice, 1978); Williams Pipe Line Co., 70 LA 664, 667 (Barnhart, 1978); Farrel Corp., 43 LA 670, 675 (Fallon, 1964); Stamford Rolling Mills Co., 15 LA 611, 612 (Donnelly, 1950); New Jersey Bell Tel. Co., 14 LA 574, 591 (Martin, Lewis, Lesser, Jr., Lord, & Dunn, 1950) (interest arbitration); Carter Carburetor Corp., 11 LA 569, 573 (Hilpert, 1948); Robertshaw-Fulton Controls Co., 11 LA 1074, 1075 (Dwyer, 1948).

[302]Army & Air Force Exch. Serv., 107 LA 758 (Allen, Jr., 1996).

[303]*Id.* at 762.

[304]*Id.* at 763.

[305]Auglaize County, Ohio, Bd. of Comm'rs, 110 LA 916 (Sugerman, 1998).

[306]*Id.* at 919.

[307]Nature's Best, 110 LA 365 (Gentile, 1998).

[308]Morton Salt, 104 LA 444 (Fullmer, 1995).

[309]*Id.* at 448.

Contrarily, under an agreement that authorized pay for attendance of union representatives only at scheduled grievance meetings, an employer was found to have improperly withheld pay for time spent in performing other union duties. There, however, union officials regularly had been compensated while engaged in union business, and the employer had never denied prior requests for such time off except due to actual production constraints. These circumstances led the arbitrator to conclude that a binding past practice had been established.[310]

Where a union's proposal to appoint stewards in certain work areas was rejected by a federal agency, the actual time spent by local officers and stewards from other departments in representing the employees in the unrepresented work areas was held to be compensable.[311] However, the arbitration costs were not included in the reimbursement.[312]

Conversely, a number of decisions have denied requests to be paid for time spent on at least some aspects of union business. Thus, an employer did not have to pay its union members for time spent at a ratification meeting despite the fact that a manager initially had offered to pay employees for attending.[313] The labor contract stated that employees must be paid for "authorized work," but no evidence of relevant bargaining history or past practice was available as an interpretive aid. An arbitrator held that because the employer had no "right to control" the union meeting, the employees' attendance could not be considered "authorized work."[314] The arbitrator considered he lacked the authority to enforce the manager's oral offer to pay because it arose outside the labor contract.[315] For like reason, a union representative is not entitled to pay for the time spent in preparing his own grievance. So ruled an arbitrator for the reason that in pursuing his "pro se" grievance, the officer was not acting in a "representative capacity."[316]

The shoe was on the other foot (even though it was found not to fit) when an employer filed a grievance seeking reimbursement from a union for payments made to a union representative in negotiating a union contract covering another bargaining unit. Believing that the service would conflict with his scheduled day shift work hours, the representative had performed his regular work at night and negotiated during the day. The arbitrator held that since the federal agency employer had allowed other employees to work flexible hours for other purposes, the union representative also was entitled to have flexible work hours in order to engage in union activities,[317] and the agency could not restrict the working hours of the representative to the day shift.[318]

---

[310]Motor Wheel Corp., 102 LA 922 (Chattman, 1994).
[311]Defense Logistics Agency, 104 LA 439 (Gentile, 1995).
[312]Id. at 443.
[313]Litton Precision Gear, 107 LA 52 (Goldstein, 1996).
[314]Id. at 57.
[315]Id. at 58.
[316]San Francisco Newspaper Agency, 93 LA 322 (Koven, 1989).
[317]Department of the Air Force, 107 LA 890 (Harr, 1996).
[318]Id. at 891.

Does a union member continue to accumulate seniority while on leave to hold union office? The question arose in the context of a contractual provision stating that seniority of full-time union officers "shall be held as it existed" at the time they take office.[319] Although the arbitrator recognized that the contractual text tended to support the company's position that seniority did not accumulate during the leave, he noted that previous officers who had returned to their jobs continued to accrue seniority during the time they were on leave, and used this "past practice" to interpret the "ambiguous contract language" favorably to the union.[320]

When union leave is unavailable to cover an absence, compensable sick leave may not be resorted to as a subterfuge. An employee who sought to take sick leave to picket on behalf of an affiliated union then on strike was discharged under a contractual "no-strike" clause that prohibited union members from participating in "strikes" and "picketing" or from assisting, encouraging, or participating in any of these actions.[321] Concluding that this provision applied to the employee's activities, the arbitrator found that the company had just cause for terminating the services of the employee. Although the union president had previously been permitted to utilize union leave for the same purpose, she had not misrepresented her actions or abused sick leave. Her case therefore afforded no exculpatory precedent.[322]

In a case of collateral interest, an arbitrator struck down a state employer's requirement that union staff representatives must give 1 week's written notice before visiting work areas.[323] The collective bargaining agreement allowed union representatives to visit work areas to the extent the visits did not disrupt work activities. Since the contract did not contain any requirement for giving written advance, the state could not unilaterally impose such a restriction.[324]

E.　Leave for Jury Duty [LA CDI 100.5221; 116.204]

The vast majority of reported decisions deal not with the right to leave of absence for jury duty, but with the resultant pay problems under pertinent contract language. In the absence of such a provision, it has been held that the company is not required to pay jury duty benefits to its employees.[325]

---

[319]Public Serv. Co. of Okla., 107 LA 1080 (Allen, Jr., 1997).

[320]Id. at 1083.

[321]Merck-Medco RX Servs. of Tex. L.L.C., 110 LA 782 (Baroni, 1998).

[322]Id. at 789.

[323]State of New Hampshire, 108 LA 209 (McCausland, 1997).

[324]Id. at 211.

[325]See Ryder Truck Lines, 38 LA 113, 115 (Williams, 1961). In Ziegler Steel Service Corp., 69 LA 1102, 1103 (Tsukiyama, 1977), a contractual provision for jury pay was held inapplicable to service as a witness. Apart from contractual rights, jury duty rights against the employer may be provided by statute. For example, an Alabama statute requiring employers to pay workers excused for jury duty their regular pay "less the fee or compensation" received for serving as a juror was upheld as to constitutionality in Dean v. Gadsden Times Publ'g Corp., 412 U.S. 543, 21 WH Cases 105 (1973). The Jury System Improvements Act of 1978, 28 U.S.C. §1861 et seq., prohibits employers from discharging, threatening to discharge, coercing, or intimidating permanent employees because they are serving or are scheduled to serve on a federal jury. In NLRB v. Merrill & Ring, Inc., 731 F.2d 605, 116 LRRM 2221 (9th Cir. 1984), pay for jury duty was held to be a mandatory subject of bargaining under the NLRA.

The object of jury duty pay provisions is to "provide competent jurors through the removal of the monetary loss that would otherwise accompany jury service."[326] Thus, employees who are called for jury duty while on vacation[327] or in layoff status[328] have been held not to be entitled to jury duty pay. The key words in many contracts are "time lost," and where an employee was called to jury service but excused early, the arbitrator held that the employee had an obligation to return to work because "he could readily have returned to his home, changed to appropriate clothing, and reported for work" for the last half of his shift allowed only partial payment.[329]

Reconciling jury duty pay provisions to situations in which shift schedules did not coincide precisely with hours of jury duty, one arbitrator held that the "rule of reason" must be applied. When the hours of jury service come so close before or after the employee's scheduled shift as to give justifiable grounds for missing that shift, the employee should be excused and paid jury allowance.[330]

Under a contract providing for pay "[i]f an employee is required to absent himself from the job" for jury service, the employee's need for rest was cited as justification for jury duty pay to an employee who was scheduled to work on the night shift. The arbitrator stated that it was "clear that the Grievant was 'required' to absent herself from the job" in order to obtain needed rest.[331] However, in one case an employer required its employees who are called for jury duty to report to work before reporting to court. A labor contract provided that employees assigned to the 6:00 a.m.–2:00 p.m. shift

---

[326]Greenleaf Mfg. Co., 32 LA 1, 2 (Edelman, 1959). *See also* Union Eye Care Ctr., 76 LA 170, 171 (Dahl, 1981); Curtiss-Wright Corp., 49 LA 901, 905 (Freund, 1967); American Bakeries Co., 40 LA 1195, 1197 (Mills, 1963). *Cf.* Master Lock Co., 74 LA 865, 867 (Hutchison, 1980) (where past practice controlled the result).

[327]Columbus Auto Parts Co., 51 LA 1288, 1292 (Klein, 1968).

[328]American Airlines, 39 LA 500, 503–04 (Hill, 1962). *See also* Union Eye Care Ctr., 76 LA 170, 171 (Dahl, 1981) (employer not obligated to pay jury duty pay for 2 scheduled off days that fell during 10-day period of jury duty); FMC Corp., 65 LA 264, 267 (Warns, 1975) (employee who was on jury duty on days when plant operation was suspended due to snowfall was not entitled to jury pay from the employer for those days). *Cf.* General Elec. Co., 50 LA 852, 860 (Seinsheimer, 1967) (jury duty performed by employees during a strike called by another union).

[329]Continental Can Co., 47 LA 683, 685–86 (Dash, Jr., 1966) (awarding the employee compensation for only one-half of each of the 5 days he was released early from jury duty). *See also* Henry Vogt Mach. Co., 39 LA 763, 766 (Volz, 1962). *Cf.* McCabe-Powers Body Co., 72 LA 1057, 1059 (Bernstein, 1979); Lever Bros. Co., 65 LA 867, 868 (D'Angelo, 1975).

[330]United States Steel Corp., 36 LA 590, 595 (McDermott, 1961); United States Steel Corp., 36 LA 595, 597 (McDermott, 1961); United States Steel Corp., 36 LA 597, 599 (McDermott, 1961). Another arbitrator, while noting that these cases are not binding upon the parties in *Bethlehem Steel Corp.*, 49 LA 334, 336–37 (Seward, 1967), was "particularly impressed" by Arbitrator McDermott's analysis and wrote that he "joins Arbitrator McDermott . . . in holding that the rule of reason should govern application of the jury pay provision." In *U.S. Pipe & Foundry Co.*, 55 LA 856 (Holly, 1970), it was held that the grievants should not have been expected to report for work before reporting for jury duty since only a maximum of 1 to 2 hours could have been worked; the arbitrator stated that "the Company's position is entirely unreasonable since it places a heavy burden on the employee-juror, and the Company cannot hope to receive any significant amount of productive work from the employee." *Id.* at 858–59.

[331]Hunt Foods & Indus., 36 LA 929, 931 (McNaughton, 1961). *See also* International Nickel Co., 33 LA 508, 511–12 (Holly, 1959); Ozark Smelting & Mining Co., 27 LA 189, 189 (Schedler, 1956).

must work the difference between their regular 8 hours and the time spent in jury duty.[332] A letter written by a management representative to a union official stated that employees whose shift began prior to the jury reporting time could be required to report for work first.[333] However, an employee selected for jury service had been excused from coming into work prior to reporting to court and had not had her shift changed. When she clocked in after being released by the court, an arbitrator decided that she was entitled to overtime compensation for all work performed after 2:00 p.m. on that day.[334] In a related scenario, an arbitrator held that a collective bargaining agreement that allowed grievances to be filed regarding any "condition of employment" authorized a union to pursue a grievance for the denial of pay to a school employee who took a day off to testify in a trial.[335]

The question sometimes arises as to whether time spent in jury service should be included as time worked for purposes of other provisions of the contract. In the absence of a provision specifically covering the issue, it has been held that jury duty does not count as time worked for purposes of computing weekly overtime.[336] One arbitrator, however, held that time spent on jury duty was to be included in computing the employee's vacation time.[337]

F. Funeral Leave [LA CDI 100.5215; 116.202]

Cases involving funeral leave provisions have turned on the precise wording of the funeral leave or "bereavement" pay clause, and arbitrators appear to be inclined toward narrow interpretation of such clauses. Thus, where the contract states that a certain number of days of paid leave would be allowed to attend the funeral of a member of the employee's immediate family, arbitrators have held that the leave includes attendance at the funeral and necessary travel time, but does not contemplate absences to aid bereaved relatives or to attend to the estate.[338] Further, where the contract provides for "consecutive" days off, arbitrators interpret "consecutive" to mean calendar,

---

[332]Sacramento Reg'l Transit Dist., 110 LA 855 (Bogue, 1998).

[333]*Id.* at 857.

[334]*Id.* at 858.

[335]Cochraine-Fountain, Wis., Sch. Dist., 110 LA 324 (Dichter, 1998).

[336]*See* Cabot Corp., 52 LA 575, 577 (Ray, 1969); Coleman Co., 52 LA 357, 360 (Carter, 1969); American Bakeries Co., 40 LA 1195, 1197 (Mills, 1963).

[337]Goodyear Aerospace Corp., 51 LA 540, 546 (Lehoczky, 1968).

[338]*See* ITT Auto. Elec. Prods. Div., 70 LA 830, 833 (Hon, 1978); Reichhold Chems., 61 LA 510, 512 (Williams, 1973); Trane Co., 53 LA 1108, 1109 (Caraway, 1969); Stupp Bros. Bridge & Iron Co., 53 LA 974, 975 (Edelman, 1969); Hill Refrigeration, 48 LA 351, 352 (Hill, 1966); Warner & Swasey Co., 47 LA 438, 440 (Teple, 1966); Chicago Vitreous Corp., 45 LA 494, 495 (Daugherty, 1965); Dana Corp., 42 LA 59, 61 (Luskin, 1963); Wolf Baking Co., 40 LA 223, 224–25 (Sweeney, 1963); Gould-National Batteries, 36 LA 1077, 1078 (Wolff, 1961); Pratt & Whitney Co., 34 LA 300, 301 (Hays, 1959). *See also* Carson Mfg. Co., 73 LA 115, 117 (Berns, 1979); Litton Fin. Printing Co., 73 LA 96, 98 (Rule, 1979). *But see* Mohawk Rubber Co., 80 LA 1305, 1309 (Cantor, 1983); Bethlehem Steel Corp., 59 LA 768, 769 (Gamser, 1972); National Indus. Prods. Co., 44 LA 739, 740 (McIntosh, 1965). One arbitrator held that the company could issue a rule requiring the employee to furnish evidence of attendance at the funeral. *See* Borg-Warner Corp., 47 LA 691, 697–98 (Bradley, 1966). *See also* Amax Zinc Co., 67 LA 536, 540 (Penfield, 1976); Kentile Floors, 57 LA 951, 954 (Dolnick, 1971). *Cf.* Stauffer Chem. Co., 70 LA 693, 695–96 (Jones, Jr., 1978).

and not scheduled, workdays.[339] If the contract language refers to "pay for time lost" or a "paid leave of absence" while attending the funeral of a family member, arbitrators generally have held the provision inapplicable when the employee was already on vacation or otherwise not scheduled.[340]

However, usually a somewhat broader interpretation is given to that portion of the funeral leave clause that identifies the family members or relatives for whose funeral the leave is allowed. For example, where a contract listed "brother" among the eligible members of the family, the arbitrator, emphasizing the closeness of the relationship between the employee and his stepbrother, held that "the latter must be deemed his brother within the meaning of that term as used in the agreement."[341]

One troubling and recurring problem is whether in-laws are covered within the "family" funeral leave provision of a contract. Thus, where a collective bargaining agreement provided for leave in the event of a death in

---

[339]Gulf Printing Co., 92 LA 893 (King, 1989); Blue Grass Cooperage Co., 89 LA 385 (Sergent, Jr., 1987); Consolidation Coal Co., 89 LA 179 (Wren, 1987).

[340]Southwestern Publ'g Co., 79 LA 82 (Gibson, 1982); Murdock Mach. & Eng'g Co., 62 LA 547 (Rohman, 1974); Dayton Rogers Mfg. Co., 61 LA 382 (O'Connell, 1973).

[341]Foremost Dairies, 43 LA 616, 617 (Greenwald, 1964) (citing Singer Mfg. Co., 28 LA 469, 469–70 (Cahn, 1957), and Sylvania Elec. Prods., 26 LA 108, 110 (Shister, 1956)). For other cases in which the arbitrator favored a somewhat *broad construction* of the provision specifying the relationship requirement, see *Hartman Elec. Mfg.*, 92 LA 253, 255–56 (Rybolt, 1989) (half-brothers included in the word "brother" for purposes of funeral leave); *Georgia Pac. Corp.*, 63 LA 163, 164 (Cohen, 1974) (term "close relatives" in contract was held not to be limited to relatives by consanguinity but rather would include relatives by affinity to whom employee factually is "close"); *Alfred M. Lewis*, 62 LA 447, 451 (Petrie, 1974) (term "parents" included stepmother even though natural mother was still living); *Sheller-Globe Corp.*, 61 LA 1224, 1226 (Teple, 1973) (term "brother-in-law" included employee's husband's sister's husband); *Bergen Mach. & Tool Co.*, 54 LA 56, 58–59 (Berkowitz, 1971); *Our Own Bakeries*, 43 LA 467, 469–70 (Thompson, 1964); *Hercules Powder Co.*, 40 LA 1230, 1234 (Marshall, 1963); *Columbia Mills*, 38 LA 1029, 1031 (Kornblum, 1961); *St. Louis Flour Mills*, 31 LA 603, 606–07 (Klamon, 1958). But one arbitrator refused to extend the meaning of "brother-in-law" to include the employee's wife's sister's husband. Consumers Power Co., 49 LA 595, 601–03 (Dworkin, 1967). For other cases in which the arbitrator was inclined toward *strict construction* of the provision specifying the relationship requirement, see *Derby Cap Mfg. Co.*, 87 LA 1042, 1047 (Imundo, Jr., 1986) (definition of spouse did not include a man grievant had lived with for 25 years); *Town of Davie, Fla.*, 83 LA 1153, 1157–58 (Kanzer, 1984) (grievant's wife's grandmother not included in term "grandparent"); *Oak Rubber Co.*, 77 LA 1127, 1128–29 (Rybolt, 1981) (husband of employee's sister ceased to be employee's brother-in-law when sister died); *Fanny Farmer Candy Shops*, 76 LA 1107, 1111–12 (Dworkin, 1981); *Armstrong Cork Co.*, 73 LA 1144, 1145–46 (Eyraud, 1979) (stating that "the relationship of husband and wife is one of affinity, not consanguinity," and stating that "a relationship of affinity is broken by death or divorce," arbitrator held that the term "brother-in-law" in funeral leave clause "does not encompass the brother of a deceased wife"); *Motor Transp. Indus. Relations Bureau of Ontario, Inc.*, 71 LA 1071, 1072 (O'Shea, 1978) (father of grievant's wife ceased to be his father-in-law when grievant and his wife were divorced); *General Refractories Co.*, 71 LA 874, 876 (Chapman, 1978); *Eagle-Picher Indus.*, 71 LA 473, 475 (Yarowsky, 1978); *Houdaille Indus.*, 69 LA 1080, 1083 (Hunter, Jr., 1977); *Union Carbide Corp.*, 64 LA 1078, 1080 (Teple, 1975) (term "immediate family" did not include brother of employee's deceased wife, where employee had remarried, even though employee may have retained at least part of his emotional ties with in-laws by his first marriage); *Frito-Lay*, 63 LA 1036, 1039 (Rimer, Jr., 1974) (absent bargaining history or past practice expanding meaning of term "father," it did not include stepfather); *Sheller-Globe Corp.*, 61 LA 1224, 1226 (Teple, 1973) (term "grandparent" did not include grandmother of employee's husband); *Cincinnati Tool Co.*, 61 LA 79, 86 (Bradley, 1973); *Superior Tube Co.*, 57 LA 959, 962 (Kates, 1971); *Texaco*, 52 LA 768, 769 (Berkowitz, 1969) (wife's uncle would not qualify as employee's uncle); *Wyman-Gordon Co.*, 51 LA 289, 290 (Davis, 1968) (stepfather-in-law would not qualify as employee's immediate family").

the employee's "immediate family" and included within the definition grandparents and in-laws of the "immediate family," such as mothers-in-law, an arbitrator held that the death of a grandparent-in-law had not entitled an employee to the paid funeral leave she had received from her county employer.[342] Nevertheless, the employer's attempt to recover the payments some 7 months later was held to be untimely.[343] Fairness required that there be some time limit imposed on the county's right to dock its employees' paycheck to recoup such improvident payments, and 7 months was too long.

The definition of "immediate family" in another funeral leave provision included "father, mother, spouse, sister, brother, father-in-law, mother-in-law or child," but did not include a "wife's stepfather."[344] The omission was held to be dispositive of an employee's claim based on this relationship. Although the employer previously had granted such leave, it did so because the employee had misrepresented the relationship of the deceased, and the prior case could not serve to enlarge the scope of the contractual provision.[345]

Of course, past practice may affect the arbitrator's decision. Thus, in one case where the contract contained no funeral leave clause but did provide for maintenance of working conditions, the arbitrator ruled that the employer was required to continue an established practice of granting up to 3 days' funeral leave.[346] In another case, an existing funeral leave policy, recognized by both parties, of not including payment of such benefits during any period of paid absence from work such as vacations was deemed by the arbitrator to have carried over into the new contract provision dealing with paid funeral leave.[347] Finally, the existence of a funeral leave clause preempts the use of any other leave clause to attend the funeral of a person not within the eligible category.[348]

Turning to other issues, when asked to determine whether summer-school bus drivers working pursuant to 9-month contracts were entitled to the same bereavement leave as 12-month employees, an arbitrator held that bereavement leave was available for all employees in the bargaining unit.[349] The contract provision failed to make any distinction between the two groups, while other sections of the agreement expressly stated whether they were available to 9-month employees. The fact that secretaries, who were also on 9-month contracts, had been denied certain benefits during the summer was not deemed relevant, because secretaries were not included within the same agreement.[350]

---

[342]National Unif. Serv., 104 LA 981 (Fullmer, 1995).

[343]*Id.* at 985.

[344]Northville Pub. Sch., 104 LA 801 (Daniel, 1995).

[345]*Id.* at 802.

[346]Commercial Motor Freight, 34 LA 592, 595 (Stouffer, 1960). *See also* United States Steel Corp., 53 LA 1215, 1216 (Dybeck, 1969).

[347]Food Employers Council, 45 LA 291, 292–93 (Roberts, 1965).

[348]Seneca County, Ohio, Eng'r, 96 LA 115, 117 (Feldman, 1990) (employee cannot use emergency vacation benefit clause to attend funeral of person not defined as member of immediate family and therefore not covered under funeral leave clause).

[349]Cahokia, Ill., Sch. Dist. No. 187, 106 LA 667 (Marino, 1996).

[350]*Id.* at 670.

Employees who falsely claim bereavement leave and take the time off to attend to other matters are subject to discipline up to and including discharge. In an analogous case, an employee who had requested personal leave on short notice to attend a funeral but drove a tour bus instead was held to have been appropriately discharged after lying to his employer about his whereabouts.[351] The arbitrator rejected the employee's contention that personal days are a "private matter," such that an employer has no right to inquire into an employee's whereabouts on such days.[352] The employer had an "absolute right" to expect honesty from its employees even in the absence of a specific policy, and the employee's past misconduct obviated progressive discipline.[353]

The assignments of college faculty members typically vary during the week. On days on which there are no scheduled class hours, they are usually not required to report to work. A question arose as to whether a teacher who had been absent from work for an entire week was properly charged for a day of funeral leave when she attended the funeral of her father, which fell on a day on which she had no scheduled hours.[354] An arbitrator took cognizance of an established policy that deemed an employee to be "absent," even if she was not scheduled to teach, if that day fell between 2 or more days when she was scheduled to teach but unable to meet her classes. Relying on the parties' understanding of the definition of a "day" and a "week," as those terms appeared in the labor contract, the arbitrator found that the employer's assessment of the leave was appropriate.[355]

G. Leave for "Personal Business" [LA CDI 100.5219; 116.203]

As with other leaves of absence, arbitrators have held that management's determination to grant or deny leaves for "personal business" must be reasonable and nondiscriminatory.[356] Management must have some information

---

[351]Meijer, Inc., 108 LA 631 (Daniel, 1997).

[352]*Id.* at 636.

[353]*Id.* at 635.

[354]Jefferson Cmty. Coll., 107 LA 1166 (Franckiewicz, 1997).

[355]*Id.* at 1171.

[356]*See* Saydel, Iowa, Consol. Sch. Dist., 76 LA 673, 675–76 (Nathan, 1981); Saydel, Iowa, Consol. Sch. Dist., 75 LA 953, 957 (Belcher, 1980); Union Carbide Corp., 47 LA 531, 535 (Merrill, 1966); Hudson Pulp & Paper Co., 35 LA 581, 583 (Hill, 1960); Pittsburgh Metallurgical Co., 12 LA 95, 97 (Jaffee, 1949); Union Oil Co., 3 LA 108, 110 (Wardlaw, 1946). *See also* Geneseo Cmty. Unit Sch. Dist. No. 228 Bd. of Educ., 75 LA 131, 134–35 (Berman, 1980); Joseph Badger Bd. of Educ., 74 LA 1284, 1287–88 (Dyke, 1980). Particular language in the agreement may significantly affect the arbitrator's conclusion regarding the scope of management's right or discretion in determining whether to grant the requested leave. *See, e.g.*, Washtenaw County, Mich., Friend of the Court Unit, 80 LA 513, 515 (Daniel, 1982) (where agreement provided that leave "shall" be granted for certain specified purposes and that "personal leave" and certain other categories of leave "may be granted by the discretion of the Employer," the employer's discretion in denying personal leave was upheld since it was not arbitrary or capricious); Le Mars, Iowa, Cmty. Sch. Dist., 72 LA 1135, 1142 (Smith, 1979) (also note the discussion at 1143–44 concerning what constitutes "personal business"); Vacaville, Cal., Unified Sch. Dist., 71 LA 1026, 1028–29 (Brisco, 1978) (involving contractual clause on leave for "personal necessity"); Area Educ. Agency 13, 70 LA 555, 558 (Smith, 1978) (discussing what constitutes "personal business"); Briggs & Stratton Corp., 64 LA 1155, 1163–64 (Kossoff, 1975) (contractual provision for leave "for personal reasons" was declared to be "very broad language"). For a case dealing with the question of whether the employer must grant an employee's request to terminate leave before its term is completed, see *Ringgold Sch. Dist., Washington, Pa.*, 75 LA 1216, 1219 (Duff, 1980).

in order to make that determination intelligently, and it is not enough for the employee to state merely "personal business" as the reason for requesting such leave. Thus, the arbitrator held that the employer has the right to require the employee to give a reasonably explicit statement of reasons rather than simply stating "personal business."[357] He noted that this may result in a conflict between the employee's right to privacy with respect to his or her personal life and the employer's interest in discouraging unnecessary absences and ensuring efficient operations. However, he found support in the contract for his conclusions, not only in a general leave of absence clause requiring presentation of evidence by the employee to substantiate the request, but also in specific leave clauses relating to jury duty, voting time, and funeral leave, all of which also indicated the necessity of presenting information concerning the employee's personal affairs.[358]

Where no specific criteria are spelled out for granting personal leave, the question posed is whether the employer's denial of the leave was unreasonable or arbitrary.[359] However, where the contract specifically stated that personal leave "may not be taken contiguous to a holiday," the arbitrator refused to find unreasonable the employer's denial of a personal leave for days missed after a holiday because of snow emergency conditions.[360]

Does an employee qualify for personal leave if he is incarcerated? Under a contract provision allowing personal leave for "unusual and compelling reasons," arbitrators came to opposite conclusions. An earlier decision had ordered the company to grant leave to an employee who had been sentenced to jail for second-degree sexual assault. There the arbitrator found the absence had not caused the company any great inconvenience, the offense seemed to be wholly unrelated to the employee's work in the plant, and the employee had a 14-year record of unblemished service. But in the later case, the arbitrator held that the company had discretion to deny personal leave for an employee to serve a 14-month federal prison term for possession and intent to distribute marijuana.[361] The contract stated that an employee using an unauthorized drug "on or off the company premises" would be subject

---

[357]Union Carbide Corp., 47 LA 531, 534–35 (Merrill, 1966). *Accord* Vacaville, Cal., Unified Sch. Dist., 71 LA 1026,1028 (Brisco, 1978); Mead Corp., 51 LA 1121, 1124 (Griffin, 1968). *See also* Fremont, Cal., Unified Sch. Dist., 78 LA 890, 893 (Concepcion, 1982). *Cf.* Consolidated Papers, 79 LA 1209, 1214–15 (Yaffe, 1982) (special contract provisions significantly affected the result).

[358]Union Carbide Corp., 47 LA 531, 533 (Merrill, 1966).

[359]Lorain County, Ohio, Human Servs., 94 LA 661 (Dworkin, 1990) (employee's request for personal leave was properly denied due to staffing requirements of the department); DeBourgh Mfg. Co., 90 LA 471 (Flagler, 1987) (refusal to grant personal leave to employee with car trouble found unreasonable); Westinghouse Elec. Corp., 89 LA 1150 (Traynor, 1987) (denial of incarcerated employee's request for extended leave of absence not arbitrary or capricious); Department of the Navy, 88 LA 1269 (Nolan, 1987) (employer did not act arbitrarily by deciding to remain open during hurricane and announcing liberal leave policy rather than granting administrative leave); Hennepin, Minn., Tech. Ctrs., 86 LA 1293 (Kapsch, 1986) (denial of employee's request for leave to attend a school's grandparents' day function found arbitrary).

[360]Community Unit Sch. Dist. No. 303 Bd. of Educ., St. Charles, Ill., 88 LA 1159 (Goldstein, 1987).

[361]Dunlop Tire Corp., 106 LA 84 (Teple, 1995).

to immediate discharge.[362] Further, this employee had less than 3 years' seniority and a record of unexcused absences and was working in a plant with a history of drug-related offenses.

Where a collective bargaining agreement provided that personal leave is not to be "unreasonably withheld," an arbitrator upheld a city's denial of the request of an officer to use 1 day during his vacation period as a "personal day" instead of a "vacation day" in order to chaperone his child's class trip.[363] Although the arbitrator found that chaperoning a class trip would ordinarily be an appropriate reason for the grant of a personal day, the agreement also deferred the use of personal leave to the use of the "most appropriate" leave.[364] Because the request for a personal day came during the time the officer was on vacation, the day was more properly characterized as a vacation day.[365]

When requests for personal leave were not usually granted, the union grieved and requested that a total of 10 percent of the workforce be allowed at any one time to use personal leave.[366] Agreeing with the union that time off was not readily available when requested, the arbitrator fashioned a remedy that set the number of employees per shift who could take personal leave but correspondingly limited the number from each classification who could be absent at the same time.[367]

A contract provided that employees with "perfect attendance" during a 3-month period were to be awarded an extra "personal day" off. An employee who had been on leave of absence for 3 weeks but who otherwise had worked all his scheduled shifts was denied the award. Despite a contract provision stating that days-off work while on approved leaves of absence would not be counted against an employee for attendance control purposes, an arbitrator refused to extend this treatment to the provision for an extra personal day.[368] He concluded that allowing the personal day would undermine the purpose of the perfect attendance provision.[369]

There may be occasions when an employer may not sanction an employee for absences even when an employee has not applied for leave. Thus, a 17-year employee with a good work record who had been discharged because she was absent from work for 8 consecutive workdays without reporting off was awarded reinstatement because she was hiding from her husband, who had threatened her.[370] The employer had sent a warning letter to her home but did not require that she sign for it; thus, the employee never knew her employer was attempting to contact her or that her job was in jeopardy. Because the spousal abuse claimed by the employee was a compelling personal

---

[362]*Id.* at 88.
[363]City of Sandusky, Ohio, 104 LA 897 (Keenan, 1995).
[364]*Id.* at 900.
[365]*Id.* at 901.
[366]Wooster, Ohio, City Bd. of Educ., 108 LA 502 (Feldman, 1997).
[367]*Id.* at 505.
[368]Manor W. Health Care & Ret. Ctr., 106 LA 764 (Cohen, 1996).
[369]*Id.* at 766.
[370]Smith Fiberglass Prods., 108 LA 225 (Allen, Jr., 1997).

reason for granting a leave of absence at the time the employee left work, her failure to notify the company did not justify the discharge.[371]

An employer violated a collective bargaining agreement by forcing leave without pay on employees who were temporarily unable to work because of a non-work-related injury and who, although they had exhausted sick leave entitlements, did have unused annual leave.[372] The company was required to notify the employees that they could use their then accrued and available annual leave.[373]

One arbitrator held that if an employee's job performance is adversely affected by his employer's refusal to grant a leave of absence, the performance lapses will not justify the employee's discharge. Thus, a quality-control technician, discharged for failure to properly inspect carton seals, was reinstated where the employer's denial of a leave of absence created anxiety in the employee and contributed, in part, to his mistakes.[374] The employee had requested a leave of absence to be with his wife, who had required surgery after a miscarriage. However, because the employee previously had been disciplined for failure to report quality-control problems, the arbitrator concluded that the employee also was at fault. Consequently, his reinstatement was without back pay.[375]

What happens when an employee whose request for a leave of absence has been granted changes her mind and wants to continue to work? In a case where the labor agreement was silent as to a professional musician employee's right to seek rescission of an administrative leave after it had been granted, an arbitrator held that the employer had discretion to grant or refuse an employee's request to cancel the leave.[376] The arbitrator also ruled that in the absence of any specific contractual entitlement, the employee was not entitled to be placed on the orchestra's substitute list for recall to work during the term of her administrative leave.[377]

H. Family and Medical Leave Act Issues [LA CDI 94.503; 100.30; 100.5206; 100.5211; 100.5215; 116.202; 116.207; 116.2501 et seq.]

The Family and Medical Leave Act (FMLA)[378] provides that collective bargaining agreements that allow greater benefits to employees than those available under the FMLA are to be given effect. Thus, where a contract permitted leaves for good cause without length-of-service requirements, the FMLA's 1-year minimum was not controlling.[379]

FMLA leave is not available for an employee to care for a live-in companion, since the FMLA does not treat such a "significant other" as a spousal

---

[371]*Id.* at 229.
[372]Johnson Controls World Servs., 104 LA 336 (Goodstein, 1995).
[373]*Id.* at 343.
[374]Dial Corp., 107 LA 879 (Robinson, 1997).
[375]*Id.* at 882.
[376]Pacific Symphony Ass'n, 108 LA 85 (Gentile, 1997).
[377]*Id.* at 89.
[378]29 U.S.C. §2611 et seq.
[379]Enesco Corp., 107 LA 513 (Berman, 1996).

equivalent. Specific mutual obligations arise from the marital relationship that are notably absent from mere cohabitation.[380]

Furthermore, the FMLA does not preclude termination of an employee for failure to comply with contractual medical leave requirements. If an employee on FMLA leave does not return to work when scheduled and does not provide timely responses to requests for further information, the employee may be discharged.[381]

Failure of an employer to give notice to an ill or injured employee that any unpaid leave taken under the employer's leave policies "counts" as FMLA leave does not automatically entitle the employee to an additional 12 weeks of FMLA leave.[382] As a result of this decision, the continued viability of arbitration awards holding that an employer violates the FMLA by discharging an employee who did not return to work upon expiration of the leave, because it failed to properly notify her that her leave time was being charged as FMLA, is questionable.[383]

The accurate calculation of FMLA leave utilization becomes particularly important in cases where an employee who has apparently exhausted FMLA leave entitlements faces termination under an employer's "no-fault" attendance policy. In one decision where the union belatedly questioned the company's accounting of FMLA time, an arbitrator held that the union had the burden of proving error and the company was not required to prove that the termination was proper.[384]

4. "MOONLIGHTING" AND OUTSIDE BUSINESS INTERESTS
[LA CDI 118.6482; 124.45]

Employees sometimes engage in "moonlighting," i.e., holding a second job during off hours, or they may own or conduct independent business.[385] In cases involving such "off hours" activity, unions argue for the right of employees to do what they please during their free time, and to use their knowledge and skill to augment income.[386]

The general rule recognized by arbitrators has been succinctly formulated:

> It is well established that the time of an employee outside his regular hours of work and outside the overtime sometimes incidental thereto belongs to him and may be used for recreation and work, provided the employee does

---

[380]Morgan Foods, 106 LA 833, 836 (Goldman, 1996).
[381]Big River Zinc Corp., 108 LA 692, 698 (Draznin, 1997).
[382]Ragsdale v. Wolverine Worldwide, 535 U.S. 81, 27 EB Cases 1865 (2002).
[383]Apcoa, Inc., 107 LA 705 (Daniel, 1996).
[384]General Mills, 107 LA 472 (Feldman, 1996).
[385]Broadly, the term "moonlighting" may be considered to encompass all remunerative activity engaged in during off hours, whether a second job or a business interest.
[386]For example, these arguments were presented (but to no avail because of the facts involved) in *Firestone Retread Shop*, 38 LA 600, 601 (McCoy, 1962), and *Capital-Chrysler Plymouth*, 53 LA 1247, 1250 (Sembower, 1969). For related discussion, see Chapter 13, section 17., "Workplace Rules," and Chapter 15, section 3.A., "Off-Duty Misconduct."

not engage in practices or occupations that are detrimental or clearly prejudicial to the business and interests with which his duties in the service of his regular employer are connected.[387]

Consequently, the bare fact that an employee holds a second job does not constitute grounds for discipline or discharge. Thus, if the primary employer has no set policy forbidding outside employment and it is not shown that the employee's work for that employer has suffered, or if it is not shown that the employee misused confidential employer information for the employee's own business benefit, or for that of a competitor of the employer, the employee may not be subject to sanction.[388]

However, if the primary employer's right to regular attendance by the employee or the right to receive a full measure of productiveness during the employee's hours of work for the company has been compromised,[389] or if the primary employer's right to loyalty free from the employee's competitive activity or other activity resulting in a conflict of interest has been violated,[390] or if the primary employer otherwise has been adversely affected by the employee's second job, disciplinary action is deemed proper.[391]

---

[387]Janitorial Serv., 33 LA 902, 907–08 (Whelan, 1959). *See also* Microdot, Inc., 66 LA 177, 180 (Kelliher, 1976). In *Armstrong Rubber Co.*, 58 LA 827, 829 (Williams, 1972), the arbitrator stated in reference to the employee's weekend work as an ambulance driver that "the Company cannot forbid an employee to work at a second job during his off-duty hours, so long as it does not impair his job performance for the Company"; but in reference to the employee's full-time work as a private-duty nurse for another employer, the arbitrator upheld discharge since this work violated the agreement's express prohibition against "working on another job while on leave of absence."

[388]*See* Mercoid Corp., 63 LA 941, 945 (Kossoff, 1974); Budd Co., 52 LA 1290, 1296 (Keefe, 1969) (grievant refused to work overtime so that he could meet the obligations of his second job; penalty reduced because of extenuating circumstances); Cincinnati Tool Co., 52 LA 818, 820–21 (Kates, 1969) (leave of absence was obtained by deceit and the employee went to work for his other employer; reinstated without back pay); Harvard Mfg. Co., 51 LA 1098, 1101–02 (Kates, 1968) (same); Wood County Tel. Co., 46 LA 175, 179 (Lee, 1966) (no detriment to the employer was shown; employee reinstated with back pay); United Eng'g & Foundry Co., 37 LA 1095, 1098 (Kates, 1962) (employee reinstated with back pay); Janitorial Serv., 33 LA 902, 908 (Whelan, 1959) (there was a somewhat competitive situation but there was no rule and no detriment shown to the employer; employee reinstated with back pay); Branch River Wool Combing Co., 31 LA 547, 551 (Pigors, 1958) (same); Armen Berry Casing Co., 17 LA 179, 182–83 (Smith, 1950) (somewhat competitive situation and grievant "did not exhibit the fidelity to his employer which his job required"; reinstated without back pay). *See also* Alameda-Contra Costa Transit Dist., 76 LA 770, 771 (Koven, 1981); City of Rockville, Md., 76 LA 140, 141 (Levitan, 1981); Rock Hill Printing & Finishing Co., 64 LA 856, 858 (Whyte, 1975); W.R. Grace & Co., 62 LA 779, 780, 784 (Boals, 1974); M. Pascale Trucking, 59 LA 47, 51 (Rodio, 1972).

[389]*See, e.g.*, Safeway Stores, 49 LA 400, 402 (Caraway, 1967).

[390]*See* Jacksonville Shipyards, 74 LA 1066, 1072 (Taylor, 1980); William Feather Co., 68 LA 13, 16 (Shanker, 1977) (upholding employer rule that requires employees to reveal outside employment so that employer "can investigate to determine whether such employment raises conflict of interest possibilities, or the potentiality for competitive disadvantage to it"); Phillips Petroleum Co., 47 LA 372, 374 (Caraway, 1966); F.E. Myers & Bro., 43 LA 338, 340 (Teple, 1964); Ravens-Metal Prods., 39 LA 404, 409 (Dworkin, 1962); Cummins Diesel Sales Corp., 34 LA 636, 642 (Gorsuch, 1960). *See also* University of Cal., San Diego, 78 LA 1032, 1037 (Ross, 1982); Northwest Airlines, 59 LA 69, 71 (Koven, 1972).

[391]*See* Cincinnati Tool Co., 52 LA 818, 820–21 (Kates, 1969); Harvard Mfg. Co., 51 LA 1098, 1101–02 (Kates, 1968); Ravens-Metal Prods., 39 LA 404, 409 (Dworkin, 1962); Mechanical Handling Sys., 26 LA 401, 403 (Keller, 1956). *See also* Bowaters S. Paper Corp., 38 LA 965, 971 (Hon, 1962); Rock Hill Printing & Finishing Co., 37 LA 254, 257–58 (Jaffee, 1961).

Obviously the employee may be prohibited from working for a competing company or carrying on a business of the same nature as that of the primary employer. However, arbitrators consistently have held that such competition must be "more than minimal." One arbitrator observed that "per se rules are to be avoided" in favor of a "rule of reason" that examines the particularized facts of the case.[392] Applying that reasoning, where a reporter for a newspaper wrote articles for a monthly magazine, the arbitrator held that the two employers were not "in competition" because they had different markets, different topical coverage areas, and different advertisers.[393] Conversely, a data systems analyst was held to have been properly discharged where he was also working for his wife's computer company, which was involved in the same areas of business as his primary employer, and the primary employer's investigation revealed that the employee had been performing services for his wife's company during his work hours for the primary employer.[394]

But, even if the activity is not competitive, it still may result in a conflict of interest.[395] In a number of cases, the asserted incompatibility of dual employment arose from circumstances other than the existence of economic competition between a primary and a secondary employer. Discharges of lawyers[396] and paralegals[397] employed by legal aid organizations have been upheld where their secondary employment violated their organization's charter and jeopardized the status of the legal services program. Of course, an ownership interest as well as an employment status can give rise to a prohibited conflict of interest. Thus, bank examiners may be prohibited from purchasing stock in banks over which their employer agency had regulatory authority.[398] The discharge penalty in such cases is likely to be up-

---

[392]Copley Newspapers & Waukegan News-Sun, 107 LA 310, 313–14 (Stallworth, 1996).

[393]*Id.* at 314–16.

[394]Michigan Employment Sec. Agency, 109 LA 178, 183–84 (Brodsky, 1997).

[395]*See* Tribune Publ'g Co., 42 LA 504, 506–07 (Kagel, 1963) (a drama critic for a newspaper obtained outside work as a press agent for a summer theater). *See also* New York Post Corp., 62 LA 225, 227 (Friedman, 1974) (newspaper sports reporter accepted part ownership of a horse that raced at tracks on his reportorial beat, "which patently conflicts with his ability to do his job properly").

[396]UAW Legal Servs. Plan, 104 LA 312, 321–22 (Imundo, Jr., 1995).

[397]Texas Rural Legal Aid, 108 LA 411, 415 (Bankston, 1997).

[398]Federal Deposit Ins. Corp., 104 LA 277, 281 (McGury, 1995).

held,[399] especially where the conflict involves the primary employer's trade secrets.[400]

The absence of a contractual provision prohibiting "moonlighting" activities does not bar an employer's disciplinary action for inappropriate off-duty employment. As one arbitrator emphasized:

> Labor agreements must be read in a reasonable manner and to reflect a sense of fair dealing and good faith. Thus, labor agreements lacking in extensive express prohibitions or constraints will be read to implicitly contain certain clauses. Within the employment relationship the quid pro quo for employment and subsequent wages is the duty of loyalty and an agreement not to compete with the Employer's business. These obligations are, in the opinion of the undersigned, so fundamental to the employment relationship that they need not be expressly stated.[401]

Arbitrators are divided as to whether an actionable conflict of interest exists where an employee's spouse or other close relative is employed in a competing or potentially competitive business. One arbitrator upheld a telecommunications company's requirement that an employee's wife discontinue her affiliation with Amway or face discharge because Amway also sold telephone equipment.[402] The arbitrator noted that the employee himself occa-

---

[399]*See* Jacksonville Shipyards, 74 LA 1066, 1072 (Taylor, 1980); Alaska Sales & Serv. Co., 73 LA 164, 165–66 (Axon, 1979); United Fuel Gas Co., 54 LA 942, 946–47 (Whyte, 1971); Capital-Chrysler Plymouth, 53 LA 1247, 1251–52 (Sembower, 1969); Utility Tree Serv., 53 LA 1176, 1180 (Karasick, 1969); Safeway Stores, 49 LA 400, 401–02 (Caraway, 1967); Tribune Publ'g Co., 42 LA 504, 506–07 (Kagel, 1963); John Thomas Motors, Inc., 40 LA 1293, 1295 (Jenkins, 1963); Cummins Diesel Sales Corp., 34 LA 636, 642–43 (Gorsuch, 1960). *See also* Arroyo Foods, 67 LA 985, 988 (Darrow, 1976); Dispatch Servs., 67 LA 632, 635 (Matten, 1976); New York Cent. R.R., 44 LA 552, 553 (Wyckoff, 1965). *Cf.* Heinrich Motors, 68 LA 1224, 1229 (Hildebrand, 1977); Airport Ground Transp., 58 LA 1296, 1299 (Rohman, 1972). For cases holding that the company may promulgate a rule prohibiting outside work in competition with it, see *United Fuel Gas Co.*, 54 LA 942, 945–46 (Whyte, 1971); *F.E. Myers & Bro.*, 43 LA 338, 340–41 (Teple, 1964); *Ravens-Metal Prods.*, 39 LA 404, 409 (Dworkin, 1962); *Cummins Diesel Sales Corp.*, 34 LA 636, 642–43 (Gorsuch, 1960); *American Monorail Co.*, 27 LA 540, 542 (Kates, 1956); *Mechanical Handling Sys.*, 26 LA 401, 403 (Keller, 1956). In upholding the reasonableness of such rules, arbitrators have pointed out that the prohibition did not apply to work in other areas of endeavor. *See* Phillips Petroleum Co., 47 LA 372, 374 (Caraway, 1966); John Thomas Motors, Inc., 40 LA 1293, 1295 (Jenkins, 1963); Cummins Diesel Sales Corp., 34 LA 636, 642 (Gorsuch, 1960); Mechanical Handling Sys., 26 LA 401, 403 (Keller, 1956).

[400]*See* Pipe Coupling Mfrs., Inc., 46 LA 1009, 1010–11 (McCoy, 1966) ("the Company had the right to lock the stable door before the horse was stolen"); Firestone Retread Shop, 38 LA 600, 601 (McCoy, 1962); Ravens-Metal Prods., 39 LA 404, 409–10 (Dworkin, 1962); E.B. Sewall Mfg. Co., 3 LA 113, 115 (Updegraff, 1946). *See also* Phillips Petroleum Co., 47 LA 372, 375 (Caraway, 1966) (the grievant was reinstated because he had not known of the rule prohibiting outside activity that conflicts with the company's best interest, but he was required to refrain from such activities in the future); American Monorail Co., 27 LA 540, 542–43 (Kates, 1956) (the company's right to discharge for violating a rule against working for a competitor was upheld, but the grievant was reinstated (without back pay) because he gave 2 weeks' notice of resignation to his second employer the day the rule went into effect).

[401]Country Club Mkts., 85 LA 286, 289 (Bognanno, 1985). *But see* Northern Rebuilders Co., 96 LA 1 (Kanner, 1990) (there must be notice to the employees of a specific rule prohibiting competition before disciplinary action can occur).

[402]Southwestern Bell Tel. Co., 107 LA 662, 667–68 (Heinsz, 1996).

sionally sold telephone equipment, and although his wife did not herself sell telecommunication supplies for Amway, the distributors, for whose sales the wife was accountable, might do so.[403] However, in another case, an arbitrator refused to sustain the discharge of an employee whose father worked for the company's prime competitor, even though the company was concerned that the employee might disclose a newly developed secret process to his father.[404] The employee did not work directly with the secret process, had not done anything that would indicate a lack of loyalty to the company, and saw his father infrequently, and the company had not attempted to implement a less severe option than discharge, such as requiring the employee to execute a nondisclosure agreement.[405]

In finding overly broad a city's requirement that a construction inspector and his spouse cease selling real estate within the city because of potential conflicts of interest, an arbitrator observed:

> The application, in an individual case, of the conflict of interest policy requires the city to be ready to make reasonable accommodations to preserve the employee's job rights and for the employee to be prepared to accept reasonable restrictions to preserve the integrity of the public service, even for just appearance's sake.[406]

Performance of renumerative work while on leave of absence is not necessarily an abuse of the leave. In a case where the contract provided for termination if the employee "without the consent of the Company engages in employment with another employer or organization while on leave of absence," the arbitrator observed:

> The decisions are not in harmony as to whether [the term "another"] includes working for oneself. They are, however, in agreement that the usual prohibition against working while on leave of absence does not apply to the continuation of work which the employee had been doing during off hours on a part-time basis before leave was granted, commonly referred to as "moonlighting," provided that the nature of the work is not inconsistent with treatment of his or her injury or sickness and would not prolong the period of leave.[407]

Arbitrators uphold discipline up to and including discharge for employees who take time off from work for the purpose of working a second job, but who misrepresent the reason for the leave to their primary employer. An arbitrator found that the company had just cause to discharge an employee who requested personal leave to attend a funeral but who instead drove a tour bus for his second employer and then lied about his whereabouts when questioned later about the matter.[408] Further, an employee who had been

---

[403]*Id.* at 668.

[404]Chrome Deposit Corp., 102 LA 733, 736 (Bethel, 1994).

[405]*Id.* at 735–36.

[406]City of Rochester Hills, Mich., 90 LA 237, 242 (Daniel, 1987).

[407]Alcan Aluminum Corp., 90 LA 16, 19 (Volz, 1987). *See* Foster Food Prods., 88 LA 337, 337 (Riker, 1986) (provision providing for termination if employee "accepts work at another job, or at any other company, while on a leave of absence" did not preclude grievant's working while on workers' compensation leave in absence of evidence that leave was fraudulently obtained).

[408]Meijer, Inc., 108 LA 631, 635–36 (Daniel, 1997). See also section 3.F., "Funeral Leave," above.

granted extended sick leave for a supposed parasitic intestinal infection was found to have been properly discharged where he gained weight during the leave and was regularly seen at the site of a family business.[409] Conversely, another arbitrator refused to uphold the discharge of an employee who was on leave to attend college courses where the employee worked in an unpaid capacity for the family business while attending the courses.[410]

If the secondary employment indicates a conflict of interest, there is no need to prove an actual detriment to the primary employer:

> [I]t is not necessarily required that the employer convincingly establish that a business detriment or financial loss has in fact resulted; it is sufficient if the off-duty relationship is such as would reasonably suggest that the outside employment would lead to a disclosure to the competitor of information and skills acquired by the employee . . . .[411]

5. PERSONAL APPEARANCE: HAIR AND CLOTHES

A. Overview [LA CDI 100.552529; 118.639]

The personal appearance of employees in private life, away from their place of employment, is a matter for their own determination, at least so long as no harm results to the employer.[412] Employees tend to object to broad

---

[409]Cincinnati, Ohio, Mine Mach. Co., 106 LA 284, 287–88 (Heekin, 1996).

[410]Flamingo Hilton Hotel/Casino, 104 LA 673, 674 (Draznin, 1995).

[411]Ravens-Metal Prods., 39 LA 404, 409–10 (Dworkin, 1962). *See also* Cummins Diesel Sales Corp., 34 LA 636, 643 (Gorsuch, 1960); Mechanical Handling Sys., 26 LA 401, 403 (Keller, 1956). *Cf.* Hearst Corp., 79 LA 1129, 1133 (Shister, 1982); Great Atl. & Pac. Tea Co., 75 LA 640, 642 (Calhoon, 1980); Albertson's, Inc., 65 LA 1042, 1046 (Christopher, 1975).

[412]*See* Chapter 15, section 3.A., "Off-Duty Misconduct." This is a developing area of law. *See, e.g.*, CAL. LAB. CODE §96(k) (allows "[c]laims for loss of wages as the result of demotion, suspension, or discharge from employment for lawful conduct occurring during nonworking hours away from the employer's premises"). For discussion of court and EEOC decisions relating to the possibility that employee dress and grooming policies in certain cases may constitute sex, race, or religious discrimination in violation of Title VII of the Civil Rights Act, see Annotation, *Employer's Enforcement of Dress or Grooming Policy as Unlawful Employment Practice Under §703(a) of the Civil Rights Act of 1964*, 27 A.L.R. FED. 274 (1976); McGuckin, *Employee Hair Styles: Recent Judicial and Arbitral Decisions*, 26 LAB. L.J. 174 (1975). The Supreme Court upheld dress and hair rules for county police officers against challenge under the Fourteenth Amendment. Kelley v. Johnson, 425 U.S. 238, 1 IER Cases 54 (1976). *See* Maloney, *Suits for the Hirsute: Defending Against America's Undeclared War on Beards in the Workplace*, 63 FORDHAM L. REV. 1203 (1995) (arguing that the decision to wear a beard is a protected First Amendment freedom of expression and criticizing *Kelley* for providing almost no protection of that freedom). The *Kelley* decision was discussed and applied in *City of Cincinnati, Ohio*, 75 LA 1261, 1264–65 (Seifer, 1980). For other arbitration decisions touching on constitutional questions, see *Lloyd Ketcham Oldsmobile*, 77 LA 953, 959 (Hilgert, 1981) (leaving constitutional questions to the courts); *General Foods Corp.*, 76 LA 532, 535 (Denson, 1981); *Pay 'n Save Corp.*, 60 LA 1191, 1196–97 (Jacobs, 1973); *Allied Employers*, 55 LA 1020, 1025 (Kleinsorge, 1970); *Pepsi Cola Gen. Bottlers*, 55 LA 663, 667 (Volz, 1970); *Pacific Gas & Elec. Co.*, 55 LA 459, 460 (Eaton, 1970); *Economy Super Mart*, 54 LA 816, 819 (Elson, 1971); *City of Waterbury, Conn.*, 54 LA 439, 441 (Stutz, 1971) (leaving constitutional questions to the courts); *Western Air Lines*, 52 LA 1282, 1284 (Steese, 1969). For general discussion of arbitration decisions in dress and grooming cases, see Gerhart, *Employee Privacy Rights in the United States*, 17 COMP. LAB. L. 175 (1995); Tucker, *Arbitration of Labor Disputes Involving Hair*, 10 WILLAMETTE L.J. 258 (1974); Valtin, *Changing Life Styles and Problems of Authority in the Plant, I. Hair and Beards in Arbitration, in* LABOR

company prohibitions or requirements that they feel infringe upon their personal right to dress and wear their hair or beards as they please. Management historically has been concerned with the personal appearance of its employees, both from the standpoint of the company's public "image" and safety and health concerns.[413]

Recognizing expressly or implicitly the right of employees to choose their clothing or hairstyle, arbitrators nonetheless point out that such right may be limited by the nature of the employment,[414] but not for the purpose of requiring conformity to the employer's preference on such matters.[415] Arbitrators recognize that:

> The prevailing theory is that the Company has the right to require its employees to cut their hair and shave when long hair and beards can reasonably threaten the Company's relations with its customers or other employees, or a real question of health or safety is involved.[416]

With regard to the image presented by employees to the public, an arbitrator elaborated:

> The arbitrator holds to the view that an employer should be free, reasonably to regulate, and to prescribe standards of, personal appearance for its employees so as to require of them a certain degree of conventionality and approximate conformation to the norm. The employer should be permitted, for instance, to prohibit extra long shoulder-length hair or extreme clothing on

---

Arbitration at the Quarter-Century Mark, Proceedings of the 25th Annual Meeting of NAA 235–52 (Somers & Dennis eds., BNA Books 1973); McDermott, *II. Drugs, Bombs and Bomb Scares, and Personal Attire, id.* at 252–53, 266–72; Cohen, *III. Arbitrators and Changing Life Styles—Establishment or Impartial?, id.* at 272–81.

[413]Weighing these respective positions, the arbitrator upheld as reasonable and clear one company's grooming regulations, stating further that they represented "a middle ground between the concern of the Company to protect and improve its image with the public and the preference of an employee for self-expression and individuality through hair styling." Pepsi Cola Gen. Bottlers, 55 LA 663, 666 (Volz, 1970). Of course, safety, health, and "image" considerations are not necessarily the only possible justifications for employer dress and grooming requirements. For example, in *Greater Harlem Nursing Home*, 76 LA 680, 684 (Marx, 1981), male and female employees could be required to wear differing uniforms to provide ready identification for nursing home patients, who, the arbitrator stated, are entitled to know the sex of the nursing attendant by whom they are being served. *See also* County of Cattaraugus, N.Y., 77 LA 1027, 1029 (Denson, 1981) (employer specified different colors of clothing "to help patients and others identify various levels of" nursing home personnel).

[414]*See* City of Erie, Pa., 73 LA 605, 606–07 (Kreimer, 1979); Pepsi Cola Gen. Bottlers, 55 LA 663, 666 (Volz, 1970); Economy Super Mart, 54 LA 816, 819–20 (Elson, 1971); City of Waterbury, Conn., 54 LA 439, 440 (Stutz, 1971); Badger Concrete Co., 50 LA 901, 908–09 (Krinsky, 1968); Stop & Shop, 49 LA 867, 868 (Johnson, 1967).

[415]*See* Union Tribune Publ'g Co., 70 LA 266, 269 (Richman, 1978); City of Racine, Wis., 68 LA 473, 475 (Schoenfeld, 1977); Dravo-Doyle Co., 54 LA 604, 605 (Krimsly, 1971); City of Waterbury, Conn., 54 LA 439, 441 (Stutz, 1971); Springday Co., 53 LA 627, 628 (Bothwell, 1969); United Parcel Serv., 52 LA 1068, 1069 (Kotin, 1969); Western Air Lines, 52 LA 1282, 1284 (Steese, 1969); Marhoefer Packing Co., 51 LA 983, 988–89 (Bradley, 1968); Northwest Publications, 48 LA 120, 123 (Neville, 1966).

[416]Dravo-Doyle Co., 54 LA 604, 606 (Krimsly, 1971). *See also* Alpha Beta Co., 93 LA 855, 858 (Horowitz, 1989) (hairstyle found inappropriate under "good grooming" rule that is entitled to "considerable deference" for store located in small farming community). *But see* Lucky Stores, 91 LA 624, 628 (Ross, 1988) (no cause to discipline grocery clerk where hairstyle was in accord with current styles and had not changed substantially in 2 years, employee had cut hair 3 times in attempt to comply with company's rules, sun-bleached appearance of hair was natural, and there was no evidence of customer complaints).

male employees, full beards on younger men, scanty or sexually . . . [suggestive] dress on the part of female employees. It should be able to expect that its employees will practice personal hygiene and will clothe themselves in a neat manner, at least where the employees meet the public.[417]

However, there must be a showing of a reasonable relation between the company's image or health and safety considerations and the regulation of employee appearance.[418] As stated by one arbitrator:

Companies providing a service to the public still have the right to protect their image. To the degree that the image is based upon the appearance of its employees dealing with the public, the company has the right to establish rules and standards of personal appearance. This right has long been recognized by unions. The right, however, is not absolute. Its exercise in any specific manner may be challenged as arbitrary, capricious or inconsistent with the objective for which the right is being exercised.[419]

The application of otherwise reasonable grooming rules to ban the wearing of certain articles of clothing[420] was successfully contested where the rules were not consistently enforced. In a case involving an employee who wore a shirt at work from the "Hooters" restaurant chain, the arbitrator found that the shirt was "indecent" within the common meaning of the word and the wearing of it violated the prohibition contained in the company's dress code.[421] Nevertheless, the arbitrator set aside the discipline because the employee had worn, or brought, vulgar and sexually explicit clothes and items into the workplace previously without having been disciplined.[422]

---

[417]Northwest Publications, 48 LA 120, 122 (Neville, 1966). *See also* Southern Bell Tel. & Tel. Co., 74 LA 1115, 1116 (Duff, 1980).

[418]*See* Alpha Beta Co., 93 LA 855, 858–59 (Horowitz, 1989); E.&J. Gallo Winery, 80 LA 765, 770 (Killion, 1983); Big Star No. 35, 73 LA 850, 856–57 (Murphy, 1979); Pacific Gas & Elec. Co., 55 LA 459, 463 (Eaton, 1970); Economy Super Mart, 54 LA 816, 820 (Elson, 1971); City of Waterbury, Conn., 54 LA 439, 441 (Stutz, 1971); Badger Concrete Co., 50 LA 901, 908–09 (Krinsky, 1968) (particularly where rules "infringe on an individual's personal life"). It also must be established that company rules were adequately communicated to the employees and uniformly enforced. *See* Hotel Employers Council of L.A., 55 LA 531, 535 (Neblett, 1970); Northwest Publications, 48 LA 120, 123 (Neville, 1966); Lawrence Bros., 28 LA 83, 87 (Davis, 1957). *See also* Honeywell, Inc., 74 LA 918, 920 (Belshaw, 1980) (employer, objecting to long fingernails that impede production, must clearly indicate to employee how long the nails reasonably may be). In *Hillview Sand & Gravel,* 39 LA 35, 40 (Somers, 1962), there were no company rules prohibiting beards, but the arbitrator stated that if the employee's actions caused the company loss, it "would be well within its rights" in suspending him for continual refusal to shave off his beard. *See also* City of Erie, Pa., 73 LA 605, 607 (Kreimer, 1979); Arden-Mayfair, 71 LA 200, 203 (Kaufman, 1978).

[419]United Parcel Serv., 52 LA 1068, 1069 (Kotin, 1969). These points apply as well to management's right to regulate for health and safety purposes. *See also* United Parcel Serv., 53 LA 126, 128 (Kotin, 1969) (standards set forth clarifying company rules as to what constitutes satisfactory appearance for employees). In *Lucky Stores,* 91 LA 624, 628 (Ross, 1988), the arbitrator pointed out that management must provide evidence of "the grooming's negative impact on customers because of the contractual requirement that employees can only be disciplined for just cause." In *Pacific Gas & Elec. Co.,* 55 LA 464, 469 (Eaton, 1970), the arbitrator formulated rules to supplant company rules about permissible facial hair.

[420]Board of Educ. of Bethlehem-Center, Pa., Sch. Dist., 105 LA 285, 288 (Talarico, 1995) (both the banning of specific apparel and the application of a subjective standard such as "professional attire" raise grievable issues).

[421]Clarion Sintered Metals, 110 LA 770, 773–74 (Cohen, 1998).

[422]*Id.* at 776.

Employees often attempt to justify their failure to observe their employer's grooming rules on the ground of religious requirement or cultural expression.[423] One arbitrator found discharge of an employee inappropriate where the employee had refused an order to tuck in his shirt on the ground that his Muslim faith prohibited obedience with this requirement of his employer's dress code. The arbitrator concluded that the employee should have first been allowed an opportunity to prove his contention.[424] However, a Hispanic employee who had contact with the public and who wore a nose ring contrary to the employer's regulations was found to have been appropriately disciplined despite her contention that the wearing of the nose ring was part of her "cultural heritage."[425] The arbitrator, following a U.S. Court of Appeals for the Ninth Circuit decision,[426] observed that it is axiomatic that an employee must often sacrifice individual self-expression during working hours, and held that there was nothing in Title VII that requires a private employer to allow employees to express their cultural identity.[427]

Arbitrators have generally recognized that an employer has the right to order an employee to discontinue wearing attire that might give offense not only to its customers but also to coworkers and might cause disruption of the work environment. For instance, where a Hispanic employee wore a West African head scarf to work and numerous African-American employees complained that the employee's attire was disrespectful, the arbitrator ruled that the company had "not only the right but an obligation" to instruct the employee to remove the scarf.[428]

Although employees' Section 7 rights under the National Labor Relations Act to wear clothing proclaiming support of a union cannot be restricted or interfered with by a dress code, one arbitrator found that an employer "can restrict 'T' shirts, buttons, and other 'solidarity' messages that genuinely disrupt its business and its authority to manage."[429] In such cases, the

---

[423]An in-depth treatment of federal and state constitutional and statutory protection against discrimination in employment is beyond the scope of this volume. See, however, section 6., "Non-Safety-Related Accommodation of Employee Religious Beliefs," below. *See also* Pergament, *It's Not Just Hair: Historical and Cultural Considerations for an Emerging Technology*, 75 Chi.-Kent L. Rev. 41, 58 (1999) (arguing that courts continue to ignore the social meaning of hair and decline to hold that individuals have an absolute right to assert their identity and reveal personal information through hair rituals or grooming).

[424]Liberty Med. Ctr., 109 LA 609, 614 (Harkless, 1997).

[425]Colonial Baking Co., 104 LA 988, 992 (Strasshofer, Jr., 1995).

[426]Garcia v. Spun Steak Co., 998 F.2d 1480, 62 FEP Cases 525 (9th Cir. 1993), *cert. denied*, 512 U.S. 1228 (1994).

[427]Colonial Baking Co., 104 LA 988, 992 (Strasshofer, Jr., 1995). *But see* Turner, *The Braided Uproar: A Defense of My Sister's Hair and a Contemporary Indictment of* Rogers v. American Airlines, 7 Cardozo Women's L.J. 115 (2001) (arguing for broadening the protections of Title VII to make actionable discrimination claims by black women challenging the wearing of braided hairstyles reflective of their culture and history).

[428]USCP-Wesco, 109 LA 225, 229 (Grabuskie, 1997) (discharge for refusing to remove the scarf was held to be too severe, and the employee was reinstated without back pay).

[429]Reed Mfg. Co., 102 LA 1, 6 (Dworkin, 1993). *See also* Intertec Sys. LLC, 114 LA 1785, 1787 (Skulina, 2000) (finding reasonable work rule prohibiting the wearing of apparel with remarks that are disrespectful or reflect unfavorably on company, but stating that "[i]f someone would be disciplined for wearing a UAW button, short shrift would be made for such an invasion of an employee's individual rights").

needs of the company and the employee must be balanced. Complete prohibitions on pro-union attire cannot be enforced when options providing reasonable accommodation could include having employees bring in clothes to cover up pro-union attire when customers tour the workplace.[430] Even when a work rule banning pro-union attire ultimately is deemed arbitrary or in conflict with labor legislation, employees who engage in self-help rather than complying with work orders and then grieving are not likely to escape discipline.[431]

Divergent male and female grooming standards often are challenged. For example, a male airline flight attendant with long hair grieved his employer's short-hair requirement, claiming sex discrimination because females were not subject to the same restrictions. The arbitrator denied the grievance, concluding that the airline was not arbitrary, capricious, or inconsistent in establishing different grooming standards for the two sexes.[432]

B. Grooming and the Employer's Image [LA CDI 100.552529; 118.639]

An employer's requirement that employees who interact with the public conform to reasonable, albeit special, grooming rules typically is upheld by arbitrators. The decisive question is whether the employee has contact with the public. The employer's public image is a matter of particular concern where the company offers services to the public or where the employee comes in contact with the company's customers.[433] Arbitrators have emphasized that "an employee who deals with the public or who solicits sales has an added responsibility for presenting a pleasing appearance."[434] For example, an arbitrator upheld a company's work rule requiring short hair for its truck drivers who had client contact, despite the fact that there was no such rule for

---

[430]Reed Mfg. Co., 102 LA 1, 7–8 (Dworkin, 1993).

[431]Park Mansions, 105 LA 849, 852 (Duff, 1995); USCP-Wesco, 109 LA 225, 230 (Grabuskie, 1997).

[432]Southwest Airlines, 107 LA 270, 275 (Jennings, 1996). See also section 5.B., "Grooming and the Employer's Image," below.

[433]The employees themselves may recognize this fact. For example, the *New York Times Service* reported in March 1971 that TWA's pilots had embarked on a program to help restore the company's earning power; the first step of the program was for the pilots to avoid "extreme styles of personal appearance" and to dress so that "any potential customer" is not offended. The pilots thus expressed recognition that employee appearance and mode of dress can produce an adverse public reaction detrimental to the employer's operations. Even apart from the interest that employees share with the employer for successful operations, employees may have strong interests of their own in making a favorable public impression. *See, e.g.,* Federal Aviation Admin., 70 LA 226, 229 (Duff, 1978) (stating in part that if the grievants "cling to their goal of using clothing to express their individuality by working in casual attire," they may not violate the collective bargaining agreement, "but they will bear the costly risk that those people who observe them will not be impressed by the important nature of the air traffic control function they perform").

[434]Pepsi Cola Gen. Bottlers, 55 LA 663, 666 (Volz, 1970). *See also* Allied Employers, 55 LA 1020, 1024 (Kleinsorge, 1970). Customer disapproval or complaints regarding the personal appearance of employees may be a significant factor supporting the employer's position before an arbitrator. *See, e.g.,* Hotel Bancroft, 78 LA 819, 819 (Wolff, 1982); Aslesen Co., 74 LA 1017, 1019 (Fogelberg, 1980); Grocers Supply Co., 72 LA 1055, 1056 (Williams, 1979); Arden-Mayfair, 71 LA 200, 202 (Kaufman, 1978). *Cf.* Roskam Baking Co., 79 LA 993, 997–98 (Beitner, 1982).

warehouse employees who did not have such interaction.[435] Similarly, a male airline flight attendant who came into contact with the public could be required to keep his long hair tucked under his cap so as to maintain the employer's image.[436] There are numerous similar cases in which protection or advancement of the employer's public image was a significant and sometimes controlling factor in upholding dress and grooming policies imposed on employees by the employer.[437]

The same requirements obtain in public-sector employment. One arbitrator upheld a prohibition against detectives not in uniform because "[t]he main import . . . appears to be that officers not in uniform maintain a professional appearance."[438]

The issue extends beyond grooming and dress to tidiness and cleanliness. For example, where a flight attendant arrived late for her scheduled flight and was disheveled in appearance, the arbitrator noted that passengers judge the airline primarily by the flight attendants who are the main

---

[435]Albertson's, Inc., 102 LA 641, 644–45 (Darrow, 1994).

[436]Southwest Airlines, 107 LA 270, 274–75 (Jennings, 1996) (quoting ELKOURI & ELKOURI, HOW ARBITRATION WORKS 765–66 (BNA Books 4th ed. 1985)).

[437]*See, e.g.*, Mister A's Rest., 80 LA 1104, 1105 (Christopher, 1983) (in keeping with a restaurant's image of fine European dining, waitresses could be required to wear gowns of Roman or Grecian mode and to wear their hair blond and upswept). *Cf.* Snaden, *Baring It All at the Workplace: Who Bears the Responsibility?*, 28 CONN. L. REV. 1225 (1996) (discussing issues of sexual harassment and dress codes in the workplace and concluding that harassing conduct on the basis of a dress code should be actionable, even if the employee knew of the provocative dress code in advance). *See also* Coca-Cola Bottling Co., 79 LA 835, 836–37 (Larkin, 1982) (no-beard rule newly adopted to enhance company's image was upheld, recognizing employer's right "to issue new rules dealing with old matters not prohibited by some language of" the agreement); Hotel Bancroft, 78 LA 819, 819 (Wolff, 1982) (hotel could require employees working in lobby to wear clean shirt, tie, jacket, trousers, and shoes, instead of more casual dress such as jeans, sweatshirts, and sneakers); Lloyd Ketcham Oldsmobile, 77 LA 953, 958–59 (Hilgert, 1981) (although finding the employer's dress and grooming policies "rather conservative by today's contemporary standards," arbitrator upheld a "no facial hair" rule that the employer had uniformly enforced for many years in order to project a favorable image to its customers, and where the penalized grievant fully understood the rule and the consequences of not complying with it); Albertsons, Inc., 77 LA 705, 706 (Hulsey, 1981) (upholding a well-established no-beard rule for drivers who have contact with the public while making deliveries to retail stores); Southern Bell Tel. & Tel. Co., 74 LA 1115, 1116–17 (Duff, 1980) (telephone company in Florida could prohibit its coin telephone collectors from wearing shorts while on duty in an effort to project an attractive company image to the public; arbitrator concluding that the "minor inconvenience of a Collector being less comfortable than he desires is overbalanced by his duty to his employer to project an acceptable appearance"); Aslesen Co., 74 LA 1017, 1019 (Fogelberg, 1980) (supplier of food products upheld in barring driver from working until he removed beard); Randall Foods No. 2, 74 LA 729, 732 (Sembower, 1980) (upholding grocery store no-beard rule since the employer seeks "maintenance of a reasonable image," arbitrator commented that "[u]nder other circumstances, such as perhaps in staging a rock band, the very opposite might be desired, and beards indeed might be required"); Arden-Mayfair, 71 LA 200, 202–03 (Kaufman, 1978) (upholding grocery store no-beard policy); Page Airways of Mich., 69 LA 141, 144 (Rinaldo, 1977) (upholding an airline's no-beard rule, but also recognizing that "[a]s fashion styles and public image concerns change, rules and regulations such as these will continue to be tested," and that "each case will have to be determined on the facts peculiar to it"). In the latter regard, other arbitrators also have stressed that in reviewing the reasonableness of employer dress and grooming policies, each case must be considered on the basis of its particular facts and circumstances. *See, e.g.*, Southern Bell Tel. & Tel. Co., 74 LA 1115, 1116 (Duff, 1980); Pacific Southwest Airlines, 73 LA 1209, 1213 (Christopher, 1979).

[438]Town of Ossining, N.Y., 114 LA 1761, 1765 (Henner, 2000).

contact between the airline and a "fickle public"; he held that "the appearance of a tardy and disheveled Stewardess on the ramp is conduct prejudicial to the Carrier."[439] Another arbitrator likewise stressed the company's image and upheld its right to protect its image of giving better service through its neat, clean employees. Under the mores prevailing at that time, he opined that the "vast majority of the public" associated long hair and beards with irresponsibility.[440]

Arbitrators have been somewhat more skeptical when at issue is a message on employee clothing. So, for example, an arbitrator reversed the discharge of a grievant who was terminated for not removing his hard hat that had a lewd message where the employer had no rule or policy concerning any writing on hard hats and many coworkers continued to wear hard hats with equally lewd or sexually suggestive messages.[441] But where the employer had a rule that prohibited the "wearing of apparel with remarks or pictures which are disrespectful or reflect unfavorably on the company or its employees," employees were subject to discipline for violating the work rule, so long as the employer did not *"misuse"* the work rule in a manner that would invade an employee's individual rights.[442]

In a case involving a public employer, an arbitrator found that a change in the dress code to require the wearing of ties and jackets was a change in "working conditions" and was, therefore, subject to the "meet and confer" process of the collective bargaining agreement.[443]

There are many arbitration cases in which consideration of "image" was recognized as a valid factor but the image was not shown to have been tarnished under the particular facts so as to justify an employer's interference with an employee's dress and grooming choices.[444] For example, where an

---

[439]Western Air Lines, 37 LA 130, 133–34 (Wyckoff, 1961) (holding, however, that discharge was too severe and reducing the penalty to 7 months' suspension without pay). In *Trans World Airlines*, 46 LA 611, 612 (Wallen, 1965), it was held that "management must be accorded the right to verify compliance with clothing, hair length and appearance regulations in a manner which imposes no unreasonable or undignified demands on the employee," and that requiring "such verification is neither improper nor unreasonable"; therefore, the airline had the right to require a hostess to demonstrate that she was not wearing a wig.

[440]Western Air Lines, 52 LA 1282, 1284 (Steese, 1969) (upholding discharge for refusal to comply with rule prohibiting long hair and beards). *See also* Safeway Trails, 57 LA 994, 995 (Dugan, 1971); Great Atl. & Pac. Tea Co., 57 LA 789, 794–95 (Casselman, 1971); Washington Gas Light Co., 57 LA 453, 456 (Daly, 1971); Allied Employers, 55 LA 1020, 1025 (Kleinsorge, 1970); Pepsi Cola Gen. Bottlers, 55 LA 663, 666–67 (Volz, 1970); Stop & Shop, 49 LA 867, 868 (Johnson, 1967) (supermarket employee wore his hair long for his second job in a rock-and-roll band). For cases upholding or assessing a lesser penalty for refusal to comply with appearance regulations, see *Jax Beer Co.*, 52 LA 1116, 1118 (Caraway, 1969); *United Parcel Serv.*, 51 LA 292, 292 (Turkus, 1968); *American Export-Isbrandten Lines*, 47 LA 1182, 1182 (Turkus, 1967).

[441]ARMCO, Inc., 93 LA 561 (Strongin, 1989).

[442]Intertec Sys. LLC, 114 LA 1785, 1785 (Skulina, 2000).

[443]County of Riverside, Cal., 92 LA 1242 (Gentile, 1989).

[444]*See, e.g.*, Roskam Baking Co., 79 LA 993, 997–98 (Beitner, 1982) (grievants had limited contact with the public and there was inadequate proof "that the Company's image was adversely affected by allowing employees to wear hair nets instead of cutting their hair," as formerly had been permitted); Missouri Pub. Serv. Co., 77 LA 973, 977 (Maniscalco, 1981) (no-beard policy held unreasonable and arbitrary where utility employer failed to show "any reasonable relationship between its announced 'New Public Image Policy' and the real attitudes of the public it serves"); Milwaukee Transp. Serv., 77 LA 807, 813–14 (Jones, Jr., 1981) (stating that transportation employer had not adequately established that its "prohibition

employee refused to cut his long hair and shave his beard to comply with a company rule, the arbitrator found that since the employee worked in an isolated area where contact with customers and other employees was extremely rare, the application of the rule to him was unreasonable. The arbitrator further noted at the hearing that, although the grievant's hair was long and he had sideburns and a short Vandyke beard, the grievant's general appearance was one of "cleanliness and neatness."[445]

The concern of management with its image is keyed to public acceptance of the clothing and hairstyles adopted by its employees. As mores change and the acceptability of given attire and hairstyles is no longer questioned by the general public, industry has likewise accepted the fashion. The evolution of the acceptability of certain attire of female employees illustrates the point. In the 1930s, women were not permitted to wear slacks in some plants because of potential distraction of male employees.[446] In the 1940s, many plants *required* women to wear slacks rather than dresses as a safety precaution as they worked around industrial machinery. In the 1950s and 1960s,

---

against mirror-type sun glasses is related to its legitimate objectives of increasing ridership," and finding "substantial evidence of community acceptance of the type of sun glasses in issue"); Safeway Stores, 75 LA 798, 801 (Madden, 1980) (grocery store discharged employee who refused to shave beard prohibited by store's grooming standards; the discharge was overruled because the employee suffers from a skin condition that becomes worse if any type of razor is used to shave beard); Pacific Southwest Airlines, 73 LA 1209, 1213–15 (Christopher, 1979) (refusing to uphold an airline's absolute prohibition on beards for flight attendants where the airline failed to produce convincing evidence that a neatly trimmed beard would damage its "public image or otherwise have a detrimental effect on its business activities"); Rome Cable Communications, 70 LA 28, 32 (Dallas, 1978) (overruling discharge for refusing to cut long hair, the arbitrator stated that grievant's hairstyle "is similar to the hair styles worn by a large proportion of young men in his age group throughout the country," and "in the arbitrator's opinion should not be detrimental to the Company's image or sales"). In *Hughes Air Corp.*, 72 LA 588, 590–91 (Bloch, 1979), the arbitrator collected many cases reflecting "great diversity among arbitral responses" to the "sensitive issue" of beards, mustaches, and hair length, and he reviewed his own previous decision that had upheld an airline no-beard rule; he refused to uphold a similar rule in the present case but explained that "the decision in this case is limited to the finding that, in light of changes effected by deregulation, one may no longer assume, absent proof, that passengers' preferences concerning beards will be of demonstrable import in their choice of carrier." In *Department of Health, Educ. & Welfare*, 69 LA 44, 48 (Zack, 1977), the arbitrator found that most government and private business offices do not require employees to wear neckties, so he held that the employer may encourage but may not require the wearing of neckties under an agreement specifying that mode of dress "shall be consistent with accepted standards of business offices dealing with the public."

[445]Dravo-Doyle Co., 54 LA 604, 605–07 (Krimsly, 1971). *See also* Badger Concrete Co., 50 LA 901, 908–09 (Krinsky, 1968) (company can enforce the rule as to some classes of employees or employees performing certain jobs, for safety or other reasons connected with the company's operations); Hillview Sand & Gravel, 39 LA 35, 39–40 (Somers, 1962) (an employee can look neat and shave daily (in compliance with a company rule) and still retain a beard). For additional cases in which the arbitrator refused to uphold the employer's rule or assessment of discipline as to long hair, see *Big Star No. 35*, 73 LA 850, 856–57 (Murphy, 1979) (but cautioning grievants "that upon their return to their job that their hair must be kept clean and neat and orderly and well combed"); *Production Finishing Corp.*, 57 LA 1017, 1019 (Forsythe, 1971) (employee could use wig to cover long hair); *Roger Wilco Stores*, 57 LA 963, 969–70 (Jacobs, 1971); *San Diego Gas & Elec. Co.*, 57 LA 821, 824 (Leonard, 1971); *Sentry Food Stores*, 57 LA 410, 414 (Somers, 1971); *Trailways Serv.*, 57 LA 197, 199 (Strong, 1971).

[446]*See* Mitchell-Bentley Corp., 45 LA 1071, 1073 (Ryder, 1965) (involving the wearing of shorts by female workers).

slacks for women gained wide acceptability. By 1970, slacks, often in the form of "pant suits" or "pant dresses," came to be viewed by many employers as the preferable attire for women, gaining approval not only in industrial plants, but also commercial and government offices, retail establishments, and hospitals.[447]

One arbitrator urged that "[c]ustom and fashion in dress and behavior change from time to time, and employees should be permitted to conform reasonably with these changes."[448] So long as no detriment results to the company and no safety or health hazard is involved, conformity to current fashion should not be objectionable if the style followed is not extreme.[449]

C. Grooming and Safety and Health Considerations
[LA CDI 100.552529; 118.639; 118.659; 124.70]

Safety, health, and sanitation reasons also have been advanced in imposing restrictions on employees' apparel, hairstyle, or wearing of beards.[450] Questions of safety may be raised where loose-fitting clothing, dangling jewelry, and long unprotected hair are worn while operating machinery. Management may be expected to object when an employee operating machinery wears a loose shirt with the tail hanging out, or a dangling bracelet or necklace. Indeed, even a wedding ring may be a hazard in some situations.[451] Long hair that may become caught or entangled in the machinery also may be banished. Under a safety rule restricting the wearing of loose apparel and

---

[447]Admittedly, many employers found the pant suits or pant dresses preferable to the "mini" dress, which, for instance, led many employers to feel compelled to add "modesty shields" at the front of secretary desks. In *School District of Kingsley, Michigan*, 56 LA 1138, 1145 (Howlett, 1971), a school board's notice prohibiting teachers from wearing pant suits was held to be "null and void." Stating that "pant-suits [for women] now are an acceptable mode of dress in many of our medical care facilities," another arbitrator required a nursing home to modify its dress code "so as to permit the wearing of dresses or pant-suits." Oxford Nursing Home, 75 LA 1300, 1301–02 (Wolff, 1980).

[448]Springday Co., 53 LA 627, 629 (Bothwell, 1969).

[449]A discharged shipping clerk was described as "wearing boots, tight clinging orange-brown pants (with a wide oversized belt and buckle) and a flowing hirsute cranial adornment characteristic of the Beatles." But since his past record was good and since he demonstrated a willingness to cooperate by appearing at the hearing "shorn of his flowing locks, and presenting the very epitome of the more mundane accepted norm," he was reinstated without back pay on condition that he continue to maintain such appearance. American Export-Isbrandten Lines, 47 LA 1182, 1182 (Turkus, 1967).

[450]*See* Ashland Oil, 97 LA 226, 231–32 (Volz, 1991); Mississippi Power & Light Co., 92 LA 1161, 1166–67 (Taylor, 1989); New Cumberland Army Depot, 78 LA 630, 631 (Mount, 1982); Lozier Corp., 72 LA 164, 167–68 (Ferguson, 1979); Colt Indus., 71 LA 22, 25–26 (Rutherford, 1978); Laclede Steel Co., 57 LA 1036, 1038 (Mattice, 1971); Economy Super Mart, 54 LA 816, 819–20 (Elson, 1971); City of Waterbury, Conn., 54 LA 439, 441 (Stutz, 1971); Springday Co., 53 LA 627, 628–29 (Bothwell, 1969); Marhoefer Packing Co., 51 LA 983, 988–90 (Bradley, 1968); Badger Concrete Co., 50 LA 901, 908 (Krinsky, 1968). *See also* Bethlehem Steel Corp., 74 LA 921, 922 (Fishgold, 1980); Lawrence Bros., 28 LA 83, 87 (Davis, 1957). For general considerations of safety and health matters, see Chapter 16, "Safety and Health."

[451]*See* Doe Run Co., 95 LA 705 (Heinsz, 1990) (rule prohibiting smelter employees from wearing any kind of ring unreasonable as applied to employees wearing safety gloves but reasonable otherwise); General Foods Corp., 76 LA 532, 535 (Denson, 1981); Bethlehem Mines Corp., 48 LA 765, 766 (Strongin, 1967). *See also* Babcock & Wilcox, 73 LA 443, 447 (Strasshofer, 1979).

long unprotected hair, management was upheld in refusing to permit an employee to continue work unless he trimmed his beard. The arbitrator ruled:

> It is properly the function of management personnel who directly supervise employees to determine the conditions under which a beard constitutes a safety hazard. The individual employee cannot decide how safety rules are to apply to him, or whether or not he should obey a particular safety rule in a particular situation. . . .
>
> . . .
>
> The arbitrator cannot determine whether a particular beard constitutes a safety hazard. This must be done on a day to day basis by supervision in the industrial plant. Only if such decisions by supervision are clearly unreasonable should the arbitrator intervene.[452]

The arbitrator stated further that "[t]he employee is not being unreasonably restrained in his conduct or dress so long as there is a reasonable relation between what is required and safety."[453]

In regard to the "reasonable relation" requirement, arbitrators have upheld rules restricting the wearing of beards or other facial hair where the restriction is necessary for the proper functioning of respirators needed for safety purposes.[454] The Department of Labor's Occupational Safety and Health Administration (OSHA) promulgated workplace safety rules requiring that

---

[452]Springday Co., 53 LA 627, 628–29 (Bothwell, 1969) (the company did not prohibit the wearing of beards but only regulated them for safety purposes). Another arbitrator would not lay down guidelines as to the point where "face hair becomes hirsute and unacceptable" from a safety standpoint, stating that "each mustache and each pair of sideburns . . . will have to be measured against the safety factor and treated accordingly." City of Waterbury, Conn., 54 LA 439, 441 (Stutz, 1971).

[453]Springday Co., 53 LA 627, 629 (Bothwell, 1969). A reasonable relationship was found where facial hair, often treated with tonics, salves, or sprays that contain inflammable materials, "may well ignite if touched by a very hot spark" of the type present in the work of the employees. Phoenix Forging Co., 71 LA 879, 882 (Dash, Jr., 1978). A reasonable relationship was not found where the employee (operating machinery) wore a protective cap over his long hair. Challenge-Cook Bros., 55 LA 517, 520–21 (Roberts, 1970). For a statement regarding reasonableness in finding the existence of a safety hazard, and reasonableness in determining whether a perceived safety hazard necessitates the restriction upon employee choice as to dress or grooming, see Babcock & Wilcox, 73 LA 443, 445 (Strasshofer, 1979) (quoting U.S. Steel (McDermott, 1962) (unpublished)).

[454]See Ashland Oil, 97 LA 226 (Volz, 1991). In this case the arbitrator upheld an employer policy requiring employees regularly exposed to toxic atmospheres to be clean-shaven for safe use of respirators, despite grievant's argument that he suffered from a skin ailment, folliculitis barbae, that made his face unsuited for shaving. This case illustrates the possibility for tension between contractual employee rights, occupational safety and health requirements, and the application of civil rights legislation such as the Americans with Disabilities Act. Because most sufferers of folliculitis barbae are African-American, there is also the potential for application of Title VII of the Civil Rights Act of 1964 under an "adverse impact" theory. See, e.g., EEOC v. Greyhound Lines, 635 F.2d 188, 24 FEP Cases 7 (3d Cir. 1980) (rejecting a claim of race discrimination based on the alleged adverse impact on the predominantly African-American sufferers of folliculitis barbae because of the company rule requiring employees to be clean-shaven). See also Riceland Foods v. Carpenters Local 2381, 737 F.2d 758, 116 LRRM 2948 (8th Cir. 1984); Bhatia v. Chevron U.S.A., 734 F.2d 1382, 34 FEP Cases 1816 (9th Cir. 1984) (discussed below in this subtopic); E.I. DuPont de Nemours & Co., 78 LA 327, 330 (Light, 1982); Pacific Southwest Airlines, 77 LA 320, 329–30 (Jones, Jr., 1981); Arkansas Glass Container Corp., 76 LA 841, 843–44 (Teple, 1981); Hess Oil V.I. Corp., 75 LA 770, 774 (Johnston, 1980); Niagara Mohawk Power Corp., 74 LA 58, 62–63 (Markowitz, 1980); American Smelting & Ref. Co., 69 LA 824, 826 (Hutcheson, 1977); J.R. Simplot Co., 68 LA 912, 915–16 (Conant, 1977). Cf. International Minerals & Chem. Corp., 78 LA 682, 685–86 (Jones, Jr., 1982).

respirators be provided to protect employees from "occupational diseases caused by breathing air contaminated with harmful dusts, fogs, fumes, mists, gases, smokes, sprays, or vapors."[455] The regulations prohibit "respirators with tight-fitting facepieces to be worn by employees who have: (A) Facial hair that comes between the sealing surface of the facepiece and the face, or that interferes with valve function. . . ."[456] In one case, employees who were engaged in the production of chemicals were sometimes required to use respirators. The employer adopted a "no-beards" policy in order to ensure improved respiratory protection based on its belief that the applicable OSHA regulations required such a policy. Interpreting statutory law to the extent that it was relevant to the issues presented in the arbitration, the arbitrator found that the company was correct and denied the grievance.[457]

Another arbitrator also upheld the discharge of an employee who on four separate occasions refused to shave off his beard for an annual respirator fit test. He observed that the respiratory policy had been negotiated with the union and was legitimately related to the safety program.[458]

However, arbitrators have not upheld no-beard rules as to employees who have no real need for the use of a respirator or whose need is too remote and conjectural.[459] Likewise, in one case, a company sought to apply a general rule against growing beards to the grievant, a mechanic, because it believed beards contributed to dermatitis caused by handling the company's product. The company's concerns were found to be unwarranted because the grievant had little or no contact with the product.[460] In another case, an arbitrator found a company's prohibition against the wearing of beards in its dairy plant unreasonable where beards had not been prohibited by any governmental regulation, the industry had not adopted or sponsored a uniform beard ban practice, and there was no evidence of a problem within the plant creating the need for such a policy. Further, the company had allowed the wearing of mustaches of any length, and had failed to show that alternatives, such as beard covers, were unworkable. The arbitrator stressed that

---

[455]29 C.F.R. §1910.134(a)(1) (2002).

[456]*Id.* §1910.134(q)(1)(A). *See* Maloney, *Suits for the Hirsute: Defending Against American's Undeclared War on Beards in the Workplace*, 63 FORDHAM L. REV. 1203, 1232–41 (1995) (arguing that the regulation itself, and not the private employer's enforcement of it, should be challenged on First Amendment free expression grounds).

[457]Dyno Nobel, 104 LA 376 (Hilgert, 1995).

[458]Central Contra Costa County, Cal., Sanitary Dist., 93 LA 801 (Silver, 1989). Decisions of the National Labor Relations Board have found that facial hair regulations are a mandatory subject of collective bargaining under §8(a)(5) of the National Labor Relations Act, and therefore may not be imposed by the employer, even in an attempt to comply with OSHA regulations, without first satisfying the employer's bargaining obligations. *See, e.g.,* Equitable Gas Co., 303 NLRB 925, 138 LRRM 1001 (1991) (finding unilateral imposition of "appearance guidelines" that banned beards to be an unfair labor practice); Hanes Corp., 260 NLRB 557, 563, 109 LRRM 1185 (1982) (finding unilateral ban on beards to achieve OSHA compliance to be an unfair labor practice, given that the alternative respirator types could achieve same degree of protection without ban on beards).

[459]*See* Union Carbide Corp., 82 LA 1084, 1087–88 (Goldman, 1984); E.&J. Gallo Winery, 80 LA 765, 770 (Killion, 1983).

[460]Badger Concrete Co., 50 LA 901, 908 (Krinsky, 1968).

the policy invaded the private life of employees by effectively regulating their off-duty appearance.[461]

Employers may attempt to ban employee hirsuteness for sanitation reasons. A supermarket argued for such a ban, but the arbitrator, while recognizing that "[t]he maintenance of a meat department, so as to give a clean and sanitary appearance, is essential to its proper operation," concluded that sideburns, "even somewhat fuzzier" than those worn by the grievant at the hearing, did not present a reasonable basis for concern.[462] In contrast, another arbitrator emphasized that "[a]lthough hair styles have changed, sanitation needs have not."[463] He upheld the discharge of an employee who wore sideburns longer than permitted by company rule, because the regulation was directed at protecting the company's products from hair contamination rather than at regulating employees' appearance.

Wigs and hair pieces may likewise be the subjects of company rules. In one case, the arbitrator held that for sanitation reasons a meat packing company could prohibit the wearing of wigs and hair pieces in the plant. The arbitrator considered such items to be in the same category as hats and other "street clothing" that were barred from the work areas of the plant as sources of contamination by a company rule and by a U.S. Department of Agriculture regulation.[464]

Sometimes dress or grooming policies adopted for safety, health, or sanitation reasons are opposed by individual employees on religious grounds. In one such case, a safety rule required employees to wear pants, but a female employee, whose religion had a tenet against women wearing men's clothing, insisted upon wearing a dress or skirt and was discharged. The arbitrator explained his conclusion that it was permissible for an employer "to give greater weight to safety considerations than to religious preferences" in certain circumstances:

> The Arbitrator must let safety considerations prevail if the Employer has made an objective determination that a certain rule is necessary based on demonstrated facts and reasonable inferences. This is not to say that freedom of religion or religious expression is ignored or not a part of the total fabric of the so-called "common law of the shop." There are other places to express religious preferences but there is no other place to practice on the job safety except the work site. Safety rules affect and inure to the benefit of all employees. The fact that the rules are most frequently originated by the Employer does not destroy the benefit which flows to employees. In any event, safety on the job is a law-

---

[461]Fairmont-Zarda Dairy, 106 LA 583 (Rohlik, 1995).
[462]Economy Super Mart, 54 LA 816, 820 (Elson, 1971).
[463]Kellogg Co., 55 LA 84, 88 (Shearer, 1970).
[464]Marhoefer Packing Co., 51 LA 983, 988–90 (Bradley, 1968) (with much discussion of evidence comparing natural hair with wigs, and noting in particular that in contrast with natural hair, wigs become brittle and break and that dust and dirt settling on a wig can fall off or be blown away more easily). Safety rather than sanitation was involved in *Babcock & Wilcox*, 79 LA 443, 444, 447 (Strasshofer, 1979), where "the evidence did not prove the alleged safety hazards"; it was not "proven that there is any particularly significant increase in safety risks to the employee or anyone else created by a wig under a hard hat, as opposed to natural hair under a hard hat."

fully mandated federal requirement under the Occupational Safety and Health Act, and, in this specific case safety is also a contractually mandated requirement under Article XIII.[465]

In a similar case, a hospital employer required all operating room personnel to wear pants to lower the incidence of infection. When an operating room technician refused to wear pants in accordance with a tenet of her religion, she was transferred to another position. The collective agreement contained a clause expressly prohibiting "discrimination as to . . . creed." Looking to Title VII of the Civil Rights Act for aid of the clause, the arbitrator concluded that the employer must show that no acceptable alternative existed. The award specified steps to be taken for designing an operating room uniform that would conform to the infection control program without violating the employee's religious beliefs.[466] However, the employee then rejected the alternative uniform that was designated pursuant to the award for the same religious reason. In subsequent proceedings, the arbitrator ruled that the employer could transfer her "to a job which she is able to perform and not be required to wear slacks."[467]

6. NON-SAFETY-RELATED ACCOMMODATION OF EMPLOYEE RELIGIOUS BELIEFS
[LA CDI 100.33; 106.20]

Safety interests of an employee are not the only employer interests that may clash with the religious faith of an employee. Sometimes employees also

---

[465]Colt Indus., 71 LA 22, 25 (Rutherford, 1978). The employer made the required showing of necessity and the discharge was held to be for just cause, but the award provided that "in view of the delicate balance between safety considerations and religious beliefs which the case presents," the employee "should be allowed to return to work without any back pay but without any loss of seniority whenever she decides that she will comply with the Employer's safety related dress code." *Id.* at 26. In *Alameda-Contra Costa, California, Transit District*, 75 LA 1273, 1282 (Randall, 1980), the employee's belief in the particular religious tenet on which she relied was found not to be sincere and her discharge for violating the employer's dress code was upheld. In *Louisville Water Co.*, 80 LA 957, 962 (Hunter, 1983), the employee's belief in the particular religious tenet on which she relied was found to be sincere but her discharge for refusing to wear a jumpsuit uniform nonetheless was upheld on the basis of estoppel—she had accepted the jumpsuit requirement as a condition of employment for several years until she adopted a religion whose beliefs prevented her from wearing men's clothing. The arbitrator stated that his jurisdiction was limited to the contract and that the question "[w]hether or not she is estopped under the Civil Rights Act of 1964" was not before him.

[466]Hurley Hosp., 70 LA 1061, 1063–66 (Roumell, Jr., 1978).

[467]Hurley Hosp., 71 LA 1013, 1015 (Roumell, Jr., 1978) (award providing also that "[s]he shall be paid the rate of said new job"). An employer's adherence to a safety policy was upheld over an employee's adherence to a tenet of his religion in *Bhatia v. Chevron U.S.A.*, 734 F.2d 1382, 34 FEP Cases 1816 (9th Cir. 1984), where the employer was held to have reasonably accommodated the employee under Title VII in transferring him to a lower-paying job after the employee's religion resulted in his refusal to shave as required for wearing a gas mask needed on the job. The court said the employer would suffer undue hardship by retaining the employee on the job: to subject the employee to toxic fumes would render the employer liable under state law, and to relieve the employee of the duties involving exposure to toxic fumes would necessitate revamping an entire system of duty assignments and would require coworkers to assume the employee's share of potentially hazardous work.

have complained that their freedom of religion was violated by the scheduling of work on the Sabbath or on other religious holidays, claiming that they
had been discriminated against when the employer required them to work
on such days or disciplined them for their failure to do so. However, before
1972, when Title VII of the Civil Rights Act was amended to impose an obligation on management to make reasonable accommodations for employee
religious beliefs, arbitrators generally had held that the employer was not
required to accommodate individual requests for scheduling work so that
the employee could observe religious holidays. Consequently, the discharge
or discipline of the employees who had refused to work as scheduled for such
reason was upheld.[468] Arbitrators emphasized the company's right to maintain efficient industrial operations, and they noted the disruption that would
result if the company were required to accommodate the religious beliefs of
individual employees.[469]

Another problem with employer accommodation of employee religious
beliefs was perceived to be the resultant apparent discrimination against
other employees.[470] So in one case, a foreman discontinued a special schedule
for one employee when other employees complained that such arrangement
was discriminatory. The employee grieved when he was told that he would
have to work his regular schedule or become subject to discipline. Ruling for
the company, the arbitrator stated: "This simply is not a case involving discrimination *against* grievant because of his religious beliefs. Rather, it is he
who seeks a special privilege which is not accorded to other employees."[471]

---

[468]*See* Avco Corp., 52 LA 707, 708 (Turkus, 1969); Smith Plastics, 50 LA 375, 380 (Walt,
1967); Combustion Eng'g, 49 LA 204, 206 (Daugherty, 1967); United States Steel Corp., 48
LA 1340, 1342–43 (Garrett, 1967); Univac Div., 48 LA 619, 620–21 (Cahn, 1967); Stanley
Works, 39 LA 374, 378–79 (Summers, 1962) (stating that "[i]n spite of the high value placed
on religious freedom in our society, employers have commonly scheduled work on days which
are the sabbath for various employees and are generally considered entitled to dismiss employees who refuse to work for religious reasons"); Mucon Corp., 29 LA 77, 79 (Stark, 1957);
International Shoe Co., 15 LA 121, 123 (Kelliher, 1950).

[469]*See* Avco Corp., 52 LA 707, 708 (Turkus, 1969); Smith Plastics, 50 LA 375, 380 (Walt,
1967); Combustion Eng'g, 49 LA 204, 206 (Daugherty, 1967); Univac Div., 48 LA 619, 621
(Cahn, 1967). *See also* Mucon Corp., 29 LA 77, 79 (Stark, 1957). *Cf.* Spiegel, Inc., 55 LA 653,
657 (Luskin, 1970) (involving a de minimis situation).

[470]Thus, where the contract contained a provision prohibiting discrimination, it was observed that to treat an employee differently for religious reasons would be to discriminate
against other employees in violation of the contract. Avco Corp., 52 LA 707, 708 (Turkus,
1969); Combustion Eng'g, 49 LA 204, 206 (Daugherty, 1967). Also, the company argued in
United States Steel Corp., 56 LA 694, 695 (McDaniel, 1971), that should it permit such differential treatment for religious reasons, it might be subject to a charge of "reverse discrimination" or favoritism. The contract in this case, however, contained a requirement that the
joint Committee on Civil Rights "shall review matters involving Civil Rights," and the arbitrator set aside the discharge pending such review. *Id.* at 696–97.

[471]United States Steel Corp., 48 LA 1340, 1341, 1343 (Garrett, 1967). *See also* Georgia
Power Co., 94 LA 1303 (Baroni, 1990) (employee properly discharged when refused to work
two Saturdays during "power outage" emergency, where company had allowed him 75 Saturdays off through shift-swapping and allowing him two Saturdays off would have caused
employer "undue hardship"). But in another case, discipline of an employee for refusal to
work on Sunday for religious reasons was held to constitute discrimination in violation of
the contract where the company had habitually shown consideration for the religious scruples
of other employees in the plant. Goodyear Tire & Rubber Co., 1 LA 121, 122–23 (McCoy,
1945). *See also* International Shoe Co., 2 LA 201, 205–06 (Klamon, 1946).

A third problem arose from employers requiring employees to take time off on religious days, thereby imposing upon them the observance found appropriate by management. One arbitrator ruled that to do so would be an arbitrary use of the contractual right to relieve employees from duty.[472]

Even prior to the amendment of Title VII of the Civil Rights Act of 1964, the Equal Employment Opportunity Commission guidelines stated that the duty imposed by Title VII not to discriminate on religious grounds "includes an obligation on the part of the employer to make reasonable accommodations to the religious needs of employees . . . where such accommodations can be made without hardship on the conduct of the employer's business." In *Dewey v. Reynolds Metals Co.*,[473] the discharge of an employee who refused to work on Sundays or to induce others to work in his place was upheld. The court held that the employer had made "reasonable accommodation" to the employee's religious needs when it gave him the opportunity to secure replacements for his Sunday overtime assignments.

Under Title VII of the Civil Rights Act as amended by the Equal Employment Opportunity Act of 1972, employers must make reasonable accommodations for employee religious beliefs in the scheduling of work and the like, unless the employer demonstrates that doing so would result in "undue hardship on the conduct of the employer's business."[474] The Supreme Court's

---

[472]Eagle Elec. Mfg. Co., 31 LA 1038, 1039 (Robins, 1957). *See also* Eagle Elec. Mfg. Co., 29 LA 489, 491 (Gamser, 1957) (finding a violation of the seniority provisions under like circumstances).

[473]429 F.2d 324, 2 FEP Cases 687 (6th Cir. 1970), *aff'd*, 402 U.S. 689, 3 FEP Cases 508 (1971) (4–4 decision).

[474]Section 701(j) provides in full:

The term "religion" includes all aspects of religious observance and practice, as well as belief, unless an employer demonstrates that he is unable to reasonably accommodate to an employee's or prospective employee's religious observance or practice without undue hardship on the conduct of the employer's business.

As analyzed in the March 6, 1972, *Congressional Record*, this subsection requires employers to make reasonable accommodations for religious practices "which differ from the employer's or potential employer's requirements regarding standards, schedules, or other business-related employment conditions." That source also states that "[t]he purpose of this subsection is to provide the statutory basis for EEOC to formulate guidelines on discrimination because of religion such as those challenged in *Dewey v. Reynolds Metals Company*." The EEOC's Guidelines on Discrimination Because of Religion are published in 29 C.F.R. Part 1605. For discussion of what constitutes a "religious belief," see Hill, *Reasonable Accommodation and Religious Discrimination Under Title VII: A Practitioner's Guide*, 34 ARB. J. No. 4, at 19, 20, 24–25 (1979). Also note the statement in *Edwards v. City of Norton, Va., School Board*, 483 F. Supp. 620, 21 FEP Cases 1375, 1377 (W.D. Va. 1980), that:

A religious belief excludes mere personal preference grounded upon a non-theological basis, such as personal choice deduced from economic or social ideology. Rather, it must consider man's nature or the scheme of his existence as it relates in a theological framework. Furthermore, the belief must have an institutional quality about it and must be sincerely held by plaintiff.

In *Building Owners & Managers Ass'n of San Francisco*, 67 LA 1031, 1033–34 (Griffin, 1976), a Roman Catholic employee's discharge for refusing to work on Sunday was upheld since the employer had the right to assign Sunday work and the Roman Catholic religion does not forbid its faithful to work on Sunday. The arbitrator stated that the employee "has the unfettered personal right to impose his own standards regarding Sunday work, even when those individual standards exceed those required by the faith he professes," but "the exercise of that right is not without possible peril." In this case the arbitrator did not expressly mention Title VII, but he did conclude that the employee's discharge "was violative of neither his contractual, nor religious civil rights." For other cases drawing a distinction

1977 decision in *Trans World Airlines v. Hardison*[475] considered both the provision for reasonable accommodation of religious beliefs under Section 701(j) of the Act and the protection of bona fide seniority systems under Section 703(h). In this case, an employee had insufficient seniority to avoid working on Saturdays, violating a tenet of his religion, which considered Saturdays as the Sabbath. He eventually was discharged for refusing to work on Saturdays. Accepting the district court's view that TWA had done all that could reasonably be expected within the bounds of the seniority system, the Supreme Court held that "absent a discriminatory purpose, the operation of a seniority system cannot be an unlawful employment practice even if the system has some discriminatory consequences."[476]

The court of appeals had believed that TWA could have accommodated the employee without undue hardship on the business (1) by permitting him to work a 4-day week, utilizing in his place a supervisor or another worker on duty elsewhere; (2) by filling his shift with another employee at premium overtime pay; or (3) by arranging a "swap between Hardison and another employee either for another shift or for the Sabbath days." The Supreme Court disagreed, and in doing so the Court explained its rejection of alternative (3) first:

---

between personal preference or the individual's conscience on the one hand, and the actual requirements of the Catholic Church on the other, see *Livonia Public Schools*, 71 LA 937, 941 (Kanner, 1978), and *City & County of Denver, Colorado, School District No. 1*, 68 LA 1056, 1060 (Yarowsky, 1977), both cases involving the construction of contractual leave provisions. *See also* Atlantic Richfield Co., 70 LA 707, 714 (Fox, Jr., 1978) (employee failed to establish either that the asserted religious belief was sincerely held or that the action requested by the employer would violate any tenet of the asserted religious faith); Reynolds & Reynolds Co., 63 LA 157, 159 (High, 1974) (employee "indicated that there would be no serious impairment of the fulfillment of his religious obligations to arrive" late at religious meetings, "but that he personally felt it important to be punctual"); Walker Mfg. Co., 60 LA 525, 532 (Simon, 1973) (stressing that it was the grievant's "own *personal* conviction that one should not perform work on Sunday"). In *Social Security Administration*, 79 LA 449, 449–55 (Mittelman, 1982), a statute provided that federal employees "whose personal religious beliefs require the abstention from work during certain periods of time, may elect to engage in overtime work for time lost for meeting those religious requirements." The arbitrator concluded that "neither the statute nor the constitution precludes an employer from making a reasonable inquiry to ascertain whether an employee in fact has a personal religious belief which requires him or her to refrain from work."

[475]432 U.S. 63, 14 FEP Cases 1697 (1977), referred to below in this topic as the *TWA* decision. The Supreme Court noted TWA's actions to accommodate as had been summarized by the district court:

It held several meetings with plaintiff at which it attempted to find a solution to plaintiff's problems. It did accommodate plaintiff's observance of his special religious holidays [which could reasonably be done since they fell on days that most other employees preferred to work]. It authorized the union steward to search for someone who would swap shifts, which apparently was normal procedure.

Id. at 77 (quoting Hardison v. Trans World Airlines, 375 F. Supp. 877, 890–91, 10 FEP Cases 502 (W.D. Mo. 1974)). The Supreme Court also noted that "TWA itself attempted without success to find Hardison another job." *Id.* Furthermore, the Court considered that the seniority system "itself represented a significant accommodation to the needs, both religious and secular, of all of TWA's employees"—it "represents a neutral way of minimizing the number of occasions when an employee must work on a day that he would prefer to have off"; and "recognizing that weekend work schedules are the least popular, the company made further accommodation by reducing its work force to a bare minimum on those days." *Id.* at 78.

[476]*Id.* at 77, 82.

> TWA itself cannot be faulted for having failed to work out a shift or job swap for Hardison. Both the union and TWA had agreed to the seniority system; the union was unwilling to entertain a variance over the objections of men senior to Hardison; and for TWA to have arranged unilaterally for a swap would have amounted to a breach of the collective-bargaining agreement.[477]

Then the Supreme Court explained its rejection of alternatives (1) and (2):

> Both of these alternatives would involve costs to TWA, either in the form of lost efficiency in other jobs or higher wages.
>
> To require TWA to bear more than a de minimis cost in order to give Hardison Saturdays off is an undue hardship. Like abandonment of the seniority system, to require TWA to bear additional costs when no such costs are incurred to give other employees the days off that they want would involve unequal treatment of employees on the basis of their religion. . . .
>
> . . . [T]he paramount concern of Congress in enacting Title VII was the elimination of discrimination in employment. In the absence of clear statutory language or legislative history to the contrary, we will not readily construe the statute to require an employer to discriminate against some employees in order to enable others to observe their Sabbath.[478]

The conflict between workplace policies and required religious observances of employees was reviewed once more by the Supreme Court in 1986 in *Ansonia Board of Education v. Philbrook*.[479] There, the employee, a high school instructor, was unable to pursue his employment on certain holy days designated by the church to which he belonged. The Board of Education, which employed the instructor, maintained a detailed, rigid policy with respect to paid leaves of absence. Under the collective bargaining agreement, up to 3 days annually could be authorized as leave for observance of mandatory religious holidays. In addition, up to 3 days per year could be used for necessary personal business. Use of these personal days, however, had to be limited to purposes other than those for which the contract provided specific leave periods. Other such leaves were listed in the contract for illness, death in the family, weddings, and acting as a delegate to certain conventions. The employee's observances of holy days usually amounted to 6 days per year, but only the first 3 days could be paid under the leave policy. The Board of Education in no way threatened the instructor with a loss of employment. However, he was seeking a greater degree of accommodation in order to avoid the loss of pay for unauthorized religious leaves.

The Supreme Court ruled that Title VII of the Civil Rights Act of 1964 as amended does not require an employer to implement an accommodation plan that is most beneficial to the employee as long as the employer avoids

---

[477]*Id.* at 78–79, where the Court said it did "not believe that the duty to accommodate requires TWA to take steps inconsistent with the otherwise valid agreement." *Id.* at 79. The Court did believe that "the strong congressional policy against discrimination in employment argues against interpreting the statute to require the abrogation of the seniority rights of some employees in order to accommodate the religious needs of others." *Id.* at n.12.

[478]*Id.* at 84–85. In *City of Auburn, Maine, Police Department*, 78 LA 537, 541 (Chandler, 1982), the *TWA* decision was cited in connection with the arbitrator's conclusion that the employer had improperly discriminated against one employee in order to accommodate the religious needs of another.

[479]479 U.S. 60, 42 FEP Cases 359 (1986).

undue hardship. The Court observed that the "undue hardship" consideration comes into play only when the employer is unable to offer any reasonable accommodation. In this case, the leave policy itself was offered by the employer as reasonable accommodation to the employee's required religious observances. Additionally, the Court conceded that such an accommodation plan generally would be reasonable. However, unpaid leave is not a reasonable accommodation if paid leaves are available for every purpose except religious purposes, because such an arrangement would be discriminatory and clearly unreasonable. The Court held that the development of additional facts concerning the administration of the agreement was necessary to make a determination of the reasonableness of the accommodation. Accordingly, the case was remanded to the district court.

In applying the standards announced by the Supreme Court, the federal courts focus on whether the employment practice at issue is "neutral"[480] and whether an accommodation would require a breach of a collective bargaining agreement or otherwise impose an undue hardship on the employer.[481] However, the showing that an employer must make to establish reasonable accommodation of religious beliefs remains unsettled.[482]

Arbitration decisions have, to a large extent, followed the lead of the federal decisions. In one case, a Seventh Day Adventist, who was discharged for refusing to work a Saturday schedule, sought to have her termination set aside on the ground that her religion precluded her from working on Saturdays. Citing *Hardison* in support of a decision that Title VII does not require the company to violate its collective bargaining agreement in order to accommodate the religious beliefs of its employees,[483] an arbitrator upheld the discharge. In another decision, an arbitrator found that Title VII does not require an employer to permit an employee to use paid leave in order to observe religious holidays. However, the arbitrator went on to find that the grievant was entitled to 2 days' paid leave under the collective bargaining agreement.[484]

Utilizing the "reasonable accommodation–undue hardship" standards set out in the *Philbrook*, an arbitrator found that an employer had improperly discharged a grocery store cashier for refusing on religious grounds to

---

[480]Beadle v. Hillsborough County Sheriff's Dep't, 29 F.3d 589, 65 FEP Cases 1069 (11th Cir. 1994) (employer offered reasonable accommodation for employee disadvantaged by neutral shift rotation system when it offered to allow him to swap shifts with other employees and to provide him with an employee roster).

[481]Lee v. ABF Freight Sys., 22 F.3d 1019, 64 FEP Cases 896 (10th Cir. 1994) (adjustment in call-in procedure would violate collective bargaining agreement and thus constituted an undue hardship); Brown v. Polk County, Iowa, 61 F.3d 650, 68 FEP Cases 648 (8th Cir. 1995) (employer not required to allow employee to print Bible notes on employer's word processor on ground of undue hardship).

[482]*Compare* Cook v. Chrysler Corp., 981 F.2d 336, 141 LRRM 3038 (8th Cir. 1992) (the cost of excusing the absences of a Seventh Day Adventist would constitute undue hardship), *with* EEOC v. Ithaca Indus., 849 F.2d 116, 46 FEP Cases 1730 (4th Cir. 1988) (the burden is on the employer to seek a reasonable accommodation with a worker who refuses on religious grounds to perform Sunday work).

[483]Moonlight Mushrooms, 101 LA 421 (Dean, Jr., 1993).

[484]Vicksburg Cmty. Sch., 101 LA 771 (Daniel, 1993).

sell state lottery tickets. [485] Although her retention in the same position without ticket-selling duties would have constituted an undue hardship on operations, the employer failed to explore some other accommodation, such as transfer to another position.

Also applying the Supreme Court approved standard, another arbitrator found that just cause existed to discharge a power company maintenance mechanic for his refusal to work on two Saturdays because of his religious

---

[485]Lucky Stores, 88 LA 841 (Gentile, 1987) (discussing Ansonia Bd. of Educ. v. Philbrook, 479 U.S. 60, 42 FEP Cases 359 (1986), and Trans World Airlines v. Hardison, 432 U.S. 63, 14 FEP Cases 1697 (1977)). *See also* Helburn & Hill, *The Arbitration of Religious Practice Grievances*, 39 ARB. J. 3 (1984). For cases where there was a showing of reasonable accommodation and/or undue hardship, see *Kansas City Area Transp. Auth.*, 79 LA 299, 303–06 (Belkin, 1982) (sustaining discharge for absences due to inability to work weekends because of religion, the arbitrator found reasonable accommodation by the employer's willingness to permit the employee to bid another job, although at significantly lower wages, and found also that the accommodation proposed by the employee would involve scheduling difficulties, would subject the employer to greater than de minimis increase in costs, and would disregard resentment expressed by other employees against any preferential scheduling, which consequences create undue hardship under the standards adopted in the *TWA* decision); *Oolite Indus.*, 77 LA 838, 843–45 (Green, 1981) (relying extensively on the *TWA* decision, the arbitrator concluded that the employer did not discriminate against grievant in discharging him for failing to make a necessary delivery on Friday afternoon and leaving work 5 hours early that day to prepare for Sabbath before sundown as required by his religion; but in light of mitigating factors, the award left a possibility open for the employee to obtain reinstatement); *General Foods Corp.*, 72 LA 505, 509–10 (Conant, 1979) (the parties requested a determination of grievant's rights under the agreement and the Civil Rights Act; the arbitrator pointed to special needs of the business and concluded that the employer's decision to transfer the grievant to another department where she could be scheduled off on Sundays and thus accommodate her religion "was the most sensible option" under all the circumstances, although it meant her loss of "a preferred kind of work"). *See also* Naval Amphibious Base, 74 LA 1131, 1132 (Gregg, 1980); School Dist. of Beloit, 73 LA 1146, 1148 (Greco, 1979) (stating that the Title VII reasonable accommodation provision "does not go to the extent of requiring" the employer to provide leave with pay, the arbitrator held that paid leave for religious holidays was not required where not required by the agreement); Norris Indus., 70 LA 936, 939 (Gentile, 1978) (citing the *TWA* decision, the arbitrator concluded that the employer could have asserted undue hardship and thus need not have granted the request of 36% of the workforce for religious leave on Good Friday; granting such request resulted in a shortage of personnel that led to the layoff of the remaining workforce without being given the contractually required 48-hour notice). For cases where there was no showing of reasonable accommodation and/or undue hardship, see *Alabama By-Products Corp.*, 79 LA 1320, 1325–26 (Clarke, 1982) (the agreement prohibited discrimination on the basis of "creed," and an EEOC guideline provided that "where there is more than one means of accommodation which would not cause undue hardship, the employer . . . must offer the alternative which least disadvantages the individual"; the arbitrator held that "under the facts of this case giving the Grievant an opportunity to take a personal or sick leave" rather than giving him an excused absence on the day of his absence to preach at a funeral was not a reasonable accommodation); *United States Steel Corp.*, 70 LA 1131, 1135–38 (Dunsford, 1978) (noting that the parties had agreed that Title VII standards would control his decision, and having analyzed and distinguished the *TWA* decision, he stated that the "reasonable accommodation of which the Act speaks refers not only to efforts to satisfy the employee's religious needs within the confines of his present job, but also a serious examination of whether there are alternative positions which the employee might fill without violating the terms of" the collective agreement); *American Forest Prods. Corp.*, 65 LA 650, 653–54 (Jacobs, 1975) (noting that this case "involves the breaking of an employee's seniority on recall because he could not accept a job which was available on the swing shift because of his religious convictions," and finding that the employer could have made reasonable accommodation since there were other laid-off employees who were qualified to perform the work on the swing shift, the arbitrator declared that the agreement's recall/forfeiture provision "cannot . . . be construed in such fashion as to violate rights guaranteed by Title VII").

belief.[486] Here, the arbitrator found that the grievant's absence caused an undue hardship because a power outage left no one with whom he could swap shifts and unforeseen equipment failures during the power outage created an emergency condition. It was noted that the grievant had been allowed 75 consecutive Saturdays off through shift-swapping.

As discussed earlier in this text, however, some arbitrators believe that their jurisdiction does not extend to determining compliance with legislation such as Title VII, but is restricted to the bare terms of the collective bargaining agreement. One arbitrator noted the problem in a decision where he determined that the term "religious holiday," as used in a contract providing for paid leave for such occasions, was restricted to holidays where adherence to the employee's faith made it impossible, rather than merely a matter of preference or conscience, to attend work.[487]

When attempting to accommodate the religious beliefs of an employee under the *Philbrook* standard, an employer must also avoid violating the contract by discriminating against others. If an employer does offer a religious accommodation that discriminates against other employees, it will be invalidated. Thus, after noting that the Supreme Court had indicated in *Hardison* that a neutral seniority system could not constitute an unlawful employment practice even if the system produced discriminatory effects, one arbitrator held that an employer had violated the collective bargaining agreement by excusing an employee from a Sunday work requirement.[488] In another case a Seventh Day Adventist successfully challenged management's policy requiring employees to recruit their own replacement for mandatory Saturday work as being in violation of the overtime distribution provisions of the bargaining agreement.[489]

The reasonableness of an offered accommodation is often at issue. By way of illustration, an employer's proposal to allow a worker to become a part-time employee and work a split shift was reasonable under *Hardison*, despite the fact that the worker did not wish to be classified as a part-time employee.[490]

---

[486]Georgia Power Co., 94 LA 1303, 1306–09 (Baroni, 1990).

[487]Denver, Colo., Pub. Sch., 98 LA 1163, 1168 (Hogler, 1992). *See* Timken Co., 75 LA 801, 804–05 (Morgan, 1980) (noting the *TWA* decision's statement that to require the employer to incur more than de minimis cost constitutes an undue hardship, but refusing to determine whether undue hardship existed in the present case, the arbitrator held for the employer solely on the basis of his finding that the employer had not violated the agreement in refusing holiday pay to an employee who failed to work the last scheduled workday before the holiday because that workday fell on his Sabbath); Kentile Floors, 66 LA 933, 935 (Larkin, 1976) (employee who was also a minister was discharged for unauthorized absence from job while attending a religious conference; upholding the discharge, the arbitrator stated that his role was to administer the agreement rather than the statute, but he did point out that "the grievant was not asking for time off to attend religious services," the purpose of the conference being to raise funds for a church-affiliated college); Walker Mfg. Co., 60 LA 525, 531–33 (Simon, 1973) (the arbitrator stated that his role was only to interpret the agreement, but he did find that the employer had "tried to accommodate the employee's request but could not do so").

[488]Cleveland, Ohio, Pub. Library, 105 LA 781 (Smith, 1995).

[489]U.S. Playing Card Co., 87 LA 937 (Duda, Jr., 1986).

[490]United Parcel Serv., 103 LA 1143 (Winograd, 1994).

A special problem arises when an employee is asked to perform work offensive to his religion beliefs. An employer was deemed to have failed to reasonably accommodate an employee's religious beliefs under Title VII by requiring the objecting employee to erect a Christmas tree despite the fact that other employees could have been used to complete the task at the same cost.[491]

Where no accommodation is available that would prevent undue hardship on an employer's business, the employer is not required to compromise its ability to get work done. Thus, an employer may not be compelled to obtain replacements at premium rates in order to accommodate an employee who wanted Sundays off for religious reasons.[492]

The issue of whether an offered accommodation is reasonable is reached only after determining that the employee's position was truly based upon a religious requirement. A Jehovah's Witness who refused to sell lottery tickets was found to be motivated by a sincerely held religious conviction and not merely a personal philosophical preference, despite the fact that another Jehovah's Witness in the same workplace had agreed to sell the ticket while maintaining his religious faith.[493] However, a Catholic employee who refused to work on Good Friday was properly subject to disciplinary penalties, because neither attendance at religious services nor avoidance of work on Good Friday was found to be a religious obligation. The arbitrator held that the grievant's decision to attend services was a matter of religious preference rather than an obligation.[494]

Similarly, the grievance of an employee who had been discharged for living in her husband's residence outside the city limits in violation of a city college's stated policy was denied because the employee had presented no evidence that her religion required her to cohabit with her husband.[495] But, assuming the validity of the claimed religious requirement, employers are not bound to accept the employee's choice of accommodation.[496]

Arbitrators have disapproved of disparate enforcement of employer prohibitions of religious signs. One arbitrator found that the employer violated

---

[491]Clallam County, Wash., Pub. Hosp. Dist. 1, 105 LA 609 (Calhoun, 1995).

[492]Goodyear Tire & Rubber Co., 107 LA 193 (Sergent, 1996). *See also* United Parcel Serv., 103 LA 1143 (Winograd, 1994).

[493]Lucky Stores, 88 LA 841 (Gentile, 1987). In this case, testimony was received from an elder in grievant's congregation indicating that selling lottery tickets was not clearly prohibited by their religion. Many parts of scripture could be consulted by an individual seeking guidance. In the final analysis, however, a person's choice of action would have to be based upon his or her "God-given conscience," and two Jehovah's Witnesses may reach different decisions regarding the moral correctness of selling lottery tickets. The arbitrator, in deciding not to become an arbiter of varying scriptural interpretations, relied on *Thomas v. Review Board of the Indiana Employment Security Division*, 450 U.S. 707, 25 FEP Cases 629 (1981). The grievant's sincerity in her religious convictions was sufficient in this case.

[494]Bronx-Lebanon Hosp. Ctr., 90 LA 1216 (Babiskin, 1988).

[495]City Colls., 104 LA 86 (Eagle, 1995).

[496]Rodriguez v. City of Chicago, 156 F.3d 771, 77 FEP Cases 1421 (7th Cir. 1998) (police department's offer to allow officer to transfer to precinct that did not contain an abortion clinic was a reasonable accommodation, despite the fact that the officer preferred to stay in the same precinct and be permanently exempted from guarding an abortion clinic).

the contract in instructing an employee to remove a poster stating, "MES-SAGE FROM ALLAH—DON'T DO THE DEVIL'S WORK," while allowing another employee to leave a sign stating, "May God grant the serenity to accept the things I cannot change."[497]

Even sincere religious beliefs may not excuse actions damaging to the employer's interests. An arbitrator reinstated without back pay a grievant who had inserted religious tracts into random packages of the company's product; the reinstatement was contingent on the employee's agreement to reimburse the employer for the cost of finding and repackaging the altered product containers.[498]

One emerging issue is whether the employer is subject to liability for failure to prevent supervisors or coworkers from harassing an employee be-cause of his religious beliefs. In one arbitration, the grievant, a born-again Christian, had been exposed to scatological language regularly uttered by a coworker. Although he was especially sensitive to this foul language, he had not been singled out because of his religion, since the entire workforce had been similarly targeted.[499]

7. Protection Against Sexual Harassment

A. What Constitutes Sexual Harrassment in the Workplace
[LA CDI 100.552510; 118.640]

Preliminary understanding of what is or may be involved in "sexual ha-rassment" in the workplace is aided by a 1981 report prepared by the Merit Systems Protection Board (MSPB) at the request of Congress. The report was based on an extensive survey of the views of federal employees, along with an intensive study of literature and case law on the subject of sexual harassment.[500]

The MSPB survey of federal employees indicated general agreement by male and female respondents that the following behaviors, ranked in order of agreement, constitute sexual harassment: (1) letters, phone calls, or mate-rials of a sexual nature; (2) pressure for sexual favors; (3) touching, leaning over, cornering, or pinching; and, deemed less severe than the aforemen-tioned behaviors, (4) pressure for dates. But general agreement was not found concerning (5) sexually suggestive looks or gestures, or (6) sexual teasing, jokes, remarks, or questions. Concerning behaviors (5) and (6), the survey indicated that "men were less likely to think that 'sexual looks' and 'sexual comments,' the more ambiguous and prevalent forms of sexual behavior on the job, were sexual harassment, particularly when perpetrated by a co-worker." In the latter regard, "men and women were more likely to think

---

[497]Department of Labor, 96 LA 5 (Feigenbaum, 1990).
[498]Eureka Co., 93 LA 513 (Wolff, 1989).
[499]Champion Int'l Corp., 105 LA 429 (Fullmer, 1995).
[500]Merit Systems Protection Board, Sexual Harassment in the Federal Workplace: Is It a Problem? (1981).

that a behavior was sexual harassment if the perpetrator was a supervisor rather than a co-worker."[501]

Concerning the underlying nature of sexual harassment, the report found to be "valid under some circumstances" the view that "sexual harassment is a form of power that is exercised by those in control, usually men, over low-status employees, usually women" (referred to also in the report as an "abuse of power"). The report found similarly valid the view that "individuals with certain low-power characteristics, such as youth and low salaries, are more subject to sexual harassment than others." But the report rejected the view that "sexual harassment is an expression of personal attraction between men and women that is widespread and cannot and should not be stopped."[502] The MSPB report stated the belief, among other conclusions, that "sexual harassment is a problem encountered by a significant number of women," and that the "experience frequently has a negative emotional and physical effect on the victim and may diminish job performance."[503]

It is now established that under certain conditions sexual harassment constitutes a type of sex discrimination prohibited by Title VII of the Civil Rights Act of 1964. The Equal Employment Opportunity Commission[504] and the federal courts have recognized two distinct types of sexual harassment—

---

[501]*Id.* at 4. The report further states that writers and researchers seem to agree that "sexual harassment is nonreciprocal behavior and does not include mutually satisfactory, no-job-related-strings-attached relationships in the office." *Id.* at G-4. Also, regarding what does *not* constitute sexual harassment:

> A cause of action does not arise [under the Civil Rights Act] from an isolated incident or a mere flirtation. These may be more properly characterized as an attempt to establish personal relationships than an endeavor to tie employment to sexual submission. Title VII should not be interpreted as reaching into sexual relationships which may arise during the course of employment, but which do not have a substantial effect on that employment. In general, we would limit Title VII claims in this area, as suggested by one commentator, to "repeated, unwelcome sexual advances" which impact as a term or condition of employment.

Heelan v. Johns-Manville Corp., 451 F. Supp. 1382, 1388–89, 20 FEP Cases 251, 255 (D. Colo. 1978).

[502]MSPB REPORT, at 101.

[503]*Id.* at G-8 and G-9, where a portion of the Report's "Conclusion" states:

> What has been established is that sexual harassment is a problem encountered by a significant number of women. The most common forms of harassment are comments and nonverbal behaviors such as gesturing and touching; far less common are instances of attempted or actual rape or sexual assault. It is not uncommon for harassment to be in the form of demands tied to negative job consequences if rejected or to positive consequences if accepted.
>
> Victims often are young and working in low-status occupations, but it is clear that women of all ages, both married and unmarried and working at all levels in a range of jobs, experience harassment. Victims respond in a variety of ways, most often by ignoring the behavior, attempting to avoid the harasser, and/or asking the harasser to stop; some leave the situation altogether by transferring or quitting. Few victims report the incidents or file formal complaints; those who do get little help and sometimes suffer negative consequences as a result. The experience frequently has a negative emotional and physical effect on the victim and may diminish job performance.
>
> Little is known about the harassment of men or same-sex harassment. Nor is much known about the way different factors in the workplace influence the incidence and nature of harassment.

[504]In 1999, the EEOC rescinded that portion of its Guidelines on Sexual Harassment, which set forth the standard of employer liability for harassment by supervisors. That section (29 C.F.R. §1604.11(c)) was no longer valid in light of the Supreme Court decisions in

"quid pro quo" harassment and "hostile environment" harassment. The former occurs when an employment benefit or continuing employment is expressly or implicitly conditioned on an employee's acquiescence to the sexual advances or sexual conduct of another person, usually a supervisor or manager. Hostile-environment sexual harassment occurs when an employee is subjected to a pattern of unwelcome sexually related conduct in the workplace that interferes with an individual's work performance or creates a hostile, intimidating, or offensive work environment.[505]

i. Hostile Environment Harassment [LA CDI 100.552510; 118.640]

In *Meritor Savings Bank v. Vinson*,[506] the Supreme Court recognized the hostile-environment theory of sexual harassment. In that case, the Court held that Title VII protects employees from discriminatory intimidation, ridicule, and insult, even though such conduct does not result in any economic

---

Burlington Industries v. Ellerth, 524 U.S. 742, 77 FEP Cases 1 (1998), and *Faragher v. City of Boca Raton*, 524 U.S. 775, 77 FEP Cases 14 (1998). The EEOC has issued a policy document that examines the *Faragher* and *Ellerth* decisions and provides detailed guidance on the issue of vicarious liability for harassment by supervisors. EEOC Enforcement Guidance: Vicarious Employer Liability for Unlawful Harassment by Supervisors (6/18/99), EEOC Compliance Manual (BNA), N:4075 [Binder 3]; 45 Fed. Reg. 74677 (Nov. 10, 1980), as amended at 64 Fed. Reg. 58334 (Oct. 29, 1999).

[505]For cases illustrating the distinctions and requirements for establishing a Title VII violation of quid pro quo sexual harassment or hostile-environment sexual harassment, see *Jones v. Flagship Int'l*, 793 F.2d 714, 41 FEP Cases 358 (5th Cir. 1986) (sexual advances by a supervisor on three occasions and a sexually offensive decoration at an office party did not create a pervasive atmosphere of sexually hostile conduct); *Downes v. Federal Aviation Admin.*, 775 F.2d 288, 39 FEP Cases 70 (Fed. Cir. 1985) (sporadic instances of offensive behavior over a 3-year period did not constitute an illegal pattern of sexual harassment); *Henson v. City of Dundee*, 682 F.2d 897, 29 FEP Cases 787 (11th Cir. 1982) (court distinguished between quid pro quo sexual harassment and hostile-environment sexual harassment); *Broderick v. Ruder*, 685 F. Supp. 1269, 46 FEP Cases 1272 (D.D.C. 1988) (conduct of consensual sexual relationships between three male office managers and certain female employees, which resulted in promotions and benefits to females, constituted illegal sexually hostile environment although not involving plaintiff personally); *Priest v. Rotary*, 634 F. Supp. 571, 40 FEP Cases 208 (N.D. Cal. 1986) (conduct of male employer who grabbed a female employee, touched intimate parts of her body, tried to kiss her, rubbed his body against hers, picked her up, and carried her across the room constituted illegal sexual harassment).

For cases illustrating that illegal sexual harassment may be found where an employee is subjected to conduct creating a hostile working environment for the employee, see *Katz v. Dole*, 709 F.2d 251, 31 FEP Cases 1521 (4th Cir. 1983) (the Federal Aviation Administration was held responsible for the sexual harassment of a female air traffic controller who had been subjected to extremely vulgar and offensive sexually related epithets by fellow controllers and supervisory personnel); *Bundy v. Jackson*, 641 F.2d 934, 24 FEP Cases 1155 (D.C. Cir. 1981) (victim of sexual harassment did not have to prove that she resisted the harassment or that any resistance caused a loss or denial of tangible job benefits); *Continental Can Co. v. Minnesota*, 297 N.W.2d 241, 22 FEP Cases 1808 (Minn. 1980) (among other abuses, male coworkers had made sexually derogatory statements and verbal sexual advances to a female employee, a violation of the Minnesota Human Rights Act being found by application of principles developed under Title VII of the Civil Rights Act of 1964). In *Goodwin v. Circuit Court of St. Louis County, Mo.*, 729 F.2d 541, 34 FEP Cases 347 (8th Cir. 1984), a judge's derogatory statements about women in the workplace, *even if made in jest*, were weighty evidence in finding that a female hearing officer was discriminatorily transferred.

[506]477 U.S. 57, 40 FEP Cases 1822 (1986). *See* Monat & Gomez, *Sexual Harassment: The Impact of* Meritor Savings Bank v. Vinson *on Grievances and Arbitration Decisions*, 41 ARB. J. 24 (1986).

loss to the employee. The Court in *Meritor* did establish a two-part definition of what constitutes a hostile working environment. The complainant must show that the conduct was (1) sufficiently severe or pervasive to alter the conditions of the victim's employment and create an abusive working environment, and (2) unwelcome.[507]

In a unanimous decision, *Harris v. Forklift Systems,*[508] the Supreme Court determined that an employee claiming sexual harassment because of a hostile or abusive work environment need not show severe psychological injury to prevail. A discriminatory abusive work environment, even one that does not seriously affect an employee's psychological well-being or cause an injury, can detract from an employee's job performance. Even without regard to the tangible effect of impact on job performance, the very fact that the discriminatory conduct is so severe as to create an environment abusive to employees based on gender is contrary to the mandate of Title VII for workplace equality. The *Harris* case went beyond *Meritor* to further delineate the factors to be considered when determining if the environment is hostile or abusive:

> But we can say that whether an environment is "hostile" or "abusive" can be determined only by looking at all the circumstances. These may include the frequency of the discriminatory conduct; its severity; whether it is physically threatening or humiliating, or a mere offensive utterance; and whether it unreasonably interferes with an employee's work performance. The effect on the employee's psychological well-being is, of course, relevant to determining whether the plaintiff actually found the environment abusive. But while psychological harm, like any other relevant factor, may be taken into account, no single factor is required.[509]

In the context of a suit alleging male-upon-male sexual harassment, *Oncale v. Sundowner Offshore Services,*[510] a unanimous Supreme Court further defined the elements that, under an objective "reasonable person" standard,[511] make up a hostile work environment. The Court also made clear that Title VII is not a general civility code that seeks to regulate genuine, but innocuous, differences in the ways men and women routinely interact with members of the same sex and of the opposite sex. It forbids only behavior so objectively offensive as to alter the conditions of the victim's employment. "'Conduct that is not severe or pervasive enough to create an objectively hostile or abusive work environment—an environment that a reasonable person would find hostile or abusive—is beyond Title VII's purview.'"[512]

The opinion proceeded to caution that courts and juries should not mistake ordinary socializing in the workplace, such as male-on-male horseplay

---

[507]477 U.S. at 67–68.

[508]510 U.S. 17, 63 FEP Cases 225 (1993).

[509]*Id.* at 23.

[510]523 U.S. 75, 76 FEP Cases 221 (1998). Preceding the *Oncale* decision, an arbitrator held that male-on-male horseplay with sexual undertones violated the company's sexual harassment program. Coca-Cola Bottling Co. of N. Ohio, 106 LA 776 (Borland, 1996). See section 7.C., "Same-Sex Harassment," below.

[511]523 U.S. at 81 (the behavior is to be "judged from the perspective of a reasonable person in the plaintiff's position, considering 'all the circumstances'").

[512]*Id.* (quoting Harris v. Forklift Sys., 510 U.S. 17, 21, 63 FEP Cases 225 (1993)).

or intersexual flirtation, for discriminatory "conditions of employment." The Court cited the following example:

> A professional football player's working environment is not severely or pervasively abusive, for example, if the coach smacks him on the buttocks as he heads onto the field—even if the same behavior would reasonably be experienced as abusive by the coach's secretary (male or female) back at the office.[513]

The conduct, the Court continued, must be viewed not in a vacuum, but within "a constellation of surrounding circumstances, expectations, and relationships which are not fully captured by a simple recitation of the words used or the physical acts performed." Further, as one arbitrator trenchantly observed, it should be borne in mind that "sexual jokes, posters, propositions and the like that were loosely tolerated as the workplace norm twenty years ago are unacceptable and illegal today."[514]

For employment in the federal public sector, the Office of Personnel Management (OPM) issued a government-wide policy statement describing sexual harassment both as a prohibited personnel practice and as a form of employee misconduct.[515] Sexual harassment is equally subject to censure in state public-sector employment.[516]

ii. *Distinguishing Between Acceptable and Inappropriate Conduct* [LA CDI 100.552510; 118.640]

The line between acceptable conduct and unacceptable sexual harassment can be a very fine one. Employees spend a great deal of their daily time in the company of other employees. It is inevitable that propinquity between employees can lead to the development of various types of social relationships. How one manifests inappropriate conduct, considering such a relationship, is not subject to easy definition.

One arbitrator attempted the line-drawing task by establishing some specific rules:

---

[513]*Id.*

[514]International Mill Serv., 104 LA 779, 782 (Marino, 1995).

[515]Merit Systems Protection Board, Sexual Harassment in the Federal Workplace: Is It a Problem?, at F-1 (1981), which (1) defined sexual harassment as "deliberate or repeated unsolicited verbal comments, gestures, or physical contact of a sexual nature which are unwelcome," and (2) declared that "sexual harassment is unacceptable conduct in the workplace and will not be condoned." In *U.S. Army Signal Center*, 78 LA 120, 128 (Hall, 1982), the arbitrator declared that "[s]exual harassment should not be tolerated any place"; in this case the arbitrator upheld the discipline of a male instructor who was charged by female soldiers with touching their breasts in a manner that each thought to be more than accidental while giving instructions.

[516]*See, e.g.*, University of Mo. Health Sciences Ctr., 78 LA 417, 423–24 (Yarowsky, 1982) (upholding discharge of supervisor for putting his arm around the waist of one female employee, looking and smacking his lips and commenting on the attractiveness of a second employee, and casting penetrating looks at a third employee to the point that the employee imagined herself "undressed"; the supervisor's conduct created stress and anxiety among the female employees that affected their mental health and interfered with their job performance).

It is friendly to tell a co-worker that she looks particularly pretty this morning. It is unacceptable to tell a co-worker who is not a personal friend that you are attracted to her. It is unavoidable and healthy that one's eyes should be drawn to a sexually attractive person. It is unacceptable to deliberately stare to the point which the other persons feels uncomfortable.[517]

When one party to a relationship ends that relationship, sexually oriented conduct that had been consensual in the past is no longer consensual, and, if continued over objection, may constitute sexual harassment.[518] But not all harassment of an employee of the opposite sex constitutes "sexual harassment." In one case following the break-up of a consensual social relationship, the rejected employee made a series of "hang-up" phone calls to the rejecting employee. The arbitrator refused to uphold a charge of sexual harassment.[519]

After another such break-up, a female employee became uncomfortable working with her former boyfriend, and the company determined that they could no longer work together. Both were said to have been at fault for the deterioration of requisite workplace civility and cooperation. The female employee was removed from her classification and shift with adverse financial consequences. The union complained that even if the company was correct, it acted improperly, since, if there was equal fault, there should have been equal treatment. The company replied that, as a matter of past practice, it had handled shift and classification removals based on seniority and pointed out that the female worker was the junior of the two employees. The arbitrator found the agreement could not be interpreted to allow removal of the complainant and that the past practice was inapplicable since the prior transfers were not occasioned by charges of sexual harassment. Accordingly, the grievant was ordered reinstated to her former shift and classification.[520] The arbitrator observed:

> Whether sexual harassment complaints have merit or not, it is important that the complainant be protected from retaliation. Otherwise legitimate complaints will remain buried because the complainants will be afraid to come forward. Also, rightly or wrongly, there is a perception in some circles that women are frequently penalized for making complaints of sexual harassment.[521]

Prior to the reasonable person standard announced by the Supreme Court in *Oncale* to measure whether workplace behavior created a hostile work environment, a diversity of standards had been fashioned by arbitrators and the courts to determine whether contested conduct amounted to sexual harassment. Many arbitrators endorsed the U.S. Court of Appeals for the Ninth Circuit's "reasonable woman" test set forth in *Ellison v. Brady.*[522] Others adopted a subjective criterion such as the "most sensitive woman." These decisions should now be reassessed in light of the *Oncale* opinion.

---

[517]Norfolk Naval Shipyard, 104 LA 991, 992 (Bernhardt, 1995).
[518]Hughes Family Mkts., 107 LA 331 (Prayzich, 1996).
[519]City of Austin, Minn., 95-1 ARB ¶5082 (Fogelberg, 1994).
[520]Champion Int'l Corp., 105 LA 429 (Fullmer, 1995).
[521]*Id.* at 434.
[522]974 F.2d 812, 55 FEP Cases 111 (9th Cir. 1991).

Those arbitrators who have endorsed the *Ellison* rationale have emphasized that the test "what is offensive to the reasonable woman" is appropriate because men and women perceive shop talk differently.[523] In one such case, after investigating a noninvolved employee's tip, a company discharged a male Spanish-speaking, newly hired employee for making lewd remarks about female coworkers' body parts and inquiring about their sexual activities. However, he had gone out of his way to be helpful to these employees by carrying heavy boxes for them, and several of the women claimed not to be offended by his behavior. Adopting the reasonable woman standard because the sex-blind reasonable-person standard tends to be male-biased, the arbitrator selected one of the female witnesses who he concluded was a "reasonable target" of such conduct as the most credible.[524] The arbitrator opined that the allegations of sexual harassment were to be judged from the perspective of this alleged victim. Since this reasonable target had failed to report the employee and testified that she did not feel the grievant "had crossed the line," and considering the grievant's overall helpful behavior to female employees, the arbitrator ordered the grievant to be reinstated, but without back pay.[525]

Some arbitrators look to the other end of the spectrum and base their determination whether an employee had engaged in sexual harassment upon the reactions of the most sensitive of the affected employees. Thus, in one situation a male employee told "dirty" sexual jokes, showed sexually suggestive cartoons, and simulated a penis with a broom handle to other male employees. Most employees, including female employees, did not find this conduct offensive, but two young women found his actions shocking. Applying a "sexual harassment is in the eyes of the beholder standard," the arbitrator condemned the conduct.[526]

However, often the conduct that was found to have constituted sexual harassment under one standard would be condemned under any standard.[527]

---

[523]As one arbitrator stated:

Sexual harassment issues often turn on the context of words and conduct. The same words and conduct that can be perceived as innocent and friendly in one context, can be perceived as predatory and threatening in another, and of course, this often occurs in "shop talk" cases and in cases of insubordination. It must be understood that men and women are socialized differently. They use language differently, interpret verbal and physical symbols differently, and use and respond to humor differently.

International Mill Serv., 104 LA 779, 781–82 (Marino, 1995).

[524]T.J. Maxx, 107 LA 78 (Richman, 1996) (summarizing workplace conduct and appropriate discipline).

[525]*Id.* at 83.

[526]Safeway, Inc., 108 LA 787 (Staudohar, 1997). It is of interest that, following grievant's discharge, 23 employees wrote letters of protest to the employer, 17 of those employees being female. It was conceded that grievant had not solicited the letters.

[527]In *International Mill Service*, 104 LA 779 (Marino, 1995), the arbitrator upheld the discipline of a male employee who had repeatedly asked the female victim to go to bed with him, promised her a good time if she slept with him, asked her to take off her clothes and roll around on the floor with him, and touched her legs and buttocks with his hands, books, and pieces of construction material. Although this conduct was judged under the "reasonable woman" standard, the conduct would likely be found sanctionable under the "reasonable person" test.

Thus, one arbitrator rejected the defense of a disciplined employee that he did not know that his behavior was actionable, ruling that the grievant should have known.[528] Sexually offensive conduct can be so egregious that arbitrators uphold the sanction without specifying either the standard of review or the burden of proof.[529] In one case, where the grievant was discharged for threatening a coworker with bodily harm, allegations of sexual harassment were successfully used as a defense.[530]

iii. Burden of Proof [LA CDI 94.60509; 100.0775]

The growing body of reported arbitration decisions involving sexual harassment reflect numerous important substantive and evidentiary issues that remain to be resolved.[531] First, the burden of proof placed on an employer who has discharged an employee for sexual harassment is unclear. Some arbitrators treat cases involving discipline for sexual harassment in similar fashion to any other case involving discipline for misconduct and, often without specifically mentioning a burden of proof, appear to require the employer to establish sexual harassment by a preponderance of the evidence.[532] However, other arbitrators have stated that an employer must prove that the disciplined employee engaged in sexual harassment by "clear and convincing evidence."[533] Finally, some arbitrators require that an employer prove "beyond a reasonable doubt" that the grievant engaged in sexual harassment.[534] In justifying this stricter standard, one arbitrator stated:

---

[528]Potlatch Corp., 104 LA 691 (Moore, 1995).

[529]AMG Indus., 106 LA 322 (Donnelly, 1996) (after an argument between two employees, a male employee turned on the plant intercom system and directed a message to the victim— "suck me!"); International Extrusion Corp., 106 LA 371 (Brisco, 1996) (grievant told a female coworker that she had such nice buttocks and she should give some to other female employees who did not have enough, and he found her so exciting that he had to go to the bathroom to masturbate); Simkins Indus., 106 LA 551 (Fullmer, 1996) (grievant's conduct included patting female employee on the buttocks while saying "I need a good dirty woman for Saturday night—I'd pay ten dollars for it," making tongue displays, thrusting hips, looking down her shirt, rubbing his fingers up her back, and using words and actions of similar nature).

[530]United Indus., 88 LA 547 (Baron, 1986) (arbitrator determined that grievant had made threat because he was upset about his marital troubles and because threatened coemployee had repeatedly provoked him by engaging in conduct amounting to sexual harassment, including making lewd remarks and gestures implying that grievant was a homosexual). *See also* EZ Communications, 91 LA 1097 (Talarico, 1988) (female radio newscaster terminated for flagrant neglect of duty after walking off job successfully proved that 2-year campaign of outrageous, lewd on-air remarks directed at her constituted hostile work environment that justified her actions).

[531]*See* Monat & Gomez, *Decisional Standards Used by Arbitrators in Sexual Harassment Cases*, 37 Lab. L.J. 712 (1986); Nelson, *Sexual Harassment, Title VII, and Labor Arbitration*, 40 Arb. J. 55 (1985).

[532]Superior Coffee & Foods, 103 LA 609 (Alleyne, 1994); Heublein, Inc., 88 LA 1292 (Ellmann, 1987); Porter Equip. Co., 86 LA 1253 (Lieberman, 1986); New Indus. Techniques, 84 LA 915 (Gray, 1985); Veterans Admin. Med. Ctr., 82 LA 25 (Dallas, 1984). For a case in which preponderance of evidence is mentioned as a standard, see *Veterans Admin. Med. Ctr.*, 87 LA 405 (Yarowsky, 1986).

[533]GTE Fla., 92 LA 1090 (Cohen, 1989); Clover Park Sch. Dist., Tacoma, Wash., 89 LA 76 (Boedecker, 1987); Sugardale Foods, 86 LA 1017, 1020 (Duda, Jr., 1986); Washington Scientific Indus., 83 LA 824, 828 (Kapsch, 1984).

[534]Defense Logistics Agency, 91 LA 1391 (Duda, Jr., 1989); King Soopers, 86 LA 254, 258 (Sass, 1985); Hyatt Hotels Palo Alto, Cal., 85 LA 11, 15 (Oestreich, 1985).

The charge of sexual harassment clearly involves an accusation of moral turpitude. . . . The charges . . . also carry enormous social stigma. . . . [I]t is not overly dramatic to say, as another witness said, that the Grievant's very life is on the line. All that he is: his marriage, his relationship with his children . . . ; his standing in the community; his relationships with other employees—all of this is on the line. In such case, the company has the burden of proving, *beyond a reasonable doubt*, that the Grievant is guilty of the conduct he is charged with. Once this is done, the company still must establish that the conduct provides just and sufficient cause for the discipline that is imposed in the case.[535]

iv. Penalties [LA CDI 100.552510; 118.640]

Once sexual harassment has been established, an arbitrator must still consider the seriousness of the sexual harassment and the propriety of the penalty imposed by the employer.

Many arbitrators have upheld discharge or discipline as assessed by the employer against employees for behavior that constitutes sexual harassment under the standards noted above.[536] In other cases, misconduct in the form of

---

[535]King Soopers, Inc., 86 LA 254, 258 (Sass, 1985).

[536]For cases upholding discharge, see *Container Corp. of Am.*, 100 LA 568 (Byars, 1993) (employee addressed abusive language to one female coworker and touched another in a manner that made her uncomfortable and afraid); *Plain Dealer Publ'g Co.*, 99 LA 969 (Fullmer, 1992) (manager sexually harassed married gas station clerk); *Central Mich. Univ.*, 99 LA 134, 140–43 (McDonald, 1992) (custodian sexually harassed two female students on several occasions, including trapping one student in a women's restroom with him and refusing to let her out); *McDonnell Douglas Corp.*, 94 LA 585 (Woolf, 1989) (male employee disobeyed manager's order to avoid work area of female coworker with whom he had been ordered to have no contact inside or outside plant); *Flexsteel Indus.*, 94 LA 497 (Briggs, 1990) (grievant referred to female coworker in lewd, sexually demeaning terms); *Hannaford Bros.*, 93 LA 721 (Chandler, 1989) (grievant harassed coworkers by name-calling, military and ethnic slurs, ridicule, obscene gestures, and comments regarding sexual preference); *Can-Tex Indus.*, 90 LA 1230 (Shearer, 1988) (grievant persistently made crude advances to female coworker and frequently grabbed at her breasts); *Tampa Elec. Co.*, 88 LA 791 (Vause, 1986) (grievant used crude, explicit language in describing to married female coworker his sexual fantasies about her despite her, rejection of his advances in the past); *Porter Equip. Co.*, 86 LA 1253 (Lieberman, 1986) (grievant pulled the hand of a female coworker and forced her to touch his exposed sex organ; evidence established that coworker suffered an intense emotional reaction); *Rockwell Int'l Corp.*, 85 LA 246 (Feldman, 1985) (grievant touched the bodies of three female coworkers without any authorization and used body language that made them uncomfortable); *Nabisco Foods Co.*, 82 LA 1186 (Allen, Jr., 1984) (grievant made sexual propositions and engaged in other forms of customer abuse for several years at retail stores in many locations to which he delivered company products, in spite of repeated warnings about such behavior); *United Elec. Supply Co.*, 82 LA 921, 922–23, 925 (Madden, 1984) (male employee with poor work record made persistent and continued advances to several female coworkers, creating offensive working environment and causing loss of work time in their efforts to avoid him); *Zia Co.*, 82 LA 640, 641–42 (Daughton, 1984) (grabbing, hugging, and kissing coworker on three separate occasions; the grievant had an unblemished work record, but he knew prior to engaging in this behavior that company policy did not tolerate sexual harassment); *Borg-Warner Corp.*, 78 LA 985, 998–99 (Neas, 1982) (calling female supervisor an obscene name and making obscene gesture toward her; grievant had a poor disciplinary record and he had failed to respond to corrective discipline); *Anaconda Copper Co.*, 78 LA 690, 694–96 (Cohen, 1982) (grievant relentlessly harassed female coworker about twice his age through obscene gestures and demeaning slurs); *St. Regis Paper Co.*, 74 LA 1281, 1282–84 (Kaufman, 1980) (threat to rape coworker; there had been prior incidents involving physical touching of females by grievant and his record afforded "virtually no mitigating factors"); *CPC Int'l*, 62 LA 1272, 1272, 1274 (Larkin, 1974) (grievant made sexual advances to co-employee in elevator on 2 successive days, and he was guilty of similar conduct toward another female employee on a previous occasion). For cases upholding a lesser penalty as assessed by the employer, see *Social Sec. Admin.*, 81 LA 459, 460 (Cox, 1983) (grievant boasted

sexual harassment was found but the penalty was reduced by the arbitrator on the basis of mitigating factors or as having been excessive under the circumstances of the offense.[537] In still other cases, the employer failed to carry the burden of proof, and no penalty was permitted against the employee charged with sexual harassment.[538]

---

to coworker of having touched the coworker's girlfriend, another coworker, on the breast and rump); *Fisher Foods*, 80 LA 133, 134–35 (Abrams, 1983) (breast-touching incident); *Monsanto Chem. Intermediates Co.*, 75 LA 592, 596 (Penefield, 1980) (physical restraint of female employee by grievants). Discharge for sexual harassment of customers also has been upheld. *See* United Parcel Serv., 104 LA 417 (Byars, 1995) (employee told dirty jokes and made lewd remarks to customers); Pepsi Cola Bottling Co. of St. Louis 108 LA 993 (Thornell, 1997) (a customer's employee was sexually harassed by the grievant); Nabisco Foods Co., 82 LA 1186, 1191–92 (Allen, Jr., 1984) (citing other cases also upholding discharge for such misconduct). For further research on sexual harassment in the arbitration context, see Crow & Koen, *Sexual Harassment: New Challenges for Labor Arbitrators?*, 47 ARB. J. 6 (Dec. 1992); Meredith, *Using Fact Finders to Probe Workplace Claims of Sexual Harassment*, 47 ARB. J. 61 (Dec. 1992); Nowlin, *Sexual Harassment in the Workplace: How Arbitrators Rule*, 43 ARB. J. 31 (Dec. 1988).

[537]For cases holding discharge or discipline inappropriate or too severe, see: *Ralphs Grocery Co.*, 100 LA 63 (Kaufman, 1992) (reference to one female employee's nipples and forceful tugging at sweatpants of another); *Honeywell, Inc.*, 95 LA 1097 (Gallagher, 1990) (discharge reduced to suspension for continued harassment of two female guards after warnings, where he gave a "spontaneous birthday kiss" on one female guard's cheek); *Dow Chem. Co.*, 95 LA 510 (Sartain, 1990) (discharge too severe for black male employee despite proof that he sexually harassed three female coworkers after being warned, where later misconduct was limited to kidding with sexual innuendo and second warning letter did not constitute clear and forceful "final warning"); *County of Oakland, Mich.*, 94 LA 451 (Daniel, 1990) (no sexual harassment or discrimination where grievant, female booking clerk in a jail, was frequently exposed to male nudity and obscene gestures by inmates since jail cells had been relocated due to state requirement for continued observation of inmates); *GTE Fla.*, 92 LA 1090 (Cohen, 1989) (discharge too severe for male employee who physically removed female employee of subcontractor from a ladder, bent her backwards over a desk, and put his face near the woman's neck in a nuzzling fashion); *Boys Mkts.*, 88 LA 1304 (Wilmoth, 1987) (discharge too severe for employee who allegedly moved his finger in upward movement between buttocks of female coworker, since "mainstream of arbitral thinking" calls for a less severe penalty); *Sugardale Foods*, 86 LA 1017 (Duda, Jr., 1986) (discharge reduced to long-term suspension where grievant hovered around a female coemployee for 10 minutes in a semidark room, briefly touched employee, and obviously made her uncomfortable and nervous; discipline reduced where employee handbook did not address sexual harassment specifically); *County of Ramsey, Minn.*, 86 LA 249 (Gallagher, 1986) (discharge of guidance counselor for sexual comments to client was too severe because lesser discipline than discharge is sufficient to prevent repetition of conduct); *Hyatt Hotels Palo Alto*, 85 LA 11 (Oestreich, 1985) (discharge of employee for exposing himself to female coemployee during working hours reduced to 15-day suspension where employer failed to show that grievant could not be rehabilitated, grievant was not coemployee's supervisor, grievant received no warning about likely consequences of his misconduct, and employer did not have clear sexual harassment policy that had been reasonably disseminated); *Meijer, Inc.*, 83 LA 570 (Ellmann, 1984) (penalty of discharge was too severe for employee who admittedly embraced fellow employee and gave "little bit of a hump motion," where incident may have been provoked by fellow employee and grievant had a good work record); *Dayton Power & Light Co.*, 80 LA 19, 21–22 (Heinsz, 1982) (incident involving touching of breast and making kissing sounds; discharge reduced to 7-month suspension); *Consolidation Coal Co.*, 79 LA 940, 942–43 (Stoltenberg, 1982) (entering women's bathhouse; discharge reduced to 60-day suspension without accrual of seniority); *Perfection Am. Co.*, 73 LA 520, 522 (Flannagan, 1979) (entering women's restroom; discharge was too severe for the offense and was reduced to suspension for period from discharge until reinstatement); *Powermatic Houdaille*, 71 LA 54, 56 (Cocalis, 1978) (sexually offensive words and gesture; discharge reduced to suspension for period from discharge until reinstatement).

[538]*See* Devry Inst. of Tech., 87 LA 1149 (Berman, 1986) (grievant improperly terminated for alleged sexual harassment that took place before he received a written warning after a prior offense that subsequent substantiated allegations of sexual harassment would result in discharge); Kidde, Inc., 86 LA 681 (Dunn, 1985) (grievant improperly suspended without

In reviewing whether the degree of discipline imposed under the "just cause" standard is excessive, some arbitrators compare sexual harassment with criminal offenses, noting that such behavior should be considered in the nature of a misdemeanor rather than a felony.[539]

One arbitrator has adopted five areas of inquiry in evaluating this issue:

(1) Did the employer have a sexual harassment policy at the time the incident(s) occurred? Was it written? Was it specific enough to make employees understand what constitutes sexual harassment and what the consequences of the infractions of this policy would be? Was the sexual harassment policy adequately disseminated to employees?

(2) Does the employer have an effective vehicle for employees to bring complaints of sexual harassment to the attention of management? Is the work environment such that it discourages employees from making formal or informal complaints?

(3) Did management know, or should it have known, of the sexual harassment practice(s) that occurred?

(4) Was the sexual harassment committed by a supervisor of the harassed employee or a person on whom the employee was dependent for employment, work assignment, promotion, performance ratings, and/or salary increases?

(5) What is the *personal* relationship between the person accused of sexual harassment and the person(s) considered to be the "victim(s)"?[540]

A unique evidentiary question that has arisen in arbitrations involving employees disciplined for conduct constituting sexual harassment is the relevance of allegations of past sexual harassment by the grievant against other individuals. Such evidence has been considered relevant by one arbitrator to the extent that the prior conduct established a pattern of conduct that was consistent with the accusations of the current sexual harassment victim.[541] However, in another case, an arbitrator found that the employer had improperly considered prior incidents of alleged sexual harassment in determining that the grievant was guilty of the current charges.[542]

In a "reverse discipline" case, an arbitrator held that an employee was improperly suspended for allegedly making a false claim of sexual harass-

---

adequate notice and without any opportunity to defend himself); King Soopers, 86 LA 254 (Sass, 1985); Washington Scientific Indus., 83 LA 824 (Kapsch, 1984) (grievant improperly discharged for telling a female coemployee whom he perceived as being "down" that he did not think that she would even enjoy sex; grievant's comment was neither obscene nor abusive in the context in which it was uttered); Louisville Gas & Elec. Co., 81 LA 730, 733 (Stonehouse, 1983); Godchaux-Henderson Sugar Co., 75 LA 377, 380 (Barnhart, 1980). For further research on the issue of burdens of proof, see Kelly, *The Burden of Proof in Criminal Cases of "Moral Turpitude Cases,"* 46 Arb. J. 45 (1991); Sinicropi, *Remedies and Arbitration Decision Making: Responses to Change*, 42 Lab. L.J. 545 (1991).

[539]Safeway Inc., 109 LA 768, 774 (DiFalco, 1997) (Sexual harassment is not as serious misconduct as workplace violence or theft, and a "zero tolerance program" does not mandate discharge. "It is generally considered that sexual harassment is a learned behavior of varying degrees of seriousness, and it can be unlearned through the appropriate imposition of sanctions to correct that behavior, at least in most instances." Hence, a discharge was reduced to a suspension without pay.). For a similar comparison to "major and minor crimes," see *Firestone Synthetic Rubber & Latex Co.*, 107 LA 276 (Koenig, Jr., 1996).

[540]Hyatt Hotels Palo Alto, 85 LA 11, 15 (Oestreich, 1985) (emphasis in original). *See also* GTE Fla., 92 LA 1090 (Cohen, 1989); Ohio Dep't of Transp., 90 LA 783 (Duda, Jr., 1988).

[541]King Soopers, 86 LA 254, 255 (Sass, 1985).

[542]Kidde, Inc., 86 LA 681, 683 (Dunn, 1985).

ment by a coworker, where the grievant, who previously had been raped, may have exaggerated one claim and inaccurately stated the other but did not intentionally mean to deceive or defraud.[543] In another case, an arbitrator upheld a female employee's suspension for falsely accusing a male of sexual harassment.[544]

B. Harassment in Schools [LA CDI 100.552510]

Because teachers are in an authority position with respect to their students, charges of sexual harassment of juveniles typically result in high-profile publicity. However, even if the evidence confirms that the complained-of conduct actually occurred, it may not constitute sexual harassment.[545] For example, a student, citing four incidents, reported that she was being sexually harassed by her teacher. First, in a conversation with the student, the teacher indicated he would assist her if she did something for him. The student asked him what he meant, and he answered, "I don't know, but I'll think of something."[546] Although the teacher stated it was an innocent remark, the student inferred that his comment contained a sexual innuendo. The second episode took place in front of 30 other students and involved the teacher's embracing the student and rubbing her arm. The teacher asserted he did so only to stop the student from braiding another's hair, behavior that the teacher considered inappropriate in the classroom. The third incident consisted of the teacher's grabbing the student's bag after she boarded a city bus. The teacher averred he did so only to get her attention so that he could greet her. In the fourth encounter, the teacher stopped by the student's father's car, in which she was a passenger, and stared inside as they drove away. The teacher maintained that he thought he recognized the passenger as a student and simply wanted to see who it was.

Noting that the incidents in the bus and automobile were devoid of sexual connotations, the arbitrator concluded that sexual harassment requires more than feeling "uncomfortable" in encounters with a male teacher.[547] Nevertheless, the arbitrator found that the teacher's initial verbal offer of assistance amounted to an inappropriate double-entendre. Consequently, his discharge was reduced to a suspension.

Under similarly ambiguous circumstances, a teacher who asked a student to get up on her desk and perform in her cheerleading outfit to gain the attention of the class may have engaged in "advertising through sex appeal," but his conduct, according to an arbitrator, was not necessarily improper. However, he went too far in making comments admittedly containing "sexual innuendos." Nonetheless, citing the absence of an applicable school district policy concerning such behavior, the arbitrator reduced the teacher's disciplinary suspension to a warning.[548]

---

[543]Department of Defense, 92 LA 653 (Cohen, 1989).
[544]City of Forth Worth, Tex., 114 LA 440 (Moore, 2000).
[545]District of Columbia Pub. Sch., 105 LA 1037 (Johnson, 1995).
[546]*Id.* at 1038–39.
[547]*Id.* at 1040.
[548]Fairfield City Sch. Dist. of Butler County, Ohio, 107 LA 669 (Duff, 1996).

C. Same-Sex Harassment [LA CDI 100.552510; 118.640]

The Supreme Court, in *Oncale v. Sundowner Offshore Service, Inc.*,[549] held that "same-sex" harassment is a cognizable violation of Title VII. Several arbitrators similarly have viewed such misconduct as embraced within a contractual anti-sexual harassment policy.

In one such case, a new employee was pretentiously called into an office, where the door was closed and lights turned off. He was then assaulted by a pair of coworkers who tugged at his shorts and encouraged each other to "get him." The perpetrators initially were discharged, but an arbitrator ordered them reinstated without back pay, finding, as mitigating circumstances, the fact that there was no actual sexual act and no intent to cause physical injury, but only "horseplay," which had been tolerated in the past by management.[550]

Another company's sexual harassment policy stated in part:

> Unwelcome sexual advances, requests for sexual favors, and other physical, verbal, or visual conduct based on sex constitutes sexual harassment when . . . the conduct has the purpose or effect of unreasonably interfering with an individual's work performance or creating an intimidating, hostile, or offensive environment.

Interpreting this policy, an arbitrator found just cause to discharge a gay employee who repeatedly related in explicit detail his sexual experiences to other male employees, after being told that his coworkers found his remarks offensive. The arbitrator rejected the grievant's claim that he was being discriminated against on account of his sexual orientation.[551]

8. Fraternization, Intermarriage of Employees, Employment of Relatives, Married Employees [LA CDI 100.15; 118.656]

Management sometimes promulgates rules prohibiting fraternization among its employees, intermarriage of employees, employment of relatives of its employees, and employment after marriage of certain employees. Arbitrators appear to subject such rules to close scrutiny, but uphold them when justification is shown.[552]

---

[549]523 U.S. 75, 76 FEP Cases 221 (1998).

[550]Coca-Cola Bottling Co. of N. Ohio, 106 LA 776 (Borland, 1996).

[551]Hughes Aircraft Co., 102 LA 353 (Bickner, 1993).

[552]Regarding federal employment, 5 U.S.C. §7202(a) authorizes the President to "[p]rescribe rules which shall prohibit, *as nearly as conditions of good administration warrant*, discrimination because of marital status" in federal employment (emphasis added). The ambivalence with which Congress thus approached the matter of "marital status" discrimination often may be equaled by that of arbitrators called upon to decide private-sector cases involving intermarriage of employees, employment of relatives, and the like, since arbitrators also recognize that company rules on such matters hold the potential both for good and for bad. The body of court decisions and statutory law, both federal and state, bearing on these types of matters appears to be fairly extensive but also fairly fragmented. *See* Edelman, *Marital Status Discrimination: A Survey of Federal Case Law*, 85 W. Va. L. Rev. 347 (1983); Wexler, *Husbands and Wives: The Uneasy Case for Antinepotism Rules*, 62 B.U. L. Rev. 75 (1982); Kovarsky & Hauck, *The No-Spouse Rule, Title VII, and Arbitration*, 32 Lab. L.J. 366 (1981).

Fraternization between an employee and his or her supervisor may have a serious adverse effect on the morale within the workforce if it gives rise to the belief that the employee is being accorded preferential treatment. It also creates a risk that a claim of sexual harassment may be made if the relationship should end. Fraternization that involves a sexual relationship during work hours may afford grounds for discharge.[553] However, preferential treatment based on a consensual relationship between a supervisor and employee does not constitute a cognizable sex discrimination cause of action under Title VII.[554]

In one case, a company promulgated a rule prohibiting male and female employees from fraternizing after a "love triangle" of employees ended in a shooting incident. Upholding the discharge of an employee who likewise became involved in a love triangle situation, the arbitrator held that the rule was reasonable under the facts.[555] Similarly, discipline was upheld when an airline pilot violated a rule prohibiting dating between male crew members and hostesses, the arbitrator stating that the company has a right to establish and enforce regulations prohibiting practices "which could reasonably result in detriment, damage, and even disaster" in the areas of safety and comfort of passengers in flight, the company's good name, and the reputation of its hostesses.[556]

However, anti-fraternization work rules may be unenforceable if the subject employees are married. Marital status has been accorded varying degrees of protection by legislation in 31 states.[557] The California statute, for example, places marital status in the same protected category as race, religious creed, color, national origin, ancestry, physical disability, mental disability, medical condition, and gender. However, the statute specifically permits employers to reasonably regulate or preclude the assignment of spouses to the same department, division, or facility for reasons of supervision, safety, security, or morale.[558]

A contractual provision prohibiting discrimination based on marital status was not violated by a school district's failure to coordinate the benefits of a married couple who had chosen the same health insurance plan.[559] Similarly, cohabiting couples may not be eligible for spousal benefits provided for under a collective bargaining agreement. In one case, an arbitrator de-

---

[553]Wyndham Franklin Plaza Hotel, 105 LA 186 (Duff, 1995) (employee and her supervisor locked themselves into the banquet office of the headquarters of a hotel during a business conference and proceeded to engage in passionate sexual congress recorded by security cameras).

[554]Womack v. Runyon, 147 F.3d 1298, 77 FEP Cases 769 (11th Cir. 1998).

[555]Alterman Foods, 45 LA 459, 460–61 (Woodruff, 1965).

[556]Braniff Airways, 29 LA 487, 489 (Yeager, 1957). *See also* City of Duncanville, Tex., 100 LA 795 (Allen, Jr., 1993).

[557]FEP MAN. §451:55 (BNA).

[558]CAL. GOV'T CODE §12940(a)(3)(A) (Lexis 2003)

[559]Elgin Sch. Dist. U-46, 104 LA 405 (Briggs, 1995).

clined to include live-in persons as relatives under the collective bargaining agreement.[560]

As to a company nepotism policy against hiring or continuing the employment of relatives, it has been held that, in the absence of special circumstances or a showing that intermarriage of employees created a particular problem or had an adverse effect on the operation of the plant, a rule requiring the resignation or termination of one of the employees could not stand.[561] But another arbitrator upheld a company policy not to hire the spouse of an incumbent employee (male or female); in the interest of a harmonious working relationship in the bargaining unit and to maintain order and efficiency

---

[560]City of McAlestar, Okla., 114 LA 1180, 1184 (Crow, 2000) (the grievant's testimony under oath "with a straight face that the woman who has lived with him for years," slept with him, "borne him a son, and who continues to live" with him "is neither his legal nor his common law wife or spouse," juxtaposed with his simultaneous claim that she is in fact his relative under the contract, amounts to a "Kafka-like absurdity").

[561]Hayes Indus., 44 LA 820, 823 (Teple, 1965) (the policy was not clearly stated or consistently followed). For other instances in which the arbitrator sustained a grievance protesting some type of adverse treatment of the grievant based on company policy restricting the hiring or continued employment of relatives, see *Distribution Ctr. of Columbus*, 83 LA 163, 165 (Seidman, 1984) (overruling discharge of employee for marrying coworker with whom he had lived for 6 months; rule prohibiting employment of relatives was unjustly applied since both employees had been with the company for about 6 years during which time they "clearly demonstrated that they were capable employees, had no attendance problems, were loyal to the Company, presented no problems with respect to the scheduling of work, and demonstrated maturity in their personal relationships with fellow employees"; the inchoate threat that they would become entirely different employees the day after their marriage was not a sufficient basis for discharge in the face of this actual record of service, attendance, and loyalty to the employer); *Safeway Stores*, 74 LA 886, 888 (Peterschmidt, 1980) (employer could not bar senior employee's bid for a job because he would be reporting directly to a relative; the policy asserted by the employer had not been posted or communicated to the employees, and the collective bargaining agreement established seniority and qualifications as the only factors limiting the right to bid for jobs); Ritchie Indus., 74 LA 650, 657–58 (Roberts, 1980) (employer's recently adopted policy against hiring spouses could not be reasonably interpreted to apply to employees who subsequently marry, nor did the employer establish that the policy is related to its business needs so as to justify intrusion into the personal lives of employees after hire); Food Basket Stores, 71 LA 959, 962–63 (Ross, 1978) (company policy against employment of a relative in the same department or under the supervision of a relative was improperly applied to grievant since the policy had not been adequately communicated to the employees and had been inconsistently applied, but apart from these deficiencies the arbitrator inferred that the policy probably could be justified by business needs); Public Serv. Co. of N.M., 70 LA 788, 791–92 (Springfield, 1978) (company rule stated that "should any two employees become married, either the husband or wife will be required to resign"; this rule was adopted "before the changing life-style of the next decade gave rise to a more general acceptance of living together," and the rule accordingly should not "be construed to include 'cohabitation' as being equivalent to 'becoming married'"); World Airways, 64 LA 276, 278 (Steese, 1975); Western Air Lines, 53 LA 1238, 1240 (Wyckoff, 1969). *See also* Sears Mfg. Co., 70 LA 719, 724–25 (Roberts, 1978) (discharge of union representative who married company president's daughter was improper, the daughter having resigned her position in personnel office, thus removing possibility of conflict of interest in making available to grievant confidential information to which she had access); Ralph M. Parsons Co., 69 LA 290, 293 (Rule, 1977) (company admitted that one reason for denying grievant a promotion as senior employee was his father's managerial position with the company; the company had no general policy against the employment or promotion of relatives, and without such a policy uniformly enforced, the company's action in the present case "must be considered an unreasonable action if not a discriminatory one," notwithstanding the possibility that some employee "might complain or even grieve about nepotism if the Grievant were promoted").

the arbitrator placed the burden on the union to show the unreasonableness of the policy.[562]

Although another arbitrator upheld the right of a company to adopt a policy prohibiting relatives from working on the same shift in the same department, he placed the burden on the company to justify the application of the one it adopted:

> The Company has made a strong case to demonstrate that its so-called "Relative Policy" is based on sound practice. Certainly it is recognized that actual conflicts can result when employees have to make a decision concerning their relatives. Favoritism, disharmony, etc., among relatives could prove disruptive to the working force. That is why I believe that an anti-nepotism rule, as long as it is consistently and fairly applied, is a proper exercise of sound management.
>
> . . .
>
> . . . [T]he Company is not proscribed from promulgating such a policy even though it was unilaterally adopted by Management. Invoking the rule, however, must be demonstrably related to the efficient operation of the plant or necessary to the management of the business. And this is what the Company has failed to prove [in the present instance].[563]

A no-marriage policy for airline stewardesses and women employees in other industries has been the subject of many arbitration cases. While upholding such a policy as reasonable in earlier cases, arbitrators have been reluctant to uphold such a policy in later years. They cite the fact that "times have changed and views have been altered by experience."[564] In holding such

---

[562]Studebaker Corp., 49 LA 105, 110 (Davey, 1967). For other cases upholding the employer's policy regarding relatives, see *Florida Power & Light Co.*, 90 LA 195, 198–200 (Holliday, Dees, & Sloane, 1987); *County of Riverside, Cal.*, 86 LA 903, 906–07 (Gentile, 1985); *Indianapolis Power & Light Co.*, 73 LA 512, 516 (Kossoff, 1979) (upholding discharge for falsely answering "no" to question in employment application asking whether applicant had relatives employed by the company, the arbitrator stated that the company "had a rational policy which made the hiring of relatives the exception rather than the rule," that it "is a policy which, although not uniformly followed in industry, is not uncommon among employers," and that the management rights clause expressly reserved the company's right to manage the business "according to its best judgment"); *National Tea Co.*, 69 LA 509, 511 (Kelliher, 1977) (retail company had right to transfer clerk in one store to another store located four miles away following his marriage to coworker, the policy against relatives working in same store being "based upon prior experiences and problems encountered in the management of the stores" such as the unlikelihood of one spouse testifying against another where removal of company product is involved, scheduling problems when both spouses need to be off at the same time, and the possibility that marital disharmony might be carried over onto store premises); *American Mach. & Foundry Co.*, 68 LA 1309, 1314 (Novak, 1977) (finding that "the Company has experienced problems with married couples taking simultaneous sick leaves and concomitant personal leaves leaving vacancies on the production line," the arbitrator concluded "that the Company was completely within its rights to establish the rule that they will not hire a spouse of a present employee or a partner living with an employee").

[563]Temple-Eastex, 69 LA 782, 786 (Taylor, 1977). In that case, the arbitrator also stated:

> I have found no showing . . . that the transfer [requested by grievant] would have had an adverse effect on the operations of the business or that the performance of his duties would have been adversely affected. He would not have been working in such close proximity to his brother as to create a legitimate Company concern. There was no evidence that one would exercise supervisory functions over the other. Quite simply, there were no insurmountable difficulties. Thus, my reasoning is not to invalidate the rule, only that I find that it is not enforceable in this particular instance.

[564]Southern Airways, 47 LA 1135, 1141 (Wallen, 1966). *See also* Braniff Airways, 48 LA 769, 770 (Gray, 1965).

a rule unreasonable in an airline stewardess case, an arbitrator found that its justification as a safety measure is minimal, its value as a sales promotion device is doubtful, and it is not in conformity with modern attitudes and trends of thought.[565] Even where the contract gave the company the right to terminate 6 months after marriage, the right was held to be limited to exercising the option by using good-faith judgment and discretion (with respect to individual stewardesses) to determine whether the employee's performance of her duties was adversely affected by her marriage.[566]

In another industry, the contract in the case specified certain grounds for the termination of employees, but did not include marriage or pregnancy. The arbitrator held that marriage or pregnancy per se was not cause for discharge. However, as a matter of safety and health, management may "promulgate certain rules relating to layoff when pregnancy is advanced to a point where hazards arise to the employee, the unborn infant, and perhaps other employees."[567]

The U.S. Court of Appeals for the Sixth Circuit held that an exogamy rule established by a public employer withstood the rational basis that "a rule interfering with the right of marital association under the First Amendment must advance a legitimate governmental interest and must not be an unreasonable means of advancing that legitimate governmental interest."[568] In another public-sector case, a district court upheld an arbitrator's decision that the discharge of a township police officer who was having an affair with the estranged wife of a fellow officer was appropriate. Even though the affair did not fall under a nepotism policy, adultery is not a protected interest and the effects of the relationship gravely affected the operation and efficiency of the force.[569] Likewise, under New York law, an employer can discharge an employee under an unwritten anti-nepotism policy even if the relationship has no effect on either employee's work. The U.S. Court of Appeals for the Second Circuit concluded that an employer does not have to show an adverse effect on work because romantic dating is not a protected recreational activity.[570]

In a matter of collateral interest, an arbitrator held that an employer's conflict-of-interest rules also may extend beyond the workplace and reach an employee whose spouse is employed by a competitor.[571]

---

[565]Southern Airways, 47 LA 1135, 1141 (Wallen, 1966). *See also* Braniff Airways, 48 LA 769, 770 (Gray, 1965); Allegheny Airlines, 48 LA 734, 737–38 (Kelliher, 1967). *Cf.* United Air Lines, 48 LA 727, 733–34 (Kahn, 1967).

[566]American Airlines, 48 LA 705, 723–24, 727 (Seitz, 1967).

[567]Alwin Mfg. Co., 38 LA 632, 638–39 (Sembower, 1962). *See also* Tennessee Coal, Iron & R.R., 11 LA 1062, 1065 (Seward, 1948). Where the contract provided that marriage would not disqualify a stewardess from employment with the company but that pregnancy would, the employer properly discharged a stewardess who had concealed her pregnancy and falsely secured sick leave. Western Air Lines, 54 LA 600, 603 (Wyckoff, 1971).

[568]Vaughn v. Lawrenceburg Power Sys., 269 F.3d 703, 712, 87 FEP Cases 107 (6th Cir. 2001).

[569]Mecure v. Van Buren Twp., 81 F. Supp. 2d 814 (E.D. Mich. 2000).

[570]McCavitt v. Swiss Reinsurance Am. Corp., 237 F.3d 166, 17 IER Cases 161 (2d Cir. 2001).

[571]Southwestern Bell Tel. Co., 107 LA 662 (Heinsz, 1996) (employee's wife sold products in direct competition with her husband's employer's products; husband subject to discharge unless wife divested herself of her dealership). See section 4., "'Moonlighting' and Outside Business Interests," above.

9. STATUS OF DOMESTIC PARTNERS [LA CDI 100.5915; 116.6005]

The extension of employee benefits to "domestic partners," whether of the same or opposite sex, is becoming more common. Among the companies extending benefits to same-sex partners are Walt Disney, Coca-Cola Co., AT&T, Boeing, and IBM.[572] However, in the absence of statutory recognition of the status of a same-sex partner or an express contractual obligation, an employer need not extend spousal benefits to the partner. Thus, an employer was held not to have violated the anti-discrimination provisions of the collective bargaining agreement when it refused to extend the employee's health insurance coverage to an employee's same-sex live-in partner.[573] So in the absence of a specific contractual provision, cohabitating couples may not be eligible for spousal benefits provided for under a collective bargaining agreement.

10. PRIVACY, DIGNITY, AND PEACE OF MIND

In management's direction of the enterprise, situations sometimes occur in which employees allege an invasion of their right of privacy or an infringement upon their dignity or peace of mind. Arbitrators have attempted to strike a balance between the personal rights of the employee and the rights of the company in the conduct of the business, considering such factors as whether there was a legitimate business need for management's action or rule,[574] whether there were reasonable safeguards for employee rights,[575] and whether management's action resulted in a substantial change in working conditions.[576]

A. Disclosure of Information to Employer

Employees sometimes claim a right of privacy in resisting the employer's requirement to disclose certain information for company records. However, where such information is reasonably necessary for the proper conduct of

---

[572]A more extensive list of companies extending benefits to same-sex partners is available at <http://www.hrc.org/worknet> (Human Rights Campaign's WorkNet project).

[573]Kent State Univ., 103 LA 338 (Strasshofer, Jr., 1994). *See* Youngstown State Univ., 115 LA 852 (Heekin, 2001); City of McAlestar, Okla., 114 LA 1180 (Crow, 2000).

[574]*See, e.g.*, City of Minneapolis, Minn., 78 LA 504, 507–08 (Karlins, 1982); Briggs & Stratton Corp., 77 LA 233, 236 (Mueller, 1981); City of Boston, 55 LA 910, 915–16 (Stutz, 1970); Michigan Consol. Gas Co., 53 LA 525, 530 (Keefe, 1969); National Broad. Co., 53 LA 312, 317–20 (Scheiber, 1969); Wyandotte Chems. Corp., 52 LA 755, 758 (Seinsheimer, 1969); International Nickel Co., 50 LA 65, 67–68 (Shister, 1967); FMC Corp., 46 LA 335, 338 (Mittenthal, 1966); EICO, Inc., 44 LA 563, 564 (Delaney, 1965).

[575]*See, e.g.*, Cagle's Poultry & Egg Co., 73 LA 34, 45–48 (Roberts, 1979); Mead Corp., 51 LA 1121, 1124 (Griffin, 1968); Aldens, Inc., 51 LA 469, 470 (Kelliher, 1968).

[576]*See, e.g.*, City of Minneapolis, Minn., 78 LA 504, 508 (Karlins, 1982); Pilgrim Liquor, 66 LA 19, 24 (Fleischli, 1976); City of Boston, 55 LA 910, 914–16 (Stutz, 1970) (safety and health clause); Michigan Consol. Gas Co., 53 LA 525, 530 (Keefe, 1969) (maintenance of working conditions clause); EICO, Inc., 44 LA 563, 564 (Delaney, 1965) (same).

the business, management is held entitled to require the disclosure. Thus, a company was upheld when it required an employee to disclose his unlisted phone number so that he could be contacted for necessary overtime assignments. The arbitrator stated:

> It is my opinion that it is not an invasion of privacy for the Company to have an employee's phone number, any more than it could be considered an invasion of privacy to have his home address, or for that matter, to talk to the employee. If being able to call an employee on the telephone could be considered an invasion of his privacy, then so could just talking to him be so considered, and this is obviously just plain unadulterated nonsense.[577]

In another case, a broadcasting company, as part of its conflict-of-interest policy, was held entitled to require members of its news staff to fill out a questionnaire regarding their financial interests. Regarding the claimed right of privacy, the arbitrator wrote:

> The litmus test of a careful examination makes it clear that the right of privacy is, at best, a limited right which, in general, protects the individual from having his name, picture, actions and statements commercially made public and exploited without his consent. This right, however, only safeguards him from the publication of his private statements or actions.[578]

The arbitrator concluded that the rule was a reasonable method of supervising employees and that the information was sought for the legitimate and limited business reason of ensuring the absence of bias in reporting the news and did not trespass upon their right of privacy since there was no public disclosure of private facts.[579]

But in ordering the reinstatement of employees who had been discharged for refusing to complete a fidelity bond application form that would require them to reveal their indebtedness, sources of income, and ownership of property, the arbitrator declared:

> The requirement that the employees complete and sign the fidelity bond application form constituted a substantial intrusion into their privacy and caused them to assume obligations which are greater than those otherwise imposed by law on employees who are accused of dishonesty. It was more than a mere work rule. It constituted a substantial change in the conditions of employment in the very real sense that their continued employment hinged on their willingness to complete and sign the form.[580]

In another case, an employee was found to be justified in refusing to sign a form authorizing the release of medical records that the employer had sought

---

[577]Wyandotte Chems. Corp., 52 LA 755, 758 (Seinsheimer, 1969). *See also* Tinker Air Force Base, Okla., 86 LA 1249 (Nelson, 1986). In *Amoco Oil Co.*, 64 LA 511 (Brown, 1975), company policy regarding exposure to toxic substances required female employees of childbearing age to notify the company doctor without delay when they had reason to believe they were pregnant. The arbitrator noted several important interests of the company served by the policy, and he stated that the "crucial question is whether those interests can be adequately protected in some manner less invasive of an employee's privacy than that embodied in" the policy. *Id.* at 513. There being "no showing in the record that they can be so protected," *id.*, he upheld the policy and the discharge of an employee who had violated it.

[578]National Broad. Co., 53 LA 312, 317 (Scheiber, 1969).

[579]*Id.* at 317–20 (the question of self-incrimination was also discussed). *See also* Scheiber, *Tests and Questionnaires in the Labor-Management Relationship*, 20 Lab. L.J. 695, 697–702 (1969).

[580]Pilgrim Liquor, 66 LA 19, 24 (Fleischli, 1976).

in order to check the truthfulness of the employee's employment application. The arbitrator found the form "so lacking in specificity and so broad in its application and coverage" as to be "a license for a fishing expedition into his private affairs."[581] Similarly, a county employer that had disciplined a corrections officer for failing to disclose plans to marry an inmate in the separate state prison system was held to have violated the officer's privacy rights where the county failed to demonstrate a compelling "need to know" about the marriage.[582]

Privacy issues also are implicated when an employer attempts to obtain information about an employee from outside sources, or to publicly disseminate information about an employee. Public employers, in particular, must be concerned about invading the privacy of their employees because public employees are protected by the Constitution against unreasonable searches and seizures.[583]

In the public employment cases, it appears that arbitrators typically employ a balancing test that weighs the employee's expectation of privacy against management's need to have the information or to otherwise regulate the employee's behavior. As one arbitrator has observed: "The crucial question often will be whether the interest of the company can be adequately served in a manner that is as noninvasive of an employee's rights as is reasonably possible."[584] For example, a city policy requiring all employees out of work for more than 3 months to submit to fingerprinting was found to be unreasonable because the employees had already been fingerprinted when they first began work, and the city could not present a compelling rationale for the refingerprinting.[585] In contrast, an arbitrator found that having a handwriting expert examine samples of employees' writings to determine the author of a sexually harassing job evaluation memorandum outweighed employees' privacy rights.[586] But where an employer did not have a preexisting policy requiring off-duty officers to submit to blood tests after being involved in traffic accidents, an off-duty officer could not be disciplined for refusing to undergo such a test.[587]

In the context of disseminating private information, a federal agency violated a police officer's right to privacy when the police chief, in responding to a citizen complaint against the officer, informed the citizen that action would be taken against the officer.[588]

---

[581]Bondtex Corp., 68 LA 476, 478 (Coburn, 1977). *See also* Chemetco, 71 LA 457, 459–60 (Gibson, 1978). Where an employee had used her diary to refresh her recollection prior to testifying, the company "was entitled to see those entries in the diary that were relevant to the proceedings and presumably reviewed by" the employee, but the company "was not entitled to insist on inspection of the full diary by its own counsel." Pacific Northwest Bell Tel. Co., 81 LA 297, 300 (Gaunt, 1983).

[582]County of Napa, Cal., 102 LA 590, 593–94 (Knowlton, 1994).

[583]*See also* Privacy Protection Act of 1980, 42 U.S.C. §2000aa et seq.; Privacy Act of 1974, 5 U.S.C. §552 et seq.

[584]City of Chicago, 109 LA 360, 368 (Goldstein, 1997) (quoting Goldstein & Kenis, *Spying Eyes: Management Rights Versus Employees' Right of Privacy*, in LABOR ARBITRATION CONFERENCE 1997, 100 (Labor Arbitration Inst. 1997)).

[585]City of Chicago, 109 LA 360, 367 (Goldstein, 1997).

[586]Michigan Dep't of Transp., 104 LA 1196, 1198 (Kelman, 1995).

[587]City of El Paso, Tex., 110 LA 411, 415 (Moore, 1998).

[588]Veterans Affairs Med. Ctr., 103 LA 74, 79 (Gentile, 1994).

In two discharge cases involving accusations of falsifying employment applications, arbitrators ordered reinstatement because the grievants reasonably believed their criminal records had been expunged. In the first case, the grievant answered no to the question: "Have you ever been convicted of a crime which has not been expunged or sealed by a court?" After the employee was hired, the employer discovered that the worker had a lengthy juvenile record, an assault conviction, and a driving-while-intoxicated conviction. The arbitrator found that the grievant reasonably considered his juvenile record to fall within the expungement exception because juvenile records typically are not considered permanent criminal records. His assault conviction was also rightfully omitted in light of a statement submitted by the trial judge negating a criminal record. Finally, although the DWI conviction could not be considered a routine traffic violation, in the past the company had taken inconsistent positions on whether traffic violations had to be mentioned in the employment application.[589] In a similar case involving a public employee, the grievant was found to have been unjustly terminated for falsifying his employment application, because the evidence was not "clear and convincing" that the grievant had intentionally lied in order to mislead.[590]

What happens if a candidate for employment who is awaiting trial on criminal charges answers no to a prior-convictions question on the application form, but thereafter, before being hired, pleads guilty to a lesser charge? In one such case, an employee, who had been terminated when his conviction was discovered, was reinstated because of the absence of a company rule requiring applicants to update the information on their application forms to the dates of their actual hire.[591]

As to a requirement that an employee submit to psychological evaluation and testing, an arbitrator stated that such compulsory testing did not infringe upon an employee's privacy rights, and that an employee could be disciplined for refusing to undergo the examination, provided the employee has been properly warned of the consequences of such refusal. In that case the grievant was sent to a psychologist for "mediation," but she did not understand that the process would include such testing and hence her suspension was set aside.[592]

B. Name Tags

In two cases, arbitrators considered the question of whether management can require employees to wear their surnames on their uniforms, and reached different conclusions. One case involved city police while the other involved service employees of a gas company. In both cases, the union argued that adding the employee's surname to his uniform was a change in working conditions and that the employer was required to bargain on the

---

[589]Freightliner Corp., 103 LA 123 (Galambos, 1994).
[590]City of Minneapolis, Minn., 106 LA 564 (Bard, 1996).
[591]Avis Rent-A-Car Sys., 107 LA 197 (Shanker, 1996).
[592]Cass Clay Creamery, 95 LA 41 (Eisele, 1990).

issue. In both cases, the unions also argued that the wearing of surnames on their uniforms would subject the employees and their families to harassment and invaded their privacy.

The arbitrator in the police case found (1) that the duty to bargain had been complied with; (2) that while individual officers and their families had received harassing, threatening, and indecent phone calls, the evidence did not support a conclusion that increased harassment resulted from the use of name tags; and (3) that issuing the name tag order, to improve the police-community relationship, was reasonable.[593]

The arbitrator in the gas company case, however, found no legitimate business need. His decision recited:

> The protested surname display constitutes a recognizable and material change in the working conditions of employees which can believably be expected, under entirely plausible and predictable circumstances, to have adverse reactions on the peace-of-mind, personal security and family privacy of at least certain individuals, thereby subjecting them to unjustifiable and avoidable hardship and inconvenience—if not outright personal hazard.[594]

C. Observing Employees at Work

"Management is properly concerned with the employee's work performance, what he does on the job and whether he obeys the plant's rules and regulations."[595] Such matters are regularly noted by supervisors. However, employees have sometimes alleged that management has gone beyond the proper limits of its right to observe them for these purposes.[596] Thus, in one case employees complained that intensive observations by a production engineer in cooperation with the foreman created undue "alarm and annoyance" and "fear and apprehension." The arbitrator found that the engineer was performing a proper management function, and he noted that "[a]lthough emotional tranquility is a condition much to be desired in labor relations, it is not one of the rights guaranteed by law or by the contract between the parties."[597]

---

[593]City of Boston, 55 LA 910, 915–16 (Stutz, 1970) (the arbitrator, notwithstanding such findings, stated that if harassment should increase, and the increase can be attributed to the name tags, the union would have a sound basis for demanding that the use of name tags be abandoned). This decision was considered "persuasive authority" and was quoted with clear approval in *City of Minneapolis, Minn.*, 78 LA 504, 509 (Karlins, 1982), where a requirement that police officers wear name tags on their uniforms was upheld. In *Briggs & Stratton Corp.*, 77 LA 233, 236 (Mueller, 1981), the company had the right to institute an employee identification program requiring the employee's picture, Social Security number, and date of birth; legitimate business interests (computerized payroll and clocking in and out procedures) were served by including the Social Security number and date of birth on identification cards, which interests "outweigh the alleged potential harm and inconvenience that may befall an employee" if the card is lost.

[594]Michigan Consol. Gas Co., 53 LA 525, 529 (Keefe, 1969).

[595]FMC Corp., 46 LA 335, 338 (Mittenthal, 1966).

[596]For related discussion, see Chapter 8, section 7.H., "Evidence Obtained by Allegedly Improper Methods."

[597]Picker X-Ray Corp., 39 LA 1245, 1246 (Kates, 1962). *See also* F&M Schaefer Brewing Co., 40 LA 199, 200–01 (Turkus, 1963) (upholding management's right to conduct time studies and finding that in doing so management was "neither 'spying on employees' nor improperly 'maintaining them under surveillance'").

In two cases involving the installation of closed circuit television to observe workers, arbitrators reached opposite conclusions. In one, where there had been loss of material and equipment, the surveillance was upheld:

> One of the supervisor's principal functions is to observe employees at work. Surely, such supervision cannot be said to interfere with an employee's right of privacy. The same conclusion should apply in this case. For all the Company has done is to add a different method of supervision to the receiving room—an electronic eye (i.e., the television camera) in addition to the human eye. Regardless of the type of supervision (a camera, a supervisor, or both), the employee works with the knowledge that supervision may be watching him at any time. He has a much better chance of knowing when he is being watched where there is no camera. But this is a difference in degree, not a difference in kind. For these reasons, I find there has been no interference with the employee's right of privacy.[598]

A maintenance-of-working-conditions clause was crucial to the other case, in which there was no indication of any need to supplement the already adequate supervision.[599] Ruling that the television cameras must be removed, the arbitrator stated:

> While I do not base my opinion on the Union's argument of the employees' legal "right of privacy," nor on the argument advanced by it on unlawful "surveillance" and "spying," I do agree that this argument cannot be totally overlooked since I find that the TV equipment does vitally affect the employees' working conditions.[600]

These cases were decided before the National Labor Relations Board ruled that the installation and use of surveillance cameras in the workplace is a mandatory subject of bargaining, notwithstanding an employer's desire to maintain secrecy in the placement of such cameras in the workplace,[601] and in neither case was the issue raised.

In a situation where the installation of surveillance cameras was deemed appropriate, an arbitrator found that the company could impose discipline on an employee whose sexual frolics were caught on videotape, despite the fact that the surveillance cameras were not installed for the purpose of detecting such activity. However, the discharge was overturned because the

---

[598]FMC Corp., 46 LA 335, 338 (Mittenthal, 1966) (emphasizing that an individual's right of privacy serves to protect him against the publication of his *private* statements or *private* actions and that an employee's actions during working hours are not private actions). The *FMC* decision was quoted with approval in *Cooper Carton Corp.*, 61 LA 697, 699–700 (Kelliher, 1973), upholding the employer's right to install two television cameras to enable its vice president and production manager, both of whom had heart conditions, to observe operations being run by foremen; the arbitrator pointed to the broad management clause, to the absence of any provision requiring the maintenance of conditions that are beneficial to employees, and to the fact that "[n]o employee has been disciplined based on these T.V. observations." In *Colonial Baking Co.*, 62 LA 586, 591 (Elson, 1974), the arbitrator noted the company's statement that the TV camera installation there was for security and not for disciplinary purposes, and he limited his holding to approving the surveillance system for security purposes only.

[599]EICO, Inc., 44 LA 563, 564 (Delaney, 1965).

[600]*Id.* at 563 (finding that while the company must have a good deal of discretion in carrying on its operations, use of the TV system imposed an "appreciable and intolerable burden" on the employees).

[601]Colgate-Palmolive Co., 323 NLRB 515, 155 LRRM 1034 (1997).

employer refused to permit the employee to have a union representative present at the investigatory interview.[602] In an analogous nonemployment context, the installation of surveillance cameras in the corridors of a high school was held not to have violated the privacy rights of students where the cameras were installed to identify students who were spraying perfumes and other fragrances outside the door of a teacher who had a hypersensitivity to these substances.[603]

Secret surveillance has been upheld in two cases. One involved the right of the employer to hire private checkers (whose identity need not be revealed) to follow and check the work performance of delivery truck drivers.[604] The other case involved a telephone company's use of remote listening devices to monitor secretly the telephone operators' performances. There, the union argued that the use of information gathered by secret and remote observations for disciplinary purposes would produce tensions upon the subject employees, and that their performance would vastly improve if they were assured that such surveillance would not be so used. However, the arbitrator observed that such considerations "are more pertinent for collective bargaining than to the arbitral forum." He explained:

> I do not mean to suggest that "policy considerations" will under no circumstances be relevant to a determination of the extent of management's right to make use of techniques for keeping employees under surveillance. Modern electronics has produced a variety of possibilities which, if used to the fullest extent, could disclose, surreptitiously, an employee's every move and every conversation while in the plant, whether directly work related or not. This could, allegedly, be the "Brave New World" of Huxley or Orwell's world of 1984! Some of these developments in employee surveillance might well raise the important question whether there is not, indeed, a "right of privacy" which employees may invoke to protect some, at least, aspects of their industrial life.[605]

But he concluded that in the case before him no such issue was actually presented for decision, and he made no determination as to the existence or extent of the grievant's right of privacy.[606]

D. Clocking In and Out for Personal Reasons

It has been held that the right of employees to absent themselves from their work area to use restrooms or for rest periods was not violated by the employer's requirement that they sign a "check-out" list. An arbitrator found that the rule was not unreasonable and that the evidence did not establish that management had invaded the employees' privacy by using the lists as a basis for improper questions regarding the personal habits of individual

---

[602]Wyndham Franklin Plaza Hotel, 105 LA 186, 188 (Duff, 1995).

[603]Culver City, Cal., Unified Sch. Dist., 110 LA 519, 527 (Hoh, 1997).

[604]Kroger Co., 40 LA 316, 317–18 (Reid, 1963). The union had argued that the "secret agents" following the drivers in unmarked cars on unfrequented highways at night put the drivers under an "intolerable strain." Id. at 317. For discussion on the evidential use of "spotters," see Chapter 8, section 4.A., "Right of Cross-Examination: Anonymous Witnesses and Confidential Documents."

[605]Michigan Bell Tel. Co., 45 LA 689, 695 (Smith, 1965).

[606]Id. at 696.

employees.[607] Similarly, a requirement that employees sign a slip to be placed in a special box when their foreman is unavailable to give them permission to leave was held reasonable since it implemented a long-standing rule that employees must obtain permission to leave their workplaces.[608]

While the company may require "clocking out and in" when an employee leaves the work station for personal reasons, the application of such rule must be reasonable and nondiscriminatory. So stated one arbitrator who found the rule before him to be unreasonable to the extent that it was a "source of embarrassment" to female employees who were required to have their male foremen note the reason for the "clock-out." He also found the rule to be discriminatory in that it was applied unevenly in different parts of the plant.[609] While the company was ordered to revoke the rule, it was given an opportunity (after a waiting period of 30 days) to devise an alternate method of accounting for restroom time or to reinstate the "clock-out" method, but with proper safeguards to eliminate discrimination, protect the individual's privacy, and avoid undue embarrassment.[610]

Another arbitrator likewise did not quarrel with the company's right to issue a check-out rule directed at abuse-of-relief privileges, but he found the rule before him to be unreasonable in that it was vague and imprecise in several important respects; he stated further that even if the rule could be assumed to achieve its objective of eliminating abuses, "it does so at a considerable price in terms of actual or threatened invasion of modesty and the ordinary amenities."[611]

---

[607]Elgin Instrument Co., 37 LA 1064, 1068 (Roberts, 1961) (employees had abused the rest period privilege). *See also* A.R.A. Mfg. Co., 85 LA 549, 552 (Heinsz, 1985) (where company instituted rule requiring employees to fill out time card noting times they were unproductive, discharge of employee who failed to comply with rule was proper). In *Cagle's Poultry & Egg Co.*, 73 LA 34, 48 (Roberts, 1979), it was held that management had the right to install a special time clock outside restrooms and to require employees to punch their time cards on entering and leaving, under guidelines instituted to prevent abuse of emergency use of restrooms; the number of emergency visits generally could be limited to 20 times in any 4-week period. In this case it was also found, however, that the guidelines had not been administered in a reasonable manner, and this was ordered to be corrected.

[608]Certain-Teed Prods. Corp., 38 LA 46, 48 (Sembower, 1962).

[609]Gremar Mfg. Co., 46 LA 215, 219 (Teele, 1965). Concerning the invasion of privacy issue, the arbitrator stated: "Whether the routine involved an invasion of personal privacy probably boils down to a matter of degree, and it is sufficient, perhaps, to find affirmatively as to embarrassment." He cited other cases dealing with check-out rules and drew certain general conclusions from them. *Id.* at 218–19.

[610]*Id.* at 220. In *Schmidt Cabinet Co.*, 75 LA 397, 400 (Berns, 1980), the employer adopted a rule requiring employees to "punch out before entering restroom (except at breaks and noon) and punch back in before returning to" the job. The rule cautioned that "[e]xcessive trips or too long trips may cause disciplinary action." Pointing out that there were no female supervisors in the plant and that monitoring of the rule by male supervisors resulted in embarrassment of female employees, the arbitrator struck the rule down as being unreasonable. In doing so, he declared that while "no one can blame the Company for wanting to curb the wasteful practices of a small number of loiterers," other "[m]ethods can surely be found to reduce the incidence of loitering without loading on all employees an onerous and humiliating timekeeping procedure which is seldom used in industrial practice."

[611]Detroit Gasket & Mfg. Co., 27 LA 717, 722 (Crane, 1956). In another case, *Chris-Craft Corp.*, 45 LA 117, 118–19 (Autrey, 1965), the employer approached the problem of loitering in restrooms and defacing of toilet doors by removing the doors to the toilets, later agreeing to replace them when the union agreed to cooperate in trying to prevent such loitering and defacing. The case went to arbitration when a modest employee, who felt the doorless toilets were "not decent or proper," was discharged for leaving his department to use the restroom (with doors intact) in another department. He was reinstated without back pay (a loss of 6½ months).

E. Employer Inspection of Employee Belongings

"Reasonableness," as determined on a case-by-case basis under the factual context and applicable contract provisions, guides arbitral decisions regarding the propriety of employer inspections of employee personal items and lockers. Adequate notice that employees are subject to such inspections and a reasonable basis to conduct an inspection consistently have been found to be necessary conditions.

Thus, where correction officers were required to submit to a search of "their person, or automobile, or place of assignment on government property, when such search is required by the Director or Administrator," an officer who had submitted to a routine search on entering the facility was suspended for refusing to permit a search of a personal bag that he had retrieved from his truck after beginning duty. The questioned search had been ordered first by a security officer, then by the acting shift commander, and eventually by the acting assistant administrator, but not the "Director or Administrator." The discipline was upheld in arbitration because the grievant had engaged in self-help, and especially since security issues were implicated, he should have obeyed the order and grieved later.[612]

In several cases, where management had serious problems with thefts or where it had other reasonable cause, a rule or practice requiring employees to submit purses, briefcases, or lockers for inspection was upheld.[613] The

---

[612]District of Columbia Dep't of Corr., 105 LA 468 (Rogers, 1995).

[613]See Pacific Southwest Airlines, 87 LA 701, 706 (Rothschild, 1986); Kawneer Co., 86 LA 297, 300 (Alexander, 1985); Lake Park of Oakland, Cal., 83 LA 27, 30 (Griffin, 1984); Kraft, Inc., 82 LA 360, 365 (Denson, 1984); Shell Oil Co., 81 LA 1205, 1208 (Brisco, 1983); McGraw-Edison Co., 76 LA 249, 253 (Sergent, Jr., 1981); B.F. Goodrich, 70 LA 326, 329 (Oppenheim, 1978) (upholding the company's right to inspect lockers; "as long as the employee is notified that an inspection will take place and he will not be taken by surprise and that a Union representative is present as a member of the inspection team, there is no necessity for the locker holder to be present"); AMF Harley-Davidson Motor Co., 68 LA 811, 816–17 (Martin, 1977); Aldens, Inc., 51 LA 469, 470 (Kelliher, 1968); International Nickel Co., 50 LA 65, 67–68 (Shister, 1967); Friedrich Refrigerators, 39 LA 934, 936–37 (Williams, 1962). But see Anchor Hocking Corp., 66 LA 480, 481 (Emerson, 1976). In Fruehauf Corp., 49 LA 89, 90–91 (Daugherty, 1967), a past practice of inspecting outgoing employees' lunch buckets for possible pilfered company property was found to support the company in searching incoming employees' buckets for liquor on a preholiday shift where drinking on the job had been a problem on such shifts in the past. For cases involving other security or search measures taken by management, see Michigan Consol. Gas Co., 80 LA 693, 696–97 (Keefe, 1983) (employee suspected of selling drugs possibly prevented discovery of evidence by violating direct order not to flush toilet; discharge upheld); General Paint & Chem. Co., 80 LA 413, 417–18 (Kossoff, 1983) (upholding metal detector and random inspection procedures adopted to guard against theft and violence; employees had been informed of the procedures and this "removes any likelihood that any employee will be forced to incriminate himself"); Prestige Stamping Co., 74 LA 163, 165 (Keefe, 1980) (upholding discharge for insubordination in refusing to produce newspaper in which grievant had folded plastic bag suspected of containing narcotics); Aldens, Inc., 73 LA 396, 398 (Martin, 1979) (upholding discharge of employee who refused to raise pant leg to reveal nature of bulges that guard had observed). Cf. Chemicals, Inc., 69 LA 217, 222–23 (Bode, 1977) (upholding ban on use of large drink coolers as lunch boxes since such use could facilitate bringing alcohol into plant and removing employer's property from plant); Orgill Bros. & Co., 68 LA 797, 803–04 (Simon, 1977) (upholding rule requiring warehouse employees to wear slacks and to place shirt inside belt waist before entering and leaving warehouse, the rule being justified to remedy a serious theft problem); Orgill Bros. & Co., 66 LA 307, 310–11 (Ross, 1976) (upholding discharge for refusing to allow search of box-shaped bulge on back of leg while leaving plant); Dow Chem. Co., 65 LA 1295, 1298–99 (Lipson, 1975). For related discussion, see Chapter 8, section 4.H., "Failure of Griev-

arbitrator in a purse inspection case emphasized that employees are entitled to reasonable safeguards of privacy, but have a duty to cooperate. He found that the company took all reasonable procedural precautions to protect the employee's privacy and dignity when the security guard exhibited her badge and asked the employee to come to a closed room where the inspection would be made only by the female security guard.[614]

Another arbitrator cautioned that the company must not act in a discriminatory, capricious, arbitrary, or unreasonable fashion but must have a reasonable basis for its search of employee lockers. In that case, the company had a legitimate reason for the search—to locate missing company property—and the manner of conducting the search was found to be proper.[615]

Discipline imposed for refusing to submit to a search is proper only when the order is reasonable and when the employee understands both the order and the consequences for refusing to obey the order.[616] In a private-sector case, an arbitrator held that the standard used in determining the reasonableness of such an order need not be determined under the "probable cause" standard adopted to satisfy the Constitution's Fourth Amendment prohibition of unreasonable searches and seizures.[617] However, even in private-sector cases, arbitrators have considered both the motivation for the search and the circumstances under which it was conducted.[618] In so doing, arbitrators have looked to how a search was conducted and have balanced the legitimate interests of the employer with the personal dignity of the employee.

In a case concerning an employee's expectation of privacy with respect to the contents of his toolbox, an arbitrator found that it was the past practice of the company to open the boxes either to remove tools needed for other employees or to protect against theft.[619] However, because of increased theft, the company had recently required employees to purchase their own locks. The arbitrator held that this requirement had endowed the toolboxes with a half-private and a half-company characterization that gave the employees an increased expectation of privacy.[620] Consequently, since there was no express rule allowing the employer to search the boxes, the employer could

---

ant to Testify," section 7.H., "Evidence Obtained by Allegedly Improper Methods," and section 9.C., "The Lie Detector." *See also* Craver, *The Inquisitorial Process in Private Employment*, 63 CORNELL L. REV. 1 (1977).

[614]Aldens, Inc., 51 LA 469, 470 (Kelliher, 1968). Regarding privacy for female employees, cf. *AMF Harley-Davidson Motor Co.*, 68 LA 811, 816–17 (Martin, 1977).

[615]International Nickel Co., 50 LA 65, 68 (Shister, 1967). *See also* General Paint & Chem. Co., 80 LA 413, 418–19 (Kossoff, 1983). For cases involving demands to be paid for time lost by employees in connection with employer searches, see *Naval Ordnance Station*, 74 LA 1055, 1058 (Fitch, 1980); *Curtis Mathes Mfg. Co.*, 73 LA 103, 106–07 (Allen, Jr., 1979); *U.S. Marine Corps Supply Ctr.*, 65 LA 59, 61–62 (King, 1975).

[616]Kraft, Inc., 82 LA 360, 364 (Denson, 1984).

[617]Kawneer Co., 86 LA 297, 300 (Alexander, 1985).

[618]Kraft, Inc., 82 LA 360 (Denson, 1984); Shell Oil Co., 81 LA 1205 (Brisco, 1983).

[619]Kawneer Co., 86 LA 297, 300, 301 (Alexander, 1985).

[620]*Id.* at 301.

search them only if it had a reasonable basis for believing that a violation of a promulgated and published rule of conduct had occurred.[621]

Employer searches of employee automobiles also have been upheld where there is a reasonable basis for conducting them. One arbitrator held that company security guards, whose essential function is to safeguard company property, did not abuse their authority when they approached a company employee and asked him to allow them to examine his car and trunk after receiving an anonymous telephone call informing them that the employee had stolen masking tape in the car's trunk. In upholding the discharge of the employee for theft, the arbitrator rejected the union's contention that the search of the employee's car was unreasonable because it was conducted without giving the employee a prior opportunity to obtain union representation.[622]

In another case, trained drug-sniffing dogs had been deployed near the grievant's car and had, according to disputed testimony, signaled the possible presence of drugs in the vehicle. Upon being directed to permit a search of his vehicle on pain of discharge, the grievant consented, and traces of marijuana were found. He was thereafter discharged. The arbitrator opined that the standard for determining whether a search by a private employer was proper, although not identical to that applicable to governmental searches and seizures under the Fourth Amendment, required the private employer to show that it "had reasonable cause to search the Grievant's vehicle and did so in a manner which complied with fundamental fairness."[623] However, although the arbitrator found the conduct of the search with police dogs to be within the general authority of the employer, he believed there had been insufficient notice of the policy regarding searches of automobiles. Accordingly, the arbitrator directed that the grievant be reinstated with back pay.[624]

Reinstatement without back pay was directed for an employee who had been discharged for refusing to consent to the search of his vehicle to ascertain whether he had brought a firearm onto the company parking lot.[625] A promulgated company policy gave clear notice that personal property of employees was subject to search, and the company had received an anonymous letter alleging that the grievant and another employee were bringing concealed weapons into the premises in their automobiles. Although the arbitrator found the search order to have been proper and acknowledged that

---

[621]*Id.* Because there was a reasonable basis to search the toolbox in this case—namely, a company rule prohibiting gambling—and grievant had been observed by a supervisor exchanging currency with another employee for a small piece of paper that was suspected to be a lottery ticket, the arbitrator held that the search was not improper. *See also* Lake Park of Oakland, Cal., 83 LA 27 (Griffin, 1984) (the arbitrator upheld the discharge of an employee for refusing to permit a search of her purse after she had clocked out, the search having been attempted in response to recent incidents of missing food items).
[622]General Elec. Co., 98 LA 355 (Stutz, 1991).
[623]Anheuser-Busch, 107 LA 1183 (Weckstein, 1996).
[624]*Id.* at 1192. *See also* Georgia Power Co., 93 LA 846 (Holley, Jr., 1989).
[625]Folsom Return to Custody, Inc., 101 LA 837 (Staudohar, 1993).

"the carrying of a gun onto facility property is a serious matter," he determined that the penalty of discharge was excessive under the circumstances.[626]

No mitigating circumstances were found in the case of an employee who was discharged following a search of his automobile that disclosed what appeared to be an item of company property in his vehicle.[627] The search was prompted by a tip from a coworker that the grievant was stealing company property, and a subsequent observation revealed the grievant carrying a covered object to his car.

Can an employer ever justify a nonconsensual search of an employee's residence? One arbitrator thought so. He upheld the discharge of an employee for theft of company property that had come to light when the employee's ex-spouse, who had control over their residence after the employee had moved out, reported the presence of stolen items to the company and asked the company to remove them.[628]

F. Misuse of E-Mail

A public school librarian received a written reprimand after using school equipment to access an e-mail system to send a critical and sarcastic note to 37 other librarians in her state regarding proposed curriculum and class changes. The note came to the supervising school principal's attention after he received a copy from another principal. The librarian claimed that the message was motivated by her need for assistance, but the principal contended that her "editorializing" was improper. The arbitrator, despite finding that the librarian's tone was inappropriate, concluded that there was no clear-cut or blatant misuse of the e-mail system. Rather, he deemed it a situation where an appropriate utilization was intermixed with improper personal opinion. Because the school district admittedly had no rules or regulations concerning use of its e-mail system, the arbitrator found the employee was not subject to discipline because she could not have known that she did not have the right to use e-mail in a "quasi-personal" manner.[629]

11. Use of Personal Radios

It has been stated that "[a]bsent any privilege on the part of the employees which would amount to a contractual right to bring radios into the shop and using them in an unrestricted manner," the company can promulgate rules absolutely or partially restricting employee use of personal radios in the plant so long as such rules are not arbitrary, unreasonable, or discriminatory.[630] Thus, a company restriction on use of radios may be found proper

---

[626]*Id.* at 843. The grievant was the president of the union and had been engaged in heated labor negotiations with the company representative. The arbitrator opined that even though the offense was serious, the employer had improperly considered the grievant's union office as a factor in the termination decision.

[627]Tyson Foods, 105 LA 1119 (Moore, 1996).

[628]Exxon Co. U.S.A., 101 LA 777 (Baroni, 1993).

[629]Conneaut, Pa., Sch. Dist., 104 LA 909 (Talarico, 1995).

[630]Anaconda Aluminum Co., 51 LA 281, 283–84 (Dolson, 1968) (finding no established practice to support the alleged right and finding that the company's restrictions were reasonable and proper, but also finding that the rules were discriminatorily applied).

if it is based on adequate reasons, such as ensuring the quality and quantity of production and promoting safety in the shop.[631]

The introduction of a ban on radio playing has been held to be improper where there is a well-established practice of allowing employees to play their radios. Thus, in the absence of proof of misuse of the radios or an adverse effect on the employees' work, a company was not justified in discontinuing a long-time practice of playing radios, but it could promulgate reasonable rules to control the type of program as well as the volume of sound.[632] In a case where a radio provided background music for nuclear plant control operators for 15 years, and both the union and the employer viewed its presence as beneficial, an arbitrator concluded that a binding past practice had been created that precluded the employer from unilaterally removing the radio from the control room even though the Nuclear Regulatory Commission had "urged" and "strongly" suggested its removal.[633]

However, where relevant circumstances had changed, an arbitrator held that even a long-standing privilege of listening to personal radios on the shop floor was reasonably subject to a rule limiting employees to using "Walkman" radios with earphones. The company had moved to a larger facility and the old practice created traffic safety concerns.[634] In another case, an absolute ban on radios playing in a plant, which had a "well established traditional right of employees to play radios," was deemed invalid. However, the arbitrator observed that the employer retained the "ULTIMATE authority to ban employee radios when such a ban appears to be—after suitable alternatives have been tried—the only practical ('reasonable') solution."[635]

Laxity in enforcing a stated long-standing policy restricting the use of radios to certain times and areas did not bar a plant manager from reactivating the enforcement policy after issuing a memorandum reaffirming the company's policy restricting radio use. The sporadic nonuse of this contractually validated management right did not amount to the relinquishment of the right, and the issuance of the memorandum was an appropriate exercise

---

[631]*See* Weyerhaeuser Co., 76 LA 561, 562 (Lynch, 1981); Transportation Enters., 75 LA 1226, 1231–32 (Johnson, 1980) (bus company could prohibit drivers from using radios while performing their duties after it received passenger complaints about loud volume causing them to miss their stops); McGraw-Edison Power Sys. Div., 53 LA 1024, 1026–27 (Lewis, 1969); Anaconda Aluminum Co., 51 LA 281, 283–84 (Dolson, 1968). *See also* Eastern Air Lines, 44 LA 1034, 1040 (Yagoda, 1965). *Cf.* Social Sec. Admin., 71 LA 963, 968–69 (Ables, 1978) (federal agency employer did not have right to require employee to discontinue watching her battery-powered TV at desk in her work station during lunch break).

[632]Minnesota Mining & Mfg. Co., 49 LA 332, 334 (Jensen, 1967) (20-year practice of permitting radios during nonworking time); Bangor Punta Operations, 48 LA 1275, 1276 (Kates, 1967) (the practice of playing radios during working time was recognized but the company could also substitute "piped-in" music or company-provided radios at reasonable locations). In *FWD Corp.*, 71 LA 929, 931–32 (Lynch, 1978), it was held that the employer improperly discontinued a past practice of allowing employees to play their radios; the employer was directed to reinstate the prior practice and to bargain with the union to agreement or impasse prior to changing the practice.

[633]Northern States Power Co., 87 LA 1077 (Fogelberg, 1986).

[634]Creative Prods., 89 LA 777, 780 (McDonald, 1987).

[635]Square D Co., 66–1 ARB ¶8134, at 3493 (Kahn, 1963) (finding that a "reasonable procedure" would include efforts by supervision to discuss the problem of objectionable radio playing with the offending employee, and, if that failed, to discuss it with the union).

of management's right to direct its workforce.[636] In another case, where permission always had been required to bring in radios, the arbitrator held that "the practice existed only subject to management permission, modification, or prohibition," and that the employer could properly refuse to permit it to spread to a newly opened building.[637] The arbitrator opined that "it is relevant that the use of personal radios seems to come closer to the area of traditional and conventional management discretion concerning productive factors and influences, than to that of employee rights not so intimately connected with the productive process."[638]

12. Coffee in the Workplace

As to employee use of coffee-making equipment in work areas, management has been held entitled to prohibit the use in the absence of an express recognition of the privilege in the agreement or a showing of a well-established practice.[639] Such a showing was made in a case where the collective bargaining agreement had a maintenance-of-practices clause and the employees had been allowed to brew their coffee for a long period. The company's installation of coffee vending machines and removal of employees' coffee-making equipment was held to violate the contract, but the company was permitted to impose requirements for the "orderly and reasonable use of the equipment for coffee and related beverage making." Employees using this equipment could also be made responsible for "orderly housekeeping practices and accountable for spending excessive time in the process."[640]

An established practice of supplying free coffee to employees during coffee breaks or lunch periods may not be unilaterally discontinued,[641] but the company is free to change the manner in which it supplies the coffee.[642]

---

[636]Southern Ind. Gas & Elec. Co., 88 LA 132 (Franke, 1986).

[637]Eastern Air Lines, 44 LA 1034, 1038, 1040 (Yagoda, 1965) (the contract contained a clause maintaining privileges so long as they are not abused).

[638]*Id.* at 1040.

[639]Electronics Communications, 52 LA 571, 574 (Belcher, 1969) (the alleged practice was not approved but was intermittent and sometimes surreptitious); Ohio Power Co., 50 LA 501, 504 (Teple, 1967) ("The kind of equipment which can be brought onto the Company's premises, and the use of Company time to operate such equipment, would appear to be well within the general authority and control of management" unless the agreement expressly recognizes the particular privilege).

[640]Sheridan Mach. Co., 37 LA 831, 832–33 (Gomberg, 1961) (holding that management could "protect itself against the erosion of its rights" by employee extension of the coffee-making privilege to using sandwich grills and frying and cooking pans). A binding practice was also found in *Wallace Murray Corp.*, 72 LA 470, 474–75 (Abrams, 1979) (practice allowing employees to drink coffee in work area during working hours); *FWD Corp.*, 71 LA 929, 931 (Lynch, 1978) (practice allowing employees to use their personal coffee pots).

[641]Beech-Nut Life Savers, 39 LA 1188, 1191 (Handsaker, 1962); Cushmans Sons, 37 LA 381, 383, 385 (Scheiber, 1961).

[642]Pillsbury Co., 34 LA 615, 616 (McIntosh, 1960).

13. DANGEROUS WEAPONS ON COMPANY PROPERTY
[LA CDI 100.552510; 118.640]

An employer has a duty to protect the health and safety of its employees. This duty includes "maintaining the right kind of environment where employees can be trusted not to commit acts of violence against other employees."[643] To this end, the employer may promulgate and enforce rules dealing with dangerous weapons.[644] Discharge or discipline has been upheld when an employee was found guilty of violating a no-weapons rule.[645]

Thus, the National Labor Relations Board found discharge to be proper where a striking employee carried a gun in the vicinity of the plant entrance used by nonstriking employees. The Board determined that this could reasonably tend to coerce or intimidate nonstriking employees in the exercise of their Section 7 rights.[646] However, discharge was not warranted for an employee who participated in picketing the employer's premises with a sheathed hunting knife on his belt where it was reasonable to infer that employees at a shipyard were accustomed to seeing sheathed knives on fellow employees, and the striker's mode of dress, unaccompanied by threatening gestures, could not reasonably be interpreted as tending to coerce nonstriking employees.[647]

The discharge of an employee was found to be proper where a loaded .22 caliber pistol was discovered in the employee's pickup truck in the company parking lot. Although the employee had not fired the weapon or threatened anyone with it, the employer's rule against possession of firearms was consistently enforced and sufficiently communicated to the employee, and was justified by the potential threat to the life and health of the employees.[648] Even when significant mitigating factors were present, the discharge of a long-service employee was upheld in a case where an employer had strictly enforced a well-publicized "no weapons on company property" rule. In that case, during the course of a drug search, the company found a loaded handgun and several half-empty bottles of alcoholic beverages in the grievant's car parked in a company lot. The grievant had inadvertently left the liquor and the gun in his car after a family gathering, and there was no indication that the grievant was an alcohol abuser or posed any threat of danger to others. In rejecting these factors as a defense, the arbitrator held that the

---

[643]Albritton Eng'g Corp., 46 LA 857, 859 (Hughes, 1966). *See also* Michigan Standard Alloys, 53 LA 511, 513 (Forsythe, 1969).

[644]*See* Brodie Indus. Trucks, 50 LA 112, 114 (Teele, 1968); Campbell Soup Co., 2 LA 27, 31 (Lohman, 1946).

[645]*See* Van Wold-Stevens Co., 79 LA 645, 648–49 (Flagler, 1982); Transit Auth. of River City, 79 LA 508, 511–12 (Staudter, 1982); Stroh Brewery Co., 53 LA 1028, 1029–30 (Ryder, 1969); Mid-States Metal Prods., 53 LA 545, 546–47 (Williams, 1969); Brown & Williamson Tobacco Corp., 50 LA 403, 412 (Willingham, 1968) (many cases cited); Brodie Indus. Trucks, 50 LA 112, 114–15 (Teele, 1968); Temco Elecs., 61–3 ARB ¶8665 (Larson, 1961). But the evidence of such infraction must be convincing. *See* Michigan Standard Alloys, 53 LA 511, 513 (Forsythe, 1969). In *Navy Exch.*, 52 LA 1142, 1144 (Williams, 1969), it was found that the grievant was not the aggressor but drew a knife in a "defensive posture."

[646]KECO Indus., 276 NLRB 1469, 120 LRRM 1269 (1985).

[647]Newport News Shipbuilding & Dry Dock Co. v. NLRB, 738 F.2d 1404, 116 LRRM 3042 (4th Cir. 1984).

[648]Goodyear Aerospace Corp., 86 LA 403 (Fullmer, 1985).

company was within its management rights in promulgating an absolute no-weapons, no-alcohol rule on its premises and strictly enforcing this rule without exception.[649]

Even where there is no express written rule prohibiting firearms or knives on company premises, an employer can discipline employees for bringing such weapons on to company premises. "Some conduct is so obviously contrary to good sense, notice of that fact by all employees may be assumed."[650] However, arbitrators may overturn or mitigate the severity of penalties imposed if a company has failed to enforce the prohibition consistently. It was for this reason that an employer's failure to consistently enforce a "no-weapons rule" resulted in the reinstatement without back pay of a firefighter who not only brought a shotgun into the firehouse in contravention of the rule, but accidentally discharged the gun into the floor while in the firehouse.[651]

Despite written rules against weapons possession, where a company had sent a "mixed message" in applying them, an employee was reinstated who, following a police search related to a protracted traffic stop commencing on company property, had been discharged for having a loaded handgun in his automobile glove box. The grievant had credibly testified that the gun belonged to his wife and he did not know it was there. Moreover, the arbitrator found it significant that the company had been lax in its enforcement, to the point of even allowing one supervisor to post a "gun for sale" sign and complete the transaction on the premises. However, since the company had committed itself to eliminating guns from its workplace, the company was entitled to enforce its rule prospectively.[652]

Lax enforcement brought about a similar result in another case, where an employee/hunter was found to have been improperly discharged for having an unloaded rifle in this truck. The plant was in an area where hunting was a passion of local residents, including, undoubtedly, the majority of the employees at the plant. There had been no other discharges for unauthorized weapons possession on company property during the previous 20 years, and the arbitrator did not find it believable that no other employee had been

---

[649]Marathon Petroleum Co., 93 LA 1082 (Marlatt, 1989). *See also* Indianapolis Pub. Transp. Corp., 98 LA 557 (Doering, 1991).

[650]Ross-Meehan Foundries, 55 LA 1078, 1080 (King, 1970) (nevertheless holding that discharge was too severe under the peculiar circumstances (grievant's son had been shot by a fellow employee), and reinstating grievant with only 2 days' disciplinary suspension). *Accord* Brown & Williamson Tobacco Corp., 50 LA 403, 412 (Willingham, 1968). Discharge was upheld in *International Harvester Co.*, 50 LA 766, 767–68 (Doyle, 1968) (citing many cases); *Inland Container Corp.*, 28 LA 312, 314 (Ferguson, 1957). Discharge was reduced to a long suspension in the absence of a rule in *Owens-Corning Fiberglas Corp.*, 54 LA 419, 420 (Reid, 1971); *American Synthetic Rubber Corp.*, 46 LA 1161, 1163–65 (Dolson, 1966) (involving other charges as well). For cases where the company alleged a work-related incident occurring off the company premises, see *International Paper Co.*, 52 LA 1266, 1269 (Jenkins, 1969); *Bird & Son*, 30 LA 948, 950–51 (Sembower, 1958).

[651]City of Tarpon Springs, Fla., 107 LA 230, 236 (Deem, 1996) ("Under normal circumstances I would find that discharge is a proper disciplinary action for even a first offense [because employers are responsible for the safety of their employees]. However, in this particular case I cannot allow the city to make an example of the grievant when they have not put their house in order as it regards this issue.").

[652]Luxfer USA, 102 LA 783 (Kaufman, 1994).

found to have a gun or bow and arrow on plant property.[653] In another case where "conditions of permissiveness" existed, an arbitrator reduced a discharge to a 5-months' disciplinary suspension. The arbitrator emphasized, however, that if the company had warned the employees about a new rule prohibiting firearms and if there had been a "line of demarcation between the . . . permissiveness and a new strict policy," the discharge would have been upheld.[654]

Evidence that a discharged bus driver employee had not intended to bring his pistol with him in his personal bag when he began driving his route did not constitute sufficient mitigation to persuade an arbitrator to reinstate him, where a clear rule prohibiting weapons had been promulgated and the employee had failed to take proper corrective steps upon realizing that he had the firearm with him.[655] In another case, a company published a new rule extending a prohibition against bringing weapons into the facility to employee automobiles parked on company premises, but it failed to comply with a contractual requirement that proposed rule changes be discussed with the union before being issued. The peremptory issuance of the rule had been motivated by the shooting of two employees by a third employee who had retrieved a gun from his car. An arbitrator held that the rule was enforceable as an emergency measure, although it did not comply with the contract.[656]

14. COMPANY LIABILITY FOR EMPLOYEE'S DAMAGED OR STOLEN PROPERTY
[LA CDI 124.05]

When an employee's tools or other personal property are damaged or stolen while on company premises, the question arises whether the employee is entitled to recompense from the company. In some cases the company was held liable for all or part of the loss.[657] In many other cases the company was

---

[653]USS, Div. of USX Corp., 106 LA 708 (Neyland, 1996). *See also* City of Tarpon Springs, Fla., 107 LA 230 (Deem, 1996).

[654]Bright-O, Inc., 54 LA 498, 500 (Mullin, Jr., 1971).

[655]Bi-State Dev. Agency, 104 LA 460 (Bailey, 1995). Other arbitrators, however, have found that an employee's freedom from malice may mitigate the penalty. *See, e.g.*, Interstate Brands Corp., 104 LA 993, 996 (Gentile, 1995) (employee who had brought a gun onto company premises intending to sell it to another employee reinstated, because "[t]here is a fine line between poor judgment and the willful and knowing violation of a posted and communicated policy").

[656]Packaging Corp. of Am., 106 LA 122, 125–26 (Nicholas, Jr., 1996) ("While my findings here uphold Union's argument that it is to be advised and be made a party to discussions on a rule change prior to Company taking final action, I am nevertheless convinced that such action was necessary and that Company has established a proper foundation for the use of the rule today.").

[657]*See* ACF Indus., 79 LA 487, 491–93 (Williams, 1982) (employer ordered to reimburse employees for stolen tools, "[b]ased purely upon its failure to communicate" to employees its policy that they could take their tools home or leave the tools on company premises at their own risk); Sharpe-Saunders Constr., 79 LA 153, 157–58 (Goodman, 1982); Logemann Bros., 75 LA 615, 621–23 (Bard, 1980); Chemineer, Inc., 72 LA 568, 576–78 (Ruben, 1979); Wilson Mfg. Co., 70 LA 994, 995–96 (Tyer, 1978); Consolidation Coal Co., 67 LA 358, 360–61 (Ipavec, 1976) (employer must reimburse employees for vandalism damage to their vehicles parked near job site, the employer having failed to provide adequate parking on job site as required by the agreement); Campbell Indus., 61 LA 1245, 1248–49 (Richman, 1973); Plough, Inc., 54

not held liable.[658] The elements argued by the parties or considered by the arbitrator included: (1) whether the contract's safety and health provision was applicable; (2) whether a bailment relationship existed between the parties; (3) whether the company had exercised reasonable care or had been negligent in regard to the employee's property; (4) whether the contract contained language, express or implied, to impose liability upon the company; and (5) whether there had been contract negotiations on the subject.

Most arbitrators have rejected the contention that the safety and health provision of the contract applies in cases where an employee's equipment or personal property is stolen or damaged while on company premises. One arbitrator concluded that this type of provision "clearly relates to the employees themselves, and not to their equipment or personal possessions."[659] Another arbitrator thought that "to apply provisions of the working agreement to issues here is reaching way out, for it would take an extremely liberal interpretation of the working agreement to read into it a duty of the Company to insure against loss of the personal effects of an employee under any circumstances."[660] A third arbitrator stated that it "would be a strained interpretation" of the safety clause to hold the company responsible for the safekeeping of all personal belongings stored in company-provided lockers.[661] And, finally, a fourth arbitrator wrote: "Nor do safety clauses as used in labor agreements generally provide for damage suits unless there is a spe-

---

LA 430, 432 (Amis, 1971); Sargent-Fletcher Co., 49 LA 76, 79–80 (Lennard, 1967); Drake Bakeries, 43 LA 114, 115 (Cohen, 1964); Best Mfg. Co., 22 LA 482, 483–84 (Handsaker, 1954); Standard Oil Co., 14 LA 641, 644 (Luskin, 1950). For two cases in which the arbitrator mentioned the matter of insurance carried by the employee, neither arbitrator considering this to be a relevant factor in determining the employer's obligation, see *Litton Microwave Cooking Prods.*, 75 LA 724, 727 (O'Connell, 1980), and *Consolidation Coal Co.*, 67 LA 358, 361 (Ipavec, 1976). *See also* Greenville, Mich., Pub. Sch., 77 LA 57, 57–58 (Roumell, Jr., 1981).

[658]*See* United States Steel Corp., 81 LA 224, 227 (Neyland, 1983); Grocers Supply Co., 79 LA 179, 180 (Allen, Jr., 1982); Bush/Hog Cont'l Gin Co., 77 LA 1145, 1150–51 (Griffin, 1981); Pettibone Corp., 74 LA 525, 528 (Dennis, 1980); American Petrofina Oil & Refinery, 71 LA 852, 855–56 (Mewhinney, 1978); Berea City Sch. Dist., 71 LA 679, 683–84 (Cohen, 1978); Chicago Bridge & Iron Co., 70 LA 584, 586–87 (Harrison, 1978) (employee not entitled to reimbursement for cost of protective jacket stolen from locker, the determining factor being that the garment, though "a quite desirable piece of protective clothing," was not required by the employer); Arden Mayfair Co., 63 LA 76, 78 (Whaley, 1974); United States Steel Corp., 59 LA 826, 828 (McDaniel, 1972); Standard Prods. Co., 55 LA 700, 703–04 (Teple, 1970); Commercial Motor Freight Co., 54 LA 240, 242–43 (Kesselman, 1971); Litton Indus., 53 LA 963, 964 (Jenkins, Jr., 1969); Pullman, Inc., 69–2 ARB ¶8750 (Gorsuch, 1969); Lockheed Aircraft Corp., 51 LA 636, 638 (Cahn, 1968); Fruehauf Corp., 50 LA 348, 350–51 (Hampton, 1968); Kennecott Copper Corp., 66–1 ARB ¶8362 (Leonard, 1966); American Potash & Chem. Corp., 47 LA 574, 575 (Block, 1966); Trans World Airlines, 41 LA 727, 729 (Beatty, Stone, & Bernson, 1963); Bethlehem Steel Co., 37 LA 195, 196 (Valtin, 1961); Bethlehem Steel, 32 LA 124, 125–26 (Valtin & Seward, 1959); Curtiss-Wright Corp., 36 LA 1136, 1137 (Crawford, 1961).

[659]Standard Prods. Co., 55 LA 700, 704 (Teple, 1970). *Accord* Owens-Corning Fiber-Glas Corp., 85 LA 305, 307 (Madden, 1985); Chemineer, Inc., 72 LA 568, 574 (Ruben, 1979); Commercial Motor Freight Co., 54 LA 240, 243 (Kesselman, 1971); Paragon Bridge & Steel Co., 46 LA 106, 108 (Stouffer, 1966). *See also* Fruehauf Corp., 50 LA 348, 350 (Hampton, 1968).

[660]Trans World Airlines, 41 LA 727, 729 (Beatty, Stone, & Bernson, 1963) (where the union argued for the application of the safety and health provision and a general provision requiring cooperation between the company and the union).

[661]Bethlehem Steel, 32 LA 124, 126 (Valtin & Seward, 1959). *Accord* Logemann Bros., 75 LA 615, 620 (Bard, 1980).

cific provision to that effect."[662] So, under the federal Labor Management Relations Act,[663] an arbitrator found that claims for property damage to employees' parked cars were too attenuated to qualify as related to employment. He viewed a grievance seeking such compensation as a tort claim falling outside the scope of the grievance procedure.

However, in addition to the traditional legal remedies available to an employee,[664] a number of arbitrators have imposed employer liability for lost, stolen, or damaged property of employees by implication arising under a collective bargaining agreement. Thus, although recognizing a past practice pursuant to which the company declined to pay "for missing or lost tools where actual theft has not been established or admitted," one decision found liability arising from the company's noncontractual requirement that employees provide their own tools and leave them at the plant.[665] The employer's negligence was manifest where it had discontinued furnishing a caged and locked area for the overnight storage of the employees' tools, and the grievant's tools were stolen from the new, unsecured area the company had provided.

> Where, as here, an employer requires employees to furnish and use their own tools in performing their work for the employer, to the benefit of the employer, and are required to leave those tools overnight with the employer, again for their mutual benefit, the employer has an implied obligation to provide a safe and secure place for the employees' tools. . . . [I]t is also reasonable to imply as part of that condition of employment, that the Company will be liable if the tools are stolen as the result of its negligence.[666]

One arbitrator commented: "While I believe that it is true general safety clauses are designed primarily to safeguard the health and personal security of employees, such clauses should not be held to exclude *all* items of personal property."[667] He postulated that "eyeglasses, hearing aids, [and] items of clothing actually being worn by employees while at work seem almost to be extensions of the employee's person."[668] He also noted that such items, as well as tools the employee is required to furnish to make possible the proper performance of the employee's work, further management's inter-

---

[662]Curtiss-Wright Corp., 36 LA 1136, 1137 (Crawford, 1961) (an employee claimed damages for the cost of replacing eyeglasses broken because of the company's alleged negligence regarding defective machinery). *See also* United States Steel Corp., 81 LA 224, 227 (Neyland, 1983) (concluding that the safety and health clause did not "either directly or implicitly" contemplate that the arbitrator "is to engage in the resolution of claims for damages based on negligence theories brought by employees against the Company").

[663]5 U.S.C. §141 et seq.

[664]For example, regulations promulgated under the federal Military Personnel and Civilian Employees' Claims Act of 1964 (31 U.S.C. §240 et seq.) provide that a covered claim is allowable "only" if (1) the damage or loss was not caused wholly or partly by the negligent or wrongful act of the claimant, claimant's agent, a member of claimant's family, or claimant's private employee (the standard to be applied is that of reasonable care under the circumstances); (2) the possession of the property damaged or lost and the quantity possessed is determined to have been reasonable, useful, or proper under the circumstances; and (3) the claim is substantiated by proper and convincing evidence. *See* 5 C.F.R. §180.104(a).

[665]Litton Precision Gear, 104 LA 151, 155 (Wolff, 1994) (citing ELKOURI & ELKOURI, HOW ARBITRATION WORKS (BNA Books 4th ed. 1985)).

[666]*Id.* at 155.

[667]Sargent-Fletcher Co., 49 LA 76, 78 (Lennard, 1967) (emphasis in original).

[668]*Id.*

ests. These circumstances, he felt, justified interpreting the contractual safety clause to cover such personal effects and employee-owned tools.

However, the arbitrator cautioned that nothing in his decision "should be construed as holding or even suggesting that this employer is, or must become, an insurer of employees' tools," but rather that his decision was directed to the company's obligation to observe an adequate standard of care where locked toolboxes were left on the plant premises in the exclusive custody of the employer while their owners were away from the plant.[669] Yet, in some cases it was emphasized either that contract language protecting the employees had been sought unsuccessfully by the union in negotiations or that the problem of tool thefts was so widely recognized in the industry that the parties would have provided protection if they had so intended.[670]

The applicability of "bailment" concepts is sometimes considered by arbitrators in determining the responsibility of the company for the safekeeping of employee property left or stored on plant premises. In this regard one arbitrator noted two schools of thought, with arbitrators of one school suggesting that

> a bailment relationship for the mutual benefit of both parties has been created by the Company's requirement that the mechanics furnish their own hand tools for the Company's benefit and by the Company's awareness of and acquiescence to having the tools stored on its premises due to the physical problem of removing them each night.[671]

Under this rationale, if a bailment relationship does exist in a given case, it is then proper for the arbitrator to determine whether the company has been negligent in safeguarding the property in question. Arbitrators of the other school of thought reason as follows: (1) The arbitrator's duty is to interpret the parties' agreement, which is the law in every case before him. (2) A bailment relationship is a legal one that may or may not be incorporated into the contract—if it is, it should be enforced by the arbitrator. (3) If a bailment

---

[669]*Id.* at 80.

[670]*See* Niagara Frontier Transit Metro Sys., 90 LA 1171, 1174 (Fullmer, 1988) (union had proposed, then dropped, tool-theft insurance during contract negotiations); Owens-Corning Fiber-Glas Corp., 85 LA 305, 308 (Madden, 1985) (union had failed in two attempts to include contract provision requiring company to replace lost tools); Arden Mayfair Co., 63 LA 76, 78 (Whaley, 1974); Litton Indus., 53 LA 963, 964 (Jenkins, Jr., 1969); American Motors Sales Corp., 48 LA 1040, 1043–44 (Yagoda, 1967) ("Silence on this subject has significance here as an absence of intent, because of the fact that the subject of protection of employees of this kind against loss of tools is a well-known one to negotiators in this industry. It has been dealt with in other contracts by the same Union bargainers."); American Potash & Chem. Corp., 47 LA 574, 575 (Block, 1966); Kennecott Copper Corp., 66–1 ARB ¶8362 (Leonard, 1966) (contract provision obligating the company to replace employee tools that "have been broken, lost or worn out in the performance of work for the Company" held not to apply to stolen tools in view of union's unsuccessful attempt in two previous negotiations to have the term "stolen" inserted in the clause). *See also* Berea City Sch. Dist., 71 LA 679, 683–84 (Cohen, 1978).

[671]Commercial Motor Freight Co., 54 LA 240, 243–44 (Kesselman, 1971) (citing arbitrators for both lines of reasoning). For later cases finding bailment, negligence, and consequent employer liability, see *Logemann Bros.*, 75 LA 615, 620–22 (Bard, 1980); Chemineer, Inc., 72 LA 568, 576–77 (Ruben, 1979). In *Arden Mayfair Co.*, 63 LA 76, 78 (Whaley, 1974), the arbitrator stated that "as an arbitrator, my concern is with the language in the contract between the parties, not with whether a bailment existed between" the employee and the company.

relationship is not a part of the contract, the arbitrator has no authority to enforce it or to rule on the question of negligence, because such a ruling cannot be enforced by the arbitrator.[672] Arbitrators following this reasoning have found the grievance to be nonarbitrable, and some have referred the grievant to a civil court remedy.[673]

Without mentioning the bailment-contract provision controversy, some arbitrators have cited the company's negligence in ruling for the employee,[674] while other arbitrators have found for the company since it had made a reasonable effort to protect the employee's property.[675] In any event, where an employee is negligent in safeguarding his or her tools, the company will not

---

[672]Commercial Motor Freight Co., 54 LA 240, 244 (Kesselman, 1971).

[673]See Reyco Indus., 85 LA 1034, 1040 (Newmark, 1985) (grievance held nonarbitrable absent relevant contract language requiring employer to reimburse employees); Transamerica Delaval, 85 LA 321, 324–25 (Bridgewater, 1985) ("no specific mutually agreed to contract language" indicating a "clear contractual intent" that employer indemnify employees for lost or stolen tools); United States Steel Corp., 81 LA 224, 227 (Neyland, 1983); Grocers Supply Co., 79 LA 179, 180 (Allen, Jr., 1982); Standard Prods. Co., 55 LA 700, 703 (Teple, 1970) (arbitrator "firmly believes that the Company cannot properly be held to be an insurer of property of employees left or stored upon the plant premises unless the collective agreement contains express terms imposing such broad liability"); Commercial Motor Freight Co., 54 LA 240, 243–44 (Kesselman, 1971); Litton Indus., 53 LA 693, 964 (Jenkins, Jr., 1969); Lockheed Aircraft Corp., 51 LA 636, 637–38 (Cahn, 1968) (finding a bailment relationship and a possible *legal* obligation on the company, but no contract violation); Paragon Bridge & Steel Co., 46 LA 106, 108 (Stouffer, 1966); Curtiss-Wright Corp., 36 LA 1136, 1137 (Crawford, 1961); Trans World Airlines, 41 LA 727, 729 (Beatty, Stone, & Bernson, 1963) (rejecting the union's bailment argument).

[674]See Wilson Mfg. Co., 70 LA 994, 996 (Tyer, 1978); Sargent-Fletcher Co., 49 LA 76, 79–80 (Lennard, 1967) (company did not provide a locked area for toolboxes or a system to safeguard toolbox keys left with the guard); Drake Bakeries, 43 LA 114, 115 (Cohen, 1964) (others had access to locked storage area); Best Mfg. Co., 22 LA 482, 483–84 (Handsaker, 1954); Standard Oil Co., 14 LA 641, 644 (Luskin, 1950). In *Sharpe-Saunders Constr.*, 79 LA 153, 155 (Goodman, 1982), the agreement required the employer to "provide an adequate tool house or storage room for the safekeeping of the employee's tools," and this was held to "impose a higher standard than that of reasonable care"; the employer was liable for loss of employee tools by theft where it "did not take every reasonable precaution," as evidenced by the fact that it provided greater security for its own tools than for those of the employee. In *Plough, Inc.*, 54 LA 430, 432 (Amis, 1971), the contract required the company to furnish and maintain satisfactory lockers, and while grievants were out on strike the company emptied their lockers (piling the contents in boxes) to make lockers available for employees hired to replace the strikers. The arbitrator held that the company failed to exercise reasonable care and therefore was required to compensate the grievants for damage to and loss of their property. Sargent-Fletcher Co., 49 LA 76, 79 (Lennard, 1967); Drake Bakeries, Inc., 43 LA 114, 115 (Cohen, 1964) (commenting on the advantage to the company from the presence of employee tools on the premises, the arbitrator noted that the company's obligation varies from exercising greater care when the employee's property is in its exclusive custody to exercising lesser care when the custody is shared or is almost exclusively in the employee).

[675]See Grocers Supply Co., 79 LA 179, 180 (Allen, Jr., 1982); Bush/Hog Cont'l Gin Co., 77 LA 1145, 1150 (Griffin, 1981); Pettibone Corp., 74 LA 525, 528 (Dennis, 1980); Standard Prods. Co., 55 LA 700, 704 (Teple, 1970) (fence with barbed wire on top, locked gate, guards); Pullman, Inc., 69–2 ARB ¶8750 (Gorsuch, 1969); Paragon Bridge & Steel Co., 46 LA 106, 108 (Stouffer, 1966); Bethlehem Steel Co., 37 LA 195, 196 (Valtin, 1961) (new locks on locker-room doors, janitors instructed to keep doors locked, employees invited to report suspicious behavior, locker rooms included in rounds of plant guards); Bethlehem Steel, 32 LA 124, 125–26 (Valtin & Seward, 1959). In *Fruehauf Corp.*, 50 LA 348, 350–51 (Hampton, 1968), where a company rule held employees responsible for 50% of the value of company tools lost while in their possession, it was ruled that since the employer and employees each took reasonable security precautions, neither was required to compensate the other for loss of tools by theft.

be held liable. For example, a grievant was denied reimbursement of $1,500 for tools missing from his personal toolbox that he left at the plant after he sustained an on-duty injury, and was ultimately terminated. The grievant had merely told a coworker to "keep an eye" on his tools, and he did not attempt to retrieve them for 2 years after he was discharged.[676]

If the collective bargaining agreement does contain a provision for the replacement of tools under certain circumstances, arbitrators generally will not extend any recovery to an employee beyond those items specified in the contract. In one case, the agreement provided merely that the employer must replace tools that are worn out or broken on the job.[677] The arbitrator held that the inclusion of such a provision indicates the parties' intent to exclude liability for stolen or misplaced tools and that the arbitrator has no authority to add to the obligation to replace worn out or broken tools the obligation to replace missing tools.

15. Union Bulletin Boards [LA CDI 2.25]

Collective bargaining agreements often contain clauses stating that the company will provide a bulletin board for the posting of union notices, usually specifying notices of union meetings, elections, social activities, and general union business.[678] Such clauses also may contain a proviso that the notices must be "approved," "signed," or "notated" by the company. In some cases, disagreement has arisen between company and union as to whether company approval was wrongly withheld or whether the notices the union sought to post were proper notices within the meaning of the contract.

Thus, the issue before the arbitrator ordinarily concerns the *content* of the employee communication, as distinguished from the *time* or *place* of the communication.[679] In contrast, the issues in cases involving employee com-

---

[676]John Fabick Tractor Co., 98 LA 438, 439–40 (Thornell, 1992). *See* Southern Clay, 92 LA 731 (Odom, Jr., 1989) (employee not entitled to reimbursement because toolbox not locked at time of theft).

[677]Centrex Corp., 95 LA 1154 (Rybolt, 1990).

[678]*See* U.S. Army Soldier Support Ctr., 91 LA 1201, 1202 (Wolff, 1988) (contract language prohibited the posting of "any derogatory remarks" or "personal attacks on individuals"); Webb Furniture, 275 NLRB 1305, 120 LRRM 1034 (1985) (the Board found that the company violated §8(a)(1) of the National Labor Relations Act (NLRA) by disparately applying its no-posting rule to prohibit union posting while permitting nonunion-related postings); Roadway Express, 272 NLRB 895, 117 LRRM 1436 (1984). Even where the agreement did not contain a bulletin board clause, the union had a right under the NLRA to use the plant bulletin board, because the employer had discriminatorily denied its use to the union while permitting it for personal messages of employees and for group notices by other organizations. NLRB v. Honeywell, Inc., 722 F.2d 405, 114 LRRM 3658 (8th Cir. 1983). In another case, a union's action was in a sense a discriminatory denial of bulletin board use, where the union whose collective bargaining agreement gave it the right to use a bulletin board for official union business violated the NLRA by removing material that a dissident member had posted criticizing union actions and policies. Helton v. NLRB, 656 F.2d 883, 107 LRRM 2819 (D.C. Cir. 1981) (court holding, in disagreement with the NLRB, that the union's action did "restrain or coerce" the employee in violation of §8(b)(1)(A) of the NLRA).

[679]There should be no issue about place, the place of the communication being the contractually provided bulletin board. There could be a time issue if the employer seeks to regulate even the minimal use of time required for the physical act of posting or seeks to restrict the time for bulletin board viewing. Where the communication is achieved not by use of the bulletin board but by some other method, such as distribution of handbills, a stronger possi-

munications under the National Labor Relations Act very well may be concerned with *time and place,* as well as *content.*[680] However, in one arbitration case that did concern the location of a bulletin board, the arbitrator allowed the employer to relocate a bulletin board unilaterally where the contract required that the union be provided one bulletin board in the department, but did not specify the location. The board often contained disloyal, critical, scatological, and obscene material, and the employer felt that this material was inappropriate for public view, especially since the company recently had

---

bility exists for the arbitrator to be confronted with a time and/or place issue. *See, e.g.*, Social Sec. Admin., 81 LA 311, 317–18 (King, 1983) (federal-sector employees have "no statutory right to distribute literature in work areas during work time, and absent agreement by an agency and bargaining representative, an agency may validly prohibit such distribution"); American Cyanamid Co., 74 LA 1270, 1272 (O'Connell, 1980); Hygrade Food Prods. Corp., 74 LA 99, 104 (O'Neill, 1980) (upholding discharge of employee who distributed literature during working time); Master Lock Co., 71 LA 999, 1003 (Seidman, 1978); Associated Hosps. of S.F., 67 LA 323, 326 (Koven, 1976); North Am. Mfg. Co., 62 LA 1219, 1220 (Hutcheson, 1974).

[680]Regarding *time* and *place* of employee communications under the NLRA, the Supreme Court has upheld the NLRB's rule that, absent special circumstances, an employer's restriction on employee solicitation during nonworking time and distribution during such time in nonworking areas is presumptively an unreasonable interference with employee rights under the Act. Beth Israel Hosp. v. NLRB, 437 U.S. 483, 492–93, 98 LRRM 2727 (1978) (holding that a hospital improperly prohibited distribution of an employee publication in its cafeteria, which was patronized primarily by employees; publication was objectionable to the employer because it disparaged the hospital's ability to provide adequate patient care due to understaffing, but the content of the publication was not the question considered by the Court in this case). For other cases dealing with time and place of employee communications under the NLRA, see *NLRB v. Baptist Hosp.*, 442 U.S. 773, 101 LRRM 2556 (1979); *Republic Aviation Corp. v. NLRB*, 324 U.S. 793, 16 LRRM 620 (1945). Regarding plant access by nonemployee union organizers for the purpose of communicating with employees, see *Hudgens v. NLRB*, 424 U.S. 507, 91 LRRM 2489 (1976) (holding that it is under the NLRA rather than the First or Fourteenth Amendments that labor may have a right of access to the private property of another person); *NLRB v. Babcock & Wilcox Co.*, 356 U.S. 581, 38 LRRM 2001 (1956). Regarding the *content* of employee communications under the NLRA, the Supreme Court did deal directly with the matter of *content* in *Eastex, Inc. v. NLRB*, 437 U.S. 556, 98 LRRM 2717 (1978). In this case, the employer prohibited distribution of a union newsletter in nonworking areas of the plant because the newsletter contained material (making appeals in respect to right-to-work and minimum wage legislation) that the employer found objectionable and that the employer said was unrelated to the employer-union relationship. The Court found "no warrant for [the employer's] view that employees lose their protection under the 'mutual aid or protection' clause [of NLRA §7] when they seek to improve terms and conditions of employment or otherwise improve their lot as employees through channels outside the immediate employee-employer relationship." *Id.* at 565. In holding the employer's prohibition improper, the Court stressed that the employer did not show that management interests would be prejudiced by distribution of the literature. The Court would not attempt to delineate precisely the boundaries of the "mutual aid or protection" clause, a task for the NLRB to perform in the first instance as it considers the wide variety of cases that come before it. The Court did indicate, however, that distribution of literature could be prohibited if its content is inflammatory to the point of threatening disorder or interruption of the normal functioning of the business. The Court also noted that the NLRB had accepted employer disallowance of "purely political" literature even though the election of any political candidate may have an ultimate effect on employment conditions. In *Auto Workers Local 174 v. NLRB (Firestone Steel Prods. Co.)*, 645 F.2d 1151, 106 LRRM 2561 (D.C. Cir. 1981), the NLRB's view that purely political literature is not protected activity under §7 was upheld. In *Timpte, Inc. v. NLRB*, 590 F.2d 871, 873, 100 LRRM 2479 (10th Cir. 1979), the court upheld the discharge of an employee for refusing to stop distributing union campaign literature containing "vulgar and indecent" language; in denying enforcement of an NLRB order, the court held that the "combination of profanity and filthy language" in the employee's disparagement of coworkers, union stewards, and management was "indefensible" and unprotected by NLRA §7.

begun conducting tours for school children. The arbitrator held that such changed conditions overrode past practice and, therefore, the employer was allowed to move the board to a remote hallway corner on the edge of the department.[681]

Arbitrators have upheld the refusal of employers to approve the posting of notices on the basis of inappropriate content such as a list of wages paid at another of the company's plants and at a rival company's plant along with some controversial and political material that would allegedly involve the company in an unfair labor practice suit,[682] an announcement of the terms of a strike settlement at another company,[683] and a letter that praised and defended the union's activity but derogated and maligned the company.[684]

When the agreement prohibited "solicitations," an arbitrator found the union's posting of membership campaign materials entitled "Effects of Being Nonunion" and "Why Join the Union" to be in violation of the contract.[685] The same result followed where a contract provided for the posting of "official announcements and notices concerning meetings of the union, scheduling and results of election, appointments to office, social, educational and recreational affairs," and the company refused to allow use of the bulletin board to provide information about long-term disability benefits. Since the purpose was not plainly within the scope of that detailed contract clause, the company's exclusion was found proper.[686] But a contrary result was reached in a similar case,[687] where the arbitrator found that the contractual listing of specific topics had been expanded by implication because supervisors allowed an additional category of information, hourly pay schedules of village employees, to remain on the bulletin board for 7 months, and had removed the material to copy for their own use and then reposted it.[688]

Employers have been upheld in disciplining employees who have deliberately disobeyed management's order not to post certain political and con-

---

[681]News-Sun, 91 LA 1324 (Goldstein, 1988).

[682]Reynolds Metals Co., 13 LA 278, 280 (Kleinsorge, 1949).

[683]Danly Mach. Co., 13 LA 499, 500–01 (Luskin, 1949) (finding that "the announcement contained material that is not customarily and generally considered an official Union announcement of the kind and character usually posted on bulletin boards where the bulletin boards are controlled by the Company"). *See also* Rebsamen Cos., 66 LA 449, 451–52 (Oppenheim, 1976) (posting of newspaper advertisement concerning strike by another union against another company could be prohibited by employer based on its objection that the appeal was inflammatory); Wisconsin Dep't of Transp., 63 LA 588, 593 (McCormick, 1974) (employer could remove poster urging boycott of another employer's product).

[684]General Elec. Co., 31 LA 924, 925 (LaCugna, undated). The contract provided that company approval would "not be unreasonably withheld," and the arbitrator found that the company's refusal to approve the letter was not unreasonable in view of its controversial and derogatory tone. *See also* Ottaway Newspapers, 61 LA 750, 753 (Eisenberg, 1973).

[685]Leggett & Platt, 104 LA 1048 (Statham, 1995).

[686]Arcata Graphics/Kingsport, 102 LA 429 (Frost, 1993).

[687]Village of Woodridge, Ill., 104 LA 806 (Wolff, 1995).

[688]*See also* Leggett & Platt, 104 LA 1048 (Statham, 1995) (company-imposed limitations on postings to the categories provided for in the contract approved, but company directed to develop a procedure to ensure uniform administration of posting requests in light of evidence that the same postings had been treated differently in different company facilities).

troversial materials on the union bulletin board.[689] In one case, an employee (after being warned) repeatedly posted on the union bulletin board items that were "inflammatory and defamatory," including a diatribe charging the company with practicing favoritism and nepotism in job promotions. The employee was discharged and in response to his grievance charging that his right of free speech was violated, the arbitrator wrote:

> In my opinion, although an employee while at work in his employer's plant may not be muzzled, he nevertheless has no unhampered right to voice opinions about his employer at the plant during his working time of such kind and in such manner as clearly to tend to disrupt employee morale or interfere with the orderly and efficient operation of the plant.[690]

However, even though a contract provides for company approval of notices to be posted, the company does not have "an unrestricted right to edit and reject" union notices, and it may not arbitrarily, unreasonably, or capriciously withhold its approval. One arbitrator stated, however, that the company can "reject and refuse to approve for posting notices which contain statements that are derogatory to it and its Supervision, those containing obscene or immoral statements, and those which are patently detrimental or disloyal to the Company, its Management and/or its business."[691] The notice considered by this arbitrator announced a meeting to hear a report of contract negotiations at another plant of the employer, and the arbitrator noted that while the company may have considered the purpose of the meeting to be adverse to its interests, it was not warranted in rejecting the notice.

In two of three cases where the contracts provided for union bulletin boards for the posting of "official" notices but did not require company approval, it was held that the company could remove or require the union to remove a notice containing the names of nonunion employees of the company. The arbitrator in one of these cases considered the notice to be detrimental to workplace discipline and likely to produce an inflammatory response.[692] The arbitrator in the second case found not only that the list of names was not "official business" of the union, but they also "tended to incite

---

[689]Cypress Gardens Citrus Prods., 50 LA 1183, 1186 (Christon, 1968) (stating that "[t]he substance of the particular material which the Union posted was completely unrelated to the plant's operations, or to the Union's activities, either in or out of the plant"). *See also* Kimberly-Clark of Can., 59 LA 513, 515 (Brown, 1972) (upholding suspension of union president who did not seek permission from employer before posting notice urging boycott of employer's product; the notice, which was posted at request of another union engaged in a strike at another plant of the employer, was contrary to the interest of the employer and did not pertain to normal union business); Bethlehem Steel Corp., 53 LA 228, 228 (Seward, 1969) (where, after express warning, an employee deliberately violated a long-standing company rule barring the posting of notices without management's permission). *Cf.* Wright Mach. Co., 64 LA 593, 595 (Calhoon, 1975).

[690]Beaver Precision Prods., 51 LA 853, 854–55 (Kates, 1968) (where there was no express contractual provision pertaining to bulletin boards, but the company as a matter of practice provided some for the union's use). *See also* Union Carbide Corp., 44 LA 554, 561 (Stouffer, 1965).

[691]Conn Organ Corp., 42 LA 1198, 1200 (Stouffer, 1964). *See also* Greyhound Food Mgmt., 87 LA 619 (Ellmann, 1985) (a posting was found to be legitimate union business even though it could be considered to be inflammatory).

[692]Quaker Oats Co., 64–3 ARB ¶8986 (Bauder, 1964).

prejudice, animosity, hatred, discrimination and intimidation against certain employees of the Company because of their Non-Union affiliation. . . . Such conclusion is not predicated on a baseless assumption—any ordinary, reasonable man could predict such a resulting effect."[693]

However, in the third case where a company removed from the bulletin board a notice urging union members to support a strike by another union against another employer, the arbitrator noted that the company had been unsuccessful in its attempt to negotiate a contractual restriction on the subject matter of bulletin board notices, the company having obtained only a commitment during negotiations that the union would "try to cooperate." He declared that there "is nothing in the words 'try to cooperate' which binds the Union to accept the Company's determination of what is an appropriate or inappropriate subject of a notice to be posted on the bulletin board." Finding convincing the union's argument that another union's strike "does raise the issue of trade union solidarity," so that it fell within "the legitimate business interests" of the union in the present case "to communicate with its members concerning a constituent policy position that the local union has taken to support the striking members of another union," the arbitrator held the company's action to be improper.[694]

Another arbitrator, interpreting a company approval clause, stated that "[t]he Company cannot be arbitrary or capricious in making its determination of whether to post a particular notice . . . but has the right to exercise some judgment concerning its approval or willingness for posting a notice."[695] The case resulted from the return of two supervisors to the bargaining unit, which contributed to the layoff of unit employees. The notice in question charged that such action violated the agreement and that the action was taken by the company in order to cause a wildcat strike so that it could discharge strike participants, thereby breaking the union. However, the notice also stated that the union had not authorized a wildcat strike and would fight the employer's action through legal means. The company contended that the notice was inflammatory, but offered to post it if objectional portions were omitted. The arbitrator, while acknowledging that the notice had some "rather harsh words," held that the notice referred to union business within the meaning of the union bulletin board provision and that its "main purpose seemed to be to avert a work stoppage." He concluded that the company should have posted the notice, and volunteered that the company could have posted its own notice and volunteered that it intended to encourage a wildcat strike.[696]

---

[693]Union Carbide Corp., 44 LA 554, 561 (Stouffer, 1965).

[694]Wisconsin Tissue Mills, 73 LA 271, 273–74 (Flagler, 1979). In *Warren City Manufacturing Co.*, 7 LA 202, 206 (Abernethy, 1947), the new contract dropped the company approval requirement and the arbitrator interpreted the bulletin board provision strictly, stating that the contract does not give the company authority to refuse to post "union material submitted by the union" or to remove from bulletin boards "union material posted there by the authorized officials of the union."

[695]Fruehauf Corp., 54 LA 1096, 1098 (Marshall, 1971).

[696]*Id.* at 1098–99. For another case in which an employer omission was a factor in holding for the union even though its notice "was in poor taste," see *Bureau of Prisons*, 65 LA 1240, 1244–45 (Hall, 1975).

In instances where notices are allowed to be posted on union bulletin boards under the terms of the contract but cause disruptive behavior among employees, the NLRB has held that absent evidence of special circumstances showing that the posting caused employee behavior that amounts to a serious threat to discipline in the workplace, the union will be permitted to keep the notice posted.[697]

In arbitration cases, the following kinds of notices have been found to relate to appropriate union business concerns: a notice of a meeting at which a strike vote would be taken,[698] a union version of the plant seniority list,[699] campaign material promoting union membership and characterizing management as being an unfair exacting overseer,[700] and a notice requiring union members to report any management contacts with respect to promotion out of the unit.[701]

In summary, the cases noted above indicate that the content of notices to be posted on union bulletin boards (1) may not stray in subject matter from the reasonable concept of what constitutes union business at the particular plant; (2) may not be of such nature as to have a detrimental effect on employee morale, or of such nature as to inflame employees against each other or against the employer, and (3) may not contain statements that defame or are patently detrimental or disloyal to the employer. It seems reasonable to expect that similar critera would be followed in arbitration cases concerning employee communications by handbills, newsletters, and other methods not involving the use of bulletin boards.[702] Finally, while public-sector employees enjoy a measure of freedom of speech protection against censorship of their communications by their employer under the First and Fourteenth Amendments,[703] private-sector employees do not. The Supreme

---

[697]Southwestern Bell Tel. Co., 276 NLRB 1053, 120 LRRM 1145, 1147 (1985). In this instance, NLRB Chairman Donald L. Dotson disagreed with his colleagues, holding that the company had the right to "prevent the deleterious consequences the posting might reasonably be expected to produce under the circumstances" and that where a notice was likely to provoke confrontation, the company should not have to wait until an actual confrontation or breakdown of discipline has already occurred before special circumstances warranting the prohibition of the posting are deemed to be present.

[698]Fairchild Engine & Airplane Corp., 16 LA 678, 681 (Jaffee, 1951).

[699]Lennox Furnace Co., 20 LA 788, 789 (Johannes, 1953).

[700]Wisconsin Dep't of Transp., 63 LA 588, 590, 593 (McCormick, 1974).

[701]Walker Mfg. Co. of Wis., 31 LA 80, 81–82 (Luskin, 1958).

[702]For some of the relatively few arbitration cases involving such other methods of employee communications, see Southern Bell Tel. & Tel. Co., 78 LA 812, 813–15 (Wolff, 1982) (discussing criteria relevant to the wearing of union buttons); Rohr Indus., 76 LA 273, 278 (Weiss, 1980) (upholding discharge for distributing purely political literature in plant after being warned); Huron Forge & Mach. Co., 75 LA 83, 96–97 (Roumell, Jr., 1980) (upholding discharge for distribution of inflammatory literature); Gold Kist, 70 LA 342, 344 (Morris, 1978); R.H. Buhrke Co., 68 LA 1170, 1173–74 (Nicholas, Jr., 1977) (employer improperly prohibited wearing of t-shirts with slogan urging repeal of state's right-to-work law); Social Sec. Admin., 67 LA 249, 250, 254 (Rose, 1976) (union leaflet maligned management official); International Harvester Co., 59 LA 219, 223 (Block, 1972) (employer could prohibit protest signs on toolboxes that were of such nature as to create an unfavorable impression upon customers in the plant).

[703]See Givhan v. Western Line Consol. Sch. Dist., 439 U.S. 410, 413–15, 18 FEP Cases 1424 (1979) (citing other Supreme Court decisions on such rights). See also Social Sec. Admin., 81 LA 311, 318 (King, 1983); Wayne-Westland, Mich., Cmty. Sch., 62 LA 1098, 1101–02 (Sembower, 1974). Cf. Garden Grove Unified Sch. Dist., 73 LA 274, 276–77 (Rule, 1979).

Court has held that "'the First and Fourteenth Amendments safeguard the rights of free speech and assembly by limitations on *state* action, not on action by the owner of private property used nondiscriminatorily for private purposes only . . . .'"[704]

16. CHANGE IN TIME OR METHOD OF PAY [LA CDI 100.45; 114.14]

Changes in the time or method of payment of wages sometimes lead to disputes between unions and employers. However, arbitrators agree that unless restricted by the contract, the employer may change the time of payment of wages. Thus, arbitrators have upheld a change from weekly to biweekly paydays even though the paydays had been on a weekly basis for many years.[705] However, one arbitrator held that an employer did not have the right to change from weekly to biweekly pay periods where the contract defined the payroll period as the "seven day period from 12:01 a.m. Sunday through midnight the following Saturday," and there was a long-standing past practice of paying employees weekly.[706] In this case, even though the company offered good business reasons as justification for the change, the arbitrator found that its unilateral action was violative of the collective bargaining agreement and that any change in the pay period should come through the process of negotiations with the union.[707] Similarly, a successor employer was found to have violated a local agreement by changing a 12-year practice of paying on a weekly basis. The arbitrator held that the union had given up seniority rights as a quid pro quo for the weekly pay schedule, and the fact that the company no longer desired the benefits gained under the agreement was not determinative.[708]

Arbitrators also have upheld changing the day of the week on which employees are paid, despite the fact that employees had been paid on a particular day for many years.[709] In the absence of contractual restriction, arbi-

---

[704]Hudgens v. NLRB, 424 U.S. 507, 519, 91 LRRM 2489 (1976) (quoting Lloyd Corp. v. Tanner, 407 U.S. 551, 567 (1972)). *See also* Rohr Indus., 76 LA 273 (Weiss, 1980); Huron Forge & Mach. Co., 75 LA 83, 90–91 (Roumell, Jr., 1980); Metropolitan Hosp. & Health Ctrs., 63 LA 378, 382 (Roumell, Jr., 1974); Jones Dairy Farm, 72 LA 968, 971 (Maslanka, 1979); Gold Kist, 70 LA 342, 343 (Morris, 1978).

[705]*See* Westlake Moving & Storage, 50 LA 125, 127–28 (Roberts, 1968); United States Steel Corp., 66–1 ARB ¶8323 (Flarey, 1966) (not a local working condition protected by contract); Cone Mills Corp., 30 LA 100, 104 (Barrett, 1958).

[706]Creative Data Servs., 87 LA 962 (Hilgert, 1986).

[707]*Id.* at 964. The arbitrator found no merit in the company's contention that it did not in fact change the payroll period, but merely paid employees for two payroll periods in each paycheck rather than one.

[708]Arch of W. Va., 90 LA 891 (Stoltenberg, 1988). *But see* Midwest Dental Prods. Corp., 94 LA 467, 470–72 (Wies, 1990) (held that the employer's new owner properly changed from a weekly to biweekly pay program and eliminated advance vacation checks contrary to a 20-year practice; the contract provided that vacation checks would be issued "only when vacation is actually taken," rights not exercised by management were not waived, and a zipper clause precluded consideration of past practices).

[709]*See* Samuel Bingham Co., 51 LA 577, 578–79 (McCoy, 1968) (payday held not to be a "condition of employment" within the meaning of the contract provision requiring bargaining on all conditions of employment); Glamorgan Pipe & Foundry Co., 46 LA 1007, 1008 (Dugan, 1966) (finding no binding past practice); FMC Corp., 40 LA 417, 422 (Gorsuch, 1993); Kennecott Copper Corp., 30 LA 964, 966 (Kadish, 1958).

trators have approved the payment of wages by check, with arrangements to permit employees to cash their checks, even though payment had been made in cash for many years.[710] However, where the contract provided that employees were to receive "[p]ay checks . . . in sealed envelopes," an arbitrator denied the company the right to implement a direct deposit system for payment of its employees' wages. The arbitrator held that this was the only form of payment of wages permitted by the contract and could not be changed by the company, notwithstanding the increased efficiency and convenience associated with the direct deposit system.[711]

In another case, past practice was found to be the decisive factor in denying a company the right to change from hand delivery on company premises to mail delivery of payroll checks. The arbitrator said that this function was not one that fell within the scope of the management-rights clause, as it was not a question of scheduling production or determining processes of manufacturing. He concluded: "As to their pay fully accrued, employees have rights as creditors, so that decision as to the place where check delivery is to be made is not the exclusive function of management."[712]

17. UNILATERAL CHANGES IN HEALTH INSURANCE TERMS
[LA CDI 100.5965; 116.6019]

Section 8(a)(5) of the NLRA requires employers to "bargain collectively with the representatives of his employees" as to wages, hours, and other terms and conditions of employment.[713] Therefore, any refusal to bargain or unilateral action with respect to any mandatory subject of bargaining is a violation of the Act.[714] The terms of a health insurance plan are a mandatory subject of bargaining.[715]

---

[710]United States Steel Corp., 36 LA 220, 221–22 (McDermott, 1961); Diamond Alkali Co., 38 LA 1055, 1057 (Rubin, 1962) ("Nor is the method of wage payment, whether in cash or by check, a type of benefit guarded by the principle of accepted past practice.").

[711]Mid-Continent Bottlers, 95 LA 1003, 1004 (Reynolds, 1990). *See also* Pickands Mather & Co., 87 LA 1071 (Garrett, 1986) (held that the unilateral requirement that all paychecks be directly deposited into employee-designated banks was improper; the practice of allowing certain employees to refuse to authorize direct deposit was a "benefit" for employees and should be protected as a local working condition).

[712]Manitowoc Shipbuilding, 39 LA 907, 909 (Kovenock, 1962). *See also* Peoples Gas Light & Coke Co., 39 LA 224, 225–26 (Davis, 1962) (a "firmly established" past practice was "created" based on a grievance settlement under which the employer agreed to pay "cash supper allowance," thus precluding the employer from changing to check payments for the period of the current contract). In *Union Oil Co. of Cal.*, 65 LA 1278, 1280 (Coburn, 1975), the company was not liable for late receipt of wages where "the delay was caused solely by the untimely delivery of the paycheck by the U.S. Postal Service and not through any negligence of the Company." However, in *National Automatic Sprinkler & Fire Control Ass'n*, 80 LA 800, 803 (Wright, 1983), the agreement expressly provided for 8 hours' pay when a paycheck is received late and this provision was strictly enforced where delayed payment resulted from a computer breakdown. *See also* Mi-Ka Prods., 76 LA 1203, 1211 (Christopher, 1981). *Cf.* Bethlehem Steel Corp., 69 LA 1100, 1101 (Sharnoff, 1977).

[713]29 U.S.C. §158(a)(5). *See also* Fibreboard Paper Prods. Corp. v. NLRB, 379 U.S. 203, 210, 57 LRRM 2609 (1964).

[714]NLRB v. Katz, 369 U.S. 736, 743, 50 LRRM 2177 (1962).

[715]SAE Young Westmont-Chicago, LLC., 333 NLRB No. 59, 169 LRRM 1157 (2001).

Most arbitrators would agree that a change in health insurance occurs when employee monthly premium contributions increase, coverage of illnesses decreases, or copay and deductible amounts increase.[716] However, if the employer simply adds a plan option that alters the procedure for determining when a treatment is medically necessary[717] or changes a plan administrator, arbitrators have found that no "change" has occurred in the terms of the health insurance plan.[718]

The collective bargaining agreement controls how changes can be made in the health insurance plan. One scenario is that the contract is silent as to changes in health insurance. Such was the case in *Browning-Ferris*.[719] Despite the existence of one plan for all the employees, the company unilaterally implemented two other plans as choices for the employees with different levels of coverage. The new plans resulted in monthly out-of-pocket expenses for employees based upon their experience levels and the union grieved, claiming an impermissible unilateral change in the health insurance terms. The arbitrator found no violation of the contract. Since the parties had specified benefits for other insurance policies, but chose not to do so for health insurance, the arbitrator concluded that the imposition of out-of-pocket costs was not prohibited.[720]

At the other extreme, a collective bargaining agreement may specifically dictate the terms and conditions of health insurance. The terms can be incorporated directly into the agreement through the explicit language of the contract, past practice,[721] or reference to the details of the insurance plan.[722] In such cases, if the unilateral change results in noncompliance with those specific provisions, the employer will be held to have violated the contract.[723]

In *Union Foundry Co.*,[724] the contract required the company to pay premium rates up to a maximum dollar amount. Increased utilization resulted in a deficit in the reserve account, and premium rates needed to be raised. Negotiations with the union were unsuccessful in producing agreement on sharing responsibility for payment of the increase. As a consequence, the company unilaterally implemented a new plan. The arbitrator found that the contract had been violated; however, he did not grant the union's request for reinstatement of the old health insurance plan because that would have

---

[716]*See* Town of Oconomowoc, Wis., 115 LA 169 (Petersen, 2000).

[717]Town of Plymouth, Case No. MUP-9829, 1997 WL 338452 (Dumont, 1997) (no violation of state employment act in unilaterally implementing such changes).

[718]Stark County, Ohio, Sheriff, 108 LA 394 (Heekin, 1997).

[719]114 LA 1424 (Briggs, 2000).

[720]*Id.* at 1428–29. *See also* Chicago Bd. of Educ., 104 LA 679 (Nicholas, Jr., 1995) (no violation where contract did not contain provision allowing waiting period for new employees prior to health insurance coverage).

[721]Joy Mining Mach., 114 LA 1097 (Coyne, 2000) (violation for employees not to be able to choose own physician as past practice dictated).

[722]Excel Corp., 106 LA 1069 (Thornell, 1996) (copay and maximum out-of-pocket cost levels written into agreement through details of plan that was incorporated into collective bargaining agreement).

[723]Union Foundry Co., 113 LA 63 (Baroni, 1999) (violation of contract requiring specific dollar amount of premiums of $394.07 when new plan implemented, so parties ordered to negotiate new language).

[724]*Id.*

resulted in the amendment of the terms of the contract by requiring the employer to pay more than the stipulated dollar amount. Therefore, the arbitrator ordered the parties to reopen negotiations with the proviso that if impasse was reached, then the employer could implement a reasonable insurance plan under its management rights powers.[725]

In some cases, a collective bargaining agreement will allow a change in insurance, but also place restrictions on the change. For example, in *Friedrich Air Conditioning*,[726] the contract provided the company had sole discretion to change the health care plan as long as the deductible for the employees remained the same. When the company implemented a copay for prescription drugs, the arbitrator found no contract violation because the deductible had remained constant.[727]

The contract may require that the same level of benefits be maintained. Such was the situation in *City of Norman, Oklahoma*,[728] where the city decided to self-insure, which resulted in reduced benefit levels. Despite the city's argument that the management-rights clause of the contract allowed such action, the arbitrator found the contract language requiring the same level of benefits governed the situation directly, and therefore sustained the grievance.[729]

The collective bargaining agreement also may contain a "me-too" clause, which dictates that if the provisions of the health insurance plan of another bargaining unit are changed, then the insurance of the "me-too" bargaining unit is changed correspondingly. The contract in *Wantagh, New York, Union Free School District*[730] provided that if the teachers' benefits are changed, then the clerical employees' benefits are equally changed. As a result of the changes in the teachers' contract, the district reduced its contribution to health insurance on behalf of the clerical employees from 95 percent to 90 percent. The arbitrator denied the clerical employees' grievance, both because of the specific contract language allowing such a change and because the district had in the past made changes to the clerical unit's health insurance based upon changes in the teacher unit's insurance plan.[731]

The parties may also agree to cost containment provisions, allowing the employer to take action to reduce the cost of health insurance. In *Palm Beach County, Florida*,[732] the contract allowed the employer to lower its contribu-

---

[725]*Id.* at 67–68.

[726]112 LA 907 (Halter, 1999).

[727]*Id.* at 909.

[728]115 LA 827 (McReynolds, 2001).

[729]*Id.* at 832. *See also* City of Duluth, Minn., 114 LA 975 (Neigh, 2000) (not same level of benefits provided when change in health insurance resulted in employees being required to obtain authorization prior to obtaining service outside of the network); Springfield, Ohio, Bd. of Educ., 114 LA 1429 (Talarico, 2000) (bargaining history, past practice, and lack of discussion during last round of negotiations established that all benefits shall remain unchanged); Town of Oconomowoc, Wis., 115 LA 169 (Petersen, 2000) (violation of contract requiring equivalent benefits as of date of change, when changing of carriers resulted in increased emergency room copay and increased payment for prescription drugs).

[730]106 LA 741 (Liebowitz, 1996). *See also* Copper & Brass Sales, 105 LA 730 (Nelson, 1995) (contract required that employees receive same health insurance as other employees, however, grievance was filed and decided based on other reasons).

[731]*Id.* at 744–45.

[732]106 LA 15 (Cohen, 1995).

tion on behalf of the employees by up to some 7½ percent as long as it was based on an actuarial study. The employer implemented changes within the cap, but without the benefit of an actuarial study, which was still being prepared. The arbitrator found the actuarial study was not essential.[733] The contract also may require that the employer pay up to a maximum amount per month toward the cost of coverage. In *Masonite Corp.*,[734] when the cost of insurance rose above the cap, the employer properly required the employees to pay the increase if they wanted to retain coverage.[735]

The most common contractual provision governing health insurance changes allows a unilateral change in the health insurance coverage as long as the benefits of the new plan are "substantially similar" or "comparable" to the previous benefits. As an example, in *Whayne Supply Co.*,[736] the contract allowed changes to health insurance as long as the coverage remained substantially similar. The employer changed to a preferred provider network program, which increased the deductible and maximum out-of-pocket expenses. The arbitrator found these changes did not violate the contract because the union was unable to show any difference in the level of care.[737]

But, in *Excel Corp.*,[738] the contract stated that the employer "shall install cost containment programs designed to control and reduce employee and employer health care cost."[739] Based on this language, the employer installed a preferred provider network plan. The new plan reduced the copayments and maximum out-of-pocket expenses for employees who used providers within the network. However, if the employees used out-of-network providers, they would be subject to an increase in the amount of copayments and out-of-pocket expenses. Interpreting the term "benefits" to include copayments and out-of-pocket expenses, the arbitrator concluded that

---

[733]*Id.* at 19.

[734]104 LA 121 (Nicholas, Jr., 1995).

[735]*Id.* at 124–25. *See also* Township of Brownstown, Mich., 114 LA 166 (Allen, 2000) (contract violation when employer simply notified union rather than bargained with union as required by contract when costs of insurance increased above 6%); Glasgow, Mont., Pub. Sch. Dist., 105 LA 1004 (1996) (Prayzich, 1996) (excess contributed over maximum by employer to health insurance is to be applied to payment for next year, as required by parties' intention).

[736]111 LA 940 (Imundo, Jr., 1998).

[737]*Id.* at 943–44. *See also* Stark County, Ohio, Sheriff, 108 LA 394 (Heekin, 1997) (administrative problems resulting in no unpaid claims is not a violation of a contract requiring similar coverage); City of Palm Beach Gardens, Fla., 112 LA 1153 (Hoffman, 1999) (no substantial benefit reduction when actuarial calculations concluded an increase in benefits in the new coverage of 12.5%, and wide interests of employees were favored). *But see* Town of Oconomowoc, Wis., 115 LA 169 (Petersen, 2000) (no equivalent benefits when increased copay for emergency room visits and increased prescription drug payments); City of Norman, Okla., 115 LA 827 (McReynolds, 2001) (not same level of benefits when self-insurance resulted in reduced benefit levels); Joy Mining Mach., 114 LA 1097 (Coyne, 2000) (no comparable benefits when new coverage does not allow employees to select personal physician and previous coverage allowed selection of personal physician); City of Duluth, Minn., 114 LA 975 (Neigh, 2000) (not same level of benefits when employees now required to obtain authorization prior to obtaining service outside of proposed network); Springfield Bd. of Educ., 114 LA 1429 (Talarico, 2000) (not same benefits level when employer refused to cover infertility treatment when previous coverage allowed such treatment).

[738]106 LA 1069 (Thornell, 1996).

[739]*Id.* at 1070.

the new plan reduced benefits for those employees who received services outside the network.[740] The employer was ordered not to reduce benefits for employees using out-of-network providers. Even if the contract contains no specific language requiring provision of substantially similar or comparable benefits in the event of changes in the insurance plan, such conditions may be implied through past practice or interpretation of other contractual language.[741]

Representations made at an informational meeting concerning changes in the insurance program may be binding upon an employer.[742] However, the union may be held to have waived its right to object to a change if it remains silent at such a meeting. In *City of Peshtigo, Wisconsin*,[743] the contract allowed the city to change health insurance carriers as long as the benefits were better or equal to the existing benefits. During the course of changing its coverage, the city held two informational meetings with the union and employees. Although the union never objected to the new coverage at the informational meetings, it filed a grievance after the new coverage was implemented. The arbitrator concluded that the union had had an opportunity to reject the new coverage, but chose not to voice its objections, and was therefore deemed to have accepted the change.[744] Finally, if the contract does not allow the employer to change health insurance coverage, the employer is obligated to bargain in good faith to impasse over the subject because it is a mandatory subject of bargaining under the NLRA.[745]

---

[740]*Id.* at 1072.

[741]Washington County, Ohio, Child Support, 111 LA 644 (Fullmer, 1998) (contractual language requiring employer to pay 80% of the "coverage" refers to the coverage in effect at the time the agreement was signed, thus, the new coverage must be substantially equivalent to the previous coverage); Jacuzzi Bros., 115 LA 588 (Allen, Jr., 2001) (past practice required maintenance of at least the same benefit coverage).

[742]Copper & Brass Sales, 105 LA 730 (Nelson, 1995) (contract required benefits be given as stated by the employer at its presentation; however, arbitrator found no conclusive testimony that employer made promise at presentation).

[743]104 LA 968 (Dichter, 1995).

[744]*Id.* at 970–71.

[745]Loral Def. Sys.-Akron v. NLRB, 200 F.3d 436, 162 LRRM 3025 (6th Cir. 1999).

Chapter 18

Remedies in Arbitration

Arbitral remedies may considered from two standpoints: (1) whether the arbitrator has the power to award a specific remedy, and (2) whether, assuming that the arbitrator has the power, the remedy is warranted in the particular case.[1]

1. SCOPE OF REMEDY POWER

In *Steelworkers v. Enterprise Wheel & Car Corp.*,[2] the U.S. Supreme Court spoke of the remedy power of arbitrators:

---

[1]For discussions of the remedy power in arbitration, see HILL & SINICROPI, REMEDIES IN ARBITRATION (BNA Books 2d ed. 1991); Berry, Cornelius v. Nutt *and the Current State of Arbitral Remedial Authority in the Federal Sector*, 40 OKLA. L. REV. 559 (1987); Feller, *Remedies: New and Old Problems: I. Remedies in Arbitration: Old Problems Revisited*, PROCEEDINGS OF THE 34TH ANNUAL MEETING OF NAA 109 (Stern & Dennis eds., BNA Books 1982); Sinicropi, *II. Remedies: Another View of New and Old Problems*, *id.* at 134; Katz, *Comment*, *id.* at 171; Harter, *Tenure and the Nonrenewal of Probationary Teachers*, 34 ARB. J. No. 1, at 22 (1979); Stevens, *Arbitrability and the Illinois Courts*, 31 ARB. J. 1 (1976) (relating to the public sector); Wolff, *Remedies in Arbitration: II. The Power of the Arbitrator to Make Monetary Awards*, *in* LABOR ARBITRATION: PERSPECTIVES AND PROBLEMS, PROCEEDINGS OF THE 17TH ANNUAL MEETING OF NAA 176 (Kahn ed., BNA Books 1964); Sirefman, *Rights Without Remedies in Labor Arbitration*, 18 ARB. J. 17 (1963); Stutz, *Arbitrators and the Remedy Power*, *in* LABOR ARBITRATION AND INDUSTRIAL CHANGE, PROCEEDINGS OF THE 16TH ANNUAL MEETING OF NAA 54 (Kahn ed., BNA Books 1963); Fleming, *Arbitrators and the Remedy Power*, 48 VA. L. REV. 1199 (1962); Stein, *Remedies in Labor Arbitration*, *in* CHALLENGES TO ARBITRATION, PROCEEDINGS OF THE 13TH ANNUAL MEETING OF NAA 39 (McKelvey ed., BNA Books 1960); Note, *Protecting Intangible Expectations Under Collective Bargaining Agreements—Overcoming the Proscription of Arbitral Penalties*, 61 MINN. L. REV. 127 (1976).
[2]363 U.S. 593, 46 LRRM 2423 (1960). For cases deferring to an arbitrator's broad remedy power, see *Molders Local 120 v. Brooks Foundry*, 892 F.2d 1283, 133 LRRM 2280 (6th Cir. 1990); *Communications Workers v. Southeastern Elec. Coop.*, 882 F.2d 467, 132 LRRM 2381 (10th Cir. 1989); *Dispatch Printing Co. v. Teamsters Local 284*, 782 F. Supp. 1201, 142 LRRM 2163 (S.D. Ohio 1991). For discussion of arbitration remedial powers, see Nicolau, *The Arbitrator's Remedial Powers: Part I.*, *in* ARBITRATION 1990: PERSPECTIVES ON OLD ISSUES, PROCEEDINGS OF THE 43D ANNUAL MEETING OF NAA 73 (Gruenberg ed., BNA Books 1991); Simons, *Part II.*, *id.* at 88.

> When an arbitrator is commissioned to interpret and apply the collective bargaining agreement, he is to bring his informed judgment to bear in order to reach a fair solution of a problem. This is especially true when it comes to formulating remedies. There the need is for flexibility in meeting a wide variety of situations. The draftsmen may never have thought of what specific remedy should be awarded to meet a particular contingency. Nevertheless, an arbitrator is confined to interpretation and application of the collective bargaining agreement; he does not sit to dispense his own brand of industrial justice. He may of course look for guidance from many sources, yet his award is legitimate only so long as it draws its essence from the collective bargaining agreement. When the arbitrator's words manifest an infidelity to this obligation, courts have no choice but to refuse enforcement of the award.[3]

This assertion of a broad, but nonetheless circumscribed, arbitral remedy power was perhaps meant to be deliberately obscure, leaving specific guidelines to be developed through the case-by-case testing process.[4] This open-textured pronouncement has led one federal court to hold that arbitrators have power to choose any appropriate remedy unless it is expressly precluded by the agreement,[5] while another federal court has limited arbitral remedial authority even when the contract is silent.[6]

It is noteworthy that broad remedial authority is granted to arbitrators under the Uniform Arbitration Act,[7] in force in a majority of states, which specifies that "the fact that the relief was such that it could not or would not be granted by a court of law or equity is not ground for vacating or refusing to confirm the award."[8]

Arbitrators differ among themselves as to how broad their remedial power is or should be.[9] For instance, in awarding an increased rate for a changed job, one arbitrator explained:

> As arbitration is a process to resolve industrial differences without resort to work stoppage, lockout and other economic measures, it necessarily implies

---

[3]*Enterprise Wheel & Car*, 363 U.S. at 597, 46 LRRM at 2425.

[4]The *Steelworkers* decision has been criticized as "invit[ing] a reviewing court to set aside an award 'because the judge is not satisfied that the award has a basis in a particular provision of the contract,'" contrary to the wide latitude an arbitrator has to form a remedy. Hill, *Remedies in Arbitration, in* The Common Law of the Workplace: The Views of Arbitrators 325, 330 (St. Antoine ed., BNA Books 1998).

[5]Bakery & Confectionery Workers Local 369 v. Cotton Baking Co., 514 F.2d 1235, 1237, 89 LRRM 2665 (5th Cir. 1975), *cert. denied*, 423 U.S. 1055 (1976); Machinists Lodge 12 v. Cameron Iron Works, 292 F.2d 112, 119, 48 LRRM 2516 (5th Cir.), *cert. denied*, 368 U.S. 926 (1961). *See also* General Tel. Co. of Ohio v. Communications Workers, 648 F.2d 452, 107 LRRM 2361, 2364–65 (6th Cir. 1981); Lynchburg Foundry Co. Div. v. Steelworkers Local 2556, 404 F.2d 259, 261, 69 LRRM 2878 (4th Cir. 1968).

[6]Teamsters Local 784 v. Ulry-Talbert Co., 330 F.2d 562, 565, 55 LRRM 2979 (8th Cir. 1964); Leather Goods Workers Local 66 v. Neevel Luggage Mfg. Co., 325 F.2d 992, 993–94, 55 LRRM 2153 (8th Cir. 1964). *See also* Retail Clerks Local 782 v. Sav-On Groceries, 508 F.2d 550, 88 LRRM 3205, 3206–07 (10th Cir. 1975). *Cf.* Capital City Tel. Co. v. Communications Workers, 575 F.2d 655, 98 LRRM 2438, 2440 (8th Cir. 1978).

[7]7 U.L.A. §5 (1955).

[8]*Id.* §12(a)(5). The Uniform Arbitration Act is not preempted by the Federal Arbitration Act, 9 U.S.C. §§1–14, in private-sector arbitrations to the extent that its terms are not in conflict with the Federal Arbitration Act and the parties agree to be governed by its provisions. While it is not clear at this writing whether the Federal Arbitration Act is applicable to disputes arising under collective bargaining agreements, its provisions may be looked to for guidance in the development of federal labor law under Section 301 of the Labor Management Relations Act.

[9]For related discussion, see Chapter 9, section 3., "'Legislation' Versus 'Interpretation.'"

power in the arbitrator, exclusive of specific contractual prohibitions, to settle and dispose of the corpus of the grievance. In this case the corpus of the grievance is, in essence, what pay grade is applicable to the jobs with changed content resulting from the banking of machines. Accordingly, the answer to the third issue is that the arbitrator is empowered to establish the Labor Grade applicable to the grievance herein.[10]

In contrast, another arbitrator responded to a suggestion that arbitrators have power under the *Steelworkers Trilogy*[11] to achieve justice in situations not contemplated, or not adequately covered, by the collective bargaining agreement:

> The present arbitrator does not share this expansive view of arbitral jurisdiction. Arbitrators are constrained by contracts in the same manner as the parties themselves. I do not believe in blank check arbitration of the "philosopher king" type, as I have made clear in numerous decisions and journal articles.
>
> I am fully aware that denial of these grievances, while required on contractual grounds, does not solve the equitability question that both management and the Union recognize in their earlier efforts to work out some mutually satisfactory treatment of the seniority problem posed by the two groups of employees now working in the same warehouse. My authority as arbitrator, however, does not extend to development of a Solomon-like solution to be imposed upon both parties as final and binding. My authority is limited to deciding whether the grievances have contractual merit. The ruling must be that they do not.[12]

If a given type of remedy has been used widely by arbitrators, an exceedingly strong case may be made in support of an arbitrator's right to use the remedy absent an express denial in the agreement or submission. The theory is that the parties may be presumed to have knowledge of arbitral practice, and their silence in their agreement on the subject implies their consent.

---

[10]U.S. Slicing Mach. Co., 41 LA 1076, 1081–82 (Willingham, 1963). For other assertions of broad remedy power, see *Sylvania, Ohio, Sch. Bd. of Educ.* 88 LA 683 (Fullmer, 1987); *Brooklyn Dressing Corp.*, 80 LA 457, 463 (Kramer, 1983) ("it cannot be gainsaid, given a violation, that the remedy should be as broad as justice dictates, provided of course, that the Arbitrator's conclusions are drawn from the intent of the collective agreement"); *Pabst Brewing Co.*, 78 LA 772, 776 (Wolff, 1982); *Dispatch Printing Co.*, 70 LA 104, 107 (Kanner, 1978); *Cincinnati Post & Times Star*, 68 LA 129, 142 (Chalfie, 1977); *Cudahy Packing Co.*, 51 LA 822, 836 (Somers, 1968); *Savoy Laundry & Linen Supply*, 48 LA 760, 763 (Summers, 1967); *Union Carbide Corp.*, 46 LA 607, 608 (Turkus, 1966); *Shell Oil Co.*, 44 LA 1219, 1221–22 (Turkus, 1965). *See also* Philadelphia Orchestra Ass'n, 46 LA 513, 517 (Gill, 1966); J.W. Wells Lumber Co., 42 LA 678, 680–82 (Howlett, 1964). In *Nassau County, Fla., Sch. Bd.*, 76 LA 1044 (Sweeney, 1981), the arbitrator stated that it "is ultimately for the arbitrator to frame a remedy if the parties are unable to agree upon a resolution of their differences," *id.* at 1045, and "rejected the employer argument that for the arbitrator to grant a remedy other than sought in the grievance form constitutes an amendment or altering of the collective bargaining agreement." *Id.* at 1048.

[11]Steelworkers v. American Mfg. Co., 363 U.S. 564, 46 LRRM 2414 (1960); Steelworkers v. Warrior & Gulf Navigation Co., 363 U.S. 574, 46 LRRM 2416 (1960); Steelworkers v. Enterprise Wheel & Car Corp., 363 U.S. 593, 46 LRRM 2423 (1960).

[12]Lagomarcino-Grupe Co., 43 LA 453, 460 (Davey, 1964) (employees of Company A who were terminated when its warehouse was closed had no right to carry their seniority with them when they were hired at Company B's warehouse, even though both companies could be regarded as one from a labor relations standpoint and the same union had contracts with both companies). For other arbitrators taking a similarly narrow "contractual" view of the remedy power, see *Klein Tools*, 90 LA 1150 (Poindexter, 1988); *Metromedia, Inc.*, 77 LA 424, 427–28 (Brisco, 1981); *Dorsey Trailers*, 69 LA 334, 336 (Williams, 1977); *Waycross Sportswear*, 53 LA 1061, 1062 (Marshall, 1969); *Welded Wire Prods.*, 48 LA 1121, 1121–22 (McIn-

The award of compensatory damages to employees who have suffered financial loss from an employer's violation of their contractual rights provides the most prominent illustration:[13]

> Many—perhaps most—labor-management contracts in this nation do not specifically authorize an arbitrator to award damages. But in hundreds of such contracts year after year arbitrators do, in fact, award damages. This is done with full knowledge of the parties, who in many cases have had decades in which to rewrite their contracts if they did not so intend them. The Arbitrator submits that under those circumstances the authority of an arbitrator to award damages is as truly and integrally a part of the contract as if it were written there in unmistakable English and boldface type.[14]

The fact is that most agreements are silent as to the scope of an arbitrator's power to remedy a violation of the agreement.[15] Of course, the parties can expressly deal with the issue in their agreement, the submission, or by stipulation at the hearing. Although in such instances the arbitrator's remedy power may sometimes be restricted,[16] usually the arbitrator's discretionary remedial authority is recognized, as, for example, by stipulation authorizing the arbitrator to determine "what shall the remedy be" in the event a violation is found.[17]

---

tosh, 1967); *American-St. Gobian Corp.*, 43 LA 1228, 1231 (Shister, 1965) (the arbitrator derives authority from the contract, is a prisoner of the contract, and is not freed from this imprisonment by the *Steelworkers Trilogy*); *Safeway Stores*, 42 LA 353, 355 (Ross, 1964) (it remains true that grievance arbitration is essentially contractual interpretation—the *Warrior & Gulf* decision "does not enthrone the arbitrator as a law maker nor permit him to impose new obligations or restrictions which cannot fairly be wrung from the contract as the parties negotiated it").

[13]For full discussion of damages in arbitration, see section 3., "Principles of Damages," below.

[14]Jeffrey Mfg. Co., 34 LA 814, 825 (Kuhn, 1960). *See also* Farrell Lines, 86 LA 36 (Hockenberry, 1986); Aetna Portland Cement Co., 41 LA 219, 222 (Dworkin, 1963).

[15]One of the apparently few aspects of the remedy power (apart from the common prohibition against adding to, subtracting from, or modifying the agreement) fairly commonly treated in the collective bargaining agreement concerns the retroactive application of the award. *See Major Collective Bargaining Agreements: Arbitration Procedures* 77–80 (U.S. Dep't of Labor Bull. No. 1425-6, 1966). Where the agreement did specify a remedy for a given type of violation, the arbitrator used it and rejected a request for an additional remedy. Ralphs Grocery Co., 70 LA 1001, 1003 (Roberts, 1978). *But see* General Tel. Co. of Ohio v. Communications Workers, 648 F.2d 452, 107 LRRM 2361, 2364–65 (6th Cir. 1981).

[16]*See* Lone Star Steel Co., 48 LA 1094, 1098 n.6 (Jenkins, 1967) (in a footnote, the arbitrator suggested what remedy he would have awarded had his authority not been limited). In *Globe-Union*, 42 LA 713, 721 (Prasow, 1963), the arbitrator outlined choices open to the parties as to the remedy power, including reservation of the power to themselves. *See also* Stevens Shipping & Terminal Co., 86 LA 373 (Anderson, 1985); McHenry Cmty. High Sch. Dist. 156 Bd. of Educ., 85 LA 976 (Craver, 1985) (the arbitrator was limited by the parties to making a decision without providing a remedy and the remedy was stipulated by the parties).

[17]*See* Amana Refrigeration, 86 LA 827 (Kulkis, 1986); Robertshaw Controls Co., 85 LA 538 (Williams, 1985); Rheem Mfg. Co., 75 LA 701, 703 (Woolf, 1980); Nestle Co., 74 LA 89, 89 (Craver, 1980); General Elec. Co., 69 LA 707, 707 (Jedel, 1977); Petro-Tex Chem. Corp., 69 LA 181, 183 (Helburn, 1977); Sonic Knitting Indus., 65 LA 453, 455, 467 (Helfeld, 1975); General Slicing Mach. Co., 49 LA 823, 826 (Yagoda, 1967); Shell Chem. Co., 47 LA 1178, 1178 (Rohman, 1967); Allied Chem. Corp., 47 LA 554, 554 (Daugherty, 1966); Pacific Maritime Ass'n, 46 LA 1146, 1146 (Gray, 1966); Gremar Mfg. Co., 46 LA 215, 215, 218 (Teele, 1965). In *Taystee Bread Co.*, 52 LA 677, 677, 680–81 (Purdom, 1969), the parties stipulated that the arbitrator was free to fashion a remedy as he saw fit based on the merits and that he was not bound by the restrictive language of the agreement.

A. Should an Available Remedy Be Imposed?

Even those arbitrators who believe their remedy power is, and should be, very broad are quick to caution that there is "a great difference between the possession of power and the occasion for its exercise,"[18] and that arbitrators should proceed with great care, particularly in devising new remedies.[19] Arbitrators who agree that, absent restrictive contract language, broad remedial power should be deemed to inhere in the arbitrator, also agree that the power is not unlimited. The following guidelines for the formulation of remedies have been proposed:

1. In form the remedy should be one that would appear to most directly effectuate the intent and purposes of that provision in the labor agreement in connection with which the right was contracted.
2. The party called upon to give [the] remedy should not be subjected to well-founded surprise by the form, nature, extent and degree of the remedy. What is awarded should be within the realm of conceivable and reasonable remedial expectation by the party in error or by other parties were they to be similarly circumstanced.
3. Remedies that are punitive in monetary or exemplary nature should be avoided, on the ground that parties bargaining collectively in a more or less perpetual relationship should not seek that one or the other partner be punished for a mistake. To so seek and to obtain punishment is putting a mortgage on the future happiness of the joint relationship. . . .
4. Remedies that are novel in form should be avoided, again for reasons of unexpectedness or possible well-based surprise. A novel remedy might bring with it unforeseen contractual and other impacts on one or both of the parties and create uncertainty as to what may result from future submissions to arbitration. The concept of the arbitrator having an "arsenal" of forms of relief, with the parties in a position of uncertainty rather than expectation, should be avoided in what is a private litigation seeking to resolve a dispute. Suspense in a private relationship might subvert the efficacy of that relationship.[20]

---

[18]Stein, *Remedies in Labor Arbitration*, *in* CHALLENGES TO ARBITRATION, PROCEEDINGS OF THE 13TH ANNUAL MEETING OF NAA 39, 46 (McKelvey ed., BNA Books 1960).

[19]*Id.* at 45–47. *See also* Shell Oil Co., 44 LA 1219, 1221–22 (Turkus, 1965) (power is a heady wine that carries with it an equally potent obligation to exercise care in its use).

[20]Ryder, *Arbitrators and the Remedy Power: Discussion*, *in* LABOR ARBITRATION AND INDUSTRIAL CHANGE, PROCEEDINGS OF THE 16TH ANNUAL MEETING OF NAA 68–69 (Kahn ed., BNA Books 1963). *See also* Osborn & Ulland, 68 LA 1146, 1152–53 (Beck, 1977) (refusing to order any "extraordinary" remedy); Swanson-Dean Corp., 68 LA 682 (Jackson, 1977) (although the arbitrator had been authorized expressly to determine "what should be the remedy," *id.* at 683, and although he stated that regarding "the form of remedy, the arbitrator's authority is broader than a court's," *id.* at 686, he stated also that the "remedy that is most suitable and equitable is that which was in the contemplation of the parties," *id.*). In *Madison Bus Co.*, 52 LA 723, 727–28 (Mueller, 1969), the arbitrator stated that although the union was subjected to arbitration costs as a result of the company's violation of the agreement, an award for such costs would constitute a novel remedy not within the reasonable expectations of the parties and accordingly would not be granted. *See also* Kroger Co., 85 LA 1198 (St. Antoine, 1985). But such an award was made in *Cameron Iron Works*, 73 LA 878, 882 (Marlatt, 1979);

Of course, not every case will fit into some existing mold or be capable of disposition by some relatively simple formula. Thus, a remedy sometimes will be complex, multifaceted, or otherwise uniquely fashioned by the arbitrator in one or more of its major aspects.[21]

As already observed, parties frequently frame the remedial question in the phrase, "If so, what shall the remedy be?" This broad remedial power should not be wielded to fashion a remedy that transcends the underlying grievance or that imposes the arbitrator's own brand of workplace justice. Consider, for instance, the following notice that an arbitrator ordered a public employer to post:

> [A]ny verified infraction of the Attorney General's rules and regulations concerning prohibition of misuse of [information] system[s] for personal reason from the date of posting the notice, forward, is a discharge infraction which shall not be remitted for any reason of seniority or outstanding service record.[22]

In some cases, where an arbitrator has found a violation of the agreement, the case has been returned to the parties to allow them to negotiate the terms of the remedy. One arbitrator deemed this procedure essential where he had "received no guidance at the hearing with respect to a remedy should the grievance be sustained."[23] In another case, the arbitrator offered the parties a contingent remedy, to be used unless they could agree "upon an alternative solution" within 60 days from the date of the award.[24]

Sonic Knitting Indus., 65 LA 453, 468–69 (Helfeld, 1975); Ralph Rogers & Co., 48 LA 40, 43 (Getman, 1966).

[21]Illustrating the use of a complex and multifaceted award, see George Ellis Co., 68 LA 261, 270–71 (Sacks, 1977). Illustrating that a situation can arise in which the arbitrator feels that a novel remedy is "peculiarly appropriate," see Social Sec. Admin., 87 LA 1026 (Wolff, 1986); Gamble-Skogmd, Inc., 71 LA 1151, 1154 (Weiss, 1978). See also E. Keeler Co., 77 LA 693, 694 (Florey, 1981); Immigration & Naturalization Serv., 77 LA 633, 636 (Grossman, 1981); General Servs. Admin., 76 LA 1028, 1033 (Rothschild, 1981); Southern Ohio Coal Co., 66 LA 446, 449 (Lubow, 1976).

[22]City of Sterling Heights, Mich., 89 LA 420, 426 (Keefe, 1987).

[23]United States Steel Corp., 45 LA 104, 107 (Florey, 1965). See also Consumers Mkts., 88 LA 985 (Belcher, 1987); United States Steel Corp., 86 LA 197 (Dybeck, 1985); County of Alameda, Cal., 86 LA 20 (Letter, 1985); Pacific Tel. & Tel. Co., 75 LA 1112, 1119 (Rothschild, 1980); General Foods Corp., 71 LA 969, 977 (Witney, 1978); Chesterfield Steel Serv. Co., 69 LA 1159, 1167 (Young, 1977); USM Corp., 69 LA 1051, 1056–57 (Gregory, 1977); Union Tank Car Co., 55 LA 170, 182 (Platt, 1970); Carling Brewing Co., 52 LA 93, 97 (Talent, 1968); Westinghouse Elec. Corp., 45 LA 161, 174 (Feinberg, 1965). In some cases, the arbitrator concluded that the appropriate remedy was negotiations, which the arbitrator ordered. See Utah Army Nat'l Guard, 74 LA 770, 775 (Wiggins, 1980); United States Steel Corp., 69 LA 740, 751 (Garrett, 1977); International Harvester Co., 65 LA 178, 182 (Caraway, 1975). Cf. Typographical Union No. 23 (Milwaukee) v. Newspapers, Inc., 639 F.2d 386, 106 LRRM 2317, 2322–23 (7th Cir. 1981). In Weyerhaeuser Co., 64 LA 869, 874 (Barnhart, 1975), the arbitrator's award stated: "The Union is requested to submit a more particularized request for relief than is presented by the suggested formula in its brief. The request for interest and for damages will be ruled upon when the Arbitrator perfects a final award." For related discussion, see Chapter 7, section 4.E., "Split Hearings and Interim or Partial Awards."

[24]Lehman Bros., 51 LA 1063, 1067 (Hill, 1968). In Ulene v. Murray Millman, Inc., 33 LA 531, 534–35 (Cal. Dist. Ct. App. 1959), an award was not rendered unenforceable merely because it contained an election provision in respect to the remedy.

B. Scope of Remedy Power When the Agreement Is Silent

As previously noted, most collective bargaining agreements leave a "gaping void" on the topic of arbitral remedies,[25] and, in the absence of language limiting the scope of a remedy in the agreement itself, arbitrators generally have been considered to possess broad discretion to fashion an appropriate remedy.[26]

One method of determining the appropriate remedy when an agreement does not address the arbitrator's remedial power is through the application of gap-filling rules that have developed over time. One such rule suggests that the arbitrator assess the remedial needs of the parties against the backdrop of the legal context in which the agreement came into existence.[27] Another rule suggests that "'unless the contrary is stated in the agreement . . . the primary authority implicitly granted to the arbitrator is the authority to award specific performance of the provisions of the agreement.'"[28] However, as discussed earlier, the arbitrator may find it appropriate to remand the case to the parties to allow them the opportunity to negotiate a remedy.[29] As will be discussed later in this chapter,[30] arbitrators generally are not given contractual authority to order the discipline of supervisors or to award damages for pain and suffering.[31]

---

[25]*See generally* Snow, *Make-Whole and Statutory Remedies: I. Informing the Silent Remedial Gap, in* Arbitration 1995: New Challenges and Expanding Responsibilities, Proceedings of the 48th Annual Meeting of NAA 150, 152 (Najita ed., BNA Books 1996).

[26]Gilmore Envelope Corp., 110 LA 1036, 1041 (Ross, 1998) ("Arbitrators have universally held that even though a contract is silent as to remedy, the arbitrator has the authority to fashion a remedy, including a monetary award, in order to make whole the party damaged by the violation.").

[27]Snow, NAA 48th Proceedings, at 158 ("By taking into account the legal context in which the parties created their agreement, an arbitrator comes closer to understanding expectations of the parties with regard to fashioning an appropriate remedy. The agreement emerged from the parties' legal-economic relationship, and arbitral remedies should be fashioned within that same context."). With respect to the application of external law to arbitration and mediation, see *Appendix B., A Due Process Protocol for Mediation and Arbitration of Statutory Disputes Arising Out of the Employment Relationship,* NAA 48th Proceedings, at 298.

[28]Snow, NAA 48th Proceedings, at 161 (quoting Feller, *Remedies: New and Old Problems: I. Remedies in Arbitration: Old Problems Revisited, in* Arbitration Issues for the 1980s, Proceedings of the 34th Annual Meeting of NAA 109, 116 (Stern & Dennis eds., BNA Books 1982)). Arbitral monetary awards are characterized as compensation to the grievant for the time gap between the contract breach and the award of specific performance requiring adherence to the contract's terms. Snow, NAA 48th Proceedings, at 161–62 (citing Feller, at 117–18).

[29]Clark County, Nev., 114 LA 1608 (Silver, 2000); Anaconda Cmty. Hosp., 114 LA 132 (Pool, 2000); San Francisco, Cal., Unified Sch. Dist., 113 LA 1505 (Bogue, 2000); Naval Aviation Depot N. Island, 113 LA 1065 (Gentile, 2000); USS, Div. of USX Corp., 113 LA 939 (Das, 1999); Los Angeles County, Cal., Metro. Transp. Auth., 108 LA 301, 304–05 (Gentile, 1997); American Red Cross, 104 LA 68 (Garrett, 1995).

[30]See section 3.C., "Mental Distress Damages," and section 4.C., "Reinstatement in Sexual Harassment Cases," below.

[31]Union Camp Corp., 104 LA 295, 300–02 (Nolan, 1995).

C. Scope of Remedy Power Limited by the Agreement

Parties can limit the arbitrator's scope of remedy power considerably through the language of the agreement itself.[32] In *Tower Automotive*,[33] the arbitrator refused to grant the union's request for more bargaining-unit employees because "the provisions of the contract prohibit me from ordering the Company to hire additional bargaining unit colleagues."[34]

Some collective bargaining agreements provide that if the arbitrator finds a party had no reasonable grounds for its position in the arbitration, that party may be ordered to pay the arbitrator's fee.[35]

Many agreements limit the authority of the arbitrator to interpreting and applying the collective bargaining agreement and deny the arbitrator the power to add to or modify the agreement. In such an instance, the award must be based on what is, or is not, required by the agreement, and there is only limited room, if any at all, for application of "equity."[36] For example, in refusing to follow a prior award that had been based on equitable grounds, the arbitrator declared:

> I cannot agree with that decision, which was based on so-called "equitable" grounds. When it becomes customary and legitimate for arbitrators to amend

---

[32]Tower Auto., 115 LA 51, 57 (Kenis, 2000). *See also* Municipality of Anchorage, Alaska, 115 LA 190, 195 (Landau, 2000).

[33]115 LA 51 (Kenis, 2000).

[34]*Id.* at 57; Municipality of Anchorage, Alaska, 115 LA 190, 195 (Landau, 2000) (where a contract contains specific restrictions, an arbitrator is more constrained and must be guided by established principles of contract interpretation and is precluded from weighing the equities); Keokuk County, Iowa, 112 LA 221, 227 (Kubie, 1999) (an arbitrator cannot award fees and costs when the agreement states that costs will be shared equally between the employer and the union); Danis-Shook Joint Venture #25, 111 LA 1095, 1100 (Klein, 1999) (arbitrator was limited by language in the agreement stating that the arbitrator "shall have no power to add to, subtract from, or modify this Agreement in any way, but shall instead be limited to the application of the terms of this Agreement in determining the dispute").

[35]H. Meyer Dairy Co., 105 LA 583, 588–89 (Sugerman, 1995). *See also* Community Counseling Ctr., 101 LA 1213, 1217 (Feldman, 1993) (arbitrator ordered his fee to be split between the parties despite loser-pay clause, where the union prevailed on procedural issue and the employer prevailed on merit issue). For a full discussion of discipline and discharge, see Chapter 15, "Discipline and Discharge."

[36]*See* City of Cuba City, Wis., School Dist., 87 LA 1294 (Yaffe, 1986); Akron Coca-Cola Bottling Co., 87 LA 622 (Dworkin, 1986); City of St. Paul Pub. Hous. Agency, 87 LA 33 (Gallagher, 1986); City of Mayfield, Ohio, City Sch. Dist. Bd. of Educ., 71 LA 1044, 1046–47 (Siegel, 1978); Okonite Co., 68 LA 1191, 1194–95 (Ludlow, 1977); Givaudan Corp., 68 LA 337, 342 (Brent, 1977); Pierz, Minn., Indep. Sch. Dist. No. 484, 68 LA 325, 330 (Conway, 1977); Greenlee Bros. & Co., 48 LA 938, 940 (Davis, 1967); Hotel Bancroft, 48 LA 481, 485 (Cole, 1967); Corte Constr. Co., 48 LA 463, 478 (Lugar, 1967); Brady Mfg. Co., 46 LA 970, 972 (Davis, 1966); R&K Plastic Indus. Co., 46 LA 11, 15 (McCoy, 1966); Alexandria Water Co., 45 LA 1165, 1166 (McCoy, 1965); Westinghouse Elec. Corp., 45 LA 131, 139 (Hebert, 1965); Marsh Wall Prods., 65–2 ARB ¶8774 (Kagel, 1965); National Rose Co., 43 LA 1066, 1070 (Autrey, 1964); Lagomarcino-Grupe Co., 43 LA 453, 460 (Davey, 1964); General Portland Cement Co., 43 LA 120, 125–26 (Dworkin, 1963); Firestone Tire & Rubber Co., 29 LA 469, 473 (Hebert, 1957); Babcock & Wilcox Co., 21 LA 133, 139 (Dworkin, 1953); Erwin Mills, 16 LA 466, 472 (Barrett, 1950). *Cf.* Alabama By-Prods. Corp., 68 LA 992, 994 (Grooms, Jr., 1977); Consolidation Coal Co., 68 LA 469, 472 (Cantor, 1977); Trumbull Asphalt Co., 41 LA 631, 635–36 (Sembower, 1963); Fedders-Quigan Corp., 15 LA 209, 210 (Handsaker, 1950). Certainly, the parties generally want the agreement applied as written. *See* Eaton, *Labor Arbitration in the San Francisco Bay Area*, 48 LA 1381, 1390 (1967).

and add to contracts according to their sense of equity, i.e., what the contract *ought* to provide, then I shall fall in line.[37]

However, arbitrators occasionally do make purely advisory recommendations based on equitable considerations. In some of these cases, where the grievance could be sustained only by adding to or modifying the agreement or by otherwise exceeding the arbitrator's authority, but where the arbitrator is convinced that the grievance has merit from the standpoint of equity, he or she will deny the grievance (or dismiss it) and at the same time make an advisory recommendation as to how the grievance should be disposed of in the best interests of both parties.[38] In doing this, one arbitrator explained:

> Since the Arbitration Board must rule according to the so-called "contractual approach" to the issue, it has no alternative but to deny the grievance. But while the Board's authority to *rule* is so circumscribed, its powers of *recommendation* are considerably broader. For in making such recommendations it can avail itself of the guideposts afforded by what one might term, "Industrial relations equity."[39]

Similarly, where an arbitrator concludes that the dispute essentially involves "interests" rather than "rights" under the existing agreement, so that a sustaining award would in effect be legislating for the parties, the claim may be denied or remanded, with the suggestion that the matter be negotiated by the parties.[40] But the arbitrator may formulate some specific

---

[37]Esso Standard Oil Co., 16 LA 73, 75 (McCoy, Reber, & Daniel, 1951) (emphasis in original). *See also* Town of N. Castle, N.Y., 116 LA 153 (Gregory, 2001) (an arbitrator does not have the authority to alter the collective bargaining agreement).

[38]*See* P.P.G. Indus., 90 LA 479, 481 (Sedwick, 1987); Spartek, Inc., 89 LA 594, 597 (Johnson, 1987); Cottage Grove, Minn., Indep. Sch. Dist. No. 833, 88 LA 713, 716 (Gallagher, 1987) (recommending a remedy that the arbitrator considered beyond his authority to order); Ohio State Univ., 69 LA 1004, 1011 (Bell, 1977); Geuder, Paeschke & Frey Co., 69 LA 871, 876 (Wyman, 1977); Orgill Bros. & Co., 68 LA 797, 804 (Simon, 1977); Simmonds Precision Prods., 51 LA 761, 764 (Kerrison, 1968); Texaco, Inc., 50 LA 951, 955 (Reid, 1968); A.O. Smith Corp., 47 LA 443, 448 (Stouffer, 1966); Brady Mfg. Co., 46 LA 970, 972 (Davis, 1966); National Rose Co., 43 LA 1066, 1070 (Autrey, 1964); Revlon Corp., 42 LA 1067, 1071 (Prasow, 1964); Yale & Towne Mfg. Co., 41 LA 913, 917 (Russell, 1963); Firestone Tire & Rubber Co., 29 LA 469, 476 (Hebert, 1957); National Lead Co., 28 LA 470, 477 (Roberts, Stony, London, Miller, & Davenport, 1957); John Deere Des Moines Works, 25 LA 394, 397 (Davey, 1955); International Harvester Co., 21 LA 444, 446 (Kelliher, 1953); Morris Paper Mills, 20 LA 653, 658 (Anrod, 1953); Southern Cal. Edison Co., 15 LA 162, 168 (Aaron, 1950). *See also* Veterans Admin. Hosp., 69 LA 822, 824 (Cox, 1977); Dearborn Brass Co., 66 LA 602, 604 (Sinicropi, 1976); Fleetwood-Airflow, Inc., 15 LA 229, 233 (Copelof, 1950). Similarly, where the grievance is sustained the arbitrator may suggest that the winner not demand the full measure of its rights under the award. *See* TPI Corp., 72 LA 288, 293 (Carson, Jr., 1979); Precision Castings Co., 49 LA 791, 797 (Shister, 1967); City of Norwalk, Conn., 48 LA 835, 837 (Johnson, 1967); Savoy Laundry & Linen Supply, 48 LA 760, 762–63 (Summers, 1967).

[39]General Aniline & Film Corp., 25 LA 50, 54 (Shister, 1955) (emphasis in original). *Cf.* National Carbon Co., 23 LA 263, 264 (Shister, 1954).

[40]*See* Peabody Coal Co., 83 LA 561, 563 (Nicholas, Jr., 1984); Bethlehem Steel, 26 LA 646, 648 (Seward, 1956); McDonnell Aircraft Corp., 26 LA 48, 54 (Klamon, 1956); New Haven Pulp & Board Co., 18 LA 486, 489 (Copelof, 1952); Youngstown Sheet & Tube Co., 16 LA 394, 396 (Kelliher, 1951); North Am. Aviation, 16 LA 303, 307 (Komaroff, 1951). *Cf.* Philadelphia Orchestra Ass'n, 46 LA 513, 515–17 (Gill, 1966); Wooster Sportswear Co., 46 LA 9, 11 (Dworkin, 1965). *See also* Chapter 9, section 2., "Ambiguity and the Exclusion of Extrinsic Evidence," and section 3., "'Legislation' Versus 'Interpretation'"; Chapter 10, section 7., "Contract Principles."

provision and recommend its adoption,[41] or may undertake to decide the dispute by "legislating" for the parties if that is what both parties want and have authorized the arbitrator to do.[42]

2. INJUNCTIONS BY ARBITRATORS [LA CDI 94.559]

The judicial power to issue an injunction to preserve the status quo and prevent irreparable harm does not have an exact counterpart in the arbitration process, because the arbitrator is called on to remedy past contractual violations and lacks enforcement power. However, an arbitrator's authority to fashion an appropriate remedy when there is a violation of an agreement oftentimes requires the arbitrator to extend his or her analysis beyond the "four corners" of the agreement to find one.[43] The quest may lead the arbitrator to issue quasi-injunctive relief by ordering a party to "cease and desist" from continuing to do some specified act that the arbitrator has ruled violative of the collective bargaining agreement.[44] For example, in *City of Orange,*

---

[41]Liquid Carbonic Corp., 84 LA 704, 707 (Richman, 1985).

[42]*See* Colonial Provision Co., 16 LA 176, 178–79 (Copelof, 1951). For related discussion, see Chapter 3, section 3.C. "Rights Arbitration Contract Clauses."

[43]Inland Container Corp., 74 LA 110 (Boals, 1980) (the nature of the process requires an equitable determination outside the contract because a different time and changed circumstances exist at the time of the remedy).

[44]For some instances in which arbitrators in granting relief have spoken in terms of an injunction or a cease-and-desist order, see: Midtown Realty Co. v. Bevona, 161 LRRM 2673 (S.D.N.Y. 1999) (district court confirmed arbitration award ordering plaintiff to cease and desist assigning work to non-bargaining-unit members); Lowell Sch. Comm. v. United Teachers of Lowell Local 495, 2001 Mass. Super. LEXIS 10, 2001 WL 13626 (Mass. Super. Ct. Jan. 2, 2001) (Massachusetts court affirmed award ordering school committee to cease and desist from refusing to hear grievance); Cincinnati Bd. of Educ., 2001 WL 574325 (Keenan, 2001) (school board directed to cease and desist requiring teachers to work more hours than provided for in the contract); Hughes Electron Dynamics, 115 LA 473 (Richman, 2001) (company ordered to cease and desist from subcontracting work normally done by bargaining-unit members); U.S. Geological Survey, 115 LA 276 (Hoffman, 2000) (agency ordered to cease and desist paying per diem travel rate lower than rate set by federal regulations); Hook-Up, Inc., Case No. WP043, 1999 WL 416374 (Daniel, Parr, & Zuckerman, 1999) (employer ordered to cease and desist subcontracting work to a nonbargaining unit); Mission Foods, 111 LA 501 (Snider, 1998) (company to cease and desist enforcing clean-shaven policy once new policy consistent with the collective bargaining agreement is promulgated); Madison Teachers, Case No. AP/M-97-605, 1998 WL 409546 (Flaten, 1988) (employer directed to cease and desist from assigning supervisory duties to teachers other than in accordance with memorandum); Lucent Techs., Case No. 97-09027, 1998 WL 1548019 (Lalka, 1998) (employer ordered to cease and desist from assigning bargaining-unit work to non-bargaining-unit personnel); Nauvoo-Colusa, Ill., Cmty. Unit Sch. Dist. 325, 106 LA 62 (Nathan, 1996) (school board ordered to cease and desist from prohibiting, discouraging, or intimidating employees from exercising their rights under the contract); Monitor Sugar Co., 1996 WL 808298 (McDonald, 1996) (employer ordered to cease and desist issuing general ban on vacations during certain times in violation of the contract); Maple Valley Educ. Ass'n, 1996 WL 607224 (Kanner, 1996) (school ordered to cease and desist violating contract by changing elementary teachers' schedules); Otis Elevator Co., Case No. 95-17437, 1996 WL 785393 (Nicholas, Jr., 1996) (employees ordered to cease and desist from turning off pagers when they are subject to callback); Stone Container Corp., 95 LA 729 (Nolan, 1990); Donaldson Mining Co., 91 LA 471 (Zobrak, 1988); District of Columbia Dep't of Fin. & Revenue, 91 LA 1 (Hockenberry, Jr., 1988); Dynamic Corp. of Am., 90 LA 377 (Zirkel, 1987); Lufkin Indus., 90 LA 301 (Nicholas, Jr., 1988); Sexton's Steak House, 76 LA 576, 579 (Ross, 1981); Mine Health & Safety Admin., 75 LA 369, 376 (Cantor, 1980) (ordering a federal-sector employer to cease and desist); Durant, Iowa, Cmty. Sch. Dist., 74 LA 934, 939 (Nathan, 1980) (ordering a state-sector

Texas,[45] the arbitrator determined that the city improperly assigned the task of trimming trees to firefighters to clear the way for fire trucks because such a task was not so "closely connected" to firefighter duties as to warrant assignment by management. As a remedy, the arbitrator directed the city to rescind the tree-trimming work order issued to the firefighters and cease and desist from assigning such work to them in the future. Other arbitrators recognize the cease and desist authority, but refer to it by other names.[46]

Courts have also recognized the significant authority of arbitrators to grant quasi-injunctive relief. The New York Court of Appeals observed that, "[t]raditionally, arbitrators have been licensed to direct such conduct of the parties as is necessary to the settlement of the matters in dispute."[47] The court upheld an award containing an injunction where the collective bargaining agreement did not directly affirm or deny power in the arbitrator to use such remedy, and where nothing short of an injunction would have accomplished the intent of the parties for speedy relief against the prohibited activity.[48] Moreover, the court also held that the New York Anti-Injunction

---

employer to cease and desist); San Antonio Air Logistics Ctr., 73 LA 455, 463 (LeBaron, 1979) (federal sector); Naval Air Rework Facility, 72 LA 129, 133 (Kaufman, 1979) (same); C. Iber & Sons, 69 LA 697, 705 (Gibson, 1977); Buchholz Mortuaries, 69 LA 623, 630 (Roberts, 1977); San Antonio Packing Co., 68 LA 893, 897–98 (Bailey, 1977); West Allis-West Milwaukee, Wis., Joint City Sch. Dist. No. 1, 68 LA 644, 651 (Yaffe, 1977) (state sector); Philadelphia Newspapers, 68 LA 401, 405 (Jaffee, 1977); Sonic Knitting Indus., 65 LA 453, 471 (Helfeld, 1975) (agreement expressly authorized such remedy); United States Steel Corp., 62 LA 743, 748–49 (Fisfis, 1974); Kentile Floors, 52 LA 771, 772 (Kornblum, 1969); Liebman Breweries, 35 LA 384, 386 (Kornblum, 1960); Hotel Employers Ass'n, 47 LA 873, 888 (Burns, 1966); Publishers' Ass'n of New York City, 66–1 ARB ¶8284 (Turkus, 1966); Macy's N.Y., 40 LA 954, 958 (Scheiber, 1962); Wyandotte Chem. Corp., 37 LA 824, 830 (Williams, 1961). Discussing injunctions by arbitrators, see Crane, *The Use and Abuse of Arbitral Power*, in Labor Arbitration at the Quarter-Century Mark, Proceedings of the 25th Annual Meeting of NAA 66, 72–74 (Dennis & Somers eds., BNA Books 1973) (arguing against such remedy); Bernstein, *Comment, id.* at 76, 79–80; Vladeck, *Comment, id.* at 81, 84–85 (defending the use of such remedy); Stein, *Remedies in Labor Arbitration*, in Challenges to Arbitration, Proceedings of the 13th Annual Meeting of NAA 39, 47 (McKelvey ed., BNA Books 1960) (arguing against such remedy). The reluctance of many arbitrators to issue injunctions or cease-and-desist orders is illustrated in *Beth Energy Mines*, 87 LA 577 (Hewitt, 1986); *Saginaw News-Booth Newspapers*, 61 LA 1205, 1213 (Platt, 1973); *Allied Paper Co.*, 53 LA 226, 227–28 (Holly, 1969); *Allied Chem. Corp.*, 47 LA 686, 691 (Hilpert, 1966); *Jos. Schlitz Brewing Co.*, 42 LA 931, 935 (Bernstein, 1964); *Budd Co.*, 34 LA 176, 178 (Gill, 1959). *See also* E.W. Bliss Co., 50 LA 191, 194 (Kates, 1967). Foreseeably, there will be even greater reluctance by arbitrators to issue a temporary restraining order pending determination of the merits of a dispute. *See* Armour & Co., 68 LA 1076, 1077 (Goetz, 1977). For related discussion, see section 1., "Scope of Remedy Power," above.

[45]103 LA 1121 (Nicholas, Jr., 1994).

[46]Ashland Chem. Co., 81 LA 881, 887 (Williams, 1983) ("'Since an arbitration award does not have the force of law, the term 'injunction' as applied to labor arbitration may be misleading. It is nevertheless settled that an arbitrator, in the exercise of his power, may include injunctive-type relief in the award,'" quoting Hill & Sinicropi, Remedies in Arbitration 309 (BNA Books 2d ed. 1991)); International Comfort Prods. Corp., 1998 WL 1033427 (Howell, 1998).

[47]*In re Ruppert*, 29 LA 775, 776–77 (N.Y. Ct. App. 1958).

[48]*Id.* An arbitrator's cease-and-desist order was also enforced in *F.&M. Schaefer Brewing Co.*, 53 LA 676 (N.Y. Sup. Ct. 1969). The New York arbitration statute does not deal specifically with injunctions by the arbitrator. An arbitrator's injunction was enforced by a court in Illinois, a Uniform Arbitration Act state. Ford Motor Co., 41 LA 621, 621 (Ill. Cir. Ct. 1963). In *Cranston Teachers Ass'n v. School Comm. City of Cranston*, 416 A.2d 1180, 1183 (R.I. 1980), the court said that a contempt motion is "an appropriate means by which a party may seek another's compliance with a judgment conforming to a confirmed arbitration award [containing an injunction]," but the court held that an arbitrator's award ordering the com-

Act did not forbid the enforcement of injunctions issued by arbitrators, even though the New York Anti-Injunction Act severely limited the jurisdiction of the courts to issue injunctions in labor disputes.[49]

It is also clear that under federal law the courts can enforce injunctive-type orders issued by arbitrator, for example, to halt strikes in breach of the collective bargaining agreement.[50] The Supreme Court held in *Boys Markets*[51] that the Norris-LaGuardia Anti-Injunction Act[52] does not bar court injunctive relief against such strikes. However, it has been noted that a cease-and-desist order may not be awarded if the agreement would prohibit it,[53] or, in the federal sector, if the order conflicted with a constitutional or statutory right.[54] The U.S. Court of Appeals for the Eighth Circuit affirmed the vacation of an award ordering the employer to cease and desist from hiring outside workers because the award did not draw its essence from the contract.[55]

Moreover, when an arbitrator issues an order commanding the employer to cease and desist from some procedure that the arbitrator has found to violate the collective bargaining agreement, the award may not necessarily bind a subsequent arbitrator faced with the same substantive issue under the agreement.[56]

However, awards in the nature of "mandatory injunctions" that command a party to take some affirmative action, such as an award ordering the employer to reinstate an employee, are very common.[57]

---

pany to "cease any implementation of the agreement contrary to this award" did not have the effect of an injunction subject to enforcement by contempt proceedings, since it did not indicate precisely what was expected of the company in "clear, certain and specific terms."

[49]*Ruppert*, 29 LA at 777. *See also In re* Griffin, 42 LA 511 (N.Y. Sup. Ct. 1964).

[50]*See* General Dynamics Corp. v. Marine & Shipbuilding Workers Local 5, 469 F.2d 848, 81 LRRM 2746 (1st Cir. 1972); Pacific Maritime Ass'n v. Longshoremen (ILWU), 454 F.2d 262, 79 LRRM 2116 (9th Cir. 1971); New Orleans S.S. Ass'n v. Longshoremen (ILA) Local 1418, 389 F.2d 369, 67 LRRM 2430 (5th Cir. 1968); Philadelphia Marine Trade Ass'n v. Longshoremen (ILA) Local 1291, 365 F.2d 295, 62 LRRM 2791 (3d Cir. 1966), *rev'd on other grounds*, 389 U.S. 64, 66 LRRM 2433 (1967). The arbitrator's injunction may not be a feasible remedy where quick action is needed unless the agreement provides for an expedited arbitration procedure. *See* Fairweather, *N.Y.U. 18th Annual Conference on Labor*, 58 LRR 240 (1965).

[51]Boys Mkts. v. Retail Clerks Local 770, 398 U.S. 235, 74 LRRM 2257 (1970). For more as to the substance of this decision, see Chapter 2, section 2.A.ii.c., "Post-*Trilogy*: Enforcement of Agreements to Arbitrate and Review of Arbitration Awards." For a comprehensive discussion of court enforcement of arbitrator injunctions see Meyer, *Enforcement of Arbitrator's Labor Injunctions in the Federal Courts*, 7 How. L.J. 17 (1961) (written prior to *Boys Markets* but still very useful). *See also* Stutz, *Arbitrators and the Remedy Power*, in Labor Arbitration and Industrial Change, Proceedings of the 16th Annual Meeting of NAA 54, 65–66 (Kahn ed., BNA Books 1963).

[52]29 U.S.C. §101 et seq.

[53]Hill & Sinicropi, Remedies in Arbitration 311 (BNA Books 2d ed. 1991).

[54]*Id.* at 326. An example would be a cease-and-desist order that violated a union's First Amendment rights.

[55]International Paper Co. v. Paperworkers, 215 F.3d 815, 164 LRRM 2513 (8th Cir. 2000).

[56]*See* Connecticut Light & Power Co. v. Electrical Workers (IBEW) Local 420, 718 F.2d 14, 114 LRRM 2770, 2775 (2d Cir. 1983).

[57]Ashland Chem. Co., 81 LA 881, 887 (Williams, 1983) (arbitrators seldom issue prohibitive injunctions restricting a party from carrying out a specific act, but often issue mandatory injunctions compelling a party to take affirmative action). For other illustrations of the use of mandatory injunctions, see *Georgia-Pacific Corp.*, 115 LA 1452 (Vonhof, 2001); *Davis Wire Corp.*, 114 LA 1345 (Olson, Jr., 2000); *Simeus Foods Int'l*, 114 LA 436 (Moreland IV, 2000); *Mead Corp.*, 113 LA 1169 (Franckiewicz, 2000); *Veterans Admin. Med. Ctr.*, 90 LA 964 (Byars, 1988); *Knapheide Mfg. Co.*, 90 LA 862 (Cohen, 1987); *Miami Valley Ready-Mixed*

3. Principles of Damages

In empowering the arbitrator to resolve their dispute, parties are generally considered to have given authority to grant adequate monetary relief for contract violations where the arbitrator finds that the grievance has merit, even though the contract does not specifically authorize this remedy.[58] In this regard, arbitrator and former Secretary of Labor W. Willard Wirtz emphasized that to restrict arbitrators to remedies specifically set forth in the contract would negate arbitration as a method of dispute settlement or would result in cluttering contracts with numerous liquidated damages provisions that would invite more trouble than they could prevent.[59]

Despite the broad scope of remedy power, arbitrators often limit themselves to granting a remedy requested in the grievance.[60] "The general ratio-

---

Concrete Ass'n, 71 LA 524, 535 (Barone, 1978); *San Francisco, Cal., Unified Sch. Dist.*, 70 LA 1159, 1168 (Barrett, 1978); *Hempstead Pub. Sch. Bd. of Educ.*, 69 LA 808, 811 (Gootnick, 1977); *Phillips Petroleum Co.*, 50 LA 522, 529 (Allen, Jr., 1968); *International Paper Co.*, 50 LA 344, 347 (Prewett, 1968); *General Fireproofing Co.*, 48 LA 819, 825 (Teple, 1967); *Hoover Chem. Prods. Div.*, 48 LA 373, 379 (Keefe, 1967); *Interstate Indus.*, 46 LA 879, 881–82 (Howlett, 1966); *American Bakeries Co.*, 46 LA 769, 773 (Hon, 1966); *Union Carbide Corp.*, 46 LA 195, 198 (Cahn, 1966); *San Diego Gas & Elec. Co.*, 43 LA 414, 426 (Somers, 1964); *Paragon Bridge & Steel Co.*, 42 LA 339, 343 (Gross, 1964).

[58]*See* Levernier Constr., 113 LA 152, 159 (Gallagher, 1999); Macon Kraft, 93 LA 642 (Mathews, 1989); Cadillac Gage Co., 87 LA 853 (Van Pelt, 1986); Farrell Lines, 86 LA 36 (Hockenberry, 1986); Wolff, *Remedies in Arbitration: I. The Power of the Arbitrator to Make Monetary Awards, in* Labor Arbitration: Perspectives and Problems, Proceedings of the 17th Annual Meeting of NAA 176 (Kahn ed., BNA Books 1964). *But see* City of Wilmington, Del., 111 LA 1159, 1166 (Collins, 1998) (remedy requested was beyond arbitrator's authority because it would have added to or modified the agreement); Seminole County, Fla., Sch. Bd., 98 LA 966 (Weston, 1992) (no authority to grant monetary damages to school bus driver interviewed by sheriff's deputy following allegation of intoxication); Vermont State Colls., 96 LA 24 (McHugh, 1990) (no authority to grant additional remedy where employer rescinded letter of reprimand that gave rise to the grievance); All Am. Gourmet Co., 94 LA 361 (Stoltenberg, 1990) (no authority to order payment of interest on a credit union loan to wrongfully discharged employee); Department of Labor, 93 LA 105 (Thornell, 1989) (arbitrator cannot grant monetary remedy prohibited by the contract and a provision of the Federal Employees Pay Act, 5 U.S.C. §5542(b)(2)(B)(IV)); FMC Corp., 92 LA 1246 (Stoltenberg, 1989) (arbitrator declined to fashion a remedy that would have required interpretation of an agreement other than the collective bargaining agreement).

[59]International Harvester Co., 9 LA 894, 896 (Wirtz, 1947). *Accord* San Antonio Air Logistic Ctr., 73 LA 1074, 1082–83 (Caraway, 1979); Aetna Portland Cement Co., 41 LA 219, 222 (Dworkin, 1963); Publishers Ass'n of New York City, 37 LA 509, 518 (Seitz, 1961); Jeffrey Mfg. Co., 34 LA 814, 825 (Kuhn, 1960); Mississippi Aluminum Corp., 27 LA 625, 628 (Reynard, 1956); Patterson-Sargent Co., 23 LA 21, 23 (Willcox, 1954); Donaldson Co., 21 LA 254, 259 (Louisell, 1953); Phillips Chem. Co., 17 LA 721, 722–23 (Emery, 1951). *See also* Canadian Gen. Elec. Co., 18 LA 925, 926 (Laskin, 1952); American Mach. & Foundry Co., 15 LA 822, 827 (Wolff, 1950). *Cf.* Berea City Sch. Dist., 71 LA 679, 683, 685 (Cohen, 1978). Regarding monetary awards against public-sector employers, compare the following court cases involving such awards: Waterbury Bd. of Educ. v. Teachers Ass'n, 174 Conn. 123, 384 A.3d 350, 97 LRRM 2401 (Conn. 1977) (upholding the award where the submission expressly empowered the arbitrator to award damages); Wayne County Bd. of Comm'rs v. Police Officers Local 502-M, 254 N.W.2d 896, 95 LRRM 3396 (Mich. Ct. App. 1977) (upholding the award even though the agreement was silent on remedies); Boston Teachers Local 66 v. Boston Sch. Comm., 350 N.E.2d 707, 93 LRRM 2205 (Mass. 1976) (holding the arbitrator could not award damages for a purpose for which public funds could not be expended, and stating in dictum that, even as to a proper purpose, an arbitrator cannot award damages in excess of amounts that have been lawfully appropriated for the particular purpose).

[60]Tower Auto., 115 LA 51, 56–57 (Kenis, 2000). *See also* Klosterman Baking Co., 106 LA 257 (Beckjord, 1996) (arbitrator does not have jurisdiction to calculate additional remedies, where grievance only asked that company pay full cost of health insurance); Howland Town-

nale is that an arbitrator's function is to decide questions which the parties themselves have tried to settle without success. The usefulness and integrity of the process is lost when a new issue or requested remedy is raised for the first time at arbitration."[61]

Furthermore, arbitrators do not always award monetary damages to remedy contract violations, and are reluctant to reward employees for time not worked. Thus, extra pay for grieving employees was denied in *Georgia-Pacific Corp.*,[62] despite a clear subcontracting violation, because no employee was laid off or sent home early and there was no monetary injury.

The arbitrator in *GTE North*,[63] however, awarded affected employees one-half of the $150,000 the company had saved by contracting out bargaining-unit work while engaged in downsizing layoffs. Another arbitrator applied the seamen's common law of "maintenance and cure" in awarding unearned wages and maintenance payments in *Marriott International*.[64]

Sometimes the monetary award may be in a form other than back pay or extra pay. In *Piney Point Transportation Co.*,[65] the arbitrator awarded lump-sum front pay and benefits instead of reinstatement and back pay to a wrongfully discharged employee.

A. Compensatory Damages: Make-Whole Awards [LA CDI 94.559]

i. Monetary Awards

Monetary damages in arbitration should "normally correspond to specific monetary losses suffered."[66] One arbitrator explained:

> The ordinary rule at common law and in the developing law of labor relations is that an award of damages should be limited to the amount necessary to make the injured whole. Unless the agreement provides that some other rule should be followed, this rule must apply.[67]

---

ship Trs., 99 LA 158 (Rybolt, 1992) (arbitrator without authority to grant overtime requested at arbitration where the grievance made no such demand); Town of Lee, Mass., 95 LA 114 (McAuliffe, 1990) (arbitrator declined to order contractually justified monetary remedy in absence of request for damages); Richfield, Minn., Indep. Sch. Dist. 280, 91 LA 346 (Rotenberg, 1988) (arbitrator cannot reach issue of seniority and back pay, where written complaint did not change violation of seniority clause or seek back pay). *See also* HILL & SINICROPI, REMEDIES IN ARBITRATION 483–84 (BNA Books 2d ed. 1991).

[61]Tower Auto., 115 LA 51, 56 (Kenis, 2000).
[62]106 LA 980 (Moore, 1996).
[63]106 LA 1115 (Coyne, 1996).
[64]106 LA 403 (Wilkinson, 1996).
[65]103 LA 1117 (Crable, 1994).
[66]Patterson-Sargent Co., 23 LA 21, 23 (Willcox, 1954). *See also* Continental Can Co., 39 LA 821, 822–23 (Sembower, 1962); Canadian Gen. Elec. Co., 18 LA 925, 926 (Laskin, 1952); Phillips Chem. Co., 17 LA 721, 723 (Emery, 1951). Collective bargaining agreements often leave the matter of retroactivity of damages to the arbitrator, but with a limitation on the period of retroactivity. *See Major Collective Bargaining Agreements: Arbitration Procedures* 77–78 (U.S. Dep't of Labor Bull. No. 1425-6, 1966). *See also* Ingalls Shipbuilding Div., 69 LA 294, 302 (Bailey, 1977); Lady Balt. Bakery Co., 47 LA 8, 11 (Koven, 1966). Where a grievant was now deceased, damages were awarded to his estate or next of kin. Phelps Dodge Aluminum Prods. Corp., 52 LA 375, 382 (Howlett, 1969).

[67]International Harvester Co., 15 LA 1, 1 (Seward, 1950). An employee is entitled to be made whole regardless of the employer's financial problems. *See* Providence, R.I., Sch. Comm., 53 LA 207, 215–16 (MacLeod, 1969); Marathon City Brewing Co., 45 LA 453, 455 (McCormick,

In accord with this view, arbitrators adhere to the principle that on finding a contract violation, arbitrators have inherent power under a contract to award monetary damages to place the parties in the position they would have been in had there been no violation.[68]

Make-whole awards may include recovery of lost overtime, premium, or other special pay;[69] payment of a contract-signing bonus paid while the grievant was laid off;[70] and pay as "time worked" for additional travel to the location of a temporary[71] or special[72] assignment. Make-whole remedial awards

---

1965). Nonetheless, where a large sum possibly was involved, the arbitrator in *Swanson-Dean Corp.*, 68 LA 682, 687 (Jackson, 1977), was "loath to grant a monetary award without having knowledge" concerning "the approximate amount of money that may be required to be paid should the employer be ordered to make full payment" for the violation. He directed the parties to submit information needed in determining the amount involved, along with "any facts or arguments" the party "may have why the full amount . . . should or should not be paid by the employer." *Id.* The arbitrator stated that "[n]othing appears to warrant dilution of the liability of the employer for the breach unless it be extreme and unexpected onerousness of the remedy." *Id. See* Valley-Todeco, Inc., 75 LA 661, 664 (Anderson, 1980) (the grievance of an employee protesting unequal pay and asking for a similar higher rate was resolved by ordering the employer to recoup the excess that had erroneously been paid to another employee); Braniff Airways, 45 LA 453, 455 (McCormick, 1965); Hillman's, 32 LA 453, 458–59 (Drake, 1959) (new employee was hired at a higher rate than the contractual rate being paid other employees in the same classification; the arbitrator refused to increase the rate of said other employees for the future, but he did award back pay in the amount of the difference between their pay and that of the new employee for the disputed period). As to the remedies in *Valley-Todeco, Inc.* and *Hillman's,* cf. *Matthew* 20:1–16 (King James) (parable); Molders & Allied Workers Local 120 v. Brooks Foundry, 892 F.2d 1283, 133 LRRM 2280 (6th Cir. 1990) (upholding arbitrator's $13,000 award that took into account the injury to the union as well as the employer's ability to pay).

[68]Cadillac Gage Co., 87 LA 853 (Van Pelt, 1986). *But see* Seminole County, Fla., Sch. Bd., 98 LA 966 (Weston, 1992) (arbitrator stated he had no authority to award damages in the absence of specific provision in the contract). Arbitrators have granted monetary rather than equalization relief in overtime violation cases, where the contract is silent as to specific remedy. Vigo County, Ind., Sch. Corp., 98 LA 988 (Brookins, 1992); Michigan Dep't of State Police, 98 LA 572 (Roumell, Jr., 1992); American Cyanamid Co., 93 LA 361 (Bernstein, 1989); Georgia-Pacific Corp., 93 LA 4 (Thornell, 1989).

[69]Akzo Nobel Salt, 113 LA 645 (Goldberg, 1999); McDowell Tire Co., 108 LA 196 (Berger, 1997); Steel Mining Co., 108 LA 1 (Das, 1996); Chicago Bd. of Educ., 107 LA 999 (Kenis, 1996); American Drug Stores, 107 LA 985 (Richman, 1996) (shift premium); Clark County, Wash., Pub. Util. Dist. 1, 107 LA 713 (Paull, 1996); Hughes Aircraft Co., 107 LA 157 (Richman, 1996); George Koch Sons, 107 LA 153 (Murphy, 1996); City of Frederick, Okla., 106 LA 298 (Neas, 1996); U.S. Steel Mining Co., 105 LA 524 (Roberts, 1995); San Benito Health Found., 105 LA 263 (Levy, 1995) (vacation/sick leave); Vicksburg, Mich., Cmty. Sch., 101 LA 771 (Daniel, 1993) (business leave); Naval Surface Warfare Ctr., 101 LA 640 (Shearer, 1993) (overtime); Cambria County, Pa., Laurel Crest Manor, 101 LA 330 (D'Eletto, 1993) (weekend or holiday premium); Quantum Chem. Corp./USI Div., 101 LA 26 (Caraway, 1993) (severance pay); Hold Family Hosp., 99 LA 1122 (Tilbury, 1992); Guernsey County, Ohio, Bd. of Mental Retardation & Developmental Disabilities, 99 LA 937 (Dworkin, 1992) (assault leave); Stow City, Ohio, Sch. Dist. Bd. of Educ., 99 LA 871 (Dworkin, 1992) (same); Veterans Admin., 99 LA 229 (Duff, 1992) (environmental differential pay); St. Louis Post-Dispatch, 99 LA 98 (Berger, 1992) (employer claims of "pyradmiding" rejected); Coast Indus., 99 LA 38 (Tilbury, 1992) (jury pay supplement); Avesta Sandvik Tube, 98 LA 662 (Crane, 1992) (profit sharing); City of E. Detroit, Mich., 98 LA 485 (Girolamo, 1992) (shift differential); Ohio Dep't of National Res., 98 LA 245 (Graham, 1992) (hazardous duty); Anoka-Hennepin, Minn., Indep. Sch. Dist. 11, 97 LA 169 (Gallagher, 1991) (extra student credit for teaching load); Lawrence Paper Co., 96 LA 297 (Berger, 1991) (incentive bonus); Youngstown, Ohio, Developmental Ctr., 93 LA 1155 (Sharpe, 1989) (holiday pay).

[70]S&S Meat Co., 97 LA 873 (Murphy, 1991).

[71]Pacific Bell, 93 LA 1199 (Freeman, 1989).

[72]City of Cortland, 108 LA 406 (Skulina, 1997) (reimburse travel expenses incurred by firefighter to take paramedic training); Combined Communications Corp., 100 LA 17 (Gallagher, 1992).

have been made in cases of improper layoffs,[73] sexual harassment,[74] age discrimination,[75] discipline for refusal to obey an order under the safety exception to the "self-help" rule,[76] work stoppages permitted by the contract,[77] failure to recognize the super-sensiority rights of union stewards,[78] and constructive discharges following picketing in protected concerted activity.[79] Compensatory awards also have been used where an employer unilaterally initiates changes in the terms and conditions of employment or in benefits established by contract,[80] or improperly subcontracts or "contracts-out" bargaining-unit work.[81]

---

[73]Yale Hoists, 113 LA 1101 (Nicholas, Jr., 1999); Lackawanna Leather, 113 LA 603 (Pelofsky, 1999).

[74]Department of Labor, 98 LA 1129 (Barnett, 1992).

[75]Hamden, Conn., Bd. of Educ., 98 LA 1209 (Meredith, 1992).

[76]Beverly Enters., 100 LA 522 (Berquist, 1993); USS, Div. of USX Corp., 98 LA 72 (Neumeier, 1991).

[77]Peter Bove Constr., 99 LA 605 (Freedman, 1992).

[78]Johnson Controls, 98 LA 1183 (Bethel, 1992); Sullivan & Cozart, Inc., 97 LA 792 (Florman, 1991). *See also* Mechanical Contractors Ass'n, 100 LA 320 (Feldman, 1992) (steward performing contractual duty).

[79]Granite Constr. Co., 100 LA 585 (Richman, 1993).

[80]Accurate Forging Corp., 113 LA 597, 603 (Imundo, Jr., 1999); Eastern Associated Coal Co, 112 LA 333 (Feldman, 1999) (overtime to be calculated per contract and not under unilaterally issued procedures); Madison Warehouse Corp., 112 LA 300 (Suardi, 1998) (profit bonus); Diamond Brands, 112 LA 265 (Jacobowski, 1999) (sickness & accident benefits improperly denied under new policy); Scrupples, Inc., 111 LA 1209 (Evans, 1999) (loss of benefits tied to change in hours); Cargill Inc., 111 LA 571 (Moreland IV, 1998) (unilaterally implemented absenteeism policy); Cesiwid Inc., 111 LA 223 (Fullmer, 1998) (successor who changed policy was ordered to make retirees whole and to provide insurance coverage); Fina Oil & Chem. Co., 111 LA 107 (Bankston, 1998) (pay was awarded for time spent using pager under unilaterally issued improper procedures); Premier Private Sec., 108 LA 270 (Chumley, 1997) (company attempted unilaterally to change from cash allowances paid to employees to plans selected by company for health and pension benefit programs); Dayton's, 108 LA 113 (Jacobowski, 1997) (back pay instead of future makeup work is proper remedy for overtime violation); Goodman Beverage Co., 108 LA 37 (Morgan, Jr., 1997) (termination of an employee as a "quit" for not changing preapproved vacation for which he had paid in advance and could not get refund); Phelps Dodge Magnet Wire Co., 108 LA 21 (Curry, Jr., 1996) (failure to provide light duty for employee injured off duty); Dubovsky & Sons, 108 LA 19 (Marx, Jr., 1996) (layoff of permanent employees instead of temporary vacation replacements); Schnuck Mkts., 107 LA 739 (Cipolla, 1996) (employer given 60 days to correct a flawed contracting-out violation system and the union was ordered not to file grievances about the system during that period); Enesco Corp., 107 LA 513, 518 (Berman, 1996) (company denied pregnant employee's request for leave under contract's "good cause shown" clause); Washington Mould Co., 106 LA 1139 (Imundo, Jr., 1996) (employer attempted unilateral change in health or medical insurance coverage); Excel Corp., 106 LA 1069 (Thornell, 1996); Copperweld Steel Co., 106 LA 918 (Duda, Jr., 1996) (company wrongfully broke continuous service of employee off work because of work-related injury); Albertson's, Inc., 106 LA 897 (Kaufman, 1996) (employer denied negotiated annual pay raise to above-scale employees); Tucson, Ariz., Unified Sch. Dist., 106 LA 202 (Oberstein, 1996) (school district denied a contractual extra stipend to teacher acting as department chair); Lightning Indus., 105 LA 417 (Mikrut, Jr., 1995); Fina Oil & Chem. Co., 104 LA 343 (Nicholas, Jr., 1995) (employer delayed return to work of an employee injured on the job by requiring a third doctor's opinion in violation of contract language); ITT Sheraton/Sheraton Bal Harbour Resort, 102 LA 903 (Hoffman, 1994) (hotel instituted automatic tipping policy applicable to some, but not all, employees in server and bartender job classifications); Burlington Med. Ctr., 101 LA 843 (Bailey, 1993) (violation of weekend work schedule agreement by requiring registered nurse to take off "low census" days to provide hours for part-time nurse); Helix Elec., 101 LA 649 (Kaufman, 1993) (violation of manning-ratio agreement); Hilite Indus., 100 LA 604 (Allen, Jr., 1993); Omnisource Corp. 100 LA 120 (Ellmann, 1992); Stuart Mfg., 100 LA 100 (Klein, 1992); Weyerhaeuser Co., 95 LA 834 (Allen, Jr., 1990); City of Cape Coral, Fla., 95 LA 563 (Abrams, 1990).

[81]Fairmont Gen. Hosp., 112 LA 655 (Neigh, 1999); Huntsman Petrochemical Corp., 112 LA 399 (Bankston, 1999) (employer ordered to hire two employees to do work subcontracted

In *City of Akron, Ohio*,[82] the grievant was awarded 1 week's pay because the employer failed to notify the union that he would be relieved from duty. The employer was ordered to set aside the grievant's discharge, treat that time off from work as unpaid medical leave, and reinstate him to his former position if he obtained proper medical clearance. In *Copley Newspapers*,[83] the arbitrator ordered the employer to pay a reporter $600 as a "make-whole" remedy for wrongful refusal of permission to write an article for a "non-competitive" magazine. In a less serious vein, the arbitrator in *Oakland University*[84] ordered the school to reissue a parking permit to the union president and to reimburse him for costs of parking violations incurred while the permit was withheld. In *North Greene School District*,[85] the arbitrator ordered the employer to stop interfering with the issuance of passes by an athletic conference to teachers and to reimburse each teacher the price of admission to each event attended for which the teacher paid admission during a designated school year. In *City of Cortland, Ohio*,[86] the employer was required to reimburse travel expenses incurred by a firefighter to take paramedic training. In *Atlantic Southeast Airlines*,[87] the employer that had refused to allow an employee to withdraw a resignation was ordered to reinstate and make the employee whole. In *Southwestern Electric Power Co.*,[88] the employer was ordered to compensate linemen required to work overtime outdoors in the rain on nonemergency work by paying them for 4 hours at overtime rates in addition to the pay already received.

Arbitrators have also relied on external law as authority to award monetary damages. One arbitrator enforced the Federal Employees Part-Time Career Employment Act of 1978[89] in *Defense Commissary Agency*[90] and another arbitrator relied on the Back Pay Act[91] in *Federal Aviation Administration*.[92]

---

after employees who had previously done work retired); Cooper Energy Servs. Corp., 111 LA 155 (Skulina, 1998) (reestablished position improperly subcontracted); City of Toledo, Ohio, 106 LA 1005 (Sharpe, 1996) (uses of non-bargaining-unit employees); Montgomery Ward & Co., 106 LA 902 (Daly, 1996); Automatic Sprinkler Corp. of Am., 106 LA 19 (Wahl, 1995) (subcontract to nonunion contractor in violation of national agreement); Fingerhut, 105 LA 1146 (Lundberg, 1995) (use of temporary employees before recalling laid-off permanent employees); Hexcel Corp., 101 LA 700 (Silver, 1993); Tennessee Valley Auth., 101 LA 218 (Bankston, 1993) (second supplemental award, following employer refusal to comply with earlier awards, ordered the employer to increase the size of the bargaining unit to its presubcontracting level, ordered the employees made whole, and ordered the employer to pay the union $25,000 for costs, expenses, and lost dues); James River Corp., 100 LA 387 (Massey, 1992); Bethlehem Steel Corp., 98 LA 703 (Kahn, 1992); Teledyne Ryan Aeronautical, 95 LA 1072 (Weiss, 1990); W.R. Grace Co., 95 LA 841 (Chandler, 1990).
    [82]105 LA 787 (Kasper, 1995).
    [83]Copley Newspapers & Waukegan News-Sun, 107 LA 310 (Stallworth, 1996).
    [84]106 LA 872 (Daniel, 1996).
    [85]North Greene, Ill., Unit Sch. Dist. No. 3 Bd. of Educ., 107 LA 284 (Nathan, 1996).
    [86]108 LA 406 (Skulina, 1997).
    [87]102 LA 656 (Feigenbaum, 1994).
    [88]94 LA 443 (Nelson, 1990).
    [89]5 U.S.C. §3401 et seq.
    [90]101 LA 850 (Wren, 1993).
    [91]5 U.S.C. §5596.
    [92]101 LA 886 (Bognanno, 1993).

Ordinarily, the amount of damages should be limited to the amount necessary to make the injured party whole, unless the contract states otherwise.[93] In *Levernier Construction*,[94] the arbitrator extended the monetary remedy only to those union members who had suffered financial damages as a direct result of the employer's wrongful violation of the labor agreement.

ii. *Other Types of Awards* [LA CDI 94.559]

Make-whole recovery may extend beyond proven out-of-pocket costs and money losses, often relying on an assumption that an employee would have done something or reached some status if the opportunity had been available. For example, in one case, an employee was awarded an attendance bonus and pay for equalized overtime as part of back pay without loss of benefits, even though he resigned and did not return to work following his reinstatement from wrongful discharge.[95] In another case, the employer was ordered to review the grievant's performance appraisals to determine whether a suspension, set aside on procedural grounds in the nature of double jeopardy, had negatively affected the appraisals and, if so, to correct them. Of particular significance are a pair of cases involving plant relocations. In *Rubbermaid Office Products*,[96] the company closed its California plant and moved the work to Tennessee without offering its employees an opportunity to relocate there. The company was ordered to pay terminated employees the wages they would have earned from the date of termination through the duration of the labor agreement. In *Kuhlman Electric Corp.*,[97] the company had moved its equipment to a Mississippi installation. The arbitrator ordered the company to return sufficient equipment and assign available work to its Kentucky plant to permit employment of at least 30 employees during the remainder of the contract. However, some such make-whole awards have been conditioned on the occurrence of some future event, such as a demonstration of the ability and qualification to perform designated work.[98]

---

[93]Curry Transfer & Storage Co., 112 LA 866, 871 (Harlan, 1999); Matanuska Elec. Ass'n, 111 LA 596, 602 (Landau, 1998) (monetary relief inappropriate where none of the unit members that could potentially be affected by the violation actually lost work or suffered any reduction in their normal work hours). *See generally* Kelsey-Hayes Co., 85 LA 774 (Thomson, 1985).

[94]113 LA 152, 159 (Gallagher, 1999) (the purpose of a monetary remedy is not to extend payment to anyone who has not suffered a monetary loss, nor is it intended to enrich any individual through payment beyond that which is justified by actual losses).

[95]Air Force, 107 LA 1089 (Stephens, 1997); Vision-Ease, 102 LA 1106 (Mathews, 1994). *See also* City of Omaha, Neb., 101 LA 476 (Bard, 1993) (employer was ordered to grant a merit pay increase to an employee with no negative work history who had missed work for a considerable portion of the performance evaluation period because of injury because evidence indicated merit increases were essentially automatic for employees without negative work histories).

[96]107 LA 161 (Alleyne, 1996).

[97]106 LA 429 (Duda, Jr., 1996).

[98]Darling Store Fixtures, 108 LA 183 (Allen, Jr., 1997) (90-day "last chance"); Apcoa, Inc., 107 LA 705 (Daniel, 1996) (12 weeks to provide medical certification of ability to return to work); Mesa Distrib. Co., 106 LA 1166 (Rule, 1996) (pass physical examination and drug screen); J.W. Costello Beverage Co., 106 LA 356 (Bickner, 1996) (60 days to prove ability); Miami Sys. Corp., 99 LA 506 (Curry, Jr., 1992); Schuylkill Metals Corp., 94 LA 562 (Pratte, 1990).

iii. Awards Denied or Reduced

Often, back-pay awards in suspension and discharge cases have been denied or reduced in consideration of the grievant's fault[99] or the grievant's responsibility for creating the problem.[100]

In *Michigan Milk Producers Ass'n*,[101] the arbitrator held that an agreement allows for compensatory relief to innocent victims; thus, if a violation is known, the aggrieved must act in a prudent manner to the limit the extent of damages. Mitigating circumstances also may lessen an award to either party. One arbitrator stated that "if consideration has not been given to mitigating circumstances, no matter why the fault, there is a legitimate basis for arbitral concern."[102]

iv. Interim Back-Pay Awards

Interim back-pay relief has been awarded to employees denied temporary promotions to jobs that they were not entitled to fill on a permanent basis,[103] and in disciplinary cases where nonprejudicial procedural or so-called "technical" errors occurred even though the discharge or suspension was

---

[99]Smith Fiberglass Prods., 108 LA 225 (Allen, Jr., 1997) (unauthorized personal leave—hiding from husband); Weyerhaeuser Co. Forest Prods., 108 LA 26 (Levak, 1997) (refusal to take drug test); Avis Rent-A-Car Sys., 107 LA 197 (Shanker, 1996) (prior criminal conviction not disclosed on employment application); Tenneco Packaging Corp., 106 LA 606 (Franckiewicz, 1996) (insubordination); Nabisco Brands, 106 LA 422 (Wolff, 1996) (fighting); Exxon Chem. Ams., 105 LA 1011 (Allen, Jr., 1996) (falsification of company document to conceal drunken driving conviction); Democratic Printing & Lithographing Co., 103 LA 327 (Weisbrod, 1994) ("atrocious" attendance record); Smurfit Recycling Co., 103 LA 243 (Richman, 1994) (safety rule violation); Greschlers, Inc., 103 LA 135 (Nadelbach, 1994) (clerk's improper conduct toward customer of a retail store); Maryvale Samaritan Med. Ctr., 103 LA 90, 98 (White, 1994) (grievant who ignored orders was "her own worst enemy"); Georgia-Pacific Corp., 99 LA 361 (Allen, Jr., 1992) (employee had been suspended indefinitely pending criminal charges involving drug offenses that authorities later elected not to prosecute).

[100]Lincoln Lutheran, 113 LA 72, 77 (Kessler, 1999) (back pay was withheld because grievant had refused to tell her side of the story); Rexam Graphics, 111 LA 1176, 1185–86 (Gangle, 1998) (back pay was denied because grievant lied at unemployment compensation and arbitration hearings); Manchester Plastics, 110 LA 169 (Knott, 1997); Bruce Hardwood Floors, 108 LA 115 (Allen, Jr., 1997) (long-term employee with no history of drug use failed random drug test after mistakenly taking wife's medication); Facility Mgmt. of La., 106 LA 879 (O'Grady, 1996) (grievant in jail for non-work-related offense); Cone Mills Corp., 106 LA 23 (Nolan, 1995) (grievant unavailable for work because of illness and personal travel); Norfolk Shipbuilding & Drydock Corp. (NORSHIPCO), 105 LA 529 (Hockenberry, 1995); Buckeye Steel Castings Co., 104 LA 825 (Weatherspoon, 1995) (refusal of job assignment); Ogden Support Servs., 104 LA 432 (Weisheit, 1995) (refusal to accept comparable job following reinstatement from gross negligence discharge); Crown Divs. of Allen Group, 103 LA 378 (Klein, 1994) (reduction in back pay by amount of property damage caused by grievant's carelessness for which she had been discharged); AT&T, 102 LA 931 (Kanner, 1994) (back pay was denied where grievant's refusal to answer questions impeded investigation); Grace Indus., 102 LA 119 (Knott, 1993) (failure to grieve demotion, which was a factor in ultimate discharge); Burlington N. R.R., 101 LA 144 (Massey, 1993) (employee responsible for much of delay in reaching arbitration); Moss Supermarket, 99 LA 408 (Grupp, 1992) (one-half back pay to employee who precipitated the problem).

[101]114 LA 1652, 1658 (Allen, 2000) (employee is obligated to call attention to an error in payment of his or her wages when the error is first discovered or when a reasonably prudent person should have first discovered the error).

[102]Department of Veterans Affairs, 114 LA 733, 743 (Moore, 2000).

[103]Peoria, Ill., Sch. Dist. 150, 95 LA 329 (Draznin, 1990); Bell Helicopter Textron, 93 LA 233 (Morris, 1989).

sustained.[104] But, where the procedural or administrative errors were deemed to be substantial, discipline has been set aside and the grievant awarded full back pay.[105]

The following cases are illustrative: In *Gaylord Container Corp.*,[106] the arbitrator set aside a disciplinary demotion, replaced it with a minor suspension, and awarded back pay for the difference in pay rates where the company had not followed progressive discipline principles. In *Atlantic Southeast Airlines*,[107] a flight attendant who was wrongfully discharged for "refusing" to take a drug test later failed such a test after being returned to work. She was denied reinstatement but awarded back pay for the period between the wrongful discharge and the assumed date, 10 months later, when she used the marijuana found in the failed test. In *Renton, Washington, School District*,[108] a disciplinary demotion involving alleged sexual harassment was upheld but the demoted employee was awarded the difference in pay up to commencement of the arbitration hearing because the employer had refused to disclose to the employee the names of his accusers. In *Mason & Hangar-Silas Mason Co.*,[109] a discharge for failing a drug test was upheld, but back pay was awarded because the employer's discharge procedure violated applicable federal regulations. In *United States Can Co.*,[110] partial back pay was awarded, but reinstatement was denied a chronically ill employee terminated after compiling an extensive record of absenteeism. In *Rodeway*

---

[104]United States Can Co., 104 LA 863 (Briggs, 1995); Mason & Hanger-Silas Mason Co., 103 LA 371 (Cipolla, 1994) (back pay awarded even though discharge was upheld, where employer violated federal drug-testing procedures); Renton, Wash., Sch. Dist., 102 LA 854 (Wilkinson, 1994) (an employee who was demoted for alleged sexual harassment was awarded back pay because of the employer's refusal to provide names of the accusers); Atlantic Southeast Airlines, 101 LA 515 (Nolan, 1993); Montana State Hosp., 99 LA 551 (McCurdy, 1992) (untimely investigation and decision); Bi-State Dev. Agency, 96 LA 1090 (Cipolla, 1991) (denial of union representation and opportunity to defend); United States Steel Corp., 95 LA 566, 568 (Talarico, 1990) (failure to comply with "justice and dignity" clause); Allied Health Care Prods., 94 LA 178 (Cipolla, 1990) (failure to investigate before discharge). *See also* Interstate Brands Corp., 97 LA 293 (Canestraight, 1991) (discharge for falsification of records sustained, but discharge for dishonesty dismissed and grievant granted 2 months' back pay).

[105]Kroger Co., 108 LA 417 (Baroni, 1997) (absence of predischarge hearing and investigation); Alaska Dep't of Transp., 108 LA 339 (Levak, 1997) (discipline reduced because of procedural and/or administrative errors); Anheuser-Busch, Inc., 107 LA 1183 (Weckstein, 1996) (insufficient involvement of union and notice to employees in development of drug-abuse policy); CR/PL Ltd. P'ship (Crane Plumbing), 107 LA 1084 (Fullmer, 1996) (no investigation); Southern Frozen Foods, 107 LA 1030 (Giblin, 1996) (lack of due process; no investigation); Ken Meyer Meats, 107 LA 1017 (Sergent, 1996) (failure to investigate before imposing discipline); Kasle Steel Corp., 107 LA 1006 (Kerner, 1996); City of Newark, Ohio, 107 LA 775 (Kindig, 1996) (lack of predisciplinary conference); S&J Ranch, 103 LA 350 (Bogue, 1994); Boeing Co., 101 LA 240 (Staudohar, 1993) (failure to give appropriate notice under the Worker Adjustment and Retraining Notification Act, 29 U.S.C. §2101 et seq.); Weber Aircraft, 100 LA 417 (Jennings, 1992); Port of Tacoma, Wash., 99 LA 1151 (Smith, 1992) (double jeopardy); Hoover-Hanes Rubber Custom Mixing Corp., 99 LA 466 (Byars, 1992); Hughes Asphalt Co., 99 LA 445 (Donald, 1992); Reynolds Metals Co./Alreco Metals, 99 LA 239 (Kahn, 1992); Montgomery County, Md., Gov't, 99 LA 111 (Hockenberry, 1992); Huntingdon Borough, 99 LA 88 (Hewitt, 1992) (double jeopardy); Purina Mills, 98 LA 504 (Jacobs, 1992) (failure to notify union); United States Steel Corp., 95 LA 610, 613 (Das, 1990) (blatant violation of "justice and dignity" clause).

[106]107 LA 1138 (Allen, Jr., 1997).

[107]101 LA 515 (Nolan, 1993).

[108]102 LA 854 (Wilkinson, 1994).

[109]103 LA 371 (Cipolla, 1994).

[110]104 LA 863 (Briggs, 1995).

Inn,[111] another arbitrator set aside a discharge and awarded full back pay but declined to reinstate the employee into a "volatile" situation. In lieu of reinstatement, the grievant was awarded 6 months' severance pay.

v.   *Future Loss*

Awards in compensatory damage cases often extend beyond strict monetary relief if the loss will continue into the future. For example, arbitrators have modified the effective date and the type of disciplinary action so that an employee might qualify for pension benefits[112] and have ordered restoration of special services once provided to employees.[113]

vi.   *Additional Employer Requirements*

Make-whole awards frequently impose additional requirements on the employer[114] in order to implement the intended remedy, such as providing special training, instructions, or equipment,[115] ordering reimbursement of special expenses,[116] restoring of contractual benefits,[117] reimbursing the cost

---

[111]102 LA 1003 (Goldberg, 1994).

[112]Town of Southington, Conn., 100 LA 67 (Halperin, 1992); Cyprus Bagdad Copper Corp., 99 LA 841 (White, 1992).

[113]GTE Hawaiian Tel. Co., 98 LA 832 (Najita, 1991) (taxi service for night switchboard operators); Transportation Mgmt. of Tenn., 93 LA 73 (Holley, Jr., 1989) (uniform pants-pressing shop).

[114]Guernsey County, Ohio, Bd. of Mental Retardation & Developmental Disabilities, 99 LA 937 (Dworkin, 1992) (assault leave); Stow City, Ohio, Sch. Dist. Bd. of Educ., 99 LA 871 (Dworkin, 1992) (same); Veterans Admin., 99 LA 229 (Duff, 1992) (environmental differential pay); Coast Indus., 99 LA 38 (Tilbury, 1992) (jury pay supplement); Avesta Sandvik Tube, 98 LA 662 (Crane, 1992) (profit sharing); City of E. Detroit, Mich., 98 LA 485 (Girolamo, 1992) (shift differential); Ohio Dep't of Natural Res., 98 LA 245 (Graham, 1992) (hazardous duty); Anoka-Hennepin, Minn., Indep. Sch. Dist. 11, 97 LA 169 (Gallagher, 1991) (extra student credit for teaching load); Lawrence Paper Co., 96 LA 297 (Berger, 1991) (incentive bonus); Youngstown, Ohio, Developmental Ctr., 93 LA 1155 (Sharpe, 1989) (holiday pay).

[115]Mount Sinai Hosp., 105 LA 1047, 1050 (Duff, 1995) (training "appropriate to polish her interpersonal skills"); Iowa Elec. Light & Power Co., 100 LA 393 (Pelofsky, 1993) (tailored test instructions for employee with learning disability); International Bus. Servs., 98 LA 1116 (Bernhardt, 1991) (determine insurability of bus driver); City of Brook Park, Ohio, 98 LA 758 (Nelson, 1992) (supply hypoallergenic gloves for emergency medical technician work); Tanner Cos., 98 LA 530 (Parent, 1991) (training to drive cement mixer truck); Jefferson County, Ky., Bd. of Educ., 97 LA 549 (Murphy, 1991) (professional staff services to help teacher correct deficiencies); Bethlehem Steel Corp., 95 LA 719 (Witt, 1990) (skills training for lower-rated employees in clerical pool).

[116]Accurate Forging Corp., 113 LA 597, 603 (Imundo, Jr., 1999) (lost insurance benefits); Department of Def. Dependents Sch., 112 LA 198 (Herzog, 1999) (reimbursement of costs of educational workshop); Engelhard Corp., 100 LA 238 (Duda, Jr., 1993) (medical insurance and expenses); Conneaut Sch. Dist. Bd. of Educ., Linesville, Pa., 99 LA 1010 (Duff, 1992) (dental services); Norwalk, Ohio, City Sch. Dist. Bd. of Educ., 99 LA 825 (Miller, 1992) (driving skills test ordered by employer); East Detroit, Mich., Pub. Sch., 99 LA 235 (Daniel, 1992) (attending mandatory high school classes); Fraenkel Co., 99 LA 1 (Odom, Jr., 1992) (substance dependency program required by employer); Valley Hosp. Ass'n, 97 LA 661 (Calhoun, 1991) (health insurance premium balance); Town of East Haven, Conn., 97 LA 108 (Orlando, 1991) (medical expenses); Flexible Corp., 95 LA 1049 (Duda, Jr., 1990) ("fine" for loss of plastic time card).

[117]Tubetech, Inc., 113 LA 1025 (Richard, 1999) (past overdue annual cash bonuses); City of St. Marys, Pa., 113 LA 708, 712 (Talarico, 1999) (tuition reimbursement); City of Lebanon, Ohio, 112 LA 53, 58 (Fullmer, 1999) (reimbursement for sick leave, vacation, and compensatory time that was used when injury leave was improperly denied); Evergreen, Ohio, Local Bd. of Educ., 111 LA 1070 (Paolucci, 1998) (restore sick leave bank, where assault leave was improperly denied); Stone Container Corp., 108 LA 249 (Hilgert, 1997) (protective eyewear); Clark County, Wash., Pub. Util. Dist. 1, 107 LA 713 (Paull, 1996) (meal allowance); Kent

of lost benefits, such as medical and dental expenses,[118] health insurance premiums,[119] tool claims,[120] protective eyewear,[121] tuition,[122] or other positive action.[123] In *Mount Sinai Hospital*,[124] the arbitrator ordered an employee reinstated with training "appropriate to polish her interpersonal skills."[125]

vii. Proving Damage Claims

Arbitrators generally require a party to prove its claim for damage,[126] and, where no grievant suffers any monetary loss as a result of the employer's violation, no damages will be awarded.[127]

Worldwide Mach. Works, 107 LA 455 (Duda, Jr., 1996) (dental claims, tool claims, and Christmas bonus); State of Oregon, 107 LA 138 (Downing, 1996) (tuition reimbursement); Doss Aviation, 107 LA 39 (Ferree, 1996) (accrued sick leave); BP Oil Co., 106 LA 976 (Hewitt, 1996); Klosterman Baking Co., 106 LA 257 (Beckjord, 1996) (health insurance premiums); City of Benton Harbor, Mich., 106 LA 847 (Ellmann, 1996) (various benefits denied temporarily disabled employee assigned to light duty while on worker's compensation); San Benito Health Found., 105 LA 263 (Levy, 1995) (medical expenses); Ohio Edison Co., 102 LA 717 (Sergent, 1994) (meal allowance); City of Omaha, Neb., 101 LA 476 (Bard, 1993) (merit increase); Rome Hosp., 99 LA 1001 (Wesman, 1992) (sick leave); Guernsey County, Ohio, Bd. of Mental Retardation & Developmental Disabilities, 99 LA 937 (Dworkin, 1992) (same); Riverside Osteopathic Hosp., 98 LA 1044 (McDonald, 1992) (medical benefits); Weinstein Wholesale Meat, 98 LA 636 (Eagle, 1992) (vacation pay); Oakland Univ., 98 LA 466 (Daniel, 1991) (longevity pay); Town of Woodbridge, Conn., 98 LA 10 (Pittocco, 1991) (supplementary disability benefits).

[118]San Benito Health Found., 105 LA 263 (Levy, 1995); Engelhard Corp., 100 LA 238 (Duda, Jr., 1993) (medical insurance and expenses); Conneaut Sch. Dist., Bd. of Educ., 99 LA 1010 (Duff, 1992) (dental services); Town of East Haven, Conn., 97 LA 108 (Orlando, 1991) (medical expenses). *See also* U.S. Sugar Corp., 112 LA 967, 973 (Chandler, 1999).

[119]BP Oil Co., 106 LA 976 (Hewitt, 1996); Klosterman Baking Co., 106 LA 257 (Beckjord, 1996); Valley Hosp. Ass'n, 97 LA 661 (Calhoun, 1991) (health insurance premium balance).

[120]Kent Worldwide Mach. Works, 107 LA 455 (Duda, Jr., 1996).

[121]Stone Container Corp., 108 LA 249 (Hilgert, 1997).

[122]State of Oregon, 107 LA 138 (Downing, 1996).

[123]City of Los Angeles, Cal., 103 LA 1075 (Bergeson, 1994) (employer ordered to change retroactively absence without approved leave to approved vacation time); Rodeway Inn, 102 LA 1003 (Goldberg, 1994) (formal apology to grievant, posting of notice to employees of award, and meeting on company time for union to discuss matter with employees); District of Columbia Bd. of Educ. 101 LA 691 (Modjeska, 1993) (employees transferred to different sites offered opportunity to return to original posts); Internal Revenue Serv., 101 LA 341 (Donnelly, 1993); Liberty Ctr. Local Bd. of Educ., 99 LA 574 (Feldman, 1992) (issue contract to teach); Bethlehem Steel Corp., 98 LA 1134 (McDermott, 1992) (reopen shut down part of plant); International Paper Co., 94 LA 409 (Mathews, 1990) (reinstate and transfer disabled employee).

[124]105 LA 1047 (Duff, 1995).

[125]*Id.* at 1050.

[126]Belcor, Inc., 77 LA 23, 28 (McKay, 1981) (because "there is not sufficient evidence to determine who suffered a loss or the extent of the loss suffered," the "arbitrator cannot grant specific relief for lost wages"); Storer Broad. Co., 76 LA 409, 411–12 (Feldman, 1981); Bureau of Census, 75 LA 1194, 1201 (Mittelman, 1980); General Tel. Co. of Cal., 74 LA 931, 934 (Bickner, 1980); Aztec Plumbing Corp., 74 LA 633, 640 (Ross, 1980); C. Schmidt Co., 69 LA 80, 85 (Albrechta, 1977); Smitty's Glass & Lock Serv., 68 LA 1102, 1108 (Conway, 1977); H.J. Madore, Inc., 47 LA 698, 703 (Callaghan, 1966) (it "is not the duty of the arbitrator to research the damages allegedly incurred . . . except insofar as the arbitrator may review the substantiation offered for specific damages demanded by one of the parties"). But where the wrongdoer is in a better position to provide evidence as to damages, the arbitrator might place the burden on that person. *See* Akers Motor Lines, 51 LA 955, 965 (Dunau, 1968). *See also* General Cable Corp., 52 LA 229, 232 (Feller, 1968).

[127]Union Carbide Corp., 113 LA 538, 544 (Woolf, 1999); Fantasy-Blanke Baer Corp., 111 LA 1057 (Marino, 1999) (no monetary damages for improper subcontracting because nobody was laid off); City of Henderson, Nev., 91 LA 941, 944 (Morris, 1988); West Penn Power Co., 87 LA 669, 673 (Dworkin, 1986); Columbia Pictures Indus., 80 LA 1030, 1032 (Christopher, 1983); Edward Kraemer & Sons, 72 LA 684, 691 (Martin, 1979); Internal Revenue Serv., 71

Thus, for example, where an employer violates the agreement by utilizing junior employees, damages will be due only to those employees whose seniority would have entitled them to the work had the employer acted in accordance with the agreement.[128]

B. Speculative Damages

Generally, arbitrators deny monetary relief where the injury is too speculative.[129] Thus, no remedial order was granted where the arbitrator found too many "variables" in the evidence to justify relief.[130]

LA 1018, 1021 (Harkless, 1978); Anaheim Union High Sch. Dist., 70 LA 645, 648 (Grenig, 1978); Beyerl Chevrolet, 68 LA 343, 346 (Bolte, 1977). *But see* Celanese Fibers Co., 72 LA 271, 276 (Foster, 1979); Merck & Co., 52 LA 243, 247 (Crawford, 1969). In *Courier Journal*, 93 LA 227, 232 (Tharp, 1989), the arbitrator applied the legal concept of *injuria absque damno*, "wrong without damage." A wrong without damage will not sustain an action. Kroger Co., 105 LA 856 (Katz, 1996). *See also* Holiday Inn of E. Peoria, 93 LA 180 (Draznin, 1989); Alpha Beta Co., 90 LA 1081 (Ross, 1988); Monterey Coal Co., 89 LA 989 (Fullmer, 1987); U.S. Playing Card Co., 87 LA 937 (Duda, Jr., 1986); Shell Oil Co./Shell Chem. Co., 87 LA 473 (Nicholas, Jr., 1986); Kroger Co., 85 LA 1198 (St. Antoine, 1985); Columbia Pictures Indus., 80 LA 1030 (Christopher, 1983). For later cases as to absence of injury, see *TGS Tech.*, 99 LA 988 (Miller, 1992); *Kahler Corp.*, 97 LA 895 (Imes, 1991); *Day & Zimmermann, Inc.*, 94 LA 112 (Talent, 1990).

[128]El Al Israel Airlines, 91 LA 121, 126 (Kramer, 1988); Aerojet-General Corp., 49 LA 1073, 1076–77 (Killion, 1967); California Metal Trades Ass'n, 41 LA 1204, 1208–09 (Ross, 1963); Northwest Airlines, 38 LA 207, 209 (Schedler, 1961); Cook Mach. Co., 35 LA 845, 850 (Boles, 1960); Kennecott Copper Corp., 32 LA 300, 304 (Cross, 1958); Corn Prods. Ref. Co., 21 LA 105, 108 (Gilden, 1953); Republic Steel Corp., 17 LA 709, 710 (Marshall, 1951); Fruehauf Trailer Co., 11 LA 495, 498 (Whiting, 1948); St. Regis Paper Co., 4 LA 786, 787 (Copelof, 1946). *See also* Wyandotte Chems. Corp., 35 LA 783, 787–88 (Wollett, 1960); Motch & Merryweather Mach. Co., 32 LA 492, 501 (Kates, 1959). *Cf.* Farmlea Dairy, 50 LA 357, 361 (Wolf, 1968); United States Radium Corp., 36 LA 1067, 1070 (Loucks, 1961); Allegheny Ludlum Steel Corp., 36 LA 855, 856 (Shipman, 1960). In *Columbus Auto Parts Co.*, 43 LA 546, 553–54 (Klein, 1964), the company asserted that the named grievants did not have sufficient seniority to make them proper claimants for damages, but this assertion came too late because it was first made in the post-hearing brief. Similarly, damages were due only to those employees whose qualifications would have entitled them to the work had the employer acted in accordance with the agreement. For related discussion as concerns the federal sector, see Chapter 20, section 5.D., "Comptroller General's Role," and section 5.E., "Arbitral Remedies and the Back Pay Act."

[129]Morton Salt, 113 LA 969, 973 (Allen, 1999); Gilmore Envelope Corp., 110 LA 1036, 1042 (Ross, 1998) (arbitrator was "loath to award damages based on speculation"); Potomac Edison Co. (Allegheny Power), 110 LA 420, 425 (Talarico, 1997) (arbitrator sustained the grievance but failed to award damages because "it would be near impossible or highly speculative for an employee to even attempt to establish that he would have been able to respond to a call-out"). Georgia-Pacific, 106 LA 980 (Moore, 1996) (extra pay denied where subcontracting violation did not cause lay off and there was no monetary injury); Union Camp Corp., 104 LA 295 (Nolan, 1995) ("mental distress" damages were not compensated because there was no evidence of injury and any such award would be "purely speculative"); Kaiser Eng'g, 102 LA 1189 (Minni, 1994) (back pay calculated at only straight time because at this installation the opportunity for overtime was "highly speculative"); TGS Tech., 99 LA 988 (Miller, 1992); Genex, 99 LA 559 (Bard, 1992); Armstrong Air Conditioning, 99 LA 540 (Harlan, 1992); Kahler Corp., 97 LA 895; Dyna Gel, 97 LA 510 (Yaney, 1991); Harbison-Walker Refractories Div., 95 LA 885 (Dworkin, 1990); MacMillan Bloedel Containers, 94 LA 992 (Nicholas, Jr., 1990); Virginian Metal Prods. Co., 94 LA 798 (Jones, 1990); Day & Zimmermann Inc., 94 LA 112 (Talent, 1990); McElroy Coal Co., 93 LA 566, 570 (McIntosh, 1989); Holiday Inn of E. Peoria, 93 LA 180 (Draznin, 1989); Alpha Beta Co., 90 LA 1081 (Ross, 1988); Knapheide Mfg. Co., 90 LA 862, 865 (Cohen, 1987); Monterey Coal Co., 89 LA 989 (Fullmer, 1987); U.S. Playing Card Co., 87 LA 937 (Duda, Jr., 1986); Shell Oil Co./Shell Chem. Co., 87 LA 473 (Nicholas, Jr., 1986); Kroger Co., 85 LA 1198 (St. Antoine, 1985); Columbia Pictures Indus., 80 LA 1030 (Christopher, 1983); Permutit Co., 19 LA 599, 600 (Trotta, 1952).

[130]Freeman Decorating Co., 102 LA 149 (Baroni, 1994).

However, damages will not be denied merely because the amount is difficult to determine.[131] When difficulty is encountered, the simplest fair method available for determining the amount will be used.[132] One possible solution in this type of situation is for the arbitrator to make a finding as to liability and provide that, in the light of the difficulty of determining the exact amount of damages, the liability may be discharged by a lump-sum settlement if the parties can reach one. This was done, for instance, where a time-consuming and expensive process of reviewing records covering a 5-year period would have been necessary to determine the precise amount due.[133]

Where no other solution is available, the arbitrator "is bound to resort to his own good sense and judgment, and after considering all the pertinent facts and circumstances make a reasonable approximation."[134]

In a few instances monetary damages were denied because they were not expressly requested in the grievance,[135] but in many other instances no such express request was found to be required.[136] If the grievance requests

---

[131]Five Star Hardware & Elec. Corp., 44 LA 944, 946 (Wolff, 1965); Plumbing, Heating & Piping Employees Council, 39 LA 513, 522 (Ross, 1962) ("The wrongdoer must bear the risk of uncertainty. At the same time the plaintiff is obliged to make a reasonable estimate of damages, supported by the evidence in the case."). See also Towns of Niagara, Wheatfield, Lewiston, & Cambria Cent. Sch. Dist. No. 1 Bd. of Educ. v. Niagara-Wheatfield Teachers Ass'n, 46 N.Y.2d 553, 415 N.Y.S.2d 790, 101 LRRM 2258, 2259 (1979); Village Meats, 91 LA 1023, 1027 (Shanker, 1988); Lorimar-Telepictures Prods., 90 LA 1115, 1118 (Christopher, 1988). Cf. Fred Meyer, Inc., 70 LA 608, 613–14 (Sinclitico, 1978).

[132]News Am. Publ'ns v. Typographical Union Local 103 (Newark), 918 F.2d 21, 135 LRRM 2979 (3d Cir. 1990); Kaiser Eng'g, 102 LA 1189 (Minni, 1994) (back pay calculated at only straight time because at this installation the opportunity for overtime was "highly speculative"); Parsons Contractors, 91 LA 73, 77 (DiLauro, 1988); Lorimar-Telepictures Prods., 90 LA 1115 (Christopher, 1988); Eagle-Picher Mining & Smelting Co., 6 LA 544, 549 (Elson, 1947).

[133]Corn Prods. Ref. Co., 7 LA 125, 132–33 (Updegraff, 1947). See also T.J. Maxx, 113 LA 533, 538 (Richman, 1999) (lost overtime hours were ordered to be paid because it was impossible to construct a make-up remedy); Bethlehem Steel, 16 LA 926, 931–32 (Feinberg, 1951). In Armco Steel Corp., 52 LA 108, 112 (Sembower, 1969), the burden of examining past records was minimized by limiting the period of retroactivity for damages. Where a basis existed for determining the total damages for a violation, the difficulty of determining the entitled individuals was circumvented by directing payment of the damages into a fund "to be used for a mutually agreed upon benefit for all employees of the bargaining unit," and this solution withstood court challenge. Newark Wire Cloth Co. v. Steelworkers, 339 F. Supp. 1207, 80 LRRM 2094, 2095 (D.N.J. 1972). Cf. Boston Teachers Local 66 v. School Comm. of Boston, 350 N.E.2d 707, 93 LRRM 2205, 2210–11 (Mass. 1976).

[134]American Mach. & Foundry Co., 15 LA 822, 827–28 (Wolff, 1950). A liquidated-damages approach was similarly used in: Jefferson City Cabinet Co., 50 LA 621, 624 (Dworkin, 1967); Pullman-Standard, 36 LA 1042, 1044 (McCoy, 1961). Some collective bargaining agreements specifically provide for liquidated damages for violation thereof. Discussing such provisions, see Mi-Ka Prods., 76 LA 1203, 1210–11 (Christopher, 1981). See also Transportation Mgmt. of Tenn., 93 LA 73, 80 (Holley, Jr., 1989); Village Meats, 91 LA 1023, 1027 (Shanker, 1988); Lorimar-Telepictures Prods., 90 LA 1115, 1118 (Christopher, 1988); Capital Decorating Co., 25 LA 424, 426 (Slavney, 1955).

[135]Richfield, Minn., Indep. Sch. Dist. 280, 91 LA 346, 351 (Rotenberg, 1988); Joffe Bros., 73 LA 965, 968 (Rothchild, 1979); Wright Mach. Co., 49 LA 64, 66 (Daly, 1967); Orr & Sembower, Inc., 43 LA 33, 35 (Seidenberg, 1964); Ohio Fuel Gas Co., 35 LA 330, 337 (Haughton, 1960). Where a contract violation was found but no damages were requested or awarded, a separate claim for damages was subsequently brought to a second arbitrator but was rejected. John Deere Co., 70 LA 997, 998 (Grether, 1978) (the "policy to avoid a multiplicity of law suits and have no more than one trial unless there is some very good reason to have more than one trial is based on the reasoning that it is wasteful to society and harassing to the adversary to have more than one trial").

[136]West Va. Pulp & Paper Co., 39 LA 163, 166–67 (Stark, 1962); Bethlehem Steel, 17 LA 295, 300 (Selekman, 1951) (past practice controlled the result).

back pay, but the award merely states that the grievance is sustained, the award of such damages may be implied.[137]

C. Mental Distress Damages

Arbitrators refrain from awarding mental distress damages even when there is no question of actual injury to the grievant.[138] This position has been explained as follows:

> While mental distress damages are now recoverable in some breach-of-contract actions, in the labor arbitration context there is strong argument that an arbitrator should never award damages for mental distress, even when there is no question of actual injury to the grievant. The question is not one of power generally, but rather whether it can reasonably be concluded that the parties, in negotiating their agreement, contemplated that such relief could be secured in the arbitral forum. The absence of reported decisions in the area arguably indicates that the better rule is to refrain altogether from making awards for emotional distress arising out of an employer's breach of contract. Such relief is better left to the expertise of the courts than the labor arbitrator.[139]

However, in sexual harassment grievances, where the labor agreements incorporate state and federal antidiscrimination law, arbitrators have been forced to reconsider whether mental distress damages should be available.[140]

D. Damages Payable to Employer or Union

The vast majority of arbitral awards for damages are concerned with indemnifying employees. In some cases, however, it is asserted that the company has suffered damage because of union violations of the agreement, or that the union has suffered damage because of company violations. Occasionally the award will be made to the union on behalf of a group of grievants[141] or because the identity of the injured party was not clear from the grievance.[142]

---

[137]California Metal Trades Ass'n, 41 LA 1204, 1207 (Ross, 1963). *See also* Glover Bottled Gas Corp./Synergy Gas Corp., 91 LA 77, 90 (Simons, 1987); Dayton Malleable Iron Co., 11 LA 1175, 1179–80 (Platt, 1949).

[138]Champlain Cable Corp., 108 LA 449, 453 (Sweeney, 1997); Kaiser Permanente Med. Care Program, 89 LA 841, 842 (Alleyne, 1987). *See also* Union Camp Corp., 104 LA 295, 300–02 (Nolan, 1995) (agreement does not authorize damage awards for pain and suffering as a remedy for sexual harassment).

[139]Hill & Sinicropi, Remedies in Arbitration 490 (BNA Books 2d ed. 1991) (footnotes omitted).

[140]In *Union Camp Corp.*, 104 LA 295 (Nolan, 1995), the arbitrator declined to award mental distress damages to grievants who proved by a preponderance of the evidence that they had been sexually harassed by their supervisor. The arbitrator explained that even though the agreement prohibited sex discrimination "as provided by law," this language was insufficient to rest "a theory of full incorporation." *Id.* at 301. The employer did not mean to vest arbitrators with all the powers of a federal judge, including the award of compensatory and punitive damages.

[141]GTE N., 106 LA 1115 (Coyne, 1996) ($75,000 to be paid to the union to distribute to employees for subcontracting violations); American Red Cross, 105 LA 240, 247 (Garrett, 1995); Helix Elec., 101 LA 649, 654 (Kaufman, 1993); Hughes Aircraft Co., 101 LA 226, 232 (Richman, 1993); Sea-Land Freight Serv., 87 LA 633 (D'Spain, 1986) (42 grievants awarded a total of $476,524.55 for improper subcontracting by the employer).

[142]Cadillac Gage Co., 87 LA 853, 856 (Van Pelt, 1986) (arbitrator ordered money paid to union be used as union determined proper, where grievance did not provide the identity of

i. Union Violations

Company claims for damages against the union for illicit work stoppages have not been uncommon. Many arbitrators have awarded damages for breach of no-strike clauses where the authority to do so was not expressly denied by the agreement (in some of these decisions, the arbitrator itemized the elements of damages).[143] A few arbitrators have ruled, however, that express contractual authority is required to empower the arbitrator to award damages for no-strike violations.[144]

ii. Employer Violations

Claims for damages in favor of the union as an entity have been based on injury caused by company violation of contract provisions respecting union representational rights,[145] union-security clauses,[146] and contractual viola-

---

the employee to receive the pay but alleged that the "company had deprived the union of one-half hour of bargaining unit work").

[143]Farrell Lines, 86 LA 36, 40 (Hockenberry, 1986) ("[A]n award of damages for illegal work stoppage is a proper performance of an arbitrator's duties and inherent in his or her office. . . . Such authority of the arbitrator to fashion a remedy to a labor dispute is critical to the ultimate resolution of the parties' differences, and should be sustained absent contrary language in the agreement."); Rust Eng'g Co., 77 LA 488, 490 (Williams, 1981); Rust Eng'g Co., 75 LA 189, 196–97 (Eigenbrod, 1980); Mercer, Fraser Co., 54 LA 1125, 1129–30 (Eaton, 1971); Vulcan Mold & Iron Co. Div., 53 LA 869, 872–76 (Kates, 1969); Associated Gen. Contractors of Am., 53 LA 542, 544–45 (Wyckoff, 1969) (an arbitrator "has the inherent power to award damages for breach of a collective bargaining agreement unless the agreement expressly prohibits such an award"); Foster Grading Co., 52 LA 197, 198, 200 (Jarvis, 1968); S.J. Groves & Sons Co., 52 LA 74, 78 (Scheib, 1969); PPG Indus., 51 LA 500, 503–04 (Vadakin, 1968); Master Builders' Ass'n, 50 LA 1018, 1020–22 (McDermott, 1968); Hartford Gen. Contractors Ass'n, 50 LA 35, 36 (Johnson, 1967); Cleveland Newspaper Publishers Ass'n, 49 LA 1043, 1044, 1051–52 (Klein, 1967); Publishers' Ass'n of N.Y. City, 42 LA 95, 95–96 (Berkowitz, 1964); Publishers' Ass'n of N.Y. City, 37 LA 509, 518–20 (Seitz, 1961); Oregonian Publ'g Co., 33 LA 574, 585 (Kleinsorge, 1959); Newark Newsdealer's Supply Co., 20 LA 476, 476–77 (Cahn, 1953); Canadian Gen. Elec. Co., 18 LA 925, 926–29 (Laskin, 1952); Brynmore Press, 7 LA 648, 654–57 (Rains, 1947). For a case upholding arbitral authority to award damages for a no-strike breach where the submission did not contain any clause denying such authority, see *Moran Towing & Transp. Co. v. Longshoremen Local 333* (ILA), 591 F.2d 1331 (2d Cir. 1978) (unpublished opinion). Cases involving claims against unions for failure to make reasonable efforts to prevent or terminate unauthorized work stoppages are cited in Chapter 5, section 14.A., "Use of Grievance Procedure Versus Self-Help," where the Supreme Court's *Carbon Fuel Co. v. Mine Workers*, 444 U.S. 212, 102 LRRM 3017 (1979), decision on the subject is also noted. For cases in which employers were awarded damages for union newsletter statements asking employees not to cooperate in surveys properly being conducted by the employer, see *San Antonio Air Logistic Ctr.*, 73 LA 1074, 1082–83 (Caraway, 1979); *San Antonio Air Logistics Ctr.*, 73 LA 455, 463 (LeBaron, 1979). *Cf.* Navy Exch., 73 LA 1016, 1020 (Bailer, 1979).

[144]Alpha Beta Co., 90 LA 1081, 1086 (Ross, 1988); High Standard Mfg. Corp., 38 LA 509, 513–15 (Dash, Jr., 1961); Baldwin-Lima-Hamilton Corp., 30 LA 1061, 1065 (Crawford, 1958); Hillbro Newspaper Printing Co. Div., 28 LA 769, 774 (Hildebrand, 1957); Colonial Provision Co., 17 LA 610, 623 (Copelof, 1951).

[145]*See* Morton Salt, 104 LA 444 (Fullmer, 1995); Defense Logistics Agency, 104 LA 439, 443 (Gentile, 1995).

[146]Dana Corp., 76 LA 125, 132 (Mittenthal, 1981); Pinehaven Sanitorium, 49 LA 991, 995–96 (Singer, 1967); Savoy Laundry & Linen Supply Co., 48 LA 760, 763 (Summers, 1967); Judy Lynn Frocks, 37 LA 360, 364 (Dash, 1961).

tions regarding plant removals, discontinuance of a department, and sub-contracting.[147]

However, where an employer stayed open on a holiday contrary to a contract provision and the employees who worked did so voluntarily and were paid at the required holiday rate, the union was held not to be entitled to damages from the employer.[148] The violation was the first of its kind committed by an employer, and the contract contained no provision for such damages. In another case, where an employer violated the subcontracting provision of the parties' collective bargaining agreement,[149] the employer was required to increase the size of the bargaining unit, pay damages to the union for lost dues, and pay the union's expenses.

A city that violated a labor contract by requiring firefighters to assist a private contractor with collection of hazardous material was required to bill the contractor for the cost of those services and pay the recovery into the Fire Fighters Relief and Welfare Fund.[150]

E. The "De Minimis" Rule

In denying grievances, arbitrators sometimes apply the rule of de minimis non curat lex, under which trifling or immaterial matters will not be taken into account.[151] Often in applying this principle the arbitrator concludes that the action complained of is such a slight departure from what is

---

[147]Lorimar-Telepictures Prods., 90 LA 1115, 1118 (Christopher, 1988); Advertiser Co., 89 LA 71, 76 (Baroni, 1987); Celanese Fibers Co., 72 LA 271, 276 (Foster, 1979); Verifine Dairy Prods. Corp. of Sheboygan, 51 LA 884, 891–92 (Lee, 1968); Yale & Towne, Inc., 46 LA 4, 9 (Duff, 1965); Sidele Fashions, 36 LA 1364, 1384–86 (Dash, Jr., 1961); Meilman, 34 LA 771, 774–76 (Gray, 1960). *See also* Bakery & Confectionery Workers Local 369 v. Cotton Baking Co., 514 F.2d 1235, 89 LRRM 2665, 2667 (5th Cir. 1975) (upholding an arbitrator's award of damages to the union, where the union had been monetarily damaged and the job security of all members had been indirectly affected by the employer's improper assignment of work outside the bargaining unit).
[148]Great Atl. & Pac. Tea Co., 88 LA 430 (Lipson, 1986).
[149]Tennessee Valley Auth., 101 LA 218 (Bankston, 1993) (the employer was ordered to pay $25,000 to the union for its costs, expenses, and lost union dues); Brutoco Eng'g Constr., 92 LA 33 (Ross, 1988). Employers committing contract violations have been ordered to remit amounts of back pay, lost pay, and lost wages to unions for distribution among affected employees or credit to their individual health, welfare, and retirement accounts. Grinnell Corp., 100 LA 78 (Chumley, 1992); Golden W. Broadcasters, 93 LA 699 (Jones, Jr., 1989); Golden W. Broadcasters, 93 LA 691 (Jones, Jr., 1989); Macon Kraft, 93 LA 642 (Mathews, 1989).
[150]City of Springfield, Ill., 97 LA 116 (O'Grady, 1991).
[151]City of Wilmington, Del., 111 LA 1159, 1165 (Collins, 1998); AGCO Corp., 111 LA 296, 303 (Stallworth, 1998); Induron Protective Coatings, 107 LA 412, 415 (Grooms, Jr., 1996); City of Toledo, Ohio, 106 LA 1005, 1012 (Sharpe, 1996); Sysco Food Servs. of L.A., 106 LA 524, 528 (Gentile, 1996); Associated Univs., 105 LA 1041, 1043–45 (Liebowitz, 1995); Elida Local Sch., 105 LA 173, 179 (Fullmer, 1995); Curtis Mathes Mfg. Co., 73 LA 103, 106–07 (Allen, Jr., 1979); Dierks Paper Co., 47 LA 761, 766–67 (Hebert, 1966); Dierks Paper Co., 47 LA 756, 760 (Morgan, 1966); Stubnitz Spring Div., 46 LA 557, 559 (Stouffer, 1966); Oxford Paper Co., 45 LA 609, 611–12 (Cahn, 1965); American Oil Co., 43 LA 1159, 1162 (Heliker, 1965); Celotex Corp., 64–3 ARB ¶9221 (Bauder, 1964); Reliance Elec. & Eng'g Co., 41 LA 1045, 1049 (Klein, 1963); International Paper Co., 27 LA 553, 556 (Swanson, 1956); Derby Gas & Elec. Co., 21 LA 681, 682 (Donnelly, 1953); Bethlehem Steel Co., 17 LA 76, 79 (Shipman, 1951); Mrs. Conkling's Bakery, 15 LA 168, 172 (Aaron, 1950); Continental Can Co., 12 LA 422, 426–27 (Cheney, 1948).

generally required by the agreement that the action must be viewed either as a permissible exception or as not creating an injury at all.[152]

Where the offending party has demonstrated that the violation was committed in good faith and no person was shown to have been injured, arbitrators refuse to award damages, referring to the lapse as a "technical violation" only.[153] For example, one arbitrator held that changing the payroll week, "although emotionally disturbing to employees, had only a de minim[i]s effect on the members of the Union."[154]

The de minimis concept has sometimes been applied, for example, in denying grievances protesting the performance by management personnel of small amounts of bargaining-unit work where a unit employee was not readily available. Thus, performing 15 minutes (but not 1 hour and 15 minutes) of bargaining-unit work each day by a supervisor was considered a de minimis contract violation.[155] Similarly, the one-time use of non-bargaining-unit employees to assist in completing important work on an overtime day was said to have had only a de minimis effect on the bargaining unit.[156]

The following kinds of contract violations were held not to be de minimis: failure of an employer to give the union proper advance notice of a layoff,[157] improper detailing of employees,[158] and changing conditions of employment by the removal of personal fans from the work area.[159]

While falsification of expense reimbursement claims by the auditor was not a de minimis rule violation and warranted his discharge,[160] the remedy for theft by a 17-year school custodian of a small amount of cash was reduced to a suspension under de minimis principles.[161] Similarly, in one case of improper picketing and handbilling of retail stores, the activities, although an "irritant," were of such minimal consequences that only a cease-and-desist order was issued and damages were denied.[162] A similar result also was

---

[152]For a narrow view as to what constitutes a true de minimis situation, see *Olin Mathieson Chem. Corp.*, 47 LA 238, 242 (Hilpert, 1966).

[153]Vermont Am. Corp., 70 LA 1041, 1043 (Moran, 1978); Gimbel Bros., 69 LA 847, 852–53 (Lubow, 1977); International Paper Co., 50 LA 344, 347 (Prewett, 1968); Dwyer Prods. Corp., 48 LA 1031, 1034–35 (Larkin, 1967); Gisholt Mach. Co., 44 LA 840, 845 (McDermott, 1965); National Lead Co., 36 LA 962, 964–65 (Marshall, 1961); Art Metal Constr. Co., 36 LA 458, 462 (Reid, 1961); Hearst Consol. Publ'ns, 26 LA 723, 726 (Gray, 1956); Universal Glass Prods. Corp., 24 LA 623, 625 (Duff, undated). *See also* C. Schmidt Co., 69 LA 80, 85 (Albrechta, 1977); Oneita Knitting Mills, 48 LA 609, 614 (Seitz, 1967); Lorraine Mfg. Co., 22 LA 390, 392 (Horvitz, 1954); Marlin-Rockwell Corp., 17 LA 254, 256 (Shister, 1951). *Cf.* Day & Zimmermann, Inc., 91 LA 669, 675 (Williams, 1988). In some cases, it appears that the good faith of the offending party was the reason for not awarding damages notwithstanding any loss suffered. *See* Gibraltar Bd. of Educ., 87 LA 1067 (McDonald, 1986); K-P Mfg. Co., 74 LA 1046, 1048 (Grabb, 1980); ICI Ams., 71 LA 587, 589 (Raffaele, 1978); Ingalls Shipbuilding Div., 69 LA 294, 302 (Bailey, 1977). *See also* Capital City Tel. Co. v. Communications Workers, 97 LRRM 2394, 2398 (W.D. Mo. 1977), *aff'd*, 575 F.2d 655, 98 LRRM 2438 (8th Cir. 1978).

[154]A.C. Humko Corp., 114 LA 664, 667 (Kindig, 2000).

[155]Safeway Stores, 93 LA 457 (Cohen, 1989).

[156]Monon Corp., 97 LA 893 (Belshaw, 1991).

[157]York Int'l Corp., 93 LA 1107 (Schwartz, 1989).

[158]Department of Health & Human Servs., 96 LA 346 (Rosen, 1990).

[159]Pierce Co., 95 LA 557 (Deitsch, 1990).

[160]State of Minnesota, 97 LA 1107 (Ver Ploeg, 1991).

[161]Deer Lakes, Pa., Sch. Dist., 94 LA 334 (Hewitt, 1989).

[162]Lucky Stores, 100 LA 262 (Gentile, 1992).

reached in a temporary job assignment violation.[163] However, a specific contract violation, no matter how insignificant, is not necessarily "de minimis."[164]

Application of the de minimis rule has been rejected where "the amount has been small but the principle large."[165] One arbitrator explained that no hard and fast mathematical line should be drawn between "minimal" on the one hand, and "substantial" on the other, but rather that each case should be decided in terms of its own circumstances.[166]

F. Punitive Damages

Even though a party is found to have violated the agreement, the arbitrator may be expected to refuse to award any relief that would, in essence, be an award of punitive damages, unless there is evidence of such bad faith as to shock the conscience of the arbitrator.[167] One arbitrator observed: "The concept of punishment, that is awarding punitive damages, is disruptive to the promotion of an amicable, and a continuing relationship that must exist between the employer and the union for years into the future."[168] Nevertheless, he would sanction the award of punitive damages for situations that cannot be corrected by other remedies, and to ensure that future violations will not occur.

While noting that some state and federal courts have disagreed as to the power of arbitrators to award punitive damages, an arbitrator added: "Power

[163]County of Middlesex, N.J., 99 LA 293 (DiLauro, 1992).
[164]Citicasters Co. WKRC-TV, 114 LA 1367, 1373 (Lewis, 2000).
[165]Bethlehem-Sparrows Point Shipyard, 26 LA 483, 490 (Feinberg, 1956). See also Customs Serv., 91 LA 630 (Finston, 1988). The rule is also said to be inapplicable, where a "continuing" activity is involved, Union Carbide Corp., 46 LA 195, 198 (Cahn, 1966), and where the arbitration involves "a test case brought seriously to obtain a ruling on a disputed point of contractual interpretation." Tenneco Oil Co., 44 LA 1121, 1128 (Merrill, 1965).
[166]John Deere Planter Works, 29 LA 328, 331 (Davey, 1957). See also Westinghouse Elec. Corp., 43 LA 84, 89–90 (Altieri, 1964) (discussion of the de minimis concept and problems of its application).
[167]Lake, Ohio, Local Bd. of Educ., 114 LA 839, 843 (Murphy, 2000); Ralphs Grocery Co., 108 LA 718, 723 (Prayzich, 1997); Stone Container Corp., 102 LA 219, 220 (Thornell, 1994). See Mason & Hanger Corp., 111 LA 60, 64 (Caraway, 1998); E.A. Norris Plumbing Co., 90 LA 462 (Christopher, 1987); Cadillac Gage Co., 87 LA 853, 856 (Van Pelt, 1986); Orchids Paper Prods. Concel, 76 LA 101, 103 (Ross, 1980); Bureau of Census, 75 LA 1194, 1201 (Mittelman, 1980); Social Sec. Admin., 75 LA 628, 632 (House, 1980); Beecher Peck & Lewis, 74 LA 489, 494 (Lipson, 1980); Cleveland Cliffs Iron Co., 73 LA 1148, 1156 (Garrett, 1980); Minnesota Dep't of Natural Res., 71 LA 754, 761 (O'Connell, 1978); Indian Head, Inc., 71 LA 82, 86 (Rimer, Jr., 1978); Buchholz Mortuaries, 69 LA 623, 630 (Roberts, 1977); Osborn & Ulland, Inc., 68 LA 1146, 1152 (Beck, 1977); Providence Med. Ctr., 68 LA 663, 668 (Conant, 1977). But see Tennessee Valley Auth., 101 LA 218, 226 (Bankston, 1993); Morton Salt, 113 LA 969, 972 (Allen, 1999). In A.C.&C. Co., 24 LA 538, 541 (Scheiber, 1955), the arbitrator denied the union's demand that a penalty payment be made by the employer to a charity, where no employee had suffered loss from the employer's violation. Similarly refusing to award a penalty payment where no employee had suffered loss due to the employer's violation of the agreement, see Dubuque Packing Co., 69 LA 999, 1003 (Carter, 1977); Seaboard World Airlines, 53 LA 1056, 1060 (Turkus, 1969). Several arbitrators, have declined to award interest, because it was deemed "punitive." See City of Bridgeport, Conn., 94 LA 975, 978 (Stewart, 1990); Griffin Pipe Prods. Co., 87 LA 283, 286–87 (Yarowsky, 1986); Farnsworth, Punitive Damages in Arbitration, 20 Stetson L. Rev. 395 (1991); Hill, Traditional and Innovative Remedies in Arbitration: Punitive Awards, Interest, and Conditional Remedies, 11 Whittier L. Rev. 617 (1989).
[168]Morton Salt, 113 LA 969, 972 (Allen, 1999).

to award punitive damages is a heady wine, however, which carries with it an equally potent obligation and abiding responsibility to invoke the remedy with great care and extreme caution in the situations where otherwise the ends of justice would be defeated or unconscionably denied."[169] Some arbitrators have felt justified in awarding punitive damages on a showing that the contractual violation was knowing and repeated,[170] or willful and flagrant,[171] or in bad faith or intended for the purpose of delay,[172] or otherwise "egregiously wrongful."[173]

Because of the heavy burden the federal courts place on those who attempt to overturn an arbitral award on the ground that the arbitrator has exceeded his or her authority,[174] most courts have been reluctant to set aside arbitral punitive damage awards.[175] Further, although some state courts have held that public policy prohibits arbitrators from awarding punitive damages, if the contractual arbitration provision permits the award of punitive damages, the provision will be enforced by federal courts despite contrary state law or policy.[176]

However, despite the existence of repeated violations, an arbitrator may not award punitive damages that were not requested in the grievance.[177]

---

[169]Seaboard World Airlines, 53 LA 1056, 1060 (Turkus, 1969). *See also* Hackett, *Punitive Damages in Arbitration: The Search for a Workable Rule*, 63 Cornell L. Rev. 272 (1978).

[170]Mallinckrodt Chem. Works, 50 LA 933, 935–40 (Goldberg, 1968). *See also* Stuart Hall Co., 48 LA 582, 585 (Yarowsky, 1967); Lamb Elec., 46 LA 450, 455 (Klein, 1966); Phillip Carey Mfg. Co., 37 LA 134, 136 (Gill, 1961).

[171]Five Star Hardware & Elec. Corp., 44 LA 944, 946 (Wolff, 1965). *See also* Milwaukee, Wis., Bd. of Sch. Dirs., 77 LA 344, 348 (Yaffe, 1981); John Morrell & Co., 69 LA 264, 278, 281 (Conway, 1977).

[172]Ralphs Grocery Co., 108 LA 718, 723 (Prayzich, 1997).

[173]National Gypsum Co., Case No. 95-19685, 1997 WL 901848 (Bankston, 1997).

[174]Pullman Power Prods. Corp. v. Plumbers & Pipe Fitters Local 403, 856 F.2d 1211, 129 LRRM 2500 (9th Cir. 1988).

[175]Machinists v. Northwest Airlines, 858 F.2d 427, 129 LRRM 2588 (8th Cir. 1988); Bonar v. Dean Witter Reynolds, 835 F.2d 1378 (11th Cir. 1988); Electrical Workers (UE) Local 1139 v. Litton Microwave Cooking Prods., 704 F.2d 393, 113 LRRM 2015 (8th Cir. 1983), *on reh'g*, 728 F.2d 970, 115 LRRM 2633 (8th Cir. 1984). *See* Clothing Workers, Baltimore Reg'l Joint Bd. v. Webster Clothes, 596 F.2d 95, 100 LRRM 3225, 3227 (4th Cir. 1979) (award invalid as punitive rather than compensatory); Georgia Power Co. v. Electrical Workers (IBEW) Local 84, 825 F. Supp. 1023, 140 LRRM 2572 (N.D. Ga. 1992); Bethlehem Steel Corp. v. Steelworkers, 138 LRRM 2091 (D. Md. 1991); Desert Palace v. Local Joint Executive Bd. of Las Vegas, 486 F. Supp. 675, 105 LRRM 3053, 3060 (D. Nev. 1980) (arbitrator exceeded his authority in awarding punitive damages, where that remedy had not been requested); Sheet Metal Workers Local 416 v. Helgesteel Corp., 335 F. Supp. 812, 80 LRRM 2113, 2115–16 (E.D. Wis. 1971) (the court stated that an award of punitive damages is not per se improper, and that the question is whether the award draws its essence from the agreement and is reasonable in light of the arbitrator's findings); Sidney Wanzer & Sons v. Teamsters Local 753, 249 F. Supp. 664, 61 LRRM 2376, 2381 (D. Ill. 1966) (the arbitrator's remedial power under the Labor Management Relations Act, 29 U.S.C. §301, includes punitive awards, but that such power is extraordinary and should be reserved for situations that cannot be pacified by other remedies).

[176]Belko v. AVX Corp., 251 Cal. Rptr. 557 (Ct. App. 1988); Shaw v. Kuhnel & Assocs., 102 N.M. 607, 609, 698 P.2d 880, 882 (1985); Willoughby Roofing & Supply v. Kajima Int'l, 598 F. Supp. 353, 360 (N.D. Ala. 1984), *aff'd*, 776 F.2d 269 (11th Cir. 1985).

[177]Tower Auto., 115 LA 51 (Kenis, 2000). *See also* Matanuska Elec. Ass'n, 109 LA 508 (Henner, 1997) (punitive damages and attorney fees were denied because the demand for these remedies was not included in the original grievance, the collective bargaining contract had no express authority for such an award, and the employer's conduct was not extremely outrageous).

G. Interest on Award [LA CDI 117.178; 118.807]

The question of whether interest should be allowed on the principal sum awarded has arisen frequently. In an early award, one arbitrator, after observing that neither the collective bargaining agreement nor the submission expressly authorized him to order the payment of interest, said that "it is not customary in arbitrations for the arbitrator to grant interest on claims which he finds owing."[178] Following this dictum, a number of other arbitrators have refused to award interest.[179] However, as noted by two other arbitrators, the "no interest" doctrine may have originated from the "one-time and now-aban-

---

[178]Intermountain Operators League, 26 LA 149, 154 (Kadish, 1956). *See also* Lithonia Hi Tek—Vermilion, 109 LA 775 (Franckiewicz, 1997); Laidlaw Transit, 109 LA 647 (Landau, 1997).

[179]East Lake Fire & Rescue, Case No. 99-15084, 2001 WL 339159 (Abrams, 2001) (violation was found not to be deliberate and egregious); Coca-Cola Bottling Co. of Mid-America, 114 LA 1153, 1157 (Bernstein, 2000) (no interest on back-pay award because grievant saved work-related expenses, such as fuel and food, which he would have paid had he continued to work); Safeway Stores, 114 LA 1551 (DiFalco, 2000) (interest not awarded; no showing of bad faith, egregious conduct, or undue delay by employer); Te-Khi Truck & Auto Plaza, Case No. 99-12117, 2000 WL 296162 (Chiesa, 2000) (no provision for interest in collective bargaining agreement); Valspar Corp., 113 LA 1111, 1120 (Hayford, 1999); Southeast Local Sch. Dist., 112 LA 833, 838 (Goldberg, 1999); City Mkt., 112 LA 726, 733 (Watkins, 1999); Lincoln County Employees Ass'n, Case No. 79 L 390 00076 97, 1998 WL 1033376 (Robinson, 1998); Lithonia Hi Tek—Vermilion, 109 LA 775; Machinists, 109 LA 339 (Bernhardt, 1997); Ralphs Grocery Co., 108 LA 718 (Prayzich, 1997); Willamette Indus., 107 LA 1213, 1216 (Kaufman, 1997); Doss Aviation, 107 LA 39, 52 (Ferree, 1996) (the union was also somewhat at fault); County of Santa Clara, Cal., 106 LA 1092, 1095 (Levy, 1996); Exxon Chem. Ams., 105 LA 1011, 1019 (Allen, Jr., 1996); Lightning Indus., 105 LA 417 (Mikrut, Jr., 1995) (the union did not request interest); San Benito Health Found., 105 LA 263 (Levy, 1995); West Co., 103 LA 452 (Murphy, 1994) (the 1-year delay was not due to employer bad faith); Burlington Med. Ctr., 101 LA 843, 849–50 (Bailey, 1993) (hospital employer did not act egregiously); Helix Elec., 101 LA 649, 654 (Kaufman, 1993); Tennessee Valley Auth., 98 LA 1090 (Bankston, 1992) (the delay was neither deliberate nor unreasonable); Cosentino Price Chopper, 98 LA 819, 827 (Mikrut, Jr., 1991) (the agreement was silent); City of Chillicothe, Ohio, 96 LA 657 (DiLeone, 1991); Builders Plumbing Supply, 95 LA 351 (Briggs, 1990) (the violation of the agreement was neither malicious nor intentional); Housing Auth. of Louisville, Ky., 95 LA 97, 104 (Wren, 1990) (the employer had acted in good faith); City of Bridgeport, Conn., 94 LA 975, 978 (Stewart, 1990) (arbitration is restorative, not punitive); Kings County, Cal., Truck Lines, 94 LA 875 (Prayzich, 1990) (the agreement was silent, and the employer was not shown to have been dilatory); Niemand Indus., 94 LA 669 (Nolan, 1990) (the issue was not raised until the remedy hearing, and the employer was not shown to have been dilatory); Hoffman (Or.)-Marmolejo, 93 LA 132 (Levak, 1989); Springfield, Ill., Sch. Dist. 186, 91 LA 1300 (Malin, 1988); Springfield, Ill., Sch. Dist. 186, 91 LA 1293 (Malin, 1988); Stone Container Corp., 91 LA 1186 (Ross, 1988); City of Pontiac, Mich., Fire Dep't, 91 LA 830, 835 (Kahn, 1988) (interest had not been a part of prior remedies); Shell Oil Co./Shell Chem. Co., 87 LA 473 (Nicholas, Jr., 1986); Griffin Pipe Prods. Co., 87 LA 283, 286–87 (Yarowsky, 1986) (an award of interest would be a penalty in the circumstances); City of Vallejo, Cal., 86 LA 1082 (Bogue, 1986) (the employer's miscalculation of a wage increase had been in good faith); Cowlitz Redi-Mix, 85 LA 745, 753 (Boedecker, 1985) (denied as to money due from prior award because no evidence demonstrated the employer's actions in the interim to be egregious enough to warrant interest being charged); Oil Transp. Co. & Gypsum Transp., 79 LA 1285, 1293–94 (Carter, 1982) (refusing to award interest where the violation was not "willful, capricious and arbitrary"); Great Atl. & Pac. Tea Co., 74 LA 422, 432 (Dean, 1980); Furr's Inc., 74 LA 121, 125 (Sartain, 1980); Prairie Heights High Sch. Bd. of Educ., 72 LA 890, 892 (Eagle, 1979); City of Anderson, 72 LA 757, 759 (Michelstetter, 1979); East Orange, N.J., Bd. of Educ., 69 LA 674, 677 (Spencer, 1977); Contract Carpets, 68 LA 1022, 1032 (Finston, 1977); Kaiser Steel Corp., 68 LA 192, 197 (Christopher, 1977); Gregory Galvanizing & Metal Processing, 48 LA 782, 788 (Willingham, 1967); Dover Corp., 45 LA 705, 706 (Dolson, 1965); American S.S. Co., 44 LA 530, 540 (Keefe, 1965); Blaw-Knox Co., 43 LA 247, 249 (Crawford,

doned practice of the NLRB [National Labor Relations Board], of not award-ing interest on back-pay awards."[180] The NLRB changed its position in 1962.[181] Furthermore, the award of interest is now authorized by statute in arbitra-tion cases involving federal agencies.[182]

The modern view is that the award of interest is within the inherent power of an arbitrator,[183] and in fashioning a "make-whole" remedy it ap-pears that a growing number of arbitrators are willing to exercise the discre-tion to award interest where appropriate.[184] Thus, one arbitrator, after not-

---

1964); Diamond Nat'l Corp., 41 LA 1310, 1313–14 (Koven, 1963); American Meter Co., 41 LA 856, 862 (Di Leone, 1963); Hampton Corp., 39 LA 177, 179 (Davis, 1962). In *Westinghouse Elec. Corp.*, 47 LA 621, 629 (Altrock, 1966), a request for interest on back pay awarded in the reversal of discipline was rejected, the arbitrator adhering to the view that interest should be allowed only where the discipline was "willful, capricious, arbitrary and unconscionable." Regarding the federal public sector, interest cannot be awarded absent statutory authoriza-tion. *See* Social Sec. Admin., 80 LA 46, 53 (Aronin, 1982); Portsmouth Naval Shipyard, 7 FLRA 30 (1981).

[180]HILL & SINICROPI, REMEDIES IN ARBITRATION 450 (BNA Books 2d ed. 1991).

[181]Isis Plumbing Co., 138 NLRB 716, 51 LRRM 1122, 1124 (1962), *rev'd on other grounds*, 322 F.2d 913, 54 LRRM 2235 (9th Cir. 1963). *See also* Florida Steel Corp., 231 NLRB 651, 96 LRRM 1070 (1977) (adoption by the NLRB of Internal Revenue Service's adjusted prime interest rate).

[182]Defense Commissary Agency, 101 LA 850 (Wren, 1993) (interest was awarded under the Back Pay Act); Department of the Navy, 112 LA 513 (Nolan, 1999); Social Sec. Admin., 80 LA 46, 53 (Aronin, 1982); Portsmouth Naval Shipyard, 7 FLRA 30 (1981).

[183]Falstaff Brewing Corp. v. Teamsters Local 153, 479 F. Supp. 850, 103 LRRM 2008 (D.N.J. 1978).

[184]Davis Wire Corp., 2001 WL 207553 (Peck, 2001) (awarded on back pay of improperly terminated employee); Geological Survey, 115 LA 276 (Hoffman, 2000) (awarded on back pay to federal employees pursuant to federal law); Department of Veterans Affairs, 115 LA 198 (Cornelius, 2000) (awarded pursuant to Civil Service Reform Act of 1978, 5 USC §5596(b)(2)); Jefferson Smurfit Corp., 114 LA 358 (Kaufman, 2000) (interest awarded on back pay not punitive, but for purpose of granting a full remedy to grievant); Lawton Philharmonic Soc'y, 113 LA 764, 769 (Goodstein, 1999) (to begin if the award is not paid within 5 days of the award); Boeing-Irving Co., 113 LA 699, 704 (Bankston, 1999) (interest on back-pay award granted due to "egregiousness of the situation"); Boeing-Irving Co., 113 LA 554, 559 (Bankston, 1999) (same); Sheet Metal Workers Local 20, Case No. 98-12344, 1999 WL 1331153 (Brunner, 1999); Hoechst Celanese Celco Plant, 111 LA 760, 763 (Duff, 1998); Lerch Bros., 111 LA 609 (Jay, 1998) (awarded on amount of shortfall due to improper pension calculation); KSTW-TV, 111 LA 94, 100 (Lundberg, 1998); Laidlaw Transit, 109 LA 647 (Landau, 1997) (em-ployer delay); USAir Shuttle, 108 LA 496 (Hockenberry, 1997) (to compensate wrongfully discharged grievant for loss of use of reduced income); Champlain Cable Corp., 108 LA 449, 453–54 (Sweeney, 1997) (interest granted because it is the natural result of a breach of contract, NLRB's practice, and the employer's bad faith); National Gypsum Co., Case No. 95-19685, 1997 WL 901848 (Bankston, 1997) (employer's conduct was egregious); Kent World-wide Mach. Works, 107 LA 455 (Duda, Jr., 1996) (employer refused to pay wages owed to employees for 2 years); Southern Cal. Permanente Med. Group, 106 LA 1033, 1042 (Bickner, 1996); San Benito Health Found., 105 LA 263, 264 (Levy, 1995) (arbitrator said interest would be awarded if employer delayed payment); WJA Realty, 104 LA 1157, 1162–64 (Haemmel, 1995) (NLRB's practice and the employer's bad faith); Kaiser Eng'g, 102 LA 1189, 1193 (Minni, 1994); Atlantic Southeast Airlines, 102 LA 656, 660 (Feigenbaum, 1994) (inter-est is routinely awarded by the courts and the NLRB); River Falls Area Sch. Dist., 99 LA 1223 (Kessler, 1992) (employer had benefited by withholding the grievant's severance pay); Wohlert Corp., 99 LA 852, 858–59 (House, 1992) (vacation pay had been improperly with-held for 5 months to help ease an employer cash flow problem); Bekins Moving & Storage Co., 98 LA 1087 (Madden, 1992); Central State Univ., 97 LA 1167 (Strasshofer, 1991); Clearfield County, Pa., Vocational Technical Sch. Bd. of Dirs., 97 LA 275, 282 (Mayer, 1991); Crane Plumbing, 95 LA 942 (Bell, 1990) (medical claims paid by the grievant); National R.R. Passenger Corp., 95 LA 617, 631 (Simons, 1990) (awarding interest because grievant was denied timely use of the money and because of the NLRB practice); Hoffman (Or.)-Marmolejo, 93 LA 132 (Levak, 1989) (arbitrator reserved the right to award interest in the event of

ing that interest was seldom requested and cautioning that interest should not be used as punishment, concluded that because of the time value of money, the awarding of interest was necessary to make a grievant whole.[185]

---

undue delay by the employer in complying with the award); Texas Util. Generating Div., 92 LA 1308, 1314 (McDermott, 1989); Dayco Prods., 92 LA 876, 882 (Fowler, 1989) (to make whole where lump-sum pension payment had been delayed for 3 years); Glasgow, Mont., Sch. Dist. No. 1-1A Bd. of Trs., 92 LA 281 (Corbett, 1988) (to make whole); EZ Communications, 91 LA 1097, 1101 (Talarico, 1988) (outrageous, lewd, on-air remarks by disc jockeys had caused the grievant to resign); Marin Tug & Barge, 91 LA 499, 505 (Huffcut, 1988); Clarion-Limestone, Pa., Area Sch. Dist., 90 LA 281, 286 (Creo, 1988); Duquesne Club, 89 LA 1302 (Talarico, 1987) (money advanced to grievant is allowed as offset, with interest, against back-pay award); Dutko Wall Sys., 89 LA 1215, 1221 (Weisinger, 1987) (awarded on delinquent contributions to benefits funds); Kaiser Permanente Med. Care Program, 89 LA 841, 845 (Alleyne, 1987) (interest granted on ground that NLRB routinely awards interest on back pay and no reason for arbitral distinction); Vermont Dep't of Corr., 89 LA 383, 384–85 (McHugh, 1987) (to make whole); Sterling Colo. Beef Co., 86 LA 866, 873 (Smith, 1986) (to make whole and to prevent employer from being unjustly enriched); St. Joseph County, Mich., Mental Health Facility, 86 LA 683, 685–86 (Girolamo, 1985) (interest awarded on the amount employer failed to roll over to retirement annuity); City of Westland, Mich., 86 LA 305, 308 (Howlett, 1985); Pacific Southwest Airlines, 82 LA 1036, 1038 (Stashower, 1984) (to make whole); Hercules Prods., 81 LA 191, 193 (Goodman, 1983); Coppes, Inc., 80 LA 1058, 1059–60 (Kossoff, 1983) (although the arbitrator never before had awarded interest, he felt special facts called for it here); Washington Metal Trades, 80 LA 1, 7 (Keltner, 1982); Auto Workers Local 594, 77 LA 370, 372 (Ellmann, 1981); Mi-Ka Prods., 76 LA 1203, 1212 (Christopher, 1981) (the original claim was for a determined sum and interest thus was appropriate from the date such liquidated damages first became due); Geneseo, Ill., Cmty. Unit Sch. Dist. No. 228 Bd. of Educ., 75 LA 131, 135 (Berman, 1980); Western Airlines, 74 LA 923, 926–27 (Richman, 1980) (the circumstances were appropriate for awarding interest because an additional hardship had been suffered by grievant due to the employer's action); Markle Mfg. Co., 73 LA 1292, 1300–02 (Williams, 1980) (employer's dilatory tactics in reinstating an employee pursuant to an earlier award); Shore Manor, 71 LA 1238, 1243 (Katz, 1978); Osborn & Ulland, Inc., 68 LA 1146, 1153 (Beck, 1977) (special circumstances justified an award of interest); Ideal Basic Indus., 68 LA 928, 931 (Eckhardt, 1977); Farmer Bros. Co., 66 LA 354, 356 (Jones, Jr., 1976) (employer's dilatory tactics in reinstating an employee pursuant to an earlier award); Hollander & Co., 64 LA 816, 821–22 (Edelman, 1975) (sufficient arbitral precedent exists for an award of interest, "but even more important, there is justification for so doing especially here"); Safeway Stores, 64 LA 563, 571 (Gould, 1975); Sunshine Convalescent Hosp., 62 LA 276, 279 (Lennard, 1974); Allied Chem. Corp., 47 LA 686, 690 (Hilpert, 1966); Oscar Joseph Stores, 41 LA 567, 567–68 (Whiting, 1963); General Elec. Co., 39 LA 897, 906–07 (Hilpert, 1962). Some arbitrators have awarded interest to begin running from the date of the award. *See* Skaggs Pay Less Drug Stores, 52 LA 1082, 1087 (Killion, 1969); Sears, Roebuck & Co., 35 LA 757, 782 (Miller, 1960).

[185]Atlantic Southeast Airlines, 101 LA 515, 525–26 (Nolan, 1993). *See also* City of Huber Heights, Ohio, Case No. 93-10820, 1996 WL 808508 (Imundo, Jr., 1996); Kaiser Eng'g, 102 LA 1189, 1193 (Minni, 1994); Atlantic Southeast Airlines, 102 LA 656, 660 (Feigenbaum, 1994); Bekins Moving & Storage Co., 98 LA 1087(Madden, 1992); Central State Univ., 97 LA 1167 (Strasshofer, 1991); Clearfield County, Pa., Vocational Technical Sch. Bd. of Dirs., 97 LA 275, 282 (Mayer, 1991); Glasgow, Mont., Sch. Dist. No. 1-1A Bd. of Trs., 92 LA 281 (Corbett, 1988) (to make whole); Marin Tug & Barge, 91 LA 499, 505 (Huffcut, 1988); Clarion-Limestone, Pa., Area Sch. Dist., 90 LA 281, 286 (Creo, 1988); Kaiser Permanente Med. Care Program, 89 LA 841, 845 (Alleyne, 1987) (interest granted on the ground that the NLRB routinely awards interest on back pay and there is no reason for arbitral distinction); Vermont Dep't of Corr., 89 LA 383, 384–85 (McHugh, 1987) (to make whole); Sterling Colo. Beef Co., 86 LA 866, 873 (Smith, 1986) (to make whole and to prevent employer from being unjustly enriched); Pacific Southwest Airlines, 82 LA 1036, 1038 (Stashower, 1984) (to make whole); Hercules Prods., 81 LA 191, 193 (Goodman, 1983); Washington Metal Trades, 80 LA 1, 7 (Keltner, 1982); Geneseo, Ill., Cmty. Unit Sch. Dist. No. 228 Bd. of Educ., 75 LA 131, 135 (Berman, 1980); Western Airlines, 74 LA 923, 926–27 (Richman, 1980) (the circumstances were appropriate for awarding interest, because an additional hardship had been suffered by the grievant due to the employer's action). *Cf.* Duquesne Club, 89 LA 1302 (Talarico, 1987) (money advanced to the grievant is allowed as offset, with interest, against back-pay award).

Interest also has been granted when there are special circumstances such as an employer's dilatory conduct on unnecessary delay in the grievance process,[186] or bad faith.[187]

H. Attorneys' Fees and Arbitration Expense

i.   *Attorneys' Fees* [LA CDI 94.65; 100.0780]

Under the so-called "American Rule," each party in litigation bears its own attorneys' fees in the absence of bad faith in the proceedings or unless a statute or public policy permits shifting the cost to the losing party, or shifting the cost would fairly distribute the cost of obtaining a "common fund" or "common benefit." Although, absent statutory or contractual authorization,[188] it is not customary to award attorneys' fees against the offending party in private-sector arbitration,[189] a request for attorneys' fees may be granted for

---

[186]Laidlaw Transit, 109 LA 647, 651 (Landau, 1997) (grievant entitled to interest on back pay from date of first scheduled arbitration hearing where employer ignored union's repeated requests to resume arbitration); San Benito Health Found., 105 LA 263, 264 (Levy, 1995) (arbitrator said interest would be awarded if the employer delayed payment); Atlantic Southeast Airlines, 101 LA 515 (Nolan, 1993); River Falls Area Sch. Dist., 99 LA 1223 (Kessler, 1992) (employer had benefited by withholding the grievant's severance pay); Wohlert Corp., 99 LA 852, 858–59 (House, 1992) (vacation pay had been improperly withheld for 5 months to help ease an employer cash flow problem); Crane Plumbing, 95 LA 942 (Bell, 1990) (medical claims paid by the grievant); National R.R. Passenger Corp., 95 LA 617, 631 (Simons, 1990) (awarding interest because grievant was denied timely use of the money and because of NLRB practice); Hoffman (Or.)-Marmolejo, 93 LA 132 (Levak, 1989) (arbitrator reserved the right to award interest in the event of undue delay by the employer in complying with the award); Texas Util. Generating Div., 92 LA 1308, 1314 (McDermott, 1989); Dayco Prods., 92 LA 876, 882 (Fowler, 1989) (to make whole where lump-sum pension payment had been delayed for 3 years); Dutko Wall Sys., 89 LA 1215, 1221 (Weisinger, 1987) (awarded on delinquent contributions to benefits funds); St. Joseph County, Mich., Mental Health Facility, 86 LA 683, 685–86 (Girolamo, 1985) (interest awarded on amount employer failed to roll over to retirement annuity); City of Westland, Mich., 86 LA 305, 308 (Howlett, 1985); Mi-Ka Prods., 76 LA 1203, 1212 (Christopher, 1981) (the original claim was for a determined sum and interest thus was appropriate fro the date such liquidated damages first became due); Markle Mfg., 73 LA 1292, 1300, 1302 (Williams, 1980) (employer's dilatory tactics in reinstating an employee pursuant to an earlier award); Farmer Bros., 66 LA 354, 356 (Jones, Jr., 1976) (same).

[187]Boeing-Irving Co., 113 LA 699, 704 (Bankston, 1999) (interest on back-pay award granted due to "egregiousness of the situation"); Boeing-Irving Co., 113 LA 554, 559 (Bankston, 1999) (same); Chaplain Cable Corp., 108 LA 449, 453–54 (Sweeney, 1997) (interest granted because it is the natural result of a breach of contract, NLRB practice, and the employer's bad faith); EZ Communications, 91 LA 1097, 1101 (Talarico, 1988) (outrageous, lewd, on-air remarks by disc jockeys had caused the grievant to resign); Coppes, Inc., 80 LA 1058, 1059–60 (Kossoff, 1983) (although the arbitrator never before had awarded interest, he felt special facts called for it here); Auto Workers Local 594, 77 LA 370, 372 (Ellmann, 1981).

[188]H. Meyer Dairy Co., 105 LA 583, 588–89 (Sugerman, 1995).

[189]KQ Servs., Case No. 00-06566, 2000 WL 33275145 (Kohler, 2000); Catlettsburg Ref., Case No. 98-11, 2000 WL 871877 (Feldman, 2000) (employer denied attorneys' fees on fourth decision on same issue, because the contract had not provided for penalties); USAir Shuttle, 108 LA 496, 502 (Hockenberry, 1997); Champlain Cable Corp., 108 LA 449, 453 (Sweeney, 1997) (the evidence was insufficient to prove the employer's malice); Apcoa, Inc., 107 LA 705, 713 (Daniel, 1996); Pennsylvania State Univ., 101 LA 890, 894 (Duff, 1993) (university policy fails to authorize the arbitrator to grant attorneys' fees); Atlantic Southeast Airlines, 101 LA 515, 526 (Nolan, 1993); City of Long Beach, Cal., 100 LA 267, 278 (Brisco, 1992) (even though the grievance was like a Fair Labor Standards Act, 29 U.S.C. §201 et seq., case, the parties were still in arbitration); Teledyne Ryan Aeronautical, 95 LA 1072, 1075–76 (Weiss, 1990)

the same reasons as a punitive damage award: bad faith, or egregious, flagrant, willful, and repeated violations of the contract.[190] Courts have sanctioned the award of attorneys' fees where a party unjustifiably refuses to abide by an arbitrator's award[191] or challeges the award without justification.[192]

An arbitrator also may choose awarding of attorneys' fees to make a grievant whole.[193] However, such a showing requires that the prevailing party meet a high standard of proof.[194]

(the employer had not acted in bad faith in violating a prior arbitration award); Department of Defense Dependents Sch., 95 LA 107 (Wilkinson, 1990) (a federal agency had reasonably relied on instructions, even though the instructions were contrary to unambiguous regulations). *See, e.g.*, Chrysler Motors Corp. v. Industrial Workers (AIW), 959 F.2d 685, 139 LRRM 2865 (7th Cir. 1992); Greyhound Exposition Servs., 113 LA 1070, 1080 (Wolff, 2000); Waste Mgmt. of Ohio, 113 LA 353, 362 (Franckiewicz, 1999) (such an award would be punitive); Tenneco Packaging, 112 LA 761, 768 (Kessler, 1999); A.I.M. Corp., 111 LA 463, 468 (Florman, 1998); Schnuck Mkts., 111 LA 288, 295–96 (Hilgert, 1998); Matanuska Elec. Ass'n, 109 LA 508 (Henner, 1997); H. Meyer Dairy Co., 105 LA 583; Stone Container Corp., 91 LA 1186, 1192 (Ross, 1988); Florida Staff Org., 91 LA 1094, 1096 (Mase, 1988); University of N. Iowa, 91 LA 868, 879 (Wolff, 1988); Pontiac, Mich., Fire Dep't, 91 LA 830 (Kahn, 1988); Ecoscience, Inc., 81 LA 132, 140–41 (Gentile, 1983); Mantua Chem. Terminal, 79 LA 732, 737 (Mitrani, 1982); Delta Air Lines, 72 LA 458, 470 (Platt, 1979); Leavenworth Times, 71 LA 396, 409–11 (Bothwell, 1978); Westinghouse Transp. Leasing Corp., 69 LA 1210, 1214–15 (Sergent, Jr., 1977); Providence Med. Ctr., 68 LA 663, 668–69 (Conant, 1977); George Ellis Co., 68 LA 261, 269–70 (Sacks, 1977) (refusing to award attorney fees to the union, absent any provision for it in the agreement, even if the company's violation of the agreement was willful and deliberate); Montgomery County Cmty. Action Agency, 62 LA 1278, 1281 (Dworkin, 1974); Leona Lee Corp., 60 LA 1310, 1319 (Gorsuch, 1973). Refusing to order reimbursement for attorneys' fees expended by a party in court proceedings connected with the grievance, see *Minnesota Dep't of Natural Res.*, 71 LA 754, 761 (O'Connell, 1978); *City of San Antonio, Tex.*, 69 LA 541, 547 (Caraway, 1977); *Vancouver Plywood Co.*, 62 LA 133, 139 (Williams, 1974). But awarding such reimbursement, see *Theatrical Stage Employees Local 646*, Case No. 96-08948, 1996 WL 658930 (Chandler, 1996) (attorneys' fees were awarded pursuant to the contract); *Rust Eng'g Co.*, 77 LA 488, 490–91 (Williams, 1981); *Jacuzzi Bros.*, 49 LA 760, 767 (Bothwell, 1967).

[190]Waste Mgmt. of Ohio, 113 LA 353, 362 (Franckiewicz, 1999); Synergy Gas Co., 91 LA 77 (Simmons, 1987), *aff'd*, 853 F.2d 59, 129 LRRM 2041 (2d Cir. 1988) (employer failed to comply with reinstatement with back-pay order). Department of the Navy, 113 LA 1214 (Lubic, 2000) (functus officio doctrine did not preclude arbitrator from considering request for attorney fees); Quality Long Term Care of Nev., 112 LA 423, 432 (Robinson, 1999); Champlain Cable Corp., 108 LA 449, 453 (Sweeney, 1997); Detroit Bd. of Educ., 101 LA 1199 (Daniel, 1993) (the employer continued to violate the agreement); Goddard Space Flight Ctr., 91 LA 1105 (Berkeley, 1988); Customs Serv., 91 LA 630 (Finston, 1988); National Gallery of Art, 91 LA 335 (Craver), *aff'd*, 853 F.2d 59 (2d Cir. 1988); John Morrell & Co., 69 LA 264, 282 (Conway, 1977); Sonic Knitting Indus., 65 LA 453, 468–69, 471 (Helfeld, 1975); Basic Vegetable Prods., 64 LA 620, 625 (Gould, 1975); Sunshine Convalescent Hosp., 62 LA 276, 279 (Lennard, 1974). *But see* Arizona Bank, 91 LA 772 (Fine, 1988).

[191]Food & Commercial Workers Local 342-50 v. Y&P Israel Glatt, 1998 U.S. Dist. LEXIS 14849 (E.D.N.Y. 1998); Georgia-Pacific Corp. v. Graphic Communications Dist. Council, 1999 U.S. Dist. LEXIS 6904 (N.D. Cal. 1999).

[192]National Gypsum Co. v. Oil, Chem. & Atomic Workers, 1997 U.S. Dist. LEXIS 8929 (E.D. La. 1997).

[193]Vandenberg Air Force Base, 106 LA 107 (Feldman, 1996) (attorneys' fees awarded to union where employer discharged employee although blood type in drug sample did not match); Port of Tacoma, Wash., 99 LA 1151 (Smith, 1992) (employer to pay employee's attorneys' fees incurred in gender discrimination lawsuit against her supervisor); Department of Agric., 93 LA 920 (Seidman, 1989); Glover Bottled Gas Corp./Synergy Gas Corp., 91 LA 77 (Simons, 1987) (employer failed to comply with prior reinstatement and back-pay award), *aff'd*, 853 F.2d 59, 129 LRRM 2041 (2d Cir. 1988).

[194]Internal Revenue Serv., 113 LA 425, 428 (Snow, 1999) (union failed to establish that an award of attorneys' fees was warranted in the interest of justice).

In grievances arising under federal-sector contracts, the Civil Service Reform Act of 1978[195] does make provision for awarding attorneys' fees to the prevailing party.[196]

The U.S. District Court for the Southern District of New York vacated an arbitration award denying attorneys' fees in a discrimination case under Title VII of the Civil Rights Act of 1964.[197] Although the Civil Rights Act provides that "the court, in its discretion, may allow the prevailing party . . . a reasonable attorney's fee,"[198] the court found that the law established a presumptive entitlement to an award of attorneys' fees, and failing to so award in this case was held to be an example of manifest disregard of the law.[199] In another case, a discharge for misuse of a government computer was reduced to a suspension, but the union was awarded attorneys' fees because the federal employer had failed to conduct a proper investigation, and the union had to respond to the unfounded charges.[200]

---

[195]Codified as amended in scattered sections of 5 U.S.C.

[196]5 U.S.C. §§5506, 7701(g). *See* Department of Veterans Affairs, 115 LA 198 (Cornelius, 2000) (employee improperly discharged for alleged sexual harassment); Department of Defense Dependents Sch., 114 LA 641 (Feldman, 2000) (union entitled to attorneys' fees under Back Pay Act). The Civil Service Reform Act of 1978 made provision for awarding attorneys' fees to federal employees in connection with the processing of their unjustified personnel action grievance through a negotiated grievance procedure. *See* 5 U.S.C. §§5506, 7701(g). For discussion, see Bufe & Ferris, *A Second View of Awarding Attorney's Fees in Federal Sector Arbitration*, 38 ARB. J. No. 1, at 21 (1983); Moore, *Awarding Attorney's Fees in Federal Sector Arbitration*, 37 ARB. J. No. 4, at 38 (1982); Kagel, *Grievance Arbitration in the Federal Service: Still Hardly Final and Binding?, in* ARBITRATION ISSUES FOR THE 1980S, PROCEEDINGS OF THE 34TH ANNUAL MEETING OF NAA 178, 193 (Stern & Dennis eds., BNA Books 1982). Denying a request for attorney fees in *Customs Serv.*, 77 LA 1001, 1003 (Merrifield, 1981), the arbitrator did not find an award of attorneys' fees to be "warranted in the interest of justice on the facts" of the case. Attorney fees were awarded in *Customs Serv.*, 77 LA 1113, 1121 (Rocha, Jr., 1981). In *Customs Serv.*, 79 LA 284, 289–90 (Rocha, Jr., 1982), in further proceedings, the arbitrator decided both (1) what was a "reasonable" fee, and (2) that the union was entitled to it although it had used its in-house counsel to represent the grievant. *See also* Gilmore Envelope Corp., 110 LA 1036 (Ross, 1998); Tennessee Valley Auth., 101 LA 218 (Bankston, 1993); Glover Bottled Gas Corp./Synergy Gas Corp., 91 LA 77 (Simons, 1987), *aff'd*, 853 F.2d 59, 129 LRRM 2041 (2d Cir. 1988). *But see* Howard P. Foley Co. v. Electrical Workers (IBEW) Local 639, 789 F.2d 1421, 122 LRRM 2471 (9th Cir. 1986); Department of the Navy, 113 LA 1214 (Lubic, 2000); Department of Def. Dependents Sch., 112 LA 457 (Blum, 1999); Internal Revenue Serv., 109 LA 805 (Richard, 1997); Customs Serv., 109 LA 746 (Blum, 1997); Department of Agric., 107 LA 621 (Wolff, 1996); Vandenberg Air Force Base, 106 LA 107 (Feldman, 1996) (the grievant's blood type did not match the drug test sample); Department of Agric., 93 LA 920, 929–31 (Seidman, 1989); Arizona Bank, 91 LA 772 (Fine, 1988) (a federal agency had failed to conduct a proper investigation and had filed unnecessary motions); Federal Corr. Inst., 90 LA 942 (White, 1987); Veterans Admin., 88 LA 554 (Byars, 1986); Hines Veterans Admin. Hosp., 85 LA 239 (Wolff, 1985). Denying attorney fees, see *Internal Revenue Serv.*, 113 LA at 427–28 (where the employer did not know that a witness would not testify); *Department of Def. Dependents Sch.*, 95 LA 107 (Wilkinson, 1990) (a federal agency had reasonably relied on instructions, even though the instructions were contrary to unambiguous regulations).

[197]DeGaetano v. Smith Barney, Inc., 983 F. Supp. 459, 75 FEP Cases 579 (S.D.N.Y. 1997).

[198]42 U.S.C. § 2000e-5(k).

[199]The court distinguished this case from *DiRussa v. Dean Witter Reynolds Inc.*, 121 F.3d 818, 74 FEP Cases 726 (2d Cir. 1997), where the award was not vacated for the failure to award attorneys' fees because the claimant had failed to advise the arbitration panel that the ADEA provides for the mandatory award of attorneys' fees.

[200]Department of Agric., 93 LA 920 (Seidman, 1989).

ii.   Arbitration Expense [LA CDI 94.65; 100.0780]

Where a procedural defect caused by an employer resulted in the need for arbitration, the employer was assessed the costs of the proceeding.[201]

I.   Mitigating Damages—Deduction of Outside Compensation
[LA CDI 100.559525; 118.806]

When awarding back pay to an employee, particularly in discharge or discipline cases, arbitrators allow the employer's liability to be reduced by the amount of unemployment compensation or compensation from other employment paid to the employee during the relevant period,[202] provided

---

[201]Union Oil Co. of Cal., 91 LA 1206 (Klein, 1988). *See also* Indiana Convention Ctr. & Hoosier Dome, 98 LA 713 (Wolff, 1992) (employer failed to have a steward present during a disciplinary interview of an employee preceding his discharge and was ordered to reimburse the union for its share of arbitration costs and expenses, even though the discharge was upheld in arbitration); National R.R. Passenger Corp., 95 LA 617 (Simons, 1990) (employer was ordered to reimburse the union for its reasonable expenses in representing a discharged employee, the employer having committed "egregious breaches" of its duty to investigate the charges and to furnish relevant information requested by the union).

[202]Interlake Conveyors, 113 LA 1120, 1126 (Lalka, 2000); GTE N., 113 LA 1047, 1052 (Daniel, 1999); U.S. Graphite, 113 LA 319 (Ellmann, 1999) (no offset for earnings where contract only mentions unemployment compensation as an offset); Akron City Hosp., 113 LA 146, 152 (Chattman, 1999); Aeronca, 112 LA 1063, 1072 (Duda, Jr., 1999); Elkhart County, Ind., Gov't, 112 LA 936, 941 (Cohen, 1999) (less earnings but not less unemployment compensation); Howmedica, Inc., 112 LA 587, 591 (Liebowitz, 1999); Coca Cola USA, 112 LA 193, 198 (Rezler, 1999); Bunge Corp., 111 LA 1201, 1209 (Hilgert, 1998); Gunite Corp., 111 LA 897 (Cohen, 1999); Safelite Glass Corp., 111 LA 561, 564 (Bain, 1998); Mid-America Packaging, 111 LA 129, 133 (Bankston, 1998); Gemala Trailer Corp., 108 LA 565, 572 (Nicholas, Jr., 1997); Quala Sys., 108 LA 284, 288 (Weston, 1997); Goodman Beverage Co., 108 LA 37, 43 (Morgan, Jr., 1997); Southern Frozen Foods, 107 LA 1030, 1037 (Giblin, 1996); Ken Meyer Meats, 107 LA 1017, 1023 (Sergent, 1996); Barnstead-Thermolyne Corp., 107 LA 645, 654 (Pelofsky, 1996); Webcraft Games, 107 LA 560, 566 (Ellmann, 1996); Marshfield, Wis., Nursing & Rehab. Ctr., 107 LA 188, 192 (Cerone, 1996); HDS Servs., 107 LA 27, 30 (Hodgson, 1996); Birmingham Sash & Door Co., 106 LA 180, 185 (Bain, 1996); Pismo-Oceano Vegetable Exch., 106 LA 132, 136 (Kaufman, 1996); Johnson Controls World Servs., 105 LA 1194, 1201 (Poole, 1996); City of Evansville, Ind., 105 LA 673, 681 (Brookins, 1995); Hickory Vinyl Corp., 105 LA 572, 576 (Hayford, 1995); County of Hennepin, Minn., 105 LA 391 (Imes, 1995); Toledo Edison, 104 LA 933, 940–41 (Shanker, 1995); State of Ohio, 104 LA 486, 494 (Feldman, 1995); Fina Oil & Chem. Co., 104 LA 343, 348 (Nicholas, Jr., 1995); County of Butler, Pa., 104 LA 131, 136 (Talarico, 1994); Clermont County Dep't of Human Servs., 102 LA 1024, 1031 (Donnelly, 1994); Oroweat Foods Co., 102 LA 910, 917 (DiFalco, 1993); Chrome Deposit Corp., 102 LA 733, 736 (Bethel, 1994); Orpack-Stone Corp., 102 LA 545, 555 (Hilgert, 1994); Michigan Dep't of Corr., 102 LA 280, 285 (VanAuken-Haight, 1993); GTE N., 102 LA 154, 160 (Kenis, 1993); T.W. Recreational Servs., 93 LA 302 (Richard, 1989); Flying Tigers Line, 91 LA 647 (Concepcion, 1988); Cowlitz Redi-Mix, 85 LA 745 (Boedecker, 1985); Yoh Sec., 85 LA 196 (Goldsmith, 1985). *See also* Lockheed Aircraft Serv. Co., 90 LA 297 (Kaufman, 1987); Boise Cascade Paper Group, 86 LA 177 (Marlatt, 1985); Vaco Prods. Co., 77 LA 432, 438 (Lewis, 1981); Zapata Indus., 76 LA 467, 473 (Woolf, 1981); Wehr Corp., 76 LA 399, 403 (Hunter, 1981) (arbitrator adjusted the unemployment compensation amount upward "by 25% to reflect their nontaxable status," and thus their "true offset value"); Southern Cal. Rapid Transit Dist., 76 LA 144, 152 (Sabo, 1980); Pepsi Cola Bottling Co., 76 LA 54, 56 (Siegel, 1980); S.A.C. Corp., 71 LA 1109, 1113 (Perry, 1978); Hygrade Food Prods. Corp., 69 LA 414, 419 (Harter, 1977); General Tel. Co. of Ky., 69 LA 351, 355 (Bowles, 1977); Bucyrus-Erie Co., 69 LA 93, 102 (Lipson, 1977); Dan-Van Rubber, 68 LA 217, 221 (Rothschild, 1977) (ordering deduction of "all welfare or other unemployment or union benefits received"); Vancouver Plywood Co., 68 LA 204, 211 (Marcus, 1977) (additionally ordering deduction of benefits from other governmental programs). *But see* O'Keefe's Aluminum Prods., 92 LA 215 (Koven, 1987) (arbitrator accepted grievant's excuse for failing to mitigate loss). In *General*

such income was not a normal part of the grievant's income prior to discharge.[203] Indeed, there is general agreement by courts, arbitrators, and the NLRB that outside earnings properly are deducted from back pay.[204] Because the objective is to make the employee whole for loss of wages, failure to take into account such other earnings results in overcompensation.

Many arbitrators hold that an employee who has been wronged by an employer has an affirmative duty to mitigate, so far as reasonable, the amount of the loss.[205] The duty to mitigate has been explained as follows:

> A discharged employee should be required to make a reasonable effort to mitigate "damages" by seeking substantially equivalent employment. The reasonableness of his effort should be evaluated in light of the individual's qualifications and the relevant job market. His burden is not onerous, and does not require that he be successful in mitigating his "damages." Further, the burden of proving lack of diligence or an honest, good faith effort on the employee's part is on management.[206]

Even where the agreement provided that an unjustly discharged employee "shall be . . . paid for all time lost,"[207] an arbitrator explained that a duty to attempt to mitigate damages existed:

> It is commonly and generally recognized that the purpose of a contract provision calling for payment of "all time lost," when disciplinary action or discharge has been found to be without justifiable cause is to compensate and indemnify the injured employee and make him whole for loss of earnings suffered by him as a result of the inappropriate exercise of judgment by the Com-

---

Felt Indus., 74 LA 972, 977 (Carnes, 1979), the arbitrator ordered deduction of unemployment compensation but also ordered that "in the event that Grievants are required to repay any amount of unemployment compensation because of their reinstatement, the Company shall reimburse them for such amounts as they may be required to repay." Also providing for the contingency that the state might recapture the benefits, see *Alvey, Inc.*, 74 LA 835, 840 (Roberts, 1980); *Schnuck Mkts.*, 73 LA 829, 832 (Holman, 1979); *Marathon Pipe Line Co.*, 69 LA 555, 563 (Brown, 1977). In allowing a deduction in favor of the employer, some arbitrators ordered the employer to reimburse the unemployment compensation commission. *See* American Bakeries Co., 43 LA 1106, 1111 (Purdom, 1964); Hub City Jobbing Co., 43 LA 907, 911 (Gundermann, 1964); Sanna Dairies, 43 LA 16, 20 (Rice, 1964). Permitting deduction of workers' compensation benefits received by grievant as a result of injury while working for another employer after his discharge, see *Champion Int'l Corp.*, 76 LA 942, 945–46 (Nicholas, Jr., 1981).

[203]United Parcel Serv., 113 LA 225, 231 (Allen, Jr., 1999) (less earnings that were not a part of predischarge income); Ryder Student Transp. Servs., 108 LA 1124 (Franckiewicz, 1997) (no deduction for earnings from second job held while working for employer); Mansfield Foundry Corp., 105 LA 353, 356 (Coyne, 1995) (no offset of earnings from previously owned pizza business); American Nat'l Can Co., 104 LA 191, 192 (McGury, 1994); Merico, Inc., 98 LA 122, 125 (Silver, 1992) (no offset for earnings from a doughnut shop); Alumax Aluminum Corp., 92 LA 28 (Allen, Jr., 1988). *But see* Dyncorp., 97 LA 572, 577–78 (Cantor, 1991) (the arbitrator allowed the employer to reduce back pay by the amount earned from a part-time job that had been worked concurrently with the employee's job with the employer).

[204]For an indication of National Railroad Adjustment Board practice as to outside earnings, see *National Ry. Labor Conference*, 53 LA 555, 563 (Seward, Howlett, & Livernash, 1969).

[205]Foster Wheeler Envtl. Corp., 116 LA 120 (Calhoun, 2001); Jackson Gen. Hosp., 113 LA 1040, 1047 (Sharpe, 2000). *See also* Wayne State Univ., 111 LA 906, 908 (Daniel, 1998) (the obligation to mitigate damages is clearly established); Zinc Corp. of Am., 101 LA 643, 646 (Nicholas, Jr., 1993) ("arbitrator's inherent obligation to see that damages are mitigated"); Gase Baking Co., 86 LA 206 (Block, 1985).

[206]HILL & SINICROPI, REMEDIES IN ARBITRATION 216 (BNA Books 2d ed. 1991).

[207]Love Bros., 45 LA 751, 752 (Solomon, 1965).

pany. The loss of earnings is usually to be measured by the wages he would have earned for the period they were improperly denied to him, subject, however, to a recognized duty and responsibility reposed in the employee to mitigate, so far as reasonable, the amount of that loss. If, as a result of employee's action or inaction, he has failed to mitigate the loss, then to the degree of such failure he is himself partially responsible.[208]

For this reason back pay may be wholly or partially denied where the employee has failed to take advantage of reasonable employment opportunities.[209] This view, however, is not universally accepted. As one arbitrator stated, "while it

---

[208]*Id.* at 756. *See also* S&C Constr. Co., 89 LA 445, 446 (Strasshofer, 1987); Orlando Transit Co., 71 LA 897, 900 (Serot, 1978). In *Continental Can Co.*, 39 LA 821, 822–23 (Sembower, 1962), outside earnings and unemployment compensation were deducted where the agreement stated the grievant was to be paid the amount "he would have earned." *Id.* at 823. *But see* United States Steel, 40 LA 1036, 1039–41 (McDermott, 1963).

[209]*See* United Int'l Investigative Serv., 114 LA 620, 626 (Maxwell, 2000) ("[I]n this day and age and with grievant's skill and training . . ., Grievant could certainly have found part-time employment . . . . By failing to make at least a reasonable effort to do so, Grievant should not be awarded back pay at the expense of the Company."); Jackson Gen. Hosp., 113 LA 1040, 1047 (Sharpe, 2000) (remand to parties, where evidence of mitigation was unclear); U.S. Graphite, 113 LA 319, 320 (Ellmann, 1999) (awards should be reduced if the grievant fails to mitigate damages); S.D. Warren Co., 113 LA 272, 278–89 (Daniel, 1999) (grievant failed to contact any employers or agencies); Lithibar Matik, 112 LA 957 (Sugerman, 1999) (back pay reduced, where grievant concealed amount of interim earnings); Bonar Packaging, 112 LA 370 (Moore, 1999); Wayne State Univ., 111 LA 906, 908 (Daniel, 1998); Matanuska Elec. Ass'n, 109 LA 1197, 1201 (Landau, 1998) (deducting interim pay received by grievant to mitigate damages); Ralphs Grocery Co., 108 LA 718 (Prayzich, 1997) (did not look for work); Avis Rent-A-Car Sys., 107 LA 197, 202 (Shanker, 1996) (grievant did not seek employment diligently); Cone Mills Corp., 106 LA 23 (Nolan, 1995); Buckeye Steel Castings Co., 104 LA 825, 828 (Weatherspoon, 1995) (grievant refused job assignment); Ogden Support Servs., 104 LA 432 (Weisheit, 1995) (grievant refused comparable employment); Atlantic Southeast Airlines, 103 LA 1179 (Nolan, 1994) (grievant had not applied for work as had been claimed); Babcock & Wilcox Co., 102 LA 104 (Nicholas, Jr., 1994); Eagle Point, Or., Sch. Dist., 100 LA 496 (Wilkinson, 1992); Memphis, Tenn., Light, Gas & Water Div., 100 LA 291, 295 (Caraway, 1993); Square D Co., 99 LA 879, 884 (Goodstein, 1992) (grievant refused corrective surgery that could have hastened his return to work); Tanner Cos., 98 LA 530 (Parent, 1991) (denied for the period when grievant refused training); Marathon Oil Co., 97 LA 1145, 1151 (Massey, 1991) (grievant repeatedly refused tutoring); Airtel, Inc., 97 LA 297 (Prayzich, 1991) (grievant refused to return to work); A.O. Thompson Lumber Co., 96 LA 585 (Berger, 1991) (reduced because grievant refused reinstatement); Quemetco, Inc., 96 LA 134 (Darrow, 1990) (reduced by amount that could have been earned in refused job); Kings County, Cal., Truck Lines, 94 LA 875 (Prayzich, 1990) (reduced by amount that would have been earned had grievant not quit an interim job); T.W. Recreational Servs., 93 LA 302, 310 (Richard, 1989); City of Rochester Hills, Mich., 90 LA 237 (Daniel, 1987); Cleveland Pneumatic Co., 89 LA 1071, 1075 (Sharpe, 1987); Mare Island Naval Shipyard, 89 LA 861, 865 (Wilcox, 1987); Roskam Baking Co., 79 LA 993, 999 (Beitner, 1982); St. Regis Paper Co., 75 LA 737, 742 (Andersen, 1980) (grievant "made only a minimal effort to obtain other employment"); Good Hope Refineries, 73 LA 1171, 1174 (LeBaron, 1979) ("Grievant's testimony does not reflect reasonable diligence in seeking interim employment."); Borg-Warner Corp., 72 LA 184, 189–90 (Allen Jr., 1979); Public Serv. Co. of N.M., 70 LA 788, 793 (Springfield, 1978); Pepsi Cola Bottling Co., 70 LA 428, 430 (Rinaldo, 1978); Palm Desert Greens Ass'n, 69 LA 191, 193 (Draznin, 1977); Rohm & Haas Tex., 68 LA 498, 503 (White, 1977); Permanente Med. Group, 52 LA 217, 221 (Block, 1968) (the arbitrator made an "educated guess" as to time reasonably necessary for grievant to find other work). *See also* Youngstown Developmental Ctr., 93 LA 1155, 1159 (Sharpe, 1989) (starting a new business satisfied the duty to mitigate damages). *But see* Steamship Trade Ass'n of Balt., 103 LA 1015 (Wahl, 1994) (grievant did not need to register for work when no work was available); AVR Inc., 95 LA 926 (Bard, 1990) (reading newspaper want ads was sufficient, where employer did not show that filing an application with state unemployment office would have resulted in finding employment); MacMillan Bloedel Containers, 94 LA 992 (Nicholas, Jr., 1990) (back pay was not reduced because the employer offered no proof as to the reason the grievant quit).

may be proper to deduct from a back pay award sums actually earned by an employee before reinstatement, or sums received indirectly from his employer, as through unemployment compensation, no authority exists in an Arbitrator to penalize an employee financially for failing to have earnings."[210]

Even arbitrators who recognize the duty to mitigate damages may qualify the obligation. For example, some arbitrators require the employer to introduce affirmative evidence to show that failure of the employee to minimize damages was inexcusable.[211] Others require only that the employee use more than "ordinary diligence" to obtain other work.[212] An employee is not required to apply for each and every job that might exist, he or she need only make a reasonable effort.[213] Furthermore, the employee may not be required to accept unsuitable or lower rated work during the pendency of the appeal,[214] and may be given credit for the added expense involved in actually getting and working at interim employment.[215] In one case, the grievant's duty to mitigate damages was satisfied by expanding his prior farm operations. In that case the arbitrator also concluded that only the extra income from farm work during the grievant's regular working hours with his employer should be deducted.[216]

When an arbitrator concludes that the grievant's outside compensation is to be deducted in the computation of back pay, the grievant has a duty to reveal the facts concerning his or her outside income. Some arbitrators have

---

[210]Shakespeare & Shakespeare Prods. Co., 9 LA 813, 817–18 (Platt, 1948). In *Bell Helicopter Textron*, 71 LA 799, 801 (Johannes, 1978), the arbitrator denied back pay for the period during which the grievant was incarcerated and thus unavailable for work; a requirement of pay for the period of incarceration "would be to go beyond making him whole and take on the attributes of a punitive remedy against the Company." Also denying back pay for a period of incarceration, see *New Albany Concrete Serv.*, 76 LA 44, 46 (Fitch, 1981). Regarding strike periods, see *Markle Mfg. Co.*, 73 LA 1292, 1295–96 (Williams, 1980).

[211]American Bakeries Co., 77 LA 530, 535 (Modjeska, 1981); Orlando Transit Co., 71 LA 897, 900 (Serot, 1978); Quick Serv. Laundry & Cleaners, 52 LA 121, 127–28 (Merrill, 1968); Armour & Co., 11 LA 600, 605 (Gilden, 1948).

[212]Standard Transformer Co., 51 LA 1110, 1113 (Gibson, 1968). Reporting periodically to the unemployment office, answering newspaper job advertisements, and applying directly for jobs were considered to constitute "reasonable" or "diligent" efforts to mitigate damages in Orlando Transit Co., 71 LA 897, 900–03 (Serot, 1978), where the arbitrator also discussed the significance of grievant's enrolling in school, moving, and spending time working on his house.

[213]Foster Wheeler Envtl. Corp., 116 LA 120, 123 (Calhoun, 2001) (employee is not obliged to explore every possibility or devote every day to a search for work). *See also* Atlantic Southeast Airlines, 103 LA 1179, 1182 (Nolan, 1994).

[214]American Bakeries Co., 77 LA 530, 535 (Modjeska, 1981); Corwell-Collier Broad. Corp., 45 LA 635, 640 (Jones, 1965); McLouth Steel Corp., 23 LA 640, 642 (Parker, 1954); Airequipment Co., 10 LA 162, 164 (Aaron, 1948). *Cf.* Rohm & Haas Tex., 68 LA 498, 499, 503 (White, 1977).

[215]Ingalls Shipbuilding Corp., 37 LA 953, 956 (Murphy, 1961).

[216]American-International Aluminum Corp., 49 LA 728, 730 (Howlett, 1967). *See also* Youngstown Developmental Ctr., 93 LA 1155, 1159 (Sharpe, 1989) (starting a new business satisfied the duty to mitigate damages); Trailways, Inc., 88 LA 1073, 1083 (Goodman, 1987); DeVry Inst. of Tech., 87 LA 1149 (Berman, 1986); Dunfy Hotel Corp., 80 LA 1161, 1173 (Bard, 1983) (income from work outside grievant's regular working hours with his employer not deducted); Markle Mfg. Co., 73 LA 1292, 1298–99 (Williams, 1980) (grievant mitigated damages by expanding his part-time work with another employer); American-International Aluminum Corp., 48 LA 283, 288 (Howlett, 1967).

ordered the grievant to submit notarized proof of outside earnings,[217] and in one case arbitral relief was conditioned on the grievant's authorizing the release of information disclosing the public assistance payments he had received.[218]

J. Other Avoidable Damages; Delayed Arbitration [LA CDI 94.57]

In some cases, back pay has been denied or reduced because the grievant could have avoided the problem by speaking up to explain his or her situation and actions, but failed to do so.[219] The concept of avoidable damages also was applied against the employer in one case, where he was ordered to pay all arbitration costs because the need for arbitration might have been obviated had he explained his rationale to the union prior to arbitration.[220]

Delay in moving a grievance to arbitration extends the period of lost wages and potential employer liability. One arbitrator reduced an employer's

---

[217]Enesco Corp., 107 LA 513, 519 (Berman, 1996) (union directed to produce evidence); New Boston Coke Corp., 107 LA 325, 328 (Kilroy, 1996); Advance Transp. Co., 105 LA 1089, 1094 (Briggs, 1995); ABM Space Care, 105 LA 199, 204 (Cohen, 1995); Ashtabula County Nursing Home, 104 LA 1006, 1012 (Feldman, 1995); American Nat'l Can Co., 104 LA 191, 192 (McGury, 1994); West Co., 103 LA 452 (Murphy, 1994) (statement of earnings from interim employer was accepted); Van Waters & Rogers, 102 LA 609, 612 (Feldman, 1993) (affidavits); United Parcel Serv., 101 LA 589, 598 (Briggs, 1993); Western Steel Group, 94 LA 1177 (Bittel, 1990) (approved an employer demand to see the tax returns of a reinstated employee and upheld the employee's discharge for refusing to comply with the request); Johnson Controls Battery Group, 113 LA 769 (Cantor, 1999) (provide pay record under oath); Dayton, Ohio, Metro. Hous. Auth., 111 LA 784, 788 (Cohen, 1998) (affidavit); Albertson's, Inc., 111 LA 630, 637 (Eisenmenger, 1998) (provide credible and reasonable documentary evidence); Morton Thiokol, 89 LA 572 (Nicholas, Jr., 1987); Georgia-Pacific Corp., 87 LA 217, 224 (Cohen, 1986); Overly Mfg. Co. of Cal., 68 LA 1343, 1346 (Jones, Jr., 1977); Evening News Ass'n, 68 LA 1314, 1318 (Volz, 1977) (additionally requiring grievant to submit copies of his federal income tax returns "and permit the arbitrator in private to compare them with the information included in the notarized statement or affidavit"); Cincinnati Post & Times Star, 68 LA 129, 142 (Chalfie, 1977); Penn Jersey Boiler & Constr. Co., 50 LA 177, 181 (Buckwalter, 1967); Western Air Lines, 37 LA 700, 704 (Jones, Jr., 1961). *See also* Southern Cal. Rapid Transit Dist., 76 LA 144, 152 (Sabo, 1980).

[218]United States Steel Corp., 52 LA 1210, 1212 (Dybeck, 1969) (agreement called for deduction of "such earnings or other amounts as [employee] would not have received except for such suspension or discharge"). In *Orlando Transit Co.*, 71 LA 897, 903 (Serot, 1978), the agreement required deduction of "any unemployment or other compensation from any source"; benefits under the G.I. bill were not deemed "compensation" to be deducted under this provision.

[219]Fitzsimons Mfg. Co., 92 LA 609, 616 (Roumell, Jr., 1989); Simplex Prods. Div., 91 LA 356, 360 (Byars, 1988); Continental White Cap, 90 LA 1119, 1123 (Staudohar, 1988); Ohio Dep't of Aging, 90 LA 423, 426 (Cohen, 1987); Southeastern Mich. Gas Co., 90 LA 307, 311 (Daniel, 1987); Renaissance Ctr. P'ship, 76 LA 379, 386 (Daniel, 1981); Keystone Steel & Wire Co., 72 LA 780, 783–84 (Elson, 1979); Rountree Transp. Co., 69 LA 132, 135 (Naehring, 1977); William Feather Co., 68 LA 13, 17–18 (Shanker, 1977); Ralston Purina Co., 61 LA 14, 16 (Krislov, 1973); Koehring Co., 51 LA 234, 240–41 (Stouffer, 1968); Exact Weight Scale Co., 50 LA 8, 9 (McCoy, 1967); Oklahoma Furniture Mfg. Co., 24 LA 522, 526 (Merrill, 1955); Packers By-Products Co., 8 LA 248, 250 (Wardlaw, 1947). In *Checker Motors Corp.*, 70 LA 805, 808–09 (Allen, Jr., 1978), the "failure to raise a vital defense prior to arbitration" led to the denial of back pay for a grievant whose reinstatement was ordered.

[220]Indiana Hosp., 110 LA 693, 699 (Dean, Jr., 1998); Ralph Rogers & Co., 48 LA 40, 43 (Getman, 1966). *But see* Madison Bus Co., 52 LA 723, 727–28 (Mueller, 1969). In *Thorsen Mfg. Co.*, 55 LA 581, 585 (Koven, 1970), the arbitrator upheld a discharge but awarded some back pay because the company unreasonably complicated and prolonged the proceedings, leaving the grievant in doubt as to his status for a substantial period. *See also* Union Oil Co. of Cal., 91 LA 1206, 1210 (Klein, 1988); Mobay Chem. Corp., 77 LA 219, 222 (Lubow, 1981).

liability for back pay because the employee or the union had caused or contributed to delay in the arbitration process,[221] but no such reduction was allowed where responsibility for the unreasonable delay in the arbitration process could not be placed on either the employee or the union.[222] Some arbitrators generally will not sustain a remedy for delayed arbitration absent time limitations in the collective bargaining agreement.[223]

Where a delay in the arbitration process was caused by the failure of a company to respond, the arbitrator denied the union's request that the company bear the expense of the second arbitration hearing, because the agreement stated that the expense of arbitration was to be borne equally by both parties.[224]

K. Remedies for Mistake

In contract interpretation cases, one or both parties may claim that a mistake was made so that the text does not actually represent their agreement. The alleged mistake may take one of three forms: mutual mistake, unilateral mistake, or calculation error. The approach to each type of mistake differs, and each is susceptible to different treatment.

i. *Mutual Mistake* [LA CDI 24.15; 94.68]

The remedy of reformation to correct a mutual mistake in a contract is well established and has been consistently recognized by arbitrators.[225] This remedy seeks to revise the text to conform to the mutual intentions of the parties. In fact, reformation may be granted even where the evidence of mis-

---

[221]University of Minn., 111 LA 774 (Daly, 1998); MetroHealth Med. Ctr., 108 LA 974 (Franckiewicz, 1997); Kodiak Elec. Ass'n, 104 LA 1112 (Peck, 1995); S&J Ranch, 103 LA 350, 362 (Bogue, 1994); Alford Packaging, 102 LA 508 (Cluster, 1994); Indianapolis Water Co., 102 LA 316, 320 (Duff, 1994); Burlington N. R.R., 101 LA 144, 153–54 (Massey, 1993); University of Pa., 99 LA 353, 360 (DiLauro, 1992); Food Barn Stores, 96 LA 266, 273–74 (Hilgert, 1990); Ohio Masonic Home, 94 LA 447, 451 (Volz, 1990); Genstar Bldg. Materials Co., 89 LA 1265, 1268 (Weisbrod, 1987); Great Lakes Carbon Corp., 88 LA 644, 651 (Singer, 1987); City of Gainesville, Fla., 72 LA 1248, 1250 (Taylor, 1979); Niles, Shepard, Crane & Hoist Corp., 71 LA 828, 832 (Alutto, 1978); Roy E. Hanson, Jr., Mfg. Co., 68 LA 1354, 1359 (Roberts, 1977) (the union was ordered to pay a portion of the back pay because of its delay in processing the case to arbitration); Hussmann Refrigerator Co., 68 LA 565, 571 (Mansfield, 1977); Appalachian Reg'l Hosps., 54 LA 680, 683 (Reid, 1970); Jacuzzi Bros., 49 LA 760, 766–67 (Bothwell, 1967); Minnesota Mining & Mfg. Co., 42 LA 1, 13 (Solomon, 1964); Yale & Towne Mfg. Co., 39 LA 1156, 1162–63 (Hill, Horlacher, & Seitz, 1962) (full discussion of the matter); Laupahoehoe Sugar Co., 38 LA 404, 413 (Tsukiyama, 1961). *Cf.* West Va. Pulp & Paper Co., 39 LA 163, 166–67 (Stark, 1962).

[222]Acme Fast Freight, 37 LA 163, 166 (Warns, 1961). *See also* Henry B. Gilpin Co., 72 LA 981, 987 (Stone, 1979). But in *Indian Head, Inc.*, 71 LA 82, 86 (Rimer, Jr., 1978), the arbitrator did "not attempt to assess the cause or causes" of the long delay in processing the case through the grievance procedure; in light of the delay, and considering the relatively short service of the grievant, he concluded that an award of back pay "would be clearly punitive."

[223]PQ Corp., 116 LA 137, 141 (Bognanno, 2001); Gulfport Shipbuilding Corp., 43 LA 1053, 1056 (Ray, 1964).

[224]Regional Transp. Dist., 87 LA 630 (Feldman, 1986). *But see* Michigan Dep't of Transp., 89 LA 551 (Borland, 1987); Denver, Colo., Pub. Sch., 88 LA 507 (Watkins, 1986).

[225]The concept is discussed in *Seattle Prof'l Eng'g Employees Ass'n v. Boeing*, 139 Wash. 2d 824, 991 P.2d 1126, 1130–31, 5 WH Cases 2d 1686 (2000). *See* Borden Chems. & Plastics, 113 LA 1080 (Pratte, 1999) (mutual mistake regarding OSHA requirements permitted refor-

take falls short of that which a court of equity would require, if the arbitrator is persuaded that "fairness and justice" require this kind of relief.[226] In some cases, rather than impose new language on the parties, arbitrators have remanded the matter and ordered the parties to reach an acceptable revision through bargaining.[227]

Whether an arbitrator will reform a contract depends on the circumstances of the mutual mistake. Obviously, if the mutual mistake produces contract language that results in an improved description of the parties' agreement, reformation is inappropriate.[228] In *East Lake, Florida, Fire & Rescue*,[229] the arbitrator was called on to analyze whether the employer violated the collective bargaining agreement by refusing to pay a flat rate increase. The arbitrator held that there was no meeting of the minds on several issues and reformed the contract to reflect the true intent of the parties.

Arbitrators will grant reformation to correct a mutual mistake even where one of the parties had accepted the other party's inappropriately drafted language without realizing the full ramifications of the provision.[230] However, the terms of an agreement will not be subject to reformation merely because at the time of signing the agreement, one party did not understand the implications of the provision proposed by the other.[231]

---

mation); Digital Domain Prods., 111 LA 137 (Gentile, 1998) (mutual mistake gives rise to reformation, not invalidation); Golden Eagle Constr. Co., 109 LA 1057 (Miles, 1997) (where there is a mutual mistake, arbitrator is obliged to reform contract to reflect parties' actual intent); Hibbing Ready Mix, 97 LA 248 (Imes, 1991); AT&T Techs., 96 LA 1001 (Levy, 1991). *See also* Dalfort Aviation Servs., 94 LA 1136 (Allen, Jr., 1990) (mutual mistake, parties ordered back to bargaining table); Gates Rubber Co., 93 LA 637 (Cohen, 1989) (even though substantial paragraph left out of the printed contract, arbitrator found a clerical error and gave effect to initialed draft of the negotiators); St. Louis Post-Dispatch, 92 LA 23 (Heinsz, 1988) (burden of proof on party claiming mistake to prove it by clear and convincing evidence); Cleveland Pneumatic Co., 91 LA 428 (Oberdank, 1988) (apparent clerical error in cost of living index figure in contract); Food Employers Council, 87 LA 514, 517 (Kaufman, 1986) (in correcting a 12-year-old typographical error, the arbitrator held, "[T]he Arbitrator's function in reforming an agreement is not to effect a change in the parties' agreement but to give effect to the parties' original intention"). However, one arbitrator refused to reform the contract on the ground that mutual mistakes were a necessary evil in the process of collective bargaining. Fors Farms, 112 LA 33, 39 (Cavanaugh, 1999).

[226]IOOF Home of Ohio, 115 LA 1517, 1521 (Florman, 2001) (arbitrator has the right to modify and mitigate unintended language to avoid an absurd result and give effect to the true intentions of the parties). *See also* Huntsville Mfg. Co., 6 LA 515, 516–17 (McCoy, 1947). Where an arbitrator was not so persuaded, the arbitrator insisted that, "Only under rare, unusual and compelling circumstances should a labor arbitrator exercise authority not expressly conferred upon him by modifying or reforming a labor agreement of long standing." Sidney Wanzer & Sons, 47 LA 708, 710–11 (Kamin, 1966).

[227]John F. Kennedy Ctr. for the Performing Arts, 101 LA 174 (Ables, 1993).

[228]Doss Aviation, 107 LA 39 (Ferree, 1996).

[229]114 LA 813, 815 (Abrams, 2000).

[230]*See, e.g.*, Guernsey County, Ohio, Dist. Pub. Library, 107 LA 435 (Sergent, 1996) (good-faith acceptance by the union of revised language proposed by the company did not change the mistake from unilateral to mutual); West Contra Costa, Cal., Unified Sch. Dist., 107 LA 109 (Henner, 1996) (unilateral mistake was caused by a scrivener's error); Kansas City Power & Light Co., 105 LA 518 (Berger, 1995) (both parties misunderstood application of Fair Labor Standards Act to overtime hours covered by contract); United Distillers Mfg., 104 LA 600 (Tharp, 1995) (employer unilaterally relied on erroneous cost information supplied by trustee bank in proposing conversion from profit-sharing to multiple-option plan for employees). *But see* Summit County, Ohio, Brewers & Distribs. Ass'n, 84 LA 840 (Kates, 1985).

[231]For cases, see Chapter 9, section 1.A., "Misunderstanding and the 'Mutual Assent' or 'Meeting of the Minds' Concept."

ii.   Unilateral Mistake [LA CDI 24.15; 94.68]

Unilateral mistake—that is, a misunderstanding by one of the parties as to the import of a term—rarely constitutes sufficient cause for altering an agreement or otherwise offering relief.[232] Occasionally, in such circumstances arbitrators will allow rescission of the contract.[233] However, arbitrators will not rescind a contract simply because it has become more burdensome or difficult to perform.[234] Rescission as a remedy for a unilateral mistake is usually available only if the mistake was basic to the agreement, and the other party knew of the other party's mistake and took advantage of it.[235]

iii.   Calculation Error [LA CDI 94.68]

Another type of "mistake" in arbitration involves the overpayment or underpayment of money due a party because of incorrect calculations. Although not remedial under traditional contract theories, arbitrators will occasionally allow correction of those errors. In one case, for instance, employ-

---

[232]Occidental Chem. Corp., 114 LA 1660 (Brunner, 2000); East Lake Fire & Rescue, 114 LA 813 (Abrams, 2000) (where the parties spent over 1 ½ months cleaning up a copy of the draft agreement for signature, the employer should have caught the error "if it was an error"; it is too late to do that in arbitration); Marley Cooling Tower Co., 110 LA 1171 (Berger, 1998); City of Fergus Falls, Minn., 110 LA 961 (Daly, 1998) (employer must live with unilateral mistake); T.J. Maxx, 105 LA 470, 473–74 (Richman, 1995) (employer's mistake in believing its proposal became part of the contract under the doctrine of acceptance by silence was unilateral and nonbinding); National Linen Serv., 95 LA 829 (Abrams, 1990) (union had chance at the time of reviewing the draft and the actual signing to correct the alleged mistake; written contract stands); Pillowtex Corp., 92 LA 321 (Goldstein, 1989); Klein Tools, 90 LA 1150 (Poindexter, 1988); Cleo Wrap, 90 LA 768 (Welch, 1988) (typographical error did not reflect the intention of the parties; hence no meeting of the minds); Maple Heights, Ohio, Bd. of Educ., 86 LA 338 (Van Pelt, 1985); Summit County, Ohio, Brewers & Distribs. Ass'n, 84 LA 840 (Kates, 1985). See also Certain Members of Printing Indus. of Twin Cities, 80 LA 96, 102–03 (Boyer, 1982); Paramount Pictures Corp., 76 LA 345, 347 (Gentile, 1981); Tennessee Dressed Beef Co., 74 LA 1229, 1235 (Hardin, 1980); Colorado-Ute, 71 LA 1128, 1133–34 (Goodman, 1978); Servomation Corp., 68 LA 1294, 1299 (Perry, 1977); Scott Paper Co., 68 LA 838, 841 (Marcus, 1977); W.R. Grace & Co., 66 LA 517, 520 (Hebert, 1976); Aro Corp., 54 LA 1265, 1268 (Sembower, 1971); Journal-Tribune Publ'g Co. of Sioux City, Iowa, 51 LA 606, 611–12 (Erbs, 1968); Distillers Co., 50 LA 877, 881 (Gould, 1968); Emhart Corp., 48 LA 1185, 1186 (Williams, 1967); Del E. Webb Corp., 48 LA 164, 167 (Koven, 1967); Bethlehem Steel Corp., 47 LA 549, 551 (Seward, 1966); Amax Specialty Metals, 67–2 ARB ¶8452 (Holly, 1967); United Biscuit Co., 43 LA 913, 917–18 (Howlett, 1964); Wyandotte Chems. Corp., 23 LA 746, 749 (Bowles, 1954); Bond Clothes, 7 LA 708, 711–12 (Platt, 1947); Goodyear Tire & Rubber Co. of Ala., 3 LA 257, 259 (McCoy, 1946). A reformation may be granted to effectuate the true intent of the parties, where that intent is not reflected in the agreement as a result of typographical error. See Mohawk Beverages, 50 LA 298, 300 (Moran, 1968). See also Southern Mich. Cold Storage, 80 LA 53, 64–65 (House, 1982). For related discussion, see Chapter 9, section 2.A.ii., "Exceptions."

[233]See, e.g., American Airlines, 48 LA 705, 717–18 (Seitz, 1967). In Overhead Door Corp., 61 LA 1229, 1232 (Duff, 1973), the arbitrator found that the parties, in adopting a provision, had acted under "mutual mistake of fact," and, though not using the term "rescission," his remedy was to "excise" the provision from the agreement and to direct the parties "to promptly return to the bargaining table."

[234]Michigan Dep't of Transp., 112 LA 1179, 1182 (Allen, 1999) (hardships or extra costs are not acceptable excuses for rescinding a validly executed agreement).

[235]For a thorough discussion of mistake as a basis for rescission, see United Drill & Tool Corp., 28 LA 677, 687–89 (Cox, 1957); Glendale Mfg. Co., 28 LA 298, 300–01 (Maggs, 1957). See also International Harvester Co., 17 LA 592, 594 (Forrester, 1951); A.C.L. Haase Co., 17 LA 472, 478 (Townsend, 1951).

ees recovered sums that their employer owed them but had mistakenly failed to pay.[236] Where an employer makes an error in favor of employees, despite full knowledge of the facts, any monies paid out may not be recovered.[237] However, the employer will be permitted to correct mathematical or clerical errors in wage computation, where the payment has not yet been made, and in some cases recoupment by the employer may be allowed of excess payments made before the error was detected.[238] Where the clerical error concerns an employee's rate (or its basis) and has continued for some time, the employer still may be permitted to correct it for the future if, on discovery of the error, prompt action is taken, but the arbitrator may be less inclined to permit recoupment. [238A] Where the error in pay rate set forth in the contract was mutual, the arbitrator will enforce the actual agreement, despite the different rate in the contract. [238B]

The union bears responsibility for correctly presenting calculations relating to the employer's wage and benefit proposals to its members. In one case, a company's final offer contained a modification of a fund contribution formula that was accepted by the union. The union, however, inadvertently presented the new contract for ratification with the old clause instead of the revised formula. The error was held to warrant the granting of relief.[239]

L. Remedies for Unjust Enrichment

The principle of unjust enrichment holds that "one shall not unjustly enrich himself at the expense of another."[240] One arbitrator elaborated:

---

[236]A.D. Juilliard & Co., 20 LA 579, 582–83 (Maggs, 1953). *See also* Carlynton Sch. Dist., 73 LA 1183, 1185 (Duff, 1979).

[237]"[M]oney paid under a mistake of fact or a mutual mistake may be recovered, . . . money paid under a mistake of law or of judgment may not be recovered." Olin Corp., 86 LA 1193, 1197 (Penfield, 1986). *Compare* Eastern Airlines, 48 LA 1005, 1009 (Seidenberg, 1967), *with* Northern Ohio Tel. Co., 48 LA 773, 775 (Kates, 1966). *See also* Rand-Whitney Midwest Packaging Corp., 80 LA 994, 999 (Lipson, 1983).

[238]Recoupment permitted in whole or in part: Appalachian Reg'l Hosps., 69 LA 794, 799–800 (Cantor, 1977); Universal Foundry Co., 56 LA 1270, 1275 (Schurke, 1971); General Tel. Co. of Ill., 49 LA 493, 498 (Kesselman, 1967); Defoe Shipbuilding Co., 49 LA 206, 210 (Walsh, 1967); Northern Ohio Tel. Co., 48 LA 773, 775 (Kates, 1966) (dictum); Columbus Bottlers, 44 LA 397, 401 (Stouffer, 1965); Hammermill Paper Co., 42 LA 1084, 1986–87 (Williams, 1964) (practice supported it); United States Steel Corp., 41 LA 10, 13–14 (McDermott, 1963) (same); United States Steel Corp., 36 LA 385, 387 (Garrett, 1960); Nickles Bakery, 33 LA 564, 566–67 (Duff, 1959). *Cf.* Air Force Logistics Command, 90 LA 481 (Koven, 1988) (disallowing recoupment by withholding but not ruling out other methods of collecting); Borg-Warner Corp., 40 LA 442, 444 (Willingham, 1963) (no recoupment permitted). Permitting recoupment of overpayment caused by Bureau of Labor Statistics error in consumer price index, see *Kennecott Copper Corp.*, 69 LA 52, 59 (Platt, 1977); *Kaiser Aluminum & Chem. Corp.*, 68 LA 970, 973 (Roberts, 1977); not permitting recoupment, see *Food Employers Council*, 64 LA 862, 864 (Karasick, 1975).

[238A]*See* Department of the Navy, 70 LA 779, 783 (Margolin, 1978); Wooster Sportswear Co., 45 LA 1015, 1017–18 (Dworkin, 1965); J.I. Holcomb Mfg. Co., 40 LA 91, 94 (Willingham, 1963); Raytheon Co., 39 LA 640, 642 (Pigors, 1962); United Eng'g & Foundry Co., 33 LA 333, 335 (Coleman, 1959). In *Valley-Todeco*, 75 LA 661, 664 (Anderson, 1980), recoupment was *required* under the circumstances involved. *But see* Hillman's, 32 LA 453, 458–59 (Drake, 1959).

[238B]*See* Golden Eagle Constr. Co., 109 LA 1057 (Miles, 1997) (higher rate in contract was mutual mistake determined by the parties' intent and actions, and the arbitrator was obligated to reform the agreement).

[239]Bay Meadows Racing Ass'n, 90 LA 770 (Christopher, 1988).

[240]Bouvier's Law Dictionary 3376 (8th ed. 1994).

The general principle of unjust enrichment is that one person should not be permitted to enrich himself unjustly at the expense of another, but the party so enriched should be required to make restitution for property or benefits received, where it is just and equitable, and where such action involves no violation or frustration of the law.[241]

In a number of cases, arbitrators have applied the doctrine.[242] However, the "unjustly at the expense of another" element is not always present when a person receives an apparent "windfall."

Thus, even though an employer was enriched by an employee's handiwork, the principle of unjust enrichment was not applied, and the employee's grievance was denied, because there was no proof of any fraud, duress, mistake, or other inequitable condition.[243] Similarly, an arbitrator upheld the right of a family to double insurance coverage by reason of separate insurance programs covering both spouses furnished by their separate employers. In the absence of a contractual provision to the contrary, the double family benefit was a legitimate result of the family's double employment.[244]

In other contexts, however, it may well be considered improper for an individual to secure double benefits for himself or herself. Such was the case where an employee secured unemployment compensation covering a period for which he also received workers' compensation.[245]

4. SCOPE OF ARBITRAL REMEDIES IN DISCIPLINE AND DISCHARGE CASES

A. Formulating a Remedy [LA CDI 100.559501; 118.801]

On finding that an employer did not have cause for discipline or discharge, arbitrators must formulate an appropriate remedy. The remedy to

---

[241]Cyclops Corp., 51 LA 613, 616 (Marshall, 1968) (also stating that reliance upon the doctrine "must be supported by clear and convincing evidence," which did not exist in that case).

[242]See Village Meats, 91 LA 1023, 1026 (Shanker, 1988); Aeolian Corp., 72 LA 1178, 1180 (Eyraud, Jr., 1979); General Tire & Rubber Co., 71 LA 813, 816 (Richman, 1978); Cudahy Packing Co., 51 LA 822, 835 (Somers, 1968); Memphis Publ'g Co., 48 LA 931, 933 (Cantor, 1967). In American Maize Prods. Co., 37 LA 673, 675 (Sembower, 1961), the employer was required to pay an employee under the "quantum meruit" principle for the value of services performed by the employee, where the employer knew of it and did nothing to halt the work. See also California State Univ., 91 LA 1079, 1082 (Jones, Jr., 1988); Stockton Unified Sch. Dist., 89 LA 754, 759 (Gallagher, 1987). Cf. McDonnell Douglas Helicopter Co., 93 LA 429, 433 (Cloke, 1989); City of Chi., Ill., 91 LA 1077, 1078 (Cox, 1988).

[243]Amherst Coal Co., 84 LA 1181 (Wren, 1985).

[244]Hawthorn-Mellody Farms, 52 LA 557, 560–61 (Kates, 1969). Accord Potlatch Forests, 51 LA 589, 592 (Williams, 1968); Columbus Plastic Prods., 67–1 ARB ¶8390 (Nichols, 1967); Goodyear Atomic Corp., 66–2 ARB ¶8567 (Seinsheimer, 1966). Cf. McDonnell Aircraft Corp., 68–1 ARB ¶6210 (Bothwell, 1967); Massachusetts Leather Mfrs. Ass'n, 41 LA 1321, 1322 (Wallen, 1962). For cases in which a "coordination of benefits" provision was present so as to prevent double benefits, see C.H. Stuart & Co., 54 LA 335, 337 (Shister, 1971); George L. Mesker Steel Corp., 47 LA 1142, 1149 (Klamon, 1967); Babcock & Wilcox Co., 39 LA 136, 138 (Uible, 1962); Minnesota Mining & Mfg. Co., 38 LA 245, 248 (Graff, 1962). For cases involving the scope of coverage where both spouses are employed by the same company, see Union Welding Co., 49 LA 612, 612 (Blistein, 1967); Minnesota Mining & Mfg. Co., 32 LA 843, 847 (Thompson, 1959).

[245]National Union Elec. Corp., 77 LA 815, 818–19 (Traynor, 1981). See also Bethlehem Steel Corp., 73 LA 264, 266 (Strongin, 1979); Louisiana-Pacific Corp., 68 LA 638, 643–44 (Kenaston, 1977); Consolidated Aluminum Corp., 62 LA 480, 481 (Williams, 1974).

be fashioned will be fact-specific, dependent on the terms of the labor agreement, the subject matter giving rise to the discipline, as well as other factors, including aggravating and mitigating circumstances.

Courts have upheld an arbitrator's consideration of mitigating factors in determining whether there is just cause for discharge unless the collective bargaining agreement clearly and unambiguously prohibits the arbitrator from doing so.[246] Courts will not hesitate in setting aside an arbitrator's decision, however, when the language of the collective bargaining agreement prohibits the arbitrator from fashioning remedies once "just cause" for an employer's action is found.[247] Post-discharge misconduct also can be a factor when formulating a remedy. Arbitrators have regarded aggressive post-discharge behavior as rendering the discharged employee unfit for further employment.[248]

The traditional remedies used by arbitrators in discipline and discharge cases are reinstatement and conditional reinstatement, back pay, reducing discipline when the penalty is too severe for the offense, execution of last-chance agreements, and specially formulated remedies used in drug and alcohol abuse cases, sexual harassment cases, and cases involving violation of an employee's procedural rights.

As set forth above, in some instances the arbitrator will remand the case to the parties for them to negotiate a remedy.[249]

The more common remedies utilized by arbitrators in modifying managerial actions in discharge and discipline cases have been summarized as follows:

i. Reducing the Penalty Imposed [LA CDI 100.559565]

Arbitrators also may reduce the penalty imposed by management if, given the facts of the case, including the grievant's seniority and work record, it is

---

[246]Teamsters Local 968 v. Sysco Food Servs., 838 F.2d 794, 127 LRRM 2925 (5th Cir. 1988); Industrial Mut. Ass'n v. Amalgamated Workers Local 383, 725 F.2d 406, 115 LRRM 2503, 2507 (6th Cir. 1984); Lynchburg Foundry Co. v. Steelworkers Local 2556, 404 F.2d 259, 261 (4th Cir. 1968); Teamsters Local 330 v. Elgin Eby-Brown Co., 670 F. Supp. 1393, 127 LRRM 2950 (N.D. Ill. 1987); GSX Corp. of Mo. v. Teamsters Local 610, 658 F. Supp. 124, 127 LRRM 2391 (E.D. Mo. 1987); Hilton Int'l Co. v. Union de Trabajadores de la Industria Gastronomica de P.R., 600 F. Supp. 1446, 119 LRRM 2011 (D.P.R. 1985).

[247]Container Prods. v. Steelworkers, 873 F.2d 818, 131 LRRM 2623 (5th Cir. 1989); Georgia-Pacific Corp. v. Paperworkers Local 27, 864 F.2d 940, 130 LRRM 2208 (1st Cir. 1988); S.D. Warren v. Paperworkers, 846 F.2d 827, 128 LRRM 2432 (1st Cir. 1988); S.D. Warren v. Paperworkers, 845 F.2d 3, 128 LRRM 2175 (1st Cir. 1988); Tootsie Roll Indus. v. Bakery, Confectionery, & Tobacco Workers Local 1, 832 F.2d 81, 126 LRRM 2700 (7th Cir. 1987); Dobbs, Inc. v. Teamsters Local 614, 813 F.2d 85, 124 LRRM 2827 (6th Cir. 1987) (the U.S. Court of Appeals for the Sixth Circuit, applying the plain-meaning rule, found the arbitrator exceeded his authority by ordering reinstatement with back pay when the contract plainly and unambiguously recognized the employer's right to discharge employees for proper cause); Pennsylvania v. Independent State Stores Union, 553 A.2d 948, 130 LRRM 2780 (Pa. 1989).

[248]Jackson Gen. Hosp., 113 LA 1040, 1047 (Sharpe, 2000) (grievant's failure to deny post-discharge threatening statements to coworker made reinstatement inappropriate).

[249]Clark County, Nev., 114 LA 1608 (Silver, 2000); Anaconda Cmty. Hosp. & Nursing Home of Anaconda, 114 LA 132 (Pool, 2000); Department of the Navy, 113 LA 1065 (Gentile, 2000); USS, Div. of USX Corp., 113 LA 939 (Das, 1999); San Francisco, Cal., Unified Sch. Dist., 113 LA 140 (Bogue, 2000); Los Angeles County, Cal., Metro. Transp. Auth. (MTA), 108 LA 301, 304–05 (Gentile, 1997); American Red Cross, 104 LA 68 (Garrett, 1995).

clearly out of line with generally accepted industrial standards of discipline. The oft-included language denying the arbitrator the power to "[a]dd or subtract from or modify any of the terms of" the agreement does not preclude arbitral discretion to reduce the penalty imposed.[250]

If a penalty of discharge is modified through arbitration, the award will typically order a "make-whole" remedy such as reinstatement of the employee,[251] either with back pay,[252] without back pay,[253] or with partial back pay,[254] and often will further order that other rights and privileges remain unimpaired. The arbitrator may also commute the discharge to a suspension for a specified period,[255] or even to a reduced penalty of only a reprimand or warning.[256]

Where a penalty of suspension assessed by management is upset through arbitration, the award will usually either void the suspension completely, sometimes substituting a reprimand or warning, or will simply reduce the length of time the employee is to be deemed suspended.[257] In any event, the make-whole remedy, including back pay, will be ordered consistent with the shortened or eliminated period of suspension.

ii.   Back-Pay Awards [LA CDI 100.559505; 118.806]

1. *Back Pay Awarded, But Not Reinstatement.* Infrequently, an arbitrator may award back pay, but not reinstate the grievant because of other considerations. One arbitrator, who found an employee discharged without just cause for leaving her post, awarded back pay but not reinstatement because the grievant lied on her application for unemployment benefits and at the arbitration hearing.[258] "The employer-employee relationship has clearly deteriorated to the point where it is no longer viable because the Grievant cannot be trusted."[259] Other arbitrators have awarded back pay, but not reinstatement in similar situations.[260]

---

[250]Lima Elec. Co., 63 LA 94, 97 (Albrechta, 1974).

[251]Michigan Dep't of Corr., 102 LA 280 (VanAuken-Haight, 1993) (discharge reduced to 5-day suspension with seniority and back pay).

[252]UPMC Presbyterian, 114 LA 986 (Bernhardt, 2000) (discharge commuted to reinstatement with unpaid suspension).

[253]Toledo Edison, 104 LA 933 (Shanker, 1995) (discharge reduced to suspension without back pay); Yellow Freight Sys., 103 LA 731 (Stix, 1994) (same).

[254]Burlington N. R.R., 101 LA 144 (Massey, 1993) (partial back pay, where employee was responsible for the delay in arbitration).

[255]Blue Cross/Blue Shield, 104 LA 634 (House, 1995) (discharge commuted to reinstatement with unpaid suspension).

[256]Kimberly-Clark Corp., 107 LA 554 (Byars, 1996) (reinstatement and penalty reduced to written warning).

[257]Oak Forest, Ill., Hosp. of Cook County, 114 LA 115 (Wolff, 2000) (29-day suspension reduced to 15-day suspension).

[258]Rexam Graphics, 111 LA 1176, 1185–86 (Gangle, 1998).

[259]*Id.* at 1186.

[260]In *Food & Commercial Workers Local 7*, 114 LA 274, 279 (Watkins, 1999), the arbitrator offered the union a choice between rehiring a staffer it discharged or modifying his termination to a voluntary separation with 4 months' pay where the working relationship between the parties deteriorated, making it virtually impossible to be productive. *See also* Safeway Stores, 64 LA 563 (Gould, 1975).

2. *Reductions in Back Pay for Employee Fault.* Arbitrators will reduce an award of back pay to ensure that the make-whole remedy does not penalize the employer and sufficiently warns the grievant that his or her misconduct should not be repeated. Arbitrators also reduce or deny back pay because of an employee's dishonesty, even after discharge.[261] Where an employee deliberately conceals his or her interim earnings, arbitrators have reduced the award of back pay.[262]

iii. Reinstatement of Discharged Employee
[LA CDI 100.559501 et seq.; 118.801 et seq.]

Reinstatement of a discharged employee may be awarded, but with significant limitations, such as the following:

1. *Loss of seniority.* Some employees have been ordered reinstated but not credited with any seniority for the period between discharge and reinstatement.[263] Loss of all or part of seniority that had accrued prior to the discharge is also a possibility.[264]
2. *Loss of other benefits under the agreement.* In denying seniority credit for the period between discharge and reinstatement, arbitrators have also prohibited the accumulation of other agreement-provided benefits during this period.[265]

---

[261]Lockheed Martin Space Sys. Co., 114 LA 481, 482 (Gentile, 2000) (employee discharged without cause for sexual harassment reinstated without back pay, where he showed poor judgment telling female employee she was "beautiful" and another that "I could stare at you all day"); Panhandle E. Pipeline Co., 88 LA 725 (Yarowsky, 1987) (arbitrator halved back pay on the theory of "comparative fault").

[262]Lithibar Matik, 112 LA 957 (Sugerman, 1999).

[263]City of Massillon, Ohio, 92 LA 1303, 1305 (Elkin, 1989); City of Tampa, Fla., 92 LA 256, 258 (Rains, 1989); Burton Mfg. Co., 82 LA 1228 (Holley, Jr., 1984). *See also* Masonite Corp., 80 LA 815, 825 (Ruben, 1983); Montgomery Ward & Co., 80 LA 321, 326 (Dobry, 1983); Bisbee Hosp. Ass'n, 79 LA 977, 978 (Weizenbaum, 1982); J.T. Baker Chem. Co., 79 LA 689, 693 (Sloane, 1982); Stylemaster, Inc., 79 LA 76, 79 (Winton, 1982); Renaissance Ctr. P'ship, 76 LA 379, 386 (Daniel, 1981); Ethyl Corp., 74 LA 953, 958 (Hart, 1980); George A. Hormel & Co., 71 LA 1090, 1095 (Wyman, 1978); Weirton Steel Div., 71 LA 1082, 1084 (Kates, 1978); Western Auto Supply Co., 71 LA 710, 716 (Ross, 1978); Delta Concrete Prods. Co., 71 LA 538, 543 (Bailey, 1978); Aeronca, Inc., 71 LA 452, 454 (Smith, Jr., 1978); Furr's, Inc., 70 LA 1036, 1041 (Gorsuch, 1978); Global Assocs., 68 LA 1300, 1305 (Marcus, 1977); Gamble Bros., 68 LA 72, 75 (Krislov, 1977); Intalco Aluminum Co., 68 LA 66, 67 (LaCugna, 1977); Safeway Stores, 65 LA 1177, 1182 (Smith, 1975). In *Warner & Swasey Co.*, 71 LA 158, 161 (Siegel, 1978), the employee lost seniority but it could be regained by meeting a specified condition. Under a strike settlement agreement, economic strikers did not acquire any seniority for the period of the strike. Reden Corp., 50 LA 413, 414 (Roberts, 1968).

[264]*See* Cincinnati Gas & Elec. Co., 90 LA 841, 843 (Katz, chair, 1988); Atlantic Parachute Corp., 19 LA 437, 439 (Copelof, 1952); American Car & Foundry Co., 10 LA 324, 335 (Hilpert, 1948); Sears, Roebuck & Co., 6 LA 211, 213 (Cheney, 1946). *See also* Duval Sulphur & Potash Co., 21 LA 560, 565 (Merrill, 1953); Aleo Mfg. Co., 15 LA 715, 725 (Jaffee, 1950); Pennsylvania Greyhound Lines, 3 LA 880, 884 (Brandschain, 1946) (temporary loss of accrued seniority). *Contra* Lone Star Steel Co., 30 LA 519, 527 (Kelliher, 1958).

[265]Moss Supermarket, 99 LA 408 (Grupp, 1992) (employee who was constructively discharged, reinstated with only half pay due to her refusal to accept different job); City of Massillon, Ohio, 92 LA 1303, 1305 (Elkin, 1989); Binswanger Glass Co., 92 LA 1153 (Nicholas, Jr., 1989); Rustco Prods. Co., 92 LA 1048 (Watkins, 1989); City of Tampa, Fla., 92 LA 256 (Rains, 1989); Meyer Prods., 91 LA 690 (Dworkin, 1988); Sahara Coal Co., 89 LA 1257 (O'Grady, 1987); Northwest Airlines, 89 LA 943 (Nicolau, 1984); Mare Island Naval Ship-

3. *Probation or final warning.* Some discharged employees have been
reinstated on a probationary basis, with the probationary conditions
and the probationary periods varying from award to award,[266] or
with a final warning that any repetition of the offense will justify
immediate discharge.[267]

4. *Reinstatement conditioned on some special act or promise by the
employee.* Reinstatement has been ordered on the condition that the
employee resign an outside job,[268] agree to avoid further unauthorized
absences,[269] sign an agreement promising to comply with company
safety rules,[270] lose weight and quit smoking cigarettes,[271] provide
an updated medical report setting forth his or her medical restrictions

---

yard, 89 LA 861 (Wilcox, 1987); Delta Air Lines, 89 LA 408 (Kahn, 1987); Georgia-Pacific
Corp., 88 LA 244 (Byars, 1987); Philips Indus., 87 LA 1122 (Rezler, 1986); Olin Corp., 86 LA
1096 (Seidman, 1986); G. Heileman Brewing Co., 83 LA 829 (Hilgert, 1984); American Packaging Corp., 83 LA 369 (Laybourne, 1984); Burton Mfg. Co., 82 LA 1228 (Holley, Jr., 1984).

[266]County of Hennepin, Minn., 105 LA 391 (Imes, 1995) (probationary reinstatement with
back pay while employer trains employee); Anchorage, Alaska, Sch. Dist., 105 LA 281 (Tilbury,
1995) (probationary reinstatement without back pay while employee completes anger management sessions); Town of Cromwell, Conn., 101 LA 388 (Stewart, 1993) (suspension of
police officer reduced to written warning and probation while employee undergoes training
for drawing firearms); Store Kraft Mfg. Co., 100 LA 666, 671 (Bailey, 1993); Murcole, Inc., 99
LA 378, 381–82 (Darrow, 1992) (6 months' strict probation); SK Hand Tool Corp., 98 LA 643,
648 (Hodgson, 1992) (30 days' probation); Payless Stores, 95 LA 1, 6–7 (Yarowsky, 1990)
(grievant to be given 6 months to try to meet employer's standards); Duquesne Light Co., 90
LA 696 (Probst, 1988) (6 months' probation); San Francisco, Cal., Bd. of Supervisors, 90 LA
469 (Riker, 1988) (1-year probation); S.E. Rykoff & Co., 90 LA 233 (Angelo, 1987) (same);
Sanford Corp., 89 LA 968 (Wies, 1987) (same); Philips Indus., 87 LA 1122 (Rezler, 1986) (6
months' probation); Drexel Univ., 85 LA 579 (Kramer, 1985) (90 days' probation); Golden
Eagle Distribs., 85 LA 279 (D'Spain, 1985) (1-year probation).

[267]Washington Dep't of Printing, 98 LA 440, 443 (Griffin, 1992); San Francisco Newspa-
per Agency, 93 LA 322 (Koven, 1989) (discharge for filing spurious overtime claim reduced to
final warning subject to suspension or discharge for any future rule violation); GTE Fla., 92
LA 1090 (Cohen, 1989); U.C. Agric. Prods. Co., 89 LA 432 (Anderson, 1987); University of
Cincinnati, 89 LA 388 (Wren, 1987); Internal Revenue Serv., 89 LA 59 (Gallagher, 1987);
U.S. Plywood Corp., 88 LA 275 (Mathews, 1986); Food Mktg. Corp., 88 LA 98 (Doering, 1986);
Lockheed Corp., 83 LA 1018 (Taylor, 1984); Pittsburgh Testing Lab., 83 LA 159 (Herrick,
1984). Where parties had agreed to reinstatement of an employee on probation or with a
final warning, such agreement was strictly enforced (i.e., subsequent discharge for breach of
the probation or conditions of final warning sustained). McDonnell Douglas Corp., 79 LA 34,
36 (Blum, 1982); Kaiser Steel Corp., 73 LA 956, 958 (Randall, 1979); Crown Cork & Seal Co.,
73 LA 896, 898–99 (Dash, Jr., 1979); Wolpin Co., 69 LA 589, 594 (Burwell, 1977).

[268]Climate Control/McQuay, 89 LA 1062 (Cromwell, 1987) (employee to resign from second job within 2 weeks); Kansas City Star Co., 12 LA 1202, 1206 (Ridge, 1949). *See also* John
Deere Tractor Co., 4 LA 161, 163, 166 (Updegraff, 1946).

[269]Ohio Lime Co., 96 LA 38 (Bressler, 1990) (reinstatement conditioned on employee submitting medical fitness certificate and agreeing that similar unauthorized absence may result in termination).

[270]Bunker Hill Co., 43 LA 1253, 1256 (Luckerath, 1964). *See also* Colt Indus., 71 LA 22,
27 (Rutherford, 1978). In *International Harvester Co.*, 53 LA 1197, 1202–03 (Seinsheimer,
1969), the condition required two employees to sign an agreement stating that they would
not threaten or molest each other or any other employee, and that violation of the agreement
would subject them to immediate discharge.

[271]Taystee Bread Co., 52 LA 677, 680 (Purdom, 1969) (the arbitrator was given broad
latitude as to the remedy). *See also* Reynolds Metals Co., 71 LA 1099, 1102 (Bothwell, 1978).

for determining job placement,[272] accept some kind of counseling,[273] or comply with some other specified condition.[274]

5. *Written waiver required.* Where the collective bargaining agreement arguably might have required back pay in the event of reinstatement after discharge, a condition to reinstatement was imposed in the form of a requirement that the employee agree in writing to waive certain conditions or back pay.[275]

6. *Reinstatement conditioned on proof of mental or physical fitness.* Employees discharged for misconduct somehow connected with physical or psychological disability sometimes have been ordered reinstated on the condition that they be physically and/or mentally fit for the job as determined by physicians or psychiatrists, as the case may be.[276] Arbitrators may reinstate an employee on the condition that the employee is placed on disability leave if the arbitrator is unsure whether the employee is fit to return to work.[277]

---

[272]Sherwin-Williams Co., 113 LA 1184 (Statham, 2000).

[273]Flushing Cmty. Sch., 100 LA 444, 449–50 (Daniel, 1992) (grievant ordered to undergo counseling prior to return to work and to continue counseling after return to work for as long as needed); Lakeside Jubilee Foods, 95 LA 358, 367 (Berquist, 1990) (grievant ordered to undergo counseling for 8 months); Rustco Prods. Co., 92 LA 1048 (Watkins, 1989) (employee to complete a program of counseling in race relations at his own expense); Lever Bros. Co., 87 LA 260 (Traynor, 1986) (consult with psychiatrist, be evaluated, and submit to treatment).

[274]East Liverpool, Ohio, Bd. of Educ., 105 LA 161 (Duda, Jr., 1995) (discharge for $1.00 theft reduced to suspension if employee admits responsibility and promises no further misconduct); Laidlaw Transit, 104 LA 302 (Concepcion, 1995) (reinstatement of employee suffering from depression on agreement to take medicine as prescribed); Chardon Rubber Co., 97 LA 750, 753 (Hewitt, 1991) (grievant ordered to sign apology to be placed on company bulletin board); Federal Bureau of Prisons, 91 LA 276 (Statham, 1988) (employee to offer official and personal apology for his racial comment and to thank fellow employee for his restraint and control during incident); U.S. Postal Serv., 89 LA 1269 (Talmadge, 1985) (attend Gamblers Anonymous meetings and not gamble).

[275]International Harvester Co., 2 LA 158, 163 (Gilden, 1946). *See also* Lone Star Steel Co., 30 LA 519, 528 (Kelliher, 1958). For other attached conditions in the general nature of a waiver, see *United Parcel Serv.*, 78 LA 836, 842 (McAllister, 1982) (employee must affirm in writing his or her understanding that the award holds that a certain work procedure is not unsafe); *Apollo Merchandisers Corp.*, 70 LA 614, 620 (Roumell, Jr., 1978) (reinstatement was conditioned on retention of information in the employee's file for a longer period than permitted by the literal language of the agreement); *New York State Dep't of Corr. Servs.*, 69 LA 344, 350–51 (Kornblum, 1977) (employee must waive in writing the right as a peace officer to carry firearms while off duty).

[276]City of Akron, Ohio, 105 LA 787 (Kasper, 1995) (employee who requested demotion due to health to be reinstated on submission of evidence of mental and physical ability to perform); Cessna Aircraft Co., 104 LA 985 (Thornell, 1995) (reinstatement conditioned on passing a functional capacity exam); General Mills, 99 LA 143 (Stallworth, 1992) (employee suffering from seasonal depression disorder conditionally reinstated; mutually selected physician to determine fitness for duty, parties to agree on plan to reasonably accommodate employee without undue hardship on employer); Kansas City Area Transp. Auth., 98 LA 57, 65 (Cohen, 1991); James River Corp., 96 LA 1174 (McDonald, 1991) (employee suffering anxiety and depression reinstated on clearance from treating psychologist and employer's medical expert); Firestone Tire & Rubber Co., 93 LA 381 (Cohen, 1989); Delta-Macon Brick & Tile Co., 92 LA 837 (O'Grady, 1989); Westinghouse Elec. Corp., 91 LA 685 (Talarico, 1988); Pacific Bell, 91 LA 653 (Kaufman, 1988); S.E. Rykoff & Co., 90 LA 233 (Angelo, 1987); U.C. Agric. Prods. Co., 89 LA 432 (Anderson, 1987); Alton Packaging Corp., 83 LA 1318 (Talent, 1984). Sometimes reinstatement has been similarly conditioned where the employee had been discharged for alleged physical disability (*see* Habuda Coal & Supply Co., 53 LA 334, 338 (Teple, 1969)), or for poor workmanship connected with the employee's physical condition (*see* New Tronics Corp., 46 LA 365, 368–69 (Kates, 1966)).

[277]East Ohio Gas Co., 91 LA 366, 374 (Dworkin, 1988).

7. *Reinstatement conditioned on the employee's not holding union office.* Under the circumstances of some cases, the arbitrator has concluded that the discharged employee should be reinstated, but only on the condition that the employee be disqualified from holding union office permanently or for a stated period.[278]

8. *Reinstatement to a different job.* In disciplinary discharge cases where the arbitrator concludes that the grievant should be reinstated, but some strong reason exists for denying reinstatement to the former job (e.g., the employee's physical condition, a need for screening from contact with the public, or personality conflicts), reinstatement may be ordered to some other job that does not involve the conditions or impediments responsible for the disqualification from the former job.[279] In one case, an employee who had been discharged for engaging in a slowdown was ordered reinstated, but with the proviso that the company could place him on any job it might wish.[280]

Reinstatement can be problematic when the grievant's former position has been eliminated.[281] It has been recommended that a

---

[278]Freeman Decorating Co., 108 LA 887 (Baroni, 1997) (employee who had disrupted construction work while acting as shop steward prohibited from serving as steward in the future). *See* Devon Apparel, 85 LA 645, 646 (Rock, 1985); Inglis Ltd., 66 LA 812, 818 (Shime, 1976); Consolidated Edison Co. of N.Y., 54 LA 488, 492 (Crowley, 1971); Lawndale Indus., 46 LA 220, 224 (McGury, 1966); Phillips Petroleum Co., 33 LA 103, 107–08 (Hayes, 1959); Lockheed Aircraft Serv., 32 LA 690, 695 (Phelps, 1959) (the award was modified in *Arterberry v. Lockheed Aircraft Serv.*, 33 LA 292, 293 (Cal. Super. Ct. 1959), by striking the condition against holding union office); Bauman Bros. Furniture Mfg. Co., 10 LA 79, 83 (Miller, 1948); Johnson-Stephens & Shinkle Shoe Co., 7 LA 422, 424 (Klamon, 1947); Sinclair Ref. Co., 6 LA 965, 968 (Whiting, 1947). In *Kankakee Elec. Steel Co.*, 53 LA 178, 184 (Sembower, 1969), the arbitrator stated that he lacked authority to tell the union whom it might choose as representatives, but he did "recommend that the Grievant not be given further duties as a grievanceman." Another arbitrator twice imposed the penalty of disqualification from holding union office, once for which he was commended and once for which he was castigated. *See* Whiting, *Arbitration and the Remedy Power: Discussion*, *in* Labor Arbitration and Industrial Change, Proceedings of the 16th Annual Meeting of NAA 70, 73 (Kahn ed., BNA Books 1963). Use of this remedy has been questioned. Crane, *The Use and Abuse of Arbitral Power*, *in* Labor Arbitration at the Quarter-Century Mark, Proceedings of the 25th Annual Meeting of NAA 66, 75 (Dennis & Somers eds., BNA Books 1973); Kearns, *Comment*, *id.* at 87.

[279]Bonar Packaging, 112 LA 370 (Moore, 1999) (senior operator reinstated to lower position due to work-related transgressions); Summit County, Ohio, Bd. of Mental Retardation & Developmental Disabilities, 100 LA 4 (Dworkin, 1992) (reassignment of teacher accused of sexual misconduct conditioned on psychological finding of fitness); Eastwood Printing Co., 99 LA 957 (Winograd, 1992) (employee placed on medical leave after sustaining temporary disability reinstated to a prior position he had held in the past so as not to displace employee who replaced him); Kaiser Permanente, 99 LA 490 (Henner, 1992) (discharge reduced to suspension and transfer to more suitable position, where absenteeism was due to seizures); Colonial Sch. Dist., 96 LA 1122 (DiLauro, 1991) (suspension and transfer to different bus route for driver accused of making improper advances toward female passengers); Transit Auth. of River City, Louisville, Ky., 95 LA 137, 147–48 (Dworkin, 1990); International Paper Co., 94 LA 409 (Mathews, 1990) (transfer in lieu of termination for employee suffering permanent partial disability); Sanford Corp., 89 LA 968 (Wies, 1987) (1-year probation); Weyerhaeuser Co., 88 LA 270 (Kapsch, 1987); Social Sec. Admin., 84 LA 1100 (Weinstein, 1985).

[280]Dirilyte Co. of Am., 18 LA 882, 884 (Ferguson, 1952); Armstrong Tire & Rubber Co., 18 LA 544, 548–50 (Ralston, 1952).

[281]In *City of Kittitas, Wash.*, 108 LA 833, 840 (Smith, 1997), the arbitrator reinstated an improperly discharged public works employee to the same or substantially similar position, with back pay calculated as amount the employee's rate was until the date the position was abolished, after which back pay was the rate the replacement was paid.

grievant may fare better when management is ordered to "reinstate [the grievant] to employment" as opposed to being "reinstated to his former position."[282]

9. *Last-Chance Agreements.* Arbitrators may reinstate a discharged grievant on condition that the employee sign a "last-chance agreement,"[283] which typically provides that any further infraction within a defined period will automatically result in the termination of employment.

10. *Other Uncommon Remedies.* Still other infrequently used remedies have been tailored by arbitrators to fit the circumstances of the particular discharge or discipline case.[284] Some of these variations

---

[282]*See* The Common Law of the Workplace: The Views of Arbitrators 340 (St. Antoine ed., BNA Books 1998).

[283]Anchor Hocking Glass Co., 114 LA 1334 (Hewitt, 2000) (employee charged with early quitting reinstated with a 2-year last-chance agreement); Borden Italian Foods Co., 113 LA 13 (Marino, 1999); City of Las Vegas, Nev., Hous. Auth., 112 LA 259, 263 (Monat, 1999); Montgomery County, Md., Gov't, 109 LA 513, 518 (Hockenberry, 1997) (discharged employee reinstated with last-chance agreement); Zeon Chems. Ky., 105 LA 648, 654 (Wren, 1995) (conditional last-chance agreement designed and imposed to guarantee employee never again loses temper); Copperweld Steel Co., 103 LA 719 (Duda, Jr., 1994) (reinstated with last-chance probation for 3 years regarding absenteeism problem). For related discussion, see Chapter 15, section 3.F.iii., "Last-Chance Agreements."

[284]Public Util. Dist. No. 1, Clark County, Wash., 103 LA 1066 (Paull, 1994) (written warning for active participants in improper work stoppage, oral warning for passive participants); Hendrickson Turner Co., 101 LA 919 (Dworkin, 1993) (discharge changed to voluntary quit under last-chance agreement); Veterans Affairs Med. Ctr., 99 LA 951 (Fowler, 1992) (union ordered to publish correction in its newsletter following derogatory article about supervisor); Ashtabula County, Ohio, Bd. of Mental Retardation & Developmental Disabilities, 94 LA 303 (Sharpe, 1990) (employer ordered to provide more information showing basis for supervisor's conclusions regarding employee's performance); Union-Tribune Publ'g Co., 93 LA 617, 618 (McBrearty, 1989) (discharge upheld for possession of drugs but employee entitled to severance pay, which may be withheld only for "gross misconduct or for willful neglect of duty," and employee's addiction rendered conduct not "willful"); Rustco Prods. Co., 92 LA 1048 (Watkins, 1989) (employer may bar employee driver from bidding on a route that would require delivery to particular customer, where employee used racial epithet and vulgar language on dock); Rohm & Haas Tex., 92 LA 850 (Allen, Jr., 1989) (employee can be promoted only at the sole discretion of management); Cincinnati Gas & Elec. Co., 90 LA 841 (Katz, 1988) (no opportunity to be promoted to any job with significant customer contact); Boise Cascade Corp., 90 LA 791 (Nicholas, Jr., 1988) (company directed to allow grievant to engage in drug rehabilitation and to reinstate him when completed); City of Pomona, Cal., 90 LA 457 (Rule, 1988) (remand to grievance procedure); U.S. Postal Serv., 89 LA 1269 (Talmadge, 1985) (60-day medical leave of absence); Peoples' Gas Light & Coke Co., 89 LA 786, 795 (Smith, 1987) (parties to negotiate "reinstatement agreement"); Morton Thiokol, Inc., 89 LA 572 (Nicholas, Jr., 1987) (to qualify for back pay, grievant must submit affidavit to company disclosing all income received during his interim discharge period); Northwest Airlines, 89 LA 268 (Flagler, 1987) (employer may withhold grievant from flight assignments and offer grievant option of referral to chemical dependency diagnosis, or termination); Kansas Power & Light Co., 87 LA 867 (Belcher, 1986) (amount of back pay to be reduced if grievant did not earnestly seek other employment during period of termination to mitigate damages); Nuodex, Inc., 87 LA 256 (Millious, 1986) (grievant to submit medical report); Harbor Furniture Mfg. Co., 85 LA 359 (Richman, 1985) (employee reinstated with 85% back pay).

include forced apologies,[285] unrecorded suspension,[286] and treating the grievant's mental anguish as a penalty.[287]

11. *Remedies for Procedural Violations.* Arbitrators have upheld the imposition of discipline on an employee, but nevertheless have found the employee entitled to a back-pay remedy because the employer failed to comply with a procedural or due process requirement,[288] or to conduct a proper investigation.[289] When such management errors do not require the overturning of a discharge, the options utilized by arbitrators have included back pay from the date of the grievance to the date of the arbitral award because the employer violated its discharge procedure;[290] 1 week's back pay for failing to give notice;[291] back pay from the date of discharge to the date of the Step 2 grievance meeting, which was the first time the employee was afforded union representation;[292] back pay and benefits from the date of discharge to the day after the arbitration hearing because of failure to advise the employee of the specific charges prior to the discharge;[293] and 1 month's back pay for the employer's failure to obtain union representation before administering a drug test.[294]

B. Reinstatement in Drug and Alcohol Use Cases [LA CDI 118.815]

In cases where drug and/or alcohol use was a factor leading to discharge and the arbitrator has decided that reinstatement is appropriate,[295] a vari-

---

[285]AFG Indus., 110 LA 661 (Holley, Jr., 1998) (employee and supervisor must apologize to each other). *See* City of Berkeley, Cal., 93 LA 1161, 1166 (Riker, 1989) (employer to apologize to grievant and to award commendation); Stylemaster, Inc., 79 LA 76, 79 (Winton, 1982); Maust Transfer Co., 78 LA 780, 783 (LaCugna, 1982); St. Regis Paper Co., 75 LA 819, 822 (Rezler, 1980); Anaconda Aluminum Co., 59 LA 1147, 1150 (Erbs, 1972); Four Wheel Drive Auto Co., 20 LA 823, 826 (Rauch, 1953); Crawford Clothes, 19 LA 475, 481–82 (Kramer, 1952). But some arbitrators have spoken strongly against forced apologies. *See* Armstrong Cork Co., 38 LA 781, 784 (Jensen, 1962); General Cable Corp., 35 LA 381, 383 (Dworet, 1960); Reynolds Metals Co., 22 LA 528, 534 (Klamon, 1954). *See also* Veterans Admin. Med. Ctr., 81 LA 201, 213–14 (Imundo, Jr., 1983); Social Sec. Admin., 80 LA 46, 53 (Aronin, 1982).

[286]Fort Pitt Bridge Works, 30 LA 633, 635 (Lehoczky, 1958) (suspension was upheld, but all reference to it was ordered stricken from the employees' personnel records). *See also* Ironrite, Inc., 28 LA 394, 398 (Haughton, 1956).

[287]Dayton Steel Foundry Co., 29 LA 137, 142 (Young, 1957); Ashland Oil & Ref. Co., 28 LA 874, 878–79 (Bradley, 1957).

[288]Kroger Co., 108 LA 417 (Baroni, 1997) (reinstatement due to employers failure to provide due process protections); Webster Indus., 107 LA 147 (Statham, 1996) (same). For related discussion, see Chapter 15, section 3.F.ii., "Due Process and Procedural Requirements."

[289]Immigration & Naturalization Serv., 114 LA 872 (Neas, 2000) (failure to interview witnesses and determine grievant's guilt); Kodiak Elec. Ass'n, 104 LA 1112 (Peck, 1995) (reinstatement of employee due to improper investigation); Department of Agric., 93 LA 920 (Seidman, 1989).

[290]Poplar, Mont., Pub. Sch., Dist. 9 & 9B, 111 LA 863, 872 (Calhoun, 1999); Mason & Hanger-Silas Mason Co., 103 LA 371 (Cipolla, 1994).

[291]City of Akron, Ohio, 105 LA 787 (Kasper, 1995).

[292]Bi-State Dev. Agency, 96 LA 1090 (Cipolla, 1991).

[293]Chromalloy Am. Corp., 93 LA 828 (Woolf, 1989).

[294]Bi-State Dev. Agency, 105 LA 319 (Bailey, 1995).

[295]Dyncorp, 114 LA 458 (Kilroy, 2000) (improper discharge for alcohol odor without proof of impairment); Vons Cos., 106 LA 740 (Darrow, 1996) (employee's discharge for alcohol

ety of remedies have been formulated. In such cases, one or more of the following conditions is usually placed on the employee's reinstatement:

1. Employee must pass a drug and/or alcohol screen before returning to work.[296]
2. Employee must present evidence from a medical practitioner that he or she is able to return to work.[297]
3. Employee will be subject to random drug and/or alcohol testing for a period of time after returning to work.[298]
4. Employee is to receive treatment for substance abuse or is to attend meetings of a support group.[299]

When reinstatement is not deemed appropriate, other "less than make whole" remedies may be formulated in drug and alcohol cases.[300]

C. Reinstatement in Sexual Harassment Cases [LA CDI 118.815]

Remedies in sexual harassment cases have included: (1) ordering a supervisory employee to keep away from females "to the maximum extent," although the arbitrator lacked authority to require the employer to discipline the supervisor, order him to apologize, or award damages for pain and suffering;[301] (2) reinstating a teacher under a "no touching" agreement regarding female students;[302] (3) ordering an employer to investigate harassment and discrimination charges and report its findings;[303] (4) demoting the employee, but with back pay from the date of demotion to the date of arbitration because the employer failed to disclose the accusers' names until the

---

reduced to suspension); Chardon Rubber Co., 97 LA 750 (Hewitt, 1991) (discharge for insubordination and reporting to work under the influence of alcohol reduced to suspension if employee posts apology on bulletin board). For related discussion, see Chapter 13, section 17.F.iii., "Drug and Alcohol Policies," and section 26.F., "Drug and Alcohol Testing"; Chapter 14, section 7.D.xiv., "Drug Abuse as a Factor"; Chapter 16, section 2.A., "Alcohol and/or Drug Use and Testing"; Chapter 19, section 4., "Privacy, Search and Seizure Protection, and Compulsory Drug and Alcohol Testing"; and Chapter 21, section 2.C.ii., "Illicit Drug Use and Possession."

[296]Aeronca, Inc., 112 LA 1063, 1072 (Duda, Jr., 1999); Metropolitan Transit Auth., 94 LA 857 (Nicholas, Jr., 1990) (discharge for positive drug test reduced to conditional reinstatement including drug screening and rehabilitation); Aeronca, Inc., 93 LA 782, 789 (Doering, 1989); Southern Cal. Rapid Transit Dist., 93 LA 20, 24 (Christopher, 1989).

[297]City of Kankakee, Ill., 97 LA 564, 572 (Wolff, 1991); Ohio State Highway Patrol, 96 LA 613, 618 (Bittel, 1991).

[298]Aeronca, Inc., 112 LA 1063, 1072 (Duda, Jr., 1999); Aeroquip Corp., 95 LA 31, 33–34 (Stieber, 1990); Metropolitan Transit Auth., 94 LA 857, 861–62 (Nicholas, Jr., 1990) (grievant also required to pass physical exam and drug screen prior to return to work).

[299]Eaton Corp., 99 LA 331, 337 (Lewis, 1992); Metropolitan Transit Auth., 94 LA 857, 861–62 (Nicholas, Jr., 1990); Metropolitan Transit Auth., 93 LA 477, 479 (Allen, Jr., 1989) (employer not required to pay for treatment).

[300]Union-Tribune Publ'g Co., 93 LA 617, 618 (McBrearty, 1989) (discharge upheld for possession of drugs but employee entitled to severance pay, which may be withheld only for "gross misconduct or for willful neglect of duty," and employee's addiction rendered conduct not "willful").

[301]Union Camp Corp., 104 LA 295 (Nolan, 1995). For related discussion, see Chapter 10, section 3.A.i., "Title VII of the Civil Rights Act," and Chapter 17, section 7., "Protection Against Sexual Harassment."

[302]Pine Island, Minn., Indep. Sch. Dist. 255, 102 LA 993 (Daly, 1994).

[303]Great Lakes Naval Training Ctr., 102 LA 827 (Yaney, 1994).

hearing;[304] and (5) ordering the employer to post the terms of an arbitration award and to discuss sexual harassment with its employees.[305] Reinstatement from discharge in sexual harassment cases may be awarded without back pay.[306]

5. ARBITRAL REMEDIES IN SPECIFIC SITUATIONS

A. Improper Subcontracting [LA CDI 117.395]

In some cases, the arbitrator is asked only to rule on the permissibility of subcontracting, and opinion is limited as to whether past or contemplated subcontracting is sanctioned by the agreement.[307] An arbitrator who is called on to remedy improper subcontracting may select one or more forms of relief as justified by the particular case. Remedies have included: (1) an order prohibiting further subcontracting so long as bargaining-unit members are available to do the work, combined with a monetary award to unit members as restitution for lost earnings;[308] (2) an order that the employer cease and desist from subcontracting, but without monetary damages, because the subcontracting was done in good faith;[309] (3) an award of damages to the union where it was impossible to identify the individual workers who were displaced by the improper subcontracting;[310] (4) a make-whole order based on the number of hours charged by the subcontractor, rather than on the number of hours subcontractor employees actually worked;[311] and (5) a cease-and-desist order, but without any monetary award because the aggrieved employees had ample work.[312]

One arbitrator found that employees discharged as a result of improper subcontracting had a duty to mitigate their losses. However, the arbitrator also held that the back pay to be awarded should not be reduced by the amount of employment compensation received.[313]

---

[304]Renton, Wash., Sch. Dist., 102 LA 854 (Wilkinson, 1994).

[305]Rodeway Inn, 102 LA 1003 (Goldberg, 1994).

[306]Escalade Sports, 115 LA 311 (Allen, 2000).

[307]See, e.g., Mead Corp., 75 LA 665, 668 (Gross, 1980) (the grievant had left the company and the union sought "a ruling only on the Company's right to subcontract under the circumstances of this case"); West Va. Pulp & Paper Co., 51 LA 842, 849 (Seinsheimer, 1968); Sealtest Foods Div., 48 LA 797, 802 (Valtin, 1966).

[308]See American Crystal Sugar Co., 116 LA 916, 920 (Jacobowski, 2002) (where it was too impractical and/or disruptive for the employer to immediately terminate its relationship with the subcontractor, the arbitrator decided simply to preclude renewal of the subcontract; additionally, the employer was ordered to reimburse those laid-off employees who could have performed the subcontracted work (mud-trucking work)); USS, Div. of USX, 115 LA 1473, 1476 (Petersen, 2001); MSB Mfg. Co., 92 LA 841 (Bankston, 1989).

[309]Trane Co., 89 LA 1112 (McIntosh, 1987).

[310]Brutoco Eng'g Constr., 92 LA 33 (Ross, 1988). However, the union must present evidence of injury to employees. Northstar Fire Prot., 115 LA 1062 (Giblin, 2002).

[311]USS, Div. of USX Corp., 96 LA 867, 869 (Beilstein, 1991).

[312]USS/Kobe Steel Co., 98 LA 13, 15 (Amis, 1991).

[313]Builders Plumbing Supply, 95 LA 351, 353 (Briggs, 1990).

B. Improper Deprivation of "Work Opportunities" [LA CDI 117.395]

In some cases, the arbitrator is asked to decide only whether the agreement was violated by the assignment of bargaining-unit work to persons outside the unit.[314] Where the arbitrator also is called on to remedy the improper assignment of bargaining-unit work to outsiders, a frequently utilized remedy is a monetary award of damages to unit employees for lost work.[315] In some cases, the arbitrator has ordered the employer to cease and desist from the improper assignment[316] or has ordered the employer to assign the work to employees in the bargaining unit.[317] Of course, the circumstances of the particular case may justify yet other remedies, possibly to be used in combination with one or more of the foregoing remedies.[318]

C. Violation of Right to Overtime [LA CDI 117.3279]

Unquestionably the most frequently utilized remedy where an employee's contractual right to overtime work has been violated is a monetary award (generally at the overtime rate) for the overtime in question.[319] In some cases,

---

[314]*See* Smith's Food King, 76 LA 601, 601, 603 (Steinberg, 1981). For related discussion, see Chapter 13, section 16., "Assigning Work Out of the Bargaining Unit."

[315]*See* Louisville Cement Co., 79 LA 584, 587 (Archer, 1982); Tenneco Oil Co., 79 LA 336, 340 (Mann, 1982); Chromalloy-American Corp., 78 LA 324, 327 (Stix, 1982); GM&W Coal Co., 76 LA 665, 666 (Duff, 1981); Metropolitan Warehouse, 76 LA 14, 18 (Darrow, 1981); NCR-Worldwide Serv. Parts Ctr., 74 LA 224, 235–36 (Mathews, 1980); United Indus. Corp., 73 LA 480, 482 (Thomson, 1979); Roberts & Schaefer Co., 72 LA 624, 626 (Cantor, 1979); Board of Water Works, Pueblo, Colo., 71 LA 637, 647 (Aisenberg, 1978); Leavenworth Times, 71 LA 396, 411 (Bothwell, 1978). However, where no employee suffered damage as a result of the improper assignment, no damages were awarded in *Kahler Corp.*, 97 LA 895, 902–03 (Imes, 1991); *Michigan Dep't of Mgmt. & Budget*, 78 LA 1268, 1272 (Daniel, 1982); *Evergreen Indus.*, 76 LA 535, 540 (Beck, 1981); *Albany Steel & Iron Supply Co.*, 71 LA 1263, 1266 (Hazell, 1978); *Valley Camp Coal Co.*, 71 LA 267, 271 (Wren, 1978); *Beyerl Chevrolet*, 68 LA 343, 346 (Bolte, 1977). In *Celanese Fibers Co.*, 72 LA 271, 275 (Foster, 1979), damages were awarded to the union because "the company's behavior . . . lacked even a colorable excuse." For related discussion, see section 3., "Principles of Damages," above, and section 5.A., "Improper Subcontracting," above.

[316]*See* Tenneco Oil Co., 79 LA 336, 340 (Mann, 1982); Evergreen Indus., 76 LA 535, 540 (Beck, 1981); Wetterau Inc., 75 LA 540, 543 (May, 1980).

[317]*See* Bessire & Co., 77 LA 594, 599 (Sergent, 1981) (if the work is to be performed, it shall be assigned to the bargaining unit); Leavenworth Times, 71 LA 396, 411 (Bothwell, 1978); Valley Camp Coal Co., 71 LA 267, 271 (Wren, 1978). This remedy was denied, where granting it would have sacrificed efficiency without benefiting the bargaining unit. Label Processing Corp., 77 LA 352, 358 (Neufeld, 1981).

[318]For example, where employees had been downgraded in connection with the improper assignment of bargaining-unit work to persons outside the unit, one arbitrator ordered that the downgraded employees be reinstated to their former positions with back pay. Board of Water Works, Pueblo, Colo., 71 LA 637, 647 (Aisenberg, 1978).

[319]*See* Georgia-Pacific Corp., 93 LA 4, 5 (Thornell, 1989); ARCO Chem. Corp., 82 LA 146, 149 (Nicholas, 1984); Pope Maint., 78 LA 1157, 1160 (Yancy, 1981); Globe-Union, 78 LA 299, 302 (Tamoush, 1982); Dundee Cement Co., 77 LA 884, 888 (Ross, 1981); Dayton-Walther Corp., 77 LA 853, 854 (Modjeska, 1981); Overhead Door Corp., 77 LA 619, 622 (Herrick, 1981); Zachary Confections, 77 LA 464, 467 (Epstein, 1981); Inland Container Corp., 74 LA 110, 115 (Boals, 1980); Colt Indus. Operating Corp., 73 LA 1087, 1091–92 (Belshaw, 1979); ASG Indus., 70 LA 1225, 1229 (Cantor, 1978); Donn Prods., 70 LA 430, 432 (Siegel, 1978); Southern Can Co., 68 LA 1183, 1191 (Jedel, 1977); Martin-Brower Co., 67 LA 778, 780 (Fields, 1976); Alabama Metal Indus. Corp., 66 LA 1065, 1067 (King, 1976). One arbitrator empha-

however, arbitrators have considered makeup overtime within a reasonable time to be the appropriate remedy.[320]

In using the makeup overtime remedy, one arbitrator stated that, in the absence of specific contract language, a monetary award for violation of overtime rights must be based on a "clearly established past practice or upon a showing that the grievant-claimant actually did suffer damages rather than temporary postponement of an overtime work opportunity."[321]

In contrast, one arbitrator declared, in *John Deere Dubuque Tractor Works*,[322] that the only proper remedy for violation of overtime rights is a monetary award:

> Offering an employee an opportunity to make up improperly lost hours at a later date is not an adequate remedy. He is entitled to work those hours at the time they are available, to know when he may expect his turn, and not be expected to work at some time more convenient to the employer, or at the personal whim of a foreman.
>
> . . .
>
> The one sure way of putting an end to foremen's inadvertent errors, or their favoritism in making overtime assignments under the round-robin system, is to hold the Company liable for these breaches of contract by awarding pay to the employee who failed to get his proper assignment.[323]

In this case, the improper overtime assignment had been made to an employee within the overtime equalization unit. However, some arbitrators would consider makeup overtime to be the preferred remedy where the im-

---

sized that a monetary award is the only proper remedy if the alternative remedy of makeup overtime would unjustly and adversely affect either the grievant or any other employee. Giant Tiger Super Stores Co., 43 LA 1243, 1246 (Kates, 1965). For a case involving the determination of compensation for an incentive employee's loss of an overtime opportunity, see *Joy Mfg. Co.*, 77 LA 683, 687–89 (Richard, 1981). For related discussion, see Chapter 13, section 14., "Overtime."

[320]*See* Lithonia Lighting, 89 LA 781, 783–86 (Chandler, 1987); Price Bros. Co., 76 LA 10, 13 (Shanker, 1980) (in the absence of "special circumstances" justifying a monetary award, makeup overtime is the more equitable remedy because, without penalizing the employer, the employee "is made whole, and it should not make that much difference whether the overtime to which he is entitled is worked on an earlier rather than a later date"); Menasco Mfg. Co., 69 LA 759, 762–63 (Bergeson, 1977); Kaiser Aluminum & Chem. Corp., 54 LA 613, 617 (Bothwell, 1971); Massey-Ferguson, Inc., 53 LA 616, 619 (Edes, 1969); McCall Corp., 49 LA 933, 939–41 (Stouffer, 1967); A.O. Smith Corp., 33 LA 365, 366 (Updegraff, 1959); Goodyear Atomic Corp., 27 LA 634, 636 (Shister, 1956); Celanese Corp. of Am., 24 LA 168, 172–73 (Justin, 1954); Goodyear Tire & Rubber Co. of Ala., 5 LA 30, 32 (McCoy, 1946). In *Giant Tiger Super Stores Co.*, 43 LA 1243, 1246 (Kates, 1965), the award was 50% back pay and 50% makeup overtime. An apportionment was also made in *Bridgeport Brass Co.*, 19 LA 690, 693 (Donnelly, 1952). In *City of S. Portland, Me., Pub. Works Dep't*, 78 LA 1172, 1176 (Chandler, 1982), the sole remedy used was a cease-and-desist order.

[321]A.O. Smith Corp., 33 LA 365, 366 (Updegraff, 1959). Also indicating that past practice may be a factor in selecting the remedy, see *Georgia-Pacific Corp.*, 93 LA 4, 5 (Thornell, 1989); *Johnson Controls*, 84 LA 553, 559–61 (Dworkin, 1985); *Kaiser Aluminum & Chem. Corp.*, 54 LA 613, 617 (Bothwell, 1971); *McCall Corp.*, 49 LA 933, 940 (Stouffer, 1967). Refusing to consider past practice as a relevant factor, see *Goodrich-Gulf Chems.*, 41 LA 1065, 1069–70 (Abernethy, 1963); *Cities Serv. Petroleum Co.*, 37 LA 888, 891 (Edes, 1961).

[322]35 LA 495 (Larkin, 1960).

[323]*Id.* at 498. *See also* Globe-Union, 78 LA 299, 302 (Tamoush, 1982). Some arbitrators have indicated that they would issue a monetary award if management's action was deliberate but that the makeup overtime remedy might be appropriate (if other considerations permit it) if inadvertent error produced the violation. *See* Diamond Nat'l Corp., 52 LA 33, 36 (Chalfie, 1969); McCall Corp., 49 LA 933, 939 (Stouffer, 1967); Giant Tiger Super Stores Co., 43 LA 1243, 1246 (Kates, 1965); United States Rubber Co., 34 LA 643, 651–52 (Hebert,

proper assignment of overtime was made within the equalization unit or other group entitled to the overtime, but a monetary award essential where the improper assignment was made to employees outside such unit or group. They reason that if the overtime was assigned within the entitled unit or group, it is possible to make it up because the employee who received the improperly assigned overtime is charged with it and will receive that much less future overtime. But, if the improper assignment of overtime was made to employees outside the unit or group, it is impossible to make it up because it can never be recovered and the only logical remedy is a monetary award.[324]

In deciding which remedy to use, an arbitrator stated that the remedy selected will differ from company to company based on the frequency with which overtime is worked:

> Many arbitrators will see the equity in simply providing an additional work opportunity to an individual on overtime rather than cash compensation where overtime is sporadic. In that way, the employer does get something for the money paid and the employee has the satisfaction of working for his wages. However, where a plant . . . works substantial overtime and individuals, such as the grievant, are regularly scheduled, it is difficult to tell with any certainty when "overtime opportunities" offered in lieu of wages are anything other than simply overtime that the individual would have been working anyway at a future time.[325]

When overtime violations occur in a plant with substantial overtime opportunities, the preferred remedy is monetary compensation, not only for the reason stated above, but also to prevent interference with another employee's right to overtime in proper turn under the agreement.[326]

One arbitrator noted that management must be careful not to offer remedial overtime work outside the bargaining unit.[327] "[Employees] should not have to be exposed directly or indirectly to terms and conditions of employment that are not subject to collective bargaining in order to receive compliance under their own agreement."[328] However, if a senior employee has a contractual right of first refusal of overtime, the arbitrator may be

---

1960). Even where the contract specified use of the makeup remedy, a monetary award was used where the violation was deliberate. *See* Diamond Nat'l Corp., 52 LA 33, 36 (Chalfie, 1969); Kimberly-Clark Corp., 39 LA 216, 220 (Hon, 1962).

[324]*See* Kaiser Aluminum & Chem. Corp., 54 LA 613, 617–18 (Bothwell, 1971); Massey-Ferguson, Inc., 53 LA 616, 619 (Edes, 1969); Trane Co., 52 LA 1144, 1145 (Cahn, 1969); Duquesne Light Co., 48 LA 848, 853 (Shister, 1967); Morton Salt Co., 42 LA 525, 531–32 (Hebert, 1964); Aetna Portland Cement Co., 41 LA 219, 223 (Dworkin, 1963); Vulcan Mold & Iron Co., 41 LA 59, 62–63 (Brecht, 1963); Bendix Aviation Corp., 26 LA 540, 541 (Kelliher, 1956). In one case, where the erroneous assignment was within the entitled group, the arbitrator awarded makeup overtime but specified that it must be on work that would not otherwise have been performed at overtime rates. Morton Salt Co., 42 LA 525, 531 (Hebert, 1964). *See also* American Viscose Corp., 38 LA 70, 73–74 (Crawford, 1962).

[325]Decker Mfg. Corp., Case No. 97-25679, 1998 WL 1013431, at *9 (Daniel, 1998).

[326]*Id.*

[327]U.S. Chem. & Plastics, Case No. 00-01532, 2000 WL 1613727, at *17 (Richard, 2000) (arbitrator ordered that the employer assign a "makeup" opportunity of performing functions that were normal to the grievant's classification but which are to be performed "in the furtherance of suitable work not normally assigned to bargaining unit employees," and to which the grievant does not have any contractual right to an assignment on an overtime basis).

[328]*Id.* at *16.

compelled to either issue a monetary award or allow the employer to provide work outside the unit.[329]

D. When the Employer Violates the Agreement in Jurisdictional Disputes

Where the company has not properly assigned work to a group of workers, the normal remedy is an order commanding the employer to assign the work to the appropriate group of employees.[330] The order may or may not be accompanied with a back-pay remedy.[331]

In an AFL-CIO Internal Disputes Plan proceeding, the usual remedy is a finding that one union violated Article XX of the AFL-CIO Constitution.[332] Pursuant to Section 14 of Article XX, the AFL-CIO president will tell a non-complying union what action it must undertake to come into compliance with the constitution.[333]

E. The Back Pay Act [LA CDI 100.559501 et seq.]

Mirroring judicial review of private-sector arbitration, the FLRA has adopted a policy that arbitral awards will not be overturned merely because of disagreement with the arbitrator's findings of fact, reasoning, and conclusions drawn from the evidence. However, unlike private-sector arbitration, arbitrators in the federal sector must consider not only the terms of the parties' agreement, but also the provisions of statutes and regulations that may apply to the grievance before them. This issue of conformance with law and regulation frequently arises in review of arbitral remedies. One example of this is the application of the Back Pay Act to arbitral awards.

The Back Pay Act of 1966 was amended in 1978 to make it expressly applicable in the disposition of grievances under collective bargaining agreements.[334]

An award of back pay under the Back Pay Act[335] is authorized only when an arbitrator finds that: (1) the aggrieved employee was affected by an unjustified or unwarranted personnel action; and (2) the personnel action directly resulted in the withdrawal or the reduction of an employee's pay, allowances, or differentials.[336] A violation of a collective bargaining agreement

---

[329]*Id.*

[330]Cooper T. Smith Stevedoring Co., 84 LA 94 (Baroni, 1984); Fruehauf Trailer Co., 40 LA 360 (Childs, 1963) (ordering the company to cease and desist from misassigning the disputed work); Westinghouse Elec. Corp., 12 LA 462 (Wyckoff, 1949) (finding a contract violation that is tantamount to ordering the company to reassign the disputed work to the appropriate group of employees).

[331]Fruehauf Trailer Co., 40 LA 360 (Childs, 1963) (the workers deprived of the work are entitled to back pay at the overtime rate); Higgins, Inc., 37 LA 297 (Mordant, 1961) (no monetary damages when the grieving union did not prove that its members suffered any economic loss). For related discussion, see Chapter 13, section 9.C., "Jurisdictional Disputes."

[332]Longshoremen (ILA), 102 LA 200 (Lesnick, 1994).

[333]AFL-CIO CONST, art. XX, §14.

[334]5 U.S.C. §5596(b).

[335]*Id.*

[336]Social Sec. Admin., 57 FLRA 538 (2001) (citing Department of Health & Human Servs., 54 FLRA 1210, 1218 (1998)).

constitutes an unjustified or unwarranted personnel action under the Back Pay Act.[337]

The FLRA has revised or modified arbitrators' awards involving application of the Back Pay Act where the arbitrator:

1. Failed to find a causal relationship between the violation and the remedy;[338]
2. Awarded overtime back pay to an employee without a finding that but for the violation, the employee would have received the overtime;[339]
3. Awarded payment of additional commuting expenses;[340]
4. Ordered an employee promoted without first finding that but for the improper failure to promote, the employee would have been promoted;[341]
5. Awarded back pay for a temporary promotion that predated the effective date of the agreement;[342]
6. Credited sick leave that was not a part of pay and allowances;[343]
7. Awarded per diem expenses;[344] and
8. Failed to award, or to compute in accordance with the Internal Revenue Service, interest on back pay.[345]

There has been considerable litigation as to what constitutes back pay under the Back Pay Act. The Back Pay Act does not contain a statute of limitations, but back pay may not be limited to the time period of the contract.[346] However, only the individual grievant may be awarded back pay.[347] Strict compliance with the provisions of the Back Pay Act is required. The FLRA set aside an arbitrator's monetary award to a grievant as violative of the Back Pay Act when the award did not state which provision of the contract was violated.[348]

---

[337]Social Sec. Admin., 57 FLRA 538 (2001) (citing Department of Def. Dependents Schs., 54 FLRA 773, 785 (1998)).

[338]National Marine Fisheries Serv., 22 FLRA 443 (1986).

[339]Government Employees (AFGE) Local 1857, 35 FLRA 325 (1990); Naval Air Rework Facility, 21 FLRA 410 (1986). See also Griffith v. FLRA, 842 F.2d 487, 489–90, 127 LRRM 3148 (D.C. Cir. 1988). Cf. Social Sec. Admin., 57 FLRA 538 (2001).

[340]Customs Serv., 23 FLRA 366 (1986). But see Department of Health & Human Servs., 54 FLRA 1210 (1998) (after passage of the Federal Employees Clean Air Incentives Act of 1990, 5 U.S.C. §7901 et seq., transit subsidies may constitute compensation covered under the Back Pay Act).

[341]Department of Commerce, Patent & Trademark Office, 21 FLRA 397 (1986).

[342]Social Sec. Admin., 20 FLRA 684 (1985).

[343]Department of the Air Force, 19 FLRA 260 (1985).

[344]Community Servs. Admin., 7 FLRA 206 (1981).

[345]Department of the Interior, 55 FLRA 152 (1999); Department of the Army, 44 FLRA 1548 (1992); Department of Def. Dependents Sch., 39 FLRA 13 (1991).

[346]Allen Park Veterans Admin. Med. Ctr., 34 FLRA 1091 (1990). See also Veterans Admin. Med. Ctr., 24 FLRA 902 (1986) (an award of hazardous duty pay to employees exposed to asbestos constituted back pay under the Back Pay Act).

[347]Department of the Interior, Bureau of Reclamation, 42 FLRA 902 (1991). But see Government Employees (AFGE) Local 3882 v. FLRA, 994 F.2d 20, 143 LRRM 2629 (D.C. Cir. 1993) (union awarded fees for work by attorneys related to court proceedings in pursuit of fees for prevailing grievant).

[348]Department of the Army, Pine Bluff Arsenal, 47 FLRA 626 (1993).

When awarding attorneys' fees, an arbitrator is required to fully articulate the basis for the award.[349] The FLRA has stated:

> As previously recognized by the Authority, a threshold requirement for entitlement to attorney fees under the Back Pay Act is a finding that the grievant has been affected by an unjustified or unwarranted personnel action which has resulted in the withdrawal or reduction of the grievant's pay, allowances, or differentials. Department of Defense Dependents School and Overseas Education Association, 3 FLRA 259, 263 (1980). Further, a reading of the Back Pay Act indicates that an award of attorney fees must be in conjunction with an award of backpay to the grievant on correction of the personnel action, that the award of attorney fees must be reasonable and related to the personnel action, and that the award of attorney fees must be in accordance with the standards established under 5 U.S.C. 7701(g). Section 7701(g) prescribes that for an employee to be eligible for an award of attorney fees, the employee must be the prevailing party. Section 7701(g)(1), which applies to all cases except those of discrimination, requires that an award of attorney fees must be warranted "in the interest of justice," that the amount must be reasonable, and that the fees must have been incurred by the employee. . . .
>
> The standards established under section 7701(g) further require a fully articulated, reasoned decision setting forth the specific findings supporting the determination on each pertinent statutory requirement, including the basis upon which the reasonableness of the amount was determined . . . .[350]

Generally, once an arbitrator's award is issued, the arbitrator lacks the authority to amend, alter, change, or otherwise add to or delete from the award.[351]

The arbitrator is not functus officio, however, where an award of attorneys' fees is involved, the arbitrator may properly retain jurisdiction to award attorneys' fees after the issuance of an award on the merits.[352] The arbitrator's decision must strictly comply with the Back Pay Act, Section 7121(f).[353] Thus, awards of attorneys' fees in arbitrally determined discrimination cases cannot be made solely under the provisions of the Civil Rights Act of 1964. They must be:

- issued only in conjunction with a back-pay award to correct unwarranted or unjustified personnel action(s);
- reasonable and related to the personnel action; and
- rendered in accordance with the standards established under Section 7701(g).[354]

The statutory provision for "reasonable attorney fees" applies where the employee is the prevailing party, and payment of attorneys' fees by the agency "is warranted in the interest of justice, including any case in which a prohib-

---

[349]5 U.S.C. §7701(g).

[350]Electrical Workers (IBEW), 14 FLRA 680, 683–84 (1984) (footnote omitted).

[351]See generally Leahy, *Federal Sector Grievance Arbitration: The Concept of Functus Officio*, 93 FLRR 8B (May 31, 1993).

[352]Philadelphia Naval Shipyard, 32 FLRA 417 (1988).

[353]Government Employees (AFGE) Council of Prison Locals, 55 FLRA 192 (1999); Philadelphia Naval Shipyard, 32 FLRA 417 (1988).

[354]Department of the Navy, Norfolk Naval Shipyard, 34 FLRA 725 (1990). *See* Celmer, *Attorney Fee Awards in Discrimination Cases*, 93 FLRRI 4B (Apr. 5, 1993). This provision of §7701(g)(2) is illustrated in *Labor Investigators*, 46 FLRA 1311 (1993).

ited personnel practice was engaged in by the agency or any case in which the agency's action was clearly without merit."[355]

The Back Pay Act was amended in 1989 to provide for interest on back-pay awards.[356] The formula for application of interest is included in the statute. The requirement for interest has been held nondiscretionary. In other words, even if the union does not raise the question of interest in its exceptions, if interest is due according to the statute, the FLRA will modify an arbitrator's award to include it.[357]

---

[355]5 U.S.C. §7701(g).
[356]*Id.* §5596(b).
[357]Department of the Army, Ft. Polk, 44 FLRA 1548 (1992); Department of Def. Dependents Sch., 39 FLRA 13 (1991).

Chapter 19

Constitutional Issues in Public-Sector Arbitration

1. INTRODUCTION

In contrast to the private sector, the labor relations, collective bargaining, and arbitration processes in the public sector are governed by comprehensive and highly detailed statutory and regulatory provisions that, among other features, may more narrowly circumscribe the scope of negotiations,

1251

restrict or prohibit altogether recourse to the strike weapon, and delimit the remedial powers of arbitrators.

However, public-sector employees, whether attached to federal, state, or local governmental agencies, all enjoy additional protections against unfair disciplinary or other adverse employer action under federal and state constitutional provisions that their private-sector counterparts do not.

The First Amendment guarantees of freedom of speech and assembly and the free exercise of religion, the Fourth Amendment's ban on unreasonable searches and seizures, and the Fifth Amendment's protection of due process and equal protection are all operative when the federal government is the employer, and, through the Fourteenth Amendment, when the state or a municipality is the employer. Counterpart state constitutional provisions, which may be interpreted more broadly, provide an additional layer of protection against offensive state and municipal personnel actions.

Although many disputes involving an alleged violation of constitutional rights will go directly to the courts, when arbitrating an employment dispute arising in the public sector, arbitrators, as a threshold inquiry, will also determine if the constitutional rights of a public-sector employee have been violated by his or her employer. The U.S. Supreme Court has long held that although an arbitrator's decision on a constitutional issue does not bind a court in subsequent litigation,[1] "[w]here an arbitral determination gives full consideration to an employee's statutory or constitutional rights, a court may properly accord it great weight."[2]

However, simply because a public employee has constitutional rights, any discipline imposed is not necessarily a violation of those rights. Though it is important for public employers and arbitrators alike to recognize and properly consider the constitutional protections afforded to public employees in the workplace as their first step in assessing the appropriateness of disciplining an employee for misconduct, "the Constitution is not an employment manual" and will not be applied to every minute work rule in the public sector.[3]

Public employees do not enjoy any constitutional right to be employed by the government. As the arbitrator pointed out in *City of Wooster, Ohio*,[4] "when citizens enter into an employment relationship with the government, they voluntarily acknowledge and accept that in its role as employer the government is endowed with all rights normally reserved to employers, including the rights to maintain discipline and promote morale, harmony, and efficiency in the work place."[5] Thus,

> [w]hile it is clear that public employees do not lose constitutional protections as a result of working for a public employer, neither does the Constitution shield

---

[1]*See* Air Line Pilots v. Miller, 523 U.S. 866, 880, 158 LRRM 2321 (1998) (Breyer, J., and Stevens, J., dissenting) ("'arbitrator's decision would not receive preclusive effect in any subsequent §1983 action'") (quoting American Fed'n of Teachers Local 1 (Chicago) v. Hudson, 475 U.S. 292, 308 n.21, 121 LRRM 2793 (1986)).

[2]McDonald v. City of W. Branch, Mich., 466 U.S. 284, 292, 115 LRRM 3646 (1984) (citing Alexander v. Gardner-Denver Co., 415 U.S. 36, 60, 7 FEP Cases 81 (1974)).

[3]Swank v. Smart, 898 F.2d 1247, 1252, 5 IER Cases 323 (7th Cir. 1990).

[4]111 LA 1167 (Richard, 1999).

[5]*Id.* at 1172.

employees from discipline if exercising typical constitutional rights undermines a significant governmental interest. Despite constitutional protections, conduct that interferes with the ability of a public employer to maintain discipline or to accomplish its statutory objectives may result in disciplinary action.[6]

2. First Amendment Freedom of Speech

While employees of the government retain First Amendment rights, when their exercise of those rights creates disruption in the work place it collides with the government's rights as an employer. If the repeated exercise of the employee's First Amendment rights hinders efficiency in the work place and rises to the level of employee misconduct, it may constitute just cause for termination of the employment relationship, but never for termination of the right to free speech. Employees are therefore sometimes faced with a choice between the exercise of their constitutional rights and the retention of their employment.[7]

In determining if the exercise of First Amendment rights constitutes just cause for discipline, courts often adhere to the following principle: speech that is disruptive of the workplace or demoralizing and reflects the expression of a private complaint is not protected speech, whereas commenting on a matter of public interest is protected speech, but must be balanced against the government's interest in the effective and efficient fulfillment of its responsibilities to the public.[8] Factors for consideration include the content,[9] context, manner, time, and place of the employee's expression.[10] The balance tips in favor of protection "unless the employer shows that some restriction is necessary to prevent the disruption of official functions or to insure effective performance by the employee."[11]

Arbitrators examine these same factors. In *Department of Correctional Services*,[12] the arbitrator noted that the basis for arbitral off-duty conduct standards pertaining to free speech rights involved "whether the [expression] impairs discipline by superiors or harmony among co-workers, has a detrimental impact on close working relationships for which personal loyalty and confidence are necessary, or impedes the performance of the speaker's duties or interferes with the regular operation of the enterprise."[13]

---

[6]Snow, *The Long Arm of the Boss: Employee Off-Duty Conduct and the Reputation of the Employer*, 15 LERC Monograph Series 9, 23 (1998).

[7]City of Wooster, Ohio, 111 LA 1167 1172 (Richard, 1999).

[8]*See* Connick v. Myers, 461 U.S. 138, 1 IER Cases 178 (1983); Pickering v. Board of Educ., 391 U.S. 563, 568, 1 IER Cases 8 (1968) (determining the applicability of First Amendment protection in determining justifiable discipline of a public employee requires "a balance between the interests of the [employee], as a citizen, in commenting upon matters of public concern and the interest of the State, as an employer, in promoting the efficiency of the public services it performs through its employees").

[9]*Connick*, 461 U.S. at 152–53. "When employee expression cannot be fairly considered as relating to any matter of political, social, or other concern to the community, government officials should enjoy wide latitude in managing their offices, without intrusive oversight by the judiciary in the name of the First Amendment." *Id.* at 146.

[10]*Id.* at 146.

[11]Childers v. Independent Sch. Dist. No. 1, Bryan County, 676 F.2d 1338, 1341 (10th Cir. 1982).

[12]Department of Corr. Servs., Naponoch, N.Y., 114 LA 1533 (Simmelkjaer, 1997).

[13]*Id.* at 1540 (citing Rankin v. McPherson, 483 U.S. 378, 388, 2 IER Cases 247 (1987)).

3. PROCEDURAL DUE PROCESS

Procedural due process rights, grounded in the Fifth and Fourteenth Amendments of the U.S. Constitution, arise in the context of the discharge of public employees. Public employees have procedural due process rights if they have a property interest in their job.[14] Whether such property interest exists is determined by the state laws governing the public employment position.[15] The Supreme Court has held that an employee will have a qualifying property interest if the employee has a statutory or contractual right to his or her continued employment.[16]

Arbitrators find less judicial guidance when there is no clear statutory or contractual statement of an employee's entitlement to job tenure. In the absence of any such guidance, courts are split as to whether public employees may have a property interest in their jobs. While some courts have ruled that an employer-promulgated employee handbook did not create contract rights,[17] and that a state agency's practice of terminating employees only for cause did not amount to a property right where a statute provided for at-will discharges of public employees,[18] other courts have found such property rights stemming from handbook language[19] or common practices in the workplace.[20]

On finding that a discharged employee had a property right in his or her job, an arbitrator is constrained by the employee's procedural due process rights in the same way he or she is constrained by the grievance procedure terms detailed in a collective bargaining agreement.

A public employee who has a property interest in his or her job cannot be terminated without the opportunity to respond to the employer's reasons for dismissal and to rebut the charges on which the dismissal is based.[21] If due process is not accorded, an arbitrator's determination and analysis of other factors is irrelevant and the discharge cannot be upheld.

---

[14]*See* Logan v. Zimmerman Brush Co., 455 U.S. 422, 28 FEP Cases 9 (1982). In addition, procedural due process issues also may arise in the context of denying a public employee his or her protected liberty interest when, "in connection with the employee's discharge, a government official makes [public] accusations that seriously damage the employee's standing in the community or foreclose other employment opportunities." Mercer v. City of Cedar Rapids, 104 F. Supp. 2d 1130, 1149, 84 FEP Cases 335 (N.D. Iowa 2000). However, this is not a common issue before arbitrators in cases of public employee discipline for off-duty misconduct, in part because employers tend to take disciplinary action only after a clear indication that the misconduct occurred and caused or potentially will cause a negative impact on their agency, and in part because, due to the desire not to undermine public confidence in the agency, a public employer is likely to try to minimize publicity of such misconduct and not to draw attention to the employee's connection to the employer.

[15]In many states, such as Virginia and Pennsylvania, for example, public employees are at-will employees and, thus, do not have a property interest in their employment absent express legislative language to the contrary.

[16]*See* Board of Regents v. Roth, 408 U.S. 564, 1 IER Cases 23 (1972).

[17]*See* Pivarnik v. Pennsylvania Dep't of Transp., 82 Pa. Cmwlth. 425, 474 A.2d 732, 117 LRRM 2961 (1984).

[18]*See* Batterton v. Texas Gen. Land Office, 789 F.2d 316, 1 IER Cases 918 (5th Cir. 1986).

[19]*See* Whitfield v. Finn, 731 F.2d 1506, 1 IER Cases 1794 (11th Cir. 1984).

[20]*See* McLaurin v. Fischer, 768 F.2d 98, 41 FEP Cases 1012 (6th Cir. 1985).

[21]*See* Cleveland Bd. of Educ. v. Loudermill, 470 U.S. 532, 1 IER Cases 424 (1985).

A. Predisciplinary Due Process: Notice and an Opportunity to Be Heard

i.   The Loudermill Rule [LA CDI 100.5520; 100.5523]

Public-sector employees who are found to have more than a unilateral expectation of continued employment are said to have a property interest in their employment, which may not be taken away without procedural due process.[22] This procedural due process requires two key elements: notice and an opportunity to be heard.[23] But what is required to satisfy these due process concerns? In *Cleveland Board of Education v. Loudermill*,[24] the Supreme Court provided guidance. The *Loudermill* Court explained that a public employee with a property interest is, at a minimum, entitled to "oral or written notice of the charges against him, an explanation of the employer's evidence, and an opportunity to present his side of the story" before the proposed action is taken.[25]

Though public employers may provide a full-scale evidentiary post-disciplinary hearing at which an employee may request a review and reconsideration of the tangible job action, that process cannot satisfy the public employee's interest in presenting his or her side of the case before an adverse job action is taken,[26] and the employer's position may have hardened. The government's interest in the expeditious removal of unsatisfactory employees and the avoidance of administrative burdens simply does not outweigh the employee's interest in this regard.[27]

The minimal predisciplinary due process protections established by the Court—notice of the charge and an opportunity to be heard—take into consideration the fact that a government employer cannot arrange a full hearing prior to every adverse job action. In essence, then, the *Loudermill* hearing serves as an initial check against a mistaken decision.[28]

However, the *Loudermill* decision stresses that the predisciplinary due process rights of a public employee with a property interest are not inflex-

---

[22]The "just cause" provision of a labor agreement has been held to create such a protectible property interest. Moffit v. Town of Bergfeld, 950 F.2d 880 (2d Cir. 1991); Smith v. Milwaukee County, 954 F. Supp. 1314 (E.D. Wis. 1997); Curry v. Pennsylvania Tpk. Comm'n, 843 F. Supp. 988, 9 FEP Cases 348 (E.D. Pa. 1994); *In re* Gregoire, 689 A.2d 431, 154 LRRM 2656 (Vt. 1996). However, probationary employees generally do not have such protection. *See, e.g.*, Board of Regents v. Roth, 408 U.S. 564, 1 IER Cases 23 (1972); Ratliff v. City of Milwaukee, 795 F.2d 612, 41 FEP Cases 296 (7th Cir. 1986). For a more thorough review of due process rights of public employees, see McGuiness, *Procedural Due Process Rights of Public Employees: Basic Rules and a Rationale for a Return to Rule-Oriented Process*, 33 NEW ENG. L. REV. 931 (1999).

[23]Mullane v. Central Hanover Bank & Trust Co., 339 U.S. 306, 313 (1950).

[24]470 U.S. 532, 1 IER Cases 424 (1985).

[25]*Id.* at 546.

[26]*Id.* at 543.

[27]*Id.*

[28]*Id.* at 543. In this regard, the *Loudermill* Court quoted a prior Supreme Court decision: "Providing 'effective notice and informal hearing permitting the [employee] to give his version of the events will provide a meaningful hedge against erroneous action. At least the [employer] will be alerted to the existence of disputes about facts and arguments about cause and effect. . . . [H]is discretion will be more informed, and we think the risk of error substantially reduced.'" *Id.* at 543 n.8 (quoting Goss v. Lopez, 419 U.S. 565, 583–84 (1975)).

ible. Rather, the due process protection can vary depending on the circumstances. The more elaborate the post-disciplinary procedures in place, the less elaborate the predisciplinary procedures need be.[29] Absent special circumstances, however, there can never be a complete elimination of predisciplinary due process.[30]

ii.   *Oral or Written Notice*   [LA CDI 100.5520]

Since the *Loudermill* decision, courts have attempted to define more precisely the due process requirements for public employees with property interests in their positions. Courts have held that oral notice and oral explanation of the employer's evidence are sufficient to satisfy *Loudermill*'s notice requirements.[31] But courts have also noted that the notice, whether oral or written, must sufficiently explain the charges against the employee.[32] A vague, boilerplate generic accusation will not suffice.[33] At the same time, the notice need not set forth each specific fact being considered by the employer.[34] Some courts have held that the notice also should include an explanation of the proposed disciplinary action to be taken.[35] In any event, the set of allegations

---

[29]*Loudermill*, 470 U.S. at 546; Locurto v. Safir, 264 F.3d 154, 174–75, 17 IER Cases 1569 (2d Cir. 2001); Whartenby v. Winnisquam Reg'l Sch. Dist., 2001 WL 274748, at *6, 2001 U.S. Dist. LEXIS 4578 (D.N.H. Mar. 14, 2001) ("Minimal pre-termination process is acceptable . . . when coupled with more thorough post-termination process.").

[30]D'Acquisto v. Washington, 640 F. Supp. 594, 616 (N.D. Ill. 1986) (noting that "the promise of an eventual full hearing means that the procedural requirements of the first stage may be somewhat relaxed. They do not say that an essential element of that first stage . . . can simply be left out"). See *infra* notes 48–51, and accompanying text, discussing special circumstances for the elimination of predisciplinary due process.

[31]Powell v. Mikulecky, 891 F.2d 1454 (10th Cir. 1989); Riggins v. Board of Regents, Univ. of Neb., 790 F.2d 707 (8th Cir. 1986); Brasslett v. Cota, 761 F.2d 827 (1st Cir. 1985); Brown v. Youth Ctr., at Topeka, 883 F. Supp. 572 (D. Kan. 1995).

[32]It should be noted that the oral or written notice must actually notify the employee against whom it is directed. Jefferson County Bd. of Educ., 99 LA 740 (Smith, Jr., 1992) (placing disciplinary report in employee's file violated due process, where employee was not informed of the report or given an opportunity to respond).

[33]Gorman v. Robinson, 977 F.2d 350 (7th Cir. 1992). *But see* Buckner v. City of Highland Park, 901 F.2d 491, 495 (6th Cir. 1990) (finding sufficient notice, where employee "knew the gist of the allegations against him"); Copeland v. Philadelphia Police Dept., 840 F.2d 1139, 1145, 4 IER Cases 352 (3d Cir.), *cert. denied*, 490 U.S. 1004 (1989) (police officer who was terminated for failing urinalysis test was sufficiently made aware of the evidence against him prior to his termination, where he knew what the urinalysis test was for and he had been informed he failed it); Palm Beach County, Fla., School Bd., 107 LA 363 (Hoffman, 1996) (although predisciplinary notification sent to employee vaguely referred to his "alleged behavior" as grounds for discipline, when read in combination with other documents provided to employee, it sufficiently notified him of charges against him).

[34]Head v. Chicago Sch. Reform Bd. of Trustees, 225 F.3d 794, 804, 16 IER Cases 1519 (7th Cir. 2000) ("[N]otice is constitutionally adequate if it is reasonably calculated to apprise interested parties of the proceeding and afford them an opportunity to present their objections."). *But see* Renton, Wash., Sch. Dist., 102 LA 854 (Wilkinson, 1994) (employee was entitled to know in predisciplinary notice the identities of the individuals who accused him of sexual harassment).

[35]Cotnoir v. University of Me. Sys., 35 F.3d 6 (1st Cir. 1994); Calhoun v. Gaines, 982 F.2d 1470, 1476 & n.6 (10th Cir. 1992). *But see* Hawaii Dep't of Health, 109 LA 289 (Nauyokas, 1997) (where it was generally known that possession of marijuana was illegal in the state and against company policy, employee was already sufficiently aware of the possible disciplinary consequences that could result from its use on the job without employer providing such information).

to which the employee expects to respond should bear some relationship to the allegations to which he or she is actually permitted to respond.[36]

Affording advance notice of charges and an opportunity to be heard on them prevents a "fishing expedition" by the employer to sustain a discipline.[37] Also, intentionally failing to provide notice of charges in order to manufacture an arbitrability defense was held to violate a federal employee's procedural due process rights.[38] Furthermore, a meeting called for other than a disciplinary purpose may not be converted into a "notice" session once commenced.[39]

iii.   Predisciplinary Hearing [LA CDI 100.5523]

To be more than "window dressing," a predisciplinary hearing should be offered before the employer has reached its disciplinary decision.[40] However, an employer may make a preliminary decision to terminate an employee prior to a meeting with that employee, as long as the employer is prepared to reconsider that decision if the employee contests the grounds for termination.[41] The time interval between the notice and the hearing need not be substantial,[42] but the converse, waiting too long before allowing the employee to respond, may violate due process.[43]

The question as to who may be present at the predisciplinary meeting has arisen frequently. There is no requirement that the supervisor officiat-

---

[36]Staples v. City of Milwaukee, 142 F.3d 383, 13 IER Cases 1527 (7th Cir. 1998); Bonsall, Cal., Union Sch. Dist., 103 LA 777 (Kaufman, 1994). *But see* DeMarco v. Cuyahoga County Dep't of Human Servs., 12 F. Supp. 2d 715, 719 (N.D. Ohio 1998) (where written notice to employee cited different grounds for discipline than the grounds ultimately found, court held: "[T]here is no constitutional right to predisciplinary notice of the grounds used to support discipline."); Community Coll. Dist. 508, Bd. of Trustees, Cook County, Ill., 109 LA 1050 (Rubin, 1997) (notice not insufficient, where written statement mistakenly alleged sexual harassment instead of the proper allegation of sex discrimination).

[37]Port of Tacoma, Wash., 99 LA 1151, 1159 n.14 (Smith, 1992).

[38]U.S. Customs Serv. Region IV, 95 LA 1311, 1317–18 (Williams, 1990).

[39]Calhoun v. Gaines, 982 F.2d 1470 (10th Cir. 1992). Also, giving an employee the choice of signing a resignation or being terminated violates due process, because the employee is not given an opportunity to rebut charges. Ellis v. City of Lakewood, 789 P.2d 449 (Colo. Ct. App. 1989).

[40]D'Acquisto v. Washington, 640 F. Supp. 594 (N.D. Ill. 1986); Everett, Wash., Cmty. Coll., 110 LA 1102, 1104 (de Grasse, 1998) (sustaining grievance, where evidence showed that "management had concluded that the grievant was culpable before his story was heard"). *But see infra* notes 48–50, and accompanying text (discussing emergency situations).

[41]O'Neill v. Baker, 210 F.3d 41, 48 (1st Cir. 2000).

[42]Edmundson v. Borough of Kent Square, 4 F.3d 186 (3d Cir. 1993); Powell v. Mikulecky, 891 F.2d 1454 (10th Cir. 1989); Reyes-Pagan v. Benitez, 910 F. Supp. 38 (D.P.R. 1995). *But see* McDaniels v. Flick, 59 F.3d 446, 457–58 (3d Cir. 1995) (intimating that it was significant that the employee was given more than 10 days after his notice meeting to respond to allegations, but declining to determine "what amount of time for 'cooling off,' if any, must be allowed for an employee to respond to charges").

[43]Rogers v. Masem, 788 F.2d 1288, 1295, 40 FEP Cases 773 (8th Cir. 1985). *But see* State of Fla., 108 LA 994 (Soll, 1997) (no specific time limit mandated for initiation of predisciplinary investigation or for taking disciplinary action). Further, in the context of a collective bargaining agreement, a public employer must be mindful of its timing obligations under the contract. City of Newark, Ohio, 107 LA 775 (Kindig, 1996) (where city contracted to hold predisciplinary conference within certain time period, failure to follow time requirements resulted in due process violation).

ing in the predisciplinary meeting be impartial,[44] so long as adequate post-disciplinary procedures are in place. Nor is it necessary for the supervisor presiding over the hearing to have the authority to discharge the employee.[45]

The predisciplinary meeting is not an evidentiary hearing. The employee does not have the right to counsel at a predisciplinary meeting[46] or a right to present or cross-examine witnesses.[47]

a. Situations Where a Predisciplinary Hearing Is Not Required
[LA CDI 100.5523]

The *Loudermill* court nevertheless recognized that there can be "emergency" situations in which a public employer may find it necessary to take immediate action against an employee without providing a predisciplinary due process meeting. The Court suggested that the proper response in such situations would be to suspend the employee with pay prior to the full post-disciplinary hearing.[48] Nevertheless, in the absence of a statutory prohibition, emergency suspensions without pay have been upheld.[49] But a payless suspension, especially for an indefinite period of time, has been rejected by some reviewing courts.[50]

It should be noted that in *Gilbert v. Homar*,[51] the Court held that a predisciplinary hearing was not required prior to issuing a short suspension to a police officer who had been arrested.

Arbitrators generally have considered the *Loudermill* principle as incorporated into the concept of "just cause" as applied to government employees involved in predisciplinary investigations.[52]

If the employer has failed to afford the required *Loudermill* hearing in a discharge case, and the arbitrator sustains the grievance for lack of due process under the just cause provision, the employer cannot simply hold a hear-

---

[44]Locurto v. Safir, 264 F.3d 154, 17 IER Cases 1569 (2d Cir. 2001); Panozzo v. Rhoads, 905 F.2d 135 (7th Cir. 1990); Duchesne v. Williams, 849 F.2d 1004, 3 IER Cases 715 (6th Cir. 1988) (en banc); City of Stillwater, Okla., 103 LA 684 (Neas, 1994).

[45]Los Angeles Police Protective League v. Gates, 907 F.2d 879 (9th Cir. 1990).

[46]Panozzo v. Rhoads, 905 F.2d 135 (7th Cir. 1990); Buschi v. Kirven, 775 F.2d 1240, 1 IER Cases 1726 (4th Cir. 1985); University of Mich., 103 LA 401 (Daniel, 1994).

[47]Catlett v. Woodfin, 2001 U.S. App. LEXIS 14848, at *9, 2001 WL 741730 (7th Cir. 2001) (unpublished) ("[D]ue process does not require that the employer provide the employee . . . the right to cross-examine witnesses or present witnesses in the employee's defense."). *But see* City of Bremerton, Wash., 97 LA 937 (Calhoun, 1991) (discharge overturned, where city refused to provide employee with names of persons interviewed during internal investigation into employee's alleged drug possession).

[48]Cleveland Bd. of Educ. v. Loudermill, 470 U.S 532, 544–45, 1 IER Cases 424 (1985).

[49]Gilbert v. Homar, 520 U.S. 924, 12 IER Cases 1473 (1997). Although there are no set guidelines regarding what constitutes an "emergency," courts have accepted emergency suspensions for the removal of dangerous employees and employees accused of sexual harassment. *Id.* (employee suspended without pay immediately on being arrested by police on felony drug charges; lack of due process acceptable due to circumstances). *See also* Macklin v. Huffman, 976 F. Supp. 1090 (W.D. Mich. 1997) (emergency suspension without due process acceptable, where employee was accused of sexually harassing inmates).

[50]Ayio v. Parish of W. Baton Rouge, 569 So. 2d 234 (La. Ct. App. 1990).

[51]520 U.S. 924, 12 IER Cases 1473 (1997).

[52]In the case of private-sector employees, it has been held that *Loudermill* rights to a predisciplinary hearing applied only to public-sector employees, and summary suspension of school bus driver for joy riding was permissible under *Gilbert* in any event. SBS Transit Corp., 108 LA 1134 (Skulina, 1997).

ing to cure the defect and reinstitute the original charges.[53] The resolution of the original charges is barred by the doctrine of res judicata.[54]

iv.   Application to Other Management Actions

The application of these due process principles to other actions by management is the subject of frequent litigation.[55]

Nondisciplinary reductions in force are not entirely exempt from the predisciplinary due process requirement.[56] Obviously, a reduction in force may not be used to conceal a "for-cause" termination in an attempt to escape the general due process obligations.[57]

While predisciplinary due process has been a frequent arbitration issue, post-disciplinary due process has not, presumably because courts have held that a collective bargaining agreement's grievance procedure generally satisfies the requirements of due process if it affords a meaningful hearing.[58]

v.   Adequacy of the Process Provided   [LA CDI 100.5501 et seq.]

When management provides some process prior to taking disciplinary action, arbitrators have been called on to analyze the sufficiency of the procedural safeguards afforded. For instance, in *Jefferson County Sheriff's Office*,[59] the arbitrator rejected the union's contention that the grievant, a discharged corrections officer, was denied due process at a predisciplinary conference concerning the allegation that he fondled female inmates when no witnesses and evidence were presented by the employer and, therefore, he could not cross-examine his accusers. After discussing numerous court cases rejecting the right to cross-examination under these circumstances, the arbitrator held that due process was afforded because grievant was given de-

---

[53]City of Benton Harbor, Mich., 103 LA 816 (Allen, 1994).
[54]*Id.*
[55]Various courts have held that property rights were implicated for purposes of *Loudermill* for a variety of personnel decisions affecting government employment. Greene v. Barrett, 174 F.3d 1136, 14 IER Cases 1821 (10th Cir. 1999) (demotion); Delahoussaye v. City of Iberia, 937 F.2d 144 (5th Cir. 1991) (involuntary removal from recall list); Bailey v. Kirk, 777 F.2d 567 (10th Cir. 1985) (unpaid suspension); Coffran v. Board of Trs., New York City Pension Fund, 842 F. Supp. 723, 17 EB Cases 2816 (S.D.N.Y. 1994) (involuntary disability retirement); Prue v. Hunt, 558 N.Y.S.2d 1016 (1990) (discharge). Lesser sanctions and actions, however, such as reprimand, reclassification, nondisciplinary transfer, psychiatric exams, performance evaluation, refusal to hire, and denial of promotions, may not implicate *Loudermill. See* 1 Silver, Public Employee Discharge & Discipline §17.05, at 1146–49, and accompanying notes (3d ed. 2001).
[56]Lalvani v. Cook County, 269 F.3d 785, 87 FEP Cases 180 (7th Cir. 2001) (citing UDC Chairs Chapter, American Ass'n of Univ. Professors v. Board of Trs., 56 F.3d 1469, 1474 (D.C. Cir. 1995) (explaining that layoffs are less stigmatizing because "the individual characteristics, qualifications or reputations of the [employees] are not at issue")).
[57]*Lalvani*, 269 F.3d 785.
[58]Dykes v. Southeastern Pa. Transp. Auth., 68 F.3d 1564, 150 LRRM 2769 (3d Cir. 1995), *cert. denied*, 517 U.S. 1142 (1996); Pedersen v. South Williamsport Area Sch. Dist., 677 F.2d 312, 316, 110 LRRM 2361 (3d Cir.), *cert. denied*, 459 U.S. 972 (1982). However, in *Parret v. City of Connersville*, 737 F.2d 690 (7th Cir.), *cert. denied*, 469 U.S. 284 (1984), the court considered arbitration in contract too slow and its remedies too limited.
[59]Jefferson County Sheriff's Office, Steubenville, Ohio, 114 LA 1508, 1515 (Klein, 2000).

tailed charges explaining the evidence and had an opportunity to tell his side of the story.[60] But if the grievant is never afforded the opportunity to cross-examine his or her accusers, even at a post-disciplinary arbitration hearing, due process has been violated.[61]

Where the labor agreement fully defines in a fair and objective fashion what process was due, it is unnecessary for the arbitrator to go any further to apply *Loudermill* doctrine.[62] Indeed, where a contract mandated that the names of persons interviewed in an internal affairs investigation into police use of marijuana must be disclosed to the grievant, a city could not defend its failure to do so on the ground that it had complied with the *Loudermill* requirements.[63]

Some arbitration cases have examined predisciplinary safeguards in unusual settings where disciplinary considerations arguably are an undercurrent. For instance, *Loudermill* safeguards have been required where a merit increase was denied to bargaining-unit employees for failure to meet an absenteeism standard.[64] However, *Loudermill* has been held inapplicable to the placing of an employee on an unpaid medical leave of absence for psychotherapy after a compelled psychological evaluation, where reasonable cause existed to require the evaluation.[65]

In addition to nullification of the discipline,[66] the remedy for violation of the *Loudermill* standards may include reduction of the penalty.[67]

vi. Protection Against Compelled Self-Incrimination

The principle that the government employee has a Fifth Amendment right against compulsory self-incrimination in the employment context has

---

[60]*Id.* (arbitrator read contractual guarantee of cross-examination as applying only when witnesses *were* presented). *Accord* Vermont Dep't of Corr., 102 LA 701, 707 (McHugh, 1994) (discharge of corrections officer upheld despite lack or opportunity to discover and obtain discovery of psychiatric evaluation of alleged victim of sexual harassment, where grievant was allowed to fully discover and challenge the diagnosis of the alleged victim at a later hearing). *See also* Portland, Me., Water Dist., 111 LA 673 (Shieber, 1998) (employee discharged for abuse of sick leave was afforded due process by virtue of meeting with district director at which union steward was present, and his account of the events confirmed the charges against him).

[61]City of Pembroke Pines, Fla., 93 LA 365 (Cantor, 1989) (reprimand issued to male officer must be rescinded, where city did not call as witnesses female dispatchers who accused grievant of sexual harassment and instead relied on sworn statements that could not be cross-examined).

[62]Palm Beach County, Fla., Sch. Bd., 107 LA 363, 368 (Hoffman, 1996) (though grievant was not given detailed charges, source documents satisfied laying out the allegations complied with contractual definition of due process, where record showed grievant understood charges from the outset based on his articulate responses to the charges, and where grievant made no objection to the lack of a face-to-face meeting).

[63]City of Bremerton, Wash., 97 LA 937 (Calhoun, 1991) (discharge overturned as outcome of disciplinary hearing might have been different if names had been given).

[64]City of Omaha, Neb., 98 LA 931 (Eisler, 1992) (no proper notice given prior to depriving employees of merit pay based on existing standards).

[65]City of Chicago, Ill., 97 LA 20 (Goldstein, 1990) (*Loudermill* inapplicable because grievant was not terminated).

[66]Cleveland Bd. of Educ. v. Loudermill, 470 U.S. 532, 1 IER Cases 424 (1985); D'Acquisto v. Washington, 640 F. Supp. 594, 616 (N.D. Ill. 1986).

[67]Merced Irrigation Dist., 86 LA 851 (Riker, 1986) (discharge for marijuana cultivation reduced to a suspension).

been firmly established by the Supreme Court over the years.[68] In a post-*Garrity*[69] case, the Court explained the doctrine as follows:

> [T]he Fifth Amendment not only protects the individual against being involuntarily called as a witness against himself in a criminal prosecution, but also privileges him not to answer official questions put to him in any other proceeding, civil or criminal, formal or informal, where the answers might incriminate him in future criminal proceedings.[70]

Many public employers require their employees to participate in investigations that are related to the performance of their job duties. In some instances, where misconduct is alleged, an investigation may lead to or coincide with the bringing of criminal charges. What happens when an employee's prediscplinary meeting requires him or her to choose between responding to evidence gathered by the employer while a criminal charge is pending, or potentially in the offing, or losing his or her job for failing to participate in the investigation? In such a situation, the Fifth Amendment right against self-incrimination has the potential to collide with the procedural due process required under *Loudermill*.[71]

In *Garrity v. New Jersey*,[72] an investigation into alleged ticket-fixing involved the interrogation of many police officers. The officers questioned during the investigation were offered the choice of answering the questions asked or being removed from office. Terming the police officers' choice as one "between a rock and the whirlpool," the Supreme Court held that under the Fifth Amendment, incriminating evidence elicited under the threat of discharge could not be admitted in a subsequent criminal proceeding.[73] When an employee is given the option of either forfeiting his or her job or incriminating himself or herself, there is no free choice, the Court concluded, and the Fifth Amendment is thereby violated.[74] The solution, the Court counseled, is to extend immunity to those individuals who do incriminate themselves by participating in the investigation.[75]

Although *Garrity* prohibits the use of compelled testimony in criminal proceedings, it does not prohibit interdepartmental inquiries or discipline, including discharge.[76] *Garrity* prohibits only the compulsion of testimony that has not been immunized. Thus, employees may not be both compelled to make a statement and required to waive their Fifth Amendment rights.[77] However, compelled testimony may be used in subsequent civil and administrative proceedings, and public employees may be fired either for refusing to cooperate or on the basis of the statements that they provide.[78]

---

[68]Lefkowitz v. Cunningham, 431 U.S. 801 (1974); Lefkowitz v. Turley, 414 U.S. 70 (1973); Sanitation Men v. Commissioner of Sanitation, New York City, 392 U.S. 280 (1968); Gardner v. Broderick, 392 U.S. 273 (1968).
[69]Garrity v. New Jersey, 385 U.S. 493 (1967).
[70]Lefkowitz v. Turley, 414 U.S. 70, 77 (1973).
[71]Cleveland Bd. of Educ. v. Loudermill, 470 U.S. 532, 1 IER Cases 424 (1985).
[72]385 U.S. 493 (1967).
[73]*Id.* at 496, 498, 500.
[74]*Id.* at 497–98.
[75]*Id.* at 500.
[76]Lefkowitz v. Turley, 414 U.S. 70, 84 (1973).
[77]*Id.* at 82–83. *See also* Gardner v. Broderick, 392 U.S. 273, 276–77 (1968).
[78]*Turley*, 414 U.S. at 81.

In determining the applicability of *Garrity*, several courts consider whether (1) the defendant subjectively believed that he or she was compelled to give a statement under threat of the loss of job, and (2) whether this belief was objectively reasonable at the time it was made.[79] The threat may be express or implied, but the belief must derive from actions by the state.[80]

It is not altogether clear when the *Garrity* protection attaches. *Garrity* obviously applies during an internal investigation; however, it is less certain whether *Garrity* protections may be triggered during the routine reporting of their job activities or in completing routine job reports. For example, police officers have argued that, because reports prepared in their normal course of duties were required by their departments, the reports were "compelled." In this type of situation, two socially important interests are in conflict: On the one hand, the criminal justice system has an interest in ensuring that police officers report their official actions, and, on the other hand, police officers have the right not to incriminate themselves.

Several courts have rejected police officers' attempts to suppress their reports, and seemingly have limited *Garrity* and its progeny to preclude the use of reports prepared because of, rather than just during, actual internal and criminal investigations.[81]

---

[79]*See, e.g.,* Minnesota v. Murphy, 465 U.S. 420 (1984); United States v. Friedrick, 842 F.2d 382, 395 (D.C. Cir. 1988); United States v. Indorato, 628 F.2d 711, 715–17 (1st Cir. 1980) (police officer had subjective belief, but it was not objectively reasonable because there was no express threat or departmental policy requiring cooperation); United States v. Solomon, 509 F.2d 863, 870–72 (2d Cir. 1975); United States v. Najarian, 915 F. Supp. 1460 (D. Minn. 1996); United States v. Camacho, 739 F. Supp. 1504 (S.D. Fla. 1990); Colorado v. Sapp, 934 P.2d 1367, 1373–74, 12 IER Cases 1268 (Colo. 1997) (holding that subjective fear of discipline, as opposed to termination, is insufficient); Illinois v. Bynum, 159 Ill. App. 3d 713, 512 N.E.2d 826, 827 (1987) (finding no direct threat because evidence "indicated that dismissal would be possible but would not necessarily follow").

[80]Hester v. City of Milledgeville, 777 F.2d 1492, 1495 (11th Cir. 1985); Womer v. Hampton, 496 F.2d 99, 108 (5th Cir. 1974); United States v. Najarian, 915 F. Supp. 1460, 1479 (D. Minn. 1996) (refusing to apply *Garrity* absent a privilege-waiving statute, regulation, or rule, or some other "operative mandate that required the interrogee to allow official questioning, or face a job termination"); United States v. Camacho, 739 F. Supp. 1504, 1515 (S.D. Fla. 1990) (noting that the state must be more coercive than requiring that the witness testify truthfully); Colorado v. Sapp, 934 P.2d 1367, 1372–74 (Colo. 1997).

[81]*See, e.g.,* Devine v. Goodstein, 680 F.2d 243, 247, 110 LRRM 2887 (D.C. Cir. 1982) (upholding suspension of immigration inspector for failing to prepare a report after a complaint of inappropriate behavior because the inspector "did not believe and could not have reasonably believed that his written report could be used in a criminal prosecution" (footnote omitted)); United States v. Ruiz, 579 F.2d 670, 675 (1st Cir. 1978) (use of an officer's arrest report in his criminal trial did not violate *Garrity* because the "fifth amendment proscribes self-incrimination, not incriminating statements"); Watson v. County of Riverside, 976 F. Supp. 951, 954–55 (C.D. Cal 1997) (arrest report was an ordinary job requirement and was not compelled self-incrimination); Commonwealth v. Harvey, 397 Mass. 351, 491 N.E.2d 607, 611 (1986) (upholding use, in criminal trial, of officer's statement during an administrative investigation because "the fact that there existed the possibility of adverse consequences from the defendant's failure to cooperate does not demonstrate that the defendant was 'compelled' to incriminate himself"); Commonwealth v. Ziegler, 503 Pa. 555, 560–61, 470 A.2d 560 (1983) (upholding use of statements given in routine, though mandatory, administrative investigation because officer was not being held as a defendant and had no reason to believe that he was being held as a suspect or defendant); State v. Falco, 60 N.J. 570, 584, 292 A.2d 13 (1972) (distinguishing *Garrity*, in which officers were questioned for suspected misconduct, from case in which officer failed to perform specific duties expected of all officers and was required to prepare a report). *See also* Myers, *Code of Silence: Police Shootings and the Right to Remain Silent*, 26 Golden Gate U. L. Rev. 497 (1996) (contending that employees' routine reports should be admissible in subsequent criminal trials).

In *Gardner v. Broderick*,[82] the Supreme Court held that a police officer who was subjected to questioning as part of a corruption probe could not be discharged for refusing to waive the immunity guaranteed by his Fifth Amendment right against self-incrimination. However, the Court noted that if an officer has not been compelled to sign an immunity waiver with respect to the use of his or her answers or the "fruits" thereof in a criminal case, the privilege against self-incrimination would not bar dismissal for refusing to answer questions "specifically, directly, and narrowly relating to the performance of his official duties . . . ."[83] Hence, in order to properly compel a government employee to answer questions in an investigation of misconduct, it is necessary to: 1) order the employee to answer under threat of discipline; 2) question the employee only on matters specifically, directly, and narrowly tailored to the employee's duties; and 3) advise the employee that the answers obtained will not be used against the person in a criminal proceeding. By affording such a guarantee of "use immunity" under these circumstances, the employer properly may discipline the employee for insubordination if the employee does not cooperate and answer the questions propounded.

With increasing frequency, arbitrators have confronted issues stemming from the *Garrity* ruling. In *Ohio Department of Public Safety*,[84] the arbitrator held that the state did not violate the labor agreement's *Garrity* language when it failed to advise law enforcement personnel of the immunity from self-incrimination during a criminal investigation of a high-speed car chase that resulted in the suspect committing suicide. Because the officers were not under criminal investigation themselves and were further told they were not the subject of administrative investigation, *Garrity* protection was not required so long as the routine investigation into the "use of force" was conducted in a fashion that was limited in scope and in good faith.

The *Garrity* immunity process has apparently caused some confusion among management and employees alike. For instance, in *Ohio Bureau of Workers' Compensation*,[85] the arbitrator ruled that an employee who was terminated for refusing to answer questions about "fixing" workers' compensation cases, and who was also the subject of a criminal investigation, was entitled to reinstatement where the state had given a *Garrity* immunity form guaranteeing the right to an attorney, but then denied such counsel at the interview.[86] Because the employee was rightly confused about his right to counsel by virtue of the form itself, and later offered to answer questions at a subsequent meeting, the discharge was inappropriate.

---

[82]392 U.S. 273 (1968).

[83]*Id.* at 278 (footnote omitted).

[84]Ohio Dep't of Pub. Safety, 114 LA 1040 (Ruben, 2000).

[85]Ohio Bureau of Workers' Comp., 110 LA 986 (Nelson, 1998).

[86]While it has been held that the employee may not have a right to counsel before giving such immunized statements, the employee would have the right to union representation if he or she was being investigated for disciplinary reasons. NLRB v. J. Weingarten, Inc., 420 U.S. 251, 88 LRRM 2689 (1975). See the discussion of *Weingarten* rights in section 3.B., "Due Process and the Right to Union Representation During an Investigatory Meeting," below. *But see* District of Columbia Dep't of Corr., 105 LA 843 (Rogers, 1996) (correction officer denied union representation during disciplinary interview implicating *Garrity* where collective bargaining agreement did not afford such right and grievant did not request it, though shop steward sought to be present).

Grievants have fared worse where they have claimed that they refused to answer questions based on the erroneous advice of counsel.[87] In this connection, it should be noted that the state has no duty to provide an attorney to the public employee in the investigatory proceeding, not even under a contractual indemnification clause requiring defense of the employee in "legal proceedings."[88]

The importance of an accurate understanding of *Garrity* rights led an arbitrator in an interest arbitration of a police contract to hold that the textual explanation of *Garrity* in the collective bargaining agreement should be retained because it spelled out important rights, and management had proposed no alternatve text, only deletion of the existing language.[89]

The level of discipline imposed for refusal to answer questions in an investigatory interrogation has been considered as well. In *Ohio Department of Natural Resources*,[90] the arbitrator ruled that there was nothing in *Garrity* requiring an employee to be removed for refusal to answer questions. Because the agency's own policy did not mandate termination for insubordination for a first offense, the grievant's discharge was reduced to a 6-month suspension.[91]

In another case, despite the fact that a police officer admitted to falsifying an arrest report about the timing of the discovery of cocaine on a suspect's person, the discharge of the officer was set aside where the city's interrogators promised that if he were truthful on his report given under *Garrity* immunity, he would receive only minor discipline.[92]

As noted in *Ohio Department of Public Safety*,[93] *Garrity* creates an "exclusionary rule" that simply prohibits a public employee's statements obtained under threat of removal from being used in a subsequent criminal proceeding.[94] Hence, where in a sexual harassment investigation management did not use statements obtained at a first meeting at which no *Garrity* immunity was given, the arbitrator held that there was no procedural bar to considering the merits of the disciplinary action against the grievant.[95]

Although the *Garrity* situation commonly arises in the course of internal police investigations,[96] every public employee has "*Garrity* rights." These

---

[87]Ohio Dep't of Natural Res., 113 LA 577, 582 (Murphy, 1999) (erroneous advice of counsel on refusal to answer questions was no defense to an insubordination charge where management had painstakingly and repeatedly given the employee information on *Garrity* rights. However, the arbitrator was careful to add that "[t]his . . . opinion should not be read to support the proposition that erroneous advice by a Union representative or private attorney can never be a basis to restore a job to an employee fired for refusing to answer questions based upon that advice"). *Compare* City of Carrollton, Tex., 90 LA 276 (Stephens, 1988) (erroneous advice of counsel to refrain from taking internal affairs polygraph test after full *Garrity* notice given was no defense to insubordination charge).

[88]University of Mich., 103 LA 401 (Daniel, 1994).

[89]City of Sallisaw, Okla., 111 LA 657 (Baroni, 1998).

[90]113 LA 577 (Murphy, 1999).

[91]*Id.* at 583.

[92]City of Tampa, Fla., 109 LA 453 (Soll, 1997) (discipline reduced).

[93]114 LA 1040 (Ruben, 2000).

[94]*Id.* at 1048. *Accord* City of Miami, 92 LA 175, 180 (Abrams, 1989) (rejecting union's argument that grievant's Fifth Amendment rights under *Garrity* "were violated by terminating him for failing to report his own involvement in" trafficking in narcotics, as this was not a criminal proceeding but a civil labor arbitration).

[95]Metropolitan Transit Comm'n, 106 LA 360, 362 (Imes, 1996).

[96]For a police force–specific treatment of *Garrity* immunity, see Clymer, *Compelled Statements From Police Officers and* Garrity *Immunity*, 76 N.Y.U. L. Rev. 1309 (2001); Bloch,

rights come into play whenever a public employee is ordered to answer questions by a superior under threat of termination.

There is no absolute requirement that *Garrity* immunity be offered in every potentially incriminating interrogation. All that is required is that the employee's choice not be limited to incrimination or termination.[97] Thus, an employer may question an employee without offering *Garrity* immunity, but in such a situation the employee may not be terminated for exercising his or her Fifth Amendment rights.[98] But, if the employee is not offered *Garrity* immunity and chooses to exercise Fifth Amendment rights, there is no prohibition against a public employer using evidence other than the employee's silence as a reason for his or her termination.[99]

B. Due Process and the Right to Union Representation During an Investigatory Meeting

i. *Substance of the Right to Union Representation*
[LA CDI 100.0705]

Private-sector employees have the right to be represented by a coworker or union representative during an investigatory meeting that they reasonably believe could lead to discipline. In *NLRB v. J. Weingarten, Inc.*,[100] the

---

Police Officers Accused of Crime: Prosecutorial and Fifth Amendment Risks Posed by Police-Elicited "Use Immunized" Statements, 1992 U. ILL. L. REV. 625 (1992).

[97]Harrison v. Wille, 132 F.3d 679, 13 IER Cases 1066 (11th Cir. 1998). It is established that a public employee may not be given the choice between waiving *Garrity* immunity and losing his or her job. Sanitation Men Ass'n v. Commissioner of Sanitation, New York City, 392 U.S. 280 (1968); Gardner v. Broderick, 392 U.S. 273 (1968). However, an employee may be given the choice between answering questions with *Garrity* immunity and losing his or her job. Jones v. Franklin County Sheriff, 52 Ohio St. 3d 40, 555 N.E.2d 940 (1990) (employee's refusal to answer questions regarding her conduct even after being afforded the requisite immunity constituted insubordination, and employee's discharge for insubordination did not violate the Fifth Amendment); Williams v. Pima County, 791 P.2d 1053 (Ariz. Ct. App. 1989) (employee was advised his statements would not be used against him in criminal proceedings; employee still refused to answer and was terminated; court found his termination for refusal to answer questions did not violate the Fifth Amendment).

[98]Washoe County, Nev., 97 LA 393 (Concepcion, 1991).

[99]Harrison v. Wille, 132 F.3d 679, 13 IER Cases 1066 (11th Cir. 1998). In *Harrison*, a deputy was suspected of stealing items from an evidence room and was questioned about the stolen items. The deputy was interviewed three times and was given his *Garrity* rights. Thereafter, the deputy was placed on leave with pay and notified of his predisciplinary conference. At the conference, the deputy was informed that no statements were being compelled (i.e., no *Garrity* immunity was offered). Therefore, the deputy exercised his Fifth Amendment right to remain silent. Eventually the deputy was terminated. When he sued for violation of the Fifth Amendment, the U.S. Court of Appeals for the Eleventh Circuit found no such violation, noting that the deputy was never faced with the choice of making a statement or being fired; moreover, there was no evidence that he was terminated solely for exercising his Fifth Amendment rights. *Id.* at 683. Indeed, noted the court, there was plenty of evidence incriminating the deputy to warrant a termination. Accordingly, the deputy's termination did not offend the constitutional principles in *Garrity*. *Id. See also* Buckner v. City of Highland Park, 901 F.2d 491 (6th Cir.), *cert. denied*, 498 U.S. 848 (1990) (similar facts; no Fifth Amendment violation where discipline was based on evidence other than employee's silence); Peiffer v. Lebanon Sch. Dist., 848 F.2d 44 (3d Cir. 1988) (school employee terminated based on incriminating evidence against him, not because he exercised his Fifth Amendment rights); Northmont, Ohio, City Sch. Dist., 110 LA 27 (Goldberg, 1998) (employer could not use employee's silence against her where it did not offer immunity; employee's discharge upheld based on evidence from other witnesses, however).

[100]420 U.S. 251, 88 LRRM 2689 (1975).

Supreme Court, affirming a decision of the National Labor Relations Board (NLRB, or the Board), held that a union employee may insist on union representation during an *investigatory* interview that the employee believes may reasonably result in disciplinary action.[101] A private-sector employer, therefore, violates Section 8(a)(1) of the National Labor Relations Act[102] by depriving employees of their *Weingarten* rights.

Even before *Weingarten*, arbitrators recognized an employee's right to union representation during an investigatory interview. Unlike the NLRB and the courts, however, arbitrators have granted employees subjected to a *Weingarten* violation substantive remedies, such as reinstatement and back pay.[103]

For public-sector employees, the right to union representation is not constitutionally guaranteed as an element of procedural due process, but rather is derived from statute. Several states have by legislation extended *Weingarten* rights to governmental employees,[104] and, in some others, a state agency has granted *Weingarten* rights without judicial or legislative authorization.[105] But other states have explicitly declined to do so,[106] and the issue remains open in several other states.[107]

In the federal sector, *Weingarten* rights have also been recognized by arbitrators.[108]

---

[101]Reversing precedent, the NLRB, in *Epilepsy Foundation of Northeast Ohio,* 331 NLRB 676, 164 LRRM 1233 (2000), extended *Weingarten* rights to nonunion employees. The NLRB has applied *Epilepsy Foundation* retroactively, so that employers that did not permit a nonunion employee to have a representative present may be guilty of an unfair labor practice even though, at the time of the alleged offense, *Epilepsy Foundation* was not the law.

[102]29 U.S.C. §151 et seq.

[103]*See, e.g.,* City of Lansing, Mich., 106 LA 761 (Ellmann, 1996) (finding that cause did not exist and overturning suspension due to *Weingarten* violation); Cook County Hosp., 105 LA 974 (Wolff, 1995) (reducing suspension); Maui Pineapple Co., 86 LA 907, 910 (Tsukiyama, 1986) ("[T]he trend of arbitral authority regards the 'Weingarten right' as an implied requirement of procedural 'just cause' in management's disciplinary process."); Kraft, Inc., 82 LA 360, 365–66 (Denson, 1984) (balancing just cause and management rights and reducing discharge to suspension). For a comparison of statutory *Weingarten* rights and arbitral *Weingarten* rights, see generally Silverman, *Special Topics in Labor Relations: The Role of Arbitration in Collective Bargaining Dispute Proceedings: Comment: The Differing Nature of the* Weingarten *Right to Union Representation in the NLRB and Arbitral Forums,* 44 U. Miami. L. Rev. 467 (1989).

[104]*See, e.g.,* Alaska (Munson v. Alaska Dep't of Corr., Alaska Labor Relations Agency, Dec. & Order No. 206 (1996)); California (Rio Hondo Cmty. Coll. Dist., 7 Cal. Pub. Empl. Rep. (LRP) ¶14,028 (1982)); Florida (Seitz v. Duval County. Sch. Bd., 4 Fla. Pub. Empl. Rep. (LRP) ¶4154 (1978)); Indiana (North Montgomery Teachers Ass'n, 26 Ind. Pub. Emp. Rep. (LRP) ¶32,012 (2001)); Iowa (Fuller v. Iowa Dep't of Human Servs., 576 N.W.2d 324, 8 AD Cases 1855 (Iowa 1998)); Massachusetts (Massachusetts, 9 Mass. Lab. Comm'n 1567, 1571 (1983)); Michigan (University of Mich., 1997 Michigan Employment Relations Comm'n, Labor Opinion 496); New Jersey (East Brunswick Bd. of Educ., 5 N.J. Pub. Empl. Rep. (LRP) ¶398, 399 (1979)); Ohio (*In re* Davenport, 13 Ohio Pub. Empl. Rep. (LRP) ¶1193 (1995)); Pennsylvania (Pennsylvania v. Pennsylvania Labor Relations Bd., 768 A.2d 1201 (Pa. Commw. Ct. 2001)).

[105]*See, e.g.,* Illinois (Illinois Dep't of Corr., 16 Ill. Pub. Emp. Rep. (LRP) ¶2023 (2000)).

[106]*See, e.g.,* Swiger v. Civil Serv. Comm'n, 179 W. Va. 133, 365 S.E.2d 797 (1987).

[107]*See, e.g.,* New York (Westhampton Beach Union Free Sch. Dist., 34 N.Y. Pub. Emp. Rep. (LRP) ¶4571 (2001)); Vermont (Dube v. Teamsters Local 597, 139 Vt. 394, 430 A.2d 440, 111 LRRM 2350 (1981)).

[108]Department of Treasury, 82 LA 1209 (Kaplan, 1984); Department of the Air Force, 75 LA 994 (Hart, 1980) (federal sector arbitrators are bound to apply external law).

ii.   Limitations on the Right to Union Representation
[LA CDI 100.0705]

Weingarten rights are, however, subject to significant limitations. In order for *Weingarten* rights to be triggered, the employee must request the representation. But, even if the employee requests a representative, the employer may simply forgo the meeting, and the employee will lose any benefit he or she may have derived from the meeting. An employer does not have to offer the representation or postpone a meeting when the requested representative is unable to attend the meeting, as long as another representative is able to attend. In addition, employers do not have to bargain with the employee's representative during the meeting. Rather, employers fulfill their *Weingarten* obligations simply by permitting the representative to attend the meeting. The employer may also carry on its inquiry and/or investigation without interviewing the employee.

Weingarten does not apply where the employer already has made its decision before the meeting and is simply announcing, without asking questions or investigating, a disciplinary decision.

Importantly, unless the employee was discharged for actually asserting such rights (as opposed to being discharged based on other reasons, such as what was uncovered during the interview in which the employee was wrongfully denied representation), the Board's remedy for a *Weingarten* violation is *not* reinstatement and back pay. Rather, the typical remedy for a *Weingarten* violation involves a cease-and-desist order, along with a mandatory posting of a notice of violation to employees.[109]

iii.   Situations Where the Right to Union Representation Exists
[LA CDI 100.0705]

The question of just what types of interactions with management warrant union intervention frequently has arisen in arbitration. For instance, in *Ohio Department of Public Safety*,[110] the arbitrator held that the state did not violate the labor agreement when three law enforcement officers were subject to routine criminal investigation following the apparent suicide of a theft suspect after a high-speed car chase. Because the officers were told they were not the subject of any administrative investigation, the criminal probe was conducted in good faith and narrowly tailored to the task of investigating the suspect's crime. No *Weingarten* right was implicated. Likewise, union representation was not required at a routine parent-teacher-principal conference.[111] Nor were *Weingarten* rights implicated where a warden requested an employee to resign because of allegations of drug trafficking.[112]

---

[109]Taracorp Indus., 273 NLRB 221, 223, 117 LRRM 1497 (1984).
[110]114 LA 1040 (Ruben, 2000).
[111]Lancaster City Sch., 81 LA 1024 (Abrams, 1983) (stressing that *Weingarten* was a statutory right not incorporated into the collective bargaining agreement).
[112]Ohio Dep't of Rehab. & Corr., 110 LA 655 (Florman, 1998).

It further has been held that "counselings" about performance deficiencies do not trigger the *Weingarten* guarantee.[113] Similarly, where management merely issues a minor "admonishment," outside an investigatory context, the right to have a representative present does not attach.[114] The absence of the "investigation" element has led arbitrators to refuse to require representation to be granted in the context of reprimands[115] and performance evaluations.[116]

Arbitrators also have rejected claims that union representation was necessary for legitimate medical scrutiny of an employee. So no union representative could be present during a psychiatric evaluation[117] or for a medical exam to detect drugs.[118]

iv. Need for the Employee to Exercise This Right [LA CDI 100.0705]

Though some cases have held that the employer has an affirmative duty to warn an employee about his or her *Weingarten* rights,[119] the weight of authority is that the employee must request such representation.[120] However, in *Cook County Hospital*,[121] the arbitrator held that the employer "has the initial burden of advising the employee of the nature and purpose of the meeting so that the employee is sufficiently informed as to whether he can or should exercise his right to Union representation."[122]

Of course, because it is a protected right, an employee cannot be disciplined for exercising it,[123] even when making a private call to secure a stew-

---

[113]City of Independence, Mo., 113 LA 83 (Hilgert, 1999). *But see* Department of the Air Force, 75 LA 994 (Hart, 1980) (though law did not require union representation in "discussion" meeting concerning length of grievant's sideburns, contract did).

[114]U.S. Air Force, 80 LA 1140 (White, 1983) (grievant was insubordinate by breaking off meeting over "oral admonishment" to obtain unnecessary union steward, where no investigation was to take place).

[115]Army Indus. Operations Command, 106 LA 148 (Kohn, 1995).

[116]Anoka County, Minn., 84 LA 516 (Jacobowski, 1985).

[117]City of Chicago, Ill., 96 LA 876 (Goldstein, 1990); City of Milwaukee, 78 LA 89 (Yaffe, 1982) (arbitrator declines to rule on issue of whether grievant was properly disciplined for refusal to submit to urine test for intoxicants, when there was no definitive ruling by state labor board).

[118]Birmingham-Jefferson County Transit Auth., 84 LA 1272 (Statham, 1985) (meeting to order exam was not investigatory).

[119]Department of Treasury, 82 LA 1209, 1214 (Kaplan, 1984) (subjective belief of grievant is standard to determine if grievant believed discipline may result from meeting); City of Lansing, Mich., 106 LA 761 (Ellmann, 1996); City of Sterling Heights, 80 LA 825 (Ellmann, 1983).

[120]Benjamin Logan, Ohio, Bd. of Educ., 105 LA 1168 (Fullmer, 1995); District of Columbia Dep't of Corr., 105 LA 843, 845 (Rogers, 1996); Bi-State Dev. Agency, 105 LA 319 (Bailey, 1995); City of Havre, Mont., 100 LA 866 (Levak, 1992) (grievant an experienced shop steward); Grand Blanc, Mich., Cmty. Sch., 97 LA 162 (Kerner, 1991) (grievant did not request steward until after making damaging statement); Calcasieu Parish Police Jury, 86 LA 350 (Nicholas, Jr., 1985).

[121]105 LA 974, 979 (Wolff, 1995) (5-day suspension reduced to 1-day suspension). *See also* Borough of Carlisle, Pa., 82 LA 1 (Woy, 1984) (rights of union president not violated because he should be aware of rights).

[122]Cook County Hosp., 105 LA 974, 979–80 (Wolff, 1995).

[123]Springfield Ass'n of Retarded Citizens, 103 LA 1136, 1141 (Hoh, 1994).

ard.[124] Occasionally, overzealous stewards have been disciplined in this context, however.[125]

v. Arbitral Remedies for Employer Breach of This Right
[LA CDI 100.0705]

Arbitrators do not follow Board policy in formulating a remedy for breach of *Weingarten* rights. In *Norwalk City School District of Education*,[126] the arbitrator nullified a verbal warning where union representation was denied. In *Pottsville Area School District*,[127] the arbitrator excluded from his consideration evidence "clouded" by lack of a grant of representation. In *Department of the Air Force*,[128] the arbitrator issued a cease-and-desist order and nullified the discipline. In *Bi-State Development Agency*,[129] the arbitrator sustained the discharge for an employee who failed a drug test but granted 1-month's back pay as a remedy to "penalize" the employer for breach of the employee's *Weingarten* rights. An arbitrator has even required an employer to pay $250 in attorney fees for interference with the employee's union representation right by calling a steward as a witness in arbitration.[130]

While in *City of Edina, Minnesota*,[131] the arbitrator believed she had no power to compel a fire chief to retract his statement that union representation was not warranted under the circumstances, in *Defense Mapping Agency*,[132] the arbitrator required the essence of the award to be publicized.

In an interest arbitration, the importance of the *Weingarten* right in the police context was evident in *City of Sallisaw, Oklahoma*.[133] There, the arbitrator retained contract language on the right and rejected management's attempts to remove it entirely from the contract.

4. Privacy, Search and Seizure Protection, and Compulsory Drug and Alcohol Testing [LA CDI 100.552545]

The Fourth Amendment's limitation on unreasonable searches and seizures, as incorporated into the Fourteenth Amendment and applied to the states, extends to public-sector employment.[134] Subject to limited exceptions,

---

[124]City of Kittitas, Wash., 108 LA 833 (Smith, 1997). *Compare* U.S. Air Force, 80 LA 1140 (White, 1983) (breaking off meeting to get steward at noninvestigatory meeting warranted reprimand).

[125]Corpus Christi Army Depot, 108 LA 1006 (Halter, 1997) (restraining employee from taking drug test and giving gum to mask alcohol); Shelby County, Tenn., Gov't, 100 LA 284 (Harvey, 1992) (steward refusing direct order to return to post discharged).

[126]City of Norwalk, Ohio, Dist. Bd. of Educ., 99 LA 825 (Miller, 1992).

[127]Pottsville, Pa., Area Sch. Dist., 91 LA 515, 519 (Mayer, 1988). *Accord* Internal Revenue Serv., 78 LA 1016, 1021 (Render, 1982) ("tainted" statements of grievant denied representation would be excluded).

[128]Department of the Air Force, 75 LA 994 (Hart, 1980).

[129]Bi-State Dev. Agency, 105 LA 319 (Bailey, 1995).

[130]Port of Tacoma, Wash., 99 LA 1151 (Smith, 1992).

[131]90 LA 209 (Ploeg, 1987).

[132]88 LA 651 (Hilgert, 1986).

[133]111 LA 657 (Baroni, 1998).

[134]O'Connor v. Ortega, 480 U.S. 709, 1 IER Cases 1617 (1987).

the Fourth Amendment prohibits the government from undertaking an unconsented-to search and seizure absent individualized suspicion of wrongdoing.[135] The taking of a urine or blood sample for analysis constitutes a seizure and search under the Fourth Amendment, because these tests invade reasonable expectations of privacy.[136]

These searches, therefore, must be reasonable under the circumstances.[137] In determining reasonableness, the interest of the government must be weighed against the privacy interest of the employee. That privacy interest encompasses the desire to be free both from mandatory testing and from an intrusive procedure.[138] The Supreme Court has found that governmental "special needs" for testing of body fluids may outweigh the employee's privacy interest,[139] particularly when safety-sensitive positions are at issue.

In *Skinner v. Railway Labor Executives' Ass'n*,[140] for example, the Court stated:

> The Government's interest in regulating the conduct of railroad employees to ensure safety, like its supervision of probationers or regulated industries, or its operation of a government office, school, or prison,
> "likewise presents 'special needs' beyond normal law enforcement that may justify the departures from the usual warrant and probable cause requirements."[141]

Then, in *Treasury Employees v. Von Raab*,[142] the Court upheld the Customs Service's urinalysis drug test for employees applying for promotions or positions involving illegal drug interdiction and requiring the carrying of a firearm.

The Supreme Court has been less inclined, however, to permit random drug testing for positions that do not implicate significant safety concerns. In *Chandler v. Miller*,[143] the Court struck down, on Fourth Amendment grounds, a Georgia statute requiring candidates for state offices to certify that they had tested negative in a drug urinalysis. The Court distinguished *Von Raab*, in part, by noting that candidates for office do not perform high-risk tasks.[144] The Court also emphasized that there was no evidence of a significant drug problem among public office candidates and that ordinary law enforcement techniques were likely adequate to apprehend these individuals, who typically face intensive public scrutiny.[145]

---

[135]*See, e.g.*, Chandler v. Miller, 520 U.S. 305, 12 IER Cases 1233 (1997); Vernonia Sch. Dist. 47J v. Acton, 515 U.S. 646 (1995).

[136]Treasury Employees v. Von Raab, 489 U.S. 656, 665–66, 4 IER Cses 246 (1989). For related discussion, see Chapter 16, section 2.A., "Alcohol and/or Drug Use and Testing."

[137]United States v. Montoya de Hernandez, 473 U.S. 531 (1985).

[138]Vernonia Sch. Dist. 47J v. Acton, 515 U.S. 646, 652–54 (1995).

[139]New Jersey v. T.L.O., 469 U.S. 325 (1985) (Court first articulating special needs exception).

[140]489 U.S. 602, 130 LRRM 2857 (1989).

[141]*Id.* at 620 (quoting Griffin v. Wisconsin, 483 U.S. 868, 873–74 (1987)).

[142]489 U.S. 656, 4 IER Cases 246 (1989).

[143]520 U.S. 305, 12 IER Cases 1233 (1997).

[144]*Id.* at 319–20.

[145]*Id.* at 321.

Decisions from lower courts have been mixed, with some courts holding considerably less expansive views on the right to privacy in drug testing. The U.S. Court of Appeals for the Sixth Circuit, for example, upheld a compulsory pre-employment drug urinalysis of all prospective teachers, teacher aides, substitute teachers, secretaries, bus drivers, and school principals.[146] Although noting that teaching is not the prototypical "safety-sensitive" type of position, the court nevertheless compared teachers with the Customs agents in *Von Raab*, stating:

> We can imagine few governmental interests more important to a community than that of insuring the safety and security of its children while they are entrusted to the care of teachers and administrators. . . . [T]eachers occupy a singularly critical and unique role in our society in that for a great portion of a child's life, they occupy a position of immense direct influence on a child, with the potential for both good and bad.[147]

In the face of lack of evidence that educational staff members were prone to drug use, the court opined that even a "'momentary lapse of attention'" by a teacher could have "'disastrous consequences'" for the children.[148] In weighing the educators' privacy interest against this concern, the court emphasized that the test was performed in a nonpublic, confidential setting, and that because people become educators "understanding that [the field] is heavily regulated as to the conduct expected of people in that field, as well as the responsibilities that they undertake toward students . . ." they therefore had a lessened expectation of privacy.[149]

Going a step further, the U.S. Court of Appeals for the Fifth Circuit rejected a school custodian's Fourth Amendment challenge to being included in a school district's mandatory random testing of employees in safety-sensitive positions.[150] The custodian cleaned bathrooms using various chemicals, mowed grass, trimmed trees, maintained and repaired furniture and equipment, and was constantly in the presence of children.[151] Although the court did not address drug testing of teachers, it held that a special need existed to protect children from the "potentially dangerous actions of adults, including school employees, who may have interaction with or influence upon [children.]"[152] In addressing the individual's privacy interest, the court considered that the custodian could reasonably have anticipated being subject to

---

[146]Knox County Educ. Ass'n v. Knox County Bd. of Educ., 158 F.3d 361, 367, 14 IER Cases 609 (6th Cir. 1998), *cert. denied*, 528 U.S. 812 (1999).

[147]*Id.* at 374–75.

[148]*Id.* at 377 (quoting Skinner v. Railway Labor Executives' Ass'n, 489 U.S. 602, 628, 130 LRRM 2857 (1989)).

[149]*Id.* at 384. The *Knox* decision was criticized in Ruben, *The Top Ten Judicial Decisions Affecting Labor Relations in Public Education During the Decade of the 1990's: The Verdict of Quiescent Years*, 30 J.L. & EDUC. 247, 258–62 (2001).

[150]Aubrey v. School Bd., Lafayette Parish, 148 F.3d 559, 14 IER Cases 375 (5th Cir. 1998). *See also* Pierce v. Smith, 117 F.3d 866, 13 IER Cases 8 (5th Cir. 1997) (upholding suspicionless drug testing of a medical resident). *But see* United Teachers of New Orleans v. Orleans Parish Sch. Bd., 142 F.3d 853, 13 IER Cases 1835 (5th Cir. 1998) (striking down suspicionless drug testing for all school teachers and employees injured in the course of employment).

[151]*Aubrey*, 148 F.3d at 561.

[152]*Id.* at 565.

the drug tests, the specimen was collected in private, the sample was tested only for drugs, and any individual failing the test was simply ordered to attend a substance abuse program.[153]

The New York Court of Appeals, however, held unconstitutional the compulsory random urinalysis testing of all probationary teachers eligible for tenure.[154] The court emphasized that suspicionless drug testing by the state would be closely scrutinized, and concluded that the school district's interest in drug-free teachers did not overcome the teachers' privacy interests.[155]

Based on the foregoing decisions, it appears that the following factors are relevant when arbitrators weigh the government's "special needs" against an individual's privacy interests in determining the validity of a suspicionless drug testing policy: (1) Are the positions safety sensitive? (2) Do individuals in the positions at issue have considerable and direct contact with, and responsibility for, children? (3) Has the targeted group exhibited a pronounced drug problem? (4) Do individuals seeking the positions at issue understand that they will be closely scrutinized? (5) What is the magnitude of harm that could result from the use of illicit drugs on the job? (6) To what degree is the industry in question regulated? (7) How intrusive is the drug test—for example, the privacy of the test, the methodology employed, and the substances subject to the screen? and (8) What is the penalty for failing a test?

---

[153]*Id.* at 564. *See also* Wilcher v. City of Wilmington, 139 F.3d 366, 13 IER Cases 1345 (3d Cir. 1998) (upholding direct observation drug testing of firefighters); Stigile v. Clinton, 110 F.3d 801, 12 IER Cases 1246 (D.C. Cir. 1997), *cert. denied*, 522 U.S. 1147 (1998) (permitting random drug testing of employees with permanent passes to the Old Executive Office Building); Rushton v. Nebraska Pub. Power Dist., 844 F.2d 562, 3 IER Cases 257 (8th Cir. 1988) (upholding drug testing of nuclear power engineers); Loder v. City of Glendale, 14 Cal. 4th 846, 927 P.2d 1200, 59 Cal. Rptr. 2d 696, 12 IER Cases 545 (1997) (permitting suspicionless drug testing of employment candidates, but not of current employees offered a promotion).

[154]Patchogue-Medford Cong. of Teachers v. Patchogue-Medford Union Free Sch. Dist. Bd. of Educ., 70 N.Y.2d 57, 510 N.E.2d 325, 517 N.Y.S.2d 456, 2 IER Cases 198 (1987). *See also* Georgia Ass'n of Educators v. Harris, 749 F. Supp. 1110, 5 IER Cases 1377 (N.D. Ga. 1990); Bangert v. Hodel, 705 F. Supp. 643, 4 IER Cases 12 (D.D.C. 1989).

[155]*Patchogue-Medford*, 70 N.Y.2d. at 70. *See also* 19 Solid Waste Dep't Mechanics v. City of Albuquerque, 156 F.3d 1068, 14 IER Cases 629 (10th Cir. 1998) (affirming district court's overturning of City's suspicionless drug-testing policy); Baron v. City of Hollywood, 93 F. Supp. 2d 1337 (S.D. Fla. 2000) (holding unconstitutional city policy requiring post-offer drug testing for employment candidates).

Chapter 20

Legal Status of Arbitration in the Federal Sector

1. Preliminary Observations: Federal and Private Sectors Compared

Much of the vast body of substantive and procedural principles developed by private-sector labor-management arbitration in the United States is equally applicable to the federal sector. While it is true that many activities and fact situations in the federal sector differ from those in private industry, the principles being applied in federal and other public-sector arbitration generally are the same time-tested principles that evolved through the years in private-sector arbitration. This is not surprising, even apart from the fact that quite commonly a given arbitrator serves both the public and private sectors. Nor is it surprising that arbitration proceedings are no less adversarial in the public sector than in the private sector.[1]

The significant differences that do exist between federal-sector and private-sector arbitration relate principally to the scope of the duty to bargain; the status of management rights; the degree of required adherence by the arbitrator to laws, rules, and regulations; and the scope of review of the arbitrator's decision.[2] The differences in these areas also may affect the arbitrability of issues and the scope of the arbitrator's remedy power. An understanding of the role of contractual grievance procedures and arbitration in the federal sector is aided by an understanding of the historical development of collective bargaining rights in federal employment.

---

[1]For an illustration of the extremely adversarial nature of some public-sector grievance disputes and their handling, see *National Labor Relations Bd.*, 68 LA 279 (Sinicropi, 1977).

[2]Even so, it is "eminently sensible" to apply existing principles of private-sector arbitration law to disputes in the public sector unless special reason exists for not doing so, as one court explained:

> The functions served by grievance and arbitration procedures in the private sector are almost identical to those served by such procedures in the public sector. In both instances, grievances and arbitration procedures provide a relatively speedy and inexpensive method of resolving labor disputes, give the employee the satisfaction of knowing that the resolution of any dispute he may have with his employer lies with a neutral party and not with his employer, and preserve judicial resources by establishing a method for resolving labor disputes independent of the courts. In the private sector, arbitration helps to maintain industrial peace by giving employees an alternative to the strike. In the public sector, arbitration helps to preserve industrial peace by giving employees some recourse when a dispute arises.

> Given all these similarities plus the existence of a well-developed body of federal common law, we conclude that it is eminently sensible to apply existing principles of arbitration law to labor disputes involving TVA [Tennessee Valley Authority]. Our conclusion is reenforced by the fact that state courts increasingly are applying principles developed in the private sector to public employee labor disputes.

Salary Police Employee Panel v. Tennessee Valley Auth., 731 F.2d 325, 330–31, 115 LRRM 3550, 3554 (6th Cir. 1984) (holding existing principles of private-sector arbitration law applicable to Tennessee Valley Authority (TVA) labor disputes, even though the unique TVA labor relations program is authorized by the agency's enabling act and is not regulated by the Taft-Hartley Act (Labor Management Relations Act (LMRA), 29 U.S.C. §141 et seq.) or any governmentwide labor statute)). For a sampling of federal-sector issues and disputes, see Lanphear, Bogdanow, & Murphy, *Federal Employment Decisions of the Federal Circuit in 1988*, 38 Am. U. L. Rev. 1257 (1989).

2. THE EXECUTIVE ORDERS AND THE CIVIL SERVICE
REFORM ACT OF 1978[3]

In 1962, federal employees were granted organizational and bargaining rights by President Kennedy's Executive Order 10,988. These rights were further advanced by President Nixon's Executive Order 11,491 of 1969, which made certain changes to coordinate, strengthen, and clarify the civil service.

Executive Order 10,988 permitted the use of advisory, but not binding, arbitration for representation, bargaining unit, and grievance issues in the federal employment context. Executive Order 11,491 provided for representation disputes, grievances, and contract-negotiation disputes as follows:

1. Representation elections were conducted under the supervision of the Assistant Secretary of Labor for Labor-Management Relations, who also decided questions concerning the appropriate unit.
2. Procedures for the arbitration of employee grievances and of disputes over the interpretation or application of collective bargaining agreements between federal agencies and labor organizations could be negotiated. Either party could file exceptions to an arbitrator's award with the Federal Labor Relations Council.
3. Arbitration or third-party factfinding could be used to resolve negotiation impasses, but only when authorized by the Federal Service Impasses Panel (FSIP) (which itself could make a final decision on the impasse).

Prior to the promulgation of the executive orders and continuing throughout their periods of enforcement, the U.S. Civil Service Commission exercised broad statutory jurisdiction over federal employment. The Commission had executive, rulemaking, and quasi-judicial functions. Its judicial function related to adjudicating claims by federal employees that the rights accorded them under the merit system had been violated. The Commission also had responsibility for enforcement of the Civil Rights Act of 1964[4] and several other statutes prohibiting discrimination in federal employment. Thus, federal employees could obtain remedies from the Civil Service Commission for both merit system and discrimination grievances. Under the executive orders, these statutory remedies were made exclusive for claims within their purview and preempted and foreclosed pursuit of alternative contractual grievance and arbitration remedies.

Major changes in employee dispute resolutions were made by Presidential Reorganization Plan No. 2 of 1978 (which automatically became law when neither House of Congress disapproved the plan within the specified time) and the Civil Service Reform Act (CSRA). The Civil Service Commission was abolished and replaced by two agencies: the Office of Personnel Management (OPM) and the Merit Systems Protection Board (MSPB). The MSPB was charged with the "hearing, adjudication, and appeals functions" of the former Civil Service Commission (except with respect to examination rat-

---

[3]Codified as amended in scattered sections of 5 U.S.C.
[4]42 U.S.C. §2000e et seq.

ings). The OPM was established to perform the other functions of the former Civil Service Commission.[5]

The Federal Labor Relations Council established by Executive Order 11,491 was replaced by the Federal Labor Relations Authority (FLRA) with statutory status,[6] while the Federal Service Impasses Panel established by Executive Order 11,491 was continued and given statutory status.[7] Thus, the labor-management relations and dispute-settlement program that had existed for federal employment under the Executive Orders has now been codified with major changes.[8]

Responsibility for enforcement of the policy against discrimination in federal employment was transferred from the Civil Service Commission and certain other agencies or officials to the Equal Employment Opportunity Commission (EEOC) by Presidential Reorganization Plan No. 1 of 1978 (which also became law automatically when it was not disapproved by either House of Congress within the specified time).[9]

In 1993, Executive Order 12,871 established the National Partnership Council, composed of federal union presidents, agency officials, and government labor and personnel experts, and directed individual agencies to establish their own counterpart councils. The order also directed agencies to bargain with unions on those subjects identified by Section 7106(b)(1) of the CSRA as permissive, or at management's option.[10]

3. The Agencies and Their Roles

A. Office of Personnel Management (OPM)

"The Office of Personnel Management is an independent establishment in the executive branch."[11] The OPM succeeded to Civil Service Commission

---

[5]5 U.S.C. §1101 et seq. (Reorganization Plan No. 2 is published with the annotations to §1101).

[6]*Id.* §§7104, 7105.

[7]*Id.* §7119.

[8]However, 5 U.S.C. §7135 provides that Exec. Order No. 11,491 and certain other executive orders "shall remain in full force and effect until revised or revoked by the President, or unless superseded by specific provisions of [the CSRA] or by regulations or decisions issued pursuant to [the Act]." For books on the federal-sector program, see Celmar & Creo, Federal Arbitration Advocate's Handbook (LRP Publ'ns 2d ed. 1993); Federal Civil Service Law and Procedures: A Basic Guide (Bussey ed., BNA Books 2d ed. 1990). *See also* Ingrassia, *Arbitration Forums Revisited: Part III. Federal Sector Arbitration: A Management Viewpoint, in* Arbitration 1990: New Perspectives on Old Issues, Proceedings of the 43d Annual Meeting of NAA 203 (Gruenberg ed., BNA Books 1991); Hodges, *The Interplay of Civil Service Law and Collective Bargaining Law in Public Sector Employee Discipline Cases*, 32 B.C. L. Rev. 95 (1990); Luneburg, *The Federal Personnel Complaint, Appeal, and Grievance Systems: A Structural Overview and Proposed Revisions*, 78 Ky. L.J. 1 (1989); Brower, *The Duty of Fair Representation Under the Civil Service Reform Act: Judicial Power to Protect Employee Rights*, 30 Okla. L. Rev. 361 (1987).

[9]Reorganization Plan No. 1 is published in the annotations to 42 U.S.C.A. §2000e-4. On discrimination complaints in federal employment, see Martin, *Equal Employment Opportunity Complaint Procedures and Federal Union-Management Relations: A Field Study*, 34 Arb. J. 34 (1979), where many articles on the subject are collected.

[10]Exec. Order No. 12,871, 58 Fed. Reg. 52,201 (1993).

[11]5 U.S.C. §1101.

functions relating to recruitment, measurement, ranking, and selection of individuals for initial appointment and competitive promotion in federal employment.[12] As its name suggests, the OPM's functions are essentially executive or managerial in nature. It is the MSPB, rather than the OPM, that now adjudicates appeals relating to federal employee grievances.

B. Merit Systems Protection Board (MSPB)

The CSRA of 1978 gave the MSPB jurisdiction over a broad range of grievance issues involving federal agency actions affecting employees, including discrimination claims that may be combined or mixed with merit system claims.[13]

The MSPB has authority to review rules and regulations issued by the OPM and to declare any rule or regulation invalid if the rule or regulation or its implementation would violate or lead to violation of any prohibited personnel practice adversely affecting employees (certain personnel practices are prohibited by statute because they are contrary to merit system principles).[14]

C. Federal Labor Relations Authority (FLRA)

The FLRA succeeded the Federal Labor Relations Council and performs a variety of important functions in federal labor-management relations,[15] among which are:

1. To "provide leadership in establishing policies and guidance relating to" labor-management relations matters under Title VII of the CSRA;
2. To determine appropriate units and to conduct representation elections for collective bargaining under the CSRA;[16]
3. To prescribe criteria and resolve issues relating to consultation rights under the CSRA;
4. To resolve issues relating to the duty to bargain;
5. To prescribe criteria and resolve issues relating to the determination of "compelling need" for agency rules or regulations (the duty to bargain extends to any matter that is the subject of rules or regulations of any agency or national subdivision thereof *only if* the FLRA has

---

[12]These functions are enumerated at 5 C.F.R. §300.101.

[13]Regarding the MSPB's composition, its special counsel, and its powers and functions, see 5 U.S.C. §§1201–1205, 7701, 7702. For merit system principles and protections that may become involved in employee claims before the MSPB, see 5 U.S.C. §§2301, 2302. The MSPB was initially established by Reorganization Plan No. 2 of 1978 to exercise "the hearing, adjudication, and appeals functions" of the Civil Service Commission.

[14]*See* 5 U.S.C. §§1205(e) (review authority), 2301 (merit system principles), 2302 (prohibited personnel practices).

[15]*See* 5 U.S.C. §§7104 (appointment of FLRA members and general counsel), 7105 (FLRA functions). See also the U.S. Supreme Court's summary of FLRA's role in *Bureau of Alcohol, Tobacco, & Firearms v. FLRA*, 464 U.S. 89, 107–08, 114 LRRM 3393 (1983), in which decision the Court considered the appropriate standard of court review of FLRA decisions interpreting the CSRA.

[16]The National Labor Relations Board (NLRB), rather than the FLRA, handles representation matters for the U.S. Postal Service. *See* 39 U.S.C. §§1202–1204.

determined that "no compelling need" exists for the rule or regulation; this becomes an important consideration in the arbitration of some grievances);

6. To resolve unfair labor practice complaints; and
7. To resolve exceptions to arbitration awards.

D. Equal Employment Opportunity Commission (EEOC)

The Civil Rights Act of 1964 established the EEOC and placed basic responsibility on it for implementation and enforcement of the Civil Rights Act's prohibitions against discriminatory employment practices.[17] Reorganization Plan No. 1 of 1978 transferred to the EEOC the responsibility for equal opportunity in federal employment that had been vested in the Civil Service Commission pursuant to Section 717 of the Civil Rights Act of 1964; it also transferred enforcement functions for age discrimination, equal pay, and federal employment of handicapped individuals to the EEOC from the agency or official previously exercising those responsibilities.

E. General Accounting Office (GAO)

The GAO has the authority to assure compliance with executive branch and competitive service personnel regulations and to evaluate the managerial effectiveness: "[I]f considered necessary by the Comptroller General, the General Accounting Office shall conduct audits and reviews to assure compliance with the laws, rules, and regulations governing employment in the executive branch and in the competitive service and to assess the effectiveness and soundness of Federal Personnel management."[18]

F. Federal Service Impasses Panel (FSIP)

By statute, the "Federal Service Impasses Panel is an entity within the [Federal Labor Relations] Authority, the function of which is to provide assistance in resolving negotiation impasses between agencies and exclusive representatives."[19] The statute provides that if an impasse is not resolved by the Federal Mediation and Conciliation Service (FMCS) or by other third-party mediation, either party may request the FSIP to consider the matter, or the parties may agree to a procedure for binding arbitration (but only if the procedure is approved by the FSIP). If the parties do not reach a settlement after assistance by the FSIP, the FSIP may conduct hearings on the

---

[17]*See* 42 U.S.C. §§2000e-4, 2000e-5.

[18]5 U.S.C. §2304. Section 2304 also specifies that the General Accounting Office (GAO) shall submit an annual report to the President and Congress on MSPB and OPM activities, including an analysis of whether OPM actions conform to merit system principles and are free from prohibited personnel practices. See also section 5.D., "Comptroller General's Role," below.

[19]5 U.S.C. §7119. Different statutory provisions exist for the U.S. Postal Service. See 39 U.S.C. §1207, which specifies use of a "factfinding panel" and arbitration under the auspices of the Federal Mediation and Conciliation Service (FMCS).

matter and resolve the impasse by action that is binding on the parties during the term of the agreement.[20]

In reviewing FSIP decisions, the FLRA differentiates between the provisions of an agreement that have been imposed by a final order of the FSIP, and those resulting from interest-arbitration awards issued by FSIP mediators/arbitrators. An agency head is authorized to review for legal sufficiency the provisions of a collective bargaining agreement imposed by FSIP decisions and orders.[21] The U.S. Court of Appeals for the Fourth Circuit has held, in part agreeing with the FLRA, that agreement provisions imposed by the FSIP or by a designee of the Panel may be reviewed by the agency head pursuant to 5 U.S.C. §7114(c).[22] If the agency head disapproves, review of that disapproval may be sought through negotiations or an unfair labor practice proceeding.[23]

Interest-arbitration awards, which have been issued based on management's voluntary agreement, are not subject to agency head review, and must be challenged by filing exceptions to the award.[24]

4. Channels for Processing Federal-Sector Grievances

The channels for processing federal-sector grievances vary depending on the subject of the grievance and the grievant's choice of statutory options. Channels and options are outlined in the chart on the following page. Reference must be made to the statutory sections cited to determine the time periods within which action is to be taken or decision rendered. When using the chart, the explanatory notes (a through i) must be considered carefully.

---

[20]Certain collective bargaining agreements strongly urge arbitrators to try to mediate a settlement of a grievance. This process is called mediation-arbitration (med-arb). For example, the Internal Revenue Service and National Treasury Employees Union National Agreement provides for the use of med-arb in expedited cases. Art. 43, §4C. However, in med-arb, the arbitrator still has the authority to issue a final and binding decision if the parties do not settle the matter.

[21]5 U.S.C. §7114(c); Interpretation and Guidance, 15 FLRA 564 (1984), aff'd sub nom. Government Employees (AFGE) v. FLRA, 778 F.2d 850, 121 LRRM 2247 (D.C. Cir. 1985). See generally Federal Civil Service Law and Procedures: A Basic Guide (Bussey ed., BNA Books 2d ed. 1990); Broida, A Guide to Federal Labor Relations Authority Law and Practice 1979–2003 (16th ed. 2003).

[22]Department of Def. Dependents Sch. v. FLRA, 852 F.2d 779, 128 LRRM 3104 (4th Cir. 1988). See also Panama Canal Comm'n v. FLRA, 867 F.2d 905, 130 LRRM 2930 (5th Cir. 1989).

[23]5 U.S.C. §7117 provides a procedure by which an exclusive representative can contest an agency's declaration that particular proposals are nonnegotiable. 5 U.S.C. §7118 provides for unfair labor practice proceedings.

[24]Department of Def., Office of Dependents Sch. v. FLRA, 879 F.2d 1220, 131 LRRM 3042 (9th Cir. 1989); Department of Agric. v. FLRA, 879 F.2d 655, 131 LRRM 3162 (9th Cir. 1989); Department of Def. Dependents Sch., 27 FLRA 586 (1987), aff'd in part, 852 F.2d 779, 128 LRRM 3104 (4th Cir. 1988). See also Air Force Logistics Command, 15 FLRA 151 (1984), aff'd sub nom. Department of the Air Force v. FLRA, 775 F.2d 727 (6th Cir. 1985). 5 U.S.C. §7122 provides that either party may file exceptions to an arbitration award with the FLRA, which can review the award and modify it on the basis that it is contrary to law, rule, or regulation, or for "other grounds similar to those applied by Federal courts in private sector labor-management relations . . . ."

Channels for Processing Federal-Sector Grievances*

	Grievance Subject	Processing Channels
Category I	All subjects (issues) except those included below in Categories II, III, and IV or those the parties have excluded from the grievance procedure or that are expressly excluded by 5 U.S.C. §7121.[a] *Statutes:* 5 U.S.C. §§7121, 7122, 7123.	Grievance Procedure → Arbitration → FLRA[b] (FLRA decision is final except that the U.S. Court of Appeals review of the FLRA final orders is available if an unfair labor practice issue is involved.)
Category II	Reduction in grade or removal for unacceptable performance. Removal, suspension for more than 14 days, reduction in grade or pay, furlough of 30 days or less. *Statutes:* 5 U.S.C. §§4303, 7121, 7122, 7512, 7701, 7703 (court review standards stated here); 28 U.S.C. §1295(a)(9).	Grievance Procedure → Arbitration[c] → U.S. Court of Appeals for the Federal Circuit[c] *Or,* at the employee's option MSPB → U.S. Court of Appeals for the Federal Circuit[c] ——— [commencing one channel bars the other]
Category III	Discrimination (race, color, religion, sex, national origin, age, sex/equal pay, handicapped condition, to the extent that any such discrimination is prohibited by federal statute).[d] *Statutes:* 5 U.S.C. §§2302, 7121; 42 U.S.C. §§2000e-5, 2000e-16[e]; Reorganization Plan No. 1 of 1978.	Grievance Procedure → Arbitration → FLRA → EEOC → U.S. District Court[e] *Or,* at the employee's option Complaint to the employee's agency → EEOC → U.S. District Court (employee has option to omit appeal to EEOC and go directly to U.S. District Court from employee's agency)[e] ——— [commencing one channel bars the other, but the employee can reach the EEOC by either]
Category IV	Mixture of a discrimination issue and other issue.[f] *Statutes:* 5 U.S.C. §§7121, 7702, 7703(b)(2).	Grievance Procedure → Arbitration → FLRA[g] or MSPB[h] → U.S. District Court[i] *Or,* at the employee's option Complaint to employee's agency → MSPB[h] → U.S. District Court[i] (employee also has option to omit appeal to MSPB and go directly to U.S. District Court[i]) ——— [by either channel employee can reach the MSPB and can petition the EEOC]

*See footnote explanations on the following page.

Channels for Processing Federal-Sector Grievances

Chart Abbreviations

MSPB: Merit Systems Protection Board
FLRA: Federal Labor Relations Authority
EEOC: Equal Employment Opportunity Commission

Notes

[a]If the issue is excluded from the grievance procedure or if the employee is outside the bargaining unit, then any statutory remedy (such as consideration by the MSPB) would be used.

[b]What FLRA ultimately does in its review may be at least indirectly affected by the role and actions of the Comptroller General. See section 5.D., "Comptroller General's Role," in the text.

[c]For Category II issues, the arbitrator is governed by the same criteria and standards that would govern the MSPB. See 5 U.S.C. §§7121(e)(2), 7701(c)(1) & (2). Under 28 U.S.C. §1295(a)(9), the U.S. Court of Appeals for the Federal Circuit, which was established in 1982 with jurisdiction limited by subject matter but not by geography, has "exclusive" jurisdiction to review MSPB decisions. By 5 U.S.C. §7121(f), arbitration decisions in Category II cases are subject to review "in the same manner and under the same conditions as if the matter had been decided by" the MSPB; thus, the court also has exclusive jurisdiction to review arbitration decisions.

[d]Section 2302 also prohibits marital status or political affiliation discrimination to the extent prohibited by any law, rule, or regulation; the remedy here would be the grievance procedure or the MSPB. See §7121(d).

[e]The U.S. District Court action specified by these sections is an original action and, thus, is a less restricted form of judicial proceeding than that indicated above for Category II grievances, for which the statute specifies limited grounds on which the court may disturb results reached below. Also, the U.S. District Court proceedings indicated below for Category IV grievances are similarly less restricted than the judicial review on limited grounds that applies to Category II grievances.

[f]The channels indicated for this category apply where the employee's agency takes action appealable to the MSPB and the employee alleges discrimination as a basis for the agency's action. A Category III issue combined with a Category II issue would qualify, as would a Category III issue combined with any other issue appealable to the MSPB. MSPB has jurisdiction over many agency actions affecting employees in addition to those in Category II. However, if the contractual grievance procedure covers a matter not involving a Category II subject and/or discrimination, the channel indicated under Category I is the only one available.

[g]If the arbitration award involves one of the subjects included under Category II, it would not be appealable to the FLRA but would go from arbitration directly to the MSPB.

[h]Instead of going directly to court from the MSPB, the employee has the option of petitioning the EEOC to consider the MSPB decision. If such a request is denied, the employee proceeds to U.S. District Court.[i] If the request is granted but the EEOC concurs with the MSPB, the matter is returned to the MSPB, and (depending on whether the MSPB adopts the EEOC decision) from there it goes either directly to U.S. District Court[i] or to a Special Panel and then to U.S. District Court.[i]

[i]In the U.S. District Court in these "mixed" cases, the employee has the right to a trial de novo. 5 U.S.C. §§7702(e)(3), 7703(c). Moreover, if a grievance is taken to the employee's agency and no decision issues within the statutory time limit, the employee may either proceed to the MSPB or commence an original action in U.S. District Court; if a grievance is taken to the MSPB or to the EEOC and no decision issues within the statutory time limit, the employee may commence an original action in U.S. District Court. 5 U.S.C. §7702(e)(1) & (2).

A. Federal-Sector Bargaining

i.   *Role and Scope of the Federal-Sector Grievance Procedure and Arbitration* [LA CDI 100.0701 et seq.]

The basic function of the grievance procedure and arbitration in private employment is to ensure compliance with the collective bargaining agreement. While this is also a key function of the grievance-arbitration procedure in the federal sector, the federal-sector procedure performs a second and also very important function, namely, to review and police compliance by federal agency employers and employees alike[25] with controlling laws, rules, and regulations.

This dual role of the grievance and arbitration procedure probably was a principal factor in the congressional decision (1) to specify that each collective bargaining agreement in the federal sector "shall" provide a grievance procedure with arbitration, (2) to specify that all grievances "shall" be subject to the grievance and arbitration procedures except those specifically excluded by the collective bargaining agreement or statute, and (3) to define the term "grievance" very broadly.

Arbitral disposition of federal-sector grievances often is governed or materially affected by laws, rules, and regulations apart from the collective bargaining agreement. For example, statutory provisions confide certain subjects to management's exclusive control. Therefore, unlike the private sector, the collective bargaining agreement and custom cannot be made the controlling "law of the shop."

Each collective bargaining agreement in the federal sector is statutorily required to "provide procedures for the settlement of grievances, including questions of arbitrability."[26] The statute also requires that each agreement also must "provide that any grievance not satisfactorily settled under the negotiated grievance procedure shall be subject to binding arbitration which may be invoked by either" the union or the federal agency employer.

With only two exceptions, the contractual grievance-arbitration procedure is "the exclusive procedure for resolving grievances which fall within its coverage."[27] The two exceptions involve certain subjects or issues for which

---

[25]For cases illustrating this role of the grievance procedure and arbitration in the federal sector, see *Department of Justice v. FLRA*, 727 F.2d 481, 115 LRRM 3499 (5th Cir. 1984); *Department of the Navy, Naval Weapons Support Ctr.*, 40 FLRA 1016 (1991); *Social Sec. Admin.*, 17 FLRA 959 (1985).

[26]5 U.S.C. §7121. The U.S. Postal Service statute states that the collective bargaining agreement "may" provide grievance and arbitration procedures. 39 U.S.C. §1206(b).

[27]If the union decides not to arbitrate and the issue is one that can only be addressed through the contractual grievance and arbitration procedures (see Category I in the chart), the employee may be left with no remedy unless some duty of fair representation issue exists. In the latter regard, the duty of fair representation applies in the federal sector just as it does in private employment. *See* Treasury Employees v. FLRA (Bureau of Alcohol, Tobacco, & Firearms), 800 F.2d 1165, 123 LRRM 2129 (D.C. Cir. 1986); Treasury Employees v. FLRA, 721 F.2d 1402, 114 LRRM 3440, 3443 (D.C. Cir. 1983). Note that federal employees have no private cause of action for breach of their union's duty of fair representation. Exclusive enforcement authority over this duty was vested in the FLRA. Karahalios v. Federal Employees (NFFE) Local 1263, 489 U.S. 527, 130 LRRM 2737 (1989). For some issues (Category I), an employee not in the bargaining unit may have a statutory MSPB remedy not available to a unit employee. The statute recognizes the right of individual employee griev-

employees are given the option of using either (but not both) the contractual grievance and arbitration procedure or certain purely statutory procedures. These issues and options are included in the chart as Categories II and III (see also Category IV).[28] The rule concerning "coverage" of the contractual grievance procedure is simple. All grievances are automatically covered by the grievance procedure and can go to arbitration unless excluded by agreement of the parties or unless specifically excluded by statute.[29] The statute provides in substance that:[30]

1. Any collective bargaining agreement may exclude any matter from the application of the agreement's grievance procedure.
2. Grievances concerning the following subjects or issues are specifically excluded from the grievance procedure and arbitration: (1) political activities; (2) retirement, life insurance, or health insurance; (3) suspension or removal for national security; (4) examination, cer-

---

ance adjustment with representation of the individual's own choosing and with "grievance or appellate rights established by law, rule, or regulation; except in the case of grievance or appeal procedures negotiated" in the collective bargaining agreement. 5 U.S.C. §7114(a)(5). Even if the collective bargaining agreement itself authorizes individual employee use of the grievance procedure, the authorization may not be broad enough to include all grievances or to include the right to arbitration. *See, e.g.*, Department of the Air Force, 71 LA 463, 465–66 (Jackson, 1978).

[28]Actually there is a third exception to the "exclusive" status of the grievance and arbitration procedures. Another section of the CSRA provides that, except for certain stated matters, "issues which can be raised under a grievance procedure may, in the discretion of the aggrieved party, be raised under the grievance procedure or as an unfair labor practice under this section [7116], but not under both procedures," 5 U.S.C. §7116(d). This provision was applied in *Department of Defense Dependents Sch.*, 78 LA 815, 818–19 (Gilson, 1982) (issuance of an unfair labor practice decision by the FLRA precluded consideration of the merits of a grievance that had been submitted to the arbitrator).

[29]Concerning the determination of arbitrability of an issue, the fact that the CSRA states in 5 U.S.C. §7121 that collective bargaining agreements in the federal sector "shall provide procedures for the settlement of grievances, including questions of arbitrability" indicates that, in their agreement, the parties are to specify who is to determine arbitrability; presumably, questions of arbitrability will be decided by the arbitrator (subject to FLRA review) if the parties do not specify otherwise. For illustrative cases in which the arbitrator, in ruling on arbitrability, clearly indicated the existence of express authority from the parties to do so, see *Veterans Admin.*, 90 LA 1086 (Madden, 1988); *Department of the Air Force*, 82 LA 593, 595, 597 (Wann, 1984); *Department of the Air Force*, 77 LA 1159, 1161, 1166 (Imundo, Jr., 1981); *Veterans Admin. Med. Ctr.*, 77 LA 725, 725, 728 (Weiss, 1981). For illustrative cases in which the arbitrator ruled on arbitrability without clearly indicating the existence of express authority to do so (but also without indicating that any party had challenged the existence of such authority), see *Veterans Admin. Med. Ctr.*, 81 LA 325, 330 (Gentile, 1983); *Department of Labor*, 78 LA 636, 640 (Rossman, 1982); *Equal Employment Opportunity Comm'n*, 78 LA 165, 171–72 (Bennett, 1982); *Federal Corr. Inst.*, 77 LA 518, 521 (Goldman, 1981); *Social Sec. Admin.*, 77 LA 136, 139 (Atleson, 1981); *National Weather Serv.*, 75 LA 712, 715–16 (Nolan, 1980); *U.S. Army Safety Ctr.*, 75 LA 238, 239 (Dallas, 1980). However, another provision that may be relevant to the determination of arbitrability in some cases is 5 U.S.C. §7117(c), which provides that if an agency employer "alleges that the duty to bargain in good faith does not extend to any matter," the union may appeal the allegation to the FLRA under procedures specified in that subsection. As concerns procedural arbitrability, the FLRA has held that this is for the arbitrator to determine. A similar rule, relied on by the FLRA in articulating this doctrine, was established in the private sector by the Supreme Court in *John Wiley & Sons v. Livingston*, 376 U.S. 543, 55 LRRM 2769 (1964). Under 5 U.S.C. §7122(a), the FLRA will only review an arbitration award to determine whether it is contrary to "any law, rule, or regulation." The FLRA adheres to a policy of deferring to arbitrators' decisions concerning procedural arbitrability in most cases. Department of the Army, 35 FLRA 1187 (1990).

[30]5 U.S.C. §7121.

tification, or appointment;[31] (5) classification of any position if the classification does not result in the reduction in grade or pay of an employee.

What can qualify as a "grievance" in federal employment? The term "grievance" is defined very broadly as follows:

> "grievance" means any complaint—
>   (A) by any employee concerning any matter relating to the employment of the employee;
>   (B) by any labor organization concerning any matter relating to the employment of any employee; or
>   (C) by any employee, labor organization, or agency concerning—
>   (i) the effect or interpretation, or a claim of breach, of a collective bargaining agreement; or
>   (ii) any claimed violation, misinterpretation, or misapplication of any law, rule, or regulation affecting conditions of employment.[32]

However, an employee may elect not to submit a grievance to arbitration but rather may pursue a statutory appeal. In that case the union is not obligated to represent the employee. The obligation of the union is limited to those matters arising out of collective bargaining.[33] But, if the employee submits the grievance to the grievance procedure, the union has an obligation to process the grievance in good faith. If the union fails to process the grievance in good faith, an employee may enforce the duty to arbitrate by filing an unfair labor practice charge with the FLRA. A federal agency also may bring such a charge on behalf of an employee. Under 5 C.F.R. §2421.4, any "person" may file an unfair labor practice charge, and 5 U.S.C. §7103(a)(1) defines the term "person" to include a federal agency.[34]

Contrary to the private sector, the aggrieved employee may not institute a lawsuit in federal district court pursuant to 28 U.S.C. §1331 or 1346. The unfair labor practice procedure of the CSRA provides the exclusive statutory remedy. The Supreme Court ruled in 1989 that the unfair labor practice procedure of the CSRA was the exclusive remedy of an employee who asserted that the union had breached its duty of fair representation.[35]

---

[31]In *James A. Haley Veterans Hosp.*, 82 LA 973 (Wahl, 1984), the FLRA found that, because the probationary period is part of the examination, certification, and appointment process, which is excluded from arbitration by statute, grievances involving probationary employees are not grievable or arbitrable. *See also* Department of the Air Force, 82 LA 593 (Wann, 1984).

[32]5 U.S.C. §7103(a)(9).

[33]Treasury Employees v. FLRA (Bureau of Alcohol, Tobacco, & Firearms), 800 F.2d 1165, 1171, 123 LRRM 2129 (D.C. Cir. 1986). Electing to utilize the unfair labor practice route rather than the grievance arbitration procedure may, in some circumstances, result in the aggrieved party being denied a forum in which to litigate the merits of its dispute. Under the *Harry S. Truman Veterans Hosp.*, 11 FLRA 516 (1983), line of cases, the FLRA will dismiss unfair labor practice charges where the dispute results from contractual interpretation and there has been no clear repudiation of any contractual provisions. If an unfair labor practice charge based on contract interpretation is dismissed by the FLRA after the time limit for the filing of a grievance has passed, the aggrieved party may be left without a remedy. *See also* Frazier, *Arbitration in the Federal Sector*, 41 Arb. J. 70 (1986).

[34]Treasury Employees, 10 FLRA 519 (1982), *aff'd*, 721 F.2d 1402, 114 LRRM 3440 (D.C. Cir. 1983).

[35]Karahalios v. Federal Employees (NFFE) Local 1263, 489 U.S. 527, 130 LRRM 2737 (1989).

With respect to the treatment of nonmembers of the union, under 5 U.S.C. §7114(a)(1), a union must represent all bargaining-unit members "without discrimination and without regard to labor organization membership." In addition, a union cannot require dues or service fees. Despite the fact that nonmembers make no financial contribution for their representation costs, a union may not require only nonmembers to pay arbitration costs.[36] In *Treasury Employees,*[37] the FLRA found that a union's policy of making attorneys available to represent members, but only stewards to represent nonmembers, was discriminatory under the CSRA.

Finally, a union is not required under the duty of fair representation to arbitrate a grievance where the weight of arbitral precedent indicates that the union would have a very difficult time prevailing.[38]

The FLRA considers a grievance to be duplicative and, therefore, prohibited by Section 7116(d) of the CSRA, when: (1) the issue in the grievance and the unfair labor practice charge is the same; (2) the issue was presented in a prior unfair labor practice charge; and (3) the choice to file the unfair labor practice charge was at the aggrieved party's discretion.[39] The FLRA has held that the pivotal point for purposes of Section 7116(d) takes place when the election of forum occurs. Thus, if an employee files an unfair labor practice charge, the employee is precluded from thereafter filing a grievance concerning the same issue.

Even if an unfair labor practice charge is withdrawn before adjudication, a subsequent grievance will not be permitted under the CSRA.[40] The FLRA has held that once an employee has raised an issue under one procedure, the employee is barred from using the other procedure, regardless of whether the matter was resolved on the merits.[41] If an arbitrator considers a grievance, contrary to Section 7116(d), the arbitrator's award will be reversed by the FLRA on appeal. If an unfair labor practice charge involving contract interpretation is dismissed by the FLRA after the time limit for the filing of a grievance has expired, the aggrieved party may not have any remedy.[42]

ii. Scope of Federal-Sector Bargaining and Management-Rights Safeguards [LA CDI 100.021501 et seq.; 100.03]

Although the term "grievance" is defined broadly, and although the door to the grievance procedure and arbitration may be wide indeed, strong protection exists against the narrowing of federal agency managerial authority and against disregard of certain laws, rules, and regulations. Both Executive Order 11,491 and the CSRA contain strong management-rights safe-

---

[36]Government Employees (AFGE) Local 1778, 10 FLRA 346 (1982).

[37]10 FLRA 519 (1982), *aff'd*, 721 F.2d 1402, 114 LRRM 3440 (D.C. Cir. 1983).

[38]Miller v. U.S. Postal Serv., 825 F.2d 62, 44 FEP Cases 1049 (5th Cir. 1987).

[39]*See, e.g.*, Department of Health & Human Servs., Social Sec. Admin., 36 FLRA 448 (1990).

[40]Machinists Lodge 39, 44 FLRA 1291 (1992).

[41]*Id.*

[42]Army Fin. & Accounting Ctr., 38 FLRA 1345 (1991), *aff'd sub nom.* Government Employees (AFGE) Local 1411 v. FLRA, 960 F.2d 176, 139 LRRM 2953 (D.C. Cir. 1992). *See also* Frazier, *Arbitration in the Federal Sector*, 41 Arb. J. 70 (1986).

guards. Collective bargaining is prohibited or merely permitted on numerous important matters in the federal sector that are mandatory subjects of bargaining in the private sector. Nor does the duty to bargain extend to any matter that is the subject of certain rules or regulations. The end result of these prohibitions and limitations is that no grievance may be sustained if the grievance is based on a contract provision dealing with a subject excluded from bargaining by statute, or one that infringes on a statutorily safeguarded management right, or if sustaining the grievance would infringe on any of certain laws, rules, or regulations.

a. Management Rights—Prohibited Bargaining Items [LA CDI 100.021501]

"Except as otherwise provided" by Title VII of the CSRA, federal-sector employees have the right "to engage in collective bargaining with respect to conditions of employment."[43] Bargaining on certain subjects is in effect prohibited by the management-rights section of the CSRA, which states that "nothing" in Title VII "shall affect the authority of any management official of any agency" (the authority thus being reserved or retained in management):

   (1) To determine the mission, budget, organization, number of employees, and internal security practices of the agency; and

   (2) in accordance with applicable laws—

      (A) to hire, assign, direct, layoff, and retain employees in the agency, or to suspend, remove, reduce in grade or pay, or take other disciplinary action against such employees;

      (B) to assign work, to make determinations with respect to contracting out, and to determine the personnel by which agency operations shall be conducted;

      (C) with respect to filling positions, to make selections for appointments from—

         (i) among properly ranked and certified candidates for promotion; or

         (ii) any other appropriate source; and

      (D) to take whatever actions may be necessary to carry out the agency mission during emergencies.[44]

The statutory words "in accordance with applicable laws" do limit management rights, and this limitation would appear to be properly enforceable by contractual grievance and arbitration procedures.[45] Apart from this, however, the statutory reservation of management rights necessarily reduces

---

[43]5 U.S.C. §7102. "Collective bargaining" is defined by §7103(12) to mean "the performance of the mutual obligation of the representative of an agency and the exclusive representative of employees in an appropriate unit in the agency to meet at reasonable times and to consult and bargain in a good-faith effort to reach agreement with respect to the conditions of employment affecting such employees and to execute, if requested by either party, a written document incorporating any collective bargaining agreement reached, but the obligation referred to in this paragraph does not compel either party to agree to a proposal or to make a concession."

[44]5 U.S.C. §7106(a).

[45]Under the first prong of the two-prong test that the FLRA uses to resolve allegations that an arbitration award violates management's rights under §7106(a) of the CSRA, the FLRA considers, in part, whether the award provides a remedy for a violation of an applicable law within the meaning of §7106(a)(2). Department of the Treasury, Bureau of Engraving & Printing, 53 FLRA 146, 151–54 (1997).

the scope of the grievance procedure or arbitral authority to disturb actions taken by agency management officials.

Contract clauses inconsistent with management's reserved rights under the CSRA are not enforceable.[46] *Government Employees (AFGE) Local 1712*[47] illustrates arbitral recognition of the overriding force of federal-sector management rights and the fact that they cannot be bargained away. The FLRA also will set aside or modify remedies imposed by arbitrators that infringe on management's statutory rights.[48]

An award finding arbitrable a grievance seeking to enforce a contract provision denying the agency the right to make a contracting-out decision was set aside because it violated the employer's right to contract out under 5 U.S.C. §7106(a). Also, a proposal barring contracting out until the grievance procedure was fully exhausted was ruled not negotiable.[49] However, the provisions in 5 U.S.C. §7106(a), stating that management rights are to be exercised "in accordance with applicable laws," may limit management's right to contract out. In *EEOC v. FLRA*,[50] the U.S. Court of Appeals for the District of Columbia Circuit affirmed the negotiability of a proposal that would mandate that the EEOC comply with the procedures set forth in Office of Management and Budget (OMB) Circular A-76 in deciding whether to contract out. An arbitrator may find that management failed to comply with OMB Circular A-76 and may require that the process be rerun. The decision to contract out is not per se subject to review,[51] but the arbitrator may not, however, cancel a procurement action.[52]

In contrast to the general statutory policy of safeguarding management rights in the federal sector, the Postal Reorganization Act's[53] grant of certain specified rights to the U.S. Postal Service (similar to the statutory management rights quoted above for federal-sector agencies) is accompanied by significant words of limitation—the U.S. Postal Service has the rights "*consistent with* . . . applicable laws, regulations, and *collective-bargaining agreements*."[54]

---

[46]A union may not have the right to grieve a job change based on the employee's seniority because that contention was inconsistent with management rights under 5 U.S.C. §7106. *See* Veterans Admin. Med. Ctr., 83 LA 1219 (Rotenberg, 1984).

[47]6 FLRA 466 (1981). *See also* Veterans Admin. Med. Ctr., 25 FLRA 520 (1987) (management's right to assign employees); 438 Air Base Group, 22 FLRA 12 (1986) (management's right to assign work); Defense Contract Admin., 20 FLRA 783 (1985) (management's right to make selections from any appropriate source).

[48]Professional Air Traffic Controllers Org., 5 FLRA 763 (1981) (management's right to take disciplinary action). *See also* Social Sec. Admin., 46 FLRA 1404 (1993) (management's right to make selections for promotions).

[49]*See* Congressional Research Employees Ass'n, 23 FLRA 137 (1986). *See also* Department of the Treasury, Internal Revenue Serv. v. FLRA, 862 F.2d 880, 130 LRRM 2024 (D.C. Cir. 1988), *rev'd*, 494 U.S. 922, 133 LRRM 3066 (1990).

[50]744 F.2d 842, 117 LRRM 2625 (D.C. Cir. 1984), *cert. dismissed*, 476 U.S. 19, 122 LRRM 2081 (1986) (Justices White and Stevens dissented from the Supreme Court's dismissal of certiorari).

[51]*Id.* at 851. *See also* Department of Health & Human Servs. v. FLRA, 822 F.2d 430, 125 LRRM 2976 (4th Cir. 1987). *But see* Defense Language Inst. v. FLRA, 767 F.2d 1398, 120 LRRM 2013 (9th Cir. 1985), *cert. dismissed*, 476 U.S. 1110 (1986).

[52]Headquarters, 97th Combat Support Group, 22 FLRA 656 (1986).

[53]39 U.S.C. §101 et seq.

[54]*Id.* §1001(e) (emphasis added). For another indication of the particularly strong status of U.S. Postal Service collective bargaining agreements, see 39 U.S.C. §1005(a)(1)(A). For a

b. Management Rights—Permitted Bargaining Items [LA CDI 100.021515]

The statutory management-rights limitation on bargaining subject matter is qualified, however, by a subsection stating that nothing in the section shall "preclude" any agency and union from negotiating:[55]

> (1) at the election of the agency, on the numbers, types, and grades of employees or positions assigned to any organizational subdivision, work project, or tour of duty, or on the technology, methods, and means of performing work;
> (2) procedures which management officials of the agency will observe in exercising any authority under this section; or
> (3) appropriate arrangements for employees adversely affected by the exercise of any authority under this section by such management officials.[56]

The question is whether a proposal relates to procedural or substantive management rights. The former is negotiable, the latter is not. Where and how to draw the line is a subject of frequent litigation. While the courts have concluded such a decision is best left to the FLRA, the U.S. Court of Appeals for the District of Columbia Circuit declined to defer to the FLRA's interpretation of Executive Order 12,871.[57] The FLRA had ruled that three federal agencies that refused to bargain over matters covered by Section 7106(b)(1) of the Federal Service Labor-Management Relations statute, 5 U.S.C. §7106(b)(1), did not commit unfair labor practices despite language in Executive Order 12,871 directing heads of agencies and their subordinates to negotiate on (b)(1) matters. The court, in upholding the FLRA's decision, found that the language of the Executive Order does not constitute a Section 7106(b)(1) election, but rather the President's direction to subordinates to take certain action.[58] One of the thorniest questions under Section 7106(b)(1)

---

convincing example of the fact that the U.S. Postal Service management rights must be exercised in a manner consistent with the collective bargaining agreement, and illustrating the broad possibility that the U.S. Postal Service may bargain away management rights, see *U.S. Postal Serv.*, 71 LA 1188, 1195–97 (Garrett, 1978) (the national collective bargaining agreement effectively imposed significant restrictions on management rights).

[55]A finding that a proposal is negotiable means only that it is a permissible subject of bargaining. It does not mean the proposal should or must be implemented. Treasury Employees Ch. 83, 35 FLRA 398 (1990). *See also* Department of Justice, Immigration & Naturalization Serv. v. FLRA, 881 F.2d 636, 132 LRRM 2017 (9th Cir. 1989); Government Employees (AFGE) Local 2441 v. FLRA (Bureau of Prisons), 864 F.2d 178, 130 LRRM 2243 (D.C. Cir. 1988).

[56]5 U.S.C. §7106(b). "Method" refers to "the way an agency performs its work." Department of the Army, Army Corps of Eng'rs, 52 FLRA 813, 818 (1996) (internal quotation marks and citation omitted). "Means" refers to "any instrumentality, including an agent, tool, device, measure, plan, or policy used by an agency for the accomplishment or furtherance of the performance of its work." *Id.* The key to determining negotiability is whether the union proposals "interfere with the purpose for which an agency's technology, methods, and means were adopted . . . ." This decision by an agency depends on a number of factors, including "the degree of departure from agency policy implicit in a particular union proposal, the type of agency involved, and the agency's specific needs and requirements." It is thus a case-by-case determination. Department of Health & Human Servs., Indian Health Serv. v. FLRA, 885 F.2d 911, 917, 132 LRRM 2492, 2497 (D.C. Cir. 1989). Management's election not to bargain on a paragraph 1 item leaves the matter for managerial decision, unless some limitation apart from the status is found applicable. Government Employees (AFGE) Int'l Council of U.S. Marshals Serv. Locals, 4 FLRA 384 (1980).

[57]Government Employees (AFGE) Def. Logistics Council v. FLRA, 810 F.2d 234, 124 LRRM 2425 (D.C. Cir. 1987).

[58]Government Employees (NAGE) v. FLRA, 179 F.3d 946, 161 LRRM 2648 (D.C. Cir. 1999).

relates to proposals that directly or indirectly affect staffing questions.[59] Two U.S. Circuit Courts of Appeals have held that the president did not intend to allow an election to bargain over the subjects set forth in Section 7106(b)(1) by stating in Executive Order 12,871[60] that "the head of each agency . . . shall . . . negotiate over the subjects set forth in 5 U.S.C. §7106(b)(1), and instruct subordinate officials to do the same." This conclusion was reached because the order is not itself an election, but rather directs those answerable to the president to take such action, and because the order states in Section 3 that it is not intended to "create any right to administrative or judicial review, or any right, substantive or procedural, enforceable by a party against the United States . . . ."[61]

Agency management may be required to bargain on *procedures* to be observed by management in exercising its rights, that is, "implementation bargaining," or on the *effect* on employees produced by the exercise of those rights, that is, "impact bargaining."[62] An agency's obligation to bargain as to the impact and implementation under 5 U.S.C. §7106(b)(2) and (3) has been limited to subjects that have more than a minimal impact on unit employees. In determining whether a union's request for impact bargaining will be validated, the FLRA stated that it will consider the effect on conditions of employment:

> We have reassessed and modified the recent *de minimis* standard. . . . In examining the record, we will place principal emphasis on such general areas of consideration as the nature and extent of the effect or reasonably foreseeable effect of the change on conditions of employment of bargaining unit employees. Equitable considerations will also be taken into account in balancing the various interests involved.[63]

The number of employees involved, however, will not be a controlling consideration. This factor will be applied primarily to expand rather than limit the number of situations where bargaining will be required. The FLRA may find that a change affecting only a few employees does not require bargaining. But, "a similar change involving hundreds of employees could, in appropriate circumstances, give rise to a bargaining obligation. The parties' bargaining history will be subject to similar limited application. As to the size of the bargaining unit, this factor will no longer be applied."[64]

---

[59]Management has a right to determine what employees are needed to perform particular work on particular shifts. However, if the proposals focus on the characteristics of the employees rather than the fact of their assignment, the proposal may be a permissible subject of bargaining under this section. *See* Government Employees (AFGE) Council of Locals 214 v. FLRA (Air Force Logistics Command), 798 F.2d 1525, 123 LRRM 2177 (D.C. Cir. 1986); Government Employees (NAGE) Local R5-184, 52 FLRA 1024 (1997).

[60]Exec. Order No. 12,871, 58 Fed. Reg. 52,201 (1993).

[61]Government Employees (AFGE) v. FLRA, 204 F.3d 1272, 163 LRRM 2641 (9th Cir. 2000); Government Employees (NAGE) v. FLRA, 179 F.3d 946, 161 LRRM 2648 (D.C. Cir. 1999).

[62]*See also* Underwood, *Collective Bargaining in the Federal Sector*, 35 A.F. L. REV. 129, 133 (1991). Agency management sometimes may feel forced to walk a legality tightrope between §7106(a) and §7106(b)(2) & (3). Note in this regard, ROBINSON, NEGOTIABILITY IN THE FEDERAL SECTOR 189 (N.Y. Sch. of Indus. Relations 1981).

[63]Department of Health & Human Servs., Social Sec. Admin., 24 FLRA 403, 407–08 (1986).

[64]*Id.* at 408.

The negotiations on impact and implementation also must relate to the change that the agency is making with respect to conditions of employment.[65] The FLRA has devised a number of standards or "tests" by which to distinguish procedural and substantive proposals. Its approach is sufficiently contextual, however, so as to provide minimal guidance or basis for generalization. Courts have upheld the FLRA's use of two different standards, the "acting at all" standard and the "direct interference" standard, in determining whether there is a duty to bargain on "procedures" proposals.[66] A proposal that "directly interferes" with management's reserved authority is deemed sufficiently substantive, although it may sound procedural, to be nonnegotiable.[67] Even proposals of "pure" procedures may be nonnegotiable if they would preclude an agency from acting at all.[68] However, as to those rights on which bargaining is prohibited, "the inclusion of a clause that infringes on a 'retained management right' renders the clause null and void."[69]

A third standard "appropriate arrangements" bargaining test is important because it allows some interference with management rights and sometimes allows the parties to bypass strict prohibitions that look toward whether there is a direct interference with management rights.[70]

What constitutes negotiable appropriate arrangements has occasioned considerable litigation. The FLRA considers five major factors when applying its "excessive interference" test: (1) the nature and extent of the impact; (2) the circumstances surrounding the effect and the extent to which it is under employee control; (3) the extent of the impact and the nature of the management right that is being affected; (4) the extent of the harm to the management right in relation to the benefit to the employee(s); and (5) the effect of the proposal on the efficient operation of government. The

---

[65]Department of the Air Force, Air Force Logistics Command, 22 FLRA 502 (1986).

[66]Department of Def., Army-Air Force Exch. Serv. v. FLRA, 659 F.2d 1140, 107 LRRM 2901 (D.C. Cir. 1981) (upheld the FLRA's acting at all test for negotiable procedural proposals), *cert. denied sub nom.* Government Employees (AFGE) v. FLRA, 455 U.S. 945 (1982). *See also* Navy Pub. Works Ctr. v. FLRA, 678 F.2d 97, 110 LRRM 2570 (9th Cir. 1982); Federal Employees (NFFE) Local 858, 47 FLRA 613 (1993) (a proposal for hiring court reporters was found to be negotiable); Treasury Employees, 47 FLRA 304 (1993) (defining negotiable procedures). The acting at all test for determining whether bargaining is mandatory was also applied to "impact" proposals in *Treasury Employees,* 2 FLRA 254, 259–62 (1979). In *Veterans Administration Medical Center v. FLRA,* 675 F.2d 260, 265–66, 110 LRRM 2465, 2469 (11th Cir. 1982), the court stated that "we concur with the Court in *Department of Defense . . . .* that the FLRA may distinguish between procedures that directly interfere with management rights—i.e., those procedures that specify the criteria pursuant to which management must exercise its rights—and procedures that indirectly affect management by outlining the *process* that management must follow when it exercises its rights pursuant to its own criteria" (emphasis in original).

[67]Federal Employees (NFFE) Local 1745 v. FLRA, 828 F.2d 834, 123 LRRM 2342 (D.C. Cir. 1987); Government Employees (AFGE) Local 1920, 47 FLRA 340 (1993).

[68]Department of Def., Army-Air Force Exch. Serv. v. FLRA, 659 F.2d 1140, 107 LRRM 2901 (D.C. Cir. 1981). There is continuing controversy over the breadth and applicability of this standard. *See* Customs Serv. v. FLRA, 854 F.2d 1414, 129 LRRM 2238 (D.C. Cir. 1988).

[69]Tobias, *The Scope of Bargaining in the Federal Sector: Collective Bargaining or Collective Consultation,* 44 Geo. Wash. L. Rev. 554, 557 (1976) (citing Federal Labor Relations Council decisions). *See also* Federal Employees (NFFE) Forest Serv. Council, 45 FLRA 242 (1992).

[70]Broida, A Guide to Federal Labor Relations Authority Law and Practice 1979–2003, at 475–76 (16th ed. 2003). For example, a proposal for installation of telephones was deemed negotiable under §7106(b)(3). Government Employees (AFGE) Local 1122, 47 FLRA 272 (1993).

FLRA also will consider any relevant past experience of the parties as part of the balance.[71]

Assuming that the substantive/procedural hurdle is surmounted, it then becomes necessary to determine when to bargain about "arrangements" that may adversely affect employees. The negative effect on employees is the trigger for Section 7106(b)(3).[72] The FLRA holds that if there is an "adverse effect," bargaining is required unless the proposed arrangement would "excessively interfere" with the exercise of management's rights. In that case, it is not negotiable.[73] An acceptable proposal can interfere with management rights, however. A proposal that impinges on a management right but which is also an "appropriate arrangement" under Section 7106(b)(3) is negotiable as long as it does not preclude the right entirely.[74]

However, the arrangement must be directed at relieving adverse effects "flowing from the exercise of a protected management right."[75] The relief must be structured so as to benefit, or compensate, only those employees suffering adverse effects resulting from the exercise of management's rights.[76] Proposals that fail to provide for application of such benefits or compensation "only to hurts arising from the exercise of management's rights" generally are outside the scope of bargaining under Section 7106(b)(3).[77]

Contractually agreed-upon Section 7106(b)(3) "arrangements" are enforceable via the contractual grievance procedure and arbitration provisions.[78] Although Section 7106(b)(3) stipulates that appropriate arrangements for adversely affected employees are negotiable, this section has been held not to carve out any exceptions to the negotiation requirements. Matters that would be deemed "inconsistent" with the law still are precluded from consideration. How this is actually applied is still unsettled.[79] Section 7106(b)(3) does not make negotiable a matter that is inconsistent with the law.[80] More-

---

[71]Government Employees (AFGE) Local 1923 v. FLRA (Department of Health & Human Servs.), 819 F.2d 306, 125 LRRM 2697 (D.C. Cir. 1987); Government Employees (AFGE) Local 513, 41 FLRA 589 (1991).

[72]Treasury Employees, 45 FLRA 1256 (1992); West Point Elementary Sch. Teachers Ass'n, 34 FLRA 1008 (1990).

[73]Government Employees (AFGE) Local 1923 v. FLRA (Department of Health & Human Servs.), 819 F.2d 306, 309 125 LRRM 2697 (D.C. Cir. 1987); Professional Airways Sys. Specialists, 56 FLRA 798 (2000); Government Employees (NAGE) Local R14-87, 21 FLRA 24 (1986).

[74]Department of the Treasury, Customs Serv., 37 FLRA 309 (1990).

[75]Department of the Treasury v. FLRA, 960 F.2d 1068, 1073, 143 LRRM 2723 (D.C. Cir. 1992).

[76]See, e.g., Government Employees (NAGE) Local R-14-23, 53 FLRA 1440, 1443–44 (1998).

[77]Government Employees (AFGE) National Border Patrol Council, 51 FLRA 1308, 1319 (1996).

[78]Marine Corps Logistics Support Base, 3 FLRA 396 (1980).

[79]Federal Employees (NFFE) Local 1655, 35 FLRA 740 (1990); Government Employees (AFGE) Local 1931, 32 FLRA 1023 (1988). For example, an arbitration award enforcing a contractual provision requiring retroactive promotion was found to infringe on management's statutory right to make decisions regarding promotion and not to be a negotiable proposal or appropriate arrangement under §7106(b)(3). Department of Health & Human Servs., Social Sec. Admin., 46 FLRA 1134 (1993). But see Federal Employees (NFFE) Local 1974, 46 FLRA 1170 (1993) (proposals concerning performance evaluations did not excessively interfere with management's rights and were negotiable arrangements under §7106(b)(3)).

[80]Government Employees (AFGE) Local 1923 v. FLRA (Department of Health & Human Servs.), 819 F.2d 306, 310, 125 LRRM 2697 (D.C. Cir. 1987).

over, in April 1993 the FLRA reversed a 1985 decision holding that proposals concerning inspector general investigations were negotiable.[81]

The FLRA also settled a dispute concerning midterm bargaining that featured conflicting views between the District of Columbia and Fourth Circuit Courts of Appeals. In 1987, the D.C. Circuit had found that an agency had an obligation to bargain over union-initiated proposals offered during the term of a collective bargaining agreement.[82] Five years later, the Fourth Circuit reached the exact opposite conclusion when it concluded that the obligation to bargain arose only to one, basic agreement and did not extend to midterm bargaining.[83] In 1996, the FLRA was asked to decide the issue of a contract term requiring union-initiated midterm bargaining.[84] The FLRA's decision finding a violation where the agency refused to bargain over a contract term requiring midterm bargaining was subsequently reviewed and reversed by the Fourth Circuit.[85] The FLRA petitioned the Supreme Court to review the Fourth Circuit's decision. The Supreme Court granted certiorari to settle the split among the Circuits and focused on the question of whether the statute imposed a duty to bargain during the term of an existing labor contract. Rejecting the view of the court below, the Court found "the Statute's language sufficiently ambiguous or open on the point as to require judicial deference to reasonable interpretation" by the FLRA.[86] The Court went on to recognize that "the Statute grants the Authority leeway . . . in answering" the question regarding midterm bargaining.[87] The Court remanded the case to permit the FLRA to consider the question of midterm bargaining. The Fourth Circuit also remanded "to the Authority for further proceedings consistent with the opinion of the Supreme Court.[88] The FLRA's decision finding a duty to engage in midterm bargaining seems to have settled this issue.[89]

c. Governmentwide Rules or Regulations

Until 1987, under the CSRA the duty to bargain did not extend to any matter that is the subject of any "Government-wide rule or regulation."[90]

In 1987 the FLRA held that "[a] government-wide regulation which essentially restates a management right under Section 7106 should not constitute a greater bar to bargaining than the statutory right itself."[91] The ques-

---

[81]Treasury Employees, 47 FLRA 370 (1993) (overruling Federal Employees (NFFE) Local 1300, 18 FLRA 789 (1985)).

[82]Treasury Employees v. FLRA, 810 F.2d 295, 124 LRRM 2489 (D.C. Cir. 1987).

[83]Social Sec. Admin. v. FLRA, 956 F.2d 1280, 139 LRRM 2691 (4th Cir. 1992).

[84]Department of the Interior, 52 FLRA 475 (1996).

[85]Department of Interior v. FLRA, 132 F.3d 157, 156 LRRM 2737 (4th Cir. 1997).

[86]Federal Employees (NFFE) Local 1309 v. Department of Interior, 526 U.S. 86, 92, 160 LRRM 2577 (1999).

[87]Id. at 100.

[88]Department of Interior v. FLRA, 174 F.3d 393, 394, 161 LRRM 2073 (4th Cir. 1999).

[89]Department of the Interior, 56 FLRA 45 (2000).

[90]5 U.S.C. §7117(a)(1). Also relevant is §7103(a)(14). Under the CSRA, collective bargaining agreements are subject to approval by the agency head within 30 days after execution of the agreement, in order to review compliance with "applicable law, rule, or regulation." 5 U.S.C. §7114(c)(1) & (2).

[91]Government Employees (AFGE) Local 32, 29 FLRA 380, 400 (1987), aff'd sub nom. Office of Pers. Mgmt. v. FLRA, 864 F.2d 165, 130 LRRM 2172 (D.C. Cir. 1988).

tion is whether the rule or regulation restates a Section 7106 management right. If not, the existence of a governmentwide rule continues to bar negotiability.[92] This interpretation has been seen as a step toward greater bargaining latitude, because inclusion under Section 7106(a) is not necessarily a bar to negotiations if it is an appropriate arrangement under Section 7106(b)(3).[93] In addition, 5 U.S.C. §7116(a)(7) makes it "an unfair labor practice for an agency . . . to enforce any rule or regulation . . . which is in conflict with any applicable collective bargaining agreement if the agreement was in effect before the date the rule or regulation was prescribed . . . ."

The FLRA has defined governmentwide rules or regulations as those that are generally applicable throughout the federal government.[94] Although many governmentwide rules and regulations were contained in the now abolished Federal Personnel Manual (FPM), many, but not all, of these rules and regulations can be found today in the Code of Federal Regulations.[95]

Arbitral awards that conflict with governmentwide regulations are not enforceable.[96] If the matters are not bargainable issues because of governmentwide rules or regulations, the union may still have consultation rights over the issues.[97] "[C]ertain unions have the privilege to engage in consultations, but not bargaining, over agency actions or regulations having national impact."[97a] "'[C]onsultation' means something different from 'bargaining' in two areas: national consultation rights under Section 7113 and Government-wide consultation rights under Section 7117(d)(1) and (2)."[98]

Regulations defining the procedures for Section 7113 are found at 5 C.F.R. §2426.1, which stipulates that an agency shall accord national consultation rights to a labor organization when a labor organization has at least 3,500 employees in the agency or 10 percent or more of the specified eligible em-

---

[92]Department of Navy, Military Sealift Command v. FLRA, 836 F.2d 1409, 127 LRRM 2332 (3d Cir. 1988) (overruling National Maritime Union, 25 FLRA 105 (1987), and giving contextual explanation to Government Employees (AFGE) v. FLRA, 653 F.2d 669, 107 LRRM 2594 (D.C. Cir. 1981)).

[93]Government Employees (NAGE), 40 FLRA 657 (1991). For a full discussion of the interrelationship of the law and negotiability determinations by the FLRA, see *Federal Employees (NFFE) Local 29*, 45 FLRA 603 (1992).

[94]Treasury Employees, 38 FLRA 1605 (1991); Marine Eng'rs Beneficial Ass'n, 26 FLRA 63 (1987).

[95]Although officially abolished as of December 1994, the FPM continues to serve as a useful source for identifying governmentwide rules and regulations. However, unless the FPM rule or regulation has been codified elsewhere, it can no longer be relied on as an authoritative source of governmentwide rules and regulations. Social Sec. Admin., 55 FLRA 834 (1999) (FPM and FLRA decisions interpreting FPM are inapplicable unless the rule or regulation is codified elsewhere). *See also* Department of the Navy, Newport News, VA, 56 FLRA 339 (2000).

[96]Department of the Army, 37 FLRA 186 (1990).

[97]5 U.S.C. §7117(d). It was stressed by the Federal Labor Relations Council under Exec. Order No. 11,491 that "[a]rbitrators should consider appropriate regulations, such as those in the Federal Personnel Manual, and ensure that their awards are consistent with them." Frazier, *Labor Arbitration in the Federal Service*, 45 GEO. WASH. L. REV. 712, 733 (1977). The obligation to consider regulations may require the arbitrator to interpret and determine the scope of the regulations. Department of Def. Dependents Sch., 4 FLRA 412 (1980). *See* Warner Robins Air Logistics Ctr., 92 LA 301 (Clarke, 1988); Fleming Foods of Mo., 89 LA 1292 (Yarowsky, 1987).

[97a]BROIDA, A GUIDE TO FEDERAL LABOR RELATIONS AUTHORITY LAW & PRACTICE ch. 5, §IX (16th ed. 2003).

[98]Oklahoma City Air Logistics Ctr., 3 FLRA 511, 522 (1980).

ployees and requests national consultation rights. The 10 percent determination is measured according to the regulation, not according to whether they are included in or eligible to be included in a collective bargaining unit.[99] Section 7117(d)(1) extends national consultation rights to governmentwide regulations issued by agencies, and 5 C.F.R. §2426.1–.13 outlines what it takes to effect these rights. "[F]or the consultation obligation . . . to apply, there must be a substantive change in conditions of employment."[100] A union's statutory consultation rights include the right to receive advance notice of proposed changes in conditions of employment, the opportunity to present views and recommendations, the right to have such views and recommendations considered by the agency before it takes final action, and the right to a written statement of the reasons for the final action taken.[101] A union may reduce its right to bargain to only "consultation" by specific waiver language in the collective bargaining agreement.[102] However, to prove a statutory violation it must be shown that the agency's actions taken without consultation effected a significant change in a condition of employment.[103] Section 7113(b) sets forth the agency's procedural obligations inherent in these rights.

d. Nongovernmentwide Rules or Regulations[104] [LA CDI 100.30]

There are no definitive answers to the questions whether the duty to bargain under the CSRA extends to matters that are the subject of any nongovernmentwide rule or regulation or whether a nongovernmentwide rule or regulation will control over a conflicting collective bargaining agreement provision. Rather, the answers to these questions appear to depend on (1) the agency level at which the rule or regulation is issued, and (2) the level and scope of the bargaining unit that produced the collective bargaining agreement provision.[105]

The statute does not state any limitation on the duty to bargain on matters that are the subject of any rule or regulation issued below the level of primary national subdivision of an agency. It appears there is a duty to bargain on matters (assuming they are otherwise proper subjects for bargaining) that are the subject only of a rule or regulation issued below the level of primary national subdivision of an agency; a collective bargaining agreement provision would control over such lower level rules or regulations where they conflict.

Between the two extremes stand those rules and regulations "issued by

---

[99]Department of Def. Dependents Sch., 37 FLRA 497 (1988).

[100]National Guard Bureau, 22 FLRA 836, 839 (1986).

[101]Aronin, *Collective Bargaining in the Federal Service: A Balanced Approach*, 44 Geo. Wash. L. Rev. 576 (1976). Regarding the distinction between the duty to consult and the duty to negotiate under the CSRA, see Robinson, Negotiability in the Federal Sector 38–39 (N.Y. Sch. of Indus. Relations 1981).

[102]Department of Health & Human Servs., Food & Drug Admin., 83 LA 883 (Edes, 1984).

[103]*See* Office of Pers. Mgmt., 18 FLRA 659 (1985).

[104]For a good description of the history of the civil service and how its structure and procedures for dealing with complaints and grievances by government workers have changed, see Luneburg, *The Federal Personnel Complaint, Appeal, and Grievance Systems: A Structural Overview and Proposed Revisions*, 78 Ky. L.J. 1 (1989).

[105]As used in this treatise, the term "nongovernmentwide" refers to government rules and regulations that are not governmentwide in application.

any agency [i.e., at the top level or headquarters of the agency] or issued by any primary national subdivision of such agency." For ready reference, these may be termed "intermediate" rules and regulations, as distinguished from "governmentwide" rules and regulations or from "lower level" rules and regulations issued below the level of primary national subdivision of an agency.

The duty to bargain extends to matters that are the subject of any "intermediate" rule or regulation only if the FLRA has determined that "no compelling need" exists for the rule or regulation, or if, under the statutory exception, the union "represents an appropriate unit including not less than a majority of the employees in the issuing agency or primary national subdivision, as the case may be, to whom the rule or regulation is applicable."[105A]

Thus, at the upper levels of the agency, where top management makes the bargaining judgments with a union speaking for at least a large segment of the agency's employees, the union has a statutory right to bargain (assuming the matter is otherwise a proper subject for bargaining) without regard to the agency's rules and regulations. However, rules and regulations issued at upper levels for broad application and for which "compelling need" exists control over conflicting collective bargaining agreements negotiated by the agency's lower level bargaining units.[106] The FLRA may make a "no compelling need" finding only through the Section 7117(b) negotiability appeal, and not through an unfair labor practice proceeding.[107]

Arbitration awards that conflict with rules or regulations that are *not* "governmentwide" may not be enforceable in such instances. However, if the collective bargaining agreement includes a provision similar to the rule, the contract takes precedence and the arbitrator's decision is binding.[108]

5. REVIEW OF ARBITRATION AWARDS

A. Review by the Federal Labor Relations Authority

One of the most significant distinctions between private-sector arbitration and arbitration in the federal sector involves scope of review. Most arbitrations in the federal sector are reviewable by the FLRA. Those that are not reviewable by the FLRA are reviewable by the MSPB and/or the EEOC, and ultimately by either the United States Court of Appeals for the Federal Circuit or the United States District Courts and then the Courts of Appeals. The Processing Channels chart on page 1280 indicates categories of issues and the processing channels for each category. If a grievance does not involve an

---

[105A]5 U.S.C. §7117(a)(3).

[106]Similar considerations may underlie the general dominance of a master agreement over a local agreement in the federal sector. *See generally* Government Employees (AFGE) Int'l Council of Marshals Serv. Locals, 11 FLRA 672 (1983) (discussing national agreements to continue to bargain at local levels). *See also* Veterans Admin. Med. Ctr., Leavenworth, 91 LA 314 (Yarowsky, 1988) (dealing with the relationship between a master agreement negotiated at the national level and agreements negotiated at the local level).

[107]FLRA v. Aberdeen Proving Ground, Dept. of the Army, 485 U.S. 409, 127 LRRM 3137 (1988).

[108]Department of Veterans Affairs, Cent. Tex. Veterans Health Care Sys., 55 FLRA 626 (1999); Department of the Air Force, Air Force Logistics Command, 43 FLRA 1397 (1992).

adverse-action issue listed under Category II, or a discrimination issue, an arbitration award resolving the grievance is subject to review only by the FLRA as indicated in the Category I segment of the chart (and the FLRA decision is final unless an unfair labor practice issue is involved).[109]

i. Grounds and Standards for Review

The CSRA, as amended in 1984, allows either party to file exceptions to any arbitration award with the FLRA (unless the award involves any issue listed under Category II of the chart above).[110] The exceptions must be filed within 30 days of the issuance of the final award, and the nonexcepting party may submit a statement in opposition.[111] If no exceptions are filed within 30 days, the award is final and binding.[112]

The statute continues:

(a)   ... If upon review the Authority finds that the award is deficient—
    (1) because it is contrary to any law, rule, or regulation; or
    (2) on other grounds similar to those applied by Federal courts in private sector labor-management relations;
    the Authority may take such action and make such recommendations concerning the award as it considers necessary, consistent with applicable laws, rules, or regulations.

(b) If no exception to an arbitrator's award is filed under subsection (a) of this section during the 30-day period beginning on the date the award is served on the party, the award shall be final and binding. An agency shall take the actions required by an arbitrator's final award. The award may include the payment of backpay (as provided in section 5596 of this Title).[113]

The FLRA regulations are as vague as the statute in articulating grounds for review of awards. The regulations state that the FLRA will review an award to determine if it is deficient because "it is contrary to any law, rule or regulation," or on "other grounds similar to those applied by Federal courts

---

[109]5 U.S.C. §7123(a)(1). In *Overseas Educ. Ass'n v. FLRA (Customs Serv.)*, 824 F.2d 61, 125 LRRM 3330 (D.C. Cir. 1987), the U.S. Court of Appeals for the District of Columbia Circuit appeared to interpret the statute, consistent with its plain language, as absolutely precluding judicial review unless an unfair labor practice was alleged. In *Griffith v. FLRA*, 842 F.2d 487, 494–96, 127 LRRM 3148 (D.C. Cir. 1988), however, the court held that because there was no explicit ban on the review of constitutional claims, the court of appeals could review decisions involving such claims even in the absence of an unfair labor practice allegation. In *Department of the Treasury, Customs Serv. v. FLRA* 43 F.3d 682, 690–91, 148 LRRM 2090 (D.C. Cir. 1994), it went a step further, finding that the court of appeals could review issues involving the FLRA's jurisdiction. This view was soundly rejected by the U.S. Court of Appeals for the Ninth Circuit in *Treasury Employees v. FLRA*, 112 F.3d 402, 405, 155 LRRM 2065 (9th Cir. 1997). *See* Pfeiffer, *Jurisdictional Restraints on the Federal Labor Relations Authority: A Split in the Circuits*, 16 HOFSTRA LAB. & EMPL. L.J. 201 (1998).

[110]Department of Health & Human Servs., Social Sec. Admin., 41 FLRA 224 (1991); Veterans Admin. Med. Ctr., 32 FLRA 1078 (1988).

[111]5 C.F.R. §2425.1(c).

[112]5 U.S.C. §7122(b); 5 C.F.R. §2425.1(b). For a discussion of when an award is final and when exceptions, including interlocutory appeals, will be considered, see *Department of the Air Force, Warner Robins Air Logistics Command*, 35 FLRA 1086 (1990). Generally, interlocutory awards, including interim decisions, are not subject to appeal. *But see* Department of the Treasury, Internal Revenue Serv., 34 FLRA 1161 (1990). When an arbitrator retains jurisdiction, the award is still considered final and appealable when rendered. Government Employees (AFGE) Local 1760, 37 FLRA 1193 (1990).

[113]5 U.S.C. §7122(a).

in private sector labor-management relations."[114] The statutory grounds for review are very similar to those adopted by the Federal Labor Relations Council under Executive Order 11,491.[115] The arbitration review procedures set forth in the statute and regulations are exclusive. Although the FLRA has held that the Federal Arbitration Act does not apply to federal public-sector awards,[116] many of the grounds on which challenges to federal-sector arbitration awards have been sustained are contained in the Federal Arbitration Act. Those grounds include:

1. The award violates a law, rule, or regulation.[117]
2. The arbitrator exceeded his or her authority.[118]
3. The award does not draw its essence from the collective bargaining agreement.[119]
4. The award is incomplete, ambiguous, or contradictory, making implementation of the award impossible.[120]
5. The award is based on a gross error of fact or a "nonfact."[121]
6. The arbitrator was biased or partial.[122]
7. The arbitrator refused to hear pertinent and material evidence.[123]
8. The arbitrator has an impermissible self-interest.[124]

The standard the FLRA uses to review a challenge depends on the ex-

---

[114]5 C.F.R. §2425.3(a). Specifically excluded from review are awards "based on unacceptable performance covered under 5 U.S.C. 4303"; "removal, suspension for more than fourteen (14) days, reduction in grade, reduction in pay, or furlough of thirty (30) days or less covered under 5 U.S.C. 7512"; and "matters similar to those covered under 5 U.S.C. 4303 and . . . 7512 which arise under other personnel systems." *Id.* §2425.3(b).

[115]*See* Frazier, *Labor Arbitration in the Federal Service*, 45 GEO. WASH. L. REV. 712, 733 (1977) (decisions are cited to illustrate the scope and application of the grounds for review under Exec. Order No. 11,491). For a concise description of the process, statutory requirements, and available avenues of appeals from the agency action, see generally Dawson & Underwood, *Overview of Labor-Management Relations in the Air Force*, 35 A.F. L. REV. 1, 12 et seq. (1991); BROIDA, A GUIDE TO FEDERAL LABOR RELATIONS AUTHORITY LAW AND PRACTICE 1979–2003 (16th ed. 2003).

[116]The jurisdiction of the FLRA is most closely analogous to the NLRB in the private sector. Among its responsibilities, the FLRA is charged with determining appropriate bargaining units; conducting representation elections; and resolving issues relating to the duty to bargain, unfair labor practice complaints, and exceptions to arbitration awards. Department of Health & Human Servs., Social Sec. Admin., 27 FLRA 706 (1987).

[117]Department of Def., Educ. Activity, 56 FLRA 985 (2000); Department of Def., Def. Logistics Agency, 56 FLRA 843 (2000); General Servs. Admin., 56 FLRA 683 (2000); Treasury Employees Ch. 143, 56 FLRA 304 (2000); Government Employees (NAGE) Local R14-143, 55 FLRA 317 (1999); Department of Def., Def. Mapping Agency, 43 FLRA 147 (1991). In reviewing a challenge based on alleged violation of law, rule, or regulation, the FLRA reviews the legal issue de novo. Treasury Employees Ch. 24, 50 FLRA 330, 332 (1995). A remand may be appropriate if the arbitrator's decision is subject to varying interpretations, one or more of which might be inconsistent with law, rule, or regulation. *Id.*

[118]Department of Def., Educ. Activity, 56 FLRA 887 (2000) (arbitrator was not found to exceed his authority); Department of Justice, Immigration & Naturalization Serv., 43 FLRA 927 (1992); Patent & Trademark Office, 32 FLRA 1168 (1988) (arbitrator did exceed his authority).

[119]Department of Labor, 34 FLRA 573 (1990).

[120]Department of Labor, Mine Safety & Health Admin., 40 FLRA 937 (1991).

[121]International Org. of Masters, Mates & Pilots, 39 FLRA 707 (1991).

[122]National Labor Relations Bd., 35 FLRA 421 (1990).

[123]Health Care Fin. Admin., 26 FLRA 860 (1987).

[124]Equal Employment Opportunity Comm'n, 52 FLRA 465 (1999).

ception filed.[125] For example, exceptions relating to violations of law, rule, or regulation are reviewed de novo.[126] The FLRA's role in reviewing arbitration awards depends on the nature of the appealing party's exceptions.[127]

The award is contrary to law. The FLRA resolves questions of law according to the law in effect at the time that a case is heard.[128] It reviews questions of law de novo. In reviewing a decision de novo, the FLRA determines whether the arbitrator's legal conclusions are consistent with the applicable standard of law, based on the underlying factual findings. In making such a determination, the FLRA defers to the arbitrator's underlying factual findings.[129]

Under 5 U.S.C. §7122(a)(2), other grounds on which challenges to federal-sector arbitration awards have been sustained are:

The arbitrator exceeded his or her authority. "An arbitrator exceeds his or her authority when the arbitrator fails to resolve an issue submitted to arbitration, resolves an issue not submitted to arbitration, disregards specific limitations on his or her authority, or awards relief to persons who are not encompassed by the grievance."[130]

The award does not draw its essence from the collective bargaining agreement. The FLRA will grant an exception to an arbitration award for failing to draw its essence from the collective bargaining agreement if it is established that the award: (1) cannot in any rational way be derived from the agreement; (2) is so unfounded in reason and fact and so unconnected with the wording and purposes of the agreement as to manifest an infidelity to the obligation of an arbitrator; (3) does not represent a plausible interpretation of the agreement; or (4) evidences a manifest disregard of the agreement.[131]

The award is based on a gross error of fact or a "nonfact." In order to demonstrate successfully that an award is based on a nonfact, the appealing party must show that a central fact underlying the award is clearly erroneous. The excepting party must show that "but for" the acceptance of the erroneous fact, the arbitrator would have reached a different result. The FLRA will not find an award deficient on the basis of an arbitrator's determination on any factual matter that the parties disputed at hearing.[132] In order to maintain the appropriate deference to arbitrators' factual findings, "[t]he mere fact that the appealing party disputes an arbitral finding does not provide a basis for finding that an award is based on a nonfact."[133] Additionally,

---

[125]Department of Def., Def. Logistics Agency, 56 FLRA 62 (2000).

[126]Department of Health & Human Servs., Indian Health Serv., 56 FLRA 535 (2000).

[127]Department of the Navy, Naval Sea Sys. Command, 57 FLRA 543 (2001).

[128]Department of Commerce, National Oceanic & Atmospheric Admin., 57 FLRA 559 (2001).

[129]Government Employees (AFGE) Local 2274, 57 FLRA 586 (2001).

[130]Social Sec. Admin., 57 FLRA 530, 537 (2001). *See also* Department of Justice, Immigration & Naturalization Serv., 43 FLRA 927 (1992).

[131]Department of Def., Def. Logistics Agency, 55 FLRA 1303, 1307 (2000) (concurrence), *cited in* Social Sec. Admin., 57 FLRA 530 (2001). *See also* Government Employees (AFGE) Local 2274, 57 FLRA 586 (2001).

[132]Department of the Air Force, Lowry Air Force Base, 48 FLRA 589, 593–94 (1993).

arbitrators' interpretations of collective bargaining agreements do not constitute matters that can be challenged as a nonfact.[134]

Failure to conduct a fair hearing. If a party can demonstrate that the arbitrator refused to hear or consider pertinent and material evidence, or that other actions in conducting the proceeding so prejudiced a party as to affect the fairness of the proceeding as a whole, the FLRA will find that the arbitrator failed to conduct a fair hearing.[135] However, the FLRA recognizes that an arbitrator has considerable latitude in conducting a hearing. The mere fact that a hearing is conducted in a manner one party finds objectionable does not, by itself, provide a basis for finding an award deficient.[136]

The award is contrary to public policy. The FLRA has adopted this extremely narrow exception to arbitration awards.[137] Following the principle laid down by the Supreme Court in *Eastern Associated Coal Corp. v. Mine Workers District 17*,[137a] the FLRA has written that, "[i]n order to find the award deficient, the public policy in question must be 'explicit,' 'well defined and dominant.' In addition, the policy is to be ascertained 'by reference to the laws and legal precedents and not from general considerations of supposed public interests.' The violation of such public policy 'must be clearly shown' if an award is to be found deficient."[138]

Other grounds on which the FLRA will reject arbitrators' awards include: when the award is incomplete, ambiguous, or contradictory, making implementation of the award impossible;[139] when it finds an arbitrator was biased or partial;[140] or if an award was procured by corruption, fraud, or undue means.[141]

ii.   Review by the Courts

An FLRA decision on exceptions to an arbitration award is final unless an unfair labor practice issue is involved. Where an unfair labor practice charge is at issue, a party may appeal the FLRA's decision to a U.S. Court of Appeals.[142]

---

[133]Government Employees (AFGE) Local 1923, 51 FLRA 576, 579 (1995), *cited in* Social Sec. Admin., 57 FLRA 530 (2001).

[134]Department of Veterans Affairs, Ralph H. Johnson Med. Ctr., 57 FLRA 489 (2001).

[135]General Servs. Admin., 56 FLRA 978, 979 (2000) (citing Government Employees (AFGE) Local 1668, 50 FLRA 124, 126 (1995)).

[136]*Id.* (citing Government Employees (AFGE) Local 22, 51 FLRA 1496, 1497–98 (1996)).

[137]U.S. Postal Serv. v. Letter Carriers, 810 F.2d 1239, 1241, 124 LRRM 2644 (D.C. Cir. 1987), *cert. dismissed*, 485 U.S. 680 (1988).

[137a]531 U.S. 57, 164 LRRM 2865 (2000).

[138]Department of Veterans Affairs, Ralph H. Jonson Med. Ctr., 57 FLRA 489, 494 (2001) (citations omitted).

[139]Department of Labor, Mine Safety & Health Admin., 40 FLRA 937 (1991); Department of Justice, Immigration & Naturalization Serv., 43 FLRA 927 (1992).

[140]Department of the Air Force, Carswell Air Force Base, 43 FLRA 1266 (1992); Health Care Fin. Admin., 26 FLRA 860 (1987).

[141]Treasury Employees Ch. 33, 44 FLRA 252 (1992).

[142]5 U.S.C. §7123(a); Begay v. Department of the Interior, 145 F.3d 1313, 1316, 158 LRRM 2329 (Fed. Cir. 1998).

iii. *Examination of Arbitrators' Decisions by the FLRA*

Prior to 1990, the primary reason for setting aside arbitrators' decisions was that they violated statutorily mandated management rights and therefore were contrary to the law. In 1990, the FLRA discarded the "excessive interference" test it had used to determine a violation of statutory management rights and substituted a "precludes from exercising" test.[143] When facing exceptions to an arbitrator's award based on a management-rights challenge (unlike and distinguished from questions of the negotiability of proposals), the FLRA first assesses whether the award affects any management right.[144] If it does, the FLRA then examines whether the contractual provision at issue: (1) constitutes an arrangement for employees adversely affected by the exercise of management's rights; and (2) if, as interpreted by the arbitrator, it abrogates the exercise of a management right.[145]

The FLRA initially determines the validity of the exceptions according to the law in effect at the time of the decision to which exception is taken.[146]

There are some matters an arbitrator may not decide, while other matters must be submitted to the arbitrator and may not be raised for the first time before the FLRA.

An arbitrator may not decide:

- negotiability,
- disputes over the scope of bargaining,
- substantive arbitrability, or
- matters contractually excluded from the grievance procedure.[147]

An arbitrator, not the FLRA or the courts, must rule on questions of:

- contract interpretation,[148]
- procedural arbitrability,[149]
- compliance with contractual midterm negotiations conditions,[150] and
- unfair labor practice issues raised before the arbitrator.[151]

---

[143]Department of the Treasury, Customs Serv., 37 FLRA 309 (1990).

[144]Department of Def., Def. Logistics Agency, 56 FLRA 62 (2000) (citing Small Bus. Admin., 55 FLRA 179, 184 (1999)).

[145]Department of the Treasury, Customs Serv., 37 FLRA 309, 314 (1990).

[146]Department of the Army, Army Reserve Pers. Ctr., 49 FLRA 95 (1994); Panama Canal Comm'n, 39 FLRA 274 (1991).

[147]Department of the Air Force, Carswell Air Force Base, 43 FLRA 1266 (1992); Veterans Admin. Hosp., 4 FLRA 432 (1980).

[148]Department of the Air Force, Oklahoma City Air Logistics Ctr., 55 FLRA 805 (1999); Department of Health & Human Servs., Social Sec. Admin., 38 FLRA 1183 (1990).

[149]Department of the Army, Reserve Pers. Ctr., 39 FLRA 402 (1991).

[150]National Border Patrol Counsel, 3 FLRA 400 (1980).

[151]Department of Health & Human Servs., 45 FLRA 737 (1992). The consideration of a grievance may be barred by an earlier filed unfair labor practice charge if the issues raised are the same in both proceedings and were, in fact, raised first in the unfair labor practice charge and the selection of the unfair labor practice charge procedures was at the discretion of the grievant. Department of Health & Human Servs., Indian Health Serv., 56 FLRA 535 (2000).

iv.   Review of Remedies

Arbitrators have great leeway in fashioning remedies.[152] The FLRA has held it will uphold a remedy that is within the arbitral jurisdiction so long as it is not a patent attempt to effect a goal not within the ambit of the statute.[153]

As with private-sector grievance arbitration, the FLRA has adopted a policy that arbitral awards will not be overturned merely because of disagreement with the arbitrator's findings of fact, reasoning, and conclusion, or conclusions drawn from the evidence.[154]

In many instances, the critical review area concerns the remedy directed by the arbitrator and its conformance with law and regulation.

> Arbitrators in the federal sector, however, must consider not only the terms of the parties' agreement, but also the provisions of statutes and regulations that may apply to the grievance with which they are presented. Federal sector agencies and unions are generally more aware than arbitrators of statutes and regulations applicable in a given situation and should advise arbitrators of the statutes and regulations that might apply to a particular grievance.[155]

The FLRA has no jurisdiction over Category II cases (called "adverse action" cases), nor does it have authority to review arbitration awards involving any Category II issue (i.e., reduction in grade or removal for unacceptable performance, removal, suspension for more than 14 days, reduction in grade or pay, furlough of 30 days or less).

B. Review by the Merit Systems Protection Board and the Equal Employment Opportunity Commission

Decisions by arbitrators involving matters under the jurisdiction of the MSPB[156] or the EEOC[157] may be reviewable directly by those agencies or by the courts.[158] Matters grieving "adverse actions" under MSPB jurisdiction that do not have claims of discrimination may be appealed by employees directly to the U.S. Court of Appeals for the Federal Circuit.[159] Grievances

---

[152]Department of the Interior, U.S. Geological Survey, 55 FLRA 30, 33 (1998). *See generally* Berry, *Cornelius v. Nutt and the Current State of Arbitral Remedial Authority in the Federal Sector*, 40 OKLA. L. REV. 559 (1987).

[153]Treasury Employees Ch. 33, 44 FLRA 252 (1992).

[154]*See* Haughton, *Arbitration in the Federal Sector*, 38 ARB. J. No. 4, at 55, 56 (1983). For a discussion of when an award is final and when exceptions will be considered, including interlocutory appeals, see *Department of the Air Force, Warner Robins Air Logistics Command*, 35 FLRA 1086 (1990). Generally, interlocutory awards, including interim decisions, are not subject to appeal. *But see* Department of the Treasury, Internal Revenue Serv., 34 FLRA 1161 (1990). When an arbitrator retains jurisdiction, the award is still considered final and appealable when rendered. Government Employees (AFGE) Local 1760, 37 FLRA 1193 (1990).

[155]Frazier, *Labor Arbitration in the Federal Service*, 45 GEO. WASH. L. REV. 712, 730 (1977).

[156]This includes issues regarding reduction in grade or removal for unacceptable performance (5 U.S.C. §4303); removal, suspension for more than 14 days, reduction in grade or pay, and furlough of 30 days or less (5 U.S.C. §7512). *See also* 5 U.S.C. §§7121, 7122, 7701, 7703; 28 U.S.C. §1295(a)(9); 5 C.F.R. §1201.3.

[157]5 U.S.C. §2302(b).

[158]*Id.* §7121(d), (f).

[159]*Id.* §7703(a)(1); 28 U.S.C. §1295(a)(9).

with a discrimination component may be appealed by the grievant to either the EEOC[160] or the MSPB.[161] Cases involving "mixed" issues (allegations of discrimination in relation to an adverse action that is appealable to the MSPB) should be appealed to the MSPB and then to the EEOC.[162] Once an arbitration decision has been reviewed by the MSPB, the MSPB decision may be appealed to the Federal Circuit Court of Appeals.[163] EEOC determinations (whether appealed to the EEOC directly from the arbitrator or from the MSPB) may be appealed by employees to a district court.[164] Appeals from adverse actions are cognizable by arbitrators or by the MSPB.

C. Review of Merit Systems Protection Board Decisions or Arbitration Awards in Adverse Action Cases

Appeals from decisions in adverse action cases—whether decided initially by an arbitrator or the MSPB—are governed by 5 U.S.C. §7703(c), which requires the court to set aside any actions, findings, or conclusions found to be:

(1) arbitrary, capricious, an abuse of discretion, or otherwise not in accordance with law;

(2) obtained without procedures required by law, rule, or regulation having been followed; or

(3) unsupported by substantial evidence.

As explained by the U.S. Court of Appeals for the District of Columbia Circuit:

> In applying this standard to arbitral decisions, Congress has, it seems clear, departed somewhat from the private sector tradition of deference in order to promote some uniformity of process and to ensure that the statutory procedures adequately protect the rights of government employees. But, consistent with private sector precedent, it has done so in a manner that leaves arbitrators' interpretations of collective bargaining agreements themselves largely unreviewable.
>
> The limited nature of this departure becomes clear when we examine the standards governing appeals by the OPM, which can be implied from the grounds on which that entity may seek judicial review of decisions of the MSPB or arbitrators. It would make nonsense of Congress' statutory scheme to allow a court considering such an appeal to consider either the sufficiency of the evidence or the arbitrator's interpretation of the collective bargaining agreement. Only if the court determines that the arbitrator erred as a matter of law in interpreting a civil service law, rule, or regulation can it upset his decision—a standard of review that is at least as deferential as the standard governing review of arbitral decisions in the private sector.
>
> We conclude, therefore, that (1) the policies favoring extremely limited judicial review of arbitrators' decisions are fully applicable in the federal sector; (2) Congress recognized the advantages of arbitration, but effected a limited departure from the private sector's tradition of deference to ensure that arbitrators' decisions, like the decisions of the MSPB, adequately protect fed-

---

[160]5 U.S.C. §7121(d); 29 C.F.R. §1614.401(d).
[161]5 U.S.C. §7702; 5 C.F.R. §1201.3(c)(3).
[162]5 U.S.C. §§7701, 7121(d); 29 C.F.R.§1614.401(d).
[163]5 U.S.C. §7703(b)(1).
[164]*Id.* §7703(b)(2); 42 U.S.C. §2000e-16(c); 29 C.F.R. §1614.407.

eral employees' rights; and (3) courts should promote arbitral resolution of disputes arising out of federal employment by considering OPM petitions for review only when the demonstrated need for review outweighs the damage to arbitration inherent in the appellate process.[165]

Where the MSPB has established a substantive rule or standard for reviewing agency actions, that standard is binding on arbitrators. Specifically, in *Cornelius v. Nutt*,[166] the Supreme Court held that arbitrators hearing cases under 5 U.S.C. §7121(e) must observe the "harmful error rule" required by 5 U.S.C. §7701(c)(2), as interpreted and defined by the MSPB. The extent to which arbitrators must follow MSPB precedent not involving statutory interpretation, however, was not specifically decided by the Court.

D. Comptroller General's Role

The Federal Labor Relations Council, the predecessor of the FLRA, sometimes requested rulings from the Comptroller General, and its acknowledgment of the authority of Comptroller General rulings was reflected in the Federal Labor Relations Council executive director's comments concerning Comptroller General application of the Back Pay Act of 1966[167] to federal agency violations of collective bargaining agreements—comments that also underscore the "but for" test or limitation on the remedy power of federal-sector arbitrators:

> Overruling his previous decisions to the contrary, the Comptroller General declared [in *National Labor Relations Board*, 54 Comp. Gen. 312 (1974),] that the Back Pay Act was appropriate statutory authority for compensating the employee for pay, allowances, or differentials he would have received *but for* violation of the agreement.
>   In accordance with the Comptroller General's interpretation of the Back Pay Act . . . , the Council upheld backpay awards which met NLRB requirements, including the *but for* test.[168]

Congress did not eliminate the Comptroller General's role in labor relations when the Civil Service Reform Act (CSRA) of 1978 was enacted. Nonetheless, other provisions of the CSRA may affect the role and actions of the Comptroller General in connection with review of federal-sector arbitration awards:

1. The statute expressly provides that an arbitrator's award "shall be final and binding" if no exceptions are filed with the FLRA within 30

---

[165]Devine v. White, 697 F.2d 421, 439–40, 112 LRRM 2374, 2387–88 (D.C. Cir. 1983). *See also* Government Employees (AFGE) Local 2578 v. General Servs. Admin., 711 F.2d 261, 264–65 (D.C. Cir. 1983) (the court gives further explanation of its decision in *Devine*). Although the decision in *Devine* was partially criticized in subsequent cases and abrogated at least in part by the Supreme Court's ruling in *Cornelius v. Nutt*, 472 U.S. 648, 119 LRRM 2905 (1985), its explanation of the MSPB appeals process remains instructive.

[166]472 U.S. 648, 119 LRRM 2905 (1985). The Court noted that *Devine* was inconsistent with its ruling in *Cornelius* "insofar as it dispenses with the requirement that harmful error have some likelihood of affecting the outcome of the agency's decision." *Id.* at 656 n.7.

[167]5 U.S.C. §5596.

[168]Frazier, *Labor Arbitration in the Federal Service*, 45 GEO. WASH. L. REV. 712, 723 (1977) (emphasis in original). Although the Back Pay Act was amended by the CSRA, no change was made in the above-quoted language on which the Comptroller General's but for test is based.

days, and that the agency "shall take the actions required by an arbitrator's final award."[169]

2. The statute now expressly provides that an arbitrator's award "may include the payment of backpay" as provided by the Back Pay Act, and the Back Pay Act was amended making it expressly applicable in the disposition of grievances under collective bargaining agreements.[170]

3. The statute provides that the FLRA may request from OPM "an advisory opinion concerning the proper interpretation of rules, regulations, or policy directives issued by the Office of Personnel Management in connection with any matter before the Authority."[171]

One commentator explained that when the CSRA was enacted, "the GAO reevaluated its statutory authority and its labor-management procedures"; that this reevaluation revealed that "[a]lmost every term and condition of employment of federal employees that involves the payment of appropriated funds was still under the GAO's statutory jurisdiction"; but that the "Comptroller General did, however, as a matter of policy, restrict the GAO's jurisdiction in certain respects."[172]

The Comptroller General believes that "the combination of a restrained jurisdictional policy by the GAO, and full access to the GAO under procedures specifically designed to meet the needs of the labor relations community has permitted the reasonable accommodation of labor law and appropriations law in the federal sector."[173]

The Comptroller General responds to joint requests for interpretation or application of a statute pertaining to labor relations matters.[174] Where the request is not jointly made, the Comptroller General has refused to assert jurisdiction where to do so would be disruptive of the grievance arbitration process.[175]

---

[169]5 U.S.C. §7122(b).

[170]*Id. See* Haughton, *Arbitration in the Federal Sector*, 38 Arb. J. No. 4, at 57; Chapter 18, section 5.E., "The Back Pay Act." *See also* Hayford, *The Impact of Law and Regulation Upon the Remedial Authority of Labor Arbitrators in the Federal Sector*, 37 Arb. J. No. 1, at 28, 30–32 (1982).

[171]5 U.S.C. §7105(i). *See also* Kagel, *Grievance Arbitration in the Federal Service: Still Hardly Final and Binding?*, *in* Arbitration Issues for the 1980s, Proceedings of the 34th Annual Meeting of NAA 178, 188–89 (Stern & Dennis eds., BNA Books 1982). For an example of FLRA citation and reliance on Comptroller General decisions, see *Department of Labor*, 10 FLRA 491, 493 (1982), where an arbitration award was set aside.

[172]Blatch, *The General Accounting Office's Jurisdiction and Federal Labor Relations Since Passage of the Civil Service Reform Act*, 39 Arb. J. No. 1, at 31, 36 (1984).

[173]*Id.* at 42. For questions of negotiability, see discussion of §7106(b)(2) and (3) in section 4.A.ii.a., "Management Rights—Permitted Bargaining Items," and section 4.A.ii.c., "Governmentwide Rules or Regulations," above.

[174]Kenneth J. Corpman et al., Comptroller General, B-214845 (slip op., Apr. 12, 1985).

[175]Valerie Pannuci Reynolds, Comptroller General, B-225918 (slip op., Mar. 19, 1987).

Chapter 21

Issues in State and Local Government Sector Arbitration

1. Legal Status of Rights Arbitration in State and Local Government Employment

Sovereignty concepts[1] provide that the responsibility of public officials to determine policy and to exercise official judgment and discretion in determining the affairs of government is nondelegable.[2] Such concepts originally led many legislatures and courts to conclude that it would be unconstitutional to share such responsibility through negotiating the terms and conditions of employment of public personnel and arbitrating disputes arising under collectively bargained contracts.

Since 1960, however, most challenges to the validity of public employee collective bargaining and grievance arbitration have been rebuffed by the courts.[3] In consequence, the majority of the states have enacted statutes authorizing, albeit often with limitations, collective bargaining in the public sector.[4] For example, California has enacted a statute legalizing collective

---

[1]Sovereignty concepts have been described as follows:

> The distinctive characteristics of State employment stem from two related factors. The first is the dual role of the State as employer and as government, which in a democratic system means it is accountable to the legislature for its actions. The second is the source of revenue for the services the State provides. Unlike private sector employers, which derive their revenue primarily from profit and are generally dependent upon maintaining a competitive position in the market in order to survive, the State derives its revenue predominantly from taxation.

Morris & Frednian, *Is There a Public/Private Labor Law Divide?*, 14 Comp. Lab. L. 115, 123 (1993).

[2]Government ability to delegate power has been explained as follows:

> State constitutional vesting clauses, which entrust certain branches of government with specified functions and powers, are the primary source of limitations on delegations. Nondelegation . . . clauses are often construed to mean that legislative powers may not be exercised by officials in other branches of government.

Vallarelli, *Note: State Constitutional Restraints on the Privatization of Education*, 72 B.U. L. Rev. 381, 391 (1992).

[3]For a general history and critique of the demise of the nondelegation doctrine, see Schoenbrod, Power Without Responsibility: How Congress Abuses the People Through Delegation (1993). *See also* Adler, *Judicial Restraint in the Administrative State: Beyond the Countermajoritarian Difficulty*, 145 U. Pa. L. Rev. 759 (1997); Befort, *Public Sector Bargaining: Fiscal Crisis and Unilateral Change*, 69 Minn. L. Rev. 1221 (1985); Westbrook, *The Use of the Non-Delegation Doctrine in Public Sector Labor Law: Lessons From Cases That Have Perpetuated an Anachronism*, 30 St. Louis U. L.J. 331, 353, 356 (1986).

[4]Partial lists of the relevant statutes are found and discussed in O'Reilly, *Collision in the Congress: Congressional Accountability, Workplace Conflict and the Separation of Powers*, 5 Geo. Mason L. Rev. 1, 21 (1996). *See also* O'Reilly, *More Magic With Less Smoke: A Ten Year Retrospective on Ohio's Collective Bargaining Law*, 19 U. Dayton L. Rev. 1, 28 (1993).

bargaining and mediation by public employers[5] and the California Supreme Court has held that public employees have a right to strike unless the strike would "seriously threaten the public health or safety."[6] Other states, like Connecticut, selectively apply the sovereignty doctrine to public employee collective bargaining.[7] Finally, some states continue to apply the sovereignty doctrine without exception.

Only North Carolina and Texas have statutes expressly prohibiting collective bargaining by public employees.[8] The states of Alabama, Arizona, Arkansas, Colorado, Louisiana, Mississippi, South Carolina, and West Virginia have not passed statutes related to public employee collective bargaining. Nevertheless, in a number of these states, some form of public employee collective bargaining is allowed.[9]

While the courts of some of these states have held that legislative authorization is not required in order for a public entity to enter into collective bargaining,[10] the Virginia Supreme Court has held that such authority is required,[11] and the Arkansas Supreme Court has declared that "collective bargaining would in effect amount to strikes against government."[12]

---

[5]CAL. GOV'T CODE §§3500-10 (West 1995).

[6]County Sanitation Dist. No. 2 of L.A. v. Los Angeles County Employees Ass'n Local 660, 38 Cal. 3d 564, 699 P.2d 835, 119 LRRM 2433, 2441 (Cal. 1985). The court reasoned that

> [t]he sovereignty concept, however, has often been criticized in recent years as a vague and outdated theory based on the assumption that "the King can do no wrong." As Judge Harry T. Edwards has cogently observed,
>
> > [T]he application of the strict sovereignty notion—that governmental power can never be opposed by employee organizations—is clearly a vestige from another era, an era of unexpanded government. . . . With rapid growth of the government, both in sheer size as well as in terms of assuming services not traditionally associated with the 'sovereign', government employees understandably no longer feel constrained by a notion that The [sic] King can do no wrong.' The distraught cries by public unions of disparate treatment merely reflect the fact that, for all intents and purposes, public employees occupy essentially the same position vis-a-vis the employer as their private counterparts.
>
> . . .
>
> . . . [T]he use of this archaic concept to justify a per se prohibition against public employee strikes is inconsistent with modern social reality and should be hereafter laid to rest.

Id. at 842.

[7]CONN. GEN. STAT. §5-279 (West 1995) (legalizing public employee collective bargaining and arbitration, but maintaining prohibition against public employee strikes).

[8]N.C. GEN. STAT. §§95-97 to 100 (1993); TEX. GOV'T CODE ANN. §617.002 (West 1997).

[9]For example, in Arizona, a county may meet and confer with a nonexclusive representative of its employees. *See* Sachen, *Collective Negotiations in Arizona's Public Schools: The Anomaly of Tolerated Illegal Activities*, 28 ARIZ. L. REV. 15 (1986). In DILTS & WALSH, COLLECTIVE BARGAINING AND IMPASSE RESOLUTION IN THE PUBLIC SECTOR 18–19 (1988), a chart of the kinds of provisions available for public employees in each state is provided.

[10]Littleton Educ. Ass'n v. Arapahoe County Sch. Dist. No. 6, 553 P.2d 793, 795, 93 LRRM 2378 (Colo. 1976). For Louisiana and West Virginia, see also *St. John & Baptist Parish Ass'n of Educators v. Brown*, 465 So. 2d 674 (La. 1985); *State, County & Mun. Employees Council 58, Local 598 v. City of Huntington*, 317 S.E.2d 167, 119 LRRM 2797 (W. Va. 1984).

[11]Virginia v. County Bd. of Arlington County, 232 S.E.2d 30, 44, 94 LRRM 2291 (Va. 1977).

[12]Czech v. Baer, 677 S.W.2d 833, 836 (Ark. 1984).

Most statutes that authorize collective bargaining also contain provisions for the establishment of grievance and arbitration procedures.[13] Statutory support for grievance arbitration has been found even though the particular arbitration statute did not expressly cover the class of public employees asserting arbitration rights.[14]

Constitutional challenges to grievance arbitration statutes based on the sovereignty concept of nondelegable duties have been rejected.[15] Indeed, significant judicial support has been expressed for the validity of grievance arbitration even in the absence of statutory authorization.[16] As the Colorado Supreme Court noted:

---

[13]*See, e.g.,* ALASKA STAT. §23.40.200 (Michie 1997); HAW. REV. STAT. §89-12 (1997); IDAHO CODE §44-1811 (1997); 5 ILL. COMP. STAT. 315/17 (West 1997); MINN. STAT. §179A.18 (1996); MONT. CODE ANN. §§39-32-110, 39-34-105 (1997); OHIO REV. CODE ANN. §§4117.15–16 (Anderson 1997); OR. REV. STAT. §243.726 (1996); 43 PA. CONS. STAT. §§1101.1001–1003, 1101.2201 (1997); VT. STAT. ANN. tit. 21 §1730 (1997); WIS. STAT. §111.70(4)(cm)(6)(c) (1995–96). *See also* PUBLIC SECTOR BARGAINING ch. 6 (2d ed., I.R.R.A. Series 1988).

[14]Teachers Union Local 958 (Providence) v. School Comm. of City of Providence, 276 A.2d 762, 77 LRRM 2530 (R.I. 1971). *See also* Community Coll. of Beaver County v. Community Coll. of Beaver County, Soc'y of the Faculty, 375 A.2d 1267, 1276, 96 LRRM 2375 (Pa. 1977); Gary Teachers Union Local No. 4 v. School City of Gary, 284 N.E.2d 108, 113–14, 80 LRRM 3090 (Ind. Ct. App. 1972). *Cf.* Westly v. Salt Lake City Corp. Bd. of City Comm'rs, 573 P.2d 1279, 97 LRRM 2580, 2581 (Utah 1978).

[15]For cases supporting public-sector grievance arbitration, see In re *Professional, Clerical, Technical Employees Ass'n (Buffalo Bd. of Educ.),* 683 N.E.2d 733 (N.Y. 1997); *City of Bethany, Okla. v. Public Employees Relations Bd.,* 904 P.2d 604, 151 LRRM 2138 (Okla. 1995); *Mayfield Hts. Fire Fighters (IAFF) Ass'n Local 1500 v. DeJohn,* 622 N.E.2d 380 (Ohio Ct. App. 1993); *Board of Educ. of Cmty. High Sch. Dist. No. 155 v. Illinois Educ. Lab. Relations Bd.,* 247 Ill. App. 3d 337, 617 N.E.2d 269, 145 LRRM 2490 (1993); *Rowry v. University of Mich.,* 441 Mich. 1, 490 N.W.2d 305 (1992); *Bloomfield Bd. of Educ. v. Bloomfield Educ. Ass'n,* 598 A.2d 517 (N.J. 1991). For related discussion, see Chapter 22, section 6., "Constitutionality of Binding Interest Arbitration."

[16]For cases supporting grievance arbitration in the absence of statutory authorization, see *Anne Arundel County v. Fraternal Order,* 313 Md. 98, 543 A.2d 841 (1988); *Stratford v. Professional & Technical Eng'rs Local 134,* 201 Conn. 577, 519 A.2d 1, 6, 125 LRRM 2052 (1986) (an arbitration award that resulted from the consent of the parties and not from the statute was upheld); *Fire Fighters (IAFF) Local 5891 v. City of Newburgh,* 116 A.D.2d 396, 501 N.Y.S.2d 369 (1986) (public policy does not exist disfavoring delegation of issues involving compensation for job-related injury or illness to an impartial third party, in this case a physician); *Dayton Classroom Teachers Ass'n v. Dayton Bd. of Educ.,* 323 N.E.2d 714, 718, 88 LRRM 3053 (Ohio 1975) (applying decisions from other states that upheld grievance arbitration without statutory authorization, including a Wisconsin Supreme Court decision that rejected the contention that "to require the city to submit to binding [grievance] arbitration is an unlawful infringement upon the legislative power of the city council and a violation of its home rule powers"); *Danville Bd. of Sch. Dirs. v. Fifield,* 315 A.2d 473, 476, 85 LRRM 2939 (Vt. 1974). *But see* Richmond Sch. Bd. v. Parham, 243 S.E.2d 468, 472 (Va. 1978) (striking down a binding grievance arbitration agreement between local school boards and their employees on the ground that it removed from the local board and transferred to others a function that was essential and indispensable to the board's exercise of its power of supervision). It appears clear that such express statutory authorization of binding grievance arbitration would be required to legalize it in any state that does not permit collective bargaining by public employers. In the latter regard, see also *City of Fairmont, W. Va.,* 73 LA 1259, 1261–63 (Lubow, 1979). For reference to the allowance of grievance arbitration in the absence of statutory authorization, particularly when collective bargaining is nevertheless approved, see *Developments in the Law—Public Employment,* 97 HARV. L. REV. 1611, 1720–21 (1984). Although favor in the public sector for grievance arbitration grows, greater scrutiny is seemingly given to the award of an arbitrator in the public sector to ensure that it complies with his or her authority. *See* Lefkowitz, *The Legal Framework of Labor Arbitration in the Public Sector, in* LABOR ARBITRATION: A PRACTICAL GUIDE FOR ADVOCATES 30 (Zimny, Dotson, & Barreca eds., BNA Books 1990). For illustrative arbitration decisions in which the arbitra-

When an arbitrator is required to interpret the provisions of an existing agreement, he acts in a judicial capacity rather than in a legislative one. . . . The authority to interpret an existing contract, therefore, does not constitute legislative authority, and the non-delegation principle is not implicated in grievance arbitration.[17]

2. ARBITRATION ISSUES IN PUBLIC EDUCATION

Collective bargaining and grievance arbitration in public education initially met with a hostile reception in some state courts.[18] These courts denied enforcement of agreements to arbitrate or vacated awards on the ground that school boards were not authorized to delegate or share their statutory authority with a private party such as a union or an arbitrator.[19] However, the passage of state public-sector collective bargaining laws with detailed procedures and substantive standards led most courts to reject constitutional challenges to public-sector arbitration.[20]

The high courts of Massachusetts, New York, and Wisconsin led the vanguard of the assault on the nondelegation doctrine.[21] In *Board of Education v. Associated Teachers of Huntington, Inc.*,[22] a school board agreed to a collective bargaining agreement that included a provision for arbitration of discharges under a just cause standard. Nevertheless, the board of education later filed suit to have that portion of the agreement declared invalid and to stay arbitration on the ground that the school board lacked authority to enter into such an agreement. The New York Court of Appeals declared the challenged provisions valid. The court found implicit legislative authority for grievance arbitration in the legislature's requirement that a public employer negotiate collectively with a recognized employee organization in the determination of, and administration of grievances arising under, the terms and conditions of employment of the public employees. Citing the U.S. Supreme Court's decision in *Steelworkers v. Warrior & Gulf Navigation Co.*,[23] the Court of Appeals noted that such grievance and arbitration provisions are commonly found in both the private and public sector as a means for resolving labor disputes. The New York court found no express or implied

---

tor concluded, because of the scope of an applicable state statute or for some other related reason, that the arbitrator lacked jurisdiction to hear a public employee grievance brought before him or her, see *Springfield, Ohio, Bd. of Educ.*, 87 LA 16 (Feldman, 1986); *City of Houston, Tex.*, 86 LA 1068 (Stephens, 1986); *City of Elyria, Ohio*, 84 LA 318 (Laybourne, 1985).

[17]City & County of Denver v. Fire Fighters (IAFF) Local 858 (Denver), 663 P.2d 1032, 1037–38 (Colo. 1983).

[18]*See, e.g.*, Commonwealth v. County Bd. of Arlington County, 217 Va. 558, 232 S.E.2d 30, 94 LRRM 2291 (1976).

[19]*See, e.g.*, Illinois Educ. Ass'n v. School Dist. 218 Bd. of Educ., 62 Ill. 2d 127, 340 N.E.2d 7 (1975).

[20]Grodin & Najita, *Judicial Response to Public-Sector Arbitration, in* PUBLIC-SECTOR BARGAINING 229 (Aaron, Najita, & Stern eds., BNA Books 2d ed. 1988).

[21]School Comm. of Danvers v. Tyman, 372 Mass. 106, 360 N.E.2d 877, 94 LRRM 3182 (1977); State, County, & Mun. Employees Local 1226 v. City of Rhinelander, 35 Wis. 2d 209, 151 N.W.2d 30, 65 LRRM 2793 (1967).

[22]30 N.Y.2d 122, 331 N.Y.S.2d 17, 282 N.E.2d 109 (1972).

[23]363 U.S. 574, 34 LA 561, 46 LRRM 2416 (1960).

legislative restriction on bargaining any of the subjects contested by the school board and rejected the school board's general argument that a school board is better qualified than an arbitrator to decide whether a teacher should be discharged for incompetence or misconduct.

A. Scope of Grievance Arbitration [LA CDI 100.0764]

In states with collective bargaining laws, the debate has shifted to determining whether arbitration of specific matters is expressly or implicitly prohibited. Where a collective bargaining agreement's arbitration clause or other provisions conflict with statutory law, the courts hold that arbitration is precluded. In *Rockford School District 205 Board of Education v. Illinois Educational Labor Relations Board*,[24] a teacher engaged in a physical altercation with two students. Following the incident, the school district issued a formal notice to the teacher to "remediate" his behavior or be terminated. An Illinois statute provides that a tenured teacher may be dismissed if he or she does not remediate within a specified time. The teacher grieved and proceeded to arbitration, contending that the notice to remediate was not fair and equitable treatment and was issued without just cause under the collective bargaining agreement. When the arbitrator issued an award directing the Board of Education to rescind the notice to remediate, the Board refused and the union filed an unfair labor practice. The Illinois Supreme Court held that the school district's noncompliance was justified. The court relied on a portion of the Illinois Educational Labor Relations Act, which provided that "[t]he parties to the collective bargaining process shall not effect or implement a provision in a collective bargaining agreement if the implementation of that provision would be in violation of, or inconsistent with, or in conflict with any statute or statutes enacted by the General Assembly of Illinois."[25] The court noted that elsewhere in the Illinois statutes the legislature had prescribed a process for dismissal that included the district's authority to issue a notice to remediate. The Illinois court characterized the power to issue a notice to remediate as an integral part of the statutory dismissal process, and hence the inconsistent arbitration award was unforceable because it conflicted with state law.

In *Board of Education v. Rockaway Township Education Ass'n*,[26] a board of education sought to enjoin a teacher and union from arbitrating a grievance that alleged that the board had interfered with the teacher's academic freedom in violation of the labor contract between the board and the union. The teacher had grieved the school superintendent's order that he not conduct a debate among his seventh grade students on the subject of abortion. New Jersey law mandated collective bargaining over terms and conditions of employment and specifically required negotiation of a grievance procedure. However, state law also declared that no agreement shall annul or modify other state statutes. The New Jersey Supreme Court rejected the

---

[24]165 Ill. 2d 80, 649 N.E.2d 369, 149 LRRM 2508 (1995).
[25]115 Ill. Comp. Stat. 5/10(b) (Michie 2002).
[26]120 N.J. Super. 564, 295 A.2d 380, 81 LRRM 2462 (1972).

union's argument that the selection of courses to be presented to, and discussed by, students was a term and condition of employment. According to the court, state law gave school boards the responsibility to adopt and alter courses of study. The court concluded that the labor agreement was unenforceable to the extent that it could be read to delegate to the teacher or the union the choice of courses of study. Accordingly, the court enjoined the arbitration.

B. Labor Relations Agency Deferral to Arbitration

Where a labor dispute is subject to both arbitration and possible labor relations agency processes, labor relations agencies must decide whether to defer to the arbitrator's decision when deciding the related statutory issues in an unfair labor practice proceeding.[27]

In the private sector, the National Labor Relations Board (NLRB) has vacillated between two competing tests for post-arbitral deferral. Initially, the NLRB considered the arbitration award to have resolved the statutory issues only when the statutory issue was both presented to and considered by the arbitrator.[28] Later, the NLRB adopted a policy of deferring when the contractual and statutory issues are factually parallel and the arbitrator generally is presented with the facts relevant to resolving the statutory issue.[29]

At least one public-sector jurisdiction follows a third, alternative approach in dealing with statutory public education issues—the administrative agency defers to the arbitrator's findings of fact and interpretations of the contract, but the agency independently decides the statutory educational questions before it.[30]

C. Off-Duty Misconduct [LA CDI 100.552505]

While issues involving off-duty misconduct arise in both private- and public-sector employment,[31] teachers and other school employees often are faced with heightened scrutiny of their personal lives because of the important role these individuals fill as educators and caretakers of children. According to one author, teachers are expected to be role models and occupy a position of special public trust.[32] Additionally, teachers generally are subject

---

[27]Feree, *National Labor Relations Board: Deferral to Arbitration*, 52 DISP. RESOL. J. 31 (1997).

[28]Suburban Motor Freight, 247 NLRB 146, 103 LRRM 1113 (1980), *overruled by* Olin Corp., 268 NLRB 573, 115 LRRM 1056 (1984).

[29]*Olin Corp.*, 268 NLRB 573.

[30]University of Ill. Bd. of Trs. (Chicago Campus), 8 Ill. Pub. Empl. Rep. (LRP) ¶1035 (Ill. Educational Lab. Rel. Bd. 1992). *See also* Berendt & Youngerman, *The Continuing Controversy Over Labor Board Deferral to Arbitration—An Alternative Approach*, 24 STETSON L. REV. 175 (1994).

[31]For related discussion in private-sector arbitration, see Chapter 15, section 3.A., "Off-Duty Misconduct."

[32]Trebilcock, *Off Campus: School Board Control Over Teacher Conduct*, 35 TULSA L.J. 445 (2000).

to specific statutes that provide broad, open-textured grounds for termination, such as "moral turpitude," "immorality," and "conduct unbecoming a teacher."[33]

In addressing the issue whether any employee may be disciplined or discharged because of off-duty conduct, the majority of arbitrators assess whether there is a nexus between the off-duty conduct and the job in question. This nexus test was explained in *W.E. Caldwell Co.*[34] According to the arbitrator, to determine whether a nexus exists, the following factors must be considered: (1) the harm to an individual employer's reputation or product, (2) the ability of an offending employee to perform assigned duties or to appear at work, and (3) the refusal or reluctance of other employees to work with the person charged with off-duty misconduct.[35]

In deciding whether the off-duty conduct of a teacher could form the basis for discipline, arbitrators and courts may employ a more detailed analysis, sometimes referred to as the *Morrison* factors. In *Morrison v. State Board of Education*,[36] the Supreme Court of California reviewed the case of a teacher who was discharged and later lost his license, because of his involvement in a limited homosexual relationship. Recognizing the inherent subjectivity of terms such as "immoral," the court stated that the focus should be on whether the teacher's conduct impacted his fitness to teach.[37] In determining whether the teacher's conduct indicated an unfitness for duty, the court examined: (1) the likelihood that the conduct may have adversely affected students or fellow teachers, (2) the degree of such adverse effect, (3) the proximity or remoteness in time of the conduct, (4) the type of teaching certificate held by the teacher, (5) any mitigating or aggravating circumstances, (6) the praiseworthiness or blameworthiness of the motives resulting in the conduct, (7) the likelihood of reoccurrence of the conduct, and (8) the extent to which punishment would affect the constitutional rights of the teacher or other teachers.[38]

i.   *Sexual Activity* [LA CDI 100.552505; 100.552510]

Off-duty sexual activity involving students typically is deemed just cause for dismissal, and terminations generally are upheld.[39] However, in limited

---

[33]*See, e.g.*, Alaska Stat. §14.20.170; Cal. Educ. Code §44932.; Fla. Stat. Ann. §231.28; Ga. Code Ann. §20-2-940; Minn. Stat. Ann. §122A.40(9) (2002); Mo. Rev. Stat. §168.114; Nev. Stat. §391.312; N.C. Gen. Stat. §115C-325; Va. Code Ann. §22.1-307; W. Va. Code §18A-2-8.

[34]28 LA 434 (Kesselman, 1957).

[35]*Id.*

[36]1 Cal. 3d 214, 461 P.2d 375, 82 Cal. Rptr. 175 (1969).

[37]*Id.*, 82 Cal. Rptr. at 186.

[38]*Id.*

[39]Sertick v. School Dist. of Pittsburgh, 584 A.2d 390 (Pa. Commw. Ct. 1990) (teacher terminated based on an affair with a student that started just prior to her graduation); Denton v. South Kitsap Sch. Dist. 402, 10 Wash. App. 69, 516 P.2d 1080 (1973) (teacher terminated based on his relationship with a female student at another school who later became pregnant, even though the parents permitted the relationship); Minneapolis, Minn., Pub. Sch., Case No. 98-PA-1031, 1998 WL 1057709 (Berquist, 1998) (education assistant was discharged for just cause for fondling the genitals of an 11-year-old mentally handicapped boy). *See also* Ulrich v. State, 555 N.E.2d 172 (Ind. Ct. App. 1990) (teaching certificate revoked for forcible rape); Strain v. Rapid City Sch. Bd., 447 N.W.2d 332 (S.D. 1989) (teacher terminated for forcible rape).

instances, courts have overturned the dismissal of teachers where the facts of the case did not establish inappropriate contact.[40]

ii. *Illicit Drug Use and Possession* [LA CDI 100.552505; 100.552545]

Arbitrators and courts frequently have upheld the termination of school employees for away-from-premises drug possession or use[41] and distribution.[42] At the same time, other cases have held that certain drug offenses, usually involving use of marijuana, did not have a reasonable nexus to a school employee's fitness for duty.[43]

iii. *Non-Drug-Related Off-Duty Criminal Offenses*
[LA CDI 100.552505; 100.552514]

Arbitrators and courts have upheld discipline and discharge of teachers who have committed criminal offenses, such as vehicular homicide,[44] grand

---

[40]Holt v. Rapides Parish Sch. Bd., 685 So. 2d 501 (La. Ct. App. 1996) (teacher reinstated, where alleged improper conduct included sleeping in the same bed with a student at a slumber party where the student and teacher were close family friends).

[41]Chicago Bd. of Educ. v. Payne, 102 Ill. App. 741, 430 N.E.2d 310 (1981) (where a teacher was charged with possession of marijuana, the court, looking at *Morrison* factors, found that the district established a nexus between the teacher's conduct and his job based on the bad effects on students and teachers, the publicity, the likelihood the behavior would recur, and the fact that the teacher could no longer function as a role model and authority figure for children); Comings v. State Bd. of Educ., 23 Cal. App. 3d 94, 100 Cal. Rptr. 73 (1972) (discharge for marijuana possession upheld); Melrose-Mindoro, Wis., Area Educ. Ass'n (Crowley, 1998), *available at* <http://www.wisbar.org/werc/ga/1998/5692.htm> (teacher termination for drug possession upheld, where his ability to teach was adversely affected because his actions were publicized and they violated district policy, and retaining him would send the wrong message to students and staff).

[42]Summers v. Vermilion Parish Sch. Bd., 493 So. 2d 1258, 1266 (La. Ct. App. 1986) (The court upheld the termination of a principal who pled guilty to possession of marijuana with intent to distribute, and stated: "Involvement with illegal drugs is a plague that most often pursues our youth, even on school grounds. The school board would be remiss in its duties if it did not properly dismiss [the principal] for his involvement with illegal drugs.").

[43]Jefferson County Bd. of Educ. v. Moore, 706 So. 2d 1147, 13 IER Cases 806 (Ala. 1997) (termination was not warranted in the case of an employee with a good work record who tested positive for marijuana in a post-accident drug test; instead, the employee was required to complete a rehabilitation program); Rogliano v. Fayette County Bd. of Educ., 347 S.E.2d 220 (W. Va. 1986) (teacher was not "immoral" and there was no nexus between possession conviction and duties); Von Durjais v. Board of Trs., 83 Cal. App. 3d 681 (1978) (possession of marijuana did not constitute immoral conduct justifying termination).

[44]West Monona, Iowa, Cmty. Sch. Dist., 93 LA 414 (Hill, 1989) (the dismissal of a guidance counselor and coach was upheld when his off-duty conduct—driving under the influence of alcohol and cocaine in his system—resulted in a car accident that caused the death of one person and the paralysis of another individual; grievant was convicted of vehicular homicide, the incident was reported in the local media, and the district established a nexus between his conduct and his job as a counselor and coach).

theft,[45] theft,[46] welfare fraud,[47] and embezzlement.[48] However, arbitrators have found that the nexus requirement was not met, or that discipline was not warranted, in situations involving driving while intoxicated,[49] shoplifting,[50] and even grand larceny.[51]

Although examination of case law and arbitral decisions confirms the lack of consensus, it seems that employees fared better where there was little publicity and where the misconduct was thought unlikely to be repeated.

D. Special Assignments for Coaching Sports and Advising Extracurricular Activities [LA CDI 100.08]

School districts routinely hire teachers and other staff to coach sports teams and sponsor extracurricular activities that take place outside the regular schoolday. Employees typically are provided an additional stipend or payment for such activities, and arrangements for these types of activities are sometimes referred to as "supplemental contracts."

One issue that frequently arises is whether disputes over the filling of coaching positions are arbitrable,[52] or whether the issuance of supplemental contracts is outside the scope of the collective bargaining contract.[53] Obvi-

---

[45]Westlake City, Ohio, Sch. Dist., 94 LA 373 (Graham, 1990) (regardless of the reasons for her plea bargain, a principal's secretary who pled guilty to grand theft was properly discharged; the wide publicity given her case affected the reputation of the school, and, considering her close and frequent contact with students, her conduct violated the high level of personal conduct to which all school personnel dealing with students must be held).

[46]Reliford v. University of Akron, 81 Ohio App. 3d 157 (1991) (university employee dismissed for theft of student property); McBroom v. Board of Educ. Dist. 205, 144 Ill. App. 3d 463, 494 N.E.2d 1191 (1986) (dismissal of teacher upheld for theft of a check from a student's locker).

[47]Perryman v. School Comm. of Boston, 458 N.E.2d 748 (Mass. App. Ct. 1983).

[48]Satterfield v. Board of Educ., 556 N.W.2d 888 (Mich. Ct. App. 1996) (teacher's dismissal for embezzlement from outside job upheld, where there was a nexus between conduct and job because retaining teacher would harm reputation of the school and it would be difficult for other staff to work with the teacher).

[49]Michigan City, Ind., Area Sch. Corp., 91 LA 1244 (Eagle, 1989) (no reasonable link between conviction and job performance was found).

[50]Independent Sch. Dist. No. 709, Duluth, Minn., Case No. 99-TD-5, 1999 WL 1066005 (Berquist, 1999) (school district improperly proposed to demote a principal who pled guilty to a misdemeanor shoplifting charge, where mitigating factors were present and the conduct did not amount to immoral behavior).

[51]Hogland v. Mt. Vernon Sch. Dist., 623 P.2d 1156 (Wash. 1981) (teacher convicted of buying a stolen motorcycle cannot be dismissed unless it is shown that the conviction materially and substantially affected ability to teach).

[52]Penn-Delco Sch. Dist. v. Penn-Delco Educ. Ass'n, 754 A.2d 51, 164 LRRM 2948 (Pa. Commw. Ct. 2000); School Dist. of City of Erie v. Erie Educ. Assn., 749 A.2d 545, 164 LRRM 3055 (Pa. Commw. Ct. 2000); Cranberry Area Sch. Dist. v. Cranberry Educ. Ass'n, 713 A.2d 726, 164 LRRM 3051 (Pa. Commw. Ct. 1998).

[53]Board of Educ. of Port Jefferson Union Free Sch. Dist. v. Port Jefferson Teachers Ass'n, 663 N.Y.S.2d 69 (App. Div. 1997) (the board's decision not to appoint a teacher to a coaching position was not arbitrable, even though the contract contained various references to terms and conditions related to such positions); School Dist. of Borough of Morrisville v. Morrisville Educ. Ass'n, 165 Pa. Commw. 96, 644 A.2d 252 (Pa. Commw. Ct. 1994) (coaching positions were not covered by the collective bargaining agreement and grievance procedure was unavailable to teachers denied positions). *See also* Clearview Educ. Ass'n v. Clearview Local Sch. Dist. Bd. of Educ., 751 N.E.2d 494, 167 LRRM 2029 (Ohio Ct. App. 2001) (overturned an arbitrator's determination regarding a coaching position, because supplemental contracts were not covered by the collective bargaining agreement); South Putnam, Ind., Classroom

ously, the contract language in a given case is of central importance. In one case, an arbitrator determined that the long-time practice of hiring both internal and external applicants for coaching positions supported the district's contention that the collective bargaining agreement did not apply to supplemental positions.[54]

Where the collective bargaining agreement is silent as to the offering of supplemental contracts, arbitrators may look to the management-rights clause in the contract and any applicable external law.[55] If the subject of supplemental contracts is referred to in the contract, but without selection guidelines, arbitrators will assess whether the school board's choice among candidates was arbitrary, capricious, or in bad faith.[56]

Commonly, supplemental contract grievances challenge the hiring of an outside individual over an internal applicant, but, in the absence of a contractually specified preference favoring bargaining-unit members, most decisions have upheld the school board's action.[57] For example, in one case[58] the school board refused to adopt a resolution awarding a supplemental contract for the position of high school girls assistant softball coach to the grievant, a certified employee, but, instead, awarded the contract to a retired former assistant softball coach without following statutorily prescribed procedures mandating the adoption of appropriate resolutions and advertising of the vacancy. The governing collective bargaining agreement provided that such supplemental salary positions had to be offered to a qualified employee applicant first before it could be offered to a qualified nonemployee applicant. The arbitrator held that the lapses of the board did not entitle the grievant to the position by default, because the evidence led to the conclusion that the board had not abused its discretion in concluding that the grievant was not qualified for the job.

However, even when the collective bargaining agreement provides for preference to be given to internal applicants, disputes arise when the contract does not address the selection criteria to be followed in choosing among multiple qualified internal applicants. In one such case, an arbitrator held that a school district was not obligated to award a coaching position to the most senior of the three qualified internal applicants.[59] In another case, the arbitrator held that a school board's decision to hire a less senior applicant must not be arbitrary, discriminatory, or taken in bad faith. Because the

---

Teachers Ass'n, Case No. 52-390-00472-00, 2001 WL 400951 (Kenis, 2001); Girard, Pa., Sch. Dist., 1996 WL 912317 (Talarico, 1996) (the mere fact that the parties had specified certain terms regarding supplemental positions did not mean they intended a specific method, such as the grievance procedure to apply to disputes).

[54]Pike-Delta-York, Ohio, Local Sch. Dist., 116 LA 432 (Lalka, 2001).

[55]Vanlue, Ohio, Local Sch. Dist. Bd. of Educ., 112 LA 1025 (Richard, 1999) (collective bargaining agreement was silent and contained a broad management-rights clause; arbitrator said if no outside statute was violated, there would be no violation of the agreement).

[56] Nordonia Hills, Ohio, City Sch. Dist. Bd. of Educ., 111 LA 582 (Skulina, 1998); Creston, Iowa, Educ. Ass'n, Case No. 96-6A-92, 1996 WL 876365 (Berquist, 1996).

[57]See, e.g., Clearview Educ. Ass'n v. Clearview Local Sch. Dist. Bd. of Educ., 751 N.E. 2d 494, 167 LRRM 2029 (Ohio Ct. App. 2001); Vanlue, Ohio, Local Sch. Dist. Bd. of Educ., 112 LA 1025 (Richard, 1999).

[58]Springfield Local Sch. Dist., AAA Case No. 53-390-00164-96 (Ruben, 1996).

[59]Harrison Hills, Ohio, City Sch. Dist., Case No. 53-390-00270-99, 1999 WL 1567632 (Fullmer, 1999).

grievant had problems controlling his temper when he had coached that sport in the past, he was properly passed over.[60] Moreover, arbitrators have held that the failure to award or renew a coaching assignment does not constitute discipline or discharge under the collective bargaining agreement.[61]

Arbitral remedies vary when a teacher has been found to have been wrongly denied a coaching position. Some arbitrators have awarded back pay for the coaching season the individual missed.[62] One arbitrator reinstated the coach for the following year, subject to a plan to assist the coach in improving his communication skills.[63]

E. Issues of Academic Freedom

"'Academic freedom' is a term that is often used, but little explained, by the federal courts."[64] Charges of violation of the academic freedom of teachers and professors often are litigated in the federal court system because of reliance on the First Amendment of the U.S. Constitution.[65] The American Association of University Professors has set forth the following standard:

> a. Teachers are entitled to full freedom in research and in the publication of the results, subject to the adequate performance of their other academic duties; . . .
> b. Teachers are entitled to freedom in the classroom in discussing their subject, but they should be careful not to introduce into their teaching controversial matter which has no relation to their subject; . . .
> c. College and university teachers are citizens, members of a learned profession, and officers of an educational institution. When they speak or write as citizens, they should be free from institutional censorship or discipline, but their special position in the community imposes special obligations. As scholars and educational officers, they should remember that the public may judge their profession and their institution by their utterances. Hence they should at all times be accurate, should exercise appropriate restraint, should show respect for the opinions of others, and should make every effort to indicate that they are not speaking for the institution.[66]

Academic freedom issues often arise in disputes over grading policies. In upholding the ability of a school district to direct a teacher to decrease the failure rate of his students, one arbitrator stated:

---

[60]Creston, Iowa, Educ. Ass'n, Case No. 96-6A-92, 1996 WL 876365 (Berquist, 1996).

[61]South Putnam, Ind., Classroom Teachers Ass'n, Case No. 52-390-00472-00, 2001 WL 400951 (Kenis, 2001).

[62]Pike-Delta-York, Ohio, Local Sch. Dist., 116 LA 432 (Lalka, 2001); Broward County, Fla., Sch. Bd., Case No 93-13644, 1994 WL 838208 (Sergent, 1994).

[63]Montgomery County Bd. of Educ., Case No. 16-390-00302-94, 1995 WL 791633 (Pritzker, 1995).

[64]Urofsky v. Gilmore, 216 F.3d 401, 410, 16 IER Cases 737, 742 (4th Cir. 2000).

[65]It should be noted that this section looks at a very narrow array of cases related to academic freedom. For a more complete review of the topic, see 4 J.A. RAPP, EDUCATION LAW §11 (2001); Daly, *Balancing Act: Teachers' Classroom Speech and the First Amendment*, 30 J.L. & EDUC. 1 (2001); Stuller, *High School Academic Freedom: Evolution of a Fish Out of Water*, 77 NEB. L. REV. 301 (1998).

[66]American Ass'n of Univ. Professors, *1940 Statement of Principles on Academic Freedom and Tenure*, available at <http://www.aaup.org/statements/Redbook/1940stat.htm>.

> The idea that a teacher should be deemed to have academic freedom in running his class and judging student performance has great appeal. Teaching is recognized as a profession and it is understood that creativity, independence, and the exercise of judgment make for effective teaching. It is self-evident that placing unnecessary constraints on a teacher's presentation and grading will have an inhibiting effect and should be avoided.[67]

However, the arbitrator went on to observe that the case must be judged in light of all the facts, including a strong management-rights clause and state law that vested in school boards the broad powers to supervise and direct the work of teachers and to "classify and control the promotion of pupils."[68]

The use of controversial teaching methods or materials also gives rise to academic freedom issues. Several arbitrators and courts have ruled that elementary and secondary schools have wide latitude to control curriculum and teaching methods.[69] The discharge or discipline of teachers has been upheld for showing controversial films in the classroom, even though the subject matter related to the topics the students were studying.[70] One arbitrator upheld the right of a school to direct a teacher to stop using a newspaper article concerning local mental health facilities in his psychology class.[71]

Teachers also have been transferred or discharged for choosing a controversial play for a student drama competition[72] and for allowing profanity or other objectionable language in the classroom.[73]

---

[67]Roseville, Mich., Cmty. Sch., 87 LA 894, 897 (Lipson, 1986).

[68]*Id. See also* Brown v. Amenti, 247 F.3d 69 (3d Cir. 2001) (grading assignments are not part of a professor's academic freedom); San Francisco, Cal., Unified Sch. Dist., 107 LA 465, 467 (Bogue, 1996) (school district did not violate the contract, which protects teachers from "unreasonable censorship or restraint," when it eliminated pluses and minuses from final end of term grades); Sylvania, Ohio, Sch. Bd. of Educ., 88 LA 683 (Fullmer, 1987) (principal's action in ordering a teacher to expunge the grades for all students who took a test was upheld because the principal felt the teacher had not prepared students adequately for test; teacher are free to teach but they must create exams that cover material for which students are prepared).

[69]*See generally* California Teachers Ass'n v. State Bd. of Educ., 263 F.3d 888 (9th Cir. 2001); Turner-Egner, *Teachers' Discretion in Selecting Instructional Materials and Methods*, 53 EDUC. L. REP. 365 (1989).

[70]Board of Educ. of Jefferson County Sch. Dist. R-1 v. Wilder, 960 P.2d 695, 14 IER Cases 111 (Colo. 1998) (court upheld the dismissal of a teacher for showing the controversial film *1900* as part of a class discussion of fascism in violation of the school's controversial materials policy); Circleville, Ohio, Bd. of Educ., 98 LA 378 (Stanton, 1991) (just cause existed to reprimand high school teacher who showed sexually explicit Madonna video to American government class as part of a discussion on censorship). *See also* Fowler v. Board of Educ. of Lincoln County, 819 F.2d 657 (6th Cir. 1987) (teacher dismissed for showing *Pink Floyd—The Wall* on the last day of class for entertainment).

[71]LaGrande, Or., Sch. Dist., 102 LA 1121, 1125 (Calhoun, 1994) (the district's order to cease using article did not violate academic freedom, because controversial material may only be introduced where it is "in no way detrimental" to education program and a student named in the article was enrolled in the class).

[72]Boring v. Buncombe County Bd. of Educ., 136 F.3d 364, 13 IER Cases 1189 (4th Cir. 1998) (play was part of the school curriculum and school officials had a legitimate concern in regulating such speech).

[73]Lacks v. Ferguson Reorganized Sch. Dist. R-2, 147 F.3d 718, 14 IER Cases 24 (8th Cir. 1998) (dismissal upheld, where teacher allowed students to use profanity in creative assignments that they performed aloud in class and such conduct violated a school policy regarding the use of profanity).

While one court held that a school district's policy regarding the teaching of sexually explicit books was not subject to arbitration,[74] another court held that a community college violated a professor's First Amendment rights when it failed to renew his contract after a student complained that he used and encouraged others to use offensive language in the context of a discussion on social deconstructionism and language.[75]

A teacher who invited an actor to her fifth grade class to speak on the environmental benefits of industrial hemp, an illegal product, was improperly terminated where the teacher followed applicable guidelines for obtaining school and parental permission before inviting the guest speaker.[76]

F. School Takeovers and Reconstitution [LA CDI 100.08]

The "takeover" or "reconstitution" of failing schools has been a frequent subject of both legislation and litigation, and ancillary arbitral review.

Generally, in a state takeover of a school system, either the state board of education, the state legislature, or a federal court chooses a designated entity, such as the mayor or the state department of education, to manage the affairs of a local school district for a limited period of time. Reconstitution is a process by which some or all of a school's staff, including administrators, teachers, custodial workers, and cafeteria workers, are replaced by new personnel.[77] In some instances, staff may reapply for their old jobs, while in other situations, staff simply have the option to apply for positions elsewhere in the district.[78] Although the words "reconstitution" and "takeover" often are used interchangeably, they describe different situations in both legal and labor relations contexts. However, both situations may fundamentally change a school and lead to arbitrations on behalf of the union as well as individual employees.

In Illinois, reconstitution is the last step after other reform processes have failed. Once it is determined that a school will be reconstituted, the principal usually is removed and all staff members must reapply for their jobs.[79] Staff members who are not rehired at the reconstituted school can apply for other employment in the district and will receive full pay for 10 months while they attempt to find another placement. Displaced teachers, known as reserve or unassigned teachers, are expected to serve as substitute teachers during this 10-month period. However, teachers who do not find a placement within this time frame may be dismissed.[80]

---

[74]School Admin. Dist. No. 58 v. Mount Abram Teachers Ass'n, 704 A.2d. 349 (Me. 1997).

[75]Hardy v. Jefferson Cmty. Coll., 260 F.3d 671, 17 IER Cases 1523 (6th Cir. 2001).

[76]Cockrel v. Shelby County Sch. Dist., 270 F.3d 1036, 18 IER Cases 65 (6th Cir. 2001).

[77]*See* Hendrie, *Reconstitution Gaining New Momentum*, Educ. Wkly. (Sept. 24, 1997).

[78] *Id.*

[79]105 Ill. Comp. Stat. 5/34-8.3 (Michie 2002).

[80]Without considering the interplay of Illinois reconstitution statutes and the teacher tenure statutes, a federal district court dismissed a 42 U.S.C. §1983 civil rights complaint by eight formerly tenured teachers who lost their jobs when their schools were reconstituted and they failed to find other positions in the system. The court held that the teachers lacked the requisite "property interest" in their jobs because they could not have had a "legitimate expectation of continued employment" in light of the fact that the state statute granted the school board plenary power to promulgate rules governing layoffs and reductions in force,

In *City of Chicago, Illinois, Public Schools Board of Education*,[81] the arbitrator sustained the grievance of a teacher who was dismissed after his school was reconstituted. In that case, a high school was reconstituted and teachers were informed that they would have to relinquish their positions and reapply for employment at the school. The teachers were informed that some may not receive reappointment, and the grievant was not selected to remain at the school. The teacher was terminated after he allegedly failed to find a permanent position after 10 months. The grievance alleged that the teacher believed he had located a permanent assignment and was entitled to such position by virtue of the contract, which provided that any reserve teacher with at least a satisfactory rating shall be permanently appointed to a position after having served in the position on an interim basis for 60 or more days. While the board of education argued that the grievant had never been assigned on an interim basis, the arbitrator found that the teacher had worked more than 60 days and received "excellent" ratings. The arbitrator further noted that the board of education neglected to provide the support services promised to teachers pursuant to school reconstitution policies.[82]

In another case, an arbitrator was called on to resolve a claimed violation of a contractual provision providing for the appointment of department heads in the event of school reconstitution.[83] The grievant had taught at a high school for 30 years, and for the last 12 of those years had served as a department head. Pursuant to a consent decree, the high school was placed in the Comprehensive School Improvement Plan, but reconstituted at the end of the school year because certain goals were not achieved.

The grievant was notified in early June that he would not be reappointed as a department head as a result of the reconstitution. However, the contract required that the district inform individuals 120 days prior to June 30 if a department head appointment might not be renewed. The school district argued that the faculty at the school were well informed regarding the possibility of reconstitution and that the teacher knew his position as a teacher, and therefore his appointment as a department head, would not be continued. The arbitrator found that nothing in the agreement required that the 120-day notice be in writing, and that the school district reasonably relied on the notice given to all high school staff as providing the grievant with notice that he may not be continued as a department head.

---

and the policy promulgated by the board did not make layoffs dependent on "person-specific issues affecting 'property' interests (that is, legitimate claims of entitlement based on contestable factual propositions to be resolved at hearings)." Shegog v. Board of Educ. of the City of Chi., 2000 WL 555504 (N.D. Ill.), *on remand from* 194 F.3d 836, 15 IER Cases 1116 (7th Cir. 1999).

[81]Case No. 51 390 00103 99, 2000 WL 33325750 (Suntrup, 2000).

[82]*Id. See also* City of Chi., Ill., Bd. of Educ., Case No. 99-09-067, 2000 WL 1670550 (Goldstein, 2000). Although the teacher in question was placed in reserve status for other reasons, the arbitrator noted that the board of education failed to follow its own policies as to reserve teachers and held that by failing to follow its own policies, its actions in terminating the teacher were arbitrary and unreasonable. Because there was insufficient evidence to conclude the teacher would have found a permanent position if the policies were followed, she was returned to status as a reserve teacher and the board of education was ordered to comply with its own policies and provide appropriate assistance.

[83]San Francisco, Cal., Unified Sch. Dist., Case No. 74-300-0047-97, 1997 WL 1098181 (Bogue, 1997).

3. ARBITRATION ISSUES INVOLVING FIREFIGHTERS,
POLICE OFFICERS, AND THEIR DEPARTMENTS

A. Scheduling and Overtime Issues Involving State or Local Government Firefighters [LA CDI 100.47; 100.4801 et seq.]

Scheduling and overtime for firefighters employed by a state or local public agency can present complex compensation issues for arbitrators because of three exemptions to the Fair Labor Standards Act (FLSA).[84] Under the first exemption,[85] a public agency that employs fewer than five firefighting personnel in a given workweek is not required to pay the firefighting employees overtime if the employees work more than 40 hours during that workweek.[86] In determining whether this exemption applies, no distinction is made between full-time or part-time employees, or between employees on duty or on leave status. All of these employees must be counted. However, volunteers as well as elected officials and their appointees are not included.[87] Because this exemption applies on a workweek basis, a public agency may have to pay firefighters overtime in some workweeks and not in others.[88]

In those workweeks in which this first exemption is not available, the public agency may have recourse to the following second exemption. Under the second exemption, which is a partial exemption,[89] a public agency is not required to pay firefighters overtime unless they work more than 212 hours in a 28-day work period. For employees whose work period is at least 7, but less than 28 consecutive days, overtime pay is required when the ratio of the number of hours worked to the number of days in the work period exceeds the ratio of 212 hours to 28 days.[90] Both of these exemptions apply to those employees who: (1) are employed by an organized fire department or fire protection district; (2) have been trained to the extent required by state statute or local ordinance; (3) have the legal authority and responsibility to engage in the prevention, control, or extinguishment of a fire of any type; and (4) perform activities that are required for, and directly concerned with, the prevention, control, or extinguishment of fires, including incidental nonfirefighting activities such as housekeeping, equipment maintenance, lecturing, attending community fire drills, and inspecting homes and schools for fire hazards.[91] All employees, regardless of their status as "trainees," "probationary," or "permanent" personnel, and regardless of their particular specialty or job title, are included. The exemption also extends to rescue and

---

[84]29 U.S.C. §201 et seq.
[85]This first exemption is a complete exemption, which is contained in §13(b)(20) of the FLSA, 29 U.S.C. §213(b)(20).
[86]29 C.F.R. §553.200(a). For a further and more detailed discussion of firefighter wage and hour issues, see *Law Enforcement/Fire Protection Employees*, Wage & Hour Man. (BNA) 191:414 (2001).
[87]29 C.F.R. §553.200(b).
[88]*Id.* §553.200(c).
[89]The second exemption is contained in §7(k) of the FLSA, 29 U.S.C. §207(k).
[90]*Id.* §553.201(a).
[91]*Id.* §553.210(a).

ambulance service personnel if they form an integral part of the public agency's fire protection activities.[92] However, the exemptions do not apply to employees of private-sector firms who provide fire protection services, even if the services are provided under contract with a public agency.[93]

The third exemption, a complete exemption,[94] applies to any employee employed in a bona fide executive, administrative, or professional capacity.[95] Arbitrators can, and have, applied this exemption to high-ranking supervisors, such as fire captains and assistant fire chiefs.[96]

Of the three exemptions, the second exemption has the broadest potential applicability. However, it is not uncommon for the work schedules favored by firefighters (e.g., 24 hours on, 48 hours off) to exceed the hours of work permitted under this exemption. This creates a dilemma for public agencies trying to limit overtime expenditures. One city,[97] whose management-rights clause allowed it to relieve firefighters from duty because of lack of work "or other reasons," attempted to address the problem creatively by relieving firefighters from any scheduled duty that would cause them to work over 212 hours in a 28-day period. Unexpectedly, because of certain provisions in the firefighters' collective bargaining agreement, the city's action resulted in more than just the elimination of overtime pay for the firefighters; it resulted in a reduction in their base pay. To mitigate for this loss, the city allowed the firefighters to use personal leave time in lieu of unpaid time off. The arbitrator concluded that the city's actions amounted to a "forced leave" in violation of the collective bargaining agreement.[98] He reasoned that if the management-rights clause could be utilized to relieve employees of duty for any reason whatsoever, then the economic provisions of the contract could be rendered ineffective.[99]

Other attempts by public agencies to utilize management-rights clauses unilaterally to bring firefighters' work schedules in compliance with the limits allowed by the second exemption also have been unsuccessful. In one such case,[100] the arbitrator declared unambiguously that the duty to comply with

---

[92]*Id.* §553.210(a). To be an integral part of the public agency's fire protection activities, the rescue and ambulance service personnel must have received training in the rescue of fire, crime, and accident victims, or firefighters or law enforcement personnel injured in the performance of their respective duties, and must be regularly dispatched to fires, crime scenes, riots, natural disasters, and accidents. *Id.* §553.215(a).

[93]*Id.* §§553.202, 553.215(c).

[94]The third exemption is contained in §13(a)(1) of the FLSA, 29 U.S.C. §213(a)(1).

[95]The determination of whether an employee is employed in one of these capacities depends, in part, on how much money the employee is paid, whether the employee is paid on an hourly or salaried basis, and whether the employee exercises independent judgment in the performance of his or her job duties and responsibilities. 29 C.F.R. part 541.

[96]City of Sapulpa, Okla., 90 LA 11, 15 (Goodstein, 1987). *See* 29 C.F.R. §553.216. *See also* City of Bethany, Okla., 87 LA 309, 311 (Levy, 1986) (fire captains and assistant fire chiefs are exempt from overtime under the FLSA, but are entitled to overtime under the terms of the collective bargaining agreement). *But see* Sylvania Township, Ohio, Bd. of Trs., 91 LA 575, 577–79 (Klein, 1988) (fire captains are not exempt from overtime under the FLSA because they are paid on an hourly, rather than a salaried, basis).

[97]City of Joliet, Ill., 88 LA 303, 307–09 (Hill, 1986).

[98]*Id.* at 309.

[99]*Id.* at 309–10.

[100]City of Warr Acres, 87 LA 126, 129–30 (Woolf, 1985).

the FLSA does not allow a public agency to change firefighter work schedules unilaterally. Instead, the public agency must use the collective bargaining process as the instrument for achieving compliance.[101]

In an interest arbitration, an arbitrator was unwilling to compel a change
in work schedules absent evidence from the public agency that its overtime
costs were comparatively excessive.[102] The parties, however, may negotiate
overtime provisions that are more generous than those required by the FLSA.
For instance, the FLSA does not require an employer to count vacation time
as hours worked for overtime purposes, but collective bargaining agreements
can, and do, allow vacation time to be counted as hours worked. As a result,
a firefighter could actually perform services for less than 212 hours in a 28-
period and still receive overtime pay.[103]

However, the collective bargaining process may not be used to circumvent FLSA overtime requirements. Thus, even though a collective bargaining agreement may not require a public agency to count time spent by
firefighters attending safety and health committee meetings as hours worked
for overtime purposes, the FLSA does require the public agency to do so when
the duties performed by the firefighters at the meeting are job-related. In
such an instance, an arbitrator concluded that the provisions of the FLSA
overrode the provisions of the collective bargaining agreement.[104]

The issue of compensation for work performed during standby or sleep
time frequently arises. In one case, the union claimed that firefighters should
be compensated at the FLSA overtime rate for actual work performed during
standby time.[105] The union argued that firefighters worked 8 hours in the
performance of their regular duties and then continued their work during
the standby time on their respective shifts. Therefore, they should be compensated at the FLSA overtime rate or night differential. The agency filed a
petition to dismiss on the basis that the claim should have been brought in
federal court and the arbitrator lacked jurisdiction to hear the grievance.
Alternatively, the agency asserted that standby time had been compensated
according to federal statutes and regulations, and that over the course of the
2-week pay period, the firefighters had been paid appropriately for their respective shifts, including the standby time. The arbitrator affirmed his jurisdiction over the dispute, but ultimately denied the grievance because the
union had not carried its burden of proof.

---

[101]*Id. See also* City of Bethany, Okla., 87 LA 309, 311–12 (Levy, 1986).

[102]City of Avon Lake, 108 LA 1049, 1053 (Smith, 1997).

[103]City of Cheyenne, Wyo., 89 LA 133, 135–36 (Allen, Jr., 1987) (firefighter who is called
back to work after last vacation shift ends, but before next regularly scheduled shift begins,
is still technically on vacation leave and is contractually entitled to be paid at an overtime
rate for the call-back shift). *See also* City of Midwest City, Okla., 96 LA 384, 388–89 (Goodstein,
1990) (collective bargaining agreement requires city to count holidays, vacation, military
leave, sick leave, and similar time off as hours worked for overtime purposes).

[104]City of Lawton, 97 LA 796, 797–99 (Weisbrod, 1991). In his decision, an arbitrator
acknowledged that, when an agreement and the law conflict, a minority of arbitrators will
respect the agreement and ignore the law. Most arbitrators, though, take the position that
arbitrators as well as judges are bound by the law. *Id.* at 798. For a further discussion of this
issue, see Chapter 10, section 2., "Range of Views as to Application of 'Law.'"

[105]Defense, Dep't of, Army, 100 Fed. Lab. Rel. Rep. 2-1131 (Lurie, 2000).

In another case,[106] firefighters contended that the agency's practice of requiring firefighters to perform nonemergency work during standby or sleep time entitled the firefighters to be compensated with FLSA overtime pay. In response, the agency asserted that substantial periods of time were spent in the designated status of sleep and standby and any of the required work done during those periods was de minimis. The arbitrator reviewed applicable federal regulations regarding compensation and concluded that if it had been intended that nonemergency work performed during sleep or standby periods was to be compensated by overtime pay, then that benefit would have been stated clearly in the comprehensive laws, rules, and regulations governing compensation. The arbitrator found no such intent and denied the grievance.

B. Residency Requirement Issues Involving Police and Firefighters [LA CDI 100.40]

Requiring police officers and/or firefighters to live in or near the jurisdiction of the employer is not a new phenomenon. Residency requirements originated in English feudal society with the Elizabethan Poor Laws.[107] The Massachusetts Bay Colony, in 1652, required members of the "watch" (the forerunner of today's police department) to be inhabitants of the constable's jurisdiction.[108] Over time, residency requirements became related to the central idea of the "spoils system" and machine politics, that is, that public employment was a reward for past political support.[109] However, residency requirements lost their popularity apparently because of five developments: the anticorruption movement of the Progressive era of the 1920s, the fear that police officers as residents might not control working class strikers, the expansion of cities, the growth of the suburbs, and the rise of unions.[110]

Early challenges to residency requirements were unsuccessful. Thus, in *Reynolds v. Lamb*,[111] the court upheld the discharge of a village manager who did not comply with a residency requirement on the ground that the requirement was not an abuse of discretion. Similarly, in *Salt Lake City Fire Fighters Local 1645 v. Salt Lake City*,[112] the court held that any inconvenience to employees was "regrettable," but that "any employer, including a city, should be able to draw from a labor pool those who live within a reasonable distance from work, or . . . within the city limits."[113] The picture changed somewhat as a result of the Supreme Court's decision in *Shapiro v. Thomp-*

---

[106]Government Employees (AFGE), 11 Fed. Lab. Rel. Rep. 2-1174 (Angelo, 1992).

[107]*See* Rhyne, Rhyne, & Elmendorf, *The Constitutionality of Residency Requirements for Municipal Officials and Employees*, NAT'L INST. OF MUN. L. OFFICERS J. RESEARCH REPORT 160 (1977) (citing 31 Eliz. 1, c. 2 (1601) (Eng.)).

[108]Johnson, Warchol, & Bumphus, *Police Residential Requirements: An Exploratory Analysis*, 26 J. COLLECTIVE NEGOTIATIONS PUB. SECTOR 43 (Winter 1997).

[109]*Id.* at 44–45.

[110]*Id.* at 45.

[111]232 A.2d 375 (R.I. 1967).

[112]449 P.2d 239 (Utah 1969).

[113]*Id.* at 240.

son,[114] where residency requirements imposed on welfare applicants were held to violate the constitutional right to travel between the states. However, subsequent challenges to residency requirements placed on applicants for employment and current employees have met with mixed success.[115]

The threshold question ordinarily has been whether residency requirements are a mandatory subject of bargaining. On this point, commentators have noted that residency requirements are in a "gray area" because they involve, on the one hand, "policy determinations" ordinarily outside the scope of bargaining, and yet, on the other hand, they impact aspects of the "terms and conditions of employment" that are, of course, bargainable.[116] Essentially, this debate has turned on whether residency requirements are considered to be "primarily related," "directly related," or "substantially related" to the terms and conditions of employment. Adjudicatory bodies have answered that question by balancing the degree to which the requirement forwards the interests of the employer against the inconvenience caused to employees.[117] Thus, for example, it has been held that residency requirements pertaining only to eligibility for hiring are not mandatory subjects of bargaining because, by definition, the condition ceases to exist once an employee is hired.[118] However, on the same basis, a continuing residency requirement has been deemed to be a mandatory subject of bargaining[119] by most adjudicatory bodies that have considered the question.[120]

In interest-arbitration proceedings, employers have argued that residency requirements promote efficiency, early response time, and the "community identity" that will result between police officers and firefighters and the citizens they serve.[121] In addition, employers have argued that residency

---

[114]394 U.S. 618 (1969).

[115]*See e.g.*, Myers, *The Constitutionality of Continuing Residency Requirements for Local Government Employees: A Second Look*, 23 Cal. W. L. Rev. 24 (Fall 1986); Rhyne, Rhyne, & Elmendorf, *The Constitutionality of Residency Requirements for Municipal Officers and Employees*, Nat'l Inst. Mun. L. Officers Research Report 160 (1977); supra; Hager, *Residency Requirements for City Employees: Important Incentives in Today's Urban Crisis*, 18 Urb. L. Ann. 197 (Summer 1980).

[116]Lynch, *Public Employment Residency Requirements and the Duty to Bargain*, J. Collective Negotiations Pub. Sector 263, 265 (Summer 1980). *See also* City of Perth Amboy, N.J., N.J. Pub. Emp. Rep. (LRP) ¶29006 (N.J. PERC 1997) (a residency requirement did not breach the duty to bargain because it did not "fix the employment condition expressly, specifically, and comprehensively").

[117]Lynch, at 270–71.

[118]Detroit Fed'n of Teachers Local 231 v. Board of Educ., 65 Mich. App. 182, 237 N.E.2d 238, 92 LRRM 2121 (1975); State, County, & Mun. Employees Local 650, 9 PERB 3058 (N.Y. 1976).

[119]Detroit Police Officers Ass'n v. City of Detroit, 391 Mich. 44, 214 N.W.2d 803 (1974). *But see* City of Auburn, N.Y., 9 PERB 3085 (N.Y. 1976).

[120]*See, e.g.*, City of Perth Amboy, N.J., 24 N.J. Pub. Emp. Rep. (LRP) ¶29006 (N.J. PERC 1997); City of Highland Park, Mich., Mich. Pub. Emp. Rep (LRP) ¶25078 (MERC 1994); City of St. Bernard, 11 Ohio Pub. Emp. Rep. (LRP) ¶1488 (Ohio Ct. App. 1994); City of Chester v. Fraternal Order of Police, Lodge 19, 23 Pa. Pub. Emp. Rep. (LRP) ¶23180 (Pa. Commw. Ct. 1992); Township of Moon v. Police Officers of Township of Moon, 508 Pa. 495, 498 A.2d 1305 (Sup. Ct. 1985); City of New Haven v. Connecticut State Bd. of Labor Relations, 410 A.2d 140 (Conn. Super. Ct. 1979).

[121]Rhyne, Rhyne, & Elmendorf, *The Constituionality of Residency Requirements for Municipal Officials and Employees*, Nat'l Inst. Mun. L. Officers Research Report 160 (1977). However, at least one commentator has observed that these arguments seem "artificial and contrived" in light of the "erratic borders of modern day cities and governmental units." Myers, *The Constitutionality of Continuing Residency Requirements for Local Government Employees: A Second Look*, 23 Cal. W. L. Rev. 24, 27 (Fall 1986).

requirements should be imposed in order to reduce local unemployment, achieve ethnic and racial balance, instill public confidence, promote safety, and benefit the local economy and tax base.[122] Opponents have contended that many of the benefits identified by employers cannot be quantified, and that a residency requirement would decrease the pool of available applicants and restrict career mobility. Further, unions argue that residency requirements are discriminatory, that police officers will be fearful if required to live in the community from which they arrest wrongdoers, and that the development of modern day transportation and communication systems and mutual aid pacts between communities render residency requirements unnecessary.[123]

Where residency requirements are already in place, many interest arbitrators are reluctant to delete them from successor agreement. For example, in *City of Warren, Michigan*,[124] the arbitrator rejected the employer's argument that a residency requirement would enhance the espirit de corps of firefighters, pointing out that unit cohesiveness is already achieved by the fact that firefighters live together while on duty. The arbitrator also noted the increasing mobility of employees, and that many of the areas outside of the city were more accessible than those within. Nonetheless, he chose the employer's final offer to maintain the status quo residency requirement in light of the fact that the union did not offer a satisfactory reason to depart from the prior practice. Similarly, in *City of Richland Center, Wisconsin*,[125] an arbitrator also chose the employer's position on residency requirements. He did so although he found that the "live where you are paid" argument was no longer persuasive in light of *Shapiro* and that the employer had failed to support its argument regarding faster response time. Rather, he found persuasive expert evidence that the residency requirement promoted health, safety, and welfare and the prevention, detection, and punishment of crimes.[126] Thus, the city's compelling interest overrode the sacrifice of police officers in surrendering their right to live where they choose.

The arbitrator in *City of Manitowoc, Wisconsin*,[127] however, held that an employer had violated the parties' collective bargaining agreement when it enacted a residency requirement. He held that the employees had a liberty interest in deciding where to live, the city's proof of perceived benefits was no more than speculative, and any enhancement to the retail trade, tax base, and economic welfare of the city was insubstantial.[128]

When Illinois first passed public-sector bargaining legislation for police officers, firefighters, and other "essential services" employees, the question of residency was expressly excluded from the list of issues arbitrable in in-

---

[122]Myers, 23 CAL. W.L. REV. at 25 (citing Ector v. City of Torrance, 10 Cal. 3d 129, 514 P.2d 433, 109 Cal. Rptr. 849 (1973)).

[123]Johnson, Warchol, & Bumphus, *Police Residential Requirements: An Exploratory Analysis*, 26 J. COLLECTIVE NEGOTIATIONS PUB. SECTOR 43, 47–48 (Winter 1997).

[124]57 LA 585 (Edwards, 1971).

[125]City of Richland Ctr., Wis., Police Dep't, 66 LA 613 (Yeager, 1976).

[126]*Id.* at 617–18.

[127]61 LA 818 (Bellman, 1973).

[128]*Id.* at 820–21. It should be noted, however, that the arbitrator did not face the issue in the context of public safety officers as he noted in his award.

terest arbitration. However, in 1997 the Illinois General Assembly amended the law to permit the parties to arbitrate the issue. Thus, in early arbitration cases, arbitrators were first confronted by the argument that by seeking to overturn residency requirements, unions were seeking to change the status quo and should therefore be held to a higher burden of proof than they otherwise might. However, arbitrators rejected that argument, holding that the existence of residency requirements prior to the amended law was, at best, a "tacit approval" of unilateral action.[129] In doing so, arbitrators reasoned that because the issue was not the product of bilateral efforts and expectations there was no base from which to consider subsequent bargaining.[130] Illinois arbitrators also faced many of the arguments that had been made historically with regard to residency. For example, the arbitrator in *City of Nashville*[131] rejected the "live where you are paid" argument, noting that there were many communities in Illinois in which employees lived outside of the community. In *City of Kankakee, Illinois*,[132] the arbitrator broadened a citywide residency requirement in light of convincing evidence that he believed established a disturbing pattern of criminal victimization and intimidation of police officers, some of which was in retaliation for the officers' performance of their duties. On a more fundamental level, the arbitrator in *Town of Cicero, Illinois*,[133] held that "projected or hypothetical needs of (the employer) cannot take precedence over the actual here-and-now freedom of the individual firefighter to exercise a basic right enjoyed by most . . . U.S. residents."[134] Even when Illinois arbitrators have upheld residency requirements, it has usually been because of unusual circumstances. Thus, in *Village of South Holland, Illinois*,[135] the arbitrator relied on a unique history of racial discrimination requiring the intervention of the U.S. Department of Justice. Similarly, in *City of Highland Park, Illinois*,[136] the arbitrator awarded the final offer of the employer because that of the union would have permitted employees to live anywhere in the state of Illinois.

C. Off-Duty Misconduct by Police Officers [LA CDI 100.552505]

Arbitrators apply the three-part workplace nexus test of *W.E. Caldwell Co.*[137] to cases involving off-duty misconduct by law enforcement officers.[138]

---

[129]City of Nashville, Case. No. S-MA-97-141 (McAlpin, 1999). The interest-arbitration awards of Illinois arbitrators are not reported by the Illinois State Labor Relations Board. Copies may be obtained by calling the Illinois Labor Relations Board in Springfield, Ill., at (217) 785-3155, or the Board's Chicago Office at (312) 793-6400.

[130]City of Lincoln, Case No. S-MA-99-140 (Perkovich, 2000).

[131]Case No. S-MA-97-141 (McAlpin, 1999).

[132]Case No. S-MA-99-137 (LeRoy, 2000).

[133]Case No. S-MA-98-230 (Berman, 1999).

[134]*Id.* at 43.

[135]Case No. S-MA-98-120 (Goldstein, 1999).

[136]Case No. S-MA-98-219 (Benn, 1999).

[137]28 LA 434 (Kesselman, 1957).

[138]Broward Co., Fla., Sheriff's Office, 115 LA 708 (Richard, 2001) (off-duty conduct shows sufficient nexus to an officer's employment and justified discharge); Jackson Township, Ohio, 112 LA 811 (Graham, 1999) (to sustain discipline for off-duty conduct, a nexus, or tangible connection between the off-duty conduct and the officer's on-duty responsibilities must exist, such as injury to the employer's business or reputation, or refusal of coworkers to work with

This test has been applied to cases involving soliciting prostitution,[139] fighting during an off-duty softball game,[140] and swearing and acting antagonistically toward a law enforcement officer from another agency.[141]

Arbitrators also recognize that law enforcement officers may be held to a higher standard by the community in which they work. In one case involving the discharge of a police officer who was convicted of the misdemeanor offense of providing alcoholic beverages to a minor, his fiancée, the arbitrator commented:

> Any intentional violation of the law by a police officer is a serious matter particularly where it is publicly done, for then disrepute and undermining of the integrity of the department is involved. This is particularly true in such a small community . . . where such incidents become widely known and notorious in the public's mind. It certainly was a violation of the professional conduct and responsibilities as stated in the manual for it was 'conduct unbecoming an officer' and it was 'likely to bring discredit to the Department.' Such is significant and inherently an obligation of police officers, even without specification in the manual; they must observe and obey all laws. That is a minimum expectation and a most reasonable requirement. The failure to do so goes directly to the capacity of an individual to serve as a law enforcement officer.[142]

The public nature of the off-duty conduct can be particularly critical in police officers' cases. For example, in a case in which an officer was charged with a misdemeanor domestic violence offense for engaging in a physical altercation with his wife at their home, the arbitrator stated, "a distinction should be made between off duty criminal acts committed in public places against members of the public, from those which take place in the privacy of a home and within the marriage relationship."[143] In another case involving an off-duty domestic altercation, the arbitrator found the officer's argument that the altercation did not warrant discharge unpersuasive partly because

---

the officer); City of El Paso, Tex., 110 LA 411, 416 (Moore, 1998) (bringing discredit or embarrassment to an officer or a police department is necessary to impose discipline for off-duty misconduct); State of Ohio, 107 LA 779, 781 (Feldman, 1996) ("[N]o doubt that off duty activity on the part of [the highway patrol officer] that may be embarrassing to the employer is subject to discipline by the employer.").

[139]Broward Co., Fla., Sheriff's Office, 115 LA 708, 710 (Richard, 2001).

[140]Jackson Township, Ohio, 112 LA 811, 812 (Graham, 1999).

[141]State of Ohio, 107 LA 779, 781 (Feldman, 1996) (highway patrol officer's suspension reduced due to absence of a physical altercation).

[142]City of Rogers City, Mich., 110 LA 92, 95 (Daniel, 1997) (discharge upheld due to an officer's intentional course of action and failure to fulfill his obligation to observe all laws). See also Township of E. Lampeter, Pa., 105 LA 133, 140 (DiLauro, 1995) ("As a public servant entrusted to protect and serve the members of the community, the grievant must realize that he is held to a public duty to uphold and abide by the law, a duty that is generally higher for police officers than those employed in the private sector."); City of Mansfield, Ohio, 105 LA 935, 937 (Shanker, 1995) (officers accept being held to higher standards of conduct by joining a police force).

[143]City of Mansfield, Ohio, 105 LA 935, 937 (Shanker, 1995) (20-day suspension reduced to 7-day suspension).

the dispute had become public.[144] Violation of a protective order to keep away from the marital residence has been found to warrant discipline.[145]

The public perception of the officer has been discussed in cases involving off-duty drinking by officers. One arbitrator stated that a municipality had not shown that an officer had brought discredit or embarrassment on himself or the police department when he was found in a bar drinking while off-duty and in civilian clothing, and that therefore discharge was inappropriate.[146] The same arbitrator reached the conclusion that a suspension was justified where the municipality established that the grievant "created the perception that he was intoxicated . . . in public."[147]

4. Limitations on Scope of Bargaining and Arbitration in State and Local Government Employment [LA CDI 100.021501 et seq.]

Significant limitations may exist on the permitted scope of bargaining and arbitration in the state and local government sector by virtue of the overriding status of (1) certain laws, rules, and regulations; and (2) certain areas of exclusive management rights.[148]

In *Liverpool*,[149] the New York Court of Appeals determined that two questions are to be answered in determining arbitrability in public-sector cases: (1) whether the law *permits* arbitration of the disputed matter, and, if so, (2) whether the parties have agreed to arbitrate the disputed matter.[150] The

---

[144]City of St. Petersburg, Fla., 104 LA 594, 595 (Thornell, 1995) (discharge upheld, where arbitrator found the incident in which an officer went to his former girlfriend's house in an intoxicated condition, was angry about being served with child support papers, struck his girlfriend in the face, injuring her, the girlfriend called 911, and the grievant took a gun from a closet and threatened to kill his girlfriend, himself, and others while brandishing the gun at others was "more than just a domestic squabble").

[145]Township of E. Lampeter, Pa., 105 LA 133, 140 (DiLauro, 1997) (by having protective order brought against him and by being arrested for violating such order, officer "risked tarnishing the image, reputation, and respect of the Township's police force").

[146]City of El Paso, Tex., 110 LA 411, 416 (Moore, 1998) (city also failed to prove that the officer was driving while intoxicated). For earlier cases applying the workplace nexus test to law enforcement officers convicted of driving while under the influence of alcohol, see *Ohio State Highway Patrol*, 96 LA 613, 617 (Bittel, 1991) ("nexus of the offense to the job is obvious" but the officer is entitled to a second chance due to significant lifestyle changes); *State of Ohio*, 94 LA 533 (Sharpe, 1990) (extensive discussion of workplace nexus test as applied to a conviction for driving while intoxicated, especially the impact of the publicity surrounding the offense on law enforcement's role in enforcing laws on drinking and driving).

[147]City of El Paso, Tex., 114 LA 225, 228 (Moore, 2000).

[148]*See* Edwards, Clark, & Craver, Labor Relations Law in the Public Sector 693 (1979); Note, *Taking the Public Out of Determining Government Policy: The Need for an Appropriate Scope of Bargaining Test in the Illinois Public Sector*, 29 J. Marshall L. Rev. 531 (1996); Blair, *State Legislative Control Over the Conditions of Public Employment: Defining the Scope of Collective Bargaining for State and Municipal Employees*, 26 Vand. L. Rev. 1 (1973).

[149]Acting Superintendent of Liverpool Cent. Sch. Dist. v. United Liverpool Faculty Ass'n, 369 N.E.2d 746, 749, 96 LRRM 2779 (N.Y. 1977).

[150]In connection with the first question, the court spoke of "overarching and fundamentally nondelegable" responsibilities of elected representatives of the public. *Id.* In a subsequent decision, the same court indicated a narrow scope for the public policy limitation on arbitration: "[A] small number of areas, interlaced with strong governmental or societal interests, restrict the power of an arbitrator to render an otherwise proper award . . . . In the public sector, this policy limitation has arisen with respect to school matters and is derived from the statutory scheme implicit in the Education Law . . . ." Binghamton Civil Serv.

Maine Supreme Court also held that two questions should be considered in determining whether a matter is subject to public-sector interest arbitration: (1) "whether the matter is within the statutorily defined scope of bargaining," and, if so, (2) "whether the matter is limited by any other existing statutory enhancements."[151]

A. Mandatory, Prohibited, and Permitted Subjects of Bargaining
[LA CDI 100.021505; 100.021515]

Matters that are mandatory subjects of bargaining in the state and local government sector ordinarily can be made arbitrable by agreement of the parties. However, some subject matter may fall outside the legal bargaining authority of state and local government sector employers because either (1) a collective bargaining statute expressly removes it from the scope of bargaining; or (2) the subject matter is regulated by some controlling statutory law, preempting regulation by bargaining; or (3) public policy requires that responsibility over the matter, because of its nature, be exercised exclusively by the public employer. Such matters thus are not proper subjects of bargaining and may be classified as prohibited or nonnegotiable subjects. A matter is not arbitrable if it is not negotiable, regardless of whether the parties have agreed to arbitrate.[152]

As to still other matters, state and local government sector employers may be permitted but not required to bargain. Management can elect to retain control over such permissible subjects of bargaining merely by refraining from bargaining or agreeing on provisions that share management's control. If a public employer does elect to bargain on a permissible subject and a clause on the subject is negotiated, grievances involving application of the clause may be made subject to arbitration.[153] At least one state has not given general recognition to the "permissible subjects of bargaining" category for the state and local government sector. New Jersey has held that in the state and local government sector (except for police and firefighters), there are only two categories of issues: "mandatory negotiable terms and conditions of employment, and nonnegotiable matters of governmental policy."[154]

Forum v. City of Binghamton, 374 N.E.2d 380, 383, 97 LRRM 3070 (N.Y. 1978).

[151]Town of Winslow Superintending Sch. Comm. v. Winslow Educ. Ass'n, 363 A.2d 229, 232, 93 LRRM 2398 (Me. 1976).

[152]Arbitrability in the public sector has been challenged on "scope of bargaining" grounds, both in suits to compel arbitration and in suits to vacate arbitration awards. Primary issues raised are discussed in *Developments in the Law—Public Employment*, 97 HARV. L. REV. 1611, 1676 (1984).

[153]*See, e.g.*, Rochester City Sch. Dist. v. Rochester Teachers Ass'n, 362 N.E.2d 977, 982, 95 LRRM 2118 (N.Y. 1977). The Massachusetts Supreme Court has held that both mandatory and permissible subjects of bargaining may be submitted to interest arbitration, but educational policy matters cannot be arbitrated. *See also* Boston Sch. Comm. v. Boston Teachers Union Local 66, 363 N.E.2d 485, 95 LRRM 2855 (Mass. 1977). *But see* School Comm. of Holbrook v. Holbrook Educ. Ass'n, 481 N.E.2d 484 (Mass. 1985) (interpreting the scope of such policy matters).

[154]Ridgefield Park Educ. Ass'n v. Ridgefield Park Bd. of Educ., 393 A.2d 278, 287, 98 LRRM 3285 (N.J. 1978). The police and firefighter exception resulted from a 1977 statutory amendment and has been narrowly construed. Paterson Police PBA Local 1 v. City of Paterson, 432 A.2d 847, 854, 112 LRRM 2205 (N.J. 1981); Board of Educ. of City of Englewood v. Englewood Teachers Ass'n, 311 A.2d 729, 732, 85 LRRM 2137 (N.J. 1973).

B. Express Statutory Removal of Matter From Bargaining
[LA CDI 100.30]

Statutes providing for collective bargaining in the state and local government sector often expressly remove some subject matters from the scope of bargaining, particularly specified areas of management rights.[155] When management rights are statutorily removed from the duty to bargain, procedures regarding the implementation of such subjects remain topics for bargaining.[156]

C. Contractual Terms Versus Statutory Law Covering Similar Matters

Collective bargaining statutes for the state and local government sector vary regarding the relationship between contractual terms and statutory law covering similar matters. Some variations are:

1. Often the collective bargaining statute is silent regarding the relationship between contract terms and statutory law covering the subject matter. This leaves for the courts the ultimate determination of any nonbargainable subject.[157]

---

[155]See, e.g., Wisconsin State Employment Labor Relations Act §§111.90, 111.91 (1995–96) (prohibiting bargaining on various specified matters including listed management rights, except that management is permitted but not required to bargain on certain of the rights). Further discussed in Rabban, Can American Labor Law Accommodate Collective Bargaining by Professional Employees?, 99 Yale L.J. 689 (1990), the Hawaii Act, which covers most public employees in the state, provides in §89-9(d) (1997) that: "The employer and the exclusive representative shall not agree to any proposal which would be inconsistent in merit principles or the principle of equal pay for equal work pursuant to [statute], or which would interfere with the rights of a public employer [to exercise any of the extensive list of management rights listed in the statute]."

[156]See, e.g., Hawaii Act, §89-(9)(d); Wisconsin State Employment Labor Relations Act, §111.91(1)(b) (1995–96).

[157]See Glendale Prof'l Policemen's Ass'n v. City of Glendale, 264 N.W.2d 594, 602, 98 LRRM 2362 (Wis. 1978). The parties may, in the collective bargaining agreement, prohibit the arbitrator from deciding whether a statute makes a term illegal in the contract, thereby leaving the question for the courts to decide. See Duluth Fed'n of Teachers Local 692 v. Independent Sch. Dist. 709, 361 N.W.2d 834, 122 LRRM 3084 (Minn. 1985). See also Krinsky, Municipal Grievance Arbitration in Wisconsin, 28 Arb. J. 50, 58 (1973). In Jefferson County Board of Education, 69 LA 890, 895 (Render, 1977), a board of education contended that statutes vesting it with broad administrative discretion precluded arbitrability of a compulsory retirement grievance, to which the arbitrator responded: "The existence of statutes dealing with the same subject matter does not necessarily preclude an arbitrator from concluding that contractual violations may also exist. . . . If the Board was allowed to successfully forestall arbitration in this case, few, if any, Association complaints could ever be resolved through the contractual grievance procedure." See also Leechburg Area Sch. Dist. v. Leechburg Educ. Ass'n, 380 A.2d 1203, 1206, 97 LRRM 2133 (Pa. 1977). It should be noted that where substantive provisions of a collective bargaining agreement are uncertain as to intent, arbitrators often do not hesitate to consider external law as an aid in determining that intent. Southern Tioga Educ. Ass'n v. Southern Tioga Sch. Dist., 668 A.2d 260 (Pa. Commw. Ct. 1995). See, e.g., Garner v. City of Tulsa, 651 P.2d 1325, 113 LRRM 3613, 3615 (Okla. 1982).

2. The statute may provide that where the agreement conflicts with statutory law, the statutory law prevails.[158]
3, Some collective bargaining statutes specifically prohibit bargaining over specified subjects covered by statutory law.[159]
4. The collective bargaining statute may provide that the agreement shall prevail against statutory law insofar as areas of legal bargaining are concerned.[160]

D. Matters Sometimes Held Nonbargainable [LA CDI 100.021501]

Some matters have been considered to fall inherently outside the scope of bargaining. Many of the challenges relate to education, an area that has produced much of the litigation.[161] Following are some of the matters that have been held outside the scope of bargaining by at least one state in state and local government sector litigation:[162]

1. Tenure—grant or denial (but procedural steps preliminary to employer's final action on tenure ordinarily are held bargainable and arbitrable),[163]

---

[158]An example is the Vermont State Employee Labor Relations Act, Vt. STAT. ANN. tit. 3 §904(a) (1997). In holding statutory authorization not to be required for school-employer bargaining, the Colorado Supreme Court stated that, in the absence of specific statutes to the contrary, collective bargaining agreements "must not conflict with existing statutes concerning the governance of the state school system." Littleton Educ. Ass'n v. Arapahoe County Sch. Dist. No. 6, 553 P.2d 793, 797, 93 LRRM 2378 (Colo. 1976). Cf. Denver Classroom Teachers Ass'n v. Denver Sch. Dist. No. 1, 911 P.2d 690 (Colo. Ct. App. 1995). A similar limitation imposed by the Ohio Supreme Court was recognized in Berea City Sch. Dist., 71 LA 679, 682, 685 (Cohen, 1978).

[159]Although those states that have comprehensive public-sector labor laws usually follow the National Labor Relations Act (NLRA), 29 U.S.C. §151 et seq., in allowing bargaining for "wages, hours and other terms and conditions of employment," most also limit or prohibit bargaining regarding civil service provisions and certain management rights. KEARNEY, LABOR RELATIONS IN THE PUBLIC SECTOR 83–84 (1992). See, e.g., HILL & SINICROPI, Legal Consideration in Negotiating Management Rights Clauses: Public-Sector Concerns: State Restrictions, in MANAGEMENT RIGHTS: A LEGAL AND ARBITRAL ANALYSIS 140–45 (BNA Books 1986); New Hampshire Public Employee Labor Relations Law, N.H. REV. STAT. ANN. §273-A:3, ¶III (1987).

[160]For example, the Wisconsin State Employment Labor Relations Act, §§111.90, 111.91, & 111.93(3) (1995–96), specifically indicates areas of mandatory bargaining, areas of permissible bargaining, and areas where bargaining is prohibited. It provides: "If a labor agreement exists between the state and a union representing a certified or recognized bargaining unit, the provisions of such agreement shall supersede such provisions of civil service and other applicable statues related to wages, hours and conditions of employment whether or not the matters contained in such statutes are set forth in such labor agreement." See also CONN. GEN. STAT. §5-278(e) (1997).

[161]For related discussion, see Holden, New Dimensions in Public-Sector Grievance Arbitration: IV. The Clash Over What Is Bargainable in the Public Schools and Its Consequences for the Arbitrator, in TRUTH, LIE DETECTORS, AND OTHER PROBLEMS IN LABOR ARBITRATION, PROCEEDINGS OF THE 31ST ANNUAL MEETING OF NAA 282 (Stern & Dennis eds., BNA Books 1979).

[162]See generally DILTS & WALSH, COLLECTIVE BARGAINING AND IMPASSE RESOLUTION IN THE PUBLIC SECTOR 29–30 (1988); Turner & Feiley, The Changing Landscape of School District Negotiations: A Practitioner's Perspective on the 1995 Amendments to the Oregon Public Employee Collective Bargaining Law, 32 WILLAMETTE L. REV. 707 (Fall 1996); Malin, Implementing the Illinois Educational Labor Relations Act, 61 CHI.-KENT L. REV. 101 (1985).

[163]A number of states have held that substantive tenure decisions or decisions not to renew a nontenured teacher's contract are both nonbargainable and nonarbitrable. Union

2. Discharge of probation officers,[164]
3. Right to inspect teacher personnel files,[165]
4. Class size,[166]

County Coll. v. Union County Coll. Chapter of AAUP, 684 A.2d 511 (N.J. 1996); School Comm. of Natick v. Education Ass'n of Natick, 666 N.E.2d 486 (Mass. 1996); University Educ. Ass'n v. Regents of Univ. of Minn., 353 N.W.2d 534, 122 LRRM 2569 (Minn. 1984). *See, e.g.,* Moravek v. Davenport Cmty. Sch. Dist., 262 N.W.2d 797, 98 LRRM 2923 (Iowa 1978); Cohoes City Sch. Dist. v. Cohoes Teachers Ass'n, 358 N.E.2d 878, 94 LRRM 2192 (N.Y. 1976) (but procedural steps are bargainable and enforceable); Town of Winslow Superintending Sch. Comm. v. Winslow Educ. Ass'n, 363 A.2d 229, 93 LRRM 2398 (Me. 1976) (discussing numerous other cases on the subject). Reaching a contrary result were: Port Huron Educ. Ass'n v. Port Huron Area Sch. Dist., 550 N.W.2d 228, 158 LRRM 2997 (Mich. 1996); Riverview Sch. Dist. v. Riverview Educ. Ass'n, 639 A.2d 974, 145 LRRM 2964 (Pa. Commw. Ct. 1994); Danville Bd. of Sch. Dirs. v. Fifield, 315 A.2d 473, 85 LRRM 2939 (Vt. 1974). See also a Hawaii Supreme Court decision covering nine disputes, *University of Haw. Prof'l Assembly v. University of Haw.,* 659 P.2d 717, 720, 729, 113 LRRM 3201, 3203 (Haw. 1983). Discharge of a teacher who *had* tenure could be submitted to arbitration in New York, according to the court in *Board of Educ. of Union Free Sch. Dist. No. 3 v. Associated Teachers of Huntington,* 282 N.E.2d 109, 79 LRRM 2881 (N.Y. 1972), where the agreement authorized arbitration of tenured teacher discharge for misconduct or incompetency. The court said: "[This provision] assures teachers with tenure that no disciplinary action will be taken against them without just cause and that any dispute as to the existence of such cause may be submitted to arbitration. It is a provision commonly found in collective bargaining agreements in the private and public sectors and carries out Federal and State policy favoring arbitration as a means of resolving labor disputes." *Id.* at 113. For a discussion of tenured teacher discharge cases submitted to arbitration in New York, see Gross, *Standards of Behavior for Tenured Teachers: The New York State Experience, in* Arbitration 1987: The Academy at Forty, Proceedings of the 40th Annual Meeting of NAA 181 (Gruenberg ed., BNA Books 1988). For a general discussion of discharge of tenured faculty in higher education, see Kruft, McDaniels v. Flick: *Terminating the Employment of Tenured Professors—What Process Is Due?,* 41 Vill. L. Rev. 607 (1996).

[164]In *Firefighters (IAFF) Local 1383 v. City of Warren,* 311 N.W.2d 702 (Mich. 1981), the court required judicial review of discharge of probation officers after finding the subject was not bargainable. Apart from special classes of employees, however, discharge of public employees is a proper subject of bargaining and arbitration. *See* Racine Educ. Ass'n v. Racine Unified Sch. Dist., 500 N.W.2d 379, 143 LRRM 3110 (Wis. Ct. App. 1993).

[165]Great Neck Union Free Sch. Dist. Bd. of Educ. v. Areman, 362 N.E.2d 943, 947–48, 95 LRRM 2165, 2169 (N.Y. 1977) ("a board of education cannot bargain away its right to inspect teacher personnel files and . . . a provision in a collective bargaining agreement which might reflect such a bargain is unenforceable as against public policy."). However, the court cautioned that "any inspection must be related to legitimate board purposes and functions." *Id.* at 947. *See also* LaRocca v. Board of Educ., 632 N.Y.S.2d 576 (N.Y. App. Div. 1995).

[166]Kenai Peninsula Borough Sch. Dist. v. Kenai Peninsula Educ. Ass'n, 557 P.2d 416, 97 LRRM 2153 (Alaska 1977) (the court provided a list of 9 nonnegotiable matters and a list of 38 negotiable matters). *See also* National Educ. Ass'n—Topeka, Inc. v. Unified Sch. Dist. 501, Shawnee County, 592 P.2d 93, 98, 101 LRRM 2611 (Kan. 1979). *But see* West Hartford Educ. Ass'n v. DeCourcy, 295 A.2d 526, 537, 80 LRRM 2422 (Conn. 1972) (class size and teacher load held mandatory subjects of bargaining). New York has held that although class size is not a mandatory bargaining subject, if a school employer voluntarily contracts on the subject, a dispute over the provision may be arbitrable. Susquehanna Valley Cent. Sch. Dist. v. Susquehanna Valley Teachers' Ass'n, 339 N.E.2d 132, 90 LRRM 3046 (N.Y. 1975). The *impact* of class size as it bears on teacher workloads was held a mandatory subject of bargaining in *City of Beloit v. Wisconsin Employment Relations Commission,* 242 N.W.2d 231, 240–41, 92 LRRM 3318, 3325 (Wis. 1976). Under a "primarily related" test, the court classified the following subjects as mandatory subjects of bargaining: teacher evaluation procedures, teacher access to their personnel files, seniority in teacher layoffs (without restricting school employer right to determine curriculum and to retain teachers qualified to teach particular subjects), school calendar and in-service days, impact of class size, and impact of reading program. *Id.* at 236–42.

5. Curriculum (courses of study),[167]
6. Classification of students according to their abilities,[168]
7. Medical disqualification standards,[169]
8. Teacher evaluations,[170]
9. School calendar,[171]
10. Reclassification of teachers,[172]
11. Decision to abolish positions,[173]
12. Hours of work of teachers,[174]

---

[167]Board of Educ. Township of Rockaway v. Rockaway Township Educ. Ass'n, 295 A.2d 380, 384, 81 LRRM 2462, 2465 (N.J. Super. Ct. Ch. Div. 1972). The court said that "if the contract is read to delegate a teacher or a teacher's union the subject of courses of study, the contract in that respect is *ultra vires* and unenforceable," and the court held nonarbitrable a grievance alleging interference with "academic freedom" (teacher was prohibited from conducting debate in seventh grade class on the subject of abortion) even though the agreement recognized that "academic freedom is essential to the fulfillment of the purposes" of the school. *Id.* at 384, 81 LRRM at 2465. Following this case, the New Jersey courts continued to hold that public-sector labor laws are superseded by and must give way to education law provisions if and when they conflict. Board of Educ. of Neptune v. Neptune Township Educ. Ass'n, 675 A.2d 611, 615, 144 N.J. 16 (N.J. 1996). *See also* the discussion of academic freedom as a policy issue in In re *University of Med. & Dentistry of N.J.*, 144 N.J. 511, 677 A.2d 721, 152 LRRM 2606 (N.J. 1996). In *Joint Sch. Dist. No. 8 v. Wisconsin Employment Relations Bd.*, 155 N.W.2d 78, 82–83 (Wis. 1967), court dictum indicated that curriculum content would not be bargainable because it was within the scope of basic educational policy, citing with approval *Teachers Local 2308 (Blackhawk) v. Wisconsin Employment Relations Comm'n*, 326 N.W.2d 247, 256, 114 LRRM 2713 (Wis. Ct. App. 1982).

[168]Rapid City Educ. Ass'n v. Rapid City Area Sch. Dist. 51-4, 376 N.W.2d 562, 120 LRRM 3424 (S.D. 1985).

[169]A Pennsylvania court declared medical standards for bus drivers to be instruments promoting public policy in favor of promoting transportation safety. Southeastern Pa. Transp. Auth. v. Transport Workers, 525 A.2d 1, 125 LRRM 3051 (Pa. Commw. Ct. 1987).

[170]Wethersfield Bd. of Educ. v. Connecticut State Bd. of Labor Relations, 519 A.2d 41, 125 LRRM 2510 (Conn. 1986).

[171]Board of Educ., Montgomery County v. Montgomery County Educ. Ass'n, 505 A.2d 905, 123 LRRM 2505 (Md. Ct. Spec. App. 1986) (the school calendar and reclassification of teachers are subjects only tenuously related to the mandatory subject of wages, hours, and working conditions and are management's prerogatives). *But see* City of Beloit v. Wisconsin Employment Relations Comm'n, 242 N.W.2d 231, 92 LRRM 3318 (Wis. 1976). *Accord* Racine Educ. Ass'n v. Wisconsin Employment Relations Comm'n, 214 Wis. 2d 353, 571 N.W.2d 887, 162 LRRM 2438 (1997). *See also* Burlington County Coll. Faculty Ass'n v. Burlington County Coll. Bd. of Trs., 64 N.J. 10, 311 A.2d 733, 84 LRRM 2857 (1973).

[172]*See* State, County, & Mun. Employees Local 128 v. City of Ishpeming, 400 N.W.2d 661, 124 LRRM 3182 (Mich. Ct. App. 1987) (there is no duty to bargain over the loss of positions through reclassification, although the impact of the elimination is a mandatory subject of bargaining). *See also* United Teachers of Flint v. Flint Sch. Dist., 404 N.W.2d 637 (Mich. Ct. App. 1986). Similarly, the merging of academic departments has been held to be nonnegotiable. Dunellen Bd. of Educ. v. Dunellen Educ. Ass'n, 311 A.2d 737, 85 LRRM 2131 (N.J. 1973).

[173]Old Bridge Township Bd. of Educ. v. Old Bridge Educ. Ass'n, 489 A.2d 159, 121 LRRM 2784 (N.J. 1985) (the decision to abolish positions is not negotiable but a provision for notice is).

[174]West Hartford Educ. Ass'n v. DeCourcy, 295 A.2d 526, 534, 80 LRRM 2422 (Conn. 1972) (hours of work of teachers not a mandatory subject of bargaining, and the court's general discussion reasons that the legislature did not intend such matters to be subjected to bargaining). But hours of work of teachers was held bargainable in *Board of Educ., City of Englewood v. Englewood Teachers Ass'n*, 311 A.2d 729, 85 LRRM 2137 (N.J. 1973).

13. Teacher transfers,[175]
14. Faculty workload, and[176]
15. Hiring of teachers.[177]

5. Relationship Between Contractual and Statutory Grievance Channels [LA CDI 100.0730]

Often statutory provisions for collective bargaining and arbitration in state and local government employment are silent regarding the relationship between contractual grievance procedures and statutory procedures, such as those under civil service laws.[178] Where a statute does deal expressly with the question, one possibility is that the employee will be given an option to use either the contractual grievance procedure or a statutory procedure.[179] However, some statutes make the contractual grievance procedure exclusive if it covers the grievance. For example, Massachusetts provides that if there is an applicable contract grievance procedure, such procedure

---

[175]*See* Tippecanoe Educ. Ass'n v. Board of Sch. Trs., 429 N.E.2d 967, 973 (Ind. Ct. App. 1981). In *Minneapolis Federation of Teachers Local 59 v. Minneapolis Special School District No. 1*, 258 N.W.2d 802, 806, 96 LRRM 2706 (Minn. 1977), the court held:

1. The decision to transfer a number of teachers is a managerial decision and not a subject for negotiation. 2. The adoption of the criteria by which individual teachers may be identified for transfer is a proper subject for negotiation, and, as such, is properly included in the collective bargaining contract. 3. To insure that individual teacher transfers conform to the negotiated contract, each individual transfer is a proper subject of grievance arbitration.

Cf. School Comm. of Lowell v. Service Employees Local 159, 679 N.E.2d 583 (Mass. Ct. App. 1997). A form of transfer of work, subcontracting out, has also been held nonnegotiable. Professional & Technical Eng'rs Local 195 v. New Jersey, 443 A.2d 187, 112 LRRM 2214, 113 LRRM 2535 (N.J. 1982). But see discussion of subsequent statutory amendments intended to limit applicability of the 1982 decision found in *New Jersey v. State Troopers Fraternal Ass'n*, 134 N.J. 393, 634 A.2d 478, 145 LRRM 2564 (1993).

[176]Tualatin Valley Bargaining Council v. Tigard Sch. Dist., 840 P.2d 657, 662 (Or. 1992). *See also* Metropolitan Technical Cmty. Coll. Educ. Ass'n v. Metropolitan Technical Cmty. Coll. Area, 281 N.W.2d 201, 102 LRRM 2142, 2146 (Neb. 1979) (certain decisions of other states were distinguishable). The allocation of nonprofessional chores to teachers was held nonbargainable and nonarbitrable in *Kenai Peninsula Educ. Ass'n v. Kenai Peninsula Sch. Dist.*, 628 P.2d 568, 569 (Alaska 1981).

[177]Bd. of Dirs. of Maine Sch. Admin. Dist. v. Teachers Ass'n, 428 A.2d 419, 110 LRRM 3361, 3364 (Me. 1981). *See also* New Bedford Sch. Comm. v. New Bedford Educators Ass'n, 405 N.E.2d 162, 165, 108 LRRM 3201, 3204–05 (Mass. App. Ct. 1980). *Cf.* School Comm. of Lowell v. Service Employees Local 159, 679 N.E.2d 583 (Mass. Ct. App. 1997). A form of transfer of work, subcontracting out, has also been held nonnegotiable. Professional & Technical Eng'rs Local 195 v. New Jersey, 443 A.2d 187, 112 LRRM 2214, 113 LRRM 2535 (N.J. 1982). But see discussion of subsequent statutory amendments intended to limit applicability of the 1982 decision found in New Jersey v. State Troopers Fraternal Ass'n, 134 N.J. 393, 634 A.2d 478, 145 LRRM 2564 (1993).

[178]For general discussion of the subject, see Rabban, *Can American Labor Law Accommodate Collective Bargaining by Professional Employees?*, 99 Yale L.J. 689 (1990); Hayford & Pegnetter, *A Comparison of Rights of Arbitration and Civil Service Appeals Procedures*, 35 Arb. J. 22 (1980); Pegnetter & Hayford, *State Employee Grievances and Due Process: An Analysis of Contract Arbitration and Civil Service Review Systems*, 29 S.C. L. Rev. 305 (1978).

[179]*See* Zelin, Annotation, *Rights of State and Municipal Public Employees in Grievance Proceedings*, 46 A.L.R. 4th 912 (1996). For an example of the statutory provision, see Minnesota Public Employment Labor Relations Act §179A.25 (1996).

shall "be exclusive and shall supersede any otherwise applicable grievance procedure provided by law."[180]

States that authorize collective bargaining and arbitration in the state and local government sector generally permit employees to adjust their grievance with the employer without intervention of the union, but the adjustment must be consistent with the terms of the collective bargaining agreement, and the union is entitled to be present.[181]

6. DETERMINING ARBITRABILITY AND COMPELLING ARBITRATION[182]

A. The Rules of Arbitrability [LA CDI 100.0765]

Many courts have struggled with and have attempted to explain the concept of arbitrability, that is, whether a collective bargaining agreement places a duty on the parties to submit a particular grievance to arbitration.[183] The principles necessary to address arbitrability issues were developed over 40 years ago in the *Steelworkers Trilogy*.[184] The concepts developed in and carried forth from the *Trilogy* have, for the most part, proven favorable for industrial relations in the private sector and have encouraged the reliance on arbitration for the resolution of disputes, ideally minimizing the necessity for strikes and lockouts.[185] The rules, as developed in the *Trilogy*, are:

1. Arbitration is a contractual matter; thus, a party cannot be required to arbitrate any dispute which he or she had not previously agreed so to submit;[186]
2. "The question of arbitrability. . . is undeniably an issue for judicial determination, unless the parties clearly and unmistakably provide otherwise . . . ;"[187]

---

[180]MASS. GEN. LAWS ANN. ch. 150E, §8 (West 1989). Another example is the Maine State Employees Labor Relations Act §979-K. In *City of Ontario, Or.*, 72 LA 1089, 1091–92 (Conant, 1979), the public employer was upheld in reprimanding an employee who bypassed the contractual grievance procedure, which was construed to provide the exclusive remedy, and carried his complaint to a city councilman; the arbitrator said that in public-sector labor relations, "'end-runs' to city officials can disrupt and impair the functioning of the bargaining process."

[181]*See, e.g.,* DEL. CODE ANN. tit. 19, §1304(b) (1974); Illinois State Labor Relations Act, 5 ILL. COMP. STAT. 315/6 (West 1997). *See* Svoboda v. Department of Mental Health & Developmental Disabilities, 515 N.E.2d 446, 127 LRRM 2971 (Ill. Ct. App. 1987).

[182]For related discussion in private-sector arbitration, see Chapter 2, section 2.A.ii.b.(1), "Determining Arbitrability and Compelling Arbitration," and Chapter 6, section 3.A., "*Trilogy* Arbitrability Criteria and the Arbitrator."

[183]AT&T Techs. v. Communications Workers, 475 U.S. 643, 649, 121 LRRM 3329 (1986).

[184]Steelworkers v. American Mfg. Co., 363 U.S. 564, 34 LA 559, 46 LRRM 2414 (1960); Steelworkers v. Warrior & Gulf Navigation Co., 363 U.S. 574, 34 LA 561, 46 LRRM 2416 (1960); Steelworkers v. Enterprise Wheel & Car Corp., 363 U.S. 593, 34 LA 569, 46 LRRM 2423 (1960).

[185]458*See AT&T Techs.*, 475 U.S. at 648.

[186]*Id.* (citing *Warrior & Gulf*, 363 U.S. at 582). *See also American Mfg. Co.*, 363 U.S. at 570–71 (Brennan, J., concurring)).

[187]*Id.* at 649 (quoting *Warrior & Gulf*, 363 U.S. at 582–83; subsequently reaffirmed in *John Wiley & Sons v. Livingston*, 376 U.S. 543, 55 LRRM 2769 (1964)).

3. When a court is determining whether the parties have previously agreed to submit a grievance to arbitration, the court must not rule on the merits of the underlying claim, even if the claim appears to be frivolous in nature;[188] and

4. If a particular contract contains an arbitration clause, a presumption of arbitrability exists.[189]

B. Applying the Rules and Compelling Arbitration [LA CDI 100.0765]

In the state and local government sector, once parties have exhausted their internal dispute resolution procedure and have reached impasse, arbitrability depends on when the impasse occured and whether the parties have complied with statutory preconditions. For example, two factors to be evaluated include whether the parties have made the requisite efforts to mediate, and the appropriateness of the filing with the applicable state agency.[190]

Arbitrability issues in the state and local government sector may reach the court in the same ways as they do in the private sector, that is, one party asks the court to compel or enjoin arbitration, or to review an arbitration award that has already been issued.

For grievances arising under a contract, and as set forth in *Trilogy* rule 2 above, arbitrability issues in the state and local government sector usually are handled similarly to arbitrability issues in the private sector: questions of substantive arbitrability are for the courts to determine unless the parties mutually agree to allow the arbitrator to address such questions,[191] and questions of procedural arbitrability are for the arbitrator, not for the courts, to

---

[188]*Id.* at 649–50 (citing *American Mfg. Co.*, 363 U.S. at 568).

[189]*Id.* at 650 (quoting *Warrior & Gulf*, 363 U.S. at 582: "[an] order to arbitrate the particular grievance should not be denied unless it may be said with positive assurance that the arbitration clause is not susceptible of an interpretation that covers the asserted dispute. Doubts should be resolved in favor of coverage." *Id.*).

[190]*See American Metal Prods. v. Sheet Metal Workers Local 104, 794 F.2d 1452, 123 LRRM 2824 (9th Cir. 1986); ACTION, 78 LA 740 (Phelan, 1982).

[191]*See AT&T Techs. v. Communications Workers, 475 U.S. 643, 121 LRRM 3329 (1986); Glendale Prof'l Policemen's Ass'n v. City of Glendale, 264 N.W.2d 594, 599, 98 LRRM 2362 (Wis. 1978); Policeman's & Fireman's Ret. Bd., City of New Haven v. Sullivan, 376 A.2d 399, 402, 95 LRRM 2351 (Conn. 1977) (the court said the parties may manifest their intent that the arbitrator determine arbitrability either by an express provision or by use of a broad arbitration clause); West Fargo Pub. Sch. Dist. No. 6 v. West Fargo Educ. Ass'n, 259 N.W.2d 612, 619, 97 LRRM 2361 (N.D. 1977). In *Teachers' Union Local 958 (Providence) v. Providence Sch. Comm.*, 433 A.2d 202, 112 LRRM 2998, 2999–3000 (R.I. 1981), both private- and public-sector cases were cited by the court in stating that: "Courts should not equate the issue of arbitrability with the deference due the arbitrator's interpretation of the contract . . . . Rather, a reviewing court must decide the question of arbitrability de novo." Abrams, *The Power Issue in Public Sector Grievance Arbitration*, 67 Minn. L. Rev. 261 (1982). *See also* Denver, Colo., Pub. Sch. 88 LA 507 (Watkins, 1986). Parties wanting to avoid circular trips through the courts to resolve such issues specifically must provide in their contract and/or submission agreement that the arbitrator is empowered to answer all arbitrability issues. *See* Kilanek v. Kim, 548 N.E.2d 598 (Ill. Ct. App. 1989).

resolve.[192] Thus, the issue of when an arbitrability issue must be raised for the first time is a procedural question answerable by the arbitrator.[193]

Some states allow arbitrability challenges to be raised directly in the courts, while others give an administrative agency or board exclusive original jurisdiction to determine arbitrability.[194]

It is possible to waive the right to arbitrate by participating in a judicial proceeding without raising the question of arbitrability.[195] Because of the "delegability" concerns, arbitrability claims are three times more likely to be raised in the state and local government sector than in the private sector.[196]

A number of states also have adopted for state and local government sector arbitration a rule similar to the rule of presumptive arbitrability that is applied in the private sector: doubts are to be resolved in favor of arbitrability.[197] However, New York has held that for state and local government sector cases under the state's Taylor Law, the courts, in determining arbitrability, "are to be guided by the principle that the agreement to arbi-

---

[192]*See* John Wiley & Sons v. Livingston, 376 U.S. 543, 55 LRRM 2769 (1964); Duquesne City Sch. Dist. v. Duquesne Educ. Ass'n, 380 A.2d 353, 356, 97 LRRM 2011 (Pa. 1977); West Fargo Pub. Sch. Dist No. 6 v. West Fargo Educ. Ass'n, 259 N.W.2d 612, 618–19, 97 LRRM 2361 (N.D. 1977). For example, as the Michigan Supreme Court noted, it "frequently looks to the federal courts' interpretation of the National Labor Relations Act in construing the PERA [public employees relations act]." Port Huron Educ. Ass'n v. Port Huron Area Sch. Dist., 452 Mich. 309, 550 N.W.2d 228, 158 LRRM 2997, 3000 n.13 (1996) (citing Kaleva-Norman-Dickson Sch. Dist. No. 6 v. Kaleva-Norman-Dickson Sch. Teachers' Ass'n, 393 Mich. 583, 227 N.W.2d 500, 89 LRRM 2078 (Mich. 1975)).

[193]This is true even under statutes that include detailed management rights clauses. *See* Department of the Navy, 38 FLRA 1509 (1991). *See also* Dick v. Dick, 534 N.W.2d 185 (Mich. Ct. App. 1995) (only the arbitrator can interpret the contract).

[194]In *School District No. 42 of City of Nashua v. Murray*, 514 A.2d 1269 (N.H. 1986), it was held that the Public Employee Labor Relations Board had exclusive original jurisdiction to determine arbitrability for purposes of collective bargaining agreement administration. *See also* Coles County Bd. of Educ. Dist. 1 v. Compton, 526 N.E.2d 149, 131 LRRM 2313 (Ill. 1988). See discussion of application of U.S. Supreme Court rulings regarding arbitrability in the states in Bethel, *Recent Supreme Court Employment Law Decisions 1990–91*, 17 DAYTON L. REV. 33, 36 (1991). The Illinois courts, for example, direct that such questions be handled by the Illinois Public Labor Relations Boards. Board of Educ., Warren Township High Sch. Dist. 121 v. Warren Township High Sch. Fed'n of Teachers Local 504, 538 N.E.2d 524 (Ill. 1989).

[195]Fire Fighters (IAFF) Local 23 v. City of East St. Louis, 571 N.E.2d 1198 (Ill. Ct. App. 1991).

[196]Naval Plant Representative Office, 91 LA 964 (Abrams, 1988).

[197]Dover Union Free Sch. Dist. Bd. of Educ. v. Dover-Wingate Teachers' Ass'n, 463 N.E.2d 32 (N.Y. 1984). *See also* City of Muskogee v. Martin, 796 P.2d 337, 134 LRRM 3265 (Okla. 1990); State, County, & Mun. Employees Dist. Council 48 (Milwaukee) v. Milwaukee County, 388 N.W.2d 630 (Wis. Ct. App. 1986); St. Clair Prosecutor v. State, County, & Mun. Employees, 388 N.W.2d 231 (Mich. 1986); Board of Trs., Community Colls. Dist. 508 v. Cook County Coll. Teachers Union Local 1600, 487 N.E.2d 956 (Ill. Ct. App. 1986); Westbrook Sch. Comm. v. Westbrook Teachers Ass'n, 404 A.2d 204, 207–08, 102 LRRM 2396, 2398 (Me. 1979); City of Jefferson Joint Sch. Dist. No. 10 v. Jefferson Educ. Ass'n, 253 N.W.2d 536, 544, 95 LRRM 3117 (Wis. 1977); Kaleva-Norman-Dickson Sch. Dist. No. 6 v. Kaleva-Norman-Dickson Sch. Teachers' Ass'n, 393 Mich. 583, 227 N.W.2d 500, 505–06, 89 LRRM 2078 (Mich. 1975). *See generally* Roumell, *Arbitration*, 1995 DET. C. L. REV. 281 (1995); Corcoran, *The Arbitrability of Labor Grievances That Arise After Expiration of the Collective Bargaining Agreement*, 43 SYRACUSE L. REV. 1073 (1992). But note that in the public sector, some matters may be held excluded from public-employer bargaining and arbitration by statutes and public policy considerations; a dispute over such matters is not arbitrable, regardless of what the collective bargaining agreement says. See section 4., "Limitations on the Scope of Bargaining and Arbitration in State and Local Government Employment," above.

trate must be express, direct and unequivocal as to the issues or disputes to be submitted to arbitration; anything less will lead to a denial of arbitration."[198]

7. Judicial Review of Arbitration Awards in State and Local Government Employment[199]

A. Statutory and Common Law Grounds for Review

Most states have enacted statutes that provide that written agreements to arbitrate are both valid and enforceable, but also provide grounds for vacating an arbitrator's decision.[200] The statutes typically are modeled after the Federal Arbitration Act[201] or the Uniform Arbitration Act.[202] A few specifically exempt employment agreements from their coverage.[203]

State statutes following the arbitral review provisions of the Uniform Arbitration Act permit vacation of arbitration awards on proof of any of five grounds:

---

[198]Acting Superintendent of Liverpool Cent. Sch. Dist. v. United Liverpool Faculty Ass'n, 369 N.E.2d 746, 747, 96 LRRM 2779 (N.Y. 1977) (the court reasoned that because arbitration is not as well established and proven in the public sector as in the private sector, stronger proof of intent to arbitrate is required). In *Liverpool*, the arbitration clause was narrow and the question whether the disputed matter fell within, or without, the clause was debatable. The court said the matter was not arbitrable because it did not fall "clearly and unequivocally within the class of claims agreed to be referred to arbitration." *Id.* at 750. Shortly after *Liverpool* was decided, the court upheld arbitrability in a case involving a broad arbitration clause, even though the clause did not specifically mention the particular matter in dispute. In *New York Bd. of Educ. v. Glaubman*, 53 N.Y.2d 781, 783, 439 N.Y.S.2d 907, 112 LRRM 2094, the court stated: "Although we noted in [*Liverpool*] that the choice of the arbitration forum should be 'express' and 'unequivocal' we did not mean to suggest that hairsplitting analysis should be used . . . to discourage or delay demands for arbitration in public sector contracts . . . ." *See* New York City Dep't of Sanitation v. MacDonald, 627 N.Y.S.2d 619 (N.Y. App. Div. 1995) (the court held that a broad interpretation is acceptable if the collective bargaining agreement gives a broad definition of arbitrability). *But see* Progressive Cas. Ins. Co. v. C.A. Reasegurador Nacional de Venez., 991 F.2d 42 (2d Cir. 1993) (denying such an interpretation).

[199]For related discussion in the private sector, see Chapter 2, section 2.A.ii.c., "Post-*Trilogy*: Enforcement of Agreements to Arbitrate and Review of Arbitration Awards."

[200]*See* Ariz. Rev. Stat. §§12-1501, 12-1512 (2000); Cal. Civ. Proc. Code §§1281, 1286.2 (2001); Colo. Rev. Stat. §§13-22-203, 13-22-214 (2001); Conn. Gen. Stat. §§52-408, 52-418 (2001); D.C. Code Ann. §§16-4301, 16-4311 (2001); Fla. Stat. ch. 682.03, 682.13; Haw. Rev. Stat. §§658-1, 658-9 (2001); 710 Ill. Comp. Stat. 5/1, 5/12 (2001); Ind. Code. Ann. §§34-57-1-1, 34-4-2-13 (2001); La. Rev. Stat. Ann. §§9:4201, 4210 (2001); Me. Rev. Stat. tit. 14. §§5927, 5938 (2000); Mass. Ann. Laws ch. 150c, §§1, 10 (2001); Minn. Stat. §§572.08, 572.19 (2000); Mo. Rev. Stat. §§435.359, 435.405 (2000). *See also Student Project: Recent Developments: The Uniform Arbitration Act*, 2000 J. Disp. Resol. 459, 478–89 (2000) (discussing court decisions interpreting state versions of the Uniform Arbitration Act, 7 U.L.A. §1 et seq.). *Cf.* Strickland, *Modern Arbitration for Alabama: A Concept Whose Time Has Come*, 25 Cumb. L. Rev. 59 (1994/1995) (criticizing Alabama for its antagonism toward arbitration and advocating the adoption of a modern state arbitration statute).

[201]9 U.S.C. §1 et seq.

[202]7 U.L.A. §1 et seq.

[203]*See* Alaska Stat. §09.43.010 (2001); Ark. Code Ann. §16-108-201 (2001); Del. Code Ann. tit. 10, §5725 (2000); Ga. Code Ann. §9-9-2 (2000); Idaho Code §7-901 (2000); Iowa Code §679A.1 (2001); Kan. Stat. Ann. §5-401 (2000); Md. Code. Ann. §3-206 (2001); Mich. Comp. Laws §600.5001.

(1) The award was procured by corruption, fraud or other undue means;

(2) There was evident partiality by an arbitrator appointed as a neutral or corruption in any of the arbitrators or misconduct prejudicing the rights of any party;

(3) The arbitrators exceeded their powers;

(4) The arbitrators refused to postpone the hearing upon sufficient cause being shown therefor or refused to hear evidence material to the controversy or otherwise so conducted the hearing, contrary to the provisions of Section 5, as to prejudice substantially the rights of a party; or

(5) There was no arbitration agreement and the issue was not adversely determined in proceedings under Section 2 and the party did not participate in the arbitration hearing without raising the objection; but the fact that the relief was such that it could not or would not be granted by a court of law or equity is not ground for vacating or refusing to confirm the award . . . .[204]

State courts also look for guidance to the common law[205] and federal courts for standards for enforcing or vacating arbitration awards.[206] In both the statutory and nonstatutory contexts, the grounds for review are influenced by the standards set forth in *Steelworkers v. American Manufacturing*

---

[204]7 U.L.A. §12 (1955 Act). The Revised Uniform Arbitration Act (2000), 7 U.L.A. §23 (Supp. 2003) is not materially dissimilar and provides:

(a) Upon [motion] to the court by a party to an arbitration proceeding, the court shall vacate an award made in the arbitration proceeding if: (1) the award was procured by corruption, fraud, or other undue means; (2) there was: (A) evident partiality by an arbitrator appointed as a neutral arbitrator; (B) corruption by an arbitrator; or (C) misconduct by an arbitrator prejudicing the rights of a party to the arbitration proceeding; (3) an arbitrator refused to postpone the hearing upon showing of sufficient cause for postponement, refused to consider evidence material to the controversy, or otherwise conducted the hearing contrary to Section 15, so as to prejudice substantially the rights of a party to the arbitration proceeding; (4) an arbitrator exceeded the arbitrator's powers; (5) there was no agreement to arbitrate, unless the person participated in the arbitration proceeding without raising the objection under Section 15(c) not later than the beginning of the arbitration hearing; or (6) the arbitration was conducted without proper notice of the initiation of an arbitration as required in Section 9 so as to prejudice substantially the rights of a party to the arbitration proceeding.

The Federal Arbitration Act similarly provides for vacation of awards:

(1) Where the award was procured by corruption, fraud, or undue means. (2) Where there was evident partiality or corruption in the arbitrators, or either of them. (3) Where the arbitrators were guilty of misconduct in refusing to postpone the hearing, upon sufficient cause shown, or in refusing to hear evidence pertinent and material to the controversy; or of any other misbehavior by which the rights of any party have been prejudiced. (4) Where the arbitrators exceeded their powers, or so imperfectly executed them that a mutual, final, and definite award upon the subject matter submitted was not made. . . .

9 U.S.C. §10.

[205]*See* Fire Fighters (IAFF) Local 1619 v. Prince George's County, 538 A.2d 329 (Md. Ct. Spec. App. 1988).

[206]*See* University of Haw. Prof'l Assembly v. University of Haw., 659 P.2d 720, 113 LRRM 3711 (Haw. 1983); Western Constr. v. Laborers (Or.-S. Idaho & Wyo. Dist. Council), 609 P.2d 1136, 1138, 105 LRRM 2081 (Idaho 1980); Iowa City Cmty. Sch. Dist. v. Iowa City Educ. Ass'n, 343 N.W.2d 139, 116 LRRM 2832 (Iowa 1983); City of Coffeyville, Kan. v. Electrical Workers (IBEW) Local 1523, 270 Kan. 322, 14 P.3d 1, 165 LRRM 3023 (2000); Orleans Parish Sch. Bd. v. United Teachers of New Orleans, 689 So. 2d 645 (4th Cir. 1997); Cape Elizabeth Sch. Bd. v. Cape Elizabeth Teachers Ass'n, 459 A.2d 166, 116 LRRM 2812 (Me. 1983).

Co.[207] Indeed, state courts generally utilize the same standard of review in both public- and private-sector cases.[208]

In light of the tradition of deference to arbitration and the policy of ensuring the finality of awards, state courts emphasize that review of arbitrators' awards is limited in scope.[209] Courts typically note that the parties bargain for an arbitrator's interpretation of their contract, not that of a court.[210] Most courts will not review the arbitrator's interpretation of the contract, or the merits of the award, even if they are believed to be erroneous,[211] and will not vacate a decision even if they would have reached a contrary decision on the facts.[212] However, some courts will conduct a more searching review and vacate an award if the arbitrator committed a "gross error" or the interpretation was "completely irrational."[213] A number of courts borrowing from fed-

---

[207]363 U.S. 564, 34 LA 559, 46 LRRM 2414 (1960).

[208]*See* University of Haw. Prof'l Assembly v. University of Haw., 659 P.2d 720, 728 n.4, 113 LRRM 3711, 3717 n.4 (Haw. 1983); City of Des Moines v. Central Iowa Pub. Employees Council, 369 N.W.2d 442, 444–45, 120 LRRM 3490, 3492 (Iowa 1985). *But see* Hodges, *Symposium on Labor Arbitration Thirty Years After the* Steelworkers Trilogy: *The* Steelworkers Trilogy *in the Public Sector,* 66 Chi-Kent L. Rev. 631, 648–55 (1990) (critiquing review of arbitration awards in the public sector).

[209]*See, e.g.,* Chicago Fire Fighters Local 2 v. City of Chi., 256 Ill. Dec. 332, 323 Ill. App. 3d 168, 751 N.E.2d 1169, 1175, 168 LRRM 2194, 2197 (2001); Fort Wayne Cmty. Sch. v. Fort Wayne Educ. Ass'n, Inc., 490 N.E.2d 337 (Ind. Ct. App. 1986); City of Coffeyville, Kans. v. Electrical Workers (IBEW) (Local 1523, 270 Kan. 322, 14 P.3d 1, 165 LRRM 3023, 3029–31 (2000); Paramount Unified Sch. Dist. v. Teachers Ass'n of Paramount, 26 Cal. App. 4th 1371, 1381, 147 LRRM 2047, 2051 (1994); Bureau of the Me. State Police v. Pratt, 568 A.2d 501, 505 (Mar. 1989); Port Huron Area Sch. Dist. v. Port Huron Educ. Ass'n, 393 N.W.2d 811, 123 LRRM 3293 (Mich. 1986).

[210]*See, e.g.,* City of Westbrook v. Teamsters Local 48, 578 A.2d 716 (Me. 1990); Transit Union Local 1593 v. Hillsborough Area Reg'l Transit Auth., 450 So. 2d 590 (Fla. Dist. Ct. App. 1984); University of Haw. Prof'l Assembly v. University of Haw., 659 P.2d 720, 728, 113 LRRM 3711, 3716 (Haw. 1983).

[211]*See, e.g.,* North Miami Educ. Ass'n v. North Miami Cmty. Sch., 736 N.E.2d 749, 165 LRRM 2738 (Ind. Ct. App. 2000); City of Coffeyville, Kan. v. Electrical Workers (IBEW) Local 1523, 14 P.3d 1, 8, 165 LRRM 3023, 3030 (mistake of law or fact not a basis for upsetting an arbitrator's decision) (2000); Sheriff of Lenawee County v. Police Officers Labor Council, 607 N.W.2d 742 (Mich. Ct. App. 1999) (same); Orleans Parish Sch. Bd. v. United Teachers of New Orleans, 689 So. 2d 645, 647 (La. Ct. App. 1997) (same); Paramount Unified Sch. Dist. v. Teachers Ass'n of Paramount, 26 Cal. App. 4th 1371, 1381, 147 LRRM 2047, 2051 (1994); Independent Sch. Dist. No. 88, New Ulm, Minn. v. School Serv. Employees Local 284, 503 N.W.2d 104, 143 LRRM 2911 (Minn. 1993) (arbitrator final judge of both law and fact); University of Haw. Prof'l Assembly v. University of Haw., 659 P.2d 720, 728, 113 LRRM 3711, 3717 (Haw. 1983); Iowa City Cmty. Sch. Dist. v. Iowa City Educ. Ass'n, 343 N.W.2d 139, 144, 116 LRRM 2832 (Iowa 1983) (same); Cape Elizabeth Sch. Bd. v. Cape Elizabeth Teacher's Ass'n., 459 A.2d 166, 116 LRRM 2812 (Me. 1983) (same).

[212]*See, e.g.,* Cedar Rapids Ass'n of Fire Fighters Local 11 v. City of Cedar Rapids, Iowa, 574 N.W.2d 313, 318, 157 LRRM 2613 (Iowa 1998); City of Westbrook v. Teamsters Local 48, 578 A.2d 716, 721 (Me. 1990); Western Constr. v. Laborers (Or.-S. Idaho & Wyo. Dist. Council), 609 P.2d 1136, 105 LRRM 2081 (Idaho 1980). The Maryland Supreme Court upheld an arbitrator's award reinstating a bus driver discharged for drunk driving where the discharge was based only on the odor of alcohol on his breath and not on a chemical test. Transit Union Div. 1300 v. Mass. Transit Admin., 504 A.2d 1132, 121 LRRM 2894 (Md. 1986).

[213]*See* Prince George's County Educators' Ass'n v. Board of Educ., Prince George's County, 486 A.2d 228, 231 (Md. Ct. Spec. App. 1985) (arbitrator's award subject to review if it is completely irrational or contains gross mistakes of law and fact), *aff'd,* 522 A.2d 931, 125 LRRM 2923 (Md. 1985).

eral doctrine hold that an arbitrator's award will not be overturned for errors of law or fact[214] unless his or her opinion evidences a "manifest disregard for the law." [215]

The specific standards most often considered by state courts in reviewing arbitrators' awards are: (1) whether the award is drawn from the "essence of the agreement,"[216] (2) whether the arbitrators exceeded the scope of their authority,[217] (3) whether the decision is arbitrary and capricious,[218] and (4) whether the award is rationally related to the collective bargaining agreement and the submission.[219] State courts often use these standards interchangeably, mentioning two or more in the same case.[220] Certain state courts rely on the explicit statutory provisions and will vacate an award only if one of the specific statutory grounds is alleged and proven.[221]

---

[214]Sylvania City Sch. Dist. Bd. of Educ. v. Sylvania Educ. Ass'n, 121 LRRM 2346 (Ohio Ct. Com. Pls. 1985).

[215]City of Madison v. Fire Fighters (IAFF) Local 311, 394 N.W.2d 766, 768, 124 LRRM 2131, 2133 (Wis. Ct. App. 1986). *Cf.* Madison Landfills v. Libby Landfill Negotiating Comm., 524 N.W.2d 883 (Wis. 1994).

[216]*See* Bureau of Special Investigations v. Coalition of Pub. Safety, 430 Mass. 601, 722 N.E.2d 441, 164 LRRM 2247 (2000); Cedar Rapids Ass'n of Fire Fighters Local 11 v. City of Cedar Rapids, Iowa, 574 N.W.2d 313, 316, 157 LRRM 2613 (Iowa 1998); Screen Actors Guild v. A. Shane Co., 225 Cal. App. 3d 260, 275 Cal. Rptr. 220 (Cal. Ct. App. 1990); City of Pontiac v. Pontiac Police Supervisors Ass'n, 450 N.W.2d 20, 21 (Mich. Ct. App. 1989); Fort Wayne Cmty. Sch. v. Fort Wayne Educ. Ass'n, 490 N.E.2d 337 (Ind. Ct. App. 1986).

[217]*See* Simmons v. City of Avon Park, 788 So. 2d 1076 (Fla. Dist. Ct. App. 2001); North Miami Educ. Ass'n v. North Miami Cmty. Sch., 736 N.E.2d 749, 165 LRRM 2738, *clarified on reh'g*, 736 N.E.2d 749, 165 LRRM 2738 (Ind. Ct. App. 2000); City of Chi. v. Water Pipe Extension, Bureau of Eng'g Laborers' Local 1092, 302 Ill. App. 3d 940, 707 N.E.2d 257, 160 LRRM 1092 (Ill. App. Ct. 1999); California Faculty Ass'n v. Superior Court of Santa Clara, 63 Cal. App. 4th 935, 159 LRRM 2097; Orleans Parish Sch. Bd. v. United Teachers of New Orleans, 689 So. 2d 645 (La. Ct. App. 1997); County of Hennepin v. Law Enforcement Labor Serv., 527 N.W.2d 821, 825, 148 LRRM 2627 (Minn. 1995); Port Huron Area Sch. Dist. v. Port Huron Educ. Ass'n, 393 N.W.2d 811, 815, 123 LRRM 3293 (Mich. 1986); South Conejos Sch. Dist. RE-10 v. Martinez, 709 P.2d 594, 121 LRRM 3515 (Colo. Ct. App. 1985); City of Des Moines v. Cent. Iowa Pub. Employees Council, 369 N.W.2d 442, 120 LRRM 3490 (Iowa 1985); Trailways Lines v. Trailways, Inc. Joint Council, No. 85-1249C (B), 1985 Mo. App. LEXIS 3878, at *18 (Mo. Ct. App. 1985).

[218]*See* State v. Council No. 81, AFL-CIO, Local 640, C.A. No. 6097, 1981 Del. Ch. Lexis 523, 1981 WL 88253 (Del. Chanc. Ct. 1981).

[219]*See* New Castle County v. Fraternal Order of Police, C.A. 154 LRRM 2272 (Del. Chan. 1996); City of Westbrook v. Teamsters Local 48, 578 A.2d 716 (Me. 1990).

[220]*See, e.g.*, Chicago Fire Fighters Local 2 v. City of Chi., 256 Ill. Dec. 332, 323 Ill. App. 3d 168, 174, 168 LRRM 2194, 2198 (2001) (scope of authority and essence of agreement); City of Coffeyville, Kan. v. Electrical Workers (IBEW) Local 1523, 270 Kan. 322, 14 P.3d 1, 10–11, 165 LRRM 3023, 3030 (2000) (same); Sheriff of Lenawee County v. Police Officers Labor Council, 607 N.W.2d 742 (Mich. Ct. App. 1999) (same); Doe v. Central Ark. Transit, 50 Ark. App. 132, 900 S.W.2d 582, 149 LRRM 2899 (1995) (essence of the agreement and scope of authority); Metropolitan Airports Comm'n v. Metropolitan Airports Police Fed'n, 443 N.W.2d 519 (Minn. 1989) (essence of the agreement and rationally related); State v. Council No. 81, AFL-CIO, Local 640, C.A. No. 6097, 1981 Del. Ch. Lexis 523, at *4–5 (scope of authority, arbitrary and capricious and rationally related standards); Western Constr. v. Laborers (Or.-S. Idaho & Wyo. Dist. Council), 609 P.2d 1136, 1138, 105 LRRM 2081, 2082–83 (Idaho 1980) (upholding an arbitrator's award as not exceeding his authority, because the award had a rational basis stemming from the agreement and therefore drew its essence from the agreement).

[221]*See* Paramount Unified Sch. Dist. v. Teachers Ass'n of Paramount, 26 Cal. App. 4th 1371, 147 LRRM 2047 (Cal. Ct. App. 1994); Eastbrook Educ. Ass'n & Eastbrook Comm. Schools Corp. v. Eastbrook Educ. Ass'n, 566 N.E.2d 63 (Ind. Ct. App. 1990).

In one case, a California court defined the standard of "exceeding an arbitrator's powers" by combining the "rational relationship" and "scope of authority" tests. The court stated that an "utterly irrational" award that amounts to a remaking of the contract exceeds the arbitrator's powers.[222] In that case, the arbitrator had awarded compensatory damages to a teacher for the school district's breach of provisions of the collective bargaining agreement regarding teacher evaluations. The school district argued that these damages were in reality back pay, which the arbitrator had no power to award. The court disagreed and refused to vacate the award, finding that the arbitrator was not irrational in his interpretation of the ambiguous clause regarding his power to award financial damages and other remedies.[223]

A Florida court concluded that an arbitrator had not exceeded his authority by considering mitigating factors in evaluating an employer's disciplinary action. This power was not spelled out explicitly in the collective bargaining agreement, but the court found the arbitrator's interpretation of the contractual power to hear "disciplinary actions" implicitly allowed him to consider additional factors in designing a remedy.[224]

In one case, a Louisiana court utilized the "scope of authority," essence of the agreement, and "rational relationship" standards in its decision. The court confirmed an arbitrator's award reinstating a coach who had been suspended, finding that this was within the arbitrator's express powers and drew its essence from the agreement. However, the court vacated that portion of the arbitrator's decision directing that the coach be given a written warning as beyond the scope of his authority because the collective bargaining agreement did not give him the power to issue written warnings in these circumstances.[225]

Maine courts will not find that an arbitrator exceeded his authority unless "'all fair and reasonable minds would agree that the construction of the contract made by the arbitrator[s] was not possible under a fair interpretation of the contract'"—a combination of the scope of authority and rational relationship tests.[226] The court upheld an award reinstating a terminated police officer where the arbitrator found that a Step 1 response issued by a supervisor had effectively reinstated the suspended officer, despite the department's contentions that the supervisor did not have the authority to reinstate. Because the contract was ambiguous regarding the authority to reinstate and the arbitrator's interpretation was reasonable, the court confirmed the award.[227]

Connecticut and Alaska employ somewhat unique standards of review that deserve individual mention. Connecticut courts will vacate an award if

---

[222]Paramount Unified Sch. Dist. v. Teachers Ass'n of Paramount, 26 Cal. App. 4th 1371, 1381, 147 LRRM 2047, 2053 (Cal. Ct. App. 1994).

[223]*Id.* at 1383, 147 LRRM at 2053–54. *See also* South Conejos Sch. Dist. RE-10 v. Martinez, 709 P.2d 594, 121 LRRM 3515 (Colo. Ct. App. 1985).

[224]Simmons v. City of Avon Park, 788 So. 2d 1076, 1077–78 (Fla. Dist. Ct. App. 2001).

[225]*See* Holmes v. Orleans Parish Sch. Bd., 698 So. 2d 429, 437 (4th Cir. 1997).

[226]Bureau of the Me. State Police v. Pratt, 568 A.2d 501, 505 (Me. 1989) (quoting Westbrook Sch. Comm. v. Westbrook Teacher's Ass'n, 404 A.2d 204, 209, 102 LRRM 2396 (Me. 1979)) (alternation in original).

[227]*See id.*

"(1) the award rules on the constitutionality of a statute . . . , (2) the award violates a clear public policy . . . or (3) the award contravenes one or more statutory proscriptions of [CONN. GEN. STAT.] § 52-418 [which sets forth grounds for vacating an arbitrator's decision]."[228] The review of an arbitrator's awards is narrow, and if the award conforms to the submission, the courts will generally find that the arbitrator has not exceeded his or her powers in violation of Section 52-418.[229] To make this determination, the court examines "the submission and the award to determine whether the award conforms to the submission."[230] Unless the submission states otherwise, arbitrators may decide factual and legal issues, and an award will not be vacated based on an arbitrator's mistake of fact or law.[231] All reasonable presumptions will be made in favor of the arbitrator's award.[232]

Alaska courts also follow a policy of deference to arbitral awards, and courts will not review the merits of a controversy in both the public and the private sectors.[233] Arbitration awards are reviewed for "gross negligence, fraud, corruption, gross error or misbehavior."[234] The cases emphasize review based on gross error, which is a mistake that is "both obvious and significant."[235] Absent such an error, a court will defer to an arbitrator's construction of a collective bargaining agreement[236] and will not substitute its own findings of fact for an arbitrator's.[237] The courts generally also will defer to an arbitrator's decisions regarding the admissibility of evidence and the testimony of witnesses.[238]

---

[228]State, County, & Mun. Employees Council 4, Local 1042 v. Board of Educ. of Norwalk, 66 Conn. App. 457, 463, 169 LRRM 2057 (2001) (citations omitted). *See also* CONN. GEN. STAT. §52-418 (2001) (arbitral award may be vacated if procured by corruption, fraud, or undue means, there has been partiality or corruption by the arbitrator, arbitrators have been guilty of certain forms of misconduct, or arbitrators have exceeded their powers).

[229]*See* Fabrics Co. v. Textile Workers Local 240, 533 A.2d 579, 126 LRRM 3336 (Conn. App. Ct. 1987). *See also* State, County, & Mun. Employees Council 4, Local 1042 v. Board of Educ. of Norwalk, 66 Conn. App. 457, 463, 169 LRRM 2057 (2001) (arbitrator was permitted to interpret ambiguous terms of the contract and because the grievant was unable to show that contract language was unambiguous, the grievant was not able to prove the award did not conform to the submission).

[230]State, County, & Mun. Employees Council 4, Local 1042 v. Board of Educ. of Norwalk, 66 Conn. App. 457, 461, 169 LRRM 2057 (2001).

[231]*See id. See also* State of Conn. v. State, County, & Mun. Employees Council 4, Local 2663, 777 A.2d 169 (Conn. 2001) (declining to review arbitrator's award based on arbitrator's alleged misinterpretation of applicable wage law, because the arbitrator's award conformed to the unrestricted submission and therefore mistakes of law were not reviewable).

[232]*See, e.g.,* State, County, & Mun. Employees Council 4, Local 1042 v. Board of Educ. of Norwalk, 66 Conn. App 457, 461, 169 LRRM 2057 (2001).

[233]*See* Alaska Pub. Employees Ass'n v. Alaska Dep't of Envtl. Conservation, 929 P.2d 662, 154 LRRM 2460 (Alaska 1996); Fairbanks Mun. Utils. Sys. v. Lees, 705 P.2d 457 (Alaska 1985).

[234]Fairbanks Mun. Utils. Sys. v. Lees, 705 P.2d 457, 460 (Alaska 1985).

[235]Nizinski v. Golden Valley Elec. Ass'n, 509 P.2d 280, 284–85 (Alaska 1973) (confirming decision of arbitrator that grievant was terminated for good cause and finding no gross error in the conduct of the proceedings, because the arbitrator was impartially selected and the grievant was given notice and an opportunity to be heard).

[236]Alaska Dep't of Pub. Safety v. Pub. Safety Employees Ass'n, 732 P.2d 1090, 125 LRRM 2116 (Alaska 1987).

[237]Alaska Pub. Employees Ass'n v. Alaska Dept of Envtl. Conservation, 929 P.2d 662, 153 LRRM 2460 (Alaska 1996).

[238]*See* Fairbanks Mun. Utils. Sys. v. Lees, 705 P.2d 457, 462–63 (the arbitrator's decision to exclude cumulative witness testimony was not a gross error).

Arbitrators have broad discretion in fashioning a remedy.[239] Various courts employ a liberal standard, allowing the arbitrator to fashion a remedy that is within the arbitrator's powers and is "rationally related" to the contract or draws its "essence" from it.[240] Courts will not enforce an award, however, that extends beyond the explicit limitations on the arbitrator's authority that are contained in the contract and relevant statutes.[241]

B. Vacation of Arbitration Awards in State and Local Government Employment on "Public Policy" Grounds [LA CDI 100.32]

Limited judicial review is also available in the state sector when an arbitration award is contrary to public policy. But, "[i]ncantations of public policy may not be advanced to overturn every arbitration award."[242] The public policy that obliges a court to refrain from enforcing an award must be clear and explicit, indeed, absolute.[243]

Following the lead of the Supreme Court in *Eastern Associated Coal Corp. v. Mine Workers District 17*,[244] state courts increasingly require that the "public policy" be found in positive law (statutes and regulations) and legal precedent.

In *Eastern Associated Coal*, a truck driver who had tested positive for marijuana in a random drug test was discharged under the employer's substance abuse policy, which required the removal of employees from any safety-

---

[239]*See, e.g.*, Fire Fighters (IAFF) Local 1619 v. Prince George's County, 538 A.2d 329 (Md. Ct. Spec. App. 1988).

[240]*See* Brooks v. City of Tallahassee, 778 So. 2d 1051 (Fla. Dist. Ct. App. 2001); Holmes v. Orleans Parish Sch. Bd., 698 So. 2d 429, 434 (La. Ct. App. 1997); Lisbon Sch. Comm. v. Lisbon Educ. Ass'n, 438 A.2d 239 (Me. 1981); Fire Fighters (IAFF) Local 1619 v. Prince George's County, 538 A.2d 329, 333 (Md. Ct. Spec. App. 1988).

[241]*See, e.g.*, California Faculty Ass'n v. Superior Court of Santa Clara County, 63 Cal. App. 4th 935, 952, 159 LRRM 2097 (1998) (vacating award, where arbitrator did not abide by restrictions and limitations imposed by the parties); City of Pontiac v. Pontiac Police Supervisors Ass'n, 450 N.W.2d 20 (Mich. Ct. App. 1989) (reversing award, where arbitrator ignored the plain language of the contract); Gray Teacher's Union Local 4 v. Gray Cmty. Sch. Corp. of Ind., 512 N.E.2d 205, 126 LRRM 2870 (Ind. Ct. App. 1987) (arbitrator exceeded authority in fashioning remedy that violated statutory limitations on teacher grievance arbitration); Transit Union Local 589 v. Massachusetts Bay Transp. Auth., 467 N.E.2d 87, 120 LRRM 3136 (Mass. 1984) (arbitrator's award was properly vacated, because it conflicted with state law limiting the transit authority's employment of part-time workers).

[242]Port Jefferson Station Teachers Ass'n v. Brookhaven-Comsewogue Union Free Sch. Dist., 383 N.E.2d 553, 99 LRRM 3438, 3439 (N.Y. 1978). To prevent enforcement of an arbitration award because it is against public policy, it must be shown that (1) the agreement to arbitrate is against public policy, and (2) the policy itself is both "well defined and dominant," that is, not merely a general public interest consideration. Board of Educ. of Sch. Dist. U-46 v. Illinois Educ. Labor Relations Bd., 576 N.E.2d 471 (Ill. Ct. App. 1991). *See* Mayes, *Labor Law—The Third Circuit Defines the Public Policy Exception to Labor Arbitration Awards—Exxon Shipping Co. v. Exxon Seamen's Union, 993 F.2d 357 (3d Cir. 1993)*, 67 Temple L. Rev. 493 (1994).

[243]In re Blackburne, 664 N.E.2d 1222, 151 LRRM 3032 (N.Y. 1996); Baltimore County v. Mayor & City Council of Balt., 621 A.2d 864 (Md. 1993); Troy Enlarged City Sch. Dist. of Troy v. Troy Teachers Ass'n, 508 N.E.2d 930 (N.Y. 1987); Transit Union Div. 1300 v. Mass Transit Admin., 504 A.2d 1132, 121 LRRM 2894 (Md. 1986).

[244]531 U.S. 57, 164 LRRM 2865 (2000). *See also* Paperworkers v. Misco, Inc., 484 U.S. 29, 126 LRRM 3113 (1987); W.R. Grace & Co. v. Rubber Workers Local 759, 461 U.S. 757, 766, 113 LRRM 2641 (1983).

sensitive position if they had tested positive for drug use. The employee was reinstated by an arbitrator subject to the employee's participation in a substance abuse program and to random drug testing for 5 years.

Approximately a year and one-half later, the employee once again tested positive for drugs, and, for a second time, the employee was discharged. Another arbitrator reduced the employee's discharge to a 3-month unpaid suspension and required him to continue participation in the substance abuse program and random testing.

The company sought to vacate the second arbitrator's award, arguing that it contravened a public policy against the operation of dangerous machinery by workers who tested positive for drugs.

The Supreme Court declined to overturn the arbitrator's decision, finding that there was no explicit, well-defined, and dominant public policy prohibiting reinstatement of a two-time drug abuser to a safety-sensitive position. Because the subject labor contract did not require termination of an employee for a second drug offense, the arbitrator did not exceed his authority in reinstating the employee.

Several state courts have reached similar conclusions. The Ohio Supreme Court[245] determined that that state had no dominant and well-defined public policy that rendered unlawful an arbitration award reinstating a safety-sensitive employee who had been terminated because he had tested positive for a controlled substance. The Ohio Supreme Court was careful to qualify its holding, however, stating that its decision did not imply that drug use may never be a basis for automatic discharge.

State courts have refused to vacate on public policy grounds arbitration awards reinstating government service employees who had been discharged for filing false expense reports,[246] using excessive force against an arrestee,[247] unauthorized accessing of confidential tax records,[248] falsifying a medical excuse for an absence,[249] requesting pay for hours not worked,[250] filing a false workers' compensation claim,[251] committing retail theft and pleading guilty to charges of driving under the influence,[252] pointing a weapon at juveniles playing basketball on school property after the school had closed,[253] incur-

---

[245]Southwest Ohio Reg'l Transit Auth. v. Transit Union Local 627, 91 Ohio St. 3d 108, 166 LRRM 2873 (2001).

[246]State Office of State Auditor v. Minnesota Ass'n of Prof'l Employees, 504 N.W.2d 751, 144 LRRM 2102 (Minn. 1993). Cf. St. Paul v. State, County, & Mun. Employees, 567 N.W.2d 524 (Minn. Ct. App. 1997).

[247]City of Minneapolis v. Police Officers Fed'n of Minneapolis, 566 N.W.2d 83 (Minn. Ct. App. 1997).

[248]Bureau of Special Investigations v. Coalition of Pub. Safety, 430 Mass. 601, 722 N.E.2d 441, 164 LRRM 2247 (2000).

[249]City of Cleveland v. State, County, & Mun. Employees Local 100, 1999 WL 58823 (Ohio Ct. App. 1999).

[250]City of Easton v. State, County, & Mun. Employees Local 447, 722 A.2d 1111 (Pa. Commw. Ct. 1998).

[251]City of Johnstown Redevelopment Auth. v. Steelworkers Local 14354, 725 A.2d 248 (Pa. Commw. Ct. 1999).

[252]Pennsylvania State Police v. Pennsylvania State Troopers Ass'n, 559 Pa. 586, 741 A.2d 1248 (1999).

[253]Town of South Windsor v. South Windsor Police Union, 255 Conn. 800, 778 A.2d 14 (2001).

ring excessive absences,[254] and using questionable force to discipline a student.[255] Some courts, however, hold that an arbitration award reinstating an employee who had been discharged after having been found guilty of a criminal offense may be overturned on "public policy grounds."[256]

---

[254]York County Transp. Auth. v. Teamsters Local 430, 746 A.2d 120 (Pa. Commw. Ct. 2000).

[255]Union River Valley Teachers' Ass'n v. LaMoine Sch. Comm., 748 A.2d 990 (Me. 2000).

[256]Town of Groton v. Steelworkers, 252 Conn. 508, 747 A.2d 1045 (2000) (employee pled nolo contendere to a charge of embezzlement of the public employer's funds); City of Easton v. State, County, & Mun. Employees Local 447, 722 A.2d 1111 (Pa. Commw. Ct. 1998).

Chapter 22

Arbitration of Interest Disputes

The preceding chapters have been concerned with the resolution of "rights" disputes—those involving issues over the interpretation and administration of the existing provisions of collective bargaining contracts. In this chapter the focus is on the resolution of "interest" disputes—those involving issues over what the terms of private-sector and public-sector collective bargaining agreements should be—and on the standards used by arbitrators in reconciling the conflicting interests of the parties to formulate those terms.

1. Purpose and Subjects of Interest Arbitration [LA CDI 100.06]

It is generally believed that the best labor-management contracts are those that are negotiated through collective bargaining without outside assistance. There are frequent instances, however, where the parties find it difficult or impossible to reach agreement by direct negotiation. In these instances, they may choose to settle the conflict by a test of strength, making use of the strike or lockout. But the use of economic weapons can be costly and injurious to both parties. Moreover, a suspension of operations may bring great hardship on others, as in the case of a cessation of public utility activities, for which neither labor nor management may wish to risk public censure. In public-sector employment, particularly in the uniformed services, strikes may be prohibited.[1]

---

[1]Only 14 states allow some classes of public employees to strike. *See* Public Employees Bargain for Excellence: A Compendium of State Public Labor Relations Law (1995); Alaska Stat. §23.40.200 (Michie 1997); Haw. Rev. Stat. §89-12 (1997); Idaho Code §44-1811 (Michie 1997); 5 Ill. Comp. Stat. 315/17 (West 1997); Minn. Stat. §179A.18 (1996); Mont. Code Ann. §§39-32-110, 39-34-105 (1997); Ohio Rev. Code Ann. §§4117.15–16 (Anderson 1997); Or. Rev. Stat. §243.726 (1996); 43 Pa. Cons. Stat. §§1101.1001–1003, 1101.2201 (1997); Vt. Stat. Ann. tit. 21 §1730 (1997); Wis. Stat. §111.70(4)(cm)(6)(c) (1995–96). *See generally Note, Reinventing a Livelihood: How United States Labor Laws, Labor-Management Cooperation Initiatives, and Privatization Influence Public Sector Labor Market*, 34 Harv. J. on Legis. 557, 567 (1997). In *County Sanitation District No. 2 v. Los Angeles County Employees' Ass'n*, 699 P.2d 835, 849–50, 119 LRRM 2433 (Cal. 1985), the California Supreme Court held public employees may not be prohibited from striking unless the strike would cause imminent dan-

In these situations, interest arbitration by impartial, competent neutrals, whether voluntary or statutorily prescribed, offers a way out of the dilemma.[2] One arbitration board, which was itself determining the provisions to be included in a utility renewal contract, stated the case for arbitration as follows:

> Arbitration should be a last resort and not an easy pillow on which to fall just because difficulties are encountered. There is some evidence that in the transit industry there has not been the fullest utilization of collective bargaining just because there has existed a ready alternative. But, on the other hand, it cannot be denied that even some minor over-use of arbitration is preferable to long and costly strikes in this vital utility.[3]

Interest arbitration clauses in private-sector contracts are enforceable in federal court under Section 301 of the Labor Management Relations Act

---

ger for public health or safety. The Colorado Supreme Court held that "under the relevant statutes employees in the public sector have a qualified right to strike subject to explicit executive and judicial controls." Martin v. Montezuma-Cortex Sch. Dist. RE-1, 841 P.2d 237, 240 (Colo. 1992). The Louisiana Supreme Court refused to enjoin a teachers' strike, holding that a public employee strike was not per se illegal. Davis v. Henry, 555 So. 2d 457, 461, 133 LRRM 2271 (La. 1990). For discussion of the judicial determination of public employee rights to strike and particularly the Louisiana court's approach, see Babin, Davis v. Henry: *One More Piece to the Public Employee Strike Rights Puzzle*, 51 LA. L. REV. 1271, 1271–78 (1991).

[2]For studies of interest arbitration and recommendations concerning its use, see section 5., "Public-Sector Interest-Arbitration Legislation," below; Chapter 1, section 4.A., "Arbitration as a Substitute for Work Stoppages." *See also* Marmo, *The Role of Fact Finding and Interest Arbitration in "Selling" a Settlement*, 24 J. COLLECTIVE NEGOTIATIONS PUB. SECTOR 77 (1995); Anderson & Krause, *Interest Arbitration: The Alternative to the Strike*, 56 FORDHAM L. REV. 153 (1987); Morris, *The Role of Interest Arbitration in a Collective Bargaining System*, *in* THE FUTURE OF LABOR ARBITRATION IN AMERICA 197 (American Arbitration Ass'n 1976); Handsaker, *Arbitration and Contract Disputes*, *in* CHALLENGES TO ARBITRATION, PROCEEDINGS OF THE 13TH ANNUAL MEETING OF NAA 78 (McKelvey ed., BNA Books 1960). For an extensive survey of past use of voluntary interest arbitration and its acceptability to the parties, see Stieber, *Voluntary Arbitration of Contract Terms*, *in* ARBITRATION AND THE EXPANDING ROLE OF NEUTRALS, PROCEEDINGS OF THE 23D ANNUAL MEETING OF NAA 71 (Somers & Dennis eds., BNA Books 1970). *See also* La Rue, *An Historical Overview of Interest Arbitration in the United States*, 42 ARB. J. No. 4, at 13 (1987).

[3]Reading St. Ry., 6 LA 860, 871 (Simkin, 1947). With this comment, the arbitration board denied the request of one party for deletion of a provision, contained in the prior agreement, for arbitration of new contract terms. *Id.* at 872. *See also* United Traction Co., 27 LA 309, 318 (Scheiber, 1956). However, in a newspaper industry case, the arbitrator refused to continue a contractual provision for interest arbitration against the wishes of one party, stating that to rule otherwise would in effect order compulsory arbitration, contrary to "our system of free collective bargaining." Public Corp., 51 LA 14, 25 (Platt, 1968). *Accord* San Joaquin Baking Co., 13 LA 115 (Haughton, 1949). This view was not always followed by subsequent arbitrators in that industry. *Cf.* Asplundh Tree Expert Co., 89 LA 183 (Allen, Jr., 1987) (granting the employer's request for removal of an interest arbitration provision, although "personally and philosophically" believing that interest arbitration is a better alternative to strikes in resolving negotiation disputes). *See* Bacheller, *The Value of Old Negotiated Language in an Interest Dispute*, *in* ARBITRATION OF INTEREST DISPUTES, PROCEEDINGS OF THE 26TH ANNUAL MEETING OF NAA 48, 48–49 (Somers & Dennis eds., BNA Books 1974). Six other experts have discussed the long history of using interest arbitration in the local transit and newspaper industries. *See* Platt, *Arbitration of Interest Disputes in the Local Transit and Newspaper Publishing Industries*, *id.* at 8; Sternstein, *Arbitration of New Contract Terms in Local Transit: The Union View*, *id* at 10; Dash, *Interest Arbitration in Public Transit*, *id.* at 21; Adair, *The Arbitration of Wage and Manning Disputes in the Newspaper Industry*, *id.* at 31; McLellan, *The Appellate Process in the International Arbitration Agreement Between the American Newspaper Publishers Association and the International Printing Pressmen*, id. at 53; Zingman, *International Appellate Arbitration*, *id.* at 58. Regarding continued use of interest arbitration for mass transit systems that have been converted to public ownership, see section 5, "Public-Sector Interest-Arbitration Legislation," below.

(LMRA),[4] and courts afford the same deference to the decisions of interest arbitrators as they do to rights arbitration decisions.[5] However, it is now well established by rulings of the National Labor Relations Board (NLRB) and the U.S. courts of appeals that inclusion of an interest arbitration provision in a collective bargaining agreement is not a mandatory subject of bargaining; a party may not legally insist on inclusion of such provisions in the agreement,[6] and an existing interest arbitration clause may not be used to perpetuate itself.[7]

Arbitration of interest disputes may be viewed more as an instrument of collective bargaining than as a process of adjudication: "Interest arbitration is a method by which an employer and union reach agreement by sending the disputed issues to an arbitrator rather than by settling them through collective bargaining and economic force."[8] Interest arbitration is most frequently found in industries where collective bargaining is well established. Some studies have hypothesized, however, that frequent use of interest arbitration may impair collective bargaining by causing "a 'narcotic effect,' i.e., dependence on arbitration in future negotiations."[9]

---

[4]29 U.S.C. §141 et seq. *See* Electrical Workers (IBEW) Local 666 v. Stokes Elec. Serv., 225 F.3d 415, 164 LRRM 3089 (4th Cir. 2000); Sheet Metal Workers Local 20 v. Baylor Heating & Air Conditioning, 877 F.2d 547, 131 LRRM 2838 (7th Cir. 1989), *abrogated on other grounds by* Operating Eng'rs Local 150 v. Rabine, 161 F.3d 427, 159 LRRM 2713 (7th Cir. 1998). Interest arbitration clauses survive the expiration of the collective bargaining agreement. *Stokes Elec.*, 225 F.3d at 422–23 (citing cases); Beach Air Conditioning & Heating v. Sheet Metal Workers Local 102, 55 F.3d 474, 476, 149 LRRM 2391 (9th Cir. 1995).

[5]Electrical Workers (IBEW) Local 257 v. Sebastian Elec., 121 F.3d 1180, 1184, 155 LRRM 2961 (8th Cir. 1997) (applying "the extreme judicial deference approved by the Supreme Court in the *Steelworkers* Trilogy [Steelworkers v. American Mfg. Co., 363 U.S. 564, 46 LRRM 2414 (1960); Steelworkers v. Warrior & Gulf Navigation Co., 363 U.S. 574, 46 LRRM 2416 (1960); Steelworkers v. Enterprise Wheel & Car Corp., 363 U.S. 593, 46 LRRM 2423 (1960)]"). *Accord* Sheet Metal Workers Local 20 v. Baylor Heating & Air Conditioning, 877 F.2d 547, 555, 131 LRRM 2838 (7th Cir. 1989). *See also* Electrical Workers (IBEW) Local 58 v. National Elec. Contractors Ass'n (Southeastern Mich. Chapter), 43 F.3d 1026, 1030, 148 LRRM 2065 (6th Cir. 1995).

[6]Laidlaw Transit, 323 NLRB 867, 156 LRRM 1029 (1997) (employer violated §8(a)(5) of the National Labor Relations Act (NLRA), 29 U.S.C. §§151–169, by insisting to impasse on arbitration clause); Sheet Metal Workers Local 359 (Madison Indus. of Ariz.), 319 NLRB 668, 150 LRRM 1303 (1995) (union violated NLRA §8(b)(3) by insisting to impasse on arbitration clause); Electrical Workers (IBEW) Local 135 (La Crosse Elec. Contractors Ass'n), 271 NLRB 250, 251, 116 LRRM 1329 (1984) (citing cases).

[7]Electrical Workers (IBEW) Local 58 v. National Elec. Contractors Ass'n (Southeastern Mich. Chapter), 43 F.3d 1026, 1032, 148 LRRM 2065 (6th Cir. 1995); Sheet Metal Workers Local 54 v. E.F. Etie Sheet Metal Co., 1 F.3d 1464, 1476, 144 LRRM 2237 (5th Cir. 1993); Graphic Arts Local 23 (Milwaukee) v. Newspapers, Inc., 586 F.2d 19, 99 LRRM 3033 (7th Cir. 1978) (citing decisions of four circuits and the NLRB in general accord). A party cannot be compelled to submit any nonmandatory subject of bargaining to interest arbitration. *National Elec. Contractors*, 43 F.3d at 1032; *E.F. Etie Sheet Metal*, 1 F.3d at 1476 (citing cases). In *Sheet Metal Workers Local 59 v. Employers Ass'n of Roofers & Sheet Metal Workers*, 430 F. Supp. 540, 95 LRRM 2149 (D. Del. 1977), enforcement of an arbitration award was refused where it had been obtained pursuant to an interest arbitration clause that the union illegally forced on the employer. For a discussion in favor of imposing a duty to bargain over interest arbitration clauses, see Scharman, *Interest Arbitration in the Private Sector*, 36 ARB. J. No. 3, at 14 (1981).

[8]Silverman v. Major League Baseball Players Relations Comm., Inc., 67 F.3d 1054, 1062 (2d Cir. 1995).

[9]Kleintop & Loewenberg, *Collective Bargaining, Compulsory Interest Arbitration and the Narcotic Effect: A Longitudinal Study of Delaware County, Pennsylvania*, 19 J. COLLECTIVE NEGOTIATIONS PUB. SECTOR 113 (1990). *See also* Graham & Perry, *Interest Arbitration in Ohio, the Narcotic Effect Revisited*, 22 J. COLLECTIVE NEGOTIATIONS PUB. SECTOR 323 (1993).

One objection commonly urged against the arbitration of interest issues is that definitive principles or standards to govern the decision are lacking. This belief is not entirely justified, however. There are a number of standards that, while not as rigorous as may be desired, are available and applied in the arbitration of such disputes. These standards are discussed later in this chapter. Moreover, it is not uncommon for parties to agree on general principles to be observed by the arbitrator, and in the public sector such criteria may be specified by statute. The arbitrator's sole task then is to apply these principles in the light of the evidence presented of record. If they choose, the parties can further limit the arbitrator's leeway by use of "final offer" arbitration.[10]

In the private sector, the subject matter of interest arbitration can be as extensive and varied as the parties choose to make it. Any subject comprehended by collective bargaining can be placed in the agreement by arbitration. In ruling on over 20,000 labor-management disputes, most of which were over the terms of new agreements, the National War Labor Board of World War II traversed practically the entire range of collective bargaining issues.

Wage issues, as would be expected, constitute the most common subject of interest arbitration.[11] Among other interest issues that have been submitted to arbitration or to emergency boards are those involving holidays,[12] va-

---

[10]For more on "final offer" arbitration, see Miller, *High Risk Final Offer Interest Arbitration in Oregon*, 28 J. COLLECTIVE NEGOTIATIONS PUB. SECTOR 265 (1999) (case studies of Oregon's adoption of a "final offer" system for public-sector interest arbitration); Stokes, *Solomon's Wisdom: An Early Analysis of the Effects of the Police and Fire Interest Arbitration Reform Act in New Jersey*, 28 J. COLLECTIVE NEGOTIATIONS PUB. SECTOR 219 (1999) (case studies of New Jersey's abandonment of such a system, to reducing arbitral wage increases).

[11]For many cases involving the arbitration of wage issues, see Chapter 18, "Remedies in Arbitration."

[12]City of Willowick, Ohio, 110 LA 1146 (Ruben, 1998); Birmingham-Jefferson County Metro Transit Auth./Metro Area Express, 103 LA 1 (Baroni, 1994); City of Renton, Wash., 71 LA 271 (Snow, 1978); Republican Co., 69 LA 1041 (Holden, Jr., 1977); Town of Manchester, 68 LA 1097 (Post, 1977); Paramus Nursing Home Corp., 48 LA 289 (Singer, 1967); Pinehaven Sanitarium, 47 LA 482 (Singer, 1966); Chatham Elecs., 37 LA 3 (Kerrison, 1961); Federal Silk Mills, 27 LA 728 (Holland, 1956); Pennsylvania R.R., 25 LA 352 (Johnson, Johnson, & O'Malley, 1955); Mt. Carmel Pub. Util. Co., 18 LA 290 (McPherson, 1952); Boller Beverage Co., 16 LA 933 (Reynolds, 1951).

cations,[13] sick leave,[14] injury leave,[15] personal leave,[16] health and hospitalization benefits,[17] life insurance plans,[18] pension and retirement benefits,[19]

---

[13]City of Willowick, Ohio, 110 LA 1146 (Ruben, 1998); City of Manitowoc, Wis., 108 LA 140 (Michelstetter, 1997); City of Garfield, N.J., 70 LA 850 (Silver, 1978); Eastalco Aluminum Co., 70 LA 793 (Whyte, 1978); Republican Co., 69 LA 1041 (Holden, Jr., 1977); St. Luke's Hosp. Ctr., 63 LA 71 (Glushien, 1974); Paramus Nursing Home, 48 LA 289 (Singer, 1967); Cleveland Transit Sys., 45 LA 905 (Kates, 1965); Appleton Coop. Ass'n, 39 LA 249 (Gundermann, 1962); Railway Express Agency, 28 LA 182 (Sanders, Begley, & Gilden, 1957); Miami Herald Publ'g Co., 24 LA 835 (Dworet, Gucker, Foy, Middendorf, & Christensen, 1955); Montaup Elec. Co., 21 LA 494 (Lynch, Green, & Borges, 1953); Los Angeles Standard Rubber, 17 LA 353 (Warren, 1951).

[14]City of Willowick, Ohio, 110 LA 1146 (Ruben, 1998); City of N. Royalton, Ohio, 109 LA 842 (Feldman, 1997); Olmsted Township, Ohio, 109 LA 237 (Ruben, 1997); St. Louis County, Minn., 108 LA 1170 (Dichter, 1997); Wooster City, Ohio, Bd. of Educ., 108 LA 502 (Feldman, 1997); Birmingham-Jefferson County Metro Transit Auth.-Metro Area Express, 103 LA 1 (Baroni, 1994); Cuyahoga County, Ohio, Sheriff's Dep't, 102 LA 143 (Strasshofer, Jr., 1993); Marathon County, Wis., 100 LA 256 (Chatman, 1992); City of Council Bluffs, 70 LA 1258 (Winton, 1978); Republican Co., 69 LA 1041 (Holden, Jr., 1977); City of Indianapolis, Ind., Dep't of Pub. Works, 58 LA 1302 (Witney, 1972); Borough of Turtle Creek, Pa., 52 LA 233 (McDermott, 1968); Paramus Nursing Home, 48 LA 289 (Singer, 1967); Pinehaven Sanitarium, 47 LA 482 (Singer, 1966); Frederick Loeser & Co., 17 LA 559 (Justin, 1951); Twin City Rapid Transit Co., 16 LA 749 (Platt, 1951); New Jersey Bell Tel. Co., 14 LA 574 (Martin, Lewis, Lesser, Jr., Lord, & Dunn, 1950); Pan Am. Airways, 13 LA 103 (Giardino, Snyder, & Smith, Jr., 1949); R.H. Macy & Co., 11 LA 450 (Cole, 1948).

[15]Olmsted Township, Ohio, 109 LA 237 (Ruben, 1997); Cuyahoga County, Ohio, Sheriff's Dep't, 102 LA 143 (Strasshofer, Jr., 1993).

[16]Northwest Kan. Educ. Serv. Ctr., 113 LA 47 (Murphy, 1999); City of Avon Lake, Ohio, 108 LA 1049 (Smith, 1997); Wooster City, Ohio, Bd. of Educ., 108 LA 502 (Feldman, 1997); West Clermont, Ohio, Local Sch. Dist. Bd. of Educ., 103 LA 1193 (Murphy, 1994); Village of Hales Corners, Wis., Police Dep't, 100 LA 789 (Krinsky, 1992).

[17]City of Willowick, Ohio, 110 LA 1146 (Ruben, 1997); Olmsted Township, Ohio, 109 LA 237 (Ruben, 1997); St. Louis County, Minn., 108 LA 1170 (Dichter, 1997); Wooster City, Ohio, Bd. of Educ., 108 LA 502 (Feldman, 1997); City of Waterville, 107 LA 1194 (Dichter, 1996); West Clermont, Ohio, Local Sch. Dist. Bd. of Educ., 103 LA 1193 (Murphy, 1994); Birmingham-Jefferson County Metro Transit Auth.-Metro Area Express, 103 LA 1 (Baroni, 1994); City of St. Paul, Minn., 101 LA 1205 (Jacobowski, 1993); ATE/Ryder, 101 LA 52 (Darrow, 1993); Marathon County, Wis., 100 LA 256 (Chatman, 1992); City of Oak Creek, Wis., 98 LA 325 (Anderson, 1991); St. Joseph's Med. Ctr., 98 LA 98 (Jacobowski, 1991); City of Mound, Minn., 93 LA 1017 (Fogelberg, 1989); Bridge Terminal Transp., 92 LA 192 (Gentile, 1988); City of Lake Worth, Fla., 91 LA 1408 (Weston, 1988); Adams County, Wis., Highway Dep't, 91 LA 1340 (Reynolds, Jr., 1988); City of Renton, Wash., 71 LA 271 (Snow, 1978); Republican Co., 69 LA 1041 (Holden, Jr., 1977); City of Burlington, Iowa, 68 LA 454 (Witney, 1977); City of Pittsburgh, Pa., 57 LA 1000 (Krimsly, 1971); Federal Labor Union Ins. Fund, 44 LA 514 (Kates, 1965); Employers Council of Cal., 26 LA 303 (Prasow, 1956); Pennsylvania R.R., 25 LA 352 (Johnson, Johnson, & O'Malley, 1955); Akron, Canton & Youngstown R.R., 22 LA 392 (Loring, Wenke, & Catherwood, 1954); Shenango Valley Transit Co., 21 LA 356 (Brecht, 1953); Boller Beverage Co., 16 LA 933 (Reynolds, 1951); R.H. Macy & Co., 11 LA 450 (Cole, 1948).

[18]City of Willowick, Ohio, 110 LA 1146 (Ruben, 1997); Wooster City, Ohio, Bd. of Educ., 108 LA 502 (Feldman, 1997); County of Clay, Minn., 107 LA 527 (Dichter, 1996); Birmingham-Jefferson County, Metro Transit Auth./Metro Area Express, 103 LA 1 (Baroni, 1994); City of Renton, Wash., 71 LA 271 (Snow, 1978); Pacific Mar. Ass'n, 28 LA 600 (Kagel, 1957); Akron, Canton & Youngstown R.R., 22 LA 392 (Loring, Wenke, & Catherwood, 1954); Window Cleaning Contractors Ass'n of Detroit, 21 LA 310 (Haughton, 1953); Twin City Rapid Transit Co., 16 LA 749 (Platt, 1951); Basic Steel Indus., 13 LA 46 (Daugherty, Cole, & Rosenman, 1949).

[19]Manitowoc, Wis., Sch. Dist., 100 LA 844 (Rice II, 1992); Asplundh Tree Expert Co., 89 LA 183 (Allen, Jr., 1987); Republican Co., 69 LA 1041 (Holden, Jr., 1977); Borough of Turtle Creek, Pa., 52 LA 233 (McDermott, 1968); General Metals Corp., 37 LA 719 (Ross, 1961); Pittsburgh Rys. Co., 33 LA 862 (Sembower, Zimring, & Drake, 1959); Rock Prods. Employers of S. Cal., 29 LA 101 (Prasow, 1957); Atlas Raincoat Mfg. Co., 25 LA 54 (Davis, 1955); Rochester Transit Corp., 19 LA 538 (Tolley, McKelvey, & Turkus, 1952); Full-Fashioned Hosiery Mfrs. of Am., 18 LA 5 (Seward, Rubin, & Leader, 1952); Full-Fashioned Hosiery Mfrs. of Am., 14 LA 321 (Taylor, Rubin, & McKeown, 1950); Felters Co., 13 LA 702 (Myers, 1949); Public

early retirement,[20] clothing and tool allowances,[21] expense reimbursements,[22] layoffs and reductions in force,[23] benefits to curb the impact of automation,[24] overtime,[25] merit increases,[26] meal periods,[27] rest periods,[28] light duty,[29] smoking rules,[30] safety equipment,[31] seniority rules,[32] longevity pay,[33] job classification,[34] work schedules and shifts,[35] premium pay,[36] standby pay,[37] length of workday or workweek,[38] released time for union work,[39] paid bargaining

---

Serv. Co-Ordinated Transp., 11 LA 1037 (Stein, Lewis, Reynolds, Syme, & Hebrank, 1948).

[20]Northwest Kan. Educ. Serv. Ctr., 113 LA 47 (Murphy, 1999); Wooster City, Ohio, Bd. of Educ., 108 LA 502 (Feldman, 1997).

[21]City of Willowick, Ohio, 110 LA 1146 (Ruben, 1997); State of Hawaii, 109 LA 873 (Pool, 1997); City of Avon Lake, Ohio, 108 LA 1049 (Smith, 1997); Birmingham-Jefferson County Metro Transit Auth./Metro Area Express, 103 LA 1 (Baroni, 1994); Borough of Indiana, Pa., 94 LA 317 (Lubow, 1989).

[22]Northwest Kan. Educ. Serv. Ctr., 113 LA 47 (Murphy, 1999); City of Willowick, Ohio, 110 LA 1146 (Ruben, 1997); Wooster City, Ohio, Bd. of Educ., 108 LA 502 (Feldman, 1997).

[23]Northwest Kan. Educ. Serv. Ctr., 113 LA 47 (Murphy, 1999); Republican Co., 69 LA 1041 (Holden, Jr., 1977).

[24]New York Shipping Ass'n, 36 LA 44 (Stein, 1960).

[25]City of Avon Lake, Ohio, 108 LA 1049 (Smith, 1997); Birmingham-Jefferson County Metro Transit Auth./Metro Area Express, 103 LA 1 (Baroni, 1994); City of Winter Haven, Fla., 65 LA 557 (Sherman, 1975).

[26]City of Winter Haven, Fla., 65 LA 557 (Sherman, 1975).

[27]Lane County Peace Officers' Ass'n, 2000 WL 995242 (Downing, 2000); County of Carlton, Minn., 104 LA 773 (Daly, 1995); Pinehaven Sanitarium, 47 LA 482 (Singer, 1966); Los Angeles Standard Rubber, 17 LA 353 (Warren, 1951); Twin City Rapid Transit Co., 16 LA 749 (Platt, 1951); West Penn Power Co., 11 LA 166 (Dash, McGivern, & Breckenridge, 1948); Atlantic City Transp. Co., 9 LA 577 (Cole, 1948); Fifth Ave. Coach Co., 4 LA 548 (Wasservogel, 1946); Railway Express Agency, 2 LA 663 (Stacy, Papp, & Sharfman, 1945).

[28]County of Carlton, Minn., 104 LA 773 (Daly, 1995); Los Angeles Standard Rubber, 17 LA 353 (Warren, 1951); Twin City Rapid Transit Co., 7 LA 845; Luckenbach S.S., 6 LA 98 (Kerr, 1946); Minneapolis-Moline Power Implement Co., 2 LA 227 (Van Fossen, Humphrey, & Prifrel, 1946).

[29]Cuyahoga County, Ohio, Sheriff's Dep't, 102 LA 143 (Strasshofer, Jr., 1993).

[30]Wooster City, Ohio, Bd. of Educ., 108 LA 502 (Feldman, 1997); Lake County Sch. Bd., 93 LA 1103 (Bairstow, 1989).

[31]Cuyahoga County, Ohio, Sheriff's Dep't, 102 LA 143 (Strasshofer, Jr., 1993).

[32]City of Waterville, 107 LA 1194 (Dichter, 1996); Williamson Cent. Sch. Dist., 63 LA 1087 (Gootnick, 1974); Pittsburgh Plate Glass Co., 32 LA 945 (Lehoczky, Fisher, & Myers, 1959).

[33]City of Willowick, Ohio, 110 LA 1146 (Ruben, 1998); City of Okla. City, Okla., 110 LA 912 (Gordon, 1998); City of N. Royalton, Ohio, 109 LA 842 (Feldman, 1997); Olmsted Township, Ohio, 109 LA 237 (Ruben, 1997); City of Avon Lake, Ohio, 108 LA 1049 (Smith, 1997); Vernon County, Wis., 103 LA 1115 (Flaten, 1995).

[34]Zia Co., 72 LA 383 (Johannes, 1979); Oxmoor Press, 68 LA 1064 (Williams, 1977).

[35]Cuyahoga County, Ohio, Sheriff's Dep't, 102 LA 143 (Strasshofer, Jr., 1993); City of Edgerton, Wis., Police Dep't, 100 LA 339 (Miller, 1992); Trenton Transit, 11 LA 501 (Stein, Curtin, & Syme, 1948); Reading St. Ry., 6 LA 860 (Simkin, 1947); United Master Barbers Ass'n, 5 LA 269 (Cahn, 1946); Bakeries of St. Paul & Minneapolis, Minn., 3 LA 804 (Peck, Berg, & Eggleston, 1946); Phoenixville Publ'g Co., 2 LA 10 (Frey, 1946).

[36]St. Louis County, Minn., 108 LA 1170 (Dichter, 1997); County of Clay, Minn., 107 LA 527 (Dichter, 1996); Cuyahoga County, Ohio, Sheriff's Dep't, 102 LA 143 (Strasshofer, Jr., 1993); 375th Mission Support Squadron/MSC, Scott Air Force Base, 99 LA 656 (Hilgert, 1992).

[37]City of Waterville, 107 LA 1194 (Dichter, 1996).

[38]City of Avon Lake, Ohio, 108 LA 1049 (Smith, 1997); Pinehaven Sanitarium, 47 LA 482 (Singer, 1966); R. Cooper, Jr., Inc., 43 LA 875 (Davis, 1964); Appleton Coop. Ass'n, 39 LA 249 (Gundermann, 1962); Pacific Mar. Ass'n, 28 LA 600 (Kagel, 1957); Birmingham News Co., 27 LA 343 (Dworet, 1956); Atlas Raincoat Mfg. Co., 25 LA 54 (Davis, 1955); Madison Bus Co., 21 LA 307 (Gooding, Fitzgibbon, & Slavney, 1953); Rochester Transit Corp., 19 LA 538 (Tolley, McKelvey, & Turkus, 1952); Detroit Inst. of Laundering, 18 LA 903 (Platt, Balwill, & Litwalk, 1952).

[39]Wooster City, Ohio, Bd. of Educ., 108 LA 502 (Feldman, 1997).

time,[40] separation pay,[41] subcontracting restrictions,[42] use of volunteers and student workers,[43] union shop,[44] agency shop,[45] check-off,[46] length of contract term,[47] management rights,[48] pay period,[49] discipline policies,[50] mandatory grievance arbitration,[51] the size of grievance committee,[52] the use of a permanent arbitrator,[53] evaluation procedures,[54] posting and filling of job vacancies,[55] and transfer and promotion provisions.[56]

Indiscriminate use of interest arbitration is to be avoided, however, for such use may impede healthy development of the labor-management relationship. In particular, parties that abdicate to arbitrators the responsibility of writing the bulk of the collective bargaining agreement risk serious disappointment.[57] The practice of leaving too many interest issues to be resolved by neutrals has been severely criticized by the neutrals themselves.[58]

---

[40]City of Renton, Wash., 71 LA 271 (Snow, 1978).

[41]City of Waterville, 107 LA 1194 (Dichter, 1996); City of St. Paul, Minn., 101 LA 1205 (Jacobowski, 1993); City of Renton, Wash., 71 LA 271 (Snow, 1978).

[42]City of Oak Creek, Wis., 98 LA 325 (Anderson, 1991); Billings Contractors' Council, 33 LA 451 (Heliker, 1959).

[43]Wooster City, Ohio, Bd. of Educ., 108 LA 502 (Feldman, 1997).

[44]A.S. Abell Co., 45 LA 801 (Cluster, Gallagher, & Kraushaar, 1965); Basic Steel Indus., 18 LA 112 (Wage Stabilization Bd., 1952); Ted's Cleaners, 16 LA 611 (Stutz, Curry, & Clark, 1951); New Jersey Bell Tel. Co., 14 LA 574 (Martin, Lewis, Lesser, Jr., Lord, & Dunn, 1950); Cuivre River Elec. Coop., 13 LA 620 (Whitlow, Schuchat, & Feldewert, 1949); Trenton Transit, 11 LA 501 (Stein, Curtin, & Syme, 1948).

[45]Ohio Tpk. Comm'n, 109 LA 215 (Feldman, 1997); Village of W. Springs, Ill., 99 LA 125 (Goldstein, 1992); Borough of Indiana, Pa., 94 LA 317 (Lubow, 1989); North Bay Reg'l Ctr., 89 LA 1181 (Concepcion, 1987); City of Newark, Ohio, 86 LA 149 (Duda, Jr., 1985).

[46]Ohio Tpk. Comm'n, 109 LA 215 (Feldman, 1997); Republican Co., 69 LA 1041 (Holden, Jr., 1977); Baptist Hosp. of Gadsden, 65 LA 248 (Moberly, 1975); Akron & Barberton Belt R.R., 17 LA 833 (Cole, Horvitz, & Osborne, 1952); New Jersey Bell Tel. Co., 14 LA 574 (Martin, Lewis, Lesser, Jr., Lord, & Dunn, 1950); Trenton Transit, 11 LA 501 (Stein, Curtin, & Syme, 1948); Kansas City Pub. Serv. Co., 8 LA 149 (Updegraff, Sawyer, Gage, Zimrign, & Hargus, 1957).

[47]City of N. Royalton, Ohio, 109 LA 842 (Feldman, 1997); Wooster City, Ohio, Bd. of Educ., 108 LA 502 (Feldman, 1997); City of Renton, Wash., 71 LA 271 (Snow, 1978); Republican Co., 69 LA 1041 (Holden, Jr., 1977); Oxmoor Press, 68 LA 1064 (Williams, 1977); Pinehaven Sanitarium, 47 LA 482 (Singer, 1966); Cleveland Transit Sys., 45 LA 905 (Kates, 1965); Port Auth. of Allegheny County, Pa., 45 LA 58 (Crawford, 1965); Billings Contractors' Council, 33 LA 451 (Heliker, 1959); Yellow Cab Co., 27 LA 468 (Prasow, 1956); Shenango Valley Transit Co., 21 LA 356 (Brecht, 1953); Hotel Employers' Ass'n, 18 LA 174 (Whitton, 1952); Patriot News Co., 15 LA 871 (Egan, 1950).

[48]Baptist Hosp. of Gadsden, 65 LA 248 (Moberly, 1975).

[49]City of Renton, Wash., 71 LA 271 (Snow, 1978); Bremer County, Iowa, Highway Dep't, 68 LA 628 (Yarowsky, 1977); City of Indianapolis, Ind., Dep't of Pub. Works, 58 LA 1302 (Witney, 1972).

[50]City of Willowick, Ohio, 110 LA 1146 (Ruben, 1998); City of Waterville, 107 LA 1194 (Dichter, 1996).

[51]Northwest Kan. Educ. Serv. Ctr., 113 LA 47 (Murphy, 1999).

[52]Republican Co., 69 LA 1041 (Holden, Jr., 1977).

[53]Id.

[54]Northwest Kan. Educ. Serv. Ctr., 113 LA 47 (Murphy, 1999).

[55]City of Oklahoma City, Okla., 110 LA 912 (Gordon, 1998); Wooster City, Ohio, Bd. of Educ., 108 LA 502 (Feldman, 1997).

[56]City of Avon Lake, Ohio, 108 LA 1049 (Smith, 1997); Carson City, Nev., Sch. Dist., 97 LA 52 (Gentile, 1991); City of Swartz Creek, Mich., 90 LA 448 (Sugerman, 1988).

[57]For examples of such disappointment, see *Internal Revenue Serv.*, 118 LA 123 (Abrams, 2003); *New England Transp. Co.*, 15 LA 126, 133 (Copelof, Zimring, & Filer, 1950); *Duquesne Light Co.*, 6 LA 470, 487, 492, 498 (Strong, Scharff, & Mueller, 1947).

[58]*See* Consumers Power Co., 18 LA 686, 688–89 (Platt, Gemrich, & Arsulowicz, 1952); Pan Am. World Airways, 17 LA 878, 881 (Shake, Gilkyson, & Grady, Jr., 1952). Similar criticism has been voiced in the public sector. *See* Ellman, *Legislated Arbitration in Michi-*

2. INTEREST ARBITRATION AND CONTRACT CLAUSES

A. Specific Provision for Interest Arbitration

Occasionally, a collective bargaining agreement will expressly provide for arbitration, at its expiration, of unsettled disputes over the terms of a new agreement.[59] A collective bargaining agreement clause providing for arbitration of future interest disputes might, for example, read as follows:

> Any differences that may arise between the company and the local union concerning wage reviews at dates specified in the agreement, or concerning amendments to the agreement at any termination date, which the representatives of the company and the local union are unable to settle, shall be submitted at the request of either party to a Board of Arbitration to be selected in a manner as specified hereinafter. The company and the local union agree that the majority decision of such Board shall be final and binding on both parties.[60]

More often, however, parties do not reach any agreement to arbitrate new contract terms until the old contract has expired and an impasse in negotiations has been reached.[61]

---

gan—A Lateral Glance, in TRUTH, LIE DETECTORS, AND OTHER PROBLEMS IN LABOR ARBITRATION, PROCEEDINGS OF THE 31ST ANNUAL MEETING OF NAA 291, 302 (Stern & Dennis eds., BNA Books 1979) (stating that some parties "have brought 40 or 50 unresolved issues to the arbitration panel" and that in such circumstances "strong chairmen have often told the parties they will simply not entertain such a multitude of issues and directed them to get back to the table and sort out the critical points of dispute"); Anderson, Lessons From Interest Arbitration in the Public Sector: The Experience of Four Jurisdictions, in ARBITRATION—1974, PROCEEDINGS OF THE 27TH ANNUAL MEETING OF NAA 59, 66 (Somers & Dennis eds., BNA Books 1975). Worthy of note is the manner in which the arbitrator and the parties handled the disposition of many interest issues in Air New Zealand, 77 LA 667, 669 (Feller, 1981), where, in addition to wages, "there were in all a total of almost thirty other issues," regarding which the arbitrator stated:

> As the [hearing] meetings progressed, and with some assistance from me when I indicated how I would probably decide, the parties were able to negotiate settlement of most of these issues. As to most of them no explanatory opinion is necessary. As to at least a few, however, I believe that the rationale for the agreement should be set forth at length. There also remained, of course, a few which proved intractable and which I was compelled to decide as an arbitrator. . . . This award, therefore, will set forth my decisions as to the award provisions which remained unresolved and the rationale for the agreement of the parties on some of the sticker issues which were settled during the conciliation process.

[59]See, e.g., Oxmoor Press, 68 LA 1064, 1064 (Williams, 1977). Of 1,717 agreements covered by one study, less than 2% provided for arbitration of such disputes. Major Collective Bargaining Agreements: Arbitration Procedures 95 (U.S. Dep't of Labor Bull. No. 1425-6, 1966). Five hundred of the agreements contained "reopening" clauses, and of these about 15% provided for arbitration if negotiations failed. Id. at 101. For related discussion, see section 5., "Public-Sector Interest-Arbitration Legislation," below; Chapter 1, Section 4.A., "Arbitration as a Substitute for Work Stoppages." In one case, the interest arbitration clause did not go into effect until negotiations for renewal of the contract went into effect. Because the union failed to give notice of its intention to reopen, the arbitration clause was never triggered and therefore was not effective. The arbitration was improperly conducted without the employer's consent. Sheet Metal Workers Local 150 v. Air Sys. Eng'g, 915 F.2d 567, 135 LRRM 2667 (9th Cir. 1990).

[60]Agreement between San Diego Gas & Elec. Co. and Electrical Workers (IBEW) (agreement has expired). For other examples, see Major Collective Bargaining Agreements: Arbitration Procedures at 98–103.

[61]For the type of instrument that may be used in such cases, see Metropolitan Tulsa Transit Auth., 63 LA 621, 622–23 (Oppenheim, 1974); A.S. Abell Co., 45 LA 801, 806–07 (Cluster, Gallagher, & Kraushaar, 1965); River Valley Tissue Mills, 3 LA 245, 246 (Blair, 1946). In Stur-Dee Health Products, 248 NLRB 1100, 104 LRRM 1012 (1980), a collective

Interest-arbitration clauses[62] are nonmandatory subjects of bargaining. Thus, a union's insistence on bargaining to impasse on inclusion of an interest-arbitration provision into a contract constitutes an unfair labor practice.[63] Most courts have held that a union cannot rely on an interest-arbitration clause in an existing contract to require an employer to agree to a similar clause in a successor contract.[64] It has been suggested that

> [t]he rationale for this result appears to be two-fold: (1) a party has a right to bargain through its own representative and therefore cannot be forced to discuss the ceding of that right to someone else; and (2) interest arbitration is a *procedure* for resolving disputes concerning terms and conditions of employment; it is not itself a term or condition of employment.[65]

Once included, however, almost every court considering the question has held that interest-arbitration provisions are entitled to the same presumptions favoring them as grievance arbitration provisions and are therefore enforceable under Section 301 of the LMRA.[66] A court's role in a Section

---

bargaining agreement barred the election petition of an outside union although the economic terms had not been set, because the employer and incumbent union had left them for determination by binding interest arbitration.

[62]For collective bargaining agreements containing specific interest-arbitration clauses, see *American Metal Prods. v. Sheet Metal Workers Local 104*, 794 F.2d 1452, 1454 n.1, 123 LRRM 2824, 2826 n.1 (9th Cir. 1986); *Sheet Metal Workers Local 57 Welfare Fund v. Tampa Sheet Metal Co.*, 786 F.2d 1459, 1460, 122 LRRM 2161, 2162 (11th Cir. 1986). In *Tampa Sheet Metal*, the interest-arbitration clause provided in part:

> In addition to the settlement of grievances arising out of interpretation or enforcement of this agreement as set forth in the preceding sections of this Article, any controversy or dispute arising out of the failure of the parties to negotiate a renewal of this agreement shall be settled as hereinafter provided:
>
> (a) Should the negotiations for the renewal of this agreement become deadlocked . . . , either party may submit the dispute to the National Joint Adjustment Board.
>
> The dispute shall be submitted to the National Joint Adjustment Board pursuant to the rules of the National Joint Adjustment Board. The unanimous decision of said Board shall be final and binding upon the parties, reduced to writing, signed and mailed to the parties as soon as possible after the decision has been reached. There shall be no cessation of work by strike or lockout unless and until said Board fails to reach a unanimous decision and the parties have received written notification of its failure.

Tampa Sheet Metal, 786 F.2d at 1459–60. *See also* Sheet Metal Workers Local 20 v. Baylor Heating & Air Conditioning, 688 F. Supp. 462, 129 LRRM 2108 (S.D. Ind. 1988), *aff'd*, 877 F.2d 547, 131 LRRM 2838 (7th Cir. 1989) (same clause); Sheet Metal Workers Local 104 v. Andrews, 119 LRRM 3516 (N.D. Cal. 1985) (same clause).

[63]Hotel & Restaurant Employees Local 703 v. Williams, 752 F.2d 1476, 118 LRRM 2600 (9th Cir. 1985) (arbitrator cannot make interest-arbitration clause self-perpetuating by including it in a new contract).

[64]Sheet Metal Workers Local 14 v. Aldrich Air Conditioning, 717 F.2d 456, 114 LRRM 2657 (8th Cir. 1983) (an interest-arbitration clause is unenforceable insofar as it applies to the inclusion of a similar clause in a new collective bargaining agreement). *See also* American Metal Prods. v. Sheet Metal Workers Local 104, 794 F.2d 1452, 123 LRRM 2824 (9th Cir. 1986); Electrical Workers (IBEW) Local 367 v. Graham County Elec. Coop., 783 F.2d 897, 121 LRRM 2924 (9th Cir. 1986); Sheet Metal Workers Local 420 v. Huggins Sheet Metal, 752 F.2d 1473, 118 LRRM 2603 (9th Cir. 1985); Sheet Metal Workers Local 263 v. Sheet Metal Contractors Labor Relations Council of Iowa (Cedar Rapids Chapter), 120 LRRM 2191 (N.D. Iowa 1984). The NLRB has taken the same position. Advice Memorandum, Sheet Metal Workers Local 162 (B.J. Heating & Air Conditioning), 109 LRRM 1205 (1981). *But see* Sheet Metal Workers Local 252 v. Standard Sheet Metal, 699 F.2d 481, 112 LRRM 2878 (9th Cir. 1983) (enforcing arbitrator's inclusion of interest-arbitration clause in a new contract).

[65]Datz, *Alternative Dispute Resolution—Interest Arbitration and the National Labor Relations Act*, 6 Lab. Law. 127 (Winter 1990) (emphasis added; footnote omitted).

[66]See cases cited in note 64, above. *But see* Bally Mfg. Corp. v. Electrical Workers (IBEW) Local 713, 605 F. Supp. 110, 120 LRRM 3166 (N.D. Ill. 1985) (court refused to enforce inter-

301 suit is to ascertain "whether the party seeking arbitration is making a claim which on its face is governed by the contract."[67] Since interest-arbitration provisions are part of a contract, courts are not hesitant to enforce them.[68]

B. Clauses Equivocal as to Interest Disputes

Some collective bargaining agreements contain provisions that on their face indicate a very broad scope of arbitration, without providing a clue as to whether the process was intended to be limited to disputes involving the interpretation of the agreement or also intended to include disputes not arising under the agreement. Such provisions may state that "any grievance or complaint" or "any difference" or "any dispute over wages, hours, or other conditions of employment" may be arbitrated. In some instances, arbitrators have held interest-type disputes to be arbitrable under such *broad* arbitration clauses,[69] but in other instances arbitrators have ruled to the contrary.[70] In one case, the arbitrator held that while a provision for arbitration of "all" unsettled disputes made a demand for amendment of the contract arbitrable in the procedural sense that the arbitrator could rule on it, the fact that granting the demand would alter the contract was a good reason for its denial, because it would be unsound and unwise for him to impose his judgment where the appropriate course of action is bilateral negotiation and agreement.[71]

Efforts of a party to arbitrate pure interest issues under *narrow* arbitration clauses often have failed. For instance, under a clause providing only for

---

est-arbitration provision because contract also contained termination provision, and to enforce interest-arbitration provision would deprive termination clause of all meaning, thus perpetuating interest-arbitration clause at expense of an equally binding termination clause). For a case dealing with the same issue but arriving at a different result, see *Sheet Metal Workers Local 420 v. Huggins Sheet Metal*, 752 F.2d 1473, 118 LRRM 2603 (9th Cir. 1985). Although interest arbitration clauses are enforceable under §301, note that these clauses cannot be enforced by the NLRB under §8(a)(5) of the NLRA. *See* Tampa Sheet Metal Co., 288 NLRB 322, 129 LRRM 1188 (1988).

[67]Steelworkers v. American Mfg. Co., 363 U.S. 564, 568, 46 LRRM 2414, 2415 (1960).

[68]Sheet Metal Workers Local 104 v. Andrews, 119 LRRM 3516 (N.D. Cal. 1985). *See also* Hotel & Restaurant Employees Local 703 v. Williams, 752 F.2d 1476, 118 LRRM 2600 (9th Cir. 1985). For an informative discussion of interest arbitration, see Datz, *Alternative Dispute Resolution—Interest Arbitration and the National Labor Relations Act*, 6 LAB. LAW. 127 (Winter 1990).

[69]*See* Rose-Derry Ohio, 49 LA 40, 44 (Kates, 1967); Country Belle Coop. Farmers, 48 LA 600, 603 (Duff, 1967); Labor Standards Ass'n, 48 LA 425, 427 (Joseph, 1967); Velvet Textile Corp., 7 LA 685, 686 (Pope, 1947); Moeller Instrument Co., 6 LA 639, 641 (Brissenden, 1947). For court decisions holding interest-type disputes arbitrable under such broad clauses, see *Associated Brick Mason Contractors of Greater N.Y. v. Harrington*, 820 F.2d 31, 125 LRRM 2648 (2d Cir. 1987); *Sheet Metal Workers Local 104 v. Huggins Sheet Metal*, 752 F.2d 1473, 118 LRRM 2603 (9th Cir. 1985); *Laundry Workers Local 93 v. Mahoney*, 491 F.2d 1029, 84 LRRM 2084 (8th Cir. 1974) (an evenly divided court upheld a lower court order for arbitration); *In re* Beech Nut Packing Co., 134 N.Y.S.2d 916, 23 LA 125 (N.Y. Sup. Ct. 1954); *Textile Workers Local 63 v. Cheney Bros.*, 141 Conn. 606, 109 A.2d 240, 22 LA 512 (Conn. 1954); *Northland Greyhound Lines v. Amalgamated Ass'n of Street, Elec. Ry., & Motor Coach Employees Div. 1150*, 66 F. Supp. 431, 3 LA 887 (D. Minn. 1946).

[70]*See* Groveton Papers Co., 41 LA 1169, 1174–76 (Gregory, 1963); Textron, Inc., 12 LA 475, 478 (Wallen, 1949); Shook Bronze Co., 9 LA 656, 657 (Lehoczky, 1948).

[71]Dictograph Prods., 8 LA 1033, 1038 (Kaplan, 1947). *See also* Chapter 18, section 1.C., "Scope of Remedy Power Limited by the Agreement."

arbitration of disputes involving the interpretation or application of the agreement, the fact that the agreement permitted reopening for consideration of general wage adjustments did not oblige the parties to agree on wage increases or, on failing to agree, to permit an arbitrator to decide for them.[72] But, the fact that a contract excepts general wage increases from arbitration does not prevent arbitration of the question of whether the wage reopening clause permits more than one reopening during the contract term, because this issue involves the interpretation of the contract, rather than a determination of a general wage increase as such.[73]

3. The Arbitrator's Function in Interest Disputes

In a very real sense, the function of an interest arbitrator is to legislate for the parties. As one arbitrator explained:

> The task is more nearly legislative than judicial. The answers are not to be found within the "four corners" of a pre-existing document which the parties have agreed shall govern their relationship. Lacking guidance of such a document which confines and limits the authority of arbitrators to a determination of what the parties had agreed to when they drew up their basic agreement, our task here is to search for what would be, in the light of all the relevant factors and circumstances, a fair and equitable answer to a problem which the parties have not been able to resolve by themselves.[74]

Another arbitrator expressed a similar view:

> [A]rbitrators in private wage disputes do not always conceive their function to be merely to discover what the parties would have agreed upon in negotiations and to decide accordingly. Quite often they view their function to be to fix a wage rate that will be fair and equitable to all concerned. Indeed, it is questionable whether any practical objective method exists of measuring the parties' bargaining strength—even when they bargain to a conclusion. In reality, an arbitrator's determination of what the parties would have agreed upon in negotiations if they had not arbitrated is his own opinion of what they should have agreed upon.[75]

A divergent concept of the function of the interest arbitrator was advanced by one arbitration board:

> Arbitration of contract terms differs radically from arbitration of grievances. The latter calls for a judicial determination of existing contract rights; the former calls for a determination, upon considerations of policy, fairness, and expediency, of what the contract rights ought to be. In submitting this case to arbitra-

---

[72]Sharples Coal Corp., 91 LA 1065 (Stoltenberg, 1988); *In re* Berger, 79 N.Y.S.2d 490, 9 LA 1048 (N.Y. Sup. Ct. 1948), *aff'd*, 81 N.Y.S.2d 196, 10 LA 929 (N.Y. App. Div. 1948). *Accord* Hughes Tool Co., 36 LA 1125, 1128 (Aaron, 1960); West Penn Power Co., 24 LA 741, 744 (McCoy, Westbrook, & Brown, 1955); Air Reduction Sales Co., 10 LA 528, 530 (Livingston, 1948). *See also* P.P. Williams Co., 24 LA 587, 589–91 (Reynard, 1955). *Cf.* Sacramento Wholesale Bakers Ass'n, 20 LA 106, 107–08 (Kerr, 1952); Lincoln Dairy Co., 14 LA 1055, 1058 (Donnelly, 1950).

[73]F.H. Hill Co., 8 LA 223, 225 (Blair, 1947). *See also* Northern Tube Co., 22 LA 261, 263–64 (Piercey, 1954); Cords, Ltd., 7 LA 748, 749 (Stein, 1947).

[74]New York Shipping Ass'n, 36 LA 44, 45 (Stein, 1960). *Accord* Zia Co., 72 LA 383, 386 (Johannes, 1979). *But see* Des Moines Transit Co., 38 LA 666, 671 (Flagler, 1962).

[75]Port Auth. of Allegheny County, 50 LA 1103, 1109 (Platt, 1968). *See also* Billings Contractors' Council, 33 LA 451, 454 (Heliker, 1959).

tion, the parties have merely extended their negotiations—they have left it to this board to determine what they should, by negotiation, have agreed upon. We take it that the fundamental inquiry, as to each issue, is: what should the parties themselves, as reasonable men, have voluntarily agreed to? . . . We believe that an unusual demand, that is, one that has not found substantial acceptance in other properties, casts upon the union the burden of showing that, because of its minor character or its inherent reasonableness, the negotiators should, as reasonable men, have voluntarily agreed to it. We would not deny such a demand merely because it had not found substantial acceptance, but it would take clear evidence to persuade us that the negotiators were unreasonable in rejecting it. We do not conceive it to be our function to impose on the parties contract terms merely because they embody our own individual economic or social theories. To repeat, our endeavor will be to decide the issues as, upon the evidence, we think reasonable negotiators, regardless of their social or economic theories might have decided them in the give and take process of bargaining. We agree with the company that the interests of stockholders and the public must be considered, and consideration of their interests will enter into our conclusions as to what the parties should reasonably have agreed on.[76]

In concluding its opinion, the arbitration board said:

We render this award not with pride but with some humility. The parties have placed upon us a tremendous task. In judging the results reached and deciding whether the award as a whole is fair, we invite the parties to consider whether, if an offer embodying this entire award had been made in bargaining, it would have been accepted as a reasonable compromise of many demands. If it would have been, we have performed the function we set for ourselves at the outset, namely, to determine what the parties, as reasonable men, should themselves have agreed to at the bargaining table.[77]

Sometimes it is possible for the parties to agree on the criteria to be observed by an arbitrator in deciding the issues submitted to arbitration. (In the public sector, criteria may be specified by statute.) But even with agreed-on points of reference, the discretion of the arbitrator ordinarily can be expected to be quite broad.[78] Interest arbitration, as part of the collective bargaining process, is essentially dynamic and fluid. A proponent may seek to move into a new field, to expand the limits of an old area, or to reduce rights previously granted. It can be expected that something new will come from

---

[76]Twin City Rapid Transit Co., 7 LA 845, 848 (McCoy, Freeman, & Goldie, 1947). Similar views have been expressed by other highly respected arbitrators. *See* North Am. Aviation, 19 LA 76, 77 (Cole, Aaron, & Wirtz, 1952). *Cf.* Printing Indus. of Metro Wash., D.C., 71 LA 838, 840 (Ables, 1978).

[77]Twin City Rapid Transit, 7 LA 845, 858 (McCoy, Freeman, & Goldie, 1947). *See also* Printing Indus. of Ind., 29 LA 7, 10 (McCoy, 1957). One professor suggested that the compulsory arbitration of interests should be called "compulsory collective bargaining" rather than arbitration. Gregory, *The Enforcement of Collective Labor Agreements by Arbitration*, 13 U. Chi. L. Rev. 445, 469–70 (1946). For various possible uses of neutrals in bargaining negotiations, see *Current Problems of Arbitration*, 35 LA 963, 965–66 (1961). With respect to combining or alternating mediation and arbitration functions in an interest-dispute neutral, see Gershenfeld, *Decision-Making in Public-Sector Interest Arbitration: II. Perceptions of the Arbitrator and the Parties, in* Truth, Lie Detectors, and Other Problems in Labor Arbitration, Proceedings of the 31st Annual Meeting of NAA 305, 314–15 (Stern & Dennis eds., BNA Books 1979) (speaking of (1) "med-arb," in which the neutral moves from mediation into arbitration, and (2) "arb-med," in which the neutral moves from arbitration into mediation); Howlett, *Contract Negotiation Arbitration in the Public Sector*, 42 U. Cin. L. Rev. 47, 70 (1973).

[78]"Final offer" arbitration is an obvious exception.

the arbitrator and that there will be some substitution of the arbitrator's judgment for that of the respective parties. It must be recognized that if the strike is to be relegated to a position of being the "very last resort, reasonable innovations must be possible through the arbitration process. Otherwise either progress would be unduly slowed or strikes invited, or both."[79]

This sense of dynamism also should infuse public-sector interest arbitration, where progress is no less needed. Indeed, the interest arbitrator's role in the public sector does not appear to be fundamentally different from that in the private sector. Obviously, since public-sector arbitration legislation varies from state to state, there will be jurisdictional differences in the limitations placed on the interest arbitrator's authority and discretion.[80]

Of course, in carrying out the arbitral function as "legislator" or as "bargainer" for the parties, the interest arbitrator must strive to achieve a workable solution:

> [The arbitrator is] not a superior sort of dictator, dispensing justice from on high, but an agent of the two sides to the collective bargain. His job is to reach a solution that will be satisfactory enough to both sides to be workable. He has to take into consideration their relative strength and their relative necessities. He has to remember not to depart so far from a possible compromise, consistent with the respective power and desires of the parties, that one or the other of them will be likely next time to prefer open hostility to peaceful settlement. He has also to remember that a decision is useless if it cannot be enforced and that the power and ability of the respective parties to administer a decision successfully is an integral part of the decision itself.
>
>   A decision which cannot be carried into effect or which will create lasting dissatisfaction is not really a decision at all. On this account a wage arbitration is not an exercise in pure reason, and a summary of merely logical arguments, accompanied by the opinion accompanying the decision, does not tell the whole story. Arbitrators frequently do not, of course, fully understand these limitations, but the more successful ones do so.[81]

In *United States Postal Service*,[82] the arbitration board took the occasion to observe:

> Arbitration of interests, as this arbitration is, sometimes may be necessary. It is never desirable. Arbitration of interests, if it becomes the practice, instead of the occasional exception, can become lethal in the long run. It is far, far better for the parties, and for American society, that the parties themselves write their own contracts. They know their own situations better than any outsiders possibly can. They must live with the contract on a daily basis after the arbitrators have left. It is also better that the parties take responsibility, not only for the terms of the contract, but also for its explanation—where explanation is

---

[79]San Diego Elec. Ry., 11 LA 458, 461 (Kerr, 1948).

[80]*See* section 5., "Public-Sector Interest-Arbitration Legislation," below. The public interest will tend to be of greater concern for the public sector. *See* Gershenfeld, NAA 31st Proceedings, at 316 ("public-sector interest-arbitrators are moving away from a pure 'creature of the parties' approach to a recognition of some public-interest role"); Morse, *Arbitration of Public-Sector Interest Disputes: Economics, Politics, and Equity: Comment, in* Arbitration—1976, Proceedings of the 29th Annual Meeting of NAA 175, 178–79 (Somers & Dennis eds., BNA Books 1976) ("with regard to the politics of arbitration, it is quite probable that arbitrators will become legislators in the public sector," and "we in public management find it difficult to accept this sort of control outside the normal public-policy process").

[81]Soule, Wage Arbitration 6–7 (1928). While this statement was made in reference to wage issues, it would appear equally applicable to other interest matters.

[82]83 LA 1105 (Kerr, Simon, Kheel, Nash, & Mahon, 1984).

needed, and even for its defense. It should be "our" contract, not the contract of a third party. This Board looks upon itself as necessary in this instance but as an evil if it should become the first in a series of such Boards.[83]

Finally, the distinction between the role of emergency boards and that of the interest arbitrator should be recognized. One emergency board, for instance, explained:

> The present Board, comprised solely of neutrals, is not empowered to make a final and binding award. Its Report, including recommendations, is designed to facilitate the subsequent and further collective bargaining of the parties. This Report is not intended to write the precise language of the collective bargaining agreement nor to determine the exact terms of settlement of the disputes between the parties. Rather, it is designed to suggest a relatively narrow area of settlement which the parties should explore constructively. The purpose of the Board is to present the facts, appropriate standards, and suggestions, in the hope that these will persuade the parties voluntarily to reach an agreement.[84]

4. Special Considerations in Public-Sector Interest Arbitration

While dispute resolution in the private sector is bilateral—between employee and employer—in the public sector, it is trilateral, with three distinctly different interests to be accommodated—the employee, the particular governmental unit or agency as employer, and the public as voter, taxpayer, and consumer of services. Justice Stewart summarized this point in *Abood v. Detroit Board of Education*:

> The government officials making decisions as the public "employer" are less likely to act as a cohesive unit than are managers in private industry, in part because different levels of public authority—department managers, budgetary officials, and legislative bodies—are involved, and in part because each official may respond to a distinctive political constituency. And the ease of negotiating a final agreement with the union may be severely limited by statutory restrictions, by the need for the approval of a higher executive authority or a legislative body, or by the commitment of budgetary decisions of critical importance to others.
> . . .
> Finally, decisionmaking by a public employer is above all a political process. The officials who represent the public employer are ultimately responsible to the electorate, which . . . can be viewed as comprising three overlapping classes of voters—taxpayers, users of particular government services, and government employees. . . .
> . . .
> Public employees are not basically different from private employees; on the whole, they have the same sort of skills, the same needs, and seek the same

---

[83]*Id.* at 1109.

[84]Railroads, 34 LA 517, 522 (Dunlop, Aaron, & Sempliner, 1960). The arbitration board also emphasized its responsibility to clarify the public interest in the dispute, to explain the dispute to the public, and thus "to bring to the bargaining table a further measure of public interest." *Id.* Another board explained that some emergency boards make recommendations only on the major subjects in dispute, while other boards deal with each submitted item. "Whatever technique is used, however, the underlying assumption is the same. The parties, following receipt of the Board's report, will be in a position to enter into a new collective bargaining contract which finally disposes of all requests of both employer and union." Pan Am. World Airways, 36 LA 1047, 1051 (Dash, Lynch, & Stark, 1961).

advantages. "The uniqueness of public employment is *not in the employees* nor in the work performed; the uniqueness is in the special character of the employer." Summers, Public Sector Bargaining: Problems of Governmental Decisionmaking, 44 U. Cin. L. Rev. 669, 670 (1975) (emphasis added).[85]

Adding the governmental body to the alternative dispute resolution mix means mechanisms such as bargaining, mediation, factfinding, and arbitration will inevitably take twists and turns that private-sector bargaining, mediation, and arbitration will not encounter. The case of *State of Florida v. Florida Police Benevolent Ass'n*[86] is instructive. In this case, the police union collectively bargained with its members' public employer for 17⅓ hours per month of annual leave and 4 hours and 20 minutes of sick leave, which was permitted pursuant to the Florida Administrative Code.[87] The agreement further permitted employees to receive cash payments for leave accumulated above 240 hours, if the employee exchanged hours above 240 hours for cash.[88] After the agreement commenced, the legislature changed the terms. The annual leave was decreased from 17⅓ hours to 13 hours per month, sick leave was increased from 4 hours and 20 minutes to 8 hours, and all hours above 240 were cancelled, thus eliminating the opportunity for cash payments in exchange for excess accumulated hours.[89] The union challenged the legislature's actions as infringing the rights its members obtained after collective bargaining.

The union succeeded at the trial and appellate level, but the Florida Supreme Court reversed. The court noted "public employee bargaining is not the same as private bargaining."[90] Although Florida precedent had held that "public employees have the same rights of collective bargaining as are granted private employees,"[91] the court noted "it would be impractical to require that collective bargaining procedures . . . be identical in the public and the private sectors."[92] The court explained that while the private-sector experience could serve as a reference, the private sector "'will not necessarily provide an infallible basis for a monolithic model for public employment.'"[93] For example, public-sector bargaining requires political activity, but private-sector bargaining does not.[94] Furthermore, private-sector employees can be bound by bargained agreements, but public-sector employees require legislative approval and discretion that cannot be bargained away.[95]

---

[85]431 U.S. 209, 228–30 (1977).

[86]613 So. 2d 415, 142 LRRM 2224 (Fla. 1993).

[87]*Id.* at 416.

[88]*Id.*

[89]*Id.*

[90]*Id.* at 417.

[91]Dade County Classroom Teachers' Ass'n v. Ryan, 225 So. 2d 903, 905 (Fla. 1969).

[92]State of Florida v. Florida Police Benevolent Ass'n, 613 So. 2d 415, 417, 142 LRRM 2224 (Fla. 1993) (quoting Pennsylvania Labor Relations Bd. v. State College Area Sch. Dist., 461 Pa. 494, 500, 337 A.2d 262, 264–65 (Pa. 1975)).

[93]*Id.* (citing Pennsylvania Labor Relations Bd. v. State Coll. Area Sch. Dist., 337 A.2d 262, 264–65 (Pa. 1975)).

[94]*Id.* (citing Antry v. Illinois Educ. Labor Relations Bd., 552 N.E.2d 313 (Ill. App. Ct. 1990)).

[95]*Id.* at 418 (citing City of Springfield v. Clouse, 206 S.W.2d 539 (Mo. 1947), and Communications Workers v. Union County Welfare Bd., 315 A.2d 709, 715 (N.J. Super. Ct. App. Div. 1974)).

States permit public-sector employee unions and public employers to engage in alternative dispute resolution as a remedy for solving bargaining impasses. As in the private sector, the most contentious issues generally involve financial interests, e.g., wages and benefits. While private-sector unions utilize alternative dispute resolution, they have the right to strike—a compelling inducement for private employers to resolve disputes before even considering whether binding alternative dispute resolution is appropriate and worthwhile. The right to strike generally does not belong to public-sector employees, because such employees provide services, often essential, to the public.[96] As a result, public-sector employers and unions may use alternative dispute resolution more than their counterparts in the private sector. Indeed, states have passed laws creating procedures for alternative dispute resolution as a remedy to reduce the incentive for employees, such as schoolteachers, to strike, or as a remedy for the inability of employees, such as police officers, to strike in the first place.[97]

Neutrals engaging in public-sector interest arbitration consider concerns that are not normally relevant in private-sector cases. One of those concerns—the need to attract and retain qualified public-sector employees in competition with the private sector—was the focus of a decision in a case involving police officers:

> [I]f the exacting requirements of police work are to be met in the near and more distant future, at least two conditions must be recognized: the level of pay must be high enough to attract able and promising young people who will be able to withstand the lure of higher wages at less dangerous work in plants in the surrounding communities in the general labor market and the compensation system should be one that will maintain the highest possible morale and esprit de corps in the present force.[98]

Another arbitrator "adopted the principle that Police Department personnel should receive compensation which is sufficient to maintain reasonable standards of health and decency without the necessity to hold alternate employment."[99]

With particular reference to firefighters, one arbitrator pointed out that "[t]he City has a fiscal interest in maintaining the quality and morale of its firefighting forces since the fire insurance rates to business and the attractiveness of doing business in Providence are influenced in part by the costs

---

[96]See Kirschner, *Labor Management Relations in the Public Sector: Introductory Overview of Organizing Activities, Bargaining Units, Scope of Bargaining, and Dispute Resolution Techniques* (American Law Inst. 1998) (noting that 38 states have no-strike laws for public employees, 22 of which specify penalties) (cited on Westlaw as SD09 ALI-ABA 271).

[97]Mukamal, *Unilateral Employer Action Under Public-Sector Binding Interest Arbitration*, 6 J. L. & Com. 107, 109–10 (1986).

[98]City of Providence, R.I., 47 LA 1036, 1039 (Seitz, 1966). *See also* City of Garfield, N.J., 70 LA 850, 855 (Silver, 1978). In *City of Birmingham, Mich.*, 55 LA 716, 723 (Roumell, Jr., 1970), the arbitrator stated that police officer compensation "should receive relative improvement as compared to other types of employees because of the changing duties and responsibilities of their jobs."

[99]City of Uniontown, Pa., 51 LA 1072, 1073 (Duff, 1968). However, this arbitrator could find no compelling reason to classify police department employees as a special group entitled to more holidays or vacation time than other city employees. *Id.* at 1075. *See* City of Providence, R.I., 47 LA 1036, 1039 (Seitz, 1966) (agreeing that "moonlighting" by police officers should be discouraged by an adequate police wage).

of fire protection."[100] The same considerations underlay a factfinder's recommendations for increases in teacher salaries. The factfinder observed that if the school district were to remain in a competitive position to attract competent, experienced teachers, retain valuable staff, and encourage the pursuit of advanced degrees and training, adequate raises had to be given.[101]

The state of Minnesota enacted a law introducing a new criterion for arbitrators to apply comparable worth. The statute requires every political subdivision to "establish equitable compensation relationships between female-dominated, male-dominated, and balanced classes of employees . . . ."[102] In all interest arbitrations, arbitrators are required to consider various "equitable compensation relationship standards," as well as "other standards appropriate to interest arbitration."[103]

This statute has been the subject of interpretation in several reported arbitral decisions. In one case, the arbitrator adopted the public employer's position on wages because it took the statute into account, while the union's position did not.[104] In another decision, the arbitrator rejected the employer's position of no wage increase partly because of a comparable worth study.[105] The arbitrator said that pay equity was only one factor to be considered and that arbitrators could not "totally ignore historical comparisons, both external and internal."[106] Yet another arbitrator ruled that the statute can be used "to decelerate the rates of increases for overcompensated employees while attempting to bring undercompensated employees to a more equitable relative position."[107]

Not all interest arbitration awards issued in public-sector impasse proceedings are binding on the governmental employer and enforceable in court. When a police union sued the city of Fairbanks during the course of negotiations for failure to comply with the terms of an earlier award, the court decided that legislative approval of collective bargaining contracts was a customary requirement, and a provision of state law to the effect that terms in labor contracts involving monetary commitments were subject to legislative approval was applicable to interest arbitration awards.[108]

---

[100]City of Providence, R.I., 42 LA 1114, 1119 (Dunlop, Pierce, & Hoban, 1963). *See also* City of Burlington, Iowa, 68 LA 454, 456 (Witney, 1977) (fire insurance rates); City of Boston, Mass., 70 LA 154, 157 (O'Brien, 1978) (speaking of the public's "interest in a well-trained, efficient and motivated fire suppression force" and recognizing the great hazards "inherent in this profession"); City of Berwyn, Ill., 66 LA 992, 998 (Sembower, 1976).

[101]Whitesboro Teachers Ass'n, 51 LA 58, 61 (Bickal, 1968). *See also* Pittsfield, Mass., Sch. Comm., 51 LA 1134, 1135–38 (Young, 1968) (teachers); Emmet County, Mich., Rd. Comm., 62 LA 1310, 1312 (Shaw, 1974) (mechanical employees); Borough of Turtle Creek, Pa., 52 LA 233, 234–35 (McDermott, 1968) (police); Green Tree Borough, Pa., 51 LA 994, 995 (Florey, 1968) (police); Paramus Nursing Home Corp., 48 LA 289, 291 (Singer, 1967) (nursing home).

[102]Minn. Stat. §471.992 subd. 1 (2002).

[103]*Id.* subd. 2. Under Minn. Stat. §471.995 (2002), a public employer must submit a report to the exclusive representatives of their employees that identifies "the female-dominated classes in the political subdivision for which compensation inequity exists, based on the comparable work value . . . ."

[104]County of Carver, Minn., 91 LA 1222 (Kanatz, 1988).

[105]City of Blaine, Minn., 90 LA 549 (Perretti, 1988).

[106]*Id.* at 551.

[107]County of Kanabec, Minn., 93 LA 479, 482 (Ver Ploeg, 1989).

[108]Fairbanks Police Dep't Chapter v. City of Fairbanks, 920 P.2d 273, 154 LRRM 2791, 2793 (Alaska 1996).

5. Public-Sector Interest-Arbitration Legislation

A. Scope of Public-Sector Arbitration Legislation

Most states have enacted legislation governing labor relations in part or all of the public sector.[109] In some states, there are also local ordinances and charter provisions authorizing the use of mediation, factfinding, and arbitration for interest disputes involving local government employees.[110]

State legislation ranges from very simple acts providing for collective bargaining rights for specific classes of employees[111] to comprehensive labor relation acts similar to (and often more complex than) the National Labor Relations Act.[112] Some apply only to limited classes of employees such as police, firefighters, teachers, hospital employees, or mass transit employees.[113] Others apply much more broadly, covering most employees of the state

---

[109]See *Validity and Construction of Statutes or Ordinances Providing for Arbitration of Labor Disputes Involving Public Employees*, 68 A.L.R.3d 885. The Maine statute provides for final and binding arbitration for judicial employees on matters other than salary, pension, and insurance. On these topics, the arbitrator can make only advisory recommendations. Me. Rev. Stat. Ann. tit. 26 §1285.4(B) (West 2002). By contrast, the Hawaii statute provides that the parties "may mutually agree" to submit their differences to final and binding arbitration if their impasse has lasted at least 30 days. Haw. Rev. Stat. Ann. §89–11(b)(3) (Michie 2002). In Illinois, "[t]he parties may, by mutual agreement, provide for arbitration of impasses resulting from their inability to agree upon wages, hours and terms and conditions of employment to be included in a collective bargaining agreement." 5 Ill. Comp. Stat. Ann. 315/7 (West 2002). *See also* Minn. Stat. §179A.16 (2002); Wash. Rev. Code Ann. §41.56.111 (West 2002). A statute specifically addressing security employees, peace officers, and firefighter disputes provides: "If any dispute has not been resolved within 15 days after the first meeting of the parties and the mediator, or within such other time limit as may be mutually agreed upon by the parties, either the exclusive representative or employer may request of the other, in writing, arbitration, and shall submit a copy of the request to the Board." 5 Ill. Comp. Stat. Ann. 315/14(a) (West 2002). For a general discussion of interest arbitration, see Howlett, *The Kenneth M. Piper Lectures: Interest Arbitration in the Public Sector*, 60 Chi.-Kent L. Rev. 815 (1984). *See also* Malin, *Public Employees' Right to Strike: Law and Experience*, 26 U. Mich. J.L. Reform 313 (1993). For a discussion of one state's experience with factfinding, see O'Reilly, *More Magic With Less Smoke: A Ten Year Retrospective on Ohio's Collective Bargaining Law*, 19 Dayton L. Rev. 1 (1993). *See also* Martin, *Fixing the Fiscal Police and Firetrap: A Critique of New Jersey's Compulsory Interest Arbitration Act*, 18 Seton Hall Legis. J. 59 (1993).

[110]For a general discussion of states that have statutory provisions expressly permitting local governments to adopt their own procedures, see Anderson & Krause, *Interest Arbitration: The Alternative to the Strike*, 56 Fordham L. Rev. 153 (1987). For a discussion on how the provisions are applied to Ohio counties through the "municipal home rule" provisions, see White, Kaplan, & Hawkins, *Ohio's Public Employee Bargaining Law: Can It Withstand Constitutional Challenge?*, 53 U. Cin. L. Rev. 1 (1984). In contrast, the Oregon statute was reportedly "easily evaded by local government employers because the statute applied to them only if the local government had petitioned the newly-created Public Employee Relations Board (now the Employment Relations Board) for determination of a bargaining unit." Drummonds, *A Case Study of the Ex Ante Veto Negotiations Process: The Derfler-Bryant Act and the 1995 Amendments to the Oregon Public Employee Collective Bargaining Law*, 32 Willamette L. Rev. 69 (1996).

[111]*E.g.*, Ga. Code Ann. tit. 25, ch. 5 (1982) (Firefighters' Mediation Act), providing for collective bargaining rights and mediation for firefighters employed by cities with a population of more than 20,000.

[112]*E.g.*, Ohio Rev. Code Ann. §4117.01 et seq. (West 2003), which addresses labor relations for all employees in the public sector.

[113]In Illinois, for example, although interest arbitration is required only for police, fire, and security personnel, it is available as a voluntary option to others. 5 Ill. Comp. Stat. Ann. §§315/7, 315/14 (West 2002). A discussion of Iowa's final-offer arbitration provisions for educators is found in Hoh, *The Effectiveness of Mediation in Public Sector Arbitration Systems: The Iowa Experience*, 39 Arb. J. 30 (1984).

or municipality.[114] Some states have two or more statutes applicable to different classes of employees and containing different provisions.

B. Dispute Resolution Procedures

i. Nonbinding Mediation

Most state labor laws provide for dispute resolution procedures in the event the parties are unable to reach agreement through collective bargaining. The most frequently encountered form of dispute resolution is nonbinding mediation. Typically, either party may request the intervention of a mediator to provide assistance in reaching agreement.[115] The mediation process is usually informal, without any structure or guidelines provided under the state law.

ii. Factfinding

Many state labor laws require factfinding if mediation fails.[116] Factfinding tends to be a more structured process than mediation and is closer to what is traditionally thought of as advisory arbitration. In a typical factfinding proceeding, parties will introduce evidence before a factfinder, who will then review the evidence and make recommendations. The factfinder's report may then be rejected or accepted by the governmental unit (by vote of the legislative body) and by the union (by ratification of majority vote of the membership). The factfinding hearing may be preceded by informal mediation efforts by the factfinder. The value in factfinding lies in the scrutiny brought to bear on the parties' positions (by both the factfinder and the parties themselves), as well as in the public pressure to accept the neutral's recommendations that result from the impartial evaluation and analysis of each party's position.

---

[114]"Iowa is the first state to grant final and binding arbitration of interest disputes . . . to every non-supervisory public employee of the state and its political subdivisions." Loihl, *Final-Offer Plus: Interest Arbitration in Iowa, in* TRUTH, LIE DETECTORS, AND OTHER PROBLEMS IN LABOR ARBITRATION, PROCEEDINGS OF THE 31ST ANNUAL MEETING OF NAA 317, 318 (Stern & Dennis eds., BNA Books 1979).

The statute provides for mediation, fact-finding, and a modified form of final-offer-by-issue arbitration, with the fact-finder's recommendation an alternate selection for the arbitrator on each issue. The arbitration proceeding is moderately rigid and judicial, not permitting amendment of final offers or mediation by the arbitrator. The results (for the first three years) are encouraging, particularly when viewed as the first full-blown experiment with legislated arbitration for public employees other than those in the "essential" services. Low usage of arbitration, particularly among teachers and other educational employees, has left a high proportion of voluntary settlements, although the time parameters have resulted in an overuse of mediation. Fact-finding shows a surprisingly high success ratio both in resolving disputes prior to arbitration and reducing the number of arbitrated issues . . . .

Id. at 340. For additional discussion of the Iowa program, see Hoh, 39 ARB. J. 30.

[115]*E.g.*, CAL. LAB. CODE §65 (Deering 2003). *Compare* OHIO REV. CODE ANN. §4117.14(C)(2) (West 2003) (state employment relations board appoints mediator if no new agreement has been reached 45 days before expiration of the collective bargaining agreement).

[116]*E.g.*, OHIO REV. CODE ANN. §4117.14(C)(3) (West 2003).

iii. Binding Interest Arbitration

The final and more formal, structured form of dispute resolution under public-sector labor laws is that of binding interest arbitration, which may be invoked when mediation and factfinding fail to bring about agreement. Final and binding interest arbitration is most frequently required for public safety forces and other classes of employees that are deemed essential for preservation of public safety and welfare.[117] The arbitration may be conducted by a third-party neutral or a panel consisting of at least one neutral. The parties will present their positions on the unresolved issues to the arbitrator, who will then render a decision that is final and binding on the parties. Some states allow the arbitrator a great deal of discretion in formulating the resolution of the issues presented.[118] More often, however, the arbitrator is limited to choosing between one of the two positions presented on each issue,[119] or even one of the two total packages presented.[120] The "final-offer arbitration" procedure requires the parties to analyze their positions before the hearing, and in theory forces adoption of a more reasonable stance before bringing the matter before the arbitrator.

iv. Last Best Offer

A number of state public-sector dispute resolution statutes require an arbitrator to choose between the "last best offer" of the parties.[121] The District of Columbia Code is illustrative.[122] In determining what is a party's

---

[117]*E.g.*, *id*. §4117.14(D)(1) (arbitrator is referred to as "conciliator").

[118]*E.g.*, ME. REV. STAT. ANN. tit. 26, §965(4) (West 2002).

[119]*E.g.*, OHIO REV. CODE ANN. §4117.14(G)(7) (West 2003).

[120]*E.g.*, DEL. CODE ANN. tit. 19, §1615 (Michie 2002).

[121]*See, e.g.*, Lane County, Or., Peace Officers' Ass'n, 2000 WL 995242 (Downing, 2000) (analyzing OR. REV. STAT. §243.746); City of Sallisaw, Okla., 111 LA 1030 (Moore, 1999); City of Oklahoma City, Okla., 110 LA 912 (Gordon, 1998).

[122]D.C. CODE ANN. §1-618.2d (Lexis 2001):

Where deemed appropriate, impasse resolution procedures may be conducted by the Board, its staff or third parties chosen either by the Board or by mutual concurrence of the parties to the dispute. Impasse resolution machinery may be invoked by either party or on application to the Board. The choice of the form(s) of impasse resolution machinery to be utilized in a particular instance shall be the prerogative of the Board, after appropriate consultation with the interested parties. In considering the appropriate award for each impasse item to be resolved, any third party shall consider at least the following criteria:

(1) Existing laws and rules and regulations which bear on the item in dispute;

(2) Ability of the District to comply with the terms of the award;

(3) The need to protect and maintain the public health, safety and welfare; and

(4) The need to maintain personnel policies that are fair, reasonable and consistent with the objectives of this chapter.

D.C. CODE ANN. §1-611.03:

(a) Compensation for all employees in the Career, Educational, Legal, Excepted, and the Management Supervisory Services shall be fixed in accordance with the following policy:

(1) Compensation shall be competitive with that provided to other public sector employees having comparable duties, responsibilities, qualifications, and working conditions by occupational groups. For purposes of this paragraph compensation shall be deemed to be competitive if it falls reasonably within the range of compensation prevailing in the Washington, D.C., Standard Metropolitan Statistical Area (SMSA); provided, that compensation levels may be examined

"last best offer," the party's preimpasse negotiating position may be considered. It is assumed that a party's demands are made in good faith, though seemingly unreasonable, so long as they are rationally connected to employee or employer interests. Demands that lack this legitimate interest on their face or are apparently made in bad faith may not be considered.[123]

A District of Columbia arbitration panel defined the parties' respective burdens of proof in "final-offer" arbitration proceedings.

> The Panel does not agree that it should impose the burden of proof on the Union by clear and convincing evidence to show a compelling reason for departure from a traditional wage relationship or bargaining pattern in the instant case for a number of reasons. However, prior to stating them, the Panel wishes to clarify what is being rejected by it and what it wishes to preserve for its decision on the merits. The Panel does not believe that last best offer arbitration imposes a burden of proof on the *Union alone*, even on issues as important as parity. The Panel believes last best offer arbitration imposes *on both parties* a burden to show by statute, by rule, and/or by traditional criteria that their final offer is best.[124]

Proposals withdrawn or beyond the scope of required bargaining should not enter into the equation.[125]

Where the issue is whether a proposal is a mandatory or a permissive subject of bargaining, an examination of past practice provides a useful guide.[126] Thus, if a labor organization has been allowed by custom and practice to bargain over what appear to be permissive bargaining subjects, and if its proposals are made pursuant to this practice, they should not be excluded from the last-best-offer process.

C. Features of Arbitration Statutes

Some of the varying features of arbitration statutes and ordinances are outlined below:[127]

---

for public and/or private employees outside the area and/or for federal government employees when necessary to establish a reasonably representative statistical basis for compensation comparisons, or when conditions in the local labor market require a larger sampling of prevailing compensation levels;

(2) Pay for the various occupations and groups of employees shall be, to the maximum extent practicable, interrelated and equal for substantially equal work . . . ;

(3) Differences in pay shall be maintained in keeping with differences in level of work and quality of performance . . . .

See also District of Columbia Office of Labor Relations & Collective Bargaining, 84 LA 713 (Rothschild, 1985).

[123]State, County, & Mun. Employees Council No. 23 v. Center Line, 414 Mich. 642, 327 N.W.2d 822, 115 LRRM 3610 (1982).

[124]District of Columbia Office of Labor Relations & Collective Bargaining, 84 LA 809, 813 (Rothschild & Deso, dissent by Klotz, 1985) (emphasis in original).

[125]First Nat'l Maintenance Corp. v. NLRB, 452 U.S. 666, 107 LRRM 2705 (1981); Fibreboard Paper Prods. Corp. v. NLRB, 379 U.S. 203, 57 LRRM 2609 (1964).

[126]District of Columbia Office of Labor Relations & Collective Bargaining, 84 LA 713 (Rothschild, 1985).

[127]For publications listing states with interest arbitration statutes for public-sector employment, see Dilts & Walsh, Collective Bargaining and Impasse Resolution in the Public Sector 18–19 (1988). *See also* Martin, *Fighting the Fiscal Police and Firetrap: A Critique of New Jersey's Compulsory Interest Arbitration Act*, 18 Seton Hall Legis. J. 59 (1993).

(1) Arbitration may be entirely voluntary, mandatory, or required only in certain circumstances.[128]

(2) Arbitration decisions may be made binding, merely advisory, or a hybrid of the two options. A number of statutes make interest arbitration both compulsory and binding.[129]

(3) Arbitrators may make their award reflect their assessment of the equities or they may be confined to accepting the "final offer" of one party or the other. If final-offer arbitration is specified, an arbitrator may be required to accept a single party's final offer as to all issues or choose final offers on an "issue-by-issue" rather than a "total package" basis.[130]

(4) Variations exist in procedural provisions such as those relating to hearings, use of transcripts, written findings of fact, and written opinions.

(5) Specific criteria or standards may or may not be specified for consideration by the arbitrators or for their guidance.[131]

(6) Safeguards against budgetary problems resulting from monetary awards may or may not be specified.[132]

---

[128]For example, although the Illinois State Labor Relations Act mandates arbitration, it may be avoided by prior successful mediation. Mediated resolutions are allowed, even if the matter has officially gone to arbitration, and can abort the arbitration procedure. 5 Ill. Comp. Stat. Ann. §315/14 (West 2002).

[129]For example, in Illinois the law applicable to security employees, peace officers, and firefighters provides that an arbitrator's decision is not final and binding on the parties until it has been accepted by the local governing authority of the public-sector entity negotiating the contract. If the local board rejects the arbitrator's award, the matter goes back to arbitration. *Id.* §315/14 (n)–(o). A different approach is taken in Iowa, where the parties "can, through joint agreement, formulate their own impasse procedure." Gallagher, *Interest Arbitration Under the Iowa Public Employment Relations Act*, 33 Arb. J. 30, 31 (1978).

[130]For a discussion of final-offer arbitration, see Feuille, *Final-Offer Arbitration and Negotiating Incentives*, 32 Arb. J. 203 (1977). *See* Martin, *Fixing the Fiscal Police and Firetrap: A Critique of New Jersey's Compulsory Interest Arbitration Act*, 18 Seton Hall Legis. J. 59 (1993). A particularly flexible variety of final-offer compulsory arbitration exists under a New Jersey statute for police and firefighter interest disputes. *See* Weitzman & Stochaj, *Attitudes of Arbitrators Toward Final-Offer Arbitration in New Jersey*, 35 Arb. J. 25 (1980). Evaluations of final-offer arbitration often reveal that it has potential utility but that both of its basic forms have problems and critics. For example, the total-package variety carries greater danger of unreasonable awards on some issues. *See* City of Oak Creek, 98 LA 325 (Anderson, 1991); City of Manitowoc, Wis., 108 LA 140 (Michelstetter, 1997). The issue-by-issue variety reduces any incentive to settle more issues prior to arbitration (a basic goal of final-offer statutes is less arbitration), because a party may believe a favorable award on favored issues will be more assured if the party offers additional issues that the arbitrators may resolve against it in formulating a balanced award on all issues. Perhaps the most novel approach to this problem is seen in the Minnesota statute, which allows parties to choose whether to limit the arbitrator to a choice between a total-package or an issue-by-issue approach. Minn. Stat. §179A.16 subd. 7 (2002). *See* Anderson & Krause, *Interest Arbitration: The Alternative to the Strike*, 56 Fordham L. Rev. 153 (1987).

[131]Virtually all statutes providing for interest arbitration include some guidelines for arbitrators. The most common major criteria include "comparability, ability to pay, cost of living changes, productivity changes, variations in job content or hazards, historical trends, equity and forces within the labor marketplace." Martin, 18 Seton Hall Legis. J. at 68–69. See also the state-by-state compilation in Anderson & Krause, 56 Fordham L. Rev. at 158–60, and Bornstein, *Interest Arbitration in Public Employment: An Arbitrator Views the Process*, 83 Lab. L.J. 77 (1978).

[132]*E.g.*, Wisconsin's Municipal Employment Relations Act, Wis. Stat. §111.70(4)(cm)7 and 7g (West 2002) (requires an interest arbitrator to give the greatest weight to the ability

(7) The arbitration tribunal's membership may be tripartite (a common requirement in public-sector interest arbitration) or it may be limited to neutrals.

D. State-by-State Summary of Public-Sector Impasse-Resolution Statutes

The following chart summarizes, on a state-by-state basis, the types of dispute resolution procedures provided under state law for public-sector labor relations.[133]

---

of the municipal employer to pay and to the economic conditions in the jurisdiction). Illinois, however, includes these factors in a list of eight different categories in its law applicable to security employees, peace officers, and firefighters. 5 ILL. COMP. STAT. ANN. §315/14(h) (West 2002), provides in pertinent part:

> [T]he arbitration panel shall base its findings, opinions and order upon the following factors, as applicable:
> (1) The lawful authority of the employer.
> (2) Stipulations of the parties.
> (3) The interests and welfare of the public and the financial ability of the unit of government to meet those costs.
> (4) Comparison of the wages, hours and conditions of employment of the employees involved in the arbitration proceeding with the wages, hours and conditions of employment of other employees performing similar services and with other employees generally:
>   (A) In public employment in comparable communities.
>   (B) In private employment in comparable communities.
> (5) The average consumer prices for goods and services, commonly known as the cost of living.
> (6) The overall compensation presently received by the employees, including direct wage compensation, vacations, holidays and other excused time, insurance and pensions, medical and hospitalization benefits, the continuity and stability of employment and all other benefits received.
> (7) Changes in any of the foregoing circumstances during the pendency of the arbitration proceedings.
> (8) Such other factors, not confined to the foregoing, which are normally or traditionally taken into consideration in the determination of wages, hours and conditions of employment through voluntary collective bargaining, mediation, fact-finding, arbitration or otherwise between the parties, in the public service or in private employment.

The statute also has specified limitations on the specific kinds of discretionary managerial determinations, which the legislature believed constituted policy determinations. *See id.* §315/14(i).

[133]For more information regarding this subject, see Kirschner, *Labor Management Relations in the Public Sector: Introductory Overview of Organizing Activities, Bargaining Units, Scope of Bargaining, and Dispute Resolution Techniques* (American Law Inst. 1998); WOLET, GRODIN, & WEISBERGER, COLLECTIVE BARGAINING IN PUBLIC EMPLOYMENT (4th ed. 1993); AARON, NAJITA, & STERN, PUBLIC SECTOR BARGAINING (BNA Books 2d ed. 1988). Additionally, BNA's *Labor Relations Reporter, State Laws,* Binders 4 and 4(a), provided invaluable assistance in compiling this survey, and contains the full text of most of the statutes cited therein.

SUMMARY OF STATES' LAWS PROVIDING FOR RESOLUTIONS
BETWEEN PUBLIC EMPLOYERS AND UNIONS OF PUBLIC EMPLOYEES[1]
WHEN THEY REACH AN IMPASSE DURING COLLECTIVE BARGAINING

STATE	STATUTE	COVERED EMPLOYEES	SUMMARY OF IMPASSE RESOLUTION PROVIDED
Alabama		None	
Alaska	Public Employment Relations Act, Alaska Statutes, Title 23, Ch. 40, §§23.40.070 to 23.40.260.	Police and fire protection employees, jail, prison and other correctional institution employees, and public hospital employees. §23.40.200(b).	The parties must submit any unresolved issues to final and binding arbitration. §23.40.200(b).
	Id.	Public utility, snow removal, sanitation, and some educational institution employees. §23.40.200(c).	Court may enjoin strike if such is shown to threaten the health, safety, and welfare of the public. Upon issuance of an injunction, the parties must resolve any impasse through binding interest arbitration. §23.40.200(c).
	Id.	School district and similar educational employees. §23.40.200(d).	The parties may submit any unresolved issues to advisory arbitration. §23.40.200(d).
Arizona		None	
Arkansas		None	

---

[1]The table will highlight which public employees are covered by a state's statute. Generally, the statutes will not include public employees with management and supervisory roles, elected officials, appointed officials, confidential employees (i.e., employees involved in the employer's labor-management relations activities), and other like persons. Because this summary is a survey, specific employees excepted from the right to belong to public sector employees' unions and, thus, the right to benefit from collective bargaining, will not be identified here. Readers are cautioned that they should consult the specific statute of each state to determine all of the public employees excepted from such coverage.

STATE	STATUTE	COVERED EMPLOYEES	SUMMARY OF IMPASSE RESOLUTION PROVIDED
California	Meyers-Milias-Brown Act, Title 1, Div. 4, Ch. 10, §§3500 to 3510.	Most employees of the political subdivisions of the state. §3501(d).	The statute provides for mediation. §3505.2.
	Title 1, Div. 4, Ch. 10.3, §§3512 to 3524.	Most employees of the state. §3513(c).	The statute provides for mediation. §3518.
	Title 1, Div. 4, Ch. 10.7, §§3540 to 3549.1.	Public school employees. §3540.1(j).	The statute provides for mediation. §3548. If mediation is unsuccessful, either party may submit the dispute to factfinding. §3548.1. The factfinder will issue an advisory finding and recommendations. §3548.3.
	Title 1, Div. 4, Ch. 12, §§3560 to 3599.	Most employees of the University of California, the Hastings College of Law, and the California State University. §3562.	The statute provides for mediation. §3590. If mediation is unsuccessful, either party may request factfinding. §3591. The factfinder will make findings of fact and issue advisory recommendations. §3593.
	Cal. Civ. Proc. Code §§1299 to 1299.9.	Police and fire employees.	The statute provides for final and binding arbitration of all economic issues upon request by the labor organization, if the parties reach impasse and mediation is unsuccessful.
Colorado	Title 8, Art. 3, §§8-3-101 et. seq.	Employees of any mass transportation system. §8-3-104.	The statute provides for mediation. §8-3-113. If mediation fails and the Director of the Div. of Labor determines that a strike would interfere with the preservation of the public peace, health, and safety, the Director may order binding arbitration. §8-3-113.
Connecticut	Labor Peace Act, Title 5, Ch. 68, §§5-270 to 5-280.	Most state employees. §5-270(a).	The statute provides for mediation. §5-276(a)(b). If mediation is unsuccessful, either party may request arbitration. §5-276(a)(c). The arbitrator's award is final and binding. §5-276(a)(e)(6). There is a limited right for the legislature to reject the findings of the arbitrator. §5-278.
	Municipal Employee Relations Act Title 7, Ch. 113, §§7-467 to 7-479	Municipal employees. §7-467(2).	The statute provides for mediation. §7-472. If mediation is unsuccessful, the parties shall submit all outstanding issues to final and binding arbitration (last best offer arbitration). §7-473(d).

STATE	STATUTE	COVERED EMPLOYEES	SUMMARY OF IMPASSE RESOLUTION PROVIDED
Connecticut *continued*	Title 10, Ch. 166, §§10-153(a) to 10-153(n).	Teachers. §10-153(a); §10-153(b).	The statute provides for mediation. §10-153(f)(b). If mediation is unsuccessful, the parties shall submit all unresolved issues to arbitration. §10-153(f)(c). There is limited right to judicial review of arbitration. §10-153(f)(c)(8).
Delaware	Public Employment Relations Act, Title 19, Part 1, Ch. 13, §1301 to 1318.	Most public employees. §1302(m).	The statute provides for mediation. §1314. If mediation is unsuccessful, the parties must submit their dispute to binding interest arbitration. §1315.
	The Public School Employment Relations Act, Title 14, Part 1, Ch. 40, §§4001 to 4019.	Most public school employees. §4002(m).	This statute provides for mediation. §4014. If mediation is unsuccessful, the parties shall submit their dispute to factfinding. §4015. The factfinder shall issue recommendations that the parties are free to accept or reject. §4015(g)–(i).
	Police Officers and Firefighters Employment Relations Act, Title 19, Part 1, Ch. 16, §§1601 to 1618.	Police and fire. §1602(k).	The statute provides for mediation. §1614. If mediation is unsuccessful, the parties shall submit their dispute to binding interest arbitration (last best offers). §1615.
District of Columbia	Dist. of Columbia Comprehensive Merit Personnel Act of 1978, Part 1, Title 1, Ch. 6.	Most public employees. §1-602.1.	The statute provides for mediation and, in the event the mediation is unsuccessful, the statute provides for final and binding arbitration of all compensation matters, §1-618.17, and rules promulgated under the statute provide for factfinding and arbitration with respect to noncompensation matters. §§527.4, 527.5, D.C. Code.

STATE	STATUTE	COVERED EMPLOYEES	SUMMARY OF IMPASSE RESOLUTION PROVIDED
Florida	Title XXXI, Part II, Ch. 447, §§447.201 to 447.609.	Most public employees. §447.203(3).	The statute provides for impasse resolution in §447.403. Mediation is the first step. If mediation is unsuccessful, a special master shall be appointed and hold hearings and make recommendations. The parties may reject the recommendations of the special master. If the recommendations are rejected, the legislative body of the employer shall hold a public hearing that will result in final resolution of all disputed impasse issues.
Georgia	Firefighters Mediation Act, Title 25, Ch. 5, §§25-5-1 to 25-5-14.	Firefighters of cities with a population of more than 20,000. §25-5.2(2).	The statute provides for nonbinding mediation. §§25-5.8; 25-5.9.
	§20, Metropolitan Atlanta Rapid Transit Authority Act of 1965.	Employees of the Metropolitan Atlanta Rapid Transit Authority.	The statute provides for factfinding. If either party rejects the factfinding recommendations, the parties may seek judicial determination of any unresolved issues in the superior courts of Fulton County or DeKalb County.
Hawaii	Title 7, Ch. 9, §§89-1 to 89-20.	Most public employees. §89-2.	The statute provides for mediation, factfinding, and final and binding arbitration, which must be by agreement of the parties. §89-11. Final and binding arbitration is mandatory for several classifications of employees, including supervisors, "white collar" employees, educational officers, personnel of the University of Hawaii and community colleges, health care workers, correctional institute workers, and public safety employees. §89-11(d).
Idaho	The Professional Negotiations Act, Title 33, Ch. 12, §§33-1271 to 33-1276.	Teachers. §33-1272.	The statute provides for mediation and factfinding. The factfinder shall make recommendations on the issues submitted, which the parties are free to accept or reject. §33-1275.

STATE	STATUTE	COVERED EMPLOYEES	SUMMARY OF IMPASSE RESOLUTION PROVIDED
Idaho *continued*	Title 44, Ch.18, §§44-1801 to 44-1811.	Firefighters. §44-1801.	The statute provides for factfinding before a factfinding commission, which issues recommendations to the parties. §44-1809.
Illinois	Illinois Public Labor Relations Act, Ch. 5, Act 315, §§5 ILCS 315/1 to 5 ILCS 315/27.	Public employees (except security employees, peace officers, and firefighters).	The statute provides for mediation and factfinding. §§5 ILCS 315/12; 5 ILCS 315/13.
	Illinois Public Labor Relations Act, Ch. 5, Act 315, §§5 ILCS 315/1 to 5 ILCS 315/27.	Security employees. peace officers and firefighters. §5 ILCS 315/14.	The statute provides initially for mediation. If mediation is unsuccessful, the matter shall proceed to final and binding arbitration. Depending on employee classification, the jurisdiction of the arbitrator may be limited with respect to certain subjects. §5 ILCS 315/14.
	Illinois Educational Labor Relations Act, Ch. 115, Act 5, §§115 ILCS 5/1 to 115 ILCS 5/20.	Educational employees. §115 ILCS 5/2.	The statute provides for mediation. The mediator may engage in factfinding and make findings and recommendations. Additionally, the parties may jointly request arbitration. §115 ILCS 5/12.
Indiana	Title 20, Art. 7.5, Ch. 1, §§20-7.5-1-1 to 20-7.5-1-14.	Public school employees. §20-7.5-1-2(e).	The statute provides for mediation and factfinding. §20-7.5-1-13.
Iowa	Iowa Public Employment Relations Act, Title I, Subtitle 8, Ch. 20, §§20.1–20.26, 20.28, and 20.31.	Most public employees. §20.3	The statute initially provides for mediation. §20.20. If mediation is unsuccessful, a factfinder will be appointed to hear evidence and make recommendations. §20.21. If factfinding recommendations are not adopted, either party may request binding arbitration. §20.22.

STATE	STATUTE	COVERED EMPLOYEES	SUMMARY OF IMPASSE RESOLUTION PROVIDED
Kansas	Kansas Professional Negotiations Act, Ch. 72, Article 54, §§72-5410 to 72-5437.	Teachers and other professional public school employees. §72-5410.	The statute initially provides for mediation. §72-5427. If mediation is unsuccessful, the parties may present their impasse before a three-member factfinding panel. §72-5428. The report of the factfinding board is made public and may be accepted or rejected by the parties. If rejected, the local board of education "shall take such action as it deems in the public interest." §72-5428(f).
	Ch. 75, Article 43, §§75-4321 to 75-4337.	Most public employees. §75-4322.	The statute provides for mediation. §75-4332. If mediation is unsuccessful, a factfinding board shall conduct a hearing, make written findings of fact, and recommendations for resolution of the dispute. *Id.* The parties need not accept the recommendations of the factfinder. If the recommendations are not acceptable, the governing body of the public employer shall take such action as it deems to be in the public interest. §75-4332(f).
Kentucky	Firefighters Collective Bargaining Act, Title XXVII, Ch. 345 §§345.010 to 345.130.	Fire employees. §§345.010(2); 345.030(1).	The statute provides for factfinding. §345.080.
Louisiana	Title 23, Ch. 8, Part V, §23:890(a)(2)(g).	Employees of public transportation facilities operated by municipalities within the state. §23.890(b).	The statute provides for final and binding arbitration. §23.890(e).
Maine	Title 26, Ch. 9A, §§961 to 974.	Employees of municipalities, counties, and certain other public employers. §962.	The statute provides for mediation. §965(2). If mediation is unsuccessful, either party may request factfinding. §965(3). Alternatively, the parties may jointly agree to pursue another procedure for resolving the dispute. *Id.* If factfinding is unsuccessful, either party may request arbitration. Arbitration is advisory with respect to any controversy involving salary, pensions, or insurance, but final and binding with respect to all other issues. §965(4).

STATE	STATUTE	COVERED EMPLOYEES	SUMMARY OF IMPASSE RESOLUTION PROVIDED
Maine *continued*	Title 26, Ch. 9B, §§979 to 979-Q.	Most state employees. §979-A(6).	The statute provides for mediation. §979-D(2). If mediation is unsuccessful (or waived) either party may request factfinding. §979-D(3). If factfinding does not resolve the dispute, the statute provides for final and binding arbitration. §979-D(4).
	Title 26, Ch. 12, §§1021 to 1035.	University and college employees. §§1022, 1023.	The statute provides for mediation. §1026(2). If mediation is unsuccessful, or waived, either party may request factfinding. §1026(3). If factfinding does not resolve the dispute, the matter shall proceed to arbitration. The arbitrators may make findings of fact and recommendations with respect to issues involving salaries, pension, and insurance. With respect to all other subjects, the determination of the arbitrators shall be final and binding. §1026(4).
Maryland	Education Article, Title 6, §§6-401 to 6-411; 6-501 to 6-510.	Public school employees. §§6-401(c); 6-501(f).	The statutes provide for factfinding. §§6-408(d); 6-510(d).
Massachusetts	Part 1, Title XXI, Ch. 150E, §§1 to 15.	Most public employees of the state and any political subdivisions. §1.	The statute initially provides for mediation. §9. If mediation is unsuccessful, either party may request factfinding proceedings. *Id.* The parties may also, by agreement, waive factfinding and proceed to final and binding interest arbitration. *Id.*
	Part 1, Title XXII, Ch. 161A, §§19 to 19G.	Employees of the Massachusetts Bay Transportation Authority. §19.	The statute provides for mediation. §19D. If mediation is unsuccessful, the matter shall proceed to final and binding arbitration. §19F.

STATE	STATUTE	COVERED EMPLOYEES	SUMMARY OF IMPASSE RESOLUTION PROVIDED
Massachusetts *continued*	§4(A), Ch. 1078, L.1973 (not codified).	Municipal police officers and firefighters.	The law establishes a committee that has responsibility for all collective bargaining negotiations involving municipal police officers and firefighters. The committee may engage in mediation and may also initiate factfinding. The committee may also require the parties to undergo arbitration, but the State Attorney General has ruled that such arbitration is not final and binding. Attorney General Op. No. 80/81-12 (2-10-81).
Michigan	Public Employment Relations Act, Ch. 423, §§423.201 to 423.217.	Most public employees of state and political subdivisions, and most public school employees. §423.201(1)(e).	The statute provides for mediation. §§423.207; 423.207(a).
	Ch. 423, §§423.271 to 423.286.	State police employees. §423.272.	The statute provides for binding arbitration. §§423.273 to 423.281.
	Ch. 423, §§423.231 to 423.246.	Municipal police and fire employees. §423.232.	The statute provides for binding arbitration. §§423.233 to 423.240.
Minnesota	Minnesota Public Employment Relations Act Ch. 179, §§179A.01 to 179A.25.	"Essential" public employees (defined to include police, fire, correctional, and certain health care and supervisory employees. §179A.03.	The statute initially provides for mediation. §179A.15. If mediation is unsuccessful, all unresolved issues must be resolved through final and binding arbitration. §179A.16.
	Id.	All other public employees. §179A.03.	Same procedure as above, except arbitration must be by mutual agreement.
Mississippi		None	
Missouri	Labor and Industrial Relations Act, Title XVIII, Ch. 295, §§295.010 to 295.210.	Anyone in the service of any public utility. §295.020(3)	The statute provides for factfinding if the parties did not agree to voluntary arbitration before reaching an impasse. §295.120(1).

STATE	STATUTE	COVERED EMPLOYEES	SUMMARY OF IMPASSE RESOLUTION PROVIDED
Montana	Collective Bargaining for Public Employees Act, Title 39, Ch. 31, §§39-31-101 to 39-31-409.	A person employed by a public employer in any capacity. §39-31-103(9)(a). §39-31-103(9)(b). A "public employer" means the State or any political subdivision, including counties, cities, towns, etc. §39-31-103(10).	The statute provides for mediation. §39-31-08. The parties may then request factfinding. §39-31-308. The parties may also agree to final and binding arbitration as an alternative to mediation and/or factfinding. §39-31-310.
	Arbitration for Firefighters Act, Title 39, Ch. 34, §§39-34-101 to 39-34-106.	Firefighters. §39-34-101.	The statute provides for final and binding arbitration. §39-34-101(2).
Nebraska	State Employee Collective Bargaining Act, Ch. 81, Article 13, Subarticle (c), §§81-1369 to 81-1390.[2]	Any employee of the State, but not any political subdivision of the State. §81-371(4) and (5).	The statute provides for mediation. §81-1381. If unsuccessful, the parties then engage in arbitration where the special master chooses the most reasonable final offer on each issue in the dispute. §81-1382.
	Industrial Relations Act, Ch. 48, Article 8, §§48-801 to 48-842.[3]	Any employee of the State or any political or governmental subdivision, except those in the State National Guard or militia. §§48-801(4) and (5).	The statute provides for the option of mediation or factfinding. §48-816(1). However, if the employer is a school district, the statute provides for arbitration where the special master chooses the most reasonable final offer on each issue in the dispute. §48-811.02.

[2]This is the "State Employees Collective Bargaining Act" and deemed "cumulative to the Industrial Relations Act" (§§48-801 to 48-842) unless otherwise specified or inconsistent. §81-1372.
[3]This is the "Industrial Relations Act."

STATE	STATUTE	COVERED EMPLOYEES	SUMMARY OF IMPASSE RESOLUTION PROVIDED
Nevada	Local Government Employee-Management Relations Act, Title 23, Ch. 288, §§288.010 to 288.280.	Any employee employed by a "local government employer," which means any political subdivision of the State, such as counties, cities, incorporated towns, school districts, etc., or any public or quasi-public corporation. §§288.050 and 288.060.	The statute provides for mediation. §288.190. If unsuccessful, the parties may submit the dispute to factfinding. §288.200.
	Id.	Police officers and firefighters. §288.215.	If mediation and factfinding is unsuccessful, the parties must submit the unresolved issues to arbitration, where the arbitrator shall select one party's entire final offer or the other party's entire final offer. §§288.215.3 and 7.
	Id.	School district employees. §288.217.	If the parties cannot reach an agreement after at least four negotiation sessions, either party may declare an impasse and submit the unresolved issues to arbitration, where the arbitrator shall select one party's entire final offer or the other party's entire final offer. §§288.217.2 and 7.
New Hampshire	Title XXIII, Ch. 273-A, §§273-A:1 to 273-A:17.	Any person employed by a "public employer," which means the State and any political subdivision thereof, any quasi-public corporation, council, commission, agency, or authority, and the State university system. §§273-A:1.IX and X.	The statute provides for mediation. §273-A.12.I. If unsuccessful, factfinding shall take place. Id. After the factfinder makes his or her recommendation, the parties may vote to accept or reject. §273-A:12.II. If either party rejects the recommendation, the relevant legislative body shall vote to accept or reject. §273-A:12.III. If the legislative body rejects the recommendation, negotiations begin again. §273-A:12.IV. The parties may then request mediation again. Id. Beyond the statute's provisions, the parties may agree to resolve impasses with arbitration or other alternatives. §273-A.12.V.[4]

[4]However, a government division may enact a charter to prevent alternatives such as binding arbitration. City of Portsmouth v. Association of Portsmouth Teachers, 134 N.H. 642, 597 A.2d 1063 (N.H. 1991) (holding a city may enact a charter amendment that makes binding interest arbitration in collective bargaining agreements impermissible).

STATE	STATUTE	COVERED EMPLOYEES	SUMMARY OF IMPASSE RESOLUTION PROVIDED
New Jersey	New Jersey Employer-Employee Relations Act, Title 34, Ch. 13A, §§34:13A-1 to 34:13A-14	Any employee employed by a "public employer," which means the State and any political subdivision thereof, or a school district, or any special district, or any authority, commission, or board, or any branch or agency of the public service. §34:13A-3.	"Whenever negotiations between a public employer and an exclusive representative concerning the terms and conditions of employment shall reach an impasse, the [Public Employment Relations Commission] . . . shall, upon the request of either party, take such steps as it may deem expedient to effect a voluntary resolution of the impasse." §34:13A-6(b). The statute provides for mediation, then factfinding if mediation fails. The commission may also arrange for one or more conferences between the parties to discuss and assist in resolving their differences. The commission may invite such parties to submit, orally or in writing, the grievances of and differences between them. §34:13A-6(c). If these measures fail, the parties may, by agreement, submit their dispute to arbitration. §34:13A-7.
	Police and Fire Public Interest Arbitration Reform Act, Title 34, Ch. 13A, §§34:13A-14a to 34:13A-16.	Employees performing firefighting and police services. §34:13A-15.	The statute, at the request of either party, provides for mediation, factfinding if mediation fails, and arbitration, if factfinding fails. §34:13A-16. The parties may agree upon different types of arbitration, e.g., conventional, single package arbitration, or issue-by-issue arbitration. *Id.* If the parties cannot agree, the commission shall use conventional arbitration, which addresses all unsettled items.
	Title 34, Ch. 13B, §§34:13B-1 to 34:13B-27.	Employees of public utilities, e.g., buses, ferries, railways, tunnel companies, electric, heat, power, gas, sewer, steam and water, telephone, etc. §34:13B-16.	The statute provides for binding arbitration. §§34:13B-20 and 23.

STATE	STATUTE	COVERED EMPLOYEES	SUMMARY OF IMPASSE RESOLUTION PROVIDED
New York—**This statute was only in effect until July 1, 1999 and has not been reenacted.**[5]	Public Employee Bargaining Act, Ch. 10, Article 7D, §10-7D-1 to 10-7D-26.	Regular nonprobationary employees of a "public employer," which means the state or any political subdivision thereof including municipalities. §§10-7D-4.P and Q. Regular probationary employees in public schools, however, are considered public employees. §10-7D-4.P.	The statute provides for mediation. §10-7D-18A.(4). If unsuccessful, factfinding shall take place. §§10-7D-18A.(5) and (6). If factfinding proves unsuccessful, the unresolved issues will be resolved through the appropriation process, which shall be the final decision. §10-7D-18A(8).

Beyond the statute's provisions, the parties may agree to resolve impasses with other alternatives. §10-7D-18.C. |
New York	Civil Service Law Article VIV, Ch. VII, Part 200, §§200 to 214.	Any person holding a position by appointment or employment in the service of a "public employer," which means the State or any other political subdivision of the state, e.g., county, city, town, village, school district, etc. §§200.6(a) and 7(a).	The statutes permit the parties to enter into written agreements that resolve issues with impartial arbitration. §209.2. If there is no such written agreement, the statute provides for mediation. §209.3(a). If mediation is unsuccessful, factfinding shall take place. §209.3(b). If factfinding is unsuccessful, the public employment relations board "shall have the power to take whatever steps it deems appropriate to resolve the dispute," including making recommendations and assisting in voluntary arbitration. §209.3(d). If the factfinding coupled with the assistance of public employment relations board cannot resolve the dispute, the recommendation from the factfinding process will go to the relevant legislative body that "shall take such action as it deems to be in the public interest, including the interest of public employees involved." §209.3(e).
	Id.	Firefighters and police officers. §209.4.	The statute provides for mediation. §209.4(a). If mediation is unsuccessful, either party may request final and binding arbitration. §§209.4(b) and (d).
	Id.	Employees of the New York City transit authority.	The parties must utilize final and binding arbitration. §§209.5(a) and (e).

---

[5]New Mexico's Public Employee Bargaining Act had a sunset clause that took effect on July 1, 1999. Although State Representative Ben Lujan has sponsored reenactment, and both the House and Senate approved reenactment in 2001, Governor Gary Johnson vetoed the law on April 5, 2001. It is possible the Public Employee Bargaining Act will return as law, thus, a summary of the law as it was in 1999 is provided here.

STATE	STATUTE	COVERED EMPLOYEES	SUMMARY OF IMPASSE RESOLUTION PROVIDED
New York *continued* (New York City)[6]	New York City Collective Bargaining Law, §§1173-1.0 to 1173-11.0.	New York City employees. §1173-3.0.e.	The local law provides for mediation, §1173-7.0.b(2), or factfinding with an impasse panel, §1173-7.0.c(2). After factfinding results in a recommendation, such recommendation may be appealed to the "board of collective bargaining" for review. §1173-7.0.c(4). The board's decision after its review shall be final and binding. §1173-7.0c(4)(f).
North Carolina	Ch. 95, Article 12, §§95-97 to 95-100.	None	Public employees may not join unions. §95-98.
North Dakota	Teachers Representation and Negotiation Act, Title 15, Ch. 15-38.1, §§15-38.1-01 to 15-38.1-14.	Teachers	The statute provides for mediation. §15-38.1-13d.2. If mediation fails, factfinding shall take place. §15-38.1-13d.2.b.(1).
Ohio	Public Employee's Collective Bargaining Act, Title XLI, Ch. 4117, §§4117.01 to 4117.23.	Any person in the service of a "public employer," which means the state or any political sub-division of the state, e.g., county, town, etc. §§4117.01(B) and (C).	The parties may agree to dispute resolution procedures not provided for in the statute. §4117.14(C). If there is no such agreement, the statute provides for mediation. §4117.14(C)(2). If mediation is unsuccessful, factfinding shall commence. §4117.14(C)(3).
	Id.	Members of the police or fire department, highway patrol, sheriff's department, employees of the state school for the deaf or for the blind, employees of the public employee retirement system, corrections officers, guards at penal or mental institutions, psychiatric attendants at mental health forensic facilities, or youth leaders at juvenile correctional facilities.	If mediation and factfinding is unsuccessful as provided in §§4117.14(C)(2) and (3), the parties must submit to final offer arbitration. The arbitrator shall resolve the dispute by selecting, on an issue-by-issue basis, between each of the party's final settlement offers. §4117.14(G)(7).

STATE	STATUTE	COVERED EMPLOYEES	SUMMARY OF IMPASSE RESOLUTION PROVIDED
Oklahoma	Public Policy of Fire and Police Arbitration Law, Title 11, Ch. 1, Article LI, §§51-101 to 51-113.	Firefighters and police officers. §51-101.	All unresolved issues shall be submitted to arbitration, upon the request of either party. §51-106. The arbitration panel shall select from the competing parties' last best offers. §51-108.4
	Title 70, Ch. 7, §§509.1 to 509.10.	School employees. §509.1.	If the parties did agree to an alternative procedure, the statute provides for factfinding. §§509.7 and 509.7.A. If either party rejects the factfinding recommendations, the parties must negotiate again. §509.7.D. If this is unsuccessful, the local board of education shall forward to the state superintendent of public instruction the factfinding recommendation report and its final disposition of the negotiations impasse. §509.7.E.
Oregon	Title 22, Ch. 243, §§243.650 to 243.782	Any employee of a "public employer," which means the State and the following political subdivisions: cities, counties, community colleges, school districts, special districts, mass transit districts, metropolitan service districts, public service corporations or municipal corporations, and public and quasi-public corporations.	The statute provides for mediation. §243.712. If mediation is unsuccessful, each party shall submit to the mediator the final offer of the party, including a cost summary of the offer. §243.712(2)(b). The parties may, however, voluntarily agree to submit any or all of the issues to final and binding arbitration pursuant to §243.746. §243.712(2)(e). After the final offers are made public, factfinding shall commence upon the joint request of both parties. §243.712(2)(c). The factfinder shall make written findings of fact and recommendations for resolution, which the parties may accept or reject. §243.722(3). If the recommendations are rejected, the factfinder shall publish his or her findings and recommendations. Id. During or after factfinding, the parties may voluntarily agree to submit any or all of the issues in dispute to final and binding arbitration. §243.722(4). The public employer shall have the right to implement all or part of its final offer if an impasse continues after factfinding or the parties did not utilize factfinding after mediation. §243.712(2)(d). The public employees shall have the right to strike. Id.

STATE	STATUTE	COVERED EMPLOYEES	SUMMARY OF IMPASSE RESOLUTION PROVIDED
Oregon *continued*	*Id.*	Police officers, firefighters, correctional institution and mental hospital guards, and 911 emergency reporting telephone workers. §243.736.	If mediation and factfinding is unsuccessful as provided in §§243.712 and 243.722, the parties must engage in final and binding arbitration. §§243.742(2) and 243.752. The arbitrator shall select only one of the last best offer packages submitted by the parties. §243.746(5).
Pennsylvania	Title 43, Ch. 19, §§1101.101 to 1101.2301.	Any individual employed by a "public employer," which means the state and its political subdivisions. §§1101.301(1) and (2).	The statute provides for mediation. §1101.801. If mediation is unsuccessful, factfinding shall commence. §1101.802. The parties may agree to voluntary binding arbitration, but the arbitration decision requires legislative enactment to become binding. §1101.804.
	Id.	Guards at prisons or mental hospitals and employees directly involved with and necessary to the functioning of the courts. §1101.805.	If mediation is unsuccessful under §1101.801, the parties must then submit to final and binding arbitration, but the arbitration decision requires legislative enactment to become binding. §1101.805.
	Title 43, Ch. 7, §§213.1 to 213.16.	Public utility employees, i.e., electric, gas, water, and steam heat services. §213.2(a).	The statute provides for mediation. §213.5. If mediation is unsuccessful, each party shall submit a final best offer to the mediator. §213.7. The bargaining unit employees shall vote whether to accept the employer's final best offer. *Id.* If the employer's offer is rejected, the parties shall participate in binding arbitration, where the arbitrators shall make findings upon the issues presented. §§213.8, 213.11, and 213.12. The arbitrators will not consider issues not identified to the mediator. §213.11.
	Title 24, Ch. 1, Article XI-A, §§11-1101-A to 11-1172-A.	Public school employees. §1101-A.	The statute provides for mediation. §1121-A. If mediation is unsuccessful, factfinding shall commence. §1122-A. If factfinding fails, final best offer arbitration shall take place. §1125-A. The parties may agree on the arbitration procedure, but if the parties cannot agree, the mediator shall select the procedure. §1125-A(c).

STATE	STATUTE	COVERED EMPLOYEES	SUMMARY OF IMPASSE RESOLUTION PROVIDED
Rhode Island	Title 36, Ch. 11 §§36-11-1 to 36-11-11.	State Employees. §36-11-1(a).	The statute provides for mediation. §36-11-7.1. If mediation is unsuccessful, conciliation and factfinding shall commence. §36-11-8. If conciliation and factfinding is unsuccessful, the parties shall engage in final and binding arbitration. §36-11-9.
	State Police Arbitration Act, Title 28, Ch. 9.5, §§28-9.5-1 to 28-9.5-17.	State police officers. §§28-9.5-1 and 28-9.5-3.	The statute provides for arbitration. §28-9.5-7.
	911 Employee's Arbitration Act, Title 28, Ch. 9.6, §§28-9.6-1 to 28-9.6-16.	Employees of the State's 911 emergency telephone system. §§28-9.6-1 and 28-9.6-3.	The statute provides for arbitration. §28-9.6-7.
	Title 28, Ch. 9.4, §§28-9.4-1 to 29.9.4-19.	Municipal employees of any political subdivision of the state, e.g., town, city, borough, district, etc. §§28-9.4-2(a) and (b). Teachers, police officers, and firefighters. §28-9.4-2(b)(3).	The statute provides for mediation and conciliation. §28-9.4-10. If mediation and conciliation fail or are not requested, either party may request arbitration. *Id.* Mediation is compulsory if negotiations have not led to an agreement 30 days before the municipal employer must appropriate money. *Id.*
	Title 28, Ch. 9.3, §28-9.3-1 to 28-9.3-16.	Teachers. §28-9.3-1.	The statute provides for mediation and conciliation. §28-9.3-9. If mediation and conciliation fail or are not requested, either party may request arbitration. *Id.* Mediation is compulsory if negotiations have not led to an agreement 30 days before the municipal employer must appropriate money. *Id.*
	Firefighters Arbitration Act, Title 28, Ch. 9.1, §28-9.1-1 to 28-9.1-17.	Firefighters. §28-9.1-1.	The statute provides for arbitration. §28-9.1-7.
	Municipal Police Arbitration Act, Title 28, Ch. 9.2, §§28-9.2-1 to 28-9.2-16.	Police officers of any department in any city or town. §§28-9.2-1 and 28-9.2-3(1).	The statute provides for arbitration. §28-9.2-7.

STATE	STATUTE	COVERED EMPLOYEES	SUMMARY OF IMPASSE RESOLUTION PROVIDED
South Carolina		None	Neither the State nor its subdivisions have the obligation or right to enter into a collective bargaining agreement with public employees. (Attorney General Opinion, issued Sept. 27, 1978).
South Dakota	Title 3, Ch. 18, §§3-18-1 to 3-18-17.	Any person employed by the State or any political subdivision thereof. §3-18-1	Either party may request the department of labor to intervene under the provisions of §§60-10-1 to 60-10-3, which provide for conciliation, factfinding, and appointment of "two capable citizens not directly connected with the dispute, one named by each party, to assist in the investigation" and make recommendations to the Secretary of Labor.
Tennessee	Education Professional Negotiations Act, Title 49, Ch. 5, §§49-5-601 to 49-5-613.	Any person employed by any local board of education that requires certification by the State department of education. §49-5-602(11).	The statute provides for mediation. §49-5-613(a). If mediation is unsuccessful, either party may request advisory arbitration. §49-5-613(b).
Texas	The Fire and Police Employee Relations Act, Ch. 174, §§174.001 to 174.007, 174.023, 174.051 to 174.055, 174.101 to 174.109, 174.251 to 174.253.	Firefighters and police officers. §174.003.	The statute provides for mediation. §174.151. The parties may request arbitration instead of mediation. §174.153. Although mediation is optional, arbitration will become mandatory at a certain point. §174.153(b).
Utah		None	Utah provides no law permitting public employees and public employers to create collective bargaining agreements.

STATE	STATUTE	COVERED EMPLOYEES	SUMMARY OF IMPASSE RESOLUTION PROVIDED
Vermont	State Employees Labor Relations Act, Title 3, Ch. 27, §§901 to 1006.	Any individual employed by the State, State colleges, or University of Vermont. §901(5).	The statute provides for mediation. §925(a). If mediation is unsuccessful, either party may request factfinding. §925(c). If factfinding is unsuccessful, each party shall submit its last best offer to the factfinding panel, which may hold hearings. §925(i). The factfinding panel shall choose between the last best offers of the parties. The panel's decision shall be binding for the University of Vermont, but the panel must recommend its choice to the State's General Assembly for appropriations. *Id.*
	Vermont Municipal Labor Relations Act, Title 21, Ch. 22, §1721 to 1735.	Any employee of a "municipal employer," which means any subdivisions of the State, e.g., city, town, village, fire district, lighting district, etc. §§1722(12) and (13).	The statute provides for mediation. §1731. If mediation is unsuccessful, factfinding shall commence. §1732. If factfinding is unsuccessful, arbitration shall commence. §1733.
	Title 16, Ch. 57, Subchapter 1, §§1981 to 2010.	Teachers. §1981(5).	The statute provides for mediation. §2006. If mediation is not selected or is unsuccessful, either party may request factfinding. §2007.
	Title 3, Ch. 28, §§1080 to 1043.	Judiciary Employees. §§1010 and 1011(8).	The statute provides for mediation. § 1018(a). If mediation is unsuccessful, the parties may request factfinding. §1018(c). If the parties do not request factfinding, the State Labor Relations Board shall appoint a factfinder. *Id.* If factfinding fails, the parties shall submit their last best offers to the board. § 1019(i). The board may hold hearings. *Id.* The board shall select between the last best of the parties. *Id.* Alternatively, the parties may agree in advance to a mediation and final and binding arbitration procedure. §1019.

STATE	STATUTE	COVERED EMPLOYEES	SUMMARY OF IMPASSE RESOLUTION PROVIDED
Virginia	Title 40.1, Ch. 4, Article 2.1, §§40.1-57.2 and 40.1-57.3.	None	No state, county, municipal, or like governing body may recognize any labor union of any public employees or collectively bargain with such union. §40.1-57.2.
Washington	Title 28B, Ch. 28B.52, §§28B.52.010 to 28B.52.900.	Academic Employees of any college district, e.g., teachers, counselors, librarians, etc. §28B.52.020.	The statute provides for mediation. §28B.52.060. If mediation is unsuccessful, either party may request the "assistance and advice" of the Public Employment Relations Commission. *Id.*
	Public Employees Collective Bargaining Act, Title 41, Ch. 41.56, §§41.56.010 to 41.56.960.	"Uniformed Personnel," which includes law enforcement officers, correctional employees, peace officers, security forces, firefighters, port district employees, dispatchers of fire or emergency medical services, and advanced life support technicians. §41.56.030(7).	The statute provides for mediation. §41.56.440. If mediation is unsuccessful, then final and binding arbitration shall commence. §41.56.450.
	Education Employment Relations Act, Title 41, Ch. 59, §§41.59.010 to 41.59.950.	Any certificated employee of a school district. §41.59.020(4).	The statute provides for mediation. §41.59.120(1). If mediation is unsuccessful, either party may request factfinding. §41.59.120(2).
	Title 47, Ch. 47.64, §§47.64.005 to 47.64.280.	Any employee of the marine transportation division of the department of transportation. §47.64.011(5).	The statute mandates that the parties attempt to agree upon an impasse procedure as the first step in bargaining. §47.64.200. If the parties cannot agree, the statute's procedures will apply. *Id.* The statute provides for mediation. §47.64.210. If mediation is unsuccessful, binding arbitration shall commence. §47.64.240(1). The arbitrators shall, by majority vote, select the most reasonable offer of the final offers submitted by each party on each impasse item. §47.64240(11).

STATE	STATUTE	COVERED EMPLOYEES	SUMMARY OF IMPASSE RESOLUTION PROVIDED
West Virginia		None	While public employees may join unions and government employers may discuss wages, hours, and working conditions with such unions, the final determination of wages, hours, and working conditions rests exclusively with the governmental authorities "and cannot be delegated away." (Attorney General Opinion, issue July 1962).
Wisconsin	Municipal Employment Relations Act, Ch. 111, Subchapter III, §§111.50 to 111.64	Any individual employed by a public utility employer, e.g., water, light, heat, gas, electric, transportation, or communication. §111.51(5)(a).	The statute provides for conciliation. §111.54. If conciliation fails after 15 days, arbitration shall commence. §111.55.
	Ch. 111, Subchapter IV, §111.70	Any individual employed by a municipal employer. §111.70(i). Law enforcement employees and firefighters are covered elsewhere.	The statute provides that the municipal employees' union and municipal employer shall exchange collective bargaining proposals. §111.70(4)(cm)2. The statute then provides for mediation. §111.70(4)(cm)3. If mediation is unsuccessful, interest arbitration is available by petition. §111.70(4)6. Before interest arbitration commences, the Employment Relations Commission shall investigate whether the parties used other available procedures, e.g., mediation, to settle the dispute. §111.70(4)6.am. During this investigation, the parties must submit their single final offers on all issues in dispute. *Id.* If impasse is not resolved prior to the completion of arbitration, the arbitrator will determine which final offer is best. §111.70(4)6.d. If an impasse is reached on economic issues between a municipal employer and a school district professional employees' union, the employer may avoid interest arbitration if the Employment Relations Commission deems that the employer's economic offer is a "qualified economic offer" as defined in the statute, which addresses, e.g., fringe benefits and raises.

STATE	STATUTE	COVERED EMPLOYEES	SUMMARY OF IMPASSE RESOLUTION PROVIDED
Wisconsin *continued*	Ch. 111, Subchapter IV, §111.77.	Fire departments' and city and county law enforcement agencies' employees. §111.77.	The statute provides for mediation. §111.77(e). If mediation is unsuccessful, compulsory, final, and binding arbitration shall commence. §111.77(f)(3). Two forms of arbitration are available. The first form shall only occur if the parties agreed to such a procedure prior to the arbitration. This procedure involves the arbitrator determining all issues involving wages, hours, and conditions of employment. §§111.77(4)(a) and (5). The second procedure involves an investigation to determine each issue in dispute and the final offer of each party. §111.77(4)(b). The arbitrator shall select the final offer of one of the parties. *Id.*
	State Employment Labor Relations Act, Ch. 111, Subchapter V, §§111.80 to 111.91.	State employees. §111.81(7).	The statute provides for mediation. §111.87. If mediation fails, factfinding shall commence. §111.88.
Wyoming	Title 27, Ch. 10, §§27-10-101 to 27-10-109.	Firefighters. §27-10-101.	The statute mandates arbitration. §27-10-105.

6. CONSTITUTIONALITY OF BINDING INTEREST ARBITRATION

Federal constitutional questions focus primarily on preemption questions, "exploring whether state laws regulating the workplace run afoul of the Supremacy Clause."[134] Binding interest arbitration has been challenged on state constitutional grounds in a number of states on delegability issues. The challenge goes to whether binding interest arbitration involves the delegation of governmental powers to private parties. The attack has succeeded in some cases but more often has failed.[135] For example, in holding binding interest arbitration for firefighters to be unconstitutional, the Utah Supreme Court explained:

> [T]he act authorizes the appointment of arbitrators, who are private citizens with no responsibility to the public, to make binding determinations affecting the quantity, quality, and cost of an essential public service. The legislature may not surrender its legislative authority to a body wherein the public interest is subjected to the interest of a group, which may be antagonistic to the public interest.
>
> Although it is not dispositive of the delegation issue, in this case the legislature failed to provide any statutory standards in the act or any protection against arbitrariness, such as hearings with procedural safeguards, legislative supervision, and judicial review.[136]

The Colorado Supreme Court similarly struck down a city charter provision for binding arbitration of police interest disputes. The court held that the provision was an unconstitutional delegation of legislative power, because "governmental decisionmaking (e.g., setting budgets, salaries, and other terms and conditions of public employment) must be accountable to the citizens," and "[b]inding arbitration removes these decisions from the aegis of elected representatives, placing them in the hands of an outside person who has no accountability to the public."[137]

---

[134]Gottesman, *Labor, Employment and Benefit Decisions of the Supreme Court's 1995–96 Term*, 12 LAB. LAW. 325 (1997). For an overview and history of state approaches to interest arbitration, see Martin, *Fixing the Fiscal Police & Firetrap: A Critique of New Jersey's Compulsory Interest Arbitration Act*, 18 SETON HALL LEGIS. J. 59, 68 (1993). *See also* Lawlor, *Validity and Construction of Statutes or Ordinances Providing for Arbitration of Labor Disputes Involving Public Employees*, 68 A.L.R. 3D 855 (1976 & Supp. 1992).

[135]The range of views can be seen in the challenges to the Ohio statute shortly after it was passed in 1984. The Ohio Supreme Court found the Ohio Public Employee's Collective Bargaining Act unconstitutional to the extent it mandated binding arbitration of disputes on municipal safety employee wages and benefits, because the provision conflicted with the city's constitutional right to local self-government. City of Rocky River v. State Employment Relations Bd., 530 N.E.2d 1, 129 LRRM 2975 (Ohio 1988). However, on reconsideration, the Ohio Supreme Court held that the Ohio Public Employee Collective Bargaining Act, Ohio Rev. Code ch. 4117, and specifically Ohio Rev. Code §4117.14(I) are constitutional as they fall within the General Assembly's authority to enact employee welfare legislation pursuant to §34, art. II, of the Ohio Constitution; the home-rule provision may not impair, limit, or negate the Act. City of Rocky River v. State Employment Relations Bd., 539 N.E.2d 103, 131 LRRM 2952, 2965 (Ohio 1989). *See also* O'Reilly, *More Magic with Less Smoke: A Ten Year Retrospective on Ohio's Collective Bargaining Law*, 19 DAYTON L. REV. 1 (1993); *Note, Binding Interest Arbitration in the Public Sector: Is It Constitutional?*, 18 WM. & MARY L. REV. 787 (1977).

[136]Salt Lake City v. Fire Fighters (IAFF) Locals 593, 1645, 1654, & 2064, 563 P.2d 786, 789, 95 LRRM 2383 (Utah 1977).

[137]Greeley Police Union v. City Council of Greeley, 553 P.2d 790, 792, 93 LRRM 2382 (Colo. 1976). In *Greeley*, the arbitration was compulsory, but it is apparent that it was the

The California Supreme Court declared that a statute that empowered unions representing safety forces to declare an impasse in contract negotiations and required the submission of unresolved economic issues to final-offer binding arbitration by a tripartite board violated the constitutional provisions prohibiting the legislature from delegating to a private body the power to control or interfere with county money and requiring that the county's governing body provide for the compensation of employees.[138]

In contrast, the New Jersey Supreme Court held a statutory provision for binding interest arbitration to be constitutional, and in doing so the court surveyed decisions of other states also upholding binding interest arbitration against constitutional challenges:

> The concept of compulsory and binding arbitration of labor negotiation as well as grievance disputes in the public sector has been coming more and more into favor. . . . The New Jersey Legislature has not only adopted this procedure in the statutory section under consideration [applying to mass transit employees], but also has recently imposed compulsory arbitration for resolution of such disputes between municipal bodies and their police and firemen. . . .
>
> The principal objection made to compulsory and binding arbitration of labor negotiation disputes in the public sector is that it constitutes an unlawful delegation of public authority and responsibility to a private person or persons. However, most of the cases that have dealt with the question have sustained the concept as an innovative way to avoid the morass of deadlocked labor disputes in the public sector. Nevertheless, in doing so, there must be excluded from the arbitration process matters involving governmental policy determinations which involve an exercise of delegated police power.
>
> Some of the cases reason that there is no improper delegation involved because the arbitrator is deemed a public official when performing functions which are public in nature. . . . Others hold that legislative delegation is not illegal as long as adequate standards and safeguards are provided. . . . Still other decisions hold that statutory provisions for compulsory arbitration of labor disputes in the public sector do not really entail the delegation of a governmental function at all, but rather in the exercise of that function, merely utilize a well-established procedure for the resolution of deadlocked labor disputes. . . . Some authorities are critical of the standards rule as applied to delegation of power. They suggest that procedural safeguards and judicial review are more important than a requirement of standards.[139]

---

binding status of the award (rather than the mere fact that use of arbitration was compulsory) that led to the holding of unconstitutionality. The Colorado Supreme Court reaffirmed its *Greeley* views in City & County of Denver v. Denver Fire Fighters, 663 P.2d 1032, 1037–40 (Colo. 1983), but distinguished binding grievance arbitration and upheld its constitutionality when limited to questions of contract interpretation. *See also* Transit Auth. of Lexington v. Transit Union Local 639, 698 S.W.2d 520 (Ky. Sup. Ct. 1985).

[138]County of Riverside v. Superior Court, 30 Cal. 4th 278, 66 P. 3d 718, 132 Cal. Rptr. 2d 713, 172 LRRM 2545 (2003).

[139]Transit Union Div. 540 v. Mercer County Improvement Auth., 386 A.2d 1290, 1293, 98 LRRM 2526 (N.J. 1978) (citations omitted). The court said that the statute contained sufficient standards to guide arbitrators in exercising their authority and contained clear procedural requirements, and that absence of an express provision for judicial review meant that one should be implied because arbitration was made compulsory. *Id.* at 1294. *See also* City of Rocky River, Ohio v. Ohio Employment Relations Bd., 43 Ohio St. 3d 1, 539 N.E.2d 103, 131 LRRM 2952 (1989); Carofano v. Bridgeport, 196 Conn. 623, 495 A.2d 1011, 1016, 123 LRRM 2408 (1985) (holding that statute set forth adequate guidance for the arbitrator as well as reasonable review procedures and, therefore, did not constitute an improper delegation of legislative authority, and stating that accountability "remains viable in the ability of the legislators to terminate or modify any delegation of legislative power that has been made"). Constitutional challenges to compulsory and binding arbitration statutes for public-sector

The following tables list state interest arbitration statutes along with court decisions about their constitutionality.

---

interest disputes have failed, inter alia, in Maine, Massachusetts, Michigan, Minnesota, New Jersey, New York, Oregon, Pennsylvania, Rhode Island, Wisconsin, and Washington, but have succeeded in California, Colorado, Ohio, South Dakota, and Utah. The constitutionality of compulsory interest arbitration was upheld by Michigan in *City of Detroit v. Police Officers Ass'n*, 294 N.W.2d 68, 105 LRRM 3083 (Mich. 1980), discussed in section 8., "Standards in Public-Sector Disputes," below. For discussion of compulsory arbitration in general, see Chapter 1, section 7.A., "Compulsory Arbitration."

Table 1: Mandatory Arbitration Statutes

State/Statute	Statutory Requirements	Key Cases
Alaska: AS 23.40.200 (2000)	Mandatory interest arbitration for all public employees; different trigger for arbitration for each of 3 classes of employees	*Anchorage v. Anchorage Police Dep't Employees' Ass'n*, 839 P.2d 1080 (Alaska 1992). Municipal charter provisions for binding interest arbitration for limited number of public sector employees was valid delegation of legislative authority, where ordinance contained sufficient standards to limit arbitrator's discretion.
Colorado: C.R.S. 8-3-112, 8-3-113 (2000)	Mandatory interest arbitration for employees of government "authorities" if collective bargaining reaches an impasse and the Director of Colorado Department of Labor denies the employee group a right to strike	*FOP v. City of Commerce City*, 996 P.2d 133 (Colo. 2000). City charter provision creating permanent panel of arbitrators for binding interest arbitration to resolve impasses in collective bargaining with police officers contained the political accountability required by constitutional prohibition against delegation of legislative power, where the elected city council appointed the panel and retained continuing authority to add or remove arbitrators.
Iowa: Iowa Code §20.17, 20.19	Mandatory interest arbitration for public employees	
Washington: Rev. Code Wash. (ARCW) §41.56.460 (2000)	Mandatory interest arbitration for uniformed public employees upon an impasse in negotiations	*Spokane v. Spokane Police Guild*, 87 Wash. 2d 457, 553 P.2d 1316 (1976). Statute providing for compulsory arbitration of public employee labor disputes, including wage increase demands, does not constitute unconstitutional delegation of legislative power, and does not violate state constitutional prohibition against legislative taxation of cities for municipal purposes; time table deadlines for conduct of arbitration would be construed as directory rather than mandatory, upon showing of good cause, in view of complex mediation, fact finding, and arbitration procedures. *City of Everett v. Fire Fighters, Local 350*, 87 Wash. 2d 572 (1976). This section does not violate the constitutional home rule powers of cities.

Table 2: Statutes Requiring Interest Arbitration at Party's Request

State/Statute	Statutory Requirements	Key Cases
Connecticut: Conn. Gen. Stat §7-474, §5-276a (1999)	Mandatory binding interest arbitration for state and municipal employees for specific issues at the request of one or both parties	
Illinois: 5 ILCS 315/14	Mandatory binding interest arbitration for firefighters and police officers at the request of one of the negotiating parties	
Maine: 26 M.R.S. §965 (1999)	Mandatory binding interest arbitration for public employees at the request of one of the negotiating parties	*Superintending School Committee v. Bangor Education Assoc.*, 433 A.2d 383 (Me. 1981). Regarding the constitutionality of the provision of the Municipal Public Employees Labor Relations Law that empowers private arbitration panels to determine in binding fashion certain disputed issues upon the request of one of the bargaining parties, standards and safeguards were adequate to meet the requirement of the state and federal constitutions. Formulation of rigid standards for the guidance of arbitrators in dealing with complex and often volatile issues would be impractical, and might destroy the flexibility necessary for the arbitrators to carry out the legislative policy of promoting the improvement of the relationship between public employers and their employees. The Act governing this arbitration affords the bargaining parties certain inherent standards and provides them with procedural safeguards which meet the constitutional tests.
Michigan: MSA §17.455(31), §17.455(33) [MCL §423.231] (2000)	Mandatory binding interest arbitration for firefighters and police officers upon request by one party to the negotiations	*Detroit v. Detroit Police Officers Ass'n*, 408 Mich. 410 (1980). Act providing for compulsory interest arbitration of municipal police and fire department disputes as amended did not impermissibly usurp constitutionally vested home rule powers. Statute providing for compulsory interest arbitration of municipal police and fire department disputes

Table 2 continued

State/Statute	Statutory Requirements	Key Cases
Michigan *continued*		did not represent unconstitutional delegation of power where statute provided reasonably precise standards to guide exercise of delegated authority. *Metropolitan Council No. 23 & Local 1277 v. Center Line,* 414 Mich. 642 (1982). The statute, which provides for compulsory arbitration in labor disputes involving municipal police and fire departments, is clearly constitutional. The standards provided are as reasonably precise as the subject matter requires or permits, and there is adequate provision for political accountability. However, the legislature did not intend to give an arbitration panel unbridled authority to compel agreement on permissive subjects of bargaining for which parties have no duty to bargain under PERA. The compulsory arbitration panel exceeded its authority in awarding the inclusion of a layoff clause. A municipal employer's initial decision to lay off employees is not a mandatory subject of bargaining, although the effect of such a decision is a mandatory subject.
New Jersey: N.J. Stat. §34:13A-16 (2000)	Mandatory binding interest arbitration for firefighters and police officers when initiated by one of the negotiating parties and approved by the labor commission	*Hillsdale PBA Local 207 v. Hillsdale,* 263 N.J. Super. 163 (1993). Unlike arbitration as normally understood, so called "interest arbitration" is not consensual arbitration, but is mandated by statute in public sector for impasse disputes between municipal public employers and police and fire fighters, and is essentially restricted to last final offer (unless all parties otherwise agree). *Amalgamated Transit Union v. Mercer County Improvement Authority,* 386 A.2d 1290 (N.J. S.Ct. 1978). Statute providing for compulsory grievance and interest arbitration of labor disputes in public sector is constitutional, given explicit statutory standards including arbitrable procedures

Table 2 continued

State/Statute	Statutory Requirements	Key Cases
New Jersey *continued*		and provision limiting scope of bargaining to wages and other conditions of employment, and given inherent standards including requirement that arbitrator consider public interest and impact of decision on public welfare; since arbitration is compulsory, judicial review is available if award is arbitrary or if arbitrator abuses powers delegated to him, and judicial review should extend to consideration of whether arbitration award is supported by substantial credible evidence.
New York: NY CLS Civ. S. §209 (2000)	Mandatory binding interest arbitration at the request of either party or the public employee relations board	*Amsterdam v. Helsby*, 27 N.Y. 2d 19, 371 N.Y.S. 2d 404 (1975). A statute requiring binding arbitration of disputes between cities and their organized fire and police forces was held not to be an unconstitutional delegation of legislative discretion or lawmaking authority. Without engaging in extensive discussion, the court pointed out that there was no constitutional prohibition against the legislative delegation of power, with reasonable safeguards and standards, to an agency or commission established to administer an enactment. In this case, the court said the legislature had delegated to a public employment relations board, and through it to ad hoc arbitration panels, its constitutional authority to regulate the compensation and working conditions of public safety employees, in the limited situation where an impasse occurs, and also established specific standards which such a panel must follow. Such delegation was both proper and reasonable, the court concluded. *Buffalo v. New York State Public Employment Relations Board*, 363 N.Y.S. 2d 896 (1975). A statute requiring binding arbitration of disputes between cities and their organized fire and police forces did not violate the city's due process rights. The statute is valid and constitutional in all respects.

Table 2 continued

State/Statute	Statutory Requirements	Key Cases
Oregon: ORS §243 et seq. (1999)	Mandatory binding arbitration for public employees at declaration of impasse by either party or mediator	*Medford Firefighters Ass'n v. Medford*, 40 Or. App. 519 (1979). Statute providing for compulsory interest-arbitration in public sector does not violate "home rule" provisions of state constitution, given predominance of substantive state policy of requiring arbitration as quid pro quo for prohibition of strikes by firemen; nor does statute constitute unconstitutional delegation of legislative power to arbitrator, since statute provides adequate statutory guidelines for precluding arbitrary or discriminatory action by arbitrator, and since arbitrator in carrying out specified statutory functions acts in public capacity.
Pennsylvania: 43 P.S. §217.4 (1999)	Mandatory binding arbitration for firefighters and police officers upon request by either of the negotiating parties	*Amalgamated Transit Union v. Port Authority of Allegheny County*, 417 Pa. 299 (1965). Where a statute provided for arbitration of labor disputes between a transit authority and its employees in the event of a failure to reach agreement on contract issues by collective bargaining, the wording of the statute being that in the event of failure to agree, the authority "shall" offer to submit such dispute to arbitration, it was held that the word "shall" in the statutory provision was imperative and required the authority to submit to arbitration.
Wisconsin: W.S.A. 111.70 et seq. (1999)	Mandatory interest arbitration for firefighters and police officers upon request of either of the negotiating parties	*Brennan v. Employment Relations Comm.*, 112 Wis. 2d 38 (1983). Statutes requiring binding interest arbitration for police and firemen in "cities of the 1st class" did not constitute violation of equal protection, even though City of Milwaukee was only city in Wisconsin in that class, where it was within legislature's power to classify cities into classes and enact legislation applicable only to various of those classes, and particularly where statutory scheme for cities such as Milwaukee was not significantly different from that applicable to municipalities not of first class.

Table 2 continued

State/Statute	Statutory Requirements	Key Cases
Wisconsin *continued*		*La Crosse Professional Police Assoc. v. City of La. Crosse*, 212 Wis. 2d 90 (1997). In interest arbitration, arbitrator exceeded his statutory authority to select final offer of one of parties and then issue award incorporating offer without modification, by accepting city employer's final offer but awarding health insurance provisions that clearly differed from wording of final offer, such that modifications went beyond mere interpretation of offer.

Table 3: Permissive Interest Arbitration Statutes

State/Statute	Statutory Requirements	Key Cases
Hawaii: HRS §89-2, §89-11 (2000)	Permissive binding interest arbitration for public employees upon procedure agreed to by the parties or by requested decision of the employment board	*Board of Educ. v. Hawaii Pub. Employment Relations Bd.*, 56 Haw. 85, 528 P.2d 809 (1974). The board, on its own motion, can declare that an impasse exists only after it reaches a determination that the party contending that an impasse exists has been bargaining in good faith.
Massachusetts: Mass. Ann. Laws ch. 150E, §9 (2000)	Permissive binding interest arbitration for public employees upon mutual request of the parties	*Town of Arlington v. Board of Conciliation and Arbitration*, 370 Mass. 769, 352 N.E.2d 914 (1976). Statute providing for binding arbitration of police and firefighter job demands does not constitute unconstitutional delegation of legislative power, does not violate home rule provisions of state constitution respecting powers of municipalities, and does not contravene "one-man, one-vote" principle applicable to units of local government with general responsibility and power for local affairs; arbitration awards relating to wages and benefits may be enforced through mandatory special appropriations by municipal finance committees and town meetings to meet arbitration awards.

7. Sources of Standards of Interest Disputes

In the private sector, the parties sometimes will specify, in their stipulation for interest arbitration, the standards or definite criteria to be observed.[140] In the public sector, the standards are likely to be set by statute. Even if the parties do not stipulate the standards to be observed, or if those specified by the legislature are not exclusive, the arbitrator generally will make an award based on one or more of the commonly accepted standards. But, even in those cases, the selection of the standards used is still determined by the parties, though indirectly, because an arbitrator generally will not apply any given standard unless evidence has been introduced to support its application. The standards used by arbitrators are neither divorced from reality nor artificially created. They are, generally speaking, the very same ones that are used by the parties in their negotiations.

The existence of a palette of commonly used standards lends a degree of predictability to interest arbitration, but the arbitrator's discretion remains quite broad. The arbitrator must determine the weight to be given to each of the standards applied in the given case.[141] Rarely will the arbitrator's consideration be limited to a single standard. The freedom to weigh the standards, to "mix the porridge," so to speak, means that the results will depend on the way the standards are applied.[142] It may not often be possible or desirable for the arbitrator to make a strict application of the relevant standards.

---

[140]*See* Air New Zealand, 77 LA 667, 674 (Feller, 1981); Munsingwear, Inc., 65 LA 997, 997–98, 1001 (Blum, 1975); University of Chicago Hosps. & Clinics, 63 LA 824, 825 (Mueller, 1974). For discussion of the pros and cons of this practice, see Handsaker, The Submission Agreement in Contract Arbitration (Univ. of Pa. Press 1952). It has been emphasized that only the parties, not an arbitrator, should place limitations in the collective bargaining agreement concerning the standards that may be observed by future interest arbitrators. United Traction Co., 27 LA 309, 317–18 (Scheiber, 1956). For a discussion of various "arbitration systems," see Gershenfeld, *Alternatives for Labor Arbitrators*, 53 Disp. Resol. J. 53 (Feb. 1998); Buckheit & Ackerman, *Arbitration Forums Revisited: I. Interest Arbitration, in* Arbitration 1990: New Perspectives on Old Issues, Proceedings of the 43d Annual Meeting of NAA 171–89 (Gruenberg ed., BNA Books 1991). For standards (some particularly interesting and unique) specified by collective bargaining agreement for use in baseball salary arbitration, and standards prohibited by the agreement, see Grebey, *Another Look at Baseball's Salary Arbitration*, 38 Arb. J. No. 4, at 24, 26 (1983).

[141]Oneida County, Wis., Sheriff's Dep't, 100 LA 581, 583 (Flaten, 1992) ("It is the arbitrator who must make the decision of determining which particular factors are more important in resolving a contested issue under the singular facts of a case.").

[142]"While there are familiar objective wage criteria to guide an arbitrator in a task of this kind, there is an area of discretion left to him in deciding which criteria are most appropriate or controlling. And persons with equal intelligence and integrity might of course differ as to the applicability of any one or number of criteria or as to the weight to be given to them." Houston Chronicle Publ'g Co., 56 LA 487, 491 (Platt, 1971). For affirmation of the arbitrator's right to decide which standards are to be accorded weight in the given case, see *In re Hopkins*, 13 LA 716 (N.Y. Sup. Ct. 1949); City of Missoula, Mont., 2002 WL 1980143 (Snow, 2002); City of Altus, Okla., 105 LA 277 (Neas, Perkins, & Riddle, 1995); Clark County, 1993 WL 790350 (Grace, 1993); Pullman Police Officers' Guild, 1992 WL 717452 (Axon, 1992); City of Mound, Minn., 93 LA 1017 (Fogelberg, 1989). Where the submission limited him to consideration of five specified factors and required him to indicate how each of the factors affected his award, the arbitrator explained his authority as follows:

As the arbitrator reads the stipulation, he is required to determine whether a wage increase is justified by considering only the factors listed therein. On the other hand, it does not appear that all of the factors must necessarily be considered of the same or equal importance. Rather, their relative importance is for the Arbitrator to determine. He is merely cautioned not to consider any other factors.

Keeping in mind the circumstances of the parties, the standards must be applied so that the end result provides a workable solution satisfactory to both sides.[143]

The weighing and balancing process is illustrated by the following statement:

> The adjudication of the various factors which are material to this determination have been carefully and conscientiously weighed by the arbitrator. This case involves a just and equitable evaluation of the totality of the considerations herein described and requires that each material factor be given its proper weight, with the final award representing a fair determination of the entire issue.[144]

Sometimes the opinion is opaque, giving no indication of what standards were considered in arriving at the award.[145] At other times it requires Delphic divination to determine the weight given by the arbitrator to any particular standard.

In the final analysis, both the relevant standards and the relative weight to be given to them depend on evidence submitted by the parties. Arbitrators are properly "unwilling to enter into the field of speculation."[146]

Several surveys of public-sector interest arbitration decisions have arrived at similar, if not identical, findings regarding the standards interest arbitrators use. A survey of 995 police salary decisions revealed that the criteria arbitrators cited most often were salary comparability, ability to pay,

---

H. Boker & Co., 12 LA 608, 610 (Feinberg, 1949). Where the New Jersey Public Utilities Disputes Act provided that decisions should be based on the five standards set forth in the statute, so far as applicable to the matter in dispute, a decision could not be based on consideration of only one of the five standards. New Jersey Bell Tel. Co., 15 LA 238, 244 (N.J. 1950). For views concerning the extent of consideration that must be given to the various standards listed in statutes covering public-sector disputes, see section 8., "Standards in Public-Sector Disputes," below.

[143]The arbitrator's freedom to fulfill this task will be restricted if final-offer arbitration is being utilized, and even more so where it is the "total package" rather than the "issue-by-issue" variety of final-offer arbitration. For related discussion, see section 5., "Public-Sector Interest-Arbitration Legislation," above. Sometimes the parties, as reasonable persons and aided by discussions and arguments made in the course of arbitration proceedings on an interest issue, may be able to dispose of the issue themselves. See, e.g., Air New Zealand, 77 LA 667, 670 (Feller, 1981). In the course of the proceedings, the parties were also able to agree on the disposition of other issues, as the arbitrator explained: "As the meetings progressed, and with some assistance from me when I indicated how I would probably decide, the parties were able to negotiate settlement of most of" the approximately 30 disputed issues. Id. at 669.

[144]Baker & Co., 7 LA 350, 353 (Kirsh, 1947). See also City of Manitowoc, Wis., 108 LA 140, 145 (Michelstetter, 1997); Blue Earth County, Minn., 90 LA 718, 720 (Rutzick, 1988); Nodak Rural Elec. Coop., 78 LA 1119, 1124 (Eisele, 1982); City of Clinton, Iowa, 72 LA 190, 196 (Winton, 1979); Oscoda Area, Mich., Sch. Bd. of Educ., 55 LA 568, 579 (Bloch, 1970); Cummins Sales, 54 LA 1069, 1074 (Seinsheimer, 1971); Town of Tiverton, R.I., 52 LA 1301, 1304 (Schmidt, Jr., 1969); Green Tree Borough, Pa., 51 LA 994, 996 (Florey, 1968); Port Auth. of Allegheny County, 50 LA 1103, 1115 (Platt, 1968); Atlanta Newspapers, Inc., 42 LA 548, 553–54 (Dworkin, 1964); San Jose Mercury & News, 29 LA 96, 100 (Ross, 1957); Mohawk Carpet Mills, 26 LA 651, 659 (Shipman, 1956).

[145]See Town of Manchester, 68 LA 1097 (Post, 1977); American Overseas Airlines, 6 LA 226 (Lewis, 1947).

[146]St. Louis Pub. Serv. Co., 8 LA 397, 405 (Holland, Anderson, & Hollingsworth, 1947). See also Sturgis Hosp., 112 LA 181, 183 (Knott, 1998); Cummins Sales, 54 LA 1069, 1072 (Seinsheimer, 1971).

and inflation/cost of living, in that order.[147] With regard to salary comparability, the arbitrators referred far more frequently to salaries in other police
departments than to salaries in other occupational groups.[148] Interviews with
interest arbitrators in Wisconsin disclosed that the arbitrators look first to
internal wage-settlement patterns. If no clear pattern of percentage increases
is observed, they next look at external comparability factors, followed by the
cost-of-living and ability-to-pay criteria.[149] Another survey found that the
criteria stressed by the parties are comparability, ability to pay, and cost of
living, "although cost of living has been given less emphasis in recent years."[150]

One study explained why arbitrators do not emphasize the ability-to-
pay criterion:

> The general conclusion [of the arbitrators interviewed] was that absent a
> specific ability-to-pay argument, the budget carried little weight on its own. . . .
> [T]he majority of arbitrators recognized the self-serving nature of such argu-
> ments. As one arbitrator noted, "any good city budget manager can manipulate
> the budget to look like the city can't afford anything—relying on this type of
> information is not bargaining."[151]

Nonetheless, when faced with serious, well-documented arguments about
a public employer's financial condition, arbitrators will evaluate them, especially if the outcome hinges on the disposition of that issue. Most arbitrators
will critically examine financial data presented to them and raise questions
about such matters as available funds and alternative priorities. An ability-
to-pay argument is likely to carry the most weight when an employer can
demonstrate that it has done everything in its power to overcome an adverse
financial position, both absolutely and in relation to what comparable public
employers have done. However, an arbitrator is more likely to rule in favor
of a union if the employer has not made sufficient taxing efforts as measured
against comparable communities.[152]

8. Standards in Public-Sector Disputes

Many of the same standards or criteria utilized by neutrals in private-
sector interest arbitration cases also have been utilized for similar cases in
the public sector.[153] Indeed, a number of states have directed arbitrators to

---

[147]Feuille & Schwochau, *The Decisions of Interest Arbitrators*, 43 Arb. J. 28, 33 (1988).
[148]*Id.*
[149]Dell'omo, *Wage Disputes in Interest Arbitration: Arbitrators Weigh the Criteria*, 44
Arb. J. 4, 8 (1989).
[150]Doherty, *Trends in Strikes and Interest Arbitration in the Public Sector*, 37 Lab. L.J.
473, 474 (1986).
[151]Dell'omo, 44 Arb. J. at 10.
[152]Krinsky, *Interest Arbitration and Ability to Pay: U.S. Public Sector Experience, in* Arbitration 1988: Emerging Issues for the 1990s, Proceedings of the 41st Annual Meeting of
NAA 197–208 (Gruenberg ed., BNA Books 1989).
[153]Many of the more recent citations for standards discussed elsewhere in this chapter
are public-sector cases. For other writings that give some consideration to standards for
public-sector cases, see Kirschner, *Labor Management Relations in the Public Sector: An
Introductory Overview of Organizing Activities, Bargaining Units, Scope of Bargaining, and
Dispute Resolution Techniques* (American Law Inst. 1998) (cited on Westlaw as SD09 ALI-
ABA 271); Wollett & Chanin, The Law and Practice of Teacher Negotiations (BNA Books
1970); Minami, *Interest Arbitration: Can the Public Sector Afford It? Developing Limitations*

consider factors traditionally taken into account by neutrals in establishing terms of employment in private industry. The Michigan Police and Firemen's Arbitration Act provides, for example:

> Sec. 9. Where there is no agreement between the parties, or where there is an agreement but the parties have begun negotiations or discussions looking to a new agreement or amendment of the existing agreement, and wage rates or other conditions of employment under the proposed new or amended agreement are in dispute, the arbitration panel shall base its findings, opinions and order upon the following factors, as applicable:
> (a)   The lawful authority of the employer.
> (b)   Stipulations of the parties.
> (c)   The interests and welfare of the public and the financial ability of the unit of government to meet those costs.
> (d)   Comparison of the wages, hours and conditions of employment of the employees involved in the arbitration proceedings with the wages, hours and conditions of employment of other employees performing similar services and with other employees generally:
>   (i)   In public employment in comparable communities.
>   (ii)   In private employment in comparable communities.
> (e)   The average consumer prices for goods and services, commonly known as the cost of living.
> (f)   The overall compensation presently received by the employees, including direct wage compensation, vacations, holidays and other excused time, insurance and pensions, medical and hospitalization benefits, the continuity and stability of employment, and all other benefits received.
> (g)   Changes in any of the foregoing circumstances during the pendency of the arbitration proceedings.
> (h)   Such other factors, not confined to the foregoing, which are normally or traditionally taken into consideration in the determination of wages, hours and conditions of employment through voluntary collective bargaining, mediation, fact-finding, arbitration or otherwise between the parties, in the public service or in private employment.[154]

---

on the Process: I. An Overview, in Arbitration Issues for the 1980s, Proceedings of the 34th Annual Meeting of NAA 241 (Stern & Dennis eds., BNA Books 1982); Ellman, Decision-Making in Public-Interest Arbitration: I. Legislative Arbitration in Michigan—A Lateral Glance, in Truth, Lie Detectors, and Other Problems in Labor Arbitration, Proceedings of the 31st Annual Meeting of NAA 291 (Stern & Dennis eds., BNA Books 1979); Morris, The Role of Interest Arbitration in a Collective Bargaining System, in The Future of Labor Arbitration in America 197, 227–50 (AAA 1976); Berkowitz, Arbitration of Public-Sector Interest Disputes: Economics, Politics, and Equity, in Arbitration—1976, Proceedings of the 29th Annual Meeting of NAA 159 (Dennis & Somers eds., BNA Books 1976); Anderson, Lessons From Interest Arbitration in the Public Sector: The Experience of Four Jurisdictions, in Arbitration—1974, Proceedings of the 27th Annual Meeting of NAA 59 (Dennis & Somers eds., BNA Books 1975); Klapper, Legislated Criteria in Arbitration of Public Safety Contract Disputes, 29 Arb. J. 115 (1974); Doering, Impasse Issues in Teacher Disputes Submitted to Fact Finding in New York, 27 Arb. J. 1 (1972); Block, Criteria in Public Sector Interest Disputes, in Arbitration and the Public Interest, Proceedings of the 24th Annual Meeting of NAA 161 (Somers & Dennis eds., BNA Books 1971); Garber, Compulsory Arbitration in the Public Sector: A Proposed Alternative, 26 Arb. J. 226 (1971); Bain, Third-Party Settlements in Education, 26 Arb. J. 41 (1971); Drotning & Lipsky, The Outcomes of Impasse Procedures in New York Schools Under the Taylor Law, 26 Arb. J. 87 (1971); Loewenberg, Compulsory Arbitration and the Arbitrator, 25 Arb. J. 248 (1970).

[154]Mich. Comp. Laws §423.239 (West 2003). In City of Detroit v. Detroit Police Officer's Ass'n, 294 N.W.2d 68, 105 LRRM 3083, 3092, 3095 (Mich. 1980), the court upheld the constitutionality of the §9 standards as being "at least as reasonably precise as the subject matter requires or permits." The court added that other jurisdictions "have sanctioned their compulsory interest arbitration schemes even though presented with less precise or even nonexplicit standards for decision." Id., 105 LRRM at 3096. Pointing to the §9 mandate that "the

One arbitrator commented on the obligation of the parties to provide information on the relevance and applicability of the statutory factors, and the inescapable exercise of judgment required of the arbitrator in attributing relative weight to them:

> True, both sides dutifully reviewed the statutory criteria which Sec. 111.77(6) Wis. Stats. directs the arbitrator to give weight to in his deliberations. Inasmuch as those statutory factors constitute a "compulsory checklist," parties to a public sector labor dispute dare not omit tying the local facts and situation to them or at least providing an explanation of why one or more of those criteria are not applicable to the situation at hand.
>
> Since the listed statutory factors are not intrinsically weighted, they cannot of themselves provide an arbitrator with an answer. It is the arbitrator who must make the decision of determining which particular factors are more important in resolving a contested issue under the singular facts of a case, although all "applicable" factors must be considered.[155]

The remainder of this chapter is largely devoted to a consideration of each of the standards used with some frequency in interest arbitration. Disputes over wages or other "economic" contract terms are the issues most frequently submitted to arbitration, and, consequently, most of the standards bear on these issues.

---

arbitration panel shall base its findings, opinions and order upon" the factors listed in §9, the court stated that the statutory factors constitute a "compulsory checklist," and the court then explained:

> Since the §9 factors are not intrinsically weighted, they cannot of themselves provide the arbitrators with an answer. It is the panel which must make the difficult decision of determining which particular factors are more important in resolving a contested issue under the singular facts of a case, although, of course, all "applicable" factors must be considered.

Id. at 3102–03. In the latter regard, the court believed that the failure of the parties to submit evidence on a given factor "did not excuse the panel's inattention to the factor." *Id.* at 3108. In *City of Boston*, 70 LA 154, 154–55, 160 (O'Brien, 1978), the arbitrator, in applying the Massachusetts statute, agreed that all statutory standards must be considered but that their respective weight in the given case is to be determined by the neutral. In *City of Winter Haven, Fla.*, 65 LA 557, 558–59, 562 (Sherman, 1975), the arbitrator considered the Florida statute, which lists various standards and emphasizes the use of comparisons with recognition of appropriate differentials, and stated that the statutory standards in his opinion "are intended to be applied only selectively depending upon the circumstances of each case," that the standards "are not to be given equal weight in every case," and that "in some cases, particular standards probably have no applicability and should not even influence the decision." The New Jersey police and firefighter statute lists standards generally similar to the Michigan standards quoted above and calls for "giving due weight to those" statutory standards "that are judged relevant for the resolution of the specific dispute." *See* 34 N.J. Stat. Ann. §§13A–16g (West 2003). As to the New Jersey statute, see also *City of Garfield, N.J.*, 70 LA 850, 851 (Silver, 1978); Lester, *Analysis of New Jersey's Flexible Arbitration System*, Arb. J., June 1989, at 14. For some other sets of statutory standards, see *City of Sallisaw, Okla.*, 111 LA 657 (Baroni, 1998); *City of Jackson, Minn.*, 105 LA 364 (Berquist, 1995); *City of Havre, Mont.*, 76 LA 789, 791 (Snow, 1981); *City of N. Las Vegas, Nev.*, 75 LA 784, 785 (Sullivan, 1980); *City of Renton, Wash.*, 71 LA 271, 272 (Snow, 1978); *County of Humboldt, Cal.*, 72 LA 63, 64 (Henderson, 1978); *City of Council Bluffs, Iowa*, 70 LA 1258, 1259 (Winton, 1978); *City of Beaumont, Tex.*, 65 LA 1048, 1049 (Bailey, 1975); *City of Kenosha, Wis.*, 63 LA 126, 131 (Rauch, 1974); *Town of Tiverton, R.I.*, 52 LA 1301, 1302 (Schmidt, Jr., 1969) (Rhode Island statute emphasizing the "comparable practice" standard with recognition of appropriate differentials). For general discussion of state statutes relating to interest arbitration in the public sector, see section 5., "Public-Sector Interest-Arbitration Legislation," above.

[155]Oneida County, Wis., Sheriff's Dep't, 100 LA 581, 583–84 (Flaten, 1992) (footnote omitted). *See also* OMRO Aides/Food Serv. Ass'n WEAC/NEA, Case No. 55513, 1998 WL 1548021 (Dichter, 1998). Wis. Stat. §111.77(6) (West 2002), cited in *Onieda County*, provides:

9. Standards Applicable in Both Private-Sector and Public-Sector Interest Arbitration

A. Prevailing Practice

Without question, the most extensively used standard in interest arbitration is "prevailing practice." In utilizing this standard, arbitrators, in effect, require the disputants indirectly to adopt the end results of the successful collective bargaining or arbitration proceedings of other similarly situated parties. The view is well illustrated by the statement of one arbitration board, which, in applying the "pattern" standard, said through its chairman:

> There is no magic formula for wage adjudication. Consequently one of the compelling considerations must be what has happened in free and successful collective bargaining. This indicates how experienced bargainers have evaluated the wage influencing factors which have evidenced themselves, and what they consider to be "just."
>
> Arbitration of primary disputes over the terms of a new contract is a substitute for successful bargaining, and the "pattern" or "package" indicates what might have evolved from successful bargaining had the parties acted like others similarly situated. Attention to the "pattern" or "package," rather than adherence to any rigid formula, also reduces the risks of parties entering wage arbitration, but also should encourage their own free settlement. It tends to afford equality of treatment for persons in comparable situations. It also provides a precise, objective figure, rather than an artificially contrived rate.[156]

If the terms of employment of a given employer are below the standard set by the prevailing practice of comparable employers, and if no basis exists for a differential, an arbitrator may conclude that an inequality exists. Many

---

(6) In reaching a decision the arbitrator shall give weight to the following factors:
    (a) The lawful authority of the employer.
    (b) Stipulations of the parties.
    (c) The interests and welfare of the public and the financial ability of the unit of government to meet these costs.
    (d) Comparison of the wages, hours and conditions of employment of the employees involved in the arbitration proceeding with wages, hours and conditions of employment of other employees performing similar services and with other employees generally:
        1. In public employment in comparable communities.
        2. In private employment in comparable communities.
    (e) The average consumer prices for goods and services, commonly known as the cost of living.
    (f) The overall compensation presently received by the employees, including direct wage compensation, vacation, holidays and excused time, insurance and pensions, medical and hospitalization benefits, the continuity and stability of employment, and all other benefits received.
    (g) Changes in any of the foregoing circumstances during the pendency of the arbitration proceedings.
    (h) Such other factors, not confined to the foregoing, which are normally or traditionally taken into consideration in the determination of wages, hours and conditions of employment through voluntary collective bargaining, mediation, fact-finding, arbitration or otherwise between the parties, in the public service or in private employment.

[156]Pacific Gas & Elec. Co., 7 LA 528, 534 (Kerr, 1947). *See also* Panama Canal Comm'n, Case No. 98-001, 1998 WL 1110338 (Nolan, 1998); Hurley Hosp., 56 LA 209, 216 (Roumell, Jr., 1971); Mercy Hosp., 53 LA 372, 374–75 (Edes, 1969); Appleton Coop. Ass'n, 39 LA 249, 253 (Gundermann, 1962). For a broader discussion, see section 3., "The Arbitrator's Function in Interest Disputes," above.

arbitration awards have undertaken to reduce or eliminate inequalities between related industries,[157] inequalities within an industry,[158] inequalities among comparable firms or work within a specific area,[159] and inequalities within the plant itself.[160]

Application of the prevailing-practice standard may involve difficulties. First, what is to be the basis of comparison? For instance, is it to be the entire industry, the particular industry within the area, or industry in general within the area? After deciding which prevailing practice is to be used, the arbitrator then must determine what that practice is.

In many cases, strong reason exists for using the prevailing practice of the same class of employers within the locality or area for the comparison. Indeed, "precedent" may be accorded arbitral stare decisis treatment and found to be the determinative factor in the selection of an appropriate comparability group. In an arbitration regarding a successor agreement between a police officers' association and the City of Waterville,[161] each party presented a list of municipalities deemed comparable. The cities proposed by the association all had industrial tax revenue bases, while Waterville was a

---

[157]See North Am. Aviation, 19 LA 76, 83 (Cole, Aaron, & Wirtz, 1952); Chicago Lighting Equip. Mfrs., 18 LA 599, 608 (Sullivan, 1952); Chesapeake & Potomac Tel. Co. of Baltimore, 7 LA 630, 641 (Jackson, Healy, & Dennis, 1947); New York Water Serv. Corp., 7 LA 30, 32–33 (Feinberg, 1947).

[158]See Yaun Welding & Mach. Works Co., 73 LA 223, 226–27 (Nicholas, Jr., 1979); Iowa Beef Processors, 62 LA 654, 657–59 (Gill, 1974); Houston Chronicle Publ'g Co., 56 LA 487, 491 (Platt, 1971); Atlanta Newspapers, Inc., 43 LA 1094, 1099 (Wallen, 1964); Mohawk Carpet Mills, 26 LA 651, 665 (Shipman, 1956). Parties sometimes seek to avoid inequalities within an industry by adoption of "most favored nation" clauses designed to equalize benefits within the industry. For cases dealing with the interpretation and application of such clauses, see Maritime Serv. Comm., 49 LA 551 (Cole, 1967); Maritime Serv. Comm., 49 LA 557 (Scheiber, 1967); Carson Linebaugh, Inc., 42 LA 1097 (Brecht, 1963).

[159]See City of Clinton, Iowa, 72 LA 190, 197 (Winton, 1979); City of Tucson, Ariz., 71 LA 113, 115 (Eckhardt, 1978); Ridgefield Park Bd. of Educ., 68 LA 163, 164 (Golob, 1977); Fountain Valley, Cal., Sch. Dist., 65 LA 1009, 1015 (Rule, 1975); City of Marquette, Mich., 54 LA 981, 987 (Barstown, Jr., 1971); Arlington Educ. Ass'n, 54 LA 492, 493 (Zack, 1971).

[160]See Pan Am World Servs., 93 LA 348, 353 (Morris, 1989) (eliminating inequalities between two classifications where arbitrator found no real differences in relative skill, ability, or types of tasks to be performed to justify differentials in compensation); City of Winter Haven, Fla., 65 LA 557, 560 (Sherman, 1975); University of Chicago Hosps. & Clinics, 63 LA 824, 827–28 (Mueller, 1974) (narrowing an existing differential to a more justifiable spread); Houston Chronicle Publ'g Co., 56 LA 487, 491 (Platt, 1971); Pittsfield, Mass., Sch. Comm., 51 LA 1134, 1138 (Young, 1968); Atlanta Newspapers, Inc., 43 LA 1094, 1099–1100 (Wallen, 1964); Birmingham News Co., 27 LA 343, 346 (Dworet, 1956); Mohawk Carpet Mills, 26 LA 651, 661 (Shipman, 1956). In City of Philadelphia, 79 LA 372 (DiLauro, Felix, & McNally, 1982), the arbitration board stated that, by the award, "economic parity has been reestablished between uniformed Fire Department employees and uniformed Police Department employees," and that:

If during the term of this Award such parity is destroyed by final decision of the highest court of competent jurisdiction or an arbitrator or board of arbitrators having jurisdiction over the City of Philadelphia, the City shall immediately restore parity for the duration of the Award.

Id. at 375. See also City of Kenosha, Wis., 63 LA 126, 132 (Rauch, 1974). Where the salary structure within a hospital had been established by careful study and with the advice of experienced consultants, an arbitrator would not lightly undertake to restructure the salary relationships within the hospital. Palo Alto-Stanford Hosp. Ctr., 50 LA 700, 705 (Mann, 1968) (under the evidence, the arbitrator was unable to find an imbalance in the internal salary structure). See also City of Tucson, Ariz., 71 LA 113, 115 (Eckhardt, 1978).

[161]City of Waterville, 107 LA 1194 (Dichter, 1996).

"bedroom community." The association's list had, however, been utilized in a prior wage award. In the successor award, the arbitrator noted that the same arguments as to which list was more appropriate had previously been made and considered. Since the budgets of the association-sponsored cities had remained in line with the budget of Waterville and there had been no change in any other material factor, there was no reason to deviate from precedent.[162]

Because employees are likely to compare their lot with that of other employees doing similar work in the area and seek parity,[163] unions have found, for instance, that the imposition of different wage scales on the same class of employers in the same locality causes competive problems for employers and discontent among the underpaid union members.[164] Sometimes, however, one party will insist on industrywide terms while the other party insists on an area comparison.

If the parties cannot reach agreement as to the basis of comparison, it is the arbitrator's responsibility to make that determination from the facts and circumstances of the case. In the final analysis, it may well be that the prevailing practice that should be used for the comparison is that of the employer's competitors, whether within or without the area, or that of other firms or industries so situated that there is a sufficient similarity of interests between them and the employer in question for it to be reasonable to use their practice as the standard.[165]

Most state interest arbitration statutes require consideration of the terms and conditions "in comparable jurisdictions." The District of Columbia Code limits "comparability" to the "occupational groups of employees in other jurisdictions in the Washington Standard Metropolitan Statistical Area [SMSA]."[166] A similar comparison also may be made on such benefits as health and life insurance, retirement, holidays, sick leave accrual, retiree health insurance, longevity pay, and overtime opportunities.[167]

---

[162]*See also* City of Edmond, Okla., 112 LA 1137 (Baroni, 1999).

[163]Condé Nash Publications, 1 ALAA ¶67,168, at 67,355 (Fleming, Jr., 1942). *See also* Houston Chronicle Publ'g Co., 56 LA 487, 490 (Platt, 1971) (quoting Hudson County Pressmen, ANPA Bull. 5067, Vol. 67, at 879 (Deibler, 1948)).

[164]Slichter, Basic Criteria Used in Wage Negotiations 28 (1947).

[165]*See generally* Cummins Sales, 54 LA 1069, 1070–71 (Seinsheimer, 1971). *See also* Nodak Rural Elec. Coop., 78 LA 1119, 1123 (Eisele, 1982); Thrifty Corp., 77 LA 1300, 1302, 1304 (Nathanson, 1982); Commonwealth Edison Co. of Ind., 72 LA 90, 92 (Goldberg, 1978). In *Houston Insulation Contractors Ass'n*, 84 LA 1245 (Williams, 1985), nonunion competition was used as one basis of comparison. In *University of Chicago Hosps. & Clinics*, 63 LA 824, 826 (Mueller, 1974), the employer was a 654-bed hospital, the employer's list of assertedly "comparable" hospitals included those ranging in size from 982 beds to 52 beds, and the union's list of assertedly "comparable" hospitals included those ranging in size from 2,173 beds to 216 beds; the arbitrator proceeded as neutrals often do where neither party's list reasonably "fits" the case under consideration—from the two lists submitted by the parties, he compiled a list of the more truly comparable employers (which in this instance included "only those hospitals within approximately 200 beds of" the employer's 654-bed operation). *See also* Town of Dedham, Mass., 67 LA 384, 386 (Holden, Jr., 1976). In *Kent Nursing Home*, 69 LA 771, 771–72 (Sabghir, 1977), the parties agreed to utilize for comparison purposes the employment terms of a single comparable employer, other comparable employers having refused to provide the data requested by the parties for use in the arbitration proceedings.

[166]D.C. Office of Labor Relations & Collective Bargaining, 84 LA 809, 813 (Rothschild, 1985).

[167]City of West Bend, Wis., 100 LA 1118, 1121 (Vernon, 1993). *See also* Sauk County, Wis., 114 LA 828 (Vernon, 2000); Northwest Kan. Educ. Serv. Ctr., 113 LA 47 (Murphy, 1999); City of Willowick, Ohio, 110 LA 1146 (Ruben, 1998); City of N. Royalton, Ohio, 109 LA 842 (Feldman, 1997).

It is not unusual for the parties to disagree on the array of communities to be considered[168] and require the arbitrator to make the determination.[169] Determining which cities are "comparable" for purposes of arbitrable resolution of a dispute between a city and its police officers has been made on the basis of the following factors: (1) proximity to a large city; (2) population; (3) size of the police force; and (4) size of the police department budget.[170] Of course, the union status of the police department also may be a factor.[171] After the cities to be used as the comparison group have been selected, one arbitrator then computed the mean, or average, value of the settlements reached by those cities' unionized police departments, determined it to represent a wage increase of 4.5 percent, and applied that percentage uniformly across the parties' wage schedule.

Selection of the "appropriate comparability group" from among 25 counties offered by the parties for purposes of resolving percentage wage increase and medical insurance contribution issues has been made on the basis of three standards of comparability. They include close geographic proximity, population and its density, and union representation. In identifying those standards, one arbitrator explained:

> [A] close geographic proximity may signal certain shared characteristics such as climate, avenues of transportation . . . and possibly socio-political values of the population. . . . [L]abor markets tend to have geographic boundaries. . . . [W]hat occurs in other counties within this range may be expected to affect the ability of Sioux County to employ or retain workers and may affect the nature of the duties of secondary road employees.
>
> . . .
>
> . . . [C]ounties with metropolitan areas will typically have a larger tax base, and may have greater diversity of industry. . . . Population therefore may be an important determinant of whether a county is comparable . . . with respect not only to ability to pay but also to the nature of duties required of secondary road employees.

---

[168]*See* City of New Berlin, Wis., 114 LA 1704, 1709 (Dichter, 2000).

[169]*See, e.g.,* Manitowoc, Wis., Sch. Dist., 100 LA 844, 846 (Rice II, 1992); City of Blaine, Minn., 90 LA 549, 551 (Perretti, 1988); City of Southfield, Mich., 78 LA 153, 155–57 (Roumell, Jr., 1982); Amphitheater Pub. Sch. Bd. of Trustees, 75 LA 268, 274 (Weizenbaum, 1980); City of Clinton, Iowa, 72 LA 190, 196–97 (Winton, 1979); City of Garfield, N.J., 70 LA 850, 852–53 (Silver, 1978); City of Boston, Mass., 70 LA 154, 158–59 (O'Brien, 1978); Sioux County, Iowa, 68 LA 1258, 1262 (Gruenberg, 1977); City of Burlington, Iowa, 68 LA 454, 459 (Witney, 1977); Port of Portland, Or., 67 LA 1034, 1035 (Dorsey, 1976); City of Winter Haven, Fla., 65 LA 557, 562–63 (Sherman, 1975); City of Birmingham, Mich., 55 LA 716, 722–23 (Roumell, Jr., 1970); City of Marquette, Mich., 54 LA 981, 986 (Barstown, Jr., 1971); Pittsfield, Mass., Sch. Comm., 51 LA 1134, 1136 (Young, 1968); Brotherhood of Saugus Police, 51 LA 208, 209–10 (Saltonstall, 1968); Sharon, Mass., Teachers' Ass'n, 50 LA 1036, 1041–42 (Siegel, 1968). In *City of Renton, Wash.,* 71 LA 271, 273–74 (Snow, 1978), the determination of what cities were "comparable" for purposes of arbitral resolution of a dispute between the city and its police officers was made on the basis of the following factors: (1) proximity to a large city, (2) population, (3) size of the police force, and (4) size of the police department budget.

[170]*See* Tuscarawas County, Ohio, Sheriff, 114 LA 307 (Feldman, 2000); City of West Bend, 100 LA 1118, 1121 (Vernon, 1993); Manitowoc, Wis., Sch. Dist., 100 LA 844, 844 (Rice II, 1992); Oneida County, Wis., Sheriff's Dep't, 100 LA 581 (Flaten, 1992); Waterloo, Iowa, Cmty. Sch. Dist., 99 LA 385 (Dilts, 1992); Lincoln County, Wis., Sheriff's Dep't, 97 LA 786 (McAlpin, 1991); City of Renton, Wash., 71 LA 271, 273–74 (Snow, 1978).

[171]City of Farmington, Minn., 85 LA 460, 464 (Bognanno, 1985).

> Employees represented by a union have an effective vehicle by which to present their views on . . . salary and fringe benefits . . . . Employees without such representation cannot be said to be similarly situated . . . .[172]

Unfortunately, developing a list of comparable communities that meets all these criteria is seldom possible. The selection process is further complicated because information relevant to disputed issues may not necessarily be available from a community that does meet the criteria. There are other times when a community that meets the criteria may still not be included on the list of comparables, because the employees in that community are not represented by a union. Such cities are often excluded because the wage rates were not the product of collective bargaining, but were unilaterally set by the employer.[173]

A 1997 factfinding report by an arbitrator for a unit of police officers contained the following observation concerning the inherent difficulties in making comparative wage rate analyses:

> Both parties submitted lengthy lists of communities deemed comparable. The Fact-Finder observes that, not unexpectedly, the City's nominees tend to include departments offering terms less favorable than those available in Willowick. In contrast, the Union's candidates included, in the main, departments providing benefits more favorable than those available in Willowick.
>
> The selection of representative communities is not easily made. This Fact-Finder believes that ideally comparable communities ought to be located nearby in the same labor market . . . be of similar territorial size and population density, draw upon similar resources and tax bases, have a similar mix of commercial, industrial and residential properties with similar need for police protection, and maintain similarly sized Police Departments.
>
> Unfortunately, developing a list of comparable communities which meets all of these criteria is seldom possible, and the selection process is further complicated because information relevant to disputed issues may not necessarily be available from a community which does meet the criteria.[174]

The terms of employment of public-sector employees may not always be compared with those of other public-sector employees.[175] The decision may be legislatively determined. As one arbitration board observed in determining the wages of postal employees:

> In its deliberations and decision-making, the board has been circumscribed by a number of constraints, two of them imposed by Acts of Congress. . . .

---

[172]Board of Supervisors, Sioux County, Iowa, 87 LA 552, 555 (Dilts, 1986).

[173]City of Farmington, Minn., 85 LA 460, 463–64 (Bognanno, 1985).

[174]City of Willowick, Ohio, 110 LA 1146, 1146 (Ruben, 1998). *See also* County of Sherburne, Minn., Sheriff's Dep't, 112 LA 889 (Bognanno, 1999).

[175]For example, see the standards specified in the Michigan Police and Fireman's Arbitration Act, quoted in section 8., "Standards in Public-Sector Disputes," above. For examples from the federal sector, see *Bonneville Power Admin.*, 73 LA 429, 432–34 (Keltner, 1979); *Government Printing Office*, 73 LA 1, 3–4, 6 (Bloch, 1979). Where multiple issues were submitted to interest arbitration under a Texas public-sector statute that permitted comparisons only with private-sector employment, and where as to some of the issues evidence submitted concerning private-sector comparability was insufficient, the arbitrator's apparent frustration was revealed by his declaration: "It must be kept in mind that, under the governing statute, our sole standard for decision is comparability of wages and benefits for similar work in the private sector in the same labor market area, an extremely restrictive standard for a case of this nature." City of Beaumont, Tex., 65 LA 1048, 1057 (Bailey, 1975).

With regard to the first of the constraints . . . it has [been] directed in two separate provisions of the Postal Reorganization Act (sections 101(c) and 1003(a)) that compensation paid to Postal Service officers and employees is to be "comparable to the rates and types of compensation paid in the private sector of the economy of the United States" and that they are to receive "compensation and benefits paid for comparable levels of work in the private sector of the economy."[176]

In affirming that the comparison ordinarily should be limited to the same or similar occupational groups, one arbitration panel rejected a "comparable worth" standard:

> It should be emphasized that in determining appropriate salaries the basis for comparison is what is paid for work in a particular profession. If the school district were hiring Engineers, Accountants, Physicists, and the like, salaries paid for those professions would presumably apply. Thus a comparison of starting salaries for teachers, who have traditionally been several thousand dollars behind the average of the other professions, may indicate the disadvantageous position of the profession in attracting competent college graduates, but it does not control in determining what should be the proper rate for entry into that profession.
>
> The same theory holds true in the Association's argument that teachers' starting salaries should be competitive with those of other professions such as Child Welfare Supervisors, or even callings such as police privates, police sergeants, bricklayers, or plumbers. Each occupation has its own rationale for wage determination, not least of which is supply and demand and control thereof.
>
> It is not the duty of this Panel to rectify years of inequity among various callings, or to impose its judgment as to the relative worth of one trade or profession over another.[177]

However, in another case the arbitrator stated that an appropriate guide in judging the pay of municipal police officers assigned to and paid directly by private concerns is "wage rate comparisons with other skilled craftsmen and semi-professionals employed to render highly responsible and skilled services in the private sector of the economy."[178]

---

[176]United States Postal Serv., 83 LA 1120, 1122 (Volz, 1985). *Compare* District of Columbia Office of Labor Relations & Collective Bargaining, 84 LA 809, 815 (Rothschild, 1985) (involving a District of Columbia statute that provided: "Compensation shall be competitive with that provided to other public sector employees having comparable duties, responsibilities, qualifications, and working conditions by occupational groups.").

[177]Arlington Educ. Ass'n, 54 LA 492, 494 (Zack, 1971). *See also* City of Havre, Mont., 76 LA 789, 792 (Snow, 1981). In *Air New Zealand,* 77 LA 667, 678 (Feller, 1981), the arbitrator resolved an important pay issue between Air New Zealand and its pilots by use of the prevailing-practice standard, utilizing the rates of pay for United Air Lines pilots as a guideline. He refused to follow the lead of another neutral in an earlier case who had compared increases requested by New Zealand pilots "with the salaries paid to the Chief Justice of New Zealand, the Prime Minister and other senior civil servants." The arbitrator stated that he did "not think that the relativity between the pay of airline pilots and that of the Prime Minister and other government officials is meaningful."

[178]Town of Tiverton, R.I., 52 LA 1301, 1303 (Schmidt, Jr., 1969). Moreover, the mere fact that an occupational group across the public sector has been underpaid in the past does not mean that interest arbitrators will disregard the occupation's claim to fair and equitable recognition for the future. *See, e.g.,* Borough of Turtle Creek, Pa., 52 LA 233, 234–35 (McDermott, 1968); Green Tree Borough, Pa., 51 LA 994, 995–96 (Florey, 1968); City of Easton, Pa., 51 LA 879, 882 (Handsaker, 1968); City of Providence, R.I., 47 LA 1036, 1039 (Seitz, 1966). In this general regard, some public-sector statutes clearly are not intended to restrict comparisons absolutely to the same occupational group. For example, under the limited evidence presented in one case subject to the Michigan statute quoted in section 8., "Standards in Public-Sector Disputes," above, the arbitrator found it "difficult if not impossible" to make a comparison between Detroit police and police in other communities for purposes of resolv-

Where the arbitrator relies on the prevailing practice in other communities or goes outside the immediate workforce for a basis of determination, it is known as "external comparison."[179] By contrast, "internal comparison" involves an examination of the employer's treatment of its other employees. Generally, arbitrators give greater weight to externals in wage disputes, unless it can be shown that a clear pattern has been established for the internal bargaining units.[180]

Benefits issues, such as health insurance benefits, are often resolved through a review of internal comparables. Applying the internal-comparison standard to determine the appropriate health insurance package, one arbitrator explained:

> [B]ecause of risk pooling, economies of scale and the lack of quality data about the coverage, contribution levels and the costs of health insurance benefits to external communities, most Arbitrators give heavy weight to evidence about the instant Employer's internal structure of health insurance coverage/contributions as opposed to what external practices are in these areas. Clearly, one cannot expect the Employer to offer a different health insurance package to each of its different work groups. By pooling risk and by "spreading" costs, the individual Employer can buy insurance protection at a far more reasonable price. Hence, in the health area the comparison focus shifts from the "external" to the "internal." This conclusion applies to dental insurance as well.[181]

In another instance, where the dominating issue was an association's request for paid health insurance for retirees, the arbitrator found that the favored position of the internal comparables was not to provide such insurance, whereas the external comparables favored the position of the association. In agreeing with the employer's position, the arbitrator found that the "internal comparables reveal that the Employer's other employees would not be getting equity if the arbitrator granted the Association's request for paid health insurance for the retirees."[182]

Similarly, in *City of West Bend*[183] the matter of comparables, both internal and external, were considered, with the union arguing that the wage increase was necessary "in order to catch up to the external comparables," and the city "argu[ing] for adherence to the internal pattern of a pair of 4% increases." In holding that the city's proposal was the more reasonable, the arbitrator explained: "[W]here there is a well-established internal pattern among the bargaining units in a city or county, the internal pattern shall prevail unless adherence to the internal pattern results in unacceptable wage level relationships between the unit at bar and its external comparables."[184]

If the case involves the setting of terms for an entire industry, the comparison may be with a similar industry. In determining whether a signifi-

---

ing the "residency requirement" issue involved in the proceedings; however, he stated that "[o]f special significance . . . are the residency requirements contained in the recent collective bargaining agreements negotiated between the City" and unions representing its firefighters. City of Detroit, Mich., 65 LA 293, 312 (Platt, 1975).

[179]*See, e.g.*, City of Edmond, Okla., 112 LA 1137 (Baroni, 1999).

[180]Monroe County, Wis., 113 LA 933, 936 (Dichter, 1999).

[181]City of Farmington, Minn., 85 LA 460, 464 (Bognanno, 1985). *See also* Sauk County, Wis., 114 LA 828 (Vernon, 2000); OMRO Aides/Food Service Ass'n, Case No. 55513, 1998 WL 1548021 (Dichter, 1998); Sibley County, Minn., Sheriff's Dep't, 111 LA 795 (Bognanno, 1998); Zia Co., 87 LA 28 (Dunn, 1986); Birmingham Bd. of Educ., 86 LA 462 (Frost, 1985).

[182]Manitowoc, Wis., Sch. Dist., 100 LA 844, 848 (Rice II, 1992).

[183]100 LA 1118, 1121 (Vernon, 1993).

[184]*Id.* at 1121. *See also* Monroe County, Wis., 113 LA 933 (Dichter, 1999).

cant and close relationship exists between two industries, a wide variety of factors may be considered. Such a relationship has been found to exist between two industries on the basis of the following factors:

> Both are engaged in handling essentially the same products. There is a marked similarity of operations, job titles, job classifications, job duties, and products handled. There is considerable overlapping of union representation . . . . There is competition between the two industries for raw materials as well as for employees. The products of one industry are used almost exclusively by the other.[185]

The telephone industry was found related to the telegraph industry on the basis of the following factors: their products were similar, frequently interdependent, and partially competitive; skills required in key jobs were similar; and requirements in many auxiliary occupations, such as clerical and accounting, were virtually identical.[186]

In any use of area practice, the geographical limits of the appropriate area must be determined.[187] Also, if the prevailing practice of industry in general within the area is to be used, there is the task of selecting the firms whose practice is to be considered in determining the prevailing area practice.[188] Arbitrators frequently use for comparison the prevailing practice of the particular industry (or public-sector occupational group) in question, as opposed to industry in general, within the area.[189]

Where each of various comparisons had some validity, an arbitrator concluded that he should give the greatest weight to those comparisons that the parties themselves had considered significant in free collective bargaining, especially in the recent past.[190] The selection of the employers whose practices are to determine the standard must, in wage cases, be followed by an

---

[185]Yakima Cement Prods. Corp., 3 LA 793, 795 (Prasow, 1946).

[186]Western Union Tel. Co., 4 LA 251, 259–60 (Wallen, Cahn, & Donahue, 1946). For guides developed by the National Wage Stabilization Board in 1946 for determining whether industries were related, see the policy statement of that Board, *Procedure: Administration of Wage Standards Under Executive Order 9697*, 2 LA xiii (1946).

[187]North Shore Water Comm'n, 111 LA 321 (Dichter, 1998). Frequently the metropolitan area or the state is used. In newspaper industry disputes, comparisons of operations in comparable cities across the nation were used to determine the prevailing practice in that industry. Newark Morning Ledger Co. v. Typographical Union Local No. 103 (Newark), 797 F.2d 162, 123 LRRM 2283 (3d Cir. 1986). In consideration of national wage stabilization policy, the National War Labor Board favored area comparison for the establishment of wage rates. Basic Steel Cos., 19 War Lab. Rep. 568 (1944). One arbitrator found significant the fact that one of the proposed communities for inclusion drew its labor pool from within the county involved in the dispute and visa-versa. County of Sherburne, Minn., Sheriff's Dep't, 112 LA 889 (Bognanno, 1999).

[188]Comparison with rates for industry in general within the area may be deemed of relatively little value unless adequate data are submitted with respect to the kind of industries being cited and the skill levels of the employees involved. *See* Florida E. Coast Ry., 41 LA 1001, 1008–09 (Platt, Bok, & Guthrie, 1963). For other considerations that may be relevant in making inter-industry comparisons, see *Railroads*, 34 LA 517, 530–32 (Dunlop, Aaron, & Sempliner, 1960).

[189]*See* Kewaunee City, Wis., Employees, Local 1470-B AFSCME, Case No. 57380, 2000 WL 1513588 (Dichter, 2000); Hurley Hosp., 56 LA 209, 214 (Roumell, Jr., 1971); City of Birmingham, Mich., 55 LA 716, 722 (Roumell, Jr., 1970); City of Marquette, Mich., 54 LA 981, 987 (Barstown, Jr., 1971); Printing Indus. of Ind., 29 LA 7, 11 (McCoy, 1957).

[190]Rochester Transit Corp., 15 LA 263, 270 (Cornsweet, 1950). *See also* San Francisco Elec. Contractors Ass'n, 60 LA 1, 7–8 (Feller, 1973); Labor Standards Ass'n, 27 LA 295, 296 (Horlacher, 1956). *But see* Houston Chronicle Publ'g Co., 56 LA 487, 489–91 (Platt, 1971). For related discussion, see section 9.L., "Past Practice and Bargaining History," below.

analysis of jobs for comparability. Mere job titles often are not reliable and are by no means conclusive. It is incumbent upon the parties to supply reliable job descriptions in order to establish a basis for comparison.[191]

Where the task involves setting the proper wage rate for newly created positions, other considerations may arise. An initial determination may be whether a "new department" or "new work" has in fact been created. Concluding that a new or changed job had been established, an arbitration board described its task as follows:

> The more difficult question is how can an arbitration board decide whether the rates set by the Company are appropriate or fair . . . .
>
> . . . [T]he labor contract has provided no standard to guide the board, and . . . therefore an implied standard should be applied [to be fair and consistent, and not to be arbitrary, capricious, or discriminatory, in setting the wage rates]. . . .
>
> . . .
>
> . . . Interest arbitration . . . requires the arbitrator to set the rates that the negotiators couldn't agree on. Perhaps the most accepted method of proof . . . is to have industrial engineer types study the jobs on the basis of skill, effort, responsibility and working conditions. This is usually done by awarding points to each of the elements of the job based on a nationally recognized manual. Each side presents its expert with differing evaluations; the arbitrator makes the decision based on this kind of evidence.
>
> Another method of proof in interest arbitration is to compare the jobs with the same jobs for other employers . . . .
>
> A third method is to try to fit the new jobs into an existing scale based on written job descriptions and verbal testimony as to the actual day to day activities of the jobs being compared.[192]

In addition to basic wage rates, the following types of issues have been resolved in some cases largely (and sometimes entirely) on the basis of the prevailing-practice standard: holidays,[193] vacations,[194] sick leave,[195] paternity leave,[196] hospitalization benefits,[197] health insurance,[198] pensions and retirement,[199] meal periods,[200] uniform allowance,[201] union security provisions,[202]

---

[191]Illustrating that a misleading picture may result in wage comparisons where job descriptions are incorrect, see City of Marquette, Mich., 54 LA 981, 986–87 (Barstown, Jr., 1971).

[192]West Penn Power Co., 86 LA 1217, 1225 (Lubow, Shrum, & Ricker, 1986).

[193]See City of Renton, Wash., 71 LA 271 (Snow, 1978); City of Winter Haven, Fla., 65 LA 557 (Sherman, 1975); City of Birmingham, Mich., 55 LA 716 (Roumell, Jr., 1970); Mercy Hosp., 53 LA 372 (Edes, 1969); National Gypsum Co., 52 LA 1030 (Bothwell, 1969).

[194]See Monroe County, Wis., 113 LA 933 (Dichter, 1999); Bremer County, Iowa, Highway Dep't, 68 LA 628 (Yarowsky, 1977); Metropolitan Tulsa Transit Auth., 65 LA 938 (Sater, 1975); St. Luke's Hosp. Ctr., 63 LA 71 (Glushien, 1974); City of Birmingham, Mich., 55 LA 716, 716 (Roumell, Jr., 1970); Mercy Hosp., 53 LA 372, 372 (Edes, 1969); Pinehaven Sanitarium, 47 LA 482 (Singer, 1966).

[195]See City of Westlake, Ohio, 111 LA 740 (Feldman, 1998); City of Winter Haven, Fla., 65 LA 557, 557 (Sherman, 1975); Mercy Hosp., 53 LA 372, 372 (Edes, 1969).

[196]City of Moses Lake, Wash., 114 LA 744 (Smith, 2000).

[197]See City of Renton, Wash., 71 LA 271, 271 (Snow, 1978); Worcester County, Md., Teachers' Ass'n, 54 LA 796 (Seidenberg, 1971).

[198]Sauk County, Wis., 114 LA 828 (Vernon, 2000).

[199]See Rochester Transit Corp., 19 LA 538, 541–42 (Tolley, McKelvey, & Turkus, 1952).

[200]See Sturgis Hosp., 112 LA 181 (Knott, 1998); Los Angeles Standard Rubber, 17 LA 353 (Warren, 1951).

[201]City of Willowick, Ohio, 110 LA 1146 (Ruben, 1998).

[202]See Baptist Hosp. of Gadsden, 65 LA 248 (Moberly, 1975); Ferris State Coll., 57 LA 613 (Edwards, 1971); City of Birmingham, Mich., 55 LA 671 (St. Antoine, 1970); City of Southgate, Mich., 54 LA 901 (Roumell, Jr., 1971); Mercy Hosp., 53 LA 372 (Edes, 1969); A.S. Abell Co., 45 LA 801 (Cluster, Gallagher, & Kraushaar, 1965).

length of workday or workweek,[203] shift differentials,[204] work schedules and shifts,[205] overtime provisions,[206] premium pay for Sundays and holidays,[207] and length of contract term.[208] In addition to these issues, a variety of other interest issues in the public sector have been resolved with the aid of the prevailing-practice standard.[209]

B. Differentials and "Minor" Standards

There may be reasons why a differential should exist among the wage terms of an employer and those of other employers (or among different groups of employees within the same company) with whom a comparison is made in applying the prevailing-practice standard.[210] Sometimes an arbitrator is asked to institute a new differential, and sometimes to perpetuate a differential that has existed in the past. Differentials serve a constructive purpose when supported by sound reasons.

---

[203]*See* Bremer County, Iowa, Highway Dep't, 68 LA 628 (Yarowsky, 1977); City of Mount Vernon, N.Y., 49 LA 1229 (McFadden, Gould, & Karow, 1968); Pinehaven Sanitarium, Inc., 47 LA 482 (Singer, 1966); Birmingham News Co., 27 LA 343 (Dworet, 1956); Rochester Transit Corp., 19 LA 538, 541–42 (Tolley, McKelvey, & Turkus, 1952).

[204]*See* City of Renton, Wash., 71 LA 271 (Snow, 1978); City of Southgate, Mich., 54 LA 901 (Roumell, Jr., 1971); Mercy Hosp., 53 LA 372, 372 (Edes, 1969); Palo Alto-Stanford Hosp. Ctr., 50 LA 700 (Mann, 1968).

[205]*See* R. Cooper, Jr., Inc., 43 LA 875 (Davis, 1964).

[206]*See* Area Educ. Agency 12, 72 LA 916 (Sembower, 1979); Sioux County, Iowa, 68 LA 1258 (Gruenberg, 1977); City of Berwyn, Ill., 66 LA 992 (Sembower, 1976); City of Winter Haven, Fla., 65 LA 557 (Sherman, 1975); Town of Tiverton, R.I., 52 LA 1301 (Schmidt, Jr., 1969).

[207]*See* City of Westlake, Ohio, 118 LA 199 (Van Pelt, 2002); City of Amherst, Ohio, Case No. 00-MED-10-1127, 2002 WL 32075102 (Ruben, 2002); Sibley County, Minn., Sheriff's Dept., 111 LA 795 (Bognanno, 1998); Oak Creek Water Utility Comm'n, Case No. 45289, 1992 WL 725741 (Kerkman, 1992); Terminal Ry. Ass'n of St. Louis, 8 LA 700 (Erickson, 1947); Charleston & W. Carolina Ry. Co., 6 LA 269 (Yeager, 1946); Minneapolis-Moline Power Implement Co., 2 LA 227 (Van Fossen, Humphrey, & Prifrel, 1946).

[208]*See* Oxmoor Press, 68 LA 1064 (Williams, 1977); Hurley Hosp., 56 LA 209 (Roumell, Jr., 1971); Palo Alto-Stanford Hosp. Ctr., 50 LA 700 (Mann, 1968); Pinehaven Sanitarium, Inc., 47 LA 482 (Singer, 1966); Port Auth. of Allegheny County, Pa., 45 LA 58 (Crawford, 1965); Yellow Cab Co., 27 LA 468 (Prasow, 1956).

[209]*See, e.g.,* City of Syracuse, 25 LAIS 3175 (Selchick, 1997); Area Educ. Agency 12, 72 LA 916, 918, 925–27 (Sembower, 1979); City of Renton, Wash., 71 LA 271, 276 (Snow, 1978); City of Birmingham, Mich., 55 LA 716, 723–26 (Roumell, Jr., 1970); Town of Tiverton, R.I., 52 LA 1301, 1302–04 (Schmidt, Jr., 1969); City of Uniontown, Pa., 51 LA 1072, 1074 (Duff, 1968). The standard also has been utilized in awarding "rights" arbitration provisions for public employees. *See* City of Birmingham, Mich., 55 LA 671, 672 (St. Antoine, 1970); City of Marquette, Mich., 54 LA 981, 984 (Barstown, Jr., 1971); Triborough Bridge & Tunnel Auth., 49 LA 1212, 1226–28 (Wolf, Feinberg, & Stockman, 1968); Lowell Sch. Comm., 48 LA 1044, 1049 (Wallen, 1967); City of Providence, R.I., 42 LA 1114, 1118–19 (Dunlop, Pierce, & Hoban, 1963).

[210]Economist Sumner H. Slichter classified wage differentials as follows: "1. Differentials which equalize the attractiveness of jobs in different occupations, industries, and places. 2. Differentials which reflect the efficiency of men in different occupations and of individuals within an occupation." SLICHTER, BASIC CRITERIA USED IN WAGE NEGOTIATIONS 41 (1947). *See also* Hill, Jr. & DeLacenserie, *Interest Criteria in Fact-Finding and Arbitration: Evidentiary and Substantive Considerations*, 74 MARQ. L. REV. 399, 422 (1991).

i.   Skill and Training

Arbitrators recognize that wages should be to some degree responsive to the general level of skill and experience required in the plant.[211]

ii.   Responsibility

Differentials have been justified, in part at least, on the basis of greater responsibility placed on one group of employees as compared with that placed on another.[212]

iii.   Steadiness of Employment

Differences in the steadiness of employment may justify differences in wage rates. Wage rates for seasonal workers and workers who otherwise have limited job security frequently are set above those of workers with steady employment.[213]

iv.   Hazards and Other Undesirable Conditions of Work

Differentials often justifiably exist in favor of employees who perform hazardous work or who work outside during inclement weather or under other undesirable conditions.[214] "Internal" comparables may prove more compelling than "external" ones in a wage increase arbitration when "hazardous duty" is a factor to be considered. Such was the case when the city of Madison, Wisconsin, firefighters assigned to a hazardous waste emergency response team asked for a premium of 3 percent of their base hourly wage rates.[215] In support of its final offer, the city had urged the arbitrator to com-

---

[211]See U.S. Postal Serv., 83 LA 1105, 1110–11 (Kerr, 1984), where the arbitrator stated:

Congress, when it established the USPS in 1970, was very concerned with career opportunities. We find, however, that the wage structure has become very compressed since that date. This compression occurred primarily through across-the-board dollar increases over a period when the cost of living rose very rapidly. Today, the most skilled and long service employees receive only fifty percent more than the least skilled and newest hires. The wage structure that Congress had established had a spread of 150 percent.

[212]See Town of Union City, Okla., 117 LA 1544 (Woolf, Woods, & Moore, 2002); County of Sherburne, Minn., 112 LA 889 (Bognanno, 1999); County of Clay, Minn., 107 LA 527 (Dichter, 1996); City of Madison, Wis., 106 LA 1059 (Flaten, 1996); Royster Guano Co., 41 LA 372, 375 (Black, 1963) (a difference in the number of duties that employees have may justify a difference in wage rates); Birmingham News Co., 27 LA 343, 347 (Dworet, 1956).

[213]See Metro Area Express, 103 LA 1 (Baroni, 1994); St. Croix Falls, Wis., Sch. Dist., Case No. 24 INT/ARB 5410, 1991 WL 693181 (Flagler, 1991); Nassau Bus Lines, Inc., 23 LA 4, 5 (Rubin, 1954); Reading St. Ry., 6 LA 860, 865 (Simkin, 1947); Consolidated Edison Sys. Cos. of N.Y., 6 LA 830, 834 (Taylor, 1947).

[214]See Government Printing Office, 73 LA 1, 7–8 (1979) (Bloch, 1979); Kent Nursing Home, 69 LA 771, 773 (Sabghir, 1977) (the work in question required "much more constant and acute attention from employees" than did the work of employees whose wages were being utilized for comparison purposes); Iowa Beef Processors, 62 LA 654, 657 (Gill, 1974); Memphis Publ'g Co., 26 LA 381, 382 (Hepburn, 1956); Kendall Ref. Co., 13 LA 454, 455 (Blair, 1949).

[215]City of Madison, Wis., 106 LA 1059 (Flaten, 1996).

pare the wages of its firefighters with those of public employees performing the same services in comparable communities throughout the state. But the arbitrator considered "internal" considerations addressed by the union to be more compelling. These included the city's history of similar percentage-based pay to its other emergency workers, the higher number of hazardous spills in the area, the greater amount of manufacture and transport of hazardous materials within the region, and the location of the region as an important traffic bridge between other major cities.

v. Geographic Differentials

Although the individual worker does not always understand why higher wages should be paid to another worker doing the same work but in a different area, there is believed to be sound reason for geographic differentials. As simply stated by one arbitration board: "[E]veryone knows our country cousins, workmen, professional men, all, on the average, earn less than urbanites; and need less. They get on the whole more comforts, services, and commodities for their dollars."[216]

vi. Fringe Benefits

Basic wages are not the only "money" benefits that employees may receive. Terms of employment include other pecuniary benefits, such as pensions, holidays and vacations with pay, sick leave, shift premiums, social and health insurance, and bonuses. These fringe benefits must be taken into account in making wage comparisons.[217]

In a public-sector case, a school board asserted that the smaller class sizes and fewer clerical duties of its teachers constituted working conditions "sufficiently preferable to offset any difference in salary compared to other communities." The arbitrator stated, however, that it was unrealistic to attach a specific dollar figure to the value of such working conditions and that, in any event, such working conditions did not justify the employer in asking its teachers to absorb increases in the cost of living for which other teachers in the area had received adjustments.[218]

---

[216]Chesapeake & Potomac Tel. Co. of Balt., 7 LA 630, 641 (Jackson, Healy, & Dennis, 1947). See also City of West Bend, Wis., 100 LA 1118 (Vernon, 1993); City of Lake Worth, Fla., 91 LA 1408 (Weston, 1988); U.S. Postal Serv., 83 LA 1233 (Peer, dissenting, 1985); U.S. Postal Serv., 83 LA 1120 (Volz, 1985).

[217]That fringes should be included was emphasized in Des Moines Transit Co., 38 LA 666, 672–73 (Flagler, 1962), where data pertaining to nine selected fringe benefits was secured from each of the 10 companies with which comparison was being made. See also City of Sallisaw, Okla., 111 LA 657 (Baroni, 1998); Iowa Beef Processors, 62 LA 654, 657 (Gill, 1974). However, fringe benefits were disregarded where the parties failed to provide evidence about the comparability of the benefits. Cummins Sales, 54 LA 1069, 1072 (Seinsheimer, 1971). In City of Marquette, Mich., 54 LA 981, 987 (Barstown, Jr., 1971), the arbitrator noted that many fringe benefits "are extremely difficult to translate into dollar terms," but he was "unable to determine any clear evidence of imbalance among fringes" of similar occupational groups in the area, and he concluded that the fringe benefits being compared were "roughly similar in total value," although "differences in detail abound." In City of Providence, R.I., 47 LA 1036, 1038 (Seitz, 1966), the arbitrator found that there was such a "wide diversity of working conditions and fringes among the cities ranked" that the prevailing-practice standard itself was rendered of little utility.

[218]Arlington Educ. Ass'n, 54 LA 492, 494–95 (Zack, 1971).

When an interest arbitration involves the subject of insurance, arbitrators generally agree that internal comparables are most germane. This is especially so where the contribution rates prevailing in comparable communities lack uniformity. Thus, one arbitrator refused to adopt a police officer association's proposal that its employers pay 100 percent of yearly insurance premiums when the city's two other bargaining units still paid part of the cost.[219] However, he did order an increase in the maximum employer contribution. The arbitrator took into account the fact that the contracts for the other bargaining units would expire during the term of the police officers' contract, and the city's contribution to the cost of its police officers' insurance had been unchanged for four years. "Externalities" were not entirely ignored, however. The arbitrator also considered significant the fact that two of the comparable cities had raised their contribution levels.

vii. Wage Leadership

A differential that has existed in the past by virtue of the employer's position as a wage leader may be the basis of an award of wage rates higher than those paid by prevailing practice.[220] Companies that in the past have set the prevailing wage may be looked to for further leadership when the trend is toward a higher level of wages.[221] It has been emphasized, however, that the lead occasionally passes from one company to another and that wage adjustments need not always wait upon agreement of the parties who usually provide the lead.[222]

viii. Historical Differentials

Arbitrators are sometimes reluctant to eliminate historical differentials[223] or those that initially were established by collective bargaining.[224] This reflects a hesitancy to disturb a stabilized situation except on compelling grounds.[225]

---

[219]City of Waterville, 107 LA 1194, 1197 (Dichter, 1996).

[220]*See* City of Renton, Wash., 71 LA 271, 281 (Snow, 1978); Connecticut Power Co., 26 LA 904, 907 (Donnelly, Curry, & Mottram, 1956); Duquesne Light Co., 11 LA 1023, 1033 (Whiting, 1948); Cleveland Elec. Illuminating Co., 8 LA 597, 606 (Cornsweet, 1947). *See also* Iowa Beef Processors, 62 LA 654, 658 (Gill, 1974). *But see* Commonwealth Edison Co. of Ind., 72 LA 90, 93 (Goldberg, 1978); Pacific Gas & Elec. Co., 7 LA 528, 532 (Kerr, 1947). A related question arising out of wage leadership is whether the leader's rate should be included in the sample used for determining the prevailing rate.

[221]But the leader may be relieved of this responsibility if its ability to pay weakens. Des Moines Transit Co., 38 LA 666, 674 (Flagler, 1962).

[222]Tribune Publ'g Co., 28 LA 477, 480 (Ross, 1957).

[223]*See* Air New Zealand, 77 LA 667, 674 (Feller, 1981); City of Renton, Wash., 71 LA 271, 280–81 (Snow, 1978); Port Auth. of Allegheny County, Pa., 45 LA 58, 61 (Crawford, 1965); Atlanta Newspapers, Inc., 43 LA 410, 411, 414 (Seibel, 1964); San Jose Mercury & News, 29 LA 96, 99 (Ross, 1957). *See also* U.S. Smelting Co., 18 LA 676, 677 (Wage Stabilization Bd. 1952). *Cf.* American Fisheries Co., 5 LA 220, 222 (Cheney, 1946); Fifth Ave. Coach Co., 4 LA 548, 575 (Wasservogel, 1946).

[224]*See* Atlanta Newspapers, 42 LA 548, 555 (Dworkin, 1964); Atlanta Newspapers, 39 LA 207, 212 (Holly, 1962); Connecticut Power Co., 26 LA 904, 907 (Donnelly, Curry, & Mottram, 1956); Rochester Transit Corp., 15 LA 263, 270–71 (Cornsweet, 1950). *See also* Capitol Broad. Co., 20 LA 610, 613 (McCoy, 1953).

[225]Newark Call Printing & Publ'g Co., 3 LA 318, 320–21 (Horvitz, 1946). In *Houston Chronicle Publishing Co.*, 56 LA 487, 490–91 (Platt, 1971), the importance of not making too

C. No Prevailing Practice

Where there is no prevailing practice, arbitrators will require a party seeking a novel change to justify it by strong evidence establishing its reasonableness and soundness. Moreover, the absence of prevailing practice may be taken to show that a demand has not yet been adequately justified by labor within the industry or area.[226] Arbitrators generally agree that demands for unusual types of contract provisions preferably should be negotiated.[227] This view was elaborated on by a chairman of a board of arbitration:

> We believe that an unusual demand, that is, one that has not found substantial acceptance in other properties, casts upon the union the burden of showing that, because of its minor character or its inherent reasonableness, the negotiators should, as reasonable men, have voluntarily agreed to it. We would not deny such a demand merely because it had not found substantial acceptance, but it would take clear evidence to persuade us that the negotiators were unreasonable in rejecting it.[228]

New provisions, however, are often included in the recommendations of factfinding boards.[229]

The outcome of a disputed pay rate issue may be determined by a balance of internal considerations, such as the special hardship created by a specific work assignment and the past treatment of the issue by the parties, where no discernible prevailing practice among external comparables exists. In deciding on the proper increase for "standby pay" for police officers, the arbitrator pointed out that police officers on standby status experienced a special hardship because they had to remain sufficiently close to the station during their lengthy standby shifts to arrive within 15 minutes from the time of the call-in. Further, the unusual length of the standby status was attributable, at least in part, to the city's having chosen to operate its department with one less police officer than it previously had employed. While granting a larger increase than that proposed by the city, the arbitrator did

---

large an award (though such award be otherwise justified to fully eliminate an intercity or interemployer inequity) was stressed in view of the need to protect "intra-plant harmony." *See also* Dallas Publishers, 50 LA 367, 368–69 (Elkouri, 1968). In *Area Education Agency 12*, 72 LA 916, 919 (Sembower, 1979), the arbitrator rejected a union wage proposal that could not be adopted "without distorting the comparability picture" of the area education group in question "in relation with the other" state area education groups "and in relationship generally with the education community." *See also* City of Quincy, Ill., 81 LA 352, 357 (Block, 1982) (refusing to increase certain wages where "a sudden increase of these wages could easily throw these jobs out of line with other jobs").

[226]*See* Fifth Ave. Coach Co., 4 LA 548, 579 (Wasservogel, 1946).

[227]*But see* Village of W. Springs, Ill., 99 LA 125 (Goldstein, 1992) (arbitrator concluded general rule against granting an unprecedented contract provision should not apply, where union was seeking to add fair share provision to initial agreement because employer's "fair but firm" bargaining position prevented genuine bargaining or quid pro quo exchange on the issue).

[228]Twin City Rapid Transit Co., 7 LA 845, 848 (McCoy, Freeman, & Goldie, 1947). *See also* City of Edgerton, Wis., 100 LA 339 (Miller, 1992); Pullman Police Officers' Guild, 1992 WL 717452 (Axon, 1992); Algoma, Wis., Sch. Dist., Case No. 46716, 1992 WL 725782 (Petrie, 1992); City of S. Milwaukee, Wis., Case No. 44236, 1991 WL 693184 (Petrie, 1991); Asplundh Tree Expert Co., 89 LA 183 (Allen, Jr., 1987); R.H. Macy & Co., 11 LA 450, 453–54 (Cole, 1948); Tampa Transit Lines, Inc., 3 LA 194, 196 (Hepburn, 1945).

[229]*See, e.g.*, Minnesota State Highway Patrol, 56 LA 697, 699 (Gleeson, 1971); General Motors Corp., 1 LA 125, 137 (Garrison, Eisenhower, & Stacy, 1946).

not award the full amount requested by the union. He found its demand to be excessive in light of the past compensation history of the parties.[230]

D. Wage "Patterns" [LA CDI 100.06; 100.45]

A "pattern" may be defined as a particular kind of solution for collective bargaining issues that has been used on a wide enough scale to be distinctly identified. The pattern standard is obviously closely related to the prevailing-practice standard and could be reasonably considered as merely one of its aspects. However, it is often spoken of as if it were a distinct criterion.

A pattern in wage arbitration may be defined in terms of a specific number of cents per hour, or it may be stated as a percentage wage increase. For instance, the pattern standard would recognize that where companies or industries A, B, and C have granted general wage increases of 10 cents per hour, related company or industry D should grant a 10 cent increase also. In the application of this standard, stress is placed on the granting of the same amount or percentage of increase granted by others, rather than on the granting of the same total wage that is paid by comparable employers.

Among other possibilities, the pattern observed may be a national pattern for the industry in general,[231] a national pattern for the particular industry or for related industries,[232] a pattern for general industry in the area,[233] or a pattern for the particular industry in the area.[234] The national pattern may be rejected where a grant of the national figure would upset the trend set by the local area pattern.[235] Patterns do not always call for wage increases. Rather, the pattern may be for wage decreases,[236] or, when the economy so justifies, for maintenance of the status quo.

---

[230]City of Waterville, 107 LA 1194 (Dichter, 1996).

[231]For example, where an arbitrator recognized a "pattern of increases" of about 6% to have been "widespread in American industry." City of Easton, Pa., 51 LA 879, 880 (Handsaker, 1968). *See also* County of Sherburne, Minn., Sheriff's Dep't, 112 LA 889 (Bognanno, 1999); Port Auth. of Allegheny County, Pa., 50 LA 1103, 1114 (Platt, 1968).

[232]*See* National Ry. Labor Conference, 53 LA 555 (Seward, 1969); Florida E. Coast Ry., 41 LA 1001 (Platt, Bok, & Guthrie, 1963); New York Harbor Carriers, 35 LA 628 (Whiting, Roberts, & Coburn, 1960); Railroads, 34 LA 517 (Dunlop, Aaron, & Sempliner, 1960); Railroads, 28 LA 110 (Cayton, Robertson, & Coffey, 1957). *See also* Furniture Negotiation Group, 26 LA 14 (Reid, 1956). In *Iowa Beef Processors*, 62 LA 654, 657–58 (Gill, 1974), an express objective of the arbitrator's award was to establish a pattern for the industry.

[233]Viloco Mach. Co., 3 LA 867, 870–71 (Ziegler, 1946). A settlement by a large employer in a given area may have strong impact on other industries within that area, as did a General Motors settlement. Hurley Hosp., 56 LA 209, 213–15 (Roumell, Jr., 1971).

[234]*See* Arizona Pub. Serv. Co., 63 LA 1189, 1196 (Platt, 1974); San Jose Mercury & News, 29 LA 96, 99 (Ross, 1957); Missouri Pub. Serv. Co., 23 LA 429, 434 (Howard, 1954); Liquid Carbonic Corp., 14 LA 655, 660–61 (Haughton, 1950). *See also* San Francisco Elec. Contractors Ass'n, 60 LA 1, 6–7 (Feller, 1973). It could even be a pattern for one company only, as where a pattern resulting from agreements between an employer and several unions was applied to some of the employees represented by still another union. Memphis Publ'g Co., 26 LA 381, 382 (Hepburn, 1956). *See also* Commonwealth Edison Co. of Ind., 72 LA 90, 92 (Goldberg, 1978); Oxmoor Press, 68 LA 1064, 1066–67 (Williams, 1977); Labor Standards Ass'n, 48 LA 425, 428–29 (Joseph, 1967). In *United States Postal Service*, 83 LA 1120, 1122 (Volz, 1985), the arbitration board chairman spoke of the "need to stay within, or close to, the monetary benefits" awarded to other employees of the same employer by another arbitration board in *United States Postal Service*, 83 LA 1105 (Kerr, Simon, Kheel, Nash, & Mahon, 1984).

[235]Jamaica Buses, 4 LA 225, 227 (Cahn, 1946).

[236]City of Detroit, Mich., 102 LA 764 (Lipson, 1993); Houston Insulation Contractors Ass'n, 84 LA 1245 (Williams, 1985); Cheney Bros., 21 LA 159, 163–65 (Scheiber, 1953); Portland Woolen Mills, Inc., 24 LA 38, 44 (Kleinsorge, 1955).

In one railroad emergency board proceeding, the use of the industry pattern was vigorously challenged by the railroad shopcrafts, which insisted that their wage claims should be considered on their merits regardless of the terms to which other railroad unions had agreed. The emergency board responded:

> Again, . . . this Board is trapped in the "pattern" dilemma faced by the parties and by many previous Emergency Boards. The Organizations are asked to accept a general wage increase which was established at bargaining tables at which they were not represented, a wage increase agreement which is thus not of their making. The frustration of the Organizations at being locked into an established pattern is understandable, but, equally understandable is the Carriers' unwillingness to break and upset . . . a wage agreement voluntarily negotiated in good faith at an earlier date. Late settlements above a pattern earlier established penalize employees involved in the earlier voluntary negotiations. This is destructive of the broader system of collective bargaining in the industry. Until and unless the structure of bargaining is modified in the industry there can be no improved approach to this difficult problem. Under these circumstances this Board cannot recommend departure from the wage pattern already in effect for some 77 percent of all railroad employees.[237]

Arbitrators look to wage patterns that have developed both within and outside a jurisdiction. "Internal patterns" refer to relationships among employee units of the same employer with respect to their terms of employment. "External patterns" refer to relationships between the terms of employment of one unit of an employer and those for units of employees of one or more other jurisdictions performing similar jobs.[238] The longer a set of internal linkages is found to have existed, the greater the weight given to maintenance of the pattern.

A well-established internal pattern generally is given greater consideration by arbitrators than external patterns.[239] Exceptions may be found where giving deference to the established internal relationships would result in anomalous disparities between the treatment of the employees in question and those of relevant counterpart units in other jurisdictions,[240] or where there are other compelling or extenuating circumstances. In the absence of an established internal pattern, maintenance of an existing external pat-

---

[237]National Ry. Lab. Conference, 53 LA 555, 559–60 (Seward, Howlett, & Livernash, 1969). In *Arizona Public Service Co.*, 63 LA 1189 (Platt, 1974), the arbitrator stated:

> In a wage dispute, a Board of Arbitration is bound to an important degree by evidence of a developing or established pattern of wage adjustments in the industry or area under consideration, especially when the adjustments have been reached through collective bargaining. For, as the Chairman has had occasion to note in previous cases, it is almost axiomatic that, if arbitration is to function successfully as a dispute-settling process, it must not yield substantially different results than could be obtained by the parties through bargaining.

Id. at 1196. For a vigorous effort by an employer to escape the "pattern," see *Florida E. Coast Ry.*, 41 LA 1001, 1010–13 (Platt, Bok, & Guthrie, 1963). Though historically following the prevailing pattern, the employer escaped it in *Franklin Woolen Mills*, 37 LA 270, 272 (Fallon, 1961).

[238]City of Altus, Okla., 105 LA 277 (Neas, 1995) (in order to establish a pattern, the jobs, as well as the jurisdictions, must be "comparable").

[239]City of West Bend, Wis., 100 LA 1118 (Vernon, 1993); City of St. Paul, Minn., 101 LA 1205 (Jacobowski, 1993).

[240]City of West Bend, 100 LA 1118 (Vernon, 1993); Oneida County, Wis., Sheriff's Dep't, 100 LA 581 (Flaten, 1992).

tern is given greatest consideration in determining an appropriate wage increase for a unit. In some cases, where the wages paid by the subject employer have failed to keep pace with those offered by the comparable jurisdictions, and thus the subject employer's "rank" has become lower, arbitrators may allow increases during the contract period greater than those offered in the comparable communities in order to allow the subject employees to catch up.[241]

E. Cost of Living

The cost-of-living standard is frequently advanced in collective bargaining and arbitration during periods characterized by pronounced changes in living costs, but, while a consideration, it is not usually a controlling factor.[242] The use of this standard has an obvious appearance of fairness, but it is not without criticism. For instance, it is said that a rising cost of living means that the demand for goods at existing prices is outrunning the supply, and that increases in wages would simply aggravate the problem except as they reflect increased production through improvements in technique or in employee efficiency.[243]

One answer given to this criticism is that the readjustment of wages has often been the result rather than the primary cause of increased living costs. Inflationary pressures more often arise from governmental monetary and fiscal policies or international developments such as cartel action increasing the price of oil.[244] A criticism that labor registers against the cost-of-living standard is that its rigid application would result in a stationary real wage rather than a higher standard of living.[245] But despite these criticisms, the

---

[241]West Clermont, Ohio, Local Sch. Dist. Bd. of Educ., 103 LA 1193 (Murphy, 1994).

[242]County of Clay, Minn., 107 LA 527 (Dichter, 1996).

[243]SLICHTER, BASIC CRITERIA USED IN WAGE NEGOTIATIONS 15 (1947).

[244]Satter, *Principles of Arbitration in Wage Rate Disputes*, 1 INDUS. & LAB. REL. REV. 363, 367 (1948). A thought-provoking statement concerning the causes and effects of a related phenomenon, inflation, was offered in *Celotex Corp.*, 68 LA 672 (Boals, 1977):

Inflation is a tremendously complicated subject, but perhaps some of the primary reasons for the predicament should be mentioned. Prices in general have increased primarily because of government deficit financing, a rapid increase in the supply of money and credit. Politicians seem to have caught-on to a unique technique: With inflation, they have an automatic way to increase taxes without passing tax laws, as the income tax takes a larger percentage of higher money incomes. This is a cruel but hidden tax on savings. In turn, they have more money which they can dispense to programs that can please their constituency. The result is that few in Congress are unseated nowadays. Other reasons for general inflation include: rising energy and raw material costs; over-regulation of business by EEOC, OSHA, ICC, EPA and other such agencies; slow increases of late in man-hour productivity; and high-prices administered by firms with market power and import cartels. There are many other reasons, and the inflationary process is dynamic and complex, involving *anticipated* price changes by all sellers, buyers and employees. In addition, many have the incorrect belief of a long-run trade-off between unemployment and inflation.

Id. at 674–75. The arbitrator also made a detailed statement specifically concerning the inflationary spiral of costs in the medical care and health insurance fields. *Id.* at 675–76.

[245]The criticism led one arbitrator to largely disregard the cost-of-living standard, the arbitrator stating that the "uncritical use of the cost-of-living formula often involves the false assumption that all is well when real wages remain constant." 195 Broadway Corp., 7 LA 516, 519 (Meyer, 1947). *See also* City of Edmond, Okla., 112 LA 1137 (Baroni, 1999); Lincoln County, Wis., Sheriff's Dep't, 97 LA 786 (McAlpin, 1991).

very frequent use of this standard is strong evidence that it is generally regarded to be of much value, and in recent decades it has held an important place in the national economy.[246]

In applying the cost-of-living standard, arbitrators rely heavily on the Consumer Price Index (CPI) issued by the Bureau of Labor Statistics of the U.S. Department of Labor. As the result of a major revision that was commenced in 1970 and completed in 1978, the CPI in fact is now a group of separate indexes.[247] Where the particular separate index to be utilized for the given arbitration case has not been mutually specified by the parties, the arbitrator will decide which index best serves the case.[248]

The CPI (which will be referred to below merely as the index) reflects the cost of living as of a date about six weeks prior to its issuance.[249] By use of the index, it is possible to measure changes in retail costs of services and commodities and the resulting effect on the purchasing power of the income of workers in the larger cities. Essentially, the index is the ratio of the current cost of a specified market basket of goods and services to the average cost of the same market basket during some designated past period. The

---

[246]The case in its favor was strengthened in 1951 by the Wage Stabilization Board's adoption of it as a ground for wage increases without the need of official approval.

[247]The sole national index prior to the revision was the "Consumer Price Index for Urban Wage Earners and Clerical Workers." The revision replaced this index with two national indexes: (1) the "Consumer Price Index for All Urban Consumers (CPI-U)," and (2) the "Consumer Price Index for Urban Wage Earners and Clerical Workers (Revised series) (CPI-W)." *The Consumer Price Index Revision–1978*, at 1 (U.S. Dep't of Labor, Bureau of Labor Statistics, 1978) provides a detailed comparison of the old index and each of its two replacements. Among other features common to each of the three indexes is the fact of monthly issuance and the use of the same base period, i.e., the 1982–1984 average = 100. The need for broader population coverage than was provided by the old index was explained as follows:

> The previous index represented only wage earners and clerical workers and therefore was, strictly speaking, appropriate for only that group. A more comprehensive consumer price index was needed to reflect expenditures for the many population groups other than wage earners and clerical workers whose income payments are now being escalated and to measure inflation and guide monetary and fiscal policy for the Nation as a whole.

THE CONSUMER PRICE INDEX: CONCEPTS AND CONTENT OVER THE YEARS 6 (U.S. Dep't of Labor, Bureau of Labor Statistics Report 517, 1977) also explains that, along with the new "Index for All Urban Consumers," the revision increased the number of city indexes and established regional indexes:

> (1) A new index representing all urban consumers—80 percent of the population—has been issued in addition to the index for wage earners and clerical workers which represents roughly half of the urban population; (2) monthly or bimonthly indexes are published for 28 cities compared with 24 monthly or quarterly indexes formerly published; (3) regional indexes are available for urban areas of different population sizes. . . .

Id. at 5. But it is also significant that "[a]lthough many changes in scope, coverage, frequency, and publication format have occurred over the years, the index has continued to measure changes in the price of a fixed market basket of goods and services." *Id.* at 3.

[248]For example, in *Commonwealth Edison Co. of Indiana*, 72 LA 90, 94 (Goldberg, 1978), the arbitrator noted data from the Chicago metropolitan area index and data from the national index, and he explained why he chose the former: "Inasmuch . . . as all . . . employees live in or near the Chicago metropolitan area, Chicago data are more meaningful than nation-wide data." *See also* Port of Portland, 67 LA 1034, 1035–36 (Dorsey, 1976).

[249]For one type of interpretative problem that this time gap can produce, see *Duriron Co.*, 54 LA 124, 127–28 (Kates, 1971).

base period is updated periodically, and since 1988 the base period for the index is the average for the years 1982–1984 (1982–1984 avg. = 100).[250]

The Bureau of Labor Statistics does not hold that its index is an exact measurement of changes in the cost of living, but arbitrators can be expected to give it considerable weight. For example, the index was held in one instance to be an appropriate measure of the change in living costs, although the union claimed that it underestimated the change and the company claimed that it overestimated the change; neither party presented sufficient evidence to support an adjustment of the index figures, which the arbitrator said at least carried apparent and official certitude.[251]

An appropriate base period must be selected in applying the cost-of-living standard. The base period that is selected determines the real wage that is to be maintained by the standard. Generally the date of the last arbitration award or of the parties' last wage negotiations is used as the base date.[252]

The determination of any adjustment to be made on the basis of a change in the cost of living requires a comparison of the percentage of change in the cost of living with the percentage of change in wages between the base period and the date of the wage adjustment.[253] In determining whether wages have kept pace with the cost of living, basic wage rates, rather than take-home pay, are generally used for the comparison.[254] The use of take-home

---

[250]For current and some historical CPI data, see BNA's *Labor Relations Reporter*, LRX 430:701 et seq. Historical data based on prior base periods are available from the Bureau of Labor Statistics. For an explanation that it is possible to continue the use of indexes utilizing earlier base periods such as the 1967 = 100 index, and that "the percentage increases shown by each Index would be identical," see *National Cleaning Contractors*, 70 LA 917, 920–21, 925 (Dworkin, 1978) (explaining also that "current information is still collected and made available for former Indexes, all the way back . . . .").

[251]R.H. Macy & Co., 9 LA 305, 308 (Shulman, 1947). In *City of Havre, Montana*, 76 LA 789, 793 (Snow, 1981), the arbitrator stated:

The difficulty with the Consumer Price Index is that it provides no insight concerning differences in cost of living from one city to another in Montana. Consequently, one does not know what the Consumer Price Index is for Havre, Montana. Nor does the Index give us insight into the standard of living that particular individuals can sustain on a given income. The point is that such price indices do not provide the precision many want to give them credit for providing. But the Employer offered no rebuttal to the Association's contention . . . [concerning the increase in cost of living reflected by the Consumer Price Index].

Regarding index shortcomings, see *Government Printing Office*, 73 LA 1, 5 (Bloch, 1979). Sometimes errors occur in the index. For cases permitting recoupment of overpayment caused by Bureau of Labor Statistics error in the index, see *Kennecott Copper Corp.*, 69 LA 52, 59 (Platt, 1977); *Kaiser Aluminum & Chem. Corp.*, 68 LA 970, 973 (Roberts, 1977). For a case not permitting recoupment, see *Food Employers Council*, 64 LA 862, 864 (Karasick, 1975).

[252]*See* Los Angeles Transit Lines, 11 LA 118, 130 (Aaron, 1948); New York City Omnibus Corp., 7 LA 794, 802 (Cole, 1947). But a date other than that of the last negotiations may be selected as the base period. For some years after World War II, for instance, January 1, 1941, was often used by arbitrators. The use of this date was initiated by the National War Labor Board of World War II. Bethlehem Steel Corp., 1 WAR LAB. REP. 325 (1942). The 1941 date was deemed clearly outmoded in *Publishers Ass'n of N.Y. City*, 22 LA 35, 41–42 (Seward, Slocum, & Meany, 1954), a later date having been established under a subsequent governmental wage control program.

[253]Regarding the determination and application of the percentage increase in cost of living, see *National Cleaning Contractors*, 70 LA 917, 921–22 (Dworkin, 1978); *Babcock & Wilcox*, 70 LA 223, 225–26 (Sembower, 1978); *Dallas Publishers*, 50 LA 367, 374 (Elkouri, 1968).

[254]Waterfront Employers Ass'n of the Pac. Coast, 5 LA 758, 761 (Kerr, 1946); Bee Line, Inc., 1 ALAA ¶67,161 (Cahn, 1946).

pay for the comparison would lead to a distortion of the normal relationship of earnings to hours worked.[255] In making the comparison, some changes in wages have been held not to be material. Among these are increases resulting from greater skill and effort,[256] increases granted for the sole purpose of eliminating inequities within the industry,[257] and pay raises for length of service or promotions.[258] The following, however, may be taken into consideration in making the comparison: increased earnings of incentive workers that result from a simplification of the work or any other increase not the result of increased efforts of the workers,[259] and reclassification adjustments general enough to affect the whole wage structure and thus to be considered general increases instead of merit increases.[260] The use of basic wage rates instead of take-home pay for the comparison eliminates from consideration vacation, holiday, and other fringe benefits granted to employees since the base date.[261]

F. Escalator and Wage Reopening Clauses
[LA CDI 24.657; 100.06; 100.45]

Many collective bargaining agreements contain escalator clauses that provide for automatic changes in wage rates in response to specified changes in the cost of living.[262] The use of such a clause may justify a longer basic term for the agreement.[263]

An alternative to the use of escalator clauses is to provide for wage reopening during the term of the agreement.[264] A wage reopening clause may

---

[255]Waterfront Employers Ass'n of Pac. Coast, 9 LA 172, 177 (Miller, 1947); Waterfront Employers Ass'n of the Pac. Coast, 5 LA 758, 761 (Kerr, 1946).

[256]McGlynn Hays Indus., 10 LA 360, 361 (Lesser, 1948).

[257]Atlantic & Gulf Coast Shippers, 6 LA 700, 704 (Kleinsorge, 1947).

[258]Trans World Airlines, 19 LA 308, 323 (Wenke, Boyd, & Sharfman, 1952); Fifth Ave. Coach Co., 1 ALAA ¶67,423 (Croxton, 1946). *See also* Madwed Mfg. Co., 20 LA 718, 719–20 (Stutz, 1953); Keyport Wood Working Co., 17 LA 914, 916 (Lesser, 1952).

[259]Associated Dress Mfrs. Ass'n, 6 LA 24, 27 (Copelof, 1946).

[260]Puget Sound Navigation Co., 11 LA 1100, 1107 (Haughton, 1948).

[261]*See* Bee Line, Inc., 1 ALAA ¶67,161 (Cahn, 1946).

[262]*See, e.g.*, Fabsteel Co., 72 LA 1214, 1215 (Bothwell, 1979) (provision included a "cap" limiting the adjustment in hourly rate to no more than 15 cents each year); Durkee-Atwood Co., 70 LA 765 (Grabb, 1978); Babcock & Wilcox, 70 LA 223, 224 (Sembower, 1978). Another possibility is to provide for automatic wage adjustments at specified intervals. *See, e.g.*, Auburn Foundry, 81 LA 274, 274–75 (Katz, 1983); Oil Transp. Co., 81 LA 272, 272–73 (Shearer, 1983); Fruehauf Corp., 71 LA 1186, 1187 (Moski, 1978); Koppel Photo Co., 56 LA 1085, 1086 (Zack, 1971). For the matters that should be covered in escalator clauses, see *Tile Contractors Ass'n of N. Cal.*, 25 LA 9, 11 (Ross, 1955). *See also* Iowa Beef Processors, 62 LA 654, 658–59 (Gill, 1974); Port Auth. of Allegheny County, Pa., 50 LA 1103, 1111 (Platt, 1968). Regarding "rounding off" fractions to the nearest cent in making adjustments, see *Fruehauf Corp.*, 71 LA 1186, 1187–88 (Moski, 1978); *Durkee-Atwood Co.*, 70 LA 765, 766–67 (Grabb, 1978). For information on the use of the Consumer Price Index in an escalation clause, see Using the Consumer Price Index for Escalation (U.S. Dep't of Labor, Bureau of Labor Statistics Report 761, 1988).

[263]*See* Port Auth. of Allegheny County, Pa., 45 LA 58, 62 (Crawford, 1965).

[264]*See* CSR & Nev. Ready Mix, 109 LA 887 (Prayzich, 1997); City of Winona, Minn., 95 LA 708, 709 (Berquist, 1990); City of Marquette, Mich., 54 LA 981, 988 (Barstown, Jr., 1971). *See also* League of Voluntary Hosps., 67 LA 293, 299 (Gootnick, 1976) (awarding a "reopener on wages" with provision for use of interest arbitration if needed). Of 1,717 contracts examined in one survey, nearly 500 contained provisions for renegotiation of economic issues during the contract term and about 15% of these provided for arbitration should negotia-

provide for the negotiation of new wage terms when the cost of living changes by a specified percentage, when there has been a "substantial" change,[265] or simply at specified intervals.[266]

In the arbitration of contract reopening disputes, the cost-of-living standard is relevant in many instances. Furthermore, in some reopening disputes, the arbitrator asserted the authority to consider all relevant standards unless restricted by the agreement or the submission, all wage-determining factors being deemed equally applicable whether it be a reopening or a new contract dispute.[267] However, in other instances the arbitrator recognized the limitation that weight may be given only to those factors for which the evidence indicates there has been a change since the agreement was signed (sometimes called the "erosion doctrine," limiting the function of reopening to "restoring the bargain" that the parties made when the agreement was signed).[268]

A clause in a collective bargaining agreement providing for an automatic wage increase equal to the increase in the cost of living has been held not to survive the expiration of the agreement, despite the fact that the parties had agreed to continue the terms of the agreement pending the negotiation of a

---

tions fail. *Major Collective Bargaining Agreements: Arbitration Procedures* 101 (U.S. Dep't of Labor Bull. No. 1425-6, 1966) (indicating also that demands for general wage changes were the predominant issues subject to arbitration). For other statistics as to use of reopening (and escalator) clauses, see Stieber, *Voluntary Arbitration of Contract Terms, in* Arbitration and the Expanding Role of Neutrals, Proceedings of the 23d Annual Meeting of NAA 71 (Somers & Dennis eds., BNA Books 1970). In *State of Connecticut*, 77 LA 729, 746–47 (Healy & Seibel, 1981), the arbitrators explained that in the public sector a significant number of retirement programs "have some form of COLA [cost of living adjustment] protection despite its high cost"; that the programs "generally do not fully adjust pension benefits to keep pace with inflation"; but that a "significant number of states provide a method for some ad hoc COLA increases in addition to any guaranteed COLAs provided for in their retirement programs." They explained further that the ad hoc "type of protection becomes particularly important in periods of high inflation during which one may also assume that the earnings from the assets of the retirement program will exceed the assumed rate of return." *Id.* at 747.

[265]Concerning what might be considered "substantial," see *Minnegasco Energy Ctr.*, 82 LA 210, 211 (Gallagher, 1984); *Keyport Woodworking Co.*, 17 LA 914, 916 (Lesser, 1952); *Steinway & Sons*, 17 LA 31, 33 (Justin, 1951); *National Zinc Co.*, 16 LA 944, 949 (Granoff, 1951).

[266]See CSR & Nev. Ready Mix, 109 LA 887 (Prayzich, 1997); Prescription Health Servs., 89 LA 663, 664 (Darrow, 1987); *Major Collective Bargaining Agreements: Arbitration Procedures*, at 101 (U.S. Dep't of Labor Bull. No. 1425-6, 1966).

[267]See Houston Chronicle Publ'g Co., 56 LA 487, 491 (Platt, 1971); Atlanta Newspapers, Inc., 43 LA 1094, 1099 (Wallen, 1964) (stating that a de novo wage determination was permitted); Atlanta Newspapers, 42 LA 548, 553 (Dworkin, 1964); Mohawk Carpet Mills, 26 LA 651, 659 (Shipman, 1956); New York Times, 22 LA 297, 298–99 (Shulman, 1954); National Chair Co., 17 LA 114, 116 (Lesser, 1951). *See also* Pacific Mar. Ass'n, 35 LA 185, 187–88 (Ross, 1960); Pittsburgh Rys. Co., 14 LA 662, 669–70 (Dash, Jr., 1950). In *Rose-Derry Ohio*, 49 LA 40, 43 (Kates, 1967), a clause permitting wage reopening when the cost-of-living index changes 2.5% was deemed to specify the time of reopening but not to specify how much of a wage adjustment may be negotiated when a reopening is triggered.

[268]See Labor Standards Ass'n, 36 LA 171, 177 (Roberts, 1960); Birmingham News Co., 23 LA 629, 639–40 (Dworet, 1954). *See also* Labor Standards Ass'n, 36 LA 201, 203–04 (Luskin, 1960); American Woolen Co., 20 LA 437, 439 (O'Connell, 1952). An objective similar to that of "restoring the bargain" was found in connection with a clause for automatic wage adjustments at specified intervals in *Auburn Foundry*, 81 LA 274, 276 (Katz, 1983), the arbitrator stating that "based on the purpose of such clauses, absent specific language limiting the right to decrease cost of living allowances, the allowance should increase or decrease depending on the Consumer Price Index." *See also* Oil Transp. Co., 81 LA 272, 274 (Shearer, 1983).

successor agreement.[269] Where the financial outlook for an employer or the prospects for a future government regulation or program impacting the issue are uncertain, arbitrators may permit a limited reopener to establish future benefit levels rather than fix the amounts for the duration of the contract.[270]

G. Living Wage

The living-wage standard is related to, but not the same as, the cost-of-living standard. The living-wage standard is in some respects based on the ideal that the standard of living of American workers should be raised to the highest level possible,[271] but a more realistic basis for it is the belief that "employees are entitled to wages and salaries sufficient to enable them, through the exercise of thrift and reasonable economy, to maintain themselves and [their] families in decency and comfort and to make reasonable provision for old age,"[272] including home ownership.[273]

An important difference exists between the cost-of-living and the living-wage standards. While the cost-of-living standard is used to keep the standard of living of employees at the status quo, the living-wage standard (which is not directly tied to changes in the cost of living) is invoked to raise the wages of employees to the point that will allow them a decent standard of living. Application of the living-wage standard may well result in a wage increase greater than that which is indicated by the change in cost of living.

A major disadvantage of the living-wage standard is its indefiniteness.[274] What may be considered a decent standard of living is largely dependent on time and circumstances. Even with the necessary information, a number of broad policy decisions would have to be made by agreement of the parties. The most important of these decisions are:

> (1) whether the size of the family alone . . . or the composition of the family, including size and other characteristics, should be used; (2) whether the necessary income should come only from earnings of the employee or whether income from all sources should be considered; (3) whether income from earnings should be computed on the basis of 2,080 hours (52 x 40 hours) at straight-time, without incentive earnings or "fringe" benefits, . . . or on the basis of earnings

---

[269]Nome Joint Utils. Bd., 103 LA 313 (Carr, 1994).

[270]Cuyahoga County, Ohio, Sheriff's Dep't, 102 LA 143 (Strasshofer, Jr., 1993).

[271]Atlantic & Gulf Coast Shippers, 6 LA 700, 702 (Kleinsorge, 1947).

[272]San Francisco Employers Council, 7 LA 35, 38 (Wyckoff, 1946). *See also* Pinehaven Sanitarium, 47 LA 482, 486 (Singer, 1966).

[273]City of West Bend, Wis., 100 LA 1118, 1122 (Vernon, 1993); Waterloo, Iowa, Cmty. Sch. Dist., 99 LA 385, 388 (Dilts, 1992).

[274]In *Port Authority of Allegheny County, Pa.*, 50 LA 1103, 1112–13 (Platt, 1968), the parties referred to the City Worker's Family Budget, but the arbitrator deemed it of little significance to the case. He commented:

> To properly evaluate this criterion would involve consideration of many collateral questions to which there are no answers in the record. Indeed, as Professor Alfred Kuhn observed in his monograph on Arbitration in Transit, the living wage criterion, because of its vagueness and intangibility, provides a sort of glittering generality which "has never been and does not seem destined to become an important wage determinant in the transit industry."

See also Commonwealth Edison Co. of Ind., 72 LA 90, 95 (Goldberg, 1978).

from overtime plus incentive earnings and "fringe" benefits, as well as straight-time earnings; (4) whether the resulting increase should be related only to the job performed or should also vary with number of dependents of individual employees.[275]

H. Ability to Pay

In the private sector, an employer's lack of ability to pay a proposed wage increase is an issue often raised in interest arbitration. In one case, the employer's inability to pay was the event that triggered arbitration. The parties had agreed that the employer would open its books to a union auditor and if, on inspection, the auditor determined that the wages sought by the union could not be paid, arbitration would follow.[276]

Although it is a generally recognized principle that large profits do not alone justify demands for wages substantially higher than those that are standard within an industry and that small profits do not justify the payment of substandard wages,[277] the ability-to-pay criterion is of great importance in the determination of wage rates and other contract benefits. This importance lies largely in the fact that, while an employer's ability to pay is not, in and of itself, a sufficient basis for change in wages, it is a significant element properly to be taken into account in determining the weight to be attached to other criteria.[278]

To determine wages exclusively on the basis of ability to pay would lead to wage scales that vary from company to company, and would require a new determination of the wage scale with each rise or fall in profits. The existence of unequal wage levels among different companies would be incompatible with union programs for the equalization of wage rates among companies in the same industry or area. If inability to pay were used as the sole or absolute basis for wage cuts, inefficient producers would receive the benefit of having a lower wage scale than that of efficient ones, regardless of the fact that the value of the services rendered by the employees of each is the same.[279] One arbitration board indicated three different degrees of weight that may be given to the ability-to-pay factor. Speaking through its chairman, that board outlined the three situations as follows: (1) "[i]n the case of properties which have been highly profitable over a period of years, the wage rate would normally be increased slightly over the levels indicated by other standards"; (2) "in the case of persistently unprofitable firms, the wage rate would nor-

---

[275]Meat Packing Indus., 9 LA 978, 998–99 (Feinsinger, Davis, & Schaefer, 1948).

[276]ATE/Ryder, 101 LA 52 (Darrow, 1993).

[277]*See* Third Ave. Transit Corp., 1 LA 321, 325 (Hays, 1946); Galveston Model Laundry, 26 WAR LAB. REP. 224 (1943). *Cf.* Munsingwear, Inc., 65 LA 997, 1001–02 (Blum, 1975). In *City of Southfield, Mich.*, 78 LA 153, 155 (Roumell, Jr., 1982) (quoting Killingsworth), the arbitrator quoted another arbitrator to the effect that "the employer's ability to pay may probably be taken into consideration only within the limits of a 'zone of reasonableness.'"

[278]City of Tucson, Ariz., 111 LA 1078 (Halter, 1998); General Motors Corp., 1 LA 125, 145 (Garrison, Eisenhower, & Stacy, 1946). *See also* Waterloo, Iowa, Cmty. Sch. Dist., 99 LA 385, 389 (Dilts, 1992) (ability to pay the decisive issue); Yellow Cab Co., 27 LA 468, 473 (Prasow, 1956).

[279]The employer paying lower scales would, of course, ultimately tend to get less efficient labor.

mally be reduced slightly from the levels indicated by other standards"; and (3) "in the case of the companies whose financial record over a period of years falls between these extremes, the wage rate level would be determined largely by other standards."[280]

An arbitrator may give recognition to an employer's weak financial position by ordering that a needed increase be made gradually,[281] or not at all.[282] Sometimes an arbitrator will award an increase but will recognize the inability-to-pay factor at least to the extent of limiting or denying retroactivity,[283] or of ordering a review of the employer's financial situation after a specified period.[284] Thus, appropriate relief can be granted to the employer based on operations under the award during the specified period.[285] But mere temporary inability to pay generally is not sufficient to cut down an increase warranted by other criteria. Moreover, consideration generally will not be given to short-run variations in profits.[286] Thus, for example, extensive nonrecurring losses charged to current operations were rejected as the basis for a lower wage adjustment.[287] A probable future decline in ability to pay sometimes will be taken into account by arbitrators "as a moderating influence on the amount of the increase recommended."[288] Also to be considered is the extent to which the other party contributed to reduce costs or to provide a quid pro quo.[289]

Inability to pay may be given slight consideration where the employer's rates are substandard or inequitable in comparison with other rates in the industry or area.[290] While there is a duty to stockholders to make profits,

---

[280]Twin City Rapid Transit Co., 10 LA 581, 594 (Dunlop, Zimring, & Willauer, 1948).

[281]See Hurley Hosp., 56 LA 209, 218 (Roumell, Jr., 1971).

[282]Kimstock, Inc., 94 LA 387 (Gentile, 1990).

[283]See Asplundh Tree Expert Co., 89 LA 183 (Allen, Jr., 1987); Florida E. Coast Ry., 41 LA 1001, 1014 (Platt, Bok, & Guthrie, 1963); Felt Cos., 16 LA 881, 883 (Lesser, 1951). The National War Labor Board considered ability to pay in determining retroactivity of its orders. James L. Whitaker, 14 War Lab. Rep. 401 (1944). It also considered this factor in certain special cases, such as where an employer was unable to pay because of inability to get sufficient oil to operate profitably. Consumers Oil & Ref. Co., 9 War Lab. Rep. 407 (1943).

[284]Detroit, Mich., Sch. Bd., 93 LA 648 (Gould IV, 1989); International Braid Co., 6 LA 911, 913 (Brown, 1947).

[285]Acme Sign Co., 94 LA 505 (Barker, 1990); Associated Food Shops, 7 LA 870, 872–73 (Baskind, 1947).

[286]Florida E. Coast Ry., 41 LA 1001, 1011–13 (Platt, Bok, & Guthrie, 1963). A railroad emergency board explained the "interaction between wages and ability to pay," stating in part:

> Financial distress or high profits do not tend in large-scale industry to affect wages in the very short period. The relationship between wages and financial conditions in large-scale industry is typically more gradual. Erosion of financial conditions and the decline in long-run prospects, or a series of profitable years with continuing good prospects, influence wage setting. The financial experience of the railroads over a series of recent years and their prospects for the next several years are most significant to current decisions on wages.

Railroads, 34 LA 517, 534 (Dunlop, Aaron, & Sempliner, 1960).

[287]U.S. Sugar Co., 5 LA 314, 319 (France, 1946).

[288]Greyhound Bus Co., 1 LA 596, 609 (Simkin, Freidin, & Wallen, 1946). See also Village of Pulaski, Wis., Case No. 44884, 1992 WL 717330 (Petrie, 1992); Prescription Health Servs., 89 LA 663 (Darrow, 1987); American Woolen Co., 11 LA 1132, 1134–35 (Murray, 1949).

[289]Manitowoc, Wis., Sch. Dist., 100 LA 844, 849 (Rice II, 1992).

[290]See City of Canton, Ohio, 96 LA 259, 264–65 (Duda, Jr., 1990); Detroit, Mich., Sch. Bd., 93 LA 648, 656–57 (Gould IV, 1989); Hendel Petroleum Co., 27 LA 85, 87 (Donnelly, 1956).

there also is a duty to employees to pay "fair" wages.[291] It has been said that a company "does not expect price concessions from suppliers because of inability to pay, and must recognize its duty to its employees to pay them fair wages."[292] If, however, an increase in wage rates would put the rates above the industry or area standard, the inability-to-pay factor will be given considerable weight.[293]

Sometimes an increase in wage rates, if granted, would endanger the solvency of the employer. While the basic risk of business belongs to management, not to the employees,[294] "high wage rates have no value to employees when layoffs are caused thereby."[295] Arbitrators take the view that "a clear showing that proposed increases would destroy a business or cause the discontinuance of a service would ordinarily be an important and perhaps a controlling factor in an arbitration decision."[296]

i. *Proof of Inability to Pay*

Employers who have pleaded inability to pay have been held to have the burden of producing sufficient evidence to support the plea. The alleged inability must be more than "speculative,"[297] and failure to produce sufficient evidence will result in a rejection of the plea.[298] The payment of reasonable dividends to stockholders and of reasonable salaries to top management has been held to render invalid a plea of inability to pay.[299] Management should

---

[291]*See* Geelan-Kilmartin Co., 40 LA 282, 284 (Stutz, 1963) ("employees should not be expected to underwrite the employer's losses"); Hendel Petroleum Co., 27 LA 85, 87 (Donnelly, 1956); Birmingham Elec. Co., 7 LA 673, 676 (Strong, 1947). In *Textile Maintenance Ass'n of Greater Kansas City*, 63 LA 197, 202 (Sinicropi, 1974), the employers argued that "the employees must suffer because they are in a declining industry [laundry and dry cleaning]," to which argument the arbitrator responded that "[l]ikewise the employers must suffer."

[292]Birmingham Elec. Co., 7 LA 673, 676 (Strong, 1947). *See also* Intermountain Transp. Co., 23 LA 733, 740 (Kleinsorge, 1954).

[293]Western Union Tel. Co., 4 LA 251, 263 (Wallen, Cahn, & Donahue, 1946).

[294]Village of Pulaski, Wis., Case No. 44884, 1992 WL 717330 (Petrie, 1992); Capital Transit Co., 9 LA 666, 684 (Taylor, 1947); Atlantic City Transp. Co., 9 LA 577, 580 (Cole, 1948).

[295]Prairie DuChien Woolen Mills Co., 10 LA 73, 75 (Rauch, 1948). *See also* Kimstock, Inc., 94 LA 387, 388–89 (Gentile, 1990); League of Voluntary Hosps., 67 LA 293, 303 (Gootnick, 1976).

[296]CSR & Nev. Ready Mix, 109 LA 887 (Prayzich, 1997) (an employer pleading inability to pay must carry its burden of producing sufficient evidence to support that plea and the inability to pay must be more than speculative); Georgia Power Co., 8 LA 691, 695 (Hepburn, 1947). *See also* Kimstock, Inc., 94 LA 387, 388 (Gentile, 1990).

[297]Restaurant-Hotel Employers' Council of San Diego, 11 LA 469, 477 (Aaron, 1948).

[298]*See* Florida E. Coast Ry., 41 LA 1001, 1013 (Platt, Bok, & Guthrie, 1963). *See also* City of Clinton, Iowa, 72 LA 190, 196 (Winton, 1979) (proceeding on the assumption that the municipal employer was "in reasonably good financial condition," because "[n]o evidence to the contrary was presented"); Textile Maint. Ass'n of Greater Kan. City, 63 LA 197, 201 (Sinicropi, 1974) (pointing to certain inadequacies of income tax returns as evidence of the employer's economic status). From the standpoint of the duty to bargain under the National Labor Relations Act, substantiating evidence to support a plea of inability to pay need not always be furnished, but refusal to furnish such evidence on request is one of the factors that may be considered in determining whether the employer has refused to bargain in good faith. Truitt Mfg. Co. v. NLRB, 351 U.S. 149, 38 LRRM 2042 (1956).

[299]Employees Transit Lines, 4 LA 748, 752 (Copelof, 1946). In *City of Havre, Montana*, 76 LA 789, 794–97 (Snow, 1981), the arbitrator stated it to be "his obligation to test the basic proposition of the Employer that 'severe financial hardships' prevent the City from funding what the arbitrator has concluded is a reasonable wage demand." Pointing to recent equipment acquisitions and capital improvements, which were nice but not imperative, and not-

be prepared to disclose its financial records in support of a plea of inability to pay. Arbitrators should provide any safeguards needed to protect the confidential nature of such evidence. Failure of management specifically to plead inability to pay may be considered sufficient to establish ability to pay up to the maximum demanded by the union.[300]

While an employer who claims "inability to pay" has the burden of proof on the issue, if the financial exigency appears to be continuing and the employer is using its reserves to pay for current costs, arbitrators will temper any wage increase.[301] But even if past dismal financial results support the employer's position, the claim may be discounted if the evidence shows that the employer's fiscal prospects are improving.[302]

ii. *Public Utilities' Ability to Pay*

Special considerations are involved in the application of the ability-to-pay standard in public utility disputes. It is recognized that because a public utility produces a basic necessity of life and because the public regulatory body must ensure the opportunity for a fair return, capacity to pay generally will exist, potentially at least, and almost any conceivable level of wages could be paid and a "fair profit" still returned to the stockholders. However, not only "fair wages" and "fair profits" are involved—a "fair price" to the consumer also enters the picture. Thus, the ability to pay should not be made the primary consideration in determining public utility wage rates.[303]

An arbitrator may give some weight to the fact that a company is unable, under the terms of its franchise, to seek an increase in the price of its service to the public. This was done by one arbitrator despite the contention of the union that it should not be made a party to the "straightjacket" in which the company had placed itself.[304] However, an arbitrator may refuse to grant the request of a public utility that any wage increase awarded should be conditioned on the company's securing a rate increase for its services. One arbitrator, speaking as chairman of an arbitration board, explained the view behind such refusal:

> In public utilities, including the railroads, there appears to be a long tradition of separation of wage and rate setting. This does not mean that rates and prices are irrelevant to wage setting, but rather that wage rates have tended to be fixed with some general reference to financial capacity and then these costs in turn have been taken into account by the rate or fare making body. Such has been the actual relation between collective bargaining or emergency boards determining wage rates and the Inter-State Commerce Commission setting railroad rates and fares. The transit industry has tended to follow an analogous practice.

---

ing that the city had not taken advantage of the full potential of revenue sources, he concluded that the city had failed to meet its burden of proving financial hardship in relation to the reasonable wage demand of the employees. *See also* City of Quincy, Ill., 81 LA 352, 357 (Block, 1982).

[300]Oil Indus., 1 LA 168, 176 (Graham, Eliel, & Beyer, 1946).

[301]Independent Sch. Dist. 361, 104 LA 323 (Berquist, 1995).

[302]Cuyahoga County, Ohio, Sheriff's Dep't, 102 LA 143 (Strasshofer, Jr., 1993).

[303]Pacific Gas & Elec. Co., 7 LA 528, 531 (Kerr, 1947). *See also* Nodak Rural Elec. Coop., 78 LA 1119, 1122–24 (Eisele, 1982) (note the company's position and its discussion by the arbitrator); Head of the Lakes Elec. Coop. Ass'n, 65 LA 839, 844 (Sembower, 1975); Arizona Pub. Serv. Co., 63 LA 1189, 1196 (Platt, 1974).

[304]New York City Omnibus Corp., 7 LA 794, 809 (Cole, 1947).

The majority of the Arbitration Board believes it can follow no other precedent in this case. . . . When the Arbitration Board has fixed the wage rates, the appropriate fare making body should then set fares, in accordance with proper standards, including the wage rates set by this Arbitration Board as costs. No other procedure in the fixing of wages and fares, which are necessarily interdependent, by different bodies can be workable.[305]

iii. Other Public-Sector Entities' Ability to Pay

In the public sector, with the necessity of continuing to provide adequate public service as a given, "going out of business" is not an option, and an employer's inability to pay can be the decisive factor in a wage award notwithstanding that comparable employers in the area have agreed to higher wage scales.[306] The city of Detroit had been experiencing recurrent deficits, and the future revenue picture did not appear any brighter. The benefits in the contract were already greater than the average in the community. The arbitrator concluded that the only way to balance the budget was to cut wages by 10 percent.

However, the entire burden of budget deficits cannot be placed on a union. In one case, the Metro Area Express was unquestionably experiencing continuing deficits, but a number of employees had already been laid off, and the arbitrator concluded that cutting wages would have unfairly increased the burden on the employees remaining.[307] Resort to tax or service charge increases or solicitation of additional inter-governmental transfers or subsidies may be required.

Disputes over the financial condition of a governmental employer are common.[308] For example, this issue surfaced in an impasse proceeding between a county sheriff's department and its employees. The county auditor's report showed a general fund balance of $80,924, but the sheriff claimed only $13,677. The factfinder gave the auditor's calculations greater probative value and found the sheriff could afford to elevate wages to equal those paid in comparable counties.[309]

Governmental employers often do not have significant sources of revenue apart from the taxing power, and that power may be limited as to subjects and its exercise dependent on vote of the electorate.[310] In one case, the arbitrator noted the dilemma of a board of education, as employer, that was

---

[305]Indianapolis Rys., 9 LA 319, 330 (Dunlop, 1947). In recognition of the problem implied here, it has sometimes been suggested that the whole job should be done by the same agency, i.e., that the rate-making body should also have jurisdiction to determine wage rates. It has also sometimes been suggested that wage awards should bind the utility commission. In any event, one arbitrator in effect asked that the regulatory commission grant a rate increase to accommodate the wage increase granted by his award. *See* Twin City Rapid Transit Co., 16 LA 749, 760 (Platt, 1951).

[306]City of Detroit, Mich., 102 LA 764 (Lipson, 1993).

[307]Birmingham-Jefferson County Metro Transit Auth./Metro Area Express, 103 LA 1 (Baroni, 1994).

[308]*See, e.g.*, City of Detroit, Mich., 102 LA 764 (Lipson, 1993).

[309]Cuyahoga County, Ohio, Sheriff's Dep't, 102 LA 143 (Strasshofer, Jr., 1993).

[310]For discussion of various special considerations that may be involved, see Miscimarra, *Inability to Pay: The Problem of Contract Enforcement in Public Sector Collective Bargaining*, 43 U. PITT. L. REV. 703 (1982); Mulcahy, *Ability to Pay: The Public Employee Dilemma*, 31 ARB. J. 90 (1976). In *Hamtramck, Mich., Board of Education*, 54 LA 162, 162–63 (Gould,

confronted by wage demands from teachers in spite of recent defeats of tax proposals for school purposes:

> The Board of Education is placed squarely in the middle in all these financing problems. On the one hand, they must provide for the citizenry the best possible education for the children of the area. On the other hand, they must answer to those same citizens for the use of the tax dollars. Unfortunately, millage issues seem to be the area where already-overtaxed voters get their revenge. Unless the Oscoda area constituents soon realize the importance of their support, their children will have no classrooms in which to learn. The burden of supporting the capital expenditures of a school system should not fall totally upon the teachers, although some restraint in wage demands is advisable.[311]

In granting a wage increase to police officers to bring them generally in line with police in other communities, an arbitration board recognized the

---

1971), the dispute was submitted by the parties with the understanding that the neutral should not make any recommendations that would result in a deficit budget for the public employer. In *City of North Las Vegas, Nevada*, 75 LA 784, 789 (Sullivan, 1980), the arbitrator stated that by statute his recommendations or award must be based upon "facts" in evidence and that "anticipated, but not yet appropriated, certain or guaranteed" federal revenue-sharing funds accordingly could not be considered in determining the public-sector employer's financial ability to pay the full increase demanded by the union. For discussion of interest arbitration and state "cap" laws limiting increases in public spending, see Minami, *Interest Arbitration: Can the Public Sector Afford It? Developing Limitations on the Process: I. An Overview, in* ARBITRATION ISSUES FOR THE 1980S, PROCEEDINGS OF THE 34TH ANNUAL MEETING OF NAA 241 (Stern & Dennis eds., BNA Books 1982); Clark, *Interest Arbitration: Can the Public Sector Afford It? Developing Limitations on the Process: II. A Management Perspective, in id.* at 248; Fallon, *Interest Arbitration: Can the Public Sector Afford It? Developing Limitations on the Process: III. An Arbitrator's Viewpoint, in id.* at 259.

[311]Oscoda, Mich., Area Sch. Board of Educ., 55 LA 568, 578 (Bloch, 1970). *See also* City of Burlington, Iowa, 68 LA 454, 457 (Witney, 1977) (stating that the municipal employer was "faced with serious financial problems resulting from economic conditions over which it has no control," and that while the arbitrator's observations concerning the employer's financial situation "will not comfort" the employees, "they are economic realities"); Town of Dedham, Mass., 67 LA 384, 387 (Holden, Jr., 1976); Pellston, Mich., Pub. Sch., 66 LA 249, 250 (Bychinsky, 1976); Metropolitan Tulsa Transit Auth., 63 LA 621, 624–25 (Oppenheim, 1974); City of Kenosha, Wis., 63 LA 126, 131–32 (Rauch, 1974); Worcester County, Md., Teachers' Ass'n, 54 LA 796, 799 (Seidenberg, 1971) ("the salaries must come from public revenues which are not limitless, and while teachers should not be expected to subsidize the community in its efforts to obtain quality education, their salary requests must be viewed in light of the total county demands for public funds"); Arlington Educ. Ass'n, 54 LA 492, 495 (Zack, 1971); South Hackensack, N.J., Bd. of Educ., 52 LA 1169, 1176 (Kerrison, 1969) (noting budget limitations and the fact that the budget had been approved at the polls); Parma Educ. Ass'n, 52 LA 800, 802 (Teple, 1969) (community refused to support higher levy needed for teacher salary increase; the arbitrator recommended no increase for balance of school year because the employer had no source of revenue for payment of any increase, rejecting a suggestion that an increase be paid even if the school must close early for lack of funds). Legislation enacted to implement California's Proposition 13 was involved in *County of Humboldt, Cal.*, 72 LA 63, 66 (Henderson, 1978), where the award merely stated that "the County is *not* in a position to finance the economic request of the Sheriff's Department, even though based upon the [Consumer Price Index] and other factors a salary increase may well be justified." For other examples of statutory obligation imposed upon neutrals to give substantial or controlling weight to the public-sector employer's inability to pay, see *City of N. Las Vegas, Nev.*, 75 LA 784, 785 (Sullivan, 1980) (involving a Nevada statute providing that a finding must first be made regarding financial ability to pay, and that if ability to pay is found, then the neutral "shall use normal criteria for interest disputes"); Gershenfeld & Gershenfeld, *Significant Developments in Public Employment Disputes Settlement During 1978, in* ARBITRATION OF SUBCONTRACTING AND WAGE INCENTIVE DISPUTES, PROCEEDINGS OF THE 32D ANNUAL MEETING OF NAA 215, 221–22 (Stern & Dennis eds., BNA Books 1980) (discussing the Financial Emergency Act for the city of New York as amended in 1978 to require neutrals to accord substantial weight to the factor of ability to pay; the amendment defined ability to pay as the "financial ability . . . to pay the cost of any increase in wages or fringe benefits without requiring an increase in the level of city taxes existing" when the impasse proceeding commenced).

financial problems of the city resulting from temporarily reduced property valuations during an urban redevelopment program, but the board stated that a police officer should be treated as a skilled employee whose wages reflect the caliber of the work expected from such employees. The board declared that it "cannot accept the conclusion that the Police Department must continue to suffer until the redevelopment program is completed."[312] However, the board did give definite weight to the city's budget limitations by denying a request for improved vacation benefits, additional insurance, a shift differential, and a cost-of-living escalator clause.[313] In another case, involving police officers and firefighters, an arbitrator awarded a 6 percent wage increase (which he recognized as the prevailing pattern in private industry) despite the city's financial problems. He limited the increase to this figure, though a larger increase was deserved, in order to keep the city within the statutory taxing limit and in light of the impact of the award on the wages of other city employees.[314]

In some cases, neutrals have expressly asserted an obligation of public employers to make added efforts to obtain additional funds to finance improved terms of employment found to be justified.[315] In one case, the neutral refused to excuse a public employer from its obligation to pay certain automatic increases that the employer had voluntarily contracted to pay, the neutral ordering the employer to "take all required steps to provide the funds necessary to implement" his award in favor of the employees.[316]

---

[312]Borough of Turtle Creek, Pa., 52 LA 233, 235 (McDermott, Zollner, & Hutskow, 1968). *See also* City of Southfield, Mich., 78 LA 153, 155 (Roumell, Jr., 1982) (quoting Arbitrator Gabriel Alexander).

[313]Borough of Turtle Creek, Pa., 52 LA 233, 235, 237 (McDermott, Zollner, & Hutskow, 1968). In *City of Uniontown, Pa.*, 51 LA 1072, 1074 (Duff, 1968), some improved fringe benefits were awarded to police department employees in lieu of awarding a salary increase larger than that necessary to place them "on parity with salaries paid by municipalities of comparable size."

[314]City of Easton, Pa., 51 LA 879, 881–82 (Handsaker, 1968). In *City of Mount Vernon, N.Y.*, 49 LA 1229, 1232–33 (McFadden, Gould, & Karow, 1968), involving police and firefighters, factfinders would "not ignore" the city's ability to pay, but they declared that they must make recommendations that are fair and equitable to the employees, the public employer, and the public itself. They added: "In the final analysis, the City . . . must raise whatever revenues are necessary in the manner which it deems best. The electorate must then pass on these decisions and, inferentially, this Board's recommendations." The factfinders construed the New York public employee statute as contemplating budgetary action subsequent to factfinding, and they suggested that the budgetary action already taken by the city should not be deemed so final as to preclude implementation of the board's recommendations. For another case where the neutral balanced the interests of the employees (firefighters), the city (particularly as to financial resources), and the public, see *City of Providence, R.I.*, 42 LA 1114, 1118–19 (Dunlop, Pierce, & Hoban, 1963). *See also* City of Philadelphia, 79 LA 372, 373 (DiLauro, 1982).

[315]*See* Fountain Valley, Cal., Sch. Dist., 65 LA 1009, 1015 (Rule, 1975) (outlining several steps that the employer might consider for the purpose of financing the full wage increase recommended for teachers); Minnesota State Highway Patrol, 56 LA 697, 699 (Gleeson, 1971) (the parties should urge the legislature to appropriate funds); City of Southgate, Mich., 54 LA 901, 908–10 (Roumell, Jr., 1971); City of Providence, R.I., 47 LA 1036, 1040 (Seitz, 1966). In *Amphitheater Public School Board of Trustees*, 75 LA 268, 274–75 (Weizenbaum, 1980), the arbitrator's wage recommendation was made with due recognition that it was "a time when careful planning and paring of dollars from the budget is essential," but the door was left ajar for possible additional benefits, her award stating that the parties "agree to reopen renegotiations if the Arizona legislature makes changes in school finance after an agreement is reached."

[316]City of Cleveland, 57 LA 781, 787–89 (Dworkin, 1971). *Cf.* City of Rialto, 67 LA 654, 657–58 (Gentile, 1976).

Finally, where one city submitted information regarding its revenues and expenditures to support its claim of inability to pay an otherwise justified wage increase, the arbitrator responded that the "information is interesting, but is not really relevant to the issues," and explained:

> The *price of labor* must be viewed like any other commodity which needs to be purchased. If a new truck is needed, the City does not plead poverty and ask to buy the trade for 25% of its established price. It can shop various dealers and makes of truck to get the best possible buy. But in the end the City either pays the asked price or gets along without a new truck.[317]

It should be recognized that the employer was a "home rule" city and that the arbitrator did not indicate the existence of any legal debt limitation on the city.[318]

I. Competition

A factor that often must be given consideration in interest arbitration is the competitive nature of the employer's business.[319] In some respects this is related to the ability-to-pay standard. In other respects it is related to the prevailing-practice standard. For these reasons it generally is not considered as an independent standard. Where, however, an employer is engaged in a highly competitive business or is faced with special competitive problems, the arbitrator may specifically point out the competitive nature of the employer's business as a factor to be given special consideration in setting contract terms (sometimes even justifying a wage reduction).[320] Another consideration is the proximity of a large city and suburbs and their effect on the competitive labor market.[321]

J. Productivity

The productivity standard is frequently advanced for consideration by arbitrators of wage disputes. Proponents of this standard urge that increases in productivity should be reflected by increases in wages. It has been recognized that there is a close relationship between the general level of productivity and the general level of wages,[322] and that both an increase in wage

---

[317]City of Quincy, Ill., 81 LA 352, 356 (Block, 1982).

[318]As a "home rule" city under the state constitution, the city was permitted to "exercise any power and perform any function pertaining to its government and affairs; and to protect the general health, morals, safety and welfare of its citizens." *Id.* at 353.

[319]CSR, 111 LA 487 (Prayzich, 1998).

[320]*See* W.T. Congleton Co., 66 LA 158, 160 (Stout, Jr., 1976); Iowa Beef Processors, 62 LA 654, 655 (Gill, 1974); Royster Guano Co., 41 LA 372, 375 (Black, 1963); Appleton Coop. Ass'n, 39 LA 249, 253 (Gundermann, 1962); Portland Woolen Mills, Inc., 24 LA 38, 44 (Kleinsorge, 1955); Wurtzel & Gordon Co., 23 LA 843, 844 (Donnelly, 1955); Massachusetts Leather Mfrs. Ass'n, 23 LA 762, 773 (Hogan, 1954); Botany Mills, Inc., 22 LA 653, 654 (Knowlton, 1954); Fall River Textile Mfrs. Ass'n, 18 LA 774, 775 (Gellhorn, 1952); Bates Mfg. Co., 18 LA 631, 644–45 (Simkin, 1952); Spear & Co., 9 LA 567, 569 (Singer, 1948); Bloomingdale Bros., 8 LA 194, 195 (Wolff, 1947); Baker & Co., 7 LA 350, 353 (Kirsh, 1947).

[321]City of West Bend, Wis., 100 LA 1118, 1122 (Vernon, 1993).

[322]Slichter, Basic Criteria Used in Wage Negotiations 21 (1947). In a December 1970 speech to the National Association of Manufacturers, U.S. Secretary of Labor James D. Hodgson noted the growing interest in improving what might be termed the quality of life and suggested that the problem is whether this can be achieved without sacrificing some-

rates and a reduction in hours may be warranted by increased productivity measured in terms of added output per employee-hour.[323]

In one case, the union advanced figures to show that productivity had been rising over an extended period of time within the plant, and argued that real wages should be increased commensurately. The arbitration board considered productivity to be an "influential but not decisive" factor and, speaking through its chairman, said:

> Normally wages rise somewhat more rapidly in those industries where productivity is rising rapidly and less rapidly where productivity is rising slowly or not at all or even declining. Thus productivity is an influential but not controlling factor. For the whole economy it is of more significance, perhaps, than for the individual plant or industry. Real wages can rise significantly in the long run only as physical productivity increases. To tie wages rigidly in each minor segment of the economy to changes in physical productivity in that segment would, however, cause greater distortion as between and among progressive, static and regressive industries than could be sustained.[324]

In another case, a factfinding board for the steel industry stated the belief that wage rates in a particular industry should not be tied directly to productivity in that industry, but, rather, should be related to the general industrial rise in productivity; moreover, the board said, any excesses of productivity in any one industry over the general average should provide primarily the means of reducing the prices of the products of that industry.[325]

Increases in productivity can result in increased wages, decreased prices, increased profits, or some combination of the three. If the increase in output per employee-hour is due to greater effort and greater skill, there would appear to be no doubt that the gain should accrue to the benefit of the employees. But if the increase is the result of technological progress or better management, several considerations must be taken into account.

While arbitrators may give weight to the productivity factor when increased production is used as the basis of a demand for an increase, they are not likely to give the factor much consideration when an employer defends against an increase by alleging that its employees have a lower per capita output than is standard. For instance, low productivity has been held not to

---

thing in the quantity or quality of goods and services; in his view, increased productivity or production efficiency is the answer.

[323]General Motors Corp., 1 LA 125, 130 (Garrison, Eisenhower, & Stacy, 1946).

[324]Pacific Gas & Elec. Co., 7 LA 528, 530 (Kerr, 1947). Some weight was also given to productivity in *City of Havre, Mont.*, 76 LA 789, 793–94 (Snow, 1981) (finding that there were fewer employees than formerly, the arbitrator stated that it "is not simply a matter of the same number of employees performing more work, but fewer employees are accomplishing the job for the Employer"); *Government Printing Office*, 73 LA 1, 4–5 (Bloch, 1979); *Arizona Pub. Serv. Co.*, 63 LA 1189, 1192, 1196 (Platt, 1974); *Pacific Mar. Ass'n*, 28 LA 600, 606 (Kagel, 1957). *See also* Houston Chronicle Publ'g Co., 56 LA 487, 488 (Platt, 1971). No weight was given to this factor where the evidence was skimpy. Atlanta Newspapers, 39 LA 207, 209 (Holly, 1962).

[325]Basic Steel Indus., 13 LA 46, 50 (Daugherty, Cole, & Rosenman, 1949). *See also* New York Shipping Ass'n, 20 LA 75, 82–83 (Hays, 1952). *Cf.* Basic Steel Indus., 18 LA 112, 117 (Wage Stabilization Bd., 1952). In *Railroads*, 34 LA 517, 533 (Dunlop, Aaron, & Sempliner, 1960), the board stated:

> The relevance of increases in productivity to wage rates in a particular industry depends in part upon the ratio of labor costs to total costs; the competitive character of the industry, which influences whether such gains are transmitted rapidly into price and quality changes; the methods of wage payment; and other factors.

justify the denial of a pattern increase, because employees' efficiency and output are largely within the control of the employer and the employer should be able, by extending the incentive system, to put the business on a "reasonable competitive basis" in relation to production costs.[326]

A board of arbitration held that an allegedly great reduction in labor efficiency, which the board found to be true to some extent, did not justify the denial of a cost-of-living increase where the inefficiency and high costs in the industry were caused by a variety of factors, including out-of-date technology, the high cost of materials, and a shortage of skilled craftsmen.[327] In another case, the arbitrator granted a cost-of-living increase without giving weight to the employer's complaint that productivity was low, on the ground that there was a failure to establish a decline in productivity after the execution of the contract.[328]

Numerous reasons exist for the refusal of arbitrators to make productivity a decisive factor in wage determination. The rate of change in productivity varies from firm to firm and even from department to department within a plant. Thus, exclusive use of the productivity standard for wage adjustments would soon lead to a chaotic wage structure within a single plant or industry.[329] Moreover, the measurement of productivity presents highly difficult problems of economic analysis and statistical measurement,[330] although assistance may be available under the U.S. Department of Labor productivity measurement program (which issues industry indices of output per employee-hour).[331] Even after a change in productivity has been measured, the problem still remains of determining whether it was caused by increased skill and effort of employees or by better management or improved technol-

---

[326]Watson Elevator Co., 8 LA 386, 389 (Copelof, 1947). In *Dallas Publishers*, 50 LA 367, 373 (Elkouri, 1968), the employees failed to establish any special claim to a wage increase based on their productivity, but the arbitrator acknowledged the economic vitality of the city in which they work to be another type of productivity that had some relevance, under the facts, to the request for increased wages.

[327]Associated Gen. Contractors, 9 LA 201, 226–27 (Aaron, 1947). *See also* Asplundh Tree Expert Co., 89 LA 183 (Allen, Jr., 1987); Dallas, Tex., Newspaper Publishers, 22 LA 88, 93 (Abernethy, 1954).

[328]Waterfront Employers Ass'n of Pac. Coast, 9 LA 172, 178 (Miller, 1947). But declining productivity was one of the factors considered by the arbitrator in refusing to award a greater wage increase than that offered by the company in *Yaun Welding & Machinery Works Co.*, 73 LA 223, 227 (Nicholas, Jr., 1979), stating that "[i]n the face of such declining productivity, Management may rightly demand evidence that an additional increase will prove worthwhile." In this case the arbitrator did note and agree with the union's view that "low wages undoubtedly serve to generate high turnover costs, especially among skilled employees, lowering the productivity of labor." *Id.* But he also noted that the union had rejected management's effort to meet the problem by use of a percentage rather than across-the-board dollar increase (a percentage increase would have meant a larger dollar increase for skilled employees and thus would reduce their turnover rate).

[329]Dunlop, *The Economics of Wage-Dispute Settlement*, 12 Law & Contemp. Probs. 281, 286–87 (1947). *See also* Allen, Updated Notes on the Interindustry Wage Structure, 1890–1990 (Cornell Univ. 1995).

[330]Dunlop, at 287–88. For an example of the difficulty involved in proving productivity changes, see *Waterfront Employers Ass'n of Pac. Coast*, 9 LA 172, 177–78 (Miller, 1947). *See also* Aurora Beacon News, Case No. 94-21494, 1995 WL 862332 (Goldstein, 1995); Labor Standards Ass'n, 27 LA 295, 299 (Horlacher, 1956); Consumers Power Co., 18 LA 686, 690 (Platt, Gemrich, & Arsulowicz,1952).

[331]*See Productivity for Selected Industries, 1997 Edition* (U.S. Dep't Lab., Bureau of Labor Statistics Bull. No. 2491, 1997). Two Bureau of Labor Statistics programs develop productivity and costs data for elements of the U.S. economy. The major sector Productivity and Costs Program produces quarterly and annual output per hour and unit labor costs for the

ogy. The arbitrator also must face the problem of assigning a value to the change in productivity; evidence of changes in productivity is not readily transformed into cents-per-hour wage adjustments.[332]

A powerful factor giving impetus to consideration of productivity as an element in determining wage increases came into being with the agreement of General Motors Corporation in 1950 to grant an annual "improvement factor" increase, amounting to 4 cents per hour. The figure was based on an estimated 3 percent annual improvement in productivity throughout all industry, a figure that the company stated it expected to surpass.[333] The 1979 General Motors agreement specified improvement factor increases (ranging from 25 cents to 45 cents per hour depending on the employee's wage rate) and stated:

> The improvement factor provided herein recognizes that a continuing improvement in the standard of living of employees depends upon technological progress, better tools, methods, processes and equipment, and a cooperative attitude on the part of all parties in such progress. It further recognizes the principle that to produce more with the same amount of human effort is a sound economic and social objective.[334]

K. Take-Home Pay

Maintenance of take-home pay emerged at the end of World War II as a means of "cushioning the shock" of the transition from an economy of war to one of peace.[335] Sudden and extensive reductions in weekly earnings throughout industry as a result of reduction of hours, especially overtime, became a matter of national concern at the end of the war while living costs were still rising. Labor demanded wage increases to maintain take-home pay as hours

---

U.S. business, non-farm business, and manufacturing sectors. Industry productivity data were last published in book form in *Bulletin 2491, Productivity for Selected Industries, 1997.* Since then, such data is available only through press releases or on the BLS website. *See* <http://www.bls.gov/schedule/archives/prod_nr.htm>. The Industry Productivity Program publishes annual measures for output per hour and unit labor costs for over 500 3- and 4-digit Standard Industrial Classification (SIC) industries in the United States, featuring complete coverage in manufacturing and in retail trade, as well as some coverage in other sectors. *See* <http://www.bls.gov/lpc/iprdata1.htm>. BLS maintains and makes available, upon request, unpublished labor productivity measures for over 200 additional industries.

[332]Dunlop, 12 Law & Contemp. Probs. at 288. *See also* New York Shipping Ass'n, 20 LA 75, 82–83 (Hays, 1952); San Diego Gas & Elec. Co., 12 LA 245, 255–56 (Aaron, 1949). For a discussion of productivity and its relation to vacation pay, see *Monroe County, Wis.*, 113 LA 933 (Dichter, 1999).

[333]Regarding the influence of this General Motors step, see *Union R.R.*, 20 LA 219, 224 (Gilden, 1953). While granting an increase partly on the basis of the "annual improvement factor," an arbitrator emphasized that an increase on the basis of this factor is not due automatically in every case, but that the factor is one of the considerations to be taken into account along with other factors. Printing Indus. of Ind., 29 LA 7, 11 (McCoy, 1957). In *Labor Standards Ass'n*, 36 LA 171, 178 (Roberts, 1960), the union sought to introduce a productivity factor that had been adopted in other industries, but the arbitrator stated that "it has never been integrated into the wage bargain of these parties and should not be imposed by an arbitrator."

[334]1979 Contract Between General Motors Corporation and United Auto Workers Regarding Productivity or Improvement Wage Factors.

[335]Another type of situation in which need may exist to "cushion the shock" concerns automation. *See, e.g.*, New York Shipping Ass'n, 36 LA 44 (Stein, 1960) (interest arbitration to determine whether and to what extent royalties should be paid by ship owners to cushion the labor displacement impact of the use of cargo containers).

of work were reduced. In considering these demands, arbitrators and factfinding boards were guided by the national wage-price policy laid down in executive orders, regulations under the Wage Stabilization Act, and an address by the President to the nation.

The maintenance of the take-home pay standard has been given consideration in numerous cases. Although it generally has not been the only standard considered, it has been responsible at least for a part of the increase granted in those cases.[336] In the application of this standard, potential[337] or probable[338] loss of take-home pay may be considered as well as present loss. Application of other standards may preclude the maintenance of take-home pay. For instance, lack of ability to pay was deemed a sufficient reason for permitting the discontinuance of overtime work without at the same time granting a wage increase to maintain take-home pay.[339]

L. Past Practice and Bargaining History [LA CDI 24.351; 24.37; 100.06]

The past practice of the parties has sometimes, although infrequently, been considered to be a standard for interest arbitration. This standard is of special significance when parties are engaged in their initial negotiations. One arbitrator stated:

> The arbitrator considers past practice a primary factor. It is standard form to incorporate past conditions into collective bargaining contracts, whether these contracts are developed by negotiation or arbitration. The fact of unionization creates no basis for the withdrawal of conditions previously in effect. If they were justified before, they remain justified after the event of union affiliation. It is almost axiomatic that the existing conditions be perpetuated. Some contracts even blanket them in through a general "catch-all" clause.[340]

In arbitrating the terms of a renewal contract, one arbitrator would consider seriously "what the parties have agreed upon in their past collective bargaining, as affected by intervening economic events . . . ."[341] The past

---

[336]*See* Bremer County, Iowa, Highway Dep't, 68 LA 628, 631–32 (Yarowsky, 1977); Printing Indus. of Ind., 29 LA 7, 10–11 (McCoy, 1957); Madison Bus Co., 21 LA 307, 309 (Gooding, Fitzgibbon, & Slavney, 1953); Rochester Transit Corp., 19 LA 538, 551–53 (Tolley, McKelvey, & Turkus, 1952); Birmingham S. R.R., 15 LA 524, 525–26 (Payne, 1950); Railway Express Agency, Inc., 12 LA 507, 515 (Cole, Horovitz, & Edwards, 1949); Twin City Rapid Transit Co., 10 LA 581, 596 (Dunlop, Zimring, & Willauer, 1948); F.W. Woolworth Co., 4 LA 502, 506 (Gellhorn, Paley, & Miller, 1946); Washington Gas Light & Suburban Gas Cos., 3 LA 566, 569 (Copelof, 1946); Full-Fashioned Hosiery Mfrs. of Am., 3 LA 639, 645 (Wallen, 1946); Armour & Co., 1 LA 333, 338–39 (Witte, Kerr, & Starr, 1946); General Motors Corp., 1 LA 125, 130, 133 (Garrison, Eisenhower, & Stacy, 1946).

[337]Waterloo, Iowa, Cmty. Sch. Dist., 99 LA 385, 389 (Dilts, 1992); F.W. Woolworth Co., 4 LA 502, 506 (Gellhorn, Paley, & Miller, 1946).

[338]Waterloo, Iowa, Cmty. Sch. Dist., 99 LA 385, 389 (Dilts, 1992) (also reason for denial of union's request for additional benefits); General Motors Corp., 1 LA 125, 133 (Garrison, Eisenhower, & Stacy, 1946).

[339]Roberts Pressure Valve Co., 8 LA 665, 667 (Singer, 1947). *See also* Railroads, 14 LA 688 (McDonough, O'Malley, & Watkins, 1950).

[340]Luckenbach S.S., 6 LA 98, 101 (Kerr, 1946). *See also* Panama Canal Commission, Case No. 98-001, 1998 WL 1110338 (Nolan, 1998); Winnebago County Sheriff's Department, Case No. 45197, 1992 WL 726598 (Petrie, 1992); City of Fort Dodge, Iowa, 86 LA 1178 (Dilts, 1986); St. Paul Dep't Stores, 2 LA 52 (Johnston, Gydeson, & Harmon, 1946).

[341]United Traction Co., 27 LA 309, 315 (Scheiber, 1956).

bargaining history of the parties, including the criteria that they used, has provided a helpful guide to other interest arbitrators.[342]

M. Prearbitration Negotiations

It has been said that the award in a wage dispute seldom falls outside the area of "probable expectancy," and that this area is the normal resultant product of the parties' negotiations and bargaining prior to submitting their differences to arbitration.[343] In this regard, too, one arbitration board concluded:

> An examination of the wealth of evidence submitted in this matter in conjunction with the provisions of settlement worked out by the parties indicates that the most satisfactory award which the Board could render would be one in general agreement with those terms on which the parties were able at one time to substantially agree. Obviously, these terms are not what either party wanted. They represent compromise by both parties. However, since the general terms indicate a meeting of the minds, the Board considers that they hold the basis of a just award.[344]

While observing that interest arbitrators usually can make a more useful award if they have knowledge of the bargaining positions of the parties prior to the arbitration stage, one group of arbitrators suggested that if at least one of the parties wishes to exclude consideration of prearbitral offers,

---

[342]This aid was used, as specified by a public-sector statute, in *Hurley Hospital*, 56 LA 209, 212–15 (Roumell, Jr., 1971). *See also* Sioux County, 68 LA 1258, 1263 (Gruenberg, 1977); Town of Dedham, 67 LA 384, 386 (Holden, Jr., 1976). It was used in private-sector arbitration in *Commonwealth Edison Co. of Ind.*, 72 LA 90, 95 (Goldberg, 1978); *Republican Co.*, 69 LA 1041, 1048 (Holden, 1977); *Oxmoor Press*, 68 LA 1064, 1067–68 (Williams, 1977); *National Elec. Contractors Ass'n*, 65 LA 1016, 1018–19 (Griffin, 1975); *Munsingwear, Inc.*, 65 LA 997, 1002 (Blum, 1975); *San Francisco Elec. Contractors Ass'n*, 60 LA 1, 7 (Feller, 1973); *Dallas Publishers*, 50 LA 367, 370 (Elkouri, 1968); *Appleton Coop. Ass'n*, 39 LA 249, 251 (Gundermann, 1962); *Des Moines Transit Co.*, 38 LA 666, 671 (Flagler, 1962); *Labor Standards Ass'n*, 36 LA 201, 202–03 (Luskin, 1960). In *Volunteer Electrical Cooperative*, 78 LA 352, 256 (Hamby, Jr., 1982), the arbitrator refused to disturb certain contractual obligations that initially had been negotiated by the parties and subsequently were perpetuated by another interest arbitrator. In *Bonneville Power Administration*, 73 LA 429, 435 (Keltner, 1979), the wage increase awarded was determined on "the basis of the historical tandem relationships" existing between the employer and eight other utilities in the area, the arbitrator stating that "the rate of increase should be consistent with the past practice of paying the average of the prevailing rates." *See also* Government Printing Office, 73 LA 1, 4 (Bloch, 1979). In *City of New Berlin, Wisconsin*, 114 LA 1704 (Dichter, 2000), the union contended that its proposal was simply a memorialization of an existing practice and that no quid pro quo was required for incorporating it into the agreement. The arbitrator held that in this circumstance, the practice could not be established in such a short time.

[343]Justin, *Arbitrating a Wage Dispute Case*, 3 ARB. J. (n.s.) 228 (1948). *See also* Bates Mfg. Co., 18 LA 631, 643 (Simkin, 1952). It is also said that parties sometimes agree on contract terms but for political reasons want an arbitrator to order them. *Current Problems of Arbitration, American Unionism*, 29 LA 880, 883 (1958).

[344]Durso & Geelan Co., 17 LA 748, 749 (Donnelly, Curry, & Clark, 1951). *See also* Sharon Teachers' Ass'n, 50 LA 1036, 1042–43 (Siegel, 1968); Royster Guano Co., 41 LA 372, 375–76 (Black, 1963). In "many instances intangible factors such as the indicated bids or offers by the parties in private bargaining . . . will be of considerable importance" in the arbitrator's consideration of the case. BACKMAN, ECONOMIC DATA UTILIZED IN WAGE ARBITRATION 3 (1952). In *Palo Alto-Stanford Hospital Center*, 50 LA 700, 701 (Mann, 1968), the submission agreement expressly confined the arbitrator to the limits of the parties' original proposals. *See also* A.S. Abell Co., 45 LA 801, 806 (Cluster, Gallagher, & Kraushaar, 1965). In *Eastalco Aluminum Co.*, 70 LA 793, 795 (Whyte, 1978), the arbitrator acknowledged the limitation without clearly indicating that it was imposed by the submission agreement.

it may be sound policy for the arbitrator to do so lest future bargaining be inhibited.[345] However, the members of one board of inquiry declared that its function was such that tentative agreements, as well as offers and counter-offers, of the parties during the negotiation stage could not be ignored completely by the board, even though one of the parties protested any consideration of such matters.[346]

N. Public Interest [LA CDI 94.64; 100.06; 100.32]

The question arises as to how far arbitrators should go in considering the public-interest aspects of interest disputes. The public, although not a direct party, has a vital interest in the settlement of some disputes. Factfinding boards do give strong consideration to the public welfare in making recommendations. For instance, a factfinding board for General Motors Corporation would recommend only such wage increases as it believed would not have inflationary price consequences.[347]

The public interest is an important consideration in public utility disputes, and equally so in disputes directly involving the public sector.[348] For example, some state statutes provide that the "interest and welfare of the public" is a factor to be given consideration by arbitrators of interest disputes in the public sector.[349]

i. *Public Utility Disputes and the Public Interest*

As discussed earlier, a utility's "ability to pay" cannot be the determining criterion in wage determination.[350] Instead, the public-interest standard often is invoked for public utility disputes. Several considerations are generally involved. The first is that services of public utilities, being constant necessities of life, should be made available to consumers at a fair price. Because wages paid by a utility will directly affect the cost of its services to the public, the amount of any wage increase granted may be affected by the arbitrator's conclusion about the probable effect of the increase on the price of the service involved, and, therefore, the arbitrator will keep in mind the

---

[345]Guides for Labor Arbitration 9–10 (1953) (published by a group of arbitrators in the Philadelphia area). *See also* Head of the Lakes Elec. Coop. Ass'n, 65 LA 839, 842 (Sembower, 1975).

[346]Rochester Transit Corp., 19 LA 538, 541–42 (Tolley, McKelvey, & Turkus, 1952). In *Cummins Sales*, 54 LA 1069, 1072 (Seinsheimer, 1971), the arbitrator gave significant weight to the employer's offer in negotiations.

[347]General Motors Corp., 1 LA 125, 128 (Garrison, Eisenhower, & Stacy, 1946). *See also* Government Printing Office, 73 LA 1, 6 (Bloch, 1979).

[348]See section 8., "Standards in Public-Sector Disputes," and section 9.H.iii., "Other Public-Sector Entities' Ability to Pay," above. It has been stated that public policy must be considered much more in public-sector disputes than in those in the private sector. Jones, *The Role of Arbitration in State and National Policy, in* Arbitration and the Public Interest, Proceedings of the 24th Annual Meeting of NAA 42, 60 (Somers & Dennis eds., BNA Books 1971).

[349]*See* City of Burlington, Iowa, 68 LA 454, 454, 456 (Witney, 1977); City of Detroit, Mich., 65 LA 293, 303, 306–08, 312 (Platt, 1975); City of Birmingham, Mich., 55 LA 716, 721 (Roumell, Jr., 1970); Town of Tiverton, R.I., 52 LA 1301, 1302, 1304 (Schmidt, Jr., 1969).

[350]See section 9.H.ii., "Public Utilities' Ability to Pay," above.

needs of the consumers.[351] The second consideration recognizes that the public has a paramount interest in continuity of operations of public utilities. The public expects utilities to provide uninterrupted service. Indeed, in one case the arbitrator stated that "most of the unions and most of the employees engaged in the essential public utilities" had "long recognized that their responsibilities required uninterrupted service to the public."[352]

Because public utility employees are under a very strong obligation not to strike, there has been considerable public discussion of the need for a wage policy that will ensure equitable treatment to these employees. Emphasis usually has been placed on the desirability of ensuring them rates and conditions of work that are as good as or better than those available for comparable work anywhere in the area.[353] In recognizing these several considerations, one arbitrator stated that, while they present a meritorious argument, it is difficult to put them into practice in specific terms.[354] But another arbitrator declared that an effort should be made to ensure utility workers "both as high or higher absolute levels and as favorable or more favorable relative changes in wages as other workers generally in the community."[355] A third arbitrator expressed preference for the view that utility employees should expect to enjoy substantially the same wages, hours, and working conditions—no better and no worse—as those enjoyed by other workers living in the area; thus, utility employment should be made to conform to local conditions, not to blaze new trails.[356]

ii.   *Governmental Wage Stabilization*

In times of wage stabilization, interest arbitrators, emergency boards, and factfinders must take cognizance of governmental stabilization regulations that may apply to the parties.[357] In some cases, awards or recommended

---

[351]*See* Consumers Power Co., 18 LA 686, 690 (Platt, Gemrich, & Arsulowicz, 1952); St. Louis Pub. Serv. Co., 8 LA 397, 402 (Holland, Anderson, & Hollingsworth, 1947). *Cf.* Volunteer Elec. Coop., 78 LA 352, 357 (Hamby, Jr., 1982) (arbitrator stated that "although the plight of [the public utility's] customers whose incomes are below the so-called 'poverty level' is regrettable, it is the opinion of the arbitrator that this consideration is not a valid one on which to base less than reasonable wage rates" for the utility's employees).

[352]Capital Transit Co., 9 LA 666, 679 (Taylor, 1947).

[353]Consolidated Edison Sys. Cos. of N.Y., 6 LA 830, 834 (Taylor, 1947).

[354]*Id.*

[355]Pacific Gas & Elec. Co., 7 LA 528, 531 (Kerr, 1947). *See also* Consumers Power Co., 24 LA 581, 584 (Smith, Howlett, & Sorensen, 1955).

[356]Cleveland Elec. Illuminating Co., 8 LA 597, 600, 605 (Cornsweet, 1947). While this view had been advanced earlier by Lee H. Hill, a management spokesman, in the instant case it was approved, but interpreted differently, by both the labor and employer arbitrators.

[357]Another aspect of governmental wage stabilization programs concerns their possible lingering effect after the regulatory agency ceases to be viable. In *Colorado Contractors Association*, 63 LA 702, 707 (Elkouri, 1974), the union argued that in no event can any agreement entered into by parties under government compulsion continue to bind them after the government power to coerce has terminated, while the employers argued that the purpose of wage and price controls is to stabilize the economy and reduce inflation, and that this purpose "would be almost completely nullified" if the parties after termination of the program's legal authority "were able to return to the same level which they would have been at had the Act [which established the program] never been in effect." For discussion of governmental wage stabilization programs, see Weber, *Labor-Management Relations in a Controlled and Rationed Economy, in* ARBITRATION—1974, PROCEEDINGS OF THE 27TH ANNUAL MEETING OF NAA 163 (Dennis & Somers eds., BNA Books 1975); Bloch, *Wage Controls and Interest Arbitration*

terms have been made subject to approval by wage stabilization authorities.[358] Sometimes arbitrators have ordered one party to join the other in seeking such approval.[359] Then the arbitrator might examine stabilization regulations and reach a conclusion as to the permissibility of requested increases.[360]

---

in the Public Sector, 52 J. Urb. L. 203 (1974); Tiernan, *The Pay Board*, *in* Labor Arbitration at the Quarter-Century Mark, Proceedings of the 25th Annual Meeting of NAA 229 (Dennis & Somers eds., BNA Books 1973). Coverage of state and local government employees by the Economic Stabilization Act of 1970 was upheld as constitutional in *Fry v. United States*, 421 U.S. 542, 22 WH Cases 284 (1975).

[358]*See* Los Angeles Standard Rubber, 17 LA 353, 354, 361 (Warren, 1951); Felt Cos., 16 LA 881, 882 (Lesser, 1951).

[359]*See* Durso & Geelan Co., 17 LA 748, 750–51 (Donnelly, Curry, & Clark, 1951). *See also* New York Shipping Ass'n, 20 LA 75, 76 (Hays, 1952).

[360]*See* Frederick Loeser & Co., 16 LA 399, 404 (Justin, 1951). In one case, the arbitrator did this at the request of the parties after they had agreed as to increases. City of Cheboygan, Mich., 57 LA 1090, 1091 (Keefe, 1971). *See also* Macy's N.Y., 57 LA 1115, 1118 (Stark, 1971) (arbitrator ruled as to the permissibility under wage stabilization regulations of certain automatic wage increases). *But see* Clarkstown, N.Y., Cent. Sch. Dist. No. 1, Bd. of Educ., 58 LA 191, 193 (Markowitz, 1972).

Titles of NAA Proceedings 1948–2003

The Profession of Labor Arbitration, Selected Papers From the First Seven Annual Meetings of the National Academy of Arbitrators, 1948–1954 (McKelvey ed., BNA Books 1957).

Arbitration Today, Proceedings of the 8th Annual Meeting, National Academy of Arbitrators (McKelvey ed., BNA Books 1955).

Management Rights and the Arbitration Process, Proceedings of the 9th Annual Meeting, National Academy of Arbitrators (McKelvey ed., BNA Books 1956).

Critical Issues in Labor Arbitration, Proceedings of the 10th Annual Meeting, National Academy of Arbitrators (McKelvey ed., BNA Books 1957).

The Arbitrator and the Parties, Proceedings of the 11th Annual Meeting, National Academy of Arbitrators (McKelvey ed., BNA Books 1958).

Arbitration and the Law, Proceedings of the 12th Annual Meeting, National Academy of Arbitrators (McKelvey ed., BNA Books 1959).

Challenges to Arbitration, Proceedings of the 13th Annual Meeting, National Academy of Arbitrators (McKelvey ed., BNA Books 1960).

Arbitration and Public Policy, Proceedings of the 14th Annual Meeting, National Academy of Arbitrators (Pollard ed., BNA Books 1961).

Collective Bargaining and the Arbitrator's Role, Proceedings of the 15th Annual Meeting, National Academy of Arbitrators (Kahn ed., BNA Books 1962).

Labor Arbitration and Industrial Change, Proceedings of the 16th Annual Meeting, National Academy of Arbitrators (Kahn ed., BNA Books 1963).

Labor Arbitration: Perspectives and Problems, Proceedings of the 17th Annual Meeting, National Academy of Arbitrators (Kahn ed., BNA Books 1964).

Proceedings of the 18th Annual Meeting of the National Academy of Arbitrators, 1965 (Jones ed., BNA Books 1965).

Problems of Proof in Arbitration, Proceedings of the 19th Annual Meeting, National Academy of Arbitrators (Jones ed., BNA Books 1967).

The Arbitrator, the NLRB, and the Courts, Proceedings of the 20th Annual Meeting, National Academy of Arbitrators (Jones ed., BNA Books 1967).

Developments in American and Foreign Arbitration, Proceedings of the 21st Annual Meeting, National Academy of Arbitrators (Rehmus ed., BNA Books 1968).

Arbitration and Social Change, Proceedings of the 22nd Annual Meeting, National Academy of Arbitrators (Somers & Dennis eds., BNA Books 1970).

Arbitration and the Expanding Role of Neutrals, Proceedings of the 23rd Annual Meeting, National Academy of Arbitrators (Somers & Dennis eds., BNA Books 1970).

Arbitration and the Public Interest, Proceedings of the 24th Annual Meeting, National Academy of Arbitrators (Somers & Dennis eds., BNA Books 1971).

Labor Arbitration at the Quarter-Century Mark, Proceedings of the 25th Annual Meeting, National Academy of Arbitrators (Dennis & Somers eds., BNA Books, 1973).

Arbitration of Interest Disputes, Proceedings of the 26th Annual Meeting, National Academy of Arbitrators (Dennis & Somers eds., BNA Books 1974).

Arbitration—1974, Proceedings of the 27th Annual Meeting, National Academy of Arbitrators (Dennis & Somers eds., BNA Books 1975).

Arbitration—1975, Proceedings of the 28th Annual Meeting, National Academy of Arbitrators (Dennis & Somers eds., BNA Books 1976).

Arbitration—1976, Proceedings of the 29th Annual Meeting, National Academy of Arbitrators (Dennis & Somers eds., BNA Books 1976).

Arbitration—1977, Proceedings of the 30th Annual Meeting, National Academy of Arbitrators (Dennis & Somers eds., BNA Books 1978).

Truth, Lie Detectors, and Other Problems in Labor Arbitration, Proceedings of the 31st Annual Meeting, National Academy of Arbitrators (Stern & Dennis eds., BNA Books 1979).

Arbitration of Subcontracting and Wage Incentive Disputes, Proceedings of the 32nd Annual Meeting, National Academy of Arbitrators (Stern & Dennis eds., BNA Books 1980).

Decisional Thinking of Arbitrators and Judges, Proceedings of the 33rd Annual Meeting, National Academy of Arbitrators (Stern & Dennis eds., BNA Books 1981).

Arbitration Issues for the 1980s, Proceedings of the 34th Annual Meeting, National Academy of Arbitrators (Stern & Dennis eds., BNA Books 1982).

Arbitration 1982: Conduct of the Hearing, Proceedings of the 35th Annual Meeting, National Academy of Arbitrators (Stern & Dennis eds., BNA Books 1983).

Arbitration—Promise and Performance, Proceedings of the 36th Annual Meeting, National Academy of Arbitrators (Stern & Dennis eds., BNA Books 1984).

Arbitration 1984: Absenteeism, Recent Law, Panels, and Published Decisions, Proceedings of the 37th Annual Meeting, National Academy of Arbitrators (Gershenfeld ed., BNA Books 1985).

Arbitration 1985: Law and Practice, Proceedings of the 38th Annual Meeting, National Academy of Arbitrators (Gershenfeld ed., BNA Books 1986).

Arbitration 1986: Current and Expanding Roles, Proceedings of the 39th Annual Meeting, National Academy of Arbitrators (Gershenfeld ed., BNA Books 1987).

Arbitration 1987: The Academy at Forty, Proceedings of the 40th Annual Meeting, National Academy of Arbitrators (Gruenberg ed., BNA Books 1988).

Arbitration 1988: Emerging Issues for the 1990s, Proceedings of the 41st Annual Meeting, National Academy of Arbitrators (Gruenberg ed., BNA Books 1989).

Arbitration 1989: The Arbitrator's Discretion During and After the Hearing, Proceedings of the 42nd Annual Meeting, National Academy of Arbitrators (Gruenberg ed., BNA Books 1990).

Arbitration 1990: New Perspectives on Old Issues, Proceedings of the 43rd Annual Meeting, National Academy of Arbitrators (Gruenberg ed., BNA Books 1991).

Arbitration 1991: The Changing Face of Arbitration in Theory and Practice, Proceedings of the 44th Annual Meeting, National Academy of Arbitrators (Gruenberg ed., BNA Books 1992).

Arbitration 1992: Improving Arbitral and Advocacy Skills, Proceedings of the 45th Annual Meeting, National Academy of Arbitrators (Gruenberg ed., BNA Books 1993).

Arbitration 1993: Arbitration and the Changing World of Work, Proceedings of the 46th Annual Meeting, National Academy of Arbitrators (Gruenberg ed., BNA Books 1994).

Arbitration 1994: Controversy and Continuity, Proceedings of the 47th Annual Meeting, National Academy of Arbitrators (Gruenberg ed., BNA Books 1994).

Arbitration 1995: New Challenges and Expanding Responsibilities, Proceedings of the 48th Annual Meeting, National Academy of Arbitrators (Najita ed., BNA Books 1996).

Arbitration 1996: At the Crossroads, Proceedings of the 49th Annual Meeting, National Academy of Arbitrators (Najita ed., BNA Books 1997).

Arbitration 1997: The Next Fifty Years, Proceedings of the 50th Annual Meeting, National Academy of Arbitrators (Najita ed., BNA Books 1998).

Arbitration 1998: The Changing World of Dispute Resolution, Proceedings of the 51st Annual Meeting, National Academy of Arbitrators (Briggs & Grenig eds., BNA Books 1999).

Arbitration 1999: Quo Vadis? The Future of Arbitration and Collective Bargaining, Proceedings of the 52nd Annual Meeting, National Academy of Arbitrators (Grenig & Briggs eds., BNA Books 2000).

Arbitration 2000: Workplace Justice and Efficiency in the Twenty-First Century, Proceedings of the 53rd Annual Meeting, National Academy of Arbitrators (Briggs & Grenig eds., BNA Books 2001).

Arbitration 2001: Arbitrating in an Evolving Legal Environment, Proceedings of the 54th Annual Meeting, National Academy of Arbitrators (Grenig & Briggs eds., BNA Books 2002).

Arbitration 2002: Workplace Arbitration: A Process in Evolution, Proceedings of the 55th Annual Meeting, National Academy of Arbitrators (Coleman ed., BNA Books 2003).

Arbitration 2003: Arbitral Decision-Making: Confronting Current and Recurrent Issues, Proceedings of the 56th Annual Meeting, National Academy of Arbitrators (Coleman ed., BNA Books 2004).

Table of Arbitrators

This table lists the names of arbitrators from awards cited within the footnotes. No distinction is made between arbitrators with the same last name. References are to footnote numbers within the chapters (e.g., **13:** 229, 432 refer to footnotes 229 and 432 in Chapter 13).

Table of Arbitration Awards

*This table is alphabetized letter-by-letter (e.g., "Hubbell Metals" precedes "Hub City Jobbing Co."). The name of the arbitrator is given in the parenthetical at the end of the cite. All of the arbitrators are listed alphabetically in the separate Table of Arbitrators. References are to chapter and footnote number (e.g., **14:** 234, 278 refers to footnotes 234 and 278 in Chapter 14).*

A

AAA Case No. 16-300-00014-93 (Aronin, Aug. 9, 1996) (unpublished) **5:** 52

AAFES Distrib., 107 LA 290 (Marcus, 1996) **8:** 350; **13:** 972, 978; **15:** 284

A&E Plasti Pak Co., 76 LA 142 (Modjeska, 1980) **14:** 431

Aaxico Airlines, 47 LA 289 (Platt, 1966) **7:** 167

A.B.A. Diesel Parts & Serv. Co., 62 LA 660 (Harter, Jr., 1974) **17:** 73

Abbott Linen Supply Co., 35 LA 12 (Schmidt, 1960) **15:** 315

Abbott-Northwestern Hosp.
75 LA 1238 (Heneman, 1980) **13:** 380
94 LA 621 (Berquist, 1990) **8:** 207, 427
95 LA 258 (Miller, 1989) **10:** 259, 308

A.B.C. Cartage & Trucking Co., 42 LA 55 (Whelan, 1963) **7:** 156

A.B. Chance Co., 57 LA 725 (Florey, 1971) **15:** 77

ABC Rail Prods. Corp., 110 LA 574 (Kenis, 1998) **8:** 45, 120; **10:** 105

Abex Corp.
47 LA 441 (Kates, 1966) **13:** 795
64 LA 721 (Rybolt, 1975) **15:** 40
71 LA 1171 (Cohen, 1978) **14:** 306
75 LA 137 (Feldman, 1980) **5:** 138
80 LA 490 (As, 1983) **14:** 115

ABM Space Care, 105 LA 199 (Cohen, 1995) **18:** 217

ABTCO, Inc., 104 LA 551 (Kanner, 1995) **13:** 14, 789; **15:** 247

A.C.&C. Co., 24 LA 538 (Scheiber, 1955) **8:** 101; **15:** 319; **18:** 167

ACCO U.S.A., 112 LA 101 (Gross, 1998) **13:** 831

Accurate Forging Corp., 113 LA 597 (Imundo, Jr., 1999) **18:** 80, 116

ACF Indus.
39 LA 1051 (Williams, 1962) **17:** 65
79 LA 487 (Williams, 1982) **17:** 657
82 LA 459 (Maniscalco, 1984) **15:** 375

Acheson Dispersed Pigments Co., 36 LA 578 (Hale, 1960) **13:** 683

A.C. Humko Corp., 114 LA 664 (Kindig, 2000) **18:** 154

A.C. Krebs Co., 64 LA 791 (White, Jr., 1975) **17:** 69, 76

A.C.L. Haase Co., 17 LA 472 (Townsend, 1951) **13:** 210, 218; **18:** 235

Acme Boot Co., 52 LA 1047 (Oppenheim, 1969) **5:** 348; **15:** 384

Acme Boot Mfg. Co., 9 LA 442 (Hepburn, 1948) **13:** 869

Acme Elec. Corp., 69 LA 176 (Croft, 1977) **11:** 84; **15:** 60

Acme Eng'g & Mfg. Corp., 81 LA 564 (Schedler, 1983) **15:** 292

Acme Fast Freight, 37 LA 163 (Warns, 1961) **18:** 222

Acme Foundry Co., 45 LA 1025 (Altieri, 1965) **10:** 52

Acme Galvanizing Co., 19 LA 575 (Gooding, 1952) **14:** 16

Acme-Newport Steel Co., 31 LA 1002 (Schmidt, 1959) **14:** 234, 278

Acme Sign Co., 94 LA 505 (Barker, 1990) **22:** 285

Acme Steel Co., 9 LA 432 (Gregory, 1947) **14:** 188, 338

Acorn Bldg. Components, 92 LA 68 (Roumell, Jr., 1988) **13:** 762

Acro Wire, Inc., 44 LA 910 (Belsky, 1965) **17:** 127, 146

Barnstead-Thermolyne Corp., 107 LA 645
(Pelofsky, 1996) *13:* 763, 764, 768; *18:*
202
Barrett Paving Materials, 78 LA 819
(Murphy, 1982) *12:* 97
Barrett Transp., 52 LA 169 (Koven, 1969)
17: 80
Bartelt Eng'g Co., 51 LA 582 (Sembower,
1968) *7:* 195; *10:* 337
Barth Smelting & Ref. Co., 42 LA 374
(Berkowitz, 1964) *13:* 998
Barton Salt Co., 46 LA 503 (Merrill, 1966)
8: 139; *9:* 13; *13:* 420
BASF Corp., 116 LA 1676 (Crider, 2002) *13:*
804; *17:* 218
BASF Wyandotte Corp.
  77 LA 492 (Liebowitz, 1981) *9:* 108
  84 LA 1055 (Caraway, 1985) *9:* 20; *10:*
  49; *12:* 120
  85 LA 602 (Nicholas, Jr., 1985) *4:* 233; *6:*
  38
Basic Inc., 82 LA 1065 (Dworkin, 1984) *3:*
142
Basic Magnesia, 69 LA 737 (Manson, 1977)
8: 383, 389
Basic Steel Cos., 19 War Lab. Rep. 568
(1944) *22:* 187
Basic Steel Indus.
  13 LA 46 (Daugherty, Cole, & Rosenman,
  1949) *22:* 18, 325
  18 LA 112 (Wage Stabilization Bd., 1952)
  22: 44, 325
Basic Vegetable Prods., 64 LA 620 (Gould,
1975) *18:* 190
Basin Coop. Servs., 105 LA 1070 (Cohen,
1996) *16:* 51
Basin Elec. Power Coop., 91 LA 675
(MacLean, 1988) *9:* 174
Baskin Robbins, 111 LA 554 (Richman,
1998) *10:* 106
Basler Elec. Co.
  47 LA 870 (Stix, 1966) *11:* 85
  49 LA 1100 (Sembower, 1968) *15:* 319
  94 LA 888 (Canestraight, 1990) *12:* 26;
  13: 736
Bassick Co.
  13 LA 135 (Lane, 1949) *13:* 661
  26 LA 627 (Kheel, 1956) *12:* 81; *13:* 944
  38 LA 278 (Seitz, 1962) *14:* 168
Bastian-Morley Co., 3 LA 412 (Epstein,
1946) *9:* 21; *13:* 944
Bates Container, 68 LA 1006 (Sisk, 1977)
8: 134; *11:* 87, 94
Bates Mfg. Co., 18 LA 631 (Simkin, 1952)
22: 320, 343
Batesville Mfg. Co., 55 LA 261 (Roberts,
1970) *13:* 894, 896, 910; *14:* 269, 295, 321
Baton Rouge Sheet Metal Workers Pension
Plan, Case No. 98-0942B, 1998 WL

1033434 (Nicholas, Jr., 1998) *10:* 222
Bauer Bros. Co.
  21 LA 529 (Brown, 1953) *5:* 305
  23 LA 696 (Dworkin, 1954) *15:* 186
  48 LA 861 (Kates, 1967) *13:* 748; *16:* 63
Baugh & Sons Co., 23 LA 177 (Dash, 1954)
4: 87
Bauman Bros. Furniture Mfg. Co., 10 LA
79 (Miller, 1948) *18:* 278
Baur Bros. Bakery, 36 LA 1422 (Joseph,
1961) *5:* 74
Bay City, Mich., City of, 111 LA 1124 (Allen,
1998) *9:* 18; *12:* 47
Bayer Corp.
  108 LA 316 (Zobrak, 1997) *13:* 773, 776,
  777
  110 LA 924 (Miles, 1998) *16:* 77, 82
Bayer, Inc., 105 LA 100 (Duff, 1995) *12:* 72
Bay Meadows Racing Ass'n, 90 LA 770
(Christopher, 1988) *9:* 34; *18:* 239
Bayshore Concrete Prods. Co., 92 LA 311
(Hart, 1989) *15:* 350
Bazor Express, 46 LA 307 (Duff, 1966) *15:*
76
B.B.D. Transp. Co., 66 LA 64 (Manos, Sr.,
1976) *17:* 33
Beacon Journal Publ'g Co., 55 LA 329
(Larkin, 1970) *13:* 18, 944
Bean, Morris, & Co., 54 LA 418 (McIntosh,
1971) *13:* 228
Bearfoot Corp., 65 LA 1208 (Marshall, 1975)
9: 174
Beatrice Foods Co.
  45 LA 540 (Stouffer, 1965) *9:* 164
  54 LA 998 (McKenna, 1971) *13:* 907, 911
  55 LA 933 (Young, 1970) *13:* 20, 949, 950
  74 LA 1008 (Gradwohl, 1980) *15:* 37
Beatrice/Hunt-Wesson, Inc.
  89 LA 710 (Bickner, 1987) *8:* 428; *15:* 206
  92 LA 383 (Brisco, 1989) *6:* 24
Beaumont, Tex., City of, 65 LA 1048 (Bailey,
1975) *22:* 154, 175
Beaumont Concrete Co., 76 LA 228 (Gentile, 1981) *10:* 138, 152
Beaunit Fibers, 49 LA 423 (McCoy, 1967)
12: 6, 20, 65
Beaunit Mills, 20 LA 784 (Williams, 1953)
11: 112
Beaver Local Sch. Dist. Bd. of Educ., Case
No. 97-25809, 1998 WL 1110777 (Ruben,
1998) *10:* 231
Beaver Precision Prods., 51 LA 853 (Kates,
1968) *17:* 690
Bechtel Civil & Minerals, 87 LA 153 (Beck,
1986) *7:* 15, 24; *9:* 212
Becker, Minn., County of, 93 LA 673 (Neigh,
1989) *17:* 253
Beckering Constr. Co., 43 LA 514 (Howlett,
1964) *10:* 276

C

Carey Salt Co., 17 LA 669 (Ralston, 1951)
13: 695
Cargill, Inc.
39 LA 929 (Williams, 1962) **13:** 577
111 LA 571 (Moreland IV, 1998) **18:** 80
Cargo & Tankship Mgmt. Corp., 38 LA 602
(Gellhorn, 1962) **13:** 1054
Carhart Refractories Co., 39 LA 138 (Volz,
1962) **13:** 995
Carl Bolander & Sons Co., 100 LA 1
(Reynolds, 1992) **15:** 200
Carl Fischer, Inc., 24 LA 674 (Rosenfarb,
1955) **15:** 186
Carlile & Doughty, 9 LA 239 (Brandschain,
1947) **9:** 23, 65; **10:** 309, 310
Carling Brewing Co.
46 LA 715 (Kates, 1966) **9:** 106, 187; **17:**
30, 42
52 LA 93 (Talent, 1968) **18:** 23
Carling Nat'l Breweries
71 LA 476 (Harkless, 1978) **14:** 155
83 LA 385 (Lewis, 1984) **14:** 428
84 LA 503 (Van Wart, 1985) **17:** 107
Carlisle, Iowa, Cmty. Sch. Dist., 77 LA 701
(Yarowsky, 1981) **17:** 224
Carlisle, Pa., Borough of, 82 LA 1 (Woy,
1984) **5:** 187; **19:** 121
Carlisle Tire & Rubber Co., 99 LA 893
(McMillen, 1992) **9:** 251
Carlon, 99 LA 677 (Hoffman, 1992) **8:** 50;
15: 113
Carlton Coll., 113 LA 786 (Daly, 2000) **14:**
220
Carlton, Minn., County of, 104 LA 773 (Daly,
1995) **22:** 27, 28
Carlyle Tile Co., 29 LA 787 (Dworkin, 1958)
13: 195, 201, 207, 413
Carlynton Sch. Dist., 73 LA 1183 (Duff,
1979) **18:** 236
Carnation Co.
3 LA 229 (Updegraff, 1946) **9:** 20, 205
34 LA 345 (Marshall, 1960) **12:** 43; **13:**
495
38 LA 270 (Peck, 1962) **9:** 152
42 LA 568 (Miller, 1964) **15:** 319
79 LA 679 (de Grasse, 1982) **13:** 1018
84 LA 80 (Wright, 1985) **5:** 283
89 LA 853 (Madden, 1987) **8:** 109
Carnation Pet Foods Div., 89 LA 1288
(Berger, 1987) **14:** 186, 213
Carnegie-Illinois Steel Corp.
5 LA 378 (Blumer, 1946) **9:** 21
5 LA 402 (Blumer, 1946) **13:** 516
5 LA 712 (Blumer, 1946) **13:** 236
12 LA 810 (Seward, 1949) **13:** 562
16 LA 794 (Sturges, 1951) **5:** 110
17 LA 328 (Morgan, 1951) **13:** 904
Caro Ctr., 104 LA 1092 (Kanner, 1995) **15:**
177–79

Carolina Coach Co., 20 LA 451 (Livengood,
1953) **8:** 290, 291; **15:** 117
Carolina Concrete Pipe Co., 76 LA 626 (Fos-
ter, 1981) **5:** 108; **14:** 208; **17:** 222
Carolina Tel. & Tel. Co., 97 LA 653 (Nolan,
1991) **15:** 343
Carol Mgmt. Co., 97 LA 503 (Freedman,
1991) **15:** 210
Carpenter Funds Admin. Office of N. Cal.,
72 LA 410 (Maloney, 1979) **13:** 489
Carpenters Dist. Council (Chicago) (Polk
Bros.), 90 LA 745 (Hockenberry, 1988) **5:**
369
Carpenters Dist. Council San Diego County,
76 LA 513 (Kaufman, 1981) **14:** 427
Carpenters' Funds Trustees, 90 LA 1097
(Nicholas, Jr., 1988) **1:** 87
Carpenter Steel Co., 44 LA 1185 (Kerrison,
1965) **5:** 391
Carr, Adams, & Collier Co., 27 LA 656
(Graff, 1956) **13:** 268
Carrier Air Conditioning Co., 54 LA 434
(Owen, 1971) **14:** 267
Carrier Corp.
103 LA 891 (Lipson, 1994) **15:** 125
110 LA 1064 (Ipavec, 1998) **15:** 370; **16:**
42, 43, 67, 71
Carrollton, Tex., City of, 90 LA 276
(Stephens, 1988) **19:** 87
Carson City, Nev., Sch. Dist., 97 LA 52 (Gen-
tile, 1991) **22:** 56
Carson Elec. Co., 24 LA 667 (Howard, 1955)
17: 117, 182
Carson Linebaugh, Inc., 42 LA 1097 (Brecht,
1963) **22:** 158
Carson Mfg. Co., 73 LA 115 (Berns, 1979)
17: 338
Carter Carburetor Corp., 11 LA 569 (Hilpert,
1948) **17:** 289, 301
Carter Prods., 45 LA 724 (Kerrison, 1965)
8: 275; **14:** 392
Carus Corp., 71 LA 624 (Kossoff, 1978) **9:**
13
Carver, Minn., County of, 91 LA 1222
(Kanatz, 1988) **22:** 104
Cascade Corp., 82 LA 313 (Bressler, 1984)
10: 308; **13:** 825
Cascade Steel Rolling Mills, 74 LA 199
(Lovell, 1980) **17:** 209
Cass Clay Creamery, 95 LA 41 (Eisele, 1990)
17: 592
Casting Eng'rs
71 LA 949 (Petersen, 1978) **8:** 152
76 LA 939 (Petersen, 1981) **8:** 302
Castle & Cooke Terminals
40 LA 62 (Kagel, 1962) **13:** 210
76 LA 1099 (Gilson, 1981) **13:** 439, 459
Castle Dome Copper Co., 17 LA 644 (Prasow,
1951) **13:** 863

I

L

Mead Chilpaco Mill, 106 LA 1066 (Feldman, 1996) *15:* 381

Mead Containerboard, 105 LA 1068 (Goodman, 1995) *13:* 754

Mead Containers, 35 LA 349 (Dworkin, 1960) *14:* 238, 242, 263

Mead Corp.
　41 LA 1038 (Strong, 1963) *13:* 224
　42 LA 224 (Marshall, 1963) *14:* 417
　42 LA 643 (Hawley, 1964) *12:* 93
　43 LA 391 (Halley, 1964) *14:* 417
　43 LA 661 (Dunau, 1964) *11:* 68
　64-3 ARB ¶9169 (Fallon, 1964) *13:* 439, 446, 450
　45 LA 881 (Wood, 1965) *12:* 19
　46 LA 70 (King, 1966) *4:* 64; *13:* 410, 412
　46 LA 459 (Klamon, 1966) *13:* 574, 589
　46 LA 641 (Hilpert, 1966) *13:* 575
　51 LA 1121 (Griffin, 1968) *17:* 357, 575
　54 LA 1218 (Porter, Jr., 1971) *13:* 553
　57 LA 1217 (Seinsheimer, 1971) *17:* 193
　61 LA 797 (Marcus, 1973) *13:* 285
　64 LA 421 (Ferguson, 1975) *13:* 278
　75 LA 665 (Gross, 1980) *13:* 596, 608; *18:* 307
　79 LA 464 (Williams, 1982) *15:* 185
　80 LA 713 (Milentz, 1983) *15:* 358
　84 LA 875 (Sergent, Jr., 1985) *5:* 371; *13:* 277, 440, 442
　86 LA 201 (Ipavec, 1985) *13:* 958; *16:* 258
　104 LA 161 (Krislov, 1995) *10:* 309
　113 LA 1169 (Franckiewicz, 2000) *8:* 252; *18:* 57
　114 LA 1753 (Nathan, 2000) *13:* 847

Mead Johnson Terminal Corp., 54 LA 886 (Witney, 1971) *13:* 653

Meadow Gold Dairies, 110 LA 865 (Bognanno, 1998) *10:* 326

Mead Paper
　70 LA 186 (McIntosh, 1978) *17:* 56
　91 LA 52 (Curry, Jr., 1988) *13:* 1000
　Chilpaco Mill, 113 LA 203 (Sharpe, 1999) *14:* 248

Mead Prods.
　104 LA 730 (Borland, 1994) *13:* 225, 385
　114 LA 1753 (Nathan, 2000) *10:* 336; *14:* 78

Means Stamping Co., 46 LA 324 (Cole, 1966) *13:* 931

Meat Packing Indus., 9 LA 978 (Feinsinger, Davis, & Schaefer, 1948) *22:* 275

Mechanical & Sheet Metal Contractors of Kan., 71 LA 286 (Yarowsky, 1978) *10:* 68

Mechanical Contractors Ass'n, 100 LA 320 (Feldman, 1992) *18:* 78

Mechanical Handling Sys., Inc., 26 LA 401 (Keller, 1956) *13:* 748; *17:* 391, 399, 411

Mechanical Prods., Inc.
　73 LA 569 (Shaw, 1979) *9:* 226

91 LA 977 (Roumell, Jr., 1988) *12:* 62, 63; *13:* 707, 740, 750

Medalist Indus., 57 LA 503 (Solomon, 1971) *13:* 924

Medart Co., 18 LA 701 (Klamon, 1952) *13:* 853

Meier Metal Servicenters, 100 LA 816 (Morgan, Jr., 1993) *13:* 958

Meijer, Inc.
　83 LA 570 (Ellmann, 1984) *17:* 537
　103 LA 834 (Daniel, 1994) *8:* 350; *10:* 49, 59, 119; *15:* 284
　108 LA 631 (Daniel, 1997) *17:* 351–53, 408
　114 LA 1048 (Fullmer, 2000) *13:* 272

Meilman, 34 LA 771 (Gray, 1960) *13:* 704; *18:* 147

Melbourne, City of
　91 LA 1210 (Baroni, 1988) *5:* 110; *9:* 28, 158, 164
　Case No. 98-00353, 1998 WL 1048334 (Cohen, 1998) *15:* 316

Melbourne Beach, Fla., Town of, 91 LA 280 (Frost, 1988) *8:* 25, 391

Meletron Corp., 36 LA 315 (Jones, Jr., 1961) *5:* 56, 57

Melrose-Mindoro, Wis., Area Educ. Ass'n (Crowley, 1998), available at http://www.wisbar.org/werc/ga/1998/5692.htm *21:* 41

Memphis Light, Gas, & Water Div.
　69 LA 687 (Simon, 1977) *12:* 72; *13:* 247
　100 LA 291 (Caraway, 1993) *15:* 107, 200; *18:* 209

Memphis Publ'g Co.
　26 LA 381 (Hepburn, 1956) *22:* 214, 234
　48 LA 554 (Oppenheim, 1967) *17:* 234
　48 LA 931 (Cantor, 1967) *10:* 325; *18:* 242
　50 LA 186 (Duff, 1967) *13:* 427
　110 LA 438 (Grooms, Jr., 1998) *12:* 36

Menasco Mfg. Co.
　30 LA 264 (Neff, 1958) *13:* 241
　30 LA 465 (Boles, 1958) *13:* 505
　31 LA 33 (Prasow, 1958) *13:* 241
　45 LA 502 (Boles, 1965) *6:* 46; *13:* 803
　50 LA 265 (Ray, 1968) *5:* 373
　69 LA 759 (Bergeson, 1977) *11:* 115; *13:* 580; *18:* 320
　71 LA 696 (Gowan, Jr., 1978) *13:* 14; *17:* 220, 222, 288

Menasha Corp.
　64 LA 307 (Kabaker, 1975) *14:* 234
　84 LA 989 (Duff, 1985) *13:* 275
　90 LA 427 (Clark, 1987) *13:* 798; *15:* 350
　108 LA 308 (Ellmann, 1997) *13:* 225, 385

Mengel Co., 18 LA 392 (Klamon, Hannah, & Connolly, 1952) *14:* 390

Mission Mfg. Co., 30 LA 365 (Boles, 1958) **14:** 210

Mississippi Aluminum Corp., 27 LA 625 (Reynard, 1956) **13:** 510; **18:** 59

Mississippi Lime Co.
29 LA 559 (Updegraff, 1957) **15:** 119
32 LA 1013 (Hilpert, 1959) **6:** 35; **11:** 73

Mississippi Power & Light Co.
38 LA 838 (Wissner, 1962) **13:** 882
92 LA 1161 (Taylor, 1989) **13:** 745; **16:** 101; **17:** 450

Mississippi Power Co., 90 LA 220 (Jewett, 1987) **8:** 196, 414

Mississippi Valley Gas Co., 41 LA 745 (Hebert, 1963) **15:** 173

Mississippi Valley Structural Steel Co., 55 LA 23 (Boothe, 1970) **5:** 102

Missoula, Mont., City of, 2002 WL 1980143 (Snow, 2002) **22:** 142

Missouri Minerals Processing, 85 LA 939 (Talent, 1985) **13:** 958

Missouri Pac. R.R., 55 LA 193 (Sembower, 1970) **14:** 405, 412

Missouri Power & Light Co., 80 LA 297 (Westbrook, 1982) **13:** 537; **15:** 102

Missouri Pub. Serv. Co.
23 LA 429 (Howard, 1954) **4:** 63; **22:** 234
77 LA 973 (Maniscalco, 1981) **11:** 98; **17:** 444

Missouri Research Labs., 55 LA 197 (Erbs, 1970) **13:** 708

Missouri Rolling Mill Corp., 88 LA 1179 (Newmark, 1987) **8:** 384

Missouri Utils. Co., 68 LA 379 (Erbs, 1977) **14:** 218

Missouri Valley, 82 LA 1018 (Yaney, 1984) **13:** 530, 544

Mister A's Rest., 80 LA 1104 (Christopher, 1983) **13:** 706; **17:** 437

Mitchell-Bentley Corp., 45 LA 1071 (Ryder, 1965) **3:** 32; **17:** 446

Mitchell Bros. Truck Line, 48 LA 953 (Peck, 1967) **8:** 335; **15:** 275

M.M. Sundt Constr. Co., 81 LA 432 (Zechar, 1983) **15:** 34

Mobay Chem. Corp.
64 LA 259 (Tharp, 1975) **13:** 479
77 LA 219 (Lubow, 1981) **8:** 346; **15:** 278; **18:** 220

Mobil Chem. Co.
50 LA 80 (Kesselman, 1968) **13:** 801
51 LA 363 (Witney, 1968) **13:** 587
71 LA 535 (May, 1978) **16:** 56

Mobile Video Servs., 83 LA 1009 (Hockenberry, 1984) **5:** 95; **13:** 960

Mobilization for Youth, 49 LA 1124 (Wolff, 1967) **14:** 340

Mobil Oil Co.
61-4 ARB ¶8069 (Willingham, 1961) **13:** 412, 451
42 LA 102 (Forsythe, 1963) **17:** 78, 192, 199
43 LA 1287 (Turkus, 1965) **6:** 37
46 LA 140 (Hebert, 1966) **4:** 62; **7:** 113; **11:** 67; **12:** 133; **13:** 411, 437
63 LA 263 (Sinclitico, 1974) **10:** 276
69 LA 828 (Ray, 1977) **16:** 110
76 LA 3 (Allen, Jr., 1981) **11:** 107
95 LA 162 (Allen, Jr., 1990) **15:** 76, 95

Modecraft Co.
38 LA 1236 (Dall, 1961) **17:** 82
44 LA 1045 (Jaffee, 1965) **9:** 178; **17:** 2, 103

Mode O'Day Corp.
1 LA 490 (Cheney, 1946) **9:** 263, 264
85 LA 297 (Thornell, 1985) **14:** 93; **15:** 46

Modern Bakeries, 39 LA 939 (Koven, 1962) **13:** 195, 207, 210, 289

Modern Coach Corp., 24 LA 810 (Holden, 1955) **13:** 748

Modernfold Indus., 60 LA 1200 (Warns, 1973) **17:** 69, 74

Modine Mfg. Co.
23 LA 243 (Porter, 1954) **5:** 304
39 LA 624 (Smith, 1962) **5:** 380

Moe Levy & Sons, 4 LA 708 (Platt, 1946) **9:** 20

Moeller Instrument Co., 6 LA 639 (Brissenden, 1947) **22:** 69

Mohawk Airlines, 49 LA 290 (McKelvey, 1967) **1:** 99

Mohawk Beverages, 50 LA 298 (Moran, 1968) **18:** 232

Mohawk Carpet Mills, 26 LA 651 (Shipman, 1956) **22:** 144, 158, 160, 267

Mohawk Rubber Co.
80 LA 1305 (Cantor, 1983) **17:** 338
86 LA 679 (Groshong, 1986) **7:** 30
93 LA 777 (Aronin, 1989) **10:** 290

Monarch Mach. Tool Co.
27 LA 640 (Ferguson, 1956) **7:** 147
51 LA 391 (Sembower, 1968) **15:** 281
54 LA 1084 (Seinsheimer, 1971) **16:** 106
74 LA 854 (Gibson, 1980) **10:** 282, 336

Monarch Rubber Co., 44 LA 246 (McCoy, 1965) **12:** 135

Monarch Tile, 101 LA 585 (Hooper, 1993) **17:** 150

Monfort Packing Co.
40 LA 388 (Gorsuch, 1963) **14:** 120
66 LA 286 (Goodman, 1976) **15:** 173

Monitor Sugar Co., 1996 WL 808298 (McDonald, 1996) **18:** 44

Monmouth, Ill., City of, 105 LA 724 (Wolff, 1995) **13:** 1027

N

P

Q

106 LA 481 (McGury, 1996) *16:* 88
Thermolite, Inc., 46 LA 974 (Klein, 1966) *8:* 383; *15:* 173
Thiokol Chem. Corp.
    27 LA 432 (Williams, 1956) *13:* 1042, 1056
    52 LA 1254 (Williams, 1969) *15:* 315
Thiokol Corp., 65 LA 1265 (Williams, 1975) *14:* 176, 308
Third Ave. Transit Corp., 1 LA 321 (Hays, 1946) *22:* 277
Thomas Indus., 61 LA 627 (Dallas, 1973) *17:* 212
Thomas/Sysco Food Servs.
    90 LA 1036 (Wren, 1988) *8:* 134; *9:* 111
    97 LA 483 (Katz, 1991) *17:* 138
Thomas Truck & Caster Co., 74 LA 1276 (Cohen, 1980) *17:* 208
Thomasville Chair Co., 8 LA 792 (Waynick, 1947) *13:* 810
Thombert, Inc., 91 LA 1275 (Yarowsky, 1988) *13:* 810
Thompson Bros. Boat Mfg. Co., 55 LA 69 (Moberly, 1970) *13:* 898, 901, 911; *14:* 379
Thompson Fuel Serv., 42 LA 62 (Kerrison, 1964) *7:* 156
Thompson Mahogany Co., 5 LA 397 (Brandschain, 1946) *13:* 200, 384
Thor Corp.
    13 LA 319 (Baab, 1949) *13:* 845
    14 LA 512 (Baab, 1950) *14:* 266, 270
Thorn Apple Valley, 98 LA 183 (Kanner, 1991) *15:* 347
Thorsen Mfg. Co.
    44 LA 1049 (Koven, 1965) *7:* 50
    55 LA 581 (Koven, 1970) *18:* 220
3M Co.
    70 LA 587 (Mueller, 1978) *15:* 40
    72 LA 949 (Grabb, 1979) *8:* 179
375th Mission Support Squadron/MSC, Scott Air Force Base, 99 LA 656 (Hilgert, 1992) *22:* 36
Thriftimart, Inc., 61 LA 992 (Irwin, Jr., 1973) *13:* 541
Thrifty Corp.
    72 LA 898 (Barrett, 1979) *10:* 54; *11:* 81
    77 LA 1300 (Nathanson, 1982) *22:* 166
    85 LA 780 (Gentile, 1985) *12:* 72
Thrifty Drug Stores Co.
    50 LA 1253 (Jones, Jr., 1968) *8:* 152, 188
    88 LA 822 (Ross, 1987) *9:* 263
Thunderbird Hotel, 69 LA 10 (Weiss, 1977) *8:* 134; *9:* 21, 96
Thunderbird Inn, 77 LA 849 (Armstrong, 1981) *15:* 392
Tibbetts Plumbing-Heating Co., 46 LA 124 (Stouffer, 1966) *7:* 140; *15:* 93
Tide Water Associated Oil Co.
    21 LA 604 (Shipman, Fillhower, & Pelowitz, 1953) *14:* 14, 87

21 LA 682 (Shipman, 1953) *14:* 119, 127
Tide Water Oil Co., 17 LA 829 (Wyckoff, 1952) *12:* 120
Tiger Maint. Corp., 89 LA 276 (Hockenberry, 1987) *9:* 20, 25
Tile Contractors Ass'n of N. Cal., 25 LA 9 (Ross, 1955) *22:* 262
Times Journal Publ'g Co.
    72 LA 971 (Williams, 1979) *10:* 147
    75 LA 939 (Williams, 1980) *7:* 100
Times Publ'g Co., 40 LA 1054 (Dworkin, 1963) *13:* 907
Timex Corp.
    54 LA 1185 (Seitz, 1971) *15:* 321
    63 LA 758 (Gruenberg, 1974) *14:* 306
Timken Co.
    75 LA 801 (Morgan, 1980) *17:* 125, 487
    79 LA 142 (Morgan, 1982) *14:* 16
    85 LA 377 (Morgan, 1985) *13:* 233
Timken-Detroit Axle Co., 21 LA 196 (Smith, 1953) *9:* 226
Timken Roller Bearing Co.
    6 LA 979 (Lehoczky, 1947) *13:* 247, 253
    7 LA 239 (Harter, 1947) *8:* 209
    32 LA 595 (Boehm, 1958) *11:* 49; *14:* 14
    51 LA 101 (Dworkin, 1968) *13:* 246
Timkin Co., 108 LA 422 (Kindig, 1996) *13:* 767; *16:* 78
Tinker Air Force Base, Okla.
    72 LA 358 (Davis, 1979) *17:* 275
    86 LA 1249 (Nelson, 1986) *17:* 577
Tin Processing Corp.
    15 LA 568 (Smith, 1950) *17:* 48
    16 LA 48 (Emery, 1951) *13:* 1056
    17 LA 193 (Smith, 1951) *14:* 272, 284
    17 LA 461 (Emery, 1951) *17:* 29
    20 LA 227 (Boles, 1953) *9:* 11
    20 LA 362 (Johannes, 1953) *9:* 65; *10:* 309, 310
    20 LA 458 (Emery, 1953) *9:* 148
    28 LA 321 (Hawley, 1957) *13:* 695
Tipp City, City of, 88 LA 315 (Imundo, Jr., 1987) *9:* 21
Titanium Metals Corp. of Am.
    49 LA 1144 (Block, 1967) *13:* 914; *14:* 401
    55 LA 690 (Block, 1970) *5:* 341
Titan Wheel Int'l, 97 LA 514 (Smith, 1991) *13:* 271
Titus Mfg. Corp., 50 LA 133 (Hughes, 1968) *15:* 281
Tiverton, R.I., Town of, 52 LA 1301 (Schmidt, Jr., 1969) *22:* 144, 154, 178, 206, 209, 349
T.J. Maxx
    105 LA 470 (Richman, 1995) *10:* 309; *12:* 19; *18:* 232
    107 LA 78 (Richman, 1996) *8:* 362; *10:* 248; *17:* 524, 525

W

Table of Cases

*References are to chapters and footnote numbers (e.g., **2:** 237, 244 refers to footnotes 237 and 234 in Chapter 2). Union locals and other subdivisions are included with the parent unions, which are sorted by popular name (e.g., Teamsters not United Brotherhood of Teamsters). Alphabetization is letter-by-letter (e.g., "Eastbrook" precedes "East Brunswick").*

N

Najarian; United States v., 915 F. Supp. 1460 (D. Minn. 1996) **19:** 79, 80

Nasca v. State Farm Mut. Auto. Ins. Co., 12 P.3d 346 (Col. Ct. App. 2000) **4:** 253

Nash County Bd. of Educ. v. Biltmore Co., 1980-81 Trade Cases ¶63,715 (4th Cir. 1981) **11:** 49

National Border Patrol Council, 3 FLRA 400 (1980) **20:** 150

National Broad. Co.; NLRB v., 798 F.2d 75, 123 LRRM 2182 (2d Cir. 1986) **5:** 268

National Cash Register Co. v. Wilson, 35 LA 646 (N.Y. Ct. App. 1960) **6:** 53

National Coal Operator's Ass'n v. Kleppe, 423 U.S. 388 (1976) **16:** 53

National Dairy Prods. Corp., 126 NLRB 434, 45 LRRM 1332 (1960) **13:** 152

National Educ. Ass'n-Topeka, Inc. v. Unified Sch. Dist. 501, Shawnee County, 592 P.2d 93, 101 LRRM 2611 (Kan. 1979) **21:** 166

National Elevator Indus. v. Elevator Constructors, 647 F. Supp. 976, 125 LRRM 2169 (S.D. Tex. 1986) **11:** 118, 119

National Furniture Mfg. Co.; NLRB v., 315 F.2d 280, 52 LRRM 2451 (7th Cir. 1963) **8:** 335; **15:** 275

National Gallery of Art
33 FLRA 859 (1989) **5:** 131
91 LA 335 (Craver, 1988), aff'd, 853 F.2d 59 (2d Cir. 1988) **18:** 190

National Grinding Wheel Co., 75 NLRB 905, 21 LRRM 1095 (1948) **13:** 67

National Guard Bureau, 22 FLRA 836 (1986) **20:** 100

National Gypsum Co. v. Oil, Chem. & Atomic Workers
147 F.3d 399, 158 LRRM 2853 (5th Cir. 1998) **7:** 24, 29
1997 U.S. Dist. LEXIS 8929 (E.D. La. 1997) **18:** 192

National Labor Relations Bd., 35 FLRA 421 (1990) **20:** 122

National Marine Fisheries Serv., 22 FLRA 443 (1986) **18:** 338

National Mar. Union, 25 FLRA 105 (1987) **20:** 92

National Oceanic & Atmospheric Admin., 57 FLRA 559 (2001) **20:** 128

National Radio Co., 198 NLRB 527, 80 LRRM 1718 (1972) **10:** 189

National R.R. Passenger Corp. v. Boston & Me. Corp., 850 F.2d 756 (D.C. Cir. 1988) **2:** 38

National Wrecking Co. v. Teamsters Local 731, 990 F.2d 957, 143 LRRM 2046 (7th Cir. 1993) **3:** 92

Nationsway Transp. Serv., 327 NLRB 1033, 164 LRRM 1339 (1999) **10:** 196

Naval Air Rework Facility, 21 FLRA 410 (1986) **18:** 339

Naval Plant Representative Office, 34 FLRA 234 (1990) **5:** 107

Navy, Dep't of
38 FLRA 1509 (1991) **21:** 193
Military Sealift Command v. FLRA, 836 F.2d 1409, 127 LRRM 2332 (3d Cir. 1988) **20:** 92
Naval Sea Sys. Command, 57 FLRA 543 (2001) **20:** 127
Naval Weapons Support Ctr., 40 FLRA 1016 (1991) **20:** 25
Newport News, Va., 56 FLRA 339 (2000) **20:** 95
Norfolk Naval Shipyard, 34 FLRA 725 (1990) **18:** 354
Pub. Works Ctr. v. FLRA, 678 F.2d 97, 110 LRRM 2570 (9th Cir. 1982) **20:** 66

NCR Corp. v. Machinists Dist. 70, 906 F.2d 1499, 134 LRRM 2694 (10th Cir. 1990) **3:** 45

N.D. Peters & Co., 327 NLRB 922, 167 LRRM 1335 (1999) **10:** 183

Neal v. Lanier Prof'l Servs., 2001 U.S. Dist. LEXIS 15719 (N.D. Tex. Sept. 28, 2001) **2:** 213

Nelson v. Electrical Workers (IBEW) Local 46, 899 F.2d 1557, 134 LRRM 2118 (9th Cir. 1990) **10:** 136

Neptune Bd. of Educ. v. Neptune Township Educ. Ass'n, 675 A.2d 611, 144 N.J. 16 (N.J. 1996) **21:** 167

Nevada Dep't of Human Res. v. Hibbs, 123 S.Ct. 1972, 8 WH Cases 2d 1221 (2003) **10:** 100a

Newark Morning Ledger Co. v. Typographical Union Local No. 103 (Newark), 797 F.2d 162, 123 LRRM 2283 (3d Cir. 1986) **22:** 187

Newark Wire Cloth Co. v. Steelworkers, 339 F. Supp. 1207, 80 LRRM 2094 (D.N.J. 1972) **18:** 133

New Assocs. dba Hospitality Care Ctr., 310 NLRB 1209 (1993) **13:** 726

New Bedford Sch. Comm. v. New Bedford Educators Ass'n, 405 N.E.2d 162, 108 LRRM 3201 (Mass. App. Ct. 1980) **21:** 177

Newberry v. Pacific Racing Ass'n, 854 F.2d 1142, 129 LRRM 2047 (9th Cir. 1988) **2:** 270

Sam Kane Packing Co. v. Meat Cutters Local 171, 477 F.2d 1128, 83 LRRM 2298 (5th Cir. 1973) *4:* 54; *7:* 159

San Antonio Portland Cement Co., 277 NLRB 338, 121 LRRM 1234 (1985) *5:* 190

Sands Mfg. Co.; NLRB v., 306 U.S. 332, 4 LRRM 530 (1939) *13:* 129

Sanford Home for Adults v. Health Prof'ls Local 6, 665 F. Supp. 312, 126 LRRM 3149 (S.D.N.Y. 1987) *1:* 136; *2:* 160

Sanitation Men Ass'n v. Commissioner of Sanitation, New York City, 392 U.S. 280 (1968) *19:* 68, 97

Sanko S.S. Co. v. Cook Indus., 495 F.2d 1260 (2d Cir. 1973) *1:* 134

San Martine Co. de Navegacion, S.A. v. Saguenay Terminals, 293 F.2d 796 (9th Cir. 1961) *10:* 17

Santos v. American Broad. Co., 866 F.2d 892, 130 LRRM 2515 (6th Cir. 1989) *5:* 210

Sartorius, Inc., 323 NLRB 1275, 158 LRRM 1060 (1997) *13:* 106

Satterfield v. Board of Educ., 556 N.W.2d 888 (Mich. Ct. App. 1996) *21:* 48

Schlacter-Jones v. General Tel. of Cal., 936 F.2d 435, 6 IER Cases 897 (9th Cir. 1991) *9:* 242

Schmidt
v. Finberg, 942 F.2d 1571 (11th Cir. 1991) *7:* 93
v. Genessee County Road Comm'n, 1996 U.S. Dist. LEXIS 17727 (E.D. Mich. 1996) *14:* 75

Schneider Moving & Storage Co. v. Robbins, 466 U.S. 364, 115 LRRM 3641 (1984) *2:* 28; *5:* 161

School Admin. Dist. No. 58 v. Mount Abram Teachers Ass'n, 704 A.2d. 349 (Me. 1997) *21:* 74

School Comm. of Danvers v. Tyman, 372 Mass. 106, 360 N.E.2d 877, 94 LRRM 3182 (1977) *21:* 21

School Comm. of Holbrook v. Holbrook Educ. Ass'n, 481 N.E.2d 484 (Mass. 1985) *21:* 153

School Comm. of Lowell v. Service Employees Local 159, 679 N.E.2d 583 (Mass. Ct. App. 1997) *21:* 175, 177

School Comm. of Natick v. Education Ass'n of Natick, 666 N.E.2d 486 (Mass. 1996) *21:* 163

School Dist. No. 42 of City of Nashua v. Murray, 514 A.2d 1269 (N.H. 1986) *21:* 194

School Dist. of Borough of Morrisville v. Morrisville Educ. Ass'n, 165 Pa. Commw.

96, 644 A.2d 252 (Pa. Commw. Ct. 1994) *21:* 53

School Dist. of City of Erie v. Erie Educ. Assn., 749 A.2d 545, 164 LRRM 3055 (Pa. Commw. Ct. 2000) *21:* 52

School Dist. U-46 Bd. of Educ. v. Illinois Educ. Lab. Relations Bd., 576 N.E.2d 471 (Ill. Ct. App. 1991) *21:* 242

Schur v. Storage Tech. Corp., 878 P.2d 51 (Colo. Ct. App. 1994) *15:* 13

Screen Actors Guild v. A. Shane Co., 225 Cal. App. 3d 260, 275 Cal. Rptr. 220 (Cal. Ct. App. 1990) *21:* 216

S.D. Warren Co. v. Paperworkers Local 1069
845 F.2d 3, 128 LRRM 2175 (1st Cir.), *cert. denied,* 488 U.S. 992 (1988) *2:* 112; *15:* 126, 140, 149; *18:* 247
846 F.2d 827, 128 LRRM 2432 (1st Cir.), *cert. denied,* 488 U.S. 992 (1988) *2:* 112; *15:* 149; *18:* 247

Seafarers v. National Marine Servs., 639 F. Supp. 1283 (E.D. La. 1986), *rev'd,* 820 F.2d 148, 125 LRRM 3069 (5th Cir.), *cert. denied,* 484 U.S. 953 (1987) *3:* 54, 112, 148

Sea-Land Serv. v. Longshoremen (ILWU) Local 13, 939 F.2d 866, 138 LRRM 2057 (9th Cir. 1991) *7:* 55

Sears, Roebuck & Co.
274 NLRB 230, 118 LRRM 1329 (1985) *5:* 173
v. Teamsters Local 243, 683 F.2d 154, 110 LRRM 3175 (6th Cir. 1982) *13:* 595

Seattle Prof'l Eng'g Employees Ass'n v. Boeing, 139 Wash. 2d 824, 991 P.2d 1126, 5 WH Cases 2d 1686 (2000) *18:* 225

Seitz v. Duval County. Sch. Bd., 4 Fla. Pub. Empl. Rep. (LRP) ¶4154 (1978) *19:* 104

S.E.L. Maduro (Fla.) v. Longshoremen (ILA) Local 1416, 765 F.2d 1057, 120 LRRM 2036 (11th Cir. 1985) *11:* 120

Serrano v. Delmonico's Hotel, 123 Lab. Cas. (CCH) ¶10,400 (S.D.N.Y. 1992) *5:* 210

Sertick v. School Dist. of Pittsburgh, 584 A.2d 390 (Pa. Commw. Ct. 1990) *21:* 39

Servair, Inc. v. NLRB, 726 F.2d 1435 (9th Cir. 1984) *10:* 201

Serv-Air; NLRB v., 401 F.2d 363, 69 LRRM 2476 (10th Cir. 1968) *5:* 143

Service Employees Local 106 v. Evergreen Cemetery, 708 F. Supp. 917, 133 LRRM 2336 (N.D. Ill. 1989) *2:* 45; *3:* 113

Seus v. John Nuveen & Co., 146 F.3d 175, 77 FEP Cases 751 (3d Cir. 1998), *cert. denied,* 525 U.S. 1139 (1999) *1:* 187; *2:* 245

Table of Statutes

Index

Alphabetization is word-by-word (e.g., "Age of retirement" precedes "Agency fee dispute"). The index contains a few well-known cases, but for a complete list of cases, see the Table of Cases, and for arbitration decisions, see the Table of Arbitration Awards. A separate index also lists all federal acts cited.

A

AAA. *See* American Arbitration Association

ABA. *See* American Bar Association

Ability determination. *See* Fitness and ability determination

Ability-to-pay standard, 1429–36. *See also* Interest arbitration

Absenteeism. *See also* Leaves of absence; Sick leave
excessive absence, grounds for discipline and discharge, 822–24, 933
fitness and ability factor, 906–07
holiday pay, effect of part-day absence on surrounding day, 1070–71
illness, excessive absence due to, 822–24
loss of seniority, 871

Absurd results
avoidance of, in contract interpretation, 470–72

Abuse of grievance procedures, 204–05

Academic freedom, right to, 1316–18

Accents, 905

Access to personnel records, 902

Accommodation of disability. *See* Reasonable accommodation of disability

Accommodation of religion. *See* Religious accommodation

Accountability of arbitrators
reporting of awards, 568–73

ACLU (American Civil Liberties Union)
Due Process Protocol for Mediation and Arbitration of Statutory Disputes, 35–36

Acts of God, 730
defined, 736

Ad hoc arbitrators, 143–44

Ad hoc compulsory arbitration, 24

ADA. *See* Americans with Disabilities Act

ADEA. *See* Age Discrimination in Employment Act

Administrative law judges
evidentiary standards, analogy to arbitration context, 346–47

Administrative Procedure Act (APA)
evidence, admissibility under, 346–47

Administrative proceedings
influence on arbitrators, 544–47
preclusive effect on subsequent arbitration, 390–91
res judicata and collateral estoppel, 386–87

Admissibility of evidence, 343–44, 403–13
affidavits of nonpresent witnesses, 368
after-acquired evidence, 407–12
disparate treatment, post-discharge evidence of, 411–12
post-disciplinary conduct, 408–11
post-hearing submission of evidence, 412
predisciplinary misconduct, 407
confessions from forced employee interviews, 372–76
confidential information, 348, 363–65
contemporaneous written notes, 369
e-mail obtained by monitoring or interception, 402
entire board to hear evidence, 412
grievance proceeding, evidence admissible when not used at, 403
guilty pleas, 373–74
improperly obtained documents, 403
informal records, 371
new evidence at hearings, 403–06

1733